MR. WILLIAM
SHAKESPEARES
COMEDIES,
HISTORIES, &
TRAGEDIES.

MR. WILLIAM

SHAKESPEARES

COMEDIES,
HISTORIES, &
TRAGEDIES.

A Facsimile of the First Folio, 1623.

INTRODUCTION BY DOUG MOSTON

ROUTLEDGE
NEW YORK LONDON

Published in 1998 by
Routledge
29 West 35th Street
New York, NY 10001

Published in Great Britain by
Routledge
11 New Fetter Lane
London EC4P 4EE

Printed in the United States of America on acid-free paper.

Library of Congress Cataloging-in-Publication Data

Shakespeare, William, 1564–1616
[Plays]
Mr. William Shakespeares comedies, histories, and tragedies : a facsimile of the first folio, 1623 / edited and with an introduction by Doug Moston.
p. cm.
Includes bibliographical references.
ISBN 0-87830-088-0 (pbk.)
1. Shakespeare, William, 1564–1616 — Bibliography — Folios. 1623 — Facsimiles. I. Moston, Doug. II. Title.
PR2751.A15 1998
822.3'3—dc21 98-12047
CIP

For you, Diana.

MR. WILLIAM
SHAKESPEARES
COMEDIES,
HISTORIES, &
TRAGEDIES.

ACKNOWLEDGMENTS

It was Talia Rodgers who alerted Bill Germano to the idea of publishing the First Folio in an affordable facsimile for actors. Thanks to both of them and the wonderful people at Routledge.

Special thanks also to Stuart Vaughan for his advice, counsel, and patience in helping me with the manuscript.

Thank you to Dean James Lipton of The School of Dramatic Arts at The New School MFA program for putting me together with some of the best actors anyone could hope to work with.

To Dr. David Krasner at Yale University for kind words, deeds and extraordinary support.

Also thank you to Frank Ventura and Eliza Ventura, two exceptional artists who founded and operate Collaborative Arts Project 21 (CAP21), and all of the Tisch School of the Arts students from New York University who attend my classes there.

To Virginia L. Bartow, Curator of Rare Books and the Arents Collections, and the staff at The New York Public Library, including John Rathé, Miriam Mandelbaum, Stephen Crook of the Berg Collection, and Daniel Tierney for his helpful report on the Library's six Folios.

To Dr. Anna Lou Ashby, Associate Curator of Printed Books at The Pierpont Morgan Library, Dr. M.J. Jannetta, Curator of English Antiquarian Collections at The British Library, and Dr. Rachel Doggett, Curator of Books at the Folger Shakespeare Library for their generosity with time, help, and advice.

Thank you to Patrick Tucker who introduced me to the concept of playing Shakespeare from cue scripts based on Folio text.

Thanks must also be given to Arthur Penn, President of The Actors Studio and Frank Corsaro, its former Artistic Director, and Patty Ewald, its former Executive Director for giving me the opportunity to explore this work further in the Shakespeare Workshops I lead for the members.

Thanks also to all of the actors who have worked with me in classes and workshops who were willing to risk playing Shakespeare in continuously changing ways.

Finally I thank Diana Moston, who endured and edited the many versions of this introduction.

"Reade him, therefore; and againe, and againe:
And if then you doe not like him, surely you are
in some manifest danger, not to understand him."

John Heminge and Henrie Condell,
To the great Variety of Readers
from their original introductory material to the First Folio.

PREFACE

This photographic facsimile of the First Folio of Shakespeare's plays is designed for use in production. It is intended to preserve the integrity of a vital Shakespeare on stage.

William Shakespeare was an actor. He wrote his plays with an actor's sensibilities. He pursued truth in the theatre using a logic that created real characters with dimension and depth for the first time on the Elizabethan stage. As a playwright, he used verse and prose to provide direction for actors to perform before an audience.

It is important for modern artists to have access to the First Folio because it is the closest version we have to Shakespeare's original performance texts. Many actors today are reaping benefits from acting Shakespeare from Folio text without the directorial interventions of editors. While editors often illuminate the text for the armchair playgoer, they inadvertently direct it as well. The changes that they incorporate into their edited texts follow their own logic of story telling narrative. The logic found in the Folio is frequently different. When Folio logic is explored through theatrical action and instruction, it often leads to new interpretations. While scholars have years to devote to solving textual problems and the printing habits of the various compositors, actors whose task it is to play Shakespeare's characters have a comparatively limited amount of time to perfect their performances.

We continually adjust our perceptions of reality to fit our own patterns of logic. In a vain attempt to control what we may not understand, or what may frighten us, we skew the organic logic of life to fit a logic that comforts our individual egos. When an artist such as Shakespeare reflects truth back to us, he reacquaints us with that original logic, and in so doing gives us a clearer, truer picture than we are often capable of seeing for ourselves. He gives us a pure truth that entertains and enlightens, inspiring the artist within us all.

Introduction

To the great Variety of Actors

Of the approximately 250 extant copies of Shakespeare's First Folio, virtually none are available to the public except as facsimiles. Even facsimiles, from time to time, are rare or unobtainable. Of the facsimiles that began to emerge from the middle of the nineteenth century to the present, all were introduced by and intended primarily for interested scholars and readers of great literature. Because William Shakespeare was an actor, this photographic facsimile, originally introduced by J.O. Halliwell-Phillipps in 1876, is designed as an affordable tool for actors and theatre people to preserve a vital Shakespeare in production.

The book is properly entitled *Mr. William Shakespeares Comedies, Histories, & Tragedies*. It has come to be known simply as the First Folio. It is said by many to be one of the two most important books ever published in the English language, the other being The King James version of the Bible published in 1611.

The First Folio of Shakespeare is not an anthology of plays, it is an anthology of scripts; there is a difference between a script and a play. A script is just one component of a play or production; it needs actors and an audience, at the very least, to become a play.

Because we read these *scripts* thinking of them as *plays* we often miss what might have been Shakespeare's actual intentions for the productions that he conceived.

When we read a script we use a frame of reference that immediately and unconsciously compares it to literature. Indeed, most of us would agree that Shakespeare's plays are the pinnacle of great literature.

When we read literature, a novel or short story for example, the entire experience the author presents us with unfolds in our minds. All the elements of the story, descriptions of behavior, subtext, and so forth, are laid out for us. Not so with a script.

A script is different. A script, in addition to providing us with a thematic story and plot, is actually a set of instructions. When followed by actors, designers, a director, and an audience, the script gives birth to the production of a play, and "the play's the thing."

Reading a script once can be satisfying and rewarding but it is hardly enough to identify the elements necessary to realize a play on the stage. When an actor or a director first reads a script, he or she will comprehend the story, plot, adventure, emotions, theme, and so on. But he will have to read it again and again to uncover the clues that will enable him to collaborate in a full production. In the pages that follow, I offer a brief overview of how actors and directors can find and use Shakespeare's clues.

The First Folio

Shakespeare was an actor, a poet (as playwrights then called themselves), and a producer. He was a shareholder in the Globe Theatre and the Lord Chamberlain's Men, and subsequently the King's Men. Shakespeare penned his scripts in order to have the final output of his art realized onstage, in full production before a paying audience. He never wanted his plays published. The plays represented the companies' assets. He wanted his audience to pay to attend them, not merely read them.

John Heminge and Henry Condell were actors who were also shareholders in the Globe Playhouse and business managers of its acting companies. In 1623, seven years after Shakespeare's death, they became the overseers or editors, if you will, of the first printed collection of their friend and colleague William Shakespeare's plays. They assembled thirty-six of them (*Pericles* was omitted for some unknown reason, perhaps to do with securing rights) and, with the help of Edward Blount and William and Isaac Jaggard, published the plays in a large volume described in printers' terms as a "folio," each large leaf being folded once, lengthwise, and yielding four printed pages, two on each side of the leaf.

Heminge and Condell were remarkable men. John Heminge was granted the title of "London Gent. of long tyme Servant to Queen Elizabeth of happie Memory, also to King

James hir Royal Successor and to King Charles [1629]," a title that Shakespeare's father John had applied for twice, once in 1570 when it was denied and again almost thirty years later in 1599, when it was granted.

Henry Condell was not an original shareholder in the Globe in 1599 but subsequently acquired an interest. He was an original sharer in the Second Blackfriars in 1608 where many of Shakespeare's plays were produced indoors during the colder months.[1] Fellow actors, Alexander Cooke, Augustine Phillips, and Nicholas Tooley remembered him in their wills by bequeathing to him money and trusteeships, and designating him executor of Tooley's estate. William Shakespeare bequeathed to him a memorial ring. In 1599 he settled with his family in St. Mary Aldermanbury, where he was a church warden. In July of 1896 a memorial to Heminge and Condell was unveiled with the inscription: "To the memory of John Heminge And Henry Condell, fellow actors and personal friends of Shakespeare. They lived many years in this parish, and are buried here. To their disinterested efforts the world owes all that it calls Shakespeare. They alone collected his dramatic writings, regardless of pecuniary loss, and, without the hope of any profit, gave them to the world. They thus merit the gratitude of mankind."

In the Preface to the First Folio, Heminge and Condell themselves address "*the great Variety of Readers*":

> . . . It had bene a thing, we confesse, worthie to have bene wished, that the Author himselfe had liv'd to have set forth, and overseen his owne writings; But since it hath bin ordain'd otherwise, and he by death departed from that right, we pray you do not envie his Friends, the office of their care, and paine, to have collected & publish'd them; and so to have publish'd them, as where (before) you were abus'd with diverse stolne, and surreptitious copies, maimed, and deformed by the frauds and stealthes of injurious impostors, that expos'd them: even those, are now offer'd to your view cur'd, and perfect of their limbes; and all the rest, absolute in their numbers, as he conceived the[m].

Folios Two, Three, Four, and More

Nine years after the Folio was published, there was enough demand to make a second impression. The Second Folio of 1632 had some changes made to it, some improvements and, inevitably, some errors as well. The problem was that the improvements were being made by people who no longer had any direct connection to the company. Henry Condell had died five years prior to the publication of the Second Folio and John Heminge died in 1630.

When the Second Folio sold out, a third was printed in 1663. It sold for almost a year when it was revised, or further "improved" upon, this time with the addition of seven new plays including *Pericles,* better late than never. The other six, *The London Prodigal*, *The Life and Death of Thomas Lord Cromwell*, *The History of Sir John Oldcastle*, *The Puritan, or The Widow of Watling Street*, *A Yorkshire Tragedy*, and *The Tragedy of Locrine* were not even written by Shakespeare. There are several accounts of plays, whose authorship is unknown, being attributed to Shakespeare because it sold plays.

In 1685 the fourth and final folio was printed. It retained the seven "new" plays and was further edited. After the publication of the Fourth Folio the next collection of Shakespeare's plays was edited by Nicholas Rowe in 1709. Rowe was a playwright. He edited the plays from the Fourth Folio, added pictures and retained the seven "new" plays.

Each edition of the plays became further removed from playhouse manuscript authority. The editors made some legitimate and useful improvements but also inadvertently tampered with the sound, tempo, and theatrical direction that were inherent in the First Folio.

A century of modern Shakespeare criticism hasn't settled — from a scholar's point of view — questions of accuracy and meaning in the Folio. But actors can find in the Folio their best available link to the playwright's intentions. As actors, Heminge and Condell knew what the plays sounded like in performance. They knew what worked and what didn't. If they spelled words by sound to suit the moment, the likelihood is great that they also set down the plays as they remembered hearing them and performing them after some eighteen years of experience with many of them. They also knew the personalities, talents, strengths, and limitations of their colleagues. They knew, better than anyone else at the time, what made these plays work. The First Folio is the best record we have of what they themselves heard and played. It is the best point of departure for any modern exploration of the plays being rehearsed for production today.

Printing the First Folio

It wasn't too long ago that the common wisdom held that the First Folio was too full of errors to rely on for performance or reading. The typesetters, or compositors, were called everything from unreliable and unskilled to drunk. Recent scholarship suggests otherwise. The Folger Shakespeare Library, for example, has a page from *Antony and Cleopatra* (original folio page 352, not part of a folio but a fragment) that contains proofreaders' marks showing errors that were corrected in Folio 68, page 352.[2] But there is considerable scholarly debate regarding this proofreading issue. Although some scholars assert that the Folio was not proofread simply because it contained errors, Blayney and McKenzie show conclusively that the Folio was not only proofread *at press*, but before going to press as well. (The reader is invited to consult Hinman and Blayney's introduction to the second edition of the Norton Facsimile [pp. xxx–xxxii] and D.F. McKenzie's *Printers of the Mind* [Studies in Bibliography 22, 1969, pp. 42–49].) I believe, and this is the reason for this book, that the First Folio is by no means so error ridden as has been argued and, more to the point, that however the scholarship advances from decade to decade, the text in the Folio is eminently more actable than in any later edited editions.

It was thought that the Folio was printed by two men, compositors A and B. Charlton Hinman reports in his study, *The Printing and Proof-Reading of the First Folio of Shakespeare* (Oxford University Press, 1963), that there were actually five compositors. The latest scholarship suggests that compositor A was actually the work of five, bringing the total to nine compositors now thought to have composed the type for the printing of the Folio.[3] [4]

Prior to 1955, Hinman reports, it was always thought that the Folio was printed "in seriatim," that is, in a conventional manner beginning with page one, two, and so on. It was actually printed in "formes." One piece of paper had two pages printed on one side and two on the reverse. The side facing the reader was called the "inner forme." After it was dried and proofread, it went back to the press for a second "pull" to imprint the other side. This second side, which faced away from the reader, was called the "outer forme." This was done in sets of three. There was a stack of three sheets of paper totaling twelve printed pages. These three pieces of printed paper, stacked and folded lengthwise in half were referred to as a "quire." Each quire was signed at the bottom of the page. B2, D3, gg3, etc., were the various "signatures" marking the quires. So if you opened one quire, looking at the inner forme of the top piece of paper in the stack, the pages you saw would be numbered six and seven. If you turned that top page over, the numbers would be pages five and eight. The middle page would be numbered four and nine for the inner forme and pages three and ten on the reverse of the paper. The bottom sheet in the quire would be numbered pages two and eleven, with pages one and twelve on the outer forme at the very bottom of the quire. The reader can simply hold pages one through six of this book in his left hand and grasp pages seven through twelve in his right hand to see how it works. However, that was not the most complicated part of all this. Because the Folio was printed this way, the compositors had to work out how to distribute the type evenly over each of the twelve, two-column pages. When one page looked as if it might have too much type, that page had to be reconfigured before composing. Disposing of, or redistributing the extra type was called "casting off." Once the type was properly "copyfit" onto the appropriate pages, the pages printed and the printed pages stacked into a quire, the quires were then stacked to be either bound into a book or sent to the local booksellers to be sold unbound. According to Blayney, a Folio might sell for about fifteen shillings unbound, about one pound (20 shillings) bound. It was not unusual for Elizabethans to buy books unbound to have them bound themselves, as London booksellers charged a fifty percent markup for binding.[5]

The Quartos

About half of Shakespeare's plays made their appearance in print well before the publication of the First Folio. If a play proved popular it might be published in a single play paperback edition called a *quarto*. This is a printer's term for a book that was made of pages that had been folded in half once, like a folio, then in half again. This produced a leaf with four pages on each side.

When a quarto was printed, the person holding the rights could produce the play, outside London. When an actor was jobbed in to play a certain part(s) he, or possibly some of his cronies in the audience, could take down various parts in a kind of shorthand or, as some say, memorial reconstruction, and get the play published in quarto. These editions were usually highly inaccurate. Because they were poorly rendered shadows of the originals they might cause the play to be less well attended, especially if people had read it and thought it might not be worth the price of admission.

To set the record straight, Shakespeare's company, who owned the plays, would sometimes issue a corrected quarto. We know they did this in the cases of *Romeo and Juliet*, *Hamlet* and, some believe, *Love's Labour's Lost*. The title page of *Romeo and Juliet* says, "Newly corrected, augmented, and amended:" The second quarto of *Hamlet* (1604) says, "Newly imprinted and enlarged to almost as much againe as it was, according to the true and perfect Coppie." The cover of the *Love's Labour's Lost* quarto of 1598 reads, "Newly corrected and augmented by W. Shakespere." The Lord Chamberlain's Men issued quartos for *Henry V*, *The Merry Wives of Windsor*, *Pericles* (which for some unknown reason never made it to the Folio), and the *Henry the Sixth* plays for which there were no "bad" quartos to correct. Some speculate that the company may have done this because they needed money to build the Globe. In any case, these editions sold for around sixpence a copy, and although some call these cheap editions, one could attend the play for one penny and the bear baiting for half a penny. The penny's purchasing power then was prodigious.

The Shakespeare plays first published as "bad" quartos were:

2 Henry VI (1594)
3 Henry VI (1595)
Romeo and Juliet (1597)
Henry V (1600)
The Merry Wives of Windsor (1602)
Hamlet (1603)
Pericles (1609)[6]

Here is how the most famous speech in the English language world is rendered in *Hamlet* (III, i) from "Q1," or the first, or "bad" quarto of 1603:[7]

To be, or not to be, I there's the point,
To Die, to sleepe, is that all? I all:
No, to sleepe, to dreame, I mary there it goes,
For in that dreame of death, when wee awake,
And borne before an euerlasting Iudge,
From whence no passenger euer retur'nd,
The vndiscouered country, at whose sight
The happy smile, and the accursed damn'd.
But for this, the ioyfull hope of this,
Whol'd beare the scornes and flattery of the world,
Scorned by the right rich, the rich cursssed of the poore?
The widow being oppressed, the orphan wrong'd,
The taste of hunger a tirants raigne,
And thousand more calamities besides,
To grunt and sweate vnder this wery life,
When that he may his full *Quiteus* Make,
With a bare bodkin, who would this indure,
But for a hope of something after death?
Which pusles the braine, and doth confound the sence,
Which makes vs rather beare those euilles we have,
Than flie to others that we know not of.
I that, O this conscience makes cowardes of vs all,
Lady in thy orizons, be all my sinnes remembred.

It sounds vaguely familiar, and comical too, because the speech is now so famous. Whoever reproduced this, either by memory or by stenography, omitted a great deal. What happened to "The Slings and Arrowes of outragious Fortune," "Or to take Armes against a Sea of troubles," and "The Oppressors wrong, the poore mans Contumely"?[8] When Hamlet says, "There's the respect—That makes Calamity of so long life," the pirate gives us, "And thousand more calamities besides," possibly confusing "quality" with "quantity," or "and the thousand Naturall shockes" with "calamities." Where Shakespeare writes "Puzels the will," the copyist has it as "pusles the braine" which, perhaps, is autobiographical on the pirate's part. The Quartos did not have act and scene divisions; but the pirate has moved the scene from approximately Act III to Act II. It is interesting, however, to see which key phrases survive.

An example from the *Hamlet* quarto of 1604 is Hamlet's speech (II, ii):

O what a rogue and pesant slave am I.
Is it not monstrous that this player heere
But in a fixion, in a dreame of passion
Could force his soule so to his owne conceit
That from her working all the visage wand,
Teares in his eyes, distraction in his aspect,
A broken voyce, an his whole function suting
With formes to his conceit; and all for nothing,
For *Hecuba.*

Q1 of 1603 has it as:

Why what a dunghill idiote slave am I?
Why these Players here draw water from eyes:
For Hecuba, why what is Hecuba to him, or he
to Hecuba? What would he do and if he had
my losse?

Of the thirty-six plays printed in the First Folio, the following were first printed in "good" quartos and are considered to be authoritative texts:

Titus Andronicus (1594)
Richard II (1597)
Love's Labour's Lost (1598)
1 Henry IV (1598)
Romeo and Juliet, Q2 (1599)
A Midsummer Night's Dream (1600)
The Merchant of Venice (1600)
Much Ado About Nothing (1600)
King Lear (1608)
Othello (1622)

Also published in "good" quartos were *2 Henry IV*, *Hamlet*, and *Troilus and Cressida.* There are questions as to whether the text of *2 Henry IV* was set from a manuscript or a corrected copy of a quarto. Hinman says, in his Introduction to the Norton Facsimile, that *2 Henry IV* was set from both, and that "for both *Hamlet* and *Troilus and Cressida* the good quarto text is again the soundest, but here the Folio has considerable authority too."[9]

Plays appearing in print for the first time (first editions) in the Folio are:

The Tempest
King John
The Two Gentlemen of Verona
1 Henry VI
Measure for Measure
Henry VIII
The Comedy of Errors
Coriolanus
As You Like It
Timon of Athens
The Taming of the Shrew
Julius Cæsar
All's Well that Ends Well
Macbeth
Twelfth Night
Antony and Cleopatra
The Winter's Tale
Cymbeline

Elizabethan Daytime Drama

When an acting troupe arrived in town they used the center courtyard of an inn, or inn yard. They erected a platform of boards at one end to use as a stage and gathered payment as they could from those who stood in the yard or sat in the surrounding windows above. They had access to the inn yards three days a week. These spaces had to be shared with the carters, who brought freight and mail into London weekly.[10] There must have been difficulties with props and costume, both lacking adequate storage and changing facilities.

In 1576, James Burbage, Richard's father, took the gamble and opened an inn yard (without the inn) north of London. This was the first building designed primarily for the presentation of plays. Mr. Burbage called it The Theatre.

This building, unlike the inn yards, was round so that the audience could see and hear better. There was a dressing room upstage center for changing one's attire, called the tiring house. The stage could be made larger than those of the inns, and extend half way into the yard. It could have traps for special effect entrances and exits of ghosts, or grave digging scenes, etc. It could feature a portico-like structure over the stage to protect the actors from rain. The audience would be protected by a thatched cover, too. In such a structure, it would be much easier to "gather" moneys for admission. With an audience of two to three thousand, paying from a penny to stand in the yard as a "groundling," all the way up to sixpence to sit on a cushion in the lord's room over the stage, the Globe could turn a pretty penny for a partnership of players. And they could play every day, except, of course, on Sunday.

The Theatre was a success for the next twenty-one years. The Burbages owned the building but not the land, and the lease to the land had just run out. The Burbages, this time Richard and his brother Cuthbert, had inherited the building from James who died in 1596. The Burbages had the contractual right "at any time or times before the end of the said term of one and twenty years, to have, take down, and carry away to his own proper use" the building called The Theatre. Sometime after the contract had run out, that is precisely what they did. They dismantled The Theatre and brought the timbers by boat across the Thames. Their intention was to rebuild it, but where would they get the money to do it? The Burbages went to other actors for the money. They combined their resources with William Shakespeare, John Heminge, Augustine Phillips, William Kempe, and Thomas Pope to create a shared ownership of the new theatre, built with the help of a carpenter in London called Peter Streete. The building was constructed on the bankside, south of the Thames in Southwark, made from the timbers of the original Theatre. Regarded by the London theatre-going public as "the glory of the Bank," it opened in the summer of 1599 when its playing flag, depicting Atlas shouldering the world, was hoisted high overhead, and it was called, simply, the Globe.

"Give me some Light"

(*Hamlet*, III, ii)

Plays were presented six days a week, at around one or two in the afternoon. The audience could see the actors clearly from virtually all seats. More importantly, the actors could see the audience, as plain as day. This was a truly interactive theatre. Shakespeare, who wrote opportunities for actors to create some of the most truthful behavior ever, would most likely not ask an audience to believe that Hamlet was talking to himself with "To be, or not to be." That Hamlets today do so is a function of theatrical evolution. Indoor staging with indoor lighting keeps the audience in the dark and reduces their role to that of spectators, non-participating observers. In 1600, Richard Burbage could turn this famous soliloquy into a scene between himself and the audience. He could explain to them, enlist their support for what would happen next. He could directly bring the audience up to the level of his character. He could include them in the play, not ignore them by pretending that they were not there. Even those of us who talk to ourselves today don't do it in iambic pentameter.

Every Day a Different Play

Very near the Globe was its rival company, the Lord Admiral's Men. Their home was the Rose Playhouse, their leading actor, Edward Alleyn. Burbage's acting style was noted for being natural. Alleyn's style was named after the padding or stuffing that was used to puff out the fashions of the day: it was called bombast.

The Rose, like the Globe, was also a partnership. Alleyn was partners with, and the son-in-law of, Philip Henslowe, who owned the Rose, some brothels, and other businesses near the Globe. Much of what is known about the Elizabethan theatre comes from the fact that Henslowe kept a journal. *Henslowe's Diary*, or *papers* as they are sometimes called, lists his expenses, the dates and plays performed, and moneys taken in for each performance. According to this diary, the Lord Admiral's Men acted a different five-act play every day.

In the fifteen-week summer season of 1596 the Admiral's Men gave eighty-five performances of twenty-five plays, seven of which were brand new.[11] When a company would repeat a play it would be anywhere from seven days to a month or more from the last time they had played it. It is remarkably similar to the job today's television actors have playing daytime soap operas. Playing one or more different characters in a different play daily might require a different method of production.

"Come, come, wee'le prompt you"

(*Coriolanus*, III, ii)

When a playwright completed the final draft of his play he would either copy it over again to make a clean copy or give it over to a scrivener (or scribe) to make it ready for use as a prompt book. The plays from which the clean copies were made were referred to as "foul papers" because they had corrections and blots dirtying the script throughout. When a play was copied by the scribe (most of Shakespeare's were prepared by Ralph Crane) for use as a prompt script, they became known as "fair papers." Heminge and Condell write of Shakespeare:

> . . . And what he thought, he uttered with that easinesse, that wee have scarse received from him a blot in his papers . . .

Once a play became a prompt book it meant that the playwright had relinquished his ownership of the property. If he was not a "sharer" in a company as Shakespeare was, he had no say in what would happen to his work. It was sold to the company outright and, if need be, could be changed and improved upon to quickly raise it to production level. Other "poets" might be enlisted to collaborate on making the play ready to play. One such playwright, Anthony Munday, was considered the Elizabethan "script doctor" of his time. He was considered "our best plotter" by his contemporaries and collaborated on numerous plays by various writers.

The prompt books were the assets of the company. They were kept under lock and key and entrusted to the company member with the most seniority, lest they be pirated to make a later appearance as a "bad" quarto. During production the prompt book was held by the book holder, or book keeper. Some say he sat directly onstage. This is difficult to believe. It seems unlikely that Shakespeare would want his carefully created scenes distracted by an omnipresent prompter. Andrew Gurr puts the book holder upstage in one of the rooms of the tiring house. He cites the *induction* in *Cynthia's Revels*, by Ben Jonson. One of the boys speaks Jonson's words:

> wee are not so officiously befriended by him, as to have his presence in the tiring-house, to prompt us aloud, stampe at the book-holder, sweare for our properties, curse the poore tire-man, raile the musicke out of tune, and sweat for everie veniall trespasse we commit.[12]

In a recent production of *The Taming of the Shrew*, the director placed a book holder above (a small balcony in one of the houses in Padua) and downstage left. Occasionally calling out, in character, cues and corrections, the book holder nearly stole the show.

"every one according to his cue"

(*A Midsomer night's Dreame*, III, i)

Lacking modern copying devices, companies could not equip actors with full texts of each play every day. Each actor was given his own "part" of the play, or parts, if he was playing more than one character. These were called "part scripts," or "cue scripts." Each contained the actor's part only, plus the last three or four words of the character who spoke prior, indicating his cue. Each page was headed with the name of the character and its page number (Orlando 1, Orlando 2, etc.). The pages were then attached, with the bottom of the first page overlapping an inch or so of the top of the next page, obscuring the heading. The whole part was then rolled into a scroll. Each actor would be give his roll, or role, for the next performance. Edward Alleyn's roll of Orlando, in Robert Greene's *Orlando Furioso*, is in the Wodehouse Library at Dulwich College. Interesting things happen when actors play their parts from cue scripts. For one, they don't "act" listening, they really have to listen.

Sometimes Shakespeare, who knew his actors' personalities very well, could really have some fun by writing scenes for two or more actors, knowing how each might respond to the genuine surprises that emerge from playing this way. Remember, each actor did not have the whole play to refer to. The principals, or shareholders, would have had the play read to them by the playwright before the performance. But how much of *Hamlet, Othello,* or *Lear* might an actor remember upon hearing it once?

In *As You Like It* (V, ii), we have a very funny scene. Orlando and Rosalind, who is dressed as a boy named Ganymed, are joined by Silvius and Phebe.

> *Phe.* Good shepheard, tell this youth what 'tis
> to love
> *Sil.* It is to be all made of sighs and teares,
> And so am I for *Phebe.*
> *Phe.* And I for *Ganimed.*
> *Orl.* And I for *Rosalind.*
> *Ros.* And I for no woman.
> *Sil.* It is to be all made of fantasie,
> All made of passion, and all made of wishes,
> All adoration, dutie, and observance,
> All humbleness, all patience, and impatience,
> All puritie, all triall, all observance:
> And so am I for *Phebe.*
> *Phe.* And so am I for *Ganimed.*
> *Orl.* And so am I for *Rosalind.*
> *Ros.* And so am I for no woman.
> *Phe.* If this be so, why blame you me to love
> you?
> *Sil.* If this be so, why blame you me to love
> you?
> *Orl.* If this be so, why blame you me to love
> you?
> *Ros.* Why do you speake too, Why blame you
> mee to love you.
> *Orl.* To her, that is not heere, nor doth not
> heare.
> *Ros.* Pray you no more of this, 'tis like the
> howling of Irish Wolves against the
> Moone: I will help you if I can: . . .

In this scene many of the cues are the same. It's a wonderful way to put the actor in the same position as the character. Give them the same cue and let's see what happens. When Phebe hears Rosalind say, "And so am I for no woman," it is her cue to say, "If this be so, why blame you me to love you?" Which means that Silvius, Orlando, and Rosalind have the same cue, "to love you?" And they speak simultaneously. Now, when Rosalind says, "'tis like the howling of Irish Wolves against the Moone," it really is.

Another example, of which there are many, is in *Macbeth* (II, ii). Macbeth finds Lady Macbeth after he has "done the deed." Lady's cue is when Macbeth says, "sleepe no more":

> *Macb.* Me thought I heard a voyce cry, Sleep no
> more:
> *Macbeth* does murther Sleepe, the innocent
> Sleepe,
> Sleepe that knits up the ravel'd Sleeve of Care,
> The Death of each dayes Life, sore Labors Bath,
> Balme of hurt Mindes, great Natures second
> Course,
> Chief nourisher in Life's Feast.
> *Lady.* What doe you meane?
> *Macb.* Still it cry'd, <u>Sleepe no more</u> to all the
> House:
> *Glamis* hath murther'd Sleepe, and therefore
> *Cawdor*
> Shall <u>sleepe no more</u>: *Macbeth* shall <u>sleepe no
> more</u>.
> *Lady.* Who was it, that thus cry'd?why worthy
> *Thane,*
> You doe unbend your Noble strength, to thinke
> So braine-sickly of things: Goe get some water,
> And wash this filthie Witnesse from your Hand.

It is an eerie night scene between two terrified people. Shakespeare directs it beautifully. Could he possibly have given Lady a different cue? Might he have avoided using her cue in his speech? When Macbeth says "sleepe no more," Lady only hears her cue. She speaks. He stops her by continuing, for he knows he has more to say. Could the boy actor playing opposite Burbage have been momentarily confused, frightened, tentative? Again she hears him say her cue and again it is wrong. What is happening here, she might have wondered? Now a third time, the cue. Perhaps she waits this time to be certain. Silence, he has no more to say. Then: "Who was it, that thus cry'd?"

The scenes were written with the knowledge that the actors played from cue scripts. These examples cannot and do not happen when these plays are acted from complete texts.

The Platt Thickens

The third and final part of the Elizabethan play is a large chart that plotted out the action of the play. This was hung on a peg in the tiring house and supplied everything the actors needed to know that wasn't in their cue scripts. Here is a short example from *The Second Parte of The Seven Deadlie Sinns*:

> Henry Awaking Enter A Keeper J Sincler to him a servant T Belt to him Lidgate and the Keeper. Exit then enter againe. Then Envy passeth over the stag Lidgate speakes.

The platt gives written direction and it sometimes contains more information than one would get from simply reading the play. For example, in *The Second Parte of The Seven Deadlie Sinns* it just says, "Enter *Sardanapulus*." But the platt direction says:

> Enter Sardanapalus w[ith] as many Jewels, robes and Gold as he can cary.

Actors might receive some "direction" from the book holder but the platt was there for all actors to know who they were in which scene, which costumes they needed, and which props to take. When an actor is playing many parts, all with different costumes and props, in six different plays a week, the platt, or plott, becomes a vital part of Elizabethan play production.

"Were met together to rehearse a Play"

(*A Midsomer night's Dreame*, III, i)

There are only two documents that give us a picture of what Shakespeare's rehearsals might have been like. One, a player's contract between an actor called Robert Dawes, and Philip Henslowe, which says among other things, that:

> . . . he the said Robert Dawes shall and will at all tymes during the said terme duly attend all suche rehearsall, which shall the night before the rehearsall be given publickly out; and if that the saide Robert Dawes shall at any tyme faile to come at the hower appoynted, then he shall and will pay to the said Phillipp Henslowe and Jacob Meade, their executors or assignes, Twelve pence; and if he come not before the saide rehearsall is ended, then the said Robert Dawes is contented to pay Twoe shillings; and further that if the said Robert Dawes . . .

There were further penalties for Mr. Dawes should he not be "readily apparrelled" or if he "should happen to be overcome with drinck at the tyme when he [ought to] play."

In *A Midsummer Night's Dream* there is a rehearsal for *Piramus and Thysbie*. But their rehearsal, comedy aside, bears little resemblance to a rehearsal we might have for a production today. They decide whether Piramus will kill himself with a sword, lest it displease the ladies. They also discuss whether the Lion will upset the same ladies. They must then figure out if the moon will shine that night and how to bring it in to the chamber, because Piramus and Thysbie meet by moonlight. When they actually do rehearse, they plan their entrances and exits:

> *Peter Quince:* Come, sit downe every mother sonne, and rehearse your parts. *Piramus,* you begin; when you have spoken your speech, enter into that Brake, and so every one according to his cue.

Judging from *Henslowe's Diary*, there couldn't have been very much time available for rehearsal. How many plays might an actor have kept in his head, ready to perform? Some modern actors claim they have acted three or four plays in repertory. But fifteen to twenty five-act plays? There are teachers and directors who believe that Shakespeare's company didn't rehearse at all. Rather, they used their cue script rolls onstage with the writing on the outside of the scroll. Many companies have staged entire plays this way. The improvisational results of these performances delight audiences. But in speaking to professionals who acted from cue scripts in the 1950s out of necessity, they hated them. "They were just for learning lines," says the director Stuart Vaughan.[13] "You couldn't really listen to the other actor because you were too busy listening for your cue. It didn't allow for the same in-depth exploration of a character one has the opportunity to do, and must do today."

Also, when Shakespeare's company worked

with a minimum of rehearsal, they were thoroughly adept at using rhetorical figures and gestures to play their parts. They were the best actors in London. Many actors today study an acting technique arising from a particular school of thought, or philosophy. While the philosophy or technique is sound, the student may develop less than adequate facility using it. That Shakespeare's plays have been tempered with time indicates that time temperance is a vital element in modern production, lest we take a purist approach and succeed only in dusting off technically correct museum pieces with little or no relevance to contemporary life.

That was then, this is how

We can discuss acting Folio text from two different technical perspectives, external and internal, and the necessary balance of both in the final performance.

Many British actors think the American Method is too self-indulgent, "emotive," and internal. Many American actors feel that the British approach is too broad, stagey, and external. There is obviously eminently good acting on both sides of the pond. What seems needed is a weaving together of the best of both schools to create a stronger fabric than either does by itself. Fiery actors (from any continent) who, like powerful locomotives, belch smoke, pushing ahead, unsupported by the railroad track structure of a verse technique, inhibit the audiences' comprehension just as much as the actors who speak Shakespeare's verse with technical perfection, but without fire. However, if we combine the best of internal and external techniques they will complete each other, transporting us great distances in record time.

"as you are well exprest By all externall warrants"

(*Measure for Measure*, II, iv)

Before an actor even reads his role, he can draw some conclusions by just looking at the "shape" of the text. Some blocks of text will have the first words in each line capitalized with the right-hand margins ragged, or unjustified—this is verse. Others will have their sentences arranged in the same manner as the text you are reading now, with even margins left and right, justified—this is prose.

By seeing the verse or prose as theatrical direction, an actor can draw certain conclusions about playing the text. If the text is written in prose, the actor has latitude. He can be free to experiment with alliteration, assonance, double entendre, sexual innuendo, and puns (see Glossary), but he need not be bound by them. Nor must he be concerned with matters of prosody.

Verse, being a heightened form of language, could suggest that the character is in a heightened state of emotion. Or perhaps he may be consciously deciding to speak in heightened language for rhetorical reasons. This, however, is true of prose as well. The main theatrical reason Shakespeare directs his characters to speak in verse, as we will see below, is for precision. In speaking prose the actor can stress syllables and inflect as he chooses. Verse will make the actor inflect, intonate, and breathe as Shakespeare directs.

In *The Tragedie of Julius Cæsar* (III, ii), Brutus speaks to the crowd in prose until the point when Antony carries Caesar's body onstage. He then shifts to verse for just seven of forty-one lines before he exits. Antony then addresses the crowd in verse with the famous "Friends, Romans, Countrymen" speech. Listen to the effect:

> *Brutus.* Be patient till the last [6 beats]. Romans [2 beats], Countrey-men [3 beats], and Lovers [3 beats], heare me for my cause [5 beats], and be silent [4 beats], that you may heare [4 beats].

Even though beats are not used in prose, look at the tempo, or rather the lack of one. Tap out his first two lines and listen to it: 6, 2, 3, 3, 5, 4, 4.

Contrast that with Antony speaking his first line in verse and hear what happens:

> *Antony.* Friends [1], Romans [2], Countrymen
> [3], lend me your ears [4]:

It is an arithmetic progression. Shakespeare writes direction for Antony to build, in tempo, on his first line. It has an immediate effect on the crowd.

Again, Brutus addresses the crowd in matter-of-fact prose, appealing to their sensibility and wisdom: "Censure me in your Wisdom, and awake your Senses, that you may the better Judge."

Antony counters in verse with:

You all did love him once, not without cause,
What cause with-holds you then, to mourne for
him?
O Judgement! thou are fled to brutish Beasts,
And Men have lost their Reason. Beare with me,
My heart is in the Coffin there with Cæsar,
And I must pawse, till it come backe to me.

When one reads this speech as prose, Shakespeare's stresses and pauses are missed. The meter, the tool he uses for precise direction, is absent:

You all did love him once, not without cause, what cause with-holds you then, to mourne for him? O Judgement! thou are fled to brutish beasts, and men have lost their reason. Beare with me, my heart is in the coffin there with Cæsar, and I must pawse, till it come backe to me.

There is an incongruity between words and behavior. We may believe the actor's behavior but we become confused because the behavior no longer supports the text. The actor may be suiting the text to himself rather than suiting himself to the text.

For many actors, verse is easier to memorize. When one speaks a line of poetry, there is a cadence and usually a natural stress on the last word in a line, regardless of whether it is the last word in a sentence or thought.

To mee Shee speakes, shee moves me for her
theame;
What, was I married to her in my dreame?
Or sleepe I now, and thinke I heare all this?
What error drives our eies and eares amisse?
The Comedie of Errors (II, ii), Antipholus

Notice the small emphasis, or "choice," given to the last syllable in each line. Shakespeare carefully chose the words he put at the end of a line to indicate further meaning, emotion, and/or character. In many instances, the last word in a line of verse falls in the middle of a sentence, or of a thought. In *The Taming of the Shrew* (III, ii), Petruchio says:

That have beheld me give away my selfe
To this most patient, sweet, and vertuous wife,

It is not necessary to emphasize the last word in a line in order to "choose" it. For instance, simply take a breath after "my selfe" and continue to speak the thought, "To this most," or say the word "selfe" louder, or softer, in order to choose it. Not only does this preserve the integrity of the verse, but it shows how Shakespeare "directed" it.

The line is also rhythmical. Shakespeare most often wrote in rhythm called iambic pentameter, or five iambs per line. An iamb, or iambus, is an unstressed syllable followed by a stressed syllable, "De-DUM." Words such as *begin*, *result*, *today*, and *complete* are iambic. If Shakespeare wanted to convey a vastly different character he could do it by changing the poetical rhythm, as he did in order to create the feeling of the witches in *Macbeth* (IV, i):

Double, double, toile and trouble;
Fire burne, and Cauldron bubble.

Here the verse is scanned in trochees, or one stressed syllable followed by an unstressed one: "DUM-de." There are only four to the line, creating a line of verse called trochaic tetrameter. Regardless of whether the actor understands scansion, defined as "the analysis of verse to show its meter,"[14] he can be aware of the rhythm. If the character is speaking verse and the actor tries to smooth it out by playing it as if he were speaking colloquially, a certain incongruity in speech and action results. We may believe the actor's behavior but we doubt or misunderstand the words that accompany that behavior.

The Elements of Shakespearean Style

Another point for actors to consider is the difference between a simple, or straightforward line, and a line that is complex. In this context, complex means both intellectually and linguistically complicated. If it is written simply, the actor can say it simply. If it is complex, the actor needs to make theatrical choices to use the verbal involutions. Some actors respond to this advice by saying, "It's already written, I'll simply say what's there." However, actors often speak verse written in rhyming couplets without being aware that the character is choosing to rhyme. They read what is there, but they may appear not to know what they're talking about.

These verbal involutions, or, as they are sometimes termed, "verbal conceits," can be in the form of a metaphor, simile, double entendre, sexual innuendo, alliteration, assonance, and puns or plays on words as in prose. When Macbeth speaks to Lady Macbeth (II, ii) his words are simple:

> *Macbeth:*
> Ile goe no more:
> I am afraid to thinke what I have done:
> Look on't againe, I dare not.

When Lady Macbeth responds she begins simply and then gets complicated:

> *Lady Macbeth*:
> Infirme of purpose:
> Give me the daggers: the sleeping, and the dead,
> Are but as Pictures: 'tis the Eye of Child-hood,
> That feares a painted Devill. If he doe bleed,
> Ile guild the Faces of the Groomes withall,
> For it must seeme their Guilt.

"Give me the daggers" is as simple as it gets. But the next thought or sentence is a simile. Then comes "If he doe bleed," with the *ee* sound in "bleed" assonating with the *ee* in "he." The word "bleed" gets an extra "choice." "Choice" in this instance does not only mean emphasis, or stressing the word or syllable, although that is certainly one way of choosing the complicating element in the line. Another choice might be to say the word more softly, or to put a pause before or after it. The main point is that the actor does not ignore it, but does something theatrical with it to make a point. Now comes,

> Ile *g*uild the Faces of the *G*roomes withall,
> For it must seeme their *G*uilt.

First there are three different "G" sounds alliterating with one another, *guild*, *Groomes*, and *Guilt*, the last two being capitalized. There is a play on words with *guild* and *Guilt.* If the actor simply chooses, or builds on the "G" sounds, the audience will get the pun.

When a speech ends in a rhyming couplet the actor should choose the rhyme. That is, the actor should find a real reason to use rhyme in order to accomplish his objective. In *The Merchant of Venice* (II, vi), Gratiano says:

> I am glad on't, I desire no more delight
> Then to be under saile, and gone to night.

Sometimes the rhyme is really exaggerated. The note from Shakespeare would then be to exaggerate it, as in *A Midsummer Night's Dream* (III, ii) at the culmination of the scene between the four lovers. Helena and Hermia say:

> *Her.* You Mistris, all this coyle is long of you.
> Nay, goe not backe.
> *Hel.* I will not trust you I,
> Nor longer stay in your curst companie.
> your hands then mine, are quicker for a fray,
> My legs are longer though to runne away.
> *Her.* I am amaz'd, and know not what to say.
> *Exit.*

Helena's last two lines, if delivered by the actor as the exaggerated rhyming couplet it is, provides a comic moment. Now the audience has the opportunity to laugh or groan. Hermia's last line is printed here as it appeared in Q1 of 1600. It was not, for whatever reason, reproduced in the Folio. Yet it is another way to theatricalize the story.

Suppose, for instance, you notice alliteration (<u>s</u>everal, <u>s</u>ame-<u>s</u>ounding con<u>s</u>onant<u>s</u>) in your first section of verse. You notice a number of words beginning with the letter "S." Choose to do something theatrical with the "S" sound when you say the words. First, simply sibilate the S's. Listen. A feeling, an attitude, may be stirred within you just from keying in on the intentional repetition of the sound. Shakespeare has asked his character to repeat the sounds. Discover what happens when you ask the same of your character. Find your own theatrical reason for choosing that sound. Perhaps you are expressing frustration, sarcasm, or disdain as

Lady Anne does in *Richard the Third* (I, ii) when she says:

> Wife to thy *Edward,* to thy slaughtered Sonne,
> Stab'd by the selfesame hand that made these
> wounds.
> Loe, in these windowes that let forth thy life, . . .

In *The Tragedie of Julius Cæsar* (II, i), look at the conspiracy scene where Caesar's assassination is planned. Here are sections of verse with a preponderance of S's. For instance, Cassius greets and introduces the conspirators to Brutus and says:

> *Cassius:* This, *Decius Brutus.*
> *Brutus:* He is welcome too.
> *Cassius:* This, *Caska;* this, *Cinna*; and this, *Metellus Cymber,* . . .

Count the number of "s" sounds (including the letter "c" when it is to be pronounced as an "s"); eleven S's alliterate in just three short lines of verse. Now say Cassius's lines aloud. Choose the "s" sound. Not the letter, the sound. See what happens. Again, if you don't notice it yet, give yourself a good acting reason, a *justification* if you will, to point up the "s" sound. Is this Shakespeare's way of creating the conspiracy aurally? Can you close your eyes and imagine a group of men whispering about murder? Which consonants do you hear most? Again in the same section we hear Caska say:

> *Caska:*
> You shall confesse, that you are both deceiv'd:
> Heere, as I point my Sword, the Sunne arises,
> Which is a great way of growing on the South,
> Weighing the youthfull Season of the yeare.

This passage has six "s" sounds, eleven if you use the "s" sounds that are properly pronounced as "z." It is not important or suggested that you count these sounds, whatever the alliterative letter might be. It is important to be aware of them, to notice them. Then again, ask your character to choose these sounds by saying them out loud. Listen to what happens. Don't think about what it means at this point. Just speak. Trust that the words will take you in the direction that Shakespeare intended.

"For it is a figure in Rhetoricke,"

(*As You Like It,* V, i)

A "rhetorical question," I was told, is a question for which no answer is required. Today the word *rhetoric* is often used as a pejorative during political debates to minimize or dismiss. Rhetoric is a set of verbal devices and relationships used in the art and study of writing and oration. It is the arrangement of words and sentence structure for use in persuasion and dissuasion. Two thousand years ago Cicero wrote a handbook about it for Roman lawyers. No doubt he based much of it on the rhetorical principles practiced by the ancient Greeks.

It is easy to view the study of rhetoric as some effete, archaic, way of learning language. Of what real use is it today? What makes us try a new brand of an old product? What makes us regularly visit franchised restaurants to eat food that we know is not like the picture representing it? What separates us daily from our hard-earned money? One answer is Madison Avenue with its idea people, think tanks, image-makers and wordsmiths. They use words and pictures to persuade and dissuade. They tell us things in a way that make us believe and buy. Rhetoric is alive and well in newspapers, magazines, television, and radio, on the road, in mass transit, even in the sky. There are ways of using words that can help people with myriad frames of reference understand complex concepts. There are figures of speech that can move us to action. The advertising industry knows this, politicians and their speech writers know this, the clergy knows this, and so too did Shakespeare.

Shakespeare did not attend the university. His education by most accounts would have included Latin, some Greek, and Rhetoric. Elizabethan audiences appreciated rhetoric, listened for it, and there is ample evidence in the texts that Shakespeare was a master at writing it. Dr. Johnson defines "rhetorick" as, "The art of speaking not merely with propriety, but with art and elegance. *Dryden.* The power of persuasion; oratory. *Shakespeare.*" It was necessary to a proper education to learn how to structure an argument with logic, passion, and entertainment, balancing word with gesture to make vital points. If an Elizabethan was granted an audience with the Queen to plead for the monopoly on wine he had to present a strong case. He did it with words, or rhetorical "figures" and gesture arranged in the form of rhetoric.

Figures of Speech

If Shakespeare is creating a character who pursues objectives using rhetoric, then the actor who spots and uses the rhetorical figures is not only using the given circumstances of the play, but following Shakespeare's original direction as well.

The rhetorical figures most familiar to us are, alliteration, assonance, antithesis, metaphor, simile, oxymoron, irony or double entendre, and hyperbole. Not so common, but equally useful for an actor to recognize, are figures like: asyndeton, polysyndeton, anaphora, epistrophe or antistrophe, epanalepsis, hypophora, paronomasia, and zeugma. The names may be more unsettling than the actual figures they represent. Paronomasia, for example, is a pun.

These "rhetorical figures" illustrate that rhetoric is the performance. But for rhetoric to be effective, passion must inform content or we will end up with a dry, technical exercise that neither entertains, persuades, nor interests anyone.

Punctuating Rhythm

Like road signs on a journey, punctuation marks guide us in speaking Shakespeare's prose and verse. A period marks the end of a sentence containing at least one complete thought. It is the same with a question mark and an exclamation point. All an actor needs to do is heed them. Almost. When there is a period, inflect the voice down or drop the voice to let the listener know that you have finished your thought. If it's a question mark be sure to intone the asking of a question.

"Oh what a Rogue and Pesant slave am I?" is a question that many Hamlets never ask. One reason they don't is because the edited editions usually punctuate the line with an exclamation point. Consider the difference in meaning and communication to the audience. The actor playing Hamlet knows that the audience has just witnessed his set up of Claudius using the Player to act "some dosen or sixteen lines, which I would set downe, and insert in't? Could ye not?" Hamlet has to get the audience to conspire with him. If they should judge him, characterize him as a rogue, peasant, or slave, he cannot effectively execute his plans. When he is alone he says to them:

> Oh, what a Rogue and Pesant slave am I?
> Is it not monstrous that this Player heere,
> But in a Fixion, in a dreame of Passion, . . .

Elizabethans had a general mistrust of actors, who were seen as vagabonds roving from town to town, dressing in clothes above their station and pretending to be women and Kings. Hamlet is asking a rhetorical question. The question mark is not a point of grammar, it is a theatrical direction from Shakespeare the director, to the actor. It tells him that the whole first unit of thought is a question that doesn't stop the thought, but carries it through to the next line.

It happens again in Act I, i of *Love's Labour's Lost.* Berowne says:

> Why! all delights are vain, but that most vain
> Which, with pain purchas'd, doth inherit pain:
> As, painfully to pore upon a book
> To seek the light of truth, while truth the while
> Doth falsely blind the eyesight of his look.

Another edition punctuates the first line this way:

> Why, all delights are vain; but that most vain
> Which, with pain purchas'd, doth inherit pain:

The Folio prints it like this:

> Why? all delights are vain, but that most vain
> Which, with paine purchas'd, doth inherit pain,

Editors have agreed that in the first lines of these monologues the characters are either making declarative or exclamatory statements. The Folio says they are asking a question, rhetorical or otherwise. Which is right? The answer is: play them both aloud. Listen to them both. Which of these choices makes the best theatre, informing story, character and communication between actor and audience? The question mark works well if you use it as a direction rather than solely as grammatical punctuation.

An exclamation point carries more emotional weight than a period. Interestingly enough, the Folio does use exclamation points. But, there are few. Editors frequently add more than ten times the number of exclamation points than occur in the Folio. Give an actor an exclamation point and you have given a theatrical direction.

Watching a rehearsal for an outdoor production of *Julius Cæsar* illustrates the exclamation point. In Act I, scene ii, we meet Caesar for the first time. The scene begins:

Enter Cæsar, Antony for the Course, Calphurnia, Portia, Decius, Cicero, Brutus, Cassius, Caska, a Soothsayer; after them Murellus and Flavius.
Cæs. Calphurnia.
Cask. Peace ho, *Cæsar* speaks.
Cæs. Calphurnia.
Calp. Heere my Lord.
Cæs. Stand you directly in *Antonio's* way,
When he doth run his course. *Antonio.*
Ant. Cæsar, my Lord.
Cæs. Forget not in your speed *Antonio,*
To touch *Calphurnia*: for our Elders say,
The Barren touched in this holy chace,
Shake off their sterrile curse.
Ant. I shall remember,
When *Cæsar* sayes, Do this: it is perform'd.
Cæs. Set on, and leave no Ceremony out.

So we have our first view of Caesar in a triumphant, ceremonial procession. The actor playing Caesar calls out, "*Calphurnia*!" Caska responds, "Peace, ho! *Cæsar* speaks." Again Caesar calls, "*Calphurnia*!" Finally she responds and Caesar calls for Antony. In one edited edition Caesar speaks to Calphurnia and Antony and it is printed this way:

Cæs. Stand you directly in Antonius' way
When he doth run the course. *Antonius.*

When the actors played the scene it looked ordinary. The director seemed concerned, as if he thought something was missing. After consulting several editions he looked at the Folio version.

"When you call for Calphurnia, why do you shout?" he asked the actor playing Caesar.

"It's a large crowd," he answered. "How is anyone to hear me?" This struck the actor as a ridiculous question. The director had noticed the lack of an exclamation point in the Folio text and requested the actor to simply say the line. Caesar said, in a quieter voice, almost overdoing it to make a point to the director, "Calphurnia." Caska said, also in a quiet voice, "Peace ho, Caesar speaks." The director informed the actor playing Caska that "Peace ho" was a command and required volume regardless of punctuation. In the performance the scene played like this:

Cæs. Calphurnia.
[spoken in normal volume]
Cask. Peace ho, *Cæsar* speaks.
[a loud order]
[Cæsar instinctively fires a look at Caska as if to say "quiet you" and repeats, as if to illustrate that he wants all of this private]
Cæs. Calphurnia.
Calp. Heere my Lord.
[quietly, as well]
Cæs. Stand you directly in *Antonio's* way,
[It is easier for him to say "Antonio's" than "Antonius's"]
When he doth run his course. *Antonio.*
Ant. Cæsar, my Lord.
Cæs. Forget not in your speed *Antonio,*
[He said this quietly, earnestly]
To touch *Calphurnia*: for our Elders say,
The Barren touched in this holy chace,
Shake off their sterrile curse.
Ant. I shall remember,
When *Cæsar* sayes, Do this: it is perform'd.
Cæs. Set on, and leave no Ceremony out.
[Now that he has finished his private conversation he commands loudly, "Set on"]

What we in the audience saw was the Emperor of Rome, not as a victorious hero, but as a man who could not have children. We meet him stepping away from the public to remedy an apparent fertility problem. This was private business not for public ears. We leaned forward in our seats paying close attention although we could hear every word plainly. It had a profound effect on how we witnessed Caesar's assassination in Act III.

Within a sentence there is often more than

one clause. They are graphically separated by commas, colons, and semicolons. If we view seventeenth-century punctuation with a twentieth-century understanding of grammar and usage we may be tempted to change the original punctuation, or what many believe to be mostly original punctuation. The Elizabethan rules of punctuation were different from ours. Spelling then was a matter of sounds and taste; it is most likely that punctuation followed the same standard. How does a modern actor deal with punctuation that is used differently from ours; one that arose from text that was intended to be heard, not seen? Heminge and Condell punctuated the plays in print to correspond to what they knew they sounded like in performance. Folio punctuation marks can now be thought of as instructions to actors as to how to say the lines and play the lines.

A comma is simply a pause. It is now and it was then. To signify a pause, we usually instinctively inflect upwards, lifting the voice in pitch, as a way of signaling to the listener that we are going to say more. Or, that we haven't finished our thought.

> *John.* I thanke you, I am not of many words,
> but I thanke you.

In this small example from Act I, i of *Much Ado*, the first comma might actually make the actor inflect downwards in pitch, dropping his voice, but he must do it in a manner that tells the listener that more is coming. In fact, some edited editions have replaced the first comma with a period, making it two thoughts. Interestingly enough, if this were being performed in 1600, the actors would be working from part script rolls with only their parts and three or so words of the cue. That would mean that Leonato might easily interrupt John the bastard, after the first "I thanke you" with:

> *Leonato.* Please it your grace leade on?

John, knowing he will say this twice, will have a chance to override Leonato in order to finish his line thereby giving Leonato his cue a second time. It is a subtle but interesting dynamic between the Governor of Messina and the bastard brother of the Prince of Arragon.

There are many semicolons in Shakespeare. The mark itself is a period resting atop a comma. Visually and theatrically the actor might drop his voice, but in a way that says "I have more to say." More simply put, he may take a longer pause than he might for a comma. Often the pause is longer for some stage business, as in Act III, scene i of *Julius Cæsar*, when Antony shakes the bloody hand of each conspirator:

> *Antony.* First *Marcus Brutus* will I shake with you ;
> Next *Caius Cassius* do I take your hand ;
> Now *Decius Brutus* yours ; now yours *Metellus ;*
> Yours *Cinna* ; and my valiant *Caska* yours ;

Colons afford even more opportunity for the actor. A colon, as printed in the Folio, has spaces on both sides. We are accustomed to seeing colons printed: this way. In the folio they are most always printed : like this. The compositor actually had to set a lead blank space before and after the colon. There is a graphic long pause. The actor can do more than just pause a bit longer than he would for either a comma or a semicolon. He can theatrically "shift gears." He is moving in the same direction pursuing his objectives, but because the terrain is changing, he performs a gear shift, adjusting his tempo, his volume, or perhaps his pitch. He can play "ante" colon faster or louder and the "post" colon slower or softer. Or, he can reverse those choices. The actor will make his own choices, but he is given the opportunity to build rhetorical levels or emotional color into his speeches by playing a gear change before and after the colons. In Act III, scene i of *Hamlet*, Hamlet says good-bye to Rosincrance and Guildenstern, then talks directly to the audience.

> *Hamlet.* I so, God buy'ye : Now I am alone.

The dialogue before the colon might be loud and, after the colon, softer for the audience (who would hear everything easily given the excellent acoustics in the Globe). Or, the first part might be said faster and the second part said slower. The gear change is up to the actor. The note is to play each side of the colon differently.

Sometimes actors are given a road map of punctuation. Look at this speech of Biondello's in III, ii of *The Taming of the Shrew*.

Biondello. Why *Petruchio* is comming, in a new hat and an old jerkin, a paire of olde breeches thrice turn'd ; a paire of bootes that have beene candle-cases, one buckled, another lac'd : an olde rusty sword tane out of the Towne Armory, with a broken hilt, and chapelesse : with two broken points : his horse hip'd with an olde mothy saddle, and stirrops of no kindred : besides possest with the glanders, and like to mose in the chine, troubled with the Lampasse, infected with the fashions, full of Windegalls, sped with Spavins, raid with the Yellowes, past cure of the fives, starke spoyl'd with the Staggers, begnawne with the Bots, Waid in the backe, and shoulder-shotten, neere leg'd before, and with a half-chekt Bitte & a headstall of sheepes leather, which being restrain'd to keepe him from stumbling, hath been often burst, and now reparied with knots : one girth sixe times peec'd, and a womans Crupper of velure, which hath two letters for her name, fairely set lo down in studs, and heere and there peec'd with packthred.

The speech as printed in the Folio is nineteen lines. It is basically all one sentence, all one thought, and a hilarious one: if the actor plays the punctuation.

Lineation Delineated

Lineation, or line division, in the Folio is also a clue to playing Shakespeare. Once again, editors have changed the line divisions in the Folio, "regularizing" the verse, making it conform to proper poetical structure as in the plays of Ben Jonson, Christopher Marlowe, etc.

In Act I, scene i of *Hamlet,* every edition I have seen prints it this way:

Barnardo : Last night of all,
When yond same star that's westward from the pole
Had made his course t' illume that part of heaven
Where it now burns, Marcellus and myself,
The bell then beating one—
Enter the Ghost.
Marcellus. Peace, break thee off! Look where it comes again!
Bar. In the same figure like the King that's dead.

The Folio directs the ghost to enter later and divides Marcellus's lines like this:

The Bell then beating one.
Mar. Peace, break thee of : *Enter the Ghost.*
Looke where it comes again.
Bar. In the same figure, like the King that's dead.

The question becomes, does the ghost enter before or after Marcellus's line, "Peace, break thee off: "? If you believe, as the editors do, that "Peace, break thee off: " is a response to seeing the ghost, then it makes sense to divide the lines and assign the ghost's entrance as all editions do, after Marcellus's line. Richard Flatter, however, in his book, *Shakespeare's Producing Hand*, W.W. Norton, 1948 (p. 88), makes the case that because this scene was staged in daylight, at one or two o'clock in the afternoon, Shakespeare must first create a verbal night. Shakespeare does this with various references: "Tis now strook twelve, get thee to bed Francisco," "Give you goodnight," "the minutes of this night," etc. Then Barnardo, Marcellus, and Horatio, sitting on the floor ("Sit downe a while," "Well, sit we downe"), become aware of the ghost because, it being daylight, he would cast a shadow. Marcellus sees the shadow of the ghost and says, "Peace, break thee off." The ghost enters and he then says, "Looke where it comes again." A wonderful device it would be too. To respond to a ghostly shadow after a verbal invocation of the night. But suppose it was overcast? Would Shakespeare have written *Hamlet* to be played solely on sunny days? Also, there is now photographic evidence that the *heavens* above the Globe's stage cast a shadow that covered all of the stage and most of the yard from one to two p.m., and after two, nearly all of the Globe was covered in shadow.[15] No, what happens here is set up subtly by Francisco when he says,

Fran. I thinke I heare them. Stand : who's there?

It is quiet, it is night; we are being conditioned to listen. The Ghost, whom many believe was played by Shakespeare himself, was costumed in full armor, carrying a truncheon, "beaver" (face protector) up. Whether the ghost entered through the stage trap or the tiring house door, as Flatter suggests, they would have had to hear him before they saw him. Shakespeare would have to incorporate the sound first as the ghost's precursor. The sound of clanging armor, echoing the unknown, cues the line, "Peace, breake thee of" (the Folio says "of" which seems like a mistake, but an actor could play the fear and make a dramatic case for not finishing the word "off," or it might be an incomplete sentence). What wonderful opportunities Shakespeare gives his actors! To create cold and darkness in the middle of the afternoon. Listening to the sounds that portend all our real ghosts come to haunt. And finally to be witness to the horrific sight of a dead King—their dead King—in full battle array. For an Elizabethan, open to the supernatural, living under a powerful monarch, a not infrequent victim of crime (Globe audiences would be familiar with reports of bands of marauders who regularly came down from the North to rape, murder, and pillage in the English countryside, and some of them might even be among the victims), *Hamlet*'s first scene was likely more deeply frightening than we may today easily replicate, even in a contemporary setting.

Another example of variant line divisions and stage instructions occurs in *Macbeth*, II, ii. The editors divide the lines like this:

> *Lady M.* That which hath made them drunk hath made me bold ;
> What hath quench'd them hath given me fire.
> Hark!
> Peace!
> It was the owl that shriek'd, the fatal bellman,
> Which gives the stern'st good-night. He is about it :
> The doors are open ; and the surfeited grooms
> Do mock their charge with snores. I have drugged their possets,
> That death and nature do contend about them,
> Whether they live or die.
> *Macb.* [*Within*] Who's there? What ho?
> *Lady M.* Alack, I am afraid they have awak'd.
> And 'tis not done ; th' attempt, and not the deed,
> Confounds us. Hark! I laid their daggers ready,
> He could not miss 'em. Had he not resembled
> My father as he slept, I had done't.
> *Enter* MACBETH.
> My husband!
> *Macb.* I have done the deed. Didst thou not hear a noise?
> *Lady M.* I heard the owl scream and the crickets cry.
> Did not you speak?
> *Macb.* When?
> *Lady M.* Now.
> *Macb.* As I descended?
> *Lady M.* Ay.
> *Macb.* Hark! Who lies i' th' second chamber?
> *Lady M.* Donalbain.
> *Macb.* This is a sorry sight
> [*Looking at his hands.*]
> *Lady M.* A foolish thought, to say a sorry sight.

Note that the words "Hark, Peace" have been tacked on to the end of Lady Macbeth's second line. This might reduce its effectiveness if it weren't for the added exclamation points which signal the actor to raise her voice. Then the editors direct Macbeth to say his lines from offstage, from "within." Then, in the middle of an extremely important line, the editors have Macbeth enter.

> My father as he slept, I had done't.
> *Enter* MACBETH.
> My husband!

Now the actor playing Macbeth must take two different thoughts and cram them together in one line with absolutely no pause between them.

> *Macb.* I have done the deed. Didst thou not hear a noise?

When Macbeth proclaims this a "sorry sight" we are informed that Macbeth looks at his hands. Is that the only meaning of the line? Could a great leader and his wife quaking in the dark in their own castle also be considered a sorry sight? Might not the whole situation be considered a sorry sight? By playing only one interpretation we lose theatrical ambiguity and we miss rhetorical irony.

Here is how the scene is reproduced in the Folio:

> *Enter* LADY.
> La. That which hath made the[m] drunk, hath made me bold :

What hath quench'd them hath given me fire.
Hearke, peace : It was the Owl that shriek'd,
The fatall Bell-man, which gives the stern'st good-night.
He is about it, the Doores are open :
And the surfeted Groomes doe mock their charge
With snores. I have drugg'd their Possets,
That Death and Nature doe contend about them,
Whether they live, or dye.

Enter MACBETH.

Macb. Who's there? what hoa?
Lady. Alack, I am afraid they have awak'd,
And 'tis not done : th' attempt, and not the deed,
Confounds vs : hearke : I lay'd their Daggers ready,
He could not misse 'em. Had he not resembled
My Father as he slept, I had don't.
My husband?
Macb. I have done the deed :
Didst thou not heare a noyse?
Lady. I heard the Owle schreame, and the Crickets cry.
Did not you speake?
Macb. When?
Lady. Now.
Macb. As I descended?
Lady. I.
Macb. Hearke, who lyes i'th'second Chamber?
Lady. Donalbaine.
Macb. This is a sorry sight
Lady. A foolish thought, to say a sorry sight.

The differences in this text represent opportunities for actors and directors. Lady Macbeth creates the given circumstance. Once again it is night. She is so terrified she says she has taken a drink. She tells us the effects of the drink in contrast to its effects on "them." If the actor plays "bold" and "fiery" we will have theatrical redundancy. The Lady must talk herself (and us) into courage. Shakespeare gives us no sound cue for an owl as he does with the bell at the end of the previous scene. But she hears the "Owle schreame"; not just an owl, but an Elizabethan icon for death. The next line begins with, "The fatall Bell-man, which gives the stern'st good-night," referring to the midnight bell tolling the completion of the executioner's task. Even if the audience is unaware of the owl/bellman symbolism, the actor in creating these circumstances will respond accordingly. This method of "delegated effect," as Flatter identifies it, creates the stimulus for us by showing the response in the actor.[16]

I won't take the time to point out the significance of every variation in line division here. But there are some that stand out. The Folio has Macbeth entering right after the Lady's first speech. He doesn't have to say his line from within, as presumed by the editors, because they can't see each other. It is dark. Macbeth can enter and not see who it is. In 1606 Richard Burbage might have come downstage to hide behind one of the two stage posts, being clearly visible to the audience but not to Lady Macbeth, yet.[17]

Editors frequently take two half lines and move the second half line to the top, joining it to the first, making a whole line. In the example above Macbeth says:

I have done the deed :
Didst thou not heare a noyse?

The Folio divides the lines into two, ending the first line with a colon which gives the actor a chance to pause for some stage business; to look around, to listen, prolonging a very suspenseful moment.

The edited versions move the second half line up to make one whole line. This becomes a different note to an actor, he can't pause if he is to maintain the integrity of the line of verse. We lose the pause, we lose the suspense.

"and make but an Interiour survey of your good selves"

(*Coriolanus*, II, i)

Again, there is no one way to act. Each actor will bring his or her own uniqueness to Shakespeare's characters if we are to preserve an essential and creative Shakespearean theatre.

The teaching of acting techniques has evolved considerably over the last four centuries. But an actor uses and represents human nature, and human nature has basically remained the same. Human beings are insatiable animals driven by whatever needs, desires, beliefs, and goals shape their individualities. And this is certainly no less true in the theatre. For instance, there will always be actors who approach characters from a personal intellectual view of reality. They will *decide* what they *think* will work theatrically. Unfortunately, they will often do this regardless of what is actually taking place on the stage. In doing this, they violate the theatrical metaphor of truth that is their contract with the audience.

Other actors have a different way of applying their skills and talents to the character. These actors use intuition and instinct to make their characters and the circumstances of the play believable to themselves and their audience. When these actors believe their surroundings, when they believe they are kings, working class, ladies, gentlemen, maidens, etc., they pursue their characters' goals as if they were their own. Constantin Stanislavski referred to the actual *doings* of these characters as his "method of physical actions."

"For they are actions that a man might play"

(*Hamlet*, I, ii)

Good acting is about creating truthful behavior. Whether it is Sophocles, Shakespeare, Williams, or Mamet, audiences need to believe the actors' behavior, on some level, in order to suspend disbelief long enough to enter into the events of the play.

Some actors don't see a difference between what is natural, what is real, and what is truthful. Many try to make Shakespeare's verse believable by trying to make it sound "natural." Their idea of "natural" is usually based on their contemporary frames of reference. The choices they employ to create various characters may reflect their own geographical origins, thinking, class, or education.

Then there is the "if it's real, it has to be truthful" school of acting. If Kate actually slaps Bianca as hard as she can from real anger, the audience will forget the play momentarily, and concern themselves with the well-being of the actor playing Bianca. That kind of "reality" is the quickest way to kill truth. On the other hand, if Kate uses a stage slap, she is conveying the character's truth without being "real." The audience can stay involved with the play.

What is real onstage is the reality of doing. The actor chooses the best things to do to the characters he is interacting with in order to pursue his character's objectives. If the actor is onstage alone about to deliver a soliloquy, then he works out who his audience is to him, and what he is doing to them.

Figuring out what the character is doing, however, is not always as simple as it seems. Is the actor portraying a drunk by trying to appear drunk, or is he doing what the drunk might actually be doing—trying to maintain his balance in order to appear sober? Is the actor who is playing a woman at a funeral going to make herself cry because that is what her character is doing? Or will she recognize that the character might be trying to distance herself from the pain of grief and, because she is unable to, she cries? When the actor creates the circumstances so that she truly responds to them, when she has a reason that is personal, one that makes her want to fight for her character's objectives as if they were her own, truthful behavior results.

"not in Pleasure, but in Passion"

(*The First Part of King Henry the Fourth*, II, iv)

Or, "unpacke my heart with words"

(*Hamlet*, III, i)

We have often seen a good actor give a Shakespearean performance that is filled with powerful, intense behavior. The performance is a *tour de force.* We are amazed and moved by what the actor has done. But the difficulty arises when we realize that we don't understand what he has said, or what actually happened in the play. And, as in the story of the emperor's new clothes, we feel that we can't say we didn't understand it because the performance we just witnessed was dazzling. It must be that there is something wrong with us; it can't be him. But sometimes the problem does belong to the performer. The actor's passions are misplaced. He confuses his own feelings and actions with the character's. It is as though the actor is saying to himself, "Hamlet is angry. What am I like when I'm angry?" Instead, he should be asking, "What am I like if I'm Hamlet, and angry?" Shakespeare, after all, didn't write the story about the actor, he wrote it about the character.

But the problem of communicability and Shakespeare acting is not limited to misguided approaches to character. There is the very real issue of language. Classical characters think complex thoughts. They express those thoughts verbally, using articulate and complex language. Time has changed that for most of us today. Now we are encouraged to spit out and digest sound bites. All too often, we speak our minds using shorthand clichés, expressing ourselves with verbal icons instead of creative language. Many people don't know how to construct a rhetorical argument that is lucid, engaging, and thought provoking. The word "sucked" no longer only means "to draw into the mouth through a suction force," it's apt to be a monosyllabic review of the latest action movie. From the essentially oral and aural medium of the stage, we have moved to the visual world of the large and small screens to find our entertainment. Creative rhetoric is consigned to public television. Not so in Shakespeare's day.

The Elizabethan grammar school curriculum included lessons in rhetoric, speech, or "the art of pronunciation." In *Acting Shakespeare* (New York: Theatre Arts Books, 1960, p. 8), Bertram Joseph writes, "From a boy's first days at school steps were taken to start him on the systematic drill which would eventually equip him to make of himself an instrument which could embody the exact quality of the words he was speaking, as music and movement, and as meaning."

Later in this discussion I will look at some ways that modern actors can technically negotiate complex texts. For now, it will be more useful to explore the driving force that powers the technical choices an actor may make.

There are certain hallmarks to great performances that endure over time. The criteria may change in terms of acceptable performance styles but in any given production we are more likely to keep our eyes trained on one actor over the others. While Edward Alleyn's acting was noted for bombast, Richard Burbage, and most of Shakespeare's company, were noted for being "natural," whatever that may have meant then. If we could go back in time to see one of Shakespeare's plays at the Globe, what kind of acting would we see? The answer to this question has a direct bearing on how to play—and to read—Shakespeare. Was the author's intention to create a style that should be played with bombast, rhetoric, or other oratorical skills? Or did Shakespeare write to take full advantage of naturalistic acting? Contemporaneous descriptions frequently use the words "personate" and "nature" to describe an ideal performance. In 1610, an academic spectator who had seen a performance of *Othello* by the King's Men at Oxford wrote:

> not only by their speech but also by their deeds they draw tears.—But indeed Desdemona, killed by her husband, although she always acted the matter very well, in her death moved us still more greatly ; when lying in bed she implored the pity of those watching with her countenance alone.[18]

This audience member not only refers to the actor playing Desdemona as "she," but uses the word "deeds" to describe what we know today as theatrical "action." We have various letters describing what it was like to attend performances; they are divided as to positive and negative experiences. It is therefore a simple task to report on a preponderance of one editorial point of view over another. Both camps still employ the concept of "natural" as a benchmark. Behaving "naturally" was Burbage's intuitive way of achieving believability. Anyone engaged to "personate" a character would, first and foremost, want to be believed. Hamlet's advice to the players (III, ii) is usually cited as an example of what Shakespeare thought of as convincing, or "good acting":

> do not saw the Ayre too much [with] your hand thus, but use all gently ; for in the verie Torment, Tempest, and (as I may say) the Whirle-winde of Passion, you must acquire and beget a Temperance that may give it Smoothnesse. . . . Be not too tame neyther : But let your owne Discretion be your Tutor. Sute the Action to the Word, the Word to the Action, with this speciall observance : That you ore-step not the modestie of Nature ; for any thing so over-done, is fro[m] the purpose of Playing , whole and both at the first and now, was and is, to hold as 'twer the Mirrour up to Nature ; to shew Vertue her owne Feature, Scorne her owne Image, and the

verie Age and Bodie of the Time, his forme and pressure. . . .

This is what Shakespeare wanted Hamlet to express in order to "catch the Conscience of the King." The speech should be on the mirror of every actor's dressing room.

Styles change, fashions come and go. Styles and fashions in playing Shakespeare are no exception. It was not too long ago that one heard great Shakespearean acting delivered in a singsong style that was admired and praised by experts. Today, such a performance looks feigned and pretentious. Today's actors have adjusted their performance style to reflect changes in what we now think of as "natural."

How then do we ask an actor to do what the character does if what the character is doing includes speaking passionately, rhetorically, and fighting for what she truly believes she needs?

Many student actors will choose to communicate with subtext much more readily than with any set of verbal skills which would necessitate their articulating the complexities of their thinking. Indeed, they have rarely experienced the expression of their own complex thoughts and some believe that they don't even have them.

Several actors' exercises can provide an antidote to the problem. One that is extremely effective, called a "passion workout," gives the actor an opportunity to speak to a class or group about a topic that she feels passionately about. Because the actor must speak at length, and because she is personally affected by what she is saying, the actor finds that she naturally employs rhetoric in much the same way that Shakespeare's characters do.

When we are confronted with long texts filled with arcane words and usages, it becomes too easy to convince ourselves that we don't speak that way today. Yet we find that we actually do. We may not use sixteenth-century language, but we do use rhetoric and strive for articulation in order to make our points. We use rhythm, tempo, irony, and double entendre, all in an attempt to keep our listeners' attention with as many examples and ideas we feel we need before we trust that they understand us. If we are to play characters who are adept at articulating their thoughts eloquently, rhetorically, easily, then we must find ways to do that too.

"for the bawdy hand of the Dyall is now upon the pricke of Noone"

(*The Tragedie of Romeo and Juliet*, II, iv)

How to hold the attention of gallants and groundlings, Lords and Ladies, Nobles and nasties? Sexual innuendo, or bawdy bits of burlesque is one method Shakespeare used often. Innuendo is the insinuation, or hint, of a different meaning from that which may seem obvious. To play sexual innuendo the actor must acknowledge the double meaning, one of which has a bawdy connotation. There are words, metaphors, similes, and images that Elizabethans recognized as sexually charged, that now have tamer or contemporary meanings. The words "pride" and "proud," for example, can indicate the male sexual organ in its tumescent state, i.e. sonnet 151:

But rysing at thy name doth point out thee,
As his triumphant prize, proud of this pride,
He is contented thy poore drudge to be
To stand in thy affaires, fall by thy side.
  No want of conscience hold it that I call,
  Her love, for whose deare love I rise and fall.

Corresponding to *pride*, was the word *fish* as the female counterpart. According to Eric Partridge's *Shakespeare's Bawdy* (New York: Dutton, 1969, p.113), *fish* was "a girl or a woman, viewed sexually; especially a prostitute." See *Romeo and Juliet*, (I, iii):

Nurse : The fish lives in the Sea, and 'tis much pride
For faire without, the faire within to hide :

Many other words, including "will," in addition to "wish," or "desire," also meant sexual wish and sexual desire.

There are audience members, actors, directors, teachers, who cannot believe that there is bawdry in Shakespeare. "He can't have meant that!" they will say. An actor must explore every opportunity to find the "Easter eggs," the hidden treasures, that delight audiences while providing chances for actors to theatricalize even more action.

Here is the Servant in *The Winters Tale*, (IV, iv):

Ser. He hath songs for man , or woman, of all sizes : No Milliner can so fit his customers with Gloves : he has the prettiest Love-songs for Maids, so with out bawdrie (which is strange,) with such delicate burthens of Dildo's and Fadings : Jump-her, and thump-her; and where some stretch-mouth'd Rascall, would (as it were) meane mischeefe, and breake a fowle gap into the Matter, hee makes the maid to answere, whoop, doe me no harme good man : put's him off, flights him, with *whoop, doe me no harme good man.*

Polixenes. This is a brave fellow.

Frankie Rubinstein reminds us, in *A Dictionary of Shakespeare's Sexual Puns and their Significance* (New York: Macmillan Press, 1984), that there were dildos made of wax, horn, leather, or glass in use. The word *fit* was a reference to coitus; *burthen*, or *burden* was frequently used by Shakespeare to pun the weight of a man in intercourse, as in *Romeo and Juliet*, (II, v):

Nurse : I am the drudge, and toile in your delight :
But you shall beare the burthen soone at night.

There are more sexually resonant words and metaphors, to be sure. When the actor finds them through innate understanding or research, he must incorporate them into his choices. Even if the audience has lost the original references due to the passage of time, the actor should still make choices that serve the original actions.

Will's World Wide Web

We can never know what was in Heminge's and Condell's minds when they decided to create a folio of their friend's plays. We do know that it was an exhausting undertaking. Because we know that they were actors in the company, we can assume that they would oversee the printing using performance as a frame of reference. Printing was barely a century old. Spelling was not standardized. Words were commonly spelled differently within a document, and this is certainly true in the Folio. This phenomenon is happening today in cyberspace on computer BBSs and on-line chatrooms around the world. In the fervor of trying to communicate live, spelling is not only sacrificed much of the time, but misspellings can actually contribute a clearer understanding of the writer's message. One can sense the speed at which the other person is communicating and can draw inferences about them and what they are saying based on spelling and sometimes line division. For example:

poet-99: Ive heard theres a pic facsimile of Lear in a gd qarto on the web
thespiann: kewl!!! r u sure. do you no the url?
poet-99: huh?
thespiann: th websyt.
poet-99: I would be most appreciative for any and alll info.:)
Bardolator: the site you want is no longr up/system down—
poet-99: thnx
thespiann: :(

Like our language, this method of communicating is changing every day.

There are excellent study resources available on the World Wide Web. Whole plays can be downloaded. There is information on music, songs, dances of the period, and how to create an authentic Elizabethan accent. Many of the best Shakespeare, and Shakespeare-related, websites are appended to the Bibliography.

About Fixed Line Numbers

There are several systems of line numbering in use today. The most common is that used in the Globe edition of 1864.[19] There is a different system used by the Oxford Facsimile or "Lee Collotype" based on the Oxford Shakespeare of 1892. Most recently, a line numbering system was used in the Norton Facsimile developed by Charlton Hinman called TLN, or Through Line Numbering.

The page numbers of the original Folio are inconsistent and inaccurate partly because the Folio was arranged according to the sections of Comedies, Histories, and Tragedies, and each section was numbered separately. For instance, page 80 could be Act V of *Measure for Measure, The Second Part of King Henry the Fourth*, or *Timon of Athens* in addition to *Troylus and Cressida*, which except for pages 79 and 80, are unnumbered altogether.

I have prepared a new numbering system called Fixed Line Numbering, or FLN. This system will make it easier and faster to reference specific lines of text. Each Folio page is printed in two columns of 66 lines each. Each of those lines is numbered in the margins every ten lines, with the same numbers repeated on all pages. At the bottom of each page of this volume there is a facsimile page number which starts on the first page of the Folio and ends on the last page. In addition, the original Globe designators have been included for cross reference. To find a particular line one needs only the facsimile page number and the line number, i.e. 367/43. Each line will always be at the same fixed point on any given page, thereby facilitating quick reference.

"what's past is Prologue;"

(*The Tempest*, II, i)

An understanding of how and why Shakespeare wrote what he wrote may enlighten us. Esoteric facts may prove interesting bits of trivia. What do we do with this understanding of the exigencies of Elizabethan theatre? If Shakespeare's plays have endured and evolved for four hundred years, what does the millennium hold for future productions? We will continue to see and be seen in "concept Shakespeare," productions which will be staged on Western sets, space stations, or costumed in the manner of whatever political group may be active. This is all good. It evinces choice, which is the point and the process of art. Asking questions and making choices are the beginnings of process. The answers to be discerned by the audience.

In the final analysis, the First Folio is but another edited version of what most of us believe Shakespeare wrote. But this one is closest to the original. If the early editors changed the text to suit their respective audiences' understanding, then it may be necessary for us to do likewise. As changes are made from decade to decade, Shakespeare's words and ideas change from the original. Whose text will we use to make our own changes? An editor's text from 1864 with "improvements" that were relevant to his time? What happened on the boards in 1598 has set the stage for what will happen in 1998 and beyond.

The First Folio of Shakespeare's plays gives us more insight into Elizabethan production, and pronunciation. More understanding of what Shakespeare might have meant before the various editors gave us their versions. The more stimuli we receive from Shakespeare in the form of clues from the text, the more opportunities we have to express ourselves as actors communicating more fully with our audiences. We don't have Shakespeare's handwritten manuscripts, but our next best, closest record is the First Folio. By going back to the Folio we get closer than any other way possible to William Shakespeare, actor, playwright. We enjoy a direct communication with a creativity that originated in the past, perpetuating the prologue that is the challenge for the present.

January, 1998
Doug Moston

GLOSSARY

accent — How and where one chooses to stress a particular word, or syllable. In Shakespeare some words were accented differently four hundred years ago. Words like *révenue*, which we accent on the first syllable, were then accented on the second, *revénue. Míscon-strued* was also accented on the second syllable, *miscónstrued.* If we say those words the way Elizabethans were used to hearing them, modern audiences will hear the word but miss the communication.

In *Shakespeare Aloud*, E.S. Brubaker says (pp. 12–13), "accent helps the ear to identify the function and grammatical relationship of words, the key to the meaning of the sentence."

There is also a difference in the strength applied to each accented syllable. The word *réinfórcement*, for example, is accented on the first and third syllable with the third syllable having a bit more strength.

alexandrine — Six feet, or twelve beats to a line of verse. If a regular line, or a line with a masculine ending, is ten beats (when in iambic pentameter), then a six foot line (twelve beats) or alexandrine, may be a case of the character trying to fit more into the line than it can comfortably contain. There is the sense of trying to empty quickly the contents of a large bottle through a small opening. It often indicates discomfort on the part of the speaker.

In *Measure for Measure* (II, ii), Angelo informs Isabella that her brother is condemned to death.

— / — / — /
It should be thus with him:
/ — / — / —
he must die to morrow. (12 beats)

alliteration — When two or more consonant sounds repeat.

anaphora — The repetition of the same word, or words, at the beginning of successive phrases, clauses, or sentences.† See, For example, *The Comedie of Errors* (IV, ii), Antipholus of Siracusa:

Some tender monie to me, some invite me;
Some other give me thankes for kindnesses;
Some offer me Commodities to buy.

antidiplosis — A figure that repeats the last word of one phrase, clause, or sentence at or very near the beginning of the next.† In *Hamlet* (II, ii), Polonius says:

That he is mad, 'tis true: 'Tis true 'tis pittie,
And pittie it is true: A foolish figure,
But fare well it: for I will use no Art.

antimetabole — A figure that reverses the order of repeated words or phrases to intensify the final formulation, to present alternatives, or to show contrast.†

Hamlet. I do repent: but heaven hath
pleas'd it so,
To punish me with this, and this with me,
That I must be their Scourge and Minister.

In this scene from *Hamlet* (II, ii), Polonius says:

Madam I sweare I use no Art at all:
That he is mad, 'tis true: 'Tis true 'tis pittie,
And pittie it is true: A foolish figure,
But farewell it: for I will use no Art.

antithesis — A rhetorical figure contrasting two ideas, or theses, by means of parallel arrangements of words, clauses, or sentences. Opposites. "That's awfully good." In *Julius Cæsar* (II, i):

Let's kill him Boldly, but not Wrathfully:
Let's carve him, as a Dish fit for the Gods,
Not hew him as a Carkasse fit for Hounds:
And let our Hearts, as subtle Masters do,
Stirre up their Servants to an acte of
Rage, . . .

Or, in *Romeo and Juliet* (II, i), when Romeo says:

It is the East, and *Juliet* is the Sunne,
Arise faire Sun and kill the envious Moone, . . .

When these "opposites" are spotted it is a note to "play" them, setting them off "the one against the other."

assonance — When two or more vowel sounds repeat as in the First Witch's opening line of *Macbeth*: "When shall we three meet again."

asyndeton — Omitting conjunctions between words, phrases, or clauses. Often used in lists to give a feeling of being unplanned.†

Hamlet: . . . a Bawdy villaine,
Remorselesse, Treacherous, Letcherous,
Kindles villaine!

caesura — A pause within a line of verse. It has been described as occurring often between the third and fourth foot of a line of verse. Some have described it as a way to allow the audience to "catch up" to what is being said. Named after Caesar because his epilepsy paused his speech from time to time.

catachresis — An implied metaphor using words in an alien or unusual way, sometimes substituting nouns for verbs, verbs for nouns, nouns for adjectives, etc.†

Hamlet. out-*Herod's Herod.* Pray you avoid it.

elision — When a two-syllable word is meant to be pronounced as one syllable, the first syllable eliding with the second. Often these words contain the letter "v" as in "seven," "eleven," and "heaven."

end jamming — Literally jamming the end of one line into the start of the next, reading the text as sentences, turning verse into prose.

end stopping — Ending your thought by stopping (inflecting downwards) at the end of a line of verse, when the thought is meant to continue.

epanalepsis — A rhetorical figure that repeats the beginning word of a clause or sentence at the end.†

Richard the Third: A horse, a Horse, my
Kingdome for a Horse.

epistrophe — The repetition of the same word, or words at the end of successive phrases, clauses, or sentences. Counterpart to anaphora.†

Hamlet. Oh Villaine, Villaine, smiling damned
Villaine!
My Tables, my Tables; meet it is I set it downe,
That one may smile, and smile and be a
Villaine ;

feminine ending — A line of iambic pentameter with eleven beats. The extra beat is said to weaken the line.

Hamlet. To be, or not to be, that is the Question:
Whether 'tis Nobler in the the minde to suffer
The Slings and Arrowes of outragious
Fortune,
Or to take Armes against a Sea of troubles,
And by opposing end them: to dye, to sleepe
No more ; and by a sleepe, to say we end

Here the first five lines of Hamlet's famous speech are written with feminine endings, creating a character who may be tentative, cautious, or perhaps, confused depending on the actor's choice. Only in the sixth line do we have a contrast with a regular line of ten beats.

half line — Or an incomplete line, is often Shakespeare's way of saying "come in on cue" to the next actor who speaks. It may also indicate a pause for some stage business.

hypophora — A rhetorical figure for raising one or more questions and then proceeding to answer them, usually at some length.†

Hamlet. What's *Hecuba* to him, or he to her,
That he should weepe for her? what would he
doe
Had he the motive, and that for passion
That I have?
He would drowne the Stage with teares,
And cleave the generall eare with horrid
speech :
Make mad the guilty, and apale the free.

iambic pentameter — An iambus, or iamb, is one unstressed syllable followed by a stressed syllable, such as, *today*, *forget*, and *resolve*. The two syllables form a metric foot. Five iambic feet to a line of verse is iambic pentameter. Much of Shakespeare's verse is written in iambic pentameter as this is the closest to the natural rhythm of our English speech. See also *scansion.*

imagery — Shakespeare's use of imagery can serve as a kind of Rorschach test in revealing to the actor a clear picture of the thoughts that motivate a character's actions. When we discern the thoughts, we understand the character's objectives. Once we know the objectives, we can choose the actions that best accomplish them. In her extraordinary book, *Shakespeare's Imagery and what it tells us,* Caroline Spurgeon defines imagery as covering every kind of compressed simile and metaphor. Shakespeare's prodigious use of imagery is one of his greatest and most poetic ways of communicating analogy. See also, *metaphor* and *simile*.

incomplete line — See *half line*, above.

irony — An ambiguous word, line, or thought. Irony must be searched for in the play. When it is found the actor must find ways of expressing both meanings. If a word has more than one meaning how can the character use both meanings to convey his intentions? See also, *antithesis*, above.

irregular line — A line of iambic pentameter that deviates from a regular line of ten beats to the line. A line of verse that has eleven (feminine ending), twelve (alexandrine), or thirteen (feminine alexandrine) beats to the line.

lineage — How the lines of verse are divided. Also called line division.

masculine ending — A line of verse containing five iambic feet, or ten beats.

metaphor — A figure of speech that substitutes one idea or object with another, suggesting a similarity between them.

> *Romeo and Juliet* (II, i, 796): *Rom.* It is the East, and *Juliet* is the Sunne.

mid-line ending — When the thought ends in the middle of the line. For the actor it means that even though you have finished your thought don't pause here, but move straight ahead to the beginning of your next thought. You may take your breath, or pause at the end of the line, inflecting your voice upward or downward as appropriate.

onomatopoeia — A word that sounds like what it is. In II, i of *The Taming of the Shrew*:

> *Kate*: And yet as heavie as my waight should be.
> *Petruchio*: Shold be, should: buzze.
> *Kate*: Well tane, and like a buzzard.

oxymoron — A kind of "mini-antithesis" where a phrase is created using opposite terms in order to convey a meaning that is different from either extreme, e.g. cruel kindness. See *Romeo and Juliet* (III, ii):

> *Juliet.* Beautifull Tyrant, fiend Angelicall :
> Ravenous Dove-feather'd Reven,
> Wolvish-ravening Lambe,

parenthesis — Actors can play parenthesis (which is another rhetorical figure) as an aside. The actor must do something vocally and/or physically different in rendering the line and contrasting the parenthesis. The Folio has more phrases enclosed in parentheses than the edited editions. Note the differences in *Twelfth Night* (I, ii) as it is printed in the Riverside and the Folio:

Riverside

> *Vio.* What country, friends, is this?

First Folio

> *Vio.* What Country (friends) is this?

paronomasia — A play on words, or more simply a pun.

pause — Indicates a beat, or beats, where nothing is being spoken. This doesn't mean that nothing is happening. A pause must be a continuation of theatrical action or it will slow down the metrical tempo and skew the verse. Often a half line, or an incomplete line, is Shakespeare's way of giving the actor a pause for stage business. For example, see Act I, i of *Much Adoe About Nothing*, John and Leonato's exchange cited earlier.

polysyndeton — The use of a conjunction between each word, phrase, or clause. The opposite of asyndeton.† See *Romeo and Juliet* (II, vi):

> *Nurse.* . . . Romeo, no not he though his face be better than any mans, yet his legs excels all mens, and for a hand, and a foote, and a body though they be not to talkt on, . . .

pronunciation — The spelling in the Folio provides us with clues as to how words might have been pronounced by the Elizabethans. The Elizabethans spelled words using homophones. In *Julius Cæsar*, Antony says (III, i):

> Cry havocke, and let slip the Dogges of Warre,

The original pronunciation makes use of the rolled "r" in "warre."

regular line — A line of iambic pentameter with ten beats or five iambic feet.

rhetoric — Learning to build a speech through the emphasis of key words, and writing a speech using careful punctuation was taught and written about by John Bulwer, Thomas Wright, and others. This was not a mechanical exercise but a way of expressing passion clearly and precisely. Gesture and speech went together so that students learned early on how to "Suite the action to the word, the word to the action." See Bergram Joseph, *Acting Shakespeare.*

Also *A Handbook of Rhetorical Devices* by Robert Harris at Southern California College (Costa Mesa, 1997) and to be found on the World Wide Web at: http://www.sccu.edu/faculty/R_Harris/rhetoric.htm.

rhyme — A rhyme, or rhyming couplet is intentional. The actor must make a deliberate choice to pursue his objective by asking his character to play fully the rhyme which is present—not to ignore it.

scansion — According to *Webster's*, scansion is "the analysis of verse to show its meter."

A metric line of verse is made up of metric feet. Some different types of metric feet are:

Anapest:	—/	Two stressed syllables followed by an unstressed one.
Dactyl:	/—	One stressed syllable followed by two unstressed.
Trochee:	/-	One stressed followed by one unstressed.
Iamb:	-/	One unstressed followed by one stressed.
Spondee:	//	Two syllables stressed equally.
Amphibrach:	-/-	One stressed syllable between two unstressed syllables.

Metric feet can be grouped in specific numbers per line. E.g. Five iambs per line would be called "iambic pentameter."

O migh - ty Cæ - sar! Dost - thou lye - so lowe?

Four trochees per line would be trochaic tetrameter, etc.

Double, - double - toil and - trouble;
Fire - burn and - cauldron - bubble.

sexual innuendo — Some words, phrases, or lines, carry a sexual connotation which, if played as if it is the only meaning, reduce the passage to mere vulgarity. The actor must find a way of pursuing his objective by playing the character who is clever enough to extract both meanings from the line. Then it isn't the actor who said it "dirty," it's the listener who heard it so. Today late night television talk show hosts routinely use sexual innuendo to get by the network censors. Elizabethan playwrights had the same problems and used the same solutions.

simile — A rhetorical figure that compares an idea or object with another. See *metaphor.*

speech — American standard speech can be as vocally sound as "mid Atlantic" or modern standard British speech. Proper speech opens the throat, frees the jaw, and gives the tongue flexiblity allowing for breath support. These qualities produce clarity, and enhance audience comprehension. If you were not born in Great Britain don't feel that you must speak Shakespeare in a contemporary London accent. An American accent from Appalachia or specifically from Tangier Island in the Chesapeake Bay is much closer in sound to the Warwickshire dialect that Shakespeare and many of his actors would have spoken. Folio spelling was based on phonemes, or how the words sounded. It gives us a sense of how the words sounded: "Oh for a muse of fire," in a modern English dialect would pronounce "Oh" as a long "O" and "fire" as one syllable with just a mere hint of the "r" sound. In a Warwickshire accent, "Oh" or "O", would be pronounced as "awe." Or, it might just indicate a sound as in Hamlet's death scene:

Hamlet: The rest is silence. O,o,o,o. *Dyes.*

Fire, which was spelled "fier" was pronounced with two syllables rolling the "r"; "fier" or "fy-errh," as in, "Awe fer a myooze of fy-errh." An American accent naturally articulates the "r," preserving more of the original old Warwickshire speech.

Sometimes Shakespeare will spell words phonetically to indicate a dialect or class relationship. In *Romeo and Juliet* (I, v), Capulet and Cousin Capulet talk of when they last masqued together.

1. *Capu.* How long 'ist now since last your selfe and I
Were in a Maske?
2. *Capu.* Berlady thirty yeares.

Editors change this to, "By'r lady, thirty years," leading an actor to contract the words "by our lady." But there is a different sound to "Berlady." There are myriad "r" sounds in the rest of 2. Capulet's speech as well:

> 'Tis more, 'tis more, his Sonne is elder sir:
> His Sonne is thirty.

When the actor playing 2. Capulet rolls his r's, we hear a rural accent. If Old Capulet is from the country we know that the Capulets are nouveau riche. Now we understand Capulet's need for Juliet to marry the County Paris.

stichomythia — Rapidly alternating lines of dialogue between two actors especially in an altercation.

zeugma — A grammatically correct yoking together of two or more parts of speech by another part of speech. There are several varieties. *Hypozeugma*, which yokes adjectives, or adjective phrases. *Prozeugma*, where the yoking word precedes the words yoked. A more important version is *diazeugma* which has a single subject with multiple verbs, as in this example from *The Life of King Henry the Eight* (IV, i), when the *Third Gentleman* describes the coronation of Anne Boleyn, Henry's second wife.†

> At length, her Grace rose, and with modest paces
> Came to the Altar, where she kneel'd,and Saint-like
> Cast her faire eyes to Heaven, and pray'd devoutly.

† These definitions are from Robert Harris's *A Handbook of Rhetorical Devices* and Ross Scaife's websites. They are used with permission.

SELECTED BIBLIOGRAPHY, READING LIST, AND WEBSITES

Adams, J.C., *The Globe Playhouse: Its Design and Equipment* (Cambridge: Harvard University Press, 1942)

Baldwin, T.W., *SHAKESPERE'S Love's Labor's Won, new evidence from the account books of an Elizabethan Bookseller* (Carbondale, Illinois: Southern Illinois University Press, 1957)

Barton, John, *Playing Shakespeare* (London: Methuen, Ltd, 1984; New York: Methuen, Inc., 1984)

Berry, Cicely, *The Actor and His Text* (New York: Macmillan Publishing Company, 1987)

Blatherwick, Simon, and Andrew Gurr, with additonal comments by John Orrell, *SHAKESPEARE'S GLOBE, Evaluating the archaeological evidence from the 1989 and 1992 digs at the site of the Globe.* (London: Shakespeare Globe Museum, 1992)

Blayney, Peter W.M., *The First Folio of Shakespeare,* (Washington, D.C.: Folger Library Publications)

Brubaker, E.S., *Shakespeare Aloud* (Lancaster, Pennsylvania: Edward S. Brubaker, 1976)

Bucknell, Peter A., *Entertainment and Ritual 600 to 1600* (London: Stainer and Bell Limited, 1979)

Burgess, Anthony, *Shakespeare* (New York: Alfred A. Knopf, 1970)

Chute, Marchette, *Shakespeare of London* (New York: E.P. Dutton & Co., Inc., 1949)

Clurman, Harold, *On Directing* (New York: Macmillan Publishing Co., Inc., 1974)

Flatter, Richard, *Shakespeare's Producing Hand* (New York: W.W. Norton & Co., 1948)

Giroux, Robert, *The Book Known as Q* (New York: Atheneum, 1982)

Granville-Barker, Harley, *Prefaces to Shakespeare* (Princeton: Princeton University Press, 1952), 2 volumes.

Greg, Walter, *Henslowe's Diary* (London: A.H. Bullen, 1904), 2 volumes.

Greg, Walter, *The Shakespeare First Folio* (Oxford: Oxford University Press, 1955)

Gurr, Andrew, *The Shakespearean Stage, 1574–1642,* 2nd and 3rd editions (Cambridge: Cambridge University Press, 1980, 1992)

Gurr, Andrew, with John Orrell, *Rebuilding Shakespeare's Globe* (New York: Routledge, 1989)

Halliday, F.E., *Shakespeare: a pictorial biography* (New York: The Viking Press, 1961)

Hamilton, Charles, *In Search of Shakespeare* (New York: Harcourt Brace Jovanovich, Publishers, 1985)

Hamilton, Charles, *Shakespeare, with John Fletcher—CARDENIO or The Second Maiden's*

Tragedy (Lakewood: Glenbridge Publishing Ltd., 1994)

Harbage, Alfred, *Shakespeare's Audience* (New York: Columbia University Press, 1941)

Harbage, Alfred, *Annals of English Drama, 975–1700*, revised by S. Schoenbaum (London: Methuen & Co., Ltd, 1964)

Hinman, Charlton, *Printing and Proof-Reading of the First Folio of Shakespeare* (Oxford: Oxford University Press, 1963)

Joseph, Bertram, *Acting Shakespeare* (New York: Theatre Arts Books, 1960)

Linklater, Kristin, *Freeing the Natural Voice* (New York: Drama Book Publishers, 1976)

Macrone, Michael, *Brush Up Your Shakespeare* (New York: Harper & Row, Publishers, 1990)

Mahood, M.M., *Shakespeare's Wordplay* (London: Methuen & Co., Ltd, 1957)

Matus, Irvin Liegh, *Shakespeare, IN FACT* (New York: The Continuum Publishing Company, 1994)

McKenzie, D.F. "Printers of the Mind," *Studies in Bibliography* 22 (1969), pp. 42–49.

Meres, Francis, *Palladis Tamia: Wits Treasuray* (1598) (New York: Scholars' Facsimile & Reprints, 1938)

Moston, Doug, *Coming to Terms with Acting* (New York: Drama Book Publishers, 1993)

Nungezer, Edwin, *A Dictionary of Actors* (New York: Greenwood Press Publishers, 1968)

Onions, C.T., *A Shakespeare Glossary*, revised by Robert D. Eagleson (Oxford: Oxford University Press, 1986)

Oxford English Dictionary, The Compact Edition (Oxford: Oxford University Press, 1971)

Papp, Joseph and Elizabeth Kirkland, *Shakespeare Alive!* (New York: Bantam Books, 1988)

Partridge, Eric, *Shakespeare's Bawdy* (New York: E.P. Dutton & Co., Inc., 1969)

Prosser, Eleanor, *Shakespeare's Anonymous Editors: Scribe and Compositor in the Folio Text of 2 Henry IV* (Stanford: Stanford University Préss, 1981)

Rubenstein, Frankie, *Dictionary of Shakespeare's Sexual Puns and Their Significance* (London: The Macmillan Press, Ltd, 1984)

Rutter, Carol, *Documents of the Rose Playhouse* (Cambridge: Cambridge University Press, 1984)

Schmidt, Alexander, *Shakespeare Lexicon and Quotation Dictionary*, 2 volumes (New York: Dover Publications, Inc., 1971)

Schoenbaum, S., *Shakespeare: The Globe and the World* (New York: Oxford University Press, © Folger Shakespeare Library, 1979)

Spurgeon, Caroline F.E., *Shakespeare's Imagery and what it tells us* (Boston: Beacon Press, 1958)

Stokes, Francis Griffin, *Who's Who in Shakespeare* (New York: Crescent Books, © Bracken Books, 1989)

Styan, J.L., *Shakespeare's Stagecraft* (Cambridge: Cambridge University Press, 1967)

Vaughan, Stuart, *Directing Plays* (New York: Longman, 1993)

Watkins, Ronald, *On Producing Shakespeare* (New York: The Citadel Press, 1965)

Wells, Stanley and Gary Taylor, *William Shakespeare, A Textual Companion* (W.W. Norton and Company, 1997)

Merriam Webster's Collegiate® Dictionary, 10th Edition (Springfield, MA: G. & C. Merriam Co., 1993)

Original Texts

Shakespeare, William, *Mr. William Shakespeare's Comedies, Histories, & Tragedies*, The First Folio, copy number 1 (known as "Lenox B"), The New York Public Library (London: Isaac Jaggard and Ed. Blount, 1623)

Shakespeare, William, *Mr. William Shakespeare's Comedies, Histories, & Tragedies*, The First Folio, copy number 2 ("The Mary Stillwell Harkness copy"), The New York Public Library (London: Isaac Jaggard and Ed. Blount, 1623). One in a set of four volumes comprising the Harkness copies: Shakespeare's First, Second, Third, and Fourth Folios.

Shakespeare, William, *Mr. William Shakespeare's Comedies, Histories, & Tragedies*, The First Folio, copy number 3 ("Lenox A"), The New York Public Library (London: Isaac Jaggard and Ed. Blount, 1623)

Shakespeare, William, *Mr. William Shakespeare's Comedies, Histories, & Tragedies*, The First Folio, copy number 4 ("Astor copy"), The New York Public Library (London: Isaac Jaggard and Ed. Blount, 1623)

Shakespeare, William, *Mr. William Shakespeare's Comedies, Histories, & Tragedies*, The First Folio, copy number 5 ("Tilden copy"), The New York Public Library (London: Isaac Jaggard and Ed. Blount, 1623)

Shakespeare, William, *Mr. William Shakespeare's Comedies, Histories, & Tragedies*, The First Folio, copy number 6 ("Colonel Edward George Hibbert Dean Sage copy"). The only Folio not housed in Rare Books and Manuscripts; part of The Berg Collection at The New York Public Library (London: Isaac Jaggard and Ed. Blount, 1623)

Shakespeare, William, *Mr. William Shakespeare's Comedies, Histories, & Tragedies*, The First Folio, copy A, The Pierpont Morgan Library.

Shakespeare, William, *Mr. William Shakespeare's Comedies, Histories, & Tragedies*, The First Folio, copy B, belonged to Robert Sydney, 1st earl of Leicester (1563–1636), The Pierpont Morgan Library.

Shakespeare, William, *Mr. William Shakespeare's Comedies, Histories, & Tragedies, The Second Impression* (London: Tho[mas] Cotes, for Robert Allot, 1632). Collophone reads, "Printed at London by Thomas Cotes, for John Smethwick, William Aspley, Richard Hawkins, Richard Meighen, and Robert Allot, 1632."

Shakespeare, William, *Mr. William Shakespeare's Comedies, Histories, & Tragedies, The Third Impression* (London: for Philip Chetwinde, 1663.)

Shakespeare, William, *Mr. William Shakespeare's Comedies, Histories, & Tragedies, The Fourth Impression* (London, printed for H. Herringman, and are to be sold by *Joseph Knight*, and *Francis Saunders* at the Anchor in the Lower Walk of the *New Exchange*, 1685.)

Facsimiles

Allen, Michael J.B. and Kenneth Muir, *Shakespeare's Plays in Quarto* (Berkeley: University of California Press, 1981)

Halliwell-Phillipps, J.O., *The First Folio of Shakespeare, 1623, in Reduced Facsimil* (New York: Funk & Wagnalls, Publishers, 1886)

Hinman, Charlton, and Peter W.M. Blayney, *The Norton Facsimile of The First Folio of Shakespeare* (New York: W.W. Norton & Co., 1968 and 1996)

Kodama, Mitsuo, *Mr. William Shakespeare's Comedies, Histories, & Tragedies* (Tokyo: Meisei University Press, 1985)

Kökeritz, Helge and Charles Tyler Prouty, *Mr. William Shakespeare's Comedies, Histories, & Tragedies*, a photographic facsimile of the First Folio edition (New Haven: Yale University Press, 1954)

Lee, Sidney, *The First Folio of Shakespeare*, 1623 (Oxford: Clarendon Press, 1902)

Shakespeare, William, *The Tragicall Historie of Hamlet Prince of Denmarke*, 1603. The Bodley Head Quartos, G.B. Harrison, editor. (London: John Lane, The Bodley Head, Ltd and E.P. Dutton & Company, New York, 1923). The original is in the British Library (C. 34. k. 1)

Staunton, Howard, *The First Folio of Shakespeare* (London: Day & Son, 1866)

Edited Texts

Cross, Wilbur L., and Tucker Brooke, *The Yale Shakespeare* (New York: Barnes & Noble Books, 1993)

Evans, G. Blakemore, *The Riverside Shakespeare* (Boston: Houghton Mifflin Company, 1974)

Furness, Horace Howard, *New Variorum Editions, Hamlet, Romeo and Juliet, As You Like It, Midsummer Night's Dream*, first published by J.B. Lippincott & Company, 1890 (New York: Dover Publications, Inc., 1963)

Shakespeare, William, *Antony and Cleopatra*, The Arden Shakespeare, edited by M.R. Ridley, general editor, Richard Proudfoot (London & New York: Routledge, 1991)

Shakespeare, William, *Henry V*, New Penguin edited by A.R. Humphreys (New York: Penguin Books, 1968)

Shakespeare, William, *Henry V*, The Signet Classic Shakespeare, edited by John Russell Brown, general editor, Sylvan Barnett (New York: New American Library, Inc., 1988)

Shakespeare, William, *The Life of Henry the Fifth*, The Pelican Shakespeare, edited by Alfred Harbage (New York: Penguin Books, Inc., 1966)

Shakespeare, William, *King Henry the Fifth*, The New Cambridge Shakespeare, edited by Andrew Gurr, general editor, Brian Gibbons (Cambridge: Cambridge University Press, 1992)

Shakespeare, William, *Henry the Fifth*, Oxford Shakespeare, edited by Gary Taylor, general editor, Stanley Wells (Oxford: Oxford University Press, 1994)

Shakespeare, William, *King Henry V*, The Arden Shakespeare, edited by J.H. Walter and general editors, Richard Proudfoot and Anne Thompson (London & New York: Routledge, 1993)

Shakespeare, William, *Henry V*, The Folger Library Shakespeare, edited by Louis B. Wright and Virginia A. LaMar (New York: Simon & Schuster, 1960)

Shakespeare, William, *Henry V*, Bantam Classic, edited by David Bevington (New York: Bantam Books, 1980)

Shakespeare, William, *Measure for Measure*, The Signet Classic Shakespeare, edited by S. Nagarajan, general editor, Sylvan Barnett (New York: New American Library, Inc., 1964)

Shakespeare, William, *The Merchant of Venice*, Bantam Classic, edited by David Bevington (New York: Bantam Books, 1980)

Shakespeare, William, *A Midsummer Night's Dream*, The Pelican Shakespeare, edited by Madeleine Doran, general editor, Alfred Harbage (New York: Penguin Books, 1971)

Shakespeare, William, *The Complete Works of William Shakespeare, corrected by the manuscript emendations contained in the recently discovered Folio of 1632*. The Jewett's Collier's Edition, edited by J. Payne Collier, Esq., F.S.A. and John L. Jewett (New York: George F. Cooledge & Brother, 1855).

Tucker, Patrick, and Michael Holden, editors, *The Shakespeare's Globe Acting Editions*, Available in single play editions. The editors reprint First Folio text in modern typeface with corrections and revisions noted and discussed. Each edition contains "cue scripts" for each character and a reconstruction of the "platt" appropriate for performance and/or study (London: MH Publications). Available from MH Publications, 17 West Heath Drive, London, NW11 7QG.

Shakespeare On-line:

http://the-tech.mit.edu/Shakespeare/works.html. — The Complete Works of Wm Shakespeare

http://www.cc.emory.edu/ENGLISH/classes/Shakespeare_Illustrated/Shakespeare.html — Shakespeare Illustrated, a work in progress, explores nineteenth-century paintings, criticism, and productions of Shakespeare's plays and their influences on one another. The Introduction to Shakespeare Illustrated. The plays of Shakespeare are listed alphabetically. Under each play is a list of paintings based on that particular work. The artists are also listed alphabetically. Under the name of each artist is a list of paintings based on various plays by Shakespeare. The bibliography lists the works cited in Shakespeare Illustrated.

http://www.rdg.ac.uk./globe/—Website of Shakespeare's Globe in UK

http://www.bcpl.lib.md.us/~tross/ws/will.html—The Shakespeaere Authorship Page Dedicated to the Proposition that Shakesp wrote Shksper

http://www2.pbs.org/wgbh/pages/frontline/shakespeare/index.html — The Shakespeare Mystery. The Oxfordians and the Stratfordians as presented on PBS's Frontline in April of 1989.

http://www.ludweb.com/msff/sonnets/—The Sonnets

http://www.ludweb.com/msff/sonnets/links.html — Shakespearean Links on the Web

http://www.gh.cs.su.oz.au/~matty/Shakespeare/Shakespeare.html — Collected works and a highly useful Shakespeare Search engine (Matty Farrow's excellent site from Australia)

http://www.shakespeare.com/ http://www.resort.com/~banshee/Faire/Language/language.html— Proper Elizabethan Accents

http://www.palomar.edu/Library/SHBEST.HTM—Best of the Web Shakespeare sites

http://www.library.upenn.edu/etext/furness/lear1619/index.html#TOC—From the University of Pennsylvania come remarkable photographs of each page of the 1619 quarto of King Lear.

http://www.newschool.edu/library/theatre.htm— From the Library at The New School for Social Research comes Theatre Resources, a very useful site for actors.

http://www.sccu.edu/faculty/R_Harris/rhetoric.htm.—*A Handbook of Rhetorical Devices* by Robert Harris at Southern California College.

http://www.uky.edu/ArtsSciences/Classics/rhetoric.html

http://www.uky.edu/ArtsSciences/Classics/lexindex.html — Two useful sites for the study of rhetoric created by Ross Scaife at the University of Kentucky.

Notes

1. Nungezer, Edward, *A Dictionary of Actors* (New Haven: Yale University Press, 1929), pp. 98–101.
2. Hinman, Charlton, *The Norton Facsimile of The First Folio of Shakespeare* (New York: W.W. Norton and Company, 1968). Appendix A.
3. See Wells, Stanley and Gary Taylor, *William Shakespeare, A Textual Companion*, (New York: W.W. Norton and Company, 1997), p. 43.
4. Hinman, Charlton, and Peter W.M. Blayney, *The Norton Facsimile of The First Folio of Shakespeare*, (New York: W.W. Norton & Co., 1968 and 1996). See in particular Blayney's Introduction to the 2nd ed. pp. xxxiii–xxxiv.
5. Blayney, Peter W.M., *The First Folio of Shakespaere* (Washington, D.C.: Folger Library Publications, 199), p. 29.
6. *Pericles*, the only play not published in the First Folio. The "bad" quarto is the sole authoritative text.
7. Allen, J.B., and Kenneth Muir, *Shakespeare's Plays in Quarto* (Berkeley: University of California Press, 1981), p. 592.
8. This is quoted from F1 although most edited editions print it as it appears in Q2, the "good" quarto of 1604 which has it as "the proude mans contumely."
9. Hinman and Blayney, *The Norton Facsimile of The First Folio*, 2nd ed., p. xv.
10. Chute, Marchette, *Shakespeare of London* (New York: E.P. Dutton, 1949), p. 26.
11. Rutter, Carol Chillington, *Documents of the Rose Playhouse*, (Manchester: Manchester University Press, 1984), p. 99.
12. Gurr, Andrew, *The Shakespearean Stage 1574–1642*, 3rd ed., (Cambridge University Press: Cambridge, 1992), p. 209.
13. Telephone interview, September 21, 1997.
14. *Merriam Webster's Collegiate® Dictionary*, 10th ed. (Springfield, MA: G. & C. Merriam Co., 1993), p. 1042.
15. Gurr, Andrew and John Orrell, *Rebuilding Shakespeare's Globe* (New York and London: Routledge/Theatre Arts Books, 1989), p. 22.
16. Flatter, Richard, *Shakepeare's Producing Hand* (New York: W.W. Norton & Co., 1948), p. 92.
17. See Mulryne, J.R. and Margaret Shewring, eds., *Shakespeare's Globe Rebuilt* (Cambridge: Cambridge University Press, 1997).
18. Gurr, *The Shakespearean Stage*, p. 226 (as quoted by G. Tillotson, *Times Literary Supplement*, 20 July 1933, p. 494.
19. Clark, W.G., W.A. Wright and J. Glover, *The Globe Edition* (New York: Harcourt, Brace and Company, 1864). A single volume edition based on the nine volume *Cambridge Edition*, 1863–6, by the same editors.

To the Reader.

This Figure, that thou here seest put,
It was for gentle Shakespeare cut;
Wherein the Grauer had a strife
with Nature, to out-doo the life:
O, could he but haue drawne his wit
As well in brasse, as he hath hit
His face, the Print would then surpasse
All, that was euer writ in brasse.
But, since he cannot, Reader, looke
Not on his Picture, but his Booke.

B. I.

MR. WILLIAM
SHAKESPEARES
COMEDIES, HISTORIES, & TRAGEDIES.

Publiſhed according to the True Originall Copies.

LONDON

Printed by Iſaac Iaggard, and Ed. Blount. 1623.

TO THE MOST NOBLE AND INCOMPARABLE PAIRE OF BRETHREN.

WILLIAM
Earle of Pembroke, &c. Lord Chamberlaine to the *Kings most Excellent Maiesty.*

AND

PHILIP
Earle of Montgomery, &c. Gentleman of his Maiesties Bed-Chamber. Both Knights of the most Noble Order of the Garter, and our singular good LORDS.

Right Honourable,

WHilst we studie to be thankful in our particular, for the many fauors we haue receiued from your L.L. we are falne vpon the ill fortune, to mingle two the most diuerse things that can bee, feare, and rashnesse; rashnesse in the enterprize, and feare of the successe. For, when we valew the places your H.H. sustaine, we cannot but know their dignity greater, then to descend to the reading of these trifles: and, vvhile we name them trifles, we haue depriu'd our selues of the defence of our Dedication. But since your L.L. haue beene pleas'd to thinke these trifles some-thing, heeretofore; and haue prosequuted both them, and their Authour liuing, with so much fauour: we hope, that (they out-liuing him, and he not hauing the fate, common with some, to be exequutor to his owne writings) you will vse the like indulgence toward them, you haue done

A 2 vnto

vnto their parent. There is a great difference, vvhether any Booke choose his Patrones, or finde them: This hath done both. For, so much were your L L. likings of the seuerall parts, vvhen they were acted, as before they vvere published, the Volume ask'd to be yours. We haue but collected them, and done an office to the dead, to procure his Orphanes, Guardians; vvithout ambition either of selfe-profit, or fame: onely to keepe the memory of so worthy a Friend, & Fellow aliue, as was our SHAKESPEARE, *by humble offer of his playes, to your most noble patronage. Wherein, as we haue iustly obserued, no man to come neere your L.L. but vvith a kind of religious addresse; it hath bin the height of our care, vvho are the Presenters, to make the present worthy of your H.H. by the perfection. But, there we must also craue our abilities to be considerd, my Lords. We cannot go beyond our owne powers. Country hands reach foorth milke, creame, fruites, or what they haue: and many Nations (we haue heard) that had not gummes & incense, obtained their requests with a leauened Cake. It vvas no fault to approch their Gods, by what meanes they could: And the most, though meanest, of things are made more precious, when they are dedicated to Temples. In that name therefore, we most humbly consecrate to your H.H. these remaines of your seruant* Shakespeare; *that what delight is in them, may be euer your L.L. the reputation his, & the faults ours, if any be committed, by a payre so carefull to shew their gratitude both to the liuing, and the dead, as is*

Your Lordſhippes moſt bounden,

IOHN HEMINGE.
HENRY CONDELL.

To the great Variety of Readers.

FRom the most able, to him that can but spell: There you are number'd. We had rather you were weighd. Especially, when the fate of all Bookes depends vpon your capacities: and not of your heads alone, but of your purses. Well! It is now publique, & you wil stand for your priuiledges wee know: to read, and censure. Do so, but buy it first. That doth best commend a Booke, the Stationer saies. Then, how odde soeuer your braines be, or your wisedomes, make your licence the same, and spare not. Iudge your sixe-pen'orth, your shillings worth, your fiue shillings worth at a time, or higher, so you rise to the iust rates, and welcome. But, what euer you do, Buy. Censure will not driue a Trade, or make the Iacke go. And though you be a Magistrate of wit, and sit on the Stage at *Black-Friers*, or the *Cock-pit*, to arraigne Playes dailie, know, these Playes haue had their triall alreadie, and stood out all Appeales; and do now come forth quitted rather by a Decree of Court, then any purchas'd Letters of commendation.

It had bene a thing, we confesse, worthie to haue bene wished, that the Author himselfe had liu'd to haue set forth, and ouerseen his owne writings; But since it hath bin ordain'd otherwise, and he by death departed from that right, we pray you do not envie his Friends, the office of their care, and paine, to haue collected & publish'd them; and so to haue publish'd them, as where (before) you were abus'd with diuerse stolne, and surreptitious copies, maimed, and deformed by the frauds and stealthes of iniurious impostors, that expos'd them: euen those, are now offer'd to your view cur'd, and perfect of their limbes; and all the rest, absolute in their numbers, as he conceiued thē. Who, as he was a happie imitator of Nature, was a most gentle expresser of it. His mind and hand went together: And what he thought, he vttered with that easinesse, that wee haue scarse receiued from him a blot in his papers. But it is not our prouince, who onely gather his works, and giue them you, to praise him. It is yours that reade him. And there we hope, to your diuers capacities, you will finde enough, both to draw, and hold you: for his wit can no more lie hid, then it could be lost. Reade him, therefore; and againe, and againe: And if then you doe not like him, surely you are in some manifest danger, not to vnderstand him. And so we leaue you to other of his Friends, whom if you need, can bee your guides: if you neede them not, you can leade your selues, and others And such Readers we wish him.

A 3

Iohn Heminge.
Henrie Condell.

To the memory of my beloued, The AVTHOR Mr. William Shakespeare: And what he hath left vs.

*To draw no enuy (*Shakespeare*) on thy name,*
Am I thus ample to thy Booke, and Fame:
While I confesse thy writings to be such,
As neither Man, *nor* Muse, *can praise too much.*
'Tis true, and all mens suffrage. But these wayes
were not the paths I meant vnto thy praise:
For seeliest Ignorance on these may light,
Which, when it sounds at best, but eccho's right;
Or blinde Affection, which doth ne're aduance
The truth, but gropes, and vrgeth all by chance;
Or crafty Malice, might pretend this praise,
And thinke to ruine, where it seem'd to raise.
These are, as some infamous Baud, or Whore,
Should praise a Matron. What could hurt her more?
But thou art proofe against them, and indeed
Aboue th'ill fortune of them, or the need.
I, therefore will begin. Soule of the Age!
The applause! delight! the wonder of our Stage!
My Shakespeare, *rise; I will not lodge thee by*
Chaucer, *or* Spenser, *or bid* Beaumont *lye*
A little further, to make thee a roome:
Thou art a Moniment, without a tombe,
And art aliue still, while thy Booke doth liue,
And we haue wits to read, and praise to giue.
That I not mixe thee so, my braine excuses;
I meane with great, but disproportion'd Muses
For, if I thought my iudgement were of yeeres,
I should commit thee surely with thy peeres,
And tell, how farre thou didstst our Lily *out-shine,*
Or sporting Kid, *or* Marlowes *mighty line.*
And though thou hadst small Latine, *and lesse* Greeke,
From thence to honour thee, I would not seeke
For names; but call forth thund'ring Æschilus,
Euripides, *and* Sophocles *to vs,*
Paccuuius, Accius, *him of* Cordoua *dead,*
To life againe, to heare thy Buskin tread,
And shake a Stage: Or, when thy Sockes were on,
Leaue thee alone, for the comparison

Of all, that insolent Greece, *or haughtie* Rome
sent forth, or since did from their ashes come.
Triumph, my Britaine, *thou hast one to showe,*
To whom all Scenes of Europe *homage owe.*
He was not of an age, but for all time!
And all the Muses *still were in their prime,*
when like Apollo *he came forth to warme*
Our eares, or like a Mercury *to charme!*
Nature her selfe was proud of his designes,
And ioy'd to weare the dressing of his lines!
which were so richly spun, and wouen so fit,
As, since, she will vouchsafe no other Wit.
The merry Greeke, *tart* Aristophanes,
Neat Terence, *witty* Plautus, *now not please;*
But antiquated, and deserted lye
As they were not of Natures family.
Yet must I not giue Nature all: Thy Art,
My gentle Shakespeare, *must enioy a part.*
For though the Poets *matter, Nature be,*
His Art doth giue the fashion. And, that he,
Who casts to write a liuing line, must sweat,
(such as thine are) and strike the second heat
Vpon the Muses *anuile: turne the same,*
(And himselfe with it) that he thinkes to frame;
Or for the lawrell, he may gaine a scorne,
For a good Poet's *made, as well as borne.*
And such wert thou. Looke how the fathers face
Liues in his issue, euen so, the race
Of Shakespeares *minde, and manners brightly shines*
In his well torned, and true-filed lines:
In each of which, he seemes to shake a Lance,
As brandish't at the eyes of Ignorance.
Sweet Swan of Auon! *what a sight it were*
To see thee in our waters yet appeare,
And make those flights vpon the bankes of Thames,
That so did take Eliza, *and our* Iames!
But stay, I see thee in the Hemisphere
Aduanc'd, and made a Constellation there!
Shine forth, thou Starre of Poets, *and with rage,*
Or influence, chide, or cheere the drooping Stage;
Which, since thy flight frō hence, hath mourn'd like night,
And despaires day, but for thy Volumes light.

BEN: IONSON.

Vpon the Lines and Life of the Famous Scenicke Poet, Master WILLIAM SHAKESPEARE.

Hose hands, which you so clapt, go now, and wring
You *Britaines* braue; for done are *Shakespeares* dayes:
His dayes are done, that made the dainty Playes,
Which made the Globe of heau'n and earth to ring.
Dry'de is that veine, dry'd is the *Thespian* Spring,
Turn'd all to teares, and *Phœbus* clouds his rayes:
That corp's, that coffin now besticke those bayes,
Which crown'd him *Poet* first, then *Poets* King.
If *Tragedies* might any *Prologue* haue,
All those he made, would scarse make one to this:
Where *Fame*, now that he gone is to the graue
(Deaths publique tyring-house) the *Nuncius* is.
For though his line of life went soone about,
The life yet of his lines shall neuer out.

HVGH HOLLAND.

TO THE MEMORIE
of the deceaſed Authour Maiſter W. SHAKESPEARE.

SHake-ſpeare, *at length thy pious fellowes giue*
The world thy Workes: thy Workes, by which, out-liue
Thy Tombe, thy name muſt when that ſtone is rent,
And Time diſſolues thy Stratford *Moniment,*
Here we aliue ſhall view thee ſtill. This Booke,
When Braſſe and Marble fade, ſhall make thee looke
Freſh to all Ages: when Poſteritie
Shall loath what's new, thinke all is prodegie
That is not Shake-ſpeares *; eu'ry Line, each Verſe*
Here ſhall reuiue, redeeme thee from thy Herſe.
Nor Fire, nor cankring Age, as Naſo *ſaid,*
Of his, thy wit-fraught Booke ſhall once inuade.
Nor ſhall I e're beleeue, or thinke thee dead
(Though miſt) vntill our bankrout Stage be ſped
(Impoſsible) with ſome new ſtraine t'out-do
Paſsions of Iuliet, *and her* Romeo;
Or till I heare a Scene more nobly take,
Then when thy half-Sword parlying Romans *ſpake.*
Till theſe, till any of thy Volumes reſt
Shall with more fire, more feeling be expreſt,
Be ſure, our Shake-ſpeare, *thou canſt neuer dye,*
But crown'd with Lawrell, liue eternally.

L. Digges.

To the memorie of M. *W. Shake-ſpeare.*

VVEE *wondred* (Shake-ſpeare) *that thou went'ſt ſo ſoone*
From the Worlds-Stage, to the Graues-Tyring-roome.
Wee thought thee dead, but this thy printed worth,
Tels thy Spectators, that thou went'ſt but forth
To enter with applauſe. An Actors Art,
Can dye, and liue, to acte a ſecond part.
That's but an Exit *of* Mortalitie;
This, a Re-entrance to a Plaudite.

I. M.

The Workes of William Shakespeare,

containing all his Comedies, Histories, and Tragedies: Truely set forth, according to their first ORIGINALL.

The Names of the Principall Actors in all these Playes.

William Shakespeare.

Richard Burbadge.

John Hemmings.

Augustine Phillips

William Kempt.

Thomas Poope.

George Bryan.

Henry Condell.

William Slye.

Richard Cowly.

John Lowine.

Samuell Crosse.

Alexander Cooke.

Samuel Gilburne.

Robert Armin.

William Ostler.

Nathan Field.

John Underwood.

Nicholas Tooley.

William Ecclestone.

Joseph Taylor.

Robert Benfield.

Robert Goughe.

Richard Robinson.

Iohn Shancke.

Iohn Rice.

A CATALOGVE

of the ſeuerall Comedies, Hiſtories, and Tragedies contained in this Volume.

COMEDIES.

The Tempeſt. Folio 1.

The two Gentlemen of Verona. 20

The Merry Wiues of Windſor. 38

Meaſure for Meaſure. 61

The Comedy of Errours. 85

Much adoo about Nothing. 101

Loues Labour loſt. 122

Midſommer Nights Dreame. 145

The Merchant of Venice. 163

As you Like it. 185

The Taming of the Shrew. 208

All is well, that Ends well. 230

Twelfe-Night, or what you will. 255

The Winters Tale. 304

HISTORIES.

The Life and Death of King John. Fol. 1.

The Life & death of Richard the ſecond. 23

The Firſt part of King Henry the fourth. 46

The Second part of K. Henry the fourth. 74

The Life of King Henry the Fift. 69

The Firſt part of King Henry the Sixt. 96

The Second part of King Hen. the Sixt. 120

The Third part of King Henry the Sixt. 147

The Life & Death of Richard the Third. 173

The Life of King Henry the Eight. 205

TRAGEDIES.

The Tragedy of Coriolanus. Fol. 1.

Titus Andronicus. 31

Romeo and Juliet. 53

Timon of Athens. 80

The Life and death of Julius Cæſar. 109

The Tragedy of Macbeth. 131

The Tragedy of Hamlet. 152

King Lear. 283

Othello, the Moore of Venice. 310

Anthony and Cleopater. 346

Cymbeline King of Britaine. 369

THE TEMPEST.

Actus primus, Scena prima.

A tempestuous noise of Thunder and Lightning heard: Enter a Ship-maſter, and a Boteſwaine.

Maſter.

Bote-ſwaine.

Boteſ. Heere Maſter: What cheere?

Maſt. Good: Speake to th'Mariners: fall too't, yarely, or we run our ſelues a ground, beſtirre, beſtirre. *Exit.*

Enter Mariners.

Boteſ. Heigh my hearts, cheerely, cheerely my harts: yare, yare: Take in the toppe-ſale: Tend to th'Maſters whiſtle: Blow till thou burſt thy winde, if roome enough.

Enter Alonſo, Sebaſtian, Anthonio, Ferdinando, Gonzalo, and others.

Alon. Good Boteſwaine haue care: where's the Maſter? Play the men.

Boteſ. I pray now keepe below.

Anth. Where is the Maſter, Boſon?

Boteſ. Do you not heare him? you marre our labour, Keepe your Cabines: you do aſsiſt the ſtorme.

Gonz. Nay, good be patient.

Boteſ. When the Sea is: hence, what cares theſe roarers for the name of King? to Cabine; ſilence: trouble vs not.

Gon. Good, yet remember whom thou haſt aboord.

Boteſ. None that I more loue then my ſelfe. You are a Counſellor, if you can command theſe Elements to ſilence, and worke the peace of the preſent, wee will not hand a rope more, vſe your authoritie: If you cannot, giue thankes you haue liu'd ſo long, and make your ſelfe readie in your Cabine for the miſchance of the houre, if it ſo hap. Cheerely good hearts: out of our way I ſay. *Exit.*

Gon. I haue great comfort from this fellow: methinks he hath no drowning marke vpon him, his complexion is perfect Gallowes: ſtand faſt good Fate to his hanging, make the rope of his deſtiny our cable, for our owne doth little aduantage: If he be not borne to bee hang'd, our caſe is miſerable. *Exit.*

Enter Boteſwaine.

Boteſ. Downe with the top-Maſt: yare, lower, lower, bring her to Try with Maine-courſe. A plague——
A cry within. *Enter Sebaſtian, Anthonio & Gonzalo.*
vpon this howling: they are lowder then the weather, or our office: yet againe? What do you heere? Shal we giue ore and drowne, haue you a minde to ſinke?

Sebaſ. A poxe o'your throat, you bawling, blaſphemous incharitable Dog.

Boteſ. Worke you then.

Anth. Hang cur, hang, you whoreſon inſolent Noyſemaker, we are leſſe afraid to be drownde, then thou art.

Gonz. I'le warrant him for drowning, though the Ship were no ſtronger then a Nutt-ſhell, and as leaky as an vnſtanched wench.

Boteſ. Lay her a hold, a hold, ſet her two courſes off to Sea againe, lay her off.

Enter Mariners wet.

Mari. All loſt, to prayers, to prayers, all loſt.

Boteſ. What muſt our mouths be cold?

Gonz. The King, and Prince, at prayers, let's aſſiſt them, for our caſe is as theirs.

Sebaſ. I'am out of patience.

An. We are meerly cheated of our liues by drunkards, This wide-chopt-raſcall, would thou mightſt lye drowning the waſhing of ten Tides.

Gonz. Hee'l be hang'd yet,
Though euery drop of water ſweare againſt it,
And gape at widſt to glut him. *A confuſed noyſe within.*
Mercy on vs.
We ſplit, we ſplit, Farewell my wife and children,
Farewell brother: we ſplit, we ſplit, we ſplit.

Anth. Let's all ſinke with' King

Seb. Let's take leaue of him. *Exit.*

Gonz. Now would I giue a thouſand furlongs of Sea, for an Acre of barren ground: Long heath, Browne firrs, any thing; the wills aboue be done, but I would faine dye a dry death. *Exit.*

Scena Secunda.

Enter Proſpero and Miranda.

Mira. If by your Art (my deereſt father) you haue
Put the wild waters in this Rore; alay them:
The skye it ſeemes would powre down ſtinking pitch,
But that the Sea, mounting to th' welkins cheeke,
Daſhes the fire out. Oh! I haue ſuffered
With thoſe that I ſaw ſuffer: A braue veſſell

A (Who

(Who had no doubt some noble creature in her)
Dash'd all to peeces : O the cry did knocke
Against my very heart : poore soules,they perish'd.
Had I byn any God of power,I would
Haue suncke the Sea within the Earth, or ere
It should the good Ship so haue swallow'd,and
The fraughting Soules within her.
Pros. Be collected,
No more amazement : Tell your pitteous heart
there's no harme done.
Mira. O woe,the day.
Pros. No harme:
I haue done nothing,but in care of thee
(Of thee my deere one; thee my daughter) who
Art ignorant of what thou art. naught knowing
Of whence I am : nor that I am more better
Then *Prospero*,Master of a full poore cell,
And thy no greater Father.
Mira. More to know
Did neuer medle with my thoughts.
Pros. 'Tis time
I should informe thee farther : Lend thy hand
And plucke my Magick garment from me: So,
Lye there my Art: wipe thou thine eyes,haue comfort,
The direfull spectacle of the wracke which touch'd
The very vertue of compassion in thee:
I haue with such prouision in mine Art
So safely ordered,that there is no soule
No not so much perdition as an hayre
Betid to any creature in the vessell
Which thou heardst cry, which thou saw'st sinke : Sit
For thou must now know farther. [downe,
Mira. You haue often
Begun to tell me what I am, but stopt
And left me to a bootelesse Inquisition,
Concluding,stay: not yet.
Pros. The howr's now come
The very minute byds thee ope thine eare,
Obey,and be attentiue. Canst thou remember
A time before we came vnto this Cell?
I doe not thinke thou canst,for then thou was't not
Out three yeeres old.
Mira. Certainely Sir, I can.
Pros. By what? by any other house,or person?
Of any thing the Image,tell me,that
Hath kept with thy remembrance.
Mira. 'Tis farre off:
And rather like a dreame,then an assurance
That my remembrance warrants: Had I not
Fowre,or fiue women once,that tended me?
Pros. Thou hadst; and more *Miranda*: But how is it
That this liues in thy minde? What seest thou els
In the dark-backward and Abisme of Time?
Yf thou remembrest ought ere thou cam'st here,
How thou cam'st here thou maist.
Mira. But that I doe not.
Pros. Twelue yere since(*Miranda*)twelue yere since,
Thy father was the Duke of *Millaine* and
A Prince of power:
Mira. Sir, are not you my Father?
Pros. Thy Mother was a peece of vertue, and
She said thou wast my daughter; and thy father
Was Duke of *Millaine*,and his onely heire,
And Princesse; no worse Issued.
Mira. O the heauens,
What fowle play had we,that we came from thence?
Or blessed was't we did?
Pros. Both,both my Girle.
By fowle-play (as thou saist) were we heau'd thence,
But blessedly holpe hither.
Mira. O my heart bleedes
To thinke oth' teene that I haue turn'd you to,
Which is from my remembrance,please you,farther;
Pros. My brother and thy vncle,call'd *Anthonio*:
I pray thee marke me, that a brother should
Be so perfidious : he, whom next thy selfe
Of all the world I lou'd,and to him put
The mannage of my state, as at that time
Through all the signories it was the first,
And *Prospero*,the prime Duke, being so reputed
In dignity; and for the liberall Artes,
Without a paralell; those being all my studie,
The Gouernment I cast vpon my brother,
And to my State grew stranger,being transported
And rapt in secret studies,thy false vncle
(Do'st thou attend me?)
Mira. Sir,most heedefully.
Pros. Being once perfected how to graunt suites,
how to deny them : who t'aduance,and who
To trash for ouer-topping; new created
The creatures that were mine,I say,or chang'd 'em,
Or els new form'd 'em; hauing both the key,
Of Officer,and office,set all hearts i'th state
To what tune pleas'd his eare,that now he was
The Iuy which had hid my princely Trunck,
And suckt my verdure out on't : Thou attend'st not?
Mira. O good Sir, I doe.
Pros. I pray thee marke me:
I thus neglecting worldly ends,all dedicated
To closenes,and the bettering of my mind
with that,which but by being so retir'd
Ore-priz'd all popular rate:in my false brother
Awak'd an euill nature,and my trust
Like a good parent,did beget of him
A falsehood in it's contrarie,as great
As my trust was,which had indeede no limit,
A confidence sans bound. He being thus Lorded,
Not onely with what my reuenew yeelded,
But what my power might els exact. Like one
Who hauing into truth,by telling of it,
Made such a synner of his memorie
To credite his owne lie,he did beleeue
He was indeed the Duke,out o'th' Substitution
And executing th'outward face of Roialtie
With all prerogatiue:hence his Ambition growing:
Do'st thou heare?
Mira. Your tale,Sir, would cure deafenesse.
Pros. To haue no Schreene between this part he plaid,
And him he plaid it for,he needes will be
Absolute *Millaine*, Me (poore man) my Librarie
Was Dukedome large enough : of temporall roalties
He thinks me now incapable. Confederates
(so drie he was for Sway) with King of *Naples*
To giue him Annuall tribute,doe him homage
Subiect his Coronet,to his Crowne and bend
The Dukedom yet vnbow'd (alas poore *Millaine*)
To most ignoble stooping.
Mira. Oh the heauens:
Pros. Marke his condition,and th'euent,then tell me
If this might be a brother.
Mira. I should sinne
To thinke but Noblie of my Grand-mother,
Good

Good wombes haue borne bad ſonnes.
Pro. Now the Condition.
This King of *Naples* being an Enemy
To me inueterate, hearkens my Brothers ſuit,
Which was, That he in lieu o'th premiſes,
Of homage, and I know not how much Tribute,
Should preſently extirpate me and mine
Out of the Dukedome, and confer faire *Millaine*
With all the Honors, on my brother: Whereon
A treacherous Armie leuied, one mid-night
Fated to th' purpoſe, did *Anthonio* open
The gates of *Millaine*, and ith' dead of darkeneſſe
The miniſters for th' purpoſe hurried thence
Me, and thy crying ſelfe.
Mir. Alack, for pitty:
I not remembring how I cride out then
Will cry it ore againe: it is a hint
That wrings mine eyes too't.
Pro. Heare a little further,
And then I'le bring thee to the preſent buſineſſe
Which now's vpon's: without the which, this Story
Were moſt impertinent.
Mir. Wherefore did they not
That howre deſtroy vs?
Pro. Well demanded, wench:
My Tale prouokes that queſtion: Deare, they durſt not,
So deare the loue my people bore me: nor ſet
A marke ſo bloudy on the buſineſſe; but
With colours fairer, painted their foule ends.
In few, they hurried vs a-boord a Barke,
Bore vs ſome Leagues to Sea, where they prepared
A rotten carkaſſe of a Butt, not rigg'd,
Nor tackle, ſayle, nor maſt, the very rats
Inſtinctiuely haue quit it: There they hoyſt vs
To cry to th' Sea, that roard to vs; to ſigh
To th' windes, whoſe pitty ſighing backe againe
Did vs but louing wrong.
Mir. Alack, what trouble
Was I then to you?
Pro. O, a Cherubin
Thou was't that did preſerue me; Thou didſt ſmile,
Infuſed with a fortitude from heauen,
When I haue deck'd the ſea with drops full ſalt,
Vnder my burthen groan'd, which raiſ'd in me
An vndergoing ſtomacke, to beare vp
Againſt what ſhould enſue.
Mir. How came we a ſhore?
Pro. By prouidence diuine,
Some food, we had, and ſome freſh water, that
A noble *Neopolitan Gonzalo*
Out of his Charity, (who being then appointed
Maſter of this deſigne) did giue vs, with
Rich garments, linnens, ſtuffs, and neceſſaries
Which ſince haue ſteeded much, ſo of his gentleneſſe
Knowing I lou'd my bookes, he furniſhd me
From mine owne Library, with volumes, that
I prize aboue my Dukedome.
Mir. Would I might
But euer ſee that man.
Pro. Now I ariſe,
Sit ſtill, and heare the laſt of our ſea-ſorrow:
Heere in this Iland we arriu'd, and heere
Haue I, thy Schoolemaſter, made thee more profit
Then other Princeſſe can, that haue more time
For vainer howres; and Tutors, not ſo carefull.
Mir. Heuens thank you for't. And now I pray you Sir,
For ſtill 'tis beating in my minde; your reaſon
For rayſing this Sea-ſtorme?
Pro. Know thus far forth,
By accident moſt ſtrange, bountifull *Fortune*
(Now my deere Lady) hath mine enemies
Brought to this ſhore: And by my preſcience
I finde my *Zenith* doth depend vpon
A moſt auſpitious ſtarre, whoſe influence
If now I court not, but omit; my fortunes
Will euer after droope: Heare ceaſe more queſtions,
Thou art inclinde to ſleepe: 'tis a good dulneſſe,
And giue it way: I know thou canſt not chuſe:
Come away, Seruant, come; I am ready now,
Approach my *Ariel*. Come. *Enter Ariel.*
Ari. All haile, great Maſter, graue Sir, haile: I come
To anſwer thy beſt pleaſure; be't to fly,
To ſwim, to diue into the fire: to ride
On the curld clowds: to thy ſtrong bidding, taske
Ariel, and all his Qualitie.
Pro. Haſt thou, Spirit,
Performd to point, the Tempeſt that I bad thee.
Ar. To euery Article.
I boorded the Kings ſhip: now on the Beake,
Now in the Waſte, the Decke, in euery Cabyn,
I flam'd amazement, ſometime I'ld diuide
And burne in many places; on the Top-maſt,
The Yards and Bore-ſpritt, would I flame diſtinctly,
Then meete, and ioyne. *Ioues* Lightning, the precurſers
O'th dreadfull Thunder-claps more momentarie
And ſight out-running were not; the fire, and cracks
Of ſulphurous roaring, the moſt mighty *Neptune*
Seeme to beſiege, and make his bold waues tremble,
Yea, his dread Trident ſhake.
Pro. My braue Spirit,
Who was ſo firme, ſo conſtant, that this coyle
Would not infect his reaſon?
Ar. Not a ſoule
But felt a Feauer of the madde, and plaid
Some tricks of deſperation; all but Mariners
Plung'd in the foaming bryne, and quit the veſſell;
Then all a fire with me the Kings ſonne *Ferdinand*
With haire vp-ſtaring (then like reeds, not haire)
Was the firſt man that leapt; cride hell is empty,
And all the Diuels are heere.
Pro. Why that's my ſpirit:
But was not this nye ſhore?
Ar. Cloſe by, my Maſter.
Pro. But are they (*Ariell*) ſafe?
Ar. Not a haire periſhd:
On their ſuſtaining garments not a blemiſh,
But freſher then before: and as thou badſt me,
In troops I haue diſperſd them 'bout the Iſle:
The Kings ſonne haue I landed by himſelfe,
Whom I left cooling of the Ayre with ſighes,
In an odde Angle of the Iſle, and ſitting
His armes in this ſad knot.
Pro. Of the Kings ſhip,
The Marriners, ſay how thou haſt diſpoſd,
And all the reſt o'th' Fleete?
Ar. Safely in harbour
Is the Kings ſhippe, in the deepe Nooke, where once
Thou calldſt me vp at midnight to fetch dewe
From the ſtill-vext *Bermoothes*, there ſhe's hid;
The Marriners all vnder hatches ſtowed,
Who, with a Charme ioynd to their ſuffred labour
I haue left aſleep: and for the reſt o'th' Fleet

A 2 Which

(Which I diſpers'd) they all haue met againe,
And are vpon the *Mediterranian* Flote
Bound ſadly home for *Naples*,
Suppoſing that they ſaw the Kings ſhip wrackt,
And his great perſon periſh.
Pro. *Ariel*, thy charge
Exactly is perform'd; but there's more worke:
What is the time o'th'day?
Ar. Paſt the mid ſeaſon.
Pro. At leaſt two Glaſſes: the time 'twixt ſix & now
Muſt by vs both be ſpent moſt preciouſly.
Ar. Is there more toyle? Since ẏ doſt giue me pains,
Let me remember thee what thou haſt promis'd,
Which is not yet perform'd me.
Pro. How now? moodie?
What is't thou canſt demand?
Ar. My Libertie.
Pro. Before the time be out? no more:
Ar. I prethee,
Remember I haue done thee worthy ſeruice,
Told thee no lyes, made thee no miſtakings, ſerv'd
Without or grudge, or grumblings; thou did promiſe
To bate me a full yeere.
Pro. Do'ſt thou forget
From what a torment I did free thee? *Ar.* No.
Pro. Thou do'ſt: & thinkſt it much to tread ẏ Ooze
Of the ſalt deepe;
To run vpon the ſharpe winde of the North,
To doe me buſineſſe in the veines o'th' earth
When it is bak'd with froſt.
Ar. I doe not Sir.
Pro. Thou lieſt, malignant Thing: haſt thou forgot
The fowle Witch *Sycorax*, who with Age and Enuy
Was growne into a hoope? haſt thou forgot her?
Ar. No Sir.
Pro. Thou haſt: where was ſhe born? ſpeak: tell me:
Ar. Sir, in *Argier*.
Pro. Oh, was ſhe ſo: I muſt
Once in a moneth recount what thou haſt bin,
Which thou forgetſt. This damn'd Witch *Sycorax*
For miſchiefes manifold, and ſorceries terrible
To enter humane hearing, from *Argier*
Thou know'ſt was baniſh'd: for one thing ſhe did
They wold not take her life: Is not this true? *Ar.* I, Sir.
Pro. This blew ey'd hag, was hither brought with
And here was left by th' Saylors; thou my ſlaue, (child,
As thou reportſt thy ſelfe, was then her ſeruant,
And for thou waſt a Spirit too delicate
To act her earthy, and abhord commands,
Refuſing her grand heſts, ſhe did confine thee
By helpe of her more potent Miniſters,
And in her moſt vnmittigable rage,
Into a clouen Pyne, within which rift
Impriſon'd, thou didſt painefully remaine
A dozen yeeres: within which ſpace ſhe di'd,
And left thee there: where thou didſt vent thy groanes
As faſt as Mill-wheeles ſtrike: Then was this Iſland
(Saue for the Son, that he did littour heere,
A frekelld whelpe, hag-borne) not honour'd with
A humane ſhape.
Ar. Yes: *Caliban* her ſonne.
Pro. Dull thing, I ſay ſo: he, that *Caliban*
Whom now I keepe in ſeruice, thou beſt know'ſt
What torment I did finde thee in; thy grones
Did make wolues howle, and penetrate the breaſts
Of euer-angry Beares; it was a torment
To lay vpon the damn'd, which *Sycorax*
Could not againe vndoe: it was mine Art,
When I arriu'd, and heard thee, that made gape
The Pyne, and let thee out.
Ar. I thanke thee Maſter.
Pro. If thou more murmur'ſt, I will rend an Oake
And peg-thee in his knotty entrailes, till
Thou haſt howl'd away twelue winters.
Ar. Pardon, Maſter,
I will be correſpondent to command
And doe my ſpryting, gently.
Pro. Doe ſo: and after two daies
I will diſcharge thee.
Ar. That's my noble Maſter:
What ſhall I doe? ſay what? what ſhall I doe?
Pro. Goe make thy ſelfe like a Nymph o'th' Sea,
Be ſubiect to no ſight but thine, and mine: inuiſible
To euery eye-ball elſe: goe take this ſhape
And hither come in't: goe: hence
With diligence. *Exit.*
Pro. Awake, deere hart awake, thou haſt ſlept well,
Awake.
Mir. The ſtrangenes of your ſtory, put
Heauineſſe in me.
Pro. Shake it off: Come on,
Wee'll viſit *Caliban*, my ſlaue, who neuer
Yeelds vs kinde anſwere.
Mir. 'Tis a villaine Sir, I doe not loue to looke on.
Pro. But as 'tis
We cannot miſſe him: he do's make our fire,
Fetch in our wood, and ſerues in Offices
That profit vs: What hoa: ſlaue: *Caliban*:
Thou Earth, thou: ſpeake.
Cal, within. There's wood enough within.
Pro. Come forth I ſay, there's other buſines for thee:
Come thou Tortoys, when? *Enter Ariel like a water-*
Fine appariſion: my queint *Ariel*, *Nymph.*
Hearke in thine eare.
Ar. My Lord, it ſhall be done. *Exit.*
Pro. Thou poyſonous ſlaue, got by ẏ diuell himſelfe
Vpon thy wicked Dam; come forth. *Enter Caliban.*
Cal. As wicked dewe, as ere my mother bruſh'd
With Rauens feather from vnwholeſome Fen
Drop on you both: A Southweſt blow on yee,
And bliſter you all ore.
Pro. For this be ſure, to night thou ſhalt haue cramps,
Side-ſtitches, that ſhall pen thy breath vp, Vrchins
Shall for that vaſt of night, that they may worke
All exerciſe on thee: thou ſhalt be pinch'd
As thicke as hony-combe, each pinch more ſtinging
Then Bees that made 'em.
Cal. I muſt eat my dinner:
This Iſland's mine by *Sycorax* my mother,
Which thou tak'ſt from me: when thou cam'ſt firſt
Thou ſtroakſt me, & made much of me: wouldſt giue me
Water with berries in't: and teach me how
To name the bigger Light, and how the leſſe
That burne by day, and night: and then I lou'd thee
And ſhew'd thee all the qualities o'th' Iſle,
The freſh Springs, Brine-pits; barren place and fertill,
Curs'd be I that did ſo: All the Charmes
Of *Sycorax*: Toades, Beetles, Batts light on you:
For I am all the Subiects that you haue,
Which firſt was min owne King: and here you ſty-me
In this hard Rocke, whiles you doe keepe from me
The reſt o'th' Iſland.
Pro. Thou

Pro. Thou most lying slaue,
Whom stripes may moue, not kindnes: I haue vs'd thee
(Filth as thou art) with humane care, and lodg'd thee
In mine owne Cell, till thou didst seeke to violate
The honor of my childe.
Cal. Oh ho, oh ho, would't had bene done:
Thou didst preuent me, I had peopel'd else
This Isle with *Calibans.*
Mira. Abhorred Slaue,
Which any print of goodnesse wilt not take,
Being capable of all ill: I pittied thee,
Took pains to make thee speak, taught thee each houre
One thing or other: when thou didst not (Sauage)
Know thine owne meaning; but wouldst gabble, like
A thing most brutish, I endow'd thy purposes
With words that made them knowne: But thy vild race
(Tho thou didst learn) had that in't, which good natures
Could not abide to be with; therefore wast thou
Deseruedly confin'd into this Rocke, who hadst
Deseru'd more then a prison.
Cal. You taught me Language, and my profit on't
Is, I know how to curse: the red-plague rid you
For learning me your language.
Pros. Hag-seed, hence:
Fetch vs in Fewell, and be quicke thou'rt best
To answer other businesse: shrug'st thou (Malice)
If thou neglectst, or dost vnwillingly
What I command, Ile racke thee with old Crampes,
Fill all thy bones with Aches, make thee rore,
That beasts shall tremble at thy dyn.
Cal. No, 'pray thee.
I must obey, his Art is of such pow'r,
It would controll my Dams god *Setebos,*
And make a vassaile of him.
Pro. So slaue, hence. *Exit Cal.*
Enter Ferdinand & Ariel, inuisible playing & singing.
Ariel Song. *Come vnto these yellow sands,*
and then take hands:
Curtsied when you haue, and kist
the wilde waues whist:
Foote it featly heere, and there, and sweete Sprights beare
the burthen. Burthen dispersedly.
Harke, harke, bowgh wawgh: the watch-Dogges barke,
bowgh-wawgh
Ar. *Hark, hark, I heare, the straine of strutting Chanticlere*
cry cockadidle-dowe.
Fer. Where shold this Musick be? I'th aire, or th'earth?
It sounds no more: and sure it waytes vpon
Some God 'oth' Iland, sitting on a banke,
Weeping againe the King my Fathers wracke.
This Musicke crept by me vpon the waters,
Allaying both their fury, and my passion
With it's sweet ayre: thence I haue follow'd it
(Or it hath drawne me rather) but 'tis gone.
No, it begins againe.
Ariell Song. *Full fadom fiue thy Father lies,*
Of his bones are Corrall made:
Those are pearles that were his eies,
Nothing of him that doth fade,
But doth suffer a Sea-change
Into something rich, & strange:
Sea-Nimphs hourly ring his knell.
Burthen: ding dong.
Harke now I heare them, ding-dong bell.
Fer. The Ditty do's remember my drown'd father,
This is no mortall busines, nor no sound
That the earth owes: I heare it now aboue me.
Pro. The fringed Curtaines of thine eye aduance,
And say what thou see'st yond.
Mira. What is't a Spirit?
Lord, how it lookes about: Beleeue me sir,
It carries a braue forme. But 'tis a spirit.
Pro. No wench, it eats, and sleeps, & hath such senses
As we haue: such. This Gallant which thou seest
Was in the wracke: and but hee's something stain'd
With greefe (that's beauties canker) ỳ might'st call him
A goodly person; he hath lost his fellowes,
And strayes about to finde 'em.
Mir. I might call him
A thing diuine, for nothing naturall
I euer saw so Noble.
Pro. It goes on I see
As my soule prompts it: Spirit, fine spirit, Ile free thee
Within two dayes for this.
Fer. Most sure the Goddesse
On whom these ayres attend: Vouchsafe my pray'r
May know if you remaine vpon this Island,
And that you will some good instruction giue
How I may beare me heere: my prime request
(Which I do last pronounce) is (O you wonder)
If you be Mayd, or no?
Mir. No wonder Sir,
But certainly a Mayd.
Fer. My Language? Heauens:
I am the best of them that speake this speech,
Were I but where 'tis spoken.
Pro. How? the best?
What wer't thou if the King of *Naples* heard thee?
Fer. A single thing, as I am now, that wonders
To heare thee speake of *Naples*: he do's heare me,
And that he do's, I weepe: my selfe am *Naples,*
Who, with mine eyes (neuer since at ebbe) beheld
The King my Father wrack't.
Mir. Alacke, for mercy.
Fer. Yes faith, & all his Lords, the Duke of *Millaine*
And his braue sonne, being twaine.
Pro. The Duke of *Millaine*
And his more brauer daughter, could controll thee
If now 'twere fit to do't: At the first sight
They haue chang'd eyes: Delicate *Ariel,*
Ile set thee free for this. A word good Sir,
I feare you haue done your selfe some wrong: A word.
Mir. Why speakes my father so vngently? This
Is the third man that ere I saw; the first
That ere I sigh'd for: pitty moue my father
To be enclin'd my way.
Fer. O, if a Virgin,
And your affection not gone forth, Ile make you
The Queene of *Naples.*
Pro. Soft sir, one word more.
They are both in eythers pow'rs: But this swift busines
I must vneasie make, least too light winning
Make the prize light. One word more: I charge thee
That thou attend me: Thou do'st heere vsurpe
The name thou ow'st not, and hast put thy selfe
Vpon this Island, as a spy, to win it
From me, the Lord on't.
Fer. No, as I am a man.
Mir. Ther's nothing ill, can dwell in such a Temple
If the ill-spirit haue so fayre a house,
Good things will striue to dwell with't
Pro. Follow me.

A3

Pros. Speake not you for him: hee's a Traitor: come,
Ile manacle thy necke and feete together:
Sea water shalt thou drinke: thy food shall be
The fresh-brooke Mussels, wither'd roots, and huskes
Wherein the Acorne cradled. Follow.
Fer. No,
I will resist such entertainment, till
Mine enemy ha's more pow'r.
He drawes, and is charmed from mouing.
Mira. O deere Father,
Make not too rash a triall of him, for
Hee's gentle, and not fearfull.
Pros. What I say,
My foote my Tutor? Put thy sword vp Traitor,
Who mak'st a shew, but dar'st not strike: thy conscience
Is so possest with guilt: Come, from thy ward,
For I can heere disarme thee with this sticke,
And make thy weapon drop.
Mira. Beseech you Father.
Pros. Hence: hang not on my garments.
Mira. Sir haue pity,
Ile be his surety.
Pros. Silence: One word more
Shall make me chide thee, if not hate thee: What,
An aduocate for an Impostor? Hush:
Thou think'st there is no more such shapes as he,
(Hauing seene but him and *Caliban:*) Foolish wench,
To th'most of men, this is a *Caliban*,
And they to him are Angels.
Mira. My affections
Are then most humble: I haue no ambition
To see a goodlier man.
Pros. Come on, obey:
Thy Nerues are in their infancy againe.
And haue no vigour in them.
Fer. So they are:
My spirits, as in a dreame, are all bound vp:
My Fathers losse, the weaknesse which I feele,
The wracke of all my friends, nor this mans threats,
To whom I am subdude, are but light to me,
Might I but through my prison once a day
Behold this Mayd: all corners else o'th'Earth
Let liberty make vse of: space enough
Haue I in such a prison.
Pros. It workes: Come on.
Thou hast done well, fine *Ariell:* follow me,
Harke what thou else shalt do mee.
Mira. Be of comfort,
My Fathers of a better nature (Sir)
Then he appeares by speech: this is vnwonted
Which now came from him.
Pros. Thou shalt be as free
As mountaine windes; but then exactly do
All points of my command.
Ariell. To th'syllable.
Pros. Come follow: speake not for him. *Exeunt.*

Actus Secundus. Scœna Prima.

Enter Alonso, Sebastian, Anthonio, Gonzalo, Adrian, Francisco, and others.

Gonz. Beseech you Sir, be merry; you haue cause,
(So haue we all) of ioy; for our escape
Is much beyond our losse; our hint of woe
Is common, euery day, some Saylors wife,
The Masters of some Merchant, and the Merchant
Haue iust our Theame of woe: But for the miracle,
(I meane our preseruation) few in millions
Can speake like vs: then wisely (good Sir) weigh
Our sorrow, with our comfort.
Alons. Prethee peace.
Seb. He receiues comfort like cold porredge.
Ant. The Visitor will not giue him ore so.
Seb. Looke, hee's winding vp the watch of his wit,
By and by it will strike.
Gon. Sir.
Seb. One: Tell.
Gon. When euery greefe is entertaind,
That's offer'd comes to th'entertainer.
Seb. A dollor.
Gon. Dolour comes to him indeed, you haue spoken truer then you purpos'd.
Seb. You haue taken it wiselier then I meant you should.
Gon. Therefore my Lord.
Ant. Fie, what a spend-thrift is he of his tongue.
Alon. I pre-thee spare.
Gon. Well, I haue done: But yet
Seb. He will be talking.
Ant. Which, of he, or Adrian, for a good wager,
First begins to crow?
Seb. The old Cocke.
Ant. The Cockrell.
Seb. Done: The wager?
Ant. A Laughter.
Seb. A match.
Adr. Though this Island seeme to be desert.
Seb. Ha, ha, ha.
Ant. So: you'r paid.
Adr. Vninhabitable, and almost inaccessible.
Seb. Yet
Adr. Yet
Ant. He could not misse't.
Adr. It must needs be of subtle, tender, and delicate temperance.
Ant. *Temperance* was a delicate wench.
Seb. I, and a subtle, as he most learnedly deliuer'd.
Adr. The ayre breathes vpon vs here most sweetly.
Seb. As if it had Lungs, and rotten ones.
Ant. Or, as 'twere perfum'd by a Fen.
Gon. Heere is euery thing aduantageous to life.
Ant. True, saue meanes to liue.
Seb. Of that there's none, or little.
Gon. How lush and lusty the grasse lookes?
How greene?
Ant. The ground indeed is tawny.
Seb. With an eye of greene in't.
Ant. He misses not much.
Seb. No: he doth but mistake the truth totally.
Gon. But the rariety of it is, which is indeed almost beyond credit.
Seb. As many voucht rarieties are.
Gon. That our Garments being (as they were) drencht in the Sea, hold notwithstanding their freshnesse and glosses, being rather new dy'de then stain'd with salte water.
Ant. If but one of his pockets could speake, would it not say he lyes?
Seb. I, or very falsely pocket vp his report.
Gon.

Gon. Me thinkes our garments are now as freſh as
when we put them on firſt in Affricke, at the marriage
of the kings faire daughter *Claribel* to the king of *Tunis.*
Seb. 'Twas a ſweet marriage, and we proſper well in
our returne.
Adri. Tunis was neuer grac'd before with ſuch a Pa-
ragon to their Queene.
Gon. Not ſince widdow *Dido's* time.
Ant. Widow? A pox o'that: how came that Wid-
dow in? Widdow *Dido!*
Seb. What if he had ſaid Widdower *Æneas* too?
Good Lord, how you take it?
Adri. Widdow *Dido* ſaid you? You make me ſtudy
of that: She was of *Carthage*, not of *Tunis*.
Gon. This *Tunis* Sir was *Carthage*.
Adri. Carthage? *Gon.* I aſſure you *Carthage*.
Ant. His word is more then the miraculous Harpe.
Seb. He hath rais'd the wall, and houſes too.
Ant. What impoſſible matter wil he make eaſy next?
Seb. I thinke hee will carry this Iſland home in his
pocket, and giue it his ſonne for an Apple.
Ant. And ſowing the kernels of it in the Sea, bring
forth more Iſlands.
Gon. I. *Ant.* Why in good time.
Gon. Sir, we were talking, that our garments ſeeme
now as freſh as when we were at *Tunis* at the marriage
of your daughter, who is now Queene.
Ant. And the rareſt that ere came there.
Seb. Bate (I beſeech you) widdow *Dido*.
Ant. O Widdow *Dido*? I, Widdow *Dido*.
Gon. Is not Sir my doublet as freſh as the firſt day I
wore it? I meane in a ſort.
Ant. That ſort was well fiſh'd for.
Gon. When I wore it at your daughters marriage.
Alon. You cram theſe words into mine eares, againſt
the ſtomacke of my ſenſe: would I had neuer
Married my daughter there: For comming thence
My ſonne is loſt, and (in my rate) ſhe too,
Who is ſo farre from *Italy* remoued,
I ne're againe ſhall ſee her: O thou mine heire
Of *Naples* and of *Millaine*, what ſtrange fiſh
Hath made his meale on thee?
Fran. Sir he may liue,
I ſaw him beate the ſurges vnder him,
And ride vpon their backes; he trod the water
Whoſe enmity he flung aſide: and breſted
The ſurge moſt ſwolne that met him: his bold head
'Boue the contentious waues he kept, and oared
Himſelfe with his good armes in luſty ſtroke
To th'ſhore; that ore his waue-worne baſis bowed
As ſtooping to releeue him: I not doubt
He came aliue to Land.
Alon. No, no, hee's gone.
Seb. Sir you may thank your ſelfe for this great loſſe,
That would not bleſſe our Europe with your daughter,
But rather looſe her to an Affrican,
Where ſhe at leaſt, is baniſh'd from your eye,
Who hath cauſe to wet the greefe on't.
Alon. Pre-thee peace.
Seb. You were kneel'd too, & importun'd otherwiſe
By all of vs: and the faire ſoule her ſelfe
Waigh'd betweene loathneſſe, and obedience, at
Which end o'th'beame ſhould bow: we haue loſt your
I feare for euer: *Millaine* and *Naples* haue (ſon,
Mo widdowes in them of this buſineſſe making,
Then we bring men to comfort them:
The faults your owne.
Alon. So is the deer'ſt oth' loſſe
Gon. My Lord *Sebaſtian*,
The truth you ſpeake doth lacke ſome gentleneſſe,
And time to ſpeake it in: you rub the ſore,
When you ſhould bring the plaiſter.
Seb. Very well. *Ant.* And moſt Chirurgeonly.
Gon. It is foule weather in vs all, good Sir,
When you are cloudy.
Seb. Fowle weather? *Ant.* Very foule.
Gon. Had I plantation of this Iſle my Lord.
Ant. Hee'd ſow't vvith Nettle-ſeed.
Seb. Or dockes, or Mallowes.
Gon. And were the King on't, what vvould I do?
Seb. Scape being drunke, for want of Wine.
Gon. I'th'Commonwealth I vvould (by contraries)
Execute all things: For no kinde of Trafficke
Would I admit: No name of Magiſtrate:
Letters ſhould not be knowne: Riches, pouerty,
And vſe of ſeruice, none: Contract, Succeſsion,
Borne, bound of Land, Tilth, Vineyard none:
No vſe of Mettall, Corne, or Wine, or Oyle:
No occupation, all men idle, all:
And Women too, but innocent and pure:
No Soueraignty.
Seb. Yet he vvould be King on't.
Ant. The latter end of his Common-wealth forgets
the beginning.
Gon. All things in common Nature ſhould produce
Without ſweat or endeuour: Treaſon, fellony,
Sword, Pike, Knife, Gun, or neede of any Engine
Would I not haue: but Nature ſhould bring forth
Of it owne kinde, all foyzon, all abundance
To feed my innocent people.
Seb. No marrying 'mong his ſubiects?
Ant. None (man) all idle; Whores and knaues,
Gon. I vvould vvith ſuch perfection gouerne Sir:
T'Excell the Golden Age.
Seb. 'Saue his Maieſty. *Ant.* Long liue *Gonzalo*.
Gon. And do you marke me, Sir? (me.
Alon. Pre-thee no more: thou doſt talke nothing to
Gon. I do vvell beleeue your Highneſſe, and did it
to miniſter occaſion to theſe Gentlemen, who are of
ſuch ſenſible and nimble Lungs, that they alwayes vſe
to laugh at nothing.
Ant. 'Twas you vve laugh'd at.
Gon. Who, in this kind of merry fooling am nothing
to you: ſo you may continue, and laugh at nothing ſtill.
Ant. What a blow vvas there giuen?
Seb. And it had not falne flat-long.
Gon. You are Gentlemen of braue mettal: you would
lift the Moone out of her ſpheare, if ſhe would continue
in it fiue weekes vvithout changing.

Enter Ariell playing ſolemne Muſicke.

Seb. We vvould ſo, and then go a Bat-fowling.
Ant. Nay good my Lord, be not angry.
Gon. No I warrant you, I vvill not aduenture my
diſcretion ſo weakly: Will you laugh me aſleepe, for I
am very heauy.
Ant. Go ſleepe, and heare vs.
Alon. What, all ſo ſoone aſleepe? I wiſh mine eyes
Would (with themſelues) ſhut vp my thoughts,
I finde they are inclin'd to do ſo.
Seb. Pleaſe you Sir,
Do not omit the heauy offer of it:
It ſildome viſits ſorrow, when it doth, it is a Comforter.
Ant.

Ant. We two my Lord, will guard your person,
While you take your rest, and watch your safety.
Alon. Thanke you: Wondrous heauy.
Seb. What a strange drowsines possesses them?
Ant. It is the quality o'th' Clymate.
Seb. Why
Doth it not then our eye-lids sinke? I finde
Not my selfe dispos'd to sleep.
Ant. Nor I, my spirits are nimble:
They fell together all, as by consent
They dropt, as by a Thunder-stroke: what might
Worthy *Sebastian*? O, what might? no more:
And yet, me thinkes I see it in thy face,
What thou should'st be: th'occasion speaks thee, and
My strong imagination see's a Crowne
Dropping vpon thy head.
Seb. What? art thou waking?
Ant. Do you not heare me speake?
Seb. I do, and surely
It is a sleepy Language; and thou speak'st
Out of thy sleepe: What is it thou didst say?
This is a strange repose, to be asleepe
With eyes wide open: standing, speaking, mouing:
And yet so fast asleepe.
Ant. Noble *Sebastian*,
Thou let'st thy fortune sleepe: die rather: wink'st
Whiles thou art waking.
Seb. Thou do'st snore distinctly,
There's meaning in thy snores.
Ant. I am more serious then my custome: you
Must be so too, if heed me: which to do,
Trebbles thee o're.
Seb. Well: I am standing water.
Ant. Ile teach you how to flow.
Seb. Do so: to ebbe
Hereditary Sloth instructs me.
Ant. O!
If you but knew how you the purpose cherish
Whiles thus you mocke it: how in stripping it
You more inuest it: ebbing men, indeed
(Most often) do so neere the bottome run
By their owne feare, or sloth.
Seb. 'Pre-thee say on,
The setting of thine eye, and cheeke proclaime
A matter from thee; and a birth, indeed,
Which throwes thee much to yeeld.
Ant. Thus Sir:
Although this Lord of weake remembrance; this
Who shall be of as little memory
When he is earth'd, hath here almost perswaded
(For hee's a Spirit of perswasion, onely
Professes to perswade) the King his sonne's aliue,
'Tis as impossible that hee's vndrown'd,
As he that sleepes heere, swims.
Seb. I haue no hope
That hee's vndrown'd.
Ant. O, out of that no hope,
What great hope haue you? No hope that way, Is
Another way so high a hope, that euen
Ambition cannot pierce a winke beyond
But doubt discouery there. Will you grant with me
That *Ferdinand* is drown'd.
Seb. He's gone.
Ant. Then tell me, who's the next heire of *Naples*?
Seb. *Claribell*.
Ant. She that is Queene of *Tunis*: she that dwels
Ten leagues beyond mans life: she that from *Naples*
Can haue no note, vnlesse the Sun were post:
The Man i'th Moone's too slow, till new-borne chinnes
Be rough, and Razor-able: She that from whom
We all were sea-swallow'd, though some cast againe,
(And by that destiny) to performe an act
Whereof, what's past is Prologue; what to come
In yours, and my discharge.
Seb. What stuffe is this? How say you?
'Tis true my brothers daughter's Queene of *Tunis*,
So is she heyre of *Naples*, 'twixt which Regions
There is some space.
Ant. A space, whose eu'ry cubit
Seemes to cry out, how shall that *Claribell*
Measure vs backe to *Naples*? keepe in *Tunis*,
And let *Sebastian* wake. Say, this were death
That now hath seiz'd them, why they were no worse
Then now they are: There be that can rule *Naples*
As well as he that sleepes: Lords, that can prate
As amply, and vnnecessarily
As this *Gonzallo*: I my selfe could make
A Chough of as deepe chat: O, that you bore
The minde that I do; what a sleepe were this
For your aduancement? Do you vnderstand me?
Seb. Me thinkes I do.
Ant. And how do's your content
Tender your owne good fortune?
Seb. I remember
You did supplant your Brother *Prospero*.
Ant. True:
And looke how well my Garments sit vpon me,
Much feater then before: My Brothers seruants
Were then my fellowes, now they are my men.
Seb. But for your conscience.
Ant. I Sir: where lies that? If 'twere a kybe
'Twould put me to my slipper: But I feele not
This Deity in my bosome: 'Twentie consciences
That stand 'twixt me, and *Millaine*, candied be they,
And melt ere they mollest: Heere lies your Brother,
No better then the earth he lies vpon,
If he were that which now hee's like (that's dead)
Whom I with this obedient steele (three inches of it)
Can lay to bed for euer: whiles you doing thus,
To the perpetuall winke for aye might put
This ancient morsell: this Sir Prudence, who
Should not vpbraid our course: for all the rest
They'l take suggestion, as a Cat laps milke,
They'l tell the clocke, to any businesse that
We say befits the houre.
Seb. Thy case, deere Friend
Shall be my president: As thou got'st *Millaine*,
I'le come by *Naples*: Draw thy sword, one stroke
Shall free thee from the tribute which thou paiest,
And I the King shall loue thee.
Ant. Draw together:
And when I reare my hand, do you the like
To fall it on *Gonzalo*.
Seb. O, but one word.

Enter Ariell with Musicke and Song.

Ariel. My Master through his Art foresees the danger
That you (his friend) are in, and sends me forth
(For else his proiect dies) to keepe them liuing.

Sings in Gonzaloes eare.

While you here do snoaring lie,
Open-ey'd Conspiracie
His time doth take:

If

If of Life you keepe a care,
Shake off slumber and beware.
Awake, awake.

Ant. Then let vs both be sodaine.
Gon. Now, good Angels preserue the King.
Alo. Why how now hoa; awake? why are you drawn?
Wherefore this ghastly looking?
Gon. What's the matter?
Seb. Whiles we stood here securing your repose,
(Euen now) we heard a hollow burst of bellowing
Like Buls, or rather Lyons, did't not wake you?
It strooke mine eare most terribly.
Alo. I heard nothing.
Ant. O, 'twas a din to fright a Monsters eare;
To make an earthquake: sure it was the roare
Of a whole heard of Lyons.
Alo. Heard you this *Gonzalo*?
Gon. Vpon mine honour, Sir, I heard a humming,
(And that a strange one too) which did awake me:
I shak'd you Sir, and cride: as mine eyes opend,
I saw their weapons drawne: there was a noyse,
That's verily: 'tis best we stand vpon our guard;
Or that we quit this place: let's draw our weapons.
Alo. Lead off this ground & let's make further search
For my poore sonne.
Gon. Heauens keepe him from these Beasts:
For he is sure i'th Island.
Alo. Lead away. (done.
Ariell. *Prospero* my Lord, shall know what I haue
So (King) goe safely on to seeke thy Son. *Exeunt.*

Scœna Secunda.

Enter Caliban, *with a burthen of Wood (a noyse of Thunder heard)*

Cal. All the infections that the Sunne suckes vp
From Bogs, Fens, Flats, on *Prosper* fall, and make him
By ynch-meale a disease: his Spirits heare me,
And yet I needes must curse. But they'll nor pinch,
Fright me with Vrchyn-shewes, pitch me i'th mire,
Nor lead me like a fire-brand, in the darke
Out of my way, vnlesse he bid em; but
For euery trifle, are they set vpon me,
Sometime like Apes, that moe and chatter at me,
And after bite me: then like Hedg-hogs, which
Lye tumbling in my bare-foote way, and mount
Their pricks at my foot-fall: sometime am I
All wound with Adders, who with clouen tongues
Doe hisse me into madnesse: Lo, now Lo, *Enter*
Here comes a Spirit of his, and to torment me *Trinculo.*
For bringing wood in slowly: I'le fall flat,
Perchance he will not minde me.

Tri. Heres neither bush, nor shrub to beare off any weather at all: and another Storme brewing, I heare it sing ith' winde: yond same blacke cloud, yond huge one, lookes like a foul bumbard that would shed his licquor: if it should thunder, as it did before, I know not where to hide my head: yond same cloud cannot choose but fall by paile-fuls. What haue we here, a man, or a fish? dead or aliue? a fish, hee smels like a fish: a very ancient and fish-like smell: a kinde of, not of the newest poore-Iohn: a strange fish: were I in *England* now (as once I was) and had but this fish painted; not a holiday-foole there but would giue a peece of siluer: there, would this Monster, make a man: any strange beast there, makes a man: when they will not giue a doit to relieue a lame Begger, they will lay out ten to see a dead *Indian*: Leg'd like a man; and his Finnes like Armes: warme o' my troth: I doe now let loose my opinion; hold it no longer; this is no fish, but an Islander, that hath lately suffered by a Thunderbolt: Alas, the storme is come againe: my best way is to creepe vnder his Gaberdine: there is no other shelter hereabout: Misery acquaints a man with strange bedfellowes: I will here shrowd till the dregges of the storme be past.

Enter Stephano singing.

Ste. *I shall no more to sea, to sea, here shall I dye ashore.*
This is a very scuruy tune to sing at a mans
Funerall: well, here's my comfort. *Drinkes.*
Sings. *The Master, the Swabber, the Boate-swaine & I;*
The Gunner, and his Mate
Lou'd Mall, Meg, and Marrian, and Margerie,
But none of vs car'd for Kate.
For she had a tongue with a tang,
Would cry to a Sailor goe hang:
She lou'd not the sauour of Tar nor of Pitch,
Yet a Tailor might scratch her where ere she did itch.
Then to Sea Boyes, and let her goe hang.
This is a scuruy tune too:
But here's my comfort. *drinks.*
Cal. Doe not torment me: oh.
Ste. What's the matter?
Haue we diuels here?
Doe you put trickes vpon's with Saluages, and Men of Inde? ha? I haue not scap'd drowning, to be afeard now of your foure legges: for it hath bin said; as proper a man as euer went on foure legs, cannot make him giue ground: and it shall be said so againe, while *Stephano* breathes at' nostrils.

Cal. The Spirit torments me: oh.

Ste. This is some Monster of the Isle, with foure legs; who hath got (as I take it) an Ague: where the diuell should he learne our language? I will giue him some reliefe if it be but for that: if I can recouer him, and keepe him tame, and get to *Naples* with him, he's a Present for any Emperour that euer trod on Neates-leather.

Cal. Doe not torment me 'prethee: I'le bring my wood home faster.

Ste. He's in his fit now; and doe's not talke after the wisest: hee shall taste of my Bottle: if hee haue neuer drunke wine afore, it will goe neere to remoue his Fit: If I can recouer him, and keepe him tame, I will not take too much for him; hee shall pay for him that hath him, and that soundly.

Cal. Thou do'st me yet but little hurt; thou wilt anon, I know it by thy trembling: Now *Prosper* workes vpon thee.

Ste. Come on your wayes. open your mouth: here is that which will giue language to you Cat; open your mouth; this will shake your shaking, I can tell you, and that soundly: you cannot tell who's your friend; open your chaps againe.

Tri. I should know that voyce:
It should be,

But.

But hee is dround; and these are diuels; O defend me.

Ste. Foure legges and two voyces; a most delicate Monster: his forward voyce now is to speake well of his friend; his backward voice, is to vtter foule speeches, and to detract: if all the wine in my bottle will recouer him, I will helpe his Ague: Come: Amen, I will poure some to thy other mouth.

Tri. Stephano.

Ste. Doth thy other mouth call me? Mercy, mercy: This is a diuell, and no Monster: I will leaue him, I haue no long Spoone.

Tri. *Stephano*: if thou beest *Stephano* touch me, and speake to me: for I am *Trinculo*; be not afeard, thy good friend *Trinculo*.

Ste. If thou bee'st *Trinculo*: come foorth: I'le pull thee by the lesser legges: if any be *Trinculo's* legges, these are they: Thou art very *Trinculo* indeede: how cam'st thou to be the siege of this Moone-calfe? Can he vent *Trinculo's*?

Tri. I tooke him to be kil'd with a thunder-strok; but art thou not dround *Stephano*: I hope now thou art not dround: Is the Storme ouer-blowne? I hid mee vnder the dead Moone-Calfes Gaberdine, for feare of the Storme: And art thou liuing *Stephano*? O *Stephano*, two *Neapolitanes* scap'd?

Ste. 'Prethee doe not turne me about, my stomacke is not constant.

Cal. These be fine things, and if they be not sprights: that's a braue God, and beares Celestiall liquor: I will kneele to him.

Ste. How did'st thou scape? How cam'st thou hither? Sweare by this Bottle how thou cam'st hither: I escap'd vpon a But of Sacke, which the Saylors heaued o're-boord, by this Bottle which I made of the barke of a Tree, with mine owne hands, since I was cast a-shore.

Cal. I'le sweare vpon that Bottle, to be thy true subiect, for the liquor is not earthly.

St. Heere: sweare then how thou escap'dst.

Tri. Swom ashore (man) like a Ducke: I can swim like a Ducke i'le be sworne.

Ste. Here, kisse the Booke. Though thou canst swim like a Ducke, thou art made like a Goose.

Tri. O *Stephano*, ha'st any more of this?

Ste. The whole But (man) my Cellar is in a rocke by th'sea-side, where my Wine is hid: How now Moone-Calfe, how do's thine Ague?

Cal. Ha'st thou not dropt from heauen?

Ste. Out o'th Moone I doe assure thee. I was the Man ith' Moone, when time was.

Cal. I haue seene thee in her: and I doe adore thee: My Mistris shew'd me thee, and thy Dog, and thy Bush.

Ste. Come, sweare to that: kisse the Booke: I will furnish it anon with new Contents: Sweare.

Tri. By this good light, this is a very shallow Monster: I afeard of him? a very weake Monster: The Man ith Moone? A most poore creadulous Monster: Well drawne Monster, in good sooth.

Cal. Ile shew thee euery fertill ynch 'oth Island: and I will kisse thy foote. I prethee be my god.

Tri. By this light, a most perfidious, and drunken Monster, when's god's a sleepe he'll rob his Bottle.

Cal. Ile kisse thy foot. Ile sweare my selfe thy Subiect.

Ste. Come on then: downe and sweare.

Tri. I shall laugh my selfe to death at this puppi-headed Monster: a most scuruie Monster: I could finde in my heart to beate him.

Ste. Come, kisse.

Tri. But that the poore Monster's in drinke: An abhominable Monster.

Cal. I'le shew thee the best Springs: I'le plucke thee Berries: I'le fish for thee; and get thee wood enough. A plague vpon the Tyrant that I serue; I'le beare him no more Stickes, but follow thee, thou wondrous man.

Tri. A most rediculous Monster, to make a wonder of a poore drunkard.

Cal. I'prethee let me bring thee where Crabs grow; and I with my long nayles will digge thee pig-nuts; show thee a Iayes nest, and instruct thee how to snare the nimble Marmazet: I'le bring thee to clustring Philbirts, and sometimes I'le get thee young Scamels from the Rocke: Wilt thou goe with me?

Ste. I pre'thee now lead the way without any more talking. *Trinculo*, the King, and all our company else being dround, wee will inherit here: Here; beare my Bottle: Fellow *Trinculo*; we'll fill him by and by againe.

Caliban Sings drunkenly.

Farewell Master; farewell, farewell.

Tri. A howling Monster: a drunken Monster.

Cal. No more dams I'le make for fish,
Nor fetch in firing, at requiring,
Nor scrape trenchering, nor wash dish,
Ban' ban' Cacal, ban
Has a new Master, get a new Man.

Freedome, high-day, high-day freedome, freedome high-day, freedome.

Ste. O braue Monster; lead the way. *Exeunt.*

Actus Tertius. Scœna Prima.

Enter Ferdinand (bearing a Log.)

Fer. There be some Sports are painfull; & their labor
Delight in them set off: Some kindes of basenesse
Are nobly vndergon; and most poore matters
Point to rich ends: this my meane Taske
Would be as heauy to me, as odious, but
The Mistris which I serue, quickens what's dead,
And makes my labours, pleasures: O She is
Ten times more gentle, then her Father's crabbed;
And he's compos'd of harshnesse. I must remoue
Some thousands of these Logs, and pile them vp,
Vpon a sore iniunction; my sweet Mistris
Weepes when she sees me worke, & saies, such basenes
Had neuer like Executor: I forget:
But these sweet thoughts, doe euen refresh my labours,
Most busie lest, when I doe it. *Enter Miranda and Prospero.*

Mir. Alas, now pray you
Worke not so hard: I would the lightning had
Burnt vp those Logs that you are enioynd to pile:
Pray set it downe, and rest you: when this burnes
'Twill weepe for hauing wearied you: my Father
Is hard at study; pray now rest your selfe,

He's

Hee's safe for these three houres.
Fer. O most deere Mistris,
The Sun will set before I shall discharge
What I must striue to do.
Mir. If you'l sit downe
Ile beare your Logges the while: pray giue me that,
Ile carry it to the pile.
Fer. No precious Creature,
I had rather cracke my sinewes, breake my backe,
Then you should such dishonor vndergoe,
While I sit lazy by.
Mir. It would become me
As well as it do's you; and I should do it
With much more ease: for my good will is to it,
And yours it is against.
Pro. Poore worme thou art infected,
This visitation shewes it.
Mir. You looke wearily.
Fer. No, noble Mistris, 'tis fresh morning with me
When you are by at night: I do beseech you
Cheefely, that I might set it in my prayers
What is your name?
Mir. *Miranda*, O my Father,
I haue broke your hest to say so.
Fer. Admir'd *Miranda*,
Indeede the top of Admiration, worth
What's deerest to the world: full many a Lady
I haue ey'd with best regard, and many a time
Th'harmony of their tongues, hath into bondage
Brought my too diligent eare: for seuerall vertues
Haue I lik'd seuerall women, neuer any
VVith so full soule, but some defect in her
Did quarrell with the noblest grace she ow'd,
And put it to the foile. But you, O you,
So perfect, and so peetlesse, are created
Of euerie Creatures best.
Mir. I do not know
One of my sexe; no womans face remember,
Saue from my glasse, mine owne: Nor haue I seene
More that I may call men, then you good friend,
And my deere Father: how features are abroad
I am skillesse of; but by my modestie
(The iewell in my dower) I would not wish
Any Companion in the world but you:
Nor can imagination forme a shape
Besides your selfe, to like of: but I prattle
Something too wildely, and my Fathers precepts
I therein do forget.
Fer. I am, in my condition
A Prince (*Miranda*) I do thinke a King
(I would not so) and would no more endure
This wodden slauerie, then to suffer
The flesh-flie blow my mouth: heare my soule speake.
The verie instant that I saw you, did
My heart flie to your seruice, there resides
To make me slaue to it, and for your sake
Am I this patient Logge-man.
Mir. Do you loue me?
Fer. O heauen; O earth, beare witnes to this sound,
And crowne what I professe with kinde euent
If I speake true: if hollowly, inuert
VVhat best is boaded me, to mischiefe: I,
Beyond all limit of what else i'th world
Do loue, prize, honor you.
Mir. I am a foole
To weepe at what I am glad of.
Pro. Faire encounter
Of two most rare affections: heauens raine grace
On that which breeds betweene 'em.
Fer. VVherefore weepe you?
Mir. At mine vnworthinesse, that dare not offer
VVhat I desire to giue; and much lesse take
VVhat I shall die to want: But this is trifling,
And all the more it seekes to hide it selfe,
The bigger bulke it shewes. Hence bashfull cunning,
And prompt me plaine and holy innocence.
I am your wife, if you will marrie me;
If not, Ile die your maid: to be your fellow
You may denie me, but Ile be your seruant
VVhether you will or no.
Fer. My Mistris (deerest)
And I thus humble euer.
Mir. My husband then?
Fer. I, with a heart as willing
As bondage ere of freedome: heere's my hand.
Mir. And mine, with my heart in't; and now farewel
Till halfe an houre hence.
Fer. A thousand, thousand. *Exeunt.*
Pro. So glad of this as they I cannot be,
VVho are surpriz'd with all; but my reioyeing
At nothing can be more: Ile to my booke,
For yet ere supper time, must I performe
Much businesse appertaining. *Exit.*

Scœna Secunda.

Enter Caliban, Stephano, and Trinculo.

Ste. Tell not me, when the But is out we will drinke water, not a drop before; therefore beare vp, & boord em' Seruant Monster, drinke to me.

Trin. Seruant Monster? the folly of this Iland, they say there's but fiue vpon this Isle; we are three of them, if th'other two be brain'd like vs, the State totters.

Ste. Drinke seruant Monster when I bid thee, thy eies are almost set in thy head.

Trin. VVhere should they bee set else? hee were a braue Monster indeede if they were set in his taile.

Ste. My man-Monster hath drown'd his tongue in sacke: for my part the Sea cannot drowne mee, I swam ere I could recouer the shore, fiue and thirtie Leagues off and on, by this light thou shalt bee my Lieutenant Monster, or my Standard.

Trin. Your Lieutenant if you list, hee's no standard.

Ste. VVeel not run Monsieur Monster.

Trin. Nor go neither; but you'l lie like dogs, and yet say nothing neither.

Ste. Moone-calfe, speak once in thy life, if thou beest a good Moone-calfe.

Cal. How does thy honour? Let me licke thy shooe: Ile not serue him, he is not valiant.

Trin. Thou liest most ignorant Monster, I am in case to iustle a Constable: why, thou debosh'd Fish thou, was there euer man a Coward, that hath drunk so much Sacke as I to day? wilt thou tell a monstrous lie, being but halfe a Fish, and halfe a Monster?

Cal. Loe, how he mockes me, wilt thou let him my Lord?

Cal.

Trin. Lord, quoth he? that a Monſter ſhould be ſuch
a Naturall?
Cal. Loe, loe againe: bite him to death I prethee.
Ste. *Trinculo*, keepe a good tongue in your head: If
you proue a mutineere, the next Tree: the poore Mon-
ſter's my ſubiect, and he ſhall not ſuffer indignity.
Cal. I thanke my noble Lord. Wilt thou be pleas'd
to hearken once againe to the ſuite I made to thee?
Ste. Marry will I: kneele, and repeate it,
I will ſtand, and ſo ſhall *Trinculo.*

Enter Ariell inuiſible.

Cal. As I told thee before, I am ſubiect to a Tirant,
A Sorcerer, that by his cunning hath cheated me
Of the Iſland.
Ariell. Thou lyeſt.
Cal. Thou lyeſt, thou ieſting Monkey thou:
I would my valiant Maſter would deſtroy thee.
I do not lye.
Ste. *Trinculo*, if you trouble him any more in's tale,
By this hand, I will ſupplant ſome of your teeth.
Trin. Why, I ſaid nothing.
Ste. Mum then, and no more: proceed.
Cal. I ſay by Sorcery he got this Iſle
From me, he got it. If thy Greatneſſe will
Reuenge it on him, (for I know thou dar'ſt)
But this Thing dare not.
Ste. That's moſt certaine.
Cal. Thou ſhalt be Lord of it, and Ile ſerue thee.
Ste. How now ſhall this be compaſt?
Canſt thou bring me to the party?
Cal. Yea, yea my Lord, Ile yeeld him thee aſleepe,
Where thou maiſt knocke a naile into his head.
Ariell. Thou lieſt, thou canſt not.
Cal. What a py'de Ninnie's this? Thou ſcuruy patch:
I do beſeech thy Greatneſſe giue him blowes,
And take his bottle from him: When that's gone,
He ſhall drinke nought but brine, for Ile not ſhew him
Where the quicke Freſhes are.
Ste. *Trinculo*, run into no further danger:
Interrupt the Monſter one word further, and by this
hand, Ile turne my mercie out o'doores, and make a
Stockfiſh of thee.
Trin. Why, what did I? I did nothing:
Ile go farther off.
Ste. Didſt thou not ſay he lyed?
Ariell. Thou lieſt.
Ste. Do I ſo? Take thou that,
As you like this, giue me the lye another time.
Trin. I did not giue the lie: Out o'your wittes, and
hearing too?
A pox o'your bottle, this can Sacke and drinking doo:
A murren on your Monſter, and the diuell take your
fingers.
Cal. Ha, ha, ha.
Ste. Now forward with your Tale: prethee ſtand
further off.
Cal. Beate him enough: after a little time
Ile beate him too.
Ste. Stand farther: Come proceede.
Cal. Why, as I told thee, 'tis a cuſtome with him
I'th afternoone to ſleepe: there thou maiſt braine him,
Hauing firſt ſeiz'd his bookes: Or with a logge
Batter his ſkull, or paunch him with a ſtake,
Or cut his wezand with thy knife. Remember
Firſt to poſſeſſe his Bookes; for without them
Hee's but a Sot, as I am; nor hath not
One Spirit to command: they all do hate him
As rootedly as I. Burne but his Bookes,
He ha's braue Vtenſils (for ſo he calles them)
Which when he ha's a houſe, hee'l decke withall.
And that moſt deeply to conſider, is
The beautie of his daughter: he himſelfe
Cals her a non-pareill: I neuer ſaw a woman
But onely *Sycorax* my Dam, and ſhe;
But ſhe as farre ſurpaſſeth *Sycorax*,
As great'ſt do's leaſt.
Ste. Is it ſo braue a Laſſe?
Cal. I Lord, ſhe will become thy bed, I warrant,
And bring thee forth braue brood.
Ste. Monſter, I will kill this man: his daughter and
I will be King and Queene, ſaue our Graces: and *Trin-
culo* and thy ſelfe ſhall be Vice-royes:
Doſt thou like the plot *Trinculo*?
Trin. Excellent.
Ste. Giue me thy hand, I am ſorry I beate thee:
But while thou liu'ſt keepe a good tongue in thy head.
Cal. Within this halfe houre will he be aſleepe,
Wilt thou deſtroy him then?
Ste. I on mine honour.
Ariell. This will I tell my Maſter.
Cal. Thou mak'ſt me merry: I am full of pleaſure,
Let vs be iocond. Will you troule the Catch
You taught me but whileare?
Ste. At thy requeſt Monſter, I will do reaſon,
Any reaſon: Come on *Trinculo*, let vs ſing.

Sings.

Flout'em, and cout'em: and skowt'em, and flout'em.
Thought is free.

Cal. That's not the tune.

Ariell plaies the tune on a Tabor and Pipe.

Ste. What is this ſame?
Trin. This is the tune of our Catch, plaid by the pic-
ture of No-body.
Ste. If thou beeſt a man, ſhew thy ſelfe in thy likenes:
If thou beeſt a diuell, take't as thou liſt.
Trin. O forgiue me my ſinnes.
Ste. He that dies payes all debts: I defie thee;
Mercy vpon vs.
Cal. Art thou affeard?
Ste. No Monſter, not I.
Cal. Be not affeard, the Iſle is full of noyſes,
Sounds, and ſweet aires, that giue delight and hurt not:
Sometimes a thouſand twangling Inſtruments
Will hum about mine eares; and ſometime voices,
That if I then had wak'd after long ſleepe,
Will make me ſleepe againe, and then in dreaming,
The clouds methought would open, and ſhew riches
Ready to drop vpon me, that when I wak'd
I cri'de to dreame againe.
Ste. This will proue a braue kingdome to me,
Where I ſhall haue my Muſicke for nothing.
Cal. When *Proſpero* is deſtroy'd.
Ste. That ſhall be by and by:
I remember the ſtorie.
Trin. The ſound is going away,
Lets follow it, and after do our worke.
Ste. Leade Monſter,
Wee'l follow: I would I could ſee this Taborer,
He layes it on.
Trin. Wilt come?
Ile follow *Stephano*. *Exeunt.*

Scena

Scena Tertia.

Enter Alonſo, Sebaſtian, Anthonio, Gonzallo, Adrian, Franciſco, &c.

Gon. By'r lakin, I can goe no further, Sir,
My old bones akes: here's a maze trod indeede
Through fourth rights, & Meanders: by your patience
I needes muſt reſt me.
Al. Old Lord, I cannot blame thee,
Who, am my ſelfe attach'd with wearineſſe
To th'dulling of my ſpirits: Sit downe, and reſt:
Euen here I will put off my hope, and keepe it
No longer for my Flatterer: he is droun'd
Whom thus we ſtray to finde, and the Sea mocks
Our fruſtrate ſearch on land: well, let him goe.
Ant. I am right glad, that he's ſo out of hope:
Doe not for one repulſe forgoe the purpoſe
That you reſolu'd t'effect.
Seb. The next aduantage will we take throughly.
Ant. Let it be to night,
For now they are oppreſs'd with trauaile, they
Will not, nor cannot vſe ſuch vigilance
As when they are freſh.

Solemne and ſtrange Muſicke: and Proſper on the top (inuiſible:) Enter ſeuerall ſtrange ſhapes, bringing in a Banket; and dance about it with gentle actions of ſalutations, and inuiting the King, &c. to eate, they depart.

Seb. I ſay to night: no more.
Al. What harmony is this? my good friends, harke.
Gon. Maruellous ſweet Muſicke.
Alo. Giue vs kind keepers, heaues: what were theſe?
Seb. A liuing *Drollerie*: now I will beleeue
That there are Vnicornes: that in *Arabia*
There is one Tree, the Phœnix throne, one Phœnix
At this houre reigning there.
Ant. Ile beleeue both:
And what do's elſe want credit, come to me
And Ile beſworne 'tis true: Trauellers nere did lye,
Though fooles at home condemne em.
Gon. If in *Naples*
I ſhould report this now, would they beleeue me?
If I ſhould ſay I ſaw ſuch Iſlands;
(For certes, theſe are people of the Iſland)
Who though they are of monſtrous ſhape, yet note
Their manners are more gentle, kinde, then of
Our humaine generation you ſhall finde
Many, nay almoſt any.
Pro. Honeſt Lord,
Thou haſt ſaid well: for ſome of you there preſent;
Are worſe then diuels.
Al. I cannot too much muſe
Such ſhapes, ſuch geſture, and ſuch ſound expreſſing
(Although they want the vſe of tongue) a kinde
Of excellent dumbe diſcourſe.
Pro. Praiſe in departing.
Fr. They vaniſh'd ſtrangely.
Seb. No matter, ſince (macks.
They haue left their Viands behinde; for wee haue ſto-
Wilt pleaſe you taſte of what is here?
Alo. Not I. (Boyes
Gon. Faith Sir, you neede not feare: when wee were
Who would beleeue that there were Mountayneeres,
Dew-lapt, like Buls, whoſe throats had hanging at'em
Wallets of fleſh? or that there were ſuch men
Whoſe heads ſtood in their breſts? which now we finde
Each putter out of fiue for one, will bring vs
Good warrant of.
Al. I will ſtand to, and feede,
Although my laſt, no matter, ſince I feele
The beſt is paſt: brother: my Lord, the Duke,
Stand too, and doe as we.

Thunder and Lightning. Enter Ariell (like a Harpey) claps his wings vpon the Table, and with a quient deuice the Banquet vaniſhes.

Ar. You are three men of ſinne, whom deſtiny
That hath to inſtrument this lower world,
And what is in't: the neuer ſurfeited Sea,
Hath caus'd to belch vp you; and on this Iſland,
Where man doth not inhabit, you 'mongſt men,
Being moſt vnfit to liue: I haue made you mad;
And euen with ſuch like valour, men hang, and drowne
Their proper ſelues: you fooles, I and my fellowes
Are miniſters of Fate, the Elements
Of whom your ſwords are temper'd, may as well
Wound the loud windes, or with bemockt-at-Stabs
Kill the ſtill cloſing waters, as diminiſh
One dowle that's in my plumbe: My fellow miniſters
Are like-invulnerable: if you could hurt,
Your ſwords are now too maſſie for your ſtrengths,
And will not be vplifted: But remember
(For that's my buſineſſe to you) that you three
From *Millaine* did ſupplant good *Proſpero*,
Expos'd vnto the Sea (which hath requit it)
Him, and his innocent childe: for which foule deed,
The Powres, delaying (not forgetting) haue
Incens'd the Seas, and Shores; yea, all the Creatures
Againſt your peace: Thee of thy Sonne, *Alonſo*
They haue bereft; and doe pronounce by me
Lingring perdition (worſe then any death
Can be at once) ſhall ſtep, by ſtep attend
You, and your wayes, whoſe wraths to guard you from,
Which here, in this moſt deſolate Iſle, elſe fals
Vpon your heads, is nothing but hearts-ſorrow,
And a cleere life enſuing.

He vaniſhes in Thunder: then (to ſoft Muſicke.) Enter the ſhapes againe, and daunce (with mockes and mowes) and carrying out the Table.

Pro. Brauely the figure of this *Harpie*, haſt thou
Perform'd (my *Ariell*) a grace it had deuouring:
Of my Inſtruction, haſt thou nothing bated
In what thou had'ſt to ſay: ſo with good life,
And obſeruation ſtrange, my meaner miniſters
Their ſeuerall kindes haue done: my high charmes work,
And theſe (mine enemies) are all knit vp
In their diſtractions: they now are in my powre;
And in theſe fits, I leaue them, while I viſit
Yong *Ferdinand* (whom they ſuppoſe is droun'd)
And his, and mine lou'd darling.
Gon. I'th name of ſomething holy, Sir, why ſtand you
In this ſtrange ſtare?
Al. O, it is monſtrous: monſtrous:
Me thought the billowes ſpoke, and told me of it,
The windes did ſing it to me: and the Thunder
(That deepe and dreadfull Organ-Pipe) pronounc'd
The name of *Proſper*: it did baſe my Treſpaſſe,
Therefore my Sonne i'th Ooze is bedded; and
I'le ſeeke him deeper then ere plummet ſounded,
And with him there lye mudded. *Exit.*
Seb. But one feend at a time,
Ile fight their Legions ore.

B *Ant.*

Ant. Ile be thy Second. *Exeunt.*
Gon. All three of them are deſperate: their great guilt
(Like poyſon giuen to worke a great time after)
Now gins to bite the ſpirits: I doe beſeech you
(That are of ſuppler ioynts) follow them ſwiftly,
And hinder them from what this extaſie
May now prouoke them to.
Ad. Follow, I pray you. *Exeunt omnes.*

Actus Quartus. Scena Prima.

Enter Proſpero, Ferdinand, and Miranda.
Pro. If I haue too auſterely puniſh'd you,
Your compenſation makes amends, for I
Haue giuen you here, a third of mine owne life,
Or that for which I liue: who, once againe
I tender to thy hand: All thy vexations
Were but my trials of thy loue, and thou
Haſt ſtrangely ſtood the teſt: here, afore heauen
I ratifie this my rich guift: O *Ferdinand*,
Doe not ſmile at me, that I boaſt her of,
For thou ſhalt finde ſhe will out-ſtrip all praiſe
And make it halt, behinde her.
Fer. I doe beleeue it
Againſt an Oracle.
Pro. Then, as my gueſt, and thine owne acquiſition
Worthily purchas'd, take my daughter: But
If thou do'ſt breake her Virgin-knot, before
All ſanctimonious ceremonies may
With full and holy right, be miniſtred,
No ſweet aſperſion ſhall the heauens let fall
To make this contract grow; but barraine hate,
Sower-ey'd diſdaine, and diſcord ſhall beſtrew
The vnion of your bed, with weedes ſo loathly
That you ſhall hate it both: Therefore take heede,
As Hymens Lamps ſhall light you.
Fer. As I hope
For quiet dayes, faire Iſſue, and long life,
With ſuch loue, as 'tis now the murkieſt den,
The moſt opportune place, the ſtrongſt ſuggeſtion,
Our worſer *Genius* can, ſhall neuer melt
Mine honor into luſt, to take away
The edge of that dayes celebration,
When I ſhall thinke, or *Phœbus* Steeds are founderd,
Or Night kept chain'd below.
Pro. Fairely ſpoke;
Sit then, and talke with her, ſhe is thine owne;
What *Ariell*; my induſtrious ſeruãt *Ariell*. *Enter Ariell.*
Ar. What would my potent maſter? here I am.
Pro. Thou, and thy meaner fellowes, your laſt ſeruice
Did worthily performe: and I muſt vſe you
In ſuch another tricke: goe bring the rabble
(Ore whom I giue thee powre) here, to this place:
Incite them to quicke motion, for I muſt
Beſtow vpon the eyes of this yong couple
Some vanity of mine Art: it is my promiſe,
And they expect it from me.
Ar. Preſently?
Pro. I: with a twincke.
Ar. Before you can ſay come, and goe,
And breathe twice; and cry, ſo, ſo:
Each one tripping on his Toe,
Will be here with mop, and mowe.
Doe you loue me Maſter? no?
Pro. Dearely, my delicate *Ariell*: doe not approach
Till thou do'ſt heare me call.
Ar. Well: I conceiue. *Exit.*
Pro. Looke thou be true: doe not giue dalliance
Too much the raigne: the ſtrongeſt oathes, are ſtraw
To th'fire ith' blood: be more abſtenious,
Or elſe good night your vow.
Fer. I warrant you, Sir,
The white cold virgin Snow, vpon my heart
Abates the ardour of my Liuer.
Pro. Well.
Now come my *Ariell*, bring a Corolary,
Rather then want a Spirit; appear, & pertly. *Soft muſick.*
No tongue: all eyes; be ſilent. *Enter Iris.*
Ir. Ceres, moſt bounteous Lady, thy rich Leas
Of Wheate, Rye, Barley, Fetches, Oates and Peaſe;
Thy Turphie-Mountaines, where liue nibling Sheepe,
And flat Medes thetchd with Stouer, them to keepe:
Thy bankes with pioned, and twilled brims
Which ſpungie *Aprill*, at thy heſt betrims;
To make cold Nymphes chaſt crownes; & thy broome-
Whoſe ſhadow the diſmiſſed Batchelor loues, (groues;
Being laſſe-lorne: thy pole-clipt vineyard,
And thy Sea-marge ſtirrile, and rockey-hard,
Where thou thy ſelfe do'ſt ayre, the Queene o'th Skie,
Whoſe watry Arch, and meſſenger, am I.
Bids thee leaue theſe, & with her ſoueraigne grace, *Iuno*
Here on this graſſe-plot, in this very place *deſcends.*
To come, and ſport: here Peacocks flye amaine:
Approach, rich *Ceres*, her to entertaine. *Enter Ceres.*
Cer. Haile, many-coloured Meſſenger, that nere
Do'ſt diſobey the wife of *Iupiter*:
Who, with thy ſaffron wings, vpon my flowres
Diffuſeſt hony drops, refreſhing ſhowres,
And with each end of thy blew bowe do'ſt crowne
My boskie acres, and my vnſhrubd downe,
Rich ſcarph to my proud earth: why hath thy Queene
Summond me hither, to this ſhort gras'd Greene?
Ir. A contract of true Loue, to celebrate,
And ſome donation freely to eſtate
On the bleſ'd Louers.
Cer. Tell me heauenly Bowe,
If *Venus* or her Sonne, as thou do'ſt know,
Doe now attend the Queene? ſince they did plot
The meanes, that duskie *Dis*, my daughter got,
Her, and her blind-Boyes ſcandald company,
I haue forſworne.
Ir. Of her ſocietie
Be not afraid: I met her deitie
Cutting the clouds towards *Paphos*: and her Son
Doue drawn with her: here thought they to haue done
Some wanton charme, vpon this Man and Maide,
Whoſe vowes are, that no bed-right ſhall be paid
Till *Hymens* Torch be lighted: but in vaine,
Marſes hot Minion is returnd againe,
Her waſpiſh headed ſonne, has broke his arrowes,
Swears he will ſhoote no more, but play with Sparrows,
And be a Boy right out.
Cer. Higheſt Queene of State,
Great *Iuno* comes, I know her by her gate.
Iu. How do's my bounteous ſiſter? goe with me
To bleſſe this twaine, that they may proſperous be,
And honourd in their Iſſue. *They Sing.*
Iu. Honor, riches, marriage, bleſſing,
Long continuance, and encreaſing,
Hourely ioyes, be ſtill vpon you,
Iuno

Iuno sings her blessings on you.
Earths increase, foyzon plentie,
Barnes, and Garners, neuer empty.
Vines, with clustring bunches growing,
Plants, with goodly burthen bowing:
Spring come to you at the farthest,
In the very end of Haruest.
Scarcity and want shall shun you,
Ceres blessing so is on you.

Fer. This is a most maiesticke vision, and
Harmonious charmingly: may I be bold
To thinke these spirits?

Pro. Spirits, which by mine Art
I haue from their confines call'd to enact
My present fancies.

Fer. Let me liue here euer,
So rare a wondred Father, and a wise
Makes this place Paradise.

Pro. Sweet now, silence:
Iuno and *Ceres* whisper seriously,
There's something else to doe: hush, and be mute
Or else our spell is mar'd.

Iuno *and* Ceres *whisper, and send* Iris *on employment.*

Iris. You Nimphs cald *Nayades* of ỳ windring brooks,
With your sedg'd crownes, and euer-harmelesse lookes,
Leaue your crispe channels, and on this greene-Land
Answere your summons, *Iuno* do's command.
Come temperate *Nimphes*, and helpe to celebrate
A Contract of true Loue: be not too late.

Enter Certaine Nimphes.

You Sun-burn'd Sicklemen of August weary,
Come hether from the furrow, and be merry,
Make holly day: your Rye-straw hats put on,
And these fresh Nimphes encounter euery one
In Country footing.

Enter certaine Reapers (properly habited:) they ioyne with the Nimphes, in a gracefull dance, towards the end whereof, Prospero *starts sodainly and speakes, after which to a strange hollow and confused noyse, they heauily vanish.*

Pro. I had forgot that foule conspiracy
Of the beast *Calliban*, and his confederates
Against my life: the minute of their plot
Is almost come: Well done, auoid: no more.

Fer. This is strange: your fathers in some passion
That workes him strongly.

Mir. Neuer till this day
Saw I him touch'd with anger, so distemper'd.

Pro. You doe looke (my son) in a mou'd sort,
As if you were dismaid: be cheerefull Sir,
Our Reuels now are ended: These our actors,
(As I foretold you) were all Spirits, and
Are melted into Ayre, into thin Ayre,
And like the baselesse fabricke of this vision
The Clowd-capt Towres, the gorgeous Pallaces,
The solemne Temples, the great Globe it selfe,
Yea, all which it inherit, shall dissolue,
And like this insubstantiall Pageant faded
Leaue not a racke behinde: we are such stuffe
As dreames are made on; and our little life
Is rounded with a sleepe: Sir, I am vext,
Beare with my weakenesse, my old braine is troubled:
Be not disturb'd with my infirmitie,
If you be pleas'd, retire into my Cell,
And there repose, a turne or two, Ile walke
To still my beating minde.

Fer. Mir. We wish your peace. *Exit.*

Pro. Come with a thought; I thank thee *Ariell*: come.

Enter Ariell.

Ar. Thy thoughts I cleaue to, what's thy pleasure?

Pro. Spirit: We must prepare to meet with *Caliban*.

Ar. I my Commander, when I presented *Ceres*
I thought to haue told thee of it, but I fear'd
Least I might anger thee.

Pro. Say again, where didst thou leaue these varlots?

Ar. I told you Sir, they were red-hot with drinking,
So full of valour, that they smote the ayre
For breathing in their faces: beate the ground
For kissing of their feete; yet alwaies bending
Towards their proiect: then I beate my Tabor,
At which like vnback't colts they prickt their eares,
Aduanc'd their eye-lids, lifted vp their noses
As they smelt musicke, so I charm'd their eares
That Calfe-like, they my lowing follow'd, through
Tooth'd briars, sharpe firzes, pricking gosse, & thorns,
Which entred their fraile shins: at last I left them
I'th' filthy mantled poole beyond your Cell,
There dancing vp to th'chins, that the fowle Lake
Ore-stunck their feet.

Pro. This was well done (my bird)
Thy shape inuisible retaine thou still:
The trumpery in my house, goe bring it hither
For stale to catch these theeues. *Ar.* I go, I goe. *Exit.*

Pro. A Deuill, a borne-Deuill, on whose nature
Nurture can neuer sticke: on whom my paines
Humanely taken, all, all lost, quite lost,
And, as with age, his body ouglier growes,
So his minde cankers: I will plague them all,
Euen to roaring: Come, hang on them this line.

Enter Ariell, *loaden with glistering apparell, &c. Enter* Caliban, Stephano, *and* Trinculo, *all wet.*

Cal. Pray you tread softly, that the blinde Mole may
not heare a foot fall: we now are neere his Cell.

St. Monster, your Fairy, ẇ you say is a harmles Fairy,
Has done little better then plaid the Iacke with vs.

Trin. Monster, I do smell all horse-pisse, at which
My nose is in great indignation.

Ste. So is mine. Do you heare Monster: If I should
Take a displeasure against you: Looke you.

Trin. Thou wert but a lost Monster.

Cal. Good my Lord, giue me thy fauour stil,
Be patient, for the prize Ile bring thee too
Shall hudwinke this mischance: therefore speake softly,
All's husht as midnight yet.

Trin. I, but to loose our bottles in the Poole.

Ste. There is not onely disgrace and dishonor in that
Monster, but an infinite losse.

Tr. That's more to me then my wetting:
Yet this is your harmlesse Fairy, Monster.

Ste. I will fetch off my bottle,
Though I be o're eares for my labour.

Cal. Pre-thee (my King) be quiet. Seest thou heere
This is the mouth o'th Cell: no noise, and enter:
Do that good mischeefe, which may make this Island
Thine owne for euer, and I thy *Caliban*
For aye thy foot-licker.

Ste. Giue me thy hand,
I do begin to haue bloody thoughts.

Trin. O King *Stephano*, O Peere: O worthy *Stephano*,
Looke what a wardrobe heere is for thee.

Cal. Let it alone thou foole, it is but trash.

Tri. Oh, ho, Monster: wee know what belongs to a
frippery, O King *Stephano*.

Ste. Put off that gowne (*Trinculo*) by this hand Ile haue that gowne.

Tri. Thy grace shall haue it.

Cal. The dropsie drowne this foole, what doe you (meane
To doate thus on such luggage? let's alone
And doe the murther first: if he awake,
From toe to crowne hee'l fill our skins with pinches,
Make vs strange stuffe.

Ste. Be you quiet (Monster) Mistris line, is not this my Ierkin? now is the Ierkin vnder the line: now Ierkin you are like to lose your haire, & proue a bald Ierkin.

Trin. Doe, doe; we steale by lyne and leuell, and't like your grace.

Ste. I thank thee for that iest; heer's a garment for't: Wit shall not goe vn-rewarded while I am King of this Country: Steale by line and leuell, is an excellent passe of pate: there's another garment for't.

Tri. Monster, come put some Lime vpon your fingers, and away with the rest.

Cal. I will haue none on't: we shall loose our time,
And all be turn'd to Barnacles, or to Apes
With foreheads villanous low.

Ste. Monster, lay to your fingers: helpe to beare this away, where my hogshead of wine is, or Ile turne you out of my kingdome: goe to, carry this.

Tri. And this.

Ste. I, and this.

A noyse of Hunters heard. Enter diuers Spirits in shape of Dogs and Hounds, hunting them about: Prospero and Ariel setting them on.

Pro. Hey *Mountaine*, hey.

Ari. *Siluer*: there it goes, *Siluer*.

Pro. Fury, Fury: there Tyrant, there: harke, harke.
Goe, charge my Goblins that they grinde their ioynts
With dry Conuultions, shorten vp their sinewes
With aged Cramps, & more pinch-spotted make them,
Then Pard, or Cat o' Mountaine.

Ari. Harke, they rore.

Pro. Let them be hunted soundly: At this houre
Lies at my mercy all mine enemies:
Shortly shall all my labours end, and thou
Shalt haue the ayre at freedome: for a little
Follow, and doe me seruice. *Exeunt.*

Actus quintus: Scœna Prima.

Enter Prospero (*in his Magicke robes*) *and* Ariel.

Pro. Now do's my Proiect gather to a head:
My charmes cracke not: my Spirits obey, and Time
Goes vpright with his carriage: how's the day?

Ar. On the sixt hower, at which time, my Lord
You said our worke should cease.

Pro. I did say so,
When first I rais'd the Tempest: say my Spirit,
How fares the King, and 's followers?

Ar. Confin'd together
In the same fashion, as you gaue in charge,
Iust as you left them; all prisoners Sir
In the *Line-groue* which weather-fends your Cell,
They cannot boudge till your release: The King,
His Brother, and yours, abide all three distracted,
And the remainder mourning ouer them,
Brim full of sorrow, and dismay: but chiefly
Him that you term'd Sir, the good old Lord *Gonzallo*,
His teares runs downe his beard like winters drops
From eaues of reeds: your charm so strongly works 'em
That if you now beheld them, your affections
Would become tender.

Pro. Dost thou thinke so, Spirit?

Ar. Mine would, Sir, were I humane.

Pro. And mine shall.
Hast thou (which art but aire) a touch, a feeling
Of their afflictions, and shall not my selfe,
One of their kinde, that rellish all as sharpely,
Passion as they, be kindlier mou'd then thou art?
Thogh with their high wrongs I am strook to th' quick,
Yet, with my nobler reason, gainst my furie
Doe I take part: the rarer Action is
In vertue, then in vengeance: they, being penitent,
The sole drift of my purpose doth extend
Not a frowne further: Goe, release them *Ariell*,
My Charmes Ile breake, their sences Ile restore,
And they shall be themselues.

Ar. Ile fetch them, Sir. *Exit.*

Pro. Ye Elues of hils, brooks, stāding lakes & groues,
And ye, that on the sands with printlesse foote
Doe chase the ebbing-*Neptune*, and doe flie him
When he comes backe: you demy-Puppets, that
By Moone-shine doe the greene sowre Ringlets make,
Whereof the Ewe not bites: and you, whose pastime
Is to make midnight-Mushrumps, that reioyce
To heare the solemne Curfewe, by whose ayde
(Weake Masters though ye be) I haue bedymn'd
The Noone-tide Sun, call'd forth the mutenous windes,
And twixt the greene Sea, and the azur'd vault
Set roaring warre: To the dread ratling Thunder
Haue I giuen fire, and rifted *Ioues* stowt Oke
With his owne Bolt: The strong bass'd promontorie
Haue I made shake, and by the spurs pluckt vp
The Pyne, and Cedar. Graues at my command
Haue wak'd their sleepers, op'd, and let 'em forth
By my so potent Art. But this rough Magicke
I heere abiure: and when I haue requir'd
Some heauenly Musicke (which euen now I do)
To worke mine end vpon their Sences, that
This Ayrie-charme is for, I'le breake my staffe,
Bury it certaine fadomes in the earth,
And deeper then did euer Plummet sound
Ile drowne my booke. *Solemne musicke.*

Heere enters Ariel *before: Then* Alonso *with a franticke gesture, attended by* Gonzalo. Sebastian *and* Anthonio *in like manner attended by* Adrian *and* Francisco: *They all enter the circle which* Prospero *had made, and there stand charm'd: which* Prospero *obseruing, speakes.*

A solemne Ayre, and the best comforter,
To an vnsetled fancie, Cure thy braines
(Now vselesse) boile within thy skull: there stand
For you are Spell-stopt.
Holy *Gonzallo*, Honourable man,
Mine eyes ev'n sociable to the shew of thine
Fall fellowly drops: The charme dissolues apace,
And as the morning steales vpon the night
(Melting the darkenesse) so their rising sences
Begin to chace the ignorant fumes that mantle
Their cleerer reason. O good *Gonzallo*
My true preseruer, and a loyall Sir,
To him thou follow'st; I will pay thy graces
Home both in word, and deede: Most cruelly

Didst

Did thou *Alonso*, vse me, and my daughter:
Thy brother was a furtherer in the Act,
Thou art pinch'd for't now *Sebastian*. Flesh, and bloud,
You, brother mine, that entertaine ambition,
Expelld remorse, and nature, whom, with *Sebastian*
(Whose inward pinches therefore are most strong)
Would heere haue kill'd your King: I do forgiue thee,
Vnnaturall though thou art: Their vnderstanding
Begins to swell, and the approching tide
Will shortly fill the reasonable shore
That now ly foule, and muddy: not one of them
That yet lookes on me, or would know me: *Ariell*,
Fetch me the Hat, and Rapier in my Cell,
I will discase me, and my selfe present
As I was sometime *Millaine*: quickly Spirit,
Thou shalt ere long be free.

Ariell sings, and helps to attire him.

Where the Bee sucks, there suck I,
In a Cowslips bell, I lie,
There I cowch when Owles doe crie,
On the Batts backe I doe flie
after Sommer merrely.
Merrely, merrily, shall I liue now,
Vnder the blossom that hangs on the Bow.

Pro. Why that's my dainty *Ariell*: I shall misse
Thee, but yet thou shalt haue freedome: so, so, so.
To the Kings ship, inuisible as thou art,
There shalt thou finde the Marriners asleepe
Vnder the Hatches: the Master and the Boat-swaine
Being awake, enforce them to this place;
And presently, I pre'thee.

Ar. I drinke the aire before me, and returne
Or ere your pulse twice beate. *Exit.*

Gon. All torment, trouble, wonder, and amazement
Inhabits heere: some heauenly power guide vs
Out of this fearefull Country.

Pro. Behold Sir King
The wronged Duke of *Millaine*, *Prospero*:
For more assurance that a liuing Prince
Do's now speake to thee, I embrace thy body,
And to thee, and thy Company, I bid
A hearty welcome.

Alo. Where thou bee'st he or no,
Or some inchanted trifle to abuse me,
(As late I haue beene) I not know: thy Pulse
Beats as of flesh, and blood: and since I saw thee,
Th'affliction of my minde amends, with which
I feare a madnesse held me: this must craue
(And if this be at all) a most strange story.
Thy Dukedome I resigne, and doe entreat
Thou pardon me my wrongs: But how shold *Prospero*
Be liuing, and be heere?

Pro. First, noble Frend,
Let me embrace thine age, whose honor cannot
Be measur'd, or confin'd.

Gonz. Whether this be,
Or be not, I'le not sweare.

Pro. You doe yet taste
Some subtleties o'th'Isle, that will nor let you
Beleeue things certaine: Wellcome, my friends all,
But you, my brace of Lords, were I so minded
I heere could plucke his Highnesse frowne vpon you
And iustifie you Traitors: at this time
I will tell no tales.

Seb. The Diuell speakes in him:

Pro. No:
For you (most wicked Sir) whom to call brother
Would euen infect my mouth, I do forgiue
Thy rankest fault; all of them: and require
My Dukedome of thee, which, perforce I know
Thou must restore.

Alo. If thou beest *Prospero*
Giue vs particulars of thy preseruation,
How thou hast met vs heere, whom three howres since
Were wrackt vpon this shore? where I haue lost
(How sharp the point of this remembrance is)
My deere sonne *Ferdinand*.

Pro. I am woe for't, Sir.

Alo. Irreparable is the losse, and patience
Saies, it is past her cure.

Pro. I rather thinke
You haue not sought her helpe, of whose soft grace
For the like losse, I haue her soueraigne aid,
And rest my selfe content.

Alo. You the like losse?

Pro As great to me, as late, and supportable
To make the deere losse, haue I meanes much weaker
Then you may call to comfort you; for I
Haue lost my daughter.

Alo. A daughter?
Oh heauens, that they were liuing both in *Nalpes*
The King and Queene there, that they were, I wish
My selfe were mudded in that oo-zie bed
Where my sonne lies: when did you lose your daughter?

Pro. In this last Tempest. I perceiue these Lords
At this encounter doe so much admire,
That they deuoure their reason, and scarce thinke
Their eies doe offices of Truth: Their words
Are naturall breath: but howsoeu'r you haue
Beene iustled from your sences, know for certain
That I am *Prospero*, and that very Duke
Which was thrust forth of *Millaine*, who most strangely
Vpon this shore (where you were wrackt) was landed
To be the Lord on't: No more yet of this,
For 'tis a Chronicle of day by day,
Not a relation for a break-fast, nor
Befitting this first meeting: Welcome, Sir;
This Cell's my Court: heere haue I few attendants,
And Subiects none abroad: pray you looke in:
My Dukedome since you haue giuen me againe,
I will requite you with as good a thing,
At least bring forth a wonder, to content ye
As much, as me my Dukedome.

Here Prospero discouers Ferdinand and Miranda, playing at Chesse.

Mir. Sweet Lord, you play me false.

Fer. No my dearest loue,
I would not for the world. (wrangle,

Mir. Yes, for a score of Kingdomes, you should
And I would call it faire play.

Alo. If this proue
A vision of the Island, one deere Sonne
Shall I twice loose.

Seb. A most high miracle.

Fer. Though the Seas threaten they are mercifull,
I haue curs'd them without cause.

Alo. Now all the blessings
Of a glad father, compasse thee about:
Arise, and say how thou cam'st heere.

Mir. O wonder!
How many goodly creatures are there heere?
How beauteous mankinde is? O braue new world

B 2 That

That has ſuch people in't.
Pro. 'Tis new to thee. (play?
Alo. What is this Maid, with whom thou was't at
Your eld'ſt acquaintance cannot be three houres:
Is ſhe the goddeſſe that hath ſeuer'd vs,
And brought vs thus together?
Fer. Sir, ſhe is mortall;
But by immortall prouidence, ſhe's mine;
I choſe her when I could not aske my Father
For his aduiſe: nor thought I had one: She
Is daughter to this famous Duke of *Millaine*,
Of whom, ſo often I haue heard renowne,
But neuer ſaw before: of whom I haue
Receiu'd a ſecond life; and ſecond Father
This Lady makes him to me.
Alo. I am hers.
But O, how odly will it ſound, that I
Muſt aske my childe forgiueneſſe?
Pro. There Sir ſtop,
Let vs not burthen our remembrances, with
A heauineſſe that's gon.
Gon. I haue inly wept,
Or ſhould haue ſpoke ere this: looke downe you gods
And on this couple drop a bleſſed crowne;
For it is you, that haue chalk'd forth the way
Which brought vs hither.
Alo. I ſay Amen, *Gonzallo.*
Gon. Was *Millaine* thruſt from *Millaine*, that his Iſſue
Should become Kings of *Naples*? O reioyce
Beyond a common ioy, and ſet it downe
With gold on laſting Pillers: In one voyage
Did *Claribell* her husband finde at *Tunis*,
And *Ferdinand* her brother, found a wife,
Where he himſelfe was loſt: *Proſpero*, his Dukedome
In a poore Iſle: and all of vs, our ſelues,
When no man was his owne.
Alo. Giue me your hands:
Let griefe and ſorrow ſtill embrace his heart,
That doth not wiſh you ioy.
Gon. Be it ſo, Amen.

Enter Ariell, with the Maſter and Boatſwaine amazedly following.

O looke Sir, looke Sir, here is more of vs:
I propheſi'd, if a Gallowes were on Land
This fellow could not drowne: Now blaſphemy,
That ſwear'ſt Grace ore-boord, not an oath on ſhore,
Haſt thou no mouth by land?
What is the newes?
Bot. The beſt newes is, that we haue ſafely found
Our King, and company: The next: our Ship,
Which but three glaſſes ſince, we gaue out ſplit,
Is tyte, and yare, and brauely rig'd, as when
We firſt put out to Sea.
Ar. Sir, all this ſeruice
Haue I done ſince I went.
Pro. My trickſey Spirit.
Alo. Theſe are not naturall euens, they ſtrengthen
From ſtrange, to ſtranger: ſay, how came you hither?
Bot. If I did thinke, Sir, I were well awake,
I'ld ſtriue to tell you: we were dead of ſleepe,
And (how we know not) all clapt vnder hatches,
Where, but euen now, with ſtrange, and ſeuerall noyſes
Of roring, ſhreeking, howling, gingling chaines,
And mo diuerſitie of ſounds, all horrible.
We were awak'd: ſtraight way, at liberty;
Where we, in all our trim, freſhly beheld
Our royall, good, and gallant Ship: our Maſter
Capring to eye her: on a trice, ſo pleaſe you,
Euen in a dreame, were we diuided from them,
And were brought moaping hither.
Ar. Was't well done?
Pro. Brauely (my diligence) thou ſhalt be free.
Alo. This is as ſtrange a Maze, as ere men trod,
And there is in this buſineſſe, more then nature
Was euer conduct of: ſome Oracle
Muſt rectifie our knowledge.
Pro. Sir, my Leige,
Doe not infeſt your minde, with beating on
The ſtrangeneſſe of this buſineſſe, at pickt leiſure
(Which ſhall be ſhortly ſingle) I'le reſolue you,
(Which to you ſhall ſeeme probable) of euery
Theſe happend accidents: till when, be cheerefull
And thinke of each thing well: Come hither Spirit,
Set *Caliban*, and his companions free:
Vntye the Spell: How fares my gracious Sir?
There are yet miſſing of your Companie
Some few odde Lads, that you remember not

Enter Ariell, driuing in Caliban, Stephano, and Trinculo in their ſtolne Apparell.

Ste. Euery man ſhift for all the reſt, and let
No man take care for himſelfe; for all is
But fortune: *Coragio* Bully-Monſter *Corasio.*
Tri. If theſe be true ſpies which I weare in my head, here's a goodly ſight.
Cal. O *Setebos*, theſe be braue Spirits indeede
How fine my Maſter is? I am afraid
He will chaſtiſe me.
Seb. Ha, ha:
What things are theſe, my Lord *Anthonio*?
Will money buy em?
Ant. Very like: one of them
Is a plaine Fiſh, and no doubt marketable.
Pro. Marke but the badges of theſe men, my Lords,
Then ſay if they be true: This miſhapen knaue;
His Mother was a Witch, and one ſo ſtrong
That could controle the Moone; make flowes, and ebs
And deale in her command, without her power:
Theſe three haue robd me, and this demy-diuell;
(For he's a baſtard one) had plotted with them
To take my life: two of theſe Fellowes, you
Muſt know, and owne, this Thing of darkeneſſe, I
Acknowledge mine.
Cal. I ſhall be pincht to death.
Alo. Is not this *Stephano*, my drunken Butler?
Seb. He is drunke now;
Where had he wine?
Alo. And *Trinculo* is reeling ripe: where ſhould they
Finde this grand Liquor that hath gilded 'em?
How cam'ſt thou in this pickle?
Tri. I haue bin in ſuch a pickle ſince I ſaw you laſt,
That I feare me will neuer out of my bones:
I ſhall not feare fly-blowing.
Seb. Who how now *Stephano*?
Ste. O touch me not, I am not *Stephano*, but a Cramp.
Pro. You'ld be King o'the Iſle, Sirha?
Ste. I ſhould haue bin a ſore one then.
Alo. This is a ſtrange thing as ere I look'd on.
Pro. He is as diſproportion'd in his Manners
As in his ſhape: Goe Sirha, to my Cell,
Take with you your Companions: as you looke
To haue my pardon, trim it handſomely.
Cal. I that I will: and Ile be wiſe hereafter,

And

And ſeeke for grace : what a thrice double Aſſe
Was I to take this drunkard for a god ?
And worſhip this dull foole?
Pro. Goe to, away.
Alo. Hence, and beſtow your luggage where you (found it.
Seb. Or ſtole it rather.
Pro. Sir, I inuite your Highneſſe, and your traine
To my poore Cell : where you ſhall take your reſt
For this onenight, which part of it, Ile waſte
With ſuch diſcourſe, as I not doubt, ſhall make it
Goe quicke away : The ſtory of my liſe,
And the particular accidents, gon by
Since I came to this Iſle : And in the morne
I'le bring you to your ſhip, and ſo to *Naples*,
Where I haue hope to ſee the nuptiall
Of theſe our deere-belou'd, ſolemnized,
And thence retire me to my *Millaine*, where
Euery third thought ſhall be my graue.
Alo. I long
To heare the ſtory of your life ; which muſt
Take the eare ſtarngely.
Pro. I'le deliuer all,
And promiſe you calme Seas, auſpicious gales,
And ſaile, ſo expeditious, that ſhall catch
Your Royall fleete farre off : My *Ariel* ; chicke
That is thy charge : Then to the Elements
Be free, and fare thou well : pleaſe you draw neere.
Exeunt omnes.

EPILOGVE,
ſpoken by *Proſpero*.

Now my Charmes are all ore-throwne,
And what ſtrength I haue's mine owne.
Which is moſt faint : now 'tis true
I muſt be heere confinde by you,
Or ſent to Naples, *Let me not*
Since I haue my Dukedome got,
And pardon'd the deceiuer, dwell
In this bare Iſland, by your Spell,
But releaſe me from my bands
with the helpe of your good hands :
Gentle breath of yours, my Sailes
Muſt fill, or elſe my proiect failes,
which was to pleaſe : Now I want
Spirits to enforce : Art to inchant,
And my ending is deſpaire,
Vnleſſe I be relieu'd by praier
Which pierces ſo, that it aſſaults
Mercy it ſelfe, and frees all faults.
As you from crimes would pardon'd be,
Let your Indulgence ſet me free. Exit.

The Scene, an vn-inhabited Iſland

Names of the Actors.

Alonſo, K. of Naples:
Sebaſtian his Brother.
Proſpero, the right Duke of Millaine.
Anthonio his brother, the vſurping Duke of Millaine
Ferdinand, Son to the King of Naples.
Gonzalo, an honeſt old Councellor.
Adrian, & Franciſco, Lords.
Caliban, a ſaluage and deformed ſlaue.
Trinculo, a Ieſter.
Stephano, a drunken Butler.
Maſter of a Ship.
Boate-Swaine
Marriners.
Miranda, daughter to Proſpero.
Ariell, an ayrie ſpirit.
Iris, *Ceres*, *Iuno*, *Nymphes*, *Reapers* — *Spirits.*

FINIS.

THE

THE
Two Gentlemen of Verona.

Actus primus, Scena prima.

Valentine: Protheus, and Speed.

Valentine.

CEase to perswade, my louing *Protheus*;
Home-keeping-youth, haue euer homely wits,
Wer't not affection chaines thy tender dayes
To the sweet glaunces of thy honour'd Loue,
I rather would entreat thy company,
To see the wonders of the world abroad,
Then (liuing dully sluggardiz'd at home)
Weare out thy youth with shapelesse idlenesse.
But since thou lou'st; loue still, and thriue therein,
Euen as I would, when I to loue begin.

Pro. Wilt thou be gone? Sweet *Valentine* adew,
Thinke on thy *Protheus*, when thou (hap'ly) seest
Some rare note-worthy obiect in thy trauaile.
Wish me partaker in thy happinesse,
When thou do'st meet good hap; and in thy danger,
(If euer danger doe enuiron thee)
Commend thy grieuance to my holy prayers,
For I will be thy beades-man, *Valentine*

Val. And on a loue-booke pray for my successe?

Pro. Vpon some booke I loue, I'le pray for thee.

Val. That's on some shallow Storie of deepe loue,
How yong *Leander* crost the *Hellespont*.

Pro That's a deepe Storie, of a deeper loue,
For he was more then ouer-shooes in loue.

Val. 'Tis true; for you are ouer-bootes in loue,
And yet you neuer swom the *Hellespont*

Pro. Ouer the Bootes? nay giue me not the Boots.

Val. No, I will not; for it boots thee not

Pro What?

Val. To be in loue; where scorne is bought with (grones:
Coy looks, with hart-sore sighes: one fading moments
With twenty watchfull, weary, tedious nights; (mirth,
If hap'ly won, perhaps a haplesse gaine;
If lost, why then a grieuous labour won,
How euer: but a folly bought with wit,
Or else a wit, by folly vanquished

Pro So, by your circumstance, you call me foole

Val. So, by your circumstance, I feare you'll proue

Pro. 'Tis Loue you cauill at, I am not Loue

Val. Loue is your master, for he masters you;
And he that is so yoked by a foole,
Me thinkes should not be chronicled for wise.

Pro Yet Writers say; as in the sweetest Bud,
The eating Canker dwels; so eating Loue
Inhabits in the finest wits of all

Val. And Writers say; as the most forward Bud
Is eaten by the Canker ere it blow,
Euen so by Loue, the yong, and tender wit
Is turn'd to folly, blasting in the Bud,
Loosing his verdure, euen in the prime,
And all the faire effects of future hopes.
But wherefore waste I time to counsaile thee
That art a votary to fond desire?
Once more adieu: my Father at the Road
Expects my comming, there to see me ship'd.

Pro And thither will I bring thee *Valentine*.

Val. Sweet *Protheus*, no: Now let vs take our leaue:
To *Millaine* let me heare from thee by Letters
Of thy successe in loue; and what newes else
Betideth here in absence of thy Friend:
And I likewise will visite thee with mine.

Pro. All happinesse bechance to thee in *Millaine*.

Val. As much to you at home: and so farewell. *Exit.*

Pro. He after Honour hunts, I after Loue;
He leaues his friends, to dignifie them more;
I loue my selfe, my friends, and all for loue:
Thou *Iulia* thou hast metamorphis'd me.
Made me neglect my Studies, loose my time;
Warre with good counsaile, set the world at nought;
Made Wit with musing, weake; hart sick with thought.

Sp. Sir *Protheus*: 'saue you: saw you my Master?

Pro. But now he parted hence to embarque for *Millain*.

Sp. Twenty to one then, he is ship'd already,
And I haue plaid the Sheepe in loosing him.

Pro. Indeede a Sheepe doth very often stray,
And if the Shepheard be awhile away.

Sp. You conclude that my Master is a Shepheard then, and I Sheepe?

Pro. I doe.

Sp. Why then my hornes are his hornes, whether I wake or sleepe.

Pro. A silly answere, and fitting well a Sheepe.

Sp. This proues me still a Sheepe.

Pro. True: and thy Master a Shepheard.

Sp. Nay, that I can deny by a circumstance.

Pro. It shall goe hard but ile proue it by another.

Sp The Shepheard seekes the Sheepe, and not the Sheepe the Shepheard; but I seeke my Master, and my Master seekes not me: therefore I am no Sheepe

Pro. The Sheepe for fodder follow the Shepheard, the Shepheard for foode followes not the Sheepe: thou for wages followest thy Master, thy Master for wages followes not thee: therefore thou art a Sheepe

Sp. Such another proofe will make me cry baâ.

Pro. But do'st thou heare: gau'st thou my Letter to *Iulia*?

Sp. I

Sp. I Sir: I (a lost-Mutton) gaue your Letter to her (a lac'd-Mutton) and she (a lac'd-Mutton) gaue mee (a lost-Mutton) nothing for my labour.

Pro. Here's too small a Pasture for such store of Muttons.

Sp. If the ground be ouer-charg'd, you were best sticke her.

Pro. Nay, in that you are astray: 'twere best pound you.

Sp. Nay Sir, lesse then a pound shall serue me for carrying your Letter.

Pro. You mistake; I meane the pound, a Pinfold.

Sp. From a pound to a pin? fold it ouer and ouer,
'Tis threefold too little for carrying a letter to your louer

Pro. But what said she?

Sp. I.

Pro. Nod-I, why that's noddy.

Sp. You mistooke Sir: I say she did nod;
And you aske me if she did nod, and I say I.

Pro. And that set together is noddy.

Sp. Now you haue taken the paines to set it together, take it for your paines.

Pro. No, no, you shall haue it for bearing the letter.

Sp. Well, I perceiue I must be faine to beare with you.

Pro. Why Sir, how doe you beare with me?

Sp. Marry Sir, the letter very orderly,
Hauing nothing but the word noddy for my paines.

Pro. Beshrew me, but you haue a quicke wit.

Sp. And yet it cannot ouer-take your slow purse.

Pro. Come, come, open the matter in briefe; what said she.

Sp. Open your purse, that the money, and the matter may be both at once deliuered.

Pro. Well Sir: here is for your paines: what said she?

Sp. Truely Sir, I thinke you'll hardly win her.

Pro. Why? could'st thou perceiue so much from her?

Sp. Sir, I could perceiue nothing at all from her;
No, not so much as a ducket for deliuering your letter:
And being so hard to me, that brought your minde;
I feare she'll proue as hard to you in telling your minde.
Giue her no token but stones, for she's as hard as steele.

Pro. What said she, nothing?

Sp. No, not so much as take this for thy pains: (me;
To testifie your bounty, I thank you, you haue cestern'd
In requital whereof, henceforth, carry your letters your
selfe; And so Sir, I'le commend you to my Master.

Pro. Go, go, be gone, to saue your Ship from wrack,
Which cannot perish hauing thee aboarde,
Being destin'd to a drier death on shore:
I must goe send some better Messenger,
I feare my *Iulia* would not daigne my lines,
Receiuing them from such a worthlesse post.

Scœna Secunda.

Enter Iulia and Lucetta.

Iul. But say *Lucetta* (now we are alone)
Would'st thou then counsaile me to fall in loue?

Luc. I Madam, so you stumble not vnheedfully.

Iul. Of all the faire resort of Gentlemen,
That euery day with par'le encounter me,
In thy opinion which is worthiest loue?

Lu. Please you repeat their names, ile shew my minde,
According to my shallow simple skill.

Iu. What thinkst thou of the faire sir *Eglamoure*?

Lu. As of a Knight, well-spoken, neat, and fine;
But were I you he neuer should be mine.

Iu. What think'st thou of the rich *Mercatio*?

Lu. Well of his wealth; but of himselfe, so, so.

Iu. What think'st thou of the gentle *Protheus*?

Lu. Lord, Lord: to see what folly raignes in vs.

Iu. How now? what meanes this passion at his name?

Lu. Pardon deare Madam, 'tis a passing shame,
That I (vnworthy body as I am)
Should censure thus on louely Gentlemen.

Iu. Why not on *Protheus*, as of all the rest?

Lu. Then thus: of many good, I thinke him best.

Iul. Your reason?

Lu. I haue no other but a womans reason:
I thinke him so, because I thinke him so.

Iul. And would'st thou haue me cast my loue on him?

Lu. I: if you thought your loue not cast away.

Iul. Why he, of all the rest, hath neuer mou'd me.

Lu. Yet he, of all the rest, I thinke best loues ye.

Iul. His little speaking, shewes his loue but small.

Lu. Fire that's closest kept, burnes most of all.

Iul. They doe not loue, that doe not shew their loue.

Lu. Oh, they loue least, that let men know their loue.

Iul. I would I knew his minde.

Lu. Peruse this paper Madam.

Iul. To *Iulia*: say, from whom?

Lu. That the Contents will shew.

Iul. Say, say: who gaue it thee?

Lu. Sir *Valentines* page: & sent I think from *Protheus*;
He would haue giuen it you, but I being in the way,
Did in your name receiue it: pardon the fault I pray.

Iul. Now (by my modesty) a goodly Broker:
Dare you presume to harbour wanton lines?
To whisper, and conspire against my youth?
Now trust me, 'tis an office of great worth,
And you an officer fit for the place:
There: take the paper: see it be return'd,
Or else returne no more into my sight.

Lu. To plead for loue, deserues more fee, then hate.

Iul. Will ye be gon?

Lu. That you may ruminate. *Exit.*

Iul. And yet I would I had ore-look'd the Letter;
It were a shame to call her backe againe,
And pray her to a fault, for which I chid her.
What 'foole is she, that knowes I am a Maid,
And would not force the letter to my view?
Since Maides, in modesty, say no, to that,
Which they would haue the profferer construe, I.
Fie, fie: how way-ward is this foolish loue;
That (like a testie Babe) will scratch the Nurse,
And presently, all humbled kisse the Rod?
How churlishly, I chid *Lucetta* hence,
When willingly, I would haue had her here?
How angerly I taught my brow to frowne,
When inward ioy enforc'd my heart to smile?
My pennance is, to call *Lucetta* backe
And aske remission, for my folly past.
What hoe: *Lucetta*.

Lu. What would your Ladiship

Iul. Is't neere dinner time?

Lu. I would it were,
That you might kill your stomacke on your meat,
And

And not vpon your Maid.
Iu. What is't that you
Tooke vp so gingerly?
Lu. Nothing.
Iu. Why didst thou stoope then?
Lu. To take a paper vp, that I let fall.
Iul. And is that paper nothing?
Lu. Nothing concerning me.
Iul. Then let it lye, for those that it concernes.
Lu. Madam, it will not lye where it concernes,
Vnlesse it haue a false Interpreter.
Iul. Some loue of yours, hath writ to you in Rime.
Lu. That I might sing it (Madam) to a tune:
Giue me a Note, your Ladiship can set
Iul. As little by such toyes, as may be possible:
Best sing it to the tune of *Light O, Loue.*
Lu. It is too heauy for so light a tune.
Iu. Heauy? belike it hath some burden then?
Lu. I: and melodious were it, would you sing it,
Iu. And why not you?
Lu. I cannot reach so high.
Iu. Let's see your Song
How now Minion?
Lu. Keepe tune there still; so you will sing it out:
And yet me thinkes I do not like this tune.
Iu You doe not?
Lu. No (Madam) tis too sharpe.
Iu. You (Minion) are too saucie.
Lu. Nay, now you are too flat;
And marre the concord, with too harsh a descant:
There wanteth but a Meane to fill your Song.
Iu. The meane is dround with you vnruly base.
Lu. Indeede I bid the base for *Protheus.*
Iu. This babble shall not henceforth trouble me;
Here is a coile with protestation:
Goe, get you gone: and let the papers lye:
You would be fingring them, to anger me.
Lu. She makes it strãge, but she would be best pleas'd
To be so angred with another Letter.
Iu. Nay, would I were so angred with the same:
Oh hatefull hands, to teare such louing words;
Iniurious Waspes, to feede on such sweet hony,
And kill the Bees that yeelde it, with your stings;
Ile kisse each seuerall paper, for amends:
Looke, here is writ, kinde *Iulia*: vnkinde *Iulia*,
As in reuenge of thy ingratitude,
I throw thy name against the bruzing-stones,
Trampling contemptuously on thy disdaine.
And here is writ, *Loue wounded Protheus.*
Poore wounded name: my bosome, as a bed,
Shall lodge thee till thy wound be throughly heal'd;
And thus I search it with a soueraigne kisse
But twice, or thrice, was *Protheus* written downe:
Be calme (good winde) blow not a word away,
Till I haue found each letter, in the Letter,
Except mine own name: That, some whirle-winde beare
Vnto a ragged, fearefull, hanging Rocke,
And throw it thence into the raging Sea.
Loe, here in one line is his name twice writ:
Poore forlorne Protheus, passionate Protheus:
To the sweet Iulia: that ile teare away:
And yet I will not, sith so prettily
He couples it, to his complaining Names;
Thus will I fold them, one vpon another;
Now kisse, embrace, contend, doe what you will.
Lu. Madam: dinner is ready. and your father staies.
Iu. Well, let vs goe.
Lu. What, shall these papers lye, like Tel-tales here?
Iu. If you respect them; best to take them vp.
Lu. Nay, I was taken vp, for laying them downe.
Yet here they shall not lye, for catching cold.
Iu. I see you haue a months minde to them.
Lu. I (Madam) you may say what sights you see;
I see things too, although you iudge I winke.
Iu. Come, come, wilt please you goe. *Exeunt.*

Scœna Tertia.

Enter Antonio and Panthino. Protheus.

Ant. Tell me *Panthino*, what sad talke was that,
Wherewith my brother held you in the Cloyster?
Pan. 'Twas of his Nephew *Protheus*, your Sonne.
Ant. Why? what of him?
Pan. He wondred that your Lordship
Would suffer him, to spend his youth at home,
While other men, of slender reputation
Put forth their Sonnes, to seeke preferment out.
Some to the warres, to try their fortune there;
Some, to discouer Islands farre away:
Some, to the studious Vniuersities;
For any, or for all these exercises,
He said, that *Protheus*, your sonne, was meet;
And did request me, to importune you
To let him spend his time no more at home;
Which would be great impeachment to his age,
In hauing knowne no trauaile in his youth.
Ant. Nor need'st thou much importune me to that
Whereon, this month I haue bin hamering.
I haue consider'd well, his losse of time,
And how he cannot be a perfect man,
Not being tryed, and tutord in the world:
Experience is by industry atchieu'd,
And perfected by the swift course of time.
Then tell me, whether were I best to send him?
Pan. I thinke your Lordship is not ignorant
How his companion, youthfull *Valentine*,
Attends the Emperour in his royall Court.
Ant. I know it well. (thither.
Pan. 'Twere good, I thinke, your Lordship sent him
There shall he practise Tilts, and Turnaments;
Heare sweet discourse, conuerse with Noble-men,
And be in eye of euery Exercise
Worthy his youth, and noblenesse of birth.
Ant. I like thy counsaile: well hast thou aduis'd:
And that thou maist perceiue how well I like it,
The execution of it shall make knowne;
Euen with the speediest expedition,
I will dispatch him to the Emperors Court.
Pan. To morrow, may it please you, *Don Alphonso*,
With other Gentlemen of good esteeme
Are iournying, to salute the *Emperor*,
And to commend their seruice to his will.
Ant. Good company: with them shall *Protheus* go:
And in good time: now will we breake with him.
Pro. Sweet Loue, sweet lines, sweet life,
Here is her hand, the agent of her heart;
Here is her oath for loue, her honors paune;

O that our Fathers would applaud our loues
To seale our happinesse with their consents.

Pro. Oh heauenly *Iulia.*

Ant. How now? What Letter are you reading there?

Pro. May't please your Lordship, 'tis a word or two
Of commendations sent from *Valentine*;
Deliuer'd by a friend, that came from him.

Ant. Lend me the Letter: Let me see what newes.

Pro. There is no newes (my Lord) but that he writes
How happily he liues, how well-belou'd,
And daily graced by the Emperor;
Wishing me with him, partner of his fortune.

Ant. And how stand you affected to his wish?

Pro. As one relying on your Lordships will,
And not depending on his friendly wish.

Ant. My will is something sorted with his wish:
Muse not that I thus sodainly proceed;
For what I will, I will, and there an end:
I am resolu'd, that thou shalt spend some time
With *Valentinus*, in the Emperors Court:
What maintenance he from his friends receiues,
Like exhibition thou shalt haue from me,
To morrow be in readinesse, to goe,
Excuse it not: for I am peremptory.

Pro. My Lord I cannot be so soone prouided,
Please you deliberate a day or two.

Ant. Look what thou want'st shalbe sent after thee:
No more of stay: to morrow thou must goe;
Come on *Panthmo*; you shall be imployd,
To hasten on his Expedition.

Pro. Thus haue I shund the fire, for feare of burning
And drench'd me in the sea, where I am drown'd.
I fear'd to shew my Father *Iulias* Letter,
Least he should take exceptions to my loue,
And with the vantage of mine owne excuse
Hath he excepted most against my loue.
Oh, how this spring of loue resembleth
The vncertaine glory of an Aprill day,
Which now shewes all the beauty of the Sun,
And by and by a clowd takes all away.

Pan. Sir *Protheus*, your Fathers call's for you,
He is in hast, therefore I pray you go.

Pro. Why this it is: my heart accords thereto,
And yet a thousand times it answer's no.

Exeunt. Finis.

Actus secundus: Scœna Prima.

Enter Valentine, Speed, Siluia.

Speed. Sir, your Gloue.

Valen. Not mine: my Gloues are on.

Sp. Why then this may be yours: for this is but one

Val. Ha? Let me see: I, giue it me, it's mine:
Sweet Ornament, that deckes a thing diuine,
Ah *Siluia, Siluia.*

Speed. Madam *Siluia*: Madam *Siluia.*

Val. How now Sirha?

Speed. Shee is not within hearing Sir.

Val. Why sir, who bad you call her?

Speed. Your worship sir, or else I mistooke.

Val. Well: you'll still be too forward.

Speed. And yet I was last chidden for being too slow.

Val. Goe to, sir, tell me: do you know Madam *Siluia*?

Speed. Shee that your worship loues?

Val. Why, how know you that I am in loue?

Speed. Marry by these speciall markes: first, you haue learn'd (like Sir *Protheus*) to wreath your Armes like a Male-content: to rellish a Loue-song, like a *Robin*-redbreast: to walke alone like one that had the pestilence: to sigh, like a Schoole-boy that had lost his *A. B. C.* to weep like a yong wench that had buried her Grandam: to fast, like one that takes diet: to watch, like one that feares robbing: to speake puling, like a beggar at Hallow-Masse: You were wont, when you laughed, to crow like a cocke; when you walk'd, to walke like one of the Lions: when you fasted, it was presently after dinner: when you look'd sadly, it was for want of money: And now you are Metamorphis'd with a Mistris, that when I looke on you, I can hardly thinke you my Master.

Val. Are all these things perceiu'd in me?

Speed. They are all perceiu'd without ye.

Val. Without me? they cannot.

Speed. Without you? nay, that's certaine: for without you were so simple, none else would: but you are so without these follies, that these follies are within you, and shine through you like the water in an Vrinall: that not an eye that sees you, but is a Physician to comment on your Malady.

Val. But tell me: do'st thou know my Lady *Siluia*?

Speed. Shee that you gaze on so, as she sits at supper?

Val. Hast thou obseru'd that? euen she I meane.

Speed. Why sir, I know her not.

Val. Do'st thou know her by my gazing on her, and yet know'st her not?

Speed. Is she not hard-fauour'd, sir?

Val. Not so faire (boy) as well fauour'd.

Speed. Sir, I know that well enough.

Val. What dost thou know?

Speed. That shee is not so faire, as (of you) well-fauourd?

Val. I meane that her beauty is exquisite,
But her fauour infinite.

Speed. That's because the one is painted, and the other out of all count.

Val. How painted? and how out of count?

Speed. Marry sir, so painted to make her faire, that no man counts of her beauty.

Val. How esteem'st thou me? I account of her beauty.

Speed. You neuer saw her since she was deform'd.

Val. How long hath she beene deform'd?

Speed. Euer since you lou'd her.

Val. I haue lou'd her euer since I saw her,
And still I see her beautifull.

Speed. If you loue her, you cannot see her.

Val. Why?

Speed. Because Loue is blinde: O that you had mine eyes, or your owne eyes had the lights they were wont to haue, when you chidde at Sir *Protheus*, for going vngarter'd.

Val. What should I see then?

Speed. Your owne present folly, and her passing deformitie: for hee beeing in loue, could not see to garter his hose; and you, beeing in loue, cannot see to put on your hose.

Val. Belike (boy) then you are in loue, for last morning
You could not see to wipe my shooes.

Speed. True sir: I was in loue with my bed, I thanke you, you swing'd me for my loue, which makes mee the bolder

bolder to chide you, for yours
Val In concluſion, I ſtand affected to her.
Speed. I would you were ſet, ſo your affection would ceaſe.
Val. Laſt night ſhe enioyn'd me,
To write ſome lines to one ſhe loues.
Speed. And haue you?
Val. I haue.
Speed. Are they not lamely writt?
Val. No (Boy) but as well as I can do them
Peace, here ſhe comes.
Speed. Oh excellent motion; oh exceeding Puppet:
Now will he interpret to her.
Val. Madam & Miſtres, a thouſand good-morrows.
Speed. Oh, 'giue ye-good-ev'n: heer's a million of manners
Sil. Sir *Valentine*, and ſeruant, to you two thouſend
Speed. He ſhould giue her intereſt: & ſhe giues it him.
Val. As you inioynd me; I haue writ your Letter
Vnto the ſecret, nameles friend of yours:
Which I was much vnwilling to proceed in,
But for my duty to your Ladiſhip. (done.
Sil. I thanke you (gentle Seruant) 'tis very Clerkly-
Val. Now truſt me (Madam) it came hardly-off:
For being ignorant to whom it goes,
I writ at randome, very doubtfully.
Sil. Perchance you think too much of ſo much pains?
Val. No (Madam) ſo it ſteed you, I will write
(Pleaſe you command) a thouſand times as much:
And yet ——
Sil. A pretty period: well: I gheſſe the ſequell;
And yet I will not name it: and yet I care not.
And yet, take this againe: and yet I thanke you:
Meaning henceforth to trouble you no more.
Speed. And yet you will: and yet, another yet,
Val. What meanes your Ladiſhip?
Doe you not like it?
Sil. Yes, yes: the lines are very queintly writ,
But (ſince vnwillingly) take them againe.
Nay, take them.
Val. Madam, they are for you.
Silu. I, I: you writ them Sir, at my requeſt,
But I will none of them: they are for you:
I would haue had them writ more mouingly:
Val. Pleaſe you, Ile write your Ladiſhip another.
Sil. And when it's writ: for my ſake read it ouer,
And if it pleaſe you, ſo: if not: why ſo:
Val. If it pleaſe me, (Madam?) what then?
Sil. Why if it pleaſe you, take it for your labour;
And ſo good-morrow Seruant. *Exit. Sil.*
Speed. Oh Ieſt vnſeene: inſcrutible: inuiſible,
As a noſe on a mans face, or a Wethercocke on a ſteeple
My Maſter ſues to her: and ſhe hath taught her Sutor,
He being her Pupill, to become her Tutor.
Oh excellent deuiſe, was there euer heard a better?
That my maſter being ſcribe,
To himſelfe ſhould write the Letter?
Val. How now Sir?
What are you reaſoning with your ſelfe?
Speed. Nay: I was riming: 'tis you ỳ haue the reaſon.
Val. To doe what?
Speed. To be a Spokeſ-man from Madam *Siluia*.
Val. To whom?
Speed. To your ſelfe: why, ſhe woes you by a figure.
Val. What figure?
Speed. By a Letter, I ſhould ſay
Val. Why ſhe hath not writ to me?
Speed. What need ſhe,
When ſhee hath made you write to your ſelfe?
Why, doe you not perceiue the ieſt?
Val. No, beleeue me.
Speed. No beleeuing you indeed ſir:
But did you perceiue her earneſt?
Val. She gaue me none, except an angry word.
Speed. Why ſhe hath giuen you a Letter.
Val. That's the Letter I writ to her friend.
Speed. And ỳ letter hath ſhe deliuer'd, & there an end.
Val. I would it were no worſe.
Speed. Ile warrant you, 'tis as well:
For often haue you writ to her: and ſhe in modeſty,
Or elſe for want of idle time, could not againe reply,
Or fearing els ſome meſſenger, ỳ might her mind diſcouer
Her ſelf hath taught her Loue himſelf, to write vnto her
All this I ſpeak in print, for in print I found it. (louer.
Why muſe you ſir, 'tis dinner time.
Val. I haue dyn'd.
Speed. I, but hearken ſir: though the Cameleon Loue can feed on the ayre, I am one that am nouriſh'd by my victuals: and would faine haue meate: oh bee not like your Miſtreſſe, be moued, be moued. *Exeunt.*

Scœna ſecunda.

Enter Protheus, Iulia, Panthion.

Pro. Haue patience, gentle *Iulia*:
Iul. I muſt where is no remedy.
Pro. When poſſibly I can, I will returne.
Iul. If you turne not: you will return the ſooner:
Keepe this remembrance for thy *Iulia's* ſake.
Pro. Why then wee'll make exchange;
Here, take you this.
Iul. And ſeale the bargaine with a holy kiſſe.
Pro. Here is my hand, for my true conſtancie:
And when that howre ore-ſlips me in the day,
Wherein I ſigh not (*Iulia*) for thy ſake,
The next enſuing howre, ſome foule miſchance
Torment me for my Loues forgetfulneſſe:
My father ſtaies my comming: anſwere not:
The tide is now; nay, not thy tide of teares,
That tide will ſtay me longer then I ſhould,
Iulia, farewell: what, gon without a word?
I, ſo true loue ſhould doe: it cannot ſpeake,
For truth hath better deeds, then words to grace it.
Panth. Sir *Protheus*: you are ſtaid for.
Pro. Goe: I come, I come
Alas, this parting ſtrikes poore Louers dumbe.
Exeunt.

Scœna Tertia.

Enter Launce, Panthion.

Launce. Nay, 'twill bee this howre ere I haue done weeping: all the kinde of the *Launces*, haue this very fault: I haue receiu'd my proportion, like the prodigious ſonne,

Sonne, and am going with Sir *Protheus* to the Imperialls Court : I thinke *Crab* my dog , be the sowrest natured dogge that liues : My Mother weeping : my Father wayling : my Sister crying : our Maid howling : our Catte wringing her hands, and all our house in a great perplexitie, yet did not this cruell-hearted Curre shedde one teare : he is a stone, a very pibble stone, and has no more pitty in him then a dogge : a Iew would haue wept to haue seene our parting : why my Grandam hauing no eyes, looke you, wept her selfe blinde at my parting: nay, Ile shew you the manner of it. This shooe is my father : no, this left shooe is my father; no, no, this left shooe is my mother : nay, that cannot bee so neyther : yes; it is so, it is so : it hath the worser sole: this shooe with the hole in it, is my mother : and this my father: a veng'ance on't, there 'tis : Now sir, this staffe is my sister : for, looke you, she is as white as a lilly , and as small as a wand : this hat is *Nan* our maid : I am the dogge : no, the dogge is himselfe, and I am the dogge: oh, the dogge is me, and I am my selfe : I ; so, so : now come I to my Father ; Father, your blessing : now should not the shooe speake a word for weeping : now should I kisse my Father ; well, hee weepes on: Now come I to my Mother : Oh that she could speake now , like a would-woman : well, I kisse her : why there 'tis ; heere's my mothers breath vp and downe: Now come I to my sister ; marke the moane she makes : now the dogge all this while sheds not a teare : nor speakes a word : but see how I lay the dust with my teares.

Panth. *Launce*, away, away : a Boord : thy Master is ship'd, and thou art to post after with oares ; what's the matter ? why weep'st thou man ? away asse, you'l loose the Tide, if you tarry any longer.

Laun. It is no matter if the tide were lost, for it is the vnkindest Tide, that euer any man tide.

Panth. What's the vnkindest tide ?

Lau. Why, he that's tide here, *Crab* my dog.

Pant. Tut, man : I meane thou'lt loose the flood, and in loosing the flood, loose thy voyage, and in loosing thy voyage, loose thy Master, and in loosing thy Master, loose thy seruice, and in loosing thy seruice : —— why dost thou stop my mouth ?

Laun. For feare thou shouldst loose thy tongue.

Panth. Where should I loose my tongue ?

Laun. In thy Tale.

Panth. In thy Taile.

Laun. Loose the Tide, and the voyage , and the Master, and the Seruice, and the tide: why man, if the Riuer were drie, I am able to fill it with my teares : if the winde were downe, I could driue the boate with my sighes.

Panth. Come : come away man , I was sent to call thee.

Lau. Sir : call me what thou dar'st.

Pant. Wilt thou goe ?

Laun. Well, I will goe.

Exeunt.

Scena Quarta.

Enter Valentine, Siluia, Thurio, Speed, Duke, Protheus.

Sil. Seruant.

Val. Mistris.

Spee. Master, Sir *Thurio* frownes on you.

Val. I Boy, it's for loue.

Spee. Not of you.

Val. Of my Mistresse then.

Spee. 'Twere good you knockt him.

Sil. Seruant, you are sad.

Val. Indeed, Madam, I seeme so.

Thu. Seeme you that you are not ?

Val. Hap'ly I doe.

Thu. So doe Counterfeyts.

Val. So doe you.

Thu. What seeme I that I am not ?

Val. Wise.

Thu. What instance of the contrary ?

Val. Your folly.

Thu. And how quoat you my folly ?

Val. I quoat it in your Ierkin.

Thu. My Ierkin is a doublet.

Val. Well then, Ile double your folly.

Thu. How ?

Sil. What, angry, Sir *Thurio*, do you change colour ?

Val. Giue him leaue, Madam, he is a kind of *Camelion.*

Thu. That hath more minde to feed on your bloud, then liue in your ayre.

Val. You haue said Sir.

Thu. I Sir, and done too for this time.

Val. I know it wel sir, you alwaies end ere you begin.

Sil. A fine volly of words, gentlemẽ, & quickly shot off

Val. 'Tis indeed, Madam, we thank the giuer.

Sil. Who is that Seruant ?

Val. Your selfe (sweet Lady) for you gaue the fire,
Sir *Thurio* borrows his wit from your Ladiships lookes,
And spends what he borrowes kindly in your company.

Thu. Sir, if you spend word for word with me, I shall make your wit bankrupt.

Val. I know it well sir : you haue an Exchequer of (words,
And I thinke, no other treasure to giue your followers:
For it appeares by their bare Liueries
That they liue by your bare words.

Sil. No more, gentlemen, no more:
Here comes my father.

Duk. Now, daughter *Siluia*, you are hard beset.
Sir *Valentine*, your father is in good health,
What say you to a Letter from your friends
Of much good newes ?

Val. My Lord, I will be thankfull,
To any happy messenger from thence.

Duk. Know ye *Don Antonio*, your Countriman ?

Val. I, my good Lord, I know the Gentleman
To be of worth, and worthy estimation,
And not without desert so well reputed.

Duk. Hath he not a Sonne ?

Val. I, my good Lord, a Son, that well deserues
The honor, and regard of such a father.

Duk. You know him well ?

Val. I knew him as my selfe : for from our Infancie
We haue conuerst, and spent our howres together,
And though my selfe haue beene an idle Trewant,
Omitting the sweet benefit of time
To cloath mine age with Angel-like perfection :
Yet hath Sir *Protheus* (for that's his name)
Made vse, and faire aduantage of his daies :
His yeares but yong, but his experience old.
His head vn-mellowed, but his Iudgement ripe
And in a word (for far behinde his worth
Comes all the praises that I now bestow.)

C He

He is compleat in feature, and in minde,
With all good grace, to grace a Gentleman.
Duk. Beſhrew me ſir, but if he make this good
He is as worthy for an Empreſſe loue,
As meet to be an Emperors Councellor:
Well, Sir: this Gentleman is come to me
With Commendation from great Potentates,
And heere he meanes to ſpend his time a while,
I thinke 'tis no vn-welcome newes to you.
Val. Should I haue wiſh'd a thing, it had beene he.
Duk. Welcome him then according to his worth:
Siluia, I ſpeake to you, and you Sir *Thurio*,
For *Valentine*, I need not cite him to it,
I will ſend him hither to you preſently.
Val. This is the Gentleman I told your Ladiſhip
Had come along with me, but that his Miſtreſſe
Did hold his eyes, lockt in her Chriſtall lookes.
Sil. Be-like that now ſhe hath enfranchis'd them
Vpon ſome other pawne for fealty.
Val. Nay ſure, I thinke ſhe holds them priſoners ſtil.
Sil. Nay then he ſhould be blind, and being blind
How could he ſee his way to ſeeke out you?
Val. Why Lady, Loue hath twenty paire of eyes.
Thur. They ſay that Loue hath not an eye at all.
Val. To ſee ſuch Louers, *Thurio*, as your ſelfe,
Vpon a homely obiect, Loue can winke.
Sil. Haue done, haue done: here comes ỹ gentleman.
Val. Welcome, deer *Protheus*: Miſtris, I beſeech you
Confirme his welcome, with ſome ſpeciall fauor.
Sil. His worth is warrant for his welcome hether,
If this be he you oft haue wiſh'd to heare from.
Val. Miſtris, it is: ſweet Lady, entertaine him
To be my fellow-ſeruant to your Ladiſhip.
Sil. Too low a Miſtres for ſo high a ſeruant.
Pro. Not ſo, ſweet Lady, but too meane a ſeruant
To haue a looke of ſuch a worthy a Miſtreſſe.
Val. Leaue off diſcourſe of diſabilitie:
Sweet Lady, entertaine him for your Seruant.
Pro. My dutie will I boaſt of, nothing elſe.
Sil. And dutie neuer yet did want his meed.
Seruant, you are welcome to a worthleſſe Miſtreſſe.
Pro. Ile die on him that ſaies ſo but your ſelfe.
Sil. That you are welcome?
Pro. That you are worthleſſe. (you.
Thur. Madam, my Lord your father wold ſpeak with
Sil. I wait vpon his pleaſure: Come Sir *Thurio*,
Goe with me: once more, new Seruant welcome;
Ile leaue you to confer of home affaires,
When you haue done, we looke too heare from you.
Pro. Wee'll both attend vpon your Ladiſhip.
Val. Now tell me: how do al from whence you came?
Pro. Your frends are wel, & haue the much comended.
Val. And how doe yours?
Pro. I left them all in health.
Val. How does your Lady? & how thriues your loue?
Pro. My tales of Loue were wont to weary you,
I know you ioy not in a Loue-diſcourſe.
Val. I *Protheus*, but that life is alter'd now,
I haue done pennance for contemning Loue,
Whoſe high emperious thoughts haue puniſh'd me
With bitter faſts, with penitentiall grones,
With nightly teares, and daily hart-ſore ſighes,
For in reuenge of my contempt of loue,
Loue hath chas'd ſleepe from my enthralled eyes,
And made them watchers of mine owne hearts ſorrow.
O gentle *Protheus*, Loue's a mighty Lord,
And hath ſo humbled me, as I confeſſe
There is no woe to his correction,
Nor to his Seruice, no ſuch ioy on earth:
Now, no diſcourſe, except it be of loue
Now can I breake my faſt, dine, ſup, and ſleepe,
Vpon the very naked name of Loue.
Pro. Enough; I read your fortune in your eye:
Was this the Idoll, that you worſhip ſo?
Val. Euen She; and is ſhe not a heauenly Saint
Pro. No; But ſhe is an earthly Paragon.
Val. Call her diuine.
Pro. I will not flatter her.
Val. O flatter me: for Loue delights in praiſes.
Pro. When I was ſick, you gaue me bitter pils,
And I muſt miniſter the like to you.
Val. Then ſpeake the truth by her; if not diuine,
Yet let her be a principalitie,
Soueraigne to all the Creatures on the earth.
Pro. Except my Miſtreſſe.
Val. Sweet: except not any,
Except thou wilt except againſt my Loue.
Pro. Haue I not reaſon to prefer mine owne?
Val. And I will help thee to prefer her to:
Shee ſhall be dignified with this high honour,
To beare my Ladies traine, leſt the baſe earth
Should from her veſture chance to ſteale a kiſſe,
And of ſo great a fauor growing proud,
Diſdaine to roote the Sommer-ſwelling flowre,
And make rough winter euerlaſtingly.
Pro. Why *Valentine*, what Bragadiſme is this?
Val. Pardon me (*Protheus*) all I can is nothing,
To her, whoſe worth, make other worthies nothing;
Shee is alone.
Pro. Then let her alone.
Val. Not for the world: why man, ſhe is mine owne,
And I as rich in hauing ſuch a Iewell
As twenty Seas, if all their ſand were pearle,
The water, Nectar, and the Rocks pure gold.
Forgiue me, that I doe not dreame on thee,
Becauſe thou ſeeſt me doate vpon my loue:
My fooliſh Riuall that her Father likes
(Onely for his poſſeſſions are ſo huge)
Is gone with her along, and I muſt after,
For Loue (thou know'ſt is full of iealouſie.)
Pro. But ſhe loues you? (howre,
Val. I, and we are betroathd: nay more, our mariage
With all the cunning manner of our flight
Determin'd of: how I muſt climbe her window,
The Ladder made of Cords, and all the meanes
Plotted, and 'greed on for my happineſſe.
Good *Protheus* goe with me to my chamber,
In theſe affaires to aid me with thy counſaile.
Pro. Goe on before: I ſhall en quire you forth:
I muſt vnto the Road, to diſ-embarque
Some neceſſaries, that I needs muſt vſe,
And then Ile preſently attend you.
Val. Will you make haſte? *Exit.*
Pro. I will.
Euen as one heate, another heate expels,
Or as one naile, by ſtrength driues out another.
So the remembrance of my former Loue
Is by a newer obiect quite forgotten,
It is mine, or *Valentines* praiſe?
Her true perfection, or my falſe tranſgreſſion?
That makes me reaſonleſſe, to reaſon thus?
Shee is faire; and ſo is *Iulia* that I loue,
(That

(That I did loue, for now my loue is thaw'd,
Which like a waxen Image 'gainſt a fire
Beares no impreſſion of the thing it was.)
Me thinkes my zeale to *Valentine* is cold,
And that I loue him not as I was wont:
O, but I loue his Lady too-too much,
And that's the reaſon I loue him ſo little.
How ſhall I doate on her with more aduice,
That thus without aduice begin to loue her?
'Tis but her picture I haue yet beheld,
And that hath dazel'd my reaſons light:
But when I looke on her perfections,
There is no reaſon, but I ſhall be blinde.
If I can checke my erring loue, I will,
If not, to compaſſe her Ile vſe my skill.

Exeunt.

Scena Quinta.

Enter Speed *and* Launce.

Speed. *Launce*, by mine honeſty welcome to *Padua*.

Laun. Forſweare not thy ſelfe, ſweet youth, for I am not welcome. I reckon this alwaies, that a man is neuer vndon till hee be hang'd, nor neuer welcome to a place, till ſome certaine ſhot be paid, and the Hoſteſſe ſay welcome.

Speed. Come-on you mad-cap: Ile to the Ale-houſe with you preſently; where, for one ſhot of fiue pence, thou ſhalt haue fiue thouſand welcomes: But ſirha, how did thy Maſter part with Madam *Iulia*?

Lau. Marry after they cloas'd in earneſt, they parted very fairely in ieſt.

Spee. But ſhall ſhe marry him?

Lau. No.

Spee. How then? ſhall he marry her?

Lau. No, neither.

Spee. What, are they broken?

Lau. No; they are both as whole as a fiſh.

Spee. Why then, how ſtands the matter with them?

Lau. Marry thus, when it ſtands well with him, it ſtands well with her.

Spee. What an aſſe art thou, I vnderſtand thee not.

Lau. What a blocke art thou, that thou canſt not? My ſtaffe vnderſtands me?

Spee. What thou ſaiſt?

Lau. I, and what I do too: looke thee, Ile but leane, and my ſtaffe vnderſtands me.

Spee. It ſtands vnder thee indeed.

Lau. Why, ſtand-vnder: and vnder-ſtand is all one.

Spee. But tell me true, wil't be a match?

Lau. Aske my dogge, if he ſay I, it will: if hee ſay no, it will: if hee ſhake his taile, and ſay nothing, it will.

Spee. The concluſion is then, that it will.

Lau. Thou ſhalt neuer get ſuch a ſecret from me, but by a parable.

Spee. 'Tis well that I get it ſo: but *Launce*, how ſaiſt thou that that my maſter is become a notable Louer?

Lau. I neuer knew him otherwiſe.

Spee. Then how?

Lau. A notable Lubber: as thou reporteſt him to bee.

Spee. Why, thou whorſon Aſſe, thou miſtak'ſt me.

Lau. Why Foole, I meant not thee, I meant thy Maſter.

Spee. I tell thee, my Maſter is become a hot Louer.

Lau. Why, I tell thee I care not, though hee burne himſelfe in Loue. If thou wilt goe with me to the Alehouſe: if not, thou art an Hebrew, a Iew, and not worth the name of a Chriſtian.

Spee. Why?

Lau Becauſe thou haſt not ſo much charity in thee as to goe to the Ale with a Chriſtian: Wilt thou goe?

Spee. At thy ſeruice.

Exeunt.

Scœna Sexta.

Enter Protheus *ſolus.*

Pro. To leaue my *Iulia*; ſhall I be forſworne?
To loue faire *Siluia*; ſhall I be forſworne?
To wrong my friend, I ſhall be much forſworne.
And ev'n that Powre which gaue me firſt my oath
Prouokes me to this three-fold periurie.
Loue bad mee ſweare, and Loue bids me for-ſweare;
O ſweet-ſuggeſting Loue, if thou haſt ſin'd,
Teach me (thy tempted ſubiect) to excuſe it.
At firſt I did adore a twinkling Starre,
But now I worſhip a celeſtiall Sunne:
Vn-heedfull vowes may heedfully be broken,
And he wants wit, that wants reſolued will,
To learne his wit, t'exchange the bad for better;
Fie, fie, vnreuerend tongue, to call her bad,
Whoſe ſoueraignty ſo oft thou haſt preferd,
With twenty thouſand ſoule-confirming oathes.
I cannot leaue to loue; and yet I doe:
But there I leaue to loue, where I ſhould loue.
Iulia I looſe, and *Valentine* I looſe,
If I keepe them, I needs muſt looſe my ſelfe:
If I looſe them, thus finde I by their loſſe,
For *Valentine*, my ſelfe: for *Iulia*, *Siluia*.
I to my ſelfe am deerer then a friend,
For Loue is ſtill moſt precious in it ſelfe,
And *Siluia* (witneſſe heauen that made her faire)
Shewes *Iulia* but a ſwarthy Ethiope.
I will forget that *Iulia* is aliue,
Remembring that my Loue to her is dead.
And *Valentine* Ile hold an Enemie,
Ayming at *Siluia* as a ſweeter friend.
I cannot now proue conſtant to my ſelfe,
Without ſome treachery vs'd to *Valentine*.
This night he meaneth with a Corded-ladder
To climbe celeſtiall *Siluia's* chamber window,
My ſelfe in counſaile his competitor.
Now preſently Ile giue her father notice
Of their diſguiſing and pretended flight.
Who (all inrag'd) will baniſh *Valentine*:
For *Thurio* he intends ſhall wed his daughter,
But *Valentine* being gon, Ile quickely croſſe
By ſome ſlie tricke, blunt *Thurio's* dull proceeding.
Loue lend me wings, to make my purpoſe ſwift
As thou haſt lent me wit, to plot this drift.

Exit.

Scœna septima.

Enter Iulia *and* Lucetta.

Iul Counsaile, *Lucetta*, gentle girle assist me,
And eu'n in kinde loue, I doe coniure thee,
Who art the Table wherein all my thoughts
Are visibly Character'd, and engrau'd,
To lesson me, and tell me some good meane
How with my honour I may vndertake
A iourney to my louing *Protheus*.
Luc. Alas, the way is wearisome and long.
Iul. A true-deuoted Pilgrime is not weary
To measure Kingdomes with his feeble steps,
Much lesse shall she that hath Loues wings to flie,
And when the flight is made to one so deere,
Of such diuine perfection as Sir *Protheus*
Luc. Better forbeare, till *Protheus* make returne.
Iul. Oh, know'st ye not, his looks are my soules food?
Pitty the dearth that I haue pined in,
By longing for that food so long a time.
Didst thou but know the inly touch of Loue,
Thou wouldst as soone goe kindle fire with snow
As seeke to quench the fire of Loue with words.
Luc. I doe not seeke to quench your Loues hot fire,
But qualifie the fires extreame rage,
Lest it should burne aboue the bounds of reason.
Iul. The more thou dam'st it vp, the more it burnes:
The Current that with gentle murmure glides
(Thou know'st) being stop'd, impatiently doth rage:
But when his faire course is not hindered,
He makes sweet musicke with th'enameld stones,
Giuing a gentle kisse to euery sedge
He ouer-taketh in his pilgrimage.
And so by many winding nookes he straies
With willing sport to the wilde Ocean.
Then let me goe, and hinder not my course:
Ile be as patient as a gentle streame,
And make a pastime of each weary step,
Till the last step haue brought me to my Loue,
And there Ile rest, as after much turmoile
A blessed soule doth in *Elizium*.
Luc. But in what habit will you goe along?
Iul. Not like a woman, for I would preuent
The loose encounters of lasciuious men:
Gentle *Lucetta*, fit me with such weedes
As may beseeme some well reputed Page.
Luc. Why then your Ladiship must cut your haire.
Iul. No girle, Ile knit it vp in silken strings,
With twentie od-conceited true-loue knots:
To be fantastique, may become a youth
Of greater time then I shall shew to be. (ches
Luc. What fashion (Madam) shall I make your bree-
Iul That fits as well, as tell me (good my Lord)
What compasse will you weare your Farthingale?
Why eu'n what fashion thou best likes (*Lucetta*.)
Luc. You must needs haue thē with a cod-peece (Ma
Iul. Out, out, (*Lucetta*) that wilbe illfauourd (dam)
Luc. A round hose (Madam) now's not worth a pin
Vnlesse you haue a cod-peece to stick pins on.
Iul. *Lucetta*, as thou lou'st me let me haue
What thou think'st meet, and is most mannerly.
But tell me (wench) how will the world repute me
For vndertaking so vnstaid a iourney?
I feare me it will make me scandaliz'd.
Luc. If you thinke so, then stay at home, and go not.
Iul. Nay, that I will not.
Luc. Then neuer dreame on Infamy, but go:
If *Protheus* like your iourney, when you come,
No matter who's displeas'd, when you are gone:
I feare me he will scarce be pleas'd with all.
Iul. That is the least (*Lucetta*) of my feare:
A thousand oathes, an Ocean of his teares,
And instances of infinite of Loue,
Warrant me welcome to my *Protheus*.
Luc. All these are seruants to deceitfull men.
Iul. Base men, that vse them to so base effect;
But truer starres did gouerne *Protheus* birth,
His words are bonds, his oathes are oracles,
His loue sincere, his thoughts immaculate,
His teares, pure messengers, sent from his heart,
His heart, as far from fraud, as heauen from earth.
Luc. Pray heau'n he proue so when you come to him.
Iul. Now, as thou lou'st me, do him not that wrong,
To beare a hard opinion of his truth:
Onely deserue my loue, by louing him,
And presently goe with me to my chamber
To take a note of what I stand in need of,
To furnish me vpon my longing iourney:
All that is mine I leaue at thy dispose,
My goods, my Lands, my reputation,
Onely, in lieu thereof, dispatch me hence:
Come; answere not: but to it presently,
I am impatient of my tarriance.

Exeunt.

Actus Tertius, Scena Prima.

Enter Duke, Thurio, Protheus, Valentine, Launce, Speed.

Duke Sir *Thurio*, giue vs leaue (I pray) a while,
We haue some secrets to confer about.
Now tell me *Protheus*, what's your will with me?
Pro. My gracious Lord, that which I wold discouer,
The Law of friendship bids me to conceale,
But when I call to minde your gracious fauours
Done to me (vndeseruing as I am)
My dutie pricks me on to vtter that
Which else, no worldly good should draw from me.
Know (worthy Prince) Sir *Valentine* my friend
This night intends to steale away your daughter:
My selfe am one made priuy to the plot.
I know you haue determin'd to bestow her
On *Thurio*, whom your gentle daughter hates,
And should she thus be stolne away from you,
It would be much vexation to your age.
Thus (for my duties sake) I rather chose
To crosse my friend in his intended drift,
Then (by concealing it) heap on your head
A pack of sorrowes, which would presse you downe
(Being vnpreuented) to your timelesse graue.
Duke. *Protheus*, I thank thee for thine honest care,
Which to requite, command me while I liue.
This loue of theirs, my selfe haue often seene,
Haply when they haue iudg'd me fast asleepe,
And oftentimes haue purpos'd to forbid

Sir

Sir *Valentine* her companie, and my Court.
But fearing lest my iealous ayme might erre,
And so (vnworthily) disgrace the man
(A rashnesse that I euer yet haue shun'd)
I gaue him gentle lookes, thereby to finde
That which thy selfe hast now disclos'd to me.
And that thou maist perceiue my feare of this,
Knowing that tender youth is soone suggested,
I nightly lodge her in an vpper Towre,
The key whereof, my selfe haue euer kept:
And thence she cannot be conuay'd away.
Pro. Know (noble Lord) they haue deuis'd a meane
How he her chamber-window will ascend,
And with a Corded-ladder fetch her downe:
For which, the youthfull Louer now is gone,
And this way comes he with it presently.
Where (if it please you) you may intercept him.
But (good my Lord) doe it so cunningly
That my discouery be not aimed at:
For, loue of you, not hate vnto my friend,
Hath made me publisher of this pretence.
Duke. Vpon mine Honor, he shall neuer know
That I had any light from thee of this.
Pro. Adiew, my Lord, Sir *Valentine* is comming.
Duk. Sir *Valentine*, whether away so fast?
Val. Please it your Grace, there is a Messenger
That stayes to beare my Letters to my friends,
And I am going to deliuer them.
Duk. Be they of much import?
Val. The tenure of them doth but signifie
My health, and happy being at your Court.
Duk. Nay then no matter: stay with me a while,
I am to breake with thee of some affaires
That touch me neere: wherein thou must be secret.
'Tis not vnknown to thee, that I haue sought
To match my friend Sir *Thurio*, to my daughter.
Val. I know it well (my Lord) and sure the Match
Were rich and honourable: besides, the gentleman
Is full of Vertue, Bounty, Worth, and Qualities
Beseeming such a Wife, as your faire daughter:
Cannot your Grace win her to fancie him?
Duk. No, trust me, She is peeuish, sullen, froward,
Prowd, disobedient, stubborne, lacking duty,
Neither regarding that she is my childe,
Nor fearing me, as if I were her father:
And may I say to thee, this pride of hers
(Vpon aduice) hath drawne my loue from her,
And where I thought the remnant of mine age
Should haue beene cherish'd by her child-like duty,
I now am full resolu'd to take a wife,
And turne her out, to who will take her in:
Then let her beauty be her wedding dowre:
For me, and my possessions she esteemes not.
Val. What would your Grace haue me to do in this?
Duk. There is a Lady in *Verona* heere
Whom I affect: but she is nice, and coy,
And naught esteemes my aged eloquence.
Now therefore would I haue thee to my Tutor
(For long agone I haue forgot to court,
Besides the fashion of the time is chang'd)
How, and which way I may bestow my selfe
To be regarded in her sun-bright eye.
Val. Win her with gifts, if she respect not words,
Dumbe Iewels often in their silent kinde
More then quicke words, doe moue a womans minde.
Duk. But she did scorne a present that I sent her,
Val. A woman somtime scorns what best cōtents her.
Send her another: neuer giue her ore,
For scorne at first, makes after-loue the more.
If she doe frowne, 'tis not in hate of you,
But rather to beget more loue in you.
If she doe chide, 'tis not to haue you gone,
For why, the fooles are mad, if left alone.
Take no repulse, what euer she doth say,
For, get you gon, she doth not meane away.
Flatter, and praise, commend, extoll their graces:
Though nere so blacke, say they haue Angells faces,
That man that hath a tongue, I say is no man,
If with his tongue he cannot win a woman.
Duk. But she I meane, is promis'd by her friends
Vnto a youthfull Gentleman of worth,
And kept seuerely from resort of men,
That no man hath accesse by day to her.
Val. Why then I would resort to her by night.
Duk. I, but the doores be lockt, and keyes kept safe,
That no man hath recourse to her by night.
Val. What letts but one may enter at her window?
Duk. Her chamber is aloft, far from the ground,
And built so sheluing, that one cannot climbe it
Without apparant hazard of his life.
Val. Why then a Ladder quaintly made of Cords
To cast vp, with a paire of anchoring hookes,
Would serue to scale another *Hero's* towre,
So bold *Leander* would aduenture it.
Duk. Now as thou art a Gentleman of blood
Aduise me, where I may haue such a Ladder.
Val. When would you vse it? pray sir, tell me that.
Duk. This very night; for Loue is like a childe
That longs for euery thing that he can come by.
Val. By seauen a clock, Ile get you such a Ladder.
Duk. But harke thee: I will goe to her alone,
How shall I best conuey the Ladder thither?
Val. It will be light (my Lord) that you may beare it
Vnder a cloake, that is of any length.
Duk. A cloake as long as thine will serue the turne?
Val. I my good Lord.
Duk. Then let me see thy cloake,
Ile get me one of such another length.
Val. Why any cloake will serue the turn (my Lord)
Duk. How shall I fashion me to weare a cloake?
I pray thee let me feele thy cloake vpon me.
What Letter is this same? what's here? to *Siluia*?
And heere an Engine fit for my proceeding,
Ile be so bold to breake the seale for once.

My thoughts do harbour with my Siluia nightly,
And slaues they are to me, that send them flying.
Oh, could their Master come, and goe as lightly,
Himselfe would lodge where (senceles) they are lying.
My Herald Thoughts, in thy pure bosome rest-them,
While I (their King) that thither them importune
Doe curse the grace, that with such grace hath blest them,
Because my selfe doe want my seruants fortune.
I curse my selfe, for they are sent by me,
That they should harbour where their Lord should be.

What's here? *Siluia, this night I will enfranchise thee.*
Tis so: and heere's the Ladder for the purpose.
Why *Phaeton* (for thou art *Merops* sonne)
Wilt thou aspire to guide the heauenly Car?
And with thy daring folly burne the world?
Wilt thou reach stars, because they shine on thee?

Goe base Intruder, ouer-weening Slaue,
Bestow thy fawning smiles on equall mates,
And thinke my patience, (more then thy desert)
Is priuiledge for thy departure hence.
Thanke me for this, more then for all the fauors
Which (all too-much) I haue bestowed on thee.
But if thou linger in my Territories
Longer then swiftest expedition
Will giue thee time to leaue our royall Court,
By heauen, my wrath shall farre exceed the loue
I euer bore my daughter, or thy selfe.
Be gone, I will not heare thy vaine excuse,
But as thou lou'st thy life, make speed from hence.

Val. And why not death, rather then liuing torment?
To die, is to be banisht from my selfe,
And *Siluia* is my selfe: banish'd from her
Is selfe from selfe. A deadly banishment:
What light, is light, if *Siluia* be not seene?
What ioy is ioy, if *Siluia* be not by?
Vnlesse it be to thinke that she is by
And feed vpon the shadow of perfection.
Except I be by *Siluia* in the night,
There is no musicke in the Nightingale.
Vnlesse I looke on *Siluia* in the day,
There is no day for me to looke vpon.
Shee is my essence, and I leaue to be;
If I be not by her faire influence
Foster'd, illumin'd, cherish'd, kept aliue.
I flie not death, to flie his deadly doome,
Tarry I heere, I but attend on death,
But flie I hence, I flie away from life.

Pro. Run (boy) run, run, and seeke him out.

Lau. So-hough, Soa hough

Pro. What seest thou?

Lau. Him we goe to finde,
There's not a haire on's head, but 'tis a *Valentine.*

Pro. *Valentine?*

Val. No.

Pro. Who then? his Spirit?

Val. Neither,

Pro. What then?

Val. Nothing

Lan. Can nothing speake? Master, shall I strike?

Pro. Who wouldst thou strike?

Lan. Nothing.

Pro. Villaine, forbeare.

Lan. Why Sir, Ile strike nothing: I pray you.

Pro. Sirha, I say forbeare: friend *Valentine*, a word.

Val. My eares are stopt, & cannot hear good newes,
So much of bad already hath possest them.

Pro. Then in dumbe silence will I bury mine,
For they are harsh, vn-tuneable, and bad.

Val. Is *Siluia* dead?

Pro. No, *Valentine.*

Val. No *Valentine* indeed, for sacred *Siluia*,
Hath she forsworne me?

Pro. No, *Valentine.*

Val. No *Valentine*, if *Siluia* haue forsworne me.
What is your newes?

Lan. Sir, there is a proclamation, ẏ you are vanished.

Pro. That thou art banish'd: oh that's the newes,
From hence, from *Siluia*, and from me thy friend.

Val. Oh, I haue fed vpon this woe already,
And now excesse of it will make me surfet.
Doth *Siluia* know that I am banish'd?

Pro. I, I: and she hath offered to the doome
(Which vn-reuerst stands in effectuall force)
A Sea of melting pearle, which some call teares;
Those at her fathers churlish feete she tendred,
With them vpon her knees, her humble selfe,
Wringing her hands, whose whitenes so became them,
As if but now they waxed pale for woe:
But neither bended knees, pure hands held vp,
Sad sighes, deepe grones, nor siluer-shedding teares
Could penetrate her vncompassionate Sire;
But *Valentine*, if he be tane, must die.
Besides, her intercession chaf'd him so,
When she for thy repeale was suppliant,
That to close prison he commanded her,
With many bitter threats of biding there.

Val. No more: vnles the next word that thou speak'st
Haue some malignant power vpon my life:
If so: I pray thee breath it in mine eare,
As ending Antheme of my endlesse dolor.

Pro. Cease to lament for that thou canst not helpe,
And study helpe for that which thou lament'st,
Time is the Nurse, and breeder of all good;
Here, if thou stay, thou canst not see thy loue;
Besides, thy staying will abridge thy life:
Hope is a louers staffe, walke hence with that
And manage it, against despairing thoughts:
Thy letters may be here, though thou art hence,
Which, being writ to me, shall be deliuer'd
Euen in the milke-white bosome of thy Loue.
The time now serues not to expostulate,
Come, Ile conuey thee through the City-gate.
And ere I part with thee, confer at large
Of all that may concerne thy Loue-affaires:
As thou lou'st *Siluia* (though not for thy selfe)
Regard thy danger, and along with me.

Val. I pray thee *Launce*, and if thou seest my Boy
Bid him make haste, and meet me at the North-gate.

Pro. Goe sirha, finde him out: Come *Valentine.*

Val. Oh my deere *Siluia*; haplesse *Valentine.*

Launce. I am but a foole, looke you, and yet I haue the wit to thinke my Master is a kinde of a knaue: but that's all one, if he be but one knaue: He liues not now that knowes me to be in loue, yet I am in loue, but a Teeme of horse shall not plucke that from me: nor who 'tis I loue: and yet 'tis a woman; but what woman, I will not tell my selfe: and yet 'tis a Milke-maid: yet 'tis not a maid: for shee hath had Gossips: yet 'tis a maid, for she is her Masters-maid, and serues for wages. Shee hath more qualities then a Water-Spaniell, which is much in a bare Christian: Heere is the Cate-log of her Condition. *Inprimis.* Shee can fetch and carry: why a horse can doe no more; nay, a horse cannot fetch, but onely carry, therefore is shee better then a Iade. *Item.* She can milke, looke you, a sweet vertue in a maid with cleane hands.

Speed. How now Signior *Launce*? what newes with your Mastership?

La. With my Mastership? why, it is at Sea:

Sp. Well, your old vice still: mistake the word: what newes then in your paper?

La. The black'st newes that euer thou heard'st.

Sp. Why man? how blacke?

La. Why, as blacke as Inke.

Sp. Let me read them?

La. Fie on thee Iolt-head, thou canst not read.

Sp. Thou lyest: I can.

La. I will try thee: tell me this: who begot thee?

Sp. Marry,

Sp. Marry, the son of my Grand-father.

La. Oh illiterate loyterer; it was the sonne of thy Grand-mother: this proues that thou canst not read.

Sp. Come foole, come: try me in thy paper.

La. There: and S.*Nicholas* be thy speed.

Sp. Inprimis she can milke.

La. I that she can.

Sp. Item, she brewes good Ale.

La. And thereof comes the prouerbe: (*Blessing of your heart, you brew good Ale.*)

Sp. Item, she can sowe.

La. That's as much as to say (*Can she so?*)

Sp. Item she can knit.

La. What neede a man care for a stock with a wench,
When she can knit him a stocke?

Sp. Item, she can wash and scoure.

La. A speciall vertue: for then shee neede not be wash'd, and scowr'd.

Sp. Item, she can spin.

La. Then may I set the world on wheeles, when she can spin for her liuing.

Sp. Item, she hath many namelesse vertues.

La. That's as much as to say *Bastard-vertues*: that indeede know not their fathers; and therefore haue no names.

Sp. Here follow her vices.

La. Close at the heeles of her vertues.

Sp. Item, shee is not to be fasting in respect of her breath.

La. Well: that fault may be mended with a breakfast: read on.

Sp. Item, she hath a sweet mouth.

La. That makes amends for her soure breath.

Sp. Item, she doth talke in her sleepe.

La. It's no matter for that; so shee sleepe not in her talke.

Sp. Item, she is slow in words.

La. Oh villaine, that set this downe among her vices;
To be slow in words, is a womans onely vertue:
I pray thee out with't, and place it for her chiefe vertue.

Sp. Item, she is proud.

La. Out with that too:
It was *Eues* legacie, and cannot be t'ane from her.

Sp. Item, she hath no teeth.

La. I care not for that neither: because I loue crusts.

Sp. Item, she is curst.

La. Well: the best is, she hath no teeth to bite.

Sp. Item, she will often praise her liquor.

La. If her liquor be good, she shall: if she will not, I will; for good things should be praised.

Sp. Item, she is too liberall.

La. Of her tongue she cannot; for that's writ downe she is slow of: of her purse, shee shall not, for that ile keepe shut: Now, of another thing shee may, and that cannot I helpe. Well, proceede.

Sp. Item, shee hath more haire then wit, and more faults then haires, and more wealth then faults.

La. Stop there: Ile haue her: she was mine, and not mine, twice or thrice in that last Article: rehearse that once more.

Sp. Item, she hath more haire then wit.

La. More haire then wit: it may be ile proue it: The couer of the salt, hides the salt, and therefore it is more then the salt; the haire that couers the wit, is more then the wit; for the greater hides the lesse: What's next?

Sp. And more faults then haires.

La. That's monstrous: oh that that were out.

Sp. And more wealth then faults.

La. Why that word makes the faults gracious: Well, ile haue her: and if it be a match, as nothing is impossible.

Sp. What then?

La. Why then, will I tell thee, that thy Master staies for thee at the *North gate*.

Sp. For me?

La. For thee? I, who art thou? he hath staid for a better man then thee.

Sp. And must I goe to him?

La. Thou must run to him; for thou hast staid so long, that going will scarce serue the turne.

Sp. Why didst not tell me sooner? 'pox of your loue Letters.

La. Now will he be swing'd for reading my Letter;
An vnmannerly slaue, that will thrust himselfe into secrets: Ile after, to reioyce in the boyes correctio. *Exeunt.*

Scena Secunda.

Enter Duke, Thurio, Protheus.

Du. Sir *Thurio*, feare not, but that she will loue you
Now *Valentine* is banish'd from her sight.

Th. Since his exile she hath despis'd me most,
Forsworne my company, and rail'd at me,
That I am desperate of obtaining her.

Du. This weake impresse of Loue, is as a figure
Trenched in ice, which with an houres heate
Dissolues to water, and doth loose his forme.
A little time will melt her frozen thoughts,
And worthlesse *Valentine* shall be forgot.
How now sir *Protheus*, is your countriman
(According to our Proclamation) gon?

Pro. Gon, my good Lord.

Du. My daughter takes his going grieuously?

Pro. A little time (my Lord) will kill that griefe.

Du. So I beleeue: but *Thurio* thinkes not so:
Protheus, the good conceit I hold of thee,
(For thou hast showne some signe of good desert)
Makes me the better to confer with thee.

Pro. Longer then I proue loyall to your Grace,
Let me not liue, to looke vpon your Grace.

Du. Thou know'st how willingly, I would effect
The match betweene sir *Thurio*, and my daughter?

Pro. I doe my Lord.

Du. And also, I thinke, thou art not ignorant
How she opposes her against my will?

Pro. She did my Lord, when *Valentine* was here.

Du. I, and peruersly, she perseuers so:
What might we doe to make the girle forget
The loue of *Valentine*, and loue sir *Thurio*?

Pro. The best way is, to slander *Valentine*,
With falsehood, cowardize, and poore discent:
Three things, that women highly hold in hate.

Du. I, but she'll thinke, that it is spoke in hate.

Pro. I, if his enemy deliuer it.
Therefore it must with circumstance be spoken
By one, whom she esteemeth as his friend.

Du. Then you must vndertake to slander him.

Pro.

Pro. And that (my Lord) I ſhall be loath to doe:
'Tis an ill office for a Gentleman,
Eſpecially againſt his very friend.
Du. Where your good word cannot aduantage him,
Your ſlander neuer can endamage him;
Therefore the office is indifferent,
Being intreated to it by your friend.
Pro. You haue preuail'd (my Lord) if I can doe it
By ought that I can ſpeake in his diſpraiſe,
She ſhall not long continue loue to him:
But ſay this weede her loue from *Valentine*,
It followes not that ſhe will loue ſir *Thurio*.
Th. Therefore, as you vnwinde her loue from him;
Leaſt it ſhould rauell, and be good to none,
You muſt prouide to bottome it on me:
Which muſt be done, by praiſing me as much
As you, in worth diſpraiſe, ſir *Valentine*.
Du. And *Protheus*, we dare truſt you in this kinde,
Becauſe we know (on *Valentines* report)
You are already loues firme votary,
And cannot ſoone reuolt, and change your minde.
Vpon this warrant, ſhall you haue acceſſe,
Where you, with *Siluia*, may conferre at large.
For ſhe is lumpiſh, heauy, mellancholly,
And (for your friends ſake) will be glad of you;
Where you may temper her, by your perſwaſion,
To hate yong *Valentine*, and loue my friend.
Pro. As much as I can doe, I will effect:
But you ſir *Thurio*, are not ſharpe enough:
You muſt lay Lime, to tangle her deſires
By walefull Sonnets, whoſe compoſed Rimes
Should be full fraught with ſeruiceable vowes.
Du. I, much is the force of heauen-bred Poeſie.
Pro. Say that vpon the altar of her beauty
You ſacrifice your teares, your ſighes, your heart:
Write till your inke be dry: and with your teares
Moiſt it againe: and frame ſome feeling line,
That may diſcouer ſuch integrity:
For *Orpheus* Lute, was ſtrung with Poets ſinewes,
Whoſe golden touch could ſoften ſteele and ſtones;
Make Tygers tame, and huge *Leuiathans*
Forſake vnſounded deepes, to dance on Sands.
After your dire-lamenting Elegies,
Viſit by night your Ladies chamber-window
With ſome ſweet Conſort; To their Inſtruments
Tune a deploring dumpe: the nights dead ſilence
Will well become ſuch ſweet complaining grieuance:
This, or elſe nothing, will inherit her.
Du. This diſcipline, ſhowes thou haſt bin in loue.
Th. And thy aduice, this night, ile put in practiſe:
Therefore, ſweet *Protheus*, my direction-giuer,
Let vs into the City preſently
To ſort ſome Gentlemen, well skil'd in Muſicke.
I haue a Sonnet, that will ſerue the turne
To giue the on-ſet to thy good aduiſe.
Du. About it Gentlemen.
Pro. We'll wait vpon your Grace, till after Supper,
And afterward determine our proceedings.
Du. Euen now about it, I will pardon you. *Exeunt.*

Actus Quartus. Scœna Prima.

Enter Valentine, Speed, and certaine Out-lawes.

1.Out-l. Fellowes, ſtand faſt: I ſee a paſſenger.
2.Out. If there be ten, ſhrinke not, but down with'em.
3.Out. Stand ſir, and throw vs that you haue about'ye.
If not: we'll make you ſit, and rifle you.
Sp. Sir we are vndone; theſe are the Villaines
That all the Trauailers doe feare ſo much.
Val. My friends.
1.Out. That's not ſo, ſir: we are your enemies.
2.Out. Peace: we'll heare him.
3.Out. I by my beard will we: for he is a proper man.
Val. Then know that I haue little wealth to looſe;
A man I am, croſs'd with aduerſitie:
My riches, are theſe poore habiliments,
Of which, if you ſhould here diſfurniſh me,
You take the ſum and ſubſtance that I haue.
2.Out. Whether trauell you?
Val. To *Verona.*
1.Out. Whence came you?
Val. From *Millaine.*
3.Out. Haue you long ſoiourn'd there? (ſtaid,
Val. Some ſixteene moneths, and longer might haue
If crooked fortune had not thwarted me.
1.Out. What, were you baniſh'd thence?
Val. I was.
2.Out. For what offence?
Val. For that which now torments me to rehearſe;
I kil'd a man, whoſe death I much repent,
But yet I ſlew him manfully, in fight,
Without falſe vantage, or baſe treachery.
1.Out. Why nere repent it, if it were done ſo;
But were you baniſht for ſo ſmall a fault?
Val. I was, and held me glad of ſuch a doome.
2.Out. Haue you the Tongues?
Val. My youthfull trauaile, therein made me happy,
Or elſe I often had beene often miſerable.
3.Out. By the bare ſcalpe of *Robin Hoods* fat Fryer,
This fellow were a King, for our wilde faction.
1.Out. We'll haue him: Sirs, a word.
Sp. Maſter, be one of them:
It's an honourable kinde of theeuery.
Val. Peace villaine.
2.Out. Tell vs this: haue you any thing to take to?
Val. Nothing but my fortune.
3.Out. Know then, that ſome of vs are Gentlemen,
Such as the fury of vngouern'd youth
Thruſt from the company of awfull men.
My ſelfe was from *Verona* baniſhed,
For practiſing to ſteale away a Lady,
And heire and Neece, allide vnto the Duke.
2.Out. And I from *Mantua*, for a Gentleman,
Who, in my moode, I ſtab'd vnto the heart.
1.Out. And I, for ſuch like petty crimes as theſe.
But to the purpoſe: for we cite our faults,
That they may hold excus'd our lawleſſe liues;
And partly ſeeing you are beautifide
With goodly ſhape; and by your owne report,
A Linguiſt, and a man of ſuch perfection,
As we doe in our quality much want.
2.Out. Indeede becauſe you are a baniſh'd man,
Therefore, aboue the reſt, we parley to you:
Are you content to be our Generall?
To make a vertue of neceſſity,
And liue as we doe in this wilderneſſe?
3.Out. What ſaiſt thou? wilt thou be of our conſort?
Say I, and be the captaine of vs all:
We'll doe thee homage, and be rul'd by thee,
Loue thee, as our Commander, and our King.

1.Out

1.Out. But if thou scorne our curtesie,thou dyest.
2.Out. Thou shalt not liue,to brag what we haue of-
Val. I take your offer,and will liue with you, (fer'd.
Prouided that you do no outrages
On silly women,or poore passengers.
3.Out. No,we detest such vile base practises.
Come,goe with vs,we'll bring thee to our Crewes,
And show thee all the Treasure we haue got;
Which,with our selues,all rest at thy dispose. *Exeunt.*

Scœna Secunda.

Enter Protheus,Thurio, Iulia,Host,Musitian,Siluia.

Pro. Already haue I bin false to *Valentine*,
And now I must be as vniust to *Thurio*,
Vnder the colour of commending him,
I haue accesse my owne loue to prefer.
But *Siluia* is too faire,too true,too holy,
To be corrupted with my worthlesse guifts;
When I protest true loyalty to her,
She twits me with my falsehood to my friend;
When to her beauty I commend my vowes,
She bids me thinke how I haue bin forsworne
In breaking faith with *Iulia*,whom I lou'd;
And notwithstanding all her sodaine quips,
The least whereof would quell a louers hope:
Yet (Spaniel-like) the more she spurnes my loue,
The more it growes,and fawneth on her still;
But here comes *Thurio*; now must we to her window,
And giue some euening Musique to her eare.
Th. How now,sir *Protheus*,are you crept before vs?
Pro. I gentle *Thurio*,for you know that loue
Will creepe in seruice,where it cannot goe.
Th. I,but I hope,Sir,that you loue not here.
Pro. Sir,but I doe: or else I would be hence.
Th. Who,*Siluia*?
Pro. I,*Siluia*,for your sake.
Th. I thanke you for your owne: Now Gentlemen
Let's tune: and to it lustily a while.
Ho. Now,my yong guest; me thinks your' allycholly
I pray you why is it?
Iu. Marry (mine *Host*) because I cannot be merry.
Ho. Come,we'll haue you merry: ile bring you where
you shall heare Musique, and see the Gentleman that
you ask'd for.
Iu. But shall I heare him speake.
Ho. I that you shall.
Iu. That will be Musique.
Ho. Harke,harke.
Iu. Is he among these?
Ho. I: but peace, let's heare'm.

Song. Who is Siluia? what is she?
That all our Swaines commend her?
Holy,faire,and wise is she,
The heauen such grace did lend her,
that she might admired be.
Is she kinde as she is faire?
For beauty liues with kindnesse:
Loue doth to her eyes repaire,
To helpe him of his blindnesse:
And being help'd,inhabits there.
Then to Siluia,let vs sing,
That Siluia is excelling;
She excels each mortall thing
Vpon the dull earth dwelling.
To her let vs Garlands bring.

Ho. How now? are you sadder then you were before;
How doe you, man? the Musicke likes you not.
Iu. You mistake: the Musitian likes me not.
Ho. Why,my pretty youth?
Iu. He plaies false (father.)
Ho. How,out of tune on the strings.
Iu. Not so; but yet
So false that he grieues my very heart-strings.
Ho. You haue a quicke eare (heart.
Iu. I,I would I were deafe: it makes me haue a slow
Ho. I perceiue you delight not in Musique.
Iu. Not a whit, when it iars so.
Ho. Harke,what fine change is in the Musique.
Iu. I: that change is the spight.
Ho. You would haue them alwaies play but one thing.
Iu. I would alwaies haue one play but one thing.
But Host doth this Sir *Protheus*,that we talke on,
Often resort vnto this Gentlewoman?
Ho. I tell you what *Launce* his man told me;
He lou'd her out of all nicke.
Iu. Where is *Launce*?
Ho. Gone to seeke his dog,which to morrow,by his
Masters command, hee must carry for a present to his
Lady.
Iu. Peace,stand aside,the company parts.
Pro. Sir *Thurio*,feare not you,I will so pleade,
That you shall say,my cunning drift excels.
Th. Where meete we?
Pro. At Saint *Gregories* well.
Th. Farewell.
Pro. Madam: good eu'n to your Ladiship.
Sil. I thanke you for your Musique (Gentlemen)
Who is that that spake?
Pro. One (Lady) if you knew his pure hearts truth,
You would quickly learne to know him by his voice.
Sil. Sir *Protheus*, as I take it.
Pro. Sir *Protheus* (gentle Lady) and your Seruant.
Sil. What's your will?
Pro. That I may compasse yours.
Sil. You haue your wish: my will is euen this,
That presently you hie you home to bed:
Thou subtile,periur'd,false, disloyall man:
Think'st thou I am so shallow,so conceitlesse,
To be seduced by thy flattery,
That has't deceiu'd so many with thy vowes?
Returne,returne and make thy loue amends:
For me (by this pale queene of night I sweare)
I am so farre from granting thy request,
That I despise thee,for thy wrongfull suite,
And by and by intend to chide my selfe,
Euen for this time I spend in talking to thee.
Pro. I grant (sweet loue) that I did loue a Lady,
But she is dead.
Iu. 'Twere false,if I should speake it;
For I am sure she is not buried.
Sil. Say that she be: yet *Valentine* thy friend
Suruiues; to whom (thy selfe art witnesse)
I am betroth'd; and art thou not asham'd
To wrong him,with thy importunacy?
Pro.

Pro. I likewise heare that *Valentine* is dead.
Sil. And so suppose am I; for in her graue
Assure thy selfe, my loue is buried.
Pro. Sweet Lady, let me take it from the earth.
Sil. Goe to thy Ladies graue and call hers thence,
Or at the least, in hers, sepulcher thine.
Iul. He heard not that.
Pro. Madam: if your heart be so obdurate:
Vouchsafe me yet your Picture for my loue,
The Picture that is hanging in your chamber:
To that ile speake, to that ile sigh and weepe:
For since the substance of your perfect selfe
Is else deuoted, I am but a shadow;
And to your shadow, will I make true loue.
Iul. If 'twere a substance you would sure deceiue it,
And make it but a shadow, as I am.
Sil. I am very loath to be your Idoll Sir;
But, since your falsehood shall become you well
To worship shadowes, and adore false shapes,
Send to me in the morning, and ile send it:
And so, good rest.
Pro. As wretches haue ore-night
That wait for execution in the morne.
Iul. *Host*, will you goe?
Ho. By my hallidome, I was fast asleepe.
Iul. Pray you, where lies Sir *Protheus*?
Ho. Marry, at my house:
Trust me, I thinke 'tis almost day.
Iul. Not so: but it hath bin the longest night
That ere I watch'd, and the most heauiest.

Scœna Tertia.

Enter Eglamore, Siluia.

Eg. This is the houre that Madam *Siluia*
Entreated me to call, and know her minde
Ther's some great matter she'ld employ me in.
Madam, Madam.
Sil. Who cals?
Eg. Your seruant, and your friend;
One that attends your Ladiships command.
Sil. Sir *Eglamore*, a thousand times good morrow.
Eg. As many (worthy Lady) to your selfe:
According to your Ladiships impose,
I am thus early come, to know what seruice
It is your pleasure to command me in.
Sil. Oh *Eglamoure*, thou art a Gentleman:
Thinke not I flatter (for I sweare I doe not)
Valiant, wise, remorse-full, well accomplish'd.
Thou art not ignorant what deere good will
I beare vnto the banish'd *Valentine*:
Nor how my father would enforce me marry
Vaine *Thurio* (whom my very soule abhor'd.)
Thy selfe hast lou'd, and I haue heard thee say
No griefe did euer come so neere thy heart,
As when thy Lady, and thy true-loue dide,
Vpon whose Graue thou vow'dst pure chastitie:
Sir *Eglamoure*: I would to *Valentine*
To *Mantua*, where I heare, he makes aboad;
And for the waies are dangerous to passe,
I doe desire thy worthy company,
Vpon whose faith and honor, I repose.
Vrge not my fathers anger (*Eglamoure*)
But thinke vpon my griefe (a Ladies griefe)
And on the iustice of my flying hence,
To keepe me from a most vnholy match,
Which heauen and fortune still rewards with plagues.
I doe desire thee, euen from a heart
As full of sorrowes, as the Sea of sands,
To beare me company, and goe with me:
If not, to hide what I haue said to thee,
That I may venture to depart alone.
Egl. Madam, I pitty much your grieuances,
Which, since I know they vertuously are plac'd,
I giue consent to goe along with you,
Wreaking as little what betideth me,
As much, I wish all good befortune you.
When will you goe?
Sil. This euening comming.
Eg. Where shall I meete you?
Sil. At Frier *Patrickes* Cell,
Where I intend holy Confession.
Eg. I will not faile your Ladiship:
Good morrow (gentle Lady.)
Sil. Good morrow, kinde Sir *Eglamoure*. *Exeunt.*

Scena Quarta.

Enter Launce, Protheus, Iulia, Siluia.

Lau. When a mans seruant shall play the Curre with him (looke you) it goes hard: one that I brought vp of a puppy: one that I sau'd from drowning, when three or foure of his blinde brothers and sisters went to it: I haue taught him (euen as one would say precisely, thus I would teach a dog) I was sent to deliuer him, as a present to Mistris *Siluia*, from my Master; and I came no sooner into the dyning-chamber, but he steps me to her Trencher, and steales her Capons-leg: O, 'tis a foule thing, when a Cur cannot keepe himselfe in all companies: I would haue (as one should say) one that takes vpon him to be a dog indeede, to be, as it were, a dog at all things. If I had not had more wit then he, to take a fault vpon me that he did, I thinke verily hee had bin hang'd for't: sure as I liue he had suffer'd for't: you shall iudge: Hee thrusts me himselfe into the company of three or foure gentleman-like-dogs, vnder the Dukes table: hee had not bin there (blesse the marke) a pissing while, but all the chamber smelt him: out with the dog (saies one) what cur is that (saies another) whip him out (saies the third) hang him vp (saies the Duke.) I hauing bin acquainted with the smell before, knew it was Crab; and goes me to the fellow that whips the dogges: friend (quoth I) you meane to whip the dog: I marry doe I (quoth he) you doe him the more wrong (quoth I) 'twas I did the thing you wot of: he makes me no more adoe, but whips me out of the chamber: how many Masters would doe this for his Seruant? nay, ile be sworne I haue sat in the stockes, for puddings he hath stolne, otherwise he had bin executed: I haue stood on the Pillorie for Geese he hath kil'd, otherwise he had sufferd for't: thou think'st not of this now: nay, I remember the tricke you seru'd me, when I tooke my leaue of Madam *Siluia*: did not

not I bid thee ſtill marke me,and doe as I do; when did'ſt thou ſee me heaue vp my leg, and make water againſt a Gentlewomans farthingale? did'ſt thou euer ſee me doe ſuch a tricke?

Pro. *Sebaſtian* is thy name: I like thee well,
And will imploy thee in ſome ſeruice preſently.
Iu. In what you pleaſe,Ile doe what I can.
Pro. I hope thou wilt.
How now you whor-ſon pezant,
Where haue you bin theſe two dayes loytering?
La. Marry Sir, I carried Miſtris *Siluia* the dogge you bad me.
Pro. And what ſaies ſhe to my little Iewell?
La. Marry ſhe ſaies your dog was a cur,and tels you curriſh thanks is good enough for ſuch a preſent.
Pro. But ſhe receiu'd my dog?
La. No indeede did ſhe not.
Here haue I brought him backe againe
Pro. What,didſt thou offer her this from me?
La. I Sir,the other Squirrill was ſtolne from me
By the Hangmans boyes in the market place,
And then I offer'd her mine owne, who is a dog
As big as ten of yours,& therefore the guift the greater
Pro. Goe,get thee hence,and finde my dog againe,
Or nere returne againe into my ſight.
Away,I ſay: ſtayeſt thou to vexe me here;
A Slaue,that ſtill an-end,turnes me to ſhame:
Sebaſtian, I haue entertained thee,
Partly that I haue neede of ſuch a youth,
That can with ſome diſcretion doe my buſineſſe:
For 'tis no truſting to yond fooliſh Lowt,
But chiefely, for thy face,and thy behauiour,
Which (if my Augury deceiue me not)
Witneſſe good bringing vp, fortune,and truth:
Therefore know thee,for this I entertaine thee.
Go preſently,and take this Ring with thee
Deliuer it to Madam *Siluia*,
She lou'd me well,deliuer'd it to me
Iul. It ſeemes you lou'd not her,not leaue her token:
She is dead belike?
Pro. Not ſo: I thinke ſhe liues.
Iul. Alas.
Pro. Why do'ſt thou cry alas?
Iul. I cannot chooſe but pitty her.
Pro. Wherefore ſhould'ſt thou pitty her?
Iul. Becauſe,methinkes that ſhe lou'd you as well
As you doe loue your Lady *Siluia*.
She dreames on him,that has forgot her loue,
You doate on her, that cares not for your loue.
'Tis pitty Loue,ſhould be ſo contrary:
And thinking on it,makes me cry alas.
Pro. Well: giue her that Ring,and therewithall
This Letter: that's her chamber: Tell my Lady,
I claime the promiſe for her heauenly Picture:
Your meſſage done,hye home vnto my chamber,
Where thou ſhalt finde me ſad,and ſolitarie.
Iul. How many women would doe ſuch a meſſage?
Alas poore *Protheus*,thou haſt entertain'd
A Foxe,to be the Shepheard of thy Lambs;
Alas,poore foole,why doe I pitty him
That with his very heart deſpiſeth me?
Becauſe he loues her,he deſpiſeth me,
Becauſe I loue him,I muſt pitty him.
This Ring I gaue him,when he parted from me,
To binde him to remember my good will:
And now am I (vnhappy Meſſenger)
To plead for that, which I would not obtaine;
To carry that,which I would haue refus'd;
To praiſe his faith,which I would haue diſprais'd.
I am my Maſters true confirmed Loue,
But cannot be true ſeruant to my Maſter,
Vnleſſe I proue falſe traitor to my ſelfe.
Yet will I woe for him,but yet ſo coldly,
As (heauen it knowes) I would not haue him ſpeed.
Gentlewoman,good day: I pray you be my meane
To bring me where to ſpeake with Madam *Siluia*.
Sil. What would you with her,if that I be ſhe?
Iul. If you be ſhe, I doe intreat your patience
To heare me ſpeake the meſſage I am ſent on.
Sil. From whom?
Iul. From my Maſter, Sir *Protheus*, Madam.
Sil. Oh: he ſends you for a Picture?
Iul. I, Madam.
Sil. *Vrſula*, bring my Picture there,
Goe,giue your Maſter this: tell him from me
One *Iulia*,that his changing thoughts forget
Would better fit his Chamber,then this Shadow.
Iul. Madam, pleaſe you peruſe this Letter;
Pardon me (Madam) I haue vnaduis'd
Deliuer'd you a paper that I ſhould not;
This is the Letter to your Ladiſhip.
Sil. I pray thee let me looke on that againe.
Iul. It may not be: good Madam pardon me.
Sil. There, hold:
I will not looke vpon your Maſters lines:
I know they are ſtuft with proteſtations,
And full of new-found oathes,which he will breake
As eaſily as I doe teare his paper.
Iul. Madam, he ſends your Ladiſhip this Ring.
Sil. The more ſhame for him,that he ſends it me;
For I haue heard him ſay a thouſand times,
His *Iulia* gaue it him,at his departure:
Though his falſe finger haue prophan'd the Ring,
Mine ſhall not doe his *Iulia* ſo much wrong.
Iul. She thankes you.
Sil. What ſai'ſt thou?
Iul. I thanke you Madam, that you tender her:
Poore Gentlewoman, my Maſter wrongs her much.
Sil. Do'ſt thou know her?
Iul. Almoſt as well as I doe know my ſelfe.
To thinke vpon her woes, I doe proteſt
That I haue wept a hundred ſeuerall times.
Sil. Belike ſhe thinks that *Protheus* hath forſook her?
Iul. I thinke ſhe doth: and that's her cauſe of ſorrow.
Sil. Is ſhe not paſſing faire?
Iul. She hath bin fairer (Madam) then ſhe is,
When ſhe did thinke my Maſter lou'd her well;
She,in my iudgement,was as faire as you.
But ſince ſhe did neglect her looking-glaſſe,
And threw her Sun-expelling Maſque away,
The ayre hath ſtaru'd the roſes in her cheekes,
And pinch'd the lilly-tincture of her face,
That now ſhe is become as blacke as I.
Sil. How tall was ſhe?
Iul. About my ſtature: for at *Pentecoſt*,
When all our Pageants of delight were plaid,
Our youth got me to play the womans part,
And I was trim'd in Madam *Iulias* gowne,
Which ſerued me as fit,by all mens iudgements,
As if the garment had bin made for me:
Therefore I know ſhe is about my height,
And at that time I made her weepe a good,

For

For I did play a lamentable part.
(Madam) 'twas *Ariadne*, passioning
For *Thesus* periury,and vniust flight;
Which I so liuely acted with my teares:
That my poore Mistris moued therewithall,
Wept bitterly: and would I might be dead,
If I in thought felt not her very sorrow.
Sil. She is beholding to thee (gentle youth)
Alas (poore Lady) desolate,and left;
I weepe my selfe to thinke vpon thy words.
Here youth: there is my purse; I giue thee this (well.
For thy sweet Mistris sake,because thou lou'st her. Fare-
Iul. And she shall thanke you for't, if ere you know
A vertuous gentlewoman,milde,and beautifull. (her.
I hope my Masters suit will be but cold,
Since she respects my Mistris loue so much.
Alas,how loue can trifle with it selfe:
Here is her Picture: let me see,I thinke
If I had such a Tyre, this face of mine
Were full as louely,as is this of hers;
And yet the Painter flatter'd her a little,
Vnlesse I flatter with my selfe too much.
Her haire is *Aburne*,mine is perfect *Yellow*,
If that be all the difference in his loue,
Ile get me such a coulour'd Perrywig:
Her eyes are grey as glasse,and so are mine:
I, but her fore-head's low,and mine's as high:
What should it be that he respects in her,
But I can make respectiue in my selfe?
If this fond Loue,were not a blinded god.
Come shadow, come, and take this shadow vp,
For'tis thy riuall: O thou senceless forme,
Thou shalt be worship'd,kiss'd,lou'd,and ador'd;
And were there sence in his Idolatry,
My substance should be statue in thy stead.
Ile vse thee kindly,for thy Mistris sake
That vs'd me so: or else by *Ioue*,I vow,
I should haue scratch'd out your vnseeing eyes,
To make my Master out of loue with thee. *Exeunt.*

Actus Quintus. Scœna Prima.

Enter Eglamoure, Siluia.

Egl. The Sun begins to guild the westerne skie.
And now it is about the very houre
That *Siluia*,at Fryer *Patricks* Cell should meet me,
She will not faile; for Louers breake not houres,
Vnlesse it be to come before their time,
So much they spur their expedition.
See where she comes: Lady a happy euening.
Sil. Amen,Amen: goe on (good *Eglamoure*)
Out at the Posterne by the Abbey wall;
I feare I am attended by some Spies.
Egl. Feare not: the Forrest is not three leagues off,
If we recouer that,we are sure enough. *Exeunt.*

Scœna Secunda.

Enter Thurio,Protheus,Iulia,Duke.

Th. Sir *Protheus*,what saies *Siluia* to my suit?
Pro. Oh Sir,I finde her milder then she was,
And yet she takes exceptions at your person.
Thu. What? that my leg is too long?
Pro. No,that it is too little. (der.
Thu. Ile weare a Boote, to make it somewhat roun-
Pro. But loue will not be spurd to what it loathes.
Thu. What saies she to my face?
Pro. She saies it is a faire one.
Thu. Nay then the wanton lyes: my face is blacke
Pro. But Pearles are faire; and the old saying is,
Blacke men are Pearles,in beauteous Ladies eyes.
Thu. 'Tis true,such Pearles as put out Ladies eyes,
For I had rather winke, then looke on them.
Thu. How likes she my discourse?
Pro. Ill, when you talke of war.
Thu. But well,when I discourse of loue and peace.
Iul. But better indeede,when you hold you peace.
Thu. What sayes she to my valour?
Pro. Oh Sir,she makes no doubt of that.
Iul. She needes not, when she knowes it cowardize.
Thu. What saies she to my birth?
Pro. That you are well deriu'd.
Iul. True: from a Gentleman, to a foole.
Thu. Considers she my Possessions?
Pro. Oh, I: and pitties them.
Thu. Wherefore?
Iul. That such an Asse should owe them.
Pro. That they are out by Lease.
Iul. Here comes the Duke.
Du. How now sir *Protheus*; how now *Thurio*?
Which of you saw *Eglamoure* of late?
Thu. Not I.
Pro. Nor I.
Du. Saw you my daughter?
Pro. Neither.
Du. Why then
She's fled vnto that pezant, *Valentine*,
And *Eglamoure* is in her Company;
'Tis true: for Frier *Laurence* met them both
As he,in pennance wander'd through the Forrest:
Him he knew well: and guesd that it was she,
But being mask'd, he was not sure of it.
Besides she did intend Confession
At *Patricks* Cell this euen,and there she was not.
These likelihoods confirme her flight from hence;
Therefore I pray you stand,not to discourse,
But mount you presently, and meete with me
Vpon the rising of the Mountaine foote
That leads toward *Mantua*,whether they are fled:
Dispatch (sweet Gentlemen) and follow me.
Thu. Why this it is,to be a peeuish Girle,
That flies her fortune when it followes her:
Ile after; more to be reueng'd on *Eglamoure*,
Then for the loue of reck-lesse *Siluia*.
Pro. And I will follow, more for *Siluias* loue
Then hate of *Eglamoure*,that goes with her.
Iul. And I will follow,more to crosse that loue
Then hate for *Siluia*,that is gone for loue. *Exeunt.*

Scena Tertia.

Siluia, Out-lawes.

1.Out. Come, come be patient:
We

We must bring you to our Captaine.
Sil. A thousand more mischances then this one
Haue learn'd me how to brooke this patiently.
2 Out. Come, bring her away.
1 Out. Where is the Gentleman that was with her?
3 Out. Being nimble footed, he hath out-run vs.
But *Moyses* and *Valerius* follow him:
Goe thou with her to the West end of the wood,
There is our Captaine: Wee'll follow him that's fled,
The Thicket is beset, he cannot scape.
1 Out. Come, I must bring you to our Captains caue.
Feare not: he beares an honourable minde,
And will not vse a woman lawlesly.
Sil. O *Valentine*: this I endure for thee.
Exeunt.

Scœna Quarta.

Enter Valentine, Protheus, Siluia, Iulia, Duke, Thurio, Out-lawes.

Val. How vse doth breed a habit in a man?
This shadowy desart, vnfrequented woods
I better brooke then flourishing peopled Townes:
Here can I sit alone, vn-seene of any,
And to the Nightingales complaining Notes
Tune my distresses, and record my woes.
O thou that dost inhabit in my brest,
Leaue not the Mansion so long Tenant-lesse,
Lest growing ruinous, the building fall,
And leaue no memory of what it was,
Repaire me, with thy presence, *Siluia*:
Thou gentle Nimph, cherish thy for-lorne swaine.
What hallowing, and what stir is this to day?
These are my mates, that make their wills their Law,
Haue some vnhappy passenger in chace;
They loue me well: yet I haue much to doe
To keepe them from vnciuill outrages.
Withdraw thee *Valentine*: who's this comes heere?
Pro. Madam, this seruice I haue done for you
(Though you respect not aught your seruant doth)
To hazard life, and reskew you from him,
That would haue forc'd your honour, and your loue,
Vouchsafe me for my meed, but one faire looke:
(A smaller boone then this I cannot beg,
And lesse then this, I am sure you cannot giue)
Val. How like a dreame is this? I see, and heare:
Loue, lend me patience to forbeare a while.
Sil. O miserable, vnhappy that I am.
Pro. Vnhappy were you (Madam) ere I came:
But by my comming, I haue made you happy.
Sil. By thy approach thou mak'st me most vnhappy.
Iul. And me, when he approcheth to your presence.
Sil. Had I beene ceazed by a hungry Lion,
I would haue beene a break-fast to the Beast,
Rather then haue false *Protheus* reskue me:
Oh heauen be iudge how I loue *Valentine*,
Whose life's as tender to me as my soule,
And full as much (for more there cannot be)
I doe detest false periur'd *Protheus*:
Therefore be gone, sollicit me no more.
Pro. What dangerous action, stood it next to death
Would I not vndergoe, for one calme looke:
Oh tis the curse in Loue, and still approu'd
When women cannot loue, where they're belou'd.
Sil. When *Protheus* cannot loue, where he's belou'd:
Read ouer *Iulia's* heart, (thy first best Loue)
For whose deare sake, thou didst then rend thy faith
Into a thousand oathes; and all those oathes,
Descended into periury, to loue me,
Thou hast no faith left now, vnlesse thou'dst two,
And that's farre worse then none: better haue none
Then plurall faith, which is too much by one:
Thou Counterfeyt, to thy true friend.
Pro. In Loue,
Who respects friend?
Sil. All men but *Protheus*.
Pro. Nay, if the gentle spirit of mouing words
Can no way change you to a milder forme;
Ile wooe you like a Souldier, at armes end,
And loue you gainst the nature of Loue: force ye.
Sil. Oh heauen.
Pro. Ile force thee yeeld to my desire.
Val. Ruffian: let goe that rude vnciuill touch,
Thou friend of an ill fashion.
Pro. *Valentine.*
Val. Thou cōmon friend, that's without faith or loue,
For such is a friend now: treacherous man,
Thou hast beguil'd my hopes; nought but mine eye
Could haue perswaded me: now I dare not say
I haue one friend aliue; thou wouldst disproue me:
Who should be trusted, when ones right hand
Is periured to the bosome? *Protheus*
I am sorry I must neuer trust thee more,
But count the world a stranger for thy sake:
The priuate wound is deepest: oh time, most accurst:
'Mongst all foes that a friend should be the worst?
Pro. My shame and guilt confounds me;
Forgiue me *Valentine*: if hearty sorrow
Be a sufficient Ransome for offence,
I tender't heere: I doe as truely suffer,
As ere I did commit.
Val. Then I am paid:
And once againe, I doe receiue thee honest;
Who by Repentance is not satisfied,
Is not of heauen, nor earth; for these are pleas'd:
By Penitence th'Eternalls wrath's appeas'd:
And that my loue may appeare plaine and free,
All that was mine, in *Siluia*, I giue thee.
Iul. Oh me vnhappy.
Pro. Looke to the Boy.
Val. Why, Boy!
Why wag: how now? what's the matter? look vp: speak.
Iul. O good sir, my master charg'd me to deliuer a ring
to Madam *Siluia*: w (out of my neglect) was neuer done.
Pro. Where is that ring? boy?
Iul. Heere 'tis: this is it.
Pro. How? let me see.
Why this is the ring I gaue to *Iulia*.
Iul. Oh, cry you mercy sir, I haue mistooke:
This is the ring you sent to *Siluia*.
Pro. But how cam'st thou by this ring? at my depert
I gaue this vnto *Iulia*.
Iul. And *Iulia* her selfe did giue it me,
And *Iulia* her selfe hath brought it hither.
Pro. How? *Iulia*?
Iul. Behold her, that gaue ayme to all thy oathes,
And entertain'd 'em deepely in her heart.
How oft hast thou with periury cleft the roote?
Oh *Protheus*, let this habit make thee blush.

D Be

Be thou asham'd that I haue tooke vpon me
Such an immodest rayment; if shame liue
In a disguise of loue?
It is the lesser blot modesty findes
Women to change their shapes, then men their minds.
Pro. Then men their minds? tis true: oh heuen, were man
But Constant, he were perfect; that one error
Fils him with faults: makes him run through all th'sins;
Inconstancy falls-off, ere it begins:
What is in *Siluia's* face, but I may spie
More fresh in *Iulia's*, with a constant eye?
Val. Come, come: a hand from either:
Let me be blest to make this happy close:
'Twere pitty two such friends should be long foes.
Pro. Beare witnes (heauen) I haue my wish for euer.
Iul. And I mine.
Out-l. A prize: a prize: a prize.
Val. Forbeare, forbeare I say: It is my Lord the *Duke*.
Your Grace is welcome to a man disgrac'd,
Banished *Valentine*.
Duke. Sir *Valentine*?
Thu. Yonder is *Siluia*: and *Siluia's* mine.
Val. *Thurio* giue backe; or else embrace thy death:
Come not within the measure of my wrath:
Doe not name *Siluia* thine: if once againe,
Verona shall not hold thee: heere she stands,
Take but possession of her, with a Touch:
I dare thee, but to breath vpon my Loue.
Thur. Sir *Valentine*, I care not for her, I:
I hold him but a foole that will endanger
His Body, for a Girle that loues him not:
I claime her not, and therefore she is thine.
Duke. The more degenerate and base art thou
To make such meanes for her, as thou hast done,
And leaue her on such slight conditions.
Now, by the honor of my Ancestry,
I doe applaud thy spirit, *Valentine*,
And thinke thee worthy of an Empresse loue:
Know then, I heere forget all former greefes,
Cancell all grudge, repeale thee home againe,
Plead a new state in thy vn-riual'd merit,
To which I thus subscribe: Sir *Valentine*,
Thou art a Gentleman, and well deriu'd,
Take thou thy *Siluia*, for thou hast deseru'd her.
Val. I thank your Grace, ŷ gift hath made me happy:
I now beseech you (for your daughters sake)
To grant one Boone that I shall aske of you.
Duke. I grant it (for thine owne) what ere it be.
Val. These banish'd men, that I haue kept withall,
Are men endu'd with worthy qualities:
Forgiue them what they haue committed here,
And let them be recall'd from their Exile:
They are reformed, ciuill, full of good,
And fit for great employment (worthy Lord.)
Duke. Thou hast preuaild, I pardon them and thee:
Dispose of them, as thou knowst their deserts.
Come, let vs goe, we will include all iarres,
With Triumphes, Mirth, and rare solemnity.
Val. And as we walke along, I dare be bold
With our discourse, to make your Grace to smile.
What thinke you of this Page (my Lord?)
Duke. I think the Boy hath grace in him, he blushes.
Val. I warrant you (my Lord) more grace, then Boy.
Duke. What meane you by that saying?
Val. Please you, Ile tell you, as we passe along,
That you will wonder what hath fortuned:
Come *Protheus*, 'tis your pennance, but to heare
The story of your Loues discouered.
That done, our day of marriage shall be yours,
One Feast, one house, one mutuall happinesse. *Exeunt.*

The names of all the Actors.

***Duke:** Father to* Siluia.
***Valentine.** }*
***Protheus.** } the two Gentlemen.*
***Anthonio:** father to Protheus.*
***Thurio:** a foolish riuall to Valentine.*
***Eglamoure:** Agent for Siluia in her escape.*
***Host:** where Iulia lodges.*
***Out-lawes** with Valentine.*
***Speed:** a clownish seruant to Valentine.*
***Launce:** the like to Protheus.*
***Panthion:** seruant to Antonio.*
***Iulia:** beloued of Protheus.*
***Siluia:** beloued of Valentine.*
***Lucetta:** waighting-woman to Iulia.*

FINIS.

THE

THE Merry VViues of Windsor.

Actus primus, Scena prima.

Enter Iustice Shallow, Slender, *Sir* Hugh Euans, *Master* Page, Falstoffe, Bardolph, Nym, Pistoll, Anne Page, *Mistresse* Ford, *Mistresse* Page, Simple.

Shallow.

SIr *Hugh*, perswade me not: I will make a Star-Chamber matter of it, if hee were twenty Sir *Iohn Falstoffs*, he shall not abuse *Robert Shallow* Esquire. (Coram.

Slen. In the County of *Glocester*, Iustice of Peace and

Shal. I (Cosen *Slender*) and *Cust-alorum*.

Slen. I, and *Rato lorum* too; and a Gentleman borne (Master Parson) who writes himselfe *Armigero*, in any Bill, Warrant, Quittance, or Obligation, *Armigero*.

Shal. I that I doe, and haue done any time these three hundred yeeres.

Slen. All his successors (gone before him) hath don't: and all his Ancestors (that come after him) may: they may giue the dozen white Luces in their Coate.

Shal. It is an olde Coate.

Euans. The dozen white Lowses doe become an old Coat well: it agrees well passant: It is a familiar beast to man, and signifies Loue.

Shal. The Luse is the fresh fish, the salt-fish, is an old Coate.

Slen. I may quarter (Coz).

Shal. You may, by marrying.

Euans. It is marring indeed, if he quarter it.

Shal. Not a whit.

Euan. Yes per-lady: if he ha's a quarter of your coat, there is but three Skirts for your selfe, in my simple coniectures; but that is all one: if Sir *Iohn Falstaffe* haue committed disparagements vnto you, I am of the Church and will be glad to do my beneuolence, to make attonements and compremises betweene you.

Shal. The Councell shall heare it, it is a Riot.

Euan. It is not meet the Councell heare a Riot: there is no feare of Got in a Riot: The Councell (looke you) shall desire to heare the feare of Got, and not to heare a Riot: take your viza-ments in that.

Shal. Ha; o'my life, if I were yong againe, the sword should end it.

Euans. It is petter that friends is the sword, and end it: and there is also another deuice in my praine, which peraduenture prings goot discretions with it. There is *Anne Page*, which is daughter to Master *Thomas Page* which is pretty virginity.

Slen. *Mistris Anne Page*? she has browne haire, and speakes small like a woman.

Euans. It is that ferry person for all the orld, as iust as you will desire, and seuen hundred pounds of Moneyes, and Gold, and Siluer, is her Grand-sire vpon his deaths-bed, (Got deliuer to a ioyfull resurrections) giue, when she is able to ouertake seuenteene yeeres old. It were a goot motion, if we leaue our pribbles and prabbles, and desire a marriage betweene Master *Abraham*, and Mistris *Anne Page*.

Slen. Did her Grand-sire leaue her seauen hundred pound?

Euan. I, and her father is make her a petter penny.

Slen. I know the young Gentlewoman, she has good gifts.

Euan. Seuen hundred pounds, and possibilities, is goot gifts.

Shal. Wel, let vs see honest Mr *Page*: is *Falstaffe* there?

Euan. Shall I tell you a lye? I doe despise a lyer, as I doe despise one that is false, or as I despise one that is not true: the Knight Sir *Iohn* is there, and I beseech you be ruled by your well-willers: I will peat the doore for Mr. *Page*. What hoa? Got-plesse your house heere.

Mr. Page. Who's there?

Euan. Here is go't's plessing and your friend, and Iustice *Shallow*, and heere yong Master *Slender*: that peraduentures shall tell you another tale, if matters grow to your likings.

M. Page. I am glad to see your Worships well: I thanke you for my Venison Master *Shallow*.

Shal. Master *Page*, I am glad to see you: much good doe it your good heart: I wish'd your Venison better, it was ill killd: how doth good Mistresse *Page*? and I thank you alwaies with my heart, la: with my heart.

M. Page. Sir, I thanke you.

Shal. Sir, I thanke you: by yea, and no I doe.

M. Pa. I am glad to see you, good Master *Slender*.

Slen. How do's your fallow Greyhound, Sir, I heard say he was out-run on *Cotsall*.

M. Pa. It could not be iudg'd, Sir.

Slen. You'll not confesse: you'll not confesse.

Shal. That he will not, 'tis your fault, 'tis your fault: 'tis a good dogge.

M. Pa. A Cur, Sir.

Shal. Sir: hee's a good dog, and a faire dog, can there be more said? he is good, and faire. Is Sir *Iohn Falstaffe* heere?

M. Pa. Sir, hee is within: and I would I could doe a good office be tweene you.

Euan. It is spoke as a Christians ought to speake.

Shal. He hath wrong'd me (Master *Page*.)

M. Pa. Sir, he doth in some sort confesse it.

D 2 *Shal.*

Shal. If it be confessed, it is not redressed; is not that so (*M. Page?*) he hath wrong'd me, indeed he hath, at a word he hath: beleeue me, *Robert Shallow* Esquire, saith he is wronged.

Ma.Pa. Here comes Sir *Iohn.*

Fal. Now, Master *Shallow*, you'll complaine of me to the King?

Shal. Knight, you haue beaten my men, kill'd my deere, and 'oke open my Lodge.

Fal. But not kiss'd your Keepers daughter?

Shal. Tut, a pin: this shall be answer'd.

Fal. I will answere it strait, I haue done all this: That is now answer'd.

Shal. The Councell shall know this.

Fal. 'Twere better for you if it were known in councell: you'll be laugh'd at.

Eu. Pauca verba; (Sir *Iohn*) good worts.

Fal. Good worts? good Cabidge; *Slender*, I broke your head: what matter haue you against me?

Slen. Marry sir, I haue matter in my head against you, and against your cony-catching Rascalls, *Bardolf, Nym*, and *Pistoll.*

Bar. You Banbery Cheese.

Slen. I, it is no matter.

Pist. How now, *Mephostophilus?*

Slen. I, it is no matter.

Nym. Slice, I say; *pauca, pauca:* Slice, that's my humor.

Slen. Where's *Simple* my man? can you tell, Cosen?

Eua. Peace, I pray you: now let vs vnderstand: there is three Vmpires in this matter, as I vnderstand; that is, Master *Page* (fidelicet Master *Page*,) & there is my selfe, (fidelicet my selfe) and the three party is (lastly, and finally) mine Host of the Gater.

Ma.Pa. We three to hear it, & end it between them.

Euan. Ferry goo't, I will make a priefe of it in my note-booke, and we wil afterwards orke vpon the cause, with as great discreetly as we can.

Fal. Pistoll.

Pist. He heares with eares.

Euan. The Teuill and his Tam: what phrase is this? he heares with eare? why, it is affectations.

Fal. Pistoll, did you picke M. *Slenders* purse?

Slen. I, by these gloues did hee, or I would I might neuer come in mine owne great chamber againe else, of seauen groates in mill-sixpences, and two *Edward* Shouelboords, that cost me two shilling and two pence a peece of *Yead Miller*: by these gloues.

Fal. Is this true, *Pistoll?*

Euan. No, it is false, if it is a picke-purse.

Pist. Ha, thou mountaine Forreyner: Sir *Iohn*, and Master mine, I combat challenge of this Latine Bilboe: word of deniall in thy *labras* here; word of denial: froth, and scum thou liest.

Slen. By these gloues, then 'twas he.

Nym. Be auis'd sir, and passe good humours: I will say marry trap with you, if you runne the nut-hooks humor on me, that is the very note of it.

Slen. By this hat, then he in the red face had it: for though I cannot remember what I did when you made me drunke, yet I am not altogether an asse.

Fal. What say you *Scarlet*, and *Iohn?*

Bar. Why sir, (for my part) I say the Gentleman had drunke himselfe out of his fiue sentences.

Eu. It is his fiue sences: fie, what the ignorance is.

Bar. And being fap, sir, was (as they say) casheerd: and so conclusions past the Car-eires.

Slen. I, you spake in Latten then to: but 'tis no matter; Ile nere be drunk whilst I liue againe, but in honest, ciuill, godly company for this tricke: if I be drunke, Ile be drunke with those that haue the feare of God, and not with drunken knaues.

Euan. So got-udge me, that is a vertuous minde.

Fal. You heare all these matters deni'd, Gentlemen; you heare it.

M. Page. Nay daughter, carry the wine in, wee'll drinke within.

Slen. Oh heauen: This is Mistresse *Anne Page.*

Mr. Page How now Mistris *Ford?*

Fal. Mistris Ford, by my troth you are very wel met: by your leaue good Mistris.

Mr. Page. Wife, bid these gentlemen welcome: come, we haue a hot Venison pasty to dinner; Come gentlemen, I hope we shall drinke downe all vnkindnesse.

Slen. I had rather then forty shillings I had my booke of Songs and Sonnets heere: How now *Simple*, where haue you beene? I must wait on my selfe, must I? you haue not the booke of Riddles about you, haue you?

Sim. Booke of Riddles? why did you not lend it to *Alice Short-cake* vpon Alhallowmas last, a fortnight afore Michaelmas.

Shal. Come Coz, come Coz, we stay for you: a word with you Coz: marry this, Coz: there is as 'twere a tender, a kinde of tender, made a farre-off by Sir *Hugh* here: doe you vnderstand me?

Slen. I Sir, you shall finde me reasonable; if it be so, I shall doe that that is reason.

Shal. Nay, but vnderstand me.

Slen. So I doe Sir.

Euan. Giue eare to his motions; (Mr. *Slender*) I will description the matter to you, if you be capacity of it.

Slen. Nay, I will doe as my Cozen *Shallow* saies: I pray you pardon me, he's a Iustice of Peace in his Countrie, simple though I stand here.

Euan. But that is not the question: the question is concerning your marriage.

Shal. I, there's the point Sir.

Eu. Marry is it: the very point of it, to Mi. *An Page.*

Slen. Why if it be so; I will marry her vpon any reasonable demands.

Eu. But can you affection the 'o-man, let vs command to know that of your mouth, or of your lips: for diuers Philosophers hold, that the lips is parcell of the mouth: therefore precisely, ca you carry your good wil to ẏ maid?

Sh. Cosen *Abraham Slender*, can you loue her?

Slen. I hope sir, I will do as it shall become one that would doe reason.

Eu. Nay, got's Lords, and his Ladies, you must speake possitable, if you can carry-her your desires towards her.

Shal. That you must: Will you, (vpon good dowry) marry her?

Slen. I will doe a greater thing then that, vpon your request (Cosen) in any reason.

Shal. Nay conceiue me, conceiue mee, (sweet Coz): what I doe is to pleasure you (Coz:) can you loue the maid?

Slen. I will marry her (Sir) at your request; but if there bee no great loue in the beginning, yet Heauen may decrease it vpon better acquaintance, when wee are married, and haue more occasion to know one another: I hope vpon familiarity will grow more content: but if you say mary-her, I will mary-her, that I am freely dissolued, and dissolutely.

Ea. It

Eu. It is a fery discetion-answere; saue the fall is in the'ord, dissolutely: the ort is (according to our meaning) resolutely: his meaning is good.

Sh. I: I thinke my Cosen meant well.

Sl. I, or else I would I might be hang'd (la.)

Sh. Here comes faire Mistris *Anne*; would I were yong for your sake, Mistris *Anne*.

An. The dinner is on the Table, my Father desires your worships company.

Sh. I will wait on him, (faire Mistris *Anne*.)

Eu. Od's plessed-wil: I wil not be absẽce at the grace.

An. Wil't please your worship to come in, Sir?

Sl. No, I thank you forsooth, hartely; I am very well.

An. The dinner attends you, Sir.

Sl. I am not a-hungry, I thanke you, forsooth: goe Sirha, for all you are my man, goe wait vpon my Cosen *Shallow*: a Iustice of peace sometime may be beholding to his friend, for a Man; I keepe but three Men, and a Boy yet, till my Mother be dead: but what though, yet I liue like a poore Gentleman borne.

An. I may not goe in without your worship: they will not sit till you come.

Sl. I faith, ile eate nothing: I thanke you as much as though I did.

An. I pray you Sir walke in.

Sl. I had rather walke here (I thanke you) I bruiz'd my shin th'other day, with playing at Sword and Dagger with a Master of Fence (three veneys for a dish of stew'd Prunes) and by my troth, I cannot abide the smell of hot meate since. Why doe your dogs barke so? be there Beares ith' Towne?

An. I thinke there are, Sir, I heard them talk'd of.

Sl. I loue the sport well, but I shall as soone quarrell at it, as any man in *England*: you are afraid if you see the Beare loose, are you not?

An. I indeede Sir.

Sl. That's meate and drinke to me now: I haue seene *Sackerson* loose, twenty times, and haue taken him by the Chaine: but (I warrant you) the women haue so cride and shrekt at it, that it past: But women indeede, cannot abide'em, they are very ill-fauour'd rough things.

Ma. Pa. Come, gentle M. *Slender*, come; we stay for you.

Sl. Ile eate nothing, I thanke you Sir.

Ma. Pa. By cocke and pie, you shall not choose, Sir: come, come.

Sl. Nay, pray you lead the way.

Ma. Pa. Come on, Sir.

Sl. Mistris *Anne*: your selfe shall goe first.

An. Not I Sir, pray you keepe on.

Sl. Truely I will not goe first: truely-la: I will not doe you that wrong.

An. I pray you Sir.

Sl. Ile rather be vnmannerly, then troublesome: you doe your selfe wrong indeede-la. *Exeunt.*

Scena Secunda.

Enter Euans, and Simple.

Eu. Go your waies, and aske of Doctor *Caius* house, which is the way; and there dwels one Mistris *Quickly*; which is in the manner of his Nurse; or his dry-Nurse; or his Cooke; or his Laundry; his Washer, and his Ringer.

Si. Well Sir.

Eu. Nay, it is petter yet: giue her this letter; for it is a'oman that altogeathers acquaintace with Mistris *Anne Page*; and the Letter is to desire, and require her to solicite your Masters desires, to Mistris *Anne Page*: I pray you be gon: I will make an end of my dinner; ther's Pippins and Cheese to come. *Exeunt.*

Scena Tertia.

Enter Falstaffe, Host, Bardolfe, Nym, Pistoll, Page.

Fal. Mine Host of the *Garter*?

Ho. What saies my Bully Rooke? speake schollerly, and wisely.

Fal. Truely mine *Host*; I must turne away some of my followers.

Ho. Discard, (bully *Hercules*) casheere; let them wag; trot, trot.

Fal. I sit at ten pounds a weeke.

Ho. Thou'rt an Emperor (*Cesar, Keiser* and *Pheazar*) I will entertaine *Bardolfe*: he shall draw; he shall tap; said I well (bully *Hector*?)

Fa. Doe so (good mine *Host*.

Ho. I haue spoke: let him follow: let me see thee froth, and liue: I am at a word: follow.

Fal. *Bardolfe*, follow him: a *Tapster* is a good trade: an old Cloake, makes a new Ierkin: a wither'd Seruingman, a fresh Tapster: goe, adew.

Ba. It is a life that I haue desir'd: I will thriue.

Pist. O base hungarian wight: wilt ỳ the spigot wield.

Ni. He was gotten in drink: is not the humor cõceited?

Fal. I am glad I am so acquit of this Tinderbox: his Thefts were too open: his filching was like an vnskilfull Singer, he kept not time.

Ni. The good humor is to steale at a minutes rest.

Pist. Conuay: the wise it call: Steale? foh: a fico for the phrase.

Fal. Well sirs, I am almost out at heeles.

Pist. Why then let Kibes ensue.

Fal. There is no remedy: I must conicatch, I must shift.

Pist. Yong Rauens must haue foode.

Fal. Which of you know *Ford* of this Towne?

Pist. I ken the wight: he is of substance good.

Fal. My honest Lads, I will tell you what I am about.

Pist. Two yards, and more.

Fal. No quips now *Pistoll*: (Indeede I am in the waste two yards about: but I am now about no waste: I am about thrift) briefely: I doe meane to make loue to *Fords* wife: I spie entertainment in her: shee discourses: shee carues: she giues the leere of inuitation: I can construe the action of her familier stile, & the hardest voice of her behauior (to be english'd rightly) is, *I am Sir Iohn Falstafs*.

Pist. He hath studied her will; and translated her will: out of honesty, into English.

Ni. The Anchor is deepe: will that humor passe?

Fal. Now, the report goes, she has all the rule of her husbands Purse: he hath a legend of Angels.

Pist. As many diuels entertaine: and to her Boy say I.

Ni. The humor rises: it is good: humor me the angels.

Fal. I haue writ me here a letter to her: & here another to *Pages* wife, who euen now gaue mee good eyes too; examind my parts with most iudicious illiads: sometimes the beame of her view, guilded my foote: sometimes my portly belly.

D 2 Pist.

Pist. Then did the Sun on dung-hill shine.

Ni. I thanke thee for that humour.

Fal. O she did so course o're my exteriors with such a greedy intention, that the appetite of her eye, did seeme to scorch me vp like a burning-glasse: here's another letter to her: She beares the Purse too: She is a Region in *Guiana*: all gold, and bountie: I will be Cheaters to them both, and they shall be Exchequers to mee: they shall be my East and West Indies, and I will trade to them both: Goe, beare thou this Letter to Mistris *Page*; and thou this to Mistris *Ford*: we will thriue (Lads) we will thriue.

Pist. Shall I Sir *Pandarus* of *Troy* become,
And by my side weare Steele? then Lucifer take all.

Ni. I will run no base humor: here take the humor-Letter; I will keepe the hauior of reputation.

Fal. Hold Sirha, beare you these Letters tightly,
Saile like my Pinnasse to these golden shores.
Rogues, hence, auaunt, vanish like haile-stones; goe,
Trudge; plod away ith' hoofe: seeke shelter, packe:
Falstaffe will learne the honor of the age,
French-thrift, you Rogues, my selfe, and skirted *Page*.

Pist. Let Vultures gripe thy guts: for gourd, and Fullam holds: & high and low beguiles the rich & poore,
Tester ile haue in pouch when thou shalt lacke,
Base *Phrygian* Turke.

Ni. I haue opperations,
Which be humors of reuenge.

Pist. Wilt thou reuenge?

Ni. By Welkin, and her Star.

Pist. With wit, or Steele?

Ni. With both the humors, I:
I will discusse the humour of this Loue to *Ford*.

Pist. And I to *Page* shall eke vnfold
How *Falstaffe* (varlet vile)
His Doue will proue: his gold will hold,
And his soft couch defile.

Ni. My humour shall not coole: I will incense *Ford* to deale with poyson: I will possesse him with yallownesse, for the reuolt of mine is dangerous: that is my true humour.

Pist. Thou art the *Mars* of *Malecontents*: I second thee: troope on. *Exeunt.*

Scœna Quarta.

Enter Mistris Quickly, Simple, Iohn Rugby, Doctor, Caius, Fenton.

Qu. What, *Iohn Rugby*, I pray thee goe to the Casement and see if you can see my Master, Master Docter *Caius* comming: if he doe (I'faith) and finde any body in the house; here will be an old abusing of Gods patience, and the Kings English.

Ru. Ile goe watch.

Qu Goe, and we'll haue a posset for't soone at night, (in faith) at the latter end of a Sea-cole-fire: An honest, willing, kinde fellow, as euer seruant shall come in house withall: and I warrant you, no tel-tale, nor no breede-bate: his worst fault is that he is giuen to prayer; hee is something peeuish that way: but no body but has his fault: but let that passe. *Peter Simple*, you say your name is?

Si. I: for fault of a better.

Qu. And Master *Slender's* your Master?

Si. I forsooth.

Qu. Do's he not weare a great round Beard, like a Glouers pairing-knife?

Si. No forsooth: he hath but a little wee-face; with a little yellow beard: a Caine colourd Beard.

Qu. A softly-sprighted man, is he not?

Si. I forsooth: but he is as tall a man of his hands, as any is betweene this and his head: he hath fought with a Warrener.

Qu. How say you: oh, I should remember him: do's he not hold vp his head (as it were?) and strut in his gate?

Si. Yes indeede do's he.

Qu. Well, heauen send *Anne Page*, no worse fortune: Tell Master Parson *Euans*, I will doe what I can for your Master: *Anne* is a good girle, and I wish —

Ru. Out alas: here comes my Master.

Qu. We shall all be shent: Run in here, good young man: goe into this Closset: he will not stay long: what *Iohn Rugby*? *Iohn*: what *Iohn* I say? goe *Iohn*, goe enquire for my Master, I doubt he be not well, that hee comes not home: *(and downe, downe, adowne'a. &c.*

Ca. Vat is you sing? I doe not like des-toyes: pray you goe and vetch me in my Closset, vnboyteene verd: a Box, a greene-a-Box: do intend vat I speake? a greene-a-Box.

Qu. I forsooth ile fetch it you:
I am glad hee went not in himselfe: if he had found the yong man he would haue bin horne-mad.

Ca. *Fe, fe, fe, fe, mai foy, il fait for ehando, Ie man voi a le Court la grand affaires.*

Qu. Is it this Sir?

Ca. *Ouy mette le au mon pocket, de-peech quickly*: Vere is dat knaue *Rugby*?

Qu. What *Iohn Rugby*, *Iohn*?

Ru. Here Sir.

Ca. You are *Iohn Rugby*, aad you are *Iacke Rugby*: Come, take-a-your Rapier, and come after my heele to the Court.

Ru. 'Tis ready Sir, here in the Porch.

Ca. By my trot: I tarry too long: od's-me: *que ay ie oublie*: dere is some Simples in my Closset, dat I vill not for the varld I shall leaue behinde.

Qu. Ay-me, he'll finde the yong man there, & be mad.

Ca. O *Diable, Diable*: vat is in my Closset? Villanie, La-roone: *Rugby*, my Rapier.

Qu. Good Master be content.

Ca. Wherefore shall I be content-a?

Qu. The yong man is an honest man.

Ca. What shall de honest man do in my Closset: dere is no honest man dat shall come in my Closset.

Qu. I beseech you be not so flegmaticke: heare the truth of it. He came of an errand to mee, from Parson *Hugh*.

Ca. Vell.

Si. I forsooth: to desire her to —

Qu. Peace, I pray you.

Ca. Peace-a-your tongue: speake-a-your Tale.

Si. To desire this honest Gentlewoman (your Maid) to speake a good word to Mistris *Anne Page*, for my Master in the way of Marriage.

Qu. This is all indeede-la: but ile nere put my finger in the fire, and neede not.

Ca. Sir *Hugh* send-a you? *Rugby*, ballow mee some paper: tarry you a littell-a-while.

Qu. I

Qui. I am glad he is ſo quiet: if he had bin throughly moued,you ſhould haue heard him ſo loud,and ſo melancholly: but notwithſtanding man, Ile doe yoe your Maſter what good I can: and the very yea,& the no is,ẏ French Doctor my Maſter, (I may call him my Maſter, looke you,for I keepe his houſe; and I waſh,ring, brew, bake, ſcowre,dreſſe meat and drinke,make the beds,and doe all my ſelfe.)

Simp. 'Tis a great charge to come vnder one bodies hand.

Qui. Are you a-uis'd o'that? you ſhall finde it a great charge: and to be vp early,and down late: but notwithſtanding,(to tell you in your eare, I wold haue no words of it) my Maſter himſelfe is in loue with Miſtris *Anne Page*: but notwithſtanding that I know *Ans* mind,that's neither heere nor there.

Caius. You, Iack'Nape: giue-a this Letter to Sir *Hugh*, by gar it is a ſhallenge: I will cut his troat in de Parke, and I will teach a ſcuruy Iack-a-nape Prieſt to meddle, or make: —— you may be gon: it is not good you tarry here: by gar I will cut all his two ſtones: by gar, he ſhall not haue a ſtone to throw at his dogge.

Qui. Alas: he ſpeakes but for his friend.

Caius. It is no matter'a ver dat: do not you tell-a-me dat I ſhall haue *Anne Page* for my ſelfe? by gar, I vill kill de Iack-Prieſt: and I haue appointed mine Hoſt of de Iarteer to meaſure our weapon: by gar,I wil my ſelfe haue *Anne Page*.

Qui. Sir, the maid loues you, and all ſhall bee well: We muſt giue folkes leaue to prate: what the good-ier.

Caius. *Rugby*, come to the Court with me: by gar, if I haue not *Anne Page*, I ſhall turne your head out of my dore: follow my heeles,*Rugby*.

Qui. You ſhall haue *An*-fooles head of your owne: No, I know *Ans* mind for that: neuer a woman in *Windſor* knowes more of *Ans* minde then I doe, nor can doe more then I doe with her,I thanke heauen.

Fenton. Who's with in there, hoa?

Qui. Who's there, I troa? Come neere the houſe I pray you.

Fen. How now(good woman)how doſt thou?

Qui. The better that it pleaſes your good Worſhip to aske?

Fen. What newes? how do's pretty Miſtris *Anne*?

Qui. In truth Sir, and ſhee is pretty, and honeſt, and gentle, and one that is your friend, I can tell you that by the way, I praiſe heauen for it.

Fen. Shall I doe any good thinkſt thou? ſhall I not looſe my ſuit?

Qui. Troth Sir, all is in his hands aboue: but notwithſtanding (Maſter *Fenton*) Ile be ſworne on a booke ſhee loues you: haue not your Worſhip a wart aboue your eye?

Fen. Yes marry haue I, what of that?

Qui. Wel, thereby hangs a tale: good faith,it is ſuch another *Nan*; (but (I deteſt) an honeſt maid as euer broke bread: wee had an howres talke of that wart; I ſhall neuer laugh but in that maids company: but (indeed) ſhee is giuen too much to Allicholy and muſing: but for you —— well — goe too——

Fen. Well: I ſhall ſee her to day: hold, there's money for thee: Let mee haue thy voice in my behalfe: if thou ſeeſt her before me, commend me ——

Qui. Will I? I faith that wee will: And I will tell your Worſhip more of the Wart,the next time we haue confidence,and of other wooers.

Fen. Well, fare-well, I am in great haſte now.

Qui. Fare-well to your Worſhip: truely an honeſt Gentleman: but *Anne* loues him not: for I know *Ans* minde as well as another do's: out vpon't: what haue I forgot. *Exit.*

Actus Secundus. Scœna Prima.

Enter Miſtris Page, *Miſtris* Ford, *Maſter* Page, *Maſter* Ford, Piſtoll, Nim, Quickly, Hoſt, Shallow.

Miſt Page. What, haue ſcap'd Loue-letters in the holly-day-time of my beauty, and am I now a ſubiect for them? let me ſee?

Aske me no reaſon why I loue you, for though Loue vſe Reaſon for his precyſian, hee admits him not for his Counſailour. you are not yong, no more am I: goe to then, there's ſimpathie: you are merry, ſo am I. ha, ha, then there's more ſimpathie: you loue ſacke, and ſo do I: would you deſire better ſimpathie? Let it ſuffice thee (Miſtris Page) at the leaſt if the Loue of Souldier can ſuffice, that I loue thee: I will not ſay pitty mee, 'tis not a Souldier-like phraſe; but I ſay, loue me:

By me, thine owne true Knight, by day or night;
Or any kinde of light, with all his might,
For thee to fight. *Iohn Falſtaffe.*

What a *Herod* of *Iurie* is this? O wicked,wicked world:
One that is well-nye worne to peeces with age
To ſhow himſelfe a yong Gallant? What an vnwaied
Behauiour hath this Flemiſh drunkard picke (with
The Deuills name) out of my conuerſation,that he dares
In this manner aſſay me? why, hee hath not beene thrice
In my Company: what ſhould I ſay to him? I was then
Frugall of my mirth: (heauen forgiue mee:) why Ile
Exhibit a Bill in the Parliament for the putting downe
of men: how ſhall I be reueng'd on him? for reueng'd I
will be? as ſure as his guts are made of puddings.

Miſ Ford. *Miſtris Page*, truſt me,I was going to your houſe.

Miſ.Page. And truſt me,I was comming to you: you looke very ill.

Miſ.Ford. Nay, Ile nere beleeee that; I haue to ſhew to the contrary.

Miſ.Page. 'Faith but you doe in my minde.

Miſ.Ford. Well: I doe then: yet I ſay, I could ſhew you to the contrary: O Miſtris *Page*, giue mee ſome counſaile.

Miſ.Page. What's the matter, woman?

Mi.Ford. O woman: if it were not for one trifling reſpect, I could come to ſuch honour.

Mi.Page. Hang the trifle (woman) take the honour: what is it? diſpence with trifles: what is it?

Mi.Ford. If I would but goe to hell, for an eternall moment,or ſo: I could be knighted.

Mi.Page. What thou lieſt? Sir *Alice Ford*? theſe Knights will hacke,and ſo thou ſhouldſt not alter the article of thy Gentry.

Mi.Ford. Wee burne day-light: heere, read,read: perceiue how I might bee knighted, I ſhall thinke the worſe of fat men, as long as I haue an eye to make difference of mens liking: and yet hee would not ſweare: praiſe

praiſe

praise womens modesty: and gaue such orderly and wel-behaued reproofe to al vncomelinesse, that I would haue sworne his disposition would haue gone to the truth of his words: but they doe no more adhere and keep place together, then the hundred Psalms to the tune of Green-sleeues: What tempest (I troa) threw this Whale, (with so many Tuns of oyle in his belly) a'shoare at Windsor? How shall I bee reuenged on him? I thinke the best way were, to entertaine him with hope, till the wicked fire of lust haue melted him in his owne greace: Did you e-uer heare the like?

Mis.Page. Letter for letter; but that the name of *Page* and *Ford* differs: to thy great comfort in this my-stery of ill opinions, heere's the twyn-brother of thy Let-ter: but let thine inherit first, for I protest mine neuer shall: I warrant he hath a thousand of these Letters, writ with blancke-space for different names (sure more): and these are of the second edition: hee will print them out of doubt: for he cares not what hee puts into the presse, when he would put vs two: I had rather be a Giantesse, and lye vnder Mount *Pelion*: Well; I will find you twen-tie lasciuious Turtles ere one chaste man

Mis.Ford. Why this is the very same · the very hand: the very words · what doth he thinke of vs?

Mis.Page Nay I know not: it makes me almost rea-die to wrangle with mine owne honesty: Ile entertaine my selfe like one that I am not acquainted withall: for sure vnlesse hee know some straine in mee, that I know not my selfe, hee would neuer haue boorded me in this furie.

Ms. Ford. Boording, call you it? Ile bee sure to keepe him aboue decke

Ms.Page. So will I: if hee come vnder my hatches, Ile neuer to Sea againe: Let's bee reueng'd on him: let's appoint him a meeting: giue him a show of comfort in his Suit, and lead him on with a fine baited delay, till hee hath pawn'd his horses to mine Host of the Garter.

Mi.Ford. Nay, I wil consent to act any villany against him, that may not sully the charinesse of our honesty: oh that my husband saw this Letter: it would giue eternall food to his iealousie.

Mis.Page. Why look where he comes; and my good man too: hee's as farre from iealousie, as I am from gi-uing him cause, and that (I hope) is an vnmeasurable di-stance.

Mis.Ford. You are the happier woman.

Mis.Page. Let's consult together against this greasie Knight: Come hither.

Ford. Well: I hope, it be not so

Pist. Hope is a curtall-dog in some affaires.
Sir *Iohn* affects thy wife.

Ford. Why sir, my wife is not young.

Pist. He wooes both high and low, both rich & poor, both yong and old, one with another (*Ford*) he loues the Gally-mawfry (*Ford*) perpend.

Ford. Loue my wife?

Pist. With liuer, burning hot: preuent:
Or goe thou like Sir *Acteon* he, with
Ring-wood at thy heeles: O, odious is the name.

Ford. What name Sir?

Pist. The horne I say: Farewell:
Take heed, haue open eye, for theeues doe foot by night.
Take heed, ere sommer comes, or Cuckoo-birds do sing
Away sir Corporall *Nim*
Beleeue it (*Page*) he speakes sence.

Ford. I will be patient: I will find out this.

Nim. And this is true: I like not the humor of lying: hee hath wronged mee in some humors: I should haue borne the humour'd Letter to her: but I haue a sword: and it shall bite vpon my necessitie: he loues your wife; There's the short and the long: My name is Corporall *Nim*: I speak, and I auouch; 'tis true: my name is *Nim*: and *Falstaffe* loues your wife: adieu, I loue not the hu-mour of bread and cheese: adieu.

Page. The humour of it (quoth'a?) heere's a fellow frights English out of his wits.

Ford. I will seeke out *Falstaffe*.

Page. I neuer heard such a drawling-affecting rogue.

Ford. If I doe finde it: well.

Page. I will not beleeue such a *Cataian*, though the Priest o'th'Towne commended him for a true man.

Ford. 'Twas a good sensible fellow: well.

Page. How now *Meg*?

Mist.Page. Whether goe you (*George*?) harke you.

Mis Ford. How now (sweet *Frank*) why art thou me-lancholy?

Ford I melancholy? I am not melancholy:
Get you home · goe.

Mis.Ford. Faith, thou hast some crochets in thy head, Now: will you goe *Mistris Page*?

Mis.Page. Haue with you you'll come to dinner *George*? Looke who comes yonder shee shall bee our Messenger to this paltrie Knight.

Mis.Ford. Trust me, I thought on her: shee'll fit it.

Mis.Page. You are come to see my daughter *Anne*?

Qui. I forsooth: and I pray how do's good Mistresse *Anne*?

Mis.Page. Go in with vs and see: we haue an houres talke with you.

Page. How now Master Ford?

For. You heard what this knaue told me, did you not?

Page. Yes, and you heard what the other told me?

Ford. Doe you thinke there is truth in them?

Pag. Hang em slaues: I doe not thinke the Knight would offer it: But these that accuse him in his intent towards our wiues, are a yoake of his discarded men: ve-ry rogues, now they be out of seruice.

Ford. Were they his men?

Page. Marry were they.

Ford. I like it neuer the beter for that,
Do's he lye at the Garter?

Page. I marry do's he: if hee should intend this voy-age toward my wife, I would turne her loose to him; and what hee gets more of her, then sharpe words, let it lye on my head.

Ford. I doe not misdoubt my wife: but I would bee loath to turne them together: a man may be too confi-dent: I would haue nothing lye on my head: I cannot be thus satisfied.

Page. Looke where my ranting-Host of the Garter comes: there is eyther liquor in his pate, or mony in his purse, when hee lookes so merrily. How now mine Host?

Host. How now Bully-Rooke · thou'rt a Gentleman Caueleiro Iustice, I say

Shal. I follow, (mine Host) I follow Good-euen, and twenty (good Master *Page*.) Master *Page*, wil you go with vs? we haue sport in hand

Host Tell him Caueleiro-Iustice: tell him Bully-Rooke.

Shall. Sir, there is a fray to be fought, betweene Sir *Hugh* the Welch Priest, and *Caius* the French Doctor.

Ford. Good

Ford. Good mine Hoſt o'th Garter: a word with you.

Hoſt. What ſaiſt thou, my Bully-Rooke?

Shal. Will you goe with vs to behold it? My merry Hoſt hath had the meaſuring of their weapons; and (I thinke) hath appointed them contrary places: for (beleeue mee) I heare the Parſon is no Ieſter: harke, I will tell you what our ſport ſhall be.

Hoſt. Haſt thou no ſuit againſt my Knight? my gueſt-Caualeire?

Shal. None, I proteſt: but Ile giue you a pottle of burn'd ſacke, to giue me recourſe to him, and tell him my name is *Broome*: onely for a ieſt.

Hoſt. My hand, (Bully:) thou ſhalt haue egreſſe and regreſſe, (ſaid I well?) and thy name ſhall be *Broome.* It is a merry Knight: will you goe An-heires?

Shal. Haue with you mine Hoſt.

Page. I haue heard the French-man hath good skill in his Rapier.

Shal. Tut ſir: I could haue told you more: In theſe times you ſtand on diſtance: your Paſſes, Stoccado's, and I know not what: 'tis the heart (Maſter *Page*) 'tis heere, 'tis heere: I haue ſeene the time, with my long-ſword, I would haue made you fowre tall fellowes skippe like Rattes.

Hoſt. Heere boyes, heere, heere: ſhall we wag?

Page. Haue with you: I had rather heare them ſcold, then fight.

Ford. Though *Page* be a ſecure foole, and ſtands ſo firmely on his wiues frailty; yet, I cannot put-off my opinion ſo eaſily: ſhe was in his company at *Pages* houſe: and what they made there, I know not. Well, I wil looke further into't, and I haue a diſguiſe, to ſound *Falſtaffe*; if I finde her honeſt, I looſe not my labor: if ſhe be otherwiſe, 'tis labour well beſtowed. *Exeunt.*

Scœna Secunda.

Enter Falſtaffe, Piſtoll, Robin, Quickly, Bardolffe, Ford.

Fal. I will not lend thee a penny.

Piſt. Why then the world's mine Oyſter, which I, with ſword will open.

Fal. Not a penny: I haue beene content (Sir,) you ſhould lay my countenance to pawne: I haue grated vpon my good friends for three Repreeues for you, and your Coach-fellow *Nim*; or elſe you had look'd through the grate, like a Geminy of Baboones: I am damn'd in hell, for ſwearing to Gentlemen my friends, you were good Souldiers, and tall-fellowes. And when Miſtreſſe *Briget* loſt the handle of her Fan, I took't vpon mine honour thou hadſt it not.

Piſt. Didſt not thou ſhare? hadſt thou not fifteene pence?

Fal. Reaſon, you roague, reaſon: thinkſt thou Ile endanger my ſoule, *gratis*? at a word, hang no more about mee, I am no gibbet for you: goe, a ſhort knife, and a throng, to your Mannor of *Pickt-hatch*: goe, you'll not beare a Letter for mee you roague? you ſtand vpon your honor: why, (thou vnconfinable baſeneſſe) it is as much as I can doe to keepe the termes of my honor preciſe: I, I, I my ſelfe ſometimes, leauing the feare of heauen on the left hand, and hiding mine honor in my neceſſity, am faine to ſhuffle: to hedge, and to lurch, and yet, you Rogue, will en-ſconce your raggs; your Cat-a-Mountaine-lookes, your red-lattice phraſes, and your bold-beating-oathes, vnder the ſhelter of your honor? you will not doe it? you?

Piſt. I doe relent: what would thou more of man?

Robin. Sir, here's a woman would ſpeake with you.

Fal. Let her approach.

Qui. Giue your worſhip good morrow.

Fal. Good-morrow, good-wife.

Qui. Not ſo and't pleaſe your worſhip.

Fal. Good maid then.

Qui. Ile be ſworne,
As my mother was the firſt houre I was borne.

Fal. I doe beleeue the ſwearer; what with me?

Qui. Shall I vouch-ſafe your worſhip a word, or two?

Fal. Two thouſand (faire woman) and ile vouchſafe thee the hearing.

Qui. There is one Miſtreſſe *Ford*, (Sir) I pray come a little neerer this waies: I my ſelfe dwell with M. Doctor *Caius*:

Fal. Well, on; Miſtreſſe *Ford*, you ſay.

Qui. Your worſhip ſaies very true: I pray your worſhip come a little neerer this waies.

Fal. I warrant thee, no-bodie heares: mine owne people, mine owne people.

Qui. Are they ſo? heauen-bleſſe them, and make them his Seruants.

Fal. Well; Miſtreſſe *Ford*, what of her?

Qui. Why, Sir; ſhee's a good-creature; Lord, Lord, your Worſhip's a wanton: well: heauen forgiue you, and all of vs, I pray———.

Fal. Miſtreſſe *Ford*: come, Miſtreſſe *Ford.*

Qui. Marry this is the ſhort, and the long of it: you haue brought her into ſuch a Canaries, as 'tis wonderfull: the beſt Courtier of them all (when the Court lay at *Windſor*) could neuer haue brought her to ſuch a Canarie: yet there has beene Knights, and Lords, and Gentlemen, with their Coaches; I warrant you Coach after Coach, letter after letter, gift after gift, ſmelling ſo ſweetly; all Muske, and ſo ruſhling, I warrant you, in ſilke and golde, and in ſuch alligant termes, and in ſuch wine and ſuger of the beſt, and the faireſt, that would haue wonne any womans heart: and I warrant you, they could neuer get an eye-winke of her: I had my ſelfe twentie Angels giuen me this morning, but I defie all Angels (in any ſuch ſort, as they ſay) but in the way of honeſty: and I warrant you, they could neuer get her ſo much as ſippe on a cup with the prowdeſt of them all, and yet there has beene Earles: nay, (which is more) Pentioners, but I warrant you all is one with her.

Fal. But what ſaies ſhee to mee? be briefe my good ſhee-*Mercurie.*

Qui. Marry, ſhe hath receiu'd your Letter: for the which ſhe thankes you a thouſand times; and ſhe giues you to notifie, that her husband will be abſence from his houſe, betweene ten and eleuen.

Fal. Ten, and eleuen.

Qui. I, forſooth: and then you may come and ſee the picture (ſhe ſayes) that you wot of: Maſter *Ford* her husband will be from home: alas, the ſweet woman leades an ill life with him: hee's a very iealouſie-man; ſhe leads a very frampold life with him, (good hart.)

Fal. Ten, and eleuen.

Women

Woman, commend me to her, I will not faile her.

Qui. Why, you ſay well: But I haue another meſſenger to your worſhip: Miſtreſſe *Page* hath her heartie commendations to you to: and let mee tell you in your eare, ſhee's as fartuous a ciuill modeſt wife, and one (I tell you) that will not miſſe you morning nor euening prayer, as any is in *Windſor*, who ere bee the other: and ſhee bade me tell your worſhip, that her husband is ſeldome from home, but ſhe hopes there will come a time. I neuer knew a woman ſo doate vpon a man; ſurely I thinke you haue charmes, la: yes in truth.

Fal. Not I, I aſſure thee; ſetting the attraction of my good parts aſide, I haue no other charmes.

Qui. Bleſſing on your heart for't.

Fal. But I pray thee tell me this: has *Fords* wife, and *Pages* wife acquainted each other, how they loue me?

Qui. That were a ieſt indeed: they haue not ſo little grace I hope, that were a tricke indeed: But Miſtris *Page* would deſire you to ſend her your little Page of al loues: her husband has a maruellous infectio to the little Page: and truely Maſter *Page* is an honeſt man: neuer a wife in *Windſor* leades a better life then ſhe do's: doe what ſhee will, ſay what ſhe will, take all, pay all, goe to bed when ſhe liſt, riſe when ſhe liſt, all is as ſhe will: and truly ſhe deſerues it; for if there be a kinde woman in *Windſor*, ſhe is one: you muſt ſend her your Page, no remedie.

Fal. Why, I will.

Qu. Nay, but doe ſo then, and looke you, hee may come and goe betweene you both: and in any caſe haue a nay-word, that you may know one anothers minde, and the Boy neuer neede to vnderſtand any thing; for 'tis not good that children ſhould know any wickednes: olde folkes you know, haue diſcretion, as they ſay, and know the world.

Fal. Farethee-well, commend mee to them both: there's my purſe, I am yet thy debter: Boy, goe along with this woman, this newes diſtracts me.

Piſt. This Puncke is one of *Cupids* Carriers,
Clap on more ſailes, purſue: vp with your fights:
Giue fire: ſhe is my prize, or Ocean whelme them all.

Fal. Saiſt thou ſo (old *Iacke*) go thy waies: Ile make more of thy olde body then I haue done: will they yet looke after thee? wilt thou after the expence of ſo much money, be now a gainer? good Body, I thanke thee: let them ſay 'tis groſſely done, ſo it bee fairely done, no matter.

Bar. Sir *Iohn*, there's one Maſter *Broome* below would faine ſpeake with you, and be acquainted with you; and hath ſent your worſhip a mornings draught of Sacke.

Fal. *Broome* is his name?

Bar. I Sir.

Fal. Call him in: ſuch *Broomes* are welcome to mee, that ore'flowes ſuch liquor: ah ha, Miſtreſſe *Ford* and Miſtreſſe *Page*, haue I encompaſs'd you? goe to, *via*.

Ford. 'Bleſſe you ſir.

Fal. And you ſir: would you ſpeake with me?

Ford. I make bold, to preſſe, with ſo little preparation vpon you.

Fal. You'r welcome, what's your will? giue vs leaue Drawer.

Ford. Sir, I am a Gentleman that haue ſpent much, my name is *Broome*.

Fal. Good Maſter *Broome*, I deſire more acquaintance of you.

Ford. Good Sir *Iohn*, I ſue for yours: not to charge you, for I muſt let you vnderſtand, I thinke my ſelfe in better plight for a Lender, then you are: the which hath ſomething emboldned me to this vnſeaſon'd intruſion: for they ſay, if money goe before, all waies doe lye open.

Fal. Money is a good Souldier (Sir) and will on.

Ford. Troth, and I haue a bag of money heere troubles me: if you will helpe to beare it (Sir *Iohn*) take all, or halfe, for eaſing me of the carriage.

Fal. Sir, I know not how I may deſerue to bee your Porter.

Ford. I will tell you ſir, if you will giue mee the hearing.

Fal. Speake (good Maſter *Broome*) I ſhall be glad to be your Seruant.

Ford. Sir, I heare you are a Scholler: (I will be briefe with you) and you haue been a man long knowne to me, though I had neuer ſo good means as deſire, to make my ſelfe acquainted with you. I ſhall diſcouer a thing to you, wherein I muſt very much lay open mine owne imperfection: but (good Sir *Iohn*) as you haue one eye vpon my follies, as you heare them vnfolded, turne another into the Regiſter of your owne, that I may paſſe with a reproofe the eaſier, ſith you your ſelfe know how eaſie it is to be ſuch an offender.

Fal. Very well *Sir*, proceed.

Ford. There is a Gentlewoman in this Towne, her husbands name is *Ford*.

Fal. Well Sir.

Ford. I haue long lou'd her, and I proteſt to you, beſtowed much on her: followed her with a doating obſeruance: Ingroſs'd opportunities to meete her: fee'd euery ſlight occaſion that could but nigardly giue mee ſight of her: not only bought many preſents to giue her, but haue giuen largely to many, to know what ſhee would haue giuen: briefly, I haue purſu'd her, as Loue hath purſued mee, which hath beene on the wing of all occaſions: but whatſoeuer I haue merited, either in my minde, or in my meanes, meede I am ſure I haue receiued none, vnleſſe Experience be a Iewell, that I haue purchaſed at an infinite rate, and that hath taught mee to ſay this,

" *Loue like a ſhadow flies, when ſubſtance Loue purſues,*
" *Purſuing that that flies, and flying what purſues.*

Fal. Haue you receiu'd no promiſe of ſatisfaction at her hands?

Ford. Neuer.

Fal. Haue you importun'd her to ſuch a purpoſe?

Ford. Neuer.

Fal. Of what qualitie was your loue then?

Ford. Like a fair houſe, built on another mans ground, ſo that I haue loſt my edifice, by miſtaking the place, where I erected it.

Fal. To what purpoſe haue you vnfolded this to me?

For. When I haue told you that, I haue told you all: Some ſay, that though ſhe appeare honeſt to mee, yet in other places ſhee enlargeth her mirth ſo farre, that there is ſhrewd conſtruction made of her. Now (Sir *Iohn*) here is the heart of my purpoſe: you are a gentleman of excellent breeding, admirable diſcourſe, of great admittance, authenticke in your place and perſon, generally allow'd for your many war-like, court-like, and learned preparations.

Fal. O Sir.

Ford. Beleeue it, for you know it: there is money, ſpend it, ſpend it, ſpend more; ſpend all I haue, onely

giue

giue me so much of your time in exchange of it, as to lay an amiable siege to the honesty of this *Fords* wife: vse your Art of wooing; win her to consent to you: if any man may, you may as soone as any.

Fal. Would it apply well to the vehemency of your affection that I should win what you would enioy? Methinkes you prescribe to your selfe very preposterously.

Ford. O, vnderstand my drift: she dwells so securely on the excellency of her honor, that the folly of my soule dares not present it selfe: shee is too bright to be look'd against. Now, could I come to her with any detection in my hand; my desires had instance and argument to commend themselues, I could driue her then from the ward of her purity, her reputation, her marriage-vow, and a thousand other her defences, which now are too-too strongly embattaild against me: what say you too't, Sir *Iohn*?

Fal. Master *Broome*, I will first make bold with your money: next, giue mee your hand: and last, as I am a gentleman, you shall, if you will, enioy *Fords* wife.

Ford. O good Sir.

Fal. I say you shall.

Ford. Want no money (Sir *Iohn*) you shall want none.

Fal. Want no *Mistresse Ford* (Master *Broome*) you shall want none: I shall be with her (I may tell you) by her owne appointment, euen as you came in to me, her assistant, or goe-betweene, parted from me: I say I shall be with her betweene ten and eleuen: for at that time the iealious-rascally-knaue her husband will be forth: come you to me at night, you shall know how I speed.

Ford. I am blest in your acquaintance: do you know *Ford* Sir?

Fal. Hang him (poore Cuckoldly knaue) I know him not: yet I wrong him to call him poore: They say the iealous wittolly-knaue hath masses of money, for the which his wife seemes to me well-fauourd: I will vse her as the key of the Cuckoldly-rogues Coffer, & ther's my haruest-home.

Ford. I would you knew *Ford*, sir, that you might auoid him, if you saw him.

Fal. Hang him, mechanicall-salt-butter rogue; I wil stare him out of his wits: I will awe-him with my cudgell: it shall hang like a Meteor ore the Cuckolds horns: Master *Broome*, thou shalt know, I will predominate ouer the pezant, and thou shalt lye with his wife. Come to me soone at night: *Ford*'s a knaue, and I will aggrauate his stile: thou (Master *Broome*) shalt know him for knaue, and Cuckold. Come to me soone at night.

Ford. What a damn'd Epicurian-Rascall is this? my heart is ready to cracke with impatience: who saies this is improuident iealousie? my wife hath sent to him, the howre is fixt, the match is made: would any man haue thought this? see the hell of hauing a false woman: my bed shall be abus'd, my Coffers ransack'd, my reputation gnawne at, and I shall not onely receiue this villanous wrong, but stand vnder the adoption of abhominable termes, and by him that does mee this wrong: Termes, names: *Amaimon* sounds well: *Lucifer*, well: *Barbason*, well: yet they are Diuels additions, the names of fiends: But Cuckold, Wittoll, Cuckold? the Diuell himselfe hath not such a name. *Page* is an Asse, a secure Asse; hee will trust his wife, hee will not be iealous: I will rather trust a *Fleming* with my butter, Parson *Hugh* the *Welshman* with my Cheese, an *Irish-man* with my Aqua-vitæ-bottle, or a Theefe to walke my ambling gelding, then my wife with her selfe. Then she plots, then shee ruminates, then shee deuises: and what they thinke in their hearts they may effect; they will breake their hearts but they will effect. Heauen bee prais'd for my iealousie: eleuen o' clocke the howre, I will preuent this, detect my wife, bee reueng'd on *Falstaffe*, and laugh at *Page*. I will about it, better three houres too soone, then a mynute too late: fie, fie, fie: Cuckold, Cuckold, Cuckold.

Exti.

Scena Tertia.

Enter Caius, Rugby, Page, Shallow, Slender, Host.

Caius. *Iacke Rugby.*

Rug. Sir.

Caius. Vat is the clocke, *Iack*

Rug. 'Tis past the howre (Sir) that Sir *Hugh* promis'd to meet.

Cai. By gar, he has saue his soule, dat he is no-come: hee has pray his Pible well, dat he is no-come: by gar (*Iack Rugby*) he is dead already, if he be come.

Rug. Hee is wise Sir: hee knew your worship would kill him if he came.

Cai. By gar, de herring is no dead, so as I vill kill him: take your Rapier, (*Iacke*) I vill tell you how I vill kill him.

Rug. Alas sir, I cannot fence.

Cai. Villanie, take your Rapier.

Rug. Forbeare: heer's company.

Host. 'Blesse thee, bully-Doctor.

Shal. 'Saue you Mr. Doctor *Caius*.

Page. Now, good Mr. Doctor.

Slen. 'Giue you good-morrow, sir.

Caius. Vat be all you one, two, tree, fowre, come for?

Host. To see thee fight, to see thee foigne, to see thee trauerse, to see thee heere, to see thee there, to see thee passe thy puncto, thy stock, thy reuerse, thy distance, thy montant: Is he dead, my Ethiopian? Is he dead, my Francisco? ha Bully? what saies my *Esculapius*? my *Galien*? my heart of Elder? ha? is he dead bully-Stale? is he dead?

Cai. By gar, he is de Coward-Iack-Priest of de vorld: he is not show his face.

Host. Thou art a Castalion king-Vrinall: *Hector* of *Greece* (my Boy)

Cai. I pray you beare witnesse, that me haue stay, sixe or seuen, two tree howres for him, and hee is no-come.

Shal. He is the wiser man (M. Docto) he is a curer of soules, and you a curer of bodies: if you should fight, you goe against the haire of your professions: is it not true, Master *Page*?

Page. Master *Shallow*; you haue your selfe beene a great fighter, though now a man of peace.

Shal. Body-kins M. *Page*, though I now be old, and of the peace; if I see a sword out, my finger itches to make one: though wee are Iustices, and Doctors, and Church-men (M. *Page*) wee haue some salt of our youth in vs, we are the sons of women (M. *Page*.)

Page. 'Tis true, Mr. *Shallow*.

Shal. It wil be found so, (M. *Page*:) M. Doctor *Caius*, I am come to fetch you home: I am sworn of the peace: you haue show'd your selfe a wise Physician, and Sir *Hugh* hath showne himselfe a wise and patient Churchman: you must goe with me, M. Doctor.

Host. Par-

Host. Pardon, Guest-Iustice; a Mounseur Mocke-water.

Cai. Mock-vater? vat is dat?

Host. Mock-water, in our English tongue, is Valour (Bully.)

Cai. By gar, then I haue as much Mock-vater as de Englishman: scuruy-Iack-dog-Priest: by gar, mee vill cut his eares.

Host. He will Clapper-claw thee tightly (Bully.)

Cai. Clapper-de-claw? vat is dat?

Host. That is, he will make thee amends.

Cai. By-gar, me doe looke hee shall clapper-de-claw me, for by-gar, me vill haue it.

Host. And I will prouoke him to't, or let him wag.

Cai. Me tanck you for dat.

Host. And moreouer, (Bully) but first, Mr. Ghuest, and M. *Page*, & eeke Caualeiro *Slender*, goe you through the Towne to *Frogmore*.

Page. Sir *Hugh* is there, is he?

Host. He is there, see what humor he is in: and I will bring the Doctor about by the Fields: will it doe well?

Shal. We will doe it.

All. Adieu, good M. Doctor.

Cai. By-gar, me vill kill de Priest, for he speake for a Iack-an-Ape to *Anne Page*.

Host. Let him die: sheath thy impatience: throw cold water on thy Choller: goe about the fields with mee through *Frogmore*, I will bring thee where Mistris *Anne Page* is, at a Farm-house a Feasting: and thou shalt wooe her: Cride-game, said I well?

Cai. By-gar, mee dancke you vor dat: by gar I loue you: and I shall procure 'a you de good Guest: de Earle, de Knight, de Lords, de Gentlemen, my patients.

Host. For the which, I will be thy aduersary toward *Anne Page*: said I well?

Cai. By-gar, 'tis good: vell said.

Host. Let vs wag then.

Cai. Come at my heeles, *Iack Rugby*.

Exeunt.

Actus Tertius. Scœna Prima.

Enter Euans, Simple, Page, Shallow, Slender, Host, Caius, Rugby.

Euans. I pray you now, good Master *Slenders* seruing-man, and friend *Simple* by your name; which way haue you look'd for Master *Caius*, that calls himselfe Doctor of Phisicke.

Sim. Marry Sir, the pittie-ward, the Parke-ward: euery way: olde *Windsor* way, and euery way but the Towne-way.

Euan. I most fehemently desire you, you will also looke that way.

Sim. I will sir.

Euan. 'Plesse my soule: how full of Chollers I am, and trempling of minde: I shall be glad if he haue deceiued me: how melancholies I am? I will knog his Vrinalls about his knaues costard, when I haue good oportunities for the orke: 'Plesse my soule: *To shallow Riuers to whose falls: melodious Birds sings Madrigalls: There will we make our Peds of Roses: and a thousand fragrant posies. To shallow:* 'Mercie on mee, I haue a great dispositions to cry. *Melodious birds sing Madrigalls: — When as I sat in Pabilon: and a thousand vagram Posies. To shallow, &c.*

Sim. Yonder he is comming, this way, Sir *Hugh*.

Euan. Hee's welcome: *To shallow Riuers, to whose fals:* Heauen prosper the right: what weapons is he?

Sim. No weapons, Sir: there comes my Master, Mr. *Shallow*, and another Gentleman; from *Frogmore*, ouer the stile, this way.

Euan. Pray you giue mee my gowne, or else keepe it in your armes.

Shal. How now Master Parson? good morrow good Sir *Hugh*: keepe a Gamester from the dice, and a good Studient from his booke, and it is wonderfull.

Slen. Ah sweet *Anne Page*.

Page. 'Saue you, good Sir *Hugh*.

Euan. 'Plesse you from his mercy-sake, all of you.

Shal. What? the Sword, and the Word? Doe you study them both, Mr. Parson?

Page. And youthfull still, in your doublet and hose, this raw-rumaticke day?

Euan. There is reasons, and causes for it.

Page. We are come to you, to doe a good office, Mr. Parson.

Euan. Fery-well: what is it?

Page. Yonder is a most reuerend Gentleman; who (be-like) hauing receiued wrong by some person, is at most odds with his owne grauity and patience, that euer you saw.

Shal. I haue liued foure-score yeeres, and vpward: I neuer heard a man of his place, grauity, and learning, so wide of his owne respect.

Euan. What is he?

Page. I thinke you know him: Mr. Doctor *Caius* the renowned French Physician.

Euan. Got's-will, and his passion of my heart: I had as lief you would tell me of a messe of porredge.

Page. Why?

Euan. He has no more knowledge in *Hibocrates* and *Galen*, and hee is a knaue besides: a cowardly knaue, as you would desires to be acquainted withall.

Page. I warrant you, hee's the man should fight with him.

Slen. O sweet *Anne Page*.

Shal. It appeares so by his weapons: keepe them asunder: here comes Doctor *Caius*.

Page. Nay good Mr. Parson, keepe in your weapon.

Shal. So doe you, good Mr. Doctor.

Host. Disarme them, and let them question: let them keepe their limbs whole, and hack our English.

Cai. I pray you let-a-mee speake a word with your eare; vherefore vill you not meet-a me?

Euan. Pray you vse your patience in good time.

Cai. By-gar, you are de Coward: de Iack dog: Iohn Ape.

Euan. Pray you let vs not be laughing-stocks to other mens humors: I desire you in friendship, and I will one way or other make you amends: I will knog your Vrinal about your knaues Cogs-combe.

Cai. *Diable: Iack Rugby*: mine *Host de Iarteer*: haue I not stay for him, to kill him? haue I not at de place I did appoint?

Euan. As I am a Christians-soule, now looke you: this is the place appointed, Ile bee iudgement by mine *Host of the Garter*.

Host. Peace, I say, *Gallia* and *Gaule*, *French* & *Welsh*, Soule-Curer, and Body-Curer.

Cai. I,

Cai. I, dat is very good, excellant.

Host. Peace, I say: heare mine Host of the Garter, Am I politicke? Am I subtle? Am I a Machiuell? Shall I loose my Doctor? No, hee giues me the Potions and the Motions. Shall I loose my Parson? my Priest? my Sir *Hugh*? No, he giues me the Prouerbes, and the No-verbes. Giue me thy hand (Celestiall) so: Boyes of Art, I haue deceiu'd you both: I haue directed you to wrong places: your hearts are mighty, your skinnes are whole, and let burn'd Sacke be the issue: Come, lay their swords to pawne: Follow me, Lad of peace, follow, follow, follow.

Shal. Trust me, a mad Host: follow Gentlemen, follow.

Slen. O sweet *Anne Page.*

Cai. Ha'do I perceiue dat? Haue you make-a-de-sot of vs, ha, ha?

Euan. This is well, he has made vs his vlowting-stog: I desire you that we may be friends: and let vs knog our praines together to be reuenge on this same scall-scuruy-cogging-companion the Host of the Garter.

Cai. By gar, with all my heart: he promise to bring me where is *Anne Page*: by gar he deceiue me too.

Euan. Well, I will smite his noddles: pray you follow.

Scena Secunda.

Mist. Page, Robin, Ford, Page, Shallow, Slender, Host, Euans, Caius.

Mist. Page. Nay keepe your way (little Gallant) you were wont to be a follower, but now you are a Leader: whether had you rather lead mine eyes, or eye your masters heeles?

Rob. I had rather (forsooth) go before you like a man, then follow him like a dwarfe.

M. Pa. O you are a flattering boy, now I see you'l be a Courtier.

Ford. Well met mistris *Page*, whether go you.

M. Pa. Truly Sir, to see your wife, is she at home?

Ford. I, and as idle as she may hang together for want of company: I thinke if your husbands were dead, you two would marry.

M. Pa. Be sure of that, two other husbands.

Ford. Where had you this pretty weather-cocke?

M. Pa. I cannot tell what (the dickens) his name is my husband had him of, what do you cal your Knights name sirrah?

Rob. Sir *Iohn Falstaffe.*

Ford. Sir *Iohn Falstaffe.*

M. Pa. He, he, I can neuer hit on's name; there is such a league betweene my goodman, and he: is your Wife at home indeed?

Ford. Indeed she is.

M. Pa. By your leaue sir, I am sicke till I see her.

Ford. Has *Page* any braines? Hath he any eies? Hath he any thinking? Sure they sleepe, he hath no vse of them: why this boy will carrie a letter twentie mile as easie, as a Canon will shoot point-blanke twelue score: hee peeces out his wiues inclination: he giues her folly motion and aduantage: and now she's going to my wife, & *Falstaffes* boy with her: A man may heare this showre sing in the winde; and *Falstaffes* boy with her: good plots, they are laide, and our reuolted wiues share damnation together. Well, I will take him, then torture my wife, plucke the borrowed vaile of modestie from the so-seeming Mist. *Page*, diuulge *Page* himselfe for a secure and wilfull *Acteon*, and to these violent proceedings all my neighbors shall cry aime. The clocke giues me my Qu, and my assurance bids me search, there I shall finde *Falstaffe*: I shall be rather praisd for this, then mock'd, for it is as possitiue, as the earth is firme, that *Falstaffe* is there: I will go.

Shal. Page, &c. Well met Mr *Ford.*

Ford. Trust me, a good knotte; I haue good cheere at home, and I pray you all go with me.

Shal. I must excuse my selfe Mr *Ford.*

Slen. And so must I Sir,
We haue appointed to dine with Mistris *Anne*,
And I would not breake with her for more mony
Then Ile speake of.

Shal. We haue linger'd about a match betweene *An Page*, and my cozen *Slender*, and this day wee shall haue our answer.

Slen. I hope I haue your good will Father *Page.*

Pag. You haue Mr *Slender*, I stand wholly for you,
But my wife (Mr Doctor) is for you altogether.

Cai. I be-gar, and de Maid is loue-a-me: my nursh-a-Quickly tell me so mush.

Host. What say you to yong Mr *Fenton*? He capers, he dances, he has eies of youth: he writes verses, hee speakes holliday, he smels April and May, he wil carry't, he will carry't, 'tis in his buttons, he will carry't.

Page. Not by my consent I promise you. The Gentleman is of no hauing, hee kept companie with the wilde Prince, and *Pointz*: he is of too high a Region, he knows too much: no, hee shall not knit a knot in his fortunes, with the finger of my substance: if he take her, let him take her simply: the wealth I haue waits on my consent, and my consent goes not that way.

Ford. I beseech you heartily, some of you goe home with me to dinner: besides your cheere you shall haue sport, I will shew you a monster: Mr Doctor, you shal go, so shall you Mr *Page*, and you Sir *Hugh.*

Shal. Well, fare you well:
We shall haue the freer woing at Mr *Pages.*

Cai. Go home *Iohn Rugby*, I come anon.

Host. Farewell my hearts, I will to my honest Knight *Falstaffe*, and drinke Canarie with him.

Ford. I thinke I shall drinke in Pipe-wine first with him, Ile make him dance. Will you go, Gentles?

All. Haue with you, to see this Monster. *Exeunt*

Scena Tertia.

Enter M. Ford, M. Page, Seruants, Robin, Falstaffe, Ford, Page, Caius, Euans.

Mist. Ford. What *Iohn*, what *Robert.*

M. Page. Quickly, quickly: Is the Buck-basket——

Mis Ford. I warrant. What *Robin* I say.

Mis. Page. Come, come, come.

Mist. Ford. Heere, set it downe.

M. Pag. Giue your men the charge, we must be briefe.

M. Ford. Marrie, as I told you before (*Iohn* & *Robert*) be ready here hard-by in the Brew-house, & when I sodainly call you, come forth, and (without any pause, or staggering) take this basket on your shoulders: ỳ done, trudge with it in all hast, and carry it among the Whitsters in *Dotchet* Mead, and there empty it in the muddie ditch, close by the Thames side.

M. Page. You will do it?

M. Ford. I ha told them ouer and ouer, they lacke no direction.

Be gone, and come when you are call'd.

M.Page. Here comes little *Robin.*

Mist.Ford. How now my Eyas-Musket, what newes with you?

Rob. My M. Sir *Iohn* is come in at your backe doore (Mist. *Ford*, and requests your company.

M.Page. You litle Iack-a-lent, haue you bin true to vs

Rob. I, Ile be sworne: my Master knowes not of your being heere: and hath threatned to put me into euerlasting liberty, if I tell you of it: for he sweares he'll turne me away.

Mist.Pag. Thou 'rt a good boy: this secrecy of thine shall be a Tailor to thee, and shal make thee a new doublet and hose. Ile go hide me.

Mi.Ford. Do so: go tell thy Master, I am alone: Mistris *Page*, remember you your *Qu.*

Mist.Pag. I warrant thee, if I do not act it, hisse me.

Mist.Ford. Go-too then: we'l vse this vnwholsome humidity, this grosse-watry Pumpion; we'll teach him to know Turtles from Iayes.

Fal. Haue I caught thee, my heauenly Iewell? Why now let me die, for I haue liu'd long enough: This is the period of my ambition: O this blessed houre.

Mist.Ford. O sweet Sir *Iohn.*

Fal. Mistris *Ford*, I cannot cog, I cannot prate (Mist. *Ford*) now shall I sin in my wish; I would thy Husband were dead, Ile speake it before the best Lord, I would make thee my Lady.

Mist.Ford. I your Lady Sir *Iohn*? Alas, I should bee a pittifull Lady.

Fal. Let the Court of France shew me such another: I see how thine eye would emulate the Diamond: Thou hast the right arched-beauty of the brow, that becomes the Ship-tyre, the Tyre-valiant, or any Tire of Venetian admittance.

Mist.Ford. A plaine Kerchiefe, Sir *Iohn*:
My browes become nothing else, nor that well neither.

Fal. Thou art a tyrant to say so: thou wouldst make an absolute Courtier, and the firme fixture of thy foote, would giue an excellent motion to thy gate, in a semicircled Farthingale. I see what thou wert if Fortune thy foe, were not Nature thy friend: Come, thou canst not hide it.

Mist.Ford. Beleeue me, ther's no such thing in me.

Fal. What made me loue thee? Let that perswade thee. Ther's something extraordinary in thee: Come, I cannot cog, and say thou art this and that, like a-manie of these lisping-hauthorne buds, that come like women in mens apparrell, and smell like Bucklers-berry in simple time: I cannot, but I loue thee, none but thee; and thou deseru'st it.

M.Ford. Do not betray me sir, I fear you loue *M.Page.*

Fal. Thou mightst as well say, I loue to walke by the Counter-gate, which is as hatefull to me, as the reeke of a Lime-kill.

Mis Ford. Well, heauen knowes how I loue you,
And you shall one day finde it.

Fal. Keepe in that minde, Ile deserue it.

Mist Ford. Nay, I must tell you, so you doe;
Or else I could not be in that minde.

Rob. Mistris *Ford*, Mistris *Ford*: heere's Mistris *Page* at the doore, sweating, and blowing and looking wildely, and would needs speake with you presently.

Fal. She shall not see me, I will ensconce mee behinde the Arras.

M.Ford. Pray you do so, she's a very tatling woman. Whats the matter? How now?

Mist.Page. O mistris *Ford* what haue you done?
You'r sham'd, y'are ouerthrowne, y'are vndone for euer.

M.Ford. What's the matter, good mistris *Page*?

M.Page. O weladay, mist. *Ford*, hauing an honest man to your husband, to giue him such cause of suspition.

M.Ford. What cause of suspition?

M.Page. What cause of suspition? Out vpon you:
How am I mistooke in you?

M.Ford. Why (alas) what's the matter?

M.Page. Your husband's comming hether (Woman) with all the Officers in Windsor, to search for a Gentleman, that he sayes is heere now in the house; by your consent to take an ill aduantage of his absence: you are vndone.

M.Ford. 'Tis not so, I hope.

M.Page. Pray heauen it be not so, that you haue such a man heere: but 'tis most certaine your husband's comming, with halfe Windsor at his heeles, to serch for such a one, I come before to tell you: If you know your selfe cleere, why I am glad of it: but if you haue a friend here, conuey, conuey him out. Be not amaz'd, call all your senses to you, defend your reputation, or bid farwell to your good life for euer.

M.Ford. What shall I do? There is a Gentleman my deere friend: and I feare not mine owne shame so much, as his perill. I had rather then a thousand pound he were out of the house.

M.Page. For shame, neuer stand (you had rather, and you had rather:) your husband's heere at hand, bethinke you of some conueyance: in the house you cannot hide him. Oh, how haue you deceiu'd me? Looke, heere is a basket, if he be of any reasonable stature, he may creepe in heere, and throw fowle linnen vpon him, as if it were going to bucking: Or it is whiting time, send him by your two men to *Datchet*-Meade.

M.Ford. He's too big to go in there: what shall I do?

Fal. Let me see't, let me see't, O let me see't:
Ile in, Ile in: Follow your friends counsell, Ile in.

M.Page. What Sir *Iohn Falstaffe*? Are these your Letters, Knight?

Fal. I loue thee, helpe mee away: let me creepe in heere: ile neuer———

M.Page. Helpe to couer your master (Boy:) Call your men (Mist. *Ford.*) You dissembling Knight.

M.Ford. What *Iohn*, *Robert*, *Iohn*; Go, take vp these cloathes heere, quickly: Wher's the Cowle-staffe? Look how you drumble? Carry them to the Landresse in Datchet mead: quickly, come.

Ford. 'Pray you come nere: if I suspect without cause,
Why then make sport at me, then let me be your iest,
I deserue it: How now? Whether beare you this?

Ser. To the Landresse forsooth?

M.Ford. Why, what haue you to doe whether they beare it? You were best meddle with buck-washing.

Ford. Bucke? I would I could wash my selfe of ẏ Bucke:
Bucke, bucke, bucke, I bucke: I warrant you Bucke,
And of the season too; it shall appeare.
Gentlemen, I haue dream'd to night, Ile tell you my dreame: heere, heere, heere bee my keyes, ascend my Chambers, search, seeke, finde out: Ile warrant wee'le vnkennell the Fox. Let me stop this way first: so, now vncape.

Page. Good master *Ford*, be contented:
You wrong your selfe too much.

Ford. True (master *Page*) vp Gentlemen.
You shall see sport anon:

Follow

Follow me Gentlemen.

Euans. This is fery fantasticall humors and iealousies.

Caius. By gar, 'tis no-the fashion of France: It is not iealous in France.

Page. Nay follow him (Gentlemen) see the yssue of his search.

Mist. Page Is there not a double excellency in this?

Mist. Ford. I know not which pleases me better, That my husband is deceiued, or Sir *Iohn*

Mist. Page. What a taking was hee in, when your husband askt who was in the basket?

Mist. Ford. I am halfe affraid he will haue neede of washing: so throwing him into the water, will doe him a benefit.

Mist. Page. Hang him dishonest rascall: I would all of the same straine, were in the same distresse.

Mist. Ford. I thinke my husband hath some speciall suspition of *Falstaffs* being heere: for I neuer saw him so grosse in his iealousie till now

Mist. Page. I will lay a plot to try that, and wee will yet haue more trickes with *Falstaffe*: his dissolute disease will scarse obey this medicine.

Mis. Ford Shall we send that foolishion Carion, Mist. *Quickly* to him, and excuse his throwing into the water, and giue him another hope, to betray him to another punishment?

Mist. Page. We will do it: let him be sent for to morrow eight a clocke to haue amends.

Ford. I cannot finde him: may be the knaue bragg'd of that he could not compasse.

Mis. Page. Heard you that?

Mis. Ford. You vse me well, M. Ford? Do you?

Ford. I, I do so.

M. Ford. Heauen make you better then your thoghts

Ford. Amen.

Mi. Page. You do your selfe mighty wrong (M. Ford)

Ford. I, I: I must beare it.

Eu. If there be any body in the house, & in the chambers, and in the coffers, and in the presses: heauen forgiue my sins at the day of iudgement

Caius. Be gar, nor I too: there is no-bodies

Page Fy, fy, M. *Ford*, are you not asham'd? What spirit, what diuell suggests this imagination? I wold not ha your distemper in this kind, for ẏ welth of *Windsor castle*.

Ford. 'Tis my fault (M. Page) I suffer for it.

Euans. You suffer for a pad conscience: your wife is as honest a o'mans, as I will desires among fiue thousand, and fiue hundred too.

Cai. By gar, I see 'tis an honest woman.

Ford. Well, I promisd you a dinner: come, come, walk in the Parke, I pray you pardon me: I wil hereafter make knowne to you why I haue done this. Come wife, come Mi. *Page*, I pray you pardon me. Pray hartly pardon me.

Page. Let's go in Gentlemen, but (trust me) we'l mock him: I doe inuite you to morrow morning to my house to breakfast: after we'll a Birding together, I haue a fine Hawke for the bush. Shall it be so.

Ford. Any thing.

Eu. If there is one, I shall make two in the Companie

Ca. If there be one, or two, I shall make-a-theturd.

Ford. Pray you go, M. *Page*.

Eua. I pray you now remembrance to morrow on the lowsie knaue, mine Host.

Cai. Dat is good by gar, withall my heart.

Eua. A lowsie knaue, to haue his gibes, and his mockeries. *Exeunt.*

Scœna Quarta.

Enter Fenton, Anne, Page, Shallow, Slender, Quickly, Page, Mist. Page.

Fen: I see I cannot get thy Fathers loue,
Therefore no more turne me to him (sweet Nan.)

Anne. Alas, how then?

Fen. Why thou must be thy selfe.
He doth obiect, I am too great of birth,
And that my state being gall'd with my expence,
I seeke to heale it onely by his wealth.
Besides these, other barres he layes before me,
My Riots past, my wilde Societies,
And tels me 'tis a thing impossible
I should loue thee, but as a property.

An. May be he tels you true

Fen. No, heauen so speed me in my time to come,
Albeit I will confesse, thy Fathers wealth
Was the first motiue that I woo'd thee (*Anne*:)
Yet wooing thee, I found thee of more valew
Then stampes in Gold, or summes in sealed bagges,
And 'tis the very riches of thy selfe,
That now I ayme at.

An Gentle M. *Fenton*,
Yet seeke my Fathers loue, still seeke it sir,
If opportunity and humblest suite
Cannot attaine it, why then harke you hither.

Shal. Breake their talke Mistris *Quickly*,
My Kinsman shall speake for himselfe.

Slen. Ile make a shaft or a bolt on't, slud, tis but venturing.

Shal. Be not dismaid.

Slen. No, she shall not dismay me:
I care not for that, but that I am affeard.

Qui. Hark ye, M. *Slender* would speak a word with you

An. I come to him. This is my Fathers choice:
O what a world of vilde ill-fauour'd faults
Lookes handsome in three hundred pounds a yeere?

Qui. And how do's good Master *Fenton*?
Pray you a word with you.

Shal. Shee's comming; to her Coz:
O boy, thou hadst a father.

Slen. I had a father (*M An*) my vncle can tel you good iests of him: pray you Vncle, tel Mist. *Anne* the iest how my Father stole two Geese out of a Pen, good Vnckle.

Shal. Mistris *Anne*, my Cozen loues you.

Slen. I that I do, as well as I loue any woman in Glocestershire.

Shal. He will maintaine you like a Gentlewoman.

Slen. I that I will, come cut and long-taile, vnder the degree of a Squire.

Shal. He will make you a hundred and fiftie pounds ioynture.

Anne. Good Maister *Shallow* let him woo for himselfe.

Shal. Marrie I thanke you for it: I thanke you for that good comfort: she cals you (Coz) Ile leaue you.

Anne. Now Master *Slender*.

Slen. Now good Mistris *Anne*.

Anne. What is your will?

Slen. My will? Odd's-hart-lings, that's a prettie iest indeede: I ne're made my Will yet (I thanke Heauen:) I am not such a sickely creature, I giue Heauen praise.

E 2 *An.*

Anne. I meane (M. *Slender*) what wold you with me?

Slen. Truely, for mine owne part, I would little or nothing with you; your father and my vncle hath made motions: if it be my lucke, ſo; if not, happy man bee his dole, they can tell you how things go, better then I can: you may aske your father, heere he comes.

Page. Now Mr *Slender*; Loue him daughter *Anne.*
Why how now? What does Mr *Fenter* here?
You wrong me Sir, thus ſtill to haunt my houſe.
I told you Sir, my daughter is diſpoſd of.

Fen. Nay Mr *Page*, be not impatient.

Miſt.Page. Good M. *Fenton*, come not to my child.

Page. She is no match for you.

Fen. Sir, will you heare me?

Page. No, good M. *Fenton.*
Come M. *Shallow*: Come ſonne *Slender*, in;
Knowing my minde, you wrong me (M. *Fenton.*)

Qui. Speake to Miſtris *Page.*

Fen. Good Miſt. *Page*, for that I loue your daughter
In ſuch a righteous faſhion as I do,
Perforce, againſt all checkes, rebukes, and manners,
I muſt aduance the colours of my loue,
And not retire. Let me haue your good will.

An. Good mother, do not marry me to yond foole.

Miſt.Page. I meane it not, I ſeeke you a better huſband.

Qui. That's my maſter, M. Doctor.

An. Alas I had rather be ſet quick i'th earth,
And bowl'd to death with Turnips.

Miſt.Page. Come, trouble not your ſelfe good M.
Fenton, I will not be your friend, nor enemy:
My daughter will I queſtion how ſhe loues you,
And as I finde her, ſo am I affected:
Till then, farewell Sir, ſhe muſt needs go in,
Her father will be angry.

Fen. Farewell gentle Miſtris: farewell *Nan.*

Qui. This is my doing now: Nay, ſaide I, will you caſt away your childe on a Foole, and a Phyſitian: Looke on M. *Fenton*, this is my doing.

Fen. I thanke thee: and I pray thee once to night,
Giue my ſweet *Nan* this Ring: there's for thy paines.

Qui. Now heauen ſend thee good fortune, a kinde heart he hath: a woman would run through fire & water for ſuch a kinde heart. But yet, I would my Maiſter had Miſtris *Anne*, or I would M. *Slender* had her: or (in ſooth) I would M. *Fenton* had her; I will do what I can for them all three, for ſo I haue promiſd, and Ile bee as good as my word, but ſpeciouſly for M. *Fenton*. Well, I muſt of another errand to Sir *Iohn Falſtaffe* from my two Miſtreſſes: what a beaſt am I to ſlacke it. *Exeunt*

Scena Quinta.

Enter Falſtaffe, Bardolfe, Quickly, Ford.

Fal. Bardolfe I ſay.

Bar. Heere Sir.

Fal. Go, fetch me a quart of Sacke, put a toſt in't. Haue I liu'd to be carried in a Basket like a barrow of butchers Offall? and to be throwne in the Thames? Wel, if I be ſeru'd ſuch another tricke, Ile haue my braines 'tane out and butter'd, and giue them to a dogge for a New-yeares gift. The rogues ſlighted me into the riuer with as little remorſe, as they would haue drown'de a blinde bitches Puppies, fifteene i'th litter: and you may know by my ſize, that I haue a kinde of alacrity in ſinking: if the bottome were as deepe as hell, I ſhold down. I had beene drown'd, but that the ſhore was ſheluy and ſhallow: a death that I abhorre: for the water ſwelles a man; and what a thing ſhould I haue beene, when I had beene ſwel'd? I ſhould haue beene a Mountaine of Mummie.

Bar. Here's M. *Quickly* Sir to ſpeake with you.

Fal. Come, let me poure in ſome Sack to the Thames water: for my bellies as cold as if I had ſwallow'd ſnowbals, for pilles to coole the reines. Call her in.

Bar. Come in woman.

Qui. By your leaue: I cry you mercy?
Giue your worſhip good morrow.

Fal. Take away theſe Challices:
Go, brew me a pottle of Sacke finely.

Bard. With Egges, Sir?

Fal. Simple of it ſelfe: Ile no Pullet-Sperſme in my brewage. How now?

Qui. Marry Sir, I come to your worſhip from M. *Ford.*

Fal. *Miſt. Ford?* I haue had Ford enough: I was thrown into the Ford; I haue my belly full of Ford.

Qui. Alas the day, (good-heart) that was not her fault: ſhe do's ſo take on with her men; they miſtooke their erection.

Fal. So did I mine, to build vpon a fooliſh Womans (promiſe.

Qui. Well, ſhe laments Sir for it, that it would yern your heart to ſee it: her husband goes this morning a birding; ſhe deſires you once more to come to her, betweene eight and nine: I muſt carry her word quickely, ſhe'll make you amends I warrant you.

Fal. Well, I will viſit her, tell her ſo; and bidde her thinke what a man is: Let her conſider his frailety, and then iudge of my merit.

Qui. I will tell her.

Fal. Do ſo. Betweene nine and ten ſaiſt thou?

Qui. Eight and nine Sir.

Fal. Well, be gone: I will not miſſe her.

Qui. Peace be with you Sir.

Fal. I meruaile I heare not of Mr *Broome*: he ſent me word to ſtay within: I like his money well. Oh, heere he comes.

Ford. Bleſſe you Sir.

Fal. Now M. *Broome*, you come to know
What hath paſt betweene me, and *Fords* wife.

Ford. That indeed (Sir *Iohn*) is my buſineſſe.

Fal. M. *Broome* I will not lye to you,
I was at her houſe the houre ſhe appointed me.

Ford. And ſped you Sir?

Fal. very ill-fauouredly M. *Broome.*

Ford. How ſo ſir, did ſhe change her determination?

Fal. No (M. *Broome*) but the peaking Curnuto her huſband (M. *Broome*) dwelling in a continual larum of ielouſie, coms me in the inſtant of our encounter, after we had embraſt, kiſt, proteſted, & (as it were) ſpoke the prologue of our Comedy: and at his heeles, a rabble of his companions, thither prouoked and inſtigated by his diſtemper, and (forſooth) to ſerch his houſe for his wiues Loue.

Ford. What? While you were there?

Fal. While I was there.

For. And did he ſearch for you, & could not find you?

Fal. You ſhall heare. As good lucke would haue it, comes in one *Miſt. Page*, giues intelligence of *Fords* approch: and in her inuention, and *Fords* wiues diſtraction, they conuey'd me into a bucke basket.

Ford

Ford. A Buck-basket?

Fal Yes: a Buck-basket: ram'd mee in with foule Shirts and Smockes, Socks, foule Stockings, greaſie Napkins, that (Maſter *Broome*) there was the rankeſt compound of villanous ſmell, that euer offended noſtrill.

Ford. And how long lay you there?

Fal. Nay, you ſhall heare (Maſter *Broome*) what I haue ſufferd, to bring this woman to euill, for your good: Being thus cram'd in the Basket, a couple of *Fords* knaues, his Hindes, were cald forth by their Miſtris, to carry mee in the name of foule Cloathes to *Datchet-lane*: they tooke me on their ſhoulders: met the iealous knaue their Maſter in the doore; who ask'd them once or twice what they had in their Baſket? I quak'd for feare leaſt the Lunatique Knaue would haue ſearch'd it: but Fate (ordaining he ſhould be a Cuckold) held his hand: well, on went hee, for a ſearch, and away went I for foule Cloathes: But marke the ſequell (Maſter *Broome*) I ſuffered the pangs of three ſeuerall deaths: Firſt, an intollerable fright, to be detected with a iealious rotten Bell-weather: Next to be compaſs'd like a good Bilbo in the circumference of a Pecke, hilt to point, heele to head. And then to be ſtopt in like a ſtrong diſtillation with ſtinking Cloathes, that fretted in their owne greaſe: thinke of that, a man of my Kidney; thinke of that, that am as ſubiect to heate as butter; a man of continuall diſſolution, and thaw: it was a miracle to ſcape ſuffocation. And in the height of this Bath (when I was more then halfe ſtew'd in greaſe (like a Dutch-diſh) to be throwne into the Thames, and coold, glowing-hot, in that ſerge like a Horſe-ſhoo; thinke of that; hiſſing hot: thinke of that (Maſter *Broome*.)

Ford. In good ſadneſſe Sir, I am ſorry, that for my ſake you haue ſufferd all this.
My ſuite then is deſperate: You'll vndertake her no more?

Fal. Maſter *Broome*: I will be throwne into *Etna*, as I haue beene into Thames, ere I will leaue her thus; her Husband is this morning gone a Birding: I haue receiued from her another ambaſſie of meeting: 'twixt eight and nine is the houre (Maſter *Broome*.)

Ford. 'Tis paſt eight already Sir.

Fal. Is it? I will then addreſſe mee to my appointment: Come to mee at your conuenient leiſure, and you ſhall know how I ſpeede: and the concluſion ſhall be crowned with your enioying her: adiew: you ſhall haue her (Maſter *Broome*) Maſter *Broome*, you ſhall cuckold *Ford*.

Ford. Hum: ha? Is this a viſion? Is this a dreame? doe I ſleepe? Maſter *Ford* awake, awake Maſter *Ford*: ther's a hole made in your beſt coate (Maſter *Ford*:) this 'tis to be married; this 'tis to haue Lynnen, and Buck-baskets: Well, I will proclaime my ſelfe what I am: I will now take the Leacher: hee is at my houſe: hee cannot ſcape me: 'tis impoſſible hee ſhould: hee cannot creepe into a halfe-penny purſe, nor into a Pepper-Boxe: But leaſt the Diuell that guides him, ſhould aide him, I will ſearch impoſſible places: though what I am, I cannot auoide; yet to be what I would not, ſhall not make me tame: If I haue hornes, to make one mad, let the prouerbe goe with me, Ile be horne-mad. *Exeunt.*

Actus Quartus. Scœna Prima.

Enter Miſtris Page, Quickly, William, Euans.

Miſt. Pag. Is he at M. *Fords* already think'ſt thou?

Qui. Sure he is by this; or will be preſently; but truely he is very couragious mad, about his throwing into the water. Miſtris *Ford* deſires you to come ſodainely.

Miſt. Pag. Ile be with her by and by: Ile but bring my yong-man here to Schoole: looke where his Maſter comes; 'tis a playing day I ſee: how now Sir *Hugh*, no Schoole to day?

Eua. No: Maſter *Slender* is let the Boyes leaue to play.

Qui 'Bleſſing of his heart.

Miſt Pag. Sir *Hugh*, my husband ſaies my ſonne profits nothing in the world at his Booke: I pray you aske him ſome queſtions in his Accidence.

Eu. Come hither *William*; hold vp your head; come.

Miſt. Pag. Come-on Sirha; hold vp your head; anſwere your Maſter, be not afraid.

Eua. William, how many Numbers is in Nownes?

Will. Two.

Qui. Truely, I thought there had bin one Number more, becauſe they ſay od's-Nownes.

Eua. Peace, your tatlings. What is (*Faire*) *William*?

Will. Pulcher.

Qu. Powlcats? there are fairer things then Powlcats, ſure.

Eua. You are a very ſimplicity o'man: I pray you peace. What is (*Lapis*) *William*?

Will. A Stone.

Eua. And what is a Stone (*William*?)

Will. A Peeble.

Eua. No; it is *Lapis*: I pray you remember in your praine.

Will. Lapis.

Eua. That is a good *William*: what is he (*William*) that do's lend Articles.

Will. Articles are borrowed of the Pronoune; and be thus declined. *Singulariter nominatiuo hic hac, hoc.*

Eua. Nominatiuo hig, hag, hog: pray you marke: *genitiuo huius*: Well, what is your *Accuſatiue-caſe*?

Will. Accuſatiuo hinc.

Eua. I pray you haue your remembrance (childe) *Accuſatiuo hing, hang, hog.*

Qu. Hang-hog, is latten for Bacon, I warrant you.

Eua. Leaue your prables (o'man) What is the *Focatiue caſe* (*William*?)

Will. O, Vocatiuo, O.

Eua. Remember *William, Focatiue*, is *caret*.

Qu. And that's a good roote.

Eua. O'man, forbeare.

Miſt. Pag. Peace.

Eua: What is your *Genitiue caſe plurall* (*William*?)

Will. Genitiue caſe?

Eua. I.

Will. Genitiue horum, harum, horum.

Qu. 'Vengeance of Ginyes caſe; fie on her; neuer name her (childe) if ſhe be a whore.

Eua. For ſhame o'man.

Qu. You doe ill to teach the childe ſuch words: hee teaches him to hic, and to hac; which they'll doe faſt enough of themſelues, and to call *horum*; fie vpon you.

E 3 *Eua.* 'Oman

Euans. O'man, art thou Lunatics? Haſt thou no vnderſtandings for thy Caſes, & the numbers of the Genders? Thou art as fooliſh Chriſtian creatures, as I would deſires.

Mi. Page. Pre'thee hold thy peace.

Eu. Shew me now (*William*) ſome declenſions of your Pronounes.

Will. Forſooth, I haue forgot.

Eu. It is *Qui, que, quod*; if you forget your *Quies*, your *Ques*, and your *Quods*, you muſt be preeches: Goe your waies and play, go.

M. Pag. He is a better ſcholler then I thought he was.

Eu. He is a good ſprag-memory: Farewel *Mis. Page.*

Miſ. Page. Adieu good Sir *Hugh*:
Get you home boy, Come we ſtay too long. *Exeunt.*

Scena Secunda.

Enter Falſtoffe, Miſt. Ford, Miſt. Page, Seruants, Ford, Page, Caius, Euans, Shallow.

Fal. Mi. *Ford*, Your ſorrow hath eaten vp my ſufferance; I ſee you are obſequious in your loue, and I profeſſe requitall to a haires bredth, not onely Miſt. *Ford*, in the ſimple office of loue, but in all the accuſtrement, complement, and ceremony of it: But are you ſure of your husband now?

Miſ. Ford. Hee's a birding (ſweet Sir *Iohn.*)

Miſ. Page. What hoa, goſſip *Ford*: what hoa.

Miſ. Ford. Step into th' chamber, Sir *Iohn.*

Miſ. Page. How now (ſweete heart) whoſe at home beſides your ſelfe?

Miſ Ford Why none but mine owne people.

Miſ Page. Indeed?

Miſ. Ford. No certainly: Speake louder.

Miſt. Pag. Truly, I am ſo glad you haue no body here.

Miſt. Ford. Why?

Miſ Page. Why woman, your husband is in his olde lines againe: he ſo takes on yonder with my husband, ſo railes againſt all married mankinde; ſo curſes all *Eues* daughters, of what complexion ſoeuer; and ſo buffettes himſelfe on the for-head: crying peere-out, peere-out, that any madneſſe I euer yet beheld, ſeem'd but tameneſſe, ciuility, and patience to this his diſtemper he is in now: I am glad the fat Knight is not heere.

Miſt. Ford. Why, do's he talke of him?

Miſt. Page. Of none but him, and ſweares he was caried out the laſt time hee ſearch'd for him, in a Basket: Proteſts to my husband he is now heere, & hath drawne him and the reſt of their company from their ſport, to make another experiment of his ſuſpition: But I am glad the Knight is not heere; now he ſhall ſee his owne foolerie.

Miſt. Ford. How neere is he Miſtris *Page*?

Miſt. Pag. Hard by, at ſtreet end; he wil be here anon.

Miſt. Ford. I am vndone, the Knight is heere.

Miſt. Page. Why then you are vtterly ſham'd, & hee's but a dead man. What a woman are you? Away with him, away with him: Better ſhame, then murther.

Miſt. Ford. Which way ſhould he go? How ſhould I beſtow him? Shall I put him into the basket againe?.

Fal. No, Ile come no more i'th Basket;
May I not go out ere he come?

Miſt. Page. Alas: three of Mr. *Fords* brothers watch the doore with Piſtols, that none ſhall iſſue out: otherwiſe you might ſlip away ere hee came: But what make you heere?

Fal. What ſhall I do? Ile creepe vp into the chimney.

Miſt. Ford. There they alwaies vſe to diſcharge their Birding-peeces: creepe into the Kill-hole.

Fal. Where is it?

Miſt. Ford. He will ſeeke there on my word: Neyther Preſſe, Coffer, Cheſt, Trunke, Well, Vault, but he hath an abſtract for the remembrance of ſuch places, and goes to them by his Note: There is no hiding you in the houſe.

Fal. Ile go out then.

Miſt. Ford. If you goe out in your owne ſemblance, you die Sir *Iohn*, vnleſſe you go out diſguis'd.

Miſt. Ford. How might we diſguiſe him?

Miſt. Page. Alas the day I know not, there is no womans gowne bigge enough for him: otherwiſe he might put on a hat, a muffler, and a kerchiefe, and ſo eſcape.

Fal. Good hearts, deuiſe ſomething: any extremitie, rather then a miſchiefe.

Miſt. Ford. My Maids Aunt the fat woman of *Brainford*, has a gowne aboue.

Miſt. Page. On my word it will ſerue him: ſhee's as big as he is: and there's her thrum'd hat, and her muffler too: run vp Sir *Iohn.*

Miſt. Ford. Go, go, ſweet Sir *Iohn*: *Miſtris Page* and I will looke ſome linnen for your head.

Miſt. Page. Quicke, quicke, wee'le come dreſſe you ſtraight: put on the gowne the while.

Miſt. Ford. I would my husband would meete him in this ſhape: he cannot abide the old woman of Brainford; he ſweares ſhe's a witch, forbad her my houſe, and hath threatned to beate her.

Miſt. Page. Heauen guide him to thy husbands cudgell: and the diuell guide his cudgell afterwards.

Miſt Ford. But is my husband comming?

Miſt. Page. I in good ſadneſſe is he, and talkes of the basket too, howſoeuer he hath had intelligence.

Miſt. Ford. Wee'l try that: for Ile appoint my men to carry the basket againe, to meete him at the doore with it, as they did laſt time.

Miſt. Page. Nay, but hee'l be heere preſently: let's go dreſſe him like the witch of *Brainford.*

Miſt. Ford. Ile firſt direct direct my men, what they ſhall doe with the basket: Goe vp, Ile bring linnen for him ſtraight.

Miſt. Page Hang him diſhoneſt Varlet,
We cannot miſuſe enough:
We'll leaue a proofe by that which we will doo,
Wiues may be merry, and yet honeſt too:
We do not acte that often, ieſt, and laugh,
'Tis old, but true, Still Swine eats all the draugh.

Miſt. Ford. Go Sirs, take the basket againe on your ſhoulders: your Maſter is hard at doore: if hee bid you ſet it downe, obey him: quickly, diſpatch.

1 Ser. Come, come, take it vp.

2 Ser. Pray heauen it be not full of Knight againe.

1 Ser. I hope not, I had liefe as beare ſo much lead.

Ford. I, but if it proue true (Mr. *Page*) haue you any way then to vnfoole me againe. Set downe the basket villaine: ſome body call my wife: Youth in a basket: Oh you Panderly Raſcals, there's a knot: a gin, a packe, a conſpiracie againſt me: Now ſhall the diuel be ſham'd. What wife I ſay: Come, come forth: behold what honeſt

neſt cloathes you ſend forth to bleaching.

Page. Why, this paſſes M. *Ford*: you are not to goe looſe any longer, you muſt be pinnion'd.

Euans. Why, this is Lunaticks: this is madde, as a mad dogge.

Shall. Indeed *M. Ford*, thi is not well indeed.

Ford. So ſay I too Sir, come hither Miſtris *Ford*, Miſtris *Ford*, the honeſt woman, the modeſt wife, the vertuous creature, that hath the iealious foole to her husband: I ſuſpect without cauſe (Miſtris) do I?

Miſt. Ford. Heauen be my witneſſe you doe, if you ſuſpect me in any diſhoneſty.

Ford. Well ſaid Brazon-face, hold it out: Come forth ſirrah.

Page. This paſſes.

Miſt.Ford. Are you not aſham'd, let the cloths alone.

Ford. I ſhall finde you anon.

Eua. 'Tis vnreaſonable; will you take vp your wiues cloathes? Come, away.

Ford. Empty the basket I ſay.

M. Ford. Why man, why?

Ford. Maſter *Page*, as I am a man, there was one conuay'd out of my houſe yeſterday in this basket: why may not he be there againe, in my houſe I am ſure he is: my Intelligence is true, my iealouſie is reaſonable, pluck me out all the linnen.

Miſt.Ford. If you find a man there, he ſhall dye a Fleas death.

Page. Heer's no man.

Shal. By my fidelity this is not well Mr. *Ford*: This wrongs you.

Euans. Mr Ford, you muſt pray, and not follow the imaginations of your owne heart: this is iealouſies.

Ford. Well, hee's not heere I ſeeke for.

Page. No, nor no where elſe but in your braine.

Ford. Helpe to ſearch my houſe this one time: if I find not what I ſeeke, ſhew no colour for my extremity: Let me for euer be your Table-ſport: Let them ſay of me, as iealous as *Ford*, that ſearch'd a hollow Wall-nut for his wiues Lemman. Satisfie me once more, once more ſerch with me.

M. Ford. What hoa (Miſtris *Page*,) come you and the old woman downe: my husband will come into the Chamber.

Ford. Old woman? what old womans that?

M.Ford. Why it is my maids Aunt of *Brainford*.

Ford. A witch, a Queane, an olde couzening queane: Haue I not forbid her my houſe. She comes of errands do's ſhe? We are ſimple men, wee doe not know what's brought to paſſe vnder the profeſſion of Fortune-telling. She workes by Charmes, by Spels, by th'Figure, & ſuch dawbry as this is, beyond our Element: wee know nothing. Come downe you Witch, you Hagge you, come downe I ſay.

Miſt.Ford. Nay, good ſweet husband, good Gentlemen, let him ſtrike the old woman.

Miſt.Page. Come mother *Prat*, Come giue me your hand.

Ford. Ile *Prat*-her: Out of my doore, you Witch, you Ragge, you Baggage, you Poulcat, you Runnion, out, out: Ile coniure you, Ile fortune-tell you.

Miſt.Page. Are you not aſham'd?
I thinke you haue kill'd the poore woman.

Miſt.Ford. Nay he will do it, 'tis a goodly credite for you.

Ford. Hang her witch.

Eua. By yea, and no, I thinke the o'man is a witch indeede: I like not when a o'man has a great peard; I ſpie a great peard vnder his muffler.

Ford. Will you follow Gentlemen, I beſeech you follow: ſee but the iſſue of my iealouſie: If I cry out thus vpon no traile, neuer truſt me when I open againe.

Page. Let's obey his humour a little further: Come Gentlemen.

Miſt.Page. Truſt me he beate him moſt pittifully.

Miſt.Ford. Nay by th'Maſſe that he did not: he beate him moſt vnpittifully, me thought.

Miſt.Page. Ile haue the cudgell hallow'd, and hung ore the Altar, it hath done meritorious ſeruice.

Miſt.Ford. What thinke you? May we with the warrant of woman hood, and the witneſſe of a good conſcience, purſue him with any further reuenge?

M.Page. The ſpirit of wantonneſſe is ſure ſcar'd out of him, if the diuell haue him not in fee-ſimple, with fine and recouery, he will neuer (I thinke) in the way of waſte, attempt vs againe.

Miſt.Ford. Shall we tell our husbands how wee haue ſeru'd him?

Miſt.Page. Yes, by all meanes: if it be but to ſcrape the figures out of your husbands braines: if they can find in their hearts, the poore vnuertuous fat Knight ſhall be any further afflicted, wee two will ſtill bee the miniſters.

Miſt.Ford. Ile warrant, they'l haue him publiquely ſham'd, and me thinkes there would be no period to the ieſt, ſhould he not be publikely ſham'd.

Miſt.Page. Come, to the Forge with it, then ſhape it: I would not haue things coole. *Exeunt*

Scena Tertia.

Enter Hoſt and Bardolfe.

Bar. Sir, the Germane deſires to haue three of your horſes: the Duke himſelfe will be to morrow at Court, and they are going to meet him.

Hoſt. What Duke ſhould that be comes ſo ſecretly? I heare not of him in the Court: let mee ſpeake with the Gentlemen, they ſpeake Engliſh?

Bar. I Sir? Ile call him to you.

Hoſt. They ſhall haue my horſes, but Ile make them pay: Ile ſauce them, they haue had my houſes a week at commaund: I haue turn'd away my other gueſts, they muſt come off, Ile ſawce them, come. *Exeunt*

Scena Quarta.

Enter Page, Ford, Miſtris Page, Miſtris Ford, and Euans.

Eua. 'Tis one of the beſt diſcretions of a o'man as euer I did looke vpon.

Page. And did he ſend you both theſe Letters at an inſtant?

Miſt.Page. VVithin a quarter of an heure.

Ford. Pardon me (wife) henceforth do what yͧ wilt:
I rather will ſuſpect the Sunne with gold,
Then thee with wantonnes: Now doth thy honor ſtand
(In

(In him that was of late an Heretike)
As firme as faith.

Page. Tis well, 'tis well, no more:
Be not as extreme in submission, as in offence,
But let our plot go forward: Let our wiues
Yet once againe (to make vs publike sport)
Appoint a meeting with this old fat-fellow,
Where we may take him, and disgrace him for it.

Ford. There is no better way then that they spoke of.

Page. How? to send him word they'll meete him in the Parke at midnight? Fie, fie, he'll neuer come.

Eu. You say he has bin throwne in the Riuers: and has bin greeuously peaten, as an old o'man: me-thinkes there should be terrors in him, that he should not come: Me-thinkes his flesh is punish'd, hee shall haue no desires.

Page. So thinke I too.

M.Ford. Deuise but how you'l vse him whē he comes,
And let vs two deuise to bring him thether.

Mis Page. There is an old tale goes, that *Herne* the
Hunter (sometime a keeper heere in Windsor Forrest)
Doth all the winter time, at still midnight
Walke round about an Oake, with great rag'd-hornes,
And there he blasts the tree, and takes the cattle,
And make milch-kine yeeld blood, and shakes a chaine
In a most hideous and dreadfull manner.
You haue heard of such a Spirit, and well you know
The superstitious idle-headed-Eld
Receiu'd, and did deliuer to our age
This tale of *Herne* the Hunter, for a truth.

Page. Why yet there want not many that do feare
In deepe of night to walke by this Hernes Oake:
But what of this?

Mist.Ford. Marry this is our deuise,
That *Falstaffe* at that Oake shall meete with vs.

Page. Well, let it not be doubted but he'll come,
And in this shape, when you haue brought him thether,
What shall be done with him? What is your plot?

Mist.Pa. That likewise haue we thoght vpon: & thus:
Nan Page (my daughter) and my little sonne,
And three or foure more of their growth, wee'l dresse
Like Vrchins, Ouphes, and Fairies, greene and white,
With rounds of waxen Tapers on their heads,
And rattles in their hands; vpon a sodaine,
As *Falstaffe*, she, and I, are newly met,
Let them from forth a saw-pit rush at once
With some diffused song: Vpon their sight
We two, in great amazednesse will flye:
Then let them all encircle him about,
And Fairy-like to pinch the vncleane Knight;
And aske him why that houre of Fairy Reuell,
In their so sacred pathes, he dares to tread
In shape prophane.

Ford. And till he tell the truth,
Let the supposed Fairies pinch him, sound,
And burne him with their Tapers.

Mist.Page. The truth being knowne,
We'll all present our selues; dis-horne the spirit,
And mocke him home to Windsor.

Ford. The children must
Be practis'd well to this, or they'l neu'r doo't.

Eua. I will teach the children their behauiours: and I will be like a Iacke-an-Apes also, to burne the Knight with my Taber.

Ford. That will be excellent,
Ile go buy them vizards.

Mist.Page. My *Nan* shall be the Queene of all the
Fairies, finely attired in a robe of white.

Page. That silke will I go buy, and in that time
Shall M. *Slender* steale my *Nan* away,
And marry her at *Eaton*: go, send to *Falstaffe* straight.

Ford. Nay, Ile to him againe in name of *Broome*,
Hee'l tell me all his purpose: sure hee'l come.

Mist.Page. Feare not you that: Go get vs properties
And tricking for our Fayries.

Euans. Let vs about it,
It is admirable pleasures, and ferry honest knaueries.

Mis.Page Go *Mist.Ford*,
Send quickly to Sir *Iohn*, to know his minde:
Ile to the Doctor, he hath my good will,
And none but he to marry with *Nan Page*:
That *Slender* (though well landed) is an Ideot:
And he, my husband best of all affects:
The Doctor is well monied, and his friends
Potent at Court: he, none but he shall haue her,
Though twenty thousand worthier come to craue her.

Scena Quinta.

Enter Host, Simple, Falstaffe, Bardolfe, Euans, Caius, Quickly.

Host. What wouldst thou haue? (Boore) what? (thick skin) speake, breathe, discusse: breefe, short, quicke, snap.

Simp. Marry Sir, I come to speake with Sir *Iohn Falstaffe* from M. *Slender*.

Host. There's his Chamber, his House, his Castle, his standing-bed and truckle-bed: 'tis painted about with the story of the Prodigall, fresh and new: go, knock and call: hee'l speake like an Anthropophaginian vnto thee: Knocke I say.

Simp. There's an olde woman, a fat woman gone vp into his chamber: Ile be so bold as stay Sir till she come downe: I come to speake with her indeed.

Host. Ha? A fat woman? The Knight may be robb'd: Ile call. Bully-Knight, Bully Sir *Iohn*: speake from thy Lungs Military: Art thou there? It is thine Host, thine Ephesian cals.

Fal. How now, mine Host?

Host. Here's a Bohemian-Tartar taries the comming downe of thy fat-woman: Let her descend (Bully) let her descend: my Chambers are honourable: Fie, priuacy? Fie.

Fal. There was (mine Host) an old-fat-woman euen now with me, but she's gone.

Simp. Pray you Sir, was't not the Wise-woman of *Brainford*?

Fal. I marry was it (Mussel-shell) what would you with her?

Simp. My Master (Sir) my master *Slender*, sent to her seeing her go thorough the streets, to know (Sir) whether one *Nim* (Sir) that beguil'd him of a chaine, had the chaine, or no.

Fal. I spake with the old woman about it.

Sim. And what sayes she, I pray Sir?

Fal. Marry shee sayes, that the very same man that beguil'd Master *Slender* of his Chaine, cozon'd him of it.

Simp. I would I could haue spoken with the Woman her

her selfe, I had other things to haue spoken with her too, from him.

Fal. What are they? let vs know

Host. I: come: quicke.

Fal. I may not conceale them (Sir.)

Host. Conceale them, or thou di'st.

Sim. Why sir, they were nothing but about Mistris *Anne Page*, to know if it were my Masters fortune to haue her, or no.

Fal. 'Tis, 'tis his fortune.

Sim. What Sir?

Fal. To haue her, or no: goe; say the woman told me so.

Sim. May I be bold to say so Sir?

Fal. I Sir: like who more bold.

Sim. I thanke your worship: I shall make my Master glad with these tydings.

Host. Thou are clearkly: thou art clearkly (Sir *Iohn*) was there a wise woman with thee?

Fal. I that there was (mine *Host*) one that hath taught me more wit, then euer I learn'd before in my life: and I paid nothing for it neither, but was paid for my learning.

Bar. Out alas (Sir) cozonage: meere cozonage.

Host. Where be my horses? speake well of them varletto.

Bar. Run away with the cozoners: for so soone as I came beyond *Eaton*, they threw me off, from behinde one of them, in a slough of myre; and set spurres, and away; like three *Germane*-diuels; three *Doctor Faustasses*.

Host. They are gone but to meete the Duke (villaine) doe not say they be fled: *Germanes* are honest men.

Euan. Where is mine *Host*?

Host. What is the matter Sir?

Euan. Haue a care of your entertainments: there is a friend of mine come to Towne, tels mee there is three Cozen-Iermans, that has cozend all the *Hosts* of *Readins*, of *Maidenhead*; of *Cole-brooke*, of horses and money: I tell you for good will (looke you) you are wise, and full of gibes, and vlouting-stocks: and 'tis not conuenient you should be cozoned. Fare you well.

Cai. Ver'is mine *Host de Iarteere*?

Host. Here (Master *Doctor*) in perplexitie, and doubtfull delemma.

Cai. I cannot tell vat is dat: but it is tell-a-me, dat you make grand preparation for a Duke *de Iamanie*: by my trot: der is no Duke that the Court is know, to come: I tell you for good will: adieu.

Host. Huy and cry, (villaine) goe: assist me Knight, I am vndone: fly, run: huy, and cry (villaine) I am vndone.

Fal. I would all the world might be cozond, for I haue beene cozond and beaten too: if it should come to the eare of the Court, how I haue beene transformed; and how my transformation hath beene washd, and cudgeld, they would melt mee out of my fat drop by drop, and liquor Fishermens-boots with me: I warrant they would whip me with their fine wits, till I were as crest-falne as a dride-peare: I neuer prosper'd, since I forswore my selfe at *Primero*: well, if my winde were but long enough; I would repent: Now? Whence come you?

Qui. From the two parties forsooth.

Fal. The Diuell take one partie, and his Dam the other: and so they shall be both bestowed; I haue suffer'd more for their sakes; more then the villanous inconstancy of mans disposition is able to beare.

Qui. And haue not they suffer'd? Yes, I warrant; speciously one of them; Mistris *Ford* (good heart) is beaten blacke and blew, that you cannot see a white spot about her.

Fal. What tell'st thou mee of blacke, and blew? I was beaten my selfe into all the colours of the Raine-bow: and I was like to be apprehended for the Witch of *Braineford*, but that my admirable dexteritie of wit, my counterfeiting the action of an old woman deliuer'd me, the knaue Constable had set me ith' Stocks, ith' common Stocks, for a Witch.

Qu. Sir: let me speake with you in your Chamber, you shall heare how things goe, and (I warrant) to your content: here is a Letter will say somewhat: (good-hearts) what a-doe here is to bring you together? Sure, one of you do's not serue heauen well, that you are so cross'd.

Fal. Come vp into my Chamber. *Exeunt.*

Scena Sexta.

Enter Fenton, Host.

Host. Master *Fenton*, talke not to mee, my minde is heauy: I will giue ouer all.

Fen. Yet heare me speake: assist me in my purpose,
And (as I am a gentleman) ile giue thee
A hundred pound in gold, more then your losse.

Host. I will heare you (Master *Fenton*) and I will (at the least) keepe your counsell.

Fen. From time to time, I haue acquainted you
With the deare loue I beare to faire *Anne Page*,
Who, mutually, hath answer'd my affection,
(So farre forth, as her selfe might be her chooser)
Euen to my wish; I haue a letter from her
Of such contents, as you will wonder at;
The mirth whereof, so larded with my matter,
That neither (singly) can be manifested
Without the shew of both: fat *Falstaffe*
Hath a great Scene; the image of the iest
Ile show you here at large (harke good mine *Host*:)
To night at *Hernes-Oke*, iust 'twixt twelue and one,
Must my sweet *Nan* present the *Faerie-Queene*;
The purpose why, is here: in which disguise
VVhile other Iests are something ranke on foote,
Her father hath commanded her to slip
Away with *Slender*, and with him, at *Eaton*
Immediately to Marry: She hath consented: Now Sir,
Her Mother, (euen strong against that match
And firme for Doctor *Caius*) hath appointed
That he shall likewise shuffle her away,
While other sports are tasking of their mindes,
And at the *Deanry*, where a *Priest* attends
Strait marry her: to this her Mothers plot
She seemingly obedient) likewise hath
Made promise to the *Doctor*: Now, thus it rests,
Her Father meanes she shall be all in white;
And in that habit, when *Slender* sees his time
To take her by the hand, and bid her goe,
She shall goe with him: her Mother hath intended
(The better to deuote her to the *Doctor*;
For they must all be mask'd, and vizarded)

That

That quaint in greene, ſhe ſhall be looſe en-roab'd,
With Ribonds-pendant, flaring 'bout her head;
And when the Doctor ſpies his vantage ripe,
To pinch her by the hand, and on that token,
The maid hath giuen conſent to go with him.

Hoſt. Which meanes ſhe to deceiue? Father, or Mother.

Fen. Both (my good Hoſt) to go along with me:
And heere it reſts, that you'l procure the Vicar
To ſtay for me at Church, 'twixt twelue, and one,
And in the lawfull name of marrying,
To giue our hearts vnited ceremony.

Hoſt. Well, husband your deuice; Ile to the Vicar,
Bring you the Maid, you ſhall not lacke a Prieſt.

Fen. So ſhall I euermore be bound to thee;
Beſides, Ile make a preſent recompence. *Exeunt*

Actus Quintus. Scœna Prima.

Enter Falſtoffe, Quickly, and Ford.

Fal. Pre'thee no more pratling: go, Ile hold, this is the third time: I hope good lucke lies in odde numbers: Away, go, they ſay there is Diuinity in odde Numbers, either in natiuity, chance, or death: away.

Qui. Ile prouide you a chaine, and Ile do what I can to get you a paire of hornes.

Fall. Away I ſay, time weares, hold vp your head & mince. How now M. *Broome*? Maſter *Broome*, the matter will be knowne to night, or neuer. Bee you in the Parke about midnight, at Hernes-Oake, and you ſhall ſee wonders.

Ford. Went you not to her yeſterday (Sir) as you told me you had appointed?

Fal. I went to her (Maſter *Broome*) as you ſee, like a poore-old-man, but I came from her (Maſter *Broome*) like a poore-old-woman; that ſame knaue (*Ford* hir husband) hath the fineſt mad diuell of iealouſie in him (Maſter *Broome*) that euer gouern'd Frenſie. I will tell you, he beate me greeuouſly, in the ſhape of a woman: (for in the ſhape of Man (Maſter *Broome*) I feare not Goliah with a Weauers beame, becauſe I know alſo, life is a Shuttle) I am in haſt, go along with mee, Ile tell you all (Maſter *Broome*:) ſince I pluckt Geeſe, plaide Trewant, and whipt Top, I knew not what 'twas to be beaten, till lately. Follow mee, Ile tell you ſtrange things of this knaue *Ford*, on whom to night I will be reuenged, and I will deliuer his wife into your hand. Follow, ſtraunge things in hand (M. *Broome*) follow. *Exeunt.*

Scena Secunda.

Enter Page, Shallow, Slender.

Page. Come, come: wee'll couch i'th Caſtle-ditch, till we ſee the light of our Fairies. Remember ſon *Slender*, my

Slen. I forſooth, I haue ſpoke with her, & we haue a nay-word, how to know one another. I come to her in white, and cry Mum; ſhe cries Budget, and by that we know one another.

Shal. That's good too: But what needes either your Mum, or her Budget? The white will decipher her well enough. It hath ſtrooke ten a'clocke.

Page. The night is darke, Light and Spirits will become it wel: Heauen proſper our ſport. No man means euill but the deuill, and we ſhal know him by his hornes. Lets away: follow me. *Exeunt.*

Scena Tertia.

Enter Miſt. Page, Miſt. Ford, Caius.

Miſt. Page. Mr Doctor, my daughter is in green, when you ſee your time, take her by the hand, away with her to the Deanerie, and diſpatch'it quickly: go before into the Parke: we two muſt go together.

Cai. I know vat I haue to do, adieu.

Miſt. Page. Fare you well (Sir.) my husband will not reioyce ſo much at the abuſe of *Falſtaffe*, as he will chafe at the Doctors marrying my daughter: But 'tis no matter; better a little chiding, then a great deale of heart-breake.

Miſt. Ford. Where is *Nan* now? and her troop of Fairies? and the Welch-deuill Herne?

Miſt. Page. They are all couch'd in a pit hard by Hernes Oake, with obſcur'd Lights; which at the very inſtant of *Falſtaffes* and our meeting, they will at once diſplay to the night.

Miſt. Ford. That cannot chooſe but amaze him.

Miſt. Page. If he be not amaz'd he will be mock'd: If he be amaz'd, he will euery way be mock'd.

Miſt. Ford. Wee'll betray him finely.

Miſt. Page. Againſt ſuch Lewdſters, and their lechery,
Thoſe that betray them, do no treachery.

Miſt. Ford. The houre drawes-on: to the Oake, to the Oake. *Exeunt,*

Scena Quarta.

Enter Euans and Fairies.

Euans. Trib, trib Fairies: Come, and remember your parts: be pold (I pray you) follow me into the pit, and when I giue the watch-'ords, do as I pid you: Come, come, trib, trib. *Exeunt*

Scena Quinta.

Enter Falſtaffe, Miſtris Page, Miſtris Ford, Euans, Anne Page, Fairies, Page, Ford, Quickly, Slender, Fenton, Caius, Piſtoll.

Fal. The Windſor-bell hath ſtroke twelue: the Minute drawes-on: Now the hot-bloodied-Gods aſſiſt me: Remember Ioue, thou was't a Bull for thy *Europa*, Loue ſet on thy hornes. O powerfull Loue, that in ſome reſpects makes a Beaſt a Man: in ſom other, a Man a beaſt. You were alſo (Iupiter) a Swan, for the loue of *Leda*: O omnipotent

omnipotent Loue, how nere the God drew to the complexion of a Goose: a fault done first in the forme of a beast, (O Ioue, a beastly fault:) and then another fault in the semblance of a Fowle, thinke on't (Ioue) a fowle-fault. When Gods haue hot backes, what shall poore men do? For me, I am heere a Windsor Stagge, and the fattest (I thinke) i'th Forrest. Send me a coole rut-time (Ioue) or who can blame me to pisse my Tallow? Who comes heere? my Doe?

M.Ford. Sir *Iohn?* Art thou there (my Deere?)
My male-Deere?

Fal. My Doe, with the blacke Scut? Let the skie raine Potatoes: let it thunder, to the tune of Greene-sleeues, haile-kissing Comfits, and snow Eringoes: Let there come a tempest of prouocation, I will shelter mee heere.

M. Ford. Mistris *Page* is come with me (sweet hart.)

Fal. Diuide me like a brib'd-Bucke, each a Haunch: I will keepe my sides to my selfe, my shoulders for the fellow of this walke; and my hornes I bequeath your husbands: Am I a Woodman, ha? Speake I like *Herne* the Hunter? Why, now is Cupid a child of conscience, he makes restitution. As I am a true spirit, welcome.

M.Page. Alas, what noise?

M.Ford. Heauen forgiue our sinnes.

Fal. What should this be?

M.Ford.M.Page. Away, away.

Fal. I thinke the diuell wil not haue me damn'd,
Least the oyle that's in me should set hell on fire;
He would neuer else crosse me thus.

Enter Fairies.

Qui. Fairies blacke, gray, greene, and white,
You Moone-shine reuellers, and shades of night.
You Orphan heires of fixed destiny,
Attend your office, and your quality.
Crier Hob-goblyn, make the Fairy Oyes.

Pist. Elues, list your names: Silence you aiery toyes
Cricket, to Windsor-chimnies shalt thou leape;
Where fires thou find'st vnrak'd, and hearths vnswept,
There pinch the Maids as blew as Bill-berry,
Our radiant Queene, hates Sluts, and Sluttery.

Fal. They are Fairies, he that speaks to them shall die,
Ile winke, and couch: No man their workes must eie.

Eu. Wher's *Bede*? Go you, and where you find a maid
That ere she sleepe has thrice her prayers said,
Raise vp the Organs of her fantasie,
Sleepe she as sound as carelesse infancie,
But those as sleepe, and thinke not on their sins,
Pinch them armes, legs, backes, shoulders, sides, & shins.

Qu. About, about:
Search Windsor Castle (Elues) within, and out.
Strew good lucke (Ouphes) on euery sacred roome,
That it may stand till the perpetuall doome,
In state as wholsome, as in state 'tis fit,
Worthy the Owner, and the Owner it.
The seuerall Chaires of Order, looke you scowre
With iuyce of Balme; and euery precious flowre,
Each faire Instalment, Coate, and seu'rall Crest,
With loyall Blazon, euermore be blest.
And Nightly-meadow-Fairies, looke you sing
Like to the *Garters*-Compasse, in a ring,
Th'expressure that it beares: Greene let it be,
Mote fertile-fresh then all the Field to see:
And, *Hony Soit Qui Mal-y-Pence*, write
In Emrold-tuffes, Flowres purple, blew, and white,
Like Saphire-pearle, and rich embroiderie,
Buckled below faire Knight-hoods bending knee.
Fairies vse Flowres for their characterie.
Away, disperse: But till 'tis one a clocke,
Our Dance of Custome, round about the Oke
Of *Herne* the Hunter, let vs not forget.

Euan. Pray you lock hand in hand: your selues in order (set:
And twenty glow-wormes shall our Lanthornes bee
To guide our Measure round about the Tree.
But stay, I smell a man of middle earth.

Fal. Heauens defend me from that Welsh Fairy,
Least he transforme me to a peece of Cheese.

Pist. Vilde worme, thou wast ore-look'd euen in thy birth.

Qu. With Triall-fire touch me his finger end:
If he be chaste, the flame will backe descend
And turne him to no paine: but if he start,
It is the flesh of a corrupted hart.

Pist. A triall, come.

Eua. Come: will this wood take fire?

Fal. Oh, oh, oh.

Qui. Corrupt, corrupt, and tainted in desire.
About him (Fairies) sing a scornfull rime,
And as you trip, still pinch him to your time.

The Song.

Fie on sinnefull phantasie: Fie on Lust, and Luxurie:
Lust is but a bloudy fire, kindled with vnchaste desire,
Fed in heart whose flames aspire,
As thoughts do blow them higher and higher.
Pinch him (Fairies) mutually: Pinch him for his villanie.
Pinch him, and burne him, and turne him about,
Till Candles, & Star-light, & Moone-shine be out.

Page. Nay do not flye, I thinke we haue watcht you now: VVill none but *Herne* the Hunter serue your turne?

M. Page. I pray you come, hold vp the iest no higher.
Now (good Sir *Iohn*) how like you *Windsor* wiues?
See you these husband? Do not these faire yoakes
Become the Forrest better then the Towne?

Ford. Now Sir, whose a Cuckold now?
Mr *Broome*, *Falstaffes* a Knaue, a Cuckoldly knaue,
Heere are his hornes Master *Broome*:
And Master *Broome*, he hath enioyed nothing of *Fords*, but his Buck-basket, his cudgell, and twenty pounds of money, which must be paid to Mr *Broome*, his horses are arrested for it, Mr *Broome*.

M.Ford. Sir *Iohn*, we haue had ill lucke: wee could neuer meete: I will neuer take you for my Loue againe, but I will alwayes count you my Deere.

Fal. I do begin to perceiue that I am made an Asse.

Ford. I, and an Oxe too: both the proofes are extant.

Fal. And these are not Fairies:
I was three or foure times in the thought they were not Fairies, and yet the guiltinesse of my minde, the sodaine surprize of my powers, droue the grossenesse of the foppery into a receiu'd beleefe, in despight of the teeth of all rime and reason, that they were Fairies. See now how wit may be made a Iacke-a-Lent, when 'tis vpon ill imployment.

Euans. Sir *Iohn Falstaffe*, serue Got, and leaue your desires, and Fairies will not pinse you.

Ford. VVell said Fairy *Hugh*.

Euans. And leaue you your iealouzies too, I pray you.

Ford.

Ford. I will neuer mistrust my wife againe, till thou art able to woo her in good English.

Fal. Haue I laid my braine in the Sun, and dri'de it, that it wants matter to preuent so grosse ore-reaching as this? Am I ridden with a Welch Goate too? Shal I haue a Coxcombe of Frize? Tis time I were choak'd with a peece of toasted Cheese.

Eu. Seese is not good to giue putter; your belly is al putter.

Fal. Seese, and Putter? Haue I liu'd to stand at the taunt of one that makes Fritters of English? This is enough to be the decay of lust and late-walking through the Realme.

Mist.Page. Why Sir *Iohn*, do you thinke though wee would haue thrust vertue out of our hearts by the head and shoulders, and haue giuen our selues without scruple to hell, that euer the deuill could haue made you our delight?

Ford. What, a hodge-pudding? A bag of flax?

Mist.Page. A puffe man?

Page. Old, cold, wither'd, and of intollerable entrailes?

Ford. And one that is as slanderous as Sathan?

Page. And as poore as Iob?

Ford. And as wicked as his wife?

Euan. And giuen to Fornications, and to Tauernes, and Sacke, and Wine, and Metheglins, and to drinkings and swearings, and starings? Pribles and prables?

Fal. Well, I am your Theame: you haue the start of me, I am deiected: I am not able to answer the Welch Flannell, Ignorance it selfe is a plummet ore me, vse me as you will.

Ford. Marry Sir, wee'l bring you to Windsor to one Mr *Broome*, that you haue cozon'd of money, to whom you should haue bin a Pander: ouer and aboue that you haue suffer'd, I thinke, to repay that money will be a biting affliction.

Page. Yet be cheerefull Knight: thou shalt eat a posset to night at my house, wher I will desire thee to laugh at my wife, that now laughes at thee: Tell her Mr *Slender* hath married her daughter.

Mist.Page. Doctors doubt that;
If *Anne Page* be my daughter, she is (by this) Doctour *Caius* wife.

Slen. Whoa hoe, hoe, Father *Page*.

Page. Sonne? How now? How now Sonne,
Haue you dispatch'd?

Slen. Dispatch'd? Ile make the best in Glostershire know on't: would I were hang'd la, else.

Page. Of what sonne?

Slen. I came yonder at *Eaton* to marry Mistris *Anne Page*, and she's a great lubberly boy. If it had not bene i'th Church, I would haue swing'd him, or hee should haue swing'd me. If I did not thinke it had beene *Anne Page*, would I might neuer stirre, and 'tis a Post-masters Boy.

Page. Vpon my life then, you tooke the wrong.

Slen. What neede you tell me that? I think so, when I tooke a Boy for a Girle: If I had bene married to him, (for all he was in womans apparrell) I would not haue had him.

Page. Why this is your owne folly,
Did not I tell you how you should know my daughter,
By her garments?

Slen. I went to her in greene, and cried Mum, and she cride budget, as *Anne* and I had appointed, and yet it was not *Anne*, but a Post-masters boy.

Mist.Page. Good *George* be not angry, I knew of your purpose: turn'd my daughter into white, and indeede she is now with the Doctor at the Deanrie, and there married.

Cai. Ver is Mistris *Page*: by gar I am cozoned, I ha married oon Garsoon, a boy; oon pesant, by gar. A boy, it is not *An Page*, by gar, I am cozened.

M.Page. VVhy? did you take her in white?

Cai. I bee gar, and 'tis a boy: be gar, Ile raise all Windsor.

Ford. This is strange: Who hath got the right *Anne*?

Page. My heart misgiues me, here comes Mr *Fenton*.
How now Mr *Fenton*?

Anne Pardon good father, good my mother pardon

Page. Now Mistris:
How chance you went not with Mr *Slender*?

M.Page. Why went you not with Mr Doctor, maid?

Fen. You do amaze her: heare the truth of it.
You would haue married her most shamefully,
Where there was no proportion held in loue:
The truth is, she and I (long since contracted)
Are now so sure that nothing can dissolue vs:
Th'offence is holy, that she hath committed,
And this deceit looses the name of craft,
Of disobedience, or vnduteous title.
Since therein she doth euitate and shun
A thousand irreligious cursed houres
Which forced marriage would haue brought vpon her.

Ford. Stand not amaz'd, here is no remedie:
In Loue, the heauens themselues do guide the state,
Money buyes Lands, and wiues are sold by fate.

Fal. I am glad, though you haue tane a special stand to strike at me, that your Arrow hath glanc'd.

Page. Well, what remedy? *Fenton*, heauen giue thee ioy, what cannot be eschew'd, must be embrac'd.

Fal. When night-dogges run, all sorts of Deere are chac'd.

Mist.Page. Well, I will muse no further: Mr *Fenton*,
Heauen giue you many, many merry dayes:
Good husband, let vs euery one go home,
And laugh this sport ore by a Countrie fire.
Sir *Iohn* and all.

Ford. Let it be so (Sir *Iohn*:)
To Master *Broome*, you yet shall hold your word,
For he, to night, shall lye with Mistris *Ford*: *Exeunt*

FINIS.

MEASVRE, For Measure.

Actus primus, Scena prima.

Enter Duke, Escalus, Lords.

Duke.
ESCALUS.
Esc. My Lord. (fold,
Duk. Of Gouernment, the properties to vn-
Would seeme in me t'affect speech & discourse,
Since I am put to know, that your owne Science
Exceedes (in that) the lists of all aduice
My strength can giue you: Then no more remaines
But that, to your sufficiency, as your worth is able,
And let them worke: The nature of our People,
Our *Cities Institutions*, and the Termes
For Common Iustice, y'are as pregnant in
As Art, and practise, hath inriched any
That we remember: There is our Commission,
From which, we would not haue you warpe; call hither,
I say, bid come before vs *Angelo*:
What figure of vs thinke you, he will beare.
For you must know, we haue with speciall soule
Elected him our absence to supply;
Lent him our terror, drest him with our loue,
And giuen his Deputation all the Organs
Of our owne powre: What thinke you of it?
Esc. If any in *Vienna* be of worth
To vndergoe such ample grace, and honour,
It is Lord *Angelo*.

Enter Angelo.

Duk. Looke where he comes.
Ang. Alwayes obedient to your Graces will,
I come to know your pleasure.
Duke. Angelo:
There is a kinde of Character in thy life,
That to th'obseruer, doth thy history
Fully vnfold: Thy selfe, and thy belongings
Are not thine owne so proper, as to waste
Thy selfe vpon thy vertues; they on thee:
Heauen doth with vs, as we, with Torches doe,
Not light them for themselues: For if our vertues
Did not goe forth of vs, 'twere all alike
As if we had them not: Spirits are not finely touch'd
But to fine issues: nor nature neuer lends
The smallest scruple of her excellence,
But like a thrifty goddesse, she determines
Her selfe the glory of a creditour,
Both thanks, and vse; but I do bend my speech
To one that can my part in him aduertise;
Hold therefore *Angelo*:
In our remoue, be thou at full, our selfe:
Mortallitie and Mercie in *Vienna*
Liue in thy tongue, and heart: Old *Escalus*
Though first in question, is thy secondary.
Take thy Commission.
Ang. Now good my Lord
Let there be some more test, made of my mettle,
Before so noble, and so great a figure
Be stamp't vpon it.
Duk. No more euasion:
We haue with a leauen'd, and prepared choice
Proceeded to you; therefore take your honors:
Our haste from hence is of so quicke condition,
That it prefers it selfe, and leaues vnquestion'd
Matters of needfull value: We shall write to you
As time, and our concernings shall importune,
How it goes with vs, and doe looke to know
What doth befall you here. So fare you well:
To th' hopefull execution doe I leaue you,
Of your Commissions.
Ang. Yet giue leaue (my Lord,)
That we may bring you something on the way.
Duk. My haste may not admit it,
Nor neede you (on mine honor) haue to doe
With any scruple: your scope is as mine owne,
So to inforce, or qualifie the Lawes
As to your soule seemes good: Giue me your hand,
Ile priuily away: I loue the people,
But doe not like to stage me to their eyes:
Though it doe well, I doe not rellish well
Their lowd applause, and Aues vehement:
Nor doe I thinke the man of safe discretion
That do's affect it. Once more fare you well.
Ang. The heauens giue safety to your purposes.
Esc. Lead forth, and bring you backe in happi-
nesse. *Exit.*
Duk. I thanke you, fare you well.
Esc. I shall desire you, Sir, to giue me leaue
To haue free speech with you; and it concernes me
To looke into the bottome of my place:
A powre I haue, but of what strength and nature,
I am not yet instructed.
Ang. 'Tis so with me: Let vs with-draw together,
And we may soone our satisfaction haue
Touching that point.
Esc. Ile wait vpon your honor. *Exeunt.*

F *Scæna*

Scena Secunda.

Enter Lucio, and two other Gentlemen.

Luc. If the *Duke*, with the other Dukes, come not to composition with the King of *Hungary*, why then all the Dukes fall vpon the King.

1. Gent. Heauen grant vs its peace, but not the King of *Hungaries*.

2. Gent. Amen.

Luc. Thou conclud'st like the Sanctimonious Pirat, that went to sea with the ten Commandements, but scrap'd one out of the Table.

2. Gent. Thou shalt not Steale?

Luc. I, that he raz'd.

1. Gent. Why? 'twas a commandement, to command the Captaine and all the rest from their functions: they put forth to steale: There's not a Souldier of vs all, that in the thanks-giuing before meate, do rallish the petition well, that praies for peace.

2. Gent. I neuer heard any Souldier dislike it.

Luc. I beleeue thee: for I thinke thou neuer was't where Grace was said.

2. Gent. No? a dozen times at least.

1. Gent. What? In meeter?

Luc. In any proportion. or in any language.

1. Gent. I thinke, or in any Religion.

Luc. I, why not? Grace, is Grace, despight of all controuersie: as for example; Thou thy selfe art a wicked villaine, despight of all Grace.

1. Gent. Well: there went but a paire of sheeres betweene vs.

Luc. I grant: as there may betweene the Lists, and the Veluet. Thou art the List.

1. Gent. And thou the Veluet; thou art good veluet; thou'rt a three pild-peece I warrant thee: I had as liefe be a Lyst of an English Kersey, as be pil'd, as thou art pil'd, for a French Veluet. Do I speake feelingly now?

Luc. I thinke thou do'st: and indeed with most painfull feeling of thy speech: I will, out of thine owne confession, learne to begin thy health; but, whilst I liue forget to drinke after thee.

1. Gen. I think I haue done my selfe wrong, haue I not?

2. Gent. Yes, that thou hast; whether thou art tainted, or free. *Enter Bawde.*

Luc. Behold, behold, where Madam *Mitigation* comes.
I haue purchas'd as many diseases vnder her Roofe,
As come to

2. Gent. To what, I pray?

Luc. Iudge.

2. Gent. To three thousand Dollours a yeare.

1. Gent. I, and more.

Luc. A French crowne more.

1. Gent. Thou art alwayes figuring diseases in me; but thou art full of error, I am sound.

Luc. Nay, not (as one would say) healthy: but so sound, as things that are hollow; thy bones are hollow; Impiety has made a feast of thee.

1. Gent. How now, which of your hips has the most profound Ciatica?

Bawd. Well, well: there's one yonder arrested, and carried to prison, was worth fiue thousand of you all.

2. Gent. Who's that I pray'thee?

Bawd. Marry Sir, that's *Claudio*, Signior *Claudio*.

1. Gent. *Claudio* to prison? 'tis not so.

Bawd. Nay, but I know 'tis so: I saw him arrested: saw him carried away: and which is more, within these three daies his head to be chop'd off.

Luc. But, after all this fooling, I would not haue it so: Art thou sure of this?

Bawd. I am too sure of it: and it is for getting Madam *Iulietta* with childe.

Luc. Beleeue me this may be: he promis'd to meete me two howres since, and he was euer precise in promise keeping.

2. Gent. Besides you know, it drawes somthing neere to the speech we had to such a purpose.

1. Gent. But most of all agreeing with the proclamatiõ.

Luc. Away: let's goe learne the truth of it. *Exit.*

Bawd. Thus, what with the war; what with the sweat, what with the gallowes, and what with pouerty, I am Custom-shrunke. How now? what's the newes with you. *Enter Clowne.*

Clo. Yonder man is carried to prison.

Baw. Well: what has he done?

Clo. A Woman.

Baw. But what's his offence?

Clo. Groping for Trowts, in a peculiar Riuer.

Baw. What? is there a maid with child by him?

Clo. No: but there's a woman with maid by him: you haue not heard of the proclamation, haue you?

Baw. What proclamation, man?

Clow. All howses in the Suburbs of *Vienna* must bee pluck'd downe.

Bawd. And what shall become of those in the Citie?

Clow. They shall stand for seed: they had gon down to, but that a wise Burger put in for them.

Bawd. But shall all our houses of resort in the Suburbs be puld downe?

Clow. To the ground, Mistris.

Bawd. Why heere's a change indeed in the Commonwealth: what shall become of me?

Clow. Come; feare not you: good Counsellors lacke no Clients: though you change your place, you neede not change your Trade: Ile bee your Tapster still; courage, there will bee pitty taken on you; you that haue worne your eyes almost out in the seruice, you will bee considered.

Bawd. What's to doe heere, *Thomas* Tapster? let's withdraw?

Clo. Here comes Signior *Claudio*, led by the Prouost to prison: and there's Madam *Iuliet*. *Exeunt.*

Scena Tertia.

Enter Prouost, Claudio, Iuliet, Officers, Lucio, & 2. Gent.

Cla. Fellow, why do'st thou show me thus to th'world?
Beare me to prison, where I am committed.

Pro. I do it not in euill disposition,
But from Lord *Angelo* by speciall charge.

Clau. Thus can the demy-god (Authority)
Make vs pay downe, for our offence, by waight
The words of heauen; on whom it will, it will,
On whom it will not (soe) yet still 'tis iust.

Luc. Why how now *Claudio*? whence comes this restraint.

Cla. From too much liberty, (my *Lucio*) Liberty
As surfet is the father of much fast,
So euery Scope by the immoderate vse
Turnes to restraint: Our Natures doe pursue

Like

Like Rats that rauyn downe their proper Bane,
A thirsty euill, and when we drinke, we die.

Luc. If I could speake so wisely vnder an arrest, I would send for certaine of my Creditors: and yet, to say the truth, I had as lief haue the foppery of freedome, as the mortality of imprisonment: what's thy offence, *Claudio*?

Cla. What (but to speake of) would offend againe.

Luc. What, is't murder?

Cla. No.

Luc. Lecherie?

Cla. Call it so.

Pro. Away, Sir, you must goe.

Cla. One word, good friend
Lucio, a word with you.

Luc. A hundred:
If they'll doe you any good: Is *Lechery* so look'd after?

Cla. Thus stands it with me: vpon a true contract
I got possession of *Iuliet*as bed,
You know the Lady, she is fast my wife,
Saue that we doe the denunciation lacke
Of outward Order. This we came not to,
Onely for propogation of a Dowre
Remaining in the Coffer of her friends,
From whom we thought it meet to hide our Loue
Till Time had made them for vs. But it chances
The stealth of our most mutuall entertainment
With Character too grosse, is writ on *Iuliet*.

Luc. With childe, perhaps?

Cla. Vnhappely, euen so.
And the new Deputie, now for the Duke,
Whether it be the fault and glimpse of newnes
Or whether that the body publique, be
A horse whereon the Gouernor doth ride,
Who newly in the Seate, that it may know
He can command; lets it strait feele the spur:
Whether the Tirranny be in his place,
Or in his Eminence that fills it vp
I stagger in: But this new Gouernor
Awakes me all the inrolled penalties
Which haue (like vn-scowr'd Armor) hung by th'wall
So long, that nineteene Zodiacks haue gone round,
And none of them beene worne; and for a name
Now puts the drowsie and neglected Act
Freshly on me: 'tis surely for a name.

Luc. I warrant it is: And thy head stands so tickle on thy shoulders, that a milke-maid, if she be in loue, may sigh it off: Send after the Duke, and appeale to him.

Cla. I haue done so, but hee's not to be found.
I pre'mee (*Lucio*) doe me this kinde seruice:
This day, my sister should the Cloyster enter,
And there receiue her approbation.
Acquaint her with the danger of my state,
Implore her, in my voice, that she make friends
To the strict deputie: bid her selfe assay him,
I haue great hope in that: for in her youth
There is a prone and speechlesse dialect,
Such as moue men: beside, she hath prosperous Art
When she will play with reason, and discourse,
And well she can perswade.

Luc. I pray shee may; aswell for the encouragement of the like, which else would stand vnder greeuous imposition: as for the enioying of thy life, who I would be sorry should bee thus foolishly lost, at a game of ticke-tacke: Ile to her.

Cla. I thanke you good friend *Lucio*.

Luc. Within two houres.

Cla. Come Officer, away. *Exeunt.*

Scena Quarta.

Enter Duke and Frier Thomas.

Duk. No: holy Father, throw away that thought,
Beleeue not that the dribling dart of Loue
Can pierce a compleat bosome: why, I desire thee
To giue me secret harbour, hath a purpose
More graue, and wrinkled, then the aimes, and ends
Of burning youth.

Fri. May your Grace speake of it?

Duk. My holy Sir, none better knowes then you
How I haue euer lou'd the life remoued
And held in idle price, to haunt assemblies
Where youth, and cost, witlesse brauery keepes.
I haue deliuerd to Lord *Angelo*
(A man of stricture and firme abstinence)
My absolute power, and place here in *Vienna*,
And he supposes me trauaild to *Poland*,
(For so I haue strewd it in the common eare)
And so it is receiu'd: Now (pious Sir)
You will demand of me, why I do this.

Fri. Gladly, my Lord.

Duk. We haue strict Statutes, and most biting Laws,
(The needfull bits and curbes to headstrong weedes,)
Which for this foureteene yeares, we haue let slip
Euen like an ore-growne Lyon in a Caue
That goes not out to prey: Now, as fond Fathers,
Hauing bound vp the threatning twigs of birch,
Onely to sticke it in their childrens sight
For terror, not to vse: in time the rod
More mock'd, then fear'd: so our Decrees,
Dead to infliction, to themselues are dead,
And libertie, plucks Iustice by the nose;
The Baby beates the Nurse, and quite athwart
Goes all decorum.

Fri. It rested in your Grace
To vnloose this tyde-vp Iustice, when you pleas'd:
And it in you more dreadfull would haue seem'd
Then in Lord *Angelo*.

Duk. I doe feare: too dreadfull:
Sith 'twas my fault, to giue the people scope,
'T would be my tirrany to strike and gall them,
For what I bid them doe: For, we bid this be done
When euill deedes haue their permissiue passe,
And not the punishment: therefore indeede (my father)
I haue on *Angelo* impos'd the office,
Who may in th'ambush of my name, strike home,
And yet, my nature neuer in the fight
To do in slander: And to behold his sway
I will, as 'twere a brother of your Order,
Visit both Prince, and People: Therefore I pre'thee
Supply me with the habit, and instruct me
How I may formally in person beare
Like a true *Frier*: Moe reasons for this action
At our more leysure, shall I render you;
Onely, this one: Lord *Angelo* is precise,
Stands at a guard with Enuie: scarce confesses
That his blood flowes: or that his appetite
Is more to bread then stone: hence shall we see
If power change purpose: what our Seemers be. *Exit.*

Scena Quinta.

Enter Isabell and Francisca a Nun.

Isa. And haue you *Nuns* no farther priuiledges?
Nun. Are not these large enough?
Isa. Yes truely; I speake not as desiring more,
But rather wishing a more strict restraint
Vpon the Sisterstood, the Votarists of Saint *Clare.*

Lucio within.

Luc. Hoa? peace be in this place.
Isa. Who's that which cals?
Nun. It is a mans voice: gentle *Isabella*
Turne you the key, and know his businesse of him;
You may; I may not: you are yet vnsworne:
When you haue vowd, you must not speake with men,
But in the presence of the *Prioresse*;
Then if you speake, you must not show your face;
Or if you show your face, you must not speake:
He cals againe: I pray you answere him.
Isa. Peace and prosperitie: who is't that cals?
Luc. Haile Virgin, (if you be) as those cheeke-Roses
Proclaime you are no lesse: can you so steed me,
As bring me to the sight of *Isabella*,
A Nouice of this place, and the faire Sister
To her vnhappie brother *Claudio*?
Isa. Why her vnhappy Brother? Let me aske,
The rather for I now must make you know
I am that *Isabella*, and his Sister.
Luc. Gentle & faire: your Brother kindly greets you;
Not to be weary with you; he's in prison.
Isa. Woe me; for what?
Luc. For that, which if my selfe might be his Iudge,
He should receiue his punishment, in thankes:
He hath got his friend with childe.
Isa. Sir, make me not your storie.
Luc. 'Tis true; I would not, though 'tis my familiar sin,
With Maids to seeme the Lapwing, and to iest
Tongue, far from heart: play with all Virgins so:
I hold you as a thing en-skied, and sainted,
By your renouncement, an imortall spirit
And to be talk'd with in sincerity,
As with a Saint.
Isa. You doe blaspheme the good, in mocking me.
Luc. Doe not beleeue it: fewnes, and truth; 'tis thus,
Your brother, and his louer haue embrac'd;
As those that feed, grow full: as blossoming Time
That from the seednes, the bare fallow brings
To teeming foyson: euen so her plenteous wombe
Expresseth his full Tilth, and husbandry.
Isa. Some one with childe by him? my cosen *Iuliet*?
Luc. Is she your cosen?
Isa. Adoptedly, as schoole-maids change their names
By vaine, though apt affection.
Luc. She it is.
Isa. Oh, let him marry her.
Luc. This is the point.
The Duke is very strangely gone from hence;
Bore many gentlemen (my selfe being one)
In hand, and hope of action: but we doe learne,
By those that know the very Nerues of State,
His giuing-out, were of an infinite distance
From his true meant designe: vpon his place,
(And with full line of his authority)
Gouernes Lord *Angelo*; A man, whose blood
Is very snow-broth: one, who neuer feeles
The wanton stings, and motions of the sence;
But doth rebate, and blunt his naturall edge
With profits of the minde: Studie, and fast
He (to giue feare to vse, and libertie,
Which haue, for long, run-by the hideous law,
As Myce, by Lyons) hath pickt out an act,
Vnder whose heauy sence, your brothers life
Fals into forfeit: he arrests him on it,
And followes close the rigor of the Statute
To make him an example: all hope is gone,
Vnlesse you haue the grace, by your faire praier
To soften *Angelo*: And that's my pith of businesse
'Twixt you, and your poore brother.
Isa. Doth he so,
Seeke his life?
Luc. Has censur'd him already,
And as I heare, the Prouost hath a warrant
For's execution.
Isa. Alas: what poore
Abilitie's in me, to doe him good.
Luc. Assay the powre you haue.
Isa. My power? alas, I doubt.
Luc. Our doubts are traitors
And makes vs loose the good we oft might win,
By fearing to attempt: Goe to Lord *Angelo*
And let him learne to know, when Maidens sue
Men giue like gods: but when they weepe and kneele,
All their petitions, are as freely theirs
As they themselues would owe them.
Isa. Ile see what I can doe.
Luc. But speedily.
Isa. I will about it strait;
No longer staying, but to giue the Mother
Notice of my affaire: I humbly thanke you:
Commend me to my brother: soone at night
Ile send him certaine word of my successe.
Luc. I take my leaue of you.
Isa. Good sir, adieu. *Exeunt.*

Actus Secundus. Scœna Prima.

Enter Angelo, Escalus, and seruants, Iustice.

Ang. We must not make a scar-crow of the Law,
Setting it vp to feare the Birds of prey,
And let it keepe one shape, till custome make it
Their pearch, and not their terror.
Esc. I, but yet
Let vs be keene, and rather cut a little
Then fall, and bruise to death: alas, this gentleman
Whom I would saue, had a most noble father,
Let but your honour know
(Whom I beleeue to be most strait in vertue)
That in the working of your owne affections,
Had time coheard with Place, or place with wishing,
Or that the resolute acting of our blood
Could haue attaind th'effect of your owne purpose,
Whether you had not sometime in your life
Er'd in this point, which now you censure him,
And puld the Law vpon you.
Ang. 'Tis one thing to be tempted (*Escalus*)
Another

Another thing to fall: I not deny
The Iury passing on the Prisoners life
May in the sworne-twelue haue a thiefe, or two
Guiltier then him they try; what's open made to Iustice,
That Iustice ceizes; What knowes the Lawes
That theeues do passe on theeues? Tis very pregnant,
The Iewell that we finde, we stoope, and take't,
Because we see it; but what we doe not see,
We tread vpon, and neuer thinke of it.
You may not so extenuate his offence,
For I haue had such faults; but rather tell me
When I, that censure him, do so offend,
Let mine owne Iudgement patterne out my death,
And nothing come in partiall. Sir, he must dye.

Enter Prouost.

Esc. Be it as your wisedome will.

Ang. Where is the *Prouost*?

Pro. Here if it like your honour.

Ang. See that *Claudio*
Be executed by nine to morrow morning,
Bring him his Confessor, let him be prepar'd,
For that's the vtmost of his pilgrimage.

Esc. Well: heauen forgiue him; and forgiue vs all:
Some rise by sinne, and some by vertue fall:
Some run from brakes of Ice, and answere none,
And some condemned for a fault alone.

Enter Elbow, Froth, Clowne, Officers.

Elb. Come, bring them away: if these be good people in a Common-weale, that doe nothing but vse their abuses in common houses, I know no law: bring them away.

Ang. How now Sir, what's your name? And what's the matter?

Elb. If it please your honour, I am the poore Dukes Constable, and my name is *Elbow*; I doe leane vpon Iustice Sir, and doe bring in here before your good honor, two notorious Benefactors.

Ang. Benefactors? Well: What Benefactors are they? Are they not Malefactors?

Elb. If it please your honour, I know not well what they are: But precise villaines they are, that I am sure of. and void of all prophanation in the world, that good Christians ought to haue.

Esc. This comes off well: here's a wise Officer.

Ang. Goe to: What quality are they of? *Elbow* is your name?
Why do'st thou not speake *Elbow*?

Clo. He cannot Sir: he's out at Elbow.

Ang. What are you Sir?

Elb. He Sir: a Tapster Sir: parcell Baud: one that serues a bad woman: whose house Sir was (as they say) pluckt downe in the Suborbs: and now shee professes a hot-house; which, I thinke is a very ill house too.

Esc. How know you that?

Elb. My wife Sir? whom I detest before heauen, and your honour.

Esc. How? thy wife?

Elb. I Sir: whom I thanke heauen is an honest woman.

Esc. Do'st thou detest her therefore?

Elb. I say sir, I will detest my selfe also, as well as she, that this house, if it be not a Bauds house, it is pitty of her life, for it is a naughty house.

Esc, How do'st thou know that, Constable?

Elb. Marry sir, by my wife, who, if she had bin a woman Cardinally giuen, might haue bin accus'd in fornication, adultery, and all vncleanlinesse there.

Esc. By the womans meanes?

Elb. I sir, by Mistris *Ouer-dons* meanes: but as she spit in his face, so she defide him.

Clo. Sir, if it please your honor, this is not so.

Elb. Proue it before these varlets here, thou honorable man, proue it.

Esc. Doe you heare how he misplaces?

Clo. Sir, she came in great with childe: and longing (sauing your honors reuerence) for stewd prewyns; sir, we had but two in the house, which at that very distant time stood, as it were in a fruit dish (a dish of some three pence; your honours haue seene such dishes) they are not China-dishes, but very good dishes.

Esc. Go too: go too: no matter for the dish sir.

Clo. No indeede sir not of a pin; you are therein in the right: but, to the point: As I say, this Mistris *Elbow*, being (as I say) with childe, and being great bellied, and longing (as I said) for prewyns: and hauing but two in the dish (as I said) Master *Froth* here, this very man, hauing eaten the rest (as I said) & (as I say) paying for them very honestly: for, as you know Master *Froth*, I could not giue you three pence againe.

Fro. No indeede.

Clo. Very well: you being then (if you be remembred) cracking the stones of the foresaid prewyns.

Fro. I, so I did indeede.

Clo. Why, very well: I telling you then (if you be remembred) that such a one. and such a one, were past cure of the thing you wot of, vnlesse they kept very good diet, as I told you.

Fro. All this is true.

Clo. Why very well then.

Esc. Come: you are a tedious foole: to the purpose: what was done to *Elbowes* wife, that hee hath cause to complaine of? Come me to what was done to her.

Clo. Sir, your honor cannot come to that yet.

Esc. No sir, nor I meane it not.

Clo. Sir, but you shall come to it, by your honours leaue: And I beseech you, looke into Master *Froth* here sir, a man of foure score pound a yeare; whose father died at *Hallowmas*: Was't not at *Hallowmas* Master *Froth*?

Fro. Allhallond-Eue.

Clo. Why very well: I hope here be truthes: he Sir, sitting (as I say) in a lower chaire, Sir, 'twas in the bunch of Grapes, where indeede you haue a delight to sit, haue you not?

Fro. I haue so, because it is an open roome, and good for winter.

Clo. Why very well then: I hope here be truthes.

Ang. This will last out a night in *Russia*
When nights are longest there: Ile take my leaue,
And leaue you to the hearing of the cause;
Hoping youle finde good cause to whip them all. *Exit.*

Esc I thinke no lesse: good morrow to your Lordship. Now Sir, come on: What was done to *Elbowes* wife, once more?

Clo. Once Sir? there was nothing done to her once.

Elb. I beseech you Sir, aske him what this man did to my wife.

Clo. I beseech your honor, aske me.

Esc. Well sir, what did this Gentleman to her?

Clo. I beseech you sir, looke in this Gentlemans face: good Master *Froth* looke vpon his honor; 'tis for a good purpose: doth your honor marke his face?

Eſc. I ſir, very well.

Clo. Nay, I beſeech you marke it well.

Eſc. Well, I doe ſo.

Clo. Doth your honor ſee any harme in his face?

Eſc. Why no.

Clo. Ile be ſuppos'd vpon a booke, his face is the worſt thing about him: good then: if his face be the worſt thing about him, how could Maſter *Froth* doe the Conſtables wife any harme? I would know that of your honour.

Eſc. He's in the right (Conſtable) what ſay you to it?

Elb. Firſt, and it like you, the houſe is a reſpected houſe; next, this is a reſpected fellow; and his Miſtris is a reſpected woman.

Clo. By this hand Sir, his wife is a more reſpected perſon then any of us all.

Elb. Varlet, thou lyeſt; thou lyeſt wicked varlet: the time is yet to come that ſhee was euer reſpected with man, woman, or childe.

Clo Sir, ſhe was reſpected with him, before he married with her.

Eſ.. Which is the wiſer here; *Iuſtice* or *Iniquitie*? Is this true?

Elb. O thou caytiffe: O thou varlet: O thou wicked *Hanniball*; I reſpected with her, before I was married to her? If euer I was reſpected with her, or ſhe with me, let not your worſhip thinke mee the poore *Dukes* Officer: proue this, thou wicked *Hanniball*, or ile haue mine action of battry on thee.

Eſc. If he tooke you a box 'oth' eare, you might haue your action of ſlander too.

Elb. Marry I thanke your good worſhip for it: what is't your Worſhips pleaſure I ſhall doe with this wicked Caitiffe?

Eſc. Truly Officer, becauſe he hath ſome offences in him, that thou wouldſt diſcouer, if thou couldſt, let him continue in his courſes, till thou knowſt what they are.

Elb. Marry I thanke your worſhip for it: Thou ſeeſt thou wicked varlet now, what's come vpon thee. Thou art to continue now thou Varlet, thou art to continue.

Eſc. Where were you borne, friend?

Froth. Here in *Vienna*, Sir.

Eſc. Are you of fourescore pounds a yeere?

Froth. Yes, and 't pleaſe you ſir.

Eſc. So: what trade are you of, ſir?

Clo. A Tapſter, a poore widdowes Tapſter.

Eſc. Your Miſtris name?

Clo. Miſtris *Ouer-don.*

Eſc. Hath ſhe had any more then one husband?

Clo. Nine, ſir: *Ouer-don* by the laſt.

Eſc. Nine? come hether to me, Maſter *Froth*; Maſter *Froth*, I would not haue you acquainted with Tapſters; they will draw you Maſter *Froth*, and you wil hang them: get you gon, and let me heare no more of you.

Fro. I thanke your worſhip: for mine owne part, I neuer come into any roome in a Tap-houſe, but I am drawne in.

Eſc. Well: no more of it Maſter *Froth*: farewell: Come you hether to me, Mr. Tapſter: what's your name Mr. Tapſter?

Clo. *Pompey.*

Eſc. What elſe?

Clo. *Bum*, Sir.

Eſc. Troth, and your bum is the greateſt thing about you, ſo that in the beaſtlieſt ſence, you are *Pompey* the great; *Pompey*, you are partly a bawd, *Pompey*; howſoeuer you colour it in being a Tapſter, are you not? come, tell me true, it ſhall be the better for you.

Clo. Truly ſir, I am a poore fellow that would liue.

Eſc. How would you liue *Pompey*? by being a bawde what doe you thinke of the trade *Pompey*? is it a lawfull trade?

Clo. If the Law would allow it, ſir.

Eſc. But the Law will not allow it *Pompey*; nor it ſhall not be allowed in *Vienna.*

Clo. Do's your Worſhip meane to geld and ſplay all the youth of the City?

Eſc. No, *Pompey.*

Clo. Truely Sir, in my poore opinion they will too't then: if your worſhip will take order for the drabs and the knaues, you need not to feare the bawds.

Eſc. There is pretty orders beginning I can tell you: It is but heading, and hanging.

Clo. If you head, and hang all that offend that way but for ten yeare together; you'll be glad to giue out a Commiſſion for more heads: if this law hold in *Vienna* ten yeare, ile rent the faireſt houſe in it after three pence a Bay: If you liue to ſee this come to paſſe, ſay *Pompey* told you ſo.

Eſc. Thanke you good *Pompey*; and in requitall of your propheſie, harke you: I aduiſe you let me not finde you before me againe vpon any complaint whatſoeuer; no, not for dwelling where you doe: if I doe *Pompey*, I ſhall beat you to your Tent, and proue a ſhrewd *Cæſar* to you: in plaine dealing *Pompey*, I ſhall haue you whipt; ſo for this time, *Pompey*, fare you well.

Clo. I thanke your Worſhip for your good counſell; but I ſhall follow it as the fleſh and fortune ſhall better determine. Whip me? no, no, let Carman whip his Iade,
The valiant heart's not whipt out of his trade. *Exit.*

Eſc. Come hether to me, Maſter *Elbow*: come hither Maſter Conſtable: how long haue you bin in this place of Conſtable?

Elb. Seuen yeere, and a halfe ſir.

Eſc. I thought by the readineſſe in the office, you had continued in it ſome time: you ſay ſeauen yeares together.

Elb. And a halfe ſir.

Eſc. Alas, it hath beene great paines to you: they do you wrong to put you ſo oft vpon't. Are there not men in your Ward ſufficient to ſerue it?

Elb. 'Faith ſir, few of any wit in ſuch matters: as they are choſen, they are glad to chooſe me for them; I do it for ſome peece of money, and goe through with all.

Eſc. Looke you bring mee in the names of ſome ſixe or ſeuen, the moſt ſufficient of your pariſh.

Elb. To your Worſhips houſe ſir?

Eſc. To my houſe: fare you well: what's a clocke, thinke you?

Iuſt. Eleuen, Sir.

Eſc. I pray you home to dinner with me.

Iuſt. I humbly thanke you.

Eſc. It grieues me for the death of *Claudio*
But there's no remedie:

Iuſt. Lord *Angelo* is ſeuere.

Eſc. It is but needfull.
Mercy is not it ſelfe, that oft lookes ſo,
Pardon is ſtill the nurſe of ſecond woe:
But yet, poore *Claudio*; there is no remedie.
Come Sir. *Exeunt.*

Scena

Scena Secunda.

Enter Prouost, Seruant.

Ser. Hee's hearing of a Cause; he will come straight.
I'le tell him of you.
Pro. 'Pray you doe; Ile know
His pleasure, may be he will relent; alas
He hath but as offended in a dreame,
All Sects, all Ages smack of this vice, and he
To die for't?

Enter Angelo.

Ang. Now, what's the matter *Prouost*?
Pro. Is it your will *Claudio* shall die to morrow?
Ang. Did not I tell thee yea? hadst thou not order?
Why do'st thou aske againe?
Pro. Lest I might be too rash:
Vnder your good correction, I haue seene
When after execution, Iudgement hath
Repented ore his doome.
Ang. Goe to; let that be mine,
Doe you your office, or giue vp your Place,
And you shall well be spar'd.
Pro. I craue your Honours pardon:
What shall be done Sir, with the groaning *Iuliet*?
Shee's very neere her howre.
Ang. Dispose of her
To some more fitter place; and that with speed.
Ser. Here is the sister of the man condemn'd,
Desires accesse to you.
Ang. Hath he a Sister?
Pro. I my good Lord, a very vertuous maid,
And to be shortlie of a Sister-hood,
If not alreadie.
Ang. Well: let her be admitted,
See you the Fornicatresse be remou'd,
Let her haue needfull, but not lauish meanes,
There shall be order for't.

Enter Lucio and Isabella.

Pro. 'Saue your Honour. (will?
Ang. Stay a little while: y'are welcome: what's your
Isab. I am a wofull Sutor to your Honour,
'Please but your Honor heare me.
Ang. Well; what's your suite.
Isab. There is a vice that most I doe abhorre,
And most desire should meet the blow of Iustice;
For which I would not plead, but that I must,
For which I must not plead, but that I am
At warre, twixt will, and will not.
Ang. Well: the matter?
Isab. I haue a brother is condemn'd to die,
I doe beseech you let it be his fault,
And not my brother.
Pro. Heauen giue thee mouing graces.
Ang. Condemne the fault, and not the actor of it,
Why euery fault's condemnd ere it be done:
Mine were the verie Cipher of a Function
To fine the faults, whose fine stands in record,
And let goe by the Actor.
Isab. Oh iust, but seuere Law:
I had a brother then; heauen keepe your honour.
Luc. Giue't not ore so: to him againe, entreat him,
Kneele downe before him, hang vpon his gowne,
You are too cold: if you should need a pin,
You could not with more tame a tongue desire it:
To him, I say.
Isab. Must he needs die?
Ang. Maiden, no remedie.
Isab. Yes: I doe thinke that you might pardon him,
And neither heauen, nor man grieue at the mercy.
Ang. I will not doe't.
Isab. But can you if you would?
Ang. Looke what I will not, that I cannot doe.
Isab. But might you doe't & do the world no wrong
If so your heart were touch'd with that remorse,
As mine is to him?
Ang Hee's sentenc'd, tis too late.
Luc. You are too cold.
Isab. Too late? why no: I that doe speak a word
May call it againe: well, beleeue this
No ceremony that to great ones longs,
Not the Kings Crowne; nor the deputed sword,
The Marshalls Truncheon, nor the Iudges Robe
Become them with one halfe so good a grace
As mercie does: If he had bin as you, and you as he,
You would haue slipt like him, but he like you
Would not haue beene so sterne.
Ang. Pray you be gone.
Isab. I would to heauen I had your potencie,
And you were *Isabell*: should it then be thus?
No: I would tell what 'twere to be a Iudge,
And what a prisoner.
Luc. I, touch him: there's the vaine.
Ang. Your Brother is a forfeit of the Law,
And you but waste your words.
Isab. Alas, alas:
Why all the soules that were, were forfeit once,
And he that might the vantage best haue tooke,
Found out the remedie: how would you be,
If he, which is the top of Iudgement, should
But iudge you, as you are? Oh, thinke on that,
And mercie then will breathe within your lips
Like man new made.
Ang. Be you content, (faire Maid)
It is the Law, not I, condemne your brother,
Were he my kinsman, brother, or my sonne,
It should be thus with him: he must die to morrow.
Isab. To morrow? oh, that's sodaine,
Spare him, spare him:
Hee's not prepar'd for death; euen for our kitchins
We kill the fowle of season: shall we serue heauen
With lesse respect then we doe minister
To our grosse-selues? good, good my Lord, bethink you;
Who is it that hath di'd for this offence?
There's many haue committed it.
Luc. I, well said.
Ang. The Law hath not bin dead, thogh it hath slept
Those many had not dar'd to doe that euill
If the first, that did th' Edict infringe
Had answer'd for his deed. Now 'tis awake,
Takes note of what is done, and like a Prophet
Lookes in a glasse that shewes what future euils
Either now, or by remissenesse, new conceiu'd,
And so in progresse to be hatc'hd, and borne,
Are now to haue no successiue degrees,
But here they liue to end.
Isab. Yet shew some pittie.
Ang. I shew it most of all, when I show Iustice;
For then I pittie those I doe not know,
Which a dismis'd offence, would after gaule

And

And doe him right, that answering one foule wrong
Liues not to act another. Be satisfied;
Your Brother dies to morrow; be content.
Isab. So you must be ÿ first that giues this sentence,
And hee, that suffers: Oh, it is excellent
To haue a Giants strength: but it is tyrannous
To vse it like a Giant.
Luc. That's well said.
Isab. Could great men thunder
As *Ioue* himselfe do's, *Ioue* would neuer be quiet
For euery pelting petty Officer
Would vse his heauen for thunder;
Nothing but thunder: Mercifull heauen,
Thou rather with thy sharpe and sulpherous bolt
Splits the vn-wedgable and gnarled Oke,
Then the soft Mertill: But man, proud man,
Drest in a little briefe authoritie,
Most ignorant of what he's most assur'd,
(His glassie Essence) like an angry Ape
Plaies such phantastique tricks before high heauen,
As makes the Angels weepe: who with our spleenes,
Would all themselues laugh mortall.
Luc. Oh, to him, to him wench: he will relent,
Hee's comming: I perceiue't.
Pro. Pray heauen she win him.
Isab. We cannot weigh our brother with our selfe,
Great men may iest with Saints: tis wit in them,
But in the lesse fowle prophanation.
Luc. Thou'rt i'th right (Girle) more o'that.
Isab. That in the Captaine's but a chollericke word,
Which in the Souldier is flat blasphemie.
Luc. Art auis'd o'that? more on't.
Ang. Why doe you put these sayings vpon me?
Isab. Because Authoritie, though it erre like others,
Hath yet a kinde of medicine in it selfe
That skins the vice o'th top; goe to your bosome,
Knock there, and aske your heart what it doth know
That's like my brothers fault: if it confesse
A naturall guiltinesse, such as is his,
Let it not sound a thought vpon your tongue
Against my brothers life.
Ang. Shee speakes, and 'tis such sence
That my Sence breeds with it; fare you well.
Isab. Gentle my Lord, turne backe.
Ang. I will bethinke me: come againe to morrow.
Isa. Hark, how Ile bribe you: good my Lord turn back.
Ang. How? bribe me?
Is. I, with such gifts that heauen shall share with you.
Luc. You had mar'd all else.
Isab. Not with fond Sickles of the tested-gold,
Or Stones, whose rate are either rich, or poore
As fancie values them: but with true prayers,
That shall be vp at heauen, and enter there
Ere Sunne rise: prayers from preserued soules,
From fasting Maides, whose mindes are dedicate
To nothing temporall.
Ang. Well: come to me to morrow.
Luc. Goe to: 'tis well; away.
Isab. Heauen keepe your honour safe.
Ang. Amen.
For I am that way going to temptation,
Where prayers crosse.
Isab. At what hower to morrow,
Shall I attend your Lordship?
Ang. At any time 'fore-noone.
Isab. 'Saue your Honour.
Ang. From thee: euen from thy vertue.
What's this? what's this? is this her fault, or mine?
The Tempter, or the Tempted, who sins most? ha?
Not she: nor doth she tempt: but it is I,
That, lying by the Violet in the Sunne,
Doe as the Carrion do's, not as the flowre,
Corrupt with vertuous season: Can it be,
That Modesty may more betray our Sence
Then womans lightnesse? hauing waste ground enough,
Shall we desire to raze the Sanctuary
And pitch our euils there? oh fie, fie, fie:
What dost thou? or what art thou *Angelo*?
Dost thou desire her fowly, for those things
That make her good? oh, let her brother liue:
Theeues for their robbery haue authority,
When Iudges steale themselues: what, doe I loue her,
That I desire to heare her speake againe?
And feast vpon her eyes? what is't I dreame on?
Oh cunning enemy, that to catch a Saint,
With Saints dost bait thy hooke: most dangerous
Is that temptation, that doth goad vs on
To sinne, in louing vertue: neuer could the Strumpet
With all her double vigor, Art, and Nature
Once stir my temper: but this vertuous Maid
Subdues me quite: Euer till now
When men were fond, I smild, and wondred how. *Exit.*

Scena Tertia.

Enter Duke and Prouost.

Duke. Haile to you, *Prouost*, so I thinke you are.
Pro. I am the Prouost: whats your will, good Frier?
Duke. Bound by my charity, and my blest order,
I come to visite the afflicted spirits
Here in the prison: doe me the common right
To let me see them: and to make me know
The nature of their crimes, that I may minister
To them accordingly.
Pro. I would do more then that, if more were needfull
Enter Iuliet.
Looke here comes one: a Gentlewoman of mine,
Who falling in the flawes of her owne youth,
Hath blisterd her report: She is with childe,
And he that got it, sentenc'd: a yong man,
More fit to doe another such offence,
Then dye for this.
Duk. When must he dye?
Pro. As I do thinke to morrow.
I haue prouided for you, stay a while
And you shall be conducted.
Duk. Repent you (faire one) of the sin you carry?
Iul. I doe; and beare the shame most patiently.
Du. Ile teach you how you shal araign your consciẽce
And try your penitence, if it be sound,
Or hollowly put on.
Iul. Ile gladly learne.
Duk. Loue you the man that wrong'd you?
Iul. Yes, as I loue the woman that wrong'd him.
Duk. So then it seemes your most offence full act
Was mutually committed.
Iul. Mutually.
Duk. Then was your sin of heauier kinde then his.
Iul. I doe confesse it, and repent it (Father.)
Du. 'Tis

Duke. 'Tis meet so (daughter) but least you do repent
As that the sin hath brought you to this shame,
Which sorrow is alwaies toward our selues, not heauen,
Showing we would not spare heauen, as we loue it,
But as we stand in feare.
Iul. I doe repent me, as it is an euill,
And take the shame with ioy.
Duke. There rest:
Your partner (as I heare) must die to morrow,
And I am going with instruction to him:
Grace goe with you, *Benedicite.* *Exit.*
Iul. Must die to morrow? oh iniurious Loue
That respits me a life, whose very comfort
Is still a dying horror.
Pro. 'Tis pitty of him. *Exeunt.*

Scena Quarta.

Enter Angelo.

An. When I would pray, & think, I thinke, and pray
To seuerall subiects: heauen hath my empty words,
Whilst my Inuention, hearing not my Tongue,
Anchors on *Isabell*: heauen in my mouth,
As if I did but onely chew his name,
And in my heart the strong and swelling euill
Of my conception: the state whereon I studied
Is like a good thing, being often read
Growne feard, and tedious: yea, my Grauitie
Wherein (let no man heare me) I take pride,
Could I, with boote, change for an idle plume
Which the ayre beats for vaine: oh place, oh forme,
How often dost thou with thy case, thy habit
Wrench awe from fooles, and tye the wiser soules
To thy false seeming? Blood, thou art blood,
Let's write good Angell on the Deuills horne
'Tis not the Deuills Crest: how now? who's there?

Enter Seruant.

Ser. One *Isabell*, a Sister, desires accesse to you.
Ang. Teach her the way: oh, heauens
Why doe's my bloud thus muster to my heart,
Making both it vnable for it selfe,
And dispossessing all my other parts
Of necessary fitnesse?
So play the foolish throngs with one that swounds,
Come all to help him, and so stop the ayre
By which hee should reuiue: and euen so
The generall subiect to a wel-wisht King
Quit their owne part, and in obsequious fondnesse
Crowd to his presence, where their vn-taught loue
Must needs appear offence: how now faire Maid.

Enter Isabella.

Isab. I am come to know your pleasure. (me,
An. That you might know it, wold much better please
Then to demand what tis: your Brother cannot liue.
Isab. Euen so: heauen keepe your Honor.
Ang. Yet may he liue a while: and it may be
As long as you, or I: yet he must die.
Isab. Vnder your Sentence?
Ang. Yea.
Isab. When, I beseech you: that in his Reprieue
(Longer, or shorter) he may be so fitted
That his soule sicken not.
Ang. Ha? fie, these filthy vices: It were as good
To pardon him, that hath from nature stolne
A man already made, as to remit
Their sawcie sweetnes, that do coyne heauens Image
In stamps that are forbid: 'tis all as easie,
Falsely to take away a life true made,
As to put mettle in restrained meanes
To make a false one.
Isab. 'Tis set downe so in heauen, but not in earth.
Ang. Say you so: then I shall poze you quickly.
Which had you rather, that the most iust Law
Now tooke your brothers life, and to redeeme him
Giue vp your body to such sweet vncleannesse
As she that he hath staind?
Isab. Sir, beleeue this.
I had rather giue my body, then my soule.
Ang. I talke not of your soule: our compel'd sins
Stand more for number, then for accompt.
Isab. How say you?
Ang. Nay Ile not warrant that: for I can speake
Against the thing I say: Answere to this,
I (now the voyce of the recorded Law)
Pronounce a sentence on your Brothers life,
Might there not be a charitie in sinne,
To saue this Brothers life?
Isab. Please you to doo't,
Ile take it as a perill to my soule,
It is no sinne at all, but charitie.
Ang. Pleas'd you to doo't, at perill of your soule
Were equall poize of sinne, and charitie.
Isab. That I do beg his life, if it be sinne
Heauen let me beare it: you granting of my suit,
If that be sin, Ile make it my Morne-praier,
To haue it added to the faults of mine,
And nothing of your answere.
Ang. Nay, but heare me,
Your sence pursues not mine: either you are ignorant,
Or seeme so crafty; and that's not good.
Isab. Let be ignorant, and in nothing good,
But graciously to know I am no better.
Ang. Thus wisdome wishes to appeare most bright,
When it doth taxe it selfe: As these blacke Masques
Proclaime an en-shield beauty ten times louder
Then beauty could displaied: But marke me,
To be receiued plaine, Ile speake more grosse:
Your Brother is to dye.
Isab. So.
Ang. And his offence is so, as it appeares,
Accountant to the Law, vpon that paine.
Isab. True.
Ang. Admit no other way to saue his life
(As I subscribe not that, nor any other,
But in the losse of question) that you, his Sister,
Finding your selfe desir'd of such a person,
Whose creadit with the Iudge, or owne great place,
Could fetch your Brother from the Manacles
Of the all-building-Law: and that there were
No earthly meane to saue him, but that either
You must lay downe the treasures of your body,
To this supposed, or else to let him suffer:
What would you doe?
Isab. As much for my poore Brother, as my selfe;
That is: were I vnder the tearmes of death,
Th'impression of keene whips, I'ld weare as Rubies,
And strip my selfe to death, as to a bed,
That longing haue bin sicke for, ere I'ld yeeld
My body vp to shame.

Ang. That

Ang. Then must your brother die.
Isa. And 'twer the cheaper way:
Better it were a brother dide at once,
Then that a sister, by redeeming him
Should die for euer.
Ang. Were not you then as cruell as the Sentence,
That you haue slander'd so?
Isa. Ignomie in ransome, and free pardon
Are of two houses: lawfull mercie,
Is nothing kin to fowle redemption.
Ang. You seem'd of late to make the Law a tirant,
And rather prou'd the sliding of your brother
A merriment, then a vice.
Isa. Oh pardon me my Lord, it oft fals out
To haue, what we would haue,
We speake not what vve meane;
I something do excuse the thing I hate,
For his aduantage that I dearely loue.
Ang. We are all fraile.
Isa. Else let my brother die,
If not a fedarie but onely he
Owe, and succeed thy weaknesse.
Ang. Nay, women are fraile too.
Isa. I, as the glasses where they view themselues,
Which are as easie broke as they make formes:
Women? Helpe heauen; men their creation marre
In profiting by them: Nay, call vs ten times fraile,
For we are soft, as our complexions are,
And credulous to false prints.
Ang. I thinke it well:
And from this testimonie of your owne sex
(Since I suppose we are made to be no stronger
Then faults may shake our frames) let me be bold;
I do arrest your words. Be that you are,
That is a woman; if you be more, you'r none.
If you be one (as you are well exprest
By all externall warrants) shew it now,
By putting on the destin'd Liuerie.
Isa. I haue no tongue but one; gentle my Lord,
Let me entreate you speake the former language.
Ang. Plainlie conceiue I loue you.
Isa. My brother did loue *Iuliet*,
And you tell me that he shall die for't.
Ang. He shall not *Isabell* if you giue me loue.
Isa. I know your vertue hath a licence in't,
Which seemes a little fouler then it is,
To plucke on others.
Ang. Beleeue me on mine Honor,
My words expresse my purpose.
Isa. Ha? Little honor, to be much beleeu'd,
And most pernitious purpose: Seeming, seeming.
I will proclaime thee *Angelo*, looke for't.
Signe me a present pardon for my brother,
Or with an out-stretcht throate Ile tell the world aloud
What man thou art.
Ang. Who will beleeue thee *Isabell*?
My vnsoild name, th'austeerenesse of my life,
My vouch against you, and my place i'th State,
Will so your accusation ouer-weigh,
That you shall stifle in your owne report,
And smell of calumnie. I haue begun,
And now I giue my sensuall race, the reine,
Fit thy consent to my sharpe appetite,
Lay by all nicetie, and prolixious blushes
That banish what they sue for: Redeeme thy brother,
By yeelding vp thy bodie to my will,
Or else he must not onelie die the death,
But thy vnkindnesse shall his death draw out
To lingring sufferance: Answer me to morrow,
Or by the affection that now guides me most,
Ile proue a Tirant to him. As for you,
Say what you can; my false, ore-weighs your true. *Exit*
Isa. To whom should I complaine? Did I tell this,
Who would beleeue me? O perilous mouthes
That beare in them, one and the selfesame tongue,
Either of condemnation, or approofe,
Bidding the Law make curtsie to their will,
Hooking both right and wrong to th'appetite,
To follow as it drawes. Ile to my brother,
Though he hath falne by prompture of the blood,
Yet hath he in him such a minde of Honor,
That had he twentie heads to tender downe
On twentie bloodie blockes, hee'ld yeeld them vp,
Before his sister should her bodie stoope
To such abhord pollution.
Then *Isabell* liue chaste, and brother die;
"More then our Brother, is our Chastitie.
Ile tell him yet of *Angelo's* request,
And fit his minde to death, for his soules rest. *Exit.*

Actus Tertius. Scena Prima.

Enter Duke, Claudio, and Prouost.

Du. So then you hope of pardon from Lord *Angelo*?
Cla. The miserable haue no other medicine
But onely hope: I'haue hope to liue, and am prepar'd to die.
Duke. Be absolute for death: either death or life
Shall thereby be the sweeter. Reason thus with life:
If I do loose thee, I do loose a thing
That none but fooles would keepe: a breath thou art,
Seruile to all the skyie-influences,
That dost this habitation where thou keepst
Hourely afflict: Meerely, thou art deaths foole,
For him thou labourst by thy flight to shun,
And yet runst toward him still. Thou art not noble,
For all th'accommodations that thou bearst,
Are nurst by basenesse: Thou'rt by no meanes valiant,
For thou dost feare the soft and tender forke
Of a poore worme: thy best of rest is sleepe,
And that thou oft prouoakst, yet grosselie fearst
Thy death, which is no more. Thou art not thy selfe,
For thou exists on manie a thousand graines
That issue out of dust. Happie thou art not,
For what thou hast not, still thou striu'st to get,
And what thou hast forgetst. Thou art not certaine,
For thy complexion shifts to strange effects,
After the Moone: If thou art rich, thou'rt poore,
For like an Asse, whose backe with Ingots bowes;
Thou bearst thy heauie riches but a iournie,
And death vnloads thee; Friend hast thou none.
For thine owne bowels which do call thee, sire
The meere effusion of thy proper loines
Do curse the Gowt, Sapego, and the Rheume
For ending thee no sooner. Thou hast nor youth, nor age
But as it were an after-dinners sleepe
Dreaming on both, for all thy blessed youth
Becomes as aged, and doth begge the almes
Of palsied-Eld: and when thou art old, and rich
Thou

Thou hast neither heate, affection, limbe, nor beautie
To make thy riches pleasant: what's yet in this
That beares the name of life? Yet in this life
Lie hid moe thousand deaths; yet death we feare
That makes these oddes, all euen.
Cla. I humblie thanke you.
To sue to liue, I finde I seeke to die,
And seeking death, finde life: Let it come on.
Enter Isabella.
Isab. What hoa? Peace heere; Grace, and good companie.
Pro. Who's there? Come in, the wish deserues a welcome.
Duke. Deere sir, ere long Ile visit you againe.
Cla. Most holie Sir, I thanke you.
Isa. My businesse is a word or two with *Claudio.*
Pro. And verie welcom: looke Signior, here's your sister.
Duke. Prouost, a word with you.
Pro. As manie as you please.
Duke. Bring them to heare me speak, where I may be conceal'd.
Cla. Now sister, what's the comfort?
Isa. Why,
As all comforts are: most good, most good indeede,
Lord *Angelo* hauing affaires to heauen
Intends you for his swift Ambassador,
Where you shall be an euerlasting Leiger;
Therefore your best appointment make with speed,
To Morrow you set on.
Clau. Is there no remedie?
Isa. None, but such remedie, as to saue a head
To cleaue a heart in twaine:
Clau. But is there anie?
Isa. Yes brother, you may liue;
There is a diuellish mercie in the Iudge,
If you'l implore it, that will free your life,
But fetter you till death.
Cla. Perpetuall durance?
Isa. I iust, perpetuall durance, a restraint
Through all the worlds vastiditie you had
To a determin'd scope.
Clau. But in what nature?
Isa. In such a one, as you consenting too't,
Would barke your honor from that trunke you beare,
And leaue you naked.
Clau. Let me know the point.
Isa. Oh, I do feare thee *Claudio*, and I quake,
Least thou a feauorous life shouldst entertaine,
And six or seuen winters more respect
Then a perpetuall Honor. Dar'st thou die?
The sence of death is most in apprehension,
And the poore Beetle that we treade vpon
In corporall sufferance, finds a pang as great,
As when a Giant dies.
Cla. Why giue you me this shame?
Thinke you I can a resolution fetch
From flowrie tendernesse? If I must die,
I will encounter darknesse as a bride,
And hugge it in mine armes.
Isa. There spake my brother: there my fathers graue
Did vtter forth a voice. Yes, thou must die:
Thou art too noble, to conserue a life
In base appliances. This outward sainted Deputie,
Whose setled visage, and deliberate word
Nips youth i'th head, and follies doth emmew
As Falcon doth the Fowle, is yet a diuell:
His filth within being cast, he would appeare
A pond, as deepe as hell.
Cla. The prenzie, *Angelo*?
Isa. Oh 'tis the cunning Liuerie of hell,
The damnest bodie to inuest, and couer
In prenzie gardes; dost thou thinke *Claudio*,
If I would yeeld him my virginitie
Thou might'st be freed?
Cla. Oh heauens, it cannot be.
Isa. Yes, he would giu't thee; from this rank offence
So to offend him still. This night's the time
That I should do what I abhorre to name,
Or else thou diest to morrow.
Clau. Thou shalt not do't.
Isa. O, were it but my life,
I'de throw it downe for your deliuerance
As frankely as a pin.
Clau. Thankes deere *Isabell.*
Isa. Be readie *Claudio*, for your death to morrow.
Clau. Yes. Has he affections in him,
That thus can make him bite the Law by th'nose,
When he would force it? Sure it is no sinne,
Or of the deadly seuen it is the least.
Isa. Which is the least?
Cla. If it were damnable, he being so wise,
Why would he for the momentarie tricke
Be perdurablie fin'de? Oh *Isabell.*
Isa. What saies my brother?
Cla. Death is a fearefull thing.
Isa. And shamed life, a hatefull.
Cla. I, but to die, and go we know not where,
To lie in cold obstruction, and to rot,
This sensible warme motion, to become
A kneaded clod; And the delighted spirit
To bath in fierie floods, or to recide
In thrilling Region of thicke-ribbed Ice,
To be imprison'd in the viewlesse windes
And blowne with restlesse violence round about
The pendant world: or to be worse then worst
Of those, that lawlesse and incertaine thought,
Imagine howling, 'tis too horrible.
The weariest, and most loathed worldly life
That Age, Ache, periury, and imprisonment
Can lay on nature, is a Paradise
To what we feare of death.
Isa. Alas, alas.
Cla. Sweet Sister, let me liue.
What sinne you do, to saue a brothers life,
Nature dispenses with the deede so farre,
That it becomes a vertue.
Isa. Oh you beast,
Oh faithlesse Coward, oh dishonest wretch,
Wilt thou be made a man, out of my vice?
Is't not a kinde of Incest, to take life
From thine owne sisters shame? What should I thinke,
Heauen shield my Mother plaid my Father faire:
For such a warped slip of wildernesse
Nere issu'd from his blood. Take my defiance,
Die, perish: Might but my bending downe
Repreeue thee from thy fate, it should proceede.
Ile pray a thousand praiers for thy death,
No word to saue thee.
Cla. Nay heare me *Isabell.*
Isa. Oh fie, fie, fie:
Thy sinn's not accidentall, but a Trade;

Mercie

Mercy to thee would proue it selfe a Bawd,
'Tis best that thou diest quickly.

Cla. Oh heare me *Isabella*.

Duk. Vouchsafe a word, yong sister, but one word.

Isa. What is your Will.

Duk. Might you dispense with your leysure, I would by and by haue some speech with you: the satisfaction I would require, is likewise your owne benefit.

Isa. I haue no superfluous leysure, my stay must be stolen out of other affaires: but I will attend you a while.

Duke. Son, I haue ouer-heard what hath past between you & your sister. *Angelo* had neuer the purpose to corrupt her; onely he hath made an assay of her vertue, to practise his iudgement with the disposition of natures. She (hauing the truth of honour in her) hath made him that gracious deniall, which he is most glad to receiue: I am Confessor to *Angelo*, and I know this to be true, therfore prepare your selfe to death: do not satisfie your resolution with hopes that are fallible, to morrow you must die, goe to your knees, and make ready.

Cla. Let me ask my sister pardon, I am so out of loue with life, that I will sue to be rid of it.

Duke. Hold you there: farewell. *Prouost*, a word with you.

Pro. What's your will (father?)

Duk. That now you are come, you wil be gone: leaue me a while with the Maid, my minde promises with my habit, no losse shall touch her by my company.

Pro. In good time. *Exit.*

Duk. The hand that hath made you faire, hath made you good: the goodnes that is cheape in beauty, makes beauty briefe in goodnes; but grace being the soule of your complexion, shall keepe the body of it euer faire: the assault that *Angelo* hath made to you, Fortune hath conuaid to my vnderstanding; and but that frailty hath examples for his falling, I should wonder at *Angelo*: how will you doe to content this Substitute, and to saue your Brother?

Isab. I am now going to resolue him: I had rather my brother die by the Law, then my sonne should be vnlawfullie borne. But (oh) how much is the good Duke deceiu'd in *Angelo*: if euer he returne, and I can speake to him, I will open my lips in vaine, or discouer his gouernment.

Duke. That shall not be much amisse: yet, as the matter now stands, he will auoid your accusation: he made triall of you onelie. Therefore fasten your eare on my aduisings, to the loue I haue in doing good; a remedie presents it selfe. I doe make my selfe beleeue that you may most vprighteously do a poor wronged Lady a merited benefit; redeem your brother from the angry Law; doe no staine to your owne gracious person, and much please the absent Duke, if peraduenture he shall euer returne to haue hearing of this businesse.

Isab. Let me heare you speake farther; I haue spirit to do any thing that appeares not fowle in the truth of my spirit.

Duke. Vertue is bold, and goodnes neuer fearefull: Haue you not heard speake of *Mariana* the sister of *Fredericke* the great Souldier, who miscarried at Sea?

Isa. I haue heard of the Lady, and good words went with her name.

Duke. Shee should this *Angelo* haue married: was affianced to her oath, and the nuptiall appointed: between which time of the contract, and limit of the solemnitie, her brother *Fredericke* was wrackt at Sea, hauing in that perished vessell, the dowry of his sister: but marke how heauily this befell to the poore Gentlewoman, there she lost a noble and renowned brother, in his loue toward her, euer most kinde and naturall: with him the portion and sinew of her fortune, her marriage dowry: with both, her combynate-husband, this well-seeming *Angelo*.

Isab. Can this be so? did *Angelo* so leaue her?

Duke. Left her in her teares, & dried not one of them with his comfort: swallowed his vowes whole, pretending in her, discoueries of dishonor: in few, bestow'd her on her owne lamentation, which she yet weares for his sake: and he, a marble to her teares, is washed with them, but relents not.

Isab. What a merit were it in death to take this poore maid from the world? what corruption in this life, that it will let this man liue? But how out of this can shee auaile?

Duke. It is a rupture that you may easily heale: and the cure of it not onely saues your brother, but keepes you from dishonor in doing it.

Isab. Shew me how (good Father.)

Duk. This fore-named Maid hath yet in her the continuance of her first affection: his vniust vnkindenesse (that in all reason should haue quenched her loue) hath (like an impediment in the Current) made it more violent and vnruly: Goe you to *Angelo*, answere his requiring with a plausible obedience, agree with his demands to the point: onely referre your selfe to this aduantage; first, that your stay with him may not be long: that the time may haue all shadow, and silence in it: and the place answere to conuenience: this being granted in course, and now followes all: wee shall aduise this wronged maid to steed vp your appointment, goe in your place: if the encounter acknowledge it selfe heereafter, it may compell him to her recompence; and heere, by this is your brother saued, your honor vntainted, the poore *Mariana* aduantaged, and the corrupt Deputy scaled. The Maid will I frame, and make fit for his attempt: if you thinke well to carry this as you may, the doublenes of the benefit defends the deceit from reproofe. What thinke you of it?

Isab. The image of it giues me content already, and I trust it will grow to a most prosperous perfection.

Duk. It lies much in your holding vp: haste you speedily to *Angelo*, if for this night he intreat you to his bed, giue him promise of satisfaction: I will presently to S. *Lukes*, there at the moated-Grange recides this dejected *Mariana*; at that place call vpon me, and dispatch with *Angelo*, that it may be quickly.

Isab. I thank you for this comfort: fare you well good father. *Exit.*

Enter Elbow, Clowne, Officers.

Elb. Nay, if there be no remedy for it, but that you will needes buy and sell men and women like beasts, we shall haue all the world drinke browne & white bastard.

Duk. Oh heauens, what stuffe is heere.

Clow. Twas neuer merry world since of two vsuries the merriest was put downe, and the worser allow'd by order of Law: a fur'd gowne to keepe him warme; and furd with Foxe and Lamb-skins too, to signifie, that craft being richer then Innocency, stands for the facing.

Elb. Come your way sir: 'blesse you good Father Frier.

Duk. And you good Brother Father; what offence hath this man made you, Sir?

Elb. Marry

Elb. Marry Sir, he hath offended the Law; and Sir, we take him to be a Theefe too Sir. for wee haue found vpon him Sir, a strange Pick-lock, which we haue sent to the Deputie.

Duke. Fie, sirrah, a Bawd, a wicked bawd,
The euill that thou causest to be done,
That is thy meanes to liue. Do thou but thinke
What 'tis to cram a maw, or cloath a backe
From such a filthie vice: say to thy selfe,
From their abhominable and beastly touches
I drinke, I eate away my selfe, and liue
Canst thou beleeue thy liuing is a life,
So stinkingly depending? Go mend, go mend.

Clo. Indeed, it do's stinke in some sort, Sir:
But yet Sir I would proue

Duke. Nay, if the diuell haue giuen thee proofs for sin
Thou wilt proue his. Take him to prison Officer:
Correction, and Instruction must both worke
Ere this rude beast will profit.

Elb. He must before the Deputy Sir, he ha's giuen him warning: the Deputy cannot abide a Whore-master: if he be a Whore-monger, and comes before him, he were as good go a mile on his errand.

Duke. That we were all, as some would seeme to bee
From our faults, as faults from seeming free.

Enter Lucio.

Elb His necke will come to your wast, a Cord sir.

Clo. I spy comfort, I cry baile: Here's a Gentleman, and a friend of mine.

Luc. How now noble *Pompey*? What, at the wheels of *Cæsar*? Art thou led in triumph? What is there none of *Pigmalions* Images newly made woman to bee had now, for putting the hand in the pocket, and extracting clutch'd? What reply? Ha? What saist thou to this Tune, Matter, and Method? Is't not drown'd i'th last raine? Ha? What saist thou Trot? Is the world as it was Man? Which is the vvay? Is it sad, and few words? Or how? The tricke of it?

Duke. Still thus, and thus: still vvorse?

Luc. How doth my deere Morsell, thy Mistris? Procures she still? Ha?

Clo. Troth sir, shee hath eaten vp all her beefe, and she is her selfe in the tub.

Luc. Why 'tis good: It is the right of it: it must be so. Euer your fresh Whore, and your pouder'd Baud, an vnshun'd consequence, it must be so. Art going to prison *Pompey*?

Clo. Yes faith sir

Luc. Why 'tis not amisse *Pompey*: farewell: goe say I sent thee thether: for debt *Pompey*? Or how?

Elb. For being a baud, for being a baud.

Luc. Well, then imprison him: If imprisonment be the due of a baud, why 'tis his right. Baud is he doubtlesse, and of antiquity too: Baud borne. Farwell good *Pompey*: Commend me to the prison *Pompey*, you will turne good husband now *Pompey*, you vvill keepe the house.

Clo. I hope Sir, your good Worship wil be my baile?

Luc. No indeed vvil I not *Pompey*, it is not the wear: I will pray (*Pompey*) to encrease your bondage if you take it not patiently: Why, your mettle is the more: Adieu trustie *Pompey*.
Blesse you Friar.

Duke. And you.

Luc. Do's *Bridget* paint still, *Pompey*? Ha?

Elb. Come your waies sir, come.

Clo. You will not baile me then Sir?

Luc. Then *Pompey*, nor now: what newes abroad *Frier*? What newes?

Elb. Come your waies sir, come.

Luc. Goe to kennell (*Pompey*) goe:
What newes Frier of the Duke?

Duke. I know none: can you tell me of any?

Luc. Some say he is with the Emperor of *Russia*: other some, he is in *Rome*: but where is he thinke you?

Duke. I know not where: but wheresoeuer, I wish him well.

Luc. It was a mad fantasticall tricke of him to steale from the State, and vsurpe the beggerie hee was neuer borne to: Lord *Angelo* Dukes it well in his absence: he puts transgression too't.

Duke. He do's well in't.

Luc. A little more lenitie to Lecherie would doe no harme in him. Something too crabbed that way, *Frier*.

Duk. It is too general a vice, and seueritie must cure it.

Luc. Yes in good sooth, the vice is of a great kindred; it is vvell allied, but it is impossible to extirpe it quite, Frier, till eating and drinking be put downe. They say this *Angelo* vvas not made by Man and Woman, after this downe-right vvay of Creation: is it true, thinke you?

Duke. How should he be made then?

Luc. Some report, a Sea-maid spawn'd him. Some, that he vvas begot betweene two Stock-fishes. But it is certaine, that when he makes water, his Vrine is congeal'd ice, that I know to bee true: and he is a motion generatiue, that's infallible.

Duke. You are pleasant sir, and speake apace.

Luc. Why, what a ruthlesse thing is this in him, for the rebellion of a Cod-peece, to take away the life of a man? Would the Duke that is absent haue done this? Ere he vvould haue hang'd a man for the getting a hundred Bastards, he vvould haue paide for the Nursing a thousand. He had some feeling of the sport, hee knew the seruice, and that instructed him to mercie.

Duke. I neuer heard the absent Duke much detected for Women, he was not enclin'd that vvay.

Luc. Oh Sir, you are deceiu'd.

Duke. 'Tis not possible.

Luc. Who, not the Duke? Yes, your beggar of fifty: and his vse was, to put a ducket in her Clack-dish; the Duke had Crochets in him. Hee would be drunke too, that let me informe you.

Duke. You do him wrong, surely.

Luc. Sir, I vvas an inward of his: a shie fellow vvas the Duke, and I beleeue I know the cause of his vvithdrawing.

Duke. What (I prethee) might be the cause?

Luc. No, pardon: 'Tis a secret must bee lockt within the teeth and the lippes: but this I can let you vnderstand, the greater file of the subiect held the Duke to be vvise.

Duke. Wise? Why no question but he was.

Luc. A very superficiall, ignorant, vnweighing fellow

Duke. Either this is Enuie in you, Folly, or mistaking: The very streame of his life, and the businesse he hath helmed, must vppon a warranted neede, giue him a better proclamation. Let him be but testimonied in his owne bringings forth, and hee shall appeare to the enuious, a Scholler, a Statesman, and a Soldier: therefore you speake vnskilfully: or, if your knowledge bee more, it is much darkned in your malice.

G *Luc.*

Luc. Sir, I know him, and I loue him.

Duke. Loue talkes with better knowledge, & knowledge with deare loue.

Luc. Come Sir, I know what I know

Duke. I can hardly beleeue that, since you know not what you speake. But if euer the Duke returne (as our praiers are he may) let mee desire you to make your answer before him; if it bee honest you haue spoke, you haue courage to maintaine it; I am bound to call vppon you, and I pray you your name?

Luc. Sir my name is *Lucio*, wel known to the Duke.

Duke. He shall know you better Sir, if I may liue to report you.

Luc. I feare you not

Duke. O you hope the Duke will returne no more: or you imagine me to vnhurtfull an opposite: but indeed I can doe you little harme: You'll for-sweare this againe?

Luc. Ile be hang'd first. Thou art deceiu'd in mee Friar. But no more of this Canst thou tell if *Claudio* die to morrow, or no?

Duke. Why should he die Sir?

Luc. Why? For filling a bottle with a Tunner dish: I would the Duke we talke of were return'd againe: this vngenitur'd Agent will vn-people the Prouince with Continencie. Sparrowes must not build in his house-eeues, because they are lecherous: The Duke yet would haue darke deeds darkelie answered, hee would neuer bring them to light: would hee were return'd. Marrie this *Claudio* is condemned for vntrussing. Farwell good Friar, I prethee pray for me: The Duke (I say to thee againe) would eate Mutton on Fridaies. He's now past it, yet (and I say to thee) hee would mouth with a beggar, though she smelt browne-bread and Garlicke: say that I said so: Farewell. *Exit.*

Duke. No might, nor greatnesse in mortality
Can censure scape: Back wounding calumnie
The whitest vertue strikes. What King so strong
Can tie the gall vp in the slanderous tong?
But who comes heere?

Enter Escalus, Prouost, and Bawd.

Esc. Go, away with her to prison.

Bawd. Good my Lord be good to mee, your Honor is accounted a mercifull man: good my Lord.

Esc. Double, and trebble admonition, and still forfeite in the same kinde? This would make mercy sweare and play the Tirant.

Pro. A Bawd of eleuen yeares continuance, may it please your Honor.

Bawd. My Lord, this is one *Lucio*'s information against me, Mistris *Kate Keepe-downe* was with childe by him in the Dukes time, he promis'd her marriage: his Childe is a yeere and a quarter olde come *Philip* and *Iacob*: I haue kept it my selfe; and see how hee goes about to abuse me.

Esc. That fellow is a fellow of much License: Let him be call'd before vs. Away with her to prison: Goe too, no more words. Prouost, my Brother *Angelo* will not be alter'd, *Claudio* must die to morrow: Let him be furnish'd with Diuines, and haue all charitable preparation. If my brother wrought by my pitie, it should not be so with him.

Pro. So please you, this Friar hath beene with him, and aduis'd him for th'entertainment of death.

Esc. Good' euen, good Father

Duke. Blisse, and goodnesse on you.

Esc. Of whence are you?

Duke. Not of this Countrie, though my chance is now
To vse it for my time: I am a brother
Of gracious Order, late come from the Sea,
In speciall businesse from his Holinesse.

Esc. What newes abroad i'th World?

Duke. None, but that there is so great a Feauor on goodnesse, that the dissolution of it must cure it. Noueltie is onely in request, and as it is as dangerous to be aged in any kinde of course, as it is vertuous to be constant in any vndertaking. There is scarse truth enough aliue to make Societies secure, but Securitie enough to make Fellowships accurst: Much vpon this riddle runs the wisedome of the world: This newes is old enough, yet it is euerie daies newes. I pray you Sir, of what disposition was the Duke?

Esc. One, that aboue all other strifes,
Contended especially to know himselfe.

Duke. What pleasure was he giuen to?

Esc. Rather reioycing to see another merry, then merrie at anie thing which profest to make him reioice. A Gentleman of all temperance. But leaue wee him to his euents, with a praier they may proue prosperous, & let me desire to know, how you finde *Claudio* prepar'd? I am made to vnderstand, that you haue lent him visitation.

Duke. He professes to haue receiued no sinister measure from his Iudge, but most willingly humbles himselfe to the determination of Iustice: yet had he framed to himselfe (by the instruction of his frailty) manie deceyuing promises of life, which I (by my good leisure) haue discredited to him, and now is he resolu'd to die.

Esc. You haue paid the heauens your Function, and the prisoner the verie debt of your Calling. I haue labour'd for the poore Gentleman, to the extremest shore of my modestie, but my brother-Iustice haue I found so seuere, that he hath forc'd me to tell him, hee is indeede Iustice.

Duke. If his owne life,
Answere the straitnesse of his proceeding,
It shall become him well: wherein if he chance to faile
he hath sentenc'd himselfe.

Esc. I am going to visit the prisoner, Fare you well.

Duke. Peace be with you,
He who the sword of Heauen will beare,
Should be as holy, as seueare:
Patterne in himselfe to know,
Grace to stand, and Vertue go:
More, nor lesse to others paying,
Then by selfe-offences weighing.
Shame to him, whose cruell striking,
Kils for faults of his owne liking:
Twice trebble shame on *Angelo*,
To vveede my vice, and let his grow.
Oh, what may Man within him hide,
Though Angel on the outward side?
How may likenesse made in crimes,
Making practise on the Times,
To draw with ydle Spiders strings
Most ponderous and substantiall things?
Craft against vice, I must applie.
With *Angelo* to night shall lye
His old betroathed (but despised:)
So disguise shall by th'disguised
Pay with falshood, false exacting,
And performe an olde contracting. *Exit*

Actus

Actus Quartus. Scœna Prima.

Enter Mariana, and Boy singing.

Song. *Take, oh take those lips away,*
that so sweetly were forsworne,
And those eyes: the breake of day
lights that doe mislead the Morne;
But my kisses bring againe, bring againe,
Seales of loue, but seal'd in vaine, seal'd in vaine.

Enter Duke.

Mar. Breake off thy song, and haste thee quick away,
Here comes a man of comfort, whose aduice
Hath often still'd my brawling discontent.
I cry you mercie, Sir, and well could wish
You had not found me here so musicall.
Let me excuse me, and beleeue me so,
My mirth it much displeas'd, but pleas'd my woe.

Duk. 'Tis good; though Musick oft hath such a charme
To make bad, good; and good prouoake to harme.
I pray you tell me, hath any body enquir'd for mee here to day; much vpon this time haue I promis'd here to meete.

Mar. You haue not bin enquir'd after: I haue sat here all day.

Enter Isabell.

Duk. I doe constantly beleeue you: the time is come euen now. I shall craue your forbearance alittle, may be I will call vpon you anone for some aduantage to your selfe.

Mar. I am alwayes bound to you. *Exit.*

Duk. Very well met, and well come:
What is the newes from this good Deputie?

Isab. He hath a Garden circummur'd with Bricke,
Whose westerne side is with a Vineyard back't;
And to that Vineyard is a planched gate,
That makes his opening with this bigger Key:
This other doth command a little doore,
Which from the Vineyard to the Garden leades,
There haue I made my promise, vpon the
Heauy midle of the night, to call vpon him.

Duk. But shall you on your knowledge find this way?

Isab. I haue t'ane a due, and wary note vpon't,
With whispering, and most guiltie diligence,
In action all of precept, he did show me
The way twice ore.

Duk. Are there no other tokens
Betweene you 'greed, concerning her obseruance?

Isab. No: none but onely a repaire ith' darke,
And that I haue possest him, my most stay
Can be but briefe: for I haue made him know,
I haue a Seruant comes with me along
That staies vpon me; whose perswasion is,
I come about my Brother.

Duk. 'Tis well borne vp.
I haue not yet made knowne to *Mariana*

Enter Mariana.

A word of this: what hoa, within; come forth,
I pray you be acquainted with this Maid,
She comes to doe you good.

Isab. I doe desire the like.

Duk. Do you perswade your selfe that I respect you?

Mar. Good Frier, I know you do, and haue found it.

Duke. Take then this your companion by the hand
Who hath a storie readie for your eare:
I shall attend your leisure, but make haste
The vaporous night approaches.

Mar. Wilt please you walke aside. *Exit.*

Duke. Oh Place, and greatnes: millions of false eies
Are stucke vpon thee: volumes of report
Run with these false, and most contrarious Quest
Vpon thy doings: thousand escapes of wit
Make thee the father of their idle dreame,
And racke thee in their fancies. Welcome, how agreed?

Enter Mariana and Isabella.

Isab. Shee'll take the enterprize vpon her father,
If you aduise it.

Duke. It is not my consent,
But my entreaty too.

Isa. Little haue you to say
When you depart from him, but soft and low,
Remember now my brother.

Mar. Feare me not.

Duk. Nor gentle daughter, feare you not at all:
He is your husband on a pre-contract:
To bring you thus together 'tis no sinne,
Sith that the Iustice of your title to him
Doth flourish the deceit. Come, let vs goe,
Our Corne's to reape, for yet our Tithes to sow. *Exeunt.*

Scena Secunda.

Enter Prouost and Clowne.

Pro. Come hither sirha; can you cut off a mans head?

Clo. If the man be a Bachelor Sir, I can. But if he be a married man, he's his wiues head, And I can neuer cut off a womans head.

Pro. Come sir, leaue me your snatches, and yeeld mee a direct answere. To morrow morning are to die *Claudio* and *Barnardine*: heere is in our prison a common executioner, who in his office lacks a helper, if you will take it on you to assist him, it shall redeeme you from your Gyues: if not, you shall haue your full time of imprisonment, and your deliuerance with an vnpittied whipping; for you haue beene a notorious bawd.

Clo. Sir, I haue beene an vnlawfull bawd, time out of minde, but yet I will bee content to be a lawfull hangman: I would bee glad to receiue some instruction from my fellow partner.

Pro. What hoa, *Abhorson*: where's *Abhorson* there?

Enter Abhorson.

Abh. Doe you call sir?

Pro. Sirha, here's a fellow will helpe you to morrow in your execution: if you thinke it meet, compound with him by the yeere, and let him abide here with you, if not, vse him for the present, and dismisse him, hee cannot plead his estimation with you: he hath beene a Bawd.

Abh. A Bawd Sir? fie vpon him, he will discredit our mysterie.

Pro. Goe too Sir, you waigh equallie: a feather will turne the Scale. *Exit.*

Clo. Pray sir, by your good fauor: for surely sir, a good fauor you haue, but that you haue a hanging look: Doe you call sir, your occupation a Mysterie?

G 2 *Abh.* I.

Abb. I Sir, a Misterie.

Clo. Painting Sir, I haue heard say, is a Misterie; and your Whores sir, being members of my occupation, vsing painting, do proue my Occupation, a Misterie: but what Misterie there should be in hanging, if I should be hang'd, I cannot imagine.

Abb. Sir, it is a Misterie.

Clo. Proofe.

Abh. Euerie true mans apparrell fits your Theefe.

Clo. If it be too little for your theefe, your true man thinkes it bigge enough. If it bee too bigge for your Theefe, your Theefe thinkes it little enough: So euerie true mans apparrell fits your Theefe.

Enter Prouost.

Pro. Are you agreed?

Clo. Sir, I will serue him: For I do finde your Hangman is a more penitent Trade then your Bawd: he doth oftner aske forgiuenesse.

Pro. You sirrah, prouide your blocke and your Axe to morrow, foure a clock.

Abh. Come on (Bawd) I will instruct thee in my Trade: follow.

Clo. I do desire to learne sir: and I hope, if you haue occasion to vse me for your owne turne, you shall finde me y'are. For truly sir, for your kindnesse, I owe you a good turne. *Exit*

Pro. Call hether *Barnardine* and *Claudio*:
Th'one has my pitie; not a iot the other,
Being a Murtherer, though he were my brother.

Enter Claudio.

Looke, here's the Warrant *Claudio*, for thy death,
'Tis now dead midnight, and by eight to morrow
Thou must be made immortall. Where's *Barnardine*.

Cla. As fast lock'd vp in sleepe, as guiltlesse labour,
When it lies starkely in the Trauellers bones,
He will not wake.

Pro. Who can do good on him?
Well, go, prepare your selfe. But harke, what noise?
Heauen giue your spirits comfort: by, and by,
I hope it is some pardon, or repreeue
For the most gentle *Claudio*. Welcome Father.

Enter Duke.

Duke. The best, and wholsomst spirits of the night,
Inuellop you, good Prouost: who call'd heere of late?

Pro. None since the Curphew rung.

Duke. Not *Isabell*?

Pro. No.

Duke. They will then er't be long.

Pro. What comfort is for *Claudio*?

Duke. There's some in hope.

Pro. It is a bitter Deputie.

Duke. Not so, not so: his life is paralel'd
Euen with the stroke and line of his great Iustice:
He doth with holie abstinence subdue
That in himselfe, which he spurres on his powre
To qualifie in others: were he meal'd with that
Which he corrects, then were he tirrannous,
But this being so, he's iust. Now are they come.
This is a gentle Prouost, sildome when
The steeled Gaoler is the friend of men:
How now? what noise? That spirit's possest with hast,
That wounds th'vnsisting Posterne with these strokes.

Pro. There he must stay vntil the Officer
Arise to let him in: he is call'd vp.

Duke. Haue you no countermand for *Claudio* yet?
But he must die to morrow?

Pro. None Sir, none.

Duke. As neere the dawning Prouost as it is,
You shall heare more ere Morning.

Pro. Happely
You something know: yet I beleeue there comes
No countermand: no such example haue we:
Besides, vpon the verie siege of Iustice,
Lord *Angelo* hath to the publike eare
Profest the contrarie.

Enter a Messenger.

Duke. This is his Lords man.

Pro. And heere comes *Claudio*'s pardon.

Mess. My Lord hath sent you this note,
And by mee this further charge;
That you swerue not from the smallest Article of it,
Neither in time, matter, or other circumstance.
Good morrow: for as I take it, it is almost day.

Pro. I shall obey him.

Duke. This is his Pardon purchas'd by such sin,
For which the Pardoner himselfe is in:
Hence hath offence his quicke celeritie,
When it is borne in high Authority.
When Vice makes Mercie; Mercie's so extended,
That for the faults loue, is th'offender friended.
Now Sir, what newes?

Pro. I told you:
Lord *Angelo* (be-like) thinking me remisse
In mine Office, awakens mee
With this vnwonted putting on, methinks strangely:
For he hath not vs'd it before.

Duk. Pray you let's heare.

The Letter.

Whatsoeuer you may heare to the contrary, let Claudio *be executed by foure of the clocke and in the afternoone* Bernardine: *For my better satisfaction, let mee haue* Claudios *head sent me by fiue. Let this be duely performed with a thought that more depends on it, then we must yet deliver. Thus faile not to doe your Office, as you will answere it at your perill.*

What say you to this Sir?

Duke. What is that *Barnardine*, who is to be executed in th'afternoone?

Pro. A Bohemian borne: But here nurst vp & bred, One that is a prisoner nine yeeres old.

Duke. How came it, that the absent Duke had not either deliuer'd him to his libertie, or executed him? I haue heard it was euer his manner to do so.

Pro. His friends still wrought Repreeues for him: And indeed his fact till now in the gouernment of Lord *Angelo*, came not to an vndoubtfull proofe.

Duke. It is now apparant?

Pro. Most manifest, and not denied by himselfe.

Duke. Hath he borne himselfe penitently in prison? How seemes he to be touch'd?

Pro. A man that apprehends death no more dreadfully, but as a drunken sleepe, carelesse, wreaklesse, and fearelesse of what's past, present, or to come: insensible of mortality, and desperately mortall.

Duke. He wants aduice.

Pro. He wil heare none: he hath euermore had the liberty of the prison: giue him leaue to escape hence, hee would not. Drunke many times a day, if not many daies entirely drunke. We haue verie oft awak'd him, as if to carrie him to execution, and shew'd him a seeming warrant for it, it hath not moued him at all.

Duke.

Duke. More of him anon: There is written in your brow Prouost, honesty and constancie; if I reade it not truly, my ancient skill beguiles me: but in the boldnes of my cunning, I will lay my selfe in hazard: *Claudio*, whom heere you haue warrant to execute, is no greater forfeit to the Law, then *Angelo* who hath sentenc'd him. To make you vnderstand this in a manifested effect, I craue but foure daies respit: for the which, you are to do me both a present, and a dangerous courtesie.

Pro. Pray Sir, in what?

Duke. In the delaying death.

Pro. Alacke, how may I do it? Hauing the houre limited, and an expresse command, vnder penaltie, to deliuer his head in the view of *Angelo*? I may make my case as *Claudio's*, to crosse this in the smallest.

Duke. By the vow of mine Order, I warrant you,
If my instructions may be your guide,
Let this *Barnardine* be this morning executed,
And his head borne to *Angelo*.

Pro. *Angelo* hath seene them both,
And will discouer the fauour.

Duke. Oh, death's a great disguiser, and you may adde to it; Shaue the head, and tie the beard, and say it was the desire of the penitent to be so bar'de before his death: you know the course is common. If any thing fall to you vpon this, more then thankes and good fortune, by the Saint whom I professe, I will plead against it with my life.

Pro. Pardon me, good Father, it is against my oath.

Duke. Were you sworne to the Duke, or to the Deputie?

Pro. To him, and to his Substitutes.

Duke. You will thinke you haue made no offence, if the Duke auouch the iustice of your dealing?

Pro. But what likelihood is in that?

Duke. Not a resemblance, but a certainty; yet since I see you fearfull, that neither my coate, integrity, nor perswasion, can with ease attempt you, I wil go further then I meant, to plucke all feares out of you. Looke you Sir, heere is the hand and Seale of the Duke: you know the Charracter I doubt not, and the Signet is not strange to you?

Pro. I know them both.

Duke. The Contents of this, is the returne of the Duke; you shall anon ouer-reade it at your pleasure: where you shall finde within these two daies, he wil be heere. This is a thing that *Angelo* knowes not, for hee this very day receiues letters of strange tenor, perchance of the Dukes death, perchance entering into some Monasterie, but by chance nothing of what is writ. Looke, th'vnfolding Starre calles vp the Shepheard; put not your selfe into amazement, how these things should be; all difficulties are but easie vvhen they are knowne. Call your executioner, and off with *Barnardines* head: I will giue him a present shrift, and aduise him for a better place. Yet you are amaz'd, but this shall absolutely resolue you: Come away, it is almost cleere dawne. *Exit*.

Scena Tertia.

Enter Clowne.

Clo. I am as well acquainted heere, as I was in our house of profession: one would thinke it vvere Mistris *Ouer-dons* owne house, for heere be manie of her olde Customers. First, here's yong Mr *Rash*, hee's in for a commoditie of browne paper, and olde Ginger, nine score and seuenteene pounds, of which hee made fiue Markes readie money: marrie then, Ginger was not much in request, for the olde Women vvere all dead. Then is there heere one Mr *Caper*, at the suite of Master *Three-Pile* the Mercer, for some foure suites of Peach-colour'd Satten, which now peaches him a beggar. Then haue vve heere, yong *Dizie*, and yong Mr *Deepe-vow*, and Mr *Copperspurre*, and Mr *Starue-Lackey* the Rapier and dagger man, and yong *Drop-heire* that kild lustie *Pudding*, and Mr *Forthlight* the Tilter, and braue Mr *Shootie* the great Traueller, and wilde *Halfe-Canne* that stabb'd Pots, and I thinke fortie more, all great doers in our Trade, and are now for the Lords sake.

Enter Abhorson.

Abh. Sirrah, bring *Barnardine* hether.

Clo. Mr *Barnardine*, you must rise and be hang'd, Mr *Barnardine*.

Abh. What hoa *Barnardine*.

Barnardine within.

Bar. A pox o'your throats: who makes that noyse there? What are you?

Clo. Your friends Sir, the Hangman:
You must be so good Sir to rise, and be put to death.

Bar. Away you Rogue, away, I am sleepie.

Abh. Tell him he must awake,
And that quickly too.

Clo: Pray Master *Barnardine*, awake till you are executed, and sleepe afterwards.

Ab. Go in to him, and fetch him out.

Clo. He is comming Sir, he is comming: I heare his Straw russle.

Enter Barnardine.

Abh. Is the Axe vpon the blocke, sirrah?

Clo. Verie readie Sir.

Bar. How now *Abhorson*?
What's the newes vvith you?

Abh. Truly Sir, I would desire you to clap into your prayers: for looke you, the Warrants come.

Bar. You Rogue, I haue bin drinking all night,
I am not fitted for't.

Clo. Oh, the better Sir: for he that drinkes all night, and is hanged betimes in the morning, may sleepe the sounder all the next day.

Enter Duke.

Abh. Looke you Sir, heere comes your ghostly Father: do we iest now thinke you?

Duke. Sir, induced by my charitie, and hearing how hastily you are to depart, I am come to aduise you,
Comfort you, and pray with you.

Bar. Friar, not I: I haue bin drinking hard all night, and I will haue more time to prepare mee, or they shall beat out my braines with billets: I will not consent to die this day, that's certaine.

Duke. Oh sir, you must: and therefore I beseech you
Looke forward on the iournie you shall go.

Bar. I sweare I will not die to day for anie mans perswasion.

Duke. But heare you:

Bar. Not a word: if you haue anie thing to say to me, come to my Ward: for thence will not I to day. *Exit*

Enter Prouost.

Duke. Vnfit to liue, or die: oh grauell heart.

After him (Fellowes) bring him to the blocke.
Pro. Now Sir, how do you finde the prisoner?
Duke. A creature vnpre-par'd, vnmeet for death,
And to transport him in the minde he is,
Were damnable.
Pro. Heere in the prison, Father,
There died this morning of a cruell Feauor,
One *Ragozine*, a most notorious Pirate,
A man of *Claudio's* yeares: his beard, and head
Iust of his colour. What if we do omit
This Reprobate, til he were wel enclin'd,
And satisfie the Deputie with the visage
Of *Ragozine*, more like to *Claudio*?
Duke. Oh, 'tis an accident that heauen prouides:
Dispatch it presently, the houre drawes on
Prefixt by *Angelo*: See this be done,
And sent according to command, whiles I
Perswade this rude wretch willingly to die.
Pro. This shall be done (good Father) presently:
But *Barnardine* must die this afternoone,
And how shall we continue *Claudio*,
To saue me from the danger that might come,
If he were knowne aliue?
Duke. Let this be done,
Put them in secret holds, both *Barnardine* and *Claudio*,
Ere twice the Sun hath made his iournall greeting
To yond generation, you shal finde
Your safetie manifested.
Pro. I am your free dependant. *Exit.*
Duke. Quicke, dispatch, and send the head to *Angelo*
Now wil I write Letters to *Angelo*,
(The Prouost he shal beare them) whose contents
Shal witnesse to him I am neere at home:
And that by great Iniunctions I am bound
To enter publikely: him Ile desire
To meet me at the consecrated Fount,
A League below the Citie: and from thence,
By cold gradation, and weale-ballanc'd forme.
We shal proceed with *Angelo*.

Enter Prouost.

Pro. Heere is the head, Ile carrie it my selfe.
Duke. Conuenient is it: Make a swift returne,
For I would commune with you of such things,
That want no eare but yours.
Pro. Ile make all speede. *Exit*

Isabell within.

Isa. Peace hoa, be heere.
Duke. The tongue of *Isabell*. She's come to know,
If yet her brothers pardon be come hither:
But I will keepe her ignorant of her good,
To make her heauenly comforts of dispaire,
When it is least expected.

Enter Isabella.

Isa. Hoa, by your leaue.
Duke. Good morning to you, faire, and gracious daughter.
Isa. The better giuen me by so holy a man,
Hath yet the Deputie sent my brothers pardon?
Duke. He hath releasd him, *Isabell*, from the world,
His head is off, and sent to *Angelo*.
Isa. Nay, but it is not so.
Duke. It is no other,
Shew your wisedome daughter in your close patience.
Isa. Oh, I wil to him, and plucke out his eies.
Duk. You shal not be admitted to his sight.
Isa. Vnhappie *Claudio*, wretched *Isabell*,
Iniurious world, most damned *Angelo*.
Duke. This nor hurts him, nor profits you a iot,
Forbeare it therefore, giue your cause to heauen,
Marke what I say, which you shal finde
By euery sillable a faithful veritie.
The Duke comes home to morrow: nay drie your eyes,
One of our Couent, and his Confessor
Giues me this instance: Already he hath carried
Notice to *Escalus* and *Angelo*,
Who do prepare to meete him at the gates,
There to giue vp their powre: If you can pace your wisdome,
In that good path that I would wish it go,
And you shal haue your bosome on this wretch,
Grace of the Duke, reuenges to your heart,
And general Honor.
Isa. I am directed by you.
Duk. This Letter then to Friar *Peter* giue,
'Tis that he sent me of the Dukes returne:
Say, by this token, I desire his companie
At *Mariana's* house to night. Her cause, and yours
Ile perfect him withall, and he shal bring you
Before the Duke; and to the head of *Angelo*
Accuse him home and home. For my poore selfe,
I am combined by a sacred Vow,
And shall be absent. Wend you with this Letter:
Command these fretting waters from your eies
With a light heart; trust not my holie Order
If I peruert your course: whose heere?

Enter Lucio.

Luc. Good 'euen;
Frier, where's the Prouost?
Duke. Not within Sir.
Luc. Oh prettie *Isabella*, I am pale at mine heart, to see thine eyes so red: thou must be patient; I am faine to dine and sup with water and bran: I dare not for my head fill my belly. One fruitful Meale would set mee too't: but they say the Duke will be heere to Morrow. By my troth *Isabell* I lou'd thy brother, if the olde fantastical Duke of darke corners had bene at home, he had liued.
Duke. Sir, the Duke is marueilous little beholding to your reports, but the best is, he liues not in them.
Luc. Friar, thou knowest not the Duke so wel as I do: he's a better woodman then thou tak'st him for.
Duke. Well: you'l answer this one day. Fare ye well.
Luc. Nay tarrie, Ile go along with thee,
I can tel thee pretty tales of the Duke.
Duke. You haue told me too many of him already sir if they be true: if not true, none were enough.
Lucio. I was once before him for getting a Wench with childe.
Duke. Did you such a thing?
Luc. Yes marrie did I; but I was faine to forswear it,
They would else haue married me to the rotten Medler.
Duke. Sir your company is fairer then honest, rest you well.
Lucio. By my troth Ile go with thee to the lanes end: if baudy talke offend you, we'el haue very litle of it: nay Friar, I am a kind of Burre, I shal sticke. *Exeunt*

Scena Quarta.

Enter Angelo & Escalus.

Esc. Euery Letter he hath writ, hath disuouch'd other.

Ang.

An. In most vneuen and distracted manner, his actions show much like to madnesse, pray heauen his wisedome bee not tainted : and why meet him at the gates and reliuer ou rauthorities there?

Esc. I ghesse not.

Ang. And why should wee proclaime it in an howre before his entring, that if any craue redresse of iniustice, they should exhibit their petitions in the street?

Esc. He showes his reason for that: to haue a dispatch of Complaints, and to deliuer vs from deuices heereafter, which shall then haue no power to stand against vs.

Ang. Well : I beseech you let it bee proclaim'd betimes i'th' morne, Ile call you at your house : giue notice to such men of sort and suite as are to meete him.

Esc. I shall sir : fareyouwell. *Exit.*

Ang. Good night.
This deede vnshapes me quite, makes me vnpregnant
And dull to all proceedings. A deflowred maid,
And by an eminent body, that enforc'd
The Law against it? But that her tender shame
Will not proclaime against her maiden losse,
How might she tongue me? yet reason dares her no
For my Authority beares of a credent bulke,
That no particular scandall once can touch
But it confounds the breather. He should haue liu'd
Saue that his riotous youth with dangerous sense
Might in the times to come haue ta'ne reuenge
By so receiuing a dishonor'd life
With ransome of such shame : would yet he had liued
Alack, when once our grace we haue forgot
Nothing goes right, we would, and we would not. *Exit.*

Scena Quinta.

Enter Duke and Frier Peter.

Duke. These Letters at fit time deliuer me.
The Prouost knowes our purpose and our plot,
The matter being a foote, keepe your instruction
And hold you euer to our speciall drift,
Though sometimes you doe blench from this to that
As cause doth minister : Goe call at *Flauia's* house,
And tell him where I stay : giue the like notice
To *Valencius*, *Rowland*, and to *Crassus*,
And bid them bring the Trumpets to the gate :
But send me *Flauius* first.

Peter. It shall be speeded well.

Enter Varrius.

Duke. I thank thee *Varrius*, thou hast made good hast,
Come, we will walke : There's other of our friends
Will greet vs heere anon : my gentle *Varrius.* *Exeunt.*

Scena Sexta.

Enter Isabella and Mariana.

Isab. To speak so indirectly I am loath,
I would say the truth, but to accuse him so
That is your part, yet I am aduis'd to doe'it.
He saies, to vaile full purpose.

Mar. Be rul'd by him.

Isab. Besides he tells me, that if peraduenture
He speake against me on the aduerse side,
I should not thinke it strange, for 'tis a physicke
That's bitter, to sweet end.

Enter Peter.

Mar. I would *Frier Peter*

Isab. Oh peace, the *Frier* is come.

Peter. Come I haue found you out a stand most fit,
Where you may haue such vantage on the *Duke*
He shall not passe you :
Twice haue the Trumpets sounded.
The generous, and grauest Citizens
Haue hent the gates, and very neere vpon
The *Duke* is entring :
Therefore hence away. *Exeunt.*

Actus Quintus. Scœna Prima.

Enter Duke, Varrius, Lords, Angelo, Esculus, Lucio, Citizens at seuerall doores.

Duk. My very worthy Cosen, fairely met,
Our old, and faithfull friend, we are glad to see you

Ang. Esc. Happy returne be to yont royall grace

Duk. Many and harty thankings to you both :
We haue made enquiry of you, and we heare
Such goodnesse of your Iustice, that our soule
Cannot but yeeld you forth to publique thankes
Forerunning more requitall.

Ang. You make my bonds still greater.

Duk. Oh your desert speaks loud, & I should wrong it
To locke it in the wards of couert bosome
When it deserues with characters of brasse
A forted residence 'gainst the tooth of time,
And razure of obliuion : Giue we your hand
And let the Subiect see, to make them know
That outward curtesies would faine proclaime
Fauours that keepe within : Come *Escalus*.
You must walke by vs, on our other hand.
And good supporters are you.

Enter Peter and Isabella.

Peter. Now is your time
Speake loud, and kneele before him.

Isab. Iustice, O royall *Duke*, vaile your regard
Vpon a wrong'd (I would faine haue said a Maid)
Oh worthy Prince, dishonor not your eye
By throwing it on any other obiect,
Till you haue heard me, in my true complaint,
And giuen me Iustice, Iustice, Iustice, Iustice.

Duk. Relate your wrongs;
In what, by whom? be briefe :
Here is Lord *Angelo* shall giue you Iustice,
Reueale your selfe to him.

Isab. Oh worthy *Duke*,
You bid me seeke redemption of the diuell,
Heare me your selfe : for that which I must speake
Must either punish me, not being beleeu'd,
Or wring redresse from you :
Heare me : oh heare me, heere.

Ang. My Lord, her wits I feare me are not firme :
She hath bin a suitor to me, for her Brother
Cut off by course of Iustice.

Isab. By course of Iustice.

Ang. And she will speake most bitterly, and strange.

Isab. Most

Iſab. Moſt ſtrange: but yet moſt truely wil I ſpeake,
That *Angelo's* forſworne, is it not ſtrange?
That *Angelo's* a murtherer, is't not ſtrange?
That *Angelo* is an adulterous thiefe,
An hypocrite, a virgin violator,
Is it not ſtrange? and ſtrange?
Duke. Nay it is ten times ſtrange?
Iſa. It is not truer he is *Angelo*,
Then this is all as true, as it is ſtrange;
Nay, it is ten times true, for truth is truth
To th'end of reckning.
Duke. Away with her: poore ſoule
She ſpeakes this in th'infirmity of ſence.
Iſa. Oh Prince, I coniure thee as thou beleeu'ſt
There is another comfort, then this world,
That thou neglect me not, with that opinion
That I am touch'd with madneſſe: make not impoſſible
That which but ſeemes vnlike, 'tis not impoſſible
But one, the wickedſt caitiffe on the ground
May ſeeme as ſhie, as graue, as iuſt, as abſolute:
As *Angelo*, euen ſo may *Angelo*
In all his dreſſings, caracts, titles, formes,
Be an arch-villaine: Beleeue it, royall Prince
If he be leſſe, he's nothing, but he's more,
Had I more name for badneſſe.
Duke. By mine honeſty
If ſhe be mad, as I beleeue no other,
Her madneſſe hath the oddeſt frame of ſenſe,
Such a dependancy of thing, on thing,
As ere I heard in madneſſe.
Iſab. Oh gracious *Duke*
Harpe not on that; nor do not baniſh reaſon
For inequality, but let your reaſon ſerue
To make the truth appeare, where it ſeemes hid,
And hide the falſe ſeemes true.
Duk. Many that are not mad
Haue ſure more lacke of reaſon:
What would you ſay?
Iſab. I am the Siſter of one *Claudio*,
Condemnd vpon the Act of Fornication
To looſe his head, condemn'd by *Angelo*,
I, (in probation of a Siſterhood)
Was ſent to by my Brother; one *Lucio*
As then the Meſſenger.
Luc. That's I, and't like your Grace:
I came to her from *Claudio*, and deſir'd her,
To try her gracious fortune with Lord *Angelo*
For her poore Brothers pardon.
Iſab. That's he indeede.
Duk. You were not bid to ſpeake.
Luc No, my good Lord,
Nor wiſh'd to hold my peace.
Duk. I wiſh you now then,
Pray you take note of it: and when you haue
A buſineſſe for your ſelfe: pray heauen you then
Be perfect.
Luc. I warrant your honor.
Duk. The warrant's for your ſelfe: take heede to't.
Iſab. This Gentleman told ſomewhat of my Tale.
Luc. Right.
Duk. It may be right, but you are i'the wrong
To ſpeake before your time: proceed,
Iſab. I went
To this pernicious Caitiffe Deputie.
Duk. That's ſomewhat madly ſpoken.
Iſab. Pardon it,
The phraſe is to the matter.
Duke. Mended againe: the matter: proceed.
Iſab. In briefe, to ſet the needleſſe proceſſe by:
How I perſwaded, how I praid, and kneel'd,
How he refeld me, and how I replide
(For this was of much length) the vild concluſion
I now begin with griefe, and ſhame to vtter.
He would not, but by gift of my chaſte body
To his concupiſcible intemperate luſt
Releaſe my brother; and after much debatement,
My ſiſterly remorſe, confutes mine honour,
And I did yeeld to him: But the next morne betimes,
His purpoſe ſurfetting, he ſends a warrant
For my poore brothers head.
Duke. This is moſt likely.
Iſab. Oh that it were as like as it is true. (ſpeak'ſt,
Duk. By heauen (fond wretch) $\overset{u}{y}$ knowſt not what thou
Or elſe thou art ſuborn'd againſt his honor
In hatefull practiſe: firſt his Integritie
Stands without blemiſh: next it imports no reaſon,
That with ſuch vehemency he ſhould purſue
Faults proper to himſelfe: if he had ſo offended
He would haue waigh'd thy brother by himſelfe,
And not haue cut him off: ſome one hath ſet you on:
Confeſſe the truth, and ſay by whoſe aduice
Thou cam'ſt heere to complaine.
Iſab. And is this all?
Then oh you bleſſed Miniſters aboue
Keepe me in patience, and with ripened time
Vnfold the euill, which is heere wrapt vp
In countenance: heauen ſhield your Grace from woe
As I thus wrong'd, hence vnbeleeued goe.
Duke. I know you'ld faine be gone: An Officer:
To priſon with her: Shall we thus permit
A blaſting and a ſcandalous breath to fall,
On him ſo neere vs? This needs muſt be a practiſe;
Who knew of your intent and comming hither?
Iſa. One that I would were heere. *Frier Lodowick*.
Duk. A ghoſtly Father, belike:
Who knowes that *Lodowicke*?
Luc. My Lord, I know him, tis a medling Fryer,
I doe not like the man: had he been Lay my Lord,
For certaine words he ſpake againſt your Grace
In your retirment, I had ſwing'd him ſoundly.
Duke. Words againſt mee? this 'a good Fryer belike
And to ſet on this wretched woman here
Againſt our Subſtitute: Let this Fryer be found.
Luc. But yeſternight my Lord, ſhe and that Fryer
I ſaw them at the priſon: a ſawcy Fryar,
A very ſcuruy fellow.
Peter. Bleſſed be your Royall Grace:
I haue ſtood by my Lord, and I haue heard
Your royall eare abus'd: firſt hath this woman
Moſt wrongfully accus'd your Subſtitute,
Who is as free from touch, or ſoyle with her
As ſhe from one vngot.
Duke. We did beleeue no leſſe.
Know you that Frier *Lodowick* that ſhe ſpeakes of?
Peter. I know him for a man diuine and holy,
Not ſcuruy, nor a temporary medler
As he's reported by this Gentleman:
And on my truſt, a man that neuer yet
Did (as he vouches) miſ-report your Grace.
Luc. My Lord, moſt villanouſly, beleeue it.
Peter. Well: he in time may come to cleere himſelfe:
But at this inſtant he is ſicke, my Lord:
Of

Of a ſtrange Feauor : vpon his meere requeſt
Being come to knowledge, that there was complaint
Intended 'gainſt Lord *Angelo*, came I hether
To ſpeake as from his mouth, what he doth know
Is true, and falſe : And what he with his oath
And all probation will make vp full cleare
Whenſoeuer he's conuented : Firſt for this woman,
To iuſtifie this worthy Noble man,
So vulgarly and perſonally accus'd,
Her ſhall you heare diſproued to her eyes,
Till ſhe her ſelfe confeſſe it.

Duk. Good Frier, let's heare it :
Doe you not ſmile at this, Lord *Angelo*?
Oh heauen, the vanity of wretched fooles.
Giue vs ſome ſeates, Come coſen *Angelo*,
In this I'll be impartiall : be you Iudge
Of your owne Cauſe : Is this the Witnes Frier?

Enter Mariana.

Firſt, let her ſhew your face, and after, ſpeake.

Mar. Pardon my Lord, I will not ſhew my face
Vntill my husband bid me.

Duke. What, are you married?

Mar. No my Lord.

Duke. Are you a Maid?

Mar. No my Lord.

Duk. A Widow then?

Mar. Neither, my Lord.

Duk. Why you are nothing then: neither Maid, Widow, nor Wife?

Luc. My Lord, ſhe may be a Puncke : for many of them, are neither Maid, Widow, nor Wife.

Duk. Silence that fellow : I would he had ſome cauſe to prattle for himſelfe.

Luc. Well my Lord.

Mar. My Lord, I doe confeſſe I nere was married,
And I confeſſe beſides, I am no Maid,
I haue known my husband, yet my husband
Knowes not, that euer he knew me.

Luc. He was drunk then, my Lord, it can be no better.

Duk. For the benefit of ſilence, would thou wert ſo to.

Luc. Well, my Lord.

Duk. This is no witneſſe for Lord *Angelo*.

Mar. Now I come to't, my Lord.
Shee that accuſes him of Fornication,
In ſelfe-ſame manner, doth accuſe my husband,
And charges him, my Lord, with ſuch a time,
When I'le depoſe I had him in mine Armes
With all th'effect of Loue.

Ang. Charges ſhe moe then me?

Mar. Not that I know.

Duk. No? you ſay your husband

Mar. Why iuſt, my Lord, and that is *Angelo*,
Who thinkes he knowes, that he nere knew my body,
But knows, he thinkes, that he knowes *Iſabels*.

Ang. This is a ſtrange abuſe : Let's ſee thy face.

Mar. My husband bids me, now I will vnmaske.
This is that face, thou cruell *Angelo*
Which once thou ſworſt, was worth the looking on :
This is the hand, which with a vowd contract
Was faſt belockt in thine : This is the body
That tooke away the match from *Iſabell*,
And did ſupply thee at thy garden-houſe
In her Imagin'd perſon.

Duke. Know you this woman?

Luc. Carnallie ſhe ſaies,

Duk. Sirha, no more.

Luc. Enoug my Lord.

Ang. My Lord, I muſt confeſſe, I know this woman,
And fiue yeres ſince there was ſome ſpeech of marriage
Betwixt my ſelfe, and her : which was broke off,
Partly for that her promis'd proportions
Came ſhort of Compoſition : But in chiefe
For that her reputation was diſ-valued
In leuitie : Since which time of fiue yeres
I neuer ſpake with her, ſaw her, nor heard from her
Vpon my faith, and honor.

Mar. Noble Prince,
As there comes light from heauen, and words frō breath,
As there is ſence in truth, and truth in vertue,
I am affianced this mans wife, as ſtrongly
As words could make vp vowes : And my good Lord,
But Tueſday night laſt gon, in's garden houſe,
He knew me as a wife. As this is true,
Let me in ſafety raiſe me from my knees,
Or elſe for euer be confixed here
A Marble Monument.

Ang. I did but ſmile till now,
Now, good my Lord, giue me the ſcope of Iuſtice,
My patience here is touch'd : I doe perceiue
Theſe poore informall women, are no more
But inſtruments of ſome more mightier member
That ſets them on. Let me haue way, my Lord
To finde this practiſe out.

Duke. I, with my heart,
And puniſh them to your height of pleaſure.
Thou fooliſh Frier, and thou pernicious woman
Compact with her that's gone : thinkſt thou, thy oathes,
Though they would ſwear downe each particular Saint,
Were teſtimonies againſt his worth, and credit
That's ſeald in approbation? you, Lord *Eſcolus*
Sit with my Cozen, lend him your kinde paines
To finde out this abuſe, whence 'tis deriu'd.
There is another Frier that ſet them on,
Let him be ſent for.

Peter. Would he were here, my Lord, for he indeed
Hath ſet the women on to this Complaint;
Your Prouoſt knowes the place where he abides,
And he may fetch him.

Duke. Goe, doe it inſtantly :
And you, my noble and well-warranted Coſen
Whom it concernes to heare this matter forth,
Doe with your iniuries as ſeemes you beſt
In any chaſtiſement ; I for a while
Will leaue you ; but ſtir not you till you haue
Well determin'd vpon theſe Slanderers. *Exit.*

Eſc. My Lord, wee'll doe it throughly : Signior *Lucio*, did not you ſay you knew that Frier *Lodowick* to be a diſhoneſt perſon?

Luc. *Cucullus non facit Monachum*, honeſt in nothing but in his Clothes, and one that hath ſpoke moſt villanous ſpeeches of the Duke.

Eſc. We ſhall intreat you to abide heere till he come, and inforce them againſt him : we ſhall finde this Frier a notable fellow.

Luc. As any in *Vienna*, on my word.

Eſc. Call that ſame *Iſabell* here once againe, I would ſpeake with her : pray you, my Lord, giue mee leaue to queſtion, you ſhall ſee how Ile handle her.

Luc. Not better then he, by her owne report.

Eſc. Say you?

Luc. Marry ſir, I thinke, if you handled her priuately

ſhee

She would sooner confesse,perchance publikely she'll be asham'd.

Enter Duke,Prouost,Isabella.

Esc. I will goe darkely to worke with her.
Luc. That's the way: for women are light at midnight.
Esc. Come on Mistris, here's a Gentlewoman,
Denies all that you haue said.
Luc. My Lord, here comes the rascall I spoke of,
Here, with the *Prouost.*
Esc. In very good time: speake not you to him, till we call vpon you.
Luc. Mum.
Esc. Come Sir, did you set these women on to slander Lord *Angelo*? they haue confes'd you did.
Duk. 'Tis false.
Esc. How? Know you where you are?
Duk. Respect to your great place; and let the diuell
Be sometime honour'd, for his burning throne.
Where is the *Duke*? 'tis he should heare me speake.
Esc. The *Duke's* in vs: and we will heare you speake,
Looke you speake iustly.
Duk. Boldly,at least. But oh poore soules,
Come you to seeke the Lamb here of the Fox;
Good night to your redresse: Is the *Duke* gone?
Then is your cause gone too: The *Duke's* vniust,
Thus to retort your manifest Appeale,
And put your triall in the villaines mouth,
Which here you come to accuse.
Luc. This is the rascall: this is he I spoke of.
Esc. Why thou vnreuerend, and vnhallowed Fryer:
Is't not enough thou hast suborn'd these women,
To accuse this worthy man? but in foule mouth,
And in the witnesse of his proper eare,
To call him villaine; and then to glance from him,
To th' *Duke* himselfe, to taxe him with Iniustice?
Take him hence; to th' racke with him: we'll towze you
Ioynt by ioynt, but we will know his purpose:
What? vniust?
Duk. Be not so hot: the *Duke* dare
No more stretch this finger of mine, then he
Dare racke his owne: his Subiect am I not,
Nor here Prouinciall: My businesse in this State
Made me a looker on here in *Vienna,*
Where I haue seene corruption boyle and bubble,
Till it ore-run the Stew: Lawes, for all faults,
But faults so countenanc'd, that the strong Statutes
Stand like the forfeites in a Barbers shop,
As much in mocke, as marke.
Esc. Slander to th' State:
Away with him to prison.
Ang. What can you vouch against him Signior *Lucio*?
Is this the man that you did tell vs of?
Luc. 'Tis he, my Lord: come hither goodman baldpate, doe you know me?
Duk. I remember you Sir, by the sound of your voice, I met you at the Prison, in the absence of the *Duke.*
Luc. Oh, did you so? and do you remember what you said of the *Duke.*
Duk. Most notedly Sir.
Luc. Do you so Sir: And was the *Duke* a flesh-monger, a foole, and a coward, as you then reported him to be?
Duk. You must (Sir) change persons with me, ere you make that my report: you indeede spoke so of him, and much more, much worse.
Luc. Oh thou damnable fellow: did not I plucke thee by the nose, for thy speeches?
Duk. I protest, I loue the *Duke*, as I loue my selfe.
Ang. Harke how the villaine would close now, after his treasonable abuses.
Esc. Such a fellow is not to be talk'd withall: Away with him to prison: Where is the *Prouost*? away with him to prison: lay bolts enough vpon him: let him speak no more: away with those Giglets too, and with the other confederate companion.
Duk. Stay Sir, stay a while.
Ang. What, resists he? helpe him *Lucio.*
Luc. Come sir, come sir, come sir: foh sir, why you bald-pated lying rascall: you must be hooded must you? show your knaues visage with a poxe to you: show your sheepe-biting face, and be hang'd an houre: will't not off?
Duk. Thou art the first knaue, that ere mad'st a *Duke.*
First *Prouost*, let me bayle these gentle three:
Sneake not away Sir, for the Fryer, and you,
Must haue a word anon: lay hold on him.
Luc. This may proue worse then hanging.
Duk. What you haue spoke, I pardon: sit you downe,
We'll borrow place of him; Sir, by your leaue:
Ha'st thou or word, or wit, or impudence,
That yet can doe thee office? If thou ha'st
Rely vpon it, till my tale be heard,
And hold no longer out.
Ang. Oh, my dread Lord,
I should be guiltier then my guiltinesse,
To thinke I can be vndiscerneable,
When I perceiue your grace, like powre diuine,
Hath look'd vpon my passes. Then good Prince,
No longer Session hold vpon my shame,
But let my Triall, be mine owne Confession:
Immediate sentence then, and sequent death,
Is all the grace I beg.
Duk. Come hither *Mariana,*
Say: was't thou ere contracted to this woman?
Ang. I was my Lord.
Duk. Goe take her hence, and marry her instantly.
Doe you the office (*Fryer*) which consummate,
Returne him here againe: goe with him *Prouost.* *Exit.*
Esc. My Lord, I am more amaz'd at his dishonor,
Then at the strangenesse of it.
Duk. Come hither *Isabell,*
Your *Frier* is now your Prince: As I was then
Aduertysing, and holy to your businesse,
(Not changing heart with habit) I am still,
Atturnied at your seruice.
Isab. Oh giue me pardon
That I, your vassaile, haue imploid, and pain'd
Your vnknowne Soueraigntie.
Duk. You are pardon'd *Isabell*:
And now, deere Maide, be you as free to vs.
Your Brothers death I know sits at your heart:
And you may maruaile, why I obscur'd my selfe,
Labouring to saue his life: and would not rather
Make rash remonstrance of my hidden powre,
Then let him so be lost: oh most kinde Maid,
It was the swift celeritie of his death,
Which I did thinke, with slower foot came on,
That brain'd my purpose: but peace be with him,
That life is better life past fearing death,
Then that which liues to feare: make it your comfort,
So

So happy is your Brother.
Enter Angelo, Maria, Peter, Prouost.
Isab. I doe my Lord.
Duk. For this new-maried man, approaching here,
Whose salt imagination yet hath wrong'd
Your well defended honor: you must pardon
For *Mariana's* sake: But as he adiudg'd your Brother,
Being criminall, in double violation
Of sacred Chastitie, and of promise-breach,
Thereon dependant for your Brothers life,
The very mercy of the Law cries out
Most audible, euen from his proper tongue.
An *Angelo* for *Claudio*, death for death.
Haste still paies haste, and leasure, answers leasure;
Like doth quit like, and *Measure* still for *Measure*:
Then *Angelo*, thy fault's thus manifested;
Which though thou would'st deny, denies thee vantage.
We doe condemne thee to the very Blocke
Where *Claudio* stoop'd to death, and with like haste.
Away with him.
Mar. Oh my most gracious Lord,
I hope you will not mocke me with a husband?
Duk. It is your husband mock't you with a husband,
Consenting to the safe-guard of your honor,
I thought your marriage fit: else Imputation,
For that he knew you, might reproach your life,
And choake your good to come: For his Possessions,
Although by confutation they are ours;
We doe en-state, and widow you with all,
To buy you a better husband.
Mar. Oh my deere Lord,
I craue no other, nor no better man.
Duke. Neuer craue him, we are definitiue.
Mar. Gentle my Liege.
Duke. You doe but loose your labour.
Away with him to death: Now Sir, to you.
Mar. Oh my good Lord, sweet *Isabell*, take my part,
Lend me your knees, and all my life to come,
I'll lend you all my life to doe you seruice.
Duke. Against all sence you doe importune her,
Should she kneele downe, in mercie of this fact,
Her Brothers ghost, his paued bed would breake,
And take her hence in horror.
Mar. Isabell:
Sweet *Isabel*, doe yet but kneele by me,
Hold vp your hands, say nothing: I'll speake all.
They say best men are moulded out of faults,
And for the most, become much more the better
For being a little bad: So may my husband.
Oh *Isabel*: will you not lend a knee?
Duke. He dies for *Claudio's* death.
Isab. Most bounteous Sir.
Looke if it please you, on this man condemn'd,
As if my Brother liu'd: I partly thinke,
A due sinceritie gouerned his deedes,
Till he did looke on me: Since it is so,
Let him not die: my Brother had but Iustice,
In that he did the thing for which he dide.
For *Angelo*, his Act did not ore-take his bad intent,
And must be buried but as an intent
That perish'd by the way: thoughts are no subiects
Intents, but meerely thoughts.
Mar. Meerely my Lord.
Duk. Your suite's vnprofitable: stand vp I say:
I haue bethought me of another fault.
Prouost, how came it *Claudio* was beheaded
At an vnusuall howre?
Pro. It was commanded so.
Duke. Had you a speciall warrant for the deed?
Pro. No my good Lord: it was by priuate message.
Duk. For which I doe discharge you of your office,
Giue vp your keyes.
Pro. Pardon me, noble Lord,
I thought it was a fault, but knew it not,
Yet did repent me after more aduice,
For testimony whereof, one in the prison
That should by priuate order else haue dide,
I haue reseru'd aliue.
Duk. What's he?
Pro. His name is *Barnardine*.
Duke. I would thou hadst done so by *Claudio*:
Goe fetch him hither, let me looke vpon him.
Esc. I am sorry, one so learned, and so wise
As you, Lord *Angelo*, haue stil appear'd,
Should slip so grosselie, both in the heat of bloud
And lacke of temper'd iudgement afterward.
Ang. I am sorrie, that such sorrow I procure,
And so deepe sticks it in my penitent heart,
That I craue death more willingly then mercy,
'Tis my deseruing, and I doe entreat it.
Enter Barnardine and Prouost, Claudio, Iulietta.
Duke. Which is that *Barnardine*?
Pro. This my Lord.
Duke. There was a Friar told me of this man.
Sirha, thou art said to haue a stubborne soule
That apprehends no further then this world,
And squar'st thy life according: Thou'rt condemn'd,
But for those earthly faults, I quit them all,
And pray thee take this mercie to prouide
For better times to come: Frier aduise him,
I leaue him to your hand. What muffeld fellow's that?
Pro. This is another prisoner that I sau'd,
Who should haue di'd when *Claudio* lost his head,
As like almost to *Claudio*, as himselfe.
Duke. If he be like your brother, for his sake
Is he pardon'd, and for your louelie sake
Giue me your hand, and say you will be mine,
He is my brother too: But fitter time for that:
By this Lord *Angelo* perceiues he's safe,
Methinkes I see a quickning in his eye:
Well *Angelo*, your euill quits you well.
Looke that you loue your wife: her worth, worth yours
I finde an apt remission in my selfe:
And yet heere's one in place I cannot pardon,
You sirha, that knew me for a foole, a Coward,
One all of Luxurie, an asse, a mad man:
Wherein haue I so deseru'd of you
That you extoll me thus?
Luc. 'Faith my Lord, I spoke it but according to the trick: if you will hang me for it you may: but I had rather it would please yon, I might be whipt.
Duke. Whipt first, sir, and hang'd after.
Proclaime it Prouost round about the Citie,
If any woman wrong'd by this lewd fellow
(As I haue heard him sweare himselfe there's one
whom he begot with childe) let her appeare,
And he shall marry her: the nuptiall finish'd,
Let him be whipt and hang'd.
Luc. I beseech your Highnesse doe not marry me to a Whore: your Highnesse said euen now I made you a Duke, good my Lord do not recompence me, in making me a Cuckold.

Duk. Vpon

Duke. Vpon mine honor thou shalt marrie her.
Thy slanders I forgiue, and therewithall
Remit thy other forfeits : take him to prison,
And see our pleasure herein executed.
Luc. Marrying a punke my Lord, is pressing to death,
Whipping and hanging.
Duke. Slandering a Prince deserues it.
She *Claudio* that you wrong'd, looke you restore.
Ioy to you *Mariana*, loue her *Angelo* :
I haue confes'd her, and I know her vertue.
Thanks good friend, *Escalus*, for thy much goodnesse,
There's more behinde that is more gratulate.
Thanks *Prouost* for thy care, and secrecie,
We shall imploy thee in a worthier place.
Forgiue him *Angelo*, that brought you home
The head of *Ragozine* for *Claudio's*,
Th'offence pardons it selfe. Deere *Isabell*,
I haue a motion much imports your good,
Whereto if you'll a willing eare incline ;
What's mine is yours, and what is yours is mine
So bring vs to our Pallace, where wee'll show
What's yet behinde, that meete you all should know.

The Scene Vienna.

The names of all the Actors.

Vincentio : the Duke.
Angelo, the Deputie.
Escalus, an ancient Lord.
Claudio, a yong Gentleman.
Lucio, a fantastique.
2. Other like Gentlemen.
Prouost.
Thomas. } *2. Friers.*
Peter. }
Elbow, a simple Constable.
Froth, a foolish Gentleman.
Clowne.
Abhorson, an Executioner.
Barnardine, a dissolute prisoner.
Isabella, sister to Claudio.
Mariana, betrothed to Angelo
Iuliet, beloued of Claudio.
Francisca, a Nun.
Mistris Ouer-don, a Bawd.

FINIS.

The Comedie of Errors.

Actus primus, Scena prima.

Enter the Duke of Ephesus, with the Merchant of Siracusa, Iaylor, and other attendants.

Marchant.

PRoceed *Solinus* to procure my fall,
And by the doome of death end woes and all.
Duke. Merchant of *Siracusa*, plead no more.
I am not partiall to infringe our Lawes;
The enmity and discord which of late
Sprung from the rancorous outrage of your Duke,
To Merchants our well-dealing Countrimen,
Who wanting gilders to redeeme their liues,
Haue seal'd his rigorous statutes with their blouds,
Excludes all pitty from our threatning lookes:
For since the mortall and intestine iarres
Twixt thy seditious Countrimen and vs,
It hath in solemne Synodes beene decreed,
Both by the *Siracusians* and our selues,
To admit no trafficke to our aduerse townes:
Nay more, if any borne at *Ephesus*
Be seene at any *Siracusian* Marts and Fayres:
Againe, if any *Siracusian* borne
Come to the Bay of *Ephesus*, he dies:
His goods confiscate to the Dukes dispose,
Vnlesse a thousand markes be leuied
To quit the penalty, and to ransome him:
Thy substance, valued at the highest rate,
Cannot amount vnto a hundred Markes,
Therefore by Law thou art condemn'd to die.
Mer. Yet this my comfort, when your words are done,
My woes end likewise with the euening Sonne.
Duk. Well *Siracusian*; say in briefe the cause
Why thou departedst from thy natiue home?
And for what cause thou cam'st to *Ephesus*
Mer. A heauier taske could not haue beene impos'd,
Then I to speake my griefes vnspeakeable:
Yet that the world may witnesse that my end
Was wrought by nature, not by vile offence,
Ile vtter what my sorrow giues me leaue.
In *Syracusa* was I borne, and wedde
Vnto a woman, happy but for me,
And by me; had not our hap beene bad:
With her I liu'd in ioy, our wealth increast
By prosperous voyages I often made
To *Epidamium*, till my factors death,
And he great care of goods at randone left,
Drew me from kinde embracements of my spouse;
From whom my absence was no sixe moneths olde,
Before her selfe (almost at fainting vnder
The pleasing punishment that women beare)
Had made prouision for her following me,
And soone, and safe, arriued where I was:
There had she not beene long, but she became
A ioyfull mother of two goodly sonnes:
And, which was strange, the one so like the other,
As could not be distinguish'd but by names.
That very howre, and in the selfe-same Inne,
A meane woman was deliuered
Of such a burthen Male, twins both alike:
Those, for their parents were exceeding poore,
I bought, and brought vp to attend my sonnes.
My wife, not meanely prowd of two such boyes,
Made daily motions for our home returne:
Vnwilling I agreed, alas, too soone wee came aboord.
A league from *Epidamium* had we saild
Before the alwaies winde-obeying deepe
Gaue any Tragicke Instance of our harme:
But longer did we not retaine much hope;
For what obscured light the heauens did grant,
Did but conuay vnto our fearefull mindes
A doubtfull warrant of immediate death,
Which though my selfe would gladly haue imbrac'd,
Yet the incessant weepings of my wife,
Weeping before for what she saw must come,
And pitteous playnings of the prettie babes
That mourn'd for fashion, ignorant what to feare,
Forst me to seeke delayes for them and me,
And this it was: (for other meanes was none)
The Sailors sought for safety by our boate,
And left the ship then sinking ripe to vs
My wife, more carefull for the latter borne,
Had fastned him vnto a small spare Mast,
Such as sea-faring men prouide for stormes:
To him one of the other twins was bound,
Whil'st I had beene like heedfull of the other.
The children thus dispos'd, my wife and I,
Fixing our eyes on whom our care was fixt,
Fastned our selues at eyther end the mast,
And floating straight, obedient to the streame,
Was carried towards *Corinth*, as we thought.
At length the sonne gazing vpon the earth,
Disperst those vapours that offended vs,
And by the benefit of his wished light
The seas waxt calme, and we discouered
Two shippes from farre, making amaine to vs:
Of *Corinth* that, of *Epidarus* this,
But ere they came, oh let me say no more,
Gather the sequell by that went before.
Duk. Nay forward old man, doe not breake off so,

H For

For we may pitty, though not pardon thee.
Merch. Oh had the gods done so, I had not now
Worthily tearm'd them mercilesse to vs:
For ere the ships could meet by twice fiue leagues,
We were encountred by a mighty rocke,
Which being violently borne vp,
Our helpefull ship was splitted in the midst;
So that in this vniust diuorce of vs,
Fortune had left to both of vs alike,
What to delight in, what to sorrow for,
Her part, poore soule, seeming as burdened
With lesser waight, but not with lesser woe,
Was carried with more speed before the winde,
And in our sight they three were taken vp
By Fishermen of *Corinth*, as we thought.
At length another ship had seiz'd on vs,
And knowing whom it was their hap to saue,
Gaue healthfull welcome to their ship-wrackt guests,
And would haue reft the Fishers of their prey,
Had not their backe beene very slow of saile;
And therefore homeward did they bend their course.
Thus haue you heard me seuer'd from my blisse,
That by misfortunes was my life prolong'd,
To tell sad stories of my owne mishaps.
Duke. And for the sake of them thou sorrowest for
Doe me the fauour to dilate at full,
What haue befalne of them and they till now.
Merch. My yongest boy, and yet my eldest care,
At eighteene yeeres became inquisitiue
After his brother; and importun'd me
That his attendant, so his case was like,
Reft of his brother, but retain'd his name,
Might beare him company in the quest of him:
Whom whil'st I laboured of a loue to see,
I hazarded the losse of whom I lou'd.
Fiue Sommers haue I spent in farthest *Greece*,
Roming cleane through the bounds of *Asia*,
And coasting homeward, came to *Ephesus*:
Hopelesse to finde, yet loth to leaue vnsought
Or that, or any place that harbours men:
But heere must end the story of my life,
And happy were I in my timelie death,
Could all my trauells warrant me they liue.
Duke. Haplesse *Egeon* whom the fates haue marke
To beare the extremitie of dire mishap:
Now trust me, were it not against our Lawes,
Against my Crowne, my oath, my dignity,
Which Princes would they may not disanull,
My soule should sue as aduocate for thee:
But though thou art adiudged to the death,
And passed sentence may not be recal'd
But to our honours great disparagement:
Yet will I fauour thee in what I can;
Therefore Marchant, Ile limit thee this day
To seeke thy helpe by beneficiall helpe,
Try all the friends thou hast in *Ephesus*,
Beg thou, or borrow, to make vp the summe,
And liue: if no, then thou art doom'd to die:
Iaylor, take him to thy custodie.
Iaylor. I will my Lord.
Merch. Hopelesse and helpelesse doth *Egean* wend,
But to procrastinate his liuelesse end. *Exeunt*

Enter Antipholis Erotes, a Marchant, and Dromio

Mer. Therefore giue out you are of *Epidamium*,
Lest that your goods too soone be confiscate:
This very day a *Syracusian* Marchant
Is apprehended for a riuall here,
And not being able to buy out his life,
According to the statute of the towne,
Dies ere the wearie sunne set in the West:
There is your monie that I had to keepe.
Ant. Goe beare it to the Centaure, where we host,
And stay there *Dromio*, till I come to thee;
Within this houre it will be dinner time,
Till that Ile view the manners of the towne,
Peruse the traders, gaze vpon the buildings,
And then returne and sleepe within mine Inne,
For with long trauaile I am stiffe and wearie.
Get thee away.
Dro. Many a man would take you at your word,
And goe indeede, hauing so good a meane.
Exit Dromio.
Ant. A trustie villaine sir, that very oft,
When I am dull with care and melancholly,
Lightens my humour with his merry iests:
What will you walke with me about the towne,
And then goe to my Inne and dine with me?
E.Mar. I am inuited sir to certaine Marchants,
Of whom I hope to make much benefit:
I craue your pardon, soone at fiue a clocke,
Please you, Ile meete with you vpon the Mart,
And afterward consort you till bed time
My present businesse cals me from you now.
Ant. Farewell till then: I will goe loose my selfe,
And wander vp and downe to view the Citie.
E.Mar. Sir, I commend you to your owne content.
Exeunt.
Ant. He that commends me to mine owne content,
Commends me to the thing I cannot get:
I to the world am like a drop of water,
That in the Ocean seekes another drop,
Who falling there to finde his fellow forth,
(Vnseene, inquisitiue) confounds himselfe.
So I, to finde a Mother and a Brother,
In quest of them (vnhappie a) loose my selfe.

Enter Dromio of Ephesus.

Here comes the almanacke of my true date:
What now? How chance thou art return'd so soone
E.Dro. Return'd so soone, rather approacht too late:
The Capon burnes, the Pig fals from the spit;
The clocke hath strucken twelue vpon the bell:
My Mistris made it one vpon my cheeke:
She is so hot because the meate is colde:
The meate is colde, because you come not home:
You come not home, because you haue no stomacke:
You haue no stomacke, hauing broke your fast:
But we that know what 'tis to fast and pray,
Are penitent for your default to day.
Ant. Stop in your winde sir, tell me this I pray?
Where haue you left the mony that I gaue you.
E.Dro. Oh sixe pence that I had a wensday last,
To pay the Sadler for my Mistris crupper:
The Sadler had it Sir, I kept it not.
Ant. I am not in a sportiue humor now:
Tell me, and dally not, where is the monie?
We being strangers here, how dar'st thou trust
So great a charge from thine owne custodie.
E.Dro. I pray you iest sir as you sit at dinner:
I from my Mistris come to you in post:
If I returne I shall be post indeede.

For ſhe will ſcoure your fault vpon my pate:
Me thinkes your maw, like mine, ſhould be your cooke,
And ſtrike you home without a meſſenger.
Ant. Come Dromio, come, theſe ieſts are out of ſeaſon,
Reſerue them till a merrier houre then this:
Where is the gold I gaue in charge to thee?
E.Dro. To me ſir? why you gaue no gold to me?
Ant. Come on ſir knaue, haue done your fooliſhnes,
And tell me how thou haſt diſpos'd thy charge.
E.Dro. My charge was but to fetch you frõ the Mart
Home to your houſe, the Phœnix ſir, to dinner;
My Miſtris and her ſiſter ſtaies for you.
Ant. Now as I am a Chriſtian anſwer me,
In what ſafe place you haue beſtow'd my monie;
Or I ſhall breake that merrie ſconce of yours
That ſtands on tricks, when I am vndiſpos'd:
Where is the thouſand Markes thou hadſt of me?
E.Dro. I haue ſome markes of yours vpon my pate:
Some of my Miſtris markes vpon my ſhoulders:
But not a thouſand markes betweene you both.
If I ſhould pay your worſhip thoſe againe,
Perchance you will not beare them patiently.
Ant. Thy Miſtris markes? what Miſtris ſlaue haſt thou?
E.Dro. Your worſhips wife, my Miſtris at the Phœnix;
She that doth faſt till you come home to dinner:
And praies that you will hie you home to dinner.
Ant. What wilt thou flout me thus vnto my face
Being forbid? There take you that ſir knaue.
E.Dro. What meane you ſir, for God ſake hold your
Nay, and you will not ſir, Ile take my heeles. (hands:
Exeunt Dromio Ep.
Ant. Vpon my life by ſome deuiſe or other,
The villaine is ore-wrought of all my monie.
They ſay this towne is full of coſenage:
As nimble Iuglers that deceiue the eie:
Darke working Sorcerers that change the minde:
Soule-killing Witches, that deforme the bodie:
Diſguiſed Cheaters, prating Mountebankes;
And manie ſuch like liberties of ſinne:
If it proue ſo, I will be gone the ſooner:
Ile to the Centaur to goe ſeeke this ſlaue,
I greatly feare my monie is not ſafe. Exit.

Actus Secundus.

Enter Adriana, wife to Antipholis Sereptus, with Luciana her Siſter.

Adr. Neither my husband nor the ſlaue return'd,
That in ſuch haſte I ſent to ſeeke his Maſter?
Sure Luciana it is two a clocke.
Luc. Perhaps ſome Merchant hath inuited him,
And from the Mart he's ſomewhere gone to dinner:
Good Siſter let vs dine, and neuer fret;
A man is Maſter of his libertie:
Time is their Maſter, and when they ſee time,
They'll goe or come; if ſo, be patient Siſter.
Adr. Why ſhould their libertie then ours be more?
Luc. Becauſe their buſineſſe ſtill lies out adore.
Adr. Looke when I ſerue him ſo, he takes it thus.
Luc. Oh, know he is the bridle of your will.
Adr. There's none but aſſes will be bridled ſo.
Luc. Why, headſtrong liberty is laſht with woe:
There's nothing ſituate vnder heauens eye,
But hath his bound in earth, in ſea, in skie.
The beaſts, the fiſhes, and the winged fowles
Are their males ſubiects, and at their controules:
Man more diuine, the Maſter of all theſe,
Lord of the wide world, and wilde watry ſeas,
Indued with intellectuall ſence and ſoules,
Of more preheminence then fiſh and fowles,
Are maſters to their females, and their Lords:
Then let your will attend on their accords.
Adri. This ſeruitude makes you to keepe vnwed.
Luci. Not this, but troubles of the marriage bed.
Adr. But were you wedded, you wold bear ſome ſway
Luc. Ere I learne loue, Ile practiſe to obey.
Adr. How if your husband ſtart ſome other where?
Luc. Till he come home againe, I would forbeare.
Adr. Patience vnmou'd, no maruel though ſhe pauſe,
They can be meeke, that haue no other cauſe:
A wretched ſoule bruis'd with aduerſitie,
We bid be quiet when we heare it crie.
But were we burdned with like waight of paine,
As much, or more, we ſhould our ſelues complaine:
So thou that haſt no vnkinde mate to greeue thee,
With vrging helpeleſſe patience would releeue me;
But if thou liue to ſee like right bereft,
This foole-beg'd patience in thee will be left.
Luci. Well, I will many one day but to trie:
Heere comes your man, now is your husband nie.

Enter Dromio Eph.

Adr. Say, is your tardie maſter now at hand?
E.Dro. Nay, hee's at too hands with mee, and that my two eares can witneſſe.
Adr. Say, didſt thou ſpeake with him? knowſt thou his minde?
E. Dro. I, I, he told his minde vpon mine eare,
Beſhrew his hand, I ſcarce could vnderſtand it.
Luc. Spake hee ſo doubtfully, thou couldſt not feele his meaning.
E. Dro. Nay, hee ſtrooke ſo plainly, I could too well feele his blowes; and withall ſo doubtfully, that I could ſcarce vnderſtand them.
Adri. But ſay, I prethee, is he comming home?
It ſeemes he hath great care to pleaſe his wife.
E.Dro. Why Miſtreſſe, ſure my Maſter is horne mad.
Adri. Horne mad, thou villaine?
E.Dro. I meane not Cuckold mad,
But ſure he is ſtarke mad:
When I deſir'd him to come home to dinner,
He ask'd me for a hundred markes in gold:
'Tis dinner time, quoth I; my gold, quoth he:
Your meat doth burne, quoth I: my gold quoth he:
Will you come, quoth I: my gold, quoth he;
Where is the thouſand markes I gaue thee villaine?
The Pigge quoth I, is burn'd: my gold, quoth he
My miſtreſſe, ſir, quoth I: hang vp thy Miſtreſſe:
I know not thy miſtreſſe, out on thy miſtreſſe.
Luci. Quoth who?
E.Dr. Quoth my Maſter, I know quoth he, no houſe, no wife, no miſtreſſe: ſo that my arrant due vnto my tongue, I thanke him, I bare home vpon my ſhoulders: for in concluſion, he did beat me there.
Adri. Go back againe, thou ſlaue, & fetch him home.
Dro. Goe backe againe, and be new beaten home?
For Gods ſake ſend ſome other meſſenger.

Adri. Backe ſlaue, or I will breake thy pate a-croſſe.
Dro. And he will bleſſe ÿ croſſe with other beating:
Betweene you, I ſhall haue a holy head.
Adri. Hence prating peſant, fetch thy Maſter home.
Dro. Am I ſo round with you, as you with me,
That like a foot-ball you doe ſpurne me thus:
You ſpurne me hence, and he will ſpurne me hither,
If I laſt in this ſeruice, you muſt caſe me in leather.
Luci. Fie how impatience lowreth in your face.
Adri. His company muſt do his minions grace,
Whil'ſt I at home ſtarue for a merrie looke:
Hath homelie age th'alluring beauty tooke
From my poore cheeke? then he hath waſted it.
Are my diſcourſes dull? Barren my wit,
If voluble and ſharpe diſcourſe be mar'd,
Vnkindneſſe blunts it more then marble hard.
Doe their gay veſtments his affections baite?
That's not my fault, hee's maſter of my ſtate.
What ruines are in me that can be found,
By him not ruin'd? Then is he the ground
Of my defeatures. My decayed faire,
A ſunnie looke of his, would ſoone repaire.
But, too vnruly Deere, he breakes the pale,
And feedes from home; poore I am but his ſtale.
Luci. Selfe-harming Iealouſie; fie beat it hence.
Ad. Vnfeeling fools can with ſuch wrongs diſpence:
I know his eye doth homage other-where,
elſe, what lets it but he would be here?
Siſter, you know he promis'd me a chaine,
Would that alone, a loue he would detaine,
So he would keepe faire quarter with his bed:
I ſee the Iewell beſt enameled
Will looſe his beautie: yet the gold bides ſtill
That others touch, and often touching will.
Where gold and no man that hath a name,
By falſhood and corruption doth it ſhame:
Since that my beautie cannot pleaſe his eie,
Ile weepe (what's left away) and weeping die.
Luci. How manie fond fooles ſerue mad Ielouſie?
Exit.

Enter Antipholis Errotis.

Ant. The gold I gaue to *Dromio* is laid vp
Safe at the *Centaur*, and the heedfull ſlaue
Is wandred forth in care to ſeeke me out
By computation and mine hoſts report.
I could not ſpeake with *Dromio*, ſince at firſt
I ſent him from the Mart? ſee here he comes.

Enter Dromio Siracuſia.

How now ſir, is your merrie humor alter'd?
As you loue ſtroakes, ſo ieſt with me againe:
You know no *Centaur*? you receiu'd no gold?
Your Miſtreſſe ſent to haue me home to dinner?
My houſe was at the *Phœnix*? Waſt thou mad,
That thus ſo madlie thou did didſt anſwere me?
S.Dro. What anſwer ſir? when ſpake I ſuch a word?
E.Ant. Euen now, euen here, not halfe an howre ſince.
S.Dro. I did not ſee you ſince you ſent me hence
Home to the *Centaur* with the gold you gaue me.
Ant. Villaine, thou didſt denie the golds receit,
And toldſt me of a Miſtreſſe, and a dinner,
For which I hope thou feltſt I was diſpleas'd.
S.Dro: I am glad to ſee you in this merrie vaine,
What meanes this ieſt, I pray you Maſter tell me?
Ant. Yea, doſt thou ieere & flowt me in the teeth?
Thinkſt ŷ I ieſt? hold, take thou that, & that. *Beats Dro.*
S.Dr. Hold ſir, for Gods ſake, now your ieſt is earneſt,
Vpon what bargaine do you giue it me?
Antiph. Becauſe that I familiarlie ſometimes
Doe vſe you for my foole, and chat with you,
Your ſawcineſſe will ieſt vpon my loue,
And make a Common of my ſerious howres,
When the ſunne ſhines, let fooliſh gnats make ſport,
But creepe in crannies, when he hides his beames:
If you will ieſt with me, know my aſpect,
And faſhion your demeanor to my lookes,
Or I will beat this method in your ſconce.

S.Dro. Sconce call you it? ſo you would leaue battering, I had rather haue it a head, and you vſe theſe blows long, I muſt get a ſconce for my head, and Inſconce it to, or elſe I ſhall ſeek my wit in my ſhoulders, but I pray ſir, why am I beaten?

Ant. Doſt thou not know?

S.Dro. Nothing ſir, but that I am beaten.

Ant. Shall I tell you why?

S.Dro. I ſir, and wherefore; for they ſay, euery why hath a wherefore.

Ant. Why firſt for flowting me, and then wherefore, for vrging it the ſecond time to me.

S.Dro. Was there euer anie man thus beaten out of ſeaſon, when in the why and the wherefore, is neither rime nor reaſon. Well ſir, I thanke you.

Ant. Thanke me ſir, for what?

S.Dro. Marry ſir, for this ſomething that you gaue me for nothing.

Ant. Ile make you amends next, to giue you nothing for ſomething. But ſay ſir, is it dinner time?

S.Dro. No ſir, I thinke the meat wants that I haue.

Ant. In good time ſir: what's that?

S.Dro. Baſting.

Ant. Well ſir, then 'twill be drie.

S.Dro. If it be ſir, I pray you eat none of it.

Ant. Your reaſon?

S.Dro. Leſt it make you chollericke, and purchaſe me another drie baſting.

Ant. Well ſir, learne to ieſt in good time, there's a time for all things.

S.Dro. I durſt haue denied that before you vvere ſo chollericke.

Anti. By what rule ſir?

S.Dro. Marry ſir, by a rule as plaine as the plaine bald pate of Father time himſelfe.

Ant. Let's heare it.

S.Dro. There's no time for a man to recouer his haire that growes bald by nature.

Ant. May he not doe it by fine and recouerie?

S.Dro. Yes, to pay a fine for a perewig, and recouer the loſt haire of another man.

Ant. Why, is Time ſuch a niggard of haire, being (as it is) ſo plentifull an excrement?

S.Dro. Becauſe it is a bleſſing that hee beſtowes on beaſts, and what he hath ſcanted them in haire, hee hath giuen them in wit.

Ant. Why, but theres manie a man hath more haire then wit.

S.Dro. Not a man of thoſe but he hath the wit to loſe his haire.

Ant. Why thou didſt conclude hairy men plain dealers without wit.

S.Dro. The plainer dealer, the ſooner loſt; yet he looſeth it in a kinde of iollitie.

An. For what reaſon.

S.Dro. For two, and ſound ones to.

An. Nay

An. Nay not sound I pray you.

S.Dro. Sure ones then.

An. Nay, not sure in a thing falsing.

S.Dro. Certaine ones then.

An. Name them.

S.Dro. The one to saue the money that he spends in trying: the other, that at dinner they should not drop in his porrage.

An. You would all this time haue prou'd, here is no time for all things.

S.Dro. Marry and did sir: namely, in no time to recouer haire lost by Nature.

An. But your reason was not substantiall, why there is no time to recouer.

S.Dro. Thus I mend it: Time himselfe is bald, and therefore to the worlds end, will haue bald followers.

An. I knew 'twould be a bald conclusion: but soft, who wafts vs yonder.

Enter Adriana and Luciana.

Adri. I, I, *Antipholus*, looke strange and frowne,
Some other Mistresse hath thy sweet aspects:
I am not *Adriana*, nor thy wife.
The time was once, when thou vn-vrg'd wouldst vow,
That neuer words were musicke to thine eare,
That neuer obiect pleasing in thine eye,
That neuer touch well welcome to thy hand,
That neuer meat sweet-sauour'd in thy taste,
Vnlesse I spake, or look'd, or touch'd, or caru'd to thee.
How comes it now, my Husband, oh how comes it,
That thou art then estranged from thy selfe?
Thy selfe I call it, being strange to me:
That vndiuidable Incorporate
Am better then thy deere selfes better part.
Ah doe not teare away thy selfe from me;
For know my loue: as easie maist thou fall
A drop of water in the breaking gulfe,
And take vnmingled thence that drop againe
Without addition or diminishing,
As take from me thy selfe, and not me too.
How deerely would it touch thee to the quicke,
Shouldst thou but heare I were licencious?
And that this body consecrate to thee,
By Ruffian Lust should be contaminate?
Wouldst thou not spit at me, and spurne at me,
And hurle the name of husband in my face,
And teare the stain'd skin of my Harlot brow,
And from my false hand cut the wedding ring,
And breake it with a deepe-diuorcing vow?
I know thou canst, and therefore see thou doe it.
I am possest with an adulterate blot,
My bloud is mingled with the crime of lust:
For if we two be one, and thou play false,
I doe digest the poison of thy flesh,
Being strumpeted by thy contagion
Keepe then faire league and truce with thy true bed,
I liue distain'd, thou vndishonoured.

Antip. Plead you to me faire dame? I know you not:
In *Ephesus* I am but two houres old.
As strange vnto your towne, as to your talke,
Who euery word by all my wit being scan'd,
Wants wit in all, one word to vnderstand.

Luci. Fie brother, how the world is chang'd with you:
When were you wont to vse my sister thus?
She sent for you by *Dromio* home to dinner.

Ant. By *Dromio*? *Drom*. By me.

Adr. By thee, and this thou didst returne from him.
That he did buffet thee, and in his blowes,
Denied my house for his, me for his wife.

Ant. Did you conuerse sir with this gentlewoman:
What is the course and drift of your compact?

S.Dro. I sir? I neuer saw her till this time.

Ant. Villaine thou liest, for euen her verie words,
Didst thou deliuer to me on the Mart.

S.Dro. I neuer spake with her in all my life.

Ant. How can she thus then call vs by our names?
Vnlesse it be by inspiration.

Adri. How ill agrees it with your grauitie,
To counterfeit thus grosely with your slaue,
Abetting him to thwart me in my moode;
Be it my wrong, you are from me exempt,
But wrong not that wrong with a more contempt.
Come I will fasten on this sleeue of thine:
Thou art an Elme my husband, I a Vine:
Whose weaknesse married to thy stranger state,
Makes me with thy strength to communicate:
If ought possesse thee from me, it is drosse,
Vsurping Iuie, Brier, or idle Mosse,
Who all for want of pruning, with intrusion,
Infect thy sap, and liue on thy confusion.

Ant. To mee shee speakes, shee moues mee for her theame;
What, was I married to her in my dreame?
Or sleepe I now, and thinke I heare all this?
What error driues our eies and eares amisse?
Vntill I know this sure vncertaintie,
Ile entertaine the free'd fa'lacie.

Luc. *Dromio*, goe bid the seruants spred for dinner.

S.Dro. Oh for my beads, I crosse me for a sinner.
This is the Fairie land, oh spight of spights,
We talke with Goblins, Owles and Sprights;
If we obay them not, this will insue:
They'll sucke our breath, or pinch vs blacke and blew.

Luc. Why prat'st thou to thy selfe, and answer'st not?
Dromio, thou *Dromio*, thou snaile, thou slug, thou sot.

S.Dro. I am transformed Master, am I not?

Ant. I thinke thou art in minde, and so am I.

S.Dro. Nay Master, both in minde, and in my shape.

Ant. Thou hast thine owne forme.

S.Dro. No, I am an Ape.

Luc. If thou art chang'd to ought, 'tis to an Asse.

S.Dro. 'Tis true she rides me, and I long for grasse.
'Tis so, I am an Asse, else it could neuer be,
But I should know her as well as she knowes me.

Adr. Come, come, no longer will I be a foole,
To put the finger in the eie and weepe;
Whil'st man and Master laughes my woes to scorne:
Come sir to dinner, *Dromio* keepe the gate:
Husband Ile dine aboue with you to day,
And shriue you of a thousand idle prankes:
Sirra, if any aske you for your Master,
Say he dines forth, and let no creature enter:
Come sister, *Dromio* play the Porter well.

Ant. Am I in earth, in heauen, or in hell?
Sleeping or waking, mad or well aduisde:
Knowne vnto these, and to my selfe disguisde:
Ile say as they say, and perseuer so:
And in this mist at all aduentures go.

S.Dro. Master, shall I be Porter at the gate?

Adr. I, and let none enter, least I breake your pate

Luc. Come, come, *Antipholus*, we dine to late.

H 2 *Actus*

Actus Tertius. Scena Prima.

Enter Antipholus of Ephesus, his man Dromio, Angelo the Goldsmith, and Balthaser the Merchant.

E. Anti. Good signior *Angelo* you must excuse vs all,
My wife is shrewish when I keepe not howres;
Say that I lingerd with you at your shop
To see the making of her Carkanet,
And that to morrow you will bring it home.
But here's a villaine that would face me downe
He met me on the Mart, and that I beat him,
And charg'd him with a thousand markes in gold,
And that I did denie my wife and house;
Thou drunkard thou, what didst thou meane by this?

E. Dro. Say what you wil sir, but I know what I know,
That you beat me at the Mart I haue your hand to show;
If ÿ skin were parchment, & ÿ blows you gaue were ink,
Your owne hand-writing would tell you what I thinke.

E. Ant. I thinke thou art an asse.

E. Dro. Marry so it doth appeare
By the wrongs I suffer, and the blowes I beare,
I should kicke being kickt, and being at that passe,
You would keepe from my heeles, and beware of an asse.

E. An. Y'are sad signior *Balthazar*, pray God our cheer
May answer my good will, and your good welcom here.

Bal. I hold your dainties cheap sir, & your welcom deer.

E. An. Oh signior *Balthazar*, either at flesh or fish,
A table full of welcome, makes scarce one dainty dish.

Bal. Good meat sir is comon that euery churle affords.

Anti. And welcome more common, for thats nothing but words.

Bal. Small cheere and great welcome, makes a merrie feast.

Anti. I, to a niggardly Host, and more sparing guest:
But though my cates be meane, take them in good part,
Better cheere may you haue, but not with better hart.
But soft, my doore is lockt; goe bid them let vs in.

E. Dro. *Maud, Briget, Marian, Cisley, Gillian, Ginn.*

S. Dro. Mome, Malthorse, Capon, Coxcombe, Idiot, Patch,
Either get thee from the dore, or sit downe at the hatch:
Dost thou coniure for wenches, that ÿ calst for such store,
When one is one too many, goe get thee from the dore.

E. Dro. What patch is made our Porter? my Master stayes in the street.

S. Dro. Let him walke from whence he came, lest hee catch cold on's feet.

E. Ant. Who talks within there? hoa, open the dore.

S. Dro. Right sir, Ile tell you when, and you'll tell me wherefore.

Ant. Wherefore? for my dinner: I haue not din'd to day.

S Dro. Not to day here you must not come againe when you may.

Anti. What art thou that keep'st mee out from the howse I owe?

S. Dro. The Porter for this time Sir, and my name is *Dromio*.

E. Dro. O villaine, thou hast stolne both mine office and my name,
The one nere got me credit, the other mickle blame
If thou hadst beene *Dromio* to day in my place,
Thou wouldst haue chang'd thy face for a name, or thy name for an asse.

Enter Luce.

Luce. What a coile is there *Dromio*? who are those at the gate?

E. Dro. Let my Master in *Luce*.

Luce. Faith no, hee comes too late, and so tell your Master.

E. Dro. O Lord I must laugh, haue at you with a Prouerbe,
Shall I set in my staffe.

Luce. Haue at you with another, that's when? can you tell?

S. Dro. If thy name be called *Luce*, *Luce* thou hast answer'd him well.

Anti. Doe you heare you minion, you'll let vs in I hope?

Luce. I thought to haue askt you

S. Dro. And you said no

E. Dro. So come helpe, well strooke, there was blow for blow.

Anti. Thou baggage let me in.

Luce. Can you tell for whose sake?

E. Drom. Master, knocke the doore hard,

Luce. Let him knocke till it ake.

Anti. You'll crie for this minion, if I beat the doore downe.

Luce What needs all that, and a paire of stocks in the towne?

Enter Adriana.

Adr. Who is that at the doore ÿ keeps all this noise?

S. Dro. By my troth your towne is troubled with vnruly boies.

Anti. Are you there Wife? you might haue come before.

Adri. Your wife sir knaue? go get you from the dore.

E. Dro. If you went in paine Master, this knaue wold goe sore.

Angelo. Heere is neither cheere sir, nor welcome, we would faine haue either.

Baltz. In debating which was best, wee shall part with neither.

E. Dro. They stand at the doore, Master, bid them welcome hither

Anti. There is something in the winde, that we cannot get in.

E. Dro. You would say so Master, if your garments were thin.
Your cake here is warme within: you stand here in the cold.
It would make a man mad as a Bucke to be so bought and sold.

Ant. Go fetch me something, Ile break ope the gate.

S. Dro. Breake any breaking here, and Ile breake your knaues pate.

E. Dro. A man may breake a word with your sir, and words are but winde:
I and breake it in your face, so he break it not behinde.

S. Dro. It seemes thou want'st breaking, out vpon thee hinde.

E. Dro. Here's too much out vpon thee, I pray thee let me in.

S. Dro. I, when fowles haue no feathers, and fish haue no fin

Ant Well, Ile breake in: go borrow me a crow.

E. Dro. A crow without feather, Master meane you so;
For

For a fiſh without a finne, ther's a fowle without a fether,
If a crow help vs in ſirra, wee'll plucke a crow together.
Ant. Go, get thee gon, fetch me an iron Crow.
Balth. Haue patience ſir, oh let it not be ſo,
Heerein you warre againſt your reputation,
And draw within the compaſſe of ſuſpect
Th'vnuiolated honor of your wife.
Once this your long experience of your wiſedome,
Her ſober vertue, yeares, and modeſtie,
Plead on your part ſome cauſe to you vnknowne;
And doubt not ſir, but ſhe will well excuſe
Why at this time the dores are made againſt you.
Be rul'd by me, depart in patience,
And let vs to the Tyger all to dinner,
And about euening come your ſelfe alone,
To know the reaſon of this ſtrange reſtraint:
If by ſtrong hand you offer to breake in
Now in the ſtirring paſſage of the day,
A vulgar comment will be made of it;
And that ſuppoſed by the common rowt
Againſt your yet vngalled eſtimation,
That may with foule intruſion enter in,
And dwell vpon your graue when you are dead;
For ſlander liues vpon ſucceſſion;
For euer hows'd, where it gets poſſeſſion.
Anti. You haue preuail'd, I will depart in quiet,
And in deſpight of mirth meane to be merrie:
I know a wench of excellent diſcourſe,
Prettie and wittie; wilde, and yet too gentle;
There will we dine: this woman that I meane
My wife (but I proteſt without deſert)
Hath oftentimes vpbraided me withall:
To her will we to dinner, get you home
And fetch the chaine, by this I know 'tis made,
Bring it I pray you to the *Porpentine*,
For there's the houſe: That chaine will I beſtow
(Be it for nothing but to ſpight my wife)
Vpon mine hoſteſſe there, good ſir make haſte:
Since mine owne doores refuſe to entertaine me,
Ile knocke elſe-where, to ſee if they'll diſdaine me.
Ang. Ile meet you at that place ſome houre hence.
Anti. Do ſo, this ieſt ſhall coſt me ſome expence.
Exeunt.

Enter Iuliena, with Antipholus of Siracuſia.

Iulia. And may it be that you haue quite forgot
A husbands office? ſhall *Antipholus*
Euen in the ſpring of Loue, thy Loue-ſprings rot?
Shall loue in buildings grow ſo ruinate?
If you did wed my ſiſter for her wealth,
Then for her wealths-ſake vſe her with more kindneſſe:
Or if you like elſe-where doe it by ſtealth,
Muffle your falſe loue with ſome ſhew of blindneſſe:
Let not my ſiſter read it in your eye:
Be not thy tongue thy owne ſhames Orator:
Looke ſweet, ſpeake faire, become diſloyaltie:
Apparell vice like vertues harbenger:
Beare a faire preſence, though your heart be tainted,
Teach ſinne the carriage of a holy Saint,
Be ſecret falſe: what need ſhe be acquainted?
What ſimple thiefe brags of his owne attaine?
Tis double wrong to truant with your bed,
And let her read it in thy lookes at boord:
Shame hath a baſtard fame, well managed,
Ill deeds is doubled with an euill word:
Alas poore women, make vs not beleeue
(Being compact of credit) that you loue vs,
Though others haue the arme, ſhew vs the ſleeue:
We in your motion turne, and you may moue vs.
Then gentle brother get you in againe;
Comfort my ſiſter, cheere her, call her wiſe;
'Tis holy ſport to be a little vaine,
When the ſweet breath of flatterie conquers ſtrife.
S. Anti. Sweete Miſtris, what your name is elſe I know not;
Nor by what wonder you do hit of mine:
Leſſe in your knowledge, and your grace you ſhow not,
Then our earths wonder, more then earth diuine.
Teach me deere creature how to thinke and ſpeake:
Lay open to my earthie groſſe conceit:
Smothred in errors, feeble, ſhallow, weake,
The foulded meaning of your words deceit:
Againſt my ſoules pure truth, why labour you,
To make it wander in an vnknowne field?
Are you a god? would you create me new?
Transforme me then, and to your powre Ile yeeld.
But if that I am I, then well I know,
Your weeping ſiſter is no wife of mine,
Nor to her bed no homage doe I owe:
Farre more, farre more, to you doe I decline:
Oh traine me not ſweet Mermaide with thy note,
To drowne me in thy ſiſter floud of teares:
Sing Siren for thy ſelfe, and I will dote:
Spread ore the ſiluer waues thy golden haires;
And as a bud Ile take thee, and there lie:
And in that glorious ſuppoſition thinke,
He gaines by death, that hath ſuch meanes to die:
Let Loue being light, be drowned if ſhe ſinke.
Luc. What are you mad, that you doe reaſon ſo?
Ant. Not mad, but mated, how I doe not know.
Luc. It is a fault that ſpringeth from your eie.
Ant. For gazing on your beames faire ſun being by.
Luc. Gaze when you ſhould, and that will cleere your ſight.
Ant. As good to winke ſweet loue, as looke on night.
Luc. Why call you me loue? Call my ſiſter ſo.
Ant. Thy ſiſters ſiſter.
Luc. That's my ſiſter.
Ant. No: it is thy ſelfe, mine owne ſelfes better part:
Mine eies cleere eie, my deere hearts deerer heart;
My foode, my fortune, and my ſweet hopes aime;
My ſole earths heauen, and my heauens claime.
Luc. All this my ſiſter is, or elſe ſhould be.
Ant. Call thy ſelfe ſiſter ſweet, for I am thee:
Thee will I loue, and with thee lead my life;
Thou haſt no husband yet, nor I no wife:
Giue me thy hand.
Luc. Oh ſoft ſir, hold you ſtill:
Ile fetch my ſiſter to get her good will. *Exit.*

Enter Dromio, Siracuſia.

Ant. Why how now *Dromio*, where run'ſt thou ſo faſt?
S.Dro. Doe you know me ſir? Am I *Dromio*? Am I your man? Am I my ſelfe?
Ant. Thou art *Dromio*, thou art my man, thou art thy ſelfe.
Dro. I am an aſſe, I am a womans man, and beſides my ſelfe.
Ant. What womans man? and how beſides thy ſelfe?
Dro. Marrie ſir, beſides my ſelfe, I am due to a woman: One that claimes me, one that haunts me, one that will haue me.

Ant. What

Anti. What claime laies she to thee?

Dro. Marry sir, such claime as you would lay to your horse, and she would haue me as a beast, not that I beeing a beast she would haue me, but that she being a verie beastly creature layes claime to me.

Anti. What is she?

Dro. A very reuerent body: I such a one, as a man may not speake of, without he say sir reuerence, I haue but leane lucke in the match, and yet is she a wondrous fat marriage

Anti. How dost thou meane a fat marriage?

Dro. Marry sir, she's the Kitchin wench, & al grease, and I know not what vse to put her too, but to make a Lampe of her, and run from her by her owne light. I warrant, her ragges and the Tallow in them, will burne a *Poland* Winter: If she liues till doomesday, she'l burne a weeke longer then the whole World

Anti. What complexion is she of?

Dro. Swart like my shoo, but her face nothing like so cleane kept: for why? she sweats a man may goe ouer-shooes in the grime of it.

Anti. That's a fault that water will mend.

Dro. No sir, 'tis in graine, *Noahs* flood could not do it

Anti. What's her name?

Dro. *Nell* Sir: but her name is three quarters, that's an Ell and three quarters, will not measure her from hip to hip.

Anti. Then she beares some bredth?

Dro. No longer from head to foot, then from hippe to hippe: she is sphericall, like a globe: I could find out Countries in her.

Anti. In what part of her body stands *Ireland*?

Dro. Marry sir in her buttockes, I found it out by the bogges.

Ant. Where *Scotland*?

Dro. I found it by the barrennesse, hard in the palme of the hand.

Ant. Where *France*?

Dro. In her forhead, arm'd and reuerted, making warre against her heire.

Ant. Where *England*?

Dro. I look'd for the chalkle Cliffes, but I could find no whitenesse in them. But I guesse, it stood in her chin by the salt rheume that ranne betweene *France*, and it.

Ant. Where *Spaine*?

Dro. Faith I saw it not: but I felt it hot in her breth.

Ant. Where *America*, the *Indies*?

Dro. Oh sir, vpon her nose, all ore embellished with Rubies, Carbuncles, Saphires, declining their rich Aspect to the hot breath of Spaine, who sent whole Armadoes of Carrects to be ballast at her nose.

Anti. Where stood *Belgia*, the *Netherlands*?

Dro. Oh sir, I did not looke so low. To conclude, this drudge or Diuiner layd claime to mee, call'd mee *Dromio*, swore I was assur'd to her, told me what priuie markes I had about mee, as the marke of my shoulder, the Mole in my necke, the great Wart on my left arme, that I amaz'd ranne from her as a witch. And I thinke, if my brest had not beene made of faith, and my heart of steele, she had transform'd me to a Curtull dog, & made me turne i'th wheele.

Anti. Go hie thee presently post to the rode,
And if the winde blow any way from shore,
I will not harbour in this Towne to night.
If any Barke put forth, come to the Mart,
Where I will walke till thou returne to me:
If euerie one knowes vs, and we know none,
'Tis time I thinke to trudge, packe, and be gone.

Dro. As from a Beare a man would run for life,
So flie I from her that would be my wife. *Exit*

Anti. There's none but Witches do inhabite heere,
And therefore 'tis hie time that I were hence:
She that doth call me husband, euen my soule
Doth for a wife abhorre. But her faire sister
Possest with such a gentle soueraigne grace,
Of such inchanting presence and discourse,
Hath almost made me Traitor to my selfe:
But least my selfe be guilty to selfe wrong,
Ile stop mine eares against the Mermaids song

Enter Angelo with the Chaine.

Ang. Mr *Antipholus.*

Anti. I that's my name.

Ang. I know it well sir, loe here's the chaine,
I thought to haue tane you at the *Porpentine*,
The chaine vnfinish'd made me stay thus long.

Anti What is your will that I shal do with this?

Ang What please your selfe sir: I haue made it for you.

Anti Made it for me sir, I bespoke it not.

Ang. Not once, nor twice, but twentie times you haue:
Go home with it, and please your Wife withall,
And soone at supper time Ile visit you,
And then receiue my money for the chaine.

Anti. I pray you sir receiue the money now,
For feare you ne're see chaine, nor mony more.

Ang. You are a merry man sir, fare you well. *Exit.*

Ant. What I should thinke of this, I cannot tell
But this I thinke, there's no man is so vaine,
That would refuse so faire an offer'd Chaine
I see a man heere needs not liue by shifts,
When in the streets he meetes such Golden gifts:
Ile to the Mart, and there for *Dromio* stay,
If any ship put out, then straight away *Exit*

Actus Quartus. Scœna Prima.

Enter a Merchant, Goldsmith, and an Officer.

Mar. You know since Pentecost the sum is due,
And since I haue not much importun'd you,
Nor now I had not, but that I am bound
To *Persia*, and want Gilders for my voyage
Therefore make present satisfaction,
Or Ile attach you by this Officer.

Gold. Euen iust the sum that I do owe to you,
Is growing to me by *Antipholus*,
And in the instant that I met with you,
He had of me a Chaine, at fiue a clocke
I shall receiue the money for the same.
Pleaseth you walke with me downe to his house,
I will discharge my bond, and thanke you too

Enter Antipholus Ephes. Dromio from the Courtizans.

Offi. That labour may you saue: See where he comes.

Ant. While I go to the Goldsmiths house, go thou

And

And buy a ropes end, that will I bestow
Among my wife, and their confederates,
For locking me out of my doores by day:
But soft I see the Goldsmith; get thee gone,
Buy thou a rope, and bring it home to me.
Dro. I buy a thousand pound a yeare, I buy a rope.
Exit Dromio
Eph.Ant. A man is well holpe vp that trusts to you,
I promised your presence, and the Chaine,
But neither Chaine nor Goldsmith came to me:
Belike you thought our loue would last too long
If it were chain'd together: and therefore came not.
Gold. Sauing your merrie humor: here's the note
How much your Chaine weighs to the vtmost charect,
The finenesse of the Gold, and chargefull fashion,
Which doth amount to three odde Duckets more
Then I stand debted to this Gentleman,
I pray you see him presently discharg'd,
For he is bound to Sea, and stayes but for it.
Anti. I am not furnish'd with the present monie:
Besides I haue some businesse in the towne,
Good Signior take the stranger to my house,
And with you take the Chaine, and bid my wife
Disburse the summe, on the receit thereof,
Perchance I will be there as soone as you.
Gold. Then you will bring the Chaine to her your selfe.
Anti. No beare it with you, least I come not time enough.
Gold. Well sir, I will? Haue you the Chaine about you?
Ant. And if I haue not sir, I hope you haue:
Or else you may returne without your money.
Gold. Nay come I pray you sir, giue me the Chaine:
Both winde and tide stayes for this Gentleman,
And I too blame haue held him heere too long.
Anti. Good Lord, you vse this dalliance to excuse
Your breach of promise to the *Porpentine*,
I should haue chid you for not bringing it,
But like a shrew you first begin to brawle.
Mar. The houre steales on, I pray you sir dispatch.
Gold. You heare how he importunes me, the Chaine.
Ant. Why giue it to my wife, and fetch your mony.
Gold. Come, come, you know I gaue it you euen now.
Either send the Chaine, or send me by some token.
Ant. Fie, now you run this humor out of breath,
Come where's the Chaine, I pray you let me see it.
Mar. My businesse cannot brooke this dalliance,
Good sir say, whe'r you'l answer me, or no:
If not, Ile leaue him to the Officer.
Ant. I answer you? What should I answer you.
Gold. The monie that you owe me for the Chaine.
Ant. I owe you none, till I receiue the Chaine.
Gold. You know I gaue it you halfe an houre since.
Ant. You gaue me none, you wrong mee much to say so.
Gold. You wrong me more sir in denying it.
Consider how it stands vpon my credit.
Mar. Well Officer, arrest him at my suite.
Offi. I do, and charge you in the Dukes name to obey me.
Gold. This touches me in reputation.
Either consent to pay this sum for me,
Or I attach you by this Officer.
Ant. Consent to pay thee that I neuer had:
Arrest me foolish fellow if thou dar'st.
Gold. Heere is thy fee, arrest him Officer.
I would not spare my brother in this case,
If he should scorne me so apparantly.
Offic. I do arrest you sir, you heare the suite.
Ant. I do obey thee, till I giue thee baile.
But sirrah, you shall buy this sport as deere,
As all the mettall in your shop will answer.
Gold. Sir, sir, I shall haue Law in *Ephesus*,
To your notorious shame, I doubt it not.

Enter Dromio Sira. from the Bay.

Dro. Master, there's a Barke of *Epidamium*,
That staies but till her Owner comes aboord,
And then sir she beares away. Our fraughtage sir,
I haue conuei'd aboord, and I haue bought
The Oyle, the *Balsamum*, and Aqua-vitæ.
The ship is in her trim, the merrie winde
Blowes faire from land: they stay for nought at all,
But for their Owner, Master, and your selfe.
An. How now? a Madman? Why thou peeuish sheep
What ship of *Epidamium* staies for me.
S.Dro. A ship you sent me too, to hier waftage.
Ant. Thou drunken slaue, I sent thee for a rope,
And told thee to what purpose, and what end.
S.Dro. You sent me for a ropes end as soone,
You sent me to the Bay sir, for a Barke.
Ant. I will debate this matter at more leisure
And teach your eares to list me with more heede:
To *Adriana* Villaine hie thee straight:
Giue her this key, and tell her in the Deske
That's couer'd o're with Turkish Tapistrie,
There is a purse of Duckets, let her send it:
Tell her, I am arrested in the streete,
And that shall baile me: hie thee slaue, be gone,
On Officer to prison, till it come. *Exeunt*
S. Dromio. To *Adriana*, that is where we din'd,
Where Dowsaball did claime me for her husband,
She is too bigge I hope for me to compasse,
Thither I must, although against my will:
For seruants must their Masters mindes fulfill. *Exit*

Enter Adriana and Luciana.

Adr. Ah *Luciana*, did he tempt thee so?
Might'st thou perceiue austeerely in his eie,
That he did plead in earnest, yea or no:
Look'd he or red or pale, or sad or merrily?
What obseruation mad'st thou in this case?
Oh, his hearts Meteors tilting in his face.
Luc. First he deni'de you had in him no right.
Adr. He meant he did me none: the more my spight
Luc. Then swore he that he was a stranger heere.
Adr. And true he swore, though yet forsworne hee were.
Luc. Then pleaded I for you.
Adr. And what said he?
Luc. That loue I begg'd for you, he begg'd of me.
Adr. With what perswasion did he tempt thy loue?
Luc. With words, that in an honest suit might moue.
First, he did praise my beautie, then my speech.
Adr. Did'st speake him faire?
Luc. Haue patience I beseech.
Adr. I cannot, nor I will not hold me still,
My tongue, though not my heart, shall haue his will.
He is deformed, crooked, old, and sere,
Ill-fac'd, worse bodied, shapelesse euery where:
Vicious, vngentle, foolish, blunt, vnkinde,

Stigma-

Stigmaticall in making w orse in minde.
Luc. Who would be iealous then of such a one?
No euill lost is wail'd, when it is gone.
Adr. Ah but I thinke him better then I say:
And yet would herein others eies were worse:
Farre from her nest the Lapwing cries away;
My heart praies for him, though my tongue doe curse.

Enter S.Dromio.

Dro. Here goe: the deske, the purse, sweet now make haste.
Luc. How hast thou lost thy breath?
S.Dro. By running fast.
Adr. Where is thy Master *Dromio*? Is he well?
S.Dro. No, he's in Tartar limbo, worse then hell:
A diuell in an euerlasting garment hath him;
On whose hard heart is button'd vp with steele:
A Feind, a Fairie, pittilesse and ruffe:
A Wolfe, nay worse, a fellow all in buffe:
A back friend, a shoulder-clapper, one that countermãds
The passages of allies, creekes, and narrow lands:
A hound that runs Counter, and yet draws drifoot well,
One that before the Iudgmẽt carries poore soules to hel.
Adr. Why man, what is the matter?
S.Dro. I doe not know the matter, hee is rested on the case.
Adr. What is he arrested? tell me at whose suite?
S.Dro. I know not at whose suite he is arested well; but is in a suite of buffe which rested him, that can I tell, will you send him Mistris redemption, the monie in his deske.
Adr. Go fetch it Sister: this I wonder at.
Exit Luciana.
Thus he vnknowne to me should be in debt:
Tell me, was he arested on a band?
S.Dro. Not on a band, but on a stronger thing:
A chaine, a chaine, doe you not here it ring.
Adria. What, the chaine?
S.Dro. No, no, the bell, 'tis time that I were gone:
It was two ere I left him, and now the clocke strikes one.
Adr. The houres come backe, that did I neue here.
S.Dro. Oh yes, if any houre meete a Serieant, a turnes backe for verie feare.
Adri. As if time were in debt: how fondly do'st thou reason?
S.Dro. Time is a verie bankerout, and owes more then he's worth to season.
Nay, he's a theefe too: haue you not heard men say,
That time comes stealing on by night and day?
If I be in debt and theft, and a Serieant in the way,
Hath he not reason to turne backe an houre in a day?

Enter Luciana.

Adr. Go *Dromio*, there's the monie, beare it straight,
And bring thy Master home imediately.
Come sister, I am prest downe with conceit:
Conceit, my comfort and my iniurie. *Exit.*

Enter Antipholus Siracusia.

There's not a man I meete but doth salute me
As if I were their well acquainted friend,
And euerie one doth call me by my name:
Some tender monie to me, some inuite me;
Some other giue me thankes for kindnesses;
Some offer me Commodities to buy.
Euen now a tailor cal'd me in his shop,
And show'd me Silkes that he had bought for me,
And therewithall tooke measure of my body.
Sure these are but imaginarie wiles,
And lapland Sorcerers inhabite here.

Enter Dromio. Sir.

S.Dro. Master, here's the gold you sent me for: what haue you got the picture of old *Adam* new apparel'd?
Ant What gold is this? What *Adam* do'st thou meane?
S.Dro. Not that *Adam* that kept the Paradise: but that *Adam* that keepes the prison; hee that goes in the calues-skin, that was kil'd for the Prodigall: hee that came behinde you sir, like an euill angel, and bid you forsake your libertie.
Ant. I vnderstand thee not.
S.Dro. No? why 'tis a plaine case: he that went like a Base-Viole in a case of leather; the man sir, that when gentlemen are tired giues them a sob, and rests them: he sir, that takes pittie on decaied men, and giues them suites of durance: he that sets vp his rest to doe more exploits with his Mace, then a Moris Pike.
Ant. What thou mean'st an officer?
S.Dro. I sir, the Serieant of the Band: he that brings any man to answer it that breakes his Band: one that thinkes a man alwaies going to bed, and saies, God giue you good rest.
Ant. Well sir, there rest in your foolerie:
Is there any ships puts forth to night? may we be gone?
S.Dro. Why sir, I brought you word an houre since, that the Barke *Expedition* put forth to night, and then were you hindred by the Serieant to tarry for the *Hoy Delay*: Here are the angels that you sent for to deliuer you.
Ant. The fellow is distract, and so am I,
And here we wander in illusions:
Some blessed power deliuer vs from hence.

Enter a Curtizan.

Cur. Well met, well met, Master *Antipholus*:
I see sir you haue found the Gold-smith now:
Is that the chaine you promis'd me to day.
Ant. Sathan auoide, I charge thee tempt me not.
S.Dro. Master, is this Mistris *Sathan*?
Ant. It is the diuell.
S.Dro. Nay, she is worse, she is the diuels dam:
And here she comes in the habit of a light wench, and thereof comes, that the wenches say God dam me, That's as much to say, God make me a light wench: It is written, they appeare to men like angels of light, light is an effect of fire, and fire will burne: *ergo*, light wenches will burne, come not neere her.
Cur. Your man and you are maruailous merrie sir.
Will you goe with me, wee'll mend our dinner here?
S.Dro. Master, if do expect spoon-meate, or bespeake a long spoone.
Ant. Why *Dromio*?
S.Dro. Marrie he must haue a long spoone that must eate with the diuell.
Ant. Auoid then fiend, what tel'st thou me of supping?
Thou art, as you are all a sorceresse:
I coniure thee to leaue me, and be gon.
Cur. Giue me the ring of mine you had at dinner,
Or for my Diamond the Chaine you promis'd,
And Ile be gone sir, and not trouble you.
S.Dro. Some diuels aske but the parings of ones naile,

a rush, a haire, a drop of blood, a pin, a nut, a cherrie-stone: but she more couetous, wold haue a chaine: Master be wise, and if you giue it her, the diuell will shake her Chaine, and fright vs with it.

Cur. I pray you sir my Ring, or else the Chaine,
I hope you do not meane to cheate me so?

Ant. Auant thou witch: Come *Dromio* let vs go.

S.Dro. Flie pride saies the Pea-cocke, Mistris that you know. *Exit.*

Cur. Now out of doubt *Antipholus* is mad,
Else would he neuer so demeane himselfe,
A Ring he hath of mine worth fortie Duckets,
And for the same he promis'd me a Chaine,
Both one and other he denies me now:
The reason that I gather he is mad,
Besides this present instance of his rage,
Is a mad tale he told to day at dinner,
Of his owne doores being shut against his entrance.
Belike his wife acquainted with his fits,
On purpose shut the doores against his way:
My way is now to hie home to his house,
And tell his wife, that being Lunaticke,
He rush'd into my house, and tooke perforce
My Ring away. This course I fittest choose,
For fortie Duckets is too much to loose.

Enter Antipholus Ephes. with a Iailor.

An. Feare me not man, I will not breake away,
Ile giue thee ere I leaue thee so much money
To warrant thee as I am rested for.
My wife is in a wayward moode to day,
And will not lightly trust the Messenger,
That I should be attach'd in *Ephesus*,
I tell you 'twill sound harshly in her eares.

Enter Dromio Eph. with a ropes end.

Heere comes my Man, I thinke he brings the monie.
How now sir? Haue you that I sent you for?

E.Dro. Here's that I warrant you will pay them all.

Anti. But where's the Money?

E.Dro. Why sir, I gaue the Monie for the Rope.

Ant. Fiue hundred Duckets villaine for a rope?

E. Dro. Ile serue you sir fiue hundred at the rate.

Ant. To what end did I bid thee hie thee home?

E.Dro. To a ropes end sir, and to that end am I return'd.

Ant. And to that end sir, I will welcome you.

Offi. Good sir be patient.

E.Dro. Nay 'tis for me to be patient, I am in aduersitie.

Offi. Good now hold thy tongue.

E.Dro. Nay, rather perswade him to hold his hands.

Anti. Thou whoreson senselesse Villaine.

E.Dro. I would I were senselesse sir, that I might not feele your blowes.

Anti. Thou art sensible in nothing but blowes, and so is an Asse.

E.Dro. I am an Asse indeede, you may prooue it by my long eares. I haue serued him from the houre of my Natiuitie to this instant, and haue nothing at his hands for my seruice but blowes. When I am cold, he heates me with beating: when I am warme, he cooles me with beating: I am wak'd with it when I sleepe, rais'd with it when I sit, driuen out of doores with it when I goe from home, welcom'd home with it when I returne, nay I beare it on my shoulders, as a begger woont her brat: and I thinke when he hath lam'd me, I shall begge with it from doore to doore.

Enter Adriana, Luciana, Courtizan, and a Schoole-master, call'd Pinch.

Ant. Come goe along, my wife is comming yonder

E.Dro. Mistris *respice finem*, respect your end, or rather the prophesie like the Parrat, beware the ropes end.

Anti. Wilt thou still talke? *Beats Dro.*

Curt. How say you now? Is not your husband mad?

Adri. His inciuility confirmes no lesse:
Good Doctor *Pinch*, you are a Coniurer,
Establish him in his true sence againe,
And I will please you what you will demand.

Luc. Alas how fiery, and how sharpe he lookes.

Cur. Marke, how he trembles in his extasie.

Pinch. Giue me your hand, and let mee feele your pulse.

Ant. There is my hand, and let it feele your eare.

Pinch. I charge thee Sathan, hous'd within this man,
To yeeld possession to my holie praiers,
And to thy state of darknesse hie thee straight,
I coniure thee by all the Saints in heauen.

Anti. Peace doting wizard, peace; I am not mad.

Adr. Oh that thou wer't not, poore distressed soule.

Anti. You Minion you, are these your Customers?
Did this Companion with the saffron face
Reuell and feast it at my house to day,
Whil'st vpon me the guiltie doores were shut,
And I denied to enter in my house.

Adr. O husband, God doth know you din'd at home
Where would you had remain'd vntill this time,
Free from these slanders, and this open shame.

Anti. Din'd at home? Thou Villaine, what sayest thou?

Dro. Sir sooth to say, you did not dine at home.

Ant. Were not my doores lockt vp, and I shut out?

Dro. Perdie, your doores were lockt, and you shut out.

Anti. And did not she her selfe reuile me there?

Dro. *Sans* Fable, she her selfe reuil'd you there.

Anti. Did not her Kitchen maide raile, taunt, and scorne me?

Dro. *Certis* she did, the kitchin vestall scorn'd you.

Ant. And did not I in rage depart from thence?

Dro. In veritie you did, my bones beares witnesse,
That since haue felt the vigor of his rage.

Adr. Is't good to sooth him in these crontraries?

Pinch. It is no shame, the fellow finds his vaine,
And yeelding to him, humors well his frensie.

Ant. Thou hast subborn'd the Goldsmith to arrest mee.

Adr. Alas, I sent you Monie to redeeme you,
By *Dromio* heere, who came in hast for it.

Dro. Monie by me? Heart and good will you might
But surely Master not a ragge of Monie.

Ant. Wentst not thou to her for a purse of Duckets.

Adri. He came to me, and I deliuer'd it.

Luci. And I am witnesse with her that she did:

Dro. God and the Rope-maker beare me witnesse,
That I was sent for nothing but a rope.

Pinch. Mistris, both Man and Master is possest,
I know it by their pale and deadly lookes,

They

They muſt be bound and laide in ſome darke roome.

Ant. Say wherefore didſt thou locke me forth to day,
And why doſt thou denie the bagge of gold?

Adr. I did not gentle husband locke thee forth.

Dro. And gentle Mr I receiu'd no gold :
But I confeſſe ſir, that we were lock'd out.

Adr. Diſſembling Villain, thou ſpeak'ſt falſe in both

Ant. Diſſembling harlot, thou art falſe in all,
And art confederate with a damned packe,
To make a loathſome abiect ſcorne of me :
But with theſe nailes, Ile plucke out theſe falſe eyes,
That would behold in me this ſhamefull ſport.

Enter three or foure, and offer to binde him: Hee ſtriues.

Adr. Oh binde him, binde him, let him not come neere me.

Pinch. More company, the fiend is ſtrong within him

Luc. Aye me poore man, how pale and wan he looks.

Ant. What will you murther me, thou Iailor thou? I am thy priſoner, wilt thou ſuffer them to make a reſcue?

Offi. Maſters let him go : he is my priſoner, and you ſhall not haue him.

Pinch. Go binde this man, for he is franticke too.

Adr. What wilt thou do, thou peeuiſh Officer?
Haſt thou delight to ſee a wretched man
Do outrage and diſpleaſure to himſelfe?

Offi. He is my priſoner, if I let him go,
The debt he owes will be requir'd of me.

Adr. I will diſcharge thee ere I go from thee,
Beare me forthwith vnto his Creditor,
And knowing how the debt growes I will pay it.
Good Maſter Doctor ſee him ſafe conuey'd
Home to my houſe, oh moſt vnhappy day.

Ant. Oh moſt vnhappie ſtrumpet.

Dro. Maſter, I am heere entred in bond for you.

Ant. Out on thee Villaine, wherefore doſt thou mad mee?

Dro. Will you be bound for nothing, be mad good Maſter, cry the diuell.

Luc. God helpe poore ſoules, how idlely doe they talke.

Adr. Go beare him hence, ſiſter go you with me:
Say now, whoſe ſuite is he arreſted at?

Exeunt. Manet Offic. Adri. Luci. Courtizan

Off. One *Angelo* a Goldſmith, do you know him?

Adr. I know the man : what is the ſumme he owes?

Off. Two hundred Duckets.

Adr. Say, how growes it due.

Off. Due for a Chaine your husband had of him.

Adr. He did beſpeake a Chain for me, but had it not.

Cur. When as your husband all in rage to day
Came to my houſe, and tooke away my Ring,
The Ring I ſaw vpon his finger now,
Straight after did I meete him with a Chaine.

Adr. It may be ſo, but I did neuer ſee it.
Come Iailor, bring me where the Goldſmith is,
I long to know the truth heereof at large

Enter Antipholus Siracuſia with his Rapier drawne, and Dromio Sirac.

Luc. God for thy mercy, they are looſe againe.

Adr. And come with naked ſwords,
Let's call more helpe to haue them bound againe.

Runne all out.

Off. Away, they'l kill vs.

Exeunt omnes, as faſt as may be, frighted.

S. Ant. I ſee theſe Witches are affraid of ſwords.

S. Dro. She that would be your wife, now ran from you.

Ant. Come to the Centaur, fetch our ſtuffe from thence :
I long that we were ſafe and ſound aboord.

Dro. Faith ſtay heere this night, they will ſurely do vs no harme : you ſaw they ſpeake vs faire, giue vs gold: me thinkes they are ſuch a gentle Nation, that but for the Mountaine of mad fleſh that claimes mariage of me, I could finde in my heart to ſtay heere ſtill, and turne Witch.

Ant. I will not ſtay to night for all the Towne,
Therefore away, to get our ſtuffe aboord. *Exeunt*

Actus Quintus. Scœna Prima.

Enter the Merchant and the Goldſmith.

Gold. I am ſorry Sir that I haue hindred you,
But I proteſt he had the Chaine of me,
Though moſt diſhoneſtly he doth denie it.

Mar. How is the man eſteem'd heere in the Citie?

Gold. Of very reuerent reputation ſir,
Of credit infinite, highly belou'd,
Second to none that liues heere in the Citie :
His word might beare my wealth at any time.

Mar Speake ſoftly, yonder as I thinke he walkes.

Enter Antipholus and Dromio againe.

Gold. 'Tis ſo : and that ſelfe chaine about his necke,
Which he forſwore moſt monſtrouſly to haue.
Good ſir draw neere to me, Ile ſpeake to him :
Signior *Antipholus*, I wonder much
That you would put me to this ſhame and trouble,
And not without ſome ſcandall to your ſelfe,
With circumſtance and oaths, ſo to denie
This Chaine, which now you weare ſo openly.
Beſide the charge, the ſhame, impriſonment,
You haue done wrong to this my honeſt friend,
Who but for ſtaying on our Controuerſie,
Had hoiſted ſaile, and put to ſea to day:
This Chaine you had of me, can you deny it?

Ant. I thinke I had, I neuer did deny it.

Mar. Yes that you did ſir, and forſwore it too.

Ant. Who heard me to denie it or forſweare it?

Mar. Theſe eares of mine thou knowſt did hear thee :
Fie on thee wretch, 'tis pitty that thou liu'ſt
To walke where any honeſt men reſort.

Ant. Thou art a Villaine to impeach me thus,
Ile proue mine honor, and mine honeſtie
Againſt thee preſently, if thou dar'ſt ſtand:

Mar. I dare and do defie thee for a villaine.

They draw. Enter Adriana, Luciana, Courtezan, & others.

Adr. Hold, hurt him not for God ſake, he is mad,
Some get within him, take his ſword away :
Binde *Dromio* too, and beare them to my houſe.

S. Dro. Runne maſter run, for Gods ſake take a houſe,
This is ſome Priorie, in, or we are ſpoyl'd.

Exeunt to the Priorie.

Enter

Enter Ladie Abbesse

Ab. Be quiet people, wherefore throng you hither?
Adr. To fetch my poore distracted husband hence,
Let vs come in, that we may binde him fast,
And beare him home for his recouerie.
Gold. I knew he vvas not in his perfect wits.
Mar. I am sorry now that I did draw on him.
Ab. How long hath this possession held the man.
Adr. This weeke he hath beene heauie, sower sad,
And much different from the man he was:
But till this afternoone his passion
Ne're brake into extremity of rage.
Ab. Hath he not lost much wealth by wrack of sea,
Buried some deere friend, hath not else his eye
Stray'd his affection in vnlawfull loue,
A sinne preuailing much in youthfull men,
Who giue their eies the liberty of gazing.
Which of these sorrowes is he subiect too?
Adr. To none of these, except it be the last,
Namely, some loue that drew him oft from home.
Ab. You should for that haue reprehended him.
Adr. Why so I did.
Ab. I but not rough enough.
Adr. As roughly as my modestie would let me.
Ab. Haply in priuate.
Adr. And in assemblies too.
Ab. I, but not enough.
Adr. It was the copie of our Conference.
In bed he slept not for my vrging it,
At boord he fed not for my vrging it:
Alone, it was the subiect of my Theame:
In company I often glanced it:
Still did I tell him, it was vilde and bad.
Ab. And thereof came it, that the man was mad.
The venome clamors of a iealous woman,
Poisons more deadly then a mad dogges tooth.
It seemes his sleepes were hindred by thy railing,
And thereof comes it that his head is light.
Thou saist his meate was sawc'd with thy vpbraidings,
Vnquiet meales make ill digestions,
Thereof the raging fire of feauer bred,
And what's a Feauer, but a fit of madnesse?
Thou sayest his sports were hindred by thy bralles.
Sweet recreation barr'd, what doth ensue
But moodie and dull melancholly,
Kinsman to grim and comfortlesse dispaire,
And at her heeles a huge infectious troope
Of pale distemperatures, and foes to life?
In food, in sport, and life-preseruing rest
To be disturb'd, would mad or man, or beast:
The consequence is then, thy iealous fits
Hath scar'd thy husband from the vse of wits.
Luc. She neuer reprehended him but mildely,
When he demean'd himselfe, rough, rude, and wildly,
Why beare you these rebukes, and answer not?
Adri. She did betray me to my owne reproofe,
Good people enter, and lay hold on him.
Ab. No not a creature enters in my house.
Ad. Then let your seruants bring my husband forth
Ab. Neither: he tooke this place for sanctuary,
And it shall priuiledge him from your hands,
Till I haue brought him to his wits againe,
Or loose my labour in assaying it.
Adr. I will attend my husband, be his nurse,
Diet his sicknesse, for it is my Office,
And will haue no atturney but my selfe,
And therefore let me haue him home with me.
Ab. Be patient, for I will not let him stirre,
Till I haue vs'd the approoued meanes I haue,
With wholsome sirrups, drugges, and holy prayers
To make of him a formall man againe:
It is a branch and parcell of mine oath,
A charitable dutie of my order,
Therefore depart, and leaue him heere with me.
Adr. I will not hence, and leaue my husband heere:
And ill it doth beseeme your holinesse
To separate the husband and the wife.
Ab. Be quiet and depart, thou shalt not haue him.
Luc. Complaine vnto the Duke of this indignity
Adr. Come go, I will fall prostrate at his feete,
And neuer rise vntill my teares and prayers
Haue won his grace to come in person hither,
And take perforce my husband from the Abbesse.
Mar. By this I thinke the Diall points at fiue:
Anon I'me sure the Duke himselfe in person
Comes this way to the melancholly vale;
The place of depth, and sorrie execution,
Behinde the ditches of the Abbey heere.
Gold. Vpon what cause?
Mar. To see a reuerent *Siracusian* Merchant,
Who put vnluckily into this Bay
Against the Lawes and Statutes of this Towne,
Beheaded publikely for his offence.
Gold. See where they come, we wil behold his death
Luc. Kneele to the Duke before he passe the Abbey.

Enter the Duke of Ephesus, and the Merchant of Siracuse bare head, with the Headsman, & other Officers.

Duke. Yet once againe proclaime it publikely,
If any friend will pay the summe for him,
He shall not die, so much we tender him.
Adr. Iustice most sacred Duke against the Abbesse.
Duke. She is a vertuous and a reuerend Lady,
It cannot be that she hath done thee wrong.
Adr. May it please your Grace, *Antipholus* my husbad,
Who I made Lord of me, and all I had,
At your important Letters this ill day,
A most outragious fit of madnesse tooke him:
That desp'rately he hurried through the streete,
With him his bondman, all as mad as he,
Doing displeasure to the Citizens,
By rushing in their houses: bearing thence
Rings, Iewels, any thing his rage did like.
Once did I get him bound, and sent him home,
Whil'st to take order for the wrongs I went,
That heere and there his furie had committed,
Anon I wot not, by what strong escape
He broke from those that had the guard of him,
And with his mad attendant and himselfe,
Each one with irefull passion, with drawne swords
Met vs againe, and madly bent on vs
Chac'd vs away: till raising of more aide
We came againe to binde them: then they fled
Into this Abbey, whether we pursu'd them,
And heere the Abbesse shuts the gates on vs,
And will not suffer vs to fetch him out,
Nor send him forth, that we may beare him hence.

I Therefore

Therefore most gracious Duke with thy command,
Let him be brought forth,and borne hence for helpe.
Duke. Long since thy husband seru'd me in my wars
And I to thee ingag'd a Princes word,
When thou didst make him Master of thy bed,
To do him all the grace and good I could.
Go some of you, knocke at the Abbey gate,
And bid the Lady Abbesse come to me:
I will determine this before I stirre.

Enter a Messenger.

Oh Mistris,Mistris, shift and saue your selfe,
My Master and his man are both broke loose,
Beaten the Maids a-row, and bound the Doctor,
Whose beard they haue sindg'd off with brands of fire,
And euer as it blaz'd, they threw on him
Great pailes of puddled myre to quench the haire;
My M' preaches patience to him, and the while
His man with Cizers nickes him like a foole:
And sure (vnlesse you send some present helpe)
Betweene them they will kill the Coniurer.
Adr. Peace foole, thy Master and his man are here,
And that is false thou dost report to vs.
Mess. Mistris, vpon my life I tel you true,
I haue not breath'd almost since I did see it.
He cries for you, and vowes if he can take you,
To scorch your face, and to disfigure you:

Cry within.

Harke, harke, I heare him Mistris: flie, be gone.
Duke. Come stand by me,feare nothing: guard with Halberds.
Adr. Ay me, it is my husband: witnesse you,
That he is borne about inuisible,
Euen now we hous'd him in the Abbey heere.
And now he's there,past thought of humane reason.

Enter Antipholus, and E. Dromio of Ephesus.

E.Ant. Iustice most gracious Duke,oh grant me iustice,
Euen for the seruice that long since I did thee,
When I bestrid thee in the warres, and tooke
Deepe scarres to saue thy life; euen for the blood
That then I lost for thee, now grant me iustice.
Mar.Fat. Vnlesse the feare of death doth make me dote, I see my sonne *Antipholus* and *Dromio.*
E.Ant. Iustice(sweet Prince)against ỳ Woman there:
She whom thou gau'st to me to be my wife;
That hath abused and dishonored me,
Euen in the strength and height of iniurie:
Beyond imagination is the wrong
That she this day hath shamelesse throwne on me.
Duke. Discouer how, and thou shalt finde me iust.
E.Ant. This day (great Duke) she shut the doores vpon me,
While she with Harlots feasted in my house.
Duke. A greeuous fault: say woman, didst thou so?
Adr. No my good Lord. My selfe,he,and my sister,
To day did dine together: so befall my soule,
As this is false he burthens me withall.
Luc. Nere may I looke on day,nor sleepe on night,
But she tels to your Highnesse simple truth.
Gold. O periur'd woman! They are both forsworne,
In this the Madman iustly chargeth them.
E,Ant. My Liege, I am aduised what I say,
Neither disturbed with the effect of Wine,
Nor headie-rash prouoak'd with raging ire,
Albeit my wrongs might make one wiser mad.
This woman lock'd me out this day from dinner;
That Goldsmith there, were he not pack'd with her,
Could witnesse it: for he was with me then,
Who parted with me to go fetch a Chaine,
Promising to bring it to the Porpentine,
Where *Balthasar* and I did dine together.
Our dinner done, and he not comming thither,
I went to seeke him. In the street I met him,
And in his companie that Gentleman.
There did this periur'd Goldsmith sweare me downe,
That I this day of him receiu'd the Chaine,
Which God he knowes, I saw not. For the which,
He did arrest me with an Officer.
I did obey, and sent my Pesant home
For certaine Duckets: he with none return'd.
Then fairely I bespoke the Officer
To go in person with me to my house.
By th'way, we met my wife,her sister,and a rabble more
Of vilde Confederates: Along with them
They brought one *Pinch*, a hungry leane-fac'd Villaine;
A meere Anatomie, a Mountebanke,
A thred-bare Iugler, and a Fortune-teller,
A needy-hollow-ey'd-sharpe-looking-wretch;
A liuing dead man. This pernicious slaue,
Forsooth tooke on him as a Coniurer:
And gazing in mine eyes, feeling my pulse,
And with no-face (as 'twere) out-facing me,
Cries out, I was possest. Then altogether
They fell vpon me, bound me, bore me thence,
And in a darke and dankish vault at home
There left me and my man, both bound together,
Till gnawing with my teeth my bonds in sunder,
I gain'd my freedome; and immediately
Ran hether to your Grace, whom I beseech
To giue me ample satisfaction
For these deepe shames, and great indignities.
Gold. My Lord, in truth, thus far I witnes with him:
That he din'd not at home, but was lock'd out.
Duke. But had he such a Chaine of thee, or no?
Gold. He had my Lord,and when he ran in heere,
These people saw the Chaine about his necke.
Mar. Besides, I will be sworne these eares of mine,
Heard you confesse you had the Chaine of him,
After you first forswore it on the Mart,
And thereupon I drew my sword on you,
And then you fled into this Abbey heere,
From whence I thinke you are come by Miracle.
E.Ant. I neuer came within these Abbey wals,
Nor euer didst thou draw thy sword on me:
I neuer saw the Chaine, so helpe me heauen:
And this is false you burthen me withall.
Duke. Why what an intricate impeach is this?
I thinke you all haue drunke of *Circes* cup:
If heere you hous'd him, heere he would haue bin.
If he were mad, he would not pleade so coldly:
You say he din'd at home, the Goldsmith heere
Denies that saying. Sirra, what say you?
E.Dro. Sir he din'de with her there,at the Porpentine.
Cur. He did, and from my finger snacht that Ring.
E.Anti. Tis true (my Liege) this Ring I had of her.
Duke. Saw'st thou him enter at the Abbey heere?
Curt. As sure (my Liege) as I do see your Grace.
Duke. Why this is straunge: Go call the Abbesse hither.
I thinke you are all mated, or starke mad.

Exit

Exit one to the Abbesse.

Fa. Most mighty Duke, vouchsafe me speak a word:
Haply I see a friend will saue my life,
And pay the sum that may deliuer me.

Duke. Speake freely *Siracusian* what thou wilt.

Fath. Is not your name sir call'd *Antipholus*?
And is not that your bondman *Dromio*?

E. Dro. Within this houre I was his bondman sir,
But he I thanke him gnaw'd in two my cords,
Now am I *Dromio*, and his man, vnbound.

Fath. I am sure you both of you remember me.

Dro. Our selues we do remember sir by you:
For lately we were bound as you are now.
You are not *Pinches* patient, are you sir?

Father. Why looke you strange on me? you know me well.

E. Ant. I neuer saw you in my life till now.

Fa. Oh! griefe hath chang'd me since you saw me last,
And carefull houres with times deformed hand,
Haue written strange defeatures in my face:
But tell me yet, dost thou not know my voice?

Ant. Neither.

Fat. *Dromio*, nor thou?

Dro. No trust me sir, nor I.

Fa. I am sure thou dost?

E. Dromio. I sir, but I am sure I do not, and whatsoeuer a man denies, you are now bound to beleeue him.

Fath. Not know my voice, oh times e tremity
Hast thou so crack'd and splitted my poore tongue
In seuen short yeares, that heere my onely sonne
Knowes not my feeble key of vntun'd cares?
Though now this grained face of mine be hid
In sap-consuming Winters drizled snow,
And all the Conduits of my blood froze vp:
Yet hath my night of life some memorie:
My wasting lampes some fading glimmer left;
My dull deafe eares a little vse to heare:
All these old witnesses, I cannot erre.
Tell me, thou art my sonne *Antipholus*.

Ant. I neuer saw my Father in my life.

Fa. But seuen yeares since, in *Siracusa* boy
Thou know'st we parted, but perhaps my sonne,
Thou sham'st to acknowledge me in miserie.

Ant. The Duke, and all that know me in the City,
Can witnesse with me that it is not so.
I ne're saw *Seracusa* in my life

Duke. I tell thee *Siracusian*, twentie yeares
Haue I bin Patron to *Antipholus*,
During which time, he ne're saw *Siracusa*:
I see thy age and dangers make thee dote.

Enter the Abbesse with Antipholus Siracusa, and Dromio Sir.

Abbesse. Most mightie Duke, behold a man much wrong'd.

All gather to see them.

Adr. I see two husbands, or mine eyes deceiue me

Duke. One of these men is *genius* to the other:
And so of these, which is the naturall man,
And which the spirit? Who deciphers them?

S. Dromio. I Sir am *Dromio*, command him away.

E. Dro. I Sir am *Dromio*, pray let me stay.

S. Ant. *Egeon* art thou not? or else his ghost.

S. Drom. Oh my olde Master, who hath bound him heere?

Abb. Who euer bound him, I will lose his bonds,
And gaine a husband by his libertie:
Speake olde *Egeon*, if thou bee'st the man
That hadst a wife once call'd *Æmilia*,
That bore thee at a burthen two faire sonnes?
Oh if thou bee'st the same *Egeon*, speake:
And speake vnto the same *Æmilia*.

Duke. Why heere begins his Morning storie right:
These two *Antipholus*, these two so like,
And these two *Dromio's*, one in semblance:
Besides her vrging of her wracke at sea,
These are the parents to these children,
Which accidentally are met together.

Fa. If I dreame not, thou art *Æmilia*,
If thou art she, tell me, where is that sonne
That floated with thee on the fatall rafte.

Abb. By men of *Epidamium*, he, and I,
And the twin *Dromio*, all were taken vp;
But by and by, rude Fishermen of *Corinth*
By force tooke *Dromio*, and my sonne from them,
And me they left with those of *Epidamium*.
What then became of them, I cannot tell:
I, to this fortune that you see mee in.

Duke. *Antipholus* thou cam'st from *Corinth* first.

S. Ant. No sir, not I, I came from *Siracuse*.

Duke. Stay, stand apart, I know not which is which.

E. Ant. I came from *Corinth* my most gracious Lord

E. Dro. And I with him.

E. Ant. Brought to this Town by that most famous Warriour,
Duke *Menaphon*, your most renowned Vnckle.

Adr. Which of you two did dine with me to day?

S. Ant. I, gentle Mistris.

Adr. And are not you my husband?

E. Ant. No, I say nay to that.

S. Ant. And so do I, yet did she call me so:
And this faire Gentlewoman her sister heere
Did call me brother. What I told you then,
I hope I shall haue leisure to make good,
If this be not a dreame I see and heare.

Goldsmith. That is the Chaine sir, which you had of mee.

S. Ant. I thinke it be sir, I denie it not.

E. Ant. And you sir for this Chaine arrested me.

Gold. I thinke I did sir, I deny it not.

Adr. I sent you monie sir to be your baile
By *Dromio*, but I thinke he brought it not.

E. Dro No, none by me.

S. Ant. This purse of Duckets I receiu'd from you,
And *Dromio* my man did bring them me:
I see we still did meete each others man,
And I was tane for him, and he for me,
And thereupon these errors are arose.

E. Ant. These Duckets pawne I for my father heere.

Duke. It shall not neede, thy father hath his life.

Cur. Sir I must haue that Diamond from you.

E. Ant. There take it, and much thanks for my good cheere.

Abb. Renowned Duke, vouchsafe to take the paines
To go with vs into the Abbey heere
And heare at large discoursed all our fortunes
And all that are assembled in this place:
That by this simpathized one daies error
Haue suffer'd wrong. Goe, keepe vs companie,

And

And we shall make fu ll satisfaction.
Thirtie three yeares h aue I but gone in trauaile ;
Of you my sonnes, an d till this present houre
My heauie burthen ar e deliuered :
The Duke my husband, and my children both,
And you the Kalenders of their Natiuity,
Go to a Gossips feast, and go with mee,
After so long greefe such Natiuitie.

Duke. With all my heart, Ile Gossip at this feast.

Exeunt omnes. Manet the two Dromio's and two Brothers.

S.Dro. Mast.shall I fetch your stuffe from shipbord?

E An.Dromio, what stuffe of mine hast thou imbarkt

S Dro. Your goods that lay at host sir in the Centaur.

S.Ant. He speakes to me, I am your master *Dromio.*
Come go with vs, wee'l looke to that anon,
Embrace thy brother there, reioyce with him. *Exit*

S.Dro. There is a fat friend at your masters house,
That kitchin'd me for you to day at dinner :
She now shall be my sister, not my wife,

E.D. Me thinks you are my glasse,& not my brother :
I see by you, I am a sweet-fac'd youth,
Will you walke in to see their gossipping?

S.Dro. Not I sir, you are my elder.

E.Dro. That's a question, how shall we trie it.

S.Dro. Wee l draw Cuts for the Signior, till then, lead thou first.

E.Dro. Nay then thus :
We came into the world like brother and brother :
And now let's go hand in hand, not one before another

Exeunt

FINIS.

Much adoe about Nothing.

Actus primus, Scena prima.

Enter Leonato Gouernour of Meſſina, Innogen his wife, Hero his daughter, and Beatrice his Neece, with a meſſenger.

Leonato.

I Learne in this Letter, that *Don Peter* of *Arragon*, comes this night to *Meſſina*.

Meſſ. He is very neere by this: he was not three Leagues off when I left him

Leon. How many Gentlemen haue you loſt in this action?

Meſſ. But few of any ſort, and none of name.

Leon. A victorie is twice it ſelfe, when the atchieuer brings home full numbers: I finde heere, that Don *Peter* hath beſtowed much honor on a yong *Florentine*, called *Claudio*.

Meſſ. Much deſeru'd on his part, and equally remembred by Don *Pedro*, he hath borne himſelfe beyond the promiſe of his age, doing in the figure of a Lambe, the feats of a Lion, he hath indeede better bettred expectation, then you muſt expect of me to tell you how.

Leo. He hath an Vnckle heere in *Meſſina*, wil be very much glad of it.

Meſſ. I haue alreadie deliuered him letters, and there appeares much ioy in him, euen ſo much, that ioy could not ſhew it ſelfe modeſt enough, without a badg of bitterneſſe.

Leo. Did he breake out into teares?

Meſſ. In great meaſure

Leo. A kinde ouerflow of kindneſſe, there are no faces truer, then thoſe that are ſo waſh'd, how much better is it to weepe at ioy, then to ioy at weeping?

Bea. I pray you, is Signior *Mountanto* return'd from the warres, or no?

Meſſ. I know none of that name, Lady, there was none ſuch in the armie of any ſort.

Leon. What is he that you aſke for Neece?

Hero. My couſin meanes Signior Benedick of *Padua*

Meſſ. O he's return'd, and as pleaſant as euer he was.

Beat. He ſet vp his bils here in *Meſſina*, & challeng'd Cupid at the Flight: and my Vnckles foole reading the Challenge, ſubſcrib'd for Cupid, and challeng'd him at the Burbolt. I pray you, how many hath hee kil'd and eaten in theſe warres? But how many hath he kil'd? for indeed, I promis'd to eate all of his killing.

Leon. 'Faith Neece, you taxe Signior Benedicke too much, but hee'l be meet with you, I doubt it not

Meſſ. He hath done good ſeruice Lady in theſe wars.

Beat. You had muſty victuall, and he hath holpe to eaſe it: he's a very valiant Trencher-man, hee hath an excellent ſtomacke.

Meſſ. And a good ſouldier too Lady.

Beat. And a good ſouldier to a Lady. But what is he to a Lord?

Meſſ. A Lord to a Lord, a man to a man, ſtuft with all honourable vertues.

Beat. It is ſo indeed, he is no leſſe then a ſtuft man: but for the ſtuffing well, we are all mortall.

Leon. You muſt not (ſir) miſtake my Neece, there is a kind of merry war betwixt Signior Benedick, & her: they neuer meet, but there's a skirmiſh of wit between them.

Bea. Alas, he gets nothing by that. In our laſt conflict, foure of his fiue wits went halting off, and now is the whole man gouern'd with one: ſo that if hee haue wit enough to keepe himſelfe warme, let him beare it for a difference betweene himſelfe and his horſe: For it is all the wealth that he hath left, to be knowne a reaſonable creature. Who is his companion now? He hath euery month a new ſworne brother.

Meſſ. I'ſt poſſible?

Beat. Very eaſily poſſible: he weares his faith but as the faſhion of his hat, it euer changes with ỹ next block.

Meſſ. I ſee (Lady) the Gentleman is not in your bookes.

Bea. No, and he were, I would burne my ſtudy. But I pray you, who is his companion? Is there no young ſquarer now, that will make a voyage with him to the diuell?

Meſſ. He is moſt in the company of the right noble *Claudio*.

Beat. O Lord, he will hang vpon him like a diſeaſe: he is ſooner caught then the peſtilence, and the taker runs preſently mad. God helpe the noble *Claudio*, if hee haue caught the Benedict, it will coſt him a thouſand pound ere he be cur'd.

Meſſ. I will hold friends with you Lady.

Bea. Do good friend.

Leo. You'l ne're run mad Neece.

Bea. No, not till a hot Ianuary.

Meſſ. *Don Pedro* is approach'd.

Enter don Pedro, Claudio, Benedicke, Balthaſar, and Iohn the baſtard.

Pedro. Good Signior *Leonato*, you are come to meet your trouble: the faſhion of the world is to auoid coſt, and you encounter it.

Leon. Neuer came trouble to my houſe in the likeneſſ of your Grace: for trouble being gone, comfort ſhould remaine: but when you depart from me, ſorrow abides, and happineſſe takes his leaue.

Pedro. You embrace your charge too willingly: I thinke this is your daughter.

Leonato. Her mother hath many times told me ſo.

Bened. Were you in doubt that you askt her?

Leonato. Signior Benedicke, no, for then were you a childe.

Pedro. You haue it full Benedicke, we may gheſſe by this, what you are, being a man, truely the Lady fathers her ſelfe: be happie Lady, for you are like an honorable father.

Ben. If Signior *Leonato* be her father, ſhe would not haue his head on her ſhoulders for al Meſſina, as like him as ſhe is.

Beat. I wonder that you will ſtill be talking, ſignior Benedicke, no body markes you.

Ben. What my deere Ladie Diſdaine! are you yet liuing?

Beat. Is it poſſible Diſdaine ſhould die, while ſhee hath ſuch meete foode to feede it, as Signior Benedicke? Curteſie it ſelfe muſt conuert to Diſdaine, if you come in her preſence.

Bene. Then is curteſie a turne-coate, but it is certaine I am loued of all Ladies, onely you excepted: and I would I could finde in my heart that I had not a hard heart, for truely I loue none.

Beat. A deere happineſſe to women, they would elſe haue beene troubled with a pernitious Suter, I thanke God and my cold blood, I am of your humour for that, I had rather heare my Dog barke at a Crow, than a man ſweare he loues me.

Bene. God keepe your Ladiſhip ſtill in that minde, ſo ſome Gentleman or other ſhall ſcape a predeſtinate ſcratcht face.

Beat. Scratching could not make it worſe, and 'twere ſuch a face as yours were.

Bene. Well, you are a rare Parrat teacher.

Beat. A bird of my tongue, is better than a beaſt of your.

Ben. I would my horſe had the ſpeed of your tongue, and ſo good a continuer, but keepe your way a Gods name, I haue done.

Beat. You alwaies end with a Iades tricke, I know ou of old.

Pedro. This is the ſumme of all: *Leonato*, ſignior *Claudio*, and ſignior *Benedicke*; my deere friend *Leonato*, hath inuited you all, I tell him we ſhall ſtay here, at the leaſt a moneth, and he heartily praies ſome occaſion may detaine vs longer: I dare ſweare hee is no hypocrite, but praies from his heart.

Leon. If you ſweare, my Lord, you ſhall not be forſworne, let mee bid you welcome, my Lord, being reconciled to the Prince your brother: I owe you all duetie.

Iohn. I thanke you, I am not of many words, but I thanke you.

Leon. Pleaſe it your grace leade on?

Pedro. Your hand *Leonato*, we will goe together.

Exeunt. Manet Benedicke and Claudio.

Clau. *Benedicke*, didſt thou note the daughter of ſignior *Leonato*?

Bene. I noted her not, but I lookt on her.

Clau. Is ſhe not a modeſt yong Ladie?

Bene. Doe you queſtion me as an honeſt man ſhould doe, for my ſimple true iudgement? or would you haue me ſpeake after my cuſtome, as being a profeſſed tyrant to their ſexe?

Clau. No, I pray thee ſpeake in ſober iudgement.

Bene. Why yfaith me thinks ſhee's too low for a hie praiſe, too browne for a faire praiſe, and too little for a great praiſe, onely this commendation I can affoord her, that were ſhee other then ſhe is, ſhe were vnbandſome, and being no other, but as ſhe is, I doe not like her.

Clau. Thou think'ſt I am in ſport, I pray thee tell me truely how thou lik'ſt her.

Bene. Would you buie her, that you enquier after her?

Clau. Can the world buie ſuch a iewell?

Ben. Yea, and a caſe to put it into, but ſpeake you this with a ſad brow? Or doe you play the flowting iacke, to tell vs Cupid is a good Hare-finder, and Vulcan a rare Carpenter: Come, in what key ſhall a man take you to goe in the ſong?

Clau. In mine eie, ſhe is the ſweeteſt Ladie that euer I lookt on.

Bene. I can ſee yet without ſpectacles, and I ſee no ſuch matter: there's her coſin, and ſhe were not poſſeſt with a furie, exceedes her as much in beautie, as the firſt of Maie doth the laſt of December: but I hope you haue no intent to turne husband, haue you?

Clau. I would ſcarce truſt my ſelfe, though I had ſworne the contrarie, if *Hero* would be my wife.

Bene. Iſt come to this? in faith hath not the world one man but he will weare his cap with ſuſpition? ſhall I neuer ſee a batcheller of three ſcore againe? goe to yfaith, and thou wilt needes thruſt thy necke into a yoke, weare the print of it, and ſigh away ſundaies: looke, *don Pedro* is returned to ſeeke you.

Enter don Pedro, Iohn the baſtard.

Pedr. What ſecret hath held you here, that you followed not to *Leonatoes*?

Bened. I would your Grace would conſtraine mee to tell.

Pedro. I charge thee on thy allegeance.

Ben. You heare, Count *Claudio*, I can be ſecret as a dumbe man, I would haue you thinke ſo (but on my allegiance, marke you this, on my allegiance) hee is in loue, With who? now that is your Graces part: marke how ſhort his anſwere is, with *Hero*, *Leonatoes* ſhort daughter.

Clau. If this were ſo, ſo were it vttred.

Bened. Like the old tale, my Lord, it is not ſo, nor 'twas not ſo: but indeede, God forbid it ſhould be ſo.

Clau. If my paſſion change not ſhortly, God forbid it ſhould be otherwiſe.

Pedro. Amen, if you loue her, for the Ladie is verie well worthie.

Clau. You ſpeake this to fetch me in, my Lord.

Pedr. By my troth I ſpeake my thought.

Clau. And in faith, my Lord, I ſpoke mine.

Bened. And by my two faiths and troths, my Lord, I ſpeake mine.

Clau. That I loue her, I feele.

Pedr. That ſhe is worthie, I know.

Bened. That I neither feele how ſhee ſhould be loued, nor know how ſhee ſhould be worthie, is the opinion that fire cannot melt out of me, I will die in it at the ſtake.

Pedr. Thou waſt euer an obſtinate heretique in the deſpight of Beautie.

Clau. And neuer could maintaine his part, but in the force of his will.

Bene. That

Ben. That a woman conceiued me, I thanke her: that ſhe brought mee vp, I likewiſe giue her moſt humble thankes; but that I will haue a rechate winded in my forehead, or hang my bugle in an inuiſible baldricke, all women ſhall pardon me: becauſe I will not do them the wrong to miſtruſt any, I will doe my ſelfe the right to truſt none: and the fine is, (for the which I may goe the finer) I will liue a Batchellor.

Pedro. I ſhall ſee thee ere I die, looke pale with loue.

Bene. With anger, with ſickneſſe, or with hunger, my Lord, not with loue: proue that euer I looſe more blood with loue, then I will get againe with drinking, picke out mine eyes with a Ballet-makers penne, and hang me vp at the doore of a brothel-houſe for the ſigne of blinde Cupid.

Pedro. Well, if euer thou dooſt fall from this faith, thou wilt proue a notable argument.

Bene. If I do, hang me in a bottle like a Cat, & ſhoot at me, and he that hit's me, let him be clapt on the ſhoulder, and cal'd *Adam*.

Pedro. Well, as time ſhall trie: In time the ſauage Bull doth beare the yoake.

Bene. The ſauage bull may, but if euer the ſenſible *Benedicke* beare it, plucke off the bulles hornes, and ſet them in my forehead, and let me be vildely painted, and in ſuch great Letters as they write, heere is good horſe to hire: let them ſignifie vnder my ſigne, here you may ſee *Benedicke* the married man.

Clau. If this ſhould euer happen, thou wouldſt bee horne mad.

Pedro. Nay, if Cupid haue not ſpent all his Quiuer in Venice, thou wilt quake for this ſhortly.

Bene. I looke for an earthquake too then.

Pedro. Well, you will temporize with the houres, in the meane time, good Signior *Benedicke*, repaire to *Leonatoes*, commend me to him, and tell him I will not faile him at ſupper, for indeede he hath made great preparation.

Bene. I haue almoſt matter enough in me for ſuch an Embaſſage, and ſo I commit you.

Clau. To the tuition of God. From my houſe, if I had it.

Pedro. The ſixt of Iuly. Your louing friend, *Benedick*.

Bene. Nay mocke not, mocke not; the body of your diſcourſe is ſometime guarded with fragments, and the guardes are but ſlightly baſted on neither, ere you flout old ends any further, examine your conſcience, and ſo I leaue you. *Exit.*

Clau. My Liege, your Highneſſe now may doe mee good.

Pedro. My loue is thine to teach, teach it but how,
And thou ſhalt ſee how apt it is to learne
Any hard Leſſon that may do thee good.

Clau. Hath *Leonato* any ſonne my Lord?

Pedro. No childe but *Hero*, ſhe's his onely heire.
Doſt thou affect her *Claudio*?

Clau. O my Lord,
When you went onward on this ended action,
I look'd vpon her with a ſouldiers eie,
That lik'd, but had a rougher taske in hand
Than to driue liking to the name of loue:
But now I am return'd, and that warre-thoughts
Haue left their places vacant: in their roomes
Come thronging ſoft and delicate deſires,
All prompting mee how faire yong *Hero* is,
Saying I lik'd her ere I went to warres.

Pedro. Thou wilt be like a louer preſently,
And tire the hearer with a booke of words:
If thou doſt loue faire *Hero*, cheriſh it,
And I will breake with her: waſt not to this end,
That thou beganſt to twiſt ſo fine a ſtory?

Clau. How ſweetly doe you miniſter to loue,
That know loues griefe by his complexion!
But leſt my liking might too ſodaine ſeeme,
I would haue ſalu'd it with a longer treatiſe.

Ped. What need ẏ bridge much broder then the flood?
The faireſt graunt is the neceſſitie:
Looke what will ſerue, is fit: 'tis once, thou loueſt,
And I will fit thee with the remedie,
I know we ſhall haue reuelling to night,
I will aſſume thy part in ſome diſguiſe,
And tell faire *Hero* I am *Claudio*,
And in her boſome Ile vnclaſpe my heart,
And take her hearing priſoner with the force
And ſtrong incounter of my amorous tale:
Then after, to her father will I breake,
And the concluſion is, ſhee ſhall be thine,
In practiſe let vs put it preſently. *Exeunt.*

Enter Leonato and an old man, brother to Leonato.

Leo. How now brother, where is my coſen your ſon: hath he prouided this muſicke?

Old. He is very buſie about it, but brother, I can tell you newes that you yet dreamt not of.

Lo. Are they good?

Old. As the euents ſtamps them, but they haue a good couer: they ſhew well outward, the Prince and Count *Claudio* walking in a thick pleached alley in my orchard, were thus ouer-heard by a man of mine: the Prince diſcouered to *Claudio* that hee loued my niece your daughter, and meant to acknowledge it this night in a dance, and if hee found her accordant, hee meant to take the preſent time by the top, and inſtantly breake with you of it.

Leo. Hath the fellow any wit that told you this?

Old. A good ſharpe fellow, I will ſend for him, and queſtion him your ſelfe.

Leo. No, no; wee will hold it as a dreame, till it appeare it ſelfe: but I will acquaint my daughter withall, that ſhe may be the better prepared for an anſwer, if per aduenture this bee true: goe you and tell her of it: coſins, you know what you haue to doe, O I crie you mercie friend, goe you with mee and I will vſe your skill, good coſin haue a care this buſie time. *Exeunt.*

Enter Sir Iohn the Baſtard, and Conrade his companion.

Con. What the good yeere my Lord, why are you thus out of meaſure ſad?

Ioh. There is no meaſure in the occaſion that breeds, therefore the ſadneſſe is without limit.

Con. You ſhould heare reaſon.

Iohn. And when I haue heard it, what bleſſing bringeth it?

Con. If not a preſent remedy, yet a patient ſufferance.

Ioh. I wonder that thou (being as thou ſaiſt thou art borne vnder *Saturne*) goeſt about to apply a morall medicine, to a mortifying miſchiefe: I cannot hide what I am: I muſt bee ſad when I haue cauſe, and ſmile at no mans ieſts, eat when I haue ſtomacke, and wait for no mans leiſure: ſleepe when I am drowſie, and tend on no mans buſineſſe, laugh when I am merry, and claw no man in his humor.

Con. Yea, but you muſt not make the full ſhow of this, till you may doe it without controllment, you haue of late

late ſtood out againſt your brother, and hee hath tane you newly into his grace, where it is impoſſible you ſhould take root, but by the faire weather that you make your ſelfe, it is needful that you frame the ſeaſon for your owne harueſt.

Iohn. I had rather be a canker in a hedge, then a roſe in his grace, and it better fits my bloud to be diſdain'd of all, then to faſhion a carriage to rob loue from any: in this (though I cannot be ſaid to be a flattering honeſt man) it muſt not be denied but I am a plaine dealing villaine, I am truſted with a muſſell, and enfranchiſde with a clog, therefore I haue decreed, not to ſing in my cage: if I had my mouth, I would bite: if I had my liberty, I would do my liking. in the meane time, let me be that I am, and ſeeke not to alter me.

Con. Can you make no vſe of your diſcontent?

Iohn. I will make all vſe of it, for I vſe it onely. Who comes here? what newes *Borachio*?

Enter Borachio.

Bor. I came yonder from a great ſupper, the Prince your brother is royally entertained by *Leonato*, and I can giue you intelligence of an intended marriage.

Iohn. Will it ſerue for any Modell to build miſchiefe on? What is hee for a foole that betrothes himſelfe to vnquietneſſe?

Bor. Mary it is your brothers right hand.

Iohn. Who, the moſt exquiſite *Claudio*?

Bor. Euen he!

Iohn. A proper ſquier, and who, and who, which way lookes he?

Bor. Mary on *Hero*, the daughter and Heire of *Leonato*.

Iohn. A very forward March-chicke, how came you to this?

Bor. Being entertain'd for a perfumer, as I was ſmoaking a muſty roome, comes me the Prince and *Claudio*, hand in hand in ſad conference: I whipt behind the Arras, and there heard it agreed vpon, that the Prince ſhould wooe *Hero* for himſelfe, aud hauing obtain'd her, giue her to Count *Claudio*.

Iohn. Come, come, let vs thither, this may proue food to my diſpleaſure, that young ſtart-vp hath all the glorie of my ouerthrow: if I can croſſe him any way, I bleſſe my ſelfe euery way, you are both ſure, and will aſſiſt mee?

Conr. To the death my Lord.

Iohn. Let vs to the great ſupper, their cheere is the greater that I am ſubdued, would the Cooke were of my minde: ſhall we goe proue whats to be done?

Bor. Wee'll wait vpon your Lordſhip.

Exeunt.

Actus Secundus.

Enter Leonato, his brother, his wife, Hero his daughter, and Beatrice his neece, and a kinſman.

Leonato. Was not Count *Iohn* here at ſupper?

Brother. I ſaw him not.

Beatrice. How tartly that Gentleman lookes, I neuer can ſee him, but I am heart-burn'd an howre after.

Hero. He is of a very melancholy diſpoſition.

Beatrice. Hee were an excellent man that were made iuſt in the mid-way betweene him and *Benedicke*, the one is too like an image and ſaies nothing, and the other too like my Ladies eldeſt ſonne, euermore tatling

Leon. Then halfe ſignior *Benedicks* tongue in Count *Iohns* mouth, and halfe Count *Iohns* melancholy in Signior *Benedicks* face.

Beat. With a good legge, and a good foot vnckle, and money enough in his purſe, ſuch a man would winne any woman in the world, if he could get her good will.

Leon. By my troth Neece, thou wilt neuer get thee a husband, if thou be ſo ſhrewd of thy tongue.

Brother. Infaith ſhee's too curſt.

Beat. Too curſt is more then curſt, I ſhall leſſen Gods ſending that way: for it is ſaid, God ſends a curſt Cow ſhort hornes, but to a Cow too curſt he ſends none.

Leon. So, by being too curſt, God will ſend you no hornes.

Beat. Iuſt, if he ſend me no husband, for the which bleſſing, I am at him vpon my knees euery morning and euening: Lord, I could not endure a husband with a beard on his face, I had rather lie in the woollen.

Leonato. You may light vpon a husband that hath no beard.

Batrice. What ſhould I doe with him? dreſſe him in my apparell, and make him my waiting gentlewoman? he that hath a beard, is more then a youth: and he that hath no beard, is leſſe then a man: and hee that is more then a youth, is not for mee: and he that is leſſe then a man, I am not for him: therefore I will euen take ſixepence in earneſt of the Berrord, and leade his Apes into hell.

Leon. Well then, goe you into hell.

Beat. No, but to the gate, and there will the Deuill meete mee like an old Cuckold with hornes on his head, and ſay get you to heauen *Beatrice*, get you to heauen, heere's no place for you maids, ſo deliuer I vp my Apes, and away to S. *Peter*: for the heauens, hee ſhewes mee where the Batchellers ſit, and there liue wee as merry as the day is long.

Brother. Well neece, I truſt you will be rul'd by your father.

Beatrice. Yes faith, it is my coſens dutie to make curtſie, and ſay, as it pleaſe you: but yet for all that coſin, let him be a handſome fellow, or elſe make an other curſie, and ſay, father, as it pleaſe me.

Leonato. Well neece, I hope to ſee you one day fitted with a husband.

Beatrice. Not till God make men of ſome other mettall then earth, would it not grieue a woman to be ouermaſtred with a peece of valiant duſt? to make account of her life to a clod of waiward marle? no vnckle, ile none: *Adams* ſonnes are my brethren, and truly I hold it a ſinne to match in my kinred.

Leon. Daughter, remember what I told you, if the Prince doe ſolicit you in that kinde, you know your anſwere.

Beatrice. The fault will be in the muſicke coſin, if you be not woed in good time: if the Prince bee too important, tell him there is meaſure in euery thing, & ſo dance out the anſwere, for heare me *Hero*, wooing, wedding, & repenting, is as a Scotch iigge, a meaſure, and a cinquepace: the firſt ſuite is hot and haſty like a Scotch iigge (and full as fantaſticall) the wedding manerly modeſt, (as a meaſure) full of ſtate & aunchentry, and then comes repentance, and with his bad legs falls into the cinquepace faſter and faſter, till he ſinkes into his graue.

Leonato.

Leonata. Cosin you apprehend passing shrewdly.

Beatrice. I haue a good eye vnckle, I can see a Church by daylight.

Leon. The reuellers are entring brother, make good roome.

Enter Prince, Pedro, Claudio, and Benedicke, and Balthasar, or dumbe Iohn, Maskers with a drum.

Pedro. Lady, will you walke about with your friend?

Hero. So you walke softly, and looke sweetly, and say nothing, I am yours for the walke, and especially when I walke away

Pedro. With me in your company.

Hero. I may say so when I please.

Pedro. And when please you to say so?

Hero. When I like your fauour, for God defend the Lute should be like the case.

Pedro My visor is *Philemons* roofe, within the house is Loue.

Hero. Why then your visor should be thatcht.

Pedro. Speake low if you speake Loue.

Bene. Well, I would you did like me

Mar. So would not I for your owne sake, for I haue manie ill qualities.

Bene. Which is one?

Mar. I say my prayers alowd.

Ben. I loue you the better, the hearers may cry Amen.

Mar. God match me with a good dauncer.

Balt. Amen.

Mar. And God keepe him out of my sight when the daunce is done: answer Clarke.

Balt. No more words the Clarke is answered.

Vrsula. I know you well enough, you are Signior *Anthonio.*

Anth. At a word, I am not.

Vrsula. I know you by the wagling of your head.

Anth. To tell you true, I counterfet him.

Vrsu. You could neuer doe him so ill well, vnlesse you were the very man: here's his dry hand vp & down, you are he, you are he.

Anth. At a word I am not.

Vrsula. Come, come, doe you thinke I doe not know you by your excellent wit? can vertue hide it selfe? goe to, mumme, you are he, graces will appeare, and there's an end.

Beat. Will you not tell me who told you so?

Bene. No, you shall pardon me.

Beat. Nor will you not tell me who you are?

Bened. Not now.

Beat. That I was disdainfull, and that I had my good wit out of the hundred merry tales; well, this was Signior *Benedicke* that said so.

Bene. What's he?

Beat. I am sure you know him well enough.

Bene. Not I, beleeue me.

Beat. Did he neuer make you laugh?

Bene. I pray you what is he?

Beat. Why he is the Princes ieaster, a very dull foole, onely his gift is, in deuising impossible slanders, none but Libertines delight in him, and the commendation is not in his witte, but in his villanie, for hee both pleaseth men and angers them, and then they laugh at him, and beat him: I am sure he is in the Fleet, I would he had boorded me.

Bene. When I know the Gentleman, Ile tell him what you say.

Beat. Do, do, hee'l but breake a comparison or two on me, which peraduenture (not markt, or not laugh'd at) strikes him into melancholly, and then there's a Partridge wing saued, for the foole will eate no supper that night. We must follow the Leaders.

Ben. In euery good thing.

Bea. Nay, if they leade to any ill, I will leaue them at the next turning. *Exeunt*

Musicke for the dance.

Iohn Sure my brother is amorous on *Hero*, and hath withdrawne her father to breake with him about it: the Ladies follow her, and but one visor remaines.

Borachio. And that is *Claudio*, I know him by his bearing.

Iohn. Are not you signior *Benedicke*?

Clau. You know me well, I am hee.

Iohn. Signior, you are verie neere my Brother in his loue, he is enamor'd on *Hero*, I pray you disswade him from her, she is no equall for his birth: you may do the part of an honest man in it.

Claudio. How know you he loues her?

Iohn. I heard him sweare his affection,

Bor. So did I too, and he swore he would marrie her to night.

Iohn. Come, let vs to the banquet. *Ex. manet Clau.*

Clau. Thus answere I in name of Benedicke,
But heare these ill newes with the eares of *Claudio*:
'Tis certaine so, the Prince woes for himselfe:
Friendship is constant in all other things,
Saue in the Office and affaires of loue:
Therefore all hearts in loue vse their owne tongues.
Let euerie eye negotiate for it selfe,
And trust no Agent: for beautie is a witch,
Against whose charmes, faith melteth into blood:
This is an accident of hourely proofe,
Which I mistrusted not. Farewell therefore *Hero.*

Enter Benedicke.

Ben. Count *Claudio.*

Clau. Yea, the same.

Ben. Come, will you go with me?

Clau. Whither?

Ben. Euen to the next Willow, about your own businesse, Count. What fashion will you weare the Garland off? About your necke, like an Vsurers chaine? Or vnder your arme, like a Lieutenants scarfe? You must weare it one way, for the Prince hath got your *Hero.*

Clau. I wish him ioy of her.

Ben. Why that's spoken like an honest Drouier, so they sel Bullockes: but did you thinke the Prince wold haue serued you thus?

Clau. I pray you leaue me.

Ben. Ho now you strike like the blindman, 'twas the boy that stole your meate, and you'l beat the post.

Clau. If it will not be, Ile leaue you. *Exit*

Ben. Alas poore hurt fowle, now will he creepe into sedges: But that my Ladie *Beatrice* should know me, & not know me: the Princes foole! Hah? It may be I goe vnder that title, because I am merrie: yea but so I am apt to do my selfe wrong: I am not so reputed, it is the base (though bitter) disposition of *Beatrice*, that putt's the world into her person, and so giues me out: well, Ile be reuenged as I may.

Enter the Prince.

Pedro. Now Signior, where's the Count, did you see him?

Ben

Bene. Troth my Lord, I haue played the part of Lady Fame, I found him heere as melancholy as a Lodge in a Warren, I told him, and I thinke, told him true, that your grace had got the will of this young Lady, and I offered him my company to a willow tree, either to make him a garland, as being forſaken, or to binde him a rod, as being worthy to be whipt.

Pedro. To be whipt, what's his fault?

Bene. The flat tranſgreſſion of a Schoole-boy, who being ouer-ioyed with finding a birds neſt, ſhewes it his companion, and he ſteales it.

Pedro. Wilt thou make a truſt, a tranſgreſſion? the tranſgreſſion is in the ſtealer.

Ben. Yet it had not beene amiſſe the rod had beene made, and the garland too, for the garland he might haue worne himſelfe, and the rod hee might haue beſtowed on you, who (as I take it) haue ſtolne his birds neſt.

Pedro. I will but teach them to ſing, and reſtore them to the owner.

Bene. If their ſinging anſwer your ſaying, by my faith you ſay honeſtly.

Pedro. The Lady *Beatrice* hath a quarrell to you, the Gentleman that daunſt with her, told her ſhee is much wrong'd by you.

Bene. O ſhe miſuſde me paſt the indurance of a block: an oake but with one greene leafe on it, would haue anſwered her: my very viſor began to aſſume life, and ſcold with her: ſhee told mee, not thinking I had beene my ſelfe, that I was the Princes Ieſter, and that I was duller then a great thaw, hudling ieſt vpon ieſt, with ſuch impoſſible conueiance vpon me, that I ſtood like a man at a marke, with a whole army ſhooting at me: ſhee ſpeakes poynyards, and euery word ſtabbes: if her breath were as terrible as terminations, there were no liuing neere her, ſhe would infect to the north ſtarre; I would not marry her, though ſhe were indowed with all that *Adam* had left him before he tranſgreſt, ſhe would haue made *Hercules* haue turnd ſpit, yea, and haue cleft his club to make the fire too: come, talke not of her, you ſhall finde her the infernall Ate in good apparell. I would to God ſome ſcholler would coniure her, for certainely while ſhe is heere, a man may liue as quiet in hell, as in a ſanctuary, and people ſinne vpon purpoſe, becauſe they would goe thither, ſo indeed all diſquiet, horror, and perturbation followes her.

Enter Claudio and Beatrice, Leonato, Hero.

Pedro. Looke heere ſhe comes.

Bene. Will your Grace command mee any ſeruice to the worlds end? I will goe on the ſlighteſt arrand now to the Antypodes that you can deuiſe to ſend me on: I will fetch you a tooth-picker now from the furtheſt inch of Aſia: bring you the length of *Preſter Iohns* foot: fetch you a hayre off the great *Chams* beard: doe you any embaſſage to the Pigmies, rather then hould three words conference, with this Harpy: you haue no employment for me?

Pedro. None, but to deſire your good company.

Bene. O God ſir, heeres a diſh I loue not, I cannot indure this Lady tongue. *Exit.*

Pedr. Come Lady, come, you haue loſt the heart of Signior *Benedicke*.

Beatr. Indeed my Lord, hee lent it mee a while, and I gaue him vſe for it, a double heart for a ſingle one, marry once before he wonne it of mee, with falſe dice, therefore your Grace may well ſay I haue loſt it.

Pedro. You haue put him downe Lady, you haue put him downe.

Beat. So I would not he ſhould do me, my Lord, leſt I ſhould prooue the mother of fooles: I haue brought Count *Claudio*, whom you ſent me to ſeeke.

Pedro. Why how now Count, wherfore are you ſad?

Claud. Not ſad my Lord.

Pedro. How then? ſicke?

Claud. Neither, my Lord.

Beat. The Count is neither ſad, nor ſicke, nor merry, nor well: but ciuill Count, ciuill as an Orange, and ſomething of a iealous complexion.

Pedro. Iſaith Lady, I thinke your blazon to be true, though Ile be ſworne, if hee be ſo, his conceit is falſe: heere *Claudio*, I haue wooed in thy name, and faire *Hero* is won, I haue broke with her father, and his good will obtained, name the day of marriage, and God giue thee ioy.

Leona. Count, take of me my daughter, and with her my fortunes: his grace hath made the match, & all grace ſay, Amen to it.

Beatr. Speake Count, tis your Qu.

Claud. Silence is the perfecteſt Herault of ioy, I were but little happy if I could ſay, how much? Lady, as you are mine, I am yours, I giue away my ſelfe for you, and doat vpon the exchange.

Beat. Speake coſin, or (if you cannot) ſtop his mouth with a kiſſe, and let not him ſpeake neither.

Pedro. Infaith Lady you haue a merry heart.

Beatr. Yea my Lord I thanke it, poore foole it keepes on the windy ſide of Care, my cooſin tells him in his eare that he is in my heart.

Clau. And ſo ſhe doth cooſin.

Beat. Good Lord for alliance: thus goes euery one to the world but I, and I am ſun-burn'd, I may ſit in a corner and cry, heigh ho for a husband.

Pedro. Lady *Beatrice*, I will get you one.

Beat. I would rather haue one of your fathers getting: hath your Grace ne're a brother like you? your father got excellent husbands, if a maid could come by them.

Prince. Will you haue me? Lady.

Beat. No, my Lord, vnleſſe I might haue another for working-daies, your Grace is too coſtly to weare euerie day: but I beſeech your Grace pardon mee, I was borne to ſpeake all mirth, and no matter.

Prince. Your ſilence moſt offends me, and to be merry, beſt becomes you, for out of queſtion, you were born in a merry howre.

Beatr. No ſure my Lord, my Mother cried, but then there was a ſtarre daunſt, and vnder that was I borne: coſins God giue you ioy.

Leonato. Neece, will you looke to thoſe things I told you of?

Beat. I cry you mercy Vncle, by your Graces pardon. *Exit Beatrice.*

Prince. By my troth a pleaſant ſpirited Lady.

Leon. There's little of the melancholy element in her my Lord, ſhe is neuer ſad, but when ſhe ſleepes, and not euer ſad then: for I haue heard my daughter ſay, ſhe hath often dreamt of vnhappineſſe, and wakt her ſelfe with laughing.

Pedro. Shee cannot indure to heare tell of a husband.

Leonato. O, by no meanes, ſhe mocks all her wooers out of ſuite.

Prince. She were an excellent wiſe for *Benedick*.

Leonato. O Lord, my Lord, if they were but a weeke married,

married, they would talke themselues madde.

Prince. Counte *Claudio*, when meane you to goe to Church?

Clau. To morrow my Lord, Time goes on crutches, till Loue haue all his rites.

Leonata. Not till monday, my deare sonne, which is hence a iust seuen night, and a time too briefe too, to haue all things answer minde.

Prince. Come, you shake the head at so long a breathing, but I warrant thee *Claudio*, the time shall not goe dully by vs, I will in the *interim*, vndertake one of *Hercules* labors, which is, to bring Signior *Benedicke* and the Lady *Beatrice* into a mountaine of affection, th'one with th'other, I would faine haue it a match, and I doubt not but to fashion it, if you three will but minister such assistance as I shall giue you direction.

Leonata. My Lord, I am for you, though it cost mee ten nights watchings.

Claud. And I my Lord.

Prin. And you to gentle *Hero*?

Hero. I will doe any modest office, my Lord, to helpe my cosin to a good husband.

Prin. And *Benedick* is not the vnhopefullest husband that I know: thus farre can I praise him, hee is of a noble straine, of approued valour, and confirm'd honesty, I will teach you how to humour your cosin, that shee shall fall in loue with *Benedicke*, and I, with your two helpes, will so practise on *Benedicke*, that in despight of his quicke wit, and his queasie stomacke, hee shall fall in loue with *Beatrice*: if wee can doe this, *Cupid* is no longer an Archer, his glory shall be ours, for wee are the onely loue-gods, goe in with me, and I will tell you my drift. *Exit.*

Enter Iohn and Borachio.

Ioh. It is so, the Count *Claudio* shal marry the daughter of *Leonato*.

Bora. Yea my Lord, but I can crosse it.

Iohn. Any barre, any crosse, any impediment, will be medicinable to me, I am sicke in displeasure to him, and whatsoeuer comes athwart his affection, ranges euenly with mine, how canst thou crosse this marriage?

Bor. Not honestly my Lord, but so couertly, that no dishonesty shall appeare in me.

Iohn. Shew me breefely how.

Bor. I thinke I told your Lordship a yeere since, how much I am in the fauour of *Margaret*, the waiting gentlewoman to *Hero*.

Iohn. I remember.

Bor. I can at any vnseasonable instant of the night, appoint her to look out at her Ladies chamber window.

Iohn. What life is in that, to be the death of this marriage?

Bor. The poyson of that lies in you to temper, goe you to the Prince your brother, spare not to tell him, that hee hath wronged his Honor in marrying the renowned *Claudio*, whose estimation do you mightily hold vp, to a contaminated stale, such a one as *Hero*.

Iohn. What proofe shall I make of that?

Bor. Proofe enough, to misuse the Prince, to vexe *Claudio*, to vndoe *Hero*, and kill *Leonato*, looke you for any other issue?

Iohn. Onely to despight them, I will endeauour any thing.

Bor. Goe then, finde me a meete howre, to draw on *Pedro* and the Count *Claudio* alone, tell them that you know that *Hero* loues me, intend a kinde of zeale both to the Prince and *Claudio* (as in a loue of your brothers honor who hath made this match) and his friends reputation, who is thus like to be cosen'd with the semblance of a maid, that you haue discouer'd thus: they will scarcely beleeue this without triall: offer them instances which shall beare no lesse likelihood, than to see mee at her chamber window, heare me call *Margaret*, *Hero*; heare *Margaret* terme me *Claudio*, and bring them to see this the very night before the intended wedding, for in the meane time, I will so fashion the matter, that *Hero* shall be absent, and there shall appeare such seeming truths of *Heroes* disloyaltie, that iealousie shall be cal'd assurance, and all the preparation ouerthrowne.

Iohn. Grow this to what aduerse issue it can, I will put it in practise: be cunning in the working this, and thy fee is a thousand ducates.

Bor. Be thou constant in the accusation, and my cunning shall not shame me.

Iohn. I will presentlie goe learne their day of marriage. *Exit.*

Enter Benedicke alone.

Bene. Boy.

Boy. Signior.

Bene. In my chamber window lies a booke, bring it hither to me in the orchard.

Boy. I am heere already sir. *Exit.*

Bene. I know that, but I would haue thee hence, and heere againe. I doe much wonder, that one man seeing how much another man is a foole, when he dedicates his behauiours to loue, will after hee hath laught at such shallow follies in others, become the argument of his owne scorne, by falling in loue, & such a man is *Claudio*, I haue known when there was no musicke with him but the drum and the fife, and now had hee rather heare the taber and the pipe: I haue knowne when he would haue walkt ten mile afoot, to see a good armor, and now will he lie ten nights awake caruing the fashion of a new dublet: he was wont to speake plaine, & to the purpose (like an honest man & a souldier) and now is he turn'd orthography, his words are a very fantasticall banquet, iust so many strange dishes: may I be so conuerted, & see with these eyes? I cannot tell, I thinke not: I will not bee sworne, but loue may transforme me to an oyster, but Ile take my oath on it, till he haue made an oyster of me, he shall neuer make me such a foole: one woman is faire, yet I am well: another is wise, yet I am well: another vertuous, yet I am well: but till all graces be in one woman, one woman shall not come in my grace: rich shee shall be, that's certaine: wise, or Ile none: vertuous, or Ile neuer cheapen her: faire, or Ile neuer looke on her: milde, or come not neere me: Noble, or not for an Angell: of good discourse: an excellent Musitian, and her haire shal be of what colour it please God, hah! the Prince and Monsieur Loue, I will hide me in the Arbor.

Enter Prince, Leonato, Claudio, and Iacke Wilson.

Prin. Come, shall we heare this musicke?

Claud. Yea my good Lord: how still the euening is,
As husht on purpose to grace harmonie.

Prin. See you where *Benedicke* hath hid himselfe?

Clau. O very well my Lord: the musicke ended,
Wee'll fit the kid-foxe with a penny worth.

Prince. Come *Balthasar*, wee'll heare that song again.

Balth. O good my Lord, taxe not so bad a voyce,
To slander musicke any more then once.

Prin. It is the witnesse still of excellency,

To

To slander Musicke any more then once.

Prince. It is the witnesse still of excellencie,
To put a strange face on his owne perfection,
I pray thee sing, and let me woe no more.

Balth. Because you talke of wooing, I will sing,
Since many a wooer doth commence his suit,
To her he thinkes not worthy, yet he wooes,
Yet will he sweare he loues.

Prince. Nay pray thee come,
Or if thou wilt hold longer argument,
Doe it in notes.

Balth. Note this before my notes,
Theres not a note of mine that's worth the noting.

Prince. Why these are very crotchets that he speaks,
Note notes forsooth, and nothing.

Bene. Now diuine aire, now is his soule rauisht, is it not strange that sheepes guts should hale soules out of mens bodies? well, a horne for my money when all's done.

The Song.

Sigh no more Ladies, sigh no more,
Men were deceiuers euer,
One foote in Sea, and one on shore,
To one thing constant neuer,
Then sigh not so, but let them goe,
And be you blithe and bonnie,
Conuerting all your sounds of woe,
Into hey nony nony.

Sing no more ditties, sing no moe,
Of dumps so dull and heauy,
The fraud of men were euer so,
Since summer first was leauy,
Then sigh not so, &c.

Prince. By my troth a good song.

Balth. And an ill singer, my Lord.

Prince. Ha, no, no faith, thou singst well enough for a shift.

Ben. And he had been a dog that should haue howld thus, they would haue hang'd him, and I pray God his bad voyce bode no mischiefe, I had as liefe haue heard the night-rauen, come what plague could haue come after it.

Prince. Yea marry, dost thou heare *Balthasar*? I pray thee get vs some excellent musick: for to morrow night we would haue it at the Lady *Heroes* chamber window.

Balth. The best I can, my Lord. *Exit Balthasar.*

Prince. Do so, farewell. Come hither *Leonato*, what was it you told me of to day, that your Niece *Beatrice* was in loue with signior *Benedicke*?

Cla. O I, stalke on, stalke on, the foule sits. I did neuer thinke that Lady would haue loued any man.

Leon. No, nor I neither, but most wonderful, that she should so dote on Signior *Benedicke*, whom shee hath in all outward behauiours seemed euer to abhorre.

Bene. Is't possible? sits the winde in that corner?

Leo. By my troth my Lord, I cannot tell what to thinke of it, but that she loues him with an inraged affection, it is past the infinite of thought.

Prince. May be she doth but counterfeit.

Claud. Faith like enough.

Leon. O God! counterfeit? there was neuer counterfeit of passion, came so neere the life of passion as she discouers it.

Prince. Why what effects of passion shewes she

Claud. Baite the hooke well, this fish will bite.

Leon. What effects my Lord? shee will sit you, you heard my daughter tell you how

Clau. She did indeed.

Prin. How, how I pray you? you amaze me, I would haue thought her spirit had beene inuincible against all assaults of affection.

Leo. I would haue sworne it had my Lord, especially against *Benedicke*.

Bene. I should thinke this a gull, but that the white-bearded fellow speakes it: knauery cannot sure hide himselfe in such reuerence.

Claud. He hath tane th' infection, hold it vp.

Prince. Hath shee made her affection known to *Benedicke*?

Leonato. No, and sweares she neuer will, that's her torment.

Claud. 'Tis true indeed, so your daughter saies: shall I, saies she, that haue so oft encountred him with scorne, write to him that I loue him?

Leo. This saies shee now when shee is beginning to write to him, for shee'll be vp twenty times a night, and there will she sit in her smocke, till she haue writ a sheet of paper: my daughter tells vs all.

Clau. Now you talke of a sheet of paper, I remember a pretty iest your daughter told vs of.

Leon. O when she had writ it, & was reading it ouer, she found *Benedicke* and *Beatrice* betweene the sheete.

Clau. That.

Leon. O she tore the letter into a thousand halfpence, raild at her self, that she should be so immodest to write, to one that shee knew would flout her: I measure him, saies she, by my owne spirit, for I should flout him if hee writ to mee, yea though I loue him, I should.

Clau. Then downe vpon her knees she falls, weepes, sobs, beates her heart, teares her hayre, praies, curses, O sweet *Benedicke*, God giue me patience.

Leon She doth indeed, my daughter saies so, and the extasie hath so much ouerborne her, that my daughter is somtime afeard she will doe a desperate out-rage to her selfe, it is very true.

Prine. It were good that *Benedicke* knew of it by some other, if she will not discouer it.

Clau. To what end? he would but make a sport of it, and torment the poore Lady worse.

Prin. And he should, it were an almes to hang him, shee's an excellent sweet Lady, and (out of all suspition,) she is vertuous.

Claudio. And she is exceeding wise.

Prince. In euery thing, but in louing *Benedicke*.

Leon. O my Lord, wisedome and bloud combating in so tender a body, we haue ten proofes to one, that bloud hath the victory, I am sorry for her, as I haue iust cause being her Vncle, and her Guardian.

Prince. I would shee had bestowed this dotage on mee, I would haue daft all other respects, and made her halfe my selfe: I pray you tell *Benedicke* of it, and heare what he will say.

Leon. Were it good thinke you?

Clau. *Hero* thinkes surely she wil die, for she saies she will die, if hee loue her not, and shee will die ere shee make her loue knowne, and she will die if hee wooe her, rather than shee will bate one breath of her accustomed crossenesse.

Prin. She doth well, if she should make tender of her loue,

loue, 'tis very poſſible hee'l ſcorne it, for the man (as you know all) hath a contemptible ſpirit.

Clau. He is a very proper man.

Prin. He hath indeed a good outward happines.

Clau. 'Fore God, and in my minde very wiſe.

Prin. He doth indeed ſhew ſome ſparkes that are like wit.

Leon. And I take him to be valiant.

Prin. As *Hector*, I aſſure you, and in the managing of quarrels you may ſee hee is wiſe, for either hee auoydes them with great diſcretion, or vndertakes them with a Chriſtian-like feare.

Leon. If hee doe feare God, a muſt neceſſarilie keepe peace, if hee breake the peace, hee ought to enter into a quarrell with feare and trembling.

Prin. And ſo will he doe, for the man doth fear God, howſoeuer it ſeemes not in him, by ſome large ieaſts hee will make: well, I am ſorry for your niece, ſhall we goe ſee *Benedicke*, and tell him of her loue.

Claud. Neuer tell him, my Lord, let her weare it out with good counſell.

Leon. Nay that's impoſſible, ſhe may weare her heart out firſt.

Prin Well, we will heare further of it by your daughter, let it coole the while, I loue *Benedicke* well, and I could wiſh he would modeſtly examine himſelfe, to ſee how much he is vnworthy to haue ſo good a Lady.

Leon. My Lord, will you walke? dinner is ready.

Clau. If he do not doat on her vpon this, I wil neuer truſt my expectation.

Prin. Let there be the ſame Net ſpread for her, and that muſt your daughter and her gentlewoman carry: the ſport will be, when they hold one an opinion of anothers dotage, and no ſuch matter, that's the Scene that I would ſee, which will be meerely a dumbe ſhew: let vs ſend her to call him into dinner. *Exeunt.*

Bene. This can be no tricke, the conference was ſadly borne, they haue the truth of this from *Hero*, they ſeeme to pittie the Lady: it ſeemes her affections haue the full bent: loue me? why it muſt be requited: I heare how I am cenſur'd, they ſay I will beare my ſelfe proudly, if I perceiue the loue come from her: they ſay too, that ſhe will rather die than giue any ſigne of affection: I did neuer thinke to marry, I muſt not ſeeme proud, happy are they that heare their detractions, and can put them to mending: they ſay the Lady is faire, 'tis a truth, I can beare them witneſſe: and vertuous, tis ſo, I cannot reprooue it, and wiſe, but for louing me, by my troth it is no addition to her witte, nor no great argument of her folly; for I wil be horribly in loue with her, I may chance haue ſome odde quirkes and remnants of witte broken on mee, becauſe I haue rail'd ſo long againſt marriage: but doth not the appetite alter? a man loues the meat in his youth, that he cannot indure in his age. Shall quips and ſentences, and theſe paper bullets of the braine awe a man from the careere of his humour? No, the world muſt be peopled. When I ſaid I would die a batcheler, I did not think I ſhould liue till I were maried, here comes *Beatrice*: by this day, ſhee's a faire Lady, I doe ſpie ſome markes of loue in her.

Enter Beatrice

Beat. Againſt my wil I am ſent to bid you come in to dinner.

Bene. Faire *Beatrice*, I thanke you for your paines.

Beat. I tooke no more paines for thoſe thankes, then you take paines to thanke me, if it had been painefull, I would not haue come.

Bene. You take pleaſure then in the meſſage.

Beat. Yea iuſt ſo much as you may take vpon a kniues point, and choake a daw withall: you haue no ſtomacke ſignior, fare you well. *Exit.*

Bene. Ha, againſt my will I am ſent to bid you come into dinner: there's a double meaning in that: I tooke no more paines for thoſe thankes then you tooke paines to thanke me, that's as much as to ſay, any paines that I take for you is as eaſie as thankes: if I do not take pitty of her I am a villaine, if I doe not loue her I am a Iew, I will goe get her picture. *Exit.*

Actus Tertius.

Enter Hero and two Gentlemen, Margaret, and Vrſula.

Hero Good *Margaret* runne thee to the parlour,
There ſhalt thou finde my Coſin *Beatrice*,
Propoſing with the Prince and *Claudio*,
Whiſper her eare, and tell her I and *Vrſula*,
Walke in the Orchard, and our whole diſcourſe
Is all of her, ſay that thou ouer-heardſt vs,
And bid her ſteale into the pleached bower,
Where hony-ſuckles ripened by the ſunne,
Forbid the ſunne to enter: like fauourites,
Made proud by Princes, that aduance their pride,
Againſt that power that bred it, there will ſhe hide her
To liſten our purpoſe, this is thy office,
Beare thee well in it, and leaue vs alone.

Marg. Ile make her come I warrant you preſently.

Hero. Now *Vrſula*, when *Beatrice* doth come,
As we do trace this alley vp and downe,
Our talke muſt onely be of *Benedicke*,
When I doe name him, let it be thy part,
To praiſe him more then euer man did merit,
My talke to thee muſt be how *Benedicke*
Is ſicke in loue with *Beatrice*: of this matter,
Is little *Cupids* crafty arrow made,
That onely wounds by heare-ſay: now begin,

Enter Beatrice.

For looke where *Beatrice* like a Lapwing runs
Cloſe by the ground, to heare our conference.

Vrſ. The pleaſant'ſt angling is to ſee the fiſh
Cut with her golden ores the ſiluer ſtreame,
And greedily deuoure the treacherous baite:
So angle we for *Beatrice*, who euen now,
Is couched in the wood-bine couerture,
Feare you not my part of the Dialogue.

Her. Then go we neare her that her eare looſe nothing,
Of the falſe ſweete baite that we lay for it:
No truely *Vrſula*, ſhe is too diſdainfull,
I know her ſpirits are as coy and wilde,
As Haggerds of the rocke.

Vrſula. But are you ſure,
That *Benedicke* loues *Beatrice* ſo intirely?

Her. So ſaies the Prince, and my new trothed Lord.

Vrſ. And did they bid you tell her of it, Madam?

Her. They did intreate me to acquaint her of it,
But I perſwaded them, if they lou'd *Benedicke*,

K To

To wish him wrastle with affection,
And neuer to let *Beatrice* know of it,
Vrsula. Why did you so, doth not the Gentleman
Deserue as full as fortunate a bed,
As euer *Beatrice* shall couch vpon?
Hero. O God of loue! I know he doth deserue,
As much as may be yeelded to a man.
But Nature neuer fram'd a womans heart,
Of prowder stuffe then that of *Beatrice*:
Disdaine and Scorne ride sparkling in her eyes,
Mis-prizing what they looke on, and her wit
Values it selfe so highly, that to her
All matter else seemes weake: she cannot loue,
Nor take no shape nor proiect of affection,
Shee is so selfe indeared
Vrsula. Sure I thinke so,
And therefore certainely it were not good
She knew his loue, lest she make sport at it
Hero. Why you speake truth, I neuer yet saw man,
How wise, how noble, yong, how rarely featur'd.
But she would spell him backward: if faire fac'd,
She would sweare the gentleman should be her sister:
If blacke, why Nature drawing of an anticke,
Made a foule blot: if tall, a launce ill headed:
If low, an agot very vildlie cut:
If speaking, why a vane blowne with all windes.
If silent, why a blocke moued with none
So turnes she euery man the wrong side out,
And neuer giues to Truth and Vertue, that
Which simplenesse and merit purchaseth.
Vrsu. Sure, sure, such carping is not commendable.
Hero. No, not to be so odde, and from all fashions,
As *Beatrice* is, cannot be commendable,
But who dare tell her so? if I should speake,
She would mocke me into ayre, O she would laugh me
Out of my selfe, presse me to death with wit,
Therefore let *Benedicke* like couered fire,
Consume away in sighes, waste inwardly:
It were a better death, to die with mockes,
Which is as bad as die with tickling.
Vrsu. Yet tell her of it heare what shee will say.
Hero. No, rather I will goe to *Benedicke*,
And counsaile him to fight against his passion,
And truly Ile deuise some honest slanders,
To staine my cosin with, one doth not know,
How much an ill word may impoison liking.
Vrsu. O doe not doe your cosin such a wrong,
She cannot be so much without true iudgement,
Hauing so swift and excellent a wit
As she is prisde to haue, as to refuse
So rare a Gentleman as signior *Benedicke*.
Hero. He is the onely man of Italy,
Alwaies excepted, my deare *Claudio*.
Vrsu. I pray you be not angry with me, Madame,
Speaking my fancy: Signior *Benedicke*,
For shape, for bearing argument and valour,
Goes formost in report through Italy.
Hero. Indeed he hath an excellent good name.
Vrsu. His excellence did earne it ere he had it:
When are you married Madame?
Hero. Why euerie day to morrow, come goe in,
Ile shew thee some attires, and haue thy counsell,
Which is the best to furnish me to morrow.
Vrsu. Shee's tane I warrant you,
We haue caught her Madame?
Hero. If it proue so, then louing goes by haps,
Some *Cupid* kills with arrowes, some with traps. *Exit.*
Beat. What fire is in mine eares? can this be true?
Stand I condemn'd for pride and scorne so much?
Contempt, farewell, and maiden pride, adew,
No glory liues behinde the backe of such.
And *Benedicke*, loue on, I will requite thee,
Taming my wilde heart to thy louing hand:
If thou dost loue, my kindenesse shall incite thee
To binde our loues vp in a holy band.
For others say thou dost deserue, and I
Beleeue it better then reportingly. *Exit.*

Enter Prince, Claudio, Benedicke, and Leonato.

Prince. I doe but stay till your marriage be consummate, and then go I toward Arragon.

Clau. Ile bring you thither my Lord, if you'l vouchsafe me.

Prin. Nay, that would be as great a soyle in the new glosse of your marriage, as to shew a childe his new coat and forbid him to weare it, I will onely bee bold with *Benedicke* for his companie, for from the crowne of his head, to the sole of his foot, he is all mirth, he hath twice or thrice cut *Cupids* bow-string, and the little hang-man dare not shoot at him, he hath a heart as sound as a bell, and his tongue is the clapper, for what his heart thinkes, his tongue speakes.

Bene. Gallants, I am not as I haue bin.

Leo. So say I, methinkes you are sadder

Claud. I hope he be in loue.

Prin. Hang him truant, there's no true drop of bloud in him to be truly toucht with loue, if he be sad, he wants money.

Bene. I haue the tooth-ach.

Prin. Draw it.

Bene. Hang it.

Claud. You must hang it first, and draw it afterwards.

Prin. What? sigh for the tooth-ach.

Leon. Where is but a humour or a worme.

Bene. Well, euery one cannot master a griefe, but hee that has it.

Clau. Yet say I, he is in loue.

Prin. There is no appearance of fancie in him, vnlesse it be a fancy that he hath to strange disguises, as to bee a Dutchman to day, a Frenchman to morrow: vnlesse hee haue a fancy to this foolery, as it appeares hee hath, hee is no foole for fancy, as you would haue it to appeare he is.

Clau. If he be not in loue vvith some vvoman, there is no beleeuing old signes, a brushes his hat a mornings, What should that bode?

Prin. Hath any man seene him at the Barbers?

Clau. No, but the Barbers man hath beene seen with him, and the olde ornament of his cheeke hath alreadie stuft tennis balls.

Leon. Indeed he lookes yonger than hee did, by the losse of a beard.

Prin. Nay a rubs himselfe vvith Ciuit, can you smell him out by that?

Clau. That's as much as to say, the sweet youth's in loue.

Prin. The greatest note of it is his melancholy

Clau. And vvhen vvas he vvont to vvash his face?

Prin. Yea, or to paint himselfe? for the which I heare vvhat they say of him.

Clau. Nay, but his iesting spirit, vvhich is now crept into a lute-string, and now gouern'd by stops

Prince.

Prin. Indeed that tels a heauy tale for him: conclude, he is in loue.

Clau. Nay, but I know who loues him.

Prince. That would I know too, I warrant one that knowes him not.

Cla. Yes, and his ill conditions, and in despight of all, dies for him

Prin. Shee shall be buried with her face vpwards.

Bene. Yet is this no charme for the tooth-ake, old signior, walke aside with mee, I haue studied eight or nine wise words to speake to you, which these hobby-horses must not heare.

Prin. For my life to breake with him about *Beatrice*:

Clau. 'Tis euen so, *Hero* and *Margaret* haue by this played their parts with *Beatrice*, and then the two Beares will not bite one another when they meete.

Enter Iohn the Bastard.

Bast. My Lord and brother, God saue you.

Prin. Good den brother.

Bast. If your leisure seru'd, I would speake with you.

Prince. In priuate?

Bast. If it please you, yet Count *Claudio* may heare, for what I would speake of, concernes him.

Prin What's the matter?

Basta. Meanes your Lordship to be married to morrow?

Prin. You know he does.

Bast. I know not that when he knowes what I know.

Clau. If there be any impediment, I pray you discouer it.

Bast You may thinke I loue you not, let that appeare hereafter, and ayme better at me by that I now will manifest, for my brother (I thinke, he holds you well, and in dearenesse of heart) hath holpe to effect your ensuing marriage: surely sute ill spent, and labour ill bestowed.

Prin. Why, what's the matter?

Bastard. I came hither to tell you, and circumstances shortned, (for she hath beene too long a talking of) the Lady is disloyall.

Clau. Who *Hero*?

Bast. Euen shee, *Leonatoes Hero*, your *Hero*, euery mans *Hero*.

Clau. Disloyall?

Bast. The word is too good to paint out her wickednesse, I could say she were worse, thinke you of a worse title, and I will fit her to it: wonder not till further warrant: goe but with mee to night, you shal see her chamber window entred, euen the night before her wedding day, if you loue her, then to morrow wed her: But it would better fit your honour to change your minde.

Claud. May this be so?

Princ. I will not thinke it.

Bast. If you dare not trust that you see, confesse not that you know: if you will follow mee, I will shew you enough, and when you haue seene more, & heard more, proceed accordingly.

Clau. If I see any thing to night, why I should not marry her to morrow in the congregation, where I shold wedde, there will I shame her.

Prin. And as I wooed for thee to obtaine her, I will ioyne with thee to disgrace her.

Bast. I will disparage her no farther, till you are my witnesses, beare it coldly but till night, and let the issue show it selfe

Prin. O day vntowardly turned!

Claud. O mischiefe strangelie thwarting!

Bastard. O plague right well preuented! so will you say, when you haue seene the sequele. *Exit.*

Enter Dogbery and his compartner with the watch.

Dog. Are you good men and true?

Verg. Yea, or else it were pitty but they should suffer saluation body and soule.

Dogb. Nay, that were a punishment too good for them, if they should haue any allegiance in them, being chosen for the Princes watch.

Verges. Well, giue them their charge, neighbour *Dogbery*.

Dog. First, who thinke you the most desartlesse man to be Constable?

Watch.1 *Hugh Ote-cake* sir, or *George Sea-coale*, for they can write and reade.

Dogb. Come hither neighbour Sea-coale, God hath blest you with a good name: to be a wel-fauoured man, is the gift of Fortune, but to write and reade, comes by Nature.

Watch 2. Both which Master Constable

Dogb. You haue: I knew it would be your answere: well, for your fauour sir, why giue God thankes, & make no boast of it, and for your writing and reading, let that appeare when there is no need of such vanity, you are thought heere to be the most senslesse and fit man for the Constable of the watch: therefore beare you the lanthorne: this is your charge: You shall comprehend all vagrom men, you are to bid any man stand in the Princes name.

Watch 2. How if a will not stand?

Dogb. Why then take no note of him, but let him go, and presently call the rest of the Watch together, and thanke God you are ridde of a knaue.

Verges. If he will not stand when he is bidden, hee is none of the Princes subiects.

Dogb. True, and they are to meddle with none but the Princes subiects: you shall also make no noise in the streetes: for, for the Watch to babble and talke, is most tollerable, and not to be indured.

Watch. We will rather sleepe than talke, wee know what belongs to a Watch.

Dog. Why you speake like an ancient and most quiet watchman, for I cannot see how sleeping should offend: only haue a care that your bills be not stolne: well, you are to call at all the Alehouses, and bid them that are drunke get them to bed.

Watch. How if they will not?

Dogb. Why then let them alone till they are sober, if they make you not then the better answere, you may say, they are not the men you tooke them for.

Watch. Well sir.

Dogb. If you meet a theefe, you may suspect him, by vertue of your office, to be no true man: and for such kinde of men, the lesse you meddle or make with them, why the more is for your honesty.

Watch. If wee know him to be a thiefe, shall wee not lay hands on him.

Dogb. Truly by your office you may, but I think they that touch pitch will be defil'd: the most peaceable way for you, if you doe take a theefe, is, to let him shew himselfe what he is, and steale out of your company.

Ver. You haue bin alwaies cal'd a merciful mā partner.

Dog. Truely I would not hang a dog by my will, much more a man who hath anie honestie in him.

Verges. If you heare a child crie in the night you must call to the nurse, and bid her still it.

Watch. How if the nurse be asleepe and will not heare vs?

Dog. Why then depart in peace, and let the childe wake her with crying, for the ewe that will not heare her Lambe when it baes, will neuer answere a calfe when he bleates.

Verges. 'Tis verie true.

Dog. This is the end of the charge: you constable are to present the Princes owne person, if you meete the Prince in the night, you may staie him.

Verges. Nay birladie that I thinke a cannot.

Dog. Fiue shillings to one on't with anie man that knowes the Statues, he may staie him, marrie not without the prince be willing, for indeed the watch ought to offend no man, and it is an offence to stay a man against his will.

Verges. Birladie I thinke it be so.

Dog. Ha, ah ha, well masters good night, and there be anie matter of weight chances, call vp me, keepe your fellowes counsailes, and your owne, and good night, come neighbour.

Watch. Well masters, we heare our charge, let vs go sit here vpon the Church bench till two, and then all to bed.

Dog. One word more, honest neighbors. I pray you watch about signior *Leonatoes* doore, for the wedding being there to morrow, there is a great coyle to night, adiew, be vigitant I beseech you. *Exeunt.*

Enter Borachio and Conrade.

Bor What, *Conrade?*

Watch. Peace, stir not.

Bor. *Conrade* I say.

Con. Here man, I am at thy elbow.

Bor. Mas and my elbow itcht, I thought there would a scabbe follow.

Con, I will owe thee an answere for that, and now forward with thy tale.

Bor. Stand thee close then vnder this penthouse, for it drissels raine, and I will, like a true drunkard, vtter all to thee.

Watch. Some treason masters, yet stand close.

Bor. Therefore know, I haue earned of *Don Iohn* a thousand Ducates.

Con. Is it possible that anie villanie should be so deare?

Bor. Thou should'st rather aske if it were possible anie villanie should be so rich? for when rich villains haue neede of poore ones, poore ones may make what price they will,

Con. I wonder at it.

Bor. That shewes thou art vnconfirm'd, thou knowest that the fashion of a doublet, or a hat, or a cloake, is nothing to a man.

Con. Yes, it is apparell.

Bor. I meane the fashion.

Con. Yes the fashion is the fashion.

Bor. Tush, I may as well say the foole's the foole, but seest thou not what a deformed theefe this fashion is?

Watch. I know that deformed, a has bin a vile theefe, this vii. yeares, a goes vp and downe like a gentle man: I remember his name.

Bor. Did'st thou not heare some bodie?

Con. No, 'twas the vaine on the house.

Bor Seest thou not (I say) what a deformed thiefe this fashion is, how giddily a turnes about all the Hot-bloods, betweene foureteene & fiue & thirtie, sometimes fashioning them like *Pharaoes* souldiours in the rechie painting, sometime like god Bels priests in the old Church window, sometime like the shauen *Hercules* in the smircht worm-eaten tapestrie, where his cod-peece seemes as massie as his club.

Con. All this I see, and see that the fashion weares out more apparrell then the man; but art not thou thy selfe giddie with the fashion too that thou hast shifted out of thy tale into telling me of the fashion?

Bor. Not so neither, but know that I haue to night wooed *Margaret* the Lady *Heroes* gentle-woman, by the name of *Hero*, she leanes me out at her mistris chamber-vvindow, bids me a thousand times good night: I tell this tale vildly. I should first tell thee how the Prince *Claudio* and my Master planted, and placed, and possessed by my Master *Don Iohn*, saw a far off in the Orchard this amiable incounter.

Con. And thought thy *Margaret* was *Hero?*

Bor. Two of them did, the Prince and *Claudio*, but the diuell my Master knew she was *Margaret* and partly by his oathes, which first possest them, partly by the darke night which did deceiue them, but chiefely, by my villanie, which did confirme any slander that *Don Iohn* had made, away vvent *Claudio* enraged, swore hee vvould meete her as he was apointed next morning at the Temple, and there, before the whole congregation shame her with vvhat he saw o're night, and send her home againe vvithout a husband.

Watch. 1. We charge you in the Princes name stand.

Watch. 2. Call vp the right master Constable, vve haue here recouered the most dangerous peece of lechery, that euer vvas knowne in the Common-wealth.

Watch. 1. And one Deformed is one of them. I know him, a vveares a locke.

Conr. Masters, masters.

Watch. 2. Youle be made bring deformed forth I warrant you,

Conr. Masters, neuer speake, vve charge you, let vs obey you to goe vvith vs.

Bor. We are like to proue a goodly commoditie, being taken vp of these mens bils.

Conr. A commoditie in question I warrant you, come vveele obey you. *Exeunt.*

Enter Hero, and Margaret, and Ursula.

Hero. Good *Vrsula* wake my cosin *Beatrice*, and desire her to rise..

Ursu. I will Lady.

Her And bid her come hither.

Vrs. Well.

Mar. Troth I thinke your other rebato were better.

Bero. No pray thee good *Meg*, Ile vveare this.

Marg. By my troth's not so good, and I vvarrant your cosin vvill say so.

Bero. My cosin's a foole, and thou art another, ile vveare none but this.

Mar. I like the new tire vvithin excellently, if the haire vvere a thought browner: and your gown's a most rare fashion yfaith, I saw the Dutchesse of *Millaines* gowne that they praise so.

Bero. O that exceedes they say.

Mar. By my troth's but a night-gowne in respect of yours, cloth a gold and cuts, and lac'd with siluer, set with pearles, downe sleeues, side sleeues, and skirts, round vnderborn with a blewish tinsel, but for a fine queint grace-full and excellent fashion, yours is worth ten on't.

Bero. God

Hero. God giue mee ioy to weare it, for my heart is exceeding heauy.

Marga. 'Twill be heauier soone, by the waight of a man.

Hero. Fie vpon thee, art not asham'd?

Marg. Of what Lady? of speaking honourably? is not marriage honourable in a beggar? is not your Lord honourable without marriage? I thinke you would haue me say, sauing your reuerence a husband: and bad thinking doe not wrest true speaking, Ile offend no body, is there any harme in the heauier for a husband? none I thinke, and it be the right husband, and the right wife, otherwise 'tis light and not heauy, aske my Lady *Beatrice* else, here she comes.

Enter Beatrice.

Hero. Good morrow Coze.

Beat. Good morrow sweet *Hero.*

Hero. Why how now? do you speake in the sick tune?

Beat. I am out of all other tune, me thinkes.

Mar. Claps into Light a loue, (that goes without a burden,) do you sing it and Ile dance it.

Beat. Ye Light aloue with your heeles, then if your husband haue stables enough, you'll looke he shall lacke no barnes.

Mar. O illegitimate construction! I scorne that with my heeles.

Beat. 'Tis almost fiue a clocke cosin, 'tis time you were ready, by my troth I am exceeding ill, hey ho.

Mar. For a hauke, a horse, or a husband?

Beat. For the letter that begins them all, H.

Mar. Well, and you be not turn'd Turke, there's no more sayling by the starre.

Beat. What meanes the foole trow?

Mar. Nothing I, but God send euery one their harts desire.

Hero. These gloues the Count sent mee, they are an excellent perfume.

Beat. I am stuft cosin, I cannot smell.

Mar. A maid and stuft! there's goodly catching of colde.

Beat. O God helpe me, God help me, how long haue you profest apprehension?

Mar. Euer since you left it, doth not my wit become me rarely?

Beat. It is not seene enough, you should weare it in your cap, by my troth I am sicke.

Mar. Get you some of this distill'd *carduus benedictus* and lay it to your heart, it is the onely thing for a qualm.

Hero. There thou prickst her with a thissell.

Beat. *Benedictus*, why *benedictus?* you haue some morall in this *benedictus.*

Mar. Morall? no by my troth, I haue no morall meaning, I meant plaine holy thissell, you may thinke perchance that I thinke you are in loue, nay birlady I am not such a foole to thinke what I list, nor I list not to thinke what I can, nor indeed I cannot thinke, if I would thinke my hart out of thinking, that you are in loue, or that you will be in loue, or that you can be in loue: yet *Benedicke* was such another, and now is he become a man, he swore hee would neuer marry, and yet now in despight of his heart he eates his meat without grudging, and how you may be conuerted I know not, but me thinkes you looke with your eies as other women doe.

Beat. What pace is this that thy tongue keepes.

Mar. Not a false gallop.

Enter Vrsula.

Vrsula. Madam, withdraw, the Prince, the Count, signior *Benedicke*, Don *Iohn*, and all the gallants of the towne are come to fetch you to Church.

Hero. Helpe to dresse mee good coze, good *Meg*, good *Vrsula.*

Enter Leonato, and the Constable, and the Headborough.

Leonato. What would you with mee, honest neighbour?

Const. Dog. Mary sir I would haue some confidence with you, that decernes you nearely.

Leon. Briefe I pray you, for you see it is a busie time with me.

Const. Dog. Mary this it is sir.

Headb. Yes in truth it is sir.

Leon. What is it my good friends?

Con. Do. Goodman Verges sir speakes a little of the matter, an old man sir, and his wits are not so blunt, as God helpe I would desire they were, but infaith honest as the skin betweene his browes.

Head. Yes I thank God, I am as honest as any man liuing, that is an old man, and no honester then I.

Con. Dog. Comparisons are odorous, palabras, neighbour Verges.

Leon. Neighbours, you are tedious.

Con. Dog. It pleases your worship to say so, but we are the poore Dukes officers, but truely for mine owne part, if I were as tedious as a King I could finde in my heart to bestow it all of your worship.

Leon. All thy tediousnesse on me, ah?

Const. Dog. Yea, and 'twere a thousand times more than 'tis, for I heare as good exclamation on your Worship as of any man in the Citie, and though I bee but a poore man, I am glad to heare it.

Head. And so am I.

Leon. I would faine know what you haue to say.

Head. Marry sir our watch to night, excepting your worships presence, haue tane a couple of as arrant knaues as any in Messina.

Con. Dog A good old man sir, hee will be talking as they say, when the age is in the wit is out, God helpe vs, it is a world to see: well said yfaith neighbour *Verges*, well, God's a good man, and two men ride of a horse, one must ride behinde, an honest soule yfaith sir, by my troth he is, as euer broke bread, but God is to bee worshipt, all men are not alike, alas good neighbour.

Leon. Indeed neighbour he comes too short of you.

Con. Do. Gifts that God giues.

Leon. I must leaue you.

Con. Dog. One word sir, our watch sir haue indeede comprehended two aspitious persons, & we would haue them this morning examined before your worship.

Leon. Take their examination your selfe, and bring it me, I am now in great haste, as may appeare vnto you.

Const. It shall be suffigance (*Exit.*

Leon. Drinke some wine ere you goe: fare you well.

Messenger. My Lord, they stay for you to giue your daughter to her husband.

Leon. Ile wait vpon them, I am ready.

Dogb. Goe good partner, goe get you to *Francis Seacoale*, bid him bring his pen and inkehorne to the Gaole: we are now to examine those men.

Verges. And we must doe it wisely.

Dogb. Wee will spare for no witte I warrant you:

heere's that ſhall driue ſome of them to a non-come, only get the learned writer to ſet downe our excommunication, and meet me at the Iaile. *Exeunt.*

Actus Quartus.

Enter Prince, Baſtard, Leonato, Frier, Claudio, Benedicke, Hero, and Beatrice.

Leonato. Come Frier *Francis*, be briefe, onely to the plaine forme of marriage, and you ſhal recount their particular duties afterwards.

Fran. You come hither, my Lord, to marry this Lady.

Clau. No.

Leo. To be married to her: Frier, you come to marrie her.

Frier. Lady, you come hither to be married to this Count.

Hero. I doe.

Frier. If either of you know any inward impediment why you ſhould not be conioyned, I charge you on your ſoules to vtter it.

Claud. Know you anie, *Hero?*

Hero. None my Lord.

Frier. Know you anie, Count?

Leon. I dare make his anſwer, None.

Clau. O what men dare do! what men may do! what men daily do!

Bene. How now! interiections? why then, ſome be of laughing, as ha, ha, he.

Clau. Stand thee by Frier, father, by your leaue,
Will you with free and vnconſtrained ſoule
Giue me this maid your daughter?

Leon. As freely ſonne as God did giue her me.

Cla. And what haue I to giue you back, whoſe worth
May counterpoiſe this rich and precious gift?

Prin. Nothing, vnleſſe you render her againe.

Clau. Sweet Prince, you learn me noble thankfulnes:
There *Leonato*, take her backe againe,
Giue not this rotten Orenge to your friend,
Shee's but the ſigne and ſemblance of her honour:
Behold how like a maid ſhe bluſhes heere!
O what authoritie and ſhew of truth
Can cunning ſinne couer it ſelfe withall!
Comes not that bloud, as modeſt euidence,
To witneſſe ſimple Vertue? would you not ſweare
All you that ſee her, that ſhe were a maide,
By theſe exterior ſhewes? But ſhe is none:
She knowes the heat of a luxurious bed:
Her bluſh is guiltineſſe, not modeſtie.

Leonato. What doe you meane, my Lord?

Clau. Not to be married,
Not to knit my ſoule to an approued wanton.

Leon. Deere my Lord, if you in your owne proofe,
Haue vanquiſht the reſiſtance of her youth,
And made defeat of her virginitie. (her,

Clau. I know what you would ſay: if I haue knowne
You will ſay, ſhe did imbrace me as a husband,
And ſo extenuate the forehand ſinne: No *Leonato*
I neuer tempted her with word too large,
But as a brother to his ſiſter, ſhewed
Baſhfull ſinceritie and comely loue.

Hero. And ſeem'd I euer otherwiſe to you?

Clau. Out on thee ſeeming, I will write againſt it,
You ſeeme to me as *Diane* in her Orbe,
As chaſte as is the budde ere it be blowne:
But you are more intemperate in your blood,
Than *Venus*, or thoſe pampred animalls,
That rage in ſauage ſenſualitie.

Hero. Is my Lord well, that he doth ſpeake ſo wide?

Leon Sweete Prince, why ſpeake not you?

Prin. What ſhould I ſpeake?
I ſtand diſhonour'd that haue gone about,
To linke my deare friend to a common ſtale.

Leon. Are theſe things ſpoken, or doe I but dreame?

Baſt. Sir, they are ſpoken, and theſe things are true.

Bene. This lookes not like a nuptiall.

Hero. True, O God!

Clau. *Leonato*, ſtand I here?
Is this the Prince? is this the Princes brother?
Is this face *Heroes*? are our eies our owne?

Leon. All this is ſo, but what of this my Lord?

Clau. Let me but moue one queſtiou to your daugh-
And by that fatherly and kindly power, (ter,
That you haue in her, bid her anſwer truly.

Leo I charge thee doe, as thou art my childe.

Hero. O God defend me how am I beſet,
What kinde of catechizing call you this?

Clau. To make you anſwer truly to your name.

Hero. Is it not *Hero*? who can blot that name
With any iuſt reproach?

Claud. Marry that can *Hero*,
Hero it ſelfe can blot out *Heroes* vertue.
What man was he, talkt with you yeſternight,
Out at your window betwixt twelue and one?
Now if you are a maid, anſwer to this.

Hero. I talkt with no man at that howre my Lord

Prince. Why then you are no maiden. *Leonato*,
I am ſorry you muſt heare: vpon mine honor,
My ſelfe, my brother, and this grieued Count
Did ſee her, heare her, at that howre laſt night,
Talke with a ruffian at her chamber window,
Who hath indeed moſt like a liberall villaine,
Confeſt the vile encounters they haue had
A thouſand times in ſecret.

Iohn. Fie, fie, they are not to be named my Lord,
Not to be ſpoken of,
There is not chaſtitie enough in language,
Without offence to vtter them: thus pretty Lady
I am ſorry for thy much miſgouernment.

Claud. O *Hero*! what a *Hero* hadſt thou beene
If halfe thy outward graces had beene placed
About thy thoughts and counſailes of thy heart?
But fare thee well, moſt foule, moſt faire, farewel!
Thou pure impiety, and impious puritie,
For thee Ile locke vp all the gates of Loue,
And on my eie-lids ſhall Coniecture hang,
To turne all beauty into thoughts of harme,
And neuer ſhall it more be gracious.

Leon. Hath no mans dagger here a point for me?

Beat. Why how now coſin, wherfore ſink you down?

Baſt. Come, let vs go: theſe things come thus to light,
Smother her ſpirits vp.

Bene. How doth the Lady?

Beat. Dead I thinke, helpe vncle,
Hero, why *Hero* Vncle, Signor *Benedicke*, Frier.

Leonato. O Fate! take not away thy heauy hand.
Death is the faireſt couer for her ſhame
That may be wiſht for.

Beat. How

Beatr. How now coſin *Hero*?
Fri. Haue comfort Ladie.
Leon. Doſt thou looke vp?
Frier. Yea, wherefore ſhould ſhe nôt?
Leon. Wherfore? Why doth not euery earthly thing
Cry ſhame vpon her? Could ſhe heere denie
The ſtorie that is printed in her blood?
Do not liue *Hero*, do not ope thine eyes:
For did I thinke thou wouldſt not quickly die,
Thought I thy ſpirits were ſtronger then thy ſhames,
My ſelfe would on the reward of reproaches
Strike at thy life Grieu'd I, I had but one?
Chid I, for that at frugal Natures frame?
O one too much by thee: why had I one?
Why euer was't thou louelie in my eies?
Why had I not with charitable hand
Tooke vp a beggars iſſue at my gates,
Who ſmeered thus, and mir'd with infamie,
I might haue ſaid, no part of it is mine:
This ſhame deriues it ſelfe from vnknowne loines,
But mine, and mine I lou'd, and mine I prais'd,
And mine that I was proud on mine ſo much,
That I my ſelfe, was to my ſelfe not mine:
Valewing of her, why ſhe, O ſhe is falne
Into a pit of Inke, that the wide ſea
Hath drops too few to waſh her cleane againe,
And ſalt too little, which may ſeaſon giue
To her foule tainted fleſh.
Ben. Sir, ſir, be patient: for my part, I am ſo attired in wonder, I know not what to ſay.
Bea. O on my ſoule my coſin is belied.
Ben. Ladie, were you her bedfellow laſt night?
Bea. No truly: not although vntill laſt night,
I haue this tweluemonth bin her bedfellow.
Leon. Confirm'd, confirm'd, O that is ſtronger made
Which was before barr'd vp with ribs of iron
Would the Princes lie, and *Claudio* lie,
Who lou'd her ſo, that ſpeaking of her foulneſſe,
Waſh'd it with teares? Hence from her, let her die.
Fri. Heare me a little, for I haue onely bene ſilent ſo long, and giuen way vnto this courſe of fortune, by noting of the Ladie, I haue markt.
A thouſand bluſhing apparitions,
To ſtart into her face, a thouſand innocent ſhames,
In Angel whiteneſſe beare away thoſe bluſhes,
And in her eie there hath appear'd a fire
To burne the errors that theſe Princes hold
Againſt her maiden truth. Call me a foole,
Truſt not my reading, nor my obſeruations,
Which with experimental ſeale doth warrant
The tenure of my booke: truſt not my age,
My reuerence, calling, nor diuinitie,
If this ſweet Ladie lye not guiltleſſe heere,
Vnder ſome biting error.
Leo. Friar, it cannot be:
Thou ſeeſt that all the Grace that ſhe hath left,
Is, that ſhe wil not adde to her damnation,
A ſinne of periury, ſhe not denies it:
Why ſeek'ſt thou then to couer with excuſe,
That which appeares in proper nakedneſſe?
Fri. Ladie, what man is he you are accus'd of?
Hero. They know that do accuſe me, I know none:
If I know more of any man aliue
Then that which maiden modeſtie doth warrant,
Let all my ſinnes lacke mercy. O my Father,
Proue you that any man with me conuerſt,
At houres vnmeete, or that I yeſternighe
Maintain'd the change of words with any creature,
Refuſe me, hate me, torture me to death.
Fri. There is ſome ſtrange miſpriſion in the Princes.
Ben. Two of them haue the verie bent of honor,
And if their wiſedomes be miſled in this:
The practiſe of it liues in *Iohn* the baſtard,
Whoſe ſpirits toile in frame of villanies.
Leo. I know not: if they ſpeake but truth of her,
Theſe hands ſhall teare her: If they wrong her honour,
The proudeſt of them ſhall wel heare of it.
Time hath not yet ſo dried this bloud of mine,
Nor age ſo eate vp my inuention,
Nor Fortune made ſuch hauocke of my meanes,
Nor my bad life reft me ſo much of friends,
But they ſhall finde, awak'd in ſuch a kinde,
Both ſtrength of limbe, and policie of minde,
Ability in meanes, and choiſe of friends,
To quit me of them throughly.
Fri. Pauſe awhile:
And let my counſell ſway you in this caſe,
Your daughter heere the Princeſſe (left for dead)
Let her awhile be ſecretly kept in,
And publiſh it, that ſhe is dead indeed:
Maintaine a mourning oſtentation,
And on your Families old monument,
Hang mournfull Epitaphes, and do all rites,
That appertaine vnto a buriall.
Leon. What ſhall become of this? What wil this do?
Fri. Marry this wel carried, ſhall on her behalfe,
Change ſlander to remorſe, that is ſome good,
But not for that dreame I on this ſtrange courſe,
But on this trauaile looke for greater birth:
She dying, as it muſt be ſo maintain'd,
Vpon the inſtant that ſhe was accus'd,
Shal be lamented, pittied, and excus'd
Of euery hearer: for it ſo fals out,
That what we haue, we prize not to the worth,
Whiles we enioy it; but being lack'd and loſt,
Why then we racke the value, then we finde
The vertue that poſſeſsion would not ſhew vs
Whiles it was ours, ſo will it fare with *Claudio*:
When he ſhal heare ſhe dyed vpon his words,
Th'Idea of her life ſhal ſweetly creepe
Into his ſtudy of imagination.
And euery louely Organ of her life,
Shall come apparel'd in more precious habite:
More mouing delicate, and ful of life,
Into the eye and proſpect of his ſoule
Then when ſhe liu'd indeed: then ſhal he mourne,
If euer Loue had intereſt in his Liuer,
And wiſh he had not ſo accuſed her:
No, though he thought his accuſation true:
Let this be ſo, and doubt not but ſucceſſe
Wil faſhion the euent in better ſhape,
Then I can lay it downe in likelihood.
But if all ayme but this be leuelld falſe,
The ſuppoſition of the Ladies death,
Will quench the wonder of her infamie.
And if it ſort not well, you may conceale her,
As beſt befits her wounded reputation,
In ſome recluſiue and religious life,
Out of all eyes, tongnes, mindes and iniuries.
Bene. Signior *Leonato*, let the Frier aduiſe you,
And though you know my inwardneſſe and loue
Is very much vnto the Prince and *Claudio*.

Yet

Yet, by mine honor, I will deale in this,
As secretly and iustlie, as your soule
Should with your bodie.

Leon. Being that I flow in greefe,
The smallest twine may lead me.

Frier. 'Tis well consented, presently away,
For to strange sores, strangely they straine the cure,
Come Lady, die to liue, this wedding day
Perhaps is but prolong'd, haue patience & endure. *Exit*

Bene. Lady *Beatrice*, haue you wept all this while?

Beat. Yea, and I will weepe a while longer.

Bene. I will not desire that.

Beat. You haue no reason, I doe it freely.

Bene. Surelie I do beleeue your fair cosin is wrong'd.

Beat. Ah, how much might the man deserue of mee that would right her!

Bene. Is there any way to shew such friendship?

Beat. A verie euen way, but no such friend.

Bene. May a man doe it?

Beat. It is a mans office, but not yours.

Bene. I doe loue nothing in the world so well as you, is not that strange?

Beat. As strange as the thing I know not, it were as possible for me to say, I loued nothing so well as you, but beleeue me not, and yet I lie not, I confesse nothing, nor I deny nothing, I am sorry for my cousin.

Bene. By my sword *Beatrice* thou lou'st me.

Beat. Doe not sweare by it and eat it.

Bene. I will sweare by it that you loue mee, and I will make him eat it that sayes I loue not you.

Beat. Will you not eat your word?

Bene. With no sawce that can be deuised to it, I protest I loue thee.

Beat. Why then God forgiue me.

Bene. What offence sweet Beatrice?

Beat. You haue stayed me in a happy howre, I was about to protest I loued you.

Bene. And doe it with all thy heart.

Beat. I loue you with so much of my heart, that none is left to protest.

Bened. Come, bid me doe any thing for thee.

Beat. Kill *Claudio*.

Bene. Ha, not for the wide world.

Beat. You kill me to denie, farewell.

Bene. Tarrie sweet *Beatrice*.

Beat. I am gone, though I am heere, there is no loue in you, nay I pray you let me goe.

Bene. Beatrice.

Beat. Infaith I will goe.

Bene. Wee'll be friends first

Beat. You dare easier be friends with mee, than fight with mine enemy.

Bene. Is *Claudio* thine enemie?

Beat. Is a not approued in the height a villaine, that hath slandered, scorned, dishonoured my kinswoman? O that I were a man! what, beare her in hand vntill they come to take hands, and then with publike accusation vncouered slander, vnmittigated rancour? O God that I were a man! I would eat his heart in the market-place.

Bene. Heare me *Beatrice*.

Beat. Talke with a man out at a window, a proper saying.

Bene. Nay but *Beatrice*.

Beat. Sweet *Hero*, she is wrong'd, shee is slandered, she is vndone.

Bene. Beat?

Beat. Princes and Counties! surelie a Princely testimonie, a goodly Count, Comfect, a sweet Gallant surelie, O that I were a man for his sake! or that I had any friend would be a man for my sake! But manhood is melted into cursies, valour into complement, and men are onelie turned into tongue, and trim ones too: he is now as valiant as *Hercules*, that only tells a lie, and sweares it: I cannot be a man with wishing, therfore I will die a woman with grieuing.

Bene. Tarry good *Beatrice*, by this hand I loue thee.

Beat. Vse it for my loue some other way then swearing by it.

Bened. Thinke you in your soule the Count *Claudio* hath wrong'd *Hero*?

Beat. Yea, as sure as I haue a thought, or a soule.

Bene. Enough, I am engagde, I will challenge him, I will kisse your hand, and so leaue you: by this hand *Claudio* shall render me a deere account: as you heare of me, so thinke of me: goe comfort your coosin, I must say she is dead, and so farewell.

Enter the Constables, Borachio, and the Towne Clerke in gownes.

Keeper. Is our whole dissembly appeard?

Cowley. O a stoole and a cushion for the Sexton.

Sexton. Which be the malefactors?

Andrew. Marry that am I, and my partner.

Cowley. Nay that's certaine, wee haue the exhibition to examine.

Sexton. But which are the offenders that are to be examined, let them come before master Constable.

Kemp. Yea marry, let them come before mee, what is your name, friend?

Bor. Borachio.

Kem. Pray write downe *Borachio*. Yours sirra.

Con. I am a Gentleman sir, and my name is *Conrade*.

Kee. Write downe Master gentleman *Conrade*: maisters, doe you serue God: maisters, it is proued alreadie that you are little better than false knaues, and it will goe neere to be thought so shortly, how answer you for your selues?

Con. Marry sir, we say we are none.

Kemp. A maruellous witty fellow I assure you, but I will goe about with him: come you hither sirra, a word in your eare sir, I say to you, it is thought you are false knaues.

Bor. Sir, I say to you, we are none.

Kemp. Well, stand aside, 'fore God they are both in a tale: haue you writ downe that they are none?

Sext. Master Constable, you goe not the way to examine, you must call forth the watch that are their accusers.

Kemp. Yea marry, that's the eftest way, let the watch come forth: masters, I charge you in the Princes name, accuse these men.

Watch 1. This man said sir, that *Don Iohn* the Princes brother was a villaine.

Kemp. Write down, Prince *Iohn* a villaine: why this is flat periurie, to call a Princes brother villaine.

Bora. Master Constable.

Kemp. Pray thee fellow peace, I do not like thy looke I promise thee.

Sexton. What heard you him say else?

Watch 2. Mary that he had receiued a thousand Dukates of *Don Iohn*, for accusing the Lady *Hero* wrongfully.

Kem.

Kemp. Flat Burglarie as euer was committed.
Const. Yea by th'masse that it is.
Sexton. What else fellow?
Watch 1. And that Count *Claudio* did meane vpon his words, to disgrace *Hero* before the whole assembly, and not marry her.
Kemp. O villaine! thou wilt be condemn'd into euerlasting redemption for this.
Sexton. What else?
Watch. This is all.
Sexton. And this is more masters then you can deny, Prince *Iohn* is this morning secretly stolne away: *Hero* was in this manner accus'd, in this very manner refus'd, and vpon the griefe of this sodainely died: Master Constable, let these men be bound, and brought to *Leonato*, I will goe before, and shew him their examination.
Const. Come, let them be opinion'd.
Sex. Let them be in the hands of *Coxcombe*.
Kem. Gods my life, where's the Sexton? let him write downe the Princes Officer *Coxcombe*: come, binde them thou naughty varlet.
Couley. Away, you are an asse, you are an asse.
Kemp. Dost thou not suspect my place? dost thou not suspect my yeeres? O that hee were heere to write mee downe an asse! but masters, remember that I am an asse: though it be not written down, yet forget not ỳ I am an asse: No thou villaine, ỳ art full of piety as shall be prou'd vpon thee by good witnesse, I am a wise fellow, and which is more, an officer, and which is more, a houshoulder, and which is more, as pretty a peece of flesh as any in Messina, and one that knowes the Law, goe to, & a rich fellow enough, goe to, and a fellow that hath had losses, and one that hath two gownes, and euery thing handsome about him: bring him away: O that I had been writ downe an asse! *Exit*

Actus Quintus.

Enter Leonato and his brother.

Brother. If you goe on thus, you will kill your selfe,
And 'tis not wisedome thus to second griefe,
Against your selfe.
Leon. I pray thee cease thy counsaile,
Which falls into mine eares as profitlesse,
As water in a siue: giue not me counsaile,
Nor let no comfort delight mine eare,
But such a one whose wrongs doth sute with mine.
Bring me a father that so lou'd his childe,
Whose ioy of her is ouer-whelmed like mine,
And bid him speake of patience,
Measure his woe the length and bredth of mine,
And let it answere euery straine for straine,
As thus for thus, and such a griefe for such,
In euery lineament, branch, shape, and forme:
If such a one will smile and stroke his beard,
And sorrow, wagge, crie hem, when he should grone,
Patch griefe with prouerbs, make misfortune drunke,
With candle-wasters: bring him yet to me,
And I of him will gather patience:
But there is no such man, for brother, men
Can counsaile, and speake comfort to that griefe,
Which they themselues not feele, but tasting it,
Their counsaile turnes to passion, which before,
Would giue preceptiall medicine to rage,
Fetter strong madnesse in a silken thred,
Charme ache with ayre, and agony with words,
No, no, 'tis all mens office, to speake patience
To those that wring vnder the load of sorrow:
But no mans vertue nor sufficiencie
To be so morall, when he shall endure
The like himselfe: therefore giue me no counsaile,
My griefs cry lowder then aduertisement.
Broth. Therein do men from children nothing differ.
Leonato. I pray thee peace, I will be flesh and bloud,
For there was neuer yet Philosopher,
That could endure the tooth-ake patiently,
How euer they haue writ the stile of gods,
And made a push at chance and sufferance.
Brother. Yet bend not all the harme vpon your selfe,
Make those that doe offend you, suffer too.
Leon. There thou speak'st reason, nay I will doe so,
My soule doth tell me, *Hero* is belied,
And that shall *Claudio* know, so shall the Prince,
And all of them that thus dishonour her.

Enter Prince and Claudio.

Brot. Here comes the *Prince* and *Claudio* hastily.
Prin. Good den, good den.
Clau. Good day to both of you.
Leon. Heare you my Lords?
Prin. We haue some haste *Leonato*.
Leo. Some haste my Lord! wel, fareyouwel my Lord,
Are you so hasty now? well, all is one.
Prin. Nay, do not quarrell with vs, good old man.
Brot. If he could rite himselfe with quarrelling,
Some of vs would lie low.
Claud. Who wrongs him?
Leon. Marry ỳ dost wrong me, thou dissembler, thou:
Nay, neuer lay thy hand vpon thy sword,
I feare thee not.
Claud. Marry beshrew my hand,
If it should giue your age such cause of feare,
Infaith my hand meant nothing to my sword.
Leonato. Tush, tush, man, neuer fleere and iest at me,
I speake not like a dotard, nor a foole,
As vnder priuiledge of age to bragge,
What I haue done being youg, or what would doe,
Were I not old, know *Claudio* to thy head,
Thou hast so wrong'd my innocent childe and me,
That I am forc'd to lay my reuerence by,
And with grey haires and bruise of many daies,
Doe challenge thee to triall of a man,
I say thou hast belied mine innocent childe
Thy slander hath gone through and through her heart,
And she lies buried with her ancestors
O in a tombe where neuer scandall slept,
Saue this of hers, fram'd by thy villanie.
Claud. My villany?
Leonato. Thine *Claudio*, thine I say.
Prin. You say not right old man.
Leon. My Lord, my Lord,
Ile proue it on his body if he dare,
Despight his nice fence, and his actiue practise,
His Maie of youth, and bloome of lustihood.
Claud. Away, I will not haue to do with you
Leo. Canst thou so daffe me? thou hast kild my child,
If thou kilst me, boy, thou shalt kill a man.
Bro. He shall kill two of vs, and men indeed,
But that's no matter, let him kill one first:

Win

Win me and weare me, let him answere me,
Come follow me boy, come sir boy, come follow me
Sir boy, ile whip you from your foyning fence,
Nay, as I am a gentleman, I will.

Leon. Brother.

Brot. Content your self, God knows I lou'd my neece,
And she is dead, slander d to death by villaines,
That dare as well answer a man indeede,
As I d are take a serpent by the tongue.
Boyes apes, braggarts, Iackes, milke-sops.

Leon Brother *Anthony.*

Brot. Hold you content, what man I know them, yea
And what they weigh, euen to the vtmost scruple,
Scambling, out-facing, fashion-monging boyes,
That lye, and cog and flout, depraue, and slander,
Goe antiquely and show outward hidiousnesse,
And speake of halfe a dozen dang'rous words,
How they might hurt their enemies, if they durst,
And this is all.

Leon. But brother *Anthonie.*

Ant. Come, tis no matter,
Do not you meddle, let me deale in this.

Pri. Gentlemen both, we will not wake your patience
My heart is sorry for your daughters death:
But on my honour she was charg'd with nothing
But what was true, and very full of proofe.

Leon. My Lord, my Lord.

Prin. I will not heare you

Enter Benedicke.

Leo. No come brother, away, I will be heard.

Exeunt ambo.

Bro. And shall, or some of vs will smart for it.

Prin. See, see, here comes the man we went to seeke.

Clau. Now signior, what newes?

Ben. Good day my Lord.

Prin. Welcome signior, you are almost come to part almost a fray.

Clau. Wee had likt to haue had our two noses snapt off with two old men without teeth.

Prin. Leonato and his brother, what think'st thou? had wee fought, I doubt we should haue beene too yong for them.

Ben. In a false quarrell there is no true valour, I came to seeke you both.

Clau. We haue beene vp and downe to seeke thee, for we are high proofe melancholly, and would faine haue it beaten away, wilt thou vse thy wit?

Ben. It is in my scabberd, shall I draw it?

Prin. Doest thou weare thy wit by thy side?

Clau. Neuer any did so, though verie many haue been beside their wit, I will bid thee drawe, as we do the minstrels, draw to pleasure vs.

Prin. As I am an honest man he lookes pale, art thou sicke, or angrie?

Clau. What, courage man: what though care kil'd a cat, thou hast mettle enough in thee to kill care.

Ben. Sir, I shall meete your wit in the careere, and you charge it against me, I pray you chuse another subiect.

Clau. Nay then giue him another staffe, this last was broke crosse.

Prin. By this light, he changes more and more, I thinke he be angrie indeede.

Clau. If he be, he knowes how to turne his girdle.

Ben. Shall I speake a word in your eare?

Clau. God blesse me from a challenge.

Ben. You are a villaine, I iest not, I will make it good how you dare, with what you dare, and when you dare: do me right, or I will protest your cowardise: you haue kill'd a sweete Ladie, and her death shall fall heauie on you, let me heare from you.

Clau. Well, I will meete you, so I may haue good cheare.

Prin. What, a feast a feast?

Clau. I faith I thanke him, he hath bid me to a calues head and a Capon, the which if I doe not carue most curiously, say my knife's naught, shall I not finde a woodcocke too?

Ben. Sir, your wit ambles well, it goes easily.

Prin. Ile tell thee how *Beatrice* prais d thy wit the other day: I said thou hadst a fine wit: true saies she, a fine little one: no said I, a great wit. right saies shee, a great grosse one: nay said I, a good wit: iust said she, it hurts no body: nay said I, the gentleman is wise: certain said she, a wise gentleman: nay said I, he hath the tongues: that I beleeue said shee, for hee swore a thing to me on munday night, which he forswore on tuesday morning: there's a double tongue, there's two tongues: thus did shee an howre together trans-shape thy particular vertues, yet at last she concluded with a sigh, thou wast the properst man in Italie.

Claud. For the which she wept heartily, and said shee car'd not.

Prin. Yea that she did, but yet for all that, and if shee did not hate him deadlie, shee would loue him dearely, the old mans daughter told vs all.

Clau. All, all, and moreouer, God saw him vvhen he was hid in the garden.

Prin. But when shall we set the sauage Bulls hornes on the sensible *Benedicks* head?

Clau. Yea and text vnder-neath, heere dwells *Benedicke* the married man.

Ben. Fare you well, Boy, you know my minde, I will leaue you now to your gossep-like humor, you breake iests as braggards do their blades, which God be thanked hurt not: my Lord, for your manie courtesies I thank you, I must discontinue your companie, your brother the Bastard is fled from *Messina*: you haue among you, kill'd a sweet and innocent Ladie: for my Lord Lackebeard there, he and I shall meete, and till then peace be with him.

Prin. He is in earnest.

Clau. In most profound earnest, and Ile warrant you, for the loue of Beatrice.

Prin. And hath challeng'd thee.

Clau. Most sincerely.

Prin. What a prettie thing man is, when he goes in his doublet and hose, and leaues off his wit.

Enter Constable, Conrade, and Borachio.]

Clau. He is then a Giant to an Ape, but then is an Ape a Doctor to such a man.

Prin. But soft you, let me be, plucke vp my heart, and be sad, did he not say my brother was fled?

Const. Come you sir, if iustice cannot tame you, shee shall nere weigh more reasons in her ballance, nay, and you be a cursing hypocrite once, you must be lookt to.

Prin. How now, two of my brothers men bound? *Borachio* one.

Clau. Harken after their offence my Lord.

Prin. Officers, what offence haue these men done?

Con. Marrie

Const. Marrie sir, they haue committed false report, moreouer they haue spoken vntruths, secondarily they are slanders, sixt and lastly, they haue belyed a Ladie, thirdly, they haue verified vniust things, and to conclude they are lying knaues.

Prin. First I aske thee what they haue done, thirdlie I aske thee vvhat's their offence, sixt and lastlie why they are committed, and to conclude, what you lay to their charge.

Clau. Rightlie reasoned, and in his owne diuision, and by my troth there's one meaning vvell suted.

Prin. Who haue you offended masters, that you are thus bound to your answer? this learned Constable is too cunning to be vnderstood, vvhat s your offence?

Bor. Sweete Prince, let me go no farther to mine answere: do you heare me, and let this Count kill mee: I haue deceiued euen your verie eies: vvhat your wisedomes could not discouer, these shallow fooles haue brought to light, vvho in the night ouerheard me confessing to this man, how *Don Iohn* your brother incensed me to slander the Ladie *Hero*, how you were brought into the Orchard, and saw me court *Margaret* in *Heroes* garments, how you disgrac'd her vvhen you should marrie her: my villanie they haue vpon record, vvhich I had rather seale vvith my death, then repeate ouer to my shame: the Ladie is dead vpon mine and my masters false accusation: and briefelie, I desire nothing but the reward of a villaine.

Prin. Runs not this speech like yron through your bloud?

Clau. I haue drunke poison whiles he vtter'd it.

Prin. But did my Brother set thee on to this?

Bor. Yea, and paid me richly for the practise of it.

Prin. He is compos'd and fram'd of treacherie,
And fled he is vpon this villanie.

Clau. Sweet Hero, now thy image doth appeare
In the rare semblance that I lou'd it first.

Const. Come, bring away the plaintiffes, by this time our *Sexton* hath reformed *Signior Leonato* of the matter: and masters, do not forget to specifie when time & place shall serue, that I am an Asse.

Con. 2. Here, here comes master *Signior Leonato*, and the *Sexton* too.

Enter Leonato.

Leon. Which is the villaine? let me see his eies,
That when I note another man like him,
I may auoide him: vvhich of these is he?

Bor. If you vvould know your wronger, looke on me.

Leon. Art thou thou the slaue that with thy breath
hast kild mine innocent childe?

Bor. Yea, euen I alone.

Leo. No, not so villaine, thou beliest thy selfe,
Here stand a paire of honourable men,
A third is fled that had a hand in it:
I thanke you Princes for my daughters death,
Record it with your high and worthie deedes,
'Twas brauely done, if you bethinke you of it.

Clau. I know not how to pray your patience,
Yet I must speake, choose your reuenge your selfe,
Impose me to what penance your inuention
Can lay vpon my sinne, yet sinn'd I not,
But in mistaking.

Prin. By my soule nor I,
And yet to satisfie this good old man,
I vvould bend vnder anie heauie vvaight,
That heele enioyne me to.

Leon. I cannot bid you bid my daughter liue,
That vvere impossible, but I praie you both,
Possesse the people in *Messina* here,
How innocent she died, and if your loue
Can labour aught in sad inuention,
Hang her an epitaph vpon her toomb,
And sing it to her bones, sing it to night:
To morrow morning come you to my house,
And since you could not be my sonne in law,
Be yet my Nephew: my brother hath a daughter,
Almost the copie of my childe that's dead,
And she alone is heire to both of vs,
Giue her the right you should haue giu'n her cosin,
And so dies my reuenge.

Clau. O noble sir!
Your ouerkindnesse doth wring teares from me,
I do embrace your offer, and dispose
For henceforth of poore *Claudio*.

Leon. To morrow then I will expect your comming,
To night I take my leaue, this naughtie man
Shall face to face be brought to *Margaret*,
Who I beleeue was packt in all this wrong,
Hired to it by your brother.

Bor. No by my soule she was not,
Nor knew not what she did when she spoke to me,
But alwaies hath bin iust and vertuous,
In anie thing that I do know by her.

Const. Moreouer sir, which indeede is not vnder white and black, this plaintiffe here, the offendour did call mee asse, I beseech you let it be remembred in his punishment, and also the vvatch heard them talke of one Deformed, they say he weares a key in his eare and a lock hanging by it, and borrowes monie in Gods name, the which he hath vs'd so long, and neuer paied, that now men grow hard-harted and will lend nothing for Gods sake: praie you examine him vpon that point.

Leon. I thanke thee for thy care and honest paines.

Const. Your vvorship speakes like a most thankefull and reuerend youth, and I praise God for you.

Leon. There's for thy paines.

Const. God saue the foundation.

Leon. Goe, I discharge thee of thy prisoner, and I thanke thee.

Const. I leaue an arrant knaue vvith your vvorship, which I beseech your worship to correct your selfe, for the example of others: God keepe your vvorship, I wish your worship vvell, God restore you to health, I humblie giue you leaue to depart, and if a merrie meeting may be wisht, God prohibite it: come neighbour.

Leon. Vntill to morrow morning, Lords, farewell.

Exeunt.

Brot. Farewell my Lords, vve looke for you to morrow.

Prin. We will not faile.

Clau. To night ile mourne with *Hero*.

Leon. Bring you these fellowes on, weel talke vvith *Margaret*, how her acquaintance grew vvith this lewd fellow. *Exeunt.*

Enter Benedicke and Margaret.

Ben. Praie thee sweete Mistris *Margaret*, deserue vvell at my hands, by helping mee to the speech of *Beatrice*.

Mar. Will

Mar. Will you then write me a Sonnet in praise of my beautie?

Bene. In so high a stile *Margaret*, that no man liuing shall come ouer it, for in most comely truth thou deseruest it.

Mar. To haue no man come ouer me, why, shall I alwaies keepe below staires?

Bene. Thy wit is as quicke as the grey-hounds mouth, it catches.

Mar. And yours, as blunt as the Fencers foiles, which hit, but hurt not.

Bene. A most manly wit *Margaret*, it will not hurt a woman: and so I pray thee call *Beatrice*, I giue thee the bucklers.

Mar. Giue vs the swords, wee haue bucklers of our owne.

Bene. If you vse them *Margaret*, you must put in the pikes with a vice, and they are dangerous weapons for Maides.

Mar. Well, I will call *Beatrice* to you, who I thinke hath legges. *Exit Margarite.*

Ben. And therefore will come. The God of loue that sits aboue, and knowes me, and knowes me, how pittifull I deserue. I meane in singing, but in louing, Leander the good swimmer, Troilous the first imploier of pandars, and a whole booke full of these quondam carpet-mongers, whose name yet runne smoothly in the euen rode of a blanke verse, why they were neuer so truely turned ouer and ouer as my poore selfe in loue: marrie I cannot shew it rime, I haue tried, I can finde out no rime to Ladie but babie, an innocent rime: for scorne, horne, a hard time: for schoole foole, a babling time: verie ominous endings, no, I was not borne vnder a riming Plannet, for I cannot wooe in festiuall tearmes:

Enter Beatrice.

sweete *Beatrice* would'st thou come when I cal'd thee?

Beat. Yea Signior, and depart when you bid me.

Bene. O stay but till then.

Beat. Then, is spoken: fare you well now, and yet ere I goe, let me goe with that I came, which is, with knowing what hath past betweene you and *Claudio*.

Bene. Onely foule words, and thereupon I will kisse thee.

Beat. Foule words is but foule wind, and foule wind is but foule breath, and foule breath is noisome, therefore I will depart vnkist.

Bene. Thou hast frighted the word out of his right sence, so forcible is thy wit, but I must tell thee plainely, *Claudio* vndergoes my challenge, and either I must shortly heare from him, or I will subscribe him a coward, and I pray thee now tell me, for which of my bad parts didst thou first fall in loue with me?

Beat. For them all together, which maintain'd so politique a state of euill, that they will not admit any good part to intermingle with them: but for which of my good parts did you first suffer loue for me?

Bene. Suffer loue! a good epithite, I do suffer loue indeede, for I loue thee against my will.

Beat. In spight of your heart I think, alas poore heart, if you spight it for my sake, I will spight it for yours, for I will neuer loue that which my friend hates.

Bened. Thou and I are too wise to wooe peaceablie.

Bea. It appeares not in this confession, there's not one wise man among twentie that will praise himselfe.

Bene. An old, an old instance *Beatrice*, that liu'd in the time of good neighbours, if a man doe not erect in this age his owne tombe ere he dies, hee shall liue no longer in monuments, then the Bels ring, & the Widdow weepes.

Beat. And how long is that thinke you

Ben. Question, why an hower in clamour and a quarter in rhewme, therfore is it most expedient for the wise, if Don worme (his conscience) finde no impediment to the contrarie, to be the trumpet of his owne vertues, as I am to my selfe so much for praising my selfe, who I my selfe will beare witnesse is praise worthie, and now tell me, how doth your cosin?

Beat. Verie ill.

Bene. And how doe you?

Beat. Verie ill too.

Enter Vrsula.

Bene. Serue God, loue me, and mend, there will I leaue you too, for here comes one in haste.

Vrs. Madam, you must come to your Vncle, yonders old coile at home, it is prooued my Ladie *Hero* hath bin falselie accusde, the *Prince* and *Claudio* mightilie abusde, and *Don Iohn* is the author of all, who is fled and gone: will you come presentlie?

Beat. Will you go heare this newes Signior?

Bene. I will liue in thy heart, die in thy lap, and be buried in thy eies: and moreouer, I will goe with thee to thy Vncles. *Exeunt.*

Enter Claudio, Prince, and three or foure with Tapers.

Clau. Is this the monument of *Leonato*?
Lord. It is my Lord. *Epitaph.*
Done to death by slanderous tongues,
Was the Hero that here lies:
Death in guerdon of her wrong,
Giues her fame which neuer dies:
So the life that dyed with shame,
Liues in death with glorious fame.
Hang thou there vpon the tombe,
Praising her when I am dombe.
Clau. Now musick sound & sing your solemn hymne

Song.

Pardon goddesse of the night,
Those that slew thy virgin knight,
For the which with songs of woe,
Round about her tombe they goe:
Midnight assist our mone, helpe vs to sigh and grone.
Heauily, heauily.
Graues yawne and yeelde your dead,
Till death be vttered,
Heauenly, heauenly.

(this right.
Lo. Now vnto thy bones good night, yeerely will I do
Prin. Good morrow masters, put your Torches out,
The wolues haue preied, and looke, the gentle day
Before the wheeles of Phœbus, round about
Dapples the drowsie East with spots of grey:
Thanks to you all, and leaue vs, fare you well.
Clau. Good morrow masters, each his seuerall way.
Prin. Come let vs hence, and put on other weedes,
And then to *Leonatoes* we will goe.
Clau. And Hymen now with luckier issue speeds,
Then

Then this for whom we rendred vp this woe. *Exeunt.*
Enter Leonato, Bene. Marg. Vrsula, old man, Frier, Hero.
Frier. Did I not tell you she was innocent?
Leo. So are the *Prince* and *Claudio* who accus'd her,
Vpon the errour that you heard debated:
But *Margaret* was in some fault for this,
Although against her will as it appeares,
In the true course of all the question.
Old. Well, I am glad that all things sort so well.
Bene. And so am I, being else by faith enforc'd
To call young *Claudio* to a reckoning for it.
Leo. Well daughter, and you gentlewomen all,
Withdraw into a chamber by your selues,
And when I send for you, come hither mask'd:
The *Prince* and *Claudio* promis'd by this howre
To visit me, you know your office Brother,
You must be father to your brothers daughter,
And giue her to young *Claudio.* *Exeunt Ladies.*
Old. Which I will doe with confirm'd countenance.
Bene. Frier, I must intreat your paines, I thinke.
Frier. To doe what Signior?
Bene. To binde me, or vndoe me, one of them:
Signior *Leonato*, truth it is good Signior,
Your neece regards me with an eye of fauour.
Leo. That eye my daughter lent her, 'tis most true.
Bene. And I doe with an eye of loue requite her.
Leo. The sight whereof I thinke you had from me,
From *Claudio*, and the *Prince*, but what's your will?
Bened. Your answer sir is Enigmaticall,
But for my will, my will is, your good will
May stand with ours, this day to be conioyn'd,
In the state of honourable marriage,
In which (good Frier) I shall desire your helpe.
Leon. My heart is with your liking.
Frier. And my helpe.
Enter Prince and Claudio, with attendants.
Prin. Good morrow to this faire assembly.
Leo. Good morrow *Prince*, good morrow *Claudio*:
We heere attend you, are you yet determin'd,
To day to marry with my brothers daughter?
Claud. Ile hold my minde were she an Ethiope.
Leo. Call her forth brother, heres the Frier ready.
Prin. Good morrow *Benedike*, why what's the matter?
That you haue such a Februarie face,
So full of frost, of storme, and clowdinesse.
Claud. I thinke he thinkes vpon the sauage bull:
Tush, feare not man, wee'll tip thy hornes with gold,
And all Europa shall reioyce at thee,
As once *Europa* did at lusty *Ioue*,
When he would play the noble beast in loue.
Ben. Bull *Ioue* sir, had an amiable low,
And some such strange bull leapt your fathers Cow,
A got a Calfe in that same noble feat,
Much like to you, for you haue iust his bleat.
Enter brother, Hero, Beatrice, Margaret, Vrsula.
Cla. For this I owe you: here comes other reckonings.
Which is the Lady I must seize vpon?
Leo. This same is she, and I doe giue you her.
Cla. Why then she's mine, sweet let me see your face.
Leon. No that you shal not, till you take her hand,
Before this Frier, and sweare to marry her.
Clau. Giue me your hand before this holy Frier,
I am your husband if you like of me.
Hero. And when I liu'd I was your other wife,
And when you lou'd, you were my other husband.
Clau. Another *Hero*?
Hero. Nothing certainer.
One *Hero* died, but I doe liue,
And surely as I liue, I am a maid.
Prin. The former *Hero*, *Hero* that is dead.
Leon. Shee died my Lord, but whiles her slander liu'd
Frier. All this amazement can I qualifie,
When after that the holy rites are ended,
Ile tell you largely of faire *Heroes* death:
Meane time let wonder seeme familiar,
And to the chappell let vs presently.
Ben. Soft and faire Frier, which is *Beatrice*?
Beat. I answer to that name, what is your will?
Bene. Doe not you loue me?
Beat. Why no, no more then reason.
Bene. Why then your Vncle, and the Prince, & *Claudio*, haue beene deceiued, they swore you did.
Beat. Doe not you loue mee?
Bene. Troth no, no more then reason.
Beat. Why then my Cosin *Margaret* and *Vrsula*
Are much deceiu'd, for they did sweare you did.
Bene. They swore you were almost sicke for me.
Beat. They swore you were wel-nye dead for me.
Bene. 'Tis no matter, then you doe not loue me?
Beat. No truly, but in friendly recompence.
Leon. Come Cosin, I am sure you loue the gentlema.
Clau. And Ile be sworne vpon't, that he loues her,
For heres a paper written in his hand,
A halting sonnet of his owne pure braine,
Fashioned to *Beatrice*.
Hero. And heeres another,
Writ in my cosins hand, stolne from her pocket
Containing her affection vnto *Benedicke*.
Bene. A miracle, here's our owne hands against our hearts: come I will haue thee, but by this light I take thee for pittie.
Beat. I would not denie you, but by this good day, I yeeld vpon great perswasion, & partly to saue your life, for I was told, you were in a consumption
Leon. Peace I will stop your mouth.
Prin. How dost thou *Benedicke* the married man?
Bene. Ile tell thee what Prince: a Colledge of witte-crackers cannot flout mee out of my humour, dost thou think I care for a Satyre or an Epigram? no, if a man will be beaten with braines, a shall weare nothing handsome about him: in briefe, since I do purpose to marry, I will thinke nothing to any purpose that the world can say against it, and therefore neuer flout at me, for I haue said against it: for man is a giddy thing, and this is my conclusion: for thy part *Claudio*, I did thinke to haue beaten thee, but in that thou art like to be my kinsman, liue vnbruis'd, and loue my cousin.
Cla. I had well hop'd ŷ wouldst haue denied *Beatrice*, ŷ I might haue cudgel'd thee out of thy single life, to make thee a double dealer, which out of questiõ thou wilt be, if my Cousin do not looke exceeding narrowly to thee.
Bene. Come, come, we are friends, let's haue a dance ere we are married, that we may lighten our own hearts, and our wiues heeles.
Leon. Wee'll haue dancing afterward.
Bene. First, of my vvord, therfore play musick. *Prince*, thou art sad, get thee a vvife, get thee a vvife, there is no staff more reuerend then one tipt with horn. *Enter. Mes.*
Messen. My Lord, your brother *Iohn* is tane in flight, And brought with armed men backe to *Messina*.
Bene. Thinke not on him till to morrow, ile deuise thee braue punishments for him: strike vp Pipers. *Dance.*

L *FINIS.*

Loues Labour's lost.

Actus primus.

Enter Ferdinand King of Nauarre, Berowne, Longauill, and Dumane.

Ferdinand.

Et *Fame*, that all hunt after in their liues,
Liue registred vpon our brazen Tombes,
And then grace vs in the disgrace of death.
when spight of cormorant deuouring Time,
Th endeuour of this present breath may buy:
That honour which shall bate his sythes keene edge,
And make vs heyres of all eternitie
Therefore braue Conquerours, for so you are,
That warre against your owne affections,
And the huge Armie of the worlds desires.
Our late edict shall strongly stand in force,
Nauar shall be the wonder of the world.
Our Court shall be a little Achademe,
Still and contemplatiue in liuing Art
You three, *Berowne, Dumaine*, and *Longauill*,
Haue sworne for three yeeres terme, to liue with me:
My fellow Schollers, and to keepe those statutes
That are recorded in this scedule heere.
Your oathes are past, and now subscribe your names:
That his owne hand may strike his honour downe,
That violates the smallest branch heerein:
If you are arm'd to doe, as sworne to do,
Subscribe to your deepe oathes, and keepe it to.

Longauill. I am resolu'd, 'tis but a three yeeres fast:
The minde shall banquet, though the body pine,
Fat paunches haue leane pates: and dainty bits,
Make rich the ribs, but bankerout the wits.

Dumane. My louing Lord, *Dumane* is mortified,
The grosser manner of these worlds delights,
He throwes vpon the grosse worlds baser slaues:
To loue, to wealth, to pompe, I pine and die,
With all these liuing in Philosophie.

Berowne. I can but say their protestation ouer,
So much, deare Liege, I haue already sworne,
That is, to liue and study heere three yeeres.
But there are other strict obseruances:
As not to see a woman in that terme,
Which I hope well is not enrolled there.
And one day in a weeke to touch no foode:
And but one meale on euery day beside:
The which I hope is not enrolled there
And then to sleepe but three houres in the night,
And not be seene to winke of all the day.
When I was wont to thinke no harme all night,
And make a darke night too of halfe the day:
Which I hope well is not enrolled there.
O, these are barren taskes, too hard to keepe,
Not to see Ladies, study, fast, not sleepe.

Ferd. Your oath is past, to passe away from these.

Berow. Let me say no my Liedge, and if you please,
I onely swore to study with your grace,
And stay heere in your Court for three yeeres space.

Longa. You swore to that *Berowne*, and to the rest.

Berow. By yea and nay sir, than I swore in iest.
What is the end of study, let me know?

Fer. Why that to know which else wee should not know.

Ber. Things hid & bard (you meane) frō cōmon sense.

Ferd. I, that is studies god-like recompence.

Bero. Come on then, I will sweare to studie so,
To know the thing I am forbid to know:
As thus, to study where I well may dine,
When I to fast expressely am forbid.
Or studie where to meet some Mistresse fine,
When Mistresses from common sense are hid.
Or hauing sworne too hard a keeping oath,
Studie to breake it, and not breake my troth.
If studies gaine be thus, and this be so,
Studie knowes that which yet it doth not know,
Sweare me to this, and I will nere say no

Ferd. These be the stops that hinder studie quite,
And traine our intellects to vaine delight.

Ber. Why? all delights are vaine, and that most vaine
Which with paine purchas'd, doth inherit paine,
As painefully to poare vpon a Booke,
To seeke the light of truth, while truth the while
Doth falsely blinde the eye-sight of his looke:
Light seeking light, doth light of light beguile:
So ere you finde where light in darkenesse lies,
Your light growes darke by losing of your eyes.
Studie me how to please the eye indeede,
By fixing it vpon a fairer eye,
Who dazling so, that eye shall be his heed,
And giue him light that it was blinded by.
Studie is like the heauens glorious Sunne,
That will not be deepe search'd with sawcy lookes:
Small haue continuall plodders euer wonne,
Saue base authoritie from others Bookes.
These earthly Godfathers of heauens lights,
That giue a name to euery fixed Starre,
Haue no more profit of their shining nights,
Then those that walke and wot not what they are.
Too much to know, is to know nought but fame:
And euery Godfather can giue a name.

Fer. How well hee's read, to reason against reading.

Dum.

Dum. Proceeded well, to stop all good proceeding.
Lon. Hee weedes the corne, and still lets grow the weeding.
Ber. The Spring is neare when greene geesse are a breeding.
Dum How followes that?
Ber. Fit in his place and time.
Dum In reason nothing.
Ber. Something then in rime.
Ferd. *Berowne* is like an enuious sneaping Frost,
That bites the first borne infants of the Spring.
Ber. Wel, say I am, why should proud Summer boast,
Before the Birds haue any cause to sing?
Why should I ioy in any abortiue birth?
At Christmas I no more desire a Rose,
Then wish a Snow in Mayes new fangled showes:
But like of each thing that in season growes.
So you to studie now it is too late,
That were to clymbe ore the house to vnlocke the gate.
Fer. Well, sit you out: go home *Berowne*: adue.
Ber. No my good Lord, I haue sworn to stay with you.
And though I haue for barbarisme spoke more,
Then for that Angell knowledge you can say,
Yet confident Ile keepe what I haue sworne,
And bide the pennance of each three yeares day.
Giue me the paper, let me reade the same,
And to the strictest decrees Ile write my name.
Fer. How well this yeelding rescues thee from shame.
Ber. *Item.* That no woman shall come within a mile of my Court
Hath this bin proclaimed?
Lon. Foure dayes agoe.
Ber. Let's see the penaltie.
On paine of loosing her tongue.
Who deuis'd this penaltie?
Lon. Marry that did I
Ber. Sweete Lord, and why?
Lon. To fright them hence with that dread penaltie,
A dangerous law against gentilitie.
Item, If any man be seene to talke with a woman within the tearme of three yeares, hee shall indure such publique shame as the rest of the Court shall possibly deuise.
Ber. This Article my Liedge your selfe must breake,
For well you know here comes in Embassie
The *French* Kings daughter, with your selfe to speake:
A Maide of grace and compleate maiestie,
About surrender vp of *Aquitaine*.
To her decrepit, sicke, and bed-rid Father
Therefore this Article is made in vaine,
Or vainly comes th'admired Princesse hither.
Fer. What say you Lords?
Why, this was quite forgot
Ber. So Studie euermore is ouershot,
While it doth study to haue what it would,
It doth forget to doe the thing it should:
And when it hath the thing it hunteth most,
'Tis won as townes with fire, so won, so lost.
Fer. We must of force dispence with this Decree,
She must lye here on meere necessitie.
Ber. Necessity will make vs all forsworne
Three thousand times within this three yeeres space:
For euery man with his affects is borne,
Not by might mastred, but by speciall grace.
If I breake faith, this word shall breake for me,
I am forsworne on meere necessitie.
So to the Lawes at large I write my name,
And he that breakes them in the least degree,
Stands in attainder of eternall shame.
Suggestions are to others as to me:
But I beleeue although I seeme so loth,
I am the last that will last keepe his oth.
But is there no quicke recreation granted?
Fer. I that there is, our Court you know is hanted
With a refined trauailer of *Spaine*,
A man in all the worlds new fashion planted,
That hath a mint of phrases in his braine:
One, who the musicke of his owne vaine tongue,
Doth rauish like inchanting harmonie:
A man of complements whom right and wrong
Haue chose as vmpire of their mutinie.
This childe of fancie that *Armado* hight,
For interim to our studies shall relate,
In high-borne words the worth of many a Knight:
From tawnie *Spaine* lost in the worlds debate.
How you delight my Lords, I know not I,
But I protest I loue to heare him lie,
And I will vse him for my Minstrelsie.
Bero. *Armado* is a most illustrious wight,
A man of fire, new words, fashions owne Knight.
Lon. *Costard* the swaine and he, shall be our sport,
And so to studie, three yeeres is but short.

Enter a Constable with Costard with a Letter

Const. Which is the Dukes owne person.
Ber. This fellow, What would'st?
Con. I my selfe reprehend his owne person, for I am his graces Tharborough: But I would see his own person in flesh and blood.
Ber. This is he.
Con. Signeor *Arme, Arme* commends you:
Ther's villanie abroad, this letter will tell you more.
Clow. Sir the Contempts thereof are as touching mee.
Fer. A letter from the magnificent *Armado*.
Ber. How low soeuer the matter, I hope in God for high words.
Lon. A high hope for a low heauen, God grant vs patience.
Ber. To heare, or forbeare hearing.
Lon. To heare meekely sir, and to laugh moderately, or to forbeare both.
Ber. Well sir, be it as the stile shall giue vs cause to clime in the mertinesse.
Clo. The matter is to me sir, as concerning *Iaquenetta*. The manner of it is, I was taken with the manner.
Ber. In what manner?
Clo. In manner and forme following sir all those three. I was seene with her in the Mannor house, sitting with her vpon the Forme, and taken following her into the Parke: which put to gether, is in manner and forme following. Now sir for the manner; It is the manner of a man to speake to a woman, for the forme in some forme.
Ber. For the following sir.
Clo. As it shall follow in my correction, and God defend the right.
Fer. Will you heare this Letter with attention?
Ber. As we would heare an Oracle
Clo. Such is the simplicitie of man to harken after the flesh.

L 2 *Fer.* Great

Ferdinand.

GReat Deputie, the Welkins Vicegerent, and sole dominator of Nauar, *my soules earths God, and bodies fostring patrone:*

Cost. Not a vvord of *Costard* yet.

Ferd. *So it is.*

Cost. It may be so: but if he say it is so, he is in telling true: but so.

Ferd. Peace,

Clow. Be to me, and euery man that dares not fight.

Ferd. No words,

Clow. Of other mens secrets I beseech you.

Ferd. *So it is besieged with sable coloured melancholie, I did commend the blacke oppressing humour to the most wholesome Physicke of thy health-giuing ayre: And as I am a Gentleman, betooke my selfe to walke: the time When? about the sixt houre, When beasts most grase, birds best pecke, and men sit downe to that nourishment which is called supper: So much for the time When. Now for the ground Which? which I meane I walkt vpon, it is ycliped, Thy Parke. Then for the place Where? where I meane I did encounter that obscene and most preposterous euent that draweth from my snow-white pen the ebon coloured Inke, which heere thou viewest, beholdest, suruayest, or seest. But to the place Where? It standeth North North-east and by East from the West corner of thy curious knotted garden; There did I see that low spirited Swaine, that base Minow of thy myrth,* (*Clown.* Mee?) *that vnletered small knowing soule,* (*Clow* Me?) *that shallow vassall* (*Clow.* Still mee?) *which as I remember, hight* Costard, (*Clow.* O me) *sorted and consorted contrary to thy established proclaymed Edict and Continet, Cannon: Which with, ô with, but with this I passion to say wherewith:*

Clo. With a Wench.

Ferd. *With a childe of our Grandmother Eue, a female; or for thy more sweet vnderstanding a woman: him, I (as my euer esteemed dutie prickes me on) haue sent to thee, to receiue the meed of punishment by thy sweet Graces Officer* Anthony Dull, *a man of good repute, carriage, bearing, & estimation.*

Anth. Me, an't shall please you? I am *Anthony Dull.*

Ferd. *For* Iaquenetta *(so is the weaker vessell called) which I apprehended with the aforesaid Swaine, I keeper her as a vessell of thy Lawes furie, and shall at the least of thy sweet notice, bring her to triall. Thine in all complements of deuoted and heart-burning heat of dutie.*

Don Adriana de Armado.

Ber. This is not so well as I looked for, but the best that euer I heard.

Fer I the best, for the worst But sirra, What say you to this?

Clo. Sir I confesse the Wench

Fer. Did you heare the Proclamation?

Clo. I doe confesse much of the hearing it, but little of the marking of it.

Fer. It was proclaimed a yeeres imprisoment to bee taken with a Wench.

Clow I was taken with none sir, I was taken vvith a Damosell.

Fer. Well, it was proclaimed Damosell.

Clo. This was no Damosell neyther sir, shee was a Virgin.

Fer It is so varried to, for it was proclaimed Virgin.

Clo. If it were, I denie her Virginitie: I was taken with a Maide.

Fer. This Maid will not serue your turne sir.

Clo. This Maide will serue my turne sir.

Kin. Sir I will pronounce your sentence: You shall fast a Weeke with Branne and water.

Clo. I had rather pray a Moneth with Mutton and Porridge.

Kin And *Don Armado* shall be your keeper.
My Lord *Berowne*, see him deliuer'd ore,
And goe we Lords to put in practice that,
Which each to other hath so strongly sworne.

Bero. Ile lay my head to any good mans hat,
These oathes and lawes will proue an idle scorne:
Sirra, come on.

Clo. I suffer for the truth sir: for true it is, I was taken with *Iaquenetta*, and *Iaquenetta* is a true girle, and therefore welcome the sowre cup of prosperitie, affliction may one day smile againe, and vntill then sit downe sorrow. *Exit.*

Enter Armado and Moth his Page.

Arma. Boy, What signe is it when a man of great spirit growes melancholy?

Boy. A great signe sir, that he will looke sad.

Brag. Why? sadnesse is one and the selfe-same thing deare impe.

Boy. No no, O Lord sir no.

Brag. How canst thou part sadnesse and melancholy my tender *Iuuenall?*

Boy. By a familiar demonstration of the working, my tough signeur.

Brag. Why tough signeur? Why tough signeur?

Boy Why tender *Iuuenall?* Why tender *Iuuenall?*

Brag. I spoke it tender *Iuuenall*, as a congruent apathaton, appertaining to thy young daies, which we may nominate tender.

Boy. And I tough signeur, as an appertinent title to your olde time, which we may name tough.

Brag. Pretty and apt.

Boy. How meane you sir, I pretty, and my saying apt? or I apt, and my saying prettie?

Brag. Thou pretty because little.

Boy. Little pretty, because little: wherefore apt?

Brag And therefore apt, because quicke.

Boy. Speake you this in my praise Master?

Brag. In thy condigne praise.

Boy. I will praise an Eele with the same praise.

Brag. What? that an Eele is ingenuous.

Boy. That an Eeele is quicke.

Brag. I doe say thou art quicke in answeres. Thou heat'st my bloud.

Boy. I am answer'd sir.

Brag. I loue not to be crost.

Boy. He speakes the meere contrary, crosses loue not (him.

Br. I haue promis'd to study iij. yeres with the Duke.

Boy. You may doe it in an houre sir.

Brag. Impossible.

Boy. How many is one thrice told?

Bra. I am ill at reckning, it fits the spirit of a Tapster.

Boy. You are a gentleman and a gamester sir.

Brag. I confesse both, they are both the varnish of a compleat man.

Boy. Then I am sure you know how much the grosse summe of deus-ace amounts to.

Brag. It doth amount to one more then two.

Boy. Which the base vulgar call three.

Br. True. *Boy.* Why sir is this such a peece of study? Now here's three studied, ere you'll thrice wink, & how easie it is to put yeres to the word three, and study three yeeres in two words, the dancing horse will tell you.

Brag. A

Brag. A most fine Figure.

Boy. To proue you Cypher.

Brag. I will heereupon confesse I am in loue: and as it is base for a Souldier to loue; so am I in loue with a base wench. If drawing my sword against the humour of affection, would deliuer mee from the reprobate thought of it, I would take Desire prisoner, and ransome him to any French Courtier for a new deuis'd curtsie. I thinke scorne to sigh, me thinkes I should out-sweare *Cupid.* Comfort me Boy, What great men haue beene in loue?

Boy. Hercules Master.

Brag. Most sweete *Hercules*: more authority deare Boy, name more; and sweet my childe let them be men of good repute and carriage.

Boy. Sampson Master, he was a man of good carriage, great carriage: for hee carried the Towne-gates on his backe like a Porter: and he was in loue.

Brag. O well-knit *Sampson*, strong ioynted *Sampson*; I doe excell thee in my rapier as much as thou didst mee in carrying gates. I am in loue too. Who was *Sampsons* loue my deare *Moth*?

Boy. A Woman, Master.

Brag. Of what complexion?

Boy. Of all the foure, or the three, or the two, or one of the foure.

Brag. Tell me precisely of what complexion?

Boy. Of the sea-water Greene sir.

Brag. Is that one of the foure complexions?

Boy. As I haue read sir, and the best of them too.

Brag. Greene indeed is the colour of Louers: but to haue a Loue of that colour, methinkes *Sampson* had small reason for it. He surely affected her for her wit.

Boy. It was so sir, for she had a greene wit.

Brag. My Loue is most immaculate white and red.

Boy. Most immaculate thoughts Master, are mask'd vnder such colours.

Brag. Define, define, well educated infant.

Boy. My fathers witte, and my mothers tongue assist mee.

Brag. Sweet inuocation of a childe, most pretty and patheticall.

Boy. If shee be made of white and red,
Her faults will nere be knowne:
For blush-in cheekes by faults are bred,
And feares by pale white showne:
Then if she feare, or be to blame,
By this you shall not know,
For still her cheekes possesse the same,
Which natiue she doth owe:
A dangerous rime master against the reason of white and redde.

Brag. Is there not a ballet Boy, of the King and the Begger?

Boy. The world was very guilty of such a Ballet some three ages since, but I thinke now tis not to be found: or if it were, it would neither serue for the writing, nor the tune.

Brag. I will haue that subiect newly writ ore, that I may example my digression by some mighty president. Boy, I doe loue that Countrey girle that I tooke in the Parke with the rationall hinde *Costard*: she deserues well.

Boy. To bee whip'd: and yet a better loue then my Master.

Brag. Sing Boy, my spirit grows heauy in loue.

Boy. And that's great maruell, louing a light wench.

Brag. I say sing.

Boy. Forbeare till this company be past.

Enter Clowne, Constable, and Wench.

Const. Sir, the Dukes pleasure, is that you keepe *Costard* safe, and you must let him take no delight, nor no penance, but hee must fast three daies a weeke: for this Damsell, I must keepe her at the Parke, shee is alowd for the Day-woman. Fare you well. *Exit.*

Brag. I do betray my selfe with blushing: Maide.

Maid. Man.

Brag. I wil visit thee at the Lodge.

Maid. That's here by.

Brag. I know where it is situate.

Mai. Lord how wise you are!

Brag. I will tell thee wonders.

Ma. With what face?

Brag. I loue thee.

Mai. So I heard you say.

Brag. And so farewell.

Mai. Faire weather after you.

Clo. Come *Iaquenetta*, away. *Exeunt.*

Brag. Villaine, thou shalt fast for thy offences ere thou be pardoned.

Clo. Well sir, I hope when I doe it, I shall doe it on a full stomacke.

Brag. Thou shalt be heauily punished.

Clo. I am more bound to you then your fellowes, for they are but lightly rewarded.

Clo. Take away this villaine, shut him vp.

Boy. Come you transgressing slaue, away.

Clow. Let mee not bee pent vp sir, I will fast being loose.

Boy. No sir, that were fast and loose: thou shalt to prison.

Clow. Well, if euer I do see the merry dayes of desolation that I haue seene, some shall see.

Boy. What shall some see?

Clow. Nay nothing, Master *Moth*, but what they looke vpon. It is not for prisoners to be silent in their words, and therefore I will say nothing: I thanke God, I haue as little patience as another man, and therefore I can be quiet. *Exit.*

Brag. I doe affect the very ground (which is base) where her shooe (which is baser) guided by her foote (which is basest) doth tread. I shall be forsworn (which is a great argument of falshood) if I loue. And how can that be true loue, which is falsly attempted? Loue is a familiar, Loue is a Diuell. There is no euill Angell but Loue, yet *Sampson* was so tempted, and he had an excellent strength: Yet was *Salomon* so seduced, and hee had a very good witte. *Cupids* Butshaft is too hard for *Hercules* Clubbe, and therefore too much ods for a Spaniards Rapier: The first and second cause will not serue my turne: the *Passado* hee respects not, the *Duello* he regards not; his disgrace is to be called Boy, but his glorie is to subdue men. Adue Valour, rust Rapier, bee still Drum, for your manager is in loue; yea hee loueth. Assist me some extemporall god of Rime, for I am sure I shall turne Sonnet. Deuise Wit, write Pen, for I am for whole volumes in folio. *Exit.*

Finis Actus Primus.

Actus Secunda.

Enter the Princeſſe of France, with three attending Ladies and three Lords.

Boyet. Now Madam ſummon vp your deareſt ſpirits
Conſider who the King your father ſends
To whom he ſends, and what's his Embaſſie
Your ſelfe, held precious in the worlds eſteeme,
To parlee with the ſole inheritour
Of all perfections that a man may owe,
Matchleſſe *Nauarre*, the plea of no leſſe weight
Then *Aquitaine*, a Dowrie for a Queene.
Be now as prodigall of all deare grace,
As Nature was in making Graces deare,
When ſhe did ſtarue the generall world beſide,
And prodigally gaue them all to you.
Queen. Good L. *Boyet*, my beauty though but mean,
Needs not the painted flouriſh of your praiſe
Beauty is bought by iudgement of the eye,
Not vttred by baſe ſale of chapmens tongues
I am leſſe proud to heare you tell my worth,
Then you much wiling to be counted wiſe,
In ſpending your wit in the praiſe of mine.
But now to taske the tasker, good *Boyet*,
Prin. You are not ignorant all-telling fame
Doth noyſe abroad *Nauar* hath made a vow,
Till painefull ſtudie ſhall out-weare three yeares,
No woman may approach his ſilent Court:
Therefore to's ſeemeth it a needfull courſe,
Before we enter his forbidden gates,
To know his pleaſure, and in that behalfe
Bold of your worthineſſe, we ſingle you,
As our beſt mouing faire ſoliciter:
Tell him, the daughter of the King of France,
On ſerious buſineſſe crauing quicke diſpatch,
Importunes perſonall conference with his grace
Haſte, ſignifie ſo much while we attend,
Like humble viſag'd ſuters his high will.
Boy. Proud of imployment, willingly I goe. *Exit.*
Prin. All pride is willing pride, and yours is ſo:
Who are the Votaries my louing Lords, that are vow-fellowes with this vertuous Duke?
Lor. *Longauill* is one.
Princ. Know you the man?
1 *Lady.* I know him Madame at a marriage feaſt,
Betweene L. *Perigort* and the beautious heire
Of *Iaques Fauconbridge* ſolemnized.
In *Normandie* ſaw I this *Longauill*,
A man of ſoueraigne parts he is eſteem'd:
Well fitted in Arts, glorious in Armes:
Nothing becomes him ill that he would well.
The onely ſoyle of his faire vertues gloſſe,
If vertues gloſſe will ſtaine with any ſoile,
Is a ſharp wit match'd with too blunt a Will.
Whoſe edge hath power to cut whoſe will ſtill wills,
It ſhould none ſpare that come within his power.
Prin. Some merry mocking Lord belike, iſt ſo?
Lad. 1. They ſay ſo moſt, that moſt his humors know.
Prin. Such ſhort liu'd wits do wither as they grow.
Who are the reſt?
2. *Lad.* The yong *Dumaine*, a well accompliſht youth,
Of all that Vertue loue, for Vertue loued.
Moſt power to doe moſt harme, leaſt knowing ill:
For he hath wit to make an ill ſhape good,
And ſhape to win grace though ſhe had no wit.
I ſaw him at the Duke *Alanſoes* once,
And much too little of that good I ſaw,
Is my report to his great worthineſſe.
Roſſa. Another of theſe Students at that time,
Was there with him, as I haue heard a truth.
Berowne they call him, but a merrier man,
Within the limit of becomming mirth,
I neuer ſpent an houres talke withall.
His eye begets occaſion for his wit,
For euery obiect that the one doth catch
The other turnes to a mirth-mouing ieſt.
Which his faire tongue (conceits expoſitor)
Deliuers in ſuch apt and gracious words,
That aged eares play treuant at his tales,
And yonger hearings are quite rauiſhed.
So ſweet and voluble is his diſcourſe
Prin. God bleſſe my Ladies, are they all in loue?
That euery one her owne hath garniſhed,
With ſuch bedecking ornaments of praiſe
Ma. Heere comes *Boyet*.

Enter Boyet.

Prin. Now, what admittance Lord?
Boyet. *Nauar* had notice of your faire approach,
And he and his competitors in oath,
Were all addreſt to meete you gentle Lady
Before I came: Marrie thus much I haue learnt,
He rather meanes to lodge you in the field,
Like one that comes heere to beſiege his Court,
Then ſeeke a diſpenſation for his oath:
To let you enter his vnpeopled houſe.

Enter Nauar, Longauill, Dumaine, and Berowne.

Heere comes *Nauar*.
Nau. Faire Princeſſe, welcom to the Court of *Nauar*
Prin. Faire I giue you backe againe, and welcome I haue not yet: the roofe of this Court is too high to bee yours, and welcome to the wide fields, too baſe to be mine.
Nau. You ſhall be welcome Madam to my Court.
Prin. I wil be welcome then, Conduct me thither.
Nau. Heare me deare Lady, I haue ſworne an oath.
Prin. Our Lady helpe my Lord, he'll be forſworne.
Nau. Not for the world faire Madam, by my will.
Prin. Why, will ſhall breake it will, and nothing els
Nau. Your Ladiſhip is ignorant what it is.
Prin. Were my Lord ſo, his ignorance were wiſe,
Where now his knowledge muſt proue ignorance.
I heare your grace hath ſworne out Houſeekeeping:
Tis deadly ſinne to keepe that oath my Lord,
And ſinne to breake it:
But pardon me, I am too ſodaine bold,
To teach a Teacher ill beſeemeth me.
Vouchſafe to read the purpoſe of my comming,
And ſodainly reſolue me in my ſuite.
Nau. Madam, I will, if ſodainly I may.
Prin. You will the ſooner that I were away,
For you'll proue periur'd if you make me ſtay.
Berow. Did not I dance with you in *Brabant* once?
Roſa. Did not I dance with you in *Brabant* once?

Ber. I

Ber. I know you did.
Rosa. How needlesse was it then to ask the question?
Ber. You must not be so quicke.
Rosa. Tis long of you ẏ spur me with such questions.
Ber. Your wit's too hot, it speeds too fast, 'twill tire.
Rosa. Not till it leaue the Rider in the mire.
Ber. What time a day?
Rosa. The howre that fooles should aske.
Ber. Now faire befall your maske.
Rosa. Faire fall the face it couers.
Ber. And send you many louers.
Rosa. Amen, so you be none.
Ber. Nay then will I be gone.
Kin. Madame, your father heere doth intimate,
The paiment of a hundred thousand Crownes,
Being but th one halfe, of an intire summe,
Disbursed by my father in his warres.
But say that he, or we, as neither haue
Receiu'd that summe; yet there remaines vnpaid
A hundred thousand more: in surety of the which,
One part of *Aquitaine* is bound to vs,
Although not valued to the moneys worth.
If then the King your father will restore
But that one halfe which is vnsatisfied,
We will giue vp our right in *Aquitaine*,
And hold faire friendship with his Maiestie:
But that it seemes he little purposeth,
For here he doth demand to haue repaie,
An hundred thousand Crownes, and not demands
One paiment of a hundred thousand Crownes,
To haue his title liue in *Aquitaine*.
Which we much rather had depart withall,
And haue the money by our father lent,
Then *Aquitane*, so guelded as it is.
Deare Princesse, were not his requests so farre
From reasons yeelding, your faire selfe should make
A yeelding 'gainst some reason in my brest,
And goe well satisfied to *France* againe.
Prin. You doe the King my Father too much wrong,
And wrong the reputation of your name,
In so vnseeming to confesse receyt
Of that which hath so faithfully beene paid.
Kin. I doe protest I neuer heard of it,
And if you proue it, Ile repay it backe,
Or yeeld vp *Aquitaine*.
Prin. We arrest your word:
Boyet, you can produce acquittances
For such a summe, from speciall Officers,
Of *Charles* his Father.
Kin. Satisfie me so.
Boyet. So please your Grace, the packet is not come
Where that and other specialties are bound,
To morrow you shall haue a sight of them.
Kin. It shall suffice me; at which enterview,
All liberall reason would I yeeld vnto:
Meane time, receiue such welcome at my hand,
As Honour, without breach of Honour may
Make tender of, to thy true worthinesse.
You may not come faire Princesse in my gates,
But heere without you shall be so receiu'd,
As you shall deeme your selfe lodg'd in my heart,
Though so deni'd farther harbour in my house:
Your owne good thoughts excuse me, and farewell,
To morrow we shall visit you againe.
Prin. Sweet health & faire desires consort your grace.
Kin. Thy own wish wish I thee, in euery place. *Exit*.

Boy. Lady, I will commend you to my owne heart,
La.Ro. Pray you doe my commendations,
I would be glad to see it.
Boy. I would you heard it grone.
La.Ro. Is the soule sicke?.
Boy. Sicke at the heart.
La.Ro. Alacke, let it bloud.
Boy. Would that doe it good?
La.Ro. My Phisicke saies I.
Boy. Will you prick't with your eye.
La.Ro. *No poynt*, with my knife.
Boy. Now God saue thy life.
La.Ro. And yours from long liuing.
Ber. I cannot stay thanks-giuing. *Exit*.

Enter Dumane.

Dum. Sir, I pray you a word: What Lady is that same?
Boy. The heire of *Alanson*, *Rosalin* her name.
Dum. A gallant Lady, Mounsier fare you well.
Long. I beseech you a word: what is she in the white?
Boy. A woman somtimes, if you saw her in the light.
Long. Perchance light in the light: I desire her name
Boy. Shee hath but one for her selfe,
To desire that were a shame.
Long. Pray you sir, whose daughter?
Boy. Her Mothers, I haue heard.
Long. Gods blessing a your beard.
Boy. Good sir be not offended,
Shee is an heyre of *Faulconbridge*.
Long. Nay, my choller is ended:
Shee is a most sweet Lady. *Exit Long*.
Boy. Not vnlike sir, that may be.

Enter Beroune.

Ber. What's her name in the cap.
Boy. *Katherine* by good hap.
Ber. Is she wedded, or no.
Boy. To her will sir, or so.
Ber. You are welcome sir, adiew.
Boy. Fare well to me sir, and welcome to you: *Exit*.
La.Ma. That last is *Beroune*, the mery mad-cap Lord.
Not a word with him, but a iest.
Boy. And euery iest but a word.
Pri. It was well done of you to take him at his word.
Boy. I was as willing to grapple, as he was to boord
La.Ma. Two hot Sheepes marie:
And wherefore not Ships? (lips.
Boy. No Sheepe (sweet Lamb) vnlesse we feed on your
La. You Sheep & I pasture: shall that finish the iest?
Boy. So you grant pasture for me.
La. Not so gentle beast.
My lips are no Common, though seuerall they be.
Bo. Belonging to whom?
La. To my fortunes and me.
Prin. Good wits wil be iangling, but gentles agree.
This ciuill warre of wits were much better vsed
On *Nauar* and his bookemen, for heere 'tis abus'd.
Bo. If my obseruation (which very seldome lies
By the hearts still rhetoricke, disclosed with eyes)
Deceiue me not now, *Nauar* is infected.
Prin. With what?
Bo. With that which we Louers intitle affected.
Prin. Your reason.
Bo. Why all his behauiours doe make their retire,
To the court of his eye, peeping thorough desire.
His hart like an Agot with your print impressed,
Proud

Proud with his forme, in his eie pride expressed.
His tongue all impatient to speake and not see,
Did stumble with haste in his eie-sight to be,
All sences to that sence did make their repaire,
To feele onely looking on fairest of faire:
Me thought all his sences were lockt in his eye,
As Iewels in Christall for some Prince to buy. (glast,
Who tendring their own worth from whence they were
Did point out to buy them along as you past
His faces owne margent did coate such amazes,
That all eyes saw his eies inchanted with gazes.
Ile giue you *Aquitaine*, and all that is his,
And you giue him for my sake, but one louing Kisse.

Prin. Come to our Pauillion, *Boyet* is disposde.

Bro. But to speak that in words, which his eie hath dis-
I onelie haue made a mouth of his eie, (clos'd.
By adding a tongue, which I know will not lie.

Lad.Ro. Thou art an old Loue-monger, and speakest skilfully.

Lad.Ma. He is *Cupids* Grandfather, and learnes news of him.

Lad.2. Then was *Venus* like her mother, for her father is but grim.

Boy. Do you heare my mad wenches?

La.1. No.

Boy. What then, do you see?

Lad.2. I, our way to be gone.

Boy. You are too hard for me. *Exeunt omnes.*

Actus Tertius.

Enter Broggart and Boy.

Song.

Bra. Warble childe, make passionate my sense of hearing.

Boy. Concolinel.

Brag. Sweete Ayer, go tendernesse of yeares: take this Key, giue enlargement to the swaine, bring him festinatly hither: I must imploy him in a letter to my Loue.

Boy. Will you win your loue with a French braule?

Bra. How meanest thou, brauling in French?

Boy. No my compleat master, but to Iigge off a tune at the tongues end, canarie to it with the feete, humour it with turning vp your eie: sigh a note and sing a note, sometime through the throate: if you swallowed loue with singing, loue sometime through: nose as if you snuft vp loue by smelling loue with your hat penthouse-like ore the shop of your eies, with your armes crost on your thinbellie doublet, like a Rabbet on a spit, or your hands in your pocket, like a man after the old painting, and keepe not too long in one tune, but a snip and away: these are complements, these are humours, these betraie nice wenches that would be betraied without these, and make them men of note: do you note men that most are affected to these?

Brag. How hast thou purchased this experience?

Boy. By my penne of obseruation.

Brag. But O, but O.

Boy. The Hobbie-horse is forgot.

Bra. Cal st thou my loue Hobbi-horse.

Boy. No Master, the Hobbie-horse is but a Colt, and and your Loue perhaps, a Hacknie: But haue you forgot your Loue?

Brag. Almost I had.

Boy. Negligent student, learne her by heart.

Brag. By heart, and in heart Boy.

Boy. And out of heart Master: all those three I will proue.

Brag. What wilt thou proue?

Boy. A man, if I liue (and this) by, in, and without, vpon the instant: by heart you loue her, because your heart cannot come by her: in heart you loue her, because your heart is in loue with her: and out of heart you loue her, being out of heart that you cannot enioy her.

Brag. I am all these three.

Boy. And three times as much more, and yet nothing at all.

Brag. Fetch hither the Swaine, he must carrie mee a letter.

Boy. A message well simpathis'd, a Horse to be embassadour for an Asse.

Brag. Ha, ha, What saiest thou?

Boy. Marrie sir, you must send the Asse vpon the Horse for he is verie slow gated: but I goe.

Brag. The way is but short, away.

Boy. As swift as Lead sir.

Brag. Thy meaning prettie ingenious, is not Lead a mettall heauie, dull, and slow?

Boy. *Minnime* honest Master, or rather Master no.

Brad. I say Lead is slow.

Boy. You are too swift sir to say so.
Is that Lead slow which is fir'd from a Gunne?

Brag. Sweete smoke of Rhetorike,
He reputes me a Cannon, and the Bullet that's he:
I shoote thee at the Swaine.

Boy. Thump then, and I flee.

Bra. A most acute Iuuenall, voluble and free of grace,
By thy fauour sweet Welkin, I must sigh in thy face.
Most rude melancholie, Valour giues thee place.
My Herald is return'd.

Enter Page and Clowne.

Pag. A wonder Master, here's a *Costard* broken in a shin.

Ar. Some enigma, some riddle, come, thy *Lenuoy* begin.

Clo. No egma, no riddle, no *lenuoy*, no salue, in thee male sir. Or sir, Plantan, a plaine Plantan: no *lenuoy*, no *lenuoy*, no Salue sir, but a Plantan.

Ar. By vertue thou inforcest laughter, thy sillie thought, my spleene, the heauing of my lunges prouokes me to rediculous smyling: O pardon me my stars, doth the inconsiderate take *salue* for *lenuoy*, and the word *lenuoy* for a *salue*?

Pag. Doe the wise thinke them other, is not *lenuoy* a *salue*? (plaine,

Ar. No *Page*, it is an epilogue or discourse to make
Some obscure precedence that hath tofore bin saine
Now will I begin your morrall, and do you follow with my *lenuoy*.
The Foxe, the Ape, and the Humble-Bee,
Were still at oddes, being but three.

Arm. Vntill the Goose came out of doore,
Staying the oddes by adding foure.

Pag. A good *Lenuoy*, ending in the Goose: would you desire more?

Clo. The Boy hath sold him a bargaine, a Goose, that's flat

Sir, your penny-worth is good, and your Goose be fat
To sell a bargaine well is as cunning as fast and loose:
Let me see a fat *Lenuoy*, I that's a fat Goose.
Ar. Come hither, come hither:
How did this argument begin?
Boy. By saying that a *Costard* was broken in a shin.
Then cal'd you for the *Lenuoy*
Clow. True, and I for a Plantan:
Thus came your argument in
Then the Boyes fat *Lenuoy*, the Goose that you bought,
And he ended the market.
Ar. But tell me: How was there a *Costard* broken in a shin?
Pag. I will tell you sencibly.
Clow. Thou hast no feeling of it *Moth*,
I will speake that *Lenuoy*.
I *Costard* running out, that was safely within,
Fell ouer the threshold, and broke my shin
Arm. We will talke no more of this matter.
Clow. Till there be more matter in the shin.
Arm. Sirra *Costard*, I will infranchise thee.
Clow. O, marrie me to one *Francis*, I smell some *Lenuoy*, some Goose in this.
Arm. By my sweete soule, I meane, setting thee at libertie. Enfreedoming thy person: thou wert emured, restrained, captiuated, bound.
Clow. True, true, and now you will be my purgation, and let me loose
Arm. I giue thee thy libertie, set thee from durance, and in lieu thereof, impose on thee nothing but this: Beare this significant to the countrey Maide *Iaquenetta*: there is remuneration, for the best ward of mine honours is rewarding my dependants. *Moth*, follow.
Pag. Like the sequell I.
Signeur *Costard* adew. *Exit.*
Clow. My sweete ounce of mans flesh, my in-conie Iew: Now will I looke to his remuneration. Remuneration, O, that's the Latine word for three-farthings: Three-farthings remuration, What's the price of this yncle? i.d. no, Ile giue you a remuneration: Why? It carries it remuneration: Why? It is a fairer name then a French-Crowne. I will neuer buy and sell out of this word.

Enter Berowne.

Ber. O my good knaue *Costard*, exceedingly well met
Clow. Pray you sir, How much Carnation Ribbon may a man buy for a remuneration?
Ber. What is a remuneration?
Cost. Marrie sir, halfe pennie farthing.
Ber. O, Why then threefarthings worth of Silke.
Cost. I thanke your worship, God be wy you.
Ber. O stay slaue, I must employ thee:
As thou wilt win my fauour, good my knaue,
Doe one thing for me that I shall intreate.
Clow. When would you haue it done sir?
Ber. O this after-noone.
Clo. Well, I will doe it sir: Fare you well.
Ber. O thou knowest not what it is.
Clo. I shall know sir, when I haue done it.
Ber. Why villaine thou must know first.
Clo. I wil come to your worship to morrow morning.
Ber. It must be done this after-noone,
Harke slaue, it is but this:
The Princesse comes to hunt here in the Parke,
And in her traine there is a gentle Ladie:
When tongues speak sweetly, then they name her name,
And *Rosaline* they call her, aske for her:
And to her white hand see thou do commend
This seal'd-vp counsaile. Ther's thy guerdon: goe.
Clo. Gardon, O sweete gardon, better then remuneration, a leuenpence-farthing better: most sweete gardon. I will doe it sir in print: gardon, remuneration.
Exit.
Ber. O, and I forsooth in loue,
I that haue beene loues whip?
A verie Beadle to a humerous sigh: A Criticke,
Nay, a night-watch Constable.
A domineering pedant ore the Boy,
Then whom no mortall so magnificent.
This wimpled, whyning, purblinde waiward Boy,
This signior *Iunios* gyant drawfe, don *Cupid*,
Regent of Loue-rimes, Lord of folded armes,
Th'annointed soueraigne of sighes and groanes:
Liedge of all loyterers and malecontents:
Dread Prince of Placcats, King of Codpeeces
Sole Emperator and great generall
Of trotting Parrators (O my little heart.)
And I to be a Corporall of his field,
And weare his colours like a Tumblers hoope.
What? I loue, I sue, I seeke a wife,
A woman that is like a Germane Cloake,
Still a repairing: euer out of frame,
And neuer going a right, being a Watch:
But being watcht, that it may still goe right.
Nay, to be periurde, which is worst of all.
And among three, to loue the worst of all,
A whitly wanton, with a veluet brow.
With two pitch bals stucke in her face for eyes.
I, and by heauen, one that will doe the deede,
Though *Argus* were her Eunuch and her garde
And I to sigh for her, to watch for her,
To pray for her, go to: it is a plague
That *Cupid* will impose for my neglect,
Of his almighty dreadfull little might.
Well, I will loue, write, sigh, pray, shue, grone,
Some men must loue my Lady, and some Ione.

Actus Quartus.

Enter the Princesse, a Forrester, her Ladies, and her Lords.

Qu. Was that the King that spurd his horse so hard,
Against the steepe vprising of the hill?
Boy. I know not, but I thinke it was not he.
Qu. Who ere a was, a shew'd a mounting minde:
Well Lords, to day we shall haue our dispatch,
On Saterday we will returne to *France*.
Then *Forrester* my friend, Where is the Bush
That we must stand and play the murtherer in?
For Hereby vpon the edge of yonder Coppice,
A Stand where you may make the fairest shoote.
Qu. I thanke my beautie, I am faire that shoote,
And thereupon thou speak'st the fairest shoote.
For. Pardon me Madam, for I meant not so.
Qu. What, what? First praise me, & then again say no,
O short liu'd pride. Not faire? alacke for woe.
For. Yes

For. Yes Madam faire.
Qu. Nay, neuer paint me now,
Where faire is not, praise cannot mend the brow.
Here (good my glasse) take this for telling true:
Faire paiment for foule words, is more then due.
For. Nothing but faire is that which you inherit.
Qu. See, see, my beautie will be sau'd by merit.
O heresie in faire, fit for these dayes,
A giuing hand, though foule, shall haue faire praise.
But come, the Bow: Now Mercie goes to kill,
And shooting well, is then accounted ill:
Thus will I saue my credit in the shoote,
Not wounding, pittie would not let me do't:
If wounding, then it was to shew my skill,
That more for praise, then purpose meant to kill.
And out of question, so it is sometimes:
Glory growes guiltie of detested crimes,
When for Fames sake, for praise an outward part,
We bend to that, the working of the hart.
As I for praise alone now seeke to spill
The poore Deeres blood, that my heart meanes no ill.
Boy. Do not curst wiues hold that selfe-soueraigntie
Onely for praise sake, when they striue to be
Lords ore their Lords?
Qu. Onely for praise, and praise we may afford,
To any Lady that subdewes a Lord.

Enter Clowne.

Boy. Here comes a member of the common-wealth.
Clo. God dig-you-den all, pray you which is the head Lady?
Qu. Thou shalt know her fellow, by the rest that haue no heads.
Clo. Which is the greatest Lady, the highest?
Qu. The thickest, and the tallest.
Clo. The thickest, & the tallest: it is so, truth is truth.
And your waste Mistris, were as slender as my wit,
One a these Maides girdles for your waste should be fit.
Are not you the chiefe womã? You are the thickest here?
Qu. What's your will sir? What's your will?
Clo. I haue a Letter from Monsier *Berowne*,
To one Lady *Rosaline*.
Qu O thy letter, thy letter: He's a good friend of mine.
Stand a side good bearer.
Boyet, you can carue,
Breake vp this Capon.
Boyet. I am bound to serue.
This Letter is mistooke: it importeth none here:
It is writ to *Iaquenetta*.
Qu. We will reade it, I sweare.
Breake the necke of the Waxe, and euery one giue eare.

Boyet reades.

BY heauen, that thou art faire, is most infallible: true that thou art beauteous, truth it selfe that thou art louely: more fairer then faire, beautifull then beautious, truer then truth it selfe: haue comiseration on thy heroicall Vassall. The magnanimous and most illustrate King *Cophetua* set eie vpon the pernicious and indubitate Begger *Zenelophon*: and he it was that might rightly say, *Veni, vidi, vici*: Which to annothanize in the vulgar, O base and obscure vulgar; *videliset*, He came, See, and ouercame: hee came one; see, two; couercame three: Who came? the King. Why did he come? to see. Why did he see? to ouercome. To whom came he? to the Begger. What saw he? the Begger. Who ouercame he? the Begger. The conclusion is victorie: On whose side? the King: the captiue is inricht: On whose side? the Beggers. The catastrophe is a Nuptiall: on whose side? the Kings: no, on both in one, or one in both. I am the King (for so stands the comparison) thou the Begger, for so witnesseth thy lowlinesse. Shall I command thy loue? I may. Shall I enforce thy loue? I could. Shall I entreate thy loue? I will. What, shalt thou exchange for ragges, roabes: for tittles titles, for thy selfe mee. Thus expecting thy reply, I prophane my lips on thy foote, my eyes on thy picture, and my heart on thy euerie part.

Thine in the dearest designe of industrie,

Don Adriana de Armatho.

Thus dost thou heare the Nemean Lion roare,
Gainst thee thou Lambe, that standest as his pray:
Submissiue fall his princely feete before,
And he from forrage will incline to play.
But if thou striue (poore soule) what art thou then?
Foode for his rage, repasture for his den.

Qu. What plume of feathers is hee that indited this Letter? What veine? What Wethercocke? Did you euer heare better?
Boy. I am much deceiued, but I remember the stile.
Qu. Else your memorie is bad, going ore it erewhile.
Boy. This *Armado* is a *Spaniard* that keeps here in court
A Phantasime, a Monarcho, and one that makes sport
To the Prince and his Booke-mates.
Qu Thou fellow, a word.
Who gaue thee this Letter?
Clow. I told you, my Lord.
Qu. To whom should'st thou giue it?
Clo. From my Lord to my Lady.
Qu. From which Lord, to which Lady?
Clo. From my Lord *Berowne*, a good master of mine,
To a Lady of *France*, that he call'd *Rosaline*.
Qu. Thou hast mistaken his letter. Come Lords away.
Here sweete, put vp this, 'twill be thine another day.
Exeunt.

Boy. Who is the shooter? Who is the shooter?
Rosa, Shall I teach you to know.
Boy. I my continent of beautie.
Rosa. Why she that beares the Bow. Finely put off.
Boy. My Lady goes to kill hornes, but if thou marrie,
Hang me by the necke, if hornes that yeare miscarrie.
Finely put on.
Rosa. Well then, I am the shooter.
Boy. And who is your Deare?
Rosa. If we choose by the hornes, your selfe come not neare. Finely put on indeede.
Maria. You still wrangle with her *Boyet*, and shee strikes at the brow.
Boyet. But she her selfe is hit lower:
Haue I hit her now.
Rosa. Shall I come vpon thee with an old saying, that was a man when King *Pippin* of *France* was a little boy, as touching the hit it.
Boyet. So I may answere thee with one as old that was a woman when Queene *Guinouer* of *Brittaine* was a little wench, as touching the hit it.

Rosa. Thou

Rosa. Thou canst not hit it,hit it,hit it,
Thou canst not hit it my good-man.

Boy. I cannot, cannot, cannot :
And I cannot,another can. *Exit.*

Clo. By my troth most pleasant,how both did fit it.

Mar. A marke marueilous well shot, for they both did hit.

Boy. A mark,O marke but that marke : a marke saies my Lady.
Let the mark haue a pricke in't,to meat at, if it may be.

Mar. Wide a'th bow hand, yfaith your hand is out.

Clo. Indeede a'must shoote nearer, or heele ne're hit the clout.

Boy. And if my hand be out, then belike your hand is in.

Clo. Then will shee get the vpshoot by cleauing the is in.

Ma. Come,come,you talke greasely, your lips grow foule

Clo. She's too hard for you at pricks,sir challenge her to boule.

Boy. I feare too much rubbing : good night my good Oule.

Clo. By my soule a Swaine,a most simple Clowne.
Lord,Lord, how the Ladies and I haue put him downe.
O my troth most sweete iests,most inconie vulgar wit,
When it comes so smoothly off,so obscenely,as it were, so fit.
Armathor ath to the side,O a most dainty man.
To see him walke before a Lady,and to beare her Fan.
To see him kisse his hand, and how most sweetly a' will sweare :
And his Page atother side,that handfull of wit,
Ah heauens,it is most patheticall nit.
Sowla,sowla. *Exeunt.*

Shoote within.

Enter Dull,Holofernes,the Pedant and Nathaniel.

Nat. Very reuerent sport truely,and done in the testimony of a good conscience.

Ped. The Deare was(as you know)sanguis in blood, ripe as a Pomwater,who now hangeth like a Iewell in the eare of *Celo* the skie ; the welken the heauen, and anon falleth like a Crab on the face of *Terra*,the soyle,the land,the earth.

Curat.Nath. Truely M.*Holofernes*,the epythithes are sweetly varied like a scholler at the least: but sir I assure ye, it was a Bucke of the first head.

Hol. Sir *Nathaniel*, *haud credo.*

Dul. 'Twas not a *haud credo*,'twas a Pricket.

Hol. Most barbarous intimation : yet a kinde of insinuation,as it were *in via*,in way of explication *facere* : as it were replication,or rather *ostentare*,to show as it were his inclination after his vndressed,vnpolished, vneducated,vnpruned,vntrained,or rather vnlettered, or ratherest vnconfirmed fashion,to insert againe my *haud credo* for a Deare.

Dul. I said the Deare was not a *haud credo*, 'twas a Pricket.

Hol. Twice sod simplicitie, *bis coctus*, O thou monster Ignorance, how deformed doost thou looke.

Nath. Sir hee hath neuer fed of the dainties that are bred in a booke.
He hath not eate paper as it were :
He hath not drunke inke.
His intellect is not replenished, hee is onely an animall onely sensible in the duller parts: and such barren plants are set before vs,that we thankfull should be : which we taste and feeling,are for those parts that doe fructifie in vs more then he.
For as it would ill become me to be vaine,indiscreet,or a foole ;
So were there a patch set on Learning, to see him in a Schoole.
But *omne bene* say I,being of an old Fathers minde,
Many can brooke the weather,that loue not the winde.

Dul. You two are book-men: Can you tell by your wit,What was a month old at *Cains* birth; that's not fiue weekes old as yet?

Hol. *Dictisima* goodman Dull, *dictisima* goodman Dull.

Dul. What is *dictima*?

Nath. A title to *Phebe*,to *Luna*,to the *Moone*.

Hol. The Moone was a month old when *Adam* was no more. (score.
And wrought not to fiue-weekes when he came to fiue-
Th'allusion holds in the Exchange.

Dul. 'Tis true indeede, the Collusion holds in the Exchange.

Hol. God comfort thy capacity,I say th'allusion holds in the Exchange.

Dul. And I say the polusion holds in the Exchange : for the Moone is neuer but a month old : and I say beside that, twas a Pricket that the Princesse kill'd.

Hol. Sir *Nathaniel*, will you heare an extemporall Epytaph on the death of the Deare, and to humour the ignorant call d the Deare, the Princesse kill'd a Pricket.

Nath. *Perge*, good M. *Holofernes*, *perge*, so it shall please you to abrogate scurilitie.

Hol I will something affect the letter, for it argues facilitie.

The prayfull Princesse pearst and pricks
a prettie pleasing Pricket,
Some say a Sore,but not a sore,
till now made sore with shooting
The Dogges did yell,put ell to Sore,
then Sorell iumps from thicket :
Or Pricket-sore, or else Sorell,
the people fall a hooting.
If Sore be sore,then ell to Sore,
makes fiftie sores O sorell :
Of one sore I an hundred make
by adding but one more L.

Nath. A rare talent.

Dul. If a talent be a claw, looke how he clawes him with a talent.

Nath. This is a gift that I haue simple: simple,a foolish extrauagant spirit,full of formes,figures,shapes,obiects,Ideas,apprehensions,motions,reuolutions. These are begot in the ventricle of memorie, nourisht in the wombe of primater,and deliuered vpon the mellowing of occasion : but the gift is good in those in whom it is acute,and I am thankfull for it.

Hol. Sir, I praise the Lord for you, and so may my parishioners, for their Sonnes are well tutor'd by you, and their Daughters profit very greatly vnder you : you are a good member of the common-wealth.

Nath. *Me hercle*, If their Sonnes be ingennious, they shall

shall want no instruction: If their Daughters be capable, I will put it to them. But *Vir sapis qui pauca loquitur*, a soule Feminine saluteth vs.

Enter Iaquenetta and the Clowne.

Iaqu. God giue you good morrow M. *Person.*

Nath. Master Person, *quasi* Person? And if one should be perst, Which is the one?

Clo. Marry M. Schoolemaster, hee that is likest to a hogshead.

Nath. Of persing a Hogshead, a good luster of conceit in a turph of Earth, Fire enough for a Flint, Pearle enough for a Swine: 'tis prettie, it is well.

Iaqu. Good Master Parson be so good as reade mee this Letter, it was giuen mee by *Costard*, and sent mee from *Don Armatho*: I beseech you reade it.

Nath. *Facile precor gellide, quando pecas omnia sub vmbra ruminat*, and so forth. Ah good old *Mantuan*, I may speake of thee as the traueiler doth of *Venice, vemchie, vencha, que non te vnde, que non te perreche.* Old *Mantuam*, old *Mantuan*. Who vnderstandeth thee not, *vt re sol la mi fa*: Vnder pardon sir, What are the contents? or rather as *Horrace* sayes in his, What my soule verses.

Hol. I sir, and very learned.

Nath. Let me heare a staffe, a stanze, a verse, *Lege domine.*

If Loue make me forsworne, how shall I sweare to loue?
Ah neuer faith could hold, if not to beautie vowed.
Though to my selfe forsworn, to thee Ile faithfull proue.
Those thoughts to mee were Okes, to thee like Osiers bowed.
Studie his byas leaues, and makes his booke thine eyes.
Where all those pleasures liue, that Art would comprehend.
If knowledge be the marke, to know thee shall suffice.
Well learned is that tongue, that well can thee comend.
All ignorant that soule, that sees thee without wonder.
Which is to me some praise, that I thy parts admire;
Thy eye *Ioues* lightning beares, thy voyce his dreadfull thunder.
Which not to anger bent, is musique, and sweet fire.
Celestiall as thou art, Oh pardon loue this wrong,
That sings heauens praise, with such an earthly tongue.

Ped. You finde not the apostraphas, and so misse the accent. Let me superuise the cangenet.

Nath. Here are onely numbers ratified, but for the elegancy, facility, & golden cadence of poesie *caret*: *Ouiddius Naso* was the man. And why in deed *Naso*, but for smelling out the odoriferous flowers of fancy? the ierkes of inuention imitarie is nothing: So doth the Hound his master, the Ape his keeper, the tyred Horse his rider: But *Damosella virgin*, Was this directed to you?

Iaq. I sir from one mounsier *Berowne*, one of the strange Queenes Lords.

Nath. I will ouerglance the superscript.

To the snow-white hand of the most beautious Lady Rosaline.

I will looke againe on the intellect of the Letter, for the nomination of the partie written to the person written vnto.

Your Ladiships in all desired imployment, Berowne.

Per. Sir *Holofernes*, this *Berowne* is one of the Votaries with the King, and here he hath framed a Letter to a sequent of the stranger Queenes: which accidentally, or by the way of progression, hath miscarried. Trip and goe my sweete, deliuer this Paper into the hand of the King, it may concerne much: stay not thy complement, I forgiue thy duetie, adue.

Maid. Good *Costard* go with me:
Sir God saue your life.

Cost. Haue with thee my girle. *exit.*

Hol. Sir you haue done this in the feare of God very religiously: and as a certaine Father saith

Ped. Sir tell not me of the Father, I do feare colourable colours. But to returne to the Verses, Did they please you sir *Nathaniel*?

Nath. Maruellous well for the pen.

Peda. I do dine to day at the fathers of a certaine Pupill of mine, where if (being repast) it shall please you to gratifie the table with a Grace. I will on my priuiledge I haue with the perents of the foresaid Childe or Pupill, vndertake your *bien vonuto*, where I will proue those Verses to be very vnlearned, neither sauouring of Poetrie, Wit, nor Inuention. I beseech your Societie.

Nat. And thanke you to: for societie (saith the text) is the happinesse of life.

Peda. And certes the text most infallibly concludes it. Sir I do inuite you too, you shall not say me nay: *pauca verba.*

Away, the gentles are at their game, and we will to our recreation. *Exeunt.*

Enter Berowne with a Paper in his hand, alone.

Bero. The King he is hunting the Deare,
I am coursing my selfe.

They haue pitcht a Toyle, I am toyling in a pytch, pitch that defiles; defile, a foule word: Well, set thee downe sorrow; for so they say the foole said, and so say I, and I the foole: Well proued wit. By the Lord this Loue is as mad as *Aiax*, it kils sheepe, it kils mee, I a sheepe: Well proued againe a my side. I will not loue; If I do hang me: yfaith I will not. O but her eye: by this light, but for her eye, I would not loue her; yes, for her two eyes. Well, I doe nothing in the world but lye, and lye in my throate. By heauen I doe loue, and it hath taught mee to Rime, and to be mallicholie: and here is part of my Rime, and heere my mallicholie. Well, she hath one a my Sonnets already, the Clowne bore it, the Foole sent it, and the Lady hath it: sweet Clowne, sweeter Foole, sweetest Lady. By the world, I would not care a pin, if the other three were in. Here comes one with a paper, God giue him grace to grone.

He stands aside. *The King entreth.*

Kin. Ay mee!

Ber. Shot by heauen: proceede sweet *Cupid*, thou hast thumpt him with thy Birdbolt vnder the left pap: in faith secrets.

King. So sweete a kisse the golden Sunne giues not,
To those fresh morning drops vpon the Rose,
As thy eye beames, when their fresh rayse haue smot.
The night of dew that on my cheekes downe flowes.
Nor shines the siluer Moone one halfe so bright;
Through the transparent bosome of the deepe,
As doth thy face through teares of mine giue light:
Thou shin'st in euery teare that I doe weepe,
No drop, but as a Coach doth carry thee:
So ridest thou triumphing in my woe.
Do but behold the teares that swell in me,
And they thy glory through my griefe will show:

But

But doe not loue thy selfe, then thou wilt keepe
My teares for glasses, and still make me weepe.
O Queene of Queenes, how farre dost thou excell,
No thought can thinke, nor tongue of mortall tell.
How shall she know my griefes? Ile drop the paper.
Sweet leaues shade folly. Who is he comes heere?

Enter Longauile. *The King steps aside.*

What *Longauill*, and reading: listen eare.
Ber. Now in thy likenesse, one more foole appeare.
Long. Ay me, I am forsworne.
Ber. Why he comes in like a periure, wearing papers.
Long. In loue I hope, sweet fellowship in shame.
Ber. One drunkard loues another of the name.
Lon. Am I the first ẏ haue been periur'd so? (know,
Ber. I could put thee in comfort, not by two that I
Thou makest the triumphery, the corner cap of societie,
The shape of Loues Tiburne, that hangs vp simplicitie.
Lon. I feare these stubborn lines lack power to moue.
O sweet *Maria*, Empresse of my Loue,
These numbers will I teare, and write in prose.
Ber. O Rimes are gards on wanton *Cupids* hose,
Disfigure not his Shop.
Lon. This same shall goe. *He reades the Sonnet.*
Did not the heauenly Rhetoricke of thine eye,
Gainst whom the world cannot hold argument,
Perswade my heart to this false periurie?
Vowes for thee broke deserue not punishment.
A Woman I forswore, but I will proue,
Thou being a Goddesse, I forswore not thee.
My Vow was earthly, thou a heauenly Loue.
Thy grace being gain'd, cures all disgrace in me.
Vowes are but breath, and breath a vapour is.
Then thou faire Sun, which on my earth doest shine,
Exhalest this vapor-vow, in thee it is:
If broken then, it is no fault of mine:
If by me broke, What foole is not so wise
To loose an oath, to win a Paradise?
Ber. This is the liuer veine, which makes flesh a deity.
A greene Goose, a Coddesse, pure pure Idolatry.
God amend vs, God amend, we are much out o'th'way.

Enter Dumaine.

Lon. By whom shall I send this (company?) Stay.
Bero. All hid, all hid, an old infant play,
Like a demie God, here sit I in the skie,
And wretched fooles secrets heedfully ore-eye.
More Sacks to the myll. O heauens I haue my wish,
Dumaine transform'd, foure Woodcocks in a dish.
Dum. O most diuine *Kate.*
Bero. O most prophane coxcombe.
Dum. By heauen the wonder of a mortall eye.
Bero. By earth she is not, corporall, there you lye.
Dum. Her Amber haires for foule hath amber coted.
Ber. An Amber coloured Rauen was well noted.
Dum. As vpright as the Cedar.
Ber. Stoope I say her shoulder is with-child.
Dum. As faire as day.
Ber. I as some daies, but then no sunne must shine.
Dum. O that I had my wish?
Lon. And I had mine.
Kin. And mine too good Lord.
Ber. Amen, so I had mine: Is not that a good word?
Dum. I would forget her, but a Feuer she
Raignes in my bloud, and will remembred be.
Ber. A Feuer in your bloud, why then incision
Would let her out in Sawcers, sweet misprision.
Dum. Once more Ile read the Ode that I haue writ.
Ber. Once more Ile marke how Loue can varry Wit.

Dumane reades his Sonnet.

On a day, alack the day:
Loue, whose Month is euery May,
Spied a blossome passing faire,
Playing in the wanton ayre:
Through the Veluet, leaues the winde,
All vnseene, can passage finde.
That the Louer sicke to death,
Wish himselfe the heauens breath.
Ayre (quoth he) thy cheekes may blowe,
Ayre, would I might triumph so.
But alacke my hand is sworne,
Nere to plucke thee from thy throne:
Vow alacke for youth vnmeete,
Youth so apt to plucke a sweet.
Doe not call it sinne in me,
That I am forsworne for thee.
Thou for whom Ioue would sweare,
Iuno but an Æthiop were,
And denie himselfe for Ioue.
Turning mortall for thy Love.

This will I send, and something else more plaine.
That shall expresse my true-loues fasting paine.
O would the *King, Berowne* and *Longauill*,
Were Louers too, ill to example ill,
Would from my forehead wipe a periur'd note:
For none offend, where all alike doe dote.
Lon. *Dumaine*, thy Loue is farre from charitie,
That in Loues griefe desir'st societie:
You may looke pale, but I should blush I know,
To be ore-heard, and taken napping so.
Kin. Come sir, you blush: as his, your case is such,
You chide at him, offending twice as much.
You doe not loue *Maria*? *Longauile*,
Did neuer Sonnet for her sake compile;
Nor neuer lay his wreathed armes athwart
His louing bosome, to keepe downe his heart.
I haue beene closely shrowded in this bush,
And markt you both, and for you both did blush.
I heard your guilty Rimes, obseru'd your fashion:
Saw sighes reeke from you, noted well your passion.
Aye me, sayes one! O *Ioue*, the other cries!
On her haires were Gold, Christall the others eyes
You would for Paradise breake Faith and troth,
And *Ioue* for your Loue would infringe an oath.
What will *Berowne* say when that he shall heare
Faith infringed, which such zeale did sweare.
How will he scorne? how will he spend his wit?
How will he triumph, leape, and laugh at it?
For all the wealth that euer I did see,
I would not haue him know so much by me.
Bero. Now step I forth to whip hypocrisie.
Ah good my Liedge, I pray thee pardon me.
Good heart, What grace hast thou thus to reproue
These wormes for louing, that art most in loue?
Your eyes doe make no couches in your teares,
There is no certaine Princesse that appeares.
You'll not be periur'd, 'tis a hatefull thing:
Tush, none but Minstrels like of Sonnetting.
But are you not asham'd? nay, are you not

M All

All three of you, to be thus much ore'ſhot?
You found his Moth, the King your Moth did ſee:
But I a Beame doe finde in each of three.
O what a Scene of fool'ry haue I ſeene.
Of ſighes, of grones, of ſorrow, and of teene:
O me, with what ſtrict patience haue I ſat,
To ſee a King transformed to a Gnat?
To ſee great *Hercules* whipping a Gigge,
And profound *Salomon* tuning a Iygge?
And *Neſtor* play at puſh-pin with the boyes,
And Critticke *Tymon* laugh at idle toyes.
Where lies thy griefe? O tell me good *Dumaine*;
And gentle *Longauill*, where lies thy paine?
And where my Liedges? all about the breſt:
A Candle hoa!
Kin. Too bitter is thy ieſt.
Are wee betrayed thus to thy ouer-view?
Ber. Not you by me, but I betrayed to you.
I that am honeſt, I that hold it ſinne
To breake the vow I am ingaged in.
I am betrayed by keeping company
With men, like men of inconſtancie.
When ſhall you ſee me write a thing in rime?
Or grone for *Ioane*? or ſpend a minutes time,
In pruning mee, when ſhall you heare that I will praiſe a hand, a foot, a face, an eye: a gate, a ſtate, a brow, a breſt, a waſte, a legge, a limme.
Kin. Soft, Whither a-way ſo faſt?
A true man, or a theefe, that gallops ſo.
Ber. I poſt from Loue, good Louer let me go

Enter Iaquenetta and Clowne.

Iaqu. God bleſſe the King.
Kin. What Preſent haſt thou there?
Clo. Some certaine treaſon.
Kin. What makes treaſon heere?
Clo. Nay it makes nothing ſir.
Kin. If it marre nothing neither,
The treaſon and you goe in peace away together
Iaqu. I beſeech your Grace let this Letter be read,
Our perſon miſ-doubts it: it was treaſon he ſaid.
Kin. *Berowne*, read it ouer. *He reades the Letter.*
Kin. Where hadſt thou it?
Iaqu. Of *Coſtard*.
King. Where hadſt thou it?
Coſt. Of *Dun Adramadio, Dun Adramadio*.
Kin. How now, what is in you? why doſt thou tear it?
Ber. A toy my Liedge, a toy: your grace needes not feare it.
Long. It did moue him to paſſion, and therefore let's heare it.
Dum. It is *Berowns* writing, and heere is his name.
Ber. Ah you whoreſon loggerhead, you were borne to doe me ſhame.
Guilty my Lord, guilty: I confeſſe, I confeſſe.
Kin. What?
Ber. That you three fooles, lackt mee foole, to make vp the meſſe.
He, he, and you: and you my Liedge, and I,
Are picke-purſes in Loue, and we deſerue to die.
O diſmiſſe this audience, and I ſhall tell you more.
Dum. Now the number is euen
Berow. True true, we are fowre: will theſe Turtles be gone?
Kin. Hence ſirs, away.
Clo. Walk aſide the true folke, & let the traytors ſtay.
Ber. Sweet Lords, ſweet Louers, O let vs imbrace,
As true we are as fleſh and bloud can be,
The Sea will ebbe and flow, heauen will ſhew his face:
Young bloud doth not obey an old decree.
We cannot croſſe the cauſe why we are borne:
Therefore of all hands muſt we be forſworne.
King. What, did theſe rent lines ſhew ſome loue of thine?
Ber. Did they, quoth you? Who ſees the heauenly *Roſaline*,
That (like a rude and ſauage man of *Inde*.)
At the firſt opening of the gorgeous Eaſt,
Bowes not his vaſſall head, and ſtrooken blinde.
Kiſſes the baſe ground with obedient breaſt
What peremptory Eagle-ſighted eye
Dares looke vpon the heauen of her brow,
That is not blinded by her maieſtie?
Kin. What zeale, what furie, hath inſpir'd thee now?
My Loue (her Miſtres) is a gracious Moone,
Shee (an attending Starre) ſcarce ſeene a light.
Ber. My eyes are then no eyes, nor I *Berowne*.
O, but for my Loue, day would turne to night,
Of all complexions the cul'd ſoueraignty,
Doe meet as at a faire in her faire cheeke,
Where ſeuerall Worthies make one dignity,
Where nothing wants, that want it ſelfe doth ſeeke.
Lend me the flouriſh of all gentle tongues,
Fie painted Rethoricke, O ſhe needs it not,
To things of ſale, a ſellers praiſe belongs:
She paſſes prayſe, then prayſe too ſhort doth blot.
A withered Hermite, fiueſcore winters worne,
Might ſhake off fiftie, looking in her eye:
Beauty doth varniſh Age, as if new borne,
And giues the Crutch the Cradles infancie.
O 'tis the Sunne that maketh all things ſhine.
King. By heauen, thy Loue is blacke as Ebonie.
Berow. Is Ebonie like her? O word diuine?
A wife of ſuch wood were felicitie.
O who can giue an oth? Where is a booke?
That I may ſweare Beauty doth beauty lacke,
If that ſhe learne not of her eye to looke:
No face is faire that is not full ſo blacke.
Kin. O paradoxe, Blacke is the badge of hell,
The hue of dungeons, and the Schoole of night:
And beauties creſt becomes the heauens well.
Ber. Diuels ſooneſt tempt reſembling ſpirits of light.
O if in blacke my Ladies browes be deckt,
It mournes, that painting vſurping haire
Should rauiſh doters with a falſe aſpect:
And therfore is ſhe berne to make blacke, faire.
Her fauour turnes the faſhion of the dayes,
For natiue bloud is counted painting now:
And therefore red that would auoyd diſpraiſe,
Paints it ſelfe blacke, to imitate her brow.
Dum. To look like her are Chimny-ſweepers blacke.
Lon. And ſince her time, are Colliers counted bright.
King. And *Æthiops* of their ſweet complexion crake.
Dum. Dark needs no Candles now, for dark is light.
Ber. Your miſtreſſes dare neuer come in raine,
For feare their colours ſhould be waſht away.
Kin. 'Twere good yours did: for ſir to tell you plaine,
Ile finde a fairer face not waſht to day.
Ber. Ile proue her faire, or talke till dooms-day here.
Kin. No Diuell will fright thee then ſo much as ſhee.
Duma. I neuer knew man hold vile ſtuffe ſo deere.
Lon. Looke, heer's thy loue, my foot and her face ſee.
Ber. O if the ſtreets were paued with thine eyes,
Her

Her feet were much too dainty for such tread.
Dumai. O vile, then as she goes what vpward lyes?
The street should see as she walk'd ouer head.
Kin. But what of this, are we not all in loue?
Ber. O nothing so sure, and thereby all forsworne.
Kin. Then leaue this chat, & good *Berown* now proue
Our louing lawfull, and our fayth not torne.
Dum. I marie there, some flattery for this euill.
Long. O some authority how to proceed,
Some tricks, some quillets, how to cheat the diuell.
Dum. Some salue for periurie.
Ber. O 'tis more then neede.
Haue at you then affections men at armes,
Consider what you first did sweare vnto:
To fast, to study, and to see no woman:
Flat treason against the Kingly state of youth.
Say, Can you fast? your stomacks are too young:
And abstinence ingenders maladies.
And where that you haue vow'd to studie (Lords)
In that each of you haue forsworne his Booke.
Can you still dreame and pore, and thereon looke.
For when would you my Lord, or you, or you,
Haue found the ground of studies excellence,
Without the beauty of a womans face;
From womens eyes this doctrine I deriue,
They are the Ground, the Bookes, the Achadems,
From whence doth spring the true *Promethean* fire.
Why, vniuersall plodding poysons vp
The nimble spirits in the arteries,
As motion and long during action tyres
The sinnowy vigour of the trauailer.
Now for not looking on a womans face,
You haue in that forsworne the vse of eyes:
And studie too, the causer of your vow.
For where is any Author in the world,
Teaches such beauty as a womans eye:
Learning is but an adiunct to our selfe,
And where we are, our Learning likewise is.
Then when our selues we see in Ladies eyes,
With our selues.
Doe we not likewise see our learning there?
O we haue made a Vow to studie, Lords,
And in that vow we haue forsworne our Bookes:
For when would you (my Leege) or you, or you?
In leaden contemplation haue found out
Such fiery Numbers as the prompting eyes,
Of beauties tutors haue inrich'd you with:
Other slow Arts intirely keepe the braine:
And therefore finding barraine practizers,
Scarce shew a haruest of their heauy toyle.
But Loue first learned in a Ladies eyes,
Liues not alone emured in the braine:
But with the motion of all elements,
Courses as swift as thought in euery power,
And giues to euery power a double power,
Aboue their functions and their offices.
It addes a precious seeing to the eye:
A Louers eyes will gaze an Eagle blinde.
A Louers eare will heare the lowest sound
When the suspicious head of theft is stopt.
Loues feeling is more soft and sensible,
Then are the tender hornes of Cockled Snayles.
Loues tongue proues dainty, *Bachus* grosse in taste,
For Valour, is not Loue a *Hercules*?
Still climing trees in the *Hesperides*.
Subtill as *Sphinx*, as sweet and musicall,
As bright *Apollo's* Lute, strung with his haire.
And when Loue speakes, the voyce of all the Gods,
Make heauen drowsie with the harmonie.
Neuer durst Poet touch a pen to write,
Vntill his Inke were tempred with Loues sighes:
O then his lines would rauish sauage eares,
And plant in Tyrants milde humilitie.
From womens eyes this doctrine I deriue.
They sparcle still the right promethean fire,
They are the Bookes, the Arts, the Achademes,
That shew, containe, and nourish all the world.
Else none at all in ought proues excellent.
Then fooles you were these women to forsweare:
Or keeping what is sworne, you will proue fooles,
For Wisedomes sake, a word that all men loue:
Or for Loues sake, a word that loues all men.
Or for Mens sake, the author of these Women.
Or Womens sake, by whom we men are Men.
Let's once loose our oathes to finde our selues,
Or else we loose our selues, to keepe our oathes:
It is religion to be thus forsworne.
For Charity it selfe fulfills the Law:
And who can seuer loue from Charity.
Kin. Saint *Cupid* then, and Souldiers to the field.
Ber. Aduance your standards, & vpon them Lords.
Pell, mell, downe with them: but be first aduis'd,
In conflict that you get the Sunne of them.
Long. Now to plaine dealing, Lay these glozes by,
Shall we resolue to woe these girles of France?
Kin. And winne them too, therefore let vs deuise,
Some entertainment for them in their Tents.
Ber. First from the Park let vs conduct them thither,
Then homeward euery man attach the hand
Of his faire Mistresse, in the afternoone
We will with some strange pastime solace them:
Such as the shortnesse of the time can shape,
For Reuels, Dances, Maskes, and merry houres,
Fore-runne faire Loue, strewing her way with flowres.
Kin. Away, away, no time shall be omitted,
That will be time, and may by vs be fitted.
Ber. Alone, alone sowed Cockell, reap'd no Corne,
And Iustice alwaies whirles in equall manure:
Light Wenches may proue plagues to men forsworne,
If so, our Copper buyes no better treasure. *Exeunt.*

Actus Quartus.

Enter the Pedant, Curate and Dull.

Pedant. *Satis quid sufficit.*

Curat. I praise God for you sir, your reasons at dinner haue beene sharpe & sententious: pleasant without scurrillity, witty without affection, audacious without impudency, learned without opinion, and strange without heresie: I did conuerse this *quondam* day with a companion of the kings, who is intituled, nominated, or called, *Don Adriano de Armatho.*

Ped. *Noui hominum tanquam te,* His humour is lofty, his discourse peremptorie: his tongue filed, his eye ambitious, his gate maiesticall, and his generall behauiour vaine, ridiculous, and thrasonicall. He is too picked, too spruce, too affected, too odde, as it were, too peregrinat, as I may call it.

M 3 *Curat*

Curat. A most singular and choise Epithat,

Draw out his Table-booke.

Peda. He draweth out the thred of his verbositie, finer then the staple of his argument. I abhor such phanaticall phantasims, such insociable and poynt deuise companions, such rackers of ortagriphie, as to speake dout fine, when he should say doubt; det, when he shold pronounce debt; d e b t, not det: he clepeth a Calf, Caufe: halfe, haufe: neighbour *vocatur* nebour; neigh abreuiated ne: this is abhominable, which he would call abhominable: it insinuateth me of infamie: *ne inteligis domine,* to make franticke, lunaticke?

Cura. Laus deo, bene intelligo.

Peda. Bome boon for boon prescian, a little scratcht, 'twil serue.

Enter Bragart, Boy.

Curat. Vides ne quis venit?

Peda. Video, & gaudio.

Brag. Chirra.

Peda. Quari Chirra, not Sirra?

Brag. Men of peace well incountred.

Ped. Most millitarie sir salutation.

Boy. They haue beene at a great feast of Languages, and stolne the scraps.

Clow. O they haue liu'd long on the almes-basket of words. I maruell thy M. hath not eaten thee for a word, for thou art not so long by the head as honorificabilitudinitatibus: Thou art easier swallowed then a flapdragon.

Page. Peace, the peale begins.

Brag. Mounsier, are you not lettred?

Page. Yes, yes, he teaches boyes the Horne-booke: What is Ab speld backward with the horn on his head?

Peda. Ba, *puericia* with a horne added.

Pag. Ba most seely Sheepe, with a horne: you heare his learning.

Peda. Quis quis, thou Consonant?

Pag. The last of the fiue Vowels if You repeat them, or the fift if I.

Peda. I will repeat them: a e I.

Pag. The Sheepe, the other two concludes it o u.

Brag. Now by the salt waue of the mediteranium, sweet tutch, a quicke vene we of wit, snip snap, quick & home, it reioyceth my intellect, true wit.

Page. Offered by a childe to an olde man: which is wit-old.

Peda. What is the figure? What is the figure?

Page. Hornes.

Peda. Thou disputes like an Infant: goe whip thy Gigge.

Pag. Lend me your Horne to make one, and I will whip about your Infamie *vnum cita* a gigge of a Cuckolds horne.

Clow. And I had but one penny in the world, thou shouldst haue it to buy Ginger bread: Hold, there is the very Remuneration I had of thy Maister, thou halfpenny purse of wit, thou Pidgeon-egge of discretion. O & the heauens were so pleased, that thou wert but my Bastard; What a ioyfull father wouldst thou make mee? Goe to, thou hast it *ad dungil,* at the fingers ends, as they say.

Peda. Oh I smell false Latine, *dunghel* for *unguem.*

Brag. Arts-man preambulat, we will bee singled from the barbarous. Do you not educate youth at the Charghouse on the top of the Mountaine?

Peda. Or *Mons* the hill.

Brag. At your sweet pleasure, for the Mountaine.

Peda. I doe *sans question.*

Bra. Sir, it is the Kings most sweet pleasure and affection, to congratulate the Princesse at her Pauilion, in the *posteriors* of this day, which the rude multitude call the after-noone.

Ped. The *posterior* of the day, most generous sir, is liable, congruent, and measurable for the after-noone: the word is well culd, chose, sweet, and apt I doe assure you sir, I doe assure.

Brag. Sir, the King is a noble Gentleman, and my familiar, I doe assure ye very good friend: for what is inward betweene vs, let it passe. I doe beseech thee remember thy curtesie. I beseech thee apparell thy head: and among other importunate & most serious designes, and of great import indeed too: but let that passe, for I must tell thee it will please his Grace (by the world) sometime to leane vpon my poore shoulder, and with his royall finger thus dallie with my excrement, with my mustachio: but sweet heart let that passe. By the world I recount no fable, some certaine speciall honours it pleaseth his greatnesse to impart to *Armado* a Souldier, a man of trauell, that hath seene the world: but let that passe; the very all of all is: but sweet heart, I do implore secrecie, that the King would haue mee present the Princesse (sweet chucke) with some delightfull ostentation, or show, or pageant, or anticke, or fire-worke: Now, vnderstanding that the Curate and your sweet self are good at such eruptions, and sodaine breaking out of myrth (as it were) I haue acquainted you withall, to the end to craue your assistance.

Peda. Sir, you shall present before her the Nine Worthies. Sir *Holofernes,* as concerning some entertainment of time, some show in the posterior of this day, to bee rendred by our assistants the Kings command: and this most gallant, illustrate and learned Gentleman, before the Princesse: I say none so fit as to present the Nine Worthies.

Curat. Where will you finde men worthy enough to present them?

Peda. Iosua, your selfe: my selfe, and this gallant gentleman *Iudas Machabeus;* this Swaine (because of his great limme or ioynt) shall passe *Pompey* the great, the Page *Hercules.*

Brag. Pardon sir, error: He is not quantitie enough for that Worthies thumb, hee is not so big as the end of his Club.

Peda. Shall I haue audience? he shall present *Hercules* in minoritie: his *enter* and *exit* shall bee strangling a Snake; and I will haue an Apologie for that purpose.

Pag. An excellent deuice: so if any of the audience hisse, you may cry, Well done *Hercules,* now thou crushest the Snake; that is the way to make an offence gracious, though few haue the grace to doe it.

Brag. For the rest of the Worthies?

Peda. I will play three my selfe.

Pag. Thrice worthy Gentleman.

Brag. Shall I tell you a thing?

Peda. We attend.

Brag. We will haue, if this fadge not, an Antique. I beseech you follow.

Ped. Via good-man *Dull,* thou hast spoken no word all this while.

Dull. Nor vnderstood none neither sir.

Ped. Alone, we will employ thee.

Dull. Ile make one in a dance, or so: or I will play

on

on the taber to the Worthles, & let them dance the hey.
Ped. Most *Dull*, honest *Dull*, to our sport away. *Exit.*

Enter Ladies.

Qu. Sweet hearts we shall be rich ere we depart,
If fairings come thus plentifully in.
A Lady wal'd about with Diamonds: Look you, what I
haue from the louing King.
Rosa. Madam, came nothing else along with that?
Qu. Nothing but this: yes as much loue in Rime,
As would be cram'd vp in a sheet of paper
Writ on both sides the leafe, margent and all,
That he was faine to seale on *Cupids* name.
Rosa. That was the way to make his god-head wax:
For he hath beene fiue thousand yeeres a Boy.
Kath. I, and a shrewd vnhappy gallowes too.
Ros. You'll nere be friends with him, a kild your sister.
Kath. He made her melancholy, sad, and heauy, and
so she died: had she beene Light like you, of such a mer-
rie nimble stirring spirit, she might a bin a Grandam ere
she died. And so may you: For a light heart liues long.
Ros. What's your darke meaning mouse, of this light
word?
Kat. A light condition in a beauty darke.
Ros. We need more light to finde your meaning out
Kat. You'll marre the light by taking it in snuffe:
Therefore Ile darkely end the argument.
Ros. Look what you doe, you doe it stil i'th darke.
Kat. So do not you, for you are a light Wench.
Ros. Indeed I waigh not you, and therefore light.
Ka. You waigh me not, O that's you care not for me.
Ros. Great reason: for past care, is still past cure.
Qu. Well bandied both, a set of Wit well played.
But *Rosaline*, you haue a Fauour too?
Who sent it? and what is it?
Ros. I would you knew.
And if my face were but as faire as yours,
My Fauour were as great, be witnesse this.
Nay, I haue Verses too, I thanke *Berowne*,
The numbers true, and were the numbring too
I were the fairest goddesse on the ground.
I am compar'd to twenty thousand fairs.
O he hath drawne my picture in his letter.
Qu. Any thing like?
Ros. Much in the letters, nothing in the praise.
Qu. Beauteous as Incke: a good conclusion.
Kat. Faire as a text B. in a Coppie booke.
Ros. Ware pensals. How? Let me not die your debtor,
My red Dominicall, my golden letter.
O that your face were full of Oes.
Qu. A Pox of that iest, and I beshrew all Shrowes:
But *Katherine*, what was sent to you
From faire *Dumaine*?
Kat. Madame, this Gloue.
Qu. Did he not send you twaine?
Kat. Yes Madame: and moreouer,
Some thousand Verses of a faithfull Louer.
A huge translation of hypocrisie,
Vildly compiled, profound simplicitie.
Mar. This, and these Pearls, to me sent *Longauile*
The Letter is too long by halfe a mile.
Qu. I thinke no lesse: Dost thou wish in heart
The Chaine were longer, and the Letter short.
Mar. I, or I would these hands might neuer part.
Quee. We are wise girles to mocke our Louers so.
Ros. They are worse fooles to purchase mocking so.
That same *Berowne* ile torture ere I goe.
O that I knew he were but in by th'weeke,
How I would make him fawne, and begge, and seeke,
And wait the season, and obserue the times,
And spend his prodigall wits in booteles rimes.
And shape his seruice wholly to my deuice,
And make him proud to make me proud that iests.
So pertaunt like would I o'resway his state,
That he shold be my foole, and I his fate.
Qu. None are so surely caught, when they are catcht,
As Wit turn'd foole, follie in Wisedome hatch'd:
Hath wisedoms warrant, and the helpe of Schoole,
And Wits owne grace to grace a learned Foole?
Ros. The bloud of youth burns not with such excesse,
As grauities reuolt to wantons be.
Mar. Follie in Fooles beares not so strong a note,
As fool'ry in the Wise, when Wit doth dote:
Since all the power thereof it doth apply,
To proue by Wit, worth in simplicitie.

Enter Boyet.

Qu. Heere comes *Boyet*, and mirth in his face.
Boy. O I am stab'd with laughter, Wher's her Grace?
Qu. Thy newes *Boyet*?
Boy. Prepare Madame, prepare.
Arme Wenches arme, incounters mounted are,
Against your Peace, Loue doth approach, disguis'd:
Armed in arguments, you'll be surpriz'd.
Muster your Wits, stand in your owne defence,
Or hide your heads like Cowards, and flie hence.
Qu. Saint *Dennis* to S. *Cupid*: What are they,
That charge their breath against vs? Say scout say.
Boy. Vnder the coole shade of a Siccamore,
I thought to close mine eyes some halfe an houre:
When lo to interrupt my purpos'd rest,
Toward that shade I might behold addrest,
The King and his companions: warely
I stole into a neighbour thicket by,
And ouer-heard, what you shall ouer-heare:
That by and by disguis'd they will be heere.
Their Herald is a pretty knauish Page:
That well by heart hath con'd his embassage,
Action and accent did they teach him there.
Thus must thou speake, and thus thy body beare.
And euer and anon they made a doubt,
Presence maiesticall would put him out:
For quoth the King, an Angell shalt thou see:
Yet feare not thou, but speake audaciously.
The Boy reply'd, An Angell is not euill:
I should haue fear'd her, had she beene a deuill.
With that all laugh'd, and clap'd him on the shoulder,
Making the bold wagg by their praises bolder.
One rub'd his elboe thus, and fleer'd, and swore,
A better speech was neuer spoke before.
Another with his finger and his thumb,
Cry'd *via*, we will doo't, come what will come.
The third he caper'd and cried, All goes well.
The fourth turn'd on the toe, and downe he fell:
With that they all did tumble on the ground,
With such a zelous laughter so profound,
That in this spleene ridiculous appeares,
To checke their folly passions solemne teares.
Quee. But what, but what, come they to visit vs?
Boy. They do, they do; and are apparel'd thus,
Like *Muscouites*, or *Russians*, as I gesse.
Their purpose is to parlee, to court, and dance,

M3 And

And euery one his Loue-feat will aduance,
Vnto his seuerall Mistresse: which they'll know
By fauours seuerall, which they did bestow.
Queen. And will they so? the Gallants shall be taskt:
For Ladies; we will euery one be maskt,
And not a man of them shall haue the grace
Despight of sute, to see a Ladies face.
Hold *Rosaline*, this Fauour thou shalt weare,
And then the King will court thee for his Deare:
Hold, take thou this my sweet, and giue me thine,
So shall *Berowne* take me for *Rosaline*.
And change your Fauours too, so shall your Loues
Woo contrary, deceiu'd by these remoues.
Rosa. Come on then, weare the fauours most in sight.
Kath. But in this changing, What is your intent?
Queen. The effect of my intent is to crosse theirs:
They doe it but in mocking merriment,
And mocke for mocke is onely my intent.
Their seuerall counsels they vnbosome shall,
To Loues mistooke, and so be mockt withall.
Vpon the next occasion that we meete,
With Visages displayd to talke and greete.
Ros. But shall we dance, if they desire vs too't?
Quee. No, to the death we will not moue a foot,
Nor to their pen'd speech render we no grace:
But while 'tis spoke, each turne away his face.
Boy. Why that contempt will kill the keepers heart,
And quite diuorce his memory from his part.
Quee. Therefore I doe it, and I make no doubt,
The rest will ere come in, if he be out.
Theres no such sport, as sport by sport orethrowne:
To make theirs ours, and ours none but our owne.
So shall we stay mocking entended game,
And they well mockt, depart away with shame. *Sound.*
Boy. The Trompet sounds, be maskt, the maskers come.

Enter Black moores with musicke, the Boy with a speech, and the rest of the Lords disguised.

Page. *All haile, the richest Beauties on the earth.*
Ber. Beauties no richer then rich Taffata.
Pag. *A holy parcell of the fairest dames that euer turn'd their backes to mortall viewes.*
The Ladies turne their backes to him.
Ber. Their eyes villaine, their eyes.
Pag. *That euer turn'd their eyes to mortall viewes.*
Out
Boy. True, out indeed.
Pag. *Out of your fauours heauenly spirits vouchsafe*
Not to beholde.
Ber. Once to behold, rogue.
Pag *Once to behold with your Sunne beamed eyes,*
With your Sunne beamed eyes.
Boy. They will not answer to that Epythite,
You were best call it Daughter beamed eyes.
Pag They do not marke me, and that brings me out.
Bero Is this your perfectnesse? be gon you rogue.
Rosa. What would these strangers?
Know their mindes *Boyet*.
If they doe speake our language, 'tis our will
That some plaine man recount their purposes.
Know what they would?
Boyet What would you with the Princes?
Ber. Nothing but peace, and gentle visitation.
Ros. What would they, say they?
Boy. Nothing but peace, and gentle visitation.
Rosa. Why that they haue, and bid them so be gon.
Boy. She saies you haue it, and you may be gon.
Kin. Say to her we haue measur'd many miles,
To tread a Measure with you on the grasse.
Boy. They say that they haue measur'd many a mile,
To tread a Measure with you on this grasse.
Rosa. It is not so. Aske them how many inches
Is in one mile? If they haue measur'd manie,
The measure then of one is easlie told.
Boy. If to come hither, you haue measur'd miles,
And many miles: the Princesse bids you tell,
How many inches doth fill vp one mile?
Ber. Tell her we measure them by weary steps.
Boy. She heares her selfe.
Rosa. How manie wearie steps,
Of many wearie miles you haue ore-gone,
Are numbred in the trauell of one mile?
Bero. We number nothing that we spend for you,
Our dutie is so rich, so infinite,
That we may doe it still without accompt.
Vouchsafe to shew the sunshine of your face,
That we (like sauages) may worship it.
Rosa. My face is but a Moone and clouded too.
Kin. Blessed are clouds, to doe as such clouds do.
Vouchsafe bright Moone, and these thy stars to shine,
(Those clouds remooued) vpon our waterie eyne.
Rosa. O vaine peticioner, beg a greater matter,
Thou now requests but Mooneshine in the water.
Kin. Then in our measure, vouchsafe but one change.
Thou bidst me begge, this begging is not strange.
Rosa. Play musicke then: nay you must doe it soone.
Not yet no dance: thus change I like the Moone.
Kin. Will you not dance? How come you thus estranged?
Rosa. You tooke the Moone at full, but now shee's changed?
Kin. Yet still she is the Moone, and I the Man.
Rosa. The musick playes, vouchsafe some motion to it: Our eares vouchsafe it.
Kin. But your legges should doe it.
Ros. Since you are strangers, & come here by chance,
Wee'll not be nice, take hands, we will not dance.
Kin. Why take you hands then?
Rosa. Onelie to part friends.
Curtsie sweet hearts, and so the Measure ends.
Kin. More measure of this measure be not nice.
Rosa. We can afford no more at such a price.
Kin. Prise your selues: What buyes your companie?
Rosa. Your absence onelie.
Kin. That can neuer be.
Rosa. Then cannot we be bought: and so adue,
Twice to your Visore, and halfe once to you.
Kin. If you denie to dance, let's hold more chat.
Ros. In priuate then.
Kin. I am best pleas'd with that.
Be. White handed Mistris, one sweet word with thee.
Qu. Hony, and Milke, and Suger: there is three.
Ber. Nay then two treyes, an if you grow so nice
Metheglin, Wort, and Malmsey; well runne dice:
There's halfe a dozen sweets.
Qu. Seuenth sweet adue, since you can cogg,
Ile play no more with you.
Ber. One word in secret.
Qu. Let it not be sweet.
Ber Thou greeu'st my gall.

Queen.

Qu. Gall,bitter.
Ber. Therefore meete.
Du. Will you vouchsafe with me to change a word?
Mar. Name it.
Dum. Faire Ladie:
Mar. Say you so? Faire Lord:
Take you that for your faire Lady.
Du. Please it you,
As much in priuate, and Ile bid adieu.
Mar. What,was your vizard made without a tong?
Long. I know the reason Ladie why you aske.
Mar. O for your reason,quickly sir, I long.
Long. You haue a double tongue within your mask.
And would affoord my speechlesse vizard halfe.
Mar. Veale quoth the Dutch-man: is not Veale a Calfe?
Long. A Calfe faire Ladie?
Mar. No,a faire Lord Calfe.
Long. Let's part the word.
Mar. No, Ile not be your halfe:
Take all and weane it, it may proue an Oxe.
Long. Looke how you but your selfe in these sharpe mockes.
Will you giue hornes chast Ladie? Do not so.
Mar. Then die a Calfe before your horns do grow.
Lon. One word in priuate with you ere I die.
Mar. Bleat softly then, the Butcher heares you cry.
Boyet. The tongues of mocking wenches are as keen
As is the Razors edge, inuisible:
Cutting a smaller haire then may be seene,
Aboue the sense of sence so sensible:
Seemeth their conference,their conceits haue wings,
Fleeter then arrows,bullets wind,thoght,swifter things
Rosa. Not one word more my maides, breake off, breake off.
Ber. By heauen, all drie beaten with pure scoffe.
King. Farewell madde Wenches, you haue simple wits. *Exeunt.*
Qu. Twentie adieus my frozen Muscouits.
Are these the breed of wits so wondred at?
Boyet. Tapers they are, with your sweete breathes puft out.
Rosa. Wel-liking wits they haue,grosse,grosse,fat,fat.
Qu. O pouertie in wit,Kingly poore flout.
Will they not (thinke you) hang themselues to night?
Or euer but in vizards shew their faces:
This pert *Berowne* was out of count'nance quite.
Rosa. They were all in lamentable cases.
The King was vveeping ripe for a good word.
Qu. *Berowne* did sweare himselfe out of all suite.
Mar *Dumaine* was at my seruice, and his sword:
No point (quoth I:) my seruant straight vvas mute.
Ka. Lord *Longauill* said I came ore his hart:
And trow you vvhat he call'd me?
Qu. Qualme perhaps.
Kat. Yes in good faith.
Qu. Go sicknesse as thou art.
Ros. Well,better wits haue worne plain statute caps,
But vvil you heare; the King is my loue sworne.
Qu. And quicke *Berowne* hath plighted faith to me.
Kat. And *Long-uill* was for my seruice borne.
Mar. *Dumaine* is mine as sure as barke on tree.
Boyet. Madam,and prettie mistresses giue eare,
Immediately they will againe be heere
In their owne shapes: for it can neuer be,
They will digest this harsh indignitie.

Qu. Will they returne?
Boy. They will they will,God knowes,
And leape for ioy, though they are lame with blowes:
Therefore change Fauours, and when they repaire,
Blow like sweet Roses, in this summer aire.
Qu. How blovv? how blovv? Speake to bee vnderstood.
Boy. Faire Ladies maskt,are Roses in their bud:
Dismaskt, their damaske sweet commixture showne,
Are Angels vailing clouds, or Roses blowne.
Qu. Auant perplexitie: What shall vve do,
If they returne in their owne shapes to wo?
Rosa. Good Madam, if by me you'l be aduis'd,
Let's mocke them still as well knowne as disguis'd:
Let vs complaine to them vvhat fooles were heare,
Disguis'd like Muscouites in shapelesse geare:
And wonder what they were, and to what end
Their shallow showes, and Prologue vildely pen'd:
And their rough carriage so ridiculous,
Should be presented at our Tent to vs.
Boyet. Ladies, withdraw: the gallants are at hand.
Quee. Whip to our Tents, as Roes runnes ore Land. *Exeunt.*

Enter the King and the rest.

King. Faire sir,God saue you. Wher's the Princesse?
Boy. Gone to her Tent.
Please it your Maiestie command me any seruice to her?
King. That she vouchsafe me audience for one word.
Boy. I will,and so will she, I know my Lord. *Exit.*
Ber. This fellow pickes vp wit as Pigeons pease,
And vtters it againe, when *Ioue* doth please.
He is Wits Pedler,and retailes his Wares,
At Wakes, and Wassels, Meetings, Markets, Faires.
And we that sell by grosse, the Lord doth know,
Haue not the grace to grace it with such show.
This Gallant pins the Wenches on his sleeue.
Had he bin *Adam*, he had tempted *Eue*.
He can carue too, and lispe: Why this is he,
That kist away his hand in courtesie.
This is the Ape of Forme, Monsieur the nice,
That when he plaies at Tables,chides the Dice
In honorable tearmes: Nay he can sing
A meane most meanly, and in Vshering
Mend him who can: the Ladies call him sweete.
The staires as he treads on them kisse his feete.
This is the flower that smiles on euerie one,
To shew his teeth as white as Whales bone.
And consciences that wil not die in debt,
Pay him the dutie of honie-tongued *Boyet*.
King. A blister on his sweet tongue with my hart,
That put *Armathoes* Page out of his part.

Enter the Ladies.

Ber. See where it comes. Behauiour what wer't thou,
Till this madman shew'd thee? And what art thou now?
King. All haile sweet Madame,and faire time of day.
Qu. Faire in all Haile is foule,as I conceiue.
King. Construe my speeches better, if you may.
Qu. Then wish me better, I wil giue you leaue.
King. We came to visit you,and purpose now
To leade you to our Court, vouchsafe it then.
Qu. This field shal hold me, and so hold your vow:
Nor God, nor I, delights in periur'd men.
King. Rebuke me not for that which you prouoke:
The

The vertue of your eie must breake my oth.
Q. You nickname vertue: vice you should haue spoke:
For vertues office neuer breakes men troth.
Now by my maiden honor, yet as pure
As the vnsallied Lilly, I protest,
A world of torments though I should endure,
I would not yeeld to be your houses guest:
So much I hate a breaking cause to be
Of heauenly oaths, vow'd with integritie.
Kin. O you haue liu'd in desolation heere,
Vnseene, vnuisited, much to our shame.
Qu. Not so my Lord, it is not so I sweare,
We haue had pastimes heere, and pleasant game,
A messe of Russians left vs but of late.
Kin. How Madam? Russians?
Qu I in truth, my Lord.
Trim gallants, full of Courtship and of state.
Rosa. Madam speake true. It is not so my Lord:
My Ladie (to the manner of the daies)
In curtesie giues vndeseruing praise.
We foure indeed confronted were with foure
In Russia habit: Heere they stayed an houre,
And talk'd apace: and in that houre (my Lord)
They did not blesse vs with one happy word.
I dare not call them fooles; but this I thinke,
When they are thirstie, fooles would faine haue drinke.
Ber. This iest is drie to me. Gentle sweete,
Your wits makes wise things foolish when we greete
With eies best seeing, heauens fierie eie:
By light we loose light; your capacitie
Is of that nature, that to your huge stoore,
Wise things seeme foolish, and rich things but poore.
Ros. This proues you wise and rich: for in my eie
Ber. I am a foole, and full of pouertie.
Ros. But that you take what doth to you belong,
It were a fault to snatch words from my tongue.
Ber. O, I am yours and all that I possesse.
Ros. All the foole mine.
Ber. I cannot giue you lesse.
Ros. Which of the Vizards what it that you wore?
Ber. Where? when? What Vizard?
Why demand you this?
Ros. There, then, that vizard, that superfluous case,
That hid the worse, and shew'd the better face.
Kin. We are discried,
They'l mocke vs now downeright.
Du. Let vs confesse, and turne it to a iest.
Que. Amaz'd my Lord? Why lookes your Highnes sadde?
Rosa Helpe hold his browes, hee'l sound: why looke you pale?
Sea-sicke I thinke comming from Muscouie.
Ber. Thus poure the stars down plagues for periury.
Can any face of brasse hold longer out?
Heere stand I, Ladie dart thy skill at me,
Bruise me with scorne, confound me with a flout.
Thrust thy sharpe wit quite through my ignorance
Cut me to peeces with thy keene conceit:
And I will wish thee neuer more to dance,
Nor neuer more in Russian habit waite.
O! neuer will I trust to speeches pen'd,
Nor to the motion of a Schoole-boies tongue
Nor neuer come in vizard to my friend,
Nor woo in rime like a blind-harpers songue,
Taffata phrases, silken tearmes precise,
Three-pil'd Hyperboles, spruce affection;
Figures pedanticall, these summer flies,
Haue blowne me full of maggot ostentation
I do forsweare them, and I heere protest,
By this white Gloue (how white the hand God knows)
Henceforth my woing minde shall be exprest
In russet yeas, and honest kersie noes.
And to begin Wench, so God helpe me law,
My loue to thee is sound *sans* cracke or flaw
Rosa. Sans, sans, I pray you.
Ber. Yet I haue a tricke
Of the old rage: beare with me, I am sicke.
Ile leaue it by degrees: soft, let vs see,
Write *Lord haue mercie on vs,* on those three,
They are infected, in their hearts it lies
They haue the plague, and caught it of your eyes:
These Lords are visited, you are not free:
For the Lords tokens on you do I see.
Qu. No, they are free that gaue these tokens to vs.
Ber. Our states are forfeit, seeke not to vndo vs.
Ros. It is not so; for how can this be true,
That you stand forfeit, being those that sue.
Ber. Peace, for I will not haue to do with you.
Ros. Nor shall not, if I do as I intend.
Ber. Speake for your selues, my wit is at an end.
King. Teach vs sweete Madame, for our rude trans-
gression, some faire excuse.
Qu. The fairest is confession.
Were you not heere but euen now, disguis'd?
Kin. Madam, I was.
Qu. And were you well aduis'd?
Kin. I was faire Madam.
Qu. When you then were heere,
What did you whisper in your Ladies eare?
King. That more then all the world I did respect her
Qu. When shee shall challenge this, you will reiect her
King. Vpon mine Honor no,
Qu. Peace peace, forbeare:
your oath once broke, you force not to forsweare.
King. Despise me when I breake this oath of mine.
Qu. I will, and therefore keepe it. *Rosaline,*
What did the Russian whisper in your eare?
Ros Madam, he swore that he did hold me deare
As precious eye-sight, and did value me
Aboue this World: adding thereto moreouer,
That he vvould Wed me, or else die my Louer.
Qu. God giue thee ioy of him: the Noble Lord
Most honorably doth vphold his word.
King. What meane you Madame?
By my life, my troth,
I neuer swore this Ladie such an oth.
Ros. By heauen you did; and to confirme it plaine,
you gaue me this: But take it sir againe.
King. My faith and this, the Princesse I did giue,
I knew her by this Iewell on her sleeue.
Qu. Pardon me sir, this Iewell did she weare,
And Lord *Berowne* (I thanke him) is my deare
What? Will you haue me, or your Pearle againe?
Ber. Neither of either, I remit both twaine.
I see the tricke on't: Heere was a consent,
Knowing aforehand of our merriment,
To dash it like a Christmas Comedie.
Some carry-tale, some please-man, some slight Zanie,
Some mumble-newes, some trencher-knight, som Dick
That smiles his cheeke in yeares, and knowes the trick
To make my Lady laugh, when shes dispos'd;
Told

Told our intents before: which once disclos'd,
The Ladies did change Fauours; and then we
Following the signes, woo'd but the signe of she.
Now to our periurie, to adde more terror,
We are againe forsworne in will and error.
Much vpon this tis: and might not you
Forestall our sport, to make vs thus vntrue?
Do not you know my Ladies foot by'th squier?
And laugh vpon the apple of her eie?
And stand betweene her backe sir, and the fire,
Holding a trencher, iesting merrilie?
You put our Page out: go, you are alowd.
Die when you will, a smocke shall be your shrowd.
You leere vpon me, do you? There's an eie
Wounds like a Leaden sword.

Boy. Full merrily hath this braue manager, this carreere bene run.

Ber. Loe, he is tilting straight. Peace, I haue don.

Enter Clowne.

Welcome pure wit, thou part'st a faire fray.

Clo. O Lord sir, they would kno,
Whether the three worthies shall come in, or no.

Ber. What, are there but three?

Clo. No sir, but it is vara fine,
For euerie one pursents three.

Ber. And three times thrice is nine.

Clo. Not so sir, vnder correction sir, I hope it is not so. You cannot beg vs sir, I can assure you sir, we know what we know: I hope sir three times thrice sir.

Ber. Is not nine.

Clo. Vnder correction sir, wee know where-vntill it doth amount.

Ber. By Ioue, I alwaies tooke three threes for nine.

Clow. O Lord sir, it were pittie you should get your liuing by reckning sir.

Ber. How much is it?

Clo. O Lord sir, the parties themselues, the actors sir will shew where-vntill it doth amount: for mine owne part, I am (as they say, but to perfect one man in one poore man) *Pompion* the great sir.

Ber. Art thou one of the Worthies?

Clo. It pleased them to thinke me worthie of *Pompey* the great: for mine owne part, I know not the degree of the Worthie, but I am to stand for him.

Ber. Go, bid them prepare. *Exit.*

Clo. We will turne it finely off sir, we wil take some care.

King. *Berowne*, they will shame vs:
Let them not approach.

Ber. We are shame-proofe my Lord: and 'tis some policie, to haue one shew worse then the Kings and his companie.

Kin. I say they shall not come.

Qu. Nay my good Lord, let me ore-rule you now;
That sport best pleases, that doth least know how.
Where Zeale striues to content, and the contents
Dies in the Zeale of that which it presents:
Their forme confounded, makes most forme in mirth,
When great things labouring perish in their birth.

Ber. A right description of our sport my Lord.

Enter Braggart.

Brag. Annointed, I implore so much expence of thy royall sweet breath, as will vtter a brace of words.

Qu. Doth this man serue God?

Ber. Why aske you?

Qu. He speak's not like a man of God's making.

Brag. That's all one my faire sweet honie Monarch: For I protest, the Schoolmaster is exceeding fantasticall: Too too vaine, too too vaine. But we wil put it (as they say) to *Fortuna delaguar*, I wish you the peace of minde most royall cupplement.

King. Here is like to be a good presence of Worthies; He presents *Hector* of Troy, the Swaine *Pompey* ŷ great, the Parish Curate *Alexander*, *Armadoes* Page *Hercules*, the Pedant *Iudas Machabeus*: And if these foure Worthies in their first shew thriue, these foure will change habites, and present the other fiue.

Ber. There is fiue in the first shew.

Kin. You are deceiued, tis not so.

Ber. The Pedant, the Braggart, the Hedge-Priest, the Foole, and the Boy,
Abate throw at Nouum, and the whole world againe,
Cannot pricke out fiue such, take each one in's vaine.

Kin. The ship is vnder saile, and here she coms amain.

Enter Pompey.

Clo. *I Pompey am.*

Ber. You lie, you are not he.

Clo. *I Pompey am.*

Boy. With Libbards head on knee.

Ber. Well said old mocker,
I must needs be friends with thee.

Clo. *I Pompey am, Pompey surnam'd the big.*

Du. The great.

Clo. It is great sir: *Pompey surnam'd the great:*
That oft in field, with Targe and Shield,
did make my foe to sweat:
And trauailing along this coast, I heere am come by chance,
And lay my Armes before the legs of this sweet Lasse of France.
If your Ladiship would say thankes *Pompey*, I had done.

La. Great thankes great *Pompey*

Clo. Tis not so much worth: but I hope I was perfect. I made a little fault in great.

Ber. My hat to a halfe-penie, Pompey prooues the best Worthie.

Enter Curate for Alexander.

Curat. *When in the world I liu'd, I was the worldes Commander:*
By East, West, North, & South, I spred my conquering might
My Scutcheon plaine declares that I am Alisander.

Boiet. Your nose saies no, you are not:
For it stands too right.

Ber. Your nose smels no, in this most tender smelling Knight.

Qu. The Conqueror is dismaid:
Proceede good *Alexander*.

Cur. *When in the world I liued, I was the worldes Commander.*

Boiet. Most true, 'tis right: you were so *Alisander*.

Ber. Pompey the great.

Clo. your seruant and *Costard*.

Ber. Take away the Conqueror, take away *Alisander*

Clo. O sir, you haue ouerthrowne *Alisander* the conqueror: you will be scrap'd out of the painted cloth for this.

this: your Lion that holds his Pollax sitting on a close stoole, will be giuen to Aiax. He will be the ninth worthie. A Conqueror, and affraid to speake? Runne away for shame *Alisander*. There an't shall please you: a foolish milde man, an honest man, looke you, & soon dasht He is a maruellous good neighbour insooth, and a verie good Bowler: but for *Alisander*, alas you see, how 'tis a little ore-parted But there are Worthies a comming, will speake their minde in some other sort. *Exit Cu.*

Qu. Stand aside good Pompey.

Enter Pedant for Iudas, and the Boy for Hercules.

Ped. Great *Hercules* is presented by this Impe,
Whose Club kil'd *Cerberus* that three-headed *Canus*,
And when he was a babe, a childe, a shrimpe,
Thus did he strangle Serpents in his *Manus*:
Quoniam, he seemeth in minoritie,
Ergo, I come with this Apologie.
Keepe some state in thy exit, and vanish. *Exit Boy*

Ped. Iudas *I am.*

Dum. A Iudas?

Ped. Not Iscariot sir.
Iudas I am, ycliped Machabeus.

Dum. Iudas Machabeus clipt, is plaine Iudas.

Ber. A kissing traitor. How art thou prou'd *Iudas*?

Ped. Iudas I am.

Dum The more shame for you *Iudas*.

Ped. What meane you sir?

Bos. To make *Iudas* hang himselfe.

Ped. Begin sir, you are my elder.

Ber. Well follow'd, *Iudas* was hang'd on an Elder.

Ped. I will not be put out of countenance.

Ber. Because thou hast no face.

Ped What is this?

Boi. A Citterne head.

Dum. The head of a bodkin.

Ber. A deaths face in a ring

Lon. The face of an old Roman coine, scarce seene

Boi. The pummell of *Cæsars* Faulchion.

Dum. The caru'd-bone face on a Flaske.

Ber. S. Georges halfe cheeke in a brooch.

Dum. I, and in a brooch of Lead.

Ber. I, and worne in the cap of a Tooth-drawer
And now forward, for we haue put thee in countenance

Ped. You haue put me out of countenance.

Ber. False, we haue giuen thee faces.

Ped. But you haue out-fac'd them all.

Ber. And thou wer't a Lion, we would do so.

Boy. Therefore as he is, an Asse, let him go:
And so adieu sweet *Iude*. Nay, why dost thou stay?

Dum. For the latter end of his name.

Ber. For the *Asse* to the *Iude*: giue it him. *Iud-as* away.

Ped. This is not generous, not gentle, not humble.

Boy. A light for monsieur *Iudas*, it growes darke, he may stumble.

Que. Alas poore *Machabeus*, how hath hee beene baited.

Enter Braggart.

Ber. Hide thy head *Achilles*, heere comes *Hector* in Armes.

Dum. Though my mockes come home by me, I will now be merrie.

King *Hector* was but a Troyan in respect of this.

Boi. But is this *Hector*?

Kin. I thinke *Hector* was not so cleane timber'd

Lon. His legge is too big for *Hector*.

Dum. More Calfe certaine

Boi. No, he is best indued in the small.

Ber This cannot be *Hector*.

Dum. He's a God or a Painter, for he makes faces.

Brag *The Armipotent Mars, of Launces the almighty, gaue* Hector *a gift.*

Dum. A gilt Nutmegge.

Ber. A Lemmon.

Lon. Stucke with Cloues.

Dum. No clouen.

Brag. *The Armipotent Mars of Launces the almighty,*
Gaue Hector *a gift, the heire of Illion;*
A man so breathed, that certaine he would fight. yea
From morne till night, out of his Pauillion
I am that Flower

Dum. That Mint.

Long. That Cullambine.

Brag Sweet Lord *Longauill* reine thy tongue

Lon. I must rather giue it the reine: for it runnes against *Hector*

Dum. I, and *Hector's* a Grey-hound

Brag. The sweet War-man is dead and rotten,
Sweet chuckes, beat not the bones of the buried
But I will forward with my deuice;
Sweet Royaltie bestow on me the sence of hearing.

Berowne steppes forth.

Qu. Speake braue Hector, we are much delighted

Brag. I do adore thy sweet Graces slipper.

Boy. Loues her by the foot.

Dum He may not by the yard

Brag. *Thus* Hector *farre surmounted Hanniball.*
The partie is gone.

Clo. Fellow *Hector*, she is gone; she is two moneths on her way.

Brag. What meanest thou?

Clo. Faith vnlesse you play the honest Troyan, the poore Wench is cast away: she's quick, the child brags in her belly alreadie: tis yours.

Brag. Dost thou infamonize me among Potentates? Thou shalt die.

Clo. Then shall Hector be whipt for *Iaquenetta* that is quicke by him, and hang'd for *Pompey*, that is dead by him.

Dum. Most rare *Pompey*.

Boi. Renowned *Pompey*

Ber. Greater then great, great, great, great *Pompey*: *Pompey* the huge.

Dum Hector trembles.

Ber. *Pompey* is moued, more Atees more Atees stirre them, or stirre them on.

Dum. Hector will challenge him.

Ber. I, if a'haue no more mans blood in's belly, then will sup a Flea.

Brag. By the North-pole I do challenge thee

Clo. I wil not fight with a pole like a Northern man; Ile slash, Ile do it by the sword: I pray you let mee borrow my Armes againe.

Dum. Roome for the incensed Worthies.

Clo. Ile do it in my shirt.

Dum Most resolute *Pompey*.

Page. Master, let me take you a button hole lower; Do you not see *Pompey* is vncasing for the combat: what meane

meane you? you will lose your reputation.

Brag. Gentlemen and Souldiers pardon me, I will not combat in my shirt.

Du. You may not denie it, *Pompey* hath made the challenge.

Brag. Sweet bloods, I both may, and will.

Ber. What reason haue you for't?

Brag. The naked truth of it is, I haue no shirt,
I go woolward for penance.

Ber. True, and it was inioyned him in *Rome* for want of Linnen: since when, Ile be sworne he wore none, but a dishclout of *Iaquenettas*, and that hee weares next his heart for a fauour.

Enter a Messenger, Monsieur Marcade.

Mar. God saue you Madame.

Qu. Welcome *Marcade*, but that thou interruptest our merriment.

Marc. I am sorrie Madam, for the newes I bring is heauie in my tongue. The King your father

Qu. Dead for my life.

Mar. Euen so: My tale is told.

Ber. Worthies away, the Scene begins to cloud.

Brag. For mine owne part, I breath free breath: I haue seene the day of wrong, through the little hole of discretion, and I will right my selfe like a Souldier.

Exeunt Worthies

Kin. How fare's your Maiestie?
Qu. *Boyet* prepaire, I will away to night.
Kin. Madame not so, I do beseech you stay.
Qu. Prepare I say. I thanke you gracious Lords
For all your faire endeuours and entreats:
Out of a new sad-soule, that you vouchsafe,
In your rich wisedome to excuse, or hide,
The liberall opposition of our spirits,
If ouer-boldly we haue borne our selues,
In the conuerse of breath (your gentlenesse
Was guiltie of it.) Farewell worthie Lord:
A heauie heart beares not a humble tongue.
Excuse me so, comming so short of thankes,
For my great suite, so easily obtain'd.
Kin. The extreme parts of time, extremelie formes
All causes to the purpose of his speed:
And often at his verie loose decides
That, which long processe could not arbitrate.
And though the mourning brow of progenie
Forbid the smiling curtesie of Loue:
The holy suite which faine it would conuince,
Yet since loues argument was first on foote,
Let not the cloud of sorrow iustle it
From what it purpos'd: since to waile friends lost,
Is not by much so wholsome profitable,
As to reioyce at friends but newly found.
Qu. I vnderstand you not, my greefes are double.
Ber. Honest plain words, best pierce the ears of griefe
And by these badges vnderstand the King,
For your faire sakes haue we neglected time,
Plaid foule play with our oaths: your beautie Ladies
Hath much deformed vs, fashioning our humors
Euen to the opposed end of our intents.
And what in vs hath seem'd ridiculous:
As Loue is full of vnbefitting straines,
All wanton as a childe, skipping and vaine.
Form'd by the eie, and therefore like the eie.
Full of straying shapes, of habits, and of formes
Varying in subiects as the eie doth roule,
To euerie varied obiect in his glance:
Which partie-coated presence of loose loue
Put on by vs, if in your heauenly eies,
Haue misbecom'd our oathes and grauities.
Those heauenlie eies that looke into these faults
Suggested vs to make: therefore Ladies
Our loue being yours, the error that Loue makes
Is likewise yonrs. We to our selues proue false,
By being once false, for euer to be true
To those that make vs both, faire Ladies you.
And euen that falshood in it selfe a sinne,
Thus purifies it selfe, and turnes to grace.
Qu. We haue receiu'd your Letters, full of Loue:
Your Fauours, the Ambassadors of Lone.
And in our maiden counsaile rated them
At courtship, pleasant iest, and curtesie,
As bumbast and as lining to the time:
But more deuout then these are our respects
Haue we not bene, and therefore met your loues
In their owne fashion, like a merriment.
Du. Our letters Madam, shew'd much more then iest
Lon. So did our lookes.
Rosa. We did not coat them so.
Kin. Now at the latest minute of the houre,
Grant vs your loues.
Qu. A time me thinkes too short,
To make a world-without-end bargaine in;
No, no my Lord, your Grace is periur'd much,
Full of deare guiltinesse, and therefore this:
If for my Loue (as there is no such cause)
You will do ought, this shall you do for me.
Your oth I will not trust: but go with speed
To some forlorne and naked Hermitage,
Remote from all the pleasures of the world:
There stay, vntill the twelue Celestiall Signes
Haue brought about their annuall reckoning.
If this austere insociable life,
Change not your offer made in heate of blood:
If frosts, and fasts, hard lodging, and thin weeds
Nip not the gaudie blossomes of your Loue,
But that it beare this triall, and last loue:
Then at the expiration of the yeare,
Come challenge me, challenge me by these deserts,
And by this Virgin palme, now kissing thine,
I will be thine: and till that instant shut
My wofull selfe vp in a mourning house,
Raining the teares of lamentation,
For the remembrance of my Fathers death.
If this thou do denie, let our hands part,
Neither intiteled in the others hart.
Kin. If this or more then this, I would denie,
To flatter vp these powers of mine with rest,
The sodaine hand of death close vp mine eie.
Hence euer then, my heart is in thy brest.
Ber. And what to me my Loue? and what to me?
Ros. You must be purged too, your sins are rack'd.
You are attaint with faults and periurie:
Therefore if you my fauor meane to get,
A tweluemonth shall you spend, and neuer rest,
But seeke the wearie beds of people sicke.
Du. But what to me my loue? but what to me?
Kat. A wife? a beard, faire health, and honestie,
With three-fold loue, I wish you all these three.
Du. O shall I say, I thanke you gentle wife?
Kat. Not so my Lord, a twelnemonth and a day,

Ile

Ile marke no words that smoothfac'd wooers say.
Come when the King doth to my Ladie come:
Then if I haue much loue, Ile giue you some.
Dum. Ile serue thee true and faithfully till then.
Kath. Yet sweare not, least ye be forsworne agen.
Lon. What saies *Maria*?
Mari. At the tweluemonths end,
Ile change my blacke Gowne, for a faithfull friend.
Lon. Ile stay with patience: but the time is long.
Mari. The liker you, few taller are so yong.
Ber. Studies my Ladie? Mistresse, looke on me,
Behold the window of my heart, mine eie:
What humble suite attends thy answer there,
Impose some seruice on me for my loue.
Ros. Oft haue I heard of you my Lord *Berowne*,
Before I saw you: and the worlds large tongue
Proclaimes you for a man repleate with mockes,
Full of comparisons, and wounding floutes:
Which you on all estates will execute,
That lie within the mercie of your wit.
To weed this Wormewood from your fruitfull braine,
And therewithall to win me, if you please,
Without the which I am not to be won:
You shall this tweluemonth terme from day to day,
Visite the speechlesse sicke, and still conuerse
With groaning wretches: and your taske shall be,
With all the fierce endeuour of your wit,
To enforce the pained impotent to smile.
Ber. To moue wilde laughter in the throate of death?
It cannot be, it is impossible.
Mirth cannot moue a soule in agonie.
Ros. Why that's the way to choke a gibing spirit,
Whose influence is begot of that loose grace,
Which shallow laughing hearers giue to fooles:
A iests prosperitie, lies in the eare
Of him that heares it, neuer in the tongue
Of him that makes it: then, if sickly eares,
Deaft with the clamors of their owne deare grones,
Will heare your idle scornes; continue then,
And I will haue you, and that fault withall.
But if they will not throw away that spirit,
And I shal finde you emptie of that fault,
Right ioyfull of your reformation.
Ber. A tweluemonth? Well: befall what will befall,
Ile iest a tweluemonth in an Hospitall.
Qu. I sweet my Lord, and so I take my leaue.
King. No Madam, we will bring you on your way.
Ber. Our woing doth not end like an old Play:
Iacke hath not Gill: these Ladies courtesie
Might wel haue made our sport a Comedie.
Kin. Come sir, it wants a tweluemonth and a day,
And then 'twill end.
Ber. That's too long for a play.

Enter Breggart.

Brag. Sweet Maiesty vouchsafe me.
Qu. Was not that Hector?
Dum. The worthie Knight of Troy.
Brag. I wil kisse thy royal finger, and take leaue.

I am a Votarie, I haue vow'd to *Iaquenetta* to holde the Plough for her sweet loue three yeares. But most esteemed greatnesse, wil you heare the Dialogue that the two Learned men haue compiled, in praise of the Owle and the Cuckow? It should haue followed in the end of our shew.

Kin. Call them forth quickely, we will do so.
Brag. Holla, Approach.

Enter all.

This side is *Hiems*, Winter.
This *Ver*, the Spring: the one maintained by the Owle,
Th'other by the Cuckow.
Ver, begin.

The Song.

When Dasies pied, and Violets blew,
And Cuckow-buds of yellow hew:
And Ladie-smockes all siluer white,
Do paint the Medowes with delight.
The Cuckow then on euerie tree,
Mockes married men, for thus sings he,
Cuckow.
Cuckow, Cuckow: O word of feare,
Vnpleasing to a married eare.

When Shepheards pipe on Oaten strawes,
And merrie Larkes are Ploughmens clockes:
When Turtles tread, and Rookes and Dawes,
And Maidens bleach their summer smockes:
The Cuckow then on euerie tree
Mockes married men; for thus sings he,
Cuckow.
Cuckow, Cuckow: O word of feare,
Vnpleasing to a married eare.

Winter.

When Isicles hang by the wall,
And Dicke the Sphepheard blowes his naile;
And Tom beares Logges into the hall,
And Milke comes frozen home in paile:
When blood is nipt, and waies be fowle,
Then nightly sings the staring Owle
Tu-whit to-who.
A merrie note,
While greasie Ione doth keele the pot.

When all aloud the winde doth blow,
And coffing drownes the Parsons saw:
And birds sit brooding in the snow,
And Marrians nose lookes red and raw:
When roasted Crabs hisse in the bowle,
Then nightly sings the staring Owle,
Tu-whit to who:
A merrie note,
While greasie Ione doth keele the pot.

Brag. The Words of Mercurie,
Are harsh after the songs of Apollo:
You that way; we this way.

Exeunt omnes.

FINIS.

A MIDSOMMER Nights Dreame.

Actus primus.

Enter Theſeus, Hippolita, with others.

Theſeus.

NOw faire Hippolita, our nuptiall houre
Drawes on apace: foure happy daies bring in
Another Moon: but oh, me thinkes, how ſlow
This old Moon wanes; She lingers my deſires
Like to a Step-dame, or a Dowager,
Long withering out a yong mans reuennew.
Hip. Foure daies wil quickly ſteep thẽſelues in nights
Foure nights wil quickly dreame away the time:
And then the Moone, like to a ſiluer bow,
Now bent in heauen, ſhal behold the night
Of our ſolemnities.
The. Go *Philoſtrate*,
Stirre vp the Athenian youth to merriments,
Awake the pert and nimble ſpirit of mirth,
Turne melancholy forth to Funerals:
The pale companion is not for our pompe,
Hippolita, I woo'd thee with my ſword,
And wonne thy loue, doing thee iniuries:
But I will wed thee in another key,
With pompe, with triumph, and with reuelling.

Enter Egeus and his daughter Hermia, Lyſander, and Demetrius.

Ege. Happy be *Theſeus*, our renowned Duke.
The. Thanks good *Egeus*: what's the news with thee?
Ege. Full of vexation, come I, with complaint
Againſt my childe, my daughter Hermia.
Stand forth Demetrius.
My Noble Lord,
This man hath my conſent to marrie her.
Stand forth Lyſander
And my gracious Duke,
This man hath bewitch'd the boſome of my childe.
Thou, thou *Lyſander*, thou haſt giuen her rimes,
And interchang'd loue-tokens with my childe:
Thou haſt by Moone-light at her window ſung,
With faining voice, verſes of faining loue,
And ſtolne the impreſſion of her fantaſie,
With bracelets of thy haire, rings, gawdes, conceits,
Knackes, trifles, Noſe-gaies, ſweet meats (meſſengers
Of ſtrong preuailment in vnhardned youth)
With cunning haſt thou filch'd my daughters heart,
Turn'd her obedience (which is due to me)
To ſtubborne harſhneſſe. And my gracious Duke,
Be it ſo ſhe will not heere before your Grace,
Conſent to marrie with *Demetrius*,
I beg the ancient priuiledge of Athens;
As ſhe is mine, I may diſpoſe of her;
Which ſhall be either to this Gentleman,
Or to her death, according to our Law,
Immediately prouided in that caſe.
The. What ſay you Hermia? be aduis'd faire Maide
To you your Father ſhould be as a God;
One that compos'd your beauties; yea and one
To whom you are but as a forme in waxe
By him imprinted: and within his power,
To leaue the figure, or disfigure it:
Demetrius is a worthy Gentleman.
Her. So is *Lyſander*.
The. In himſelfe he is.
But in this kinde, wanting your fathers voyce.
The other muſt be held the worthier.
Her. I would my father look'd but with my eyes.
The. Rather your eies muſt with his iudgment looke.
Her. I do entreat your Grace to pardon me.
I know not by what power I am made bold,
Nor how it may concerne my modeſtie
In ſuch a preſence heere to pleade my thoughts:
But I beſeech your Grace, that I may know
The worſt that may befall me in this caſe,
If I refuſe to wed *Demetrius*.
The. Either to dye the death, or to abiure
For euer the ſociety of men.
Therefore faire Hermia queſtion your deſires,
Know of your youth, examine well your blood,
Whether (if you yeeld not to your fathers choice)
You can endure the liuerie of a Nunne,
For aye to be in ſhady Cloiſter mew'd,
To liue a barren ſiſter all your life,
Chanting faint hymnes to the cold fruitleſſe Moone,
Thrice bleſſed they that maſter ſo their blood,
To vndergo ſuch maiden pilgrimage,
But earthlier happie is the Roſe diſtil'd,
Then that which withering on the virgin thorne,
Growes, liues, and dies, in ſingle bleſſedneſſe.

N Her.

Her So will I grow, so liue, so die my Lord,
Ere I will yeeld my virgin Patent vp
Vnto his Lordship, whose vnwished yoake,
My soule consents not to giue soueraignty.
The. Take time to pause, and by the next new Moon
The sealing day betwixt my loue and me,
For euerlasting bond of fellowship:
Vpon that day either prepare to dye,
For disobedience to your fathers will,
Or else to wed *Demetrius* as hee would,
Or on *Dianaes* Altar to protest
For aie, austerity, and single life.
Dem. Relent sweet *Hermia*, and *Lysander*, yeelde
Thy crazed title to my certaine right.
Lys. You haue her fathers loue, *Demetrius*:
Let me haue *Hermiaes*: do you marry him.
Egeus. Scornfull *Lysander*, true, he hath my Loue;
And what is mine, my loue shall render him.
And she is mine, and all my right of her,
I do estate vnto *Demetrius*.
Lys. I am my Lord, as well deriu'd as he,
As well possest: my loue is more then his:
My fortunes euery way as fairely ranck'd
(If not with vantage) as *Demetrius*:
And (which is more then all these boasts can be)
I am belou'd of beauteous *Hermia*.
Why should not I then prosecute my right?
Demetrius, Ile auouch it to his head,
Made loue to *Nedars* daughter, *Helena*,
And won her soule: and she (sweet Ladie) dotes,
Deuoutly dotes, dotes in Idolatry,
Vpon this spotted and inconstant man.
The. I must confesse, that I haue heard so much,
And with *Demetrius* thought to haue spoke thereof:
But being ouer-full of selfe-affaires,
My minde did lose it. But *Demetrius* come,
And come *Egeus*, you shall go with me,
I haue some priuate schooling for you both.
For you faire *Hermia*, looke you arme your selfe,
To fit your fancies to your Fathers will;
Or else the Law of Athens yeelds you vp
(Which by no meanes we may extenuate)
To death, or to a vow of single life.
Come my *Hippolita*, what cheare my loue?
Demetrius and *Egeus* go along:
I must imploy you in some businesse
Against our nuptiall, and conferre with you
Of something, neerely that concernes your selues.
Ege. With dutie and desire we follow you. *Exeunt*
Manet Lysander and Hermia.
Lys. How now my loue? Why is your cheek so pale?
How chance the Roses there do fade so fast?
Her. Belike for want of raine, which I could well
Beteeme them, from the tempest of mine eyes
Lys. For ought that euer I could reade,
Could euer heare by tale or historie,
The course of true loue neuer did run smooth,
But either it was different in blood.
Her. O crosse! too high to be enthral'd to loue.
Lys. Or else misgraffed, in respect of yeares
Her. O spight! too old to be ingag'd to yong
Lys. Or else it stood vpon the choise of merit.
Her. O hell! to choose loue by anothers eie.
Lys. Or if there were a simpathie in choise,
Warre, death, or sicknesse, did lay siege to it;
Making it momentarie, as a sound:
Swift as a shadow, short as any dreame,
Briefe as the lightning in the collied night,
That (in a spleene) vnfolds both heauen and earth;
And ere a man hath power to say, behold,
The iawes of darknesse do deuoure it vp:
So quicke bright things come to confusion
Her. If then true Louers haue beene euer crost,
It stands as an edict in destinie:
Then let vs teach our triall patience,
Because it is a customarie crosse,
As due to loue, as thoughts, and dreames, and sighes,
Wishes and teares; poore Fancies followers.
Lys. A good perswasion; therefore heare me *Hermia*,
I haue a Widdow Aunt, a dowager,
Of great reuennew, and she hath no childe,
From Athens is her house remou'd seuen leagues,
And she respects me, as her onely sonne:
There gentle *Hermia*, may I marrie thee,
And to that place, the sharpe Athenian Law
Cannot pursue vs. If thou lou'st me, then
Steale forth thy fathers house to morrow night
And in the wood, a league without the towne,
(Where I did meete thee once with *Helena*,
To do obseruance for a morne of May)
There will I stay for thee
Her. My good *Lysander*,
I sweare to thee, by Cupids strongest bow,
By his best arrow with the golden head,
By the simplicitie of Venus Doues,
By that which knitteth soules, and prospers loue,
And by that fire which burn'd the Carthage Queene,
When the false Troyan vnder saile was seene,
By all the vowes that euer men haue broke,
(In number more then euer women spoke)
In that same place thou hast appointed me,
To morrow truly will I meete with thee.
Lys. Keepe promise loue. looke here comes *Helena*.

Enter Helena.

Her. God speede faire *Helena*, whither away?
Hel. Cal you me faire? that faire againe vnsay,
Demetrius loues you faire: O happie faire!
Your eyes are loadstarres, and your tongues sweet ayre
More tuneable then Larke to shepheards eare,
When wheate is greene, when hauthorne buds appeare,
Sicknesse is catching: O were fauor so,
Your words I catch, faire *Hermia* ere I go,
My eare should catch your voice, my eye, your eye,
My tongue should catch your tongues sweet melodie,
Were the world mine, *Demetrius* being bated,
The rest Ile giue to be to you translated
O teach me how you looke, and with what art
you sway the motion of *Demetrius* hart.
Her. I frowne vpon him, yet he loues me still.
Hel. O that your frownes would teach my smiles
such skil.
Her. I giue him curses, yet he giues me loue.
Hel. O that my prayers could such affection moue.
Her. The more I hate, the more he followes me.
Hel. The more I loue, the more he hateth me.
Her. His folly Helena is none of mine
Hel. None but your beauty, wold that fault wer mine
Her. Take comfort: he no more shall see my face,
Lysander and my selfe will flie this place.
Before the time I did *Lysander* see,
Seem'd Athens like a Paradise to mee.

O then, what graces in my Loue do dwell,
That he hath turn'd a heauen into hell.
Lys. *Helen*, to you our mindes we will vnfold,
To morrow night, when *Phœbe* doth behold
Her siluer visage, in the watry glasse,
Decking with liquid pearle, the bladed grasse
(A time that Louers flights doth still conceale)
Through *Athens* gates, haue we deuis'd to steale.
Her. And in the wood, where often you and I,
Vpon faint Primrose beds, were wont to lye,
Emptying our bosomes, of their counsell sweld:
There my *Lysander*, and my selfe shall meete,
And thence from *Athens* turne away our eyes
To seeke new friends and strange companions,
Farwell sweet play-fellow, pray thou for vs,
And good lucke grant thee thy *Demetrius*.
Keepe word *Lysander* we must starue our sight,
From louers foode, till morrow deepe midnight.
Exit Hermia.
Lys. I will my *Hermia*. *Helena* adieu,
As you on him, *Demetrius* dotes on you. *Exit Lysander.*
Hele. How happy some, ore othersome can be?
Through *Athens* I am thought as faire as she.
But what of that? *Demetrius* thinkes not so:
He will not know, what all, but he doth know,
And as hee erres, doting on *Hermias* eyes;
So I, admiring of his qualities:
Things base and vilde, holding no quantity,
Loue can transpose to forme and dignity,
Loue lookes not with the eyes, but with the minde,
And therefore is wing'd *Cupid* painted blinde.
Nor hath loues minde of any iudgement taste:
Wings and no eyes, figure, vnheedy haste.
And therefore is Loue said to be a childe,
Because in choise he is often beguil'd,
As waggish boyes in game themselues forsweare;
So the boy Loue is periur'd euery where.
For ere *Demetrius* lookt on *Hermias* eyne,
He hail'd downe oathes that he was onely mine.
And when this Haile some heat from *Hermia* felt,
So he dissolu'd, and showres of oathes did melt,
I will goe tell him of faire *Hermias* flight:
Then to the wood will he, to morrow night
Pursue her; and for his intelligence,
If I haue thankes, it is a deere expence:
But heerein meane I to enrich my paine,
To haue his sight thither, and backe againe. *Exit.*

Enter Quince the Carpenter, Snug the Ioyner, Bottome the Weauer, Flute the bellowes-mender, Snout the Tinker, and Starueling the Taylor.

Quin. Is all our company heere?

Bot. You were best to call them generally, man by man, according to the scrip.

Qui. Here is the scrowle of euery mans name, which is thought fit through all *Athens*, to play in our Enterlude before the Duke and the Dutches, on his wedding day at night.

Bot. First, good *Peter Quince*, say what the play treats on: then read the names of the Actors: and so grow on to a point.

Quin. Marry our play is the most lamentable Comedy, and most cruell death of *Pyramus* and *Thisbie*.

Bot. A very good peece of worke I assure you, and a merry. Now good *Peter Quince*, call forth your Actors by the scrowle. Masters spread your selues.

Quince. Answere as I call you. *Nick Bottome* the Weauer.

Bottome. Ready; name what part I am for, and proceed.

Quince. You *Nicke Bottome* are set downe for *Pyramus*.

Bot. What is *Pyramus*, a louer, or a tyrant?

Quin. A Louer that kills himselfe most gallantly for loue.

Bot. That will aske some teares in the true performing of it: if I do it, let the audience looke to their eies: I will mooue stormes; I will condole in some measure. To the rest yet, my chiefe humour is for a tyrant. I could play *Ercles* rarely, or a part to teare a Cat in, to make all split the raging Rocks; and shiuering shocks shall break the locks of prison gates, and *Phibbus* carre shall shine from farre, and make and marre the foolish Fates. This was lofty. Now name the rest of the Players. This is *Ercles* vaine, a tyrants vaine: a louer is more condoling.

Quin *Francis Flute* the Bellowes-mender.

Flu. Heere *Peter Quince*.

Quin. You must take *Thisbie* on you.

Flut What is *Thisbie*, a wandring Knight?

Quin. It is the Lady that *Pyramus* must loue.

Flut. Nay faith, let not mee play a woman, I haue a beard comming.

Qui. That's all one, you shall play it in a Maske, and you may speake as small as you will.

Bot. And I may hide my face, let me play *Thisbie* too: Ile speake in a monstrous little voyce; *Thisne, Thisne*, ah *Pyramus* my louer deare, thy *Thisbie* deare, and Lady deare.

Quin. No no, you must play *Pyramus*, and *Flute*, you *Thisby*.

Bot. Well, proceed.

Qu. *Robin Starueling* the Taylor.

Star. Heere *Peter Quince*.

Quince. *Robin Starueling*, you must play *Thisbies* mother?

Tom Snowt, the Tinker.

Snowt. Heere *Peter Quince*.

Quin. You, *Pyramus* father; my self, *Thisbies* father; *Snugge* the Ioyner, you the Lyons part: and I hope there is a play fitted.

Snug. Haue you the Lions part written? pray you if be, giue it me, for I am slow of studie.

Quin. You may doe it *extemporie*, for it is nothing but roaring.

Bot. Let mee play the Lyon too, I will roare that I will doe any mans heart good to heare me. I will roare, that I will make the Duke say, Let him roare againe, let him roare againe.

Quin. If you should doe it too terribly, you would fright the Dutchesse and the Ladies, that they would shrike, and that were enough to hang vs all.

All. That would hang vs euery mothers sonne.

Bottome. I graunt you friends, if that you should fright the Ladies out of their Wittes, they would haue no more discretion but to hang vs: but I will aggrauate my voyce so, that I will roare you as gently as any sucking Doue; I will roare and 'twere any Nightingale.

Quin. You can play no part but *Piramus*, for *Piramus*

mus is a ſweet-fac'd man, a proper man as one ſhall ſee in a ſummers day; a moſt louely Gentleman-like man, therfore you muſt needs play *Pyramus*.

Bot. Well, I will vndertake it. What beard were I beſt to play it in?

Quin. Why, what you will.

Bot. I will diſcharge it, in either your ſtraw-colour beard, your orange tawnie beard, your purple in graine beard, or your French-crowne colour'd beard, your perfect yellow.

Quin. Some of your French Crownes haue no haire at all, and then you will play bare-fac'd. But maſters here are your parts, and I am to intreat you, requeſt you, and deſire you, to con them by too morrow night: and meet me in the palace wood, a mile without the Towne, by Moone-light, there we will rehearſe: for if we meete in the Citie, we ſhalbe dog'd with company, and our deuiſes knowne. In the meane time, I wil draw a bil of properties, ſuch as our play wants. I pray you faile me not.

Bottom. We will meete, and there we may rehearſe more obſcenely and couragiouſly. Take paines, be perfect, adieu.

Quin. At the Dukes oake we meete.

Bot. Enough, hold or cut bow-ſtrings. *Exeunt*

Actus Secundus.

Enter a Fairie at one doore, and Robin goodfellow at another.

Rob. How now ſpirit, whether wander you?

Fai. Ouer hil, ouer dale, through buſh, through briar,
Ouer parke, ouer pale, through flood, through fire,
I do wander euerie where, ſwifter then ẏ Moons ſphere;
And I ſerue the Fairy Queene, to dew her orbs vpon the (green.
The Cowſlips tall, her penſioners bee,
In their gold coats, ſpots you ſee,
Thoſe be Rubies, Fairie fauors,
In thoſe freckles, liue their ſauors,
I muſt go ſeeke ſome dew drops heere,
And hang a pearle in euery cowſlips eare.
Farewell thou Lob of ſpirits, Ile be gon,
Our Queene and all her Elues come heere anon.

Rob. The King doth keepe his Reuels here to night,
Take heed the Queene come not within his ſight,
For *Oberon* is paſſing fell and wrath,
Becauſe that ſhe, as her attendant, hath
A louely boy ſtolne from an Indian King,
She neuer had ſo ſweet a changeling,
And iealous *Oberon* would haue the childe
Knight of his traine, to trace the Forreſts wilde.
But ſhe (perforce) with holds the loued boy,
Crownes him with flowers, and makes him all her ioy.
And now they neuer meete in groue, or greene,
By fountaine cleere, or ſpangled ſtar-light ſheene,
But they do ſquare, that all their Elues for feare
Creepe into Acorne cups and hide them there.

Fai. Either I miſtake your ſhape and making quite,
Or elſe you are that ſhrew'd and knauiſh ſpirit
Cal'd Robin Good-fellow. Are you not hee,
That frights the maidens of the Villagree,
Skim milke, and ſometimes labour in the querne,
And bootleſſe make the breathleſſe huſwife cherne,
And ſometime make the drinke to beare no barme,
Miſleade night-wanderers, laughing at their harme,
Thoſe that Hobgoblin call you, and ſweet Pucke,
You do their worke, and they ſhall haue good lucke.
Are not you he?

Rob. Thou ſpeak'ſt aright;
I am that merrie wanderer of the night:
I ieſt to *Oberon*, and make him ſmile,
When I a fat and beane-fed horſe beguile,
Neighing in likeneſſe of a ſilly foale,
And ſometime lurke I in a Goſſips bole,
In very likeneſſe of a roaſted crab:
And when ſhe drinkes, againſt her lips I bob,
And on her withered dewlop poure the Ale.
The wiſeſt Aunt telling the ſaddeſt tale,
Sometime for three-foot ſtoole, miſtaketh me,
Then ſlip I from her bum, downe topples ſhe,
And tailour cries, and fals into a coffe.
And then the whole quire hold their hips, and loffe,
And waxen in their mirth, and neeze, and ſweare,
A merrier houre vvas neuer waſted there.
But roome Fairy, heere comes *Oberon*

Fair. And heere my Miſtris:
Would that he vvere gone.

Enter the King of Fairies at one doore with his traine, and the Queene at another with hers.

Ob. Ill met by Moone-light,
Proud *Tytania*.

Qu. What, iealous *Oberon*? Fairy skip hence.
I haue forſworne his bed and companie.

Ob. Tarrie raſh Wanton; am not I thy Lord?

Qu. Then I muſt be thy Lady: but I know
When thou vvaſt ſtolne away from Fairy Land,
And in the ſhape of *Corin*, ſate all day,
Playing on pipes of Corne, and verſing loue
To amorous *Phillida*. Why art thou heere
Come from the fartheſt ſteepe of *India*?
But that forſooth the bouncing *Amazon*
Your buskin'd Miſtreſſe, and your Warrior loue,
To *Theſeus* muſt be Wedded; and you come,
To giue their bed ioy and proſperitie.

Ob. How canſt thou thus for ſhame *Tytania*,
Glance at my credite, vvith *Hippolita*?
Knowing I knovv thy loue to *Theſeus*?
Didſt thou not leade him through the glimmering night
From *Peregenia*, whom he rauiſhed?
And make him vvith faire Eagles breake his faith
With *Ariadne*, and *Atiopa*?

Que. Theſe are the forgeries of iealouſie,
And neuer ſince the middle Summers ſpring
Met vve on hil, in dale, forreſt, or mead,
By paued fountaine, or by ruſhie brooke,
Or in the beached margent of the ſea,
To dance our ringlets to the whiſtling Winde,
But vvith thy braules thou haſt diſturb'd our ſport.
Therefore the Windes, piping to vs in vaine,
As in reuenge, haue ſuck'd vp from the ſea
Contagious fogges: Which falling in the Land,
Hath euerie petty Riuer made ſo proud,
That they haue ouer-borne their Continents
The Oxe hath therefore ſtretch'd his yoake in vaine,
The Ploughman loſt his ſweat, and the greene Corne
Hath rotted, ere his youth attain'd a beard:
The fold ſtands empty in the drowned field,
And Crowes are fatted vvith the murrion flocke,

The

The nine mens Morris is fild vp with mud,
And the queint Mazes in the wanton greene,
For lacke of tread are vndistinguishable.
The humane mortals want their winter heere,
No night is now with hymne or caroll blest;
Therefore the Moone (the gouernesse of floods)
Pale in her anger, washes all the aire;
That Rheumaticke diseases doe abound.
And through this distemperature, we see
The seasons alter; hoared headed frosts
Fall in the fresh lap of the crimson Rose,
And on old *Hyems* chinne and Icie crowne,
An odorous Chaplet of sweet Sommer buds
Is as in mockry set. The Spring, the Sommer,
The childing Autumne, angry Winter change
Their wonted Liueries, and the mazed world,
By their increase, now knowes not which is which;
And this same progeny of euills,
Comes from our debate, from our dissention,
We are their parents and originall.
Ober. Do you amend it then, it lies in you,
Why should *Titania* crosse her *Oberon*?
I do but beg a little changeling, boy,
To be my Henchman.
Qu. Set your heart at rest,
The Fairy land buyes not the childe of me,
His mother was a Votresse of my Order,
And in the spiced *Indian* aire, by night
Full often hath she gossipt by my side,
And sat with me on *Neptunes* yellow sands,
Marking th' embarked traders on the flood,
When we haue laught to see the sailes conceiue,
And grow big bellied with the wanton winde:
Which she with pretty and with swimming gate,
Following (her wombe then rich with my yong squire)
Would imitate, and saile vpon the Land,
To fetch me trifles, and returne againe,
As from a voyage, rich with merchandize.
But she being mortall, of that boy did die,
And for her sake I doe reare vp her boy,
And for her sake I will not part with him.
Ob. How long within this wood intend you stay?
Qu. Perchance till after *Theseus* wedding day.
If you will patiently dance in our Round,
And see our Moone-light reuels, goe with vs;
If not, shun me and I will spare your haunts.
Ob. Giue me that boy, and I will goe with thee.
Qu. Not for thy Fairy Kingdome. Fairies away:
We shall chide downe right, if I longer stay. *Exeunt.*
Ob. Wel, go thy way: thou shalt not from this groue,
Till I torment thee for this iniury.
My gentle *Pucke* come hither; thou remembrest
Since once I sat vpon a promontory,
And heard a Meare-maide on a Dolphins backe,
Vttering such dulcet and harmonious breath,
That the rude sea grew ciuill at her song,
And certaine starres shot madly from their Spheares,
To heare the Sea-maids musicke.
Puc. I remember.
Ob. That very time I say (but thou couldst not)
Flying betweene the cold Moone and the earth,
Cupid all arm'd; a certaine aime he tooke
At a faire Vestall, throned by the West,
And loos'd his loue-shaft smartly from his bow,
As it should pierce a hundred thousand hearts,
But I might see young *Cupids* fiery shaft
Quencht in the chaste beames of the watry Moone;
And the imperiall Votresse passed on,
In maiden meditation, fancy free.
Yet markt I where the bolt of *Cupid* fell.
It fell vpon a little westerne flower;
Before, milke-white; now purple with loues wound,
And maidens call it, Loue in idlenesse.
Fetch me that flower; the hearb I shew'd thee once,
The iuyce of it, on sleeping eye-lids laid,
Will make or man or woman madly dote
Vpon the next liue creature that it sees.
Fetch me this hearbe, and be thou heere againe,
Ere the *Leuiathan* can swim a league.
Pucke. Ile put a girdle about the earth, in forty minutes.
Ober. Hauing once this iuyce,
Ile watch *Titania*, when she is asleepe,
And drop the liquor of it in her eyes:
The next thing when she waking lookes vpon,
(Be it on Lyon, Beare, or Wolfe, or Bull,
On medling Monkey, or on busie Ape)
Shee shall pursue it, with the soule of loue.
And ere I take this charme off from her sight,
(As I can take it with another hearbe)
Ile make her render vp her Page to me.
But who comes heere? I am inuisible,
And I will ouer-heare their conference.

Enter Demetrius, Helena following him.

Deme. I loue thee not, therefore pursue me not,
Where is *Lysander*, and faire *Hermia*?
The one Ile stay, the other stayeth me.
Thou toldst me they were stolne into this wood;
And heere am I, and wood within this wood,
Because I cannot meet my *Hermia*.
Hence, get thee gone, and follow me no more.
Hel. You draw me, you hard-hearted Adamant,
But yet you draw not Iron, for my heart
Is true as steele. Leaue you your power to draw,
And I shall haue no power to follow you.
Deme. Do I entice you? do I speake you faire?
Or rather doe I not in plainest truth,
Tell you I doe not, nor I cannot loue you?
Hel. And euen for that doe I loue thee the more;
I am your spaniell, and *Demetrius*,
The more you beat me, I will fawne on you.
Vse me but as your spaniell; spurne me, strike me,
Neglect me, lose me; onely giue me leaue
(Vnworthy as I am) to follow you.
What worser place can I beg in your loue,
(And yet a place of high respect with me)
Then to be vsed as you doe your dogge.
Dem. Tempt not too much the hatred of my spirit,
For I am sicke when I do looke on thee.
Hel. And I am sicke when I looke not on you.
Dem. You doe impeach your modesty too much,
To leaue the City, and commit your selfe
Into the hands of one that loues you not,
To trust the opportunity of night,
And the ill counsell of a desert place,
With the rich worth of your virginity.
Hel. Your vertue is my priuiledge: for that
It is not night when I doe see your face.
Therefore I thinke I am not in the night,
Nor doth this wood lacke worlds of company,

For you in my reſpect are all the world.
Then how can it be ſaid I am alone,
When all the world is heere to looke on me?
Dem. Ile run from thee, and hide me in the brakes,
And leaue thee to the mercy of wilde beaſts.
Hel. The wildeſt hath not ſuch a heart as you;
Runne when you will, the ſtory ſhall be chang'd:
Apollo flies, and *Daphne* holds the chaſe;
The Doue purſues the Griffin, the milde Hinde
Makes ſpeed to catch the Tyger. Bootleſſe ſpeede,
When cowardiſe purſues, and valour flies.
Demet. I will not ſtay thy queſtions, let me go;
Or if thou follow me, doe not beleeue,
But I ſhall doe thee miſchiefe in the wood.
Hel. I, in the Temple in the Towne, and Field
You doe me miſchiefe. Fye *Demetrius*,
Your wrongs doe ſet a ſcandall on my ſexe:
We cannot fight for loue, as men may doe;
We ſhould be woo'd, and were not made to wooe.
I follow thee, and make a heauen of hell,
To die vpon the hand I loue ſo well. *Exit.*
Ob. Fare thee well Nymph, ere he do leaue this groue,
Thou ſhalt flie him, and he ſhall ſeeke thy loue.
Haſt thou the flower there? Welcome wanderer.

Enter Pucke.

Puck. I, there it is.
Ob. I pray thee giue it me.
I know a banke where the wilde time blowes,
Where Oxſlips and the nodding Violet growes,
Quite ouer-cannoped with luſcious woodbine,
With ſweet muske roſes, and with Eglantine;
There ſleepes *Tytania*, ſometime of the night,
Lul'd in theſe flowers, with dances and delight.
And there the ſnake throwes her enammel'd skinne,
Weed wide enough to rap a Fairy in.
And with the iuyce of this Ile ſtreake her eyes,
And make her full of hatefull fantaſies.
Take thou ſome of it, and ſeek through this groue;
A ſweet *Athenian* Lady is in loue
With a diſdainefull youth: annoint his eyes,
But doe it when the next thing he eſpies,
May be the Lady. Thou ſhalt know the man,
By the *Athenian* garments he hath on.
Effect it with ſome care, that he may proue
More fond on her, then ſhe vpon her loue;
And looke thou meet me ere the firſt Cocke crow.
Pu. Feare not my Lord, your ſeruant ſhall do ſo. *Exit.*

Enter Queene of Fairies, with her traine.

Queen. Come, now a Roundell, and a Fairy ſong;
Then for the third part of a minute hence,
Some to kill Cankers in the muske roſe buds,
Some warre with Reremiſe, for their leathern wings,
To make my ſmall Elues coates, and ſome keepe backe
The clamorous Owle that nightly hoots and wonders
At our queint ſpirits: Sing me now aſleepe.
Then to your offices, and let me reſt.

Fairies Sing.

You ſpotted Snakes with double tongue,
Thorny Hedgehogges be not ſeene,
Newts and blinde wormes do no wrong,
Come not neere our Fairy Queene.
Philomele with melodie,
Sing in your ſweet Lullaby.
Lulla, lulla, lullaby, lulla, lulla, lullaby,
Neuer harme, nor ſpell, nor charme,
Come our louely Lady nye,
So good night with Lullaby.
2. *Fairy. Weauing Spiders come not heere,*
Hence you long leg'd Spinners, hence.
Beetles blacke approach not neere;
Worme nor Snayle doe no offence.
Philomele with melody, &c.
1. *Fairy. Hence away, now all is well;*
One aloofe, ſtand Centinell. *Shee ſleepes.*

Enter Oberon.

Ober. What thou ſeeſt when thou doſt wake,
Doe it for thy true Loue take:
Loue and languiſh for his ſake.
Be it Ounce, or Catte, or Beare,
Pard, or Boare with briſtled haire,
In thy eye that ſhall appeare,
When thou wak'ſt, it is thy deare,
Wake when ſome vile thing is neere.

Enter Liſander and Hermia.

Liſ. Faire loue, you faint with wandring in þe woods
And to ſpeake troth I haue forgot our way:
Wee'll reſt vs *Hermia*, if you thinke it good,
And tarry for the comfort of the day.
Her. Be it ſo *Lyſander*; finde you out a bed,
For I vpon this banke will reſt my head.
Lyſ. One turfe ſhall ſerue as pillow for vs both,
One heart, one bed, two boſomes, and one troth.
Her. Nay good *Lyſander*, for my ſake my deere
Lie further off yet, doe not lie ſo neere.
Lyſ. O take the ſence ſweet, of my innocence,
Loue takes the meaning, in loues conference,
I meane that my heart vnto yours is knit,
So that but one heart can you make of it.
Two boſomes interchanged with an oath,
So then two boſomes, and a ſingle troth.
Then by your ſide, no bed-roome me deny,
For lying ſo, *Hermia*, I doe not lye.
Her. *Lyſander* riddles very prettily;
Now much beſhrew my manners and my pride,
If *Hermia* meant to ſay, *Lyſander* lied.
But gentle friend, for loue and courteſie
Lie further off, in humane modeſty,
Such ſeparation, as may well be ſaid,
Becomes a vertuous batchelour, and a maide,
So farre be diſtant, and good night ſweet friend;
Thy loue nere alter, till thy ſweet life end.
Lyſ. Amen, amen, to that faire prayer, ſay I,
And then end life, when I end loyalty:
Heere is my bed, ſleepe giue thee all his reſt.
Her. With halfe that wiſh, the wiſhers eyes be preſt.

Enter Pucke. *They ſleepe.*

Puck. Through the Forreſt haue I gone,
But *Athenian* finde I none,
One whoſe eyes I might approue
This flowers force in ſtirring loue.
Night and ſilence: who is heere?
Weedes of *Athens* he doth weare:
This is he (my maſter ſaid)
Deſpiſed the *Athenian* maide:
And heere the maiden ſleeping ſound,

On

On the danke and durty ground
Pretty soule, she durst not lye
Neere this lacke-loue, this kill-curtesie.
Churle, vpon thy eyes I throw
All the power this charme doth owe:
When thou wak'st, let loue forbid
Sleepe his seate on thy eye-lid.
So awake when I am gone:
For I must now to *Oberon*. *Exit.*

Enter Demetrius and Helena running.

Hel Stay, though thou kill me, sweete *Demetrius*
De. I charge thee hence, and do not haunt me thus.
Hel. O wilt thou darkling leaue me? do not so.
De. Stay on thy perill, I alone will goe.
Exit Demetrius

Hel. O I am out of breath, in this fond chace,
The more my prayer, the lesser is my grace,
Happy is *Hermia*, wheresoere she lies;
For she hath blessed and attractiue eyes.
How came her eyes so bright? Not with salt teares.
If so, my eyes are oftner washt then hers.
No, no, I am as vgly as a Beare;
For beasts that meete me, runne away for feare,
Therefore no maruaile, though *Demetrius*
Doe as a monster, flie my presence thus.
What wicked and dissembling glasse of mine,
Made me compare with *Hermias* sphery eyne?
But who is here? *Lysander* on the ground;
Deade or asleepe? I see no bloud, no wound,
Lysander, if you liue, good sir awake.
Lys. And run through fire I will for thy sweet sake.
Transparent *Helena*, nature her shewes art,
That through thy bosome makes me see thy heart.
Where is *Demetrius*? oh how fit a word
Is that vile name, to perish on my sword!
Hel. Do not say so *Lysander*, say not so:
What though he loue your *Hermia*? Lord, what though?
Yet *Hermia* still loues you; then be content.
Lys. Content with *Hermia*? No, I do repent
The tedious minutes I with her haue spent.
Not *Hermia*, but *Helena* now I loue;
Who will not change a Rauen for a Doue?
The will of man is by his reason sway'd:
And reason saies you are the worthier Maide.
Things growing are not ripe vntill their season;
So I being yong, till now ripe not to reason,
And touching now the point of humane skill,
Reason becomes the Marshall to my will,
And leades me to your eyes, where I orelooke
Loues stories, written in Loues richest booke.
Hel. Wherefore was I to this keene mockery borne?
When at your hands did I deserue this scorne?
Ist not enough, ist not enough, yong man,
That I did neuer, no nor neuer can,
Deserue a sweete looke from *Demetrius* eye,
But you must flout my insufficiency?
Good troth you do me wrong (good-sooth you do)
In such disdainfull manner, me to wooe.
But fare you well; perforce I must confesse,
I thought you Lord of more true gentlenesse.
Oh, that a Lady of one man refus'd,
Should of another therefore be abus'd *Exit.*
Lys. She sees not *Hermia*: *Hermia* sleepe thou there,
And neuer maist thou come *Lysander* neere;
For as a surfeit of the sweetest things
The deepest loathing to the stomacke brings:
Or as the heresies that men do leaue,
Are hated most of those that did deceiue:
So thou, my surfeit, and my heresie,
Of all be hated; but the most of me;
And all my powers addresse your loue and might,
To honour *Helen*, and to be her Knight. *Exit*
Her. Helpe me *Lysander*, helpe me; do thy best
To plucke this crawling serpent from my brest.
Aye me, for pitty; what a dreame was here?
Lysander looke, how I do quake with feare:
Me-thought a serpent eate my heart away,
And yet sat smiling at his cruell prey.
Lysander, what remoou'd? *Lysander*, Lord,
What, out of hearing, gone? No sound, no word?
Alacke where are you? speake and if you heare
Speake of all loues; I sound almost with feare.
No, then I well perceiue you are not nye,
Either death or you Ile finde immediately. *Exit.*

Actus Tertius.

Enter the Clownes.

Bot. Are we all met?

Quin. Pat, pat, and here's a maruailous conuenient place for our rehearsall. This greene plot shall be our stage, this hauthorne brake our tyring house, and we will do it in action, as we will do it before the Duke.

Bot. Peter quince?

Peter. What saist thou, bully *Bottome*?

Bot. There are things in this Comedy of *Piramus* and *Thisby*, that will neuer please. First *Piramus* must draw a sword to kill himselfe; which the Ladies cannot abide. How answere you that?

Snout. Berlaken, a parlous feare.

Star. I beleeue we must leaue the killing out, when all is done.

Bot. Not a whit, I haue a deuice to make all well. Write me a Prologue, and let the Prologue seeme to say, we will do no harme with our swords, and that *Pyramus* is not kill'd indeede: and for the more better assurance, tell them, that I *Piramus* am not *Piramus*, but *Bottome* the Weauer; this will put them out of feare.

Quin. Well, we will haue such a Prologue, and it shall be written in eight and sixe.

Bot. No, make it two more, let it be written in eight and eight.

Snout. Will not the Ladies be afear'd of the Lyon?

Star. I feare it, I promise you.

Bot. Masters, you ought to consider with your selues, to bring in (God shield vs) a Lyon among Ladies, is a most dreadfull thing. For there is not a more fearefull wilde foule then your Lyon liuing: and wee ought to looke to it.

Snout. Therefore another Prologue must tell he is not a Lyon.

Bot. Nay, you must name his name, and halfe his face must be seene through the Lyons necke, and he himselfe must speake through, saying thus, or to the same defect; Ladies, or faire Ladies, I would wish you, or I would request

request you, or I would entreat you, not to feare, not to tremble: my life for yours. If you thinke I come hither as a Lyon, it were pitty of my life. No, I am no such thing, I am a man as other men are; and there indeed let him name his name, and tell him plainly hee is *Snug* the ioyner.

Quin. Well, it shall be so; but there is two hard things, that is, to bring the Moone-light into a chamber: for you know, *Piramus* and *Thisby* meete by Moone-light.

Sn. Doth the Moone shine that night wee play our play?

Bot. A Calender, a Calender, looke in the Almanack, finde out Moone-shine, finde out Moone-shine.

Enter Pucke.

Quin. Yes, it doth shine that night.

Bot. Why then may you leaue a casement of the great chamber window (where we play) open, and the Moone may shine in at the casement.

Quin. I, or else one must come in with a bush of thorns and a lanthorne, and say he comes to disfigure, or to present the person of Moone-shine. Then there is another thing, we must haue a wall in the great Chamber; for *Piramus* and *Thisby* (saies the story) did talke through the chinke of a wall.

Sn. You can neuer bring in a wall. What say you *Bottome*?

Bot. Some man or other must present wall, and let him haue some Plaster, or some Lome, or some rough cast about him, to signifie wall; or let him hold his fingers thus; and through that cranny, shall *Piramus* and *Thisby* whisper.

Quin. If that may be, then all is well. Come, sit downe euery mothers sonne, and rehearse your parts. *Piramus*, you begin; when you haue spoken your speech, enter into that Brake, and so euery one according to his cue.

Enter Robin.

Rob. What hempen home-spuns haue we swaggering here,
So neere the Cradle of the Faerie Queene?
What, a Play toward? Ile be an auditor,
An Actor too perhaps, if I see cause.

Quin. Speake *Piramus*: *Thisby* stand forth.

Pir. *Thisby*, the flowers of odious sauors sweete.

Quin. Odours, odours.

Pir. Odours sauors sweete,
So hath thy breath, my dearest *Thisby* deare.
But harke, a voyce: stay thou but here a while,
And by and by I will to thee appeare. *Exit. Pir.*

Puck. A stranger *Piramus*, then ere plaid here.

This. Must I speake now?

Pet. I marry must you. For you must vnderstand he goes but to see a noyse that he heard, and is to come againe.

Thys. Most radiant *Piramus*, most Lilly white of hue,
Of colour like the red rose on triumphant bryer,
Most brisky Iuuenall, and eke most louely Iew,
As true as truest horse, that yet would neuer tyre,
Ile meete thee *Piramus*, at *Ninnies* toombe.

Pet. *Ninus* toombe man: why, you must not speake that yet; that you answere to *Piramus*: you speake all your part at once, cues and all. *Piramus* enter, your cue is past; it is neuer tyre.

Thys. O, as true as truest horse, that yet would neuer tyre:

Pir. If I were faire, *Thisby* I were onely thine.

Pet. O monstrous. O strange. We are hanted; pray masters, flye masters, helpe.

The Clownes all Exit.

Puk. Ile follow you, Ile leade you about a Round,
Through bogge, through bush, through brake, through bryer,
Sometime a horse Ile be, sometime a hound:
A hogge, a headlesse beare, sometime a fire,
And neigh, and barke, and grunt, and rore, and burne,
Like horse, hound, hog, beare, fire, at euery turne. *Exit.*

Enter Piramus with the Asse head.

Bot. Why do they run away? This is a knauery of them to make me afeard. *Enter Snowt.*

Sn. O *Bottom*, thou art chang'd; What doe I see on thee?

Bot. What do you see? You see an Asse-head of your owne, do you?

Enter Peter Quince.

Pet. Blesse thee *Bottome*, blesse thee; thou art translated. *Exit.*

Bot. I see their knauery; this is to make an asse of me, to fright me if they could; but I will not stirre from this place, do what they can. I will walke vp and downe here, and I will sing that they shall heare I am not afraid.
The Woosell cocke, so blacke of hew,
With Orenge-tawny bill.
The Throstle, with his note so true,
The Wren and little quill.

Tyta. What Angell wakes me from my flowry bed?

Bot. The Finch, the Sparrow, and the Larke,
The plainsong Cuckow gray;
Whose note full many a man doth marke,
And dares not answere, nay.
For indeede, who would set his wit to so foolish a bird? Who would giue a bird the lye, though he cry Cuckow, neuer so?

Tyta. I pray thee gentle mortall, sing againe.
Mine eare is much enamored of thy note;
On the first view to say, to sweare I loue thee.
So is mine eye enthralled to thy shape.
And thy faire vertues force (perforce) doth moue me.

Bot. Me-thinkes mistresse, you should haue little reason for that: and yet to say the truth, reason and loue keepe little company together, now-adayes. The more the pittie, that some honest neighbours will not make them friends. Nay, I can gleeke vpon occasion.

Tyta. Thou art as wise, as thou art beautifull.

Bot. Not so neither: but if I had wit enough to get out of this wood, I haue enough to serue mine owne turne.

Tyta. Out of this wood, do not desire to goe,
Thou shalt remaine here, whether thou wilt or no.
I am a spirit of no common rate:
The Summer still doth tend vpon my state,
And I doe loue thee; therefore goe with me,
Ile giue thee Fairies to attend on thee;
And they shall fetch thee Iewels from the deepe,
And sing, while thou on pressed flowers dost sleepe:
And I will purge thy mortall grossenesse so,
That thou shalt like an airie spirit go.

Enter Pease-blossome, Cobweb, Moth, Mustard-seede, and foure Fairies.

Fai. Ready; and I, and I, and I. Where shall we go?

Tita. Be

Tita. Be kinde and curteous to this Gentleman,
Hop in his walkes, and gambole in his eies,
Feede him with Apricocks, and Dewberries,
With purple Grapes, greene Figs, and Mulberries,
The honie-bags steale from the humble Bees,
And for night-tapers crop their waxen thighes,
And light them at the fierie-Glow-wormes eyes,
To haue my loue to bed, and to arise:
And plucke the wings from painted Butterflies,
To fan the Moone-beames from his sleeping eies
Nod to him Elues, and doe him curtesies.

1.Fai. Haile mortall, haile.

2.Fai. Haile.

3.Fai. Haile.

Bot. I cry your worships mercy hartily; I beseech your worships name.

Cob. *Cobweb.*

Bot. I shall desire you of more acquaintance, good Master *Cobweb*: if I cut my finger, I shall make bold with you. Your name honest Gentleman?

Peas. *Pease blossome.*

Bot. I pray you commend mee to mistresse *Squash*, your mother, and to master *Peascod* your father. Good master *Pease-blossome*, I shal desire of you more acquaintance to. Your name I beseech you sir?

Mus. *Mustard-seede.*

Peas. *Pease-blossome.*

Bot. Good master *Mustard seede*, I know your patience well: that same cowardly gyant-like Oxe beefe hath deuoured many a gentleman of your house. I promise you, your kindred hath made my eyes water ere now. I desire you more acquaintance, good Master *Mustard-seede.*

Tita. Come waite vpon him, lead him to my bower.
The Moone me-thinks, lookes with a watrie eie,
And when she weepes, weepe euerie little flower,
Lamenting some enforced chastitie.
Tye vp my louers tongue, bring him silently. *Exit.*

Enter King of Pharies, solus.

Ob. I wonder if *Titania* be awak't;
Then what it was that next came in her eye,
Which she must dote on, in extremitie.

Enter Pucke.

Here comes my messenger: how now mad spirit,
What night-rule now about this gaunted groue?

Puck. My Mistris with a monster is in loue,
Neere to her close and consecrated bower,
While she was in her dull and sleeping hower,
A crew of patches, rude Mechanicals,
That worke for bread vpon *Athenian* stals,
Were met together to rehearse a Play,
Intended for great *Theseus* nuptiall day:
The shallowest thick-skin of that barren sort,
Who *Piramus* presented, in their sport,
Forsooke his Scene, and entred in a brake,
When I did him at this aduantage take,
An Asses nole I fixed on his head.
Anon his *Thisbie* must be answered,
And forth my Mimmick comes: when they him spie,
As Wilde-geese, that the creeping Fowler eye,
Or russed-pated choughes, many in sort
(Rising and cawing at the guns report)
Seuer themselues, and madly sweepe the skye:
So at his sight, away his fellowes flye,
And at our stampe, here ore and ore one fals;
He murther cries, and helpe from *Athens* cals.
Their sense thus weake, lost with their fears thus strong,
Made senselesse things begin to do them wrong.
For briars and thornes at their apparell snatch,
Some sleeues, some hats, from yeelders all things catch,
I led them on in this distracted feare,
And left sweete *Piramus* translated there:
When in that moment (so it came to passe)
Tytania waked, and straightway lou'd an Asse.

Ob. This fals out better then I could deuise:
But hast thou yet lacht the *Athenians* eyes,
With he loue iuyce, as I did bid thee doe?

Rob. I tooke him sleeping (that is finisht
And the *Athenian* woman by his side,
That when he wak't, of force she must be eyde.

Enter Demetrius and Hermia.

Ob. Stand close, this is the same *Athenian.*

Rob. This is the woman, but not this the man.

Dem. O why rebuke you him that loues you so?
Lay breath so bitter on your bitter foe.

Her. Now I but chide, but I should vse thee worse.
For thou (I feare) hast giuen me cause to curse,
If thou hast slaine *Lysander* in his sleepe,
Being ore shooes in bloud, plunge in the deepe, and kill me too:
The Sunne was not so true vnto the day,
As he to me. Would he haue stollen away,
From sleeping *Hermia*? Ile beleeue as soone
This whole earth may be bord, and that the Moone
May through the Center creepe, and so displease
Her brothers noonetide, with th' *Antipodes.*
It cannot be but thou hast murdred him,
So should a murtherer looke, so dead, so grim.

Dem. So should the murderer looke, and so should I,
Pierst through the heart with your stearne cruelty.
Yet you the murderer looks as bright as cleare,
As yonder *Venus* in her glimmering spheare.

Her. What's this to my *Lysander*? where is he?
Ah good *Demetrius*, wilt thou giue him me?

Dem. I'de rather giue his carkasse to my hounds.

Her. Out dog, out cur, thou driu'st me past the bounds
Of maidens patience. Hast thou slaine him then?
Henceforth be neuer numbred among men.
Oh, once tell true, euen for my sake,
Durst thou a lookt vpon him, being awake?
And hast thou kill'd him sleeping? O braue tutch:
Could not a worme, an Adder do so much?
An Adder did it: for with doubler tongue
Then thine (thou serpent) neuer Adder stung.

Dem. You spend your passion on a mispris'd mood,
I am not guiltie of *Lysanders* blood:
Nor is he dead for ought that I can tell.

Her. I pray thee tell me then that he is well.

Dem. And if I could, what should I get therefore?

Her. A priuiledge, neuer to see me more;
And from thy hated presence part I: see me no more
Whether he be dead or no. *Exit.*

Dem. There is no following her in this fierce vaine,
Here therefore for a while I will remaine.
So sorrowes heauinesse doth heauier grow:
For debt that bankrout slip doth sorrow owe,
Which now in some slight measure it will pay,

If

Iſ for his tender here I make ſome ſtay. *Lie downe.*
Ob. What haſt thou done? Thou haſt miſtaken quite
And laid the loue iuyce on ſome true loues ſight:
Of thy miſpriſion, muſt perforce enſue
Some true loue turn'd, and not a falſe turn'd true.
Rob. Then fate ore-rules, that one man holding troth,
A million faile, confounding oath on oath.
Ob. About the wood, goe ſwifter then the winde,
And *Helena* of *Athens* looke thou finde.
All fancy ſicke ſhe is, and pale of cheere,
With ſighes of loue, that coſts the freſh bloud deare.
By ſome illuſion ſee thou bring her heere,
Ile charme his eyes againſt ſhe doth appeare.
Robin. I go, I go, looke how I goe,
Swifter then arrow from the *Tartars* bowe. *Exit.*
Ob. Flower of this purple die,
Hit with *Cupids* archery,
Sinke in apple of his eye,
When his loue he doth eſpie,
Let her ſhine as glorиouſly
As the *Venus* of the sky.
When thou wak'ſt if ſhe be by,
Beg of her for remedy.

Enter Pucke.

Puck. Captaine of our Fairy band,
Helena is heere at hand,
And the youth, miſtooke by me,
Pleading for a Louers fee.
Shall we their fond Pageant ſee?
Lord, what fooles theſe mortals be!
Ob. Stand aſide: the noyſe they make,
Will cauſe *Demetrius* to awake.
Puck. Then will two at once wooe one,
That muſt needs be ſport alone:
And thoſe things doe beſt pleaſe me,
That befall prepoſterouſly.

Enter Lyſander and Helena.

Lyſ. Why ſhould you think ẏ I ſhould wooe in ſcorn?
Scorne and deriſion neuer comes in teares:
Looke when I vow I weepe; and vowes ſo borne,
In their natiuity all truth appeares.
How can theſe things in me, ſeeme ſcorne to you?
Bearing the badge of faith to proue them true.
Hel. You doe aduance your cunning more & more,
When truth kils truth, O diueliſh holy fray!
Theſe vowes are *Hermias*. Will you giue her ore?
Weigh oath with oath, and you will nothing weigh.
Your vowes to her, and me, (put in two ſcales)
Will euen weigh, and both as light as tales.
Lyſ. I had no iudgement, when to her I ſwore.
Hel. Nor none in my minde, now you giue her ore.
Lyſ. *Demetrius* loues her, and he loues not you. *Awa.*
Dem. O *Helen*, goddeſſe, nimph, perfect, diuine,
To what my loue, ſhall I compare thine eyne.
Chriſtall is muddy, O how ripe in ſhow,
Thy lips, thoſe kiſſing cherries, tempting grow!
That pure congealed white, high *Taurus* ſnow,
Fan'd with the Eaſterne winde, turnes to a crow,
When thou holdſt vp thy hand. O let me kiſſe
This Princeſſe of pure white, this ſeale of bliſſe.
Hell. O ſpight! O hell! I ſee you are all bent
To ſet againſt me, for your merriment:
If you were ciuill, and knew curteſie,
You would not doe me thus much iniury.
Can you not hate me, as I know you doe,
But you muſt ioyne in ſoules to mocke me to?
If you are men, as men you are in ſhow,
You would not vſe a gentle Lady ſo;
To vow, and ſweare, and ſuperpraiſe my parts,
When I am ſure you hate me with your hearts.
You both are Riuals, and loue *Hermia*;
And now both Riuals to mocke *Helena*.
A trim exploit, a manly enterprize,
To coniure teares vp in a poore maids eyes,
With your deriſion; none of noble ſort,
Would ſo offend a Virgin, and extort
A poore ſoules patience, all to make you ſport.
Lyſa. You are vnkind *Demetrius*; be not ſo,
For you loue *Hermia*; this you know I know;
And here with all good will, with all my heart,
In *Hermias* loue I yeeld you vp my part;
And yours of *Helena*, to me bequeath,
Whom I do loue, and will do to my death.
Hel. Neuer did mockers waſt more idle breth.
Dem. *Lyſander*, keep thy *Hermia*, I will none:
If ere I lou'd her, all that loue is gone.
My heart to her, but as gueſt-wiſe ſoiourn'd,
And now to *Helen* it is home return'd,
There to remaine.
Lyſ. It is not ſo.
De. Diſparage not the faith thou doſt not know,
Leſt to thy perill thou abide it deare.
Looke where thy Loue comes, yonder is thy deare.

Enter Hermia.

Her. Dark night, that from the eye his function takes,
The eare more quicke of apprehenſion makes.
Wherein it doth impaire the ſeeing ſenſe,
It paies the hearing double recompence.
Thou art not by mine eye, *Lyſander* found,
Mine eare (I thanke it) brought me to that ſound.
But why vnkindly didſt thou leaue me ſo?
Lyſan. Why ſhould hee ſtay whom Loue doth preſſe (to go?
Her. What loue could preſſe *Lyſander* from my ſide?
Lyſ. *Lyſanders* loue (that would not let him bide)
Faire *Helena*; who more engilds the night,
Then all yon fierie oes, and eies of light.
Why ſeek'ſt thou me? Could not this make thee know,
The hate I bare thee, made me leaue thee ſo?
Her. You ſpeake not as you thinke; it cannot be.
Hel. Loe, ſhe is one of this confederacy,
Now I perceiue they haue conioyn'd all three,
To faſhion this falſe ſport in ſpight of me.
Iniurious Hermia, moſt vngratefull maid,
Haue you conſpir'd, haue you with theſe contriu'd
To baite me, with this foule deriſion?
Is all the counſell that we two haue ſhar'd,
The ſiſters vowes, the houres that we haue ſpent,
When wee haue chid the haſty footed time,
For parting vs; O, is all forgot?
All ſchooledaies friendſhip, child-hood innocence?
We Hermia, like two Artificiall gods,
Haue with our needles, created both one flower,
Both on one ſampler, ſitting on one cuſhion,
Both warbling of one ſong, both in one key;
As if our hands, our ſides, voices, and mindes
Had beene incorporate. So we grew together,
Like to a double cherry, ſeeming parted,
But yet a vnion in partition,

Two

Two louely berries molded on one ſtem,
So with two ſeeming bodies, but one heart,
Two of the firſt life coats in Heraldry,
Due but to one and crowned with one creſt.
And will you rent our ancient loue aſunder,
To ioyne with men in ſcorning your poore friend?
It is not friendly,'tis not maidenly.
Our ſexe as well as I,may chide you for it,
Though I alone doe feele the iniurie.
Her. I am amazed at your paſſionate words,
I ſcorne you not; It ſeemes that you ſcorne me.
Hel. Haue you not ſet *Lyſander*,as in ſcorne
To follow me,and praiſe my eies and face?
And made your other loue,*Demetrius*
(Who euen but now did ſpurne me with his foote)
To call me goddeſſe,nimph,diuine,and rare.
Precious,celeſtiall? Wherefore ſpeakes he this
To her he hates? And wherefore doth *Lyſander*
Denie your loue(ſo rich within his ſoule)
And tender me (forſooth) affection,
But by your ſetting on,by your conſent?
What though I be not ſo in grace as you,
So hung vpon with loue,ſo fortunate?
(But miſerable moſt,to loue vnlou'd)
This you ſhould pittie,rather then deſpiſe.
Her. I vnderſtand not what you meane by this.
Hel. I,doe,perſeuer,counterfeit ſad lookes,
Make mouthes vpon me when I turne my backe,
Winke each at other,hold the ſweete ieſt vp:
This ſport well carried,ſhall be chronicled.
If you haue any pittie,grace,or manners,
You would not make me ſuch an argument:
But fare ye well,'tis partly mine owne fault,
Which death or abſence ſoone ſhall remedie.
Lyſ. Stay gentle *Helena*,heare my excuſe,
My loue,my life,my ſoule,faire *Helena*.
Hel. O excellent!
Her. Sweete,do not ſcorn her ſo.
Dem. If ſhe cannot entreate,I can compell.
Lyſ. Thou canſt compell,no more then ſhe entreate.
Thy threats haue no more ſtrength then her weak praiſe.
Helen,I loue thee,by my life I doe;
I ſweare by that which I will loſe for thee,
To proue him falſe,that ſaies I loue thee not.
Dem. I ſay,I loue thee more then he can do.
Lyſ. If thou ſay ſo,with-draw and proue it too.
Dem. Quick,come.
Her. *Lyſander*,whereto tends all this?
Lyſ. Away,you *Ethiope*.
Dem. No,no,Sir,ſeeme to breake looſe;
Take on as you would follow,
But yet come not: you are a tame man,go.
Lyſ. Hang off thou cat,thou bur;vile thing let looſe,
Or I will ſhake thee from me like a ſerpent.
Her Why are you growne ſo rude?
What change is this ſweete Loue?
Lyſ. Thy loue? out tawny *Tartar*,out;
Out loathed medicine; O hated poiſon hence.
Her. Do you not ieſt?
Hel. Yes ſooth,and ſo do you.
Lyſ. *Demetrius*:I will keepe my word with thee.
Dem. I would I had your bond: for I perceiue
A weake bond holds you; Ile not truſt your word.
Lyſ. What,ſhould I hurt her,ſtrike her, kill her dead?
Although I hate her, Ile not harme her ſo.
Her. What,can you do me greater harme then hate?
Hate me,wherefore? O me,what newes my Loue?
Am not I *Hermia*? Are not you *Lyſander*?
I am as faire now,as I was ere while.
Since night you lou'dme;yet ſince night you left me.
Why then you left me (O the gods forbid
In earneſt, ſhall I ſay?
Lyſ. I,by my life;
And neuer did deſire to ſee thee more.
Therefore be out of hope,of queſtion,of doubt;
Be certaine,nothing truer: tis no ieſt,
That I doe hate thee,and loue *Helena*.
Her. O me,you iugler,you canker bloſſome,
You theefe of love; What,haue you come by night,
And ſtolne my loues heart from him?
Hel. Fine yfaith:
Haue you no modeſty,no maiden ſhame,
No touch of baſhfulneſſe? What,will you teare
Impatient anſwers from my gentle tongue?
Fie,fie,you counterfeit,you puppet,you.
Her Puppet? why ſo? I,that way goes the game.
Now I perceiue that ſhe hath made compare
Betweene our ſtatures,ſhe hath vrg'd her height,
And with her perſonage,her tall perſonage,
Her height (forſooth) ſhe hath preuail'd with him.
And are you growne ſo high in his eſteeme,
Becauſe I am ſo dwarfiſh, and ſo low?
How low am I, thou painted May-pole? Speake,
How low am I? I am not yet ſo low,
But that my nailes can reach vnto thine eyes.
Hel. I pray you though you mocke me,gentlemen,
Let her not hurt me; I was neuer curſt:
I haue no gift at all in ſhrewiſhneſſe;
I am a right maide for my cowardize;
Let her not ſtrike me: you perhaps may thinke,
Becauſe ſhe is ſomething lower then my ſelfe,
That I can match her.
Her. Lower? harke againe.
Hel. Good *Hermia*,do not be ſo bitter with me,
I euermore did loue you *Hermia*,
Did euer keepe your counſels,neuer wronged you,
Saue that in loue vnto *Demetrius*,
I told him of your ſtealth vnto this wood.
He followed you,for loue I followed him,
But he hath chid me hence,and threatned me
To ſtrike me,ſpurne me,nay to kill me too;
And now,ſo you will let me quiet go,
To *Athens* will I beare my folly backe,
And follow you no further. Let me go.
You ſee how ſimple,and how fond I am.
Her. Why get you gone: who iſt that hinders you?
Hel. A fooliſh heart,that I leaue here behinde.
Her. What,with *Lyſander*?
Her. With *Demetrius*.
Lyſ. Be not afraid,ſhe ſhall not harme thee *Helena*.
Dem. No ſir,ſhe ſhall not, though you take her part.
Hel. O when ſhe's angry,ſhe is keene and ſhrewd,
She was a vixen when ſhe went to ſchoole,
And though ſhe be but little,ſhe is fierce.
Her. Little againe? Nothing but low and little?
Why will you ſuffer her to flout me thus?
Let me come to her.
Lyſ. Get you gone you dwarfe,
You *minimus*, of hindring knot-graſſe made,
You bead,you acorne.
Dem. You are too officious,
In her behalfe that ſcornes your ſeruices.

Let

Let her alone, ſpeake not of *Helena*,
Take not her part. For if thou doſt intend
Neuer ſo little ſhew of loue to her,
Thou ſhalt abide it.

Lyſ. Now ſhe holds me not,
Now follow if thou dar'ſt, to try whoſe right,
Of thine or mine is moſt in *Helena*.

Dem. Follow? Nay, Ile goe with thee cheeke by iowle *Exit Lyſander and Demetrius.*

Her. You Miſtris, all this coyle is long of you.
Nay, goe not backe.

Hel. I will not truſt you I,
Nor longer ſtay in your curſt companie.
Your hands then mine, are quicker for a fray,
My legs are longer though to runne away.

Enter Oberon and Pucke.

Ob. This is thy negligence, ſtill thou miſtak'ſt,
Or elſe committ'ſt thy knaueries willingly.

Puck. Beleeue me, King of ſhadowes, I miſtooke,
Did not you tell me, I ſhould know the man,
By the *Athenian* garments he hath on?
And ſo farre blameleſſe proues my enterpize,
That I haue nointed an Athenians eies,
And ſo farre am I glad, it ſo did ſort,
As this their iangling I eſteeme a ſport.

Ob. Thou ſeeſt theſe Louers ſeeke a place to fight,
Hie therefore *Robin*, ouercaſt the night,
The ſtarrie Welkin couer thou anon,
With drooping fogge as blacke as *Acheron*,
And lead theſe teſtie Riuals ſo aſtray,
As one come not within anothers way.
Like to *Lyſander*, ſometime frame thy tongue,
Then ſtirre *Demetrius* vp with bitter wrong;
And ſometime raile thou like *Demetrius*;
And from each other looke thou leade them thus,
Till ore their browes, death-counterfeiting, ſleepe
With leaden legs, and Battie-wings doth creepe;
Then cruſh this hearbe into *Lyſanders* eie,
Whoſe liquor hath this vertuous propertie,
To take from thence all error, with his might,
And make his eie-bals role with wonted ſight.
When they next wake, all this deriſion
Shall ſeeme a dreame, and fruitleſſe viſion,
And backe to *Athens* ſhall the Louers wend
With league, whoſe date till death ſhall neuer end.
Whiles I in this affaire do thee imply,
Ile to my Queene, and beg her *Indian* Boy;
And then I will her charmed eie releaſe
From monſters view, and all things ſhall be peace.

Puck. My Fairie Lord, this muſt be done with haſte,
For night-ſwift Dragons cut the Clouds full faſt,
And yonder ſhines *Auroras* harbinger
At whoſe approach Ghoſts wandring here and there,
Troope home to Church-yards; damned ſpirits all,
That in croſſe-waies and floods haue buriall,
Alreadie to their wormie beds are gone;
For feare leaſt day ſhould looke their ſhames vpon,
They wilfully themſelues dxile from light,
And muſt for aye conſort with blacke browd night.

Ob. But we are ſpirits of another ſort:
I, with the mornings loue haue oft made ſport,
And like a Forreſter, the groues may tread,
Euen till the Eaſterne gate all fierie red,
Opening on *Neptune*, with faire bleſſed beames,
Turnes into yellow gold, his ſalt greene ſtreames.
But notwithſtanding haſte, make no delay
We may effect this buſineſſe, yet ere day.

Puck. Vp and downe, vp and downe, I will leade them vp and downe: I am fear'd in field and towne. *Goblin*, lead them vp and downe: here comes one.

Enter Lyſander.

Lyſ. Where art thou, proud *Demetrius*?
Speake thou now.

Rob Here villaine, drawne & readie. Where art thou?

Lyſ. I will be with thee ſtraight.

Rob. Follow me then to plainer ground.

Enter Demetrius.

Dem. *Lyſander*, ſpeake againe;
Thou runaway, thou coward, art thou fled?
Speake in ſome buſh: Where doſt thou hide thy head?

Rob. Thou coward, art thou bragging to the ſtars,
Telling the buſhes that thou look'ſt for wars,
And wilt not come? Come recreant, come thou childe,
Ile whip thee with a rod. He is defil'd
That drawes a ſword on thee.

Dem. Yea, art thou there?

Ro. Follow my voice, we'l try no manhood here. *Exit.*

Lyſ. He goes before me, and ſtill dares me on,
When I come where he cals, then he's gone.
The villaine is much lighter heel'd then I:
I followed faſt, but faſter he did flye; *ſhifting places.*
That fallen am I in darke vneuen way,
And here wil reſt me. Come thou gentle day: *lye down.*
For if but once thou ſhew me thy gray light,
Ile finde *Demetrius*, and reuenge this ſpight.

Enter Robin and Demetrius.

Rob. Ho, ho, ho; coward, why com'ſt thou not?

Dem. Abide me, if thou dar'ſt. For well I wot,
Thou runſt before me, ſhifting euery place,
And dar'ſt not ſtand, nor looke me in the face.
Where art thou?

Rob. Come hither, I am here.

Dem. Nay then thou mock'ſt me; thou ſhalt buy this deere,
If euer I thy face by day-light ſee.
Now goe thy way: faintneſſe conſtraineth me,
To meaſure out my length on this cold bed,
By daies approach looke to be viſited.

Enter Helena.

Hel. O weary night, O long and tedious night,
Abate thy houres, ſhine comforts from the Eaſt,
That I may backe to *Athens* by day-light,
From theſe that my poore companie deteſt;
And ſleepe that ſometime ſhuts vp ſorrowes eie,
Steale me a while from mine owne companie. *Sleepe.*

Rob. Yet but three? Come one more,
Two of both kindes makes vp foure.
Here ſhe comes, curſt and ſad,
Cupid is a knauiſh lad,

Enter Hermia.

Thus to make poore females mad.

Her. Neuer ſo wearie neuer ſo in woe,
Bedabbled with the dew, and torne with briars,
I can no further crawle, no further goe;
My legs can keepe no pace with my deſires.
Here will I reſt me till the breake of day,
Heauens ſhield *Lyſander*, if they meane a fray.

Rob. On the ground ſleepe ſound,
Ile apply your eie gentle louer, remedy.
When thou wak'ſt, thou tak'ſt
True delight in the ſight of thy former Ladies eye,

And

And the Country Prouerb knowne,
That euery man ſhould take his owne,
In your waking ſhall be ſhowne.
Iacke ſhall haue *Iill*, nought ſhall goe ill,
The man ſhall haue his Mare againe, and all ſhall bee well.

They ſleepe all the Act.

Actus Quartus.

Enter Queene of Fairies, and Clowne, and Fairies, and the King behinde them.

Tita. Come, ſit thee downe vpon this flowry bed,
While I thy amiable cheekes doe coy,
And ſticke muske roſes in thy ſleeke ſmoothe head,
And kiſſe thy faire large eares, my gentle ioy.

Clow. Where's *Peaſe bloſſome?*

Peaſ. Ready.

Clow. Scratch my head, *Peaſe-bloſſome.* Wher's Mounſieuer *Cobweb.*

Cob. Ready.

Clowne. Mounſieur *Cobweb*, good Mounſier get your weapons in your hand, & kill me a red hipt humble-Bee, on the top of a thiſtle; and good Mounſieur bring mee the hony bag. Doe not fret your ſelfe too much in the action, Mounſieur; and good Mounſieur haue a care the hony bag breake not, I would be loth to haue yon ouerflowne with a hony-bag ſigniour. Where's Mounſieur *Muſtardſeed?*

Muſ. Ready.

Clo. Giue me your neaſe, Mounſieur *Muſtardſeed.* Pray you leaue your courteſie good Mounſieur.

Muſ. What's your will?

Clo. Nothing good Mounſieur, but to help Caualery *Cobweb* to ſcratch. I muſt to the Barbers Mounſieur, for me-thinkes I am maruellous hairy about the face. And I am ſuch a tender aſſe, if my haire do but tickle me, I muſt ſcratch.

Tita. What, wilt thou heare ſome muſicke, my ſweet loue.

Clow. I haue a reaſonable good eare in muſicke. Let vs haue the tongs and the bones.

Muſicke Tongs, Rurall Muſicke.

Tita. Or ſay ſweete Loue, what thou deſireſt to eat.

Clowne. Truly a pecke of Prouender; I could munch your good dry Oates. Me-thinkes I haue a great deſire to a bottle of hay: good hay, ſweete hay hath no fellow.

Tita. I haue a venturous Fairy,
That ſhall ſeeke the Squirrels hoard,
And fetch thee new Nuts.

Clowne. I had rather haue a handfull or two of dried peaſe. But I pray you let none of your people ſtirre me, I haue an expoſition of ſleepe come vpon me.

Tyta. Sleepe thou, and I will winde thee in my arms,
Fairies be gone, and be alwaies away.
So doth the woodbine, the ſweet Honiſuckle,
Gently entwiſt; the female Iuy ſo
Enrings the barky fingers of the Elme.
O how I loue thee! how I dote on thee!

Enter Robin goodfellow and Oberon.

Ob. Welcome good *Robin*:
Seeſt thou this ſweet ſight?
Her dotage now I doe begin to pitty.
For meeting her of late behinde the wood,
Seeking ſweet ſauors for this hatefull foole,
I did vpbraid her, and fall out with her.
For ſhe his hairy temples then had rounded,
With coronet of freſh and fragrant flowers.
And that ſame dew which ſomtime on the buds,
Was wont to ſwell like round and orient pearles;
Stood now within the pretty flouriets eyes,
Like teares that did their owne diſgrace bewaile.
When I had at my pleaſure taunted her,
And ſhe in milde termes beg'd my patience,
I then did aske of her, her changeling childe,
Which ſtraight ſhe gaue me, and her Fairy ſent
To beare him to my Bower in Fairy Land.
And now I haue the Boy, I will vndoe
This hatefull imperfection of her eyes.
And gentle *Pucke* take this transformed ſcalpe,
From off the head of this *Athenian* ſwaine;
That he awaking when the other doe,
May all to *Athens* backe againe repaire,
And thinke no more of this nights accidents,
But as the fierce vexation of a dreame.
But firſt I will releaſe the Fairy Queene.

Be thou as thou waſt wont to be;
See as thou waſt wont to ſee.
Dians bud, or Cupids flower,
Hath ſuch force and bleſſed power

Now my *Titania* wake you my ſweet Queene.

Tita. My *Oberon*, what viſions haue I ſeene!
Me-thought I was enamoured of an Aſſe.

Ob. There lies your loue.

Tita. How came theſe things to paſſe?
Oh, how mine eyes doth loath this viſage now!

Ob. Silence a while. *Robin* take off his head:
Titania muſick call, and ſtrike more dead
Then common ſleepe; of all theſe, fine the ſenſe.

Tita. Muſicke, ho muſicke, ſuch as charmeth ſleepe.

Muſick ſtill.

Rob. When thou wak'ſt, with thine owne fooles eies peepe. (me

Ob. Sound muſick; come my Queen, take hands with
And rocke the ground whereon theſe ſleepers be.
Now thou and I are new in amity,
And will to morrow midnight, ſolemnly
Dance in Duke *Theſeus* houſe triumphantly,
And bleſſe it to all faire poſterity.
There ſhall the paires of faithfull Louers be
Wedded, with *Theſeus*, all in iollity.

Rob. Faire King attend, and marke,
I doe heare the morning Larke.

Ob. Then my Queene in ſilence ſad,
Trip we after the nights ſhade;
We the Globe can compaſſe ſoone,
Swifter then the wandring Moone.

Tita. Come my Lord, and in our flight,
Tell me how it came this night,
That I ſleeping heere was found,

Sleepers Lye ſtill.

O With

With these mortals on the ground. *Exeunt.*

Winde Hornes.

Enter Theseus, Egeus, Hippolita and all his traine.

Thes. Goe one of you, finde out the Forrester,
For now our obseruation is perform'd;
And since we haue the vaward of the day,
My Loue shall heare the musicke of my hounds.
Vncouple in the Westerne valley, let them goe;
Dispatch I say, and finde the Forrester.
We will faire Queene, vp to the Mountaines top,
And marke the musicall confusion
Of hounds and eccho in coniunction.

Hip. I was with *Hercules* and *Cadmus* once,
When in a wood of *Creete* they bayed the Beare
With hounds of *Sparta*; neuer did I heare
Such gallant chiding. For besides the groues,
The skies, the fountaines, euery region neere,
Seeme all one mutuall cry. I neuer heard
So musicall a discord, such sweet thunder.

Thes. My hounds are bred out of the *Spartan* kinde,
So flew'd, so sanded, and their heads are hung
With eares that sweepe away the morning dew,
Crooke kneed, and dew-lapt, like *Thessalian* Buls,
Slow in pursuit, but match'd in mouth like bels,
Each vnder each. A cry more tuneable
Was neuer hallowed to, nor cheer'd with horne,
In *Creete*, in *Sparta*, nor in *Thessaly*;
Judge when you heare. Bnt soft, what nimphs are these?

Egeus. My Lord, this is my daughter heere asleepe,
And this *Lysander*, this *Demetrius* is,
This *Helena*, olde *Nedars Helena*,
I wonder of this being heere together.

The. No doubt they rose vp early, to obserue
The right of May; and hearing our intent,
Came heere in grace of our solemnity.
But speake *Egeus*, is not this the day
That *Hermia* should giue answer of her choice?

Egeus. It is, my Lord.

Thes. Goe bid the hunts-men wake them with their hornes.

Hornes and they wake.

Shout within, they all start vp.

Thes. Good morrow friends: Saint *Valentine* is past,
Begin these wood birds but to couple now?

Lys. Pardon my Lord.

Thes. I pray you all stand vp.
I know you two are Riuall enemies.
How comes this gentle concord in the world,
That hatred is is so farre from iealousie,
To sleepe by hate, and feare no enmity.

Lys. My Lord, I shall reply amazedly,
Halfe sleepe, halfe waking. But as yet, I sweare,
I cannot truly say how I came heere.
But as I thinke (for truly would I speake)
And now I doe bethinke me, so it is;
I came with *Hermia* hither. Our intent
Was to be gone from *Athens*, where we might be
Without the perill of the *Athenian* Law.

Ege. Enough, enough, my Lord: you haue enough;
I beg the Law, the Law, vpon his head:
They would haue stolne away, they would *Demetrius*,
Thereby to haue defeated you and me:
You of your wife, and me of my consent;
Of my consent, that she should be your wife.

Dem. My Lord, faire *Helen* told me of their stealth,
Of this their purpose hither, to this wood,
And I in furie hither followed them;
Faire *Helena*, in fancy followed me.
But my good Lord, I wot not by what power,
(But by some power it is) my loue
To *Hermia* (melted as the snow)
Seems to me now as the remembrance of an idle gaude,
Which in my childehood I did doat vpon:
And all the faith, the vertue of my heart,
The obiect and the pleasure of mine eye,
Is onely *Helena*. To her, my Lord,
Was I betroth'd, ere I see *Hermia*,
But like a sickenesse did I loath this food,
But as in health, come to my naturall taste,
Now doe I wish it, loue it, long for it,
And will for euermore be true to it.

Thes. Faire Louers, you are fortunately met;
Of this discourse we shall heare more anon.
Egeus, I will ouer-beare your will;
For in the Temple, by and by with vs,
These couples shall eternally be knit.
And for the morning now is something worne,
Our purpos'd hunting shall be set aside.
Away, with vs to *Athens*; three and three,
Wee'll hold a feast in great solemnitie.
Come *Hippolita*. *Exit Duke and Lords.*

Dem. These things seeme small & vndistinguishable,
Like farre off mountaines turned into Clouds.

Her. Me-thinks I see these things with parted eye,
When euery things seemes double.

Hel. So me-thinkes:
And I haue found *Demetrius*, like a iewell,
Mine owne, and not mine owne.

Dem. It seemes to mee,
That yet we sleepe, we dreame. Do not you thinke,
The Duke was heere, and bid vs follow him?

Her. Yea, and my Father.

Hel. And *Hippolita*.

Lys. And he bid vs follow to the Temple.

Dem. Why then we are awake; lets follow him, and by the way let vs recount our dreames.

Bottome wakes. *Exit Louers.*

Clo. When my cue comes, call me, and I will answer. My next is, most faire *Piramus*. Hey ho *Peter Quince*? *Flute* the bellowes-mender? *Snout* the tinker? *Starueling*? Gods my life! Stolne hence, and left me asleepe: I haue had a most rare vision. I had a dreame, past the wit of man, to say, what dreame it was. Man is but an Asse, if he goe about to expound this dreame. Me-thought I was, there is no man can tell what. Me-thought I was, and me-thought I had. But man is but a patch'd foole, if he will offer to say, what me-thought I had. The eye of man hath not heard, the eare of man hath not seen, mans hand is not able to taste, his tongue to conceiue, nor his heart to report, what my dreame was. I will get *Peter Quince* to write a ballet of this dreame, it shall be called *Bottomes Dream*, because it hath no bottome; and I will sing it in the latter end of a play, before the Duke. Peraduenture, to make it the more gracious, I shall sing it at her death. *Exit.*

Enter Quince, Flute, Thisbie, Snout, and Starueling.

Quin. Haue you sent to *Bottomes* house? Is he come home yet?

Staru. He cannot be heard of. Out of doubt hee is transported.

This. If

Thif. If he come not, then the play is mar'd. It goes not forward, doth it?

Quin. It is not possible: you haue not a man in all *Athens*, able to discharge *Piramus* but he.

Thif. No hee hath simply the best wit of any handy-craft man in *Athens*.

Quin. Yea, and the best person too, and hee is a very Paramour, for a sweet voyce.

Thif. You must say, Paragon. A Paramour is (God blesse vs) a thing of nought.

Enter Snug the Ioyner.

Snug. Masters, the Duke is comming from the Temple, and there is two or three Lords & Ladies more married: If our sport had gone forward, we had all bin made men.

Thif. O sweet bully *Bottome*: thus hath he lost sixepence a day, during his life; he could not haue scaped sixpence a day. And the Duke had not giuen him sixpence a day for playing *Piramus*, Ile be hang'd. He would haue deserued it. Sixpence a day in *Piramus*, or nothing.

Enter Bottome.

Bot. Where are these Lads? Where are these hearts?

Quin. *Bottome*, ô most couragious day! O most happie houre!

Bot. Masters, I am to discourse wonders; but ask me not what. For if I tell you, I am no true *Athenian*. I will tell you euery thing as it fell out.

Qu. Let vs heare, sweet *Bottome*.

Bot. Not a word of me: all that I will tell you, is, that the Duke hath dined. Get your apparell together, good strings to your beards, new ribbands to your pumps, meete presently at the Palace, euery man looke ore his part: for the short and the long is, our play is preferred: In any case let *Thisby* haue cleane linnen: and let not him that playes the Lion, paire his nailes, for they shall hang out for the Lions clawes. And most deare Actors, eate no Onions, nor Garlicke; for wee are to vtter sweete breath, and I doe not doubt but to heare them say, it is a sweet Comedy. No more words: away, go away.

Exeunt.

Actus Quintus.

Enter Theseus, Hippolita, Egeus and his Lords.

Hip. 'Tis strange my *Theseus*, ẏ these louers speake of.

The. More strange then true. I neuer may beleeue
These anticke fables, nor these Fairy toyes,
Louers and mad men haue such seething braines,
Such shaping phantasies, that apprehend more
Then coole reason euer comprehends.
The Lunaticke, the Louer, and the Poet,
Are of imagination all compact.
One sees more diuels then vaste hell can hold;
That is the mad man. The Louer, all as franticke,
Sees *Helens* beauty in a brow of *Egipt*.
The Poets eye in a fine frenzy rolling, doth glance
From heauen to earth, from earth to heauen.
And as imagination bodies forth the forms of things
Vnknowne; the Poets pen turnes them to shapes,
And giues to aire nothing, a locall habitation,
And a name. Such tricks hath strong imagination,
That if it would but apprehend some ioy,
It comprehends some bringer of that ioy.
Or in the night, imagining some feare,
How easie is a bush suppos'd a Beare?

Hip. But all the storie of the night told ouer,
And all their minds transfigur'd so together,
More witnesseth than fancies images,
And growes to something of great constancie;
But howsoeuer, strange, and admirable.

Enter louers, Lysander, Demetrius, Hermia, and Helena.

The. Heere come the louers, full of ioy and mirth:
Ioy, gentle friends, ioy and fresh dayes
Of loue accompany your hearts.

Lys. More then to vs, waite in your royall walkes, your boord, your bed.

The. Come now, what maskes, what dances shall we haue,
To weare away this long age of three houres,
Between our after supper, and bed-time?
Where is our vsuall manager of mirth?
What Reuels are in hand? Is there no play,
To ease the anguish of a torturing houre?
Call *Egeus*.

Ege. Heere mighty *Theseus*.

The. Say, what abridgement haue you for this euening?
What maske? What musicke? How shall we beguile
The lazie time, if not with some delight?

Ege. There is a breefe how many sports are rife:
Make choise of which your Highnesse will see first.

Lis. The battell with the Centaurs to be sung
By an Athenian Eunuch, to the Harpe.

The. Wee'l none of that. That haue I told my Loue
In glory of my kinsman Hercules.

Lis. The riot of the tipsie Bachanals,
Tearing the Thracian singer, in their rage?

The. That is an old deuice, and it was plaid
When I from *Thebes* came last a Conqueror.

Lis. The thrice three Muses, mourning for the death
of learning, late deceast in beggerie.

The. That is some Satire keene and criticall,
Not sorting with a nuptiall ceremonie.

Lis. A tedious breefe Scene of yong *Piramus*,
And his loue *Thisby*; very tragicall mirth.

The. Merry and tragicall? Tedious, and briefe? That is, hot ice, and wondrous strange snow. How shall wee finde the concord of his discord?

Ege. A play there is, my Lord, some ten words long,
Which is as breefe, as I haue knowne a play;
But by ten words, my Lord, it is too long;
Which makes it tedious. For in all the play,
There is not one word apt, one Player fitted.
And tragicall my noble Lord it is: for *Piramus*
Therein doth kill himselfe. Which when I saw
Rehearst, I must confesse, made mine eyes water:
But more merrie teares, the passion of loud laughter
Neuer shed.

Thes. What are they that do play it?

Ege. Hard handed men, that worke in Athens heere,
Which neuer labour'd in their mindes till now;
And now haue toyled their vnbreathed memories
With this same play, against your nuptiall.

The. And we will heare it.

O 2 Phil.

Phi. No,my noble Lord,it is not for you. I haue heard
It ouer,and it is nothing, nothing in the world;
Vnlesse you can finde sport in their intents,
Extreamely stretcht,and cond with cruell paine,
To doe you seruice.
Thes. I will heare that play. For neuer any thing
Can be amisse, when simplenesse and duty tender it.
Goe bring them in,and take your places, Ladies.
Hip. I loue not to see wretchednesse orecharged;
And duty in his seruice perishing.
Thes. Why gentle sweet,you shall see no such thing.
Hip. He saies,they can doe nothing in this kinde.
Thes. The kinder we,to giue them thanks for nothing
Our sport shall be,to take what they mistake;
And what poore duty cannot doe, noble respect
Takes it in might, not merit.
Where I haue come,great Clearkes haue purposed
To greete me with premeditated welcomes;
Where I haue seene them shiuer and looke pale,
Make periods in the midst of sentences,
Throttle their practiz'd accent in their feares,
And in conclusion,dumbly haue broke off,
Not paying me a welcome. Trust me sweete,
Out of this silence yet, I pickt a welcome:
And in the modesty of fearefull duty,
I read as much,as from the ratling tongue
Of saucy and audacious eloquence.
Loue therefore, and tongue-tide simplicity,
In least,speake most, to my capacity.
Egeus. So please your Grace,the Prologue is addrest.
Duke. Let him approach. *Flor. Trum.*

Enter the Prologue. Quince.

Pro. If we offend,it is with our good will.
That you should thinke,we come not to offend,
But with good will. To shew our simple skill
That is the true beginning of our end.
Consider then, we come but in despight.
We do not come, as minding to content you
Our true intent is. All for your delight,
We are not heere. That you should here repent you,
The Actors are at hand; and by their show,
You shall know all, that you are like to know.
Thes. This fellow doth not stand vpon points.
Lys. He hath rid his Prologue, like a rough Colt: he knowes not the stop. A good morall my Lord. It is not enough to speake, but to speake true.
Hip. Indeed hee hath plaid on his Prologue, like a childe on a Recorder,a sound,but not in gouernment.
Thes. His speech was like a tangled chaine: nothing impaired,but all disordered. Who is next?

Tawyer with a Trumpet before them.

Enter Pyramus and Thisby, Wall, Moone-shine, and Lyon.

Prol. Gentles,perchance you wonder at this show,
But wonder on,till truth make all things plaine.
This man is *Piramus,* if you would know;
This beauteous Lady, *Thisby* is certaine.
This man, with lyme and rough-cast,doth present
Wall, that vile wall, which did these louers sunder:
And through walls chink(poor soules) they are content
To whisper. At the which, let no man wonder.
This man,with Lanthorne,dog,and bush of thorne,
Presenteth moone-shine. For if you will know,
By moone-shine did these Louers thinke no scorne
To meet at *Ninus* toombe,there, there to wooe:
This grizy beast (which Lyon hight by name)
The trusty *Thisby,* comming first by night,
Did scarre away, or rather did affright:
And as she fled, her mantle she did fall;
Which Lyon vile with bloody mouth did staine.
Anon comes *Piramus,* sweet youth and tall,
And findes his *Thisbies* Mantle slaine;
Whereat, with blade, with bloody blamefull blade,
He brauely broacht his boiling bloudy breast,
And *Thisby,* tarrying in Mulberry shade,
His dagger drew,and died. For all the rest,
Let *Lyon, Moone-shine, Wall,* and Louers twaine,
At large discourse,while here they doe remaine.

Exit all but Wall.

Thes. I wonder if the Lion be to speake.
Deme. No wonder, my Lord: one Lion may, when many Asses doe.

Exit Lyon, Thisbie, and Mooneshine.

Wall. In this same Interlude, it doth befall,
That I, one *Snowt* (by name) present a wall:
And such a wall, as I vvould haue you thinke,
That had in it a crannied hole or chinke:
Through which the Louers, *Piramus* and *Thisbie*
Did whisper often, very secretly.
This loame, this rough-cast, and this stone doth shew,
That I am that same Wall; the truth is so.
And this the cranny is,right and sinister,
Through which the fearefull Louers are to whisper.
Thes. Would you desire Lime and Haire to speake better?
Deme. It is the vvittiest partition, that euer I heard discourse, my Lord.
Thes. *Pyramus* drawes neere the Wall, silence.

Enter Pyramus.

Pir. O grim lookt night, ô night with hue so blacke,
O night, which euer art, when day is not:
O night, ô night, alacke, alacke, alacke,
I feare my *Thisbies* promise is forgot.
And thou ô vvall, thou sweet and louely vvall,
That stands betweene her fathers ground and mine,
Thou vvall, ô vvall, ô sweet and louely vvall,
Shew me thy chinke, to blinke through vvith mine eine.
Thankes courteous vvall. *Ioue* shield thee vvell for this.
But vvhat see I? No *Thisbie* doe I see.
O vvicked vvall, through vvhom I see no blisse,
Curst be thy stones for thus deceiuing mee.
Thes. The vvall me-thinkes being sensible, should curse againe.
Pir. No in truth sir,he should not. *Deceiuing me,*
Is *Thisbies* cue; she is to enter, and I am to spy
Her through the vvall. You shall see it vvill fall.

Enter Thisbie.

Pat as I told you; yonder she comes.
This. O vvall, full often hast thou heard my mones,
For parting my faire *Piramus,* and me.
My cherry lips haue often kist thy stones;
Thy stones vvith Lime and Haire knit vp in thee.
Pyra. I see a voyce; now vvill I to the chinke,
To spy and I can heare my *Thisbies* face. *Thisbie?*
This. My Loue thou art, my Loue I thinke.
Pir. Thinke vvhat thou vvilt, I am thy Louers grace,
And like *Limander* am I trusty still.
This. And like *Helen* till the Fates me kill.
Pir. Not *Shafalus* to *Procrus,* was so true.
This. As *Shafalus* to *Procrus,* I to you.

Pir. O

Pir. O kiſſe me through the hole of this vile wall.
Thiſ. I kiſſe the wals hole, not your lips at all.
Pir. Wilt thou at *Ninnies* tombe meete me ſtraight way?
Thiſ. Tide life, tide death, I come without delay.
Wall. Thus haue I *Wall*, my part diſcharged ſo;
And being done, thus *Wall* away doth go. *Exit Clow.*

Du. Now is the morall downe betweene the two Neighbors.

Dem. No remedie my Lord, when Wals are ſo wilfull, to heare without vvarning.

Dut. This is the ſillieſt ſtuffe that ere I heard.

Du. The beſt in this kind are but ſhadowes, and the worſt are no worſe, if imagination amend them.

Dut. It muſt be your imagination then, & not theirs.

Duk. If wee imagine no worſe of them then they of themſelues, they may paſſe for excellent men. Here com two noble beaſts, in a man and a Lion.

Enter Lyon and Moone-ſhine.

Lyon. You Ladies, you (whoſe gentle harts do feare
The ſmalleſt monſtrous mouſe that creepes on floore)
May now perchance, both quake and tremble heere,
When Lion rough in wildeſt rage doth roare.
Then know that I, one *Snug* the Ioyner am
A Lion fell, nor elſe no Lions dam:
For if I ſhould as Lion come in ſtriſe
Into this place, 'twere pittie of my liſe.

Du. A verie gentle beaſt, and of a good conſcience.

Dem. The verie beſt at a beaſt, my Lord, ÿ ere I ſaw.

Liſ. This Lion is a verie Fox for his valor.

Du. True, and a Gooſe for his diſcretion.

Dem. Not ſo my Lord: for his valor cannot carrie his diſcretion, and the Fox carries the Gooſe.

Du. His diſcretion I am ſure cannot carrie his valor: for the Gooſe carries not the Fox. It is well; leaue it to his diſcretion, and let vs hearken to the Moone.

Moon. This Lanthorne doth the horned Moone preſent.

De. He ſhould haue worne the hornes on his head.

Du. Hee is no creſcent, and his hornes are inuiſible, within the circumference.

Moon. This lanthorne doth the horned Moone preſent: My ſelfe, the man i'th Moone doth ſeeme to be.

Du. This is the greateſt error of all the reſt; the man ſhould be put into the Lanthorne. How is it els the man i'th Moone?

Dem. He dares not come there for the candle.
For you ſee, it is already in ſnuffe.

Dut. I am vvearie of this Moone; vvould he would change.

Du. It appeares by his ſmal light of diſcretion, that he is in the wane: but yet in courteſie, in all reaſon, vve muſt ſtay the time.

Lyſ. Proceed Moone.

Moon. All that I haue to ſay, is to tell you, that the Lanthorne is the Moone; I, the man in the Moone; this thorne buſh, my thorne buſh; and this dog, my dog.

Dem. Why all theſe ſhould be in the Lanthorne: for they are in the Moone. But ſilence, heere comes *Thisby*.

Enter Thisby.

Thiſ. This is old *Ninnies* tombe: where is my loue?

Lyon. Oh.

The Lion roares, Thisby runs off.

Dem. Well roar'd Lion.

Du. Well run *Thisby*.

Dut. Well ſhone Moone.
Truly the Moone ſhines with a good grace.

Du. Wel mouz'd Lion.

Dem. And then came *Piramus*.

Lyſ. And ſo the Lion vaniſht.

Enter Piramus.

Pyr. Sweet Moone, I thank thee for thy ſunny beames,
I thanke thee Moone, for ſhining now ſo bright:
For by thy gracious, golden, glittering beames,
I truſt to taſte of trueſt *Thisbies* ſight.
But ſtay: O ſpight! but marke, poore Knight,
What dreadful dole is heere?
Eyes do you ſee! How can it be.
O dainty Ducke: O Deere:
Thy mantle good; what ſtaind with blood!
Approch you Furies fell:
O Fates! come, come: Cut thred and thrum,
Quaile, cruſh, conclude, and quell.

Du. This paſſion, and the death of a deare friend,
Would go neere to make a man looke ſad.

Dut. Beſhrew my heart, but I pittie the man.

Pir. O wherefore Nature, did'ſt thou Lions frame?
Since Lion vilde hath heere deflour'd my deere:
Which is: no, no, which was the faireſt Dame
That liu'd, that lou'd, that lik'd, that look'd with cheere.
Come teares, confound: Out ſword, and wound
The pap of *Piramus*:
I, that left pap, where heart doth hop;
Thus dye I, thus, thus, thus.
Now am I dead, now am I fled, my ſoule is in the sky,
Tongue loſe thy light, Moone take thy flight,
Now dye, dye, dye, dye, dye.

Dem. No Die, but an ace for him; for he is but one.

Liſ. Leſſe then an ace man. For he is dead, he is nothing.

Du. With the helpe of a Surgeon, he might yet recouer, and proue an Aſſe.

Dut. How chance Moone-ſhine is gone before?
Thisby comes backe, and findes her Louer.

Enter Thisby.

Duke. She wil finde him by ſtarre-light.
Heere ſhe comes, and her paſſion ends the play.

Dut. Me thinkes ſhee ſhould not vſe a long one for ſuch a *Piramus*: I hope ſhe will be breefe.

Dem. A Moth wil turne the ballance, which *Piramus* which *Thisby* is the better.

Lyſ. She hath ſpyed him already, with thoſe ſweete (eyes.

Dem. And thus ſhe meanes, *videlicit*.

This. Aſleepe my Loue? What, dead my Doue?
O *Piramus* ariſe:
Speake, Speake. Quite dumbe? Dead, dead? A tombe
Muſt couer thy ſweet eyes.
Theſe Lilly Lips, this cherry noſe,
Theſe yellow Cowſlip cheekes
Are gone, are gone: Louers make mone:
His eyes were greene as Leekes.
O ſiſters three, come, come to mee,
With hands as pale as Milke,
Lay them in gore, ſince you haue ſhore
With ſheeres, his thred of ſilke.
Tongue not a word: Come truſty ſword:
Come blade, my breſt imbrue:

O 3 And

And farwell friends, thus *Thubie* ends;
Adieu, adieu, adieu.

Duk. Moon-shine & Lion are left to burie the dead.

Deme. I, and Wall too.

Bot. No, I assure you, the wall is downe, that parted their Fathers. Will it please you to see the Epilogue, or to heare a Bergomask dance, betweene two of our company?

Duk. No Epilogue, I pray you; for your play needs no excuse. Neuer excuse; for when the plaiers are all dead, there need none to be blamed. Marry, if hee that writ it had plaid *Piramus*, and hung himselfe in *Thisbies* garter, it would haue beene a fine Tragedy: and so it is truely, and very notably discharg'd. But come, your Burgomaske; let your Epilogue alone.

The iron tongue of midnight hath old twelue.
Louers to bed, 'tis almost Fairy time.
I feare we shall out-sleepe the comming morne,
As much as we this night haue ouer-watcht.
This palpable grosse play hath well beguil'd
The heauy gate of night. Sweet friends to bed.
A fortnight hold we this solemnity.
In nightly Reuels; and new iollitie. *Exeunt.*

Enter Pucke.

Puck Now the hungry Lyons rores,
And the Wolfe beholds the Moone:
Whilest the heauy ploughman snores,
All with weary taske fore-done.
Now the wasted brands doe glow,
Whil'st the scritch-owle, scritching loud,
Puts the wretch that lies in woe,
In remembrance of a shrowd.
Now it is the time of night,
That the graues, all gaping wide,
Euery one lets forth his spright,
In the Church-way paths to glide.
And we Fairies, that do runne,
By the triple *Hecates* teame,
From the presence of the Sunne,
Following darkenesse like a dreame,
Now are frollicke; not a Mouse
Shall disturbe this hallowed house.
I am sent with broome before,
To sweep the dust behinde the doore.

Enter King and Queene of Fairies, with their traine.

Ob. Through the house giue glimmering light,
By the dead and drowsie fier,
Euerie Elfe and Fairie spright,
Hop as light as bird from brier,
And this Ditty after me, sing and dance it trippinglie.

Tita. First rehearse this song by roate,
To each word a warbling note.
Hand in hand, with Fairie grace,
Will we sing and blesse this place.

The Song.

Now untill the breake of day,
Through this house each Fairy stray.
To the best Bride-bed will we,
Which by vs shall blessed be:
And the issue there create,
Euer shall be fortunate:
So shall all the couples three,
Euer true in louing be:
And the blots of Natures hand,
Shall not in their issue stand.
Neuer mole, harelip, nor scarre,
Nor marke prodigious, such as are
Despised in Natiuitie,
Shall vpon their children be.
With this field dew consecrate,
Euery Fairy take his gate,
And each seuerall chamber blesse,
Through this Pallace with sweet peace,
Euer shall in safety rest,
And the owner of it blest.
Trip away, make no stay;
Meet me all by breake of day.

Robin. If we shadowes haue offended,
Thinke but this (and all is mended)
That you haue but slumbred heere,
While these visions did appeare.
And this weake and idle theame,
No more yeelding but a dreame,
Centles, doe not reprehend.
If you pardon, we will mend.
And as I am an honest *Pucke*,
If we haue vnearned lucke,
Now to scape the Serpents tongue,
We will make amends ere long:
Else the *Pucke* a lyar call.
So good night vnto you all.
Giue me your hands, if we be friends,
And *Robin* shall restore amends.

FINIS.

The Merchant of Venice.

Actus primus.

Enter Anthonio, Salarino, and Salanio.

Anthonio.

IN sooth I know not why I am so sad,
It wearies me: you say it wearies you;
But how I caught it, found it, or came by it,
What stuffe 'tis made of, whereof it is borne,
I am to learne: and such a Want-wit sadnesse makes of mee,
That I haue much ado to know my selfe.

Sal. Your minde is tossing on the Ocean,
There where your Argosies with portly saile
Like Signiors and rich Burgers on the flood,
Or as it were the Pageants of the sea,
Do ouer-peere the pettie Traffiquers
That curtsie to them, do them reuerence
As they flye by them with their wouen wings.

Salar. Beleeue me sir, had I such venture forth,
The better part of my affections, would
Be with my hopes abroad. I should be still
Plucking the grasse to know where sits the winde,
Peering in Maps for ports, and peers, and rodes:
And euery obiect that might make me feare
Misfortune to my ventures, out of doubt
Would make me sad.

Sal. My winde cooling my broth,
Would blow me to an Ague, when I thought
What harme a winde too great might doe at sea.
I should not see the sandie houre-glasse runne,
But I should thinke of shallows, and of flats,
And see my wealthy *Andrew* docks in sand,
Vailing her high top lower then her ribs
To kisse her buriall; should I goe to Church
And see the holy edifice of stone,
And not bethinke me straight of dangerous rocks,
Which touching but my gentle Vessels side
Would scatter all her spices on the streame,
Enrobe the roring waters with my silkes,
And in a word, but euen now worth this,
And now worth nothing. Shall I haue the thought
To thinke on this, and shall I lacke the thought
That such a thing bechaunc'd would make me sad?
But tell not me, I know *Anthonio*
Is sad to thinke vpon his merchandize.

Anth. Beleeue me no, I thanke my fortune for it,
My ventures are not in one bottome trusted,
Nor to one place; nor is my whole estate
Vpon the fortune of this present yeere:
Therefore my merchandize makes me not sad.

Sola. Why then you are in loue.

Anth. Fie, fie.

Sola. Not in loue neither: then let vs say you are sad
Because you are not merry; and 'twere as easie
For you to laugh and leape, and say you are merry
Because you are not sad. Now by two-headed *Ianus*,
Nature hath fram'd strange fellowes in her time:
Some that will euermore peepe through their eyes,
And laugh like Parrats at a bag-piper.
And other of such vineger aspect,
That they'll not shew their teeth in way of smile,
Though *Nestor* sweare the iest be laughable.

Enter Bassanio, Lorenso, and Gratiano.

Sola. Heere comes *Bassanio*,
Your most noble Kinsman,
Gratiano, and *Lorenso*. Faryewell,
We leaue you now with better company.

Sala. I would haue staid till I had made you merry,
If worthier friends had not preuented me.

Ant. Your worth is very deere in my regard.
I take it your owne busines calls on you,
And you embrace th'occasion to depart.

Sal. Good morrow my good Lords. (when?

Bass. Good signiors both, when shall we laugh? say,
You grow exceeding strange: must it be so?

Sal. Wee'll make our leysures to attend on yours.

Exeunt Salarino, and Solanio.

Lor. My Lord *Bassanio*, since you haue found *Anthonio*
We two will leaue you, but at dinner time
I pray you haue in minde where we must meete.

Bass. I will not faile you.

Grat. You looke not well signior *Anthonio*,
You haue too much respect vpon the world:
They loose it that doe buy it with much care,
Beleeue me you are maruellously chang'd.

Ant. I hold the world but as the world *Gratiano*,
A stage, where euery man must play a part,
And mine a sad one.

Grati. Let me play the foole,
With mirth and laughter let old wrinckles come,
And let my Liuer rather heate with wine,
Then my heart coole with mortifying grones.
Why should a man whose bloud is warme within,
Sit like his Grandsire, cut in Alablaster?
Sleepe when he wakes? and creep into the Iaundies

By

By being peeuiſh? I tell thee what *Anthonio*,
I loue thee, and it is my loue that ſpeakes:
There are a ſort of men, whoſe viſages
Do creame and mantle like a ſtanding pond,
And do a wilfull ſtilneſſe entertaine,
With purpoſe to be dreſt in an opinion
Of wiſedome, grauity, profound conceit,
As who ſhould ſay, I am ſir an Oracle,
And when I ope my lips, let no dogge barke.
O my *Anthonio*, I do know of theſe
That therefore onely are reputed wiſe,
For ſaying nothing; when I am verie ſure
If they ſhould ſpeake, would almoſt dam thoſe eares
Which hearing them would call their brothers fooles:
Ile tell thee more of this another time.
But fiſh not with this melancholly baite
For this foole Gudgin, this opinion:
Come good *Lorenzo*, faryewell a while,
Ile end my exhortation after dinner.

Lor. Well, we will leaue you then till dinner time.
I muſt be one of theſe ſame dumbe wiſe men,
For *Gratiano* neuer let's me ſpeake.

Gra. Well, keepe me company but two yeares mo,
Thou ſhalt not know the ſound of thine owne tongue.

Ant. Far you well, Ile grow a talker for this geare.

Gra. Thankes iſaith, for ſilence is onely commendable
In a neats tongue dri'd, and a maid not vendible. *Exit.*

Ant. It is that any thing now.

Baſ. *Gratiano* ſpeakes an infinite deale of nothing, more then any man in all Venice, his reaſons are two graines of wheate hid in two buſhels of chaffe: you ſhall ſeeke all day ere you finde them, & when you haue them they are not worth the ſearch.

An. Well: tel me now, what Lady is the ſame
To whom you ſwore a ſecret Pilgrimage
That you to day promis'd to tel me of?

Baſ. Tis not vnknowne to you *Anthonio*
How much I haue diſabled mine eſtate,
By ſomething ſhewing a more ſwelling port
Then my faint meanes would grant continuance:
Nor do I now make mone to be abridg'd
From ſuch a noble rate, but my cheefe care
Is to come fairely off from the great debts
Wherein my time ſomething too prodigall
Hath left me gag'd: to you *Anthonio*
I owe the moſt in money, and in loue,
And from your loue I haue a warrantie
To vnburthen all my plots and purpoſes,
How to get cleere of all the debts I owe.

An. I pray you good *Baſſanio* let me know it,
And if it ſtand as you your ſelfe ſtill do,
Within the eye of honour, be aſſur'd
My purſe, my perſon, my extreameſt meanes
Lye all vnlock'd to your occaſions.

Baſſ. In my ſchoole dayes, when I had loſt one ſhaft
I ſhot his fellow of the ſelfeſame flight
The ſelfeſame way, with more aduiſed watch
To finde the other forth, and by aduenturing both,
I oft found both. I vrge this child-hoode proofe,
Becauſe what followes is pure innocence.
I owe you much, and like a wilfull youth,
That which I owe is loſt: but if you pleaſe
To ſhoote another arrow that ſelfe way
Which you did ſhoot the firſt, I do not doubt,
As I will watch the ayme: Or to finde both,
Or bring your latter hazard backe againe,
And thankfully reſt debter for the firſt.

An. You know me well, and herein ſpend but time
To winde about my loue with circumſtance,
And out of doubt you doe more wrong
In making queſtion of my vttermoſt
Then if you had made waſte of all I haue:
Then doe but ſay to me what I ſhould doe
That in your knowledge may by me be done,
And I am preſt vnto it: therefore ſpeake.

Baſſ. In *Belmont* is a Lady richly left,
And ſhe is faire, and fairer then that word,
Of wondrous vertues, ſometimes from her eyes
I did receiue faire ſpeechleſſe meſſages:
Her name is *Portia*, nothing vndervallewd
To *Cato's* daughter, *Brutus Portia*,
Nor is the wide world ignorant of her worth,
For the foure windes blow in from euery coaſt
Renowned ſutors, and her ſunny locks
Hang on her temples like a golden fleece,
Which makes her ſeat of *Belmont Cholchos* ſtrond,
And many *Iaſons* come in queſt of her.
O my *Anthonio*, had I but the meanes
To hold a riuall place with one of them,
I haue a minde preſages me ſuch thrift,
That I ſhould queſtionleſſe be fortunate.

Anth. Thou knowſt that all my fortunes are at ſea,
Neither haue I money, nor commodity
To raiſe a preſent ſumme, therefore goe forth
Try what my credit can in *Venice* doe,
That ſhall be rackt euen to the vttermoſt,
To furniſh thee to *Belmont* to faire *Portia*.
Goe preſently enquire, and ſo will I
Where money is, and I no queſtion make
To haue it of my truſt, or for my ſake. *Exeunt.*

Enter Portia with her waiting woman Neriſſa.

Portia. By my troth *Nerriſſa*, my little body is a wearie of this great world.

Ner. You would be ſweet Madam, if your miſeries were in the ſame abundance as your good fortunes are: and yet for ought I ſee, they are as ſicke that ſurfet with too much, as they that ſtarue with nothing; it is no ſmal happineſſe therefore to bee ſeated in the meane, ſuperfluitie comes ſooner by white haires, but competencie liues longer.

Portia. Good ſentences, and well pronounc'd.

Ner. They would be better if well followed.

Portia. If to doe were as eaſie as to know what were good to doe, Chappels had beene Churches, and poore mens cottages Princes Pallaces: it is a good Diuine that followes his owne inſtructions; I can eaſier teach twentie what were good to be done, then be one of the twentie to follow mine owne teaching: the braine may deuiſe lawes for the blood, but a hot temper leapes ore a colde decree, ſuch a hare is madneſſe the youth, to skip ore the meſhes of good counſaile the cripple; but this reaſon is not in faſhion to chooſe me a husband: O mee, the word chooſe, I may neither chooſe whom I would, nor refuſe whom I diſlike, ſo is the wil of a liuing daughter curb'd by the will of a dead father: it is not hard *Nerriſſa*, that I cannot chooſe one, nor refuſe none.

Ner. Your father was euer vertuous, and holy men at their death haue good inſpirations, therefore the lotterie that hee hath deuiſed in theſe three cheſts of gold, ſiluer, and leade, whereof who chooſes his meaning, chooſes

chooſes you, wil no doubt neuer be choſen by any rightly, but one who you ſhall rightly loue: but what warmth is there in your affection towards any of theſe Princely ſuters that are already come?

Por. I pray thee ouer-name them, and as thou nameſt them, I will deſcribe them, and according to my deſcription leuell at my affection.

Ner. Firſt there is the Neopolitane Prince.

Por. I that's a colt indeede, for he doth nothing but talke of his horſe, and hee makes it a great appropriation to his owne good parts that he can ſhoo him himſelfe: I am much afraid my Ladie his mother plaid falſe with a Smyth.

Ner. Than is there the Countie Palentine.

Por. He doth nothing but frowne (as who ſhould ſay, and you will not haue me, choose: he heares merrie tales and ſmiles not, I feare hee will proue the weeping Phyloſopher when he growes old, being ſo full of vnmannerly ſadneſſe in his youth.) I had rather to be married to a deaths head with a bone in his mouth, then to either of theſe: God defend me from theſe two.

Ner. How ſay you by the French Lord, Mounſier *Le Boune*?

Pro. God made him, and therefore let him paſſe for a man, in truth I know it is a ſinne to be a mocker, but he, why he hath a horſe better then the Neopolitans, a better bad habite of frowning then the Count Palentine, he is euery man in no man, if a Traſſell ſing, he fals ſtraight a capring, he will fence with his own ſhadow. If I ſhould marry him, I ſhould marry twentie husbands: if hee would deſpiſe me, I would forgiue him, for if he loue me to madneſſe, I ſhould neuer requite him.

Ner. What ſay you then to *Fauconbridge*, the yong Baron of *England*?

Por. You know I ſay nothing to him, for hee vnderſtands not me, nor I him: he hath neither *Latine*, *French*, nor *Italian*, and you will come into the Court & ſweare that I haue a poore pennie-worth in the *Engliſh*: hee is a proper mans picture, but alas who can conuerſe with a dumbe ſhow? how odly he is ſuited, I thinke he bought his doublet in *Italie*, his round hoſe in *France*, his bonnet in *Germanie*, and his behauiour euery where.

Ner. What thinke you of the other Lord his neighbour?

Por. That he hath a neighbourly charitie in him, for he borrowed a boxe of the eare of the *Engliſhman*, and ſwore he would pay him againe when hee was able: I thinke the *Frenchman* became his ſuretie, and ſeald vnder for another.

Ner. How like you the yong *Germaine*, the Duke of *Saxonies* Nephew?

Por. Very vildely in the morning when hee is ſober, and moſt vildely in the afternoone when hee is drunke: when he is beſt, he is a little worſe then a man, and when he is worſt, he is little better then a beaſt: and the worſt fall that euer fell, I hope I ſhall make ſhift to goe without him.

Ner. If he ſhould offer to choose, and chooſe the right Casket, you ſhould refuſe to performe your Fathers will, if you ſhould refuſe to accept him.

Por. Therefore for feare of the worſt, I pray thee ſet a deepe glaſſe of Reiniſh-wine on the contrary Casket, for if the diuell be within, and that temptation without, I know he will chooſe it. I will doe any thing *Nerriſſa* ere I will be married to a ſpunge.

Ner. You neede not feare Lady the hauing any of theſe Lords, they haue acquainted me with their determinations, which is indeede to returne to their home, and to trouble you with no more ſuite, vnleſſe you may be won by ſome other ſort then your Fathers impoſition, depending on the Caskets.

Por. If I liue to be as olde as *Sibilla*, I will dye as chaſte as *Diana*: vnleſſe I be obtained by the manner of my Fathers will: I am glad this parcell of wooers are ſo reaſonable, for there is not one among them but I doate on his verie abſence: and I wiſh them a faire departure.

Ner. Doe you not remember Ladie in your Fathers time, a *Venecian*, a Scholler and a Souldior that came hither in companie of the Marqueſſe of *Mountferrat*?

Por. Yes, yes, it was *Baſſanio*, as I thinke, ſo was hee call'd.

Ner. True Madam, hee of all the men that euer my fooliſh eyes look'd vpon, was the beſt deſeruing a faire Lady.

Por. I remember him well, and I remember him worthy of thy praiſe.

Enter a Seruingman.

Ser. The foure Strangers ſeeke you Madam to take their leaue: and there is a fore-runner come from a fift, the Prince of *Moroco*, who brings word the Prince his Maiſter will be here to night.

Por. If I could bid the fift welcome with ſo good heart as I can bid the other foure farewell, I ſhould be glad of his approach: if he haue the condition of a Saint, and the complexion of a diuell, I had rather hee ſhould ſhriue me then wiue me. Come *Nerriſſa*, ſirra go before; whiles wee ſhut the gate vpon one wooer, another knocks at the doore. *Exeunt.*

Enter Baſſanio with Shylocke the Iew.

Shy. Three thouſand ducates, well.

Baſſ. I ſir, for three months.

Shy. For three months, well.

Baſſ. For the which, as I told you, *Anthonio* ſhall be bound.

Shy. *Anthonio* ſhall become bound, well.

Baſſ. May you ſted me? Will you pleaſure me? Shall I know your anſwere.

Shy. Three thouſand ducats for three months, and *Anthonio* bound.

Baſſ. Your anſwere to that.

Shy. *Anthonio* is a good man.

Baſſ. Haue you heard any imputation to the contrary.

Shy. Ho no, no, no, no: my meaning in ſaying he is a good man, is to haue you vnderſtand me that he is ſufficient, yet his meanes are in ſuppoſition: he hath an Argoſie bound to Tripolis, another to the Indies, I vnderſtand moreouer vpon the Ryalta, he hath a third at Mexico, a fourth for England, and other ventures hee hath ſquandred abroad, but ſhips are but boords, Saylers but men, there be land rats, and water rats, water theeues, and land theeues, I meane Pyrats, and then there is the perrill of waters, windes, and rocks: the man is notwithſtanding ſufficient, three thouſand ducats, I thinke I may take his bond.

Baſ. Be aſſured you may.

Iew. I

Iew. I will be aſſured I may: and that I may be aſſured, I will bethinke mee, may I ſpeake with *Anthonio*?
Baſſ. If it pleaſe you to dine with vs.
Iew. Yes, to ſmell porke, to eate of the habitation which your Prophet the Nazarite coniured the diuell into: I will buy with you, ſell with you, talke with you, walke with you, and ſo following: but I will not eate with you, drinke with you, nor pray with you. What newes on the Ryalta, who is he comes here?

Enter Anthonio.

Baſſ. This is ſignior *Anthonio*.
Iew. How like a fawning publican he lookes.
I hate him for he is a Chriſtian:
But more, for that in low ſimplicitie
He lends out money gratis, and brings downe
The rate of vſance here with vs in *Venice*.
If I can catch him once vpon the hip,
I will feede fat the ancient grudge I beare him.
He hates our ſacred Nation, and he railes
Euen there where Merchants moſt doe congregate
On me, my bargaines, and my well-worne thrift,
Which he cals intereſt: Curſed be my Trybe
If I forgiue him.
Baſſ. *Shylock*, doe you heare.
Shy. I am debating of my preſent ſtore,
And by the neere geſſe of my memorie
I cannot inſtantly raiſe vp the groſſe
Of full three thouſand ducats: what of that?
Tuball a wealthy Hebrew of my Tribe
Will furniſh me; but ſoft, how many months
Doe you deſire? Reſt you faire good ſignior,
Your worſhip was the laſt man in our mouthes.
Ant. *Shylocke*, albeit I neither lend nor borrow
By taking, nor by giuing of exceſſe,
Yet to ſupply the ripe wants of my friend,
Ile breake a cuſtome: is he yet poſſeſt
How much he would?
Shy. I, I, three thouſand ducats.
Ant. And for three months.
Shy. I had forgot, three months, you told me ſo.
Well then, your bond: and let me ſee, but heare you,
Me thoughts you ſaid, you neither lend nor borrow
Vpon aduantage.
Ant. I doe neuer vſe it.
Shy. When *Iacob* graz'd his Vncle *Labans* ſheepe,
This *Iacob* from our holy *Abram* was
(As his wiſe mother wrought in his behalfe)
The third poſſeſſer; I, he was the third.
Ant. And what of him, did he take interreſt?
Shy. No, not take intereſt, not as you would ſay
Directly intereſt, marke what *Iacob* did,
When *Laban* and himſelfe were compremyz'd
That all the eanelings which were ſtreakt and pied
Should fall as *Iacobs* hier, the Ewes being rancke,
In end of Autumne turned to the Rammes,
And when the worke of generation was
Betweene theſe woolly breeders in the act,
The skilfull ſhepheard pil'd me certaine wands,
And in the dooing of the deede of kinde,
He ſtucke them vp before the fulſome Ewes,
Who then conceauing, did in eaning time
Fall party-colour'd lambs, and thoſe were *Iacobs*.
This was a way to thriue, and he was bleſt:
And thrift is bleſſing if men ſteale it not.
Ant. This was a venture ſir that *Iacob* ſeru'd for,
A thing not in his power to bring to paſſe,
But ſway'd and faſhion'd by the hand of heauen.
Was this inſerted to make interreſt good?
Or is your gold and ſiluer Ewes and Rams?
Shy. I cannot tell, I make it breede as faſt,
But note me ſignior.
Ant. Marke you this *Baſſanio*,
The diuell can cite Scripture for his purpoſe,
An euill ſoule producing holy witneſſe,
Is like a villaine with a ſmiling cheeke,
A goodly apple rotten at the heart.
O what a goodly outſide falſehood hath.
Shy. Three thouſand ducats, 'tis a good round ſum.
Three months from twelue, then let me ſee the rate.
Ant. Well *Shylocke*, ſhall we be beholding to you?
Shy. Signior *Anthonio*, many a time and oft
In the Ryalto you haue rated me
About my monies and my vſances:
Still haue I borne it with a patient ſhrug,
(For ſuffrance is the badge of all our Tribe.)
You call me misbeleeuer, cut-throate dog,
And ſpet vpon my Iewiſh gaberdine,
And all for vſe of that which is mine owne.
Well then, it now appeares you neede my helpe:
Goe to then, you come to me, and you ſay,
Shylocke, we would haue moneyes, you ſay ſo:
You that did voide your rume vpon my beard,
And foote me as you ſpurne a ſtranger curre
Ouer your threſhold, moneyes is your ſuite.
What ſhould I ſay to you? Should I not ſay,
Hath a dog money? Is it poſſible
A curre ſhould lend three thouſand ducats? or
Shall I bend low, and in a bond-mans key
With bated breath, and whiſpring humbleneſſe,
Say this: Faire ſir, you ſpet on me on Wedneſday laſt;
You ſpurn'd me ſuch a day; another time
You cald me dog: and for theſe curteſies
Ile lend you thus much moneyes.
Ant. I am as like to call thee ſo againe,
To ſpet on thee againe, to ſpurne thee too.
If thou wilt lend this money, lend it not
As to thy friends, for when did friendſhip take
A breede of barraine mettall of his friend?
But lend it rather to thine enemie,
Who if he breake, thou maiſt with better face
Exact the penalties.
Shy. Why looke you how you ſtorme,
I would be friends with you, and haue your loue,
Forget the ſhames that you haue ſtaind me with,
Supplie your preſent wants, and take no doite
Of vſance for my moneyes, and youle not heare me,
This is kinde I offer.
Baſſ. This were kindneſſe.
Shy. This kindneſſe will I ſhowe,
Goe with me to a Notarie, ſeale me there
Your ſingle bond, and in a merrie ſport
If you repaie me not on ſuch a day,
In ſuch a place, ſuch ſum or ſums as are
Expreſt in the condition, let the forfeite
Be nominated for an equall pound
Of your faire fleſh, to be cut off and taken
In what part of your bodie it pleaſeth me.
Ant. Content infaith, Ile ſeale to ſuch a bond,
And ſay there is much kindneſſe in the Iew.
Baſſ. You

Baſſ. You ſhall not ſeale to ſuch a bond for me,
Ile rather dwell in my neceſſitie.
Ant. Why feare not man, I will not forfaite it,
Within theſe two months, that's a month before
This bond expires, I doe expect returne
Of thrice three times the valew of this bond.
Shy. O father *Abram*, what theſe Chriſtians are,
Whoſe owne hard dealings teaches them ſuſpect
The thoughts of others: Praie you tell me this,
If he ſhould breake his daie, what ſhould I gaine
By the exaction of the forfeiture?
A pound of mans fleſh taken from a man,
Is not ſo eſtimable, profitable neither
As fleſh of Muttons, Beefes, or Goates, I ſay
To buy his fauour, I extend this friendſhip,
If he will take it, ſo: if not adiew,
And for my loue I praie you wrong me not.
Ant. Yes *Shylocke*, I will ſeale vnto this bond.
Shy. Then meete me forthwith at the Notaries,
Giue him direction for this merrie bond,
And I will goe and purſe the ducats ſtraite.
See to my houſe left in the fearefull gard
Of an vnthriftie knaue: and preſentlie
Ile be with you. *Exit.*
Ant. Hie thee gentle *Iew*. This Hebrew will turne
Chriſtian, he growes kinde.
Baſſ. I like not faire teames, and a villaines minde.
Ant. Come on, in this there can be no diſmaie,
My Shippes come home a month before the daie.
Exeunt.

Actus Secundus.

Enter Morochus a tawnie Moore all in white, and three or foure followers accordingly, with Portia, Nerriſſa, and their traine. Flo. Cornets.

Mor. Miſlike me not for my complexion,
The ſhadowed liuerie of the burniſht ſunne,
To whom I am a neighbour, and neere bred.
Bring me the faireſt creature North-ward borne,
Where *Phœbus* fire ſcarce thawes the yſicles,
And let vs make incision for your loue,
To proue whoſe blood is reddeſt, his or mine.
I tell thee Ladie this aſpect of mine
Hath feard the valiant, (by my loue I ſweare)
The beſt regarded Virgins of our Clyme
Haue lou'd it to: I would not change this hue,
Except to ſteale your thoughts my gentle Queene.
Por. In tearmes of choiſe I am not ſolie led
By nice direction of a maidens eies:
Beſides, the lottrie of my deſtenie
Bars me the right of voluntarie chooſing:
But if my Father had not ſcanted me,
And hedg'd me by his wit to yeelde my ſelfe
His wife, who wins me by that meanes I told you;
Your ſelfe (renowned Prince) than ſtood as faire
As any commer I haue look'd on yet
For my affection.
Mor. Euen for that I thanke you,
Therefore I pray you leade me to the Caskets
To trie my fortune: By this Symitare
That ſlew the Sophie, and a Perſian Prince
That won three fields of Sultan Solyman,
I would ore-ſtare the ſterneſt eies that looke:
Out-braue the heart moſt daring on the earth:
Plucke the yong ſucking Cubs from the ſhe Beare,
Yea, mocke the Lion when he rores for pray
To win the Ladie. But alas, the while
If *Hercules* and *Lychas* plaie at dice
Which is the better man, the greater throw
May turne by fortune from the weaker hand:
So is *Alcides* beaten by his rage,
And ſo may I, blinde fortune leading me
Miſſe that which one vnworthier may attaine,
And die with grieuing.
Port. You muſt take your chance,
And either not attempt to chooſe at all,
Or ſweare before you chooſe, if you chooſe wrong
Neuer to ſpeake to Ladie afterward
In way of marriage, therefore be aduis'd.
Mor. Nor will not, come bring me vnto my chance.
Por. Firſt forward to the temple, after dinner
Your hazard ſhall be made.
Mor. Good fortune then, *Cornets.*
To make me bleſt or curſed'ſt among men. *Exeunt.*

Enter the Clowne alone.

Clo. Certainely, my conſcience will ſerue me to run from this Iew my Maiſter: the fiend is at mine elbow, and tempts me, ſaying to me, *Iobbe, Launcelet Iobbe*, good *Launcelet*, or good *Iobbe*, or good *Launcelet Iobbe*, vſe your legs, take the ſtart, run awaie: my conſcience ſaies no; take heede honeſt *Launcelet*, take heed honeſt *Iobbe*, or as afore-ſaid honeſt *Launcelet Iobbe*, doe not runne, ſcorne running with thy heeles; well, the moſt coragious fiend bids me packe, *fia* ſaies the fiend, away ſaies the fiend, for the heauens rouſe vp a braue minde ſaies the fiend, and run; well, my conſcience hanging about the necke of my heart, ſaies verie wiſely to me: my honeſt friend *Launcelet*, being an honeſt mans ſonne, or rather an honeſt womans ſonne, for indeede my Father did ſomething ſmack, ſomething grow too; he had a kinde of taſte; wel, my conſcience ſaies *Lancelet* bouge not, bouge ſaies the fiend, bouge not ſaies my conſcience, conſcience ſay I you counſaile well, fiend ſay I you counſaile well, to be rul'd by my conſcience I ſhould ſtay with the *Iew* my Maiſter, (who God bleſſe the marke) is a kinde of diuell; and to run away from the *Iew* I ſhould be ruled by the fiend, who ſauing your reuerence is the diuell himſelfe: certainely the *Iew* is the verie diuell incarnation, and in my conſcience, my conſcience is a kinde of hard conſcience, to offer to counſaile me to ſtay with the *Iew*; the fiend giues the more friendly counſaile: I will runne fiend, my heeles are at your commandement, I will runne.

Enter old Gobbo with a Basket.

Gob. Maiſter yong-man, you I praie you, which is the waie to Maiſter *Iewes*?
Lan. O heauens, this is my true begotten Father, who being more then ſand-blinde, high grauel blinde, knows me not, I will trie confuſions with him.
Gob. Maiſter yong Gentleman, I praie you which is the waie to Maiſter *Iewes*.
Laun. Turne vpon your right hand at the next turning

ning, but at the next turning of all on your left; marrie at the verie next turning, turne of no hand, but turn down indirectlie to the *Iewes* houſe.

Gob. Be Gods ſonties 'twill be a hard waie to hit, can you tell me whether one *Launcelet* that dwels with him, dwell with him or no.

Laun. Talke you of yong Maſter *Launcelet*, marke me now, now will I raiſe the waters; talke you of yong Maiſter *Launcelet*?

Gob. No Maiſter ſir, but a poore mans ſonne, his Father though I ſay't is an honeſt exceeding poore man, and God be thanked well to liue.

Lan. Well, let his Father be what a will, wee talke of yong Maiſter *Launcelet*.

Gob. Your worſhips friend and *Launcelet*

Laun. But I praie you *ergo* old man, *ergo* I beſeech you, talke you of yong Maiſter *Launcelet*

Gob. Of *Launcelet*, ant pleaſe your maiſterſhip.

Lan. Ergo Maiſter *Lancelet* talke not of maiſter *Lancelet* Father, for the youg gentleman according to fates and deſtinies, and ſuch odde ſayings, the ſiſters three, & ſuch branches of learning, is indeede deceaſed, or as you would ſay in plaine tearmes, gone to heauen.

Gob. Marrie God forbid, the boy was the verie ſtaffe of my age, my verie prop.

Lan. Do I look like a cudgell or a houell-poſt, a ſtaffe or a prop: doe you know me Father.

Gob Alacke the day, I know you not yong Gentleman, but I praie you tell me, is my boy God reſt his ſoule aliue or dead.

Lan. Doe you not know me Father.

Gob. Alacke ſir I am ſand blinde, I know you not.

Lan. Nay, indeede if you had your eies you might faile of the knowing me: it is a wiſe Father that knowes his owne childe. Well, old man, I will tell you newes of your ſon, giue me your bleſſing, truth will come to light, murder cannot be hid long, a mans ſonne may, but in the end truth will out.

Gob. Praie you ſir ſtand vp, I am ſure you are not *Lancelet* my boy.

Lan. Praie you let's haue no more fooling about it, but giue mee your bleſſing: I am *Lancelet* your boy that was, your ſonne that is, your childe that ſhall be.

Gob. I cannot thinke you are my ſonne.

Lan. I know not what I ſhall thinke of that: but I am *Lancelet* the *Iewes* man, and I am ſure *Margerie* your wife is my mother.

Gob. Her name is *Margerie* indeede, Ile be ſworne if thou be *Lancelet*, thou art mine owne fleſh and blood: Lord worſhipt might he be, what a beard haſt thou got; thou haſt got more haire on thy chin, then Dobbin my philhorſe has on his taile

Lan It ſhould ſeeme then that Dobbins taile growes backeward. I am ſure he had more haire of his taile then I haue of my face when I loſt ſaw him.

Gob. Lord how art thou chang'd: how dooſt thou and thy Maſter agree, I haue brought him a preſent; how gree you now?

Lan. Well, well, but for mine owne part, as I haue ſet vp my reſt to run awaie, ſo I will not reſt till I haue run ſome ground: my Maiſter's a verie *Iew*, giue him a preſent, giue him a halter, I am famiſht in his ſeruice. You may tell euerie finger I haue with my ribs: Father I am glad you are come, giue me your preſent to one Maiſter *Baſſanio*, who indeede giues rare new Liueries, if I ſerue not him, I will run as far as God has anie ground. O rare fortune, here comes the man, to him Father, for I am a *Iew* if I ſerue the *Iew* anie longer.

Enter Baſſanio with a follower or two

Baſſ You may doe ſo, but let it be ſo haſted that ſupper be readie at the fartheſt by fiue of the clocke: ſee theſe Letters deliuered, put the Liueries to making, and deſire *Gratiano* to come anone to my lodging

Lan. To him Father.

Gob. God bleſſe your worſhip

Baſſ. Gramercie, would'ſt thou ought with me.

Gob. Here's my ſonne ſir, a poore boy.

Lan. Not a poore boy ſir, but the rich *Iewes* man that would ſir as my Father ſhall ſpecifie.

Gob. He hath a great infection ſir, as one would ſay to ſerue.

Lan. Indeede the ſhort and the long is, I ſerue the *Iew*, and haue a deſire as my Father ſhall ſpecifie

Gob. His Maiſter and he (ſauing your worſhips reuerence) are ſcarce catercoſins

Lan. To be briefe, the verie truth is, that the *Iew* hauing done me wrong, doth cauſe me as my Father being I hope an old man ſhall frutifie vnto you.

Gob. I haue here a diſh of Doues that I would beſtow vpon your worſhip, and my ſuite is.

Lan. In verie briefe, the ſuite is impertinent to my ſelfe, as your worſhip ſhall know by this honeſt old man, and though I ſay it, though old man, yet poore man my Father

Baſſ. One ſpeake for both, what would you?

Lan Serue you ſir.

Gob That is the verie defect of the matter ſir.

Baſſ. I know thee well, thou haſt obtain'd thy ſuite,
Shylocke thy Maiſter ſpoke with me this daie,
And hath prefer'd thee, if it be preferment
To leaue a rich *Iewes* ſeruice, to become
The follower of ſo poore a Gentleman.

Clo. The old prouerbe is verie well parted betweene my Maiſter *Shylocke* and you ſir, you haue the grace of God ſir, and he hath enough.

Baſſ. Thou ſpeak'ſt it well; go Father with thy Son,
Take leaue of thy old Maiſter, and enquire
My lodging out, giue him a Liuerie
More garded then his fellowes: ſee it done.

Clo. Father in, I cannot get a ſeruice, no, I haue nere a tongue in my head, well: if anie man in *Italie* haue a fairer table which doth offer to ſweare vpon a booke, I ſhall haue good fortune; goe too, here's a ſimple line of life, here's a ſmall trifle of wiues, alas, fifteene wiues is nothing, a leuen widdowes and nine maides is a ſimple comming in for one man, and then to ſcape drowning thrice, and to be in perill of my life with the edge of a featherbed, here are ſimple ſcapes: well, if Fortune be a woman, ſhe's a good wench for this gere: Father come, Ile take my leaue of the *Iew* in the twinkling.

Exit Clowne.

Baſſ. I praie thee good *Leonardo* thinke on this,
These things being bought and orderly beſtowed
Returne in haſte, for I doe feaſt to night
My beſt eſteemd acquaintance, hie thee goe

Leon. My beſt endeuors ſhall be done herein. *Exit.Le.*

Enter Gratiano.

Gra. Where's your Maiſter.

Leon. Yonder

Leon. Yonder ſir he walkes.
Gra. Signior *Baſſanio.*
Baſ. *Gratiano.*
Gra. I haue a ſute to you.
Baſſ. You haue obtain'd it.
Gra. You muſt not denie me, I muſt goe with you to Belmont.
Baſſ. Why then you muſt: but heare thee *Gratiano,*
Thou art to wilde, to rude, and bold of voyce,
Parts that become thee happily enough,
And in ſuch eyes as ours appeare not faults;
But where they are not knowne, why there they ſhow
Something too liberall, pray thee take paine
To allay with ſome cold drops of modeſtie
Thy skipping ſpirit, leaſt through thy wilde behauiour
I be miſconſterd in the place I goe to,
And looſe my hopes.
Gra. Signor *Baſſanio,* heare me,
If I doe not put on a ſober habite,
Talke with reſpect, and ſweare but now and than,
Weare prayer bookes in my pocket, looke demurely,
Nay more, while grace is ſaying hood mine eyes
Thus with my hat, and ſigh and ſay Amen:
Vſe all the obſeruance of ciuillitie
Like one well ſtudied in a ſad oſtent
To pleaſe his Grandam, neuer truſt me more.
Baſ. Well, we ſhall ſee your bearing
Gra. Nay but I barre to night, you ſhall not gage me
By what we doe to night.
Baſ. No that were pittie,
I would intreate you rather to put on
Your boldeſt ſuite of mirth, for we haue friends
That purpoſe merriment: but far you well,
I haue ſome buſineſſe.
Gra. And I muſt to *Lorenſo* and the reſt,
But we will viſite you at ſupper time. *Exeunt.*

Enter Ieſſica and the Clowne.

Ieſ. I am ſorry thou wilt leaue my Father ſo,
Our houſe is hell, and thou a merrie diuell
Did'ſt rob it of ſome taſte of tediouſneſſe;
But far thee well, there is a ducat for thee,
And *Lancelet,* ſoone at ſupper ſhalt thou ſee
Lorenzo, who is thy new Maiſters gueſt,
Giue him this Letter, doe it ſecretly,
And ſo farwell: I would not haue my Father
See me talke with thee.
Clo. Adue, teares exhibit my tongue, moſt beautifull Pagan, moſt ſweete Iew, if a Chriſtian doe not play the knaue and get thee, I am much deceiued; but adue, theſe fooliſh drops doe ſomewhat drowne my manly ſpirit: adue. *Exit*
Ieſ. Farewell good *Lancelet.*
Alacke, what hainous ſinne is it in me
To be aſhamed to be my Fathers childe,
But though I am a daughter to his blood,
I am not to his manners: O *Lorenzo,*
If thou keepe promiſe I ſhall end this ſtrife,
Become a Chriſtian, and thy louing wife. *Exit*

Enter Gratiano, Lorenzo, Slarino, and Salanio.

Lor. Nay, we will ſlinke away in ſupper time,
Diſguiſe vs at my lodging, and returne all in an houre.
Gra. We haue not made good preparation.
Sal. We haue not ſpoke vs yet of Torch-bearers.
Sol. 'Tis vile vnleſſe it may be quaintly ordered,
And better in my minde not vndertooke.
Lor. 'Tis now but foure of clock, we haue two houres
To furniſh vs; friend *Lancelet* what's the newes.

Enter Lancelet with a Letter.

Lan. And it ſhall pleaſe you to breake vp this, ſhall it ſeeme to ſignifie.
Lor. I know the hand, in faith 'tis a faire hand
And whiter then the paper it writ on,
I the faire hand that writ.
Gra. Loue newes in faith.
Lan. By your leaue ſir.
Lor. Whither goeſt thou?
Lan. Marry ſir to bid my old Maſter the *Iew* to ſup to night with my new Maſter the Chriſtian.
Lor. Hold here, take this, tell gentle *Ieſſica*
I will not faile her, ſpeake it priuately;
Go Gentlemen, will you prepare you for this Maske to night,
I am prouided of a Torch-bearer. *Exit. Clowne.*
Sal. I marry, ile be gone about it ſtrait.
Sol. And ſo will I.
Lor. Meete me and *Gratiano* at *Gratianos* lodging
Some houre hence.
Sal. 'Tis good we do ſo. *Exit*
Gra. Was not that Letter from faire *Ieſſica?*
Lor. I muſt needes tell thee all, ſhe hath directed
How I ſhall take her from her Fathers houſe,
What gold and iewels ſhe is furniſht with,
What Pages ſuite ſhe hath in readineſſe
If ere the *Iew* her Father come to heauen,
It will be for his gentle daughters ſake;
And neuer dare misfortune croſſe her foote,
Vnleſſe ſhe doe it vnder this excuſe,
That ſhe is iſſue to a faithleſſe *Iew:*
Come goe with me, peruſe this as thou goeſt,
Faire *Ieſſica* ſhall be my Torch-bearer. *Exit.*

Enter Iew, and his man that was the Clowne.

Iew. Well, thou ſhall ſee, thy eyes ſhall be thy iudge,
The difference of old *Shylocke* and *Baſſanio;*
What *Ieſſica,* thou ſhalt not gurmandize
As thou haſt done with me: what *Ieſſica?*
And ſleepe, and ſnore, and rend apparrell out.
Why *Ieſſica* I ſay.
Clo. Why *Ieſſica.*
Shy. Who bids thee call? I do not bid thee call.
Clo. Your worſhip was wont to tell me
I could doe nothing without bidding.

Enter Ieſſica.

Ieſ. Call you? what is your will?
Shy. I am bid forth to ſupper *Ieſſica,*
There are my Keyes: but wherefore ſhould I go?
I am not bid for loue, they flatter me,
But yet Ile goe in hate, to feede vpon
The prodigall Chriſtian. *Ieſſica* my girle,
Looke to my houſe, I am right loath to goe,
There is ſome ill a bruing towards my reſt,
For I did dreame of money bags to night.
Clo. I beſeech you ſir goe, my yong Maſter
Doth expect your reproach.
Shy. So doe I his.
Clo. And they haue conſpired together, I will not ſay you ſhall ſee a Maske, but if you doe, then it was not for nothing that my noſe fell a bleeding on blacke monday laſt,

P

last,at six a clocke ith morning, falling out that yeere on ashwensday was foure yeere in th'afternoone

Shy. What are their maskes? heare you me *Iessica*,
Lock vp my doores,and when you heare the drum
And the vile squealing of the wry-neckt Fife,
Clamber not you vp to the casements then,
Nor thrust your head into the publique streete
To gaze on Christian fooles with varnisht faces:
But stop my houses eares, I meane my casements,
Let not the sound of shallow fopperie enter
My sober house. By *Iacobs* staffe I sweare,
I haue no minde of feasting forth to night:
But I will goe: goe you before me sirra,
Say I will come.

Clo. I will goe before sir.
Mistris looke out at window for all this;
There will come a Christian by,
Will be worth a Iewes eye.

Shy. What saies that foole of *Hagars* off-spring? ha.

Ies. His words were farewell mistris,nothing else.

Shy. The patch is kinde enough,but a huge feeder:
Snaile-slow in profit,but he sleepes by day
More then the wilde-cat: drones hiue not with me,
Therefore I part with him,and part with him
To one that I would haue him helpe to waste
His borrowed purse. Well *Iessica* goe in,
Perhaps I will returne immediately;
Doe as I bid you, shut dores after you, fast binde, fast finde,
A prouerbe neuer stale in thriftie minde. *Exit.*

Ies. Farewell,and if my fortune be not crost,
I haue a Father,you a daughter lost. *Exit.*

Enter the Maskers, Gratiano and Salino.

Gra. This is the penthouse vnder which *Lorenzo*
Desired vs to make a stand.

Sal. His houre is almost past.

Gra. And it is meruaile he out-dwels his houre,
For louers euer run before the clocke.

Sal. O ten times faster *Venus* Pidgions flye
To steale loues bonds new made,then they are wont
To keepe obliged faith vnforfaited.

Gra. That euer holds,who riseth from a feast
With that keene appetite that he sits downe?
Where is the horse that doth vntread againe
His tedious measures with the vnbated fire,
That he did pace them first: all things that are,
Are with more spirit chased then enioy'd.
How like a yonger or a prodigall
The skarfed barke puts from her natiue bay,
Hudg'd and embraced by the strumpet winde:
How like a prodigall doth she returne
With ouer-wither'd ribs and ragged sailes,
Leane,rent,and begger'd by the strumpet winde?

Enter Lorenzo.

Salino. Heere comes *Lorenzo*, more of this hereafter.

Lor. Sweete friends, your patience for my long abode,
Not I,but my affaires haue made you wait:
When you shall please to play the theeues for wiues
Ile watch as long for you then: approach
Here dwels my father Iew. Hoa,who's within?

Iessica aboue.

Ies. Who are you?tell me for more certainty,
Albeit Ile sweare that I do know your tongue.

Lor. *Lorenzo*,and thy Loue.

Ies. *Lorenzo* certaine,and my loue indeed,
For who loue I so much? and now who knowes
But you *Lorenzo*,whether I am yours?

Lor. Heauen and thy thoughts are witness that thou art.

Ies. Heere,catch this casket,it is worth the paines,
I am glad 'tis night,you do not looke on me,
For I am much asham'd of my exchange:
But loue is blinde, and louers cannot see
The pretty follies that themselues commit,
For if they could, *Cupid* himselfe would blush
To see me thus transformed to a boy.

Lor. Descend,for you must be my torch-bearer.

Ies. What, must I hold a Candle to my shames?
They in themselues goodsooth are too too light.
Why, 'tis an office of discouery Loue,
And I should be obscur'd.

Lor. So you are sweet,
Euen in the louely garnish of a boy:but come at once,
For the close night doth play the run-away,
And we are staid for at *Bassanio's* feast.

Ies. I will make fast the doores and guild my selfe
With some more ducats,and be with you straight.

Gra. Now by my hood, a gentle,and no Iew.

Lor. Beshrew me but I loue her heartily.
For she is wise, if I can iudge of her,
And faire she is, if that mine eyes be true,
And true she is,as she hath prou'd her selfe:
And therefore like her selfe,wise,faire,and true,
Shall she be placed in my constant soule.

Enter Iessica.

What, art thou come? on gentlemen, away,
Our masking mates by this time for vs stay. *Exit.*

Enter Anthonio.

Ant. Who's there?

Gra. Signior *Anthonio*?

Ant. Fie,fie,*Gratiano*,where are all the rest?
'Tis nine a clocke, our friends all stay for you,
No maske to night,the winde is come about,
Bassanio presently will goe aboord,
I haue sent twenty out to seeke for you.

Gra. I am glad on't, I desire no more delight
Then to be vnder saile,and gone to night. *Exeunt.*

Enter Portia with Morrocho, and both their traines.

Por. Goe,draw aside the curtaines, and discouer
The seuerall Caskets to this noble Prince:
Now make your choyse.

Mor. The first of gold,who this inscription beares,
Who chooseth me, shall gaine what men desire.
The second siluer,which this promise carries
Who chooseth me, shall get as much as he deserues.
This third,dull lead,with warning all as blunt,
Who chooseth me,must giue and hazard all he hath.
How shall I know if I doe choose the right?

Por. The

How shall I know if I doe choose the right.
Por. The one of them containes my picture Prince,
If you choose that, then I am yours withall.
Mor. Some God direct my iudgement, let me see,
I will suruay the inscriptions, backe againe:
What saies this leaden casket?
Who chooseth me, must giue and hazard all he hath.
Must giue, for what? for lead, hazard for lead?
This casket threatens men that hazard all
Doe it in hope of faire aduantages:
A golden minde stoopes not to showes of drosse,
Ile then nor giue nor hazard ought for lead.
What saies the Siluer with her virgin hue?
Who chooseth me, shall get as much as he deserues.
As much as he deserues; pause there *Morocho*,
And weigh thy value with an euen hand,
If thou beest rated by thy estimation
Thou doost deserue enough, and yet enough
May not extend so farre as to the Ladie:
And yet to be afeard of my deseruing,
Were but a weake disabling of my selfe.
As much as I deserue, why that's the Lady.
I doe in birth deserue her, and in fortunes,
In graces, and in qualities of breeding:
But more then these, in loue I doe deserue.
What if I strai'd no farther, but chose here?
Let's see once more this saying grau'd in gold.
Who chooseth me shall gaine what many men desire:
Why that's the Lady, all the world desires her:
From the foure corners of the earth they come
To kisse this shrine, this mortall breathing Saint.
The Hircanion deserts, and the vaste wildes
Of wide Arabia are as throughfares now
For Princes to come view faire *Portia*.
The waterie Kingdome, whose ambitious head
Spets in the face of heauen, is no barre
To stop the forraine spirits, but they come
As ore a brooke to see faire *Portia*.
One of these three containes her heauenly picture.
Is't like that Lead containes her? 'twere damnation
To thinke so base a thought, it were too grose
To rib her searecloath in the obscure graue:
Or shall I thinke in Siluer she's immur'd
Being ten times vndervalued to tride gold;
O sinfull thought, neuer so rich a Iem
Was set in worse then gold! They haue in England
A coyne that beares the figure of an Angell
Stampt in gold, but that's insculpt vpon:
But here an Angell in a golden bed
Lies all within. Deliuer me the key:
Here doe I choose, and thriue I as I may.
Por. There take it Prince, and if my forme lye there
Then I am yours.
Mor. O hell! what haue we here, a carrion death,
Within whose emptie eye there is a written scroule;
Ile reade the writing.

All that glisters is not gold,
Often haue you heard that told;
Many a man his life hath sold
But my out side to behold;
Guilded timber doe wormes infold:
Had you beene as wise as bold,
Yong in limbs, in iudgement old,
Your answere had not beene inscrold,
Fareyouwell, your suite is cold,

Mor. Cold indeede, and labour lost,
Then farewell heate, and welcome frost:
Portia adew, I haue too grieu'd a heart
To take a tedious leaue: thus loosers part. *Exit.*
Por. A gentle riddance: draw the curtaines, go:
Let all of his complexion choose me so. *Exeunt.*

Enter Salarino and Solanio.

Flo. Cornets.

Sal. Why man I saw *Bassanio* vnder sayle,
With him is *Gratiano* gone along;
And in their ship I am sure *Lorenzo* is not.
Sol. The villaine *Iew* with outcries raisd the Duke.
Who went with him to search *Bassanios* ship.
Sal. He comes too late, the ship was vndersaile;
But there the Duke was giuen to vnderstand
That in a Gondilo were seene together
Lorenzo and his amorous *Iessica*.
Besides, *Anthonio* certified the Duke
They were not with *Bassanio* in his ship.
Sol. I neuer heard a passion so confusd,
So strange, outragious, and so variable,
As the dogge *Iew* did vtter in the streets;
My daughter, O my ducats, O my daughter,
Fled with a Christian, O my Christian ducats
Iustice, the law, my ducats, and my daughter;
A sealed bag, two sealed bags of ducats,
Of double ducats, stolne from me by my daughter,
And iewels, two stones, two rich and precious stones,
Stolne by my daughter: iustice, finde the girle,
She hath the stones vpon her, and the ducats.
Sal. Why all the boyes in Venice follow him,
Crying his stones, his daughter, and his ducats.
Sol. Let good *Anthonio* looke he keepe his day
Or he shall pay for this.
Sal. Marry well remembred,
I reason'd with a Frenchman yesterday,
Who told me, in the narrow seas that part
The French and English, there miscaried
A vessell of our countrey richly fraught:
I thought vpon *Anthonio* when he told me,
And wisht in silence that it were not his.
Sol. Yo were best to tell *Anthonio* what you heare.
Yet doe not suddainely, for it may grieue him.
Sal. A kinder Gentleman treads not the earth,
I saw *Bassanio* and *Anthonio* part,
Bassanio told him he would make some speede
Of his returne: he answered, doe not so,
Slubber not businesse for my sake *Bassanio*,
But stay the very riping of the time,
And for the *Iewes* bond which he hath of me,
Let it not enter in your minde of loue:
Be merry, and imploy your chiefest thoughts
To courtship, and such faire ostents of loue
As shall conueniently become you there;
And euen there his eye being big with teares,
Turning his face, he put his hand behinde him,
And with affection wondrous sencible
He wrung *Bassanios* hand, and so they parted.
Sol. I thinke he onely loues the world for him,
I pray thee let vs goe and finde him out
And quicken his embraced heauinesse
With some delight or other.
Sal. Doe we so. *Exeunt.*

Enter Nerrissa and a Seruiture.

Ner. Quick, quick I pray thee, draw the curtain strait,

P 2 The

The Prince of Arragon hath tane his oath,
And comes to his election presently.

Enter Arragon, his traine, and Portia.
Flor. Cornets.

Por. Behold, there stand the caskets noble Prince,
If you choose that wherein I am contain'd,
Straight shall our nuptiall rights be solemniz'd:
But if thou faile, without more speech my Lord,
You must be gone from hence immediately.
Ar. I am enioynd by oath to obserue three things;
First, neuer to vnfold to any one
Which casket 'twas I chose; next, if I faile
Of the right casket, neuer in my life
To wooe a maide in way of marriage:
Lastly, if I doe faile in fortune of my choyse,
Immediately to leaue you, and be gone.
Por. To these iniunctions euery one doth sweare
That comes to hazard for my worthlesse selfe.
Ar. And so haue I addrest me, fortune now
To my hearts hope: gold, siluer, and base lead.
Who chooseth me must giue and hazard all he hath.
You shall looke fairer ere I giue or hazard.
What saies the golden chest, ha, let me see:
Who chooseth me, shall gaine what many men desire:
What many men desire, that many may be meant
By the foole multitude that choose by show,
Not learning more then the fond eye doth teach,
Which pries not to th'interior, but like the Martlet
Builds in the weather on the outward wall,
Euen in the force and rode of casualtie.
I will not choose what many men desire,
Because I will not iumpe with common spirits,
And ranke me with the barbarous multitudes.
Why then to thee thou Siluer treasure house,
Tell me once more, what title thou doost beare;
Who chooseth me shall get as much as he deserues:
And well said too; for who shall goe about
To cosen Fortune, and be honourable
Without the stampe of merrit, let none presume
To weare an vndeserued dignitie:
O that estates, degrees, and offices,
Were not deriu'd corruptly, and that cleare honour
Were purchast by the merrit of the wearer;
How many then should couer that stand bare?
How many be commanded that command?
How much low pleasantry would then be gleaned
From the true seede of honor? And how much honor
Pickt from the chaffe and ruine of the times,
To be new varnisht: Well, but to my choise.
Who chooseth me shall get as much as he deserues.
I will assume desert; giue me a key for this,
And instantly vnlocke my fortunes here.
Por. Too long a pause for that which you finde there.
Ar. What's here, the portrait of a blinking idiot
Presenting me a scedule, I will reade it:
How much vnlike art thou to *Portia*?
How much vnlike my hopes and my deseruings?
Who chooseth me, shall haue as much as he deserues.
Did I deserue no more then a fooles head,
Is that my prize, are my deserts no better?
Por. To offend and iudge are distinct offices,
And of opposed natures.
Ar. What is here?

The fier seauen times tried this,
Seauen times tried that iudement is,
That did neuer choose amis,
Some there be that shadowes kisse,
Such haue but a shadowes blisse:
There be fooles aliue Iwis
Siluer'd o're, and so was this:
Take what wife you will to bed,
I will euer be your head:
So be gone, you are sped.

Ar. Still more foole I shall appeare
By the time I linger here,
With one fooles head I came to woo,
But I goe away with two.
Sweet adue, Ile keepe my oath,
Patiently to beard my wroath.
Por. Thus hath the candle sing'd the moath:
O these deliberate fooles when they doe choose,
They haue the wisdome by their wit to loose.
Ner. The ancient saying is no heresie,
Hanging and wiuing goes by destinie.
Por. Come draw the curtaine *Nerrissa.*

Enter Messenger.

Mes. Where is thy Lady?
Por. Here, what would my Lord?
Mes. Madam, there is a-lighted at your gate
A yong Venetian, one that comes before
To signifie th'approaching of his Lord,
From whom he bringeth sensible regreets;
To wit (besides commends and curteous breath)
Gifts of rich value; yet I haue not seene
So likely an Embassador of loue.
A day in Aprill neuer came so sweete
To show how costly Sommer was at hand,
As this fore-spurrer comes before his Lord.
Por. No more I pray thee, I am halfe a-feard
Thou wilt say anone he is some kin to thee,
Thou spend'st such high-day wit in praising him:
Come, come *Nerryssa*, for I long to see
Quicke *Cupids* Post, that comes so mannerly.
Ner. Bassanio Lord, loue if thy will it be. *Exeunt.*

Actus Tertius

Enter Solanio and Salarino.

Sol. Now, what newes on the Ryalto?

Sal. Why yet it liues there vncheckt, that *Anthonio* hath a ship of rich lading wrackt on the narrow Seas; the Goodwins I thinke they call the place, a very dangerous flat, and fatall, where the carcasses of many a tall ship, lye buried, as they say, if my gossips report be an honest woman of her word.

Sol. I would she were as lying a gossip in that, as euer knapt Ginger, or made her neighbours beleeue she wept for the death of a third husband: but it is true, without any slips of prolixity, or crossing the plaine high-way of talke, that the good *Anthonio*, the honest *Anthonio*; o that I had a title good enough to keepe his name company!

Sal. Come, the full stop.

Sol. Ha, what sayest thou, why the end is, he hath lost a ship.

Sal. I

Sal. I would it might proue the end of his loſſes.

Sol. Let me ſay Amen betimes, leaſt the diuell croſſe my praier, for here he comes in the likenes of a *Iew*. How now *Shylocke*, what newes among the Merchants?

Enter Shylocke.

Shy. You knew none ſo well, none ſo well as you, of my daughters flight.

Sal. That's certaine, I for my part knew the Tailor that made the wings ſhe flew withall.

Sol. And *Shylocke* for his own part knew the bird was fledg'd, and then it is the complexion of them al to leaue the dam.

Shy. She is damn'd for it.

Sal. That's certaine, if the diuell may be her Iudge.

Shy. My owne fleſh and blood to rebell.

Sol. Out vpon it old carrion, rebels it at theſe yeeres.

Shy. I ſay my daughter is my fleſh and bloud.

Sal. There is more difference betweene thy fleſh and hers, then betweene Iet and Iuorie, more betweene your bloods, then there is betweene red wine and reniſh: but tell vs, doe you heare whether *Anthonio* haue had anie loſſe at ſea or no?

Shy. There I haue another bad match, a bankrout, a prodigall, who dare ſcarce ſhew his head on the Ryalto, a begger that was vſd to come ſo ſmug vpon the Mart: let him look to his bond, he was wont to call me Vſurer, let him looke to his bond, he was wont to lend money for a Chriſtian curtſie, let him looke to his bond.

Sal. Why I am ſure if he forfaite, thou wilt not take his fleſh, what's that good for?

Shy. To baite fiſh withall, if it will feede nothing elſe, it will feede my reuenge; he hath diſgrac'd me, and hindred me halfe a million, laught at my loſſes, mockt at my gaines, ſcorned my Nation, thwarted my bargaines, cooled my friends, heated mine enemies, and what's the reaſon? I am a *Iewe*: Hath not a *Iew* eyes? hath not a *Iew* hands, organs, dementions, ſences, affections, paſſions, fed with the ſame foode, hurt with the ſame weapons, ſubiect to the ſame diſeaſes, healed by the ſame meanes, warmed and cooled by the ſame Winter and Sommmer as a Chriſtian is: if you pricke vs doe we not bleede? if you tickle vs, doe we not laugh? if you poiſon vs doe we not die? and if you wrong vs ſhall we not reuenge? if we are like you in the reſt, we will reſemble you in that. If a *Iew* wrong a *Chriſtian*, what is his humility, reuenge? If a *Chriſtian* wrong a *Iew*, what ſhould his ſufferance be by Christian example, why reuenge? The villanie you teach me I will execute, and it ſhall goe hard but I will better the inſtruction.

Enter a man from Anthonio.

Gentlemen, my maiſter *Anthonio* is at his houſe, and deſires to ſpeake with you both.

Sal. We haue beene vp and downe to ſeeke him.

Enter Tuball.

Sol. Here comes another of the Tribe, a third cannot be matcht, vnleſſe the diuell himſelfe turne *Iew*.

Exeunt Gentlemen.

Shy. How now *Tuball*, what newes from *Genowa*? haſt thou found my daughter?

Tub. I often came where I did heare of her, but cannot finde her.

Shy. Why there, there, there, there, a diamond gone coſt me two thouſand ducats in Franckford, the curſe neuer fell vpon our Nation till now, I neuer felt it till now, two thouſand ducats in that, and other precious, precious iewels: I would my daughter were dead at my foot, and the iewels in her eare: would ſhe were hearſt at my foote, and the duckets in her coffin: no newes of them, why ſo? and I know not how much is ſpent in the ſearch: why thou loſſe vpon loſſe; the theefe gone with ſo much, and ſo much to finde the theefe, and no ſatisfaction, no reuenge, nor no ill luck ſtirring but what lights a my ſhoulders, no ſighes but a my breathing, no teares but a my ſhedding.

Tub. Yes, other men haue ill lucke too, *Anthonio* as I heard in Genowa?

Shy. What, what, what, ill lucke, ill lucke.

Tub. Hath an Argoſie caſt away comming from Tripolis.

Shy. I thanke God, I thanke God, is it true, is it true?

Tub. I ſpoke with ſome of the Saylers that eſcaped the wracke.

Shy. I thanke thee good *Tuball*, good newes, good newes: ha, ha, here in Genowa.

Tub. Your daughter ſpent in Genowa, as I heard, one night foureſcore ducats.

Shy. Thou ſtick'ſt a dagger in me, I ſhall neuer ſee my gold againe, foureſcore ducats at a ſitting, foureſcore ducats.

Tub. There came diuers of *Anthonios* creditors in my company to Venice, that ſweare hee cannot choose but breake.

Shy. I am very glad of it, ile plague him, ile torture him, I am glad of it.

Tub. One of them ſhewed me a ring that hee had of your daughter for a Monkie.

Shy. Out vpon her, thou tortureſt me *Tuball*, it was my Turkies, I had it of *Leah* when I was a Batcheler: I would not haue giuen it for a wilderneſſe of Monkies.

Tub. But *Anthonio* is certainely vndone.

Shy. Nay, that's true, that's very true, goe *Tuball*, fee me an Officer, beſpeake him a fortnight before, I will haue the heart of him if he forfeit, for were he out of Venice, I can make what merchandize I will: goe *Tuball*, and meete me at our Sinagogue, goe good *Tuball*, at our Sinagogue *Tuball*. *Exeunt.*

Enter Baſſanio, Portia, Gratiano, and all their traine.

Por. I pray you tarrie, pauſe a day or two
Before you hazard, for in chooſing wrong
I looſe your companie; therefore forbeare a while,
There's ſomething tels me (but it is not loue)
I would not looſe you, and you know your ſelfe,
Hate counſailes not in ſuch a quallitie;
But leaſt you ſhould not vnderſtand me well,
And yet a maiden hath no tongue, but thought,
I would detaine you here ſome month or two
Before you venture for me. I could teach you
How to chooſe right, but then I am forſworne,
So will I neuer be, ſo may you miſſe me,
But if you doe, youle make me wiſh a ſinne,
That I had beene forſworne: Beſhrow your eyes,
They haue ore-lookt me and deuided me,
One halfe of me is yours, the other halfe yours,
Mine owne I would ſay: but of mine then yours,
And ſo all yours; O theſe naughtie times
Puts bars betweene the owners and their rights.
And ſo though yours, not yours (proue it ſo)
Let Fortune goe to hell for it, not I.
I ſpeake too long, but 'tis to peize the time,
To ich it, and to draw it out in length,
To ſtay you from election.

Baſſ. Let me chooſe,
For as I am, I liue vpon the racke.
Por. Vpon the racke *Baſſanio*, then confeſſe
What treaſon there is mingled with your loue.
Baſſ. None but that vglie treaſon of miſtruſt,
Which makes me feare the enioying of my loue:
There may as well be amitie and life,
'Tweene ſnow and fire, as treaſon and my loue.
Por. I, but I feare you ſpeake vpon the racke,
Where men enforced doth ſpeake any thing.
Baſſ. Promiſe me life, and ile confeſſe the truth.
Por. Well then, confeſſe and liue.
Baſſ. Confeſſe and loue
Had beene the verie ſum of my confeſſion:
O happie torment, when my torturer
Doth teach me anſwers for deliuerance:
But let me to my fortune and the caskets.
Por. Away then, I am lockt in one of them,
If you doe loue me, you will finde me out.
Nerryſſa and the reſt, ſtand all aloofe,
Let muſicke ſound while he doth make his choiſe,
Then if he looſe he makes a Swan-like end,
Fading in muſique. That the compariſon
May ſtand more proper, my eye ſhall be the ſtreame
And watrie death-bed for him: he may win,
And what is muſique than? Than muſique is
Euen as the flouriſh, when true ſubiects bowe
To a new crowned Monarch: Such it is,
As are thoſe dulcet ſounds in breake of day,
That creepe into the dreaming bride-groomes eare,
And ſummon him to marriage. Now he goes
With no leſſe preſence, but with much more loue
Then yong *Alcides*, when he did redeeme
The virgine tribute, paied by howling *Troy*
To the Sea-monſter: I ſtand for ſacrifice,
The reſt aloofe are the Dardanian wiues:
With bleared viſages come forth to view
The iſſue of th'exploit: Goe Hercules,
Liue thou, I liue with much more diſmay
I view the fight, then thou that mak'ſt the fray.

Here Muſicke.

A Song the whilſt Baſſanio *comments on the Caskets to himſelfe.*

Tell me where is fancie bred,
Or in the heart, or in the head:
How begot, how nouriſhed. *Replie, replie.*
It is engendred in the eyes,
With gazing fed, and Fancie dies,
In the cradle where it lies:
Let vs all ring Fancies knell.
Ile begin it.
Ding, dong, bell.
All. *Ding, dong, bell.*

Baſſ. So may the outward ſhowes be leaſt themſelues
The world is ſtill deceiu'd with ornament.
In Law, what Plea ſo tanted and corrupt,
But being ſeaſon'd with a gracious voice,
Obſcures the ſhow of euill? In Religion,
What damned error, but ſome ſober brow
Will bleſſe it, and approue it with a text,
Hiding the groſeneſſe with faire ornament:
There is no voice ſo ſimple, but aſſumes
Some marke of vertue on his outward parts;
How manie cowards, whoſe hearts are all as falſe
As ſtayers of ſand, weare yet vpon their chins
The beards of *Hercules* and frowning *Mars*,
Who inward ſearcht, haue lyuers white as milke,
And theſe aſſume but valors excrement,
To render them redoubted. Looke on beautie,
And you ſhall ſee 'tis purchaſt by the weight,
Which therein workes a miracle in nature,
Making them lighteſt that weare moſt of it:
So are thoſe criſped ſnakie golden locks
Which makes ſuch wanton gambols with the winde
Vpon ſuppoſed faireneſſe, often knowne
To be the dowrie of a ſecond head,
The ſcull that bred them in the Sepulcher.
Thus ornament is but the guiled ſhore
To a moſt dangerous ſea: the beautious ſcarfe
Vailing an Indian beautie; In a word,
The ſeeming truth which cunning times put on
To intrap the wiſeſt. Therefore then thou gaudie gold,
Hard food for *Midas*, I will none of thee,
Nor none of thee thou pale and common drudge
'Tweene man and man: but thou, thou meager lead
Which rather threatneſt then doſt promiſe ought,
Thy paleneſſe moues me more then eloquence,
And here chooſe I, ioy be the conſequence.
Por. How all the other paſſions fleet to ayre,
As doubtfull thoughts, and raſh imbrac'd deſpaire:
And ſhudding feare, and greene-eyed iealouſie.
O loue be moderate, allay thy extaſie,
In meaſure raine thy ioy, ſcant this exceſſe,
I feele too much thy bleſſing, make it leſſe,
For feare I ſurfeit.
Baſ. What finde I here?
Faire *Portias* counterfeit. What demie God
Hath come ſo neere creation? moue theſe eies?
Or whether riding on the bals of mine
Seeme they in motion? Here are ſeuer'd lips
Parted with ſuger breath, ſo ſweet a barre
Should ſunder ſuch ſweet friends: here in her haires
The Painter plaies the Spider, and hath wouen
A golden meſh t'intrap the hearts of men
Faſter then gnats in cobwebs: but her eies,
How could he ſee to doe them? hauing made one,
Me thinkes it ſhould haue power to ſteale both his
And leaue it ſelfe vnfurniſht: Yet looke how farre
The ſubſtance of my praiſe doth wrong this ſhadow
In vnderpriſing it, ſo farre this ſhadow
Doth limpe behinde the ſubſtance. Here's the ſcroule,
The continent, and ſummarie of my fortune.

You that chooſe not by the view
Chance as faire, and chooſe as true:
Since this fortune fals to you,
Be content, and ſeeke no new.
If you be well pleaſd with this,
And hold your fortune for your bliſſe,
Turne you where your Lady is,
And claime her with a louing kiſſe.

Baſſ. A gentle ſcroule: Faire Lady, by your leaue,
I come by note to giue, and to receiue,
Like one of two contending in a prize
That thinks he hath done well in peoples eies:
Hearing applauſe and vniuerſall ſhout,
Giddie in ſpirit, ſtill gazing in a doubt
Whether thoſe peales of praiſe be his or no.

So

So thrice faire Lady stand I euen so,
As doubtfull whether what I see be true,
Vntill confirm'd, sign'd, ratified by you.
Por. You see my Lord *Bassiano* where I stand,
Such as I am; though for my selfe alone
I would not be ambitious in my wish,
To wish my selfe much better, yet for you,
I would be trebled twenty times my selfe,
A thousand times more faire, ten thousand times
More rich, that onely to stand high in your account,
I might in vertues, beauties, liuings, friends,
Exceed account: but the full summe of me
Is sum of nothing: which to terme in grosse,
Is an vnlessoned girle, vnschool'd, vnpractiz'd,
Happy in this, she is not yet so old
But she may learne: happier then this,
Shee is not bred so dull but she can learne;
Happiest of all, is that her gentle spirit
Commits it selfe to yours to be directed,
As from her Lord, her Gouernour, her King.
My selfe, and what is mine, to you and yours
Is now conuerted. But now I was the Lord
Of this faire mansion, master of my seruants,
Queene ore my selfe: and euen now, but now,
This house, these seruants, and this same my selfe
Are yours, my Lord, I giue them with this ring,
Which when you part from, loose, or giue away,
Let it presage the ruine of your loue,
And be my vantage to exclaime on you
Bass. Maddam, you haue bereft me of all words,
Onely my bloud speakes to you in my vaines,
And there is such confusion in my powers,
As after some oration fairely spoke
By a beloued Prince, there doth appeare
Among the buzzing pleased multitude,
Where euery something being blent together,
Turnes to a wilde of nothing, saue of ioy
Exprest, and not exprest: but when this ring
Parts from this finger, then parts life from hence,
O then be bold to say *Bassanio's* dead.
Ner. My Lord and Lady, it is now our time
That haue stood by and seene our wishes prosper,
To cry good ioy, good ioy my Lord and Lady.
Gra. My Lord *Bassanio*, and my gentle Lady,
I wish you all the ioy that you can wish:
For I am sure you can wish none from me:
And when your Honours meane to solemnize
The bargaine of your faith: I doe beseech you
Euen at that time I may be married too.
Bass. With all my heart, so thou canst get a wife.
Gra. I thanke your Lordship, you gave got me one.
My eyes my Lord can looke as swift as yours:
You saw the mistres, I beheld the maid:
You lou'd, I lou'd for intermission,
No more pertaines to me my Lord then you;
Your fortune stood vpon the caskets there,
And so did mine too, as the matter falls:
For wooing heere vntill I swet againe,
And swearing till my very rough was dry
With oathes of loue, at last, if promise last,
I got a promise of this faire one heere
To haue her loue: prouided that your fortune
Achieu'd her mistresse.
Por. Is this true *Nerrissa*?
Ner. Madam it is so, so you stand pleas'd withall.
Bass. And doe you *Gratiano* meane good faith?
Gra. Yes faith my Lord.
Bass. Our feast shall be much honored in your marriage.
Gra. Weele play with them the first boy for a thousand ducats.
Ner. What and stake downe?
Gra. No, we shal nere win at that sport, and stake downe.
But who comes heere? *Lorenzo* and his Infidell?
What and my old Venetian friend *Salerio*?

Enter Lorenzo, Iessica, and Salerio.

Bas. *Lorenzo* and *Salerio*, welcome hether,
If that the youth of my new interest heere
Haue power to bid you welcome: by your leaue
I bid my verie friends and Countrimen
Sweet *Portia* welcome.
Por. So do I my Lord, they are intirely welcome
Lor. I thanke your honor; for my part my Lord,
My purpose was not to haue seene you heere,
But meeting with *Salerio* by the way,
He did intreate mee past all saying nay
To come with him along.
Sal. I did my Lord,
And I haue reason for it, Signior *Anthonio*
Commends him to you.
Bass. Ere I ope his Letter
I pray you tell me how my good friend doth.
Sal. Not sicke my Lord, vnlesse it be in minde,
Nor wel, vnlesse in minde: his Letter there
Wil shew you his estate.

Opens the Letter.

Gra. *Nerrissa*, cheere yond stranger, bid her welcom.
Your hand *Salerio*, what's the newes from Venice?
How doth that royal Merchant good *Anthonio*;
I know he wil be glad of our successe,
We are the *Iasons*, we haue won the fleece.
Sal. I would you had won the fleece that hee hath lost.
Por. There are some shrewd contents in yond same Paper,
That steales the colour from *Bassianos* cheeke,
Some deere friend dead, else nothing in the world
Could turne so much the constitution
Of any constant man. What, worse and worse?
With leaue *Bassanio* I am halfe your selfe,
And I must freely haue the halfe of any thing
That this same paper brings you.
Bass. O sweet *Portia*,
Heere are a few of the vnpleasant'st words
That euer blotted paper. Gentle Ladie
When I did first impart my loue to you,
I freely told you all the wealth I had
Ran in my vaines: I was a Gentleman,
And then I told you true: and yet deere Ladie,
Rating my selfe at nothing, you shall see
How much I was a Braggart, when I told you
My state was nothing, I should then haue told you
That I was worse then nothing: for indeede
I haue ingag'd my selfe to a deere friend,
Ingag'd my friend to his meere enemie
To feede my meanes. Heere is a Letter Ladie,
The paper as the bodie of my friend,
And euerie word in it a gaping wound
Issuing life blood. But is it true *Salerio*,

Hath

Hath all his ventures faild, what not one hit,
From Tripolis, from Mexico and England,
From Lisbon, Barbary, and India,
And not one veſſell ſcape the dreadfull touch
Of Merchant-marring rocks?
Sal. Not one my Lord.
Beſides, it ſhould appeare, that if he had
The preſent money to diſcharge the Iew,
He would not take it: neuer did I know
A creature that did beare the ſhape of man
So keene and greedy to confound a man.
He plyes the Duke at morning and at night,
And doth impeach the freedome of the ſtate
If they deny him iuſtice. Twenty Merchants,
The Duke himſelfe, and the Magnificoes
Of greateſt port haue all perſwaded with him,
But none can driue him from the enuious plea
Of forfeiture, of iuſtice, and his bond.
Ieſſi. When I was with him, I haue heard him ſweare
To *Tuball* and to *Chus*, his Countri-men,
That he would rather haue *Anthonio's* fleſh,
Then twenty times the value of the ſumme
That he did owe him: and I know my Lord,
If law, authoritie, and power denie not,
It will goe hard with poore *Anthonio*.
Por. Is it your deere friend that is thus in trouble?
Baſſ. The deereſt friend to me, the kindeſt man,
The beſt condition'd, and vnwearied ſpirit
In doing curteſies: and one in whom
The ancient Romane honour more appeares
Then any that drawes breath in Italie.
Por. What ſumme owes he the Iew?
Baſſ. For me three thouſand ducats.
Por. What, no more?
Pay him ſixe thouſand, and deface the bond:
Double ſixe thouſand, and then treble that,
Before a friend of this deſcription
Shall loſe a haire through *Baſſano's* fault.
Firſt goe with me to Church, and call me wife,
And then away to Venice to your friend:
For neuer ſhall you lie by *Portias* ſide
With an vnquiet ſoule. You ſhall haue gold
To pay the petty debt twenty times ouer.
When it is payd, bring your true friend along,
My maid *Nerriſſa*, and my ſelfe meane time
Will liue as maids and widdowes; come away,
For you ſhall hence vpon your wedding day:
Bid your friends welcome, ſhow a merry cheere,
Since you are deere bought, I will loue you deere.
But let me heare the letter of your friend.

Sweet Baſſanio, *my ſhips haue all miſcarried, my Creditors grow cruell, my eſtate is very low, my bond to the Iew is forfeit, and ſince in paying it, it is impoſſible I ſhould liue, all debts are cleerd betweene you and I, if I might ſee you at my death: notwithſtanding, vſe your pleaſure, if your loue doe not perſwade you to come, let not my letter.*

Por. O loue! diſpach all buſines and be gone.
Baſſ. Since I haue your good leaue to goe away,
I will make haſt; but till I come againe,
No bed ſhall ere be guilty of my ſtay,
Nor reſt be interpoſer twixt vs twaine. *Exeunt.*

Enter the Iew, and Solanio, and Anthonio, and the Iaylor.

Iew. Iaylor, looke to him, tell not me of mercy,
This is the foole that lends out money *gratis*.
Iaylor, looke to him.
Ant. Heare me yet good *Shylok*.
Iew. Ile haue my bond, ſpeake not againſt my bond,
I haue ſworne an oath that I will haue my bond:
Thou call'dſt me dog before thou hadſt a cauſe,
But ſince I am a dog, beware my phangs,
The Duke ſhall grant me iuſtice, I do wonder
Thou naughty Iaylor, that thou art ſo fond
To come abroad with him at his requeſt.
Ant. I pray thee heare me ſpeake.
Iew. Ile haue my bond, I will not heare thee ſpeake,
Ile haue my bond, and therefore ſpeake no more.
Ile not be made a ſoft and dull ey'd foole,
To ſhake the head, relent, and ſigh, and yeeld
To Chriſtian interceſſors: follow not,
Ile haue no ſpeaking, I will haue my bond. *Exit Iew.*
Sol. It is the moſt impenetrable curre
That euer kept with men.
Ant. Let him alone,
Ile follow him no more with bootleſſe prayers:
He ſeekes my life, his reaſon well I know;
I oft deliuer'd from his forfeitures
Many that haue at times made mone to me,
Therefore he hates me.
Sol. I am ſure the Duke will neuer grant
this forfeiture to hold.
An. The Duke cannot deny the courſe of law
For the commoditie that ſtrangers haue
With vs in Venice, if it be denied,
Will much impeach the iuſtice of the State,
Since that the trade and profit of the citty
Conſiſteth of all Nations. Therefore goe,
Theſe greefes and loſſes haue ſo bated mee,
That I ſhall hardly ſpare a pound of fleſh
To morrow, to my bloudy Creditor.
Well Iaylor, on, pray God *Baſſanio* come
To ſee me pay his debt, and then I care not. *Exeunt.*

Enter Portia, Nerriſſa, Lorenzo, Ieſſica, and a man of Portias.

Lor. Madam, although I ſpeake it in your preſence,
You haue a noble and a true conceit
Of god-like amity, which appeares moſt ſtrongly
In bearing thus the abſence of your Lord.
But if you knew to whom you ſhew this honour,
How true a Gentleman you ſend releefe,
How deere a louer of my Lord your husband,
I know you would be prouder of the worke
Then cuſtomary bounty can enforce you.
Por. I neuer did repent for doing good,
Nor ſhall not now: for in companions
That do conuerſe and waſte the time together,
Whoſe ſoules doe beare an egal yoke of loue,
There muſt be needs a like proportion
Of lyniaments, of manners, and of ſpirit;
Which makes me thinke that this *Anthonio*
Being the boſome louer of my Lord,
Muſt needs be like my Lord. If it be ſo,
How little is the coſt I haue beſtowed
In purchaſing the ſemblance of my ſoule;
From out the ſtate of helliſh cruelty,
This comes too neere the praiſing of my ſelfe,
Therefore no more of it: heere other things
Lorenſo I commit into your hands,

The

The husbandry and mannage of my house,
Vntill my Lords returne; for mine owne part
I haue toward heauen breath'd a secret vow,
To liue in prayer and contemplation,
Onely attended by *Nerrissa* heere,
Vntill her husband and my Lords returne:
There is a monastery too miles off,
And there we will abide. I doe desire you
Not to denie this imposition,
The which my loue and some necessity
Now layes vpon you.

Lorens. Madame, with all my heart,
I shall obey you in all faire commands.

Por. My people doe already know my minde,
And will acknowledge you and *Iessica*
In place of Lord *Bassanio* and my selfe.
So far you well till we shall meete againe.

Lor. Faire thoughts & happy houres attend on you.

Iessi. I wish your Ladiship all hearts content.

Por. I thanke you for your wish, and am well pleas'd
To wish it backe on you: faryouwell *Iessica*. *Exeunt.*
Now *Balthaser*, as I haue euer found thee honest true,
So let me finde thee still: take this same letter,
And vse thou all the indeauor of a man,
In speed to Mantua, see thou render this
Into my cosins hand, Doctor *Belario*,
And looke what notes and garments he doth giue thee,
Bring them I pray thee with imagin'd speed
Vnto the Tranect, to the common Ferrie
Which trades to Venice; waste no time in words,
But get thee gone, I shall be there before thee.

Balth. Madam, I goe with all conuenient speed.

Por. Come on *Nerissa*, I haue worke in hand
That you yet know not of; wee'll see our husbands
Before they thinke of vs?

Nerrissa. Shall they see vs?

Portia. They shall *Nerrissa*: but in such a habit,
That they shall thinke we are accomplished
With that we lacke; Ile hold thee any wager
When we are both accoutered like yong men,
Ile proue the prettier fellow of the two,
And weare my dagger with the brauer grace,
And speake betweene the change of man and boy,
With a reede voyce, and turne two minsing steps
Into a manly stride; and speake of frayes
Like a fine bragging youth: and tell quaint lyes
How honourable Ladies sought my loue,
Which I denying, they fell sicke and died.
I could not doe withall: then Ile repent,
And wish for all that, that I had not kil'd them;
And twentie of these punie lies Ile tell,
That men shall sweare I haue discontinued schoole
Aboue a twelue moneth: I haue within my minde
A thousand raw tricks of these bragging Iacks,
Which I will practise.

Nerris. Why, shall wee turne to men?

Portia. Fie, what a questions that?
If thou wert nere a lewd interpreter:
But come, Ile tell thee all my whole deuice
When I am in my coach, which stayes for vs
At the Parke gate; and therefore haste away,
For we must measure twentie miles to day. *Exeunt.*

Enter Clowne and Iessica.

Clown. Yes truly; for looke you, the sinnes of the Father are to be laid vpon the children, therefore I promise you, I feare you, I was alwaies plaine with you, and so now I speake my agitation of the matter: therfore be of good cheere, for truly I thinke you are damn'd, there is but one hope in it that can doe you anie good, and that is but a kinde of bastard hope neither.

Iessica. And what hope is that I pray thee?

Clow. Marrie you may partlie hope that your father got you not, that you are not the Iewes daughter

Ies. That were a kinde of bastard hope indeed, so the sins of my mother should be visited vpon me.

Clow. Truly then I feare you are damned both by father and mother: thus when I shun *Scilla* your father, I fall into *Charibdis* your mother; well, you are gone both waies.

Ies. I shall be sau'd by my husband, he hath made me a Christian.

Clow. Truly the more to blame he, we were Christians enow before, e'ne as many as could wel liue one by another: thus making of Christians will raise the price of Hogs, if wee grow all to be porke-eaters, wee shall not shortlie haue a rasher on the coales for money.

Enter Lorenzo.

Ies. Ile tell my husband *Lanceles* what you say, heere he comes.

Loren. I shall grow iealous of you shortly *Lancelet*, if you thus get my wife into corners?

Ies. Nay, you need not feare vs *Lorenzo*, *Launcelet* and I are out, he tells me flatly there is no mercy for mee in heauen, because I am a Iewes daughter: and hee saies you are no good member of the common wealth, for in conuerting Iewes to Christians, you raise the price of Porke.

Loren. I shall answere that better to the Commonwealth, than you can the getting vp of the Negroes bellie: the Moore is with childe by you *Launcelet*?

Clow. It is much that the Moore should be more then reason: but if she be lesse then an honest woman, shee is indeed more then I tooke her for.

Loren. How euerie foole can play vpon the word, I thinke the best grace of witte will shortly turne into silence, and discourse grow commendable in none onely but Parrats: goe in sirra, bid them prepare for dinner?

Clow. That is done sir, they haue all stomacks?

Loren. Goodly Lord, what a witte-snapper are you, then bid them prepare dinner

Clow. That is done to sir, onely couer is the word

Loren. Will you couer than sir?

Clow. Not so sir neither, I know my dutie.

Loren. Yet more quarrelling with occasion, wilt thou shew the whole wealth of thy wit in an instant; I pray thee vnderstand a plaine man in his plaine meaning: goe to thy fellowes, bid them couer the table, serue in the meat, and we will come in to dinner.

Clow. For the table sir, it shall be seru'd in, for the meat sir, it shall bee couered, for your comming in to dinner sir, why let it be as humors and conceits shall gouerne. *Exit Clowne.*

Lor. O deare discretion, how his words are suted,
The foole hath planted in his memory
An Armie of good words, and I doe know
A many fooles that stand in better place,
Garnisht like him, that for a tricksie word
Defie the matter: how cheer'st thou *Iessica*,
And now good sweet say thy opinion,

How

How doſt thou like the Lord *Baſſiano's* wife?
Ieſſi. Paſt all expreſſing, it is very meete
The Lord *Baſſanio* liue an vpright life
For hauing ſuch a bleſſing in his Lady,
He findes the ioyes of heauen heere on earth,
And if on earth he doe not meane it, it
Is reaſon he ſhonld neuer come to heauen?
Why, if two gods ſhould play ſome heauenly match,
And on the wager lay two earthly women,
And *Portia* one: there muſt be ſomething elſe
Paund with the other, for the poore rude world
Hath not her fellow.
Loren. Euen ſuch a husband
Haſt thou of me, as ſhe is for a wife.
Ieſ. Nay, but aske my opinion to of that?
Lor. I will anone, firſt let vs goe to dinner?
Ieſ. Nay, let me praiſe you while I haue a ſtomacke?
Lor. No pray thee, let it ſerue for table talke,
Then how ſom ere thou ſpeakſt 'mong other things,
I ſhall digeſt it?
Ieſſi. Well, Ile ſet you forth. *Exeunt.*

Actus Quartus.

Enter the Duke, the Magnificoes, Anthonio, Baſſanio, and Gratiano.

Duke. What, is *Anthonio* heere?
Ant. Ready, ſo pleaſe your grace?
Duke. I am ſorry for thee, thou art come to anſwere
A ſtonie aduerſary, an inhumane wretch,
Vncapable of pitty, voyd, and empty
From any dram of mercie.
Ant. I haue heard
Your Grace hath tane great paines to qualifie
His rigorous courſe: but ſince he ſtands obdurate,
And that no lawful meanes can carrie me
Out of his enuies reach, I do oppoſe
My patience to his fury, and am arm'd
To ſuffer with a quietneſſe of ſpirit,
The very tiranny and rage of his.
Du. Go one and cal the Iew into the Court.
Sal. He is ready at the doore, he comes my Lord.

Enter Shylocke.

Du. Make roome, and let him ſtand before our face.
Shylocke the world thinkes, and I thinke ſo to
That thou but leadeſt this faſhion of thy mallice
To the laſt houre of act, and then 'tis thought
Thou'lt ſhew thy mercy and remorſe more ſtrange,
Than is thy ſtrange apparant cruelty;
And where thou now exact'ſt the penalty,
Which is a pound of this poore Merchants fleſh,
Thou wilt not onely looſe the forfeiture,
But touch'd with humane gentleneſſe and loue:
Forgiue a moytie of the principall,
Glancing an eye of pitty on his loſſes
That haue of late ſo hudled on his backe,
Enow to preſſe a royall Merchant downe;
And plucke commiſeration of his ſtate
From braſſie boſomes, and rough hearts of flints,
From ſtubborne Turkes and Tarters neuer traind
To offices of tender curteſie,
We all expect a gentle anſwer Iew?
Iew. I haue poſſeſt your grace of what I purpoſe,
And by our holy Sabbath haue I ſworne
To haue the due and forfeit of my bond.
If you denie it, let the danger light
Vpon your Charter, and your Cities freedome.
You'l aske me why I rather chooſe to haue
A weight of carrion fleſh, then to receiue
Three thouſand Ducats? Ile not anſwer that:
But ſay it is my humor; Is it anſwered?
What if my houſe be troubled with a Rat,
And I be pleas'd to giue ten thouſand Ducates
To haue it bain'd? What, are you anſwer'd yet?
Some men there are loue not a gaping Pigge:
Some that are mad, if they behold a Cat:
And others, when the bag-pipe ſings i'th noſe,
Cannot containe their Vrine for affection.
Maſters of paſſion ſwayes it to the moode
Of what it likes or loaths, now for your anſwer:
As there is no firme reaſon to be rendred
Why he cannot abide a gaping Pigge?
Why he a harmleſſe neceſſarie Cat?
Why he a woollen bag-pipe: but of force
Muſt yeeld to ſuch ineuitable ſhame,
As to offend himſelfe being offended:
So can I giue no reaſon, nor I will not,
More then a lodg'd hate, and a certaine loathing
I beare *Anthonio*, that I follow thus
A looſing ſuite againſt him? Are you anſwered?
Baſſ. This is no anſwer thou vnfeeling man,
To excuſe the currant of thy cruelty.
Iew. I am not bound to pleaſe thee with my anſwer.
Baſſ. Do all men kil the things they do not loue?
Iew. Hates any man the thing he would not kill?
Baſſ. Euerie offence is not a hate at firſt.
Iew. What wouldſt thou haue a Serpent ſting thee twice?
Ant. I pray you thinke you queſtion with the Iew:
You may as well go ſtand vpon the beach,
And bid the maine flood baite his vſuall height,
Or euen as well vſe queſtion with the Wolfe,
The Ewe bleate for the Lambe:
You may as well forbid the Mountaine Pines
To wagge their high tops, and to make no noiſe
When they are fretted with the guſts of heauen:
You may as well do any thing moſt hard,
As ſeeke to ſoften that, then which what harder?
His Iewiſh heart. Therefore I do beſeech you
Make no more offers, vſe no farther meanes,
But with all briefe and plaine conueniencie
Let me haue iudgement, and the Iew his will.
Baſ. For thy three thouſand Ducates heere is ſix.
Iew. If euerie Ducat in ſixe thouſand Ducates
Were in ſixe parts, and euery part a Ducate,
I would not draw them, I would haue my bond?
Du. How ſhalt thou hope for mercie, rendring none?
Iew. What iudgement ſhall I dread doing no wrong?
You haue among you many a purchaſt ſlaue,
Which like your Aſſes, and your Dogs and Mules,
You vſe in abiect and in ſlauiſh parts,
Becauſe you bought them. Shall I ſay to you,
Let them be free, marrie them to your heires?
Why ſweate they vnder burthens? Let their beds
Be made as ſoft as yours: and let their pallats
Be ſeaſon'd with ſuch Viands: you will anſwer
The

The ſlaues are ours. So do I anſwer you.
The pound of fleſh which I demand of him
Is deerely bought,'tis mine,and I will haue it.
If you deny me; fie vpon your Law,
There is no force in the decrees of Venice;
I ſtand for iudgement, anſwer, Shall I haue it?
Du. Vpon my power I may diſmiſſe this Court,
Vnleſſe *Bellario* a learned Doctor,
Whom I haue ſent for to determine this,
Come heere to day.
Sal. My Lord, heere ſtayes without
A Meſſenger with Letters from the Doctor,
New come from Padua.
Du Bring vs the Letters, Call the Meſſengers.
Baſſ. Good cheere *Anthonio.* What man,corage yet:
The Iew ſhall haue my fleſh, blood,bones,and all,
Ere thou ſhalt looſe for me one drop of blood.
Ant. I am a tainted Weather of the flocke,
Meeteſt for death, the weakeſt kinde of fruite
Drops earlieſt to the ground, and ſo let me;
You cannot better be employ'd *Baſſanio*,
Then to liue ſtill,and write mine Epitaph.

Enter Nerriſſa.

Du. Came you from Padua from *Bellario*?
Ner. From both.
My Lord *Bellario* greets your Grace.
Baſ. Why doſt thou whet thy knife ſo earneſtly?
Iew. To cut the forfeiture from that bankrout there.
Gra. Not on thy ſoale: but on thy ſoule harſh Iew
Thou mak'ſt thy kniſe keene: but no mettall can,
No, not the hangmans Axe beare halfe the keenneſſe
Of thy ſharpe enuy. Can no prayers pierce thee?
Iew. No, none that thou haſt wit enough to make.
Gra. O be thou damn'd, inexecrable dogge,
And for thy life let iuſtice be accus'd:
Thou almoſt mak'ſt me wauer in my faith;
To hold opinion with *Pythagoras*,
That ſoules of Animals infuſe themſelues
Into the trunkes of men. Thy curriſh ſpirit
Gouern'd a Wolfe, who hang'd for humane ſlaughter,
Euen from the gallowes did his fell ſoule fleet;
And whil'ſt thou layeſt in thy vnhallowed dam,
Infus'd it ſelfe in thee: For thy deſires
Are Woluiſh, bloody, ſteru'd,and rauenous.
Iew. Till thou canſt raile the ſeale from off my bond
Thou but offend'ſt thy Lungs to ſpeake ſo loud:
Repaire thy wit good youth, or it will fall
To endleſſe ruine. I ſtand heere for Law.
Du. This Letter from *Bellario* doth commend
A yong and Learned Doctor in our Court;
Where is he?
Ner. He attendeth heere hard by
To know your anſwer,whether you'l admit him.
Du. With all my heart. Some three or four of you
Go giue him curteous conduct to this place,
Meane time the Court ſhall heare *Bellarioes* Letter.

Your Grace ſhall vnderſtand, that at the receite of your Letter I am very ſicke: but in the inſtant that your meſſenger came, in louing viſitation, was with me a young Doctor of Rome, his name is Balthaſar: *I acquainted him with the cauſe in Controuerſie, betweene the Iew and* Anthonio *the Merchant: We turn'd ore many Bookes together: hee is furniſhed with my opinion, which bettred with his owne learning, the greatneſſe whereof I cannot enough commend, comes with him at my importunity, to fill vp your Graces requeſt in my ſted. I beſeech you, let his lacke of years be no impediment to let him lacke a reuerend eſtimation: for I neuer knewe ſo yong a body, with ſo old a head I leaue him to your gracious acceptance, whoſe trial ſhall better publiſh his commendation.*

Enter Portia for Balthazar

Duke. You heare the learn'd *Bellario* what he writes,
And heere (I take it) is the Doctor come.
Giue me your hand: Came you from old *Bellario*?
Por. I did my Lord
Du. You are welcome: take your place;
Are you acquainted with the difference
That holds this preſent queſtion in the Court.
Por. I am enformed throughly of the cauſe.
Which is the Merchant heere? and which the Iew?
Du. *Anthonio* and old *Shylocke*, both ſtand forth.
Por. Is your name *Shylocke*?
Iew. *Shylocke* is my name.
Por. Of a ſtrange nature is the ſute you follow,
Yet in ſuch rule, that the Venetian Law
Cannot impugne you as you do proceed.
You ſtand within his danger, do you not?
Ant. I, ſo he ſayes.
Por. Do you confeſſe the bond?
Ant. I do.
Por. Then muſt the Iew be mercifull.
Iew. On what compulſion muſt I? Tell me that.
Por The quality of mercy is not ſtrain'd,
It droppeth as the gentle raine from heauen
Vpon the place beneath. It is twice bleſt,
It bleſſeth him that giues, and him that takes,
Tis mightieſt in the mightieſt, it becomes
The throned Monarch better then his Crowne.
His Scepter ſhewes the force of temporall power,
The attribute to awe and Maieſtie,
Wherein doth ſit the dread and feare of Kings:
But mercy is aboue this ſceptred ſway,
It is enthroned in the hearts of Kings,
It is an attribute to God himſelfe;
And earthly power doth then ſhew likeſt Gods
When mercie ſeaſons Iuſtice. Therefore Iew,
Though Iuſtice be thy plea, conſider this.
That in the courſe of Iuſtice, none of vs
Should ſee ſaluation: we do pray for mercie,
And that ſame prayer, doth teach vs all to render
The deeds of mercie. I haue ſpoke thus much
To mittigate the iuſtice of thy plea:
Which if thou follow, this ſtrict courſe of Venice
Muſt needes giue ſentence 'gainſt the Merchant there.
Shy. My deeds vpon my head, I craue the Law,
The penaltie and forfeite of my bond.
Por. Is he not able to diſcharge the money
Baſ. Yes, heere I tender it for him in the Court
Yea, twice the ſumme, if that will not ſuffice,
I will be bound to pay it ten times ore,
On forfeit of my hands, my head, my heart
If this will not ſuffice, it muſt appeare
That malice beares downe truth. And I beſeech you
Wreſt once the Law to your authority,
To do a great right, do a little wrong,
And curbe this cruell diuell of his will.
Por. It muſt not be, there is no power in Venice
Can alter a decree eſtabliſhed:
'Twill be recorded for a Preſident,

And

And many an error by the same example,
Will rush into the state: It cannot be.
Iew. A *Daniel* come to iudgement, yea a *Daniel*.
O wise young Iudge, how do I honour thee.
Por. I pray you let me looke vpon the bond.
Iew. Heere 'tis most reuerend Doctor, heere it is.
Por. *Shylocke*, there's thrice thy monie offered thee.
Shy An oath, an oath, I haue an oath in heauen:
Shall I lay periurie vpon my soule?
No not for Venice.
Por. Why this bond is forfeit,
And lawfully by this the Iew may claime
A pound of flesh, to be by him cut off
Neerest the Merchants heart; be mercifull,
Take thrice thy money, bid me teare the bond
Iew When it is paid according to the tenure.
It doth appeare you are a worthy Iudge:
you know the Law, your exposition
Hath beene most sound. I charge you by the Law,
Whereof you are a well-deseruing pillar,
Proceede to iudgement: By my soule I sweare,
There is no power in the tongue of man
To alter me: I stay heere on my bond.
An. Most heartily I do beseech the Court
To giue the iudgement.
Por. Why then thus it is:
you must prepare your bosome for his knife.
Iew O noble Iudge, O excellent yong man.
Por. For the intent and purpose of the Law
Hath full relation to the penaltie,
Which heere appeareth due vpon the bond.
Iew. Tis verie true: O wise and vpright Iudge,
How much more elder art thou then thy lookes?
Por. Therefore lay bare your bosome.
Iew. I, his brest,
So sayes the bond, doth it not noble Iudge?
Neerest his heart, those are the very words.
Por It is so: Are there ballance heere to weigh the flesh?
Iew. I haue them ready.
Por. Haue by some Surgeon *Shylock* on your charge
To stop his wounds, least he should bleede to death.
Iew It is not nominated in the bond?
Por. It is not so exprest: but what of that?
Twere good you do so much for charitie.
Iew. I cannot finde it, 'tis not in the bond.
Por. Come Merchant, haue you any thing to say?
Ant. But little: I am arm'd and well prepar'd.
Giue me your hand *Bassanio*, fare you well.
Greeue not that I am falne to this for you:
For heerein fortune shewes her selfe more kinde
Then is her custome. It is still her vse
To let the wretched man out-liue his wealth,
To view with hollow eye, and wrinkled brow
An age of pouerty. From which lingring penance
Of such miserie, doth she cut me off:
Commend me to your honourable Wife,
Tell her the processe of *Anthonio's* end:
Say how I lou'd you; speake me faire in death:
And when the tale is told, bid her be iudge,
Whether *Bassanio* had not once a Loue:
Repent not you that you shall loose your friend,
And he repents not that he payes your debt.
For if the Iew do cut but deepe enough,
Ile pay it instantly, with all my heart.
Bas. *Anthonio*, I am married to a wife,
Which is as deare to me as life it selfe,
But life it selfe, my wife, and all the world,
Are not with me esteem'd aboue thy life.
I would loose all, I sacrifice them all
Heere to this deuill, to deliuer you
Por Your wife would giue you little thanks for that
If she were by to heare you make the offer.
Gra. I haue a wife whom I protest I loue,
I would she were in heauen, so she could
Intreat some power to change this currish Iew.
Ner 'Tis well you offer it behinde her backe,
The wish would make else an vnquiet house.
Iew. These be the Christian husbands: I haue a daugh-(ter
Would any of the stocke of *Barrabas*
Had beene her husband, rather then a Christian.
We trifle time, I pray thee pursue sentence.
Por. A pound of that same marchants flesh is thine,
The Court awards it, and the law doth giue it.
Iew Most rightfull Iudge.
Por. And you must cut this flesh from off his breast.
The Law allowes it, and the Court awards it.
Iew. Most learned Iudge, a sentence, come prepare.
Por. Tarry a little, there is something else,
This bond doth giue thee heere no iot of bloud,
The words expresly are a pound of flesh:
Then take thy bond, take thou thy pound of flesh,
But in the cutting it, if thou dost shed
One drop of Christian bloud, thy lands and goods
Are by the Lawes of Venice confiscate
Vnto the state of Venice.
Gra. O vpright Iudge,
Marke Iew, o learned Iudge.
Shy. Is that the law
Por. Thy selfe shall see the Act:
For as thou vrgest iustice, be assur'd
Thou shalt haue iustice more then thou desirest.
Gra. O learned Iudge, mark Iew, a learned Iudge.
Iew. I take this offer then, pay the bond thrice,
And let the Christian goe.
Bass. Heere is the money.
Por. Soft, the Iew shall haue all iustice, soft, no haste,
He shall haue nothing but the penalty.
Gra. O Iew, an vpright Iudge, a learned Iudge.
Por. Therefore prepare thee to cut off the flesh,
Shed thou no bloud, nor cut thou lesse nor more
But iust a pound of flesh: if thou tak'st more
Or lesse then a iust pound, be it so much
As makes it light or heauy in the substance,
Or the deuision of the twentieth part
Of one poore scruple, nay if the scale doe turne
But in the estimation of a hayre,
Thou diest, and all thy goods are confiscate.
Gra A second *Daniel*, a *Daniel* Iew,
Now infidell I haue thee on the hip.
Por. Why doth the Iew pause, take thy forfeiture.
Shy. Giue me my principall, and let me goe.
Bass. I haue it ready for thee, heere it is.
Por. He hath refus'd it in the open Court,
He shall haue meerly iustice and his bond.
Gra. A *Daniel* still say I, a second *Daniel*,
I thanke thee Iew for teaching me that word.
Shy Shall I not haue barely my principall?
Por. Thou shalt haue nothing but the forfeiture,
To be taken so at thy perill Iew.
Shy. Why then the Deuill giue him good of it
Ile stay no longer question.
Por. Tarry

Por. Tarry Iew,
The Law hath yet another hold on you.
It is enacted in the Lawes of Venice,
If it be proued against an Alien,
That by direct, or indirect attempts
He seeke the life of any Citizen,
The party gainst the which he doth contriue,
Shall seaze one halfe his goods, the other halfe
Comes to the priuie coffer of the State,
And the offenders life lies in the mercy
Of the Duke onely, gainst all'other voice.
In which predicament I say thou standst:
For it appeares by manifest proceeding,
That indirectly, and directly to;
Thou hast contriu'd against the very life
Of the defendant: and thou hast incur'd
The danger formerly by me rehearst.
Downe therefore, and beg mercy of the Duke.
Gra. Beg that thou maist haue leaue to hang thy selfe,
And yet thy wealth being forfeit to the state,
Thou hast not left the value of a cord,
Therefore thou must be hang'd at the states charge.
Duk. That thou shalt see the difference of our spirit,
I pardon thee thy life before thou aske it:
For halfe thy wealth, it is *Anthonio's*,
The other ha fe comes to the generall state,
Which humblenesse may driue vnto a fine.
Por. I for the state, not for *Anthonio*.
Shy. Nay, take my life and all, pardon not that,
You take my house, when you do take the prop
That doth sustaine my house: you take my life
When you doe take the meanes whereby I liue.
Por. What mercy can you render him *Anthonio*?
Gra. A halter *gratis*, nothing else for Gods sake
Ant. So please my Lord the Duke, and all the Court
To quit the fine for one halfe of his goods,
I am content: so he will let me haue
The other halfe in vse, to render it
Vpon his death, vnto the Gentleman
That lately stole his daughter.
Two things prouided more, that for this fauour
He presently become a Christian:
The other, that he doe record a gift
Heere in the Court of all he dies possest
Vnto his sonne *Lorenzo*, and his daughter.
Duk. He shall doe this, or else I doe recant
The pardon that I late pronounced heere.
Por. Art thou contented Iew? what dost thou say?
Shy. I am content.
Por. Clarke, draw a deed of gift.
Shy. I pray you giue me leaue to goe from hence,
I am not well, send the deed after me,
And I will signe it.
Duke. Get thee gone, but doe it.
Gra. In christning thou shalt haue two godfathers,
Had I been iudge, thou shouldst haue had ten more,
To bring thee to the gallowes, not to the font. *Exit.*
Du. Sir I intreat you with me home to dinner.
Por. I humbly doe desire your Grace of pardon,
I must away this night toward Padua,
And it is meete I presently set forth.
Duk. I am sorry that your leysure serues you not:
Anthonio, gratifie this gentleman,
For in my minde you are much bound to him.
Exit Duke and his traine.
Bass. Most worthy gentleman, I and my friend
Haue by your wisedome beene this day acquitted
Of greeuous penalties, in lieu whereof,
Three thousand Ducats due vnto the Iew
We freely cope your curteous paines withall.
An. And stand indebted ouer and aboue
In loue and seruice to you euermore.
Por. He is well paid that is well satisfied,
And I deliuering you, am satisfied,
And therein doe account my selfe well paid,
My minde was neuer yet more mercinarie.
I pray you know me when we meete againe,
I wish you well, and so I take my leaue.
Bass. Deare sir, of force I must attempt you further,
Take some remembrance of vs as a tribute,
Not as fee: grant me two things, I pray you
Not to denie me, and to pardon me.
Por. You presse mee farre, and therefore I will yeeld,
Giue me your gloues, Ile weare them for your sake,
And for your loue Ile take this ring from you,
Doe not draw backe your hand, ile take no more,
And you in loue shall not deny me this?
Bass. This ring good sir, alas it is a trifle,
I will not shame my selfe to giue you this.
Por. I wil haue nothing else but onely this,
And now methinkes I haue a minde to it.
Bas There's more depends on this then on the valew,
The dearest ring in Venice will I giue you,
And finde it out by proclamation,
Onely for this I pray you pardon me.
Por. I see sir you are liberall in offers,
You taught me first to beg, and now me thinkes
You teach me how a beggar should be answer'd.
Bas. Good sir, this ring was giuen me by my wife,
And when she put it on, she made me vow
That I should neither sell, nor giue, nor lose it.
Por. That scuse serues many men to saue their gifts,
And if your wife be not a mad woman,
And know how well I haue deseru'd this ring,
Shee would not hold out enemy for euer
For giuing it to me: well, peace be with you. *Exeunt.*
Ant. My L. *Bassanio*, let him haue the ring,
Let his deseruings and my loue withall
Be valued against your wiues commandement.
Bass. Goe *Gratiano*, run and ouer-take him,
Giue him the ring, and bring him if thou canst
Vnto *Anthonios* house, away, make haste. *Exit Grati.*
Come, you and I will thither presently,
And in the morning early will we both
Flie toward *Belmont*, come *Anthonio*. *Exeunt.*

Enter Portia and Nerrissa.

Por. Enquire the Iewes house out, giue him this deed,
And let him signe it, wee'll away to night,
And be a day before our husbands home:
This deed will be well welcome to *Lorenzo*.

Enter Gratiano.

Gra. Faire sir, you are well ore-tane:
My L. *Bassanio* vpon more aduice,
Hath sent you heere this ring, and doth intreat
Your company at dinner.
Por. That cannot be;
His ring I doe accept most thankfully,
And so I pray you tell him: furthermore,
I pray you shew my youth old *Shylockes* house.
Gra. That will I doe.
Ner. Sir, I would speake with you:

Q Ile

Ile ſee if I can get my husbands ring
Which I did make him ſweare to keepe for euer.
Por. Thou maiſt I warrant, we ſhal haue old ſwearing
That they did giue the rings away to men;
But weele out-face them, and out-ſweare them to:
Away, make haſte, thou know'ſt where I will tarry.
Ner. Come good ſir, will you ſhew me to this houſe.
Exeunt.

Actus Quintus.

Enter Lorenzo and Ieſſica.

Lor. The moone ſhines bright. In ſuch a night as this,
When the ſweet winde did gently kiſſe the trees,
And they did make no noyſe, in ſuch a night
Troylus me thinkes mounted the Troian walls,
And ſigh'd his ſoule toward the Grecian tents
Where *Creſſed* lay that night.
Ieſ. In ſuch a night
Did *Thisbie* fearefully ore-trip the dewe,
And ſaw the Lyons ſhadow ere himſelfe,
And ranne diſmayed away.
Loren. In ſuch a night
Stood *Dido* with a Willow in her hand
Vpon the wilde ſea bankes, and waft her Loue
To come againe to Carthage.
Ieſ. In ſuch a night
Medea gathered the inchanted hearbs
That did renew old *Eſon.*
Loren. In ſuch a night
Did *Ieſſica* ſteale from the wealthy Iewe,
And with an Vnthrift Loue did runne from Venice,
As farre as Belmont.
Ieſ. In ſuch a night
Did young *Lorenzo* ſweare he lou'd her well,
Stealing her ſoule with many vowes of faith
And nere a true one.
Loren. In ſuch a night
Did pretty *Ieſſica* (like a little ſhrow)
Slander her Loue, and he forgaue it her.
Ieſſi. I would out-night you did no body come:
But harke, I heare the footing of a man.

Enter Meſſenger.

Lor. Who comes ſo faſt in ſilence of the night?
Meſ. A friend. (friend?
Loren. A friend, what friend? your name I pray you
Meſ. *Stephano* is my name, and I bring word
My Miſtreſſe will before the breake of day
Be heere at Belmont, ſhe doth ſtray about
By holy croſſes where ſhe kneeles and prayes
For happy wedlocke houres.
Loren. Who comes with her?
Meſ. None but a holy Hermit and her maid:
I pray you is my Maſter yet returnd?
Loren. He is not, nor we haue not heard from him,
But goe we in I pray thee *Ieſſica*,
And ceremoniouſly let vs prepare
Some welcome for the Miſtreſſe of the houſe,

Enter Clowne.

Clo. Sola, ſola: wo ha ho, ſola, ſola.
Loren. Who calls?
Clo. Sola, did you ſee M. *Lorenzo*, & M. *Lorenzo*, ſola,
Lor. Leaue hollowing man, heere. (ſola.
Clo. Sola, where, where?
Lor. Heere?
Clo. Tel him ther's a Poſt come from my Maſter, with his horne full of good newes, my Maſter will be here ere morning ſweet ſoule.
Loren. Let's in, and there expect their comming.
And yet no matter: why ſhould we goe in?
My friend *Stephen*, ſignifie pray you
Within the houſe, your Miſtreſſe is at hand,
And bring your muſique foorth into the ayre.
How ſweet the moone-light ſleepes vpon this banke,
Heere will we ſit, and let the ſounds of muſicke
Creepe in our eares ſoft ſtilnes, and the night
Become the tutches of ſweet harmonie:
Sit *Ieſſica*, looke how the floore of heauen
Is thicke inlayed with pattens of bright gold,
There's not the ſmalleſt orbe which thou beholdſt
But in his motion like an Angell ſings,
Still quiring to the young eyed Cherubins;
Such harmonie is in immortall ſoules,
But whilſt this muddy veſture of decay
Doth groſly cloſe in it, we cannot heare it:
Come hoe, and wake *Diana* with a hymne,
With ſweeteſt tutches pearce your Miſtreſſe eare,
And draw her home with muſicke.
Ieſſi. I am neuer merry when I heare ſweet muſique.
Play muſicke.
Lor. The reaſon is, your ſpirits are attentiue:
For doe but note a wilde and wanton heard
Or race of youthful and vnhandled colts,
Fetching mad bounds, bellowing and neighing loud,
Which is the hot condition of their bloud,
If they but heare perchance a trumpet ſound,
Or any ayre of muſicke touch their eares,
You ſhall perceiue them make a mutuall ſtand,
Their ſauage eyes turn'd to a modeſt gaze,
By the ſweet power of muſicke: therefore the Poet
Did faine that *Orpheus* drew trees, ſtones, and floods.
Since naught ſo ſtockiſh, hard, and full of rage,
But muſicke for time doth change his nature,
The man that hath no muſicke in himſelfe,
Nor is not moued with concord of ſweet ſounds,
Is fit for treaſons, ſtratagems, and ſpoyles,
The motions of his ſpirit are dull as night,
And his affections darke as *Erobus*,
Let no ſuch man be truſted: marke the muſicke.

Enter Portia and Nerriſſa.

Por. That light we ſee is burning in my hall:
How farre that little candell throwes his beames,
So ſhines a good deed in a naughty world. (dle?
Ner. When the moone ſhone we did not ſee the can
Por. So doth the greater glory dim the leſſe,
A ſubſtitute ſhines brightly as a King
Vntill a King be by, and then his ſtate
Empties it ſelfe, as doth an inland brooke
Into the maine of waters: muſique, harke. *Muſicke.*
Ner. It is your muſicke Madame of the houſe.
Por. Nothing is good I ſee without reſpect,
Methinkes it ſounds much ſweeter then by day?
Ner. Silence beſtowes that vertue on it Madam.
Por. The Crow doth ſing as ſweetly as the larke
When

When neither is attended : and I thinke
The Nightingale if ſhe ſhould ſing by day
When euery Gooſe is cackling, would be thought
No better a Muſician then the Wren :
How many things by ſeaſon, ſeaſon'd are
To their right praiſe, and true perfection :
Peace, how the Moone ſleepes with Endimion,
And would not be awak'd
Muſicke ceaſes.
Lor. That is the voice,
Or I am much deceiu'd of *Portia.*
Por. He knowes me as the blinde man knowes the
Cuckow by the bad voice ?
Lor. Deere Lady welcome home ?
Por. We haue bene praying for our huſbands welfare
Which ſpeed we hope the better for our words,
Are they return'd?
Lor. Madam, they are not yet :
But there is come a Meſſenger before
To ſignifie their comming.
Por. Go in *Nerriſſa*,
Giue order to my ſeruants, that they take
No note at all of our being abſent hence,
Nor you *Lorenzo*, *Ieſſica* nor you.
A Tucket ſounds.
Lor. Your husband is at hand, I heare his Trumpet,
We are no tell-tales Madam, feare you not.
Por. This night methinkes is but the daylight ſicke,
It lookes a little paler, 'tis a day,
Such as the day is, when the Sun is hid.

Enter Baſſanio, Anthonio, Gratiano, and their Followers.

Baſ. We ſhould hold day with the Antipodes,
If you would walke in abſence of the ſunne.
Por. Let me giue light, but let me not be light,
For a light wife doth make a heauie husband,
And neuer be *Baſſanio* ſo for me,
But God ſort all: you are welcome home my Lord.
Baſſ. I thanke you Madam, giue welcom to my friend
This is the man, this is *Anthonio*,
To whom I am ſo infinitely bound.
Por. You ſhould in all ſence be much bound to him,
For as I heare he was much bound for you.
Anth. No more then I am wel acquitted of.
Por. Sir, you are verie welcome to our houſe :
It muſt appeare in other waies then words,
Therefore I ſcant this breathing curteſie.
Gra. By yonder Moone I ſweare you do me wrong,
Infaith I gaue it to the Iudges Clearke,
Would he were gelt that had it for my part,
Since you do take it Loue ſo much at hart.
Por. A quarrel hoe alreadie, what's the matter ?
Gra. About a hoope of Gold, a paltry Ring
That ſhe did giue me, whoſe Poeſie was
For all the world like Cutlers Poetry
Vpon a knife ; *Loue mee, and leaue mee not.*
Ner. What talke you of the Poeſie or the valew:
You ſwore to me when I did giue it you,
That you would weare it til the houre of death,
And that it ſhould lye with you in your graue,
Though not for me, yet for your vehement oaths,
You ſhould haue beene reſpectiue and haue kept it.
Gaue it a Iudges Clearke: but wel I know
The Clearke wil nere weare haire on's face that had it.
Gra. He wil, and if he liue to be a man.
Nerriſſa. I, if a Woman liue to be a man.
Gra. Now by this hand I gaue it to a youth,
A kinde of boy, a little ſcrubbed boy,
No higher then thy ſelfe, the Iudges Clearke,
A prating boy that begg'd it as a Fee,
I could not for my heart deny it him.
Por. You were too blame, I muſt be plaine with you,
To part ſo ſlightly with your wiues firſt gift,
A thing ſtucke on with oathes vpon your finger,
And ſo riueted with faith vnto your fleſh.
I gaue my Loue a Ring, and made him ſweare
Neuer to part with it, and heere he ſtands :
I dare be ſworne for him, he would not leaue it,
Nor plucke it from his finger, for the wealth
That the world maſters. Now in faith *Gratiano*,
You giue your wife too vnkinde a cauſe of greefe,
And 'twere to me I ſhould be mad at it.
Baſſ. Why I were beſt to cut my left hand off,
And ſweare I loſt the Ring defending it.
Gre. My Lord *Baſſanio* gaue his Ring away
Vnto the Iudge that beg'd it, and indeede
Deſeru'd it too : and then the Boy his Clearke
That tooke ſome paines in writing, he begg'd mine,
And neyther man nor maſter would take ought
But the two Rings.
Por. What Ring gaue you my Lord ?
Not that I hope which you receiu'd of me.
Baſſ. If I could adde a lie vnto a fault,
I would deny it : but you ſee my finger
Hath not the Ring vpon it, it is gone.
Por. Euen ſo voide is your falſe heart of truth.
By heauen I wil nere come in your bed
Vntil I ſee the Ring.
Ner. Nor I in yours, til I againe ſee mine.
Baſſ. Sweet *Portia*,
If you did know to whom I gaue the Ring,
If you did know for whom I gaue the Ring,
And would conceiue for what I gaue the Ring,
And how vnwillingly I left the Ring,
When nought would be accepted but the Ring,
You would abate the ſtrength of your diſpleaſure?
Por. If you had knowne the vertue of the Ring,
Or halfe her worthineſſe that gaue the Ring,
Or your owne honour to containe the Ring,
You would not then haue parted with the Ring :
What man is there ſo much vnreaſonable,
If you had pleas'd to haue defended it
With any termes of Zeale : wanted the modeſtie
To vrge the thing held as a ceremonie :
Nerriſſa teaches me what to beleeue,
Ile die for't, but ſome Woman had the Ring ?
Baſſ. No by mine honor Madam, by my ſoule
No Woman had it, but a ciuill Doctor,
Which did refuſe three thouſand Ducates of me,
And beg'd the Ring; the which I did denie him,
And ſuffer'd him to go diſpleas'd away :
Euen he that had held vp the verie life
Of my deere friend. What ſhould I ſay ſweete Lady?
I was inforc'd to ſend it after him,
I was beſet with ſhame and curteſie,
My honor would not let ingratitude
So much beſmeare it. Pardon me good Lady,
And by theſe bleſſed Candles of the night,
Had you bene there, I thinke you would haue beg'd
The Ring of me, to giue the worthie Doctor ?

Por. Let not that Doctor ere come neere my house,
Since he hath got the iewell that I loued,
And that which you did sweare to keepe for me,
I will become as liberall as you,
Ile not deny him any thing I haue,
No, not my body, nor my husbands bed:
Know him I shall, I am well sure of it.
Lie not a night from home. Watch me like Argos,
If you doe not, if I be left alone,
Now by mine honour which is yet mine owne,
Ile haue the Doctor for my bedfellow.
Nerrissa. And I his Clarke: therefore be well aduis'd
How you doe leaue me to mine owne protection.
Gra. Well, doe you so: let not me take him then,
For if I doe, ile mar the yong Clarks pen.
Ant. I am th'vnhappy subiect of these quarrels.
Por. Sir, grieue not you,
You are welcome notwithstanding.
Bas. *Portia*, forgiue me this enforced wrong,
And in the hearing of these manie friends
I sweare to thee, euen by thine owne faire eyes
Wherein I see my selfe
Por. Marke you but that?
In both my eyes he doubly sees himselfe:
In each eye one, sweare by your double selfe,
And there's an oath of credit.
Bas. Nay, but heare me.
Pardon this fault, and by my soule I sweare
I neuer more will breake an oath with thee.
Anth. I once did lend my bodie for thy wealth,
Which but for him that had your husbands ring
Had quite miscarried. I dare be bound againe,
My soule vpon the forfeit, that your Lord
Will neuer more breake faith aduisedlie.
Por. Then you shall be his suretie: giue him this,
And bid him keepe it better then the other.
Ant. Heere Lord *Bassanio*, swear to keep this ring.
Bass. By heauen it is the same I gaue the Doctor
Por. I had it of him: pardon *Bassanio*,
For by this ring the Doctor lay with me.
Ner. And pardon me my gentle *Gratiano*,
For that same scrubbed boy the Doctors Clarke
In liew of this, last night did lye with me
Gra. Why this is like the mending of high waies
In Sommer, where the waies are faire enough:
What, are we Cuckolds ere we haue deseru'd it.
Por. Speake not so grossely, you are all amaz'd;
Heere is a letter, reade it at your leysure,
It comes from Padua from *Bellario*,
There you shall finde that *Portia* was the Doctor,
Nerrissa there her Clarke. *Lorenzo* heere
Shall witnesse I set forth as soone as you,
And but eu'n now return'd: I haue not yet
Entred my house. *Anthonio* you are welcome,
And I haue better newes in store for you
Then you expect: vnseale this letter soone,
There you shall finde three of your Argosies
Are richly come to harbour sodainlie.
You shall not know by what strange accident
I chanced on this letter.
Antho. I am dumbe.
Bass. Were you the Doctor, and I knew you not?
Gra. Were you the Clark that is to make me cuckold.
Ner. I, but the Clark that neuer meanes to doe it,
Vnlesse he liue vntill he be a man.
Bass. (Sweet Doctor) you shall be my bedfellow,
When I am absent, then lie with my wife.
An. (Sweet Ladie) you haue giuen me life & liuing;
For heere I reade for certaine that my ships
Are safelie come to Rode.
Por. How now *Lorenzo*?
My Clarke hath some good comforts to for you
Ner. I, and Ile giue them him without a fee
There doe I giue to you and *Iessica*
From the rich Iewe, a speciall deed of gift
After his death, of all he dies possess'd of.
Loren. Faire Ladies you drop Manna in the way
Of starued people.
Por. It is almost morning,
And yet I am sure you are not satisfied
Of these euents at full. Let vs goe in,
And charge vs there vpon intergatories,
And we will answer all things faithfully.
Gra. Let it be so, the first intergatory
That my *Nerrissa* shall be sworne on, is,
Whether till the next night she had rather stay,
Or goe to bed, now being two houres to day,
But were the day come, I should wish it darke,
Till I were couching with the Doctors Clarke.
Well, while I liue, Ile feare no other thing
So sore, as keeping safe *Nerrissas* ring.

Exeunt.

FINIS.

As you Like it.

Actus primus. Scœna Prima.

Enter Orlando and Adam.

Orlando.

As I remember *Adam*, it was vpon this faſhion bequeathed me by will, but poore a thouſand Crownes, and as thou ſaiſt, charged my brother on his bleſſing to breed mee well : and there begins my ſadneſſe : My brother *Iaques* he keepes at ſchoole, and report ſpeakes goldenly of his profit : for my part, he keepes me ruſtically at home, or (to ſpeak more properly) ſtaies me heere at home vnkept : for call you that keeping for a gentleman of my birth, that differs not from the ſtalling of an Oxe? his horſes are bred better, for beſides that they are faire with their feeding, they are taught their mannage, and to that end Riders deerely hir'd : but I (his brother) gaine nothing vnder him but growth, for the which his Animals on his dunghils are as much bound to him as I : beſides this nothing that he ſo plentifully giues me, the ſomething that nature gaue mee, his countenance ſeemes to take from me : hee lets mee feede with his Hindes, barres mee the place of a brother, and as much as in him lies, mines my gentility with my education. This is it *Adam* that grieues me, and the ſpirit of my Father, which I thinke is within mee, begins to mutinie againſt this ſeruitude. I will no longer endure it, though yet I know no wiſe remedy how to auoid it.

Enter Oliuer.

Adam. Yonder comes my Maſter, your brother.

Orlan. Goe a-part *Adam*, and thou ſhalt heare how he will ſhake me vp.

Oli. Now Sir, what make you heere?

Orl. Nothing : I am not taught to make any thing.

Oli. What mar you then ſir?

Orl. Marry ſir, I am helping you to mar that which God made, a poore vnworthy brother of yours with idleneſſe.

Oliuer. Marry ſir be better employed, and be naught a while.

Orlan. Shall I keepe your hogs, and eat huskes with them? what prodigall portion haue I ſpent, that I ſhould come to ſuch penury?

Oli. Know you where you are ſir?

Orl. O ſir, very well: heere in your Orchard.

Oli. Know you before whom ſir?

Orl. I, better then him I am before knowes mee : know you are my eldeſt brother, and in the gentle condition of bloud you ſhould ſo know me: the courteſie of nations allowes you my better, in that you are the firſt borne, but the ſame tradition takes not away my bloud, were there twenty brothers betwixt vs : I haue as much of my father in mee, as you, albeit I confeſſe your comming before me is neerer to his reuerence.

Oli. What Boy.

Orl. Come, come elder brother, you are too yong in this.

Oli. Wilt thou lay hands on me villaine?

Orl. I am no villaine : I am the yongeſt ſonne of Sir *Rowland de Boys*, he was my father, and he is thrice a villaine that ſaies ſuch a father begot villaines : wert thou not my brother, I would not take this hand from thy throat, till this other had puld out thy tongue for ſaying ſo, thou haſt raild on thy ſelfe.

Adam. Sweet Maſters bee patient, for your Fathers remembrance, be at accord.

Oli. Let me goe I ſay.

Orl. I will not till I pleaſe : you ſhall heare mee : my father charg'd you in his will to giue me good education : you haue train'd me like a pezant, obſcuring and hiding from me all gentleman-like qualities : the ſpirit of my father growes ſtrong in mee, and I will no longer endure it : therefore allow me ſuch exerciſes as may become a gentleman, or giue mee the poore allottery my father left me by teſtament, with that I will goe buy my fortunes.

Oli. And what wilt thou do? beg when that is ſpent? Well ſir, get you in. I will not long be troubled with you : you ſhall haue ſome part of your will, I pray you leaue me.

Orl. I will no further offend you, then becomes mee for my good.

Oli. Get you with him, you olde dogge.

Adam. Is old dogge my reward : moſt true, I haue loſt my teeth in your ſeruice : God be with my olde maſter, he would not haue ſpoke ſuch a word. *Ex. Orl. Ad.*

Oli. Is it euen ſo, begin you to grow vpon me? I will phyſicke your ranckeneſſe, and yet giue no thouſand crownes neyther : holla *Dennis*

Enter Dennis.

Den. Calls your worſhip?

Oli. Was not *Charles* the Dukes Wraſtler heere to ſpeake with me?

Den. So pleaſe you, he is heere at the doore, and importunes acceſſe to you.

Oli. Call him in : 'twill be a good way: and to morrow the wraſtling is.

Enter Charles.

Cha. Good morrow to your worſhip.

Oli. Good Mounſier *Charles* : what's the new newes at the new Court?

Charles. There's no newes at the Court Sir, but the olde newes: that is, the old Duke is baniſhed by his yonger brother the new Duke, and three or foure louing

Q3 Lords

Lords haue put themſelues into voluntary exile with him, whoſe lands and reuenues enrich the new Duke, therefore he giues them good leaue to wander

Oli. Can you tell if *Roſalind* the Dukes daughter bee baniſhed with her Father?

Cha. O no; for the Dukes daughter her Coſen ſo loues her, being euer from their Cradles bred together, that hee would haue followed her exile, or haue died to ſtay behind her; ſhe is at the Court, and no leſſe beloued of her Vncle, then his owne daughter, and neuer two Ladies loued as they doe.

Oli. Where will the old Duke liue?

Cha. They ſay hee is already in the Forreſt of *Arden*, and a many merry men with him; and there they liue like the old *Robin Hood* of *England*: they ſay many yong Gentlemen flocke to him euery day, and fleet the time careleſly as they did in the golden world.

Oli. What, you wraſtle to morrow before the new Duke.

Cha. Marry doe I ſir: and I came to acquaint you with a matter: I am giuen ſir ſecretly to vnderſtand, that your yonger brother *Orlando* hath a diſpoſition to come in diſguis'd againſt mee to try a fall: to morrow ſir I wraſtle for my credit, and hee that eſcapes me without ſome broken limbe, ſhall acquit him well: your brother is but young and tender, and for your loue I would bee loth to foyle him, as I muſt for my owne honour if hee come in: therefore out of my loue to you, I came hither to acquaint you withall, that either you might ſtay him from his intendment, or brooke ſuch diſgrace well as he ſhall runne into, in that it is a thing of his owne ſearch, and altogether againſt my will.

Oli. *Charles*, I thanke thee for thy loue to me, which thou ſhalt finde I will moſt kindly requite: I had my ſelfe notice of my Brothers purpoſe heerein, and haue by vnder-hand meanes laboured to diſſwade him from it; but he is reſolute. Ile tell thee *Charles*, it is the ſtubborneſt yong fellow of France, full of ambition, an enuious emulator of euery mans good parts, a ſecret & villanous contriuer againſt mee his naturall brother: therefore vſe thy diſcretion, I had as liefe thou didſt breake his necke as his finger. And thou wert beſt looke to't; for if thou doſt him any ſlight diſgrace, or if hee doe not mightilie grace himſelfe on thee, hee will practiſe againſt thee by poyſon, entrap thee by ſome treacherous deuiſe, and neuer leaue thee till he hath tane thy life by ſome indirect meanes or other: for I aſſure thee, (and almoſt with teares I ſpeake it) there is not one ſo young, and ſo villanous this day liuing. I ſpeake but brotherly of him, but ſhould I anathomize him to thee, as hee is, I muſt bluſh, and weepe, and thou muſt looke pale and wonder.

Cha. I am heartily glad I came hither to you: if hee come to morrow, Ile giue him his payment: if euer hee goe alone againe, Ile neuer wraſtle for prize more: and ſo God keepe your worſhip. *Exit.*

Farewell good *Charles*. Now will I ſtirre this Gameſter: I hope I ſhall ſee an end of him; for my ſoule (yet I know not why) hates nothing more then he: yet hee's gentle, neuer ſchool'd, and yet learned, full of noble deuiſe, of all ſorts enchantingly beloued, and indeed ſo much in the heart of the world, and eſpecially of my owne people, who beſt know him, that I am altogether miſpriſed: but it ſhall not be ſo long, this wraſtler ſhall cleare all: nothing remaines, but that I kindle the boy thither, which now Ile goe about. *Exit.*

Scœna Secunda.

Enter Roſalind, and Cellia.

Cel. I pray thee *Roſalind*, ſweet my Coz, be merry.

Roſ. Deere *Cellia*; I ſhow more mirth then I am miſtreſſe of, and would you yet were merrier: vnleſſe you could teach me to forget a baniſhed father, you muſt not learne mee how to remember any extraordinary pleaſure.

Cel. Heerein I ſee thou lou'ſt mee not with the full waight that I loue thee; if my Vncle thy baniſhed father had baniſhed thy Vncle the Duke my Father, ſo thou hadſt beene ſtill with mee, I could haue taught my loue to take thy father for mine; ſo wouldſt thou, if the truth of thy loue to me were ſo righteouſly temper'd, as mine is to thee.

Roſ. Well, I will forget the condition of my eſtate, to reioyce in yours

Cel. You know my Father hath no childe, but I, nor none is like to haue; and truely when he dies, thou ſhalt be his heire; for what hee hath taken away from thy father perforce, I will render thee againe in affection: by mine honor I will, and when I breake that oath, let mee turne monſter: therefore my ſweet *Roſe*, my deare *Roſe*, be merry

Roſ. From henceforth I will Coz, and deuiſe ſports: let me ſee, what thinke you of falling in Loue?

Cel. Marry I prethee doe, to make ſport withall: but loue no man in good earneſt, nor no further in ſport neyther, then with ſafety of a pure bluſh, thou maiſt in honor come off againe.

Roſ. What ſhall be our ſport then?

Cel. Let vs ſit and mocke the good houſwife *Fortune* from her wheele, that her gifts may henceforth bee beſtowed equally.

Roſ. I would wee could doe ſo: for her benefits are mightily miſplaced, and the bountifull blinde woman doth moſt miſtake in her gifts to women.

Cel. 'Tis true, for thoſe that ſhe makes faire, ſhe ſcarce makes honeſt, & thoſe that ſhe makes honeſt, ſhe makes very illfauouredly.

Roſ. Nay now thou goeſt from Fortunes office to Natures: Fortune reignes in gifts of the world, not in the lineaments of Nature.

Enter Clowne

Cel. No; when Nature hath made a faire creature, may ſhe not by Fortune fall into the fire? though nature hath giuen vs wit to flout at Fortune, hath not Fortune ſent in this foole to cut off the argument?

Roſ. Indeed there is fortune too hard for nature, when fortune makes natures naturall, the cutter off of natures witte.

Cel. Peraduenture this is not Fortunes work neither, but Natures, who perceiueth our naturall wits too dull to reaſon of ſuch goddeſſes, hath ſent this Naturall for our whetſtone: for alwaies the dulneſſe of the foole, is the whetſtone of the wits. How now Witte, whether wander you?

Clow. Miſtreſſe, you muſt come away to your father.

Cel. Were you made the meſſenger?

Clo. No by mine honor, but I was bid to come for you

Roſ.

Roſ. Where learned you that oath foole?

Clo. Of a certaine Knight, that ſwore by his Honour they were good Pan-cakes, and ſwore by his Honor the Muſtard was naught: Now Ile ſtand to it, the Pancakes were naught, and the Muſtard was good, and yet was not the Knight forſworne.

Cel. How proue you that in the great heape of your knowledge?

Roſ. I marry, now vnmuzzle your wiſedome.

Clo. Stand you both forth now: ſtroke your chinnes, and ſweare by your beards that I am a knaue.

Cel. By our beards (if we had them) thou art.

Clo. By my knauerie (if I had it) then I were: but if you ſweare by that that is not, you are not forſworn: no more was this knight ſwearing by his Honor, for he neuer had anie; or if he had, he had ſworne it away, before euer he ſaw thoſe Pancakes, or that Muſtard.

Cel. Prethee, who is't that thou means't?

Clo. One that old *Fredericke* your Father loues.

Roſ. My Fathers loue is enough to honor him enough; ſpeake no more of him, you'l be whipt for taxation one of theſe daies.

Clo. The more pittie that fooles may not ſpeak wiſely, what Wiſemen do fooliſhly.

Cel. By my troth thou ſaieſt true: For, ſince the little wit that fooles haue was ſilenced, the little foolerie that wiſe men haue makes a great ſhew; Heere comes Monſieur the *Beu.*

Enter le Beau.

Roſ. With his mouth full of newes.

Cel. Which he vvill put on vs, as Pigeons feed their young.

Roſ. Then ſhal we be newes-cram'd.

Cel. All the better: we ſhalbe the more Marketable. *Boon-iour Monſieur le Beu,* what's the newes?

Le Beu. Faire Princeſſe,
you haue loſt much good ſport.

Cel. Sport: of what colour?

Le Beu. What colour Madame? How ſhall I aunſwer you?

Roſ. As wit and fortune will.

Clo. Or as the deſtinies decrees.

Cel. Well ſaid, that was laid on with a trowell.

Clo. Nay, if I keepe not my ranke.

Roſ. Thou looſeſt thy old ſmell.

Le Beu. You amaze me Ladies: I would haue told you of good wraſtling, which you haue loſt the ſight of.

Roſ. Yet tell vs the manner of the Wraſtling.

Le Beu. I wil tell you the beginning: and if it pleaſe your Ladiſhips, you may ſee the end, for the beſt is yet to doe, and heere where you are, they are comming to performe it.

Cel. Well, the beginning that is dead and buried.

Le Beu. There comes an old man, and his three ſons.

Cel. I could match this beginning with an old tale.

Le Beu. Three proper yong men, of excellent growth and preſence.

Roſ. With bils on their neckes: Be it knowne vnto all men by theſe preſents.

Le Beu. The eldeſt of the three, wraſtled with *Charles* the Dukes Wraſtler, which *Charles* in a moment threw him, and broke three of his ribbes, that there is little hope of life in him: So he ſeru'd the ſecond, and ſo the third: yonder they lie, the poore old man their Father, making ſuch pittiful dole ouer them, that all the beholders take his part with weeping.

Roſ. Alas.

Clo. But what is the ſport Monſieur, that the Ladies haue loſt?

Le Beu. Why this that I ſpeake of.

Clo. Thus men may grow wiſer euery day. It is the firſt time that euer I heard breaking of ribbes was ſport for Ladies.

Cel. Or I, I promiſe thee.

Roſ. But is there any elſe longs to ſee this broken Muſicke in his ſides? Is there yet another doates vpon rib-breaking? Shall we ſee this wraſtling Coſin?

Le Beu. You muſt if you ſtay heere, for heere is the place appointed for the wraſtling, and they are ready to performe it.

Cel. Yonder ſure they are comming. Let vs now ſtay and ſee it.

Flouriſh. Enter Duke, Lords, Orlando, Charles, and Attendants.

Duke. Come on, ſince the youth will not be intreated
His owne perill on his forwardneſſe.

Roſ. Is yonder the man?

Le Beu. Euen he, Madam.

Cel. Alas, he is too yong: yet he looks ſucceſſefully

Du. How now daughter, and Couſin:
Are you crept hither to ſee the wraſtling?

Roſ. I my Liege, ſo pleaſe you giue vs leaue.

Du. You wil take little delight in it, I can tell you there is ſuch oddes in the man: In pitie of the challengers youth, I would faine diſſwade him, but he will not bee entreated. Speake to him Ladies, ſee if you can mooue him.

Cel. Call him hether good Monſieuer *Le Beu.*

Duke. Do ſo: Ile not be by.

Le Beu. Monſieur the Challenger, the Princeſſe cals for you.

Orl. I attend them with all reſpect and dutie.

Roſ. Young man, haue you challeng'd *Charles* the Wraſtler?

Orl. No faire Princeſſe: he is the generall challenger, I come but in as others do, to try with him the ſtrength of my youth.

Cel. Yong Gentleman, your ſpirits are too bold for your yeares: you haue ſeene cruell proofe of this mans ſtrength, if you ſaw your ſelfe with your eies, or knew your ſelfe with your iudgment, the feare of your aduenture would counſel you to a more equall enterpriſe. We pray you for your owne ſake to embrace your own ſafetie, and giue ouer this attempt.

Roſ. Do yong Sir, your reputation ſhall not therefore be miſpriſed: we wil make it our ſuite to the Duke, that the wraſtling might not go forward.

Orl. I beſeech you, puniſh mee not with your harde thoughts, wherein I confeſſe me much guiltie to denie ſo faire and excellent Ladies anie thing. But let your faire eies, and gentle wiſhes go with mee to my triall; wherein if I bee foil'd, there is but one ſham'd that vvas neuer gracious: if kil'd, but one dead that is willing to be ſo: I ſhall do my friends no wrong, for I haue none to lament me: the world no iniurie, for in it I haue nothing: onely in the world I fil vp a place, which may bee better ſupplied, when I haue made it emptie.

Roſ. The little ſtrength that I haue, I would it vvere with you.

Cel

Cel. And mine to eeke out hers.
Roſ. Fare you well: praie heauen I be deceiu'd in you.
Cel. Your hearts deſires be with you.
Char. Come, where is this yong gallant, that is ſo
deſirous to lie with his mother earth?
Orl. Readie Sir, but his will hath in it a more modeſt
working.
Duk. You ſhall trie but one fall.
Cha. No, I warrant your Grace you ſhall not entreat
him to a ſecond, that haue ſo mightilie perſwaded him
from a firſt.
Orl. You meane to mocke me after: you ſhould not
haue mockt me before: but come your waies.
Roſ. Now Hercules, be thy ſpeede yong man.
Cel. I would I were inuiſible, to catch the ſtrong fel-
low by the legge. *Wraſtle*
Roſ. Oh excellent yong man.
Cel. If I had a thunderbolt in mine eie, I can tell who
ſhould downe. *Shout*
Duk. No more, no more.
Orl. Yes I beſeech your Grace, I am not yet well
breath'd.
Duk. How do'ſt thou *Charles?*
Le Beu. He cannot ſpeake my Lord.
Duk. Beare him awaie:
What is thy name yong man?
Orl. *Orlando* my Liege, the yongeſt ſonne of Sir *Ro-
land de Boys.*
Duk. I would thou hadſt beene ſon to ſome man elſe,
The world eſteem'd thy father honourable,
But I did finde him ſtill mine enemie:
Thou ſhould'ſt haue better pleas'd me with this deede,
Hadſt thou deſcended from another houſe:
But fare thee well, thou art a gallant youth,
I would thou had'ſt told me of another Father.
Exit Duke.
Cel. Were I my Father (Coze) would I do this?
Orl. I am more proud to be Sir *Rolands* ſonne,
His yongeſt ſonne, and would not change that calling
To be adopted heire to *Fredricke.*
Roſ. My Father lou'd Sir *Roland* as his ſoule,
And all the world was of my Fathers minde,
Had I before knowne this yong man his ſonne,
I ſhould haue giuen him teares vnto entreaties,
Ere he ſhould thus haue ventur'd.
Cel. Gentle Coſen,
Let vs goe thanke him, and encourage him.
My Fathers rough and enuious diſpoſition
Sticks me at heart: Sir, you haue well deſeru'd,
If you doe keepe your promiſes in loue;
But iuſtly as you haue exceeded all promiſe,
Your Miſtris ſhall be happie.
Roſ. Gentleman,
Weare this for me: one out of ſuites with fortune
That could giue more, but that her hand lacks meanes.
Shall we goe Coze?
Cel. I: fare you well faire Gentleman.
Orl. Can I not ſay, I thanke you? My better parts
Are all throwne downe, and that which here ſtands vp
Is but a quintine, a meere liueleſſe blocke.
Roſ. He cals vs back: my pride fell with my fortunes,
Ile aske him what he would: Did you call Sir?
Sir, you haue wraſtled well, and ouerthrowne
More then your enemies.
Cel. Will you goe Coze?
Roſ. Haue with you: fare you well. *Exit.*
Orl. What paſſion hangs theſe waights vpō my toong?
I cannot ſpeake to her, yet ſhe vrg'd conference.

Enter Le Beu.

O poore *Orlando*! thou art ouerthrowne
Or Charles, or ſomething weaker maſters thee.
Le Beu. Good Sir, I do in friendſhip counſaile you
To leaue this place; Albeit you haue deſeru'd
High commendation, true applauſe, and loue;
Yet ſuch is now the Dukes condition,
That he miſconſters all that you haue done:
The Duke is humorous, what he is indeede
More ſuites you to conceiue, then I to ſpeake of.
Orl. I thanke you Sir; and pray you tell me this,
Which of the two was daughter of the Duke,
That here was at the Wraſtling?
Le Beu. Neither his daughter, if we iudge by manners,
But yet indeede the taller is his daughter,
The other is daughter to the baniſh'd Duke,
And here detain'd by her vſurping Vncle
To keepe his daughter companie, whoſe loues
Are deerer then the naturall bond of Siſters.
But I can tell you, that of late this Duke
Hath tane diſpleaſure 'gainſt his gentle Neece,
Grounded vpon no other argument,
But that the people praiſe her for her vertues,
And pittie her, for her good Fathers ſake;
And on my life his malice 'gainſt the Lady
Will ſodainly breake forth: Sir, fare you well,
Hereafter in a better world then this,
I ſhall deſire more loue and knowledge of you.
Orl. I reſt much bounden to you: fare you well.
Thus muſt I from the ſmoake into the ſmother,
From tyrant Duke, vnto a tyrant Brother.
But heauenly *Roſaline.* *Exit*

Scena Tertius.

Enter Celia and Roſaline.

Cel. Why Coſen, why *Roſaline*: *Cupid* haue mercie,
Not a word?
Roſ. Not one to throw at a dog.
Cel. No, thy words are too precious to be caſt away
vpon curs, throw ſome of them at me; come lame mee
with reaſons.
Roſ. Then there were two Coſens laid vp, when the
one ſhould be lam'd with reaſons, and the other mad
without any.
Cel. But is all this for your Father?
Roſ. No, ſome of it is for my childes Father: Oh
how full of briers is this working day world.
Cel. They are but burs, Coſen, throwne vpon thee
in holiday foolerie, if we walke not in the trodden paths
our very petty-coates will catch them.
Roſ. I could ſhake them off my coate, theſe burs are
in my heart.
Cel. Hem them away.
Roſ. I would try if I could cry hem, and haue him.
Cel. Come, come, wraſtle with thy affections.
Roſ. O they take the part of a better wraſtler then
my ſelfe.
Cel. O, a good wiſh vpon you: you will trie in time
in

in dispight of al all: but turning these iests out of seruice, let vs talke in good earnest: Is it possible on such a sodaine, you should fall into so strong a liking with old Sir *Roulands* yongest sonne?

Ros. The Duke my Father lou'd his Father deerelie.

Cel. Doth it therefore ensue that you should loue his Sonne deerelie? By this kinde of chase, I should hate him, for my father hated his father deerely; yet I hate not *Orlando.*

Ros. No faith, hate him not for my sake.

Cel Why should I not? doth he not deserue well?

Enter Duke with Lords.

Ros. Let me loue him for that, and do you loue him
Because I doe. Looke, here comes the Duke.
Cel. With his eies full of anger.
Duk. Mistris, dispatch you with your safest haste,
And get you from our Court.
Ros. Me Vncle.
Duk You Cosen,
Within these ten daies if that thou beest found
So neere our publike Court as twentie miles,
Thou diest for it.
Ros. I doe beseech your Grace
Let me the knowledge of my fault beare with me:
If with my selfe I hold intelligence,
Or haue acquaintance with mine owne desires,
If that I doe not dreame, or be not franticke,
(As I doe trust I am not) then deere Vncle,
Neuer so much as in a thought vnborne,
Did I offend your highnesse.
Duk. Thus doe all Traitors,
If their purgation did consist in words,
They are as innocent as grace it selfe;
Let it suffice thee that I trust thee not
Ros. Yet your mistrust cannot make me a Traitor;
Tell me whereon the likelihoods depends?
Duk. Thou art thy Fathers daughter, there's enough.
Ros. So was I when your highnes took his Dukdome,
So was I when your highnesse banisht him;
Treason is not inherited my Lord,
Or if we did deriue it from our friends,
What's that to me, my Father was no Traitor,
Then good my Leige, mistake me not so much,
To thinke my pouertie is treacherous.
Cel. Deere Soueraigne heare me speake.
Duk. I *Celia*, we staid her for your sake,
Else had she with her Father rang'd along.
Cel. I did not then intreat to haue her stay,
It was your pleasure, and your owne remorse,
I was too yong that time to value her,
But now I know her: if she be a Traitor,
Why so am I: we still haue slept together,
Rose at an instant, learn'd, plaid, eate together,
And wheresoere we went, like *Iunos* Swans,
Still we went coupled and inseperable.
Duk. She is too subtile for thee, and her smoothnes;
Her verie silence, and per patience,
Speake to the people, and they pittie her:
Thou art a foole, she robs thee of thy name,
And thou wilt show more bright, & seem more vertuous
When she is gone: then open not thy lips
Firme, and irreuocable is my doombe,
Which I haue past vpon her, she is banish'd.
Cel. Pronounce that sentence then on me my Leige,
I cannot liue out of her companie.
Duk. You are a foole: you Neice prouide your selfe,
If you out-stay the time, vpon mine honor,
And in the greatnesse of my word you die.
Exit Duke, &c.
Cel. O my poore *Rosaline*, whether wilt thou goe?
Wilt thou change Fathers? I will giue thee mine:
I charge thee be not thou more grieu'd then I am.
Ros. I haue more cause.
Cel. Thou hast not Cosen,
Prethee be cheerefull; know'st thou not the Duke
Hath banish'd me his daughter?
Ros. That he hath not
Cel. No, hath not? *Rosaline* lacks then the loue
Which teacheth thee that thou and I am one,
Shall we be sundred? shall we part sweete girle?
No, let my Father seeke another heire:
Therefore deuise with me how we may flie
Whether to goe, and what to beare with vs,
And doe not seeke to take your change vpon you,
To beare your griefes your selfe, and leaue me out
For by this heauen, now at our sorrowes pale;
Say what thou canst, Ile goe along with thee.
Ros. Why, whether shall we goe?
Cel. To seeke my Vncle in the Forrest of *Arden*
Ros. Alas, what danger will it be to vs,
(Maides as we are) to trauell forth so farre?
Beautie prouoketh theeues sooner then gold.
Cel. Ile put my selfe in poore and meane attire,
And with a kinde of vmber smirch my face,
The like doe you, so shall we passe along,
And neuer stir assailants.
Ros. Were it not better,
Because that I am more then common tall,
That I did suite me all points like a man,
A gallant curtelax vpon my thigh,
A bore-speare in my hand, and in my heart
Lye there what hidden womans feare there will,
Weele haue a swashing and a marshall outside,
As manie other mannish cowards haue,
That doe outface it with their semblances.
Cel. What shall I call thee when thou art a man?
Ros. Ile haue no worse a name then *Ioues* owne Page,
And therefore looke you call me *Ganimed.*
But what will you by call'd?
Cel. Something that hath a reference to my state:
No longer *Celia*, but *Aliena.*
Ros. But Cosen, what if we assaid to steale
The clownish Foole out of your Fathers Court:
Would he not be a comfort to our trauaile?
Cel. Heele goe along ore the wide world with me,
Leaue me alone to woe him; Let's away
And get our Iewels and our wealth together,
Deuise the fittest time, and safest way
To hide vs from pursuite that will be made
After my flight: now goe in we content
To libertie, and not to banishment. *Exeunt.*

Actus Secundus. Scœna Prima.

Enter Duke Senior: Amyens, and two or three Lords like Forresters.

Duk. Sen. Now my Coe-mates, and brothers in exile:
Hath not old custome made this life more sweete
Then

Then that of painted pompe? Are not theſe woods
More free from perill then the enuious Court?
Heere feele we not the penaltie of *Adam*,
The ſeaſons difference, as the Icie phange
And churliſh chiding of the winters winde,
Which when it bites and blowes vpon my body
Euen till I ſhrinke with cold, I ſmile, and ſay
This is no flattery: theſe are counſellors
That feelingly perſwade me what I am:
Sweet are the vſes of aduerſitie
Which like the toad, ougly and venemous,
Weares yet a precious Iewell in his head:
And this our life exempt from publike haunt,
Findes tongues in trees, bookes in the running brookes,
Sermons in ſtones, and good in euery thing.

Amien. I would not change it, happy is your Grace
That can tranſlate the ſtubbornneſſe of fortune
Into ſo quiet and ſo ſweet a ſtile.

Du.Sen. Come, ſhall we goe and kill vs veniſon?
And yet it irkes me the poore dapled fooles
Being natiue Burgers of this deſert City,
Should in their owne confines with forked heads
Haue their round hanches goard.

1.Lord. Indeed my Lord
The melancholy *Iaques* grieues at that,
And in that kinde ſweares you doe more vſurpe
Then doth your brother that hath baniſh'd you:
To day my Lord of *Amiens*, and my ſelfe,
Did ſteale behinde him as he lay along
Vnder an oake, whoſe anticke roote peepes out
Vpon the brooke that brawles along this wood,
To the which place a poore ſequeſtred Stag
That from the Hunters aime had tane a hurt,
Did come to languiſh; and indeed my Lord
The wretched annimall heau'd forth ſuch groanes
That their diſcharge did ſtretch his leatherne coat
Almoſt to burſting, and the big round teares
Cours'd one another downe his innocent noſe
In pitteous chaſe: and thus the hairie foole,
Much marked of the melancholie *Iaques*,
Stood on th'extremeſt verge of the ſwift brooke,
Augmenting it with teares.

Du.Sen. But what ſaid *Iaques*?
Did he not moralize this ſpectacle?

1.Lord. O yes, into a thouſand ſimilies.
Firſt, for his weeping into the needleſſe ſtreame;
Poore Deere quoth he, thou mak'ſt a teſtament
As worldlings doe, giuing thy ſum of more
To that which had too muſt: then being there alone,
Left and abandoned of his veluet friend;
'Tis right quoth he, thus miſerie doth part
The Fluxe of companie: anon a careleſſe Heard
Full of the paſture, iumps along by him
And neuer ſtaies to greet him: I quoth *Iaques*,
Sweepe on you fat and greazie Citizens,
'Tis iuſt the faſhion; wherefore doe you looke
Vpon that poore and broken bankrupt there?
Thus moſt inuectiuely he pierceth through
The body of Countrie, Citie, Court,
Yea, and of this our life, ſwearing that we
Are meere vſurpers, tyrants, and whats worſe
To fright the Annimals, and to kill them vp
In their aſſign'd and natiue dwelling place.

D.Sen. And did you leaue him in this contemplation?

2.Lord. We did my Lord, weeping and commenting
Vpon the ſobbing Deere.

Du.Sen. Show me the place,
I loue to cope him in theſe ſullen fits,
For then he's full of matter.

1.Lor. Ile bring you to him ſtrait. *Exeunt.*

Scena Secunda.

Enter Duke, with Lords.

Duk. Can it be poſſible that no man ſaw them?
It cannot be, ſome villaines of my Court
Are of conſent and ſufferance in this.

1.Lo. I cannot heare of any that did ſee her,
The Ladies her attendants of her chamber
Saw her a bed, and in the morning early,
They found the bed vntreaſur'd of their Miſtris.

2.Lor. My Lord, the royniſh Clown, at whom ſo
Your Grace was wont to laugh is alſo miſſing,
Hiſperia the Princeſſe Gentlewoman
Confeſſes that ſhe ſecretly ore-heard
Your daughter and her Coſen much commend
The parts and graces of the Wraſtler
That did but lately foile the ſynowie *Charles*,
And ſhe beleeues where euer they are gone
That youth is ſurely in their companie.

Duk. Send to his brother, fetch that gallant hither,
If he be abſent, bring his Brother to me,
Ile make him finde him: do this ſodainly;
And let not ſearch and inquiſition quaile,
To bring againe theſe fooliſh runawaies. *Exunt.*

Scena Tertia.

Enter Orlando and Adam.

Orl. Who's there?

Ad. What my yong Maſter, oh my gentle maſter,
Oh my ſweet maſter, O you memorie
Of old Sir *Rowland*; why, what make you here?
Why are you vertuous? Why do people loue you?
And wherefore are you gentle, ſtrong, and valiant?
Why would you be ſo fond to ouercome
The bonnie priſer of the humorous Duke?
Your praiſe is come too ſwiftly home before you.
Know you not Maſter, to ſeeme kinde of men,
Their graces ſerue them but as enemies,
No more doe yours: your vertues gentle Maſter
Are ſanctified and holy traitors to you:
Oh what a world is this, when what is comely
Enuenoms him that beares it?
Why, what's the matter?

Ad. O vnhappie youth,
Come not within theſe doores: within this roofe
The enemie of all your graces liues
Your brother, no, no brother, yet the ſonne
(Yet not the ſon, I will not call him ſon)
Of him I was about to call his Father,
Hath heard your praiſes, and this night he meanes,
To burne the lodging where you vſe to lye,
And you within it: if he faile of that

He

He will haue othet meanes to cut you off,
I ouerheard him: and his practises:
This is no place, this house is but a butcherie,
Abhorre it, feare it, doe not enter it.

Ad. Why whether *Adam* would'st thou haue me go?

Ad. No matter whether, so you come not here.

Orl. What, would'st thou haue me go & beg my food,
Or with a base and boistrous Sword enforce
A theeuish liuing on the common rode?
This I must do, or know not what to do:
Yet this I will not do, do how I can,
I rather will subiect me to the malice
Of a diuerted blood, and bloudie brother.

Ad. But do not so: I haue fiue hundred Crownes,
The thriftie hire I saued vnder your Father,
Which I did store to be my foster Nurse,
When seruice should in my old limbs lie lame,
And vnregarded age in corners throwne,
Take that, and he that doth the Rauens feede,
Yea prouidently caters for the Sparrow,
Be comfort to my age: here is the gold,
All this I giue you, let me be your seruant,
Though I looke old, yet I am strong and lustie;
For in my youth I neuer did apply
Hot, and rebellious liquors in my bloud,
Nor did not with vnbashfull forehead woe,
The meanes of weaknesse and debilitie,
Therefore my age is as a lustie winter,
Frostie, but kindely; let me goe with you,
Ile doe the seruice of a yonger man
In all your businesse and necessities.

Orl. Oh good old man, how well in thee appeares
The constant seruice of the antique world,
When seruice sweate for dutie, not for meede:
Thou art not for the fashion of these times,
Where none will sweate, but for promotion,
And hauing that do choake their seruice vp,
Euen with the hauing, it is not so with thee:
But poore old man, thou prun'st a rotten tree,
That cannot so much as a blossome yeelde,
In lieu of all thy paines and husbandrie,
But come thy waies, weele goe along together,
And ere we haue thy youthfull wages spent,
Weele light vpon some setled low content.

Ad. Master goe on, and I will follow thee
To the last gaspe with truth and loyaltie,
From seauentie yeeres, till now almost fourescore
Here liued I, but now liue here no more
At seauenteene yeeres, many their fortunes seeke
But at fourescore, it is too late a weeke,
Yet fortune cannot recompence me better
Then to die well, and not my Masters debter. *Exeunt.*

Scena Quarta.

Enter Rosaline for Ganimed, Celia for Aliena, and Clowne, alias Touchstone.

Ros. O *Iupiter*, how merry are my spirits?

Clo I care not for my spirits, if my legges were not wearie.

Ros. I could finde in my heart to disgrace my mans apparell, and to cry like a woman: but I must comfort the weaker vessell, as doublet and hose ought to show it selfe coragious to petty-coate; therefore courage, good *Aliena.*

Cel. I pray you beare with me, I cannot goe no further.

Clo. For my part, I had rather beare with you, then beare you: yet I should beare no crosse if I did beare you, for I thinke you haue no money in your purse.

Ros. Well, this is the Forrest of *Arden.*

Clo. I, now am I in *Arden*, the more foole I, when I was at home I was in a better place, but Trauellers must be content.

Enter Corin and Siluius.

Ros. I, be so good *Touchstone*: Look you, who comes here, a yong man and an old in solemne talke.

Cor. That is the way to make her scorne you still.

Sil. Oh *Corin*, that thou knew'st how I do loue her.

Cor. I partly guesse: for I haue lou'd ere now.

Sil. No *Corin*, being old, thou canst not guesse,
Though in thy youth thou wast as true a louer
As euer sigh'd vpon a midnight pillow:
But if thy loue were euer like to mine,
As sure I thinke did neuer man loue so:
How many actions most ridiculous,
Hast thou beene drawne to by thy fantasie?

Cor. Into a thousand that I haue forgotten.

Sil. Oh thou didst then neuer loue so hartily
If thou remembrest not the slightest folly,
That euer loue did make thee run into,
Thou hast not lou'd.
Or if thou hast not sat as I doe now,
Wearing thy hearer in thy Mistris praise,
Thou hast not lou'd.
Or if thou hast not broke from companie,
Abruptly as my passion now makes me,
Thou hast not lou'd.
O *Phebe, Phebe, Phebe.* *Exit.*

Ros. Alas poore Shepheard searching of they would,
I haue by hard aduenture found mine owne.

Clo. And I mine: I remember when I was in loue, I broke my sword vpon a stone, and bid him take that for comming a night to *Iane Smile*, and I remember the kissing of her batler, and the Cowes dugs that her prettie chopt hands had milk'd; and I remember the wooing of a peascod instead of her, from whom I tooke two cods, and giuing her them againe, said with weeping teares, weare these for my sake: wee that are true Louers, runne into strange capers; but as all is mortall in nature, so is all nature in loue, mortall in folly.

Ros. Thou speak'st wiser then thou art ware of.

Clo. Nay, I shall nere be ware of mine owne wit, till I breake my shins against it.

Ros. *Ioue, Ioue*, this Shepherds passion,
Is much vpon my fashion.

Clo. And mine, but it growes something stale with mee.

Cel. I pray you, one of you question yon'd man,
If he for gold will giue vs any foode,
I faint almost to death.

Clo. Holla; you Clowne.

Ros. Peace foole, he's not thy kinsman.

Cor. Who cals?

Clo. Your betters Sir.

Cor. Else are they very wretched.

Ros. Peace

Ros. Peace I say; good euen to your friend.
Cor. And to you gentle Sir, and to you all.
Ros. I prethee Shepheard, if that loue or gold
Can in this desert place buy entertainment,
Bring vs where we may rest our selues, and feed:
Here's a yong maid with trauaile much oppressed,
And faints for succour.
Cor. Faire Sir, I pittie her,
And wish for her sake more then for mine owne,
My fortunes were more able to releeue her:
But I am shepheard to another man,
And do not sheere the Fleeces that I graze:
My master is of churlish disposition,
And little wreakes to finde the way to heauen
By doing deeds of hospitalitie.
Besides his Coate, his Flockes, and bounds of feede
Are now on sale, and at our sheep-coat now
By reason of his absence there is nothing
That you will feed on: but what is, come see,
And in my voice most welcome shall you be
Ros. What is he that shall buy his flocke and pasture?
Cor. That yong Swaine that you saw heere but erewhile,
That little cares for buying any thing.
Ros. I pray thee, if it stand with honestie,
Buy thou the Cottage, pasture, and the flocke,
And thou shalt haue to pay for it of vs.
Cel. And we will mend thy wages:
I like this place, and willingly could
Waste my time in it.
Cor. Assuredly the thing is to be sold:
Go with me, if you like vpon report,
The soile, the profit, and this kinde of life,
I will your very faithfull Feeder be,
And buy it with your Gold right sodainly. *Exeunt.*

Scena Quinta.

Enter, Amyens, Iaques, & others.

Song.

Vnder the greene wood tree,
who loues to lye with mee,
And turne his merrie Note,
vnto the sweet Birds throte
Come hither, come hither, come hither:
Heere shall he see no enemie,
But Winter and rough Weather.

Iaq. More, more, I pre'thee more.
Amy. It will make you melancholly Monsieur *Iaques*
Iaq. I thanke it: More, I prethee more,
I can sucke melancholly out of a song,
As a Weazel suckes egges: More, I pre'thee more.
Amy. My voice is ragged, I know I cannot please you.
Iaq. I do not desire you to please me,
I do desire you to sing:
Come, more, another stanzo: Cal you'em stanzo's.
Amy. What you wil Monsieur *Iaques.*
Iaq. Nay, I care not for their names, they owe mee nothing. Wil you sing?
Amy. More at your request, then to please my selfe.
Iaq Well then, if euer I thanke any man, Ile thanke you: but that they cal complement is like th'encounter of two dog-Apes. And when a man thankes me hartily, me thinkes I haue giuen him a penie, and he renders me the beggerly thankes. Come sing; and you that wil not hold your tongues.
Amy. Wel, Ile end the song. Sirs, couer the while, the Duke wil drinke vnder this tree; he hath bin all this day to looke you.
Iaq. And I haue bin all this day to auoid him.
He is too disputeable for my companie:
I thinke of as many matters as he, but I giue
Heauen thankes, and make no boast of them.
Come, warble, come

Song. *Altogether heere.*

Who doth ambition shunne,
and loues to liue i'th Sunne:
Seeking the food he eates,
and pleas'd with what he gets:
Come hither, come hither, come hither,
Heere shall he see. &c.

Iaq. Ile giue you a verse to this note,
That I made yesterday in despight of my Inuention.
Amy. And Ile sing it.
Amy. Thus it goes.
If it do come to passe, that any man turne Asse:
Leauing his wealth and ease,
A stubborne will to please,
Ducdame, ducdame, ducdame:
Heere shall he see, grosse fooles as he,
And if he will come to me.
Amy. What's that Ducdame?
Iaq. 'Tis a Greeke inuocation to call fools into a circle. Ile go sleepe if I can: if I cannot, Ile raile against all the first borne of Egypt.
Amy. And Ile go seeke the Duke,
His banket is prepar'd. *Exeunt*

Scena Sexta.

Enter Orlando, & Adam.

Adam. Deere Master, I can go no further:
O I die for food. Heere lie I downe,
And measure out my graue. Farwel kinde master.
Orl. Why how now *Adam*? No greater heart in thee:
Liue a little, comfort a little, cheere thy selfe a little.
If this vncouth Forrest yeeld any thing sauage,
I wil either be food for it, or bring it for foode to thee
Thy conceite is neerer death, then thy powers.
For my sake be comfortable, hold death a while
At the armes end: I wil heere be with thee presently,
And if I bring thee not something to eate,
I wil giue thee leaue to die: but if thou diest
Before I come, thou art a mocker of my labor.
Wel said, thou look'st cheerely,
And Ile be with thee quickly: yet thou liest
In the bleake aire. Come, I wil beare thee
To some shelter, and thou shalt not die
For lacke of a dinner,
If there liue any thing in this Desert.
Cheerely good *Adam.* *Exeunt*

Scena

Scena Septima.

Enter Duke Sen. & Lord, like Out-lawes.

Du.Sen. I thinke he be transform'd into a beaſt,
For I can no where finde him, like a man.
1. Lord. My Lord, he is but euen now gone hence,
Heere was he merry, hearing of a Song.
Du Sen. If he compact of iarres, grow Muſicall,
We ſhall haue ſhortly diſcord in the Spheares:
Go ſeeke him, tell him I would ſpeake with him.

Enter Iaques.

1.Lord. He ſaues my labor by his owne approach.
Du.Sen. Why how now Monſieur, what a life is this
That your poore friends muſt woe your companie,
What, you looke merrily.
Iaq. A Foole, a foole: I met a foole i'th Forreſt,
A motley Foole (a miſerable world:)
As I do liue by foode, I met a foole,
Who laid him downe, and bask'd him in the Sun,
And rail'd on Lady Fortune in good termes,
In good ſet termes, and yet a motley foole.
Good morrow foole (quoth I:) no Sir, quoth he,
Call me not foole, till heauen hath ſent me fortune,
And then he drew a diall from his poake,
And looking on it, with lacke-luſtre eye,
Sayes, very wiſely, it is ten a clocke:
Thus we may ſee (quoth he) how the world wagges:
'Tis but an houre agoe, ſince it was nine,
And after one houre more, 'twill be eleuen,
And ſo from houre to houre, we ripe, and ripe,
And then from houre to houre, we rot, and rot,
And thereby hangs a tale. When I did heare
The motley Foole, thus morall on the time,
My Lungs began to crow like Chanticleere,
That Fooles ſhould be ſo deepe contemplatiue:
And I did laugh, ſans intermiſſion
An houre by his diall. Oh noble foole,
A worthy foole: Motley's the onely weare.
Du.Sen. What foole is this?
Iaq. O worthie Foole: One that hath bin a Courtier
And ſayes, if Ladies be but yong, and faire,
They haue the gift to know it: and in his braine,
Which is as drie as the remainder bisket
After a voyage: He hath ſtrange places cram'd
With obſeruation, the which he vents
In mangled formes. O that I were a foole,
I am ambitious for a motley coat.
Du.Sen. Thou ſhalt haue one.
Iaq. It is my onely ſuite,
Prouided that you weed your better iudgements
Of all opinion that growes ranke in them,
That I am wiſe. I muſt haue liberty
Withall, as large a Charter as the winde,
To blow on whom I pleaſe, for ſo fooles haue:
And they that are moſt gauled with my folly,
They moſt muſt laugh: And why ſir muſt they ſo?
The why is plaine, as way to Pariſh Church:
Hee, that a Foole doth very wiſely hit,
Doth very fooliſhly, although he ſmart
Seeme ſenſeleſſe of the bob. If not,
The Wiſe-mans folly is anathomiz'd
Euen by the ſquandring glances of the foole.
Inueſt me in my motley: Giue me leaue
To ſpeake my minde, and I will through and through
Cleanſe the foule bodie of th'infected world,
If they will patiently receiue my medicine.
Du.Sen. Fie on thee. I can tell what thou wouldſt do
Iaq. What, for a Counter, would I do, but good?
Du.Sen. Moſt miſcheeuous foule ſin, in chiding ſin:
For thou thy ſelfe haſt bene a Libertine,
As ſenſuall as the brutiſh ſting it ſelfe,
And all th'imboſſed ſores, and headed euils,
That thou with licenſe of free foot haſt caught,
Would'ſt thou diſgorge into the generall world
Iaq. Why who cries out on pride,
That can therein taxe any priuate party:
Doth it not flow as hugely as the Sea,
Till that the wearie verie meanes do ebbe.
What woman in the Citie do I name,
When that I ſay the City woman beares
The coſt of Princes on vnworthy ſhoulders?
Who can come in, and ſay that I meane her,
When ſuch a one as ſhee, ſuch is her neighbor?
Or what is he of baſeſt function,
That ſayes his brauerie is not on my coſt,
Thinking that I meane him, but therein ſuites
His folly to the mettle of my ſpeech,
There then, how then, what then, let me ſee wherein
My tongue hath wrong'd him: if it do him right,
Then he hath wrong'd himſelfe: if he be free,
why then my taxing like a wild-gooſe flies
Vnclaim'd of any man But who come here?

Enter Orlando.

Orl. Forbeare, and eate no more.
Iaq. Why I haue eate none yet.
Orl. Nor ſhalt not, till neceſſity be ſeru'd.
Iaq. Of what kinde ſhould this Cocke come of?
Du.Sen. Art thou thus bolden'd man by thy diſtres?
Or elſe a rude deſpiſer of good manners,
That in ciuility thou ſeem'ſt ſo emptie?
Orl. You touch'd my veine at firſt, the thorny point
Of bare diſtreſſe, hath tane from me the ſhew
Of ſmooth ciuility: yet am I in-land bred,
And know ſome nourture: But forbeare, I ſay,
He dies that touches any of this fruite,
Till I, and my affaires are anſwered.
Iaq. And you will not be anſwer'd with reaſon,
I muſt dye.
Du.Sen What would you haue?
Your gentleneſſe ſhall force, more then your force
Moue vs to gentleneſſe.
Orl. I almoſt die for food, and let me haue it.
Du.Sen. Sit downe and feed, & welcom to our table
Orl. Speake you ſo gently? Pardon me I pray you,
I thought that all things had bin ſauage heere,
And therefore put I on the countenance
Of ſterne command'ment. But what ere you are
That in this deſert inacceſſible,
Vnder the ſhade of melancholly boughes,
Looſe, and neglect the creeping houres of time:
If euer you haue look'd on better dayes:
If euer beene where bels haue knoll'd to Church:
If euer ſate at any good mans feaſt:
If euer from your eye-lids wip'd a teare,
And know what 'tis to pittie, and be pittied:
Let gentleneſſe my ſtrong enforcement be,
In the which hope, I bluſh, and hide my Sword

R *Duke*

Du. Sen. True is it, that we haue seene better dayes
And haue with holy bell bin knowld to Church,
And sat at good mens feasts, and wip'd our eies
Of drops, that sacred pity hath engendred:
And therefore sit you downe in gentlenesse,
And take vpon command, what helpe we haue
That to your wanting may be ministred.
Orl. Then but forbeare your food a little while:
Whiles (like a Doe) I go to finde my Fawne,
And giue it food. There is an old poore man,
Who after me, hath many a weary steppe
Limpt in pure loue: till he be first suffic'd,
Opprest with two weake euils, age, and hunger,
I will not touch a bit.
Duke Sen. Go finde him out,
And we will nothing waste till you returne.
Orl. I thanke ye, and be blest for your good comfort.
Du Sen. Thou seest, we are not all alone vnhappie:
This wide and vniuersall Theater
Presents more wofull Pageants then the Sceane
Wherein we play in.
Ja. All the world's a stage,
And all the men and women, meerely Players;
They haue their *Exits* and their Entrances,
And one man in his time playes many parts,
His Acts being seuen ages. At first the Infant,
Mewling, and puking in the Nurses armes:
Then, the whining Schoole-boy with his Satchell
And shining morning face, creeping like snaile
Vnwillingly to schoole. And then the Louer,
Sighing like Furnace, with a wofull ballad
Made to his Mistresse eye-brow. Then, a Soldier,
Full of strange oaths, and bearded like the Pard,
Ielous in honor, sodaine, and quicke in quarrell,
Seeking the bubble Reputation
Euen in the Canons mouth: And then, the Iustice,
In faire round belly, with good Capon lin'd,
With eyes seuere, and beard of formall cut,
Full of wise sawes, and moderne instances,
And so he playes his part. The sixt age shifts
Into the leane and slipper'd Pantaloone,
With spectacles on nose, and pouch on side,
His youthfull hose well sau'd, a world too wide,
For his shrunke shanke, and his bigge manly voice,
Turning againe toward childish trebble pipes,
And whistles in his sound. Last Scene of all,
That ends this strange euentfull historie,
Is second childishnesse, and meere obliuion,
Sans teeth, sans eyes, sans taste, sans euery thing.

Enter Orlando with Adam.

Du Sen. Welcome: set downe your venerable burthen, and let him feede.
Orl. I thanke you most for him
Ad. So had you neede,
I scarce can speake to thanke you for my selfe.
Du. Sen. Welcome, fall too: I wil not trouble you,
As yet to question you about your fortunes:
Giue vs some Musicke, and good Cozen, sing.

Song.

Blow, blow, thou winter winde,
Thou art not so vnkinde, as mans ingratitude
Thy tooth is not so keene, because thou art not seene,
although thy breath be rude.
Heigh ho, sing heigh ho, vnto the greene holly,
Most frendship, is fayning; most Louing, meere folly:
The heigh ho, the holly,
This Life is most iolly.

Freize, freize, thou bitter skie that dost not bight so nigh
as benefitts forgot:
Though thou the waters warpe, thy sting is not so sharpe,
as freind remembred not
Heigh ho, sing, &c.

Duke Sen. If that you were the good Sir *Rowlands* son,
As you haue whisper'd faithfully you were,
And as mine eye doth his effigies witnesse,
Most truly limn'd, and liuing in your face,
Be truly welcome hither: I am the Duke
That lou'd your Father, the residue of your fortune,
Go to my Caue, and tell mee. Good old man,
Thou art right welcome, as thy masters is:
Support him by the arme: giue me your hand,
And let me all your fortunes vnderstand. *Exeunt.*

Actus Tertius. Scena Prima.

Enter Duke, Lords, & Oliuer.

Du. Not see him since? Sir, sir, that cannot be:
But were I not the better part made mercie,
I should not seeke an absent argument
Of my reuenge, thou present: but looke to it,
Finde out thy brother wheresoere he is,
Seeke him with Candle: bring him dead, or liuing
Within this tweluemonth, or turne thou no more
To seeke a liuing in our Territorie.
Thy Lands and all things that thou dost call thine,
Worth seizure, do we seize into our hands,
Till thou canst quit thee by thy brothers mouth,
Of what we thinke against thee.
Ol. Oh that your Highnesse knew my heart in this:
I neuer lou'd my brother in my life.
Duke. More villaine thou. Well push him out of dores
And let my officers of such a nature
Make an extent vpon his house and Lands:
Do this expediently, and turne him going. *Exeunt*

Scena Secunda.

Enter Orlando.

Orl. Hang there my verse, in witnesse of my loue,
And thou thrice crowned Queene of night suruey
With thy chaste eye, from thy pale spheare aboue
Thy Huntresse name, that my full life doth sway.
O *Rosalind*, these Trees shall be my Bookes,
And in their barkes my thoughts Ile charracter,
That euerie eye, which in this Forrest lookes,
Shall see thy vertue witnest euery where.
Run, run *Orlando*, carue on euery Tree,
The faire, the chaste, and vnexpressiue shee. *Exit*

Enter Corin & Clowne.

Co. And how like you this shepherds life Mr *Touchstone?*
Clo.

Clow. Truely Shepheard, in reſpect of it ſelfe, it is a good life; but in reſpect that it is a ſhepheards life, it is naught. In reſpect that it is ſolitary, I like it verie well: but in reſpect that it is priuate, it is a very vild life. Now in reſpect it is in the fields, it pleaſeth mee well: but in reſpect it is not in the Court, it is tedious. As it is a ſpare life (looke you) it fits my humor well: but as there is no more plentie in it, it goes much againſt my ſtomacke. Has't any Philoſophie in thee ſhepheard?

Cor. No more, but that I know the more one ſickens, the worſe at eaſe he is: and that hee that wants money, meanes, and content, is without three good frends. That the propertie of raine is to wet, and fire to burne: That pood paſture makes fat ſheepe: and that a great cauſe of the night, is lacke of the Sunne: That hee that hath learned no wit by Nature, nor Art, may complaine of good breeding, or comes of a very dull kindred.

Clo. Such a one is a naturall Philoſopher Was't euer in Court, Shepheard?

Cor. No truly.

Clo. Then thou art damn'd.

Cor. Nay, I hope.

Clo. Truly thou art damn'd, like an ill roaſted Egge, all on one ſide.

Cor. For not being at Court? your reaſon.

Clo. Why, if thou neuer was't at Court, thou neuer ſaw'ſt good manners: if thou neuer ſaw'ſt good maners, then thy manners muſt be wicked, and wickednes is ſin, and ſinne is damnation: Thou art in a parlous ſtate ſhepheard.

Cor. Not a whit *Touchſtone*, thoſe that are good maners at the Court, are as ridiculous in the Countrey, as the behauiour of the Countrie is moſt mockeable at the Court. You told me, you ſalute not at the Court, but you kiſſe your hands; that courteſie would be vncleanlie if Courtiers were ſhepheards.

Clo. Inſtance, briefly: come, inſtance.

Cor. Why we are ſtill handling our Ewes, and their Fels you know are greaſie.

Clo. Why do not your Courtiers hands ſweate? and is not the greaſe of a Mutton, as wholeſome as the ſweat of a man? Shallow, ſhallow: A better inſtance I ſay: Come.

Cor. Beſides, our hands are hard.

Clo. Your lips wil feele them the ſooner. Shallow agen: a more ſounder inſtance, come.

Cor. And they are often tarr'd ouer, with the ſurgery of our ſheepe: and would you haue vs kiſſe Tarre? The Courtiers hands are perfum'd with Ciuet.

Clo. Moſt ſhallow man: Thou wormes meate in reſpect of a good peece of fleſh indeed: learne of the wiſe and perpend: Ciuet is of a baſer birth then Tarre, the verie vncleanly fluxe of a Cat. Mend the inſtance Shepheard.

Cor. You haue too Courtly a wit, for me, Ile reſt.

Clo. Wilt thou reſt damn'd? God helpe thee ſhallow man: God make inciſion in thee, thou art raw.

Cor. Sir, I am a true Labourer, I earne that I eate: get that I weare; owe no man hate, enuie no mans happineſſe: glad of other mens good content with my harme: and the greateſt of my pride, is to ſee my Ewes graze, & my Lambes ſucke.

Clo. That is another ſimple ſinne in you, to bring the Ewes and the Rammes together, and to offer to get your liuing, by the copulation of Cattle, to be bawd to a Belweather, and to betray a ſhee-Lambe of a tweluemonth to a crooked-pated olde Cuckoldly Ramme, out of all reaſonable match. If thou bee'ſt not damn'd for this, the diuell himſelfe will haue no ſhepherds, I cannot ſee elſe how thou ſhouldſt ſcape.

Cor. Heere comes yong Mr *Ganimed*, my new Miſtriſſes Brother.

Enter Roſalind.

Roſ. From the eaſt to weſterne Inde,
no iewel is like Roſalinde,
Hir worth being mounted on the winde,
through all the world beares Roſalinde.
All the pictures faireſt Linde,
are but blacke to Roſalinde:
Let no face bee kept in mind,
but the faire of Roſalinde.

Clo. Ile rime you ſo, eight yeares together; dinners, and ſuppers, and ſleeping hours excepted: it is the right Butter-womens ranke to Market.

Roſ. Out Foole.

Clo. For a taſte.

If a Hart doe lacke a Hinde,
Let him ſeeke out Roſalinde:
If the Cat will after kinde,
ſo be ſure will Roſalinde:
Wintred garments muſt be linde,
ſo muſt ſlender Roſalinde:
They that reap muſt ſheafe and binde,
then to cart with Roſalinde.
Sweeteſt nut, hath ſowreſt rinde,
ſuch a nut is Roſalinde.
He that ſweeteſt roſe will finde,
muſt finde Loues pricke, & Roſalinde.

This is the verie falſe gallop of Verſes, why doe you infect your ſelfe with them?

Roſ. Peace you dull foole, I found them on a tree.

Clo. Truely the tree yeelds bad fruite.

Roſ. Ile graffe it with you, and then I ſhall graffe it with a Medler: then it will be the earlieſt fruit i'th country: for you'l be rotten ere you bee halfe ripe, and that's the right vertue of the Medler.

Clo. You haue ſaid: but whether wiſely or no, let the Forreſt iudge.

Enter Celia with a writing.

Roſ. Peace, here comes my ſiſter reading, ſtand aſide.

Cel. Why ſhould this Deſert bee,
for it is vnpeopled? Noe:
Tonges Ile hang on euerie tree,
that ſhall ciuill ſayings ſhoe.
Some, how brieſe the Life of man
runs his erring pilgrimage,
That the ſtretching of a ſpan,
buckles in his ſumme of age.
Some of violated vowes,
twixt the ſoules of friend, and friend:
But vpon the faireſt bowes,
or at euerie ſentence end;
Will I Roſalinda write,
teaching all that reade, to know
The quinteſſence of euerie ſprite,
heauen would in little ſhow.
Therefore heauen Nature charg'd,
that one bodie ſhould be fill'd
With all Graces wide enlarg'd,
nature preſently diſtill'd

R 3 *Helens*

Helens cheeke, but not his heart,
Cleopatra's *Maieſtie;*
Attalanta's *better part,*
ſad Lucrecia's *Modeſtie.*
Thus Roſalinde *of manie parts,*
by Heauenly Synode was deuis'd,
Of manie faces, eyes, and hearts,
to haue the touches deereſt pris'd.
Heauen would that ſhee theſe gifts ſhould haue,
and I to liue and die her ſlaue.

Roſ. O moſt gentle Iupiter, what tedious homilie of Loue haue you wearied your pariſhioners withall, and neuer cri'de, haue patience good people.

Cel. How now backe friends: Shepheard, go off a little: go with him ſirrah.

Clo. Come Shepheard, let vs make an honorable retreit, though not with bagge and baggage, yet with ſcrip and ſcrippage. *Exit.*

Cel. Didſt thou heare theſe verſes?

Roſ. O yes, I heard them all, and more too, for ſome of them had in them more feete then the Verſes would beare.

Cel. That's no matter: the feet might beare ÿ verſes.

Roſ. I, but the feet were lame, and could not beare themſelues without the verſe, and therefore ſtood lamely in the verſe.

Cel. But didſt thou heare without wondering, how thy name ſhould be hang'd and carued vpon theſe trees?

Roſ. I was ſeuen of the nine daies out of the wonder, before you came: for looke heere what I found on a Palme tree; I was neuer ſo berim'd ſince *Pythagoras* time that I was an Iriſh Rat, which I can hardly remember.

Cel. Tro you, who hath done this?

Roſ. Is it a man?

Cel. And a chaine that you once wore about his neck: change you colour?

Roſ. I pre'thee who?

Cel. O Lord, Lord, it is a hard matter for friends to meete; but Mountaines may bee remoou'd with Earthquakes, and ſo encounter.

Roſ. Nay, but who is it?

Cel. Is it poſſible?

Roſ. Nay, I pre'thee now, with moſt petitionary vehemence, tell me who it is.

Cel. O wonderfull, wonderfull, and moſt wonderfull wonderfull, and yet againe wonderful, and after that out of all hooping.

Roſ. Good my complection, doſt thou think though I am capariſon'd like a man, I haue a doublet and hoſe in my diſpoſition? One inch of delay more, is a South-ſea of diſcouerie. I pre'thee tell me, who is it quickely, and ſpeake apace: I would thou couldſt ſtammer, that thou might ſt powre this conceal'd man out of thy mouth, as Wine comes out of a narrow-mouth'd bottle: either too much at once, or none at all. I pre'thee take the Corke out of thy mouth, that I may drinke thy tydings.

Cel. So you may put a man in your belly.

Roſ. Is he of Gods making? What manner of man? Is his head worth a hat? Or his chin worth a beard?

Cel. Nay, he hath but a little beard.

Roſ. Why God will ſend more, if the man will bee thankful: let me ſtay the growth of his beard, if thou delay me not the knowledge of his chin.

Cel. It is yong *Orlando*, that tript vp the Wraſtlers heeles, and your heart, both in an inſtant.

Roſ. Nay, but the diuell take mocking: ſpeake ſadde brow, and true maid

Cel. I'faith (Coz) tis he.

Roſ. *Orlando?*

Cel. *Orlando.*

Roſ. Alas the day, what ſhall I do with my doublet & hoſe? What did he when thou ſaw'ſt him? What ſayde he? How look'd he? Wherein went he? What makes hee heere? Did he aske for me? Where remaines he? How parted he with thee? And when ſhalt thou ſee him againe? Anſwer me in one vvord.

Cel. You muſt borrow me Gargantuas mouth firſt: 'tis a Word too great for any mouth of this Ages ſize, to ſay I and no, to theſe particulars, is more then to anſwer in a Catechiſme.

Roſ. But doth he know that I am in this Forreſt, and in mans apparrell? Looks he as freſhly, as he did the day he Wraſtled?

Cel. It is as eaſie to count Atomies as to reſolue the propoſitions of a Louer: but take a taſte of my finding him, and relliſh it with good obſeruance. I found him vnder a tree like a drop'd Acorne.

Roſ. It may vvel be cal'd Ioues tree, when it droppes forth fruite.

Cel. Giue me audience, good Madam.

Roſ. Proceed.

Cel. There lay hee ſtretch'd along like a Wounded knight.

Roſ. Though it be pittie to ſee ſuch a ſight, it vvell becomes the ground.

Cel. Cry holla, to the tongue, I prethee: it curuettes vnſeaſonably. He was furniſh'd like a Hunter.

Roſ. O ominous, he comes to kill my Hart.

Cel. I would ſing my ſong without a burthen, thou bring'ſt me out of tune.

Roſ. Do you not know I am a woman, when I thinke, I muſt ſpeake: ſweet, ſay on.

Enter Orlando & Iaques.

Cel. You bring me out. Soft, comes he not heere?

Roſ. 'Tis he, ſlinke by, and note him.

Iaq I thanke you for your company, but good faith I had as liefe haue beene my ſelfe alone.

Orl. And ſo had I: but yet for faſhion ſake I thanke you too, for your ſocietie.

Iaq. God buy you, let's meet as little as we can.

Orl. I do deſire we may be better ſtrangers.

Iaq. I pray you marre no more trees vvith Writing Loue-ſongs in their barkes.

Orl. I pray you marre no moe of my verſes with reading them ill-fauouredly.

Iaq. *Roſalinde* is your loues name? *Orl.* Yes, Iuſt.

Iaq. I do not like her name.

Orl. There was no thought of pleaſing you when ſhe was chriſten'd.

Iaq. What ſtature is ſhe of?

Orl. Iuſt as high as my heart.

Iaq. You are ful of pretty anſwers: haue you not bin acquainted with goldſmiths wiues, & cond the out of rings

Orl. Not ſo: but I anſwer you right painted cloath, from whence you haue ſtudied your queſtions.

Iaq. You haue a nimble wit; I thinke twas made of *Attalanta's* heeles. Will you ſitte downe with me, and wee two, will raile againſt our Miſtris the world, and all our miſerie.

Orl. I wil chide no breather in the world but my ſelfe againſt

against whom I know most faults.

Iaq. The worst fault you haue, is to be in loue.

Orl. 'Tis a fault I will not change, for your best vertue: I am wearie of you.

Iaq. By my troth, I was seeking for a Foole, when I found you.

Orl. He is drown'd in the brooke, looke but in, and you shall see him.

Iaq. There I shal see mine owne figure.

Orl. Which I take to be either a foole, or a Cipher.

Iaq. Ile tarrie no longer with you, farewell good signior Loue.

Orl. I am glad of your departure: Adieu good Monsieur Melancholly.

Ros. I wil speake to him like a sawcie Lacky, and vnder that habit play the knaue with him, do you hear Forrester.

Orl. Verie wel, what would you?

Ros. I pray you, what i'st a clocke?

Orl. You should aske me what time o'day: there's no clocke in the Forrest.

Ros. Then there is no true Louer in the Forrest, else sighing euerie minute and groaning euerie houre wold detect the lazie foot of time, as wel as a clocke.

Orl. And why not the swift foote of time? Had not that bin as proper?

Ros. By no meanes sir; Time trauels in diuers paces, with diuers persons: Ile tel you who Time ambles withall, who Time trots withal, who Time gallops withal, and who he stands stil withall.

Orl. I prethee, who doth he trot withal?

Ros. Marry he trots hard with a yong maid, between the contract of her marriage, and the day it is solemnizd: if the interim be but a sennight, Times pace is so hard, that it seemes the length of seuen yeare.

Orl. Who ambles Time withal?

Ros. With a Priest that lacks Latine, and a rich man that hath not the Gowt: for the one sleepes easily because he cannot study, and the other liues merrily, because he feeles no paine: the one lacking the burthen of leane and wastefull Learning; the other knowing no burthen of heauie tedious penurie. These Time ambles withal.

Orl. Who doth he gallop withal?

Ros. With a theefe to the gallowes: for though hee go as softly as foot can fall, he thinkes himselfe too soon there.

Orl. Who staies it stil withal?

Ros. With Lawiers in the vacation: for they sleepe betweene Terme and Terme, and then they perceiue not how time moues.

Orl. Where dwel you prettie youth?

Ros. With this Shepheardesse my sister: heere in the skirts of the Forrest, like fringe vpon a petticoat.

Orl. Are you natiue of this place?

Ros. As the Conie that you see dwell where shee is kindled.

Orl. Your accent is something finer, then you could purchase in so remoued a dwelling.

Ros. I haue bin told so of many: but indeed, an olde religious Vnckle of mine taught me to speake, who was in his youth an inland man, one that knew Courtship too well: for there he fel in loue. I haue heard him read many Lectors against it, and I thanke God, I am not a Woman to be touch'd with so many giddie offences as hee hath generally tax'd their whole sex withal.

Orl. Can you remember any of the principall euils, that he laid to the charge of women?

Ros. There were none principal, they were all like one another, as halfe pence are, euerie one fault seeming monstrous, til his fellow-fault came to match it.

Orl. I prethee recount some of them.

Ros. No: I wil not cast away my physick, but on those that are sicke. There is a man haunts the Forrest, that abuses our yong plants with caruing *Rosalinde* on their barkes; hangs Oades vpon Hauthornes, and Elegies on brambles; all (forsooth) defying the name of *Rosalinde*. If I could meet that Fancie-monger, I would giue him some good counsel, for he seemes to haue the Quotidian of Loue vpon him.

Orl. I am he that is so Loue-shak'd, I pray you tel me your remedie.

Ros. There is none of my Vnckles markes vpon you: he taught me how to know a man in loue: in which cage of rushes, I am sure you art not prisoner.

Orl. What were his markes?

Ros. A leane cheeke, which you haue not: a blew eie and sunken, which you haue not: an vnquestionable spirit, which you haue not: a beard neglected, which you haue not: (but I pardon you for that, for simply your hauing in beard, is a yonger brothers reuennew) then your hose should be vngarter'd, your bonnet vnbanded, your sleeue vnbutton'd, your shoo vnti'de, and euerie thing about you, demonstrating a carelesse desolation: but you are no such man; you are rather point deuice in your accoustrements, as louing your selfe, then seeming the Louer of any other.

Orl. Faire youth, I would I could make thee beleeue I Loue.

Ros. Me beleeue it? You may assoone make her that you Loue beleeue it, which I warrant she is apter to do then to confesse she do's: that is one of the points, in the which women stil giue the lie to their consciences. But in good sooth, are you he that hangs the verses on the Trees, wherein *Rosalind* is so admired?

Orl. I sweare to thee youth, by the white hand of *Rosalind*, I am that he, that vnfortunate he.

Ros. But are you so much in loue, as your rimes speak?

Orl. Neither rime nor reason can expresse how much.

Ros. Loue is meerely a madnesse, and I tel you, deserues as wel a darke house, and a whip, as madmen do: and the reason why they are not so punish'd and cured, is that the Lunacie is so ordinarie, that the whippers are in loue too: yet I professe curing it by counsel.

Orl. Did you euer cure any so?

Ros. Yes one, and in this manner. Hee was to imagine me his Loue, his Mistris: and I set him euerie day to woe me. At which time would I, being but a moonish youth, greeue, be effeminate, changeable, longing, and liking, proud, fantastical, apish, shallow, inconstant, ful of teares, full of smiles; for euerie passion something, and for no passion truly any thing, as boyes and women are for the most part, cattle of this colour: would now like him, now loath him: then entertaine him, then forswear him: now weepe for him, then spit at him; that I draue my Sutor from his mad humor of loue, to a liuing humor of madnes, ẇ was to forsweare the ful stream of yͤ world, and to liue in a nooke meerly Monastick: and thus I cur'd him, and this way wil I take vpon mee to wash your Liuer as cleane as a sound sheepes heart, that there shal not be one spot of Loue in't.

Orl. I would not be cured, youth.

Ros. I would cure you, if you would but call me *Rosalind*, and come euerie day to my Coat, and woe me.

Orlan. Now by the faith of my loue, I will ; Tel me where it is.

Rof. Go with me to it, and Ile fhew it you : and by the way, you fhal tell me where in the Forreft you liue : Wil you go?

Orl. With all my heart, good youth.

Rof. Nay, you muft call mee *Rofalind*: Come fifter, will you go? *Exeunt*.

Scœna Tertia.

Enter Clowne, Audrey, & Iaques.

Clo Come apace good *Audrey*, I wil fetch vp your Goates, *Audrey* ; and how *Audrey* am I the man yet? Doth my fimple feature content you?

Aud. Your features, Lord warrant vs: what features?

Clo. I am heere with thee, and thy Goats, as the moft capricious Poet honeft *Ouid* was among the Gothes.

Iaq. O knowledge ill inhabited, worfe then Ioue in a thatch'd houfe.

Clo. When a mans verfes cannot be vnderftood, nor a mans good wit feconded with the forward childe, vnderftanding: it ftrikes a man more dead then a great reckoning in a little roome : truly, I would the Gods hadde made thee poeticall.

Aud. I do not know what Poetical is : is it honeft in deed and word: is it a true thing?

Clo. No truly : for the trueft poetrie is the moft faining, and Louers are giuen to Poetrie : and what they fweare in Poetrie, may be faid as Louers, they do feigne.

Aud. Do you wifh then that the Gods had made me Poeticall?

Clow. I do truly : for thou fwear'ft to me thou art honeft : Now if thou wert a Poet, I might haue fome hope thou didft feigne.

Aud. Would you not haue me honeft?

Clo. No truly, vnleffe thou wert hard fauour'd : for honeftie coupled to beautie, is to haue Honie a fawce to Sugar.

A materiall foole.

Aud. Well, I am not faire, and therefore I pray the Gods make me honeft.

Clo. Truly, and to caft away honeftie vppon a foule flut, were to put good meate into an vncleane difh.

Aud. I am not a flut, though I thanke the Goddes I am foule.

Clo. Well, praifed be the Gods, for thy foulneffe; fluttifhneffe may come heereafter. But be it, as it may bee, I wil marrie thee : and to that end, I haue bin with Sir *Oliuer Mar-text*, the Vicar of the next village, who hath promis'd to meete me in this place of the Forreft, and to couple vs.

Iaq. I would faine fee this meeting.

Aud. Wel, the Gods giue vs ioy.

Clo, Amen. A man may if he were of a fearful heart ftagger in this attempt : for heere wee haue no Temple but the wood, no affembly but horne-beafts. But what though? Courage. As hornes are odious, they are neceffarie. It is faid, many a man knowes no end of his goods; right : Many a man has good Hornes, and knows no end of them. Well, that is the dowrie of his wife, 'tis none of his owne getting ; hornes, euen fo poore men alone : No, no, the nobleft Deere hath them as huge as the Rafcall : Is the fingle m n therefore bleffed? No, as a wall'd Towne is more worthier then a village, fo is the forehead of a married man, more honourable then the bare brow of a Batcheller : and by how much defence is better then no skill, by fo much is a horne more precious then to want.

Enter Sir Oliuer Mar-text.

Heere comes Sir *Oliuer* : Sir *Oliuer Mar-text* you are wel met. Will you difpatch vs heere vnder this tree, or fhal we go with you to your Chappell?

Ol. Is there none heere to giue the woman?

Clo. I wil not take her on guift of any man.

Ol. Truly fhe muft be giuen, or the marriage is not lawfull.

Iaq. Proceed, proceede : Ile giue her.

Clo, Good euen good Mr what ye cal't: how do you Sir, you are verie well met : goddild you for your laft companie, I am verie glad to fee you, euen a toy in hand heere Sir : Nay, pray be couer'd.

Iaq. Wil you be married, Motley?

Clo. As the Oxe hath his bow fir, the horfe his curb, and the Falcon her bels, fo man hath his defires, and as Pigeons bill, fo wedlocke would be nibling.

Iaq. And wil you (being a man of your breeding) be married vnder a bufh like a begger? Get you to church, and haue a good Prieft that can tel you what marriage is, this fellow wil but ioyne you together, as they ioyne Wainfcot, then one of you wil proue a fhrunke pannell, and like greene timber, warpe, warpe.

Clo. I am not in the minde, but I were better to bee married of him then of another, for he is not like to marrie me wel : and not being wel married, it wil be a good excufe for me heereafter, to leaue my wife.

Iaq. Goe thou with mee,
And let me counfel thee.

Ol. Come fweete *Audrey*,
We muft be married, or we muft liue in baudrey :
Farewel good Mr *Oliuer* : Not O fweet *Oliuer*, O braue
Oliuer leaue me not behind thee : But winde away, bee
gone I fay, I wil not to wedding with thee.

Ol. 'Tis no matter; Ne're a fantaftical knaue of them all fhal flout me out of my calling. *Exeunt*

Scœna Quarta.

Enter Rofalind & Celia.

Rof. Neuer talke to me, I wil weepe.

Cel. Do I prethee, but yet haue the grace to confider, that teares do not become a man.

Rof. But haue I not caufe to weepe?

Cel. As good caufe as one would defire,
Therefore weepe.

Rof. His very haire
Is of the diffembling colour.

Cel. Something browner then Iudaffes :
Marrie his kiffes are Iudaffes owne children.

Rof. I'faith his haire is of a good colour.

Cel. An excellent colour :
Your Cheffenut was euer the onely colour :

Rof. And his kiffing is as ful of fanctitie,
As the touch of holy bread.

Cel.

Cel. Hee hath bought a paire of caſt lips of *Diana*: a Nun of winters ſiſterhood kiſſes not more religiouſlie, the very yce of chaſtity is in them

Roſa. But why did hee ſweare hee would come this morning, and comes not?

Cel. Nay certainly there is no truth in him.

Roſ. Doe you thinke ſo?

Cel. Yes, I thinke he is not a picke purſe, nor a horſe-ſtealer, but for his verity in loue, I doe thinke him as concaue as a couered goblet, or a Worme-eaten nut.

Roſ. Not true in loue?

Cel. Yes, when he is in, but I thinke he is not in.

Roſ. You haue heard him ſweare downright he was.

Cel. Was, is not is: beſides, the oath of Louer is no ſtronger then the word of a Tapſter, they are both the confirmer of falſe reckonings, he attends here in the forreſt on the Duke your father.

Roſ. I met the Duke yeſterday, and had much queſtion with him: he askt me of what parentage I was; I told him of as good as he, ſo he laugh'd and let mee goe. But what talke wee of Fathers, when there is ſuch a man as *Orlando*?

Cel. O that's a braue man, hee writes braue verſes, ſpeakes braue words, ſweares braue oathes, and breakes them brauely, quite trauers athwart the heart of his louer, as a puiſny Tilter, y ſpurs his horſe but on one ſide, breakes his ſtaffe like a noble gooſe; but all's braue that youth mounts, and folly guides: who comes heere?

Enter Corin.

Corin. Miſtreſſe and Maſter, you haue oft enquired
After the Shepheard that complain'd of loue,
Who you ſaw ſitting by me on the Turph,
Praiſing the proud diſdainfull Shepherdeſſe
That was his Miſtreſſe.

Cel. Well: and what of him?

Cor. If you will ſee a pageant truely plaid
Betweene the pale complexion of true Loue,
And the red glowe of ſcorne and prowd diſdaine,
Goe hence a little, and I ſhall conduct you
If you will marke it.

Roſ. O come, let vs remoue,
The ſight of Louers feedeth thoſe in loue:
Bring vs to this ſight, and you ſhall ſay
Ile proue a buſie actor in their play. *Exeunt.*

Scena Quinta.

Enter Siluius and Phebe.

Sil. Sweet *Phebe* doe not ſcorne me, do not *Phebe*
Say that you loue me not, but ſay not ſo
In bitterneſſe; the common executioner
Whoſe heart th'accuſtom'd ſight of death makes hard
Falls not the axe vpon the humbled neck,
But firſt begs pardon: will you ſterner be
Then he that dies and liues by bloody drops?

Enter Roſalind, Celia, and Corin.

Phe. I would not be thy executioner,
I flye thee, for I would not iniure thee:
Thou tell'ſt me there is murder in mine eye,
'Tis pretty ſure, and very probable,
That eyes that are the frailſt, and ſofteſt things,
Who ſhut their coward gates on atomyes,
Should be called tyrants, butchers, murtherers.
Now I doe frowne on thee with all my heart,
And if mine eyes can wound, now let them kill thee:
Now counterfeit to ſwound, why now fall downe,
Or if thou canſt not, oh for ſhame, for ſhame,
Lye not, to ſay mine eyes are murtherers:
Now ſhew the wound mine eye hath made in thee,
Scratch thee but with a pin, and there remaines
Some ſcarre of it: Leane vpon a ruſh
The Cicatrice and capable impreſſure
Thy palme ſome moment keepes: but now mine eyes
Which I haue darted at thee, hurt thee not,
Nor I am ſure there is no force in eyes
That can doe hurt.

Sil. O deere *Phebe*,
If euer (as that euer may be neere)
You meet in ſome freſh cheeke the power of fancie,
Then ſhall you know the wounds inuiſible
That Loues keene arrows make.

Phe. But till that time
Come not thou neere me: and when that time comes,
Afflict me with thy mockes, pitty me not,
As till that time I ſhall not pitty thee.

Roſ. And why I pray you? who might be your mother
That you inſult, exult, and all at once
Ouer the wretched? what though you hau no beauty
As by my faith, I ſee no more in you
Then without Candle may goe darke to bed:
Muſt you be therefore prowd and pittileſſe?
Why what meanes this? why do you looke on me?
I ſee no more in you then in the ordinary
Of Natures ſale-worke? 'ods my little life,
I thinke ſhe meanes to tangle my eies too:
No faith proud Miſtreſſe, hope not after it,
'Tis not your inkie browes, your blacke ſilke haire,
Your bugle eye-balls, nor your cheeke of creame
That can entame my ſpirits to your worſhip:
You fooliſh Shepheard, wherefore do you follow her
Like foggy South, puffing with winde and raine,
You are a thouſand times a properer man
Then ſhe a woman. 'Tis ſuch fooles as you
That makes the world full of ill-fauourd children:
'Tis not her glaſſe, but you that flatters her,
And out of you ſhe ſees her ſelfe more proper
Then any of her lineaments can ſhow her:
But Miſtris, know your ſelfe, downe on your knees
And thanke heauen, faſting, for a good mans loue;
For I muſt tell you friendly in your eare,
Sell when you can, you are not for all markets:
Cry the man mercy, loue him, take his offer,
Foule is moſt foule, being foule to be a ſcoffer.
So take her to thee Shepheard, fare you well.

Phe. Sweet youth, I pray you chide a yere together,
I had rather here you chide, then this man wooe.

Ros. Hees falne in loue with your foulneſſe, & ſhee'll
Fall in loue with my anger. If it be ſo, as faſt
As ſhe anſweres thee with frowning lookes, ile ſauce
Her with bitter words: why looke you ſo vpon me?

Phe. For no ill will I beare you.

Roſ. I pray you do not fall in loue with mee,
For I am falſer then vowes made in wine:
Beſides, I like you not: if you will know my houſe,
'Tis at the tuft of Oliues, here hard by:
Will you goe Siſter? Shepheard ply her hard:

Come

Come Sister : Shepheardesse,looke on him better
And be not proud,though all the world could see,
None could be so abus'd in sight as hee.
Come,to our flocke, *Exit.*

Phe. Dead Shepheard,now I find thy saw of might,
Who euer lov'd,that lou'd not at first sight?

Sil. Sweet *Phebe.*

Phe. Hah: what saist thou *Siluius*?

Sil. Sweet *Phebe* pitty me.

Phe. Why I am sorry for thee gentle *Siluius.*

Sil. Where euer sorrow is,reliefe would be:
If you doe sorrow at my griefe in loue,
By giuing loue your sorrow,and my griefe
Were both extermin'd.

Phe. Thou hast my loue,is not that neighbourly?

Sil. I would haue you.

Phe. Why that were couetousnesse:
Siluius; the time was,that I hated thee;
And yet it is not,that I beare thee loue,
But since that thou canst talke of loue so well,
Thy company,which erst was irkesome to me
I will endure; and Ile employ thee too:
But doe not looke for further recompence
Then thine owne gladnesse,that thou art employd.

Sil. So holy,and so perfect is my loue,
And I in such a pouerty of grace,
That I shall thinke it a most plenteous crop
To gleane the broken eares after the man
That the maine haruest reapes:loose now and then
A scattred smile,and that Ile liue vpon. (while?

Phe. Knowst thou the youth that spoke to mee yere-

Sil. Not very well,but I haue met him oft,
And he hath bought the Cottage and the bounds
That the old *Carlot* once was Master of.

Phe. Thinke not I loue him,though I ask for him,
'Tis but a peeuish boy,yet he talkes well,
But what care I for words? yet words do well
When he that speakes them pleases those that heare:
It is a pretty youth,not very prettie,
But sure hee's proud,and yet his pride becomes him;
Hee'll make a proper man: the best thing in him
Is his complexion: and faster then his tongue
Did make offence,his eye did heale it vp:
He is not very tall,yet for his yeeres hee's tall:
His leg is but so so,and yet 'tis well:
There was a pretty rednesse in his lip
A little riper,and more lustie red
Then that mixt in his cheeke: 'twas iust the difference
Betwixt the constant red,and mingled Damaske.
There be some women *Siluius*,had they markt him
In parcells as I did,would haue gone neere
To fall in loue with him: but for my part
I loue him not,nor hate him not: and yet,
Haue more cause to hate him then to loue him,
For what had he to doe to chide at me?
He said mine eyes were black,and my haire blacke,
And now I am remembred,scorn'd at me:
I maruell why I answer'd not againe,
But that's all one: omittance is no quittance:
Ile write to him a very tanting Letter,
And thou shalt beare it,wilt thou *Siluius*?

Sil. *Phebe*,with all my heart.

Phe. Ile write it strait:
The matter's in my head,and in my heart,
I will be bitter with him,and passing short;
Goe with me *Siluius*. *Exeunt.*

Actus Quartus. Scena Prima.

Enter Rosalind, and Celia, and Iaques.

Iaq. I prethee,pretty youth,let me better acquainted with thee.

Ros. They say you are a melancholly fellow.

Iaq. I am so: I doe loue it better then laughing.

Ros. Those that are in extremity of either, are abhominable fellowes, and betray themselues to euery moderne censure,worse then drunkards.

Iaq. Why,'tis good to be sad and say nothing.

Ros. Why then 'tis good to be a poste.

Iaq. I haue neither the Schollers melancholy, which is emulation: nor the Musitians, which is fantasticall; nor the Courtiers, which is proud: nor the Souldiers, which is ambitious: nor the Lawiers,which is politick: nor the Ladies, which is nice: nor the Louers, which is all these: but it is a melancholy of mine owne, compounded of many simples,extracted from many obiects, and indeed the sundrie contemplation of my trauells, in which by often rumination, wraps me in a most humorous sadnesse.

Ros. A Traueller: by my faith you haue great reason to be sad: I feare you haue sold your owne Lands, to see other mens; then to haue seene much, and to haue nothing, is to haue rich eyes and poore hands.

Iaq. Yes, I haue gain'd my experience.

Enter Orlando.

Ros. And your experience makes you sad: I had rather haue a foole to make me merrie, then experience to make me sad,and to trauaile for it too.

Orl. Good day,and happinesse,deere *Rosalind.*

Iaq. Nay then God buy you,and you talke in blanke verse.

Ros. Farewell Mounsieur Trauellor: looke you lispe,and weare strange suites; disable all the benefits of your owne Countrie: be out of loue with your natiuitie, and almost chide God for making you that countenance you are; or I will scarce thinke you haue swam in a Gundello. Why how now *Orlando*, where haue you bin all this while? you a louer? and you serue me such another tricke, neuer come in my sight more.

Orl. My faire *Rosalind*,I come within an houre of my promise.

Ros. Breake an houres promise in loue? hee that will diuide a minute into a thousand parts, and breake but a part of the thousand part of a minute in the affairs of loue, it may be said of him that *Cupid* hath clapt him oth' shoulder, but Ile warrant him heart hole.

Orl. Pardon me deere *Rosalind.*

Ros. Nay,and you be so tardie, come no more in my sight,I had as liefe be woo'd of a Snaile.

Orl. Of a Snaile?

Ros. I, of a Snaile: for though he comes slowly, hee carries his house on his head; a better ioyncture I thinke then you make a woman: besides,he brings his destinie with him

Orl. What's that?

Ros. Why hornes: w such as you are faine to be beholding to your wiues for: but he comes armed in his fortune,and preuents the slander of his wife.

Orl. Vertue

Orl. Vertue is no horne-maker: and my *Roſalind* is vertuous.

Roſ. And I am your *Roſalind.*

Cel. It pleaſes him to call you ſo: but he hath a *Roſalind* of a better leere then you.

Roſ. Come, wooe me, wooe mee: for now I am in a holy-day humor, and like enough to conſent: What would you ſay to me now, and I were your verie, verie *Roſalind?*

Orl. I would kiſſe before I ſpoke.

Roſ. Nay, you were better ſpeake firſt, and when you were grauel'd, for lacke of matter, you might take occaſion to kiſſe: verie good Orators when they are out, they will ſpit, and for louers, lacking (God warne vs) matter, the cleanlieſt ſhift is to kiſſe.

Orl. How if the kiſſe be denide?

Roſ. Then ſhe puts you to entreatie, and there begins new matter.

Orl. Who could be out, being before his beloued Miſtris?

Roſ. Marrie that ſhould you if I were your Miſtris, or I ſhould thinke my honeſtie ranker then my wit.

Orl. What, of my ſuite?

Roſ. Not out of your apparrell, and yet out of your ſuite:
Am not I your *Roſalind?*

Orl. I take ſome ioy to ſay you are, becauſe I would be talking of her.

Roſ. Well, in her perſon, I ſay I will not haue you.

Orl. Then in mine owne perſon, I die.

Roſ. No faith, die by Attorney: the poore world is almoſt ſix thouſand yeeres old, and in all this time there was not anie man died in his owne perſon (*videlicet*) in a loue cauſe: *Troilous* had his braines daſh'd out with a Grecian club, yet he did what hee could to die before, and he is one of the patternes of loue. *Leander*, he would haue liu'd manie a faire yeere though *Hero* had turn'd Nun; if it had not bin for a hot Midſomer-night, for (good youth) he went but forth to waſh him in the Helleſpont, and being taken with the crampe, was droun'd, and the fooliſh Chroniclers of that age, found it was *Hero* of Ceſtos. But theſe are all lies, men haue died from time to time, and wormes haue eaten them, but not for loue.

Orl. I would not haue my right *Roſalind* of this mind, for I proteſt her frowne might kill me.

Roſ. By this hand, it will not kill a flie: but come, now I will be your *Roſalind* in a more comming-on diſpoſition: and aske me what you will, I will grant it.

Orl. Then loue me *Roſalind.*

Roſ. Yes faith will I, fridaies and ſaterdaies, and all.

Orl. And wilt thou haue me?

Roſ. I, and twentie ſuch.

Orl. What ſaieſt thou?

Roſ. Are you not good?

Orl. I hope ſo.

Roſalind. Why then, can one deſire too much of a good thing: Come ſiſter, you ſhall be the Prieſt, and marrie vs: giue me your hand *Orlando*: What doe you ſay ſiſter?

Orl. Pray thee marrie vs.

Cel. I cannot ſay the words.

Roſ. You muſt begin, will you *Orlando.*

Cel. Goe too: wil you *Orlando*, haue to wife this *Roſalind*:

Orl. I will.

Roſ. I, but when?

Orl. Why now, as faſt as ſhe can marrie vs.

Roſ. Then you muſt ſay, I take thee *Roſalind* for wife.

Orl. I take thee *Roſalind* for wife.

Roſ. I might aske you for your Commiſſion,
But I doe take thee *Orlando* for my husband: there's a girle goes before the Prieſt, and certainely a Womans thought runs before her actions.

Orl. So do all thoughts, they are wing'd.

Roſ. Now tell me how long you would haue her, after you haue poſſeſt her?

Orl. For euer, and a day.

Roſ. Say a day, without the euer: no, no *Orlando*, men are Aprill when they woe, December when they wed: Maides are May when they are maides, but the sky changes when they are wiues: I will bee more iealous of thee, then a Barbary cocke-pidgeon ouer his hen, more clamorous then a Parrat againſt raine, more new-fangled then an ape, more giddy in my deſires, then a monkey: I will weepe for nothing, like *Diana* in the Fountaine, & I wil do that when you are diſpos'd to be merry: I will laugh like a Hyen, and that when thou art inclin'd to ſleepe.

Orl. But will my *Roſalind* doe ſo?

Roſ. By my life, ſhe will doe as I doe.

Orl. O but ſhe is wiſe.

Ros. Or elſe ſhee could not haue the wit to doe this: the wiſer, the waywarder: make the doores vpon a womans wit, and it will out at the caſement: ſhut that, and 'twill out at the key-hole: ſtop that, 'twill flie with the ſmoake out at the chimney.

Orl. A man that had a wife with ſuch a wit, he might ſay, wit whether wil't?

Roſ. Nay, you might keepe that checke for it, till you met your wiues wit going to your neighbours bed.

Orl. And what wit could wit haue, to excuſe that?

Roſa. Marry to ſay, ſhe came to ſeeke you there: you ſhall neuer take her without her anſwer, vnleſſe you take her without her tongue: ô that woman that cannot make her fault her husbands occaſion, let her neuer nurſe her childe her ſelfe, for ſhe will breed it like a foole.

Orl. For theſe two houres *Roſalinde*, I wil leaue thee.

Roſ. Alas, deere loue, I cannot lacke thee two houres.

Orl. I muſt attend the Duke at dinner, by two a clock I will be with thee againe.

Roſ. I, goe your waies, goe your waies: I knew what you would proue, my friends told mee as much, and I thought no leſſe: that flattering tongue of yours wonne me: 'tis but one caſt away, and ſo come death: two o' clocke is your howre.

Orl. I, ſweet *Roſalind.*

Roſ. By my troth, and in good earneſt, and ſo God mend mee, and by all pretty oathes that are not dangerous, if you breake one iot of your promiſe, or come one minute behinde your houre, I will thinke you the moſt patheticall breake-promiſe, and the moſt hollow louer, and the moſt vnworthy of her you call *Roſalinde*, that may bee choſen out of the groſſe band of the vnfaithfull: therefore beware my cenſure, and keep your promiſe.

Orl With no leſſe religion, then if thou wert indeed my *Roſalind*: ſo adieu.

Roſ. Well, Time is the olde Iuſtice that examines all ſuch offenders, and let time try: adieu. *Exit.*

Cel. You haue ſimply miſus'd our ſexe in your loue-prate:

prate : we muſt haue your doublet and hoſe pluckt ouer your head, and ſhew the world what the bird hath done to her owne neaſt.

Roſ. O coz,coz,coz : my pretty little coz, that thou didſt know how many fathome deepe I am in loue : but it cannot bee ſounded : my affection hath an vnknowne bottome,like the Bay of Portugall.

Cel. Or rather bottomleſſe, that as faſt as you poure affection in,in runs out.

Roſ. No,that ſame wicked Baſtard of *Venus*, that was begot of thought, conceiu'd of ſpleene, and borne of madneſſe, that blinde raſcally boy, that abuſes euery ones eyes,becauſe his owne are out, let him bee iudge, how deepe I am in loue : ile tell thee *Aliena*, I cannot be out of the ſight of *Orlando* : Ile goe finde a ſhadow, and ſigh till he come.

Cel. And Ile ſleepe. *Exeunt.*

Scena Secunda.

Enter Iaques and Lords, Forreſters.

Iaq. Which is he that killed the Deare?

Lord. Sir,it was I.

Iaq. Let's preſent him to the Duke like a Romane Conquerour, and it would doe well to ſet the Deares horns vpon his head, for a branch of victory; haue you no ſong Forreſter for this purpoſe?

Lord. Yes Sir.

Iaq. Sing it: 'tis no matter how it bee in tune, ſo it make noyſe enough.

Muſicke, Song

What ſhall he haue that kild the Deare?
His Leather skin,and hornes to weare :
Then ſing him home,the reſt ſhall beare this burthen;
Take thou no ſcorne to weare the horne,
It was a creſt ere thou waſt borne,
Thy fathers father wore it,
And thy father bore it,
The horne,the horne,the luſty horne,
Is not a thing to laugh to ſcorne. *Exeunt*

Scœna Tertia.

Enter Roſalind and Celia.

Roſ. How ſay you now,is it not paſt two a clock? And heere much *Orlando.*

Cel. I warrant you,with pure loue,& troubled brain,

Enter Silnius.

He hath t'ane his bow and arrowes,and is gone forth
To ſleepe : looke who comes heere.

Sil. My errand is to you,faire youth,
My gentle *Phebe*,did bid me giue you this :
I know not the contents, but as I gueſſe
By the ſterne brow,and waſpiſh action
Which ſhe did vſe,as ſhe was writing of it,
It beares an angry tenure; pardon me,
I am but as a guiltleſſe meſſenger.

Roſ Patience her ſelfe would ſtartle at this letter,
And play the ſwaggerer, beare this,beare all :
Shee ſaies I am not faire,that I lacke manners,
She calls me proud,and that ſhe could not loue me
Were man as rare as Phenix : od's my will,
Her loue is not the Hare that I doe hunt,
Why writes ſhe ſo to me? well Shepheard well,
This is a Letter of your owne deuice.

Sil. No, I proteſt,I know not the contents,
Phebe did write it.

Roſ. Come,come,you are a foole,
And turn'd into the extremity of loue.
I ſaw her hand,ſhe has a leatherne hand,
A freeſtone coloured hand : I verily did thinke
That her old gloues were on,but twas her hands:
She has a huſwiues hand, but that's no matter :
I ſay ſhe neuer did inuent this letter,
This is a mans inuention, and his hand.

Sil. Sure it is hers.

Roſ. Why,tis a boyſterous and a cruell ſtile,
A ſtile for challengers : why,ſhe defies me,
Like Turke to Chriſtian : vvomens gentle braine
Could not drop forth ſuch giant rude inuention,
Such Ethiop vvords, blacker in their effect
Then in their countenance : vvill you heare the letter?

Sil. So pleaſe you, for I neuer heard it yet :
Yet heard too much of *Phebes* crueltie.

Roſ. She *Phebes* me : marke how the tyrant vvrites.

Read. *Art thou god, to Shepherd turn'd?*
That a maidens heart hath burn'd.

Can a vvoman raile thus?

Sil. Call you this railing?

Roſ. Read. *Why, thy godhead laid a part,*
War'ſt thou with a womans heart?

Did you euer heare ſuch railing?

Whiles the eye of man did wooe me,
That could do no vengeance to me.

Meaning me a beaſt.

If the ſcorne of your bright eine
Haue power to raiſe ſuch loue in mine,
Alacke, in me, what ſtrange effect
Would they worke in milde aſpect?
Whiles you chid me, I did loue,
How then might your praiers moue?
He that brings this loue to thee,
Little knowes this Loue in me :
And by him ſeale vp thy minde,
Whether that thy youth and kinde
Will the faithfull offer take
Of me, and all that I can make,
Or elſe by him my loue denie,
And then Ile ſtudie how to die.

Sil. Call you this chiding?

Cel. Alas poore Shepheard.

Roſ. Doe you pitty him? No, he deſerues no pitty: wilt thou loue ſuch a woman? what to make thee an inſtrument,and play falſe ſtraines vpon thee? not to be endur'd. Well,goe your way to her; (for I ſee Loue hath made thee a tame ſnake) and ſay this to her; That if ſhe loue me, I charge her to loue thee : if ſhe will not, I will neuer haue her,vnleſſe thou intreat for her : if you bee a true louer hence,and not a word; for here comes more company. *Exit Sil.*

Enter Oliuer.

Oliu. Good morrow, faire ones : pray you, (if you know)
Where in the Purlews of this Forreſt, ſtands

A

A sheep-coat, fenc'd about with Oliue-trees.
Cel. West of this place, down in the neighbor bottom
The ranke of Oziers, by the murmuring streame
Left on your right hand, brings you to the place:
But at this howre, the house doth keepe it selfe,
There's none within.
Oli. If that an eye may profit by a tongue,
Then should I know you by description,
Such garments, and such yeeres: the boy is faire,
Of femall fauour, and bestowes himselfe
Like a ripe sister: the woman low
And browner then her brother: are not you
The owner of the house I did enquire for?
Cel. It is no boast, being ask'd, to say we are.
Oli. *Orlando* doth commend him to you both,
And to that youth hee calls his *Rosalind*,
He sends this bloudy napkin; are you he?
Ros. I am: what must we vnderstand by this?
Oli. Some of my shame, if you will know of me
What man I am, and how, and why, and where
This handkercher was stain'd.
Cel. I pray you tell it.
Oli. When last the yong *Orlando* parted from you,
He left a promise to returne againe
Within an houre, and pacing through the Forrest,
Chewing the food of sweet and bitter fancie,
Loe vvhat befell: he threw his eye aside,
And marke vvhat obiect did present it selfe
Vnder an old Oake, whose bows were moss'd with age
And high top, bald with drie antiquitie:
A wretched ragged man, ore-growne with haire
Lay sleeping on his back; about his necke
A greene and guilded snake had wreath'd it selfe,
Who with her head, nimble in threats approach'd
The opening of his mouth: but sodainly
Seeing *Orlando*, it vnlink'd it selfe,
And with indented glides, did slip away
Into a bush, vnder which bushes shade
A Lyonnesse, with vdders all drawne drie,
Lay cowching head on ground, with catlike watch
When that the sleeping man should stirre; for 'tis
The royall disposition of that beast
To prey on nothing, that doth seeme as dead:
This seene, *Orlando* did approach the man,
And found it was his brother, his elder brother.
Cel. O I haue heard him speake of that same brother,
And he did render him the most vnnaturall
That liu'd amongst men.
Oli. And well he might so doe,
For well I know he was vnnaturall.
Ros. But to *Orlando*: did he leaue him there
Food to the suck'd and hungry Lyonnesse?
Oli. Twice did he turne his backe, and purpos'd so:
But kindnesse, nobler euer then reuenge,
And Nature stronger then his iust occasion,
Made him giue battell to the Lyonnesse:
Who quickly fell before him, in which hurtling
From miserable slumber I awaked.
Cel. Are you his brother?
Ros. Was't you he rescu'd?
Cel. Was't you that did so oft contriue to kill him?
Oli. 'Twas I: but 'tis not I: I doe not shame
To tell you what I was, since my conuersion
So sweetly tastes, being the thing I am.
Ros. But for the bloody napkin?
Oli. By and by:
When from the first to last betwixt vs two,
Teares our recountments had most kindely bath'd,
As how I came into that Desert place.
I briefe, he led me to the gentle Duke,
Who gaue me fresh aray, and entertainment,
Committing me vnto my brothers loue,
Who led me instantly vnto his Caue,
There stript himselfe, and heere vpon his arme
The Lyonnesse had torne some flesh away,
Which all this while had bled; and now he fainted,
And cride in fainting vpon *Rosalinde*.
Briefe, I recouer'd him, bound vp his wound,
And after some small space, being strong at heart,
He sent me hither, stranger as I am
To tell this story, that you might excuse
His broken promise, and to giue this napkin
Died in this bloud, vnto the Shepheard youth,
That he in sport doth call his *Rosalind*.
Cel. Why how now *Ganimed*, sweet *Ganimed*.
Oli. Many will swoon when they do look on bloud.
Cel. There is more in it; Cosen *Ganimed*.
Oli. Looke, he recouers.
Ros. I would I were at home.
Cel. Wee'll lead you thither:
I pray you will you take him by the arme.
Oli. Be of good cheere youth: you a man?
You lacke a mans heart.
Ros. I doe so, I confesse it:
Ah, sirra, a body would thinke this was well counterfeited, I pray you tell your brother how well I counterfeited: heigh-ho.
Oli. This was not counterfeit, there is too great testimony in your complexion, that it was a passion of earnest.
Ros. Counterfeit, I assure you.
Oli. Well then, take a good heart, and counterfeit to be a man.
Ros. So I doe: but yfaith, I should haue beene a woman by right.
Cel. Come, you looke paler and paler: pray you draw homewards: good sir, goe with vs.
Oli. That will I: for I must beare answere backe
How you excuse my brother, *Rosalind*.
Ros. I shall deuise something: but I pray you commend my counterfeiting to him: will you goe?
Exeunt.

Actus Quintus. Scena Prima.

Enter Clowne and Awdrie.

Clow. We shall finde a time *Awdrie*, patience gentle *Awdrie*.
Awd. Faith the Priest was good enough, for all the olde gentlemans saying.
Clow. A most wicked Sir *Oliuer*, *Awdrie*, a most vile *Mar-text*. But *Awdrie*, there is a youth heere in the Forrest layes claime to you.
Awd. I, I know who 'tis: he hath no interest in mee in the world: here comes the man you meane.

Enter William.

Clo. It is meat and drinke to me to see a Clowne, by my

my troth, we that haue good wits, haue much to anſwer for: we ſhall be flouting: we cannot hold.

Will. Good eu'n *Audrey*.

Aud. God ye good eu'n *William*.

Will. And good eu'n to you Sir.

Clo. Good eu'n gentle friend. Couer thy head, couer thy head: Nay prethee bee couer'd. How olde are you Friend?

Will. Fiue and twentie Sir.

Clo. A ripe age: Is thy name *William*?

Will. *William*, ſir.

Clo. A faire name. Was't borne i'th Forreſt heere?

Will. I ſir, I thanke God.

Clo. Thanke God: A good anſwer:
Art rich?

Will. Faith ſir, ſo, ſo.

Clo. So, ſo, is good, very good, very excellent good: and yet it is not, it is but ſo, ſo:
Art thou wiſe?

Will. I ſir, I haue a prettie wit.

Clo. Why, thou ſaiſt well. I do now remember a ſaying: The Foole doth thinke he is wiſe, but the wiſeman knowes himſelfe to be a Foole. The Heathen Philoſopher, when he had a deſire to eate a Grape, would open his lips when he put it into his mouth, meaning thereby, that Grapes were made to eate, and lippes to open. You do loue this maid?

Will. I do ſir.

Clo. Giue me your hand: Art thou Learned?

Will. No ſir.

Clo. Then learne this of me, To haue, is to haue. For it is a figure in Rhetoricke, that drink being powr'd out of a cup into a glaſſe, by filling the one, doth empty the other. For all your Writers do conſent, that *ipſe* is hee: now you are not *ipſe*, for I am he.

Will. Which he ſir?

Clo. He ſir, that muſt marrie this woman: Therefore you Clowne, abandon: which is in the vulgar, leaue the ſocietie: which in the booriſh, is companie, of this female: which in the common, is woman: which together, is, abandon the ſociety of this Female, or Clowne thou periſheſt: or to thy better vnderſtanding, dyeſt; or (to wit) I kill thee, make thee away, tranſlate thy life into death, thy libertie into bondage: I will deale in poyſon with thee, or in baſtinado, or in ſteele: I will bandy with thee in faction, I will ore-run thee with police: I will kill thee a hundred and fifty wayes, therefore tremble and depart.

Aud. Do good *William*.

Will. God reſt you merry ſir. *Exit*

Enter Corin.

Cor. Our Maſter and Miſtreſſe ſeekes you: come away, away.

Clo. Trip *Audry*, trip *Audry*, I attend,
I attend. *Exeunt*

Scœna Secunda.

Enter Orlando & Oliuer.

Orl. Is't poſſible, that on ſo little acquaintance you ſhould like her? that, but ſeeing, you ſhould loue her? And louing woo? and wooing, ſhe ſhould graunt? And will you perſeuer to enioy her?

Ol. Neither call the giddineſſe of it in queſtion; the pouertie of her, the ſmall acquaintance, my ſodaine wooing, nor ſodaine conſenting: but ſay with mee, I loue *Aliena*: ſay with her, that ſhe loues mee; conſent with both, that we may enioy each other: it ſhall be to your good: for my fathers houſe, and all the reuennew, that was old Sir *Rowlands* will I eſtate vpon you, and heere liue and die a Shepherd.

Enter Roſalind.

Orl. You haue my conſent.
Let your Wedding be to morrow: thither will I
Inuite the Duke, and all's contented followers:
Go you, and prepare *Aliena*; for looke you,
Heere comes my *Roſalinde*.

Roſ. God ſaue you brother.

Ol. And you faire ſiſter.

Roſ. Oh my deere *Orlando*, how it greeues me to ſee thee weare thy heart in a ſcarfe.

Orl. It is my arme.

Roſ. I thought thy heart had beene wounded with the clawes of a Lion.

Orl. Wounded it is, but with the eyes of a Lady.

Roſ. Did your brother tell you how I counterfeyted to ſound, when he ſhew'd me your handkercher?

Orl. I, and greater wonders then that.

Roſ. O, I know where you are: nay, tis true: there was neuer any thing ſo ſodaine, but the fight of two Rammes, and *Cæſars* Thraſonicall bragge of I came, ſaw, and ouercome. For your brother, and my ſiſter, no ſooner met, but they look'd: no ſooner look'd, but they lou'd; no ſooner lou'd, but they ſigh'd: no ſooner ſigh'd but they ask'd one another the reaſon: no ſooner knew the reaſon, but they ſought the remedie: and in theſe degrees, haue they made a paire of ſtaires to marriage, which they will climbe incontinent, or elſe bee incontinent before marriage; they are in the verie wrath of loue, and they will together. Clubbes cannot part them.

Orl. They ſhall be married to morrow: and I will bid the Duke to the Nuptiall. But O, how bitter a thing it is, to looke into happines through another mans eies: by ſo much the more ſhall I to morrow be at the height of heart heauineſſe, by how much I ſhal thinke my brother happie, in hauing what he wiſhes for.

Roſ. Why then to morrow, I cannot ſerue your turne for *Roſalind*?

Orl. I can liue no longer by thinking.

Roſ. I will wearie you then no longer with idle talking. Know of me then (for now I ſpeake to ſome purpoſe) that I know you are a Gentleman of good conceit: I ſpeake not this, that you ſhould beare a good opinion of my knowledge: inſomuch (I ſay) I know you are: neither do I labor for a greater eſteeme then may in ſome little meaſure draw a beleefe from you, to do your ſelfe good, and not to grace me. Beleeue then, if you pleaſe, that I can do ſtrange things: I haue ſince I was three yeare old conuerſt with a Magitian, moſt profound in his Art, and yet not damnable. If you do loue *Roſalinde* ſo neere the hart, as your geſture cries it out: when your brother marries *Aliena*, ſhall you marrie her. I know into what ſtraights of Fortune ſhe is driuen, and it is not impoſſible to me, if it appeare not inconuenient to you,

to

to ſet her before your eyes to morrow humane as ſhe is, and without any danger.

Orl. Speak'ſt thou in ſober meanings?

Roſ. By my life I do, which I tender deerly, though I ſay I am a Magitian: Therefore put you in your beſt aray, bid your friends: for if you will be married to morrow, you ſhall: and to *Roſalind* if you will.

Enter Siluius & Phebe.

Looke, here comes a Louer of mine, and a louer of hers.

Phe. Youth, you haue done me much vngentleneſſe,
To ſhew the letter that I writ to you.

Roſ. I care not if I haue: it is my ſtudie
To ſeeme deſpightfull and vngentle to you:
you are there followed by a faithful ſhepheard,
Looke vpon him, loue him: he worſhips you.

Phe. Good ſhepheard, tell this youth what 'tis to loue

Sil. It is to be all made of ſighes and teares,
And ſo am I for *Phebe.*

Phe. And I for *Ganimed.*

Orl. And I for *Roſalind.*

Roſ And I for no woman.

Sil. It is to be all made of faith and ſeruice,
And ſo am I for *Phebe.*

Phe. And I for *Ganimed.*

Orl. And I for *Roſalind.*

Roſ. And I for no woman.

Sil. It is to be all made of fantaſie,
All made of paſſion, and all made of wiſhes,
All adoration, dutie, and obſeruance,
All humbleneſſe, all patience, and impatience,
All puritie, all triall, all obſeruance:
And ſo am I for *Phebe.*

Phe. And ſo am I for *Ganimed.*

Orl. And ſo am I for *Roſalind.*

Roſ. And ſo am I for no woman.

Phe. If this be ſo, why blame you me to loue you?

Sil. If this be ſo, why blame you me to loue you?

Orl. If this be ſo, why blame you me to loue you?

Roſ. Why do you ſpeake too, Why blame you mee to loue you.

Orl. To her, that is not heere, nor doth not heare.

Roſ. Pray you no more of this, 'tis like the howling of Iriſh Wolues againſt the Moone: I will helpe you if I can: I would loue you if I could: To morrow meet me altogether: I wil marrie you, if euer I marrie Woman, and Ile be married to morrow: I will ſatisfie you, if euer I ſatisfi'd man, and you ſhall bee married to morrow. I wil content you, if what pleaſes you contents you, and you ſhal be married to morrow: As you loue *Roſalind* meet, as you loue *Phebe* meet, and as I loue no women, Ile meet: ſo fare you wel: I haue left you commands.

Sil. Ile not faile, if I liue.

Phe. Nor I.

Orl. Nor I *Exeunt.*

Scœna Tertia.

Enter Clowne and Audrey.

Clo. To morrow is the ioyfull day *Audrey*, to morow will we be married.

Aud. I do deſire it with all my heart: and I hope it is no diſhoneſt deſire, to deſire to be a woman of ye world? Heere come two of the baniſh'd Dukes Pages.

Enter two Pages.

1.Pa. Wel met honeſt Gentleman.

Clo. By my troth well met: come, ſit, ſit, and a ſong.

2.Pa. We are for you, ſit i'th middle.

1.Pa. Shal we clap into't roundly, without hauking, or ſpitting, or ſaying we are hoarſe, which are the onely prologues to a bad voice.

2.Pa. I faith, y'faith, and both in a tune like two gipſies on a horſe.

Song.

It was a Louer, and his laſſe,
With a hey, and a ho, and a hey nonino.
That o're the greene corne feild did paſſe,
In the ſpring time, the onely pretty rang time.
When Birds do ſing, hey ding a ding, ding.
Sweet Louers loue the ſpring,
And therefore take the preſent time.
With a hey, & a ho, and a hey nonino,
For loue is crowned with the prime.
In ſpring time, &c.

Betweene the acres of the Rie,
With a hey, and a ho, & a hey nonino:
Theſe prettie Countrey folks would lie.
In ſpring time, &c.

This Carroll they began that houre,
With a hey and a ho, & a hey nonino:
How that a life was but a Flower,
In ſpring time, &c.

Clo. Truly yong Gentlemen, though there vvas no great matter in the dittie, yet ye note was very vntunable

1.Pa. you are deceiu'd Sir, we kept time, we loſt not our time.

Clo. By my troth yes: I count it but time loſt to heare ſuch a fooliſh ſong. God buy you, and God mend your voices. Come *Audrie.* *Exeunt.*

Scena Quarta.

Enter Duke Senior, Amyens, Iaques, Orlando, Oliuer, Celia.

Du.Sen. Doſt thou beleeue *Orlando*, that the boy
Can do all this that he hath promiſed?

Orl. I ſometimes do beleeue, and ſomtimes do not,
As thoſe that feare they hope, and know they feare.

Enter Roſalinde, Siluius, & Phebe.

Roſ. Patience once more, whiles our cõpact is vrg'd:
You ſay, if I bring in your *Roſalinde*,
You wil beſtow her on *Orlando* heere?

Du.Se. That would I, had I kingdoms to giue with hir.

Roſ. And you ſay you wil haue her, when I bring hir?

Orl. That would I, were I of all kingdomes King.

Roſ. You ſay, you'l marrie me, if I be willing.

Phe. That will I, ſhould I die the houre after.

Roſ. But if you do refuſe to marrie me,
You'l giue your ſelfe to this moſt faithfull Shepheard.

Phe. So is the bargaine.

Roſ. You ſay that you'l haue *Phebe* if ſhe will.

Sil. Though to haue her and death, were both one thing.

S *Roſ*

Ros. I haue promis'd to make all this matter euen:
Keepe you your word, O Duke, to giue your daughter,
You yours *Orlando*, to receiue his daughter:
Keepe you your word *Phebe*, that you'l marrie me,
Or else refusing me to wed this shepheard:
Keepe your word *Siluius*, that you'l marrie her
If she refuse me, and from hence I go
To make these doubts all euen. *Exit Ros. and Celia.*

Du.Sen. I do remember in this shepheard boy,
Some liuely touches of my daughters fauour.

Orl. My Lord, the first time that I euer saw him,
Me thought he was a brother to your daughter:
But my good Lord, this Boy is Forrest borne,
And hath bin tutor'd in the rudiments
Of many desperate studies, by his vnckle,
Whom he reports to be a great Magitian.

Enter Clowne and Audrey.

Obscured in the circle of this Forrest.

Iaq. There is sure another flood toward, and these couples are comming to the Arke. Here comes a payre of verie strange beasts, which in all tongues, are call'd Fooles.

Clo. Salutation and greeting to you all.

Iaq. Good my Lord, bid him welcome: This is the Motley-minded Gentleman, that I haue so often met in the Forrest: he hath bin a Courtier he sweares.

Clo. If any man doubt that, let him put mee to my purgation, I haue trod a measure, I haue flattred a Lady, I haue bin politicke with my friend, smooth with mine enemie, I haue vndone three Tailors, I haue had foure quarrels, and like to haue fought one.

Iaq. And how was that tane vp?

Clo. Faith we met, and found the quarrel was vpon the seuenth cause.

Iaq. How seuenth cause? Good my Lord, like this fellow.

Du.Se. I like him very well.

Clo. God'ild you sir, I desire you of the like: I presse in heere sir, amongst the rest of the Country copulatiues to sweare, and to forsweare, according as mariage binds and blood breakes: a poore virgin sir, an il-fauor'd thing sir, but mine owne, a poore humour of mine sir, to take that that no man else will: rich honestie dwels like a miser sir, in a poore house, as your Pearle in your foule oyster.

Du.Se. By my faith, he is very swift, and sententious

Clo. According to the fooles bolt sir, and such dulcet diseases.

Iaq. But for the seuenth cause. How did you finde the quarrell on the seuenth cause?

Clo. Vpon a lye, seuen times remoued: (beare your bodie more seeming *Audry*) as thus sir: I did dislike the cut of a certaine Courtiers beard; he sent me word, if I said his beard was not cut well, hee was in the minde it was: this is call'd the retort courteous. If I sent him word againe, it was not well cut, he wold send me word he cut it to please himselfe: this is call'd the quip modest. If againe, it was not well cut, he disabled my iudgment: this is called, the reply churlish. If againe it was not well cut, he would answer I spake not true: this is call'd the reproofe valiant. If againe, it was not well cut, he wold say, I lie: this is call'd the counter-checke quarrelsome: and so ro lye circumstantiall, and the lye direct.

Iaq. And how oft did you say his beard was not well cut?

Clo. I durst go no further then the lye circumstantial: nor he durst not giue me the lye direct: and so wee measur'd swords, and parted.

Iaq. Can you nominate in order now, the degrees of the lye.

Clo. O sir, we quarrel in print, by the booke: as you haue bookes for good manners: I will name you the degrees. The first, the Retort courteous: the second, the Quip-modest: the third, the reply Churlish: the fourth, the Reproofe valiant: the fift, the Countercheck quarrelsome: the sixt, the Lye with circumstance: the seauenth, the Lye direct: all these you may auoyd, but the Lye direct: and you may auoide that too, with an If. I knew when seuen Iustices could not take vp a Quarrell, but when the parties were met themselues, one of them thought but of an If; as if you saide so, then I saide so: and they shooke hands, and swore brothers. Your If, is the onely peace-maker: much vertue in if.

Iaq. Is not this a rare fellow my Lord? He's as good at any thing, and yet a foole.

Du.Se. He vses his folly like a stalking-horse, and vnder the presentation of that he shoots his wit.

Enter Hymen, Rosalind, and Celia.
Still Musicke.

Hymen. *Then is there mirth in heauen,*
When earthly things made eauen
attone together.
Good Duke receiue thy daughter,
Hymen from Heauen brought her,
Yea brought her hether.
That thou mightst ioyne his hand with his,
Whose heart within his bosome is.

Ros. To you I giue my selfe, for I am yours.
To you I giue my selfe, for I am yours.

Du.Se. If there be truth in sight, you are my daughter.

Orl. If there be truth in sight, you are my *Rosalind*.

Phe. If sight & shape be true, why then my loue adieu

Ros. Ile haue no Father, if you be not he:
Ile haue no Husband, if you be not he:.
Nor ne're wed woman, if you be not shee.

Hy. Peace hoa: I barre confusion,
'Tis I must make conclusion
Of these most strange euents:
Here's eight that must take hands,
To ioyne in *Hymens* bands,
If truth holds true contents.
You and you, no crosse shall part;
You and you, are hart in hart:
You, to his loue must accord,
Or haue a Woman to your Lord.
You and you, are sure together,
As the Winter to fowle Weather:
Whiles a Wedlocke Hymne we sing,
Feede your selues with questioning.
That reason, wonder may diminish
How thus we met, and these things finish.

Song.

Wedding is great Iunos crowne,
O blessed bond of boord and bed:
'Tis Hymen peoples euerie towne,
High wedlock then be honored:
Honor, high honor and renowne
To Hymen, God of euerie Towne.

Du.Se. O my deere Neece, welcome thou art to me,
Euen daughter welcome, in no lesse degree.

Phe.

Phe. I wil not eate my word, now thou art mine,
Thy faith, my fancie to thee doth combine.

Enter Second Brother.

2.Bro. Let me haue audience for a word or two:
I am the second sonne of old *Sir Rowland*,
That bring these tidings to this faire assembly.
Duke Frederick hearing how that euerie day
Men of great worth resorted to this forrest,
Addrest a mightie power, which were on foote
In his owne conduct, purposely to take
His brother heere, and put him to the sword:
And to the skirts of this wilde Wood he came;
Where, meeting with an old Religious man,
After some question with him, was conuerted
Both from his enterprize, and from the world:
His crowne bequeathing to his banish'd Brother,
And all their Lands restor'd to him againe
That were with him exil'd. This to be true,
I do engage my life.

Du.Se. Welcome yong man:
Thou offer'st fairely to thy brothers wedding:
To one his lands with-held, and to the other
A land it selfe at large, a potent Dukedome.
First, in this Forrest, let vs do those ends
That heere vvere well begun, and wel begot:
And after, euery of this happie number
That haue endur'd shrew'd daies, and nights with vs,
Shal share the good of our returned fortune,
According to the measure of their states.
Meane time, forget this new-falne dignitie,
And fall into our Rusticke Reuelrie:
Play Musicke, and you Brides and Bride-groomes all,
With measure heap'd in ioy, to'th Measures fall.

Iaq. Sir, by your patience: if I heard you rightly,
The Duke hath put on a Religious life,
And throwne into neglect the pompous Court.

2.Bro. He hath.

Iaq. To him will I: out of these conuertites,
There is much matter to be heard, and learn'd:
you to your former Honor, I bequeath
your patience, and your vertue, well deserues it.
you to a loue, that your true faith doth merit:
you to your land, and loue, and great allies:
you to a long, and well-deserued bed:
And you to wrangling, for thy louing voyage
Is but for two moneths victuall'd: So to your pleasures,
I am for other, then for dancing meazures.

Du.Se. Stay, *Iaques*, stay.

Iaq. To see no pastime, I: what you would haue,
Ile stay to know, at your abandon'd caue. *Exit.*

Du.Se. Proceed, proceed: wee'l begin these rights,
As we do trust, they'l end in true delights. *Exit*

Ros. It is not the fashion to see the Ladie the Epilogue: but it is no more vnhandsome, then to see the Lord the Prologue. If it be true, that good wine needs no bush, 'tis true, that a good play needes no Epilogue. Yet to good wine they do vse good bushes: and good playes proue the better by the helpe of good Epilogues: What a case am I in then, that am neither a good Epilogue, nor cannot insinuate with you in the behalfe of a good play? I am not furnish'd like a Begger, therefore to begge will not become mee. My way is to coniure you, and Ile begin with the Women. I charge you (O women) for the loue you beare to men, to like as much of this Play, as please you: And I charge you (O men) for the loue you beare to women (as I perceiue by your simpring, none of you hates them) that betweene you, and the women, the play may please. If I were a Woman, I would kisse as many of you as had beards that pleas'd me, complexions that lik'd me, and breaths that I defi'de not: And I am sure, as many as haue good beards, or good faces, or sweet breaths, will for my kind offer, when I make curt'sie, bid me farewell. *Exit.*

FINIS.

S 2

THE Taming of the Shrew.

Actus primus. Scœna Prima.

Enter Begger and Hostes, Christophero Sly.

Begger.

I Le pheeze you infaith.

Host. A paire of stockes you rogue.

Beg. Y'are a baggage, the *Slies* are no Rogues. Looke in the Chronicles, we came in with *Richard Conqueror*: therefore *Paucas pallabris*, let the world slide: Sessa.

Host. You will not pay for the glasses you haue burst?

Beg. No, not a deniere: go by S. *Ieronimie*, goe to thy cold bed, and warme thee.

Host. I know my remedie, I must go fetch the Headborough.

Beg. Third, or fourth, or fift Borough, Ile answere him by Law. Ile not budge an inch boy: Let him come, and kindly. *Falles asleepe.*

Winde hornes. Enter a Lord from hunting, with his traine.

Lo. Huntsman I charge thee, tender wel my hounds,
Brach *Meriman*, the poore Curre is imbost,
And couple *Clowder* with the deepe-mouth'd brach,
Saw'st thou not boy how *Siluer* made it good
At the hedge corner, in the couldest fault,
I would not loose the dogge for twentie pound.

Hunts. Why *Belman* is as good as he my Lord,
He cried vpon it at the meerest losse,
And twice to day pick'd out the dullest sent,
Trust me, I take him for the better dogge.

Lord. Thou art a Foole, if *Eccho* were as fleete,
I would esteeme him worth a dozen such:
But sup them well, and looke vnto them all,
To morrow I intend to hunt againe.

Hunts. I will my Lord.

Lord. What's heere? One dead, or drunke? See doth he breath?

2. Hun. He breath's my Lord. Were he not warm'd with Ale, this were a bed but cold to sleep so soundly.

Lord. Oh monstrous beast, how like a swine he lyes.
Grim death, how foule and loathsome is thine image:
Sirs, I will practise on this drunken man.
What thinke you, if he were conuey'd to bed,
Wrap'd in sweet cloathes: Rings put vpon his fingers:
A most delicious banquet by his bed,
And braue attendants neere him when he wakes,
Would not the begger then forget himselfe?

1. Hun. Beleeue me Lord, I thinke he cannot choose.

2. H. It would seem strange vnto him when he wak'd

Lord. Euen as a flatt'ring dreame, or worthles fancie.
Then take him vp, and manage well the iest:
Carrie him gently to my fairest Chamber,
And hang it round with all my wanton pictures:
Balme his foule head in warme distilled waters,
And burne sweet Wood to make the Lodging sweete:
Procure me Musicke readie when he wakes,
To make a dulcet and a heauenly sound:
And if he chance to speake, be readie straight
(And with a lowe submissiue reuerence)
Say, what is it your Honor wil command:
Let one attend him with a siluer Bason
Full of Rose-water, and bestrew'd with Flowers,
Another beare the Ewer: the third a Diaper,
And say wilt please your Lordship coole your hands.
Some one be readie with a costly suite,
And aske him what apparrel he will weare:
Another tell him of his Hounds and Horse,
And that his Ladie mournes at his disease,
Perswade him that he hath bin Lunaticke,
And when he sayes he is, say that he dreames,
For he is nothing but a mightie Lord:
This do, and do it kindly, gentle sirs,
It wil be pastime passing excellent,
If it be husbanded with modestie.

1. Hunts. My Lord I warrant you we wil play our part
As he shall thinke by our true diligence
He is no lesse then what we say he is.

Lord. Take him vp gently, and to bed with him,
And each one to his office when he wakes.

Sound trumpets.

Sirrah, go see what Trumpet 'tis that sound.
Belike some Noble Gentleman that meanes
(Trauelling some iourney) to repose him heere.

Enter Seruingman.

How now? who is it?

Ser. An't please your Honor, Players
That offer seruice to your Lordship.

Enter Players

Lord. Bid them come neere:
Now fellowes, you are welcome.

Players. We thanke your Honor

Lord. Do you intend to stay with me to night?

2. Player. So please your Lordshippe to accept our dutie.

Lord With all my heart. This fellow I remember,
Since once he plaide a Farmers eldest sonne,
'Twas where you woo'd the Gentlewoman so well:
I haue forgot your name: but sure that part

Was

Was aptly fitted, and naturally perform'd.
Sincklo. I thinke 'twas *Soto* that your honor meanes.
Lord. 'Tis verie true, thou didſt it excellent:
Well you are come to me in happie time,
The rather for I haue ſome ſport in hand,
Wherein your cunning can aſſiſt me much.
There is a Lord will heare you play to night;
But I am doubtfull of your modeſties,
Leaſt (ouer-eying of his odde behauiour,
For yet his honor neuer heard a play)
You breake into ſome merrie paſſion,
And ſo offend him: for I tell you ſirs,
If you ſhould ſmile, he growes impatient.
Plai. Feare not my Lord, we can contain our ſelues,
Were he the verieſt anticke in the world.
Lord. Go ſirra, take them to the Butterie,
And giue them friendly welcome euerie one,
Let them want nothing that my houſe affoords.
Exit one with the Players.
Sirra go you to Bartholmew my Page,
And ſee him dreſt in all ſuites like a Ladie:
That done, conduct him to the drunkards chamber,
And call him Madam, do him obeiſance:
Tell him from me (as he will win my loue)
He beare himſelfe with honourable action,
Such as he hath obſeru'd in noble Ladies
Vnto their Lords, by them accompliſhed,
Such dutie to the drunkard let him do:
With ſoft lowe tongue, and lowly curteſie,
And ſay: What is't your Honor will command,
Wherein your Ladie, and your humble wife,
May ſhew her dutie, and make knowne her loue.
And then with kinde embracements, tempting kiſſes,
And with declining head into his boſome
Bid him ſhed teares, as being ouer-ioyed
To ſee her noble Lord reſtor'd to health,
Who for this ſeuen yeares hath eſteemed him
No better then a poore and loathſome begger:
And if the boy haue not a womans guift
To raine a ſhower of commanded teares,
An Onion wil do well for ſuch a ſhift,
Which in a Napkin (being cloſe conuei'd)
Shall in deſpight enforce a waterie eie:
See this diſpatch'd with all the haſt thou canſt,
Anon Ile giue thee more inſtructions.
Exit a ſeruingman.
I know the boy will wel vſurpe the grace,
Voice, gate, and action of a Gentlewoman:
I long to heare him call the drunkard husband,
And how my men will ſtay themſelues from laughter,
When they do homage to this ſimple peaſant,
Ile in to counſell them: haply my preſence
May well abate the ouer-merrie ſpleene,
Which otherwiſe would grow into extreames.

Enter aloft the drunkard with attendants, ſome with apparel, Baſon and Ewer, & other appurtenances, & Lord.

Beg. For Gods ſake a pot of ſmall Ale
1.Ser. Wilt pleaſe your Lord drink a cup of ſacke?
2 Ser. Wilt pleaſe your Honor taſte of theſe Conſerues?
3.Ser. What raiment wil your honor weare to day.
Beg. I am *Chriſtophero Sly*, call not mee Honour nor Lordſhip: I ne're drank ſacke in my life: and if you giue me any Conſerues, giue me conſerues of Beefe: nere ask me what raiment Ile weare, for I haue no more doublets then backes: no more ſtockings then legges: nor no more ſhooes then feet, nay ſometime more feete then ſhooes, or ſuch ſhooes as my toes look through the ouer-leather.
Lord. Heauen ceaſe this idle humor in your Honor.
Oh that a mightie man of ſuch diſcent,
Of ſuch poſſeſſions, and ſo high eſteeme
Should be infuſed with ſo foule a ſpirit.
Beg. What would you make me mad? Am not I *Chriſtopher Slie*, old Sies ſonne of Burton-heath, by byrth a Pedler, by education a Cardmaker, by tranſmutation a Beare-heard, and now by preſent profeſſion a Tinker. Aske *Marrian Hacket* the fat Alewife of Wincot, if ſhee know me not: if ſhe ſay I am not xiiii.d. on the ſcore for ſheere Ale, ſcore me vp for the lyingſt knaue in Chriſten dome. What I am not beſtraught: here's———
3.Man. Oh this it is that makes your Ladie mourne.
2 Man. Oh this is it that makes your ſeruants droop.
Lord. Hence comes it, that your kindred ſhuns your
As beaten hence by your ſtrange Lunacie. (houſe
Oh Noble Lord, bethinke thee of thy birth,
Call home thy ancient thoughts from baniſhment,
And baniſh hence theſe abiect lowlie dreames:
Looke how thy ſeruants do attend on thee,
Each in his office readie at thy becke.
Wilt thou haue Muſicke? Harke Apollo plaies, *Muſick*
And twentie caged Nightingales do ſing.
Or wilt thou ſleepe? Wee'l haue thee to a Couch,
Softer and ſweeter then the luſtfull bed
On purpoſe trim'd vp for Semiramis.
Say thou wilt walke: we wil beſtrow the ground.
Or wilt thou ride? Thy horſes ſhal be trap'd,
Their harneſſe ſtudded all with Gold and Pearle.
Doſt thou loue hawking? Thou haſt hawkes will ſoare
Aboue the morning Larke. Or wilt thou hunt,
Thy hounds ſhall make the Welkin anſwer them
And fetch ſhrill ecchoes from the hollow earth.
1 Man. Say thou wilt courſe, thy gray-hounds are as
As breathed Stags: I fleeter then the Roe. (ſwift
2 M. Doſt thou loue pictures? we wil fetch thee ſtrait
Adonis painted by a running brooke,
And Citherea all in ſedges hid,
Which ſeeme to moue and wanton with her breath,
Euen as the wauing ſedges play with winde.
Lord. Wee'l ſhew thee *Io*, as ſhe was a Maid,
And how ſhe was beguiled and ſurpriz'd,
As liuelie painted, as the deede was done.
3.Man. Or *Daphne* roming through a thornie wood,
Scratching her legs, that one ſhal ſweare ſhe bleeds,
And at that ſight ſhal ſad Apollo weepe,
So workmanlie the blood and teares are drawne.
Lord. Thou art a Lord, and nothing but a Lord:
Thou haſt a Ladie farre more Beautifull,
Then any woman in this waining age.
1 Man. And til the teares that ſhe hath ſhed for thee,
Like enuious flouds ore-run her louely face,
She was the faireſt creature in the world,
And yet ſhee is inferiour to none.
Beg. Am I a Lord, and haue I ſuch a Ladie?
Or do I dreame? Or haue I dream'd till now?
I do not ſleepe: I ſee, I heare, I ſpeake:
I ſmel ſweet ſauours, and I feele ſoft things:
Vpon my life I am a Lord indeede,
And not a Tinker, nor Chriſtopher Slie.
Well, bring our Ladie hither to our ſight,
And once againe a pot o'th ſmalleſt Ale.

S3 2. M.

2. *Man.* Wilt please your mightinesse to wash your hands:
Oh how we ioy to see your wit restor'd,
Oh that once more you knew but what you are:
These fifteene yeeres you haue bin in a dreame,
Or when you wak'd, so wak'd as if you slept.
Beg. These fifteene yeeres, by my fay, a goodly nap,
But did I neuer speake of all that time.
1 *Man.* Oh yes my Lord, but verie idle words,
For though you lay heere in this goodlie chamber,
Yet would you say, ye were beaten out of doore,
And raile vpon the Hostesse of the house,
And say you would present her at the Leete,
Because she brought stone-Iugs, and no seal'd quarts:
Sometimes you would call out for Cicely Hacket
Beg. I, the womans maide of the house.
3. *man.* Why sir you know no house, nor no such maid
Nor no such men as you haue reckon'd vp,
As *Stephen Slie*, and old *Iohn Naps* of Greece,
And *Peter Turph*, and *Henry Pimpernell*,
And twentie more such names and men as these,
Which neuer were, nor no man euer saw.
Beg. Now Lord be thanked for my good amends.
All. Amen.

Enter Lady with Attendants.

Beg. I thanke thee, thou shalt not loose by it.
Lady. How fares my noble Lord?
Beg. Marrie I fare well, for heere is cheere enough
Where is my wife?
La. Heere noble Lord, what is thy will with her?
Beg. Are you my wife, and will not cal me husband?
My men should call me Lord, I am your good-man.
La. My husband and my Lord, my Lord and husband
I am your wife in all obedience.
Beg. I know it well, what must I call her?
Lord. Madam.
Beg. *Alce* Madam, or *Ione* Madam?
Lord. Madam, and nothing else, so Lords cal Ladies
Beg Madame wife, they say that I haue dream'd,
And slept aboue some fifteene yeare or more.
Lady I, and the time seeme's thirty vnto me,
Being all this time abandon'd from your bed.
Beg 'Tis much, seruants leaue me and her alone:
Madam vndresse you, and come now to bed
La. Thrice noble Lord, let me intreat of you
To pardon me yet for a night or two:
Or if not so, vntill the Sun be set.
For your Physitians haue expressely charg'd,
In perill to incurre your former malady,
That I should yet absent me from your bed
I hope this reason stands for my excuse.
Beg. I, it stands so that I may hardly tarry so long.
But I would be loth to fall into my dreames againe: I wil therefore tarrie in despight of the flesh & the blood

Enter a Messenger.

Mes. Your Honors Players hearing your amendment,
Are come to play a pleasant Comedie,
For so your doctors hold it very meete,
Seeing too much sadnesse hath congeal'd your blood,
And melancholly is the Nurse of frenzie,
Therefore they thought it good you heare a play,
And frame your minde to mirth and merriment,
Which barres a thousand harmes, and lengthens life.
Beg. Marrie I will let them play, it is not a Comontie, a Christmas gambold, or a tumbling tricke?
Lady. No my good Lord, it is more pleasing stuffe.
Beg. What, houshold stuffe.
Lady It is a kinde of history.
Beg. Well, we'l see't:
Come Madam wife sit by my side,
And let the world slip, we shall nere be yonger.

Flourish. Enter Lucentio, and his man Triano.

Luc. *Tranio*, since for the great desire I had
To see faire *Padua*, nurserie of Arts,
I am arriu'd for fruitfull *Lumbardie*,
The pleasant garden of great *Italy*,
And by my fathers loue and leaue am arm'd
With his good will, and thy good companie.
My trustie seruant well approu'd in all,
Heere let vs breath, and haply institute
A course of Learning, and ingenious studies.
Pisa renowned for graue Citizens
Gaue me my being, and my father first
A Merchant of great Trafficke through the world:
Vincentio's come of the *Bentiuolij*,
Vincentio's sonne, brough vp in *Florence*,
It shall become to serue all hopes conceiu'd
To decke his fortune with his vertuous deedes:
And therefore *Tranio*, for the time I studie,
Vertue and that part of Philosophie
Will I applie, that treats of happinesse,
By vertue specially to be atchieu'd.
Tell me thy minde, for I haue *Pisa* left,
And am to *Padua* come, as he that leaues
A shallow plash, to plunge him in the deepe,
And with facietie seekes to quench his thirst.
Tra *Me Pardonato*, gentle master mine:
I am in all affected as your selfe,
Glad that you thus continue your resolue,
To sucke the sweets of sweete Philosophie.
Onely (good master) while we do admire
This vertue, and this morall discipline,
Let's be no Stoickes, nor no stockes I pray,
Or so deuote to *Aristotles* checkes
As *Ouid*; be an out-cast quite abiur'd:
Balke Lodgicke with acquaintance that you haue,
And practise Rhetoricke in your common talke,
Musicke and Poesie vse, to quicken you,
The Mathematickes, and the Metaphysickes
Fall to them as you finde your stomacke serues you:
No profit growes, where is no pleasure tane:
In briefe sir, studie what you most affect.
Luc. Gramercies *Tranio*, well dost thou aduise,
If *Biondello* thou wert come ashore,
We could at once put vs in readinesse,
And take a Lodging fit to entertaine
Such friends (as time) in *Padua* shall beget.
But stay a while, what companie is this?
Tra. Master some shew to welcome vs to Towne.

Enter Baptista with his two daughters, Katerina & Bianca, Gremio a Pantelowne. Hortentio sister to Bianca. Lucen. Tranio, stand by.

Bap. Gentlemen, importune me no farther,
For how I firmly am resolu'd you know:
That is, not to bestow my yongest daughter,
Before I haue a husband for the elder:
If either of you both loue *Katherina*,

Because

Becauſe I know you well, and loue you well,
Leaue ſhall you haue to court her at your pleaſure.
Gre. To cart her rather. She's to rough for mee,
There,there *Hortenſio*. will you any Wife?
Kate. I pray you ſir, is it your will
To make a ſtale of me amongſt theſe mates?
Hor. Mates maid,how meane you that?.
No mates for you,
Vnleſſe you were of gentler milder mould.
Kate. I'faith ſir, you ſhall neuer neede to feare,
I wis it is not halfe way to her heart:
But if it were, doubt not, her care ſhould be,
To combe your noddle with a three-legg'd ſtoole,
And paint your face, and vſe you like a foole.
Hor. From all ſuch diuels,good Lord deliuer vs.
Gre. And me too good Lord.
Tra.Huſht maſter,heres ſome good paſtime toward;
That wench is ſtarke mad, or wonderfull froward
Lucen. But in the others ſilence do I ſee,
Maids milde behauiour and ſobrietie.
Peace *Tranio*.
Tra. Well ſaid Mr, mum,and gaze your fill
Bap. Gentlemen, that I may ſoone make good
What I haue ſaid, *Bianca* get you in,
And let it not diſpleaſe thee good *Bianca*,
For I will loue thee nere the leſſe my girle.
Kate. A pretty peate, it is beſt put finger in the eye, and ſhe knew why.
Bian. Siſter content you in my diſcontent.
Sir, to your pleaſure humbly I ſubſcribe:
My bookes and inſtruments ſhall be my companie,
On them to looke, and practiſe by my ſelfe.
Luc. Harke *Tranio*,thou maiſt heare *Minerua* ſpeak.
Hor. Signior *Baptiſta*, will you be ſo ſtrange,
Sorrie am I that our good will effects
Bianca's greefe.
Gre. Why will you mew her vp
(Signior *Baptiſta*) for this fiend of hell,
And make her beare the pennance of her tongue.
Bap. Gentlemen content ye: I am reſould:
Go in *Bianca*.
And for I know ſhe taketh moſt delight
In Muſicke, Inſtruments, and Poetry,
Schoolemaſters will I keepe within my houſe,
Fit to inſtruct her youth. If you *Hortenſio*,
Or ſignior *Gremio* you know any ſuch,
Preferre them hither: for to cunning men,
I will be very kinde and liberall
To mine owne children, in good bringing vp,
And ſo farewell: *Katherina* you may ſtay,
For I haue more to commune with *Bianca*. *Exit*.
Kate. Why, and I truſt I may go too,may I not?
What ſhall I be appointed houres, as though
(Belike) I knew not what to take,
And what to leaue? Ha *Exit*
Gre. You may go to the diuels dam: your guifts are ſo good heere's none will holde you: Their loue is not ſo great *Hortenſio*, but we may blow our nails together, and faſt it fairely out. Our cakes dough on both ſides. Farewell: yet for the loue I beare my ſweet *Bianca*, if I can by any meanes light on a fit man to teach her that wherein ſhe delights, I will wiſh him to her father.
Hor. So will I ſigniour *Gremio*: but a word I pray: Though the nature of our quarrell yet neuer brook'd parle, know now vpon aduice, it toucheth vs both: that we may yet againe haue acceſſe to our faire Miſtris, and be happie riuals in *Bianca's* loue, to labour and effect one thing ſpecially.
Gre. What's that I pray?
Hor. Marrie ſir to get a husband for her Siſter.
Gre. A husband: a diuell.
Hor. I ſay a husband.
Gre. I ſay, a diuell: Think'ſt thou *Hortenſio*,though her father be verie rich, any man is ſo verie a foole to be married to hell?
Hor. Tuſh *Gremio*: though it paſſe your patience & mine to endure her lowd alarums, why man there bee good fellowes in the world, and a man could light on them, would take her with all faults,and mony enough.
Gre. I cannot tell: but I had as lief take her dowrie with this condition; To be whipt at the hie croſſe euerie morning.
Hor. Faith (as you ſay) there's ſmall choiſe in rotten apples: but come, ſince this bar in law makes vs friends, it ſhall be ſo farre forth friendly maintain'd, till by helping *Baptiſtas* eldeſt daughter to a husband, wee ſet his yongeſt free for a husband, and then haue too t afreſh: Sweet *Bianca*, happy man be his dole: hee that runnes faſteſt, gets the Ring: How ſay you ſignior *Gremio*?
Grem I am agreed, and would I had giuen him the beſt horſe in *Padua* to begin his woing that would thoroughly woe her, wed her, and bed her, and ridde the houſe of her. Come on.
Exeunt ambo. Manet Tranio and Lucentio
Tra. I pray ſir tel me, is it poſſible
That loue ſhould of a ſodaine take ſuch hold.
Luc. Oh *Tranio*, till I found it to be true,
I neuer thought it poſſible or likely.
But ſee, while idely I ſtood looking on,
I found the effect of Loue in idleneſſe,
And now in plainneſſe do confeſſe to thee
That art to me as ſecret and as deere
As *Anna* to the Queene of Carthage was
Tranio I burne, I pine, I periſh *Tranio*,
If I atchieue not this yong modeſt gyrle:
Counſaile me *Tranio*, for I know thou canſt:
Aſſiſt me *Tranio*, for I know thou wilt.
Tra. Maſter, it is no time to chide you now,
Affection is not rated from the heart:
If loue haue touch'd you, naught remaines but ſo,
Redime te captam quam queas minimo.
Luc Gramercies Lad: Go forward, this contents,
The reſt wil comfort, for thy counſels ſound.
Tra. Maſter, you look'd ſo longly on the maide.
Perhaps you mark'd not what's the pith of all.
Luc. Oh yes, I ſaw ſweet beautie in her face,
Such as the daughter of *Agenor* had,
That made great *Ioue* to humble him to her hand,
When with his knees he kiſt the Cretan ſtrond.
Tra.Saw you no more? Mark'd you not how hir ſiſter
Began to ſcold, and raiſe vp ſuch a ſtorme,
That mortal eares might hardly indure the din.
Luc. *Tranio*, I ſaw her corrall lips to moue,
And with her breath ſhe did perfume the ayre,
Sacred and ſweet was all I ſaw in her.
Tra. Nay, then tis time to ſtirre him fro his trance:
I pray awake ſir: if you loue the Maide,
Bend thoughts and wits to atcheeue her. Thus it ſtands:
Her elder ſiſter is ſo curſt and ſhrew'd,
That til the Father rid his hands of her,
Maſter, your Loue muſt liue a maide at home,
And therefore has he cloſely meu'd her vp,
Becauſe

Because she will not be annoy'd with suters.
Luc. Ah *Tranio*, what a cruell Fathers he:
But art thou not aduis'd, he tooke some care
To get her cunning Schoolemasters to instruct her.
Tra. I marry am I sir, and now 'tis plotted.
Luc. I haue it *Tranio*.
Tra Master, for my hand
Both our inuentions meet and iumpe in one.
Luc. Tell me thine first
Tra. You will be schoole-master,
And vndertake the teaching of the maid:
That's your deuice.
Luc. It is: May it be done?
Tra. Not possible: for who shall beare your part,
And be in *Padua* heere *Vincentio's* sonne,
Keepe house, and ply his booke, welcome his friends,
Visit his Countrimen, and banquet them?
Luc. *Basta*, content thee: for I haue it full.
We haue not yet bin seene in any house,
Nor can we be distinguish'd by our faces,
For man or master: then it followes thus;
Thou shalt be master, *Tranio* in my sted:
Keepe house, and port, and seruants, as I should,
I will some other be, some *Florentine*,
Some *Neapolitan*, or meaner man of *Pisa*.
'Tis hatch'd, and shall be so: *Tranio* at once
Vncase thee: take my Conlord hat and cloake,
When *Biondello* comes, he waites on thee,
But I will charme him first to keepe his tongue.
Tra. So had you neede:
In breefe Sir, sith it your pleasure is,
And I am tyed to be obedient,
For so your father charg'd me at our parting:
Be seruiceable to my sonne (quoth he)
Although I thinke 'twas in another sence,
I am content to bee *Lucentio*,
Because so well I loue *Lucentio*.
Luc. *Tranio* be so, because *Lucentio* loues,
And let me be a slaue, t'atchieue that maide,
Whose sodaine sight hath thral'd my wounded eye.

Enter Biondello.

Heere comes the rogue. Sirra, where haue you bin?
Bion. Where haue I beene? Nay how now, where are you? Maister, ha's my fellow *Tranio* stolne your cloathes, or you stolne his, or both? Pray what's the newes
Luc. Sirra come hither, 'tis no time to iest,
And therefore frame your manners to the time
Your fellow *Tranio* heere to saue my life,
Puts my apparrell, and my countenance on,
And I for my escape haue put on his:
For in a quarrell since I came a shore,
I kil'd a man, and feare I was descried:
Waite you on him, I charge you, as becomes:
While I make way from hence to saue my life:
You vnderstand me?
Bion. I sir, ne're a whit.
Luc. And not a iot of *Tranio* in your mouth,
Tranio is chang'd into *Lucentio*.
Bion. The better for him, would I were so too.
Tra. So could I 'faith boy, to haue the next wish after, that *Lucentio* indeede had *Baptistas* yongest daughter. But sirra, not for my sake, but your masters, I aduise you vse your manners discreetly in all kind of companies: When I am alone, why then I am *Tranio*: but in all places else, you master *Lucentio*.
Luc. *Tranio* let's go:
One thing more rests, that thy selfe execute,
To make one among these wooers: if thou ask me why,
Sufficeth my reasons are both good and waighty.
Exeunt. *The Presenters aboue speakes.*
1. Man. My Lord you nod, you do not minde the play
Beg. Yes by Saint Anne do I, a good matter surely: Comes there any more of it?
Lady My Lord, 'tis but begun
Beg. 'Tis a verie excellent peece of worke, Madame Ladie: would 'twere done. *They sit and marke.*

Enter Petruchio, and his man Grumio.

Petr. *Verona*, for a while I take my leaue,
To see my friends in *Padua*; but of all
My best beloued and approued friend
Hortensio: & I trow this is his house:
Heere sirra *Grumio*, knocke I say.
Gru. Knocke sir? whom should I knocke? Is there any man ha's rebus'd your worship?
Petr. Villaine I say, knocke me heere soundly.
Gru. Knocke you heere sir? Why sir, what am I sir, that I should knocke you heere sir
Petr. Villaine I say, knocke me at this gate,
And rap me well, or Ile knocke your knaues pate
Gru. My Mr is growne quarrelsome:
I should knocke you first,
And then I know after who comes by the worst.
Petr. Will it not be?
'Faith sirrah, and you'l not knocke, Ile ring it,
Ile trie how you can *Sol*, *Fa*, and sing it.
He rings him by the eares
Gru. Helpe mistris helpe, my master is mad.
Petr. Now knocke when I bid you: sirrah villaine.
Enter Hortensio.
Hor. How now, what's the matter? My olde friend *Grumio*, and my good friend *Petruchio*? How do you all at *Verona*?
Petr. Signior *Hortensio*, come you to part the fray? *Contutti le core bene trobatto*, may I say.
Hor. *Alla nostra casa bene venuto multo honorata signior mio Petruchio.*
Rise *Grumio* rise, we will compound this quarrell
Gru Nay 'tis no matter sir, what he leges in Latine If this be not a lawfull cause for me to leaue his seruice, looke you sir. He bid me knocke him, & rap him soundly sir. Well, was it fit for a seruant to vse his master so, being perhaps (for ought I see) two and thirty, a peepe out? Whom would to God I had well knockt at first, then had not *Grumio* come by the worst
Petr. A sencelesse villaine: good *Hortensio*,
I bad the rascall knocke vpon your gate,
And could not get him for my heart to do it.
Gru. Knocke at the gate? O heauens: spake you not these words plaine? Sirra, Knocke me heere: rappe me heere: knocke me well, and knocke me soundly? And come you now with knocking at the gate?
Petr. Sirra be gone, or talke not I aduise you.
Hor. *Petruchio* patience, I am *Grumio's* pledge
Why this a heauie chance twixt him and you,
Your ancient trustie pleasant seruant *Grumio*.
And tell me now (sweet friend) what happie gale
Blowes you to *Padua* heere, from old *Verona*?
Petr. Such wind as scatters yongmen throgh y world.
To

To seeke their fortunes farther then at home,
Where small experience growes but in a few.
Signior *Hortensio*, thus it stands with me,
Antonio my father is deceast,
And I haue thrust my selfe into this maze,
Happily to wiue and thriue, as best I may:
Crownes in my purse I haue, and goods at home,
And so am come abroad to see the world.

Hor. *Petruchio*, shall I then come roundly to thee,
And wish thee to a shrew'd ill-fauour'd wife?
Thou'dst thanke me but a little for my counsell:
And yet Ile promise thee she shall be rich,
And verie rich: but th'art too much my friend,
And Ile not wish thee to her.

Petr. Signior *Hortensio*, 'twixt such friends as wee,
Few words suffice: and therefore, if thou know
One rich enough to be *Petruchio's* wife:
(As wealth is burthen of my woing dance)
Be she as foule as was *Florentius* Loue,
As old as *Sibell*, and as curst and shrow'd
As *Socrates Zentippe*, or a worse:
She moues me not, or not remoues at least
Affections edge in me. Were she is as rough
As are the swelling *Adriaticke* seas.
I come to wiue it wealthily in *Padua*:
If wealthily, then happily in *Padua*.

Gru. Nay looke you sir, hee tels you flatly what his minde is: why giue him Gold enough, and marrie him to a Puppet or an Aglet babie, or an old trot with ne're a tooth in her head, though she haue as manie diseases as two and fiftie horses. Why nothing comes amisse, so monie comes withall.

Hor. *Petruchio*, since we are stept thus farre in,
I will continue that I broach'd in iest,
I can *Petruchio* helpe thee to a wife
With wealth enough and yong and beautious,
Brought vp as best becomes a Gentlewoman.
Her onely fault, and that is faults enough,
Is, that she is intollerable curst,
And shrow'd, and froward, so beyond all measure,
That were my state farre worser then it is,
I would not wed her for a mine of Gold.

Petr. *Hortensio* peace: thou knowst not golds effect,
Tell me her fathers name, and 'tis enough:
For I will boord her, though she chide as loud
As thunder, when the clouds in Autumne cracke.

Hor. Her father is *Baptista Minola*,
An affable and courteous Gentleman,
Her name is *Katherina Minola*,
Renown'd in *Padua* for her scolding tongue.

Petr. I know her father, though I know not her,
And he knew my deceased father well:
I wil not sleepe *Hortensio* til I see her,
And therefore let me be thus bold with you,
To giue you ouer at this first encounter,
Vnlesse you wil accompanie me thither.

Gru. I pray you Sir let him go while the humor lasts. A my word, and she knew him as wel as I do, she would thinke scolding would doe little good vpon him. Shee may perhaps call him halfe a score Knaues, or so: Why that's nothing; and he begin once, hee'l raile in his rope trickes. Ile tell you what sir, and she stand him but a litle, he wil throw a figure in her face, and so disfigure hir with it, that shee shal haue no more eies to see withall then a Cat: you know him not sir.

Hor. Tarrie *Petruchio*, I must go with thee,
For in *Baptistas* keepe my treasure is:
He hath the Iewel of my life in hold,
His yongest daughter, beautiful *Bianca*,
And her with-holds from me. Other more
Suters to her, and riuals in my Loue:
Supposing it a thing impossible,
For those defects I haue before rehearst,
That euer *Katherina* wil be woo'd:
Therefore this order hath *Baptista* tane,
That none shal haue accesse vnto *Bianca*,
Til *Katherine* the Curst, haue got a husband.

Gru. *Katherine* the curst,
A title for a maide, of all titles the worst.

Hor. Now shal my friend *Petruchio* do me grace,
And offer me disguis'd in sober robes,
To old *Baptista* as a schoole-master
Well seene in Musicke, to instruct *Bianca*,
That so I may by this deuice at least
Haue leaue and leisure to make loue to her,
And vnsuspected court her by her selfe.

Enter Gremio and Lucentio disgused.

Gru. Heere's no knauerie. See, to beguile the olde-folkes, how the young folkes lay their heads together. Master, master, looke about you: Who goes there? ha.

Hor. Peace *Grumio*, it is the riuall of my Loue.
Petruchio stand by a while.

Grumio. A proper stripling, and an amorous.

Gremio. O very well, I haue perus'd the note:
Hearke you sir, Ile haue them verie fairely bound,
All bookes of Loue, see that at any hand,
And see you reade no other Lectures to her:
You vnderstand me. Ouer and beside
Signior *Baptistas* liberalitie,
Ile mend it with a Largesse. Take your paper too,
And let me haue them verie wel perfum'd;
For she is sweeter then perfume it selfe
To whom they go to: what wil you reade to her.

Luc. What ere I reade to her, Ile pleade for you,
As for my patron, stand you so assur'd,
As firmely as your selfe were still in place,
Yea and perhaps with more successefull words
Then you; vnlesse you were a scholler sir.

Gre. Oh this learning, what a thing it is.

Gru. Oh this Woodcocke, what an Asse it is.

Petru. Peace sirra.

Hor. *Grumio* mum: God saue you signior *Gremio*.

Gre. And you are wel met, Signior *Hortensio*.
Trow you whither I am going? To *Baptista Minola*,
I promist to enquire carefully
About a schoolemaster for the faire *Bianca*,
And by good fortune I haue lighted well
On this yong man: For learning and behauiour
Fit for her turne, well read in Poetrie
And other bookes, good ones, I warrant ye.

Hor. 'Tis well: and I haue met a Gentleman
Hath promist me to helpe one to another,
A fine Musician to instruct our Mistris,
So shal I no whit be behinde in dutie
To faire *Bianca*, so beloued of me.

Gre. Beloued of me, and that my deeds shal proue.

Gru. And that his bags shal proue.

Hor. *Gremio*, 'tis now no time to vent our loue,
Listen to me, and if you speake me faire,
Ile tel you newes indifferent good for either.
Heere is a Gentleman whom by chance I met

Vpon

Vpon agreement from vs to his liking,
Will vndertake to woo curſt *Katherine*,
Yea, and to marrie her, if her dowrie pleaſe.
Gre. So ſaid, ſo done, is well:
Hortenſio, haue you told him all her faults?
Petr. I know ſhe is an irkeſome brawling ſcold:
If that be all Maſters, I heare no harme.
Gre. No, ſayſt me ſo, friend? What Countreyman?
Petr. Borne in *Verona*, old *Butonios* ſonne:
My father dead, my fortune liues for me,
And I do hope, good dayes and long, to ſee.
Gre. Oh ſir, ſuch a life with ſuch a wife, were ſtrange:
But if you haue a ſtomacke, too't a Gods name,
You ſhal haue me aſſiſting you in all.
But will you woo this Wilde-cat?
Petr. Will I liue?
Gru. Wil he woo her? I: or Ile hang her.
Petr. Why came I hither, but to that intent?
Thinke you, a little dinne can daunt mine eares?
Haue I not in my time heard Lions rore?
Haue I not heard the ſea, puft vp with windes,
Rage like an angry Boare, chafed with ſweat?
Haue I not heard great Ordnance in the field?
And heauens Artillerie thunder in the skies?
Haue I not in a pitched battell heard
Loud larums, neighing ſteeds, & trumpets clangue?
And do you tell me of a womans tongue?
That giues not halfe ſo great a blow to heare,
As wil a Cheſſe-nut in a Farmers fire.
Tuſh, tuſh, feare boyes with bugs.
Gru. For he feares none.
Grem. *Hortenſio* hearke:
This Gentleman is happily arriu'd,
My minde preſumes for his owne good, and yours.
Hor. I promiſt we would be Contributors,
And beare his charge of wooing whatſoere.
Gremio. And ſo we wil, prouided that he win her.
Gru. I would I were as ſure of a good dinner.

Enter Tranio braue, and Biondello.

Tra. Gentlemen God ſaue you. If I may be bold
Tell me I beſeech you, which is the readieſt way
To the houſe of Signior *Baptiſta Minola*?
Bion. He that ha's the two faire daughters: iſt he you meane?
Tra. Euen he *Biondello*.
Gre. Hearke you ſir, you meane not her to——
Tra. Perhaps him and her ſir, what haue you to do?
Petr. Not her that chides ſir, at any hand I pray.
Tranio. I loue no chiders ſir: *Biondello*, let's away.
Luc Well begun *Tranio*.
Hor. Sir, a word ere you go:
Are you a ſutor to the Maid you talke of, yea or no?
Tra. And if I be ſir, is it any offence?
Gremio. No: if without more words you will get you hence.
Tra. Why ſir, I pray are not the ſtreets as free
For me, as for you?
Gre. But ſo is not ſhe.
Tra. For what reaſon I beſeech you.
Gre. For this reaſon if you'l kno,
That ſhe's the choiſe loue of Signior *Gremio*.
Hor. That ſhe's the choſen of ſignior *Hortenſio*.
Tra. Softly my Maſters: If you be Gentlemen
Do me this right: heare me with patience.
Baptiſta is a noble Gentleman,
To whom my Father is not all vnknowne,
And were his daughter fairer then ſhe is,
She may more ſutors haue, and me for one.
Faire *Ladaes* daughter had a thouſand wooers,
Then well one more may faire *Bianca* haue;
And ſo ſhe ſhall: *Lucentio* ſhal make one,
Though *Paris* came, in hope to ſpeed alone.
Gre. What, this Gentleman will out-talke vs all.
Luc. Sir giue him head, I know hee'l proue a Iade.
Petr. *Hortenſio*, to what end are all theſe words?
Hor. Sir, let me be ſo bold as aske you,
Did you yet euer ſee *Baptiſtas* daughter?
Tra. No ſir, but heare I do that he hath two:
The one, as famous for a ſcolding tongue,
As is the other, for beauteous modeſtie.
Petr. Sir, ſir, the firſt's for me, let her go by
Gre. Yea, leaue that labour to great *Hercules*,
And let it be more then *Alcides* twelue.
Petr. Sir vnderſtand you this of me (inſooth)
The yongeſt daughter whom you hearken for,
Her father keepes from all acceſſe of ſutors
And will not promiſe her to any man,
Vntill the elder ſiſter firſt be wed.
The yonger then is free, and not before.
Tranio. If it be ſo ſir, that you are the man
Muſt ſteed vs all, and me amongſt the reſt:
And if you breake the ice, and do this ſeeke,
Atchieue the elder: ſet the yonger free,
For our acceſſe, whoſe hap ſhall be to haue her,
Wil not ſo graceleſſe be, to be ingrate.
Hor. Sir you ſay wel, and wel you do conceiue,
And ſince you do profeſſe to be a ſutor,
You muſt as we do, gratifie this Gentleman,
To whom we all reſt generally beholding.
Tranio. Sir, I ſhal not be ſlacke, in ſigne whereof,
Pleaſe ye we may contriue this afternoone,
And quaffe carowſes to our Miſtreſſe health,
And do as aduerſaries do in law,
Striue mightily, but eate and drinke as friends.
Gru. Bion. Oh excellent motion: fellowes let's be gon
Hor. The motions good indeed, and be it ſo,
Petruchio, I ſhal be your *Been venuto*. *Exeunt*

Enter Katherina and Bianca.

Bian. Good ſiſter wrong me not, nor wrong your ſelf,
To make a bondmaide and a ſlaue of mee,
That I diſdaine: but for theſe other goods,
Vnbinde my hands, Ile pull them off my ſelfe,
Yea all my raiment, to my petticoate,
Or what you will command me, wil I do,
So well I know my dutie to my elders.
Kate. Of all thy ſutors heere I charge tel
Whom thou lou'ſt beſt: ſee thou diſſemble not.
Bianca. Beleeue me ſiſter, of all the men aliue,
I neuer yet beheld that ſpeciall face,
Which I could fancie, more then any other.
Kate. Minion thou lyeſt: Is't not *Hortenſio*?
Bian. If you affect him ſiſter, heere I ſweare
Ile pleade for you my ſelfe, but you ſhal haue him.
Kate. Oh then belike you fancie riches more,
You wil haue *Gremio* to keepe you faire.
Bian. Is it for him you do enuie me ſo?
Nay then you ieſt, and now I wel perceiue
You haue but ieſted with me all this while:
I prethee ſiſter Kate, vntie my hands.
Ka. If that be ieſt, then all the reſt was ſo. *Strikes her*
Enter

Enter Baptista.

Bap. Why how now Dame, whence growes this insolence?
Bianca stand aside, poore gyrle she weepes:
Go ply thy Needle, meddle not with her
For shame thou Hilding of a diuellish spirit,
Why dost thou wrong her, that did nere wrong thee?
When did she crosse thee with a bitter word?

Kate. Her silence flouts me, and Ile be reueng'd.

Flies after Bianca

Bap. What in my sight? *Bianca* get thee in. *Exit.*

Kate. What will you not suffer me: Nay now I see
She is your treasure, she must haue a husband,
I must dance bare-foot on her wedding day,
And for your loue to her, leade Apes in hell.
Talke not to me, I will go sit and weepe,
Till I can finde occasion of reuenge.

Bap. Was euer Gentleman thus greeu'd as I
But who comes heere.

Enter Gremio, Lucentio, in the habit of a meane man, Petruchio with Tranio, with his boy bearing a Lute and Bookes.

Gre. Good morrow neighbour *Baptista*.

Bap. Good morrow neighbour *Gremio*: God saue you Gentlemen.

Pet. And you good sir: pray haue you not a daughter, cal'd *Katerina*, faire and vertuous.

Bap. I haue a daughter sir, cal'd *Katerina*.

Gre. You are too blunt, go to it orderly.

Pet. You wrong me signior *Gremio*, giue me leaue.
I am a Gentleman of *Verona* sir,
That hearing of her beautie, and her wit,
Her affability and bashfull modestie:
Her wondrous qualities, and milde behauiour
Am bold to shew my selfe a forward guest
Within your house, to make mine eye the witnesse
Of that report, which I so oft haue heard,
And for an entrance to my entertainment,
I do present you with a man of mine
Cunning in Musicke, and the Mathematickes,
To instruct her fully in those sciences,
Whereof I know she is not ignorant,
Accept of him, or else you do me wrong,
His name is *Litio*, borne in *Mantua*.

Bap. Y'are welcome sir, and he for your good sake.
But for my daughter *Katerine*, this I know,
She is not for your turne, the more my greefe.

Pet. I see you do not meane to part with her,
Or else you like not of my companie.

Bap. Mistake me not, I speake but as I finde,
Whence are you sir? What may I call your name.

Pet. *Petruchio* is my name, *Antonio's* sonne,
A man well knowne throughout all Italy

Bap. I know him well: you are welcome for his sake.

Gre. Sauing your tale *Petruchio*, I pray let vs that are poore petitioners speake too? *Bacare*, you are meruaylous forward.

Pet. Oh, Pardon me signior *Gremio*, I would faine be doing.

Gre. I doubt it not sir. But you will curse
Your wooing neighbors: this is a guift
Very gratefull, I am sure of it, to expresse
The like kindnesse my selfe, that haue beene
Mere kindely beholding to you then any:
Freely giue vnto this yong Scholler, that hath
Beene long studying at *Rhemes*, as cunning
In Greeke, Latine, and other Languages,
As the other in Musicke and Mathematickes:
His name is *Cambio*: pray accept his seruice.

Bap. A thousand thankes signior *Gremio*:
Welcome good *Cambio*. But gentle sir,
Me thinkes you walke like a stranger,
May I be so bold, to know the cause of your comming

Tra. Pardon me sir, the boldnesse is mine owne,
That being a stranger in this Cittie heere,
Do make my selfe a sutor to your daughter,
Vnto *Bianca*, faire and vertuous:
Nor is your firme resolue vnknowne to me,
In the preferment of the eldest sister.
This liberty is all that I request,
That vpon knowledge of my Parentage,
I may haue welcome mongst the rest that woo,
And free accesse and fauour as the rest.
And toward the education of your daughters:
I heere bestow a simple instrument,
And this small packet of Greeke and Latine bookes:
If you accept them, then their worth is great:

Bap. *Lucentio* is your name, of whence I pray.

Tra. Of *Pisa* sir, sonne to *Vincentio*.

Bap. A mightie man of *Pisa* by report,
I know him well: you are verie welcome sir:
Take you the Lute, and you the set of bookes,
You shall go see your Pupils presently.
Holla, within.

Enter a Seruant.

Sirrah, leade these Gentlemen
To my daughters, and tell them both
These are their Tutors, bid them vse them well,
We will go walke a little in the Orchard,
And then to dinner: you are passing welcome,
And so I pray you all to thinke your selues.

Pet. Signior *Baptista*, my businesse asketh haste,
And euerie day I cannot come to woo,
You knew my father well, and in him me,
Left solie heire to all his Lands and goods,
Which I haue bettered rather then decreast,
Then tell me, if I get your daughters loue,
What dowrie shall I haue with her to wife.

Bap. After my death, the one halfe of my Lands,
And in possession twentie thousand Crownes.

Pet And for that dowrie, Ile assure her of
Her widdow-hood, be it that she suruiue me
In all my Lands and Leases whatsoeuer,
Let specialties be therefore drawne betweene vs,
That couenants may be kept on either hand.

Bap. I, when the speciall thing is well obtain'd,
That is her loue: for that is all in all.

Pet. Why that is nothing: for I tell you father,
I am as peremptorie as she proud minded:
And where two raging fires meete together,
They do consume the thing that feedes their furie.
Though little fire growes great with little winde,
yet extreme gusts will blow out fire and all:
So I to her, and so she yeelds to me,
For I am rough, and woo not like a babe.

Bap. Well maist thou woo, and happy be thy speed:
But be thou arm'd for some vnhappie words.

Pet. I to the proofe, as Mountaines are for windes,
That shakes not, though they blow perpetually

Enter Hortensio with his head broke.

B pa

Bap. How now my friend, why doſt thou looke ſo pale?
Hor. For feare I promiſe you, if I looke pale.
Bap. What, will my daughter proue a good Muſitian?
Hor. I thinke ſhe'l ſooner proue a ſouldier,
Iron may hold with her, but neuer Lutes.
Bap. Why then thou canſt not break her to the Lute?
Hor. Why no, for ſhe hath broke the Lute to me:
I did but tell her ſhe miſtooke her frets,
And bow'd her hand to teach her fingering,
When (with a moſt impatient diuelliſh ſpirit)
Frets call you theſe? (quoth ſhe) Ile fume with them:
And with that word ſhe ſtroke me on the head,
And through the inſtrument my pate made way,
And there I ſtood amazed for a while,
As on a Pillorie, looking through the Lute,
While ſhe did call me Raſcall, Fidler,
And twangling Iacke, with twentie ſuch vilde tearmes,
As had ſhe ſtudied to miſvſe me ſo.
Pet. Now by the world, it is a luſtie Wench,
I loue her ten times more then ere I did,
Oh how I long to haue ſome chat with her.
Bap. Wel go with me, and be not ſo diſcomfited.
Proceed in practiſe with my yonger daughter,
She's apt to learne, and thankefull for good turnes:
Signior *Petruchio*, will you go with vs,
Or ſhall I ſend my daughter *Kate* to you.
Exit. Manet Petruchio.
Pet. I pray you do. Ile attend her heere,
And woo her with ſome ſpirit when ſhe comes,
Say that ſhe raile, why then Ile tell her plaine,
She ſings as ſweetly as a Nightinghale:
Say that ſhe frowne, Ile ſay ſhe lookes as cleere
As morning Roſes newly waſht with dew:
Say ſhe be mute, and will not ſpeake a word,
Then Ile commend her volubility,
And ſay ſhe vttereth piercing eloquence.
If ſhe do bid me packe, Ile giue her thankes,
As though ſhe bid me ſtay by her a weeke:
If ſhe denie to wed, Ile craue the day
When I ſhall aske the banes, and when be married.
But heere ſhe comes, and now *Petruchio* ſpeake.
Enter Katerina.
Good morrow *Kate*, for thats your name I heare.
Kate. Well haue you heard, but ſomething hard of hearing:
They call me *Katerine*, that do talke of me.
Pet. You lye infaith, for you are call'd plaine *Kate*,
And bony *Kate*, and ſometimes *Kate* the curſt:
But *Kate*, the prettieſt *Kate* in Chriſtendome,
Kate of *Kate*-hall, my ſuper-daintie *Kate*,
For dainties are all *Kates*, and therefore *Kate*
Take this of me, *Kate* of my conſolation,
Hearing thy mildneſſe prais'd in euery Towne,
Thy vertues ſpoke of, and thy beautie ſounded,
Yet not ſo deepely as to thee belongs,
My ſelfe am moou'd to woo thee for my wife.
Kate. Mou'd, in good time, let him that mou'd you hether
Remoue you hence: I knew you at the firſt
You were a mouable.
Pet. Why, what's a mouable?
Kat. A ioyn'd ſtoole.
Pet. Thou haſt hit it: come ſit on me.
Kate. Aſſes are made to beare, and ſo are you.
Pet. Women are made to beare, and ſo are you.
Kate. No ſuch Iade as you, if me you meane.
Pet. Alas good *Kate*, I will not burthen thee,
For knowing thee to be but yong and light.
Kate. Too light for ſuch a ſwaine as you to catch,
And yet as heauie as my waight ſhould be.
Pet. Shold be, ſhould: buzze.
Kate. Well tane, and like a buzzard.
Pet. Oh ſlow wing'd Turtle, ſhal a buzard take thee?
Kat. I for a Turtle, as he takes a buzard.
Pet. Come, come you Waſpe, y'faith you are too angrie.
Kate. If I be waſpiſh, beſt beware my ſting.
Pet. My remedy is then to plucke it out.
Kate. I, if the foole could finde it where it lies.
Pet. Who knowes not where a Waſpe does weare his ſting? In his taile.
Kate. In his tongue?
Pet. Whoſe tongue.
Kate. Yours if you talke of tales, and ſo farewell.
Pet. What with my tongue in your taile.
Nay, come againe, good *Kate*, I am a Gentleman,
Kate. That Ile trie. *ſhe ſtrikes him*
Pet. I ſweare Ile cuffe you, if you ſtrike againe.
Kate. So may you looſe your armes,
If you ſtrike me, you are no Gentleman,
And if no Gentleman, why then no armes.
Pet. A Herald *Kate*? Oh put me in thy bookes.
Kate. What is your Creſt, a Coxcombe?
Pet. A combleſſe Cocke, ſo *Kate* will be my Hen.
Kate. No Cocke of mine, you crow too like a crauen
Pet. Nay come *Kate*, come: you muſt not looke ſo ſowre.
Kate. It is my faſhion when I ſee a Crab.
Pet Why heere's no crab, and therefore looke not ſowre.
Kate. There is, there is.
Pet. Then ſhew it me.
Kate. Had I a glaſſe, I would.
Pet. What, you meane my face.
Kate Well aym'd of ſuch a yong one.
Pet. Now by S. George I am too yong for you.
Kate. Yet you are wither'd.
Pet. 'Tis with cares.
Kate. I care not.
Pet. Nay heare you *Kate*. Inſooth you ſcape not ſo.
Kate. I chafe you if I tarrie. Let me go.
Pet. No, not a whit, I finde you paſſing gentle:
'Twas told me you were rough, and coy, and ſullen,
And now I finde report a very liar:
For thou art pleaſant, gameſome, paſſing courteous,
But ſlow in ſpeech: yet ſweet as ſpring-time flowers.
Thou canſt not frowne, thou canſt not looke a ſconce,
Nor bite the lip, as angry wenches will,
Nor haſt thou pleaſure to be croſſe in talke:
But thou with mildneſſe entertain'ſt thy wooers,
With gentle conference, ſoft, and affable.
Why does the world report that *Kate* doth limpe?
Oh ſland'rous world: *Kate* like the hazle twig
Is ſtraight, and ſlender, and as browne in hue
As hazle nuts, and ſweeter then the kernels:
Oh let me ſee thee walke: thou doſt not halt.
Kate. Go foole, and whom thou keep'ſt command.
Pet. Did euer *Dian* ſo become a Groue
As *Kate* this chamber with her princely gate:
O be thou *Dian*, and let her be *Kate*,

And then let *Kate* be chaſte, and *Dian* ſportfull.
Kate. Where did you ſtudy all this goodly ſpeech?
Petr. It is *extempore*, from my mother wit.
Kate. A witty mother, witleſſe elſe her ſonne.
Pet. Am I not wiſe?
Kat. Yes, keepe you warme.
Pet. Marry ſo I meane ſweet *Katherine* in my bed:
And therefore ſetting all this chat aſide,
Thus in plaine termes: your father hath conſented
That you ſhall be my wife; your dowry greed on,
And will you, nill you, I will marry you.
Now *Kate*, I am a husband for your turne,
For by this light, whereby I ſee thy beauty,
Thy beauty that doth make me like thee well,
Thou muſt be married to no man but me.

Enter Baptiſta, Gremio, Trayno.

For I am he am borne to tame you *Kate*,
And bring you from a wilde *Kate* to a *Kate*
Conformable as other houſhold *Kates*:
Heere comes your father, neuer make deniall,
I muſt, and will haue *Katherine* to my wiſe.
Bap. Now Signior *Petruchio*, how ſpeed you with my (daughter?
Pet. How but well ſirhow but well?
It were impoſſible I ſhould ſpeed amiſſe.
Bap. Why how now daughter *Katherine*, in your (dumps?
Kat. Call you me daughter? now I promiſe you
You haue ſhewd a tender fatherly regard,
To wiſh me wed to one halfe Lunaticke,
A mad-cap ruffian, and a ſwearing Iacke,
That thinkes with oathes to face the matter out.
Pet. Father, 'tis thus, your ſelfe and all the world
That talk'd of her, haue talk'd amiſſe of her:
If ſhe be curſt, it is for pollicie,
For ſhee's not froward, but modeſt as the Doue,
Shee is not hot, but temperate as the morne,
For patience ſhee will proue a ſecond *Griſſell*,
And Romane *Lucrece* for her chaſtitie:
And to conclude, we haue greed ſo well together,
That vpon ſonday is the wedding day.
Kate. Ile ſee thee hang'd on ſonday firſt.
Gre. Hark *Petruchio*, ſhe ſaies ſhee'll ſee thee hang'd (firſt.
Tra. Is this your ſpeeding? nay the godnight our part.
Pet: Be patient gentlemen, I chooſe her for my ſelfe,
If ſhe and I be pleas'd, what's that to you?
'Tis bargain'd twixt vs twaine being alone,
That ſhe ſhall ſtill be curſt in company.
I tell you 'tis incredible to beleeue
How much ſhe loues me: oh the kindeſt *Kate*,
Shee hung about my necke, and kiſſe on kiſſe
Shee vi'd ſo faſt, proteſting oath on oath,
That in a twinke ſhe won me to her loue.
Oh you are nouices, 'tis a world to ſee
How tame when men and women are alone,
A meacocke wretch can make the curſteſt ſhrew:
Giue me thy hand *Kate*, I will vnto *Venice*
To buy apparell 'gainſt the wedding day;
Prouide the feaſt father, and bid the gueſts,
I will be ſure my *Katherine* ſhall be fine.
Bap. I know not what to ſay, but giue me your hads,
God ſend you ioy, *Petruchio*, 'tis a match.
Gre. Tra. Amen ſay we, we will be witneſſes.
Pet. Father, and wife, and gentlemen adieu,
I will to *Venice*, ſonday comes apace,
We will haue rings, and things, and fine array,
And kiſſe me *Kate*, we will be married a ſonday.
Exit Petruchio and Katherine.
Gre. Was euer match clapt vp ſo ſodainly?
Bap: Faith Gentlemen now I play a marchants part,
And venture madly on a deſperate Mart.
Tra. Twas a commodity lay fretting by you,
Twill bring you gaine, or periſh on the ſeas.
Bap. The gaine I ſeeke, is quiet me the match.
Gre. No doubt but he hath got a quiet catch:
But now *Baptiſta*, to your yonger daughter,
Now is the day we long haue looked for,
I am your neighbour, and was ſuter firſt.
Tra. And I am one that loue *Bianca* more
Then words can witneſſe, or your thoughts can gueſſe.
Gre. Yongling thou canſt not loue ſo deare as I.
Tra. Gray-beard thy loue doth freeze.
Gre. But thine doth frie,
Skipper ſtand backe, 'tis age that nouriſheth.
Tra. But youth in Ladies eyes that floriſheth.
Bap. Content you gentlemen, I wil cōpound this ſtrife
'Tis deeds muſt win the prize, and he of both
That can aſſure my daughter greateſt dower,
Shall haue my *Biancas* loue.
Say ſignior *Gremio*, what can you aſſure her?
Gre. Firſt, as you know, my houſe within the City
Is richly furniſhed with plate and gold,
Baſons and ewers to laue her dainty hands:
My hangings all of *tirian* tapeſtry:
In Iuory cofers I haue ſtuft my crownes:
In Cypres cheſts my arras counterpoints,
Coſtly apparell, tents, and Canopies,
Fine Linnen, Turky cuſhions boſt with pearle,
Vallens of Venice gold, in needle worke:
Pewter and braſſe, and all things that belongs
To houſe or houſe-keeping: then at my farme
I haue a hundred milch-kine to the pale,
Sixe-ſcore fat Oxen ſtanding in my ſtalls,
And all things anſwerable to this portion.
My ſelfe am ſtrooke in yeeres I muſt confeſſe,
And if I die to morrow this is hers,
If whil'ſt I liue ſhe will be onely mine.
Tra. That only came well in: ſir, liſt to me,
I am my fathers heyre and onely ſonne,
If I may haue your daughter to my wife,
Ile leaue her houſes three or foure as good
Within rich *Piſa* walls, as any one
Old Signior *Gremio* has in *Padua*,
Beſides, two thouſand Duckets by the yeere
Of fruitfull land, all which ſhall be her ioynter.
What, haue I pincht you Signior *Gremio*?
Gre. Two thouſand Duckets by the yeere of land,
My Land amounts not to ſo much in all:
That ſhe ſhall haue, beſides an Argoſie
That now is lying in Marcellus roade:
What, haue I choakt you with an Argoſie?
Tra. *Gremio*, 'tis knowne my father hath no leſſe
Then three great Argoſies, beſides two Galliaſſes
And twelue tite Gallies, theſe I will aſſure her,
And twice as much what ere thou offreſt next.
Gre. Nay, I haue offred all, I haue no more,
And ſhe can haue no more then all I haue,
If you like me, ſhe ſhall haue me and mine.
Tra. Why then the maid is mine from all the world
By your firme promiſe, *Gremio* is out vied.
Bap. I muſt confeſſe your offer is the beſt,
And let your father make her the aſſurance,

T Shee

Shee is your owne, else you must pardon me:
If you should die before him, where's her dower?
Tra. That's but a cauill: he is olde, I young.
Gre. And may not yong men die as well as old?
Bap Well gentlemen, I am thus resolu'd,
On sonday next, you know
My daughter *Katherine* is to be married:
Now on the sonday following, shall *Bianca*
Be Bride to you, if you make this assurance:
If not, to Signior *Gremio*:
And so I take my leaue, and thanke you both. *Exit.*
Gre. Adieu good neighbour: now I feare thee not:
Sirra, yong gamester, your father were a foole
To giue thee all, and in his wayning age
Set foot vnder thy table: tut, a toy,
An olde Italian foxe is not so kinde my boy. *Exit.*
Tra. A vengeance on your crafty withered hide,
Yet I haue fac'd it with a card of ten:
Tis in my head to doe my master good:
I see no reason but suppos'd *Lucentio*
Must get a father, call'd suppos'd *Vincentio*,
And that's a wonder: fathers commonly
Doe get their children: but in this case of woing,
A childe shall get a sire, if I faile not of my cunning. *Exit*

Actus Tertia.

Enter Lucentio, Hortentio, and Bianca.
Luc. Fidler forbeare you grow too forward Sir,
Haue you so soone forgot the entertainment
Her sister *Katherine* welcom'd you withall.
Hort But wrangling pedant, this is
The patronesse of heauenly harmony:
Then giue me leaue to haue prerogatiue,
And when in Musicke we haue spent an houre,
Your Lecture shall haue leisure for as much.
Luc. Preposterous Asse that neuer read so farre,
To know the cause why musicke was ordain'd:
Was it not to refresh the minde of man
After his studies, or his vsuall paine?
Then giue me leaue to read Philosophy,
And while I pause, serue in your harmony.
Hort. Sirra, I will not beare these braues of thine.
Bianc. Why gentlemen, you doe me double wrong,
To striue for that which resteth in my choice:
I am no breeching scholler in the schooles,
Ile not be tied to howres, nor pointed times,
But learne my Lessons as I please my selfe,
And to cut off all strife: heere sit we downe,
Take you your instrument, play you the whiles,
His Lecture will be done ere you haue tun'd.
Hort. You'll leaue his Lecture when I am in tune?
Luc That will be neuer, tune your instrument.
Bian. Where left we last?
Luc. Heere Madam: *Hic Ibat Simois, hic est sigeria tellus, hic steterat Priami regia Celsa senis.*
Bian. Conster them.
Luc. *Hic Ibat*, as I told you before, *Simois*, I am Lucentio, *hic est*, sonne vnto Vincentio of Pisa, *Sigeria tellus*, disguised thus to get your loue, *hic steterat*, and that Lucentio that comes a wooing, *priami*, is my man Tranio, *regia*, bearing my port, *celsa senis* that we might beguile the old Pantalowne.
Hort. Madam, my Instrument's in tune.
Bian. Let's heare, oh fie, the treble iarres.
Luc. Spit in the hole man, and tune againe.
Bian. Now let mee see if I can conster it. *Hic ibat simois*, I know you not, *hic est sigeria tellus*, I trust you not, *hic staterat priami*, take heede he heare vs not, *regia* presume not, *Celsa senis*, despaire not.
Hort. Madam, tis now in tune.
Luc. All but the base.
Hort. The base is right, 'tis the base knaue that iars.
Luc. How fiery and forward our Pedant is,
Now for my life the knaue doth court my loue,
Pedascule, Ile watch you better yet:
In time I may beleeue, yet I mistrust.
Bian. Mistrust it not, for sure *Æacides*
Was *Aiax* cald so from his grandfather.
Hort. I must beleeue my master, else I promise you,
I should be arguing still vpon that doubt,
But let it rest, now *Litio* to you:
Good master take it not vnkindly pray
That I haue beene thus pleasant with you both.
Hort. You may go walk, and giue me leaue a while,
My Lessons make no musicke in three parts.
Luc. Are you so formall sir, well I must waite
And watch withall, for but I be deceiu'd,
Our fine Musitian groweth amorous.
Hor. Madam, before you touch the instrument,
To learne the order of my fingering,
I must begin with rudiments of Art,
To teach you gamoth in a briefer sort,
More pleasant, pithy, and effectuall,
Then hath beene taught by any of my trade,
And there it is in writing fairely drawne.
Bian. Why, I am past my gamouth long agoe.
Hor. Yet read the gamouth of *Hortentio*.
Bian. *Gamouth* I am, the ground of all accord:
Are, to plead Hortensio's passion:
Beeme, Bianca take him for thy Lord
Cfavt, that loues with all affection:
D solre, one Cliffe, two notes haue I,
Ela mi, show pitty or I die.
Call you this gamouth? tut I like it not,
Old fashions please me best, I am not so nice
To charge true rules for old inuentions.
Enter a Messenger.
Nicke. Mistresse, your father prayes you leaue your (books,
And helpe to dresse your sisters chamber vp,
You know to morrow is the wedding day.
Bian. Farewell sweet masters both, I must be gone.
Luc. Faith Mistresse then I haue no cause to stay.
Hor But I haue cause to pry into this pedant,
Methinkes he lookes as though he were in loue:
Yet if thy thoughts *Bianca* be so humble
To cast thy wandring eyes on euery stale:
Seize thee that List, if once I finde thee ranging,
Hortensio will be quit with thee by changing. *Exit.*

Enter Baptista, Gremio, Tranio, Katherine, Bianca, and others, attendants.
Bap. Signior *Lucentio*, this is the pointed day
That *Katherine* and *Petruchio* should be married,
And yet we heare not of our sonne in Law:
What will be said, what mockery will it be?
To want the Bride-groome when the Priest attends
To speake the ceremoniall rites of marriage?
What saies *Lucentio* to this shame of ours?
No

Kate. No shame but mine, I must forsooth be forst
To giue my hand oppos'd against my heart
Vnto a mad-braine rudesby, full of spleene,
Who woo'd in haste and meanes to wed at leysure:
I told you I, he was a franticke foole,
Hiding his bitter iests in blunt behauiour,
And to be noted for a merry man;
Hee'll wooe a thousand, point the day of marriage,
Make friends, inuite, and proclaime the banes,
Yet neuer meanes to wed where he hath woo'd:
Now must the world point at poore *Katherine*,
And say, loe, there is mad *Petruchio's* wife
If it would please him come and marry her.

Tra. Patience good *Katherine* and *Baptista* too,
Vpon my life *Petruchio* meanes but well,
What euer fortune stayes him from his word,
Though he be blunt, I know him passing wise
Though he be merry, yet withall he's honest.

Kate. Would *Katherine* had neuer seen him though.
Exit weeping.

Bap. Goe girle, I cannot blame thee now to weepe,
For such an iniurie would vexe a very saint,
Much more a shrew of impatient humour.

Enter Biondello.

Bion. Master, master, newes, and such newes as you
neuer heard of,

Bap. Is it new and olde too? how may that be?

Bion. Why, is it not newes to heard of *Petruchio's* comming?

Bap. Is he come?

Bion. Why no sir.

Bap. What then?

Bion. He is comming.

Bap. When will he be heere?

Bion. When he stands where I am, and sees you there.

Tra. But say, what to thine olde newes?

Bion. Why *Petruchio* is comming, in a new hat and
an old ierkin, a paire of olde breeches thrice turn'd; a
paire of bootes that haue beene candle-cases, one buckled, another lac'd: an olde rusty sword tane out of the
Towne Armory, with a broken hilt, and chapelesse: with
two broken points: his horse hip'd with an olde mothy saddle, and stirrops of no kindred: besides possest
with the glanders, and like to mose in the chine, troubled with the Lampasse, infected with the fashions, full
of Windegalls, sped with Spauins, raied with the Yellowes, past cure of the Fiues, starke spoyl'd with the
Staggers, begnawne with the Bots, Waid in the backe,
and shoulder-shotten, neere leg'd before, and with a
halfe-chekt Bitte, & a headstall of sheepes leather, which
being restrain'd to keepe him from stumbling, hath been
often burst, and now repaired with knots: one girth sixe
times peec'd, and a womans Crupper of velure, which
hath two letters for her name, fairely set down in studs,
and heere and there peec'd with packthred.

Bap. Who comes with him?

Bion. Oh sir, his Lackey, for all the world Caparison'd like the horse: with a linnen stock on one leg, and
a kersey boot-hose on the other, gartred with a red and
blew list; an old hat, & the humor of forty fancies prickt
in't for a feather: a monster, a very monster in apparell,
& not like a Christian foot-boy, or a gentlemans Lacky.

Tra. 'Tis some od humor pricks him to this fashion,
Yet oftentimes he goes but meane apparel'd.

Bap. I am glad he's come howsoere he comes.

Bion. Why sir, he comes not.

Bap. Didst thou not say hee comes?

Bion. Who, that *Petruchio* came?

Bap. I, that *Petruchio* came.

Bion. No sir, I say his horse comes with him on his backe.

Bap. Why that's all one.

Bion. Nay by S. *Iamy*, I hold you a penny a horse and
a man is more then one, and yet not many.

Enter Petruchio and Grumio.

Pet. Come, where be these gallants? who's at home

Bap. You are welcome sir.

Petr. And yet I come not well.

Bap. And yet you halt not.

Tra. Not so well apparell'd as I wish you were.

Petr. Were it better I should rush in thus:
But where is *Kate*? where is my louely Bride?
How does my father? gentles methinkes you frowne,
And wherefore gaze this goodly company,
As if they saw some wondrous monument,
Some Commet, or vnusuall prodigie?

Bap. Why sir, you know this is your wedding day
First were we sad, fearing you would not come,
Now sadder that you come so vnprouided:
Fie, doff this habit, shame to your estate,
An eye-sore to our solemne festiuall.

Tra. And tell vs what occasion of import
Hath all so long detain'd you from your wife,
And sent you hither so vnlike your selfe?

Petr. Tedious it were to tell, and harsh to heare,
Sufficeth I am come to keepe my word,
Though in some part inforced to digresse,
Which at more leysure I will so excuse,
As you shall well be satisfied with all.
But where is *Kate*? I stay too long from her,
The morning weares, 'tis time we were at Church.

Tra. See not your Bride in these vnreuerent robes,
Goe to my chamber, put on clothes of mine.

Pet. Not I, beleeue me, thus Ile visit her.

Bap. But thus I trust you will not marry her.

Pet. Good sooth euen thus: therefore ha done with words,
To me she's married, not vnto my cloathes:
Could I repaire what she will weare in me,
As I can change these poore accoutrements,
Twere well for *Kate*, and better for my selfe.
But what a foole am I to chat with you,
When I should bid good morrow to my Bride?
And seale the title with a louely kisse. *Exit.*

Tra. He hath some meaning in his mad attire,
We will perswade him be it possible,
To put on better ere he goe to Church.

Bap. Ile after him, and see the euent of this. *Exit.*

Tra. But sir, Loue concerneth vs to adde
Her fathers liking, which to bring to passe
As before imparted to your worship,
I am to get a man what ere he be,
It skills not much, weele fit him to our turne,
And he shall be *Vincentio* of *Pisa*,
And make assurance heere in *Padua*
Of greater summes then I haue promised,
So shall you quietly enioy your hope,
And marry sweet *Bianca* with consent.

Luc. Were it not that my fellow schoolemaster
Doth watch *Bianca's* steps so narrowly:
'Twere good me-thinkes to steale our marriage,
Which once perform'd, let all the world say no,
Ile keepe mine owne despite of all the world.

Tra. That by degrees we meane to looke into,

T 2 And

And watch our vantage in this businesse,
Wee'll ouer-reach the grey-beard *Gremio*,
The narrow prying father *Minola*,
The quaint Musician, amorous *Litio*,
All for my Masters sake *Lucentio*.

Enter Gremio.

Signior *Gremio*, came you from the Church?
Gre. As willingly as ere I came from schoole.
Tra. And is the Bride & Bridegroom coming home?
Gre. A bridegroome say you? 'tis a groome indeed,
A grumlling groome, and that the girle shall finde.
Tra. Curster then she, why 'tis impossible.
Gre. Why hee's a deuill, a deuill, a very fiend.
Tra. Why she's a deuill, a deuill, the deuils damme.
Gre. Tut, she's a Lambe, a Doue, a foole to him:
Ile tell you sir *Lucentio*; when the Priest
Should aske if *Katherine* should be his wife,
I, by goggs woones quoth he, and swore so loud,
That all amaz'd the Priest let fall the booke,
And as he stoop'd againe to take it vp,
This mad-brain'd bridegroome tooke him such a cuffe,
That downe fell Priest and booke, and booke and Priest,
Now take them vp quoth he, if any list.
Tra. What said the wench when he rose againe?
Gre. Trembled and shooke: for why, he stamp'd and swore, as if the Vicar meant to cozen him: but after many ceremonies done, hee calls for wine, a health quoth he, as if he had beene aboord carowsing to his Mates after a storme, quaft off the Muscadell, and threw the sops all in the Sextons face: hauing no other reason, but that his beard grew thinne and hungerly, and seem'd to aske him sops as hee was drinking: This done, hee tooke the Bride about the necke, and kist her lips with such a clamorous smacke, that at the parting all the Church did eccho: and I seeing this, came thence for very shame, and after mee I know the rout is comming, such a mad marryage neuer was before: harke, harke, I heare the minstrels play. *Musicke playes.*

Enter Petruchio, Kate, Bianca, Hortensio, Baptista.

Petr. Gentlemen & friends, I thank you for your pains,
I know you thinke to dine with me to day,
And haue prepar'd great store of wedding cheere,
But so it is, my haste doth call me hence,
And therefore heere I meane to take my leaue.
Bap. Is't possible you will away to night?
Pet. I must away to day before night come,
Make it no wonder: if you knew my businesse,
You would intreat me rather goe then stay:
And honest company, I thanke you all,
That haue beheld me giue away my selfe
To this most patient, sweet, and vertuous wife,
Dine with my father, drinke a health to me,
For I must hence, and farewell to you all.
Tra. Let vs intreat you stay till after dinner.
Pet. It may not be.
Gra. Let me intreat you.
Pet. It cannot be.
Kat. Let me intreat you.
Pet. I am content.
Kat. Are you content to stay?
Pet. I am content you shall entreat me stay,
But yet not stay, entreat me how you can.
Kat. Now if you loue me stay.
Pet. Grumio, my horse.
Gru. I sir, they be ready, the Oates haue eaten the horses.
Kate. Nay then,
Doe what thou canst, I will not goe to day,
No, nor to morrow, not till I please my selfe,
The dore is open sir, there lies your
You may be iogging whiles your bootes are greene:
For me, Ile not be gone till I please my selfe,
'Tis like you'll proue a iolly surly groome,
That take it on you at the first so roundly.
Pet. O *Kate* content thee, prethee be not angry.
Kat. I will be angry, what hast thou to doe?
Father, be quiet, he shall stay my leisure.
Gre. I marry sir, now it begins to worke.
Kat. Gentlemen, forward to the bridall dinner,
I see a woman may be made a foole
If she had not a spirit to resist.
Pet. They shall goe forward *Kate* at thy command
Obey the Bride you that attend on her.
Goe to the feast, reuell and domineere,
Carowse full measure to her maiden-head,
Be madde and merry, or goe hang your selues:
But for my bonny *Kate*, she must with me.
Nay, looke not big, nor stampe, nor stare, nor fret,
I will be master of what is mine owne,
Shee is my goods, my chattels, she is my house,
My houshold-stuffe, my field, my barne,
My horse, my oxe, my asse, my any thing,
And heere she stands, touch her who euer dare,
Ile bring mine action on the proudest he
That stops my way in *Padua*: *Grumio*
Draw forth thy weapon, we are beset with theeues,
Rescue thy Mistresse if thou be a man:
Feare not sweet wench, they shall not touch thee *Kate*,
Ile buckler thee against a Million. *Exeunt. P. Ka.*
Bap. Nay, let them goe, a couple of quiet ones.
Gre. Went they not quickly, I should die with laughing.
Tra. Of all mad matches neuer was the like.
Luc. Mistresse, what's your opinion of your sister?
Bian. That being mad her selfe, she's madly mated.
Gre. I warrant him *Petruchio* is Kated.
Bap. Neighbours and friends, though Bride & Bridegroom wants
For to supply the places at the table,
You know there wants no iunkets at the feast:
Lucentio, you shall supply the Bridegroomes place,
And let *Bianca* take her sisters roome.
Tra. Shall sweet *Bianca* practise how to bride it?
Bap. She shall *Lucentio*: come gentlemen lets goe. *Exeunt.*

Enter Grumio.

Gru: Fie, fie on all tired Iades, on all mad Masters, & all foule waies: was euer man so beaten? was euer man so raide? was euer man so weary? I am sent before to make a fire, and they are comming after to warme them: now were not I a little pot, & soone hot; my very lippes might freeze to my teeth, my tongue to the roofe of my mouth, my heart in my belly, ere I should come by a fire to thaw me, but I with blowing the fire shall warme my selfe: for considering the weather, a taller man then I will take cold: Holla, hoa *Curtis*.

Enter Curtis.

Curt. Who is that calls so coldly?
Gru. A piece of Ice: if thou doubt it, thou maist slide from my shoulder to my heele, with no greater

greater a run but my head and my necke. A fire good *Curtis*.

Cur. Is my master and his wife comming *Grumio*?

Gru. Oh I *Curtis* I, and therefore fire, fire, cast on no water.

Cur. Is she so hot a shrew as she's reported.

Gru. She was good *Curtis* before this frost: but thou know'st winter tames man, woman, and beast: for it hath tam'd my old master, and my new mistris, and my selfe fellow *Curtis*.

Gru. Away you three inch foole, I am no beast.

Gru. Am I but three inches? Why thy horne is a foo and so long am I at the least. But wilt thou make a fire or shall I complaine on thee to our mistris, whose hand (she being now at hand) thou shalt soone feele, to thy cold comfort, for being slow in thy hot office.

Cur. I prethee good *Grumio*, tell me, how goes the world?

Gru. A cold world *Curtis* in euery office but thine, & therefore fire: do thy duty, and haue thy dutie, for my Master and mistris are almost frozen to death.

Cur. There's fire readie, and therefore good *Grumio* the newes.

Gru. Why Iacke boy, ho boy, and as much newes as wilt thou.

Cur. Come, you are so full of conicatching.

Gru. Why therefore fire, for I haue caught extreme cold. Where's the Cooke, is supper ready, the house trim'd, rushes strew'd, cobwebs swept, the seruingmen in their new fustian, the white stockings, and euery officer his wedding garment on? Be the Iackes faire within, the Gils faire without, the Carpets laide, and euerie thing in order?

Cur. All readie: and therefore I pray thee newes.

Gru. First know my horse is tired, my master & mistris falne out. *Cur.* How?

Gru. Out of their saddles into the durt, and thereby hangs a tale.

Cur. Let's ha't good *Grumio*.

Gru. Lend thine eare.

Cur. Heere.

Gru. There.

Cur. This 'tis to feele a tale, not to heare a tale

Gru. And therefore 'tis cal'd a sensible tale: and this Cuffe was but to knocke at your eare, and beseech listning: now I begin, Inprimis wee came downe a fowle hill, my Master riding behinde my Mistris.

Cur. Both of one horse?

Gru. What's that to thee?

Cur. Why a horse.

Gru. Tell thou the tale: but hadst thou not crost me, thou shouldst haue heard how her horse fel, and she vnder her horse: thou shouldst haue heard in how miery a place, how she was bemoil'd, how hee left her with the horse vpon her, how he beat me because her horse stumbled, how she waded through the durt to plucke him off me: how he swore, how she prai'd, that neuer prai'd before: how I cried, how the horses ranne away, how her bridle was burst: how I lost my crupper, with manie things of worthy memorie, which now shall die in obliuion, and thou returne vnexperienc'd to thy graue.

Cur. By this reckning he is more shrew than she.

Gru. I, and that thou and the proudest of you all shall finde when he comes home. But what talke I of this? Call forth *Nathaniel, Ioseph, Nicholas, Phillip, Walter, Sugersop* and the rest: let their heads bee slickely comb'd, their blew coats brush'd, and their garters of an indifferent knit, let them curtsie with their left legges, and not presume to touch a haire of my Masters horse-taile, till they kisse their hands. Are they all readie?

Cur. They are.

Gru. Call them forth.

Cur. Do you heare ho? you must meete my master to countenance my mistris.

Gru. Why she hath a face of her owne

Cur. Who knowes not that?

Gru. Thou it seemes, that cals for company to countenance her.

Cur. I call them forth to credit her.

Enter foure or fiue seruingmen.

Gru. Why she comes to borrow nothing of them

Nat. Welcome home *Grumio*.

Phil. How now *Grumio*.

Ios. What *Grumio*.

Nick. Fellow *Grumio*.

Nat. How now old lad.

Gru. Welcome you: how now you: what you: fellow you: and thus much for greeting. Now my spruce companions, is all readie, and all things neate?

Nat. All things is readie, how neere is our master?

Gre. E'ne at hand, alighted by this: and therefore be not——Cockes passion, silence, I heare my master

Enter Petruchio and Kate.

Pet. Where be these knaues? What no man at doore
To hold my stirrop, nor to take my horse?
Where is *Nathaniel, Gregory, Phillip*.
All ser. Heere, heere sir, heere sir.
Pet. Heere sir, heere sir, heere sir, heere sir.
You logger-headed and vnpollisht groomes:
What? no attendance? no regard? no dutie?
Where is the foolish knaue I sent before?
Gru. Heere sir, as foolish as I was before.
Pet. You pezant, swain, you horson malt-horse drudg
Did I not bid thee meete me in the Parke,
And bring along these rascal knaues with thee?
Grumio. *Nathaniels* coate sir was not fully made,
And *Gabrels* pumpes were all vnpinkt i'th heele:
There was no Linke to colour *Peters* hat,
And *Walters* dagger was not come from sheathing:
There were none fine, but *Adam, Rafe*, and *Gregory*,
The rest were ragged, old, and beggerly,
Yet as they are, heere are they come to meete you.
Pet. Go rascals, go, and fetch my supper in. *Ex. Ser.*
Where is the life that late I led?
Where are those? Sit downe *Kate*,
And welcome. Soud, soud, soud, soud.

Enter seruants with supper.

Why when I say? Nay good sweete *Kate* be merrie.
Off with my boots, you rogues: you villaines, when?
It was the Friar of Orders gray,
As he forth walked on his way.
Out you rogue, you plucke my foote awrie,
Take that, and mend the plucking of the other.
Be merrie *Kate*: Some water heere: what hoa.

Enter one with water.

Where's my Spaniel *Troilus*? Sirra, get you hence,
And bid my cozen *Ferdinand* come hither:
One *Kate* that you must kisse, and be acquainted with.
Where are my Slippers? Shall I haue some water?
Come *Kate* and wash, & welcome heartily:
you horson villaine, will you let it fall?

Kate. Patience I pray you, 'twas a fault vnwilling.
Pet. A horſon beetle-headed flap-ear'd knaue:
Come *Kate* ſit downe, I know you haue a ſtomacke,
Will you giue thankes, ſweete *Kate*, or elſe ſhall I?
What's this, Mutton?
1. Ser. I.
Pet. Who brought it?
Peter. I.
Pet. 'Tis burnt, and ſo is all the meate:
What dogges are theſe? Where is the raſcall Cooke?
How durſt you villaines bring it from the dreſſer
And ſerue it thus to me that loue it not?
There, take it to you, trenchers, cups, and all:
You heedleſſe iolt-heads, and vnmanner'd ſlaues.
What, do you grumble? Ile be with you ſtraight
Kate. I pray you husband be not ſo diſquiet,
The meate was well, if you were ſo contented.
Pet. I tell thee *Kate*, 'twa burnt and dried away,
And I expreſſely am forbid to touch it:
For it engenders choller, planteth anger,
And better 'twere that both of vs did faſt
Since of our ſelues, our ſelues are chollericke,
Then feede it with ſuch ouer-roſted fleſh:
Be patient, to morrow't ſhalbe mended,
And for this night we'l faſt for companie.
Come I wil bring thee to thy Bridall chamber. *Exeunt.*

Enter Seruants ſeuerally.

Nath. Peter didſt euer ſee the like.
Peter. He kils her in her owne humor.
Grumio. Where is he?

Enter Curtis a Seruant.

Cur. In her chamber, making a ſermon of continencie to her, and railes, and ſweares, and rates, that ſhee (poore ſoule) knowes not which way to ſtand, to looke, to ſpeake, and ſits as one new-riſen from a dreame. Away, away, for he is comming hither.

Enter Petruchio.

Pet. Thus haue I politickely begun my reigne,
And 'tis my hope to end ſucceſſefully:
My Faulcon now is ſharpe, and paſſing emptie,
And til ſhe ſtoope, ſhe muſt not be full gorg'd,
For then ſhe neuer lookes vpon her lure.
Another way I haue to man my Haggard,
To make her come, and know her Keepers call:
That is, to watch her, as we watch theſe Kites,
That baite, and beate, and will not be obedient
She eate no meate to day, nor none ſhall eate.
Laſt night ſhe ſlept not, nor to night ſhe ſhall not:
As with the meate, ſome vndeſerued fault
Ile finde about the making of the bed,
And heere Ile fling the pillow, there the boulſter
This way the Couerlet, another way the ſheets:
I, and amid this hurlie I intend,
That all is done in reuerend care of her,
And in concluſion, ſhe ſhal watch all night,
And if ſhe chance to nod Ile raile and brawle,
And with the clamor keepe her ſtil awake:
This is a way to kil a Wife with kindneſſe,
And thus Ile curbe her mad and headſtrong humor:
He that knowes better how to tame a ſhrew,
Now let him ſpeake, 'tis charity to ſhew. *Exit*

Enter Tranio and Hortenſio:

Tra. Is't poſible friend *Liſio*, that miſtris *Bianca*
Doth fancie any other but *Lucentio*,
I tel you ſir, ſhe beares me faire in hand.
Luc. Sir, to ſatisfie you in what I haue ſaid,
Stand by, and marke the manner of his teaching.

Enter Bianca.

Hor. Now Miſtris, profit you in what you reade?
Bian. What Maſter reade you firſt, reſolue me that?
Hor. I reade, that I profeſſe the Art to loue.
Bian And may you proue ſir Maſter of your Art.
Luc. While you ſweet deere proue Miſtreſſe of my heart.
Hor. Quicke proceeders marry, now tel me I pray, you that durſt ſweare that your miſtris *Bianca*
Lou'd me in the World ſo wel as *Lucentio*.
Tra. Oh deſpightful Loue, vnconſtant womankind,
I tel thee *Liſio* this is wonderfull.
Hor. Miſtake no more, I am not *Liſio*,
Nor a Muſitian as I ſeeme to bee,
But one that ſcorne to liue in this diſguiſe,
For ſuch a one as leaues a Gentleman,
And makes a God of ſuch a Cullion;
Know ſir, that I am cal'd *Hortenſio*.
Tra. Signior *Hortenſio*, I haue often heard
Of your entire affection to *Bianca*,
And ſince mine eyes are witneſſe of her lightneſſe,
I wil with you, if you be ſo contented,
Forſweare *Bianca*, and her loue for euer.
Hor. See how they kiſſe and court: Signior *Lucentio*
Heere is my hand, and heere I firmly vow
Neuer to woo her more, but do forſweare her
As one vnworthie all the former fauours
That I haue fondly flatter'd them withall.
Tra. And heere I take the like vnfained oath,
Neuer to marrie with her, though ſhe would intreate,
Fie on her, ſee how beaſtly ſhe doth court him.
Hor. Would all the world but he had quite forſworn
For me, that I may ſurely keepe mine oath
I wil be married to a wealthy Widdow,
Ere three dayes paſſe, which hath as long lou'd me,
As I haue lou'd this proud diſdainful Haggard,
And ſo farewel ſignior *Lucentio*,
Kindneſſe in women, not their beauteous lookes
Shal win my loue, and ſo I take my leaue,
In reſolution, as I ſwore before.
Tra. Miſtris *Bianca*, bleſſe you with ſuch grace,
As longeth to a Louers bleſſed caſe:
Nay, I haue tane you napping gentle Loue,
And haue forſworne you with *Hortenſio*.
Bian. *Tranio* you ieſt, but haue you both forſworne mee?
Tra. Miſtris we haue.
Luc. Then we are rid of *Liſio*.
Tra. I'faith hee'l haue a luſtie Widdow now,
That ſhalbe woo'd, and wedded in a day.
Bian. God giue him ioy.
Tra. I, and hee'l tame her.
Bianca. He ſayes ſo *Tranio*.
Tra. Faith he is gone vnto the taming ſchoole.
Bian. The taming ſchoole: what is there ſuch a place?
Tra. I miſtris, and *Petruchio* is the maſter,
That teacheth trickes eleuen and twentie long,
To tame a ſhrew, and charme her chattering tongue.

Enter Biondello.

Bion. Oh Maſter, maſter I haue watcht ſo long,
That I am dogge-wearie, but at laſt I ſpied
An ancient Angel comming downe the hill,
Wil ſerue the turne.
Tra. What is he *Biondello*?
Bio. Maſter, a Marcantant, or a pedant,

I

I know not what, but formall in apparrell,
In gate and countenance surely like a Father.
Luc. And what of him *Tranio*?
Tra. If he be credulous, and trust my tale,
Ile make him glad to seeme *Vincentio*,
And giue assurance to *Baptista Minola*.
As if he were the right *Vincentio*.
Par. Take me your loue, and then let me alone.

Enter a Pedant.

Ped. God saue you sir.
Tra. And you sir, you are welcome,
Trauaile you farre on, or are you at the farthest?
Ped. Sir at the farthest for a weeke or two,
But then vp farther, and as farre as Rome,
And so to Tripolie, if God lend me life.
Tra. What Countreyman I pray?
Ped. Of *Mantua*.
Tra. Of *Mantua* Sir, marrie God forbid,
And come to Padua carelesse of your life.
Ped. My life sir? how I pray? for that goes hard.
Tra. Tis death for any one in Mantua
To come to Padua, know you not the cause?
Your ships are staid at Venice, and the Duke
For priuate quarrel 'twixt your Duke and him,
Hath publish'd and proclaim'd it openly:
'Tis meruaile, but that you are but newly come,
you might haue heard it else proclaim'd about.
Ped. Alas sir, it is worse for me then so,
For I haue bils for monie by exchange
From Florence, and must heere deliuer them.
Tra. Wel sir, to do you courtesie,
This wil I do, and this I wil aduise you,
First tell me, haue you euer beene at Pisa?
Ped. I sir, in Pisa haue I often bin,
Pisa renowned for graue Citizens.
Tra. Among them know you one *Vincentio*?
Ped. I know him not, but I haue heard of him:
A Merchant of incomparable wealth.
Tra. He is my father sir, and sooth to say,
In count'nance somewhat doth resemble you.
Bion. As much as an apple doth an oyster, & all one.
Tra. To saue your life in this extremitie,
This fauor wil I do you for his sake,
And thinke it not the worst of all your fortunes,
That you are like to Sir *Vincentio*.
His name and credite shal you vndertake,
And in my house you shal be friendly lodg'd,
Looke that you take vpon you as you should,
you vnderstand me sir: so shal you stay
Til you haue done your businesse in the Citie:
If this be court'sie sir, accept of it.
Ped. Oh sir I do, and wil repute you euer
The patron of my life and libertie.
Tra. Then go with me, to make the matter good,
This by the way I let you vnderstand,
My father is heere look'd for euerie day,
To passe assurance of a dowre in marriage
Twixt me, and one *Baptistas* daughter heere:
In all these circumstances Ile instruct you,
Go with me to cloath you as becomes you. *Exeunt.*

Actus Quartus. Scena Prima.

Enter Katherina and Grumio.

Gru. No, no forsooth I dare not for my life.
Ka. The more my wrong, the more his spite appears.
What, did he marrie me to famish me?
Beggers that come vnto my fathers doore,
Vpon intreatie haue a present almes,
If not, elsewhere they meete with charitie:
But I, who neuer knew how to intreat,
Nor neuer needed that I should intreate,
Am staru'd for meate, giddie for lacke of sleepe:
With oathes kept waking, and with brawling fed,
And that which spights me more then all these wants,
He does it vnder name of perfect loue:
As who should say, if I should sleepe or eate,
'Twere deadly sicknesse, or else present death.
I prethee go, and get me some repast,
I care not what, so it be holsome foode.
Gru. What say you to a Neats foote?
Kate. 'Tis passing good, I prethee let me haue it.
Gru. I feare it is too chollericke a meate.
How say you to a fat Tripe finely broyl'd?
Kate. I like it well, good Grumio fetch it me.
Gru. I cannot tell, I feare 'tis chollericke.
What say you to a peece of Beefe and Mustard?
Kate. A dish that I do loue to feede vpon.
Gru. I, but the Mustard is too hot a little.
Kate. Why then the Beefe, and let the Mustard rest.
Gru. Nay then I wil not, you shal haue the Mustard
Or else you get no beefe of Grumio.
Kate. Then both or one, or any thing thou wilt.
Gru. Why then the Mustard without the beefe.
Kate. Go get thee gone, thou false deluding slaue, *Beats him.*
That feed'st me with the verie name of meate.
Sorrow on thee, and all the packe of you
That triumph thus vpon my misery:
Go get thee gone, I say.

Enter Petruchio, and Hortensio with meate.

Petr. How fares my Kate, what sweeting all a-mort?
Hor. Mistris, what cheere?
Kate. Faith as cold as can be.
Pet. Plucke vp thy spirits, looke cheerfully vpon me.
Heere Loue, thou seest how diligent I am,
To dresse thy meate my selfe, and bring it thee.
I am sure sweet Kate, this kindnesse merites thankes.
What, not a word? Nay then, thou lou'st it not:
And all my paines is sorted to no proofe.
Heere take away this dish.
Kate. I pray you let it stand.
Pet. The poorest seruice is repaide with thankes,
And so shall mine before you touch the meate.
Kate. I thanke you sir.
Hor. Signior *Petruchio*, fie you are too blame:
Come Mistris Kate, Ile beare you companie.
Petr. Eate it vp all *Hortensio*, if thou louest mee:
Much good do it vnto thy gentle heart:
Kate eate apace; and now my honie Loue,
Will we returne vnto thy Fathers house,
And reuell it as brauely as the best,
With silken coats and caps, and golden Rings,
With Ruffes and Cuffes, and Fardingales, and things:
With Scarfes, and Fannes, & double change of brau'ry,
With Amber Bracelets, Beades, and all this knau'ry.
What hast thou din'd? The Tailor staies thy leasure,
To decke thy bodie with his ruffling treasure.

Enter Tailor.

Come

Come Tailor, let vs see these ornaments.
Enter Haberdasher.
Lay forth the gowne. What newes with you sir?
Fel. Heere is the cap your Worship did bespeake.
Pet. Why this was moulded on a porrenger,
A Veluet dish: Fie,fie, 'tis lewd and filthy,
Why 'tis a cockle or a walnut-shell,
A knacke, a toy, a tricke, a babies cap:
Away with it, come let me haue a bigger.
Kate. Ile haue no bigger, this doth fit the time,
And Gentlewomen weare such caps as these
Pet. When you are gentle, you shall haue one too,
And not till then.
Hor. That will not be in hast.
Kate. Why sir I trust I may haue leaue to speake,
And speake I will. I am no childe, no babe,
Your betters haue indur'd me say my minde,
And if you cannot, best you stop your eares,
My tongue will tell the anger of my heart,
Or els my heart concealing it wil breake,
And rather then it shall, I will be free,
Euen to the vttermost as I please in words,
Pet. Why thou saist true, it is paltrie cap,
A custard coffen, a bauble, a silken pie,
I loue thee well in that thou lik'st it not.
Kate. Loue me, or loue me not, I like the cap,
And it I will haue, or I will haue none.
Pet. Thy gowne, why I: come Tailor let vs see't.
Oh mercie God, what masking stuffe is heere?
Whats this? a sleeue? 'tis like demi cannon,
What, vp and downe caru'd like an apple Tart?
Heers snip, and nip, and cut, and slish and slash,
Like to a Censor in a barbers shoppe:
Why what a deuils name Tailor cal'st thou this?
Hor. I see shees like to haue neither cap nor gowne.
Tai. You bid me make it orderlie and well,
According to the fashion, and the time.
Pet. Marrie and did: but if you be remembred,
I did not bid you marre it to the time.
Go hop me ouer euery kennell home,
For you shall hop without my custome sir:
Ile none of it; hence, make your best of it.
Kate. I neuer saw a better fashion'd gowne,
More queint, more pleasing, nor more commendable:
Belike you meane to make a puppet of me.
Pet. Why true, he meanes to make a puppet of thee.
Tail. She saies your Worship meanes to make a puppet of her.
Pet. Oh monstrous arrogance.
Thou lyest, thou thred, thou thimble,
Thou yard three quarters, halfe yard, quarter, naile,
Thou Flea, thou Nit, thou winter cricket thou:
Brau'd in mine owne house with a skeine of thred:
Away thou Ragge, thou quantitie, thou remnant,
Or I shall so be-mete thee with thy yard,
As thou shalt thinke on prating whil'st thou liu'st:
I tell thee I, that thou hast marr'd her gowne.
Tail. Your worship is deceiu'd, the gowne is made
Iust as my master had direction:
Grumio gaue order how it should be done.
Gru. I gaue him no order, I gaue him the stuffe.
Tail. But how did you desire it should be made?
Gru. Marrie sir with needle and thred.
Tail. But did you not request to haue it cut?
Gru. Thou hast fac'd many things.
Tail. I haue.
Gru. Face not mee: thou hast brau'd manie men, braue not me; I will neither bee fac'd nor brau'd. I say vnto thee, I bid thy Master cut out the gowne, but I did not bid him cut it to peeces. Ergo thou liest.
Tail. Why heere is the note of the fashion to testify.
Pet. Reade it.
Gru. The note lies in's throate if he say I said so.
Tail. Inprimis, a loose bodied gowne.
Gru. Master, if euer I said loose-bodied gowne, sow me in the skirts of it, and beate me to death with a bottome of browne thred: I said a gowne.
Pet. Proceede.
Tai. With a small compast cape.
Gru. I confesse the cape.
Tai. With a trunke sleeue.
Gru. I confesse two sleeues.
Tai. The sleeues curiously cut.
Pet. I there's the villanie.
Gru. Error i'th bill sir, error i'th bill? I commanded the sleeues should be cut out, and sow'd vp againe, and that Ile proue vpon thee, though thy little finger be armed in a thimble.
Tail. This is true that I say, and I had thee in place where thou shouldst know it.
Gru I am for thee straight: take thou the bill, giue me thy meat-yard, and spare not me.
Hor. God-a-mercie *Grumio*, then hee shall haue no oddes.
Pet. Well sir in breefe the gowne is not for me.
Gru. You are i'th right sir, 'tis for my mistris.
Pet. Go take it vp vnto thy masters vse.
Gru. Villaine, not for thy life: Take vp my Mistresse gowne for thy masters vse.
Pet. Why sir, what's your conceit in that?
Gru. Oh sir, the conceit is deeper then you think for:
Take vp my Mistris gowne to his masters vse.
Oh fie, fie, fie.
Pet. *Hortensio*, say thou wilt see the Tailor paide.
Go take it hence, be gone, and say no more.
Hor. Tailor, Ile pay thee for thy gowne to morrow,
Take no vnkindnesse of his hastie words:
Away I say, commend me to thy master. *Exit Tail.*
Pet. Well, come my *Kate*, we will vnto your fathers,
Euen in these honest meane habiliments:
Our purses shall be proud, our garments poore:
For 'tis the minde that makes the bodie rich.
And as the Sunne breakes through the darkest clouds,
So honor peereth in the meanest habit.
What is the Iay more precious then the Larke?
Because his feathers are more beautifull.
Or is the Adder better then the Eele,
Because his painted skin contents the eye.
Oh no good *Kate*: neither art thou the worse
For this poore furniture, and meane array.
If thou accountedst it shame, lay it on me,
And therefore frolicke, we will hence forthwith,
To feast and sport vs at thy fathers house,
Go call my men, and let vs straight to him,
And bring our horses vnto Long-lane end,
There wil we mount, and thither walke on foote,
Let's see, I thinke 'tis now some seuen a clocke,
And well we may come there by dinner time.
Kate. I dare assure you sir, 'tis almost two,
And 'twill be supper time ere you come there.
Pet. It shall be seuen ere I go to horse:
Looke what I speake, or do, or thinke to doe,
You

You are still crossing it, sirs let't alone,
I will not goe to day, and ere I doe,
It shall be what a clock I say it is.
Hor. Why so this gallant will command the sunne.

Enter Tranio, and the Pedaut drest like Vincentio.

Tra. Sirs, this is the house, please it you that I call.
Ped. I what else, and but I be deceiued,
Signior *Baptista* may remember me
Neere twentie yeares a goe in *Genoa.*
Tra. Where we were lodgers, at the *Pegasus,*
Tis well, and hold your owne in any case
With such austeritie as longeth to a father.

Enter Biondello.

Ped. I warrant you: but sir here comes your boy,
'Twere good he were school'd.
Tra. Feare you not him: sirra *Biondello,*
Now doe your dutie throughlie I aduise you:
Imagine 'twere the right *Vincentio.*
Bion. Tut, feare not me.
Tra. But hast thou done thy errand to *Baptista.*
Bion I told him that your father was at *Venice,*
And that you look't for him this day in *Padua.*
Tra. Th'art a tall fellow, hold thee that to drinke;
Here comes *Baptista*: set your countenance sir.

Enter Baptista and Lucentio: Pedant booted and bare headed.

Tra. Signior *Baptista* you are happilie met:
Sir, this is the gentleman I told you of,
I pray you stand good father to me now,
Giue me *Bianca* for my patrimony.
Ped Soft son: sir by your leaue, hauing com to *Padua*
To gather in some debts, my son *Lucentio*
Made me acquainted with a waighty cause
Of loue betweene your daughter and himselfe:
And for the good report I heare of you,
And for the loue he beareth to your daughter,
And she to him: to stay him not too long,
I am content in a good fathers care
To haue him matcht, and if you please to like
No worse then I, vpon some agreement
Me shall you finde readie and willing
With one consent to haue her so bestowed:
For curious I cannot be with you
Signior *Baptista*, of whom I heare so well.
Bap. Sir, pardon me in what I haue to say,
Your plainnesse and your shortnesse please me well:
Right true it is your sonne *Lucentio* here
Doth loue my daughter, and she loueth him,
Or both dissemble deepely their affections:
And therefore if you say no more then this,
That like a Father you will deale with him,
And passe my daughter a sufficient dower,
The match is made, and all is done,
Your sonne shall haue my daughter with consent.
Tra. I thanke you sir, where then doe you know best
We be affied and such assurance tane,
As shall with either parts agreement stand.
Bap. Not in my house *Lucentio*, for you know
Pitchers haue eares, and I haue manie seruants,
Besides old *Gremio* is harkning still,
And happilie we might be interrupted.
Tra. Then at my lodging, and it like you,
There doth my father lie: and there this night
Weele passe the businesse priuately and well:
Send for your daughter by your seruant here,
My Boy shall fetch the Scriuener presentlie,
The worst is this that at so slender warning,
You are like to haue a thin and slender pittance.
Bap. It likes me well:
Cambio hie you home, and bid *Bianca* make her readie straight:
And if you will tell what hath hapned,
Lucentios Father is arriued in *Padua,*
And how she's like to be *Lucentios* wife.
Biond. I praie the gods she may withall my heart. *Exit.*
Tran. Dallie not with the gods, but get thee gone.

Enter Peter.

Signior *Baptista*, shall I leade the way,
We come, one messe is like to be your cheere,
Come sir, we will better it in *Pisa.*
Bap. I follow you. *Exeunt.*

Enter Lucentio and Biondello.

Bion. Cambio.
Luc. What saist thou *Biondello.*
Biond. You saw my Master winke and laugh vpon you?
Luc. *Biondello*, what of that?
Biond. Faith nothing: but has left mee here behinde to expound the meaning or morrall of his signes and tokens.
Luc. I pray thee moralize them.
Biond. Then thus: *Baptista* is safe talking with the deceiuing Father of a deceitfull sonne.
Luc. And what of him?
Biond. His daughter is to be brought by you to the supper.
Luc. And then.
Bio. The old Priest at Saint *Lukes* Church is at your command at all houres.
Luc. And what of all this.
Bion. I cannot tell, expect they are busied about a counterfeit assurance: take you assurance of her, *Cum preuilegio ad Impremendum solem*, to th' Church take the Priest, Clarke, and some sufficient honest witnesses:
If this be not that you looke for, I haue no more to say,
But bid *Bianca* farewell for euer and a day.
Luc. Hear'st thou *Biondello.*
Biond. I cannot tarry: I knew a wench maried in an afternoone as shee went to the Garden for Parseley to stuffe a Rabit, and so may you sir: and so adew sir, my Master hath appointed me to goe to Saint *Lukes* to bid the Priest be readie to come against you come with your appendix. *Exit.*
Luc. I may and will, if she be so contented:
She will be pleas'd, then wherefore should I doubt:
Hap what hap may, Ile roundly goe about her:
It shall goe hard if *Cambio* goe without her. *Exit.*

Enter Petruchio, Kate, Hortentio

Petr. Come on a Gods name, once more toward our fathers:
Good Lord how bright and goodly shines the Moone.
Kate. The Moone, the Sunne: it is not Moonelight now.
Pet. I say it is the Moone that shines so bright.
Kate. I know it is the Sunne that shines so bright.
Pet. Now by my mothers sonne, and that's my selfe,
It

It shall be moone, or starre, or what I list,
Or ere I iourney to your Fathers house:
Goe on, and fetch our horses backe againe.
Euermore crost and crost, nothing but crost.
Hort. Say as he saies, or we shall neuer goe.
Kate. Forward I pray, since we haue come so farre,
And be it moone, or sunne, or what you please:
And if you please to call it a rush Candle,
Henceforth I vowe it shall be so for me,
Petr. I say it is the Moone.
Kate. I know it is the Moone.
Petr. Nay then you lye: it is the blessed Sunne.
Kate. Then God be blest, it in the blessed sun,
But sunne it is not, when you say it is not,
And the Moone changes euen as your minde:
What you will haue it nam'd, euen that it is,
And so it shall be so for *Katherine*.
Hort. *Petruchio*, goe thy waies, the field is won.
Petr. Well, forward, forward, thus the bowle should
And not vnluckily against the Bias. (run,
But soft, Company is comming here.

Enter Vincentio.

Good morrow gentle Mistris, where away:
Tell me sweete *Kate*, and tell me truely too,
Hast thou beheld a fresher Gentlewoman:
Such warre of white and red within her cheekes:
What stars do spangle heauen with such beautie,
As those two eyes become that heauenly face?
Faire louely Maide, once more good day to thee:
Sweete *Kate* embrace her for her beauties sake.
Hort. A will make the man mad to make the woman of him.
Kate. Yong budding Virgin, faire, and fresh, & sweet,
Whether away, or whether is thy aboade?
Happy the Parents of so faire a childe;
Happier the man whom fauourable stars
A lots thee for his louely bedfellow.
Petr. Why how now *Kate*, I hope thou art not mad,
This is a man old, wrinckled, faded, withered,
And not a Maiden, as thou saist he is.
Kate. Pardon old father my mistaking eies,
That haue bin so bedazled with the sunne,
That euery thing I looke on seemeth greene:
Now I perceiue thou art a reuerent Father:
Pardon I pray thee for my mad mistaking.
Petr. Do good old grandsire, & withall make known
Which way thou trauellest, if along with vs,
We shall be ioyfull of thy companie.
Vin. Faire Sir, and you my merry Mistris,
That with your strange encounter much amasde me:
My name is call'd *Vincentio*, my dwelling *Pisa*,
And bound I am to *Padua*, there to visite
A sonne of mine, which long I haue not seene.
Petr. What is his name?
Vinc. *Lucentio* gentle sir.
Petr. Happily met, the happier for thy sonne:
And now by Law, as well as reuerent age,
I may intitle thee my louing Father,
The sister to my wife, this Gentlewoman,
Thy Sonne by this hath married: wonder not,
Nor be not grieued, she is of good esteeme,
Her dowrie wealthie, and of worthie birth;
Beside, so qualified, as may beseeme
The Spouse of any noble Gentleman:
Let me imbrace with old *Vincentio*,
And wander we to see thy honest sonne,
Who will of thy arriuall be full ioyous.
Vinc. But is this true, or is it else your pleasure,
Like pleasant trauailors to breake a Iest
Vpon the companie you ouertake?
Hort. I doe assure thee father so it is.
Petr. Come goe along and see the truth hereof,
For our first merriment hath made thee iealous. *Exeunt.*
Hor. Well *Petruchio*, this has put me in heart;
Haue to my Widdow, and if she froward,
Then hast thou taught *Hortentio* to be vntoward. *Exit.*

Enter Biondello, Lucentio and Bianca, Gremio is out before.

Biond. Softly and swiftly sir, for the Priest is ready.
Luc. I flie *Biondello*; but they may chance to neede thee at home, therefore leaue vs. *Exit.*
Biond. Nay faith, Ile see the Church a your backe, and then come backe to my mistris as soone as I can.
Gre. I maruaile *Cambio* comes not all this while.

Enter Petruchio, Kate, Vincentio, Grumio with Attendants.

Petr. Sir heres the doore, this is *Lucentios* house,
My Fathers beares more toward the Market-place,
Thither must I, and here I leaue you sir.
Vin. You shall not choose but drinke before you go,
I thinke I shall command your welcome here;
And by all likelihood some cheere is toward. *Knock.*
Grem. They're busie within, you were best knocke lowder.

Pedant lookes out of the window.

Ped. What's he that knockes as he would beat downe the gate?
Vin. Is Signior *Lucentio* within sir?
Ped. He's within sir, but not to be spoken withall.
Vinc. What if a man bring him a hundred pound or two to make merrie withall.
Ped. Keepe your hundred pounds to your selfe, hee shall neede none so long as I liue.
Petr. Nay, I told you your sonne was well beloued in *Padua*: doe you heare sir, to leaue friuolous circumstances, I pray you tell signior *Lucentio* that his Father is come from *Pisa*, and is here at the doore to speake with him.
Ped. Thou liest his Father is come from *Padua*, and here looking out at the window.
Vin. Art thou his father?
Ped. I sir, so his mother saies, if I may beleeue her.
Petr. Why how now gentleman: why this is flat knauerie to take vpon you another mans name.
Peda. Lay hands on the villaine, I beleeue a meanes to cosen some bodie in this Citie vnder my countenance.

Enter Biondello.

Bio. I haue seene them in the Church together, God send'em good shipping: but who is here? mine old Master *Vincentio*: now wee are vndone and brough to nothing.
Vin. Come hither crackhempe.
Bion. I hope I may choose Sir.
Vin. Come hither you rogue, what haue you forgot mee?
Biond. Forgot you, no sir: I could not forget you, for I neuer saw you before in all my life.
Vinc. What, you notorious villaine, didst thou neuer see thy Mistris father, *Vincentio*?
Bion. What

Bion. What my old worshipfull old master? yes marie sir see where he lookes out of the window.

Vin. Ist so indeede. *He beates Biondello.*

Bion. Helpe,helpe, helpe,here's a mad man will murder me.

Pedan. Helpe,sonne, helpe signior *Baptista*.

Petr. Pree the *Kate* let's stand aside and see the end of this controuersie.

Enter Pedant with seruants, Baptista, Tranio.

Tra. Sir, what are you that offer to beate my seruant?

Vinc. What am I sir:nay what are you sir: oh immortall Goddes : oh fine villaine, a silken doublet, a veluet hose, a scarlet cloake, and a copataine hat : oh I am vndone, I am vndone : while I plaie the good husband at home, my sonne and my seruant spend all at the vniuersitie.

Tra. How now, what's the matter?

Bapt. What is the man lunaticke?

Tra. Sir, you seeme a sober ancient Gentleman by your habit : but your words shew you a mad man : why sir, what cernes it you, if I weare Pearle and gold: I thank my good Father, I am able to maintaine it.

Vin. Thy father : oh villaine, he is a Saile-maker in *Bergamo*.

Bap. You mistake sir, you mistake sir, praie what do you thinke is his name?

Vin. His name, as if I knew not his name : I haue brought him vp euer since he was three yeeres old, and his name is *Tronio*.

Ped. Awaie,awaie mad asse, his name is *Lucentio*, and he is mine onelie sonne and heire to the Lands of me signior *Vincentio*.

Ven. *Lucentio* : oh he hath murdred his Master ; laie hold on him I charge you in the Dukes name : oh my sonne, my sonne : tell me thou villaine, where is my son *Lucentio*?

Tra. Call forth an officer : Carrie this mad knaue to the Iaile : father *Baptista*, I charge you see that hee be forth comming.

Vinc. Carrie me to the Iaile?

Gre. Staie officer, he shall not go to prison.

Bap. Talke not signior *Gremio* : I saie he shall goe to prison.

Gre. Take heede signior *Baptista*, least you be conicatcht in this businesse : I dare sweare this is the right *Vincentio*.

Ped. Sweare if thou dar'st.

Gre. Naie, I dare not sweare it.

Tran. Then thou wert best saie that I am not *Lucentio*.

Gre. Yes, I know thee to be signior *Lucentio*.

Bap. Awaie with the dotard, to the Iaile with him.

Enter Biondello, Lucentio and Bianca.

Vin. Thus strangers may be haild and abusd : oh monstrous villaine.

Bion. Oh we are spoil'd, and yonder he is, denie him, forsweare him, or else we are all vndone.

Exit Biondello, Tranio and Pedant as fast as may be.

Luc. Pardon sweete father. *Kneele.*

Vin. Liues my sweete sonne?

Bion. Pardon deere father.

Bap. How hast thou offended, where is *Lucentio*?

Luc. Here's *Lucentio*, right sonne to the right *Vincentio*,
That haue by marriage made thy daughter mine,
While counterfeit supposes bleer'd thine eine.

Gre. Here's packing with a witnesse to deceiue vs all.

Vin. Where is that damned villaine *Tranio*,
That fac'd and braued me in this matter so?

Bap. Why, tell me is not this my *Cambio*?

Bian. *Cambio* is chang'd into *Lucentio*.

Luc. Loue wrought these miracles. *Biancas* loue
Made me exchange my state with *Tranio*,
While he did beare my countenance in the towne,
And happilie I haue arriued at the last
Vnto the wished hauen of my blisse :
What *Tranio* did, my selfe enforst him to ;
Then pardon him sweete Father for my sake.

Vin. Ile slit the villaines nose that would haue sent me to the Iaile.

Bap. But doe you heare sir, haue you married my daughter without asking my good will?

Vin. Feare not *Baptista*, we will content you, goe to : but I will in to be reueng'd for this villanie. *Exit.*

Bap. And I to sound the depth of this knauerie. *Exit.*

Luc. Looke not pale *Bianca*, thy father will not frown. *Exeunt.*

Gre. My cake is doug,hbut Ile in among the rest,
Out of hope of all, but my share of the feast.

Kate. Husband let's follow, to see the end of this adoe.

Petr. First kisse me *Kate*, and we will.

Kate. What in the midst of the streete?

Petr. What art thou asham'd of me?

Kate. No sir, God forbid, but asham'd to kisse.

Petr. Why then let's home againe : Come Sirra let's awaie.

Kate. Nay, I will giue thee a kisse, now praie thee Loue staie.

Petr. Is not this well? come my sweete *Kate*.
Better once then neuer, for neuer to late. *Exeunt.*

Actus Quintus.

Enter Baptista, Vincentio, Gremio, the Pedant, Lucentio, and Bianca. Tranio, Biondello Grumio, and Widdow : The Seruingmen with Tranio bringing in a Banquet.

Luc. At last, though long, our iarring notes agree,
And time it is when raging warre is come,
To smile at scapes and perils ouerblowne :
My faire *Bianca* bid my father welcome,
While I with selfesame kindnesse welcome thine:
Brother *Petruchio*, sister *Katerina*,
And thou *Hortentio* with thy louing *Widdow* :
Feast with the best, and welcome to my house,
My Banket is to close our stomakes vp
After our great good cheere : praie you sit downe,
For now we sit to chat as well as eate.

Petr. Nothing but sit and sit, and eate and eate.

Bap. *Padua* affords this kindnesse, sonne *Petruchio*.

Petr. *Padua* affords nothing but what is kinde.

Hor. For both our sakes I would that word were true.

Pet. Now for my life *Hortentio* feares his Widow.

Wid. Then neuer trust me if I be affeard.

Petr. You are verie sencible, and yet you misse my sence :
I meane *Hortentio* is afeard of you.

Wid. He

Wid. He that is giddie thinks the world turns round.
Petr. Roundlie replied.
Kat. Mistris, how meane you that?
Wid. Thus I conceiue by him.
Petr. Conceiues by me, how likes *Hortentio* that?
Hor. My Widdow saies, thus she conceiues her tale.
Petr. Verie well mended: kisse him for that good Widdow.
Kat. He that is giddie thinkes the world turnes round,
I praie you tell me what you meant by that.
Wid. Your housband being troubled with a shrew,
Measures my husbands sorrow by his woe:
And now you know my meaning.
Kate. A verie meane meaning.
Wid. Right, I meane you
Kat. And I am meane indeede, respecting you.
Petr. To her *Kate*
Hor. To her *Widdow.*
Petr. A hundred marks, my *Kate* does put her down
Hor. That's my office
Petr. Spoke like an Officer: ha to the lad.
Drinkes to Hortentio.
Bap. How likes *Gremio* these quicke witted folkes?
Gre. Beleeue me sir, they But together well.
Bian. Head, and but an hastie witted bodie,
Would say your Head and But were head and horne.
Vin. I Mistris Bride, hath that awakened you?
Bian. I, but not frighted me, therefore Ile sleepe againe.
Petr. Nay that you shall not since you haue begun:
Haue at you for a better iest or too.
Bian. Am I your Bird, I meane to shift my bush,
And then pursue me as you draw your Bow.
You are welcome all. *Exit Bianca.*
Petr She hath preuented me, here signior *Tranio,*
This bird you aim'd at, though you hit her not,
Therefore a health to all that shot and mist.
Tri. Oh sir, *Lucentio* slipt me like his Grey-hound,
Which runs himselfe, and catches for his Master.
Petr. A good swift simile, but something currish.
Tra. 'Tis well sir that you hunted for your selfe:
Tis thought your Deere does hold you at a baie.
Bap. Oh, oh *Petruchio, Tranio* hits you now.
Luc. I thanke thee for that gird good *Tranio.*
Hor. Confesse, confesse, hath he not hit you here?
Petr. A has a little gald me I confesse:
And as the Iest did glaunce awaie from me,
'Tis ten to one it maim'd you too out right.
Bap. Now in good sadnesse sonne *Petruchio,*
I thinke thou hast the veriest shrew of all.
Petr. Well, I say no: and therefore sir assurance,
Let's each one send vnto his wife,
And he whose wife is most obedient,
To come at first when he doth send for her,
Shall win the wager which we will propose.
Hort. Content, what's the wager?
Luc. Twentie crownes.
Petr. Twentie crownes,
Ile venture so much of my Hawke or Hound,
But twentie times so much vpon my Wife.
Luc. A hundred then.
Hor. Content.
Petr. A match, 'tis done.
Hor. Who shall begin?
Luc. That will I.
Goe *Biondello*, bid your Mistris come to me.
Bio. I goe. *Exit.*
Bap. Sonne, Ile be your halfe, *Bianca* comes.
Luc. Ile haue no halues: Ile beare it all my selfe.
Enter Biondello.
How now, what newes?
Bio. Sir, my Mistris sends you word
That she is busie, and she cannot come.
Petr. How? she's busie, and she cannot come: is that an answere?
Gre. I, and a kinde one too:
Praie God sir your wife send you not a worse.
Petr. I hope better.
Hor. Sirra *Biondello*, goe and intreate my wife to come to me forthwith. *Exit. Bion.*
Pet. Oh ho, intreate her, nay then shee must needes come.
Hor. I am affraid sir, doe what you can
Enter Biondello.
Yours will not be entreated: Now, where's my wife?
Bion. She saies you haue some goodly Iest in hand,
She will not come: she bids you come to her.
Petr. Worse and worse, she will not come:
Oh vilde, intollerable, not to be indur'd:
Sirra *Grumio*, goe to your Mistris,
Say I command her come to me. *Exit.*
Hor. I know her answere.
Pet. What?
Hor. She will not.
Petr. The fouler fortune mine, and there an end.
Enter Katerina.
Bap. Now by my hollidam here comes *Katerina.*
Kat. What is your will sir, that you send for me?
Petr. Where is your sister, and *Hortensios* wife?
Kate. They sit conferring by the Parler fire.
Petr. Goe fetch them hither, if they denie to come,
Swinge me them soundly forth vnto their husbands:
Away I say, and bring them hither straight.
Luc. Here is a wonder, if you talke of a wonder.
Hor. And so it is: I wonder what it boads.
Petr. Marrie peace it boads, and loue, and quiet life,
An awfull rule, and right supremicie:
And to be short, what not, that's sweete and happie.
Bap Now faire befall thee good *Petruchio;*
The wager thou hast won, and I will adde
Vnto their losses twentie thousand crownes,
Another dowrie to another daughter,
For she is chang'd as she had neuer bin.
Petr. Nay, I will win my wager better yet,
And show more signe of her obedience,
Her new built vertue and obedience
Enter Kate, Bianca, and Widdow.
See where she comes, and brings your froward Wiues
As prisoners to her womanlie perswasion
Katerine, that Cap of yours becomes you not,
Off with that bable, throw it vnderfoote.
Wid. Lord let me neuer haue a cause to sigh,
Till I be brought to such a sillie passe
Bian. Fie what a foolish dutie call you this?
Luc. I would your dutie were as foolish too
The wisdome of your dutie faire *Bianca,*
Hath cost me fiue hundred crownes since supper time.
Bian. The more foole you for laying on my dutie.
Pet. *Katherine* I charge thee tell these head-strong women, what dutie they doe owe their Lords and husbands.
Wid. Come,

Wid. Come, come, your mocking: we will haue no telling.
Pet. Come on I say, and first begin with her.
Wid. She shall not.
Pet. I say she shall, and first begin with her.
Kate. Fie, fie, vnknit that thretaning vnkinde brow,
And dart not scornefull glances from those eies,
To wound thy Lord, thy King, thy Gouernour.
It blots thy beautie, as frosts doe bite the Meads,
Confounds thy fame, as whirlewinds shake faire budds,
And in no sence is meete or amiable.
A woman mou'd, is like a fountaine troubled,
Muddie, ill seeming, thicke, bereft of beautie,
And while it is so, none so dry or thirstie
Will daigne to sip, or touch one drop of it.
Thy husband is thy Lord, thy life, thy keeper,
Thy head, thy soueraigne: One that cares for thee,
And for thy maintenance. Commits his body
To painfull labour, both by sea and land:
To watch the night in stormes, the day in cold,
Whil'st thou ly'st warme at home, secure and safe,
And craues no other tribute at thy hands,
But loue, faire lookes, and true obedience;
Too little payment for so great a debt.
Such dutie as the subiect owes the Prince,
Euen such a woman oweth to her husband:
And when she is froward, peeuish, sullen, sowre,
And not obedient to his honest will,
What is she but a foule contending Rebell,
And gracelesse Traitor to her louing Lord?
I am asham'd that women are so simple,
To offer warre, where they should kneele for peace:
Or seeke for rule, supremacie, and sway,
When they are bound to serue, loue, and obay.
Why are our bodies soft, and weake, and smooth,
Vnapt to toyle and trouble in the world,
But that our soft conditions, and our harts,
Should well agree with our externall parts?
Come, come, you froward and vnable wormes,
My minde hath bin as bigge as one of yours,
My heart as great, my reason haplie more,
To bandie word for word, and frowne for frowne;
But now I see our Launces are but strawes:
Our strength as weake, our weakenesse past compare,
That seeming to be most, which we indeed least are.
Then vale your stomackes, for it is no boote,
And place your hands below your husbands foote:
In token of which dutie, if he please,
My hand is readie, may it do him ease.
Pet. Why there's a wench: Come on, and kisse mee *Kate*.
Luc. Well go thy waies olde Lad for thou shalt ha't.
Vin. Tis a good hearing, when children are toward.
Luc. But a harsh hearing, when women are froward,
Pet. Come *Kate*, wee'le to bed,
We three are married, but you two are sped.
'Twas I wonne the wager, though you hit the white,
And being a winner, God giue you good night.
Exit Petruchio
Horten. Now goe thy wayes, thou hast tam'd a curst Shrow.
Luc. Tis a wonder, by your leaue, she wil be tam'd so.

FINIS.

Vv

ALL'S Well, that Ends Well.

Actus primus. Scœna Prima.

Enter yong Bertram Count of Rossillion, his Mother, and Helena, Lord Lafew, all in blacke.

Mother

IN deliuering my sonne from me, I burie a second husband.

Ros. And I in going Madam, weep ore my fathers death anew; but I must attend his maiesties command, to whom I am now in Ward, euermore in subiection.

Laf. You shall find of the King a husband Madame, you sir a father. He that so generally is at all times good, must of necessitie hold his vertue to you, whose worthinesse would stirre it vp where it wanted rather then lack it where there is such abundance.

Mo. What hope is there of his Maiesties amendment?

Laf. He hath abandon'd his Phisitions Madam, vnder whose practises he hath persecuted time with hope, and finds no other aduantage in the processe, but onely the loosing of hope by time.

Mo. This yong Gentlewoman had a father, O that had, how sad a passage tis, whose skill was almost as great as his honestie, had it stretch'd so far, would haue made nature immortall, and death should haue play for lacke of worke. Would for the Kings sake hee were liuing, I thinke it would be the death of the Kings disease.

Laf. How call'd you the man you speake of Madam?

Mo. He was famous sir in his profession, and it was his great right to be so: *Gerard de Narbon.*

Laf. He was excellent indeed Madam, the King very latelie spoke of him admiringly, and mourningly: hee was skilfull enough to haue liu'd stil, if knowledge could be set vp against mortallitie.

Ros. What is it (my good Lord) the King languishes of?

Laf. A Fistula my Lord

Ros I heard not of it before

Laf. I would it were not notorious. Was this Gentlewoman the Daughter of *Gerard de Narbon?*

Mo. His sole childe my Lord, and bequeathed to my ouer looking. I haue those hopes of her good, that her education promises her dispositions shee inherits, which makes faire gifts fairer: for where an vncleane mind carries vertuous qualities, there commendations go with pitty, they are vertues and traitors too: in her they are the better for their simplenesse; she deriues her honestie, and atcheeues her goodnesse.

Lafew. Your commendations Madam get from her teares.

Mo. 'Tis the best brine a Maiden can season her praise in. The remembrance of her father neuer approches her heart, but the tirrany of her sorrowes takes all liuelihood from her cheeke. No more of this *Helena*, go too, no more least it be rather thought you affect a sorrow, then to haue.

Hell. I doe affect a sorrow indeed, but I haue it too.

Laf. Moderate lamentation is the right of the dead, excessiue greefe the enemie to the liuing.

Mo. If the liuing be enemie to the greefe, the excesse makes it soone mortall.

Ros. Maddam I desire your holie wishes

Laf. How vnderstand we that?

Mo. Be thou blest *Bertrame*, and succeed thy father
in manners as in shape: thy blood and vertue
Contend for Empire in thee, and thy goodnesse
Share with thy birth-right. Loue all, trust a few,
Doe wrong to none: be able for thine enemie
Rather in power then vse; and keepe thy friend
Vnder thy owne lifes key. Be checkt for silence,
But neuer tax'd for speech. What heauen more wil,
That thee may furnish, and my prayers plucke downe,
Fall on thy head. Farwell my Lord,
'Tis an vnseason'd Courtier, good my Lord
Aduise him.

Laf. He cannot want the best
That shall attend his loue.

Mo. Heauen blesse him: Farwell *Bertram*

Ro. The best wishes that can be forg'd in your thoghts be seruants to you: be comfortable to my mother, your Mistris, and make much of her.

Laf. Farewell prettie Lady, you must hold the credit of your father.

Hell. O were that all, I thinke not on my father,
And these great teares grace his remembrance more
Then those I shed for him. What was he like?
I haue forgott him. My imagination
Carries no fauour in't but *Bertrams*.
I am vndone, there is no liuing, none,
If *Bertram* be away. 'Twere all one,
That I should loue a bright particuler starre,
And think to wed it, he is so aboue me
In his bright radience and colaterall light,

Must

Muſt I be comforted, not in his ſphere;
Th'ambition in my loue thus plagues it ſelfe:
The hind that would be mated by the Lion
Muſt die for loue. 'Twas prettie, though a plague
To ſee him euerie houre to ſit and draw
His arched browes, his hawking eie, his curles
In our hearts table: heart too capeable
Of euerie line and tricke of his ſweet fauour.
But now he's gone, and my idolatrous fancie
Muſt ſanctifie his Reliques. Who comes heere?

Enter Parrolles.

One that goes with him: I loue him for his ſake,
And yet I know him a notorious Liar,
Thinke him a great way foole, ſolie a coward,
Yet theſe fixt euils ſit ſo fit in him,
That they take place, when Vertues ſteely bones
Lookes bleake i'th cold wind: withall full ofte we ſee
Cold wiſedome waighting on ſuperfluous follie.

Par. Saue you faire Queene.

Hel. And you Monarch.

Par. No.

Hel. And no.

Par. Are you meditating on virginitie?

Hel. I: you haue ſome ſtaine of ſouldier in you: Let mee aske you a queſtion. Man is enemie to virginitie, how may we barracado it againſt him?

Par. Keepe him out.

Hel. But he aſſailes, and our virginitie though valiant, in the defence yet is weak: vnfold to vs ſome warlike reſiſtance.

Par. There is none: Man ſetting downe before you, will vndermine you, and blow you vp.

Hel. Bleſſe our poore Virginity from vnderminers and blowers vp. Is there no Military policy how Virgins might blow vp men?

Par. Virginity beeing blowne downe, Man will quicklier be blowne vp: marry in blowing him downe againe, with the breach your ſelues made, you loſe your Citty. It is not politicke, in the Common-wealth of Nature, to preſerue virginity. Loſſe of Virginitie, is rationall encreaſe, and there was neuer Virgin goe, till virginitie was firſt loſt. That you were made of, is mettall to make Virgins. Virginitie, by beeing once loſt, may be ten times found: by being euer kept, it is euer loſt: 'tis too cold a companion: Away with't.

Hel. I will ſtand for't a little, though therefore I die a Virgin.

Par. There's little can bee ſaide in't, 'tis againſt the rule of Nature. To ſpeake on the part of virginitie, is to accuſe your Mothers; which is moſt infallible diſobedience. He that hangs himſelfe is a Virgin: Virginitie murthers it ſelfe, and ſhould be buried in highwayes out of all ſanctified limit, as a deſperate Offendreſſe againſt Nature. Virginitie breedes mites, much like a Cheeſe, conſumes it ſelfe to the very payring, and ſo dies with feeding his owne ſtomacke. Beſides, Virginitie is peeuiſh, proud, ydle, made of ſelfe-loue, which is the moſt inhibited ſinne in the Cannon. Keepe it not, you cannot chooſe but looſe by't. Out with't: within ten yeare it will make it ſelfe two, which is a goodly increaſe, and the principall it ſelfe not much the worſe. Away with't.

Hel. How might one do ſir, to looſe it to her owne liking?

Par. Let mee ſee. Marry ill, to like him that ne're it likes. 'Tis a commodity wil loſe the gloſſe with lying: The longer kept, the leſſe worth: Off with't while 'tis vendible. Anſwer the time of requeſt, Virginitie like an olde Courtier, weares her cap out of faſhion, richly ſuted, but vnſuteable, iuſt like the brooch & the toothpick, which were not now: your Date is better in your Pye and your Porredge, then in your cheeke: and your virginity, your old virginity, is like one of our French wither'd peares, it lookes ill, it eates drily, marry 'tis a wither'd peare: it was formerly better, marry yet 'tis a wither'd peare: Will you any thing with it?

Hel. Not my virginity yet:
There ſhall your Maſter haue a thouſand loues,
A Mother, and a Miſtreſſe, and a friend,
A Phenix, Captaine, and an enemy,
A guide, a Goddeſſe, and a Soueraigne,
A Counſellor a Traitoreſſe, and a Deare:
His humble ambition, proud humility:
His iarring, concord: and his diſcord, dulcet:
His faith, his ſweet diſaſter: with a world
Of pretty fond adoptious chriſtendomes
That blinking Cupid goſſips. Now ſhall he:
I know not what he ſhall, God ſend him well,
The Courts a learning place, and he is one.

Par. What one ifaith?

Hel. That I wiſh well, 'tis pitty.

Par. What's pitty?

Hel. That wiſhing well had not a body in't,
Which might be felt, that we the poorer borne,
Whoſe baſer ſtarres do ſhut vs vp in wiſhes,
Might with effects of them follow our friends,
And ſhew what we alone muſt thinke, which neuer
Returnes vs thankes.

Enter Page.

Pag. Monſieur *Parrolles*,
My Lord cals for you.

Par. Little *Hellen* farewell, if I can remember thee, I will thinke of thee at Court.

Hel. Monſieur *Parolles*, you were borne vnder a charitable ſtarre.

Par. Vnder *Mars* I.

Hel. I eſpecially thinke, vnder *Mars*.

Par. Why vnder *Mars*?

Hel. The warres hath ſo kept you vnder, that you muſt needes be borne vnder *Mars*.

Par. When he was predominant.

Hel. When he was retrograde I thinke rather.

Par. Why thinke you ſo?

Hel. You go ſo much backward when you fight.

Par. That's for aduantage.

Hel. So is running away,
When feare propoſes the ſafetie:
But the compoſition that your valour and feare makes in you, is a vertue of a good wing, and I like the weare well.

Paroll. I am ſo full of buſineſſes, I cannot anſwere thee acutely: I will returne perfect Courtier, in the which my inſtruction ſhall ſerue to naturalize thee, ſo thou wilt be capeable of a Courtiers councell, and vnderſtand what aduice ſhall thruſt vppon thee, elſe thou dieſt in thine vnthankfulnes, and thine ignorance makes thee away, farewell: When thou haſt leyſure, ſay thy praiers: when thou haſt none, remember thy Friends:

V 2 Get

Get thee a good husband, and vse him as he vses thee:
So farewell.

Hel Our remedies oft in our selues do lye,
Which we ascribe to heauen: the fated skye
Giues vs free scope, onely doth backward pull
Our slow designes, when we our selues are dull.
What power is it, which mounts my loue so hye,
That makes me see, and cannot feede mine eye?
The mightiest space in fortune, Nature brings
To ioyne like, likes; and kisse like natiue things.
Impossible be strange attempts to those
That weigh their paines in sence, and do suppose
What hath beene, cannot be. Who euer stroue
To shew her merit, that did misse her loue?
(The Kings disease) my proiect may deceiue me,
But my intents are fixt, and will not leaue me. *Exit*

Flourish Cornets.

Enter the King of France with Letters, and diuers Attendants.

King. The *Florentines* and *Senoys* are by th'eares,
Haue fought with equall fortune, and continue
A brauing warre.

1 Lo.G. So tis reported sir.

King. Nay tis most credible, we heere receiue it,
A certaintie vouch'd from our Cosin *Austria*,
With caution, that the *Florentine* will moue vs
For speedie ayde: wherein our deerest friend
Preiudicates the businesse, and would seeme
To haue vs make deniall.

1.Lo.G His loue and wisedome
Approu'd so to your Maiesty, may pleade
For amplest credence.

King. He hath arm'd our answer,
And *Florence* is deni'de before he comes:
Yet for our Gentlemen that meane to see
The *Tuscan* seruice, freely haue they leaue
To stand on either part.

2.Lo.E. It well may serue
A nursserie to our Gentrie, who are sicke
For breathing, and exploit.

King. What's he comes heere.

Enter Bertram, Lafew, and Parolles.

1 Lor.G. It is the Count *Rosignoll* my good Lord,
Yong *Bertram*.

King. Youth, thou bear'st thy Fathers face,
Franke Nature rather curious then in hast
Hath well compos'd thee: Thy Fathers morall parts
Maist thou inherit too: Welcome to *Paris*

Ber. My thankes and dutie are your Maiesties.

Kin. I would I had that corporall soundnesse now,
As when thy father, and my selfe, in friendship
First tride our souldiership: he did looke farre
Into the seruice of the time, and was
Discipled of the brauest. He lasted long,
But on vs both did haggish Age steale on,
And wore vs out of act: It much repaires me,
To talke of your good father; in his youth
He had the wit, which I can well obserue
To day in our yong Lords: but they may iest
Till their owne scorne returne to them vnnoted
Ere they can hide their leuitie in honour:
So like a Courtier, contempt nor bitternesse
Were in his pride, or sharpnesse; if they were,
His equall had awak'd them, and his honour
Clocke to it selfe, knew the true minute when
Exception bid him speake: and at this time
His tongue obey'd his hand. Who were below him,
He vs'd as creatures of another place,
And bow'd his eminent top to their low rankes,
Making them proud of his humilitie,
In their poore praise he humbled: Such a man
Might be a copie to these yonger times;
Which followed well, would demonstrate them now
But goers backward

Ber. His good remembrance sir
Lies richer in your thoughts, then on his tombe:
So in approofe liues not his Epitaph,
As in your royall speech

King. Would I were with him he would alwaies say,
(Me thinkes I heare him now) his plausiue words
He scatter'd not in eares, but grafted them
To grow there and to beare: Let me not liue,
This his good melancholly oft began
On the Catastrophe and heele of pastime
When it was out: Let me not liue (quoth hee)
After my flame lackes oyle, to be the snuffe
Of yonger spirits, whose apprehensiue senses
All but new things disdaine; whose iudgements are
Meere fathers of their garments: whose constancies
Expire before their fashions: this he wish'd
I after him, do after him wish too:
Since I nor wax nor honie can bring home,
I quickly were dissolued from my hiue
To giue some Labourers roome.

L.2.E. You'r loued Sir,
They that least lend it you, shall lacke you first.

Kin. I fill a place I know't: how long ist Count
Since the Physitian at your fathers died?
He was much fam'd.

Ber. Some six moneths since my Lord.

Kin. If he were liuing, I would try him yet.
Lend me an arme: the rest haue worne me out
With seuerall applications: Nature and sicknesse
Debate it at their leisure. Welcome Count,
My sonne's no deerer.

Ber. Thanke your Maiesty. *Exit*

Flourish.

Enter Countesse, Steward, and Clowne.

Coun. I will now heare, what say you of this gentlewoman.

Ste. Maddam the care I haue had to euen your content, I wish might be found in the Kalender of my past endeuours, for then we wound our Modestie, and make foule the clearnesse of our deseruings, when of our selues we publish them.

Coun. What doe's this knaue heere? Get you gone sirra: the complaints I haue heard of you I do not all beleeue, 'tis my slownesse that I doe not. For I know you lacke not folly to commit them, & haue abilitie enough to make such knaueries yours.

Clo. Tis not vnknown to you Madam, I am a poore fellow.

Coun. Well sir.

Clo. No maddam,
Tis not so well that I am poore, though manie of

of the rich are damn'd, but if I may haue your Ladiships good will to goe to the world, *Isbell* the woman and w will doe as we may.

Coun. Wilt thou needes be a begger?

Clo. I doe beg your good will in this case.

Cou. In what case?

Clo. In *Isbels* case and mine owne: seruice is no heritage, and I thinke I shall neuer haue the blessing of God, till I haue issue a my bodie: for they say barnes are blessings.

Cou. Tell me thy reason why thou wilt marrie?

Clo. My poore bodie Madam requires it, I am driuen on by the flesh, and hee must needes goe that the diuell driues.

Cou. Is this all your worships reason?

Clo. Faith Madam I haue other holie reasons, such as they are.

Cou. May the world know them?

Clo. I haue beene Madam a wicked creature, as you and all flesh and blood are, and indeede I doe marrie that I may repent.

Cou. Thy marriage sooner then thy wickednesse

Clo. I am out a friends Madam, and I hope to haue friends for my wiues sake.

Cou. Such friends are thine enemies knaue.

Clo. Y'are shallow Madam in great friends, for the knaues come to doe that for me which I am a wearie of: he that eres my Land, spares my teame, and giues mee leaue to Inne the crop: if I be his cuckold hee's my drudge; he that comforts my wife, is the cherisher of my flesh and blood; hee that cherishes my flesh and blood, loue my flesh and blood; he that loues my flesh and blood is my friend: *ergo*, he that kisses my wife is my friend: if men could be contented to be what they are, there were no feare in marriage, for yong *Charbon* the Puritan, and old *Poysam* the Papist, how somere their hearts are seuer'd in Religion, their heads are both one, they may ioule horns together like any Deare i'th Herd.

Cou. Wilt thou euer be a foule mouth'd and calumnious knaue?

Clo. A Prophet I Madam, and I speake the truth the next waie, for I the Ballad will repeate, which men full true shall finde, your marriage comes by destinie, your Cuckow sings by kinde.

Cou. Get you gone sir, Ile talke with you more anon.

Stew. May it please you Madam, that hee bid *Hellen* come to you, of her I am to speake.

Cou. Sirra tell my gentlewoman I would speake with her, *Hellen* I meane.

Clo. Was this faire face the cause, quoth she,
Why the Grecians sacked *Troy*,
Fond done, done, fond was this King *Priams* ioy,
With that she sighed as she stood, *bis*
And gaue this sentence then, among nine bad if one be good, among nine bad if one be good, there's yet one good in ten.

Cou. What, one good in tenne? you corrupt the song sirra.

Clo. One good woman in ten Madam, which is a purifying ath' song: would God would serue the world so all the yeere, wee'd finde no fault with the tithe woman if I were the Parson, one in ten quoth a? and wee might haue a good woman borne but ore euerie blazing starre, or at an earthquake, 'twould mend the Lotterie well, a man may draw his heart out ere a plucke one.

Cou. Youle begone sir knaue, and doe as I command you?

Clo. That man should be at womans command, and yet no hurt done, though honestie be no Puritan, yet it will doe no hurt, it will weare the Surplis of humilitie ouer the blacke-Gowne of a bigge heart: I am going forsooth, the businesse is for *Helen* to come hither.

Exit.

Cou. Well now.

Stew. I know Madam you loue your Gentlewoman intirely.

Cou. Faith I doe: her Father bequeath'd her to mee, and she her selfe without other aduantage, may lawfullie make title to as much loue as shee findes, there is more owing her then is paid, and more shall be paid her then sheele demand.

Stew. Madam, I was verie late more neere her then I thinke shee wisht mee, alone shee was, and did communicate to her selfe her owne words to her owne eares, shee thought, I dare vowe for her, they toucht not anie stranger sence, her matter was, shee loued your Sonne; Fortune shee said was no goddesse, that had put such difference betwixt their two estates: Loue no god, that would not extend his might onelie, where qualities were leuell, Queene of Virgins, that would suffer her poore Knight surpris'd without rescue in the first assault or ransome afterward: This shee deliuer'd in the most bitter touch of sorrow that ere I heard Virgin exclaime in, which I held my dutie speedily to acquaint you withall, sithence in the losse that may happen, it concernes you something to know it.

Cou. You haue discharg'd this honestlie, keepe it to your selfe, manie likelihoods inform'd mee of this before, which hung so tottring in the ballance, that I could neither beleeue nor misdoubt: praie you leaue mee, stall this in your bosome, and I thanke you for your honest care: I will speake with you further anon.

Exit Steward.

Enter Hellen.

Old.Cou. Euen so it vvas vvith me when I was yong:
If euer vve are natures, these are ours, this thorne
Doth to our Rose of youth righlie belong
Our bloud to vs, this to our blood is borne,
It is the show, and seale of natures truth,
Where loues strong passion is imprest in youth,
By our remembrances of daies forgon,
Such were our faults, or then we thought them none,
Her eie is sicke on't, I obserue her now.

Hell. What is your pleasure Madam?

Ol.Cou. You know *Hellen* I am a mother to you.

Hell. Mine honorable Mistris

Ol.Cou. Nay a mother, why not a mother? when I sed a mother
Me thought you saw a serpent, what's in mother,
That you start at it? I say I am your mother,
And put you in the Catalogue of those
That were enwombed mine, 'tis often seene
Adoption striues vvith nature, and choise breedes
A natiue slip to vs from forraine seedes:
You nere opprest me with a mothers groane,
Yet I expresse to you a mothers care,
(Gods mercie maiden) dos it curd thy blood
To say I am thy mother? vvhat's the matter,
That this distempered messenger of wet?

V 3 The

ne manie colour'd Iris rounds thine eye?
——— Why, that you are my daughter?
Hell. That I am not.
Old.Cou. I say I am your Mother.
Hell Pardon Madam.
The Count *Rosillion* cannot be my brother
I am from humble, he from honored name:
No note vpon my Parents, his all noble,
My Master, my deere Lord he is, and I
His seruant liue, and will his vassall die:
He must not be my brother.
Ol.Cou. Nor I your Mother.
Hell. You are my mother Madam, would you were
So that my Lord your sonne were not my brother,
Indeede my mother, or were you both our mothers,
I care no more for, then I doe for heauen,
So I were not his sister, cant no other,
But I your daughter, he must be my brother.
Old.Cou Yes *Hellen*, you might be my daughter in law,
God shield you meane it not, daughter and mother
So striue vpon your pulse; vvhat pale agen?
My feare hath catcht your fondnesse! now I see
The mistrie of your louelinesse, and finde
Your salt teares head, now to all sence 'tis grosse:
You loue my sonne, inuention is asham'd
Against the proclamation of thy passion
To say thou doost not: therefore tell me true,
But tell me then 'tis so, for looke, thy cheekes
Confesse it 'ton tooth to th'other, and thine eies
See it so grosely showne in thy behauiours,
That in their kinde they speake it, onely sinne
And hellish obstinacie tye thy tongue
That truth should be suspected, speake, ist so?
If it be so, you haue wound a goodly clewe:
If it be not, forsweare't how ere I charge thee,
As heauen shall worke in me for thine auaile
To tell me truelie.
Hell. Good Madam pardon me.
Cou. Do you loue my Sonne?
Hell. Your pardon noble Mistris.
Cou. Loue you my Sonne?
Hell. Doe not you loue him Madam?
Cou. Goe not about; my loue hath in't a bond
Whereof the world takes note: Come, come, disclose:
The state of your affection, for your passions
Haue to the full appeach'd.
Hell Then I confesse
Here on my knee, before high heauen and you,
That before you, and next vnto high heauen, I loue your
Sonne:
My friends were poore but honest, so's my loue:
Be not offended, for it hurts not him
That he is lou'd of me; I follow him not
By any token of presumptuous suite,
Nor would I haue him, till I doe deserue him,
Yet neuer know how that desert should be:
I know I loue in vaine, striue against hope:
Yet in this captious, and intemible Siue.
I still poure in the waters of my loue
And lacke not to loose still; thus *Indian* like
Religious in mine error, I adore
The Sunne that lookes vpon his worshipper,
But knowes of him no more. My deerest Madam,
Let not your hate incounter with my loue,
For louing where you doe; but if your selfe,
Whose aged honor cites a vertuous youth,
Did euer, in so true a flame of liking,
Wish chastly, and loue dearely, that your *Dian*
Was both her selfe and loue, O then giue pittie
To her whose state is such, that cannot choose
But lend and giue where she is sure to loose;
That seekes not to finde that, her search implies,
But riddle like, liues sweetely where she dies.
Cou Had you not lately an intent, speake truely,
To goe to *Paris*?
Hell Madam I had.
Cou Wherefore? tell true.
Hell. I will tell truth, by grace it selfe I sweare
You know my Father left me some prescriptions
Of rare and prou'd effects, such as his reading
And manifest experience, had collected
For generall soueraigntie: and that he wil'd me
In heedefull'st reseruation to bestow them,
As notes, whose faculties inclusiue were,
More then they were in note: Amongst the rest,
There is a remedie, approu'd, set downe,
To cure the desperate languishings whereof
The King is render'd lost.
Cou This was your motiue for *Paris*, was it, speake?
Hell My Lord, your sonne, made me to think of this;
Else *Paris*, and the medicine, and the King,
Had from the conuersation of my thoughts,
Happily beene absent then.
Cou But thinke you *Hellen*,
If you should tender your supposed aide,
He would receiue it? He and his Phisitions
Are of a minde, he, that they cannot helpe him:
They, that they cannot helpe, how shall they credit
A poore vnlearned Virgin, when the Schooles
Embowel'd of their doctrine, haue left off
The danger to it selfe.
Hell. There's something in't
More then my Fathers skill, which was the great'st
Of his profession, that his good receipt,
Shall for my legacie be sanctified
Byth luckiest stars in heauen, and would your honor
But giue me leaue to trie successe, I'de venture
The well lost life of mine, on his Graces cure,
By such a day, an houre.
Cou. Doo'st thou beleeue't?
Hell. I Madam knowingly.
Cou Why *Hellen* thou shalt haue my leaue and loue,
Meanes and attendants, and my louing greetings
To those of mine in Court, Ile staie at home
And praie Gods blessing into thy attempt:
Begon to morrow, and be sure of this,
What I can helpe thee to, thou shalt not misse. *Exeunt.*

Actus Secundus.

Enter the King with diuers yong Lords, taking leaue for the Florentine warre: Count, Rosse, and Parrolles. Florish Cornets.

King. Farewell yong Lords, these warlike principles
Doe not throw from you, and you my Lords farewell:
Share the aduice betwixt you, if both gaine, all
The guift doth stretch it selfe as 'tis receiu'd,
And is enough for both.
Lord.G. 'Tis our hope sir,

After

After well entred ſouldiers, to returne
And finde your grace in health.
King. No,no, it cannot be; and yet my heart
Will not confeſſe he owes the mallady
That doth my life beſiege: farwell yong Lords,
Whether I liue or die, be you the ſonnes
Of worthy French men: let higher Italy
(Thoſe bated that inherit but the fall
Of the laſt Monarchy) ſee that you come
Not to wooe honour, but to wed it, when
The braueſt queſtant ſhrinkes: finde what you ſeeke,
That fame may cry you loud: I ſay farewell.
L.G. Health at your bidding ſerue your Maieſty.
King. Thoſe girles of Italy, take heed of them,
They ſay our French lacke language to deny
If they demand: beware of being Captiues
Before you ſerue.
Bo. Our hearts receiue your warnings.
King. Farewell, come hether to me.
1.Lo.G. Oh my ſweet Lord y you wil ſtay behind vs.
Parr. 'Tis not his fault the ſpark
2.Lo.E. Oh 'tis braue warres.
Parr. Moſt admirable, I haue ſeene thoſe warres.
Roſſill. I am commanded here, and kept a coyle with,
Too young, and the next yeere, and 'tis too early.
Parr. And thy minde ſtand too't boy,
Steale away brauely.
Roſſill. I ſhal ſtay here the for-horſe to a ſmocke,
Creeking my ſhooes on the plaine Maſonry,
Till honour be bought vp, and no ſword worne
But one to dance with: by heauen, Ile ſteale away.
1.Lo.G. There's honour in the theft.
Parr. Commit it Count.
2.Lo.E. I am your acceſſary, and ſo farewell.
Roſ. I grow to you, & our parting is a tortur'd body.
1.Lo.G. Farewll Captaine.
2.Lo.E. Sweet Mounſier *Parolles.*
Parr. Noble *Heroes*; my ſword and yours are kinne, good ſparkes and luſtrous, a word good mettals. You ſhall finde in the Regiment of the Spinij, one Captaine *Spurio* his ſicatrice, with an Embleme of warre heere on his ſiniſter cheeke; it was this very ſword entrench'd it: ſay to him I liue, and obſerue his reports for me.
Lo.G. We ſhall noble Captaine.
Parr. *Mars* doate on you for his nouices, what will ye doe?
Roſſ. Stay the King.
Parr. Vſe a more ſpacious ceremonie to the Noble Lords, you haue reſtrain'd your ſelfe within the Liſt of too cold an adieu: be more expreſſiue to them; for they weare themſelues in the cap of the time, there do muſter true gate; eat, ſpeake, and moue vnder the influence of the moſt receiu'd ſtarre, and though the deuill leade the meaſure, ſuch are to be followed: after them, and take a more dilated farewell.
Roſſ. And I will doe ſo.
Parr. Worthy fellowes, and like to prooue moſt ſinewie ſword-men. *Exeunt.*

Enter Lafew.

L.Laf. Pardon my Lord for mee and for my tidings.
King. Ile ſee thee to ſtand vp. (pardon,
L.Laf. Then heres a man ſtands that has brought his
I would you had kneel'd my Lord to aske me mercy,
And that at my bidding you could ſo ſtand vp.
King. I would I had, ſo I had broke thy pate
And aske thee mercy for't.
Laf. Goodfaith a-croſſe, but my good Lord 'tis thus,
Will you be cur'd of your infirmitie?
King. No.
Laf. O will you eat no grapes my royall foxe?
Yes but you will, my noble grapes, and if
My royall foxe could reach them: I haue ſeen a medicine
That's able to breath life into a ſtone,
Quicken a rocke, and make you dance Canari
With ſprightly fire and motion, whoſe ſimple touch
Is powerfull to arayſe King *Pippen*, nay
To giue great *Charlemaine* a pen in's hand
And write to her a loue-line.
King. What her is this?
Laf. Why doctor ſhe: my Lord, there's one arriu'd,
If you will ſee her: now by my faith and honour,
If ſeriouſly I may conuay my thoughts
In this my light deliuerance, I haue ſpoke
With one, that in her ſexe, her yeeres, profeſſion,
Wiſedome and conſtancy, hath amaz'd mee more
Then I dare blame my weakeneſſe: will you ſee her?
For that is her demand, and know her buſineſſe?
That done, laugh well at me.
King. Now good *Lafew*,
Bring in the admiration, that we with thee
May ſpend our wonder too, or take off thine
By wondring how thou tookſt it.
Laf. Nay, Ile fit you,
And not be all day neither.
King. Thus he his ſpeciall nothing euer prologues.
Laf. Nay, come your waies.

Enter Hellen.

King. This haſte hath wings indeed.
Laf. Nay, come your waies,
This is his Maieſtie, ſay your minde to him,
A Traitor you doe looke like, but ſuch traitors
His Maieſty ſeldome feares, I am *Creſſeds* Vncle,
That dare leaue two together, far you well. *Exit.*
King. Now faire one, do's your buſines follow vs?
Hel. I my good Lord,
Gerard de Narbon was my father,
In what he did profeſſe, well found.
King. I knew him.
Hel. The rather will I ſpare my praiſes towards him,
Knowing him is enough: on's bed of death,
Many receits he gaue me, chieflie one,
Which as the deareſt iſſue of his practice
And of his olde experience, th'onlie darling,
He bad me ſtore vp, as a triple eye,
Safer then mine owne two: more deare I haue ſo,
And hearing your high Maieſtie is toucht
With that malignant cauſe, wherein the honour
Of my deare fathers gift, ſtands cheefe in power,
I come to tender it, and my appliance,
With all bound humbleneſſe.
King. We thanke you maiden,
But may not be ſo credulous of cure,
When our moſt learned Doctors leaue vs, and
The congregated Colledge haue concluded,
That labouring Art can neuer ranſome nature
From her inaydible eſtate: I ſay we muſt not
So ſtaine our iudgement, or corrupt our hope,
To proſtitute our paſt-cure malladie
To empericks, or to diſſeuer ſo
Our great ſelfe and our credit, to eſteeme
A ſenceleſſe helpe, when helpe paſt ſence we deeme.
Hel. My

Hell. My dutie then shall pay me for my paines:
I will no more enforce mine office on you,
Humbly intreating from your royall thoughts,
A modest one to beare me backe againe.
King. I cannot giue thee lesse to be cal'd gratefull:
Thou thoughtst to helpe me, and such thankes I giue,
As one neere death to those that wish him liue:
But what at full I know, thou knowst no part,
I knowing all my perill, thou no Art.
Hell. What I can doe, can doe no hurt to try,
Since you seevp your rest gainst remedie:
He that of greatest wo kes is finisher,
Oft does them by the weakest minister:
So holy Writ, in babes hath iudgement showne,
When Iudges haue bin babes; great flouds haue flowne
From simple sources: and great Seas haue dried
When Miracles haue by the great'st beene denied.
Oft expectation failes, and most oft there
Where most it promises: and oft it hits,
Where hope is coldest, and despaire most shifts.
King. I must not heare thee, fare thee wel kind maide
Thy paines not vs'd, must by thy selfe be paid,
Proffers not tooke, reape thanks for their reward.
Hel. Inspired Merit so by breath is bard,
It is not so with him that all things knowes
As 'tis with vs, that square our guesse by showes:
But most it is presumption in vs, when
The help of heauen we count the act of men.
Deare sir, to my endeauors giue consent,
Of heauen, not me, make an experiment.
I am not an Impostrue, that proclaime
My selfe against the leuill of mine aime,
But know I thinke, and thinke I know most sure,
My Art is not past power, nor you past cure.
King. Art thou so confident? Within what space
Hop'st thou my cure?
Hel. The greatest grace lending grace,
Ere twice the horses of the sunne shall bring
Their fiery torcher his diurnall ring,
Ere twice in murke and occidentall dampe
Moist *Hesperus* hath quench'd her sleepy Lampe:
Or foure and twenty times the Pylots glasse
Hath told the theeuish minutes, how they passe:
What is infirme, from your sound parts shall flie,
Health shall liue free, and sickenesse freely dye.
King. Vpon thy certainty and confidence,
What dar'st thou venter?
Hell. Taxe of impudence,
A strumpets boldnesse, a divulged shame
Traduc'd by odious ballads: my maidens name
Seard otherwise, ne worse of worst extended
With vildest torture, let my life be ended.
Kin. Methinks in thee some blessed spirit doth speak
His powerfull sound, within an organ weake:
And what impossibility would slay
In common sence, sence saues another way:
Thy life is deere, for all that life can rate
Worth name of life, in thee hath estimate
Youth, beauty, wisedome, courage, all
That happines and prime, can happy call:
Thou this to hazard, needs must intimate
Skill infinite, or monstrous desperate,
Sweet practiser, thy Physicke I will try,
That ministers thine owne death if I die.
Hel. If I breake time, or flinch in property
Of what I spoke, vnpittied let me die,
And well deseru'd. not helping, death's my fee,
But if I helpe, what doe you promise me.
Kin. Make thy demand.
Hel. But will you make it euen?
Kin. I by my Scepter, and my hopes of helpe.
Hel. Then shalt thou giue me with thy kingly hand
What husband in thy power I will command:
Exempted be from me the arrogance
To choose from forth the royall bloud of France,
My low and humble name to propagate
With any branch or image of thy state:
But such a one thy vassall, whom I know
Is free for me to aske, hee to bestow.
Kin. Heere is my hand, the premises obseru'd,
Thy will by my performance shall be seru'd:
So make the choice of thy owne time, for I
Thy resolv'd Patient, on thee still relye:
More should I question thee, and more I must,
Though more to know, could not be more to trust:
From whence thou cam'st, how tended on, but rest
Vnquestion'd welcome, and vndoubted blest.
Giue me some helpe heere hoa, if thou proceed,
As high as word, my deed shall match thy deed.
Florish. Exit.

Enter Countesse and Clowne.

Lady. Come on sir, I shall now put you to the height of your breeding.

Clown. I will show my selfe highly fed, and lowly taught, I know my businesse is but to the Court.

Lady. To the Court, why what place make you speciall, when you put off that with such contempt, but to the Court?

Clo. Truly Madam, if God haue lent a man any manners, hee may easilie put it off at Court: hee that cannot make a legge, put off's cap, kisse his hand, and say nothing, has neither legge, hands, lippe, nor cap; and indeed such a fellow, to say precisely, were not for the Court, but for me, I haue an answere will serue all men.

Lady. Marry that's a bountifull answere that fits all questions.

Clo. It is like a Barbers chaire that fits all buttockes, the pin buttocke, the quatch-buttocke, the brawn buttocke, or any buttocke.

Lady. Will your answere serue fit to all questions?

Clo. As fit as ten groats is for the hand of an Atturney, as your French Crowne for your taffety punke, as *Tibs* rush for *Toms* fore-finger, as a pancake for Shrouetuesday, a Morris for May-day, as the naile to his hole, the Cuckold to his horne, as a scolding queane to a wrangling knaue, as the Nuns lip to the Friers mouth, nay as the pudding to his skin.

Lady. Haue you, I say, an answere of such fitnesse for all questions?

Clo. From below your Duke, to beneath your Constable, it will fit any question.

Lady. It must be an answere of most monstrous size, that must fit all demands.

Clo. But a trifle neither in good faith, if the learned should speake truth of it: heere it is, and all that belongs to't. Aske mee if I am a Courtier, it shall doe you no harme to learne.

Lady. To be young againe if we could: I will bee a foole in question, hoping to bee the wiser by your answer.

Lady.

La. I pray you sir, are you a Courtier?

Clo. O Lord sir theres a simple putting off: more, more, a hundred of them.

La. Sir I am a poore freind of yours, that loues you.

Clo. O Lord sir, thicke, thicke, spare not me.

La. I thinke sir, you can eate none of this homely meate.

Clo. O Lord sir; nay put me too't, I warrant you.

La. You were lately whipt sir as I thinke

Clo. O Lord sir, spare not me.

La. Doe you crie O Lord sir at your whipping, and spare not me? Indeed your O Lord sir, is very sequent to your whipping: you would answere very well to a whipping if you were but bound too't.

Clo. I nere had worse lucke in my life in my O Lord sir: I see things may serue long, but not serue euer.

La. I play the noble huswife with the time, to entertaine it so merrily with a foole.

Clo. O Lord sir, why there't serues well agen.

La. And end sir to your businesse: giue *Hellen* this,
And vrge her to a present answer backe,
Commend me to my kinsmen, and my sonne,
This is not much.

Clo. Not much commendation to them.

La. Not much imployement for you, you vnderstand me.

Clo Most fruitfully, I am there, before my legegs.

La. Hast you agen. *Exeunt*

Enter Count, Lafew, and Parolles.

Ol.Laf. They say miracles are past, and we haue our Philosophicall persons, to make moderne and familiar things supernaturall and causelesse. Hence is it, that we make trifles of terrours, ensconcing our selues into seeming knowledge, when we should submit our selues to an vnknowne feare.

Par. Why 'tis the rarest argument of wonder, that hath shot out in our latter times.

Ros. And so 'tis.

Ol Laf. To be relinquisht of the Artists.

Par. So I say both of *Galen* and *Paracelsus.*

Ol Laf. Of all the learned and authenticke fellowes.

Par. Right so I say.

Ol.Laf. That gaue him out incureable.

Par. Why there 'tis, so say I too.

Ol.Laf. Not to be help'd.

Par. Right, as 'twere a man assur'd of a———

Ol.Laf. Vncertaine life, and sure death.

Par. Iust, you say well: so would I haue said.

Ol.Laf. I may truly say, it is a noueltie to the world.

Par. It is indeede if you will haue it in shewing, you shall reade it in what do ye call there.

Ol.Laf. A shewing of a heauenly effect in an earthly Actor

Par. That's it, I would haue said, the verie same

Ol.Laf. Why your Dolphin is not lustier: fore mee I speake in respect———

Par Nay 'tis strange, 'tis very straunge, that is the breefe and the tedious of it, and he's of a most facinerious spirit, that will not acknowledge it to be the———

Ol.Laf. Very hand of heauen.

Par. I, so I say.

Ol.Laf. In a most weake———

Par. And debile minister great power, great trancendence, which should indeede giue vs a further vse to be made, then alone the recou'ry of the king, as to bee

Old Laf. Generally thankfull.

Enter King, Hellen, and attendants.

Par I would haue said it, you say well: heere comes the King.

Ol.Laf. Lustique, as the Dutchman saies: Ile like a maide the Better whil'st I haue a tooth in my head: why he's able to leade her a Carranto.

Par. *Mor du vinager,* is not this *Helen?*

Ol.Laf. Fore God I thinke so.

King. Goe call before mee all the Lords in Court,
Sit my preseruer by thy patients side,
And with this healthfull hand whose banisht sence
Thou hast repeal'd, a second time receyue
The confirmation of my promis'd guift,
Which but attends thy naming.

Enter 3 or 4 Lords.

Faire Maide send forth thine eye, this youthfull parcell
Of Noble Batchellors, stand at my bestowing,
Ore whom both Soueraigne power, and fathers voice
I haue to vse; thy franke election make,
Thou hast power to choose, and they none to forsake.

Hel. To each of you, one faire and vertuous Mistris;
Fall when loue please, marry to each but one.

Old Laf. I'de giue bay curtall, and his furniture
My mouth no more were broken then these boyes,
And writ as little beard

King. Peruse them well:
Not one of those, but had a Noble father

She addresses her to a Lord.

Hel. Gentlemen, heauen hath through me, restor'd the king to health.

All. We vnderstand it, and thanke heauen for you.

Hel. I am a simple Maide, and therein wealthiest
That I protest, I simply am a Maide:
Please it your Maiestie, I haue done already:
The blushes in my cheekes thus whisper mee,
We blush that thou shouldst choose, but be refused;
Let the white death sit on thy cheeke for euer.
Wee'l nere come there againe.

King Make choise and see,
Who shuns thy loue, shuns all his loue in mee.

Hel. Now *Dian* from thy Altar do I fly,
And to imperiall loue, that God most high
Do my sighes streame: Sir, wil you heare my suite?

1.Lo And grant it.

Hel. Thankes sir, all the rest is mute

Ol.Laf. I had rather be in this choise, then throw Ames-ace for my life.

Hel The honor sir that flames in your faire eyes,
Before I speake too threatningly replies:
Loue make your fortunes twentie times aboue
Her that so wishes, and her humble loue.

2.Lo. No better if you please

Hel. My wish receiue,
Which great loue grant, and so I take my leaue.

Ol.Laf. Do all they denie her? And they were sons of mine, I'de haue them whip'd, or I would send them to'th Turke to make Eunuches of.

Hel Be not afraid that I your hand should take,
Ile neuer do you wrong for your owne sake:
Blessing vpon your vowes, and in your bed
Finde fairer fortune, if you euer wed.

Old Laf. These boyes are boyes of Ice, they'le none haue

haue heere : sure they are bastards to the English, the
French nere got em.
La. You are too young, too happie, and too good
To make your selfe a sonne out of my blood.
4.Lord. Faire one, I thinke not so.
Ol.Lord There's one grape yet, I am sure thy father
drunke wine. But if thou be'st not an asse, I am a youth
of fourteene : I haue knowne thee already.
Hel. I dare not say I take you, but I giue
Me and my seruice, euer whilst I liue
Into your guiding power : This is the man.
King. Why then young *Bertram* take her shee's thy
wife.
Ber. My wife my Leige? I shal beseech your highnes
In such a busines, giue me leaue to vse
The helpe of mine owne eies.
King. Know'st thou not *Bertram* what shee ha's
done for mee?
Ber. Yes my good Lord, but neuer hope to know
why I should marrie her.
King. Thou know'st shee ha's rais'd me from my sick-
ly bed.
Ber. But followes it my Lord, to bring me downe
Must answer for your raising? I knowe her well:
Shee had her breeding at my fathers charge:
A poore Physitians daughter my wife? Disdaine
Rather corrupt me euer.
King. Tis onely title thou disdainst in her, the which
I can build vp : strange is it that our bloods
Of colour, waight, and heat, pour'd all together,
Would quite confound distinction: yet stands off
In differences so mightie. If she bee
All that is vertuous (saue what thou dislik'st)
A poore Phisitians daughter, thou dislik'st
Of vertue for the name : but doe not so :
From lowest place, whence vertuous things proceed,
The place is dignified by th' doers deede.
Where great additions swell's, and vertue none,
It is a dropsied honour. Good alone,
Is good without a name? Vilenesse is so :
The propertie by what is is, should go,
Not by the title. Shee is young, wise, faire,
In these, to Nature shee's immediate heire :
And these breed honour : that is honours scorne,
Which challenges it selfe as honours borne,
And is not like the sire : Honours thriue,
When rather from our acts we them deriue
Then our fore-goers : the meere words, a slaue
Debosh'd on euerie tombe, on euerie graue :
A lying Trophee, and as oft is dumbe,
Where dust, and damn'd obliuion is the Tombe.
Of honour'd bones indeed, what should be saide?
If thou canst like this creature, as a maide,
I can create the rest : Vertue, and shee
Is her owne dower : Honour and wealth, from mee.
Ber. I cannot loue her, nor will striue to doo't.
King Thou wrong'st thy selfe, if thou shold'st striue
to choose.
Hel. That you are well restor'd my Lord, I'me glad:
Let the rest go.
King. My Honor's at the stake, which to defeate
I must produce my power. Heere, take her hand,
Proud scornfull boy, vnworthie this good gift,
That dost in vile misprision shackle vp
My loue, and her desert : that canst not dreame,
We poizing vs in her defectiue scale,
Shall weigh thee to the beame : That wilt not know,
It is in Vs to plant thine Honour, where
We please to haue it grow. Checke thy contempt :
Obey Our will, which trauailes in thy good :
Beleeue not thy disdaine, but presentlie
Do thine owne fortunes that obedient right
Which both thy dutie owes, and Our power claimes,
Or I will throw thee from my care for euer
Into the staggers, and the carelesse lapse
Of youth and ignorance : both my reuenge and hate
Loosing vpon thee, in the name of iustice,
Without all termes of pittie. Speake, thine answer.
Ber. Pardon my gracious Lord : for I submit
My fancie to your eies, when I consider
What great creation, and what dole of honour
Flies where you bid it : I finde that she which late
Was in my Nobler thoughts, most base : is now
The praised of the King, who so ennobled,
Is as 'twere borne so.
King. Take her by the hand,
And tell her she is thine: to whom I promise
A counterpoize : If not to thy estate,
A ballance more replete.
Ber. I take her hand.
Kin. Good fortune, and the fauour of the King
Smile vpon this Contract : whose Ceremonie
Shall seeme expedient on the now borne briefe,
And be perform'd to night : the solemne Feast
Shall more attend vpon the coming space,
Expecting absent friends. As thou lou'st her,
Thy loue's to me Religious : else, do's erre. *Exeunt*
Parolles and Lafew stay behind, commen-
ting of this wedding.
Laf. Do you heare Monsieur? A word with you.
Par. Your pleasure sir.
Laf. Your Lord and Master did well to make his re-
cantation.
Par. Recantation? My Lord? my Master?
Laf. I : Is it not a Language I speake?
Par. A most harsh one, and not to bee vnderstoode
without bloudie succeeding. My Master?
Laf. Are you Companion to the Count *Rosillion?*
Par. To any Count, to all Counts : to what is man.
Laf. To what is Counts man : Counts maister is of
another stile.
Par. You are too old sir : Let it satisfie you, you are
oo old.
Laf. I must tell thee sirrah, I write Man : to which
title age cannot bring thee.
Par. What I dare too well do, I dare not do.
Laf. I did thinke thee for two ordinaries : to bee a
prettie wise fellow, thou didst make tollerable vent of
thy trauell, it might passe : yet the scarffes and the ban-
nerets about thee, did manifoldlie disswade me from beleeuing thee a vessell of too great a burthen. I haue now
found thee, when I loose thee againe, I care not: yet art
thou good for nothing but taking vp, and that th'ourt
scarce worth.
Par. Hadst thou not the priuiledge of Antiquity vpon thee.
Laf. Do not plundge thy selfe to farre in anger, least
thou hasten thy triall : which if, Lord haue mercie on
thee for a hen, so my good window of Lettice fare thee
well, thy casement I neede not open, for I look through
thee. Giue me thy hand.
Par. My Lord, you giue me most egregious indignity.
Laf.

Laf. I with all my heart, and thou art worthy of it.

Par. I haue not my Lord deseru'd it.

Laf. Yes good faith, eu'ry dramme of it, and I will not bate thee a scruple.

Par. Well, I shall be wiser.

Laf. Eu'n as soone as thou can'st, for thou hast to pull at a smacke a'th contrarie. If euer thou bee'st bound in thy skarfe and beaten, thou shall finde what it is to be proud of thy bondage, I haue a desire to holde my acquaintance with thee, or rather my knowledge, that I may say in the default, he is a man I know.

Par. My Lord you do me most insupportable vexation.

Laf. I would it were hell paines for thy sake, and my poore doing eternall: for doing I am past, as I will by thee, in what motion age will giue me leaue. *Exit.*

Par. Well, thou hast a sonne shall take this disgrace off me; scuruy, old, filthy, scuruy Lord: Well, I must be patient, there is no fettering of authority. Ile beate him (by my life) if I can meete him with any conuenience, and he were double and double a Lord. Ile haue no more pittie of his age then I would haue of—— Ile beate him, and if I could but meet him agen.

Enter Lafew.

Laf. Sirra, your Lord and masters married, there's newes for you: you haue a new Mistris.

Par. I most vnfainedly beseech your Lordshippe to make some reseruation of your wrongs. He is my good Lord, whom I serue aboue is my master.

Laf. Who? God.

Par. I sir.

Laf. The deuill it is, that's thy master. Why dooest thou garter vp thy armes a this fashion? Dost make hose of thy sleeues? Do other seruants so? Thou wert best set thy lower part where thy nose stands. By mine Honor, if I were but two houres yonger, I'de beate thee: meethink'st thou art a generall offence, and euery man shold beate thee: I thinke thou wast created for men to breath themselues vpon thee.

Par. This is hard and vndeserued measure my Lord.

Laf. Go too sir, you were beaten in *Italy* for picking a kernell out of a Pomgranat, you are a vagabond, and no true traueller: you are more sawcie with Lordes and honourable personages, then the Commission of your birth and vertue giues you Heraldry. You are not worth another word, else I'de call you knaue. I leaue you. *Exit*

Enter Count Rossillion.

Par. Good, very good, it is so then: good, very good, let it be conceal'd awhile.

Ros. Vndone, and forfeited to cares for euer.

Par. What's the matter sweet-heart?

Rossill. Although before the solemne Priest I haue sworne, I will not bed her.

Par. What? what sweet heart?

Ros. O my *Parrolles*, they haue married me:
Ile to the *Tuscan* warres, and neuer bed her.

Par. *France* is a dog-hole, and it no more merits,
The tread of a mans foot: too'th warres.

Ros. There's letters from my mother: What th'import is, I know not yet.

Par. I that would be knowne: too'th warrs my boy, too'th warres:
He weares his honor in a boxe vnseene,
That hugges his kickie wickie heare at home,
Spending his manlie marrow in her armes
Which should sustaine the bound and high curuet
Of *Marses* fierie steed: to other Regions,
France is a stable, wee that dwell in't Iades,
Therefore too'th warre.

Ros. It shall be so, Ile send her to my house,
Acquaint my mother with my hate to her,
And wherefore I am fled: Write to the King
That which I durst not speake. His present gift
Shall furnish me to those Italian fields
Where noble fellowes strike: Warres is no strife
To the darke house, and the detected wife.

Par. Will this Caprichio hold in thee, art sure?

Ros. Go with me to my chamber, and aduice me.
Ile send her straight away: To morrow,
Ile to the warres, she to her single sorrow.

Par. Why these bals bound, ther's noise in it. Tis hard
A yong man maried, is a man that's mard:
Therefore away, and leaue her brauely: go,
The King ha's done you wrong: but hush 'tis so. *Exit*

Enter Helena and Clowne.

Hel. My mother greets me kindly, is she well?

Clo. She is not well, but yet she has her health, she's very merrie, but yet she is not well: but thankes be giuen she's very well, and wants nothing i'th world: but yet she is not well.

Hel. If she be verie wel, what do's she ayle, that she's not verie well?

Clo. Truly she's very well indeed, but for two things

Hel. What two things?

Clo. One, that she's not in heauen, whether God send her quickly: the other, that she's in earth, from whence God send her quickly

Enter Parolles.

Par Blesse you my fortunate Ladie.

Hel. I hope sir I haue your good will to haue mine owne good fortune.

Par. You had my prayers to leade them on, and to keepe them on, haue them still. O my knaue, how do's my old Ladie?

Clo. So that you had her wrinkles, and I her money, I would she did as you say.

Par. Why I say nothing.

Clo. Marry you are the wiser man: for many a mans tongue shakes out his masters vndoing: to say nothing, to do nothing, to know nothing, and to haue nothing, is to be a great part of your title, which is within a verie little of nothing.

Par. Away, th'art a knaue.

Clo. You should haue said sir before a knaue, th'art a knaue, that's before me th'art a knaue: this had beene truth sir.

Par. Go too, thou art a wittie foole, I haue found thee.

Clo. Did you finde me in your selfe sir, or were you taught to finde me?

Clo. The search sir was profitable, and much Foole may you find in you, euen to the worlds pleasure, and the encrease of laughter.

Par. A good knaue ifaith, and well fed.
Madam, my Lord will go awaie to night,

A verie serrious businesse call's on him :
The great prerogatiue and rite of loue,
Which as your due time claimes, he do's acknowledge
But puts it off to a compell'd restraint :
Whose want, and whose delay, is strew'd with sweets
Which they distill now in the curbed time,
To make the comming houre oreflow with ioy,
And pleasure drowne the brim.

Fel. What's his will else?

Par. That you will take your instant leaue a'th king,
And make this hast as your owne good proceeding,
Strengthned with what Apologie you thinke
May make it probable neede.

Hel. What more commands hee?

Par. That hauing this obtain'd, you presentlie
Attend his further pleasure.

Hel. In euery thing I waite vpon his will.

Par. I shall report it so. *Exit Par.*

Hell. I pray you come sirrah. *Exit*

Enter Lafew and Bertram.

Laf. But I hope your Lordshippe thinkes not him a souldier.

Ber. Yes my Lord and of verie valiant approofe.

Laf. You haue it from his owne deliuerance.

Ber. And by other warranted testimonie.

Laf. Then my Diall goes not true, I tooke this Larke for a bunting.

Ber. I do assure you my Lord he is very great in knowledge, and accordinglie valiant.

Laf. I haue then sinn'd against his experience, and transgrest against his valour, and my state that way is dangerous, since I cannot yet find in my heart to repent: Heere he comes, I pray you make vs freinds, I will pursue the amitie.

Enter Parolles.

Par. These things shall be done sir.

Laf. Pray you sir whose his Tailor?

Par. Sir?

Laf. O I know him well, I sir, hee sirs a good workeman, a verie good Tailor.

Ber. Is shee gone to the king?

Par. Shee is.

Ber. Will shee away to night?

Par. As you'le haue her.

Ber. I haue writ my letters, casketted my treasure,
Giuen order for our horses, and to night,
When I should take possession of the Bride,
And ere I doe begin.

Laf. A good Trauailer is something at the latter end of a dinner, but on that lies three thirds, and vses a known truth to passe a thousand nothings with, should bee once hard, and thrice beaten. God saue you Captaine.

Ber. Is there any vnkindnes betweene my Lord and you Monsieur?

Par. I know not how I haue deserued to run into my Lords displeasure.

Laf. You haue made shift to run into't, bootes and spurres and all: like him that leapt into the Custard, and out of it you'le runne againe, rather then suffer question for your residence.

Ber. It may bee you haue mistaken him my Lord.

Laf. And shall doe so euer, though I tooke him at's prayers. Fare you well my Lord, and beleeue this of me, there can be no kernell in this light Nut: the soule of this man is his cloathes: Trust him not in matter of heauie consequence: I haue kept of them tame, & know their natures. Farewell Monsieur, I haue spoken better of you, then you haue or will to deserue at my hand, but we must do good against euill.

Par. An idle Lord, I sweare.

Ber. I thinke so.

Par. Why do you not know him?

Ber. Yes, I do know him well, and common speech
Giues him a worthy passe. Heere comes my clog.

Enter Helena.

Hel. I haue sir as I was commanded from you
Spoke with the King, and haue procur'd his leaue
For present parting, onely he desires
Some priuate speech with you.

Ber. I shall obey his will.
You must not meruaile *Helen* at my course,
Which holds not colour with the time, nor does
The ministration, and required office
On my particular. Prepar'd I was not
For such a businesse, therefore am I found
So much vnsetled: This driues me to intreate you,
That presently you take your way for home,
And rather muse then aske why I intreate you,
For my respects are better then they seeme,
And my appointments haue in them a neede
Greater then shewes it selfe at the first view,
To you that know them not. This to my mother,
'Twill be two daies ere I shall see you, so
I leaue you to your wisedome.

Hel. Sir, I can nothing say,
But that I am your most obedient seruant.

Ber. Come, come, no more of that.

Hel. And euer shall
With true obseruance seeke to eeke out that
Wherein toward me my homely starres haue faild
To equall my great fortune.

Ber. Let that goe: my hast is verie great. Farwell:
Hie home.

Hel. Pray sir your pardon.

Ber. Well, what would you say?

Hel. I am not worthie of the wealth I owe,
Nor dare I say 'tis mine: and yet it is,
But like a timorous theefe, most faine would steale
What law does vouch mine owne.

Ber. What would you haue?

Hel. Something, and scarse so much: nothing indeed,
I would not tell you what I would my Lord: Faith yes,
Strangers and foes do sunder, and not kisse.

Ber. I pray you stay not, but in hast to horse.

Hel. I shall not breake your bidding, good my Lord:
Where are my other men? Monsieur, farwell. *Exit*

Ber. Go thou toward home, where I wil neuer come,
Whilst I can shake my sword, or heare the drumme:
Away, and for our flight.

Par. Brauely, Coragio.

Actus Tertius.

Flourish. Enter the Duke of Floreuce, the two Frenchmen, with a troope of Souldiers.

Duke. So that from point to point, now haue you heard
The

The fundamentall reasons of this warre,
Whose great decision hath much blood let forth
And more thirsts after.

1.Lord Holy seemes the quarrell
Vpon your Graces part: blacke and fearefull
On the opposer.

Duke. Therefore we meruaile much our Cosin France
Would in so iust a businesse, shut his bosome
Against our borrowing prayers.

French E. Good my Lord,
The reasons of our state I cannot yeelde,
But like a common and an outward man,
That the great figure of a Counsaile frames,
By selfe vnable motion, therefore dare not
Say what I thinke of it, since I haue found
My selfe in my incertaine grounds to faile
As often as I guest.

Duke. Be it his pleasure.

Fren.G. But I am sure the yonger of our nature,
That surfet on their ease, will day by day
Come heere for Physicke.

Duke. Welcome shall they bee:
And all the honors that can flye from vs,
Shall on them settle: you know your places well,
When better fall, for your auailes they fell,
To morrow to'th the field. *Flourish.*

Enter Countesse and Clowne.

Count. It hath happen'd all, as I would haue had it, saue that he comes not along with her.

Clo. By my troth I take my young Lord to be a verie melancholly man.

Count. By what obseruance I pray you.

Clo Why he will looke vppon his boote, and sing: mend the Ruffe and sing, aske questions and sing, picke his teeth, and sing: I know a man that had this tricke of melancholy hold a goodly Mannor for a song.

Lad. Let me see what he writes, and when he meanes to come.

Clow. I haue no minde to *Isbell* since I was at Court. Our old Lings, and our *Isbels* a'th Country, are nothing like your old Ling and your *Isbels* a'th Court: the brains of my Cupid's knock'd out, and I beginne to loue, as an old man loues money, with no stomacke.

Lad. What haue we heere?

Clo. In that you haue there. *exit*

A Letter.

I haue sent you a daughter-in-Law, shee hath recouered the King, and vndone me: I haue wedded her, not bedded her, and sworne to make the not eternall. You shall heare I am runne away, know it before the report come. If there bee bredth enough in the world, I will hold a long distance. My duty to you. Your vnfortunate sonne,
Bertram.

This is not well rash and vnbridled boy,
To flye the fauours of so good a King,
To plucke his indignation on thy head,
By the misprising of a Maide too vertuous
For the contempt of Empire.

Enter Clowne.

Clow. O Madam, yonder is heauie newes within betweene two souldiers, and my yong Ladie.

La. What is the matter.

Clo. Nay there is some comfort in the newes, some comfort, your sonne will not be kild so soone as I thoght he would.

La. Why should he be kill'd?

Clo. So say I Madame, if he runne away, as I heare he does, the danger is in standing too't, that's the losse of men, though it be the getting of children. Heere they come will tell you more. For my part I onely heare your sonne was run away.

Enter Hellen and two Gentlemen.

French E. Saue you good Madam.

Hel. Madam, my Lord is gone, for euer gone.

French G. Do not say so.

La. Thinke vpon patience, pray you Gentlemen,
I haue felt so many quirkes of ioy and greefe,
That the first face of neither on the start
Can woman me vntoo't. Where is my sonne I pray you

Fren.G. Madam he's gone to serue the Duke of Florence,
We met him thitherward, for thence we came:
And after some dispatch in hand at Court,
Thither we bend againe.

Hel. Looke on his Letter Madam, here's my Pasport.

When thou canst get the Ring vpon my finger, which neuer shall come off, and shew mee a childe begotten of thy bodie, that I am father too, then call me husband: but in such a (then) I write a Neuer.

This is a dreadfull sentence.

La. Brought you this Letter Gentlemen?

1.G. I Madam, and for the Contents sake are sorrie for our paines.

Old La. I prethee Ladie haue a better cheere,
If thou engrossest, all the greefes are thine,
Thou robst me of a moity: He was my sonne,
But I do wash his name out of my blood,
And thou art all my childe. Towards Florence is he?

Fren.G. I Madam.

La. And to be a souldier.

Fren.G. Such is his noble purpose, and beleeu't
The Duke will lay vpon him all the honor
That good conuenience claimes.

La. Returne you thither.

Fren.E. I Madam, with the swiftest wing of speed.

Hel. *Till I haue no wife, I haue nothing in France,*
Tis bitter.

La. Finde you that there?

Hel. I Madame.

Fren.E. 'Tis but the boldnesse of his hand haply, which is heart was not consenting too.

Lad. Nothing in France, vntill he haue no wife:
There's nothing heere that is too good for him
But onely she, and she deserues a Lord
That twenty such rude boyes might tend vpon,
And call her hourely Mistris. Who was with him?

Fren.E. A seruant onely, and a Gentleman: which I haue sometime knowne.

La. *Parolles* was it not?

Fren.E. I my good Ladie, hee.

La. A verie tainted fellow, and full of wickednesse,
My sonne corrupts a well deriued nature
With his inducement.

Fren.E. Indeed good Ladie the fellow has a deale of that, too much, which holds him much to haue.

La. Y'are welcome Gentlemen, I will intreate you when you see my sonne, to tell him that his sword can neuer winne the honor that he looses: more Ile intreate you

you written to bearealong.

Fren.G. We ſerue you Madam in that and all your worthieſt affaires.

La. Not ſo, but as we change our courteſies,
Will you draw neere? *Exit.*

Hel. Till I haue no wife I haue nothing in France.
Nothing in France vntill he has no wife:
Thou ſhalt haue none *Roſſillion*, none in France,
Then haſt thou all againe: poore Lord, is't I
That chaſe thee from thy Countrie, and expoſe
Thoſe tender limbes of thine, to the euent
Of the none-ſparing warre? And is it I,
That driue thee from the ſportiue Court, where thou
Was't ſhot at with faire eyes, to be the marke
Of ſmoakie Muskets? O you leaden meſſengers,
That ride vpon the violent ſpeede of fire,
Fly with falſe ayme, moue the ſtill-peering aire
That ſings with piercing, do not touch my Lord:
Who euer ſhoots at him, I ſet him there.
Who euer charges on his forward breſt
I am the Caitiffe that do hold him too't,
And though I kill him not, I am the cauſe
His death was ſo effected: Better 'twere
I met the rauine Lyon when he roar'd
With ſharpe conſtraint of hunger: better 'twere,
That all the miſeries which nature owes
Were mine at once. No come thou home *Roſſillion*,
Whence honor but of danger winnes a ſcarre,
As oft it looſes all. I will be gone:
My being heere it is, that holds thee hence,
Shall I ſtay heere to doo't? No, no, although
The ayre of Paradiſe did fan the houſe,
And Angles offic'd all: I will be gone,
That pittifull rumour may report my flight
To conſolate thine eare. Come night, end day,
For with the darke (poore theefe) Ile ſteale away. *Exit.*

Flouriſh. Enter the Duke of Florence, Roſſillion, drum and trumpets, ſoldiers, Parrolles.

Duke. The Generall of our horſe thou art, and we
Great in our hope, lay our beſt loue and credence
Vpon thy promiſing fortune.

Ber. Sir it is
A charge too heauy for my ſtrength, but yet
Wee'l ſtriue to beare it for your worthy ſake,
To th'extreme edge of hazard

Duke. Then go thou forth,
And fortune play vpon thy proſperous helme
As thy auſpicious miſtris

Ber. This very day
Great Mars I put my ſelfe into thy file,
Make me but like my thoughts, and I ſhall proue
A louer of thy drumme, hater of loue. *Exeunt omnes*

Enter Counteſſe & Steward.

La. Alas! and would you take the letter of her:
Might you not know ſhe would do, as ſhe has done,
By ſending me a Letter. Reade it agen.

Letter.

I am S. Iaques Pilgrim, thither gone:
Ambitious loue hath ſo in me offended,
That bare-foot plod I the cold ground vpon
With ſainted vow my faults to haue amended.
Write, write, that from the bloodie courſe of warre
My deereſt Maſter your deare ſonne, may hie,
Bleſſe him at home in peace. Whilſt I from farre,
His name with zealous feruour ſanctifie:
His taken labours bid him me forgiue:
I his deſpightfull Iuno ſent him forth,
From Courtly friends, with Camping foes to liue,
Where death and danger dogges the heeles of worth.
He is too good and faire for death, and mee,
Whom I my ſelfe embrace, to ſet him free.

Ah what ſharpe ſtings are in her mildeſt words?
Rynaldo, you did neuer lacke aduice ſo much,
As letting her paſſe ſo: had I ſpoke with her,
I could haue well diuerted her intents,
Which thus ſhe hath preuented.

Ste. Pardon me Madam,
If I had giuen you this at ouer-night,
She might haue beene ore-tane: and yet ſhe writes
Purſuite would be but vaine.

La. What Angell ſhall
Bleſſe this vnworthy husband, he cannot thriue,
Vnleſſe her prayers, whom heauen delights to heare
And loues to grant, repreeue him from the wrath
Of greateſt Iuſtice. Write, write *Rynaldo*,
To this vnworthy husband of his wife,
Let euerie word waigh heauie of her worth,
That he does waigh too light: my greateſt greefe,
Though little he do feele it, ſet downe ſharpely.
Diſpatch the moſt conuenient meſſenger,
When haply he ſhall heare that ſhe is gone,
He will returne, and hope I may that ſhee
Hearing ſo much, will ſpeede her foote againe,
Led hither by pure loue: which of them both
Is deereſt to me, I haue no skill in ſence
To make diſtinction, prouide this Meſſenger:
My heart is heauie, and mine age is weake,
Greefe would haue teares, and ſorrow bids me ſpeake.
Exeunt

A Tucket afarre off

Enter old Widdow of Florence, her daughter, Violenta and Mariana, with other Citizens.

Widdow. Nay come,
For if they do approach the Citty,
We ſhall looſe all the ſight.

Diana. They ſay, the French Count has done
Moſt honourable ſeruice.

Wid. It is reported,
That he has taken their great'ſt Commander,
And that with his owne hand he ſlew
The Dukes brother: we haue loſt our labour,
They are gone a contrarie way: harke,
you may know by their Trumpets.

Maria. Come lets returne againe,
And ſuffice our ſelues with the report of it
Well *Diana*, take heed of this French Earle,
The honor of a Maide is her name,
And no Legacie is ſo rich
As honeſtie.

Widdow. I haue told my neighbour
How you haue beene ſolicited by a Gentleman
His Companion.

Mar

Maria. I know that knaue, hang him, one *Parolles*, a filthy Officer he is in those suggestions for the young Earle, beware of them *Diana*; their promises, entisements, oathes, tokens, and all these engines of lust, are not the things they go vnder: many a maide hath beene seduced by them, and the miserie is example, that so terrible shewes in the wracke of maiden-hood, cannot for all that disswade succession, but that they are limed with the twigges that threatens them. I hope I neede not to aduise you further, but I hope your owne grace will keepe you where you are, though there were no further danger knowne, but the modestie which is so lost.

Dia. You shall not neede to feare me.

Enter Hellen.

Wid. I hope so: looke here comes a pilgrim, I know she will lye at my house, thither they send one another, Ile question her. God saue you pilgrim, whether are bound?

Hel. To S. *Iaques la grand.*
Where do the Palmers lodge, I do beseech you?

Wid. At the S. *Francis* heere beside the Port.

Hel. Is this the way? *A march afarre.*

Wid. I marrie ist. Harke you, they come this way:
If you will tarrie holy Pilgrime
But till the troopes come by,
I will conduct you where you shall be lodg'd,
The rather for I thinke I know your hostesse
As ample as my selfe.

Hel. Is it your selfe?

Wid. If you shall please so Pilgrime.

Hel. I thanke you, and will stay vpon your leisure.

Wid. you came I thinke from *France*?

Hel. I did so.

Wid. Heere you shall see a Countriman of yours
That has done worthy seruice.

Hel. His name I pray you?

Dia. The Count *Rossillion*: know you such a one?

Hel. But by the eare that heares most nobly of him:
His face I know not.

Dia. What somere he is
He's brauely taken heere. He stole from *France*
As 'tis reported: for the King had married him
Against his liking. Thinke you it is so?

Hel. I surely meere the truth, I know his Lady.

Dia. There is a Gentleman that serues the Count,
Reports but coursely of her.

Hel. What's his name?

Dia. Monsieur *Parrolles.*

Hel. Oh I beleeue with him,
In argument of praise, or to the worth
Of the great Count himselfe, she is too meane
To haue her name repeated, all her deseruing
Is a reserued honestie, and that
I haue not heard examin'd.

Dian. Alas poore Ladie,
Tis a hard bondage to become the wife
Of a detesting Lord.

Wid. I write good creature, wheresoere she is,
Her hart waighes sadly: this yong maid might do her
A shrewd turne if she pleas'd.

Hel. How do you meane?
May be the amorous Count solicites her
In the vnlawfull purpose.

Wid. He does indeede,
And brokes with all that can in such a suite
Corrupt the tender honour of a Maide:
But she is arm'd for him, and keepes her guard
In honestest defence.

Drumme and Colours.

Enter Count Rossillion, Parrolles, and the whole Armie.

Mar. The goddes forbid else.

Wid. So, now they come:
That is *Anthonio* the Dukes eldest sonne,
That *Escalus.*

Hel. Which is the Frenchman?

Dia. Hee,
That with the plume, 'tis a most gallant fellow,
I would he lou'd his wife: if he were honester
He were much goodlier. Is't not a handsom Gentleman

Hel. I like him well.

Di 'Tis pitty he is not honest: yonds that same knaue
That leades him to these places: were I his Ladie,
I would poison that vile Rascall.

Hel. Which is he?

Dia. That Iacke an-apes with scarfes. Why is hee melancholly?

Hel. Perchance he's hurt i'th battaile.

Par. Loose our drum? Well.

Mar. He's shrewdly vext at something Looke he has spyed vs.

Wid. Marrie hang you.

Mar. And your curtesie, for a ring-carrier. *Exit.*

Wid. The troope is past: Come pilgrim, I wil bring you, Where you shall host: Of inioyn'd penitents
There's foure or fiue, to great S. *Iaques* bound,
Alreadie at my house.

Hel. I humbly thanke you:
Please it this Matron, and this gentle Maide
To eate with vs to night, the charge and thanking
Shall be for me. and to requite you further,
I will bestow some precepts of this Virgin,
Worthy the note.

Both. Wee'l take your offer kindly. *Exeunt.*

Enter Count Rossillion and the Frenchmen, as at first.

Cap. E. Nay good my Lord put him too't: let him haue his way.

Cap. G. If your Lordshippe finde him not a Hilding, hold me no more in your respect.

Cap. E. On my life my Lord a bubble.

Ber. Do you thinke I am so farre
Deceiued in him.

Cap. E. Beleeue it my Lord, in mine owne direct knowledge, without any malice, but to speake of him as my kinsman, hee's a most notable Coward, an infinite and endlesse Lyar, an hourely promise-breaker, the owner of no one good qualitie, worthy your Lordships entertainment.

Cap G. It were fit you knew him, least reposing too farre in his vertue which he hath not, he might at some great and trustie businesse, in a maine daunger, fayle you.

Ber. I would I knew in what particular action to try him.

Cap. G. None better then to let him fetch off his drumme, which you heare him so confidently vndertake to do.

C. E. I with a troop of Florentines wil sodainly sur-

X2 prize

prize him; such I will haue whom I am sure he knowes not from the enemie: wee will binde and hoodwinke him so, that he shall suppose no other but that he is carried into the Leager of the aduersaries, when we bring him to our owne tents: be but your Lordship present at his examination, if he do not for the promise of his life, and in the highest compulsion of base feare, offer to betray you, and deliuer all the intelligence in his power against you, and that with the diuine forfeite of his soule vpon oath, neuer trust my iudgement in anie thing.

Cap.G. O for the loue of laughter, let him fetch his drumme, he sayes he has a stratagem for't: when your Lordship sees the bottome of this successe in't, and to what mettle this counterfeyt lump of ours will be melted if you giue him not Iohn drummes entertainement, your inclining cannot be remoued. Heere he comes.

Enter Parrolles.

Cap.E. O for the loue of laughter hinder not the honor of his designe, let him fetch off his drumme in any hand.

Ber. How now Monsieur? This drumme sticks sorely in your disposition.

Cap.G. A pox on't, let it go, 'tis but a drumme.

Par. But a drumme: Ist but a drumme? A drum so lost. There was excellent command, to charge in with our horse vpon our owne wings, and to rend our owne souldiers.

Cap.G. That was not to be blam'd in the command of the seruice: it was a disaster of warre that *Cæsar* him selfe could not haue preuented, if he had beene there to command.

Ber. Well, wee cannot greatly condemne our successe: some dishonor wee had in the losse of that drum, but it is not to be recouered.

Par. It might haue beene recouered.

Ber. It might, but it is not now.

Par. It is to be recouered, but that the merit of seruice is sildome attributed to the true and exact performer, I would haue that drumme or another, or *hic iacet.*

Ber. Why if you haue a stomacke, too't Monsieur: if you thinke your mysterie in stratagem, can bring this instrument of honour againe into his natiue quarter, be magnanimious in the enterprize and go on, I wil grace the attempt for a worthy exploit: if you speede well in it, the Duke shall both speake of it, and extend to you what further becomes his greatnesse, euen to the vtmost syllable of your worthinesse.

Par. By the hand of a souldier I will vndertake it.

Ber. But you must not now slumber in it.

Par. Ile about it this euening, and I will presently pen downe my dilemma's, encourage my selfe in my certaintie, put my selfe into my mortall preparation and by midnight looke to heare further from me.

Ber. May I bee bold to acquaint his grace you are gone about it.

Par. I know not what the successe wil be my Lord, but the attempt I vow.

Ber. I know th'art valiant,
And to the possibility of thy souldiership,
Will subscribe for thee: Farewell.

Par. I loue not many words. *Exit*

Cap.E. No more then a fish loues water. Is not this a strange fellow my Lord, that so confidently seemes to vndertake this businesse, which he knowes is not to be done, damnes himselfe to do, & dares better be damnd then to doo't.

Cap.G. You do not know him my Lord as we doe, certaine it is that he will steale himselfe into a mans fauour, and for a weeke escape a great deale of discoueries, but when you finde him out, you haue him euer after.

Ber. Why do you thinke he will make no deede at all of this that so seriouslie hee dooes addresse himselfe vnto?

Cap.E. None in the world, but returne with an inuention, and clap vpon you two or three probable lies: but we haue almost imbost him, you shall see his fall to night; for indeede he is not for your Lordshippes respect.

Cap.G. Weele make you some sport with the Foxe ere we case him. He was first smoak'd by the old Lord *Lafew*, when his disguise and he is parted, tell me what a sprat you shall finde him, which you shall see this verie night.

Cap.E. I must go looke my twigges,
He shall be caught.

Ber Your brother he shall go along with me.

Cap.G. As't please your Lordship, Ile leaue you.

Ber. Now wil I lead you to the house, and shew you
The Lasse I spoke of.

Cap.E. But you say she's honest.

Ber. That's all the fault: I spoke with hir but once,
And found her wondrous cold, but I sent to her
By this same Coxcombe that we haue i'th winde
Tokens and Letters, which she did resend,
And this is all I haue done: She's a faire creature,
Will you go see her?

Cap.E. With all my heart my Lord. *Exeunt*

Enter Hellen, and Widdow.

Hel. If you misdoubt me that I am not shee,
I know not how I shall assure you further,
But I shall loose the grounds I worke vpon.

Wid. Though my estate be falne, I was well borne,
Nothing acquainted with these businesses,
And would not put my reputation now
In any staining act.

Hel. Nor would I wish you.
First giue me trust, the Count he is my husband,
And what to your sworne counsaile I haue spoken,
Is so from word to word: and then you cannot
By the good ayde that I of you shall borrow,
Erre in bestowing it.

Wid. I should beleeue you,
For you haue shew'd me that which well approues
Y'are great in fortune.

Hel. Take this purse of Gold,
And let me buy your friendly helpe thus farre,
Which I will ouer-pay, and pay againe
When I haue found it. The Count he woes your daughter,
Layes downe his wanton siedge before her beautie,
Resolue to carrie her: let her in fine consent
As wee'l direct her how 'tis best to beare it:
Now his important blood will naught denie,
That shee'l demand: a ring the Countie weares,
That downward hath succeeded in his house

From

From sonne to sonne, some foure or fiue discents,
Since the first father wore it. This Ring he holds
In most rich choice : yet in his idle fire,
To buy his will, it would not seeme too deere,
How ere repented after.

Wid. Now I see the bottome of your purpose.

Hel. You see it lawfull then, it is no more,
But that your daughter ere she seemes as wonne,
Desires this Ring ; appoints him an encounter ;
In fine, deliuers me to fill the time,
Her selfe most chastly absent : after
To marry her, Ile adde three thousand Crownes
To what is past already.

Wid. I haue yeelded.
Instruct my daughter how she shall perseuer,
That time and place with this deceite so lawfull
May proue coherent. Euery night he comes
With Musickes of all sorts, and songs compos'd
To her vnworthinesse : It nothing steeds vs
To chide him from our eeues, for he persists
As if his life lay on't.

Hel. Why then to night
Let vs assay our plot, which if it speed,
Is wicked meaning in a lawfull deede ;
And lawfull meaning in a lawfull act,
Where both not sinne, and yet a sinfull fact.
But let's about it.

Actus Quartus.

Enter one of the Frenchmen, with fiue or sixe other souldiers in ambush.

1.Lord E. He can come no other way but by this hedge corner : when you sallie vpon him, speake what terrible Language you will : though you vnderstand it not your selues, no matter : for we must not seeme to vnderstand him, vnlesse some one among vs, whom wee must produce for an Interpreter.

1.Sol. Good Captaine, let me be th' Interpreter.

Lor.E. Art not acquainted with him ? knowes he not thy voice?

1.Sol. No sir I warrant you.

Lo.E. But what linsie wolsy hast thou to speake to vs againe.

1.Sol. E n such as you speake to me.

Lo.E. He must thinke vs some band of strangers, i'th aduersaries entertainment. Now he hath a smacke of all neighbouring Languages : therefore we must euery one be a man of his owne fancie, not to know what we speak one to another : so we seeme to know, is to know straight our purpose : Choughs language, gabble enough, and good enough. As for you interpreter, you must seeme very politicke. But couch hoa, heere hee comes, to beguile two houres in a sleepe, and then to returne & swear the lies he forges.

Enter Parrolles.

Par Ten a clocke : Within these three houres 'twill be time enough to goe home. What shall I say I haue done ? It must bee a very plausiue inuention that carries it. They beginne to smoake mee, and disgraces haue of late, knock'd too often at my doore : I finde my tongue is too foole-hardie, but my heart hath the feare of Mars before it, and of his creatures, not daring the reports of my tongue.

Lo.E. This is the first truth that ere thine own tongue was guiltie of.

Par. What the diuell should moue mee to vndertake the recouerie of this drumme, being not ignorant of the impossibility, and knowing I had no such purpose ? I must giue my selfe some hurts, and say I got them in exploit : yet slight ones will not carrie it. They will say, came you off with so little ? And great ones I dare not giue, wherefore what's the instance. Tongue, I must put you into a Butter-womans mouth, and buy my selfe another of *Baiazeths* Mule, if you prattle mee into these perilles.

Lo.E. Is it possible he should know what hee is, and be that he is

Par. I would the cutting of my garments wold serue the turne, or the breaking of my Spanish sword.

Lo.E. We cannot affoord you so.

Par. Or the baring of my beard, and to say it was in stratagem.

Lo.E. 'Twould not do.

Par. Or to drowne my cloathes, and say I was stript.

Lo.E. Hardly serue.

Par Though I swore I leapt from the window of the Citadell.

Lo.E. How deepe ?

Par. Thirty fadome.

Lo.E. Three great oathes would scarse make that be beleeued.

Par I would I had any drumme of the enemies, I would sweare I recouer'd it.

Lo.E. You shall heare one anon.

Par. A drumme now of the enemies.

Alarum within.

Lo E. *Throca mouousus, cargo, cargo, cargo.*

All. *Cargo, cargo, cargo, villianda par corbo, cargo.*

Par. O ransome, ransome,
Do not hide mine eyes.

Inter. *Boskos thromuldo boskos.*

Par I know you are the *Muskos* Regiment,
And I shall loose my life for want of language.
If there be heere German or Dane, Low Dutch,
Italian, or French, let him speake to me,
Ile discouer that, which shal vndo the Florentine.

Int *Boskos vauvado*, I vnderstand thee, & can speake thy tongue : *Kerelybonto* sir, betake thee to thy faith, for seuenteene ponyards are at thy bosome.

Par. Oh.

Inter. Oh pray, pray, pray,
Manka reuania dulche.

Lo.E. *Oscorbidulchos volivorco.*

Int. The Generall is content to spare thee yet,
And hoodwinkt as thou art, will leade thee on
To gather from thee. Haply thou mayst informe
Something to saue thy life.

Par. O let me liue,
And all the secrets of our campe Ile shew,
Their force, their purposes : Nay, Ile speake that,
Which you will wonder at.

Inter. But wilt thou faithfully ?

Par If I do not, damne me.

Inter. *Acordo linta.*
Come on, thou are granted space. *Exit*

A short Alarum within.

X 3 *Lo. E*

L.E. Go tell the Count *Rossillion* and my brother,
We haue caught the woodcocke, and will keepe him
Till we do heare from them. (mufled
Sol. Captaine I will.
L.E. A will betray vs all vnto our selues,
Informe on that.
Sol. So I will sir.
L.E. Till then Ile keepe him darke and safely lockt.
Exit

Enter Bertram, and the Maide called Diana.

Ber. They told me that your name was *Fontybell.*
Dia. No my good Lord, *Diana.*
Ber. Titled Goddesse,
And worth it with addition: but faire soule,
In your fine frame hath loue no qualitie?
If the quicke fire of youth light not your minde,
You are no Maiden but a monument
When you are dead you should be such a one
As you are now: for you are cold and sterne,
And now you should be as your mother was
When your sweet selfe w is got.
Dia. She then was honest.
Ber. So should you be.
Dia. No:
My mother did but dutie, such (my Lord)
As you owe to your wife.
Ber. No more a'that:
I prethee do not striue against my vowes:
I was compell'd to her, but I loue thee
By loues owne sweet constraint, and will for euer
Do thee all rights of seruice.
Dia. I so you serue vs
Till we serue you: But when you haue our Roses,
You barely leaue our thornes to pricke our selues,
And mocke vs with our barenesse.
Ber. How haue I sworne.
Dia. 'Tis not the many oathes that makes the truth
But the plaine single vow, that is vow'd true:
What is not holie, that we sweare not by,
But take the high'st to witnesse: then pray you tell me,
If I should sweare by Ioues great attributes,
I lou'd you deerely, would you beleeue my oathes,
When I did loue you ill? This ha's no holding
To sweare by him whom I protest to loue
That I will worke against him. Therefore your oathes
Are words and poore conditions, but vnseal'd
At lest in my opinion.
Ber. Change it, change it:
Be not so holy cruell: Loue is holie,
And my integritie ne're knew the crafts
That you do charge men with: Stand no more off,
But giue thy selfe vnto my sicke desires,
Who then recouers. Say thou art mine, and euer
My loue as it beginnes, shall so perseuer.
Dia. I see that men make ropes in such a scarre,
That wee'l forsake our selues. Giue me that Ring.
Ber. Ile lend it thee my deere; but haue no power
To giue it from me.
Dia. Will you not my Lord?
Ber. It is an honour longing to our house,
Bequeathed downe from manie Ancestors,
Which were the greatest obloquie i'th world,
In me to loose.
Dian. Mine Honors such a Ring,
My chastities the Iewell of our house,
Bequeathed downe from many Ancestors,
Which were the greatest obloquie i'th world,
In mee to loose. Thus your owne proper wisedome
Brings in the Champion honor on my part,
Against your vaine assault.
Ber. Heere, take my Ring,
My house, mine honor, yea my life be thine,
And Ile be bid by thee.
Dia. When midnight comes, knocke at my chamber window:
Ile order take, my mother shall not heare.
Now will I charge you in the band of truth,
When you haue conquer'd my yet maiden-bed,
Remaine there but an houre, nor speake to mee:
My reasons are most strong, and you shall know them,
When backe againe this Ring shall be deliuer'd:
And on your finger in the night, Ile put
Another Ring, that what in time proceeds,
May token to the future, our past deeds.
Adieu till then, then faile not: you haue wonne
A wife of me, though there my hope be done.
Ber. A heauen on earth I haue won by wooing thee.
Di. For which, liue long to thank both heauen & me,
You may so in the end.
My mother told me iust how he would woo,
As if she sate in's heart. She sayes, all men
Haue the like oathes: He had sworne to marrie me
When his wife's dead: therfore Ile lye with him
When I am buried. Since Frenchmen are so braide,
Marry that will, I liue and die a Maid:
Onely in this disguise, I think't no sinne,
To cosen him that would vniustly winne. *Exit*

Enter the two French Captaines, and some two or three Souldiours.

Cap.G. You haue not giuen him his mothers letter.

Cap.E. I haue deliu'red it an houre since, there is som thing in't that stings his nature: for on the reading it, he chang'd almost into another man.

Cap.G. He has much worthy blame laid vpon him, for shaking off so good a wife, and so sweet a Lady.

Cap.E. Especially, hee hath incurred the euerlasting displeasure of the King, who had euen tun'd his bounty to sing happinesse to him. I will tell you a thing, but you shall let it dwell darkly with you.

Cap.G. When you haue spoken it 'tis dead, and I am the graue of it.

Cap.E. Hee hath peruerted a young Gentlewoman heere in *Florence*, of a most chaste renown, & this night he fleshes his will in the spoyle of her honour: hee hath giuen her his monumentall Ring, and thinkes himselfe made in the vnchaste composition.

Cap.G. Now God delay our rebellion as we are our selues, what things are we.

Cap.E. Meerely our owne traitours. And as in the common course of all treasons, we still see them reueale themselues, till they attaine to their abhorr'd ends: so he that in this action contriues against his owne Nobility in his proper streame, ore-flowes himselfe.

Cap.G. Is it not meant damnable in vs, to be Trumpeters of our vnlawfull intents? We shall not then haue his company to night?

Cap.E. Not till after midnight: for hee is dieted to his houre

Cap.G. That approaches apace: I would gladly haue him see his company anathomiz'd, that hee might take a measure of his owne iudgements, wherein so curiously he had set this counterfeit.

Cap.E. We will not meddle with him till he come; for his presence must be the whip of the other.

Cap.C. In the meane time, what heare you of these Warres?

Cap.E. I heare there is an ouerture of peace.

Cap.G. Nay, I assure you a peace concluded.

Cap.E. What will Count *Rossillion* do then? Will he trauaile higher, or returne againe into France?

Cap.G. I perceiue by this demand, you are not altogether of his councell.

Cap.E. Let it be forbid sir, so should I bee a great deale of his act.

Cap G. Sir, his wife some two months since fledde from his house, her pretence is a pilgrimage to Saint *Iaques le grand*; which holy vndertaking, with most austere sanctimonie she accomplisht: and there residing, the tendernesse of her Nature, became as a prey to her greefe: in fine, made a groane of her last breath, & now she sings in heauen.

Cap.E. How is this iustified?

Cap.G. The stronger part of it by her owne Letters, which makes her storie true, euen to the poynt of her death: her death it selfe, which could not be her office to say, is come: was faithfully confirm'd by the Rector of the place.

Cap.E. Hath the Count all this intelligence?

Cap.G. I, and the particular confirmations, point from point, to the full arming of the veritie

Cap.E. I am heartily sorrie that hee'l bee gladde of this.

Cap.G. How mightily sometimes, we make vs comforts of our losses.

Cap.E. And how mightily some other times, wee drowne our gaine in teares, the great dignitie that his valour hath here acquir'd for him, shall at home be encountred with a shame as ample.

Cap.G. The webbe of our life, is of a mingled yarne, good and ill together: our vertues would bee proud, if our faults whipt them not, and our crimes would dispaire if they were not cherish'd by our vertues.

Enter a Messenger.

How now? Where's your master?

Ser. He met the Duke in the street sir, of whom hee hath taken a solemne leaue: his Lordshippe will next morning for France. The Duke hath offered him Letters of commendations to the King.

Cap.E. They shall bee no more then needfull there, if they were more then they can commend.

Enter Count Rossillion.

Ber. They cannot be too sweete for the Kings tartnesse, heere's his Lordship now. How now my Lord, i'st not after midnight?

Ber. I haue to night dispatch'd sixteene businesses, a moneths length a peece, by an abstract of successe: I haue congied with the Duke, done my adieu with his neerest; buried a wife, mourn'd for her, writ to my Ladie mother, I am returning, entertain'd my Conuoy, & betweene these maine parcels of dispatch, affected many nicer needs: the last was the greatest, but that I haue not ended yet.

Cap.E. If the businesse bee of any difficulty, and this morning your departure hence, it requires hast of your Lordship.

Ber. I meane the businesse is not ended, as fearing to heare of it hereafter: but shall we haue this dialogue betweene the Foole and the Soldiour. Come, bring forth this counterfet module, ha's deceiu'd mee, like a double-meaning Prophesier.

Cap.E. Bring him forth, ha's sate i'th stockes all night poore gallant knaue.

Ber. No matter, his heeles haue deseru'd it, in vsurping his spurres so long. How does he carry himselfe?

Cap.E. I haue told your Lordship alreadie: The stockes carrie him. But to answer you as you would be vnderstood, hee weepes like a wench that had shed her milke, he hath confest himselfe to *Morgan*, whom hee supposes to be a Friar, fro the time of his remembrance to this very instant disaster of his setting i'th stockes: and what thinke you he hath confest?

Ber. Nothing of me, ha's a?

Cap.E. His confession is taken, and it shall bee read to his face, if your Lordshippe be in't, as I beleeue you are, you must haue the patience to heare it.

Enter Parolles with his Interpreter.

Ber. A plague vpon him, muffeld; he can say nothing of me: hush, hush.

Cap.G. Hoodman comes: *Portotartarossa.*

Inter. He calles for the tortures, what will you say without em.

Par. I will confesse what I know without constraint, If ye pinch me like a Pasty, I can say no more.

Int. *Bosko Chimurcho.*

Cap. *Boblibindo chicurmurco.*

Int. You are a mercifull Generall: Our Generall bids you answer to what I shall aske you out of a Note.

Par. And truly, as I hope to liue.

Int. First demand of him, how many horse the Duke is strong What say you to that?

Par Fiue or sixe thousand, but very weake and vnseruiceable: the troopes are all scattered, and the Commanders verie poore rogues, vpon my reputation and credit, and as I hope to liue.

Int. Shall I set downe your answer so?

Par. Do, Ile take the Sacrament on't, how & which way you will: all's one to him.

Ber. What a past-sauing slaue is this?

Cap.G Y'are deceiu'd my Lord, this is Mounsieur *Parrolles* the gallant militarist, that was his owne phrase that had the whole theoricke of warre in the knot of his scarfe, and the practise in the chape of his dagger.

Cap.E. I will neuer trust a man againe, for keeping his sword cleane, nor beleeue he can haue euerie thing in him, by wearing his apparrell neatly.

Int. Well, that's set downe.

Par. Fiue or six thousand horse I sed, I will say true, or thereabouts set downe, for Ile speake truth.

Cap.G. He's very neere the truth in this.

Ber. But I con him no thankes for't in the nature he deliuers it.

Par. Poore rogues, I pray you say.

Int. Well, that's set downe.

Par. I humbly thanke you sir, a truth's a truth, the Rogues are maruailous poore.

Interp. Demaund of him of what strength they are a foot. What say you to that?

Par By my troth sir, if I were to liue this present houre, I will tell true. Let me see, *Spurio* a hundred & fiftie

fiftie, *Sebastian* so many, *Corambus* so many, *Iaques* so many: *Guiltian*, *Cosmo*, *Lodowicke*, and *Gratij*, two hundred fiftie each: Mine owne Company, *Chitopher*, *Vaumond*, *Bentij*, two hundred fiftie each: so that the muster file, rotten and sound, vppon my life amounts not to fifteene thousand pole, halfe of the which, dare not shake the snow from off their Cassockes, least they shake themselues to peeces.

Ber. What shall be done to him.

Cap.G. Nothing, but let him haue thankes. Demand of him my condition: and what credite I haue with the Duke.

Int. Well that's set downe: you shall demaund of him, whether one Captaine *Dumaine* bee i'th Campe, a Frenchman: what his reputation is with the Duke, what his valour, honestie, and expertnesse in warres: or whether he thinkes it were not possible with well-waighing summes of gold to corrupt him to a reuolt. What say you to this? What do you know of it?

Par. I beseech you let me answer to the particular of the intergatories. Demand them singly.

Int. Do you know this Captaine *Dumaine*?

Par. I know him, a was a Botchers Prentize in *Paris*, from whence he was whipt for getting the Shrieues fool with childe, a dumbe innocent that could not say him nay.

Ber. Nay, by your leaue hold your hands, though I know his braines are forfeite to the next tile that fals.

Int. Well, is this Captaine in the Duke of Florences campe?

Par. Vpon my knowledge he is, and lowsie.

Cap.G. Nay looke not so vpon me: we shall heare of your Lord anon.

Int. What is his reputation with the Duke?

Par. The Duke knowes him for no other, but a poore Officer of mine, and writ to mee this other day, to turne him out a'th band. I thinke I haue his Letter in my pocket.

Int. Marry we'll search.

Par. In good sadnesse I do not know, either it is there, or it is vpon a file with the Dukes other Letters, in my Tent.

Int. Heere 'tis, heere's a paper, shall I reade it to you?

Par. I do not know if it be it or no.

Ber. Our Interpreter do's it well.

Cap.G. Excellently.

Int. *Dian, the Counts a foole, and full of gold.*

Par. That is not the Dukes letter sir: that is an aduertisement to a proper maide in Florence, one *Diana*, to take heede of the allurement of one Count *Rossillion*, a foolish idle boy: but for all that very ruttish. I pray you sir put it vp againe.

Int. Nay, Ile reade it first by your fauour.

Par. My meaning in't I protest was very honest in the behalfe of the maid: for I knew the young Count to be a dangerous and lasciuious boy, who is a whale to Virginity, and deuours vp all the fry it finds.

Ber. Damnable both-sides rogue.

Int.Let. *When he sweares oathes, bid him drop gold, and take it:*
After he scores, he neuer payes the score:
Halfe won is match well made, match and well make it,
He nere payes after-debts, take it before,
And say a souldier (Dian) told thee this:
Men are to mell with, boyes are not to kis.
For count of this, the Counts a Foole I know it,
Who payes before, but not when he does owe it.

Thine as he vow'd to thee in thine eare,

Parolles.

Ber. He shall be whipt through the Armie with this rime in's forehead.

Cap.E. This is your deuoted friend sir, the manifold Linguist, and the army-potent souldier

Ber. I could endure any thing before but a Cat, and now he's a Cat to me.

Int. I perceiue sir by your Generals lookes, wee shall be faine to hang you.

Par. My life sir in any case: Not that I am afraide to dye, but that my offences beeing many, I would repent out the remainder of Nature. Let me liue sir in a dungeon, i'th stockes, or any where, so I may liue.

Int. Wee'le see what may bee done, so you confesse freely: therefore once more to this Captaine *Dumaine*: you haue answer'd to his reputation with the Duke, and to his valour. What is his honestie?

Par. He will steale sir an Egge out of a Cloister: for rapes and rauishments he paralels *Nessus*. Hee professes not keeping of oaths, in breaking em he is stronger then *Hercules*. He will lye sir, with such volubilitie, that you would thinke truth were a foole: drunkennesse is his best vertue, for he will be swine-drunke, and in his sleepe he does little harme, saue to his bed-cloathes about him: but they know his conditions, and lay him in straw. I haue but little more to say sir of his honesty, he ha's euerie thing that an honest man should not haue; what an honest man should haue, he has nothing.

Cap.G. I begin to loue him for this.

Ber. For this description of thine honestie? A pox vpon him for me, he's more and more a Cat.

Int. What say you to his expertnesse in warre?

Par. Faith sir, ha's led the drumme before the English Tragedians: to belye him I will not, and more of his souldiership I know not, except in that Country, he had the honour to be the Officer at a place there called *Mile-end*, to instruct for the doubling of files. I would doe the man what honour I can, but of this I am not certaine.

Cap.G. He hath out-villain'd villanie so farre, that the raritie redeemes him.

Ber. A pox on him, he's a Cat still.

Int. His qualities being at this poore price, I neede not to aske you, if Gold will corrupt him to reuolt.

Par. Sir, for a Cardceue he will sell the fee-simple of his saluation, the inheritance of it, and cut th'intaile from all remainders, and a perpetuall succession for it perpetually.

Int. What's his Brother, the other Captain *Dumain*?

Cap.E. Why do's he aske him of me?

Int. What's he?

Par. E'ne a Crow a'th same nest: not altogether so great as the first in goodnesse, but greater a great deale in euill. He excels his Brother for a coward, yet his Brother is reputed one of the best that is. In a retreate hee outrunnes any Lackey; marrie in comming on, hee ha's the Crampe.

Int. If your life be saued, will you vndertake to betray the Florentine.

Par. I, and the Captaine of his horse, Count *Rossillion*.

Int. Ile whisper with the Generall, and knowe his pleasure.

Par. Ile no more drumming, a plague of all drummes, onely to seeme to deserue well, and to beguile the supposition

ſition of that laſciuious yong boy the Count, haue I run into this danger: yet who would haue ſuſpected an ambuſh where I was taken?

Int. There is no remedy ſir, but you muſt dye: the Generall ſayes, you that haue ſo traitorouſly diſcouerd the ſecrets of your army, and made ſuch peſtiferous reports of men very nobly held, can ſerue the world for no honeſt vſe: therefore you muſt dye. Come headeſman, off with his head.

Par. O Lord ſir let me liue, or let me ſee my death.

Int. That ſhall you, and take your leaue of all your friends:
So, looke about you, know you any heere?

Count. Good morrow noble Captaine

Lo.E. God bleſſe you Captaine *Parolles.*

Cap.G. God ſaue you noble Captaine.

Lo.E. Captain, what greeting will you to my Lord *Lafew?* I am for *France.*

Cap.G. Good Captaine will you giue me a Copy of the ſonnet you writ to *Diana* in behalfe of the Count *Roſſillion,* and I were not a verie Coward, I de compell it of you, but far you well *Exeunt.*

Int You are vndone Captaine all but your ſcarſe, that has a knot on't yet.

Par. Who cannot be cruſh'd with a plot?

Inter. If you could finde out a Countrie where but women were that had receiued ſo much ſhame, you might begin an impudent Nation. Fare yee well ſir, I am for *France* too, we ſhall ſpeake of you there. *Exit*

Par. Yet am I thankfull: if my heart were great
'Twould burſt at this: Captaine Ile be no more,
But I will eate, and drinke, and ſleepe as ſoft
As Captaine ſhall. Simply the thing I am
Shall make me liue: who knowes himſelfe a braggart
Let him feare this; for it will come to paſſe,
That euery braggart ſhall be found an Aſſe.
Ruſt ſword, coole bluſhes, and *Parrolles* liue
Safeſt in ſhame: being fool'd, by fool'rie thriue;
There's place and meanes for euery man aliue.
Ile after them *Exit.*

Enter Hellen, Widdow, and Diana.

Hel. That you may well perceiue I haue not wrong'd you,
One of the greateſt in the Chriſtian world
Shall be my ſuretie: for whoſe throne 'tis needfull
Ere I can perfect mine intents, to kneele
Time was, I did him a deſired office
Deere almoſt as his life, which gratitude
Through flintie Tartars boſome would peepe forth,
And anſwer thankes. I duly am inform'd,
His grace is at *Marcelle,* to which place
We haue conuenient conuoy: you muſt know
I am ſuppoſed dead, the Army breaking,
My husband hies him home, where heauen ayding,
And by the leaue of my good Lord the King,
Wee'l be before our welcome.

Wid. Gentle Madam,
You neuer had a ſeruant to whoſe truſt
Your buſines was more welcome.

Hel. Nor your Miſtris
Euer a friend, whoſe thoughts more truly labour
To recompence your loue: Doubt not but heauen
Hath brought me vp to be your daughters dower,
As it hath fated her to be my motiue
And helper to a husband. But O ſtrange men,
That can ſuch ſweet vſe make of what they hate,
When ſawcie truſting of the coſin'd thoughts
Defiles the pitchy night, ſo luſt doth play
With what it loathes, for that which is away,
But more of this heereafter: you *Diana,*
Vnder my poore inſtructions yet muſt ſuffer
Something in my behalfe.

Dia. Let death and honeſtie
Go with your impoſitions, I am yours
Vpon your will to ſuffer.

Hel. Yet I pray you:
But with the word the time will bring on ſummer,
When Briars ſhall haue leaues as well as thornes,
And be as ſweet as ſharpe: we muſt away,
Our Wagon is prepar'd, and time reuiues vs,
All's well that ends well, ſtill the fines the Crowne;
What ere the courſe, the end is the renowne. *Exeunt*

Enter Clowne, old Lady, and Lafew.

Laf. No, no, no, your ſonne was miſled with a ſnipt taffata fellow there, whoſe villanous ſaffron wold haue made all the vnbak'd and dowy youth of a nation in his colour: your daughter-in-law had beene aliue at this houre, and your ſonne heere at home, more aduanc'd by the King, then by that red-tail'd humble Bee I ſpeak of

La. I would I had not knowne him, it was the death of the moſt vertuous gentlewoman, that euer Nature had praiſe for creating. If ſhe had pertaken of my fleſh and coſt mee the deereſt groanes of a mother, I could not haue owed her a more rooted loue.

Laf Twas a good Lady, 'twas a good Lady. Wee may picke a thouſand ſallets ere wee light on ſuch another hearbe.

Clo. Indeed ſir ſhe was the ſweete Margerom of the ſallet, or rather the hearbe of grace.

Laf. They are not hearbes you knaue, they are noſe-hearbes.

Clowne I am no great *Nabuchadnezar* ſir, I haue not much skill in grace.

Laf. Whether doeſt thou profeſſe thy ſelfe, a knaue or a foole?

Clo. A foole ſir at a womans ſeruice, and a knaue at a mans.

Laf. Your diſtinction.

Clo. I would couſen the man of his wife, and do his ſeruice.

Laf. So you were a knaue at his ſeruice indeed.

Clo. And I would giue his wife my bauble ſir to doe her ſeruice.

Laf. I will ſubſcribe for thee, thou art both knaue and foole.

Clo. At your ſeruice.

Laf. No, no, no.

Clo. Why ſir, if I cannot ſerue you, I can ſerue as great a prince as you are.

Laf. Whoſe that, a Frenchman?

Clo. Faith ſir a has an Engliſh maine, but his fiſnomie is more hotter in France then there.

Laf. What prince is that?

Clo. The blacke prince ſir, alias the prince of darkeneſſe, alias the diuell.

Laf. Hold thee there's my purſe, I giue thee not this to ſuggeſt thee from thy maſter thou talk'ſt off, ſerue him ſtill.

Clow

Clo. I am a woodland fellow ſir, that alwaies loued a great fire, and the maſter I ſpeak of euer keeps a good fire, but ſure he is the Prince of the world, let his Nobilitie remaine in's Court. I am for the houſe with the narrow gate, which I take to be too little for pompe to enter : ſome that humble themſelues may, but the manie will be too chill and tender, and theyle bee for the flowrie way that leads to the broad gate, and the great fire.

Laf. Go thy waies, I begin to bee a wearie of thee, and I tell thee ſo before, becauſe I would not fall out with thee. Go thy wayes, let my horſes be wel look'd too without any trickes.

Clo. If I put any trickes vpon em ſir, they ſhall bee Iades trickes, which are their owne right by the law of Nature. *exit*

Laf. A ſhrewd knaue and an vnhappie.

Lady. So a is. My Lord that's gone made himſelſe much ſport out of him, by his authoritie hee remaines heere, which he thinkes is a pattent for his ſawcineſſe, and indeede he has no pace, but runnes where he will.

Laf. I like him well, 'tis not amiſſe:and I was about to tell you, ſince I heard of the good Ladies death, and that my Lord your ſonne was vpon his returne home. I moued the King my maſter to ſpeake in the behalfe of my daughter, which in the minoritie of them both, his Maieſtie out of a ſelfe gracious remembrance did firſt propoſe, his Highneſſe hath promis'd me to doe it, and to ſtoppe vp the diſpleaſure he hath conceiued againſt your ſonne, there is no fitter matter. How do's your Ladyſhip like it?

La. With verie much content my Lord, and I wiſh it happily effected.

Laf. His Highneſſe comes poſt from *Marcellus*, of as able bodie as when he number'd thirty, a will be heere to morrow, or I am deceiu d by him that in ſuch intelligence hath ſeldome fail'd.

La It reioyces me, that I hope I ſhall ſee him ere I die. I haue letters that my ſonne will be heere to night: I ſhall beſeech your Lordſhip to remaine with mee, till they meete together.

Laf. Madam, I was thinking with what manners I might ſafely be admitted

Lad. You neede but pleade your honourable priuiledge.

Laf. Ladie, of that I haue made a bold charter, but I thanke my God, it holds yet.

Enter Clowne

Clo. O Madam, yonders my Lord your ſonne with a patch of veluet on's face, whether there bee a ſcar vnder't or no, the Veluet knowes, but 'tis a goodly patch of Veluet, his left cheeke is a cheeke of two pile and a halfe, but his right cheeke is worne bare.

Laf. A ſcarre nobly got,
Or a noble ſcarre, is a good liu'rie of honor.
So belike is that.

Clo. But it is your carbinado'd face

Laf. Let vs go ſee
your ſonne I pray you, I long to talke
With the yong noble ſouldier.

Clowne. 'Faith there's a dozen of em, with delicate fine hats, and moſt courteous feathers, which bow the head, and nod at euerie man.

Exeunt

Actus Quintus.

Enter Hellen, Widdow, and Dian , with two Attendants

Hel. But this exceeding poſting day and night
Muſt wear your ſpirits low, we cannot helpe it
But ſince you haue made the daies and nights as one,
To weare your gentle limbes in my affayres,
Be bold you do ſo grow in my requitall,
As nothing can vnroote you. In happie time,

Enter a gentle Aſtringer.

This man may helpe me to his Maieſties eare,
If he would ſpend his power. God ſaue you ſir.

Gent. And you.

Hel. Sir, I haue ſeene you in the Court of France.

Gent. I haue beene ſometimes there.

Hel. I do preſume ſir, that you are not faine
From the report that goes vpon your goodneſſe,
And therefore goaded with moſt ſharpe occaſions,
Which lay nice manners by, I put you to
The vſe of your owne vertues, for the which
I ſhall continue thankefull.

Gent. What's your will?

Hel. That it will pleaſe you
To giue this poore petition to the King,
And ayde me with that ſtore of power you haue
To come into his preſence,

Gen. The Kings not heere.

Hel. Not heere ſir?

Gen. Not indeed,
He hence remou'd laſt night, and with more haſt
Then is his vſe.

Wid. Lord how we looſe our paines

Hel. All's well that ends well yet,
Though time ſeeme ſo aduerſe, and meanes vnfit:
I do beſeech you, whither is he gone?

Gent. Marrie as I take it to *Roſſillion*,
Whither I am going.

Hel. I do beſeech you ſir
Since you are like to ſee the King before me,
Commend the paper to his gracious hand,
Which I preſume ſhall render you no blame,
But rather make you thanke your paines for it,
I will come after you with what good ſpeede
Our meanes will make vs meanes.

Gent. This Ile do for you

Hel. And you ſhall finde your ſelfe to be well thankt
what e're falles more We muſt to horſe againe, Go, go,
prouide.

Enter Clowne and Parrolles.

Par. Good M[r] Lauatch giue my Lord *Lafew* this letter, I haue ere now ſir beene better knowne to you, when I haue held familiaritie with freſher cloathes : but I am now ſir muddied in fortunes mood, and ſmell ſomewhat ſtrong of her ſtrong diſpleaſure.

Clo. Truely, Fortunes diſpleaſure is but ſluttiſh if it ſmell ſo ſtrongly as thou ſpeak'ſt of: I will henceforth eate no Fiſh of Fortunes butt'ring. Pre thee alow the winde.

Par. Nay you neede not to ſtop your noſe ſir: I ſpake but by a Metaphor

Clo. Indeed ſir, if your Metaphor ſtinke, I will ſtop my noſe, or againſt any mans Metaphor. Prethe get thee further.

Par.

Par. Pray you sir deliuer me this paper.

Clo. Foh, prethee stand away: a paper from fortunes close-stoole, to giue to a Nobleman. Looke heere he comes himselfe.

Enter Lafew.

Clo. Heere is a purre of Fortunes sir, or of Fortunes Cat, but not a Muscat, that ha's falne into the vncleane fish-pond of her displeasure, and as he sayes is muddied withall. Pray you sir, vse the Carpe as you may, for he lookes like a poore decayed, ingenious, foolish, rascally knaue. I doe pittie his distresse in my smiles of comfort, and leaue him to your Lordship.

Par. My Lord I am a man whom fortune hath cruelly scratch'd.

Laf. And what would you haue me to doe? 'Tis too late to paire her nailes now. Wherein haue you played the knaue with fortune that she should scratch you, who of her selfe is a good Lady, and would not haue knaues thriue long vnder? There's a Cardecue for you: Let the Iustices make you and fortune friends; I am for other businesse.

Par. I beseech your honour to heare mee one single word.

Laf. you begge a single peny more: Come you shall ha't, saue your word.

Par. My name my good Lord is *Parrolles*.

Laf. You begge more then word then. Cox my passion, giue me your hand: How does your drumme?

Par. O my good Lord, you were the first that found mee.

Laf. Was I insooth? And I was the first that lost thee.

Par. It lies in you my Lord to bring me in some grace for you did bring me out.

Laf. Out vpon thee knaue, doest thou put vpon mee at once both the office of God and the diuel: one brings thee in grace, and the other brings thee out. The Kings comming I know by his Trumpets. Sirrah, inquire further after me, I had talke of you last night, though you are a foole and a knaue, you shall eate, go too, follow.

Par. I praise God for you.

Flourish. Enter King, old Lady, Lafew, the two French Lords, with attendants.

Kin. We lost a Iewell of her, and our esteeme
Was made much poorer by it: but your sonne,
As mad in folly, lack'd the sence to know
Her estimation home.

Old La. 'Tis past my Liege,
And I beseech your Maiestie to make it
Naturall rebellion, done i'th blade of youth,
When oyle and fire, too strong for reasons force,
Ore-beares it, and burnes on.

Kin. My honour'd Lady,
I haue forgiuen and forgotten all,
Though my reuenges were high bent vpon him,
And watch'd the time to shoote.

Laf. This I must say,
But first I begge my pardon: the yong Lord
Did to his Maiesty, his Mother, and his Ladie,
Offence of mighty note; but to himselfe,
The greatest wrong of all. He lost a wife,
Whose beauty did astonish the suruey
Of richest eies: whose words all eares tooke captiue,
Whose deere perfection, hearts that scorn'd to serue,
Humbly call'd Mistris.

Kin. Praising what is lost,
Makes the remembrance deere. Well, call him hither,
We are reconcil'd, and the first view shall kill
All repetition: Let him not aske our pardon,
The nature of his great offence is dead,
And deeper then obliuion, we do burie
Th'incensing reliques of it. Let him approach
A stranger, no offender; and informe him
So 'tis our will he should.

Gent. I shall my Liege.

Kin. What sayes he to your daughter,
Haue you spoke?

Laf. All that he is, hath reference to your Highnes.

Kin. Then shall we haue a match. I haue letters sent me, that sets him high in fame.

Enter Count Bertram.

Laf. He lookes well on't

Kin. I am not a day of season,
For thou maist see a sun-shine, and a haile
In me at once: But to the brightest beames
Distracted clouds giue way, so stand thou forth,
The time is faire againe.

Ber. My high repented blames
Deere Soueraigne pardon to me.

Kin. All is whole,
Not one word more of the consumed time,
Let's take the instant by the forward top:
For we are old, and on our quick'st decrees
Th'inaudible, and noiselesse foot of time
Steales, ere we can effect them. You remember
The daughter of this Lord?

Ber. Admiringly my Liege, at first
I stucke my choice vpon her, ere my heart
Durst make too bold a herauld of my tongue:
Where the impression of mine eye enfixing,
Contempt his scornfull Perspectiue did lend me,
Which warpt the line, of euerie other fauour,
Scorn'd a faire colour, or exprest it stolne,
Extended or contracted all proportions
To a most hideous obiect. Thence it came,
That she whom all men prais'd, and whom my selfe,
Since I haue lost, haue lou'd; was in mine eye
The dust that did offend it.

Kin. Well excus'd:
That thou didst loue her, strikes some scores away
From the great compt: but loue that comes too late,
Like a remorsefull pardon slowly carried
To the great sender, turnes a sowre offence,
Crying, that's good that's gone: Our rash faults,
Make triuiall price of serious things we haue,
Not knowing them, vntill we know their graue.
Oft our displeasures to our selues vniust,
Destroy our friends, and after weepe their dust:
Our owne loue waking, cries to see what's don,e
While shamefull hate sleepes out the afternoone.
Be this sweet *Helens* knell, and now forget her.
Send forth your amorous token for faire *Maudlin*,
The maine consents are had, and heere wee'l stay
To see our widdowers second marriage day:
Which better then the first. O deere heauen blesse,
Or, ere they meete in me, O Nature cesse.

Laf. Come on my sonne, in whom my houses name
Must be digested: giue a fauour from you
To sparkle in the spirits of my daughter,

That

That she may quickly come. By my old beard,
And eu'rie haire that's on't, *Helen* that's dead
Was a sweet creature: such a ring as this,
The last that ere I tooke her leaue at Court,
I saw vpon her finger.
Ber. Hers it was not.
King. Now pray you let me see it. For mine eye,
While I was speaking, oft was fasten'd too't:
This Ring was mine, and when I gaue it *Hellen*,
I bad her if her fortunes euer stoode
Necessitied to helpe, that by this token
I would releeue her. Had you that craft to reaue her
Of what should stead her most?
Ber. My gracious Soueraigne,
How ere it pleases you to take it so,
The ring was neuer hers.
Old La. Sonne, on my life
I haue seene her weare it, and she reckon'd it
At her liues rate.
Laf. I am sure I saw her weare it
Ber. You are deceiu'd my Lord, she neuer saw it:
In Florence was it from a casement throwne mee,
Wrap'd in a paper, which contain'd the name
Of her that threw it: Noble she was, and thought
I stood ingag'd. but when I had subscrib'd
To mine owne fortune, and inform'd her fully,
I could not answer in that course of Honour
As she had made the ouerture, she ceast
In heauie satisfaction, and would neuer
Receiue the Ring againe.
Kin. *Platus* himselfe,
That knowes the tinct and multiplying med'cine,
Hath not in natures mysterie more science,
Then I haue in this Ring. 'Twas mine, 'twas *Helens*,
Who euer gaue it you: then if you know
That you are well acquainted with your selfe,
Confesse 'twas hers, and by what rough enforcement
You got it from her. She call'd the Saints to suretie,
That she would neuer put it from her finger,
Vnlesse she gaue it to your selfe in bed,
Where you haue neuer come: or sent it vs
Vpon her great disaster.
Ber. She neuer saw it.
Kin. Thou speak'st it falsely: as I loue mine Honor,
And mak st connecturall feares to come into me,
Which I would faine sh it out, if it should proue
That thou art so inhumane, 'twill not proue so:
And yet I know not, thou didst hate her deadly,
And she is dead, which nothing but to close
Her eyes my selfe, could win me to beleeue,
More then to see this Ring. Take him away,
My fore-past proofes, how ere the matter fall
Shall taze my feares of little vanitie,
Hauing vainly fear'd too little. Away with him,
Wee'l sift this matter further.
Ber. If you shall proue
This Ring was euer hers, you shall as easie
Proue that I husbanded her bed in Florence,
Where yet she neuer was.

Enter a Gentleman.

King. I am wrap d in dismall thinkings.
Gen. Gracious Soueraigne.
Whether I haue beene too blame or no, I know not,
Here's a petition from a Florentine,
Who hath for foure or fiue remoues come short,
To tender it her selfe. I vndertooke it,
Vanquish'd thereto by the faire grace and speech
Of the poore suppliant, who by this I know
Is heere attending: her businesse lookes in her
With an importing visage, and she told me
In a sweet verball breeze, it did concerne
Your Highnesse with her selfe.

A Letter

Vpon his many protestations to marrie mee when his wife was dead, I blush to say it, he wonne me. Now is the Count Rossillion a Widdower, his vowes are forfeited to mee, and my honors payed to him. Hee stole from Florence, taking no leaue, and I follow him to his Countrey for Iustice: Grant it me, O King, in you it best lies, otherwise a seducer flourishes, and a poore Maid is vndone.

Diana Capilet.

Laf. I will buy me a sonne in Law in a faire, and toule for this. Ile none of him.
Kin. The heauens haue thought well on thee *Lafew*,
To bring forth this discou'rie, seeke these sutors:
Go speedily, and bring againe the Count.

Enter Bertram.

I am a-feard the life of *Hellen* (Ladie)
Was fowly snatcht.
Old La. Now iustice on the doers.
King. I wonder sir, sir, wiues are monsters to you,
And that you flye them as you sweare them Lordship,
Yet you desire to marry. What woman's that?

Enter Widdow, Diana, and Parrolles.

Dia. I am my Lord a wretched Florentine,
Deriued from the ancient Capilet,
My suite as I do vnderstand you know,
And therefore know how farre I may be pittied
Wid. I am her Mother sir, whose age and honour
Both suffer vnder this complaint we bring,
And both shall cease, without your remedie.
King. Come hether Count, do you know these Women?
Ber. My Lord, I neither can nor will denie,
But that I know them, do they charge me further?
Dia. Why do you looke so strange vpon your wife?
Ber. She's none of mine my Lord.
Dia. If you shall marrie
You giue away this hand, and that is mine,
You giue away heauens vowes, and those are mine.
You giue away my selfe, which is knowne mine:
For I by vow am so embodied yours,
That she which marries you, must marrie me,
Either both or none.
Laf. your reputation comes too short for my daughter, you are no husband for her.
Ber. My Lord, this is a fond and desp rate creature,
Whom sometime I haue laugh'd with: Let your highnes
Lay a more noble thought vpon mine honour,
Then for to thinke that I would sinke it heere.
Kin. Sir for my thoughts, you haue them il to friend,
Till your deeds gaine them fairer: proue your honor,
Then in my thought it lies.
Dian. Good my Lord,
Aske him vpon his oath, if hee do's thinke
He had not my virginity.
Kin. What saist thou to her?
Ber. She's impudent my Lord,
And was a common gamester to the Campe.
Dia. He do's me wrong my Lord: If I were so,
He might haue bought me at a common price.

Do

r

Do not beleeue him. O behold this Ring,
Whose high respect and rich validitie
Did lacke a Paralell: yet for all that
He gaue it to a Commoner a'th Campe
If I be one.

Coun. He blushes, and 'tis hit:
Of sixe preceding Ancestors, that Iemme
Confer'd by testament to'th sequent issue
Hath it beene owed and worne. This is his wife,
That Ring's a thousand proofes.

King. Me thought you saide
You saw one heere in Court could witnesse it.

Dia. I did my Lord, but loath am to produce
So bad an instrument, his names *Parrolles*.

Laf. I saw the man to day, if man he bee.

Kin. Finde him, and bring him hether.

Ros. What of him:
He's quoted for a most perfidious slaue
With all the spots a'th world, taxt and debosh'd,
Whose nature sickens: but to speake a truth,
Am I, or that or this for what he'l vtter,
That will speake any thing.

Kin. She hath that Ring of yours.

Ros. I thinke she has; certaine it is I lyk'd her,
And boorded her i'th wanton way of youth
She knew her distance, and did angle for mee,
Madding my eagernesse with her restraint,
As all impediments in fancies course
Are motiues of more fancie, and in fine,
Her insuite comming with her moderne grace,
Subdu'd me to her rate, she got the Ring,
And I had that which any inferiour might
At Market price haue bought.

Dia. I must be patient:
You that haue turn'd off a first so noble wife,
May iustly dyet me. I pray you yet.
(Since you lacke vertue, I will loose a husband)
Send for your Ring, I will returne it home,
And giue me mine againe.

Ros. I haue it not.

Kin. What Ring was yours I pray you?

Dian. Sir much like the same vpon your finger.

Kin. Know you this Ring, this Ring was his of late.

Dia. And this was it I gaue him being a bed.

Kin. The story then goes false, you threw it him
Out of a Casement.

Dia. I haue spoke the truth. *Enter Parolles.*

Ros. My Lord, I do confesse the ring was hers.

Kin. You boggle shrewdly, euery feather starts you:
Is this the man you speake of?

Dia. I, my Lord.

Kin. Tell me sirrah, but tell me true I charge you,
Not fearing the displeasure of your master.
Which on your iust proceeding, Ile keepe off,
By him and by this woman heere, what know you?

Par. So please your Maiesty, my master hath bin an honourable Gentleman. Trickes hee hath had in him, which Gentlemen haue.

Kin. Come, come, to'th'purpose: Did hee loue this woman?

Par. Faith sir he did loue her, but how.

Kin. How I pray you?

Par. He did loue her sir, as a Gent. loues a Woman.

Kin. How is that?

Par. He lou'd her sir, and lou'd her not.

Kin. As thou art a knaue and no knaue, what an equiuocall Companion is this?

Par. I am a poore man and at your Maiesties command.

Laf. Hee's a good drumme my Lord, but a naughtie Orator.

Dian. Do you know he promist me marriage?

Par. Faith I know more then Ile speake.

Kin. But wilt thou not speake all thou know'st?

Par. Yes so please your Maiesty: I did goe betweene them as I said, but more then that he loued her, for indeede he was madde for her, and talkt of Sathan, and of Limbo, and of Furies, and I know not what: yet I was in that credit with them at that time, that I knewe of their going to bed, and of other motions, as promising her marriage, and things which would deriue mee ill will to speake of, therefore I will not speake what I know.

Kin. Thou hast spoken all alreadie, vnlesse thou canst say they are maried, but thou art too fine in thy euidence, therefore stand aside. This Ring you say was yours.

Dia. I my good Lord.

Kin. Where did you buy it? Or who gaue it you?

Dia. It was not giuen me, nor I did not buy it.

Kin. Who lent it you?

Dia. It was not lent me neither.

Kin. Where did you finde it then?

Dia. I found it not.

Kin. If it were yours by none of all these wayes,
How could you giue it him?

Dia. I neuer gaue it him.

Laf. This womans an easie gloue my Lord, she goes off and on at pleasure.

Kin. This Ring was mine, I gaue it his first wife.

Dia. It might be yours or hers for ought I know.

Kin. Take her away, I do not like her now,
To prison with her: and away with him,
Vnlesse thou telst me where thou hadst this Ring,
Thou diest within this houre.

Dia. Ile neuer tell you.

Kin. Take her away.

Dia. Ile put in baile my liedge.

Kin. I thinke thee now some common Customer.

Dia. By loue if euer I knew man 'twas you.

King. Wherefore hast thou accus'de him al this while.

Dia. Because he's guiltie, and he is not guilty:
He knowes I am no Maid, and hee'l sweare too't:
Ile sweare I am a Maid, and he knowes not.
Great King I am no strumpet, by my life,
I am either Maid, or else this old mans wife.

Kin. She does abuse our eares, to prison with her.

Dia. Good mother fetch my bayle. Stay Royall sir,
The Ieweller that owes the Ring is sent for,
And he shall surety me. But for this Lord,
Who hath abus'd me as he knowes himselfe,
Though yet he neuer harm'd me, heere I quit him.
He knowes himselfe my bed he hath defil'd,
And at that time he got his wife with childe:
Dead though she be, she feeles her yong one kicke:
So there's my riddle, one that's dead is quicke,
And now behold the meaning.

Enter Hellen and Widdow.

Kin. Is there no exorcist
Beguiles the truer Office of mine eyes?
Is't reall that I see?

Hel. No my good Lord,

Y Tis

Tis but the shadow of a wife you see,
The name, and not the thing.
Ros. Both, both, O pardon.
Hel. Oh my good Lord, when I was like this Maid,
I found you wondrous kinde, there is your Ring,
And looke you, heeres your letter: this it sayes,
When from my finger you can get this Ring,
And is by me with childe, &c. This is done,
Will you be mine now you are doubly wonne?
Ros. If she my Liege can make me know this clearly,
Ile loue her dearely, euer, euer dearly.
Hel. If it appeare not plaine, and proue vntrue,
Deadly diuorce step betweene me and you.
O my deere mother do I see you liuing?
Laf. Mine eyes smell Onions, I shall weepe anon:
Good Tom Drumme lend me a handkercher.
So I thanke thee, waite on me home, Ile make sport with
thee: Let thy curtsies alone, they are scuruy ones.
King Let vs from point to point this storie know,
To make the euen truth in pleasure flow:
If thou beest yet a fresh vncropped flower,
Choose thou thy husband, and Ile pay thy dower.
For I can guesse, that by thy honest ayde,
Thou keptst a wife her selfe, thy selfe a Maide
Of that and all the progresse more and lesse,
Resolduedly more leasure shall expresse:
All yet seemes well, and if it end so meete,
The bitter past, more welcome is the sweet.

Flourish.

The Kings a Begger, now the Play is done,
All is well ended, if this suite be wonne,
That you expresse Content: which we will pay,
With strift to please you, day exceeding day:
Ours be your patience then, and yours our parts,
Your gentle hands lend vs, and take our hearts. Exeunt omn.

FINIS.

Twelfe Night, Or what you will.

Actus Primus, Scæna Prima.

Enter Orsino Duke of Illyria, Curio, and other Lords.

Duke.

IF Musicke be the food of Loue, play on,
Giue me excesse of it: that surfetting,
The appetite may sicken, and so dye.
That straine agen, it had a dying fall:
O, it came ore my eare, like the sweet sound
That breathes vpon a banke of Violets;
Stealing, and giuing Odour. Enough, no more,
'Tis not so sweet now, as it was before.
O spirit of Loue, how quicke and fresh art thou,
That notwithstanding thy capacitie,
Receiueth as the Sea. Nought enters there,
Of what validity, and pitch so ere,
But falles into abatement, and low price
Euen in a minute; so full of shapes is fancie,
That it alone, is high fantasticall.
Cu. Will you go hunt my Lord?
Du. What *Curio*?
Cu. The Hart.
Du. Why so I do, the Noblest that I haue:
O when mine eyes did see *Oliuia* first,
Me thought she purg'd the ayre of pestilence;
That instant was I turn'd into a Hart,
And my desires like fell and cruell hounds,
Ere since pursue me. How now what newes from her?

Enter Valentine.

Val. So please my Lord, I might not be admitted,
But from her handmaid do returne this answer:
The Element it selfe, till seuen yeares heate,
Shall not behold her face at ample view:
But like a Cloystresse she will vailed walke,
And water once a day her Chamber round
With eye-offending brine: all this to season
A brothers dead loue, which she would keepe fresh
And lasting, in her sad remembrance.
Du. O she that hath a heart of that fine frame
To pay this debt of loue but to a brother,
How will she loue, when the rich golden shaft
Hath kill'd the flocke of all affections else
That liue in her. When Liuer, Braine, and Heart,
These soueraigne thrones, are all supply'd and fill'd
Her sweete perfections with one selfe king:
Away before me, to sweet beds of Flowres,
Loue-thoughts lye rich, when canopy'd with bowres.
Exeunt

Scena Secunda.

Enter Viola, a Captaine, and Saylors.

Vio. What Country (Friends) is this?
Cap. This is Illyria Ladie.
Vio. And what should I do in Illyria?
My brother he is in Elizium,
Perchance he is not drown'd: What thinke you saylors?
Cap. It is perchance that you your selfe were saued.
Vio. O my poore brother, and so perchance may he be.
Cap. True Madam, and to comfort you with chance,
Assure your selfe, after our ship did split,
When you, and those poore number saued with you,
Hung on our driuing boate: I saw your brother
Most prouident in perill, binde himselfe,
(Courage and hope both teaching him the practise)
To a stong Maste, that liu'd vpon the sea:
Where like *Orion* on the Dolphines backe,
I saw him hold acquaintance with the waues,
So long as I could see.
Vio. For saying so, there's Gold:
Mine owne escape vnfoldeth to my hope,
Whereto thy speech serues for authoritie
The like of him. Know'st thou this Countrey?
Cap. I Madam well, for I was bred and borne
Not three houres trauaile from this very place.
Vio. Who gouernes heere?
Cap. A noble Duke in nature, as in name.
Vio. What is his name?
Cap. *Orsino.*
Vio. *Orsino*: I haue heard my father name him.
He was a Batchellor then.
Cap. And so is now, or was so very late:
For but a month ago I went from hence,
And then 'twas fresh in murmure (as you know
What great ones do, the lesse will prattle of,)
That he did seeke the loue of faire *Oliuia*.
Vio. What's shee?
Cap. A vertuous maid, the daughter of a Count
That dide some tweluemonth since, then leauing her
In the protection of his sonne, her brother,
Who shortly also dide: for whose deere loue
(They say) she hath abiur'd the sight
And company of men.
Vio. O that I seru'd that Lady,
And might not be deliuered to the world

Till I had made mine owne occasion mellow
What my estate is.

Cap. That were hard to compasse,
Because she will admit no kinde of suite,
No, not the Dukes.

Vio. There is a faire behauiour in thee Captaine,
And though that nature, with a beauteous wall
Doth oft close in pollution: yet of thee
I will beleeue thou hast a minde that suites
With this thy faire and outward charracter.
I prethee (and Ile pay thee bounteously)
Conceale me what I am, and be my ayde,
For such disguise as haply shall become
The forme of my intent. Ile serue this Duke,
Thou shalt present me as an Eunuch to him,
It may be worth thy paines: for I can sing,
And speake to him in many sorts of Musicke,
That will allow me very worth his seruice.
What else may hap, to time I will commit,
Onely shape thou thy silence to my wit.

Cap. Be you his Eunuch, and your Mute Ile bee,
When my tongue blabs, then let mine eyes not see.

Vio. I thanke thee: Lead me on. *Exeunt.*

Scæna Tertia.

Enter Sir Toby, and Maria.

Sir To. What a plague meanes my Neece to take the death of her brother thus? I am sure care's an enemie to life.

Mar. By my troth sir *Toby*, you must come in earlyer a nights: your Cosin, my Lady, takes great exceptions to your ill houres.

To. Why let her except, before excepted.

Ma. I, but you must confine your selfe within the modest limits of order.

To. Confine? Ile confine my selfe no finer then I am: these cloathes are good enough to drinke in, and so bee these boots too: and they be not, let them hang themselues in their owne straps.

Ma. That quaffing and drinking will vndoe you: I heard my Lady talke of it yesterday: and of a foolish knight that you brought in one night here, to be hir woer.

To. Who, Sir *Andrew Ague-cheeke*?

Ma. I he.

To. He's as tall a man as any's in Illyria.

Ma. What's that to th'purpose?

To. Why he ha's three thousand ducates a yeare.

Ma. I, but hee'l haue but a yeare in all these ducates: He's a very foole, and a prodigall.

To. Fie, that you'l say so: he playes o'th Viol-de-gamboys, and speaks three or four languages word for word without booke, & hath all the good gifts of nature.

Ma. He hath indeed, almost naturall: for besides that he's a foole, he's a great quarreller: and but that hee hath the gift of a Coward, to allay the gust he hath in quarrelling, 'tis thought among the prudent, he would quickely haue the gift of a graue.

Tob. By this hand they are scoundrels and substractors that say so of him. Who are they?

Ma. They that adde moreour, hee's drunke nightly in your company.

To. With drinking healths to my Neece: Ile drinke to her as long as there is a passage in my throat, & drinke in Illyria: he's a Coward and a Coystrill that will not drinke to my Neece, till his braines turne o'th toe, like a parish top. What wench? *Castiliano vulgo*: for here coms Sir *Andrew Agueface*.

Enter Sir Andrew.

And. Sir *Toby Belch*. How now sir *Toby Belch*?

To. Sweet sir *Andrew*.

And. Blesse you faire Shrew.

Mar. And you too sir.

Tob. Accost Sir *Andrew*, accost.

And. What's that?

To. My Neeces Chamber-maid.

Ma. Good Mistris accost, I desire better acquaintance

Ma. My name is *Mary* sir.

And. Good mistris *Mary*, accost.

To. You mistake knight: Accost, is front her, boord her, woe her, assayle her.

And. By my troth I would not vndertake her in this company. Is that the meaning of Accost?

Ma. Far you well Gentlemen.

To. And thou let part so Sir *Andrew*, would thou mightst neuer draw sword agen.

And. And you part so mistris, I would I might neuer draw sword agen: Faire Lady, doe you thinke you haue fooles in hand?

Ma. Sir, I haue not you by'th hand.

An. Marry but you shall haue, and heeres my hand.

Ma. Now sir, thought is free: I pray you bring your hand to'th Buttry barre, and let it drinke.

An. Wherefore (sweet-heart?) What's your Metaphor?

Ma. It's dry sir.

And. Why I thinke so: I am not such an asse, but I can keepe my hand dry. But what's your iest?

Ma. A dry iest Sir.

And. Are you full of them?

Ma. I Sir, I haue them at my fingers ends: marry now I let go your hand, I am barren. *Exit Maria*

To. O knight, thou lack'st a cup of Canarie: when did I see thee so put downe?

An. Neuer in your life I thinke, vnlesse you see Canarie put me downe: mee thinkes sometimes I haue no more wit then a Christian, or an ordinary man ha's: but I am a great eater of beefe, and I beleeue that does harme to my wit.

To. No question.

An. And I thought that, I'de forsweare it. Ile ride home to morrow sir *Toby*.

To. *Pur-quoy* my deere knight?

An. What is *purquoy*? Do, or not do? I would I had bestowed that time in the tongues, that I haue in fencing dancing, and beare-bayting: O had I but followed the Arts.

To. Then hadst thou had an excellent head of haire.

An. Why, would that haue mended my haire?

To. Past question, for thou seest it will not coole my nature.

An. But it becoms we wel enough, dost not?

To. Excellent, it hangs like flax on a distaffe: & I hope to see a huswife take thee between her legs, & spin it off.

An. Faith Ile home to morrow sir *Toby*, your niece wil not be seene, or if she be it's four to one, she'l none of me: the Count himselfe here hard by, wooes her.

To. Shee'l none o'th Count, she'l not match aboue hir degree, neither in estate, yeares, nor wit: I haue heard her swear t. Tut there's life in't man.

And

And. Ile stay a moneth longer. I am a fellow o'th strangest minde i'th world: I delight in Maskes and Reuels sometimes altogether

To. Art thou good at these kicke-chawses Knight?

And. As any man in Illyria, whatsoeuer he be, vnder the degree of my betters, & yet I will not compare with an old man.

To. What is thy excellence in a galliard, knight?

And. Faith, I can cut a caper.

To. And I can cut the Mutton too't.

And. And I thinke I haue the backe-tricke, simply as strong as any man in Illyria.

To. Wherefore are these things hid? Wherefore haue these gifts a Curtaine before 'em? Are they like to take dust, like mistris *Mals* picture? Why dost thou not goe to Church in a Galliard, and come home in a Carranto? My verie walke should be a Iigge: I would not so much as make water but in a Sinke-a-pace: What dooest thou meane? Is it a world to hide vertues in? I did thinke by the excellent constitution of thy legge, it was form'd vnder the starre of a Galliard

And, I, 'tis strong, and it does indifferent well in a dam'd colour'd stocke. Shall we sit about some Reuels?

To. What shall we do else: were we not borne vnder Taurus?

And. Taurus? That sides and heart.

To. No sir, it is leggs and thighes: let me see thee caper. Ha, higher: ha, ha, excellent. *Exeunt*

Scena Quarta.

Enter Valentine, and Viola in mans attire.

Val. If the Duke continue these fauours towards you *Cesario*, you are like to be much aduanc'd, he hath known you but three dayes, and already you are no stranger.

Vio. You either feare his humour, or my negligence, that you call in question the continuance of his loue. Is he inconstant sir, in his fauours. *Val.* No beleeue me.

Enter Duke, Curio and Attendants.

Vio. I thanke you: heere comes the Count.

Duke. Who saw *Cesario* hoa?

Vio. On your attendance my Lord heere.

Du. Stand you a-while aloofe. *Cesario*,
Thou knowst no lesse, but all: I haue vnclasp'd
To thee the booke euen of my secret soule.
Therefore good youth, addresse thy gate vnto her,
Be not deni'de accesse, stand at her doores,
And tell them, there thy fixed foot shall grow
Till thou haue audience.

Vio. Sure my Noble Lord,
If she be so abandon'd to her sorrow
As it is spoke, she neuer will admit me.

Du. Be clamorous, and leape all ciuill bounds,
Rather then make vnprofited returne,

Vio. Say I do speake with her (my Lord) what then?

Du. O then, vnfold the passion of my loue,
Surprize her with discourse of my deere faith;
It shall become thee well to act my woes.
She will attend it better in thy youth,
Then in a Nuntio's of more graue aspect.

Vio I thinke not so, my Lord.

Du. Deere Lad, beleeue it;
For they shall yet belye thy happy yeeres,
That say thou art a man: *Dianas* lip
Is not more smooth, and rubious: thy small pipe
Is as the maidens organ, shrill, and sound,
And all is semblatiue a womans part.
I know thy constellation is right apt
For this affayre: some foure or fiue attend him,
All if you will: for I my selfe am best
When least in companie: prosper well in this,
And thou shalt liue as freely as thy Lord,
To call his fortunes thine.

Vio. Ile do my best
To woe your Lady: yet a barrefull strife,
Who ere I woe, my selfe would be his wife. *Exeunt.*

Scena Quinta.

Enter Maria, and Clowne.

Ma. Nay, either tell me where thou hast bin, or I will not open my lippes so wide as a brisle may enter, in way of thy excuse: my Lady will hang thee for thy absence.

Clo. Let her hang me: hee that is well hang'de in this world, needs to feare no colours.

Ma. Make that good.

Clo. He shall see none to feare.

Ma. A good lenton answer: I can tell thee where y saying was borne, of I feare no colours.

Clo. Where good mistris *Mary*?

Ma. In the warrs, & that may you be bolde to say in your foolerie.

Clo. Well, God giue them wisedome that haue it: & those that are fooles, let them vse their talents.

Ma. Yet you will be hang'd for being so long absent, or to be turn'd away: is not that as good as a hanging to you?

Clo. Many a good hanging, preuents a bad marriage: and for turning away, let summer beare it out.

Ma. You are resolute then?

Clo Not so neyther, but I am resolu'd on two points

Ma. That if one breake, the other will hold: or if both breake, your gaskins fall.

Clo. Apt in good faith, very apt: well go thy way, if sir *Toby* would leaue drinking, thou wert as witty a piece of *Eues* flesh, as any in Illyria

Ma. Peace you rogue, no more o'that: here comes my Lady: make your excuse wisely, you were best.

Enter Lady Oliuia, with Maluolio.

Clo. Wit, and't be thy will, put me into good fooling: those wits that thinke they haue thee, doe very oft proue fooles: and I that am sure I lacke thee, may passe for a wise man. For what saies *Quinapalus*, Better a witty foole, then a foolish wit. God blesse thee Lady.

Ol. Take the foole away.

Clo. Do you not heare fellowes, take away the Ladie.

Ol. Go too, y'are a dry foole: Ile no more of you: besides you grow dis-honest.

Clo. Two faults Madona, that drinke & good counsell wil amend: for giue the dry foole drink, then is the foole not dry: bid the dishonest man mend himself, if he mend, he is no longer dishonest; if hee cannot, let the Botcher mend him: any thing that's mended, is but patch'd: vertu that transgresses, is but patcht with sinne, and sin that amends, is but patcht with vertue. If that this simple Sillogisme will serue, so: if it will not, vvhat remedy?

As there is no true Cuckold but calamity, ſo beauties a flower; The Lady bad take away the foole, therefore I ſay againe, take her away.

Ol. Sir, I bad them take away you.

Clo. Miſpriſion in the higheſt degree. Lady, *Cucullus non facit monachum*: that's as much to ſay, as I weare not motley in my braine: good *Madona*, giue mee leaue to proue you a foole.

Ol. Can you do it?

Clo. Dexteriouſly, good Madona.

Ol. Make your proofe.

Clo. I muſt catechize you for it Madona, Good my Mouſe of vertue anſwer mee.

Ol. Well ſir, for want of other idleneſſe, Ile bide your proofe.

Clo. Good Madona, why mournſt thou?

Ol. Good foole, for my brothers death.

Clo. I thinke his ſoule is in hell, Madona.

Ol. I know his ſoule is in heauen, foole.

Clo. The more foole (Madona) to mourne for your Brothers ſoule, being in heauen. Take away the Foole, Gentlemen.

Ol. What thinke you of this foole *Maluolio*, doth he not mend?

Mal. Yes, and ſhall do, till the pangs of death ſhake him: Infirmity that decaies the wiſe, doth euer make the better foole.

Clow. God ſend you ſir, a ſpeedie Infirmity, for the better increaſing your folly: Sir *Toby* will be ſworn that I am no Fox, but he wil not paſſe his word for two pence that you are no Foole.

Ol. How ſay you to that *Maluolio*?

Mal. I maruell your Ladyſhip takes delight in ſuch a barren raſcall: I ſaw him put down the other day, with an ordinary foole, that has no more braine then a ſtone. Looke you now, he's out of his gard already: vnles you laugh and miniſter occaſion to him, he is gag'd. I proteſt I take theſe Wiſemen, that crow ſo at theſe ſet kinde of fooles, no better then the fooles Zanies.

Ol. O you are ſicke of ſelfe-loue *Maluolio*, and taſte with a diſtemper'd appetite. To be generous, guiltleſſe, and of free diſpoſition, is to take thoſe things for Bird-bolts, that you deeme Cannon bullets: There is no ſlander in an allow'd foole, though he do nothing but rayle; nor no rayling, in a knowne diſcreet man, though hee do nothing but reproue.

Clo. Now Mercury indue thee with leaſing, for thou ſpeak'ſt well of fooles.

Enter Maria.

Mar. Madam, there is at the gate, a young Gentleman, much deſires to ſpeake with you.

Ol. From the Count *Orſino*, is it?

Ma. I know not (Madam) 'tis a faire young man, and well attended.

Ol. Who of my people hold him in delay?

Ma. Sir *Toby* Madam, your kinſman.

Ol. Fetch him off I pray you, he ſpeakes nothing but madman: Fie on him. Go you *Maluolio*; If it be a ſuit from the Count, I am ſicke, or not at home. What you will, to diſmiſſe it. *Exit Maluo.*

Now you ſee ſir, how your fooling growes old, & people diſlike it.

Clo. Thou haſt ſpoke for vs (Madona) as if thy eldeſt ſonne ſhould be a foole: whoſe ſcull, Ioue cramme with braines, for heere he comes. *Enter Sir Toby.*

One of thy kin has a moſt weake *Pia-mater*.

Ol. By mine honor halfe drunke. What is he at the gate Coſin?

To. A Gentleman.

Ol. A Gentleman? What Gentleman?

To. 'Tis a Gentleman heere. A plague o'theſe pickle herring: How now Sot.

Clo. Good Sir *Toby*.

Ol. Coſin, Coſin, how haue you come ſo earely by this Lethargie?

To. Letcherie, I defie Letchery: there's one at the gate.

Ol. I marry, what is he?

To. Let him be the diuell and he will, I care not: giue me faith ſay I. Well, it's all one. *Exit*

Ol. What's a drunken man like, foole?

Clo. Like a drown'd man, a foole, and a madde man: One draught aboue heate, makes him a foole, the ſecond maddes him, and a third drownes him.

Ol. Go thou and ſeeke the Crowner, and let him ſitte o'my Coz: for he's in the third degree of drinke: hee's drown'd: go looke after him.

Clo. He is but mad yet Madona, and the foole ſhall looke to the madman.

Enter Maluolio.

Mal. Madam, yond young fellow ſweares hee will ſpeake with you. I told him you were ſicke, he takes on him to vnderſtand ſo much, and therefore comes to ſpeak with you. I told him you were aſleepe, he ſeems to haue a fore knowledge of that too, and therefore comes to ſpeake with you. What is to be ſaid to him Ladie, hee's fortified againſt any deniall.

Ol. Tell him, he ſhall not ſpeake with me.

Mal. Ha's beene told ſo: and hee ſayes hee'l ſtand at your doore like a Sheriffes poſt, and be the ſupporter to a bench, but hee'l ſpeake with you.

Ol. What kinde o'man is he?

Mal. Why of mankinde.

Ol. What manner of man?

Mal. Of verie ill manner: hee'l ſpeake with you, will you, or no.

Ol. Of what perſonage, and yeeres is he?

Mal. Not yet old enough for a man, nor yong enough for a boy: as a ſquaſh is before 'tis a peſcod, or a Codling when 'tis almoſt an Apple: 'Tis with him in ſtanding water, betweene boy and man. He is verie well-fauour'd, and he ſpeakes verie ſhrewiſhly: One would thinke his mothers milke were ſcarſe out of him.

Ol. Let him approach: Call in my Gentlewoman.

Mal. Gentlewoman, my Lady calles. *Exit.*

Enter Maria.

Ol. Giue me my vaile: come throw it ore my face,
Wee'l once more heare *Orſinos* Embaſſie.

Enter Violenta.

Vio. The honorable Ladie of the houſe, which is ſhe?

Ol. Speake to me, I ſhall anſwer for her: your will.

Vio. Moſt radiant, exquiſite, and vnmatchable beautie. I pray you tell me if this bee the Lady of the houſe, for I neuer ſaw her. I would bee loath to caſt away my ſpeech: for beſides that it is excellently well pend, I haue taken great paines to con it. Good Beauties, let mee ſuſtaine no ſcorne; I am very comptible, euen to the leaſt ſiniſter vſage.

Ol. Whence came you ſir?

Vio. I can ſay little more then I haue ſtudied, & that queſtion's out of my part. Good gentle one, giue mee modeſt aſſurance, if you be the Ladie of the houſe, that

I

may proceede in my ſpeech.
Ol. Are you a Comedian?
Vio. No my profound heart: and yet (by the verie phangs of malice, I ſweare) I am not that I play. Are you the Ladie of the houſe?
Ol. If I do not vſurpe my ſelfe, I am.
Vio. Moſt certaine, if you are ſhe, you do vſurp your ſelfe: for what is yours to beſtowe, is, not yours to reſerue. But this is from my Commiſſion: I will on with my ſpeech in your praiſe, and then ſhew you the heart of my meſſage.
Ol. Come to what is important in't: I forgiue you the praiſe.
Vio Alas, I tooke great paines to ſtudie it, and 'tis Poeticall.
Ol. It is the more like to be feigned, I pray you keep it in. I heard you were ſawcy at my gates, & allowd your approach rather to wonder at you, then to heare you. If you be not mad, be gone: if you haue reaſon, be breefe: 'tis not that time of Moone with me, to make one in ſo skipping a dialogue.
Ma. Will you hoyſt ſayle ſir, here lies your way.
Vio. No good ſwabber, I am to hull here a little longer. Some mollification for your Giant, ſweete Ladie; tell me your minde, I am a meſſenger.
Ol. Sure you haue ſome hiddeous matter to deliuer, when the curteſie of it is ſo fearefull. Speake your office.
Vio It alone concernes your eare: I bring no ouerture of warre, no taxation of homage; I hold the Olyffe in my hand: my words are as full of peace, as matter.
Ol. Yet you began rudely. What are you?
What would you?
Vio. The rudeneſſe that hath appear'd in mee, haue I learn'd from my entertainment. What I am, and what I would, are as ſecret as maiden-head: to your eares, Diuinity; to any others, prophanation.
Ol. Giue vs the place alone,
We will heare this diuinitie. Now ſir, what is your text?
Vio Moſt ſweet Ladie.
Ol A comfortable doctrine, and much may bee ſaide of it. Where lies your Text?
Vio In *Orſinoes* boſome.
Ol In his boſome? In what chapter of his boſome?
Vio To anſwer by the method, in the firſt of his hart.
Ol. O, I haue read it: it is hereſie. Haue you no more to ſay?
Vio. Good Madam, let me ſee your face.
Ol. Haue you any Commiſſion from your Lord, to negotiate with my face: you are now out of your Text: but we will draw the Curtain, and ſhew you the picture. Looke you ſir, ſuch a one I was this preſent: Iſt not well done?
Vio Excellently done, if God did all.
Ol 'Tis in graine ſir, 'twill endure winde and weather.
Vio. Tis beauty truly blent, whoſe red and white,
Natures owne ſweet, and cunning hand laid on:
Lady, you are the cruell'ſt ſhee aliue,
If you will leade theſe graces to the graue,
And leaue the world no copie.
Ol O ſir, I will not be ſo hard-hearted: I will giue out diuers ſcedules of my beautie. It ſhalbe Inuentoried and euery particle and vtenſile labell'd to my will: As, Item two lippes indifferent redde, Item two grey eyes, with lids to them: Item, one necke, one chin, & ſo forth. Were you ſent hither to praiſe me?
Vio. I ſee you what you are, you are too proud:
But if you were the diuell, you are faire:
My Lord, and maſter loues you: O ſuch loue
Could be but recompenc'd, though you were crown'd
The non-pareil of beautie.
Ol. How does he loue me?
Vio. With adorations, fertill teares,
With groanes that thunder loue, with ſighes of fire.
Ol. Your Lord does know my mind, I cannot loue him
Yet I ſuppoſe him vertuous, know him noble,
Of great eſtate, of freſh and ſtainleſſe youth;
In voyces well diuulg'd, free, learn'd, and valiant,
And in dimenſion, and the ſhape of nature,
A gracious perſon; But yet I cannot loue him:
He might haue tooke his anſwer long ago.
Vio. If I did loue you in my maſters flame,
With ſuch a ſuffring, ſuch a deadly life:
In your deniall, I would finde no ſence,
I would not vnderſtand it.
Ol. Why, what would you?
Vio. Make me a willow Cabine at your gate,
And call vpon my ſoule within the houſe,
Write loyall Cantons of contemned loue,
And ſing them lowd euen in the dead of night:
Hallow your name to the reuerberate hilles,
And make the babling Goſſip of the aire,
Cry out *Oliuia*: O you ſhould not reſt
Betweene the elements of ayre, and earth,
But you ſhould pittie me.
Ol. You might do much:
What is your Parentage?
Vio. Aboue my fortunes, yet my ſtate is well:
I am a Gentleman.
Ol Get you to your Lord:
I cannot loue him: let him ſend no more,
Vnleſſe (perchance) you come to me againe,
To tell me how he takes it: Fare you well:
I thanke you for your paines: ſpend this for mee.
Vio. I am no feede poaſt, Lady; keepe your purſe,
My Maſter, not my ſelfe, lackes recompence.
Loue make his heart of flint, that you ſhal loue,
And let your feruour like my maſters be,
Plac'd in contempt: Farwell fayre crueltie. *Exit*
Ol. What is your Parentage?
Aboue my fortunes, yet my ſtate is well,
I am a Gentleman. Ile be ſworne thou art,
Thy tongue, thy face, thy limbes, actions, and ſpirit,
Do giue thee fiue-fold blazon: not too faſt: ſoft, ſoft,
Vnleſſe the Maſter were the man. How now?
Euen ſo quickly may one catch the plague?
Me thinkes I feele this youths perfections
With an inuiſible, and ſubtle ſtealth
To creepe in at mine eyes. Well, let it be.
What hoa, *Maluolio*.

Enter Maluolio.

Mal Heere Madam, at your ſeruice.
Ol Run after that ſame peeuiſh Meſſenger
The Countes man: he left this Ring behinde him
Would I, or not: tell him, Ile none of it.
Deſire him not to flatter with his Lord,
Nor hold him vp with hopes, I am not for him:
If that the youth will come this way to morrow,
Ile giue him reaſons for't: hie thee *Maluolio*.
Mal Madam, I will. *Exit.*
Ol I do I know not what, and feare to finde
Mine eye too great a flatterer for my minde:

Fate

Fate, ſhew thy force, our ſelues we do not owe,
What is decreed, muſt be: and be this ſo.

Finis, Actus primus.

Actus Secundus, Scæna prima.

Enter Antonio & Sebaſtian.

Ant. Will you ſtay no longer: nor will you not that I go with you.

Seb. By your patience, no: my ſtarres ſhine darkely ouer me; the malignancie of my fate, might perhaps diſtemper yours; therefore I ſhall craue of you your leaue, that I may beare my euils alone. It were a bad recompence for your loue, to lay any of them on you.

An. Let me yet know of you, whither you are bound.

Seb. No ſooth ſir: my determinate voyage is meere extrauagancie. But I perceiue in you ſo excellent a touch of modeſtie, that you will not extort from me, what I am willing to keepe in: therefore it charges me in manners, the rather to expreſſe my ſelfe: you muſt know of mee then *Antonio*, my name is *Sebaſtian* (which I call'd *Rodorigo*) my father was that *Sebaſtian* of *Meſſaline*, whom I know you haue heard of. He left behinde him, my ſelfe, and a ſiſter, both borne in an houre: if the Heauens had beene pleas'd, would we had ſo ended. But you ſir, alter'd that, for ſome houre before you tooke me from the breach of the ſea, was my ſiſter drown'd.

Ant. Alas the day.

Seb. A Lady ſir, though it was ſaid ſhee much reſembled me, was yet of many accounted beautiful: but thogh I could not with ſuch eſtimable wonder ouer farre beleeue that, yet thus farre I will boldly publiſh her, ſhee bore a minde that enuy could not but call faire: Shee is drown'd already ſir with ſalt water, though I ſeeme to drowne her remembrance againe with more.

Ant. Pardon me ſir, your bad entertainment.

Seb. O good *Antonio*, forgiue me your trouble.

Ant. If you will not murther me for my loue, let mee be your ſeruant.

Seb. If you will not vndo what you haue done, that is kill him, whom you haue recouer'd, deſire it not. Fare ye well at once, my boſome is full of kindneſſe, and I am yet ſo neere the manners of my mother, that vpon the leaſt occaſion more, mine eyes will tell tales of me: I am bound to the Count *Orſino's* Court, farewell. *Exit*

Ant. The gentleneſſe of all the gods go with thee:
I haue many enemies in *Orſino's* Court,
Elſe would I very ſhortly ſee thee there:
But come what may, I do adore thee ſo,
That danger ſhall ſeeme ſport, and I will go. *Exit.*

Scæna Secunda.

Enter Viola and Maluolio, at ſeuerall doores.

Mal. Were not you eu'n now, with the Counteſſe *Oliuia*?

Vio. Euen now ſir, on a moderate pace, I haue ſince ariu'd but hither.

Mal She returnes this Ring to you (ſir) you might haue ſaued mee my paines, to haue taken it away your ſelfe. She adds moreouer, that you ſhould put your Lord into a deſperate aſſurance, ſhe will none of him. And one thing more, that you be neuer ſo hardie to come againe in his affaires, vnleſſe it bee to report your Lords taking of this: receiue it ſo.

Vio. She tooke the Ring of me, Ile none of it.

Mal. Come ſir, you peeuiſhly threw it to her: and her will is, it ſhould be ſo return'd: If it bee worth ſtooping for, there it lies, in your eye: if not, bee it his that findes it. *Exit.*

Vio. I left no Ring with her: what meanes this Lady?
Fortune forbid my out-ſide haue not charm'd her:
She made good view of me, indeed ſo much,
That me thought her eyes had loſt her tongue,
For ſhe did ſpeake in ſtarts diſtractedly.
She loues me ſure, the cunning of her paſsion
Inuites me in this churliſh meſſenger:
None of my Lords Ring? Why he ſent her none;
I am the man, if it be ſo as tis,
Poore Lady, ſhe were better loue a dreame:
Diſguiſe, I ſee thou art a wickedneſſe,
Wherein the pregnant enemie does much.
How eaſie is it, for the proper falſe
In womens waxen hearts to ſet their formes:
Alas, O frailtie is the cauſe, not wee,
For ſuch as we are made, if ſuch we bee:
How will this fadge? My maſter loues her deerely,
And I (poore monſter) fond aſmuch on him:
And ſhe (miſtaken) ſeemes to dote on me:
What will become of this? As I am man,
My ſtate is deſperate for my maiſters loue:
As I am woman (now alas the day)
What thriftleſſe ſighes ſhall poore *Oliuia* breath?
O time, thou muſt vntangle this, not I,
It is too hard a knot for me t'vnty.

Scœna Tertia.

Enter Sir Toby, and Sir Andrew.

To. Approach Sir *Andrew*: not to bee a bedde after midnight, is to be vp betimes, and *Deliculo ſurgere*, thou know'ſt.

And. Nay by my troth I know not: but I know, to be vp late, is to be vp late.

To. A falſe concluſion: I hate it as an vnfill'd Canne. To be vp after midnight, and to go to bed then is early: ſo that to go to bed after midnight, is to goe to bed betimes. Does not our liues conſiſt of the foure Elements?

And. Faith ſo they ſay, but I thinke it rather conſiſts of eating and drinking.

To. Th'art a ſcholler; let vs therefore eate and drinke *Marian* I ſay, a ſtoope of wine.

Enter Clowne.

And. Heere comes the foole yfaith.

Clo. How now my harts: Did you neuer ſee the Picture of we three?

To. Welcome aſſe, now let's haue a catch.

And. By my troth the foole has an excellent breaſt. I had rather then forty ſhillings I had ſuch a legge, and ſo ſweet a breath to ſing, as the foole has. Inſooth thou waſt in very gracious fooling laſt night, when thou ſpok'ſt of *Pigrogromitus*, of the *Vapians* paſsing the Equinoctial of *Queubus*: 'twas very good yfaith: I ſent thee ſixe pence for

for thy Lemon, hadſt it?

Clo. I did impeticos thy gratillity: for *Maluolios* noſe is no Whip-ſtocke. My Lady has a white hand, and the Mermidons are no bottle-ale houſes.

An. Excellent: Why this is the beſt fooling, when all is done: Now a ſong.

To. Come on, there is ſixe pence for you. Let's haue a ſong.

An. There's a teſtrill of me too: if one knight giue a

Clo. Would you haue a loue-ſong, or a ſong of good life?

To. A loue ſong, a loue ſong.

An. I, I. I care not for good life.

Clowne ſings.

O Miſtris mine where are you roming?
O ſtay and heare, your true loues coming,
That can ſing both high and low.
Trip no further prettie ſweeting.
Iourneys end in louers meeting,
Euery wiſe mans ſonne doth know.

An. Excellent good, ifaith.

To Good, good.

Clo. *What is loue, tis not heereafter,*
Preſent mirth, hath preſent laughter:
What's to come, is ſtill vnſure.
In delay there lies no plentie,
Then come kiſſe me ſweet and twentie:
Youths a ſtuffe will not endure.

An. A mellifluous voyce, as I am true knight.

To. A contagious breath.

An. Very ſweet, and contagious ifaith.

To. To heare by the noſe, it is dulcet in contagion. But ſhall we make the Welkin dance indeed? Shall wee rowze the night-Owle in a Catch, that will drawe three ſoules out of one Weauer? Shall we do that?

And. And you loue me, let's doo't: I am dogge at a Catch.

Clo. Byrlady ſir, and ſome dogs will catch well.

An. Moſt certaine: Let our Catch be, *Thou Knaue*

Clo. *Hold thy peace, thou Knaue* knight. I ſhall be conſtrain'd in't, to call thee knaue, Knight.

An. 'Tis not the firſt time I haue conſtrained one to call me knaue. Begin foole: it begins, *Hold thy peace.*

Clo. I ſhall neuer begin if I hold my peace.

An. Good ifaith: Come begin. *Catch ſung*

Enter Maria.

Mar. What a catterwalling doe you keepe heere? If my Ladie haue not call'd vp her Steward *Maluolio*, and bid him turne you out of doores, neuer truſt me.

To. My Lady's a *Catayan*, we are politicians, *Maluolios* a Peg-a-ramſie, and *Three merry men be wee.* Am not I conſanguinious? Am I not of her blood: tilly vally. Ladie, *There dwelt a man in Babylon, Lady, Lady.*

Clo. Beſhrew me, the knights in admirable fooling.

An. I, he do's well enough if he be diſpos'd, and ſo do I too: he does it with a better grace, but I do it more naturall.

To *O the twelfe day of December*

Mar. For the loue o God peace.

Enter Maluolio.

Mal. My maſters are you mad? Or what are you? Haue you no wit, manners, nor honeſtie, but to gabble like Tinkers at this time of night? Do yee make an Alehouſe of my Ladies houſe, that ye ſqueak out your Coziers Catches without any mitigation or remorſe of voice? Is there no reſpect of place, perſons, nor time in you?

To. We did keepe time ſir in our Catches. Snecke vp.

Mal. *Sir Toby*, I muſt be round with you. My Lady bad me tell you, that though ſhe harbors you as her kinſman, ſhe's nothing ally'd to your diſorders. If you can ſeparate your ſelfe and your miſdemeanors, you are welcome to the houſe: if not, and it would pleaſe you to take leaue of her, ſhe is very willing to bid you farewell.

To. Farewell deere heart, ſince I muſt needs be gone.

Mar. Nay good Sir *Toby.*

Clo. His eyes do ſhew his dayes are almoſt done.

Mal. Is't euen ſo?

To. But I will neuer dye.

Clo. Sir *Toby* there you lye.

Mal. This is much credit to you.

To. *Shall I bid him go.*

Clo. *What and if you do?*

To. *Shall I bid him go, and ſpare not?*

Clo. *O no, no, no, no, you dare not*

To. Out o'tune ſir, ye lye: Art any more then a Steward? Doſt thou thinke becauſe thou art vertuous, there ſhall be no more Cakes and Ale?

Clo. Yes by *S.*Anne, and Ginger ſhall bee hotte y'th mouth too.

To. Th'art i'th right. Goe ſir, rub your Chaine with crums. A ſtope of Wine *Maria.*

Mal. Miſtris Mary, if you priz'd my Ladies fauour at any thing more then contempt, you would not giue meanes for this vnciuill rule; ſhe ſhall know of it by this hand. *Exit*

Mar. Go ſhake your eares.

An. 'Twere as good a deede as to drink when a mans a hungrie, to challenge him the field, and then to breake promiſe with him, and make a foole of him.

To. Doo't knight, Ile write thee a Challenge: or Ile deliuer thy indignation to him by word of mouth.

Mar. Sweet Sir Toby be patient for to night: Since the youth of the Counts was to day with my Lady, ſhe is much out of quiet. For Monſieur Maluolio, let me alone with him: If I do not gull him into an ayword, and make him a common recreation, do not thinke I haue witte enough to lye ſtraight in my bed: I know I can do it.

To. Poſſeſſe vs, poſſeſſe vs, tell vs ſomething of him.

Mar. Marrie ſir, ſometimes he is a kinde of Puritane.

An. O, if I thought that, Ide beate him like a dogge.

To. What for being a Puritan, thy exquiſite reaſon, deere knight.

An. I haue no exquiſite reaſon for't, but I haue reaſon good enough.

Mar. The diu'll a Puritane that hee is, or any thing conſtantly but a time-pleaſer, an affection'd Aſſe, that cons State without booke, and vtters it by great ſwarths. The beſt perſwaded of himſelfe: ſo cram'd (as he thinkes) with excellencies, that it is his grounds of faith, that all that looke on him, loue him: and on that vice in him, will my reuenge finde notable cauſe to worke.

To. What wilt thou do?

Mar. I will drop in his way ſome obſcure Epiſtles of loue, wherein by the colour of his beard, the ſhape of his legge, the manner of his gate, the expreſſure of his eye, forehead, and complection, he ſhall finde himſelfe moſt feelingly perſonated. I can write very like my Ladie your Neece, on a forgotten matter wee can hardly make diſtinction of our hands.

To. Excellent, I ſmell a deuice.

An. I hau't in my noſe too.

To. He ſhall thinke by the Letters that thou wilt drop that

that they come from my Neece, and that shee's in loue with him.

Mar. My purpose is indeed a horse of that colour.

An. And your horse now would make him an Asse

Mar. Asse, I doubt not.

An. O twill be admirable.

Mar. Sport royall I warrant you: I know my Physicke will worke with him, I will plant you two, and let the Foole make a third, where he shall finde the Letter: obserue his construction of it: For this night to bed, and dreame on the euent: Farewell. *Exit*

To. Good night *Penthisilea.*

An. Before me she's a good wench.

To. She's a beagle true bred, and one that adores me: what o'that?

An. I was ador'd once too.

To. Let's to bed knight: Thou hadst neede send for more money.

An. If I cannot recouer your Neece, I am a foule way out.

To. Send for money knight, if thou hast her not i'th end, call me Cut.

An. If I do not, neuer trust me, take it how you will.

To. Come, come, Ile go burne some Sacke, tis too late to go to bed now: Come knight, come knight. *Exeunt*

Scena Quarta.

Enter Duke, Viola, Curio, and others.

Du. Giue me some Musick; Now good morow frends.
Now good *Cesario*, but that peece of song,
That old and Anticke song we heard last night;
Me thought it did releeue my passion much,
More then light ayres, and recollected termes
Of these most briske and giddy-paced times.
Come, but one verse.

Cur. He is not heere (so please your Lordshippe) that should sing it?

Du. Who was it?

Cur. *Feste* the Iester my Lord, a foole that the Ladie *Oliuiaes* Father tooke much delight in. He is about the house.

Du. Seeke him out, and play the tune the while.
Musicke playes.
Come hither Boy, if euer thou shalt loue
In the sweet pangs of it, remember me:
For such as I am, all true Louers are,
Vnstaid and skittish in all motions else,
Saue in the constant image of the creature
That is belou'd. How dost thou like this tune?

Vio. It giues a verie eccho to the seate
Where loue is thron'd.

Du. Thou dost speake masterly,
My life vpon't, yong though thou art, thine eye
Hath staid vpon some fauour that it loues:
Hath it not boy?

Vio. A little, by your fauour.

Du. What kinde of woman ist?

Vio. Of your complection.

Du. She is not worth thee then. What yeares ifaith?

Vio. About your yeeres my Lord.

Du. Too old by heauen: Let still the woman take
An elder then her selfe, so weares she to him;
So swayes she leuell in her husbands heart:
For boy, howeuer we do praise our selues,
Our fancies are more giddie and vnfirme,
More longing, wauering, sooner lost and worne,
Then womens are.

Vio. I thinke it well my Lord.

Du. Then let thy Loue be yonger then thy selfe,
Or thy affection cannot hold the bent:
For women are as Roses, whose faire flowre
Being once displaid, doth fall that verie howre.

Vio. And so they are: alas, that they are so:
To die, euen when they to perfection grow.

Enter Curio & Clowne.

Du. O fellow come, the song we had last night:
Marke it Cesario, it is old and plaine;
The Spinsters and the Knitters in the Sun,
And the free maides that weaue their thred with bones,
Do vse to chaunt it: it is silly sooth,
And dallies with the innocence of loue,
Like the old age.

Clo. Are you ready Sir?

Duke I prethee sing. *Musicke.*

The Song.

Come away, come away death,
And in sad cypresse let me be laide.
Fye away, fie away breath,
I am slaine by a faire cruell maide:
My shrowd of white, stuck all with Ew, O prepare it.
My part of death no one so true did share it.

Not a flower, not a flower sweete
On my blacke coffin, let there be strewne:
Not a friend, not a friend greet
My poore corpes, where my bones shall be throwne:
A thousand thousand sighes to saue, lay me o where
Sad true louer neuer find my graue, to weepe there.

Du. There's for thy paines

Clo. No paines sir, I take pleasure in singing sir.

Du. Ile pay thy pleasure then

Clo. Truely sir, and pleasure will be paide one time, or another.

Du. Giue me now leaue, to leaue thee.

Clo Now the melancholly God protect thee, and the Tailor make thy doublet of changeable Taffata, for thy minde is a very Opall. I would haue men of such constancie put to Sea, that their businesse might be euery thing, and their intent euerie where, for that's it, that alwayes makes a good voyage of nothing. Farewell. *Exit*

Du. Let all the rest giue place: Once more *Cesario*,
Get thee to yond same soueraigne crueltie:
Tell her my loue, more noble then the world
Prizes not quantitie of dirtie lands,
The parts that fortune hath bestow'd vpon her:
Tell her I hold as giddily as Fortune:
But 'tis that miracle, and Queene of Iems
That nature prankes her in, attracts my soule.

Vio. But if she cannot loue you sir

Du. It cannot be so answer'd.

Vio. Sooth but you must
Say that some Lady, as perhappes there is,
Hath for your loue as great a pang of heart
As you haue for *Oliuia*: you cannot loue her:
You tel her so: Must she not then be answer'd?

Du. There is no womans sides

Can

Can bide the beating of so strong a passion,
As loue doth giue my heart: no womans heart
So bigge, to hold so much, they lacke retention.
Alas, their loue may be call'd appetite,
No motion of the Liuer, but the Pallat,
That suffer surfet, cloyment, and reuolt,
But mine is all as hungry as the Sea,
And can digest as much, make no compare
Betweene that loue a woman can beare me,
And that I owe *Oliuia*.

Vio. I but I know

Du. What dost thou knowe?

Vio. Too well what loue women to men may owe:
In faith they are as true of heart, as we.
My Father had a daughter lou'd a man
As it might be perhaps, were I a woman
I should your Lordship.

Du. And what's her history?

Vio. A blanke my Lord: she neuer told her loue,
But let concealment like a worme i'th budde
Feede on her damaske cheeke: she pin'd in thought,
And with a greene and yellow melancholly,
She sate like Patience on a Monument,
Smiling at greefe. Was not this loue indeede?
We men may say more, sweare more, but indeed
Our shewes are more then will: for still we proue
Much in our vowes, but little in our loue.

Du. But di'de thy sister of her loue my Boy?

Vio. I am all the daughters of my Fathers house,
And all the brothers too: and yet I know not
Sir, shall I to this Lady?

Du. I that's the Theame,
To her in haste: giue her this Iewell: say,
My loue can giue no place, bide no denay. *exeunt*

Scena Quinta.

Enter Sir Toby, Sir Andrew, and Fabian.

To. Come thy wayes Signior *Fabian*.

Fab. Nay Ile come: if I loose a scruple of this sport, let me be boyl'd to death with Melancholly.

To. Wouldst thou not be glad to haue the niggardly Rascally sheepe-biter, come by some notable shame?

Fa. I would exult man: you know he brought me out o'fauour with my Lady, about a Beare-baiting heere.

To. To anger him wee'l haue the Beare againe, and we will foole him blacke and blew, shall we not sir *Andrew*?

An. And we do not, it is pittie of our liues.

Enter Maria.

To. Heere comes the little villaine: How now my Mettle of India?

Mar. Get ye all three into the box tree: *Maluolio's* comming downe this walke, he has beene yonder i'the Sunne practising behauiour to his own shadow this halfe houre: obserue him for the loue of Mockerie: for I know this Letter wil make a contemplatiue Ideot of him. Close in the name of ieasting, lye thou there: for heere comes the Trowt, that must be caught with tickling. *Exit*

Enter Maluolio.

Mal. 'Tis but Fortune, all is fortune. *Maria* once told me she did affect me, and I haue heard her self come thus neere, that should shee fancie, it should bee one of my complection. Besides she vses me with a more exalted respect, then any one else that followes her. What should I thinke on't?

To. Heere's an ouer-weening rogue.

Fa. Oh peace: Contemplation makes a rare Turkey Cocke of him, how he iets vnder his aduanc'd plumes.

And. Slight I could so beate the Rogue.

To. Peace I say

Mal. To be Count *Maluolio*.

To. Ah Rogue.

An. Pistoll him, pistoll him.

To. Peace, peace.

Mal. There is example for't: The Lady of the *Strachy*, married the yeoman of the wardrob

An. Fie on him Iezabel.

Fa. O peace, now he's deepely in: looke how imagination blowes him.

Mal. Hauing beene three moneths married to her, sitting in my state.

To. O for a stone-bow to hit him in the eye.

Mal. Calling my Officers about me, in my branch'd Veluet gowne: hauing come from a day bedde, where I haue left *Oliuia* sleeping

To. Fire and Brimstone.

Fa. O peace, peace.

Mal. And then to haue the humor of state: and after a demure trauaile of regard: telling them I knowe my place, as I would they should doe theirs: to aske for my kinsman *Toby*.

To. Boltes and shackles.

Fa. Oh peace, peace, peace, now, now.

Mal. Seauen of my people with an obedient start, make out for him I frowne the while, and perchance winde vp my watch, or play with my some rich Iewell: *Toby* approaches; curtsies there to me.

To. Shall this fellow liue?

Fa. Though our silence be drawne from vs with cars yet peace.

Mal. I extend my hand to him thus: quenching my familiar smile with an austere regard of controll.

To. And do's not *Toby* take you a blow o'the lippes, then?

Mal. Saying, Cosine *Toby*, my Fortunes hauing cast me on your Neece, giue me this prerogatiue of speech.

To. What, what?

Mal. You must amend your drunkennesse.

To. Out scab.

Fab. Nay patience, or we breake the sinewes of our plot?

Mal Besides you waste the treasure of your time, with a foolish knight.

And. That's mee I warrant you.

Mal. One sir *Andrew*.

And. I knew 'twas I, for many do call mee foole.

Mal. What employment haue we heere?

Fa. Now is the Woodcocke neere the gin.

To. Oh peace, and the spirit of humors intimate reading aloud to him.

Mal. By my life this is my Ladies hand: these bee her very *C's*, her *V's*, and her *T's*, and thus makes shee her great *P's*. It is in contempt of question her hand.

An. Her *C's*, her *V's*, and her *T's*: why that?

Mal. *To the vnknowne belou'd, this, and my good Wishes*: Her very Phrases: By your leaue wax. Soft, and the impressure her *Lucrece*, with which she vses to seale: tis my Lady: To whom should this be?

Fab. This winnes him, Liuer and all.

Mal.

Mal. *Ioue knowes I loue, but who, Lips do not mooue, no man must know.* No man must know. What followes? The numbers alter'd: No man must know,
If this should be thee *Maluolio*?

To. Marrie hang thee brocke.

Mal. *I may command where I adore, but silence like a Lucresse knife:*
With bloodlesse stroke my heart doth gore, M. O. A. I. doth sway my life.

Fa. A fustian riddle.

To. Excellent Wench, say I.

Mal. *M.O.A.I.* doth sway my life Nay but first let me see, let me see, let me see.

Fab. What dish a poyson has she drest him?

To. And with what wing the stallion checkes at it?

Mal. *I may command, where I adore*: Why shee may command me: I serue her, she is my Ladie. Why this is euident to any formall capacitie. There is no obstruction in this, and the end: What should that Alphabeticall position portend, if I could make that resemble something in me? Softly, *M.O.A.I.*

To O I, make vp that, he is now at a cold sent

Fab. Sowter will cry vpon't for all this, though it bee as ranke as a Fox

Mal. *M. Maluolio, M.* why that begins my name.

Fab. Did not I say he would worke it out, the Curre is excellent at faults.

Mal. *M.* But then there is no consonancy in the sequell that suffers vnder probation: *A.* should follow, but *O.* does.

Fa. And *O* shall end, I hope

To. I, or Ile cudgell him, and make him cry *O.*

Mal. And then *I.* comes behind.

Fa. I, and you had any eye behinde you, you might see more detraction at your heeles, then Fortunes before you.

Mal. *M,O,A,I.* This simulation is not as the former: and yet to crush this a little, it would bow to mee, for euery one of these Letters are in my name. Soft, here followes prose: *If this fall into thy hand, reuolue.* In my stars I am aboue thee, but be not affraid of greatnesse: Some are become great, some atcheeues greatnesse, and some haue greatnesse thrust vppon em. Thy fates open theyr hands, let thy blood and spirit embrace them, and to inure thy selfe to what thou art like to be: cast thy humble slough, and appeare fresh. Be opposite with a kinsman, surly with seruants: Let thy tongue tang arguments of state; put thy selfe into the tricke of singularitie. Shee thus aduises thee, that sighes for thee. Remember who commended thy yellow stockings, and wish'd to see thee euer crosse garter'd: I say remember, goe too, thou art made if thou desir'st to be so: If not, let me see thee a steward still, the fellow of seruants, and not woorthie to touch Fortunes fingers Farewell, Shee that would alter seruices with thee, tht fortunate vnhappy daylight and champian discouers not more: This is open, I will bee proud, I will reade politicke Authours, I will baffle Sir *Toby*, I will wash off grosse acquaintance, I will be point deuise, the very man. I do not now foole my selfe, to let imagination iade mee; for euery reason excites to this, that my Lady loues me. She did commend my yellow stockings of late, shee did praise my legge being crosse-garter'd, and in this she manifests her selfe to my loue, & with a kinde of iniunction driues mee to these habites of her liking. I thanke my starres, I am happy: I will bee strange, stout, in yellow stockings, and crosse Garter'd, euen with the swiftnesse of putting on. Ioue, and my starres be praised. Heere is yet a postscript. *Thou canst not choose but know who I am. If thou entertainst my loue, let it appeare in thy smiling, thy smiles become thee well. Therefore in my presence still smile, deere my sweete, I prethee* Ioue I thanke thee, I will smile, I wil do euery thing that thou wilt haue me. *Exit*

Fab. I will not giue my part of this sport for a pension of thousands to be paid from the Sophy.

To. I could marry this wench for this deuice.

An. So could I too.

To. And aske no other dowry with her, but such another iest.

Enter Maria.

An. Nor I neither

Fab. Heere comes my noble gull catcher.

To Wilt thou set thy foote o'my necke.

An. Or o'mine either?

To. Shall I play my freedome at tray-trip, and becom thy bondslaue?

An. Ifaith, or I either?

Tob. Why, thou hast put him in such a dreame, that when the image of it leaues him, he must run mad.

Ma. Nay but say true, do's it worke vpon him?

To. Like Aqua vite with a Midwife.

Mar. If you will then see the fruites of the sport, mark his first approach before my Lady: hee will come to her in yellow stockings, and 'tis a colour she abhorres, and crosse garter'd, a fashion shee detests: and hee will smile vpon her, which will now be so vnsuteable to her disposition, being addicted to a melancholly, as shee is, that it cannot but turn him into a notable contempt: if you wil see it follow me.

To. To the gates of Tartar, thou most excellent diuell of wit.

And Ile make one too *Exeunt.*

Finis Actus secundus

Actus Tertius, Scæna prima.

Enter Viola and Clowne.

Vio. Saue thee Friend and thy Musick: dost thou liue by thy Tabor?

Clo. No sir, I liue by the Church.

Vio. Art thou a Churchman?

Clo. No such matter sir, I do liue by the Church: For, I do liue at my house, and my house dooth stand by the Church

Vio. So thou maist say the Kings lyes by a begger, if a begger dwell neer him: or the Church stands by thy Tabor, if thy Tabor stand by the Church.

Clo. You haue said sir: To see this age: A sentence is but a cheu'rill gloue to a good witte, how quickely the wrong side may be turn'd outward.

Vio. Nay that's certaine: they that dally nicely with words, may quickely make them wanton.

Clo. I would therefore my sister had had no name Sir.

Vio. Why man?

Clo. Why sir, her names a word, and to dallie with that word, might make my sister wanton: But indeede, words are very Rascals, since bonds disgrac'd them.

Vio. Thy reason man?

Clo

Clo. Troth sir, I can yeeld you none without wordes, and wordes are growne so false, I am loath to proue reason with them.

Vio I warrant thou art a merry fellow, and car'st for nothing.

Clo. Not so sir, I do care for something: but in my conscience sir, I do not care for you: if that be to care for nothing sir, I would it would make you inuisible.

Vio. Art not thou the Lady *Oliuia s* foole?

Clo. No indeed sir, the Lady *Oliuia* has no folly, shee will keepe no foole sir, till she be married, and fooles are as like husbands, as Pilchers are to Herrings, the Husbands the bigger, I am indeede not her foole, but hir corrupter of words.

Vio. I saw thee late at the Count *Orsino s*

Clo. Foolery sir, does walke about the Orbe like the Sun, it shines euery where. I would be sorry sir, but the Foole should be as oft with your Master, as with my Mistris: I thinke I saw your wisedome there.

Vio. Nay, and thou passe vpon me, Ile no more with thee. Hold there's expences for thee.

Clo. Now Ioue in his next commodity of hayre, send thee a beard.

Vio. By my troth Ile tell thee, I am almost sicke for one, though I would not haue it grow on my chinne. Is thy Lady within?

Clo Would not a paire of these haue bred sir?

Vio. Yes being kept together, and put to vse.

Clo. I would play Lord *Pandarus* of *Phrygia* sir, to bring a *Cressida* to this *Troylus*

Vio. I vnderstand you sir, tis well begg'd.

Clo The matter I hope is not great sir; begging, but a begger: *Cressida* was a begger. My Lady is within sir. I will conster to them whence you come, who you are, and what you would are out of my welkin, I might say Element, but the word is ouer-worne. *exit*

Vio. This fellow is wise enough to play the foole,
And to do that well, craues a kinde of wit:
He must obserue their mood on whom he iests,
The quality of persons, and the time
And like the Haggard, cheeke at euery Feather
That comes before his eye. This is a practice,
As full of labour as a Wise-mans Art:
For folly that he wisely shewes, is fit;
But wisemens folly falne, quite taint their wit

Enter Sir Toby and Andrew.

To. Saue you Gentleman.

Vio. And you sir.

And. Dieu vou guard Monsieur

Vio. Et vouz ousie vostre seruiture.

An. I hope sir, you are, and I am yours.

To. Will you incounter the house, my Neece is desirous you should enter, if your trade be to her.

Vio. I am bound to your Neece sir, I meane she is the list of my voyage.

To. Taste your legges sir, put them to motion.

Vio. My legges do better vnderstand me sir, then I vnderstand what you meane by bidding me taste my legs.

To. I meane to go sir, to enter.

Vio. I will answer you with gate and entrance, but we are preuented.

Enter Oliuia, and Gentlewoman.

Most excellent accomplish'd Lady, the heauens raine Odours on you.

And. That youth's a rare Courtier, raine odours, wel.

Vio. My matter hath no voice Lady, but to your owne most pregnant and vouchsafed eare

And. Odours, pregnant, and vouchsafed: Ile get 'em all three already.

Ol. Let the Garden doore be shut, and leaue mee to my hearing. Giue me your hand sir.

Vio My dutie Madam, and most humble seruice.

Ol. What is your name?

Vio. Cesario is your seruants name, faire Princesse.

Ol. My seruant sir? 'Twas neuer merry world,
Since lowly feigning was call'd complement:
y'are seruant to the Count *Orsino* youth.

Vio And he is yours, and his must needs be yours:
your seruants seruant, is your seruant Madam.

Ol. For him, I thinke not on him: for his thoughts,
Would they were blankes, rather then fill'd with me.

Vio Madam, I come to whet your gentle thoughts
On his behalfe.

Ol. O by your leaue I pray you.
I bad you neuer speake againe of him;
But would you vndertake another suite
I had rather heare you, to solicit that,
Then Musicke from the spheares.

Vio. Deere Lady.

Ol. Giue me leaue, beseech you: I did send,
After the last enchantment you did heare,
A Ring in chace of you. So did I abuse
My selfe, my seruant, and I feare me you:
Vnder your hard construction must I sit,
To force that on you in a shamefull cunning
Which you knew none of yours. What might you think?
Haue you not set mine Honor at the stake,
And baited it with all th'vnmuzled thoughts
That tyrannous heart can think? To one of your receiuing
Enough is shewne, a Cipresse, not a bosome,
Hides my heart: so let me heare you speake.

Vio I pittie you.

Ol That's a degree to loue.

Vio. No not a grize: for tis a vulgar proofe
That verie oft we pitty enemies.

Ol Why then me thinkes 'tis time to smile agen:
O world, how apt the poore are to be proud?
If one should be a prey, how much the better
To fall before the Lion, then the Wolfe?

Clocke strikes.

The clocke vpbraides me with the waste of time:
Be not affraid good youth, I will not haue you,
And yet when wit and youth is come to haruest,
your wife is like to reape a proper man:
There lies your way, due West.

Vio. Then Westward hoe:
Grace and good disposition attend your Ladyship:
you'l nothing Madam to my Lord, by me:

Ol. Stay: I prethee tell me what thou thinkst of me?

Vio. That you do thinke you are not what you are.

Ol. If I thinke so, I thinke the same of you.

Vio. Then thinke you right: I am not what I am.

Ol. I would you were, as I would haue you be.

Vio Would it be better Madam, then I am?
I wish it might, for now I am your foole.

Ol. O what a deale of scorne, lookes beautifull?
In the contempt and anger of his lip,
A murdrous guilt shewes not it selfe more soone,
Then loue that would seeme hid: Loues night, is noone.
Cesario, by the Roses of the Spring,
By maid-hood, honor, truth, and euery thing,
I loue thee so, that maugre all thy pride,

Nor wit, nor reason, can my passion hide:
Do not extort thy reasons from this clause,
For that I woo, thou therefore hast no cause:
But rather reason thus, with reason fetter;
Loue sought, is good: but giuen vnsought, is better.
Vio. By innocence I sweare, and by my youth,
I haue one heart, one bosome, and one truth,
And that no woman has, nor neuer none
Shall mistris be of it, saue I alone.
And so adieu good Madam, neuer more,
Will I my Masters teares to you deplore.
Ol. Yet come againe: for thou perhaps mayst moue
That heart which now abhorres to like his loue. *Exeunt*

Scœna Secunda.

Enter Sir Toby, Sir Andrew, and Fabian.

And. No faith, Ile not stay a iot longer:

To. Thy reason deere venom, giue thy reason.

Fab. You must needes yeelde your reason, Sir *Andrew*?

And. Marry I saw your Neece do more fauours to the Counts Seruing-man, then euer she bestow'd vpon mee: I saw't i'th Orchard.

To. Did she see the while, old boy, tell me that.

And. As plaine as I see you now.

Fab. This was a great argument of loue in her toward you.

And. S'light; will you make an Asse o'me.

Fab. I will proue it legitimate sir, vpon the Oathes of iudgement, and reason.

To. And they haue beene grand Iurie men, since before *Noah* was a Saylor.

Fab. Shee did shew fauour to the youth in your sight, onely to exasperate you, to awake your dormouse valour, to put fire in your Heart, and brimstone in your Liuer: you should then haue accosted her, and with some excellent iests, fire-new from the mint, you should haue bangd the youth into dumbenesse: this was look'd for at your hand, and this was baulkt: the double gilt of this opportunitie you let time wash off, and you are now sayld into the North of my Ladies opinion, where you will hang like an ysickle on a Dutchmans beard, vnlesse you do redeeme it, by some laudable attempt, either of valour or policie.

And. And't be any way, it must be with Valour, for policie I hate: I had as liefe be a Brownist, as a Politician.

To. Why then build me thy fortunes vpon the basis of valour. Challenge me the Counts youth to fight with him hurt him in eleuen places, my Neece shall take note of it, and assure thy selfe, there is no loue-Broker in the world, can more preuaile in mans commendation with woman, then report of valour.

Fab. There is no way but this sir *Andrew*.

An. Will either of you beare me a challenge to him?

To Go, write it in a martial hand, be curst and briefe: it is no matter how wittie, so it bee eloquent, and full of inuention: taunt him with the license of Inke: if thou thou'st him some thrice, it shall not be amisse, and as many Lyes, as will lye in thy sheete of paper, although the sheete were bigge enough for the bedde of *Ware* in England, set 'em downe, go about it. Let there bee gaulle enough in thy inke, though thou write with a Goose-pen, no matter: about it.

And. Where shall I finde you?

To. Wee'l call thee at the Cubiculo: Go.

Exit Sir Andrew.

Fa. This is a deere Manakin to you Sir *Toby*.

To. I haue beene deere to him lad, some two thousand strong, or so.

Fa. We shall haue a rare Letter from him; but you'le not deliuer't.

To. Neuer trust me then: and by all meanes stirre on the youth to an answer. I thinke Oxen and waine-ropes cannot hale them together. For *Andrew*, if he were open'd and you finde so much blood in his Liuer, as will clog the foote of a flea, Ile eate the rest of th'anatomy.

Fab. And his opposit the youth beares in his visage no great presage of cruelty.

Enter Maria.

To. Looke where the youngest Wren of mine comes.

Mar. If you desire the spleene, and will laughe your selues into stitches, follow me; yond gull *Maluolio* is turned Heathen, a verie Renegatho; for there is no christian that meanes to be saued by beleeuing rightly, can euer beleeue such impossible passages of grossenesse. Hee's in yellow stockings.

To. And crosse garter'd?

Mar. Most villanously: like a Pedant that keepes a Schoole i'th Church: I haue dogg'd him like his murtherer. He does obey euery point of the Letter that I dropt, to betray him: He does smile his face into more lynes, then is in the new Mappe, with the augmentation of the Indies: you haue not seene such a thing as tis: I can hardly forbeare hurling things at him, I know my Ladie will strike him: if shee doe, hee'l smile, and take't for a great fauour.

To. Come bring vs, bring vs where he is.

Exeunt Omnes.

Scœna Tertia.

Enter Sebastian and Anthonio.

Seb. I would not by my will haue troubled you,
But since you make your pleasure of your paines,
I will no further chide you.
Ant. I could not stay behinde you: my desire
(More sharpe then filed steele) did spurre me forth,
And not all loue to see you (though so much
As might haue drawne one to a longer voyage)
But iealousie, what might befall your trauell,
Being skillesse in these parts: which to a stranger,
Vnguided, and vnfriended, often proue
Rough, and vnhospitable. My willing loue,
The rather by these arguments of feare
Set forth in your pursuite.
Seb. My kinde *Anthonio*,
I can no other answer make, but thankes,
And thankes: and euer oft good turnes,
Are shuffel'd off with such vncurrant pay:
But were my worth, as is my conscience firme,

You

You should finde better dealing : what's to do?
Shall we go see the reliques of this Towne?
Ant. To morrow sir, best first go see your Lodging?
Seb. I am not weary, and 'tis long to night
I pray you let vs satisfie our eyes
With the memorials, and the things of fame
That do renowne this City.
Ant. Would youl'd pardon me:
I do not without danger walke these streetes.
Once in a sea-fight 'gainst the Count his gallies,
I did some seruice, of such note indeede,
That were I tane heere, it would scarse be answer'd.
Seb. Belike you slew great number of his people.
Ant. Th offence is not of such a bloody nature,
Albeit the quality of the time, and quarrell
Might well haue giuen vs bloody argument:
It might haue since bene answer'd in repaying
What we tooke from them, which for Traffiques sake
Most of our City did. Onely my selfe stood out,
For which if I be lapsed in this place
I shall pay deere.
Seb. Do not then walke too open.
Ant. It doth not fit me: hold sir, here's my purse,
In the South Suburbes at the Elephant
Is best to lodge: I will bespeake our dyet,
Whiles you beguile the time, and feed your knowledge
With viewing of the Towne, there shall you haue me.
Seb. Why I your purse?
Ant. Haply your eye shall light vpon some toy
You haue desire to purchase: and your store
I thinke is not for idle Markets, sir.
Seb. Ile be your purse-bearer, and leaue you
For an houre.
Ant. To th'Elephant.
Seb. I do remember. *Exeunt.*

Scœna Quarta.

Enter Olivia and Maria.

Ol. I haue sent after him, he sayes hee'l come:
How shall I feast him? What bestow of him?
For youth is bought more oft, then begg'd, or borrow'd.
I speake too loud: Where's *Maluolio*, he is sad, and ciuill,
And suites well for a seruant with my fortunes,
Where is *Maluolio*?
Mar. He's comming Madame:
But in very strange manner. He is sure possest Madam.
Ol. Why what's the matter, does he raue?
Mar. No Madam, he does nothing but smile: your Ladyship were best to haue some guard about you, if hee come, for sure the man is tainted in's wits.
Ol. Go call him hither.

Enter Maluolio.

I am as madde as hee,
If sad and merry madnesse equall bee.
How now *Maluolio*?
Mal. Sweet Lady, ho, ho.
Ol. Smil'st thou? I sent for thee vpon a sad occasion.
Mal. Sad Lady, I could be sad:
This does make some obstruction in the blood:
This crosse gartering, but what of that?
If it please the eye of one, it is with me as the very true Sonnet is: Please one, and please all.
Mal. Why how doest thou man?
What is the matter with thee?
Mal. Not blacke in my minde, though yellow in my legges: It did come to his hands, and Commaunds shall be executed. I thinke we doe know the sweet Romane hand.
Ol. Wilt thou go to bed *Maluolio*?
Mal. To bed? I sweet heart, and Ile come to thee.
Ol. God comfort thee: Why dost thou smile so, and kisse thy hand so oft?
Mar. How do you *Maluolio*?
Maluo. At your request:
Yes Nightingales answere Dawes.
Mar. Why appeare you with this ridiculous boldnesse before my Lady.
Mal. Be not afraid of greatnesse: 'twas well writ.
Ol. What meanst thou by that *Maluolio*?
Mal. Some are borne great.
Ol. Ha?
Mal. Some atcheeue greatnesse.
Ol. What sayst thou?
Mal. And some haue greatnesse thrust vpon them.
Ol. Heauen restore thee.
Mal. Remember who commended thy yellow stockings.
Ol Thy yellow stockings?
Mal And wish'd to see thee crosse garter'd.
Ol. Crosse garter'd?
Mal. Go too, thou art made, if thou desir'st to be so.
Ol. Am I made?
Mal. If not, let me see thee a seruant still.
Ol. Why this is verie Midsommer madnesse.

Enter Seruant.

Ser. Madame, the young Gentleman of the Count *Orsino's* is return'd, I could hardly entreate him backe: he attends your Ladyships pleasure.
Ol. Ile come to him.
Good *Maria*, let this fellow be look d too. Where's my Cosine *Toby*, let some of my people haue a speciall care of him, I would not haue him miscarrie for the halfe of my Dowry. *exit*
Mal. Oh ho, do you come neere me now: no worse man then sir *Toby* to looke to me. This concurres directly with the Letter, she sends him on purpose, that I may appeare stubborne to him: for she incites me to that in the Letter. Cast thy humble slough sayes she: be opposite with a Kinsman, surly with seruants, let thy tongue langer with arguments of state, put thy selfe into the tricke of singularity: and consequently setts downe the manner how: as a sad face, a reuerend carriage, a slow tongue, in the habite of some Sir of note, and so foorth. I haue lymde her, but it is Ioues doing, and Ioue make me thankefull. And when she went away now, let this Fellow be look'd too: Fellow? not *Maluolio*, nor after my degree, but Fellow. Why euery thing adheres togither, that no dramme of a scruple, no scruple of a scruple, no obstacle, no incredulous or vnsafe circumstance: What can be saide? Nothing that can be, can come betweene me, and the full prospect of my hopes. Well Ioue, not I, is the doer of this, and he is to be thanked.

Enter Toby, Fabian, and Maria.

Z 2 To.

To. Which way is hee in the name of sanctity. If all the diuels of hell be drawne in little, and Legion himselfe possest him, yet Ile speake to him.

Fab. Heere he is, heere he is: how ist with you sir? How ist with you man?

Mal. Go off, I discard you: let me enioy my priuate: go off.

Mar. Lo, how hollow the fiend speakes within him; did not I tell you? Sir *Toby*, my Lady prayes you to haue a care of him.

Mal. Ah ha, does she so?

To. Go too, go too: peace, peace, wee must deale gently with him: Let me alone. How do you *Maluolio*? How ist with you? What man, defie the diuell: consider, he's an enemy to mankinde.

Mal. Do you know what you say?

Mar. La you, and you speake ill of the diuell, how he takes it at heart Pray God he be not bewitch'd.

Fab. Carry his water to th'wise woman.

Mar. Marry and it shall be done to morrow morning if I liue. My Lady would not loose him for more then ile say.

Mal. How now mistris?

Mar. Oh Lord.

To. Prethee hold thy peace, this is not the way: Doe you not see you moue him? Let me alone with him.

Fa. No way but gentlenesse, gently, gently: the Fiend is rough, and will not be roughly vs'd.

To. Why how now my bawcock? how dost ÿ chuck?

Mal. Sir.

To. I biddy, come with me. What man, tis not for grauity to play at cherrie-pit with sathan Hang him foul Colliar.

Mar. Get him to say his prayers, good sir *Toby* gette him to pray.

Mal. My prayers Minx.

Mar. No I warrant you, he will not heare of godlynesse.

Mal. Go hang your selues all: you are ydle shallowe things, I am not of your element, you shall knowe more heereafter. *Exit*

To. Ist possible?

Fa. If this were plaid vpon a stage now, I could condemne it as an improbable fiction.

To His very genius hath taken the infection of the deuice man.

Mar. Nay pursue him now, least the deuice take ayre, and taint.

Fa. Why we shall make him mad indeede.

Mar. The house will be the quieter.

To. Come, wee'l haue him in a darke room & bound. My Neece is already in the beleefe that he's mad: we may carry it thus for our pleasure, and his pennance, til our very pastime tyred out of breath, prompt vs to haue mercy on him: at which time, we wil bring the deuice to the bar and crowne thee for a finder of madmen: but see, but see.

Enter Sir Andrew.

Fa. More matter for a May morning.

An. Heere's the Challenge, reade it: I warrant there's vinegar and pepper in't.

Fab. Ist so sawcy?

And. I, ist? I warrant him: do but read.

To. Giue me.

Youth, whatsoeuer thou art, thou art but a scuruy fellow.

Fa. Good, and valiant.

To. Wonder not, nor admire not in thy minde why I doe call thee so, for I will shew thee no reason for't. (Law

Fa. A good note, that keepes you from the blow of ÿ

To. Thou com'st to the Lady Oliuia, and in my sight she vses thee kindly: but thou lyest in thy throat, that is not the matter I challenge thee for.

Fa. Very breefe, and to exceeding good sence-lesse.

To. I will way-lay thee going home, where if it be thy chance to kill me.

Fa. Good.

To. Thou kilst me like a rogue and a villaine.

Fa. Still you keepe o'th windie side of the Law: good.

Tob. Fartheewell, and God haue mercie vpon one of our soules. He may haue mercie vpon mine, but my hope is better, and so looke to thy selfe. Thy friend as thou vsest him, & thy sworne enemie, Andrew Ague-cheeke.

To. If this Letter moue him not, his legges cannot: Ile giu't him.

Mar. Yon may haue verie fit occasion fot't: he is now in some commerce with my Ladie, and will by and by depart.

To. Go sir *Andrew*: scout mee for him at the corner of the Orchard like a bum-Baylie: so soone as euer thou seest him, draw, and as thou draw'st, sweare horrible: for t comes to passe oft, that a terrible oath, with a swaggering accent sharpely twang'd off, giues manhoode more approbation, then euer proofe it selfe would haue earn'd him. Away.

And. Nay let me alone for swearing. *Exit*

To. Now will not I deliuer his Letter: for the behauiour of the yong Gentleman, giues him out to be of good capacity, and breeding: his employment betweene his Lord and my Neece, confirmes no lesse. Therefore, this Letter being so excellently ignorant, will breed no terror in the youth: he will finde it comes from a Clodde-pole. But sir, I will deliuer his Challenge by word of mouth; set vpon *Ague-cheeke* a notable report of valor, and driue the Gentleman (as I know his youth will aptly receiue it) into a most hideous opinion of his rage, skill, furie, and impetuositie. This will so fright them both, that they wil kill one another by the looke, like Cockatrices.

Enter Oliuia and Viola.

Fab. Heere he comes with your Neece, giue them way till he take leaue, and presently after him.

To I wil meditate the while vpon some horrid message for a Challenge.

Ol. I haue said too much vnto a hart of stone,
And laid mine honour too vnchary on't:
There's something in me that reproues my fault:
But such a head-strong potent fault it is,
That it but mockes reproofe.

Vio. With the same hauiour that your passion beares,
Goes on my Masters greefes.

Ol. Heere, weare this Iewell for me, tis my picture:
Refuse it not, it hath no tongue, to vex you:
And I beseech you come againe to morrow.
What shall you aske of me that Ile deny,
That honour (sau'd) may vpon asking giue.

Vio. Nothing but this, your true loue for my master.

Ol. How with mine honor may I giue him that,
Which I haue giuen to you.

Vio I will acquit you.

Ol. Well, come againe to morrow: far-thee-well,
A Fiend like thee might beare my soule to hell.

Enter Toby and Fabian.

To. Gentleman, God saue thee.

Vio.

Vio. And you sir.

To. That defence thou hast, betake the too't: of what nature the wrongs are thou hast done him, I knowe not: but thy intercepter full of despight, bloody as the Hunter, attends thee at the Orchard end: dismount thy tucke, be yare in thy preparation, for thy assaylant is quick, skilfull, and deadly.

Vio. You mistake sir I am sure, no man hath any quarrell to me: my remembrance is very free and cleere from any image of offence done to any man.

To. You'l finde it otherwise I assure you: therefore, if you hold your life at any price, betake you to your gard: for your opposite hath in him what youth, strength, skill, and wrath, can furnish man withall.

Vio. I pray you sir what is he?

To. He is knight dubb'd with vnhatch'd Rapier, and on carpet consideration, but he is a diuell in priuate brall, soules and bodies hath he diuorc'd three, and his incensement at this moment is so implacable, that satisfaction can be none, but by pangs of death and sepulcher: Hob, nob, is his word: giu't or take't.

Vio. I will returne againe into the house, and desire some conduct of the Lady. I am no fighter, I haue heard of some kinde of men, that put quarrells purposely on others, to taste their valour: belike this is a man of that quirke.

To. Sir, no: his indignation deriues it selfe out of a very computent iniurie, therefore get you on, and giue him his desire. Backe you shall not to the house, vnlesse you vndertake that with me, which with as much safetie you might answer him: therefore on, or strippe your sword starke naked: for meddle you must that's certain, or forsweare to weare iron about you.

Vio. This is as vnciuill as strange. I beseech you doe me this courteous office, as to know of the Knight what my offence to him is: it is something of my negligence, nothing of my purpose.

To. I will doe so. Signiour *Fabian*, stay you by this Gentleman, till my returne. *Exit Toby.*

Vio. Pray you sir, do you know of this matter?

Fab. I know the knight is incenst against you, euen to a mortall arbitrement, but nothing of the circumstance more.

Vio. I beseech you what manner of man is he?

Fab. Nothing of that wonderfull promise to read him by his forme, as you are like to finde him in the proofe of his valour. He is indeede sir, the most skilfull, bloudy, & fatall opposite that you could possibly haue found in anie part of Illyria: will you walke towards him, I will make your peace with him, if I can.

Vio. I shall bee much bound to you for't: I am one, that had rather go with sir Priest, then sir knight: I care not who knowes so much of my mettle. *Exeunt.*

Enter Toby and Andrew.

To. Why man hee s a verie diuell, I haue not seen such a firago: I had a passe with him, rapier, scabberd, and all: and he giues me the stucke in with such a mortall motion that it is ineuitable: and on the answer, he payes you as surely, as your feete hits the ground they step on. They say, he has bin Fencer to the Sophy.

And. Pox on't Ile not meddle with him.

To. I but he will not now be pacified,
Fabian can scarse hold him yonder.

An. Plague on't, and I thought he had beene valiant, and so cunning in Fence, I'de haue seene him damn'd ere I'de haue challeng'd him. Let him let the matter slip, and Ile giue him my horse, gray Capilet.

To. Ile make the motion: stand heere, make a good shew on't, this shall end without the perdition of soules, marry Ile ride your horse as well as I ride you.

Enter Fabian and Viola.

I haue his horse to take vp the quarrell, I haue perswaded him the youths a diuell.

Fa. He is as horribly conceited of him: and pants, & lookes pale, as if a Beare were at his heeles.

To. There's no remedie sir, he will fight with you for's oath sake: marrie hee hath better bethought him of his quarrell, and hee findes that now scarse to bee worth talking of: therefore draw for the supportance of his vowe, he protests he will not hurt you.

Vio. Pray God defend me: a little thing would make me tell them how much I lacke of a man.

Fab. Giue ground if you see him furious.

To. Come sir *Andrew*, there's no remedie, the Gentleman will for his honors sake haue one bowt with you: he cannot by the Duello auoide it: but hee has promised me, as he is a Gentleman and a Soldiour, he will not hurt you. Come on, too't.

And. Pray God he keepe his oath.

Enter Antonio.

Vio. I do assure you tis against my will.

Ant. Put vp your sword: if this yong Gentleman
Haue done offence, I take the fault on me:
If you offend him, I for him defie you.

To. You sir? Why, what are you?

Ant. One sir, that for his loue dares yet do more
Then you haue heard him brag to you he will.

To. Nay, if you be an vndertaker, I am for you.

Enter Officers.

Fab. O good sir *Toby* hold: heere come the Officers.

To. Ile be with you anon.

Vio. Pray sir, put your sword vp if you please.

And. Marry will I sir: and for that I promis'd you Ile be as good as my word. Hee will beare you easily, and raines well.

1.Off. This is the man, do thy Office.

2 Off. *Anthonio*, I arrest thee at the suit of Count *Orsino*

An. You do mistake me sir.

1.Off. No sir, no iot: I know your fauour well:
Though now you haue no sea-cap on your head:
Take him away, he knowes I know him well.

Ant. I must obey. This comes with seeking you:
But there's no remedie, I shall answer it:
What will you do: now my necessitie
Makes me to aske you for my purse. It greeues mee
Much more, for what I cannot do for you,
Then what befals my selfe: you stand amaz'd,
But be of comfort.

2 Off. Come sir away.

Ant. I must entreat of you some of that money.

Vio. What money sir?
For the fayre kindnesse you haue shew'd me heere,
And part being prompted by your present trouble,
Out of my leane and low ability
Ile lend you something: my hauing is not much,
Ile make diuision of my present with you:
Hold, there's halfe my Coffer.

Ant. Will you deny me now,
Ist possible that my deserts to you
Can lacke perswasion. Do not tempt my misery,
Least that it make me so vnsound a man
As to vpbraid you with those kindnesses

Z 3 That

That I haue done for you.

Vio. I know of none,
Nor know I you by voyce, or any feature:
I hate ingratitude more in a man,
Then lying, vainnesse, babling drunkennesse,
Or any taint of vice, whose strong corruption
Inhabites our fraile blood.

Ant. Oh heauens themselues.

2.*Off*. Come sir, I pray you go.

Ant. Let me speake a little. This youth that you see (heere,
I snatch'd one halfe out of the iawes of death,
Releeu'd him with such sanctitie of loue;
And to his image, which me thought did promise
Most venerable worth, did I deuotion.

1.*Off*. What's that to vs, the time goes by: Away.

Ant. But oh, how vilde an idoll proues this God:
Thou hast *Sebastian* done good feature, shame.
In Nature, there's no blemish but the minde:
None can be call'd deform'd, but the vnkinde.
Vertue is beauty, but the beauteous euill
Are empty trunkes, ore-flourish'd by the deuill.

1.*Off* The man growes mad, away with him:
Come, come sir.

Ant. Leade me on. *Exit*

Vio. Me thinkes his words do from such passion flye
That he beleeues himselfe, so do not I:
Proue true imagination, oh proue ttue,
That I deere brother, be now tane for you.

To. Come hither Knight, come hither *Fabian*: Weel whisper ore a couplet or two of most sage sawes.

Vio. He nam'd *Sebastian*: I my brother know
Yet liuing in my glasse: euen such, and so
In fauour was my Brother, and he went
Still in this fashion, colour, ornament,
For him I imitate: Oh if it proue,
Tempests are kinde, and salt waues fresh in loue.

To. A very dishonest paltry boy, and more a coward then a Hare, his dishonesty appeares, in leauing his frend heere in necessity, and denying him: and for his coward ship aske *Fabian*.

Fab. A Coward, a most deuout Coward, religious in it.

And. Slid Ile after him againe, and beate him.

To. Do, cuffe him soundly, but neuer draw thy sword

And. And I do not.

Fab. Come, let's see the euent.

To. I dare lay any money, twill be nothing yet. *Exit*

Actus Quartus, Scæna prima.

Enter Sebastian and Clowne.

Clo. Will you make me beleeue, that I am not sent for you?

Seb. Go too, go too, thou art a foolish fellow,
Let me be cleere of thee.

Clo. Well held out yfaith: No, I do not know you, nor I am not sent to you by my Lady, to bid you come speake with her: nor your name is not Master *Cesario*, nor this is not my nose neyther: Nothing that is so, is so.

Seb. I prethee vent thy folly some-where else, thou know st not me.

Clo. Vent my folly: He has heard that word of some great man, and now applyes it to a foole. Vent my folly: I am affraid this great lubber the World will proue a Cockney: I prethee now vngird thy strangenes, and tell me what I shall vent to my Lady? Shall I vent to hir that thou art comming?

Seb. I prethee foolish greeke depart from me, there's money for thee, if you tarry longer, I shall giue worse paiment.

Clo. By my troth thou hast an open hand: these Wisemen that giue fooles money, get themselues a good report, after foureteene yeares purchase.

Enter Andrew, Toby, and Fabian.

And. Now sir, haue I met you again: ther's for you.

Seb. Why there's for thee, and there, and there,
Are all the people mad?

To Hold sir, or Ile throw your dagger ore the house

Clo. This will I tell my Lady straight, I would not be in some of your coats for two pence.

To. Come on sir, hold.

An. Nay let him alone, Ile go another way to worke with him: Ile haue an action of Battery against him, if there be any law in Illyria: though I stroke him first, yet t's no matter for that.

Seb. Let go thy hand.

To. Come sir, I will not let you go. Come my yong souldier put vp your yron: you are well flesh'd: Come on.

Seb. I will be free from thee. What wouldst ẏ now?
If thou dar'st tempt me further, draw thy sword

To. What, what? Nay then I must haue an Ounce or two of this malapert blood from you.

Enter Olivia.

Ol. Hold *Toby*, on thy life I charge thee hold.

To. Madam.

Ol. Will it be euer thus? Vngracious wretch,
Fit for the Mountaines, and the barbarous Caues,
Where manners nere were preach'd: out of my sight.
Be not offended, deere *Cesario*:
Rudesbey be gone. I prethee gentle friend,
Let thy fayre wisedome, not thy passion sway
In this vnciuill, and vniust extent
Against thy peace. Go with me to my house,
And heare thou there how many fruitlesse prankes
This Ruffian hath botch'd vp, that thou thereby
Mayst smile at this: Thou shalt not choose but goe:
Do not denie, beshrew his soule for mee,
He started one poore heart of mine, in thee.

Seb. What rellish is in this? How runs the streame?
Or I am mad, or else this is a dreame:
Let fancie still my sense in Lethe steepe,
If it be thus to dreame, still let me sleepe.

Ol. Nay come I prethee, would thoud'st be rul'd by me

Seb. Madam, I will

Ol. O say so, and so be. *Exeunt*

Scœna Secunda.

Enter Maria and Clowne.

Mar. Nay, I prethee put on this gown, & this beard, make him beleeue thou art sir *Topas* the Curate, doe it quickly. Ile call sir *Toby* the whilst.

Clo. Well, Ile put it on, and I will dissemble my selfe in't, and I would I were the first that euer dissembled in such in ſuch a gowne. I am not tall enough to become the function well, nor leane enough to bee thought a good Studient: but to be ſaid an honeſt man and a good houſe keeper goes as fairely, as to ſay, a carefull man, & a great ſcholler. The Competitors enter.

Enter Toby.

To. Ioue bleſſe thee M. Parſon.

Clo. *Bonos dies* ſir *Toby*: for as the old hermit of *Prage* that neuer ſaw pen and inke, very wittily ſayd to a Neece of King *Gorbodacke*, that that is, is: ſo I being M. Parſon, am M. Parſon; for what is that, but that? and is, but is?

To. To him ſir *Topas*.

Clow. What hoa, I ſay, Peace in this priſon.

To. The knaue counterfets well: a good knaue.

Maluolio within.

Mal. Who cals there?

Clo. Sir *Topas* the Curate, who comes to viſit *Maluolio* the Lunaticke.

Mal. Sir *Topas*, ſir *Topas*, good ſir *Topas* goe to my Ladie.

Clo. Out hyperbolicall fiend, how vexeſt thou this man? Talkeſt thou nothing but of Ladies?

Tob. Well ſaid M. Parſon.

Mal. Sir *Topas*, neuer was man thus wronged, good ſir *Topas* do not thinke I am mad: they haue layde mee heere in hideous darkneſſe.

Clo. Fye, thou diſhoneſt ſathan: I call thee by the moſt modeſt termes, for I am one of thoſe gentle ones, that will vſe the diuell himſelfe with curteſie: ſayſt thou that houſe is darke?

Mal. As hell ſir *Topas*.

Clo. Why it hath bay Windowes tranſparant as baricadoes, and the cleere ſtores toward the South north, are as luſtrous as Ebony: and yet complaineſt thou of obſtruction?

Mal. I am not mad ſir *Topas*, I ſay to you this houſe is darke.

Clo. Madman thou erreſt: I ſay there is no darkneſſe but ignorance, in which thou art more puzel'd then the Ægyptians in their fogge.

Mal. I ſay this houſe is as darke as Ignorance, thogh Ignorance were as darke as hell; and I ſay there was neuer man thus abus'd, I am no more madde then you are, make the triall of it in any conſtant queſtion.

Clo: What is the opinion of *Pythagoras* concerning Wilde-fowle?

Mal. That the ſoule of our grandam, might happily inhabite a bird.

Clo. What thinkſt thou of his opinion?

Mal. I thinke nobly of the ſoule, and no way aproue his opinion.

Clo. Fare thee well: remaine thou ſtill in darkeneſſe, thou ſhalt hold th'opinion of *Pythagoras*, ere I will allow of thy wits, and feare to kill a Woodcocke, leſt thou diſpoſſeſſe the ſoule of thy grandam. Fare thee well.

Mal. Sir *Topas*, ſir *Topas*.

Tob. My moſt exquiſite ſir *Topas*.

Clo. Nay I am for all waters.

Mar. Thou mightſt haue done this without thy berd and gowne, he ſees thee not.

To. To him in thine owne voyce, and bring me word how thou findſt him: I would we were well ridde of this knauery. If he may bee conueniently deliuer'd, I would he were, for I am now ſo farre in offence with my Niece, that I cannot purſue with any ſafety this ſport the vppeſhot. Come by and by to my Chamber. *Exit*

Clo. Hey Robin, iolly Robin, tell me how thy Lady does.

Mal. Foole.

Clo. My Lady is vnkind, *perdie*.

Mal. Foole.

Clo. Alas why is ſhe ſo?

Mal. Foole, I ſay.

Clo. She loues another. Who calles, ha?

Mal. Good foole, as euer thou wilt deſerue well at my hand, helpe me to a Candle, and pen, inke, and paper: as I am a Gentleman, I will liue to bee thankefull to thee for't.

Clo. M. *Maluolio*?

Mal. I good Foole.

Clo. Alas ſir, how fell you beſides your fiue witts?

Mall. Foole, there was neuer man ſo notoriouſlie abus'd: I am as well in my wits (foole) as thou art.

Clo. But as well: then you are mad indeede, if you be no better in your wits then a foole.

Mal. They haue heere propertied me: keepe mee in darkeneſſe, ſend Miniſters to me, Aſſes, and doe all they can to face me out of my wits.

Clo. Aduiſe you what you ſay: the Miniſter is heere. *Maluolio, Maluolio*, thy wittes the heauens reſtore: endeauour thy ſelfe to ſleepe, and leaue thy vaine bibble babble.

Mal. Sir *Topas*

Clo. Maintaine no words with him good fellow.

Who I ſir, not I ſir. God buy you good ſir Topas: Marry Amen. I will ſir, I will.

Mal. Foole, foole, foole I ſay.

Clo. Alas ſir be patient. What ſay you ſir, I am ſhent for ſpeaking to you.

Mal. Good foole, helpe me to ſome light, and ſome paper, I tell thee I am as well in my wittes, as any man in Illyria.

Clo. Well-a-day, that you were ſir.

Mal. By this hand I am: good foole, ſome inke, paper, and light: and conuey what I will ſet downe to my Lady: it ſhall aduantage thee more, then euer the bearing of Letter did.

Clo. I will help you too't. But tel me true, are you not mad indeed, or do you but counterfeit.

Mal. Beleeue me I am not. I tell thee true.

Clo. Nay, Ile nere beleeue a madman till I ſee his brains I will fetch you light, and paper, and inke.

Mal. Foole, Ile requite it in the higheſt degree: I prethee be gone.

Clo. I am gone ſir, and anon ſir,
Ile be with you againe:
In a trice, like to the old vice,
your neede to ſuſtaine.
Who with dagger of lath, in his rage and his wrath,
cries ah ha, to the diuell:
Like a mad lad, paire thy nayles dad,
Adieu good man diuell. *Exit*

Scæna Tertia.

Enter Sebaſtian.

This is the ayre, that is the glorious Sunne,
This pearle ſhe gaue me, I do feel't, and ſee't,
And though tis wonder that enwraps me thus,
Yet

Yet 'tis not madnesse. Where's *Anthonio* then,
I could not finde him at the Elephant,
Yet there he was, and there I found this credite,
That he did range the towne to seeke me out,
His councell now might do me golden seruice,
For though my soule disputes well with my sence,
That this may be some error, but no madnesse,
Yet doth this accident and flood of Fortune,
So farre exceed all instance, all discourse,
That I am readie to distrust mine eyes,
And wrangle with my reason that perswades me
To any other trust, but that I am mad,
Or else the Ladies mad; yet if 'twere so,
She could not sway her house, command her followers,
Take, and giue backe affayres, and their dispatch,
With such a smooth, discreet, and stable bearing
As I perceiue she do's: there's something in't
That is deceiueable. But heere the Lady comes.

Enter Oliuia, and Priest.

Ol. Blame not this haste of mine: if you meane well
Now go with me, and with this holy man
Into the Chantry by: there before him,
And vnderneath that consecrated roofe,
Plight me the full assurance of your faith,
That my most iealious, and too doubtfull soule
May liue at peace. He shall conceale it
Whiles you are willing it shall come to note,
What time we will our celebration keepe
According to my birth, what do you say?

Seb. Ile follow this good man, and go with you,
And hauing sworne truth, euer will be true.

Ol. Then lead the way good father, & heauens so shine,
That they may fairely note this acte of mine. *Exeunt.*

Finis Actus Quartus.

Actus Quintus. Scena Prima.

Enter Clowne and Fabian.

Fab. Now as thou lou'st me, let me see his Letter.

Clo. Good M. *Fabian*, grant me another request.

Fab. Any thing.

Clo. Do not desire to see this Letter.

Fab. This is to giue a dogge, and in recompence desire my dogge againe.

Enter Duke, Viola, Curio, and Lords.

Duke Belong you to the Lady *Oliuia*, friends?

Clo. I sir, we are some of her trappings.

Duke. I know thee well: how doest thou my good Fellow?

Clo. Truely sir, the better for my foes, and the worse for my friends.

Du. Iust the contrary: the better for thy friends.

Clo. No sir, the worse.

Du. How can that be?

Clo. Marry sir, they praise me, and make an asse of me, now my foes tell me plainly, I am an Asse: so that by my foes sir, I profit in the knowledge of my selfe, and by my friends I am abused: so that conclusions to be as kisses, if your foure negatiues make your two affirmatiues, why then the worse for my friends, and the better for my foes.

Du. Why this is excellent.

Clo. By my troth sir, no: though it please you to be one of my friends.

Du. Thou shalt not be the worse for me, there's gold.

Clo. But that it would be double dealing sir, I would you could make it another.

Du. O you giue me ill counsell.

Clo. Put your grace in your pocket sir, for this once, and let your flesh and blood obey it.

Du. Well, I will be so much a sinner to be a double dealer: there's another.

Clo. *Primo, secundo, tertio*, is a good play, and the olde saying is, the third payes for all: the triplex sir, is a good tripping measure, or the belles of S. *Bennet* sir, may put you in minde, one, two, three.

Du. You can foole no more money out of mee at this throw: if you will let your Lady know I am here to speak with her, and bring her along with you, it may awake my bounty further.

Clo. Marry sir, lullaby to your bountie till I come agen. I go sir, but I would not haue you to thinke, that my desire of hauing is the sinne of couetousnesse: but as you say sir, let your bounty take a nappe, I will awake it anon. *Exit*

Enter Anthonio and Officers.

Vio. Here comes the man sir, that did rescue mee.

Du. That face of his I do remember well,
yet when I saw it last, it was besmear'd
As blacke as Vulcan, in the smoake of warre:
A bawbling Vessell was he Captaine of,
For shallow draught and bulke vnprizable,
With which such scathfull grapple did he make,
With the most noble bottome of our Fleete,
That very enuy, and the tongue of losse
Cride fame and honor on him: What's the matter?

1 Offi. *Orsino*, this is that *Anthonio*
That tooke the *Phoenix*, and her fraught from *Candy*,
And this is he that did the *Tiger* boord,
When your yong Nephew *Titus* lost his legge;
Heere in the streets, desperate of shame and state,
In priuate brabble did we apprehend him.

Vio. He did me kindnesse sir, drew on my side,
But in conclusion put strange speech vpon me,
I know not what 'twas, but distraction.

Du. Notable Pyrate, thou salt-water Theefe,
What foolish boldnesse brought thee to their mercies,
Whom thou in termes so bloudie, and so deere
Hast made thine enemies?

Ant. *Orsino*: Noble sir,
Be pleas'd that I shake off these names you giue mee:
Anthonio neuer yet was Theefe, or Pyrate,
Though I confesse, on base and ground enough
Orsino's enemie. A witchcraft drew me hither:
That most ingratefull boy there by your side,
From the rude seas enrag'd and foamy mouth
Did I redeeme: a wracke past hope he was:
His life I gaue him, and did thereto adde
My loue without retention, or restraint,
All his in dedication. For his sake,
Did I expose my selfe (pure for his loue)
Into the danger of this aduerse Towne,
Drew to defend him, when he was beset:
Where being apprehended, his false cunning
(Not meaning to partake with me in danger)
Taught him to face me out of his acquaintance,

And

And grew a twentie yeeres remoued thing
While one would winke: denide me mine owne purse,
Which I had recommended to his vse,
Not halfe an houre before.
. How can this be?
Du. When came he to this Towne?
Ant. To day my Lord: and for three months before,
No *intrim*, not a minutes vacancie,
Both day and night did we keepe companie.

Enter Oliuia and attendants.

Du. Heere comes the Countesse, now heauen walkes on earth:
But for thee fellow, fellow thy words are madnesse,
Three monthes this youth hath tended vpon mee,
But more of that anon. Take him aside.
Ol. What would my Lord, but that he may not haue,
Wherein *Oliuia* may seeme seruiceable?
Cesario, you do not keepe promise with me.
Vio. Madam:
Du. Gracious *Oliuia*.
Ol. What do you say *Cesario*? Good my Lord.
Vio. My Lord would speake, my dutie hushes me.
Ol. If it be ought to the old tune my Lord,
It is as fat and fulsome to mine eare
As howling after Musicke.
Du. Still so cruell?
Ol. Still so constant Lord.
Du. What to peruersenesse? you vnciuill Ladie
To whose ingrate, and vnauspicious Altars
My soule the faithfull'st offrings haue breath'd out
That ere deuotion tender'd. What shall I do?
Ol Euen what it please my Lord, that shal becom him
Du. Why should I not, (had I the heart to do it)
Like to th'Egyptian theefe, at point of death
Kill what I loue: (a sauage iealousie,
That sometime sauours nobly) but heare me this:
Since you to non-regardance cast my faith,
And that I partly know the instrument
That screwes me from my true place in your fauour:
Liue you the Marble-brested Tirant still.
But this your Minion, whom I know you loue,
And whom, by heauen I sweare, I tender deerely,
Him will I teare out of that cruell eye,
Where he sits crowned in his masters spight.
Come boy with me, my thoughts are ripe in mischiefe:
Ile sacrifice the Lambe that I do loue,
To spight a Rauens heart within a Doue.
Vio. And I most iocund, apt, and willinglie,
To do you rest, a thousand deaths would dye.
Ol. Where goes *Cesario*?
Vio. After him I loue,
More then I loue these eyes, more then my life,
More by all mores, then ere I shall loue wife.
If I do feigne, you witnesses aboue
Punish my life, for tainting of my loue.
Ol. Aye me detested, how am I beguil'd?
Vio. Who does beguile you? who does do you wrong?
Ol. Hast thou forgot thy selfe? Is it so long?
Call forth the holy Father.
Du. Come, away.
Ol. Whether my Lord? *Cesario*, Husband, stay.
Du. Husband?
Ol. I Husband. Can he that deny?
Du. Her husband, sirrah?
Vio. No my Lord, not I.
Ol. Alas, it is the basenesse of thy feare,
That makes thee strangle thy proprietie:
Feare not *Cesario*, take thy fortunes vp,
Be that thou know'st thou art, and then thou art
As great as that thou fear'st.

Enter Priest.

O welcome Father:
Father, I charge thee by thy reuerence
Heere to vnfold, though lately we intended
To keepe in darkenesse, what occasion now
Reueales before 'tis ripe: what thou dost know
Hath newly past, betweene this youth, and me.
Priest. A Contract of eternall bond of loue,
Confirm'd by mutuall ioynder of your hands,
Attested by the holy close of lippes,
Strengthned by enterchangement of your rings,
And all the Ceremonie of this compact
Seal'd in my function, by my testimony:
Since when, my watch hath told me, toward my graue
I haue trauail'd but two houres.
Du. O thou dissembling Cub: what wilt thou be
When time hath sow'd a grizzle on thy case?
Or will not else thy craft so quickely grow,
That thine owne trip shall be thine ouerthrow:
Farewell, and take her, but direct thy feete,
Where thou, and I (henceforth) may neuer meet.
Vio. My Lord, I do protest.
Ol. O do not sweare,
Hold little faith, though thou hast too much feare.

Enter Sir Andrew.

And. For the loue of God a Surgeon, send one presently to sir *Toby*.

Ol. What's the matter?

And. Has broke my head a-crosse, and has giuen Sir *Toby* a bloody Coxcombe too: for the loue of God your helpe, I had rather then forty pound I were at home.

Ol. Who has done this sir *Andrew*?

And. The Counts Gentleman, one *Cesario*: we tooke him for a Coward, but hee's the verie diuell incardinate.

Du. My Gentleman *Cesario*?

And. Od's lifelings heere he is: you broke my head for nothing, and that that I did, I was set on to do't by sir *Toby*.

Vio Why do you speake to me, I neuer hurt you:
you drew your sword vpon me without cause,
But I bespake you faire, and hurt you not.

Enter Toby and Clowne.

And. If a bloody coxcombe be a hurt, you haue hurt me: I thinke you set nothing by a bloody Coxecombe. Heere comes sir *Toby* halting, you shall heare more: but if he had not beene in drinke, hee would haue tickel'd you other gates then he did.

Du. How now Gentleman? how ist with you?

To. That's all one, has hurt me, and there's th'end on't: Sot, didst see Dicke Surgeon, sot?

Clo. O he's drunke sir *Toby* an houre agone: his eyes were set at eight i'th morning.

To. Then he's a Rogue, and a passy measures panyn: I hate a drunken rogue.

Ol. Away with him? Who hath made this hauocke with them?

And Ile helpe you sir *Toby*, because we'll be drest together.

To. Will you helpe an Asse-head, and a coxcombe, & a knaue: a thin fac'd knaue, a gull?

Ol.

Ol. Get him to bed, and let his hurt be look'd too.

Enter Sebaſtian.

Seb. I am ſorry Madam I haue hurt your kinſman:
But had it beene the brother of my blood,
I muſt haue done no leſſe with wit and ſafety.
You throw a ſtrange regard vpon me, and by that
I do perceiue it hath offended you.
Pardon me (ſweet one) euen for the vowes
We made each other, but ſo late ago.

Du. One face, one voice, one habit, and two perſons,
A naturall Perſpectiue, that is, and is not.

Seb. *Anthonio*: O my deere *Anthonio*,
How haue the houres rack'd, and tortur'd me,
Since I haue loſt thee?

Ant. *Sebaſtian* are you?

Seb. Fear'ſt thou that *Anthonio*?

Ant. How haue you made diuiſion of your ſelfe,
An apple cleft in two, is not more twin
Then theſe two creatures. Which is *Sebaſtian*?

Ol. Moſt wonderfull.

Seb. Do I ſtand there? I neuer had a brother:
Nor can there be that Deity in my nature
Of heere, and euery where. I had a ſiſter,
Whom the blinde waues and ſurges haue deuour'd:
Of charity, what kinne are you to me?
What Countreyman? What name? What Parentage?

Vio. Of *Meſſaline*: *Sebaſtian* was my Father,
Such a *Sebaſtian* was my brother too:
So went he ſuited to his watery tombe:
If ſpirits can aſſume both forme and ſuite,
You come to fright vs.

Seb. A ſpirit I am indeed,
But am in that dimenſion groſſely clad,
Which from the wombe I did participate.
Were you a woman, as the reſt goes euen,
I ſhould my teares let fall vpon your cheeke,
And ſay, thrice welcome drowned *Viola*.

Vio. My father had a moale vpon his brow.

Seb. And ſo had mine.

Vio. And dide that day when *Viola* from her birth
Had numbred thirteene yeares.

Seb. O that record is liuely in my ſoule,
He finiſhed indeed his mortall acte
That day that made my ſiſter thirteene yeares.

Vio. If nothing lets to make vs happie both,
But this my maſculine vſurp'd attyre:
Do not embrace me, till each circumſtance,
Of place, time, fortune, do co-here and iumpe
That I am *Viola*, which to confirme,
Ile bring you to a Captaine in this Towne,
Where lye my maiden weeds: by whoſe gentle helpe,
I was preſeru'd to ſerue this Noble Count:
All the occurrence of my fortune ſince
Hath beene betweene this Lady, and this Lord.

Seb. So comes it Lady, you haue beene miſtooke:
But Nature to her bias drew in that.
You would haue bin contracted to a Maid,
Nor are you therein (by my life) deceiu'd,
You are betroth'd both to a maid and man.

Du. Be not amaz'd, right noble is his blood:
If this be ſo, as yet the glaſſe ſeemes true,
I ſhall haue ſhare in this moſt happy wracke,
Boy, thou haſt ſaide to me a thouſand times,
Thou neuer ſhould'ſt loue woman like to me.

Vio. And all thoſe ſayings, will I ouer ſweare,
And all thoſe ſwearings keepe as true in ſoule,
As doth that Orbed Continent, the fire,
That ſeuers day from night.

Du. Giue me thy hand,
And let me ſee thee in thy womans weedes.

Vio. The Captaine that did bring me firſt on ſhore
Hath my Maides garments: he vpon ſome Action
Is now in durance, at *Maluolio's* ſuite,
A Gentleman, and follower of my Ladies.

Ol. He ſhall inlarge him: fetch *Maluolio* hither,
And yet alas, now I remember me,
They ſay poore Gentleman, he's much diſtract.

Enter Clowne with a Letter, and Fabian.

A moſt extracting frenſie of mine owne
From my remembrance, clearly baniſht his.
How does he ſirrah?

Cl. Truely Madam, he holds *Belzebub* at the ſtaues end as well as a man in his caſe may do: has heere writ a letter to you, I ſhould haue giuen't you to day morning. But as a madmans Epiſtles are no Goſpels, ſo it skilles not much when they are deliuer'd.

Ol. Open't, and read it.

Clo. Looke then to be well edified, when the Foole deliuers the Madman. *By the Lord Madam.*

Ol. How now, art thou mad?

Clo. No Madam, I do but reade madneſſe: and your Ladyſhip will haue it as it ought to bee, you muſt allow *Vox*.

Ol. Prethee reade i'thy right wits.

Clo. So I do Madona: but to reade his right wits, is to reade thus: therefore, perpend my Princeſſe, and giue eare.

Ol. Read it you, ſirrah.

Fab. Reads. By the Lord Madam, you wrong me, and the world ſhall know it: Though you haue put mee into darkeneſſe, and giuen your drunken Coſine rule ouer me, yet haue I the benefit of my ſenſes as well as your Ladieſhip. I haue your owne letter, that induced mee to the ſemblance I put on; with the which I doubt not, but to do my ſelfe much right, or you much ſhame: thinke of me as you pleaſe. I leaue my duty a little vnthought of, and ſpeake out of my iniury. *The madly vs'd Maluolio.*

Ol. Did he write this?

Clo. I Madame.

Du. This ſauours not much of diſtraction.

Ol. See him deliuer'd *Fabian*, bring him hither:
My Lord, ſo pleaſe you, theſe things further thought on,
To thinke me as well a ſiſter, as a wife,
One day ſhall crowne th'alliance on't, ſo pleaſe you,
Heere at my houſe, and at my proper coſt.

Du. Madam, I am moſt apt t'embrace your offer:
Your Maſter quits you: and for your ſeruice done him,
So much againſt the mettle of your ſex,
So farre beneath your ſoft and tender breeding,
And ſince you call'd me Maſter, for ſo long:
Heere is my hand, you ſhall from this time bee
your Maſters Miſtris.

Ol. A ſiſter, you are ſhe.

Enter Maluolio.

Du. Is this the Madman?

Ol. I my Lord, this ſame: How now *Maluolio*?

Mal. Madam, you haue done me wrong,
Notorious wrong.

Ol. Haue I *Maluolio*? No.

Mal. Lady you haue, pray you peruſe that Letter.
You muſt not now denie it is your hand,
Write from it if you can, in hand, or phraſe,

Or

Or say, tis not your seale, not your inuention:
You can say none of this. Well, grant it then,
And tell me in the modestie of honor,
Why you haue giuen me such cleare lights of fauour,
Bad me come smiling, and crosse-garter'd to you,
To put on yellow stockings, and to frowne
Vpon sir *Toby*, and the lighter people:
And acting this in an obedient hope,
Why haue you suffer'd me to be imprison'd,
Kept in a darke house, visited by the Priest,
And made the most notorious gecke and gull
That ere inuention plaid on? Tell me why?

Ol. Alas *Maluolio*, this is not my writing,
Though I confesse much like the Charracter
But out of question, tis *Marias* hand.
And now I do bethinke me, it was shee
First told me thou wast mad; then cam'st in smiling,
And in such formes, which heere were presuppos'd
Vpon thee in the Letter: prethee be content,
This practice hath most shrewdly past vpon thee:
But when we know the grounds, and authors of it,
Thou shalt be both the Plaintiffe and the Iudge
Of thine owne cause.

Fab. Good Madam heare me speake,
And let no quarrell, nor no braule to come,
Taint the condition of this present houre,
Which I haue wondred at. In hope it shall not,
Most freely I confesse my selfe, and *Toby*
Set this deuice against *Maluolio* heere,
Vpon some stubborne and vncourteous parts
We had conceiu'd against him. *Maria* writ
The Letter, at sir *Tobyes* great importance,
In recompence whereof, he hath married her:
How with a sportfull malice it was follow'd,
May rather plucke on laughter then reuenge,
If that the iniuries be iustly weigh'd,
That haue on both sides past

Ol. Alas poore Foole, how haue they baffel'd thee?

Clo. Why some are borne great, some atchieue greatnesse, and some haue greatnesse throwne vpon them. I was one sir, in this Enterlude, one sir *Topas* sir, but that's all one: By the Lord Foole, I am not mad: but do you remember, Madam, why laugh you at such a barren rascall, and you smile not he's gag'd: and thus the whirlegigge of time, brings in his reuenges.

Mal. Ile be reueng'd on the whole packe of you?

Ol. He hath bene most notoriously abus'd.

Du. Pursue him, and entreate him to a peace:
He hath not told vs of the Captaine yet,
When that is knowne, and golden time conuents
A solemne Combination shall be made
Of our deere soules. Meane time sweet sister,
We will not part from hence. *Cesario* come
(For so you shall be while you are a man:)
But when in other habites you are seene,
Orsino's Mistris, and his fancies Queene. *Exeunt*

Clowne sings.

When that I was and a little tine boy,
with hey, ho, the winde and the raine:
A foolish thing was but a toy,
for the raine it raineth euery day.

But when I came to mans estate,
with hey ho, &c.
Gainst Knaues and Theeues men shut their gate,
for the raine, &c.

But when I came alas to wiue,
with hey ho, &c.
By swaggering could I neuer thriue,
for the raine, &c.

But when I came vnto my beds,
with hey ho, &c
With tospottes still had drunken heades,
for the raine, &c.

A great while ago the world begon,
hey ho, &c.
But that's all one, our Play is done,
and wee'l striue to please you euery day.

FINIS.

The VVinters Tale.

Actus Primus. Scœna Prima.

Enter Camillo and Archidamus.

Arch. IF you ſhall chance (*Camillo*) to viſit *Bohemia*, on the like occaſion whereon my ſeruices are now on-foot, you ſhall ſee (as I haue ſaid) great difference betwixt our *Bohemia*, and your *Sicilia*.

Cam. I thinke, this comming Summer, the King of *Sicilia* meanes to pay *Bohemia* the Viſitation, which hee iuſtly owes him.

Arch. Wherein our Entertainment ſhall ſhame vs: we will be iuſtified in our Loues: for indeed---

Cam. 'Beſeech you---

Arch. Verely I ſpeake it in the freedome of my knowledge: we cannot with ſuch magnificence--- in ſo rare--- I know not what to ſay--- Wee will giue you ſleepie Drinkes, that your Sences (vn-intelligent of our inſufficience) may, though they cannot prayſe vs, as little accuſe vs.

Cam. You pay a great deale to deare, for what's giuen freely.

Arch. 'Beleeue me, I ſpeake as my vnderſtanding inſtructs me, and as mine honeſtie puts it to vtterance.

Cam. *Sicilia* cannot ſhew himſelfe ouer-kind to *Bohemia*: They were trayn'd together in their Child-hoods; and there rooted betwixt them then ſuch an affection, which cannot chuſe but braunch now. Since their more mature Dignities, and Royall Neceſſities, made ſeperation of their Societie, their Encounters (though not Perſonall) hath been Royally attornyed with enter-change of Gifts, Letters, louing Embaſſies, that they haue ſeem'd to be together, though abſent: ſhooke hands, as ouer a Vaſt; and embrac'd as it were from the ends of oppoſed Winds. The Heauens continue their Loues.

Arch. I thinke there is not in the World, either Malice or Matter, to alter it. You haue an vnſpeakable comfort of your young Prince *Mamillius*: it is a Gentleman of the greateſt Promiſe, that euer came into my Note.

Cam. I very well agree with you, in the hopes of him: it is a gallant Child; one, that (indeed Phyſicks the Subiect, makes old hearts freſh: they that went on Crutches ere he was borne, deſire yet their life, to ſee him a Man.

Arch. Would they elſe be content to die?

Cam. Yes; if there were no other excuſe, why they ſhould deſire to liue.

Arch. If the King had no Sonne, they would deſire to liue on Crutches till he had one. *Exeunt.*

Scœna Secunda.

Enter Leontes, Hermione, Mamillius, Polixenes, Camillo.

Pol. Nine Changes of the Watry-Starre hath been
The Shepheards Note, ſince we haue left our Throne
Without a Burthen: Time as long againe
Would be fill'd vp (my Brother) with our Thanks,
And yet we ſhould, for perpetuitie,
Goe hence in debt: And therefore, like a Cypher
(Yet ſtanding in rich place) I multiply
With one we thanke you, many thouſands moe,
That goe before it.

Leo. Stay your Thanks a while,
And pay them when you part.

Pol. Sir, that's to morrow:
I am queſtion'd by my feares, of what may chance,
Or breed vpon our abſence, that may blow
No ſneaping Winds at home, to make vs ſay,
This is put forth too truly: beſides, I haue ſtay'd
To tyre your Royaltie.

Leo. We are tougher (Brother)
Then you can put vs to't.

Pol. No longer ſtay.

Leo. One Seue'night longer.

Pol. Very ſooth, to morrow.

Leo. Wee'le part the time betweene's then: and in that
Ile no gaine-ſaying.

Pol. Preſſe me not ('beſeech you) ſo:
There is no Tongue that moues; none, none i'th' World
So ſoone as yours could win me: ſo it ſhould now,
Were there neceſſitie in your requeſt, although
'Twere needfull I deny'd it. My Affaires
Doe euen drag me home-ward: which to hinder,
Were (in your Loue) a Whip to me; my ſtay,
To you a Charge, and Trouble: to ſaue both,
Farewell (our Brother.)

Leo. Tongue-ty'd our Queene? ſpeake you.

Her. I had thought (Sir) to haue held my peace, vntill
You had drawne Oathes from him, not to ſtay: you (Sir)
Charge him too coldly. Tell him, you are ſure
All in *Bohemia's* well: this ſatisfaction,
The by-gone-day proclaym'd, ſay this to him,
He's beat from his beſt ward.

Leo. Well ſaid, *Hermione*.

Her. To tell, he longs to ſee his Sonne, were ſtrong:
But let him ſay ſo then, and let him goe;
But let him ſweare ſo, and he ſhall not ſtay,
Wee'l thwack him hence with Diſtaffes.
Yet of your Royall preſence, Ile aduenture
The borrow of a Weeke. When at *Bohemia*
You take my Lord, Ile giue him my Commiſſion,
To let him there a Moneth, behind the Geſt
Prefix'd for's parting: yet (good-deed) *Leontes*,
I loue thee not a Iarre o'th' Clock, behind

What Lady ſhe her Lord. You'le ſtay?
Pol. No, Madame.
Her. Nay, but you will?
Pol. I may not verely.
Her. Verely?
You put me off with limber Vowes: but I,
Though you would ſeek t'vnſphere the Stars with Oaths,
Should yet ſay, Sir, no going: Verely
You ſhall not goe; a Ladyes Verely' is
As potent as a Lords. Will you goe yet?
Force me to keepe you as a Priſoner,
Not like a Gueſt: ſo you ſhall pay your Fees
When you depart, and ſaue your Thanks. How ſay you?
My Priſoner? or my Gueſt? by your dread Verely,
One of them you ſhall be.
Pol. Your Gueſt then, Madame:
To be your Priſoner, ſhould import offending;
Which is for me, leſſe eaſie to commit,
Then you to puniſh.
Her. Not your Gaoler then,
But your kind Hoſteſſe. Come, Ile queſtion you
Of my Lords Tricks, and yours, when you were Boyes:
You were pretty Lordings then?
Pol. We were (faire Queene)
Two Lads, that thought there was no more behind,
But ſuch a day to morrow, as to day,
And to be Boy eternall.
Her. Was not my Lord
The veryer Wag o'th' two?
Pol. We were as twyn'd Lambs, that did friſk i'th' Sun,
And bleat the one at th'other: what we chang'd,
Was Innocence, for Innocence: we knew not
The Doctrine of ill-doing, nor dream'd
That any did: Had we purſu'd that life,
And our weake Spirits ne're been higher rear'd
With ſtronger blood, we ſhould haue anſwer'd Heauen
Boldly, not guilty; the Impoſition clear'd,
Hereditarie ours.
Her. By this we gather
You haue tript ſince.
Pol. O my moſt ſacred Lady,
Temptations haue ſince then been borne to's: for
In thoſe vnfledg'd dayes, was my Wife a Girle;
Your precious ſelfe had then not croſs'd the eyes
Of my young Play-fellow.
Her. Grace to boot:
Of this make no concluſion, leaſt you ſay
Your Queene and I are Deuils: yet goe on,
Th'offences we haue made you doe, wee'le anſwere,
If you firſt ſinn'd with vs: and that with vs
You did continue fault; and that you ſlipt not
With any, but with vs.
Leo. Is he woon yet?
Her. Hee'le ſtay (my Lord.)
Leo. At my requeſt he would not:
Hermione (my deareſt) thou neuer ſpoak'ſt
To better purpoſe.
Her. Neuer?
Leo. Neuer, but once.
Her. What? haue I twice ſaid well? when was't before?
I prethee tell me: cram's with prayſe, and make's
As fat as tame things: One good deed, dying tongueleſſe,
Slaughters a thouſand, wayting vpon that.
Our prayſes are our Wages. You may ride's
With one ſoft Kiſſe a thouſand Furlongs, ere
With Spur we heat an Acre. But to th' Goale:
My laſt good deed, was to entreat his ſtay.
What was my firſt? it ha's an elder Siſter,
Or I miſtake you: O, would her Name were *Grace*.
But once before I ſpoke to th' purpoſe? when?
Nay, let me haue't: I long.
Leo. Why, that was when
Three crabbed Moneths had ſowr'd themſelues to death,
Ere I could make thee open thy white Hand:
A clap thy ſelfe my Loue; then didſt thou vtter,
I am yours for euer.
Her. 'Tis Grace indeed.
Why lo-you now; I haue ſpoke to th' purpoſe twice:
The one, for euer earn'd a Royall Husband;
Th'other, for ſome while a Friend.
Leo. Too hot, too hot:
To mingle friendſhip farre, is mingling bloods.
I haue *Tremor Cordis* on me: my heart daunces,
But not for ioy; not ioy. This Entertainment
May a free face put on: deriue a Libertie
From Heartineſſe, from Bountie, fertile Boſome,
And well become the Agent: 't may; I graunt:
But to be padling Palmes, and pinching Fingers,
As now they are, and making practis'd Smiles
As in a Looking-Glaſſe; and then to ſigh, as 'twere
The Mort o'th'Deere: oh, that is entertainment
My Boſome likes not, nor my Browes. *Mamillius*,
Art thou my Boy?
Mam. I, my good Lord.
Leo. I'fecks:
Why that's my Bawcock: what? has't ſmutch'd thy Noſe?
They ſay it is a Coppy out of mine. Come Captaine,
We muſt be neat; not neat, but cleanly, Captaine:
And yet the Steere, the Heycfer, and the Calfe,
Are all call'd Neat. Still Virginalling
Vpon his Palme? How now (you wanton Calfe)
Art thou my Calfe?
Mam. Yes, if you will (my Lord.)
Leo Thou want'ſt a rough paſh, & the ſhoots that I haue
To be full, like me: yet they ſay we are
Almoſt as like as Egges; Women ſay ſo,
(That will ſay any thing.) But were they falſe
As o're-dy'd Blacks, as Wind, as Waters; falſe
As Dice are to be wiſh'd, by one that fixes
No borne 'twixt his and mine; yet were it true,
To ſay this Boy were like me. Come (Sir Page)
Looke on me with your Welkin eye: ſweet Villaine,
Moſt dear'ſt, my Collop: Can thy Dam, may't be
Affection? thy Intention ſtabs the Center.
Thou do'ſt make poſſible things not ſo held,
Communicat'ſt with Dreames (how can this be?)
With what's vnreall: thou coactiue art,
And fellow'ſt nothing. Then 'tis very credent,
Thou may'ſt co-ioyne with ſomething, and thou do'ſt,
(And that beyond Commiſſion) and I find it,
(And that to the infection of my Braines,
And hardning of my Browes.)
Pol. What meanes *Sicilia*?
Her. He ſomething ſeemes vnſetled.
Pol. How? my Lord?
Leo. What cheere? how is't with you, beſt Brother?
Her. You look as if you held a Brow of much diſtraction:
Are you mou'd (my Lord?)
Leo. No, in good earneſt.
How ſometimes Nature will betray it's folly?
It's tenderneſſe? and make it ſelfe a Paſtime
To harder boſomes? Looking on the Lynes
Of

Of my Boyes face, me thoughts I did requoyle
Twentie three yeeres, and saw my selfe vn-breech'd,
In my greene Veluet Coat; my Dagger muzzel'd,
Least it should bite it's Master, and so proue
(As Ornaments oft do's) too dangerous:
How like (me thought) I then was to this Kernell,
This Squash, this Gentleman. Mine honest Friend,
Will you take Egges for Money?
Mam. No (my Lord) Ile fight.
Leo. You will: why happy man be's dole. My Brother
Are you so fond of your young Prince, as we
Doe seeme to be of ours?
Pol. If at home (Sir)
He's all my Exercise, my Mirth, my Matter;
Now my sworne Friend, and then mine Enemy;
My Parasite, my Souldier: States-man; all:
He makes a Iulyes day, short as December,
And with his varying child-nesse, cures in me
Thoughts, that would thick my blood.
Leo. So stands this Squire
Offic'd with me: We two will walke (my Lord)
And leaue you to your grauer steps. *Hermione*,
How thou lou'st vs, shew in our Brothers welcome;
Let what is deare in Sicily, be cheape:
Next to thy selfe, and my young Rouer, he's
Apparant to my heart.
Her. If you would seeke vs,
We are yours i'th Garden: shall's attend you there?
Leo. To your owne bents dispose you: you'le be found,
Be you beneath the Sky: I am angling now,
(Though you perceiue me not how I giue Lyne)
Goe too, goe too
How she holds vp the Neb? the Byll to him?
And armes her with the boldnesse of a Wife
To her allowing Husband. Gone already,
Ynch-thick, knee-deepe; ore head and eares a fork'd one.
Goe play (Boy) play: thy Mother playes, and I
Play too; but so disgrac'd a part, whose issue
Will hisse me to my Graue: Contempt and Clamor
Will be my Knell. Goe play (Boy) play, there haue been
(Or I am much deceiu'd) Cuckolds ere now,
And many a man there is (euen at this present,
Now, while I speake this) holds his Wife by th'Arme,
That little thinkes she ha's been sluyc'd in's absence,
And his Pond fish'd by his next Neighbor (by
Sir *Smile*, his Neighbor:) nay, there's comfort in't,
Whiles other men haue Gates, and those Gates open'd
(As mine) against their will. Should all despaire
That haue reuolted Wiues, the tenth of Mankind
Would hang themselues. Physick for't, there's none:
It is a bawdy Planet, that will strike
Where 'tis predominant; and 'tis powrefull: thinke it:
From East, West, North, and South, be it concluded,
No Barricado for a Belly. Know't,
It will let in and out the Enemy,
With bag and baggage: many thousand on's
Haue the Disease, and feele't not. How now Boy?
Mam. I am like you say.
Leo. Why, that's some comfort.
What? *Camillo* there?
Can. I, my good Lord.
Leo. Goe play (*Mamillius*) thou'rt an honest man:
Camillo, this great Sir will yet stay longer.
Cam. You had much adoe to make his Anchor hold,
When you cast out, it still came home.
Leo. Didst note it?
Cam. He would not stay at your Petitions, made
His Businesse more materiall.
Leo. Didst perceiue it?
They're here with me already; whisp'ring, rounding:
Sicilia is a so-forth: 'tis farre gone,
When I shall gust it last. How cam't (*Camillo*)
That he did stay?
Cam. At the good Queenes entreatie.
Leo. At the Queenes be't: Good should be pertinent,
But so it is, it is not. Was this taken
By any vnderstanding Pate but thine?
For thy Conceit is soaking, will draw in
More then the common Blocks. Not noted, is't,
But of the finer Natures? by some Seueralls
Of Head-peece extraordinarie? Lower Messes
Perchance are to this Businesse purblind? say.
Cam. Businesse, my Lord? I thinke most vnderstand
Bohemia stayes here longer.
Leo. Ha?
Cam. Stayes here longer.
Leo. I, but why?
Cam. To satisfie your Highnesse, and the Entreaties
Of our most gracious Mistresse.
Leo. Satisfie?
Th'entreaties of your Mistresse? Satisfie?
Let that suffice. I haue trusted thee (*Camillo*)
With all the neerest things to my heart, as well
My Chamber-Councels, wherein (Priest-like) thou
Hast cleans'd my Bosome: I, from thee departed
Thy Penitent reform'd: but we haue been
Deceiu'd in thy Integritie, deceiu'd
In that which seemes so.
Cam. Be it forbid (my Lord.)
Leo. To bide vpon't: thou art not honest: or
If thou inclin'st that way, thou art a Coward,
Which hoxes honestie behind, restrayning
From Course requir'd: or else thou must be counted
A Seruant, grafted in my serious Trust,
And therein negligent: or else a Foole,
That seest a Game play'd home, the rich Stake drawne,
And tak'st it all for ieast.
Cam. My gracious Lord,
I may be negligent, foolish, and fearefull,
In euery one of these, no man is free,
But that his negligence, his folly, feare,
Among the infinite doings of the World,
Sometime puts forth in your affaires (my Lord.)
If euer I were wilfull-negligent,
It was my folly: if industriously
I play'd the Foole, it was my negligence,
Not weighing well the end: if euer fearefull
To doe a thing, where I the issue doubted,
Whereof the execution did cry out
Against the non-performance, 'twas a feare
Which oft infects the wisest: these (my Lord)
Are such allow'd Infirmities, that honestie
Is neuer free of. But beseech your Grace
Be plainer with me, let me know my Trespas
By it's owne visage; if I then deny it,
'Tis none of mine.
Leo. Ha' not you seene *Camillo*?
(But that's past doubt: you haue, or your eye-glasse
Is thicker then a Cuckolds Horne) or heard?
(For to a Vision so apparant, Rumor
Cannot be mute) or thought? (for Cogitation
Resides not in that man, that do's not thinke)

Aa 2 My

My Wife is ſlipperie? If thou wilt confeſſe,
Or elſe be impudently negatiue,
To haue nor Eyes, nor Eares, nor Thought, then ſay
My Wife's a Holy-Horſe, deſerues a Name
As ranke as any Flax-Wench, that puts to
Before her troth-plight: ſay't, and iuſtify't.
Cam. I would not be a ſtander-by, to heare
My Soueraigne Miſtreſſe clouded ſo, without
My preſent vengeance taken: 'ſhrew my heart,
You neuer ſpoke what did become you leſſe
Then this; which to reiterate, were ſin
As deepe as that, though true.
Leo. Is whiſpering nothing?
Is leaning Cheeke to Cheeke? is meating Noſes?
Kiſſing with in-ſide Lip? ſtopping the Cariere
Of Laughter, with a ſigh? (a Note infallible
Of breaking Honeſtie) horſing foot on foot?
Skulking in corners? wiſhing Clocks more ſwift?
Houres, Minutes? Noone, Mid-night? and all Eyes
Blind with the Pin and Web, but theirs; theirs onely,
That would vnſeene be wicked? Is this nothing?
Why then the World, and all that's in't, is nothing,
The couering Skie is nothing, *Bohemia* nothing,
My Wife is nothing, nor Nothing haue theſe Nothings,
If this be nothing.
Cam. Good my Lord, be cur'd
Of this diſeas'd Opinion, and betimes,
For 'tis moſt dangerous.
Leo. Say it be, 'tis true.
Cam. No, no, my Lord.
Leo. It is: you lye, you lye:
I ſay thou lyeſt *Camillo*, and I hate thee,
Pronounce thee a groſſe Lowt, a mindleſſe Slaue,
Or elſe a houering Temporizer, that
Canſt with thine eyes at once ſee good and euill,
Inclining to them both: were my Wiues Liuer
Infected (as her life) ſhe would not liue
The running of one Glaſſe.
Cam. Who do's infect her?
Leo. Why he that weares her like her Medull, hanging
About his neck (*Bohemia*) who, if I
Had Seruants true about me, that bare eyes
To ſee alike mine Honor, as their Profits,
(Their owne particular Thrifts) they would doe that
Which ſhould vndoe more doing: I, and thou
His Cup-bearer, whom I from meaner forme
Haue Bench'd, and rear'd to Worſhip, who may'ſt ſee
Plainely, as Heauen ſees Earth, and Earth ſees Heauen,
How I am gall'd, might'ſt be-ſpice a Cup,
To giue mine Enemy a laſting Winke:
Which Draught to me, were cordiall.
Cam. Sir (my Lord)
I could doe this, and that with no raſh Potion,
But with a lingring Dram, that ſhould not worke
Maliciouſly, like Poyſon: But I cannot
Beleeue this Crack to be in my dread Miſtreſſe
(So ſoueraignely being Honorable.)
I haue lou'd thee,
Leo Make that thy queſtion, and goe rot:
Do'ſt thinke I am ſo muddy, ſo vnſetled,
To appoint my ſelfe in this vexation?
Sully the puritie and whiteneſſe of my Sheetes
(Which to preſerue, is Sleepe; which being ſpotted,
Is Goades, Thornes, Nettles, Tayles of Waſpes)
Giue ſcandall to the blood o'th' Prince, my Sonne,
(Who I doe thinke is mine, and loue as mine)
Without ripe mouing to't? Would I doe this?
Could man ſo blench?
Cam. I muſt beleeue you (Sir)
I doe, and will fetch off *Bohemia* for't:
Prouided, that when hee's remou'd, your Highneſſe
Will take againe your Queene, as yours at firſt,
Euen for your Sonnes ſake, and thereby for ſealing
The Iniurie of Tongues, in Courts and Kingdomes
Knowne, and ally'd to yours.
Leo. Thou do'ſt aduiſe me,
Euen ſo as I mine owne courſe haue ſet downe:
Ile giue no blemiſh to her Honor, none.
Cam. My Lord,
Goe then; and with a countenance as cleare
As Friendſhip weares at Feaſts, keepe with *Bohemia*,
And with your Queene: I am his Cup-bearer,
If from me he haue wholeſome Beueridge,
Account me not your Seruant.
Leo. This is all:
Do't, and thou haſt the one halfe of my heart;
Do't not, thou ſplitt'ſt thine owne.
Cam. Ile do't my Lord.
Leo. I wil ſeeme friendly, as thou haſt aduis'd me. *Exit*
Cam. O miſerable Lady. But for me,
What caſe ſtand I in? I muſt be the poyſoner
Of good *Polixenes*, and my ground to do't,
Is the obedience to a Maſter; one,
Who in Rebellion with himſelfe, will haue
All that are his, ſo too. To doe this deed,
Promotion followes: If I could find example
Of thouſand's that had ſtruck anoynted Kings,
And flouriſh'd after, Il'd not do't: But ſince
Nor Braſſe, nor Stone, nor Parchment beares not one,
Let Villanie it ſelfe forſwear't. I muſt
Forſake the Court: to do't, or no, is certaine
To me a breake-neck. Happy Starre raigne now,
Here comes *Bohemia*. *Enter Polixenes.*
Pol. This is ſtrange: Me thinkes
My fauor here begins to warpe. Not ſpeake?
Good day *Camillo*.
Cam. Hayle moſt Royall Sir.
Pol. What is the Newes i'th' Court?
Cam. None rare (my Lord.)
Pol. The King hath on him ſuch a countenance,
As he had loſt ſome Prouince, and a Region
Lou'd, as he loues himſelfe: euen now I met him
With cuſtomarie complement, when hee
Waſting his eyes to th' contrary, and falling
A Lippe of much contempt, ſpeedes from me, and
So leaues me, to conſider what is breeding,
That changes thus his Manners.
Cam. I dare not know (my Lord.)
Pol. How, dare not? doe not? doe you know, and dare not?
Be intelligent to me, 'tis thereabouts:
For to your ſelfe, what you doe know, you muſt,
And cannot ſay, you dare not. Good *Camillo*,
Your chang'd complexions are to me a Mirror,
Which ſhewes me mine chang'd too: for I muſt be
A partie in this alteration, finding
My ſelfe thus alter'd with't.
Cam. There is a ſickneſſe
Which puts ſome of vs in diſtemper, but
I cannot name the Diſeaſe, and it is caught
Of you, that yet are well.
Pol. How caught of me?
Make me not ſighted like the Baſiliſque.
I haue

I haue look'd on thousands, who haue sped the better
By my regard, but kill'd none so: *Camillo*,
As you are certainely a Gentleman, thereto
Clerke-like experienc'd, which no lesse adornes
Our Gentry, then our Parents Noble Names,
In whose successe we are gentle: I beseech you,
If you know ought which do's behoue my knowledge,
Thereof to be inform'd, imprison't not
In ignorant concealement.

Cam. I may not answere.

Pol. A Sicknesse caught of me, and yet I well?
I must be answer'd. Do'st thou heare *Camillo*,
I coniure thee, by all the parts of man,
Which Honor do's acknowledge, whereof the least
Is not this Suit of mine, that thou declare
What incidencie thou do'st ghesse of harme
Is creeping toward me; how farre off, how neere,
Which way to be preuented, if to be:
If not, how best to beare it.

Cam. Sir, I will tell you,
Since I am charg'd in Honor, and by him
That I thinke Honorable: therefore marke my counsaile,
Which must be eu'n as swiftly followed, as
I meane to vtter it; or both your selfe, and me,
Cry lost, and so good night.

Pol. On, good *Camillo*.

Cam. I am appointed him to murther you.

Pol. By whom, *Camillo*?

Cam. By the King.

Pol. For what?

Cam. He thinkes, nay with all confidence he sweares,
As he had seen't, or beene an Instrument
To vice you to't, that you haue toucht his Queene
Forbiddenly.

Pol. Oh then, my best blood turne
To an infected Gelly, and my Name
Be yoak'd with his, that did betray the Best:
Turne then my freshest Reputation to
A sauour, that may strike the dullest Nosthrill
Where I arriue, and my approch be shun'd,
Nay hated too, worse then the great'st Infection
That ere was heard, or read.

Cam. Sweare his thought ouer
By each particular Starre in Heauen, and
By all their Influences; you may as well
Forbid the Sea for to obey the Moone,
As (or by Oath) remoue, or (Counsaile) shake
The Fabrick of his Folly, whose foundation
Is pyl'd vpon his Faith, and will continue
The standing of his Body.

Pol. How should this grow?

Cam. I know not: but I am sure 'tis safer to
Auoid what's growne, then question how 'tis borne.
If therefore you dare trust my honestie,
That lyes enclosed in this Trunke, which you
Shall beare along impawnd, away to Night,
Your Followers I will whisper to the Businesse,
And will by twoes, and threes, at seuerall Posternes,
Cleare them o'th' Citie: For my selfe, Ile put
My fortunes to your seruice (which are here
By this discouerie lost.) Be not vncertaine,
For by the honor of my Parents, I
Haue vttred Truth: which if you seeke to proue,
I dare not stand by; nor shall you be safer,
Then one condemnd by the Kings owne mouth:
Thereon his Execution sworne.

Pol. I doe beleeue thee:
I saw his heart in's face. Giue me thy hand,
Be Pilot to me, and thy places shall
Still neighbour mine. My Ships are ready, and
My people did expect my hence departure
Two dayes agoe. This Iealousie
Is for a precious Creature: as shee's rare,
Must it be great; and, as his Person's mightie,
Must it be violent: and, as he do's conceiue,
He is dishonor'd by a man, which euer
Profess'd to him: why his Reuenges must
In that be made more bitter. Feare ore-shades me:
Good Expedition be my friend, and comfort
The gracious Queene, part of his Theame; but nothing
Of his ill-ta'ne suspition. Come *Camillo*,
I will respect thee as a Father, if
Thou bear'st my life off, hence: Let vs auoid.

Cam. It is in mine authoritie to command
The Keyes of all the Posternes: Please your Highnesse
To take the vrgent houre. Come Sir, away. *Exeunt.*

Actus Secundus. Scena Prima

Enter Hermione, Mamillius, Ladies: Leontes, Antigonus, Lords.

Her. Take the Boy to you: he so troubles me,
'Tis past enduring.

Lady. Come (my gracious Lord)
Shall I be your play-fellow?

Mam. No, Ile none of you.

Lady. Why (my sweet Lord?)

Mam. You'le kisse me hard, and speake to me, as if
I were a Baby still. I loue you better.

2. Lady. And why so (my Lord?)

Mam. Not for because
Your Browes are blacker (yet black-browes they say
Become some Women best, so that there be not
Too much haire there, but in a Cemicircle,
Or a halfe-Moone, made with a Pen.)

2. Lady. Who taught 'this?

Mam. I learn'd it out of Womens faces: pray now,
What colour are your eye-browes?

Lady. Blew (my Lord.)

Mam. Nay, that's a mock: I haue seene a Ladies Nose
That ha's beene blew, but not her eye-browes.

Lady. Harke ye,
The Queene (your Mother) rounds apace: we shall
Present our seruices to a fine new Prince
One of these dayes, and then youl'd wanton with vs,
If we would haue you.

2. Lady. She is spread of late
Into a goodly Bulke (good time encounter her.)

Her. What wisdome stirs amongst you? Come Sir, now
I am for you againe: 'Pray you sit by vs,
And tell's a Tale.

Mam. Merry, or sad, shal't be?

Her. As merry as you will.

Mam. A sad Tale's best for Winter:
I haue one of Sprights, and Goblins.

Her. Let's haue that (good Sir.)
Come-on, sit downe, come-on, and doe your best,
To fright me with your Sprights: you're powrefull at it.

Mam.. There was a man.
Her. Nay, come sit downe: then on.
Mam. Dwelt by a Church-yard: I will tell it softly,
Yond Crickets shall not heare it.
Her. Come on then, and giu't me in mine eare.
Leon. Was hee met there? his Traine? *Camillo* with him?
Lord. Behind the tuft of Pines I met them, neuer
Saw I men scowre so on their way: I eyed them
Euen to their Ships.
Leo. How blest am I
In my iust Censure? in my true Opinion?
Alack, for lesser knowledge, how accurs'd,
In being so blest? There may be in the Cup
A Spider steep'd, and one may drinke; depart,
And yet partake no venome: (for his knowledge
Is not infected) but if one present
Th'abhor'd Ingredient to his eye, make knowne
How he hath drunke, he cracks his gorge, his sides
With violent Hefts: I haue drunke, and seene the Spider.
Camillo was his helpe in this, his Pandar:
There is a Plot against my Life, my Crowne;
All's true that is mistrusted: that false Villaine,
Whom I employ'd, was pre-employ'd by him:
He ha's discouer'd my Designe, and I
Remaine a pinch'd Thing; yea, a very Trick
For them to play at will: how came the Posternes
So easily open?
Lord. By his great authority,
Which often hath no lesse preuail'd, then so,
On your command.
Leo. I know't too well.
Giue me the Boy, I am glad you did not nurse him:
Though he do's beare some signes of me, yet you
Haue too much blood in him.
Her. What is this? Sport?
Leo. Beare the Boy hence, he shall not come about her,
Away with him, and let her sport her selfe
With that shee's big-with, for 'tis *Polixenes*
Ha's made thee swell thus.
Her. But Il'd say he had not;
And Ile be sworne you would beleeue my saying,
How e're you leane to th' Nay-ward.
Leo. You (my Lords)
Looke on her, marke her well: be but about
To say she is a goodly Lady, and
The iustice of your hearts will thereto adde
'Tis pitty shee's not honest: Honorable;
Prayse her but for this her without-dore-Forme,
(Which on my faith deserues high speech) and straight
The Shrug, the Hum, or Ha, (these Petty-brands
That Calumnie doth vse; Oh, I am out,
That Mercy do's, for Calumnie will seare
Vertue it selfe) these Shrugs, these Hum's, and Ha's,
When you haue said shee's goodly, come betweene,
Ere you can say shee's honest: But be't knowne
(From him that ha's most cause to grieue it should be)
Shee's an Adultresse.
Her. Should a Villaine say so,
(The most replenish'd Villaine in the World)
He were as much more Villaine: you (my Lord)
Doe but mistake.
Leo. You haue mistooke (my Lady)
Polixenes for *Leontes*: O thou Thing,
(Which Ile not call a Creature of thy place,
Least Barbarisme (making me the precedent)
Should a like Language vse to all degrees,
And mannerly distinguishment leaue out,
Betwixt the Prince and Begger:) I haue said
Shee's an Adultresse, I haue said with whom:
More; shee's a Traytor, and *Camillo* is
A Federarie with her, and one that knowes
What she should shame to know her selfe,
But with her most vild Principall: that shee's
A Bed-swaruer, euen as bad as those
That Vulgars giue bold'st Titles; I, and priuy
To this their late escape.
Her. No (by my life)
Priuy to none of this: how will this grieue you,
When you shall come to clearer knowledge, that
You thus haue publish'd me? Gentle my Lord,
You scarce can right me throughly, then, to say
You did mistake.
Leo. No: if I mistake
In those Foundations which I build vpon,
The Centre is not bigge enough to beare
A Schoole-Boyes Top. Away with her, to Prison:
He who shall speake for her, is a farre-off guiltie,
But that he speakes.
Her. There's some ill Planet raignes:
I must be patient, till the Heauens looke
With an aspect more fauorable. Good my Lords,
I am not prone to weeping (as our Sex
Commonly are) the want of which vaine dew
Perchance shall dry your pitties: but I haue
That honorable Griefe lodg'd here, which burnes
Worse then Teares drowne: 'beseech you all (my Lords)
With thoughts so qualified, as your Charities
Shall best instruct you measure me; and so
The Kings will be perform'd.
Leo. Shall I be heard?
Her. Who is't that goes with me? 'beseech your Highnes
My Women may be with me, for you see
My plight requires it. Doe not weepe (good Fooles)
There is no cause: When you shall know your Mistris
Ha's deseru'd Prison, then abound in Teares,
As I come out; this Action I now goe on,
Is for my better grace. Adieu (my Lord)
I neuer wish'd to see you sorry, now
I trust I shall: my Women come, you haue leaue.
Leo. Goe, doe our bidding: hence.
Lord. Beseech your Highnesse call the Queene againe.
Antig. Be certaine what you do (Sir) least your Iustice
Proue violence, in the which three great ones suffer,
Your Selfe, your Queene, your Sonne.
Lord. For her (my Lord)
I dare my life lay downe, and will do't (Sir)
Please you t'accept it, that the Queene is spotlesse
I'th' eyes of Heauen, and to you (I meane
In this, which you accuse her.)
Antig. If it proue
Shee's otherwise, Ile keepe my Stables where
I lodge my Wife, Ile goe in couples with her:
Then when I feele, and see her, no farther trust her
For euery ynch of Woman in the World,
I, euery dram of Womans flesh is false,
If she be.
Leo. Hold your peaces.
Lord. Good my Lord.
Antig. It is for you we speake, not for our selues.
You are abus'd, and by some putter on,
That will be damn'd for't: would I knew the Villaine,
I would

I would Land-damne him : be she honor-flaw'd,
I haue three daughters : the eldest is eleuen;
The second, and the third, nine : and some fiue :
If this proue true, they'l pay for't. By mine Honor
Ile gell'd em all : fourteene they shall not see
To bring false generations : they are co-heyres,
And I had rather glib my selfe, then they
Should not produce faire issue.

Leo. Cease, no more.
You smell this businesse with a sence as cold
As is a dead-mans nose : but I do see't, and feel't,
As you feele doing thus : and see withall
The Instruments that feele.

Antig If it be so,
We neede no graue to burie honesty.
There's not a graine of it, the face to sweeten
Of the whole dungy-earth.

Leo. What? lacke I credit ?

Lord. I had rather you did lacke then I (my Lord)
Vpon this ground : and more it would content me
To haue her Honor true, then your suspition
Be blam'd for't how you might.

Leo. Why what neede we
Commune with you of this ? but rather follow
Our forcefull instigation ? Our prerogatiue
Cals not your Counsailes, but our naturall goodnesse
Imparts this : which, if you, or stupified,
Or seeming so, in skill, cannot, or will not
Rellish a truth, like vs : informe your selues,
We neede no more of your aduice : the matter,
The losse, the gaine, the ord'ring on't,
Is all properly ours.

Antig. And I wish (my Liege)
You had onely in your silent iudgement tride it,
Without more ouerture.

Leo. How could that be ?
Either thou art most ignorant by age,
Or thou wer't borne a foole : *Camillo's* flight
Added to their Familiarity
(Which was as grosse, as euer touch'd coniecture,
That lack'd sight onely, nought for approbation
But onely seeing, all other circumstances
Made vp to'th deed) doth push-on this proceeding.
Yet, for a greater confirmation
(For in an Acte of this importance, 'twere
Most pitteous to be wilde) I haue dispatch'd in post,
To sacred *Delphos*, to *Appollo's* Temple,
Cleomines and *Dion*, whom you know
Of stuff'd-sufficiency : Now, from the Oracle
They will bring all, whose spirituall counsaile had
Shall stop, or spurre me. Haue I done well ?

Lord. Well done (my Lord.)

Leo. Though I am satisfide, and neede no more
Then what I know, yet shall the Oracle
Giue rest to th'mindes of others ; such as he
Whose ignorant credulitie, will not
Come vp to th'truth. So haue we thought it good
From our free person, she should be confinde,
Least that the treachery of the two, fled hence,
Be left her to performe. Come follow vs,
We are to speake in publique : for this businesse
Will raise vs all.

Antig To laughter, as I take it,
If the good truth, were knowne.

Exeunt

Scena Secunda.

Enter Paulina, a Gentleman, Gaoler, Emilia.

Paul The Keeper of the prison, call to him :
Let him haue knowledge who I am. Good Lady,
No Court in Europe is too good for thee,
What dost thou then in prison ? Now good Sir,
You know me, do you not ?

Gao. For a worthy Lady,
And one, who much I honour.

Pau. Pray you then,
Conduct me to the Queene.

Gao. I may not (Madam)
To the contrary I haue expresse commandment.

Pau. Here's a-do, to locke vp honesty & honour from
Th'accesse of gentle visitors. Is't lawfull pray you
To see her Women ? Any of them? *Emilia?*

Gao. So please you (Madam)
To put a-part these your attendants, I
Shall bring *Emilia* forth.

Pau. I pray now call her :
With-draw your selues.

Gao. And Madam,
I must be present at your Conference.

Pau. Well : be't so prethee.
Heere's such a-doe, to make no staine, a staine,
As passes colouring. Deare Gentlewoman,
How fares our gracious Lady ?

Emil. As well as one so great, and so forlorne
May hold together : On her frights, and greefes
(Which neuer tender Lady hath borne greater)
She is, something before her time, deliuer'd.

Pau. A boy ?

Emil. A daughter, and a goodly babe,
Lusty, and like to liue : the Queene receiues
Much comfort in't : Sayes, my poore prisoner,
I am innocent as you.

Pau I dare be sworne:
These dangerous, vnsafe Lunes i'th'King, beshrew them:
He must be told on't, and he shall : the office
Becomes a woman best. Ile take't vpon me,
If I proue hony-mouth'd, let my tongue blister.
And neuer to my red-look'd Anger bee
The Trumpet any more : pray you (*Emilia*)
Commend my best obedience to the Queene,
If she dares trust me with her little babe,
I'le shew't the King, and vndertake to bee
Her Aduocate to th'lowd'st. We do not know
How he may soften at the sight o'th'Childe :
The silence often of pure innocence
Perswades, when speaking failes.

Emil. Most worthy Madam,
your honor, and your goodnesse is so euident,
That your free vndertaking cannot misse
A thriuing yssue : there is no Lady liuing
So meete for this great errand ; please your Ladiship
To visit the next roome, Ile presently
Acquaint the Queene of your most noble offer,
Who, but to day hammered of this designe,
But durst not tempt a minister of honour
Least she should be deny'd.

Pau

Paul. Tell her (*Emilia*)
Ile vse that tongue I haue: If wit flow from't
As boldnesse from my bosome, le't not be doubted
I shall do good,
Emil. Now be you blest for it.
Ile to the Queene: please you come something neerer.
Gao. Madam, if't please the Queene to send the babe
I know not what I shall incurre, to passe it,
Hauing no warrant
Pau You neede not feare it (sir)
This Childe was prisoner to the wombe, and is
By Law and processe of great Nature, thence
Free'd, and enfranchis'd, not a partie to
The anger of the King, nor guilty of
(If any be) the trespasse of the Queene.
Gao. I do beleeue it.
Paul. Do not you feare: vpon mine honor, I
Will stand betwixt you, and danger. *Exeunt*

Scæna Tertia.

Enter Leontes, Seruants, Paulina, Antigonus, and Lords

Leo Nor night, nor day, no rest: It is but weaknesse
To beare the matter thus: meere weaknesse, if
The cause were not in being: part o'th cause,
She, th'Adultresse: for the harlot-King
Is quite beyond mine Arme, out of the blanke
And leuell of my braine: plot-proofe: but shee,
I can hooke to me: say that she were gone,
Giuen to the fire, a moity of my rest
Might come to me againe. Whose there?
Ser My Lord.
Leo. How do's the boy?
Ser. He tooke good rest to night; 'tis hop'd
His sicknesse is discharg'd
Leo To see his Noblenesse,
Conceyuing the dishonour of his Mother.
He straight declin'd, droop'd, tooke it deeply,
Fasten'd, and fix'd the shame on't in himselfe:
Threw-off his Spirit, his Appetite, his Sleepe,
And down-right languish'd. Leaue me solely: goe,
See how he fares: Fie, fie, no thought of him,
The very thought of my Reuenges that way
Recoyle vpon me: in himselfe too mightie,
And in his parties, his Alliance; Let him be,
Vntill a time may serue. For present vengeance
Take it on her: *Camillo*, and *Polixenes*
Laugh at me: make their pastime at my sorrow:
They should not laugh, if I could reach them, nor
Shall she, within my powre.
Enter Paulina.
Lord. You must not enter.
Paul. Nay rather (good my Lords) be second to me:
Feare you his tyrannous passion more (alas)
Then the Queenes life? A gracious innocent soule,
More free, then he is iealous.
Antig. That's enough.
Ser. Madam; he hath not slept to night, commanded
None should come at him.
Pau. Not so hot (good Sir)
I come to bring him sleepe. 'Tis such as you
That creepe like shadowes by him, and do sighe
At each his needlesse heauings: such as you
Nourish the cause of his awaking. I
Do, come with words, as medicinall, as true;
(Honest, as either;) to purge him of that humor
That presses him from sleepe.
Leo. Who noyse there, hoe?
Pau. No noyse (my Lord) but needfull conference,
About some Gossips for your Highnesse.
Leo. How?
Away with that audacious Lady. *Antigonus*,
I charg'd thee that she should not come about me,
I knew she would.
Ant. I told her so (my Lord)
On your displeasures perill, and on mine,
She should not visit you.
Leo. What? canst not rule her?
Paul. From all dishonestie he can: in this
(Vnlesse he take the course that you haue done)
Commit me, for committing honor, trust it,
He shall not rule me:
Ant. La-you now, you heare,
When she will take the raine, I let her run,
But shee'l not stumble.
Paul. Good my Liege, I come:
And I beseech you heare me, who professes
My selfe your loyall Seruant, your Physitian,
Your most obedient Counsailor: yet that dares
Lesse appeare so, in comforting your Euilles,
Then such as most seeme yours. I say, I come
From your good Queene.
Leo. Good Queene?
Paul. Good Queene (my Lord) good Queene,
I say good Queene,
And would by combate, make her good so, were I
A man, the worst about you.
Leo. Force her hence.
Pau Let him that makes but trifles of his eyes
First hand me: on mine owne accord, Ile off,
But first, Ile do my errand. The good Queene
(For she is good) hath brought you forth a daughter,
Heere 'tis. Commends it to your blessing.
Leo Out.
A mankinde Witch? Hence with her, out o'dore:
A most intelligencing bawd.
Paul. Not so:
I am as ignorant in that, as you,
In so entit'ling me: and no lesse honest
Then you are mad: which is enough, Ile warrant
(As this world goes) to passe for honest:
Leo. Traitors;
Will you not push her out? Giue her the Bastard,
Thou dotard, thou art woman-tyr'd: vnroosted
By thy dame *Partlet* heere. Take vp the Bastard,
Take't vp, I say: giue't to thy Croane.
Paul. For euer
Vnvenerable be thy hands, if thou
Tak'st vp the Princesse, by that forced basenesse
Which he ha's put vpon't
Leo. He dreads his Wife.
Paul. So I would you did: then 'twere past all doubt
Youl'd call your children, yours.
Leo. A nest of Traitors.
Ant. I am none, by this good light.
Pau. Not I: nor any
But one that's heere: and that's himselfe: for he,
The

The ſacred Honor of himſelfe, his Queenes,
His hopefull Sonnes, his Babes, betrayes to Slander,
Whoſe ſting is ſharper then the Swords; and will not
(For as the caſe now ſtands, it is a Curſe
He cannot be compell'd too't) once remoue
The Root of his Opinion, which is rotten,
As euer Oake, or Stone was ſound.
Leo. A Callat
Of boundleſſe tongue, who late hath beat her Husband,
And now bayts me: This Brat is none of mine,
It is the Iſſue of *Polixenes.*
Hence with it, and together with the Dam,
Commit them to the fire.
Paul. It is yours:
And might we lay th'old Prouerb to your charge,
So like you, 'tis the worſe. Behold (my Lords)
Although the Print be little, the whole Matter
And Coppy of the Father: (Eye, Noſe, Lippe,
The trick of's Frowne, his Fore-head, nay, the Valley,
The pretty dimples of his Chin, and Cheeke; his Smiles:
The very Mold, and frame of Hand, Nayle, Finger.)
And thou good Goddeſſe *Nature*, which haſt made it
So like to him that got it, if thou haſt
The ordering of the Mind too, 'mongſt all Colours
No Yellow in't, leaſt ſhe ſuſpect, as he do's,
Her Children, not her Husbands.
Leo. A groſſe Hagge:
And Lozell, thou art worthy to be hang'd,
That wilt not ſtay her Tongue.
Antig. Hang all the Husbands
That cannot doe that Feat, you'le leaue your ſelfe
Hardly one Subiect.
Leo. Once more take her hence.
Paul. A moſt vnworthy, and vnnaturall Lord
Can doe no more.
Leo. Ile ha' thee burnt.
Paul. I care not:
It is an Heretique that makes the fire,
Not ſhe which burnes in't. Ile not call you Tyrant:
But this moſt cruell vſage of your Queene
(Not able to produce more accuſation
Then your owne weake-hindg'd Fancy) ſomthing ſauors
Of Tyrannie, and will ignoble make you,
Yea ſcandalous to the World.
Leo. On your Allegeance,
Out of the Chamber with her. Were I a Tyrant,
Where were her life? ſhe durſt not call me ſo,
If ſhe did know me one. Away with her.
Paul. I pray you doe not puſh me, Ile be gone.
Looke to your Babe (my Lord) 'tis yours: *Ioue* ſend her
A better guiding Spirit. What needs theſe hands?
You that are thus ſo tender o're his Follyes,
Will neuer doe him good, not one of you.
So, ſo: Farewell, we are gone. *Exit*
Leo. Thou (Traytor) haſt ſet on thy Wife to this.
My Child? away with't? euen thou, that haſt
A heart ſo tender o're it, take it hence,
And ſee it inſtantly conſum'd with fire.
Euen thou, and none but thou. Take it vp ſtraight:
Within this houre bring me word 'tis done,
(And by good teſtimonie) or Ile ſeize thy life,
With what thou elſe call'ſt thine: if thou refuſe,
And wilt encounter with my Wrath, ſay ſo;
The Baſtard-braynes with theſe my proper hands
Shall I daſh out. Goe, take it to the fire,
For thou ſett'ſt on thy Wife.
Antig. I did not, Sir:
Theſe Lords, my Noble Fellowes, if they pleaſe,
Can cleare me in't.
Lords. We can: my Royall Liege,
He is not guiltie of her comming hither.
Leo. You're lyers all.
Lord. Beſeech your Highneſſe, giue vs better credit:
We haue alwayes truly ſeru'd you, and beſeech
So to eſteeme of vs: and on our knees we begge,
(As recompence of our deare ſeruices
Paſt, and to come) that you doe change this purpoſe,
Which being ſo horrible, ſo bloody, muſt
Lead on to ſome foule Iſſue. We all kneele.
Leo. I am a Feather for each Wind that blows:
Shall I liue on, to ſee this Baſtard kneele,
And call me Father? better burne it now,
Then curſe it then. But be it: let it liue.
It ſhall not neyther. You Sir, come you hither:
You that haue beene ſo tenderly officious
With Lady *Margerie*, your Mid-wife there,
To ſaue this Baſtards life; for 'tis a Baſtard,
So ſure as this Beard's gray. What will you aduenture,
To ſaue this Brats life?
Antig. Any thing (my Lord)
That my abilitie may vndergoe,
And Nobleneſſe impoſe: at leaſt thus much;
Ile pawne the little blood which I haue left,
To ſaue the Innocent: any thing poſſible.
Leo. It ſhall be poſſible: Sweare by this Sword
Thou wilt performe my bidding.
Antig. I will (my Lord.)
Leo. Marke, and performe it: ſeeſt thou? for the faile
Of any point in't, ſhall not onely be
Death to thy ſelfe, but to thy lewd-tongu'd Wife,
(Whom for this time we pardon) We enioyne thee,
As thou art Liege-man to vs, that thou carry
This female Baſtard hence, and that thou beare it
To ſome remote and deſart place, quite out
Of our Dominions; and that there thou leaue it
(Without more mercy) to it owne protection,
And fauour of the Climate: as by ſtrange fortune
It came to vs, I doe in Iuſtice charge thee,
On thy Soules perill, and thy Bodyes torture,
That thou commend it ſtrangely to ſome place,
Where Chance may nurſe, or end it: take it vp.
Antig. I ſweare to doe this: though a preſent death
Had beene more mercifull. Come on (poore Babe)
Some powerfull Spirit inſtruct the Kytes and Rauens
To be thy Nurſes. Wolues and Beares, they ſay,
(Caſting their ſauageneſſe aſide) haue done
Like offices of Pitty. Sir, be proſperous
In more then this deed do's require; and Bleſſing
Againſt this Crueltie, fight on thy ſide
(Poore Thing, condemn'd to loſſe.) *Exit.*
Leo. No: Ile not reare
Anothers Iſſue. *Enter a Seruant.*
Seru. Pleaſe' your Highneſſe, Poſts
From thoſe you ſent to th'Oracle, are come
An houre ſince: *Cleomines* and *Dion*,
Being well arriu'd from Delphos, are both landed,
Haſting to th' Court.
Lord. So pleaſe you (Sir) their ſpeed
Hath beene beyond accompt.
Leo. Twentie three dayes
They haue beene abſent: 'tis good ſpeed: fore-tells
The great *Apollo* ſuddenly will haue
The

The truth of this appeare: Prepare you Lords,
Summon a Session, that we may arraigne
Our most disloyall Lady: for as she hath
Been publikely accus'd, so shall she haue
A iust and open Triall. While she liues,
My heart will be a burthen to me. Leaue me,
And thinke vpon my bidding. *Exeunt.*

Actus Tertius. Scena Prima.

Enter Cleomines and Dion.

Cleo. The Clymat's delicate, the Ayre most sweet,
Fertile the Isle, the Temple much surpassing
The common prayse it beares.
Dion. I shall report,
For most it caught me, the Celestiall Habits,
(Me thinkes I so should terme them) and the reuerence
Of the graue Wearers. O, the Sacrifice,
How ceremonious, solemne, and vn-earthly
It was i'th'Offring?
Cleo. But of all, the burst
And the eare-deaff'ning Voyce o'th'Oracle,
Kin to *Ioues* Thunder, so surpriz'd my Sence,
That I was nothing.
Dio. If th'euent o'th'Iourney
Proue as successefull to the Queene (O be't so)
As it hath beene to vs, rare, pleasant, speedie,
The time is worth the vse on't.
Cleo. Great *Apollo*
Turne all to th'best: these Proclamations,
So forcing faults vpon *Hermione*,
I little like.
Dio. The violent carriage of it
Will cleare, or end the Businesse, when the Oracle
(Thus by *Apollo's* great Diuine seal'd vp)
Shall the Contents discouer: something rare
Euen then will rush to knowledge. Goe: fresh Horses,
And gracious be the issue. *Exeunt.*

Scœna Secunda.

Enter Leontes, Lords, Officers: Hermione (as to her Triall) Ladies: Cleomines, Dion.

Leo. This Sessions (to our great griefe we pronounce)
Euen pushes 'gainst our heart. The partie try'd,
The Daughter of a King, our Wife, and one
Of vs too much belou'd. Let vs be clear'd
Of being tyrannous, since we so openly
Proceed in Iustice, which shall haue due course,
Euen to the Guilt, or the Purgation:
Produce the Prisoner.
Officer. It is his Highnesse pleasure, that the Queene
Appeare in person, here in Court. *Silence.*
Leo. Reade the Indictment.
Officer. Hermione, *Queene to the worthy* Leontes, *King of Sicilia, thou art here accused and arraigned of High Treason, in committing Adultery with* Polixenes *King of Bohemia, and conspiring with* Camillo *to take away the Life of our Soueraigne Lord the King, thy Royall Husband: the pretence whereof being by circumstances partly layd open, thou* (Hermione) *contrary to the Faith and Allegeance of a true Subiect, didst counsaile and ayde them, for their better safetie, to flye away by Night.*
Her. Since what I am to say, must be but that
Which contradicts my Accusation, and
The testimonie on my part, no other
But what comes from my selfe, it shall scarce boot me
To say, Not guiltie: mine Integritie
Being counted Falsehood, shall (as I expresse it)
Be so receiu'd. But thus, if Powres Diuine
Behold our humane Actions (as they doe)
I doubt not then, but Innocence shall make
False Accusation blush, and Tyrannie
Tremble at Patience. You (my Lord) best know
(Whom least will seeme to doe so) my past life
Hath beene as continent, as chaste, as true,
As I am now vnhappy; which is more
Then Historie can patterne, though deuis'd,
And play'd, to take Spectators. For behold me,
A Fellow of the Royall Bed, which owe
A Moitie of the Throne: a great Kings Daughter,
The Mother to a hopefull Prince, here standing
To prate and talke for Life, and Honor, fore
Who please to come, and heare. For Life, I prize it
As I weigh Griefe (which I would spare:) For Honor,
'Tis a deriuatiue from me to mine,
And onely that I stand for. I appeale
To your owne Conscience (Sir) before *Polixenes*
Came to your Court, how I was in your grace,
How merited to be so: Since he came,
With what encounter so vncurrant, I
Haue strayn'd t'appeare thus; if one iot beyond
The bound of Honor, or in act, or will
That way enclining, hardned be the hearts
Of all that heare me, and my neer'st of Kin
Cry fie vpon my Graue.
Leo. I ne're heard yet,
That any of these bolder Vices wanted
Lesse Impudence to gaine-say what they did,
Then to performe it first.
Her. That's true enough,
Though 'tis a saying (Sir) not due to me.
Leo. You will not owne it.
Her. More then Mistresse of,
Which comes to me in name of Fault, I must not
At all acknowledge. For *Polixenes*
(With whom I am accus'd) I doe confesse
I lou'd him, as in Honor he requir'd:
With such a kind of Loue, as might becom
A Lady like me; with a Loue, euen such,
So, and no other, as your selfe commanded:
Which, not to haue done, I thinke had been in me
Both Disobedience, and Ingratitude
To you, and toward your Friend, whose Loue had spoke,
Euen since it could speake, from an Infant, freely,
That it was yours. Now for Conspiracie,
I know not how it tastes, though it be dish'd
For me to try how: All I know of it,
Is, that *Camillo* was an honest man;
And why he left your Court, the Gods themselues
(Wotting no more then I) are ignorant.
Leo. You knew of his departure, as you know
What you haue vnderta'ne to doe in's absence.
Her. Sir,

Her. Sir,
You ſpeake a Language that I vnderſtand not:
My Life ſtands in the leuell of your Dreames,
Which Ile lay downe.
Leo. Your Actions are my Dreames.
You had a Baſtard by *Polixenes*,
And I but dream'd it: As you were paſt all ſhame,
(Thoſe of your Fact are ſo) ſo paſt all truth;
Which to deny, concernes more then auailes: for as
Thy Brat hath been caſt out, like to it ſelfe,
No Father owning it (which is indeed
More criminall in thee, then it) ſo thou
Shalt feele our Iuſtice; in whoſe eaſieſt paſſage,
Looke for no leſſe then death.
Her. Sir, ſpare your Threats:
The Bugge which you would fright me with, I ſeeke:
To me can Life be no commoditie;
The crowne and comfort of my Life (your Fauor)
I doe giue loſt, for I doe feele it gone,
But know not how it went. My ſecond Ioy,
And firſt Fruits of my body, from his preſence
I am bar'd, like one infectious. My third comfort
(Star'd moſt vnluckily) is from my breaſt
(The innocent milke in it moſt innocent mouth)
Hal'd out to murther. My ſelfe on euery Poſt
Proclaym'd a Strumpet: With immodeſt hatred
The Child-bed priuiledge deny'd, which longs
To Women of all faſhion. Laſtly, hurried
Here, to this place, i'th' open ayre, before
I haue got ſtrength of limit. Now (my Liege)
Tell me what bleſſings I haue here aliue,
That I ſhould feare to die? Therefore proceed:
But yet heare this: miſtake me not: no Life,
(I prize it not a ſtraw) but for mine Honor,
Which I would free: if I ſhall be condemn'd
Vpon ſurmizes (all proofes ſleeping elſe,
But what your Iealouſies awake) I tell you
'Tis Rigor, and not Law. Your Honors all,
I doe referre me to the Oracle:
Apollo be my Iudge.
Lord. This your requeſt
Is altogether iuſt: therefore bring forth
(And in *Apollo's* Name) his Oracle.
Her. The Emperor of Ruſſia was my Father.
Oh that he were aliue, and here beholding
His Daughters Tryall: that he did but ſee
The flatneſſe of my miſerie; yet with eyes
Of Pitty, not Reuenge.
Officer. You here ſhal ſweare vpon this Sword of Iuſtice,
That you (*Cleomines* and *Dion*) haue
Been both at Delphos, and from thence haue brought
This ſeal'd-vp Oracle, by the Hand deliuer'd
Of great *Apollo's* Prieſt; and that ſince then,
You haue not dar'd to breake the holy Seale,
Nor read the Secrets in't.
Cleo. Dio. All this we ſweare.
Leo. Breake vp the Seales, and read.
Officer. Hermione *is chaſt,* Polixenes *blameleſſe,* Camillo *a true Subiect,* Leontes *a iealous Tyrant, his innocent Babe truly begotten, and the King ſhall liue without an Heire, if that which is loſt, be not found.*
Lords. Now bleſſed be the great *Apollo.*
Her. Prayſed.
Leo. Haſt thou read truth?
Offic. I (my Lord) euen ſo as it is here ſet downe.
Leo. There is no truth at all i'th'Oracle:
The Seſſions ſhall proceed: this is meere falſehood.
Ser. My Lord the King: the King?
Leo. What is the buſineſſe?
Ser. O Sir, I ſhall be hated to report it.
The Prince your Sonne, with meere conceit, and feare
Of the Queenes ſpeed, is gone.
Leo. How? gone?
Ser. Is dead.
Leo. *Apollo's* angry, and the Heauens themſelues
Doe ſtrike at my Iniuſtice. How now there?
Paul. This newes is mortall to the Queene: Look downe
And ſee what Death is doing.
Leo. Take her hence:
Her heart is but o're-charg'd: ſhe will recouer.
I haue too much beleeu'd mine owne ſuſpition:
'Beſeech you tenderly apply to her
Some remedies for life. *Apollo* pardon
My great prophaneneſſe 'gainſt thine Oracle.
Ile reconcile me to *Polixenes*,
New woe my Queene, recall the good *Camillo*
(Whom I proclaime a man of Truth, of Mercy:)
For being tranſported by my Iealouſies
To bloody thoughts, and to reuenge, I choſe
Camillo for the miniſter, to poyſon
My friend *Polixenes*: which had been done,
But that the good mind of *Camillo* tardied
My ſwift command: though I with Death, and with
Reward, did threaten and encourage him,
Not doing it, and being done: he (moſt humane,
And fill'd with Honor) to my Kingly Gueſt
Vnclaſp'd my practiſe, quit his fortunes here
(Which you knew great) and to the hazard
Of all Incertainties, himſelfe commended,
No richer then his Honor: How he gliſters
Through my Ruſt? and how his Pietie
Do's my deeds make the blacker?
Paul. Woe the while:
O cut my Lace, leaſt my heart (cracking it)
Breake too.
Lord. What fit is this? good Lady?
Paul. What ſtudied torments (Tyrant) haſt for me?
What Wheeles? Racks? Fires? What flaying? boyling?
In Leads, or Oyles? What old, or newer Torture
Muſt I receiue? whoſe euery word deſerues
To taſte of thy moſt worſt. Thy Tyranny
(Together working with thy Iealouſies,
Fancies too weake for Boyes, too greene and idle
For Girles of Nine) O thinke what they haue done,
And then run mad indeed: ſtarke-mad: for all
Thy by-gone fooleries were but ſpices of it.
That thou betrayed'ſt *Polixenes*, 'twas nothing,
(That did but ſhew thee, of a Foole, inconſtant,
And damnable ingratefull:) Nor was't much.
Thou would'ſt haue poyſon'd good *Camillo's* Honor,
To haue him kill a King: poore Treſpaſſes,
More monſtrous ſtanding by: whereof I reckon
The caſting forth to Crowes, thy Baby-daughter,
To be or none, or little; though a Deuill
Would haue ſhed water out of fire, ere don't:
Nor is't directly layd to thee the death
Of the young Prince, whoſe honorable thoughts
(Thoughts high for one ſo tender) cleft the heart
That could conceiue a groſſe and fooliſh Sire
Blemiſh'd his gracious Dam: this is not, no,
Layd to thy anſwere: but the laſt: O Lords,
When I haue ſaid, cry woe: the Queene, the Queene,
The

The ſweet'ſt, deer'ſt creature's dead: & vengeance for't
Not drop'd downe yet.

Lord. The higher powres forbid.

Pau. I ſay ſhe's dead: Ile ſwear't. If word, nor oath
Preuaile not, go and ſee: if you can bring
Tincture, or luſtre in her lip, her eye
Heate outwardly, or breath within, Ile ſerue you
As I would do the Gods. But, O thou Tyrant,
Do not repent theſe things, for they are heauier
Then all thy woes can ſtirre: therefore betake thee
To nothing but diſpaire. A thouſand knees,
Ten thouſand yeares together, naked, faſting,
Vpon a barren Mountaine, and ſtill Winter
In ſtorme perpetuall, could not moue the Gods
To looke that way thou wer't.

Leo. Go on, go on
Thou canſt not ſpeake too much, I haue deſeru'd
All tongues to talke their bittreſt.

Lord. Say no more;
How ere the buſineſſe goes, you haue made fault
I'th boldneſſe of your ſpeech.

Pau. I am ſorry for't;
All faults I make, when I ſhall come to know them,
I do repent: Alas, I haue ſhew'd too much
The raſhneſſe of a woman: he is toucht
To th'Noble heart. What's gone, and what's paſt helpe
Should be paſt greefe: Do not receiue affliction
At my petition; I beſeech you, rather
Let me be puniſh'd, that haue minded you
Of what you ſhould forget. Now (good my Liege)
Sir, Royall Sir, forgiue a fooliſh woman:
The loue I bore your Queene (Lo, foole againe)
Ile ſpeake of her no more, nor of your Children:
Ile not remember you of my owne Lord
(Who is loſt too:) take your patience to you,
And Ile ſay nothing

Leo. Thou didſt ſpeake but well,
When moſt the truth: which I receyue much better,
Then to be pittied of thee. Prethee bring me
To the dead bodies of my Queene, and Sonne,
One graue ſhall be for both: Vpon them ſhall
The cauſes of their death appeare (vnto
Our ſhame perpetuall) once a day, Ile viſit
The Chappell where they lye, and teares ſhed there
Shall be my recreation. So long as Nature
Will beare vp with this exerciſe, ſo long
I dayly vow to vſe it. Come, and leade me
To theſe ſorrowes.

Scæna Tertia.

Enter Antigonus, a Marriner, Babe, Sheepe-heard, and Clowne.

Ant. Thou art perfect then, our ſhip hath toucht vpon
The Deſarts of *Bohemia.*

Mar. I (my Lord) and feare
We haue Landed in ill time: the skies looke grimly,
And threaten preſent bluſters. In my conſcience
The heauens with that we haue in hand, are angry,
And frowne vpon's.

Ant. Their ſacred wil's be done: go get a-boord,
Looke to thy barke, Ile not be long before
I call vpon thee.

Mar. Make your beſt haſte, and go not
Too-farre i'th Land: 'tis like to be lowd weather,
Beſides this place is famous for the Creatures
Of prey, that keepe vpon't.

Antig. Go thou away,
Ile follow inſtantly.

Mar. I am glad at heart
To be ſo ridde o'th buſineſſe. *Exit*

Ant. Come, poore babe;
I haue heard (but not beleeu'd) the Spirits o'th'dead
May walke againe: if ſuch thing be, thy Mother
Appear'd to me laſt night: for ne're was dreame
So like a waking. To me comes a creature,
Sometimes her head on one ſide, ſome another,
I neuer ſaw a veſſell of like ſorrow
So fill'd, and ſo becomming: in pure white Robes
Like very ſanctity ſhe did approach
My Cabine where I lay: thrice bow'd before me,
And (gaſping to begin ſome ſpeech) her eyes
Became two ſpouts; the furie ſpent, anon
Did this breake from her. Good *Antigonus,*
Since Fate (againſt thy better diſpoſition)
Hath made thy perſon for the Thower-out
Of my poore babe, according to thine oath,
Places remote enough are in *Bohemia,*
There weepe, and leaue it crying: and for the babe
Is counted loſt for euer, *Perdita*
I prethee call't: For this vngentle buſineſſe
Put on thee, by my Lord, thou ne're ſhalt ſee
Thy Wife *Paulina* more: and ſo, with ſhriekes
She melted into Ayre. Affrighted much,
I did in time collect my ſelfe, and thought
This was ſo, and no ſlumber: Dreames, are toyes,
Yet for this once, yea ſuperſtitiouſly,
I will be ſquar'd by this. I do beleeue
Hermione hath ſuffer'd death, and that
Apollo would (this being indeede the iſſue
Of King *Polixenes*) it ſhould heere be laide
(Either for life, or death) vpon the earth
Of it's right Father. Bloſſome, ſpeed thee well,
There lye, and there thy charracter: there theſe,
Which may if Fortune pleaſe, both breed thee (pretty)
And ſtill reſt thine. The ſtorme beginnes, poore wretch,
That for thy mothers fault, art thus expos'd
To loſſe, and what may follow. Weepe I cannot,
But my heart bleedes: and moſt accurſt am I
To be by oath enioyn'd to this. Farewell,
The day frownes more and more: thou'rt like to haue
A lullabie too rough: I neuer ſaw
The heauens ſo dim, by day. A ſauage clamor?
Well may I get a-boord: This is the Chace,
I am gone for euer. *Exit purſued by a Beare.*

Shep. I would there were no age betweene ten and three and twenty, or that youth would ſleep out the reſt: for there is nothing (in the betweene) but getting wenches with childe, wronging the Auncientry, ſtealing, fighting, hearke you now: would any but theſe boylde-braines of nineteene, and two and twenty hunt this weather? They haue ſcarr'd away two of my beſt Sheepe, which I feare the Wolfe will ſooner finde then the Maiſter; if any where I haue them, 'tis by the ſea-ſide, brouzing of Iuy. Good-lucke (and't be thy will) what haue we heere? Mercy on's, a Barne? A very pretty barne; A boy, or a Childe I wonder? (A pretty one, a verie prettie one) ſure ſome Scape; Though I am not bookiſh, yet I can

can reade Waiting-Gentlewoman in the ſcape: this has beene ſome ſtaire-worke, ſome Trunke-worke, ſome behinde-doore worke: they were warmer that got this, then the poore Thing is heere. Ile take it vp for pity, yet Ile tarry till my ſonne come: he hallow'd but euen now. Whoa-ho-hoa.

Enter Clowne.

Clo. Hilloa, loa.

Shep. What? art ſo neere? If thou'lt ſee a thing to talke on, when thou art dead and rotten, come hither: what ayl'ſt thou, man?

Clo. I haue ſeene two ſuch ſights, by Sea & by Land: but I am not to ſay it is a Sea, for it is now the ſkie, betwixt the Firmament and it, you cannot thruſt a bodkins point.

Shep. Why boy, how is it?

Clo. I would you did but ſee how it chafes, how it rages, how it takes vp the ſhore, but that's not to the point: Oh, the moſt pitteous cry of the poore ſoules, ſometimes to ſee 'em and not to ſee 'em: Now the Shippe boaring the Moone with her maine Maſt, and anon ſwallowed with yeſt and froth, as you'ld thruſt a Corke into a hogſhead. And then for the Land-ſeruice, to ſee how the Beare tore out his ſhoulder-bone, how he cride to mee for helpe, and ſaid his name was *Antigonus*, a Nobleman: But to make an end of the Ship, to ſee how the Sea flapdragon'd it: but firſt, how the poore ſoules roared, and the ſea mock'd them: and how the poore Gentleman roared, and the Beare mock'd him, both roaring lowder then the ſea, or weather.

Shep. Name of mercy, when was this boy?

Clo. Now, now: I haue not wink'd ſince I ſaw theſe ſights: the men are not yet cold vnder water, nor the Beare halfe din'd on the Gentleman: he's at it now.

Shep. Would I had bin by, to haue help'd the olde man.

Clo. I would you had beene by the ſhip ſide, to haue help'd her; there your charity would haue lack'd footing.

Shep. Heauy matters, heauy matters: but looke thee heere boy. Now bleſſe thy ſelfe: thou met'ſt with things dying, I with things new borne. Here's a ſight for thee: Looke thee, a bearing-cloath for a Squires childe: looke thee heere, take vp, take vp (Boy:) open't: ſo, let's ſee, it was told me I ſhould be rich by the Fairies. This is ſome Changeling: open't: what's within, boy?

Clo. You're a mad olde man: If the ſinnes of your youth are forgiuen you, you're well to liue. Golde, all Gold.

Shep. This is Faiery Gold boy, and 'twill proue ſo: vp with't, keepe it cloſe: home, home, the next way. We are luckie (boy) and to bee ſo ſtill requires nothing but ſecrecie. Let my ſheepe go: Come (good boy) the next way home.

Clo. Go you the next way with your Findings, Ile go ſee if the Beare bee gone from the Gentleman, and how much he hath eaten: they are neuer curſt but when they are hungry: if there be any of him left, Ile bury it.

Shep. That's a good deed: if thou mayeſt diſcerne by that which is left of him, what he is, fetch me to th'ſight of him.

Clowne. 'Marry will I: and you ſhall helpe to put him i'th'ground.

Shep. 'Tis a lucky day, boy, and wee'l do good deeds on't.

Exeunt

Actus Quartus. Scena Prima.

Enter Time, the Chorus.

Time. I that pleaſe ſome, try all: both ioy and terror
Of good, and bad: that makes, and vnfolds error,
Now take vpon me (in the name of Time)
To vſe my wings: Impute it not a crime
To me, or my ſwift paſſage, that I ſlide
Ore ſixteene yeeres, and leaue the growth vntride
Of that wide gap, ſince it is in my powre
To orethrow Law, and in one ſelfe-borne howre
To plant, and ore-whelme Cuſtome. Let me paſſe
The ſame I am, ere ancient'ſt Order was,
Or what is now receiu'd. I witneſſe to
The times that brought them in, ſo ſhall I do
To th'freſheſt things now reigning, and make ſtale
The gliſtering of this preſent, as my Tale
Now ſeemes to it: your patience this allowing,
I turne my glaſſe, and giue my Scene ſuch growing
As you had ſlept betweene: *Leontes* leauing
Th'effects of his fond iealouſies, ſo greeuing
That he ſhuts vp himſelfe. Imagine me
(Gentle Spectators) that I now may be
In faire Bohemia, and remember well,
I mentioned a ſonne o'th'Kings, which *Florizell*
I now name to you: and with ſpeed ſo pace
To ſpeake of *Perdita*, now growne in grace
Equall with wond'ring. What of her inſues
I liſt not propheſie: but let Times newes
Be knowne when 'tis brought forth. A ſhepherds daughter
And what to her adheres, which followes after,
Is th'argument of Time: of this allow,
If euer you haue ſpent time worſe, ere now:
If neuer, yet that Time himſelfe doth ſay,
He wiſhes earneſtly, you neuer may. *Exit.*

Scena Secunda.

Enter Polixenes, and Camillo.

Pol. I pray thee (good *Camillo*) be no more importunate: 'tis a ſickneſſe denying thee any thing: a death to grant this.

Cam. It is fifteene yeeres ſince I ſaw my Countrey: though I haue (for the moſt part) bin ayred abroad, I deſire to lay my bones there. Beſides, the penitent King (my Maſter) hath ſent for me, to whoſe feeling ſorrowes I might be ſome allay, or I oreweene to thinke ſo) which is another ſpurre to my departure.

Pol. As thou lou'ſt me (*Camillo*) wipe not out the reſt of thy ſeruices, by leauing me now: the neede I haue of thee, thine owne goodneſſe hath made: better not to haue had thee, then thus to want thee, thou hauing made me Buſineſſes, (which none (without thee) can ſufficiently manage) muſt either ſtay to execute them thy ſelfe, or take away with thee the very ſeruices thou haſt done: which if I haue not enough conſidered (as too much I cannot) to bee more thankefull to thee, ſhall bee my ſtudie, and my profite therein, the heaping friendſhippes. Of that fatall Countrey Sicillia, prethee ſpeake no more, whoſe very naming, puniſhes me with the remembrance of of that penitent (as thou calſt him) and reconciled King my brother, whoſe loſſe of his moſt precious Queene & Children, are euen now to be a-freſh lamented. Say to me, when ſaw'ſt thou the Prince *Florizell* my ſon? Kings are no leſſe vnhappy, their iſſue, not being gracious, then they are in looſing them, when they haue approued their Vertues.

Cam. Sir, it is three dayes ſince I ſaw the Prince: what his happier affayres may be, are to me vnknowne: but I haue (miſsingly) noted, he is of late much retyred from Court, and is leſſe frequent to his Princely exerciſes then formerly he hath appeared.

Pol. I haue conſidered ſo much (*Camillo*) and with ſome care, ſo farre, that I haue eyes vnder my ſeruice, which looke vpon his remouedneſſe: from whom I haue this Intelligence, that he is ſeldome from the houſe of a moſt homely ſhepheard: a man (they ſay) that from very nothing, and beyond the imagination of his neighbors, is growne into an vnſpeakable eſtate.

Cam. I haue heard (ſir) of ſuch a man, who hath a daughter of moſt rare note: the report of her is extended more, then can be thought to begin from ſuch a cottage

Pol. That's likewiſe part of my Intelligence: but (I feare) the Angle that pluckes our ſonne thither. Thou ſhalt accompany vs to the place, where we will (not appearing what we are) haue ſome queſtion with the ſhepheard; from whoſe ſimplicity, I thinke it not vneaſie to get the cauſe of my ſonnes reſort thether. 'Prethe be my preſent partner in this buſines, and lay aſide the thoughts of Sicillia.

Cam. I willingly obey your command.

Pol. My beſt *Camillo*, we muſt diſguiſe our ſelues. *Exit*

Scena Tertia

Enter Autolicus ſinging.

When Daffadils begin to peere,
With heigh the Doxy ouer the dale,
Why then comes in the ſweet o'the yeere,
For the red blood raigns in ỹ winters pale.

The white ſheete bleaching on the hedge,
With hey the ſweet birds, O how they ſing:
Doth ſet my pugging tooth an edge,
For a quart of Ale is a diſh for a King.

The Larke, that tirra Lyra chaunts,
With heigh, the Thruſh and the Iay:
Are Summer ſongs for me and my Aunts
While we lye tumbling in the hay.

I haue ſeru'd Prince *Florizell*, and in my time wore three pile, but now I am out of ſeruice.

But ſhall I go mourne for that (my deere)
the pale Moone ſhines by night:
And when I wander here, and there
I then do moſt go right.
If Tinkers may haue leaue to liue,
and beare the Sow-skin Bowget,
Then my account I well may giue,
and in the Stockes auouch-it.

My Trafficke is ſheetes: when the Kite builds, looke to leſſer Linnen. My Father nam'd me *Autolicus*, who being (as I am) lytter'd vnder Mercurie, was likewiſe a ſnapper-vp of vnconſidered trifles: With Dye and drab, I purchas'd this Capariſon, and my Reuennew is the ſilly Cheate. Gallowes, and Knocke, are too powerfull on the Highway. Beating and hanging are terrors to mee: For the life to come, I ſleepe out the thought of it. A prize, a prize

Enter Clowne.

Clo. Let me ſee, euery Leauen-weather toddes, euery tod yeeldes pound and odde ſhilling: fifteene hundred ſhorne, what comes the wooll too?

Aut. If the ſprindge hold, the Cocke's mine.

Clo. I cannot do't without Compters. Let mee ſee, what am I to buy for our Sheepe-ſhearing-Feaſt? Three pound of Sugar, fiue pound of Currence, Rice: What will this ſiſter of mine do with Rice? But my father hath made her Miſtris of the Feaſt, and ſhe layes it on Shee hath made-me four and twenty Noſe-gayes for the ſhearers (three-man ſong-men, all, and very good ones) but they are moſt of them Meanes and Baſes; but one Puritan amongſt them, and he ſings Pſalmes to horne-pipes, I muſt haue Saffron to colour the Warden Pies, Mace: Dates, none: that's out of my note: Nutmegges, ſeuen; a Race or two of Ginger, but that I may begge: Foure pound of Prewyns, and as many of Reyſons o'th Sun.

Aut Oh, that euer I was borne.

Clo I'th'name of me.

Aut. Oh helpe me, helpe mee: plucke but off theſe ragges: and then, death, death.

Clo. Alacke poore ſoule, thou haſt need of more rags to lay on thee, rather then haue theſe off.

Aut. Oh ſir, the loathſomneſſe of them offend mee, more then the ſtripes I haue receiued, which are mightie ones and millions.

Clo. Alas poore man, a million of beating may come to a great matter.

Aut. I am rob'd ſir, and beaten: my money, and apparrell tane from me, and theſe deteſtable things put vpon me.

Clo. What, by a horſe-man, or a foot-man?

Aut. A footman (ſweet ſir) a footman.

Clo. Indeed, he ſhould be a footman, by the garments he has left with thee: If this bee a horſemans Coate, it hath ſeene very hot ſeruice. Lend me thy hand, Ile helpe thee. Come, lend me thy hand.

Aut. Oh good ſir, tenderly, oh.

Clo. Alas poore ſoule.

Aut. Oh good ſir, ſoftly, good ſir: I feare (ſir) my ſhoulder-blade is out.

Clo. How now? Canſt ſtand?

Aut. Softly, deere ſir: good ſir, ſoftly: you ha done me a charitable office.

Clo. Doeſt lacke any mony? I haue a little mony for thee.

Aut. No, good ſweet ſir: no, I beſeech you ſir: I haue a Kinſman not paſt three quarters of a mile hence, vnto whome I was going: I ſhall there haue money, or anie thing I want: Offer me no money I pray you, that killes my heart

Clow What manner of Fellow was hee that robb'd you?

Aut. A fellow (ſir) that I haue knowne to goe about with Troll-my-dames: I knew him once a ſeruant of the Prince: I cannot tell good ſir, for which of his Vertues it was, but hee was certainely Whipt out of the Court.

Clo.

Clo. His vices you would say: there's no vertue whipt out of the Court: they cherish it to make it stay there; and yet it will no more but abide.

Aut. Vices I would say (Sir.) I know this man well, he hath bene since an Ape-bearer, then a Processe-seruer (a Bayliffe) then hee compast a Motion of the Prodigall sonne, and married a Tinkers wife, within a Mile where my Land and Liuing lyes; and (hauing flowne ouer many knauish professions) he setled onely in Rogue: some call him *Autolicus*.

Clo. Out vpon him: Prig for my life Prig: he haunts Wakes, Faires, and Beare-baitings.

Aut. Very true sir: he sir hee: that's the Rogue that put me into this apparrell.

Clo. Not a more cowardly Rogue in all *Bohemia*; If you had but look'd bigge, and spit at him, hee'ld haue runne.

Aut. I must confesse to you (sir) I am no fighter: I am false of heart that way, & that he knew I warrant him.

Clo. How do you now?

Aut. Sweet sir, much better then I was: I can stand, and walke: I will euen take my leaue of you, & pace softly towards my Kinsmans.

Clo. Shall I bring thee on the way?

Aut. No, good fac'd sir, no sweet sir.

Clo. Then fartheewell, I must go buy Spices for our sheepe-shearing. *Exit.*

Aut. Prosper you sweet sir. Your purse is not hot enough to purchase your Spice: Ile be with you at your sheepe-shearing too: If I make not this Cheat bring out another, and the sheerers proue sheepe, let me be vnrold, and my name put in the booke of Vertue.

Song. *Iog-on, Iog-on, the foot path way,*
And merrily hent the Stile-a:
A merry heart goes all the day,
Your sad tyres in a Mile-a. *Exit.*

Scena Quarta.

Enter Florizell, Perdita, Shepherd, Clowne, Polixenes, Camillo, Mopsa, Dorcas, Seruants, Autolicus.

Flo. These your vnvsuall weeds, to each part of you
Do's giue a life: no Shepherdesse, but *Flora*
Peering in Aprils front. This your sheepe-shearing,
Is as a meeting of the petty Gods,
And you the Queene on't.

Perd. Sir: my gracious Lord,
To chide at your extreames, it not becomes me:
(Oh pardon, that I name them:) your high selfe
The gracious marke o'th'Land, you haue obscur'd
With a Swaines wearing: and me (poore lowly Maide)
Most Goddesse-like prank'd vp: But that our Feasts
In euery Messe, haue folly; and the Feeders
Digest with a Custome, I should blush
To see you so attyr'd: sworne I thinke,
To shew my selfe a glasse.

Flo. I blesse the time.
When my good Falcon, made her flight a-crosse
Thy Fathers ground

Perd. Now Ioue affoord you cause:
To me the difference forges dread (your Greatnesse
Hath not beene vs'd to feare:) euen now I tremble
To thinke your Father, by some accident
Should passe this way, as you did: Oh the Fates,
How would he looke, to see his worke, so noble,
Vildely bound vp? What would he say? Or how
Should I (in these my borrowed Flaunts) behold
The sternnesse of his presence?

Flo. Apprehend
Nothing but iollity: the Goddes themselues
(Humbling their Deities to loue) haue taken
The shapes of Beasts vpon them. Iupiter,
Became a Bull, and bellow'd: the greene Neptune
A Ram, and bleated: and the Fire-roab'd-God
Golden Apollo, a poore humble Swaine,
As I seeme now. Their transformations,
Were neuer for a peece of beauty, rarer,
Nor in a way so chaste: since my desires
Run not before mine honor: nor my Lusts
Burne hotter then my Faith.

Perd. O but Sir,
Your resolution cannot hold, when 'tis
Oppos'd (as it must be) by th'powre of the King:
One of these two must be necessities,
Which then will speake, that you must change this purpose,
Or I my life.

Flo. Thou deer'st *Perdita*,
With these forc'd thoughts, I prethee darken not
The Mirth o'th' Feast: Or Ile be thine (my Faire)
Or not my Fathers. For I cannot be
Mine owne, nor any thing to any, if
I be not thine. To this I am most constant,
Though destiny say no. Be merry (Gentle)
Strangle such thoughts as these, with any thing
That you behold the while. Your guests are comming:
Lift vp your countenance, as it were the day
Of celebration of that nuptiall, which
We two haue sworne shall come.

Perd. O Lady Fortune,
Stand you auspicious.

Flo. See, your Guests approach,
Addresse your selfe to entertaine them sprightly,
And let's be red with mirth.

Shep. Fy (daughter) when my old wife liu'd: vpon
This day, she was both Pantler, Butler, Cooke,
Both Dame and Seruant: Welcom'd all: seru'd all,
Would sing her song, and dance her turne: now heere
At vpper end o'th Table; now, i'th middle:
On his shoulder, and his: her face o'fire
With labour, and the thing she tooke to quench it
She would to each one sip. You are retyred,
As if you were a feasted one: and not
The Hostesse of the meeting: Pray you bid
These vnknowne friends to's welcome, for it is
A way to make vs better Friends, more knowne.
Come, quench your blushes, and present your selfe
That which you are, Mistris o'th'Feast. Come on,
And bid vs welcome to your sheepe-shearing,
As your good flocke shall prosper.

Perd. Sir, welcome:
It is my Fathers will, I should take on mee
The Hostesseship o'th'day: you're welcome sir.
Giue me those Flowres there (*Dorcas*.) Reuerend Sirs,
For you, there's Rosemary, and Rue, these keepe
Seeming, and sauour all the Winter long:
Grace, and Remembrance be to you both,
And welcome to our Shearing.

Bb2 *Pol.*

Pol. Shepherdeſſe,
(A faire one are you:) well you fit our ages
With flowres of Winter.
Perd. Sir, the yeare growing ancient,
Not yet on ſummers death, nor on the birth
Of trembling winter, the fayreſt flowres o'th ſeaſon
Are our Carnations, and ſtreak'd Gilly-vors,
(Which ſome call Natures baſtards) of that kind
Our ruſticke Gardens barren, and I care not
To get ſlips of them.
Pol. Wherefore (gentle Maiden)
Do you neglect them.
Perd. For I haue heard it ſaid,
There is an Art, which in their pideneſſe ſhares
With great creating-Nature.
Pol. Say there be:
Yet Nature is made better by no meane,
But Nature makes that Meane: ſo ouer that Art,
(Which you ſay addes to Nature) is an Art
That Nature makes: you ſee (ſweet Maid) we marry
A gentler Sien, to the wildeſt Stocke,
And make conceyue a barke of baſer kinde
By bud of Nobler race. This is an Art
Which do's mend Nature: change it rather, but
The Art it ſelfe, is Nature.
Perd. So it is.
Pol. Then make you Garden rich in Gilly'vors,
And do not call them baſtards.
Perd. Ile not put
The Dible in earth, to ſet one ſlip of them:
No more then were I painted, I would wiſh
This youth ſhould ſay 'twer well: and onely therefore
Deſire to breed by me. Here's flowres for you:
Hot Lauender, Mints, Sauory, Mariorum,
The Mary-gold, that goes to bed with'Sun,
And with him riſes, weeping: Theſe are flowres
Of middle ſummer, and I thinke they are giuen
To men of middle age. Y'are very welcome.
Cam. I ſhould leaue graſing, were I of your flocke,
And onely liue by gazing.
Perd. Out alas:
You'ld be ſo leane, that blaſts of January (Friend,
Would blow you through and through. Now (my fairſt
I would I had ſome Flowres o'th Spring, that might
Become your time of day: and yours, and yours,
That weare vpon your Virgin-branches yet
Your Maiden-heads growing: O *Proſerpina*,
For the Flowres now, that (frighted) thou let'ſt fall
From *Dyſſes* Waggon: Daffadils,
That come before the Swallow dares, and take
The windes of March with beauty: Violets (dim,
But ſweeter then the lids of *Iuno's* eyes,
Or *Cytherea's* breath) pale Prime-roſes,
That dye vnmarried, ere they can behold
Bright Phœbus in his ſtrength (a Maladie
Moſt incident to Maids:) bold Oxlips, and
The Crowne Imperiall: Lillies of all kinds,
(The Flowre-de-Luce being one.) O, theſe I lacke,
To make you Garlands of) and my ſweet friend,
To ſtrew him o're, and ore.
Flo. What? like a Coarſe?
Perd. No, like a banke, for Loue to lye, and play on:
Not like a Coarſe: or if: not to be buried,
But quicke, and in mine armes. Come, take your flours,
Me thinkes I play as I haue ſeene them do
In Whitſon-Paſtorals: Sure this Robe of mine
Do's change my diſpoſition:
Flo. What you do,
Still betters what is done. When you ſpeake (Sweet)
I'ld haue you do it euer: When you ſing,
I'ld haue you buy, and ſell ſo: ſo giue Almes,
Pray ſo: and for the ord'ring your Affayres,
To ſing them too. When you do dance, I wiſh you
A waue o'th Sea, that you might euer do
Nothing but that: moue ſtill, ſtill ſo:
And owne no other Function. Each your doing,
(So ſingular, in each particular)
Crownes what you are doing, in the preſent deeds,
That all your Actes, are Queenes.
Perd. O *Doricles*,
Your praiſes are too large: but that your youth
And the true blood which peepes fairely through't,
Do plainly giue you out an vnſtain'd Shepherd
With wiſedome, I might feare (my *Doricles*)
You woo'd me the falſe way.
Flo. I thinke you haue
As little skill to feare, as I haue purpoſe
To put you to't. But come, our dance I pray,
Your hand (my *Perdita*:) ſo Turtles paire
That neuer meane to part.
Perd. Ile ſweare for 'em.
Po. This is the pretieſt Low-borne Laſſe, that euer
Ran on the greene-ſord: Nothing ſhe do's, or ſeemes
But ſmackes of ſomething greater then her ſelfe,
Too Noble for this place.
Cam. He tels her ſomething
That makes her blood looke on't: Good ſooth ſhe is
The Queene of Curds and Creame.
Clo. Come on: ſtrike vp.
Dorcas. *Mopſa* muſt be your Miſtris: marry Garlick to mend her kiſſing with.
Mop. Now in good time.
Clo. Not a word, a word, we ſtand vpon our manners, Come, ſtrike vp.

Heere a Daunce of Shepheards and Shephearddeſſes.

Pol. Pray good Shepheard, what faire Swaine is this,
Which dances with your daughter?
Shep. They call him *Doricles*, and boaſts himſelfe
To haue a worthy Feeding; but I haue it
Vpon his owne report, and I beleeue it:
He lookes like ſooth: he ſayes he loues my daughter,
I thinke ſo too; for neuer gaz'd the Moone
Vpon the water, as hee'l ſtand and reade
As 'twere my daughters eyes: and to be plaine,
I thinke there is not halfe a kiſſe to chooſe
Who loues another beſt.
Pol. She dances featly.
Shep. So ſhe do's any thing, though I report it
That ſhould be ſilent: If yong *Doricles*
Do light vpon her, ſhe ſhall bring him that
Which he not dreames of. *Enter Seruant.*

Ser. O Maſter: if you did but heare the Pedler at the doore, you would neuer dance againe after a Tabor and Pipe: no, the Bag-pipe could not moue you: hee ſinges ſeuerall Tunes, faſter then you'l tell money: hee vtters them as he had eaten ballads and all mens eares grew to his Tunes.

Clo. He could neuer come better: hee ſhall come in: I loue a ballad but euen too well, if it be dolefull matter merrily ſet downe: or a very pleaſant thing indeede and ſung lamentably.

Ser.

Ser. He hath ſongs for man, or woman, of all ſizes: No Milliner can ſo fit his cnſtomers with Gloues: he has the prettieſt Loue-ſongs for Maids, ſo without bawdrie (which is ſtrange,) with ſuch delicate burthens of Dildo's and Fadings: Iump-her, and thump-her; and where ſome ſtretch-mouth'd Raſcall, would (as it were) meane miſcheefe, and breake a ſowle gap into the Matter, hee makes the maid to anſwere, *Whoop, doe me no harme good man*: put's him off, ſlights him, with *Whoop, doe mee no harme good man.*

Pol. This is a braue fellow.

Clo. Beleeee mee, thou talkeſt of an admirable conceited fellow, has he any vnbraided Wares?

Ser. Hee hath Ribbons of all the colours i'th Rainebow; Points, more then all the Lawyers in *Bohemia*, can learnedly handle, though they come to him by th'groſſe: Inckles, Caddyſſes, Cambrickes, Lawnes: why he ſings em ouer, as they were Gods, or Goddeſſes: you would thinke a Smocke were a ſhee-Angell, he ſo chauntes to the ſleeue-hand, and the worke about the ſquare on't.

Clo. Pre'thee bring him in, and let him approach ſinging.

Perd. Forewarne him, that he vſe no ſcurrilous words in's tunes.

Clow. You haue of theſe Pedlers, that haue more in them, then youl'd thinke (Siſter.)

Perd. I, good brother, or go about to thinke.

Enter Autolicus ſinging.

Lawne as white as driuen Snow,
Cypreſſe blacke as ere was Crow,
Gloues as ſweete as Damaske Roſes,
Maskes for faces, and for noſes
Bugle-bracelet, Necke-lace Amber,
Perfume for a Ladies Chamber:
Golden Quoifes, and Stomachers
For my Lads, to giue their deers:
Pins, and poaking-ſtickes of ſteele.
What Maids lacke from head to heele:
Come buy of me, come: come buy, come buy,
Buy Lads, or elſe your Laſſes cry: Come buy.

Clo. If I were not in loue with *Mopſa*, thou ſhouldſt take no money of me, but being enthrall'd as I am, it will alſo be the bondage of certaine Ribbons and Gloues.

Mop. I was promis'd them againſt the Feaſt, but they come not too late now.

Dor. He hath promis'd you more then that, or there be lyars.

Mop. He hath paid you all he promis'd you: 'May be he has paid you more, which will ſhame you to giue him againe.

Clo. Is there no manners left among maids? Will they weare their plackets, where they ſhould bear their faces? Is there not milking-time? When you are going to bed? Or kill-hole? To whiſtle of theſe ſecrets, but you muſt be tittle-tatling before all our gueſts? 'Tis well they are whiſpring: clamor your tongues, and not a word more.

Mop. I haue done; Come you promis'd me a tawdry-lace, and a paire of ſweet Gloues.

Clo. Haue I not told thee how I was cozen'd by the way, and loſt all my money.

Aut. And indeed Sir, there are Cozeners abroad, therfore it behooues men to be wary.

Clo. Feare not thou man, thou ſhalt loſe nothing here

Aut. I hope ſo ſir, for I haue about me many parcels of charge.

Clo. What haſt heere? Ballads?

Mop. Pray now buy ſome: I loue a ballet in print, life, for then we are ſure they are true

Aut. Here's one, to a very doleſull tune, how a Vſurers wife was brought to bed of twenty money baggs at a burthen, and how ſhe long'd to eate Adders heads, and Toads carbonado'd.

Mop. Is it true, thinke you?

Aut. Very true, and but a moneth old.

Dor. Bleſſe me from marrying a Vſurer.

Aut. Here's the Midwiues name to't: one Miſt. *Tale-Porter*, and fiue or ſix honeſt Wiues, that were preſent. Why ſhould I carry lyes abroad?

Mop. Pray you now buy it.

Clo. Come-on, lay it by: and let's firſt ſee moe Ballads: Wee'l buy the other things anon.

Aut. Here's another ballad of a Fiſh, that appeared vpon the coaſt, on wenſday the fourescore of April, fortie thouſand fadom aboue water, & ſung this ballad againſt the hard hearts of maids: it was thought ſhe was a Woman, and was turn'd into a cold fiſh, for ſhe wold not exchange fleſh with one that lou'd her: The Ballad is very pittifull, and as true.

Dor. Is it true too, thinke you.

Autol. Fiue Iuſtices hands at it, and witneſſes more then my packe will hold.

Clo. Lay it by too; another.

Aut. This is a merry ballad, but a very pretty one.

Mop. Let's haue ſome merry ones.

Aut. Why this is a paſſing merry one, and goes to the tune of two maids wooing a man: there's ſcarſe a Maide weſtward but ſhe ſings it: 'tis in requeſt, I can tell you.

Mop. We can both ſing it: if thou'lt beare a part, thou ſhalt heare, 'tis in three parts.

Dor. We had the tune on't, a month agoe.

Aut. I can beare my part, you muſt know 'tis my occupation: Haue at it with you:

Song *Get you hence, for I muſt goe*
Aut. *Where it fits not you to know.*
Dor. *Whether?*
Mop *O whether?*
Dor. *Whether?*
Mop. *It becomes thy oath full well,*
Thou to me thy ſecrets tell
Dor: *Me too: Le me go thether:*
Mop *Or thou goeſt to th'Grange, or Mill,*
Dor: *If to either thou doſt ill.*
Aut: *Neither.*
Dor: *What neither?*
Aut: *Neither:*
Dor: *Thou haſt ſworne my Loue to be,*
Mop *Thou haſt ſworne it more to mee.*
Then whether goeſt? Say whether?

Clo. Wee'l haue this ſong out anon by our ſelues: My Father, and the Gent. are in ſad talke, & wee'll not trouble them: Come bring away thy pack after me, Wenches Ile buy for you both: Pedler let's haue the firſt choice; folow me girles. *Aut*: And you ſhall pay well for em.

Song. *Will you buy any Tape, or Lace for your Cape?*
My dainty Ducke, my deere-a?
Any Silke, any Thred, any Toyes for your head
Of the new'ſt, and fin'ſt, fin'ſt weare-a.
Come to the Pedler, Money's a medler,
That doth vtter all mens ware-a. *Exit.*

Seruant. Mayſter, there is three Carters, three Shepherds, three Neat-herds, three Swine-herds y haue made them themselues all men of haire, they cal themselues Saltiers, and they haue a Dance, which the Wenches say is a gally-maufrey of Gambols, because they are not in't: but they themselues are o'th'minde (if it bee not too rough for some, that know little but bowling) it will please plentifully.

Shep. Away: Wee'l none on't; heere has beene too much homely foolery already. I know (Sir) wee wearie you.

Pol. You wearie those that refresh vs: pray let's see these foure-threes of Heardsmen.

Ser. One three of them, by their owne report (Sir,) hath danc'd before the King: and not the worst of the three, but iumpes twelue foote and a halfe by th'squire.

Shep. Leaue your prating, since these good men are pleas'd, let them come in: but quickly now.

Ser. Why, they stay at doore Sir.

Heere a Dance of twelue Satyres.

Pol. O Father, you'l know more of that heereafter:
Is it not too farre gone? 'Tis time to part them,
He's simple, and tels much. How now (faire shepheard)
Your heart is full of something, that do's take
Your minde from feasting. Sooth, when I was yong,
And handed loue, as you do; I was wont
To load my Shee with knackes: I would haue ransackt
The Pedlers silken Treasury, and haue powr'd it
To her acceptance: you haue let him go,
And nothing marted with him. If your Lasse
Interpretation should abuse, and call this
Your lacke of loue, or bounty, you were straited
For a reply at least, if you make a care
Of happie holding her.

Flo. Old Sir, I know
She prizes not such trifles as these are:
The gifts she lookes from me, are packt and locke
Vp in my heart, which I haue giuen already,
But not deliuer'd. O heare me breath my life
Before this ancient Sir, whom (it should seeme)
Hath sometime lou'd: I take thy hand, this hand,
As soft as Doues-downe, and as white as it,
Or Ethyopians tooth, or the fan'd snow, that's bolted
By th'Northerne blasts, twice ore.

Pol. What followes this?
How prettily th'yong Swaine seemes to wash
The hand, was faire before? I haue put you out,
But to your protestation: Let me heare
What you professe.

Flo. Do, and be witnesse too't.

Pol. And this my neighbour too?

Flo. And he, and more
Then he, and men: the earth, the heauens, and all;
That were I crown'd the most Imperiall Monarch
Thereof most worthy: were I the fayrest youth
That euer made eye swerue, had force and knowledge
More then was euer mans, I would not prize them
Without her Loue; for her, employ them all,
Commend them, and condemne them to her seruice,
Or to their owne perdition.

Pol. Fairely offer'd.

Cam. This shewes a sound affection.

Shep. But my daughter,
Say you the like to him.

Per. I cannot speake
So well, (nothing so well) no, nor meane better
By th'patterne of mine owne thoughts, I cut out
The puritie of his.

Shep. Take hands, a bargaine;
And friends vnknowne, you shall beare witnesse to't:
I giue my daughter to him, and will make
Her Portion, equall his.

Flo. O, that must bee
I'th Vertue of your daughter: One being dead,
I shall haue more then you can dreame of yet,
Enough then for your wonder: but come-on,
Contract vs fore these Witnesses.

Shep. Come, your hand:
And daughter, yours.

Pol. Soft Swaine a-while, beseech you,
Haue you a Father?

Flo. I haue: but what of him?

Pol. Knowes he of this?

Flo. He neither do's, nor shall.

Pol. Me-thinkes a Father,
Is at the Nuptiall of his sonne, a guest
That best becomes the Table: Pray you once more
Is not your Father growne incapeable
Of reasonable affayres? Is he not stupid
With Age, and altring Rheumes? Can he speake? heare?
Know man, from man? Dispute his owne estate?
Lies he not bed-rid? And againe, do's nothing
But what he did, being childish?

Flo. No good Sir:
He has his health, and ampler strength indeede
Then most haue of his age.

Pol. By my white beard,
You offer him (if this be so) a wrong
Something vnfilliall: Reason my sonne
Should choose himselfe a wife, but as good reason
The Father (all whose ioy is nothing else
But faire posterity) should hold some counsaile
In such a businesse.

Flo. I yeeld all this;
But for some other reasons (my graue Sir)
Which 'tis not fit you know, I not acquaint
My Father of this businesse.

Pol. Let him know't.

Flo. He shall not.

Pol. Prethee let him.

Flo. No, he must not.

Shep. Let him (my sonne) he shall not need to greeue
At knowing of thy choice.

Flo. Come, come, he must not:
Marke our Contract.

Pol. Marke your diuorce (yong sir)
Whom sonne I dare not call: Thou art too base
To be acknowledge. Thou a Scepters heire,
That thus affects a sheepe-hooke? Thou, old Traitor,
I am sorry, that by hanging thee, I can
but shorten thy life one weeke. And thou, fresh peece
Of excellent Witchcraft, whom of force must know
The royall Foole thou coap'st with.

Shep. Oh my heart.

Pol. Ile haue thy beauty scratcht with briers & made
More homely then thy state. For thee (fond boy)
If I may euer know thou dost but sigh,
That thou no more shalt neuer see this knacke (as neuer
I meane thou shalt) wee'l barre thee from succession,
Not hold thee of our blood, no not our Kin,
Farre then *Deucalion* off: (marke thou my words)
Follow vs to the Court. Thou Churle, for this time
(Though full of our displeasure) yet we free thee
From the dead blow of it. And you Enchantment,

Wor-

Worthy enough a Heardsman: yea him too,
That makes himselfe (but for our Honor therein)
Vnworthy thee. If euer henceforth, thou
These rurall Latches, to his entrance open,
Or hope his body more, with thy embraces,
I will deuise a death, as cruell for thee
As thou art tender to't. *Exit.*

Perd. Euen heere vndone:
I was not much a-fear'd: for once, or twice
I was about to speake, and tell him plainely,
The selfe-same Sun, that shines vpon his Court,
Hides not his visage from our Cottage, but
Lookes on alike. Wilt please you (Sir) be gone?
I told you what would come of this: Beseech you
Of your owne state take care: This dreame of mine
Being now awake, Ile Queene it no inch farther,
But milke my Ewes, and weepe.

Cam. Why how now Father,
Speake ere thou dyest.

Shep. I cannot speake, nor thinke,
Nor dare to know, that which I know: O Sir,
You haue vndone a man of fourescore three,
That thought to fill his graue in quiet: yea,
To dye vpon the bed my father dy'de,
To lye close by his honest bones; but now
Some Hangman must put on my shrowd, and lay me
Where no Priest shouels-in dust. Oh cursed wretch,
That knew'st this was the Prince, and wouldst aduenture
To mingle faith with him. Vndone, vndone:
If I might dye within this houre, I haue liu'd
To die when I desire. *Exit.*

Flo. Why looke you so vpon me?
I am but sorry, not affear'd: delaid,
But nothing altred: What I was, I am:
More straining on, for plucking backe; not following
My leash vnwillingly.

Cam. Gracious my Lord,
You know my Fathers temper: at this time
He will allow no speech: (which I do ghesse
You do not purpose to him:) and as hardly
Will he endure your sight, as yet I feare;
Then till the fury of his Highnesse settle
Come not before him.

Flo. I not purpose it:
I thinke *Camillo.*

Cam. Euen he, my Lord.

Per. How often haue I told you 'twould be thus?
How often said my dignity would last
But till 'twer knowne?

Flo. It cannot faile, but by
The violation of my faith, and then
Let Nature crush the sides o'th earth together,
And marre the seeds within. Lift vp thy lookes:
From my succession wipe me (Father) I
Am heyre to my affection.

Cam. Be aduis'd.

Flo. I am: and by my fancie, if my Reason
Will thereto be obedient: I haue reason:
If not, my sences better pleas'd with madnesse,
Do bid it welcome.

Cam. This is desperate (sir.)

Flo. So call it: but it do's fulfill my vow:
I needs must thinke it honesty. *Camillo,*
Not for *Bohemia*, nor the pompe that may
Be thereat gleaned: for all the Sun sees, or
The close earth wombes, or the profound seas, hides
In vnknowne fadomes, will I breake my oath
To this my faire belou'd: Therefore, I pray you,
As you haue euer bin my Fathers honour'd friend
When he shall misse me, as (in faith I meane not
To see him any more) cast your good counsailes
Vpon his passion: Let my selfe, and Fortune
Tug for the time to come. This you may know,
And so deliuer, I am put to Sea
With her, who heere I cannot hold on shore:
And most opportune to her neede, I haue
A Vessell rides fast by, but not prepar'd
For this designe. What course I meane to hold
Shall nothing benefit your knowledge, nor
Concerne me the reporting.

Cam. O my Lord,
I would your spirit were easier for aduice,
Or stronger for your neede.

Flo. Hearke *Perdita*,
Ile heare you by and by.

Cam. Hee's irremoueable,
Resolu'd for flight: Now were I happy if
His going, I could frame to serue my turne,
Saue him from danger, do him loue and honor,
Purchase the sight againe of deere Sicillia,
And that vnhappy King, my Master, whom
I so much thirst to see.

Flo. Now good *Camillo*,
I am so fraught with curious businesse, that
I leaue out ceremony.

Cam. Sir, I thinke
You haue heard of my poore seruices, i'th loue
That I haue borne your Father?

Flo. Very nobly
Haue you deseru'd: It is my Fathers Musicke
To speake your deeds: not little of his care
To haue them recompenc'd, as thought on.

Cam. Well (my Lord)
If you may please to thinke I loue the King,
And through him, what's neerest to him, which is
Your gracious selfe; embrace but my direction,
If your more ponderous and setled proiect
May suffer alteration. On mine honor,
Ile point you where you shall haue such receiuing
As shall become your Highnesse, where you may
Enioy your Mistris; from the whom, I see
There's no disiunction to be made, but by
(As heauens forefend) your ruine: Marry her,
And with my best endeuours, in your absence,
Your discontenting Father, striue to qualifie
And bring him vp to liking.

Flo. How *Camillo*
May this (almost a miracle) be done?
That I may call thee something more then man,
And after that trust to thee.

Cam. Haue you thought on
A place whereto you'l go?

Flo. Not any yet:
But as th'vnthought-on accident is guiltie
To what we wildely do, so we professe
Our selues to be the slaues of chance, and flyes
Of euery winde that blowes.

Cam. Then list to me:
This followes, if you will not change your purpose
But vndergo this flight; make for Sicillia,
And there present your selfe, and your fayre Princesse,
(For so I see she must be) 'fore *Leontes*;

Shee

She ſhall be habited, as it becomes
The partner of your Bed. Me thinkes I ſee
Leontes opening his free Armes, and weeping
His Welcomes forth: asks thee there Sonne forgiueneſſe,
As 'twere i'th' Fathers perſon: kiſſes the hands
Of your freſh Princeſſe; ore and ore diuides him,
'Twixt his vnkindneſſe, and his Kindneſſe: th'one
He chides to Hell, and bids the other grow
Faſter then Thought, or Time.

Flo. Worthy *Camillo,*
What colour for my Viſitation, ſhall I
Hold vp before him?

Cam. Sent by the King your Father
To greet him, and to giue him comforts. Sir,
The manner of your bearing towards him, with
What you (as from your Father) ſhall deliuer,
Things knowne betwixt vs three, Ile write you downe,
The which ſhall point you forth at euery ſitting
What you muſt ſay: that he ſhall not perceiue,
But that you haue your Fathers Boſome there,
And ſpeake his very Heart.

Flo. I am bound to you:
There is ſome ſappe in this.

Cam. A Courſe more promiſing,
Then a wild dedication of your ſelues
To vnpath'd Waters, vndream'd Shores; moſt certaine,
To Miſeries enough: no hope to helpe you,
But as you ſhake off one, to take another:
Nothing ſo certaine, as your Anchors, who
Doe their beſt office, if they can but ſtay you,
Where you'le be loth to be: beſides you know,
Proſperitie's the very bond of Loue,
Whoſe freſh complexion, and whoſe heart together,
Affliction alters.

Perd. One of theſe is true:
I thinke Affliction may ſubdue the Cheeke,
But not take-in the Mind.

Cam. Yea? ſay you ſo?
There ſhall not, at your Fathers Houſe, theſe ſeuen yeeres
Be borne another ſuch.

Flo. My good *Camillo,*
She's as forward, of her Breeding, as
She is i'th' reare 'our Birth.

Cam. I cannot ſay, 'tis pitty
She lacks Inſtructions, for ſhe ſeemes a Miſtreſſe
To moſt that teach.

Perd. Your pardon Sir, for this,
Ile bluſh you Thanks.

Flo My prettieſt *Perdita.*
But O, the Thornes we ſtand vpon: (*Camillo*)
Preſeruer of my Father, now of me,
The Medicine of our Houſe: how ſhall we doe?
We are not furniſh'd like *Bohemia's* Sonne,
Nor ſhall appeare in *Sicilia.*

Cam. My Lord,
Feare none of this: I thinke you know my fortunes
Doe all lye there: it ſhall be ſo my care,
To haue you royally appointed, as if
The Scene you play, were mine. For inſtance Sir,
That you may know you ſhall not want: one word.

Enter Autolicus.

Aut. Ha, ha, what a Foole Honeſtie is? and Truſt (his ſworne brother) a very ſimple Gentleman. I haue ſold all my Tromperie: not a counterfeit Stone, not a Ribbon, Glaſſe, Pomander, Browch, Table-booke, Ballad, Knife, Tape, Gloue, Shooe-tye, Bracelet, Horne-Ring, to keepe my Pack from faſting: they throng who ſhould buy firſt, as if my Trinkets had beene hallowed, and brought a benediction to the buyer: by which meanes, I ſaw whoſe Purſe was beſt in Picture; and what I ſaw, to my good vſe, I remembred. My Clowne (who wants but ſomething to be a reaſonable man) grew ſo in loue with the Wenches Song, that hee would not ſtirre his Petty-toes, till he had both Tune and Words, which ſo drew the reſt of the Heard to me, that all their other Sences ſtucke in Eares: you might haue pinch'd a Placket, it was ſenceleſſe; 'twas nothing to gueld a Cod-peece of a Purſe: I would haue fill'd Keyes of that hung in Chaynes: no hearing, no feeling, but my Sirs Song, and admiring the Nothing of it. So that in this time of Lethargie, I pickd and cut moſt of their Feſtiuall Purſes: And had not the old-man come in with a Whoo-bub againſt his Daughter, and the Kings Sonne, and ſcar'd my Chowghes from the Chaffe, I had not left a Purſe aliue in the whole Army.

Cam. Nay, but my Letters by this meanes being there
So ſoone as you arriue, ſhall cleare that doubt.

Flo. And thoſe that you'le procure from King *Leontes*?

Cam. Shall ſatisfie your Father.

Perd. Happy be you:
All that you ſpeake, ſhewes faire.

Cam. Who haue we here?
Wee'le make an Inſtrument of this: omit
Nothing may giue vs aide.

Aut. If they haue ouer-heard me now: why hanging.

Cam. How now (good Fellow)
Why ſhak'ſt thou ſo? Feare not (man)
Here's no harme intended to thee.

Aut. I am a poore Fellow, Sir.

Cam. Why, be ſo ſtill: here's no body will ſteale that from thee: yet for the out-ſide of thy pouertie, we muſt make an exchange; therefore diſ-caſe thee inſtantly (thou muſt thinke there's a neceſſitie in't) and change Garments with this Gentleman: Though the penny-worth (on his ſide) be the worſt, yet hold thee, there's ſome boot.

Aut. I am a poore Fellow, Sir: (I know ye well enough.)

Cam. Nay prethee diſpatch: the Gentleman is halfe fled already.

Aut. Are you in earneſt, Sir? (I ſmell the trick on't.)

Flo. Diſpatch, I prethee.

Aut. Indeed I haue had Earneſt, but I cannot with conſcience take it.

Cam. Vnbuckle, vnbuckle.
Fortunate Miſtreſſe (let my prophecie
Come home to ye:) you muſt retire your ſelfe
Into ſome Couert; take your ſweet-hearts Hat
And pluck it ore your Browes, muffle your face,
Diſ-mantle you, and (as you can) diſliken
The truth of your owne ſeeming, that you may
(For I doe feare eyes ouer) to Ship-boord
Get vndeſcry'd.

Perd. I ſee the Play ſo lyes,
That I muſt beare a part.

Cam. No remedie:
Haue you done there?

Flo. Should I now meet my Father,
He would not call me Sonne.

Cam. Nay, you ſhall haue no Hat:
Come Lady, come: Farewell (my friend.)

Aut. Adieu, Sir.

Flo. O *Perdita*: what haue we twaine forgot?

'Pray

Pray you a word.

Cam. What I doe next, shall be to tell the King
Of this escape, and whither they are bound;
Wherein, my hope is, I shall so preuaile,
To force him after: in whose company
I shall re-view *Sicilia*; for whose sight,
I haue a Womans Longing.

Flo. Fortune speed vs:
Thus we set on (*Camillo*) to th' Sea-side.

Cam. The swifter speed, the better. *Exit.*

Aut. I vnderstand the businesse, I heare it: to haue an open eare, a quick eye, and a nimble hand, is necessary for a Cut-purse; a good Nose is requisite also, to smell out worke for th'other Sences. I see this is the time that the vniust man doth thriue. What an exchange had this been, without boot? What a boot is here, with this exchange? Sure the Gods doe this yeere conniue at vs, and we may doe any thing extempore. The Prince himselfe is about a peece of Iniquitie (stealing away from his Father, with his Clog at his heeles:) if I thought it were a peece of honestie to acquaint the King withall, I would not do't: I hold it the more knauerie to conceale it; and therein am I constant to my Profession.

Enter Clowne and Shepheard.

Aside, aside, here is more matter for a hot braine: Euery Lanes end, euery Shop, Church, Session, Hanging, yeelds a carefull man worke.

Clowne. See, see: what a man you are now? there is no other way, but to tell the King she's a Changeling, and none of your flesh and blood.

Shep. Nay, but heare me.

Clow. Nay; but heare me.

Shep. Goe too then.

Clow. She being none of your flesh and blood, your flesh and blood ha's not offended the King, and so your flesh and blood is not to be punish'd by him. Shew those things you found about her (those secret things, all but what she ha's with her:) This being done, let the Law goe whistle: I warrant you.

Shep. I will tell the King all, euery word, yea, and his Sonnes prancks too; who, I may say, is no honest man, neither to his Father, nor to me, to goe about to make me the Kings Brother in Law.

Clow. Indeed Brother in Law was the farthest off you could haue beene to him, and then your Blood had beene the dearer, by I know how much an ounce.

Aut. Very wisely (Puppies.)

Shep. Well: let vs to the King: there is that in this Farthell, will make him scratch his Beard.

Aut. I know not what impediment this Complaint may be to the flight of my Master.

Clo. 'Pray heartily he be at' Pallace.

Aut. Though I am not naturally honest, I am so sometimes by chance: Let me pocket vp my Pedlers excrement. How now (Rustiques) whither are you bound?

Shep. To th' Pallace (and it like your Worship.)

Aut. Your Affaires there? what? with whom? the Condition of that Farthell? the place of your dwelling? your names? your ages? of what hauing? breeding, and any thing that is fitting to be knowne, discouer?

Clo. We are but plaine fellowes, Sir.

Aut. A Lye; you are rough, and hayrie: Let me haue no lying; it becomes none but Trades-men, and they often giue vs (Souldiers) the Lye, but wee pay them for it with stamped Coyne, not stabbing Steele, therefore they doe not giue vs the Lye.

Clo. Your Worship had like to haue giuen vs one, if you had not taken your selfe with the manner.

Shep. Are you a Courtier, and't like you Sir?

Aut. Whether it like me, or no, I am a Courtier. Seest thou not the ayre of the Court, in these enfoldings? Hath not my gate in it, the measure of the Court? Receiues not thy Nose Court-Odour from me? Reflect I not on thy Basenesse, Court-Contempt? Think'st thou, for that I insinuate, at toaze from thee thy Businesse, I am therefore no Courtier? I am Courtier *Cap-a-pe*; and one that will eyther push-on, or pluck-back, thy Businesse there: whereupon I command thee to open thy Affaire.

Shep. My Businesse, Sir, is to the King.

Aut. What Aduocate ha'st thou to him?

Shep. I know not (and't like you.)

Clo. Aduocate's the Court-word for a Pheazant: say you haue none.

Shep. None, Sir: I haue no Pheazant Cock, nor Hen.

Aut. How blessed are we, that are not simple men?
Yet Nature might haue made me as these are,
Therefore I will not disdaine.

Clo. This cannot be but a great Courtier.

Shep. His Garments are rich, but he weares them not handsomely.

Clo. He seemes to be the more Noble, in being fantasticall: A great man, Ile warrant; I know by the picking on's Teeth.

Aut. The Farthell there? What's i'th' Farthell? Wherefore that Box?

Shep. Sir, there lyes such Secrets in this Farthell and Box, which none must know but the King, and which hee shall know within this houre, if I may come to th' speech of him.

Aut. Age, thou hast lost thy labour.

Shep. Why Sir?

Aut. The King is not at the Pallace, he is gone aboord a new Ship, to purge Melancholy, and ayre himselfe: for if thou bee'st capable of things serious, thou must know the King is full of griefe.

Shep. So 'tis said (Sir:) about his Sonne, that should haue marryed a Shepheards Daughter.

Aut. If that Shepheard be not in hand-fast, let him flye; the Curses he shall haue, the Tortures he shall feele, will breake the back of Man, the heart of Monster.

Clo. Thinke you so, Sir?

Aut. Not hee alone shall suffer what Wit can make heauie, and Vengeance bitter; but those that are Iermaine to him (though remou'd fiftie times) shall all come vnder the Hang-man: which, though it be great pitty, yet it is necessarie. An old Sheepe-whistling Rogue, a Ram-tender, to offer to haue his Daughter come into grace? Some say hee shall be ston'd: but that death is too soft for him (say I:) Draw our Throne into a Sheep-Coat? all deaths are too few, the sharpest too easie.

Clo. Ha's the old-man ere a Sonne Sir (doe you heare) and't like you, Sir?

Aut. Hee ha's a Sonne: who shall be flayd aliue, then 'noynted ouer with Honey, set on the head of a Waspes Nest, then stand till he be three quarters and a dram dead: then recouer'd againe with Aquavite, or some other hot Infusion: then, raw as he is (and in the hotest day Prognostication proclaymes) shall he be set against a Brick-wall, (the Sunne looking with a South-ward eye vpon him; where hee is to behold him, with Flyesblown to death) But what talke we of these Traitorly-Rascals, whose miseries are to be smil'd at, their offences being so capitall? Tell

Tell me(for you seeme to be honest plainemen)what you haue to the King: being something gently consider'd, Ile bring you where he is aboord, tender your persons to his presence, whisper him in your behalfes: and if it be in man, besides the King, to effect your Suites, here is man shall doe it.

Clow. He seemes to be of great authoritie: close with him, giue him Gold; and though Authoritie be a stubborne Beare, yet hee is oft led by the Nose with Gold: shew the in-side of your Purse to the out-side of his hand, and no more adoe. Remember ston'd, and flay'd aliue.

Shep. And't please you(Sir)to vndertake the Businesse for vs, here is that Gold I haue: Ile make it as much more, and leaue this young man in pawne, till I bring it you.

Aut. After I haue done what I promised?

Shep. I Sir.

Aut. Well, giue me the Moitie: Are you a partie in this Businesse?

Clow. In some sort, Sir: but though my case be a pittifull one, I hope I shall not be flayd out of it.

Aut. Oh, that's the case of the Shepheards Sonne: hang him hee'le be made an example.

Clow. Comfort, good comfort: We must to the King, and shew our strange sights: he must know 'tis none of your Daughter, nor my Sister: wee are gone else. Sir, I will giue you as much as this old man do's, when the Businesse is performed, and remaine(as he sayes)your pawne till it be brought you.

Aut. I will trust you. Walke before toward the Sea-side, goe on the right hand, I will but looke vpon the Hedge, and follow you.

Clow. We are bless'd, in this man: as I may say, euen bless'd.

Shep. Let's before, as he bids vs: he was prouided to doe vs good.

Aut. If I had a mind to be honest, I see *Fortune* would not suffer mee: shee drops Booties in my mouth. I am courted now with a double occasion:(Gold, and a means to doe the Prince my Master good; which, who knowes how that may turne backe to my aduancement?) I will bring these two Moales, these blind-ones, aboord him, if he thinke it fit to shoare them againe, and that the Complaint they haue to the King, concernes him nothing, let him call me Rogue, for being so farre officious, for I am proofe against that Title, and what shame else belongs to't: To him will I present them, there may be matter in it. *Exeunt.*

Actus Quintus. Scena Prima.

Enter Leontes, Cleomines, Dion, Paulina, Seruants: Florizel, Perdita.

Cleo. Sir, you haue done enough, and haue perform'd
A Saint-like Sorrow: No fault could you make,
Which you haue not redeem'd; indeed pay'd downe
More penitence, then done trespas: At the last
Doe, as the Heauens haue done; forget your euill,
With them, forgiue your selfe.

Leo. Whilest I remember
Her, and her Vertues, I cannot forget
My blemishes in them, and so still thinke of
The wrong I did my selfe: which was so much,
That Heire-lesse it hath made my Kingdome, and
Destroy'd the sweet'st Companion, that ere man
Bred his hopes out of. true.

Paul. Too true(my Lord:)
If one by one, you wedded all the World,
Or from the All that are, tooke something good,
To make a perfect Woman; she you kill'd,
Would be vnparallell'd.

Leo. I thinke so. Kill'd?
She I kill'd? I did so: but thou strik'st me
Sorely, to say I did: it is as bitter
Vpon thy Tongue, as in my Thought. Now, good now,
Say so but seldome.

Cleo. Not at all, good Lady:
You might haue spoken a thousand things, that would
Haue done the time more benefit, and grac'd
Your kindnesse better.

Paul. You are one of those
Would haue him wed againe.

Dio. If you would not so,
You pitty not the State, nor the Remembrance
Of his most Soueraigne Name: Consider little,
What Dangers, by his Highnesse faile of Issue,
May drop vpon his Kingdome, and deuoure
Incertaine lookers on. What were more holy,
Then to reioyce the former Queene is well?
What holyer, then for Royalties repayre,
For present comfort, and for future good,
To blesse the Bed of Maiestie againe
With a sweet Fellow to't?

Paul. There is none worthy,
(Respecting her that's gone:) besides the Gods
Will haue fulfill'd their secret purposes:
For ha's not the Diuine *Apollo* said?
Is't not the tenor of his Oracle,
That King *Leontes* shall not haue an Heire,
Till his lost Child be found? Which, that it shall,
Is all as monstrous to our humane reason,
As my *Antigonus* to breake his Graue,
And come againe to me: who, on my life,
Did perish with the Infant. 'Tis your councell,
My Lord should to the Heauens be contrary,
Oppose against their wills. Care not for Issue,
The Crowne will find an Heire. Great *Alexander*
Left his to th' Worthiest: so his Successor
Was like to be the best.

Leo. Good *Paulina*,
Who hast the memorie of *Hermione*
I know in honor: O, that euer I
Had squar'd me to thy councell: then, euen now,
I might haue look'd vpon my Queenes full eyes,
Haue taken Treasure from her Lippes.

Paul. And left them
More rich, for what they yeelded.

Leo. Thou speak'st truth:
No more such Wiues, therefore no Wife: one worse,
And better vs'd, would make her Sainted Spirit
Againe possesse her Corps, and on this Stage
(Where we Offendors now appeare) Soule-vext,
And begin, why to me?

Paul. Had she such power,
She had iust such cause.

Leo. She had, and would incense me
To murther her I marryed.

Paul. I

Paul. I ſhould ſo:
Were I the Ghoſt that walk'd, Il'd bid you marke
Her eye, and tell me for what dull part in't
You choſe her: then Il'd ſhrieke, that euen your eares
Should rift to heare me, and the words that follow'd,
Should be, Remember mine.
Leo. Starres, Starres,
And all eyes elſe, dead coales: feare thou no Wife;
Ile haue no Wife, *Paulina*.
Paul. Will you ſweare
Neuer to marry, but by my free leaue?
Leo. Neuer (*Paulina*) ſo be bleſs'd my Spirit.
Paul. Then good my Lords, beare witneſſe to his Oath.
Cleo. You tempt him ouer-much.
Paul. Vnleſſe another,
As like *Hermione*, as is her Picture,
Affront his eye.
Cleo. Good Madame, I haue done.
Paul. Yet if my Lord will marry: if you will, Sir;
No remedie but you will: Giue me the Office
To chuſe your Queene: ſhe ſhall not be ſo young
As was your former, but ſhe ſhall be ſuch
As (walk'd your firſt Queenes Ghoſt) it ſhould take ioy
To ſee her in your armes.
Leo. My true *Paulina*,
We ſhall not marry, till thou bidſt vs.
Paul. That
Shall be when your firſt Queene's againe in breath:
Neuer till then.
Enter a Seruant.
Ser. One that giues out himſelfe Prince *Florizell*,
Sonne of *Polixenes*, with his Princeſſe (ſhe
The faireſt I haue yet beheld) deſires acceſſe
To your high preſence.
Leo. What with him? he comes not
Like to his Fathers Greatneſſe: his approach
(So out of circumſtance, and ſuddaine) tells vs,
'Tis not a Viſitation fram'd, but forc'd
By need, and accident. What Trayne?
Ser. But few,
And thoſe but meane.
Leo. His Princeſſe (ſay you) with him?
Ser. I: the moſt peereleſſe peece of Earth, I thinke,
That ere the Sunne ſhone bright on.
Paul. Oh *Hermione*,
As euery preſent Time doth boaſt it ſelfe
Aboue a better, gone; ſo muſt thy Graue
Giue way to what's ſeene now. Sir, you your ſelfe
Haue ſaid, and writ ſo; but your writing now
Is colder then that Theame: ſhe had not beene,
Nor was not to be equall'd, thus your Verſe
Flow'd with her Beautie once; 'tis ſhrewdly ebb'd,
To ſay you haue ſeene a better.
Ser. Pardon, Madame:
The one, I haue almoſt forgot (your pardon:)
The other, when ſhe ha's obtayn'd your Eye,
Will haue your Tongue too. This is a Creature,
Would ſhe begin a Sect, might quench the zeale
Of all Profeſſors elſe; make Proſelytes
Of who ſhe but bid follow.
Paul. How? not women?
Ser. Women will loue her, that ſhe is a Woman
More worth then any Man: Men, that ſhe is
The rareſt of all Women.
Leo. Goe *Cleomines*,
Your ſelfe (aſſiſted with your honor'd Friends)
Bring them to our embracement. Still 'tis ſtrange,
He thus ſhould ſteale vpon vs. *Exit.*
Paul. Had our Prince
(Iewell of Children) ſeene this houre, he had payr'd
Well with this Lord; there was not full a moneth
Betweene their births.
Leo. Prethee no more; ceaſe: thou know'ſt
He dyes to me againe, when talk'd-of: ſure
When I ſhall ſee this Gentleman, thy ſpeeches
Will bring me to conſider that, which may
Vnfurniſh me of Reaſon. They are come.
Enter Florizell, Perdita, Cleomines, and others.
Your Mother was moſt true to Wedlock, Prince,
For ſhe did print your Royall Father off,
Conceiuing you. Were I but twentie one,
Your Fathers Image is ſo hit in you,
(His very ayre) that I ſhould call you Brother,
As I did him, and ſpeake of ſomething wildly
By vs perform'd before. Moſt dearely welcome,
And your faire Princeſſe (Goddeſſe) oh: alas,
I loſt a couple, that 'twixt Heauen and Earth
Might thus haue ſtood, begetting wonder, as
You (gracious Couple) doe: and then I loſt
(All mine owne Folly) the Societie,
Amitie too of your braue Father, whom
(Though bearing Miſerie) I deſire my life
Once more to looke on him.
Flo. By his command
Haue I here touch'd *Sicilia*, and from him
Giue you all greetings, that a King (at friend)
Can ſend his Brother: and but Infirmitie
(Which waits vpon worne times) hath ſomething ſeiz'd
His wiſh'd Abilitie, he had himſelfe
The Lands and Waters, 'twixt your Throne and his,
Meaſur'd, to looke vpon you; whom he loues
(He bad me ſay ſo) more then all the Scepters,
And thoſe that beare them, liuing.
Leo Oh my Brother,
(Good Gentleman) the wrongs I haue done thee, ſtirre
Afreſh within me: and theſe thy offices
(So rarely kind) are as Interpreters
Of my behind-hand ſlackneſſe. Welcome hither,
As is the Spring to th'Earth. And hath he too
Expos'd this Paragon to th'fearefull vſage
(At leaſt vngentle) of the dreadfull *Neptune*,
To greet a man, not worth her paines; much leſſe,
Th'aduenture of her perſon?
Flo. Good my Lord,
She came from *Libia*.
Leo. Where the Warlike *Smalus*,
That Noble honor'd Lord, is fear'd, and lou'd?
Flo. Moſt Royall Sir,
From thence: from him, whoſe Daughter
His Teares proclaym'd his parting with her: thence
(A proſperous South-wind friendly) we haue croſs'd,
To execute the Charge my Father gaue me,
For viſiting your Highneſſe: My beſt Traine
I haue from your *Sicilian* Shores diſmiſs'd;
Who for *Bohemia* bend, to ſignifie
Not onely my ſucceſſe in *Libia* (Sir)
But my arriuall, and my Wifes, in ſafetie
Here, where we are.
Leo. The bleſſed Gods
Purge all Infection from our Ayre, whileſt you
Doe Clymate here: you haue a holy Father,
A gracefull Gentleman, againſt whoſe perſon
(So

(So facred as it is) I haue done finne,
For which, the Heauens (taking angry note)
Haue left me Iffue-leffe: and your Father's bleff'd
(As he from Heauen merits it) with you,
Worthy his goodneffe. What might I haue been,
Might I a Sonne and Daughter now haue look'd on,
Such goodly things as you?

Enter a Lord.

Lord. Moft Noble Sir,
That which I fhall report, will beare no credit,
Were not the proofe fo nigh. Pleafe you (great Sir)
Bohemia greets you from himfelfe, by me:
Defires you to attach his Sonne, who ha's
(His Dignitie, and Dutie both caft off)
Fled from his Father, from his Hopes, and with
A Shepheards Daughter.

Leo. Where's *Bohemia*? fpeake:

Lord. Here, in your Citie: I now came from him.
I fpeake amazedly, and it becomes
My meruaile, and my Meffage. To your Court
Whiles he was haftning (in the Chafe, it feemes,
Of this faire Couple) meetes he on the way
The Father of this feeming Lady, and
Her Brother, hauing both their Countrey quitted,
With this young Prince.

Flo. *Camillo* ha's betray'd me,
Whofe honor, and whofe honeftie till now,
Endur'd all Weathers.

Lord. Lay't fo to his charge:
He's with the King your Father.

Leo. Who? *Camillo*?

Lord. *Camillo* (Sir:) I fpake with him: who now
Ha's thefe poore men in queftion. Neuer faw I
Wretches fo quake: they kneele, they kiffe the Earth;
Forfweare themfelues as often as they fpeake:
Bohemia ftops his eares, and threatens them
With diuers deaths, in death.

Perd. Oh my poore Father:
The Heauen fets Spyes vpon vs, will not haue
Our Contract celebrated.

Leo. You are marryed?

Flo. We are not (Sir) nor are we like to be:
The Starres (I fee) will kiffe the Valleyes firft:
The oddes for high and low's alike.

Leo. My Lord,
Is this the Daughter of a King?

Flo. She is,
When once fhe is my Wife.

Leo. That once (I fee) by your good Fathers fpeed
Will come-on very flowly. I am forry
(Moft forry) you haue broken from his liking,
Where you were ty'd in dutie: and as forry,
Your Choife is not fo rich in Worth, as Beautie,
That you might well enioy her.

Flo. Deare, looke vp:
Though *Fortune*, vifible an Enemie,
Should chafe vs, with my Father; powre no iot
Hath fhe to change our Loues. Befeech you (Sir)
Remember, fince you ow'd no more to Time
Then I doe now: with thought of fuch Affections,
Step forth mine Aduocate: at your requeft,
My Father will graunt precious things, as Trifles.

Leo. Would he doe fo, I'ld beg your precious Miftris,
Which he counts but a Trifle.

Paul. Sir (my Liege)
Your eye hath too much youth in't: not a moneth
Fore your Queene dy'd, fhe was more worth fuch gazes,
Then what you looke on now.

Leo. I thought of her,
Euen in thefe Lookes I made. But your Petition
Is yet vn-anfwer'd: I will to your Father:
Your Honor not o're-throwne by your defires,
I am friend to them, and you: Vpon which Errand
I now goe toward him: therefore follow me,
And marke what way I make: Come good my Lord.

Exeunt.

Scœna Secunda.

Enter Autolicus, and a Gentleman.

Aut. Befeech you (Sir) were you prefent at this Relation?

Gent.1. I was by at the opening of the Farthell, heard the old Shepheard deliuer the manner how he found it: Whereupon (after a little amazedneffe) we were all commanded out of the Chamber: onely this (me thought) I heard the Shepheard fay, he found the Child.

Aut. I would moft gladly know the iffue of it.

Gent.1. I make a broken deliuerie of the Bufineffe; but the changes I perceiued in the King, and *Camillo*, were very Notes of admiration: they feem'd almoft, with ftaring on one another, to teare the Cafes of their Eyes. There was fpeech in their dumbneffe, Language in their very gefture: they look'd as they had heard of a World ranfom'd, or one deftroyed: a notable paffion of Wonder appeared in them: but the wifeft beholder, that knew no more but feeing, could not fay, if th'importance were Ioy, or Sorrow: but in the extremitie of the one, it muft needs be.

Enter another Gentleman.

Here comes a Gentleman, that happily knowes more: The Newes, *Rogero*.

Gent.2. Nothing but Bon-fires: the Oracle is fulfill'd: the Kings Daughter is found: fuch a deale of wonder is broken out within this houre, that Ballad-makers cannot be able to expreffe it.

Enter another Gentleman.

Here comes the Lady *Paulina's* Steward, hee can deliuer you more. How goes it now (Sir.) This Newes (which is call'd true) is fo like an old Tale, that the veritie of it is in ftrong fufpition: Ha's the King found his Heire?

Gent.3. Moft true, if euer Truth were pregnant by Circumftance: That which you heare, you'le fweare you fee, there is fuch vnitie in the proofes. The Mantle of Queene *Hermiones*: her Iewell about the Neck of it: the Letters of *Antigonus* found with it, which they know to be his Character: the Maieftie of the Creature, in refemblance of the Mother: the Affection of Nobleneffe, which Nature fhewes aboue her Breeding, and many other Euidences, proclayme her, with all certaintie, to be the Kings Daughter. Did you fee the meeting of the two Kings?

Gent.2. No.

Gent.3. Then haue you loft a Sight which was to bee feene, cannot bee fpoken of. There might you haue beheld one Ioy crowne another, fo and in fuch manner, that it feem'd Sorrow wept to take leaue of them: for their Ioy waded in teares. There was cafting vp of Eyes, holding vp of Hands, with Countenance of fuch diftraction, that they were to be knowne by Garment, not by Fauor.

Our

Our King being ready to leape out of himſelfe, for ioy of his found Daughter; as if that Ioy were now become a Loſſe, cryes, Oh, thy Mother, thy Mother: then askes *Bohemia* forgineneſſe, then embraces his Sonne-in-Law: then againe worryes he his Daughter, with clipping her. Now he thanks the old Shepheard (which ſtands by, like a Weather-bitten Conduit, of many Kings Reignes.) I neuer heard of ſuch another Encounter; which lames Report to follow it, and vndo's deſcription to doe it.

Gent.2. What, pray you, became of *Antigonus*, that carryed hence the Child?

Gent.3. Like an old Tale ſtill, which will haue matter to rehearſe, though Credit be aſleepe, and not an eare open; he was torne to pieces with a Beare: This auouches the Shepheards Sonne; who ha's not onely his Innocence (which ſeemes much) to iuſtifie him, but a Hand-kerchief and Rings of his, that *Paulina* knowes.

Gent.1. What became of his Barke, and his Followers?

Gent.3. Wrackt the ſame inſtant of their Maſters death, and in the view of the Shepheard: ſo that all the Inſtruments which ayded to expoſe the Child, were euen then loſt when it was found. But oh the Noble Combat, that 'twixt Ioy and Sorrow was fought in *Paulina*. Shee had one Eye declin'd for the loſſe of her Husband, another eleuated, that the Oracle was fulfill'd: Shee lifted the Princeſſe from the Earth, and ſo locks her in embracing, as if ſhee would pin her to her heart, that ſhee might no more be in danger of looſing.

Gent.1. The Dignitie of this Act was worth the audience of Kings and Princes, for by ſuch was it acted.

Gent.3. One of the prettyeſt touches of all, and that which angl'd for mine Eyes (caught the Water, though not the Fiſh) was, when at the Relation of the Queenes death (with the manner how ſhee came to't brauely confeſs'd, and lamented by the King) how attentiueneſſe wounded his Daughter, till (from one ſigne of dolour to another) ſhee did (with an *Alas*) I would faine ſay, bleed Teares; for I am ſure, my heart wept blood. Who was moſt Marble, there changed colour: ſome ſwownded, all ſorrowed: if all the World could haue ſeen't, the Woe had beene vniuerſall.

Gent.1. Are they returned to the Court?

Gent.3. No: The Princeſſe hearing of her Mothers Statue (which is in the keeping of *Paulina*) a Peece many yeeres in doing, and now newly perform'd, by that rare Italian Maſter, *Iulio Romano*, who (had he himſelfe Eternitie, and could put Breath into his Worke) would beguile Nature of her Cuſtome, ſo perfectly he is her Ape: He ſo neere to *Hermione*, hath done *Hermione*, that they ſay one would ſpeake to her, and ſtand in hope of anſwer. Thither (with all greedineſſe of affection) are they gone, and there they intend to Sup.

Gent.2. I thought ſhe had ſome great matter there in hand, for ſhee hath priuately, twice or thrice a day, euer ſince the death of *Hermione*, viſited that remoued Houſe. Shall wee thither, and with our companie peece the Reioycing?

Gent.1. Who would be thence, that ha's the benefit of Acceſſe? euery winke of an Eye, ſome new Grace will be borne: our Abſence makes vs vnthriftie to our Knowledge. Let's along. *Exit.*

Aut. Now (had I not the daſh of my former life in me) would Preferment drop on my head. I brought the old man and his Sonne aboord the Prince; told him, I heard them talke of a Farthell, and I know not what: but he at that time ouer-fond of the Shepheards Daughter (ſo he then tooke her to be) who began to be much Sea-ſick, and himſelfe little better, extremitie of Weather continuing, this Myſterie remained vndiſcouer'd. But 'tis all one to me: for had I beene the finder-out of this Secret, it would not haue relliſh'd among my other diſcredits.

Enter Shepheard and Clowne.

Here come thoſe I haue done good to againſt my will, and alreadie appearing in the bloſſomes of their Fortune.

Shep. Come Boy, I am paſt moe Children: but thy Sonnes and Daughters will be all Gentlemen borne.

Clow. You are well met (Sir.) you deny'd to fight with mee this other day, becauſe I was no Gentleman borne. See you theſe Clothes? ſay you ſee them not, and thinke me ſtill no Gentleman borne: You were beſt ſay theſe Robes are not Gentlemen borne. Giue me the Lye: doe: and try whether I am not now a Gentleman borne.

Aut. I know you are now (Sir) a Gentleman borne.

Clow. I, and haue been ſo any time theſe foure houres.

Shep. And ſo haue I, Boy.

Clow. So you haue: but I was a Gentleman borne before my Father: for the Kings Sonne tooke me by the hand, and call'd mee Brother: and then the two Kings call'd my Father Brother: and then the Prince (my Brother) and the Princeſſe (my Siſter) call'd my Father, Father; and ſo wee wept: and there was the firſt Gentleman-like teares that euer we ſhed.

Shep. We may liue (Sonne) to ſhed many more.

Clow. I: or elſe 'twere hard luck, being in ſo prepoſterous eſtate as we are.

Aut. I humbly beſeech you (Sir) to pardon me all the faults I haue committed to your Worſhip, and to giue me your good report to the Prince my Maſter.

Shep. 'Prethee Sonne doe: for we muſt be gentle, now we are Gentlemen.

Clow. Thou wilt amend thy life?

Aut. I, and it like your good Worſhip.

Clow. Giue me thy hand: I will ſweare to the Prince, thou art as honeſt a true Fellow as any is in *Bohemia*.

Shep. You may ſay it, but not ſweare it.

Clow. Not ſweare it, now I am a Gentleman? Let Boores and Francklins ſay it, Ile ſweare it.

Shep. How if it be falſe (Sonne?)

Clow. If it be ne're ſo falſe, a true Gentleman may ſweare it, in the behalfe of his Friend: And Ile ſweare to the Prince thou art a tall Fellow of thy hands, and that thou wilt not be drunke: but I know thou art no tall Fellow of thy hands, and that thou wilt be drunke: but Ile ſweare it, and I would thou would'ſt be a tall Fellow of thy hands.

Aut. I will proue ſo (Sir) to my power.

Clow. I, by any meanes proue a tall Fellow: if I do not wonder, how thou dar'ſt venture to be drunke, not being a tall Fellow, truſt me not. Harke, the Kings and the Princes (our Kindred) are going to ſee the Queenes Picture. Come, follow vs: wee'le be thy good Maſters. *Exeunt.*

Scæna Tertia.

Enter Leontes, Polixenes, Florizell, Perdita, Camillo, Paulina: Hermione (like a Statue:) Lords &c.

Leo. O graue and good *Paulina*, the great comfort That I haue had of thee?

Cc *Paul.* What

Paul. What (Soueraigne Sir)
I did not well, I meant well: all my Seruices
You haue pay'd home. But that you haue vouchſaf'd
(With your Crown'd Brother, and theſe your contracted
Heires of your Kingdomes) my poore Houſe to viſit;
It is a ſurplus of your Grace, which neuer
My life may laſt to anſwere.
Leo. O *Paulina,*
We honor you with trouble: but we came
To ſee the Statue of our Queene. Your Gallerie
Haue we paſs'd through, not without much content
In many ſingularities; but we ſaw not
That which my Daughter came to looke vpon,
The Statue of her Mother.
Paul. As ſhe liu'd peereleſſe,
So her dead likeneſſe I doe well beleeue
Excells what euer yet you look'd vpon,
Or hand of Man hath done: therefore I keepe it
Louely, apart. But here it is: prepare
To ſee the Life as liuely mock'd, as euer
Still Sleepe mock'd Death: behold, and ſay 'tis well.
I like your ſilence, it the more ſhewes-off
Your wonder: but yet ſpeake, firſt you (my Liege)
Comes it not ſomething neere:
Leo. Her naturall Poſture.
Chide me (deare Stone) that I may ſay indeed
Thou art *Hermione*; or rather, thou art ſhe,
In thy not chiding: for ſhe was as tender
As Infancie, and Grace. But yet (*Paulina*)
Hermione was not ſo much wrinckled, nothing
So aged as this ſeemes.
Pol. Oh, not by much.
Paul. So much the more our Caruers excellence,
Which lets goe-by ſome ſixteene yeeres, and makes her
As ſhe liu'd now.
Leo. As now ſhe might haue done,
So much to my good comfort, as it is
Now piercing to my Soule. Oh, thus ſhe ſtood,
Euen with ſuch Life of Maieſtie (warme Life,
As now it coldly ſtands) when firſt I woo'd her.
I am aſham'd: Do's not the Stone rebuke me,
For being more Stone then it? Oh Royall Peece:
There's Magick in thy Maieſtie, which ha's
My Euils coniur'd to remembrance; and
From thy admiring Daughter tooke the Spirits,
Standing like Stone with thee.
Perd. And giue me leaue,
And doe not ſay 'tis Superſtition, that
I kneele, and then implore her Bleſſing. Lady,
Deere Queene, that ended when I but began,
Giue me that hand of yours, to kiſſe.
Paul. O, patience:
The Statue is but newly fix'd; the Colour's
Not dry.
Cam. My Lord, your Sorrow was too ſore lay'd-on,
Which ſixteene Winters cannot blow away,
So many Summers dry: ſcarce any Ioy
Did euer ſo long liue; no Sorrow,
But kill'd it ſelfe much ſooner.
Pol. Deere my Brother,
Let him, that was the cauſe of this, haue powre
To take-off ſo much griefe from you, as he
Will peece vp in himſelfe.
Paul. Indeed my Lord,
If I had thought the ſight of my poore Image
Would thus haue wrought you (for the Stone is mine)
I'ld not haue ſhew'd it.
Leo. Doe not draw the Curtaine.
Paul. No longer ſhall you gaze on't, leaſt your Fancie
May thinke anon, it moues.
Leo. Let be, let be:
Would I were dead, but that me thinkes alreadie.
(What was he that did make it?) See (my Lord)
Would you not deeme it breath'd? and that thoſe veines
Did verily beare blood?
Pol. 'Maſterly done:
The very Life ſeemes warme vpon her Lippe.
Leo. The fixure of her Eye ha's motion in't,
As we are mock'd with Art.
Paul. Ile draw the Curtaine:
My Lord's almoſt ſo farre tranſported, that
Hee'le thinke anon it liues.
Leo. Oh ſweet *Paulina,*
Make me to thinke ſo twentie yeeres together:
No ſetled Sences of the World can match
The pleaſure of that madneſſe. Let't alone.
Paul. I am ſorry (Sir) I haue thus farre ſtir'd you: but
I could afflict you farther.
Leo. Doe *Paulina:*
For this Affliction ha's a taſte as ſweet
As any Cordiall comfort. Still me thinkes
There is an ayre comes from her. What fine Chizzell
Could euer yet cut breath? Let no man mock me,
For I will kiſſe her.
Paul Good my Lord, forbeare:
The ruddineſſe vpon her Lippe, is wet:
You'le marre it, if you kiſſe it; ſtayne your owne
With Oyly Painting: ſhall I draw the Curtaine.
Leo. No: not theſe twentie yeeres.
Perd. So long could I
Stand-by, a looker-on.
Paul. Either forbeare,
Quit preſently the Chappell, or reſolue you
For more amazement: if you can behold it,
Ile make the Statue moue indeed; deſcend,
And take you by the hand: but then you'le thinke
(Which I proteſt againſt) I am aſſiſted
By wicked Powers.
Leo. What you can make her doe,
I am content to looke on: what to ſpeake,
I am content to heare: for 'tis as eaſie
To make her ſpeake, as moue.
Paul. It is requir'd
You doe awake your Faith: then, all ſtand ſtill:
On: thoſe that thinke it is vnlawfull Buſineſſe
I am about, let them depart.
Leo. Proceed:
No foot ſhall ſtirre.
Paul. Muſick; awake her: Strike:
'Tis time: deſcend: be Stone no more: approach:
Strike all that looke vpon with meruaile: Come:
Ile fill your Graue vp: ſtirre: nay, come away:
Bequeath to Death your numneſſe (for from him,
Deare Life redeemes you) you perceiue ſhe ſtirres:
Start not: her Actions ſhall be holy, as
You heare my Spell is lawfull: doe not ſhun her,
Vntill you ſee her dye againe; for then
You kill her double: Nay, preſent your Hand:
When ſhe was young, you woo'd her: now, in age,
Is ſhe become the Suitor?
Leo. Oh ſhe's warme:
If this be Magick, let it be an Art
Law-

Lawfull as Eating.
Pol. She embraces him.
Cam. She hangs about his necke,
If ſhe pertaine to life, let her ſpeake too.
Pol. I, and make it manifeſt where ſhe ha's liu'd,
Or how ſtolne from the dead?
Paul. That ſhe is liuing,
Were it but told you, ſhould be hooted at
Like an old Tale: but it appeares ſhe liues,
Though yet ſhe ſpeake not. Marke a little while:
Pleaſe you to interpoſe (faire Madam) kneele,
And pray your Mothers bleſſing: turne good Lady,
Our *Perdita* is found.
Her. You Gods looke downe,
And from your ſacred Viols poure your graces
Vpon my daughters head: Tell me (mine owne)
Where haſt thou bin preſeru'd? Where liu'd? How found
Thy Fathers Court? For thou ſhalt heare that I
Knowing by *Paulina*, that the Oracle
Gaue hope thou waſt in being, haue preſeru'd
My ſelfe, to ſee the yſſue.
Paul. There's time enough for that,
Leaſt they deſire (vpon this puſh) to trouble
Your ioyes, with like Relation. Go together
You precious winners all: your exultation
Partake to euery one: I (an old Turtle)
Will wing me to ſome wither'd bough, and there
My Mate (that's neuer to be found againe)
Lament, till I am loſt.
Leo. O peace *Paulina*:
Thou ſhouldſt a husband take by my conſent,
As I by thine a Wife. This is a Match,
And made betweene's by Vowes. Thou haſt found mine,
But how, is to be queſtion'd: for I ſaw her
(As I thought) dead: and haue (in vaine) ſaid many
A prayer vpon her graue. Ile not ſeeke farre
(For him, I partly know his minde) to finde thee
An honourable husband. Come *Camillo*,
And take her by the hand: whoſe worth, and honeſty
Is richly noted: and heere iuſtified
By Vs, a paire of Kings. Let's from this place.
What? looke vpon my Brother: both your pardons,
That ere I put betweene your holy lookes
My ill ſuſpition: This your Son-in-law,
And Sonne vnto the King, whom heauens directing
Is troth-plight to your daughter. Good *Paulina*,
Leade vs from hence, where we may leyſurely
Each one demand, and anſwere to his part
Perform'd in this wide gap of Time, ſince firſt
We were diſſeuer'd: Haſtily lead away. *Exeunt.*

The Names of the Actors.

Leontes, King of Sicillia.
Mamillus, yong Prince of Sicillia.
Camillo.
Antigonus. } *Foure*
Cleomines. } *Lords of Sicillia.*
Dion.
Hermione, Queene to Leontes.
Perdita, Daughter to Leontes and Hermione.
Paulina, wife to Antigonus
Emilia, a Lady.
Polixenes, King of Bohemia.
Florizell, Prince of Bohemia.
Old Shepheard, reputed Father of Perdita.
Clowne, his Sonne.
Autolicus, a Rogue.
Archidamus, a Lord of Bohemia.
Other Lords, and Gentlemen, and Seruants.
Shepheards, and Shepheardeſſes.

FINIS.

The life and death of King Iohn.

Actus Primus, Scæna Prima.

Enter King Iohn, Queene Elinor, Pembroke, Eſſex, and Salisbury, with the Chattylion of France.

King Iohn.
NOw ſay *Chatillion*, what would *France* with vs?
Chat. Thus (after greeting) ſpeakes the King of France,
In my behauiour to the Maieſty,
The borrowed Maieſty of *England* heere.
Elea. A ſtrange beginning: borrowed Maieſty?
K.Iohn. Silence (good mother) heare the Embaſſie.
Chat. Philip of *France*, in right and true behalfe
Of thy deceaſed brother, *Geffreyes* ſonne,
Arthur Plantaginet, laies moſt lawfull claime
To this faire Iland, and the Territories:
To *Ireland, Poyctiers, Aniowe, Torayne, Maine*,
Deſiring thee to lay aſide the ſword
Which ſwaies vſurpingly theſe ſeuerall titles,
And put the ſame into yong *Arthurs* hand,
Thy Nephew, and right royall Soueraigne.
K. Iohn. What followes if we diſallow of this?
Chat. The proud controle of fierce and bloudy warre,
To inforce theſe rights, ſo forcibly with-held,
K.Io. Heere haue we war for war, & bloud for bloud,
Controlement for controlement: ſo anſwer *France*.
Chat. Then take my Kings defiance from my mouth,
The fartheſt limit of my Embaſſie.
K. Iohn. Beare mine to him, and ſo depart in peace,
Be thou as lightning in the eies of *France*;
For ere thou canſt report, I will be there:
The thunder of my Cannon ſhall be heard.
So hence: be thou the trumpet of our wrath,
And ſullen preſage of your owne decay:
An honourable conduct let him haue,
Pembroke looke too't: farewell *Chattillion*.
Exit Chat and Pem.
Ele. What now my ſonne, haue I not euer ſaid
How that ambitious *Conſtance* would not ceaſe
Till ſhe had kindled *France* and all the world,
Vpon the right and party of her ſonne.
This might haue beene preuented, and made whole
With very eaſie arguments of loue,
Which now the mannage of two kingdomes muſt
With fearefull bloudy iſſue arbitrate.
K Iohn. Our ſtrong poſſeſſion, and our right for vs.
Eli. Your ſtrong poſſeſsiō much more then your right,
Or elſe it muſt go wrong with you and me,
So much my conſcience whiſpers in your eare,
Which none but heauen, and you, and I, ſhall heare.
Enter a Sheriffe.
Eſſex. My Liege, here is the ſtrangeſt controuerſie
Come from the Country to be iudg'd by you
That ere I heard: ſhall I produce the men?
K.Iohn. Let them approach:
Our Abbies and our Priories ſhall pay
This expeditious charge: what men are you?
Enter Robert Faulconbridge, and Philip.
Philip. Your faithfull ſubiect, I a gentleman
Borne in *Northamptonſhire*, and eldeſt ſonne
As I ſuppoſe, to *Robert Faulconbridge*,
A Souldier by the Honor-giuing-hand
Of *Cordelion*, Knighted in the field.
K.Iohn. What art thou?
Robert. The ſon and heire to that ſame *Faulconbridge*.
K.Iohn. Is that the elder, and art thou the heyre?
You came not of one mother then it ſeemes.
Philip. Moſt certain of one mother, mighty King,
That is well knowne, and as I thinke one father:
But for the certaine knowledge of that truth,
I put you o're to heauen, and to my mother;
Of that I doubt, as all mens children may.
Eli. Out on thee rude man, ý doſt ſhame thy mother,
And wound her honor with this diffidence.
Phil. I Madame? No, I haue no reaſon for it,
That is my brothers plea, and none of mine,
The which if he can proue, a pops me out,
At leaſt from faire fiue hundred pound a yeere:
Heauen guard my mothers honor, and my Land.
K.Iohn. A good blunt fellow: why being yonger borne
Doth he lay claime to thine inheritance?
Phil. I know not why, except to get the land:
But once he ſlanderd me with baſtardy:
But where I be as true begot or no,
That ſtill I lay vpon my mothers head,
But that I am as well begot my Liege
(Faire fall the bones that tooke the paines for me)
Compare our faces, and be Iudge your ſelfe
If old Sir *Robert* did beget vs both,
And were our father, and this ſonne like him:
O old ſir *Robert* Father, on my knee
I giue heauen thankes I was not like to thee.
K.Iohn. Why what a mad-cap hath heauen lent vs here?
Elen. He hath a tricke of *Cordelions* face,
The accent of his tongue affecteth him:
Doe you not read ſome tokens of my ſonne
In the large compoſition of this man?

a K.Iohn

K.Iohn. Mine eye hath well examined his parts,
And findes them perfect *Richard*: ſirra ſpeake,
What doth moue you to claime your brothers land.
Philip. Becauſe he hath a half-face like my father:
With halfe that face would he haue all my land,
A halfe-fac'd groat, fiue hundred pound a yeere?
Rob. My gracious Liege, when that my father liu'd,
Your brother did imploy my father much.
Phil. Well ſir, by this you cannot get my land,
Your tale muſt be how he employ'd my mother.
Rob. And once diſpatch'd him in an Embaſſie
To *Germany*, there with the Emperor
To treat of high affaires touching that time:
Th'aduantage of his abſence tooke the King,
And in the meane time ſoiourn'd at my fathers;
Where how he did preuaile, I ſhame to ſpeake:
But truth is truth, large lengths of ſeas and ſhores
Betweene my father, and my mother lay,
As I haue heard my father ſpeake himſelfe
When this ſame luſty gentleman was got:
Vpon his death-bed he by will bequeath'd
His lands to me, and tooke it on his death
That this my mothers ſonne was none of his;
And if he were, he came into the world
Full fourteene weekes before the courſe of time:
Then good my Liedge let me haue what is mine,
My fathers land, as was my fathers will.
K.Iohn. Sirra, your brother is Legittimate,
Your fathers wife did after wedlocke beare him:
And if ſhe did play falſe, the fault was hers,
Which fault lyes on the hazards of all husbands
That marry wiues: tell me, how if my brother
Who as you ſay, tooke paines to get this ſonne,
Had of your father claim'd this ſonne for his,
Inſooth, good friend, your father might haue kept
This Calfe, bred from his Cow from all the world:
Inſooth he might: then if he were my brothers
My brother might not claime him, nor your father
Being none of his, refuſe him: this concludes,
My mothers ſonne did get your fathers heyre,
Your fathers heyre muſt haue your fathers land.
Rob. Shal then my fathers Will be of no force,
To diſpoſſeſſe that childe which is not his.
Phil. Of no more force to diſpoſſeſſe me ſir,
Then was his will to get me, as I think.
Eli. Whether hadſt thou rather be a *Faulconbridge*,
And like thy brother to enioy thy land:
Or the reputed ſonne of *Cordelion*,
Lord of thy preſence, and no land beſide.
Baſt. Madam, and if my brother had my ſhape
And I had his, ſir *Roberts* his like him,
And if my legs were two ſuch riding rods,
My armes, ſuch eele-skins ſtuft, my face ſo thin,
That in mine eare I durſt not ſticke a roſe,
Leſt men ſhould ſay, looke where three farthings goes,
And to his ſhape were heyre to all this land,
Would I might neuer ſtirre from off this place,
I would giue it euery foot to haue this face:
It would not be ſir nobbe in any caſe.
Elinor. I like thee well: wilt thou forſake thy fortune,
Bequeath thy land to him, and follow me?
I am a Souldier, and now bound to *France*.
Baſt. Brother, take you my land, Ile take my chance;
Your face hath got fiue hundred pound a yeere,
Yet ſell your face for fiue pence and 'tis deere:
Madam, Ile follow you vnto the death.
Elinor. Nay, I would haue you go before me thither.
Baſt. Our Country manners giue our betters way.
K.Iohn. What is thy name?
Baſt. *Philip* my Liege, ſo is my name begun,
Philip, good old Sir *Roberts* wiues eldeſt ſonne.
K.Iohn. From henceforth beare his name
Whoſe forme thou beareſt:
Kneele thou downe *Philip*, but riſe more great,
Ariſe Sir *Richard*, and *Plantagenet*.
Baſt. Brother by th'mothers ſide, giue me your hand,
My father gaue me honor, yours gaue land:
Now bleſſed be the houre by night or day
When I was got, Sir *Robert* was away.
Ele. The very ſpirit of *Plantaginet*:
I am thy grandame *Richard*, call me ſo.
Baſt. Madam by chance, but not by truth, what tho;
Something about a little from the right,
In at the window, or elſe ore the hatch:
Who dares not ſtirre by day, muſt walke by night,
And haue is haue, how euer men doe catch:
Neere or farre off, well wonne is ſtill well ſhot,
And I am I, how ere I was begot.
K.Iohn. Goe, *Faulconbridge*, now haſt thou thy deſire,
A landleſſe Knight, makes thee a landed Squire:
Come Madam, and come *Richard*, we muſt ſpeed
For *France*, for *France*, for it is more then need.
Baſt Brother adieu, good fortune come to thee,
For thou waſt got i'th way of honeſty.
Exeunt all but baſtard.

Baſt. A foot of Honor better then I was,
But many a many foot of Land the worſe.
Well, now can I make any *Ioane* a Lady,
Good den Sir *Richard*, Godamercy fellow,
And if his name be *George*, Ile call him *Peter*;
For new made honor doth forget mens names:
Tis two reſpectiue, and too ſociable
For your conuerſion, now your traueller,
Hee and his tooth-picke at my worſhips meſſe,
And when my knightly ſtomacke is ſuffis'd,
Why then I ſucke my teeth, and catechize
My picked man of Countries: my deare ſir,
Thus leaning on mine elbow I begin,
I ſhall beſeech you; that is queſtion now,
And then comes anſwer like an Abſey booke:
O ſir, ſayes anſwer, at your beſt command,
At your employment, at your ſeruice ſir:
No ſir, ſaies queſtion, I ſweet ſir at yours,
And ſo ere anſwer knowes what queſtion would,
Sauing in Dialogue of Complement,
And talking of the Alpes and Appenines,
The Perennean and the riuer *Poe*,
It drawes toward ſupper in concluſion ſo.
But this is worſhipfull ſociety,
And fits the mounting ſpirit like my ſelfe;
For he is but a baſtard to the time
That doth not ſmoake of obſeruation,
And ſo am I whether I ſmacke or no:
And not alone in habit and deuice,
Exterior forme, outward accoutrement;
But from the inward motion to deliuer
Sweet, ſweet, ſweet poyſon for the ages tooth,
Which though I will not practice to deceiue,
Yet to auoid deceit I meane to learne;
For it ſhall ſtrew the footſteps of my riſing:
But who comes in ſuch haſte in riding robes?
What

What woman poſt is this? hath ſhe no husband
That will take paines to blow a horne before her?
O me, 'tis my mother: how now good Lady,
What brings you heere to Court ſo haſtily?

Enter Lady Faulconbridge and Iames Gurney.

Lady. Where is that ſlaue thy brother? where is he?
That holds in chaſe mine honour vp and downe.
Baſt. My brother *Robert*, old Sir *Roberts* ſonne:
Colbrand the Gyant, that ſame mighty man,
Is it Sir *Roberts* ſonne that you ſeeke ſo?
Lady. Sir *Roberts* ſonne, I thou vnreuerend boy,
Sir *Roberts* ſonne? why ſcorn'ſt thou at ſir *Robert*?
He is Sir *Roberts* ſonne, and ſo art thou.
Baſt. Iames Gournie, wilt thou giue vs leaue a while?
Gour. Good leaue good *Philip*.
Baſt. Philip, ſparrow, *Iames*,
There's toyes abroad, anon Ile tell thee more.
Exit Iames.
Madam, I was not old Sir *Roberts* ſonne,
Sir *Robert* might haue eat his part in me
Vpon good Friday, and nere broke his faſt:
Sir *Robert* could doe well, marrie to confeſſe
Could get me ſir *Robert* could not doe it;
We know his handy-worke, therefore good mother
To whom am I beholding for theſe limmes?
Sir *Robert* neuer holpe to make this legge.
Lady. Haſt thou conſpired with thy brother too,
That for thine owne gaine ſhouldſt defend mine honor?
What meanes this ſcorne, thou moſt vntoward knaue?
Baſt. Knight, knight good mother, Baſiliſco-like:
What, I am dub'd, I haue it on my ſhoulder:
But mother, I am not Sir *Roberts* ſonne,
I haue diſclaim'd Sir *Robert* and my land,
Legitimation, name, and all is gone;
Then good my mother, let me know my father,
Some proper man I hope, who was it mother?
Lady. Haſt thou denied thy ſelfe a *Faulconbridge*?
Baſt. As faithfully as I denie the deuill.
Lady. King Richard Cordelion was thy father,
By long and vehement ſuit I was ſeduc'd
To make roome for him in my husbands bed:
Heauen lay not my tranſgreſſion to my charge,
That art the iſſue of my deere offence
Which was ſo ſtrongly vrg'd paſt my defence.
Baſt. Now by this light were I to get againe,
Madam I would not wiſh a better father:
Some ſinnes doe beare their priuiledge on earth,
And ſo doth yours; your fault, was not your follie,
Needs muſt you lay your heart at his diſpoſe,
Subiected tribute to commanding loue,
Againſt whoſe furie and vnmatched force,
The awleſſe Lion could not wage the fight,
Nor keepe his Princely heart from *Richards* hand:
He that perforce robs Lions of their hearts,
May eaſily winne a womans: aye my mother,
With all my heart I thanke thee for my father:
Who liues and dares but ſay, thou didſt not well
When I was got, Ile ſend his ſoule to hell.
Come Lady I will ſhew thee to my kinne,
And they ſhall ſay, when *Richard* me begot,
If thou hadſt ſayd him nay, it had beene ſinne;
Who ſayes it was, he lyes, I ſay twas not.
Exeunt.

Scæna Secunda.

Enter before Angiers, Philip King of France, Lewis, Daulphin, Auſtria, Conſtance, Arthur.

Lewis. Before *Angiers* well met braue *Auſtria*,
Arthur that great fore-runner of thy bloud,
Richard that rob'd the Lion of his heart,
And fought the holy Warres in *Paleſtine*,
By this braue Duke came early to his graue:
And for amends to his poſteritie,
At our importance hether is he come,
To ſpread his colours boy, in thy behalfe,
And to rebuke the vſurpation
Of thy vnnaturall Vncle, Engliſh *Iohn*,
Embrace him, loue him, giue him welcome hether.
Arth. God ſhall forgiue you *Cordelions* death
The rather, that you giue his off-ſpring life,
Shadowing their right vnder your wings of warre:
I giue you welcome with a powerleſſe hand,
But with a heart full of vnſtained loue,
Welcome before the gates of *Angiers* Duke.
Lewis. A noble boy, who would not doe thee right?
Auſt. Vpon thy cheeke lay I this zelous kiſſe,
As ſeale to this indenture of my loue:
That to my home I will no more returne
Till *Angiers*, and the right thou haſt in *France*,
Together with that pale, that white-fac'd ſhore,
Whoſe foot ſpurnes backe the Oceans roaring tides,
And coopes from other lands her Ilanders,
Euen till that *England* hedg'd in with the maine,
That Water-walled Bulwarke, ſtill ſecure
And confident from forreine purpoſes,
Euen till that vtmoſt corner of the Weſt
Salute thee for her King, till then faire boy
Will I not thinke of home, but follow Armes.
Conſt. O take his mothers thanks, a widdows thanks,
Till your ſtrong hand ſhall helpe to giue him ſtrength,
To make a more requitall to your loue.
Auſt. The peace of heauen is theirs yͭ lift their ſwords
In ſuch a iuſt and charitable warre.
King. Well, then to worke our Cannon ſhall be bent
Againſt the browes of this reſiſting towne,
Call for our cheefeſt men of diſcipline,
To cull the plots of beſt aduantages:
Wee'll lay before this towne our Royal bones,
Wade to the market-place in *French*-mens bloud,
But we will make it ſubiect to this boy.
Con. Stay for an anſwer to your Embaſſie,
Leſt vnaduis'd you ſtaine your ſwords with bloud,
My Lord *Chattilion* may from *England* bring
That right in peace which heere we vrge in warre,
And then we ſhall repent each drop of bloud,
That hot raſh haſte ſo indirectly ſhedde.
Enter Chattilion.
King. A wonder Lady: lo vpon thy wiſh
Our Meſſenger *Chattilion* is arriu'd,
What *England* ſaies, ſay breefely gentle Lord,
We coldly pauſe for thee, *Chatilion* ſpeake,
Chat. Then turne your forces from this paltry ſiege,
And ſtirre them vp againſt a mightier taske:
England impatient of your iuſt demands,
Hath put himſelfe in Armes, the aduerſe windes

a 2 Whoſe

Whoſe leiſure I haue ſtaid, haue giuen him time
To land his Legions all as ſoone as I:
His marches are expedient to this towne,
His forces ſtrong, his Souldiers confident:
With him along is come the Mother Queene,
An Ace ſtirring him to bloud and ſtrife,
With her her Neece, the Lady *Blanch of Spaine*,
With them a Baſtard of the Kings deceaſt,
And all th'vnſetled humors of the Land,
Raſh, inconſiderate, fiery voluntaries,
With Ladies faces, and fierce Dragons ſpleenes,
Haue ſold their fortunes at their natiue homes,
Bearing their birth-rights proudly on their backs,
To make a hazard of new fortunes heere:
In briefe, a brauer choyſe of dauntleſſe ſpirits
Then now the *Engliſh* bottomes haue waft o're,
Did neuer flote vpon the ſwelling tide,
To doe offence and ſcathe in Chriſtendome:
The interruption of their churliſh drums
Cuts off more circumſtance, they are at hand,
Drum beats.
To parlie or to fight, therefore prepare.
Kin. How much vnlook'd for, is this expedition.
Auſt. By how much vnexpected, by ſo much
We muſt awake indeuor for defence,
For courage mounteth with occaſion,
Let them be welcome then, we are prepar'd.

Enter K. of England, Baſtard, Queene, Blanch, Pembroke, and others.

K.Iohn. Peace be to *France*: If France in peace permit
Our iuſt and lineall entrance to our owne;
If not, bleede *France*, and peace aſcend to heauen.
Whiles we Gods wrathfull agent doe correct
Their proud contempt that beats his peace to heauen.
Fran. Peace be to *England*, if that warre returne
From *France* to *England*, there to liue in peace:
England we loue, and for that *Englands* ſake,
With burden of our armor heere we ſweat:
This toyle of ours ſhould be a worke of thine;
But thou from louing *England* art ſo farre,
That thou haſt vnder-wrought his lawfull King,
Cut off the ſequence of poſterity,
Out-faced Infant State, and done a rape
Vpon the maiden vertue of the Crowne:
Looke heere vpon thy brother *Geffreyes* face,
Theſe eyes, theſe browes, were moulded out of his;
This little abſtract doth containe that large,
Which died in *Geffreys* and the hand of time,
Shall draw this breefe into as huge a volume:
That *Geffrey* was thy elder brother borne,
And this his ſonne, *England* was *Geffreys* right,
And this is *Geffreyes* in the name of God:
How comes it then that thou art call'd a King,
When liuing blood doth in theſe temples beat
Which owe the crowne, that thou ore-maſtereſt?
K.Iohn. From whom haſt thou this great commiſſion
To draw my anſwer from thy Articles? (*France*
Fra. Frō that ſupernal Iudge that ſtirs good thoughts
In any beaſt of ſtrong authoritie,
To looke into the blots and ſtaines of right,
That Iudge hath made me guardian to this boy
Vnder whoſe warrant I impeach thy wrong,
And by whoſe helpe I meane to chaſtiſe it.
K. Iohn. Alack thou doſt vſurpe authoritie.
Fran. Excuſe it is to beat vſurping downe.
Queen. Who is it thou doſt call vſurper *France*?
Conſt. Let me make anſwer: thy vſurping ſonne.
Queen. Out inſolent, thy baſtard ſhall be King,
That thou maiſt be a Queen, and checke the world.
Con. My bed was euer to thy ſonne as true
As thine was to thy husband, and this boy
Liker in feature to his father *Geffrey*
Then thou and *Iohn*, in manners being as like,
As raine to water, or deuill to his damme;
My boy a baſtard? by my ſoule I thinke
His father neuer was ſo true begot,
It cannot be, and if thou wert his mother. (-ther
Queen. Theres a good mother boy, that blots thy fa-
Conſt. There's a good grandame boy
That would blot thee.
Auſt. Peace.
Baſt. Heare the Cryer.
Auſt. What the deuill art thou?
Baſt. One that wil play the deuill ſir with you,
And a may catch your hide and you alone:
You are the Hare of whom the Prouerb goes
Whoſe valour plucks dead Lyons by the beard;
Ile ſmoake your skin-coat and I catch you right,
Sirra looke too't, yfaith I will, yfaith.
Blan. O well did he become that Lyons robe,
That did diſrobe the Lion of that robe.
Baſt. It lies as ſightly on the backe of him,
As great *Alcides* ſhooes vpon an Aſſe:
But Aſſe, Ile take that burthen from your backe,
Or lay on that ſhall make your ſhoulders cracke.
Auſt. What cracker is this ſame that deafes our eares
With this abundance of ſuperfluous breath?
King *Lewis*, determine what we ſhall doe ſtrait.
Lew. Women & fooles, breake off your conference.
King *Iohn*, this is the very ſumme of all:
England and *Ireland*, *Angiers*, *Toraine*, *Maine*,
In right of *Arthur* doe I claime of thee:
Wilt thou reſigne them, and lay downe thy Armes?
Iohn. My life as ſoone: I doe defie thee *France*,
Arthur of *Britaine*, yeeld thee to my hand,
And out of my deere loue Ile giue thee more,
Then ere the coward hand of *France* can win;
Submit thee boy.
Queen. Come to thy grandame child.
Conſ. Doe childe, goe to yt grandame childe,
Giue grandame kingdome, and it grandame will
Giue yt a plum, a cherry, and a figge,
There's a good grandame.
Arthur. Good my mother peace,
I would that I were low laid in my graue,
I am not worth this coyle that's made for me. (weepes.
Qu. Mo. His mother ſhames him ſo, poore boy hee
Con. Now ſhame vpon you where ſhe does or no.
His grandames wrongs, and not his mothers ſhames
Drawes thoſe heauen-mouing pearles fro his poor eies,
Which heauen ſhall take in nature of a fee:
I, with theſe Chriſtall beads heauen ſhall be brib'd
To doe him Iuſtice, and reuenge on you.
Qu. Thou monſtrous ſlanderer of heauen and earth.
Con. Thou monſtrous Iniurer of heauen and earth,
Call not me ſlanderer, thou and thine vſurpe
The Dominations, Royalties, and rights
Of this oppreſſed boy; this is thy eldeſt ſonnes ſonne,
Infortunate in nothing but in thee:
Thy

Thy ſinnes are viſited in this poore childe,
The Canon of the Law is laide on him,
Being but the ſecond generation
Remoued from thy ſinne-conceiuing wombe.
Iohn. Bedlam haue done.
Con. I haue but this to ſay,
That he is not onely plagued for her ſin,
But God hath made her ſinne and her, the plague
On this remoued iſſue, plagued for her,
And with her plague her ſinne: his iniury
Her iniurie the Beadle to her ſinne,
All puniſh'd in the perſon of this childe,
And all for her, a plague vpon her.
Que. Thou vnaduiſed ſcold, I can produce
A Will, that barres the title of thy ſonne.
Con. I who doubts that, a Will: a wicked will,
A womans will, a cankred Grandams will.
Fra. Peace Lady, pauſe, or be more temperate,
It ill beſeemes this preſence to cry ayme
To theſe ill tuned repetitions:
Some Trumpet ſummon hither to the walles
Theſe men of Angiers, let vs heare them ſpeake,
Whoſe title they admit, *Arthurs* or *Iohns*.

Trumpet ſounds.
Enter a Citizen vpon the walles.

Cit. Who is it that hath warn'd vs to the walles?
Fra. Tis France, for England.
Iohn. England for it ſelfe:
You men of Angiers, and my louing ſubiects.
Fra. You louing men of Angiers, *Arthurs* ſubiects,
Our Trumpet call'd you to this gentle parle.
Iohn. For our aduantage, therefore heare vs firſt.
Theſe flagges of France that are aduanced heere
Before the eye and proſpect of your Towne,
Haue hither march'd to your endamagement.
The Canons haue their bowels full of wrath,
And ready mounted are they to ſpit forth
Their Iron indignation 'gainſt your walles:
All preparation for a bloody ſiedge
And merciles proceeding, by theſe French.
Comfort yours Citties eies, your winking gates:
And but for our approch, thoſe ſleeping ſtones,
That as a waſte doth girdle you about
By the compulſion of their Ordinance,
By this time from their fixed beds of lime
Had bin diſhabited, and wide hauocke made
For bloody power to ruſh vppon your peace.
But on the ſight of vs your lawfull King,
Who painefully with much expedient march
Haue brought a counter-checke before your gates,
To ſaue vnſcratch'd your Citties threatned cheekes:
Behold the French amaz'd vouchſafe a parle,
And now inſteed of bulletts wrapt in fire
To make a ſhaking feuer in your walles,
They ſhoote but calme words, folded vp in ſmoake,
To make a faithleſſe errour in your eares,
Which truſt accordingly kinde Cittizens,
And let vs in. Your King, whoſe labour'd ſpirits
Fore-wearied in this action of ſwift ſpeede,
Craues harbourage within your Citie walles.
France. When I haue ſaide, make anſwer to vs both.
Loe in this right hand, whoſe protection
Is moſt diuinely vow'd vpon the right
Of him it holds, ſtands yong *Plantagenet*,
Sonne to the elder brother of this man,
And King ore him, and all that he enioyes:
For this downe-troden equity, we tread
In warlike march, theſe greenes before your Towne,
Being no further enemy to you
Then the conſtraint of hoſpitable zeale,
In the releefe of this oppreſſed childe,
Religiouſly prouokes. Be pleaſed then
To pay that dutie which you truly owe,
To him that owes it, namely, this yong Prince,
And then our Armes, like to a muzled Beare,
Saue in aſpect, hath all offence ſeal'd vp:
Our Cannons malice vainly ſhall be ſpent
Againſt th'involuerable clouds of heauen,
And with a bleſſed and vn-vext retyre,
With vnhack'd ſwords, and Helmets all vnbruis'd,
We will beare home that luſtie blood againe,
Which heere we came to ſpout againſt your Towne,
And leaue your children, wiues, and you in peace.
But if you fondly paſſe our proffer'd offer,
Tis not the rounder of your old-fac'd walles,
Can hide you from our meſſengers of Warre,
Though all theſe Engliſh, and their diſcipline
Were harbour'd in their rude circumference:
Then tell vs, Shall your Citie call vs Lord,
In that behalfe which we haue challeng'd it?
Or ſhall we giue the ſignall to our rage,
And ſtalke in blood to our poſſeſſion?
Cit. In breefe, we are the King of Englands ſubiects
For him, and in his right, we hold this Towne.
Iohn. Acknowledge then the King, and let me in.
Cit. That can we not: but he that proues the King
To him will we proue loyall, till that time
Haue we ramm'd vp our gates againſt the world.
Iohn. Doth not the Crowne of England, prooue the King?
And if not that, I bring you Witneſſes
Twice fifteene thouſand hearts of Englands breed
Baſt. Baſtards and elſe.
Iohn. To verifie our title with their liues.
Fran. As many and as well-borne bloods as thoſe.
Baſt. Some Baſtards too.
Fran. Stand in his face to contradict his claime.
Cit. Till you compound whoſe right is worthieſt,
We for the worthieſt hold the right from both.
Iohn. Then God forgiue the ſinne of all thoſe ſoules,
That to their euerlaſting reſidence,
Before the dew of euening fall, ſhall fleete
In dreadfull triall of our kingdomes King.
Fran. Amen, Amen, mount Cheualiers to Armes.
Baſt. Saint George that ſwindg'd the Dragon,
And ere ſince ſit's on's horſebacke at mine Hoſteſſe dore
Teach vs ſome fence. Sirrah, were I at home
At your den ſirrah, with your Lioneſſe,
I would ſet an Oxe-head to your Lyons hide:
And make a monſter of you.
Auſt. Peace, no more.
Baſt. O tremble: for you heare the Lyon rore.
Iohn. Vp higher to the plaine, where we'l ſet forth
In beſt appointment all our Regiments.
Baſt. Speed then to take aduantage of the field.
Fra. It ſhall be ſo, and at the other hill
Command the reſt to ſtand. God and our right. *Exeunt*
Heere after excurſions, Enter the Herald of France with Trumpets to the gates.
F. Her. You men of Angiers open wide your gates,
And let yong *Arthur* Duke of Britaine in,

Who by the hand of France, this day hath made
Much worke for teares in many an Engliſh mother,
Whoſe ſonnes lye ſcattered on the bleeding ground :
Many a widdowes husband groueling lies,
Coldly embracing the diſcoloured earth,
And victorie with little loſſe doth play
Vpon the dancing banners of the French,
Who are at hand triumphantly diſplayed
To enter Conquerors, and to proclaime
Arthur of Britaine, Englands King, and yours.

Enter Engliſh Herald with Trumpet.

E.Har. Reioyce you men of Angiers, ring your bels,
King *Iohn*, your king and Englands, doth approach,
Commander of this hot malicious day,
Their Armours that march'd hence ſo ſiluer bright,
Hither returne all gilt with Frenchmens blood
There ſtucke no plume in any Engliſh Creſt,
That is remoued by a ſtaffe of France.
Our colours do returne in thoſe ſame hands
That did diſplay them when we firſt marcht forth
And like a Iolly troope of Huntſmen come
Our luſtie Engliſh, all with purpled hands,
Dide in the dying ſlaughter of their foes,
Open your gates, and giue the Victors way

Hubert. Heralds, from off our towres we might behold
From firſt to laſt, the on-ſet and retyre :
Of both your Armies, whoſe equality
By our beſt eyes cannot be cenſured : (blowes.
Blood hath bought blood, and blowes haue anſwerd
Strength matcht with ſtrength, and power confronted power,
Both are alike, and both alike we like.
One muſt proue greateſt. While they weigh ſo euen,
We hold our Towne for neither : yet for both.

Enter the two Kings with their powers, at ſeuerall doores.

Iohn. France, haſt thou yet more blood to caſt away?
Say, ſhall the currant of our right rome on,
Whoſe paſſage vext with thy impediment,
Shall leaue his natiue channell, and ore-ſwell
with courſe diſturb'd euen thy confining ſhores,
Vnleſſe thou let his ſiluer Water, keepe
A peacefull progreſſe to the Ocean.

Fra. England thou haſt not ſau'd one drop of blood
In this hot triall more then we of France,
Rather loſt more. And by this hand I ſweare
That ſwayes the earth this Climate ouer-lookes,
Before we will lay downe our iuſt-borne Armes,
Wee'l put thee downe, gainſt whom theſe Armes wee
Or adde a royall number to the dead : (beare,
Gracing the ſcroule that tels of this warres loſſe,
With ſlaughter coupled to the name of kings.

Baſt. Ha Maieſty : how high thy glory towres,
When the rich blood of kings is ſet on fire :
Oh now doth death line his dead chaps with ſteele,
The ſwords of ſouldiers are his teeth, his phangs,
And now he feaſts, mouſing the fleſh of men
In vndetermin'd differences of kings.
Why ſtand theſe royall fronts amazed thus :
Cry hauocke kings, backe to the ſtained field
You equall Potents, fierie kindled ſpirits,
Then let confuſion of one part confirm
The others peace : till then, blowes, blood, and death.

Iohn. Whoſe party do the Townеſmen yet admit?

Fra. Speake Citizens for England, whoſe your king.

Hub. The king of England, when we know the king.

Fra. Know him in vs, that heere hold vp his right.

Iohn. In Vs, that are our owne great Deputie,
And beare poſſeſſion of our Perſon heere,
Lord of our preſence Angiers, and of you.

Fra. A greater powre then We denies all this,
And till it be vndoubted, we do locke
Our former ſcruple in our ſtrong barr'd gates :
Kings of our feare, vntill our feares reſolu'd
Be by ſome certaine king, purg'd and depos'd.

Baſt. By heauen, theſe ſcroyles of Angiers flout you
And ſtand ſecurely on their battelments, (kings,
As in a Theater, whence they gape and point
At your induſtrious Scenes and acts of death.
Your Royall preſences be rul'd by mee,
Do like the Mutines of Ieruſalem,
Be friends a-while, and both conioyntly bend
Your ſharpeſt Deeds of malice on this Towne.
By Eaſt and Weſt let France and England mount.
Their battering Canon charged to the mouthes,
Till their ſoule-fearing clamours haue braul'd downe
The flintie ribbes of this contemptuous Citie,
I'de play inceſſantly vpon theſe Iades,
Euen till vnfenced deſolation
Leaue them as naked as the vulgar ayre :
That done, diſſeuer your vnited ſtrengths,
And part your mingled colours once againe,
Turne face to face, and bloody point to point:
Then in a moment Fortune ſhall cull forth
Out of one ſide her happy Minion,
To whom in fauour ſhe ſhall giue the day,
And kiſſe him with a glorious victory :
How like you this wilde counſell mighty States,
Smackes it not ſomething of the policie.

Iohn. Now by the sky that hangs aboue our heads,
I like it well. France, ſhall we knit our powres,
And lay this Angiers euen with the ground,
Then after fight who ſhall be king of it?

Baſt. And if thou haſt the mettle of a king,
Being wrong'd as we are by this peeuiſh Towne :
Turne thou the mouth of thy Artillerie,
As we will ours, againſt theſe ſawcie walles,
And when that we haue daſh'd them to the ground,
Why then defie each other, and pell-mell,
Make worke vpon our ſelues, for heauen or hell.

Fra. Let it be ſo : ſay, where will you aſſault?

Iohn. We from the Weſt will ſend deſtruction
Into this Cities boſome.

Auſt. I from the North.

Fran. Our Thunder from the South,
Shall raine their drift of bullets on this Towne.

Baſt. O prudent diſcipline! From North to South:
Auſtria and France ſhoot in each others mouth.
Ile ſtirre them to it : Come, away, away.

Hub. Heare vs great kings, vouchſafe awhile to ſtay
And I ſhall ſhew you peace, and faire-fac'd league :
Win you this Citie without ſtroke, or wound,
Reſcue thoſe breathing liues to dye in beds,
That heere come ſacrifices for the field.
Perſeuer not, but heare me mighty kings.

Iohn. Speake on with fauour, we are bent to heare.

Hub. That daughter there of Spaine, the Lady *Blanch*
Is neere to England, looke vpon the yeeres
Of *Lewes* the Dolphin, and that louely maid.
If luſtie loue ſhould go in queſt of beautie,

Where

Where ſhould he finde it fairer, then in *Blanch*:
If zealous loue ſhould go in ſearch of vertue,
Where ſhould he finde it purer then in *Blanch*?
If loue ambitious, ſought a match of birth,
Whoſe veines bound richer blood then Lady *Blanch*?
Such as ſhe is, in beautie, vertue, birth,
Is the yong Dolphin euery way compleat,
If not compleat of, ſay he is not ſhee,
And ſhe againe wants nothing, to name want,
If want it be not, that ſhe is not hee:
He is the halfe part of a bleſſed man,
Left to be finiſhed by ſuch as ſhee,
And ſhe a faire diuided excellence,
Whoſe fulneſſe of perfection lyes in him.
O two ſuch ſiluer currents when they ioyne
Do glorifie the bankes that bound them in:
And two ſuch ſhores, to two ſuch ſtreames made one,
Two ſuch controlling bounds ſhall you be, kings,
To theſe two Princes, if you marrie them:
This Vnion ſhall do more then batterie can
To our faſt cloſed gates: for at this match,
With ſwifter ſpleene then powder can enforce
The mouth of paſſage ſhall we fling wide ope,
And giue you entrance: but without this match,
The ſea enraged is not halfe ſo deafe,
Lyons more confident, Mountaines and rockes
More free from motion, no not death himſelfe
In mortall furie halfe ſo peremptorie,
As we to keepe this Citie.

Baſt. Heeres a ſtay,
That ſhakes the rotten carkaſſe of old death
Out of his ragges. Here's a large mouth indeede,
That ſpits forth death, and mountaines, rockes, and ſeas,
Talkes as familiarly of roaring Lyons,
As maids of thirteene do of puppi-dogges.
What Cannoneere begot this luſtie blood,
He ſpeakes plaine Cannon fire, and ſmoake, and bounce,
He giues the baſtinado with his tongue:
Our eares are cudgel'd, not a word of his
But buffets better then a fiſt of France:
Zounds, I was neuer ſo bethumpt with words,
Since I firſt cal'd my brothers father Dad.

Old Qu. Son, liſt to this coniunction, make this match
Giue with our Neece a dowrie large enough,
For by this knot, thou ſhalt ſo ſurely tye
Thy now vnſur'd aſſurance to the Crowne,
That yon greene boy ſhall haue no Sunne to ripe
The bloome that promiſeth a mightie fruite.
I ſee a yeelding in the lookes of France:
Marke how they whiſper, vrge them while their ſoules
Are capeable of this ambition,
Leaſt zeale now melted by the windie breath
Of ſoft petitions, pittie and remorſe,
Coole and congeale againe to what it was.

Hub. Why anſwer not the double Maieſties,
This friendly treatie of our threatned Towne.

Fra. Speake England firſt, that hath bin forward firſt
To ſpeake vnto this Cittie: what ſay you?

Iohn. If that the Dolphin there thy Princely ſonne,
Can in this booke of beautie read, I loue:
Her Dowrie ſhall weigh equall with a Queene:
For *Angiers*, and faire *Toraine Maine*, *Poyctiers*,
And all that we vpon this ſide the Sea,
(Except this Cittie now by vs beſiedg'd)
Finde liable to our Crowne and Dignitie,
Shall gild her bridall bed and make her rich
In titles, honors, and promotions,
As ſhe in beautie, education, blood,
Holdes hand with any Princeſſe of the world.

Fra. What ſai'ſt thou boy? looke in the Ladies face.

Dol. I do my Lord, and in her eie I find
A wonder, or a wondrous miracle,
The ſhadow of my ſelfe form'd in her eye,
Which being but the ſhadow of your ſonne,
Becomes a ſonne and makes your ſonne a ſhadow:
I do proteſt I neuer lou'd my ſelfe
Till now, infixed I beheld my ſelfe,
Drawne in the flattering table of her eie.

Whiſper: with Blanch.

Baſt. Drawne in the flattering table of her eie,
Hang'd in the frowning wrinkle of her brow,
And quarter'd in her heart, hee doth eſpie
Himſelfe loues traytor, this is pittie now;
That hang'd, and drawne, and quarter'd there ſhould be
In ſuch a loue, ſo vile a Lout as he.

Blan. My vnckles will in this reſpect is mine,
If he ſee ought in you that makes him like,
That any thing he ſee's which moues his liking,
I can with eaſe tranſlate it to my will:
Or if you will, to ſpeake more properly,
I will enforce it eaſlie to my loue.
Further I will not flatter you, my Lord
That all I ſee in you is worthie loue,
Then this, that nothing do I ſee in you,
Though churliſh thoughts themſelues ſhould bee your Iudge,
That I can finde, ſhould merit any hate.

Iohn. What ſaie theſe yong-ones? What ſay you my Neece?

Blan. That ſhe is bound in honor ſtill to do
What you in wiſedome ſtill vouchſafe to ſay.

Iohn. Speake then Prince Dolphin, can you loue this Ladie?

Dol. Nay aske me if I can refraine from loue,
For I doe loue her moſt vnfainedly.

Iohn. Then do I giue *Volqueſſen*, *Toraine*, *Maine*,
Poyctiers, and *Aniow*, theſe fiue Prouinces
With her to thee, and this addition more,
Full thirty thouſand Markes of Engliſh coyne.
Phillip of France, if thou be pleaſ'd withall,
Command thy ſonne and daughter to ioyne hands.

Fra. It likes vs well young Princes: cloſe your hands

Auſt. And your lippes too, for I am well aſſur'd,
That I did ſo when I was firſt aſſur'd.

Fra. Now Cittizens of Angires ope your gates,
Let in that amitie which you haue made,
For at Saint Maries Chappell preſently,
The rights of marriage ſhallbe ſolemniz'd.
Is not the Ladie *Conſtance* in this troope?
I know ſhe is not for this match made vp,
Her preſence would haue interrupted much.
Where is ſhe and her ſonne, tell me, who knowes?

Dol. She is ſad and paſſionate at your highnes Tent.

Fra. And by my faith, this league that we haue made
Will giue her ſadneſſe very little cure:
Brother of England, how may we content
This widdow Lady? In her right we came,
Which we God knowes, haue turn'd another way,
To our owne vantage.

Iohn. We will heale vp all,
For wee'l create yong *Arthur* Duke of Britaine
And Earle of Richmond, and this rich faire Towne

We

We make him Lord of. Call the Lady *Conſtance*,
Some ſpeedy Meſſenger bid her repaire
To our ſolemnity: I truſt we ſhall,
(If not fill vp the meaſure of her will)
Yet in ſome meaſure ſatisfie her ſo,
That we ſhall ſtop her exclamation,
Go we as well as haſt will ſuffer vs,
To this vnlook'd for vnprepared pompe. *Exeunt.*
Baſt. Mad world, mad kings, mad compoſition:
Iohn to ſtop *Arthurs* Title in the whole,
Hath willingly departed with a part,
And France, whoſe armour Conſcience buckled on,
Whom zeale and charitie brought to the field,
As Gods owne ſouldier, rounded in the eare,
With that ſame purpoſe-changer, that ſlye diuel,
That Broker, that ſtill breakes the pate of faith,
That dayly breake-vow, he that winnes of all,
Of kings, of beggers, old men, yong men, maids,
Who hauing no externall thing to looſe,
But the word Maid, cheats the poore Maide of that.
That ſmooth-fac'd Gentleman, tickling commoditie,
Commoditie, the byas of the world,
The world, who of it ſelfe is peyſed well,
Made to run euen, vpon euen ground;
Till this aduantage, this vile drawing byas,
This ſway of motion, this commoditie,
Makes it take head from all indifferency,
From all direction, purpoſe, courſe, intent.
And this ſame byas, this Commoditie,
This Bawd, this Broker, this all-changing-word,
Clap'd on the outward eye of fickle France,
Hath drawne him from his owne determin'd ayd,
From a reſolu'd and honourable warre,
To a moſt baſe and vile-concluded peace.
And why rayle I on this Commoditie?
But for becauſe he hath not wooed me yet:
Not that I haue the power to clutch my hand,
When his faire Angels would ſalute my palme,
But for my hand, as vnattempted yet,
Like a poore begger, raileth on the rich.
Well, whiles I am a begger, I will raile,
And ſay there is no ſin but to be rich:
And being rich, my vertue then ſhall be,
To ſay there is no vice, but beggerie:
Since Kings breake faith vpon commoditie,
Gaine be my Lord, for I will worſhip thee. *Exit.*

Actus Secundus

Enter Conſtance, Arthur, and Salisbury.

Con. Gone to be married? Gone to ſweare a peace?
Falſe blood to falſe blood ioyn'd. Gone to be freinds?
Shall *Lewis* haue *Blaunch*, and *Blaunch* thoſe Prouinces?
It is not ſo, thou haſt miſpoke, miſheard,
Be well aduis'd, tell ore thy tale againe.
It cannot be, thou do'ſt but ſay 'tis ſo.
I truſt I may not truſt thee, for thy word
Is but the vaine breath of a common man:
Beleeue me, I doe not beleeue thee man,
I haue a Kings oath to the contrarie.
Thou ſhalt be puniſh'd for thus frighting me,
For I am ſicke, and capeable of feares,
Oppreſt with wrongs, and therefore full of feares,
A widdow, husbandles, ſubiect to feares,
A woman naturally borne to feares;
And though thou now confeſſe thou didſt but ieſt
With my vext ſpirits, I cannot take a Truce,
But they will quake and tremble all this day.
What doſt thou meane by ſhaking of thy head?
Why doſt thou looke ſo ſadly on my ſonne?
What meanes that hand vpon that breaſt of thine?
Why holdes thine eie that lamentable rhewme,
Like a proud riuer peering ore his bounds?
Be theſe ſad ſignes confirmers of thy words?
Then ſpeake againe, not all thy former tale,
But this one word, whether thy tale be true.
Sal. As true as I beleeue you thinke them falſe,
That giue you cauſe to proue my ſaying true.
Con. Oh if thou teach me to beleeue this ſorrow,
Teach thou this ſorrow, how to make me dye,
And let beleefe, and life encounter ſo,
As doth the furie of two deſperate men,
Which in the very meeting fall, and dye.
Lewes marry *Blaunch*? O boy, then where art thou?
France friend with *England*, what becomes of me?
Fellow be gone: I cannot brooke thy ſight,
This newes hath made thee a moſt vgly man.
Sal. What other harme haue I good Lady done,
But ſpoke the harme, that is by others done?
Con. Which harme within it ſelfe ſo heynous is,
As it makes harmefull all that ſpeake of it.
Ar. I do beſeech you Madam be content.
Con. If thou that bidſt me be content, wert grim
Vgly, and ſlandrous to thy Mothers wombe,
Full of vnpleaſing blots, and ſightleſſe ſtaines,
Lame, fooliſh, crooked, ſwart, prodigious,
Patch'd with foule Moles, and eye-offending markes,
I would not care, I then would be content,
For then I ſhould not loue thee: no, nor thou
Become thy great birth, nor deſerue a Crowne.
But thou art faire, and at thy birth (deere boy)
Nature and Fortune ioyn'd to make thee great.
Of Natures guifts, thou mayſt with Lillies boaſt,
And with the halfe-blowne Roſe. But Fortune, oh,
She is corrupted, chang'd, and wonne from thee,
Sh'adulterates hourely with thine Vnckle *Iohn*,
And with her golden hand hath pluckt on France
To tread downe faire reſpect of Soueraigntie,
And made his Maieſtie the bawd to theirs.
France is a Bawd to Fortune, and king *Iohn*,
That ſtrumpet Fortune, that vſurping *Iohn*:
Tell me thou fellow, is not France forſworne?
Euenom him with words, or get thee gone,
And leaue thoſe woes alone, which I alone
Am bound to vnder-beare.
Sal. Pardon me Madam,
I may not goe without you to the kings.
Con. Thou maiſt, thou ſhalt, I will not go with thee,
I will inſtruct my ſorrowes to bee proud,
For greefe is proud, and makes his owner ſtoope,
To me and to the ſtate of my great greefe,
Let kings aſſemble: for my greefe's ſo great,
That no ſupporter but the huge firme earth
Can hold it vp: here I and ſorrowes ſit,
Heere is my Throne, bid kings come bow to it.

Actus

Actus Tertius, Scæna prima.

Enter King John, France, Dolphin, Blanch, Elianor, Philip, Austria, Constance.

Fran. 'Tis true (faire daughter) and this blessed day,
Euer in *France* shall be kept festiuall:
To solemnize this day the glorious sunne
Stayes in his course, and playes the Alchymist,
Turning with splendor of his precious eye
The meager cloddy earth to glittering gold:
The yearely course that brings this day about,
Shall neuer see it, but a holy day.
Const. A wicked day, and not a holy day.
What hath this day deseru'd? what hath it done,
That it in golden letters should be set
Among the high tides in the Kalender?
Nay, rather turne this day out of the weeke,
This day of shame, oppression, periury.
Or if it must stand still, let wiues with childe
Pray that their burthens may not fall this day,
Lest that their hopes prodigiously be crost:
But (on this day) let Sea-men feare no wracke,
No bargaines breake that are not this day made;
This day all things begun, come to ill end,
Yea, faith it selfe to hollow falshood change.
Fra. By heauen Lady, you shall haue no cause
To curse the faire proceedings of this day:
Haue I not pawn'd to you my Maiesty?
Const. You haue beguil'd me with a counterfeit
Resembling Maiesty, which being touch'd and tride,
Proues valuelesse: you are forsworne, forsworne,
You came in Armes to spill mine enemies bloud,
But now in Armes, you strengthen it with yours.
The grapling vigor, and rough frowne of Warre
Is cold in amitie, and painted peace,
And our oppression hath made vp this league:
Arme, arme, you heauens, against these periur'd Kings,
A widdow cries, be husband to me (heauens)
Let not the howres of this vngodly day
Weare out the daies in Peace; but ere Sun-set,
Set armed discord 'twixt these periur'd Kings,
Heare me, Oh, heare me.
Aust. Lady *Constance*, peace.
Const. War, war, no peace, peace is to me a warre:
O *Lymoges*, O *Austria*, thou dost shame
That bloudy spoyle: thou slaue, thou wretch, ỳ coward,
Thou little valiant, great in villanie,
Thou euer strong vpon the stronger side;
Thou Fortunes Champion, that do'st neuer fight
But when her humourous Ladiship is by
To teach thee safety: thou art periur'd too,
And sooth'st vp greatnesse. What a foole art thou,
A ramping foole, to brag, and stamp, and sweare,
Vpon my partie: thou cold blooded slaue,
Hast thou not spoke like thunder on my side?
Beene sworne my Souldier, bidding me depend
Vpon thy starres, thy fortune, and thy strength,
And dost thou now fall ouer to my foes?
Thou weare a Lyons hide, doff it for shame,
And hang a Calues skin on those recreant limbes.
Aus. O that a man should speake those words to me.
Phil. And hang a Calues-skin on those recreant limbs
Aus Thou dar'st not say so villaine for thy life.
Phil. And hang a Calues skin on those recreant limbs.
Iohn. We like not this, thou dost forget thy selfe.
Enter Pandulph.
Fra. Heere comes the holy Legat of the Pope.
Pan. Haile you annointed deputies of heauen;
To thee King *Iohn* my holy errand is:
I *Pandulph*, of faire *Millane* Cardinall,
And from Pope *Innocent* the Legate heere,
Doe in his name religiously demand
Why thou against the Church, our holy Mother,
So wilfully dost spurne; and force perforce
Keepe *Stephen Langton* chosen Arshbishop
Of *Canterbury* from that holy Sea:
This in our foresaid holy Fathers name
Pope *Innocent*, I doe demand of thee.
Iohn. What earthie name to Interrogatories
Can tast the free breath of a sacred King?
Thou canst not (Cardinall) deuise a name
So slight, vnworthy, and ridiculous
To charge me to an answere, as the Pope:
Tell him this tale, and from the mouth of *England*,
Adde thus much more, that no *Italian* Priest
Shall tythe or toll in our dominions:
But as we, vnder heauen, are supreame head,
So vnder him that great supremacy
Where we doe reigne, we will alone vphold
Without th'assistance of a mortall hand:
So tell the Pope, all reuerence set apart
To him and his vsurp'd authoritie.
Fra. Brother of *England*, you blaspheme in this.
Iohn. Though you, and all the Kings of Christendom
Are led so grossely by this medling Priest,
Dreading the curse that money may buy out,
And by the merit of vilde gold, drosse, dust,
Purchase corrupted pardon of a man,
Who in that sale sels pardon from himselfe:
Though you, and al the rest so grossely led,
This iugling witchcraft with reuennue cherish,
Yet I alone, alone doe me oppose
Against the Pope, and count his friends my foes.
Pand. Then by the lawfull power that I haue,
Thou shalt stand curst, and excommunicate,
And blessed shall he be that doth reuolt
From his Allegeance to an heretique,
And meritorious shall that hand be call'd,
Canonized and worship'd as a Saint,
That takes away by any secret course
Thy hatefull life.
Con. O lawfull let it be
That I haue roome with *Rome* to curse a while,
Good Father Cardinall, cry thou Amen
To my keene curses; for without my wrong
There is no tongue hath power to curse him right.
Pan. There's Law and Warrant (Lady) for my curse.
Cons. And for mine too, when Law can do no right.
Let it be lawfull, that Law barre no wrong:
Law cannot giue my childe his kingdome heere;
For he that holds his Kingdome, holds the Law.
Therefore since Law it selfe is perfect wrong,
How can the Law forbid my tongue to curse?
Pand. *Philip* of *France*, on perill of a curse,
Let goe the hand of that Arch-heretique,
And raise the power of *France* vpon his head,
Vnlesse he doe submit himselfe to *Rome*.
Elea. Look'st thou pale *France*? do not let go thy hand.
Con. Looke to that Deuill, lest that *France* repent,
And

And by diſioyning hands hell loſe a ſoule.
Auſt. King *Philip*, liſten to the Cardinall.
Baſt. And hang a Calues-skin on his recreant limbs.
Auſt. Well ruffian, I muſt pocket vp theſe wrongs,
Becauſe,
Baſt. Your breeches beſt may carry them.
Iohn. *Philip*, what ſaiſt thou to the Cardinall?
Con. What ſhould he ſay, but as the Cardinall?
Dolph. Bethinke you father, for the difference
Is purchaſe of a heauy curſe from *Rome*,
Or the light loſſe of *England*, for a friend:
Forgoe the eaſier.
Bla. That's the curſe of *Rome*.
Con. O *Lewis*, ſtand faſt, the deuill tempts thee heere
In likeneſſe of a new vntrimmed Bride.
Bla The Lady *Conſtance* ſpeakes not from her faith,
But from her need.
Con. Oh, if thou grant my need,
Which onely liues but by the death of faith,
That need, muſt needs inferre this principle,
That faith would liue againe by death of need:
O then tread downe my need, and faith mounts vp,
Keepe my need vp, and faith is trodden downe.
Iohn. The king is moud, and anſwers not to this.
Con. O be remou'd from him, and anſwere well.
Auſt. Doe ſo king *Philip*, hang no more in doubt.
Baſt. Hang nothing but a Calues skin moſt ſweet lout.
Fra. I am perplext, and know not what to ſay.
Pan. What canſt thou ſay, but wil perplex thee more?
If thou ſtand excommunicate, and curſt?
Fra. Good reuerend father, make my perſon yours,
And tell me how you would beſtow your ſelfe?
This royall hand and mine are newly knit,
And the coniunction of our inward ſoules
Married in league, coupled, and link'd together
With all religous ſtrength of ſacred vowes,
The lateſt breath that gaue the ſound of words
Was deepe-ſworne faith, peace, amity, true loue
Betweene our kingdomes and our royall ſelues,
And euen before this truce, but new before,
No longer then we well could waſh our hands,
To clap this royall bargaine vp of peace,
Heauen knowes they were beſmear'd and ouer-ſtaind
With ſlaughters pencill; where reuenge did paint
The fearefull difference of incenſed kings:
And ſhall theſe hands ſo lately purg'd of bloud?
So newly ioyn'd in loue? ſo ſtrong in both,
Vnyoke this ſeyſure, and this kinde regreete?
Play faſt and looſe with faith? ſo ieſt with heauen,
Make ſuch vnconſtant children of our ſelues
As now againe to ſnatch our palme from palme:
Vn-ſweare faith ſworne, and on the marriage bed
Of ſmiling peace to march a bloody hoaſt,
And make a ryot on the gentle brow
Of true ſincerity? O holy Sir
My reuerend father, let it not be ſo;
Out of your grace, deuiſe, ordaine, impoſe
Some gentle order, and then we ſhall be bleſt
To doe your pleaſure, and continue friends.
Pand. All forme is formeleſſe, Order orderleſſe,
Saue what is oppoſite to *Englands* loue.
Therefore to Armes, be Champion of our Church,
Or let the Church our mother breathe her curſe,
A mothers curſe, on her reuolting ſonne:
France thou maiſt hold a ſerpent by the tongue,
A caſed Lion by the mortal paw,
A faſting Tyger ſafer by the tooth,
Then keepe in peace that hand which thou doſt hold.
Fra. I may diſ-ioyne my hand, but not my faith.
Pand. So mak'ſt thou faith an enemy to faith,
And like a ciuill warre ſetſt oath to oath,
Thy tongue againſt thy tongue. O let thy vow
Firſt made to heauen, firſt be to heauen perform'd,
That is, to be the Champion of our Church,
What ſince thou ſworſt, is ſworne againſt thy ſelfe,
And may not be performed by thy ſelfe,
For that which thou haſt ſworne to doe amiſſe,
Is not amiſſe when it is truely done:
And being not done, where doing tends to ill,
The truth is then moſt done not doing it:
The better Act of purpoſes miſtooke,
Is to miſtake again, though indirect,
Yet indirection thereby growes direct,
And falſhood, falſhood cures, as fire cooles fire
Within the ſcorched veines of one new burn'd:
It is religion that doth make vowes kept,
But thou haſt ſworne againſt religion:
By what thou ſwear'ſt againſt the thing thou ſwear'ſt
And mak'ſt an oath the ſuretie for thy truth,
Againſt an oath the truth, thou art vnſure
To ſweare, ſweares onely not to be forſworne,
Elſe what a mockerie ſhould it be to ſweare?
But thou doſt ſweare, onely to be forſworne,
And moſt forſworne, to keepe what thou doſt ſweare,
Therefore thy later vowes, againſt thy firſt,
Is in thy ſelfe rebellion to thy ſelfe:
And better conqueſt neuer canſt thou make,
Then arme thy conſtant and thy nobler parts
Againſt theſe giddy looſe ſuggeſtions:
Vpon which better part, our prayrs come in,
If thou vouchſafe them. But if not, then know
The perill of our curſes light on thee
So heauy, as thou ſhalt not ſhake them off
But in deſpaire, dye vnder their blacke weight.
Auſt. Rebellion, flat rebellion.
Baſt. Wil't not be?
Will not a Calues-skin ſtop that mouth of thine?
Daul. Father, to Armes.
Blanch. Vpon thy wedding day?
Againſt the blood that thou haſt married?
What, ſhall our feaſt be kept with ſlaughtered men?
Shall braying trumpets, and loud churliſh drums
Clamors of hell, be meaſures to our pomp?
O husband heare me: aye, alacke, how new
Is husband in my mouth? euen for that name
Which till this time my tongue did nere pronounce;
Vpon my knee I beg, goe not to Armes
Againſt mine Vncle.
Conſt. O, vpon my knee made hard with kneeling,
I doe pray to thee, thou vertuous *Daulphin*,
Alter not the doome fore-thought by heauen.
Blan. Now ſhall I ſee thy loue, what motiue may
Be ſtronger with thee, then the name of wife?
Con. That which vpholdeth him, that thee vpholds,
His Honor, Oh thine Honor, *Lewis* thine Honor.
Dolph. I muſe your Maieſty doth ſeeme ſo cold,
When ſuch profound reſpects doe pull you on?
Pand. I will denounce a curſe vpon his head.
Fra. Thou ſhalt not need. *England*, I will fall frõ thee.
Conſt. O faire returne of baniſh'd Maieſtie.
Elea. O foule reuolt of French inconſtancy.
Eng. *France*, ÿ ſhalt rue this houre within this houre.
Baſt

Baſt. Old Time the clocke ſetter, y bald ſexton Time:
Is it as he will? well then, *France* ſhall rue.
Bla. The Sun's orecaſt with bloud: faire day adieu,
Which is the ſide that I muſt goe withall?
I am with both, each Army hath a hand,
And in their rage, I hauing hold of both,
They whurle a-ſunder, and diſmember mee.
Husband, I cannot pray that thou maiſt winne:
Vncle, I needs muſt pray that thou maiſt loſe:
Father, I may not wiſh the fortune thine:
Grandam, I will not wiſh thy wiſhes thriue:
Who-euer wins, on that ſide ſhall I loſe:
Aſſured loſſe, before the match be plaid.
Dolph. Lady, with me, with me thy fortune lies.
Bla. There where my fortune liues, there my life dies.
Iohn. Coſen, goe draw our puiſance together,
France, I am burn'd vp with inflaming wrath,
A rage, whoſe heat hath this condition;
That nothing can allay, nothing but blood,
The blood and deereſt valued bloud of *France*.
Fra. Thy rage ſhall burne thee vp, & thou ſhalt turne
To aſhes, ere our blood ſhall quench that fire:
Looke to thy ſelfe, thou art in ieopardie.
Iohn. No more then he that threats. To Arms le'ts hie.
Exeunt.

Scœna Secunda.

Allarums, Excurſions: Enter Baſtard with Auſtria's head.

Baſt. Now by my life, this day grows wondrous hot,
Some ayery Deuill houers in the skie,
And pour's downe miſchiefe. *Auſtrias* head lye there,
Enter Iohn, Arthur, Hubert.
While *Philip* breathes.
Iohn. *Hubert*, keepe this boy: *Philip* make vp,
My Mother is aſſayled in our Tent,
And tane I feare.
Baſt. My Lord I reſcued her,
Her Highneſſe is in ſafety, feare you not:
But on my Liege, for very little paines
Will bring this labor to an happy end. *Exit.*

Alarums, excurſions, Retreat. Enter Iohn, Eleanor, Arthur Baſtard, Hubert, Lords.

Iohn. So ſhall it be: your Grace ſhall ſtay behinde
So ſtrongly guarded: Coſen, looke not ſad,
Thy Grandame loues thee, and thy Vnkle will
As deere be to thee, as thy father was.
Arth. O this will make my mother die with griefe.
Iohn. Coſen away for *England*, haſte before,
And ere our comming ſee thou ſhake the bags
Of hoording Abbots, impriſoned angells
Set at libertie: the fat ribs of peace
Muſt by the hungry now be fed vpon:
Vſe our Commiſſion in his vtmoſt force.
Baſt. Bell, Booke, & Candle, ſhall not driue me back,
When gold and ſiluer becks me to come on.
I leaue your highneſſe: Grandame, I will pray
(If euer I remember to be holy)
For your faire ſafety: ſo I kiſſe your hand.
Ele. Farewell gentle Coſen.
Iohn. Coz, farewell.
Ele. Come hether little kinſman, harke, a worde.
Iohn. Come hether *Hubert*. O my gentle *Hubert*,
We owe thee much: within this wall of fleſh
There is a ſoule counts thee her Creditor,
And with aduantage meanes to pay thy loue:
And my good friend, thy voluntary oath
Liues in this boſome, deerely cheriſhed.
Giue me thy hand, I had a thing to ſay,
But I will fit it with ſome better tune.
By heauen *Hubert*, I am almoſt aſham'd
To ſay what good reſpect I haue of thee.
Hub. I am much bounden to your Maieſty.
Iohn. Good friend, thou haſt no cauſe to ſay ſo yet,
But thou ſhalt haue: and creepe time nere ſo ſlow,
Yet it ſhall come, for me to doe thee good.
I had a thing to ſay, but let it goe:
The Sunne is in the heauen, and the proud day,
Attended with the pleaſures of the world,
Is all too wanton, and too full of gawdes
To giue me audience: If the mid-night bell
Did with his yron tongue, and brazen mouth
Sound on into the drowzie race of night:
If this ſame were a Church-yard where we ſtand,
And thou poſſeſſed with a thouſand wrongs:
Or if that ſurly ſpirit melancholy
Had bak'd thy bloud, and made it heauy, thicke,
Which elſe runnes tickling vp and downe the veines,
Making that idiot laughter keepe mens eyes,
And ſtraine their cheekes to idle merriment,
A paſſion hatefull to my purpoſes:
Or if that thou couldſt ſee me without eyes,
Heare me without thine eares, and make reply
Without a tongue, vſing conceit alone,
Without eyes, eares, and harmefull ſound of words:
Then, in deſpight of brooded watchfull day,
I would into thy boſome poure my thoughts:
But (ah) I will not, yet I loue thee well,
And by my troth I thinke thou lou'ſt me well.
Hub. So well, that what you bid me vndertake,
Though that my death were adiunct to my Act,
By heauen I would doe it.
Iohn. Doe not I know thou wouldſt?
Good *Hubert*, *Hubert*, *Hubert* throw thine eye
On yon young boy: Ile tell thee what my friend,
He is a very ſerpent in my way,
And whereſoere this foot of mine doth tread,
He lies before me: doſt thou vnderſtand me?
Thou art his keeper.
Hub. And Ile keepe him ſo,
That he ſhall not offend your Maieſty.
Iohn. Death.
Hub. My Lord.
Iohn. A Graue.
Hub. He ſhall not liue.
Iohn. Enough.
I could be merry now, *Hubert*, I loue thee.
Well, Ile not ſay what I intend for thee:
Remember: Madam, Fare you well,
Ile ſend thoſe powers o're to your Maieſty.
Ele. My bleſſing goe with thee.
Iohn. For *England* Coſen, goe.
Hubert ſhall be your man, attend on you
With al true duetie: On toward *Calice*, hoe.
Exeunt.

Scena

Scæna Tertia.

Enter France, Dolphin, Pandulpho, Attendants.

Fra. So by a roaring Tempest on the flood,
A whole Armado of conuicted saile
Is scattered and dis-ioyn'd from fellowship.
Pand. Courage and comfort, all shall yet goe well.
Fra. What can goe well, when we haue runne so ill?
Are we not beaten? Is not *Angiers* lost?
Arthur tane prisoner? diuers deere friends slaine?
And bloody *England* into *England* gone,
Ore-bearing interruption spight of *France*?
Dol. What he hath won, that hath he fortified:
So hot a speed, with such aduice dispos'd,
Such temperate order in so fierce a cause,
Doth want example: who hath read, or heard
Of any kindred-action like to this?
Fra. Well could I beare that *England* had this praise,
So we could finde some patterne of our shame:
Enter Constance.
Looke who comes heere? a graue vnto a soule,
Holding th'eternall spirit against her will,
In the vilde prison of afflicted breath:
I prethee Lady goe away with me.
Con. Lo; now: now see the issue of your peace.
Fra. Patience good Lady, comfort gentle *Constance*.
Con. No, I defie all Counsell, all redresse,
But that which ends all counsell, true Redresse:
Death, death, O amiable, louely death,
Thou odoriferous stench: sound rottennesse,
Arise forth from the couch of lasting night,
Thou hate and terror to prosperitie,
And I will kisse thy detestable bones,
And put my eye-balls in thy vaultie browes,
And ring these fingers with thy houshold wormes,
And stop this gap of breath with fulsome dust,
And be a Carrion Monster like thy selfe;
Come, grin on me, and I will thinke thou smil'st,
And busse thee as thy wife: Miseries Loue,
O come to me.
Fra. O faire affliction, peace.
Con. No, no, I will not, hauing breath to cry:
O that my tongue were in the thunders mouth,
Then with a passion would I shake the world,
And rowze from sleepe that fell Anatomy
Which cannot heare a Ladies feeble voyce,
Which scornes a moderne Inuocation.
Pand. Lady, you vtter madnesse, and not sorrow.
Con. Thou art holy to belye me so,
I am not mad: this haire I teare is mine,
My name is *Constance*, I was *Geffreyes* wife,
Yong *Arthur* is my sonne, and he is lost:
I am not mad, I would to heauen I were,
For then 'tis like I should forget my selfe:
O, if I could, what griefe should I forget?
Preach some Philosophy to make me mad,
And thou shalt be Canoniz'd (Cardinall.)
For, being not mad, but sensible of greefe,
My reasonable part produces reason
How I may be deliuer'd of these woes,
And teaches mee to kill or hang my selfe:
If I were mad, I should forget my sonne,
Or madly thinke a babe of clowts were he;
I am not mad: too well, too well I feele
The different plague of each calamitie.
Fra. Binde vp those tresses: O what loue I note
In the faire multitude of those her haires;
Where but by chance a siluer drop hath falne,
Euen to that drop ten thousand wiery fiends
Doe glew themselues in sociable griefe,
Like true, inseparable, faithfull loues,
Sticking together in calamitie.
Con. To *England*, if you will.
Fra. Binde vp your haires.
Con. Yes that I will: and wherefore will I do it
I tore them from their bonds, and cride aloud,
O, that these hands could so redeeme my sonne
As they haue giuen these hayres their libertie:
But now I enuie at their libertie,
And will againe commit them to their bonds,
Because my poore childe is a prisoner.
And Father Cardinall, I haue heard you say
That we shall see and know our friends in heauen:
If that be true, I shall see my boy againe;
For since the birth of *Caine*, the first male-childe
To him that did but yesterday suspire,
There was not such a gracious creature borne:
But now will Canker-sorrow eat my bud
And chase the natiue beauty from his cheeke,
And he will looke as hollow as a Ghost,
As dim and meager as an Agues fitte,
And so hee'll dye: and rising so againe,
When I shall meet him in the Court of heauen
I shall not know him: therefore neuer, neuer
Must I behold my pretty *Arthur* more.
Pand. You hold too heynous a respect of greefe.
Const. He talkes to me, that neuer had a sonne.
Fra. You are as fond of greefe, as of your childe.
Con. Greefe fils the roome vp of my absent childe:
Lies in his bed, walkes vp and downe with me,
Puts on his pretty lookes, repeats his words,
Remembers me of all his gracious parts,
Stuffes out his vacant garments with his forme;
Then, haue I reason to be fond of griefe?
Fareyouwell: had you such a losse as I,
I could giue better comfort then you doe.
I will not keepe this forme vpon my head,
When there is such disorder in my witte:
O Lord, my boy, my *Arthur*, my faire sonne,
My life, my ioy, my food, my all the world:
My widow-comfort, and my sorrowes cure. *Exit.*
Fra. I feare some out-rage, and Ile follow her. *Exit.*
Dol. There's nothing in this world can make me ioy,
Life is as tedious as a twice-told tale,
Vexing the dull eare of a drowsie man;
And bitter shame hath spoyl'd the sweet words taste,
That it yeelds nought but shame and bitternesse
Pand. Before the curing of a strong disease
Euen in the instant of repaire and health,
The fit is strongest: Euils that take leaue
On their departure, most of all shew euill:
What haue you lost by losing of this day?
Dol. All daies of glory, ioy, and happinesse.
Pan. If you had won it, certainely you had.
No, no: when Fortune meanes to men most good,
Shee lookes vpon them with a threatning eye:
'Tis strange to thinke how much King *Iohn* hath lost
In this which he accounts so clearely wonne:
Are

Are not you grieu'd that *Arthur* is his prisoner?
Dol. As heartily as he is glad he hath him.
Pan. Your minde is all as youthfull as your blood.
Now heare me speake with a propheticke spirit:
For euen the breath of what I meane to speake,
Shall blow each dust, each straw, each little rub
Out of the path which shall directly lead
Thy foote to Englands Throne. And therefore marke:
Iohn hath seiz'd *Arthur*, and it cannot be,
That whiles warme life playes in that infants veines
The mis-plac'd-*Iohn* should entertaine an houre,
One minute, nay one quiet breath of rest.
A Scepter snatch'd with an vnruly hand,
Must be as boysterously maintain'd as gain'd.
And he that stands vpon a slipp'ry place,
Makes nice of no vilde hold to stay him vp:
That *Iohn* may stand, then *Arthur* needs must fall,
So be it, for it cannot be but so.
Dol. But what shall I gaine by yong *Arthurs* fall?
Pan. You, in the right of Lady *Blanch* your wife,
May then make all the claime that *Arthur* did.
Dol. And loose it, life and all, as *Arthur* did.
Pan. How green you are, and fresh in this old world?
Iohn layes you plots: the times conspire with you,
For he that steepes his safetie in true blood,
Shall finde but bloodie safety, and vntrue.
This Act so euilly borne shall coole the hearts
Of all his people, and freeze vp their zeale,
That none so small aduantage shall step forth
To checke his reigne, but they will cherish it.
No naturall exhalation in the skie,
No scope of Nature, no distemper'd day,
No common winde, no customed euent,
But they will plucke away his naturall cause,
And call them Meteors, prodigies, and signes,
Abbortiues, presages, and tongues of heauen,
Plainly denouncing vengeance vpon *Iohn*.
Dol. May be he will not touch yong *Arthurs* life,
But hold himselfe safe in his prisonment.
Pan. O Sir, when he shall heare of your approach,
If that yong *Arthur* be not gone alreadie,
Euen at that newes he dies: and then the hearts
Of all his people shall reuolt from him,
And kisse the lippes of vnacquainted change,
And picke strong matter of reuolt, and wrath
Out of the bloody fingers ends of *Iohn*.
Me thinkes I see this hurley all on foot;
And O, what better matter breeds for you,
Then I haue nam'd. The Bastard *Falconbridge*
Is now in England ransacking the Church,
Offending Charity: If but a dozen French
Were there in Armes, they would be as a Call
To traine ten thousand English to their side;
Or, as a little snow, tumbled about,
Anon becomes a Mountaine. O noble Dolphine,
Go with me to the King, 'tis wonderfull,
What may be wrought out of their discontent,
Now that their soules are topfull of offence,
For England go; I will whet on the King.
Dol. Strong reasons makes strange actions: let vs go,
If you say I, the King will not say no. *Exeunt.*

Actus Quartus, Scæna prima.

Enter Hubert and Executioners.

Hub. Heate me these Irons hot, and looke thou stand
Within the Arras: when I strike my foot
Vpon the bosome of the ground, rush forth
And binde the boy, which you shall finde with me
Fast to the chaire: be heedfull: hence, and watch.
Exec. I hope your warrant will beare out the deed.
Hub. Vncleanly scruples feare not you: looke too't.
Yong Lad come forth; I haue to say with you.

Enter Arthur.

Ar. Good morrow *Hubert*.
Hub Good morrow, little Prince.
Ar. As little Prince, hauing so great a Title
To be more Prince, as may be: you are sad.
Hub. Indeed I haue beene merrier.
Art. 'Mercie on me:
Me thinkes no body should be sad but I:
Yet I remember, when I was in France,
Yong Gentlemen would be as sad as night
Onely for wantonnesse: by my Christendome,
So I were out of prison, and kept Sheepe
I should be as merry as the day is long:
And so I would be heere, but that I doubt
My Vnckle practises more harme to me:
He is affraid of me, and I of him:
Is it my fault, that I was *Geffreyes* sonne?
No in deede is't not: and I would to heauen
I were your sonne, so you would loue me, Hubert.
Hub. If I talke to him, with his innocent prate
He will awake my mercie, which lies dead:
Therefore I will be sodaine, and dispatch.
Ar. Are you sicke Hubert? you looke pale to day,
Insooth I would you were a little sicke,
That I might sit all night, and watch with you.
I warrant I loue you more then you do me.
Hub. His words do take possession of my bosome.
Reade heere yong *Arthur*. How now foolish rheume?
Turning dispitious torture out of doore?
I must be breefe, least resolution drop
Out at mine eyes, in tender womanish teares.
Can you not reade it? Is it not faire writ?
Ar. Too fairely *Hubert*, for so foule effect,
Must you with hot Irons, burne out both mine eyes?
Hub. Yong Boy, I must.
Art. And will you?
Hub. And I will.
Art. Haue you the heart? When your head did but ake,
I knit my hand-kercher about your browes
(The best I had, a Princesse wrought it me)
And I did neuer aske it you againe:
And with my hand, at midnight held your head;
And like the watchfull minutes, to the houre,
Still and anon cheer'd vp the heauy time;
Saying, what lacke you? and where lies your greefe?
Or what good loue may I performe for you?
Many a poore mans sonne would haue lyen still,
And nere haue spoke a louing word to you:
But you, at your sicke seruice had a Prince:
Nay, you may thinke my loue was craftie loue,
And call it cunning. Do, and if you will,

If heauen be pleas'd that you must vse me ill,
Why then you must. Will you put out mine eyes?
These eyes, that neuer did, nor neuer shall
So much as frowne on you.
Hub. I haue sworne to do it:
And with hot Irons must I burne them out.
Ar. Ah, none but in this Iron Age, would do it:
The Iron of it selfe, though heate red hot,
Approaching neere these eyes, would drinke my teares,
And quench this fierie indignation,
Euen in the matter of mine innocence:
Nay, after that, consume away in rust,
But for containing fire to harme mine eye:
Are you more stubborne-hard, then hammer'd Iron?
And if an Angell should haue come to me,
And told me *Hubert* should put out mine eyes,
I would not haue beleeu'd him: no tongue but *Huberts*.
Hub. Come forth: Do as I bid you do.
Art. O saue me *Hubert*, saue me: my eyes are out
Euen with the fierce lookes of these bloody men.
Hub. Giue me the Iron I say, and binde him heere.
Art. Alas, what neede you be so boistrous rough?
I will not struggle, I will stand stone still.
For heauen sake *Hubert* let me not be bound:
Nay heare me *Hubert*, driue these men away,
And I will sit as quiet as a Lambe.
I will not stirre, nor winch, nor speake a word,
Nor looke vpon the Iron angerly:
Thrust but these men away, and Ile forgiue you,
What euer torment you do put me too.
Hub. Go stand within: let me alone with him.
Exec. I am best pleas'd to be from such a deede.
Art. Alas, I then haue chid away my friend,
He hath a sterne looke, but a gentle heart:
Let him come backe, that his compassion may
Giue life to yours.
Hub. Come (Boy) prepare your selfe.
Art. Is there no remedie?
Hub. None, but to lose your eyes.
Art. O heauen: that there were but a moth in yours,
A graine, a dust, a gnat, a wandering haire,
Any annoyance in that precious sense:
Then feeling what small things are boysterous there,
Your vilde intent must needs seeme horrible.
Hub. Is this your promise? Go too, hold your toong.
Art. *Hubert*, the vtterance of a brace of tongues,
Must needes want pleading for a paire of eyes:
Let me not hold my tongue: let me not *Hubert*,
Or *Hubert*, if you will cut out my tongue,
So I may keepe mine eyes. O spare mine eyes,
Though to no vse, but still to looke on you.
Loe, by my troth, the Instrument is cold,
And would not harme me.
Hub. I can heate it, Boy.
Art No, in good sooth: the fire is dead with griefe,
Being create for comfort, to be vs'd
In vndeserued extreames: See else your selfe,
There is no malice in this burning cole,
The breath of heauen, hath blowne his spirit out,
And strew'd repentant ashes on his head.
Hub. But with my breath I can reuiue it Boy.
Art. And if you do, you will but make it blush,
And glow with shame of your proceedings, *Hubert*:
Nay, it perchance will sparkle in your eyes:
And, like a dogge that is compell'd to fight,
Snatch at his Master that doth tarre him on.
All things that you should vse to do me wrong
Deny their office: onely you do lacke
That mercie, which fierce fire, and Iron extends,
Creatures of note for mercy, lacking vses.
Hub. Well, see to liue: I will not touch thine eye,
For all the Treasure that thine Vnckle owes,
Yet am I sworne, and I did purpose, Boy,
With this same very Iron, to burne them out.
Art. O now you looke like *Hubert*. All this while
You were disguis'd.
Hub. Peace: no more. Adieu,
Your Vnckle must not know but you are dead.
Ile fill these dogged Spies with false reports:
And, pretty childe, sleepe doubtlesse, and secure,
That *Hubert* for the wealth of all the world,
Will not offend thee.
Art. O heauen! I thanke you *Hubert*.
Hub. Silence, no more; go closely in with mee,
Much danger do I vndergo for thee. *Exeunt*

Scena Secunda.

Enter Iohn, Pembroke, Salisbury, and other Lordes.
Iohn. Heere once againe we sit: once against crown'd
And look'd vpon, I hope, with cheerefull eyes.
Pem. This once again (but that your Highnes pleas'd)
Was once superfluous: you were Crown'd before,
And that high Royalty was nere pluck'd off:
The faiths of men, nere stained with reuolt:
Fresh expectation troubled not the Land
With any long'd-for-change, or better State.
Sal. Therefore, to be possess'd with double pompe,
To guard a Title, that was rich before;
To gilde refined Gold, to paint the Lilly;
To throw a perfume on the Violet,
To smooth the yce, or adde another hew
Vnto the Raine-bow; or with Taper-light
To seeke the beauteous eye of heauen to garnish,
Is wastefull, and ridiculous excesse.
Pem. But that your Royall pleasure must be done,
This acte, is as an ancient tale new told,
And, in the last repeating, troublesome,
Being vrged at a time vnseasonable.
Sal. In this the Anticke, and well noted face
Of plaine old forme, is much disfigured,
And like a shifted winde vnto a saile,
It makes the course of thoughts to fetch about,
Startles, and frights consideration:
Makes sound opinion sicke, and truth suspected,
For putting on so new a fashion'd robe.
Pem. When Workemen striue to do better then wel,
They do confound their skill in couetousnesse,
And oftentimes excusing of a fault,
Doth make the fault the worse by th'excuse:
As patches set vpon a little breach,
Discredite more in hiding of the fault,
Then did the fault before it was so patch'd.
Sal. To this effect, before you were new crown'd
We breath'd our Councell: but it pleas'd your Highnes
To ouer-beare it, and we are all well pleas'd,
Since all, and euery part of what we would
Doth make a stand, at what your Highnesse will.

Iohn.

Ioh. Some reasons of this double Corronation
I haue possest you with, and thinke them strong.
And more, more strong, then lesser is my feare
I shall indue you with: Meane time, but aske
What you would haue reform'd, that is not well,
And well shall you perceiue, how willingly
I will both heare, and grant you your requests.
Pem. Then I, as one that am the tongue of these
To sound the purposes of all their hearts,
Both for my selfe, and them: but chiefe of all
Your safety: for the which, my selfe and them
Bend their best studies, heartily request
Th'infranchisement of *Arthur*, whose restraint
Doth moue the murmuring lips of discontent
To breake into this dangerous argument.
If what in rest you haue, in right you hold,
Why then your feares, which (as they say) attend
The steppes of wrong, should moue you to mew vp
Your tender kinsman, and to choake his dayes
With barbarous ignorance, and deny his youth
The rich aduantage of good exercise,
That the times enemies may not haue this
To grace occasions: let it be our suite,
That you haue bid vs aske his libertie,
Which for our goods, we do no further aske,
Then, whereupon our weale on you depending,
Counts it your weale: he haue his liberty.
Enter Hubert.
Iohn. Let it be so: I do commit his youth
To your direction: *Hubert*, what newes with you?
Pem. This is the man should do the bloody deed:
He shew'd his warrant to a friend of mine,
The image of a wicked heynous fault
Liues in his eye: that close aspect of his,
Do shew the mood of a much troubled brest,
And I do fearefully beleeue 'tis done,
What we so fear'd he had a charge to do.
Sal. The colour of the King doth come, and go
Betweene his purpose and his conscience,
Like Heralds 'twixt two dreadfull battailes set:
His passion is so ripe, it needs must breake.
Pem. And when it breakes, I feare will issue thence
The foule corruption of a sweet childes death.
Iohn. We cannot hold mortalities strong hand.
Good Lords, although my will to giue, is liuing,
The suite which you demand is gone, and dead.
He tels vs *Arthur* is deceas'd to night.
Sal. Indeed we fear'd his sicknesse was past cure.
Pem: Indeed we heard how neere his death he was,
Before the childe himselfe felt he was sicke:
This must be answer'd either heere, or hence.
Ioh. Why do you bend such solemne browes on me?
Thinke you I beare the Sheeres of destiny?
Haue I commandement on the pulse of life?
Sal. It is apparant foule-play, and 'tis shame
That Greatnesse should so grossely offer it;
So thriue it in your game, and so farewell.
Pem. Stay yet (Lord Salisbury) Ile go with thee,
And finde th'inheritance of this poore childe,
His little kingdome of a forced graue.
That blood which ow'd the bredth of all this Ile,
Three foot of it doth hold; bad world the while:
This must not be thus borne, this will breake out
To all our sorrowes, and ere long I doubt. *Exeunt*
Io. They burn in indignation: I repent: *Enter Mes.*
There is no sure foundation set on blood:
No certaine life atchieu'd by others death:
A fearefull eye thou hast. Where is that blood,
That I haue seene inhabite in those cheekes?
So foule a skie, cleeres not without a storme,
Poure downe thy weather: how goes all in France?
Mes. From France to England, neuer such a powre
For any forraigne preparation,
Was leuied in the body of a land.
The Copie of your speede is learn'd by them:
For when you should be told they do prepare,
The tydings comes, that they are all arriu'd.
Ioh. Oh where hath our Intelligence bin drunke?
Where hath it slept? Where is my Mothers care?
That such an Army could be drawne in France,
And she not heare of it?
Mes. My Liege, her eare
Is stopt with dust: the first of Aprill di'de
Your noble mother; and as I heare, my Lord,
The Lady *Constance* in a frenzie di'de
Three dayes before: but this from Rumors tongue
I idely heard: if true, or false I know not.
Iohn. With-hold thy speed, dreadfull Occasion:
O make a league with me, 'till I haue pleas'd
My discontented Peeres. What? Mother dead?
How wildely then walkes my Estate in France?
Vnder whose conduct came those powres of France,
That thou for truth giu'st out are landed heere?
Mes. Vnder the Dolphin.
Enter Bastard and Peter of Pomfret.
Ioh. Thou hast made me giddy
With these ill tydings: Now? What sayes the world
To your proceedings? Do not seeke to stuffe
My head with more ill newes: for it is full.
Bast. But if you be a-feard to heare the worst,
Then let the worst vn-heard, fall on your head.
Iohn. Beare with me Cosen, for I was amaz'd
Vnder the tide; but now I breath againe
Aloft the flood, and can giue audience
To any tongue, speake it of what it will.
Bast. How I haue sped among the Clergy men,
The summes I haue collected shall expresse:
But as I trauail'd hither through the land,
I finde the people strangely fantasied,
Possest with rumors, full of idle dreames.
Not knowing what they feare, but full of feare.
And here's a Prophet that I brought with me
From forth the streets of Pomfret, whom I found
With many hundreds treading on his heeles:
To whom he sung in rude harsh sounding rimes,
That ere the next Ascension day at noone,
Your Highnes should deliuer vp your Crowne.
Iohn. Thou idle Dreamer, wherefore didst thou so?
Pet. Fore-knowing that the truth will fall out so.
Iohn. *Hubert*, away with him: imprison him,
And on that day at noone, whereon he sayes
I shall yeeld vp my Crowne, let him be hang'd.
Deliuer him to safety, and returne,
For I must vse thee. O my gentle Cosen,
Hear'st thou the newes abroad, who are arriu'd?
Bast. The *French* (my Lord) mens mouths are ful of it:
Besides I met Lord *Bigot*, and Lord *Salisburie*
With eyes as red as new enkindled fire,
And others more, going to seeke the graue
Of *Arthur*, whom they say is kill'd to night, on your
Iohn. Gentle kinsman, go (suggestion.
And thrust thy selfe into their Companies,

I haue a way to winne their loues againe:
Bring them before me.
Bast. I will seeke them out.
Iohn. Nay, but make haste: the better foote before.
O, let me haue no subiect enemies,
When aduerse Forreyners affright my Townes
With dreadfull pompe of stout inuasion.
Be Mercurie, set feathers to thy heeles,
And flye (like thought) from them, to me againe.
Bast. The spirit of the time shall teach me speed. *Exit*
Iohn. Spoke like a sprightfull Noble Gentleman.
Go after him: for he perhaps shall neede
Some Messenger betwixt me, and the Peeres,
And be thou hee.
Mes. With all my heart, my Liege.
Iohn. My mother dead?

Enter Hubert.

Hub. My Lord, they say fiue Moones were seene to
Foure fixed, and the fift did whirle about (night:
The other foure, in wondrous motion.
Ioh. Fiue Moones?
Hub. Old men, and Beldames, in the streets
Do prophesie vpon it dangerously:
Yong *Arthurs* death is common in their mouths,
And when they talke of him, they shake their heads,
And whisper one another in the eare.
And he that speakes, doth gripe the hearers wrist,
Whilst he that heares, makes fearefull action
With wrinkled browes, with nods, with rolling eyes.
I saw a Smith stand with his hammer (thus)
The whilst his Iron did on the Anuile coole,
With open mouth swallowing a Taylors newes,
Who with his Sheeres, and Measure in his hand,
Standing on slippers, which his nimble haste
Had falsely thrust vpon contrary feete,
Told of a many thousand warlike French,
That were embattailed, and rank'd in Kent.
Another leane, vnwash'd Artificer,
Cuts off his tale, and talkes of *Arthurs* death.
Io. Why seek'st thou to possesse me with these feares?
Why vrgest thou so oft yong *Arthurs* death?
Thy hand hath murdred him: I had a mighty cause
To wish him dead, but thou hadst none to kill him.
H. No had (my Lord) why, did you not prouoke me?
Iohn. It is the curse of Kings, to be attended
By slaues, that take their humors for a warrant,
To breake within the bloody house of life,
And on the winking of Authoritie
To vnderstand a Law; to know the meaning
Of dangerous Maiesty, when perchance it frownes
More vpon humor, then aduis'd respect.
Hub. Heere is your hand and Seale for what I did.
Ioh. Oh, when the last accompt twixt heauen & earth
Is to be made, then shall this hand and Seale
Witnesse against vs to damnation.
How oft the sight of meanes to do ill deeds,
Make deeds ill done? Had'st not thou beene by
A fellow by the hand of Nature mark'd,
Quoted, and sign'd to do a deede of shame,
This murther had not come into my minde.
But taking note of thy abhorr'd Aspect,
Finding thee fit for bloody villanie:
Apt, liable to be employ'd in danger,
I faintly broke with thee of *Arthurs* death:
And thou, to be endeered to a King,
Made it no conscience to destroy a Prince.
Hub. My Lord.
Ioh. Had'st thou but shooke thy head, or made a pause
When I spake darkely, what I purposed:
Or turn'd an eye of doubt vpon my face;
As bid me tell my tale in expresse words:
Deepe shame had struck me dumbe, made me break off,
And those thy feares, might haue wrought feares in me
But, thou didst vnderstand me by my signes,
And didst in signes againe parley with sinne,
Yea, without stop, didst let thy heart consent,
And consequently, thy rude hand to acte
The deed, which both our tongues held vilde to name.
Out of my sight, and neuer see me more:
My Nobles leaue me, and my State is braued,
Euen at my gates, with rankes of forraigne powres;
Nay, in the body of this fleshly Land,
This kingdome, this Confine of blood, and breathe
Hostilitie, and ciuill tumult reignes
Betweene my conscience, and my Cosins death.
Hub. Arme you against your other enemies:
Ile make a peace betweene your soule, and you.
Yong *Arthur* is aliue: This hand of mine
Is yet a maiden, and an innocent hand.
Not painted with the Crimson spots of blood,
Within this bosome, neuer entred yet
The dreadfull motion of a murderous thought,
And you haue slander'd Nature in my forme,
Which howsoeuer rude exteriorly,
Is yet the couer of a fayrer minde,
Then to be butcher of an innocent childe.
Iohn. Doth *Arthur* liue? O hast thee to the Peeres,
Throw this report on their incensad rage,
And make them tame to their obedience.
Forgiue the Comment that my passion made
Vpon thy feature, for my rage was blinde,
And foule immaginarie eyes of blood
Presented thee more hideous then thou art
Oh, answer not; but to my Closset bring
The angry Lords, with all expedient hast,
I coniure thee but slowly: run more fast. *Exeunt*

Scœna Tertia.

Enter Arthur on the walles.

Ar. The Wall is high, and yet will I leape downe.
Good ground be pittifull, and hurt me not:
There's few or none do know me, if they did,
This Ship-boyes semblance hath disguis'd me quite.
I am afraide, and yet Ile venture it.
If I get downe, and do not breake my limbes,
Ile finde a thousand shifts to get away;
As good to dye and go; as dye, and stay.
Oh me, my Vnckles spirit is in these stones,
Heauen take my soule, and England keep my bones *Dies*

Enter Pembroke, Salisbury, & Bigot.

Sal. Lords, I will meet him at S. *Edmondsbury*,
It is our safetie, and we must embrace
This gentle offer of the perillous time.
Pem. Who brought that Letter from the Cardinall?
Sal. The Count *Meloone*, a Noble Lord of France,
Whose priuate with me of the Dolphines loue,
Is much more generall, then these lines import.
Big.

Big. To morrow morning let vs meete him then.
Sal. Or rather then set forward, for 'twill be
Two long dayes iourney (Lords) or ere we meete.

Enter Bastard.

Bast. Once more to day well met, distemper'd Lords,
The King by me requests your presence straight.
Sal. The king hath dispossest himselfe of vs,
We will not lyne his thin-bestained cloake
With our pure Honors: nor attend the foote
That leaues the print of blood where ere it walkes.
Returne, and tell him so: we know the worst.
Bast. What ere you thinke, good words I thinke were best.
Sal. Our greefes, and not our manners reason now.
Bast. But there is little reason in your greefe.
Therefore 'twere reason you had manners now.
Pem. Sir, sir, impatience hath his priuiledge.
Bast. 'Tis true, to hurt his master, no mans else.
Sal. This is the prison: What is he lyes heere?
P. Oh death, made proud with pure & princely beuty,
The earth had not a hole to hide this deede.
Sal. Murther, as hating what himselfe hath done,
Doth lay it open to vrge on reuenge.
Big. Or when he doom'd this Beautie to a graue,
Found it too precious Princely, for a graue.
Sal. Sir *Richard*, what thinke you? you haue beheld,
Or haue you read, or heard, or could you thinke?
Or do you almost thinke, although you see,
That you do see? Could thought, without this obiect
Forme such another? This is the very top,
The heighth, the Crest: or Crest vnto the Crest
Of murthers Armes: This is the bloodiest shame,
The wildest Sauagery, the vildest stroke
That euer wall-ey'd wrath, or staring rage
Presented to the teares of soft remorse.
Pem. All murthers past, do stand excus'd in this:
And this so sole, and so vnmatcheable,
Shall giue a holinesse, a puritie,
To the yet vnbegotten sinne of times;
And proue a deadly blood-shed, but a iest,
Exampled by this heynous spectacle.
Bast. It is a damned, and a bloody worke,
The gracelesse action of a heauy hand,
If that it be the worke of any hand.
Sal. If that it be the worke of any hand?
We had a kinde of light, what would ensue:
It is the shamefull worke of *Huberts* hand,
The practice, and the purpose of the king:
From whose obedience I forbid my soule,
Kneeling before this ruine of sweete life,
And breathing to his breathlesse Excellence
The Incense of a Vow, a holy Vow:
Neuer to taste the pleasures of the world,
Neuer to be infected with delight,
Nor conuersant with Ease, and Idlenesse,
Till I haue set a glory to this hand,
By giuing it the worship of Reuenge.
Pem. Big. Our soules religiously confirme thy words.

Enter Hubert.

Hub. Lords, I am hot with haste, in seeking you,
Arthur doth liue, the king hath sent for you.
Sal. Oh he is bold, and blushes not at death,
Auant thou hatefull villain, get thee gone. (the Law?
Hu. I am no villaine. *Sal.* Must I rob
Bast. Your sword is bright sir, put it vp againe.
Sal. Not till I sheath it in a murtherers skin.
Hub. Stand backe Lord Salsbury, stand backe I say:
By heauen, I thinke my sword's as sharpe as yours.
I would not haue you (Lord) forget your selfe,
Nor tempt the danger of my true defence;
Least I, by marking of your rage, forget
Your Worth, your Greatnesse, and Nobility.
Big. Out dunghill: dar'st thou braue a Nobleman?
Hub. Not for my life: But yet I dare defend
My innocent life against an Emperor.
Sal. Thou art a Murtherer.
Hub. Do not proue me so:
Yet I am none. Whose tongue so ere speakes false,
Not truely speakes: who speakes not truly, Lies.
Pem. Cut him to peeces.
Bast. Keepe the peace, I say.
Sal. Stand by, or I shall gaul you *Faulconbridge*.
Bast. Thou wer't better gaul the diuell Salsbury.
If thou but frowne on me, or stirre thy foote,
Or teach thy hastie spleene to do me shame,
Ile strike thee dead. Put vp thy sword betime,
Or Ile so maule you, and your tosting-Iron,
That you shall thinke the diuell is come from hell.
Big. What wilt thou do, renowned *Faulconbridge*?
Second a Villaine, and a Murtherer?
Hub Lord *Bigot*, I am none.
Big. Who kill'd this Prince?
Hub. 'Tis not an houre since I left him well:
I honour'd him, I lou'd him, and will weepe
My date of life out, for his sweete liues losse.
Sal. Trust not those cunning waters of his eyes,
For villanie is not without such rheume,
And he, long traded in it, makes it seeme
Like Riuers of remorse and innocencie.
Away with me, all you whose soules abhorre
Th'vncleanly sauours of a Slaughter-house,
For I am stifled with this smell of sinne.
Big. Away, toward *Burie*, to the Dolphin there.
P. There tel the king, he may inquire vs out. *Ex Lords.*
Ba. Here's a good world: knew you of this faire work?
Beyond the infinite and boundlesse reach of mercie,
(If thou didst this deed of death) art yͤ damn'd *Hubert*.
Hub Do but heare me sir.
Bast. Ha? Ile tell thee what.
Thou'rt damn'd as blacke, nay nothing is so blacke,
Thou art more deepe damn'd then Prince Lucifer:
There is not yet so vgly a fiend of hell
As thou shalt be, if thou didst kill this childe.
Hub. Vpon my soule.
Bast. If thou didst but consent
To this most cruell Act: do but dispaire,
And if thou want'st a Cord, the smallest thred
That euer Spider twisted from her wombe
Will serue to strangle thee: A rush will be a beame
To hang thee on. Or wouldst thou drowne thy selfe,
Put but a little water in a spoone,
And it shall be as all the Ocean,
Enough to stifle such a villaine vp.
I do suspect thee very greeuously.
Hub. If I in act, consent, or sinne of thought,
Be guiltie of the stealing that sweete breath
Which was embounded in this beauteous clay,
Let hell want paines enough to torture me:
I left him well.
Bast. Go, beare him in thine armes:
I am amaz'd me thinkes, and loose my way
Among the thornes, and dangers of this world

How easie dost thou take all *England* vp,
From forth this morcell of dead Royaltie?
The life, the right, and truth of all this Realme
Is fled to heauen: and *England* now is left
To tug and scamble, and to part by th'teeth
The vn-owed interest of proud swelling State:
Now for the bare-pickt bone of Maiesty,
Doth dogged warre bristle his angry crest,
And snarleth in the gentle eyes of peace:
Now Powers from home, and discontents at hom
Meet in one line: and vast confusion waites
As doth a Rauen on a sicke-falne beast,
The iminent decay of wrested pompe.
Now happy he, whose cloake and center can
Hold out this tempest. Beare away that childe,
And follow me with speed: Ile to the King:
A thousand businesses are briefe in hand,
And heauen it selfe doth frowne vpon the Land. *Exit*

Actus Quartus, Scæna prima.

Enter King Iohn and Pandolph, attendants.

K.Iohn. Thus haue I yeelded vp into your hand
The Circle of my glory.
Pan. Take againe
From this my hand, as holding of the Pope
Your Soueraigne greatnesse and authoritie.
Iohn. Now keep your holy word, go meet the *French*,
And from his holinesse vse all your power
To stop their marches 'fore we are enflam'd:
Our discontented Counties doe reuolt:
Our people quarrell with obedience,
Swearing Allegiance, and the loue of soule
To stranger-bloud, to forren Royalty;
This inundation of mistempred humor,
Rests by you onely to be qualified.
Then pause not: for the present time's so sicke,
That present medcine must be ministred,
Or ouerthrow incureable ensues.
Pand. It was my breath that blew this Tempest vp.
Vpon your stubborne vsage of the Pope:
But since you are a gentle conuertite,
My tongue shall hush againe this storme of warre,
And make faire weather in your blustring land:
On this Ascention day, remember well,
Vpon your oath of seruice to the Pope,
Goe I to make the *French* lay downe their Armes. *Exit*
Iohn. Is this Ascension day? did not the Prophet
Say, that before Ascension day at noone,
My Crowne I should giue off? euen so I haue:
I did suppose it should be on constraint,
But (heau'n be thank'd) it is but voluntary.
Enter Bastard.
Bast. All Kent hath yeelded: nothing there holds out
But Douer Castle: London hath receiu'd
Like a kinde Host, the Dolphin and his powers.
Your Nobles will not heare you, but are gone
To offer seruice to your enemy:
And wilde amazement hurries vp and downe
The little number of your doubtfull friends.
Iohn. Would not my Lords returne to me againe
After they heard yong *Arthur* was aliue?
Bast. They found him dead, and cast into the streets,
An empty Casket, where the Iewell of life
By some damn'd hand was rob'd, and tane away.
Iohn. That villaine *Hubert* told me he did liue.
Bast. So on my soule he did, for ought he knew:
But wherefore doe you droope? why looke you sad?
Be great in act, as you haue beene in thought:
Let not the world see feare and sad distrust
Gouerne the motion of a kinglye eye:
Be stirring as the time, be fire with fire,
Threaten the threatner, and out-face the brow
Of bragging horror: So shall inferior eyes
That borrow their behauiours from the great,
Grow great by your example, and put on
The dauntlesse spirit of resolution.
Away, and glister like the god of warre
When he intendeth to become the field:
Shew boldnesse and aspiring confidence:
What, shall they seeke the Lion in his denne,
And fright him there? and make him tremble there?
Oh let it not be said: forrage, and runne
To meet displeasure farther from the dores,
And grapple with him ere he come so nye.
Iohn. The Legat of the Pope hath beene with mee,
And I haue made a happy peace with him,
And he hath promis'd to dismisse the Powers
Led by the Dolphin.
Bast. Oh inglorious league:
Shall we vpon the footing of our land,
Send fayre-play-orders and make comprimise,
Insinuation, parley, and base truce
To Armes Inuasiue? Shall a beardlesse boy,
A cockred-silken wanton braue our fields,
And flesh his spirit in a warre-like soyle,
Mocking the ayre with colours idlely spred,
And finde no checke? Let vs my Liege to Armes:
Perchance the Cardinall cannot make your peace;
Or if he doe, let it at least be said
They saw we had a purpose of defence.
Iohn. Haue thou the ordering of this present time.
Bast. Away then with good courage: yet I know
Our Partie may well meet a prowder foe. *Exeunt.*

Scœna Secunda.

Enter (in Armes) Dolphin, Salisbury, Meloone, Pembroke, Bigot, Souldiers.

Dol. My Lord *Melloone*, let this be coppied out,
And keepe it safe for our remembrance:
Returne the president to those Lords againe,
That hauing our faire order written downe,
Both they and we, perusing ore these notes
May know wherefore we tooke the Sacrament,
And keepe our faithes firme and inuiolable.
Sal. Vpon our sides it neuer shall be broken.
And Noble Dolphin, albeit we sweare
A voluntary zeale, and an vn-urg'd Faith
To your proceedings: yet beleeue me Prince,
I am not glad that such a sore of Time
Should seeke a plaster by contemn'd reuolt,
And heale the inueterate Canker of one wound,

By

By making many: Oh it grieues my soule,
That I must draw this mettle from my side
To be a widdow-maker: oh, and there
Where honourable rescue, and defence
Cries out vpon the name of *Salisbury*.
But such is the infection of the time,
That for the health and Physicke of our right,
We cannot deale but with the very hand
Of sterne Iniustice, and confused wrong:
And is't not pitty, (oh my grieued friends)
That we, the sonnes and children of this Isle,
Was borne to see so sad an houre as this,
Wherein we step after a stranger, march
Vpon her gentle bosom, and fill vp
Her Enemies rankes? I must withdraw, and weepe
Vpon the spot of this inforced cause,
To grace the Gentry of a Land remote,
And follow vnacquainted colours heere:
What heere? O Nation that thou couldst remoue,
That *Neptunes* Armes who clippeth thee about,
Would beare thee from the knowledge of thy selfe,
And cripple thee vnto a Pagan shore,
Where these two Christian Armies might combine
The bloud of malice, in a vaine of league,
And not to spend it so vn-neighbourly.

Dolph. A noble temper dost thou shew in this,
And great affections wrastling in thy bosome
Doth make an earth-quake of Nobility:
Oh, what a noble combat hast fought
Between compulsion, and a braue respect:
Let me wipe off this honourable dewe,
That siluerly doth progresse on thy cheekes:
My heart hath melted at a Ladies teares,
Being an ordinary Inundation:
But this effusion of such manly drops,
This showre, blowne vp by tempest of the soule,
Startles mine eyes, and makes me more amaz'd
Then had I seene the vaultie top of heauen
Figur'd quite ore with burning Meteors.
Lift vp thy brow (renowned *Salisburie*)
And with a great heart heaue away this storme:
Commend these waters to those baby-eyes
That neuer saw the giant-world enrag'd,
Nor met with Fortune, other then at feasts,
Full warm of blood, of mirth, of gossipping:
Come, come; for thou shalt thrust thy hand as deepe
Into the purse of rich prosperity
As *Lewis* himselfe: so (Nobles) shall you all,
That knit your sinewes to the strength of mine.

Enter Pandulpho.

And euen there, methinkes an Angell spake,
Looke where the holy Legate comes apace,
To giue vs warrant from the hand of heauen,
And on our actions set the name of right
With holy breath.

Pand. Haile noble Prince of *France*:
The next is this: King *Iohn* hath reconcil'd
Himselfe to *Rome*, his spirit is come in,
That so stood out against the holy Church,
The great Metropolis and Sea of Rome:
Therefore thy threatning Colours now winde vp,
And tame the sauage spirit of wilde warre,
That like a Lion fostered vp at hand,
It may lie gently at the foot of peace,
And be no further harmefull then in shewe.

Dol. Your Grace shall pardon me, I will not backe:
I am too high-borne to be proportied
To be a secondary at controll,
Or vsefull seruing-man, and Instrument
To any Soueraigne State throughout the world.
Your breath first kindled the dead coale of warres,
Betweene this chastiz'd kingdome and my selfe,
And brought in matter that should feed this fire;
And now 'tis farre too huge to be blowne out
With that same weake winde, which enkindled it
You taught me how to know the face of right,
Acquainted me with interest to this Land,
Yea, thrust this enterprize into my heart,
And come ye now to tell me *Iohn* hath made
His peace with *Rome*? what is that peace to me?
I (by the honour of my marriage bed)
After yong *Arthur*, claime this Land for mine,
And now it is halfe conquer'd, must I backe,
Because that *Iohn* hath made his peace with *Rome*?
Am I *Romes* slaue? What penny hath *Rome* borne?
What men prouided? What munition sent
To vnder-prop this Action? Is't not I
That vnder-goe this charge? Who else but I,
And such as to my claime are liable,
Sweat in this businesse, and maintaine this warre?
Haue I not heard these Islanders shout out
Viue le Roy, as I haue bank'd their Townes?
Haue I not heere the best Cards for the game
To winne this easie match, plaid for a Crowne?
And shall I now giue ore the yeelded Set?
No, no, on my soule it neuer shall be said.

Pand. You looke but on the out-side of this worke.

Dol. Out-side or in-side, I will not returne
Till my attempt so much be glorified,
As to my ample hope was promised,
Before I drew this gallant head of warre,
And cull'd these fiery spirits from the world
To out-looke Conquest, and to winne renowne
Euen in the iawes of danger, and of death
What lusty Trumpet thus doth summon vs?

Enter Bastard.

Bast. According to the faire-play of the world,
Let me haue audience: I am sent to speake:
My holy Lord of Millane, from the King
I come to learne how you haue dealt for him:
And, as you answer, I doe know the scope
And warrant limited vnto my tongue.

Pand. The *Dolphin* is too wilfull opposite
And will not temporize with my intreaties:
He flatly saies, hee'll not lay downe his Armes.

Bast. By all the bloud that euer fury breath'd,
The youth saies well. Now heare our *English* King,
For thus his Royaltie doth speake in me:
He is prepar'd, and reason to he should,
This apish and vnmannerly approach,
This harness'd Maske, and vnaduised Reuell,
This vn-heard sawcinesse and boyish Troopes,
The King doth smile at, and is well prepar'd
To whip this dwarfish warre, this Pigmy Armes
From out the circle of his Territories.
That hand which had the strength, euen at your dore,
To cudgell you, and make you take the hatch,
To diue like Buckets in concealed Welles,
To crowch in litter of your stable plankes,
To lye like pawnes, lock'd vp in chests and truncks,
To hug with swine, to seeke sweet safety out
In vaults and prisons, and to thrill and shake,

Euen

Euen at the crying of your Nations crow,
Thinking this voyce an armed Englishman.
Shall that victorious hand be feebled heere,
That in your Chambers gaue you chasticement?
No: know the gallant Monarch is in Armes,
And like an Eagle, o're his ayerie towres,
To sowsse annoyance that comes neere his Nest;
And you degenerate, you ingrate Reuolts,
you bloudy Nero's, ripping vp the wombe
Of your deere Mother-England: blush for shame:
For your owne Ladies, and pale-visag'd Maides,
Like *Amazons*, come tripping after drummes:
Their thimbles into armed Gantlets change,
Their Needl's to Lances, and their gentle hearts
To fierce and bloody inclination.

Dol. There end thy braue, and turn thy face in peace,
We grant thou canst out-scold vs: Far thee well,
We hold our time too precious to be spent
With such a brabler.

Pan. Giue me leaue to speake.

Bast. No, I will speake.

Dol. We will attend to neyther:
Strike vp the drummes, and let the tongue of warre
Pleade for our interest, and our being heere.

Bast. Indeede your drums being beaten, wil cry out;
And so shall you, being beaten: Do but start
An eccho with the clamor of thy drumme,
And euen at hand, a drumme is readie brac'd,
That shall reuerberate all, as lowd as thine.
Sound but another, and another shall
(As lowd as thine) rattle the Welkins eare,
And mocke the deepe mouth'd Thunder: for at hand
(Not trusting to this halting Legate heere,
Whom he hath vs'd rather for sport, then neede)
Is warlike *Iohn*: and in his fore-head sits
A bare-rib'd death, whose office is this day
To feast vpon whole thousands of the French.

Dol. Strike vp our drummes, to finde this danger out.

Bast. And thou shalt finde it (Dolphin) do not doubt

Exeunt.

Scæna Tertia.

Alarums. Enter Iohn and Hubert.

Iohn. How goes the day with vs? oh tell me *Hubert.*

Hub. Badly I feare; how fares your Maiesty?

Iohn. This Feauer that hath troubled me so long,
Lyes heauie on me: oh, my heart is sicke.

Enter a Messenger.

Mes. My Lord: your valiant kinsman *Falconbridge*,
Desires your Maiestie to leaue the field,
And send him word by me, which way you go.

Iohn. Tell him toward *Swinsted*, to the Abbey there.

Mes. Be of good comfort: for the great supply,
That was expected by the Dolphin heere,
Are wrack'd three nights ago on *Goodwin* sands.
This newes was brought to *Richard* but euen now,
The French fight coldly, and retyre themselues.

Iohn. Aye me, this tyrant Feauer burnes mee vp,
And will not let me welcome this good newes.
Set on toward *Swinsted*: to my Litter straight,
Weaknesse possesseth me, and I am faint. *Exeunt.*

Scena Quarta.

Enter Salisbury, Pembroke, and Bigot.

Sal. I did not thinke the King so stor'd with friends.

Pem. Vp once againe: put spirit in the French,
If they miscarry: we miscarry too.

Sal. That misbegotten diuell *Falconbridge*,
In spight of spight, alone vpholds the day.

Pem. They say King *Iohn* sore sick, hath left the field.

Enter Meloon wounded.

Mel. Lead me to the Reuolts of England heere.

Sal. When we were happie, we had other names.

Pem. It is the Count *Meloone.*

Sal. Wounded to death.

Mel. Fly Noble English, you are bought and sold,
Vnthred the rude eye of Rebellion,
And welcome home againe discarded faith,
Seeke out King *Iohn*, and fall before his feete:
For if the French be Lords of this loud day,
He meanes to recompence the paines you take,
By cutting off your heads: Thus hath he sworne,
And I with him, and many moe with mee,
Vpon the Altar at S. *Edmondsbury*,
Euen on that Altar, where we swore to you
Deere Amity, and euerlasting loue.

Sal. May this be possible? May this be true?

Mel. Haue I not hideous death within my view,
Retaining but a quantity of life,
Which bleeds away, euen as a forme of waxe
Resolueth from his figure 'gainst the fire?
What in the world should make me now deceiue,
Since I must loose the vse of all deceite?
Why should I then be false, since it is true
That I must dye heere, and liue hence, by Truth?
I say againe, if *Lewis* do win the day,
He is forsworne, if ere those eyes of yours
Behold another day breake in the East:
But euen this night, whose blacke contagious breath
Already smoakes about the burning Crest
Of the old, feeble, and day-wearied Sunne,
Euen this ill night, your breathing shall expire,
Paying the fine of rated Treachery,
Euen with a treacherous fine of all your liues:
If *Lewis*, by your assistance win the day.
Commend me to one *Hubert*, with your King;
The loue of him, and this respect besides
(For that my Grandsire was an Englishman)
Awakes my Conscience to confesse all this.
In lieu whereof, I pray you beare me hence
From forth the noise and rumour of the Field;
Where I may thinke the remnant of my thoughts
In peace: and part this bodie and my soule
With contemplation, and deuout desires.

Sal. We do beleeue thee, and beshrew my soule,
But I do loue the fauour, and the forme
Of this most faire occasion, by the which
We will vntread the steps of damned flight,
And like a bated and retired Flood,
Leauing our ranknesse and irregular course,
Stoope lowe within those bounds we haue ore-look'd,
And calmely run on in obedience
Euen to our Ocean, to our great King *Iohn.*
My arme shall giue thee helpe to beare thee hence,

For

For I do see the cruell pangs of death
Right in thine eye. Away, my friends, new flight,
And happie newnesse, that intends old right. *Exeunt*

Scena Quinta.

Enter Dolphin, and his Traine.

Dol. The Sun of heauen (me thought) was loth to set
But staid, and made the Westerne Welkin blush,
When English measure backward their owne ground
In faint Retire: Oh brauely came we off,
When with a volley of our needlesse shot,
After such bloody toile, we bid good night,
And woon'd our tott'ring colours clearly vp,
Last in the field, and almost Lords of it.

Enter a Messenger.

Mes. Where is my Prince, the Dolphin?
Dol. Heere: what newes?
Mes. The Count *Meloone* is slaine: The English Lords
By his perswasion, are againe falne off,
And your supply, which you haue wish'd so long,
Are cast away, and sunke on *Goodwin* sands.
Dol. Ah fowle, shrew'd newes. Beshrew thy very (hart
I did not thinke to be so sad to night
As this hath made me. Who was he that said
King *John* did flie an houre or two before
The stumbling night did part our wearie powres?
Mes. Who euer spoke it, it is true my Lord.
Dol. Well: keepe good quarter, & good care to night,
The day shall not be vp so soone as I,
To try the faire aduenture of to morrow. *Exeunt*

Scena Sexta.

Enter Bastard and Hubert, seuerally.

Hub. Whose there? Speake hoa, speake quickely, or I shoote.
Bast. A Friend. What art thou?
Hub. Of the part of England.
Bast. Whether doest thou go?
Hub. What's that to thee?
Why may not I demand of thine affaires,
As well as thou of mine?
Bast. *Hubert*, I thinke.
Hub. Thou hast a perfect thought:
I will vpon all hazards well beleeue
Thou art my friend, that know'st my tongue so well:
Who art thou?
Bast. Who thou wilt: and if thou please
Thou maist be-friend me so much, as to thinke
I come one way of the *Plantagenets*.
Hub. Vnkinde remembrance: thou, & endles night,
Haue done me shame: Braue Soldier, pardon me,
That any accent breaking from thy tongue,
Should scape the true acquaintance of mine eare.
Bast. Come, come: sans complement, What newes abroad?
Hub. Why heere walke I, in the black brow of night
To finde you out.
Bast. Breefe then: and what's the newes?
Hub. O my sweet sir, newes fitting to the night,
Blacke, fearefull, comfortlesse, and horrible.
Bast. Shew me the very wound of this ill newes,
I am no woman, Ile not swound at it.
Hub. The King I feare is poyson'd by a Monke,
I left him almost speechlesse, and broke out
To acquaint you with this euill, that you might
The better arme you to the sodaine time,
Then if you had at leisure knowne of this.
Bast. How did he take it? Who did taste to him?
Hub. A Monke I tell you, a resolued villaine
Whose Bowels sodainly burst out: The King
Yet speakes, and peraduenture may recouer.
Bast Who didst thou leaue to tend his Maiesty?
Hub. Why know you not? The Lords are all come backe,
And brought Prince *Henry* in their companie,
At whose request the king hath pardon'd them,
And they are all about his Maiestie.
Bast. With hold thine indignation, mighty heauen,
And tempt vs not to beare aboue our power.
Ile tell thee *Hubert*, halfe my power this night
Passing these Flats, are taken by the Tide,
These Lincolne-Washes haue deuoured them,
My selfe, well mounted, hardly haue escap'd.
Away before: Conduct me to the king,
I doubt he will be dead, or ere I come. *Exeunt*

Scena Septima.

Enter Prince Henry, Salisburie, and Bigot.

Hen. It is too late, the life of all his blood
Is touch'd, corruptibly: and his pure braine
(Which some suppose the soules fraile dwelling house)
Doth by the idle Comments that it makes,
Fore-tell the ending of mortality.

Enter Pembroke.

Pem. His Highnesse yet doth speak, & holds beleefe,
That being brought into the open ayre,
It would allay the burning qualitie
Of that fell poison which assayleth him.
Hen. Let him be brought into the Orchard heere:
Doth he still rage?
Pem. He is more patient
Then when you left him; euen now he sung.
Hen. Oh vanity of sicknesse: fierce extreames
In their continuance, will not feele themselues.
Death hauing praide vpon the outward parts
Leaues them inuisible, and his seige is now
Against the winde, the which he prickes and wounds
With many legions of strange fantasies,
Which in their throng, and presse to that last hold,
Counfound themselues. 'Tis strange y^t death shold sing:
I am the Symet to this pale faint Swan,
Who chaunts a dolefull hymne to his owne death,
And from the organ-pipe of frailety sings
His soule and body to their lasting rest.
Sal. Be of good comfort (Prince) for you are borne
To set a forme vpon that indigest
Which he hath left so shapelesse, and so rude.

Iohn brought in.

Iohn. I marrie, now my soule hath elbow roome,
It

It would not out at windowes, nor at doores,
There is ſo hot a ſummer in my boſome,
That all my bowels crumble vp to duſt:
I am a ſcribled forme drawne with a pen
Vpon a Parchment, and againſt this fire
Do I ſhrinke vp.
Hen. How fares your Maieſty?
Ioh. Poyſon'd, ill fare: dead, forſooke, caſt off,
And none of you will bid the winter come
To thruſt his ycie fingers in my maw;
Nor let my kingdomes Riuers take their courſe
Through my burn'd boſome: nor intreat the North
To make his bleake windes kiſſe my parched lips,
And comfort me with cold. I do not aske you much,
I begge cold comfort: and you are ſo ſtraight
And ſo ingratefull, you deny me that.
Hen. Oh that there were ſome vertue in my teares,
That might releeue you.
Iohn. The ſalt in them is hot.
Within me is a hell, and there the poyſon
Is, as a fiend, confin'd to tyrannize,
On vnrepreeuable condemned blood.

Enter Baſtard.

Baſt. Oh, I am ſcalded with my violent motion
And ſpleene of ſpeede, to ſee your Maieſty.
Iohn. Oh Cozen, thou art come to ſet mine eye:
The tackle of my heart, is crack'd and burnt,
And all the ſhrowds wherewith my life ſhould ſaile,
Are turned to one thred, one little haire:
My heart hath one poore ſtring to ſtay it by,
Which holds but till thy newes be vttered,
And then all this thou ſeeſt, is but a clod,
And module of confounded royalty.
Baſt. The Dolphin is preparing hither-ward,
Where heauen he knowes how we ſhall anſwer him.
For in a night the beſt part of my powre,
As I vpon aduantage did remoue,
Were in the *Waſhes* all vnwarily,
Deuoured by the vnexpected flood.
Sal. You breath theſe dead newes in as dead an eare
My Liege, my Lord: but now a King, now thus.
Hen. Euen ſo muſt I run on, and euen ſo ſtop.
What ſurety of the world, what hope, what ſtay,
When this was now a King, and now is clay?
Baſt. Art thou gone ſo? I do but ſtay behinde,
To do the office for thee, of reuenge,
And then my ſoule ſhall waite on thee to heauen,
As it on earth hath bene thy ſeruant ſtill.
Now, now you Starres, that moue in your right ſpheres,
Where be your powres? Shew now your mended faiths,
And inſtantly returne with me againe.
To puſh deſtruction, and perpetuall ſhame
Out of the weake doore of our fainting Land:
Straight let vs ſeeke, or ſtraight we ſhall be ſought,
The Dolphine rages at our verie heeles.
Sal. It ſeemes you know not then ſo much as we,
The Cardinall *Pandulph* is within at reſt,
Who halfe an houre ſince came from the Dolphin,
And brings from him ſuch offers of our peace,
As we with honor and reſpect may take,
With purpoſe preſently to leaue this warre.
Baſt. He will the rather do it, when he ſees
Our ſelues well ſinew'd to our defence.
Sal. Nay, 'tis in a manner done already,
For many carriages hee hath diſpatch'd
To the ſea ſide, and put his cauſe and quarrell
To the diſpoſing of the Cardinall,
With whom your ſelfe, my ſelfe, and other Lords,
If you thinke meete, this afternoone will poaſt
To conſummate this buſineſſe happily.
Baſt. Let it be ſo, and you my noble Prince,
With other Princes that may beſt be ſpar'd,
Shall waite vpon your Fathers Funerall.
Hen. At Worſter muſt his bodie be interr'd,
For ſo he will'd it.
Baſt. Thither ſhall it then,
And happily may your ſweet ſelfe put on
The lineall ſtate, and glorie of the Land,
To whom with all ſubmiſſion on my knee,
I do bequeath my faithfull ſeruices
And true ſubiection euerlaſtingly.
Sal. And the like tender of our loue wee make
To reſt without a ſpot for euermore.
Hen. I haue a kinde ſoule, that would giue thankes,
And knowes not how to do it, but with teares.
Baſt. Oh let vs pay the time: but needfull woe,
Since it hath beene before hand with our greefes.
This England neuer did, nor neuer ſhall
Lye at the proud foote of a Conqueror,
But when it firſt did helpe to wound it ſelfe.
Now, theſe her Princes are come home againe,
Come the three corners of the world in Armes,
And we ſhall ſhocke them: Naught ſhall make vs rue,
If England to it ſelfe, do reſt but true.

Exeunt.

The life and death of King Richard the Second.

Actus Primus, Scæna Prima.

Enter King Richard, Iohn of Gaunt, with other Nobles and Attendants.

King Richard.

OLd *Iohn of Gaunt*, time-honoured Lancaster,
Hast thou according to thy oath and band
Brought hither *Henry* Herford thy bold son:
Heere to make good yͤ boistrous late appeale,
Which then our leysure would not let vs heare,
Against the Duke of Norfolke, *Thomas Mowbray*?

Gaunt. I haue my Liege.

King. Tell me moreouer, hast thou sounded him,
If he appeale the Duke on ancient malice,
Or worthily as a good subiect should
On some knowne ground of treacherie in him.

Gaunt. As neere as I could sift him on that argument,
On some apparant danger seene in him,
Aym'd at your Highnesse, no inueterate malice.

Kin. Then call them to our presence face to face,
And frowning brow to brow, our selues will heare
Th'accuser, and the accused, freely speake;
High stomack'd are they both, and full of ire,
In rage, deafe as the sea; hastie as fire.

Enter Bullingbrooke and Mowbray.

Bul. Many yeares of happy dayes befall
My gracious Soueraigne, my most louing Liege.

Mow. Each day still better others happinesse,
Vntill the heauens enuying earths good hap,
Adde an immortall title to your Crowne.

King. We thanke you both, yet one but flatters vs,
As well appeareth by the cause you come,
Namely, to appeale each other of high treason.
Coosin of Hereford, what dost thou obiect
Against the Duke of Norfolke, *Thomas Mowbray*?

Bul. First, heauen be the record to my speech,
In the deuotion of a subiects loue,
Tendering the precious safetie of my Prince,
And free from other misbegotten hate,
Come I appealant to this Princely presence.
Now *Thomas Mowbray* do I turne to thee,
And marke my greeting well: for what I speake,
My body shall make good vpon this earth,
Or my diuine soule answer it in heauen.
Thou art a Traitor, and a Miscreant;
Too good to be so, and too bad to liue
Since the more faire and christall is the skie,
The vglier seeme the cloudes that in it flye:
Once more, the more to aggrauate the note,
With a foule Traitors name stuffe I thy throte,
And wish (so please my Soueraigne) ere I moue,
What my tong speaks, my right drawn sword may proue

Mow. Let not my cold words heere accuse my zeale:
'Tis not the triall of a Womans warre,
The bitter clamour of two eager tongues,
Can arbitrate this cause betwixt vs twaine:
The blood is hot that must be cool'd for this.
Yet can I not of such tame patience boast,
As to be husht, and nought at all to say.
First the faire reuerence of your Highnesse curbes mee,
From giuing reines and spurres to my free speech,
Which else would post, vntill it had return'd
These tearmes of treason, doubly downe his throat.
Setting aside his high bloods royalty,
And let him be no Kinsman to my Liege,
I do defie him, and I spit at him,
Call him a slanderous Coward, and a Villaine:
Which to maintaine, I would allow him oddes,
And meete him, were I tide to runne afoote
Euen to the frozen ridges of the Alpes,
Or any other ground inhabitable,
Where euer Englishman durst set his foote.
Meane time, let this defend my loyaltie,
By all my hopes most falsely doth he lie.

Bul. Pale trembling Coward, there I throw my gage,
Disclaiming heere the kindred of a King,
And lay aside my high bloods Royalty,
Which feare, not reuerence makes thee to except.
If guilty dread hath left thee so much strength,
As to take vp mine Honors pawne, then stoope.
By that, and all the rites of Knight-hood else,
Will I make good against thee arme to arme,
What I haue spoken, or thou canst deuise.

Mow. I take it vp, and by that sword I sweare,
Which gently laid my Knight-hood on my shoulder,
Ile answer thee in any faire degree,
Or Chiualrous designe of knightly triall:
And when I mount, aliue may I not light,
If I be Traitor, or vniustly fight.

King. What doth our Cosin lay to *Mowbraies* charge?
It must be great that can inherite vs,
So much as of a thought of ill in him.

Bul. Looke what I said, my life shall proue it true,
That *Mowbray* hath receiu'd eight thousand Nobles,

In

In name of lendings for your Highnesse Soldiers,
The which he hath detain'd for lewd employments,
Like a false Traitor, and iniurious Villaine.
Besides I say, and will in battaile proue,
Or heere, or elsewhere to the furthest Verge
That euer was suruey'd by English eye,
That all the Treasons for these eighteene yeeres
Complotted, and contriued in this Land,
Fetch'd from false *Mowbray* their first head and spring.
Further I say, and further will maintaine
Vpon his bad life, to make all this good.
That he did plot the Duke of Glousters death,
Suggest his soone beleeuing aduersaries,
And consequently, like a Traitor Coward,
Sluc'd out his innocent soule through streames of blood:
Which blood, like sacrificing *Abels* cries,
(Euen from the toonglesse cauernes of the earth)
To me for iustice, and rough chasticement:
And by the glorious worth of my discent,
This arme shall do it, or this life be spent.
King. How high a pitch his resolution soares:
Thomas of Norfolke, what sayest thou to this?
Mow. Oh let my Soueraigne turne away his face,
And bid his eares a little while be deafe,
Till I haue told this slander of his blood,
How God, and good men, hate so foule a lyar.
King. *Mowbray*, impartiall are our eyes and eares,
Were he my brother, nay our kingdomes heyre,
As he is but my fathers brothers sonne;
Now by my Scepters awe, I make a vow,
Such neighbour-neerenesse to our sacred blood,
Should nothing priuiledge him, nor partialize
The vn-stooping firmenesse of my vpright soule.
He is our subiect (*Mowbray*) so art thou,
Free speech, and fearelesse, I to thee allow.
Mow. Then *Bullingbrooke*, as low as to thy heart,
Through the false passage of thy throat; thou lyest:
Three parts of that receipt I had for Callice,
Disburst I to his Highnesse souldiers;
The other part reseru'd I by consent,
For that my Soueraigne Liege was in my debt,
Vpon remainder of a deere Accompt,
Since last I went to France to fetch his Queene:
Now swallow downe that Lye. For Glousters death,
I slew him not; but (to mine owne disgrace)
Neglected my sworne duty in that case:
For you my noble Lord of *Lancaster*,
The honourable Father to my foe,
Once I did lay an ambush for your life,
A trespasse that doth vex my greeued soule:
But ere I last receiu'd the Sacrament,
I did confesse it, and exactly begg'd
Your Graces pardon, and I hope I had it.
This is my fault: as for the rest appeal'd,
It issues from the rancour of a Villaine,
A recreant, and most degenerate Traitor,
Which in my selfe I boldly will defend,
And interchangeably hurle downe my gage
Vpon this ouer-weening Traitors foote,
To proue my selfe a loyall Gentleman,
Euen in the best blood chamber'd in his bosome.
In hast whereof, most heartily I pray
Your Highnesse to assigne our Triall day.
King. Wrath-kindled Gentlemen be rul'd by me:
Let's purge this choller without letting blood:
This we prescribe, though no Physition,
Deepe malice makes too deepe incision.
Forget, forgiue, conclude, and be agreed,
Our Doctors say, This is no time to bleed.
Good Vnckle, let this end where it begun,
Wee'l calme the Duke of Norfolke; you, your son.
Gaunt. To be a make-peace shall become my age,
Throw downe (my sonne) the Duke of Norfolkes gage.
King. And Norfolke, throw downe his.
Gaunt. When *Harrie* when? Obedience bids,
Obedience bids I should not bid agen.
King Norfolke, throw downe, we bidde; there is no boote.
Mow. My selfe I throw (dread Soueraigne) at thy foot.
My life thou shalt command, but not my shame,
The one my dutie owes, but my faire name
Despight of death, that liues vpon my graue
To darke dishonours vse, thou shalt not haue.
I am disgrac'd, impeach'd, and baffel'd heere,
Pierc'd to the soule with slanders venom'd speare:
The which no balme can cure, but his heart blood
Which breath'd this poyson.
King. Rage must be withstood:
Giue me his gage: Lyons make Leopards tame.
Mo. Yea, but not change his spots: take but my shame,
And I resigne my gage. My deere, deere Lord,
The purest treasure mortall times afford
Is spotlesse reputation: that away,
Men are but gilded loame, or painted clay.
A Iewell in a ten times barr'd vp Chest,
Is a bold spirit, in a loyall brest.
Mine Honor is my life; both grow in one:
Take Honor from me, and my life is done.
Then (deere my Liege) mine Honor let me trie,
In that I liue; and for that will I die.
King. Coosin, throw downe your gage,
Do you begin.
Bul. Oh heauen defend my soule from such foule sin.
Shall I seeme Crest-falne in my fathers sight,
Or with pale beggar-feare impeach my hight
Before this out-dar'd dastard? Ere my toong,
Shall wound mine honor with such feeble wrong;
Or sound so base a parle: my teeth shall teare
The slauish motiue of recanting feare,
And spit it bleeding in his high disgrace,
Where shame doth harbour, euen in *Mowbrayes* face.
Exit Gaunt.
King. We were not borne to sue, but to command,
Which since we cannot do to make you friends,
Be readie, (as your liues shall answer it)
At Couentree, vpon S. *Lamberts* day:
There shall your swords and Lances arbitrate
The swelling difference of your setled hate:
Since we cannot attone you, you shall see
Iustice designe the Victors Chiualrie.
Lord Marshall, command our Officers at Armes,
Be readie to direct these home Alarmes. *Exeunt.*

Scæna Secunda.

Enter Gaunt, and Dutchesse of Gloucester.

Gaunt. Alas, the part I had in Glousters blood,
Doth more solicite me then your exclaimes,
To stirre against the Butchers of his life.
But

But since correction lyeth in those hands
Which made the fault that we cannot correct,
Put we our quarrell to the will of heauen,
Who when they see the houres ripe on earth,
Will raigne hot vengeance on offenders heads.

Dut. Findes brotherhood in thee no sharper spurre?
Hath loue in thy old blood no liuing fire?
Edwards seuen sonnes (whereof thy selfe art one)
Were as seuen violles of his Sacred blood,
Or seuen faire branches springing from one roote:
Some of those seuen are dride by natures course,
Some of those branches by the destinies cut:
But *Thomas*, my deere Lord, my life, my Glouster,
One Violl full of *Edwards* Sacred blood,
One flourishing branch of his most Royall roote
Is crack'd, and all the precious liquor spilt;
Is hackt downe, and his summer leafes all vaded
By Enuies hand, and Murders bloody Axe
Ah *Gaunt*! His blood was thine, that bed, that wombe,
That mettle, that selfe-mould that fashion'd thee,
Made him a man; and though thou liu'st, and breath'st,
Yet art thou slaine in him: thou dost consent
In some large measure to thy Fathers death,
In that thou seest thy wretched brother dye,
Who was the modell of thy Fathers life.
Call it not patience (*Gaunt*) it is dispaire,
In suff'ring thus thy brother to be slaughter'd,
Thou shew'st the naked path way to thy life,
Teaching sterne murther how to butcher thee:
That which in meane men we intitle patience
Is pale cold cowardice in noble brests:
What shall I say, to safegard thine owne life,
The best way is to venge my Glousters death.

Gaunt. Heauens is the quarrell: for heauens substitute
His Deputy annointed in his sight,
Hath caus'd his death, the which if wrongfully
Let heauen reuenge: for I may neuer lift
An angry arme against his Minister.

Dut. Where then (alas may I) complaint my selfe?

Gau. To heauen, the widdowes Champion to defence

Dut. Why then I will: farewell old *Gaunt*.
Thou go'st to Couentrie, there to behold
Our Cosine Herford, and fell Mowbray fight:
O sit my husbands wrongs on Herfords speare,
That it may enter butcher Mowbrayes brest:
Or if misfortune misse the first carreere,
Be Mowbrayes sinnes so heauy in his bosome,
That they may breake his foaming Coursers backe,
And throw the Rider headlong in the Lists,
A Caytiffe recreant to my Cosine Herford:
Farewell old *Gaunt*, thy sometimes brothers wife
With her companion Greefe, must end her life.

Gau. Sister farewell: I must to Couentree,
As much good stay with thee, as go with mee.

Dut. Yet one word more: Greefe boundeth where it
Not with the emptie hollownes, but weight: (falls,
I take my leaue, before I haue begun,
For sorrow ends not, when it seemeth done.
Commend me to my brother *Edmund Yorke*.
Loe, this is all: nay, yet depart not so,
Though this be all, do not so quickly go,
I shall remember more. Bid him, Oh, what?
With all good speed at Plashie visit mee.
Alacke, and what shall good old Yorke there see
But empty lodgings, and vnfurnish'd walles,
Vn-peopel'd Offices, vntroden stones?
And what heare there for welcome, but my grones?
Therefore commend me, let him not come there,
To seeke out sorrow, that dwels euery where:
Desolate, desolate will I hence, and dye,
The last leaue of thee, takes my weeping eye. *Exeunt*

Scena Tertia.

Enter Marshall, and Aumerle.

Mar. My L. *Aumerle*, is *Harry Herford* arm'd.

Aum. Yea, at all points, and longs to enter in.

Mar. The Duke of Norfolke, sprightfully and bold,
Stayes but the summons of the Appealants Trumpet.

Au. Why then the Champions, are prepar'd, and stay
For nothing but his Maiesties approach. *Flourish.*

Enter King, Gaunt, Bushy, Bagot, Greene, & others: Then Mowbray in Armor, and Harrold.

Rich. Marshall, demand of yonder Champion
The cause of his arriuall heere in Armes,
Aske him his name, and orderly proceed
To sweare him in the iustice of his cause.

Mar. In Gods name, and the Kings, say who ỹ art,
And why thou com'st thus knightly clad in Armes?
Against what man thou com'st, and what's thy quarrell,
Speake truly on thy knighthood, and thine oath,
As so defend thee heauen, and thy valour.

Mow. My name is *Tho. Mowbray*, Duke of Norfolk,
Who hither comes engaged by my oath
(Which heauen defend a knight should violate)
Both to defend my loyalty and truth,
To God, my King, and his succeeding issue,
Against the Duke of Herford, that appeales me:
And by the grace of God, and this mine arme,
To proue him (in defending of my selfe)
A Traitor to my God, my King, and me,
And as I truly fight, defend me heauen.

Tucket. Enter Hereford, and Harold.

Rich. Marshall: Aske yonder Knight in Armes,
Both who he is, and why he commeth hither,
Thus placed in habiliments of warre:
And formerly according to our Law
Depose him in the iustice of his cause.

Mar. What is thy name? and wherfore comst ỹ hither
Before King *Richard* in his Royall Lists?
Against whom com'st thou? and what's thy quarrell?
Speake like a true Knight, so defend thee heauen.

Bul. *Harry* of Herford, Lancaster, and Derbie,
Am I: who ready heere do stand in Armes,
To proue by heauens grace, and my bodies valour)
In Lists, on *Thomas Mowbray* Duke of Norfolke,
That he's a Traitor foule, and dangerous,
To God of heauen, King *Richard*, and to me,
And as I truly fight, defend me heauen.

Mar. On paine of death, no person be so bold,
Or daring hardie as to touch the Listes,
Except the Marshall, and such Officers
Appointed to direct these faire designes.

Bul. Lord Marshall, let me kisse my Soueraigns hand,
And bow my knee before his Maiestie:
For *Mowbray* and my selfe are like two men,
That vow a long and weary pilgrimage,

Then

Then let vs take a ceremonious leaue
And louing farwell of our seuerall friends.
Mar. The Appealant in all duty greets your Highnes,
And craues to kisse your hand, and take his leaue.
Rich. We will descend, and fold him in our armes.
Cosin of Herford, as thy cause is iust,
So be thy fortune in this Royall fight:
Farewell, my blood, which if to day thou shead,
Lament we may, but not reuenge thee dead.
Bull. Oh let no noble eye prophane a teare
For me, if I be gor'd with *Mowbrayes* speare:
As confident, as is the Falcons flight
Against a bird, do I with *Mowbray* fight.
My louing Lord, I take my leaue of you,
Of you (my Noble Cosin) Lord *Aumerle*;.
Not sicke, although I haue to do with death,
But lustie, yong, and cheerely drawing breath.
Loe, as at English Feasts, so I regreete
The daintiest last, to make the end most sweet.
Oh thou the earthy author of my blood,
Whose youthfull spirit in me regenerate,
Doth with a two-fold rigor lift mee vp
To reach at victory aboue my head,
Adde proofe vnto mine Armour with thy prayres,
And with thy blessings steele my Lances point,
That it may enter *Mowbrayes* waxen Coate,
And furnish new the name of *Iohn a Gaunt*,
Euen in the lusty hauiour of his sonne.
Gaunt. Heauen in thy good cause make thee prosp'rous
Be swift like lightning in the execution,
And let thy blowes doubly redoubled,
Fall like amazing thunder on the Caske
Of thy amaz'd pernicious enemy.
Rouze vp thy youthfull blood, be valiant, and liue.
Bul. Mine innocence, and S. *George* to thriue.
Mow. How euer heauen or fortune cast my lot,
There liues, or dies, true to Kings *Richards* Throne,
A loyall, iust, and vpright Gentleman:
Neuer did Captiue with a freer heart,
Cast off his chaines of bondage, and embrace
His golden vncontroul'd enfranchisement,
More then my dancing soule doth celebrate
This Feast of Battell, with mine Aduersarie.
Most mighty Liege, and my companion Peeres,
Take from my mouth, the wish of happy yeares,
As gentle, and as iocond, as to iest,
Go I to fight: Truth, hath a quiet brest.
Rich. Farewell, my Lord, securely I espy
Vertue with Valour, couched in thine eye:
Order the triall Marshall, and begin.
Mar. Harrie of Herford, Lancaster, and Derby,
Receiue thy Launce, and heauen defend thy right.
Bul. Strong as a towre in hope, I cry Amen.
Mar. Go beare this Lance to *Thomas* D. of Norfolke.
1. Har. Harry of Herford, Lancaster, and Derbie,
Stands heere for God, his Soueraigne, and himselfe,
On paine to be found false, and recreant,
To proue the Duke of Norfolke, *Thomas Mowbray*,
A Traitor to his God, his King, and him,
And dares him to set forwards to the fight.
2. Har. Here standeth *Tho: Mowbray* Duke of Norfolk
On paine to be found false and recreant,
Both to defend himselfe, and to approue
Henry of Herford, Lancaster, and Derby,
To God, his Soueraigne, and to him disloyall:
Couragiously, and with a free desire
Attending but the signall to begin. *A charge sounde*
Mar. Sound Trumpets, and set forward Combatants
Stay, the King hath throwne his Warder downe.
Rich. Let them lay by their Helmets & their Speares
And both returne backe to their Chaires againe:
Withdraw with vs, and let the Trumpets sound,
While we returne these Dukes what we decree.
A long Flourish.
Draw neere and list
What with our Councell we haue done.
For that our kingdomes earth should not be soyld
With that deere blood which it hath fostered,
And for our eyes do hate the dire aspect
Of ciuill wounds plowgh'd vp with neighbors swords,
Which so rouz'd vp with boystrous vntun'd drummes,
With harsh resounding Trumpets dreadfull bray,
And grating shocke of wrathfull yron Armes,
Might from our quiet Confines fright faire peace,
And make vs wade euen in our kindreds blood:
Therefore, we banish you our Territories.
You Cosin Herford, vpon paine of death,
Till twice fiue Summers haue enrich'd our fields,
Shall not regreet our faire dominions,
But treade the stranger pathes of banishment.
Bul. Your will be done: This must my comfort be,
That Sun that warmes you heere, shall shine on me:
And those his golden beames to you heere lent,
Shall point on me, and gild my banishment.
Rich. Norfolke: for thee remaines a heauier dombe,
Which I with some vnwillingnesse pronounce,
The slye slow houres shall not determinate
The datelesse limit of thy deere exile:
The hopelesse word, of Neuer to returne,
Breath I against thee, vpon paine of life.
Mow. A heauy sentence, my most Soueraigne Liege,
And all vnlook'd for from your Highnesse mouth:
A deerer merit, not so deepe a maime,
As to be cast forth in the common ayre
Haue I deserued at your Highnesse hands.
The Language I haue learn'd these forty yeares
(My natiue English) now I must forgo,
And now my tongues vse is to me no more,
Then an vnstringed Vyall, or a Harpe,
Or like a cunning Instrument cas'd vp,
Or being open, put into his hands
That knowes no touch to tune the harmony.
Within my mouth you haue engaol'd my tongue,
Doubly percullist with my teeth and lippes,
And dull, vnfeeling, barren ignorance,
Is made my Gaoler to attend on me:
I am too old to fawne vpon a Nurse,
Too farre in yeeres to be a pupill now:
What is thy sentence then, but speechlesse death,
Which robs my tongue from breathing natiue breath?
Rich. It boots thee not to be compassionate,
After our sentence, plaining comes too late.
Mow. Then thus I turne me from my countries ligh
To dwell in solemne shades of endlesse night.
Ric. Returne againe, and take an oath with thee,
Lay on our Royall sword, your banisht hands;
Sweare by the duty that you owe to heauen
(Our part therein we banish with your selues)
To keepe the Oath that we administer:
You neuer shall (so helpe you Truth, and Heauen)
Embrace each others loue in banishment,
Nor euer looke vpon each others face,
Nor

Nor euer write, regreete, or reconcile
This lowring tempest of your home-bred hate,
Nor euer by aduised purpose meete,
To plot, contriue, or complot any ill,
Gainst Vs, our State, our Subiects, or our Land.
Bull. I sweare.
Mow. And I, to keepe all this.
Bul. Norfolke, so fare, as to mine enemie,
By this time (had the King permitted vs)
One of our soules had wandred in the ayre,
Banish'd this fraile sepulchre of our flesh,
As now our flesh is banish'd from this Land.
Confesse thy Treasons, ere thou flye this Realme,
Since thou hast farre to go, beare not along
The clogging burthen of a guilty soule.
Mow. No *Bullingbroke*: If euer I were Traitor,
My name be blotted from the booke of Life,
And I from heauen banish'd, as from hence:
But what thou art, heauen, thou, and I do know,
And all too soone (I feare) the King shall rue.
Farewell (my Liege) now no way can I stray,
Saue backe to England, all the worlds my way. *Exit.*
Rich. Vncle, euen in the glasses of thine eyes
I see thy greeued heart: thy sad aspect,
Hath from the number of his banish'd yeares
Pluck'd foure away: Six frozen Winters spent,
Returne with welcome home, from banishment.
Bul. How long a time lyes in one little word:
Foure lagging Winters, and foure wanton springs
End in a word, such is the breath of Kings.
Gaunt. I thanke my Liege, that in regard of me
He shortens foure yeares of my sonnes exile:
But little vantage shall I reape thereby.
For ere the sixe yeares that he hath to spend
Can change their Moones, and bring their times about,
My oyle-dride Lampe, and time-bewasted light
Shall be extinct with age, and endlesse night:
My inch of Taper, will be burnt, and done,
And blindfold death, not let me see my sonne.
Rich. Why Vncle, thou hast many yeeres to liue.
Gaunt. But not a minute (King) that thou canst giue;
Shorten my dayes thou canst with sudden sorow,
And plucke nights from me, but not lend a morrow:
Thou canst helpe time to furrow me with age,
But stop no wrinkle in his pilgrimage:
Thy word is currant with him, for my death,
But dead, thy kingdome cannot buy my breath.
Ric. Thy sonne is banish'd vpon good aduice,
Whereto thy tongue a party-verdict gaue,
Why at our Iustice seem'st thou then to lowre?
Gau. Things sweet to tast, proue in digestion sowre:
You vrg'd me as a Iudge, but I had rather
you would haue bid me argue like a Father.
Alas, I look'd when some of you should say,
I was too strict to make mine owne away:
But you gaue leaue to my vnwilling tong,
Against my will, to do my selfe this wrong.
Rich. Cosine farewell: and Vncle bid him so:
Six yeares we banish him, and he shall go. *Exit.*
Flourish.
Au. Cosine farewell: what presence must not know
From where you do remaine, let paper show.
Mar. My Lord, no leaue take I, for I will ride
As farre as land will let me, by your side.
Gaunt. Oh to what purpose dost thou hord thy words,
That thou returnst no greeting to thy friends?
Bull. I haue too few to take my leaue of you
When the tongues office should be prodigall,
To breath th'abundant dolour of the heart.
Gau Thy greefe is but thy absence for a time.
Bull. Ioy absent, greefe is present for that time.
Gau. What is sixe Winters, they are quickely gone?
Bul. To men in ioy, but greefe makes one houre ten.
Gau. Call it a trauell that thou tak'st for pleasure.
Bul. My heart will sigh, when I miscall it so,
Which findes it an inforced Pilgrimage.
Gau. The sullen passage of thy weary steppes
Esteeme a soyle, wherein thou art to set
The precious Iewell of thy home returne.
Bul. Oh who can hold a fire in his hand
By thinking on the frostie *Caucasus*?
Or cloy the hungry edge of appetite,
by bare imagination of a Feast?
Or Wallow naked in December snow
by thinking on fantasticke summers heate?
Oh no, the apprehension of the good
Giues but the greater feeling to the worse:
Fell sorrowes tooth, doth euer ranckle more
Then when it bites, but lanceth not the sore.
Gau. Come, come (my son) Ile bring thee on thy way
Had I thy youth, and cause, I would not stay.
Bul. Then Englands ground farewell: sweet soil adieu,
My Mother, and my Nurse, which beares me yet:
Where ere I wander, boast of this I can,
Though banish'd, yet a true-borne Englishman.

Scœna Quarta.

Enter King, Aumerle, Greene, and Bagot.

Rich. We did obserue. Cosine *Aumerle*,
How far brought you high Herford on his way?
Aum. I brought high Herford (if you call him so)
but to the next high way, and there I left him.
Rich. And say, what store of parting tears were shed?
Aum. Faith none for me: except the Northeast wind
Which then grew bitterly against our face,
Awak'd the sleepie rhewme, and so by chance
Did grace our hollow parting with a teare.
Rich. What said our Cosin when you parted with him?
Au. Farewell: and for my hart disdained ẏ my tongue
Should so prophane the word, that taught me craft
To counterfeit oppression of such greefe,
That word seem'd buried in my sorrowes graue.
Marry, would the word Farwell, haue lengthen'd houres,
And added yeeres to his short banishment,
He should haue had a volume of Farwels,
but since it would not, he had none of me.
Rich. He is our Cosin (Cosin) but 'tis doubt,
When time shall call him home from banishment,
Whether our kinsman come to see his friends,
Our selfe, and *Bushy*: heere *Bagot* and *Greene*
Obseru'd his Courtship to the common people:
How he did seeme to diue into their hearts,
With humble, and familiar courtesie,
What reuerence he did throw away on slaues;
Wooing poore Craftes-men, with the craft of soules,
And patient vnder-bearing of his Fortune,
As 'twere to banish their affects with him.
Off goes his bonnet to an Oyster-wench,

A brace of Dray-men bid God speed him well,
And had the tribute of his supple knee,
With thankes my Countrimen, my louing friends,
As were our England in reuersion his,
And he our subiects next degree in hope.
Gr. Well, he is gone, & with him go these thoughts:
Now for the Rebels, which stand out in Ireland,
Expedient manage must be made my Liege
Ere further leysure, yeeld them further meanes
For their aduantage, and your Highnesse losse.
Ric. We will our selfe in person to this warre,
And for our Coffers, with too great a Court,
And liberall Largesse, are growne somewhat light,
We are inforc'd to farme our royall Realme,
The Reuennew whereof shall furnish vs
For our affayres in hand: if that come short
Our Substitutes at home shall haue Blanke-charters:
Whereto, when they shall know what men are rich,
They shall subscribe them for large summes of Gold,
And send them after to supply our wants:
For we will make for Ireland presently.

Enter Bushy.

Bushy, what newes?
Bu. Old *Iohn of Gaunt* is verie sicke my Lord,
Sodainly taken, and hath sent post haste
To entreat your Maiesty to visit him.
Ric. Where lyes he?
Bu. At Ely house.
Ric. Now put it (heauen) in his Physitians minde,
To helpe him to his graue immediately:
The lining of his coffers shall make Coates
To decke our souldiers for these Irish warres.
Come Gentlemen, let's all go visit him:
Pray heauen we may make hast, and come too late. *Exit.*

Actus Secundus. Scena Prima.

Enter Gaunt, sicke with Yorke.

Gau. Will the King come, that I may breath my last
In wholsome counsell to his vnstaid youth?
Yor. Vex not your selfe, nor striue not with your breth,
For all in vaine comes counsell to his eare
Gau. Oh but (they say) the tongues of dying men
Inforce attention like deepe harmony;
Where words are scarse, they are seldome spent in vaine,
For they breath truth, that breath their words in paine.
He that no more must say, is listen'd more,
Then they whom youth and ease haue taught to glose,
More are mens ends markt, then their liues before,
The setting Sun, and Musicke is the close
As the last taste of sweetes, is sweetest last,
Writ in remembrance, more then things long past;
Though *Richard* my liues counsell would not heare,
My deaths sad tale, may yet vndeafe his eare.
Yor. No, it is stopt with other flatt'ring sounds
As praises of his state: then there are sound
Lascitious Meeters, to whose venom sound
The open eare of youth doth alwayes listen,
Report of fashions in proud Italy,
Whose manners still our tardie apish Nation
Limpes after in base imitation.
Where doth the world thrust forth a vanity,
So it be new, there's no respect how vile,
That is not quickly buz'd into his eares?
That all too late comes counsell to be heard,
Where will doth mutiny with wits regard:
Direct not him, whose way himselfe will choose,
Tis breath thou lackst, and that breath wilt thou loose.
Gaunt. Me thinkes I am a Prophet new inspir'd,
And thus expiring, do foretell of him,
His rash fierce blaze of Ryot cannot last,
For violent fires soone burne out themselues,
Small showres last long, but sodaine stormes are short.
He tyres betimes, that spurs too fast betimes;
With eager feeding, food doth choake the feeder:
Light vanity, insatiate cormorant,
Consuming meanes soone preyes vpon it selfe.
This royall Throne of Kings, this sceptred Isle,
This earth of Maiesty, this seate of Mars,
This other Eden, demy paradise,
This Fortresse built by Nature for her selfe,
Against infection, and the hand of warre:
This happy breed of men, this little world,
This precious stone, set in the siluer sea,
Which serues it in the office of a wall,
Or as a Moate defensiue to a house,
Against the enuy of lesse happier Lands,
This blessed plot, this earth, this Realme, this England,
This Nurse, this teeming wombe of Royall Kings,
Fear'd by their breed, and famous for their birth,
Renowned for their deeds, as farre from home,
For Christian seruice, and true Chiualrie,
As is the sepulcher in stubborne *Iury*
Of the Worlds ransome, blessed *Maries* Sonne.
This Land of such deere soules, this deere-deere Land,
Deere for her reputation through the world,
Is now Leas'd out (I dye pronouncing it)
Like to a Tenement or pelting Farme.
England bound in with the triumphant sea,
Whose rocky shore beates backe the enuious siedge
Of watery Neptune, is now bound in with shame,
With Inky blottes, and rotten Parchment bonds.
That England, that was wont to conquer others,
Hath made a shamefull conquest of it selfe.
Ah! would the scandall vanish with my life,
How happy then were my ensuing death?

Enter King, Queene, Aumerle, Bushy, Greene, Bagot, Ros, and Willoughby.

Yor. The King is come, deale mildly with his youth,
For young hot Colts, being rag'd do rage the more.
Qu. How fares our noble Vncle Lancaster?
Ri. What comfort man? How ist with aged *Gaunt*?
Ga. Oh how that name befits my composition:
Old *Gaunt* indeed, and gaunt in being old:
Within me greefe hath kept a tedious fast,
And who abstaynes from meate, that is not gaunt?
For sleeping England long time haue I watcht,
Watching breeds leannesse, leannesse is all gaunt.
The pleasure that some Fathers feede vpon,
Is my strict fast, I meane my Childrens lookes,
And therein fasting, hast thou made me gaunt:
Gaunt am I for the graue, gaunt as a graue,
Whose hollow wombe inherits naught but bones.
Ric. Can sicke men play so nicely with their names?
Gau. No, misery makes sport to mocke it selfe:
Since thou dost seeke to kill my name in mee,
I

I mocke my name (great King) to flatter thee
Ric. Should dying men flatter those that liue?
Gau. No, no, men liuing flatter those that dye.
Rich. Thou now a dying, sayst thou flatter'st me.
Gau Oh no, thou dyest, though I the sicker be.
Rich. I am in health, I breath, I see thee ill.
Gau. Now he that made me, knowes I see thee ill:
Ill in my selfe to see, and in thee, seeing ill,
Thy death-bed is no lesser then the Land,
Wherein thou lyest in reputation sicke,
And thou too care-lesse patient as thou art,
Commit'st thy'anointed body to the cure
Of those Physitians, that first wounded thee.
A thousand flatterers sit within thy Crowne,
Whose compasse is no bigger then thy head,
And yet incaged in so small a Verge,
The waste is no whit lesser then thy Land:
Oh had thy Grandsire with a Prophets eye,
Seene how his sonnes sonne, should destroy his sonnes,
From forth thy reach he would haue laid thy shame,
Deposing thee before thou wert possest,
Which art possest now to depose thy selfe.
Why (Cosine) were thou Regent of the world,
It were a shame to let his Land by lease:
But for thy world enioying but this Land,
Is it not more then shame, to shame it so?
Landlord of England art thou, and not King:
Thy state of Law, is bondslaue to the law,
And——
Rich. And thou, a lunaticke leane-witted foole,
Presuming on an Agues priuiledge,
Dar'st with thy frozen admonition
Make pale our cheeke, chafing the Royall blood
With fury, from his natiue residence?
Now by my Seates right Royall Maiestie,
Wer't thou not Brother to great *Edwards* sonne,
This tongue that runs so roundly in thy head,
Should run thy head from thy vnreuerent shoulders.
Gau. Oh spare me not, my brothers *Edwards* sonne,
For that I was his Father *Edwards* sonne:
That blood already (like the Pellican)
Thou hast tapt out, and drunkenly carows'd
My brother Gloucester, plaine well meaning soule
(Whom faire befall in heauen 'mongst happy soules)
May be a president, and witnesse good,
That thou respect'st not spilling *Edwards* blood:
Ioyne with the present sicknesse that I haue,
And thy vnkindnesse be like crooked age,
To crop at once a too-long wither'd flowre.
Liue in thy shame, but dye not shame with thee,
These words heereafter, thy tormentors bee.
Conuey me to my bed, then to my graue,
Loue they to liue, that loue and honor haue. *Exit*
Rich. And let them dye, that age and sullens haue,
For both hast thou, and both become the graue.
Yor. I do beseech your Maiestie impute his words
To wayward sicklinesse, and age in him:
He loues you on my life, and holds you deere
As *Harry* Duke of *Herford*, were he heere.
Rich. Right, you say true: as *Herfords* loue, so his;
As theirs, so mine: and all be as it is.

Enter Northumberland.

Nor. My Liege, olde *Gaunt* commends him to your Maiestie.
Rich. What sayes he?
Nor. Nay nothing, all is said:
His tongue is now a stringlesse instrument,
Words, life, and all, old Lancaster hath spent.
Yor. Be Yorke the next, that must be bankrupt so,
Though death be poore, it ends a mortall wo.
Rich. The ripest fruit first fals, and so doth he,
His time is spent, our pilgrimage must be:
So much for that. Now for our Irish warres,
We must supplant those rough rug-headed Kernes,
Which liue like venom, where no venom else
But onely they, haue priuiledge to liue.
And for these great affayres do aske some charge
Towards our assistance, we do seize to vs
The plate, coine, reuennewes, and moueables,
Whereof our Vncle *Gaunt* did stand possest.
Yor. How long shall I be patient? Oh how long
Shall tender dutie make me suffer wrong?
Not *Glousters* death, nor *Herfords* banishment,
Nor *Gauntes* rebukes, nor Englands priuate wrongs,
Nor the preuention of poore *Bullingbrooke*,
About his marriage, nor my owne disgrace
Haue euer made me sowre my patient cheeke,
Or bend one wrinckle on my Soueraignes face:
I am the last of noble *Edwards* sonnes,
Of whom thy Father Prince of Wales was first,
In warre was neuer Lyon rag'd more fierce:
In peace, was neuer gentle Lambe more milde,
Then was that yong and Princely Gentleman,
His face thou hast, for euen so look'd he
Accomplish'd with the number of thy howers:
But when he frown'd, it was against the French,
And not against his friends: his noble hand
Did win what he did spend: and spent not that
Which his triumphant fathers hand had won:
His hands were guilty of no kindreds blood,
But bloody with the enemies of his kinne:
Oh *Richard*, *Yorke* is too farre gone with greefe,
Or else he neuer would compare betweene.
Rich. Why Vncle,
What's the matter?
Yor. Oh my Liege, pardon me if you please, if not
I pleas'd not to be pardon'd, am content with all:
Seeke you to seize, and gripe into your hands
The Royalties and Rights of banish'd Herford?
Is not *Gaunt* dead? and doth not Herford liue?
Was not *Gaunt* iust? and is not *Harry* true?
Did not the one deserue to haue an heyre?
Is not his heyre a well-deseruing sonne?
Take Herfords rights away, and take from time
His Charters, and his customarie rights:
Let not to morrow then insue to day,
Be not thy selfe. For how art thou a King
But by faire sequence and succession?
Now afore God, God forbid I say true,
If you do wrongfully seize Herfords right,
Call in his Letters Patents that he hath
By his Atturneyes generall, to sue
His Liuerie, and denie his offer'd homage,
You plucke a thousand dangers on your head,
You loose a thousand well-disposed hearts,
And pricke my tender patience to those thoughts
Which honor and allegeance cannot thinke
Ric. Thinke what you will: we seise into our hands,
His plate, his goods, his money, and his lands.
Yor. Ile not be by the while: My Liege farewell,

What will ensue heereof, there s none can tell.
But by bad courses may be vnderstood,
That their euents can neuer fall out good. *Exit.*
Rich. Go *Bushie* to the Earle of *Wiltshire* streight,
Bid him repaire to vs to *Ely* house,
To see this businesse . to morrow next
We will for *Ireland*, and 'tis time, I trow :
And we create in absence of our selfe
Our Vncle Yorke, Lord Gouernor of England :
For he is iust, and alwayes lou'd vs well
Come on our Queene, to morrow must we part,
Be merry, for our time of stay is short. *Flourish.*
Manet North. Willoughby, & Ross
Nor Well Lords, the Duke of Lancaster is dead.
Ross. And liuing too, for now his sonne is Duke.
Wil. Barely in title, not in reuennew
Nor. Richly in both, if iustice had her right.
Ross. My heart is great : but it must break with silence,
Er't be disburthen'd with a liberall tongue.
Nor. Nay speake thy mind : & let him ne'r speak more
That speakes thy words againe to do thee harme.
Wil. Tends that thou'dst speake to th' Du. of Hereford,
If it be so, out with it boldly man,
Quicke is mine eare to heare of good towards him.
Ross. No good at all that I can do for him,
Vnlesse you call it good to pitie him,
Bereft and gelded of his patrimonie.
Nor. Now afore heauen, 'tis shame such wrongs are borne,
In him a royall Prince, and many moe
Of noble blood in this declining Land ;
The King is not himselfe, but basely led
By Flatterers, and what they will informe
Meerely in hate 'gainst any of vs all,
That will the King seuerely prosecute
'Gainst vs, our liues, our children, and our heires.
Ros. The Commons hath he pil'd with greeuous taxes
And quite lost their hearts : the Nobles hath he finde
For ancient quarrels, and quite lost their hearts.
Wil. And daily new exactions are deuis'd,
As blankes, beneuolences, and I wot not what :
But what o'Gods name doth become of this?
Nor. Wars hath not wasted it, for war'd he hath not.
But basely yeelded vpon comprimize,
That which his Ancestors atchieu'd with blowes :
More hath he spent in peace, then they in warres.
Ros. The Earle of Wiltshire hath the realme in Farme.
Wil. The Kings growne bankrupt like a broken man.
Nor. Reproach, and dissolution hangeth ouer him.
Ros. He hath not monie for these Irish warres :
(His burthenous taxations notwithstanding)
But by the robbing of the banish'd Duke.
Nor. His noble Kinsman, most degenerate King :
But Lords, we heare this fearefull tempest sing,
Yet seeke no shelter to auoid the storme :
We see the winde sit sore vpon our sailes,
And yet we strike not, but securely perish.
Ros. We see the very wracke that we must suffer,
And vnauoyded is the danger now
For suffering so the causes of our wracke.
Nor. Not so : euen through the hollow eyes of death,
I spie life peering : but I dare not say
How neere the tidings of our comfort is.
Wil. Nay let vs share thy thoughts, as thou dost ours
Ros. Be confident to speake Northumberland,
We three, are but thy selfe, and speaking so,
Thy words are but as thoughts, therefore be bold.
Nor. Then thus : I haue from Port *le Blan*]
A Bay in *Britaine*, receiu'd intelligence,
That *Harry* Duke of *Herford*, *R. inald* Lord *Cobham*,
That late broke from the Duke of *Exeter*,
His brother Archbishop, late of *Canterbury*,
Sir *Thomas Erpingham*, Sir *Iohn Rainston*,
Sir *Iohn Norberie*, Sir *Robert Waterton*, & *Francis Quoint*.
All these well furnish'd by the Duke of *Britaine*,
With eight tall ships, three thousand men of warre
Are making hither with all due expedience,
And shortly meane to touch our Northerne shore :
Perhaps they had ere this, but that they stay
The first departing of the King for Ireland.
If then we shall shake off our slauish yoake,
Impe out our drooping Countries broken wing,
Redeeme from broaking pawne the blemish'd Crowne,
Wipe off the dust that hides our Scepters gilt,
And make high Maiestie looke like it selfe,
Away with me in poste to *Rauenspurgh*,
But if you faint, as fearing to do so,
Stay, and be secret, and my selfe will go.
Ros. To horse, to horse, vrge doubts to them ŷ feare
Wil. Hold out my horse, and I will first be there.
Exeunt.

Scena Secunda.

Enter Queene, Bushy, and Bagot.

Bush. Madam, your Maiesty is too much sad,
You promis'd when you parted with the King,
To lay aside selfe-harming heauinesse,
And entertaine a cheerefull disposition.
Qu. To please the King, I did : to please my selfe
I cannot do it : yet I know no cause
Why I should welcome such a guest as greefe,
Saue bidding farewell to so sweet a guest
As my sweet *Richard* ; yet againe me thinkes,
Some vnborne sorrow, ripe in fortunes wombe
Is comming towards me, and my inward soule
With nothing trembles, at something it greeues,
More then with parting from my Lord the King.
Bush. Each substance of a greefe hath twenty shadows
Which shewes like greefe it selfe, but is not so :
For sorrowes eye, glazed with blinding teares,
Diuides one thing intire, to many obiects,
Like perspectiues, which rightly gaz'd vpon
Shew nothing but confusion, ey'd awry,
Distinguish forme : so your sweet Maiestie
Looking awry vpon your Lords departure,
Finde shapes of greefe, more then himselfe to waile,
Which look'd on as it is, is naught but shadowes
Of what it is not : then thrice-gracious Queene,
More then your Lords departure weep not, more's not (seene :
Or if it be, 'tis with false sorrowes eie,
Which for things true, weepe things imaginary.
Qu. It may be so : but yet my inward soule
Perswades me it is otherwise : how ere it be,
I cannot but be sad ; so heauy sad,
As though on thinking on no thought I thinke,
Makes me with heauy nothing faint and shrinke.
Bush. 'Tis nothing but conceit (my gracious Lady.)
Queene

Qu. 'Tis nothing lesse: conceit is still deriu'd
From some fore-father greefe, mine is not so,
For nothing hath begot my something greefe,
Or something, hath the nothing that I greeue,
'Tis in reuersion that I do possesse,
But what it is, that is not yet knowne, what
I cannot name, 'tis namelesse woe I wot.

Enter Greene.

Gree. Heauen saue your Maiesty, and wel met Gentle-
I hope the King is not yet shipt for Ireland. (men:
Qu. Why hop'st thou so? Tis better hope he is:
For his designes craue hast, his hast good hope,
Then wherefore dost thou hope he is not shipt?
Gre. That he our hope, might haue retyr'd his power,
and driuen into dispaire an enemies hope,
Who strongly hath set footing in this Land.
The banish'd *Bullingbroke* repeales himselfe,
And with vp-lifted Armes is safe arriu'd
At *Rauenspurg*.
Qu. Now God in heauen forbid.
Gr. O Madam 'tis too true: and that is worse,
The L. Northumberland, his yong sonne *Henrie Percie*,
The Lords of *Rosse, Beaumond*, and *Willoughby*,
With all their powrefull friends are fled to him.
Bush. Why haue you not proclaim'd Northumberland
And the rest of the reuolted faction, Traitors?
Gre. We haue: whereupon the Earle of Worcester
Hath broke his staffe, resign'd his Stewardship,
And al the houshold seruants fled with him to *Bullinbrook*
Qu. So *Greene*, thou art the midwife of my woe,
And *Bullinbrooke* my sorrowes dismall heyre:
Now hath my soule brought forth her prodegie,
And I a gasping new deliuered mother,
Haue woe to woe, sorrow to sorrow ioyn'd.
Bush. Dispaire not Madam.
Qu. Who shall hinder me?
I will dispaire, and be at enmitie
With couzening hope; he is a Flatterer,
A Parasite, a keeper backe of death,
Who gently would dissolue the bands of life,
Which false hopes linger in extremity.

Enter Yorke

Gre. Heere comes the Duke of Yorke.
Qu. With signes of warre about his aged necke,
Oh full of carefull businesse are his lookes:
Vncle, for heauens sake speake comfortable words:
Yor. Comfort's in heauen, and we are on the earth,
Where nothing liues but crosses, care and greefe:
Your husband he is gone to saue farre off,
Whilst others come to make him loose at home:
Heere am I left to vnder-prop his Land,
Who weake with age, cannot support my selfe.
Now comes the sicke houre that his surfet made,
Now shall he try his friends that flattered him.

Enter a seruant

Ser. My Lord, your sonne was gone before I came.
Yor. He was: why so: go all which way it will:
The Nobles they are fled, the Commons they are cold,
And will I feare reuolt on Herfords side.
Sirra, get thee to Plashie to my sister Gloster,
Bid her send me presently a thousand pound,
Hold, take my Ring
Ser My Lord, I had forgot
To tell your Lordship, to day I came by, and call'd there,
But I shall greeue you to report the rest.
Yor. What is't knaue?
Ser. An houre before I came, the Dutchesse di'de.
Yor. Heau'n for his mercy, what a tide of woes
Come rushing on this wofull Land at once?
I know not what to do: I would to heauen
(So my vntruth had not prouok'd him to it)
The King had cut off my head with my brothers.
What, are there postes dispatcht for Ireland?
How shall we do for money for these warres?
Come sister (Cozen I would say) pray pardon me.
Go fellow, get thee home, poouide some Carts,
And bring away the Armour that is there.
Gentlemen, will you muster men?
If I know how, or which way to order these affaires
Thus disorderly thrust into my hands,
Neuer beleeue me. Both are my kinsmen,
Th'one is my Soueraigne, whom both my oath
And dutie bids defend: th'other againe
Is my kinsman, whom the King hath wrong'd,
Whom conscience, and my kindred bids to right:
Well, somewhat we must do: Come Cozen,
Ile dispose of you. Gentlemen, go muster vp your men,
And meet me presently at Barkley Castle:
I should to Plashy too: but time will not permit,
All is vneuen, and euery thing is left at six and seuen. *Exit*
Bush. The winde sits faire for newes to go to Ireland,
But none returnes: For vs to leuy power
Proportionable to th'enemy, is all impossible.
Gr. Besides our neerenesse to the King in loue,
Is neere the hate of those loue not the King.
Ba And that's the wauering Commons, for their loue
Lies in their purses, and who so empties them,
By so much fils their hearts with deadly hate.
Bush. Wherein the king stands generally condemn'd
Bag. If iudgement lye in them, then so do we,
Because we haue beene euer neere the King.
Gr. Well: I will for refuge straight to Bristoll Castle,
The Earle of Wiltshire is alreadie there.
Bush. Thither will I with you, for little office
Will the hatefull Commons performe for vs,
Except like Curres, to teare vs all in peeces:
Will you go along with vs?
Bag. No, I will to Ireland to his Maiestie:
Farewell, if hearts presages be not vaine,
We three here part, that neu'r shall meete againe.
Bu. That's as Yorke thriues to beate back *Bullinbroke*
Gr. Alas poore Duke, the taske he vndertakes
Is numbring sands, and drinking Oceans drie,
Where one on his side fights, thousands will flye.
Bush. Farewell at once, for once, for all, and euer.
Well, we may meete againe.
Bag. I feare me neuer. *Exit.*

Scæna Tertia.

Enter the Duke of Hereford, and Northumberland.

Bul. How farre is it my Lord to Berkley now?
Nor. Beleeue me noble Lord,
I am a stranger heere in Gloustershire,
These high wilde hilles, and rough vneeuen waies,
Drawes out our miles, and makes them wearisome:
And yet our faire discourse hath beene as sugar,
Makin

Making the hard way sweet and delectable:
But I bethinke me, what a wearie way
From Rauenspurgh to Cottshold will be found,
In *Rosse* and *Willoughby*, wanting your companie,
Which I protest hath very much beguild
The tediousnesse, and processe of my trauell:
But theirs is sweetned with the hope to haue
The present benefit that I possesse;
And hope to ioy, is little lesse in ioy,
Then hope enioy'd: By this, the wearie Lords
Shall make their way seeme short, as mine hath done,
By sight of what I haue, your Noble Companie.
Bull. Of much lesse value is my Companie,
Then your good words: but who comes here?

Enter H. Percie.

North. It is my Sonne, young *Harry Percie*,
Sent from my Brother *Worcester*: Whence soeuer.
Harry, how fares your Vnckle?
Percie. I had thought, my Lord, to haue learn'd his health of you.
North. Why, is he not with the Queene?
Percie. No, my good Lord, he hath forsook the Court,
Broken his Staffe of Office, and disperst
The Household of the King.
North. What was his reason?
He was not so resolu'd, when we last spake together.
Percie. Because your Lordship was proclaimed Traitor.
But hee, my Lord, is gone to Rauenspurgh,
To offer seruice to the Duke of Hereford,
And sent me ouer by Barkely, to discouer
What power the Duke of Yorke had leuied there,
Then with direction to repaire to Rauenspurgh.
North. Haue you forgot the Duke of Hereford (Boy.)
Percie. No, my good Lord; for that is not forgot
Which ne're I did remember: to my knowledge,
I neuer in my life did looke on him.
North. Then learne to know him now: this is the Duke.
Percie. My gracious Lord, I tender you my seruice,
Such as it is, being tender, raw, and young,
Which elder dayes shall ripen, and confirme
To more approued seruice, and desert.
Bull. I thanke thee gentle *Percie*, and be sure
I count my selfe in nothing else so happy,
As in a Soule remembring my good Friends:
And as my Fortune ripens with thy Loue,
It shall be still thy true Loues recompence,
My Heart this Couenant makes, my Hand thus seales it.
North. How farre is it to Barkely? and what stirre
Keepes good old *Yorke* there, with his Men of Warre?
Percie. There stands the Castle, by yond tuft of Trees,
Mann'd with three hundred men, as I haue heard,
And in it are the Lords of *Yorke*, *Barkely*, and *Seymor*,
None else of Name, and noble estimate.

Enter Rosse and Willoughby.

North. Here come the Lords of *Rosse* and *Willoughby*,
Bloody with spurring, fierie red with haste.
Bull. Welcome my Lords, I wot your loue pursues
A banisht Traytor; all my Treasurie
Is yet but vnfelt thankes, which more enrich'd,
Shall be your loue, and labours recompence.
Ross. Your presence makes vs rich, most Noble Lord.
Willo. And farre surmounts our labour to attaine it.
Bull. Euermore thankes, th'Exchequer of the poore,
Which till my infant-fortune comes to yeeres,
Stands for my Bountie: but who comes here?

Enter Barkely.

North. It is my Lord of Barkely, as I ghesse.
Bark. My Lord of Hereford, my Message is to you.
Bull. My Lord, my Answere is to *Lancaster*,
And I am come to seeke that Name in England,
And I must finde that Title in your Tongue,
Before I make reply to aught you say.
Bark. Mistake me not, my Lord, 'tis not my meaning
To raze one Title of your Honor out.
To you, my Lord, I come (what Lord you will)
From the most glorious of this Land,
The Duke of Yorke, to know what pricks you on
To take aduantage of the absent time,
And fright our Natiue Peace with selfe-borne Armes.

Enter Yorke.

Bull. I shall not need transport my words by you,
Here comes his Grace in Person My Noble Vnckle.
York. Shew me thy humble heart, and not thy knee,
Whose dutie is deceiuable, and false.
Bull. My gracious Vnckle.
York. Tut, tut Grace me no Grace, nor Vnckle me,
I am no Traytors Vnckle; and that word Grace,
In an vngracious mouth, is but prophane.
Why haue these banish'd, and forbidden Legges,
Dar'd once to touch a Dust of Englands Ground?
But more then why, why haue they dar'd to march
So many miles vpon her peacefull Bosome,
Frighting her pale-fac'd Villages with Warre,
And ostentation of despised Armes?
Com'st thou because th'anoynted King is hence?
Why foolish Boy, the King is left behind,
And in my loyall Bosome lyes his power.
Were I but now the Lord of such hot youth,
As when braue *Gaunt*, thy Father, and my selfe
Rescued the *Black Prince*, that yong *Mars* of men,
From forth the Rankes of many thousand French:
Oh then, how quickly should this Arme of mine,
Now Prisoner to the Palsie, chastise thee,
And minister correction to thy Fault.
Bull. My gracious Vnckle, let me know my Fault,
On what Condition stands it, and wherein?
York. Euen in Condition of the worst degree,
In grosse Rebellion, and detested Treason:
Thou art a banish'd man, and here art come
Before th'expiration of thy time,
In brauing Armes against thy Soueraigne.
Bull. As I was banish'd, I was banish'd *Hereford*,
But as I come, I come for *Lancaster*
And Noble Vnckle, I beseech your Grace
Looke on my Wrongs with an indifferent eye:
You are my Father, for me thinkes in you
I see old *Gaunt* aliue. Oh then my Father,
Will you permit, that I shall stand condemn'd
A wandring Vagabond; my Rights and Royalties
Pluckt from my armes perforce, and giuen away
To vpstart Vnthrifts? Wherefore was I borne?
If that my Cousin King, be King of England,
It must be graunted, I am Duke of Lancaster.
You haue a Sonne, *Aumerle*, my Noble Kinsman,
Had you first died, and he beene thus trod downe,
He should haue found his Vnckle *Gaunt* a Father,
To rowze his Wrongs, and chase them to the bay.
I am denyde to sue my Liuerie here,
And yet my Letters Patents giue me leaue:
My Fathers goods are all distraynd, and sold,
And these, and all, are all amisse imployd.

What

What would you haue me doe? I am a Subiect,
And challenge Law: Attorneyes are deny'd me;
And therefore personally I lay my claime
To my Inheritance of free Discent.
North. The Noble Duke hath been too much abus'd.
Ross. It stands your Grace vpon, to doe him right.
Willo. Base men by his endowments are made great.
York. My Lords of England, let me tell you this,
I haue had feeling of my Cosens Wrongs,
And labour'd all I could to doe him right:
But in this kind, to come in brauing Armes,
Be his owne Caruer, and cut out his way,
To find out Right with Wrongs, it may not be;
And you that doe abett him in this kind,
Cherish Rebellion, and are Rebels all.
North. The Noble Duke hath sworne his comming is
But for his owne; and for the right of that,
Wee all haue strongly sworne to giue him ayd,
And let him neu'r see Ioy, that breakes that Oath.
York. Well, well, I see the issue of these Armes,
I cannot mend it, I must needes confesse,
Because my power is weake, and all ill left:
But if I could, by him that gaue me life,
I would attach you all, and make you stoope
Vnto the Soueraigne Mercy of the King.
But since I cannot, be it knowne to you,
I doe remaine as Neuter. So fare you well,
Vnlesse you please to enter in the Castle,
And there repose you for this Night.
Bull. An offer Vnckle, that wee will accept:
But wee must winne your Grace to goe with vs
To Bristow Castle, which they say is held
By *Bushie*, *Bagot*, and their Complices,
The Caterpillers of the Commonwealth,
Which I haue sworne to weed, and plucke away.
York. It may be I will go with you: but yet Ile pawse,
For I am loth to breake our Countries Lawes:
Nor Friends, nor Foes, to me welcome you are,
Things past redresse, are now with me past care. *Exeunt.*

Scœna Quarta.

Enter Salisbury, and a Captaine.

Capt. My Lord of Salisbury, we haue stayd ten dayes,
And hardly kept our Countreymen together,
And yet we heare no tidings from the King;
Therefore we will disperse our selues: farewell.
Sal. Stay yet another day, thou trustie Welchman,
The King reposeth all his confidence in thee.
Capt. 'Tis thought the King is dead, we will not stay;
The Bay-trees in our Countrey all are wither'd,
And Meteors fright the fixed Starres of Heauen;
The pale-fac'd Moone lookes bloody on the Earth,
And leane-look'd Prophets whisper fearefull change;
Rich men looke sad, and Ruffians dance and leape,
The one in feare, to loose what they enioy,
The other to enioy by Rage, and Warre:
These signes fore-run the death of Kings.
Farewell, our Countreymen are gone and fled,
As well assur'd *Richard* their King is dead. *Exit.*
Sal. Ah *Richard*, with eyes of heauie mind,
I see thy Glory, like a shooting Starre,
Fall to the base Earth, from the Firmament:
Thy Sunne sets weeping in the lowly West,
Witnessing Stormes to come, Woe, and Vnrest:
Thy Friends are fled, to wait vpon thy Foes,
And crossely to thy good, all fortune goes. *Exit.*

Actus Tertius. Scena Prima.

Enter Bullingbrooke, Yorke, Northumberland, Rosse, Percie, Willoughby, with Bushie and Greene Prisoners.

Bull. Bring forth these men:
Bushie and *Greene*, I will not vex your soules,
(Since presently your soules must part your bodies)
With too much vrging your pernitious liues,
For 'twere no Charitie: yet to wash your blood
From off my hands, here in the view of men,
I will vnfold some causes of your deaths.
You haue mis-led a Prince, a Royall King,
A happie Gentleman in Blood, and Lineaments,
By you vnhappied, and disfigur'd cleane:
You haue in manner with your sinfull houres
Made a Diuorce betwixt his Queene and him,
Broke the possession of a Royall Bed,
And stayn'd the beautie of a faire Queenes Cheekes,
With teares drawn fro her eyes, with your foule wrongs.
My selfe a Prince, by fortune of my birth,
Neere to the King in blood, and neere in loue,
Till you did make him mis-interprete me,
Haue stoopt my neck vnder your iniuries,
And sigh'd my English breath in forraine Clouds,
Eating the bitter bread of banishment;
While you haue fed vpon my Seignories,
Dis-park'd my Parkes, and fell'd my Forrest Woods;
From mine owne Windowes torne my Household Coat,
Raz'd out my Impresse, leauing me no signe,
Saue mens opinions, and my liuing blood,
To shew the World I am a Gentleman.
This, and much more, much more then twice all this,
Condemnes you to the death: see them deliuered ouer
To execution, and the hand of death.
Bushie. More welcome is the stroake of death to me,
Then *Bullingbrooke* to England.
Greene. My comfort is, that Heauen will take our soules,
And plague Iniustice with the paines of Hell.
Bull. My Lord *Northumberland*, see them dispatch'd:
Vnckle, you say the Queene is at your House,
For Heauens sake fairely let her be entreated,
Tell her I send to her my kind commends;
Take speciall care my Greetings be deliuer'd.
York. A Gentleman of mine I haue dispatch'd
With Letters of your loue, to her at large.
Bull. Thankes gentle Vnckle: come Lords away,
To fight with *Glendoure*, and his Complices;
A while to worke, and after holliday.
Exeunt.

Scœna

Scena Secunda.

Drums: Flouriſh, and Colours.

Enter Richard, Aumerle, Carlile, and Souldiers.

Rich. Barkloughly Caſtle call you this at hand?
Au. Yea, my Lord: how brooks your Grace the ayre,
After your late toſſing on the breaking Seas?
Rich. Needs muſt I like it well: I weepe for ioy
To ſtand vpon my Kingdome once againe.
Deere Earth, I doe ſalute thee with my hand,
Though Rebels wound thee with their Horſes hoofes:
As a long parted Mother with her Child,
Playes fondly with her teares, and ſmiles in meeting;
So weeping, ſmiling, greet I thee my Earth,
And doe thee fauor with my Royall hands.
Feed not thy Soueraignes Foe, my gentle Earth,
Nor with thy Sweetes, comfort his rauenous ſence:
But let thy Spiders, that ſuck vp thy Venome,
And heauie-gated Toades lye in their way,
Doing annoyance to the trecherous feete,
Which with vſurping ſteps doe trample thee.
Yeeld ſtinging Nettles to mine Enemies;
And when they from thy Boſome pluck a Flower
Guard it I prethee with a lurking Adder,
Whoſe double tongue may with a mortall touch
Throw death vpon thy Soueraignes Enemies.
Mock not my ſenceleſſe Coniuration, Lords;
This Earth ſhall haue a feeling, and theſe Stones
Proue armed Souldiers, ere her Natiue King
Shall falter vnder foule Rebellious Armes.
Car. Feare not my Lord, that Power that made you King
Hath power to keepe you King, in ſpight of all.
Aum. He meanes, my Lord, that we are too remiſſe,
Whileſt *Bullingbrooke* through our ſecuritie,
Growes ſtrong and great, in ſubſtance and in friends.
Rich. Diſcomfortable Couſin, know'ſt thou not,
That when the ſearching Eye of Heauen is hid
Behind the Globe, that lights the lower World,
Then Theeues and Robbers raunge abroad vnſeene,
In Murthers and in Out-rage bloody here:
But when from vnder this Terreſtriall Ball
He fires the prowd tops of the Eaſterne Pines,
And darts his Lightning through eu'ry guiltie hole,
Then Murthers, Treaſons, and deteſted ſinnes
(The Cloake of Night being pluckt from off their backs)
Stand bare and naked, trembling at themſelues.
So when this Theefe, this Traytor *Bullingbrooke*,
Who all this while hath reuell'd in the Night,
Shall ſee vs riſing in our Throne, the Eaſt,
His Treaſons will ſit bluſhing in his face,
Not able to endure the ſight of Day;
But ſelfe-affrighted, tremble at his ſinne.
Not all the Water in the rough rude Sea
Can waſh the Balme from an anoynted King;
The breath of worldly men cannot depoſe
The Deputie elected by the Lord:
For euery man that *Bullingbrooke* hath preſt,
To lift ſhrewd Steele againſt our Golden Crowne,
Heauen for his *Richard* hath in heauenly pay
A glorious Angell: then if Angels fight,
Weake men muſt fall, for Heauen ſtill guards the right.

Enter Saliſbury.

Welcome my Lord, how farre off lyes your Power?
Saliſb. Nor neere, nor farther off, my gracious Lord,
Then this weake arme; diſcomfort guides my tongue,
And bids me ſpeake of nothing but deſpaire:
One day too late, I feare (my Noble Lord)
Hath clouded all thy happie dayes on Earth!
Oh call backe Yeſterday, bid Time returne,
And thou ſhalt haue twelue thouſand fighting men:
To day, to day, vnhappie day too late
Orethrowes thy Ioyes, Friends, Fortune, and thy State;
For all the Welchmen hearing thou wert dead,
Are gone to *Bullingbrooke*, diſperſt, and fled.
Aum. Comfort my Liege, why lookes your Grace ſo pale?
Rich. But now the blood of twentie thouſand men
Did triumph in my face, and they are fled,
And till ſo much blood thither come againe,
Haue I not reaſon to looke pale, and dead?
All Soules that will be ſafe, flye from my ſide,
For Time hath ſet a blot vpon my pride.
Aum. Comfort my Liege, remember who you are.
Rich. I had forgot my ſelfe. Am I not King?
Awake thou ſluggard Maieſtie, thou ſleepeſt:
Is not the Kings Name fortie thouſand Names?
Arme, arme my Name: a punie ſubiect ſtrikes
At thy great glory. Looke not to the ground,
Ye Fauorites of a King: are wee not high?
High be our thoughts: I know my Vnckle *Yorke*
Hath Power enough to ſerue our turne.
But who comes here? *Enter Scroope.*
Scroope. More health and happineſſe betide my Liege,
Then can my care-tun'd tongue deliuer him.
Rich. Mine eare is open, and my heart prepar'd:
The worſt is worldly loſſe, thou canſt vnfold:
Say, Is my Kingdome loſt? why 'twas my Care:
And what loſſe is it to be rid of Care?
Striues *Bullingbrooke* to be as Great as wee?
Greater he ſhall not be: If hee ſerue God,
Wee'l ſerue him too, and be his Fellow ſo.
Reuolt our Subiects? That we cannot mend,
They breake their Faith to God, as well as vs:
Cry Woe, Deſtruction, Ruine, Loſſe, Decay,
The worſt is Death, and Death will haue his day.
Scroope. Glad am I, that your Highneſſe is ſo arm'd
To beare the tidings of Calamitie.
Like an vnſeaſonable ſtormie day,
Which make the Siluer Riuers drowne their Shores,
As if the World were all diſſolu'd to teares;
So high, aboue his Limits, ſwells the Rage
Of *Bullingbrooke*, coueting your fearefull Land
With hard bright Steele, and hearts harder then Steele:
White Beares haue arm'd their thin and haireleſſe Scalps
Againſt thy Maieſtie, and Boyes with Womens Voyces,
Striue to ſpeake bigge, and clap their female ioints
In ſtiffe vnwieldie Armes: againſt thy Crowne
Thy very Beadſ-men learne to bend their Bowes
Of double fatall Eugh: againſt thy State
Yea Diſtaffe-Women manage ruſtie Bills:
Againſt thy Seat both young and old rebell,
And all goes worſe then I haue power to tell.
Rich. Too well too well thou tell'ſt a Tale ſo ill.
Where is the Earle of Wiltſhire? where is *Baget*?
What is become of *Buſhie*? where is *Greene*?

That

That they haue let the dangerous Enemie
Measure our Confines with such peacefull steps?
If we preuaile, their heads shall pay for it.
I warrant they haue made peace with *Bullingbrooke.*
Scroope. Peace haue they made with him indeede (my Lord.)
Rich. Oh Villains, Vipers, damn'd without redemption,
Dogges, easily woon to fawne on any man,
Snakes in my heart blood warm'd, that sting my heart,
Three Iudasses, each one thrice worse then *Iudas,*
Would they make peace? terrible Hell make warre
Vpon their spotted Soules for this Offence.
Scroope. Sweet Loue (I see) changing his propertie,
Turnes to the sowrest, and most deadly hate:
Againe vncurse their Soules; their peace is made
With Heads, and not with Hands: those whom you curse
Haue felt the worst of Deaths destroying hand,
And lye full low, grau'd in the hollow ground.
Aum. Is *Bushie, Greene,* and the Earle of Wiltshire dead?
Scroope. Yea all of them at Bristow lost their heads.
Aum. Where is the Duke my Father with his Power?
Rich. No matter where; of comfort no man speake:
Let's talke of Graues, of Wormes, and Epitaphs,
Make Dust our Paper, and with Raynie eyes
Write Sorrow on the Bosome of the Earth.
Let's chuse Executors, and talke of Wills:
And yet not so; for what can we bequeath,
Saue our deposed bodies to the ground?
Our Lands, our Liues, and all are *Bullingbrookes,*
And nothing can we call our owne, but Death,
And that small Modell of the barren Earth,
Which serues as Paste, and Couer to our Bones:
For Heauens sake let vs sit vpon the ground,
And tell sad stories of the death of Kings:
How some haue been depos'd, some slaine in warre,
Some haunted by the Ghosts they haue depos'd,
Some poyson'd by their Wiues, some sleeping kill'd,
All murther'd. For within the hollow Crowne
That rounds the mortall Temples of a King,
Keepes Death his Court, and there the Antique sits
Scoffing his State, and grinning at his Pompe,
Allowing him a breath, a little Scene,
To Monarchize, be fear'd, and kill with lookes,
Infusing him with selfe and vaine conceit,
As if this Flesh, which walls about our Life,
Were Brasse impregnable: and humor'd thus,
Comes at the last, and with a little Pinne
Bores through his Castle Walls, and farwell King.
Couer your heads, and mock not flesh and blood
With solemne Reuerence: throw away Respect,
Tradition, Forme, and Ceremonious dutie,
For you haue but mistooke me all this while:
I liue with Bread like you, feele Want,
Taste Griefe, need Friends: subiected thus,
How can you say to me, I am a King?
Carl. My Lord, wise men ne're waile their present woes,
But presently preuent the wayes to waile:
To feare the Foe, since feare oppresseth strength,
Giues in your weakenesse, strength vnto your Foe;
Feare, and be slaine, no worse can come to fight,
And fight and die, is death destroying death,
Where fearing, dying, payes death seruile breath.
Aum. My Father hath a Power, enquire of him,
And learne to make a Body of a Limbe.
Rich. Thou chid'st me well: proud *Bullingbrooke* I come
To change Blowes with thee, for our day of Doome:
This ague fit of feare is ouer-blowne,
An easie taske it is to winne our owne.
Say *Scroope,* where lyes our Vnckle with his Power?
Speake sweetly man, although thy lookes be sowre.
Scroope. Men iudge by the complexion of the Skie
The state and inclination of the day;
So may you by my dull and heauie Eye:
My Tongue hath but a heauier Tale to say:
I play the Torturer, by small and small
To lengthen out the worst, that must be spoken.
Your Vnckle *Yorke* is ioyn'd with *Bullingbrooke,*
And all your Northerne Castles yeelded vp,
And all your Southerne Gentlemen in Armes
Vpon his Faction.
Rich. Thou hast said enough.
Beshrew thee Cousin, which didst lead me forth
Of that sweet way I was in, to despaire:
What say you now? What comfort haue we now?
By Heauen Ile hate him euerlastingly,
That bids me be of comfort any more.
Goe to Flint Castle, there Ile pine away,
A King, Woes slaue, shall Kingly Woe obey:
That Power I haue, discharge, and let 'em goe
To eare the Land, that hath some hope to grow,
For I haue none. Let no man speake againe
To alter this, for counsaile is but vaine.
Aum. My Liege, one word.
Rich. He does me double wrong,
That wounds me with the flatteries of his tongue.
Discharge my followers: let them hence away,
From *Richards* Night, to *Bullingbrookes* faire Day.
Exeunt.

Scæna Tertia.

Enter with Drum and Colours, Bullingbrooke, Yorke, Northumberland, Attendants.

Bull. So that by this intelligence we learne
The Welchmen are dispers'd, and *Salisbury*
Is gone to meet the King, who lately landed
With some few priuate friends, vpon this Coast.
North. The newes is very faire and good, my Lord,
Richard, not farre from hence, hath hid his head.
York. It would beseeme the Lord Northumberland,
To say King *Richard:* alack the heauie day,
When such a sacred King should hide his head.
North. Your Grace mistakes: onely to be briefe,
Left I his Title out.
York. The time hath beene,
Would you haue beene so briefe with him, he would
Haue beene so briefe with you, to shorten you,
For taking so the Head, your whole heads length.
Bull. Mistake not (Vnckle) farther then you should.
York. Take not (good Cousin) farther then you should.
Least you mistake the Heauens are ore your head.
Bull. I know it (Vnckle) and oppose not my selfe
Against their will. But who comes here?
Enter Percie.
Welcome *Harry:* what, will not this Castle yeeld?
Per. The Castle royally is mann'd, my Lord,
Against thy entrance.
Bull. Roy-

Bull. Royally: Why, it containes no King?
Per. Yes (my good Lord)
It doth containe a King: King *Richard* lyes
Within the limits of yond Lime and Stone,
And with him, the Lord *Aumerle*, Lord *Salisbury*,
Sir *Stephen Scroope*, beſides a Clergie man
Of holy reuerence; who, I cannot learne.
North. Oh, belike it is the Biſhop of Carlile.
Bull. Noble Lord,
Goe to the rude Ribs of that ancient Caſtle,
Through Brazen Trumpet ſend the breath of Parle
Into his ruin'd Eares, and thus deliuer:
Henry Bullingbrooke vpon his knees doth kiſſe
King *Richards* hand, and ſends allegeance
And true faith of heart to his Royall Perſon: hither come
Euen at his feet, to lay my Armes and Power,
Prouided, that my Baniſhment repeal'd,
And Lands reſtor'd againe, be freely graunted:
If not, Ile vſe th'aduantage of my Power,
And lay the Summers duſt with ſhowers of blood,
Rayn'd from the wounds of ſlaughter'd Engliſhmen;
The which, how farre off from the mind of *Bullingbrooke*
It is, ſuch Crimſon Tempeſt ſhould bedrench
The freſh greene Lap of faire King *Richards* Land,
My ſtooping dutie tenderly ſhall ſhew.
Goe ſignifie as much, while here we march
Vpon the Graſſie Carpet of this Plaine:
Let's march without the noyſe of threatning Drum,
That from this Caſtles tatter'd Battlements
Our faire Appointments may be well peruſ'd.
Me thinkes King *Richard* and my ſelfe ſhould meet
With no leſſe terror then the Elements
Of Fire and Water, when their thundring ſmoake
At meeting teares the cloudie Cheekes of Heauen:
Be he the fire, Ile be the yeelding Water;
The Rage be his, while on the Earth I raine
My Waters on the Earth, and not on him.
March on, and marke King *Richard* how he lookes.

Parle without, and anſwere within: then a Flouriſh. Enter on the Walls, Richard, Carlile, Aumerle, Scroop, Salisbury.

See ſee, King *Richard* doth himſelfe appeare
As doth the bluſhing diſcontented Sunne,
From out the fierie Portall of the Eaſt,
When he perceiues the enuious Clouds are bent
To dimme his glory, and to ſtaine the tract
Of his bright paſſage to the Occident.
Yorke. Yet lookes he like a King: behold his Eye
(As bright as is the Eagles) lightens forth
Controlling Maieſtie: alack, alack, for woe,
That any harme ſhould ſtaine ſo faire a ſhew.
Rich. Wee are amaz'd, and thus long haue we ſtood
To watch the fearfull bending of thy knee,
Becauſe we thought our ſelfe thy lawfull King:
And if we be, how dare thy ioynts forget
To pay their awfull dutie to our preſence?
If we be not, ſhew vs the Hand of God,
That hath diſmiſ'd vs from our Stewardſhip,
For well wee know, no Hand of Blood and Bone
Can gripe the ſacred Handle of our Scepter,
Vnleſſe he doe prophane, ſteale, or vſurpe.
And though you thinke, that all, as you haue done,
Haue torne their Soules, by turning them from vs,
And we are barren, and bereft of Friends:
Yet know, my Maſter, God Omnipotent,
Is muſtring in his Clouds, on our behalfe,
Armies of Peſtilence, and they ſhall ſtrike
Your Children yet vnborne, and vnbegot,
That lift your Vaſſall Hands againſt my Head,
And threat the Glory of my precious Crowne.
Tell *Bullingbrooke*, for yond me thinkes he is,
That euery ſtride he makes vpon my Land,
Is dangerous Treaſon: He is come to ope
The purple Teſtament of bleeding Warre;
But ere the Crowne he lookes for, liue in peace,
Ten thouſand bloody crownes of Mothers Sonnes
Shall ill become the flower of Englands face,
Change the complexion of her Maid-pale Peace
To Scarlet Indignation, and bedew
Her Paſtors Graſſe with faithfull Engliſh Blood.
North. The King of Heauen forbid our Lord the King
Should ſo with ciuill and vnciuill Armes
Be ruſh'd vpon: Thy thrice-noble Couſin,
Harry Bullingbrooke, doth humbly kiſſe thy hand,
And by the Honorable Tombe he ſweares,
That ſtands vpon your Royall Grandſires Bones,
And by the Royalties of both your Bloods,
(Currents that ſpring from one moſt gracious Head)
And by the buried Hand of Warlike *Gaunt*,
And by the Worth and Honor of himſelfe,
Compriſing all that may be ſworne, or ſaid,
His comming hither hath no further ſcope,
Then for his Lineall Royalties, and to begge
Infranchiſement immediate on his knees:
Which on thy Royall partie graunted once,
His glittering Armes he will commend to'Ruſt,
His barbed Steedes to Stables, and his heart
To faithfull ſeruice of your Maieſtie:
This ſweares he, as he is a Prince, is iuſt,
And as I am a Gentleman, I credit him.
Rich. *Northumberland*, ſay thus: The King returnes,
His Noble Couſin is right welcome hither,
And all the number of his faire demands
Shall be accompliſh'd without contradiction:
With all the gracious vtterance thou haſt,
Speake to his gentle hearing kind commends.
We doe debaſe our ſelfe (Couſin) doe we not,
To looke ſo poorely, and to ſpeake ſo faire?
Shall we call back *Northumberland*, and ſend
Defiance to the Traytor, and ſo die?
Aum. No, good my Lord, let's fight with gentle words,
Till time lend friends, and friends their helpeful Swords.
Rich. Oh God, oh God, that ere this tongue of mine,
That layd the Sentence of dread Baniſhment
On yond prowd man, ſhould take it off againe
With words of ſooth: Oh that I were as great
As is my Griefe, or leſſer then my Name,
Or that I could forget what I haue beene,
Or not remember what I muſt be now:
Swell'ſt thou prowd heart? Ile giue thee ſcope to beat,
Since Foes haue ſcope to beat both thee and me.
Aum. *Northumberland* comes backe from *Bullingbrooke.*
Rich. What muſt the King doe now? muſt he ſubmit?
The King ſhall doe it: Muſt he be depos'd?
The King ſhall be contented: Muſt he looſe
The Name of King? o' Gods Name let it goe.
Ile giue my Iewels for a ſett of Beades,
My gorgeous Pallace, for a Hermitage,
My gay Apparrell, for an Almes-mans Gowne,
My figur'd Goblets, for a Diſh of Wood,
My Scepter, for a Palmers walking Staffe,
My

My Subiects, for a payre of carued Saints,
And my large Kingdome, for a little Graue,
A little little Graue, an obſcure Graue.
Or Ile be buryed in the Kings high-way,
Some way of common Trade, where Subiects feet
May howrely trample on their Soueraignes Head:
For on my heart they tread now, whileſt I liue;
And buryed once, why not vpon my Head?
Aumerle, thou weep'ſt (my tender-hearted Couſin)
Wee'le make foule Weather with deſpiſed Teares:
Our ſighes, and they, ſhall lodge the Summer Corne,
And make a Dearth in this reuolting Land.
Or ſhall we play the Wantons with our Woes,
And make ſome prettie Match, with ſhedding Teares?
As thus: to drop them ſtill vpon one place,
Till they haue fretted vs a payre of Graues,
Within the Earth: and therein lay'd there lyes
Two Kinſmen, digg'd their Graues with weeping Eyes?
Would not this ill, doe well? Well, well, I ſee
I talke but idly, and you mock at mee.
Moſt mightie Prince, my Lord *Northumberland*,
What ſayes King *Bullingbrooke*? Will his Maieſtie
Giue *Richard* leaue to liue, till *Richard* die?
You make a Legge, and *Bullingbrooke* ſayes I.
North. My Lord, in the baſe Court he doth attend
To ſpeake with you, may it pleaſe you to come downe.
Rich. Downe, downe I come, like gliſt'ring *Phaeton*,
Wanting the manage of vnruly Iades.
In the baſe Court? baſe Court, where Kings grow baſe,
To come at Traytors Calls, and doe them Grace.
In the baſe Court come down: down Court, down King,
For night-Owls ſhrike, where mouting Larks ſhould ſing.
Bull. What ſayes his Maieſtie?
North. Sorrow, and griefe of heart
Makes him ſpeake fondly, like a frantick man:
Yet he is come.
Bull. Stand all apart,
And ſhew faire dutie to his Maieſtie.
My gracious Lord.
Rich. Faire Couſin.
You debaſe your Princely Knee,
To make the baſe Earth prowd with kiſſing it.
Me rather had, my Heart might feele your Loue,
Then my vnpleas'd Eye ſee your Courteſie.
Vp Couſin, vp, your Heart is vp, I know,
Thus high at leaſt, although your Knee be low.
Bull. My gracious Lord, I come but for mine owne.
Rich. Your owne is yours, and I am yours, and all.
Bull. So farre be mine, my moſt redoubted Lord,
As my true ſeruice ſhall deſerue your loue.
Rich. Well you deſeru'd:
They well deſerue to haue,
That know the ſtrong'ſt, and ſureſt way to get.
Vnckle giue me your Hand: nay, drie your Eyes,
Teares ſhew their Loue, but want their Remedies.
Couſin, I am too young to be your Father,
Though you are old enough to be my Heire.
What you will haue, Ile giue, and willing to,
For doe we muſt, what force will haue vs doe.
Set on towards London.
Couſin, is it ſo?
Bull. Yea, my good Lord.
Rich. Then I muſt not ſay, no.
Flouriſh. Exeunt.

Scena Quarta.

Enter the Queene, and two Ladies.

Qu. What ſport ſhall we deuiſe here in this Garden,
To driue away the heauie thought of Care?
La. Madame, wee'le play at Bowles.
Qu. 'Twill make me thinke the World is full of Rubs,
And that my fortune runnes againſt the Byas.
La. Madame, wee'le Dance.
Qu My Legges can keepe no meaſure in Delight,
When my poore Heart no meaſure keepes in Griefe.
Therefore no Dancing (Girle) ſome other ſport.
La. Madame, wee'le tell Tales.
Qu. Of Sorrow, or of Griefe?
La. Of eyther, Madame.
Qu. Of neyther, Girle.
For if of Ioy, being altogether wanting,
It doth remember me the more of Sorrow:
Or if of Griefe, being altogether had,
It addes more Sorrow to my want of Ioy:
For what I haue, I need not to repeat;
And what I want, it bootes not to complaine.
La. Madame Ile ſing.
Qu. 'Tis well that thou haſt cauſe:
But thou ſhould'ſt pleaſe me better, would'ſt thou weepe.
La. I could weepe, Madame, would it doe you good.
Qu. And I could ſing, would weeping doe me good,
And neuer borrow any Teare of thee.
Enter a Gardiner, and two Seruants.
But ſtay, here comes the Gardiners,
Let's ſtep into the ſhadow of theſe Trees.
My wretchedneſſe, vnto a Rowe of Pinnes,
They'le talke of State; for euery one doth ſo,
Againſt a Change; Woe is fore-runne with Woe.
Gard. Goe binde thou vp yond dangling Apricocks,
Which like vnruly Children, make their Syre
Stoupe with oppreſſion of their prodigall weight:
Giue ſome ſupportance to the bending twigges.
Goe thou, and like an Executioner
Cut off the heads of too faſt growing ſprayes,
That looke too loftie in our Common-wealth:
All muſt be euen, in our Gouernment.
You thus imploy'd, I will goe root away
The noyſome Weedes, that without profit ſucke
The Soyles fertilitie from wholeſome flowers.
Ser. Why ſhould we, in the compaſſe of a Pale,
Keepe Law and Forme, and due Proportion,
Shewing as in a Modell our firme Eſtate?
When our Sea-walled Garden, the whole Land,
Is full of Weedes, her faireſt Flowers choakt vp,
Her Fruit-trees all vnpruin'd, her Hedges ruin'd,
Her Knots diſorder'd, and her wholeſome Hearbes
Swarming with Caterpillers.
Gard. Hold thy peace.
He that hath ſuffer'd this diſorder'd Spring,
Hath now himſelfe met with the Fall of Leafe.
The Weeds that his broad-ſpreading Leaues did ſhelter,
That ſeem'd, in eating him, to hold him vp,
Are pull'd vp, Root and all, by *Bullingbrooke*:
I meane, the Earle of Wiltſhire, *Buſhie*, *Greene*.

d *Ser.* What

Ser. What are they dead?
Gard. They are,
And *Bullingbrooke* hath seiz'd the wastefull King.
Oh, what pitty is it, that he had not so trim'd
And drest his Land, as we this Garden, at time of yeare,
And wound the Barke, the skin of our Fruit-trees,
Least being ouer-proud with Sap and Blood,
With too much riches it confound it selfe?
Had he done so, to great and growing men,
They might haue liu'd to beare, and he to taste
Their fruites of dutie. Superfluous branches
We lop away, that bearing boughes may liue:
Had he done so, himselfe had borne the Crowne,
Which waste and idle houres, hath quite thrown downe.
Ser. What thinke you the King shall be depos'd?
Gar. Deprest he is already, and depos'd
'Tis doubted he will be. Letters came last night
To a deere Friend of the Duke of Yorkes,
That tell blacke tydings.
Qu. Oh I am prest to death through want of speaking:
Thou old *Adams* likenesse, set to dresse this Garden:
How dares thy harsh rude tongue sound this vnpleasing newes
What Eue? what Serpent hath suggested thee,
To make a second fall of cursed man?
Why do'st thou say, King *Richard* is depos'd,
Dar'st thou, thou little better thing then earth,
Diuine his downfall? Say, where, when, and how
Cam'st thou by this ill-tydings? Speake thou wretch.
Gard. Pardon me Madam. Little ioy haue I
To breath these newes; yet what I say, is true;
King *Richard*, he is in the mighty hold
Of *Bullingbrooke*, their Fortunes both are weigh'd:
In your Lords Scale, is nothing but himselfe,
And some few Vanities, that make him light:
But in the Ballance of great *Bullingbrooke*,
Besides himselfe, are all the English Peeres,
And with that oddes he weighes King *Richard* downe.
Poste you to London, and you'l finde it so,
I speake no more, then euery one doth know.
Qu. Nimble mischance, that art so light of foote,
Doth not thy Embassage belong to me?
And am I last that knowes it? Oh thou think'st
To serue me last, that I may longest keepe
Thy sorrow in my breast. Come Ladies goe,
To meet at London, Londons King in woe.
What was I borne to this: that my sad looke,
Should grace the Triumph of great *Bullingbrooke*.
Gard'ner, for telling me this newes of woe,
I would the Plants thou graft'st, may neuer grow. *Exit.*
G. Poore Queen, so that thy State might be no worse,
I would my skill were subiect to thy curse:
Heere did she drop a teare, heere in this place
Ile set a Banke of Rew, sowre Herbe of Grace:
Rue, eu'n for ruth, heere shortly shall be seene,
In the remembrance of a Weeping Queene. *Exit.*

Actus Quartus. Scœna Prima.

Enter as to the Parliament, Bullingbrooke, Aumerle, Northumberland, Percie, Fitz-Water, Surrey, Carlile, Abbot of Westminster. Herauld, Officers, and Bagot.

Bullingbrooke. Call forth *Bagot*.
Now *Bagot*, freely speake thy minde,
What thou do'st know of Noble Glousters death:
Who wrought it with the King, and who perform'd
The bloody Office of his Timelesse end.
Bag. Then set before my face, the Lord *Aumerle*.
Bul. Cosin, stand forth, and looke vpon that man.
Bag. My Lord *Aumerle*, I know your daring tongue
Scornes to vnsay, what it hath once deliuer'd.
In that dead time, when Glousters death was plotted,
I heard you say, Is not my arme of length,
That reacheth from the restfull English Court
As farre as Callis, to my Vnkles head.
Amongst much other talke, that very time,
I heard you say, that you had rather refuse
The offer of an hundred thousand Crownes,
Then *Bullingbrookes* returne to England; adding withall,
How blest this Land would be, in this your Cosins death.
Aum. Princes, and Noble Lords:
What answer shall I make to this base man?
Shall I so much dishonor my faire Starres,
On equall termes to giue him chasticement?
Either I must, or haue mine honor soyl'd
With th'Attaindor of his sland'rous Lippes.
There is my Gage, the manuall Seale of death
That markes thee out for Hell. Thou lyest,
And will maintaine what thou hast said, is false,
In thy heart blood, though being all too base
To staine the temper of my Knightly sword.
Bul. *Bagot* forbeare, thou shalt not take it vp.
Aum. Excepting one, I would he were the best
In all this presence, that hath mou'd me so.
Fitz. If that thy valour stand on sympathize:
There is my Gage, *Aumerle*, in Gage to thine:
By that faire Sunne, that shewes me where thou stand'st,
I heard thee say (and vauntingly thou spak'st it)
That thou wer't cause of Noble Glousters death.
If thou deniest it, twenty times thou lyest,
And I will turne thy falshood to thy hart,
Where it was forged with my Rapiers point.
Aum. Thou dar'st not (Coward) liue to see the day.
Fitz. Now by my Soule, I would it were this houre.
Aum. *Fitzwater* thou art damn'd to hell for this.
Per. *Aumerle*, thou lye'st: his Honor is as true
In this Appeale, as thou art all vniust:
And that thou art so, there I throw my Gage
To proue it on thee, to th'extreamest point
Of mortall breathing. Seize it, if thou dar'st.
Aum. And if I do not, may my hands rot off,
And neuer brandish more reuengefull Steele,
Ouer the glittering Helmet of my Foe.
Surrey. My Lord *Fitz-water*:
I do remember well, the very time
Aumerle, and you did talke.
Fitz. My Lord,
'Tis very true: You were in presence then,
And you can witnesse with me, this is true.
Surrey. As false, by heauen,
As Heauen it selfe is true.
Fitz. Surrey, thou Lyest.
Surrey. Dishonourable Boy;
That Lye, shall lie so heauy on my Sword,
That it shall render Vengeance, and Reuenge,
Till thou the Lye-giuer, and that Lye, doe lye
In earth as quiet, as thy Fathers Scull.
In proofe whereof, there is mine Honors pawne,
Engage it to the Triall, if thou dar'st.
Fitz.

Fitzw. How fondly do'st thou spurre a forward Horse?
If I dare eate, or drinke, or breathe, or liue,
I dare meete *Surrey* in a Wildernesse,
And spit vpon him, whilest I say he Lyes,
And Lyes, and Lyes: there is my Bond of Faith,
To tye thee to my strong Correction.
As I intend to thriue in this new World,
Aumerle is guiltie of my true Appeale.
Besides, I heard the banish'd *Norfolke* say,
That thou *Aumerle* didst send two of thy men,
To execute the Noble Duke at Callis.
Aum. Some honest Christian trust me with a Gage,
That *Norfolke* lyes: here doe I throw downe this,
If he may be repeal'd, to trie his Honor.
Bull. These differences shall all rest vnder Gage,
Till *Norfolke* be repeal'd: repeal'd he shall be;
And (though mine Enemie) restor'd againe
To all his Lands and Seignories: when hee's return'd,
Against *Aumerle* we will enforce his Tryall.
Carl. That honorable day shall ne're be seene.
Many a time hath banish'd *Norfolke* fought
For Jesu Christ, in glorious Christian field
Streaming the Ensigne of the Christian Crosse,
Against black Pagans, Turkes, and Saracens:
And toyl'd with workes of Warre, retyr'd himselfe
To Italy, and there at Venice gaue
His Body to that pleasant Countries Earth,
And his pure Soule vnto his Captaine Christ,
Vnder whose Colours he had fought so long.
Bull. Why Bishop, is *Norfolke* dead?
Carl. As sure as I liue, my Lord.
Bull. Sweet peace conduct his sweet Soule
To the Bosome of good old *Abraham.*
Lords Appealants your differẽces shal all rest vnder gage,
Till we assigne you to your dayes of Tryall.

Enter Yorke.

Yorke. Great Duke of Lancaster, I come to thee
From plume-pluckt *Richard*, who with willing Soule
Adopts thee Heire, and his high Scepter yeelds
To the possession of thy Royall Hand.
Ascend his Throne, descending now from him,
And long liue *Henry*, of that Name the Fourth.
Bull. In Gods Name, Ile ascend the Regall Throne.
Carl. Mary, Heauen forbid.
Worst in this Royall Presence may I speake,
Yet best beseeming me to speake the truth.
Would God, that any in this Noble Presence
Were enough Noble, to be vpright Iudge
Of Noble *Richard*: then true Noblenesse would
Learne him forbearance from so foule a Wrong.
What Subiect can giue Sentence on his King?
And who sits here, that is not *Richards* Subiect?
Theeues are not iudg'd, but they are by to heare,
Although apparant guilt be seene in them:
And shall the figure of Gods Maiestie,
His Captaine, Steward, Deputie elect,
Anoynted, Crown'd, planted many yeeres,
Be iudg'd by subiect, and inferior breathe,
And he himselfe not present? Oh, forbid it, God,
That in a Christian Climate, Soules refin'de
Should shew so heynous, black, obscene a deed.
I speake to Subiects, and a Subiect speakes,
Stirr'd vp by Heauen, thus boldly for his King.
My Lord of Hereford here, whom you call King,
Is a foule Traytor to prowd *Herefords* King.
And if you Crowne him, let me prophecie,
The blood of English shall manure the ground,
And future Ages groane for his foule Act.
Peace shall goe sleepe with Turkes and Infidels,
And in this Seat of Peace, tumultuous Warres
Shall Kinne with Kinne, and Kinde with Kinde confound.
Disorder, Horror, Feare, and Mutinie
Shall here inhabite, and this Land be call'd
The field of Golgotha, and dead mens Sculls.
Oh, if you reare this House, against this House
It will the wofullest Diuision proue,
That euer fell vpon this cursed Earth.
Preuent it, resist it, and let it not be so,
Least Child, Childs Children cry against you, Woe.
North. Well haue you argu'd Sir: and for your paines,
Of Capitall Treason we arrest you here.
My Lord of Westminster, be it your charge,
To keepe him safely, till his day of Tryall.
May it please you, Lords, to grant the Commons Suit?
Bull. Fetch hither *Richard*, that in common view
He may surrender: so we shall proceede
Without suspition.
Yorke. I will be his Conduct. *Exit.*
Bull. Lords, you that here are vnder our Arrest,
Procure your Sureties for your Dayes of Answer:
Little are we beholding to your Loue,
And little look'd for at your helping Hands.

Enter Richard and Yorke.

Rich. Alack, why am I sent for to a King,
Before I haue shooke off the Regall thoughts
Wherewith I reign'd? I hardly yet haue learn'd
To insinuate, flatter, bowe, and bend my Knee.
Giue Sorrow leaue a while, to tuture me
To this submission. Yet I well remember
The fauors of these men: were they not mine?
Did they not sometime cry, All hayle to me?
So *Iudas* did to Christ: but he in twelue,
Found truth in all, but one; I, in twelue thousand, none.
God saue the King: will no man say, Amen?
Am I both Priest, and Clarke? well then, Amen.
God saue the King, although I be not hee:
And yet Amen, if Heauen doe thinke him mee.
To doe what seruice, am I sent for hither?
Yorke. To doe that office of thine owne good will,
Which tyred Maiestie did make thee offer:
The Resignation of thy State and Crowne
To *Henry Bullingbrooke.*
Rich. Giue me the Crown. Here Cousin, seize ŷ Crown:
Here Cousin, on this side my Hand, on that side thine.
Now is this Golden Crowne like a deepe Well,
That owes two Buckets, filling one another,
The emptier euer dancing in the ayre,
The other downe, vnseene, and full of Water:
That Bucket downe, and full of Teares am I,
Drinking my Griefes, whil'st you mount vp on high.
Bull. I thought you had been willing to resigne.
Rich My Crowne I am, but still my Griefes are mine:
You may my Glories and my State depose,
But not my Griefes; still am I King of those.
Bull Part of your Cares you giue me with your Crowne.
Rich. Your Cares set vp, do not pluck my Cares downe.
My Care, is losse of Care, by old Care done,
Your Care, is gaine of Care, by new Care wonne:
The Cares I giue, I haue, though giuen away,
They 'tend the Crowne, yet still with me they stay:
Bull. Are you contented to resigne the Crowne?

Rich. I, no; no, I: for I muſt nothing bee:
Therefore no, no, for I reſigne to thee.
Now, marke me how I will vndoe my ſelfe.
I giue this heauie Weight from off my Head,
And this vnwieldie Scepter from my Hand,
The pride of Kingly ſway from out my Heart.
With mine owne Teares I waſh away my Balme,
With mine owne Hands I giue away my Crowne,
With mine owne Tongue denie my Sacred State,
With mine owne Breath releaſe all dutious Oathes,
All Pompe and Maieſtie I doe forſweare:
My Manors, Rents, Reuenues, I forgoe;
My Acts, Decrees, and Statutes I denie:
God pardon all Oathes that are broke to mee,
God keepe all Vowes vnbroke are made to thee.
Make me, that nothing haue, with nothing grieu'd,
And thou with all pleas'd, that haſt all atchieu'd.
Long may'ſt thou liue in *Richards* Seat to ſit,
And ſoone lye *Richard* in an Earthie Pit.
God ſaue King *Henry*, vn-King'd *Richard* ſayes,
And ſend him many yeeres of Sunne-ſhine dayes.
What more remaines?
North. No more: but that you reade
Theſe Accuſations, and theſe grieuous Crymes,
Committed by your Perſon, and your followers,
Againſt the State, and Profit of this Land:
That by confeſſing them, the Soules of men
May deeme, that you are worthily depos'd.
Rich. Muſt I doe ſo? and muſt I rauell out
My weau'd-vp follyes? Gentle *Northumberland*,
If thy Offences were vpon Record,
Would it not ſhame thee, in ſo faire a troupe,
To reade a Lecture of them? If thou would'ſt,
There ſhould'ſt thou finde one heynous Article,
Contayning the depoſing of a King,
And cracking the ſtrong Warrant of an Oath,
Mark'd with a Blot, damn'd in the Booke of Heauen.
Nay, all of you, that ſtand and looke vpon me,
Whil'ſt that my wretchedneſſe doth bait my ſelfe,
Though ſome of you, with *Pilate*, waſh your hands,
Shewing an outward pittie: yet you *Pilates*
Haue here deliuer'd me to my ſowre Croſſe,
And Water cannot waſh away your ſinne.
North. My Lord diſpatch, reade o're theſe Articles.
Rich. Mine Eyes are full of Teares, I cannot ſee:
And yet ſalt-Water blindes them not ſo much,
But they can ſee a ſort of Traytors here.
Nay, if I turne mine Eyes vpon my ſelfe,
I finde my ſelfe a Traytor with the reſt:
For I haue giuen here my Soules conſent,
T'vndeck the pompous Body of a King;
Made Glory baſe; a Soueraigntie, a Slaue;
Prowd Maieſtie, a Subiect; State, a Peſant.
North. My Lord.
Rich. No Lord of thine, thou haught-inſulting man;
No, nor no mans Lord: I haue no Name, no Title;
No, not that Name was giuen me at the Font,
But 'tis vſurpt: alack the heauie day,
That I haue worne ſo many Winters out,
And know not now, what Name to call my ſelfe.
Oh, that I were a Mockerie, King of Snow,
Standing before the Sunne of *Bullingbrooke*,
To melt my ſelfe away in Water-drops.
Good King, great King, and yet not greatly good,
And if my word be Sterling yet in England,
Let it command a Mirror hither ſtraight,
That it may ſhew me what a Face I haue,
Since it is Bankrupt of his Maieſtie.
Bull. Goe ſome of you, and fetch a Looking-Glaſſe.
North. Read o're this Paper, while ẏ Glaſſe doth come.
Rich. Fiend, thou torments me, ere I come to Hell.
Bull. Vrge it no more, my Lord *Northumberland*.
North. The Commons will not then be ſatisfy'd.
Rich. They ſhall be ſatisfy'd: Ile reade enough,
When I doe ſee the very Booke indeede,
Where all my ſinnes are writ, and that's my ſelfe.
Enter one with a Glaſſe.
Giue me that Glaſſe, and therein will I reade.
No deeper wrinckles yet? hath Sorrow ſtrucke
So many Blowes vpon this Face of mine,
And made no deeper Wounds? Oh flatt'ring Glaſſe,
Like to my followers in proſperitie,
Thou do'ſt beguile me. Was this Face, the Face
That euery day, vnder his Houſe-hold Roofe,
Did keepe ten thouſand men? Was this the Face,
That like the Sunne, did make beholders winke?
Is this the Face, which fac'd ſo many follyes,
That was at laſt out-fac'd by *Bullingbrooke*?
A brittle Glory ſhineth in this Face,
As brittle as the Glory, is the Face,
For there it is, crackt in an hundred ſhiuers.
Marke ſilent King, the Morall of this ſport,
How ſoone my Sorrow hath deſtroy'd my Face.
Bull. The ſhadow of your Sorrow hath deſtroy'd
The ſhadow of your Face.
Rich. Say that againe.
The ſhadow of my Sorrow: ha, let's ſee,
'Tis very true, my Griefe lyes all within,
And theſe externall manner of Laments,
Are meerely ſhadowes, to the vnſeene Griefe,
That ſwells with ſilence in the tortur'd Soule.
There lyes the ſubſtance: and I thanke thee King
For thy great bountie, that not onely giu'ſt
Me cauſe to wayle, but teacheſt me the way
How to lament the cauſe. Ile begge one Boone,
And then be gone, and trouble you no more.
Shall I obtaine it?
Bull. Name it, faire Couſin.
Rich. Faire Couſin? I am greater then a King:
For when I was a King, my flatterers
Were then but ſubiects; being now a ſubiect,
I haue a King here to my flatterer:
Being ſo great, I haue no neede to begge.
Bull. Yet aske.
Rich. And ſhall I haue?
Bull. You ſhall.
Rich. Then giue me leaue to goe.
Bull. Whither?
Rich. Whither you will, ſo I were from your ſights.
Bull. Goe ſome of you, conuey him to the Tower.
Rich. Oh good: conuey: Conueyers are you all,
That riſe thus nimbly by a true Kings fall.
Bull. On Wedneſday next, we ſolemnly ſet downe
Our Coronation: Lords, prepare your ſelues. *Exeunt.*
Abbot. A wofull Pageant haue we here beheld.
Carl. The Woes to come, the Children yet vnborne,
Shall feele this day as ſharpe to them as Thorne.
Aum. You holy Clergie-men, is there no Plot
To rid the Realme of this pernicious Blot.
Abbot. Before I freely ſpeake my minde herein,
You ſhall not onely take the Sacrament,
To bury mine intents, but alſo to effect

What

What euer I ſhall happen to deuiſe.
I ſee your Browes are full of Diſcontent,
Your Heart of Sorrow, and your Eyes of Teares.
Come home with me to Supper, Ile lay a Plot
Shall ſhew vs all a merry day. *Exeunt.*

Actus Quintus. Scena Prima.

Enter Queene, and Ladies.

Qu. This way the King will come: this is the way
To *Iulius Cæſars* ill-erected Tower:
To whoſe flint Boſome, my condemned Lord
Is doom'd a Priſoner, by prowd *Bullingbrooke.*
Here let vs reſt, if this rebellious Earth
Haue any reſting for her true Kings Queene.

Enter Richard, and Guard.

But ſoft, but ſee, or rather doe not ſee,
My faire Roſe wither: yet looke vp; behold,
That you in pittie may diſſolue to dew,
And waſh him freſh againe with true-loue Teares.
Ah thou, the Modell where old Troy did ſtand,
Thou Mappe of Honor, thou King *Richards* Tombe,
And not King *Richard*: thou moſt beauteous Inne,
Why ſhould hard-fauor'd Griefe be lodg'd in thee,
When Triumph is become an Ale-houſe Gueſt.
Rich. Ioyne not with griefe, faire Woman, do not ſo,
To make my end too ſudden: learne good Soule,
To thinke our former State a happie Dreame,
From which awak'd, the truth of what we are,
Shewes vs but this. I am ſworne Brother (Sweet)
To grim Neceſſitie; and hee and I
Will keepe a League till Death. High thee to France,
And Cloyſter thee in ſome Religious Houſe:
Our holy liues muſt winne a new Worlds Crowne,
Which our prophane houres here haue ſtricken downe.
Qu. What, is my *Richard* both in ſhape and minde
Transform'd, and weaken'd? Hath *Bullingbrooke*
Depos'd thine Intellect? hath he beene in thy Heart?
The Lyon dying, thruſteth forth his Paw,
And wounds the Earth, if nothing elſe, with rage
To be o're-powr'd: and wilt thou, Pupill-like,
Take thy Correction mildly, kiſſe the Rodde,
And fawne on Rage with baſe Humilitie,
Which art a Lyon, and a King of Beaſts?
Rich. A King of Beaſts indeed: if aught but Beaſts,
I had beene ſtill a happy King of Men.
Good (ſometime Queene) prepare thee hence for France:
Thinke I am dead, and that euen here thou tak'ſt,
As from my Death-bed, my laſt liuing leaue.
In Winters tedious Nights ſit by the fire
With good old folkes, and let them tell thee Tales
Of wofull Ages, long agoe betide:
And ere thou bid good-night, to quit their griefe,
Tell thou the lamentable fall of me,
And ſend the hearers weeping to their Beds:
For why? the ſenceleſſe Brands will ſympathize
The heauie accent of thy mouing Tongue,
And in compaſſion, weepe the fire out:
And ſome will mourne in aſhes, ſome coale-black,
For the depoſing of a rightfull King.

Enter Northumberland.

North. My Lord, the mind of *Bullingbrooke* is chang'd.
You muſt to Pomfret, not vnto the Tower.
And Madame, there is order ta'ne for you:
With all ſwift ſpeed, you muſt away to France.
Rich. Northumberland, thou Ladder wherewithall
The mounting *Bullingbrooke* aſcends my Throne,
The time ſhall not be many houres of age,
More then it is, ere foule ſinne, gathering head,
Shall breake into corruption: thou ſhalt thinke,
Though he diuide the Realme, and giue thee halfe,
It is too little, helping him to all:
He ſhall thinke, that thou which know'ſt the way
To plant vnrightfull Kings, wilt know againe,
Being ne're ſo little vrg'd another way,
To pluck him headlong from the vſurped Throne.
The Loue of wicked friends conuerts to Feare;
That Feare, to Hate; and Hate turnes one, or both,
To worthie Danger, and deſerued Death.
North. My guilt be on my Head, and there an end:
Take leaue, and part, for you muſt part forthwith.
Rich. Doubly diuorc'd? (bad men) ye violate
A two-fold Marriage; 'twixt my Crowne, and me,
And then betwixt me, and my marryed Wife.
Let me vn-kiſſe the Oath 'twixt thee, and me;
And yet not ſo, for with a Kiſſe 'twas made.
Part vs, *Northumberland*: I, towards the North,
Where ſhiuering Cold and Sickneſſe pines the Clyme:
My Queene to France: from whence, ſet forth in pompe,
She came adorned hither like ſweet May;
Sent back like Hollowmas, or ſhort'ſt of day.
Qu. And muſt we be diuided? muſt we part?
Rich. I, hand from hand (my Loue) and heart fro heart.
Qu. Baniſh vs both, and ſend the King with me.
North. That were ſome Loue, but little Pollicy.
Qu. Then whither he goes, thither let me goe.
Rich. So two together weeping, make one Woe.
Weepe thou for me in France; I, for thee heere:
Better farre off, then neere, be ne're the neere.
Goe, count thy Way with Sighes; I, mine with Groanes.
Qu. So longeſt Way ſhall haue the longeſt Moanes.
Rich. Twice for one ſtep Ile groane, ẏ Way being ſhort,
And peece the Way out with a heauie heart.
Come, come, in wooing Sorrow let's be briefe,
Since wedding it, there is ſuch length in Griefe:
One Kiſſe ſhall ſtop our mouthes, and dumbely part;
Thus giue I mine, and thus take I thy heart.
Qu. Giue me mine owne againe: 'twere no good part
To take on me to keepe, and kill thy heart.
So, now I haue mine owne againe, be gone,
That I may ſtriue to kill it with a groane.
Rich. We make Woe wanton with this fond delay:
Once more adieu; the reſt, let Sorrow ſay. *Exeunt.*

Scœna Secunda.

Enter Yorke, and his Ducheſſe.

Duch. My Lord, you told me you would tell the reſt,
When weeping made you breake the ſtory off,
Of our two Couſins comming into London.
Yorke. Where did I leaue?
Duch. At that ſad ſtoppe, my Lord,
Where rude miſ-gouern'd hands, from Windowes tops
Threw duſt and rubbiſh on King *Richards* head.

d 3 *Yorke.* Then

Yorke. Then, as I said, the Duke, great *Bullingbrooke*,
Mounted vpon a hot and fierie Steed,
Which his aspiring Rider seem'd to know,
With slow, but stately pace, kept on his course:
While all tongues cride, God saue thee *Bullingbrooke*.
You would haue thought the very windowes spake,
So many greedy lookes of yong and old,
Through Casements darted their desiring eyes
Vpon his visage: and that all the walles,
With painted Imagery had said at once,
Iesu preserue thee, welcom *Bullingbrooke*.
Whil'st he, from one side to the other turning,
Bare-headed, lower then his proud Steeds necke,
Bespake them thus: I thanke you Countrimen:
And thus still doing, thus he past along.
Dutch. Alas poore *Richard*, where rides he the whilst?
Yorke. As in a Theater, the eyes of men
After a well grac'd Actor leaues the Stage,
Are idlely bent on him that enters next,
Thinking his prattle to be tedious:
Euen so, or with much more contempt, mens eyes
Did scowle on *Richard*: no man cride, God saue him:
No ioyfull tongue gaue him his welcome home,
But dust was throwne vpon his Sacred head,
Which with such gentle sorrow he shooke off,
His face still combating with teares and smiles
(The badges of his greefe and patience)
That had not God (for some strong purpose) steel'd
The hearts of men, they must perforce haue melted,
And Barbarisme it selfe haue pittied him.
But heauen hath a hand in these euents,
To whose high will we bound our calme contents.
To *Bullingbrooke*, are we sworne Subiects now,
Whose State, and Honor, I for aye allow.

Enter Aumerle.

Dut. Heere comes my sonne *Aumerle*.
Yor. *Aumerle* that was,
But that is lost, for being *Richards* Friend.
And Madam, you must call him *Rutland* now:
I am in Parliament pledge for his truth,
And lasting fealtie to the new-made King.
Dut. Welcome my sonne: who are the Violets now,
That strew the greene lap of the new-come Spring?
Aum. Madam, I know not, nor I greatly care not,
God knowes, I had as liefe be none, as one.
Yorke. Well, beare you well in this new-spring of time
Least you be cropt before you come to prime.
What newes from Oxford? Hold those Iusts & Triumphs?
Aum. For ought I know my Lord they do.
Yorke. You will be there I know.
Aum. If God preuent not, I purpose so.
Yor. What Seale is that that hangs without thy bosom?
Yea, look'st thou pale? Let me see the Writing.
Aum. My Lord, 'tis nothing.
Yorke. No matter then who sees it,
I will be satisfied, let me see the Writing.
Aum. I do beseech your Grace to pardon me,
It is a matter of small consequence,
Which for some reasons I would not haue seene.
Yorke. Which for some reasons sir, I meane to see:
I feare, I feare.
Dut. What should you feare?
'Tis nothing but some bond, that he is enter'd into
For gay apparrell against the Triumph.
Yorke. Bound to himselfe? What doth he with a Bond
That he is bound to? Wife, thou art a foole.
Boy, let me see the Writing.
Aum. I do beseech you pardon me, I may not shew it
Yor. I will be satisfied: let me see it I say. *Snatches it*
Treason, foule Treason, Villaine, Traitor, Slaue.
Dut. What's the matter, my Lord?
Yorke. Hoa, who's within there? Saddle my horse.
Heauen for his mercy: what treachery is heere?
Dut. Why, what is't my Lord?
Yorke. Giue me my boots, I say: Saddle my horse:
Now by my Honor, my life, my troth,
I will appeach the Villaine.
Dut. What is the matter?
Yorke. Peace foolish Woman.
Dut. I will not peace. What is the matter Sonne?
Aum. Good Mother be content, it is no more
Then my poore life must answer.
Dut. Thy life answer?

Enter Seruant with Boots.

Yor. Bring me my Boots, I will vnto the King.
Dut. Strike him *Aumerle*. Poore boy, y^t art amaz'd,
Hence Villaine, neuer more come in my sight.
Yor. Giue me my Boots, I say.
Dut. Why Yorke, what wilt thou do?
Wilt thou not hide the Trespasse of thine owne?
Haue we more Sonnes? Or are we like to haue?
Is not my teeming date drunke vp with time?
And wilt thou plucke my faire Sonne from mine Age,
And rob me of a happy Mothers name?
Is he not like thee? Is he not thine owne?
Yor. Thou fond mad woman:
Wilt thou conceale this darke Conspiracy?
A dozen of them heere haue tane the Sacrament,
And interchangeably set downe their hands
To kill the King at Oxford.
Dut. He shall be none:
Wee'l keepe him heere: then what is that to him?
Yor. Away fond woman: were hee twenty times my
Son, I would appeach him.
Dut. Hadst thou groan'd for him as I haue done,
Thou wouldest be more pittifull:
But now I know thy minde; thou do'st suspect
That I haue bene disloyall to thy bed,
And that he is a Bastard, not thy Sonne:
Sweet Yorke, sweet husband, be not of that minde:
He is as like thee, as a man may bee,
Not like to me, nor any of my Kin,
And yet I loue him.
Yorke. Make way, vnruly Woman. *Exit*
Dut. After *Aumerle*. Mount thee vpon his horse,
Spurre post, and get before him to the King,
And begge thy pardon, ere he do accuse thee,
Ile not be long behind: though I be old,
I doubt not but to ride as fast as Yorke:
And neuer will I rise vp from the ground,
Till *Bullingbrooke* haue pardon'd thee: Away be gone. *Exit*

Scæna Tertia.

Enter Bullingbrooke, Percie, and other Lords.

Bul. Can no man tell of my vnthriftie Sonne?
'Tis full three monthes since I did see him last.
If any plague hang ouer vs, 'tis he,
I would to heauen (my Lords) he might be found:
Enquire at London, 'mongst the Tauernes there:
For

For there (they say) he dayly doth frequent,
With vnrestrained loose Companions,
Euen such (they say) as stand in narrow Lanes,
And rob our Watch, and beate our passengers,
Which he, yong wanton, and effeminate Boy
Takes on the point of Honor, to support
So dissolute a crew.
Per. My Lord, some two dayes since I saw the Prince,
And told him of these Triumphes held at Oxford.
Bul. And what said the Gallant?
Per. His answer was: he would vnto the Stewes,
And from the common'st creature plucke a Gloue
And weare it as a fauour, and with that
He would vnhorse the lustiest Challenger.
Bul. As dissolute as desp'rate, yet through both,
I see some sparkes of better hope: which elder dayes
May happily bring forth. But who comes heere?

Enter Aumerle.

Aum. Where is the King?
Bul. What meanes our Cosin, that hee stares
And lookes so wildely?
Aum. God saue your Grace. I do beseech your Maiesty
To haue some conference with your Grace alone.
Bul. Withdraw your selues, and leaue vs here alone:
What is the matter with our Cosin now?
Aum. For euer may my knees grow to the earth,
My tongue cleaue to my roofe within my mouth,
Vnlesse a Pardon, ere I rise, or speake.
Bul. Intended, or committed was this fault?
If on the first, how heynous ere it bee,
To win thy after loue, I pardon thee.
Aum. Then giue me leaue, that I may turne the key,
That no man enter, till my tale me done.
Bul. Haue thy desire. *Yorke within.*
Yor. My Liege beware, looke to thy selfe,
Thou hast a Traitor in thy presence there.
Bul. Villaine, Ile make thee safe.
Aum. Stay thy reuengefull hand, thou hast no cause to feare.
Yorke. Open the doore, secure foole-hardy King:
Shall I for loue speake treason to thy face?
Open the doore, or I will breake it open.

Enter Yorke.

Bul. What is the matter (Vnkle) speak, recouer breath,
Tell vs how neere is danger,
That we may arme vs to encounter it.
Yor. Peruse this writing heere, and thou shalt know
The reason that my haste forbids me show.
Aum. Remember as thou read'st, thy promise past:
I do repent me, reade not my name there,
My heart is not confederate with my hand.
Yor. It was (villaine) ere thy hand did set it downe.
I tore it from the Traitors bosome, King.
Feare, and not Loue, begets his penitence;
Forget to pitty him, least thy pitty proue
A Serpent, that will sting thee to the heart.
Bul. Oh heinous, strong, and bold Conspiracie,
O loyall Father of a treacherous Sonne:
Thou sheere, immaculate, and siluer fountaine,
From whence this streame, through muddy passages
Hath had his current, and defil'd himselfe.
Thy ouerflow of good, conuerts to bad,
And thy abundant goodnesse shall excuse
This deadly blot, in thy digressing sonne.
Yorke. So shall my Vertue be his Vices bawd,
And he shall spend mine Honour, with his Shame;
As thriftlesse Sonnes, their scraping Fathers Gold.
Mine honor liues, when his dishonor dies,
Or my sham'd life, in his dishonor lies:
Thou kill'st me in his life, giuing him breath,
The Traitor liues, the true man's put to death.

Dutchesse within.

Dut. What hoa (my Liege) for heauens sake let me in.
Bul. What shrill-voic'd Suppliant, makes this eager cry?
Dut. A woman, and thine Aunt (great King) 'tis I.
Speake with me, pitty me, open the dore,
A Begger begs, that neuer begg'd before.
Bul. Our Scene is alter'd from a serious thing,
And now chang'd to the Begger, and the King.
My dangerous Cosin, let your Mother in,
I know she's come, to pray for your foule sin.
Yorke. If thou do pardon, whosoeuer pray,
More sinnes for this forgiuenesse, prosper may.
This fester'd ioynt cut off, the rest rests sound,
This let alone, will all the rest confound.

Enter Dutchesse.

Dut. O King, beleeue not this hard-hearted man,
Loue, louing not it selfe, none other can.
Yor. Thou franticke woman, what dost y make here,
Shall thy old dugges, once more a Traitor reare?
Dut. Sweet Yorke be patient, heare me gentle Liege.
Bul. Rise vp good Aunt.
Dut. Not yet, I thee beseech.
For euer will I kneele vpon my knees,
And neuer see day, that the happy sees,
Till thou giue ioy: vntill thou bid me ioy,
By pardoning Rutland, my transgressing Boy.
Aum. Vnto my mothers prayres, I bend my knee.
Yorke. Against them both, my true ioynts bended be.
Dut. Pleades he in earnest? Looke vpon his Face,
His eyes do drop no teares: his prayres are in iest:
His words come from his mouth, ours from our brest.
He prayes but faintly, and would be denide,
We pray with heart, and soule, and all beside:
His weary ioynts would gladly rise, I know,
Our knees shall kneele, till to the ground they grow:
His prayers are full of false hypocrisie,
Ours of true zeale, and deepe integritie:
Our prayers do out-pray his, then let them haue
That mercy, which true prayers ought to haue.
Bul. Good Aunt stand vp.
Dut. Nay, do not say stand vp.
But Pardon first, and afterwards stand vp.
And if I were thy Nurse, thy tongue to teach,
Pardon should be the first word of thy speach.
I neuer long'd to heare a word till now:
Say Pardon (King,) let pitty teach thee how.
The word is short: but not so short as sweet,
No word like Pardon, for Kings mouth's so meet.
Yorke. Speake it in French (King) say *Pardon'ne moy.*
Dut. Dost thou teach pardon, Pardon to destroy?
Ah my sowre husband, my hard-hearted Lord,
That set's the word it selfe, against the word.
Speake Pardon, as 'tis currant in our Land,
The chopping French we do not vnderstand.
Thine eye begins to speake, set thy tongue there,
Or in thy pitteous heart, plant thou thine eare,
That hearing how our plaints and prayres do pearce,
Pitty may moue thee, Pardon to rehearse.
Bul. Good Aunt, stand vp.
Dut. I do not sue to stand,
Pardon is all the suite I haue in hand.

Bul.

Bul. I pardon him, as heauen shall pardon mee.
Dut. O happy vantage of a kneeling knee:
Yet am I sicke for feare: Speake it againe,
Twice saying Pardon, doth not pardon twaine,
But makes one pardon strong.
Bul. I pardon him with all my hart.
Dut. A God on earth thou art.
Bul. But for our trusty brother-in-Law, the Abbot,
With all the rest of that consorted crew,
Destruction straight shall dogge them at the heeles:
Good Vnckle helpe to order seuerall powres
To Oxford, or where ere these Traitors are:
They shall not liue within this world I sweare,
But I will haue them, if I once know where.
Vnckle farewell, and Cosin adieu:
Your mother well hath praid, and proue you true.
Dut. Come my old son, I pray heauen make thee new.
Exeunt.

Enter Exton and Seruants.

Ext. Didst thou not marke the King what words hee spake?
Haue I no friend will rid me of this liuing feare:
Was it not so?
Ser. Those were his very words.
Ex. Haue I no Friend? (quoth he:) he spake it twice,
And vrg'd it twice together, did he not?
Ser. He did.
Ex. And speaking it, he wistly look'd on me,
As who should say, I would thou wer't the man
That would diuorce this terror from my heart,
Meaning the King at Pomfret: Come, let's goe;
I am the Kings Friend, and will rid his Foe. *Exit.*

Scæna Quarta.

Enter Richard.

Rich. I haue bin studying, how to compare
This Prison where I liue, vnto the World:
And for because the world is populous,
And heere is not a Creature, but my selfe,
I cannot do it: yet Ile hammer't out.
My Braine, Ile proue the Female to my Soule,
My Soule, the Father: and these two beget
A generation of still breeding Thoughts;
And these same Thoughts, people this Little World
In humors, like the people of this world,
For no thought is contented. The better sort,
As thoughts of things Diuine, are intermixt
With scruples, and do set the Faith it selfe
Against the Faith: as thus: Come litle ones: & then again,
It is as hard to come, as for a Camell
To thred the posterne of a Needles eye.
Thoughts tending to Ambition, they do plot
Vnlikely wonders; how these vaine weake nailes
May teare a passage through the Flinty ribbes
Of this hard world, my ragged prison walles:
And for they cannot, dye in their owne pride.
Thoughts tending to Content, flatter themselues,
That they are not the first of Fortunes slaues,
Nor shall not be the last. Like silly Beggars,
Who sitting in the Stockes, refuge their shame
That many haue, and others must sit there;
And in this Thought, they finde a kind of ease,
Bearing their owne misfortune on the backe
Of such as haue before indur'd the like.
Thus play I in one Prison, many people,
And none contented. Sometimes am I King;
Then Treason makes me wish my selfe a Beggar,
And so I am. Then crushing penurie,
Perswades me, I was better when a King;
Then am I king'd againe: and by and by,
Thinke that I am vn-king'd by *Bullingbrooke*,
And straight am nothing. But what ere I am, *Musick*
Nor I, nor any man, that but man is,
With nothing shall be pleas'd, till he be eas'd
With being nothing. Musicke do I heare?
Ha, ha? keepe time: How sowre sweet Musicke is,
When Time is broke, and no Proportion kept?
So is it in the Musicke of mens liues:
And heere haue I the daintinesse of eare,
To heare time broke in a disorder'd string:
But for the Concord of my State and Time,
Had not an eare to heare my true Time broke.
I wasted Time, and now doth Time waste me:
For now hath Time made me his numbring clocke;
My Thoughts, are minutes; and with Sighes they iarre,
Their watches on vnto mine eyes, the outward Watch,
Whereto my finger, like a Dialls point,
Is pointing still, in cleansing them from teares.
Now sir, the sound that tels what houre it is,
Are clamorous groanes, that strike vpon my heart,
Which is the bell: so Sighes, and Teares, and Grones,
Shew Minutes, Houres, and Times: but my Time
Runs poasting on, in *Bullingbrookes* proud ioy,
While I stand fooling heere, his Iacke o'th'Clocke.
This Musicke mads me, let it sound no more,
For though it haue holpe madmen to their wits,
In me it seemes, it will make wise-men mad:
Yet blessing on his heart that giues it me;
For 'tis a signe of loue, and loue to *Richard*,
Is a strange Brooch, in this all-hating world.

Enter Groome.

Groo. Haile Royall Prince.
Rich. Thankes Noble Peere,
The cheapest of vs, is ten groates too deere.
What art thou? And how com'st thou hither?
Where no man euer comes, but that sad dogge
That brings me food, to make misfortune liue?
Groo. I was a poore Groome of thy Stable (King)
When thou wer't King: who trauelling towards Yorke,
With much adoo, at length haue gotten leaue
To looke vpon my (sometimes Royall) masters face.
O how it yern'd my heart, when I beheld
In London streets, that Coronation day,
When *Bullingbrooke* rode on Roane Barbary,
That horse, that thou so often hast bestrid,
That horse, that I so carefully haue drest.
Rich. Rode he on Barbary? Tell me gentle Friend,
How went he vnder him?
Groo. So proudly, as if he had disdain'd the ground.
Rich. So proud, that *Bullingbrooke* was on his backe;
That Iade hath eate bread from my Royall hand.
This hand hath made him proud with clapping him.
Would he not stumble? Would he not fall downe
(Since Pride must haue a fall) and breake the necke
Of that proud man, that did vsurpe his backe?
Forgiuenesse horse: Why do I raile on thee,
Since thou created to be aw'd by man
Was't borne to beare? I was not made a horse,
And

And yet I beare a burthen like an Asse,
Spur-gall'd, and tyrd by iauncing *Bullingbrooke*.

Enter Keeper with a Dish.

Keep. Fellow, giue place, heere is no longer stay.

Rich. If thou loue me, 'tis time thou wer't away.

Groo. What my tongue dares not, that my heart shall say. *Exit.*

Keep. My Lord, wilt please you to fall too?

Rich. Taste of it first, as thou wer't wont to doo.

Keep. My Lord I dare not: Sir *Pierce* of Exton,
Who lately came from th'King, commands the contrary.

Rich. The diuell take *Henrie* of Lancaster, and thee;
Patience is staie, and I am weary of it.

Keep. Helpe, helpe, helpe.

Enter Exton and Seruants.

Ri. How now? what meanes Death in this rude assalt?
Villaine, thine owne hand yeelds thy deaths instrument,
Go thou and fill another roome in hell.

Exton strikes him downe.

That hand shall burne in neuer-quenching fire,
That staggers thus my person. *Exton*, thy fierce hand,
Hath with the Kings blood, stain'd the Kings own land,
Mount, mount my soule, thy seate is vp on high,
Whil'st my grosse flesh sinkes downward, heere to dye.

Exton. As full of Valor, as of Royall blood,
Both haue I spilt: Oh would the deed were good.
For now the diuell, that told me I did well,
Sayes, that this deede is chronicled in hell.
This dead King to the liuing King Ile beare,
Take hence the rest, and giue them buriall heere. *Exit.*

Scœna Quinta.

Flourish. Enter Bullingbrooke, Yorke, with other Lords & attendants.

Bul. Kinde Vnkle Yorke, the latest newes we heare,
Is that the Rebels haue consum'd with fire
Our Towne of Ciceter in Gloucestershire,
But whether they be tane or slaine, we heare not.

Enter Northumberland.

Welcome my Lord: What is the newes?

Nor. First to thy Sacred State, wish I all happinesse:
The next newes is, I haue to London sent
The heads of *Salsbury*, *Spencer*, *Blunt*, and *Kent*:
The manner of their taking may appeare
At large discoursed in this paper heere.

Bul. We thank thee gentle *Percy* for thy paines,
And to thy worth will adde right worthy gaines.

Enter Fitz-waters.

Fitz. My Lord, I haue from Oxford sent to London,
The heads of *Broccas*, and Sir *Bennet Seely*,
Two of the dangerous consorted Traitors,
That sought at Oxford, thy dire ouerthrow.

Bul. Thy paines *Fitzwaters* shall not be forgot,
Right Noble is thy merit, well I wot.

Enter Percy and Carlile.

Per. The grand Conspirator, Abbot of Westminster,
With clog of Conscience, and sowre Melancholly,
Hath yeelded vp his body to the graue:
But heere is *Carlile*, liuing to abide
Thy Kingly doome, and sentence of his pride.

Bul. *Carlile*, this is your doome:
Choose out some secret place, some reuerend roome
More then thou hast, and with it ioy thy life:
So as thou liu'st in peace, dye free from strife:
For though mine enemy, thou hast euer beene,
High sparkes of Honor in thee haue I seene.

Enter Exton with a Coffin.

Exton. Great King, within this Coffin I present
Thy buried feare. Heerein all breathlesse lies
The mightiest of thy greatest enemies
Richard of Burdeaux, by me hither brought.

Bul. *Exton*, I thanke thee not, for thou hast wrought
A deede of Slaughter, with thy fatall hand,
Vpon my head, and all this famous Land.

Ex. From your owne mouth my Lord, did I this deed.

Bul. They loue not poyson, that do poyson neede,
Nor do I thee: though I did wish him dead,
I hate the Murtherer, loue him murthered.
The guilt of conscience take thou for thy labour,
But neither my good word, nor Princely fauour.
With *Caine* go wander through the shade of night,
And neuer shew thy head by day, nor light.
Lords, I protest my soule is full of woe,
That blood should sprinkle me, to make me grow.
Come mourne with me, for that I do lament,
And put on sullen Blacke incontinent:
Ile make a voyage to the Holy-land,
To wash this blood off from my guilty hand.
March sadly after, grace my mourning heere,
In weeping after this vntimely Beere. *Exeunt.*

FINIS.

The Firſt Part of Henry the Fourth, with the Life and Death of HENRY Sirnamed HOT-SPVRRE.

Actus Primus. Scœna Prima.

Enter the King, Lord Iohn of Lancaſter, Earle of Weſtmerland, with others.

King.

SO ſhaken as we are, ſo wan with care,
Finde we a time for frighted Peace to pant,
And breath ſhortwinded accents of new broils
To be commenc'd in Stronds a-farre remote:
No more the thirſty entrance of this Soile,
Shall daube her lippes with her owne childrens blood:
No more ſhall trenching Warre channell her fields,
Nor bruiſe her Flowrets with the Armed hoofes
Of hoſtile paces. Thoſe oppoſed eyes,
Which like the Meteors of a troubled Heauen,
All of one Nature, of one Subſtance bred,
Did lately meete in the inteſtine ſhocke,
And furious cloze of ciuil Butchery,
Shall now in mutuall well-beſeeming rankes
March all one way, and be no more oppos'd
Againſt Acquaintance, Kindred, and Allies.
The edge of Warre, like an ill-ſheathed knife,
No more ſhall cut his Maſter. Therefore Friends,
As farre as to the Sepulcher of Chriſt,
Whoſe Souldier now vnder whoſe bleſſed Croſſe
We are impreſſed and ingag'd to fight,
Forthwith a power of Engliſh ſhall we leuie,
Whoſe armes were moulded in their Mothers wombe,
To chace theſe Pagans in thoſe holy Fields,
Ouer whoſe Acres walk'd thoſe bleſſed feete
Which fourteene hundred yeares ago were nail'd
For our aduantage on the bitter Croſſe.
But this our purpoſe is a tweluemonth old,
And bootleſſe 'tis to tell you we will go:
Therefore we meete not now. Then let me heare
Of you my gentle Couſin Weſtmerland,
What yeſternight our Councell did decree,
In forwarding this deere expedience.
West. My Liege: This haſte was hot in queſtion,
And many limits of the Charge ſet downe
But yeſternight: when all athwart there came
A Poſt from Wales, loaden with heauy Newes;
Whoſe worſt was, That the Noble *Mortimer*,
Leading the men of Herefordſhire to fight
Againſt the irregular and wilde *Glendower*,
Was by the rude hands of that Welſhman taken,
And a thouſand of his people butchered:
Vpon whoſe dead corpes there was ſuch miſuſe,
Such beaſtly, ſhameleſſe transformation,
By thoſe Welſhwomen done, as may not be
(Without much ſhame) re-told or ſpoken of.
King. It ſeemes then, that the tidings of this broile,
Brake off our buſineſſe for the Holy land.
West. This matcht with other like, my gracious Lord,
Farre more vneuen and vnwelcome Newes
Came from the North, and thus it did report:
On Holy-roode day, the gallant *Hotſpurre* there,
Young *Harry Percy*, and braue *Archibald*,
That euer-valiant and approoued Scot,
At *Holmeden* met, where they did ſpend
A ſad and bloody houre:
As by diſcharge of their Artillerie,
And ſhape of likely-hood the newes was told:
For he that brought them, in the very heate
And pride of their contention, did take horſe,
Vncertaine of the iſſue any way.
King. Heere is a deere and true induſtrious friend,
Sir *Walter Blunt*, new lighted from his Horſe,
Strain'd with the variation of each ſoyle,
Betwixt that *Holmeden*, and this Seat of ours:
And he hath brought vs ſmooth and welcomes newes.
The Earle of *Dowglas* is diſcomfited,
Ten thouſand bold Scots, two and twenty Knights
Balk'd in their owne blood did Sir *Walter* ſee
On *Holmedons* Plaines. Of Priſoners, *Hotſpurre* tooke
Mordake Earle of Fife, and eldeſt ſonne
To beaten *Dowglas*, and the Earle of *Atholl*,
Of *Murry*, *Angus*, and *Menteith*.
And is not this an honourable ſpoyle?
A gallant prize? Ha Coſin, is it not? Infaith it is.
West. A Conqueſt for a Prince to boaſt of.
King. Yea, there thou mak'ſt me ſad, & mak'ſt me ſin,
In enuy, that my Lord Northumberland
Should be the Father of ſo bleſt a Sonne:
A Sonne, who is the Theame of Honors tongue;
Among'ſt a Groue, the very ſtraighteſt Plant,
Who is ſweet Fortunes Minion, and her Pride:
Whil'ſt I by looking on the praiſe of him,
See Ryot and Diſhonor ſtaine the brow
Of my yong *Harry*. O that it could be prou'd,
That ſome Night-tripping-Faiery, had exchang'd
In Cradle-clothes, our Children where they lay,
And call'd mine *Percy*, his *Plantagenet*:

Then

Then would I haue his *Harry*, and he mine:
But let him from my thoughts. What thinke you Coze
Of this young *Perceies* pride? The Prisoners
Which he in this aduenture hath surpriz'd,
To his owne vse he keepes, and sends me word
I shall haue none but *Mordake* Earle of *Fife*.

West. This is his Vnckles teaching. This is Worceste
Maleuolent to you in all Aspects:
Which makes him prune himselfe and bristle vp
The crest of Youth against your Dignity.

King. But I haue sent for him to answer this:
And for this cause a-while we must neglect
Our holy purpose to Ierusalem.
Cosin, on Wednesday next, our Councell we will hold
At Windsor, and so informe the Lords:
But come your selfe with speed to vs againe,
For more is to be said, and to be done,
Then out of anger can be vttered.

West. I will my Liege. *Exeunt*

Scæna Secunda.

Enter Henry Prince of Wales, Sir Iohn Falstaffe, and Pointz.

Fal. Now *Hal*, what time of day is it Lad?

Prince Thou art so fat-witted with drinking of olde Sacke, and vnbuttoning thee after Supper, and sleeping vpon Benches in the afternoone, that thou hast forgotten to demand that truely, which thou wouldest truly know. What a diuell hast thou to do with the time of the day? vnlesse houres were cups of Sacke, and minutes Capons, and clockes the tongues of Bawdes, and dialls the signes of Leaping-houses, and the blessed Sunne himselfe a faire hot Wench in Flame-coloured Taffata; I see no reason, why thou shouldest bee so superfluous, to demaund the time of the day.

Fal. Indeed you come neere me now *Hal*, for we that take Purses, go by the Moone and seuen Starres, and not by Phœbus hee, that wand'ring Knight so faire. And I prythee sweet Wagge, when thou art King, as God saue thy Grace, Maiesty I should say, for Grace thou wilte haue none.

Prin What, none?

Fal. No, not so much as will serue to be Prologue to an Egge and Butter.

Prin. Well, how then? Come roundly, roundly.

Fal. Marry then, sweet Wagge, when thou art King, let not vs that are Squires of the Nights bodie, bee call'd Theeues of the Dayes beautie. Let vs be *Dianaes* Forresters, Gentlemen of the Shade. Minions of the Moone; and let men say, we be men of good Gouernment, being gouerned as the Sea is, by our noble and chast mistris the Moone, vnder whose countenance we steale.

Prin. Thou say'st well, and it holds well too: for the fortune of vs that are the Moones men, dooth ebbe and flow like the Sea, beeing gouerned as the Sea is, by the Moone: as for proofe. Now a Purse of Gold most resolutely snatch'd on Monday night, and most dissolutely spent on Tuesday Morning; got with swearing, Lay by: and spent with crying, Bring in: now, in as low an ebbe as the foot of the Ladder, and by and by in as high a flow as the ridge of the Gallowes.

Fal. Thou say'st true Lad: and is not my Hostesse of the Tauerne a most sweet Wench?

Prin. As is the hony, my old Lad of the Castle: and is not a Buffe Ierkin a most sweet robe of durance?

Fal. How now? how now mad Wagge? What in thy quips and thy quiddities? What a plague, haue I to doe with a Buffe-Ierkin?

Prin. Why, what a poxe haue I to doe with my Hostesse of the Tauerne?

Fal. Well, thou hast call'd her to a reck'ning many a time and oft.

Prin. Did I euer call for thee to pay thy part?

Fal. No, Ile giue thee thy due, thou hast paid al there.

Prin. Yea and elsewhere, so farre as my Coine would stretch, and where it would not, I haue vs'd my credit.

Fal. Yea, and so vs'd it, that were it heere apparant, that thou art Heire apparant. But I prythee sweet Wag, shall there be Gallowes standing in England when thou art King? and resolution thus fobb'd as it is, with the rustie curbe of old Father Anticke the Law? Doe not thou when thou art a King, hang a Theefe.

Prin. No, thou shalt.

Fal. Shall I? O rare! Ile be a braue Iudge.

Prin. Thou iudgest false already. I meane, thou shalt haue the hanging of the Theeues, and so become a rare Hangman.

Fal. Well *Hal*, well: and in some sort it iumpes with my humour, as well as waiting in the Court, I can tell you.

Prin. For obtaining of suites?

Fal. Yea, for obtaining of suites, whereof the Hangman hath no leane Wardrobe. I am as Melancholly as a Gyb-Cat, or a lugg'd Beare.

Prin. Or an old Lyon, or a Louers Lute.

Fal. Yea, or the Drone of a Lincolnshire Bagpipe.

Prin. What say'st thou to a Hare, or the Melancholly of Moore Ditch?

Fal. Thou hast the most vnsauoury smiles, and art indeed the most comparatiue rascallest sweet yong Prince. But *Hal*, I prythee trouble me no more with vanity, I wold thou and I knew, where a Commodity of good names were to be bought: an olde Lord of the Councell rated me the other day in the street about you sir; but I mark'd him not, and yet hee talk'd very wisely, but I regarded him not, and yet he talkt wisely, and in the street too.

Prin. Thou didst well: for no man regards it.

Fal. O, thou hast damnable iteration, and art indeede able to corrupt a Saint. Thou hast done much harme vnto me *Hall*, God forgiue thee for it. Before I knew thee *Hal*, I knew nothing: and now I am (if a man shold speake truly) little better then one of the wicked. I must giue ouer this life, and I will giue it ouer: and I do not, I am a Villaine. Ile be damn'd for neuer a Kings sonne in Christendome.

Prin. Where shall we take a purse to morrow, Iacke?

Fal. Where thou wilt Lad, Ile make one: and I doe not, call me Villaine, and baffle me.

Prin. I see a good amendment of life in thee: From Praying, to Purse-taking.

Fal. Why, *Hal*, 'tis my Vocation *Hal*: 'Tis no sin for a man to labour in his Vocation.

Pointz. Now shall wee know if Gads hill haue set a Watch. O, if men were to be saued by merit, what hole in Hell were hot enough for him? This is the most omnipotent Villaine, that euer cryed, Stand, to a true man.

Prin. Good morrow *Ned*.

Pointz.

Poines. Good morrow sweet *Hal.* What saies Monsieur Remorse ? What sayes Sir Iohn Sacke and Sugar : Iacke? How agrees the Diuell and thee about thy Soule, that thou soldest him on Good-Friday last, for a Cup of Madera, and a cold Capons legge?

Prin. Sir Iohn stands to his word, the diuel shall haue his bargaine, for he was neuer yet a Breaker of Prouerbs: *He will giue the diuell his due.*

Poin. Then art thou damn'd for keeping thy word with the diuell.

Prin. Else he had damn'd for cozening the diuell.

Poy. But my Lads, my Lads, to morrow morning, by foure a clocke early at Gads hill, there are Pilgrimes going to Canterbury with rich Offerings, and Traders riding to London with fat Purses. I haue vizards for you all; you haue horses for your selues: Gads-hill lyes to night in Rochester, I haue bespoke Supper to morrow in Eastcheape; we may doe it as secure as sleepe: if you will go, I will stuffe your Purses full of Crownes: if you will not, tarry at home and be hang'd.

Fal. Heare ye Yedward, if I tarry at home and go not, Ile hang you for going.

Poy. You will chops.

Fal. *Hal,* wilt thou make one?

Prin. Who, I rob? I a Theefe? Not I.

Fal. There's neither honesty, manhood, nor good fellowship in thee, nor thou cam'st not of the blood-royall, if thou dar'st not stand for ten shillings.

Prin. Well then, once in my dayes Ile be a mad-cap.

Fal. Why, that's well said.

Prin. Well, come what will, Ile tarry at home.

Fal. Ile be a Traitor then, when thou art King.

Prin. I care not.

Poyn. Sir *Iohn,* I prythee leaue the Prince & me alone, I will lay him downe such reasons for this adventure, that he shall go.

Fal. Well, maist thou haue the Spirit of perswasion; and he the eares of profiting, that what thou speakest, may moue; and what he heares may be beleeued, that the true Prince, may (for recreation sake) proue a false theefe; for the poore abuses of the time, want countenance. Farwell, you shall finde me in Eastcheape.

Prin. Farwell the latter Spring. Farewell Alhollown Summer.

Poy. Now, my good sweet Hony Lord, ride with vs to morrow. I haue a iest to execute, that I cannot mannage alone. *Falstaffe, Haruey, Rossill,* and *Gads-hill,* shall robbe those men that wee haue already way-layde, your selfe and I, wil not be there: and when they haue the booty, if you and I do not rob them, cut this head from my shoulders.

Prin. But how shal we part with them in setting forth?

Poyn. Why, we wil set forth before or after them, and appoint them a place of meeting, wherin it is at our pleasure to faile; and then will they adventure vppon the exploit themselues, which they shall haue no sooner atchieued, but wee'l set vpon them.

Prin. I, but tis like that they will know vs by our horses, by our habits, and by euery other appointment to be our selues.

Poy. Tut our horses they shall not see, Ile tye them in the wood, our vizards wee will change after wee leaue them: and sirrah, I haue Cases of Buckram for the nonce, to immaske our noted outward garments.

Prin. But I doubt they will be too hard for vs.

Poin. Well, for two of them, I know them to bee as true bred Cowards as euer turn'd backe: and for the third if he fight longer then he sees reason, Ile forswear Armes. The vertue of this Iest will be, the incomprehensible lyes that this fat Rogue will tell vs, when we meete at Supper: how thirty at least he fought with, what Wardes, what blowes, what extremities he endured; and in the reproofe of this, lyes the iest.

Prin. Well, Ile goe with thee, prouide vs all things necessary, and meete me to morrow night in Eastcheape, there Ile sup. Farewell.

Poyn. Farewell, my Lord. *Exit Pointz*

Prin. I know you all, and will a-while vphold
The vnyoak'd humor of your idlenesse:
Yet heerein will I imitate the Sunne,
Who doth permit the base contagious cloudes
To smother vp his Beauty from the world,
That when he please againe to be himselfe,
Being wanted, he may be more wondred at,
By breaking through the foule and vgly mists
Of vapours, that did seeme to strangle him.
If all the yeare were playing holidaies,
To sport, would be as tedious as to worke;
But when they seldome come, they wisht-for come,
And nothing pleaseth but rare accidents.
So when this loose behauiour I throw off,
And pay the debt I neuer promised;
By how much better then my word I am,
By so much shall I falsifie mens hopes,
And like bright Mettall on a sullen ground;
My reformation glittering o're my fault,
Shall shew more goodly, and attract more eyes,
Then that which hath no foyle to set it off.
Ile so offend, to make offence a skill,
Redeeming time, when men thinke least I will.

Scœna Tertia.

Enter the King, Northumberland, Worcester, Hotspurre, Sir Walter Blunt, and others.

King. My blood hath beene too cold and temperate,
Vnapt to stirre at these indignities,
And you haue found me; for accordingly,
You tread vpon my patience: But be sure,
I will from henceforth rather be my Selfe,
Mighty, and to be fear'd, then my condition
Which hath beene smooth as Oyle, soft as yong Downe,
And therefore lost that Title of respect,
Which the proud soule ne're payes, but to the proud.

Wor. Our house (my Soueraigne Liege) little deserues
The scourge of greatnesse to be vsed on it,
And that same greatnesse too, which our owne hands
Haue holpe to make so portly.

Nor. My Lord.

King. Worcester get thee gone: for I do see
Danger and disobedience in thine eye.
O sir, your presence is too bold and peremptory,
And Maiestie might neuer yet endure
The moody Frontier of a seruant brow,
You haue good leaue to leaue vs. When we need
Your vse and counsell, we shall send for you.
You were about to speake.

North. Yea, my good Lord.

Those

Those Prisoners in your Highnesse demanded,
Which *Harry Percy* heere at *Holmedon* tooke,
Were (as he sayes) not with such strength denied
As was deliuered to your Maiesty:
Who either through enuy, or misprision,
Was guilty of this fault; and not my Sonne.

Hot. My Liege, I did deny no Prisoners.
But, I remember when the fight was done,
When I was dry with Rage, and extreame Toyle,
Breathlesse, and Faint, leaning vpon my Sword,
Came there a certaine Lord, neat and trimly drest;
Fresh as a Bride-groome, and his Chin new reapt,
Shew'd like a stubble Land at Haruest home.
He was perfumed like a Milliner,
And 'twixt his Finger and his Thumbe, he held
A Pouncet-box: which euer and anon
He gaue his Nose, and took't away againe:
Who therewith angry, when it next came there,
Tooke it in Snuffe. And still he smil'd and talk'd:
And as the Souldiers bare dead bodies by,
He call'd them vntaught Knaues, Vnmannerly,
To bring a slouenly vnhandsome Coarse
Betwixt the Winde, and his Nobility.
With many Holiday and Lady tearme
He question'd me: Among the rest, demanded
My Prisoners, in your Maiesties behalfe.
I then, all-smarting, with my wounds being cold,
(To be so pestered with a Popingay)
Out of my Greefe, and my Impatience,
Answer'd (neglectingly) I know not what,
He should, or should not: For he made me mad,
To see him shine so briske, and smell so sweet,
And talke so like a Waiting-Gentlewoman,
Of Guns, & Drums, and Wounds: God saue the marke;
And telling me, the Soueraign'st thing on earth
Was Parmacity, for an inward bruise:
And that it was great pitty, so it was,
That villanous Salt-peter should be digg'd
Out of the Bowels of the harmlesse Earth,
Which many a good Tall Fellow had destroy'd
So Cowardly. And but for these vile Gunnes,
He would himselfe haue beene a Souldier.
This bald, vnioynted Chat of his (my Lord)
Made me to answer indirectly (as I said.)
And I beseech you, let not this report
Come currant for an Accusation,
Betwixt my Loue, and your high Maiesty.

Blunt. The circumstance considered, good my Lord,
What euer *Harry Percie* then had said,
To such a person, and in such a place,
At such a time, with all the rest retold,
May reasonably dye, and neuer rise
To do him wrong, or any way impeach
What then he said, so he vnsay it now.

King. Why yet doth deny his Prisoners,
But with Prouiso and Exception,
That we at our owne charge, shall ransome straight
His Brother-in-Law, the foolish *Mortimer*,
Who (in my soule) hath wilfully betraid
The liues of those, that he did leade to Fight,
Against the great Magitian, damn'd *Glendower*:
Whose daughter (as we heare) the Earle of March
Hath lately married. Shall our Coffers then,
Be emptied, to redeeme a Traitor home?
Shall we buy Treason, and indent with Feares,
When they haue lost and forfeyted themselues.
No: on the barren Mountaine let him sterue:
For I shall neuer hold that man my Friend,
Whose tongue shall aske me for one peny cost
To ransome home reuolted *Mortimer*.

Hot. Reuolted *Mortimer*?
He neuer did fall off, my Soueraigne Liege,
But by the chance of Warre: to proue that true,
Needs no more but one tongue. For all those Wounds,
Those mouthed Wounds, which valiantly he tooke,
When on the gentle Seuernes siedgie banke,
In single Opposition hand to hand,
He did confound the best part of an houre
In changing hardiment with great *Glendower*:
Three times they breath'd, and three times did they drink
Vpon agreement, of swift Seuernes flood;
Who then affrighted with their bloody lookes,
Ran fearefully among the trembling Reeds,
And hid his crispe-head in the hollow banke,
Blood-stained with these Valiant Combatants.
Neuer did base and rotten Policy
Colour her working with such deadly wounds;
Nor neuer could the Noble *Mortimer*
Receiue so many, and all willingly:
Then let him not be sland'red with Reuolt.

King. Thou do'st bely him *Percy*, thou dost bely him;
He neuer did encounter with *Glendower*:
I tell thee, he durst as well haue met the diuell alone,
As *Owen Glendower* for an enemy.
Art thou not asham'd? But Sirrah, henceforth
Let me not heare you speake of *Mortimer*.
Send me your Prisoners with the speediest meanes,
Or you shall heare in such a kinde from me
As will displease ye. My Lord *Northumberland*,
We License your departure with your sonne,
Send vs your Prisoners, or you'l heare of it. *Exit King.*

Hot. And if the diuell come and roare for them
I will not send them. I will after straight
And tell him so: for I will ease my heart,
Although it be with hazard of my head.

Nor. What? drunke with choller? stay & pause awhile,
Heere comes your Vnckle. *Enter Worcester.*

Hot. Speake of *Mortimer*?
Yes, I will speake of him, and let my soule
Want mercy, if I do not ioyne with him.
In his behalfe, Ile empty all these Veines,
And shed my deere blood drop by drop i'th dust,
But I will lift the downfall *Mortimer*
As high i'th Ayre, as this Vnthankfull King,
As this Ingrate and Cankred *Bullingbrooke*.

Nor. Brother, the King hath made your Nephew mad

Wor. Who strooke this heate vp after I was gone

Hot. He will (forsooth) haue all my Prisoners:
And when I vrg'd the ransom once againe
Of my Wiues Brother, then his cheeke look'd pale,
And on my face he turn'd an eye of death,
Trembling euen at the name of *Mortimer*.

Wor. I cannot blame him: was he not proclaim'd
By *Richard* that dead is, the next of blood?

Nor. He was: I heard the Proclamation,
And then it was, when the vnhappy King
(Whose wrongs in vs God pardon) did set forth
Vpon his Irish Expedition:
From whence he intercepted, did returne
To be depos'd, and shortly murthered.

Wor. And for whose death, we in the worlds wide mouth
Liue scandaliz'd, and fouly spoken of.

e *Hot.*

Hot. But soft I pray you; did King *Richard* then
Proclaime my brother *Mortimer*,
Heyre to the Crowne?
Nor. He did, my selfe did heare it.
Hot. Nay then I cannot blame his Cousin King,
That wish'd him on the barren Mountaines staru'd.
But shall it be, that you that set the Crowne
Vpon the head of this forgetfull man,
And for his sake, wore the detested blot
Of murtherous subornation? Shall it be,
That you a world of curses vndergoe,
Being the Agents, or base second meanes,
The Cords, the Ladder, or the Hangman rather?
O pardon, if that I descend so low,
To shew the Line, and the Predicament
Wherein you range vnder this subtill King.
Shall it for shame, be spoken in these dayes,
Or fill vp Chronicles in time to come,
That men of your Nobility and Power,
Did gage them both in an vniust behalfe
(As Both of you, God pardon it, haue done)
To put downe *Richard*, that sweet louely Rose,
And plant this Thorne, this Canker *Bullingbrooke*?
And shall it in more shame be further spoken,
That you are fool'd, discarded, and shooke off
By him, for whom these shames ye vnderwent?
No: yet time serues, wherein you may redeeme
Your banish'd Honors, and restore your selues
Into the good Thoughts of the world againe.
Reuenge the geering and disdain'd contempt
Of this proud King, who studies day and night
To answer all the Debt he owes vnto you,
Euen with the bloody Payment of your deaths:
Therefore I say——
Wor. Peace Cousin, say no more.
And now I will vnclaspe a Secret booke,
And to your quicke conceyuing Discontents,
Ile reade you Matter, deepe and dangerous,
As full of perill and aduenturous Spirit,
As to o're-walke a Current, roaring loud
On the vnstedfast footing of a Speare.
Hot. If he fall in, good night, or sinke or swimme:
Send danger from the East vnto the West,
So Honor crosse it from the North to South,
And let them grapple: The blood more stirres
To rowze a Lyon, then to start a Hare.
Nor. Imagination of some great exploit,
Driues him beyond the bounds of Patience.
Hot. By heauen, me thinkes it were an easie leap,
To plucke bright Honor from the pale-fac'd Moone,
Or diue into the bottome of the deepe,
Where Fadome-line could neuer touch the ground,
And plucke vp drowned Honor by the Lockes:
So he that doth redeeme her thence, might weare
Without Co-riuall, all her Dignities:
But out vpon this halfe-fac'd Fellowship.
Wor. He apprehends a World of F gures here,
Bnt not the forme of what he should attend:
Good Cousin giue me audience for a-while,
And list to me.
Hot. I cry you mercy.
Wor. Those same Noble Scottes
That are your Prisoners.
Hot. Ile keepe them all.
By heauen, he shall not haue a Scot of them:
No if a Scot would saue his Soule, he shall not.
Ile keepe them, by this Hand.
Wor. You start away,
And lend no eare vnto my purposes.
Those Prisoners you shall keepe.
Hot. Nay, I will; that's flat:
He said, he would not ransome *Mortimer*:
Forbad my tongue to speake of *Mortimer*.
But I will finde him when he lyes asleepe,
And in his eare, Ile holla *Mortimer*.
Nay, Ile haue a Starling shall be taught to speake
Nothing but *Mortimer*, and giue it him,
To keepe his anger still in motion.
Wor. Heare you Cousin: a word.
Hot. All studies heere I solemnly defie,
Saue how to gall and pinch this *Bullingbrooke*,
And that same Sword and Buckler Prince of Wales.
But that I thinke his Father loues him not,
And would be glad he met with some mischance,
I would haue poyson'd him with a pot of Ale.
Wor. Farewell Kinsman: Ile talke to you
When you are better temper'd to attend.
Nor. Why what a Waspe-tongu'd & impatient foole
Art thou, to breake into this Womans mood,
Tying thine eare to no tongue but thine owne?
Hot. Why look you, I am whipt & scourg'd with rods,
Netled, and stung with Pismires, when I heare
Of this vile Politician *Bullingbrooke*.
In *Richards* time: What de'ye call the place?
A plague vpon't, it is in Gloustershire:
'Twas, where the madcap Duke his Vncle kept,
His Vncle Yorke, where I first bow'd my knee
Vnto this King of Smiles, this *Bullingbrooke*:
When you and he came backe from Rauenspurgh.
Nor. At Barkley Castle.
Hot. You say true:
Why what a caudie deale of curtesie,
This fawning Grey-hound then did proffer me.
Looke when his infant Fortune came to age,
And gentle *Harry Percy*, and kinde Cousin:
O, the Diuell take such Couzeners, God forgiue me,
Good Vncle tell your tale, for I haue done.
Wor. Nay, if you haue not, too't againe,
Wee'l stay your leysure.
Hot. I haue done insooth.
Wor. Then once more to your Scottish Prisoners.
Deliuer them vp without their ransome straight,
And make the *Dowglas* sonne your onely meane
For powres in Scotland: which for diuers reasons
Which I shall send you written, be assur'd
Will easily be granted you, my Lord.
Your Sonne in Scotland being thus impl y'd,
Shall secretly into the bosome creepe
Of that same noble Prelate, well belou'd,
The Archbishop.
Hot. Of Yorke, is't not?
Wor. True, who beares hard
His Brothers death at *Bristow*, the Lord *Scroope*.
I speake not this in estimation,
As what I thinke might be, but what I know
Is ruminated, plotted, and set downe,
And onely stayes but to behold the face
Of that occasion that shall bring it on.
Hot. I smell it:
Vpon my life, it will do wond'rous well.
Nor. Before the game's a-foot, thou still let'st slip.
Hot. Why, it cannot choose but be a Noble plot,
And

And then the power of Scotland, and of Yorke
To ioyne with *Mortimer*, He.

Wor. And so they shall.

Hot. Infaith it is exceedingly well aym'd.

Wor. And 'tis no little reason bids vs speed,
To saue our heads, by raising of a Head:
For, beare our selues as euen as we can,
The King will alwayes thinke him in our debt,
And thinke, we thinke our selues vnsatisfied,
Till he hath found a time to pay vs home.
And see already, how he doth beginne
To make vs strangers to his lookes of loue.

Hot. He does, he does; wee'l be reueng'd on him.

Wor. Cousin, farewell. No further go in this,
Then I by Letters shall direct your course
When time is ripe, which will be sodainly:
Ile steale to *Glendower*, and loe, *Mortimer*,
Where you, and *Dowglas*, and our powres at once,
As I will fashion it, shall happily meete,
To beare our fortunes in our owne strong armes,
Which now we hold at much vncertainty.

Nor. Farewell good Brother, we shall thriue, I trust.

Hot Vncle, adieu: O let the houres be short,
Till fields, and blowes, and grones, applaud our sport. *exit*

Actus Secundus. Scena Prima.

Enter a Carrier with a Lanterne in his hand.

1. *Car* Heigh-ho, an't be not foure by the day, Ile be hang'd. *Charles waine* is ouer the new Chimney, and yet our horse not packt. What Ostler?

Ost. Anon, anon.

1. *Car.* I prethee Tom, beate Cuts Saddle, put a few Flockes in the point: the poore Iade is wrung in the withers, out of all cesse.

Enter another Carrier.

2. *Car.* Pease and Beanes are as danke here as a Dog, and this is the next way to giue poore Iades the Bottes: This house is turned vpside downe since *Robin* the Ostler dyed.

1. *Car.* Poore fellow neuer ioy'd since the price of oats rose, it was the death of him.

2. *Car.* I thinke this is the most villanous house in al London rode for Fleas: I am stung like a Teneh.

1. *Car.* Like a Tench? There is ne're a King in Christendome, could be better bit, then I haue beene since the first Cocke.

2. *Car.* Why, you will allow vs ne're a' Iourden, and then we leake in your Chimney: and your Chamber-lye breeds Fleas like a Loach.

1. *Car.* What Ostler, come away, and be hangd: come away.

2. *Car.* I haue a Gammon of Bacon, and two razes of Ginger, to be deliuered as farre as Charing-crosse.

1. *Car.* The Turkies in my Pannier are quite starued. What Ostler? A plague on thee, hast thou neuer an eye in thy head? Can'st not heare? And t'were not as good a deed as drinke, to break the pate of thee, I am a very Villaine. Come and be hang'd, hast no faith in thee?

Enter Gads-hill.

Gad Good-morrow Carriers. What's a clocke?

Car I thinke it be two a clocke.

Gad I prethee lend me thy Lanthorne to see my Gelding in the stable.

1. *Car.* Nay soft I pray ye, I know a trick worth two of that.

Gad. I prethee lend me thine.

2. *Car.* I, when, canst tell? Lend mee thy Lanthorne (quoth-a) marry Ile see thee hang'd first.

Gad. Sirra Carrier: What time do you mean to come to London?

2. *Car.* Time enough to goe to bed with a Candle, I warrant thee. Come neighbour *Mugges*, wee'll call vp the Gentlemen, they will along with company, for they haue great charge. *Exeunt*

Enter Chamberlaine.

Gad. What ho, Chamberlaine?

Cham. At hand quoth Pick-purse.

Gad. That's euen as faire, as at hand quoth the Chamberlaine: For thou variest no more from picking of Purses, then giuing direction, doth from labouring. Thou layst the plot, how.

Cham. Good morrow Master *Gads-Hill*, it holds currant that I told you yesternight. There's a Franklin in the wilde of Kent, hath brought three hundred Markes with him in Gold: I heard him tell it to one of his company last night at Supper; a kinde of Auditor, one that hath abundance of charge too (God knowes what) they are vp already, and call for Egges and Butter. They will away presently.

Gad. Sirra, if they meete not with S. Nicholas Clarks, Ile giue thee this necke.

Cham. No, Ile none of it: I prythee keep that for the Hangman, for I know thou worshipst S. Nicholas as truly as a man of falshood may.

Gad. What talkest thou to me of the Hangman? If I hang, Ile make a fat payre of Gallowes. For, if I hang, old Sir *Iohn* hangs with mee, and thou know'st hee's no Starueling. Tut, there are other Troians that yͧ dream'st not of, the which (for sport sake) are content to doe the Profession some grace; that would (if matters should bee look'd into) for their owne Credit sake, make all Whole. I am ioyned with no Poot-land-Rakers, no Long-staffe six-penny strikers, none of these mad Mustachio-purple-hu'd Maltwormes, but with Nobility, and Tranquilitie; Bourgomasters, and great Oneyers, such as can holde in, such as will strike sooner then speake; and speake sooner then drinke, and drinke sooner then pray: and yet I lye, for they pray continually vnto their Saint the Commonwealth; or rather, not to pray to her, but prey on her: for they ride vp & downe on her, and make hir their Boots.

Cham. What, the Commonwealth their Bootes? Will she hold out water in foule way?

Gad. She will, she will; Iustice hath liquor'd her. We steale as in a Castle, cocksure: we haue the receit of Fernseede, we walke inuisible.

Cham. Nay, I thinke rather, you are more beholding to the Night, then to the Fernseed, for your walking inuisible.

Gad. Giue me thy hand
Thou shalt haue a share in our purpose,
As I am a true man.

Cham. Nay, rather let mee haue it, as you are a false Theefe.

God. Goe too: *Homo* is a common name to all men. Bid the Ostler bring the Gelding out of the stable. Farewell, ye muddy Knaue. *Exeunt.*

Scæna Secunda.

Enter Prince Poynes, and Peto.

Poines. Come shelter, shelter, I haue remoued *Falstafs* Horse, and he frets like a gum'd Veluet.

Prin. Stand close.

Enter Falstaffe.

Fal. *Poines, Poines*, and be hang'd *Poines*.

Prin. Peace ye fat-kidney'd Rascall, what a brawling dost thou keepe.

Fas. What *Poines. Hal?*

Prin. He is walk'd vp to the top of the hill, Ile go seek him.

Fal. I am accurst to rob in that Theefe company: that Rascall hath remoued my Horse, and tied him I know not where. If I trauell but foure foot by the squire further a foote, I shall breake my winde. Well, I doubt not but to dye a faire death for all this, if I scape hanging for killing that Rogue, I haue forsworne his company hourely any time this two and twenty yeare, & yet I am bewitcht with the Rogues company. If the Rascall haue not giuen me medicines to make me loue him, Ile be hang'd; it could not be else: I haue drunke Medicines. *Poines, Hal*, a Plague vpon you both. *Bardolph, Peto*: Ile starue ere I rob a foote further. And 'twere not as good a deede as to drinke, to turne True-man, and to leaue these Rogues, I am the veriest Varlet that euer chewed with a Tooth. Eight yards of vneuen ground, is threescore & ten miles afoot with me: and the stony-hearted Villaines knowe it well enough. A plague vpon't, when Theeues cannot be true one to another. *They whistle.*

Whew: a plague light vpon you all. Giue my Horse you Rogues: giue me my Horse, and be hang'd.

Prin. Peace ye fat guttes, lye downe, lay thine eare close to the ground, and list if thou can heare the tread of Trauellers.

Fal. Haue you any Leauers to lift me vp again being downe? Ile not beare mine owne flesh so far afoot again, for all the coine in thy Fathers Exchequer. What a plague meane ye to colt me thus?

Prin. Thou ly'st, thou art not colted, thou art vncolted.

Fal. I prethee good Prince *Hal*, help me to my horse, good Kings sonne.

Prin. Out you Rogue, shall I be your Ostler?

Fal. Go hang thy selfe in thine owne heire-apparant-Garters: If I be tane, Ile peach for this: and I haue not Ballads made on all, and sung to filthy tunes, let a Cup of Sacke be my poyson: when a iest is so forward, & a foote too, I hate it.

Enter Gads-hill.

Gad. Stand.

Fal. So I do against my will.

Poin. O 'tis our Setter, I know his voyce. *Bardolfe*, what newes?

Bar. Case ye, case ye; on with your Vizards, there's mony of the Kings comming downe the hill, 'tis going to the Kings Exchequer.

Fal. You lie you rogue, 'tis going to the Kings Tauern.

Gad. There's enough to make vs all.

Fal. To be hang'd.

Prin. You foure shall front them in the narrow Lane: *Ned* and I, will walke lower; if they scape from your encounter, then they light on vs.

Peto. But how many be of them?

Gad. Some eight or ten.

Fal. Will they not rob vs?

Prin. What, a Coward Sir *Iohn* Paunch?

Fal. Indeed I am not *Iohn of Gaunt* your Grandfather; but yet no Coward, *Hal*.

Prin. Wee'l leaue that to the proofe.

Poin. Sirra Iacke, thy horse stands behinde the hedg, when thon need'st him, there thou shalt finde him. Farewell, and stand fast.

Fal. Now cannot I strike him, if I should be hang'd.

Prin. *Ned*, where are our disguises?

Poin. Heere hard by: Stand close.

Fal. Now my Masters, happy man be his dole, say I: euery man to his businesse.

Enter Trauellers.

Tra. Come Neighbor: the boy shall leade our Horses downe the hill: Wee'l walke a-foot a while, and ease our Legges.

Theeues. Stay.

Tra. Iesu blesse vs.

Fal. Strike: down with them, cut the villains throates a whorson Caterpillars. Bacon-fed Knaues, they hate vs youth; downe with them, fleece them.

Tra. O, we are vndone, both we and ours for euer.

Fal. Hang ye gorbellied knaues, are you vndone? No ye Fat Chuffes, I would your store were heere. On Bacons, on, what ye knaues? Yong men must liue, you are Grand Iurers, are ye? Wee'l iure ye ifaith.

Heere they rob them, and binde them. Enter the Prince and Poynes.

Prin. The Theeues haue bound the True-men: Now could thou and I rob the Theeues, and go merily to London, it would be argument for a Weeke, Laughter for a Moneth, and a good iest for euer.

Poynes. Stand close, I heare them comming.

Enter Theeues againe.

Fal. Come my Masters, let vs share, and then to horsse before day: and the Prince and Poynes bee not two arrand Cowards, there's no equity stirring. There's no moe valour in that Poynes, than in a wilde Ducke.

Prin. Your money.

Poin. Villaines.

As they are sharing, the Prince and Poynes set vpon them. They all run away, leauing the booty behind them.

Prince. Got with much ease. Now merrily to Horse: The Theeues are scattred, and possest with fear so strongly, that they dare not meet each other: each takes his fellow for an Officer. Away good *Ned*, *Falstaffe* sweates to death, and Lards the leane earth as he walkes along: wer't not for laughing, I should pitty him.

Poin. How the Rogue roar'd. *Exeunt.*

Scæna Tertia.

Enter Hotspurre solus, reading a Letter.

But for mine owne part, my Lord, I could bee well contented to be there, in respect of the loue I beare your house.

He

He could be contented: Why is he not then? in respect of the loue he beares our house. He shewes in this, he loues his owne Barne better then he loues our house.. Let me see some more. *The purpose you vndertake is dangerous.* Why that's certaine: 'Tis dangerous to take a Colde, to sleepe, to drinke: but I tell you (my Lord foole) out of this Nettle, Danger; we plucke this Flower, Safety. *The purpose you vndertake is dangerous, the Friends you haue named vncertaine, the Time it selfe vnsorted, and your whole Plot too light, for the counterpoize of so great an Opposition.* Say you so, say you so: I say vnto you againe, you are a shallow cowardly Hinde, and you Lye. What a lacke-braine is this? I protest, our plot is as good a plot as euer was laid; our Friend true and constant: A good Plotte, good Friends, and full of expectation: An excellent plot, very good Friends. What a Frosty-spirited rogue is this? Why, my Lord of Yorke commends the plot, and the generall course of the action. By this hand, if I were now by this Rascall, I could braine him with his Ladies Fan. Is there not my Father, my Vnckle, and my Selfe, Lord *Edmund Mortimer*, my Lord of *Yorke*, and *Owen Glendour*? Is there not besides, the *Dowglas*? Haue I not all their letters, to meete me in Armes by the ninth of the next Moneth? and are they not some of them set forward already? What a Pagan Rascall is this? An Infidell. Ha, you shall see now in very sincerity of Feare and Cold heart, will he to the King, and lay open all our proceedings. O, I could diuide my selfe, and go to buffets, for mouing such a dish of skim'd Milk with so honourable an Action. Hang him, let him tell the King we are prepared. I will set forwards to night.

Enter his Lady.

How now Kate, I must leaue you within these two hours.
La. O my good Lord, why are you thus alone?
For what offence haue I this fortnight bin
A banish'd woman from my *Harries* bed?
Tell me (sweet Lord) what is't that takes from thee
Thy stomacke, pleasure, and thy golden sleepe?
Why dost thou bend thine eyes vpon the earth?
And start so often when thou sitt'st alone?
Why hast thou lost the fresh blood in thy cheekes?
And giuen my Treasures and my rights of thee,
To thicke-ey'd musing, and curst melancholly
In my faint-slumbers, I by thee haue watcht,
And heard thee murmore tales of Iron Warres:
Speake tearmes of manage to thy bounding Steed,
Cry courage to the field. And thou hast talk'd
Of Sallies, and Retires; Trenches, Tents,
Of Palizadoes, Frontiers, Parapets,
Of Basiliskes, of Canon, Culuerin,
Of Prisoners ransome, and of Souldiers slaine,
And all the current of a headdy fight.
Thy spirit within thee hath beene so at Warre,
And thus hath so bestirr'd thee in thy sleepe,
That beds of sweate hath stood vpon thy Brow,
Like bubbles in a late-disturbed Streame;
And in thy face strange motions haue appear'd,
Such as we see when men restraine their breath
On some great sodaine hast. O what portents are these?
Some heauie businesse hath my Lord in hand,
And I must know it: else he loues me not.
Hot. What ho; Is *Gilliams* with the Packet gone?
Ser. He is my Lord, an houre agone.
Hot. Hath *Butler* brought those horses fro the Sheriffe?
Ser. One horse, my Lord, he brought euen now.
Hot. What Horse? A Roane, a crop eare, is it not.
Ser. It is my Lord.
Hot. That Roane shall be my Throne. Well, I will backe him straight. *Esperance*, bid *Butler* lead him forth into the Parke.
La. But heare you, my Lord.
Hot. What say'st thou my Lady?
La. What is it carries you away?
Hot. Why, my horse (my Loue) my horse.
La. Out you mad-headed Ape, a Weazell hath not such a deale of Spleene, as you are tost with. In sooth Ile know your businesse *Harry*, that I will. I feare my Brother *Mortimer* doth stirre about his Title, and hath sent for you to line his enterprize. But if you go——
Hot. So farre a foot, I shall be weary, Loue.
La. Come, come, you Paraquito, answer me directly vnto this question, that I shall aske. Indeede Ile breake thy little finger *Harry*, if thou wilt not tel me true.
Hot. Away, away you trifler: Loue, I loue thee not,
I care not for thee *Kate*: this is no world
To play with Mammets, and to tilt with lips.
We must haue bloodie Noses, and crack'd Crownes,
And passe them currant too. Gods me, my horse.
What say'st thou *Kate*? what wold'st thou haue with me?
La. Do ye not loue me? Do ye not indeed?
Well, do not then. For since you loue me not
I will not loue my selfe. Do you not loue me?
Nay, tell me if thou speak'st in iest or no.
Hot. Come, wilt thou see me ride?
And when I am a horsebacke, I will sweare
I loue thee infinitely. But hearke you *Kate*,
I must not haue you henceforth, question me,
Whether I go: nor reason whereabout.
Whether I must, I must: and to conclude,
This Euening must I leaue thee, gentle *Kate*.
I know you wise, but yet no further wise
Then *Harry Percies* wife. Constant you are,
But yet a woman: and for secrecie,
No Lady closer. For I will beleeue
Thou wilt not vtter what thou do'st not know,
And so farre wilt I trust thee, gentle Kate.
La. How so farre?
Hot. Not an inch further. But harke you *Kate*,
Whither I go, thither shall you go too:
To day will I set forth, to morrow you.
Will this content you *Kate*?
La. It must of force. *Exeunt*

Scena Quarta.

Enter Prince and Poines.

Prin. *Ned*, prethee come out of that fat roome, & lend me thy hand to laugh a little.

Poines. Where hast bene *Hall*?

Prin. With three or foure Logger-heads, amongst 3. or fourescore Hogsheads. I haue sounded the verie base string of humility. Sirra, I am sworn brother to a leash of Drawers, and can call them by their names, as *Tom Dicke*, and *Francis* They take it already vpon their confidence, that though I be but Prince of Wales, yet I am the King of Curtesie: telling me flatly I am no proud Iack like *Falstaffe*, but a Corinthian, a lad of mettle, a good boy, and when I am King of England, I shall command al the good Laddes in East-cheape. They call drinking deepe, dying Scarlet; and when you breath in your watering, then they cry hem,and bid you play it off. To conclude, I am so good a proficient in one quarter of an houre, that I can drinke with any Tinker in his owne Language duringmy life. I tell thee *Ned*,thou hast lost much honor, that thou wer't not with me in this action: but sweet *Ned*,to sweeten which name of *Ned*,I giue thee this peniworth of Sugar, clapt euen now into my hand by an vnder Skinker, one that neuer spake other English in his life, then *Eight shillings and six pence*, and, *You are welcome*: with this shril addition, *Anon, Anon sir, Score a Pint of Bastard in the Halfe Moone*,or so. But *Ned*, to driue away time till *Falstaffe* come, I prythee doe thou stand in some by-roome, while I question my puny Drawer, to what end hee gaue me the Sugar, and do neuer leaue calling *Francis*, that his Tale to me may be nothing but, Anon: step aside, and Ile shew thee a President.

Poines. Francis.

Prin. Thou art perfect.

Poin. Francis.

Enter Drawer.

Fran. Anon,anon sir; looke downe into the Pomgarnet, *Ralfe*.

Prince. Come hither *Francis*.

Fran. My Lord.

Prin. How long hast thou to serue, Francis?

Fran. Forsooth fiue yeares,and as much as to——

Poin. Francis.

Fran. Anon,anon sir.

Prin. Fiue yeares: Berlady a long Lease for the clinking of Pewter. But Francis, darest thou be so valiant, as to play the coward with thy Indenture, & shew it a faire paire of heeles,and run from it?

Fran. O Lord sir, Ile be sworne vpon all the Books in England,I could finde in my heart.

Poin. Francis.

Fran. Anon,anon sir.

Prin. How old art thou,*Francis*?

Fran. Let me see, about Michaelmas next I shalbe——

Poin. Francis.

Fran. Anon sir, pray you stay a little,my Lord.

Prin. Nay but harke you Francis, for the Sugar thou gauest me,'twas a penyworth,was't not?

Fran. O Lord sir, I would it had bene two.

Prin I will giue thee for it a thousand pound: Aske me when thou wilt,and thou shalt haue it.

Poin, Francis.

Fran, Anon,anon.

Prin. Anon Francis? No Francis,but to morrow Francis: or Francis,on thursday: or indeed Francis when thou wilt. But Francis.

Fran. My Lord.

Prin. Wilt thou rob this Leatherne Ierkin, Christall button, Not-pated, Agat ring, Puke stocking, Caddice garter, Smooth tongue,Spanish pouch.

Fran. O Lord sir,who do you meane?

Prin. Why then your browne Bastard is your onely drinke: for looke you Francis,your white Canuas doublet will sulley. In Barbary sir,it cannot come to so much.

Fran. What sir?

Poin. Francis.

Prin. Away you Rogue,dost thou heare them call?

Heere they both call him, the Drawer stands amazed, not knowing which way to go.

Enter Vintner.

Vint. What,stand'st thou still,and hear'st such a calling? Looke to the Guests within: My Lord, olde Sir *Iohn* with halfe a dozen more,are at the doore: shall I let them in?

Prin. Let them alone awhile, and then open the doore. *Poines.*

Enter Poines.

Poin. Anon,anon sir.

Prin. Sirra, *Falstaffe* and the rest of the Theeues,are at the doore,shall we be merry?

Poin. As merrie as Crickets my Lad. But hark yee, What cunning match haue you made with this iest of the Drawer? Come,what's the issue?

Prin. I am now of all humors,that haue shewed themselues humors, since the old dayes of goodman *Adam*, to the pupill age of this present twelue a clock at midnight. What's a clocke Francis?

Fran. Anon,anon sir.

Prin. That euer this Fellow should haue fewer words then a Parret, and yet the sonne of a Woman. His industry is vp-staires and down-staires, his eloquence the parcell of a reckoning. I am not yet of *Percies* mind,the Hotspurre of the North, he that killes me some sixe or seauen dozen of Scots at a Breakfast, washes his hands,and saies to his wife; Fie vpon this quiet life, I want worke. O my sweet *Harry* sayes she, how many hast thou kill'd to day? Giue my Roane horse a drench (sayes hee) and answeres, some fourteene,an houre after: a trifle,a trifle. I prethee call in *Falstaffe*, Ile play *Percy*, and that damn'd Brawne shall play Dame *Mortimer* his wife. *Rivo*,sayes the drunkard. Call in Ribs,call in Tallow.

Enter Falstaffe.

Poin. Welcome Iacke,where hast thou beene?

Fal. A plague of all Cowards I say,and a Vengeance too, marry and Amen. Giue me a cup of Sacke Boy. Ere I leade this life long, Ile sowe nether stockes, and mend them too. A plague of all cowards. Giue me a Cup of Sacke, Rogue. Is there no Vertue extant?

Prin. Didst thou neuer see Titan kisse a dish of Butter, pittifull hearted Titan that melted at the sweete Tale of the Sunne? If thou didst,then behold that compound.

Fal. You Rogue, heere's Lime in this Sacke too: there is nothing but Roguery to be found in Villanous man; yet a Coward is worse then a Cup of Sack with lime. A villanous Coward, go thy wayes old Iacke, die when thou wilt,if manhood,good manhood be not forgot vpon the face of the earth,then am I a shotten Herring: there liues not three good men vnhang'd in England, & one of them is fat,and growes old,God helpe the while,a bad world I say. I would I were a Weauer,I could sing all manner of songs. A plague of all Cowards,I say still.

Prin. How now Woolsacke,what mutter you?

Fal. A Kings Sonne? If I do not beate thee out of thy Kingdome with a dagger of Lath, and driue all thy Subiects afore thee like a flocke of Wilde-geese, Ile neuer weare haire on my face more. You Prince of Wales?

Prin. Why you horson round man?what's the matter?

Fal. Are you not a Coward? Answer me to that, and *Poines* there?

Prin. Ye fatch paunch, and yee call mee Coward, Ile stab thee.

Fal. I call thee Coward? Ile see thee damn'd ere I call the Coward: but I would giue a thousand pound I could run as fast as thou canst. You are straight enough in the shoulders, you care not who sees your backe: Call you that

that backing of your friends? a plague vpon ſuch backing: giue me them that will face me. Giue me a Cup of Sack, I am a Rogue if I drunke to day.

Prince. O Villaine, thy Lippes are ſcarce wip'd, ſince thou drunk'ſt laſt.

Falſt. All's one for that. *He drinkes.*
A plague of all Cowards ſtill, ſay I.

Prince. What's the matter?

Falſt. What's the matter? here be foure of vs, haue ta'ne a thouſand pound this Morning.

Prince. Where is it, *Iack?* where is it?

Falſt. Where is it? taken from vs, it is: a hundred vpon poore foure of vs.

Prince. What, a hundred, man?

Falſt. I am a Rogue, if I were not at halfe Sword with a dozen of them two houres together. I haue ſcaped by miracle. I am eight times thruſt through the Doublet, foure through the Hoſe, my Buckler cut through and through, my Sword hackt like a Hand-ſaw, *ecce ſignum.* I neuer dealt better ſince I was a man: all would not doe. A plague of all Cowards: let them ſpeake; if they ſpeake more or leſſe then truth, they are villaines, and the ſonnes of darkneſſe.

Prince. Speake ſirs, how was it?

Gad. We foure ſet vpon ſome dozen.

Falſt. Sixteene, at leaſt, my Lord.

Gad. And bound them.

Peto. No, no, they were not bound.

Falſt. You Rogue, they were bound, euery man of them, or I am a Iew elſe, an Ebrew Iew.

Gad. As we were ſharing, ſome ſixe or ſeuen freſh men ſet vpon vs.

Falſt. And vnbound the reſt, and then come in the other.

Prince. What, fought yee with them all?

Falſt. All? I know not what yee call all: but if I fought not with fiftie of them, I am a bunch of Radiſh: if there were not two or three and fiftie vpon poore olde *Iack*, then am I no two-legg'd Creature.

Poin. Pray Heauen, you haue not murthered ſome of them.

Falſt. Nay, that's paſt praying for, I haue pepper'd two of them: Two I am ſure I haue payed, two Rogues in Buckrom Sutes. I tell thee what, *Hal*, if I tell thee a Lye, ſpit in my face, call me Horſe: thou knoweſt my olde word: here I lay, and thus I bore my point; foure Rogues in Buckrom let driue at me.

Prince. What, foure? thou ſayd'ſt but two, euen now.

Falſt. Foure *Hal*, I told thee foure.

Poin. I, I, he ſaid foure.

Falſt. Theſe foure came all a-front, and mainely thruſt at me; I made no more adoe, but tooke all their ſeuen points in my Targuet, thus.

Prince. Seuen? why there were but foure, euen now.

Falſt. In Buckrom.

Poin. I, foure, in Buckrom Sutes.

Falſt. Seuen, by theſe Hilts, or I am a Villaine elſe.

Prin. Prethee let him alone, we ſhall haue more anon.

Falſt. Doeſt thou heare me, *Hal?*

Prin. I, and marke thee too, *Iack.*

Falſt. Doe ſo, for it is worth the liſtning too: theſe nine in Buckrom, that I told thee of.

Prin. So, two more alreadie.

Falſt. Their Points being broken.

Poin. Downe fell his Hoſe.

Falſt. Began to giue me ground: but I followed me cloſe, came in foot and hand; and with a thought, ſeuen of the eleuen I pay'd.

Prin. O monſtrous! eleuen Buckrom men growne out of two?

Falſt. But as the Deuill would haue it, three miſ-begotten Knaues, in Kendall Greene, came at my Back, and let driue at me; for it was ſo darke, *Hal*, that thou could'ſt not ſee thy Hand.

Prin. Theſe Lyes are like the Father that begets them, groſſe as a Mountaine, open, palpable. Why thou Clay-brayn'd Guts, thou Knotty-pated Foole, thou Horſon obſcene greaſie Tallow Catch.

Falſt. What, art thou mad? art thou mad? is not the truth, the truth?

Prin. Why, how could'ſt thou know theſe men in Kendall Greene, when it was ſo darke, thou could'ſt not ſee thy Hand? Come, tell vs your reaſon: what ſay'ſt thou to this?

Poin. Come, your reaſon *Iack*, your reaſon.

Falſt. What, vpon compulſion? No: were I at the Strappado, or all the Racks in the World, I would not tell you on compulſion. Giue you a reaſon on compulſion? If Reaſons were as plentie as Black-berries, I would giue no man a Reaſon vpon compulſion, I.

Prin. Ile be no longer guiltie of this ſinne. This ſanguine Coward, this Bed-preſſer, this Horſ-back-breaker, this huge Hill of Fleſh.

Falſt. Away you Starueling, you Elfe-skin, you dried Neats tongue, Bulles-piſſell, you ſtocke-fiſh: O for breth to vtter. What is like thee? You Tailors yard, you ſheath you Bow-caſe, you vile ſtanding tucke.

Prin. Well, breath a-while, and then to't againe: and when thou haſt tyr'd thy ſelfe in baſe compariſons, heare me ſpeake but thus.

Poin. Marke Iacke.

Prin. We two, ſaw you foure ſet on foure and bound them, and were Maſters of their Wealth: mark now how a plaine Tale ſhall put you downe. Then did we two, ſet on you foure, and with a word, outfac'd you from your prize, and haue it: yea, and can ſhew it you in the Houſe. And *Falſtaffe*, you caried your Guts away as nimbly, with as quicke dexteritie, and roared for mercy, and ſtill ranne and roar'd, as euer I heard Bull-Calfe. What a Slaue art thou, to hacke thy ſword as thou haſt done, and then ſay it was in fight. What trick? what deuice? what ſtarting hole canſt thou now find out, to hide thee from this open and apparant ſhame?

Poines. Come, let's heare Iacke: What tricke haſt thou now?

Fal. I knew ye as well as he that made ye. Why heare ye my Maſters, was it for me to kill the Heire apparant? Should I turne vpon the true Prince? Why, thou knoweſt I am as valiant as *Hercules*: but beware Inſtinct, the Lion will not touch the true Prince: Inſtinct is a great matter. I was a Coward on Inſtinct: I ſhall thinke the better of my ſelfe, and thee, during my life: I, for a valiant Lion, and thou for a true Prince. But Lads, I am glad you haue the Mony. Hoſteſſe, clap to the doores: watch to night, pray to morrow. Gallants, Lads, Boyes, Harts of Gold, all the good Titles of Fellowſhip come to you. What, ſhall we be merry? ſhall we haue a Play extempory.

Prin. Content, and the argument ſhall be, thy runing away.

Fal. A, no more of that *Hall*, and thou loueſt me.

Enter Hoſteſſe.

Hoſt. My Lord, the Prince?

Prin.

Prin How now my Lady the Hoſteſſe, what ſay'ſt thou to me?

Hoſteſſe. Marry, my Lord, there is a Noble man of the Court at doore would ſpeake with you: hee ſayes, hee comes from your Father.

Prin. Giue him as much as will make him a Royall man, and ſend him backe againe to my Mother.

Falſt. What manner of man is hee?

Hoſteſſe. An old man.

Falſt. What doth Grauitie out of his Bed at Midnight? Shall I giue him his anſwere?

Prin. Prethee doe *Iacke*.

Falſt. Faith, and Ile ſend him packing. *Exit.*

Prince. Now Sirs: you fought faire; ſo did you *Peto*, ſo did you *Bardol*: you are Lyons too, you ranne away vpon inſtinct: you will not touch the true Prince; no, fie.

Bard. 'Faith, I ranne when I ſaw others runne.

Prin. Tell mee now in earneſt, how came *Falſtaffes* Sword ſo hackt?

Peto. Why, he hackt it with his Dagger, and ſaid, hee would ſweare truth out of England, but hee would make you beleeue it was done in fight, and perſwaded vs to doe the like.

Bard Yea, and to tickle our Noſes with Spear-graſſe, to make them bleed, and then to beſlubber our garments with it, and ſweare it was the blood of true men. I did that I did not this ſeuen yeeres before, I bluſht to heare his monſtrous deuices.

Prin. O Villaine, thou ſtoleſt a Cup of Sacke eighteene yeeres agoe, and wert taken with the manner, and euer ſince thou haſt bluſht extempore: thou hadſt fire and ſword on thy ſide, and yet thou ranſt away; what inſtinct hadſt thou for it?

Bard. My Lord, doe you ſee theſe Meteors? doe you behold theſe Exhalations?

Prin. I doe.

Bard. What thinke you they portend?

Prin. Hot Liuers, and cold Purſes.

Bard. Choler, my Lord, if rightly taken.

Prin No, if rightly taken, Halter.

Enter Falſtaffe

Heere comes leane *Iacke*, heere comes bare-bone. How now my ſweet Creature of Bombaſt, how long is't agoe, *Iacke*, ſince thou ſaw'ſt thine owne Knee?

Falſt. My owne Knee? When I was about thy yeeres (*Hal*) I was not an Eagles Talent in the Waſte, I could haue crept into any Aldermans Thumbe-Ring: a plague of ſighing and griefe, it blowes a man vp like a Bladder. There's villanous Newes abroad: heere was Sir *Iohn Braby* from your Father; you muſt goe to the Court in the Morning. The ſame mad fellow of the North, *Percy*; and hee of Wales, that gaue *Amamon* the Baſtinado, and made *Lucifer* Cuckold, and ſwore the Deuill his true Liege-man vpon the Croſſe of a Welch-hooke; what a plague call you him?

Poin. O, *Glendower*.

Falſt. *Owen, Owen*; the ſame, and his Sonne in Law *Mortimer*, and old *Northumberland*, and the ſprightly Scot of Scots, *Dowglas*, that runnes a Horſe-backe vp a Hill perpendicular.

Prin. Hee that rides at high ſpeede, and with a Piſtoll kills a Sparrow flying.

Falſt. You haue hit it

Prin. So did he neuer the Sparrow.

Falſt. Well, that Raſcall hath good mettall in him, hee will not runne.

Prin. Why, what a Raſcall art thou then, to prayſe him ſo for running?

Falſt. A Horſe-backe (ye Cuckoe) but a foot hee will not budge a foot.

Prin. Yes *Iacke*, vpon inſtinct.

Falſt I grant ye, vpon inſtinct: Well, hee is there too, and one *Mordake*, and a thouſand blew-Cappes more. *Worceſter* is ſtolne away by Night: thy Fathers Beard is turn'd white with the Newes; you may buy Land now as cheape as ſtinking Mackrell.

Prin Then 'tis like, if there come a hot Sunne, and this ciuill buffetting hold, wee ſhall buy Maiden-heads as they buy Hob-nayles, by the Hundreds.

Falſt. By the Maſſe Lad, thou ſay'ſt true, it is like wee ſhall haue good trading that way. But tell me *Hal*, art not thou horrible afear'd? thou being Heire apparant, could the World picke thee out three ſuch Enemyes againe as that Fiend *Dowglas*, that Spirit *Percy*, and that Deuill *Glendower*? Art not thou horrible afraid? Doth not thy blood thrill at it?

Prin. Not a whit: I lacke ſome of thy inſtinct.

Falſt. Well, thou wilt be horrible chidde to morrow, when thou commeſt to thy Father: if thou doe loue me, practiſe an anſwere.

Prin. Doe thou ſtand for my Father, and examine mee vpon the particulars of my Life.

Falſt. Shall I? content: This Chayre ſhall bee my State, this Dagger my Scepter, and this Cuſhion my Crowne.

Prin. Thy State is taken for a Ioyn'd-Stoole, thy Golden Scepter for a Leaden Dagger, and thy precious rich Crowne, for a pittifull bald Crowne.

Falſt. Well, and the fire of Grace be not quite out of thee now ſhalt thou be moued. Giue me a Cup of Sacke to make mine eyes looke redde, that it may be thought I haue wept for I muſt ſpeake in paſſion, and I will doe it in King *Cambyſes* vaine.

Prin. Well, heere is my Legge.

Falſt. And heere is my ſpeech: ſtand aſide Nobilitie.

Hoſteſſe. This is excellent ſport, yfaith.

Falſt. Weepe not, ſweet Queene, for trickling teares are vaine.

Hoſteſſe. O the Father, how hee holdes his countenance?

Falſt. For Gods ſake Lords, conuey my truſtfull Queen,
For teares doe ſtop the ſloud-gates of her eyes.

Hoſteſſe. O rare, he doth it as like one of theſe harlotry Players, as euer I ſee.

Falſt. Peace good Pint-pot, peace good Tickle-braine. *Harry*, I doe not onely maruell where thou ſpendeſt thy time; but alſo, how thou art accompanied: For though the Camomile, the more it is troden, the faſter it growes; yet Youth, the more it is waſted, the ſooner it weares. Thou art my Sonne: I haue partly thy Mothers Word, partly my Opinion; but chiefely, a villanous tricke of thine Eye, and a fooliſh hanging of thy nether Lippe, that doth warrant me. If then thou be Sonne to mee, heere lyeth the point: why, being Sonne to me, art thou ſo poynted at? Shall the bleſſed Sonne of Heauen proue a Micher, and eate Black-berryes? a queſtion not to bee askt. Shall the Sonne of England proue a Theefe, and take Purſes? a queſtion to be askt. There is a thing, *Harry*, which thou haſt often heard of, and it is knowne to many

many in our Land, by the Name of Pitch: this Pitch (as ancient Writers doe report) doth defile; ſo doth the companie thou keepeſt: for *Harry*, now I doe not ſpeake to thee in Drinke, but in Teares; not in Pleaſure, but in Paſſion; not in Words onely, but in Woes alſo: and yet there is a vertuous man, whom I haue often noted in thy companie, but I know not his Name.

Prin. What manner of man, and it like your Maieſtie?

Falſt. A goodly portly man yfaith, and a corpulent, of a chearefull Looke, a pleaſing Eye, and a moſt noble Carriage, and as I thinke, his age ſome fiftie, or (byrlady) inclining to threeſcore; and now I remember mee, his Name is *Falſtaffe*: if that man ſhould be lewdly giuen, hee deceiues mee; for *Harry*, I ſee Vertue in his Lookes. If then the Tree may be knowne by the Fruit, as the Fruit by the Tree, then peremptorily I ſpeake it, there is Vertue in that *Falſtaffe*: him keepe with, the reſt baniſh. And tell mee now, thou naughtie Varlet, tell mee, where haſt thou beene this moneth?

Prin. Do'ſt thou ſpeake like a King? doe thou ſtand for mee, and Ile play my Father.

Falſt. Depoſe me: if thou do'ſt it halfe ſo grauely, ſo maieſtically, both in word and matter, hang me vp by the heeles for a Rabbet-ſucker, or a Poulters Hare.

Prin. Well, heere I am ſet.

Falſt. And heere I ſtand: iudge my Maſters.

Prin. Now *Harry*, whence come you?

Falſt. My Noble Lord, from Eaſt-cheape.

Prin. The complaints I heare of thee, are grieuous.

Falſt. Yfaith, my Lord, they are falſe: Nay, Ile tickle ye for a young Prince.

Prin. Swеareſt thou, vngracious Boy? henceforth ne're looke on me: thou art violently carryed away from Grace: there is a Deuill haunts thee, in the likeneſſe of a fat old Man; a Tunne of Man is thy Companion: Why do'ſt thou conuerſe with that Trunke of Humors, that Boulting-Hutch of Beaſtlineſſe, that ſwolne Parcell of Dropſies, that huge Bombard of Sacke, that ſtuft Cloake-bagge of Guts, that roſted Manning Tree Oxe with the Pudding in his Belly, that reuerend Vice, that grey Iniquitie, that Father Ruffian, that Vanitie in yeeres? wherein is he good, but to taſte Sacke, and drinke it? wherein neat and cleanly, but to carue a Capon, and eat it? wherein Cunning, but in Craft? wherein Craftie, but in Villanie? wherein Villanous, but in all things? wherein worthy, but in nothing.

Falſt. I would your Grace would take me with you: whom meanes your Grace?

Prince. That villanous abhominable miſ-leader of Youth, *Falſtaffe*, that old white-bearded Sathan.

Falſt. My Lord, the man I know.

Prince. I know thou do'ſt.

Falſt. But to ſay, I know more harme in him then in my ſelfe, were to ſay more then I know. That hee is olde (the more the pittie) his white hayres doe witneſſe it: but that hee is (ſauing your reuerence) a Whore-maſter, that I vtterly deny. If Sacke and Sugar bee a fault, Heauen helpe the Wicked: if to be olde and merry, be a ſinne, then many an olde Hoſte that I know, is damn'd: if to be fat, be to be hated, then *Pharaohs* leane Kine are to be loued. No, my good Lord, baniſh *Peto*, baniſh *Bardolph*, baniſh *Poines*: but for ſweete *Iacke Falſtaffe*, kinde *Iacke Falſtaffe*, true *Iacke Falſtaffe*, valiant *Iacke Falſtaffe*, and therefore more valiant, being as hee is olde *Iack Falſtaffe*, baniſh not him thy *Harryes* companie, baniſh not him thy *Harryes* companie; baniſh plumpe *Iacke* and baniſh all the World.

Prince. I doe, I will.

Enter Bardolph running.

Bard. O, my Lord, my Lord, the Sheriffe, with a moſt moſt monſtrous Watch, is at the doore.

Falſt. Out you Rogue, play out the Play: I haue much to ſay in the behalfe of that *Falſtaffe*.

Enter the Hoſteſſe.

Hoſteſſe. O, my Lord, my Lord.

Falſt. Heigh, heigh, the Deuill rides vpon a Fiddle-ſticke: what's the matter?

Hoſteſſe. The Sheriffe and all the Watch are at the doore: they are come to ſearch the Houſe, ſhall I let them in?

Falſt. Do'ſt thou heare *Hal*, neuer call a true peece of Gold a Counterfeit: thou art eſſentially made, without ſeeming ſo.

Prince. And thou a naturall Coward, without inſtinct.

Falſt. I deny your *Maior*: if you will deny the Sheriffe, ſo: if not, let him enter. If I become not a Cart as well as another man, a plague on my bringing vp: I hope I ſhall as ſoone be ſtrangled with a Halter, as another.

Prince. Goe hide thee behinde the Arras, the reſt walke vp aboue. Now my Maſters, for a true Face and good Conſcience.

Falſt. Both which I haue had: but their date is out, and therefore Ile hide me. *Exit.*

Prince. Call in the Sheriffe.

Enter Sheriffe and the Carrier.

Prince. Now Maſter Sheriffe, what is your will with mee?

She. Firſt pardon me, my Lord. A Hue and Cry hath followed certaine men vnto this houſe.

Prince. What men?

She. One of them is well knowne, my gracious Lord, a groſſe fat man.

Car. As fat as Butter.

Prince. The man, I doe aſſure you, is not heere,
For I my ſelfe at this time haue imploy'd him:
And Sheriffe, I will engage my word to thee,
That I will by to morrow Dinner time,
Send him to anſwere thee, or any man,
For any thing he ſhall be charg'd withall:
And ſo let me entreat you, leaue the houſe.

She. I will, my Lord: there are two Gentlemen
Haue in this Robberie loſt three hundred Marke.

Prince. It may be ſo: if he haue robb'd theſe men,
He ſhall be anſwerable: and ſo farewell.

She. Good Night, my Noble Lord.

Prince. I thinke it is good Morrow, is it not?

She. Indeede, my Lord, I thinke it be two a Clocke. *Exit.*

Prince. This oyly Raſcall is knowne as well as Poules: goe call him forth.

Peto. *Falſtaffe*? faſt aſleepe behinde the Arras, and ſnorting like a Horſe.

Prince. Harke, how hard he fetches breath: ſearch his Pockets.

He

He ſearcheth his Pockets, and findeth certaine Papers.

Prince. What haſt thou found?

Peto. Nothing but Papers, my Lord.

Prince. Let's ſee, what be they? reade them.

Peto. Item, a Capon. ii.s.ii.d.
Item, Sawce. iiii.d.
Item, Sacke, two Gallons. v.s.viii.d.
Item, Anchoues and Sacke after Supper. ii.s.vi.d.
Item, Bread. ob.

Prince. O monſtrous, but one halfe penny-worth of Bread to this intollerable deale of Sacke? What there is elſe, keepe cloſe, wee'le reade it at more aduantage: there let him ſleepe till day. Ile to the Court in the Morning: Wee muſt all to the Warres, and thy place ſhall be honorable. Ile procure this fat Rogue a Charge of Foot, and I know his death will be a Match of Twelue-ſcore. The Money ſhall be pay'd backe againe with aduantage. Be with me betimes in the Morning: and ſo good morrow *Peto.*

Peto. Good morrow, good my Lord. *Exeunt.*

Actus Tertius. Scena Prima.

Enter Hotſpurre, Worceſter, Lord Mortimer, Owen Glendower.

Mort. Theſe promiſes are faire, the parties ſure,
And our induction full of proſperous hope.

Hotſp. Lord *Mortimer*, and Couſin *Glendower*,
Will you ſit downe?
And Vnckle *Worceſter*; a plague vpon it,
I haue forgot the Mappe.

Glend. No, here it is:
Sit Couſin *Percy*, ſit good Couſin *Hotſpurre*:
For by that Name, as oft as *Lancaſter* doth ſpeake of you,
His Cheekes looke pale, and with a riſing ſigh,
He wiſheth you in Heauen.

Hotſp. And you in Hell, as oft as he heares *Owen Glendower* ſpoke of.

Glend. I cannot blame him: At my Natiuitie,
The front of Heauen was full of fierie ſhapes,
Of burning Creſſets: and at my Birth,
The frame and foundation of the Earth
Shak'd like a Coward.

Hotſp. Why ſo it would haue done at the ſame ſeaſon, if your Mothers Cat had but kitten'd, though your ſelfe had neuer beene borne.

Glend. I ſay the Earth did ſhake when I was borne.

Hotſp. And I ſay the Earth was not of my minde,
If you ſuppoſe, as fearing you, it ſhooke.

Glend. The Heauens were all on fire, the Earth did tremble.

Hotſp. Oh, then the Earth ſhooke
To ſee the Heauens on fire,
And not in feare of your Natiuitie.
Diſeaſed Nature oftentimes breakes forth
In ſtrange eruptions; and the teeming Earth
Is with a kinde of Collick pincht and vext,
By the impriſoning of vnruly Winde
Within her Wombe: which for enlargement ſtriuing,
Shakes the old Beldame Earth, and tombles downe
Steeples, and moſſe-growne Towers. At your Birth,
Our Grandam Earth, hauing this diſtemperature,
In paſſion ſhooke.

Glend. Couſin: of many men
I doe not beare theſe Croſſings: Giue me leaue
To tell you once againe, that at my Birth
The front of Heauen was full of fierie ſhapes,
The Goates ranne from the Mountaines, and the Heards
Were ſtrangely clamorous to the frighted fields:
Theſe ſignes haue markt me extraordinarie,
And all the courſes of my Life doe ſhew,
I am not in the Roll of common men.
Where is the Liuing, clipt in with the Sea,
That chides the Bankes of England, Scotland, and Wales,
Which calls me Pupill, or hath read to me?
And bring him out, that is but Womans Sonne,
Can trace me in the tedious wayes of Art,
And hold me pace in deepe experiments.

Hotſp. I thinke there's no man ſpeakes better Welſh:
Ile to Dinner.

Mort. Peace Couſin *Percy*, you will make him mad.

Glend. I can call Spirits from the vaſtie Deepe.

Hotſp. Why ſo can I, or ſo can any man:
But will they come, when you doe call for them?

Glend. Why, I can teach thee, Couſin, to command the Deuill.

Hotſp. And I can teach thee, Couſin, to ſhame the Deuil,
By telling truth. *Tell truth, and ſhame the Deuill.*
If thou haue power to rayſe him, bring him hither,
And Ile be ſworne, I haue power to ſhame him hence.
Oh, while you liue, tell truth, and ſhame the Deuill.

Mort. Come come, no more of this vnprofitable Chat.

Glend. Three times hath *Henry Bullingbrooke* made head
Againſt my Power: thrice from the Banks of Wye,
And ſandy-bottom'd Seuerne, haue I hent him
Bootleſſe home, and Weather-beaten backe.

Hotſp. Home without Bootes,
And in foule Weather too,
How ſcapes he Agues in the Deuils name?

Glend. Come, heere's the Mappe:
Shall wee diuide our Right,
According to our three-fold order ta'ne?

Mort. The Arch-Deacon hath diuided it
Into three Limits, very equally:
England, from Trent, and Seuerne, hitherto,
By South and Eaſt is to my part aſſign'd:
All Weſtward, Wales, beyond the Seuerne ſhore,
And all the fertile Land within that bound,
To *Owen Glendower*: And deare Couze, to you
The remnant Northward, lying off from Trent.
And our Indentures Tripartite are drawne:
Which being ſealed enterchangeably,
(A Buſineſſe that this Night may execute)
To morrow, Couſin *Percy*, you and I,
And my good Lord of Worceſter, will ſet forth,
To meete your Father, and the Scottiſh Power,
As is appointed vs at Shrewsbury.
My Father *Glendower* is not readie yet;
Nor ſhall wee neede his helpe theſe foureteene dayes:
Within that ſpace, you may haue drawne together
Your Tenants Friends and neighbouring Gentlemen.

Glend. A ſhorter time ſhall ſend me to you, Lords:
And in my Conduct ſhall your Ladies come,
From whom you now muſt ſteale, and take no leaue,
For there will be a World of Water ſhed,

Vpon

Vpon the parting of your Wiues and you.
Hotsp. Me thinks my Moity, North from Burton here,
In quantitie equals not one of yours:
See, how this Riuer comes me cranking in,
And cuts me from the best of all my Land,
A huge halfe Moone, a monstrous Cantle out.
Ile haue the Currant in this place damn'd vp,
And here the smug and Siluer Trent shall runne,
In a new Channell, faire and euenly:
It shall not winde with such a deepe indent,
To rob me of so rich a Bottome here.
Glend. Not winde? it shall, it must, you see it doth.
Mort, Yea, but marke how he beares his course,
And runnes me vp with like aduantage on the other side,
Gelding the opposed Continent as much,
As on the other side it takes from you.
Worc. Yea, but a little Charge will trench him here,
And on this North side winne this Cape of Land,
And then he runnes straight and euen.
Hotsp. Ile haue it so, a little Charge will doe it.
Glend. Ile not haue it alter'd.
Hotsp. Will not you?
Glend. No, nor you shall not.
Hotsp. Who shall say me nay?
Glend. Why, that will I.
Hotsp. Let me not vnderstand you then, speake it in Welsh.
Glend. I can speake English, Lord, as well as you:
For I was trayn'd vp in the English Court;
Where, being but young, I framed to the Harpe
Many an English Dittie, louely well,
And gaue the Tongue a helpefull Ornament;
A Vertue that was neuer seene in you.
Hotsp. Marry, and I am glad of it with all my heart,
I had rather be a Kitten, and cry mew,
Then one of these same Meeter Ballad-mongers:
I had rather heare a Brazen Candlestick turn'd,
Or a dry Wheele grate on the Axle-tree,
And that would set my teeth nothing an edge,
Nothing so much, as mincing Poetrie;
'Tis like the forc't gate of a shuffling Nagge.
Glend. Come, you shall haue Trent turn'd.
Hotsp. I doe not care: Ile giue thrice so much Land
To any well-deseruing friend;
But in the way of Bargaine, marke ye me,
Ile cauill on the ninth part of a hayre.
Are the Indentures drawne? shall we be gone?
Glend. The Moone shines faire,
You may away by Night:
Ile haste the Writer; and withall,
Breake with your Wiues, of your departure hence:
I am afraid my Daughter will runne madde,
So much she doteth on her *Mortimer*. *Exit.*
Mort. Fie, Cousin *Percy*, how you crosse my Father.
Hotsp. I cannot chuse: sometime he angers me,
With telling me of the Moldwarpe and the Ant,
Of the Dreamer *Merlin*, and his Prophecies;
And of a Dragon, and a finne-lesse Fish,
A clip-wing'd Griffin, and a moulten Rauen,
A couching Lyon, and a ramping Cat,
And such a deale of skimble-skamble Stuffe,
As puts me from my Faith. I tell you what,
He held me last Night, at least, nine howres,
In reckning vp the seuerall Deuils Names,
That were his Lacqueyes:
I cry'd hum, and well, goe too,
But mark'd him not a word. O, he is as tedious
As a tyred Horse, a rayling Wife,
Worse then a smoakie House. I had rather liue
With Cheese and Garlick in a Windmill farre,
Than feede on Cates, and haue him talke to me,
In any Summer-House in Christendome.
Mort. In faith he was a worthy Gentleman,
Exceeding well read, and profited,
In strange Concealements.
Valiant as a Lyon, and wondrous affable,
And as bountifull, as Mynes of India.
Shall I tell you, Cousin,
He holds your temper in a high respect,
And curbes himselfe, euen of his naturall scope,
When you doe crosse his humor: 'faith he does.
I warrant you, that man is not aliue,
Might so haue tempted him, as you haue done,
Without the taste of danger, and reproofe:
But doe not vse it oft, let me entreat you.
Worc. In faith, my Lord, you are too wilfull blame,
And since your comming hither, haue done enough,
To put him quite besides his patience.
You must needes learne, Lord, to amend this fault:
Though sometimes it shew Greatnesse, Courage, Blood,
And that's the dearest grace it renders you;
Yet oftentimes it doth present harsh Rage,
Defect of Manners, want of Gouernment,
Pride, Haughtinesse, Opinion, and Disdaine:
The least of which, haunting a Nobleman,
Loseth mens hearts, and leaues behinde a stayne
Vpon the beautie of all parts besides,
Beguiling them of commendation.
Hotsp. Well, I am school'd:
Good-manners be your speede;
Heere come your Wiues, and let vs take our leaue.

Enter Glendower, with the Ladies.

Mort. This is the deadly spight, that angers me,
My Wife can speake no English, I no Welsh.
Glend. My Daughter weepes, shee'le not part with you,
Shee'le be a Souldier too, shee'le to the Warres.
Mort. Good Father tell her, that she and my Aunt *Percy*
Shall follow in your Conduct speedily.

Glendower speakes to her in Welsh, and she answeres him in the same.

Glend. Shee is desperate heere;
A peeuish selfe-will'd Harlotry,
One that no perswasion can doe good vpon.

The Lady speakes in Welsh

Mort. I vnderstand thy Lookes: that pretty Welsh
Which thou powr'st down from these swelling Heauens,
I am too perfect in: and but for shame,
In such a parley should I answere thee.

The Lady againe in Welsh.

Mort. I vnderstand thy Kisses, and thou mine,
And that's a feeling disputation:
But I will neuer be a Truant, Loue,
Till I haue learn'd thy Language: for thy tongue
Makes

Makes Welsh as sweet as Ditties highly penn'd,
Sung by a faire Queene in a Summers Bowre,
With rauishing Diuision to her Lute.
Glend. Nay, if thou melt, then will she runne madde.

The Lady speakes agaime in Welsh.

Mort. O, I am Ignorance it selfe in this.
Glend. She bids you,
On the wanton Rushes lay you downe,
And rest your gentle Head vpon her Lappe,
And she will sing the Song that pleaseth you,
And on your Eye-lids Crowne the God of Sleepe,
Charming your blood with pleasing heauinesse;
Making such difference betwixt Wake and Sleepe,
As is the difference betwixt Day and Night,
The houre before the Heauenly Harneis'd Teeme
Begins his Golden Progresse in the East.
Mort. With all my heart Ile sit, and heare her sing:
By that time will our Booke, I thinke, be drawne.
Glend. Doe so:
And those Musitians that shall play to you,
Hang in the Ayre a thousand Leagues from thence;
And straight they shall be here: sit, and attend.
Hotsp. Come *Kate*, thou art perfect in lying downe:
Come, quicke, quicke, that I may lay my Head in thy Lappe
Lady. Goe, ye giddy-Goose.

The Musicke playes.

Hotsp. Now I perceiue the Deuill vnderstands Welsh,
And 'tis no maruell he is so humorous:
Byrlady hee's a good Musitian.
Lady. Then would you be nothing but Musicall,
For you are altogether gouerned by humors:
Lye still ye Theefe, and heare the Lady sing in Welsh.
Hotsp. I had rather heare (Lady) my Brach howle in Irish.
Lady. Would'st haue thy Head broken?
Hotsp. No.
Lady. Then be still
Hotsp. Neyther, 'tis a Womans fault.
Lady. Now God helpe thee.
Hotsp. To the Welsh Ladies Bed.
Lady. What's that?
Hotsp. Peace, shee sings.

Heere the Lady sings a Welsh Song.

Hotsp. Come, Ile haue your Song too.
Lady. Not mine, in good sooth.
Hotsp. Not yours, in good sooth?
You sweare like a Comfit-makers Wife:
Not you, in good sooth; and, as true as I liue;
And, as God shall mend me; and, as sure as day:
And giuest such Sarcenet suretie for thy Oathes,
As if thou neuer walk'st further then Finsbury.
Sweare me, *Kate*, like a Lady, as thou art,
A good mouth-filling Oath: and leaue in sooth,
And such protest of Pepper Ginger-bread,
To Veluet-Guards, and Sunday-Citizens.
Come, sing.
Lady. I will not sing.
Hotsp. 'Tis the next way to turne Taylor, or be Red-brest teacher: and the Indentures be drawne, Ile away within these two howres: and so come in, when yee will. *Exit.*
Glend. Come, come, Lord *Mortimer*, you are as slow,
As hot Lord *Percy* is on fire to goe.
By this our Booke is drawne: wee'le but seale,
And then to Horse immediately.
Mort. With all my heart. *Exeunt.*

Scæna Secunda.

Enter the King, Prince of Wales and others.

King. Lords, giue vs leaue:
The Prince of Wales, and I,
Must haue some priuate conference:
But be neere at hand,
For wee shall presently haue neede of you. *Exeunt Lords.*
I know not whether Heauen will haue it so,
For some displeasing seruice I haue done;
That in his secret Doome, out of my Blood,
Hee'le breede Reuengement, and a Scourge for me:
But thou do'st in thy passages of Life,
Make me beleeue, that thou art onely mark'd
For the hot vengeance, and the Rod of heauen
To punish my Mistreadings. Tell me else,
Could such inordinate and low desires,
Such poore, such bare, such lewd, such meane attempts,
Such barren pleasures, rude societie,
As thou art matcht withall, and grafted too,
Accompanie the greatnesse of thy blood,
And hold their leuell with thy Princely heart?
Prince So please your Maiesty, I would I could
Quit all offences with as cleare excuse,
As well as I am doubtlesse I can purge
My selfe of many I am charg'd withall:
Yet such extenuation let me begge,
As in reproofe of many Tales deuis'd,
Which oft the Eare of Greatnesse needes must heare,
By smiling Pick-thankes, and base Newes-mongers;
I may for some things true, wherein my youth
Hath faultie wandred, and irregular,
Finde pardon on my true submission.
King. Heauen pardon thee:
Yet let me wonder, *Harry*,
At thy affections, which doe hold a Wing
Quite from the flight of all thy ancestors.
Thy place in Councell thou hast rudely lost,
Which by thy younger Brother is supply'de;
And art almost an alien to the hearts
Of all the Court and Princes of my blood.
The hope and expectation of thy time
Is ruin'd, and the Soule of euery man
Prophetically doe fore-thinke thy fall.
Had I so lauish of my presence beene,
So common hackney'd in the eyes of men,
So stale and cheape to vulgar Company;
Opinion, that did helpe me to the Crowne,
Had still kept loyall to possession,
And left me in reputelesse banishment,
A fellow of no marke, nor likelyhood.
By being seldome seene, I could not stirre,
But like a Comet, I was wondred at,
That

That men would tell their Children, This is hee:
Others would ſay; Where, Which is *Bullingbrooke*.
And then I ſtole all Courteſie from Heauen,
And dreſt my ſelfe in ſuch Humilitie,
That I did plucke Allegeance from mens hearts,
Lowd Showts and Salutations from their mouthes,
Euen in the preſence of the Crowned King.
Thus I did keepe my Perſon freſh and new,
My Preſence like a Robe Pontificall,
Ne're ſeene, but wondred at: and ſo my State,
Seldome but ſumptuous, ſhewed like a Feaſt,
And wonne by rareneſſe ſuch Solemnitie.
The skipping King hee ambled vp and downe,
With ſhallow Ieſters, and raſh Bauin Wits,
Soone kindled, and ſoone burnt, carded his State,
Mingled his Royaltie with Carping Fooles,
Had his great Name prophaned with their Scornes,
And gaue his Countenance, againſt his Name,
To laugh at gybing Boyes, and ſtand the puſh
Of euery Beardleſſe vaine Comparatiue;
Grew a Companion to the common Streetes,
Enfeoff'd himſelfe to Popularitie:
That being dayly ſwallowed by mens Eyes,
They ſurfeted with Honey, and began to loathe
The taſte of Sweetneſſe, whereof a little
More then a little, is by much too much.
So when he had occaſion to be ſeene,
He was but as the Cuckow is in Iune,
Heard, not regarded: ſeene but with ſuch Eyes,
As ſicke and blunted with Communitie,
Affoord no extraordinarie Gaze,
Such as is bent on Sunne-like Maieſtie,
When it ſhines ſeldome in admiring Eyes:
But rather drowz'd, and hung their eye-lids downe,
Slept in his Face, and rendred ſuch aſpect
As Cloudie men vſe to doe to their aduerſaries,
Being with his preſence glutted, gorg'd, and full.
And in that very Line, *Harry*, ſtandeſt thou:
For thou haſt loſt thy Princely Priuiledge,
With vile participation. Not an Eye
But is a-wearie of thy common ſight,
Saue mine, which hath deſir'd to ſee thee more:
Which now doth that I would not haue it doe,
Make blinde it ſelfe with fooliſh tenderneſſe.
Prince. I ſhall hereafter, my thrice gracious Lord,
Be more my ſelfe.
King. For all the World,
As thou art to this houre, was *Richard* then,
When I from France ſet foot at Rauenſpurgh;
And euen as I was then, is *Percy* now:
Now by my Scepter, and my Soule to boot,
He hath more worthy intereſt to the State
Then thou, the ſhadow of Succeſſion;
For of no Right, nor colour like to Right.
He doth fill fields with Harneis in the Realme,
Turnes head againſt the Lyons armed Iawes;
And being no more in debt to yeeres, then thou,
Leades ancient Lords, and reuerent Biſhops on
To bloody Battailes, and to bruſing Armes.
What neuer-dying Honor hath he got,
Againſt renowned *Dowglas*? whoſe high Deedes,
Whoſe hot Incurſions, and great Name in Armes,
Holds from all Souldiers chiefe Maioritie,
And Militarie Title Capitall.
Through all the Kingdomes that acknowledge Chriſt,
Thrice hath the *Hotſpur Mars*, in ſwathing Clothes,
This Infant Warrior, in his Enterpriſes,
Diſcomfited great *Dowglas*, ta'ne him once,
Enlarged him, and made a friend of him,
To fill the mouth of deepe Defiance vp,
And ſhake the peace and ſafetie of our Throne.
And what ſay you to this? *Percy, Northumberland*,
The Arch-biſhops Grace of Yorke, *Dowglas, Mortimer*,
Capitulate againſt vs, and are vp.
But wherefore doe I tell theſe Newes to thee?
Why, *Harry*, doe I tell thee of my Foes,
Which art my neer'ſt and deareſt Enemie?
Thou, that art like enough, through vaſſall Feare,
Baſe Inclination, and the ſtart of Spleene,
To fight againſt me vnder *Percies* pay,
To dogge his heeles, and curtſie at his frownes,
To ſhew how much thou art degenerate.
Prince. Doe not thinke ſo, you ſhall not finde it ſo:
And Heauen forgiue them, that ſo much haue ſway'd
Your Maieſties good thoughts away from me:
I will redeeme all this on *Percies* head,
And in the cloſing of ſome glorious day,
Be bold to tell you, that I am your Sonne,
When I will weare a Garment all of Blood,
And ſtaine my fauours in a bloody Maske:
Which waſht away, ſhall ſcowre my ſhame with it.
And that ſhall be the day, when ere it lights,
That this ſame Child of Honor and Renowne,
This gallant *Hotſpur*, this all-prayſed Knight,
And your vnthought-of *Harry* chance to meet:
For euery Honor ſitting on his Helme,
Would they were multitudes, and on my head
My ſhames redoubled. For the time will come,
That I ſhall make this Northerne Youth exchange
His glorious Deedes for my Indignities:
Percy is but my Factor, good my Lord,
To engroſſe vp glorious Deedes on my behalfe:
And I will call him to ſo ſtrict account,
That he ſhall render euery Glory vp,
Yea, euen the ſleighteſt worſhip of his time,
Or I will teare the Reckoning from his Heart.
This, in the Name of Heauen, I promiſe here:
The which, if I performe, and doe ſuruiue,
I doe beſeech your Maieſtie, may ſalue
The long-growne Wounds of my intemperature:
If not, the end of Life cancells all Bands,
And I will dye a hundred thouſand Deaths,
Ere breake the ſmalleſt parcell of this Vow.
King. A hundred thouſand Rebels dye in this:
Thou ſhalt haue Charge, and ſoueraigne truſt herein.

Enter Blunt.

How now good *Blunt*? thy Lookes are full of ſpeed.
Blunt. So hath the Buſineſſe that I come to ſpeake of.
Lord *Mortimer* of Scotland hath ſent word,
That *Dowglas* and the Engliſh Rebels met
The eleuenth of this moneth, at Shrewsbury:
A mightie and a fearefull Head they are,
(If Promiſes be kept on euery hand)
As euer offered foule play in a State.
King. The Earle of Weſtmerland ſet forth to day:
With him my ſonne, Lord *Iohn* of Lancaſter,
For this aduertiſement is fiue dayes old.
On Wedneſday next, *Harry* thou ſhalt ſet forward:
On Thurſday, wee our ſelues will march.
Our meeting is Bridgenorth: and *Harry*, you ſhall march

f Through

Through Glocestershire: by which account,
Our Businesse valued some twelue dayes hence,
Our generall Forces at Bridgenorth shall meete.
Our Hands are full of Businesse: let's away,
Aduantage feedes him fat, while men delay. *Exeunt.*

Scena Tertia.

Enter Falstaffe and Bardolph.

Falst. *Bardolph*, am I not falne away vilely, since this last action? doe I not bate? doe I not dwindle? Why my skinne hangs about me like an olde Ladies loose Gowne: I am withered like an olde Apple *Iohn*. Well, Ile repent, and that suddenly, while I am in some liking: I shall be out of heart shortly, and then I shall haue no strength to repent. And I haue not forgotten what the in-side of a Church is made of, I am a Pepper-Corne, a Brewers Horse, the in-side of a Church. Company, villanous Company hath beene the spoyle of me.

Bard. Sir *Iohn*, you are so fretfull, you cannot liue long.

Falst. Why there is it: Come, sing me a bawdy Song, make me merry: I was as vertuously giuen, as a Gentleman need to be; vertuous enough, swore little, dic'd not aboue seuen times a weeke, went to a Bawdy-house not aboue once in a quarter of an houre, payd Money that I borrowed, three or foure times; liued well, and in good compasse: and now I liue out of all order, out of compasse.

Bard Why, you are so fat, Sir *Iohn*, that you must needes bee out of all compasse; out of all reasonable compasse, Sir *Iohn*.

Falst. Doe thou amend thy Face, and Ile amend thy Life: Thou art our Admirall, thou bearest the Lanterne in the Poope, but 'tis in the Nose of thee; thou art the Knight of the burning Lampe.

Bard. Why, Sir *Iohn*, my Face does you no harme.

Falst. No, Ile be sworne: I make as good vse of it, as many a man doth of a Deaths-Head, or a *Memento Mori*. I neuer see thy Face, but I thinke vpon Hell fire, and *Diues* that liued in Purple; for there he is in his Robes burning, burning. If thou wert any way giuen to vertue, I would sweare by thy Face; my Oath should bee, *By this Fire*: But thou art altogether giuen ouer; and wert indeede, but for the Light in thy Face, the Sunne of vtter Darkenesse. When thou ran'st vp Gads-Hill, in the Night, to catch my Horse, if I did not thinke that thou hadst beene an *Ignis fatuus*, or a Ball of Wild-fire, there's no Purchase in Money. O thou art a perpetuall Triumph, an euerlasting Bone-fire-Light: thou hast saued me a thousand Markes in Linkes and Torches, walking with thee in the Night betwixt Tauerne and Tauerne: But the Sack that thou hast drunke me, would haue bought me Lights as good cheape, as the dearest Chandlers in Europe. I haue maintain'd that Salamander of yours with fire, any time this two and thirtie yeeres, Heauen reward me for it.

Bard. I would my Face were in your Belly.

Falst. So should I be sure to be heart-burn'd.

Enter Hostesse.

How now, Dame *Partlet* the Hen, haue you enquir'd yet who pick'd my Pocket?

Hostesse. Why Sir *Iohn*, what doe you thinke, Sir *Iohn*? doe you thinke I keepe Theeues in my House? I haue search'd, I haue enquired, so haz my Husband, Man by Man, Boy by Boy, Seruant by Seruant: the tight of a hayre was neuer lost in my house before.

Falst. Ye lye Hostesse: *Bardolph* was shau'd, and lost many a hayre; and Ile be sw me my Pocket was pick'd: goe to, you are a Woman, goe.

Hostesse. Who I? I defie thee: I was neuer call'd so in mine owne house before.

Falst. Goe to, I know you well enough.

Hostesse. No, Sir *Iohn*, you doe not know me, Sir *Iohn*: I know you, Sir *Iohn*: you owe me Money, Sir *Iohn*, and now you picke a quarrell, to beguile me of it: I bought you a dozen of Shirts to your Backe.

Falst. Doulas, filthy Doulas: I haue giuen them away to Bakers Wiues, and they haue made Boulters of them.

Hostesse. Now as I am a true Woman, Holland of eight shillings an Ell: You owe Money here besides, Sir *Iohn*, for your Dyet, and by-Drinkings, and Money lent you, foure and twentie pounds.

Falst. Hee had his part of it, let him pay.

Hostesse. Hee? alas hee is poore, hee hath nothing.

Falst. How? Poore? Looke vpon his Face: What call you Rich? Let them coyne his Nose, let them coyne his Cheekes, Ile not pay a Denier. What, will you make a Younker of me? Shall I not take mine ease in mine Inne, but I shall haue my Pocket pick'd? I haue lost a Seale-Ring of my Grand-fathers, worth fortie Marke.

Hostesse. I haue heard the Prince tell him, I know not how oft, that that Ring was Copper.

Falst. How? the Prince is a Iacke, a Sneake-Cuppe: and if hee were heere, I would cudgell him like a Dogge, if hee would say so.

Enter the Prince marching, and Falstaffe meets him, playing on his Truncheon like a Fife.

Falst. How now Lad? is the Winde in that Doore? Must we all march?

Bard. Yea, two and two, Newgate fashion.

Hostesse. My Lord, I pray you heare me.

Prince. What say'st thou, Mistresse *Quickly*? How does thy Husband? I loue him well, hee is an honest man.

Hostesse. Good, my Lord, heare mee.

Falst. Prethee let her alone, and list to mee.

Prince. What say'st thou, *Iacke*?

Falst. The other Night I fell asleepe heere behind the Arras, and had my Pocket pickt: this House is turn'd Bawdy-house, they picke Pockets.

Prince. What didst thou lose, *Iacke*?

Falst. Wilt thou beleeue me, *Hal*? Three or foure Bonds of fortie pound apeece, and a Seale-Ring of my Grandfathers.

Prince. A Trifle, some eight-penny matter.

Host. So I told him, my Lord; and I said, I heard your Grace say so: and (my Lord) hee speakes most vilely of you, like a foule-mouth'd man as hee is, and said, hee would cudgell you.

Prince. What hee did not?

Host. There's neyther Faith, Truth, nor Woman-hood in me else.

Falst. There's

Falst. There's no more faith in thee then a stu'de Prune; nor no more truth in thee, then in a drawne Fox: and for Wooman-hood, Maid-marian may be the Deputies wife of the Ward to thee. Go you nothing: go.

Host. Say, what thing? what thing?

Falst. What thing? why a thing to thanke heauen on.

Host. I am no thing to thanke heauen on, I wold thou shouldst know it: I am an honest mans wife: and setting thy Knighthood aside, thou art a knaue to call me so.

Falst. Setting thy woman-hood aside, thou art a beast to say otherwise.

Host. Say, what beast, thou knaue thou?

Fal. What beast? Why an Otter.

Prin. An Otter, sir *Iohn*? Why an Otter?

Fal. Why? She's neither fish nor flesh; a man knowes not where to haue her.

Host. Thou art vniust man in saying so; thou, or anie man knowes where to haue me, thou knaue thou.

Prince. Thou say'st true Hostesse, and he slanders thee most grossely.

Host. So he doth you, my Lord, and sayde this other day, You ought him a thousand pound.

Prince. Sirrah, do I owe you a thousand pound?

Falst. A thousand pound *Hal*? A Million. Thy loue is worth a Million: thou ow'st me thy loue.

Host. Nay my Lord, he call'd you Iacke, and said hee would cudgell you.

Fal. Did I, *Bardolph*?

Bar. Indeed Sir *Iohn*, you said so.

Fal. Yea, if he said my Ring was Copper.

Prince. I say 'tis Copper. Dar'st thou bee as good as thy word now?

Fal. Why *Hal*? thou know'st, as thou art but a man, I dare: but, as thou art a Prince, I feare thee, as I feare the roaring of the Lyons Whelpe.

Prince. And why not as the Lyon?

Fal. The King himselfe is to bee feared as the Lyon: Do'st thou thinke Ile feare thee, as I feare thy Father? nay if I do, let my Girdle breake.

Prin. O, if it should, how would thy guttes fall about thy knees. But sirra: There's no roome for Faith, Truth, nor Honesty, in this bosome of thine: it is all fill'd vppe with Guttes and Midriffe. Charge an honest Woman with picking thy pocket? Why thou horson impudent imbost Rascall, if there were any thing in thy Pocket but Tauerne Recknings, *Memorandums* of Bawdie-houses, and one poore peny-worth of Sugar-candie to make thee long-winded: if thy pocket were enrich'd with anie other iniuries but these, I am a Villaine: And yet you will stand to it, you will not Pocket vp wrong. Art thou not asham'd?

Fal. Do'st thou heare *Hal*? Thou know'st in the state of Innocency, *Adam* fell: and what should poore *Iacke Falstaffe* do, in the dayes of Villany? Thou seest, I haue more flesh then another man, and therefore more frailty. You confesse then you pickt my Pocket?

Prin. It appeares so by the Story.

Fal. Hostesse, I forgiue thee:
Go make ready Breakfast, loue thy Husband,
Looke to thy Seruants, and cherish thy Guests:
Thou shalt find me tractable to any honest reason:
Thou seest, I am pacified still.
Nay, I prethee be gone.

Exit Hostesse.

Now *Hal*, to the newes at Court for the Robbery, Lad? How is that answered?

Prin. O my sweet Beefe:
I must still be good Angell to thee.
The Monie is paid backe againe.

Fal. O, I do not like that paying backe, 'tis a double Labour.

Prin. I am good Friends with my Father, and may do any thing.

Fal. Rob me the Exchequer the first thing thou do'st, and do it with vnwash'd hands too.

Bard. Do my Lord.

Prin. I haue procured thee *Iacke*, a Charge of Foot.

Fal. I would it had beene of Horse. Where shal I finde one that can steale well? O, for a fine theefe of two and twentie, or thereabout: I am heynously vnprouided. Wel God be thanked for these Rebels, they offend none but the Vertuous. I laud them, I praise them.

Prin. *Bardolph*.

Bar. My Lord.

Prin. Go beare this Letter to Lord *Iohn* of Lancaster
To my Brother *Iohn*. This to my Lord of Westmerland,
Go *Peto*, to horse: for thou, and I,
Haue thirtie miles to ride yet ere dinner time.
Iacke, meet me to morrow in the Temple Hall
At two a clocke in the afternoone,
There shalt thou know thy Charge, and there receiue
Money and Order for their Furniture.
The Land is burning, *Percie* stands on hye,
And either they, or we must lower lye.

Fal. Rare words! braue world.
Hostesse, my breakfast, come;
Oh, I could wish this Tauerne were my drumme.

Exeunt omnes.

Actus Quartus. Scœna Prima.

Enter Harrie Hotspurre, Worcester, and Dowglas.

Hot. Well said, my Noble Scot, if speaking truth
In this fine Age, were not thought flatterie,
Such attribution should the *Dowglas* haue,
As not a Souldiour of this seasons stampe,
Should go so generall currant through the world.
By heauen I cannot flatter: I defie
The Tongues of Soothers. But a Brauer place
In my hearts loue, hath no man then your Selfe.
Nay, taske me to my word: approue me Lord.

Dow. Thou art the King of Honor
No man so potent breathes vpon the ground,
But I will Beard him.

Enter a Messenger.

Hot. Do so, and 'tis well. What Letters hast there?
I can but thanke you.

Mess. These Letters come from your Father.

Hot. Letters from him?
Why comes he not himselfe?

Mes. He cannot come, my Lord,
He is greeuous sicke.

Hot. How? haz he the leysure to be sicke now,
In such a iustling time? Who leades his power?
Vnder whose Gouernment come they along?

f 2 *Mess*

Meſſ. His Letters beares his minde, not I his minde.
Wor. I prethee tell me, doth he keepe his Bed?
Meſſ. He did, my Lord, foure dayes ere I ſet forth:
And at the time of my departure thence,
He was much fear'd by his Phyſician.
Wor. I would the ſtate of time had firſt beene whole,
Ere he by ſickneſſe had beene viſited:
His health was neuer better worth then now.
Hotſp. Sicke now? droope now? this ſicknes doth infect
The very Life-blood of our Enterpriſe,
'Tis catching hither, euen to our Campe.
He writes me here, that inward ſickneſſe,
And that his friends by deputation
Could not ſo ſoone be drawne: nor did he thinke it meet,
To lay ſo dangerous and deare a truſt
On any Soule remou'd, but on his owne.
Yet doth he giue vs bold aduertiſement,
That with our ſmall coniunction we ſhould on,
To ſee how Fortune is diſpos'd to vs:
For, as he writes, there is no quailing now,
Becauſe the King is certainely poſſeſt
Of all our purpoſes. What ſay you to it?
Wor. Your Fathers ſickneſſe is a mayme to vs.
Hotſp. A perillous Gaſh, a very Limme lopt off:
And yet, in faith, it is not his preſent want
Seemes more then we ſhall finde it.
Were it good, to ſet the exact wealth of all our ſtates
All at one Caſt? To ſet ſo rich a mayne
On the nice hazard of one doubtfull houre,
It were not good: for therein ſhould we reade
The very Bottome, and the Soule of Hope
The very Liſt, the very vtmoſt Bound
Of all our fortunes.
Dowg. Faith, and ſo wee ſhould;
Where now remaines a ſweet reuerſion.
We may boldly ſpend, vpon the hope
Of what is to come in:
A comfort of retyrement liues in this.
Hotſp. A Randeuous, a Home to flye vnto,
If that the Deuill and Miſchance looke bigge
Vpon the Maydenhead of our Affaires.
Wor. But yet I would your Father had beene here:
The Qualitie and Heire of our Attempt
Brookes no diuiſion: It will be thought
By ſome, that know not why he is away,
That wiſedome, loyaltie, and meere diſlike
Of our proceedings, kept the Earle from hence.
And thinke, how ſuch an apprehenſion
May turne the tyde of fearefull Faction,
And breede a kinde of queſtion in our cauſe:
For well you know, wee of the offring ſide,
Muſt keepe aloofe from ſtrict arbitrement,
And ſtop all ſight-holes, euery loope, from whence
The eye of reaſon may prie in vpon vs:
This abſence of your Father drawes a Curtaine,
That ſhewes the ignorant a kinde of feare,
Before not dreamt of.
Hotſp. You ſtrayne too farre.
I rather of his abſence make this vſe:
It lends a Luſtre, and more great Opinion,
A larger Dare to your great Enterprize,
Then if the Earle were here: for men muſt thinke,
If we without his helpe, can make a Head
To puſh againſt the Kingdome; with his helpe,
We ſhall o're-turne it topſie-turuy downe:
Yet all goes well, yet all our ioynts are whole.
Dowg. As heart can thinke:
There is not ſuch a word ſpoke of in Scotland,
As this Dreame of Feare.

Enter Sir Richard Vernon.

Hotſp. My Couſin *Vernon*, welcome by my Soule.
Vern. Pray God my newes be worth a welcome, Lord.
The Earle of Weſtmerland, ſeuen thouſand ſtrong,
Is marching hither-wards, with Prince *Iohn*.
Hotſp. No harme: what more?
Vern. And further, I haue learn'd,
The King himſelfe in perſon hath ſet forth,
Or hither-wards intended ſpeedily,
With ſtrong and mightie preparation.
Hotſp. He ſhall be welcome too.
Where is his Sonne,
The nimble-footed Mad-Cap, Prince of Wales,
And his Cumrades, that daft the World aſide,
And bid it paſſe?
Vern. All furniſht, all in Armes,
All plum'd like Eſtridges, that with the Winde
Bayted like Eagles, hauing lately bath'd,
Glittering in Golden Coates, like Images,
As full of ſpirit as the Moneth of May,
And gorgeous as the Sunne at Mid-ſummer,
Wanton as youthfull Goates, wilde as young Bulls.
I ſaw young *Harry* with his Beuer on,
His Cuſhes on his thighes, gallantly arm'd,
Riſe from the ground like feathered *Mercury*,
And vaulted with ſuch eaſe into his Seat,
As if an Angell dropt downe from the Clouds,
To turne and winde a fierie *Pegaſus*,
And witch the World with Noble Horſemanſhip.
Hotſp. No more, no more,
Worſe then the Sunne in March:
This prayſe doth nouriſh Agues: let them come.
They come like Sacrifices in their trimme,
And to the fire-ey'd Maid of ſmoakie Warre,
All hot, and bleeding, will wee offer them:
The mayled *Mars* ſhall on his Altar ſit
Vp to the eares in blood. I am on fire,
To heare this rich reprizall is ſo nigh,
And yet not ours. Come, let me take my Horſe,
Who is to beare me like a Thunder-bolt,
Againſt the boſome of the Prince of Wales.
Harry to *Harry*, ſhall not Horſe to Horſe
Meete, and ne're part, till one drop downe a Coarſe?
Oh, that *Glendower* were come.
Ver. There is more newes:
I learned in Worceſter, as I rode along,
He cannot draw his Power this foureteene dayes.
Dowg. That's the worſt Tidings that I heare of yet.
Wor. I by my faith, that beares a froſty ſound.
Hotſp. What may the Kings whole Battaile reach vnto?
Ver. To thirty thouſand.
Hot. Forty let it be,
My Father and *Glendower* being both away,
The powres of vs, may ſerue ſo great a day.
Come, let vs take a muſter ſpeedily:
Doomeſday is neere; dye all, dye merrily.
Dow. Talke not of dying, I am out of feare
Of death, or deaths hand, for this one halfe yeare.
Exeunt Omnes.

Scena

Scæna Secunda.

Enter Falſtaffe and Bardolph.

Falſt. *Bardolph*, get thee before to Couentry, fill me a Bottle of Sack, our Souldiers ſhall march through: wee'le to Sutton-cop-hill to Night.

Bard. Will you giue me Money, Captaine?

Falſt. Lay out, lay out.

Bard. This Bottle makes an Angell.

Falſt. And if it doe, take it for thy labour: and if it make twentie, take them all, Ile anſwere the Coynage. Bid my Lieutenant *Peto* meete me at the Townes end.

Bard. I will Captaine: farewell. *Exit.*

Falſt. If I be not aſham'd of my Souldiers, I am a ſowc't-Gurnet: I haue miſ-vs'd the Kings Preſſe damnably. I haue got, in exchange of a hundred and fiftie Souldiers, three hundred and odde Pounds. I preſſe me none but good Houſe-holders, Yeomens Sonnes: enquire me out contracted Batchelers, ſuch as had beene ask'd twice on the Banes: ſuch a Commoditie of warme ſlaues, as had as lieue heare the Deuill, as a Drumme; ſuch as feare the report of a Caliuer, worſe then a ſtruck-Foole, or a hurt wilde-Ducke. I preſt me none but ſuch Toſtes and Butter, with Hearts in their Bellyes no bigger then Pinnes heads, and they haue bought out their ſeruices: And now, my whole Charge conſiſts of Ancients, Corporals, Lieutenants, Gentlemen of Companies, Slaues as ragged as *Lazarus* in the painted Cloth, where the Gluttons Dogges licked his Sores; and ſuch, as indeed were neuer Souldiers, but diſ-carded vniuſt Seruingmen, younger Sonnes to younger Brothers, reuolted Tapſters and Oſtlers, Trade-falne, the Cankers of a calme World, and long Peace, tenne times more diſ-honorable ragged, then an old-fac'd Ancient; and ſuch haue I to fill vp the roomes of them that haue bought out their ſeruices: that you would thinke, that I had a hundred and fiftie totter'd Prodigalls, lately come from Swine-keeping, from eating Draffe and Huskes. A mad fellow met me on the way, and told me, I had vnloaded all the Gibbets, and preſt the dead bodyes. No eye hath ſeene ſuch skar-Crowes: Ile not march through Couentry with them, that's flat. Nay, and the Villaines march wide betwixt the Legges, as if they had Gyues on; for indeede, I had the moſt of them out of Priſon. There's not a Shirt and a halfe in all my Company: and the halfe Shirt is two Napkins tackt together, and throwne ouer the ſhoulders like a Heralds Coat, without ſleeues: and the Shirt, to ſay the truth, ſtolne from my Hoſt of S. Albones, or the Red-Noſe Inne-keeper of Dauintry. But that's all one, they'le finde Linnen enough on euery Hedge.

Enter the Prince, and the Lord of Weſtmerland.

Prince. How now blowne *Iack*? how now Quilt?

Falſt. What *Hal*? How now mad Wag, what a Deuill do'ſt thou in Warwickſhire? My good Lord of Weſtmerland, I cry you mercy, I thought your Honour had already beene at Shrewsbury.

Weſt. 'Faith, Sir *Iohn*, 'tis more then time that I were there, and you too: but my Powers are there alreadie. The King, I can tell you, lookes for vs all: we muſt away all to Night.

Falſt. Tut, neuer feare me, I am as vigilant as a Cat, to ſteale Creame.

Prince. I thinke to ſteale Creame indeed, for thy theft hath alreadie made thee Butter: but tell me, *Iack*, whoſe fellowes are theſe that come after?

Falſt. Mine, *Hal*, mine.

Prince. I did neuer ſee ſuch pittifull Raſcals.

Falſt. Tut, tut, good enough to toſſe: foode for Powder, foode for Powder: they'le fill a Pit, as well as better: tuſh man, mortall men, mortall men.

Weſtm. I, but Sir *Iohn*, me thinkes they are exceeding poore and bare, too beggarly.

Falſt. Faith, for their pouertie, I know not where they had that; and for their bareneſſe, I am ſure they neuer learn'd that of me.

Prince. No, Ile be ſworne, vnleſſe you call three fingers on the Ribbes bare. But ſirra, make haſte, *Percy* is already in the field.

Falſt. What, is the King encamp'd?

Weſtm. Hee is, Sir *Iohn*, I feare wee ſhall ſtay too long.

Falſt. Well, to the latter end of a Fray, and the beginning of a Feaſt, fits a dull fighter, and a keene Gueſt. *Exeunt.*

Scœna Tertia.

Enter Hotſpur, Worceſter, Dowglas, and Vernon.

Hotſp. Wee'le fight with him to Night.
Worc. It may not be.
Dowg. You giue him then aduantage.
Vern. Not a whit.
Hotſp. Why ſay you ſo? lookes he not for ſupply?
Vern. So doe wee.
Hotſp. His is certaine, ours is doubtfull.
Worc. Good Couſin be aduis'd, ſtirre not to night.
Vern. Doe not, my Lord.
Dowg. You doe not counſaile well:
You ſpeake it out of feare, and cold heart.
Vern. Doe me no ſlander, *Dowglas*: by my Life,
And I dare well maintaine it with my Life,
If well-reſpected Honor bid me on,
I hold as little counſaile with weake feare,
As you, my Lord, or any Scot that this day liues.
Let it be ſeene to morrow in the Battell,
Which of vs feares.
Dowg. Yea, or to night.
Vern. Content.
Hotſp. To night, ſay I.
Vern. Come, come, it may not be.
I wonder much, being me of ſuch great leading as you are
That you fore-ſee not what impediments
Drag backe our expedition: certaine Horſe
Of my Couſin *Vernons* are not yet come vp,
Your Vnckle *Worceſters* Horſe came but to day,
And now their pride and mettall is aſleepe,
Their courage with hard labour tame and dull,
That not a Horſe is halfe the halfe of himſelfe.
Hotſp. So are the Horſes of the Enemie
In generall iourney bated, and brought low:
The better part of ours are full of reſt.

Worc. The number of the King exceedeth ours:
For Gods ſake, Couſin, ſtay till all come in.

The Trumpet ſounds a Parley. Enter Sir Walter Blunt.

Blunt. I come with gracious offers from the King,
If you vouchſafe me hearing, and reſpect.
Hotſp. Welcome, Sir *Walter Blunt*:
And would to God you were of our determination.
Some of vs loue you well: and euen thoſe ſome
Enuie your great deſeruings, and good name,
Becauſe you are not of our qualitie,
But ſtand againſt vs like an Enemie.
Blunt. And Heauen defend, but ſtill I ſhould ſtand ſo,
So long as out of Limit, and true Rule,
You ſtand againſt anoynted Maieſtie.
But to my Charge.
The King hath ſent to know
The nature of your Griefes, and whereupon
You coniure from the Breſt of Ciuill Peace,
Such bold Hoſtilitie, teaching his dutious Land
Audacious Crueltie. If that the King
Haue any way your good Deſerts forgot,
Which he confeſſeth to be manifold,
He bids you name your Griefes, and with all ſpeed
You ſhall haue your deſires, with intereſt;
And Pardon abſolute for your ſelfe, and theſe,
Herein mis-led, by your ſuggeſtion.
Hotſp The King is kinde:
And well wee know, the King
Knowes at what time to promiſe, when to pay.
My Father, my Vnckle, and my ſelfe,
Did giue him that ſame Royaltie he weares:
And when he was not ſixe and twentie ſtrong,
Sicke in the Worlds regard, wretched, and low,
A poore vnminded Out-law, ſneaking home,
My Father gaue him welcome to the ſhore:
And when he heard him ſweare, and vow to God,
He came but to be Duke of Lancaſter,
To ſue his Liuerie, and begge his Peace,
With teares of Innocencie, and tearmes of Zeale;
My Father, in kinde heart and pitty mou'd,
Swore him aſſiſtance, and perform'd it too.
Now, when the Lords and Barons of the Realme
Perceiu'd *Northumberland* did leane to him,
The more and leſſe came in with Cap and Knee,
Met him in Boroughs, Cities, Villages,
Attended him on Bridges, ſtood in Lanes,
Layd Gifts before him, proffer'd him their Oathes,
Gaue him their Heires, as Pages followed him,
Euen at the heeles, in golden multitudes.
He preſently, as Greatneſſe knowes it ſelfe,
Steps me a little higher then his Vow
Made to my Father, while his blood was poore,
Vpon the naked ſhore at Rauenſpurgh:
And now (forſooth) takes on him to reforme
Some certaine Edicts, and ſome ſtrait Decrees,
That lay too heauie on the Common-wealth;
Cryes out vpon abuſes, ſeemes to weepe
Ouer his Countries Wrongs: and by this Face,
This ſeeming Brow of Iuſtice, did he winne
The hearts of all that hee did angle for.
Proceeded further, cut me off the Heads
Of all the Fauorites, that the abſent King
In deputation left behinde him heere,
When hee was perſonall in the Iriſh Warre.
Blunt. Tut, I came not to heare this.
Hotſp. Then to the point.
In ſhort time after, hee depos'd the King,
Soone after that, depriu'd him of his Life:
And in the neck of that, task't the whole State.
To make that worſe, ſuffer'd his Kinſman *March*,
Who is, if euery Owner were plac'd,
Indeede his King, to be engag'd in Wales,
There, without Ranſome, to lye forfeited:
Diſgrac'd me in my happie Victories,
Sought to intrap me by intelligence,
Rated my Vnckle from the Councell-Boord,
In rage diſmiſs'd my Father from the Court,
Broke Oath on Oath, committed Wrong on Wrong,
And in concluſion, droue vs to ſeeke out
This Head of ſafetie; and withall, to prie
Into his Title: the which wee finde
Too indirect, for long continuance.
Blunt. Shall I returne this anſwer to the King?
Hotſp. Not ſo, Sir *Walter*.
Wee'le with-draw a while.
Goe to the King, and let there be impawn'd
Some ſuretie for a ſafe returne againe,
And in the Morning early ſhall my Vnckle
Bring him our purpoſe: and ſo farewell.
Blunt. I would you would accept of Grace and Loue.
Hotſp. And't may be, ſo wee ſhall.
Blunt. Pray Heauen you doe. *Exeunt.*

Scena Quarta.

Enter the Arch-Biſhop of Yorke and Sir Michell.

Arch. Hie, good Sir *Michell*, beare this ſealed Briefe
With winged haſte to the Lord Marſhall,
This to my Couſin *Scroope*, and all the reſt
To whom they are directed.
If you knew how much they doe import,
You would make haſte.
Sir Mich. My good Lord, I gueſſe their tenor.
Arch. Like enough you doe.
To morrow, good Sir *Michell*, is a day,
Wherein the fortune of ten thouſand men
Muſt bide the touch. For Sir, at Shrewsbury,
As I am truly giuen to vnderſtand,
The King, with mightie and quick-rayſed Power,
Meetes with Lord *Harry*: and I feare, Sir *Michell*,
What with the ſickneſſe of *Northumberland*,
Whoſe Power was in the firſt proportion;
And what with *Owen Glendowers* abſence thence,
Who with them was rated firmely too,
And comes not in, ouer-rul'd by Prophecies,
I feare the Power of *Percy* is too weake,
To wage an inſtant tryall with the King.
Sir Mich. Why, my good Lord, you need not feare,
There is *Douglas*, and Lord *Mortimer*.
Arch. No, *Mortimer* is not there.
Sir Mic. But there is *Mordake*, *Vernon*, Lord *Harry Percy*,
And there is my Lord of Worceſter,
And a Head of gallant Warriors,
Noble Gentlemen.
Arch. And

Arch. And ſo there is, but yet the King hath drawne
The ſpeciall head of all the Land together:
The Prince of Wales, Lord *Iohn* of Lancaſter,
The Noble Weſtmerland, and warlike *Blunt*;
And many moe Corriuals, and deare men
Of eſtimation, and command in Armes.
Sir M. Doubt not my Lord, he ſhall be well oppos'd
Arch. I hope no leſſe? Yet needfull 'tis to feare,
And to preuent the worſt, Sir *Michell* ſpeed;
For if Lord *Percy* thriue not, ere the King
Diſmiſſe his power, he meanes to viſit vs:
For he hath heard of our Confederacie,
And, 'tis but Wiſedome to make ſtrong againſt him:
Therefore make haſt, I muſt go write againe
To other Friends: and ſo farewell, Sir *Michell*. *Exeunt.*

Actus Quintus. Scena Prima.

Enter the King, Prince of Wales, Lord Iohn of Lancaſter, Earle of Weſtmerland, Sir Walter Blunt, and Falſtaffe.

King. How bloodily the Sunne begins to peere
Aboue yon busky hill: the day lookes pale
At his diſtemperature.
Prin. The Southerne winde
Doth play the Trumpet to his purpoſes,
And by his hollow whiſtling in the Leaues,
Foretels a Tempeſt, and a bluſt'ring day.
King. Then with the loſers let it ſympathize,
For nothing can ſeeme foule to thoſe that win.
The Trumpet ſounds.
Enter Worceſter.

King. How now my Lord of Worſter? 'Tis not well
That you and I ſhould meet vpon ſuch tearmes,
As now we meet. You haue deceiu'd our truſt,
And made vs doffe our eaſie Robes of Peace,
To cruſh our old limbes in vngentle Steele:
This is not well, my Lord, this is not well.
What ſay you to it? Will you againe vnknit
This churliſh knot of all-abhorred Warre?
And moue in that obedient Orbe againe,
Where you did giue a faire and naturall light,
And be no more an exhall'd Meteor,
A prodigie of Feare, and a Portent
Of broached Miſcheefe, to the vnborne Times?
Wor. Heare me, my Liege:
For mine owne part, I could be well content
To entertaine the Lagge-end of my life
With quiet houres: For I do proteſt,
I haue not ſought the day of this diſlike.
King. You haue not ſought it: how comes it then?
Fal. Rebellion lay in his way, and he found it.
Prin. Peace, Chewet, peace.
Wor. It pleas'd your Maieſty, to turne your lookes
Of Fauour, from my Selfe, and all our Houſe;
And yet I muſt remember you my Lord,
We were the firſt, and deareſt of your Friends:
For you, my ſtaffe of Office did I breake
In *Richards* time, and poaſted day and night
To meete you on the way, and kiſſe your hand,
When yet you were in place, and in account
Nothing ſo ſtrong and fortunate, as I;
It was my Selfe, my Brother, and his Sonne,
That brought you home, and boldly did out-dare
The danger of the time. You ſwore to vs,
And you did ſweare that Oath at Doncaſter,
That you did nothing of purpoſe 'gainſt the State,
Nor claime no further, then your new-falne right,
The ſeate of *Gaunt*, Dukedome of Lancaſter,
To this, we ſware our aide: But in ſhort ſpace,
It rain'd downe Fortune ſhowring on your head,
And ſuch a floud of Greatneſſe fell on you,
What with our helpe, what with the abſent King,
What with the iniuries of wanton time,
The ſeeming ſufferances that you had borne,
And the contrarious Windes that held the King
So long in the vnlucky Iriſh Warres,
That all in England did repute him dead:
And from this ſwarme of faire aduantages,
You tooke occaſion to be quickly woo'd,
To gripe the generall ſway into your hand,
Forgot your Oath to vs at Doncaſter,
And being fed by vs, you vs'd vs ſo,
As that vngentle gull the Cuckowes Bird
Vſeth the Sparrow, did oppreſſe our Neſt,
Grew by our Feeding, to ſo great a bulke,
That euen our Loue durſt not come neere your ſight
For feare of ſwallowing: But with nimble wing
We were inforc'd for ſafety ſake, to flye
Out of your ſight, and raiſe this preſent Head,
Whereby we ſtand oppoſed by ſuch meanes
As you your ſelfe, haue forg'd againſt your ſelfe,
By vnkinde vſage, dangerous countenance,
And violation of all faith and troth
Sworne to vs in yonger enterprize.
Kin. Theſe things indeede you haue articulated,
Proclaim'd at Market Croſſes, read in Churches,
To face the Garment of Rebellion
With ſome fine colour, that may pleaſe the eye
Of fickle Changelings, and poore Diſcontents,
Which gape, and rub the Elbow at the newes
Of hurly burly Innouation:
And neuer yet did Inſurrection want
Such water-colours, to impaint his cauſe:
Nor moody Beggars, ſtaruing for a time
Of pell-mell hauocke, and confuſion.
Prin. In both our Armies, there is many a ſoule
Shall pay full dearely for this encounter,
If once they ioyne in triall. Tell your Nephew,
The Prince of Wales doth ioyne with all the world
In praiſe of *Henry Percie*: By my Hopes,
This preſent enterprize ſet off his head,
I do not thinke a brauer Gentleman,
More actiue, valiant, or more valiant yong,
More daring, or more bold, is now aliue,
To grace this latter Age with Noble deeds.
For my part, I may ſpeake it to my ſhame,
I haue a Truant beene to Chiualry,
And ſo I heare, he doth account me too;
Yet this before my Fathers Maieſty,
I am content that he ſhall take the oddes
Of his great name and eſtimation,
And will, to ſaue the blood on either ſide,
Try fortune with him, in a Single Fight.
King. And Prince of Wales, ſo dare we venter thee,
Albeit, conſiderations infinite
Do

Do make against it : No good Worster, no,
We loue our people well ; euen those we loue
That are misled vpon your Cousins part :
And will they take the offer of our Grace :
Both he, and they, and you ; yea, euery man
Shall be my Friend againe, and Ile be his.
So tell your Cousin, and bring me word,
What he will do But if he will not yeeld,
Rebuke and dread correction waite on vs,
And they shall do their Office. So bee gone,
We will not now be troubled with reply,
We offer faire, take it aduisedly.

Exit Worcester.

Prin. It will not be accepted, on my life,
The *Douglas* and the *Hotspurre* both together,
Are confident against the world in Armes.

King. Hence therefore, euery Leader to his charge.
For on their answer will we set on them ;
And God befriend vs, as our cause is iust. *Exeunt.*

Manet Prince and Falstaffe.

Fal. Hal, if thou see me downe in the battell,
And bestride me, so ; 'tis a point of friendship.

Prin. Nothing but a Colossus can do thee that frendship
Say thy prayers, and farewell.

Fal. I would it were bed time *Hal*, and all well.

Prin. Why, thou ow'st heauen a death.

Falst. 'Tis not due yet : I would bee loath to pay him before his day. What neede I bee so forward with him, that call's not on me? Well, 'tis no matter, Honor prickes me on. But how if Honour pricke me off when I come on? How then? Can Honour set too a legge? No : or an arme? No : Or take away the greefe of a wound? No. Honour hath no skill in Surgerie, then? No. What is Honour? A word. What is that word Honour? Ayre : A trim reckoning. Who hath it? He that dy'de a Wednesday. Doth he feele it? No. Doth hee heare it? No. Is it insensible then? yea, to the dead. But wil it not liue with the liuing? No. Why? Detraction wil not suffer it, therfore Ile none of it. Honour is a meere Scutcheon, and so ends my Catechisme. *Exit.*

Scena Secunda.

Enter Worcester, and Sir Richard Vernon.

Wor. O no, my Nephew must not know, Sir Richard,
The liberall kinde offer of the King.

Ver. 'Twere best he did.

Wor. Then we are all vndone.
It is not possible, it cannot be,
The King would keepe his word in louing vs,
He will suspect vs still, and finde a time
To punish this offence in others faults :
Supposition, all our liues, shall be stucke full of eyes ;
For Treason is but trusted like the Foxe,
Who ne're so tame, so cherisht, and lock'd vp,
Will haue a wilde tricke of his Ancestors :
Looke how he can, or sad or merrily,
Interpretation will misquote our lookes,
And we shall feede like Oxen at a stall,
The better cherisht, still the nearer death.
My Nephewes trespasse may be well forgot,
It hath the excuse of youth, and heate of blood,
And an adopted name of Priuiledge,
A haire-brain'd *Hotspurre*, gouern'd by a Spleene.
All his offences liue vpon my head,
And on his Fathers. We did traine him on,
And his corruption being tane from vs,
We as the Spring of all, shall pay for all :
Therefore good Cousin, let not *Harry* know
In any case, the offer of the King.

Ver. Deliuer what you will, Ile say 'tis so.
Heere comes your Cosin.

Enter Hotspurre.

Hot. My Vnkle is return'd,
Deliuer vp my Lord of Westmerland.
Vnkle, what newes?

Wor. The King will bid you battell presently.

Dow. Defie him by the Lord of Westmerland.

Hot. Lord *Douglas* : Go you and tell him so.

Dow. Marry and shall, and verie willingly.

Exit Douglas.

Wor. There is no seeming mercy in the King.

Hot. Did you begge any? God forbid.

Wor. I told him gently of our greeuances,
Of his Oath-breaking : which he mended thus,
By now forswearing that he is forsworne,
He cals vs Rebels, Traitors, and will scourge
With haughty armes, this hatefull name in vs.

Enter Douglas.

Dow. Arme Gentlemen, to Armes, for I haue thrown
A braue defiance in King *Henries* teeth :
And Westmerland that was ingag'd did beare it,
Which cannot choose but bring him quickly on.

Wor. The Prince of Wales stept forth before the king,
And Nephew, challeng'd you to single fight.

Hot. O, would the quarrell lay vpon our heads,
And that no man might draw short breath to day,
But I and *Harry Monmouth*. Tell me, tell mee,
How shew'd his Talking? Seem'd it in contempt?

Ver. No, by my Soule : I neuer in my life
Did heare a Challenge vrg'd more modestly,
Vnlesse a Brother should a Brother dare
To gentle exercise, and proofe of Armes.
He gaue you all the Duties of a Man,
Trimm'd vp your praises with a Princely tongue,
Spoke your deseruings like a Chronicle,
Making you euer better then his praise,
By still dispraising praise, valew'd with you :
And which became him like a Prince indeed,
He made a blushing citall of himselfe,
And chid his Trewant youth with such a Grace,
As if he mastred there a double spirit
Of teaching, and of learning instantly :
There did he pause. But let me tell the World,
If he out-liue the enuie of this day,
England did neuer owe so sweet a hope,
So much misconstrued in his Wantonnesse.

Hot. Cousin, I thinke thou art enamored
On his Follies : neuer did I heare
Of any Prince so wilde at Liberty
But be he as he will, yet once ere night,
I will imbrace him with a Souldiers arme,
That he shall shrinke vnder my curtesie.
Arme, arme with speed. And Fellow's, Soldiers, Friends,
Better consider what you haue to do,
That I that haue not well the gift of Tongue,

Can

Can lift your blood vp with perswasion.

Enter a Messenger.

Mes. My Lord, heere are Letters for you.
Hot. I cannot reade them now.
O Gentlemen, the time of life is short;
To spend that shortnesse basely, were too long.
If life did ride vpon a Dials point,
Still ending at the arriuall of an houre,
And if we liue, we liue to treade on Kings:
If dye; braue death, when Princes dye with vs.
Now for our Consciences, the Armes is faire,
When the intent for bearing them is iust.

Enter another Messenger.

Mes. My Lord prepare, the King comes on apace.
Hot. I thanke him, that he cuts me from my tale:
For I professe not talking: Onely this,
Let each man do his best. And heere I draw a Sword,
Whose worthy temper I intend to staine
With the best blood that I can meete withall,
In the aduenture of this perillous day.
Now Esperance *Percy*, and set on:
Sound all the lofty Instruments of Warre,
And by that Musicke, let vs all imbrace:
For heauen to earth, some of vs neuer shall,
A second time do such a curtesie.

They embrace, the Trumpets sound, the King entereth with his power, alarum vnto the battell. Then enter Dowglas, and Sir Walter Blunt.

Blu. What is thy name, that in battel thus ŷ crossest me?
What honor dost thou seeke vpon my head?
Dow Know then my name is *Dowglas*,
And I do haunt thee in the battell thus,
Because some tell me, that thou art a King.
Blunt. They tell thee true.
Dow. The Lord of Stafford deere to day hath bought
Thy likenesse: for insted of thee King *Harry*,
This Sword hath ended him, so shall it thee,
Vnlesse thou yeeld thee as a Prisoner.
Blu. I was not borne to yeeld, thou haughty Scot,
And thou shalt finde a King that will reuenge
Lords Staffords death.

Fight, Blunt is slaine, then enters Hotspur.

Hot. O *Dowglas*, hadst thou fought at Holmedon thus
I neuer had triumphed o're a Scot.
Dow All's done, all's won, here breathles lies the king
Hot. Where?
Dow. Heere.
Hot. This *Dowglas*? No, I know this face full well:
A gallant Knight he was, his name was *Blunt*,
Semblably furnish'd like the King himselfe.
Dow. Ah foole: go with thy soule whether it goes,
A borrowed Title hast thou bought too deere.
Why didst thou tell me, that thou wer't a King?
Hot. The King hath many marching in his Coats.
Dow. Now by my Sword, I will kill all his Coates,
Ile murder all his Wardrobe peece by peece,
Vntill I meet the King.
Hot. Vp, and away,
Our Souldiers stand full fairely for the day. *Exeunt*

Alarum, and enter Falstaffe solus.

Fal. Though I could scape shot-free at London, I fear the shot heere: here's no scoring, but vpon the pate. Soft who are you? Sir *Walter Blunt*, there's Honour for you: here's no vanity, I am as hot as molten Lead, and as heauy too; heauen keepe Lead out of mee, I neede no more weight then mine owne Bowelles. I haue led my rag of Muffins where they are pepper'd: there's not three of my 150. left aliue, and they for the Townes end, to beg during life. But who comes heere?

Enter the Prince.

Pri. What, stand'st thou idle here? Lend me thy sword,
Many a Nobleman lies starke and stiffe
Vnder the hooues of vaunting enemies,
Whose deaths are vnreueng'd. Prethy lend me thy sword
Fal. O *Hal*, I prethee giue me leaue to breath awhile: Turke *Gregory* neuer did such deeds in Armes, as I haue done this day. I haue paid *Percy*, I haue made him sure.
Prin. He is indeed, and liuing to kill thee:
I prethee lend me thy sword.
Falst. Nay *Hal*, if *Percy* bee aliue, thou getst not my Sword; but take my Pistoll if thou wilt.
Prin. Giue it me: What, is it in the Case?
Fal. I *Hal*, 'tis hot: There's that will Sacke a City.

The Prince drawes out a Bottle of Sacke.

Prin. What, is it a time to iest and dally now. *Exit.*

Throwes it at him.

Fal. If *Percy* be aliue, Ile pierce him: if he do come in my way, so: if he do not, if I come in his (willingly) let him make a Carbonado of me. I like not such grinning honour as Sir *Walter* hath: Giue mee life, which if I can saue, so: if not, honour comes vnlook'd for, and ther's an end. *Exit*

Scena Tertia.

Alarum, excursions, enter the King, the Prince, Lord Iohn of Lancaster, and Earle of Westmerland.

King. I prethee *Harry* withdraw thy selfe, thou bleedest too much: Lord *Iohn of Lancaster*, go you with him.
P. Ioh. Not I, my Lord, vnlesse I did bleed too.
Prin. I beseech your Maiesty make vp,
Least you retirement do amaze your friends.
King. I will do so:
My Lord of Westmerland leade him to his Tent.
West. Come my Lord, Ile leade you to your Tent.
Prin. Lead me my Lord? I do not need your helpe;
And heauen forbid a shallow scratch should driue
The Prince of Wales from such a field as this,
Where stain'd Nobility lyes troden on,
And Rebels Armes triumph in massacres.
Ioh. We breath too long: Come cosin Westmerland,
Our duty this way lies, for heauens sake come.
Prin. By heauen thou hast deceiu'd me Lancaster,
I did not thinke thee Lord of such a spirit:
Before, I lou'd thee as a Brother, *Iohn*;
But now, I do respect thee as my Soule.
King. I saw him hold Lord *Percy* at the point,
With lustier maintenance then I did looke for
Of such an vngrowne Warriour.
Prin O this Boy, lends mettall to vs all. *Exit.*

Enter Dowglas.

Dow. Another King? They grow like Hydra's head:
I am the *Dowglas*, fatall to all those
That weare those colours on them. What art thou
That counterfeit'st the person of a King?
King. The King himselfe: who *Dowglas* grieues at hart
So

So many of his shadowes thou hast met,
And not the very King. I haue two Boyes
Seeke *Percy* and thy selfe about the Field:
But seeing thou fall'st on me so luckily,
I will assay thee: so defend thy selfe.
Dow. I feare thou art another counterfeit:
And yet infaith thou bear'st thee like a King:
But mine I am sure thou art, whoere thou be,
And thus I win thee. *They fight, the K. being in danger,*
Enter Prince.
Prin. Hold vp they head vile Scot, or thou art like
Neuer to hold it vp againe: the Spirits
Of valiant *Sherly, Stafford, Blunt*, are in my Armes;
It is the Prince of Wales that threatens thee,
Who neuer promiseth, but he meanes to pay.
They Fight, Douglas flyeth.
Cheerely My Lord: how fare's your Grace?
Sir *Nicholas Gawsey* hath for succour sent,
And so hath *Clifton*: Ile to *Clifton* straight.
King. Stay, and breath awhile.
Thou hast redeem'd thy lost opinion,
And shew'd thou mak'st some tender of my life
In this faire rescue thou hast brought to mee.
Prin. O heauen, they did me too much iniury,
That euer said I hearkned to your death.
If it were so, I might haue let alone
The insulting hand of *Douglas* ouer you,
Which would haue bene as speedy in your end,
As all the poysonous Potions in the world,
And sau'd the Treacherous labour of your Sonne.
K. Make vp to *Clifton* Ile to Sir *Nicholas Gausey*. *Exit*
Enter Hotspur.
Hot. If I mistake not, thou art *Harry Monmouth*.
Prin. Thou speak'st as if I would deny my name.
Hot. My name is *Harrie Percie*.
Prin. Why then I see a very valiant rebel of that name.
I am the Prince of Wales, and thinke not *Percy*,
To share with me in glory any more:
Two Starres keepe not their motion in one Sphere,
Nor can one England brooke a double reigne,
Of *Harry Percy*, and the Prince of Wales.
Hot. Nor shall it *Harry*, for the houre is come
To end the one of vs; and would to heauen,
Thy name in Armes, were now as great as mine.
Prin. Ile make it greater, ere I part from thee,
And all the budding Honors on thy Crest,
Ile crop, to make a Garland for my head.
Hot. I can no longer brooke thy Vanities. *Fight.*
Enter Falstaffe.

Fal. Well said *Hal*, to it *Hal*. Nay you shall finde no Boyes play heere, I can tell you.

Enter Dowglas, he fights with Falstaffe, who fals down as if he were dead. The Prince killeth Percie.

Hot. Oh *Harry*, thou hast rob'd me of my youth:
I better brooke the losse of brittle life,
Then those proud Titles thou hast wonne of me,
They wound my thoghts worse, then the sword my flesh:
But thought's the slaue of Life, and Life, Times foole;
And Time, that takes suruey of all the world,
Must haue a stop. O, I could Prophesie,
But that the Earth, and the cold hand of death,
Lyes on my Tongue: No *Percy*, thou art dust
And food for——
Prin. For Wormes, braue *Percy*. Farewell great heart:
Ill-weau'd Ambition, how much art thou shrunke?
When that this bodie did containe a spirit,
A Kingdome for it was too small a bound:
But now two paces of the vilest Earth
Is roome enough. This Earth that beares the dead,
Beares not aliue so stout a Gentleman.
If thou wer't sensible of curtesie,
I should not make so great a shew of Zeale.
But let my fauours hide thy mangled face,
And euen in thy behalfe, Ile thanke my selfe
For doing these fayre Rites of Tendernesse.
Adieu, and take thy praise with thee to heauen,
Thy ignomy sleepe with thee in the graue,
But not remembred in thy Epitaph.
What? Old Acquaintance? Could not all this flesh
Keepe in a little life? Poore Iacke, farewell:
I could haue better spar'd a better man.
O, I should haue a heauy misse of thee,
If I were much in loue with Vanity.
Death hath not strucke so fat a Deere to day,
Though many dearer in this bloody Fray:
Imbowell'd will I see thee by and by,
Till then, in blood, by Noble *Percie* lye. *Exit.*
Falstaffe riseth vp.

Falst. Imbowell'd? If thou imbowell mee to day, Ile giue you leaue to powder me, and eat me too to morow. 'Twas time to counterfet, or that hotte Termagant Scot, had paid me scot and lot too. Counterfeit? I am no counterfeit; to dye, is to be a counterfeit, for hee is but the counterfeit of a man, who hath not the life of a man: But to counterfeit dying, when a man thereby liueth, is to be no counterfeit, but the true and perfect image of life indeede. The better part of Valour, is Discretion; in the which better part, I haue saued my life. I am affraide of this Gun-powder *Percy* though he be dead. How if hee should counterfeit too, and rise? I am afraid hee would proue the better counterfeit: therefore Ile make him sure: yea, and Ile sweare I kill'd him. Why may not hee rise as well as I: Nothing confutes me but eyes, and no-bodie sees me. Therefore sirra, with a new wound in your thigh come you along me. *Takes Hotspurre on his backe.*

Enter Prince and Iohn of Lancaster.

Prin. Come Brother *Iohn*, full brauely hast thou flesht thy Maiden sword.

Iohn. But soft, who haue we heere?
Did you not tell me this Fat man was dead?
Prin. I did, I saw him dead,
Breathlesse, and bleeding on the ground: Art thou aliue?
Or is it fantasie that playes vpon our eye-sight?
I prethee speake, we will not trust our eyes
Without our eares. Thou art not what thou seem'st.

Fal. No, that's certaine: I am not a double man: but if I be not *Iacke Falstaffe*, then am I a Iacke: There is *Percy*, if your Father will do me any Honor, so: if not, let him kill the next *Percie* himselfe. I looke to be either Earle or Duke, I can assure you.

Prin. Why, *Percy* I kill'd my selfe, and saw thee dead.

Fal. Did'st thou? Lord, Lord, how the world is giuen to Lying? I graunt you I was downe, and out of Breath, and so was he, but we rose both at an instant, and fought a long houre by Shrewsburie clocke. If I may bee beleeued, so: if not, let them that should reward Valour, beare the sinne vpon their owne heads. Ile take't on my death I gaue him this wound in the Thigh: if the man vvere aliue, and would deny it, I would make him eate a peece of my sword.

Iohn. This is the strangest Tale that e're I heard.
Prin. This is the strangest Fellow, Brother *Iohn*.

Come

Come bring your luggage Nobly on your backe :
For my part, if a lye may do thee grace,
Ile gil d it with the happiest tearmes I haue.

A Retreat is sounded.

The Trumpets sound Retreat, the day is ours :
Come Brother, let's to the highest of the field,
To see what Friends are liuing, who are dead. *Exeunt*

Fal. Ile follow as they say, for Reward. Hee that rewards me, heauen reward him. If I do grow great again, Ile grow lesse? For Ile purge, and leaue Sacke, and liue cleanly, as a Nobleman should do. *Exi*

Scæna Quarta.

The Trumpets sound.
Enter the King, Prince of Wales, Lord Iohn of Lancaste Earle of Westmerland, with Worcester & Vernon Prisoners.

King. Thus euer did Rebellion finde Rebuke.
Ill-spirited Worcester, did we not send Grace,
Pardon, and tearmes of Loue to all of you ?
And would'st thou turne our offers contrary ?
Misuse the tenor of thy Kinsmans trust ?
Three Knights vpon our party slaine to day,
A Noble Earle, and many a creature else,
Had beene aliue this houre,
If like a Christian thou had'st truly borne
Betwixt our Armies, true Intelligence.

Wor. What I haue done, my safety vrg'd me to
And I embrace this fortune patiently,
Since not to be auoyded, it fals on mee.

King. Beare Worcester to death, and *Vernon* too :
Other Offenders we will pause vpon.

Exit Worcester and Vernon.

How goes the Field ?

Prin. The Noble Scot Lord *Dowglas*, when hee saw
The fortune of the day quite turn'd from him,
The Noble *Percy* slaine, and all his men,
Vpon the foot of feare, fled with the rest ;
And falling from a hill, he was so bruiz'd
That the pursuers tooke him. At my Tent
The *Dowglas* is, and I beseech your Grace,
I may dispose of him.

King. With all my heart.

Prin. Then Brother *Iohn* of Lancaster,
To you this honourable bounty shall belong :
Go to the *Dowglas*, and deliuer him
Vp to his pleasure, ransomlesse and free :
His Valour shewne vpon our Crests to day,
Hath taught vs how to cherish such high deeds,
Euen in the bosome of our Aduersaries.

King. Then this remaines : that we diuide our Powers.
You Sonne *Iohn*, and my Cousin Westmerland
Towards Yorke shall bend you, with your deerest speed
To meet Northumberland, and the Prelate *Scroope*,
Who (as we heare) are busily in Armes.
My Selfe, and you Sonne *Harry* will towards Wales,
To fight with *Glendower*, and the Earle of March.
Rebellion in this Land shall lose his way,
Meeting the Checke of such another day :
And since this Businesse so faire is done,
Let vs not leaue till all our owne be wonne. *Exeunt.*

FINIS.

The Second Part of Henry the Fourth, Containing his Death: and the Coronation of King Henry the Fift.

Actus Primus. Scœna Prima.

INDVCTION.

Enter Rumour.

OPen your Eares: For which of you will stop
The vent of Hearing, when loud *Rumor* speakes?
I, from the Orient, to the drooping West
(Making the winde my Post-horse) still vnfold
The Acts commenced on this Ball of Earth.
Vpon my Tongue, continuall Slanders ride,
The which, in euery Language, I pronounce,
Stuffing the Eares of them with false Reports.
I speake of Peace, while couert Enmitie
(Vnder the smile of Safety) wounds the World:
And who but *Rumour*, who but onely I
Make fearfull Musters, and prepar'd Defence,
Whil'st the bigge yeare, swolne with some other griefes,
Is thought with childe, by the sterne Tyrant, Warre,
And no such matter? *Rumour*, is a Pipe
Blowne by Surmises, Ielousies, Coniectures;
And of so easie, and so plaine a stop,
That the blunt Monster, with vncounted heads,
The still discordant, wauering Multitude,
Can play vpon it. But what neede I thus
My well-knowne Body to Anathomize
Among my houshold? Why is *Rumour* heere?
I run before King *Harries* victory,
Who in a bloodie field by Shrewsburie
Hath beaten downe yong *Hotspurre*, aud his Troopes,
Qnenching the flame of bold Rebellion,
Euen with the Rebels blood. But what meane I
To speake so true at first? My Office is
To noyse abroad, that *Harry Monmouth* fell
Vnder the Wrath of Noble *Hotspurres* Sword:
And that the King, before the *Douglas* Rage
Stoop'd his Annointed head, as low as death.
This haue I rumour'd through the peasant-Townes,
Betweene the Royall Field of Shrewsburie,
And this Worme-eaten-Hole of ragged Stone,
Where *Hotspurres* Father, old Northumberland,
Lyes crafty sicke. The Postes come tyring on,
And not a man of them brings other newes
Then they haue learn'd of Me. From *Rumours* Tongues,
They bring smooth-Comforts-false, worse then True-wrongs. *Exit.*

Scena Secunda.

Enter Lord Bardolfe, and the Porter.

L.Bar. Who keepes the Gate heere hoa?
Where is the Earle?
Por. What shall I say you are?
Bar. Tell thou the Earle
That the Lord *Bardolfe* doth attend him heere.
Por. His Lordship is walk'd forth into the Orchard,
Please it your Honor, knocke but at the Gate,
And he himselfe will answer.

Enter Northumberland.

L.Bar. Heere comes the Earle.
Nor. What newes Lord *Bardolfe*? Eu'ry minute now
Should be the Father of some Stratagem;
The Times are wilde: Contention (like a Horse
Full of high Feeding) madly hath broke loose,
And beares downe all before him.
L.Bar. Noble Earle,
I bring you certaine newes from Shrewsbury
Nor. Good, and heauen will.
L.Bar. As good as heart can wish:
The King is almost wounded to the death:
And in the Fortune of my Lord your Sonne,
Prince *Harrie* slaine out-right: and both the *Blunts*
Kill'd by the hand of *Dowglas*. Yong Prince *Iohn*,
And Westmerland, and Stafford, fled the Field,
And *Harrie Monmouth's* Brawne (the Hulke Sir *Iohn*)
Is prisoner to your Sonne. O, such a Day.
(So fought, so follow'd, and so fairely wonne)
Came not, till now, to dignifie the Times
Since *Cæsars* Fortunes.
Nor. How is this deriu'd?
Saw you the Field? Came you from Shrewsbury?
L.Bar. I spake with one (my L.) that came frō thence,
A Gentleman well bred, and of good name,
That freely render'd me these newes for true.
Nor. Heere comes my Seruant *Trauers*, whom I sent
On Tuesday last, to listen after Newes.

Enter Trauers.

L.Bar. My Lord, I ouer-rod him on the way,
And he is furnish'd with no certainties,
More then he (haply) may retaile from me.
Nor. Now *Trauers*, what good tidings comes frō you?

Tra.

Tra. My Lord, Sir *Iohn Vmfreuill* turn'd me backe
With ioyfull tydings; and (being better hors'd)
Out-rod me. After him, came spurring head
A Gentleman (almost fore-spent with speed)
That stopp'd by me, to breath his bloodied horse.
He ask'd the way to Chester: And of him
I did demand what Newes from Shrewsbury:
He told me, that Rebellion had ill lucke,
And that yong *Harry Percies* Spurre was cold.
With that he gaue his able Horse the head,
And bending forwards strooke his able heeles
Against the panting sides of his poore Iade
Vp to the Rowell head, and starting so,
He seem'd in running, to deuoure the way,
Staying no longer question.
North. Ha? Againe:
Said he yong *Harrie Perceyes* Spurre was cold?
(Of *Hot-Spurre*, cold-Spurre?) that Rebellion,
Had met ill lucke?
L.Bar. My Lord: Ile tell you what,
If my yong Lord your Sonne, haue not the day,
Vpon mine Honor, for a silken point
Ile giue my Barony. Neuer talke of it.
Nor. Why should the Gentleman that rode by *Trauers*
Giue then such instances of Losse?
L.Bar. Who, he?
He was some hielding Fellow, that had stolne
The Horse he rode-on: and vpon my life
Speake at aduenture. Looke, here comes more Newes.

Enter Morton.

Nor. Yea, this mans brow, like to a Title-leafe,
Fore-tels the Nature of a Tragicke Volume:
So lookes the Strond, when the Imperious Flood
Hath left a witnest Vsurpation.
Say *Morton*, did'st thou come from Shrewsbury?
Mor. I ran from Shrewsbury (my Noble Lord)
Where hatefull death put on his vgliest Maske
To fright our party.
North. How doth my Sonne, and Brother?
Thou trembl'st; and the whitenesse in thy Cheeke
Is apter then thy Tongue, to tell thy Errand.
Euen such a man, so faint, so spiritlesse,
So dull, so dead in looke, so woe-be-gone,
Drew *Priams* Curtaine, in the dead of night,
And would haue told him, Halfe his Troy was burn'd.
But *Priam* found the Fire, ere he his Tongue:
And I, my *Percies* death, ere thou report'st it.
This, thou would'st say: Your Sonne did thus, and thus:
Your Brother, thus. So fought the Noble *Douglas*,
Stopping my greedy eare, with their bold deeds.
But in the end (to stop mine Eare indeed)
Thou hast a Sigh, to blow away this Praise,
Ending with Brother, Sonne, and all are dead.
Mor. *Douglas* is liuing, and your Brother, yet:
But for my Lord, your Sonne.
North. Why, he is dead.
See what a ready tongue Suspition hath:
He that but feares the thing, he would not know,
Hath by Instinct, knowledge from others Eyes,
That what he feard, is chanc'd. Yet speake (*Morton*)
Tell thou thy Earle, his Diuination Lies,
And I will take it, as a sweet Disgrace,
And make thee rich, for doing me such wrong.
Mor. You are too great, to be (by me) gainsaid:
Your Spirit is too true, your Feares too certaine.
North. Yet for all this, say not that *Percies* dead.
I see a strange Confession in thine Eye:
Thou shak'st thy head, and hold'st it Feare, or Sinne,
To speake a truth. If he be slaine, say so:
The Tongue offends not, that reports his death:
And he doth sinne that doth belye the dead:
Not he, which sayes the dead is not aliue:
Yet the first bringer of vnwelcome Newes
Hath but a loosing Office: and his Tongue,
Sounds euer after as a sullen Bell
Remembred, knolling a departing Friend.
L.Bar. I cannot thinke (my Lord) your son is dead.
Mor. I am sorry, I should force you to beleeue
That, which I would to heauen, I had not seene.
But these mine eyes, saw him in bloody state,
Rend'ring faint quittance (wearied, and out-breath'd)
To *Henrie Monmouth*, whose swift wrath beate downe
The neuer-daunted *Percie* to the earth,
From whence (with life) he neuer more sprung vp.
In few; his death (whose spirit lent a fire,
Euen to the dullest Peazant in his Campe)
Being bruited once, tooke fire and heate away
From the best temper'd Courage in his Troopes.
For from his Mettle, was his Party steel'd;
Which once, in him abated, all the rest
Turn'd on themselues, like dull and heauy Lead:
And as the Thing, that's heauy in it selfe,
Vpon enforcement, flyes with greatest speede,
So did our Men, heauy in *Hotspurres* losse,
Lend to this weight, such lightnesse with their Feare,
That Arrowes fled not swifter toward their ayme,
Then did our Soldiers (ayming at their safety)
Fly from the field. Then was that Noble Worcester
Too soone ta'ne prisoner: and that furious Scot,
(The bloody *Douglas*) whose well-labouring sword
Had three times slaine th'appearance of the King,
Gan vaile his stomacke, and did grace the shame
Of those that turn'd their backes: and in his flight,
Stumbling in Feare, was tooke. The summe of all,
Is, that the King hath wonne: and hath sent out
A speedy power, to encounter you my Lord,
Vnder the Conduct of yong Lancaster
And Westmerland. This is the Newes at full.
North. For this, I shall haue time enough to mourne.
In Poyson, there is Physicke: and this newes
(Hauing beene well) that would haue made me sicke,
Being sicke, haue in some measure, made me well.
And as the Wretch, whose Feauer-weakned ioynts,
Like strengthlesse Hindges, buckle vnder life,
Impatient of his Fit, breakes like a fire
Out of his keepers armes: Euen so, my Limbes
(Weak'ned with greefe) being now inrag'd with greefe,
Are thrice themselues. Hence therefore thou nice crutch;
A scalie Gauntlet now, with ioynts of Steele
Must gloue this hand. And hence thou sickly Quoife,
Thou art a guard too wanton for the head,
Which Princes, flesh'd with Conquest, ayme to hit.
Now binde my Browes with Iron, and approach
The ragged'st houre, that Time and Spight dare bring
To frowne vpon th'enrag'd Northumberland.
Let Heauen kisse Earth: now let not Natures hand
Keepe the wilde Flood confin'd: Let Order dye,
And let the world no longer be a stage
To feede Contention in a ling'ring Act:
But let one spirit of the First-borne *Caine*

g Reigne

Reigne in all boſomes, that each heart being ſet
On bloody Courſes, the rude Scene may end.
And darkneſſe be the burier of the dead. (Honor

L.Bar. Sweet Earle, diuorce not wiſedom from you

Mor. The liues of all your louing Complices
Leane-on your health, the which if you giue-o're
To ſtormy Paſſion, muſt perforce decay.
You caſt th'euent of Warre (my Noble Lord)
And ſumm'd the accompt of Chance, before you ſaid
Let vs make head: It was your preſurmize,
That in the dole of blowes, your Son might drop.
You knew he walk'd o're perils, on an edge
More likely to fall in, then to get o're:
You were aduis'd his fleſh was capeable
Of Wounds, and Scarres; and that his forward Spirit
Would lift him, where moſt trade of danger rang'd,
Yet did you ſay go forth: and none of this
(Though ſtrongly apprehended) could reſtraine
The ſtiffe-borne Action: What hath then befalne?
Or what hath this bold enterprize bring forth,
More then that Being, which was like to be?

L.Bar. We all that are engaged to this loſſe,
Knew that we ventur'd on ſuch dangerous Seas,
That if we wrought out life, was ten to one:
And yet we ventur'd for the gaine propos'd,
Choak'd the reſpect of likely perill fear'd,
And ſince we are o're-ſet, venture againe.
Come, we will all put forth; Body, and Goods,

Mor. 'Tis more then time: And (my moſt Noble Lord)
I heare for certaine, and do ſpeake the truth:
The gentle Arch-biſhop of Yorke is vp
With well appointed Powres: he is a man
Who with a double Surety bindes his Followers.
My Lord (your Sonne) had onely but the Corpes,
But ſhadowes, and the ſhewes of men to fight.
For that ſame word (Rebellion) did diuide
The action of their bodies, from their ſoules,
And they did fight with queaſineſſe, conſtrain'd
As men drinke Potions; that their Weapons only
Seem'd on our ſide: but for their Spirits and Soules,
This word (Rebellion) it had froze them vp,
As Fiſh are in a Pond. But now the Biſhop
Turnes Inſurrection to Religion,
Suppos'd ſincere, and holy in his Thoughts:
He's follow'd both with Body, and with Minde:
And doth enlarge his Riſing, with the blood
Of faire King *Richard*, ſcrap'd from Pomfret ſtones,
Deriues from heauen, his Quarrell, and his Cauſe:
Tels them, he doth beſtride a bleeding Land,
Gaſping for life, vnder great *Bullingbrooke*,
And more, and leſſe, do flocke to follow him.

North. I knew of this before. But to ſpeake truth,
This preſent greefe had wip'd it from my minde.
Go in with me, and councell euery man
The apteſt way for ſafety, and reuenge:
Get Poſts, and Letters, and make Friends with ſpeed,
Neuer ſo few, nor neuer yet more need. *Exeunt.*

Scena Tertia.

Enter Falſtaffe and Page.

Fal. Sirra, you giant, what saies the Doct. to my water?

Pag He ſaid ſir, the water it ſelfe was a good healthy water: but for the party that ow'd it, he might haue more diſeaſes then he knew for.

Fal. Men of all ſorts take a pride to gird at mee: the braine of this fooliſh compounded Clay-man, is not able to inuent any thing that tends to laughter, more then I inuent, or is inuented on me. I am not onely witty in my ſelfe, but the cauſe that wit is in other men. I doe heere walke before thee, like a Sow, that hath o'rewhelm'd all her Litter, but one. If the Prince put thee into my Seruice for any other reaſon, then to ſet mee off, why then I haue no iudgement. Thou horſon Mandrake, thou art fitter to be worne in my cap, then to wait at my heeles. I was neuer mann'd with an Agot till now: but I will ſette you neyther in Gold, nor Siluer, but in vilde apparell, and ſend you backe againe to your Maſter, for a Iewell. The *Iuuenall* (the Prince your Maſter) whoſe Chin is not yet fledg'd, I will ſooner haue a beard grow in the Palme of my hand, then he ſhall get one on his cheeke: yet he will not ſticke to ſay, his Face is a Face-Royall. Heauen may finiſh it when he will, it is not a haire amiſſe yet: he may keepe it ſtill at a Face-Royall, for a Barber ſhall neuer earne ſix pence out of it; and yet he will be crowing, as if he had writ man euer ſince his Father was a Batchellour. He may keepe his owne Grace, but he is almoſt out of mine, I can aſſure him. What ſaid M. *Dombledon*, about the Satten for my ſhort Cloake, and Slops?

Pag. He ſaid ſir, you ſhould procure him better Aſſurance, then *Bardolfe*: he wold not take his Bond & yours, he lik'd not the Security.

Fal. Let him bee damn'd like the Glutton, may his Tongue be hotter, a horſon *Achitophel*; a Raſcally-yea-forſooth-knaue, to beare a Gentleman in hand, and then ſtand vpon Security? The horſon ſmooth-pates doe now weare nothing but high ſhoes, and bunches of Keyes at their girdles: and if a man is through with them in honeſt Taking-vp, then they muſt ſtand vpon Securitie: I had as liefe they would put Rats-bane in my mouth, as offer to ſtoppe it with Security. I look'd hee ſhould haue ſent me two and twenty yards of Satten (as I am true Knight) and he ſends me Security. Well, he may ſleep in Security, for he hath the horne of Abundance: and the lighteneſſe of his Wife ſhines through it, and yet cannot he ſee, though he haue his owne Lanthorne to light him. Where's *Bardolfe*?

Pag. He's gone into Smithfield to buy your worſhip a horſe.

Fal. I bought him in Paules, and hee'l buy mee a horſe in Smithfield. If I could get mee a wife in the Stewes, I were Mann'd, Hors'd, and Wiu'd.

Enter Chiefe Iuſtice, and Seruant.

Pag. Sir, heere comes the Nobleman that committed the Prince for ſtriking him, about *Bardolfe*.

Fal. Wait cloſe, I will not ſee him.

Ch.Iuſt. What's he that goes there?

Ser. *Falſtaffe*, and't pleaſe your Lordſhip.

Iuſt. He that was in queſtion for the Robbery?

Ser. He my Lord, but he hath ſince done good ſeruice at Shrewsbury: and (as I heare) is now going with ſome Charge, to the Lord *Iohn of Lancaſter*.

Iuſt. What to Yorke? Call him backe againe.

Ser. Sir *Iohn Falſtaffe*.

Fal. Boy, tell him, I am deafe.

Pag. You muſt ſpeake lowder, my Maſter is deafe.

Iuſt. I am ſure he is, to the hearing of any thing good. Go plucke him by the Elbow, I muſt ſpeake with him.

Ser. Sir *Iohn*.

Fal. What? a yong knaue and beg? Is there not wars? Is there not imployment? Doth not the K. lack ſubiects? Do not the Rebels want Soldiers? Though it be a ſhame to be

on

on any ſide but one, it is worſe ſhame to begge, then to be on the worſt ſide, were it worſe then the name of Rebellion can tell how to make it.

Ser. You miſtake me Sir.

Fal. Why ſir? Did I ſay you were an honeſt man? Setting my Knight-hood, and my Souldierſhip aſide, I had lyed in my throat, if I had ſaid ſo.

Ser. I pray you (Sir) then ſet your Knighthood and your Souldier-ſhip aſide, and giue mee leaue to tell you, you lye in your throat, if you ſay I am any other then an honeſt man.

Fal. I giue thee leaue to tell me ſo? I lay a-ſide that which growes to me? If thou get'ſt any leaue of me, hang me: if thou tak'ſt leaue, thou wer't better be hang'd: you Hunt-counter, hence: Auant.

Ser. Sir, my Lord would ſpeake with you.

Iuſt. Sir *Iohn Falſtaffe*, a word with you.

Fal. My good Lord: giue your Lordſhip good time of the day. I am glad to ſee your Lordſhip abroad: I heard ſay your Lordſhip was ſicke. I hope your Lordſhip goes abroad by aduiſe. Your Lordſhip (though not clean paſt your youth) hath yet ſome ſmack of age in you: ſome relliſh of the ſaltneſſe of Time, and I moſt humbly beſeech your Lordſhip, to haue a reuerend care of your health.

Iuſt. Sir *Iohn*, I ſent you before your Expedition, to Shrewsburie.

Fal. If it pleaſe your Lordſhip, I heare his Maieſtie is return'd with ſome diſcomfort from Wales.

Iuſt. I talke not of his Maieſty: you would not come when I ſent for you?

Fal. And I heare moreouer, his Highneſſe is falne into this ſame whorſon Apoplexie.

Iuſt. Well, heauen mend him. I pray let me ſpeak with (you.

Fal. This Apoplexie is (as I take it) a kind of Lethargie, a ſleeping of the blood, a horſon Tingling.

Iuſt. What tell you me of it? be it as it is.

Fal. It hath it originall from much greefe; from ſtudy and perturbation of the braine. I haue read the cauſe of his effects in *Galen*. It is a kinde of deafeneſſe.

Iuſt. I thinke you are falne into the diſeaſe: For you heare not what I ſay to you.

Fal. Very well (my Lord) very well: rather an't pleaſe you) it is the diſeaſe of not Liſtning, the malady of not Marking, that I am troubled withall.

Iuſt. To puniſh you by the heeles, would amend the attention of your eares, & I care not if I be your Phyſitian

Fal. I am as poore as *Iob*, my Lord; but not ſo Patient: your Lordſhip may miniſter the Potion of impriſonment to me, in reſpect of Pouertie: but how I ſhould bee your Patient, to follow your preſcriptions, the wiſe may make ſome dram of a ſcruple, or indeede, a ſcruple it ſelfe.

Iuſt. I ſent for you (when there were matters againſt you for your life) to come ſpeake with me.

Fal. As I was then aduiſed by my learned Councel, in the lawes of this Land-ſeruice, I did not come.

Iuſt. Wel, the truth is (ſir *Iohn*) you liue in great infamy

Fal. He that buckles him in my belt, canot liue in leſſe.

Iuſt. Your Meanes is very ſlender, and your waſt great.

Fal. I would it were otherwiſe: I would my Meanes were greater, and my waſte ſlenderer.

Iuſt. You haue miſled the youthfull Prince.

Fal. The yong Prince hath miſled mee. I am the Fellow with the great belly, and he my Dogge.

Iuſt. Well, I am loth to gall a new-heal'd wound: your daies ſeruice at Shrewsbury, hath a little gilded ouer your Nights exploit on Gads-hill. You may thanke the vnquiet time, for your quiet o're-poſting that Action.

Fal. My Lord?

Iuſt. But ſince all is wel, keep it ſo: wake not a ſleeping (Wolfe.

Fal. To wake a Wolfe, is as bad as to ſmell a Fox.

Iu. What? you are as a candle, the better part burnt out

Fal. A Waſſell-Candle, my Lord; all Tallow: if I did ſay of wax, my growth would approue the truth.

Iuſt. There is not a white haire on your face, but ſhold haue his effect of grauity.

Fal. His effect of grauy, grauy, grauy.

Iuſt You follow the yong Prince vp and downe, like his euill Angell.

Fal. Not ſo (my Lord) your ill Angell is light: but I hope, he that lookes vpon mee, will take mee without, weighing: and yet, in ſome reſpects I grant, I cannot go: I cannot tell. Vertue is of ſo little regard in theſe Coſtor-mongers, that true valor is turn'd Beare-heard. Pregnancie is made a Tapſter, and hath his quicke wit waſted in giuing Reckonings: all the other gifts appertinent to man (as the malice of this Age ſhapes them) are not woorth a Gooſeberry. You that are old, conſider not the capacities of vs that are yong: you meaſure the heat of our Liuers, with the bitternes of your gals. & we that are in the vaward of our youth, I muſt confeſſe, are wagges too.

Iuſt. Do you ſet downe your name in the ſcrowle of youth, that are written downe old, with all the Charracters of age? Haue you not a moiſt eye? a dry hand? a yellow cheeke? a white beard? a decreaſing leg? an increſing belly? Is not your voice broken? your winde ſhort? your wit ſingle? and euery part about you blaſted with Antiquity? and wil you cal your ſelfe yong? Fy, fy, fy, ſir *Iohn*.

Fal. My Lord, I was borne with a white head, & ſomthing a round belly. For my voice, I haue loſt it with hallowing and ſinging of Anthemes. To approue my youth farther, I will not: the truth is, I am onely olde in iudgement and vnderſtanding: and he that will caper with mee for a thouſand Markes, let him lend me the mony, & haue at him. For the boxe of th'eare that the Prince gaue you, he gaue it like a rude Prince, and you tooke it like a ſenſible Lord. I haue checkt him for it, and the yong Lion repents: Marry not in aſhes and ſacke-cloath, but in new Silke, and old Sacke.

Iuſt. Wel, heauen ſend the Prince a better companion.

Fal. Heauen ſend the Companion a better Prince: I cannot rid my hands of him.

Iuſt. Well, the King hath ſeuer'd you and Prince *Harry*, I heare you are going with Lord *Iohn* of Lancaſter, againſt the Archbiſhop, and the Earle of Northumberland

Fal. Yes, I thanke your pretty ſweet wit for it: but looke you pray, (all you that kiſſe my Ladie Peace, at home) that our Armies ioyn not in a hot day: for if I take but two ſhirts out with me, and I meane not to ſweat extraordinarily: if it bee a hot day, if I brandiſh any thing but my Bottle, would I might neuer ſpit white againe: There is not a daungerous Action can peepe out his head, but I am thruſt vpon it. Well, I cannot laſt euer.

Iuſt. Well, be honeſt, be honeſt, and heauen bleſſe your Expedition.

Fal. Will your Lordſhip lend mee a thouſand pound, to furniſh me forth?

Iuſt. Not a peny, not a peny: you are too impatient to beare croſſes. Fare you well. Commend mee to my Coſin Weſtmerland.

Fal. If I do, fillop me with a three-man-Beetle. A man can no more ſeparate Age and Couetouſneſſe, then he can part yong limbes and letchery: but the Gowt galles the one,

one,and the pox pinches the other ; and ſo both the Degrees preuent my curſes. Boy?

Page. Sir.

Fal. What money is in my purſe?

Page. Seuen groats,and two pence.

Fal. I can get no remedy againſt this Conſumption of the purſe. Borrowing onely lingers, and lingers it out, but the diſeaſe is incureable. Go beare this letter to my Lord of Lancaſter, this to the Prince, this to the Earle of Weſtmerland, and this to old Miſtris *Vrſula*, whome I haue weekly ſworne to marry, ſince I perceiu'd the firſt white haire on my chin. About it : you know where to finde me. A pox of this Gowt, or a Gowt of this Poxe : for the one or th'other playes the rogue with my great toe : It is no matter, if I do halt,I haue the warres for my colour,and my Penſion ſhall ſeeme the more reaſonable. A good wit will make vſe of any thing : I will turne diſeaſes to commodity. *Exeunt*

Scena Quarta.

Enter Archbiſhop, Haſtings, Mowbray, and Lord Bardolfe.

Ar. Thus haue you heard our cauſes,& kno our Means :
And my moſt noble Friends, I pray you all
Speake plainly your opinions of our hopes,
And firſt(Lord Marſhall) what ſay you to it?
Mow. I well allow the occaſion of our Armes,
But gladly would be better ſatisfied,
How (in our Meanes) we ſhould aduance our ſelues
To looke with forhead bold and big enough
Vpon the Power and puiſance of the King.
Haſt. Our preſent Muſters grow vpon the File
To fiue and twenty thouſand men of choice ;
And our Supplies, liue largely in the hope
Of great Northumberland, whoſe boſome burnes
With an incenſed Fire of Iniuries.
L.Bar. The queſtion then(Lord *Haſtings*)ſtandeth thus
Whether our preſent fiue and twenty thouſand
May hold-vp-head, without Northumberland:
Haſt. With him, we may.
L.Bar. I marry, there's the point:
But if without him we be thought to feeble,
My iudgement is, we ſhould not ſtep too farre
Till we had his Aſsiſtance by the hand.
For in a Theame ſo bloody fac'd, as this,
Coniecture, Expectation, and Surmiſe
Of Aydes incertaine, ſhould not be admitted.
Arch. 'Tis very true Lord *Bardolfe*, for indeed
It was yong *Hotſpurres* caſe, at Shrewsbury.
L.Bar. It was(my Lord)who lin'd himſelf with hope,
Eating the ayre, on promiſe of Supply,
Flatt'ring himſelfe with Proiect of a power,
Much ſmaller, then the ſmalleſt of his Thoughts,
And ſo with great imagination
(Proper to mad men) led his Powers to death,
And (winking) leap'd into deſtruction.
Haſt. But (by your leaue)it neuer yet did hurt,
To lay downe likely-hoods, and formes of hope.
L.Bar. Yes, if this preſent quality of warre,
Indeed the inſtant action: a cauſe on foot,
Liues ſo in hope : As in an early Spring,
We ſee th'appearing buds, which to proue fruite,
Hope giue not ſo much warrant, as Diſpaire
That Froſts will bite them. When we meane to build,
We firſt ſuruey the Plot, then draw the Modell,
And when we ſee the figure of the houſe,
Then muſt we rate the coſt of the Erection,
Which if we finde out-weighes Ability,
What do we then, but draw a-new the Modell
In fewer offices? Or at leaſt, deſiſt
To builde at all? Much more, in this great worke,
(Which is (almoſt) to plucke a Kingdome downe,
And ſet another vp) ſhould we ſuruey
The plot of Situation, and the Modell ;
Conſent vpon a ſure Foundation :
Queſtion Surueyors, know our owne eſtate,
How able ſuch a Worke to vndergo,
To weigh againſt his Oppoſite? Or elſe,
We fortifie in Paper, and in Figures,
Vſing the Names of men, inſtead of men :
Like one, that drawes the Modell of a houſe
Beyond his power to builde it; who(halfe through)
Giues o're, and leaues his part-created Coſt
A naked ſubiect to the Weeping Clouds,
And waſte, for churliſh Winters tyranny.
Haſt. Grant that our hopes(yet likely of faire byrth)
Should be ſtill-borne : and that we now poſſeſt
The vtmoſt man of expectation :
I thinke we are a Body ſtrong enough
(Euen as we are) to equall with the King.
L.Bar. What is the King but fiue & twenty thouſand?
Haſt. To vs no more : nay not ſo much Lord *Bardolf*.
For his diuiſions (as the Times do braul)
Are in three Heads : one Power againſt the French,
And one againſt *Glendower*: Perforce a third
Muſt take vp vs : So is the vnfirme King
In three diuided : and his Coffers ſound
With hollow Pouerty, and Emptineſſe.
Ar. That he ſhould draw his ſeuerall ſtrengths togither
And come againſt vs in full puiſſance
Need not be dreaded.
Haſt. If he ſhould do ſo,
He leaues his backe vnarm'd, the French, and Welch
Baying him at the heeles : neuer feare that.
L.Bar. Who is it like ſhould lead his Forces hither?
Haſt. The Duke of Lancaſter, and Weſtmerland :
Againſt the Welſh himſelfe, and *Harrie Monmouth*.
But who is ſubſtituted 'gainſt the French,
I haue no certaine notice.
Arch. Let vs on :
And publiſh the occaſion of our Armes.
The Common-wealth is ſicke of their owne Choice,
Their ouer-greedy loue hath ſurfetted :
An habitation giddy, and vnſure
Hath he that buildeth on the vulgar heart.
O thou fond Many, with what loud applauſe
Did'ſt thou beate heauen with bleſſing *Bullingbrooke*,
Before he was, what thou would'ſt haue him be?
And being now trimm'd in thine owne deſires,
Thou (beaſtly Feeder) art ſo full of him,
That thou prouok'ſt thy ſelfe to caſt him vp.
So, ſo, (thou common Dogge) did'ſt thou diſgorge
Thy glutton-boſome of the Royall *Richard*,
And now thou would'ſt eate thy dead vomit vp,
And howl'ſt to finde it. What truſt is in theſe Times?
They, that when *Richard* liu'd, would haue him dye,
Are now become enamour'd on his graue
Thou that threw'ſt duſt vpon his goodly head
When through proud London he came ſighing on,
After th'admired heeles of *Bullingbrooke*,
Cri'ſt now, O Earth, yeeld vs that King agiue,

And

And take thou this (O thoughts of men accurs'd)
"*Past, and to Come, seemes best; things Present, worst.*

Mow. Shall we go draw our numbers, and set on?

Hast. We are Times subiects, and Time bids, be gon.

Actus Secundus. Scœna Prima.

Enter Hostesse, with two Officers, Fang, and Snare.

Hostesse. Mr. *Fang*, haue you entred the Action?

Fang. It is enter'd.

Hostesse. Wher's your Yeoman? Is it a lusty yeoman? Will he stand to it?

Fang. Sirrah, where's *Snare*?

Hostesse. I, I, good M. *Snare*.

Snare. Heere, heere.

Fang. *Snare*, we must Arrest Sir *Iohn Falstaffe*.

Host. I good M. *Snare*, I haue enter'd him, and all.

Sn. It may chance cost some of vs our liues: he wil stab

Hostesse. Alas the day: take heed of him: he stabd me in mine owne house, and that most beastly: he cares not what mischeefe he doth, if his weapon be out. Hee will foyne like any diuell, he will spare neither man, woman, nor childe.

Fang. If I can close with him, I care not for his thrust.

Hostesse. No, nor I neither: Ile be at your elbow.

Fang. If I but fist him once: if he come but within my Vice.

Host. I am vndone with his going: I warrant he is an infinitiue thing vpon my score. Good M. *Fang* hold him sure: good M. *Snare* let him not scape, he comes continuantly to Py-Corner (sauing your manhoods) to buy a saddle, and hee is indited to dinner to the Lubbars head in Lombardstreet, to M. *Smoothes* the Silkman. I pra'ye, since my Exion is enter'd, and my Case so openly known to the world, let him be brought in to his answer: A 100. Marke is a long one, for a poore lone woman to beare: & I haue borne, and borne, and borne, and haue bin fub'd off, and fub'd-off, from this day to that day, that it is a shame to be thought on. There is no honesty in such dealing, vnles a woman should be made an Asse and a Beast, to beare euery Knaues wrong. *Enter Falstaffe and Bardolfe.* Yonder he comes, and that arrant Malmesey-Nose *Bardolfe* with him. Do your Offices, do your offices: M. *Fang*, & M. *Snare*, do me, do me, do me your Offices.

Fal. How now? whose Mare's dead? what's the matter?

Fang. Sir *Iohn*, I arrest you, at the suit of Mist. *Quickly*.

Falst. Away Varlets, draw *Bardolfe*: Cut me off the Villaines head: throw the Queane in the Channel.

Host. Throw me in the channell? Ile throw thee there. Wilt thou? wilt thou? thou bastardly rogue. Murder, murder, O thou Hony-suckle villaine, wilt thou kill Gods officers, and the Kings? O thou hony-seed Rogue, thou art a honyseed, a Man-queller, and a woman-queller.

Falst. Keep them off, *Bardolfe*. *Fang.* A rescu, a rescu.

Host. Good people bring a rescu. Thou wilt not? thou wilt not? Do, do thou Rogue: Do thou Hempseed.

Page. Away you Scullion, you Rampallian, you Fustillirian: Ile tucke your Catastrophe. *Enter. Ch. Iustice.*

Iust. What's the matter? Keepe the Peace here, hoa.

Host. Good my Lord be good to mee. I beseech you stand to me.

Ch. Iust. How now sir *Iohn*? What are you brauling here?
Doth this become your place, your time, and businesse?
You should haue bene well on your way to Yorke.
Stand from him Fellow; wherefore hang'st vpon him?

Host. Oh my most worshipfull Lord, and't please your Grace, I am a poore widdow of Eastcheap, and he is arrested at my suit. *Ch. Iust.* For what summe?

Host. It is more then for some (my Lord) it is for all: all I haue, he hath eaten me out of house and home; hee hath put all my substance into that fat belly of his: but I will haue some of it out againe, or I will ride thee o' Nights, like the Mare.

Falst. I thinke I am as like to ride the Mare, if I haue any vantage of ground, to get vp.

Ch. Iust. How comes this, Sir *Iohn*? Fy, what a man of good temper would endure this tempest of exclamation? Are you not asham'd to inforce a poore Widdowe to so rough a course, to come by her owne?

Falst. What is the grosse summe that I owe thee?

Host. Marry (if thou wer't an honest man) thy selfe, & the mony too. Thou didst sweare to mee vpon a parcell gilt Goblet, sitting in my Dolphin-chamber at the round table, by a sea-cole fire, on Wednesday in Whitson week, when the Prince broke thy head for lik'ning him to a singing man of Windsor; Thou didst sweare to me then (as I was washing thy wound) to marry me, and make mee my Lady thy wife. Canst ÿ deny it? Did not goodwife *Keech* the Butchers wife come in then, and cal me gossip *Quickly*? comming in to borrow a messe of Vinegar: telling vs, she had a good dish of Prawnes: whereby ÿ didst desire to eat some: whereby I told thee they were ill for a greene wound? And didst not thou (when she was gone downe staires) desire me to be no more familiar with such poore people, saying, that ere long they should call me Madam? And did'st ÿ not kisse me, and bid mee fetch thee 30.s? I put thee now to thy Book-oath, deny it if thou canst?

Fal. My Lord, this is a poore mad soule: and she sayes vp & downe the town, that her eldest son is like you. She hath bin in good case, & the truth is, pouerty hath distracted her: but for these foolish Officers, I beseech you, I may haue redresse against them.

Iust. Sir *Iohn*, sir *Iohn*, I am well acquainted with your maner of wrenching the true cause, the false way. It is not a confident brow, nor the throng of wordes, that come with such (more then impudent) sawcines from you, can thrust me from a leuell consideration, I know you ha' practis'd vpon the easie-yeelding spirit of this woman.

Host. Yes in troth my Lord.

Iust. Prethee peace: pay her the debt you owe her, and vnpay the villany you haue done her: the one you may do with sterling mony, & the other with currant repentance.

Fal. My Lord, I will not vndergo this sneape without reply. You call honorable Boldnes, impudent Sawcinesse: If a man wil curt'sie, and say nothing, he is vertuous: No, my Lord (your humble duty remebred) I will not be your sutor. I say to you, I desire deliu'rance from these Officers being vpon hasty employment in the Kings Affaires.

Iust. You speake, as hauing power to do wrong: But answer in the effect of your Reputation, and satisfie the poore woman.

Falst. Come hither Hostesse. *Enter M. Gower*

Ch. Iust. Now Master *Gower*; What newes?

Gow. The King (my Lord) and *Henrie* Prince of Wales
Are neere at hand: The rest the Paper telles.

Falst. As I am a Gentleman.

Host. Nay, you said so before.

Fal. As I am a Gentleman. Come, no more words of it

Host. By this Heauenly ground I tread on, I must be faine to pawne both my Plate, and the Tapistry of my dyning Chambers.

g 3 *Falst.*

Fal. Glaſſes, glaſſes, is the onely drinking: and for thy walles a pretty ſlight Drollery, or the Storie of the Prodigall, or the Germane hunting in Waterworke, is worth a thouſand of theſe Bed-hangings, and theſe Fly-bitten Tapiſtries. Let it be tenne pound (if thou canſt.) Come, if it were not for thy humors, there is not a better Wench in England. Go, waſh thy face, and draw thy Action: Come, thou muſt not bee in this humour with me, come, I know thou was't ſet on to this.

Hoſt. Prethee (Sir *Iohn*) let it be but twenty Nobles, I loath to pawne my Plate, in good earneſt la.

Fal. Let it alone, Ile make other ſhift: you'l be a fool ſtill.

Hoſt. Well. you ſhall haue it although I pawne my Gowne. I hope you'l come to Supper. You'l pay me altogether?

Fal. Will I liue? Go with her, with her: hooke-on, hooke-on.

Hoſt. Will you haue *Doll Teare-ſheet* meet you at ſupper?

Fal. No more words. Let's haue her.

Ch. Iuſt. I haue heard bitter newes.

Fal What's the newes (my good Lord?)

Ch. Iu. Where lay the King laſt night?

Meſ. At Baſingſtoke my Lord.

Fal. I hope (my Lord) all's well. What is the newes my Lord?

Ch. Iuſt. Come all his Forces backe?

Meſ. No: Fifteene hundred Foot, fiue hundred Horſe
Are march'd vp to my Lord of Lancaſter,
Againſt Northumberland, and the Archbiſhop.

Fal. Comes the King backe from Wales, my noble L?

Ch. Iuſt. You ſhall haue Letters of me preſently.
Come, go along with me, good M. *Gowre.*

Fal. My Lord.

Ch. Iuſt. What's the matter?

Fal. Maſter *Gowre*, ſhall I entreate you with mee to dinner?

Gow. I muſt waite vpon my good Lord heere.
I thanke you, good Sir *Iohn.*

Ch. Iuſt. Sir *Iohn*, you loyter heere too long being you are to take Souldiers vp, in Countries as you go.

Fal. Will you ſup with me, Maſter *Gowre?*

Ch. Iuſt. What fooliſh Maſter taught you theſe manners, Sir *Iohn?*

Fal. Maſter *Gower*, if they become mee not, hee was a Foole that taught them mee. This is the right Fencing grace (my Lord) tap for tap, and ſo part faire.

Ch. Iuſt Now the Lord lighten thee, thou art a great Foole. *Exeunt*

Scena Secunda.

Enter Prince Henry, Pointz, Bardolfe, and Page.

Prin. Truſt me, I am exceeding weary.

Poin. Is it come to that? I had thought wearines durſt not haue attach'd one of ſo high blood.

Prin. It doth me: though it diſcolours the complexion of my Greatneſſe to acknowledge it. Doth it not ſhew vildely in me, to deſire ſmall Beere?

Poin. Why, a Prince ſhould not be ſo looſely ſtudied, as to remember ſo weake a Compoſition.

Prince. Belike then, my Appetite was not Princely got: for (in troth) I do now remember the poore Creature, Small Beere. But indeede theſe humble conſiderations make me out of loue with my Greatneſſe. What a diſgrace is it to me, to remember thy name? Or to know thy face to morrow? Or to take note how many paire of Silk ſtockings ỷ haſt (Viz. theſe, and thoſe that were thy peach-colour'd ones:) Or to beare the Inuentorie of thy ſhirts, as one for ſuperfluity, and one other, for vſe. But that the Tennis-Court-keeper knowes better then I, for it is a low ebbe of Linnen with thee, when thou kept'ſt not Racket there, as thou haſt not done a great while, becauſe the reſt of thy Low Countries, haue made a ſhift to eate vp thy Holland.

Poin. How ill it followes, after you haue labour'd ſo hard, you ſhould talke ſo idlely? Tell me how many good yong Princes would do ſo, their Fathers lying ſo ſicke, as yours is?

Prin. Shall I tell thee one thing, *Peintz?*

Poin Yes: and let it be an excellent good thing.

Prin. It ſhall ſerue among wittes of no higher breeding then thine.

Poin. Go to: I ſtand the puſh of your one thing, that you'l tell.

Prin. Why, I tell thee, it is not meet, that I ſhould be ſad now my Father is ſicke: albeit I could tell to thee (as to one it pleaſes me, for fault of a better, to call my friend) I could be ſad, and ſad indeed too.

Poin Very hardly, vpon ſuch a ſubiect.

Prin. Thou think'ſt me as farre in the Diuels Booke, as thou, and *Falſtaffe*, for obduracie and perſiſtencie. Let the end try the man. But I tell thee, my hart bleeds inwardly, that my Father is ſo ſicke: and keeping ſuch vild company as thou art, hath in reaſon taken from me, all oſtentation of ſorrow.

Poin. The reaſon?

Prin. What would'ſt thou think of me, if I ſhold weep?

Poin. I would thinke thee a moſt Princely hypocrite.

Prin. It would be euery mans thought: and thou art a bleſſed Fellow, to thinke as euery man thinkes: neuer a mans thought in the world, keepes the Rode-way better then thine: euery man would thinke me an Hypocrite indeede. And what accites your moſt worſhipful thought to thinke ſo?

Poin. Why, becauſe you haue beene ſo lewde, and ſo much ingraffed to *Falſtaffe.*

Prin. And to thee.

Pointz. Nay, I am well ſpoken of, I can heare it with mine owne eares: the worſt that they can ſay of me is, that I am a ſecond Brother, and that I am a proper Fellowe of my hands: and thoſe two things I confeſſe I canot helpe. Looke, looke, here comes *Bardolfe.*

Prince. And the Boy that I gaue *Falſtaffe*, he had him from me Chriſtian, and ſee if the fat villain haue not transform'd him Ape.

Enter Bardolfe.

Bar. Saue your Grace.

Prin. And yours, moſt Noble *Bardolfe.*

Poin. Come you pernitious Aſſe, you baſhfull Foole, muſt you be bluſhing? Wherefore bluſh you now? what a Maidenly man at Armes are you become? Is it ſuch a matter to get a Pottle-pots Maiden-head?

Page. He call'd me euen now (my Lord) through a red Lattice, and I could diſcerne no part of his face from the window:

window: at last I spy'd his eyes, and me thought he had made two holes in the Ale-wiues new Petticoat, & peeped through.

Prin. Hath not the boy profited?

Bar. Away, you horson vpright Rabbet, away.

Page. Away, you rascally *Altheas* dreame, away.

Prin. Instruct vs Boy: what dreame, Boy?

Page. Marry (my Lord) *Althea* dream'd, she was deliuer'd of a Firebrand, and therefore I call him hir dream.

Prince. A Crownes-worth of good Interpretation: There it is, Boy.

Poin. O that this good Blossome could bee kept from Cankers: Well, there is six pence to preserue thee.

Bard. If you do not make him be hang'd among you, the gallowes shall be wrong'd.

Prince. And how doth thy Master, *Bardolph*?

Bar. Well, my good Lord: he heard of your Graces comming to Towne. There's a Letter for you.

Poin. Deliuer'd with good respect: And how doth the Martlemas, your Master?

Bard. In bodily health Sir.

Poin. Marry, the immortall part needes a Physitian: but that moues not him: though that bee sicke, it dyes not.

Prince. I do allow this Wen to bee as familiar with me, as my dogge: and he holds his place, for looke you he writes.

Poin.Letter. *Iohn Falstaffe Knight*: (Euery man must know that, as oft as hee hath occasion to name himselfe:) Euen like those that are kinne to the King, for they neuer pricke their finger, but they say, there is som of the kings blood spilt. How comes that (sayes he) that takes vpon him not to conceiue? the answer is as ready as a borrowed cap: I am the Kings poore Cosin, Sir.

Prince. Nay, they will be kin to vs, but they wil fetch it from *Iaphet*. But to the Letter: —*Sir Iohn Falstaffe, Knight, to the Sonne of the King, neerest his Father, Harrie Prince of Wales, greeting.*

Poin. Why this is a Certificate.

Prin. Peace.

I will imitate the honourable Romaines in breuitie.

Poin. Sure he meanes breuity in breath: short-winded. *I commend me to thee, I commend thee, and I leaue thee. Bee not too familiar with* Pointz, *for hee misuses thy Fauours so much, that he sweares thou art to marrie his Sister* Nell. *Repent at idle times as thou mayst, and so farewell.*

Thine, by yea and no: which is as much as to say, as thou vsest him. Iacke Falstaffe *with my Familiars:* Iohn *with my Brothers and Sister: & Sir* Iohn, *with all Europe.*

My Lord, I will steepe this Letter in Sack, and make him eate it.

Prin. That's to make him eate twenty of his Words. But do you vse me thus *Ned*? Must I marry your Sister?

Poin. May the Wench haue no worse Fortune. But I neuer said so.

Prin. Well, thus we play the Fooles with the time, & the spirits of the wise, sit in the clouds, and mocke vs: Is your Master heere in London?

Bard. Yes my Lord.

Prin. Where suppes he? Doth the old Bore, feede in the old Franke?

Bard. At the old place my Lord, in East-cheape.

Prin. What Company?

Page. Ephesians my Lord, of the old Church.

Prin. Sup any women with him?

Page. None my Lord, but old Mistris *Quickly*, and M. *Doll Teare-sheet*.

Prin. What Pagan may that be?

Page. A proper Gentlewoman, Sir, and a Kinswoman of my Masters.

Prin. Euen such Kin, as the Parish Heyfors are to the Towne-Bull?
Shall we steale vpon them (*Ned*) at Supper?

Poin. I am your shadow, my Lord, Ile follow you.

Prin. Sirrah, you boy, and *Bardolph*, no word to your Master that I am yet in Towne.
There's for your silence.

Bar. I haue no tongue, sir.

Page. And for mine Sir, I will gouerne it.

Prin. Fare ye well: go.
This *Doll Teare-sheet* should be some Rode.

Poin. I warrant you, as common as the way betweene S. Albans, and London.

Prin. How might we see *Falstaffe* bestow himselfe to night, in his true colours, and not our selues be seene?

Poin. Put on two Leather Ierkins, and Aprons, and waite vpon him at his Table, like Drawers.

Prin. From a God, to a Bull? A heauie declension: It was Ioues case. From a Prince, to a Prentice, a low transformation, that shall be mine: for in euery thing, the purpose must weigh with the folly. Follow me *Ned*. *Exeunt*

Scena Tertia.

Enter Northumberland, his Ladie, and Harrie Percies Ladie.

North. I prethee louing Wife, and gentle Daughter,
Giue an euen way vnto my rough Affaires:
Put not you on the visage of the Times,
And be like them to Percie, troublesome.

Wife. I haue giuen ouer, I will speak no more,
Do what you will: your Wisedome, be your guide.

North. Alas (sweet Wife) my Honor is at pawne,
And but my going, nothing can redeeme it.

La. Oh yet, for heauens sake, go not to these Warrs;
The Time was (Father) when you broke your word,
When you were more endeer'd to it, then now,
When your owne Percy, when my heart-deere-*Harry*,
Threw many a Northward looke, to see his Father
Bring vp his Powres: but he did long in vaine.
Who then perswaded you to stay at home?
There were two Honors lost; Yours, and your Sonnes.
For Yours, may heauenly glory brighten it:
For His, it stucke vpon him, as the Sunne
In the gray vault of Heauen: and by his Light
Did all the Cheualrie of England moue
To do braue Acts. He was (indeed) the Glasse
Wherein the Noble-Youth did dresse themselues.
He had no Legges, that practic'd not his Gate:
And speaking thicke (which Nature made his blemish)
Became the Accents of the Valiant.
For those that could speake low, and tardily,
Would turne their owne Perfection, to Abuse,
To seeme like him. So that in Speech, in Gate,
In Diet, in Affections of delight,
In Militarie Rules, Humors of Blood,

He

He was the Marke, and Glasse, Coppy, and Booke,
That fashion'd others. And him, O wondrous! him,
O Miracle of Men! Him did you leaue
(Second to none) vn-seconded by you,
To looke vpon the hideous God of Warre,
In dis-aduantage, to abide a field,
Where nothing but the sound of *Hotspurs* Name
Did seeme defensible: so you left him.
Neuer, O neuer doe his Ghost the wrong,
To hold your Honor more precise and nice
With others, then with him. Let them alone:
The Marshall and the Arch-bishop are strong.
Had my sweet *Harry* had but halfe their Numbers,
To day might I (hanging on *Hotspurs* Necke)
Haue talk'd of *Monmouth's* Graue.

North. Beshrew your heart,
(Faire Daughter) you doe draw my Spirits from me,
With new lamenting ancient Ouer-sights.
But I must goe, and meet with Danger there,
Or it will seeke me in another place,
And finde me worse prouided.

Wife. O flye to Scotland,
Till that the Nobles, and the armed Commons,
Haue of their Puissance made a little taste.

Lady. If they get ground, and vantage of the King,
Then ioyne you with them, like a Ribbe of Steele,
To make Strength stronger. But, for all our loues,
First let them trye themselues. So did your Sonne,
He was so suffer'd; so came I a Widow
And neuer shall haue length of Life enough,
To raine vpon Remembrance with mine Eyes,
That it may grow, and sprowt, as high as Heauen,
For Recordation to my Noble Husband.

North. Come, come, go in with me: 'tis with my Minde
As with the Tyde, swell'd vp vnto his height,
That makes a still-stand, running neyther way.
Faine would I goe to meet the Arch-bishop,
But many thousand Reasons hold me backe.
I will resolue for Scotland: there am I,
Till Time and Vantage craue my company. *Exeunt*

Scæna Quarta.

Enter two Drawers.

1. Drawer. What hast thou brought there? Apple-Iohns? Thou know'st Sir *Iohn* cannot endure an Apple-Iohn.

2. Draw. Thou say'st true: the Prince once set a Dish of Apple-Iohns before him, and told him there were fiue more Sir *Iohns*: and, putting off his Hat, said, I will now take my leaue of these sixe drie, round, old-wither'd Knights. It anger'd him to the heart: but hee hath forgot that.

1. Draw. Why then couer, and set them downe: and see if thou canst finde out *Sneakes* Noyse; Mistris *Teare-sheet* would faine haue some Musique.

2. Draw. Sirrha, heere will be the Prince, and Master *Points*, anon: and they will put on two of our Ierkins, and Aprons, and Sir *Iohn* must not know of it: *Bardolph* hath brought word.

1. Draw. Then here will be old *Vtis*: it will be an excellent stratagem.

2. Draw. Ile see if I can finde out *Sneake*. *Exit.*

Enter Hostesse, and Dol.

Host. Sweet-heart, me thinkes now you are in an excellent good temperalitie: your Pulsidge beates as extraordinarily, as heart would desire; and your Colour (I warrant you) is as red as any Rose: But you haue drunke too much Canaries, and that's a maruellous searching Wine; and it perfumes the blood, ere wee can say what's this. How doe you now?

Dol. Better then I was: Hem.

Host. Why that was well said: A good heart's worth Gold. Looke, here comes Sir *Iohn*.

Enter Falstaffe.

Falst. *When Arthur first in Court*—(emptie the Iordan) *and was a worthy King*. How now Mistris *Dol*?

Host. Sick of a Calme: yea, good-sooth.

Falst. So is all her Sect: if they be once in a Calme, they are sick.

Dol. You muddie Rascall, is that all the comfort you giue me?

Falst. You make fat Rascalls, Mistris *Dol*.

Dol. I make them? Gluttonie and Diseases make them, I make them not.

Falst. If the Cooke make the Gluttonie, you helpe to make the Diseases (*Dol*) we catch of you (*Dol*) we catch of you: Grant that, my poore Vertue, grant that.

Dol. I marry, our Chaynes, and our Iewels.

Falst. Your Brooches, Pearles, and Owches: For to serue brauely, is to come halting off: you know, to come off the Breach, with his Pike bent brauely, and to Surgerie brauely; to venture vpon the charg'd-Chambers brauely.

Host. Why this is the olde fashion: you two neuer meete, but you fall to some discord: you are both (in good troth) as Rheumatike as two drie Tostes, you cannot one beare with anothers Confirmities. What the good-yere? One must beare, and that must bee you: you are the weaker Vessell; as they say, the emptier Vessell.

Dol. Can a weake emptie Vessell beare such a huge full Hogs-head? There's a whole Marchants Venture of Burdeux-Stuffe in him: you haue not seene a Hulke better stufft in the Hold. Come, Ile be friends with thee *Iacke*: Thou art going to the Warres, and whether I shall euer see thee againe, or no, there is no body cares.

Enter Drawer.

Drawer. Sir, Ancient *Pistoll* is below, and would speake with you.

Dol. Hang him, swaggering Rascall, let him not come hither: it is the foule-mouth'dst Rogue in England.

Host. If hee swagger, let him not come here: I must liue amongst my Neighbors, Ile no Swaggerers: I am in good name, and fame, with the very best: shut the doore, there comes no Swaggerers heere: I haue not liu'd all this while, to haue swaggering now: shut the doore, I pray you.

Falst. Do'st thou heare, Hostesse?

Host. 'Pray you pacifie your selfe (Sir *Iohn*) there comes no Swaggerers heere.

Falst. Do'st

Talſt. Do'ſt thou heare? it is mine Ancient.

Hoſt. Tilly-fally (Sir *Iohn*) neuer tell me, your ancient Swaggerer comes not in my doores. I was before Maſter *Tiſick* the Deputie, the other day: and as hee ſaid to me, it was no longer agoe then Wedneſday laſt: Neighbour *Quickly* (ſayes hee;) Maſter *Dombe*, our Miniſter, was by then: Neighbour *Quickly* (ſayes hee) receiue thoſe that are Ciuill; for (ſayth hee) you are in an ill Name: now hee ſaid ſo, I can tell whereupon: for (ſayes hee) you are an honeſt Woman, and well thought on; therefore take heede what Gueſts you receiue: Receiue (ſayes hee) no ſwaggering Companions. There comes none heere. You would bleſſe you to heare what hee ſaid. No, Ile no Swaggerers.

Falſt. Hee's no Swaggerer (Hoſteſſe:) a tame Cheater, hee: you may ſtroake him as gently, as a Puppie Grey-hound: hee will not ſwagger with a Barbarie Henne, if her feathers turne backe in any ſhew of reſiſtance. Call him vp (Drawer.)

Hoſt. Cheater, call you him? I will barre no honeſt man my houſe, nor no Cheater: but I doe not loue ſwaggering; I am the worſe when one ſayes, ſwagger: Feele Maſters, how I ſhake: looke you, I warrant you.

Dol. So you doe, Hoſteſſe.

Hoſt. Doe I? yea, in very truth doe I, if it were an Aſpen Leafe: I cannot abide Swaggerers.

Enter Piſtol, and Bardolph and his Boy.

Piſt. 'Saue you, Sir *Iohn*.

Falſt. Welcome Ancient *Piſtol*. Here (*Piſtol*) I charge you with a Cup of Sacke: doe you diſcharge vpon mine Hoſteſſe.

Piſt. I will diſcharge vpon her (Sir *Iohn*) with two Bullets.

Falſt. She is Piſtoll-proofe (Sir) you ſhall hardly offend her.

Hoſt. Come, Ile drinke no Proofes, nor no Bullets: I will drinke no more then will doe me good, for no mans pleaſure, I.

Piſt. Then to you (Miſtris *Dorothie*) I will charge you.

Dol. Charge me? I ſcorne you (ſcuruie Companion) what? you poore, baſe, raſcally, cheating, lacke-Linnen-Mate: away you mouldie Rogue, away; I am meat for your Maſter.

Piſt. I know you, Miſtris *Dorothie*.

Dol. Away you Cut-purſe Raſcall, you filthy Bung, away: By this Wine, Ile thruſt my Kniſe in your mouldie Chappes, if you play the ſawcie Cuttle with me. Away you Bottle-Ale Raſcall, you Basket-hilt ſtale Iugler, you. Since when, I pray you, Sir? what, with two Points on your ſhoulder? much.

Piſt. I will murther your Ruffe, for this.

Hoſt No, good Captaine *Piſtol*: not heere, ſweete Captaine

Dol. Captaine? thou abhominable damn'd Cheater, art thou not aſham'd to be call'd Captaine? If Captaines were of my minde, they would truncheon you out, for taking their Names vpon you, before you haue earn'd them. You a Captaine? you ſlaue, for what? for tearing a poore Whores Ruffe in a Bawdy-houſe? Hee a Captaine? hang him Rogue, hee liues vpon mouldie ſtew'd-Pruines, and dry'de Cakes. A Captaine? Theſe Villaines will make the word Captaine odious: Therefore Captaines had neede looke to it.

Bard. 'Pray thee goe downe, good Ancient.

Falſt. Hearke thee hither, Miſtris *Dol*.

Piſt. Not I: I tell thee what, Corporall *Bardolph*, I could teare her: Ile be reueng'd on her.

Page. 'Pray thee goe downe.

Piſt. Ile ſee her damn'd firſt: to *Pluto's* damn'd Lake, to the Infernall Deepe, where *Erebus* and Tortures vilde alſo. Hold Hooke and Line, ſay I: Downe: downe Dogges, downe Fates: haue wee not *Hiren* here?

Hoſt. Good Captaine *Peeſel* be quiet, it is very late: I beſeeke you now, aggrauate your Choler.

Piſt. Theſe be good Humors indeede. Shall Pack-Horſes, and hollow-pamper'd Iades of Aſia, which cannot goe but thirtie miles a day, compare with *Cæſar*, and with Caniballs, and Troian Greekes? nay, rather damne them with King *Cerberus*, and let the Welkin roare: ſhall wee fall foule for Toyes?

Hoſt. By my troth Captaine, theſe are very bitter words.

Bard. Be gone, good Ancient: this will grow to a Brawle anon.

Piſt. Die men, like Dogges; giue Crownes like Pinnes: Haue we not *Hiren* here?

Hoſt. On my word (Captaine) there's none ſuch here. What the good-yere, doe you thinke I would denye her? I pray be quiet.

Piſt. Then feed, and be fat (my faire *Calipolis*.) Come, giue me ſome Sack, *Si fortune me tormente, ſperato me contente*. Feare wee broad-ſides? No, let the Fiend giue fire: Giue me ſome Sack: and Sweet-heart lye thou there: Come wee to full Points here, and are *et cetera's* nothing?

Fal. *Piſtol*, I would be quiet.

Piſt. Sweet Knight, I kiſſe thy Neaffe: what? wee haue ſeene the ſeuen Starres.

Dol. Thruſt him downe ſtayres, I cannot endure ſuch a Fuſtian Raſcall.

Piſt. Thruſt him downe ſtayres? know we not Galloway Nagges?

Fal. Quoit him downe (*Bardolph*) like a ſhoue-groat ſhilling: nay, if hee doe nothing but ſpeake nothing, hee ſhall be nothing here.

Bard. Come, get you downe ſtayres.

Piſt. What? ſhall wee haue Inciſion? ſhall wee embrew? then Death rocke me aſleepe, abridge my doleſull dayes: why then let grieuous, gaſtly, gaping Wounds, vntwin'd the Siſters three: Come *Atropos*, I ſay.

Hoſt. Here's good ſtuffe toward.

Fal. Giue me my Rapier, Boy.

Dol. I prethee *Iack*, I prethee doe not draw.

Fal. Get you downe ſtayres.

Hoſt. Here's a goodly tumult: Ile forſweare keeping houſe, before Ile be in theſe tirrits, and frights. So: Murther I warrant now. Alas, alas, put vp your naked Weapons, put vp your naked Weapons.

Dol. I prethee *Iack* be quiet, the Raſcall is gone: ah, you whorſon little valiant Villaine, you.

Hoſt. Are you not hurt i'th' Groyne? me thought hee made a ſhrewd Thruſt at your Belly.

Fal. Haue you turn'd him out of doores?

Bard. Yes Sir: the Raſcall's drunke: you haue hurt him (Sir) in the ſhoulder.

Fal. A Raſcall to braue me.

Dol. Ah, you ſweet little Rogue, you: alas, poore Ape, how thou ſweat'ſt? Come, let me wipe thy Face: Come on, you whorſon Chops: Ah Rogue, I loue thee: Thou

art

art as valorous as *Hector* of Troy, worth fiue of *Agamemnon*, and tenne times better then the nine Worthies: ah Villaine.

Fal. A rascally Slaue, I will tosse the Rogue in a Blanket.

Dol. Doe, if thou dar'st for thy heart: if thou doo'st, Ile canuas thee betweene a paire of Sheetes.

Enter Musique.

Page. The Musique is come, Sir.

Fal. Let them play: play Sirs. Sit on my Knee, *Dol.* A Rascall, bragging Slaue: the Rogue fled from me like Quick-siluer.

Dol. And thou follow'd'st him like a Church: thou whorson little tydie Bartholmew Bore-pigge, when wilt thou leaue fighting on dayes, and foyning on nights, and begin to patch vp thine old Body for Heauen?

Enter the Prince and Poines disguis'd.

Fal. Peace (good *Dol*) doe not speake like a Deaths-head: doe not bid me remember mine end.

Dol. Sirrha, what humor is the Prince of?

Fal. A good shallow young fellow: hee would haue made a good Pantler, hee would haue chipp'd Bread well.

Dol. They say *Poines* hath a good Wit.

Fal. Hee a good Wit? hang him Baboone, his Wit is as thicke as Tewksburie Mustard: there is no more conceit in him, then is in a Mallet.

Dol. Why doth the Prince loue him so then?

Fal. Because their Legges are both of a bignesse: and hee playes at Quoits well, and eates Conger and Fennell, and drinkes off Candles ends for Flap-dragons, and rides the wilde-Mare with the Boyes, and iumpes vpon Ioyn'd-stooles, and sweares with a good grace, and weares his Boot very smooth, like vnto the Signe of the Legge; and breedes no bate with telling of discreete stories: and such other Gamboll Faculties hee hath, that shew a weake Minde, and an able Body, for the which the Prince admits him; for the Prince himselfe is such another: the weight of an hayre will turne the Scales betweene their *Haber-de-pois*.

Prince. Would not this Naue of a Wheele haue his Eares cut off?

Poin. Let vs beat him before his Whore.

Prince. Looke, if the wither'd Elder hath not his Poll claw'd like a Parrot.

Poin. Is it not strange, that Desire should so many yeeres out-liue performance?

Fal. Kisse me *Dol.*

Prince. *Saturne* and *Venus* this yeere in Coniunction? What sayes the Almanack to that?

Poin. And looke whether the fierie *Trigon*, his Man, be not lisping to his Masters old Tables, his Note-Booke, his Councell-keeper?

Fal. Thou do'st giue me flatt'ring Busses.

Dol. Nay truely, I kisse thee with a most constant heart.

Fal. I am olde, I am olde.

Dol. I loue thee better, then I loue ere a scuruie young Boy of them all.

Fal. What Stuffe wilt thou haue a Kirtle of? I shall receiue Money on Thursday: thou shalt haue a Cappe to morrow. A merrie Song, come: it growes late, wee will to Bed. Thou wilt forget me, when I am gone.

Dol. Thou wilt set me a weeping, if thou say'st so: proue that euer I dresse my selfe handsome, till thy returne: well, hearken the end.

Fal. Some Sack, *Francis*.

Prin. Poin. Anon, anon, Sir.

Fal. Ha? a Bastard Sonne of the Kings? And art not thou *Poines*, his Brother?

Prince. Why thou Globe of sinfull Continents, what a Life do'st thou lead?

Fal. A better then thou: I am a Gentleman, thou art a Drawer.

Prince. Very true, Sir: and I come to draw you out by the Eares.

Host. Oh, the Lord preserue thy good Grace: Welcome to London. Now Heauen blesse that sweete Face of thine: what, are you come from Wales?

Fal. Thou whorson mad Compound of Maiestie: by this light Flesh, and corrupt Blood, thou art welcome.

Dol. How? you fat Foole, I scorne you.

Poin. My Lord, hee will driue you out of your reuenge, and turne all to a merryment, if you take not the heat.

Prince. You whorson Candle-myne you, how vildly did you speake of me euen now, before this honest, vertuous, ciuill Gentlewoman?

Host. 'Blessing on your good heart, and so shee is by my troth.

Fal. Didst thou heare me?

Prince. Yes: and you knew me, as you did when you ranne away by Gads-hill: you knew I was at your back, and spoke it on purpose, to trie my patience.

Fal. No, no, no: not so: I did not thinke, thou wast within hearing.

Prince. I shall driue you then to confesse the wilfull abuse, and then I know how to handle you.

Fal. No abuse (*Hall*) on mine Honor, no abuse.

Prince. Not to disprayse me? and call me Pantler, and Bread-chopper, and I know not what?

Fal. No abuse (*Hal.*)

Poin. No abuse?

Fal. No abuse (*Ned*) in the World: honest *Ned* none. I disprays'd him before the Wicked, that the Wicked might not fall in loue with him: In which doing, I haue done the part of a carefull Friend, and a true Subiect, and thy Father is to giue me thankes for it. No abuse (*Hal:*) none (*Ned*) none; no Boyes, none.

Prince. See now whether pure Feare, and entire Cowardise, doth not make thee wrong this vertuous Gentlewoman, to close with vs? Is shee of the Wicked? Is thine Hostesse heere, of the Wicked? Or is the Boy of the Wicked? Or honest *Bardolph* (whose Zeale burnes in his Nose) of the Wicked?

Poin. Answere thou dead Elme, answere.

Fal. The Fiend hath prickt downe *Bardolph* irrecouerable, and his Face is *Lucifers* Priuy-Kitchin, where hee doth nothing but rost Mault-Wormes: for the Boy, there is a good Angell about him, but the Deuill outbids him too.

Prince. For the Women?

Fal. For one of them, shee is in Hell alreadie, and burnes poore Soules: for the other, I owe her Money; and whether shee bee damn'd for that, I know not.

Host. No, I warrant you.

Fal. No.

Fal. No, I thinke thou art not: I thinke thou art quit for that. Marry, there is another Indictment vpon thee, for suffering flesh to bee eaten in thy house, contrary to the Law, for the which I thinke thou wilt howle.

Host. All Victuallers doe so: What is a Ioynt of Mutton, or two, in a whole Lent?

Prince. You, Gentlewoman.

Dol. What sayes your Grace?

Falst. His Grace sayes that, which his flesh rebells against.

Host. Who knocks so lowd at doore? Looke to the doore there, *Francis*?

Enter Peto.

Prince. *Peto*, how now? what newes?

Peto. The King, your Father, is at Westminster,
And there are twentie weake and wearied Postes,
Come from the North: and as I came along,
I met, and ouer-tooke a dozen Captaines,
Bare-headed, sweating, knocking at the Tauernes,
And asking euery one for Sir *Iohn Falstaffe.*

Prince. By Heauen (*Poines*) I feele me much to blame,
So idly to prophane the precious time,
When Tempest of Commotion, like the South,
Borne with black Vapour, doth begin to melt,
And drop vpon our bare vnarmed heads.
Giue me my Sword, and Cloake:
Falstaffe, good night. *Exit.*

Falst. Now comes in the sweetest Morsell of the night, and wee must hence, and leaue it vnpickt. More knocking at the doore? How now? what's the matter?

Bard. You must away to Court, Sir, presently,
A dozen Captaines stay at doore for you.

Falst. Pay the Musitians, Sirrha: farewell Hostesse, farewell *Dol.* You see (my good Wenches) how men of Merit are sought after: the vndeseruer may sleepe, when the man of Action is call'd on. Farewell good Wenches: If I be not sent away poste, I will see you againe, ere I goe.

Dol. I cannot speake: if my heart bee not readie to burst--- Well (sweete *Iacke*) haue a care of thy selfe.

Falst. Farewell, farewell. *Exit.*

Host. Well, fare thee well: I haue knowne thee these twentie nine yeeres, come Pescod-time. but an honester, and truer-hearted man---- Well, fare thee well.

Bard. Mistris *Teare-sheet.*

Host. What's the matter?

Bard. Bid Mistris *Teare-sheet* come to my Master.

Host. Oh runne *Dol*, runne: runne, good *Dol.*

Exeunt.

Actus Tertius. Scena Prima.

Enter the King, with a Page.

King. Goe, call the Earles of Surrey, and of Warwick:
But ere they come, bid them ore-reade these Letters,
And well consider of them: make good speed. *Exit.*
How many thousand of my poorest Subiects
Are at this howre asleepe? O Sleepe, O gentle Sleepe,
Natures soft Nurse, how haue I frighted thee,
That thou no more wilt weigh my eye-lids downe,
And steepe my Sences in Forgetfulnesse?
Why rather (Sleepe) lyest thou in smoakie Cribs,
Vpon vneasie Pallads stretching thee,
And huisht with bussing Night, flyes to thy slumber,
Then in the perfum'd Chambers of the Great?
Vnder the Canopies of costly State,
And lull'd with sounds of sweetest Melodie?
O thou dull God, why lyest thou with the vilde,
In loathsome Beds, and leau'st the Kingly Couch,
A Watch-case, or a common Larum-Bell?
Wilt thou, vpon the high and giddie Mast,
Seale vp the Ship-boyes Eyes, and rock his Braines,
In Cradle of the rude imperious Surge,
And in the visitation of the Windes,
Who take the Ruffian Billowes by the top,
Curling their monstrous heads, and hanging them
With deaff'ning Clamors in the slipp'ry Clouds,
That with the hurley, Death it selfe awakes?
Canst thou (O partiall Sleepe) giue thy Repose
To the wet Sea-Boy, in an houre so rude:
And in the calmest, and most stillest Night,
With all appliances, and meanes to boote,
Deny it to a King? Then happy Lowe, lye downe,
Vneasie lyes the Head, that weares a Crowne.

Enter Warwicke and Surrey.

War. Many good-morrowes to your Maiestie.

King. Is it good-morrow, Lords?

War. 'Tis One a Clock, and past.

King. Why then good-morrow to you all (my Lords:)
Haue you read o're the Letters that I sent you?

War. We haue (my Liege.)

King. Then you perceiue the Body of our Kingdome,
How foule it is: what ranke Diseases grow,
And with what danger, neere the Heart of it?

War. It is but as a Body, yet distemper'd,
Which to his former strength may be restor'd,
With good aduice, and little Medicine:
My Lord *Northumberland* will soone be cool'd.

King. Oh Heauen, that one might read the Book of Fate,
And see the reuolution of the Times
Make Mountaines leuell, and the Continent
(Wearie of solide firmenesse) melt it selfe
Into the Sea: and other Times, to see
The beachie Girdle of the Ocean
Too wide for *Neptunes* hippes; how Chances mocks
And Changes fill the Cuppe of Alteration
With diuers Liquors. 'Tis not tenne yeeres gone,
Since *Richard*, and *Northumberland*, great friends,
Did feast together; and in two yeeres after,
Were they at Warres. It is but eight yeeres since,
This *Percie* was the man, neerest my Soule,
Who, like a Brother, toyl'd in my Affaires,
And layd his Loue and Life vnder my foot:
Yea, for my sake, euen to the eyes of *Richard*
Gaue him defiance. But which of you was by
(You Cousin *Neuil*, as I may remember)
When *Richard*, with his Eye, brim-full of Teares,
(Then check'd, and rated by *Northumberland*)
Did speake these words (now prou'd a Prophecie:)
Northumberland, thou Ladder, by the which

My

My Couſin *Bullingbrooke* aſcends my Throne:
(Though then, Heauen knowes, I had no ſuch intent,
But that neceſſitie ſo bow'd the State,
That I and Greatneſſe were compell'd to kiſſe:)
The Time ſhall come (thus did hee follow it)
The Time will come, that foule Sinne gathering head,
Shall breake into Corruption: ſo went on,
Fore-telling this ſame Times Condition,
And the diuiſion of our Amitie.

War. There is a Hiſtorie in all mens Liues,
Figuring the nature of the Times deceas'd:
The which obſeru'd, a man may prophecie
With a neere ayme, of the maine chance of things,
As yet not come to Life, which in their Seedes
And weake beginnings lye entreaſured:
Such things become the Hatch and Brood of Time;
And by the neceſſarie forme of this,
King *Richard* might create a perfect gueſſe,
That great *Northumberland*, then falſe to him,
Would of that Seed, grow to a greater falſeneſſe,
Which ſhould not finde a ground to roote vpon,
Vnleſſe on you.

King. Are theſe things then Neceſſities?
Then let vs meete them like Neceſſities;
And that ſame word, euen now cryes out on vs:
They ſay, the Biſhop and *Northumberland*
Are fiftie thouſand ſtrong.

War. It cannot be (my Lord:)
Rumor doth double, like the Voice, and Eccho,
The numbers of the feared. Pleaſe it your Grace
To goe to bed, vpon my Life (my Lord)
The Pow'rs that you alreadie haue ſent forth,
Shall bring this Prize in very eaſily.
To comfort you the more, I haue receiu'd
A certaine inſtance, that *Glendour* is dead.
Your Maieſtie hath beene this fort-night ill,
And theſe vnſeaſon'd howres perforce muſt adde
Vnto your Sickneſſe.

King. I will take your counſaile:
And were theſe inward Warres once out of hand,
Wee would (deare Lords) vnto the Holy-Land.

Exeunt.

Scena Secunda.

Enter Shallow and Silence: with Mouldie, Shadow, Wart, Feeble, Bull-calfe.

Shal. Come-on, come-on, come-on: giue mee your Hand, Sir; giue mee your Hand, Sir: an early ſtirrer, by the Rood. And how doth my good Couſin *Silence*?

Sil. Good-morrow, good Couſin *Shallow*.

Shal. And how doth my Couſin, your Bed-fellow? and your faireſt Daughter, and mine, my God-Daughter *Ellen*?

Sil. Alas, a blacke Ouzell (Couſin *Shallow*.)

Shal. By yea and nay, Sir, I dare ſay my Couſin *William* is become a good Scholler? hee is at Oxford ſtill, is hee not?

Sil. Indeede Sir, to my coſt.

Shal. Hee muſt then to the Innes of Court ſhortly: I was once of *Clements* Inne; where (I thinke) they will talke of mad *Shallow* yet.

Sil. You were call'd luſtie *Shallow* then (Couſin.)

Shal. I was call'd any thing: and I would haue done any thing indeede too, and roundly too. There was I, and little *Iohn Doit* of Staffordſhire, and blacke *George Bare*, and *Francis Pick-bone*, and *Will Squele* a Cot-ſal-man, you had not foure ſuch Swindge-bucklers in all the Innes of Court againe: And I may ſay to you, wee knew where the *Bena-Roba's* were, and had the beſt of them all at commandement. Then was *Iacke Falſtaffe* (now Sir *Iohn*) a Boy, and Page to *Thomas Mowbray*, Duke of Norfolke.

Sil. This Sir *Iohn* (Couſin) that comes hither anon about Souldiers?

Shal. The ſame Sir *Iohn*, the very ſame: I ſaw him breake *Scoggan's* Head at the Court-Gate, when hee was a Crack, not thus high: and the very ſame day did I fight with one *Sampſon Stock-fiſh*, a Fruiterer, behinde Greyes-Inne. Oh the mad dayes that I haue ſpent! and to ſee how many of mine olde Acquaintance are dead?

Sil. Wee ſhall all follow (Couſin.)

Shal. Certaine: 'tis certaine: very ſure, very ſure: Death is certaine to all, all ſhall dye. How a good Yoke of Bullocks at Stamford Fayre?

Sil. Truly Couſin, I was not there.

Shal. Death is certaine. Is old *Double* of your Towne liuing yet?

Sil. Dead, Sir.

Shal. Dead? See, ſee: hee drew a good Bow: and dead? hee ſhot a fine ſhoote. *Iohn* of Gaunt loued him well, and betted much Money on his head. Dead? hee would haue clapt in the Clowt at Twelue-ſcore, and carryed you a fore-hand Shaft at foureteene, and foureteene and a halfe, that it would haue done a mans heart good to ſee. How a ſcore of Ewes now?

Sil. Thereafter as they be: a ſcore of good Ewes may be worth tenne pounds.

Shal. And is olde *Double* dead?

Enter Bardolph and his Boy.

Sil. Heere come two of Sir *Iohn Falſtaffes* Men (as I thinke.)

Shal. Good-morrow, honeſt Gentlemen.

Bard. I beſeech you, which is Iuſtice *Shallow*?

Shal. I am *Robert Shallow* (Sir) a poore Eſquire of this Countie, and one of the Kings Iuſtices of the Peace: What is your good pleaſure with me?

Bard. My Captaine (Sir) commends him to you: my Captaine, Sir *Iohn Falſtaffe*: a tall Gentleman, and a moſt gallant Leader.

Shal. Hee greetes me well: (Sir) I knew him a good Back-Sword-man. How doth the good Knight? may I aske, how my Lady his Wife doth?

Bard. Sir, pardon: a Souldier is better accommodated, then with a Wife.

Shal. It is well ſaid, Sir; and it is well ſaid, indeede, too: Better accommodated? it is good, yea indeede is it: good phraſes are ſurely, and euery where very commendable. Accommodated, it comes of *Accommodo*: very good, a good Phraſe.

Bard. Pardon, Sir, I haue heard the word. Phraſe call you it? by this Day, I know not the Phraſe: but I will maintaine the Word with my Sword, to bee a Souldier-like Word, and a Word of exceeding good Command. Accommodated: that is, when a man is (as they ſay) accommodated: or, when a man is, being whereby

whereby he thought to be accommodated, which is an excellent thing.

Enter Falstaffe.

Shal. It is very iust: Looke, heere comes good Sir *Iohn*. Giue me your hand, giue me your Worships good hand: Trust me, you looke well: and beare your yeares very well. Welcome, good Sir *Iohn*.

Fal. I am glad to see you well, good M. *Robert Shallow*: Master *Sure-card* as I thinke?

Shal. No sir *Iohn*, it is my Cosin *Silence*: in Commission with mee.

Fal. Good M. *Silence*, it well befits you should be of the peace.

Sil. Your good Worship is welcome.

Fal Fye, this is hot weather (Gentlemen) haue you prouided me heere halfe a dozen of sufficient men?

Shal. Marry haue we sir: Will you sit?

Fal. Let me see them, I beseech you.

Shal. Where's the Roll? Where's the Roll? Where's the Roll? Let me see, let me see, let me see: so, so, so, so: yea marry Sir. *Raphe Mouldie*: let them appeare as I call: let them do so, let them do so: Let mee see, Where is *Mouldie*?

Moul. Heere, if it please you.

Shal. What thinke you (Sir *Iohn*) a good limb'd fellow: yong, strong, and of good friends.

Fal. Is thy name *Mouldie*?

Moul. Yea, if it please you.

Fal. 'Tis the more time thou wert vs'd.

Shal. Ha, ha, ha, most excellent. Things that are mouldie, lacke vse: very singular good. Well saide Sir *Iohn*, very well said.

Fal. Pricke him.

Moul. I was prickt well enough before, if you could haue let me alone: my old Dame will be vndone now, for one to doe her Husbandry, and her Drudgery; you need not to haue prickt me, there are other men fitter to goe out, then I.

Fal. Go too: peace *Mouldie*, you shall goe. *Mouldie*, it is time you were spent.

Moul. Spent?

Shallow. Peace, fellow, peace; stand aside: Know you where you are? For the other sir *Iohn*: Let me see: *Simon Shadow*.

Fal. I marry, let me haue him to sit vnder: he's like to be a cold souldier.

Shal. Where's *Shadow*?

Shad. Heere sir.

Fal. *Shadow*, whose sonne art thou?

Shad. My Mothers sonne, Sir.

Falst. Thy Mothers sonne: like enough, and thy Fathers shadow: so the sonne of the Female, is the shadow of the Male: it is often so indeede, but not of the Fathers substance.

Shal. Do you like him, sir *Iohn*?

Falst. *Shadow* will serue for Summer: pricke him: For wee haue a number of shadowes to fill vppe the Muster-Booke.

Shal. *Thomas Wart*?

Falst Where's he?

Wart. Heere sir.

Falst. Is thy name *Wart*?

Wart. Yea sir.

Fal. Thou art a very ragged Wart.

Shal. Shall I pricke him downe, Sir *Iohn*?

Falst. It were superfluous: for his apparrel is built vpon his backe, and the whole frame stands vpon pins: prick him no more.

Shal. Ha, ha, ha, you can do it sir: you can doe it: I commend you well. *Francis Feeble*.

Feeble. Heere sir.

Shal. What Trade art thou *Feeble*?

Feeble. A Womans Taylor sir.

Shal. Shall I pricke him, sir?

Fal. You may:
But if he had beene a mans Taylor, he would haue prick'd you. Wilt thou make as many holes in an enemies Battaile, as thou hast done in a Womans petticote?

Feeble. I will doe my good will sir, you can haue no more.

Falst. Well said, good Womans Tailour: Well sayde Couragious *Feeble*: thou wilt bee as valiant as the wrathfull Doue, or most magnanimous Mouse. Pricke the womans Taylour well Master *Shallow*, deepe Maister *Shallow*.

Feeble. I would *Wart* might haue gone sir.

Fal. I would thou wert a mans Tailor, that ẏ might'st mend him, and make him fit to goe. I cannot put him to a priuate souldier, that is the Leader of so many thousands Let that suffice, most Forcible *Feeble*.

Feeble. It shall suffice.

Falst. I am bound to thee, reuerend *Feeble*. Who is the next?

Shal. *Peter Bulcalfe* of the Greene.

Falst. Yea marry, let vs see *Bulcalfe*.

Bul. Heere sir.

Fal. Trust me, a likely Fellow. Come, pricke me *Bulcalfe* till he roare againe.

Bul. Oh, good my Lord Captaine.

Fal. What? do'st thou roare before th'art prickt.

Bul. Oh sir, I am a diseased man.

Fal. What disease hast thou?

Bul. A whorson cold sir, a cough sir, which I caught with Ringing in the Kings affayres, vpon his Coronation day, sir.

Fal. Come, thou shalt go to the Warres in a Gowne: we will haue away thy Cold, and I will take such order, that thy friends shall ring for thee. Is heere all?

Shal. There is two more called then your number: you must haue but foure heere sir, and so I pray you go in with me to dinner.

Fal. Come, I will goe drinke with you, but I cannot tarry dinner. I am glad to see you in good troth, Master *Shallow*.

Shal. O sir *Iohn*, doe you remember since wee lay all night in the Winde mill, in S Georges Field.

Falstaffe. No more of that good Master *Shallow*: No more of that.

Shal. Ha! it was a merry night. And is *Iane Nightworke* aliue?

Fal. She liues, M. *Shallow*.

Shal. She neuer could away with me.

Fal. Neuer, neuer: she would alwayes say shee could not abide M. *Shallow*.

Shal. I could anger her to the heart: shee was then a *Bona-Roba*. Doth she hold her owne well.

Fal. Old, old, M. *Shallow*.

Shal. Nay, she must be old, she cannot choose but be old:

gg

old: certaine ſhee's old: and had *Robin Night-worke*, by old *Night-worke*, before I came to *Clements* Inne.

Sil. That's fiftie fiue yeeres agoe.

Shal. Hah, Couſin *Silence*, that thou hadſt ſeene that, that this Knight and I haue ſeene: hah, Sir *Iohn*, ſaid I well?

Falſt. Wee haue heard the Chymes at mid-night, Maſter *Shallow*.

Shal. That wee haue, that wee haue; in faith, Sir *Iohn*, wee haue: our watch-word was, Hem-Boyes. Come, let's to Dinner; come, let's to Dinner: Oh the dayes that wee haue ſeene. Come, come.

Bul. Good Maſter Corporate *Bardolph*, ſtand my friend, and heere is foure *Harry* tenne ſhillings in French Crownes for you: in very truth, ſir, I had as lief be hang'd ſir, as goe: and yet, for mine owne part, ſir, I do not care; but rather, becauſe I am vnwilling, and for mine owne part, haue a deſire to ſtay with my friends: elſe, ſir, I did not care, for mine owne part, ſo much.

Bard. Go-too: ſtand aſide.

Mould. And good Maſter Corporall Captaine, for my old Dames ſake, ſtand my friend: ſhee hath no body to doe any thing about her, when I am gone: and ſhe is old, and cannot helpe her ſelfe: you ſhall haue fortie, ſir.

Bard. Go-too: ſtand aſide.

Feeble. I care not, a man can die but once: wee owe a death. I will neuer beare a baſe minde: if it be my deſtinie, ſo: if it be not, ſo: no man is too good to ſerue his Prince: and let it goe which way it will, he that dies this yeere, is quit for the next.

Bard. Well ſaid, thou art a good fellow

Feeble. Nay, I will beare no baſe minde.

Falſt. Come ſir, which men ſhall I haue?

Shal. Foure of which you pleaſe.

Bard. Sir, a word with you: I haue three pound, to free *Mouldie* and *Bull-calfe*.

Falſt. Go-too: well.

Shal. Come, ſir *Iohn*, which foure will you haue?

Falſt. Doe you chuſe for me.

Shal. Marry then, *Mouldie*, *Bull-calfe*, *Feeble*, and *Shadow*.

Falſt. *Mouldie*, and *Bull-calfe*: for you *Mouldie*, ſtay at home, till you are paſt ſeruice: and for your part, *Bull-calfe*, grow till you come vnto it: I will none of you.

Shal. Sir *Iohn*, Sir *Iohn*, doe not your ſelfe wrong, they are your likelyeſt men, and I would haue you ſeru'd with the beſt.

Falſt. Will you tell me (Maſter *Shallow*) how to chuſe a man? Care I for the Limbe, the Thewes, the ſtature, bulke, and bigge aſſemblance of a man? giue mee the ſpirit (Maſter *Shallow*.) Where's *Wart*? you ſee what a ragged appearance it is: hee ſhall charge you, and diſcharge you, with the motion of a Pewterers Hammer: come off, and on, ſwifter then hee that gibbets on the Brewers Bucket. And this ſame halfe-fac'd fellow, *Shadow*, giue me this man: hee preſents no marke to the Enemie, the foe-man may with as great ayme leuell at the edge of a Pen-knife: and for a Retrait, how ſwiftly will this *Feeble*, the Womans Taylor, runne off. O, giue me the ſpare men, and ſpare me the great ones. Put me a Calyuer into *Warts* hand, *Bardolph*.

Bard. Hold *Wart*, Trauerſe: thus, thus, thus.

Falſt. Come, manage me your Calyuer: ſo: very well, go-too, very good, exceeding good. O, giue me alwayes a little, leane, old, chopt, bald Shot. Well ſaid *Wart*, thou art a good Scab: hold, there is a Teſter for thee.

Shal. Hee is not his Crafts-maſter, hee doth not doe it right. I remember at Mile-end-Greene, when I lay at *Clements* Inne, I was then Sir *Dagonet* in *Arthurs* Show: there was a little quiuer fellow, and hee would manage you his Peece thus: and hee would about, and about, and come you in, and come you in: Rah, tah, tah, would hee ſay, Bownce would hee ſay, and away againe would hee goe, and againe would he come: I ſhall neuer ſee ſuch a fellow.

Falſt. Theſe fellowes will doe well, Maſter *Shallow*. Farewell Maſter *Silence*, I will not vſe many wordes with you: fare you well, Gentlemen both: I thanke you: I muſt a dozen mile to night. *Bardolph*, giue the Souldiers Coates.

Shal. Sir *Iohn*, Heauen bleſſe you, and proſper your Affaires, and ſend vs Peace. As you returne, viſit my houſe. Let our old acquaintance be renewed: peraduenture I will with you to the Court.

Falſt. I would you would, Maſter *Shallow*.

Shal. Go-too: I haue ſpoke at a word. Fare you well. *Exit.*

Falſt. Fare you well, gentle Gentlemen. On *Bardolph*, leade the men away. As I returne, I will fetch off theſe Iuſtices: I doe ſee the bottome of Iuſtice *Shallow*. How ſubiect wee old men are to this vice of Lying? This ſame ſtaru'd Iuſtice hath done nothing but prate to me of the wildeneſſe of his Youth, and the Feates hee hath done about Turnball-ſtreet, and euery third word a Lye, duer pay'd to the hearer, then the Turkes Tribute. I doe remember him at *Clements* Inne, like a man made after Supper, of a Cheeſe-paring. When hee was naked, hee was, for all the world, like a forked Radiſh, with a Head fantaſtically caru'd vpon it with a Knife. Hee was ſo forlorne, that his Dimenſions (to any thicke ſight) were inuincible. Hee was the very *Genius* of Famine: hee came euer in the rere-ward of the Faſhion: And now is this Vices Dagger become a Squire, and talkes as familiarly of *Iohn* of Gaunt, as if hee had beene ſworne Brother to him: and Ile be ſworne hee neuer ſaw him but once in the Tilt-yard, and then he burſt his Head, for crowding among the Marſhals men. I ſaw it, and told *Iohn* of Gaunt, hee beat his owne Name, for you might haue truſs'd him and all his Apparrell into an Eele-skinne: the Caſe of a Treble Hoeboy was a Manſion for him: a Court: and now hath hee Land, and Beeues. Well, I will be acquainted with him, if I returne: and it ſhall goe hard, but I will make him a Philoſophers two Stones to me. If the young Dace be a Bayt for the old Pike, I ſee no reaſon, in the Law of Nature, but I may ſnap at him. Let time ſhape, and there an end. *Exeunt.*

Actus Quartus. Scena Prima.

Enter the Arch-biſhop, Mowbray, Haſtings, Weſtmerland, Coleuile.

Biſh. What is this Forreſt call'd?

Haſt. 'Tis Gualtree Forreſt, and't ſhall pleaſe your Grace.

Biſh. Here ſtand (my Lords) and ſend diſcouerers forth,
To know the numbers of our Enemies.

Haſt Wee

Haſt. Wee haue ſent forth alreadie.
Biſh. Tis well done.
My Friends, and Brethren (in theſe great Affaires)
I muſt acquaint you, that I haue receiu'd
New-dated Letters from *Northumberland:*
Their cold intent, tenure, and ſubſtance thus.
Here doth hee wiſh his Perſon, with ſuch Powers
As might hold ſortance with his Qualitie,
The which hee could not leuie: whereupon
Hee is retyr'd, to ripe his growing Fortunes,
To Scotland; and concludes in heartie prayers,
That your Attempts may ouer-liue the hazard,
And fearefull meeting of their Oppoſite.
Mow. Thus do the hopes we haue in him, touch ground,
And daſh themſelues to pieces.

Enter a Meſſenger.

Haſt. Now? what newes?
Meſſ. Weſt of this Forreſt, ſcarcely off a mile,
In goodly forme, comes on the Enemie:
And by the ground they hide, I iudge their number
Vpon, or neere, the rate of thirtie thouſand.
Mow. The iuſt proportion that we gaue them out.
Let vs ſway-on, and face them in the field.

Enter Weſtmerland.

Biſh. What well-appointed Leader fronts vs here?
Mow. I thinke it is my Lord of Weſtmerland.
Weſt. Health, and faire greeting from our Generall,
The Prince, Lord *Iohn*, and Duke of Lancaſter.
Biſh. Say on (my Lord of Weſtmerland) in peace:
What doth concerne your comming?
Weſt. Then (my Lord)
Vnto your Grace doe I in chiefe addreſſe
The ſubſtance of my Speech. If that Rebellion
Came like it ſelfe, in baſe and abiect Routs,
Led on by bloodie Youth, guarded with Rage,
And countenanc'd by Boyes, and Beggerie:
I ſay, if damn'd Commotion ſo appeare,
In his true, natiue and moſt proper ſhape,
You (Reuerend Father, and theſe Noble Lords)
Had not beene here, to dreſſe the ougly forme
Of baſe, and bloodie Inſurrection,
With your faire Honors. You, Lord Arch-biſhop,
Whoſe Sea is by a Ciuill Peace maintain'd,
Whoſe Beard, the Siluer Hand of Peace hath touch'd,
Whoſe Learning, and good Letters, Peace hath tutor'd,
Whoſe white Inueſtments figure Innocence,
The Doue, and very bleſſed Spirit of Peace.
Wherefore doe you ſo ill tranſlate your ſelfe,
Out of the Speech of Peace, that beares ſuch grace,
Into the harſh and boyſtrous Tongue of Warre?
Turning your Bookes to Graues, your Inke to Blood,
Your Pennes to Launces, and your Tongue diuine
To a lowd Trumpet, and a Point of Warre.
Biſh. Wherefore doe I this? ſo the Queſtion ſtands.
Briefely to this end: Wee are all diſeas'd,
And with our ſurfetting, and wanton howres,
Haue brought our ſelues into a burning Feuer,
And wee muſt bleede for it: of which Diſeaſe,
Our late King *Richard* (being infected) dy'd.
But (my moſt Noble Lord of Weſtmerland)
I take not on me here as a Phyſician,
Nor doe I, as an Enemie to Peace,
Troope in the Throngs of Militarie men:
But rather ſhew a while like fearefull Warre,
To dyet ranke Mindes, ſicke of happineſſe,
And purge th'obſtructions, which begin to ſtop
Our very Veines of Life: heare me more plainely.
I haue in equall ballance iuſtly weigh'd,
What wrongs our Arms may do, what wrongs we ſuffer,
And finde our Griefes heauier then our Offences.
Wee ſee which way the ſtreame of Time doth runne,
And are enforc'd from our moſt quiet there,
By the rough Torrent of Occaſion,
And haue the ſummarie of all our Griefes
(When time ſhall ſerue) to ſhew in Articles;
Which long ere this, wee offer'd to the King,
And might, by no Suit, gayne our Audience:
When wee are wrong'd, and would vnfold our Griefes,
Wee are deny'd acceſſe vnto his Perſon,
Euen by thoſe men, that moſt haue done vs wrong.
The dangers of the dayes but newly gone,
Whoſe memorie is written on the Earth
With yet appearing blood; and the examples
Of euery Minutes inſtance (preſent now)
Hath put vs in theſe ill-beſeeming Armes:
Not to breake Peace, or any Branch of it,
But to eſtabliſh here a Peace indeede,
Concurring both in Name and Qualitie.
Weſt. When euer yet was your Appeale deny'd?
Wherein haue you beene galled by the King?
What Peere hath beene ſuborn'd, to grate on you,
That you ſhould ſeale this lawleſſe bloody Booke
Of forg'd Rebellion, with a Seale diuine?
Biſh. My Brother generall, the Common-wealth,
I make my Quarrell, in particular.
Weſt. There is no neede of any ſuch redreſſe:
Or if there were, it not belongs to you.
Mow. Why not to him in part, and to vs all,
That feele the bruizes of the dayes before,
And ſuffer the Condition of theſe Times
To lay a heauie and vnequall Hand vpon our Honors?
Weſt. O my good Lord *Mowbray*,
Conſtrue the Times to their Neceſſities,
And you ſhall ſay (indeede) it is the Time,
And not the King, that doth you iniuries.
Yet for your part, it not appeares to me,
Either from the King, or in the preſent Time,
That you ſhould haue an ynch of any ground
To build a Griefe on: were you not reſtor'd
To all the Duke of Norfolkes Seignories,
Your Noble, and right well-remembred Fathers?
Mow. What thing, in Honor, had my Father loſt,
That need to be reuiu'd, and breath'd in me?
The King that lou'd him, as the State ſtood then,
Was forc'd, perforce compell'd to baniſh him:
And then, that *Henry Bullingbrooke* and hee
Being mounted, and both rowſed in their Seates,
Their neighing Courſers daring of the Spurre,
Their armed Staues in charge, their Beauers downe,
Their eyes of fire, ſparkling through ſights of Steele,
And the lowd Trumpet blowing them together:
Then, then, when there was nothing could haue ſtay'd
My Father from the Breaſt of *Bullingbrooke*;
O, when the King did throw his Warder downe,
(His owne Life hung vpon the Staffe hee threw)
Then threw hee downe himſelfe, and all their Liues,
That by Indictment, and by dint of Sword,
Haue ſince miſ-carryed vnder *Bullingbrooke*.

West. You speak (Lord *Mowbray*) now you know not what.
The Earle of Hereford was reputed then
In England the most valiant Gentleman.
Who knowes, on whom Fortune would then haue smil'd?
But if your Father had beene Victor there,
Hee ne're had borne it out of Couentry.
For all the Countrey, in a generall voyce,
Cry'd hate vpon him: and all their prayers, and loue,
Were set on *Herford*, whom they doted on,
And bless'd, and grac'd, and did more then the King.
But this is meere digression from my purpose.
Here come I from our Princely Generall,
To know your Griefes; to tell you, from his Grace,
That hee will giue you Audience: and wherein
It shall appeare, that your demands are iust,
You shall enioy them, euery thing set off,
That might so much as thinke you Enemies.
Mow. But hee hath forc'd vs to compell this Offer,
And it proceedes from Pollicy, not Loue.
West. *Mowbray*, you ouer-weene to take it so:
This Offer comes from Mercy, not from Feare.
For loe, within a Ken our Army lyes,
Vpon mine Honor, all too confident
To giue admittance to a thought of feare.
Our Battaile is more full of Names then yours,
Our Men more perfect in the vse of Armes,
Our Armor all as strong, our Cause the best;
Then Reason will, our hearts should be as good.
Say you not then, our Offer is compell'd.
Mow. Well, by my will, wee shall admit no Parley.
West. That argues but the shame of your offence:
A rotten Case abides no handling.
Hast. Hath the Prince *Iohn* a full Commission,
In very ample vertue of his Father,
To heare, and absolutely to determine
Of what Conditions wee shall stand vpon?
West. That is intended in the Generals Name:
I muse you make so slight a Question.
Bish. Then take (my Lord of Westmerland) this Schedule,
For this containes our generall Grieuances:
Each seuerall Article herein redress'd,
All members of our Cause, both here, and hence,
That are insinewed to this Action,
Acquitted by a true substantiall forme,
And present execution of our wills,
To vs, and to our purposes confin'd,
Wee come within our awfull Banks againe,
And knit our Powers to the Arme of Peace.
West. This will I shew the Generall. Please you Lords,
In sight of both our Battailes, wee may meete
At either end in peace: which Heauen so frame,
Or to the place of difference call the Swords,
Which must decide it.
Bish. My Lord, wee will doe so.
Mow. There is a thing within my Bosome tells me,
That no Conditions of our Peace can stand.
Hast. Feare you not, that if wee can make our Peace
Vpon such large termes, and so absolute,
As our Conditions shall consist vpon,
Our Peace shall stand as firme as Rockie Mountaines.
Mow. I, but our valuation shall be such,
That euery slight, and false-deriued Cause,
Yea, euery idle, nice, and wanton Reason,
Shall, to the King, taste of this Action:
That were our Royall faiths, Martyrs in Loue,
Wee shall be winnowed with so rough a winde,
That euen our Corne shall seeme as light as Chaffe,
And good from bad finde no partition.
Bish. No, no (my Lord) note this: the King is wearie
Of daintie, and such picking Grieuances:
For hee hath found, to end one doubt by Death,
Reuiues two greater in the Heires of Life.
And therefore will hee wipe his Tables cleane,
And keepe no Tell-tale to his Memorie,
That may repeat, and Historie his losse,
To new remembrance. For full well hee knowes,
Hee cannot so precisely weede this Land,
As his mis-doubts present occasion:
His foes are so en-rooted with his friends,
That plucking to vnfixe an Enemie,
Hee doth vnfasten so, and shake a friend.
So that this Land, like an offensiue wife,
That hath enrag'd him on, to offer strokes,
As he is striking, holds his Infant vp,
And hangs resolu'd Correction in the Arme,
That was vpreard to execution.
Hast. Besides, the King hath wasted all his Rods,
On late Offenders, that he now doth lacke
The very Instruments of Chasticement:
So that his power, like to a Fanglesse Lion
May offer, but not hold.
Bish. Tis very true:
And therefore be assur'd (my good Lord Marshal)
If we do now make our attonement well,
Our Peace, will (like a broken Limbe vnited)
Grow stronger, for the breaking.
Mow. Be it so:
Heere is return'd my Lord of Westmerland.

Enter Westmerland.

West. The Prince is here at hand: pleaseth your Lordship
To meet his Grace, iust distance 'tweene our Armies?
Mow. Your Grace of Yorke, in heauen's name then forward.
Bish. Before, and greet his Grace (my Lord) we come.

Enter Prince Iohn.

Iohn. You are wel encountred here (my cosin *Mowbray*)
Good day to you, gentle Lord Archbishop,
And so to you Lord *Hastings*, and to all.
My Lord of Yorke, it better shew'd with you,
When that your Flocke (assembled by the Bell)
Encircled you, to heare with reuerence
Your exposition on the holy Text,
Then now to see you heere an Iron man
Chearing a rowt of Rebels with your Drumme,
Turning the Word, to Sword; and Life to death:
That man that sits within a Monarches heart,
And ripens in the Sunne-shine of his fauor,
Would hee abuse the Countenance of the King,
Alack, what Mischiefes might hee set abroach,
In shadow of such Greatnesse? With you, Lord Bishop,
It is euen so. Who hath not heard it spoken,
How deepe you were within the Bookes of Heauen?
To vs, the Speaker in his Parliament;
To vs, th'imagine Voyce of Heauen it selfe:
The very Opener, and Intelligencer,
Betweene the Grace, the Sanctities of Heauen;
And our dull workings. O, who shall beleeue,
But you mis-vse the reuerence of your Place,
Employ the Countenance, and Grace of Heauen,
As a false Fauorite doth his Princes Name,
In deedes dis-honorable? You haue taken vp,
Vnder

Vnder the counterfeited Zeale of Heauen,
The Subiects of Heauens Substitute, my Father,
And both against the Peace of Heauen, and him,
Haue here vp-swarmed them.
Bish. Good my Lord of Lancaster,
I am not here against your Fathers Peace:
But (as I told my Lord of Westmerland)
The Time (mis-order'd) doth in common sence
Crowd vs, and crush vs, to this monstrous Forme,
To hold our safetie vp. I sent your Grace
The parcels, and particulars of our Griefe,
The which hath been with scorne shou'd from the Court:
Whereon this *Hydra*-Sonne of Warre is borne,
Whose dangerous eyes may well be charm'd asleepe,
With graunt of our most iust and right desires;
And true Obedience, of this Madnesse cur'd,
Stoope tamely to the foot of Maiestie.
Mow. If not, wee readie are to trye our fortunes,
To the last man.
Hast. And though wee here fall downe,
Wee haue Supplyes, to second our Attempt:
If they mis-carry, theirs shall second them.
And so, successe of Mischiefe shall be borne,
And Heire from Heire shall hold this Quarrell vp,
Whiles England shall haue generation.
Iohn. You are too shallow (*Hastings*)
Much too shallow,
To sound the bottome of the after-Times.
West. Pleaseth your Grace, to answere them directly,
How farre-forth you doe like their Articles.
Iohn. I like them all, and doe allow them well:
And sweare here, by the honor of my blood,
My Fathers purposes haue beene mistooke,
And some, about him, haue too lauishly
Wrested his meaning, and Authoritie.
My Lord, these Griefes shall be with speed redrest:
Vpon my Life, they shall. If this may please you,
Discharge your Powers vnto their seuerall Counties,
As wee will ours: and here, betweene the Armies,
Let's drinke together friendly, and embrace,
That all their eyes may beare those Tokens home,
Of our restored Loue, and Amitie.
Bish. I take your Princely word, for these redresses.
Iohn. I giue it you, and will maintaine my word:
And thereupon I drinke vnto your Grace.
Hast. Goe Captaine, and deliuer to the Armie
This newes of Peace: let them haue pay, and part:
I know, it will well please them.
High thee Captaine. *Exit.*
Bish. To you, my Noble Lord of Westmerland.
West. I pledge your Grace:
And if you knew what paines I haue bestow'd,
To breede this present Peace,
You would drinke freely: but my loue to ye,
Shall shew it selfe more openly hereafter.
Bish I doe not doubt you.
West. I am glad of it.
Health to my Lord, and gentle Cousin *Mowbray*.
Mow You wish me health in very happy season,
For I am, on the sodaine, something ill.
Bish Against ill Chances, men are euer merry,
But heauinesse fore-runnes the good euent.
West. Therefore be merry (Cooze) since sodaine sorrow
Serues to say thus: some good thing comes to morrow.
Bish. Beleeue me, I am passing light in spirit.
Mow. So much the worse, if your owne Rule be true.
Iohn. The word of Peace is render'd: hearke how they showt.
Mow. This had been chearefull, after Victorie.
Bish. A Peace is of the nature of a Conquest:
For then both parties nobly are subdu'd,
And neither partie looser.
Iohn. Goe (my Lord)
And let our Army be discharged too:
And good my Lord (so please you) let our Traines
March by vs, that wee may peruse the men *Exit.*
Wee should haue coap'd withall.
Bish. Goe, good Lord *Hastings*:
And ere they be dismiss'd, let them march by. *Exit.*
Iohn. I trust (Lords) wee shall lye to night together.
Enter Westmerland.
Now Cousin, wherefore stands our Army still?
West. The Leaders hauing charge from you to stand,
Will not goe off, vntill they heare you speake.
Iohn. They know their duties. *Enter Hastings.*
Hast. Our Army is dispers'd:
Like youthfull Steeres, vnyoak'd, they tooke their course
East, West, North, South: or like a Schoole, broke vp,
Each hurryes towards his home, and sporting place.
West. Good tidings (my Lord *Hastings*) for the which,
I doe arrest thee (Traytor) of high Treason:
And you Lord Arch-bishop, and you Lord *Mowbray*,
Of Capitall Treason, I attach you both.
Mow. Is this proceeding iust, and honorable?
West. Is your Assembly so?
Bish. Will you thus breake your faith?
Iohn. I pawn'd thee none:
I promis'd you redresse of these same Grieuances
Whereof you did complaine; which, by mine Honor,
I will performe, with a most Christian care.
But for you (Rebels) looke to taste the due
Meet for Rebellion, and such Acts as yours.
Most shallowly did you these Armes commence,
Fondly brought here, and foolishly sent hence.
Strike vp our Drummes, pursue the scatter'd stray,
Heauen, and not wee, haue safely fought to day.
Some guard these Traitors to the Block of Death,
Treasons true Bed, and yeelder vp of breath. *Exeunt.*
Enter Falstaffe and Colleuile.

Falst. What's your Name, Sir? of what Condition are you? and of what place, I pray?

Col. I am a Knight, Sir:
And my Name is *Colleuile* of the Dale.

Falst. Well then, *Colleuile* is your Name, a Knight is your Degree, and your Place, the Dale. *Colleuile* shall still be your Name, a Traytor your Degree, and the Dungeon your Place, a place deepe enough: so shall you be still *Colleuile* of the Dale.

Col. Are not you Sir *Iohn Falstaffe*?

Falst. As good a man as he sir, who ere I am. doe yee yeelde sir, or shall I sweate for you? if I doe sweate, they are the drops of thy Louers, and they weep for thy death, therefore rowze vp Feare and Trembling, and do obseruance to my mercy.

Col. I thinke you are Sir *Iohn Falstaffe*, & in that thought yeeld me.

Fal. I haue a whole Schoole of tongues in this belly of mine, and not a Tongue of them all, speakes anie other word but my name: and I had but a belly of any indifferencie, I were simply the most actiue fellow in Europe: my wombe, my wombe, my wombe vndoes mee. Heere comes our Generall.

gg 3 Enter

Enter Prince Iohn, and Weſtmerland.

Iohn. The heat is paſt, follow no farther now:
Call in the Powers, good Couſin *Weſtmerland*.
Now *Falſtaffe*, where haue you beene all this while?
When euery thing is ended, then you come.
Theſe tardie Tricks of yours will (on my life)
One time, or other, breake ſome Gallowes back.

Falſt. I would bee ſorry (my Lord) but it ſhould bee thus: I neuer knew yet, but rebuke and checke was the reward of Valour. Doe you thinke me a Swallow, an Arrow, or a Bullet? Haue I, in my poore and olde Motion, the expedition of Thought? I haue ſpeeded hither with the very extremeſt ynch of poſſibilitie. I haue fowndred nine ſcore and odde Poſtes: and heere (trauell-tainted as I am) haue, in my pure and immaculate Valour, taken Sir *Iohn Colleuile* of the Dale, a moſt furious Knight, and valorous Enemie: But what of that? hee ſaw mee, and yeelded: that I may iuſtly ſay with the hooke-nos'd fellow of Rome, I came, ſaw, and ouer-came.

Iohn. It was more of his Courteſie, then your deſeruing.

Falſt. I know not: heere hee is, and heere I yeeld him: and I beſeech your Grace, let it be book'd, with the reſt of this dayes deedes; or I ſweare, I will haue it in a particular Ballad, with mine owne Picture on the top of it (*Colleuile* kiſſing my foot:) To the which courſe, if I be enforc'd, if you do not all ſhew like gilt two-pences to me; and I, in the cleare Skie of Fame, o're-ſhine you as much as the Full Moone doth the Cynders of the Element (which ſhew like Pinnes-heads to her) beleeue not the Word of the Noble: therefore let mee haue right, and let deſert mount.

Iohn. Thine's too heauie to mount.

Falſt. Let it ſhine then.

Iohn. Thine's too thick to ſhine.

Falſt. Let it doe ſomething (my good Lord) that may doe me good, and call it what you will.

Iohn. Is thy Name *Colleuile*?

Col. It is (my Lord.)

Iohn. A famous Rebell art thou, *Colleuile*.

Falſt. And a famous true Subiect tooke him.

Col. I am (my Lord) but as my Betters are,
That led me hither: had they beene rul'd by me,
You ſhould haue wonne them dearer then you haue.

Falſt. I know not how they ſold themſelues, but thou like a kinde fellow, gau'ſt thy ſelfe away; and I thanke thee, for thee.

Enter Weſtmerland.

Iohn. Haue you left purſuit?

Weſt. Retreat is made, and Execution ſtay'd.

Iohn. Send *Colleuile*, with his Confederates,
To Yorke, to preſent Execution.
Blunt, leade him hence, and ſee you guard him ſure.

Exit with Colleuile.

And now diſpatch we toward the Court (my Lords)
I heare the King, my Father, is ſore ſicke.
Our Newes ſhall goe before vs, to his Maieſtie,
Which (Couſin) you ſhall beare, to comfort him:
And wee with ſober ſpeede will follow you.

Falſt. My Lord, I beſeech you, giue me leaue to goe through Glouceſterſhire: and when you come to Court, ſtand my good Lord, 'pray, in your good report.

Iohn. Fare you well, *Falſtaffe*: I, in my condition,
Shall better ſpeake of you, then you deſerue. *Exit.*

Falſt. I would you had but the wit: 'twere better then your Dukedome. Good faith, this ſame young ſober-blooded Boy doth not loue me, nor a man cannot make him laugh: but that's no maruaile, hee drinkes no Wine. There's neuer any of theſe demure Boyes come to any proofe: for thinne Drinke doth ſo ouer-coole their blood, and making many Fiſh-Meales, that they fall into a kinde of Male Greene-ſickneſſe: and then, when they marry, they get Wenches. They are generally Fooles, and Cowards; which ſome of vs ſhould be too, but for inflamation. A good Sherris-Sack hath a two-fold operation in it: it aſcends me into the Braine, dryes me there all the fooliſh, and dull, and cruddie Vapours, which enuiron it: makes it apprehenſiue, quicke, forgetiue, full of nimble, fierie, and delectable ſhapes; which deliuer'd o're to the Voyce, the Tongue, which is the Birth, becomes excellent Wit. The ſecond propertie of your excellent Sherris, is, the warming of the Blood: which before (cold, and ſetled) left the Liuer white, and pale; which is the Badge of Puſillanimitie, and Cowardize: but the Sherris warmes it, and makes it courſe from the inwards, to the parts extremes: it illuminateth the Face, which (as a Beacon) giues warning to all the reſt of this little Kingdome (Man) to Arme: and then the Vitall Commoners, and in-land pettie Spirits, muſter me all to their Captaine, the Heart; who great, and puft vp with his Retinue, doth any Deed of Courage: and this Valour comes of Sherris. So, that skill in the Weapon is nothing, without Sack (for that ſets it a-worke:) and Learning, a meere Hoord of Gold, kept by a Deuill, till Sack commences it, and ſets it in act, and vſe. Hereof comes it, that Prince *Harry* is valiant: for the cold blood hee did naturally inherite of his Father, hee hath, like leane, ſtirrill, and bare Land, manured, husbanded, and tyll'd, with excellent endeauour of drinking good, and good ſtore of fertile Sherris, that hee is become very hot, and valiant. If I had a thouſand Sonnes, the firſt Principle I would teach them, ſhould be to forſweare thinne Potations, and to addict themſelues to Sack. *Enter Bardolph.*
How now *Bardolph*?

Bard. The Armie is diſcharged all, and gone.

Falſt. Let them goe: Ile through Glouceſterſhire, and there will I viſit Maſter *Robert Shallow*, Eſquire: I haue him alreadie tempering betweene my finger and my thombe, and ſhortly will I ſeale with him. Come away.

Exeunt.

Scena Secunda.

Enter King, Warwicke, Clarence, Glouceſter.

King. Now Lords, if Heauen doth giue ſucceſſefull end
To this Debate that bleedeth at our doores,
Wee will our Youth lead on to higher Fields,
And draw no Swords, but what are ſanctify'd.
Our Nauie is addreſſed, our Power collected,
Our Subſtitutes, in abſence, well inueſted,
And euery thing lyes leuell to our wiſh;
Onely wee want a little perſonall Strength:
And pawſe vs, till theſe Rebels, now a-foot,
Come vnderneath the yoake of Gouernment.

War. Both which we doubt not, but your Maieſtie
Shall ſoone enioy.

King. Hum-

King. *Humphrey* (my Sonne of Glouceſter) where is
the Prince, your Brother?
Glo. I thinke hee's gone to hunt (my Lord) at Wind-
ſor.
King. And how accompanied?
Glo. I doe not know (my Lord.)
King. Is not his Brother, *Thomas* of Clarence, with
him?
Glo. No (my good Lord) hee is in preſence heere.
Clar. What would my Lord, and Father?
King. Nothing but well to thee, *Thomas* of Clarence.
How chance thou art not with the Prince, thy Brother?
Hee loues thee, and thou do'ſt neglect him (*Thomas.*)
Thou haſt a better place in his Affection,
Then all thy Brothers: cheriſh it (my Boy)
And Noble Offices thou may'ſt effect
Of Mediation (after I am dead)
Betweene his Greatneſſe, and thy other Brethren.
Therefore omit him not: blunt not his Loue,
Nor looſe the good aduantage of his Grace,
By ſeeming cold, or careleſſe of his will.
For hee is gracious, if hee be obſeru'd:
Hee hath a Teare for Pitie, and a Hand
Open (as Day) for melting Charitie:
Yet notwithſtanding, being incens'd, hee's Flint,
As humorous as Winter, and as ſudden,
As Flawes congealed in the Spring of day.
His temper therefore muſt be well obſeru'd:
Chide him for faults, and doe it reuerently,
When you perceiue his blood enclin'd to mirth:
But being moodie, giue him Line, and ſcope,
Till that his paſſions (like a Whale on ground)
Confound themſelues with working. Learne this *Thomas*,
And thou ſhalt proue a ſhelter to thy friends,
A Hoope of Gold, to binde thy Brothers in:
That the vnited Veſſell of their Blood
(Mingled with Venome of Suggeſtion,
As force, perforce, the Age will powre it in)
Shall neuer leake, though it doe worke as ſtrong
As *Aconitum*, or raſh Gun-powder.
Clar. I ſhall obſerue him with all care, and loue.
King. Why art thou not at Windſor with him (*Tho-
mas?*)
Clar. Hee is not there to day: hee dines in Lon-
don.
King. And how accompanyed? Canſt thou tell
that?
Clar. With *Pointz*, and other his continuall fol-
lowers.
King. Moſt ſubiect is the fatteſt Soyle to Weedes:
And hee (the Noble Image of my Youth)
Is ouer-ſpread with them: therefore my griefe
Stretches it ſelfe beyond the howre of death.
The blood weepes from my heart, when I doe ſhape
(In formes imaginarie) th'vnguided Dayes,
And rotten Times, that you ſhall looke vpon,
When I am ſleeping with my Anceſtors.
For when his head-ſtrong Riot hath no Curbe,
When Rage and hot-Blood are his Counſailors,
When Meanes and lauiſh Manners meete together;
Oh, with what Wings ſhall his Affections flye
Towards fronting Perill, and oppos'd Decay?
War. My gracious Lord, you looke beyond him quite:
The Prince but ſtudies his Companions,
Like a ſtrange Tongue: wherein, to gaine the Language,
Tis needfull, that the moſt immodeſt word
Be look'd vpon, and learn'd: which once attayn'd,
Your Highneſſe knowes, comes to no farther vſe,
But to be knowne, and hated. So, like groſſe termes,
The Prince will, in the perfectneſſe of time,
Caſt off his followers: and their memorie
Shall as a Patterne, or a Meaſure, liue,
By which his Grace muſt mete the liues of others,
Turning paſt-euills to aduantages.
King. 'Tis ſeldome, when the Bee doth leaue her Comb
In the dead Carrion.

Enter Weſtmerland.

Who's heere? *Weſtmerland?*
Weſt. Health to my Soueraigne, and new happineſſe
Added to that, that I am to deliuer.
Prince *Iohn*, your Sonne, doth kiſſe your Graces Hand:
Mowbray, the Biſhop, *Scroope*, *Haſtings*, and all,
Are brought to the Correction of your Law.
There is not now a Rebels Sword vnſheath'd,
But Peace puts forth her Oliue euery where.
The manner how this Action hath beene borne,
Here (at more leyſure) may your Highneſſe reade,
With euery courſe, in his particular.
King. O *Weſtmerland*, thou art a Summer Bird,
Which euer in the haunch of Winter ſings
The lifting vp of day.

Enter Harcourt.

Looke, heere's more newes.
Harc. From Enemies, Heauen keepe your Maieſtie:
And when they ſtand againſt you, may they fall,
As thoſe that I am come to tell you of.
The Earle *Northumberland*, and the Lord *Bardolfe*,
With a great Power of Engliſh, and of Scots,
Are by the Sherife of Yorkeſhire ouerthrowne:
The manner, and true order of the fight,
This Packet (pleaſe it you) containes at large.
King. And wherefore ſhould theſe good newes
Make me ſicke?
Will Fortune neuer come with both hands full,
But write her faire words ſtill in fouleſt Letters?
Shee eyther giues a Stomack, and no Foode,
(Such are the poore, in health) or elſe a Feaſt,
And takes away the Stomack (ſuch are the Rich,
That haue aboundance, and enioy it not.)
I ſhould reioyce now, at this happy newes,
And now my Sight fayles, and my Braine is giddie.
O me, come neere me, now I am much ill.
Glo. Comfort your Maieſtie.
Cla. Oh, my Royall Father.
Weſt. My Soueraigne Lord, cheare vp your ſelfe, looke
vp.
War. Be patient (Princes) you doe know, theſe Fits
Are with his Highneſſe very ordinarie.
Stand from him, giue him ayre:
Hee'le ſtraight be well.
Clar. No, no, hee cannot long hold out: theſe pangs,
Th'inceſſant care, and labour of his Minde,
Hath wrought the Mure, that ſhould confine it in,
So thinne, that Life lookes through, and will breake out.
Glo. The people feare me: for they doe obſerue
Vnfather'd Heires, and loathly Births of Nature:
The Seaſons change their manners, as the Yeere
Had found ſome Moneths aſleepe, and leap'd them ouer.
Clar. The Riuer hath thrice flow'd, no ebbe betweene:
And the old folke (Times doting Chronicles)
Say it did ſo, a little time before
That our great Grand-ſire *Edward* ſick'd, and dy'de.

War. Speake lower (Princes) for the King recouers.
Glo. This Apoplexie will (certaine) be his end.
King. I pray you take me vp, and beare me hence
Into some other Chamber: softly 'pray.
Let there be no noyse made (my gentle friends)
Vnlesse some dull and fauourable hand
Will whisper Musicke to my wearie Spirit.
War. Call for the Musicke in the other Roome.
King. Set me the Crowne vpon my Pillow here.
Clar. His eye is hollow, and hee changes much.
War. Lesse noyse, lesse noyse.

Enter Prince Henry.

P.Hen. Who saw the Duke of Clarence?
Clar. I am here (Brother) full of heauinesse.
P.Hen. How now? Raine within doores, and none abroad? How doth the King?
Glo. Exceeding ill.
P.Hen. Heard hee the good newes yet?
Tell it him.
Glo Hee alter'd much, vpon the hearing it.
P.Hen. If hee be sicke with Ioy,
Hee'le recouer without Physicke.
War. Not so much noyse (my Lords)
Sweet Prince speake lowe,
The King, your Father, is dispos'd to sleepe.
Clar Let vs with-draw into the other Roome.
War Wil't please your Grace to goe along with vs?
P.Hen. No: I will sit, and watch here, by the King.
Why doth the Crowne lye there, vpon his Pillow,
Being so troublesome a Bed-fellow?
O pollish'd Perturbation! Golden Care!
That keep'st the Ports of Slumber open wide,
To many a watchfull Night: sleepe with it now,
Yet not so sound, and halfe so deepely sweete,
As hee whose Brow (with homely Biggen bound)
Snores out the Watch of Night. O Maiestie!
When thou do'st pinch thy Bearer, thou do'st sit
Like a rich Armor, worne in heat of day,
That scald'st with safetie: by his Gates of breath,
There lyes a dowlney feather which stirres not:
Did hee suspire, that light and weightlesse dowlne
Perforce must moue. My gracious Lord, my Father,
This sleepe is sound indeede: this is a sleepe,
That from this Golden Rigoll hath diuorc'd
So many English Kings. Thy due, from me,
Is Teares, and heauie Sorrowes of the Blood,
Which Nature, Loue, and filiall tendernesse,
Shall (O deare Father) pay thee plenteously.
My due, from thee, is this Imperiall Crowne,
Which (as immediate from thy Place and Blood)
Deriues it selfe to me. Loe, heere it sits,
Which Heauen shall guard:
And put the worlds whole strength into one gyant Arme,
It shall not force this Lineall Honor from me.
This, from thee, will I to mine leaue,
As 'tis left to me. *Exit.*

Enter Warwicke, Gloucester, Clarence.

King. *Warwicke, Gloucester, Clarence.*
Clar Doth the King call?
War. What would your Maiestie? how fares your Grace?
King. Why did you leaue me here alone (my Lords?)
Cla. We left the Prince (my Brother) here (my Liege)
Who vndertooke to sit and watch by you.
King. The Prince of Wales? where is hee? let mee see him.
War. This doore is open, hee is gone this way.
Glo. Hee came not through the Chamber where wee stayd.
King. Where is the Crowne? who tooke it from my Pillow?
War. When wee with-drew (my Liege) wee left it heere.
King. The Prince hath ta'ne it hence:
Goe seeke him out.
Is hee so hastie, that hee doth suppose
My sleepe, my death? Finde him (my Lord of Warwick)
Chide him hither: this part of his conioynes
With my disease, and helpes to end me.
See Sonnes, what things you are:
How quickly Nature falls into reuolt,
When Gold becomes her Obiect?
For this, the foolish ouer-carefull Fathers
Haue broke their sleepes with thoughts,
Their braines with care, their bones with industry.
For this, they haue ingrossed and pyl'd vp
The canker'd heapes of strange-atchieued Gold:
For this, they haue beene thoughtfull, to inuest
Their Sonnes with Arts, and Martiall Exercises:
When, like the Bee, culling from euery flower
The vertuous Sweetes, our Thighes packt with Wax,
Our Mouthes with Honey, wee bring it to the Hiue;
And like the Bees, are murthered for our paines.
This bitter taste yeelds his engrossements,
To the ending Father.

Enter Warwicke.

Now, where is hee, that will not stay so long,
Till his Friend Sicknesse hath determin'd me?
War. My Lord, I found the Prince in the next Roome,
Washing with kindly Teares his gentle Cheekes,
With such a deepe demeanure, in great sorrow,
That Tyranny, which neuer quafft but blood,
Would (by beholding him) haue wash'd his Knife
With gentle eye-drops. Hee is comming hither.
King. But wherefore did hee take away the Crowne?

Enter Prince Henry.

Loe, where hee comes. Come hither to me (*Harry.*)
Depart the Chamber, leaue vs heere alone. *Exit.*
P Hen. I neuer thought to heare you speake againe.
King. Thy wish was Father (*Harry*) to that thought:
I stay too long by thee, I wearie thee.
Do'st thou so hunger for my emptie Chayre,
That thou wilt needes inuest thee with mine Honors,
Before thy howre be ripe? O foolish Youth!
Thou seek'st the Greatnesse, that will ouer-whelme thee.
Stay but a little: for my Cloud of Dignitie
Is held from falling, with so weake a winde,
That it will quickly drop: my Day is dimme.
Thou hast stolne that, which after some few howres
Were thine, without offence: and at my death
Thou hast seal'd vp my expectation.
Thy Life did manifest, thou lou'dst me not,
And thou wilt haue me dye assur'd of it.
Thou hid'st a thousand Daggers in thy thoughts,
Which thou hast whetted on thy stonie heart,
To stab at halfe an howre of my Life.
What? canst thou not forbeare me halfe an howre?

Then

Then get thee gone, and digge my graue thy selfe,
And bid the merry Bels ring to thy eare
That thou art Crowned, not that I am dead
Let all the Teares, that should bedew my Hearse
Be drops of Balme, to sanctifie thy head:
Onely compound me with forgotten dust.
Giue that, which gaue thee life, vnto the Wormes:
Plucke downe my Officers, breake my Decrees;
For now a time is come, to mocke at Forme.
Henry the fift is Crown'd: Vp Vanity,
Downe Royall State: All you sage Counsailors, hence:
And to the English Court, assemble now
From eu'ry Region, Apes of Idlenesse.
Now neighbor-Confines, purge you of your Scum:
Haue you a Ruffian that will sweare? drinke? dance?
Reuell the night? Rob? Murder? and commit
The oldest sinnes, the newest kinde of wayes?
Be happy, he will trouble you no more:
England, shall double gill'd, his trebble guilt.
England, shall giue him Office, Honor, Might:
For the Fift *Harry*, from curb'd License pluckes
The muzzle of Restraint; and the wilde Dogge
Shall flesh his tooth in euery Innocent.
O my poore Kingdome (sicke, with ciuill blowes)
When that my Care could not with-hold thy Ryots,
What wilt thou do, when Ryot is thy Care?
O, thou wilt be a Wildernesse againe,
Peopled with Wolues (thy old Inhabitants.

Prince. O pardon me (my Liege)
But for my Teares,
The most Impediments vnto my Speech,
I had fore-stall'd this deere, and deepe Rebuke,
Ere you (with greefe) had spoke, and I had heard
The course of it so farre. There is your Crowne,
And he that weares the Crowne immortally,
Long guard it yours. If I affect it more,
Then as your Honour, and as your Renowne,
Let me no more from this Obedience rise,
Which my most true, and inward duteous Spirit
Teacheth this prostrate, and exteriour bending.
Heauen witnesse with me, when I heere came in,
And found no course of breath within your Maiestie,
How cold it strooke my heart. If I do faine,
O let me, in my present wildenesse, dye,
And neuer liue, to shew th'incredulous World,
The Noble change that I haue purposed.
Comming to looke on you, thinking you dead,
(And dead almost (my Liege) to thinke you were)
I spake vnto the Crowne (as hauing sense)
And thus vpbraided it. The Care on thee depending,
Hath fed vpon the body of my Father,
Therefore, thou best of Gold, art worst of Gold.
Other, lesse fine in Charract, is more precious,
Preseruing life, in Med'cine potable:
But thou, most Fine, most Honour'd, most Renown'd,
Hast eate the Bearer vp.
Thus (my Royall Liege)
Accusing it, I put it on my Head,
To try with it (as with an Enemie,
That had before my face murdred my Father)
The Quarrell of a true Inheritor.
But if it did infect my blood with Ioy,
Or swell my Thoughts, to any straine of Pride,
If any Rebell, or vaine spirit of mine,
Did, with the least Affection of a Welcome,
Giue entertainment to the might of it,
Let heauen, for euer, keepe it from my head,
And make me, as the poorest Vassaile is,
That doth with awe, and terror kneele to it.

King. O my Sonne!
Heauen put it in thy minde to take it hence,
That thou might'st ioyne the more, thy Fathers loue,
Pleading so wisely, in excuse of it.
Come hither *Harrie*, sit thou by my bedde,
And heare (I thinke, the very latest Counsell
That euer I shall breath: Heauen knowes, my Sonne)
By what by-pathes, and indirect crook'd-wayes
I met this Crowne: and I my selfe know well
How troublesome it sate vpon my head.
To thee, it shall descend with better Quiet,
Better Opinion, better Confirmation:
For all the soyle of the Atchieuement goes
With me, into the Earth. It seem'd in mee,
But as an Honour snatch'd with boyst'rous hand,
And I had many liuing, to vpbraide
My gaine of it, by their Assistances,
Which dayly grew to Quarrell, and to Blood-shed,
Wounding supposed Peace.
All these bold Feares,
Thou seest (with perill) I haue answered:
For all my Reigne, hath beene but as a Scene
Acting that argument. And now my death
Changes the Moode: For what in me, was purchas'd,
Falles vpon thee, in a more Fayrer sort.
So thou, the Garland wear'st successiuely.
Yet, though thou stand'st more sure, then I could do,
Thou art not firme enough, since greefes are greene:
And all thy Friends, which thou must make thy Friends
Haue but their stings, and teeth, newly tak'n out,
By whose fell working, I was first aduanc'd,
And by whose power, I well might lodge a Feare
To be againe displac'd. Which to auoyd,
I cut them off: and had a purpose now
To leade out many to the Holy Land;
Least rest, and lying still, might make them looke
Too neere vnto my State.
Therefore (my *Harrie*)
Be it thy course to busie giddy Mindes
With Forraigne Quarrels: that Action hence borne out,
May waste the memory of the former dayes.
More would I, but my Lungs are wasted so,
That strength of Speech is vtterly deni'de mee.
How I came by the Crowne, O heauen forgiue:
And grant it may, with thee, in true peace liue.

Prince. My gracious Liege:
You wonne it, wore it: kept it, gaue it me,
Then plaine and right must my possession be;
Which I, with more, then with a Common paine,
'Gainst all the World, will rightfully maintaine.

Enter Lord Iohn of Lancaster, and Warwicke.

King. Looke, looke,
Heere comes my *Iohn* of Lancaster:

Iohn. Health, Peace, and Happinesse,
To my Royall Father.

King. Thou bring'st me happinesse and Peace (Sonne *Iohn*:
But health (alacke) with youthfull wings is flowne
From this bare, wither'd Trunke. Vpon thy sight
My worldly businesse makes a period.

Where

Where is my Lord of Warwicke?

Prin. My Lord of Warwicke.

King. Doth any name particular, belong
Vnto the Lodging, where I first did swoon'd?

War. 'Tis call'd *Ierusalem*, my Noble Lord.

King. Laud be to heauen:
Euen there my life must end.
It hath beene prophesi'de to me many yeares,
I should not dye, but in *Ierusalem*:
Which (vainly) I suppos'd the Holy-Land.
But beare me to that Chamber, there Ile lye:
In that *Ierusalem*, shall *Harry* dye. *Exeunt.*

Actus Quintus. Scœna Prima.

Enter Shallow, Silence, Falstaffe, Bardolfe, Page, and Dauie.

Shal. By Cocke and Pye, you shall not away to night. What *Dauy*, I say.

Fal. You must excuse me, M. *Robert Shallow.*

Shal I will not excuse you: you shall not be excused. Excuses shall not be admitted: there is no excuse shall serue: you shall not be excus'd. Why *Dauie*

Dauie. Heere sir.

Shal. Dauy, Dauy, Dauy, let me see (*Dauy*) let me see: *William* Cooke, bid him come hither. Sir *Iohn*, you shal not be excus'd.

Dauy. Marry sir, thus: those Precepts cannot bee seru'd. and againe sir, shall we sowe the head-land with Wheate?

Shal Withred Wheate *Dauy*. But for *William* Cook: are there no youg Pigeons?

Dauy. Yes Sir.
Heere is now the Smithes note, for Shooing,
And Plough-Irons.

Shal. Let it be cast, and payde: Sir *Iohn*, you shall not be excus'd.

Dauy Sir, a new linke to the Bucket must needes bee had: And Sir, doe you meane to stoppe any of *Williams* Wages, about the Sacke he lost the other day, at *Hinckley* Fayre?

Shal. He shall answer it:
Some Pigeons *Dauy*, a couple of short-legg'd Hennes: a ioynt of Mutton, and any pretty little tine Kickshawes, tell *William* Cooke.

Dauy. Doth the man of Warre, stay all night sir?

Shal Yes *Dauy*:
I will vse him well. A Friend i'th Court, is better then a penny in purse. Vse his men well *Dauy*, for they are arrant Knaues, and will backe-bite.

Dauy No worse then they are bitten. sir: For they haue maruellous fowle linnen.

Shallow. Well conceited *Dauy*: about thy Businesse, *Dauy.*

Dauy. I beseech you sir,
To countenance *William Visor* of Woncot, against *Clement Perkes* of the hill.

Shal. There are many Complaints *Dauy*, against that *Visor*, that *Visor* is an arrant Knaue, on my knowledge.

Dauy. I graunt your Worship, that he is a knaue Sir:) But yet heauen forbid Sir, but a Knaue should haue some Countenance, at his Friends request. An honest man sir, is able to speake for himselfe, when a Knaue is not. I haue seru'd your Worshippe truely sir, these eight yeares: and if I cannot once or twice in a Quarter beare out a knaue, against an honest man, I haue but a very litle credite with your Worshippe. The Knaue is mine honest Friend Sir, therefore I beseech your Worship, let him bee Countenanc'd.

Shal. Go too,
I say he shall haue no wrong: Looke about *Dauy*.
Where are you Sir *Iohn*? Come, off with your Boots.
Giue me your hand M. *Bardolfe.*

Bard. I am glad to see your Worship.

Shal. I thanke thee, with all my heart, kinde Master *Bardolfe*: and welcome my tall Fellow:
Come Sir *Iohn.*

Falstaffe. Ile follow you, good Master *Robert Shallow.* *Bardolfe*, looke to our Horsses. If I were saw'de into Quantities, I should make foure dozen of such bearded Hermites staues, as Master *Shallow*. It is a wonderfull thing to see the semblable Coherence of his mens spirits, and his: They, by obseruing of him, do beare themselues like foolish Iustices: Hee, by conuersing with them, is turn'd into a Iustice-like Seruingman. Their spirits are so married in Coniunction, with the participation of Society, that they flocke together in consent, like so many Wilde-Geese. If I had a suite to Mayster *Shallow*, I would humour his men, with the imputation of beeing neere their Mayster. If to his Men, I would currie with Maister *Shallow*, that no man could better command his Seruants. It is certaine, that either wise bearing, or ignorant Carriage is caught, as men take diseases, one of another: therefore, let men take heede of their Companie. I will deuise matter enough out of this *Shallow*, to keepe Prince *Harry* in continuall Laughter, the wearing out of sixe Fashions (which is foure Tearmes) or two Actions, and he shall laugh with *Interuallums.* O it is much that a Lye (with a slight Oath) and a iest (with a sadde brow) will doe, with a Fellow, that neuer had the Ache in his shoulders. O you shall see him laugh, till his Face be like a wet Cloake, ill laid vp.

Shal. Sir *Iohn.*

Falst. I come Master *Shallow*, I come Master *Shallow.* *Exeunt*

Scena Secunda.

Enter the Earle of Warwicke, and the Lord Chiefe Iustice.

Warwicke. How now, my Lord Chiefe Iustice, whether away?

Ch. Iust. How doth the King?

Warw. Exceeding well: his Cares
Are now, all ended.

Ch. Iust I hope, not dead.

Warw. Hee's walk'd the way of Nature,
And to our purposes, he liues no more.

Ch. Iust I would his Maiesty had call'd me with him,
The seruice, that I truly did his life.
Hath left me open to all iniuries.

War.

War. Indeed I thinke the yong King loues you not.
Ch.Iuſt. I know he doth not,and do arme my ſelfe
To welcome the condition of the Time,
Which cannot looke more hideouſly vpon me,
Then I haue drawne it in my fantaſie.

Enter Iohn of Lancaſter, Glouceſter, and Clarence.

War. Heere come the heauy Iſſue of dead *Harrie:*
O, that the liuing *Harrie* had the temper
Of him,the worſt of theſe three Gentlemen:
How many Nobles then, ſhould hold their places,
That muſt ſtrike ſaile, to Spirits of vilde ſort?
Ch.Iuſt. Alas, I feare,all will be ouer-turn'd.
Iohn. Good morrow Coſin Warwick,good morrow.
Glou. Cla. Good morrow, Coſin.
Iohn. We meet, like men,that had forgot to ſpeake.
War. We do remember: but our Argument
Is all too heauy, to admit much talke.
Ioh. Well: Peace be with him,that hath made vs heauy
Ch.Iuſt. Peace be with vs,leaſt we be heauier.
Glou. O, good my Lord,you haue loſt a friend indeed:
And I dare ſweare,you borrow not that face
Of ſeeming ſorrow, it is ſure your owne.
Iohn. Though no man be aſſur'd what grace to finde,
You ſtand in coldeſt expectation.
I am the ſorrier,would 'twere otherwiſe.
Cla. Wel,you muſt now ſpeake Sir *Iohn Falſtaffe* faire,
Which ſwimmes againſt your ſtreame of Quality.
Ch.Iuſt. Sweet Princes: what I did, I did in Honor,
Led by th'Imperiall Conduct of my Soule,
And neuer ſhall you ſee, that I will begge
A ragged, and fore-ſtall'd Remiſſion.
If Troth, and vpright Innocency fayle me,
Ile to the King (my Maſter) that is dead,
And tell him, who hath ſent me after him.
War. Heere comes the Prince.

Enter Prince Henrie.

Ch.Iuſt. Good morrow: and heauen ſaue your Maieſty
Prince. This new, and gorgeous Garment, Maieſty,
Sits not ſo eaſie on me, as you thinke.
Brothers, you mixe your Sadneſſe with ſome Feare:
This is the Engliſh, not the Turkiſh Court:
Not *Amurah*, an *Amurah* ſucceeds,
But *Harry, Harry*: Yet be ſad (good Brothers)
For (to ſpeake truth) it very well becomes you
Sorrow, ſo Royally in you appeares,
That I will deeply put the Faſhion on,
And weare it in my heart. Why then be ſad,
But entertaine no more of it (good Brothers)
Then a ioynt burthen, laid vpon vs all.
For me, by Heauen (I bid you be aſſur'd)
Ile be your Father, and your Brother too:
Let me but beare your Loue, Ile beare your Cares;
But weepe that *Horrie's* dead,and ſo will I.
But *Harry* liues, that ſhall conuert thoſe Teares
By number, into houres of Happineſſe.
Iohn,&c. We hope no other from your Maieſty.
Prin. You all looke ſtrangely on me: and you moſt,
You are (I thinke) aſſur'd, I loue you not.
Ch.Iuſt. I am aſſur'd (if I be meaſur'd rightly)
Your Maieſty hath no iuſt cauſe to hate mee.
Pr. No? How might a Prince of my great hopes forget
So great Indignities you laid vpon me?
What? Rate? Rebuke? and roughly ſend to Priſon
Th'immediate Heire of England? Was this eaſie?
May this be waſh'd in *Lethe*, and forgotten?
Ch.Iuſt. I then did vſe the Perſon of your Father:
The Image of his power, lay then in me,
And in th'adminiſtration of his Law,
Whiles I was buſie for the Commonwealth,
Your Highneſſe pleaſed to forget my place,
The Maieſty, and power of Law, and Iuſtice,
The Image of the King, whom I preſented,
And ſtrooke me in my very Seate of Iudgement
Whereon (as an Offender to your Father)
I gaue bold way to my Authority,
And did commit you. If the deed were ill,
Be you contented, wearing now the Garland,
To haue a Sonne, ſet your Decrees at naught?
To plucke downe Iuſtice from your awefull Bench:
To trip the courſe of Law, and blunt the Sword
That guards the peace, and ſafety of your Perſon?
Nay more, to ſpurne at your moſt Royall Image,
And mocke your workings, in a Second body?
Queſtion your Royall Thoughts, make the caſe yours:
Be now the Father, and propoſe a Sonne,
Heare your owne dignity ſo much prophan'd,
See your moſt dreadfull Lawes, ſo looſely ſlighted;
Behold your ſelfe, ſo by a Sonne diſdained:
And then imagine me, taking you part,
And in your power, ſoft ſilencing your Sonne:
After this cold conſiderance, ſentence me;
And, as you are a King, ſpeake in your State,
What I haue done, that misbecame my place,
My perſon, or my Lieges Soueraigntie.
Prin. You are right Iuſtice, and you weigh this well:
Therefore ſtill beare the Ballance, and the Sword:
And I do wiſh your Honors may encreaſe,
Till you do liue, to ſee a Sonne of mine
Offend you, and obey you, as I did.
So ſhall I liue, to ſpeake my Fathers words:
Happy am I, that haue a man ſo bold,
That dares do Iuſtice, on my proper Sonne;
And no leſſe happy, hauing ſuch a Sonne,
That would deliuer vp his Greatneſſe ſo,
Into the hands of Iuſtice. You did commit me:
For which, I do commit into your hand,
Th'vnſtained Sword that you haue vs'd to beare:
With this Remembrance; That you vſe the ſame
With the like bold, iuſt, and impartiall ſpirit
As you haue done 'gainſt me. There is my hand,
You ſhall be as a Father, to my Youth:
My voice ſhall ſound, as you do prompt mine eare,
And I will ſtoope, and humble my Intents,
To your well-practis'd, wiſe Directions
And Princes all, beleeue me, I beſeech you:
My Father is gone wilde into his Graue,
(For in his Tombe, lye my Affections)
And with his Spirits, ſadly I ſuruiue,
To mocke the expectation of the World;
To fruſtrate Propheſies, and to race out
Rotten Opinion, who hath writ me downe
After my ſeeming. The Tide of Blood in me,
Hath prowdly flow'd in Vanity, till now.
Now doth it turne, and ebbe backe to the Sea,
Where it ſhall mingle with the ſtate of Floods,
And flow henceforth in formall Maieſty.
Now call we our High Court of Parliament,
And let vs chooſe ſuch Limbes of Noble Counſaile,

That

That the great Body of our State may go
In equall ranke, with the best gouern'd Nation,
That Warre, or Peace, or both at once may be
As things acquainted and familiar to vs,
In which you (Father) shall haue formost hand.
Our Coronation done, we will accite
(As I before remembred) all our State,
And heauen (consigning to my good intents)
No Prince, nor Peere, shall haue iust cause to say,
Heauen shorten *Harries* happy life, one day. *Exeunt.*

Scena Tertia.

Enter Falstaffe, Shallow, Silence, Bardolfe, Page, and Pistoll.

Shal Nay, you shall see mine Orchard: where, in an Arbor we will eate a last yeares Pippin of my owne graffing, with a dish of Carrawayes, and so forth (Come Cosin *Silence*, and then to bed.

Fal. You haue heere a goodly dwelling, and a rich.

Shal. Barren, barren, barren: Beggers all, beggers all Sir *Iohn*: Marry, good ayre. Spread *Dauy*, spread *Dauie*: Well said *Dauie*.

Falst. This *Dauie* serues you for good vses: he is your Seruingman, and your Husband.

Shal. A good Varlet, a good Varlet, a very good Varlet, Sir *Iohn*: I haue drunke too much Sacke at Supper. A good Varlet. Now sit downe, now sit downe. Come Cosin.

Sil. Ah sirra (quoth-a) we shall doe nothing but eate, and make good cheere, and praise heauen for the merrie yeere: when flesh is cheape, and Females deere, and lustie Lads rome heere, and there: so merrily, and euer among so merrily.

Fal. There's a merry heart, good M. *Silence*, Ile giue you a health for that anon.

Shal. Good M. *Bardolfe*: some wine, *Dauie*.

Da. Sweet sir, sit: Ile be with you anon: most sweete sir, sit. Master Page, good M. Page, sit: Proface. What you want in meate, wee'l haue in drinke: but you beare, the heart's all.

Shal. Be merry M. *Bardolfe*, and my little Souldiour there, be merry.

Sil. Be merry, be merry, my wife ha's all.
For women are Shrewes, both short, and tall:
'Tis merry in Hall, when Beards wagge all;
And welcome merry Shrouetide. Be merry, be merry.

Fal. I did not thinke M. *Silence* had bin a man of this Mettle.

Sil. Who I? I haue beene merry twice and once, ere now.

Dauy. There is a dish of Lether-coats for you.

Shal. *Dauie.*

Dau. Your Worship: Ile be with you straight. A cup of Wine, sir?

Sil. A Cup of Wine, that's briske and fine, & drinke vnto the Leman mine: and a merry heart liues long-a.

Fal. Well said, M. *Silence*.

Sil. If we shall be merry, now comes in the sweete of the night.

Fal. Health, and long life to you, M. *Silence*.

Sil. Fill the Cuppe, and let it come. Ile pledge you a mile to the bottome.

Shal. Honest *Bardolfe*, welcome: If thou want'st any thing, and wilt not call, beshrew thy heart. Welcome my little tyne theefe, and welcome indeed too: Ile drinke to M. *Bardolfe*, and to all the Cauileroes about London.

Dau. I hope to see London, once ere I die.

Bar. If I might see you there, *Dauie*.

Shal. You'l cracke a quart together? Ha, will you not M. *Bardolfe*?

Bar. Yes Sir, in a pottle pot.

Shal. I thanke thee: the knaue will sticke by thee, I can assure thee that. He will not out, he is true bred.

Bar. And Ile sticke by him, sir.

Shal. Why there spoke a King: lack nothing, be merry. Looke, who's at doore there, ho: who knockes?

Fal Why now you haue done me right.

Sil. Do me right, and dub me Knight, *Samingo*. Is't not so?

Fal. Tis so.

Sil. Is't so? Why then say an old man can do somwhat.

Dau. If it please your Worshippe, there's one *Pistoll* come from the Court with newes.

Fal. From the Court? Let him come in.

Enter Pistoll.

How now Pistoll?

Pist. Sir *Iohn*, 'saue you sir.

Fal. What winde blew you hither, Pistoll?

Pist. Not the ill winde which blowes none to good, sweet Knight: Thou art now one of the greatest men in the Realme.

Sil. Indeed, I thinke he bee, but Goodman *Puffe* of Barson.

Pist. Puffe? puffe in thy teeth, most recreant Coward base. Sir *Iohn*, I am thy Pistoll, and thy Friend: helter skelter haue I rode to thee, and tydings do I bring, and luckie ioyes, and golden Times, and happie Newes of price.

Fal. I prethee now deliuer them, like a man of this World.

Pist. A footra for the World, and Worldlings base,
I speake of Affrica, and Golden ioyes.

Fal. O base Assyrian Knight, what is thy newes?
Let King *Couitha* know the truth thereof.

Sil. And Robin-hood, Scarlet, and Iohn.

Pist. Shall dunghill Curres confront the *Hellicons*?
And shall good newes be baffel'd?
Then Pistoll lay thy head in Furies lappe.

Shal. Honest Gentleman,
I know not your breeding.

Pist. Why then Lament therefore.

Shal. Giue me pardon, Sir.
If sir, you come with news from the Court, I take it, there is but two wayes, either to vtter them, or to conceale them. I am Sir, vnder the King, in some Authority.

Pist. Vnder which King?
Bezonian, speake, or dye.

Shal. Vnder King *Harry*.

Pist. *Harry* the Fourth? or Fift?

Shal *Harry* the Fourth.

Pist. A footra for thine Office.
Sir *Iohn*, thy tender Lamb-kinne, now is King.
Harry the Fift's the man, I speake the truth.
When Pistoll lyes, do this, and figge-me, like
The bragging Spaniard.

Fal.

Fal. What, is the old King dead?

Pist. As nalle in doore.
The things I speake, are iust.

Fal. Away *Bardolfe*, Sadle my Horse,
Master *Robert Shallow*, choose what Office thou wilt
In the Land, 'tis thine. *Pistol*, I will double charge thee
With Dignities.

Bard. O ioyfull day:
I would not take a Knighthood for my Fortune.

Pist. What? I do bring good newes.

Fal. Carrie Master *Silence* to bed: Master *Shallow*, my Lord *Shallow*, be what thou wilt, I am Fortunes Steward. Get on thy Boots, wee'l ride all night. Oh sweet Pistoll: Away *Bardolfe*: Come Pistoll, vtter more to mee: and withall deuise something to do thy selfe good. Boote, boote Master *Shallow*, I know the young King is sick for mee. Let vs take any mans Horsses: The Lawes of England are at my command'ment. Happie are they, which haue beene my Friendes: and woe vnto my Lord Chiefe Iustice.

Pist. Let Vultures vil'de seize on his Lungs also:
Where is the life that late I led, say they?
Why heere it is, welcome those pleasant dayes. *Exeunt*

Scena Quarta.

Enter Hostesse Quickly, Dol Teare-sheete, and Beadles.

Hostesse. No, thou arrant knaue: I would I might dy, that I might haue thee hang'd: Thou hast drawne my shoulder out of ioynt.

Off. The Constables haue deliuer'd her ouer to mee: and shee shall haue Whipping cheere enough, I warrant her. There hath beene a man or two (lately) kill'd about her.

Dol. Nut-hooke, nut-hooke, you Lye: Come on, Ile tell thee what, thou damn'd Tripe-visag'd Rascall, if the Childe I now go with, do miscarrie, thou had'st better thou had'st strooke thy Mother, thou Paper-fac'd Villaine.

Host. O that Sir *Iohn* were come, hee would make this a bloody day to some body. But I would the Fruite of her Wombe might miscarry.

Officer. If it do, you shall haue a dozen of Cushions againe, you haue but eleuen now. Come, I charge you both go with me: for the man is dead, that you and Pistoll beate among you.

Dol. Ile tell thee what, thou thin man in a Censor; I will haue you as soundly swindg'd for this, you blew-Bottel'd Rogue: you filthy famish'd Correctioner, if you be not swing'd, Ile forsweare halfe Kirtles.

Off. Come, come, you shee-Knight-arrant, come.

Host. O, that right should thus o'recome might. Wel of sufferance, comes ease.

Dol. Come you Rogue, come:
Bring me to a Iustice.

Host. Yes, come you staru'd Blood-hound.

Dol. Goodman death, goodman Bones.

Host. Thou Anatomy, thou.

Dol. Come you thinne Thing:
Come you Rascall.

Off. Very well. *Exeunt.*

Scena Quinta.

Enter two Groomes.

1.Groo. More Rushes, more Rushes.

2.Groo. The Trumpets haue sounded twice.

1.Groo. It will be two of the Clocke, ere they come from the Coronation. *Exit Groo.*

Enter Falstaffe, Shallow, Pistoll, Bardolfe, and Page.

Falstaffe. Stand heere by me, M. *Robert Shallow*, I will make the King do you Grace. I will leere vpon him, as he comes by: and do but marke the countenance that hee will giue me.

Pistol. Blesse thy Lungs, good Knight.

Falst. Come heere *Pistol*, stand behind me. O if I had had time to haue made new Liueries, I would haue bestowed the thousand pound I borrowed of you. But it is no matter, this poore shew doth better: this doth inferre the zeale I had to see him.

Shal. It doth so.

Falst. It shewes my earnestnesse in affection.

Pist. It doth so.

Fal. My deuotion.

Pist. It doth, it doth, it doth.

Fal. As it were, to ride day and night,
And not to deliberate, not to remember,
Not to haue patience to shift me.

Shal. It is most certaine.

Fal. But to stand stained with Trauaile, and sweating with desire to see him, thinking of nothing else, putting all affayres in obliuion, as if there were nothing els to bee done, but to see him.

Pist. 'Tis *semper idem*: for *obsque hoc nihil est.* 'Tis all in euery part.

Shal. 'Tis so indeed.

Pist. My Knight, I will enflame thy Noble Liuer, and make thee rage. Thy *Dol*, and *Helen* of thy noble thoghts is in base Durance, and contagious prison: Hall'd thither by most Mechanicall and durty hand. Rowze vppe Reuenge from Ebon den, with fell Alecto's Snake, for *Dol* is in. Pistol, speakes nought but troth.

Fal. I will deliuer her.

Pistol. There roar'd the Sea: and Trumpet Clangour sounds.

The Trumpets sound. Enter King Henrie the Fift, Brothers, Lord Chiefe Iustice.

Falst. Saue thy Grace, King *Hall*, my Royall *Hall*.

Pist. The heauens thee guard, and keepe, most royall Impe of Fame.

Fal. 'Saue thee my sweet Boy.

King. My Lord Chiefe Iustice, speake to that vaine man.

Ch.Iust. Haue you your wits?
Know you what 'tis you speake?

Falst. My King, my Ioue; I speake to thee, my heart.

King. I know thee not, old man: Fall to thy Prayers:
How ill white haires become a Foole, and Iester?

I haue

I haue long dream'd of such a kinde of man,
So surfeit-swell'd, so old, and so prophane:
But being awake, I do despise my dreame.
Make lesse thy body (hence) and more thy Grace,
Leaue gourmandizing; Know the Graue doth gape
For thee, thrice wider then for other men.
Reply not to me, with a Foole-borne Iest,
Presume not, that I am the thing I was,
For heauen doth know (so shall the world perceiue)
That I haue turn'd away my former Selfe,
So will I those that kept me Companie.
When thou dost heare I am, as I haue bin,
Approach me, and thou shalt be as thou was't
The Tutor and the Feeder of my Riots:
Till then, I banish thee, on paine of death,
As I haue done the rest of my Misleaders,
Not to come neere our Person, by ten mile.
For competence of life, I will allow you,
That lacke of meanes enforce you not to euill:
And as we heare you do reforme your selues,
We will according to your strength, and qualities,
Giue you aduancement. Be it your charge (my Lord)
To see perform'd the tenure of our word. Set on.

Exit King.

Fal. Master *Shallow*, I owe you a thousand pound.

Shal. I marry Sir *Iohn*, which I beseech you to let me haue home with me.

Fal. That can hardly be, M. *Shallow*, do not you grieue at this: I shall be sent for in priuate to him: Looke you, he must seeme thus to the world: feare not your aduancement: I will be the man yet, that shall make you great.

Shal. I cannot well perceiue how, vnlesse you should giue me your Doublet, and stuffe me out with Straw. I beseech you, good Sir *Iohn*, let mee haue fiue hundred of my thousand.

Fal. Sir, I will be as good as my word. This that you heard, was but a colour.

Shall. A colour I feare, that you will dye, in Sir *Iohn.*

Fal. Feare no colours, go with me to dinner:
Come Lieutenant *Pistol*, come *Bardolfe*,
I shall be sent for soone at night

Ch. Iust. Go carry Sir *Iohn Falstaffe* to the Fleete,
Take all his Company along with him.

Fal. My Lord, my Lord.

Ch. Iust. I cannot now speake, I will heare you soone:
Take them away.

Pist. *Si fortuna me tormento, spera me contento.*

Exit. Manet Lancaster and Chiefe Iustice.

Iohn. I like this faire proceeding of the Kings:
He hath intent his wonted Followers
Shall all be very well prouided for:
But all are banisht, till their conuersations
Appeare more wise, and modest to the world.

Ch. Iust. And so they are.

Iohn. The King hath call'd his Parliament,
My Lord.

Ch. Iust. He hath.

Iohn. I will lay oddes, that ere this yeere expire,
We beare our Ciuill Swords, and Natiue fire
As farre as France. I heare a Bird so sing,
Whose Musicke (to my thinking) pleas'd the King.
Come, will you hence?

Exeunt

FINIS.

EPILOGVE.

FIRST, my Feare: then, my Curtſie: laſt, my Speech. My Feare, is your Diſpleaſure: My Curtſie, my Dutie: And my ſpeech, to Begge your Pardons. If you looke for a good ſpeech now, you vndoe me: For what I haue to ſay, is of mine owne making: and what (indeed) I ſhould ſay, will (I doubt) prooue mine owne marring. But to the Purpoſe, and ſo to the Venture. Be it knowne to you (as it is very well) I was lately heere in the end of a diſpleaſing Play, to pray your Patience for it, and to promiſe you a Better: I did meane (indeede) to pay you with this, which if (like an ill Venture) it come vnluckily home, I breake; and you, my gentle Creditors loſe. Heere I promiſt you I would be, and heere I commit my Bodie to your Mercies: Bate me ſome, and I will pay you ſome, and (as moſt Debtors do) promiſe you infinitely.

If my Tongue cannot entreate you to acquit me: will you command me to vſe my Legges? And yet that were but light payment, to Dance out of your debt: But a good Conſcience, will make any poſſible ſatisfaction, and ſo will I. All the Gentlewomen heere, haue forgiuen me, if the Gentlemen will not, then the Gentlemen do not agree with the Gentlewowen, which was neuer ſeene before, in ſuch an Aſſembly.

One word more, I beſeech you: if you be not too much cloid with Fat Meate, our humble Author will continue the Story (with Sir Iohn in it) and make you merry, with faire Katherine of France: where (for any thing I know) Falſtaffe ſhall dye of a ſweat, vnleſſe already he be kill'd with your hard Opinions: For Old-Caſtle dyed a Martyr, and this is not the man. My Tongue is wearie, when my Legs are too, I will bid you good night; and ſo kneele downe before you: But (indeed) to pray for the Queene.

THE ACTORS NAMES.

RVMOVR the Presentor.
King *Henry* the Fourth.
Prince *Henry*, afterwards Crowned King *Henrie* the Fift.

Prince *Iohn* of Lancaster.
Humphrey of Gloucester.
Thomas of Clarence.
} Sonnes to *Henry* the Fourth, & brethren to *Henry* 5.

Northumberland.
The Arch Byshop of Yorke.
Mowbray.
Hastings.
Lord Bardolfe.
Trauers.
Morton.
Coleuile.
} Opposites against King *Henrie* the Fourth.

Warwicke.
Westmerland.
Surrey.
Gowre.
Harecourt.
Lord Chiefe Iustice.
} Of the Kings Partie.

Pointz.
Falstaffe.
Bardolphe.
Pistoll.
Peto.
Page.
} Irregular Humorists.

Shallow.
Silence.
} Both Country Iustices.

Dauie, Seruant to Shallow.
Phang, and Snare, 2. Serieants

Mouldie.
Shadow.
Wart.
Feeble.
Bullcalfe.
} Country Soldiers

Drawers
Beadles.
Groomes

Northumberlands Wife.
Percies Widdow.
Hostesse Quickly.
Doll Teare-sheete.
Epilogue.

The Life of Henry the Fift.

Enter Prologue.

O For a Muse of Fire, that would ascend
The brightest Heauen of Inuention:
A Kingdome for a Stage, Princes to Act,
And Monarchs to behold the swelling Scene.
Then should the Warlike Harry, *like himselfe,*
Assume the Port of Mars, *and at his heeles*
(Leasht in, like Hounds) should Famine, Sword, and Fire
Crouch for employment. But pardon, Gentles all:
The flat vnraysed Spirits, that hath dar'd,
On this vnworthy Scaffold, to bring forth
So great an Obiect. Can this Cock-Pit hold
The vastie fields of France? Or may we cramme
Within this Woodden O, the very Caskes
That did affright the Ayre at Agincourt?
O pardon: since a crooked Figure may
Attest in little place a Million,
And let vs, Cyphers to this great Accompt,
On your imaginarie Forces worke.
Suppose within the Girdle of these Walls
Are now confin'd two mightie Monarchies,
Whose high, vp-reared, and abutting Fronts,
The perillous narrow Ocean parts asunder.
Peece out our imperfections with your thoughts:
Into a thousand parts diuide one Man,
And make imaginarie Puissance.
Thinke when we talke of Horses, that you see them
Printing their prowd Hoofes i'th' receiuing Earth:
For 'tis your thoughts that now must deck our Kings,
Carry them here and there: Iumping o're Times;
Turning th'accomplishment of many yeeres
Into an Howre-glasse: for the which supplie,
Admit me Chorus *to this Historie;*
Who Prologue-like, your humble patience pray,
Gently to heare, kindly to iudge our Play. **Exit.**

Actus Primus. Scœna Prima.

Enter the two Bishops of Canterbury and Ely.

Bish. Cant.

MY Lord, Ile tell you, that selfe Bill is vrg'd,
Which in th'eleueth yere of ye last Kings reign
Was like, and had indeed against vs past,
But that the scambling and vnquiet time
Did push it out of farther question.

Bish. Ely. But how my Lord shall we resist it now?

Bish. Cant. It must be thought on: if it passe against vs,
We loose the better halfe of our Possession:
For all the Temporall Lands, which men deuout
By Testament haue giuen to the Church,
Would they strip from vs; being valu'd thus,
As much as would maintaine, to the Kings honor,
Full fifteene Earles, and fifteene hundred Knights,
Six thousand and two hundred good Esquires:
And to reliefe of Lazars, and weake age
Of indigent faint Soules, past corporall toyle,
A hundred Almes-houses, right well supply'd:
And to the Coffers of the King beside,
A thousand pounds by th'yeere. Thus runs the Bill.

Bish. Ely. This would drinke deepe.

Bish. Cant 'Twould drinke the Cup and all.

Bish. Ely. But what preuention?

Bish Cant. The King is full of grace, and faire regard.

Bish Ely. And a true louer of the holy Church.

Bish Cant. The courses of his youth promis'd it not.
The breath no sooner left his Fathers body,
But that his wildnesse, mortify'd in him,
Seem'd to dye too: yea, at that very moment,
Consideration like an Angell came,
And whipt th'offending *Adam* out of him;
Leauing his body as a Paradise,
T'inuelop and containe Celestiall Spirits.
Neuer was such a sodaine Scholler made:
Neuer came Reformation in a Flood,
With such a heady currance scowring faults:
Nor neuer *Hidra*-headed Wilfulnesse
So soone did loose his Seat; and all at once;
As in this King.

Bish Ely. We are blessed in the Change.

Bish. Cant Heare him but reason in Diuinitie;
And all-admiring, with an inward wish
You would desire the King were made a Prelate:
Heare him debate of Common-wealth Affaires;
You would say, it hath been all in all his study:
List his discourse of Warre; and you shall heare
A fearefull Battaile rendred you in Musique.

h Turne.

Turne him to any Cauſe of Pollicy,
The Gordian Knot of it he will vnlooſe,
Familiar as his Garter: that when he ſpeakes,
The Ayre, a Charter'd Libertine, is ſtill,
And the mute Wonder lurketh in mens eares,
To ſteale his ſweet and honyed Sentences:
So that the Art and Practique part of Life,
Muſt be the Miſtreſſe to this Theorique.
Which is a wonder how his Grace ſhould gleane it,
Since his addiction was to Courſes vaine,
His Companies vnletter'd, rude, and ſhallow,
His Houres fill'd vp with Ryots, Banquets, Sports;
And neuer noted in him any ſtudie,
Any retyrement, any ſequeſtration,
From open Haunts and Popularitie.
B. Ely. The Strawberry growes vnderneath the Nettle,
And holeſome Berryes thriue and ripen beſt,
Neighbour'd by Fruit of baſer qualitie:
And ſo the Prince obſcur'd his Contemplation
Vnder the Veyle of Wildneſſe, which (no doubt)
Grew like the Summer Graſſe, faſteſt by Night,
Vnſeene, yet creſſiue in his facultie.
B. Cant. It muſt be ſo; for Miracles are ceaſt:
And therefore we muſt needes admit the meanes,
How things are perfected.
B. Ely. But my good Lord:
How now for mittigation of this Bill,
Vrg'd by the Commons? doth his Maieſtie
Incline to it, or no?
B. Cant. He ſeemes indifferent:
Or rather ſwaying more vpon our part,
Then cheriſhing th'exhibiters againſt vs:
For I haue made an offer to his Maieſtie,
Vpon our Spirituall Conuocation,
And in regard of Cauſes now in hand,
Which I haue open'd to his Grace at large,
As touching France, to giue a greater Summe,
Then euer at one time the Clergie yet
Did to his Predeceſſors part withall.
B. Ely. How did this offer ſeeme receiu'd, my Lord?
B. Cant. With good acceptance of his Maieſtie:
Saue that there was not time enough to heare,
As I perceiu'd his Grace would faine haue done,
The ſeueralls and vnhidden paſſages
Of his true Titles to ſome certaine Dukedomes,
And generally, to the Crowne and Seat of France,
Deriu'd from *Edward*, his great Grandfather.
B. Ely. What was th'impediment that broke this off?
B. Cant. The French Embaſſador vpon that inſtant
Crau'd audience; and the howre I thinke is come,
To giue him hearing: Is it foure a Clock?
B. Ely. It is.
B. Cant. Then goe we in, to know his Embaſſie:
Which I could with a ready gueſſe declare,
Before the Frenchman ſpeake a word of it.
B. Ely. Ile wait vpon you, and I long to heare it.
Exeunt.

Enter the King, Humfrey, Bedford, Clarence, Warwick, Weſtmerland, and Exeter.

King. Where is my gracious Lord of Canterbury?
Exeter. Not here in preſence.
King. Send for him, good Vnckle.
Weſtm. Shall we call in th'Ambaſſador, my Liege?
King. Not yet, my Couſin: we would be reſolu'd,
Before we heare him, of ſome things of weight,
That taske our thoughts, concerning vs and France.

Enter two Biſhops.

B. Cant. God and his Angels guard your ſacred Throne,
And make you long become it.
King. Sure we thanke you.
My learned Lord, we pray you to proceed,
And iuſtly and religiouſly vnfold,
Why the Law *Salike*, that they haue in France,
Or ſhould or ſhould not barre vs in our Clayme:
And God forbid, my deare and faithfull Lord,
That you ſhould faſhion, wreſt, or bow your reading,
Or nicely charge your vnderſtanding Soule,
With opening Titles miſcreate, whoſe right
Sutes not in natiue colours with the truth:
For God doth know, how many now in health,
Shall drop their blood, in approbation
Of what your reuerence ſhall incite vs to.
Therefore take heed how you impawne our Perſon,
How you awake our ſleeping Sword of Warre;
We charge you in the Name of God take heed:
For neuer two ſuch Kingdomes did contend,
Without much fall of blood, whoſe guiltleſſe drops
Are euery one, a Woe, a ſore Complaint,
'Gainſt him, whoſe wrongs giues edge vnto the Swords,
That makes ſuch waſte in briefe mortalitie.
Vnder this Coniuration, ſpeake my Lord:
For we will heare, note, and beleeue in heart,
That what you ſpeake, is in your Conſcience waſht,
As pure as ſinne with Baptiſme.
B. Can. Then heare me gracious Soueraign, & you Peers,
That owe your ſelues, your liues, and ſeruices,
To this Imperiall Throne. There is no barre
To make againſt your Highneſſe Clayme to France,
But this which they produce from *Pharamond*,
In terram Salicam Mulieres ne ſuccedaul,
No Woman ſhall ſucceed in *Salike* Land:
Which *Salike* Land, the French vniuſtly gloze
To be the Realme of France, and *Pharamond*
The founder of this Law, and Female Barre.
Yet their owne Authors faithfully affirme,
That the Land *Salike* is in Germanie,
Betweene the Flouds of Sala and of Elue:
Where *Charles* the Great hauing ſubdu'd the Saxons,
There left behind and ſettled certaine French:
Who holding in diſdaine the German Women,
For ſome diſhoneſt manners of their life,
Eſtabliſht then this Law; to wit, No Female
Should be Inheritrix in *Salike* Land:
Which *Salike* (as I ſaid) 'twixt Elue and Sala,
Is at this day in Germanie, call'd *Meiſen*.
Then doth it well appeare, the *Salike* Law
Was not deuiſed for the Realme of France:
Nor did the French poſſeſſe the *Salike* Land,
Vntill foure hundred one and twentie yeeres
After defunction of King *Pharamond*,
Idly ſuppos'd the founder of this Law,
Who died within the yeere of our Redemption,
Foure hundred twentie ſix: and *Charles* the Great
Subdu'd the Saxons, and did ſeat the French
Beyond the Riuer Sala, in the yeere
Eight hundred fiue. Beſides, their Writers ſay,
King *Pepin*, which depoſed *Childerike*,
Did as Heire Generall, being deſcended
Of *Blithild*, which was Daughter to King *Clothair*,
Make Clayme and Title to the Crowne of France.
Hugh Capet alſo, who vſurpt the Crowne
Of

Of *Charles* the Duke of Loraine, ſole Heire male
Of the true Line and Stock of *Charlſt* the Great:
To find his Title with ſome ſhewes of truth,
Though in pure truth it was corrupt and naught,
Conuey'd himſelfe as th'Heire to th' Lady *Lingare*,
Daughter to *Charlemaine*, who was the Sonne
To *Lewes* The Emperour, and *Lewes* the Sonne
Of *Charles* the Great: alſo King *Lewes* the Tenth,
Who was ſole Heire to the Vſurper *Capet*,
Could not keepe quiet in his conſcience,
Wearing the Crowne of France, 'till ſatisfied,
That faire Queene *Iſabel*, his Grandmother,
Was Lineall of the Lady *Ermengare*,
Daughter to *Charles* the foreſaid Duke of Loraine:
By the which Marriage, the Lyne of *Charles* the Great
Was re-vnited to the Crowne of France
So, that as cleare as is the Summers Sunne,
King *Pepins* Title, and *Hugh Capets* Clayme,
King *Lewes* his ſatisfaction, all appeare
To hold in Right and Title of the Female:
So doe the Kings of France vnto this day.
Howbeit, they would hold vp this Salique Law,
To barre your Highneſſe clayming from the Female,
And rather chuſe to hide them in a Net,
Then amply to imbarre their crooked Titles,
Vſurpt from you and your Progenitors.
King. May I with right and conſcience make this claim?
Biſh.Cant. The ſinne vpon my head, dread Soueraigne:
For in the Booke of *Numbers* is it writ,
When the man dyes, let the Inheritance
Deſcend vnto the Daughter. Gracious Lord,
Stand for your owne, vnwind your bloody Flagge,
Looke back into your mightie Anceſtors:
Goe my dread Lord, to your great Grandſires Tombe,
From whom you clayme; inuoke his Warlike Spirit,
And your Great Vnckles, *Edward* the Black Prince,
Who on the French ground play'd a Tragedie,
Making defeat on the full Power of France:
Whiles his moſt mightie Father on a Hill
Stood ſmiling, to behold his Lyons Whelpe
Forrage in blood of French Nobilitie.
O Noble Engliſh, that could entertaine
With halfe their Forces, the full pride of France,
And let another halfe ſtand laughing by,
All out of worke, and cold for action.
Biſh. Awake remembrance of theſe valiant dead,
And with your puiſſant Arme renew their Feats;
You are their Heire, you ſit vpon their Throne:
The Blood and Courage that renowned them,
Runs in your Veines: and my thrice-puiſſant Liege
Is in the very May-Morne of his Youth,
Ripe for Exploits and mightie Enterpriſes.
Exe. Your Brother Kings and Monarchs of the Earth
Doe all expect, that you ſhould rowſe your ſelfe,
As did the former Lyons of your Blood. (might;
Weſt. They know your Grace hath cauſe, and means, and
So hath your Highneſſe: neuer King of England
Had Nobles richer, and more loyall Subiects,
Whoſe hearts haue left their bodyes here in England,
And lye pauillion'd in the fields of France.
Biſh.Can. O let their bodyes follow my deare Liege
With Bloods, and Sword and Fire, to win your Right:
In ayde whereof, we of the Spiritualtie
Will rayſe your Highneſſe ſuch a mightie Summe,
As neuer did the Clergie at one time
Bring in to any of your Anceſtors.
King. We muſt not onely arme t'inuade the French,
But lay downe our proportions, to defend
Againſt the Scot, who will make roade vpon vs,
With all aduantages.
Biſh.Can. They of thoſe Marches, gracious Soueraign,
Shall be a Wall ſufficient to defend
Our in-land from the pilfering Borderers.
King. We do not meane the courſing ſnatchers onely,
But feare the maine intendment of the Scot,
Who hath been ſtill a giddy neighbour to vs:
For you ſhall reade, that my great Grandfather
Neuer went with his forces into France,
But that the Scot, on his vnfurniſht Kingdome,
Came pouring like the Tyde into a breach,
With ample and brim fulneſſe of his force,
Galling the gleaned Land with hot Aſſayes,
Girding with grieuous ſiege, Caſtles and Townes:
That England being emptie of defence,
Hath ſhooke and trembled at th'ill neighbourhood.
B.Can. She hath bin thẽ more fear'd thẽ harm'd, my Liege:
For heare her but exampl'd by her ſelfe,
When all her Cheualrie hath been in France,
And ſhee a mourning Widdow of her Nobles,
Shee hath her ſelfe not onely well defended,
But taken and impounded as a Stray,
The King of Scots: whom ſhee did ſend to France,
To fill King *Edwards* fame with priſoner Kings,
And make their Chronicle as rich with prayſe,
As is the Owſe and bottome of the Sea
With ſunken Wrack, and ſum-leſſe Treaſuries.
Biſh.Ely. But there's a ſaying very old and true,
If that you will France win, then with Scotland firſt begin.
For once the Eagle (England) being in prey,
To her vnguarded Neſt, the Weazell (Scot)
Comes ſneaking, and ſo ſucks her Princely Egges,
Playing the Mouſe in abſence of the Cat,
To tame and hauocke more then ſhe can eate.
Exet. It followes then, the Cat muſt ſtay at home,
Yet that is but a cruſh'd neceſsity,
Since we haue lockes to ſafegard neceſſaries,
And pretty traps to catch the petty theeues.
While that the Armed hand doth fight abroad,
Th'aduiſed head defends it ſelfe at home:
For Gouernment, though high, and low, and lower,
Put into parts, doth keepe in one conſent,
Congreeing in a full and natural cloſe,
Like Muſicke.
Cant. Therefore doth heauen diuide
The ſtate of man in diuers functions,
Setting endeuour in continual motion:
To which is fixed as an ayme or butt,
Obedience: for ſo worke the Hony Bees,
Creatures that by a rule in Nature teach
The Act of Order to a peopled Kingdome.
They haue a King, and Officers of ſorts,
Where ſome like Magiſtrates correct at home:
Others, like Merchants venter Trade abroad:
Others, like Souldiers armed in their ſtings,
Make boote vpon the Summers Veluet buddes:
Which pillage, they with merry march bring home,
To the Tent-royal of their Emperor
Who buſied in his Maieſties ſurueyes
The ſinging Maſons building roofes of Gold,
The ciuil Citizens kneading vp the hony;
The poore Mechanicke Porters, crowding in
Their heauy burthens at his narrow gate:

The ſad-ey'd Iuſtice with his ſurly humme,
Deliuering ore to Executors pale
The lazie yawning Drone: I this inferre,
That many things hauing full reference
To one conſent, may worke contrariouſly,
As many Arrowes looſed ſeuerall wayes
Come to one marke: as many wayes meet in one towne,
As many freſh ſtreames meet in one ſalt ſea;
As many Lynes cloſe in the Dials center:
So may a thouſand actions once a foote,
And in one purpoſe, and be all well borne
Without defeat. Therefore to France, my Liege,
Diuide your happy England into foure,
Whereof, take you one quarter into France,
And you withall ſhall make all Galiia ſhake.
If we with thrice ſuch powers left at home,
Cannot defend our owne doores from the dogge,
Let vs be worried, and our Nation loſe
The name of hardineſſe and policie.
King. Call in the Meſſengers ſent from the Dolphin.
Now are we well reſolu'd, and by Gods helpe
And yours, the noble ſinewes of our power,
France being ours, wee'l bend it to our Awe,
Or breake it all to peeces. Or there wee'l ſit,
(Ruling in large and ample Emperie,
Ore France, and all her (almoſt) Kingly Dukedomes)
Or lay theſe bones in an vnworthy Vrne,
Tombleſſe, with no remembrance ouer them
Either our Hiſtory ſhall with full mouth
Speake freely of our Acts, or elſe our graue
Like Turkiſh mute, ſhall haue a tongueleſſe mouth,
Not worſhipt with a waxen Epitaph.
Enter Ambaſſadors of France.
Now are we well prepar'd to know the pleaſure
Of our faire Coſin Dolphin: for we heare,
Your greeting is from him, not from the King.
Amb. May't pleaſe your Maieſtie to giue vs leaue
Freely to render what we haue in charge:
Or ſhall we ſparingly ſhew you farre off
The Dolphins meaning, and our Embaſſie.
King. We are no Tyrant, but a Chriſtian King,
Vnto whoſe grace our paſſion is as ſubiect
As is our wretches fettred in our priſons,
Therefore with franke and with vncurbed plaineſſe,
Tell vs *Dolphins* minde
Amb. Thus than in few:
Your Highneſſe lately ſending into France,
Did claime ſome certaine Dukedomes, in the right
Of your great Predeceſſor, King *Edward* the third.
In anſwer of which claime, the Prince our Maſter
Sayes, that you ſauour too much of your youth,
And bids you be aduis'd: There's nought in France,
That can be with a nimble Galliard wonne:
You cannot reuell into Dukedomes there.
He therefore ſends you meeter for your ſpirit
This Tun of Treaſure; and in lieu of this,
Deſires you let the dukedomes that you claime
Heare no more of you. This the *Dolphin* ſpeakes.
King. What Treaſure Vncle?
Exe. Tennis balles, my Liege.
Kin. We are glad the *Dolphin* is ſo pleaſant with vs,
His Preſent, and your paines we thanke you for:
When we haue matcht our Rackets to theſe Balles,
We will in France (by Gods grace) play a ſet,
Shall ſtrike his fathers Crowne into the hazard.
Tell him, he hath made a match with ſuch a Wrangler,
That all the Courts of France will be diſturb'd
With Chaces. And we vnderſtand him well,
How he comes o're vs with our wilder dayes,
Not meaſuring what vſe we made of them.
We neuer valew'd this poore ſeate of England,
And therefore liuing hence, did giue our ſelfe
To barbarous licenſe: As 'tis euer common,
That men are merrieſt, when they are from home.
But tell the *Dolphin*, I will keepe my State,
Be like a King, and ſhew my ſayle of Greatneſſe,
When I do rowſe me in my Throne of France.
For that I haue layd by my Maieſtie,
And plodded like a man for working dayes:
But I will riſe there with ſo full a glorie,
That I will dazle all the eyes of France,
Yea ſtrike the *Dolphin* blinde to looke on vs,
And tell the pleaſant Prince, this Mocke of his
Hath turn'd his balles to Gun-ſtones, and his ſoule
Shall ſtand ſore charged, for the waſtefull vengeance
That ſhall flye with them: for many a thouſand widows
Shall this his Mocke, mocke out of their deer husbands;
Mocke mothers from their ſonnes, mock Caſtles downe:
And ſome are yet vngotten and vnborne,
That ſhal haue cauſe to curſe the *Dolphins* ſcorne.
But this lyes all within the wil of God,
To whom I do appeale, and in whoſe name
Tel you the *Dolphin*, I am comming on,
To venge me as I may, and to put forth
My rightfull hand in a wel-hallow'd cauſe.
So get you hence in peace: And tell the *Dolphin*,
His Ieſt will ſauour but of ſhallow wit,
When thouſands weepe more then did laugh at it.
Conuey them with ſafe conduct. Fare you well.
Exeunt Ambaſſadors.
Exe. This was a merry Meſſage.
King. We hope to make the Sender bluſh at it:
Therefore, my Lords, omit no happy howre,
That may giue furth'rance to our Expedition:
For we haue now no thought in vs but France,
Saue thoſe to God, that runne before our buſineſſe.
Therefore let our proportions for theſe Warres
Be ſoone collected, and all things thought vpon,
That may with reaſonable ſwiftneſſe adde
More Feathers to our Wings: for God before,
Wee'le chide this *Dolphin* at his fathers doore.
Therefore let euery man now taske his thought,
That this faire Action may on foot be brought. *Exeunt.*

Flouriſh. Enter Chorus.
Now all the Youth of England are on fire,
And ſilken Dalliance in the Wardrobe lyes:
Now thriue the Armorers, and Honors thought
Reignes ſolely in the breaſt of euery man.
They ſell the Paſture now, to buy the Horſe;
Following the Mirror of all Chriſtian Kings,
With winged heeles, as Engliſh *Mercuries.*
For now ſits Expectation in the Ayre,
And hides a Sword, from Hilts vnto the Point,
With Crownes Imperiall, Crownes and Coronets
Promis'd to *Harry*, and his followers.
The French aduis'd by good intelligence
Of this moſt dreadfull preparation,
Shake in their feare, and with pale Pollicy
Seeke to diuert the Engliſh purpoſes.
O England: Modell to thy inward Greatneſſe,
Like little Body with a mightie Heart:

What

What mighteſt thou do, that honour would thee do,
Were all thy children kinde and naturall:
But ſee, thy fault France hath in thee found out,
A neſt of hollow boſomes, which he filles
With treacherous Crownes, and three corrupted men:
One, *Richard* Earle of Cambridge, and the ſecond
Henry Lord *Scroope* of *Maſham*, and the third
Sir *Thomas Grey* Knight of Northumberland,
Haue for the Gilt of France (O guilt indeed)
Confirm'd Conſpiracy with fearefull France,
And by their hands, this grace of Kings muſt dye,
If Hell and Treaſon hold their promiſes,
Ere he take ſhip for France; and in Southampton.
Linger your patience on, and wee'l digeſt
Th'abuſe of diſtance; force a play:
The ſumme is payde, the Traitors are agreed,
The King is ſet from London, and the Scene
Is now tranſported (Gentles) to Southampton,
There is the Play-houſe now, there muſt you ſit,
And thence to France ſhall we conuey you ſafe,
And bring you backe: Charming the narrow ſeas
To giue you gentle Paſſe: for if we may,
Wee'l not offend one ſtomacke with our Play.
But till the King come forth, and not till then,
Vnto Southampton do we ſhift our Scene. *Exit*

Enter Corporall Nym, and Lieutenant Bardolfe.

Bar. Well met Corporall *Nym*.

Nym. Good morrow Lieutenant *Bardolfe*.

Bar. What, are Ancient *Piſtoll* and you friends yet?

Nym. For my part, I care not: I ſay little: but when time ſhall ſerue, there ſhall be ſmiles, but that ſhall be as it may. I dare not fight, but I will winke and holde out mine yron: it is a ſimple one, but what though? It will toſte Cheeſe, and it will endure cold, as another mans ſword will: and there's an end.

Bar. I will beſtow a breakfaſt to make you friendes, and wee'l bee all three ſworne brothers to France: Let't be ſo good Corporall *Nym*.

Nym. Faith, I will liue ſo long as I may, that's the certaine of it: and when I cannot liue any longer, I will doe as I may: That is my reſt, that is the rendeuous of it.

Bar. It is certaine Corporall, that he is marryed to *Nell Quickly*, and certainly ſhe did you wrong, for you were troth-plight to her.

Nym. I cannot tell, Things muſt be as they may: men may ſleepe, and they may haue their throats about them at that time, and ſome ſay, kniues haue edges: It muſt be as it may, though patience be a tyred name, yet ſhee will plodde, there muſt be Concluſions, well, I cannot tell.

Enter Piſtoll, & Quickly.

Bar. Heere comes Ancient *Piſtoll* and his wife: good Corporall be patient heere. How now mine Hoaſte *Piſtoll*?

Piſt. Baſe Tyke, cal'ſt thou mee Hoſte, now by this hand I ſweare I ſcorne the terme: nor ſhall my *Nel* keep Lodgers.

Hoſt. No by my troth, not long: For we cannot lodge and board a dozen or fourteene Gentlewomen that liue honeſtly by the pricke of their Needles, but it will bee thought we keepe a Bawdy-houſe ſtraight. O welliday Lady, if he be not hewne now, we ſhall ſee wilful adultery and murther commited.

Bar. Good Lieutenant, good Corporal offer nothing heere. *Nym.* Piſh.

Piſt. Piſh for thee, Iſland dogge: thou prickeard cur of Iſland.

Hoſt. Good Corporall *Nym* ſhew thy valor, and put vp your ſword.

Nym. Will you ſhogge off? I would haue you ſolus.

Piſt. Solus, egregious dog? O Viper vile; The ſolus in thy moſt meruailous face, the ſolus in thy teeth, and in thy throate, and in thy hatefull Lungs, yea in thy Maw perdy; and which is worſe, within thy naſtie mouth. I do retort the ſolus in thy bowels, for I can take, and *Piſtols* cocke is vp, and flaſhing fire will follow.

Nym. I am not *Barbaſon*, you cannot coniure mee: I haue an humor to knocke you indifferently well: If you grow fowle with me Piſtoll, I will ſcoure you with my Rapier, as I may, in fayre tearmes. If you would walke off, I would pricke your guts a little in good tearmes, as I may, and that's the humor of it.

Piſt. O Braggard vile, and damned furious wight,
The Graue doth gape, and doting death is neere,
Therefore exhale.

Bar. Heare me, heare me what I ſay: Hee that ſtrikes the firſt ſtroake, Ile run him vp to the hilts, as I am a ſoldier.

Piſt. An oath of mickle might, and fury ſhall abate.
Giue me thy fiſt, thy fore-foote to me giue: Thy ſpirites are moſt tall.

Nym. I will cut thy throate one time or other in faire termes, that is the humor of it.

Piſtoll. *Couple a gorge*, that is the word. I defie thee againe. O hound of Creet, think'ſt thou my ſpouſe to get? No, to the ſpittle goe, and from the Poudring tub of infamy, fetch forth the Lazar Kite of *Creſſids* kinde, *Doll Teare-ſheete*, ſhe by name, and her eſpouſe. I haue, and I will hold the *Quondam Quickely* for the onely ſhee: and *Pauca*, there's enough to go to.

Enter the Boy.

Boy. Mine Hoaſt *Piſtoll*, you muſt come to my Mayſter, and your Hoſteſſe: He is very ſicke, & would to bed. Good *Bardolfe*, put thy face betweene his ſheets, and do the Office of a Warming-pan: Faith, he's very ill.

Bard. Away you Rogue.

Hoſt. By my troth he'l yeeld the Crow a pudding one of theſe dayes: the King has kild his heart. Good Husband come home preſently. *Exit*

Bar. Come, ſhall I make you two friends. Wee muſt to France together: why the diuel ſhould we keep kniues to cut one anothers throats?

Piſt. Let floods ore-ſwell, and fiends for food howle on.

Nym. You'l pay me the eight ſhillings I won of you at Betting?

Piſt. Baſe is the Slaue that payes.

Nym. That now I wil haue: that's the humor of it.

Piſt. As manhood ſhal compound: puſh home. *Draw*

Bard. By this ſword, hee that makes the firſt thruſt, Ile kill him: By this ſword, I wil.

Pi. Sword is an Oath, & Oaths muſt haue their courſe

Bar. Coporall *Nym*, & thou wilt be friends be frends, and thou wilt not, why then be enemies with me to: prethee put vp.

Piſt. A Noble ſhalt thou haue, and preſent pay, and Liquor likewiſe will I giue to thee, and friendſhippe ſhall combyne, and brotherhood. Ile liue by *Nymme*, & *Nymme* ſhall liue by me, is not this iuſt? For I ſhal Sutler be vnto the Campe, and profits will accrue. Giue mee thy hand.

Nym. I shall haue my Noble?
Pist. In cash, most iustly payd.
Nym. Well, then that the humor of't.

Enter Hostesse.

Host. As euer you come of women, come in quickly to sir *Iohn*: A poore heart, hee is so shak'd of a burning quotidian Tertian, that it is most lamentable to behold. Sweet men, come to him.
Nym. The King hath run bad humors on the Knight, that's the euen of it.
Pist. *Nym*, thou hast spoke the right, his heart is fracted and corroborate.
Nym. The King is a good King, but it must bee as it may: he passes some humors, and carreeres.
Pist. Let vs condole the Knight, for (Lambekins) we will liue.

Enter Exeter, Bedford, & Westmerland.

Bed Fore God his Grace is bold to trust these traitors
Exe. They shall be apprehended by and by.
West. How smooth and euen they do bear themselues,
As if allegeance in their bosomes sate
Crowned with faith, and constant loyalty.
Bed. The King hath note of all that they intend,
By interception, which they dreame not of.
Exe. Nay, but the man that was his bedfellow,
Whom he hath dull'd and cloy'd with gracious fauours;
That he should for a forraigne purse, so sell
His Soueraignes life to death and treachery.

Sound Trumpets.

Enter the King, Scroope, Cambridge, and Gray.

King. Now sits the winde faire, and we will aboord.
My Lord of *Cambridge*, and my kinde Lord of *Masham*,
And you my gentle Knight, giue me your thoughts:
Thinke you not that the powres we beare with vs
Will cut their passage through the force of France?
Doing the execution, and the acte,
For which we haue in head assembled them.
Scro. No doubt my Liege, if each man do his best.
King. I doubt not that, since we are well perswaded
We carry not a heart with vs from hence,
That growes not in a faire consent with ours:
Nor leaue not one behinde, that doth not wish
Successe and Conquest to attend on vs.
Cam. Neuer was Monarch better fear'd and lou'd,
Then is your Maiesty; there's not I thinke a subiect
That sits in heart-greefe and vneasinesse
Vnder the sweet shade of your gouernment.
Kni. True: those that were your Fathers enemies,
Haue steep'd their gauls in hony, and do serue you
With hearts create of duty, and of zeale.
King. We therefore haue great cause of thankfulnes,
And shall forget the office of our hand
Sooner then quittance of desert and merit,
According to the weight and worthinesse.
Scro. So seruice shall with steeled sinewes toyle,
And labour shall refresh it selfe with hope
To do your Grace incessant seruices.
King. We Iudge no lesse. Vnkle of *Exeter*,
Inlarge the man committed yesterday,
That rayl'd against our person: We consider
It was excesse of Wine that set him on,
And on his more aduice, We pardon him.
Scro. That's mercy, but too much security:
Let him be punish'd Soueraigne, least example
Breed (by his sufferance) more of such a kind.
King. O let vs yet be mercifull.
Cam. So may your Highnesse, and yet punish too.
Grey. Sir, you shew great mercy if you giue him life,
After the taste of much correction.
King Alas, your too much loue and care of me,
Are heauy Orisons 'gainst this poore wretch:
If little faults proceeding on distemper,
Shall not be wink'd at, how shall we stretch our eye
When capitall crimes, chew'd, swallow'd, and digested,
Appeare before vs? Wee'l yet inlarge that man,
Though *Cambridge, Scroope*, and *Gray*, in their deere care
And tender preseruation of our person
Wold haue him punish'd. And now to our French causes,
Who are the late Commissioners?
Cam. I one my Lord,
Your Highnesse bad me aske for it to day.
Scro. So did you me my Liege.
Gray. And I my Royall Soueraigne.
King. Then *Richard* Earle of *Cambridge*, there is yours:
There yours Lord *Scroope* of *Masham*, and Sir Knight:
Gray of *Northumberland*, this same is yours:
Reade them, and know I know your worthinesse.
My Lord of *Westmerland*, and Vnkle *Exeter*,
We will aboord to night. Why how now Gentlemen?
What see you in those papers, that you loose
So much complexion? Looke ye how they change:
Their cheekes are paper. Why, what reade you there,
That haue so cowarded and chac'd your blood
Out of apparance.
Cam. I do confesse my fault,
And do submit me to your Highnesse mercy.
Gray. Scro. To which we all appeale.
King. The mercy that was quicke in vs but late,
By your owne counsaile is supprest and kill'd:
You must not dare (for shame) to talke of mercy,
For your owne reasons turne into your bosomes,
As dogs vpon their maisters, worrying you:
See you my Princes, and my Noble Peeres,
These English monsters: My Lord of *Cambridge* heere,
You know how apt our loue was, to accord
To furnish with all appertinents
Belonging to his Honour; and this man,
Hath for a few light Crownes, lightly conspir'd
And sworne vnto the practises of France
To kill vs heere in Hampton. To the which,
This Knight no lesse for bounty bound to Vs
Then Cambridge is, hath likewise sworne. But O,
What shall I say to thee Lord *Scroope*, thou cruell,
Ingratefull, sauage, and inhumane Creature?
Thou that didst beare the key of all my counsailes,
That knew'st the very bottome of my soule,
That (almost) might'st haue coyn'd me into Golde,
Would'st thou haue practis'd on me, for thy vse?
May it be possible, that forraigne hyer
Could out of thee extract one sparke of euill
That might annoy my finger? 'Tis so strange,
That though the truth of it stands off as grosse
As blacke and white, my eye will scarsely see it.
Treason, and murther, euer kept together,
As two yoake diuels sworne to eythers purpose,
Working so grossely in an naturall cause,
That admiration did not hoope at them.
But thou (gainst all proportion) didst bring in
Wonder to waite on treason, and on murther:
And whatsoeuer cunning fiend it was
That wrought vpon thee so preposterously,
Hath got the voyce in hell for excellence:
And

And other diuels that suggest by treasons,
Do botch and bungle vp damnation,
With patches, colours, and with formes being fetcht
From glist'ring semblances of piety:
But he that temper'd thee, bad thee stand vp,
Gaue thee no instance why thou shouldst do treason,
Vnlesse to dub thee with the name of Traitor.
If that same Dæmon that hath gull'd thee thus,
Should with his Lyon-gate walke the whole world,
He might returne to vastie Tartar backe,
And tell the Legions, I can neuer win
A soule so easie as that Englishmans.
Oh, how hast thou with iealousie infected
The sweetnesse of affiance? Shew men dutifull,
Why so didst thou: seeme they graue and learned:
Why so didst thou. Come they of Noble Family?
Why so didst thou. Seeme they religious?
Why so didst thou. Or are they spare in diet,
Free from grosse passion, or of mirth, or anger,
Constant in spirit, not sweruing with the blood,
Garnish'd and deck'd in modest complement,
Not working with the eye, without the eare,
And but in purged iudgement trusting neither,
Such and so finely boulted didst thou seeme:
And thus thy fall hath left a kinde of blot,
To make thee full fraught man, and best indued
With some suspition, I will weepe for thee.
For this reuolt of thine, me thinkes is like
Another fall of Man. Their faults are open,
Arrest them to the answer of the Law,
And God acquit them of their practises.

Exe. I arrest thee of High Treason, by the name of *Richard* Earle of *Cambridge*.

I arrest thee of High Treason, by the name of *Thomas* Lord *Scroope* of *Marsham*.

I arrest thee of High Treason, by the name of *Thomas Grey*, Knight of *Northumberland*.

Scro. Our purposes, God iustly hath discouer'd,
And I repent my fault more then my death,
Which I beseech your Highnesse to forgiue,
Although my body pay the price of it.

Cam. For me, the Gold of France did not seduce,
Although I did admit it as a motiue,
The sooner to effect what I intended:
But God be thanked for preuention,
Which in sufferance heartily will reioyce,
Beseeching God, and you, to pardon mee.

Gray. Neuer did faithfull subiect more reioyce
At the discouery of most dangerous Treason,
Then I do at this houre ioy ore my selfe,
Preuented from a damned enterprize;
My fault, but not my body, pardon Soueraigne.

King. God quit you in his mercy: Hear your sentence
You haue conspir'd against Our Royall person,
Ioyn'd with an enemy proclaim'd, and from his Coffers,
Receyu'd the Golden Earnest of Our death:
Wherein you would haue sold your King to slaughter,
His Princes, and his Peeres to seruitude,
His Subiects to oppression, and contempt,
And his whole Kingdome into desolation:
Touching our person, seeke we no reuenge,
But we our Kingdomes safety must so tender
Whose ruine you sought, that to her Lawes
We do deliuer you. Get you therefore hence,
(Poore miserable wretches) to your death:
The taste whereof, God of his mercy giue
You patience to indure, and true Repentance
Of all your deare offences. Beare them hence. *Exit.*
Now Lords for France: the enterprise whereof
Shall be to you as vs, like glorious.
We doubt not of a faire and luckie Warre,
Since God so graciously hath brought to light
This dangerous Treason, lurking in our way,
To hinder our beginnings. We doubt not now,
But euery Rubbe is smoothed on our way.
Then forth, deare Countreymen: Let vs deliuer
Our Puissance into the hand of God,
Putting it straight in expedition.
Chearely to Sea, the signes of Warre aduance,
No King of England, if not King of France. *Flourish.*

Enter Pistoll, Nim, Bardolph, Boy, and Hostesse.

Hostesse. 'Prythee honey sweet Husband, let me bring thee to Staines.

Pistoll. No: for my manly heart doth erne. *Bardolph*, be blythe: *Nim*, rowse thy vaunting Veines: Boy, brissle thy Courage vp: for *Falstaffe* hee is dead, and wee must erne therefore.

Bard. Would I were with him, wheresomere hee is, eyther in Heauen, or in Hell.

Hostesse. Nay sure, hee's not in Hell: hee's in *Arthurs* Bosome, if euer man went to *Arthurs* Bosome: a made a finer end, and went away and it had beene any Christome Child: a parted eu'n iust betweene Twelue and One, eu'n at the turning o'th' Tyde: for after I saw him fumble with the Sheets, and play with Flowers, and smile vpon his fingers end, I knew there was but one way: for his Nose was as sharpe as a Pen, and a Table of greene fields. How now Sir *Iohn* (quoth I?) what man? be a good cheare: so a cryed out, God, God, God, three or foure times: now I, to comfort him, bid him a should not thinke of God; I hop'd there was no neede to trouble himselfe with any such thoughts yet: so a bad me lay more Clothes on his feet: I put my hand into the Bed, and felt them, and they were as cold as any stone: then I felt to his knees, and so vp-peer'd, and vpward, and all was as cold as any stone.

Nim. They say he cryed out of Sack.

Hostesse. I, that a did.

Bard. And of Women.

Hostesse. Nay, that a did not.

Boy. Yes that a did, and said they were Deules incarnate.

Woman. A could neuer abide Carnation, 'twas a Colour he neuer lik'd.

Boy. A said once, the Deule would haue him about Women.

Hostesse. A did in some sort (indeed) handle Women: but then hee was rumatique, and talk'd of the Whore of Babylon.

Boy. Doe you not remember a saw a Flea sticke vpon *Bardolphs* Nose, and a said it was a blacke Soule burning in Hell.

Bard. Well, the fuell is gone that maintain'd that fire: that's all the Riches I got in his seruice.

Nim. Shall wee shogg? the King will be gone from Southampton.

Pist. Come, let's away. My Loue, giue me thy Lippes: Looke to my Chattels, and my Moueables: Let Sences rule: The world is, Pitch and pay: trust none: for Oathes are Strawes, mens Faiths are Wafer-Cakes, and hold-fast is the onely Dogge: My Ducke, therefore *Caueto* bee thy Counsailor. Goe, cleare thy Chrystalls. Yoke-fellowes in Armes, let vs to France, like Horse-leeches

leeches my Boyes, to sucke, to sucke, the very blood to sucke.

Boy. And that's but vnwholesome food, they say.

Pist. Touch her soft mouth, and march.

Bard. Farwell Hostesse.

Nim. I cannot kisse, that is the humor of it: but adieu.

Pist. Let Huswiferie appeare: keepe close, I thee command.

Hostesse. Farwell: adieu. *Exeunt*

Flourish.

Enter the French King, the Dolphin, the Dukes of Berry and Britaine.

King. Thus comes the English with full power vpon vs,
And more then carefully it vs concernes,
To answer Royally in our defences.
Therefore the Dukes of Berry and of Britaine,
Of Brabant and of Orleance, shall make forth,
And you Prince Dolphin, with all swift dispatch
To lyne and new repayre our Townes of Warre
With men of courage, and with meanes defendant:
For England his approaches makes as fierce,
As Waters to the sucking of a Gulfe.
It fits vs then to be as prouident,
As feare may teach vs, out of late examples
Left by the fatall and neglected English,
Vpon our fields.

Dolphin. My most redoubted Father,
It is most meet we arme vs 'gainst the Foe:
For Peace it selfe should not so dull a Kingdome,
(Though War nor no knowne Quarrel were in question)
But that Defences, Musters, Preparations,
Should be maintain'd, assembled, and collected,
As were a Warre in expectation.
Therefore I say, 'tis meet we all goe forth,
To view the sick and feeble parts of France:
And let vs doe it with no shew of feare,
No, with no more, then if we heard that England
Were busied with a Whitson Morris-dance:
For, my good Liege, shee is so idly King'd,
Her Scepter so phantastically borne,
By a vaine giddie shallow humorous Youth,
That feare attends her not.

Const. O peace, Prince Dolphin,
You are too much mistaken in this King:
Question your Grace the late Embassadors,
With what great State he heard their Embassie,
How well supply'd with Noble Councellors,
How modest in exception; and withall,
How terrible in constant resolution:
And you shall find, his Vanities fore-spent,
Were but the out-side of the Roman *Brutus*,
Couering Discretion with a Coat of Folly;
As Gardeners doe with Ordure hide those Roots
That shall first spring, and be most delicate.

Dolphin. Well, 'tis not so, my Lord High Constable.
But though we thinke it so, it is no matter:
In cases of defence, 'tis best to weigh
The Enemie more mightie then he seemes,
So the proportions of defence are fill'd:
Which of a weake and niggardly proiection,
Doth like a Miser spoyle his Coat, with scanting
A little Cloth.

King. Thinke we King *Harry* strong:
And Princes, looke you strongly arme to meet him.
The Kindred of him hath beene flesht vpon vs:
And he is bred out of that bloodie straine,
That haunted vs in our familiar Pathes:
Witnesse our too much memorable shame,
When Cressy Battell fatally was strucke,
And all our Princes captiu'd, by the hand
Of that black Name, *Edward*, black Prince of Wales:
Whiles that his Mountaine Sire, on Mountaine standing
Vp in the Ayre, crown'd with the Golden Sunne,
Saw his Heroicall Seed, and smil'd to see him
Mangle the Worke of Nature, and deface
The Patternes, that by God and by French Fathers
Had twentie yeeres been made. This is a Stem
Of that Victorious Stock: and let vs feare
The Natiue mightinesse and fate of him.

Enter a Messenger.

Mess. Embassadors from *Harry* King of England,
Doe craue admittance to your Maiestie.

King. Weele giue them present audience.
Goe, and bring them.
You see this Chase is hotly followed, friends.

Dolphin. Turne head, and stop pursuit: for coward Dogs
Most spend their mouths, whē what they seem to threaten
Runs farre before them. Good my Soueraigne
Take vp the English short, and let them know
Of what a Monarchie you are the Head:
Selfe-loue, my Liege, is not so vile a sinne,
As selfe-neglecting.

Enter Exeter.

King. From our Brother of England?

Exe. From him, and thus he greets your Maiestie:
He wills you in the Name of God Almightie,
That you deuest your selfe, and lay apart
The borrowed Glories, that by gift of Heauen,
By Law of Nature, and of Nations, longs
To him and to his Heires, namely the Crowne,
And all wide-stretched Honors, that pertaine
By Custome, and the Ordinance of Times,
Vnto the Crowne of France: that you may know
'Tis no sinister, nor no awk-ward Clayme,
Pickt from the worme-holes of long-vanisht dayes,
Nor from the dust of old Obliuion rakt,
He sends you this most memorable Lyne,
In euery Branch truly demonstratiue;
Willing you ouer-looke this Pedigree:
And when you find him euenly deriu'd
From his most fam'd, of famous Ancestors,
Edward the third; he bids you then resigne
Your Crowne and Kingdome, indirectly held
From him, the Natiue and true Challenger.

King. Or else what followes?

Exe. Bloody constraint: for if you hide the Crowne
Euen in your hearts, there will he rake for it.
Therefore in fierce Tempest is he comming,
In Thunder and in Earth-quake, like a *Ioue*:
That if requiring faile, he will compell.
And bids you, in the Bowels of the Lord,
Deliuer vp the Crowne, and to take mercie
On the poore Soules, for whom this hungry Warre
Opens his vastie Iawes: and on your head
Turning the Widdowes Teares, the Orphans Cryes,
The dead-mens Blood, the priuy Maidens Groanes,
For Husbands, Fathers, and betrothed Louers,
That shall be swallowed in this Controuersie.
This is his Clayme, his Threatning, and my Message:
Vnlesse the Dolphin be in presence here;
To whom expressely I bring greeting to.

King. For

King. For vs, we will consider of this further:
To morrow shall you beare our full intent
Back to our Brother of England.
Dolph. For the Dolphin,
I stand here for him: what to him from England?
Exe. Scorne and defiance, sleight regard, contempt,
And any thing that may not mis-become
The mightie Sender, doth he prize you at.
Thus sayes my King: and if your Fathers Highnesse
Doe not, in graunt of all demands at large,
Sweeten the bitter Mock you sent his Maiestie;
Hee'le call you to so hot an Answer of it,
That Caues and Wombie Vaultages of France
Shall chide your Trespas, and returne your Mock
In second Accent of his Ordinance.
Dolph. Say: if my Father render faire returne,
It is against my will: for I desire
Nothing but Oddes with England.
To that end, as matching to his Youth and Vanitie,
I did present him with the Paris-Balls.
Exe. Hee'le make your Paris Louer shake for it,
Were it the Mistresse Court of mightie Europe:
And be assur'd, you'le find a diff'rence,
As we his Subiects haue in wonder found,
Betweene the promise of his greener dayes,
And these he masters now: now he weighes Time
Euen to the vtmost Graine: that you shall reade
In your owne Losses, if he stay in France.
King. To morrow shall you know our mind at full.
Flourish.
Exe. Dispatch vs with all speed, least that our King
Come here himselfe to question our delay;
For he is footed in this Land already.
King. You shalbe soone dispatcht, with faire conditions.
A Night is but small breathe, and little pawse,
To answer matters of this consequence. *Exeunt.*

Actus Secundus.

Flourish. Enter Chorus.

Thus with imagin'd wing our swift Scene flyes,
In motion of no lesse celeritie then that of Thought.
Suppose, that you haue seene
The well-appointed King at Douer Peer,
Embarke his Royaltie: and his braue Fleet,
With silken Streamers, the young *Phebus* fayning;
Play with your Fancies: and in them behold,
Vpon the Hempen Tackle, Ship-boyes climbing;
Heare the shrill Whistle, which doth order giue
To sounds confus'd: behold the threaden Sayles,
Borne with th'inuisible and creeping Wind,
Draw the huge Bottomes through the furrowed Sea,
Bresting the loftie Surge. O, doe but thinke
You stand vpon the Riuage, and behold
A Citie on th'inconstant Billowes dauncing:
For so appeares this Fleet Maiesticall,
Holding due course to Harflew. Follow, follow:
Grapple your minds to sternage of this Nauie,
And leaue your England as dead Mid-night, still,
Guarded with Grandsires, Babyes, and old Women,
Eyther past, or not arriu'd to pyth and puissance:
For who is he, whose Chin is but enricht
With one appearing Hayre, that will not follow
These cull'd and choyse-drawne Caualiers to France?
Worke, worke your Thoughts, and therein see a Siege:
Behold the Ordenance on their Carriages,
With fatall mouthes gaping on girded Harflew.
Suppose th'Embassador from the French comes back:
Tells *Harry*, That the King doth offer him
Katherine his Daughter, and with her to Dowrie,
Some petty and vnprofitable Dukedomes.
The offer likes not: and the nimble Gunner
With Lynstock now the diuellish Cannon touches,
Alarum, and Chambers goe off.
And downe goes all before them. Still be kind,
And eech out our performance with your mind. *Exit.*

Enter the King, Exeter, Bedford, and Glocester.
Alarum: Scaling Ladders at Harflew.

King. Once more vnto the Breach,
Deare friends, once more;
Or close the Wall vp with our English dead:
In Peace, there's nothing so becomes a man,
As modest stillnesse, and humilitie:
But when the blast of Warre blowes in our eares,
Then imitate the action of the Tyger:
Stiffen the sinewes, commune vp the blood,
Disguise faire Nature with hard-fauour'd Rage:
Then lend the Eye a terrible aspect:
Let it pry through the portage of the Head,
Like the Brasse Cannon: let the Brow o'rewhelme it,
As fearefully, as doth a galled Rocke
O're-hang and iutty his confounded Base,
Swill'd with the wild and wastfull Ocean.
Now set the Teeth, and stretch the Nosthrill wide,
Hold hard the Breath, and bend vp euery Spirit
To his full height. On, on, you Noblish English,
Whose blood is fet from Fathers of Warre-proofe:
Fathers, that like so many *Alexanders*,
Haue in these parts from Morne till Euen fought,
And sheath'd their Swords, for lack of argument.
Dishonour not your Mothers: now attest,
That those whom you call'd Fathers, did beget you.
Be Coppy now to me of grosser blood,
And teach them how to Warre. And you good Yeomen,
Whose Lyms were made in England; shew vs here
The mettell of your Pasture: let vs sweare,
That you are worth your breeding: which I doubt not:
For there is none of you so meane and base,
That hath not Noble luster in your eyes.
I see you stand like Grey-hounds in the slips,
Straying vpon the Start. The Game's afoot:
Follow your Spirit; and vpon this Charge,
Cry, God for *Harry*, England, and S. *George*.
Alarum, and Chambers goe off.

Enter Nim, Bardolph, Pistoll, and Boy.

Bard. On, on, on, on, on, to the breach, to the breach.

Nim. 'Pray thee Corporall stay, the Knocks are too hot: and for mine owne part, I haue not a Case of Liues: the humor of it is too hot, that is the very plaine-Song of it.

Pist. The plaine-Song is most iust: for humors doe abound: Knocks goe and come: Gods Vassals drop and dye: and Sword and Shield, in bloody Field, doth winne immortall fame.

Boy. Would I were in an Ale-house in London, I would giue all my fame for a Pot of Ale, and safetie.

Pist. And

Piſt. And I: If wiſhes would preuayle with me, my purpoſe ſhould not fayle with me; but thither would I high.

Boy. As duly, but not as truly, as Bird doth ſing on bough.

Enter Fluellen.

Flu. Vp to the breach, you Dogges; auaunt you Cullions.

Piſt. Be mercifull great Duke to men of Mould: abate thy Rage, abate thy manly Rage; abate thy Rage, great Duke Good Bawcock bate thy Rage: vſe lenitie ſweet Chuck.

Nim. Theſe be good humors: your Honor wins bad humors. *Exit.*

Boy. As young as I am, I haue obſeru'd theſe three Swaſhers: I am Boy to them all three, but all they three, though they would ſerue me, could not be Man to me; for indeed three ſuch Antiques doe not amount to a man: for *Bardolph*, hee is white-liuer'd, and red-fac'd; by the meanes whereof, a faces it out, but fights not: for *Piſtoll*, hee hath a killing Tongue, and a quiet Sword; by the meanes whereof, a breakes Words, and keepes whole Weapons: for *Nim*, hee hath heard, that men of few Words are the beſt men, and therefore hee ſcornes to ſay his Prayers, leſt a ſhould be thought a Coward: but his few bad Words are matcht with as few good Deeds; for a neuer broke any mans Head but his owne, and that was againſt a Poſt, when he was drunke. They will ſteale any thing, and call it Purchaſe. *Bardolph* ſtole a Lute-caſe, bore it twelue Leagues, and ſold it for three halfepence. *Nim* and *Bardolph* are ſworne Brothers in filching: and in Callice they ſtole a fire-ſhouell. I knew by that peece of Seruice, the men would carry Coales. They would haue me as familiar with mens Pockets, as their Gloues or their Hand-kerchers: which makes much againſt my Manhood, if I ſhould take from anothers Pocket, to put into mine; for it is plaine pocketting vp of Wrongs. I muſt leaue them, and ſeeke ſome better Seruice: their Villany goes againſt my weake ſtomacke, and therefore I muſt caſt it vp. *Exit.*

Enter Gower.

Gower. Captaine *Fluellen*, you muſt come preſently to the Mynes; the Duke of Glouceſter would ſpeake with you.

Flu. To the Mynes? Tell you the Duke, it is not ſo good to come to the Mynes: for looke you, the Mynes is not according to the diſciplines of the Warre; the concauities of it is not ſufficient: for looke you, th'athuerſarie, you may diſcuſſe vnto the Duke, looke you, is dig himſelfe foure yard vnder the Countermines: by *Cheſhu*, I thinke a will plowe vp all, if there is not better directions.

Gower. The Duke of Glouceſter, to whom the Order of the Siege is giuen, is altogether directed by an Iriſh man, a very valiant Gentleman yfaith.

Welch. It is Captaine *Makmorrice*, is it not?

Gower. I thinke it be.

Welch. By *Cheſhu* he is an Aſſe, as in the World, I will verifie as much in his Beard: he ha's no more directions in the true diſciplines of the Warres, looke you, of the Roman diſciplines, then is a Puppy-dog.

Enter Makmorrice, and Captaine Iamy.

Gower. Here a comes, and the Scots Captaine, Captaine *Iamy*, with him.

Welch. Captaine *Iamy* is a maruellous falorous Gentleman, that is certain, and of great expedition and knowledge in th'aunchiant Warres, vpon my particular knowledge of his directions: by *Cheſhu* he will maintaine his Argument as well as any Militarie man in the World, in the diſciplines of the Priſtine Warres of the Romans.

Scot. I ſay gudday, Captaine *Fluellen*.

Welch. Godden to your Worſhip, good Captaine *Iames*.

Gower. How now Captaine *Mackmorrice*, haue you quit the Mynes: haue the Pioners giuen o're.

Iriſh. By Chriſh Law tiſh ill done: the Worke iſh giue ouer, the Trompet ſound the Retreat. By my Hand I ſweare, and my fathers Soule, the Worke iſh ill done: it iſh giue ouer: I would haue blowed vp the Towne, ſo Chriſh ſaue me law, in an houre. O tiſh ill done, tiſh ill done: by my Hand tiſh ill done.

Welch. Captaine *Mackmorrice*, I beſeech you now, will you voutſafe me, looke you, a few diſputations with you, as partly touching or concerning the diſciplines of the Warre, the Roman Warres, in the way of Argument, looke you, and friendly communication: partly to ſatisfie my Opinion, and partly for the ſatisfaction, looke you, of my Mind: as touching the direction of the Militarie diſcipline, that is the Point.

Scot. It ſall be vary gud, gud feith, gud Captens bath, and I ſall quit you with gud leue, as I may pick occaſion: that ſall I mary.

Iriſh. It is no time to diſcourſe, ſo Chriſh ſaue me: the day is hot, and the Weather, and the Warres, and the King, and the Dukes: it is no time to diſcourſe, the Town is beſeech'd: and the Trumpet call vs to the breech, and we talke, and be Chriſh do nothing, tis ſhame for vs all: ſo God ſa'me tis ſhame to ſtand ſtill, it is ſhame by my hand: and there is Throats to be cut, and Workes to be done, and there iſh nothing done, ſo Chriſt ſa'me law.

Scot. By the Mes, ere theiſe eyes of mine take themſelues to ſlomber, ayle de gud ſeruice, or Ile ligge i'th' grund for it; ay, or goe to death: and Ile pay't as valorouſly as I may, that ſal I ſuerly do, that is the breff and the long: mary, I wad full faine heard ſome queſtion tween you tway.

Welch. Captaine *Mackmorrice*, I thinke, looke you, vnder your correction, there is not many of your Nation.

Iriſh. Of my Nation? What iſh my Nation? Iſh a Villaine, and a Baſterd, and a Knaue, and a Raſcall. What iſh my Nation? Who talkes of my Nation?

Welch. Looke you, if you take the matter otherwiſe then is meant, Captaine *Mackmorrice*, peraduenture I ſhall thinke you doe not vſe me with that affabilitie, as in diſcretion you ought to vſe me, looke you, being as good a man as your ſelfe, both in the diſciplines of Warre, and in the deriuation of my Birth, and in other particularities.

Iriſh. I doe not know you ſo good a man as my ſelfe: ſo Chriſh ſaue me, I will cut off your Head.

Gower. Gentlemen both, you will miſtake each other

Scot. A, that's a foule fault. *A Parley.*

Gower. The Towne ſounds a Parley.

Welch. Captaine *Mackmorrice*, when there is more better oportunitie to be required, looke you, I will be ſo bold as to tell you, I know the diſciplines of Warre: and there is an end. *Exit.*

Enter the King and all his Traine before the Gates.

King. How yet reſolues the Gouernour of the Towne?
This is the lateſt Parle we will admit:

There-

Therefore to our best mercy giue your selues,
Or like to men prowd of destruction,
Defie vs to our worst: for as I am a Souldier,
A Name that in my thoughts becomes me best;
If I begin the batt'rie once againe,
I will not leaue the halfe-atchieued Harflew,
Till in her ashes she lye buryed.
The Gates of Mercy shall be all shut vp,
And the flesh'd Souldier, rough and hard of heart,
In libertie of bloody hand, shall raunge
With Conscience wide as Hell, mowing like Grasse
Your fresh faire Virgins, and your flowring Infants.
What is it then to me, if impious Warre,
Arrayed in flames like to the Prince of Fiends,
Doe with his smyrcht complexion all fell feats,
Enlynckt to wast and desolation?
What is't to me, when you your selues are cause,
If your pure Maydens fall into the hand
Of hot and forcing Violation?
What Reyne can hold licentious Wickednesse,
When downe the Hill he holds his fierce Carriere?
We may as bootlesse spend our vaine Command
Vpon th'enraged Souldiers in their spoyle,
As send Precepts to the *Leuiathan*, to come ashore.
Therefore, you men of Harflew,
Take pitty of your Towne and of your People,
Whiles yet my Souldiers are in my Command,
Whiles yet the coole and temperate Wind of Grace
O're-blowes the filthy and contagious Clouds
Of headly Murther, Spoyle and Villany.
If not: why in a moment looke to see
The blind and bloody Souldier, with foule hand
Desire the Locks of your shrill-shriking Daughters:
Your Fathers taken by the siluer Beards,
And their most reuerend Heads dasht to the Walls:
Your naked Infants spitted vpon Pykes,
Whiles the mad Mothers, with their howles confus'd,
Doe breake the Clouds; as did the Wiues of Iewry,
At *Herods* bloody-hunting slaughter-men.
What say you? Will you yeeld, and this auoyd?
Or guiltie in defence, be thus destroy'd.

Enter Gouernour.

Gouer. Our expectation hath this day an end:
The Dolphin, whom of Succours we entreated,
Returnes vs, that his Powers are yet not ready,
To rayse so great a Siege: Therefore great King,
We yeeld our Towne and Liues to thy soft Mercy:
Enter our Gates, dispose of vs and ours,
For we no longer are defensible.

King. Open your Gates: Come Vnckle *Exeter*,
Goe you and enter Harflew; there remaine,
And fortifie it strongly 'gainst the French:
Vse mercy to them all for vs, deare Vnckle.
The Winter comming on, and Sicknesse growing
Vpon our Souldiers, we will retyre to Calis.
To night in Harflew will we be your Guest,
To morrow for the March are we addrest.

Flourish, and enter the Towne.

Enter Katherine and an old Gentlewoman.

Kathe. Alice, tu as este en Angleterre, & tu bien parlas le Language.

Alice. En peu Madame.

Kath. Ie te prie m'ensigniez, il faut que ie apprend a parlen: Comient appelle vous le main en Anglois

Alice. Le main il & appelle de Hand.

Kath. De Hand.

Alice. E le doyts.

Kat. Le doyts, ma foy Ie oublie, e doyt mays, ie me souemeray le doyts ie pense qu'ils ont appelle de fingres, ou de fingres.

Alice. Le main de Hand, le doyts le Fingres, ie pense que ie suis le bon escholier.

Kath. I'ay gaynie diux mots d'Anglois vistement, coment appelle vous le ongles?

Alice. Le ongles, les appellons de Nayles.

Kath. De Nayles escoute: dites moy, si ie parle bien: de Hand, de Fingres, e de Nayles.

Alice. C'est bien dict Madame, il & fort bon Anglois.

Kath. Dites moy l'Anglois pour le bras.

Alice. De Arme, Madame.

Kath. E de coudee.

Alice. D'Elbow.

Kath. D'Elbow: Ie men fay le repiticio de touts les mots que vous maves, apprins des a present.

Alice. Il & trop difficile Madame, comme Ie pense.

Kath. Excuse moy Alice escoute, d'Hand, de Fingre, de Nayles, d'Arma, de Bilbow.

Alice. D'Elbow, Madame.

Kath. O Seigneur Dieu, ie men oublie d'Elbow, coment appelle vous le col.

Alice. De Nick, Madame.

Kath. De Nick, e le menton.

Alice. De Chin.

Kath. De Sin: le col de Nick, le menton de Sin.

Alice. Ouy. Sauf vostre honneur en verite vous pronouncies les mots ausi droict, que le Natifs d'Angleterre.

Kath. Ie ne doute point d'apprendre par de grace de Dieu, & en peu de temps.

Alice. N'aue vos y desia oublie ce que ie vous a ensignie.

Kath. Nome ie recitera a vous promptement, d'Hand, de Fingre, de Maylees.

Alice. De Nayles, Madame.

Kath. De Nayles, de Arme, de Ilbow.

Alice. Sans vostre honeus d'Elbow.

Kath. Ainsi de ie d'Elbow, de Nick, & de Sin: coment appelle vous les pied & de roba.

Alice. Le Foot Madame, & le Count.

Kath. Le Foot, & le Count: O Seignieur Dieu, il sont le mots de son mauvais corruptible grosse & impudique, & non pour le Dames de Honeur d'vser: Ie ne voudray pronouncer ce mots deuant le Seigneurs de France, pour toute le monde, fo le Foot & le Count, neant moys, Ie recitera vn autrefoys ma lecon ensembe, d'Hand, de Fingre, de Nayles, d'Arme, d'Elbow, de Nick, de Sin, de Foot, le Count.

Alice. Excellent, Madame.

Kath. C'est asses pour vne foyes, alons nous a diner.

Exit.

Enter the King of France, the Dolphin, the Constable of France, and others.

King. 'Tis certaine he hath past the Riuer Some.

Const. And if he be not fought withall, my Lord,
Let vs not liue in France: let vs quit all,
And giue our Vineyards to a barbarous People.

Dolph. O Dieu viuant: Shall a few Sprayes of vs,
The emptying of our Fathers Luxurie,
Our Syens, put in wilde and sauage Stock,
Spirt vp so suddenly into the Clouds,
And ouer-looke their Grafters?

Brit. Normans, but bastard Normans, Norman bastards:
Mort du ma vie, if they march along
Vnfought withall, but I will sell my Dukedome,

To

To buy a slobbry and a durtie Farme
In that nooke-shotten Ile of Albion.

Const. *Dieu de Battailes*, where haue they this mettell?
Is not their Clymate foggy, raw, and dull?
On whom, as in despight, the Sunne lookes pale,
Killing their Fruit with frownes. Can sodden Water,
A Drench for sur-reyn'd Iades, their Barly broth,
Decoct their cold blood to such valiant heat?
And shall our quick blood, spirited with Wine,
Seeme frostie? O, for honor of our Land,
Let vs not hang like roping Isyckles
Vpon our Houses Thatch, whiles a more frostie People
Sweat drops of gallant Youth in our rich fields:
Poore we call them, in their Natiue Lords.

Dolphin. By Faith and Honor,
Our Madames mock at vs, and plainely say,
Our Mettell is bred out, and they will giue
Their bodyes to the Lust of English Youth,
To new-store France with Bastard Warriors.

Brit. They bid vs to the English Dancing-Schooles,
And teach *Lauolta's* high, and swift *Carranto's*,
Saying, our Grace is onely in our Heeles,
And that we are most loftie Run-awayes.

King Where is *Montioy* the Herald? speed him hence,
Let him greet England with our sharpe defiance
Vp Princes, and with spirit of Honor edged,
More sharper then your Swords, high to the field:
Charles Delabreth, High Constable of France,
You Dukes of *Orleance*, *Burbon*, and of *Berry*,
Alanson, *Brabant*, *Bar*, and *Burgonie*,
Iaques Chattillion, *Rambures*, *Vandemont*,
Beumont, *Grand Pree*, *Roussi*, and *Faulconbridge*,
Loys, *Lestrale*, *Bouciquall*, and *Charaloyes*,
High Dukes, great Princes, Barons, Lords, and Kings;
For your great Seats, now quit you of great shames:
Barre *Harry* England, that sweepes through our Land
With Penons painted in the blood of Harflew:
Rush on his Hoast, as doth the melted Snow
Vpon the Valleyes, whose low Vassall Seat,
The Alpes doth spit, and void his rhewme vpon.
Goe downe vpon him, you haue Power enough,
And in a Captiue Chariot, into Roan
Bring him our Prisoner.

Const. This becomes the Great.
Sorry am I his numbers are so few,
His Souldiers sick, and famisht in their March:
For I am sure, when he shall see our Army,
Hee'le drop his heart into the sinck of feare,
And for atchieuement, offer vs his Ransome.

King. Therefore Lord Constable, hast on *Montioy*,
And let him say to England, that we send,
To know what willing Ransome he will giue.
Prince *Dolphin*, you shall stay with vs in Roan.

Dolph. Not so, I doe beseech your Maiestie.

King Be patient, for you shall remaine with vs.
Now forth Lord Constable, and Princes all,
And quickly bring vs word of Englands fall. *Exeunt.*

Enter Captaines, English and Welch, Gower and Fluellen.

Gower. How now Captaine *Fluellen*, come you from the Bridge?

Flu. I assure you, there is very excellent Seruices committed at the Bridge.

Gower. Is the Duke of Exeter safe?

Flu. The Duke of Exeter is as magnanimous as *Agamemnon*, and a man that I loue and honour with my soule and my heart, and my dutie, and my liue, and my liuing, and my vttermost power. He is not, God be praysed and blessed, any hurt in the World, but keepes the Bridge most valiantly, with excellent discipline. There is an aunchient Lieutenant there at the Pridge, I thinke in my very conscience hee is as valiant a man as *Marke Anthony*, and hee is a man of no estimation in the World, but I did see him doe as gallant seruice.

Gower. What doe you call him?

Flu. Hee is call'd aunchient *Pistoll*.

Gower. I know him not.

Enter Pistoll.

Flu. Here is the man.

Pist. Captaine, I thee beseech to doe me fauours; the Duke of Exeter doth loue thee well.

Flu. I, I prayse God, and I haue merited some loue at his hands.

Pist *Bardolph*, a Souldier firme and sound of heart, and of buxome valour, hath by cruell Fate, and giddie Fortunes furious fickle Wheele, that Goddesse blind, that stands vpon the rolling restlesse Stone.

Flu. By your patience, aunchient *Pistoll*: Fortune is painted blinde, with a Muffler afore his eyes, to signifie to you, that Fortune is blinde; and shee is painted also with a Wheele, to signifie to you, which is the Morall of it, that shee is turning and inconstant, and mutabilitie, and variation: and her foot, looke you, is fixed vpon a Sphericall Stone, which rowles, and rowles, and rowles: in good truth, the Poet makes a most excellent description of it: Fortune is an excellent Morall.

Pist. Fortune is *Bardolphs* foe, and frownes on him: for he hath stolne a Pax, and hanged must a be: a damned death: let Gallowes gape for Dogge, let Man goe free, and let not Hempe his Wind-pipe suffocate: but *Exeter* hath giuen the doome of death, for Pax of little price. Therefore goe speake, the Duke will heare thy voyce; and let not *Bardolphs* vitall thred bee cut with edge of Penny-Cord, and vile reproach. Speake Captaine for his Life, and I will thee requite.

Flu Aunchient *Pistoll*, I doe partly vnderstand your meaning.

Pist. Why then reioyce therefore.

Flu. Certainly Aunchient, it is not a thing to reioyce at: for if, looke you, he were my Brother, I would desire the Duke to vse his good pleasure, and put him to execution; for discipline ought to be vsed.

Pist Dye, and be dam'd, and *Figo* for thy friendship.

Flu. It is well.

Pist The Figge of Spaine. *Exit.*

Flu. Very good.

Gower. Why, this is an arrant counterfeit Rascall, I remember him now: a Bawd, a Cut-purse.

Flu. Ile assure you, a vtt'red as praue words at the Pridge, as you shall see in a Summers day: but it is very well: what he ha's spoke to me, that is well I warrant you, when time is serue.

Gower. Why 'tis a Gull, a Foole, a Rogue, that now and then goes to the Warres, to grace himselfe at his returne into London, vnder the forme of a Souldier: and such fellowes are perfit in the Great Commanders Names, and they will learne you by rote where Seruices were done; at such and such a Sconce, at such a Breach, at such a Conuoy: who came off brauely, who was shot, who disgrac'd, what termes the Enemy stood on: and this they conne perfitly in the phrase of Warre; which they tricke vp vp with new-tuned Oathes: and what a Beard of the Generalls Cut, and a horride Sute of the Campe, will doe among foming Bottles, and Ale-waſht Wits, is wonderfull to be thought on: but you muſt learne to know ſuch ſlanders of the age, or elſe you may be maruellouſly miſtooke.

Flu. I tell you what, Captaine *Gower*: I doe perceiue hee is not the man that hee would gladly make ſhew to the World hee is: if I finde a hole in his Coat, I will tell him my minde: hearke you, the King is comming, and I muſt ſpeake with him from the Pridge.

Drum and Colours. Enter the King and his poore Souldiers.

Flu. God pleſſe your Maieſtie.

King. How now *Fluellen*, cam'ſt thou from the Bridge?

Flu. I, ſo pleaſe your Maieſtie: The Duke of Exeter ha's very gallantly maintain'd the Pridge; the French is gone off, looke you, and there is gallant and moſt praue paſſages: marry, th'athuerſarie was haue poſſeſſion of the Pridge, but he is enforced to retyre, and the Duke of Exeter is Maſter of the Pridge: I can tell your Maieſtie, the Duke is a praue man.

King. What men haue you loſt, *Fluellen*?

Flu. The perdition of th'athuerſarie hath beene very great, reaſonnable great: marry for my part, I thinke the Duke hath loſt neuer a man, but one that is like to be executed for robbing a Church, one *Bardolph*, if your Maieſtie know the man: his face is all bubukles and whelkes, and knobs, and flames a fire, and his lippes blowes at his noſe, and it is like a coale of fire, ſometimes plew, and ſometimes red, but his noſe is executed, and his fire's out.

King. Wee would haue all ſuch offendors ſo cut off: and we giue expreſſe charge, that in our Marches through the Countrey, there be nothing compell'd from the Villages; nothing taken, but pay'd for: none of the French vpbrayded or abuſed in diſdainefull Language; for when Leuitie and Crueltie play for a Kingdome, the gentler Gameſter is the ſooneſt winner.

Tucket. Enter Mountioy.

Mountioy. You know me by my habit.

King. Well then, I know thee: what ſhall I know of thee?

Mountioy. My Maſters mind.

King. Vnfold it.

Mountioy. Thus ſayes my King: Say thou to *Harry* of England, Though we ſeem'd dead, we did but ſleepe: Aduantage is a better Souldier then raſhneſſe. Tell him, wee could haue rebuk'd him at Harflewe, but that wee thought not good to bruiſe an iniurie, till it were full ripe. Now wee ſpeake vpon our Q. and our voyce is imperiall: England ſhall repent his folly, ſee his weakeneſſe, and admire our ſufferance. Bid him therefore conſider of his ranſome, which muſt proportion the loſſes we haue borne, the ſubiects we haue loſt, the diſgrace we haue digeſted; which in weight to re-anſwer, his pettineſſe would bow vnder. For our loſſes, his Exchequer is too poore; for th'effuſion of our bloud, the Muſter of his Kingdome too faint a number; and for our diſgrace, his owne perſon kneeling at our feet, but a weake and worthleſſe ſatisfaction. To this adde defiance: and tell him for concluſion, he hath betrayed his followers, whoſe condemnation is pronounc't: So farre my King and Maſter; ſo much my Office.

King. What is thy name? I know thy qualitie.

Mount. *Mountioy.*

King. Thou doo'ſt thy Office fairely. Turne thee back,
And tell thy King, I doe not ſeeke him now,
But could be willing to march on to Callice,
Without impeachment: for to ſay the ſooth,
Though 'tis no wiſdome to confeſſe ſo much
Vnto an enemie of Craft and Vantage,
My people are with ſickneſſe much enfeebled,
My numbers leſſen'd: and thoſe few I haue,
Almoſt no better then ſo many French;
Who when they were in health, I tell thee Herald,
I thought, vpon one payre of Engliſh Legges
Did march three Frenchmen. Yet forgiue me God,
That I doe bragge thus; this your ayre of France
Hath blowne that vice in me. I muſt repent:
Goe therefore tell thy Maſter, heere I am;
My Ranſome, is this frayle and worthleſſe Trunke;
My Army, but a weake and ſickly Guard:
Yet God before, tell him we will come on,
Though France himſelfe, and ſuch another Neighbor
Stand in our way. There's for thy labour *Mountioy.*
Goe bid thy Maſter well aduiſe himſelfe.
If we may paſſe, we will: if we be hindred,
We ſhall your tawnie ground with your red blood
Diſcolour: and ſo *Mountioy*, fare you well.
The ſumme of all our Anſwer is but this:
We would not ſeeke a Battaile as we are,
Nor as we are, we ſay we will not ſhun it:
So tell your Maſter.

Mount. I ſhall deliuer ſo: Thankes to your Highneſſe.

Glouc. I hope they will not come vpon vs now.

King. We are in Gods hand, Brother, not in theirs:
March to the Bridge, it now drawes toward night,
Beyond the Riuer wee'le encampe our ſelues,
And on to morrow bid them march away. *Exeunt.*

Enter the Conſtable of France, the Lord Ramburs, Orleance, Dolphin, with others.

Conſt. Tut, I haue the beſt Armour of the World: would it were day.

Orleance. You haue an excellent Armour: but let my Horſe haue his due.

Conſt. It is the beſt Horſe of Europe.

Orleance. Will it neuer be Morning?

Dolph. My Lord of Orleance, and my Lord High Conſtable, you talke of Horſe and Armour?

Orleance. You are as well prouided of both, as any Prince in the World.

Dolph. What a long Night is this? I will not change my Horſe with any that treades but on foure poſtures: ch' ha: he bounds from the Earth, as if his entrayles were hayres: *le Cheual volante*, the Pegaſus, *chez les narines de feu.* When I beſtryde him, I ſoare, I am a Hawke: he trots the ayre: the Earth ſings, when he touches it: the baſeſt horne of his hooſe, is more Muſicall then the Pipe of *Hermes.*

Orleanee. Hee's of the colour of the Nutmeg.

Dolph. And of the heat of the Ginger. It is a Beaſt for *Perſeus*: hee is pure Ayre and Fire; and the dull Elements of Earth and Water neuer appeare in him, but only in patient ſtillneſſe while his Rider mounts him: hee is indeede a Horſe, and all other Iades you may call Beaſts.

Conſt. In.

Const. Indeed my Lord, it is a most absolute and excellent Horse.

Dolph. It is the Prince of Palfrayes, his Neigh is like the bidding of a Monarch, and his countenance enforces Homage.

Orleance. No more Cousin.

Dolph. Nay, the man hath no wit, that cannot from the rising of the Larke to the lodging of the Lambe, varie deserued prayse on my Palfray: it is a Theame as fluent as the Sea: Turne the Sands into eloquent tongues, and my Horse is argument for them all: 'tis a subiect for a Soueraigne to reason on, and for a Soueraignes Soueraigne to ride on: And for the World, familiar to vs, and vnknowne, to lay apart their particular Functions, and wonder at him, I once writ a Sonnet in his prayse, and began thus, *Wonder of Nature.*

Orleance. I haue heard a Sonnet begin so to ones Mistresse.

Dolph. Then did they imitate that which I compos'd to my Courser, for my Horse is my Mistresse.

Orleance. Your Mistresse beares well.

Dolph. Me well, which is the prescript prayse and perfection of a good and particular Mistresse.

Const. Nay, for me thought yesterday your Mistresse shrewdly shooke your back.

Dolph. So perhaps did yours.

Const. Mine was not bridled.

Dolph. O then belike she was old and gentle, and you rode like a Kerne of Ireland, your French Hose off, and in your strait Strossers.

Const. You haue good iudgement in Horsemanship.

Dolph. Be warn'd by me then: they that ride so, and ride not warily, fall into foule Boggs: I had rather haue my Horse to my Mistresse.

Const. I had as liue haue my Mistresse a Iade.

Dolph. I tell thee Constable, my Mistresse weares his owne hayre.

Const. I could make as true a boast as that, if I had a Sow to my Mistresse.

Dolph. *Le chien est retourne a son propre vemissement est la leuye lauee au bourbier:* thou mak'st vse of any thing.

Const. Yet doe I not vse my Horse for my Mistresse, or any such Prouerbe, so little kin to the purpose.

Ramb. My Lord Constable, the Armour that I saw in your Tent to night, are those Starres or Sunnes vpon it?

Const. Starres my Lord.

Dolph. Some of them will fall to morrow, I hope.

Const: And yet my Sky shall not want.

Dolph. That may be, for you beare a many superfluously, and 'twere more honor some were away.

Const. Eu'n as your Horse beares your prayses, who would trot as well, were some of your bragges dismounted.

Dolph. Would I were able to loade him with his desert. Will it neuer be day? I will trot to morrow a mile, and my way shall be paued with English Faces.

Const. I will not say so, for feare I should be fac't out of my way: but I would it were morning, for I would faine be about the eares of the English.

Ramb. Who will goe to Hazard with me for twentie Prisoners?

Const. You must first goe your selfe to hazard, ere you haue them.

Dolph. Tis Mid-night, Ile goe arme my selfe. *Exit.*

Orleance. The Dolphin longs for morning.

Ramb He longs to eate the English.

Const. I thinke he will eate all he kills.

Orleance. By the white Hand of my Lady, hee's a gallant Prince.

Const. Sweare by her Foot, that she may tread out the Oath.

Orleance. He is simply the most actiue Gentleman of France.

Const. Doing is actiuitie, and he will still be doing.

Orleance. He neuer did harme, that I heard of.

Const. Nor will doe none to morrow: hee will keepe that good name still.

Orleance. I know him to be valiant.

Const. I was told that, by one that knowes him better then you.

Orleance. What's hee?

Const. Marry hee told me so himselfe, and hee sayd hee car'd not who knew it.

Orleance. Hee needes not, it is no hidden vertue in him.

Const. By my faith Sir, but it is: neuer any body saw it, but his Lacquey: 'tis a hooded valour, and when it appeares, it will bate.

Orleance. Ill will neuer sayd well.

Const. I will cap that Prouerbe with, There is flatterie in friendship.

Orleance. And I will take vp that with, Giue the Deuill his due.

Const. Well plac't: there stands your friend for the Deuill: haue at the very eye of that Prouerbe with, A Pox of the Deuill.

Orleance. You are the better at Prouerbs, by how much a Fooles Bolt is soone shot.

Const. You haue shot ouer.

Orleance. 'Tis not the first time you were ouer-shot.

Enter a Messenger.

Mess. My Lord high Constable, the English lye within fifteene hundred paces of your Tents.

Const. Who hath measur'd the ground?

Mess. The Lord *Grandpree.*

Const. A valiant and most expert Gentleman. Would it were day? Alas poore *Harry* of England: hee longs not for the Dawning, as wee doe.

Orleance What a wretched and peeuish fellow is this King of England, to mope with his fat-brain'd followers so farre out of his knowledge.

Const. If the English had any apprehension, they would runne away.

Orleance. That they lack: for if their heads had any intellectuall Armour, they could neuer weare such heauie Head-pieces.

Ramb. That Iland of England breedes very valiant Creatures; their Mastiffes are of vnmatchable courage.

Orleance. Foolish Curres, that runne winking into the mouth of a Russian Beare, and haue their heads crusht like rotten Apples: you may as well say, that's a valiant Flea, that dare eate his breakefast on the Lippe of a Lyon.

Const. Iust, iust: and the men doe sympathize with the Mastiffes, in robustious and rough comming on, leauing their Wits with their Wiues: and then giue them great Meales of Beefe, and Iron and Steele; they will eate like Wolues, and fight like Deuils.

Orleance. I.

Orleance. I, but these English are shrowdly out of Beefe.

Const. Then shall we finde to morrow, they haue only stomackes to eate, and none to fight. Now is it time to arme : come, shall we about it ?

Orleance. It is now two a Clock: but let me see, by ten
Wee shall haue each a hundred English men. *Exeunt.*

Actus Tertius

Chorus.

Now entertaine coniecture of a time,
When creeping Murmure and the poring Darke
Fills the wide Vessell of the Vniuerse.
From Camp to Camp, through the foule Womb of Night
The Humme of eyther Army stilly sounds;
That the fixe Centinels almost receiue
The secret Whispers of each others Watch.
Fire answers fire, and through their paly flames
Each Battaile sees the others vmber'd face.
Steed threatens Steed, in high and boastfull Neighs
Piercing the Nights dull Eare : and from the Tents,
The Armourers accomplishing the Knights,
With busie Hammers closing Riuets vp,
Giue dreadfull note of preparation.
The Countrey Cocks doe crow, the Clocks doe towle:
And the third howre of drowsie Morning nam'd,
Prowd of their Numbers, and secure in Soule,
The confident and ouer-lustie French,
Doe the low-rated English play at Dice;
And chide the creeple-tardy-gated Night,
Who like a foule and ougly Witch doth limpe
So tediously away. The poore condemned English,
Like Sacrifices, by their watchfull Fires
Sit patiently, and inly ruminate
The Mornings danger : and their gesture sad,
Inuesting lanke-leane Cheekes, and Warre-worne Coats,
Presented them vnto the gazing Moone
So many horride Ghosts. O now, who will behold
The Royall Captaine of this ruin'd Band
Walking from Watch to Watch, from Tent to Tent;
Let him cry, Prayse and Glory on his head :
For forth he goes, and visits all his Hoast,
Bids them good morrow with a modest Smyle,
And calls them Brothers, Friends, and Countreymen.
Vpon his Royall Face there is no note,
How dread an Army hath enrounded him;
Nor doth he dedicate one iot of Colour
Vnto the wearie and all-watched Night:
But freshly lookes, and ouer-beares Attaint,
With chearefull semblance, and sweet Maiestie:
That euery Wretch, pining and pale before,
Beholding him, plucks comfort from his Lookes.
A Largesse vniuersall, like the Sunne,
His liberall Eye doth giue to euery one,
Thawing cold feare, that meane and gentle all
Behold, as may vnworthinesse define.
A little touch of *Harry* in the Night,
And so our Scene must to the Battaile flye:
Where, O for pitty, we shall much disgrace,
With foure or fiue most vile and ragged foyles,
(Right ill dispos'd, in brawle ridiculous)
The Name of Agincourt : Yet sit and see,
Minding true things, by what their Mock'ries bee.
Exit.

Enter the King, Bedford, and Gloucester.

King. *Gloster*, 'tis true that we are in great danger,
The greater therefore should our Courage be.
God morrow Brother *Bedford* : God Almightie,
There is some soule of goodnesse in things euill,
Would men obseruingly distill it out.
For our bad Neighbour makes vs early stirrers,
Which is both healthfull, and good husbandry.
Besides, they are our outward Consciences,
And Preachers to vs all; admonishing,
That we should dresse vs fairely for our end.
Thus may we gather Honey from the Weed,
And make a Morall of the Diuell himselfe.

Enter Erpingham.

Good morrow old Sir *Thomas Erpingham* :
A good soft Pillow for that good white Head,
Were better then a churlish turfe of France.

Erpmg. Not so my Liege, this Lodging likes me better,
Since I may say, now lye I like a King.

King. 'Tis good for men to loue their present paines,
Vpon example, so the Spirit is eased :
And when the Mind is quickned, out of doubt
The Organs, though defunct and dead before,
Breake vp their drowsie Graue and newly moue
With casted slough, and fresh legeritie.
Lend me thy Cloake Sir *Thomas* : Brothers both,
Commend me to the Princes in our Campe;
Doe my good morrow to them, and anon
Desire them all to my Pauilion.

Gloster. We shall, my Liege.

Erping. Shall I attend your Grace?

King. No, my good Knight :
Goe with my Brothers to my Lords of England:
I and my Bosome must debate a while,
And then I would no other company.

Erping. The Lord in Heauen blesse thee, Noble Harry. *Exeunt.*

King. God a mercy old Heart, thou speak'st cheare-fully. *Enter Pistoll.*

Pist. Che vous la?

King. A friend.

Pist. Discusse vnto me, art thou Officer, or art thou base, common, and popular?

King. I am a Gentleman of a Company.

Pist. Trayl'st thou the puissant Pyke?

King. Euen so: what are you?

Pist. As good a Gentleman as the Emperor.

King. Then you are a better then the King.

Pist. The King's a Bawcock, and a Heart of Gold, a Lad of Life, an Impe of Fame, of Parents good, of Fist most valiant : I kisse his durtie shooe, and from heart-string I loue the louely Bully. What is thy Name?

King. Harry le Roy.

Pist. Le Roy? a Cornish Name: art thou of Cornish Crew?

King. No, I am a Welchman.

Pist. Know'st thou *Fluellen*?

King. Yes.

Pist. Tell him Ile knock his Leeke about his Pate vpon S. *Dauies* day.

King. Doe not you weare your Dagger in your Cappe that day, least he knock that about yours.

i 2 *Pist.* Art

Pist. Art thou his friend?

King. And his Kinsman too.

Pist. The *Figo* for thee then.

King. I thanke you: God be with you.

Pist. My name is *Pistol* call'd. *Exit.*

King. It sorts well with your fiercenesse.

Manet King.

Enter Fluellen and Gower.

Gower. Captaine *Fluellen.*

Flu. 'So, in the Name of Iesu Christ, speake fewer: it is the greatest admiration in the vniuersall World, when the true and aunchient Prerogatifes and Lawes of the Warres is not kept: if you would take the paines but to examine the Warres of *Pompey* the Great, you shall finde, I warrant you, that there is no tiddle tadle nor pibble bable in *Pompeyes* Campe: I warrant you, you shall finde the Ceremonies of the Warres, and the Cares of it, and the Formes of it, and the Sobrietie of it, and the Modestie of it, to be otherwise.

Gower. Why the Enemie is lowd, you heare him all Night.

Flu. If the Enemie is an Asse and a Foole, and a prating Coxcombe; is it meet, thinke you, that wee should also, looke you, be an Asse and a Foole, and a prating Coxcombe, in your owne conscience now?

Gow. I will speake lower.

Flu. I pray you, and beseech you, that you will. *Exit.*

King. Though it appeare a little out of fashion,
There is much care and valour in this Welchman.

Enter three Souldiers, Iohn Bates, Alexander Court, and Michael Williams.

Court. Brother *Iohn Bates*, is not that the Morning which breakes yonder?

Bates. I thinke it be: but wee haue no great cause to desire the approach of day.

Williams. Wee see yonder the beginning of the day, but I thinke wee shall neuer see the end of it. Who goes there?

King. A Friend.

Williams. Vnder what Captaine serue you?

King. Vnder Sir *Iohn Erpingham.*

Williams. A good old Commander, and a most kinde Gentleman: I pray you, what thinkes he of our estate?

King. Euen as men wracke vpon a Sand, that looke to be washt off the next Tyde.

Bates. He hath not told his thought to the King?

King. No: nor it is not meet he should: for though I speake it to you, I thinke the King is but a man, as I am: the Violet smells to him, as it doth to me; the Element shewes to him, as it doth to me; all his Sences haue but humane Conditions: his Ceremonies layd by, in his Nakednesse he appeares but a man; and though his affections are higher mounted then ours, yet when they stoupe, they stoupe with the like wing: therefore, when he sees reason of feares, as we doe; his feares, out of doubt, be of the same rellish as ours are: yet in reason, no man should possesse him with any appearance of feare; least hee, by shewing it, should dis-hearten his Army.

Bates. He may shew what outward courage he will: but I beleeue, as cold a Night as 'tis, hee could wish himselfe in Thames vp to the Neck; and so I would he were, and I by him, at all aduentures, so we were quit here.

King. By my troth, I will speake my conscience of the King: I thinke hee would not wish himselfe any where, but where hee is.

Bates. Then I would he were here alone; so should he be sure to be ransomed, and a many poore mens liues saued.

King. I dare say, you loue him not so ill, to wish him here alone: howsoeuer you speake this to feele other mens minds, me thinks I could not dye any where so contented, as in the Kings company; his Cause being iust, and his Quarrell honorable.

Williams. That's more then we know.

Bates. I, or more then wee should seeke after; for wee know enough, if wee know wee are the Kings Subiects: if his Cause be wrong, our obedience to the King wipes the Cryme of it out of vs.

Williams. But if the Cause be not good, the King himselfe hath a heauie Reckoning to make, when all those Legges, and Armes, and Heads, chopt off in a Battaile, shall ioyne together at the latter day, and cry all, Wee dyed at such a place, some swearing, some crying for a Surgean; some vpon their Wiues, left poore behind them; some vpon the Debts they owe, some vpon their Children rawly left: I am afear'd, there are few dye well, that dye in a Battaile: for how can they charitably dispose of any thing, when Blood is their argument? Now, if these men doe not dye well, it will be a black matter for the King, that led them to it; who to disobey, were against all proportion of subiection.

King. So, if a Sonne that is by his Father sent about Merchandize, doe sinfully miscarry vpon the Sea; the imputation of his wickednesse, by your rule, should be imposed vpon his Father that sent him: or if a Seruant, vnder his Masters command, transporting a summe of Money, be assayled by Robbers, and dye in many irreconcil'd Iniquities; you may call the businesse of the Master the author of the Seruants damnation: but this is not so: The King is not bound to answer the particular endings of his Souldiers, the Father of his Sonne, nor the Master of his Seruant; for they purpose not their death, when they purpose their seruices. Besides, there is no King, be his Cause neuer so spotlesse, if it come to the arbitrement of Swords, can trye it out with all vnspotted Souldiers: some (peraduenture) haue on them the guilt of premeditated and contriued Murther; some, of beguiling Virgins with the broken Seales of Periurie; some, making the Warres their Bulwarke, that haue before gored the gentle Bosome of Peace with Pillage and Robberie. Now, if these men haue defeated the Law, and outrunne Natiue punishment; though they can out-strip men, they haue no wings to flye from God. Warre is his Beadle, Warre is his Vengeance: so that here men are punisht, for before breach of the Kings Lawes, in now the Kings Quarrell: where they feared the death, they haue borne life away; and where they would bee safe, they perish. Then if they dye vnprouided, no more is the King guiltie of their damnation, then hee was before guiltie of those Impieties, for the which they are now visited. Euery Subiects Dutie is the Kings, but euery Subiects Soule is his owne. Therefore should euery Souldier in the Warres doe as euery sicke man in his Bed, wash euery Moth out of his Conscience: and dying so, Death is to him aduantage; or not dying, the time was blessedly lost, wherein such preparation was gayned: and in him that escapes, it were not sinne to thinke, that making God so free an offer, he let him outliue that day, to see his Greatnesse, and to teach others how they should prepare.

Will. 'Tis

Will. 'Tis certaine, euery man that dyes ill, the ill vpon his owne head, the King is not to answer it.

Bates. I doe not desire hee should answer for me, and yet I determine to fight lustily for him.

King. I my selfe heard the King say he would not be ransom'd.

Will. I, hee said so, to make vs fight chearefully: but when our throats are cut, hee may be ransom'd, and wee ne're the wiser.

King. If I liue to see it, I will neuer trust his word after.

Will. You pay him then: that's a perillous shot out of an Elder Gunne, that a poore and a priuate displeasure can doe against a Monarch: you may as well goe about to turne the Sunne to yce, with fanning in his face with a Peacocks feather: You'le neuer trust his word after; come, 'tis a foolish saying.

King. Your reproofe is something too round, I should be angry with you, if the time were conuenient.

Will. Let it bee a Quarrell betweene vs, if you liue.

King. I embrace it.

Will. How shall I know thee againe?

King. Giue me any Gage of thine, and I will weare it in my Bonnet: Then if euer thou dar'st acknowledge it, I will make it my Quarrell.

Will. Heere's my Gloue: Giue mee another of thine.

King. There.

Will. This will I also weare in my Cap: if euer thou come to me, and say, after to morrow, This is my Gloue, by this Hand I will take thee a box on the eare.

King. If euer I liue to see it, I will challenge it.

Will. Thou dar'st as well be hang'd.

King. Well, I will doe it, though I take thee in the Kings companie.

Will. Keepe thy word: fare thee well.

Bates. Be friends you English fooles, be friends, wee haue French Quarrels enow, if you could tell how to reckon. *Exit Souldiers.*

King. Indeede the French may lay twentie French Crownes to one, they will beat vs, for they beare them on their shoulders: but it is no English Treason to cut French Crownes, and to morrow the King himselfe will be a Clipper.
Vpon the King, let vs our Liues, our Soules,
Our Debts, our carefull Wiues,
Our Children, and our Sinnes, lay on the King:
We must beare all.
O hard Condition, Twin-borne with Greatnesse,
Subiect to the breath of euery foole, whose sence
No more can feele, but his owne wringing.
What infinite hearts-ease must Kings neglect,
That priuate men enioy?
And what haue Kings, that Priuates haue not too,
Saue Ceremonie, saue generall Ceremonie?
And what art thou, thou Idoll Ceremonie?
What kind of God art thou? that suffer'st more
Of mortall griefes, then doe thy worshippers.
What are thy Rents? what are thy Commings in?
O Ceremonie, shew me but thy worth.
What? is thy Soule of Odoration?
Art thou ought else but Place, Degree, and Forme,
Creating awe and feare in other men?
Wherein thou art lesse happy, being fear'd,
Then they in fearing.
What drink'st thou oft, in stead of Homage sweet,
But poyson'd flatterie? O, be sick, great Greatnesse,
And bid thy Ceremonie giue thee cure.
Thinks thou the fierie Feuer will goe out
With Titles blowne from Adulation?
Will it giue place to flexure and low bending?
Canst thou, when thou command'st the beggers knee,
Command the health of it? No, thou prowd Dreame,
That play'st so subtilly with a Kings Repose.
I am a King that find thee: and I know,
'Tis not the Balme, the Scepter, and the Ball,
The Sword, the Mase, the Crowne Imperiall,
The enter-tissued Robe of Gold and Pearle,
The farsed Title running 'fore the King,
The Throne he sits on: nor the Tyde of Pompe,
That beates vpon the high shore of this World:
No, not all these, thrice-gorgeous Ceremonie;
Not all these, lay'd in Bed Maiesticall,
Can sleepe so soundly, as the wretched Slaue:
Who with a body fill'd, and vacant mind,
Gets him to rest, cram'd with distressefull bread,
Neuer sees horride Night, the Child of Hell:
But like a Lacquey, from the Rise to Set,
Sweates in the eye of *Phebus*; and all Night
Sleepes in *Elizium*: next day after dawne,
Doth rise and helpe *Hiperio* to his Horse,
And followes so the euer-running yeere
With profitable labour to his Graue:
And but for Ceremonie, such a Wretch,
Winding vp Dayes with toyle, and Nights with sleepe,
Had the fore-hand and vantage of a King.
The Slaue, a Member of the Countreyes peace,
Enioyes it; but in grosse braine little wots,
What watch the King keepes, to maintaine the peace;
Whose howres, the Pesant best aduantages.

Enter Erpingham.

Erp. My Lord, your Nobles iealous of your absence,
Seeke through your Campe to find you.

King. Good old Knight, collect them all together
At my Tent: Ile be before thee.

Erp. I shall doo't, my Lord. *Exit.*

King. O God of Battailes, steele my Souldiers hearts,
Possesse them not with feare: Take from them now
The sence of reckning of th'opposed numbers:
Pluck their hearts from them. Not to day, O Lord,
O not to day, thinke not vpon the fault
My Father made, in compassing the Crowne.
I *Richards* body haue interred new,
And on it haue bestowed more contrite teares,
Then from it issued forced drops of blood.
Fiue hundred poore I haue in yeerely pay,
Who twice a day their wither'd hands hold vp
Toward Heauen, to pardon blood:
And I haue built two Chauntries,
Where the sad and solemne Priests sing still
For *Richards* Soule. More will I doe:
Though all that I can doe, is nothing worth;
Since that my Penitence comes after all,
Imploring pardon.

Enter Gloucester.

Glou. My Liege.

King. My Brother *Gloucesters* voyce? I:
I know thy errand, I will goe with thee:
The day, my friend, and all things stay for me.

Exeunt.

i 3 Enter

Enter the Dolphin, Orleance, Ramburs, and Beaumont.

Orleance. The Sunne doth gild our Armour vp, my Lords.

Dolph. *Monte Cheual:* My Horſe, *Verlot Lacquay:* Ha.

Orleance. Oh braue Spirit.

Dolph. *Via les ewes & terre.*

Orleance. *Rien puis le air & feu.*

Dolph. *Cein,* Couſin *Orleance.* *Enter Conſtable.*

Now my Lord Conſtable?

Conſt. Hearke how our Steedes, for preſent Seruice neigh.

Dolph. Mount them, and make inciſion in their Hides,
That their hot blood may ſpin in Engliſh eyes,
And doubt them with ſuperfluous courage: ha.

Ram. What, wil you haue them weep our Horſes blood?
How ſhall we then behold their naturall teares?

Enter Meſſenger.

Meſſeng. The Engliſh are embattail'd, you French Peeres.

Conſt. To Horſe you gallant Princes, ſtraight to Horſe.
Doe but behold yond poore and ſtarued Band,
And your faire ſhew ſhall ſuck away their Soules,
Leauing them but the ſhales and huskes of men.
There is not worke enough for all our hands,
Scarce blood enough in all their ſickly Veines,
To giue each naked Curtleax a ſtayne,
That our French Gallants ſhall to day draw out,
And ſheath for lack of ſport. Let vs but blow on them,
The vapour of our Valour will o're-turne them
'Tis poſitiue againſt all exceptions, Lords,
That our ſuperfluous Lacquies, and our Peſants,
Who in vnneceſſarie action ſwarme
About our Squares of Battaile, were enow
To purge this field of ſuch a hilding Foe;
Though we vpon this Mountaines Baſis by,
Tooke ſtand for idle ſpeculation:
But that our Honours muſt not. What's to ſay?
A very little little let vs doe,
And all is done: then let the Trumpets ſound
The Tucket Sonuance, and the Note to mount:
For our approach ſhall ſo much dare the field,
That England ſhall couch downe in feare, and yeeld.

Enter Graundpree.

Grandpree. Why do you ſtay ſo long, my Lords of France?
Yond Iland Carrions, deſperate of their bones,
Ill-fauoredly become the Morning field:
Their ragged Curtaines poorely are let looſe,
And our Ayre ſhakes them paſſing ſcornefully.
Bigge *Mars* ſeemes banqu'rout in their begger'd Hoaſt,
And faintly through a ruſtie Beuer peepes.
The Horſemen ſit like fixed Candleſticks,
With Torch-ſtaues in their hand: and their poore Iades
Lob downe their heads, dropping the hides and hips:
The gumme downe roping from their pale-dead eyes,
And in their pale dull mouthes the Iymold Bitt
Lyes foule with chaw'd-graſſe, ſtill and motionleſſe.
And their executors, the knauiſh Crowes,
Flye o're them all, impatient for their howre.
Deſcription cannot ſute it ſelfe in words,
To demonſtrate the Life of ſuch a Battaile,
In life ſo liueleſſe, as it ſhewes it ſelfe.

Conſt. They haue ſaid their prayers,
And they ſtay for death.

Dolph. Shall we goe ſend them Dinners, and freſh Sutes,
And giue their faſting Horſes Prouender
And after fight with them?

Conſt. I ſtay but for my Guard: on
To the field, I will the Banner from a Trumpet take,
And vſe it for my haſte. Come, come away,
The Sunne is high, and we out-weare the day. *Exeunt.*

Enter Glouceſter, Bedford, Exeter, Erpingham with all his Hoaſt: Salisbury, and Weſtmerland.

Glouc. Where is the King?

Bedf. The King himſelfe is rode to view their Battaile.

Weſt. Of fighting men they haue full threeſcore thouſand.

Exe. There's fiue to one, beſides they all are freſh.

Salisb. Gods Arme ſtrike with vs, 'tis a fearefull oddes.
God buy' you Princes all; Ile to my Charge:
If we no more meet, till we meet in Heauen;
Then ioyfully, my Noble Lord of Bedford,
My deare Lord Glouceſter, and my good Lord Exeter,
And my kind Kinſman, Warriors all, adieu.

Bedf. Farwell good *Salisbury*, & good luck go with thee:
And yet I doe thee wrong, to mind thee of it,
For thou art fram'd of the firme truth of valour.

Exe. Farwell kind Lord: fight valiantly to day.

Bedf. He is as full of Valour as of Kindneſſe,
Princely in both.

Enter the King.

Weſt. O that we now had here
But one ten thouſand of thoſe men in England,
That doe no worke to day.

King. What's he that wiſhes ſo?
My Couſin *Weſtmerland*. No, my faire Couſin:
If we are markt to dye, we are enow
To doe our Countrey loſſe: and if to liue,
The fewer men, the greater ſhare of honour.
Gods will, I pray thee wiſh not one man more.
By *Ioue*, I am not couetous for Gold,
Nor care I who doth feed vpon my coſt:
It yernes me not, if men my Garments weare;
Such outward things dwell not in my deſires.
But if it be a ſinne to couet Honor,
I am the moſt offending Soule aliue.
No 'faith, my Couze, wiſh not a man from England:
Gods peace, I would not looſe ſo great an Honor,
As one man more me thinkes would ſhare from me,
For the beſt hope I haue. O, doe not wiſh one more:
Rather proclaime it (*Weſtmerland*) through my Hoaſt,
That he which hath no ſtomack to this fight,
Let him depart, his Paſport ſhall be made,
And Crownes for Conuoy put into his Purſe:
We would not dye in that mans companie,
That feares his fellowſhip, to dye with vs
This day is call'd the Feaſt of *Criſpian:*
He that out-liues this day, and comes ſafe home,
Will ſtand a tip-toe when this day is named,
And rowſe him at the Name of *Criſpian.*
He that ſhall ſee this day, and liue old age,
Will yeerely on the Vigil feaſt his neighbours,
And ſay, to morrow is Saint *Criſpian.*
Then will he ſtrip his ſleeue, and ſhew his skarres
Old men forget; yet all ſhall be forgot:
But hee'le remember, with aduantages,
What feats he did that day. Then ſhall our Names,
Familiar in his mouth as houſehold words,

Harry

Harry the King, *Bedford* and *Exeter*,
Warwick and *Talbot*, *Saliſbury* and *Glouceſter*,
Be in their flowing Cups freſhly remembred.
This ſtory ſhall the good man teach his ſonne:
And *Criſpine Criſpian* ſhall ne're goe by,
From this day to the ending of the World,
But we in it ſhall be remembred;
We few, we happy few, we band of brothers:
For he to day that ſheds his blood with me,
Shall be my brother: be he ne're ſo vile,
This day ſhall gentle his Condition.
And Gentlemen in England, now a bed,
Shall thinke themſelues accurſt they were not here,
And hold their Manhoods cheape, whiles any ſpeakes,
That fought with vs vpon Saint *Criſpines* day.

Enter Saliſbury.

Sal. My Soueraign Lord, beſtow your ſelfe with ſpeed:
The French are brauely in their battailes ſet,
And will with all expedience charge on vs.

King. All things are ready, if our minds be ſo.

Weſt. Periſh the man, whoſe mind is backward now.

King. Thou do'ſt not wiſh more helpe from England,
Couze?

Weſt. Gods will, my Liege, would you and I alone,
Without more helpe, could fight this Royall battaile.

King. Why now thou haſt vnwiſht fiue thouſand men:
Which likes me better, then to wiſh vs one.
You know your places: God be with you all.

Tucket. Enter Montioy.

Mont. Once more I come to know of thee King *Harry*,
If for thy Ranſome thou wilt now compound,
Before thy moſt aſſured Ouerthrow:
For certainly, thou art ſo neere the Gulfe,
Thou needs muſt be englutted. Beſides, in mercy
The Conſtable deſires thee, thou wilt mind
Thy followers of Repentance; that their Soules
May make a peacefull and a ſweet retyre
From off theſe fields: where (wretches) their poore bodies
Muſt lye and feſter.

King. Who hath ſent thee now?

Mont. The Conſtable of France.

King. I pray thee beare my former Anſwer back:
Bid them atchieue me, and then ſell my bones.
Good God, why ſhould they mock poore fellowes thus?
The man that once did ſell the Lyons skin
While the beaſt liu'd, was kill'd with hunting him.
A many of our bodyes ſhall no doubt
Find Natiue Graues: vpon the which, I truſt
Shall witneſſe liue in Braſſe of this dayes worke.
And thoſe that leaue their valiant bones in France,
Dying like men, though buryed in your Dunghills,
They ſhall be fam'd: for there the Sun ſhall greet them,
And draw their honors reeking vp to Heauen,
Leauing their earthly parts to choake your Clyme,
The ſmell whereof ſhall breed a Plague in France.
Marke then abounding valour in our Engliſh:
That being dead, like to the bullets craſing,
Breake out into a ſecond courſe of miſchiefe,
Killing in relapſe of Mortalitie.
Let me ſpeake prowdly: Tell the Conſtable,
We are but Warriors for the working day:
Our Gayneſſe and our Gilt are all beſmyrcht
With raynie Marching in the painefull field.
There's not a piece of feather in our Hoaſt:
Good argument (I hope) we will not flye:
And time hath worne vs into ſlouenrie.
But by the Maſſe, our hearts are in the trim:
And my poore Souldiers tell me, yet ere Night,
They'le be in freſher Robes, or they will pluck
The gay new Coats o're the French Souldiers heads,
And turne them out of ſeruice. If they doe this,
As if God pleaſe, they ſhall; my Ranſome then
Will ſoone be leuyed.
Herauld, ſaue thou thy labour:
Come thou no more for Ranſome, gentle Herauld,
They ſhall haue none, I ſweare, but theſe my ioynts:
Which if they haue, as I will leaue vm them,
Shall yeeld them little, tell the Conſtable.

Mont. I ſhall, King *Harry*. And ſo fare thee well:
Thou neuer ſhalt heare Herauld any more. *Exit.*

King. I feare thou wilt once more come againe for a Ranſome.

Enter Yorke.

Yorke. My Lord, moſt humbly on my knee I begge
The leading of the Vaward.

King. Take it, braue *Yorke*.
Now Souldiers march away,
And how thou pleaſeſt God, diſpoſe the day. *Exeunt.*

Alarum. Excurſions.

Enter Piſtoll, French Souldier, Boy.

Piſt. Yeeld Curre.

French. *Ie penſe que vous eſtes le Gentilhome de bon qualitee.*

Piſt. Qualtitie calmie custure me. Art thou a Gentleman? What is thy Name? diſcuſſe.

French. *O Seigneur Dieu.*

Piſt. O Signieur Dewe ſhould be a Gentleman: perpend my words O Signieur Dewe, and marke: O Signieur Dewe, thou dyeſt on point of Fox, except O Signieur thou doe giue to me egregious Ranſome.

French. *O prennes miſericordie aye pitez de moy.*

Piſt. Moy ſhall not ſerue, I will haue fortie Moyes: for I will fetch thy rymme out at thy Throat, in droppes of Crimſon blood.

French. *Eſt il impoſſible d'eſchapper le force de ton bras.*

Piſt. Braſſe, Curre? thou damned and luxurious Mountaine Goat, offer'ſt me Braſſe?

French. *O perdonne moy.*

Piſt. Say'ſt thou me ſo? is that a Tonne of Moyes? Come hither boy, aske me this ſlaue in French what is his Name.

Boy. *Eſcoute comment eſtes vous appelle?*

French. *Mounſieur le Fer.*

Boy. He ſayes his Name is M. Fer.

Piſt. M. Fer: Ile fer him, and firke him, and ferret him: diſcuſſe the ſame in French vnto him.

Boy. I doe not know the French for fer, and ferret, and firke.

Piſt. Bid him prepare, for I will cut his throat.

French. *Que dit il Mounſieur?*

Boy. *Il me commande a vous dire que vous faite vous preſt, car ce ſoldat icy eſt diſpoſee tout aſture de couppes voſtre gorge.*

Piſt. Owy, cuppele gorge permafoy peſant, vnleſſe thou giue me Crownes, braue Crownes; or mangled ſhalt thou be by this my Sword.

French. *O Ie vous ſupplie pour l'amour de Dieu: ma pardonner, Ie ſuis le Gentilhome de bon maiſon, garde ma vie, & Ie vous donneray deux cent eſcus.*

Piſt. What are his words?

Boy. He

Boy. He prayes you to saue his life, he is a Gentleman of a good house, and for his ransom he will giue you two hundred Crownes.

Pist. Tell him my fury shall abate, and I the Crownes will take.

Fren. *Petit Monsieur que dit il?*

Boy. *Encore qu'il et contra son Iurement, de pardonner aucune prisonner: neant-mons pour les escues que vous layt a promets, il est content a vous donnes le liberte le franchisement.*

Fre. *Sur mes genoux se vous donnes milles remercions, et Ie me estime heurex que Ie intombe, entre les main. d'vn Cheualier Ie pense le plus braue valiant et tres distinie signieur d'Angleterre.*

Pist. Expound vnto me boy.

Boy. He giues you vpon his knees a thousand thanks, and he esteemes himselfe happy, that he hath falne into the hands of one (as he thinkes) the most braue, valorous and thrice-worthy signeur of England.

Pist. As I sucke blood, I will some mercy shew. Follow mee.

Boy. *Saaue vous le grand Capitaine?* I did neuer know so full a voyce issue from so emptie a heart: but the saying is true, The empty vessel makes the greatest sound, *Bardolfe* and *Nym* had tenne times more valour, then this roaring diuell i'th olde play, that euerie one may payre his nayles with a woodden dagger, and they are both hang'd, and so would this be, if hee durst steale any thing aduenturously. I must stay with the Lackies with the luggage of our camp, the French might haue a good pray of vs, if he knew of it, for there is none to guard it but boyes. *Exit.*

Enter Constable, Orleance, Burbon, Dolphin, and Rambures.

Con. *O Diable.*

Orl. *O signeur le iour et perdia, toute et perdie.*

Dol. *Mor Dieu ma vie*, all is confounded all,
Reproach, and euerlasting shame
Sits mocking in our Plumes. *A short Alarum.*
O meschante Fortune, do not runne away.

Con. Why all our rankes are broke.

Dol. O perdurable shame, let's stab our selues:
Be these the wretches that we plaid at dice for?

Orl. Is this the King we sent too, for his ransome?

Bur. Shame, and eternall shame, nothing but shame,
Let vs dye in once more backe againe,
And he that will not follow *Burbon* now,
Let him go hence, and with his cap in hand
Like a base Pander hold the Chamber doore,
Whilst a base slaue, no gentler then my dogge,
His fairest daughter is contaminated.

Con. Disorder that hath spoyl'd vs, friend vs now,
Let vs on heapes go offer vp our liues.

Orl. We are enow yet liuing in the Field,
To smother vp the English in our throngs,
If any order might be thought vpon.

Bur. The diuell take Order now, Ile to the throng;
Let life be short, else shame will be too long. *Exit.*

Alarum. Enter the King and his trayne, with Prisoners.

King. Well haue we done, thrice-valiant Countrimen,
But all's not done, yet keepe the French the field.

Exe. The D. of York commends him to your Maiesty

King. Liues he good Vnckle: thrice within this houre
I saw him downe; thrice vp againe, and fighting,
From Helmet to the spurre, all blood he was.

Exe. In which array (braue Soldier) doth he lye,
Larding the plaine: and by his bloody side,
(Yoake-fellow to his honour-owing-wounds)
The Noble Earle of Suffolke also lyes.
Suffolke first dyed, and Yorke all hagled ouer
Comes to him, where in gore he lay insteeped,
And takes him by the Beard, kisses the gashes
That bloodily did yawne vpon his face.
He cryes aloud; Tarry my Cosin Suffolke,
My soule shall thine keepe company to heauen:
Tarry (sweet soule) for mine, then flye a-brest:
As in this glorious and well-foughten field
We kept together in our Chiualrie.
Vpon these words I came, and cheer'd him vp,
He smil'd me in the face, raught me his hand,
And with a feeble gripe, sayes: Deere my Lord,
Commend my seruice to my Soueraigne,
So did he turne, and ouer Suffolkes necke
He threw his wounded arme, and kist his lippes,
And so espous'd to death, with blood he seal'd
A Testament of Noble-ending-loue:
The prettie and sweet manner of it forc'd
Those waters from me, which I would haue stop'd,
But I had not so much of man in mee,
And all my mother came into mine eyes,
And gaue me vp to teares.

King. I blame you not,
For hearing this, I must perforce compound
With mixtfull eyes, or they will issue to. *Alarum*
But hearke, what new alarum is this same?
The French haue re-enforc'd their scatter'd men:
Then euery souldiour kill his Prisoners,
Giue the word through. *Exit*

Actus Quartus.

Enter Fluellen and Gower.

Flu. Kill the poyes and the luggage, 'Tis expressely against the Law of Armes, tis as arrant a peece of knauery marke you now, as can bee offert in your Conscience now, is it not?

Gow. Tis certaine, there's not a boy left aliue, and the Cowardly Rascalls that ranne from the battaile ha' done this slaughter: besides they haue burned and carried away all that was in the Kings Tent, wherefore the King most worthily hath caus'd euery soldiour to cut his prisoners throat. O 'tis a gallant King.

Flu. I, hee was porne at *Monmouth* Captaine *Gower*: What call you the Townes name where *Alexander* the pig was borne?

Gow. *Alexander* the Great.

Flu. Why I pray you, is not pig, great? The pig, or the great, or the mighty, or the huge, or the magnanimous, are all one reckonings, saue the phrase is a litle variations.

Gower. I thinke *Alexander* the Great was borne in *Macedon*, his Father was called *Phillip* of *Macedon*, as I take it.

Flu. I thinke it is in *Macedon* where *Alexander* is porne.

porne: I tell you Captaine, if you looke in the Maps of the Orld, I warrant you ſall finde in the compariſons betweene *Macedon* & *Monmouth*, that the ſituations looke you, is both alike. There is a Riuer in *Macedon*, & there is alſo moreouer a Riuer at *Monmouth*, it is call'd Wye at *Monmouth*: but it is out of my praines, what is the name of the other Riuer: but 'tis all one, tis alike as my fingers is to my fingers, and there is Salmons in both. If you marke *Alexanders* life well, *Harry of Monmouthes* life is come after it indifferent well, for there is figures in all things. *Alexander* God knowes, and you know, in his rages, and his furies, and his wraths, and his chollers, and his moodes, and his diſpleaſures, and his indignations, and alſo being a little intoxicates in his praines, did in his Ales and his angers (looke you) kill his beſt friend *Clytus*.

Gow. Our King is not like him in that, he neuer kill'd any of his friends.

Flu. It is not well done (marke you now) to take the tales out of my mouth, ere it is made and finiſhed. I ſpeak but in the figures, and compariſons of it: as *Alexander* kild his friend *Clytus*, being in his Ales and his Cuppes; ſo alſo *Harry Monmouth* being in his right wittes, and his good iudgements, turn'd away the fat Knight with the great belly doublet: he was full of ieſts, and gypes, and knaueries, and mockes, I haue forgot his name.

Gow. Sir *Iohn Falſtaffe*.

Flu. That is he: Ile tell you, there is good men porne at *Monmouth*.

Gow. Heere comes his Maieſty

Alarum. Enter King Harry and Burbon
with priſoners. Flouriſh.

King. I was not angry ſince I came to France,
Vntill this inſtant. Take a Trumpet Herald,
Ride thou vnto the Horſemen on yond hill:
If they will fight with vs, bid them come downe,
Or voyde the field: they do offend our ſight.
If they'l do neither, we will come to them,
And make them sker away, as ſwift as ſtones
Enforced from the old Aſſyrian ſlings:
Beſides, wee'l cut the throats of thoſe we haue,
And not a man of them that we ſhall take,
Shall taſte our mercy. Go and tell them ſo.

Enter Montioy.

Exe. Here comes the Herald of the French, my Liege
Glou. His eyes are humbler then they vs'd to be.
King. How now, what meanes this Herald? Know'ſt thou not,
That I haue fin'd theſe bones of mine for ranſome?
Com'ſt thou againe for ranſome?
Her. No great King:
I come to thee for charitable Licenſe,
That we may wander ore this bloody field,
To booke our dead, and then to bury them,
To ſort our Nobles from our common men.
For many of our Princes (woe the while)
Lye drown'd and ſoak'd in mercenary blood:
So do our vulgar drench their peaſant limbes
In blood of Princes, and with wounded ſteeds
Fret fet-locke deepe in gore, and with wilde rage
Yerke out their armed heeles at their dead maſters,
Killing them twice. O giue vs leaue great King,
To view the field in ſafety, and diſpoſe
Of their dead bodies.
Kin. I tell thee truly Herald,
I know not if the day be ours or no,
For yet a many of your horſemen peere,
And gallop ore the field.
Her. The day is yours.
Kin. Praiſed be God, and not our ſtrength for it:
What is this Caſtle call'd that ſtands hard by.
Her. They call it *Agincourt*.
King. Then call we this the field of *Agincourt*,
Fought on the day of *Criſpin Criſpianus*.

Flu. Your Grandfather of famous memory (an't pleaſe your Maieſty) and your great Vncle *Edward* the Placke Prince of Wales, as I haue read in the Chronicles, fought a moſt praue pattle here in France.

Kin. They did *Fluellen*.

Flu. Your Maieſty ſayes very true: If your Maieſties is remembred of it, the Welchmen did good ſeruice in a Garden where Leekes did grow, wearing Leekes in their *Monmouth* caps, which your Maieſty know to this houre is an honourable badge of the ſeruice: And I do beleeue your Maieſty takes no ſcorne to weare the Leeke vppon S. Tauies day.

King. I weare it for a memorable honor:
For I am Welch you know good Countriman.

Flu. All the water in Wye, cannot waſh your Maieſties Welſh plood out of your pody, I can tell you that: God pleſſe it, and preſerue it, as long as it pleaſes his Grace, and his Maieſty too.

Kin. Thankes good my Countrymen.

Flu. By Ieſhu, I am your Maieſties Countreyman, I care not who know it: I will confeſſe it to all the Orld, I need not to be aſhamed of your Maieſty, praiſed be God ſo long as your Maieſty is an honeſt man.

King. Good keepe me ſo.

Enter Williams.

Our Heralds go with him,
Bring me iuſt notice of the numbers dead
On both our parts. Call yonder fellow hither.

Exe. Souldier, you muſt come to the King.

Kin. Souldier, why wear'ſt thou that Gloue in thy Cappe?

Will: And't pleaſe your Maieſty, tis the gage of one that I ſhould fight withall, if he be aliue.

Kin. An Engliſhman?

Wil. And't pleaſe your Maieſty, a Raſcall that ſwagger'd with me laſt night: who if aliue, and euer dare to challenge this Gloue, I haue ſworne to take him a boxe a'th ere: or if I can ſee my Gloue in his cappe, which he ſwore as he was a Souldier he would weare (if aliue) I wil ſtrike it out ſoundly.

Kin. What thinke you Captaine *Fluellen*, is it fit this ſouldier keepe his oath.

Flu. Hee is a Crauen and a Villaine elſe, and't pleaſe your Maieſty in my conſcience.

King. It may bee, his enemy is a Gentleman of great ſort quite from the anſwer of his degree.

Flu. Though he be as good a Ientleman as the diuel is, as Lucifer and Belzebub himſelfe, it is neceſſary (looke your Grace) that he keepe his vow and his oath: If hee bee periur'd (ſee you now) his reputation is as arrant a villaine and a Iacke ſawce, as euer his blacke ſhoo trodd vpon Gods ground, and his earth, in my conſcience law

King. Then keepe thy vow ſirrah, when thou meet'ſt the fellow.

Wil. So, I wil my Liege, as I liue.

King. Who ſeru'ſt thou vnder?

Wil.

Will. Vnder Captaine *Gower*, my Liege.

Flu. *Gower* is a good Captaine, and is good knowledge and literatured in the Warres.

King. Call him hither to me, Souldier.

Will. I will my Liege. *Exit.*

King. Here *Fluellen*, weare thou this fauour for me, and sticke it in thy Cappe: when *Alanson* and my selfe were downe together, I pluckt this Gloue from his Helme: If any man challenge this, hee is a friend to *Alanson*, and an enemy to our Person; if thou encounter any such, apprehend him, and thou do'st me loue.

Flu. Your Grace doo's me as great Honors as can be desir'd in the hearts of his Subiects: I would faine see the man, that ha's but two legges, that shall find himselfe agreefd at this Gloue; that is all: but I would faine see it once, and please God of his grace that I might see.

King. Know'st thou *Gower?*

Flu. He is my deare friend, and please you.

King. Pray thee goe seeke him, and bring him to my Tent.

Flu. I will fetch him. *Exit.*

King. My Lord of *Warwick*, and my Brother *Gloster*,
Follow *Fluellen* closely at the heeles.
The Gloue which I haue giuen him for a fauour,
May haply purchase him a box a'th'eare.
It is the Souldiers: I by bargaine should
Weare it my selfe. Follow good Cousin *Warwick*:
If that the Souldier strike him, as I iudge
By his blunt bearing, he will keepe his word;
Some sodaine mischiefe may arise of it:
For I doe know *Fluellen* valiant,
And toucht with Choler, hot as Gunpowder,
And quickly will returne an iniurie.
Follow, and see there be no harme betweene them.
Goe you with me, Vnckle of Exeter. *Exeunt.*

Enter Gower and Williams.

Will. I warrant it is to Knight you, Captaine.

Enter Fluellen.

Flu. Gods will, and his pleasure, Captaine, I beseech you now, come apace to the King: there is more good toward you peraduenture, then is in your knowledge to dreame of.

Will. Sir, know you this Gloue?

Flu. Know the Gloue? I know the Gloue is a Gloue.

Will. I know this, and thus I challenge it. *Strikes him.*

Flu. 'Sblud, an arrant Traytor as anyes in the Vniuersall World, or in France, or in England.

Gower. How now Sir? you Villaine.

Will. Doe you thinke Ile be forsworne?

Flu. Stand away Captaine *Gower*, I will giue Treason his payment into plowes, I warrant you.

Will. I am no Traytor.

Flu. That's a Lye in thy Throat. I charge you in his Maiesties Name apprehend him, he's a friend of the Duke *Alansons.*

Enter Warwick and Glouchester.

Warw. How now, how now, what's the matter?

Flu. My Lord of Warwick, heere is, prayesed be God for it, a most contagious Treason come to light, looke you, as you shall desire in a Summers day. Heere is his Maiestie. *Enter King and Exeter.*

King. How now, what's the matter?

Flu. My Liege, heere is a Villaine, and a Traytor, that looke your Grace, ha's strooke the Gloue which your Maiestie is take out of the Helmet of *Alanson.*

Will. My Liege, this was my Gloue, here is the fellow of it: and he that I gaue it to in change, promis'd to weare it in his Cappe: I promis'd to strike him, if he did: I met this man with my Gloue in his Cappe, and I haue been as good as my word.

Flu. Your Maiestie heare now, sauing your Maiesties Manhood, what an arrant rascally, beggerly, lowsie Knaue it is: I hope your Maiestie is peare me testimonie and witnesse, and will auouchment, that this is the Gloue of *Alanson*, that your Maiestie is giue me, in your Conscience now.

King. Giue me thy Gloue Souldier;
Looke, heere is the fellow of it:
'Twas I indeed thou promised'st to strike,
And thou hast giuen me most bitter termes.

Flu. And please your Maiestie, let his Neck answere for it, if there is any Marshall Law in the World.

King. How canst thou make me satisfaction?

Will. All offences, my Lord, come from the heart: neuer came any from mine, that might offend your Maiestie.

King. It was our selfe thou didst abuse.

Will. Your Maiestie came not like your selfe: you appear'd to me but as a common man; witnesse the Night, your Garments, your Lowlinesse: and what your Highnesse suffer'd vnder that shape, I beseech you take it for your owne fault, and not mine: for had you beene as I tooke you for, I made no offence; therefore I beseech your Highnesse pardon me.

King. Here Vnckle *Exeter*, fill this Gloue with Crownes,
And giue it to this fellow. Keepe it fellow,
And weare it for an Honor in thy Cappe,
Till I doe challenge it. Giue him the Crownes:
And Captaine, you must needs be friends with him.

Flu. By this Day and this Light, the fellow ha's mettell enough in his belly: Hold, there is twelue-pence for you, and I pray you to serue God, and keepe you out of prawles and prabbles, and quarrels and dissentions, and I warrant you it is the better for you.

Will. I will none of your Money.

Flu. It is with a good will: I can tell you it will serue you to mend your shooes: come, wherefore should you be so pashfull, your shooes is not so good: 'tis a good silling I warrant you, or I will change it.

Enter Herauld.

King. Now Herauld, are the dead numbred?

Herald. Heere is the number of the slaught'red French.

King. What Prisoners of good sort are taken, Vnckle?

Exe. *Charles* Duke of Orleance, Nephew to the King,
Iohn Duke of Burbon, and Lord *Bonchiquald*:
Of other Lords and Barons, Knights and Squires,
Full fifteene hundred, besides common men.

King. This Note doth tell me of ten thousand French
That in the field lye slaine: of Princes in this number,
And Nobles bearing Banners, there lye dead
One hundred twentie six: added to these,
Of Knights, Esquires, and gallant Gentlemen,
Eight thousand and foure hundred: of the which,
Fiue hundred were but yesterday dubb'd Knights.
So that in these ten thousand they haue lost,
There are but sixteene hundred Mercenaries:
The rest are Princes, Barons, Lords, Knights, Squires,
And

And Gentlemen of bloud and qualitie.
The Names of those their Nobles that lye dead :
Charles Delabreth, High Constable of France,
Iaques of Chatilion, Admirall of France,
The Master of the Crosse-bowes, Lord *Rambures*,
Great Master of France, the braue Sir *Guichard Dolphin*,
Iohn Duke of Alanson, *Anthonie* Duke of Brabant,
The Brother to the Duke of Burgundie,
And *Edward* Duke of Barr : of lustie Earles,
Grandpree and *Roussie*, *Fauconbridge* and *Foyes*,
Beaumont and *Marle*, *Vandemont* and *Lestrale*.
Here was a Royall fellowship of death.
Where is the number of our English dead?
Edward the Duke of Yorke, the Earle of Suffolke,
Sir *Richard Ketly*, *Dauy Gam* Esquire ;
None else of name : and of all other men,
But fiue and twentie.
O God, thy Arme was heere :
And not to vs, but to thy Arme alone,
Ascribe we all : when, without stratagem,
But in plaine shock, and euen play of Battaile,
Was euer knowne so great and little losse?
On one part and on th'other, take it God,
For it is none but thine.

Exet. 'Tis wonderfull.

King. Come, goe we in procession to the Village :
And be it death proclaymed through our Hoast,
To boast of this, or take that prayse from God,
Which is his onely.

Flu. Is it not lawfull and please your Maiestie, to tell how many is kill'd?

King. Yes Captaine: but with this acknowledgement,
That God fought for vs.

Flu. Yes, my conscience, he did vs great good.

King. Doe we all holy Rights :
Let there be sung *Non nobis*, and *Te Deum*,
The dead with charitie enclos'd in Clay:
And then to Callice, and to England then,
Where ne're from France arriu'd more happy men.

Exeunt.

Actus Quintus.

Enter Chorus.

Vouchsafe to those that haue not read the Story,
That I may prompt them : and of such as haue,
I humbly pray them to admit th'excuse
Of time, of numbers, and due course of things,
Which cannot in their huge and proper life,
Be here presented. Now we beare the King
Toward Callice : Graunt him there ; there seene,
Heaue him away vpon your winged thoughts,
Athwart the Sea : Behold the English beach
Pales in the flood ; with Men, Wiues, and Boyes,
Whose shouts & claps out-voyce the deep-mouth'd Sea,
Which like a mightie Whiffler 'fore the King,
Seemes to prepare his way : So let him land,
And solemnly see him set on to London.
So swift a pace hath Thought, that euen now
You may imagine him vpon Black-Heath :
Where, that his Lords desire him, to haue borne
His bruised Helmet, and his bended Sword
Before him, through the Citie : he forbids it,
Being free from vain-nesse, and selfe-glorious pride ;
Giuing full Trophee, Signall, and Ostent,
Quite from himselfe, to God. But now behold,
In the quick Forge and working-house of Thought,
How London doth powre out her Citizens,
The Maior and all his Brethren in best sort,
Like to the Senatours of th'antique Rome,
With the Plebeians swarming at their heeles,
Goe forth and fetch their Conqu'ring *Cæsar* in :
As by a lower, but by louing likelyhood,
Were now the Generall of our gracious Empresse,
As in good time he may, from Ireland comming,
Bringing Rebellion broached on his Sword ;
How many would the peacefull Citie quit,
To welcome him? much more, and much more cause,
Did they this *Harry*. Now in London place him.
As yet the lamentation of the French
Inuites the King of Englands stay at home :
The Emperour's comming in behalfe of France,
To order peace betweene them : and omit
All the occurrences, what euer chanc't,
Till *Harryes* backe returne againe to France:
There must we bring him ; and my selfe haue play'd
The *interim*, by remembring you 'tis past
Then brooke abridgement, and your eyes aduance,
After your thoughts, straight backe againe to France.

Exit.

Enter Fluellen and Gower.

Gower. Nay, that's right : but why weare you your Leeke to day? S. *Dauies* day is past.

Flu. There is occasions and causes why and wherefore in all things : I will tell you asse my friend, Captaine *Gower* ; the rascally, scauld, beggerly, lowsie, pragging Knaue *Pistoll*, which you and your selfe, and all the World, know to be no petter then a fellow, looke you now, of no merits : hee is come to me, and prings me pread and sault yesterday, looke you, and bid me eate my Leeke : it was in a place where I could not breed no contention with him ; but I will be so bold as to weare it in my Cap till I see him once againe, and then I will tell him a little piece of my desires.

Enter Pistoll.

Gower. Why heere hee comes, swelling like a Turky-cock.

Flu. 'Tis no matter for his swellings, nor his Turky-cocks. God plesse you aunchient *Pistoll*: you scuruie lowsie Knaue, God plesse you.

Pist. Ha, art thou bedlam? doest thou thirst, base Troian, to haue me fold vp *Parcas* fatall Web? Hence; I am qualmish at the smell of Leeke.

Flu. I peseech you heartily, scuruie lowsie Knaue, at my desires, and my requests, and my petitions, to eate, looke you, this Leeke ; because, looke you, you doe not loue it, nor your affections, and your appetites and your digestions doo's not agree with it, I would desire you to eate it.

Pist. Not for *Cadwallader* and all his Goats.

Flu. There is one Goat for you. *Strikes him.* Will you be so good, scauld Knaue, as eate it?

Pist: Base Troian, thou shalt dye.

Flu. You say very true, scauld Knaue, when Gods will is : I will desire you to liue in the meane time, and eate your Victuals : come, there is sawce for it. You call'd me yesterday Mountaine-Squier, but I will make you

you to day a ſquire of low degree. I pray you fall too, if you can mocke a Leeke, you can eate a Leeke.

Gour. Enough Captaine, you haue aſtoniſht him.

Flu. I ſay, I will make him eate ſome part of my leeke, or I will peate his pate foure dayes: bite I pray you, it is good for your greene wound, and your ploodie Ooxecombe.

Piſt. Muſt I bite.

Flu. Yes certainly, and out of doubt and out of queſtion too and ambiguities.

Piſt. By this Leeke, I will moſt horribly reuenge I eate and eate I ſweare.

Flu. Eate I pray you, will you haue ſome more ſauce to your Leeke: there is not enough Leeke to ſweare by.

Piſt. Quiet thy Cudgell, thou doſt ſee I eate.

Flu. Much good do you ſcald knaue, heartily. Nay, pray you throw none away, the skinne is good for your broken Coxcombe; when you take occaſions to ſee Leekes heereafter, I pray you mocke at 'em, that is all.

Piſt. Good.

Flu. I, Leekes is good: hold you, there is a groat to heale your pate.

Piſt. Me a groat?

Flu Yes verily, and in truth you ſhall take it, or I haue another Leeke in my pocket, which you ſhall eate.

Piſt. I take thy groat in earneſt of reuenge.

Flu. If I owe you any thing, I will pay you in Cudgels, you ſhall be a Woodmonger, and buy nothing of me but cudgels: God bu'y you, and keepe you, & heale your pate. *Exit*

Piſt. All hell ſhall ſtirre for this.

Gow. Go, go, you are a counterfeit cowardly Knaue, will you mocke at an ancient Tradition began vppon an honourable reſpect, and worne as a memorable Trophee of predeceaſed valor, and dare not auouch in your deeds any of your words. I haue ſeene you gleeking & galling at this Gentleman twice or thrice. You thought, becauſe he could not ſpeake Engliſh in the natiue garb, he could not therefore handle an Engliſh Cudgell: you finde it otherwiſe, and henceforth let a Welſh correction, teach you a good Engliſh condition, fare ye well. *Exit*

Piſt. Doeth fortune play the huſwife with me now? Newes haue I that my *Doll* is dead i'th Spittle of a malady of France, and there my rendeuous is quite cut off: Old I do waxe, and from my wearie limbes honour is Cudgeld. Well, Baud Ile turne, and ſomething leane to Cut-purſe of quicke hand: To England will I ſteale, and there Ile ſteale:
And patches will I get vnto theſe cudgeld ſcarres,
And ſwore I got them in the Gallia warres. *Exit.*

Enter at one doore, King Henry, Exeter, Bedford, Warwicke, and other Lords. At another, Queene Iſabel, the King, the Duke of Bourgongne, and other French.

King. Peace to this meeting, wherefore we are met;
Vnto our brother France, and to our Siſter
Health and faire time of day: Ioy and good wiſhes
To our moſt faire and Princely Coſine *Katherine*;
And as a branch and member of this Royalty,
By whom this great aſſembly is contriu'd,
We do ſalute you Duke of *Burgogne*,
And Princes French and Peeres health to you all.

Fra. Right ioyous are we to behold your face,
Moſt worthy brother England, fairely met,
So are you Princes (Engliſh) euery one.

Quee. So happy be the Iſſue brother Ireland
Of this good day, and of this gracious meeting,
As we are now glad to behold your eyes,
Your eyes which hitherto haue borne
In them againſt the French that met them in their bent,
The fatall Balls of murthering Baſiliskes:
The venome of ſuch Lookes we fairely hope
Haue loſt their qualitie, and that this day
Shall change all griefes and quarrels into loue.

Eng. To cry Amen to that, thus we appeare.

Quee. You Engliſh Princes all, I doe ſalute you.

Burg. My dutie to you both, on equall loue.
Great Kings of France and England: that I haue labour'd
With all my wits, my paines, and ſtrong endeuors,
To bring your moſt Imperiall Maieſties
Vnto this Barre, and Royall enterview;
Your Mightineſſe on both parts beſt can witneſſe.
Since then my Office hath ſo farre preuayl'd,
That Face to Face, and Royall Eye to Eye,
You haue congreeted: let it not diſgrace me,
If I demand before this Royall view,
What Rub, or what Impediment there is,
Why that the naked, poore, and mangled Peace,
Deare Nourſe of Arts, Plentyes, and ioyfull Births,
Should not in this beſt Garden of the World,
Our fertile France, put vp her louely Viſage?
Alas, ſhee hath from France too long been chas'd,
And all her Husbandry doth lye on heapes,
Corrupting in it owne fertilitie.
Her Vine, the merry chearer of the heart,
Vnpruned, dyes: her Hedges euen pleach'd,
Like Priſoners wildly ouer-growne with hayre,
Put forth diſorder'd Twigs: her fallow Leas,
The Darnell, Hemlock, and ranke Femetary,
Doth root vpon; while that the Culter ruſts,
That ſhould deracinate ſuch Sauagery:
The euen Meade, that erſt brought ſweetly forth
The freckled Cowſlip, Burnet and greene Clouer,
Wanting the Sythe, withall vncorrected, ranke;
Conceiues by idleneſſe, and nothing teemes,
But hateſull Docks, rough Thiſtles, Kekſyes, Burres,
Looſing both beautie and vtilitie;
And all our Vineyards, Fallowes, Meades, and Hedges,
Defectiue in their natures, grow to wildneſſe.
Euen ſo our Houſes, and our ſelues, and Children,
Haue loſt, or doe not learne, for want of time,
The Sciences that ſhould become our Countrey;
But grow like Sauages, as Souldiers will,
That nothing doe, but meditate on Blood,
To Swearing, and ſterne Lookes, defus'd Attyre,
And euery thing that ſeemes vnnaturall.
Which to reduce into our former fauour,
You are aſſembled: and my ſpeech entreats,
That I may know the Let, why gentle Peace
Should not expell theſe inconueniences,
And bleſſe vs with her former qualities.

Eng. If Duke of Burgonie, you would the Peace,
Whoſe want giues growth to th'imperfections
Which you haue cited; you muſt buy that Peace
With full accord to all our iuſt demands,
Whoſe Tenures and particular effects
You haue enſchedul'd briefely in your hands.

Burg. The King hath heard them: to the which, as yet
There is no Anſwer made.

Eng. Well then: the Peace which you before ſo vrg'd,
Lyes in his Anſwer.

France. I

France: I haue but with a curselarie eye
O're-glanc't the Articles: Pleaseth your Grace
To appoint some of your Councell presently
To sit with vs once more, with better heed
To re-suruey them; we will suddenly
Passe our accept and peremptorie Answer.

England. Brother we shall. Goe Vnckle *Exeter*,
And Brother *Clarence*, and you Brother *Gloucester*,
Warwick, and *Huntington*, goe with the King,
And take with you free power, to ratifie,
Augment, or alter, as your Wisdomes best
Shall see aduantageable for our Dignitie,
Any thing in or out of our Demands,
And wee'le consigne thereto. Will you, faire Sister,
Goe with the Princes, or stay here with vs?

Quee. Our gracious Brother, I will goe with them:
Happily a Womans Voyce may doe some good,
When Articles too nicely vrg'd, be stood on.

England. Yet leaue our Cousin *Katherine* here with vs,
She is our capitall Demand, compris'd
Within the fore-ranke of our Articles.

Quee. She hath good leaue. *Exeunt omnes.*

Manet King and Katherine.

King. Faire *Katherine*, and most faire,
Will you vouchsafe to teach a Souldier tearmes,
Such as will enter at a Ladyes eare,
And pleade his Loue-suit to her gentle heart.

Kath. Your Maiestie shall mock at me, I cannot speake your England.

King. O faire *Katherine*, if you will loue me soundly with your French heart, I will be glad to heare you confesse it brokenly with your English Tongue. Doe you like me, *Kate*?

Kath. Pardonne moy, I cannot tell wat is like me.

King. An Angell is like you *Kate*, and you are like an Angell.

Kath. Que dit il que Ie suis semblable a les Anges?

Lady. Ouy verayment (sauf vostre Grace) ainsi dit il.

King. I said so, deare *Katherine*, and I must not blush to affirme it.

Kath. O bon Dieu, les langues des hommes sont plein de tromperies.

King. What sayes she, faire one? that the tongues of men are full of deceits?

Lady. Ouy, dat de tongeus of de mans is be full of deceits: dat is de Princesse.

King. The Princesse is the better English-woman: yfaith *Kate*, my wooing is fit for thy vnderstanding, I am glad thou canst speake no better English, for if thou could'st, thou would'st finde me such a plaine King, that thou wouldst thinke, I had sold my Farme to buy my Crowne. I know no wayes to mince it in loue, but directly to say, I loue you; then if you vrge me farther, then to say, Doe you in faith? I weare out my suite: Giue me your answer, yfaith doe, and so clap hands, and a bargaine: how say you, Lady?

Kath. Sauf vostre honeur, me vnderstand well.

King. Marry, if you would put me to Verses, or to Dance for your sake, *Kate*, why you vndid me: for the one I haue neither words nor measure; and for the other, I haue no strength in measure, yet a reasonable measure in strength. If I could winne a Lady at Leape-frogge, or by vawting into my Saddle, with my Armour on my backe; vnder the correction of bragging be it spoken. I should quickly leape into a Wife: Or if I might buffet for my Loue, or bound my Horse for her fauours, I could lay on like a Butcher, and sit like a Iack an Apes, neuer off. But before God *Kate*, I cannot looke greenely, nor gaspe out my eloquence, nor I haue no cunning in protestation; onely downe-right Oathes, which I neuer vse till vrg'd, nor neuer breake for vrging. If thou canst loue a fellow of this temper, *Kate*, whose face is not worth Sunne-burning? that neuer lookes in his Glasse, for loue of any thing he sees there? let thine Eye be thy Cooke. I speake to thee plaine Souldier: If thou canst loue me for this, take me? if not? to say to thee that I shall dye, is true; but for thy loue, by the L. No: yet I loue thee too. And while thou liu'st, deare *Kate*, take a fellow of plaine and vncoyned Constancie, for he perforce must do thee right, because he hath not the gift to wooe in other places: for these fellowes of infinit tongue, that can ryme themselues into Ladyes fauours, they doe alwayes reason themselues out againe. What? a speaker is but a prater, a Ryme is but a Ballad; a good Legge will fall, a strait Backe will stoope, a blacke Beard will turne white, a curl'd Pate will grow bald, a faire Face will wither, a full Eye will wax hollow: but a good Heart, *Kate*, is the Sunne and the Moone, or rather the Sunne, and not the Moone; for it shines bright, and neuer changes, but keepes his course truly. If thou would haue such a one, take me? and take me; take a Souldier: take a Souldier; take a King. And what say'st thou then to my Loue? speake my faire, and fairely, I pray thee.

Kath. Is it possible dat I sould loue de ennemie of Fraunce?

King. No, it is not possible you should loue the Enemie of France, *Kate*; but in louing me, you should loue the Friend of France: for I loue France so well, that I will not part with a Village of it; I will haue it all mine: and *Kate*, when France is mine, and I am yours; then yours is France, and you are mine.

Kath. I cannot tell wat is dat.

King. No, *Kate*? I will tell thee in French, which I am sure will hang vpon my tongue, like a new-married Wife about her Husbands Necke, hardly to be shooke off; *Ie quand sur le possession de Fraunce, & quand vous aues le possession de moy*, (Let mee see, what then? Saint *Dennis* bee my speede) *Donc vostre est Fraunce, & vous estes mienne.* It is as easie for me, *Kate*, to conquer the Kingdome, as to speake so much more French: I shall neuer moue thee in French, vnlesse it be to laugh at me.

Kath. Sauf vostre honeur, le Francois ques vous parleis, il & melieus que l'Anglois le quel Ie parle.

King. No faith is't not, *Kate*: but thy speaking of my Tongue, and I thine, most truely falsely, must needes be graunted to be much at one. But *Kate*, doo'st thou vnderstand thus much English? Canst thou loue mee?

Kath. I cannot tell.

King. Can any of your Neighbours tell, *Kate*? Ile aske them. Come, I know thou louest me: and at night when you come into your Closet, you'le question this Gentlewoman about me; and I know, *Kate*, you will to her disprayse those parts in me, that you loue with your heart: but good *Kate*, mocke me mercifully, the rather gentle Princesse, because I loue thee cruelly. If euer thou beest mine, *Kate*, as I haue a sauing Faith within me tells me thou shalt; I get thee with skambling, and thou must therefore needes proue a good Souldier-breeder: Shall not thou and I, betweene Saint *Dennis* and Saint *George*, compound a Boy, halfe French halfe English,

k that

that shall goe to Constantinople, and take the Turke by th Beard. Shall wee not? what say'st thou, my faire Flower-de-Luce.

Kate. I doe not know dat.

King. No:'tis hereafter to know, but now to promise: doe but now promise *Kate*, you will endeauour for your French part of such a Boy; and for my English moytie, take the Word of a King, and a Batcheler. How answer you, *La plus belle Katherine du monde mon trescher & deuin deesse.*

Kath. Your Maiestee aue fause Frenche enough to deceiue de most sage Damoiseil dat is en Fraunce.

King. Now fye vpon my false French: by mine Honor in true English, I loue thee *Kate*; by which Honor, I dare not sweare thou louest me, yet my blood begins to flatter me, that thou doo'st; notwithstanding the poore and vntempering effect of my Visage. Now beshrew my Fathers Ambition, hee was thinking of Ciuill Warres when hee got me, therefore was I created with a stubborne out-side, with an aspect of Iron, that when I come to wooe Ladyes, I fright them: but in faith *Kate*, the elder I wax, the better I shall appeare. My comfort is, that Old Age, that ill layer vp of Beautie, can doe no more spoyle vpon my Face. Thou hast me, if thou hast me, at the worst; and thou shalt weare me, if thou weare me, better and better: and therefore tell me, most faire *Katherine*, will you haue me? Put off your Maiden Blushes, auouch the Thoughts of your Heart with the Lookes of an Empresse, take me by the Hand, and say, *Harry* of England, I am thine: which Word thou shalt no sooner blesse mine Eare withall, but I will tell thee alowd, England is thine, Ireland is thine, France is thine, and *Henry Plantaginet* is thine; who, though I speake it before his Face, if he be not Fellow with the best King, thou shalt finde the best King of Good-fellowes. Come, your Answer in broken Musick; for thy Voyce is Musick, and thy English broken: Therefore Queene of all, *Katherine*, breake thy minde to me in broken English; wilt thou haue me?

Kath. Dat is as it shall please *de Roy mon pere.*

King. Nay, it will please him well, *Kate*; it shall please him, *Kate.*

Kath. Den it sall also content me.

King. Vpon that I kisse your Hand, and I call you my Queene.

Kath. *Laisse mon Seigneur, laisse, laisse, may foy: Ie ne veus point que vous abbaisse vostre grandeus, en baisant le main d'une nostre Seigneur indignie seruiteur excuse moy. Ie vous supplie mon tres-puissant Seigneur.*

King. Then I will kisse your Lippes, *Kate.*

Kath. *Les Dames & Damoisels pour estre baisee deuant leur nopcese il net pas le costume de Fraunce.*

King. Madame, my Interpreter, what sayes shee?

Lady. Dat it is not be de fashon pour le Ladies of Fraunce; I cannot tell wat is buisse en Anglish.

King. To kisse.

Lady. Your Maiestee *entendre bettre que moy.*

King. It is not a fashion for the Maids in Fraunce to kisse before they are marryed, would she say?

Lady. *Ouy verayment.*

King. O *Kate*, nice Customes cursie to great Kings. Deare *Kate*, you and I cannot bee confin'd within the weake Lyst of a Countreyes fashion: wee are the makers of Manners, *Kate*; and the libertie that followes our Places, stoppes the mouth of all finde-faults, as I will doe yours, for vpholding the nice fashion of your Countrey, in denying me a Kisse: therefore patiently, and yeelding. You haue Witch-craft in your Lippes, *Kate*: there is more eloquence in a Sugar touch of them, then in the Tongues of the French Councell; and they should sooner perswade *Harry* of England, then a generall Petition of Monarchs. Heere comes your Father.

Enter the French Power, and the English Lords.

Burg. God saue your Maiestie, my Royall Cousin, teach you our Princesse English?

King. I would haue her learne, my faire Cousin, how perfectly I loue her, and that is good English.

Burg. Is shee not apt?

King. Our Tongue is rough, Coze, and my Condition is not smooth: so that hauing neyther the Voyce nor the Heart of Flatterie about me, I cannot so coniure vp the Spirit of Loue in her, that hee will appeare in his true likenesse.

Burg. Pardon the franknesse of my mirth, if I answer you for that. If you would coniure in her, you must make a Circle: if coniure vp Loue in her in his true likenesse, hee must appeare naked, and blinde. Can you blame her then, being a Maid, yet ros'd ouer with the Virgin Crimson of Modestie, if shee deny the apparance of a naked blinde Boy in her naked seeing selfe? It were (my Lord) a hard Condition for a Maid to consigne to.

King. Yet they doe winke and yeeld, as Loue is blind and enforces.

Burg. They are then excus'd, my Lord when they see not what they doe.

King. Then good my Lord, teach your Cousin to consent winking.

Burg. I will winke on her to consent, my Lord, if you will teach her to know my meaning: for Maides well Summer'd, and warme kept, are like Flyes at Bartholomew-tyde, blinde, though they haue their eyes, and then they will endure handling, which before would not abide looking on.

King. This Morall tyes me ouer to Time, and a hot Summer; and so I shall catch the Flye, your Cousin, in the latter end, and shee must be blinde to.

Burg. As Loue is my Lord, before it loues.

King. It is so: and you may, some of you, thanke Loue for my blindnesse, who cannot see many a faire French Citie for one faire French Maid that stands in my way.

French King. Yes my Lord, you see them perspectiuely: the Cities turn'd into a Maid; for they are all gyrdled with Maiden Walls, that Warre hath entred.

England. Shall *Kate* be my Wife?

France. So please you.

England. I am content, so the Maiden Cities you talke of, may wait on her: so the Maid that stood in the way for my Wish, shall shew me the way to my Will.

France. Wee haue consented to all tearmes of reason.

England. Is't so, my Lords of England?

West. The King hath graunted euery Article:
His Daughter first; and in sequele, all,
According to their firme proposed natures.

Exet. Onely

Exet. Onely he hath not yet subscribed this:
Where your Maiestie demands, That the King of France hauing any occasion to write for matter of Graunt, shall name your Highnesse in this forme, and with this addition, in French: *Nostre trescher filz Henry Roy d'Angleterre Heretere de Fraunce:* and thus in Latine; *Praeclarissimus Filius noster Henricus Rex Angliae & Heres Franciae.*

France. Nor this I haue not Brother so deny'd,
But your request shall make me let it passe.

England. I pray you then, in loue and deare allyance,
Let that one Article ranke with the rest,
And thereupon giue me your Daughter.

France. Take her faire Sonne, and from her blood rayse vp
Issue to me, that the contending Kingdomes
Of France and England, whose very shoares looke pale,
With enuy of each others happinesse,
May cease their hatred; and this deare Coniunction
Plant Neighbour-hood and Christian-like accord
In their sweet Bosomes: that neuer Warre aduance
His bleeding Sword 'twixt England and faire France.

Lords. Amen.

King. Now welcome *Kate*: and beare me witnesse all
That here I kisse her as my Soueraigne Queene.

Flourish.

Quee. God, the best maker of all Marriages,
Combine your hearts in one, your Realmes in one:
As Man and Wife being two, are one in loue,
So be there 'twixt your Kingdomes such a Spousall,
That neuer may ill Office, or fell Iealousie,
Which troubles oft the Bed of blessed Marriage,
Thrust in betweene the Pation of these Kingdomes,
To make diuorce of their incorporate League:
That English may as French, French Englishmen,
Receiue each other. God speake this Amen.

All. Amen.

King. Prepare we for our Marriage: on which day,
My Lord of Burgundy wee'le take your Oath
And all the Peeres, for suretie of our Leagues.
Then shall I sweare to *Kate*, and you to me,
And may our Oathes well kept and prosp'rous be.

Senet *Exeunt*

Enter Chorus

Thus farre with rough, and all-vnable Pen,
Our bending Author hath pursu'd the Story,
In little roome confining mightie men,
Mangling by starts the full course of their glory
Small time: but in that small, most greatly liued
This Starre of England. Fortune made his Sword;
By which, the Worlds best Garden he atchieued:
And of it left his Sonne Imperiall Lord
Henry the Sixt, in Infant Bands crown'd King
Of France and England, did this King succeed:
Whose State so many had the managing,
That they lost France, and made his England bleed:
Which oft our Stage hath showne; and for their sake,
In your faire minds let this acceptance take.

FINIS.

The first Part of Henry the Sixt.

Actus Primus. Scœna Prima.

Dead March.

Enter the Funerall of King Henry the Fift, attended on by the Duke of Bedford, Regent of France; the Duke of Gloster, Protector; the Duke of Exeter Warwicke, the Bishop of Winchester, and the Duke of Somerset.

Bedford.

HVng be ỳ heauens with black, yield day to night;
Comets importing change of Times and States,
Brandish your crystall Tresses in the Skie,
And with them scourge the bad reuolting Stars,
That haue consented vnto *Henries* death:
King *Henry* the Fift, too famous to liue long,
England ne're lost a King of so much worth.
Glost. England ne're had a King vntill his time:
Vertue he had, deseruing to command,
His brandisht Sword did blinde men with his beames,
His Armes spred wider then a Dragons Wings:
His sparkling Eyes, repleat with wrathfull fire,
More dazled and droue back his Enemies,
Then mid-day Sunne, fierce bent against their faces.
What should I say? his Deeds exceed all speech:
He ne're lift vp his Hand, but conquered.
Exe. We mourne in black, why mourn we not in blood?
Henry is dead, and neuer shall reuiue:
Vpon a Wodden Coffin we attend;
And Deaths dishonourable Victorie,
We with our stately presence glorifie,
Like Captiues bound to a Triumphant Carre.
What? shall we curse the Planets of Mishap,
That plotted thus our Glories ouerthrow?
Or shall we thinke the subtile-witted French,
Coniurers and Sorcerers, that afraid of him,
By Magick Verses haue contriu'd his end.
Winch. He was a King, blest of the King of Kings.
Vnto the French, the dreadfull Iudgement-Day
So dreadfull will not be, as was his sight.
The Battailes of the Lord of Hosts he fought:
The Churches Prayers made him so prosperous
Glost. The Church? where is it?
Had not Church-men pray'd,
His thred of Life had not so soone decay'd.
None doe you like, but an effeminate Prince,
Whom like a Schoole-boy you may ouer-awe.
Winch. Gloster, what ere we like, thou art Protector,
And lookest to command the Prince and Realme.
Thy Wife is prowd, she holdeth thee in awe,
More then God or Religious Church-men may.
Glost. Name not Religion, for thou lou'st the Flesh,
And ne're throughout the yeere to Church thou go'st,
Except it be to pray against thy foes.
Bed. Cease, cease these Iarres, & rest your minds in peace:
Let's to the Altar: Heralds wayt on vs;
In stead of Gold, wee'le offer vp our Armes,
Since Armes auayle not, now that *Henry's* dead,
Posteritie await for wretched yeeres,
When at their Mothers moistned eyes, Babes shall suck,
Our Ile be made a Nourish of salt Teares,
And none but Women left to wayle the dead.
Henry the Fift, thy Ghost I inuocate:
Prosper this Realme, keepe it from Ciuill Broyles,
Combat with aduerse Planets in the Heauens;
A farre more glorious Starre thy Soule will make,
Then *Iulius Cæsar*, or bright----

Enter a Messenger.

Mess. My honourable Lords, health to you all:
Sad tidings bring I to you out of France,
Of losse, of slaughter, and discomfiture:
Guyen, Champaigne, Rheimes, Orleance,
Paris, Guysors, Poictiers, are all quite lost.
Beds. What say'st thou man, before dead *Henry's* Coarse?
Speake softly, or the losse of those great Townes
Will make him burst his Lead, and rise from death.
Glost. Is Paris lost? is Roan yeelded vp?
If *Henry* were recall'd to life againe,
These news would cause him once more yeeld the Ghost.
Exe. How were they lost? what trecherie was vs'd?
Mess. No trecherie, but want of Men and Money.
Amongst the Souldiers this is muttered,
That here you maintaine seuerall Factions:
And whil'st a Field should be dispatcht and fought,
You are disputing of your Generals.
One would haue lingring Warres, with little cost;
Another would flye swift, but wanteth Wings:
A third thinkes, without expence at all,
By guilefull faire words, Peace may be obtayn'd.
Awake, awake, English Nobilitie,
Let not slouth dimme your Honors, new begot;
Cropt are the Flower-de-Luces in your Armes
Of Englands Coat, one halfe is cut away.
Exe. Were our Teares wanting to this Funerall,
These Tidings would call forth her flowing Tides.
Bedf. Me they concerne, Regent I am of France:
Giue me my steeled Coat, Ile fight for France.
Away with these disgracefull wayling Robes;
Wounds will I lend the French, in stead of Eyes,
To weepe their intermissiue Miseries.

Enter

Enter to them another Messenger.

Mess. Lords view these Letters, full of bad mischance.
France is reuolted from the English quite,
Except some petty Townes, of no import.
The Dolphin *Charles* is crowned King in Rheimes:
The Bastard of Orleance with him is ioyn'd:
Reynold, Duke of Aniou, doth take his part,
The Duke of Alanson flyeth to his side. *Exit.*

Exe. The Dolphin crown'd King? all flye to him?
O whither shall we flye from this reproach?

Glost. We will not flye, but to our enemies throats.
Bedford, if thou be slacke, Ile fight it out.

Bed. *Gloster*, why doubtst thou of my forwardnesse?
An Army haue I muster'd in my thoughts,
Wherewith already France is ouer-run.

Enter another Messenger.

Mes. My gracious Lords, to adde to your laments,
Wherewith you now bedew King *Henries* hearse,
I must informe you of a dismall fight,
Betwixt the stout Lord *Talbot*, and the French.

Win. What? wherein *Talbot* ouercame, is't so?

3. *Mes.* O no: wherein Lord *Talbot* was o'rethrown:
The circumstance Ile tell you more at large.
The tenth of August last, this dreadfull Lord,
Retyring from the Siege of Orleance,
Hauing full scarce six thousand in his troupe,
By three and twentie thousand of the French
Was round incompassed, and set vpon:
No leysure had he to enranke his men.
He wanted Pikes to set before his Archers:
Instead whereof, sharpe Stakes pluckt out of Hedges
They pitched in the ground confusedly,
To keepe the Horsemen off, from breaking in.
More then three houres the fight continued:
Where valiant *Talbot*, aboue humane thought,
Enacted wonders with his Sword and Lance.
Hundreds he sent to Hell, and none durst stand him:
Here, there, and euery where enrag'd, he slew.
The French exclaym'd, the Deuill was in Armes,
All the whole Army stood agaz'd on him.
His Souldiers spying his vndaunted Spirit,
A *Talbot*, a *Talbot*, cry'd out amaine,
And rusht into the Bowels of the Battaile.
Here had the Conquest fully been seal'd vp,
If Sir *Iohn Falstaffe* had not play'd the Coward.
He being in the Vauward, plac't behinde,
With purpose to relieue and follow them,
Cowardly fled, not hauing struck one stroake.
Hence grew the generall wrack and massacre:
Enclosed were they with their Enemies.
A base Wallon, to win the Dolphins grace,
Thrust *Talbot* with a Speare into the Back,
Whom all France, with their chiefe assembled strength,
Durst not presume to looke once in the face.

Bedf. Is *Talbot* slaine then? I will slay my selfe,
For liuing idly here, in pompe and ease,
Whil'st such a worthy Leader, wanting ayd,
Vnto his dastard foe-men is betray'd.

3. *Mess.* O no, he liues, but is tooke Prisoner,
And Lord *Scales* with him, and Lord *Hungerford*:
Most of the rest slaughter'd, or tooke likewise.

Bedf. His Ransome there is none but I shall pay
Ile hale the Dolphin headlong from his Throne,
His Crowne shall be the Ransome of my friend:
Foure of their Lords Ile change for one of ours.
Farwell my Masters, to my Taske will I.
Bonfires in France forthwith I am to make,
To keepe our great Saint *Georges* Feast withall.
Ten thousand Souldiers with me I will take,
Whose bloody deeds shall make all Europe quake.

3. *Mess.* So you had need, for Orleance is besieg'd,
The English Army is growne weake and faint:
The Earle of Salisbury craueth supply,
And hardly keepes his men from mutinie,
Since they so few, watch such a multitude.

Exe. Remember Lords your Oathes to *Henry* sworne:
Eyther to quell the Dolphin vtterly,
Or bring him in obedience to your yoake.

Bedf. I doe remember it, and here take my leaue,
To goe about my preparation. *Exit Bedford.*

Glost. Ile to the Tower with all the hast I can,
To view th'Artillerie and Munition,
And then I will proclayme young *Henry* King.
Exit Gloster.

Exe. To Eltam will I, where the young King is,
Being ordayn'd his speciall Gouernor,
And for his safetie there Ile best deuise. *Exit.*

Winch. Each hath his Place and Function to attend:
I am left out; for me nothing remaines:
But long I will not be Iack out of Office.
The King from Eltam I intend to send,
And sit at chiefest Sterne of publique Weale.
Exit.

Sound a Flourish.

Enter Charles, Alanson, and Reigneir, marching with Drum and Souldiers.

Charles. Mars his true mouing, euen as in the Heauens,
So in the Earth, to this day is not knowne.
Late did he shine vpon the English side:
Now we are Victors, vpon vs he smiles.
What Townes of any moment, but we haue?
At pleasure here we lye, neere Orleance:
Otherwhiles, the famisht English, like pale Ghosts,
Faintly besiege vs one houre in a moneth.

Alan. They want their Porredge, & their fat Bul Beeues:
Eyther they must be dyeted like Mules,
And haue their Prouender ty'd to their mouthes,
Or pitteous they will looke, like drowned Mice.

Reigneir. Let's rayse the Siege: why liue we idly here?
Talbot is taken, whom we wont to feare:
Remayneth none but mad-brayn'd *Salisbury*,
And he may well in fretting spend his gall,
Nor men nor Money hath he to make Warre.

Charles. Sound, sound Alarum, we will rush on them.
Now for the honour of the forlorne French:
Him I forgiue my death, that killeth me,
When he sees me goe back one foot, or flye. *Exeunt.*

Here Alarum, they are beaten back by the English, with great losse.

Enter Charles, Alanson, and Reigneir.

Charles. Who euer saw the like? what men haue I?
Dogges, Cowards, Dastards: I would ne're haue fled,
But that they left me 'midst my Enemies.

Reigneir. *Salisbury* is a desperate Homicide,
He fighteth as one weary of his life:
The other Lords, like Lyons wanting foode,
Doe rush vpon vs as their hungry prey.

Alanſon. *Froyſard*, a Countreyman of ours, records,
England all *Oliuers* and *Rowlands* breed,
During the time *Edward* the third did raigne:
More truly now may this be verified;
For none but *Samſons* and *Goliaſſes*
It ſendeth forth to skirmiſh: one to tenne?
Leane raw-bon'd Raſcals, who would e're ſuppoſe,
They had ſuch courage and audacitie?

Charles. Let's leaue this Towne,
For they are hayre-brayn'd Slaues,
And hunger will enforce them to be more eager:
Of old I know them; rather with their Teeth
The Walls they'le teare downe, then forſake the Siege.

Reigneir. I thinke by ſome odde Gimmors or Deuice
Their Armes are ſet, like Clocks, ſtill to ſtrike on;
Elſe ne're could they hold out ſo as they doe:
By my conſent, wee'le euen let them alone.

Alanſon. Be it ſo.

Enter the Baſtard of Orleance.

Baſtard. Where's the Prince Dolphin? I haue newes for him.

Dolph. Baſtard of Orleance, thrice welcome to vs.

Baſt. Me thinks your looks are ſad, your chear appal'd.
Hath the late ouerthrow wrought this offence?
Be not diſmay'd, for ſuccour is at hand:
A holy Maid hither with me I bring,
Which by a Viſion ſent to her from Heauen,
Ordayned is to rayſe this tedious Siege,
And driue the Engliſh forth the bounds of France:
The ſpirit of deepe Prophecie ſhe hath,
Exceeding the nine *Sibyls* of old Rome:
What's paſt, and what's to come, ſhe can deſcry.
Speake, ſhall I call her in? beleeue my words,
For they are certaine, and vnfallible.

Dolph. Goe call her in: but firſt, to try her skill,
Reignier ſtand thou as Dolphin in my place;
Queſtion her prowdly, let thy Lookes be ſterne,
By this meanes ſhall we ſound what skill ſhe hath.

Enter Ioane Puzel.

Reigneir. Faire Maid, is't thou wilt doe theſe wondrous feats?

Puzel. *Reignier*, is't thou that thinkeſt to beguile me?
Where is the Dolphin? Come, come from behinde,
I know thee well, though neuer ſeene before.
Be not amaz'd, there's nothing hid from me;
In priuate will I talke with thee apart:
Stand back you Lords, and giue vs leaue a while.

Reigneir. She takes vpon her brauely at firſt daſh.

Puzel. Dolphin, I am by birth a Shepheards Daughter,
My wit vntrayn'd in any kind of Art:
Heauen and our Lady gracious hath it pleas'd
To ſhine on my contemptible eſtate.
Loe, whileſt I wayted on my tender Lambes,
And to Sunnes parching heat diſplay'd my cheekes,
Gods Mother deigned to appeare to me,
And in a Viſion full of Maieſtie,
Will'd me to leaue my baſe Vocation,
And free my Countrey from Calamitie:
Her ayde ſhe promis'd, and aſſur'd ſucceſſe.
In compleat Glory ſhee reueal'd her ſelfe:
And whereas I was black and ſwart before,
With thoſe cleare Rayes, which ſhee infus'd on me,
That beautie am I bleſt with, which you may ſee.
Aske me what queſtion thou canſt poſſible,
And I will anſwer vnpremeditated:
My Courage trie by Combat, if thou dar'ſt,
And thou ſhalt finde that I exceed my Sex.
Reſolue on this, thou ſhalt be fortunate,
If thou receiue me for thy Warlike Mate.

Dolph. Thou haſt aſtoniſht me with thy high termes:
Onely this proofe Ile of thy Valour make,
In ſingle Combat thou ſhalt buckle with me;
And if thou vanquiſheſt, thy words are true,
Otherwiſe I renounce all confidence.

Puzel. I am prepar'd: here is my keene-edg'd Sword,
Deckt with fine Flower-de-Luces on each ſide,
The which at Touraine, in S. *Katherines* Church-yard,
Out of a great deale of old Iron, I choſe forth.

Dolph. Then come a Gods name, I feare no woman.

Puzel. And while I liue, Ile ne're flye from a man.

Here they fight, and Ioane de Puzel ouercomes.

Dolph. Stay, ſtay thy hands, thou art an Amazon,
And fighteſt with the Sword of *Debora*.

Puzel. Chriſts Mother helpes me, elſe I were too weake.

Dolph. Who e're helps thee, 'tis thou that muſt help me:
Impatiently I burne with thy deſire,
My heart and hands thou haſt at once ſubdu'd.
Excellent *Puzel*, if thy name be ſo,
Let me thy ſeruant, and not Soueraigne be,
'Tis the French Dolphin ſueth to thee thus.

Puzel. I muſt not yeeld to any rights of Loue,
For my Profeſſion's ſacred from aboue:
When I haue chaſed all thy Foes from hence,
Then will I thinke vpon a recompence.

Dolph. Meane time looke gracious on thy proſtrate Thrall.

Reigneir. My Lord me thinkes is very long in talke.

Alanſ. Doubtleſſe he ſhriues this woman to her ſmock,
Elſe ne're could he ſo long protract his ſpeech.

Reigneir. Shall wee diſturbe him, ſince hee keepes no meane?

Alan. He may meane more then we poor men do know,
Theſe women are ſhrewd tempters with their tongues.

Reigneir. My Lord, where are you? what deuiſe you on?
Shall we giue o're Orleance, or no?

Puzel. Why no, I ſay: diſtruſtfull Recreants,
Fight till the laſt gaſpe: Ile be your guard.

Dolph. What ſhee ſayes, Ile confirme: wee'le fight it out.

Puzel. Aſſign'd am I to be the Engliſh Scourge.
This night the Siege aſſuredly Ile rayſe:
Expect Saint *Martins* Summer, *Halcyons* dayes,
Since I haue entred into theſe Warres.
Glory is like a Circle in the Water,
Which neuer ceaſeth to enlarge it ſelfe,
Till by broad ſpreading, it diſperſe to naught.
With *Henries* death, the Engliſh Circle ends,
Diſperſed are the glories it included:
Now am I like that prowd inſulting Ship,
Which *Cæſar* and his fortune bare at once.

Dolph. Was *Mahomet* inſpired with a Doue?
Thou with an Eagle art inſpired then.
Helen, the Mother of Great *Conſtantine*,
Nor yet S. *Philips* daughters were like thee.
Bright Starre of *Venus*, falne downe on the Earth,
How may I reuerently worſhip thee enough?

Alanſon. Leaue off delayes, and let vs rayſe the Siege.

Reigneir. Wo-

Reigneir. Woman, do what thou canſt to ſaue our honors,
Driue them from Orleance, and be immortaliz'd.
Dolph. Preſently wee'le try: come, let's away about it,
No Prophet will I truſt, if ſhee proue falſe. *Exeunt.*

Enter Gloſter, with his Seruing-men.

Gloſt. I am come to ſuruey the Tower this day;
Since Henries death, I feare there is Conueyance:
Where be theſe Warders, that they wait not here?
Open the Gates, 'tis Gloſter that calls.
1. Warder. Who's there, that knocks ſo imperiouſly?
Gloſt. 1. Man. It is the Noble Duke of Gloſter.
2. Warder. Who ere he be, you may not be let in.
1. Man. Villaines, anſwer you ſo the Lord Protector?
1. Warder. The Lord protect him, ſo we anſwer him,
We doe no otherwiſe then wee are will'd.
Gloſt. Who willed you? or whoſe will ſtands but mine?
There's none Protector of the Realme, but I:
Breake vp the Gates, Ile be your warrantize;
Shall I be flowted thus by dunghill Groomes?
Gloſters men ruſh at the Tower Gates, and Wooduile the Lieutenant ſpeakes within.
Wooduile. What noyſe is this? what Traytors haue wee here?
Gloſt. Lieutenant, is it you whoſe voyce I heare?
Open the Gates, here's Gloſter that would enter.
Wooduile. Haue patience Noble Duke, I may not open,
The Cardinall of Wincheſter forbids:
From him I haue expreſſe commandement,
That thou nor none of thine ſhall be let in.
Gloſt. Faint-hearted Wooduile, prizeſt him 'fore me?
Arrogant Wincheſter, that haughtie Prelate,
Whom Henry our late Soueraigne ne're could brooke?
Thou art no friend to God, or to the King:
Open the Gates, or Ile ſhut thee out ſhortly.
Seruingmen. Open the Gates vnto the Lord Protector,
Or wee'le burſt them open, if that you come not quickly.

Enter to the Protector at the Tower Gates Wincheſter and his men in Tawney Coates.

Wincheſt. How now ambitious Vmpheir, what meanes this?
Gloſt. Piel'd Prieſt, doo'ſt thou command me to be ſhut out?
Winch. I doe, thou moſt vſurping Proditor,
And not Protector of the King or Realme.
Gloſt. Stand back thou maniſeſt Conſpirator,
Thou that contriued'ſt to murther our dead Lord,
Thou that giu'ſt Whores Indulgences to ſinne,
Ile canuas thee in thy broad Cardinalls Hat,
If thou proceed in this thy inſolence.
Winch. Nay, ſtand thou back, I will not budge a foot:
This be Damaſcus, be thou curſed Cain,
To ſlay thy Brother Abel, if thou wilt.
Gloſt. I will not ſlay thee, but Ile driue thee back:
Thy Scarlet Robes, as a Childs bearing Cloth,
Ile vſe, to carry thee out of this place.
Winch. Doe what thou dar'ſt, I beard thee to thy face.
Gloſt. What? am I dar'd, and bearded to my face?
Draw men, for all this priuiledged place,
Blew Coats to Tawny Coats. Prieſt, beware your Beard,
I meane to tugge it, and to cuffe you ſoundly.
Vnder my feet I ſtampe thy Cardinalls Hat:
In ſpight of Pope, or dignities of Church,
Here by the Cheekes Ile drag thee vp and downe.
Winch. Gloſter, thou wilt anſwere this before the Pope.
Gloſt. Wincheſter Gooſe, I cry, a Rope, a Rope.
Now beat them hence, why doe you let them ſtay?
Thee Ile chaſe hence, thou Wolfe in Sheepes array.
Out Tawney-Coates, out Scarlet Hypocrite.

Here Gloſters men beat out the Cardinalls men, and enter in the hurly-burly the Maior of London, and his Officers.

Maior. Fye Lords, that you being ſupreme Magiſtrates,
Thus contumeliouſly ſhould breake the Peace.
Gloſt. Peace Maior, thou know'ſt little of my wrongs:
Here's Beauford, that regards nor God nor King,
Hath here diſtrayn'd the Tower to his vſe.
Winch. Here's Gloſter, a Foe to Citizens,
One that ſtill motions Warre, and neuer Peace,
O're-charging your free Purſes with large Fines;
That ſeekes to ouerthrow Religion,
Becauſe he is Protector of the Realme;
And would haue Armour here out of the Tower,
To Crowne himſelfe King, and ſuppreſſe the Prince.
Gloſt. I will not anſwer thee with words, but blowes.
Here they skirmiſh againe.
Maior. Naught reſts for me, in this tumultuous ſtrife,
But to make open Proclamation.
Come Officer, as lowd as e're thou canſt, cry:
All manner of men, aſſembled here in Armes this day, againſt Gods Peace and the Kings, wee charge and command you, in his Highneſſe Name, to repayre to your ſeuerall dwelling places, and not to weare, handle, or vſe any Sword, Weapon, or Dagger hence-forward, vpon paine of death.
Gloſt. Cardinall, Ile be no breaker of the Law:
But we ſhall meet, and breake our minds at large.
Winch. Gloſter, wee'le meet to thy coſt, be ſure:
Thy heart-blood I will haue for this dayes worke.
Maior. Ile call for Clubs, if you will not away:
This Cardinall's more haughtie then the Deuill.
Gloſt. Maior farewell: thou doo'ſt but what thou may'ſt.
Winch. Abhominable Gloſter, guard thy Head,
For I intend to haue it ere long. *Exeunt.*
Maior. See the Coaſt clear'd, and then we will depart.
Good God, theſe Nobles ſhould ſuch ſtomacks beare,
I my ſelfe fight not once in fortie yeere. *Exeunt.*

Enter the Maſter Gunner of Orleance, and his Boy.

M.Gunner. Sirrha, thou know'ſt how Orleance is beſieg'd,
And how the Engliſh haue the Suburbs wonne.
Boy. Father I know, and oft haue ſhot at them,
How e're vnfortunate, I miſs'd my ayme.
M.Gunner. But now thou ſhalt not. Be thou rul'd by me:
Chiefe Maſter Gunner am I of this Towne,
Something I muſt doe to procure me grace:
The Princes eſpyals haue informed me,
How the Engliſh, in the Suburbs cloſe entrencht,
Went through a ſecret Grate of Iron Barres,
In yonder Tower, to ouer-peere the Citie,
And thence diſcouer, how with moſt aduantage
They may vex vs with Shot or with Aſſault.
To intercept this inconuenience,
A Peece of Ordnance 'gainſt it I haue plac'd,
And

And euen theſe three dayes haue I watcht,
If I could ſee them. Now doe thou watch,
For I can ſtay no longer.
If thou ſpy'ſt any, runne and bring me word,
And thou ſhalt finde me at the Gouernors. *Exit.*
Boy. Father, I warrant you, take you no care,
Ile neuer trouble you, if I may ſpye them. *Exit.*

Enter Saliſbury and Talbot on the Turrets, with others.

Saliſb. Talbot, my life, my ioy, againe return'd?
How wert thou handled, being Priſoner?
Or by what meanes got's thou to be releas'd?
Diſcourſe I prethee on this Turrets top.
Talbot. The Earle of Bedford had a Priſoner,
Call'd the braue Lord *Ponton de Santrayle,*
For him was I exchang'd, and ranſom'd.
But with a baſer man of Armes by farre,
Once in contempt they would haue barter'd me:
Which I diſdaining, ſcorn'd, and craued death,
Rather then I would be ſo pil'd eſteem'd:
In fine, redeem'd I was as I deſir'd.
But O, the trecherous *Falſtaffe* wounds my heart,
Whom with my bare fiſts I would execute,
If I now had him brought into my power.
Saliſb. Yet tell'ſt thou not, how thou wert entertain'd.
Tal. With ſcoffes and ſcornes, and contumelious taunts,
In open Market-place produc't they me,
To be a publique ſpectacle to all:
Here, ſayd they, is the Terror of the French,
The Scar-Crow that affrights our Children ſo.
Then broke I from the Officers that led me,
And with my nayles digg'd ſtones out of the ground,
To hurle at the beholders of my ſhame.
My griſly countenance made others flye,
None durſt come neere, for feare of ſuddaine death.
In Iron Walls they deem'd me not ſecure:
So great feare of my Name 'mongſt them were ſpread,
That they ſuppos'd I could rend Barres of Steele,
And ſpurne in pieces Poſts of Adamant.
Wherefore a guard of choſen Shot I had,
That walkt about me euery Minute while:
And if I did but ſtirre out of my Bed,
Ready they were to ſhoot me to the heart.
Enter the Boy with a Linſtock.
Saliſb. I grieue to heare what torments you endur'd,
But we will be reueng'd ſufficiently.
Now it is Supper time in Orleance:
Here, through this Grate, I count each one,
And view the Frenchmen how they fortifie:
Let vs looke in, the ſight will much delight thee:
Sir *Thomas Gargraue,* and Sir *William Glanſdale,*
Let me haue your expreſſe opinions,
Where is beſt place to make our Batt'ry next?
Gargraue. I thinke at the North Gate, for there ſtands Lords.
Glanſdale. And I heere, at the Bulwarke of the Bridge.
Talb. For ought I ſee, this Citie muſt be famiſht,
Or with light Skirmiſhes enfeebled. *Here they ſhot, and Saliſbury falls downe.*
Saliſb. O Lord haue mercy on vs, wretched ſinners.
Gargr. O Lord haue mercy on me, wofull man.
Talb. What chance is this, that ſuddenly hath croſt vs?
Speake *Saliſbury;* at leaſt, if thou canſt, ſpeake:
How far'ſt thou, Mirror of all Martiall men?
One of thy Eyes, and thy Cheekes ſide ſtruck off?
Accurſed Tower, accurſed fatall Hand,
That hath contriu'd this wofull Tragedie.
In thirteene Battailes, *Saliſbury* o'recame:
Henry the Fift he firſt trayn'd to the Warres.
Whil'ſt any Trumpe did ſound, or Drum ſtruck vp,
His Sword did ne're leaue ſtriking in the field.
Yet liu'ſt thou *Saliſbury?* though thy ſpeech doth fayle,
One Eye thou haſt to looke to Heauen for grace.
The Sunne with one Eye vieweth all the World.
Heauen be thou gracious to none aliue,
If *Saliſbury* wants mercy at thy hands.
Beare hence his Body, I will helpe to bury it.
Sir *Thomas Gargraue,* haſt thou any life?
Speake vnto *Talbot,* nay, looke vp to him.
Saliſbury cheare thy Spirit with this comfort,
Thou ſhalt not dye whiles——
He beckens with his hand, and ſmiles on me:
As who ſhould ſay, When I am dead and gone,
Remember to auenge me on the French.
Plantaginet I will, and like thee,
Play on the Lute, beholding the Townes burne:
Wretched ſhall France be onely in my Name.
Here an Alarum, and it Thunders and Lightens.
What ſtirre is this? what tumult's in the Heauens?
Whence commeth this Alarum, and the noyſe?
Enter a Meſſenger.
Meſſ. My Lord, my Lord, the French haue gather'd head.
The Dolphin, with one *Ioane de Puzel* ioyn'd,
A holy Propheteſſe, new riſen vp,
Is come with a great Power, to rayſe the Siege.
Here Saliſbury lifteth himſelfe vp, and groanes.
Talb. Heare, heare, how dying *Saliſbury* doth groane
It irkes his heart he cannot be reueng'd.
Frenchmen, Ile be a *Saliſbury* to you.
Puzel or *Puſſel,* Dolphin or Dog-fiſh,
Your hearts Ile ſtampe out with my Horſes heeles,
And make a Quagmire of your mingled braines.
Conuey me *Saliſbury* into his tent,
And then wee'le try what theſe daſtard Frenchmen dare.
Alarum. Exeunt.

Here an Alarum againe, and Talbot purſueth the Dolphin, and driueth him: Then enter Ioane de Puzel, driuing Engliſhmen before her. Then enter Talbot.

Talb. Where is my ſtrength, my valour, and my force?
Our Engliſh Troupes retyre, I cannot ſtay them,
A Woman clad in Armour chaſeth them.
Enter Puzel.
Here, here ſhee comes. Ile haue a bowt with thee:
Deuill, or Deuils Dam, Ile coniure thee:
Blood will I draw on thee, thou art a Witch,
And ſtraightway giue thy Soule to him thou ſeru'ſt.
Puzel. Come, come, 'tis onely I that muſt diſgrace thee. *Here they fight.*
Talb. Heauens, can you ſuffer Hell ſo to preuayle?
My breſt Ile burſt with ſtraining of my courage,
And from my ſhoulders crack my Armes aſunder,
But I will chaſtiſe this high-minded Strumpet.
They fight againe.
Puzel. Talbot farwell, thy houre is not yet come,
I muſt goe Victuall Orleance forthwith:
A ſhort Alarum: then enter the Townes with Souldiers.

O're-

O're-take me if thou canſt, I ſcorne thy ſtrength.
Goe, goe, cheare vp thy hungry-ſtarued men,
Helpe *Salisbury* to make his Teſtament,
This Day is ours, as many more ſhall be. *Exit.*
Talb. My thoughts are whirled like a Potters Wheele,
I know not where I am, nor what I doe:
A Witch by feare, not force, like *Hannibal,*
Driues back our troupes, and conquers as ſhe liſts:
So Bees with ſmoake, and Doues with noyſome ſtench,
Are from their Hyues and Houſes driuen away.
They call'd vs, for our fierceneſſe, Engliſh Dogges,
Now like to Whelpes, we crying runne away.

A ſhort Alarum.

Hearke Countreymen, eyther renew the fight,
Or teare the Lyons out of Englands Coat;
Renounce your Soyle, giue Sheepe in Lyons ſtead:
Sheepe run not halfe ſo trecherous from the Wolfe,
Or Horſe or Oxen from the Leopard,
As you flye from your oft-ſubdued ſlaues.

Alarum. Here another Skirmiſh.

It will not be, retyre into your Trenches:
You all conſented vnto *Salisburies* death,
For none would ſtrike a ſtroake in his reuenge.
Puzel is entred into Orleance,
In ſpight of vs, or ought that we could doe.
O would I were to dye with *Salisbury,*
The ſhame hereof, will make me hide my head.

Exit Talbot.

Alarum, Retreat, Flouriſh.

Enter on the Walls, Puzel, Dolphin, Reigneir, Alanſon, and Souldiers.

Puzel. Aduance our wauing Colours on the Walls,
Reſcu'd is Orleance from the Engliſh.
Thus *Ioane de Puzel* hath perform'd her word.
Dolph. Diuineſt Creature, *Aſtrea's* Daughter,
How ſhall I honour thee for this ſucceſſe?
Thy promiſes are like *Adonis* Garden,
That one day bloom'd, and fruitfull were the next.
France, triumph in thy glorious Propheteſſe,
Recouer'd is the Towne of Orleance,
More bleſſed hap did ne're befall our State.
Reigneir. Why ring not out the Bells alowd,
Throughout the Towne?
Dolphin command the Citizens make Bonfires,
And feaſt and banquet in the open ſtreets,
To celebrate the ioy that God hath giuen vs.
Alanſ. All France will be repleat with mirth and ioy,
When they ſhall heare how we haue play'd the men.
Dolph. 'Tis *Ioane,* not we, by whom the day is wonne:
For which, I will diuide my Crowne with her,
And all the Prieſts and Fryers in my Realme,
Shall in proceſſion ſing her endleſſe prayſe.
A ſtatelyer Pyramis to her Ile reare,
Then *Rhodophe's* or *Memphis* euer was.
In memorie of her, when ſhe is dead,
Her Aſhes, in an Vrne more precious
Then the rich-iewel'd Coffer of *Darius,*
Tranſported, ſhall be at high Feſtiuals
Before the Kings and Queenes of France.
No longer on Saint *Dennis* will we cry,
But *Ioane de Puzel* ſhall be France's Saint.
Come in, and let vs Banquet Royally,
After this Golden Day of Victorie.

Flouriſh. Exeunt.

Actus Secundus. Scena Prima.

Enter a Sergeant of a Band, with two Sentinels.

Ser. Sirs, take your places, and be vigilant:
If any noyſe or Souldier you perceiue
Neere to the walles, by ſome apparant ſigne
Let vs haue knowledge at the Court of Guard.
Sent. Sergeant you ſhall. Thus are poore Seruitors
(When others ſleepe vpon their quiet beds)
Conſtrain'd to watch in darkneſſe, raine, and cold.

Enter Talbot, Bedford, and Burgundy, with ſcaling Ladders: Their Drummes beating a Dead March.

Tal. Lord Regent, and redoubted *Burgundy,*
By whoſe approach, the Regions of *Artoys,*
Wallon, and *Picardy,* are friends to vs:
This happy night, the Frenchmen are ſecure,
Hauing all day carows'd and banquetted,
Embrace we then this opportunitie,
As fitting beſt to quittance their deceite,
Contriu'd by Art, and balefull Sorcerie.
Bed. Coward of France, how much he wrongs his fame,
Diſpairing of his owne armes fortitude,
To ioyne with Witches, and the helpe of Hell.
Bur. Traitors haue neuer other company.
But what's that *Puzell* whom they tearme ſo pure?
Tal. A Maid, they ſay.
Bed. A Maid? And be ſo martiall?
Bur. Pray God ſhe proue not maſculine ere long:
If vnderneath the Standard of the French
She carry Armour, as ſhe hath begun.
Tal. Well, let them practiſe and conuerſe with ſpirits.
God is our Fortreſſe, in whoſe conquering name
Let vs reſolue to ſcale their flinty bulwarkes.
Bed. Aſcend braue *Talbot,* we will follow thee.
Tal. Not altogether: Better farre I gueſſe,
That we do make our entrance ſeuerall wayes:
That if it chance the one of vs do faile,
The other yet may riſe againſt their force.
Bed. Agreed; Ile to yond corner.
Bur. And I to this.
Tal. And heere will *Talbot* mount, or make his graue.
Now *Salisbury,* for thee and for the right
Of Engliſh *Henry,* ſhall this night appeare
How much in duty, I am bound to both.
Sent. Arme, arme, the enemy doth make aſſault.

Cry, S. George, A Talbot.

The French leape ore the walles in their ſhirts. Enter ſeuerall wayes, Baſtard, Alanſon, Reignier, halfe ready, and halfe vnready.

Alan. How now my Lords? what all vnreadie ſo?
Baſt. Vnready? I and glad we ſcap'd ſo well.
Reig. 'Twas time (I trow) to wake and leaue our beds,
Hearing Alarums at our Chamber doores.
Alan. Of all exploits ſince firſt I follow'd Armes,
Nere heard I of a warlike enterprize

More

More venturous, or desperate then this.
Bast. I thinke this *Talbot* be a Fiend of Hell.
Reig. If not of Hell, the Heauens sure fauour him.
Alans. Here commeth *Charles*, I maruell how he sped?

Enter Charles and Ioane.

Bast. Tut, holy *Ioane* was his defensiue Guard.
Charl. Is this thy cunning, thou deceitfull Dame?
Didst thou at first, to flatter vs withall,
Make vs partakers of a little gayne,
That now our losse might be ten times so much?
Ioane. Wherefore is *Charles* impatient with his friend?
At all times will you haue my Power alike?
Sleeping or waking, must I still preuayle,
Or will you blame and lay the fault on me?
Improuident Souldiors, had your Watch been good,
This sudden Mischiefe neuer could haue falne.
Charl. Duke of Alanson, this was your default,
That being Captaine of the Watch to Night,
Did looke no better to that weightie Charge.
Alans. Had all your Quarters been as safely kept,
As that whereof I had the gouernment,
We had not beene thus shamefully surpriz'd.
Bast. Mine was secure.
Reig. And so was mine, my Lord.
Charl. And for my selfe, most part of all this Night
Within her Quarter, and mine owne Precinct,
I was imploy'd in passing to and fro,
About relieuing of the Centinels.
Then how, or which way, should they first breake in?
Ioane. Question (my Lords) no further of the case,
How or which way; 'tis sure they found some place,
But weakely guarded, where the breach was made:
And now there rests no other shift but this,
To gather our Souldiors, scatter'd and disperc't,
And lay new Plat-formes to endammage them.
Exeunt.

Alarum. Enter a Souldier, crying, a Talbot, a Talbot: they flye, leauing their Clothes behind.

Sould. Ile be so bold to take what they haue left:
The Cry of *Talbot* serues me for a Sword,
For I haue loaden me with many Spoyles,
Vsing no other Weapon but his Name. *Exit.*

Enter Talbot, Bedford, Burgundie.

Bedf. The Day begins to breake, and Night is fled,
Whose pitchy Mantle ouer-vayl'd the Earth.
Here sound Retreat, and cease our hot pursuit. *Retreat.*
Talb. Bring forth the Body of old *Salisbury*,
And here aduance it in the Market-Place,
The middle Centure of this cursed Towne.
Now haue I pay'd my Vow vnto his Soule:
For euery drop of blood was drawne from him,
There hath at least fiue Frenchmen dyed to night.
And that hereafter Ages may behold
What ruine happened in reuenge of him,
Within their chiefest Temple Ile erect
A Tombe, wherein his Corps shall be interr'd:
Vpon the which, that euery one may reade,
Shall be engrau'd the sacke of Orleance,
The trecherous manner of his mournefull death,
And what a terror he had beene to France.
But Lords, in all our bloudy Massacre,
I muse we met not with the Dolphins Grace,
His new-come Champion, vertuous *Ioane* of Acre,
Nor any of his false Confederates.
Bedf. 'Tis thought Lord *Talbot*, when the fight began,
Rows'd on the sudden from their drowsie Beds,
They did amongst the troupes of armed men,
Leape ore the Walls for refuge in the field.
Burg. My selfe, as farre as I could well discerne,
For smoake and duskie vapours of the night,
Am sure I scar'd the Dolphin and his Trull,
When Arme in Arme they both came swiftly running,
Like to a payre of louing Turtle-Doues,
That could not liue asunder day or night.
After that things are set in order here,
Wee'le follow them with all the power we haue.

Enter a Messenger.

Mess. All hayle, my Lords: which of this Princely trayne
Call ye the Warlike *Talbot*, for his Acts
So much applauded through the Realme of France?
Talb. Here is the *Talbot*, who would speak with him?
Mess. The vertuous Lady, Countesse of Ouergne,
With modestie admiring thy Renowne,
By me entreats (great Lord) thou would'st vouchsafe
To visit her poore Castle where she lyes,
That she may boast she hath beheld the man,
Whose glory fills the World with lowd report.
Burg. Is it euen so? Nay, then I see our Warres
Will turne vnto a peacefull Comick sport,
When Ladyes craue to be encountred with.
You may not (my Lord) despise her gentle suit.
Talb. Ne're trust me then: for when a World of men
Could not preuayle with all their Oratorie,
Yet hath a Womans kindnesse ouer-rul'd:
And therefore tell her, I returne great thankes,
And in submission will attend on her.
Will not your Honors beare me company?
Bedf. No, truly, 'tis more then manners will.
And I haue heard it sayd, Vnbidden Guests
Are often welcommest when they are gone.
Talb. Well then, alone (since there's no remedie)
I meane to proue this Ladyes courtesie.
Come hither Captaine, you perceiue my minde.
Whispers.
Capt. I doe my Lord, and meane accordingly.
Exeunt.

Enter Countesse.

Count. Porter, remember what I gaue in charge,
And when you haue done so, bring the Keyes to me.
Port. Madame, I will. *Exit.*
Count. The Plot is layd, if all things fall out right,
I shall as famous be by this exploit,
As Scythian *Tomyris* by *Cyrus* death.
Great is the rumour of this dreadfull Knight,
And his atchieuements of no lesse account:
Faine would mine eyes be witnesse with mine eares,
To giue their censure of these rare reports.

Enter Messenger and Talbot.

Mess. Madame, according as your Ladyship desir'd,
By Message crau'd, so is Lord *Talbot* come.
Count. And he is welcome: what? is this the man?
Mess. Madame, it is.
Count. Is this the Scourge of France?
Is this the *Talbot*, so much fear'd abroad?
That with his Name the Mothers still their Babes?
I see Report is fabulous and false.

I

I thought I ſhould haue ſeene ſome *Hercules*,
A ſecond *Hector*, for his grim aſpect,
And large proportion of his ſtrong knit Limbes.
Alas, this is a Child, a ſilly Dwarfe:
It cannot be, this weake and writhled ſhrimpe
Should ſtrike ſuch terror to his Enemies.
Talb. Madame, I haue beene bold to trouble you:
But ſince your Ladyſhip is not at leyſure,
Ile ſort ſome other time to viſit you.
Count. What meanes he now?
Goe aske him, whither he goes?
Meſſ. Stay my Lord *Talbot*, for my Lady craues,
To know the cauſe of your abrupt departure?
Talb. Marry, for that ſhee's in a wrong beleefe,
I goe to certifie her *Talbot's* here.

Enter Porter with Keyes.

Count. If thou be he, then art thou Priſoner.
Talb. Priſoner? to whom?
Count. To me, blood-thirſtie Lord:
And for that cauſe I trayn'd thee to my Houſe.
Long time thy ſhadow hath been thrall to me,
For in my Gallery thy Picture hangs:
But now the ſubſtance ſhall endure the like,
And I will chayne theſe Legges and Armes of thine,
That haſt by Tyrannie theſe many yeeres
Waſted our Countrey, ſlaine our Citizens,
And ſent our Sonnes and Husbands captiuate.
Talb. Ha, ha, ha.
Count. Laugheſt thou Wretch?
Thy mirth ſhall turne to moane.
Talb. I laugh to ſee your Ladyſhip ſo fond,
To thinke, that you haue ought but *Talbots* ſhadow,
Whereon to practiſe your ſeueritie.
Count. Why? art not thou the man?
Talb. I am indeede.
Count. Then haue I ſubſtance too.
Talb. No, no, I am but ſhadow of my ſelfe:
You are deceiu'd, my ſubſtance is not here;
For what you ſee, is but the ſmalleſt part,
And leaſt proportion of Humanitie:
I tell you Madame, were the whole Frame here,
It is of ſuch a ſpacious loftie pitch,
Your Roofe were not ſufficient to contayn't.
Count. This is a Riddling Merchant for the nonce,
He will be here, and yet he is not here:
How can theſe contrarieties agree?
Talb. That will I ſhew you preſently.

Winds his Horne, Drummes ſtrike vp, a Peale of Ordenance: Enter Souldiors.

How ſay you Madame? are you now perſwaded,
That *Talbot* is but ſhadow of himſelfe?
Theſe are his ſubſtance, ſinewes, armes, and ſtrength,
With which he yoaketh your rebellious Neckes,
Razeth your Cities, and ſubuerts your Townes,
And in a moment makes them deſolate.
Count. Victorious *Talbot*, pardon my abuſe,
I finde thou art no leſſe then Fame hath bruited,
And more then may be gathered by thy ſhape.
Let my preſumption not prouoke thy wrath,
For I am ſorry, that with reuerence
I did not entertaine thee as thou art.
Talb. Be not diſmay'd, faire Lady, nor miſconſter
The minde of *Talbot*, as you did miſtake
The outward compoſition of his body.
What you haue done, hath not offended me:
Nor other ſatisfaction doe I craue,
But onely with your patience, that we may
Taſte of your Wine, and ſee what Cates you haue,
For Souldiers ſtomacks alwayes ſerue them well.
Count. With all my heart, and thinke me honored,
To feaſt ſo great a Warrior in my Houſe. *Exeunt.*

Enter Richard Plantagenet, Warwick, Somerſet, Poole, and others.

Yorke. Great Lords and Gentlemen,
What meanes this ſilence?
Dare no man anſwer in a Caſe of Truth?
Suff. Within the Temple Hall we were too lowd,
The Garden here is more conuenient.
York. Then ſay at once, if I maintain'd the Truth:
Or elſe was wrangling *Somerſet* in th'error?
Suff. Faith I haue beene a Truant in the Law,
And neuer yet could frame my will to it,
And therefore frame the Law vnto my will.
Som. Iudge you, my Lord of Warwicke, then betweene vs.
War. Between two Hawks, which flyes the higher pitch,
Between two Dogs, which hath the deeper mouth,
Between two Blades, which beares the better temper,
Between two Horſes, which doth beare him beſt,
Between two Girles, which hath the merryeſt eye,
I haue perhaps ſome ſhallow ſpirit of Iudgement:
But in theſe nice ſharpe Quillets of the Law,
Good faith I am no wiſer then a Daw.
York. Tut, tut, here is a mannerly forbearance:
The truth appeares ſo naked on my ſide,
That any purblind eye may find it out.
Som. And on my ſide it is ſo well apparrell'd,
So cleare, ſo ſhining, and ſo euident,
That it will glimmer through a blind-mans eye.
York. Since you are tongue-ty'd, and ſo loth to ſpeake,
In dumbe ſignificants proclayme your thoughts:
Let him that is a true-borne Gentleman,
And ſtands vpon the honor of his birth,
If he ſuppoſe that I haue pleaded truth,
From off this Bryer pluck a white Roſe with me.
Som. Let him that is no Coward, nor no Flatterer,
But dare maintaine the partie of the truth,
Pluck a red Roſe from off this Thorne with me.
War. I loue no Colours: and without all colour
Of baſe inſinuating flatterie,
I pluck this white Roſe with *Plantagenet*.
Suff. I pluck this red Roſe, with young *Somerſet*,
And ſay withall, I thinke he held the right.
Vernon. Stay Lords and Gentlemen, and pluck no more
Till you conclude, that he vpon whoſe ſide
The feweſt Roſes are cropt from the Tree,
Shall yeeld the other in the right opinion.
Som. Good Maſter *Vernon*, it is well obiected:
If I haue feweſt, I ſubſcribe in ſilence.
York. And I.
Vernon. Then for the truth, and plaineſſe of the Caſe,
I pluck this pale and Maiden Bloſſome here,
Giuing my Verdict on the white Roſe ſide.
Som. Prick not your finger as you pluck it off,
Leaſt bleeding, you doe paint the white Roſe red,
And fall on my ſide ſo againſt your will.
Vernon. If I, my Lord, for my opinion bleed,
Opinion ſhall be Surgeon to my hurt,
And keepe me on the ſide where ſtill I am.
Som. Well, well, come on, who elſe?

Lawyer. Vn-

Lawyer. Vnlesse my Studie and my Bookes be false,
The argument you held, was wrong in you;
In signe whereof, I pluck a white Rose too.
Yorke. Now *Somerset*, where is your argument?
Som. Here in my Scabbard, meditating, that
Shall dye your white Rose in a bloody red.
York. Meane time your cheeks do counterfeit our Roses:
For pale they looke with feare, as witnessing
The truth on our side.
Som. No *Plantagenet*:
'Tis not for feare, but anger, that thy cheekes
Blush for pure shame, to counterfeit our Roses,
And yet thy tongue will not confesse thy error.
Yorke. Hath not thy Rose a Canker, *Somerset*?
Som. Hath not thy Rose a Thorne, *Plantagenet*?
Yorke. I, sharpe and piercing to maintaine his truth,
Whiles thy consuming Canker eates his falsehood.
Som. Well, Ile find friends to weare my bleeding Roses,
That shall maintaine what I haue said is true,
Where false *Plantagenet* dare not be seene.
Yorke. Now by this Maiden Blossome in my hand,
I scorne thee and thy fashion, peeuish Boy.
Suff. Turne not thy scornes this way, *Plantagenet*.
Yorke. Prowd *Poole*, I will, and scorne both him and thee.
Suff. Ile turne my part thereof into thy throat.
Som. Away, away, good *William de la Poole*,
We grace the Yeoman, by conuersing with him.
Warw. Now by Gods will thou wrong'st him, *Somerset*:
His Grandfather was *Lyonel* Duke of Clarence,
Third Sonne to the third *Edward* King of England:
Spring Crestlesse Yeomen from so deepe a Root?
Yorke. He beares him on the place's Priuiledge,
Or durst not for his crauen heart say thus.
Som. By him that made me, Ile maintaine my words
On any Plot of Ground in Christendome.
Was not thy Father, *Richard*, Earle of Cambridge,
For Treason executed in our late Kings dayes?
And by his Treason, stand'st not thou attainted,
Corrupted, and exempt from ancient Gentry?
His Trespas yet liues guiltie in thy blood,
And till thou be restor'd, thou art a Yeoman.
Yorke. My Father was attached, not attainted,
Condemn'd to dye for Treason, but no Traytor;
And that Ile proue on better men then *Somerset*,
Were growing time once ripened to my will.
For your partaker *Poole*, and you your selfe,
Ile note you in my Booke of Memorie,
To scourge you for this apprehension:
Looke to it well, and say you are well warn'd.
Som. Ah, thou shalt finde vs ready for thee still:
And know vs by these Colours for thy Foes,
For these, my friends in spight of thee shall weare.
Yorke. And by my Soule, this pale and angry Rose,
As Cognizance of my blood-drinking hate,
Will I for euer, and my Faction weare,
Vntill it wither with me to my Graue,
Or flourish to the height of my Degree.
Suff. Goe forward, and be choak'd with thy ambition:
And so farwell, vntill I meet thee next. *Exit.*
Som. Haue with thee *Poole*: Farwell ambitious *Richard*. *Exit.*
Yorke. How I am brau'd, and must perforce endure it?
Warw. This blot that they obiect against your House,
Shall be whipt out in the next Parliament,
Call'd for the Truce of *Winchester* and *Gloucester*:
And if thou be not then created *Yorke*,
I will not liue to be accounted *Warwicke*.
Meane time, in signall of my loue to thee,
Against prowd *Somerset*, and *William Poole*,
Will I vpon thy partie weare this Rose.
And here I prophecie: this brawle to day,
Growne to this faction in the Temple Garden,
Shall send betweene the Red-Rose and the White,
A thousand Soules to Death and deadly Night.
Yorke. Good Master *Vernon*, I am bound to you,
That you on my behalfe would pluck a Flower.
Ver. In your behalfe still will I weare the same.
Lawyer. And so will I.
Yorke. Thankes gentle.
Come, let vs foure to Dinner: I dare say,
This Quarrell will drinke Blood another day.
Exeunt.

Enter Mortimer, brought in a Chayre, and Iaylors.

Mort. Kind Keepers of my weake decaying Age,
Let dying *Mortimer* here rest himselfe.
Euen like a man new haled from the Wrack,
So fare my Limbes with long Imprisonment:
And these gray Locks, the Pursuiuants of death,
Nestor-like aged, in an Age of Care,
Argue the end of *Edmund Mortimer*.
These Eyes, like Lampes, whose wasting Oyle is spent,
Waxe dimme, as drawing to their Exigent.
Weake Shoulders, ouer-borne with burthening Griefe,
And pyth-lesse Armes, like to a withered Vine,
That droupes his sappe-lesse Branches to the ground.
Yet are these Feet, whose strength-lesse stay is numme,
(Vnable to support this Lumpe of Clay)
Swift-winged with desire to get a Graue,
As witting I no other comfort haue.
But tell me, Keeper, will my Nephew come?
Keeper. *Richard Plantagenet*, my Lord, will come:
We sent vnto the Temple, vnto his Chamber,
And answer was return'd, that he will come.
Mort. Enough: my Soule shall then be satisfied.
Poore Gentleman, his wrong doth equall mine.
Since *Henry Monmouth* first began to reigne,
Before whose Glory I was great in Armes,
This loathsome sequestration haue I had;
And euen since then, hath *Richard* beene obscur'd,
Depriu'd of Honor and Inheritance.
But now, the Arbitrator of Despaires,
Iust Death, kinde Vmpire of mens miseries,
With sweet enlargement doth dismisse me hence:
I would his troubles likewise were expir'd,
That so he might recouer what was lost.

Enter Richard.

Keeper. My Lord, your louing Nephew now is come.
Mor. *Richard Plantagenet*, my friend, is he come?
Rich. I, Noble Vnckle, thus ignobly vs'd,
Your Nephew, late despised *Richard*, comes.
Mort. Direct mine Armes, I may embrace his Neck,
And in his Bosom spend my latter gaspe.
Oh tell me when my Lippes doe touch his Cheekes,
That I may kindly giue one fainting Kisse.
And now declare sweet Stem from *Yorkes* great Stock,
Why didst thou say of late thou wert despis'd?
Rich. First

Rich. Firſt, leane thine aged Back againſt mine Arme,
And in that eaſe, Ile tell thee my Diſeaſe.
This day in argument vpon a Caſe,
Some words there grew 'twixt *Somerſet* and me:
Among which tearmes, he vs'd his lauiſh tongue,
And did vpbrayd me with my Fathers death;
Which obloquie ſet barres before my tongue,
Elſe with the like I had requited him.
Therefore good Vnckle, for my Fathers ſake,
In honor of a true *Plantagenet*,
And for Alliance ſake, declare the cauſe
My Father, Earle of Cambridge, loſt his Head.
Mort. That cauſe (faire Nephew) that impriſon'd me,
And hath detayn'd me all my flowring Youth,
Within a loathſome Dungeon, there to pyne,
Was curſed Inſtrument of his deceaſe.
Rich. Diſcouer more at large what cauſe that was,
For I am ignorant, and cannot gueſſe.
Mort. I will, if that my fading breath permit,
And Death approach not, ere my Tale be done.
Henry the Fourth, Grandfather to this King,
Depos'd his Nephew *Richard, Edwards* Sonne,
The firſt begotten, and the lawfull Heire
Of *Edward* King, the Third of that Deſcent.
During whoſe Reigne, the *Percies* of the North,
Finding his Vſurpation moſt vniuſt,
Endeuour'd my aduancement to the Throne.
The reaſon mou'd theſe Warlike Lords to this,
Was, for that (young *Richard* thus remou'd,
Leauing no Heire begotten of his Body)
I was the next by Birth and Parentage:
For by my Mother, I deriued am
From *Lionel* Duke of Clarence, third Sonne
To King *Edward* the Third; whereas hee,
From *Iohn* of Gaunt doth bring his Pedigree,
Being but fourth of that Heroick Lyne.
But marke: as in this haughtie great attempt,
They laboured, to plant the rightfull Heire,
I loſt my Libertie, and they their Liues.
Long after this, when *Henry* the Fift
(Succeeding his Father *Bullingbrooke*) did reigne;
Thy Father, Earle of Cambridge, then deriu'd
From famous *Edmund Langley*, Duke of Yorke,
Marrying my Siſter, that thy Mother was;
Againe, in pitty of my hard diſtreſſe,
Leuied an Army, weening to redeeme,
And haue inſtall'd me in the Diademe:
But as the reſt, ſo fell that Noble Earle,
And was beheaded. Thus the *Mortimers*,
In whom the Title reſted, were ſuppreſt.
Rich. Of which, my Lord, your Honor is the laſt.
Mort. True; and thou ſeeſt, that I no Iſſue haue,
And that my fainting words doe warrant death:
Thou art my Heire; the reſt, I wiſh thee gather:
But yet be wary in thy ſtudious care.
Rich. Thy graue admoniſhments preuayle with me:
But yet me thinkes, my Fathers execution
Was nothing leſſe then bloody Tyranny.
Mort. With ſilence, Nephew, be thou pollitick,
Strong fixed is the Houſe of *Lancaſter*,
And like a Mountaine, not to be remou'd.
But now thy Vnckle is remouing hence,
As Princes doe their Courts, when they are cloy'd
With long continuance in a ſetled place.
Rich. O Vnckle, would ſome part of my young yeeres
Might but redeeme the paſſage of your Age.
Mort. Thou do'ſt then wrong me, as y ſlaughterer doth,
Which giueth many Wounds, when one will kill.
Mourne not, except thou ſorrow for my good,
Onely giue order for my Funerall.
And ſo farewell, and faire be all thy hopes,
And proſperous be thy Life in Peace and Warre. *Dyes.*
Rich. And Peace, no Warre, befall thy parting Soule.
In Priſon haſt thou ſpent a Pilgrimage,
And like a Hermite ouer-paſt thy dayes.
Well, I will locke his Councell in my Breſt,
And what I doe imagine, let that reſt.
Keepers conuey him hence, and I my ſelfe
Will ſee his Buryall better then his Life. *Exit.*
Here dyes the duskie Torch of *Mortimer*,
Choakt with Ambition of the meaner ſort.
And for thoſe Wrongs, thoſe bitter Iniuries,
Which *Somerſet* hath offer'd to my Houſe,
I doubt not, but with Honor to redreſſe.
And therefore haſte I to the Parliament,
Eyther to be reſtored to my Blood,
Or make my will th'aduantage of my good. *Exit.*

Actus Tertius. Scena Prima.

Flouriſh. Enter King, Exeter, Gloſter, Wincheſter, Warwick, Somerſet, Suffolk, Richard Plantagenet. Gloſter offers to put vp a Bill: Wincheſter ſnatches it, teares it.

Winch. Com'ſt thou with deepe premeditated Lines?
With written Pamphlets, ſtudiouſly deuis'd?
Humfrey of Gloſter, if thou canſt accuſe,
Or ought intend'ſt to lay vnto my charge,
Doe it without inuention, ſuddenly,
As I with ſudden, and extemporall ſpeech,
Purpoſe to anſwer what thou canſt obiect.
Glo. Preſumptuous Prieſt, this place cõmands my patiẽce,
Or thou ſhould'ſt finde thou haſt diſ-honor'd me.
Thinke not, although in Writing I preferr'd
The manner of thy vile outragious Crymes,
That therefore I haue forg'd, or am not able
Verbatim to rehearſe the Methode of my Penne.
No Prelate, ſuch is thy audacious wickedneſſe,
Thy lewd, peſtiferous, and diſſentious prancks,
As very Infants prattle of thy pride.
Thou art a moſt pernitious Vſurer,
Froward by nature, Enemie to Peace,
Laſciuious, wanton, more then well beſeemes
A man of thy Profeſſion, and Degree.
And for thy Trecherie, what's more maniſeſt?
In that thou layd'ſt a Trap to make my Life,
As well at London Bridge, as at the Tower.
Beſide, I feare me, if thy thoughts were ſifted,
The King, thy Soueraigne, is not quite exempt
From enuious mallice of thy ſwelling heart.
Winch. Gloſter, I doe defie thee. Lords vouchſafe
To giue me hearing what I ſhall reply.
If I were couetous, ambitious, or peruerſe,
As he will haue me: how am I ſo poore?
Or how haps it, I ſeeke not to aduance
Or rayſe my ſelfe? but keepe my wonted Calling.
And for Diſſention, who preferreth Peace
More then I doe? except I be prouok'd.
No, my good Lords, it is not that offends,
It is not that, that hath incens'd the Duke:
It is becauſe no one ſhould ſway but hee,
No one, but hee, ſhould be about the King;
And that engenders Thunder in his breaſt,

And

And makes him rore these Accusations forth.
But he shall know I am as good.
Glost. As good?
Thou Bastard of my Grandfather.
Winch. I, Lordly Sir: for what are you, I pray,
But one imperious in anothers Throne?
Glost. Am I not Protector, sawcie Priest?
Winch. And am not I a Prelate of the Church?
Glost. Yes, as an Out-law in a Castle keepes,
And vseth it, to patronage his Theft.
Winch. Vnreuerent *Glocester.*
Glost. Thou art reuerent,
Touching thy Spirituall Function, not thy Life.
Winch. Rome shall remedie this.
Warw. Roame thither then.
My Lord, it were your dutie to forbeare.
Som. I, see the Bishop be not ouer-borne:
Me thinkes my Lord should be Religious,
And know the Office that belongs to such.
Warw. Me thinkes his Lordship should be humbler,
It fitteth not a Prelate so to plead.
Som. Yes, when his holy State is toucht so neere.
Warw. State holy, or vnhallow'd, what of that?
Is not his Grace Protector to the King?
Rich. *Plantagenet* I see must hold his tongue,
Least it be said, Speake Sirrha when you should:
Must your bold Verdict enter talke with Lords?
Else would I haue a fling at *Winchester.*
King. Vnckles of *Gloster*, and of *Winchester*,
The speciall Watch-men of our English Weale,
I would preuayle, if Prayers might preuayle,
To ioyne your hearts in loue and amitie.
Oh, what a Scandall is it to our Crowne,
That two such Noble Peeres as ye should iarre?
Beleeue me, Lords, my tender yeeres can tell,
Ciuill dissention is a viperous Worme,
That gnawes the Bowels of the Common-wealth.
A noyse within, Downe with the Tawny-Coats.
King. What tumult's this?
Warw. An Vprore, I dare warrant,
Begun through malice of the Bishops men.
A noyse againe, Stones, Stones.

Enter Maior.

Maior. Oh my good Lords, and vertuous *Henry*,
Pitty the Citie of London, pitty vs:
The Bishop, and the Duke of Glosters men,
Forbidden late to carry any Weapon,
Haue fill'd their Pockets full of peeble stones;
And banding themselues in contrary parts,
Doe pelt so fast at one anothers Pate,
That many haue their giddy braynes knockt out:
Our Windowes are broke downe in euery Street,
And we, for feare, compell'd to shut our Shops.

Enter in skirmish with bloody Pates.

King. We charge you, on allegeance to our selfe,
To hold your slaughtring hands, and keepe the Peace:
Pray' Vnckle *Gloster* mittigate this strife.
1. Seruing. Nay, if we be forbidden Stones, wee'le fall to it with our Teeth.
2. Seruing. Doe what ye dare, we are as resolute.
Skirmish againe.
Glost. You of my household, leaue this peeuish broyle,
And set this vnaccustom'd fight aside.
3. Seru. My Lord, we know your Grace to be a man
Iust, and vpright; and for your Royall Birth,
Inferior to none, but to his Maiestie:
And ere that we will suffer such a Prince,
So kinde a Father of the Common-weale,
To be disgraced by an Inke-horne Mate,
Wee and our Wiues and Children all will fight,
And haue our bodyes slaughtred by thy foes.
1. Seru. I, and the very parings of our Nayles
Shall pitch a Field when we are dead.
Begin againe.
Glost. Stay, stay, I say:
And if you loue me, as you say you doe,
Let me perswade you to forbeare a while.
King. Oh, how this discord doth afflict my Soule.
Can you, my Lord of Winchester, behold
My sighes and teares, and will not once relent?
Who should be pittifull, if you be not?
Or who should study to preferre a Peace,
If holy Church-men take delight in broyles?
Warw. Yeeld my Lord Protector, yeeld *Winchester*,
Except you meane with obstinate repulse
To slay your Soueraigne, and destroy the Realme.
You see what Mischiefe, and what Murther too,
Hath beene enacted through your enmitie:
Then be at peace except ye thirst for blood.
Winch. He shall submit, or I will neuer yeeld.
Glost. Compassion on the King commands me stoupe,
Or I would see his heart out, ere the Priest
Should euer get that priuiledge of me.
Warw. Behold my Lord of Winchester, the Duke
Hath banisht moodie discontented fury,
As by his smoothed Browes it doth appeare:
Why looke you still so sterne, and tragicall?
Glost. Here *Winchester*, I offer thee my Hand.
King. Fie Vnckle *Beauford*, I haue heard you preach,
That Mallice was a great and grieuous sinne:
And will not you maintaine the thing you teach?
But proue a chiefe offendor in the same.
Warw. Sweet King: the Bishop hath a kindly gyrd:
For shame my Lord of Winchester relent;
What, shall a Child instruct you what to doe?
Winch. Well, Duke of Gloster, I will yeeld to thee
Loue for thy Loue, and Hand for Hand I giue.
Glost. I, but I feare me with a hollow Heart.
See here my Friends and louing Countreymen,
This token serueth for a Flagge of Truce,
Betwixt our selues, and all our followers:
So helpe me God, as I dissemble not.
Winch. So helpe me God, as I intend it not.
King. Oh louing Vnckle, kinde Duke of Gloster,
How ioyfull am I made by this Contract.
Away my Masters, trouble vs no more,
But ioyne in friendship, as your Lords haue done.
1. Seru. Content, Ile to the Surgeons.
2. Seru. And so will I.
3. Seru. And I will see what Physick the Tauerne affords. *Exeunt.*
Warw. Accept this Scrowle, most gracious Soueraigne,
Which in the Right of *Richard Plantagenet*,
We doe exhibite to your Maiestie.
Glo. Well vrg'd, my Lord of Warwick: for sweet Prince,
And if your Grace marke euery circumstance,
You haue great reason to doe *Richard* right,
Especially for those occasions
At Eltam Place I told your Maiestie.

King. And

King. And thoſe occaſions, Vnckle, were of force:
Therefore my louing Lords, our pleaſure is,
That *Richard* be reſtored to his Blood.
Warw. Let *Richard* be reſtored to his Blood,
So ſhall his Fathers wrongs be recompenc't.
Winch. As will the reſt, ſo willeth *Wincheſter*.
King. If *Richard* will be true, not that all alone,
But all the whole Inheritance I giue,
That doth belong vnto the Houſe of *Yorke*,
From whence you ſpring, by Lineall Deſcent.
Rich. Thy humble ſeruant vowes obedience,
And humble ſeruice, till the point of death.
King Stoope then, and ſet your Knee againſt my Foot,
And in reguerdon of that dutie done,
I gyrt thee with the valiant Sword of *Yorke*:
Riſe *Richard*, like a true *Plantagenet*,
And riſe created Princely Duke of *Yorke*.
Rich. And ſo thriue *Richard*, as thy foes may fall,
And as my dutie ſprings, ſo periſh they,
That grudge one thought againſt your Maieſty.
All. Welcome high Prince, the mighty Duke of *Yorke*.
Som. Periſh baſe Prince, ignoble Duke of *Yorke*.
Gloſt. Now will it beſt auaile your Maieſtie,
To croſſe the Seas, and to be Crown'd in France:
The preſence of a King engenders loue
Amongſt his Subiects, and his loyall Friends,
As it diſ-animates his Enemies.
King. When *Gloſter* ſayes the word, King *Henry* goes,
For friendly counſaile cuts off many Foes.
Gloſt. Your Ships alreadie are in readineſſe.
Senet. Flouriſh. Exeunt.

Manet Exeter.
Exet. I, we may march in England, or in France,
Not ſeeing what is likely to enſue:
This late diſſention growne betwixt the Peeres,
Burnes vnder fained aſhes of forg'd loue,
And will at laſt breake out into a flame,
As feſtred members rot but by degree,
Till bones and fleſh and ſinewes fall away,
So will this baſe and enuious diſcord breed.
And now I feare that fatall Prophecie,
Which in the time of *Henry*, nam'd the Fift,
Was in the mouth of euery ſucking Babe,
That *Henry* borne at Monmouth ſhould winne all,
And *Henry* borne at Windſor, looſe all:
Which is ſo plaine, that *Exeter* doth wiſh,
His dayes may finiſh, ere that hapleſſe time. *Exit.*

Scœna Secunda.

Enter Pucell diſguis'd, with foure Souldiors with Sacks vpon their backs.
Pucell. Theſe are the Citie Gates, the Gates of Roan,
Through which our Pollicy muſt make a breach.
Take heed, be wary how you place your words,
Talke like the vulgar ſort of Market men,
That come to gather Money for their Corne.
If we haue entrance, as I hope we ſhall,
And that we finde the ſlouthfull Watch but weake,
Ile by a ſigne giue notice to our friends,
That *Charles* the Dolphin may encounter them.

Souldier. Our Sacks ſhall be a meane to ſack the City,
And we be Lords and Rulers ouer Roan,
Therefore wee'le knock. *Knock.*
Watch. Che la.
Pucell. Peaſauns la pouure gens de Fraunce,
Poore Market folkes that come to ſell their Corne.
Watch. Enter, goe in, the Market Bell is rung.
Pucell. Now Roan, Ile ſhake thy Bulwarkes to the ground. *Exeunt.*
Enter Charles, Baſtard, Alanſon.
Charles. Saint *Dennis* bleſſe this happy Stratageme,
And once againe wee'le ſleepe ſecure in Roan.
Baſtard. Here entred *Pucell*, and her Practiſants:
Now ſhe is there, how will ſhe ſpecifie?
Here is the beſt and ſafeſt paſſage in.
Reig. By thruſting out a Torch from yonder Tower,
Which once diſcern'd, ſhewes that her meaning is,
No way to that (for weakneſſe) which ſhe entred.
Enter Pucell on the top, thruſting out a Torch burning.
Pucell. Behold, this is the happy Wedding Torch,
That ioyneth Roan vnto her Countreymen,
But burning fatall to the *Talbonites*.
Baſtard. See Noble *Charles* the Beacon of our friend,
The burning Torch in yonder Turret ſtands.
Charles. Now ſhine it like a Commet of Reuenge,
A Prophet to the fall of all our Foes.
Reig. Deferre no time, delayes haue dangerous ends,
Enter and cry, the Dolphin, preſently,
And then doe execution on the Watch. *Alarum.*

An Alarum. Talbot in an Excurſion.
Talb. France, thou ſhalt rue this Treaſon with thy teares,
If *Talbot* but ſuruiue thy Trecherie.
Pucell that Witch, that damned Sorcereſſe,
Hath wrought this Helliſh Miſchiefe vnawares,
That hardly we eſcap't the Pride of France. *Exit.*
An Alarum: Excurſions. Bedford brought in ſicke in a Chayre.

Enter Talbot and Burgonie without: within, Pucell, Charles, Baſtard, and Reigneir on the Walls.
Pucell. God morrow Gallants, want ye Corn for Bread?
I thinke the Duke of Burgonie will faſt,
Before hee'le buy againe at ſuch a rate.
'Twas full of Darnell: doe you like the taſte?
Burg. Scoffe on vile Fiend, and ſhameleſſe Curtizan,
I truſt ere long to choake thee with thine owne,
And make thee curſe the Harueſt of that Corne.
Charles. Your Grace may ſtarue (perhaps) before that time.
Bedf. Oh let no words, but deedes, reuenge this Treaſon.
Pucell. What will you doe, good gray-beard?
Breake a Launce, and runne a-Tilt at Death,
Within a Chayre.
Talb. Foule Fiend of France, and Hag of all deſpight,
Incompaſs'd with thy luſtfull Paramours,
Becomes it thee to taunt his valiant Age,
And twit with Cowardiſe a man halfe dead?
Damſell, Ile haue a bowt with you againe,
Or elſe let *Talbot* periſh with this ſhame.
Pucell. Are ye ſo hot, Sir: yet *Pucell* hold thy peace,
If *Talbot* doe but Thunder, Raine will follow.
They whiſper together in counſell.
God ſpeed the Parliament: who ſhall be the Speaker?
Talb. Dare

l 2

Talb. Dare yee come forth,and meet vs in the field?
Pucell. Belike your Lordſhip takes vs then for fooles,
To try if that our owne be ours,or no.
Talb. I ſpeake not to that rayling *Hecate*,
But vnto thee *Alanſon*, and the reſt.
Will ye,like Souldiors,come and fight it out?
Alanſ. Seignior no.
Talb. Seignior hang: baſe Muleters of France,
Like Peſant foot-Boyes doe they keepe the Walls,
And dare not take vp Armes,like Gentlemen.
Pucell. Away Captaines,let's get vs from the Walls,
For *Talbot* meanes no goodneſſe by his Lookes.
God b'uy my Lord, we came but to tell you
That wee are here. *Exeunt from the Walls.*
Talb. And there will we be too,ere it be long,
Or elſe reproach be *Talbots* greateſt fame.
Vow *Burgonie*, by honor of thy Houſe,
Prickt on by publike Wrongs ſuſtain'd in France,
Either to get the Towne againe,or dye.
And I,as ſure as Engliſh *Henry* liues,
And as his Father here was Conqueror;
As ſure as in this late betrayed Towne,
Great *Cordelions* Heart was buryed;
So ſure I ſweare,to get the Towne,or dye.
Burg. My Vowes are equall partners with thy Vowes.
Talb. But ere we goe,regard this dying Prince,
The valiant Duke of Bedford: Come my Lord,
We will beſtow you in ſome better place,
Fitter for ſickneſſe,and for craſie age.
Bedf. Lord *Talbot*,doe not ſo diſhonour me:
Here will I ſit,before the Walls of Roan,
And will be partner of your weale or woe.
Burg. Couragious *Bedford*,let vs now perſwade you.
Bedf. Not to be gone from hence: for once I read,
That ſtout *Pendragon*,in his Litter ſick,
Came to the field,and vanquiſhed his foes.
Me thinkes I ſhould reuiue the Souldiors hearts,
Becauſe I euer found them as my ſelfe.
Talb. Vndaunted ſpirit in a dying breaſt,
Then be it ſo: Heauens keepe old *Bedford* ſafe.
And now no more adoe, braue *Burgonie*,
But gather we our Forces out of hand,
And ſet vpon our boaſting Enemie. *Exit.*

An Alarum. Excurſions. Enter Sir Iohn Falſtaffe, and a Captaine.

Capt. Whither away Sir *Iohn Falſtaffe*,in ſuch haſte?
Falſt. Whither away? to ſaue my ſelfe by flight,
We are like to haue the ouerthrow againe.
Capt. What? will you flye,and leaue Lord *Talbot*?
Falſt. I,all the *Talbots* in the World,to ſaue my life. *Exit.*
Capt. Cowardly Knight,ill fortune follow thee. *Exit.*

Retreat. Excurſions. Pucell, Alanſon, and Charles flye.

Bedf. Now quiet Soule,depart when Heauen pleaſe,
For I haue ſeene our Enemies ouerthrow.
What is the truſt or ſtrength of fooliſh man?
They that of late were daring with their ſcoffes,
Are glad and faine by flight to ſaue themſelues.
Bedford dyes,and is carryed in by two in his Chaire.

An Alarum. Enter Talbot, Burgonie, and the reſt.

Talb. Loſt,and recouered in a day againe,
This is a double Honor, *Burgonie*:
Yet Heauens haue glory for this Victorie.
Burg. Warlike and Martiall *Talbot*, *Burgonie*
Inſhrines thee in his heart,and there erects
Thy noble Deeds,as Valors Monuments.
Talb. Thanks gentle Duke: but where is *Pucel* now?
I thinke her old Familiar is aſleepe.
Now where's the Baſtards braues,and *Charles* his glikes?
What all amort? Roan hangs her head for griefe,
That ſuch a valiant Company are fled.
Now will we take ſome order in the Towne,
Placing therein ſome expert Officers,
And then depart to Paris, to the King,
For there young *Henry* with his Nobles lye.
Burg. What wills Lord *Talbot*,pleaſeth *Burgonie*.
Talb. But yet before we goe,let's not forget
The Noble Duke of Bedford,late deceas'd,
But ſee his Exequies fulfill'd in Roan.
A brauer Souldier neuer couched Launce,
A gentler Heart did neuer ſway in Court.
But Kings and mightieſt Potentates muſt die,
For that's the end of humane miſerie. *Exeunt.*

Scæna Tertia.

Enter Charles, Baſtard, Alanſon, Pucell.

Pucell. Diſmay not (Princes) at this accident,
Nor grieue that Roan is ſo recouered:
Care is no cure,but rather corroſiue,
For things that are not to be remedy'd.
Let frantike *Talbot* triumph for a while,
And like a Peacock ſweepe along his tayle,
Wee'le pull his Plumes,and take away his Trayne,
If Dolphin and the reſt will be but rul'd.
Charles. We haue been guided by thee hitherto,
And of thy Cunning had no diffidence,
One ſudden Foyle ſhall neuer breed diſtruſt.
Baſtard. Search out thy wit for ſecret pollicies,
And we will make thee famous through the World.
Alanſ. Wee'le ſet thy Statue in ſome holy place,
And haue thee reuerenc't like a bleſſed Saint.
Employ thee then,ſweet Virgin, for our good.
Pucell. Then thus it muſt be, this doth *Ioane* deuiſe:
By faire perſwaſions,mixt with ſugred words,
We will entice the Duke of Burgonie
To leaue the *Talbot*,and to follow vs.
Charles. I marry Sweeting, if we could doe that,
France were no place for *Henryes* Warriors,
Nor ſhould that Nation boaſt it ſo with vs,
But be extirped from our Prouinces.
Alanſ. For euer ſhould they be expuls'd from France,
And not haue Title of an Earledome here.
Pucell. Your Honors ſhall perceiue how I will worke,
To bring this matter to the wiſhed end.
Drumme ſounds a farre off.
Hearke,by the ſound of Drumme you may perceiue
Their Powers are marching vnto Paris-ward.
Here ſound an Engliſh March.
There goes the *Talbot*,with his Colours ſpred,
And all the Troupes of Engliſh after him.

French

French March.

Now in the Rereward comes the Duke and his:
Fortune in fauor makes him lagge behinde.
Summon a Parley, we will talke with him.

Trumpets sound a Parley.

Charles. A Parley with the Duke of Burgonie.
Burg. Who craues a Parley with the Burgonie?
Pucell. The Princely *Charles* of France, thy Countreyman.
Burg. What say'st thou *Charles*? for I am marching hence.
Charles. Speake *Pucell*, and enchaunt him with thy words.
Pucell. Braue *Burgonie*, vndoubted hope of France,
Stay, let thy humble Hand-maid speake to thee.
Burg. Speake on, but be not ouer-tedious.
Pucell. Looke on thy Country, look on fertile France,
And see the Cities and the Townes defac't,
By wasting Ruine of the cruell Foe,
As lookes the Mother on her lowly Babe,
When Death doth close his tender-dying Eyes.
See, see the pining Maladie of France:
Behold the Wounds, the most vnnaturall Wounds,
Which thou thy selfe hast giuen her wofull Brest.
Oh turne thy edged Sword another way,
Strike those that hurt, and hurt not those that helpe
One drop of Blood drawne from thy Countries Bosome,
Should grieue thee more then streames of forraine gore.
Returne thee therefore with a floud of Teares,
And wash away thy Countries stayned Spots.
Burg. Either she hath bewitcht me with her words,
Or Nature makes me suddenly relent.
Pucell. Besides, all French and France exclaimes on thee
Doubting thy Birth and lawfull Progenie.
Who ioyn'st thou with, but with a Lordly Nation,
That will not trust thee, but for profits sake?
When *Talbot* hath set footing once in France,
And fashion'd thee that Instrument of Ill,
Who then, but English *Henry*, will be Lord,
And thou be thrust out, like a Fugitiue?
Call we to minde, and marke but this for proofe:
Was not the Duke of Orleance thy Foe?
And was he not in England Prisoner?
But when they heard he was thine Enemie,
They set him free, without his Ransome pay'd,
In spight of *Burgonie* and all his friends.
See then, thou fight'st against thy Countreymen,
And ioyn'st with them will be thy slaughter-men.
Come, come, returne; returne thou wandering Lord,
Charles and the rest will take thee in their armes.
Burg. I am vanquished:
These haughtie wordes of hers
Haue batt'red me like roaring Cannon-shot,
And made me almost yeeld vpon my knees.
Forgiue me Countrey, and sweet Countreymen:
And Lords accept this heartie kind embrace.
My Forces and my Power of Men are yours.
So farwell *Talbot*, Ile no longer trust thee.
Pucell. Done like a Frenchman: turne and turne againe.
Charles. Welcome braue Duke, thy friendship makes vs fresh.
Bastard. And doth beget new Courage in our Breasts.
Alans. *Pucell* hath brauely play'd her part in this,
And doth deserue a Coronet of Gold.
Charles. Now let vs on, my Lords,
And ioyne our Powers,
And seeke how we may preiudice the Foe. *Exeunt.*

Scœna Quarta.

Enter the King, Glocester, Winchester, Yorke, Suffolke, Somerset, Warwicke, Exeter: To them, with his Souldiors, Talbot.

Talb. My gracious Prince, and honorable Peeres,
Hearing of your arriuall in this Realme,
I haue a while giuen Truce vnto my Warres,
To doe my dutie to my Soueraigne.
In signe whereof, this Arme, that hath reclaym'd
To your obedience, fiftie Fortresses,
Twelue Cities, and seuen walled Townes of strength,
Beside fiue hundred Prisoners of esteeme;
Lets fall his Sword before your Highnesse feet:
And with submissiue loyaltie of heart
Ascribes the Glory of his Conquest got,
First to my God, and next vnto your Grace.
King. Is this the Lord *Talbot*, Vnckle *Glocester*,
That hath so long beene resident in France?
Glost. Yes, if it please your Maiestie, my Liege.
King. Welcome braue Captaine, and victorious Lord.
When I was young (as yet I am not old)
I doe remember how my Father said,
A stouter Champion neuer handled Sword.
Long since we were resolued of your truth,
Your faithfull seruice, and your toyle in Warre:
Yet neuer haue you tasted our Reward,
Or beene reguerdon'd with so much as Thanks,
Because till now, we neuer saw your face.
Therefore stand vp, and for these good deserts,
We here create you Earle of Shrewsbury,
And in our Coronation take your place.

Senet. Flourish. Exeunt.

Manet Vernon and Basset.

Vern. Now Sir, to you that were so hot at Sea,
Disgracing of these Colours that I weare,
In honor of my Noble Lord of Yorke
Dar'st thou maintaine the former words thou spak'st?
Bass. Yes Sir, as well as you dare patronage
The enuious barking of your sawcie Tongue,
Against my Lord the Duke of Somerset.
Vern. Sirrha, thy Lord I honour as he is.
Bass. Why, what is he? as good a man as *Yorke*.
Vern. Hearke ye: not so: in witnesse take ye that.

Strikes him.

Bass. Villaine, thou knowest
The Law of Armes is such,
That who so drawes a Sword, 'tis present death,
Or else this Blow should broach thy dearest Bloud.
But Ile vnto his Maiestie, and craue,
I may haue libertie to venge this Wrong,
When thou shalt see, Ile meet thee to thy cost.
Vern. Well miscreant, Ile be there as soone as you,
And after meete you, sooner then you would.

Exeunt.

Actus Quartus. Scena Prima.

Enter King, Gloceſter, Wincheſter, Yorke, Suffolke, Somerſet, Warwicke, Talbot, and Gouernor Exeter.

Glo. Lord Biſhop ſet the Crowne vpon his head.
Win. God ſaue King *Henry* of that name the ſixt.
Glo. Now Gouernour of Paris take your oath,
That you elect no other King but him;
Eſteeme none Friends, but ſuch as are his Friends,
And none your Foes, but ſuch as ſhall pretend
Malicious practiſes againſt his State:
This ſhall ye do, ſo helpe you righteous God.

Enter Falſtaffe.

Fal. My gracious Soueraigne, as I rode from Calice,
To haſte vnto your Coronation:
A Letter was deliuer'd to my hands,
Writ to your Grace, from th'Duke of Burgundy.
Tal. Shame to the Duke of Burgundy, and thee:
I vow'd (baſe Knight) when I did meete the next,
To teare the Garter from thy Crauens legge,
Which I haue done, becauſe (vnworthily)
Thou was't inſtalled in that High Degree.
Pardon me Princely *Henry*, and the reſt:
This Daſtard, at the battell of *Poictiers*,
When (but in all) I was ſixe thouſand ſtrong,
And that the French were almoſt ten to one,
Before we met, or that a ſtroke was giuen,
Like to a truſtie Squire, did run away.
In which aſſault, we loſt twelue hundred men
My ſelfe, and diuers Gentlemen beſide,
Were there ſurpriz'd, and taken priſoners.
Then iudge (great Lords) if I haue done amiſſe:
Or whether that ſuch Cowards ought to weare
This Ornament of Knighthood, yea or no?
Glo. To ſay the truth, this fact was infamous,
And ill beſeeming any common man;
Much more a Knight, a Captaine, and a Leader.
Tal. When firſt this Order was ordain'd my Lords,
Knights of the Garter were of Noble birth;
Valiant, and Vertuous, full of haughtie Courage,
Such as were growne to credit by the warres:
Not fearing Death, nor ſhrinking for Diſtreſſe,
But alwayes reſolute, in moſt extreames.
He then, that is not furniſh'd in this ſort,
Doth but vſurpe the Sacred name of Knight,
Prophaning this moſt Honourable Order,
And ſhould (if I were worthy to be Iudge)
Be quite degraded, like a Hedge-borne Swaine,
That doth preſume to boaſt of Gentle blood.
K. Staine to thy Countrymen, thou hear'ſt thy doom:
Be packing therefore, thou that was't a knight:
Henceforth we baniſh thee on paine of death.
And now Lord Protector, view the Letter
Sent from our Vnckle Duke of Burgundy.
Glo. What meanes his Grace, that he hath chaung'd his Stile?
No more but plaine and bluntly? (*To the King.*)
Hath he forgot he is his Soueraigne?
Or doth this churliſh Superſcription
Pretend ſome alteration in good will?
What's heere? *I haue vpon eſpeciall cauſe,*
Mou'd with compaſſion of my Countries wracke,
Together with the pittifull complaints
Of ſuch as your oppreſſion feedes vpon,
Forſaken your pernitious Faction,
And ioyn'd with Charles, the rightfull king of France
O monſtrous Treachery: Can this be ſo?
That in alliance, amity, and oathes,
There ſhould be found ſuch falſe diſſembling guile?
King. What? doth my Vnckle Burgundy reuolt?
Glo. He doth my Lord, and is become your foe.
King. Is that the worſt this Letter doth containe?
Glo. It is the worſt, and all (my Lord) he writes.
King. Why then Lord *Talbot* there ſhal talk with him,
And giue him chaſticement for this abuſe.
How ſay you (my Lord) are you not content?
Tal. Content, my Liege? Yes: But ẏ I am preuented,
I ſhould haue begg'd I might haue bene employd.
King. Then gather ſtrength, and march vnto him ſtraight:
Let him perceiue how ill we brooke his Treaſon,
And what offence it is to flout his Friends.
Tal. I go my Lord, in heart deſiring ſtill
You may behold confuſion of your foes.

Enter Vernon and Baſſit.

Ver. Grant me the Combate, gracious Soueraigne.
Baſ. And me (my Lord) grant me the Combate too
Yorke. This is my Seruant, heare him Noble Prince.
Som. And this is mine (ſweet *Henry*) fauour him.
King. Be patient Lords, and giue them leaue to ſpeak.
Say Gentlemen, what makes you thus exclaime,
And wherefore craue you Combate? Or with whom?
Ver. With him (my Lord) for he hath done me wrong.
Baſ. And I with him, for he hath done me wrong.
King. What is that wrong, wherof you both complain
Firſt let me know, and then Ile anſwer you.
Baſ. Croſſing the Sea, from England into France,
This Fellow heere with enuious carping tongue,
Vpbraided me about the Roſe I weare,
Saying, the ſanguine colour of the Leaues
Did repreſent my Maſters bluſhing cheekes:
When ſtubbornly he did repugne the truth,
About a certaine queſtion in the Law,
Argu'd betwixt the Duke of Yorke, and him:
With other vile and ignominious tearmes.
In confutation of which rude reproach,
And in defence of my Lords worthineſſe,
I craue the benefit of Law of Armes.
Ver. And that is my petition (Noble Lord:)
For though he ſeeme with forged queint conceite
To ſet a gloſſe vpon his bold intent,
Yet know (my Lord) I was prouok'd by him,
And he firſt tooke exceptions at this badge,
Pronouncing that the paleneſſe of this Flower,
Bewray'd the faintneſſe of my Maſters heart.
Yorke. Will not this malice Somerſet be left?
Som. Your priuate grudge my Lord of York, wil out,
Though ne're ſo cunningly you ſmother it.
King. Good Lord, what madneſſe rules in braine-ſicke men,
When for ſo ſlight and friuolous a cauſe,
Such factious æmulations ſhall ariſe?
Good Coſins both of Yorke and Somerſet,
Quiet your ſelues (I pray) and be at peace.
Yorke. Let this diſſention firſt be tried by fight,
And then your Highneſſe ſhall command a Peace.
Som. The quarrell toucheth none but vs alone,
Betwixt our ſelues let vs decide it then.
Yorke. There is my pledge, accept it Somerſet.
Ver. Nay, let it reſt where it began at firſt.

Baſſ.

Baſſ. Confirme it ſo, mine honourable Lord.
Glo. Confirme it ſo? Confounded be your ſtrife,
And periſh ye with your audacious prate,
Preſumptuous vaſſals, are you not aſham'd
With this immodeſt clamorous outrage,
To trouble and diſturbe the King, and Vs?
And you my Lords, me thinkes you do not well
To beare with their peruerſe Obiections:
Much leſſe to take occaſion from their mouthes,
To raiſe a mutiny betwixt your ſelues.
Let me perſwade you take a better courſe.
Exet. It greeues his Highneſſe,
Good my Lords, be Friends.
King. Come hither you that would be Combatants:
Henceforth I charge you, as you loue our fauour,
Quite to forget this Quarrell, and the cauſe.
And you my Lords: Remember where we are,
In France, amongſt a fickle wauering Nation:
If they perceyue diſſention in our lookes,
And that within our ſelues we diſagree;
How will their grudging ſtomackes be prouok'd
To wilfull Diſobedience, and Rebell?
Beſide, What infamy will there ariſe,
When Forraigne Princes ſhall be certified,
That for a toy, a thing of no regard,
King *Henries* Peeres, and cheefe Nobility,
Deſtroy'd themſelues, and loſt the Realme of France?
Oh thinke vpon the Conqueſt of my Father,
My tender yeares, and let vs not forgoe
That for a trifle, that was bought with blood.
Let me be Vmper in this doubtfull ſtrife:
I ſee no reaſon if I weare this Roſe,
That any one ſhould therefore be ſuſpitious
I more incline to Somerſet, than Yorke:
Both are my kinſmen, and I loue them both.
As well they may vpbray'd me with my Crowne,
Becauſe (forſooth) the King of Scots is Crown'd.
But your diſcretions better can perſwade,
Then I am able to inſtruct or teach:
And therefore, as we hither came in peace,
So let vs ſtill continue peace, and loue.
Coſin of Yorke, we inſtitute your Grace
To be our Regent in theſe parts of France:
And good my Lord of Somerſet, vnite
Your Troopes of horſemen, with his Bands of foote,
And like true Subiects, ſonnes of your Progenitors,
Go cheerefully together, and digeſt
Your angry Choller on your Enemies.
Our Selfe, my Lord Protector, and the reſt,
After ſome reſpit, will returne to Calice;
From thence to England, where I hope ere long
To be preſented by your Victories,
With *Charles*, *Alanſon*, and that Traiterous rout.
Exeunt. Manet Yorke, Warwick, Exeter, Vernon.
War. My Lord of Yorke, I promiſe you the King
Prettily (me thought) did play the Orator.
Yorke. And ſo he did, but yet I like it not,
In that he weares the badge of Somerſet.
War. Tuſh, that was but his fancie, blame him not,
I dare preſume (ſweet Prince) he thought no harme.
York. And if I wiſh he did. But let it reſt,
Other affayres muſt now be managed. *Exeunt.*
Flouriſh. Manet Exeter.
Exet Well didſt thou *Richard* to ſuppreſſe thy voice:
For had the paſſions of thy heart burſt out,
I feare we ſhould haue ſeene decipher'd there
More rancorous ſpight, more furious raging broyles,
Then yet can be imagin'd or ſuppos'd:
But howſoere, no ſimple man that ſees
This iarring diſcord of Nobilitie,
This ſhouldering of each other in the Court,
This factious bandying of their Fauourites,
But that it doth preſage ſome ill euent.
'Tis much, when Scepters are in Childrens hands:
But more, when Enuy breeds vnkinde deuiſion,
There comes the ruine, there begins confuſion. *Exit.*

Enter Talbot with Trumpe and Drumme, before Burdeaux.

Talb. Go to the Gates of Burdeaux Trumpeter,
Summon their Generall vnto the Wall. *Sounds.*
Enter Generall aloft.
English *Iohn Talbot* (Captaines) call you forth,
Seruant in Armes to *Harry* King of England,
And thus he would. Open your Citie Gates,
Be humble to vs, call my Soueraigne yours,
And do him homage as obedient Subiects,
And Ile withdraw me, and my bloody power.
But if you frowne vpon this proffer'd Peace,
You tempt the fury of my three attendants,
Leane Famine, quartering Steele, and climbing Fire,
Who in a moment, eeuen with the earth,
Shall lay your ſtately, and ayre-brauing Towers,
If you forſake the offer of their loue.
Cap. Thou ominous and fearefull Owle of death,
Our Nations terror, and their bloody ſcourge,
The period of thy Tyranny approacheth,
On vs thou canſt not enter but by death:
For I proteſt we are well fortified,
And ſtrong enough to iſſue out and fight.
If thou retire, the Dolphin well appointed,
Stands with the ſnares of Warre to tangle thee.
On either hand thee, there are ſquadrons pitcht,
To wall thee from the liberty of Flight;
And no way canſt thou turne thee for redreſſe,
But death doth front thee with apparant ſpoyle,
And pale deſtruction meets thee in the face:
Ten thouſand French haue tane the Sacrament,
To ryue their dangerous Artillerie
Vpon no Chriſtian ſoule but Engliſh *Talbot*:
Loe, there thou ſtandſt a breathing valiant man
Of an inuincible vnconquer'd ſpirit:
This is the lateſt Glorie of thy praiſe,
That I thy enemy dew thee withall:
For ere the Glaſſe that now begins to runne,
Finiſh the proceſſe of his ſandy houre,
Theſe eyes that ſee thee now well coloured,
Shall ſee thee withered, bloody, pale, and dead.
Drum a farre off.
Harke, harke, the Dolphins drumme, a warning bell,
Sings heauy Muſicke to thy timorous ſoule,
And mine ſhall ring thy dire departure out. *Exit*
Tal. He Fables not, I heare the enemie:
Out ſome light Horſemen, and peruſe their Wings.
O negligent and heedleſſe Diſcipline,
How are we park'd and bounded in a pale?
A little Heard of Englands timorous Deere,
Maz'd with a yelping kennell of French Curres.
If we be Engliſh Deere, be then in blood,
Not Raſcall-like to fall downe with a pinch,
But rather moodie mad: And deſperate Stagges,
Turne

Turne on the bloody Hounds with heads of Steele,
And make the Cowards stand aloofe at bay:
Sell euery man his life as deere as mine,
And they shall finde deere Deere of vs my Friends.
God, and S. *George*, *Talbot* and Englands right,
Prosper our Colours in this dangerous fight.

Enter a Messenger that meets Yorke. Enter Yorke with Trumpet, and many Soldiers.

Yorke. Are not the speedy scouts return'd againe,
That dog'd the mighty Army of the Dolphin?

Mess. They are return'd my Lord, and giue it out,
That he is march'd to Burdeaux with his power
To fight with *Talbot* as he march'd along.
By your espyals were discouered
Two mightier Troopes then that the Dolphin led,
Which ioyn'd with him, and made their march for (Burdeaux

Yorke. A plague vpon that Villaine Somerset,
That thus delayes my promised supply
Of horsemen, that were leuied for this siege.
Renowned *Talbot* doth expect my ayde,
And I am lowted by a Traitor Villaine,
And cannot helpe the noble Cheualier:
God comfort him in this necessity:
If he miscarry, farewell Warres in France.

Enter another Messenger.

2.Mes. Thou Princely Leader of our English strength,
Neuer so needfull on the earth of France,
Spurre to the rescue of the Noble *Talbot*,
Who now is girdled with a waste of Iron,
And hem'd about with grim destruction:
To Burdeaux warlike Duke, to Burdeaux Yorke,
Else farwell *Talbot*, France, and Englands honor.

Yorke. O God, that Somerset who in proud heart
Doth stop my Cornets, were in *Talbots* place,
So should wee saue a valiant Gentleman,
By forfeyting a Traitor, and a Coward:
Mad ire, and wrathfull fury makes me weepe,
That thus we dye, while remisse Traitors sleepe.

Mes. O send some succour to the distrest Lord.

Yorke. He dies, we loose: I breake my warlike word:
We mourne, France smiles: We loose, they dayly get,
All long of this vile Traitor Somerset.

Mes. Then God take mercy on braue *Talbots* soule,
And on his Sonne yong *Iohn*, who two houres since,
I met in trauaile toward his warlike Father;
This seuen yeeres did not *Talbot* see his sonne,
And now they meete where both their liues are done.

Yorke. Alas, what ioy shall noble *Talbot* haue,
To bid his yong sonne welcome to his Graue:
Away, vexation almost stoppes my breath,
That sundred friends greete in the houre of death.
Lucie farewell, no more my fortune can,
But curse the cause I cannot ayde the man.
Maine, *Bloys*, *Poytiers*, and *Toures*, are wonne away,
Long all of Somerset, and his delay. *Exit*

Mes. Thus while the Vulture of sedition,
Feedes in the bosome of such great Commanders,
Sleeping neglection doth betray to losse:
The Conquest of our scarse-cold Conqueror,
That euer-liuing man of Memorie,
Henrie the fift: Whiles they each other crosse,
Liues, Honours, Lands, and all, hurrie to losse.

Enter Somerset with his Armie.

Som. It is too late, I cannot send them now:
This expedition was by *Yorke* and *Talbot*,
Too rashly plotted. All our generall force,
Might with a sally of the very Towne
Be buckled with: the ouer-daring *Talbot*
Hath sullied all his glosse of former Honor
By this vnheedfull, desperate, wilde aduenture:
Yorke set him on to fight, and dye in shame,
That *Talbot* dead, great *Yorke* might beare the name.

Cap. Heere is Sir *William Lucie*, who with me
Set from our ore-matcht forces forth for ayde.

Som. How now Sir *William*, whether were you sent?

Lu. Whether my Lord, from bought & sold L. *Talbot*,
Who ring'd about with bold aduersitie,
Cries out for noble Yorke and Somerset,
To beate assayling death from his weake Regions;
And whiles the honourable Captaine there
Drops bloody swet from his warre-wearied limbes,
And in aduantage lingring lookes for rescue,
You his false hopes, the trust of Englands honor,
Keepe off aloofe with worthlesse emulation:
Let not your priuate discord keepe away
The leuied succours that should lend him ayde,
While he renowned Noble Gentleman
Yeeld vp his life vnto a world of oddes.
Orleance the Bastard, *Charles*, *Burgundie*,
Alanson, *Reignard*, compasse him about,
And *Talbot* perisheth by your default.

Som. Yorke set him on, Yorke should haue sent him ayde.

Luc. And Yorke as fast vpon your Grace exclaimes,
Swearing that you with-hold his leuied hoast,
Collected for this expidition.

Som. York lyes: He might haue sent, & had the Horse:
I owe him little Dutie, and lesse Loue,
And take foule scorne to fawne on him by sending.

Lu. The fraud of England, not the force of France,
Hath now intrapt the Noble-minded *Talbot*:
Neuer to England shall he beare his life,
But dies betraid to fortune by your strife.

Som. Come go, I will dispatch the Horsemen strait:
Within sixe houres, they will be at his ayde.

Lu. Too late comes rescue, he is tane or slaine,
For flye he could not, if he would haue fled:
And flye would *Talbot* neuer though he might.

Som. If he be dead, braue *Talbot* then adieu.

Lu. His Fame liues in the world. His Shame in you. *Exeunt.*

Enter Talbot and his Sonne.

Tal. O yong *Iohn Talbot*, I did send for thee
To tutor thee in stratagems of Warre,
That *Talbots* name might be in thee reuiu'd,
When saplesse Age, and weake vnable limbes
Should bring thy Father to his drooping Chaire.
But O malignant and ill-boading Starres,
Now thou art come vnto a Feast of death,
A terrible and vnauoyded danger:
Therefore deere Boy, mount on my swiftest horse,
And Ile direct thee how thou shalt escape
By sodaine flight. Come, dally not, be gone.

Iohn. Is my name *Talbot*? and am I your Sonne?

Shall

And shall I flye? O, if you loue my Mother,
Dishonor not her Honorable Name,
To make a Bastard, and a Slaue of me:
The World will say, he is not *Talbots* blood,
That basely fled, when Noble *Talbot* stood.
Talb. Flye, to reuenge my death, if I be slaine.
Iohn. He that flyes so, will ne're returne againe.
Talb. If we both stay, we both are sure to dye.
Iohn. Then let me stay, and Father doe you flye:
Your losse is great, so your regard should be;
My worth vnknowne, no losse is knowne in me.
Vpon my death, the French can little boast;
In yours they will, in you all hopes are lost.
Flight cannot stayne the Honor you haue wonne,
But mine it will, that no Exploit haue done.
You fled for Vantage, euery one will sweare:
But if I bow, they'le say it was for feare.
There is no hope that euer I will stay,
If the first howre I shrinke and run away:
Here on my knee I begge Mortalitie,
Rather then Life, preseru'd with Infamie.
Talb. Shall all thy Mothers hopes lye in one Tombe?
Iohn. I rather then Ile shame my Mothers Wombe.
Talb. Vpon my Blessing I command thee goe.
Iohn. To fight I will, but not to flye the Foe.
Talb. Part of thy Father may be sau'd in thee.
Iohn. No part of him, but will be shame in mee.
Talb. Thou neuer hadst Renowne, nor canst not lose it.
Iohn. Yes, your renowned Name: shall flight abuse it?
Talb. Thy Fathers charge shal cleare thee from ẏ staine.
Iohn. You cannot witnesse for me, being slaine.
If Death be so apparant, then both flye.
Talb. And leaue my followers here to fight and dye?
My Age was neuer tainted with such shame.
Iohn. And shall my Youth be guiltie of such blame?
No more can I be seuered from your side,
Then can your selfe, your selfe in twaine diuide:
Stay, goe, doe what you will, the like doe I;
For liue I will not, if my Father dye.
Talb. Then here I take my leaue of thee, faire Sonne,
Borne to eclipse thy Life this afternoone:
Come, side by side, together liue and dye,
And Soule with Soule from France to Heauen flye. *Exit.*

Alarum: Excursions, wherein Talbots Sonne is hemm'd about, and Talbot rescues him.

Talb. Saint *George*, and Victory; fight Souldiers, fight:
The Regent hath with *Talbot* broke his word,
And left vs to the rage of France his Sword.
Where is *Iohn Talbot*? pawse, and take thy breath,
I gaue thee Life, and rescu'd thee from Death.
Iohn. O twice my Father, twice am I thy Sonne:
The Life thou gau'st me first, was lost and done,
Till with thy Warlike Sword, despight of Fate,
To my determin'd time thou gau'st new date.
Talb. When frõ the *Dolphins* Crest thy Sword struck fire,
It warm'd thy Fathers heart with prowd desire
Of bold-fac't Victorie. Then Leaden Age,
Quicken'd with Youthfull Spleene, and Warlike Rage,
Beat downe *Alanson, Orleance, Burgundie*,
And from the Pride of Gallia rescued thee.
The irefull Bastard *Orleance*, that drew blood
From thee my Boy, and had the Maidenhood
Of thy first fight, I soone encountred,
And interchanging blowes, I quickly shed
Some of his Bastard blood, and in disgrace
Bespoke him thus: Contaminated, base,
And mis-begotten blood, I spill of thine,
Meane and right poore, for that pure blood of mine,
Which thou didst force from *Talbot*, my braue Boy.
Here purposing the Bastard to destroy,
Came in strong rescue. Speake thy Fathers care:
Art thou not wearie, *Iohn*? How do'st thou fare?
Wilt thou yet leaue the Battaile, Boy, and flie,
Now thou art seal'd the Sonne of Chiualrie?
Flye, to reuenge my death when I am dead,
The helpe of one stands me in little stead.
Oh, too much folly is it, well I wot,
To hazard all our liues in one small Boat.
If I to day dye not with Frenchmens Rage,
To morrow I shall dye with mickle Age.
By me they nothing gaine, and if I stay,
'Tis but the shortning of my Life one day.
In thee thy Mother dyes, our Households Name,
My Deaths Reuenge, thy Youth, and Englands Fame:
All these, and more, we hazard by thy stay;
All these are sau'd, if thou wilt flye away.
Iohn. The Sword of *Orleance* hath not made me smart,
These words of yours draw Life-blood from my Heart.
On that aduantage, bought with such a shame,
To saue a paltry Life, and slay bright Fame,
Before young *Talbot* from old *Talbot* flye,
The Coward Horse that beares me, fall and dye:
And like me to the pesant Boyes of France,
To be Shames scorne, and subiect of Mischance.
Surely, by all the Glorie you haue wonne,
And if I flye, I am not *Talbots* Sonne.
Then talke no more of flight, it is no boot,
If Sonne to *Talbot*, dye at *Talbots* foot.
Talb. Then follow thou thy desp'rate Syre of Creet,
Thou *Icarus*, thy Life to me is sweet:
If thou wilt fight, fight by thy Fathers side,
And commendable prou'd, let's dye in pride. *Exit.*

Alarum. Excursions. Enter old Talbot led.

Talb. Where is my other Life? mine owne is gone.
O, where's young *Talbot*? where is valiant *Iohn*?
Triumphant Death, smear'd with Captiuitie,
Young *Talbots* Valour makes me smile at thee.
When he perceiu'd me shrinke, and on my Knee,
His bloodie Sword he brandisht ouer mee,
And like a hungry Lyon did commence
Rough deeds of Rage, and sterne Impatience:
But when my angry Guardant stood alone,
Tendring my ruine, and assayl'd of none,
Dizzie-ey'd Furie, and great rage of Heart,
Suddenly made him from my side to start
Into the clustring Battaile of the French:
And in that Sea of Blood, my Boy did drench
His ouer-mounting Spirit; and there di'de
My *Icarus*, my Blossome, in his pride.

Enter with Iohn Talbot, borne.

Seru. O my deare Lord, loe where your Sonne is borne.
Tal. Thou antique Death, which laugh'st vs here to scorn,
Anon from thy insulting Tyrannie,
Coupled in bonds of perpetuitie,
Two *Talbots* winged through the lither Skie,
In thy despight shall scape Mortalitie.

O

O thou whoſe wounds become hard fauoured death,
Speake to thy father, ere thou yeeld thy breath,
Braue death by ſpeaking, whither he will or no:
Imagine him a Frenchman, and thy Foe.
Poore Boy, he ſmiles, me thinkes, as who ſhould ſay,
Had Death bene French, then Death had dyed to day.
Come, come, and lay him in his Fathers armes,
My ſpirit can no longer beare theſe harmes.
Souldiers adieu: I haue what I would haue,
Now my old armes are yong *Iohn Talbots* graue. *Dyes*

Enter Charles, Alanſon, Burgundie, Baſtard, and Pucell.

Char. Had Yorke and Somerſet brought reſcue in,
We ſhould haue found a bloody day of this.
Baſt. How the yong whelpe of *Talbots* raging wood,
Did fleſh his punie-ſword in Frenchmens blood.
Puc. Once I encountred him, and thus I ſaid:
Thou Maiden youth, be vanquiſht by a Maide.
But with a proud Maieſticall high ſcorne
He anſwer'd thus: Yong *Talbot* was not borne
To be the pillage of a Giglot Wench:
So ruſhing in the bowels of the French,
He left me proudly, as vnworthy fight.
Bur. Doubtleſſe he would haue made a noble Knight:
See where he lyes inherced in the armes
Of the moſt bloody Nurſer of his harmes.
Baſt. Hew them to peeces, hack their bones aſſunder,
Whoſe life was Englands glory, Gallia's wonder.
Char. Oh no forbeare: For that which we haue fled
During the life, let vs not wrong it dead.

Enter Lucie.

Lu. Herald, conduct me to the Dolphins Tent,
To know who hath obtain'd the glory of the day.
Char. On what ſubmiſſiue meſſage art thou ſent?
Lucy Submiſſion Dolphin? Tis a meere French word.
We Engliſh Warriours wot not what it meanes.
I come to know what Priſoners thou haſt tane,
And to ſuruey the bodies of the dead.
Char. For priſoners askſt thou? Hell our priſon is.
But tell me whom thou ſeek'ſt?
Luc. But where's the great Alcides of the field,
Valiant Lord *Talbot* Earle of Shrewsbury?
Created for his rare ſucceſſe in Armes,
Great Earle of *Waſhford, Waterford,* and *Valence,*
Lord *Talbot* of *Goodrig* and *Vrchinfield,*
Lord *Strange* of *Blackmere*, Lord *Verdon* of *Alton,*
Lord *Cromwell* of *Wingefield*, Lord *Furniuall* of *Sheffeild,*
The thrice victorious Lord of *Falconbridge,*
Knight of the Noble Order of *S. George,*
Worthy *S. Michael,* and the *Golden Fleece,*
Great Marſhall to *Henry* the ſixt,
Of all his Warres within the Realme of France.
Puc. Heere's a ſilly ſtately ſtile indeede:
The Turke that two and fiftie Kingdomes hath,
Writes not ſo tedious a Stile as this.
Him that thou magnifi'ſt with all theſe Titles,
Stinking and fly-blowne lyes heere at our feete.
Lucy. Is *Talbot* ſlaine, the Frenchmens only Scourge,
Your Kingdomes terror, and blacke *Nemeſis*?
Oh were mine eye-balles into Bullets turn'd,
That I in rage might ſhoot them at your faces.
Oh, that I could but call theſe dead to life,
It were enough to fright the Realme of France.
Were but his Picture left amongſt you here,
It would amaze the prowdeſt of you all.
Giue me their Bodyes, that I may beare them hence,
And giue them Buriall, as beſeemes their worth.
Pucel. I thinke this vpſtart is old *Talbots* Ghoſt,
He ſpeakes with ſuch a proud commanding ſpirit:
For Gods ſake let him haue him, to keepe them here,
They would but ſtinke, and putrifie the ayre.
Char. Go take their bodies hence.
Lucy. Ile beare them hence: but from their aſhes ſhal be reard
A Phœnix that ſhall make all France affear'd.
Char So we be rid of them, do with him what y^u^ wilt.
And now to Paris in this conquering vaine,
All will be ours, now bloody *Talbots* ſlaine. *Exit.*

Scena ſecunda.

SENNET.

Enter King, Gloceſter, and Exeter.

King. Haue you perus'd the Letters from the Pope,
The Emperor, and the Earle of Arminack?
Glo. I haue my Lord, and their intent is this,
They humbly ſue vnto your Excellence,
To haue a godly peace concluded of,
Betweene the Realmes of England, and of France.
King. How doth your Grace affect their motion?
Glo. Well (my good Lord) and as the only meanes
To ſtop effuſion of our Chriſtian blood,
And ſtabliſh quietneſſe on euery ſide.
King. I marry Vnckle, for I alwayes thought
It was both impious and vnnaturall,
That ſuch immanity and bloody ſtrife
Should reigne among Profeſſors of one Faith.
Glo. Beſide my Lord, the ſooner to effect,
And ſurer binde this knot of amitie,
The Earle of Arminacke neere knit to *Charles,*
A man of great Authoritie in France,
Proffers his onely daughter to your Grace,
In marriage, with a large and ſumptuous Dowrie.
King Marriage Vnckle? Alas my yeares are yong:
And fitter is my ſtudie, and my Bookes,
Than wanton dalliance with a Paramour.
Yet call th'Embaſſadors, and as you pleaſe,
So let them haue their anſweres euery one:
I ſhall be well content with any choyce
Tends to Gods glory, and my Countries weale.

Enter Wincheſter, and three Ambaſſadors.

Exet. What, is my Lord of *Wincheſter* inſtall'd,
And call'd vnto a Cardinalls degree?
Then I perceiue, that will be verified
Henry the Fift did ſometime propheſie.
If once he come to be a Cardinall,
Hee'l make his cap coequall with the Crowne.
King My Lords Ambaſſadors, your ſeuerall ſuites
Haue bin conſider'd and debated on,
Your purpoſe is both good and reaſonable:
And therefore are we certainly reſolu'd,
To draw conditions of a friendly peace.

Which

Which by my Lord of Winchester we meane
Shall be transported presently to France.
Glo. And for the proffer of my Lord your Master,
I haue inform'd his Highnesse so at large,
As liking of the Ladies vertuous gifts,
Her Beauty, and the valew of her Dower,
He doth intend she shall be Englands Queene.
King. In argument and proofe of which contract,
Beare her this Iewell, pledge of my affection.
And so my Lord Protector see them guarded,
And safely brought to *Douer*, wherein ship'd
Commit them to the fortune of the sea. *Exeunt.*
Win. Stay my Lord Legate, you shall first receiue
The summe of money which I promised
Should be deliuered to his Holinesse,
For cloathing me in these graue Ornaments.
Legat. I will attend vpon your Lordships leysure.
Win. Now Winchester will not submit, I trow,
Or be inferiour to the proudest Peere;
Humfrey of Gloster, thou shalt well perceiue,
That neither in birth, or for authoritie,
The Bishop will be ouer-borne by thee:
Ile either make thee stoope, and bend thy knee,
Or sacke this Country with a mutiny. *Exeunt*

Scœna Tertia.

Enter Charles, Burgundy, Alanson, Bastard, Reignier, and Ione.

Char. These newes (my Lords) may cheere our drooping spirits:
'Tis said, the stout Parisians do reuolt,
And turne againe vnto the warlike French.
Alan. Then march to Paris Royall *Charles* of France,
And keepe not backe your powers in dalliance.
Pucel. Peace be amongst them if they turne to vs,
Else ruine combate with their Pallaces.
Enter Scout.
Scout. Successe vnto our valiant Generall,
And happinesse to his accomplices.
Char. What tidings send our Scouts? I prethee speak.
Scout. The English Army that diuided was
Into two parties, is now conioyn'd in one,
And meanes to giue you battell presently.
Char. Somewhat too sodaine Sirs, the warning is.
But we will presently prouide for them.
Bur. I trust the Ghost of *Talbot* is not there:
Now he is gone my Lord, you neede not feare.
Pucel. Of all base passions, Feare is most accurst.
Command the Conquest *Charles*, it shall be thine:
Let *Henry* fret, and all the world repine.
Char. Then on my Lords, and France be fortunate.
Exeunt Alarum. Excursions.

Enter Ione de Pucell.

Puc. The Regent conquers, and the Frenchmen flye,
Now helpe ye charming Spelles and Periapts,
And ye choise spirits that admonish me,
And giue me signes of future accidents. *Thunder.*
You speedy helpers, that are substitutes
Vnder the Lordly Monarch of the North,
Appeare, and ayde me in this enterprize.
Enter Fiends.
This speedy and quicke appearance argues proofe
Of your accustom'd diligence to me.
Now ye Familiar Spirits, that are cull'd
Out of the powerfull Regions vnder earth,
Helpe me this oace, that France may get the field.
They walke, and speake not.
Oh hold me not with silenee ouer-long:
Where I was wont to feed you with my blood,
Ile lop a member off, and giue it you,
In earnest of a further benefit:
So you do condiscend to helpe me now.
They hang their heads.
No hope to haue redresse? My body shall
Pay recompence, if you will graunt my suite.
They shake their heads.
Cannot my body, nor blood-sacrifice,
Intreate you to your wonted furtherance?
Then take my soule; my body, soule, and all,
Before that England giue the French the foyle.
They depart.
See, they forsake me. Now the time is come,
That France must vale her lofty plumed Crest,
And let her head fall into Englands lappe.
My ancient Incantations are too weake,
And hell too strong for me to buckle with:
Now France, thy glory droopeth to the dust. *Exit.*

Excursions. Burgundie and Yorke fight hand to hand. French flye.

Yorke. Damsell of France, I thinke I haue you fast,
Vnchaine your spirits now with spelling Charmes,
And try if they can gaine your liberty.
A goodly prize, fit for the diuels grace.
See how the vgly Witch doth bend her browes,
As if with *Circe*, she would change my shape.
Puc. Chang'd to a worser shape thou canst not be:
Yor. Oh, *Charles* the Dolphin is a proper man,
No shape but his can please your dainty eye.
Puc A plaguing mischeefe light on *Charles*, and thee,
And may ye both be sodainly surpriz'd
By bloudy hands, in sleeping on your beds.
Yorke. Fell banning Hagge, Inchantresse hold thy tongue.
Puc. I prethee giue me leaue to curse awhile.
Yorke. Curse Miscreant, when thou comst to the stake
Exeunt.
Alarum. Enter Suffolke with Margaret in his hand.
Suff. Be what thou wilt, thou art my prisoner.
Gazes on her.
Oh Fairest Beautie, do not feare, nor flye:
For I will touch thee but with reuerend hands,
I kisse these fingers for eternall peace,
And lay them gently on thy tender side.
Who art thou, say? that I may honor thee.
Mar. *Margaret* my name, and daughter to a King,
The King of Naples, who so ere thou art.
Suff. An Earle I am, and Suffolke am I call'd
Be not offended Natures myracle,
Thou art alotted to be tane by me:
So doth the Swan her downie Signets saue,
Oh stay:

Keeping them priſoner vnderneath his wings:
Yet if this ſeruile vſage once offend,
Go, and be free againe, as Suffolkes friend. *She is going*
Oh ſtay: I haue no power to let her paſſe,
My hand would free her, but my heart ſayes no.
As playes the Sunne vpon the glaſſie ſtreames,
Twinkling another counterfetted beame,
So ſeemes this gorgeous beauty to mine eyes.
Faine would I woe her, yet I dare not ſpeake:
Ile call for Pen and Inke, and write my minde:
Fye *De la Pole*, diſable not thy ſelfe:
Haſt not a Tongue? Is ſhe not heere?
Wilt thou be daunted at a Womans ſight?
I: Beauties Princely Maieſty is ſuch,
'Confounds the tongue, and makes the ſenſes rough.
Mar. Say Earle of Suffolke, if thy name be ſo,
What ranſome muſt I pay before I paſſe?
For I perceiue I am thy priſoner.
Suf. How canſt thou tell ſhe will deny thy ſuite,
Before thou make a triall of her loue?
M. Why ſpeak'ſt thou not? What ranſom muſt I pay?
Suf. She's beautifull; and therefore to be Wooed:
She is a Woman; therefore to be Wonne.
Mar. Wilt thou accept of ranſome, yea or no?
Suf. Fond man, remember that thou haſt a wife,
Then how can *Margaret* be thy Paramour?
Mar. I were beſt to leaue him, for he will not heare.
Suf. There all is marr'd: there lies a cooling card.
Mar. He talkes at randon: ſure the man is mad.
Suf. And yet a diſpenſation may bee had.
Mar. And yet I would that you would anſwer me.
Suf. Ile win this Lady *Margaret*. For whom?
Why for my King: Tuſh, that's a woodden thing.
Mar He talkes of wood: It is ſome Carpenter.
Suf. Yet ſo my fancy may be ſatisfied,
And peace eſtabliſhed betweene theſe Realmes.
But there remaines a ſcruple in that too:
For though her Father be the King of *Naples*,
Duke of *Anion* and *Mayne*, yet is he poore,
And our Nobility will ſcorne the match.
Mar. Heare ye Captaine? Are you not at leyſure?
Suf. It ſhall be ſo, diſdaine they ne're ſo much:
Henry is youthfull, and will quickly yeeld.
Madam, I haue a ſecret to reueale.
Mar. What though I be inthral'd, he ſeems a knight
And will not any way diſhonor me.
Suf. Lady, vouchſafe to liſten what I ſay.
Mar. Perhaps I ſhall be reſcu'd by the French,
And then I need not craue his curteſie.
Suf. Sweet Madam, giue me hearing in a cauſe.
Mar. Tuſh, women haue bene captiuate ere now.
Suf. Lady, wherefore talke you ſo?
Mar. I cry you mercy, 'tis but *Quid* for *Quo*.
Suf. Say gentle Princeſſe, would you not ſuppoſe
Your bondage happy, to be made a Queene?
Mar. To be a Queene in bondage, is more vile,
Than is a ſlaue, in baſe ſeruility:
For Princes ſhould be free.
Suf. And ſo ſhall you,
If happy Englands Royall King be free.
Mar. Why what concernes his freedome vnto mee?
Suf. Ile vndertake to make thee *Henries* Queene,
To put a Golden Scepter in thy hand,
And ſet a precious Crowne vpon thy head,
If thou wilt condiſcend to be my———
Mar What?
Suf. His loue.
Mar. I am vnworthy to be *Henries* wife.
Suf. No gentle Madam, I vnworthy am
To woe ſo faire a Dame to be his wife,
And haue no portion in the choice my ſelfe.
How ſay you Madam, are ye ſo content?
Mar. And if my Father pleaſe, I am content.
Suf. Then call our Captaines and our Colours forth,
And Madam, at your Fathers Caſtle walles,
Wee'l craue a parley, to conferre with him.
Sound. Enter Reignier on the Walles.
See *Reignier* ſee, thy daughter priſoner.
Reig. To whom?
Suf. To me.
Reig. Suffolke, what remedy?
I am a Souldier, and vnapt to weepe,
Or to exclaime on Fortunes fickleneſſe.
Suf. Yes, there is remedy enough my Lord,
Conſent, and for thy Honor giue conſent,
Thy daughter ſhall be wedded to my King,
Whom I with paine haue wooed and wonne thereto:
And this her eaſie held impriſonment,
Hath gain'd thy daughter Princely libertie.
Reig. Speakes Suffolke as he thinkes?
Suf. Faire *Margaret* knowes,
That Suffolke doth not flatter, face, or faine.
Reig. Vpon thy Princely warrant, I deſcend,
To giue thee anſwer of thy iuſt demand.
Suf. And heere I will expect thy comming.

Trumpets ſound. Enter Reignier.

Reig. Welcome braue Earle into our Territories,
Command in *Anion* what your Honor pleaſes.
Suf. Thankes *Reignier*, happy for ſo ſweet a Childe,
Fit to be made companion with a King:
What anſwer makes your Grace vnto my ſuite?
Reig. Since thou doſt daigne to woe her little worth,
To be the Princely Bride of ſuch a Lord:
Vpon condition I may quietly
Enioy mine owne, the Country *Maine* and *Anion*,
Free from oppreſſion, or the ſtroke of Warre,
My daughter ſhall be *Henries*, if he pleaſe.
Suf. That is her ranſome, I deliuer her,
And thoſe two Counties I will vndertake
Your Grace ſhall well and quietly enioy.
Reig. And I againe in *Henries* Royall name,
As Deputy vnto that gracious King,
Giue thee her hand for ſigne of plighted faith.
Suf. *Reignier* of France, I giue thee Kingly thankes,
Becauſe this is in Trafficke of a King.
And yet me thinkes I could be well content
To be mine owne Atturney in this caſe.
Ile ouer then to England with this newes.
And make this marriage to be ſolemniz'd:
So farewell *Reignier*, ſet this Diamond ſafe
In Golden Pallaces as it becomes.
Reig. I do embrace thee, as I would embrace
The Chriſtian Prince King *Henrie* were he heere.
Mar. Farewell my Lord, good wiſhes, praiſe, & praiers,
Shall Suffolke euer haue of *Margaret*. *Shee is going.*
Suf. Farwell ſweet Madam: but hearke you *Margaret*,
No Princely commendations to my King.
Mar. Such commendations as becomes a Maide,
A Virgin, and his Seruant, ſay to him.
Suf. Words ſweetly plac'd, and modeſtie directed,
But

But Madame, I must trouble you againe,
No louing Token to his Maiestie?
Mar. Yes, my good Lord, a pure vnspotted heart,
Neuer yet taint with loue, I send the King.
Suf. And this withall. *Kisse her.*
Mar. That for thy selfe, I will not so presume,
To send such peeuish tokens to a King.
Suf. Oh wert thou for my selfe: but *Suffolke* stay,
Thou mayest not wander in that Labyrinth,
There Minotaurs and vgly Treasons lurke,
Solicite *Henry* with her wonderous praise.
Bethinke thee on her Vertues that surmount,
Mad naturall Graces that extinguish Art,
Repeate their semblance often on the Seas,
That when thou com'st to kneele at *Henries* feete,
Thou mayest bereaue him of his wits with wonder. *Exit*

Enter Yorke, Warwicke, Shepheard, Pucell.

Yor. Bring forth that Sorceresse condemn'd to burne.
Shep Ah *Ione*, this kils thy Fathers heart out-right,
Haue I sought euery Country farre and neere,
And now it is my chance to finde thee out,
Must I behold thy timelesse cruell death:
Ah *Ione*, sweet daughter *Ione*, Ile die with thee.
Pucel. Decrepit Miser, base ignoble Wretch,
I am descended of a gentler blood.
Thou art no Father, nor no Friend of mine.
Shep. Out, out: My Lords, and please you, 'tis not so
I did beget her, all the Parish knowes:
Her Mother liueth yet, can testifie
She was the first fruite of my Bach'ler-ship.
War. Gracelesse, wilt thou deny thy Parentage?
Yorke. This argues what her kinde of life hath beene,
Wicked and vile, and so her death concludes.
Shep. Fye *Ione*, that thou wilt be so obstacle:
God knowes, thou art a collop of my flesh,
And for thy sake haue I shed many a teare:
Deny me not, I prythee, gentle *Ione*.
Pucell. Pezant auant. You haue suborn'd this man
Of purpose, to obscure my Noble birth.
Shep. 'Tis true, I gaue a Noble to the Priest,
The morne that I was wedded to her mother.
Kneele downe and take my blessing, good my Gyrle.
Wilt thou not stoope? Now cursed be the time
Of thy natiuitie: I would the Milke
Thy mother gaue thee when thou suck'st her brest,
Had bin a little Rats-bane for thy sake.
Or else, when thou didst keepe my Lambes a-field,
I wish some rauenous Wolfe had eaten thee.
Doest thou deny thy Father, cursed Drab?
O burne her, burne her, hanging is too good. *Exit.*
Yorke. Take her away, for she hath liu'd too long,
To fill the world with vicious qualities.
Puc. First let me tell you whom you haue condemn'd;
Not me, begotten of a Shepheard Swaine,
But issued from the Progeny of Kings.
Vertuous and Holy, chosen from aboue,
By inspiration of Celestiall Grace,
To worke exceeding myracles on earth.
I neuer had to do with wicked Spirits.
But you that are polluted with your lustes,
Stain'd with the guiltlesse blood of Innocents,
Corrupt and tainted with a thousand Vices:
Because you want the grace that others haue,
You iudge it straight a thing impossible
To compasse Wonders, but by helpe of diuels.
No misconceyued, *Ione of Aire* hath beene
A Virgin from her tender infancie,
Chaste, and immaculate in very thought,
Whose Maiden-blood thus rigorously effus'd,
Will cry for Vengeance, at the Gates of Heauen.
Yorke. I, I: away with her to execution.
War. And hearke ye sirs: because she is a Maide,
Spare for no Faggots, let there be enow:
Place barrelles of pitch vpon the fatall stake,
That so her torture may be shortned.
Puc. Will nothing turne your vnrelenting hearts?
Then *Ione* discouer thine infirmity,
That warranteth by Law, to be thy priuiledge.
I am with childe ye bloody Homicides:
Murther not then the Fruite within my Wombe,
Although ye hale me to a violent death.
Yor. Now heauen forfend, the holy Maid with child?
War. The greatest miracle that ere ye wrought.
Is all your strict precisenesse come to this?
Yorke. She and the Dolphin haue bin iugling,
I did imagine what would be her refuge.
War. Well go too, we'll haue no Bastards liue.
Especially since *Charles* must Father it.
Puc. You are deceyu'd, my childe is none of his,
It was *Alanson* that inioy'd my loue.
Yorke. *Alanson* that notorious Macheuile?
It dyes, and if it had a thousand liues.
Puc. Oh giue me leaue, I haue deluded you,
'Twas neyther *Charles*, nor yet the Duke I nam'd,
But *Reignier* King of *Naples* that preuayl'd
War. A married man, that's most intollerable.
Yor. Why here's a Gyrle: I think she knowes not wel
(There were so many) whom she may accuse.
War. It's signe she hath beene liberall and free
Yor. And yet forsooth she is a Virgin pure.
Strumpet, thy words condemne thy Brat, and thee.
Vse no intreaty, for it is in vaine
Pu. Then lead me hence: with whom I leaue my curse.
May neuer glorious Sunne reflex his beames
Vpon the Countrey where you make abode:
But darknesse, and the gloomy shade of death
Inuiron you, till Mischeefe and Dispaire,
Driue you to break your necks, or hang your selues. *Exit*

Enter Cardinall.

Yorke. Breake thou in peeces, and consume to ashes,
Thou fowle accursed minister of Hell.
Car. Lord Regent, I do greete your Excellence
With Letters of Commission from the King.
For know my Lords, the States of Christendome,
Mou'd with remorse of these out-ragious broyles,
Haue earnestly implor'd a generall peace,
Betwixt our Nation, and the aspyring French;
And heere at hand, the Dolphin and his Traine
Approacheth, to conferre about some matter.
Yorke. Is all our trauell turn'd to this effect,
After the slaughter of so many Peeres,
So many Captaines, Gentlemen, and Soldiers,
That in this quarrell haue beene ouerthrowne,
And sold their bodyes for their Countryes benefit,
Shall we at last conclude effeminate peace?
Haue we not lost most part of all the Townes,
By Treason, Falshood, and by Treacherie,
Our great Progenitors had conquered:
Oh Warwicke, Warwicke, I foresee with greefe
The vtter losse of all the Realme of France.
War. Be patient Yorke, if we conclude a Peace

m It

It shall be with such strict and seuere Couenants,
As little shall the Frenchmen gaine thereby.

Enter Charles, Alanson, Bastard, Reignier.

Char. Since Lords of England, it is thus agreed,
That peacefull truce shall be proclaim'd in France,
We come to be informed by your selues,
What the conditions of that league must be.
Yorke. Speake Winchester, for boyling choller chokes
The hollow passage of my poyson'd voyce,
By sight of these our balefull enemies.
Win. *Charles*, and the rest, it is enacted thus:
That in regard King *Henry* giues consent,
Of meere compassion, and of lenity,
To ease your Countrie of distressefull Warre,
And suffer you to breath in fruitfull peace,
You shall become true Liegemen to his Crowne.
And *Charles*, vpon condition thou wilt sweare
To pay him tribute, and submit thy selfe,
Thou shalt be plac'd as Viceroy vnder him,
And still enioy thy Regall dignity.
Alan. Must he be then as shadow of himselfe?
Adorne his Temples with a Coronet,
And yet in substance and authority,
Retaine but priuiledge of a priuate man?
This proffer is absurd, and reasonlesse.
Char 'Tis knowne already that I am possest
With more then halfe the Gallian Territories,
And therein reuerenc'd for their lawfull King.
Shall I for lucre of the rest vn-vanquisht,
Detract so much from that prerogatiue,
As to be call'd but Viceroy of the whole?
No Lord Ambassador, Ile rather keepe
That which I haue, than coueting for more
Be cast from possibility of all.
Yorke. Insulting *Charles*, hast thou by secret meanes
Vs'd intercession to obtaine a league,
And now the matter growes to compremize,
Stand'st thou aloofe vpon Comparison.
Either accept the Title thou vsurp'st,
Of benefit proceeding from our King,
And not of any challenge of Desert,
Or we will plague thee with incessant Warres.
Reig. My Lord, you do not well in obstinacy,
To cauill in the course of this Contract:
If once it be neglected, ten to one
We shall not finde like opportunity.
Alan. To say the truth, it is your policie,
To saue your Subiects from such massacre
And ruthlesse slaughters as are dayly seene
By our proceeding in Hostility,
And therefore take this compact of a Truce,
Although you breake it, when your pleasure serues.
War. How sayst thou *Charles*?
Shall our Condition stand?
Char. It Shall:
Onely reseru'd, you claime no interest
In any of our Townes of Garrison.
Yor. Then sweare Allegeance to his Maiesty,
As thou art Knight, neuer to disobey,
Nor be Rebellious to the Crowne of England,
Thou nor thy Nobles, to the Crowne of England.
So, now dismisse your Army when ye please:
Hang vp your Ensignes, let your Drummes be still,
For heere we entertaine a solemne peace. *Exeunt*

Actus Quintus.

Enter Suffolke in conference with the King, Glocester, and Exeter.

King. Your wondrous rare description (noble Earle)
Of beauteous *Margaret* hath astonish'd me:
Her vertues graced with externall gifts,
Do breed Loues setled passions in my heart,
And like as rigour of tempestuous gustes
Prouokes the mightiest Hulke against the tide,
So am I driuen by breath of her Renowne,
Either to suffer Shipwracke, or arriue
Where I may haue fruition of her Loue.
Suf. Tush my good Lord, this superficiall tale,
Is but a preface of her worthy praise:
The cheefe perfections of that louely Dame,
(Had I sufficient skill to vtter them)
Would make a volume of inticing lines,
Able to rauish any dull conceit.
And which is more, she is not so Diuine,
So full replete with choice of all delights,
But with as humble lowlinesse of minde,
She is content to be at your command:
Command I meane, of Vertuous chaste intents,
To Loue, and Honor *Henry* as her Lord.
King. And otherwise, will *Henry* ne're presume:
Therefore my Lord Protector, giue consent,
That *Marg'ret* may be Englands Royall Queene.
Glo So should I giue consent to flatter sinne,
You know (my Lord) your Highnesse is betroath'd
Vnto another Lady of esteeme,
How shall we then dispense with that contract,
And not deface your Honor with reproach?
Suf. As doth a Ruler with vnlawfull Oathes,
Or one that at a Triumph, hauing vow'd
To try his strength, forsaketh yet the Listes
By reason of his Aduersaries oddes.
A poore Earles daughter is vnequall oddes,
And therefore may be broke without offence.
Gloucester. Why what (I pray) is *Margaret* more then that?
Her Father is no better than an Earle,
Although in glorious Titles he excell.
Suf. Yes my Lord, her Father is a King,
The King of Naples, and Ierusalem,
And of such great Authoritie in France,
As his alliance will confirme our peace,
And keepe the Frenchmen in Allegeance.
Glo. And so the Earle of Arminacke may doe,
Because he is neere Kinsman vnto *Charles*.
Exet Beside, his wealth doth warrant a liberal dower,
Where *Reignier* sooner will receyue, than giue.
Suf. A Dowre my Lords? Disgrace not so your King,
That he should be so abiect, base, and poore,
To choose for wealth, and not for perfect Loue.
Henry is able to enrich his Queene,
And not to seeke a Queene to make him rich,
So worthlesse Pezants bargaine for their Wiues,
As Market men for Oxen, Sheepe, or Horse.
Marriage is a matter of more worth,
Then to be dealt in by Atturney-ship:
Not whom we will, but whom his Grace affects,

Must

Must be companion of his Nuptiall bed.
And therefore Lords, since he affects her most,
Most of all these reasons bindeth vs,
In our opinions she should be preferr'd.
For what is wedlocke forced? but a Hell,
An Age of discord and continuall strife,
Whereas the contrarie bringeth blisse,
And is a patterne of Celestiall peace.
Whom should we match with *Henry* being a King,
But *Margaret*, that is daughter to a King:
Her peerelesse feature, ioyned with her birth,
Approues her fit for none, but for a King.
Her valiant courage, and vndaunted spirit,
(More then in women commonly is seene)
Will answer our hope in issue of a King.
For *Henry*, sonne vnto a Conqueror,
Is likely to beget more Conquerors,
If with a Lady of so high resolue,
(As is faire *Margaret*) he be link'd in loue.
Then yeeld my Lords, and heere conclude with mee,
That *Margaret* shall be Queene, and none but shee.
King. Whether it be through force of your report,
My Noble Lord of Suffolke: Or for that
My tender youth was neuer yet attaint
With any passion of inflaming loue,
I cannot tell: but this I am assur'd,
I feele such sharpe dissention in my breast,
Such fierce alarums both of Hope and Feare,
As I am sicke with working of my thoughts.
Take therefore shipping, poste my Lord to France,
Agree to any couenants, and procure
That Lady *Margaret* do vouchsafe to come
To crosse the Seas to England, and be crown'd
King *Henries* faithfull and annointed Queene.
For your expences and sufficient charge,
Among the people gather vp a tenth.
Be gone I say, for till you do returne,
I rest perplexed with a thousand Cares.
And you (good Vnckle) banish all offence:
If you do censure me, by what you were,
Not what you are, I know it will excuse
This sodaine execution of my will.
And so conduct me, where from company,
I may reuolue and ruminate my greefe. *Exit.*
Glo. I greefe I feare me, both at first and last.
Exit Glocester.
Suf. Thus Suffolke hath preuail'd, and thus he goes
As did the youthfull *Paris* once to Greece,
With hope to finde the like euent in loue,
But prosper better than the Troian did:
Margaret shall now be Queene, and rule the King:
But I will rule both her, the King, and Realme. *Exit*

FINIS.

m 2 The

The second Part of Henry the Sixt, with the death of the Good Duke HVMFREY.

Actus Primus. Scœna Prima.

Flourish of Trumpets: Then Hoboyes.

Enter King, Duke Humfrey, Salisbury, Warwicke, and Beauford on the one side.

The Queene, Suffolke, Yorke, Somerset, and Buckingham, on the other.

Suffolke.

AS by your high Imperiall Maiesty,
I had in charge at my depart for France,
As Procurator to your Excellence,
To marry Princes *Margaret* for your Grace;
So in the Famous Ancient City, *Toures,*
In presence of the Kings of *France,* and *Sicill,*
The Dukes of *Orleance, Calaber, Britaigne,* and *Alanson,*
Seuen Earles, twelue Barons, & twenty reuerend Bishops
I haue perform'd my Taske, and was espous'd,
And humbly now vpon my bended knee,
In sight of England, and her Lordly Peeres,
Deliuer vp my Title in the Queene
To your most gracious hands, that are the Substance
Of that great Shadow I did represent:
The happiest Gift, that euer Marquesse gaue,
The Fairest Queene, that euer King receiu'd.

King. Suffolke arise. Welcome Queene *Margaret,*
I can expresse no kinder signe of Loue
Then this kinde kisse: O Lord, that lends me life,
Lend me a heart repleate with thankfulnesse:
For thou hast giuen me in this beauteous Face
A world of earthly blessings to my soule,
If Simpathy of Loue vnite our thoughts.

Queen. Great King of England, & my gracious Lord,
The mutuall conference that my minde hath had,
By day, by night; waking, and in my dreames,
In Courtly company, or at my Beades,
With you mine *Alder liefest* Soueraigne,
Makes me the bolder to salute my King,
With ruder termes, such as my wit affoords,
And ouer ioy of heart doth minister.

King. Her sight did rauish, but her grace in Speech,
Her words yclad with wisedomes Maiesty,
Makes me from Wondring, fall to Weeping ioyes,
Such is the Fulnesse of my hearts content.
Lords, with one cheerefull voice, Welcome my Loue.

All kneel. Long liue Qu. *Margaret,* Englands happines.

Queene. We thanke you all. *Florish*

Suf. My Lord Protector, so it please your Grace,
Heere are the Articles of contracted peace,
Betweene our Soueraigne, and the French King *Charles,*
For eighteene moneths concluded by consent.

Glo. Reads. Inprimis, *It is agreed betweene the French K. Charles, and William de la Pole Marquesse of Suffolke, Ambassador for Henry King of England, That the said Henry shal espouse the Lady Margaret, daughter vnto Reignier King of Naples, Sicillia, and Ierusalem, and Crowne her Queene of England, ere the thirtieth of May next ensuing.*

Item, *That the Dutchy of Aniou, and the County of Main, shall be released and deliuered to the King her father.*

King. Vnkle, how now?

Glo. Pardon me gracious Lord,
Some sodaine qualme hath strucke me at the heart,
And dim'd mine eyes, that I can reade no further.

King. Vnckle of Winchester, I pray read on.

Win. Item, *It is further agreed betweene them, That the Dutchesse of Aniou and Maine, shall be released and deliuered ouer to the King her Father, and shee sent ouer of the King of Englands owne proper Cost and Charges, without hauing any Dowry.*

King. They please vs well. Lord Marques kneel down,
We heere create thee the first Duke of Suffolke,
And girt thee with the Sword. Cosin of Yorke,
We heere discharge your Grace from being Regent
I'th parts of France, till terme of eighteene Moneths
Be full expyr'd. Thankes Vncle Winchester,
Gloster, Yorke, Buckingham, Somerset,
Salisburie, and Warwicke.
We thanke you all for this great fauour done,
In entertainment to my Princely Queene.
Come, let vs in, and with all speede prouide
To see her Coronation be perform'd.

Exit King, Queene, and Suffolke.

Manet the rest.

Glo. Braue Peeres of England, Pillars of the State,
To you Duke *Humfrey* must vnload his greefe:
Your greefe, the common greefe of all the Land.
What? did my brother *Henry* spend his youth,
His valour, coine, and people in the warres?
Did he so often lodge in open field:
In Winters cold, and Summers parching heate,
To conquer France, his true inheritance?
And did my brother *Bedford* toyle his wits,

To

To keepe by policy what *Henrie* got:
Haue you your selues, *Somerset*, *Buckingham*,
Braue *Yorke*, *Salisbury*, and victorious *Warwicke*,
Receiud deepe scarres in France and Normandie:
Or hath mine Vnckle *Beauford*, and my selfe,
With all the Learned Counsell of the Realme,
Studied so long, sat in the Councell house,
Early and late, debating too and fro
How France and Frenchmen might be kept in awe,
And hath his Highnesse in his infancie,
Crowned in Paris in despight of foes,
And shall these Labours, and these Honours dye?
Shall *Henries* Conquest, *Bedfords* vigilance,
Your Deeds of Warre, and all our Counsell dye?
O Peeres of England, shamefull is this League,
Fatall this Marriage, cancelling your Fame,
Blotting your names from Bookes of memory,
Racing the Charracters of your Renowne,
Defacing Monuments of Conquer'd France,
Vndoing all as all had neuer bin.
Car. Nephew, what meanes this passionate discourse?
This preroration with such circumstance:
For France, 'tis ours; and we will keepe it still.
Glo. I Vnckle, we will keepe it, if we can:
But now it is impossible we should.
Suffolke, the new made Duke that rules the rost,
Hath giuen the Dutchy of *Aniou* and *Mayne*,
Vnto the poore King *Reignier*, whose large style
Agrees not with the leannesse of his purse.
Sal. Now by the death of him that dyed for all,
These Counties were the Keyes of *Normandie*:
But wherefore weepes *Warwicke*, my valiant sonne?
War. For greefe that they are past recouerie.
For were there hope to conquer them againe,
My sword should shed hot blood, mine eyes no teares.
Aniou and *Maine*? My selfe did win them both:
Those Prouinces, these Armes of mine did conquer,
And are the Citties that I got with wounds,
Deliuer'd vp againe with peacefull words?
Mort Dieu.
Yorke. For Suffolkes Duke, may he be suffocate,
That dims the Honor of this Warlike Isle:
France should haue torne and rent my very hart,
Before I would haue yeelded to this League.
I neuer read but Englands Kings haue had
Large summes of Gold, and Dowries with their wiues,
And our King *Henry* giues away his owne,
To match with her that brings no vantages.
Hum. A proper iest, and neuer heard before,
That Suffolke should demand a whole Fifteenth,
For Costs and Charges in transporting her:
She should haue staid in France, and steru'd in France
Before———
Car. My Lord of Gloster, now ye grow too hot,
It was the pleasure of my Lord the King.
Hum. My Lord of Winchester I know your minde.
'Tis not my speeches that you do mislike:
But 'tis my presence that doth trouble ye,
Rancour will out, proud Prelate, in thy face
I see thy furie: If I longer stay,
We shall begin our ancient bickerings:
Lordings farewell, and say when I am gone,
I prophesied, France will be lost ere long. *Exit Humfrey.*
Car. So, there goes our Protector in a rage:
'Tis knowne to you he is mine enemy:
Nay more, an enemy vnto you all,
And no great friend, I feare me to the King;
Consider Lords, he is the next of blood,
And heyre apparant to the English Crowne:
Had *Henrie* got an Empire by his marriage,
And all the wealthy Kingdomes of the West,
There's reason he should be displeas'd at it:
Looke to it Lords, let not his smoothing words
Bewitch your hearts, be wise and circumspect.
What though the common people fauour him,
Calling him, *Humfrey the good Duke of Gloster*,
Clapping their hands, and crying with loud voyce,
Iesu maintaine your Royall Excellence,
With God preserue the good Duke *Humfrey*:
I feare me Lords, for all this flattering glosse,
He will be found a dangerous Protector.
Buc. Why should he then protect our Soueraigne?
He being of age to gouerne of himselfe.
Cosin of Somerset, ioyne you with me,
And altogether with the Duke of Suffolke,
Wee'l quickly hoyse Duke *Humfrey* from his seat.
Car. This weighty businesse will not brooke delay,
Ile to the Duke of Suffolke presently. *Exit Cardinall.*
Som. Cosin of Buckingham, though *Humfries* pride
And greatnesse of his place be greefe to vs,
Yet let vs watch the haughtie Cardinall,
His insolence is more intollerable
Then all the Princes in the Land beside,
If Gloster be displac'd, hee'l be Protector.
Buc. Or thou, or I Somerset will be Protectors,
Despite Duke *Humfrey*, or the Cardinall.
Exit Buckingham, and Somerset.
Sal. Pride went before, Ambition followes him.
While these do labour for their owne preferment,
Behooues it vs to labor for the Realme.
I neuer saw but Humfrey Duke of Gloster,
Did beare him like a Noble Gentleman:
Oft haue I seene the haughty Cardinall,
More like a Souldier then a man o'th'Church,
As stout and proud as he were Lord of all,
Sweare like a Ruffian, and demeane himselfe
Vnlike the Ruler of a Common-weale.
Warwicke my sonne, the comfort of my age,
Thy deeds, thy plainnesse, and thy house-keeping,
Hath wonne the greatest fauour of the Commons,
Excepting none but good Duke Humfrey.
And Brother Yorke, thy Acts in Ireland,
In bringing them to ciuill Discipline:
Thy late exploits done in the heart of France,
When thou wert Regent for our Soueraigne,
Haue made thee fear'd and honor'd of the people,
Ioyne we together for the publike good,
In what we can, to bridle and suppresse
The pride of Suffolke, and the Cardinall,
With Somersets and Buckinghams Ambition,
And as we may, cherish Duke Humfries deeds,
While they do tend the profit of the Land.
War. So God helpe Warwicke, as he loues the Land,
And common profit of his Countrey.
Yor. And so sayes Yorke,
For he hath greatest cause.
Salisbury. Then lets make hast away,
And looke vnto the maine.
Warwicke. Vnto the maine?
Oh Father, *Maine* is lost,
That *Maine*, which by maine force Warwicke did winne,
And would haue kept, so long as breath did last:
m 3 Main

Main-chance father you meant, but I meant *Maine*,
Which I will win from France, or else be slaine.
Exit Warwicke, and Salisbury. Manet Yorke.
Yorke. *Aniou* and *Maine* are giuen to the French,
Paris is lost, the state of *Normandie*
Stands on a tickle point, now they are gone:
Suffolke concluded on the Articles,
The Peeres agreed, and *Henry* was well pleas'd,
To change two Dukedomes for a Dukes faire daughter.
I cannot blame them all, what is't to them?
'Tis thine they giue away, and not their owne.
Pirates may make cheape penyworths of their pillage,
And purchase Friends, and giue to Curtezans,
Still reuelling like Lords till all be gone,
While as the silly Owner of the goods
Weepes ouer them, and wrings his haplesse hands,
And shakes his head, and trembling stands aloofe,
While all is shar'd, and all is borne away,
Ready to sterue, and dare not touch his owne.
So Yorke must sit, and fret, and bite his tongue,
While his owne Lands are bargain'd for, and sold:
Me thinkes the Realmes of England, France, & Ireland,
Beare that proportion to my flesh and blood,
As did the fatall brand *Althaa* burnt,
Vnto the Princes heart of *Calidon*:
Aniou and *Maine* both giuen vnto the French?
Cold newes for me: for I had hope of France,
Euen as I haue of fertile Englands soile.
A day will come, when Yorke shall claime his owne,
And therefore I will take the *Neuils* parts,
And make a shew of loue to proud Duke *Humfrey*,
And when I spy aduantage, claime the Crowne,
For that's the Golden marke I seeke to hit:
Nor shall proud Lancaster vsurpe my right,
Nor hold the Scepter in his childish Fist,
Nor weare the Diadem vpon his head,
Whose Church-like humors fits not for a Crowne.
Then Yorke be still a-while, till time do serue:
Watch thou, and wake when others be asleepe,
To prie into the secrets of the State,
Till *Henrie* surfetting in ioyes of loue,
With his new Bride, & Englands deere bought Queen,
And *Humfrey* with the Peeres be falne at iarres:
Then will I raise aloft the Milke-white-Rose,
With whose sweet smell the Ayre shall be perfum'd,
And in my Standard beare the Armes of Yorke,
To grapple with the house of Lancaster,
And force perforce Ile make him yeeld the Crowne,
Whose bookish Rule, hath pull'd faire England downe.
Exit Yorke.

Enter Duke Humfrey and his wife Elianor.

Elia. Why droopes my Lord like ouer-ripen'd Corn,
Hanging the head at Ceres plenteous load?
Why doth the Great Duke *Humfrey* knit his browes,
As frowning at the Fauours of the world?
Why are thine eyes fixt to the sullen earth,
Gazing on that which seemes to dimme thy sight?
What seest thou there? King *Henries* Diadem,
Inchac'd with all the Honors of the world?
If so, Gaze on, and grouell on thy face,
Vntill thy head be circled with the same.
Put forth thy hand, reach at the glorious Gold.
What, is't too short? Ile lengthen it with mine,
And hauing both together heau'd it vp,
Wee'l both together lift our heads to heauen,
And neuer more abase our sight so low,
As to vouchsafe one glance vnto the ground.
Hum. O *Nell*, sweet *Nell*, if thou dost loue thy Lord,
Banish the Canker of ambitious thoughts:
And may that thought, when I imagine ill
Against my King and Nephew, vertuous *Henry*,
Be my last breathing in this mortall world.
My troublous dreames this night, doth make me sad.
Eli. What dream'd my Lord, tell me, and Ile requite it
With sweet rehearsall of my mornings dreame?
Hum. Me thought this staffe mine Office-badge in Court
Was broke in twaine: by whom, I haue forgot,
But as I thinke, it was by'th Cardinall,
And on the peeces of the broken Wand
Were plac'd the heads of *Edmond* Duke of Somerset,
And *William de la Pole* first Duke of Suffolke.
This was my dreame, what it doth bode God knowes.
Eli. Tut, this was nothing but an argument,
That he that breakes a sticke of Glosters groue,
Shall loose his head for his presumption.
But list to me my *Humfrey*, my sweete Duke:
Me thought I sate in Seate of Maiesty,
In the Cathedrall Church of Westminster,
And in that Chaire where Kings & Queens wer crownd,
Where *Henrie* and Dame *Margaret* kneel'd to me,
And on my head did set the Diadem.
Hum. Nay *Elinor*, then must I chide outright:
Presumptuous Dame, ill-nurter'd *Elianor*,
Art thou not second Woman in the Realme?
And the Protectors wife belou'd of him?
Hast thou not worldly pleasure at command,
Aboue the reach or compasse of thy thought?
And wilt thou still be hammering Treachery,
To tumble downe thy husband, and thy selfe,
From top of Honor, to Disgraces feete?
Away from me, and let me heare no more.
Elia. What, what, my Lord? Are you so chollericke
With *Elianor*, for telling but her dreame?
Next time Ile keepe my dreames vnto my selfe,
And not be check'd.
Hum. Nay be not angry, I am pleas'd againe.
Enter Messenger.
Mess. My Lord Protector, 'tis his Highnes pleasure,
You do prepare to ride vnto S. *Albons*,
Where as the King and Queene do meane to Hawke.
Hu. I go. Come *Nel* thou wilt ride with vs? *Ex. Hum*
Eli. Yes my good Lord, Ile follow presently.
Follow I must, I cannot go before,
While Gloster beares this base and humble minde.
Were I a Man, a Duke, and next of blood,
I would remoue these tedious stumbling blockes,
And smooth my way vpon their headlesse neckes.
And being a woman, I will not be slacke
To play my part in Fortunes Pageant.
Where are you there? Sir *Iohn*; nay feare not man,
We are alone, here's none but thee, & I. *Enter Hume.*
Hume. Iesus preserue your Royall Maiesty.
Elia. What saist thou? Maiesty: I am but Grace.
Hume. But by the grace of God, and *Humes* aduice,
Your Graces Title shall be multiplied.
Elia. What saist thou man? Hast thou as yet confer'd
With *Margerie Iordane* the cunning Witch,
With *Roger Bollingbrooke* the Coniurer?
And will they vndertake to do me good?
Hume. This they haue promised to shew your Highnes
A Spirit rais'd from depth of vnder ground,
That

That shall make answere to such Questions,
As by your Grace shall be propounded him.
Elianor. It is enough, Ile thinke vpon the Questions:
When from Saint *Albones* we doe make returne,
Wee'le see these things effected to the full.
Here *Hume*, take this reward, make merry man
With thy Confederates in this weightie cause.
Exit Elianor.
Hume. Hume must make merry with the Duchesse Gold:
Marry and shall: but how now, Sir *Iohn Hume*?
Seale vp your Lips, and giue no words but Mum,
The businesse asketh silent secrecie.
Dame *Elianor* giues Gold, to bring the Witch:
Gold cannot come amisse, were she a Deuill.
Yet haue I Gold flyes from another Coast:
I dare not say, from the rich Cardinall,
And from the great and new-made Duke of Suffolke;
Yet I doe finde it so: for to be plaine,
They (knowing Dame *Elianors* aspiring humor)
Haue hyred me to vnder-mine the Duchesse,
And buzze these Coniurations in her brayne.
They say, A craftie Knaue do's need no Broker,
Yet am I *Suffolke* and the Cardinalls Broker.
Hume, if you take not heed, you shall goe neere
To call them both a payre of craftie Knaues.
Well, so it stands: and thus I feare at last,
Humes Knauerie will be the Duchesse Wracke,
And her Attainture, will be *Humphreyes* fall:
Sort how it will, I shall haue Gold for all. *Exit.*

Enter three or foure Petitioners, the Armorers Man being one.

1. *Pet*. My Masters, let's stand close, my Lord Protector will come this way by and by, and then wee may deliuer our Supplications in the Quill.

2. *Pet*. Marry the Lord protect him, for hee's a good man, Iesu blesse him.

Enter Suffolke, and Queene.

Peter. Here a comes me thinkes, and the Queene with him: Ile be the first sure.

2. *Pet*. Come backe foole, this is the Duke of Suffolk, and not my Lord Protector.

Suff. How now fellow: would'st any thing with me?

1. *Pet*. I pray my Lord pardon me, I tooke ye for my Lord Protector.

Queene. To my Lord Protector? Are your Supplications to his Lordship? Let me see them: what is thine?

1. *Pet*. Mine is, and't please your Grace, against *Iohn Goodman*, my Lord Cardinals Man, for keeping my House, and Lands, and Wife and all, from me.

Suff. Thy Wife too? that's some Wrong indeede. What's yours? What's heere? Against the Duke of Suffolke, for enclosing the Commons of Melforde. How now, Sir Knaue?

2. *Pet*. Alas Sir, I am but a poore Petitioner of our whole Towneship.

Peter. Against my Master *Thomas Horner*, for saying. That the Duke of Yorke was rightfull Heire to the Crowne.

Queene. What say'st thou? Did the Duke of Yorke say, hee was rightfull Heire to the Crowne?

Peter. That my Mistresse was? No forsooth: my Master said, That he was, and that the King was an Vsurper.

Suff. Who is there?
Enter Seruant.

Take this fellow in, and send for his Master with a Purseuant presently: wee'le heare more of your matter before the King. *Exit.*

Queene. And as for you that loue to be protected
Vnder the Wings of our Protectors Grace,
Begin your Suites anew, and sue to him.
Teare the Supplication.
Away, base Cullions: *Suffolke* let them goe.
All. Come, let's be gone. *Exit.*
Queene. My Lord of Suffolke, say, is this the guise?
Is this the Fashions in the Court of England?
Is this the Gouernment of Britaines Ile?
And this the Royaltie of *Albions* King?
What, shall King *Henry* be a Pupill still,
Vnder the surly *Glosters* Gouernance?
Am I a Queene in Title and in Stile,
And must be made a Subiect to a Duke?
I tell thee *Poole*, when in the Citie *Tours*
Thou ran'st a-tilt in honor of my Loue,
And stol'st away the Ladies hearts of France;
I thought King *Henry* had resembled thee,
In Courage, Courtship, and Proportion:
But all his minde is bent to Holinesse,
To number *Aue-Maries* on his Beades:
His Champions, are the Prophets and Apostles
His Weapons, holy Sawes of sacred Writ,
His Studie is his Tilt-yard, and his Loues
Are brazen Images of Canonized Saints.
I would the Colledge of the Cardinalls
Would chuse him Pope, and carry him to Rome,
And set the Triple Crowne vpon his Head;
That were a State fit for his Holinesse.
Suff. Madame be patient: as I was cause
Your Highnesse came to England, so will I
In England worke your Graces full content.
Queene. Beside the haughtie Protector, haue we *Beauford*
The imperious Churchman; *Somerset*, *Buckingham*,
And grumbling *Yorke*: and not the least of these,
But can doe more in England then the King.
Suff. And he of these, that can doe most of all,
Cannot doe more in England then the *Neuils*:
Salisbury and *Warwick* are no simple Peeres.
Queene. Not all these Lords do vex me halfe so much,
As that prowd Dame, the Lord Protectors Wife:
She sweepes it through the Court with troups of Ladies,
More like an Empresse, then Duke *Humphreyes* Wife:
Strangers in Court, doe take her for the Queene:
She beares a Dukes Reuenewes on her backe,
And in her heart she scornes our Pouertie:
Shall I not liue to be aueng'd on her?
Contemptuous base-borne Callot as she is,
She vaunted 'mongst her Minions t'other day,
The very trayne of her worst wearing Gowne,
Was better worth then all my Fathers Lands,
Till *Suffolke* gaue two Dukedomes for his Daughter.
Suff. Madame, my selfe haue lym'd a Bush for her,
And plac't a Quier of such enticing Birds,
That she will light to listen to the Layes,
And neuer mount to trouble you againe.
So let her rest: and Madame list to me,
For I am bold to counsaile you in this;
Although we fancie not the Cardinall,
Yet must we ioyne with him and with the Lords,
Till we haue brought Duke *Humphrey* in disgrace.
As

As for the Duke of Yorke, this late Complaint
Will make but little for his benefit:
So one by one wee'le weed them all at last,
And you your selfe shall steere the happy Helme. *Exit.*

Sound a Sennet.

Enter the King, Duke Humfrey, Cardinall, Buckingham, Yorke, Salisbury, Warwicke, and the Duchesse.

King. For my part, Noble Lords, I care not which,
Or *Somerset*, or *Yorke*, all's one to me.
Yorke. If *Yorke* haue ill demean'd himselfe in France,
Then let him be denay'd the Regent-ship.
Som. If *Somerset* be vnworthy of the Place,
Let *Yorke* be Regent, I will yeeld to him.
Warw. Whether your Grace be worthy, yea or no,
Dispute not that, *Yorke* is the worthyer.
Card. Ambitious *Warwicke*, let thy betters speake.
Warw. The Cardinall's not my better in the field.
Buck. All in this presence are thy betters, *Warwicke.*
Warw. *Warwicke* may liue to be the best of all.
Salisb. Peace Sonne, and shew some reason *Buckingham*
Why *Somerset* should be preferr'd in this?
Queene. Because the King forsooth will haue it so.
Humf. Madame, the King is old enough himselfe
To giue his Censure: These are no Womens matters.
Queene. If he be old enough, what needs your Grace
To be Protector of his Excellence?
Humf. Madame, I am Protector of the Realme,
And at his pleasure will resigne my Place.
Suff. Resigne it then, and leaue thine insolence.
Since thou wert King; as who is King, but thou?
The Common-wealth hath dayly run to wrack,
The Dolphin hath preuayl'd beyond the Seas,
And all the Peeres and Nobles of the Realme
Haue beene as Bond-men to thy Soueraigntie.
Card. The Commons hast thou rackt, the Clergies Bags
Are lanke and leane with thy Extortions.
Som. Thy sumptuous Buildings, and thy Wiues Attyre
Haue cost a masse of publique Treasurie.
Buck. Thy Crueltie in execution
Vpon Offendors, hath exceeded Law,
And left thee to the mercy of the Law.
Queene. Thy sale of Offices and Townes in France,
If they were knowne, as the suspect is great,
Would make thee quickly hop without thy Head.

Exit Humfrey.

Giue me my Fanne: what, Mynion, can ye not?

She giues the Duchesse a box on the eare.

I cry you mercy, Madame: was it you?
Duch. Was't I? yea, I it was, prowd French-woman:
Could I come neere your Beautie with my Nayles,
I could set my ten Commandements in your face.
King. Sweet Aunt be quiet, 'twas against her will.
Duch. Against her will, good King? looke to't in time
Shee'le hamper thee, and dandle thee like a Baby:
Though in this place most Master weare no Breeches,
She shall not strike Dame *Elianor* vnreueng'd.

Exit Elianor.

Buck. Lord Cardinall, I will follow *Elianor*,
And listen after *Humfrey*, how he proceedes:
Shee's tickled now, her Fume needs no spurres,
Shee'le gallop farre enough to her destruction.

Exit Buckingham.

Enter Humfrey.

Humf. Now Lords, my Choller being ouer-blowne,
With walking once about the Quadrangle,
I come to talke of Common-wealth Affayres.
As for your spightfull false Obiections,
Proue them, and I lye open to the Law:
But God in mercie so deale with my Soule,
As I in dutie loue my King and Countrey.
But to the matter that we haue in hand:
I say, my Soueraigne, *Yorke* is meetest man
To be your Regent in the Realme of France.
Suff. Before we make election, giue me leaue
To shew some reason, of no little force,
That *Yorke* is most vnmeet of any man.
Yorke. Ile tell thee, *Suffolke*, why I am vnmeet.
First, for I cannot flatter thee in Pride:
Next, if I be appointed for the Place,
My Lord of Somerset will keepe me here,
Without Discharge, Money, or Furniture,
Till France be wonne into the Dolphins hands:
Last time I danc't attendance on his will,
Till Paris was besieg'd, famisht, and lost.
Warw. That can I witnesse, and a fouler fact
Did neuer Traytor in the Land commit.
Suff. Peace head-strong *Warwicke.*
Warw. Image of Pride, why should I hold my peace?

Enter Armorer and his Man.

Suff. Because here is a man accused of Treason,
Pray God the Duke of Yorke excuse himselfe.
Yorke. Doth any one accuse *Yorke* for a Traytor?
King. What mean'st thou, *Suffolke*? tell me, what are these?
Suff. Please it your Maiestie, this is the man
That doth accuse his Master of High Treason;
His words were these: That *Richard*, Duke of Yorke,
Was rightfull Heire vnto the English Crowne,
And that your Maiestie was an Vsurper.
King. Say man, were these thy words?

Armorer. And't shall please your Maiestie, I neuer sayd nor thought any such matter: God is my witnesse, I am falsely accus'd by the Villaine.

Peter. By these tenne bones, my Lords, hee did speake them to me in the Garret one Night, as wee were scowring my Lord of Yorkes Armor.

Yorke. Base Dunghill Villaine, and Mechanicall
Ile haue thy Head for this thy Traytors speech:
I doe beseech your Royall Maiestie,
Let him haue all the rigor of the Law.

Armorer. Alas, my Lord, hang me if euer I spake the words: my accuser is my Prentice, and when I did correct him for his fault the other day, he did vow vpon his knees he would be euen with me: I haue good witnesse of this; therefore I beseech your Maiestie, doe not cast away an honest man for a Villaines accusation.

King. Vnckle, what shall we say to this in law?
Humf. This doome, my Lord, if I may iudge:
Let *Somerset* be Regent o're the French,
Because in *Yorke* this breedes suspition;
And let these haue a day appointed them
For single Combat, in conuenient place,
For he hath witnesse of his seruants malice:
This is the Law, and this Duke *Humfreyes* doome.

Som. I

Som. I humbly thanke your Royall Maieſtie.

Armorer. And I accept the Combat willingly.

Peter. Alas, my Lord, I cannot fight; for Gods ſake pitty my caſe: the ſpight of man preuayleth againſt me. O Lord haue mercy vpon me, I ſhall neuer be able to fight a blow: O Lord my heart.

Humf. Sirrha, or you muſt fight, or elſe be hang'd.

King. Away with them to Priſon: and the day of Combat, ſhall be the laſt of the next moneth. Come *Somerſet*, wee'le ſee thee ſent away.

Flouriſh. Exeunt.

Enter the Witch, the two Prieſts, and Bullingbrooke.

Hume. Come my Maſters, the Ducheſſe I tell you expects performance of your promiſes.

Bulling. Maſter *Hume*, we are therefore prouided: will her Ladyſhip behold and heare our Exorciſmes?

Hume. I, what elſe? feare you not her courage.

Bulling. I haue heard her reported to be a Woman of an inuincible ſpirit: but it ſhall be conuenient, Maſter *Hume*, that you be by her aloft, while wee be buſie below; and ſo I pray you goe in Gods Name, and leaue vs.

Exit Hume.

Mother *Iordan*, be you proſtrate, and grouell on the Earth; *Iohn Southwell* reade you, and let vs to our worke.

Enter Elianor aloft

Elianor Well ſaid my Maſters, and welcome all: To this geere, the ſooner the better

Bullin. Patience, good Lady, Wizards know their times:
Deepe Night, darke Night, the ſilent of the Night,
The time of Night when Troy was ſet on fire,
The time when Screech-owles cry, and Bandogs howle,
And Spirits walke, and Ghoſts breake vp their Graues;
That time beſt fits the worke we haue in hand.
Madame, ſit you, and feare not: whom wee rayſe,
Wee will make faſt within a hallow'd Verge.

Here doe the Ceremonies belonging, and make the Circle, Bullingbrooke or Southwell reades, Coniuro te, &c. *It Thunders and Lightens terribly: then the Spirit riſeth.*

Spirit. Ad ſum.

Witch. Aſmath, by the eternall God,
Whoſe name and power thou trembleſt at,
Anſwere that I ſhall aske: for till thou ſpeake,
Thou ſhalt not paſſe from hence.

Spirit. Aske what thou wilt; that I had ſayd, and done.

Bulling. Firſt of the King: What ſhall of him become?

Spirit. The Duke yet liues, that *Henry* ſhall depoſe:
But him out-liue, and dye a violent death.

Bulling. What fates await the Duke of Suffolke?

Spirit By Water ſhall he dye, and take his end.

Bulling. What ſhall befall the Duke of Somerſet?

Spirit. Let him ſhun Caſtles,
Safer ſhall he be vpon the ſandie Plaines,
Then where Caſtles mounted ſtand.
Haue done, for more I hardly can endure.

Bulling. Diſcend to Darkneſſe, and the burning Lake:
Falſe Fiend auoide.

Thunder and Lightning. Exit Spirit.

Enter the Duke of Yorke and the Duke of Buckingham with their Guard, and breake in.

Yorke. Lay hands vpon theſe Traytors, and their traſh:
Beldam I thinke we watcht you at an ynch.
What Madame, are you there? the King & Commonweale
Are deepely indebted for this peece of paines;
My Lord Protector will, I doubt it not,
See you well guerdon'd for theſe good deſerts.

Elianor. Not halfe ſo bad as thine to Englands King,
Iniurious Duke, that threateſt where's no cauſe.

Buck. True Madame, none at all: what call you this?
Away with them, let them be clapt vp cloſe,
And kept aſunder: you Madame ſhall with vs.
Stafford take her to thee.
Wee'le ſee your Trinkets here all forth-comming.
All away. *Exit.*

Yorke. Lord *Buckingham*, me thinks you watcht her well:
A pretty Plot, well choſen to build vpon.
Now pray my Lord, let's ſee the Deuils Writ.
What haue we here? *Reades.*
The Duke yet liues, that Henry *ſhall depoſe:*
But him out-liue, and dye a violent death.
Why this is iuſt *Aio Æacida Romanos vincere poſſo.*
Well, to the reſt:
Tell me what fate awaits the Duke of Suffolke?
By Water ſhall he dye, and take his end.
What ſhall betide the Duke of Somerſet?
Let him ſhunne Caſtles,
Safer ſhall he be vpon the ſandie Plaines,
Then where Caſtles mounted ſtand.
Come, come, my Lords,
Theſe Oracles are hardly attain'd,
And hardly vnderſtood.
The King is now in progreſſe towards Saint *Albones*,
With him, the Husband of this louely Lady:
Thither goes theſe Newes,
As faſt as Horſe can carry them:
A ſorry Breakfaſt for my Lord Protector.

Buck. Your Grace ſhal giue me leaue, my Lord of York,
To be the Poſte, in hope of his reward.

Yorke. At your pleaſure, my good Lord.
Who's within there, hoe?

Enter a Seruingman.

Inuite my Lords of Salisbury and Warwick
To ſuppe with me to morrow Night. Away.

Exeunt.

Enter the King, Queene, Protector, Cardinall, and Suffolke, with Faulkners hallowing.

Queene. Beleeue me Lords, for flying at the Brooke,
I ſaw not better ſport theſe ſeuen yeeres day:
Yet by your leaue, the Winde was very high,
And ten to one, old *Ioane* had not gone out.

King. But what a point, my Lord, your Faulcon made,
And what a pytch ſhe flew aboue the reſt:
To ſee how God in all his Creatures workes,
Yea Man and Birds are fayne of climbing high.

Suff. No maruell, and it like your Maieſtie,
My Lord Protectors Hawkes doe towre ſo well,
They know their Maſter loues to be aloft,
And beares his thoughts aboue his Faulcons Pitch.

Gloſt. My Lord, tis but a baſe ignoble minde,
That mounts no higher then a Bird can ſore.

Card. I

Card. I thought as much, hee would be aboue the
Clouds.
Glost. I my Lord Cardinall, how thinke you by that?
Were it not good your Grace could flye to Heauen?
King. The Treasurie of euerlasting Ioy.
Card. Thy Heauen is on Earth, thine Eyes & Thoughts
Beat on a Crowne, the Treasure of thy Heart,
Pernitious Protector, dangerous Peere,
That smooth'st it so with King and Common-weale.
Glost. What, Cardinall?
Is your Priest-hood growne peremptorie?
Tantæne animis Cœlestibus ira, Church-men so hot?
Good Vnckle hide such mallice:
With such Holynesse can you doe it?
Suff. No mallice Sir, no more then well becomes
So good a Quarrell, and so bad a Peere.
Glost. As who, my Lord?
Suff. Why, as you, my Lord,
An't like your Lordly Lords Protectorship.
Glost. Why *Suffolke*, England knowes thine insolence.
Queene. And thy Ambition, *Gloster*.
King. I prythee peace, good Queene,
And whet not on these furious Peeres,
For blessed are the Peace-makers on Earth.
Card. Let me be blessed for the Peace I make
Against this prowd Protector with my Sword.
Glost. Faith holy Vnckle, would't were come to that.
Card. Marry, when thou dar'st.
Glost. Make vp no factious numbers for the matter,
In thine owne person answere thy abuse.
Card. I, where thou dar'st not peepe:
And if thou dar'st, this Euening,
On the East side of the Groue.
King. How now, my Lords?
Card. Beleeue me, Cousin *Gloster*,
Had not your man put vp the Fowle so suddenly,
We had had more sport.
Come with thy two-hand Sword.
Glost. True Vnckle, are ye aduis'd?
The East side of the Groue:
Cardinall, I am with you.
King. Why how now, Vnckle *Gloster*?
Glost. Talking of Hawking; nothing else, my Lord.
Now by Gods Mother, Priest,
Ile shaue your Crowne for this,
Or all my Fence shall fayle.
Card. *Medice teipsum*, Protector see to't well, protect
your selfe.
King. The Windes grow high,
So doe your Stomacks, Lords:
How irkesome is this Musick to my heart?
When such Strings iarre, what hope of Harmony?
I pray my Lords let me compound this strife.

Enter one crying a Miracle.

Glost. What meanes this noyse?
Fellow, what Miracle do'st thou proclayme?
One. A Miracle, a Miracle.
Suffolke. Come to the King, and tell him what Miracle.
One. Forsooth, a blinde man at Saint *Albones* Shrine,
Within this halfe houre hath receiu'd his sight,
A man that ne're saw in his life before.
King. Now God be prays'd, that to beleeuing Soules
Giues Light in Darknesse, Comfort in Despaire.

Enter the Maior of Saint Albones, and his Brethren, bearing the man betweene two in a Chayre.

Card. Here comes the Townes-men, on Procession,
To present your Highnesse with the man.
King. Great is his comfort in this Earthly Vale,
Although by his sight his sinne be multiplyed.
Glost. Stand by, my Masters, bring him neere the King,
His Highnesse pleasure is to talke with him.
King. Good-fellow, tell vs here the circumstance,
That we for thee may glorifie the Lord.
What, hast thou beene long blinde, and now restor'd?
Simpc. Borne blinde, and't please your Grace.
Wife. I indeede was he.
Suff. What Woman is this?
Wife. His Wife, and't like your Worship.
Glost. Hadst thou been his Mother, thou could'st haue
better told.
King. Where wert thou borne?
Simpc. At Barwick in the North, and't like your
Grace.
King. Poore Soule,
Gods goodnesse hath beene great to thee:
Let neuer Day nor Night vnhallowed passe,
But still remember what the Lord hath done.
Queene. Tell me, good-fellow,
Cam'st thou here by Chance, or of Deuotion,
To this holy Shrine?
Simpc. God knowes of pure Deuotion,
Being call'd a hundred times, and oftner,
In my sleepe, by good Saint *Albon*:
Who said; *Symon*, come; come offer at my Shrine,
And I will helpe thee.
Wife. Most true, forsooth:
And many time and oft my selfe haue heard a Voyce,
To call him so.
Card. What, art thou lame?
Simpc. I, God Almightie helpe me.
Suff. How cam'st thou so?
Simpc. A fall off of a Tree.
Wife. A Plum-tree, Master.
Glost. How long hast thou beene blinde?
Simpc. O borne so, Master.
Glost. What, and would'st climbe a Tree?
Simpc. But that in all my life, when I was a youth.
Wife. Too true, and bought his climbing very deare.
Glost. Masse, thou lou'dst Plummes well, that would'st
venture so.
Simpc. Alas, good Master, my Wife desired some
Damsons, and made me climbe, with danger of my
Life.
Glost. A subtill Knaue, but yet it shall not serue:
Let me see thine Eyes; winck now, now open them,
In my opinion, yet thou seest not well.
Simpc. Yes Master, cleare as day, I thanke God and
Saint *Albones*.
Glost. Say'st thou me so: what Colour is this Cloake
of?
Simpc. Red Master, Red as Blood.
Glost. Why that's well said: What Colour is my
Gowne of?
Simpc. Black forsooth, Coale-Black, as Iet.
King. Why then, thou know'st what Colour Iet is
of?
Suff. And yet I thinke, Iet did he neuer see.

Glost. But

Gloſt. But Cloakes and Gownes, before this day, a many.
Wife. Neuer before this day, in all his life.
Gloſt. Tell me Sirrha, what's my Name?
Simpc Alas Maſter, I know not.
Gloſt. What's his Name?
Simpc. I know not.
Gloſt. Nor his?
Simpc. No indeede, Maſter.
Gloſt. What's thine owne Name?
Simpc. *Saunder Simpcoxe*, and if it pleaſe you, Maſter.
Gloſt. Then *Saunder*, ſit there,
The lying'ſt Knaue in Chriſtendome.
If thou hadſt beene borne blinde,
Thou might'ſt as well haue knowne all our Names,
As thus to name the ſeuerall Colours we doe weare.
Sight may diſtinguiſh of Colours:
But ſuddenly to nominate them all,
It is impoſſible.
My Lords, Saint *Albone* here hath done a Miracle:
And would ye not thinke it, Cunning to be great,
That could reſtore this Cripple to his Legges againe.
Simpc. O Maſter, that you could?
Gloſt. My Maſters of Saint *Albones*,
Haue you not Beadles in your Towne,
And Things call'd Whippes?
Maior. Yes, my Lord, if it pleaſe your Grace.
Gloſt. Then ſend for one preſently.
Maior. Sirrha, goe fetch the Beadle hither ſtraight.
Exit.
Gloſt. Now fetch me a Stoole hither by and by. Now Sirrha, if you meane to ſaue your ſelfe from Whipping, leape me ouer this Stoole, and runne away.
Simpc. Alas Maſter, I am not able to ſtand alone:
You goe about to torture me in vaine.

Enter a Beadle with Whippes.

Gloſt. Well Sir, we muſt haue you finde your Legges. Sirrha Beadle, whippe him till he leape ouer that ſame Stoole.
Beadle. I will, my Lord.
Come on Sirrha, off with your Doublet, quickly.
Simpc. Alas Maſter, what ſhall I doe? I am not able to ſtand.

After the Beadle hath hit him once, he leapes ouer the Stoole, and runnes away: and they follow, and cry, A Miracle.

King. O God, ſeeſt thou this, and beareſt ſo long?
Queene. It made me laugh, to ſee the Villaine runne.
Gloſt. Follow the Knaue, and take this Drab away.
Wife. Alas Sir, we did it for pure need.
Gloſt. Let thẽ be whipt through euery Market Towne,
Till they come to Barwick, from whence they came.
Exit.
Card. Duke *Humfrey* ha's done a Miracle to day.
Suff. True: made the Lame to leape and flye away.
Gloſt. But you haue done more Miracles then I:
You made in a day, my Lord, whole Townes to flye.

Enter Buckingham.

King What Tidings with our Couſin *Buckingham*?
Buck. Such as my heart doth tremble to vnfold:
A ſort of naughtie perſons, lewdly bent,
Vnder the Countenance and Confederacie
Of Lady *Elianor*, the Protectors Wife,
The Ring-leader and Head of all this Rout,
Haue practis'd dangerouſly againſt your State,
Dealing with Witches and with Coniurers,
Whom we haue apprehended in the Fact,
Rayſing vp wicked Spirits from vnder ground,
Demanding of King *Henries* Life and Death,
And other of your Highneſſe Priuie Councell,
As more at large your Grace ſhall vnderſtand.
Card. And ſo my Lord Protector, by this meanes
Your Lady is forth-comming, yet at London.
This Newes I thinke hath turn'd your Weapons edge;
'Tis like, my Lord, you will not keepe your houre.
Gloſt. Ambitious Church-man, leaue to afflict my heart:
Sorrow and griefe haue vanquiſht all my powers;
And vanquiſht as I am, I yeeld to thee,
Or to the meaneſt Groome.
King. O God, what miſchiefes work the wicked ones?
Heaping confuſion on their owne heads thereby.
Queene. *Gloſter*, ſee here the Taincture of thy Neſt,
And looke thy ſelfe be faultleſſe, thou wert beſt.
Gloſt. Madame, for my ſelfe, to Heauen I doe appeale,
How I haue lou'd my King, and Common-weale:
And for my Wife, I know not how it ſtands,
Sorry I am to heare what I haue heard.
Noble ſhee is: but if ſhee haue forgot
Honor and Vertue, and conuers't with ſuch,
As like to Pytch, defile Nobilitie;
I baniſh her my Bed, and Companie,
And giue her as a Prey to Law and Shame,
That hath dis-honored *Gloſters* honeſt Name.
King. Well, for this Night we will repoſe vs here:
To morrow toward London, back againe,
To looke into this Buſineſſe thorowly,
And call theſe foule Offendors to their Anſweres;
And poyſe the Cauſe in Iuſtice equall Scales,
Whoſe Beame ſtands ſure, whoſe rightful cauſe preuailes.
Flouriſh. Exeunt.

Enter Yorke, Salisbury, and Warwick.

Yorke. Now my good Lords of Salisbury & Warwick,
Our ſimple Supper ended, giue me leaue,
In this cloſe Walke, to ſatisfie my ſelfe,
In crauing your opinion of my Title,
Which is infallible, to Englands Crowne.
Saliſb. My Lord, I long to heare it at full.
Warw. Sweet *Yorke* begin: and if thy clayme be good,
The *Neuills* are thy Subiects to command.
Yorke. Then thus:
Edward the third, my Lords, had ſeuen Sonnes:
The firſt, *Edward* the Black-Prince, Prince of Wales;
The ſecond, *William* of Hatfield; and the third,
Lionel, Duke of Clarence; next to whom,
Was *Iohn* of Gaunt, the Duke of Lancaſter;
The fift, was *Edmond Langley*, Duke of Yorke;
The ſixt, was *Thomas* of Woodſtock, Duke of Gloſter;
William of Windſor was the ſeuenth, a [illegible] laſt.
Edward the Black-Prince dyed before his Father,
And left behinde him *Richard*, his onely Sonne,
Who after *Edward* the third's death, raign'd as King,
Till *Henry Bullingbrooke*, Duke of Lancaſter,
The eldeſt Sonne and Heire of *Iohn* of Gaunt,
Crown'd by the Name of *Henry* the fourth,
Seiz'd on the Realme, depos'd the rightfull King,
Sent his poore Queene to France, from whence ſhe came,
And

And him to Pumfret; where,as all you know,
Harmeleſſe *Richard* was murthered traiterouſly.
Warw. Father,the Duke hath told the truth;
Thus got the Houſe of *Lancaſter* the Crowne.
Yorke. Which now they hold by force,and not by right:
For *Richard*,the firſt Sonnes Heire,being dead,
The Iſſue of the next Sonne ſhould haue reign'd.
Salisb. But *William* of Hatfield dyed without an Heire.
Yorke. The third Sonne,Duke of Clarence,
From whoſe Line I clayme the Crowne,
Had Iſſue *Phillip*, a Daughter,
Who marryed *Edmond Mortimer*,Earle of March:
Edmond had Iſſue,*Roger*,Earle of March;
Roger had Iſſue,*Edmond*,*Anne*,and *Elianor*.
Salisb. This *Edmond*,in the Reigne of *Bullingbrooke*,
As I haue read,layd clayme vnto the Crowne,
And but for *Owen Glendour*, had beene King;
Who kept him in Captiuitie,till he dyed.
But,to the reſt.
Yorke. His eldeſt Siſter,*Anne*,
My Mother,being Heire vnto the Crowne,
Marryed *Richard*,Earle of Cambridge,
Who was to *Edmond Langley*,
Edward the thirds fift Sonnes Sonne;
By her I clayme the Kingdome:
She was Heire to *Roger*,Earle of March,
Who was the Sonne of *Edmond Mortimer*,
Who marryed *Phillip*, ſole Daughter
Vnto *Lionel*,Duke of Clarence.
So,if the Iſſue of the elder Sonne
Succeed before the younger,I am King.
Warw. What plaine proceedings is more plain then this?
Henry doth clayme the Crowne from *Iohn* of Gaunt,
The fourth Sonne,*Yorke* claymes it from the third:
Till *Lionels* Iſſue fayles,his ſhould not reigne.
It fayles not yet,but flouriſhes in thee,
And in thy Sonnes,faire ſlippes of ſuch a Stock.
Then Father *Salisbury*, kneele we together,
And in this priuate Plot be we the firſt,
That ſhall ſalute our rightfull Soueraigne
With honor of his Birth-right to the Crowne.
Both. Long liue our Soueraigne *Richard*, Englands King.
Yorke. We thanke you Lords:
But I am not your King,till I be Crown'd,
And that my Sword be ſtayn'd
With heart-blood of the Houſe of *Lancaſter*:
And that's not ſuddenly to be perform'd,
But with aduice and ſilent ſecrecie.
Doe you as I doe in theſe dangerous dayes,
Winke at the Duke of Suffolkes inſolence,
At *Beaufords* Pride,at *Somerſets* Ambition,
At *Buckingham*,and all the Crew of them,
Till they haue ſnar'd the Shepheard of the Flock,
That vertuous Prince,the good Duke *Humfrey*:
'Tis that they ſeeke; and they,in ſeeking that,
Shall finde their deaths,if *Yorke* can prophecie.
Salisb. My Lord,breake we off; we know your minde at full.
Warw. My heart aſſures me,that the Earle of Warwick
Shall one day make the Duke of Yorke a King.
Yorke. And *Neuill*,this I doe aſſure my ſelfe,
Richard ſhall liue to make the Earle of Warwick
The greateſt man in England,but the King.
Exeunt.

Sound Trumpets. Enter the King and State,
with Guard,to baniſh the Ducheſſe.

King. Stand forth Dame *Elianor Cobham*,
Gloſters Wife:
In ſight of God,and vs,your guilt is great,
Receiue the Sentence of the Law for ſinne,
Such as by Gods Booke are adiudg'd to death.
You foure from hence to Priſon,back againe;
From thence,vnto the place of Execution.
The Witch in Smithfield ſhall be burnt to aſhes,
And you three ſhall be ſtrangled on the Gallowes.
You Madame,for you are more Nobly borne,
Deſpoyled of your Honor in your Life,
Shall,after three dayes open Penance done,
Liue in your Countrey here,in Baniſhment,
With Sir *Iohn Stanly*,in the Ile of Man.
Elianor. Welcome is Baniſhment,welcome were my Death.
Gloſt. *Elianor*,the Law thou ſeeſt hath iudged thee,
I cannot iuſtifie whom the Law condemnes:
Mine eyes are full of teares,my heart of griefe.
Ah *Humfrey*,this diſhonor in thine age,
Will bring thy head with ſorrow to the ground.
I beſeech your Maieſtie giue me leaue to goe;
Sorrow would ſollace,and mine Age would eaſe.
King. Stay *Humfrey*,Duke of Gloſter,
Ere thou goe,giue vp thy Staffe,
Henry will to himſelfe Protector be,
And God ſhall be my hope,my ſtay,my guide,
And Lanthorne to my feete:
And goe in peace,*Humfrey*,no leſſe belou'd,
Then when thou wert Protector to thy King.
Queene. I ſee no reaſon,why a King of yeeres
Should be to be protected like a Child,
God and King *Henry* gouerne Englands Realme:
Giue vp your Staffe,Sir,and the King his Realme.
Gloſt. My Staffe? Here,Noble *Henry*,is my Staffe:
As willingly doe I the ſame reſigne,
As ere thy Father *Henry* made it mine;
And euen as willingly at thy feete I leaue it,
As others would ambitiouſly receiue it.
Farewell good King: when I am dead,and gone,
May honorable Peace attend thy Throne.
Exit Gloſter.
Queene. Why now is *Henry* King,and *Margaret* Queen,
And *Humfrey*,Duke of Gloſter,ſcarce himſelfe,
That beares ſo ſhrewd a mayme: two Pulls at once;
His Lady baniſht,and a Limbe lopt off.
This Staffe of Honor raught,there let it ſtand,
Where it beſt fits to be,in *Henries* hand.
Suff. Thus droupes this loftie Pyne,& hangs his ſprayes,
Thus *Elianors* Pride dyes in her youngeſt dayes.
Yorke. Lords,let him goe. Pleaſe it your Maieſtie,
This is the day appointed for the Combat,
And ready are the Appellant and Defendant,
The Armorer and his Man,to enter the Liſts,
So pleaſe your Highneſſe to behold the fight.
Queene. I,good my Lord: for purpoſely therefore
Left I the Court,to ſee this Quarrell try'de.
King. A Gods Name ſee the Lyſts and all things fit,
Here let them end it,and God defend the right.
Yorke. I neuer ſaw a fellow worſe beſtead,
Or more afraid to fight,then is the Appellant,
The ſeruant of this Armorer,my Lords.

Enter

Enter at one Doore the Armorer and his Neighbors, drinking to him so much, that hee is drunke; and he enters with a Drumme before him, and his Staffe, with a Sand-bagge fastened to it: and at the other Doore his Man, with a Drumme and Sand-bagge, and Prentices drinking to him.

1. *Neighbor.* Here Neighbour *Horner*, I drinke to you in a Cup of Sack; and feare not Neighbor, you shall doe well enough.

2. *Neighbor.* And here Neighbour, here's a Cuppe of Charneco.

3. *Neighbor.* And here's a Pot of good Double-Beere Neighbor: drinke, and feare not your Man.

Armorer. Let it come yfaith, and Ile pledge you all, and a figge for *Peter.*

1 *Prent.* Here *Peter*, I drinke to thee, and be not afraid.

2. *Prent.* Be merry *Peter*, and feare not thy Master,
Fight for credit of the Prentices.

Peter. I thanke you all: drinke, and pray for me, I pray you, for I thinke I haue taken my last Draught in this World. Here *Robin*, and if I dye, I giue thee my Aporne; and *Will*, thou shalt haue my Hammer: and here *Tom*, take all the Money that I haue. O Lord blesse me, I pray God, for I am neuer able to deale with my Master, hee hath learnt so much fence already.

Salisb. Come, leaue your drinking, and fall to blowes. Sirrha, what's thy Name?

Peter. *Peter* forsooth.

Salisb. *Peter*? what more?

Peter. *Thumpe.*

Salisb. *Thumpe*? Then see thou thumpe thy Master well.

Armorer. Masters, I am come hither as it were vpon my Mans instigation, to proue him a Knaue, and my selfe an honest man: and touching the Duke of Yorke, I will take my death, I neuer meant him any ill, nor the King, nor the Queene: and therefore *Peter* haue at thee with a downe-right blow.

Yorke. Dispatch, this Knaues tongue begins to double.
Sound Trumpets, Alarum to the Combattants.

They fight, and Peter strikes him downe.

Armorer. Hold *Peter*, hold, I confesse, I confesse Treason.

Yorke. Take away his Weapon: Fellow thanke God, and the good Wine in thy Masters way.

Peter. O God, haue I ouercome mine Enemies in this presence? O *Peter*, thou hast preuayl'd in right.

King. Goe, take hence that Traytor from our sight,
For by his death we doe perceiue his guilt,
And God in Iustice hath reueal'd to vs
The truth and innocence of this poore fellow,
Which he had thought to haue murther'd wrongfully.
Come fellow, follow vs for thy Reward.

Sound a flourish. Exeunt.

Enter Duke Humfrey and his Men in Mourning Cloakes.

Glost. Thus sometimes hath the brightest day a Cloud:
And after Summer, euermore succeedes
Barren Winter, with his wrathfull nipping Cold;
So Cares and Ioyes abound, as Seasons fleet.
Sirs, what's a Clock?

Seru. Tenne, my Lord.

Glost. Tenne is the houre that was appointed me,
To watch the comming of my punisht Duchesse:
Vnneath may shee endure the Flintie Streets,
To treade them with her tender-feeling feet.
Sweet *Nell*, ill can thy Noble Minde abrooke
The abiect People, gazing on thy face,
With enuious Lookes laughing at thy shame,
That erst did follow thy prowd Chariot-Wheeles,
When thou didst ride in triumph through the streets.
But soft, I thinke she comes, and Ile prepare
My teare-stayn'd eyes, to see her Miseries.

Enter the Duchesse in a white Sheet, and a Taper burning in her hand, with the Sherife and Officers.

Seru. So please your Grace, wee'le take her from the Sherife.

Gloster. No, stirre not for your liues, let her passe by.

Elianor. Come you, my Lord, to see my open shame?
Now thou do'st Penance too. Looke how they gaze,
See how the giddy multitude doe point,
And nodde their heads, and throw their eyes on thee.
Ah *Gloster*, hide thee from their hatefull lookes,
And in thy Closet pent vp, rue my shame,
And banne thine Enemies, both mine and thine.

Glost. Be patient, gentle *Nell*, forget this griefe.

Elianor. Ah *Gloster*, teach me to forget my selfe:
For whilest I thinke I am thy married Wife,
And thou a Prince, Protector of this Land;
Me thinkes I should not thus be led along,
Mayl'd vp in shame, with Papers on my back,
And follow'd with a Rabble, that reioyce
To see my teares, and heare my deepe-fet groanes.
The ruthlesse Flint doth cut my tender feet,
And when I start, the enuious people laugh,
And bid me be aduised how I treade.
Ah *Humfrey*, can I beare this shamefull yoake?
Trowest thou, that ere Ile looke vpon the World,
Or count them happy, that enioyes the Sunne?
No: Darke shall be my Light, and Night my Day.
To thinke vpon my Pompe, shall be my Hell.
Sometime Ile say, I am Duke *Humfreyes* Wife,
And he a Prince, and Ruler of the Land:
Yet so he rul'd, and such a Prince he was,
As he stood by, whilest I, his forlorne Duchesse,
Was made a wonder, and a pointing stock
To euery idle Rascall follower.
But be thou milde, and blush not at my shame,
Nor stirre at nothing, till the Axe of Death
Hang ouer thee, as sure it shortly will.
For *Suffolke*, he that can doe all in all
With her, that hateth thee and hates vs all,
And *Yorke*, and impious *Beauford*, that false Priest,
Haue all lym'd Bushes to betray thy Wings,
And flye thou how thou canst, they'le tangle thee.
But feare not thou, vntill thy foot be snar'd,
Nor neuer seeke preuention of thy foes.

Glost. Ah *Nell*, forbeare: thou aymest all awry.
I must offend, before I be attainted:
And had I twentie times so many foes,
And each of them had twentie times their power,
All these could not procure me any scathe,
So long as I am loyall, true, and crimelesse.
Would'st haue me rescue thee from this reproach?

n Why

Why yet thy scandall were not wipt away,
But I in danger for the breach of Law.
Thy greatest helpe is quiet, gentle *Nell:*
I pray thee sort thy heart to patience,
These few dayes wonder will be quickly worne.

Enter a Herald.

Her. I summon your Grace to his Maiesties Parliament,
Holden at Bury, the first of this next Moneth.
Glost. And my consent ne're ask'd herein before?
This is close dealing. Well, I will be there.
My *Nell*, I take my leaue: and Master Sherife,
Let not her Penance exceede the Kings Commission.
Sh. And't please your Grace, here my Commission stayes:
And Sir *Iohn Stanly* is appointed now,
To take her with him to the Ile of Man.
Glost. Must you, Sir *Iohn*, protect my Lady here?
Stanly. So am I giuen in charge, may't please your Grace..
Glost. Entreat her not the worse, in that I pray
You vse her well: the World may laugh againe,
And I may liue to doe you kindnesse, if you doe it her.
And so Sir *Iohn*, farewell.
Elianor What, gone my Lord, and bid me not farewell?
Glost. Witnesse my teares, I cannot stay to speake.

Exit Gloster.

Elianor. Art thou gone to? all comfort goe with thee,
For none abides with me: my Ioy, is Death;
Death, at whose Name I oft haue beene afear'd,
Because I wish'd this Worlds eternitie.
Stanley, I prethee goe, and take me hence,
I care not whither, for I begge no fauor;
Onely conuey me where thou art commanded.
Stanley. Why, Madame, that is to the Ile of Man,
There to be vs'd according to your State.
Elianor. That's bad enough, for I am but reproach:
And shall I then be vs'd reproachfully?
Stanley. Like to a Duchesse, and Duke *Humfreyes* Lady,
According to that State you shall be vs'd.
Elianor. Sherife farewell, and better then I fare,
Although thou hast beene Conduct of my shame.
Sherife. It is my Office, and Madame pardon me.
Elianor. I, I, farewell, thy Office is discharg'd:
Come *Stanley*, shall we goe?
Stanley. Madame, your Penance done,
Throw off this Sheet,
And goe we to attyre you for our Iourney.
Elianor. My shame will not be shifted with my Sheet:
No, it will hang vpon my richest Robes,
And shew it selfe, attyre me how I can.
Goe, leade the way, I long to see my Prison. *Exeunt*

Sound a Senet. Enter King, Queene, Cardinall, Suffolke, Yorke, Buckingham, Salisbury, and Warwicke, to the Parliament.

King. I muse my Lord of Gloster is not come:
'Tis not his wont to be the hindmost man,
What e're occasion keepes him from vs now.
Queene. Can you not see? or will ye not obserue
The strangenesse of his alter'd Countenance?
With what a Maiestie he beares himselfe,
How insolent of late he is become,
How prowd, how peremptorie, and vnlike himselfe.
We know the time since he was milde and affable,
And if we did but glance a farre-off Looke,
Immediately he was vpon his Knee,
That all the Court admir'd him for submission.
But meet him now, and be it in the Morne,
When euery one will giue the time of day,
He knits his Brow, and shewes an angry Eye,
And passeth by with stiffe vnbowed Knee,
Disdaining dutie that to vs belongs.
Small Curres are not regarded when they grynne,
But great men tremble when the Lyon rores,
And *Humfrey* is no little Man in England.
First note, that he is neere you in discent,
And should you fall, he is the next will mount.
Me seemeth then, it is no Pollicie,
Respecting what a rancorous minde he beares,
And his aduantage following your decease,
That he should come about your Royall Person,
Or be admitted to your Highnesse Councell.
By flatterie hath he wonne the Commons hearts:
And when he please to make Commotion,
'Tis to be fear'd they all will follow him.
Now 'tis the Spring, and Weeds are shallow-rooted,
Suffer them now, and they'le o're-grow the Garden,
And choake the Herbes for want of Husbandry.
The reuerent care I beare vnto my Lord,
Made me collect these dangers in the Duke.
If it be fond, call it a Womans feare:
Which feare, if better Reasons can supplant,
I will subscribe, and say I wrong'd the Duke.
My Lord of Suffolke, Buckingham, and Yorke,
Reproue my allegation, if you can,
Or else conclude my words effectuall.
Suff. Well hath your Highnesse seene into this Duke:
And had I first beene put to speake my minde,
I thinke I should haue told your Graces Tale.
The Duchesse, by his subornation,
Vpon my Life began her diuellish practises:
Or if he were not priuie to those Faults,
Yet by reputing of his high discent,
As next the King, he was successiue Heire,
And such high vaunts of his Nobilitie,
Did instigate the Bedlam braine-sick Duchesse,
By wicked meanes to frame our Soueraignes fall.
Smooth runnes the Water, where the Brooke is deepe,
And in his simple shew he harbours Treason.
The Fox barkes not, when he would steale the Lambe.
No, no, my Soueraigne, *Glouster* is a man
Vnsounded yet, and full of deepe deceit.
Card. Did he not, contrary to forme of Law,
Deuise strange deaths, for small offences done?
Yorke. And did he not, in his Protectorship,
Leuie great summes of Money through the Realme,
For Souldiers pay in France, and neuer sent it?
By meanes whereof, the Townes each day reuolted.
Buck. Tut, these are petty faults to faults vnknowne,
Which time will bring to light in smooth Duke *Humfrey*.
King. My Lords at once: the care you haue of vs,
To mowe downe Thornes that would annoy our Foot,
Is worthy prayse: but shall I speake my conscience,
Our Kinsman *Gloster* is as innocent,
From meaning Treason to our Royall Person,
As is the sucking Lambe, or harmelesse Doue:
The Duke is vertuous, milde, and too well giuen,
To dreame on euill, or to worke my downefall.
Qu. Ah what's more dangerous, then this fond affiance?
Seemes he a Doue? his feathers are but borrow'd,
For hee's disposed as the hatefull Rauen.
Is he a Lambe? his Skinne is surely lent him,

For

For hee's enclin'd as is the rauenous Wolues.
Who cannot steale a shape, that meanes deceit?
Take heed, my Lord, the welfare of vs all,
Hangs on the cutting short that fraudfull man.

Enter Somerset.

Som. All health vnto my gracious Soueraigne.
King. Welcome Lord *Somerset*: What Newes from France?
Som. That all your Interest in those Territories,
Is vtterly bereft you: all is lost.
King. Cold Newes, Lord *Somerset*: but Gods will be done.
Yorke. Cold Newes for me: for I had hope of France,
As firmely as I hope for fertile England.
Thus are my Blossomes blasted in the Bud,
And Caterpillers eate my Leaues away:
But I will remedie this geare ere long,
Or sell my Title for a glorious Graue.

Enter Gloucester.

Glost. All happinesse vnto my Lord the King:
Pardon, my Liege, that I haue stay'd so long.
Suff. Nay *Gloster*, know that thou art come too soone,
Vnlesse thou wert more loyall then thou art:
I doe arrest thee of High Treason here.
Glost. Well *Suffolke*, thou shalt not see me blush,
Nor change my Countenance for this Arrest:
A Heart vnspotted, is not easily daunted.
The purest Spring is not so free from mudde,
As I am cleare from Treason to my Soueraigne.
Who can accuse me? wherein am I guiltie?
Yorke. 'Tis thought, my Lord,
That you tooke Bribes of France,
And being Protector, stay'd the Souldiers pay,
By meanes whereof, his Highnesse hath lost France.
Glost. Is it but thought so?
What are they that thinke it?
I neuer rob'd the Souldiers of their pay,
Nor euer had one penny Bribe from France.
So helpe me God, as I haue watcht the Night,
I, Night by Night, in studying good for England.
That Doyt that ere I wrested from the King,
Or any Groat I hoorded to my vse,
Be brought against me at my Tryall day.
No: many a Pound of mine owne proper store,
Because I would not taxe the needie Commons,
Haue I dis-pursed to the Garrisons,
And neuer ask'd for restitution.
Card. It serues you well, my Lord, to say so much.
Glost. I say no more then truth, so helpe me God.
Yorke. In your Protectorship, you did deuise
Strange Tortures for Offendors, neuer heard of,
That England was defam'd by Tyrannie.
Glost. Why 'tis well known, that whiles I was Protector,
Pittie was all the fault that was in me:
For I should melt at an Offendors teares,
And lowly words were Ransome for their fault:
Vnlesse it were a bloody Murtherer,
Or foule felonious Theefe, that fleec'd poore passengers,
I neuer gaue them condigne punishment.
Murther indeede, that bloodie sinne, I tortur'd
Aboue the Felon, or what Trespas else.
Suff. My Lord, these faults are easie, quickly answer'd
But mightier Crimes are lay'd vnto your charge,
Whereof you cannot easily purge your selfe.
I doe arrest you in his Highnesse Name,
And here commit you to my Lord Cardinall
To keepe, vntill your further time of Tryall.
King. My Lord of Gloster, 'tis my speciall hope,
That you will cleare your selfe from all suspence,
My Conscience tells me you are innocent.
Glost. Ah gracious Lord, these dayes are dangerous:
Vertue is choakt with foule Ambition,
And Charitie chas'd hence by Rancours hand;
Foule Subornation is predominant,
And Equitie exil'd your Highnesse Land.
I know, their Complot is to haue my Life:
And if my death might make this Iland happy,
And proue the Period of their Tyrannie,
I would expend it with all willingnesse.
But mine is made the Prologue to their Play:
For thousands more, that yet suspect no perill,
Will not conclude their plotted Tragedie.
Beaufords red sparkling eyes blab his hearts mallice,
And *Suffolks* cloudie Brow his stormie hate;
Sharpe *Buckingham* vnburthens with his tongue,
The enuious Load that lyes vpon his heart:
And dogged *Yorke*, that reaches at the Moone,
Whose ouer-weening Arme I haue pluckt back,
By false accuse doth leuell at my Life.
And you, my Soueraigne Lady, with the rest,
Causelesse haue lay'd disgraces on my head,
And with your best endeuour haue stirr'd vp
My liefest Liege to be mine Enemie:
I, all of you haue lay'd your heads together,
My selfe had notice of your Conuenticles,
And all to make away my guiltlesse Life.
I shall not want false Witnesse, to condemne me,
Nor store of Treasons, to augment my guilt:
The ancient Prouerbe will be well effected,
A Staffe is quickly found to beat a Dogge.
Card. My Liege, his rayling is intollerable.
If those that care to keepe your Royall Person
From Treasons secret Knife, and Traytors Rage,
Be thus vpbrayded, chid, and rated at,
And the Offendor graunted scope of speech,
'Twill make them coole in zeale vnto your Grace.
Suff. Hath he not twit our Soueraigne Lady here
With ignominious words, though Clarkely coucht?
As if she had suborned some to sweare
False allegations, to o'rethrow his state.
Qu. But I can giue the loser leaue to chide.
Glost. Farre truer spoke then meant: I lose indeede,
Beshrew the winners, for they play'd me false,
And well such losers may haue leaue to speake.
Buck. Hee'le wrest the sence, and hold vs here all day.
Lord Cardinall, he is your Prisoner.
Card. Sirs, take away the Duke, and guard him sure.
Glost. Ah, thus King *Henry* throwes away his Crutch,
Before his Legges be firme to beare his Body.
Thus is the Shepheard beaten from thy side,
And Wolues are gnarling, who shall gnaw thee first.
Ah that my feare were false, ah that it were;
For good King *Henry*, thy decay I feare. *Exit Gloster.*
King. My Lords, what to your wisdomes seemeth best,
Doe, or vndoe, as if our selfe were here.
Queene. What, will your Highnesse leaue the Parliament?
King. I *Margaret*: my heart is drown'd with griefe,
Whose floud begins to flowe within mine eyes;
My Body round engyrt with miserie:

n 2 For

For what's more miserable then Discontent?
Ah Vnckle *Humfrey*, in thy face I see
The Map of Honor, Truth, and Loyaltie
And yet, good *Humfrey*, is the houre to come,
That ere I prou'd thee false, or fear'd thy faith.
What lowring Starre now enuies thy estate?
That these great Lords, and *Margaret* our Queene,
Doe seeke subuersion of thy harmelesse Life.
Thou neuer didst them wrong, nor no man wrong:
And as the Butcher takes away the Calfe,
And binds the Wretch, and beats it when it strayes,
Bearing it to the bloody Slaughter-house;
Euen so remorselesse haue they borne him hence:
And as the Damme runnes lowing vp and downe,
Looking the way her harmelesse young one went,
And can doe naught but wayle her Darlings losse,
Euen so my selfe bewayles good *Glosters* case
With sad vnhelpefull teares, and with dimn'd eyes;
Looke after him, and cannot doe him good:
So mightie are his vowed Enemies.
His fortunes I will weepe, and 'twixt each groane,
Say, who's a Traytor? *Gloster* he is none. *Exit.*
Queene. Free Lords:
Cold Snow melts with the Sunnes hot Beames:
Henry, my Lord, is cold in great Affaires,
Too full of foolish pittie: and *Glosters* shew
Beguiles him, as the mournefull Crocodile
With sorrow snares relenting passengers;
Or as the Snake, roll'd in a flowring Banke,
With shining checker'd slough doth sting a Child,
That for the beautie thinkes it excellent.
Beleeue me Lords, were none more wise then I,
And yet herein I iudge mine owne Wit good;
This *Gloster* should be quickly rid the World,
To rid vs from the feare we haue of him.
Card. That he should dye, is worthie pollicie,
But yet we want a Colour for his death:
'Tis meet he be condemn'd by course of Law.
Suff. But in my minde, that were no pollicie:
The King will labour still to saue his Life,
The Commons haply rise, to saue his Life;
And yet we haue but triuiall argument,
More then mistrust, that shewes him worthy death.
Yorke. So that by this, you would not haue him dye.
Suff. Ah *Yorke*, no man aliue, so faine as I.
Yorke. 'Tis *Yorke* that hath more reason for his death.
But my Lord Cardinall, and you my Lord of Suffolke,
Say as you thinke, and speake it from your Soules:
Wer't not all one, an emptie Eagle were set,
To guard the Chicken from a hungry Kyte,
As place Duke *Humfrey* for the Kings Protector?
Queene. So the poore Chicken should be sure of death.
Suff. Madame 'tis true: and wer't not madnesse then,
To make the Fox surueyor of the Fold?
Who being accus'd a craftie Murtherer,
His guilt should be but idly posted ouer,
Because his purpose is not executed.
No: let him dye, in that he is a Fox,
By nature prou'd an Enemie to the Flock,
Before his Chaps be stayn'd with Crimson blood,
As *Humfrey* prou'd by Reasons to my Liege.
And doe not stand on Quillets how to slay him:
Be it by Gynnes, by Snares, by Subtletie,
Sleeping, or Waking, 'tis no matter how,
So he be dead; for that is good deceit,
Which mates him first, that first intends deceit.
Queene. Thrice Noble *Suffolke*, 'tis resolutely spoke.
Suff. Not resolute, except so much were done,
For things are often spoke, and seldome meant,
But that my heart accordeth with my tongue,
Seeing the deed is meritorious,
And to preserue my Soueraigne from his Foe,
Say but the word, and I will be his Priest.
Card. But I would haue him dead, my Lord of Suffolke,
Ere you can take due Orders for a Priest:
Say you consent, and censure well the deed,
And Ile prouide his Executioner,
I tender so the safetie of my Liege.
Suff. Here is my Hand, the deed is worthy doing.
Queene. And so say I.
Yorke. And I: and now we three haue spoke it,
It skills not greatly who impugnes our doome.

Enter a Poste.

Post. Great Lords, from Ireland am I come amaine,
To signifie, that Rebels there are vp,
And put the Englishmen vnto the Sword.
Send Succours (Lords) and stop the Rage betime,
Before the Wound doe grow vncurable;
For being greene, there is great hope of helpe.
Card. A Breach that craues a quick expedient stoppe.
What counsaile giue you in this weightie cause?
Yorke. That *Somerset* be sent as Regent thither:
'Tis meet that luckie Ruler be imploy'd,
Witnesse the fortune he hath had in France.
Som. If *Yorke*, with all his farre-fet pollicie,
Had beene the Regent there, in stead of me,
He neuer would haue stay'd in France so long.
Yorke. No, not to lose it all, as thou hast done.
I rather would haue lost my Life betimes,
Then bring a burthen of dis-honour home,
By staying there so long, till all were lost.
Shew me one skarre, character'd on thy Skinne,
Mens flesh preseru'd so whole, doe seldome winne.
Qu. Nay then, this sparke will proue a raging fire,
If Wind and Fuell be brought, to feed it with:
No more, good *Yorke*; sweet *Somerset* be still.
Thy fortune, *Yorke*, hadst thou beene Regent there,
Might happily haue prou'd farre worse then his.
Yorke. What, worse then naught? nay, then a shame take all.
Somerset. And in the number, thee, that wishest shame.
Card. My Lord of Yorke, trie what your fortune is:
Th'vnciuill Kernes of Ireland are in Armes,
And temper Clay with blood of Englishmen.
To Ireland will you leade a Band of men,
Collected choycely, from each Countie some,
And trie your hap against the Irishmen?
Yorke. I will, my Lord, so please his Maiestie.
Suff. Why, our Authoritie is his consent,
And what we doe establish, he confirmes:
Then, Noble *Yorke*, take thou this Taske in hand.
Yorke. I am content: Prouide me Souldiers, Lords,
Whiles I take order for mine owne affaires.
Suff. A charge, Lord *Yorke*, that I will see perform'd.
But now returne we to the false Duke *Humfrey*.
Card. No more of him: for I will deale with him,
That henceforth he shall trouble vs no more:
And so breake off, the day is almost spent,
Lord *Suffolke*, you and I must talke of that euent.

Yorke. My

Yorke. My Lord of Suffolke, within foureteene dayes
At Bristow I expect my Souldiers,
For there Ile shippe them all for Ireland.
Suff. Ile see it truly done, my Lord of Yorke. *Exeunt.*
Manet Yorke.
Yorke. Now *Yorke*, or neuer, steele thy fearfull thoughts
And change misdoubt to resolution;
Be that thou hop'st to be, or what thou art;
Resigne to death, it is not worth th'enioying:
Let pale-fac't feare keepe with the meane-borne man,
And finde no harbor in a Royall heart.
Faster the Spring-time showres, comes thoght on thoght,
And not a thought, but thinkes on Dignitie.
My Brayne, more busie then the laboring Spider,
Weaues tedious Snares to trap mine Enemies.
Well Nobles, well: 'tis politikely done,
To send me packing with an Hoast of men:
I feare me, you but warme the starued Snake,
Who cherisht in your breasts, will sting your hearts.
'Twas men I lackt, and you will giue them me;
I take it kindly: yet be well assur'd,
You put sharpe Weapons in a mad-mans hands.
Whiles I in Ireland nourish a mightie Band,
I will stirre vp in England some black Storme,
Shall blowe ten thousand Soules to Heauen, or Hell:
And this fell Tempest shall not cease to rage,
Vntill the Golden Circuit on my Head,
Like to the glorious Sunnes transparant Beames,
Doe calme the furie of this mad-bred Flawe.
And for a minister of my intent,
I haue seduc'd a head-strong Kentishman,
Iohn Cade of Ashford,
To make Commotion, as full well he can,
Vnder the Title of *Iohn Mortimer.*
In Ireland haue I seene this stubborne *Cade*
Oppose himselfe against a Troupe of Kernes,
And fought so long, till that his thighes with Darts
Were almost like a sharpe-quill'd Porpentine:
And in the end being rescued, I haue seene
Him capre vpright, like a wilde Morisco,
Shaking the bloody Darts, as he his Bells.
Full often, like a shag-hayr'd craftie Kerne,
Hath he conuersed with the Enemie,
And vndiscouer'd, come to me againe,
And giuen me notice of their Villanies.
This Deuill here shall be my substitute;
For that *Iohn Mortimer*, which now is dead,
In face, in gate, in speech he doth resemble.
By this, I shall perceiue the Commons minde,
How they affect the House and Clayme of *Yorke.*
Say he be taken, rackt, and tortured;
I know, no paine they can inflict vpon him,
Will make him say, I mou'd him to those Armes.
Say that he thriue, as 'tis great like he will,
Why then from Ireland come I with my strength,
And reape the Haruest which that Rascall sow'd.
For *Humfrey*; being dead, as he shall be,
And *Henry* put apart: the next for me. *Exit.*

Enter two or three running ouer the Stage, from the Murther of Duke Humfrey.

1\. Runne to my Lord of Suffolke: let him know
We haue dispatcht the Duke, as he commanded.
2\. Oh, that it were to doe: what haue we done?
Didst euer heare a man so penitent? *Enter Suffolke.*
1\. Here comes my Lord.
Suff. Now Sirs, haue you dispatcht this thing?
1\. I, my good Lord, hee's dead.
Suff. Why that's well said. Goe, get you to my House,
I will reward you for this venturous deed:
The King and all the Peeres are here at hand.
Haue you layd faire the Bed? Is all things well,
According as I gaue directions?
1\. 'Tis, my good Lord.
Suff. Away, be gone. *Exeunt.*

Sound Trumpets. Enter the King, the Queene, Cardinall, Suffolke, Somerset, with Attendants.

King. Goe call our Vnckle to our presence straight:
Say, we intend to try his Grace to day,
If he be guiltie, as 'tis published.
Suff. Ile call him presently, my Noble Lord. *Exit.*
King. Lords take your places: and I pray you all
Proceed no straiter 'gainst our Vnckle *Gloster,*
Then from true euidence, of good esteeme,
He be approu'd in practise culpable.
Queene. God forbid any Malice should preuayle,
That faultlesse may condemne a Noble man:
Pray God he may acquit him of suspition.
King. I thanke thee *Nell*, these wordes content mee much.

Enter Suffolke.

How now? why look'st thou pale? why tremblest thou?
Where is our Vnckle? what's the matter, *Suffolke?*
Suff. Dead in his Bed, my Lord: *Gloster* is dead.
Queene. Marry God forfend.
Card. Gods secret Iudgement: I did dreame to Night,
The Duke was dumbe, and could not speake a word.
King sounds.
Qu. How fares my Lord? Helpe Lords, the King is dead.
Som. Rere vp his Body, wring him by the Nose.
Qu. Runne, goe, helpe, helpe: Oh *Henry* ope thine eyes.
Suff. He doth reuiue againe, Madame be patient.
King. Oh Heauenly God.
Qu. How fares my gracious Lord?
Suff. Comfort my Soueraigne, gracious *Henry* comfort.
King. What, doth my Lord of Suffolke comfort me?
Came he right now to sing a Rauens Note,
Whose dismall tune bereft my Vitall powres:
And thinkes he, that the chirping of a Wren,
By crying comfort from a hollow breast,
Can chase away the first-conceiued sound?
Hide not thy poyson with such sugred words,
Lay not thy hands on me: forbeare I say,
Their touch affrights me as a Serpents sting.
Thou balefull Messenger, out of my sight:
Vpon thy eye-balls, murderous Tyrannie
Sits in grim Maiestie, to fright the World.
Looke not vpon me, for thine eyes are wounding;
Yet doe not goe away: come Basiliske,
And kill the innocent gazer with thy sight:
For in the shade of death, I shall finde ioy;
In life, but double death, now *Gloster's* dead.
Queene. Why do you rate my Lord of Suffolke thus?
Although the Duke was enemie to him,
Yet he most Christian-like laments his death:
And for my selfe, Foe as he was to me,
Might liquid teares, or heart-offending groanes,
Or blood-consuming sighes recall his Life;

n 3 I

I would be blinde with weeping, sicke with grones,
Looke pale as Prim-rose with blood-drinking sighes,
And all to haue the Noble Duke aliue.
What know I how the world may deeme of me?
For it is knowne we were but hollow Friends:
It may be judg'd I made the Duke away,
So shall my name with Slanders tongue be wounded,
And Princes Courts be fill'd with my reproach:
This get I by his death: Aye me vnhappie,
To be a Queene, and Crown'd with infamie.
King. Ah woe is me for Gloster, wretched man.
Queen. Be woe for me, more wretched then he is.
What, Dost thou turne away, and hide thy face?
I am no loathsome Leaper, looke on me.
What? Art thou like the Adder waxen deafe?
Be poysonous too, and kill thy forlorne Queene.
Is all thy comfort shut in Glosters Tombe?
Why then Dame *Elianor* was neere thy ioy.
Erect his Statue, and worship it,
And make my Image but an Ale-house signe.
Was I for this nye wrack'd vpon the Sea,
And twice by awkward winde from Englands banke
Droue backe againe vnto my Natiue Clime.
What boaded this? but well fore-warning winde
Did seeme to say, seeke not a Scorpions Nest,
Nor set no footing on this vnkinde Shore.
What did I then? But curst the gentle gusts,
And he that loos'd them forth their Brazen Caues,
And bid them blow towards Englands blessed shore,
Or turne our Sterne vpon a dreadfull Rocke:
Yet Æolus would not be a murtherer,
But left that hatefull office vnto thee.
The pretty vaulting Sea refus'd to drowne me,
Knowing that thou wouldst haue me drown'd on shore
With teares as salt as Sea, through thy vnkindnesse.
The splitting Rockes cowr'd in the sinking sands,
And would not dash me with their ragged sides,
Because thy flinty heart more hard then they,
Might in thy Pallace, perish *Elianor*.
As farre as I could ken thy Chalky Cliffes,
When from thy Shore, the Tempest beate vs backe,
I stood vpon the Hatches in the storme:
And when the duskie sky, began to rob
My earnest-gaping-sight of thy Lands view,
I tooke a costly Iewell from my necke,
A Hart it was bound in with Diamonds,
And threw it towards thy Land: The Sea receiu'd it,
And so I wish'd thy body might my Heart:
And euen with this, I lost faire Englands view,
And bid mine eyes be packing with my Heart,
And call'd them blinde and duskie Spectacles,
For loosing ken of *Albions* wished Coast.
How often haue I tempted Suffolkes tongue
(The agent of thy foule inconstancie)
To sit and watch me as *Ascanius* did,
When he to madding *Dido* would vnfold
His Fathers Acts, commenc'd in burning Troy.
Am I not witcht like her? Or thou not false like him?
Aye me, I can no more: Dye *Elinor*,
For *Henry* weepes, that thou dost liue so long.

Noyse within. Enter Warwicke, and many Commons.

War. It is reported, mighty Soueraigne,
That good Duke *Humfrey* Traiterously is murdred
By Suffolke, and the Cardinall *Beaufords* meanes:
The Commons like an angry Hiue of Bees
That want their Leader, scatter vp and downe,
And care not who they sting in his reuenge.
My selfe haue calm'd their spleenfull mutinie,
Vntill they heare the order of his death.
King. That he is dead good Warwick, 'tis too true,
But how he dyed, God knowes, not *Henry*:
Enter his Chamber, view his breathlesse Corpes,
And comment then vpon his sodaine death.
War. That shall I do my Liege; Stay Salsburie
With the rude multitude, till I returne.
King. O thou that iudgest all things, stay my thoghts:
My thoughts, that labour to perswade my soule,
Some violent hands were laid on *Humfries* life:
If my suspect be false, forgiue me God,
For iudgement onely doth belong to thee:
Faine would I go to chafe his palie lips,
With twenty thousand kisses, and to draine
Vpon his face an Ocean of salt teares,
To tell my loue vnto his dumbe deafe trunke,
And with my fingers feele his hand, vnfeeling:
But all in vaine are these meane Obsequies,
Bed put forth.
And to suruey his dead and earthy Image:
What were it but to make my sorrow greater
Warw. Come hither gracious Soueraigne, view this body.
King. That is to see how deepe my graue is made,
For with his soule fled all my worldly solace:
For seeing him, I see my life in death.
War. As surely as my soule intends to liue
With that dread King that tooke our state vpon him,
To free vs from his Fathers wrathfull curse,
I do beleeue that violent hands were laid
Vpon the life of this thrice-famed Duke.
Suf. A dreadfull Oath, sworne with a solemn tongue:
What instance giues Lord Warwicke for his vow.
War. See how the blood is setled in his face.
Oft haue I seene a timely-parted Ghost,
Of ashy semblance, meager, pale, and bloodlesse,
Being all descended to the labouring heart,
Who in the Conflict that it holds with death,
Attracts the same for aydance 'gainst the enemy,
Which with the heart there cooles, and ne're returneth,
To blush and beautifie the Cheeke againe.
But see, his face is blacke, and full of blood:
His eye-balles further out, than when he liued,
Staring full gastly, like a strangled man:
His hayre vp rear'd, his nostrils stretcht with strugling:
His hands abroad display'd, as one that graspt
And tugg'd for Life, and was by strength subdude.
Looke on the sheets his haire (you see) is sticking,
His well proportion'd Beard, made ruffe and rugged,
Like to the Summers Corne by Tempest lodged:
It cannot be but he was murdred heere,
The least of all these signes were probable.
Suf. Why Warwicke, who should do the D. to death?
My selfe and *Beauford* had him in protection,
And we I hope sir, are no murtherers.
War. But both of you were vowed D. Humfries foes,
And you (forsooth) had the good Duke to keepe:
Tis like you would not feast him like a friend,
And 'tis well seene, he found an enemy.
Queen. Than you belike suspect these Noblemen,
As guilty of Duke *Humfries* timelesse death.

War.

Warw. Who finds the Heyfer dead, and bleeding fresh,
And sees fast-by, a Butcher with an Axe,
But will suspect, 'twas he that made the slaughter?
Who finds the Partridge in the Puttocks Nest,
But may imagine how the Bird was dead,
Although the Kyte soare with vnbloudied Beake?
Euen so suspitious is this Tragedie.

Qu. Are you the Butcher, *Suffolke*? where's your Knife?
Is *Beauford* tearm'd a Kyte? where are his Tallons?

Suff. I weare no Knife, to slaughter sleeping men,
But here's a vengefull Sword, rusted with ease,
That shall be scowred in his rancorous heart,
That slanders me with Murthers Crimson Badge.
Say, if thou dar'st, prowd Lord of Warwickshire,
That I am faultie in Duke *Humfreyes* death.

Warw. What dares not *Warwick*, if false *Suffolke* dare him?

Qu. He dares not calme his contumelious Spirit,
Nor cease to be an arrogant Controller,
Though *Suffolke* dare him twentie thousand times.

Warw. Madame be still: with reuerence may I say,
For euery word you speake in his behalfe,
Is slander to your Royall Dignitie.

Suff. Blunt-witted Lord, ignoble in demeanor,
If euer Lady wrong'd her Lord so much,
Thy Mother tooke into her blamefull Bed
Some sterne vntutur'd Churle; and Noble Stock
Was graft with Crab-tree slippe, whose Fruit thou art,
And neuer of the *Neuils* Noble Race.

Warw. But that the guilt of Murther bucklers thee,
And I should rob the Deaths-man of his Fee,
Quitting thee thereby of ten thousand shames,
And that my Soueraignes presence makes me milde,
I would, false murd'rous Coward, on thy Knee
Make thee begge pardon for thy passed speech,
And say, it was thy Mother that thou meant'st,
That thou thy selfe wast borne in Bastardie;
And after all this fearefull Homage done,
Giue thee thy hyre, and send thy Soule to Hell,
Pernicious blood-sucker of sleeping men.

Suff. Thou shalt be waking, while I shed thy blood,
If from this presence thou dar'st goe with me.

Warw. Away euen now, or I will drag thee hence:
Vnworthy though thou art, Ile cope with thee,
And doe some seruice to Duke *Humfreyes* Ghost.

Exeunt.

King. What stronger Brest-plate then a heart vntainted?
Thrice is he arm'd, that hath his Quarrell iust;
And he but naked, though lockt vp in Steele,
Whose Conscience with Iniustice is corrupted.

A noyse within.

Queene. What noyse is this?

Enter Suffolke and Warwicke, with their Weapons drawne.

King. Why how now Lords?
Your wrathfull Weapons drawne,
Here in our presence? Dare you be so bold?
Why what tumultuous clamor haue we here?

Suff. The trayt'rous *Warwick*, with the men of Bury,
Set all vpon me, mightie Soueraigne.

Enter Salisbury.

Salisb Sirs stand apart, the King shall know your minde.
Dread Lord, the Commons send you word by me,
Vnlesse Lord *Suffolke* straight be done to death,
Or banished faire Englands Territories,
They will by violence teare him from your Pallace,
And torture him with grieuous lingring death.
They say, by him the good Duke *Humfrey* dy'de:
They say, in him they feare your Highnesse death;
And meere instinct of Loue and Loyaltie,
Free from a stubborne opposite intent,
As being thought to contradict your liking,
Makes them thus forward in his Banishment.
They say, in care of your most Royall Person,
That if your Highnesse should intend to sleepe,
And charge, that no man should disturbe your rest,
In paine of your dislike, or paine of death;
Yet notwithstanding such a strait Edict,
Were there a Serpent seene, with forked Tongue,
That slyly glyded towards your Maiestie,
It were but necessarie you were wak't.
Least being suffer'd in that harmefull slumber,
The mortall Worme might make the sleepe eternall.
And therefore doe they cry, though you forbid,
That they will guard you, where you will, or no,
From such fell Serpents as false *Suffolke* is;
With whose inuenomed and fatall sting,
Your louing Vnckle, twentie times his worth,
They say is shamefully bereft of life.

Commons within. An answer from the King, my Lord of Salisbury.

Suff. 'Tis like the Commons, rude vnpolisht Hindes,
Could send such Message to their Soueraigne:
But you, my Lord, were glad to be imploy'd,
To shew how queint an Orator you are.
But all the Honor *Salisbury* hath wonne,
Is, that he was the Lord Embassador,
Sent from a sort of Tinkers to the King.

Within. An answer from the King, or wee will all breake in.

King. Goe *Salisbury*, and tell them all from me,
I thanke them for their tender louing care;
And had I not beene cited so by them,
Yet did I purpose as they doe entreat:
For sure, my thoughts doe hourely prophecie,
Mischance vnto my State by *Suffolkes* meanes.
And therefore by his Maiestie I sweare,
Whose farre-vnworthie Deputie I am,
He shall not breathe infection in this ayre,
But three dayes longer, on the paine of death.

Qu. Oh *Henry*, let me pleade for gentle *Suffolke*.

King. Vngentle Queene, to call him gentle *Suffolke*.
No more I say: if thou do'st pleade for him,
Thou wilt but adde encrease vnto my Wrath.
Had I but sayd, I would haue kept my Word;
But when I sweare, it is irreuocable:
If after three dayes space thou here bee'st found,
On any ground that I am Ruler of,
The World shall not be Ransome for thy Life.
Come *Warwicke*, come good *Warwicke*, goe with mee,
I haue great matters to impart to thee. *Exit.*

Qu. Mischance and Sorrow goe along with you,
Hearts Discontent, and sowre Affliction,
Be play-fellowes to keepe you companie:
There's two of you, the Deuill make a third,
And three-fold Vengeance tend vpon your steps.

Suff. Cease, gentle Queene, these Execrations,
And let thy *Suffolke* take his heauie leaue.

Queene. Fye

Queen. Fye Coward woman, and soft harted wretch,
Hast thou not spirit to curse thine enemy.
Suf. A plague vpon them : wherefore should I cursse them?
Would curses kill, as doth the Mandrakes grone,
I would inuent as bitter searching termes,
As curst, as harsh, and horrible to heare,
Deliuer'd strongly through my fixed teeth,
With full as many signes of deadly hate,
As leane-fac'd enuy in her loathsome caue.
My tongue should stumble in mine earnest words,
Mine eyes should sparkle like the beaten Flint,
Mine haire be fixt an end, as one distract:
I, euery ioynt should seeme to curse and ban,
And euen now my burthen'd heart would breake
Should I not curse them. Poyson be their drinke.
Gall, worse then Gall, the daintiest that they taste:
Their sweetest shade, a groue of Cypresse Trees:
Their cheefest Prospect, murd'ring Basiliskes:
Their softest Touch, as smart as Lyzards stings:
Their Musicke, frightfull as the Serpents hisse,
And boading Screech-Owles, make the Consort full.
All the foule terrors in darke seated hell——
Q. Enough sweet Suffolke, thou torment'st thy selfe,
And these dread curses like the Sunne 'gainst glasse,
Or like an ouer-charged Gun, recoile,
And turnes the force of them vpon thy selfe.
Suf. You bad me ban, and will you bid me leaue?
Now by the ground that I am banish'd from,
Well could I curse away a Winters night,
Though standing naked on a Mountaine top,
Where byting cold would neuer let grasse grow,
And thinke it but a minute spent in sport.
Qu. Oh, let me intreat thee cease, giue me thy hand,
That I may dew it with my mournfull teares:
Nor let the raine of heauen wet this place,
To wash away my wofull Monuments.
Oh, could this kisse be printed in thy hand,
That thou might'st thinke vpon these by the Seale,
Through whom a thousand sighes are breath'd for thee.
So get thee gone, that I may know my greefe,
'Tis but surmiz'd, whiles thou art standing by,
As one that surfets, thinking on a want:
I will repeale thee, or be well assur'd,
Aduenrure to be banished my selfe:
And banished I am, if but from thee.
Go, speake not to me; euen now be gone.
Oh go not yet. Euen thus, two Friends condemn'd,
Embrace, and kisse, and take ten thousand leaues,
Loather a hundred times to part then dye;
Yet now farewell, and farewell Life with thee.
Suf. Thus is poore Suffolke ten times banished,
Once by the King, and three times thrice by thee.
Tis not the Land I care for, wer't thou thence,
A Wildernesse is populous enough,
So Suffolke had thy heauenly company:
For where thou art, there is the World it selfe,
With euery seuerall pleasure in the World:
And where thou art not, Desolation.
I can no more: Liue thou to ioy thy life;
My selfe no ioy in nought, but that thou liu'st.

Enter Vaux.

Queene. Whether goes *Vaux* so fast? What newes I prethee?
Vaux. To signifie vnto his Maiesty,
That Cardinall *Beauford* is at point of death:
For sodainly a greeuous sicknesse tooke him,
That makes him gaspe, and stare, and catch the aire,
Blaspheming God, and cursing men on earth.
Sometime he talkes, as if Duke *Humfrues* Ghost
Were by his side: Sometime, he calles the King,
And whispers to his pillow, as to him,
The secrets of his ouer-charged soule,
And I am sent to tell his Maiestie,
That euen now he cries alowd for him.
Qu. Go tell this heauy Message to the King. *Exit*
Aye me! What is this World? What newes are these?
But wherefore greeue I at an houres poore losse,
Omitting Suffolkes exile, my soules Treasure?
Why onely Suffolke mourne I not for thee?
And with the Southerne clouds, contend in teares?
Theirs for the earths encrease, mine for my sorrowes.
Now get thee hence, the King thou know'st is comming,
If thou be found by me, thou art but dead.
Suf. If I depart from thee, I cannot liue,
And in thy sight to dye, what were it else,
But like a pleasant slumber in thy lap?
Heere could I breath my soule into the ayre,
As milde and gentle as the Cradle-babe,
Dying with mothers dugge betweene it's lips.
Where from thy sight, I should be raging mad,
And cry out for thee to close vp mine eyes:
To haue thee with thy lippes to stop my mouth:
So should'st thou eyther turne my flying soule,
Or I should breathe it so into thy body,
And then it liu'd in sweete Elizium.
To dye by thee, were but to dye in iest,
From thee to dye, were torture more then death:
Oh let me stay, befall what may befall.
Queen. Away: Though parting be a fretfull corosiue,
It is applyed to a deathfull wound.
To France sweet Suffolke: Let me heare from thee:
For wheresoere thou art in this worlds Globe,
Ile haue an *Iris* that shall finde thee out.
Suf. I go.
Qu. And take my heart with thee.
Suf. A Iewell lockt into the wofulst Caske,
That euer did containe a thing of worth,
Euen as a splitted Barke, so sunder we:
This way fall I to death.
Qu. This way for me. *Exeunt*

Enter the King, Salisbury, and Warwicke, to the Cardinal in bed.

King. How fare's my Lord? Speake *Beauford* to thy Soueraigne.
Ca If thou beest death, Ile giue thee Englands Treasure,
Enough to purchase such another Island,
So thou wilt let me liue, and feele no paine.
King. Ah, what a signe it is of euill life,
Where death's approach is seene so terrible.
War. *Beauford* it is thy Soueraigne speakes to thee.
Beau. Bring me vnto my Triall when you will.
Dy'de he not in his bed? Where should he dye?
Can I make men liue where they will or no?
Oh torture me no more, I will confesse.
Aliue againe? Then shew me where he is,
Ile giue a thousand pound to looke vpon him.
He hath no eyes, the dust hath blinded them.

Comb

Combe downe his haire; looke, looke, it stands vpright,
Like Lime-twigs set to catch my winged soule:
Giue me some drinke, and bid the Apothecarie
Bring the strong poyson that I bought of him.
King. Oh thou eternall mouer of the heauens,
Looke with a gentle eye vpon this Wretch,
Oh beate away the busie medling Fiend,
That layes strong siege vnto this wretches soule,
And from his bosome purge this blacke dispaire.
War. See how the pangs of death do make him grin.
Sal. Disturbe him not, let him passe peaceably.
King. Peace to his soule, if Gods good pleasure be
Lord Card'nall, if thou think'st on heauens blisse,
Hold vp thy hand, make signall of thy hope.
He dies and makes no signe: Oh God forgiue him.
War. So bad a death, argues a monstrous life.
King Forbeare to iudge, for we are sinners all.
Close vp his eyes, and draw the Curtaine close,
And let vs all to Meditation. *Exeunt.*

Alarum. Fight at Sea. Ordnance goes off.

Enter Lieutenant, Suffolke, and others.

Lieu. The gaudy blabbing and remorsefull day,
Is crept into the bosome of the Sea:
And now loud houling Wolues arouse the Iades
That dragge the Tragicke melancholy night:
Who with their drowsie, slow, and flagging wings
Cleape dead-mens graues, and from their misty Iawes,
Breath foule contagious darknesse in the ayre:
Therefore bring forth the Souldiers of our prize,
For whilst our Pinnace Anchors in the Downes,
Heere shall they make their ransome on the sand,
Or with their blood staine this discoloured shore.
Maister, this Prisoner freely giue I thee,
And thou that art his Mate, make boote of this:
The other *Walter Whitmore* is thy share.
1. Gent. What is my ransome Master, let me know.
Ma. A thousand Crownes, or else lay down your head
Mate. And so much shall you giue, or off goes yours.
Lieu. What thinke you much to pay 2000. Crownes,
And beare the name and port of Gentlemen?
Cut both the Villaines throats, for dy you shall:
The liues of those which we haue lost in fight,
Be counter-poys'd with such a pettie summe.
1. Gent. Ile giue it sir, and therefore spare my life.
2. Gent. And so will I, and write home for it straight.
Whitm. I lost mine eye in laying the prize aboord,
And therefore to reuenge it, shalt thou dye,
And so should these, if I might haue my will.
Lieu. Be not so rash, take ransome, let him liue.
Suf. Looke on my George, I am a Gentleman,
Rate me at what thou wilt, thou shalt be payed.
Whit. And so am I: my name is *Walter Whitmore.*
How now? why starts thou? What doth death affright?
Suf. Thy name affrights me, in whose sound is death:
A cunning man did calculate my birth,
And told me that by Water I should dye:
Yet let not this make thee be bloody-minded,
Thy name is *Gualtier*, being rightly sounded.
Whit. *Gualtier* or *Walter*, which it is I care not,
Neuer yet did base dishonour blurre our name,
But with our sword we wip'd away the blot.
Therefore, when Merchant-like I sell reuenge,
Broke be my sword, my Armes torne and defac'd,
And I proclaim'd a Coward through the world.
Suf. Stay *Whitmore*, for thy Prisoner is a Prince,
The Duke of Suffolke, *William de la Pole.*
Whit. The Duke of Suffolke, muffled vp in ragges?
Suf. I, but these ragges are no part of the Duke.
Lieu. But Ioue was neuer slaine as thou shalt be,
Obscure and lowsie Swaine, King *Henries* blood.
Suf. The honourable blood of Lancaster
Must not be shed by such a iaded Groome:
Hast thou not kist thy hand, and held my stirrop?
Bare-headed plodded by my foot-cloth Mule,
And thought thee happy when I shooke my head.
How often hast thou waited at my cup,
Fed from my Trencher, kneel'd downe at the boord,
When I haue feasted with Queene *Margaret*?
Remember it, and let it make thee Crest-faine,
I, and alay this thy abortiue Pride:
How in our voyding Lobby hast thou stood,
And duly wayted for my comming forth?
This hand of mine hath writ in thy behalfe,
And therefore shall it charme thy riotous tongue.
Whit. Speak Captaine, shall I stab the forlorn Swain.
Lieu. First let my words stab him, as he hath me.
Suf. Base slaue, thy words are blunt, and so art thou.
Lieu. Conuey him hence, and on our long boats side,
Strike off his head. *Suf.* Thou dar'st not for thy owne
Lieu. *Poole*, Sir *Poole*? Lord,
I kennell, puddle, sinke, whose filth and dirt
Troubles the siluer Spring, where England drinkes:
Now will I dam vp this thy yawning mouth,
For swallowing the Treasure of the Realme.
Thy lips that kist the Queene, shall sweepe the ground:
And thou that smil'dst at good Duke *Humfries* death,
Against the senselesse windes shall grin in vaine,
Who in contempt shall hisse at thee againe.
And wedded be thou to the Hagges of hell,
For daring to affye a mighty Lord
Vnto the daughter of a worthlesse King,
Hauing neyther Subiect, Wealth, nor Diadem:
By diuellish policy art thou growne great,
And like ambitious Sylla ouer-gorg'd,
With gobbets of thy Mother-bleeding heart.
By thee *Aniou* and *Maine* were sold to France.
The false reuolting Normans thorough thee,
Disdaine to call vs Lord, and *Piccardie*
Hath slaine their Gouernors, surpriz'd our Forts,
And sent the ragged Souldiers wounded home.
The Princely Warwicke, and the *Neuils* all,
Whose dreadfull swords were neuer drawne in vaine,
As hating thee, and rising vp in armes.
And now the House of Yorke thrust from the Crowne,
By shamefull murther of a guiltlesse King,
And lofty proud incroaching tyranny,
Burnes with reuenging fire, whose hopefull colours
Aduance our halfe-fac'd Sunne, striuing to shine;
Vnder the which is writ, *Inuitis nubibus.*
The Commons heere in Kent are vp in armes,
And to conclude, Reproach and Beggerie,
Is crept into the Pallace of our King,
And all by thee: away, conuey him hence.
Suf. O that I were a God, to shoot forth Thunder
Vpon these paltry, seruile, abiect Drudges:
Small things make base men proud. This Villaine heere,
Being Captaine of a Pinnace, threatens more
Then *Bargulus* the strong Illyrian Pyrate.
Drones sucke not Eagles blood, but rob Bee-hiues:
It is impossible that I should dye

By

By such a lowly Vassall as thy selfe.
Thy words moue Rage, and not remorse in me:
I go of Message from the Queene to France:
I charge thee waft me safely crosse the Channell.

Lieu. Water: W. Come Suffolke, I must waft thee to thy death.

Suf. *Pine gelidus timor occupat artus*, it is thee I feare.

Wal. Thou shalt haue cause to feare before I leaue thee.
What, are ye danted now? Now will ye stoope.

1.Gent. My gracious Lord intreat him, speak him fair

Suf. Suffolkes Imperiall tongue is sterne and rough:
Vs'd to command, vntaught to pleade for fauour.
Farre be it, we should honor such as these
With humble suite: no, rather let my head
Stoope to the blocke, then these knees bow to any,
Saue to the God of heauen, and to my King:
And sooner dance vpon a bloody pole,
Then stand vncouer'd to the Vulgar Groome.
True Nobility, is exempt from feare:
More can I beare, then you dare execute.

Lieu. Hale him away, and let him talke no more:
Come Souldiers, shew what cruelty ye can.

Suf. That this my death may neuer be forgot.
Great men oft dye by vilde Bezonions.
A Romane Sworder, and Bandetto slaue
Murder'd sweet *Tully*. *Brutus* Bastard hand
Stab'd *Iulius Cæsar*. Sauage Islanders
Pompey the Great, and *Suffolke* dyes by Pyrats.

Exit Water with Suffolke.

Lieu. And as for these whose ransome we haue set,
It is our pleasure one of them depart:
Therefore come you with vs, and let him go.

Exit Lieutenant, and the rest.

Manet the first Gent. *Enter Walter with the body.*

Wal. There let his head, and liuelesse bodie lye,
Vntill the Queene his Mistris bury it. *Exit Walter.*

1.Gent. O barbarous and bloudy spectacle,
His body will I beare vnto the King:
If he reuenge it not, yet will his Friends,
So will the Queene, that liuing, held him deere.

Enter Beuis, and Iohn Holland.

Beuis. Come and get thee a sword, though made of a Lath, they haue bene vp these two dayes.

Hol. They haue the more neede to sleepe now then.

Beuis. I tell thee, *Iacke Cade* the Cloathier, meanes to dresse the Common-wealth and turne it, and set a new nap vpon it.

Hol. So he had need, for 'tis thred-bare. Well, I say, it was neuer merrie world in England, since Gentlemen came vp.

Beuis. O miserable Age: Vertue is not regarded in Handy-crafts men.

Hol. The Nobilitie thinke scorne to goe in Leather Aprons.

Beuis. Nay more, the Kings Councell are no good Workemen.

Hol. True: and yet it is said, Labour in thy Vocation: which is as much to say, as let the Magistrates be labouring men, and therefore should we be Magistrates.

Beuis. Thou hast hit it: for there's no better signe of a braue minde, then a hard hand.

Hol. I see them, I see them: There's *Bests* Sonne, the Tanner of Wingham.

Beuis. Hee shall haue the skinnes of our enemies, to make Dogges Leather of.

Hol. And Dicke the Butcher.

Beuis. Then is sin strucke downe like an Oxe, and iniquities throate cut like a Calfe.

Hol. And Smith the Weauer.

Beu. Argo, their thred of life is spun.

Hol. Come, come, let's fall in with them.

Drumme. *Enter Cade, Dicke Butcher, Smith the Weauer, and a Sawyer, with infinite numbers.*

Cade. Wee *Iohn Cade*, so tearm'd of our supposed Father.

But. Or rather of stealing a Cade of Herrings.

Cade. For our enemies shall faile before vs, inspired with the spirit of putting down Kings and Princes. Command silence.

But. Silence.

Cade. My Father was a *Mortimer*.

But. He was an honest man, and a good Bricklayer.

Cade. My mother a *Plantagenet*.

Butch. I knew her well, she was a Midwife.

Cade. My wife descended of the *Lacies*.

But. She was indeed a Pedlers daughter, & sold many Laces.

Weauer. But now of late, not able to trauell with her furr'd Packe, she washes buckes here at home.

Cade. Therefore am I of an honorable house.

But. I by my faith, the field is honourable, and there was he borne, vnder a hedge: for his Father had neuer a house but the Cage.

Cade. Valiant I am.

Weauer. A must needs, for beggery is valiant.

Cade. I am able to endure much.

But. No question of that: for I haue seene him whipt three Market dayes together.

Cade. I feare neither sword, nor fire.

Wea. He neede not feare the sword, for his Coate is of proofe.

But. But me thinks he should stand in feare of fire, being burnt i'th hand for stealing of Sheepe.

Cade. Be braue then, for your Captaine is Braue, and Vowes Reformation. There shall be in England, seuen halfe peny Loaues sold for a peny: the three hoop'd pot, shall haue ten hoopes, and I wil make it Fellony to drink small Beere. All the Realme shall be in Common, and in Cheapside shall my Palfrey go to grasse: and when I am King, as King I will be.

All. God saue your Maiesty.

Cade. I thanke you good people. There shall bee no mony, all shall eate and drinke on my score, and I will apparrell them all in one Liuery, that they may agree like Brothers, and worship me their Lord.

But. The first thing we do, let's kill all the Lawyers.

Cade. Nay, that I meane to do. Is not this a lamentable thing, that of the skin of an innocent Lambe should be made Parchment; that Parchment being scribeld ore, should vndoe a man. Some say the Bee stings, but I say, tis the Bees waxe: for I did but seale once to a thing, and I was neuer mine owne man since. How now? Who's there?

Enter a Clearke.

Weauer. The Clearke of Chartam: hee can write and reade, and cast accompt.

Cade. O monstrous.

Wea. We tooke him setting of boyes Copies.

Cade.

Cade. Here's a Villaine.

Wea. He's a Booke in his pocket with red Letters in't

Cade. Nay then he is a Coniurer.

But. Nay, he can make Obligations, and write Court hand.

Cade. I am sorry for't: The man is a proper man of mine Honour: vnlesse I finde him guilty, he shall not die. Come hither sirrah, I must examine thee: What is thy name?

Clearke. *Emanuell.*

But. They vse to writ it on the top of Letters: 'Twill go hard with you.

Cade. Let me alone: Dost thou vse to write thy name? Or hast thou a marke to thy selfe, like a honest plain dealing man?

Clearke. Sir I thanke God, I haue bin so well brought vp, that I can write my name.

All. He hath confest: away with him: he's a Villaine and a Traitor.

Cade. Away with him I say: Hang him with his Pen and Inke-horne about his necke.

Exit one with the Clearke

Enter Michael.

Mich. Where's our Generall?

Cade. Heere I am thou particular fellow.

Mich. Fly, fly, fly, Sir *Humfrey Stafford* and his brother are hard by, with the Kings Forces.

Cade. Stand villaine, stand, or Ile fell thee downe: he shall be encountred with a man as good as himselfe. He is but a Knight, is a?

Mich. No.

Cade. To equall him I will make my selfe a knight presently; Rise vp Sir *Iohn Mortimer.* Now haue at him.

Enter Sir Humfrey Stafford, and his Brother, with Drum and Soldiers.

Staf. Rebellious Hinds, the filth and scum of Kent,
Mark'd for the Gallowes: Lay your Weapons downe,
Home to your Cottages: forsake this Groome.
The King is mercifull, if you reuolt.

Bro. But angry, wrathfull, and inclin'd to blood,
If you go forward: therefore yeeld, or dye.

Cade. As for these silken-coated slaues I passe not,
It is to you good people, that I speake,
Ouer whom (in time to come) I hope to raigne:
For I am rightfull heyre vnto the Crowne.

Staff. Villaine, thy Father was a Playsterer,
And thou thy selfe a Sheareman, art thou not?

Cade. And *Adam* was a Gardiner.

Bro. And what of that?

Cade. Marry, this *Edmund Mortimer* Earle of March, married the Duke of *Clarence* daughter, did he not?

Staf. I sir.

Cade. By her he had two children at one birth.

Bro. That's false.

Cade. I, there's the question; But I say, 'tis true:
The elder of them being put to nurse,
Was by a begger-woman stolne away,
And ignorant of his birth and parentage,
Became a Bricklayer, when he came to age.
His sonne am I, deny it if you can.

But. Nay, 'tis too true, therefore he shall be King.

Wea. Sir, he made a Chimney in my Fathers house, & the brickes are aliue at this day to testifie it: therefore deny it not.

Staf. And will you credit this base Drudges Wordes, that speakes he knowes not what.

All. I marry will we: therefore get ye gone.

Bro. *Iacke Cade*, the D. of York hath taught you this.

Cade. He lyes, for I inuented it my selfe. Go too Sirrah, tell the King from me, that for his Fathers sake *Henry* the fift, (in whose time, boyes went to Span-counter for French Crownes) I am content he shall raigne, but Ile be Protector ouer him.

Butcher. And furthermore, wee'l haue the Lord *Sayes* head, for selling the Dukedome of *Maine.*

Cade And good reason: for thereby is England main'd And faine to go with a staffe, but that my puissance holds it vp. Fellow-Kings, I tell you, that that Lord *Say* hath gelded the Commonwealth, and made it an Eunuch: & more then that, he can speake French, and therefore hee is a Traitor.

Staf. O grosse and miserable ignorance.

Cade. Nay answer if you can: The Frenchmen are our enemies: go too then, I ask but this: Can he that speaks with the tongue of an enemy, be a good Councellour, or no?

All. No, no, and therefore wee'l haue his head.

Bro. Well, seeing gentle words will not preuayle,
Assaile them with the Army of the King.

Staf. Herald away, and throughout euery Towne,
Proclaime them Traitors that are vp with *Cade,*
That those which flye before the battell ends,
May euen in their Wiues and Childrens sight,
Be hang'd vp for example at their doores:
And you that be the Kings Friends follow me. *Exit.*

Cade. And you that loue the Commons, follow me:
Now shew your selues men, 'tis for Liberty.
We will not leaue one Lord, one Gentleman:
Spare none, but such as go in clouted shooen,
For they are thrifty honest men, and such
As would (but that they dare not) take our parts.

But. They are all in order, and march toward vs.

Cade. But then are we in order, when we are most out of order. Come, march forward.

Alarums to the fight, wherein both the Staffords are slaine. Enter Cade and the rest.

Cade. Where's Dicke, the Butcher of Ashford?

But. Heere sir.

Cade. They fell before thee like Sheepe and Oxen, & thou behaued'st thy selfe, as if thou hadst beene in thine owne Slaughter-house: Therfore thus will I reward thee, the Lent shall bee as long againe as it is, and thou shalt haue a License to kill for a hundred lacking one.

But. I desire no more.

Cade. And to speake truth, thou deseru'st no lesse. This Monument of the victory will I beare, and the bodies shall be dragg'd at my horse heeles, till I do come to London, where we will haue the Maiors sword born before vs.

But. If we meane to thriue, and do good, breake open the Gaoles, and let out the Prisoners.

Cade. Feare not that I warrant thee. Come, let's march towards London. *Exeunt.*

Enter the King with a Supplication, and the Queene with Suffolkes head, the Duke of Buckingham, and the Lord Say.

Queene. Oft haue I heard that greefe softens the mind,

And

And makes it fearefull and degenerate,
Thinke therefore on reuenge, and ceaſe to weepe.
But who can ceaſe to weepe, and looke on this.
Heere may his head lye on my throbbing breſt:
But where's the body that I ſhould imbrace?
Buc. What anſwer makes your Grace to the Rebells
Supplication?
King. Ile ſend ſome holy Biſhop to intreat:
For God forbid, ſo many ſimple ſoules
Should periſh by the Sword. And I my ſelfe,
Rather then bloody Warre ſhall cut them ſhort,
Will parley with *Iacke Cade* their Generall,
But ſtay, Ile read it ouer once againe.
Qu. Ah barbarous villaines: Hath this louely face,
Rul'd like a wandering Plannet ouer me,
And could it not inforce them to relent,
That were vnworthy to behold the ſame.
King. Lord *Say*, *Iacke Cade* hath ſworne to huae thy
head.
Say. I, but I hope your Highneſſe ſhall haue his.
King. How now Madam?
Still lamenting and mourning for Suffolkes death?
I feare me (Loue) if that I had beene dead,
Thou would'ſt not haue mourn'd ſo much for me.
Qu. No my Loue, I ſhould not mourne, but dye for
thee.

Enter a Meſſenger.

King. How now? What newes? Why com'ſt thou in
ſuch haſte?
Meſ. The Rebels are in Southwarke: Fly my Lord:
Iacke Cade proclaimes himſelfe Lord *Mortimer*,
Deſcended from the Duke of *Clarence* houſe,
And calles your Grace Vſurper, openly,
And vowes to Crowne himſelfe in Weſtminſter.
His Army is a ragged multitude
Of Hindes and Pezants, rude and mercileſſe:
Sir *Humfrey Stafford*, and his Brothers death,
Hath giuen them heart and courage to proceede:
All Schollers, Lawyers, Courtiers, Gentlemen,
They call falſe Catterpillers, and intend their death.
Kin. Oh graceleſſe men: they know not what they do.
Buck. My gracious Lord, retire to Killingworth,
Vntill a power be rais'd to put them downe.
Qu. Ah were the Duke of Suffolke now aliue,
Theſe Kentiſh Rebels would be ſoone appeas'd.
King. Lord *Say*, the Traitors hateth thee,
Therefore away with vs to Killingworth.
Say. So might your Graces perſon be in danger.
The ſight of me is odious in their eyes:
And therefore in this Citty will I ſtay,
And liue alone as ſecret as I may.

Enter another Meſſenger.

Meſſ. *Iacke Cade* hath gotten London-bridge.
The Citizens flye and forſake their houſes:
The Raſcall people, thirſting after prey,
Ioyne with the Traitor, and they ioyntly ſweare
To ſpoyle the City, and your Royall Court.
Buc. Then linger not my Lord, away, take horſe.
King. Come *Margaret*, God our hope will ſuccor vs.
Qu. My hope is gone, now Suffolke is deceaſt.
King. Farewell my Lord, truſt not the Kentiſh Rebels
Buc. Truſt no body for feare you betraid.
Say. The truſt I haue, is in mine innocence,
And therefore am I bold and reſolute. *Exeunt.*

Enter Lord Scales vpon the Tower walking. Then enters two or three Citizens below.

Scales. How now? Is *Iacke Cade* ſlaine?
1.Cit. No my Lord, nor likely to be ſlaine
For they haue wonne the Bridge,
Killing all thoſe that withſtand them:
The L. Maior craues ayd of your Honor from the Tower
To defend the City from the Rebels.
Scales. Such ayd as I can ſpare you ſhall command,
But I am troubled heere with them my ſelfe,
The Rebels haue aſſay'd to win the Tower.
But get you to Smithfield, and gather head,
And thither I will ſend you *Mathew Goffe*.
Fight for your King, your Countrey, and your Liues,
And ſo farwell, for I muſt hence againe. *Exeunt*

Enter Iacke Cade and the reſt, and ſtrikes his ſtaffe on London ſtone.

Cade. Now is *Mortimer* Lord of this City,
And heere ſitting vpon London Stone,
I charge and command, that of the Cities coſt
The piſſing Conduit run nothing but Clarret Wine
This firſt yeare of our raigne.
And now henceforward it ſhall be Treaſon for any,
That calles me other then Lord *Mortimer*.

Enter a Soldier running.

Soul. *Iacke Cade, Iacke Cade.*
Cade. Knocke him downe there. *They kill him.*
But. If this Fellow be wiſe, hee'l neuer call yee *Iacke Cade* more, I thinke he hath a very faire warning.
Dicke. My Lord, there's an Army gathered together in Smithfield.
Cade. Come, then let's go fight with them:
But firſt, go and ſet London Bridge on fire,
And if you can, burne downe the Tower too.
Come, let's away. *Exeunt omnes.*

Alarums. Mathew Goffe is ſlain, and all the reſt. Then enter Iacke Cade, with his Company.

Cade. So ſirs: now go ſome and pull down the Sauoy:
Others to'th Innes of Court, downe with them all.
But. I haue a ſuite vnto your Lordſhip.
Cade. Bee it a Lordſhippe, thou ſhalt haue it for that word.
But. Onely that the Lawes of England may come out of your mouth.
Iohn. Maſſe 'twill be ſore Law then, for he was thruſt in the mouth with a Speare, and 'tis not whole yet.
Smith. Nay *Iohn*, it wil be ſtinking Law, for his breath ſtinkes with eating toſted cheeſe.
Cade. I haue thought vpon it, it ſhall bee ſo. Away, burne all the Records of the Realme, my mouth ſhall be the Parliament of England.
Iohn. Then we are like to haue biting Statutes
Vnleſſe his teeth be pull'd out.
Cade. And hence-forward all things ſhall be in Common. *Enter a Meſſenger.*
Meſ. My Lord, a prize, a prize, heeres the Lord *Say*, which ſold the Townes in France. He that made vs pay one and twenty Fifteenes, and one ſhilling to the pound, the laſt Subſidie.

Enter

Enter George, with the Lord Say.

Cade. Well, hee ſhall be beheaded for it ten times: Ah thou Say, thou Surge, nay thou Buckram Lord, now art thou within point-blanke of our Iuriſdiction Regall. What canſt thou anſwer to my Maieſty, for giuing vp of Normandie vnto Mounſieur *Baſimecu*, the Dolphine of France? Be it knowne vnto thee by theſe preſence, euen the preſence of Lord *Mortimer*, that I am the Beeſome that muſt ſweepe the Court cleane of ſuch filth as thou art: Thou haſt moſt traiterouſly corrupted the youth of the Realme, in erecting a Grammar Schoole: and whereas before, our Fore-fathers had no other Bookes but the Score and the Tally, thou haſt cauſed printing to be vs'd, and contrary to the King, his Crowne, and Dignity, thou haſt built a Paper-Mill. It will be prooued to thy Face, that thou haſt men about thee, that vſually talke of a Nowne and a Verbe, and ſuch abhominable wordes, as no Chriſtian eare can endure to heare. Thou haſt appointed Iuſtices of Peace, to call poore men before them, about matters they were not able to anſwer. Moreouer, thou haſt put them in priſon, and becauſe they could not reade, thou haſt hang'd them, when (indeede) onely for that cauſe they haue beene moſt worthy to liue. Thou doſt ride in a foot-cloth, doſt thou not?

Say. What of that?

Cade. Marry, thou ought'ſt not to let thy horſe weare a Cloake, when honeſter men then thou go in their Hoſe and Doublets.

Dicke. And worke in their ſhirt to, as my ſelfe for example, that am a butcher.

Say. You men of Kent.

Dic. What ſay you of Kent.

Say. Nothing but this: 'Tis *bona terra, mala gens.*

Cade. Away with him, away with him, he ſpeaks Latine.

Say. Heare me but ſpeake, and beare mee wher'e you will:
Kent, in the Commentaries *Cæſar* writ,
Is term'd the ciuel'ſt place of all this Iſle:
Sweet is the Covntry, becauſe full of Riches,
The People Liberall, Valiant, Actiue, Wealthy,
Which makes me hope you are not void of pitty.
I ſold not *Maine*, I loſt not *Normandie*,
Yet to recouer them would looſe my life:
Iuſtice with fauour haue I alwayes done,
Prayres and Teares haue mou'd me, Gifts could neuer.
When haue I ought exacted at your hands?
Kent to maintaine, the King, the Realme and you,
Large gifts haue I beſtow'd on learned Clearkes,
Becauſe my Booke preferr'd me to the King.
And ſeeing Ignorance is the curſe of God,
Knowledge the Wing wherewith we flye to heauen.
Vnleſſe you be poſſeſt with diuelliſh ſpirits,
You cannot but forbeare to murther me:
This Tongue hath parlied vnto Forraigne Kings
For your behoofe.

Cade. Tut, when ſtruck'ſt thou one blow in the field?

Say. Great men haue reaching hands: oft haue I ſtruck
Thoſe that I neuer ſaw, and ſtrucke them dead.

Geo. O monſtrous Coward! What, to come behinde Folkes?

Say. Theſe cheekes are pale for watching for your good

Cade. Giue him a box o'th'eare, and that wil make 'em red againe.

Say. Long ſitting to determine poore mens cauſes,
Hath made me full of ſickneſſe and diſeaſes.

Cade. Ye ſhall haue a hempen Candle then, & the help of hatchet.

Dicke. Why doſt thou quiuer man?

Say. The Palſie, and not feare prouokes me.

Cade. Nay, he noddes at vs, as who ſhould ſay, Ile be euen with you. Ile ſee if his head will ſtand ſteddier on a pole, or no: Take him away, and behead him.

Say. Tell me: wherein haue I offended moſt?
Haue I affected wealth, or honor? Speake.
Are my Cheſts fill'd vp with extorted Gold?
Is my Apparrell ſumptuous to behold?
Whom haue I iniur'd, that ye ſeeke my death?
Theſe hands are free from guiltleſſe bloodſhedding,
This breaſt from harbouring foule deceitfull thoughts.
O let me liue.

Cade. I feele remorſe in my ſelfe with his words: but Ile bridle it: he ſhall dye, and it bee but for pleading ſo well for his life. Away with him, he ha's a Familiar vnder his Tongue, he ſpeakes not a Gods name. Goe, take him away I ſay, and ſtrike off his head preſently, and then breake into his Sonne in Lawes houſe, Sir *Iames Cromer*, and ſtrike off his head, and bring them both vppon two poles hither.

All. It ſhall be done.

Say. Ah Countrimen: If when you make your prair's,
God ſhould be ſo obdurate as your ſelues:
How would it fare with your departed ſoules.
And therefore yet relent, and ſaue my life.

Cade. Away with him, and do as I command ye: the proudeſt Peere in the Realme, ſhall not weare a head on his ſhoulders, vnleſſe he pay me tribute: there ſhall not a maid be married, but ſhe ſhall pay to me her Maydenhead ere they haue it: Men ſhall hold of mee in Capite. And we charge and command, that their wiues be as free as heart can wiſh, or tongue can tell.

Dicke. My Lord,
When ſhall we go to Cheapſide, and take vp commodities vpon our billes?

Cade. Marry preſently.

All. O braue.

Enter one with the heads.

Cade. But is not this brauer:
Let them kiſſe one another: For they lou'd well
When they were aliue. Now part them againe,
Leaſt they conſult about the giuing vp
Of ſome more Townes in France. Soldiers,
Deferre the ſpoile of the Citie vntill night:
For with theſe borne before vs, in ſteed of Maces,
Will we ride through the ſtreets, & at euery Corner
Haue them kiſſe. Away. *Exit*

Alarum, and Retreat. Enter againe Cade, and all his rabblement.

Cade. Vp Fiſh-ſtreete, downe Saint Magnes corner, kill and knocke downe, throw them into Thames:

Sound a parley

What noiſe is this I heare?
Dare any be ſo bold to ſound Retreat or Parley
When I command them kill?

Enter

Enter Buckingham, and old Clifford.

Buc. I heere they be, that dare and will disturb thee:
Know *Cade*, we come Ambassadors from the King
Vnto the Commons, whom thou hast misled,
And heere pronounce free pardon to them all,
That will forsake thee, and go home in peace.

Clif. What say ye Countrimen, will ye relent
And yeeld to mercy, whil'st 'tis offered you,
Or let a rabble leade you to your deaths.
Who loues the King, and will imbrace his pardon,
Fling vp his cap, and say, God saue his Maiesty.
Who hateth him, and honors not his Father,
Henry the fift, that made all France to quake,
Shake he his weapon at vs, and passe by.

All. God saue the King, God saue the King.

Cade. What Buckingham and Clifford are ye so braue? And you base Pezants, do ye beleeue him, will you needs be hang'd with your Pardons about your neckes? Hath my sword therefore broke through London gates, that you should leaue me at the White-heart in Southwarke. I thought ye would neuer haue giuen out these Armes til you had recouered your ancient Freedome. But you are all Recreants and Dastards, and delight to liue in slauerie to the Nobility. Let them breake your backes with burthens, take your houses ouer your heads, rauish your Wiues and Daughters before your faces. For me, I will make shift for one, and so Gods Cursse light vppon you all.

All Wee'l follow *Cade*,
Wee'l follow *Cade*

Clif Is *Cade* the sonne of *Henry* the fift,
That thus you do exclaime you'l go with him.
Will he conduct you through the heart of France,
And make the meanest of you Earles and Dukes?
Alas, he hath no home, no place to flye too
Nor knowes he how to liue, but by the spoile,
Vnlesse by robbing of your Friends, and vs.
Wer't not a shame, that whilst you liue at iarre,
The fearfull French, whom you late vanquished
Should make a start ore-seas, and vanquish you?
Me thinkes alreadie in this ciuill broyle,
I see them Lording it in London streets,
Crying *Villiago* vnto all they meete.
Better ten thousand base-borne *Cades* miscarry,
Then you should stoope vnto a Frenchmans mercy.
To France, to France, and get what you haue lost:
Spare England, for it is your Natiue Coast:
Henry hath mony, you are strong and manly.
God on our side, doubt not of Victorie.

All. A Clifford, a Clifford,
Wee'l follow the King, and Clifford.

Cade. Was euer Feather so lightly blowne too & fro, as this multitude? The name of Henry the fift, hales them to an hundred mischiefes, and makes them leaue mee desolate. I see them lay their heades together to surprize me. My sword make way for me, for heere is no staying: in despight of the diuels and hell, haue through the verie middest of you, and heauens and honor be witnesse, that no want of resolution in mee, but onely my Followers base and ignominious treasons, makes me betake mee to my heeles *Exit*

Buck What, is he fled? Go some and follow him,
And he that brings his head vnto the King,
Shall haue a thousand Crownes for his reward.
Exeunt some of them.

Follow me souldiers, wee'l deuise a meane,
To reconcile you all vnto the King. *Exeunt omnes.*

Sound Trumpets. Enter King, Queene, and Somerset on the Tarras.

King. Was euer King that ioy'd an earthly Throne,
And could command no more content then I?
No sooner was I crept out of my Cradle,
But I was made a King, at nine months olde.
Was neuer Subiect long'd to be a King,
As I do long and wish to be a Subiect.

Enter Buckingham and Clifford.

Buc. Health and glad tydings to your Maiesty.

Kin. Why Buckingham, is the Traitor *Cade* surpris'd?
Or is he but retir'd to make him strong?

Enter Multitudes with Halters about their Neckes

Clif. He is fled my Lord, and all his powers do yeeld,
And humbly thus with halters on their neckes,
Expect your Highnesse doome of life, or death.

King. Then heauen set ope thy euerlasting gates,
To entertaine my vowes of thankes and praise.
Souldiers, this day haue you redeem'd your liues,
And shew'd how well you loue your Prince & Countrey
Continue still in this so good a minde,
And *Henry* though he be infortunate,
Assure your selues will neuer be vnkinde.
And so with thankes, and pardon to you all,
I do dismisse you to your seuerall Countries.

All. God saue the King, God saue the King.

Enter a Messenger

Mes. Please it your Grace to be aduertised,
The Duke of Yorke is newly come from Ireland,
And with a puissant and a mighty power
Of Gallow-glasses and stout Kernes,
Is marching hitherward in proud array,
And still proclaimeth as he comes along,
His Armes are onely to remoue from thee
The Duke of Somerset, whom he tearmes a Traitor.

King. Thus stands my state, 'twixt Cade and Yorke distrest,
Like to a Ship, that hauing scap'd a Tempest,
Is straight way calme, and boorded with a Pyrate.
But now is Cade driuen backe, his men dispierc'd,
And now is Yorke in Armes, to second him.
I pray thee Buckingham go and meete him,
And aske him what's the reason of these Armes.
Tell him, Ile send Duke *Edmund* to the Tower,
And *Somerset* we will commit thee thither,
Vntill his Army be dismist from him.

Somerset. My Lord,
Ile yeelde my selfe to prison willingly,
Or vnto death, to do my Countrey good.

King. In any case, be not to rough in termes,
For he is fierce, and cannot brooke hard Language.

Buc. I will my Lord, and doubt not so to deale,
As all things shall redound vnto your good.

King. Come wife, let's in, and learne to gouern better,
For yet may England curse my wretched raigne.
Flourish. *Exeunt*

Enter

Enter Cade.

Cade. Fye on Ambitions: fie on my selfe, that haue a sword, and yet am ready to famish. These fiue daies haue I hid me in these Woods, and durst not peepe out, for all the Country is laid for me: but now am I so hungry, that if I might haue a Lease of my life for a thousand yeares, I could stay no longer. Wherefore on a Bricke wall haue I climb'd into this Garden, to see if I can eate Grasse, or picke a Sallet another while, which is not amisse to coole a mans stomacke this hot weather: and I think this word Sallet was borne to do me good. for many a time but for a Sallet, my braine-pan had bene cleft with a brown Bill; and many a time when I haue beene dry, & brauely marching, it hath seru'd me insteede of a quart pot to drinke in: and now the word Sallet must serue me to feed on.

Enter Iden.

Iden. Lord, who would liue turmoyled in the Court,
And may enioy such quiet walkes as these?
This small inheritance my Father left me,
Contenteth me, and worth a Monarchy.
I seeke not to waxe great by others warning,
Or gather wealth I care not with what enuy:
Sufficeth, that I haue maintaines my state,
And sends the poore well pleased from my gate.

Cade. Heere's the Lord of the soile come to seize me for a stray, for entering his Fee-simple without leaue. A Villaine, thou wilt betray me, and get a 1000. Crownes of the King by carrying my head to him, but Ile make thee eate Iron like an Ostridge, and swallow my Sword like a great pin ere thou and I part.

Iden. Why rude Companion, whatsoere thou be,
I know thee not, why then should I betray thee?
Is't not enough to breake into my Garden,
And like a Theefe to come to rob my grounds:
Climbing my walles inspight of me the Owner,
But thou wilt braue me with these sawcie termes?

Cade. Braue thee? I by the best blood that euer was broach'd, and beard thee to. Looke on mee well, I haue eate no meate these fiue dayes, yet come thou and thy fiue men, and if I doe not leaue you all as dead as a doore naile, I pray God I may neuer eate grasse more.

Iden. Nay, it shall nere be said, while England stands,
That *Alexander Iden* an Esquire of Kent,
Tooke oddes to combate a poore famisht man.
Oppose thy stedfast gazing eyes to mine,
See if thou canst out-face me with thy lookes:
Set limbe to limbe, and thou art farre the lesser:
Thy hand is but a finger to my fist,
Thy legge a sticke compared with this Truncheon,
My foote shall fight with all the strength thou hast,
And if mine arme be heaued in the Ayre,
Thy graue is digg'd already in the earth:
As for words, whose greatnesse answer's words,
Let this my sword report what speech forbeares.

Cade. By my Valour: the most compleate Champion that euer I heard. Steele, if thou turne the edge, or cut not out the burly bon'd Clowne in chines of Beefe, ere thou sleepe in thy Sheath, I beseech Ioue on my knees thou mayst be turn'd to Hobnailes.

Heere they Fight.

O I am slaine Famine and no other hath slaine me, let ten thousand diuelles come against me, and giue me but the ten meales I haue lost, and I'de defie them all. Wither Garden, and be henceforth a burying place to all that do dwell in this house, because the vnconquered soule of *Cade* is fled.

Iden. Is't *Cade* that I haue slain, that monstrous traitor?
Sword, I will hallow thee for this thy deede,
And hang thee o're my Tombe, when I am dead.
Ne're shall this blood be wiped from thy point,
But thou shalt weare it as a Heralds coate,
To emblaze the Honor that thy Master got.

Cade. *Iden* farewell, and be proud of thy victory: Tell Kent from me, she hath lost her best man, and exhort all the World to be Cowards: For I that neuer feared any, am vanquished by Famine, not by Valour. *Dyes.*

Id. How much thou wrong'st me, heauen be my iudge;
Die damned Wretch, the curse of her that bare thee:
And as I thrust thy body in with my sword,
So wish I, I might thrust thy soule to hell.
Hence will I dragge thee headlong by the heeles
Vnto a dunghill, which shall be thy graue,
And there cut off thy most vngracious head,
Which I will beare in triumph to the King,
Leauing thy trunke for Crowes to feed vpon. *Exit.*

Enter Yorke, and his Army of Irish, with Drum and Colours.

Yor. From Ireland thus comes York to claim his right,
And plucke the Crowne from feeble *Henries* head.
Ring Belles alowd, burne Bonfires cleare and bright
To entertaine great Englands lawfull King.
Ah *Sancta Maiestas*! who would not buy thee deere?
Let them obey, that knowes not how to Rule.
This hand was made to handle nought but Gold.
I cannot giue due action to my words,
Except a Sword or Scepter ballance it.
A Scepter shall it haue, haue I a soule,
On which Ile tosse the Fleure-de-Luce of France.

Enter Buckingham.

Whom haue we heere? Buckingham to disturbe me?
The king hath sent him sure: I must dissemble.

Buc. Yorke, if thou meanest wel, I greet thee well.

Yor. *Humfrey* of Buckingham, I accept thy greeting.
Art thou a Messenger, or come of pleasure.

Buc. A Messenger from *Henry*, our dread Liege,
To know the reason of these Armes in peace.
Or why, thou being a Subiect, as I am,
Against thy Oath, and true Allegeance sworne,
Should raise so great a power without his leaue?
Or dare to bring thy Force so neere the Court?

Yor. Scarse can I speake, my Choller is so great.
Oh I could hew vp Rockes, and fight with Flint,
I am so angry at these abiect tearmes.
And now like *Aiax Telamonius*,
On Sheepe or Oxen could I spend my furie.
I am farre better borne then is the king:
More like a King, more Kingly in my thoughts.
But I must make faire weather yet a while,
Till *Henry* be more weake, and I more strong.
Buckingham, I prethee pardon me,
That I haue giuen no answer all this while:
My minde was troubled with deepe Melancholly.
The cause why I haue brought this Armie hither,

Is to remoue proud Somerset from the King,
Seditious to his Grace, and to the State.
Buc. That is too much presumption on thy part:
But if thy Armes be to no other end,
The King hath yeelded vnto thy demand:
The Duke of Somerset is in the Tower.
Yorke. Vpon thine Honor is he Prisoner?
Buck. Vpon mine Honor he is Prisoner.
Yorke. Then Buckingham I do dismisse my Powres.
Souldiers, I thanke you all: disperse your selues:
Meet me to morrow in S. Georges Field,
You shall haue pay, and euery thing you wish.
And let my Soueraigne, vertuous *Henry*,
Command my eldest sonne, nay all my sonnes,
As pledges of my Fealtie and Loue,
Ile send them all as willing as I liue:
Lands, Goods, Horse, Armor, any thing I haue
Is his to vse, so Somerset may die.
Buc. Yorke, I commend this kinde submission,
We twaine will go into his Highnesse Tent.

Enter King and Attendants.

King. Buckingham, doth Yorke intend no harme to vs
That thus he marcheth with thee arme in arme?
Yorke. In all submission and humility,
Yorke doth present himselfe vnto your Highnesse.
K. Then what intends these Forces thou dost bring?
Yor. To heaue the Traitor Somerset from hence,
And fight against that monstrous Rebell *Cade*,
Who since I heard to be discomfited.

Enter Iden with Cades head.

Iden. If one so rude, and of so meane condition
May passe into the presence of a King:
Loe, I present your Grace a Traitors head,
The head of *Cade*, whom I in combat slew.
King. The head of *Cade*? Great God, how iust art thou?
Oh let me view his Visage being dead,
That liuing wrought me such exceeding trouble.
Tell me my Friend, art thou the man that slew him?
Iden. I was, an't like your Maiesty.
King. How art thou call'd? And what is thy degree?
Iden. *Alexander Iden*, that's my name,
A poore Esquire of Kent, that loues his King.
Buc. So please it you my Lord, 'twere not amisse
He were created Knight for his good seruice.
King. *Iden*, kneele downe, rise vp a Knight:
We giue thee for reward a thousand Markes,
And will, that thou henceforth attend on vs.
Iden. May *Iden* liue to merit such a bountie,
And neuer liue but true vnto his Liege.

Enter Queene and Somerset.

K. See Buckingham, Somerset comes with th'Queene
Go bid her hide him quickly from the Duke.
Qu. For thousand Yorkes he shall not hide his head,
But boldly stand, and front him to his face.
Yor. How now? is Somerset at libertie?
Then Yorke vnloose thy long imprisoned thoughts,
And let thy tongue be equall with thy heart.
Shall I endure the sight of Somerset?
False King, why hast thou broken faith with me,
Knowing how hardly I can brooke abuse?
King did I call thee? No: thou art not King:
Not fit to gouerne and rule multitudes,
Which dar'st not, no nor canst not rule a Traitor.
That Head of thine doth not become a Crowne:
Thy Hand is made to graspe a Palmers staffe,
And not to grace an awefull Princely Scepter.
That Gold, must round engirt these browes of mine,
Whose Smile and Frowne, like to *Achilles* Speare
Is able with the change, to kill and cure.
Heere is a hand to hold a Scepter vp,
And with the same to acte controlling Lawes:
Giue place: by heauen thou shalt rule no more
O're him, whom heauen created for thy Ruler.
Som. O monstrous Traitor! I arrest thee Yorke
Of Capitall Treason 'gainst the King and Crowne:
Obey audacious Traitor, kneele for Grace.
York. Wold'st haue me kneele? First let me ask of thee,
If they can brooke I bow a knee to man:
Sirrah, call in my sonne to be my bale:
I know ere they will haue me go to Ward,
They'l pawne their swords of my infranchisement.
Qu. Call hither *Clifford*, bid him come amaine,
To say, if that the Bastard boyes of Yorke
Shall be the Surety for their Traitor Father.
Yorke. O blood-bespotted Neopolitan,
Out-cast of *Naples*, Englands bloody Scourge,
The sonnes of Yorke, thy betters in their birth,
Shall be their Fathers baile, and bane to those
That for my Surety will refuse the Boyes.

Enter Edward and Richard.

See where they come, Ile warrant they'l make it good.

Enter Clifford.

Qu. And here comes *Clifford* to deny their baile.
Clif. Health, and all happinesse to my Lord the King.
Yor. I thanke thee *Clifford*: Say, what newes with thee?
Nay, do not fright vs with an angry looke:
We are thy Soueraigne *Clifford*, kneele againe;
For thy mistaking so, We pardon thee.
Clif. This is my King Yorke, I do not mistake,
But thou mistakes me much to thinke I do,
To Bedlem with him, is the man growne mad.
King. I Clifford, a Bedlem and ambitious humor
Makes him oppose himselfe against his King.
Clif. He is a Traitor, let him to the Tower,
And chop away that factious pate of his.
Qu. He is arrested, but will not obey:
His sonnes (he sayes) shall giue their words for him.
Yor. Will you not Sonnes?
Edw. I Noble Father, if our words will serue.
Rich. And if words will not, then our Weapons shal.
Clif. Why what a brood of Traitors haue we heere?
Yorke. Looke in a Glasse, and call thy Image so.
I am thy King, and thou a false-heart Traitor:
Call hither to the stake my two braue Beares,
That with the very shaking of their Chaines,
They may astonish these fell-lurking Curres,
Bid Salsbury and Warwicke come to me.

Enter the Earles of Warwicke, and Salisbury.

Clif. Are these thy Beares? Wee'l bate thy Bears to death,
And manacle the Berard in their Chaines,
If thou dar'st bring them to the bayting place.
Rich. Oft haue I seene a hot ore-weening Curre,
Run backe and bite, because he was with-held,
Who being suffer'd with the Beares fell paw,
Hath clapt his taile, betweene his legges and cride,
And such a peece of seruice will you do,

If

If you oppose your selues to match Lord Warwicke.
Clif. Hence heape of wrath, foule indigested lumpe,
As crooked in thy manners, as thy shape.
Yor. Nay we shall heate you thorowly anon.
Clif. Take heede least by your heate you burne your selues:
King. Why Warwicke, hath thy knee forgot to bow?
Old Salsbury, shame to thy siluer haire,
Thou mad misleader of thy brain-sicke sonne,
What wilt thou on thy death-bed play the Ruffian?
And seeke for sorrow with thy Spectacles?
Oh where is Faith? Oh, where is Loyalty?
If it be banisht from the frostie head,
Where shall it finde a harbour in the earth?
Wilt thou go digge a graue to finde out Warre,
And shame thine honourable Age with blood?
Why art thou old, and want'st experience?
Or wherefore doest abuse it, if thou hast it?
For shame in dutie bend thy knee to me,
That bowes vnto the graue with mickle age.
Sal. My Lord, I haue considered with my selfe
The Title of this most renowned Duke,
And in my conscience, do repute his grace
The rightfull heyre to Englands Royall seate.
King. Hast thou not sworne Allegeance vnto me?
Sal. I haue.
Ki. Canst thou dispense with heauen for such an oath?
Sal. It is great sinne, to sweare vnto a sinne:
But greater sinne to keepe a sinfull oath:
Who can be bound by any solemne Vow
To do a murd'rous deede, to rob a man,
To force a spotlesse Virgins Chastitie,
To reaue the Orphan of his Patrimonie,
To wring the Widdow from her custom'd right,
And haue no other reason for this wrong,
But that he was bound by a solemne Oath?
Qu. A subtle Traitor needs no Sophister.
King. Call Buckingham, and bid him arme himselfe.
Yorke. Call Buckingham, and all the friends thou hast,
I am resolu'd for death and dignitie.
Old Clif. The first I warrant thee, if dreames proue true
War. You were best to go to bed, and dreame againe,
To keepe thee from the Tempest of the field.
Old Clif. I am resolu'd to beare a greater storme,
Then any thou canst coniure vp to day:
And that Ile write vpon thy Burgonet,
Might I but know thee by thy housed Badge.
War. Now by my Fathers badge, old *Neuils* Crest,
The rampant Beare chain'd to the ragged staffe,
This day Ile weare aloft my Burgonet,
As on a Mountaine top, the Cedar shewes,
That keepes his leaues inspight of any storme,
Euen to affright thee with the view thereof.
Old Clif. And from thy Burgonet Ile rend thy Beare,
And tread it vnder foot with all contempt,
Despight the Bearard, that protects the Beare.
Yo. Clif. And so to Armes victorious Father,
To quell the Rebels, and their Complices.
Rich. Fie, Charitie for shame, speake not in spight,
For you shall sup with Iesu Christ to night.
Yo Clif. Foule stygmaticke that's more then thou canst tell.
Ric. If not in heauen, you'l surely sup in hell. *Exeunt*

Enter Warwicke.

War. Clifford of Cumberland, 'tis Warwicke calles:
And if thou dost not hide thee from the Beare,
Now when the angrie Trumpet sounds alarum,
And dead mens cries do fill the emptie ayre,
Clifford I say, come forth and fight with me,
Proud Northerne Lord, Clifford of Cumberland,
Warwicke is hoarse with calling thee to armes.

Enter Yorke.

War. How now my Noble Lord? What all a-foot.
Yor. The deadly handed Clifford slew my Steed:
But match to match I haue encountred him,
And made a prey for Carrion Kytes and Crowes
Euen of the bonnie beast he loued so well.

Enter Clifford.

War. Of one or both of vs the time is come.
Yor. Hold Warwick seek thee out some other chace
For I my selfe must hunt this Deere to death.
War. Then nobly Yorke, 'tis for a Crown thou fightst;
As I intend Clifford to thriue to day,
It greeues my soule to leaue theee vnassail'd. *Exit War.*
Clif. What seest thou in me Yorke?
Why dost thou pause?
Yorke. With thy braue bearing should I be in loue,
But that thou art so fast mine enemie.
Clif. Nor should thy prowesse want praise & esteeme,
But that 'tis shewne ignobly, and in Treason.
Yorke. So let it helpe me now against thy sword,
As I in iustice, and true right expresse it.
Clif. My soule and bodie on the action both.
Yor. A dreadfull lay, addresse thee instantly.
Clif. *La fin Corrone les eumenes.*
Yor. Thus Warre hath giuen thee peace, for ỳ art still,
Peace with his soule, heauen if it be thy will.

Enter yong Clifford.

Clif. Shame and Confusion all is on the rout,
Feare frames disorder, and disorder wounds
Where it should guard. O Warre, thou sonne of hell,
Whom angry heauens do make their minister,
Throw in the frozen bosomes of our part,
Hot Coales of Vengeance. Let no Souldier flye.
He that is truly dedicate to Warre,
Hath no selfe-loue: nor he that loues himselfe,
Hath not essentially, but by circumstance
The name of Valour. O let the vile world end,
And the premised Flames of the Last day,
Knit earth and heauen together.
Now let the generall Trumpet blow his blast,
Particularities, and pettie sounds
To cease. Was't thou ordain'd (deere Father)
To loose thy youth in peace, and to atcheeue
The Siluer Liuery of aduised Age,
And in thy Reuerence, and thy Chaire-dayes, thus
To die in Ruffian battell? Euen at this sight,
My heart is turn'd to stone: and while 'tis mine,
It shall be stony. Yorke, not our old men spares:
No more will I their Babes, Teares Virginall,
Shall be to me, euen as the Dew to Fire,
And Beautie, that the Tyrant oft reclaimes,
Shall to my flaming wrath, be Oyle and Flax:
Henceforth, I will not haue to do with pitty.
Meet I an infant of the house of Yorke,
Into as many gobbits will I cut it
As wilde *Medea* yong *Absirtis* did.
In cruelty, will I seeke out my Fame.
Come thou new ruine of olde Cliffords house:
As did *Æneas* old *Anchyses* beare,
So beare I thee vpon my manly shoulders:
But then, *Æneas* bare a liuing loade;

o 3 Nothing

Nothing so heauy as these woes of mine.

Enter Richard, and Somerset to fight.

Rich. So lye thou there:
For vnderneath an Ale-house paltry signe,
The Castle in S. *Albons*, Somerset
Hath made the Wizard famous in his death:
Sword, hold thy temper; Heart, be wrathfull still:
Priests pray for enemies, but Princes kill.

Fight. Excursions.

Enter King, Queene, and others.

Qu. Away my Lord, you are slow, for shame away.
King. Can we outrun the Heauens? Good *Margaret* stay.
Qu. What are you made of? You'l nor fight nor fly:
Now is it manhood, wisedome, and defence,
To giue the enemy way, and to secure vs
By what we can, which can no more but flye.

Alarum a farre off.

If you be tane, we then should see the bottome
Of all our Fortunes: but if we haply scape,
(As well we may, if not through your neglect)
We shall to London get, where you are lou'd,
And where this breach now in our Fortunes made
May readily be stopt.

Enter Clifford.

Clif. But that my hearts on future mischeefe set,
I would speake blasphemy ere bid you flye:
But flye you must: Vncureable discomfite
Reignes in the hearts of all our present parts.
Away for your releefe, and we will liue
To see their day, and them our Fortune giue.
Away my Lord, away. *Exeunt*

Alarum. Retreat. Enter Yorke, Richard, Warwicke, and Soldiers, with Drum & Colours.

Yorke. Of Salsbury, who can report of him,
That Winter Lyon, who in rage forgets
Aged contusions, and all brush of Time:
And like a Gallant, in the brow of youth,
Repaires him with Occasion. This happy day
Is not it selfe, nor haue we wonne one foot,
If Salsbury be lost.
Rich. My Noble Father:
Three times to day I holpe him to his horse,
Three times bestrid him: Thrice I led him off,
Perswaded him from any further act:
But still where danger was, still there I met him,
And like rich hangings in a homely house,
So was his Will, in his old feeble body,
But Noble as he is, looke where he comes.

Enter Salsbury.

Sal. Now by my Sword, well hast thou fought to day
By'th'Masse so did we all. I thanke you *Richard*
God knowes how long it is I haue to liue:
And it hath pleas'd him that three times to day
You haue defended me from imminent death.
Well Lords, we haue not got that which we haue,
'Tis not enough our foes are this time fled,
Being opposites of such repayring Nature.
York. I know our safety is to follow them,
For (as I heare) the King is fled to London,
To call a present Court of Parliament:
Let vs pursue him ere the Writs go forth.
What sayes Lord Warwicke, shall we after them?
War. After them: nay before them if we can:
Now by my hand (Lords) 'twas a glorious day.
Saint Albons battell wonne by famous Yorke,
Shall be eterniz'd in all Age to come.
Sound Drumme and Trumpets, and to London all,
And more such dayes as these, to vs befall. *Exeunt*

FINIS.

The third Part of Henry the Sixt, with the death of the Duke of YORKE.

Actus Primus. Scœna Prima.

Alarum.

Enter Plantagenet, Edward, Richard, Norfolke, Mountague, Warwicke, and Souldiers.

Warwicke.

I Wonder how the King escap'd our hands?
Pl. While we pursu'd the Horsmen of ẏ North,
He slyly stole away, and left his men:
Whereat the great Lord of Northumberland,
Whose Warlike eares could neuer brooke retreat,
Chear'd vp the drouping Army, and himselfe.
Lord *Clifford* and Lord *Stafford* all a-brest
Charg'd our maine Battailes Front: and breaking in,
Were by the Swords of common Souldiers slaine.
Edw. Lord *Staffords* Father, Duke of *Buckingham*,
Is either slaine or wounded dangerous.
I cleft his Beauer with a down-right blow:
That this is true (Father) behold his blood.
Mount. And Brother, here's the Earle of Wiltshires
Whom I encountred as the Battels ioyn'd. (blood
Rich. Speake thou for me, and tell them what I did.
Plan. *Richard* hath best deseru'd of all my sonnes:
But is your Grace dead, my Lord of Somerset?
Nor. Such hope haue all the line of *Iohn of Gaunt*.
Rich. Thus do I hope to shake King *Henries* head.
Warw. And so doe I, victorious Prince of *Yorke*.
Before I see thee seated in that Throne,
Which now the House of *Lancaster* vsurpes,
I vow by Heauen, these eyes shall neuer close.
This is the Pallace of the fearefull King,
And this the Regall Seat: possesse it *Yorke*,
For this is thine, and not King *Henries* Heires.
Plant. Assist me then, sweet *Warwick*, and I will,
For hither we haue broken in by force.
Norf. Wee'le all assist you: he that flyes, shall dye.
Plant. Thankes gentle *Norfolke*, stay by me my Lords,
And Souldiers stay and lodge by me this Night.
They goe vp.
Warw. And when the King comes, offer him no violence,
Vnlesse he seeke to thrust you out perforce.
Plant. The Queene this day here holds her Parliament,
But little thinkes we shall be of her counsaile,
By words or blowes here let vs winne our right.
Rich. Arm'd as we are, let's stay within this House.
Warw. The bloody Parliament shall this be call'd,
Vnlesse *Plantagenet*, Duke of Yorke, be King,
And bashfull *Henry* depos'd, whose Cowardize
Hath made vs by-words to our enemies.
Plant. Then leaue me not, my Lords be resolute,
I meane to take possession of my Right.
Warw. Neither the King, nor he that loues him best,
The prowdest hee that holds vp *Lancaster*,
Dares stirre a Wing, if *Warwick* shake his Bells.
Ile plant *Plantagenet*, root him vp who dares:
Resolue thee *Richard*, clayme the English Crowne.

Flourish. Enter King Henry, Clifford, Northumberland, Westmerland, Exeter, and the rest.

Henry. My Lords, looke where the sturdie Rebell sits,
Euen in the Chayre of State: belike he meanes,
Backt by the power of *Warwicke*, that false Peere,
To aspire vnto the Crowne, and reigne as King.
Earle of Northumberland, he slew thy Father,
And thine, Lord *Clifford*, & you both haue vow'd reuenge
On him, his sonnes, his fauorites, and his friends.
Northumb. If I be not, Heauens be reueng'd on me.
Clifford. The hope thereof, makes *Clifford* mourne in Steele.
Westm. What, shall we suffer this? lets pluck him down,
My heart for anger burnes, I cannot brooke it.
Henry. Be patient, gentle Earle of Westmerland.
Clifford. Patience is for Poultroones, such as he:
He durst not sit there, had your Father liu'd.
My gracious Lord, here in the Parliament
Let vs assayle the Family of *Yorke*.
North. Well hast thou spoken, Cousin be it so.
Henry. Ah, know you not the Citie fauours them,
And they haue troupes of Souldiers at their beck?
Westm. But when the Duke is slaine, they'le quickly flye.
Henry. Farre be the thought of this from *Henries* heart,
To make a Shambles of the Parliament House.
Cousin of Exeter, frownes, words, and threats,
Shall be the Warre that *Henry* meanes to vse.
Thou factious Duke of Yorke descend my Throne,
And kneele for grace and mercie at my feet,
I am thy Soueraigne.
Yorke. I am thine.
Exet. For shame come downe, he made thee Duke of Yorke.
Yorke. It was my Inheritance, as the Earledome was.
Exet. Thy

Exet. Thy Father was a Traytor to the Crowne.
Warw. *Exeter* thou art a Traytor to the Crowne,
In following this vſurping *Henry*.
Clifford. Whom ſhould hee follow, but his naturall King?
Warw. True *Clifford*, that's *Richard* Duke of Yorke.
Henry. And ſhall I ſtand, and thou ſit in my Throne?
Yorke. It muſt and ſhall be ſo, content thy ſelfe.
Warw. Be Duke of Lancaſter, let him be King.
Weſtm. He is both King, and Duke of Lancaſter,
And that the Lord of Weſtmerland ſhall maintaine.
Warw. And *Warwick* ſhall diſproue it. You forget,
That we are thoſe which chas'd you from the field,
And ſlew your Fathers, and with Colours ſpread
Marcht through the Citie to the Pallace Gates.
Northumb. Yes *Warwicke*, I remember it to my griefe,
And by his Soule, thou and thy Houſe ſhall rue it.
Weſtm. *Plantagenet*, of thee and theſe thy Sonnes,
Thy Kinſmen, and thy Friends, Ile haue more liues
Then drops of bloud were in my Fathers Veines.
Cliff. Vrge it no more, leſt that in ſtead of words,
I ſend thee, *Warwicke*, ſuch a Meſſenger,
As ſhall reuenge his death, before I ſtirre.
Warw. Poore *Clifford*, how I ſcorne his worthleſſe Threats.
Plant. Will you we ſhew our Title to the Crowne?
If not, our Swords ſhall pleade it in the field.
Henry. What Title haſt thou Traytor to the Crowne?
My Father was as thou art, Duke of Yorke,
Thy Grandfather *Roger Mortimer*, Earle of March.
I am the Sonne of *Henry* the Fift,
Who made the Dolphin and the French to ſtoupe,
And ſeiz'd vpon their Townes and Prouinces.
Warw. Talke not of France, ſith thou haſt loſt it all.
Henry. The Lord Protector loſt it, and not I:
When I was crown'd, I was but nine moneths old.
Rich. You are old enough now,
And yet me thinkes you looſe:
Father teare the Crowne from the Vſurpers Head.
Edward. Sweet Father doe ſo, ſet it on your Head.
Mount. Good Brother,
As thou lou'ſt and honoreſt Armes,
Let's fight it out, and not ſtand cauilling thus.
Richard. Sound Drummes and Trumpets, and the King will flye.
Plant. Sonnes peace.
Henry. Peace thou, and giue King *Henry* leaue to ſpeake.
Warw. *Plantagenet* ſhal ſpeake firſt: Heare him Lords,
And be you ſilent and attentiue too,
For he that interrupts him, ſhall not liue.
Hen. Think'ſt thou, that I will leaue my Kingly Throne,
Wherein my Grandſire and my Father ſat?
No: firſt ſhall Warre vnpeople this my Realme;
I, and their Colours often borne in France,
And now in England, to our hearts great ſorrow,
Shall be my Winding-ſheet. Why faint you Lords?
My Title's good, and better farre then his.
Warw. Proue it *Henry*, and thou ſhalt be King.
Hen. *Henry* the Fourth by Conqueſt got the Crowne.
Plant. 'Twas by Rebellion againſt his King.
Henry. I know not what to ſay, my Titles weake:
Tell me, may not a King adopt an Heire?
Plant. What then?
Henry. And if he may, then am I lawfull King:
For *Richard*, in the view of many Lords,
Reſign'd the Crowne to *Henry* the Fourth,
Whoſe Heire my Father was, and I am his.
Plant. He roſe againſt him, being his Soueraigne,
And made him to reſigne his Crowne perforce.
Warw. Suppoſe, my Lords, he did it vnconſtrayn'd,
Thinke you 'twere preiudiciall to his Crowne?
Exet. No: for he could not ſo reſigne his Crowne,
But that the next Heire ſhould ſucceed and reigne.
Henry. Art thou againſt vs, Duke of Exeter?
Exet. His is the right, and therefore pardon me.
Plant. Why whiſper you, my Lords, and anſwer not?
Exet. My Conſcience tells me he is lawfull King.
Henry. All will reuolt from me, and turne to him.
Northumb. *Plantagenet*, for all the Clayme thou lay'ſt,
Thinke not, that *Henry* ſhall be ſo depos'd.
Warw. Depos'd he ſhall be, in deſpight of all.
Northumb. Thou art deceiu'd:
'Tis not thy Southerne power
Of Eſſex, Norfolke, Suffolke, nor of Kent,
Which makes thee thus preſumptuous and prowd,
Can ſet the Duke vp in deſpight of me.
Clifford. King *Henry*, be thy Title right or wrong,
Lord *Clifford* vowes to fight in thy defence:
May that ground gape, and ſwallow me aliue,
Where I ſhall kneele to him that ſlew my Father.
Henry. Oh *Clifford*, how thy words reuiue my heart.
Plant. *Henry* of Lancaſter, reſigne thy Crowne:
What mutter you, or what conſpire you Lords?
Warw. Doe right vnto this Princely Duke of Yorke,
Or I will fill the Houſe with armed men,
And ouer the Chayre of State, where now he ſits,
Write vp his Title with vſurping blood.
He ſtampes with his foot, and the Souldiers ſhew themſelues.
Henry. My Lord of Warwick, heare but one word,
Let me for this my life time reigne as King.
Plant. Confirme the Crowne to me and to mine Heires,
And thou ſhalt reigne in quiet while thou liu'ſt.
Henry. I am content: *Richard Plantagenet*
Enioy the Kingdome after my deceaſe.
Clifford. What wrong is this vnto the Prince, your Sonne?
Warw. What good is this to England, and himſelfe?
Weſtm. Baſe, fearefull, and deſpayring *Henry*.
Clifford. How haſt thou iniur'd both thy ſelfe and vs?
Weſtm. I cannot ſtay to heare theſe Articles.
Northumb. Nor I.
Clifford. Come Couſin, let vs tell the Queene theſe Newes.
Weſtm. Farwell faint-hearted and degenerate King,
In whoſe cold blood no ſparke of Honor bides.
Northumb. Be thou a prey vnto the Houſe of *Yorke*,
And dye in Bands, for this vnmanly deed.
Cliff. In dreadfull Warre may'ſt thou be ouercome,
Or liue in peace abandon'd and deſpis'd.
Warw. Turne this way *Henry*, and regard them not.
Exeter. They ſeeke reuenge, and therefore will not yeeld.
Henry. Ah Exeter.
Warw. Why ſhould you ſigh, my Lord?
Henry. Not for my ſelfe Lord *Warwick*, but my Sonne,
Whom I vnnaturally ſhall diſ-inherite.
But be it as it may: I here entayle
The Crowne to thee and to thine Heires for euer,
Conditionally, that heere thou take an Oath,
To ceaſe this Ciuill Warre: and whil'ſt I liue,
To

To honor me as thy King, and Soueraigne:
And neyther by Treason nor Hostilitie,
To seeke to put me downe, and reigne thy selfe.
Plant. This Oath I willingly take, and will performe.
Warw. Long liue King *Henry*: *Plantagenet* embrace him.
Henry. And long liue thou, and these thy forward Sonnes.
Plant. Now *Yorke* and *Lancaster* are reconcil'd.
Exet. Accurst be he that seekes to make them foes.

Senet. Here they come downe.

Plant. Farewell my gracious Lord, Ile to my Castle.
Warw. And Ile keepe London with my Souldiers.
Norf. And I to Norfolke with my followers.
Mount. And I vnto the Sea, from whence I came.
Henry. And I with griefe and sorrow to the Court.

Enter the Queene.

Exeter. Heere comes the Queene,
Whose Lookes bewray her anger:
Ile steale away.
Henry. *Exeter* so will I.
Queene. Nay, goe not from me, I will follow thee.
Henry. Be patient gentle Queene, and I will stay.
Queene. Who can be patient in such extreames?
Ah wretched man, would I had dy'de a Maid?
And neuer seene thee, neuer borne thee Sonne,
Seeing thou hast prou'd so vnnaturall a Father.
Hath he deseru'd to loose his Birth-right thus?
Hadst thou but lou'd him halfe so well as I,
Or felt that paine which I did for him once,
Or nourisht him, as I did with my blood;
Thou would'st haue left thy dearest heart-blood there,
Rather then haue made that sauage Duke thine Heire,
And dis-inherited thine onely Sonne.
Prince. Father, you cannot dis-inherite me:
If you be King, why should not I succeede?
Henry. Pardon me *Margaret*, pardon me sweet Sonne,
The Earle of Warwick and the Duke enforc't me.
Quee. Enforc't thee? Art thou King, and wilt be forc't?
I shame to heare thee speake: ah timorous Wretch,
Thou hast vndone thy selfe, thy Sonne, and me,
And giu'n vnto the House of *Yorke* such head,
As thou shalt reigne but by their sufferance.
To entayle him and his Heires vnto the Crowne,
What is it, but to make thy Sepulcher,
And creepe into it farre before thy time?
Warwick is Chancelor, and the Lord of Callice,
Sterne *Falconbridge* commands the Narrow Seas,
The Duke is made Protector of the Realme,
And yet shalt thou be safe? Such safetie findes
The trembling Lambe, inuironned with Wolues.
Had I beene there, which am a silly Woman,
The Souldiers should haue toss'd me on their Pikes,
Before I would haue granted to that Act.
But thou preferr'st thy Life, before thine Honor.
And seeing thou do'st, I here diuorce my selfe,
Both from thy Table *Henry*, and thy Bed,
Vntill that Act of Parliament be repeal'd,
Whereby my Sonne is dis-inherited.
The Northerne Lords, that haue forsworne thy Colours,
Will follow mine, if once they see them spread:
And spread they shall be, to thy foule disgrace,
And vtter ruine of the House of *Yorke*.
Thus doe I leaue thee: Come Sonne, let's away,
Our Army is ready; come, wee'le after them.
Henry. Stay gentle *Margaret*, and heare me speake.
Queene. Thou hast spoke too much already: get thee gone.
Henry. Gentle Sonne *Edward*, thou wilt stay me?
Queene. I, to be murther'd by his Enemies.
Prince. When I returne with victorie to the field,
Ile see your Grace: till then, Ile follow her.
Queene. Come Sonne away, we may not linger thus.
Henry. Poore Queene,
How loue to me, and to her Sonne,
Hath made her breake out into termes of Rage.
Reueng'd may she be on that hatefull Duke,
Whose haughtie spirit, winged with desire,
Will cost my Crowne, and like an emptie Eagle,
Tyre on the flesh of me, and of my Sonne.
The losse of those three Lords torments my heart:
Ile write vnto them, and entreat them faire;
Come Cousin, you shall be the Messenger.
Exet. And I, I hope, shall reconcile them all. *Exit.*

Flourish. Enter Richard, Edward, and Mountague.

Richard. Brother, though I bee youngest, giue mee leaue.
Edward. No, I can better play the Orator.
Mount. But I haue reasons strong and forceable.

Enter the Duke of Yorke.

Yorke. Why how now Sonnes, and Brother, at a strife?
What is your Quarrell? how began it first?
Edward. No Quarrell, but a slight Contention.
Yorke. About what?
Rich. About that which concernes your Grace and vs,
The Crowne of England, Father, which is yours.
Yorke. Mine Boy? not till King *Henry* be dead.
Richard. Your Right depends not on his life, or death.
Edward. Now you are Heire, therefore enioy it now:
By giuing the House of *Lancaster* leaue to breathe,
It will out-runne you, Father, in the end.
Yorke. I tooke an Oath, that hee should quietly reigne.
Edward. But for a Kingdome any Oath may be broken:
I would breake a thousand Oathes, to reigne one yeere.
Richard. No: God forbid your Grace should be forsworne.
Yorke. I shall be, if I clayme by open Warre.
Richard. Ile proue the contrary, if you'le heare mee speake.
Yorke. Thou canst not, Sonne: it is impossible.
Richard. An Oath is of no moment, being not tooke
Before a true and lawfull Magistrate,
That hath authoritie ouer him that sweares.
Henry had none, but did vsurpe the place.
Then seeing 'twas he that made you to depose,
Your Oath, my Lord, is vaine and friuolous.
Therefore to Armes: and Father doe but thinke,
How sweet a thing it is to weare a Crowne,
Within whose Circuit is *Elizium*,
And all that Poets faine of Blisse and Ioy.
Why doe we linger thus? I cannot rest,
Vntill the White Rose that I weare, be dy'de
Euen in the luke-warme blood of *Henries* heart.
Yorke. *Richard* ynough: I will be King, or dye.
Brother, thou shalt to London presently,
And whet on *Warwick* to this Enterprise.

Thou

Thou *Richard* shalt to the Duke of Norfolke,
And tell him priuily of our intent.
You *Edward* shall vnto my Lord *Cobham*,
With whom the Kentishmen will willingly rise.
In them I trust: for they are Souldiors,
Wittie,courteous,liberall,full of spirit.
While you are thus imploy'd, what resteth more?
But that I seeke occasion how to rise,
And yet the King not priuie to my Drift,
Nor any of the House of *Lancaster*.

Enter Gabriel.

But stay, what Newes? Why comm'st thou in such poste?
Gabriel. The Queene,
With all the Northerne Earles and Lords,
Intend here to besiege you in your Castle.
She is hard by,with twentie thousand men:
And therefore fortifie your Hold,my Lord.
Yorke. I,with my Sword.
What? think'st thou,that we feare them?
Edward and *Richard*, you shall stay with me,
My Brother *Mountague* shall poste to London.
Let Noble *Warwicke*,*Cobham*,and the rest,
Whom we haue left Protectors of the King,
With powrefull Pollicie strengthen themselues,
And trust not simple *Henry*,nor his Oathes.
Mount. Brother, I goe: Ile winne them,feare it not
And thus most humbly I doe take my leaue.
Exit Mountague.

Enter Mortimer,and his Brother.

York. Sir *Iohn*,and Sir *Hugh Mortimer*,mine Vnckles
You are come to Sandall in a happie houre.
The Armie of the Queene meane to besiege vs.
Iohn. Shee shall not neede, wee'le meete her in the field.
Yorke. What,with fiue thousand men?
Richard. I,with fiue hundred,Father,for a neede.
A Woman's generall: what should we feare?
A March afarre off.
Edward. I heare their Drummes:
Let's set our men in order,
And issue forth,and bid them Battaile straight.
Yorke. Fiue men to twentie: though the oddes be great,
I doubt not, Vnckle,of our Victorie.
Many a Battaile haue I wonne in France,
When as the Enemie hath beene tenne to one:
Why should I not now haue the like successe?
Alarum. Exit.

Enter Rutland,and his Tutor.

Rutland. Ah,whither shall I flye,to scape their hands
Ah Tutor,looke where bloody *Clifford* comes.

Enter Clifford.

Clifford. Chaplaine away,thy Priesthood saues thy life.
As for the Brat of this accursed Duke,
Whose Father slew my Father,he shall dye.
Tutor. And I,my Lord,will beare him company.
Clifford. Souldiers,away with him.
Tutor. Ah *Clifford*,murther not this innocent Child,
Least thou be hated both of God and Man *Exit.*

Clifford. How now? is he dead alreadie?
Or is it feare,that makes him close his eyes?
Ile open them.
Rutland. So looks the pent-vp Lyon o're the Wretch,
That trembles vnder his deuouring Pawes:
And so he walkes,insulting o're his Prey,
And so he comes,to rend his Limbes asunder.
Ah gentle *Clifford*,kill me with thy Sword,
And not with such a cruell threatning Looke.
Sweet *Clifford* heare me speake,before I dye:
I am too meane a subiect for thy Wrath,
Be thou reueng'd on men,and let me liue.
Clifford. In vaine thou speak'st,poore Boy:
My Fathers blood hath stopt the passage
Where thy words should enter.
Rutland. Then let my Fathers blood open it againe,
He is a man,and *Clifford* cope with him.
Clifford. Had I thy Brethren here, their liues and thine
Were not reuenge sufficient for me:
No,if I digg'd vp thy fore-fathers Graues,
And hung their rotten Coffins vp in Chaynes,
It could not slake mine ire,nor ease my heart.
The sight of any of the House of *Yorke*,
Is as a furie to torment my Soule:
And till I root out their accursed Line,
And leaue not one aliue,I liue in Hell.
Therefore——
Rutland. Oh let me pray,before I take my death:
To thee I pray;sweet *Clifford* pitty me.
Clifford. Such pitty as my Rapiers point affords.
Rutland. I neuer did thee harme: why wilt thou slay me?
Clifford. Thy Father hath.
Rutland. But 'twas ere I was borne.
Thou hast one Sonne, for his sake pitty me,
Least in reuenge thereof,sith God is iust,
He be as miserably slaine as I.
Ah,let me liue in Prison all my dayes,
And when I giue occasion of offence,
Then let me dye,for now thou hast no cause.
Clifford. No cause? thy Father slew my Father:therefore dye.
Rutland. *Dij faciant laudis summa sit ista tuæ.*
Clifford. *Plantagenet*, I come *Plantagenet*:
And this thy Sonnes blood cleauing to my Blade,
Shall rust vpon my Weapon,till thy blood
Congeal'd with this,doe make me wipe off both. *Exit.*

Alarum. Enter Richard,Duke of Yorke.

Yorke. The Army of the Queene hath got the field:
My Vnckles both are slaine, in rescuing me;
And all my followers,to the eager foe
Turne back,and flye,like Ships before the Winde,
Or Lambes pursu'd by hunger-starued Wolues.
My Sonnes,God knowes what hath bechanced them:
But this I know,they haue demean'd themselues
Like men borne to Renowne,by Life or Death.
Three times did *Richard* make a Lane to me,
And thrice cry'de,Courage Father,fight it out:
And full as oft came *Edward* to my side,
With Purple Faulchion,painted to the Hilt,
In blood of those that had encountred him:
And when the hardyest Warriors did retyre,
Richard cry'de,Charge,and giue no foot of ground,
And cry'de,A Crowne,or else a glorious Tombe,

A Scepter,or an Earthly Sepulchre.
With this we charg'd againe : but out alas,
We bodg'd againe, as I haue ſeene a Swan
With bootleſſe labour ſwimme againſt the Tyde,
And ſpend her ſtrength with ouer-matching Waues.

A ſhort Alarum within.

Ah hearke,the fatall followers doe purſue,
And I am faint,and cannot flye their furie:
And were I ſtrong,I would not ſhunne their furie.
The Sands are numbred,that makes vp my Life,
Here muſt I ſtay,and here my Life muſt end.

Enter the Queene,Clifford,Northumberland,
the young Prince,and Souldiers.

Come bloody *Clifford*, rough *Northumberland*,
I dare your quenchleſſe furie to more rage .
I am your Butt,and I abide your Shot.

Northumb. Yeeld to our mercy,proud *Plantagenet.*

Clifford. I,to ſuch mercy,as his ruthleſſe Arme
With downe-right payment,ſhew'd vnto my Father.
Now *Phaeton* hath tumbled from his Carre,
And made an Euening at the Noone-tide Prick.

Yorke My aſhes,as the Phoenix,may bring forth
A Bird,that will reuenge vpon you all :
And in that hope,I throw mine eyes to Heauen,
Scorning what ere you can afflict me with.
Why come you not ? what,multitudes,and feare ?

Cliff. So Cowards fight,when they can flye no further,
So Doues doe peck the Faulcons piercing Tallons,
So deſperate Theeues,all hopeleſſe of their Liues,
Breathe out Inuectiues 'gainſt the Officers.

Yorke. Oh *Clifford*, but bethinke thee once againe,
And in thy thought ore-run my former time :
And if thou canſt,for bluſhing,view this face,
And bite thy tongue,that ſlanders him with Cowardice,
Whoſe frowne hath made thee faint and flye ere this.

Clifford. I will not bandie with thee word for word,
But buckler with thee blowes twice two for one.

Queene. Hold valiant *Clifford*, for a thouſand cauſes
I would prolong a while the Traytors Life:
Wrath makes him deafe; ſpeake thou *Northumberland.*

*Northumb.*Hold *Clifford*,doe not honor him ſo much,
To prick thy finger,though to wound his heart.
What valour were it,when a Curre doth grinne,
For one to thruſt his Hand betweene his Teeth,
When he might ſpurne him with his Foot away ?
It is Warres prize,to take all Vantages,
And tenne to one,is no impeach of Valour.

Clifford. I, I, ſo ſtriues the Woodcocke with the Gynne.

Northumb So doth the Connie ſtruggle in the Net.

York. So triumph Theeues vpon their conquer'd Booty,
So True men yeeld with Robbers,ſo o're-matcht.

Northumb. What would your Grace haue done vnto him now ?

Queene. Braue Warriors, *Clifford* and *Northumberland*,
Come make him ſtand vpon this Mole-hill here,
That raught at Mountaines with out-ſtretched Armes,
Yet parted but the ſhadow with his Hand.
What,was it you that would be Englands King ?
Was't you that reuell'd in our Parliament,
And made a Preachment of your high Deſcent ?
Where are your Meſſe of Sonnes,to back you now
The wanton *Edward*,and the luſtie *George* ?
And where's that valiant Crook-back Prodigie,
Dickie,your Boy,that with his grumbling voyce
Was wont to cheare his Dad in Mutinies ?
Or with the reſt,where is your Darling, *Rutland* ?
Looke *Yorke*, I ſtayn'd this Napkin with the blood
That valiant *Clifford*,with his Rapiers point,
Made iſſue from the Boſome of the Boy.
And if thine eyes can water for his death,
I giue thee this to drie thy Cheekes withall.
Alas poore *Yorke*, but that I hate thee deadly,
I ſhould lament thy miſerable ſtate
I prythee grieue,to make me merry,*Yorke.*
What,hath thy fierie heart ſo parcht thine entrayles,
That not a Teare can fall,for *Rutlands* death ?
Why art thou patient,man? thou ſhould'ſt be mad:
And I,to make thee mad,doe mock thee thus.
Stampe,raue,and fret,that I may ſing and dance.
Thou would'ſt be fee'd,I ſee,to make me ſport :
Yorke cannot ſpeake,vnleſſe he weare a Crowne.
A Crowne for *Yorke* ; and Lords,bow lowe to him ;
Hold you his hands,whileſt I doe ſet it on.
I marry Sir,now lookes he like a King .
I,this is he that tooke King *Henries* Chaire,
And this is he was his adopted Heire,
But how is it,that great *Plantagenet*
Is crown'd ſo ſoone,and broke his ſolemne Oath ?
As I bethinke me you ſhould not be King,
Till our King *Henry* had ſhooke hands with Death.
And will you pale your head in *Henries* Glory,
And rob his Temples of the Diademe,
Now in his Life,againſt your holy Oath ?
Oh 'tis a fault too too vnpardonable.
Off with the Crowne;and with the Crowne,his Head,
And whileſt we breathe,take time to doe him dead.

Clifford. That is my Office, for my Fathers ſake.

Queene Nay ſtay , let's heare the Orizons hee makes

Yorke. Shee-Wolfe of France,
But worſe then Wolues of France,
Whoſe Tongue more poyſons then the Adders Tooth :
How ill-beſeeming is it in thy Sex,
To triumph like an Amazonian Trull,
Vpon their Woes,whom Fortune captiuates ?
But that thy Face is Vizard-like,vnchanging,
Made impudent with vſe of euill deedes.
I would aſſay,prowd Queene,to make thee bluſh.
To tell thee whence thou cam'ſt,of whom deriu'd,
Were ſhame enough, to ſhame thee,
Wert thou not ſhameleſſe.
Thy Father beares the type of King of Naples,
Of both the Sicils,and Ieruſalem,
Yet not ſo wealthie as an Engliſh Yeoman.
Hath that poore Monarch taught thee to inſult ?
It needes not,nor it bootes thee not,prowd Queene,
Vnleſſe the Adage muſt be verify'd,
That Beggers mounted,runne their Horſe to death.
'Tis Beautie that doth oft make Women prowd,
But God he knowes,thy ſhare thereof is ſmall.
'Tis Vertue,that doth make them moſt admir'd,
The contrary,doth make thee wondred at.
Tis Gouernment that makes them ſeeme Diuine,
The want thereof,makes thee abhominable.
Thou art as oppoſite to euery good,
As the *Antipodes* are vnto vs,
Or as the South to the *Septentrion.*
Oh Tygres Heart,wrapt in a Womans Hide,

How

How could'ſt thou drayne the Life-blood of the Child,
To bid the Father wipe his eyes withall,
And yet be ſeene to beare a Womans face?
Women are ſoft, milde, pittifull, and flexible;
Thou, ſterne, obdurate, flintie, rough, remorſeleſſe.
Bidſt thou me rage? why now thou haſt thy wiſh.
Would'ſt haue me weepe? why now thou haſt thy will.
For raging Wind blowes vp inceſſant ſhowers,
And when the Rage allayes, the Raine begins.
Theſe Teares are my ſweet *Rutlands* Obſequies,
And euery drop cryes vengeance for his death,
'Gainſt thee fell *Clifford*, and thee falſe French-woman.

Northumb. Beſhrew me, but his paſſions moues me ſo,
That hardly can I check my eyes from Teares.

Yorke. That Face of his,
The hungry Caniballs would not haue toucht,
Would not haue ſtayn'd with blood:
But you are more inhumane, more inexorable,
Oh, tenne times more then Tygers of Hyrcania.
See, ruthleſſe Queene, a hapleſſe Fathers Teares:
This Cloth thou dipd'ſt in blood of my ſweet Boy,
And I with Teares doe waſh the blood away.
Keepe thou the Napkin, and goe boaſt of this,
And if thou tell'ſt the heauie ſtorie right,
Vpon my Soule, the hearers will ſhed Teares:
Yea, euen my Foes will ſhed faſt-falling Teares,
And ſay, Alas, it was a pittious deed.
There, take the Crowne, and with the Crowne, my Curſe,
And in thy need, ſuch comfort come to thee,
As now I reape at thy too cruell hand.
Hard-hearted *Clifford*, take me from the World,
My Soule to Heauen, my Blood vpon your Heads.

Northumb. Had he been ſlaughter-man to all my Kinne,
I ſhould not for my Life but weepe with him,
To ſee how inly Sorrow gripes his Soule.

Queen. What, weeping ripe, my Lord *Northumberland*?
Thinke but vpon the wrong he did vs all,
And that will quickly drie thy melting Teares.

Clifford. Heere's for my Oath, heere's for my Fathers Death.

Queene. And heere's to right our gentle-hearted King.

Yorke. Open thy Gate of Mercy, gracious God,
My Soule flyes through theſe wounds, to ſeeke out thee.

Queene. Off with his Head, and ſet it on Yorke Gates,
So *Yorke* may ouer-looke the Towne of Yorke.

Flouriſh. Exit.

A March. Enter Edward, Richard, and their power.

Edward. I wonder how our Princely Father ſcap't:
Or whether he be ſcap't away, or no,
From *Cliffords* and *Northumberlands* purſuit?
Had he been ta'ne, we ſhould haue heard the newes;
Had he beene ſlaine, we ſhould haue heard the newes:
Or had he ſcap't, me thinkes we ſhould haue heard
The happy tidings of his good eſcape.
How fares my Brother? why is he ſo ſad?

Richard. I cannot ioy, vntill I be reſolu'd
Where our right valiant Father is become.
I ſaw him in the Battaile range about,
And watcht him how he ſingled *Clifford* forth.
Me thought he bore him in the thickeſt troupe,
As doth a Lyon in a Heard of Neat,
Or as a Beare encompas'd round with Dogges:
Who hauing pincht a few, and made them cry,
The reſt ſtand all aloofe, and barke at him.
So far'd our Father with his Enemies,
So fled his Enemies my Warlike Father:
Me thinkes 'tis prize enough to be his Sonne.
See how the Morning opes her golden Gates,
And takes her farwell of the glorious Sunne.
How well reſembles it the prime of Youth,
Trimm'd like a Yonker, prauncing to his Loue?

Ed. Dazle mine eyes, or doe I ſee three Sunnes?

Rich. Three glorious Sunnes, each one a perfect Sunne,
Not ſeperated with the racking Clouds,
But ſeuer'd in a pale cleare-ſhining Skye.
See, ſee, they ioyne, embrace, and ſeeme to kiſſe,
As if they vow'd ſome League inuiolable.
Now are they but one Lampe, one Light, one Sunne:
In this, the Heauen figures ſome euent.

Edward. 'Tis wondrous ſtrange,
The like yet neuer heard of.
I thinke it cites vs (Brother) to the field,
That wee, the Sonnes of braue *Plantagenet*,
Each one alreadie blazing by our meedes,
Should notwithſtanding ioyne our Lights together,
And ouer-ſhine the Earth, as this the World.
What ere it bodes, hence-forward will I beare
Vpon my Targuet three faire ſhining Sunnes.

Richard. Nay, beare three Daughters:
By your leaue, I ſpeake it,
You loue the Breeder better then the Male.

Enter one blowing.

But what art thou, whoſe heauie Lookes fore-tell
Some dreadfull ſtory hanging on thy Tongue?

Meſſ. Ah, one that was a wofull looker on,
When as the Noble Duke of Yorke was ſlaine,
Your Princely Father, and my louing Lord.

Edward. Oh ſpeake no more, for I haue heard too much.

Richard. Say how he dy'de, for I will heare it all.

Meſſ. Enuironed he was with many foes,
And ſtood againſt them, as the hope of Troy
Againſt the Greekes, that would haue entred Troy.
But *Hercules* himſelfe muſt yeeld to oddes:
And many ſtroakes, though with a little Axe,
Hewes downe and fells the hardeſt-tymber'd Oake.
By many hands your Father was ſubdu'd,
But onely ſlaught'red by the irefull Arme
Of vn-relenting *Clifford*, and the Queene:
Who crown'd the gracious Duke in high deſpight,
Laugh'd in his face: and when with griefe he wept,
The ruthleſſe Queene gaue him, to dry his Cheekes,
A Napkin, ſteeped in the harmeleſſe blood
Of ſweet young *Rutland*, by rough *Clifford* ſlaine:
And after many ſcornes, many foule taunts,
They tooke his Head, and on the Gates of Yorke
They ſet the ſame, and there it doth remaine,
The ſaddeſt ſpectacle that ere I view'd.

Edward. Sweet Duke of Yorke, our Prop to leane vpon,
Now thou art gone, wee haue no Staffe, no Stay.
Oh *Clifford*, boyſt'rous *Clifford* thou haſt ſlaine
The flowre of Europe, for his Cheualrie,
And trecherouſly haſt thou vanquiſht him,
For hand to hand he would haue vanquiſht thee.
Now my Soules Pallace is become a Priſon:
Ah, would ſhe breake from hence, that this my body
Might

Might in the ground be closed vp in rest:
For neuer henceforth shall I ioy againe:
Neuer, oh neuer shall I see more ioy.
Rich. I cannot weepe: for all my bodies moysture
Scarse serues to quench my Furnace-burning hart:
Nor can my tongue vnloade my hearts great burthen,
For selfe-same winde that I should speake withall,
Is kindling coales that fires all my brest,
And burnes me vp with flames, that tears would quench.
To weepe, is to make lesse the depth of greefe:
Teares then for Babes; Blowes, and Reuenge for mee.
Richard, I beare thy name, Ile venge thy death,
Or dye renowned by attempting it.
Ed. His name that valiant Duke hath left with thee:
His Dukedome, and his Chaire with me is left.
Rich. Nay, if thou be that Princely Eagles Bird,
Shew thy descent by gazing 'gainst the Sunne:
For Chaire and Dukedome, Throne and Kingdome say,
Either that is thine, or else thou wer't not his.

March. Enter Warwicke, Marquesse Mountacute, and their Army.

Warwick. How now faire Lords? What faire? What newes abroad?
Rich. Great Lord of Warwicke, if we should recomp
Our balefull newes, and at each words deliuerance
Stab Poniards in our flesh, till all were told,
The words would adde more anguish then the wounds.
O valiant Lord, the Duke of Yorke is slaine.
Edw. O Warwicke, Warwicke, that *Plantagenet*
Which held thee deerely, as his Soules Redemption,
Is by the sterne Lord *Clifford* done to death.
War. Ten dayes ago, I drown'd these newes in teares
And now to adde more measure to your woes,
I come to tell you things sith then befalne.
After the bloody Fray at Wakefield fought,
Where your braue Father breath'd his latest gaspe,
Tydings, as swiftly as the Postes could runne,
Were brought me of your Losse, and his Depart.
I then in London, keeper of the King,
Muster'd my Soldiers, gathered flockes of Friends,
Marcht toward S. Albons, to intercept the Queene,
Bearing the King in my behalfe along:
For by my Scouts, I was aduertised
That she was comming with a full intent
To dash our late Decree in Parliament,
Touching King *Henries* Oath, and your Succession:
Short Tale to make, we at S. Albons met,
Our Battailes ioyn'd, and both sides fiercely fought:
But whether 'twas the coldnesse of the King,
Who look'd full gently on his warlike Queene,
That robb'd my Soldiers of their heated Spleene,
Or whether 'twas report of her successe,
Or more then common feare of *Cliffords* Rigour,
Who thunders to his Captiues, Blood and Death,
I cannot iudge: but to conclude with truth,
Their Weapons like to Lightning, came and went:
Our Souldiers like the Night-Owles lazie flight,
Or like a lazie Thresher with a Flaile,
Fell gently downe, as if they strucke their Friends.
I cheer'd them vp with iustice of our Cause,
With promise of high pay, and great Rewards:
But all in vaine, they had no heart to fight,
And we (in them) no hope to win the day,
So that we fled: the King vnto the Queene,
Lord *George*, your Brother, Norfolke, and my Selfe,
In haste, post haste, are come to ioyne with you:
For in the Marches heere we heard you were,
Making another Head, to fight againe.
Ed. Where is the Duke of Norfolke, gentle Warwick?
And when came *George* from Burgundy to England?
War. Some six miles off the Duke is with the Soldiers,
And for your Brother he was lately sent
From your kinde Aunt Dutchesse of Burgundie,
With ayde of Souldiers to this needfull Warre.
Rich. 'Twas oddes belike, when valiant Warwick fled;
Oft haue I heard his praises in Pursuite,
But ne're till now, his Scandall of Retire.
War. Nor now my Scandall *Richard*, dost thou heare:
For thou shalt know this strong right hand of mine,
Can plucke the Diadem from faint *Henries* head,
And wring the awefull Scepter from his Fist,
Were he as famous, and as bold in Warre,
As he is fam'd for Mildnesse, Peace, and Prayer.
Rich. I know it well Lord Warwick, blame me not,
'Tis loue I beare thy glories make me speake:
But in this troublous time, what's to be done?
Shall we go throw away our Coates of Steele,
And wrap our bodies in blacke mourning Gownes,
Numb'ring our Aue-Maries with our Beads?
Or shall we on the Helmets of our Foes
Tell our Deuotion with reuengefull Armes?
If for the last, say I, and to it Lords.
War. Why therefore Warwick came to seek you out,
And therefore comes my Brother *Mountague*:
Attend me Lords, the proud insulting Queene,
With *Clifford*, and the haught Northumberland,
And of their Feather, many moe proud Birds,
Haue wrought the easie-melting King, like Wax.
He swore consent to your Succession,
His Oath enrolled in the Parliament.
And now to London all the crew are gone,
To frustrate both his Oath, and what beside
May make against the house of Lancaster.
Their power (I thinke) is thirty thousand strong:
Now, if the helpe of Norfolke, and my selfe,
With all the Friends that thou braue Earle of March,
Among'st the louing Welshmen can'st procure,
Will but amount to fiue and twenty thousand,
Why Via, to London will we march,
And once againe, bestride our foaming Steeds,
And once againe cry Charge vpon our Foes,
But neuer once againe turne backe and flye.
Rich. I, now me thinks I heare great Warwick speak;
Ne're may he liue to see a Sun-shine day,
That cries Retire, if Warwicke bid him stay.
Ed. Lord Warwicke, on thy shoulder will I leane,
And when thou failst (as God forbid the houre)
Must *Edward* fall, which perill heauen forefend.
War. No longer Earle of March, but Duke of Yorke:
The next degree, is Englands Royall Throne:
For King of England shalt thou be proclaim'd
In euery Burrough as we passe along,
And he that throwes not vp his cap for ioy,
Shall for the Fault make forfeit of his head.
King *Edward*, valiant *Richard Mountague*:
Stay we no longer, dreaming of Renowne,
But sound the Trumpets, and about our Taske.
Rich. Then *Clifford*, were thy heart as hard as Steele,
As thou hast shewne it flintie by thy deeds,
I come to pierce it, or to giue thee mine.
Ed. Then strike vp Drums, God and S. George for vs

p *War*

Enter a Meſſenger.

War. How now? what newes?
Meſ. The Duke of Norfolke ſends you word by me,
The Queene is comming with a puiſſant Hoaſt,
And craues your company, for ſpeedy counſell.
War. Why then it ſorts, braue Warriors, let's away.
Exeunt Omnes.

Flouriſh. Enter the King, the Queene, Clifford, Northum- and Yong Prince, with Drumme and Trumpettes.

Qu. Welcome my Lord, to this braue town of Yorke,
Yonders the head of that Arch-enemy,
That ſought to be incompaſt with your Crowne.
Doth not the obiect cheere your heart, my Lord.
K. I, as the rockes cheare them that feare their wrack,
To ſee this ſight, it irkes my very ſoule:
With hold reuenge (deere God) 'tis not my fault,
Nor wittingly haue I infring'd my Vow.
Clif. My gracious Liege, this too much lenity
And harmfull pitty muſt be layd aſide:
To whom do Lyons caſt their gentle Lookes?
Not to the Beaſt, that would vſurpe their Den.
Whoſe hand is that the Forreſt Beare doth licke?
Not his that ſpoyles her yong before her face.
Who ſcapes the lurking Serpents mortall ſting?
Not he that ſets his foot vpon her backe.
The ſmalleſt Worme will turne, being troden on,
And Doues will pecke in ſafegard of their Brood.
Ambitious Yorke, did leuell at thy Crowne,
Thou ſmiling, while he knit his angry browes.
He but a Duke, would haue his Sonne a King,
And raiſe his iſſue like a louing Sire.
Thou being a King, bleſt with a goodly ſonne,
Did'ſt yeeld conſent to diſinherit him:
Which argued thee a moſt vnlouing Father.
Vnreaſonable Creatures feed their young,
And though mans face be fearefull to their eyes,
Yet in protection of their tender ones,
Who hath not ſeene them euen with thoſe wings,
Which ſometime they haue vs'd with fearfull flight,
Make warre with him that climb'd vnto their neſt,
Offering their owne liues in their yongs defence?
For ſhame, my Liege, make them your Preſident:
Were it not pitty that this goodly Boy
Should looſe his Birth-right by his Fathers fault,
And long heereafter ſay vnto his childe,
What my great Grandfather, and Grandſire got,
My careleſſe Father fondly gaue away.
Ah, what a ſhame were this? Looke on the Boy,
And let his manly face, which promiſeth
Succeſſefull Fortune ſteele thy melting heart,
To hold thine owne, and leaue thine owne with him.
King. Full well hath *Clifford* plaid the Orator,
Inferring arguments of mighty force:
But *Clifford* tell me, did'ſt thou neuer heare,
That things ill got, had euer bad ſucceſſe.
And happy alwayes was it for that Sonne,
Whoſe Father for his hoording went to hell:
Ile leaue my Sonne my Vertuous deeds behinde,
And would my Father had left me no more:
For all the reſt is held at ſuch a Rate,
As brings a thouſand fold more care to keepe,
Then in poſſeſſion any iot of pleaſure.
Ah Coſin Yorke, would thy beſt Friends did know,
How it doth greeue me that thy head is heere.
Qu. My Lord cheere vp your ſpirits, our foes are nye,
And this ſoft courage makes your Followers faint:
You promiſt Knighthood to our forward ſonne,
Vnſheath your ſword, and dub him preſently.
Edward, kneele downe.
King. Edward Plantagenet, ariſe a Knight,
And learne this Leſſon; Draw thy Sword in right.
Prin. My gracious Father, by your Kingly leaue,
Ile draw it as Apparant to the Crowne,
And in that quarrell, vſe it to the death.
Clif. Why that is ſpoken like a toward Prince.

Enter a Meſſenger.

Meſſ. Royall Commanders, be in readineſſe,
For with a Band of thirty thouſand men,
Comes Warwicke backing of the Duke of Yorke,
And in the Townes as they do march along,
Proclaimes him King, and many flye to him,
Darraigne your battell, for they are at hand.
Clif. I would your Highneſſe would depart the field,
The Queene hath beſt ſucceſſe when you are abſent.
Qu. I good my Lord, and leaue vs to our Fortune.
King. Why, that's my fortune too, therefore Ile ſtay.
North. Be it with reſolution then to fight.
Prin. My Royall Father, cheere theſe Noble Lords,
And hearten thoſe that fight in your defence:
Vnſheath your Sword, good Father: Cry S. George.

March. Enter Edward, Warwicke, Richard, Clarence, Norfolke, Mountague, and Soldiers.

Edw. Now periur'd *Henry*, wilt thou kneel for grace?
And ſet thy Diadem vpon my head?
Or bide the mortall Fortune of the field.
Qu. Go rate thy Minions, proud inſulting Boy,
Becomes it thee to be thus bold in termes,
Before thy Soueraigne, and thy lawfull King?
Ed. I am his King, and he ſhould bow his knee:
I was adopted Heire by his conſent.
Cla. Since when, his Oath is broke: for as I heare,
You that are King, though he do weare the Crowne,
Haue caus'd him by new Act of Parliament,
To blot out me, and put his owne Sonne in.
Clif. And reaſon too,
Who ſhould ſucceede the Father, but the Sonne.
Rich. Are you there Butcher? O, I cannot ſpeake.
Clif. I Crooke-back, here I ſtand to anſwer thee,
Or any he, the proudeſt of thy ſort.
Rich. 'Twas you that kill'd yong Rutland, was it not?
Clif. I, and old Yorke, and yet not ſatisfied.
Rich. For Gods ſake Lords giue ſignall to the fight.
War. What ſay'ſt thou *Henry*,
Wilt thou yeeld the Crowne? (you ſpeak?
Qu. Why how now long-tongu'd Warwicke, dare
When you and I, met at S. *Albons* laſt,
Your legges did better ſeruice then your hands.
War. Then 'twas my turne to fly, and now 'tis thine:
Clif. You ſaid ſo much before, and yet you fled.
War. 'Twas not your valor *Clifford* droue me thence.
Nor. No, nor your manhood that durſt make you ſtay.
Rich. Northumberland, I hold thee reuerently,
Breake off the parley, for ſcarſe I can refraine
The execution of my big-ſwolne heart
Vpon that *Clifford*, that cruell Child-killer.
Clif. I ſlew thy Father, cal'ſt thou him a Child?
Rich.

Rich. I like a Dastard, and a treacherous Coward,
As thou didd'st kill our tender Brother Rutland,
But ere Sunset, Ile make thee curse the deed:
King. Haue done with words (my Lords) and heare me speake.
Qu. Defie them then, or els hold close thy lips.
King. I prythee giue no limits to my Tongue,
I am a King, and priuiledg'd to speake.
Clif. My Liege, the wound that bred this meeting here
Cannot be cur'd by Words, therefore be still.
Rich. Then Executioner vnsheath thy sword:
By him that made vs all, I am resolu'd,
That *Cliffords* Manhood, lyes vpon his tongue.
Ed. Say *Henry*, shall I haue my right, or no:
A thousand men haue broke their Fasts to day,
That ne're shall dine, vnlesse thou yeeld the Crowne.
War. If thou deny, their Blood vpon thy head,
For Yorke in iustice put's his Armour on.
Pr.Ed. If that be right, which Warwick saies is right,
There is no wrong, but euery thing is right.
War. Who euer got thee, there thy Mother stands,
For well I wot, thou hast thy Mothers tongue.
Qu. But thou art neyther like thy Sire nor Damme,
But like a foule mishapen Stygmaticke,
Mark'd by the Destinies to be auoided,
As venome Toades, or Lizards dreadfull stings.
Rich. Iron of Naples, hid with English gilt,
Whose Father beares the Title of a King,
(As if a Channell should be call'd the Sea)
Sham'st thou not, knowing whence thou art extraught,
To let thy tongue detect thy base-borne heart.
Ed. A wispe of straw were worth a thousand Crowns,
To make this shamelesse Callet know her selfe:
Helen of Greece was fayrer farre then thou,
Although thy Husband may be *Menelaus*;
And ne're was *Agamemnons* Brother wrong'd
By that false Woman, as this King by thee.
His Father reuel'd in the heart of France,
And tam'd the King, and made the Dolphin stoope:
And had he match'd according to his State,
He might haue kept that glory to this day.
But when he tooke a begger to his bed,
And grac'd thy poore Sire with his Bridall day,
Euen then that Sun-shine brew'd a showre for him,
That washt his Fathers fortunes forth of France,
And heap'd sedition on his Crowne at home:
For what hath broach'd this tumult but thy Pride?
Had'st thou bene meeke, our Title still had slept,
And we in pitty of the Gentle King,
Had slipt our Claime, vntill another Age.
Cla. But when we saw, our Sunshine made thy Spring,
And that thy Summer bred vs no increase,
We set the Axe to thy vsurping Roote:
And though the edge hath something hit our selues,
Yet know thou, since we haue begun to strike,
Wee'l neuer leaue, till we haue hewne thee downe,
Or bath'd thy growing, with our heated bloods.
Edw. And in this resolution, I defie thee,
Not willing any longer Conference,
Since thou denied'st the gentle King to speake.
Sound Trumpets, let our bloody Colours waue,
And either Victorie, or else a Graue.
Qu. Stay *Edward*.
Ed. No wrangling Woman, wee'l no longer stay,
These words will cost ten thousand liues this day.

Exeunt omnes.

Alarum. Excursions. Enter Warwicke.

War. Fore-spent with Toile, as Runners with a Race,
I lay me downe a little while to breath:
For strokes receiu'd, and many blowes repaid,
Haue robb'd my strong knit sinewes of their strength,
And spight of spight, needs must I rest a-while.

Enter Edward running.

Ed. Smile gentle heauen, or strike vngentle death,
For this world frownes, and *Edwards* Sunne is clowded.
War. How now my Lord, what happe? what hope of good?

Enter Clarence.

Cla. Our hap is losse, our hope but sad dispaire,
Our rankes are broke, and ruine followes vs.
What counsaile giue you? whether shall we flye?
Ed. Bootlesse is flight, they follow vs with Wings,
And weake we are, and cannot shun pursuite.

Enter Richard.

Rich. Ah Warwicke, why hast thou withdrawn thy selfe?
Thy Brothers blood the thirsty earth hath drunk,
Broach'd with the Steely point of *Cliffords* Launce:
And in the very pangs of death, he cryde,
Like to a dismall Clangor heard from farre,
Warwicke, reuenge; Brother, reuenge my death.
So vnderneath the belly of their Steeds,
That stain'd their Fetlockes in his smoaking blood,
The Noble Gentleman gaue vp the ghost.
War. Then let the earth be drunken with our blood:
Ile kill my Horse, because I will not flye:
Why stand we like soft-hearted women heere,
Wayling our losses, whiles the Foe doth Rage,
And looke vpon, as if the Tragedie
Were plaid in iest, by counterfetting Actors.
Heere on my knee, I vow to God aboue,
Ile neuer pawse againe, neuer stand still,
Till either death hath clos'd these eyes of mine,
Or Fortune giuen me measure of Reuenge.
Ed. Oh Warwicke, I do bend my knee with thine,
And in this vow do chaine my soule to thine:
And ere my knee rise from the Earths cold face,
I throw my hands, mine eyes, my heart to thee,
Thou setter vp, and plucker downe of Kings:
Beseeching thee (if with thy will it stands)
That to my Foes this body must be prey,
Yet that thy brazen gates of heauen may ope,
And giue sweet passage to my sinfull soule.
Now Lords, take leaue vntill we meete againe,
Where ere it be, in heauen, or in earth.
Rich. Brother,
Giue me thy hand, and gentle Warwicke,
Let me imbrace thee in my weary armes:
I that did neuer weepe, now melt with wo,
That Winter should cut off our Spring-time so.
War. Away, away:
Once more sweet Lords farwell.
Cla. Yet let vs altogether to our Troopes,
And giue them leaue to flye, that will not stay:
And call them Pillars that will stand to vs:
And if we thriue, promise them such rewards
As Victors weare at the Olympian Games.
This may plant courage in their quailing breasts,
For yet is hope of Life and Victory:

p 2 Fore-

Foreſlow no longer, make we hence amaine. *Exeunt*

Excurſions. Enter Richard and Clifford.

Rich. Now *Clifford*, I haue ſingled thee alone,
Suppoſe this arme is for the Duke of Yorke,
And this for Rutland, both bound to reuenge,
Wer't thou inuiron'd with a Brazen wall.

Clif. Now *Richard*, I am with thee heere alone,
This is the hand that ſtabb'd thy Father Yorke,
And this the hand, that ſlew thy Brother Rutland,
And here's the heart, that triumphs in their death,
And cheeres theſe hands, that ſlew thy Sire and Brother,
To execute the like vpon thy ſelfe,
And ſo haue at thee.

They Fight, Warwicke comes, Clifford flies.

Rich. Nay Warwicke, ſingle out ſome other Chace,
For I my ſelfe will hunt this Wolfe to death. *Exeunt.*

Alarum. Enter King Henry alone.

Hen. This battell fares like to the mornings Warre,
When dying clouds contend, with growing light,
What time the Shepheard blowing of his nailes,
Can neither call it perfect day, nor night.
Now ſwayes it this way, like a Mighty Sea,
Forc'd by the Tide, to combat with the Winde:
Now ſwayes it that way, like the ſelfe-ſame Sea,
Forc'd to retyre by furie of the Winde.
Sometime, the Flood preuailes; and than the Winde:
Now, one the better: then, another beſt;
Both tugging to be Victors, breſt to breſt:
Yet neither Conqueror, nor Conquered.
So is the equall poiſe of this fell Warre.
Heere on this Mole-hill will I ſit me downe,
To whom God will, there be the Victorie:
For *Margaret* my Queene, and *Clifford* too
Haue chid me from the Battell: Swearing both,
They proſper beſt of all when I am thence.
Would I were dead, if Gods good will were ſo;
For what is in this world, but Greefe and Woe.
Oh God! me thinkes it were a happy life,
To be no better then a homely Swaine,
To ſit vpon a hill, as I do now,
To carue out Dialls queintly, point by point,
Thereby to ſee the Minutes how they runne:
How many makes the Houre full compleate,
How many Houres brings about the Day,
How many Dayes will finiſh vp the Yeare,
How many Yeares, a Mortall man may liue.
When this is knowne, then to diuide the Times:
So many Houres, muſt I tend my Flocke;
So many Houres, muſt I take my Reſt:
So many Houres, muſt I Contemplate:
So many Houres, muſt I Sport my ſelfe:
So many Dayes, my Ewes haue bene with yong:
So many weekes, ere the poore Fooles will Eane:
So many yeares, ere I ſhall ſheere the Fleece:
So Minutes, Houres, Dayes, Monthes, and Yeares,
Paſt ouer to the end they were created,
Would bring white haires, vnto a Quiet graue.
Ah! what a life were this? How ſweet? how louely?
Giues not the Hawthorne buſh a ſweeter ſhade
To Shepheards, looking on their ſilly Sheepe,
Then doth a rich Imbroider'd Canopie
To Kings, that feare their Subiects treacherie?
Oh yes, it doth; a thouſand fold it doth.
And to conclude, the Shepherds homely Curds,
His cold thinne drinke out of his Leather Bottle,
His wonted ſleepe, vnder a freſh trees ſhade,
All which ſecure, and ſweetly he enioyes,
Is farre beyond a Princes Delicates:
His Viands ſparkling in a Golden Cup,
His bodie couched in a curious bed,
When Care, Miſtruſt, and Treaſon waits on him.

Alarum. Enter a Sonne that hath kill'd his Father, at one doore: and a Father that hath kill'd his Sonne at another doore.

Son. Ill blowes the winde that profits no body,
This man whom hand to hand I ſlew in fight,
May be poſſeſſed with ſome ſtore of Crownes,
And I that (haply) take them from him now,
May yet (ere night) yeeld both my Life and them
To ſome man elſe, as this dead man doth me.
Who's this? Oh God! It is my Fathers face,
Whom in this Conflict, I (vnwares) haue kill'd:
Oh heauy times! begetting ſuch Euents.
From London, by the King was I preſt forth,
My Father being the Earle of Warwickes man,
Came on the part of Yorke, preſt by his Maſter:
And I, who at his hands receiu'd my life,
Haue by my hands, of Life bereaued him.
Pardon me God, I knew not what I did:
And pardon Father, for I knew not thee.
My Teares ſhall wipe away theſe bloody markes:
And no more words, till they haue flow'd their fill.

King. O pitteous ſpectacle! O bloody Times!
Whiles Lyons Warre, and battaile for their Dennes,
Poore harmleſſe Lambes abide their enmity.
Weepe wretched man: Ile ayde thee Teare for Teare,
And let our hearts and eyes, like Ciuill Warre,
Be blinde with teares, and break ore-charg'd with griefe

Enter Father, bearing of his Sonne.

Fa. Thou that ſo ſtoutly hath reſiſted me,
Giue me thy Gold, if thou haſt any Gold:
For I haue bought it with an hundred blowes.
But let me ſee: Is this our Foe-mans face?
Ah, no, no, no, it is mine onely Sonne.
Ah Boy, if any life be left in thee,
Throw vp thine eye: ſee, ſee, what ſhowres ariſe,
Blowne with the windie Tempeſt of my heart,
Vpon thy wounds, that killes mine Eye, and Heart.
O pitty God, this miſerable Age!
What Stragems? how fell? how Butcherly?
Erreoneous, mutinous, and vnnaturall,
This deadly quarrell daily doth beget?
O Boy! thy Father gaue thee life too ſoone,
And hath bereft thee of thy life too late.

King. Wo aboue wo: greefe, more the common greefe
O that my death would ſtay theſe ruthfull deeds:
O pitty, pitty, gentle heauen pitty:
The Red Roſe and the White are on his face,
The fatall Colours of our ſtriuing Houſes:
The one, his purple Blood right well reſembles,
The other his pale Cheekes (me thinkes) preſenteth:
Wither one Roſe, and let the other flouriſh:
If you contend, a thouſand liues muſt wither.

Son. How will my Mother, for a Fathers death
Take on with me, and ne're be ſatisfi'd?

Fa. How will my Wife, for ſlaughter of my Sonne,
Shed ſeas of Teares, and ne're be ſatisfi'd?

King. How will the Country, for theſe woful chances,
Miſ-thinke

Mis-thinke the King, and not be satisfied ?
Son. Was euer sonne, so rew'd a Fathers death?
Fath. Was euer Father so bemoan'd his Sonne?
Hen. Was euer King so greeu'd for Subiects woe?
Much is your sorrow; Mine,ten times so much.
Son. Ile beare thee hence, where I may weepe my fill.
Fath. These armes of mine shall be thy winding sheet:
My heart (sweet Boy) shall be thy Sepulcher,
For from my heart, thine Image ne're shall go.
My sighing brest, shall be thy Funerall bell ;
And so obsequious will thy Father be,
Men for the losse of thee,hauing no more,
As *Priam* was for all his Valiant Sonnes,
Ile beare thee hence,and let them fight that will,
For I haue murthered where I should not kill. *Exit*
Hen. Sad-hearted-men, much ouergone with Care;
Heere sits a King, more wofull then you are.

Alarums. Excursions. Enter the Queen,the Prince,and Exeter.

Prin. Fly Father,flye : for all your Friends are fled.
And Warwicke rages like a chafed Bull :
Away, for death doth hold vs in pursuite.
Qu. Mount you my Lord, towards Barwicke post amaine :
Edward and *Richard* like a brace of Grey-hounds,
Hauing the fearfull flying Hare in sight,
With fiery eyes,sparkling for very wrath,
And bloody steele graspt in their yrefull hands
Are at our backes,and therefore hence amaine.
Exet. Away : for vengeance comes along with them.
Nay, stay not to expostulate, make speed,
Or else come after, Ile away before.
Hen. Nay take me with thee,good sweet Exeter :
Not that I feare to stay, but loue to go
Whether the Queene intends. Forward,away. *Exeunt*

A lowd alarum. Enter Clifford Wounded.

Clif. Heere burnes my Candle out; I,heere it dies,
Which whiles it lasted, gaue King *Henry* light.
O Lancaster! I feare thy ouerthrow,
More then my Bodies parting with my Soule:
My Loue and Feare, glew'd many Friends to thee,
And now I fall. Thy tough Commixtures melts,
Impairing *Henry*, strength'ning misproud Yorke ;
And whether flye the Gnats, but to the Sunne?
And who shines now, but *Henries* Enemies?
O Phoebus! had'st thou neuer giuen consent,
That *Phaeton* should checke thy fiery Steeds,
Thy burning Carre neuer had scorch'd the earth.
And *Henry*, had'st thou sway'd as Kings should do,
Or as thy Father,and his Father did,
Giuing no ground vnto the house of Yorke,
They neuer then had sprung like Sommer Flyes :
I, and ten thousand in this lucklesse Realme,
Hed left no mourning Widdowes for our death,
And thou this day,had'st kept thy Chaire in peace.
For what doth cherrish Weeds,but gentle ayre?
And what makes Robbers bold, but too much lenity?
Bootlesse are Plaints,and Curelesse are my Wounds :
No way to flye, nor strength to hold out flight :
The Foe is mercilesse, and will not pitty :
For at their hands I haue deseru'd no pitty.
The ayre hath got into my deadly Wounds,
And much effuse of blood, doth make me faint :
Come *Yorke*,and *Richard*,*Warwicke*,and the rest,
I stab'd your Fathers bosomes; Split my brest.

Alarum & Retreat. Enter Edward,Warwicke,Richard,and Soldiers, Montague,& Clarence.

*Ed.*Now breath we Lords,good fortune bids vs pause,
And smooth the frownes of War,with peacefull lookes:
Some Troopes pursue the bloody-minded Queene,
That led calme *Henry*, though he were a King,
As doth a Saile, fill'd with a fretting Gust
Command an Argosie to stemme the Waues.
But thinke you(Lords)that Clifford fled with them?
War. No, 'tis impossible he should escape :
(For though before his face I speake the words)
Your Brother *Richard* markt him for the Graue.
And wheresoere he is, hee's surely dead. *Clifford grones*
Rich. Whose soule is that which takes hir heauy leaue?
A deadly grone, like life and deaths departing.
See who it is.
Ed. And now the Battailes ended,
If Friend or Foe, let him be gently vsed.
Rich. Reuoke that doome of mercy,for 'tis *Clifford*,
Who not contented that he lopp'd the Branch
In hewing Rutland, when his leaues put forth,
But set his murth'ring knife vnto the Roote,
From whence that tender spray did sweetly spring,
I meane our Princely Father,Duke of Yorke.
War. From off the gates of Yorke, fetch down yͤ head,
Your Fathers head,which *Clifford* placed there:
In stead whereof, let this supply the roome,
Measure for measure, must be answered.
*Ed.*Bring forth that fatall Schreechowle to our house,
That nothing sung but death, to vs and ours :
Now death shall stop his dismall threatning sound,
And his ill-boading tongue,no more shall speake.
War. I thinke is vnderstanding is bereft :
Speake *Clifford*,dost thou kuow who speakes to thee?
Darke cloudy death ore-shades his beames of life,
And he nor sees, nor heares vs,what we say.
Rich. O would he did, and so (perhaps)he doth,
Tis but his policy to counterfet,
Because he would auoid such bitter taunts
Which in the time of death he gaue our Father.
Cla If so thou think'st,
Vex him with eager Words.
Rich. *Clifford*,aske mercy,and obtaine no grace.
Ed. *Clifford*,repent in bootlesse penitence.
War. *Clifford*, deuise excuses for thy faults.
Cla. While we deuise fell Tortures for thy faults.
Rich. Thou didd'st loue Yorke,and I am son to Yorke.
Edw. Thou pittied'st Rutland,I will pitty thee.
Cla. Where's Captaine *Margaret*,to fence you now?
War. They mocke thee *Clifford*,
Sweare as thou was't wont.
Ric. What,not an Oath? Nay then the world go's hard
When *Clifford* cannot spare his Friends an oath :
I know by that he's dead,and by my Soule,
If this right hand would buy two houres life,
That I(in all despight) might rayle at him,
This hand should chop it off: & with the issuing Blood
Stifle the Villaine,whose vnstanched thirst
Yorke,and yong Rutland could not satisfie
War. I, but he's dead. Of with the Traitors head,
And reare it in the place your Fathers stands.
And now to London with Triumphant march,

P 3 There

There to be crowned Englands Royall King:
From whence, shall Warwicke cut the Sea to France,
And aske the Ladie *Bona* for thy Queene:
So shalt thou sinow both these Lands together,
And hauing France thy Friend, thou shalt not dread
The scattred Foe, that hopes to rise againe:
For though they cannot greatly sting to hurt,
Yet looke to haue them buz to offend thine eares:
First, will I see the Coronation,
And then to Britanny Ile crosse the Sea,
To effect this marriage, so it please my Lord.
Ed. Euen as thou wilt sweet Warwicke, let it bee:
For in thy shoulder do I builde my Seate;
And neuer will I vndertake the thing
Wherein thy counsaile and consent is wanting:
Richard, I will create thee Duke of Gloucester,
And *George* of Clarence; *Warwicke* as our Selfe,
Shall do, and vndo as him pleaseth best.
Rich. Let me be Duke of Clarence, *George* of Gloster,
For Glosters Dukedome is too ominous.
War. Tut, that's a foolish obseruation:
Richard, be Duke of Gloster: Now to London,
To see these Honors in possession. *Exeunt*

Enter Sinklo, and Humfrey, with Crosse-bowes in their hands.

Sink. Vnder this thicke growne brake, wee'l shrowd (our selues:
For through this Laund anon the Deere will come,
And in this couert will we make our Stand,
Culling the principall of all the Deere.
Hum. Ile stay aboue the hill, so both may shoot.
Sink. That cannot be, the noise of thy Crosse-bow
Will scarre the Heard, and so my shoot is lost:
Heere stand we both, and ayme we at the best:
And for the time shall not seeme tedious,
Ile tell thee what befell me on a day,
In this selfe-place, where now we meane to stand.
Sink. Heere comes a man, let's stay till he be past:
Enter the King with a Prayer booke.
Hen. From Scotland am I stolne euen of pure loue,
To greet mine owne Land with my wishfull sight:
No *Harry*, *Harry*, 'tis no Land of thine,
Thy place is fill'd, thy Scepter wrung from thee,
Thy Balme washt off, wherewith thou was Annointed:
No bending knee will call thee *Cæsar* now,
No humble suters prease to speake for right:
No, not a man comes for redresse of thee:
For how can I helpe them, and not my selfe?
Sink. I, heere's a Deere, whose skin's a Keepers Fee:
This is the quondam King; Let's seize vpon him.
Hen. Let me embrace the sower Aduersaries,
For Wise men say, it is the wisest course.
Hum. Why linger we? Let vs lay hands vpon him.
Sink. Forbeare a-while, wee'l heare a little more.
Hen. My Queene and Son are gone to France for aid:
And (as I heare) the great Commanding Warwicke
I: thither gone, to craue the French Kings Sister
To wife for *Edward*. If this newes be true,
Poore Queene, and Sonne, your labour is but lost:
For Warwicke is a subtle Orator:
And *Lewis* a Prince soone wonne with mouing words:
By this accont then, *Margaret* may winne him,
For she's a woman to be pittied much:
Her sighes will make a batt'ry in his brest,
Her teares will pierce into a Marble heart:
The Tyger will be milde, whiles she doth mourne;
And *Nero* will be tainted with remorse,
To heare and see her plaints, her Brinish Teares.
I, but shee's come to begge, Warwicke to giue:
Shee on his left side, crauing ayde for *Henrie*;
He on his right, asking a wife for *Edward*.
Shee Weepes, and sayes, her *Henry* is depos'd:
He Smiles, and sayes, his *Edward* is instaul'd;
That she (poore Wretch) for greefe can speake no more:
Whiles Warwicke tels his Title, smooths the Wrong,
Inferreth arguments of mighty strength,
And in conclusion winnes the King from her,
With promise of his Sister, and what else,
To strengthen and support King *Edwards* place.
O *Margaret*, thus 'twill be, and thou (poore soule)
Art then forsaken, as thou went'st forlorne.
Hum. Say, what art thou talk'st of Kings & Queens?
King. More then I seeme, and lesse then I was born to:
A man at least, for lesse I should not be:
And men may talke of Kings, and why not I?
Hum. I, but thou talk'st, as if thou wer't a King.
King. Why so I am (in Minde) and that's enough.
Hum. But if thou be a King, where is thy Crowne?
King. My Crowne is in my heart, not on my head:
Not deck'd with Diamonds, and Indian stones:
Nor to be seene: my Crowne, is call'd Content,
A Crowne it is, that sildome Kings enioy.
Hum. Well, if you be a King crown'd with Content,
Your Crowne Content, and you, must be contented
To go along with vs. For (as we thinke)
You are the king King *Edward* hath depos'd:
And we his subiects, sworne in all Allegeance,
Will apprehend you, as his Enemie.
King But did you neuer sweare, and breake an Oath.
Hum. No, neuer such an Oath, nor will not now.
King. Where did you dwell when I was K. of England?
Hum. Heere in this Country, where we now remaine.
King. I was annointed King at nine monthes old,
My Father, and my Grandfather were Kings:
And you were sworne true Subiects vnto me:
And tell me then, haue you not broke your Oathes?
Sin. No, for we were Subiects, but while you wer king
King. Why? Am I dead? Do I not breath a Man?
Ah simple men, you know not what you sweare:
Looke, as I blow this Feather from my Face,
And as the Ayre blowes it to me againe,
Obeying with my winde when I do blow,
And yeelding to another, when it blowes,
Commanded alwayes by the greater gust:
Such is the lightnesse of you, common men.
But do not breake your Oathes, for of that sinne,
My milde intreatie shall not make you guiltie.
Go where you will, the king shall be commanded,
And be you kings, command, and Ile obey.
Sinklo. We are true Subiects to the king,
King *Edward*.
King. So would you be againe to *Henrie*,
If he were seated as king *Edward* is.
Sinklo. We charge you in Gods name & the Kings,
To go with vs vnto the Officers.
King. In Gods name lead, your Kings name be obeyd,
And what God will, that let your King performe,
And what he will, I humbly yeeld vnto. *Exeunt*

Enter K. Edward, Gloster, Clarence, Lady Gray.

King. Brother of Gloster, at S. Albons field

This

This Ladyes Husband, Sir *Richard Grey*, was ſlaine,
His Land then ſeiz'd on by the Conqueror,
Her ſuit is now, to repoſſeſſe thoſe Lands,
Which wee in Iuſtice cannot well deny,
Becauſe in Quarrell of the Houſe of *Yorke*,
The worthy Gentleman did loſe his Life.

Rich. Your Highneſſe ſhall doe well to graunt her ſuit:
It were diſhonor to deny it her.

King. It were no leſſe, but yet Ile make a pawſe.

Rich. Yea, is it ſo:
I ſee the Lady hath a thing to graunt,
Before the King will graunt her humble ſuit.

Clarence. Hee knowes the Game, how true hee keepes the winde?

Rich. Silence.

King. Widow, we will conſider of your ſuit,
And come ſome other time to know our minde.

Wid. Right gracious Lord, I cannot brooke delay:
May it pleaſe your Highneſſe to reſolue me now,
And what your pleaſure is, ſhall ſatisfie me.

Rich. I Widow? then Ile warrant you all your Lands,
And if what pleaſes him, ſhall pleaſure you:
Fight cloſer, or good faith you'le catch a Blow.

Clarence. I feare her not, vnleſſe ſhe chance to fall.

Rich. God forbid that, for hee'le take vantages.

King. How many Children haſt thou, Widow? tell me.

Clarence. I thinke he meanes to begge a Child of her.

Rich Nay then whip me: hee'le rather giue her two.

Wid. Three, my moſt gracious Lord.

Rich. You ſhall haue foure, if you'le be rul'd by him.

King. 'Twere pittie they ſhould loſe their Fathers Lands.

Wid. Be pittifull, dread Lord, and graunt it then.

King. Lords giue vs leaue, Ile trye this Widowes wit.

Rich. I, good leaue haue you, for you will haue leaue
Till Youth take leaue, and leaue you to the Crutch.

King. Now tell me, Madame, doe you loue your Children?

Wid. I, full as dearely as I loue my ſelfe.

King. And would you not doe much to doe them good?

Wid. To doe them good, I would ſuſtayne ſome harme.

King. Then get your Husbands Lands, to doe them good.

Wid. Therefore I came vnto your Maieſtie.

King. Ile tell you how theſe Lands are to be got.

Wid. So ſhall you bind me to your Highneſſe ſeruice.

King. What ſeruice wilt thou doe me, if I giue them?

Wid. What you command, that reſts in me to doe.

King: But you will take exceptions to my Boone.

Wid. No, gracious Lord, except I cannot doe it.

King. I, but thou canſt doe what I meane to aske.

Wid. Why then I will doe what your Grace commands.

Rich. Hee plyes her hard, and much Raine weares the Marble.

Clar. As red as fire? nay then, her Wax muſt melt.

Wid. Why ſtoppes my Lord? ſhall I not heare my Taske?

King. An eaſie Taske, 'tis but to loue a King.

Wid. That's ſoone perform'd, becauſe I am a Subiect.

King. Why then, thy Husbands Lands I freely giue thee.

Wid. I take my leaue with many thouſand thankes.

Rich. The Match is made, ſhee ſeales it with a Curſie.

King. But ſtay thee, 'tis the fruits of loue I meane.

Wid. The fruits of Loue, I meane, my louing Liege.

King. I, but I feare me in another ſence.
What Loue, think'ſt thou, I ſue ſo much to get?

Wid. My loue till death, my humble thanks, my prayers,
That loue which Vertue begges, and Vertue graunts.

King. No, by my troth, I did not meane ſuch loue.

Wid. Why then you meane not, as I thought you did.

King. But now you partly may perceiue my minde.

Wid. My minde will neuer graunt what I perceiue
Your Highneſſe aymes at, if I ayme aright.

King. To tell thee plaine, I ayme to lye with thee.

Wid. To tell you plaine, I had rather lye in Priſon.

King. Why then thou ſhalt not haue thy Husbands Lands.

Wid. Why then mine Honeſtie ſhall be my Dower,
For by that loſſe, I will not purchaſe them.

King. Therein thou wrong'ſt thy Children mightily.

Wid. Herein your Highneſſe wrongs both them & me:
But mightie Lord, this merry inclination
Accords not with the ſadneſſe of my ſuit:
Pleaſe you diſmiſſe me, eyther with I, or no.

King. I, if thou wilt ſay I to my requeſt:
No, if thou do'ſt ſay No to my demand.

Wid. Then No, my Lord: my ſuit is at an end.

Rich. The Widow likes him not, ſhee knits her Browes.

Clarence. Hee is the blunteſt Wooer in Chriſtendome.

King. Her Looks doth argue her replete with Modeſty,
Her Words doth ſhew her Wit incomparable,
All her perfections challenge Soueraigntie,
One way, or other, ſhee is for a King,
And ſhee ſhall be my Loue, or elſe my Queene.
Say, that King *Edward* take thee for his Queene?

Wid. 'Tis better ſaid then done, my gracious Lord:
I am a ſubiect fit to ieaſt withall,
But farre vnfit to be a Soueraigne.

King. Sweet Widow, by my State I ſweare to thee,
I ſpeake no more then what my Soule intends,
And that is, to enioy thee for my Loue.

Wid. And that is more then I will yeeld vnto:
I know, I am too meane to be your Queene,
And yet too good to be your Concubine.

King. You cauill, Widow, I did meane my Queene.

Wid. 'Twill grieue your Grace, my Sonnes ſhould call you Father.

King. No more, then when my Daughters
Call thee Mother.
Thou art a Widow, and thou haſt ſome Children,
And by Gods Mother, I being but a Batchelor,
Haue other-ſome. Why, 'tis a happy thing,
To be the Father vnto many Sonnes:
Anſwer no more, for thou ſhalt be my Queene.

Rich. The Ghoſtly Father now hath done his Shrift.

Clarence. When hee was made a Shriuer, 'twas for ſhift.

King. Brothers, you muſe what Chat wee two haue had.

Rich. The Widow likes it not, for ſhee lookes very ſad.

King. You'ld thinke it ſtrange, if I ſhould marrie her.

Clarence. To who, my Lord?

King. Why *Clarence*, to my ſelfe.

Rich. That

Rich. That would be tenne dayes wonder at the least.
Clarence. That's a day longer then a Wonder lasts.
Rich. By so much is the Wonder in extremes.
King. Well, ieast on Brothers: I can tell you both,
Her suit is graunted for her Husbands Lands.

Enter a Noble man.

Nob. My gracious Lord, *Henry* your Foe is taken,
And brought your Prisoner to your Pallace Gate.
King. See that he be conuey'd vnto the Tower:
And goe wee Brothers to the man that tooke him,
To question of his apprehension.
Widow goe you along: Lords vse her honourable.

Exeunt.

Manet Richard.

Rich. I, *Edward* will vse Women honourably:
Would he were wasted, Marrow, Bones, and all,
That from his Loynes no hopefull Branch may spring,
To crosse me from the Golden time I looke for:
And yet, betweene my Soules desire, and me,
The lustfull *Edwards* Title buryed,
Is *Clarence, Henry*, and his Sonne young *Edward*,
And all the vnlook'd-for Issue of their Bodies,
To take their Roomes, ere I can place my selfe:
A cold premeditation for my purpose.
Why then I doe but dreame on Soueraigntie,
Like one that stands vpon a Promontorie,
And spyes a farre-off shore, where hee would tread,
Wishing his foot were equall with his eye,
And chides the Sea, that sunders him from thence,
Saying hee'le lade it dry, to haue his way:
So doe I wish the Crowne, being so farre off,
And so I chide the meanes that keepes me from it,
And so (I say) Ile cut the Causes off,
Flattering me with impossibilities:
My Eyes too quicke, my Heart o're-weenes too much,
Vnlesse my Hand and Strength could equall them.
Well, say there is no Kingdome then for *Richard*:
What other Pleasure can the World affoord?
Ile make my Heauen in a Ladies Lappe,
And decke my Body in gay Ornaments,
And 'witch sweet Ladies with my Words and Lookes.
Oh miserable Thought! and more vnlikely,
Then to accomplish twentie Golden Crownes.
Why Loue forswore me in my Mothers Wombe:
And for I should not deale in her soft Lawes,
Shee did corrupt frayle Nature with some Bribe,
To shrinke mine Arme vp like a wither'd Shrub,
To make an enuious Mountaine on my Back,
Where sits Deformitie to mocke my Body;
To shape my Legges of an vnequall size,
To dis-proportion me in euery part:
Like to a Chaos, or an vn-lick'd Beare-whelpe,
That carryes no impression like the Damme.
And am I then a man to be belou'd?
Oh monstrous fault, to harbour such a thought.
Then since this Earth affoords no Ioy to me,
But to command, to check, to o're-beare such,
As are of better Person then my selfe:
Ile make my Heauen, to dreame vpon the Crowne,
And whiles I liue, t'account this World but Hell,
Vntill my mis-shap'd Trunke, that beares this Head,
Be round impaled with a glorious Crowne.
And yet I know not how to get the Crowne,
For many Liues stand betweene me and home:
And I, like one lost in a Thornie Wood,
That rents the Thornes, and is rent with the Thornes,
Seeking a way, and straying from the way,
Not knowing how to finde the open Ayre,
But toyling desperately to finde it out,
Torment my selfe, to catch the English Crowne:
And from that torment I will free my selfe,
Or hew my way out with a bloody Axe.
Why I can smile, and murther whiles I smile,
And cry, Content, to that which grieues my Heart,
And wet my Cheekes with artificiall Teares,
And frame my Face to all occasions.
Ile drowne more Saylers then the Mermaid shall,
Ile slay more gazers then the Basiliske,
Ile play the Orator as well as *Nestor*,
Deceiue more slyly then *Vlisses* could,
And like a *Synon*, take another Troy.
I can adde Colours to the Camelion,
Change shapes with *Proteus*, for aduantages,
And set the murtherous *Macheuill* to Schoole.
Can I doe this, and cannot get a Crowne?
Tut, were it farther off, Ile plucke it downe. *Exit.*

Flourish.

Enter Lewis the French King, his Sister Bona, his Admirall, call'd Bourbon: Prince Edward, Queene Margaret, and the Earle of Oxford. Lewis sits, and riseth vp againe.

Lewis. Faire Queene of England, worthy *Margaret*,
Sit downe with vs: it ill befits thy State,
And Birth, that thou should'st stand, while *Lewis* doth sit.
Marg. No, mightie King of France: now *Margaret*
Must strike her sayle, and learne a while to serue,
Where Kings command. I was (I must confesse)
Great Albions Queene, in former Golden dayes:
But now mischance hath trod my Title downe,
And with dis-honor layd me on the ground,
Where I must take like Seat vnto my fortune,
And to my humble Seat conforme my selfe.
Lewis. Why say, faire Queene, whence springs this deepe despaire?
Marg. From such a cause, as fils mine eyes with teares,
And stops my tongue, while heart is drown'd in cares.
Lewis. What ere it be, be thou still like thy selfe,
And sit thee by our side. *Seats her by him.*
Yeeld not thy necke to Fortunes yoake,
But let thy dauntlesse minde still ride in triumph,
Ouer all mischance.
Be plaine, Queene *Margaret*, and tell thy griefe,
It shall be eas'd, if France can yeeld reliefe.
Marg. Those gracious words
Reuiue my drooping thoughts,
And giue my tongue-ty'd sorrowes leaue to speake.
Now therefore be it knowne to Noble *Lewis*,
That *Henry*, sole possessor of my Loue,
Is, of a King, become a banisht man,
And forc'd to liue in Scotland a Forlorne;
While prowd ambitious *Edward*, Duke of Yorke,
Vsurpes the Regall Title, and the Seat
Of Englands true anoynted lawfull King.
This is the cause that I, poore *Margaret*,
With this my Sonne, Prince *Edward*, *Henries* Heire,
Am come to craue thy iust and lawfull ayde:
And if thou faile vs, all our hope is done.
Scotland hath will to helpe, but cannot helpe:

Our

Our People, and our Peeres, are both mis-led,
Our Treasure seiz'd, our Souldiors put to flight,
And (as thou seest) our selues in heauie plight.
Lewis. Renowned Queene,
With patience calme the Storme,
While we bethinke a meanes to breake it off.
Marg. The more wee stay, the stronger growes our Foe.
Lewis. The more I stay, the more Ile succour thee.
Marg. O, but impatience waiteth on true sorrow.
And see where comes the breeder of my sorrow.

Enter Warwicke.

Lewis. What's hee approacheth boldly to our presence?
Marg. Our Earle of Warwicke, *Edwards* greatest Friend.
Lewis. Welcome braue *Warwicke*, what brings thee to France? *Hee descends. Shee ariseth.*
Marg. I now begins a second Storme to rise,
For this is hee that moues both Winde and Tyde.
Warw. From worthy *Edward*, King of Albion,
My Lord and Soueraigne, and thy vowed Friend,
I come (in Kindnesse, and vnfayned Loue)
First, to doe greetings to thy Royall Person,
And then to craue a League of Amitie:
And lastly, to confirme that Amitie
With Nuptiall Knot, if thou vouchsafe to graunt
That vertuous Lady *Bona*, thy faire Sister,
To Englands King, in lawfull Marriage.
Marg. If that goe forward, *Henries* hope is done.
Warw. And gracious Madame, *Speaking to Bona.*
In our Kings behalfe,
I am commanded, with your leaue and fauor,
Humbly to kisse your Hand, and with my Tongue
To tell the passion of my Soueraignes Heart;
Where Fame, late entring at his heedfull Eares,
Hath plac'd thy Beauties Image, and thy Vertue.
Marg. King *Lewis*, and Lady *Bona*, heare me speake,
Before you answer *Warwicke*. His demand
Springs not from *Edwards* well-meant honest Loue,
But from Deceit, bred by Necessitie:
For how can Tyrants safely gouerne home,
Vnlesse abroad they purchase great allyance?
To proue him Tyrant, this reason may suffice,
That *Henry* liueth still: but were hee dead,
Yet here Prince *Edward* stands, King *Henries* Sonne.
Looke therefore *Lewis*, that by this League and Mariage
Thou draw not on thy Danger, and Dis-honor:
For though Vsurpers sway the rule a while,
Yet Heau'ns are iust, and Time suppresseth Wrongs.
Warw. Iniurious *Margaret*.
Edw. And why not Queene?
Warw. Because thy Father *Henry* did vsurpe,
And thou no more art Prince, then shee is Queene.
Oxf. Then *Warwicke* disanulls great *Iohn* of Gaunt,
Which did subdue the greatest part of Spaine;
And after *Iohn* of Gaunt, *Henry* the Fourth,
Whose Wisdome was a Mirror to the wisest:
And after that wise Prince, *Henry* the Fift,
Who by his Prowesse conquered all France:
From these, our *Henry* lineally descends.
Warw. Oxford, how haps it in this smooth discourse,
You told not, how *Henry* the Sixt hath lost
All that, which *Henry* the Fift had gotten:
Me thinkes these Peeres of France should smile at that.
But for the rest: you tell a Pedigree
Of threescore and two yeeres, a silly time
To make prescription for a Kingdomes worth.
Oxf. Why *Warwicke*, canst thou speak against thy Liege
Whom thou obeyd'st thirtie and six yeeres,
And not bewray thy Treason with a Blush?
Warw. Can *Oxford*, that did euer fence the right,
Now buckler Falsehood with a Pedigree?
For shame leaue *Henry*, and call *Edward* King.
Oxf. Call him my King, by whose iniurious doome
My elder Brother, the Lord *Aubrey Vere*
Was done to death? and more then so, my Father,
Euen in the downe-fall of his mellow'd yeeres,
When Nature brought him to the doore of Death?
No *Warwicke*, no: while Life vpholds this Arme,
This Arme vpholds the House of *Lancaster*.
Warw. And I the House of *Yorke*.
Lewis. Queene *Margaret*, Prince *Edward*, and *Oxford*,
Vouchsafe at our request, to stand aside,
While I vse further conference with *Warwicke*.
They stand aloofe.
Marg. Heauens graunt, that *Warwickes* wordes bewitch him not.
Lew. Now *Warwicke*, tell me euen vpon thy conscience
Is *Edward* your true King? for I were loth
To linke with him, that were not lawfull chosen.
Warw. Thereon I pawne my Credit, and mine Honor.
Lewis. But is hee gracious in the Peoples eye?
Warw. The more, that *Henry* was vnfortunate.
Lewis. Then further: all dissembling set aside,
Tell me for truth, the measure of his Loue
Vnto our Sister *Bona*.
War. Such it seemes,
As may beseeme a Monarch like himselfe.
My selfe haue often heard him say, and sweare,
That this his Loue was an externall Plant,
Whereof the Root was fixt in Vertues ground,
The Leaues and Fruit maintain'd with Beauties Sunne,
Exempt from Enuy, but not from Disdaine,
Vnlesse the Lady *Bona* quit his paine.
Lewis. Now Sister, let vs heare your firme resolue.
Bona. Your graunt, or your denyall, shall be mine.
Yet I confesse, that often ere this day, *Speaks to War.*
When I haue heard your Kings desert recounted,
Mine eare hath tempted iudgement to desire.
Lewis. Then *Warwicke*, thus:
Our Sister shall be *Edwards*.
And now forthwith shall Articles be drawne,
Touching the Ioynture that your King must make,
Which with her Dowrie shall be counter-poys'd:
Draw neere, Queene *Margaret*, and be a witnesse,
That *Bona* shall be Wife to the English King.
Pr. Edw. To *Edward*, but not to the English King.
Marg. Deceitfull *Warwicke*, it was thy deuice,
By this alliance to make void my suit:
Before thy comming, *Lewis* was *Henries* friend.
Lewis. And still is friend to him, and *Margaret*.
But if your Title to the Crowne be weake,
As may appeare by *Edwards* good successe:
Then 'tis but reason, that I be releas'd
From giuing ayde, which late I promised.
Yet shall you haue all kindnesse at my hand,
That your Estate requires, and mine can yeeld.
Warw. *Henry* now liues in Scotland, at his ease;
When

Where hauing nothing, nothing can he lose.
And as for you your selfe (our quondam Queene)
You haue a Father able to maintaine you,
And better 'twere, you troubled him, then France.
Mar. Peace impudent, and shamelesse Warwicke,
Proud setter vp, and puller downe of Kings,
I will not hence, till with my Talke and Teares
(Both full of Truth) I make King *Lewis* behold
Thy slye conueyance, and thy Lords false loue,
Post blowing a horne Within.
For both of you are Birds of selfe-same Feather.
Lewes. Warwicke, this is some poste to vs, or thee.
Enter the Poste.
Post. My Lord Ambassador,
These Letters are for you. *Speakes to Warwick,*
Sent from your Brother Marquesse *Montague.*
These from our King, vnto your Maiesty. *To Lewis.*
And Madam, these for you: *To Margaret*
From whom, I know not.
They all reade their Letters.
Oxf. I like it well, that our faire Queene and Mistris
Smiles at her newes, while *Warwicke* frownes at his.
Prince Ed. Nay marke how *Lewis* stampes as he were netled. I hope, all's for the best.
Lew. Warwicke, what are thy Newes?
And yours, faire Queene.
Mar. Mine such, as fill my heart with vnhop'd ioyes.
War. Mine full of sorrow, and hearts discontent.
Lew. What? has your King married the Lady *Grey*?
And now to sooth your Forgery, and his,
Sends me a Paper to perswade me Patience?
Is this th'Alliance that he seekes with France?
Dare he presume to scorne vs in this manner?
Mar. I told your Maiesty as much before:
This proueth *Edwards* Loue, and Warwickes honesty.
War. King *Lewis*, I heere protest in sight of heauen,
And by the hope I haue of heauenly blisse,
That I am cleere from this misdeed of *Edwards*;
No more my King, for he dishonors me,
But most himselfe, if he could see his shame.
Did I forget, that by the House of Yorke
My Father came vntimely to his death?
Did I let passe th'abuse done to my Neece?
Did I impale him with the Regall Crowne?
Did I put *Henry* from his Natiue Right?
And am I guerdon'd at the last, with Shame?
Shame on himselfe, for my Desert is Honor.
And to repaire my Honor lost for him,
I heere renounce him, and returne to *Henry.*
My Noble Queene, let former grudges passe,
And henceforth, I am thy true Seruitour:
I will reuenge his wrong to Lady *Bona,*
And replant *Henry* in his former state.
Mar. Warwicke,
These words haue turn'd my Hate, to Loue,
And I forgiue, and quite forget old faults,
And ioy that thou becom'st King *Henries* Friend.
War. So much his Friend, I, his vnfained Friend,
That if King *Lewis* vouchsafe to furnish vs
With some few Bands of chosen Soldiours,
Ile vndertake to Land them on our Coast,
And force the Tyrant from his seat by Warre.
Tis not his new-made Bride shall succour him.
And as for *Clarence*, as my Letters tell me,
Hee's very likely now to fall from him,
For matching more for wanton Lust, then Honor,
Or then for strength and safety of our Country.
Bona. Deere Brother, how shall *Bona* be reueng'd,
But by thy helpe to this distressed Queene?
Mar. Renowned Prince, how shall Poore *Henry* liue,
Vnlesse thou rescue him from foule dispaire?
Bona. My quarrel, and this English Queens, are one.
War. And mine faire Lady *Bona*, ioynes with yours.
Lew. And mine, with hers, and thine, and *Margarets.*
Therefore, at last, I firmely am resolu'd
You shall haue ayde.
Mar. Let me giue humble thankes for all, at once.
Lew. Then Englands Messenger, returne in Poste,
And tell false *Edward*, thy supposed King,
That *Lewis* of France, is sending ouer Maskers
To reuell it with him, and his new Bride.
Thou seest what's past, go feare thy King withall.
Bona. Tell him, in hope hee'l proue a widower shortly
I weare the Willow Garland for his sake.
Mar. Tell him, my mourning weeds are layde aside,
And I am ready to put Armor on.
War. Tell him from me, that he hath done me wrong,
And therefore Ile vn-Crowne him, er't be long.
There's thy reward, be gone. *Exit Post.*
Lew. But Warwicke,
Thou and Oxford, with fiue thousand men
Shall crosse the Seas, and bid false *Edward* battaile:
And as occasion serues, this Noble Queen
And Prince, shall follow with a fresh Supply.
Yet ere thou go, but answer me one doubt:
What Pledge haue we of thy firme Loyalty?
War. This shall assure my constant Loyalty,
That if our Queene, and this young Prince agree,
Ile ioyne mine eldest daughter, and my Ioy,
To him forthwith, in holy Wedlocke bands.
Mar. Yes, I agree, and thanke you for your Motion.
Sonne *Edward*, she is Faire and Vertuous,
Therefore delay not, giue thy hand to Warwicke,
And with thy hand, thy faith irreuocable,
That onely Warwickes daughter shall be thine.
Prin. Ed. Yes, I accept her, for she well deserues it,
And heere to pledge my Vow, I giue my hand.
He giues his hand to Warw.
Lew. Why stay we now? These soldiers shalbe leuied,
And thou Lord Bourbon, our High Admirall
Shall waft them ouer with our Royall Fleete.
I long till *Edward* fall by Warres mischance,
For mocking Marriage with a Dame of France.
Exeunt. Manet Warwicke.
War. I came from *Edward* as Ambassador,
But I returne his sworne and mortall Foe:
Matter of Marriage was the charge he gaue me,
But dreadfull Warre shall answer his demand.
Had he none else to make a stale but me?
Then none but I, shall turne his Iest to Sorrow.
I was the Cheefe that rais'd him to the Crowne,
And Ile be Cheefe to bring him downe againe:
Not that I pitty *Henries* misery,
But seeke Reuenge on *Edwards* mockery. *Exit.*

Enter Richard, Clarence, Somerset, and Mountague.

Rich. Now tell me Brother *Clarence*, what thinke you
Of this new Marriage with the Lady *Gray*?
Hath not our Brother made a worthy choice?
Cla. Alas, you know, tis farre from hence to France,
How

How could he ſtay till *Warwicke* made returne?
Som. My Lords,forbeare this talke: heere comes the King.

Flouriſh.

Enter King Edward,Lady Grey,Penbrooke,Stafford, Haſtings: foure ſtand on one ſide, and foure on the other.

Rich. And his well-choſen Bride.
Clarence. I minde to tell him plainly what I thinke.
King. Now Brother of Clarence,
How like you our Choyce,
That you ſtand penſiue,as halfe malecontent?
Clarence. As well as *Lewis* of France,
Or the Earle of Warwicke,
Which are ſo weake of courage,and in iudgement,
That they'le take no offence at our abuſe.
King. Suppoſe they take offence without a cauſe
They are but *Lewis* and *Warwicke*,I am *Edward*,
Your King and *Warwickes*, and muſt haue my will.
Rich. And ſhall haue your will, becauſe our King:
Yet haſtie Marriage ſeldome proueth well.
King. Yea,Brother *Richard*, are you offended too?
Rich. Not I: no:
God forbid,that I ſhould wiſh them ſeuer'd,
Whom God hath ioyn'd together:
I,and 'twere pittie, to ſunder them,
That yoake ſo well together.
King. Setting your ſkornes,and your miſlike aſide,
Tell me ſome reaſon,why the Lady *Grey*
Should not become my Wife,and Englands Queene?
And you too *Somerſet*,and *Mountague*,
Speake freely what you thinke.
Clarence. Then this is mine opinion:
That King *Lewis* become your Enemie,
For mocking him about the Marriage
Of the Lady *Bona*.
Rich. And *Warwicke*,doing what you gaue in charge,
Is now diſ-honored by this new Marriage.
King. What, if both *Lewis* and *Warwick* be appeas'd,
By ſuch inuention as I can deuiſe?
Mount. Yet,to haue ioyn'd with France in ſuch alliance,
Would more haue ſtrength'ned this our Commonwealth
'Gainſt forraine ſtormes,then any home-bred Marriage.
Haſt. Why,knowes not *Mountague*,that of it ſelfe,
England is ſafe,if true within it ſelfe?
Mount. But the ſafer, when 'tis back'd with France.
Haſt. 'Tis better vſing France,then truſting France:
Let vs be back'd with God,and with the Seas,
Which he hath giu'n for fence impregnable,
And with their helpes,onely defend our ſelues:
In them,and in our ſelues,our ſafetie lyes.
Clar. For this one ſpeech, Lord *Haſtings* well deſerues
To haue the Heire of the Lord *Hungerford*.
King. I,what of that? it was my will,and graunt,
And for this once,my Will ſhall ſtand for Law.
Rich. And yet me thinks,your Grace hath not done well,
To giue the Heire and Daughter of Lord *Scales*
Vnto the Brother of your louing Bride;
Shee better would haue fitted me,or *Clarence*:
But in your Bride you burie Brotherhood.
Clar. Or elſe you would not haue beſtow'd the Heire
Of the Lord *Bonuill* on your new Wiues Sonne,
And leaue your Brothers to goe ſpeede elſewhere.
King. Alas poore *Clarence*: is it for a Wife
That thou art malecontent? I will prouide thee.
Clarence. In chuſing for your ſelfe,
You ſhew'd your iudgement:
Which being ſhallow, you ſhall giue me leaue
To play the Broker in mine owne behalfe;
And to that end,I ſhortly minde to leaue you.
King. Leaue me,or tarry, *Edward* will be King,
And not be ty'd vnto his Brothers will.
Lady Grey. My Lords, before it pleas'd his Maieſtie
To rayſe my State to Title of a Queene,
Doe me but right,and you muſt all confeſſe,
That I was not ignoble of Deſcent,
And meaner then my ſelfe haue had like fortune.
But as this Title honors me and mine,
So your diſlikes,to whom I would be pleaſing,
Doth cloud my ioyes with danger, and with ſorrow.
King. My Loue,forbeare to fawne vpon their frownes
What danger,or what ſorrow can befall thee,
So long as *Edward* is thy conſtant friend,
And their true Soueraigne,whom they muſt obey?
Nay,whom they ſhall obey,and loue thee too,
Vnleſſe they ſeeke for hatred at my hands:
Which if they doe,yet will I keepe thee ſafe,
And they ſhall feele the vengeance of my wrath.
Rich. I heare, yet ſay not much,but thinke the more.

Enter a Poſte.

King. Now Meſſenger,what Letters,or what Newes from France?
Poſt. My Soueraigne Liege,no Letters,& few words,
But ſuch,as I (without your ſpeciall pardon)
Dare not relate.
King. Goe too,wee pardon thee:
Therefore,in briefe,tell me their words,
As neere as thou canſt gueſſe them.
What anſwer makes King *Lewis* vnto our Letters?
Poſt. At my depart,theſe were his very words:
Goe tell falſe *Edward*,the ſuppoſed King,
That *Lewis* of France is ſending ouer Maskers,
To reuell it with him,and his new Bride.
King. Is *Lewis* ſo braue? belike he thinkes me *Henry*.
But what ſaid Lady *Bona* to my Marriage?
Poſt. Theſe were her words,vtt'red with mild diſdaine
Tell him,in hope hee'le proue a Widower ſhortly,
Ile weare the Willow Garland for his ſake.
King. I blame not her; ſhe could ſay little leſſe:
She had the wrong. But what ſaid *Henries* Queene?
For I haue heard,that ſhe was there in place.
Poſt. Tell him(quoth ſhe)
My mourning Weedes are done,
And I am readie to put Armour on.
King. Belike ſhe minds to play the Amazon.
But what ſaid *Warwicke* to theſe iniuries?
Poſt. He,more incens'd againſt your Maieſtie,
Then all the reſt,diſcharg'd me with theſe words:
Tell him from me,that he hath done me wrong,
And therefore Ile vncrowne him,er't be long.
King. Ha? durſt the Traytor breath out ſo prowd words?
Well,I will arme me,being thus fore-warn'd:
They ſhall haue Warres,and pay for their preſumption.
But ſay,is *Warwicke* friends with *Margaret*?
Poſt. I, gracious Soueraigne,
They are ſo link'd in friendſhip,
That yong Prince *Edward* marryes *Warwicks* Daughter.
Clarence. Belike,the elder;
Clarence will haue the younger.

Now

Now Brother King farewell, and sit you fast,
For I will hence to Warwickes other Daughter,
That though I want a Kingdome, yet in Marriage
I may not proue inferior to your selfe.
You that loue me, and Warwicke, follow me.
Exit Clarence, and Somerset followes.
Rich. Not I:
My thoughts ayme at a further matter:
I stay not for the loue of Edward, but the Crowne.
King. Clarence and Somerset both gone to Warwicke?
Yet am I arm'd against the worst can happen:
And haste is needfull in this desp'rate case.
Pembrooke and Stafford, you in our behalfe
Goe leuie men, and make prepare for Warre;
They are alreadie, or quickly will be landed:
My selfe in person will straight follow you.
Exeunt Pembrooke and Stafford.
But ere I goe, Hastings and Mountague
Resolue my doubt: you twaine, of all the rest,
Are neere to Warwicke, by bloud, and by allyance:
Tell me, if you loue Warwicke more then me;
If it be so, then both depart to him:
I rather wish you foes, then hollow friends.
But if you minde to hold your true obedience,
Giue me assurance with some friendly Vow,
That I may neuer haue you in suspect.
Mount. So God helpe Mountague, as hee proues true.
Hast. And Hastings, as hee fauours Edwards cause.
King. Now, Brother Richard, will you stand by vs?
Rich. I, in despight of all that shall withstand you.
King. Why so: then am I sure of Victorie.
Now therefore let vs hence, and lose no howre,
Till wee meet Warwicke, with his forreine powre.
Exeunt.

Enter Warwicke and Oxford in England, with French Souldiors.

Warw. Trust me, my Lord, all hitherto goes well,
The common people by numbers swarme to vs.
Enter Clarence and Somerset.
But see where Somerset and Clarence comes:
Speake suddenly, my Lords, are wee all friends?
Clar. Feare not that, my Lord.
Warw. Then gentle Clarence, welcome vnto Warwicke,
And welcome Somerset: I hold it cowardize,
To rest mistrustfull, where a Noble Heart
Hath pawn'd an open Hand, in signe of Loue;
Else might I thinke, that Clarence, Edwards Brother,
Were but a fained friend to our proceedings:
But welcome sweet Clarence, my Daughter shall be thine.
And now, what rests? but in Nights Couerture,
Thy Brother being carelessely encamp'd,
His Souldiors lurking in the Towne about,
And but attended by a simple Guard,
Wee may surprize and take him at our pleasure,
Our Scouts haue found the aduenture very easie:
That as Vlysses, and stout Diomede,
With sleight and manhood stole to Rhesus Tents,
And brought from thence the Thracian fatall Steeds;
So wee, well couer'd with the Nights black Mantle,
At vnawares may beat downe Edwards Guard,
And seize himselfe: I say not, slaughter him,
For I intend but onely to surprize him.
You that will follow me to this attempt
Applaud the Name of Henry, with your Leader.
They all cry, Henry.
Why then, let's on our way in silent sort,
For Warwicke and his friends, God and Saint George.
Exeunt.

Enter three Watchmen to guard the Kings Tent.

1. Watch. Come on my Masters, each man take his stand:
The King by this, is set him downe to sleepe.
2. Watch. What, will he not to Bed?
1. Watch. Why, no: for he hath made a solemne Vow
Neuer to lye and take his naturall Rest,
Till Warwicke, or himselfe, be quite supprest.
2. Watch. To morrow then belike shall be the day,
If Warwicke be so neere as men report.
3. Watch. But say, I pray, what Noble man is that,
That with the King here resteth in his Tent?
1. Watch. 'Tis the Lord Hastings, the Kings chiefest friend.
3. Watch. O, is it so? but why commands the King,
That his chiefe followers lodge in Townes about him,
While he himselfe keepes in the cold field?
2. Watch. 'Tis the more honour, because more dangerous.
3. Watch. I, but giue me worship, and quietnesse,
I like it better then a dangerous honor.
If Warwicke knew in what estate he stands,
'Tis to be doubted he would waken him.
1. Watch. Vnlesse our Halberds did shut vp his passage.
2. Watch. I: wherefore else guard we his Royall Tent,
But to defend his Person from Night-foes?

Enter Warwicke, Clarence, Oxford, Somerset, and French Souldiors, silent all.

Warw. This is his Tent, and see where stand his Guard:
Courage my Masters: Honor now, or neuer:
But follow me, and Edward shall be ours.
1. Watch. Who goes there?
2. Watch. Stay, or thou dyest.
Warwicke and the rest cry all, Warwicke, Warwicke, and set vpon the Guard, who flye, crying, Arme, Arme, Warwicke and the rest following them.

The Drumme playing, and Trumpet sounding. Enter Warwicke, Somerset, and the rest, bringing the King out in his Gowne, sitting in a Chaire: Richard and Hastings flyes ouer the Stage.

Som. What are they that flye there?
Warw. Richard and Hastings: let them goe, heere is the Duke.
K. Edw. The Duke?
Why Warwicke, when wee parted,
Thou call'dst me King.
Warw. I, but the case is alter'd.
When you disgrac'd me in my Embassade,
Then I degraded you from being King,
And come now to create you Duke of Yorke.
Alas, how should you gouerne any Kingdome,
That know not how to vse Embassadors,
Nor how to be contented with one Wife,
Nor how to vse your Brothers Brotherly,
Nor how to studie for the Peoples Welfare,
Nor how to shrowd your selfe from Enemies?
K. Edw. Yea,

K. Edw. Yea, Brother of Clarence,
Art thou here too?
Nay then I ſee, that *Edward* needs muſt downe.
Yet *Warwicke*, in deſpight of all miſchance,
Of thee thy ſelfe, and all thy Complices,
Edward will alwayes beare himſelfe as King:
Though Fortunes mallice ouerthrow my State,
My minde exceedes the compaſſe of her Wheele.
Warw. Then for his minde, be *Edward* Englands King.

Takes off his Crowne.

But *Henry* now ſhall weare the Engliſh Crowne,
And be true King indeede: thou but the ſhadow.
My Lord of Somerſet, at my requeſt,
See that forthwith Duke *Edward* be conuey'd
Vnto my Brother Arch-Biſhop of Yorke:
When I haue fought with *Pembrooke*, and his fellowes,
Ile follow you, and tell what anſwer
Lewis and the Lady *Bona* ſend to him.
Now for a-while farewell good Duke of Yorke.

They leade him out forcibly.

K.Ed. What Fates impoſe, that men muſt needs abide;
It boots not to reſiſt both winde and tide. *Exeunt.*
Oxf. What now remaines my Lords for vs to do,
But march to London with our Soldiers?
War. I, that's the firſt thing that we haue to do,
To free King *Henry* from impriſonment,
And ſee him ſeated in the Regall Throne. *exit.*

Enter Riuers, and Lady Gray.

Riu. Madam, what makes you in this ſodain change?
Gray. Why Brother *Riuers*, are you yet to learne
What late miſfortune is befalne King *Edward*?
Riu. What loſſe of ſome pitcht battell
Againſt *Warwicke*?
Gray. No, but the loſſe of his owne Royall perſon.
Riu. Then is my Soueraigne ſlaine?
Gray. I almoſt ſlaine, for he is taken priſoner,
Either betrayd by falſhood of his Guard,
Or by his Foe ſurpriz'd at vnawares:
And as I further haue to vnderſtand,
Is new committed to the Biſhop of Yorke,
Fell Warwickes Brother, and by that our Foe.
Riu. Theſe Newes I muſt confeſſe are full of greefe,
Yet gracious Madam, beare it as you may,
Warwicke may looſe, that now hath wonne the day.
Gray. Till then, faire hope muſt hinder liues decay:
And I the rather waine me from diſpaire
For loue of *Edwards* Off-ſpring in my wombe:
This is it that makes me bridle paſſion,
And beare with Mildneſſe my misfortunes croſſe:
I, I, for this I draw in many a teare,
And ſtop the riſing of blood-ſucking ſighes,
Leaſt with my ſighes or teares, I blaſt or drowne
King *Edwards* Fruite, true heyre to th'Engliſh Crowne.
Riu. But Madam,
Where is Warwicke then become?
Gray. I am inform'd that he comes towards London
To ſet the Crowne once more on *Henries* head,
Gueſſe thou the reſt, King *Edwards* Friends muſt downe.
But to preuent the Tyrants violence,
(For truſt not him that hath once broken Faith)
Ile hence forthwith vnto the Sanctuary,
To ſaue (at leaſt) the heire of *Edwards* right:
There ſhall I reſt ſecure from force and fraud:
Come therefore let vs flye, while we may flye,
If Warwicke take vs, we are ſure to dye. *exeunt.*

Enter Richard, Lord Haſtings, and Sir William Stanley.

Rich. Now my Lord *Haſtings*, and Sir *William Stanley*
Leaue off to wonder why I drew you hither,
Into this cheefeſt Thicket of the Parke.
Thus ſtand the caſe: you know our King, my Brother,
Is priſoner to the Biſhop here, at whoſe hands
He hath good vſage, and great liberty,
And often but attended with weake guard,
Come hunting this way to diſport himſelfe.
I haue aduertis'd him by ſecret meanes,
That if about this houre he make this way,
Vnder the colour of his vſuall game,
He ſhall heere finde his Friends with Horſe and Men,
To ſet him free from his Captiuitie.

Enter King Edward, and a Huntſman with him.

Huntſman. This way my Lord,
For this way lies the Game.
King Edw. Nay this way man,
See where the Huntſmen ſtand.
Now Brother of Gloſter, Lord Haſtings, and the reſt,
Stand you thus cloſe to ſteale the Biſhops Deere?
Rich. Brother, the time and caſe, requireth haſt,
Your horſe ſtands ready at the Parke-corner.
King Ed. But whether ſhall we then?
Haſt. To Lyn my Lord,
And ſhipt from thence to Flanders.
Rich. Wel gueſt beleeue me, for that was my meaning
K.Ed. *Stanley*, I will requite thy forwardneſſe.
Rich. But wherefore ſtay we? 'tis no time to talke.
K.Ed. Huntſman, what ſay'ſt thou?
Wilt thou go along?
Hunts. Better do ſo, then tarry and be hang'd.
Rich. Come then away, lets ha no more adoo.
K.Ed. Biſhop farwell,
Sheeld thee from *Warwickes* frowne,
And pray that I may re-poſſeſſe the Crowne. *exeunt*

Florriſh. Enter King Henry the ſixt, Clarence, Warwicke, Somerſet, young Henry, Oxford, Mountague, and Lieutenant.

K.Hen. M. Lieutenant, now that God and Friends
Haue ſhaken *Edward* from the Regall ſeate,
And turn'd my captiue ſtate to libertie,
My feare to hope, my ſorrowes vnto ioyes,
At our enlargement what are thy due Fees?
Lieu. Subiects may challenge nothing of their Sou'raigns
But, if an humble prayer may preuaile,
I then craue pardon of your Maieſtie.
K.Hen. For what, Lieutenant? For well vſing me?
Nay, be thou ſure, Ile well requite thy kindneſſe.
For that it made my impriſonment, a pleaſure:
I, ſuch a pleaſure, as incaged Birds
Conceiue; when after many moody Thoughts,
At laſt, by Notes of Houſhold harmonie,
They quite forget their loſſe of Libertie.

But *Warwicke*, after God, thou ſet'ſt me free.
And chiefely therefore, I thanke God, and thee,
He was the Author, thou the Inſtrument.
Therefore that I may conquer Fortunes ſpight,
By liuing low, where Fortune cannot hurt me,
And that the people of this bleſſed Land
May not be puniſht with my thwarting ſtarres.
Warwicke, although my Head ſtill weare the Crowne,
I here reſigne my Gouernment to thee,
For thou art fortunate in all thy deeds.

Warw. Your Grace hath ſtill beene fam'd for vertuous,
And now may ſeeme as wiſe as vertuous,
By ſpying and auoiding Fortunes malice,
For few men rightly temper with the Starres:
Yet in this one thing let me blame your Grace,
For chuſing me, when *Clarence* is in place.

Clar. No *Warwicke*, thou art worthy of the ſway,
To whom the Heau'ns in thy Natiuitie,
Adiudg'd an Oliue Branch, and Lawrell Crowne,
As likely to be bleſt in Peace and Warre:
And therefore I yeeld thee my free conſent.

Warw. And I chuſe *Clarence* onely for Protector.

King. Warwick and *Clarence*, giue me both your Hands:
Now ioyne your Hands, & with your Hands your Hearts,
That no diſſention hinder Gouernment:
I make you both Protectors of this Land,
While I my ſelfe will lead a priuate Life,
And in deuotion ſpend my latter dayes,
To ſinnes rebuke, and my Creators prayſe.

Warw. What anſweres *Clarence* to his Soueraignes will?

Clar. That he conſents, if *Warwicke* yeeld conſent,
For on thy fortune I repoſe my ſelfe.

Warw Why then, though loth, yet muſt I be content:
Wee'le yoake together, like a double ſhadow
To *Henries* Body, and ſupply his place;
I meane, in bearing weight of Gouernment,
While he enioyes the Honor, and his eaſe.
And *Clarence*, now then it is more then needfull,
Forthwith that *Edward* be pronounc'd a Traytor,
And all his Lands and Goods confiſcate.

Clar. What elſe? and that Succeſſion be determined

Warw. I, therein *Clarence* ſhall not want his part.

King But with the firſt, of all your chiefe affaires,
Let me entreat (for I command no more)
That *Margaret* your Queene, and my Sonne *Edward*,
Be ſent for, to returne from France with ſpeed:
For till I ſee them here, by doubtfull feare,
My ioy of libertie is halfe eclips'd.

Clar. It ſhall bee done, my Soueraigne, with all ſpeede.

King My Lord of Somerſet, what Youth is that,
Of whom you ſeeme to haue ſo tender care?

Somerſ. My Liege, it is young *Henry*, Earle of Richmond.

King. Come hither, Englands Hope:

Layes his Hand on his Head.

If ſecret Powers ſuggeſt but truth
To my diuining thoughts,
This prettie Lad will proue our Countries bliſſe.
His Lookes are full of peacefull Maieſtie,
His Head by nature fram'd to weare a Crowne,
His Hand to wield a Scepter, and himſelfe
Likely in time to bleſſe a Regall Throne:
Make much of him, my Lords; for this is hee
Muſt helpe you more, then you are hurt by mee.

Enter a Poſte.

Warw. What newes, my friend?

Poſte. That *Edward* is eſcaped from your Brother,
And fled (as hee heares ſince) to Burgundie.

Warw. Vnſauorie newes: but how made he eſcape?

Poſte. He was conuey'd by *Richard*, Duke of Gloſter,
And the Lord *Haſtings*, who attended him
In ſecret ambuſh, on the Forreſt ſide,
And from the Biſhops Huntſmen reſcu'd him:
For Hunting was his dayly Exerciſe.

Warw. My Brother was too careleſſe of his charge.
But let vs hence, my Soueraigne, to prouide
A ſalue for any ſore, that may betide. *Exeunt.*

Manet Somerſet, Richmond, and Oxford.

Som. My Lord, I like not of this flight of *Edwards*:
For doubtleſſe, *Burgundie* will yeeld him helpe,
And we ſhall haue more Warres befor't be long.
As *Henries* late preſaging Prophecie
Did glad my heart, with hope of this young *Richmond*:
So doth my heart miſ-giue me, in theſe Conflicts,
What may befall him, to his harme and ours.
Therefore, Lord *Oxford*, to preuent the worſt,
Forthwith wee'le ſend him hence to Brittanie,
Till ſtormes be paſt of Ciuill Enmitie.

Oxf. I: for if *Edward* re-poſſeſſe the Crowne,
'Tis like that *Richmond*, with the reſt, ſhall downe.

Som. It ſhall be ſo: he ſhall to Brittanie.
Come therefore, let's about it ſpeedily. *Exeunt.*

Flouriſh. Enter Edward, Richard, Haſtings, and Souldiers.

Edw. Now Brother *Richard*, Lord *Haſtings*, and the reſt,
Yet thus farre Fortune maketh vs amends,
And ſayes, that once more I ſhall enterchange
My wained ſtate, for *Henries* Regall Crowne.
Well haue we paſ'd, and now re-paſ'd the Seas,
And brought deſired helpe from Burgundie.
What then remaines, we being thus arriu'd
From Rauenſpurre Hauen, before the Gates of Yorke,
But that we enter, as into our Dukedome?

Rich. The Gates made faſt?
Brother, I like not this.
For many men that ſtumble at the Threſhold,
Are well fore-told, that danger lurkes within.

Edw. Tuſh man, aboadments muſt not now affright vs:
By faire or foule meanes we muſt enter in,
For hither will our friends repaire to vs.

Haſt. My Liege, Ile knocke once more, to ſummon them.

Enter on the Walls, the Maior of Yorke, and his Brethren.

Maior. My Lords,
We were fore-warned of your comming,
And ſhut the Gates, for ſafetie of our ſelues;
For now we owe allegeance vnto *Henry*.

Edw. But, Maſter Maior, if *Henry* be your King,
Yet *Edward*, at the leaſt, is Duke of Yorke.

Maior. True, my good Lord, I know you for no leſſe.

Edw. Why, and I challenge nothing but my Dukedome,
As being well content with that alone.

Rich. But

Rich. But when the Fox hath once got in his Nose,
Hee'le soone finde meanes to make the Body follow.
Hast. Why, Master Maior, why stand you in a doubt?
Open the Gates, we are King *Henries* friends.
Maior. I, say you so? the Gates shall then be opened.
He descends.
Rich. A wise stout Captaine, and soone perswaded.
Hast. The good old man would faine that all were wel,
So 'twere not long of him: but being entred,
I doubt not I, but we shall soone perswade
Both him, and all his Brothers, vnto reason.

Enter the Maior, and two Aldermen.

Edw. So, Master Maior: these Gates must not be shut,
But in the Night, or in the time of Warre.
What, feare not man, but yeeld me vp the Keyes,
Takes his Keyes.
For *Edward* will defend the Towne, and thee,
And all those friends, that deine to follow mee.

March. Enter Mountgomerie, with Drumme and Souldiers.

Rich. Brother, this is Sir *Iohn Mo ntgomerie,*
Our trustie friend, vnlesse I be deceiu'd.
Edw. Welcome Sir *Iohn*: but why come you in Armes?
Mount. To helpe King *Edward* in his time of storme,
As euery loyall Subiect ought to doe.
Edw. Thankes good *Mountgomerie*:
But we now forget our Title to the Crowne,
And onely clayme our Dukedome,
Till God please to send the rest.
Mount. Then fare you well, for I will hence againe,
I came to serue a King, and not a Duke:
Drumme strike vp, and let vs march away.
The Drumme begins to march.
Edw. Nay stay, Sir *Iohn*, a while, and wee'le debate
By what safe meanes the Crowne may be recouer'd.
Mount. What talke you of debating? in few words,
If you'le not here proclaime your selfe our King,
Ile leaue you to your fortune, and be gone,
To keepe them back, that come to succour you.
Why shall we fight, if you pretend no Title?
Rich. Why Brother, wherefore stand you on nice points?
Edw. When wee grow stronger,
Then wee'le make our Clayme:
Till then, 'tis wisdome to conceale our meaning.
Hast. Away with scrupulous Wit, now Armes must rule.
Rich. And fearelesse minds clyme soonest vnto Crowns.
Brother, we will proclaime you out of hand,
The bruit thereof will bring you many friends.
Edw. Then be it as you will: for 'tis my right,
And *Henry* but vsurpes the Diademe.
Mount. I, now my Soueraigne speaketh like himselfe,
And now will I be *Edwards* Champion.
Hast. Sound Trumpet, *Edward* shal be here proclaim'd:
Come, fellow Souldior, make thou proclamation.
Flourish. Sound.
Soul. Edward *the Fourth, by the Grace of God, King of England and France, and Lord of Ireland, &c.*
Mount. And whosoe're gainsayes King *Edwards* right,
By this I challenge him to single fight.
Throwes downe his Gauntlet.
All. Long liue *Edward* the Fourth.
Edw. Thankes braue *Mountgomery*,
And thankes vnto you all:
If fortune serue me, Ile requite this kindnesse.
Now for this Night, let's harbor here in Yorke:
And when the Morning Sunne shall rayse his Carre
Aboue the Border of this Horizon,
Wee'le forward towards *Warwicke*, and his Mates;
For well I wot, that *Henry* is no Souldier.
Ah froward *Clarence*, how euill it beseemes thee,
To flatter *Henry*, and forsake thy Brother?
Yet as wee may, wee'le meet both thee and *Warwicke*.
Come on braue Souldiors: doubt not of the Day,
And that once gotten, doubt not of large Pay. *Exeunt.*

Flourish. Enter the King, Warwicke, Mountague, Clarence, Oxford, and Somerset.

War. What counsaile, Lords? *Edward* from Belgia,
With hastie Germanes, and blunt Hollanders,
Hath pass'd in safetie through the Narrow Seas,
And with his troupes doth march amaine to London,
And many giddie people flock to him.
King. Let's leuie men, and beat him backe againe.
Clar. A little fire is quickly trodden out,
Which being suffer'd, Riuers cannot quench.
War. In Warwickshire I haue true-hearted friends,
Not mutinous in peace, yet bold in Warre,
Those will I muster vp: and thou Sonne *Clarence*
Shalt stirre vp in Suffolke, Norfolke, and in Kent,
The Knights and Gentlemen, to come with thee.
Thou Brother *Mountague*, in Buckingham,
Northampton, and in Leicestershire, shalt find
Men well enclin'd to heare what thou command'st.
And thou, braue *Oxford*, wondrous well belou'd,
In Oxfordshire shalt muster vp thy friends.
My Soueraigne, with the louing Citizens,
Like to his Iland, gyrt in with the Ocean,
Or modest *Dyan*, circled with her Nymphs,
Shall rest in London, till we come to him:
Faire Lords take leaue, and stand not to reply.
Farewell my Soueraigne.
King. Farewell my *Hector*, and my Troyes true hope.
Clar. In signe of truth, I kisse your Highnesse Hand.
King. Well-minded *Clarence*, be thou fortunate.
Mount. Comfort, my Lord, and so I take my leaue.
Oxf. And thus I seale my truth, and bid adieu.
King. Sweet *Oxford*, and my louing *Mountague*,
And all at once, once more a happy farewell.
War. Farewell, sweet Lords, let's meet at Couentry.
Exeunt.
King. Here at the Pallace will I rest a while.
Cousin of *Exeter*, what thinkes your Lordship?
Me thinkes, the Power that *Edward* hath in field,
Should not be able to encounter mine.
Exet. The doubt is, that he will seduce the rest.
King. That's not my feare, my meed hath got me fame:
I haue not stopt mine eares to their demands,
Nor posted off their suites with slow delayes,
My pittie hath beene balme to heale their wounds,
My mildnesse hath allay'd their swelling griefes,
My mercie dry'd their water-flowing teares.
I haue not been desirous of their wealth,
Nor much opprest them with great Subsidies,
Nor forward of reuenge, though they much err'd.
Then why should they loue *Edward* more then me?
No *Exeter*, these Graces challenge Grace:

q 3 And

And when the Lyon fawnes vpon the Lambe,
The Lambe will neuer ceaſe to follow him.
Shout within, A Lancaſter, A Lancaſter.
Exet. Hearke, hearke, my Lord, what Shouts are theſe?

Enter Edward and his Souldiers.

Edw. Seize on the ſhamefac'd *Henry*, beare him hence,
And once againe proclaime vs King of England.
You are the Fount that makes ſmall Brookes to flow,
Now ſtops thy Spring, my Sea ſhall ſuck them dry,
And ſwell ſo much the higher, by their ebbe.
Hence with him to the Tower, let him not ſpeake.
Exit with King Henry.
And Lords, towards Couentry bend we our courſe,
Where peremptorie *Warwicke* now remaines:
The Sunne ſhines hot, and if we vſe delay,
Cold biting Winter marres our hop'd-for Hay.
Rich. Away betimes, before his forces ioyne,
And take the great-growne Traytor vnawares:
Braue Warriors, march amaine towards Couentry.
Exeunt.

Enter Warwicke, the Maior of Couentry, two Meſſengers, and others vpon the Walls.

War. Where is the Poſt that came from valiant *Oxford*?
How farre hence is thy Lord, mine honeſt fellow?
Meſſ.1. By this at Dunſmore, marching hitherward.
War. How farre off is our Brother *Mountague*?
Where is the Poſt that came from *Mountague*?
Meſſ.2. By this at Daintry, with a puiſſant troope.
Enter Someruile.
War. Say *Somerule*, what ſayes my louing Sonne?
And by thy gueſſe, how nigh is *Clarence* now?
Someru. At Southam I did leaue him with his forces,
And doe expect him here ſome two howres hence.
War. Then *Clarence* is at hand, I heare his Drumme.
Someru. It is not his, my Lord, here Southam lyes:
The Drum your Honor heares, marcheth from *Warwicke*.
War. Who ſhould that be? belike vnlook'd for friends
Someru. They are at hand, and you ſhall quickly know.

March. Flouriſh. Enter Edward, Richard, and Souldiers.

Edw. Goe, Trumpet, to the Walls, and ſound a Parle.
Rich. See how the ſurly *Warwicke* mans the Wall.
War. Oh vnbid ſpight, is ſportfull *Edward* come?
Where ſlept our Scouts, or how are they ſeduc'd,
That we could heare no newes of his repayre.
Edw. Now *Warwicke*, wilt thou ope the Citie Gates,
Speake gentle words, and humbly bend thy Knee,
Call *Edward* King, and at his hands begge Mercy,
And he ſhall pardon thee theſe Outrages?
War. Nay rather, wilt thou draw thy forces hence,
Confeſſe who ſet thee vp, and pluckt thee downe,
Call *Warwicke* Patron, and be penitent,
And thou ſhalt ſtill remaine the Duke of Yorke.
Rich. I thought at leaſt he would haue ſaid the King,
Or did he make the Ieaſt againſt his will?
War. Is not a Dukedome, Sir, a goodly gift?
Rich. I, by my faith, for a poore Earle to giue,
Ile doe thee ſeruice for ſo good a gift.
War. 'Twas I that gaue the Kingdome to thy Brother.
Edw. Why then 'tis mine, if but by *Warwickes* gift.
War. Thou art no *Atlas* for ſo great a weight:
And Weakeling, *Warwicke* takes his gift againe,
And *Henry* is my King, *Warwicke* his Subiect.
Edw. But *Warwickes* King is *Edwards* Priſoner:
And gallant *Warwicke*, doe but anſwer this,
What is the Body, when the Head is off?
Rich. Alas, that *Warwicke* had no more fore-caſt,
But whiles he thought to ſteale the ſingle Ten,
The King was ſlyly finger'd from the Deck:
You left poore *Henry* at the Biſhops Pallace,
And tenne to one you'le meet him in the Tower.
Edw. 'Tis euen ſo, yet you are *Warwicke* ſtill.
Rich. Come *Warwicke*,
Take the time, kneele downe, kneele downe:
Nay when? ſtrike now, or elſe the Iron cooles.
War. I had rather chop this Hand off at a blow,
And with the other, fling it at thy face,
Then beare ſo low a ſayle, to ſtrike to thee.
Edw. Sayle how thou canſt,
Haue Winde and Tyde thy friend,
This Hand, faſt wound about thy coale-black hayre,
Shall, whiles thy Head is warme, and new cut off,
Write in the duſt this Sentence with thy blood,
Wind-changing *Warwicke* now can change no more.

Enter Oxford, with Drumme and Colours.

War. Oh chearefull Colours, ſee where *Oxford* comes.
Oxf. *Oxford, Oxford*, for *Lancaſter*.
Rich. The Gates are open, let vs enter too.
Edw. So other foes may ſet vpon our backs.
Stand we in good array: for they no doubt
Will iſſue out againe, and bid vs battaile;
If not, the Citie being but of ſmall defence,
Wee'le quickly rowze the Traitors in the ſame.
War. Oh welcome *Oxford*, for we want thy helpe.

Enter Mountague, with Drumme and Colours.

Mount. *Mountague, Mountague*, for *Lancaſter*.
Rich. Thou and thy Brother both ſhall buy this Treaſon
Euen with the deareſt blood your bodies beare.
Edw. The harder matcht, the greater Victorie,
My minde preſageth happy gaine, and Conqueſt.

Enter Somerſet, with Drumme and Colours.

Som. *Somerſet, Somerſet*, fot *Lancaſter*.
Rich. Two of thy Name, both Dukes of Somerſet,
Haue ſold their Liues vnto the Houſe of *Yorke*,
And thou ſhalt be the third, if this Sword hold.

Enter Clarence, with Drumme and Colours.

War. And loe, where George of Clarence ſweepes along,
Of force enough to bid his Brother Battaile:
With whom, in vpright zeale to right, preuailes
More then the nature of a Brothers Loue.
Come *Clarence*, come: thou wilt, if *Warwicke* call.
Clar. Father of Warwick, know you what this meanes?
Looke here, I throw my infamie at thee:
I will not ruinate my Fathers Houſe,
Who gaue his blood to lyme the ſtones together,
And ſet vp *Lancaſter*. Why, troweſt thou, *Warwicke*,
That *Clarence* is ſo harſh, ſo blunt, vnnaturall,
To bend the fatall Inſtruments of Warre
Againſt

Against his Brother, and his lawfull King.
Perhaps thou wilt obiect my holy Oath:
To keepe that Oath, were more impietie,
Then *Iephah*, when he sacrific'd his Daughter.
I am so sorry for my Trespas made,
That to deserue well at my Brothers hands,
I here proclayme my selfe thy mortall foe:
With resolution, wheresoe're I meet thee,
(As I will meet thee, if thou stirre abroad)
To plague thee, for thy foule mis-leading me.
And so, prowd-hearted *Warwicke*, I defie thee,
And to my Brother turne my blushing Cheekes.
Pardon me *Edward*, I will make amends:
And *Richard*, doe not frowne vpon my faults,
For I will henceforth be no more vnconstant.

Edw. Now welcome more, and ten times more belou'd,
Then if thou neuer hadst deseru'd our hate.

Rich. Welcome good *Clarence*, this is Brother-like.

Warw. Oh passing Traytor, periur d and vniust.

Edw. What *Warwicke*,
Wilt thou leaue the Towne, and fight?
Or shall we beat the Stones about thine Eares?

Warw. Alas, I am not coop d here for defence:
I will away towards Barnet presently,
And bid thee Battaile, *Edward*, if thou dar'st.

Edw. Yes *Warwicke*, *Edward* dares, and leads the way:
Lords to the field: Saint *George*, and Victorie. *Exeunt.*

March. Warwicke and his companie followes.

Alarum, and Excursions. Enter Edward bringing forth Warwicke wounded.

Edw. So, lye thou there: dye thou, and dye our feare,
For *Warwicke* was a Bugge that fear'd vs all.
Now *Mountague* sit fast, I seeke for thee,
That *Warwickes* Bones may keepe thine companie.
Exit.

Warw. Ah, who is nigh? come to me, friend, or foe,
And tell me who is Victor, *Yorke*, or *Warwicke*?
Why aske I that? my mangled body shewes,
My blood, my want of strength, my sicke heart shewes,
That I must yeeld my body to the Earth,
And by my fall, the conquest to my foe.
Thus yeelds the Cedar to the Axes edge,
Whose Armes gaue shelter to the Princely Eagle,
Vnder whose shade the ramping Lyon slept,
Whose top-branch ouer-peer'd *Ioues* spreading Tree,
And kept low Shrubs from Winters pow'rfull Winde.
These Eyes, that now are dim'd with Deaths black Veyle,
Haue beene as piercing as the Mid-day Sunne,
To search the secret Treasons of the World:
The Wrinckles in my Browes, now fill'd with blood,
Were lik'ned oft to Kingly Sepulchers:
For who liu'd King, but I could digge his Graue?
And who durst smile, when *Warwicke* bent his Brow?
Loe, now my Glory smear'd in dust and blood.
My Parkes, my Walkes, my Mannors that I had,
Euen now forsake me; and of all my Lands,
Is nothing left me, but my bodies length.
Why, what is Pompe, Rule, Reigne, but Earth and Dust?
And liue we how we can, yet dye we must.

Enter Oxford and Somerset.

Som Ah *Warwicke*, *Warwicke*, wert thou as we are,
We might recouer all our Losse againe:
The Queene from France hath brought a puissant power.
Euen now we heard the newes: ah, could'st thou flye.

Warw. Why then I would not flye. Ah *Mountague*,
If thou be there, sweet Brother, take my Hand,
And with thy Lippes keepe in my Soule a while.
Thou lou'st me not: for, Brother, if thou didst,
Thy teares would wash this cold congealed blood,
That glewes my Lippes, and will not let me speake.
Come quickly *Mountague*, or I am dead.

Som. Ah *Warwicke*, *Mountague* hath breath'd his last,
And to the latest gaspe, cry'd out for *Warwicke*:
And said, Commend me to my valiant Brother.
And more he would haue said, and more he spoke,
Which sounded like a Cannon in a Vault,
That mought not be distinguisht: but at last
I well might heare, deliuered with a groane,
Oh farewell *Warwicke*.

Warw. Sweet rest his Soule:
Flye Lords, and saue your selues,
For *Warwicke* bids you all farewell, to meet in Heauen.

Oxf. Away, away, to meet the Queenes great power.
Here they beare away his Body. Exeunt.

Flourish. Enter King Edward in triumph, with Richard, Clarence, and the rest.

King. Thus farre our fortune keepes an vpward course,
And we are grac'd with wreaths of Victorie:
But in the midst of this bright-shining Day,
I spy a black suspicious threatning Cloud,
That will encounter with our glorious Sunne,
Ere he attaine his easefull Westerne Bed:
I meane, my Lords, those powers that the Queene
Hath rays'd in Gallia, haue arriued our Coast,
And, as we heare, march on to fight with vs.

Clar. A little gale will soone disperse that Cloud,
And blow it to the Source from whence it came,
Thy very Beames will dry those Vapours vp,
For euery Cloud engenders not a Storme.

Rich. The Queene is valued thirtie thousand strong,
And *Somerset*, with *Oxford*, fled to her:
If she haue time to breathe, be well assur'd
Her faction will be full as strong as ours.

King. We are aduertis'd by our louing friends,
That they doe hold their course toward Tewksbury.
We hauing now the best at Barnet field,
Will thither straight, for willingnesse rids way,
And as we march, our strength will be augmented:
In euery Countie as we goe along,
Strike vp the Drumme, cry courage, and away. *Exeunt.*

Flourish. March. Enter the Queene, young Edward, Somerset, Oxford, and Souldiers.

Qu. Great Lords, wise men ne'r sit and waile their losse,
But chearely seeke how to redresse their harmes.
What though the Mast be now blowne ouer-boord,
The Cable broke, the holding-Anchor lost,
And halfe our Saylors swallow'd in the flood?
Yet liues our Pilot still. Is't meet, that hee
Should leaue the Helme, and like a fearefull Lad,
With tearefull Eyes adde Water to the Sea,
And giue more strength to that which hath too much,
Whiles in his moane, the Ship splits on the Rock,
Which Industrie and Courage might haue sau'd?
Ah what a shame, ah what a fault were this.
Say *Warwicke* was our Anchor: what of that?

And *Mountague* our Top-Mast: what of him?
Our slaught'red friends, the Tackles: what of these?
Why is not *Oxford* here, another Anchor?
And *Somerset*, another goodly Mast?
The friends of France our Shrowds and Tacklings?
And though vnskilfull, why not *Ned* and I,
For once allow'd the skilfull Pilots Charge?
We will not from the Helme, to sit and weepe,
But keepe our Course (though the rough Winde say no)
From Shelues and Rocks, that threaten vs with Wrack.
As good to chide the Waues, as speake them faire.
And what is *Edward*, but a ruthlesse Sea?
What *Clarence*, but a Quick-sand of Deceit?
And *Richard*, but a raged fatall Rocke?
All these, the Enemies to our poore Barke.
Say you can swim, alas 'tis but a while:
Tread on the Sand, why there you quickly sinke,
Bestride the Rock, the Tyde will wash you off,
Or else you famish, that's a three-fold Death.
This speake I (Lords) to let you vnderstand,
If case some one of you would flye from vs,
That there's no hop'd-for Mercy with the Brothers,
More then with ruthlesse Waues, with Sands and Rocks.
Why courage then, what cannot be auoided,
'Twere childish weakenesse to lament, or feare.

Prince. Me thinkes a Woman of this valiant Spirit,
Should, if a Coward heard her speake these words,
Infuse his Breast with Magnanimitie,
And make him, naked, foyle a man at Armes.
I speake not this, as doubting any here:
For did I but suspect a fearefull man,
He should haue leaue to goe away betimes,
Least in our need he might infect another,
And make him of like spirit to himselfe.
If any such be here, as God forbid,
Let him depart, before we neede his helpe.

Oxf. Women and Children of so high a courage,
And Warriors faint, why 'twere perpetuall shame.
Oh braue young Prince: thy famous Grandfather
Doth liue againe in thee; long may'st thou liue,
To beare his Image, and renew his Glories.

Som. And he that will not fight for such a hope,
Goe home to Bed, and like the Owle by day,
If he arise, be mock'd and wondred at.

Qu. Thankes gentle *Somerset*, sweet *Oxford* thankes.

Prince. And take his thankes, that yet hath nothing else.

Enter a Messenger.

Mess. Prepare you Lords, for *Edward* is at hand,
Readie to fight: therefore be resolute.

Oxf. I thought no lesse: it is his Policie,
To haste thus fast, to finde vs vnprouided.

Som. But hee's deceiu'd, we are in readinesse.

Qu. This cheares my heart, to see your forwardnesse.

Oxf. Here pitch our Battaile, hence we will not budge.

Flourish, and march. Enter Edward, Richard, Clarence, and Souldiers.

Edw. Braue followers, yonder stands the thornie Wood,
Which by the Heauens assistance, and your strength,
Must by the Roots be hew'ne vp yet ere Night.
I need not adde more fuell to your fire,
For well I wot, ye blaze, to burne them out:
Giue signall to the fight, and to it Lords.

Qu. Lords, Knights, and Gentlemen, what I should say,
My teares gaine-say: for euery word I speake,
Ye see I drinke the water of my eye.
Therefore no more but this: *Henry* your Soueraigne
Is Prisoner to the Foe, his State vsurp'd,
His Realme a slaughter-house, his Subiects slaine,
His Statutes cancell'd, and his Treasure spent:
And yonder is the Wolfe, that makes this spoyle.
You fight in Iustice: then in Gods Name, Lords,
Be valiant, and giue signall to the fight.

Alarum, Retreat, Excursions. Exeunt.

Flourish. Enter Edward, Richard, Queene, Clarence, Oxford, Somerset.

Edw. Now here a period of tumultuous Broyles.
Away with *Oxford* to Hames Castle straight:
For *Somerset*, off with his guiltie Head.
Goe beare them hence, I will not heare them speake.

Oxf. For my part, Ile not trouble thee with words.

Som. Nor I, but stoupe with patience to my fortune.

Exeunt.

Qu. So part we sadly in this troublous World,
To meet with Ioy in sweet Ierusalem.

Edw. Is Proclamation made, That who finds *Edward*,
Shall haue a high Reward, and he his Life?

Rich. It is, and loe where youthfull *Edward* comes.

Enter the Prince.

Edw. Bring forth the Gallant, let vs heare him speake.
What? can so young a Thorne begin to prick?
Edward, what satisfaction canst thou make,
For bearing Armes, for stirring vp my Subiects,
And all the trouble thou hast turn'd me to?

Prince. Speake like a Subiect, prowd ambitious *Yorke*.
Suppose that I am now my Fathers Mouth,
Resigne thy Chayre, and where I stand, kneele thou,
Whil'st I propose the selfe-same words to thee,
Which (Traytor) thou would'st haue me answer to.

Qu. Ah, that thy Father had beene so resolu'd.

Rich. That you might still haue worne the Petticoat,
And ne're haue stolne the Breech from *Lancaster*.

Prince. Let *Æsop* fable in a Winters Night,
His Currish Riddles sorts not with this place.

Rich. By Heauen, Brat, Ile plague ye for that word.

Qu. I, thou wast borne to be a plague to men.

Rich. For Gods sake, take away this Captiue Scold.

Prince. Nay, take away this scolding Crooke-backe, rather.

Edw. Peace wilfull Boy, or I will charme your tongue.

Clar. Vntutor'd Lad, thou art too malapert.

Prince. I know my dutie, you are all vndutifull:
Lasciuious *Edward*, and thou periur'd *George*,
And thou mis-shapen *Dicke*, I tell ye all,
I am your better, Traytors as ye are,
And thou vsurp'st my Fathers right and mine.

Edw. Take that, the likenesse of this Rayler here.

Stabs him.

Rich. Sprawl'st thou? take that, to end thy agonie.

Rich. stabs him.

Clar. And ther's for twitting me with periurie.

Clar. stabs him.

Qu. Oh, kill me too.

Rich. Marry, and shall. *Offers to kill her.*

Edw. Hold, *Richard*, hold, for we haue done too much.

Rich. Why

Rich. Why ſhould ſhee liue, to fill the World with words.
Edw. What? doth ſhee ſwowne? vſe meanes for her recouerie.
Rich. *Clarence* excuſe me to the King my Brother:
Ile hence to London on a ſerious matter,
Ere ye come there, be ſure to heare ſome newes.
Cla. What? what?
Rich Tower, the Tower. *Exit.*
Qu. Oh *Ned*, ſweet *Ned*, ſpeake to thy Mother Boy.
Can'ſt thou not ſpeake? O Traitors, Murtherers!
They that ſtabb'd *Cæſar*, ſhed no blood at all:
Did not offend, nor were not worthy Blame,
If this foule deed were by, to equall it.
He was a Man; this (in reſpect) a Childe,
And Men, ne're ſpend their fury on a Childe.
What's worſe then Murtherer, that I may name it?
No, no, my heart will burſt, and if I ſpeake,
And I will ſpeake, that ſo my heart may burſt.
Butchers and Villaines, bloudy Caniballes,
How ſweet a Plant haue you vntimely cropt:
You haue no children (Butchers) if you had,
The thought of them would haue ſtirr'd vp remorſe,
But if you euer chance to haue a Childe,
Looke in his youth to haue him ſo cut off
As deathſmen you haue rid this ſweet yong Prince.
King. Away with her, go beare her hence perforce.
Qu. Nay, neuer beare me hence, diſpatch me heere:
Here ſheath thy Sword, Ile pardon thee my death:
What? wilt thou not? Then *Clarence* do it thou.
Cla. By heauen, I will not do thee ſo much eaſe.
Qu. Good *Clarence* do: ſweet *Clarence* do thou do it.
Cla. Did'ſt thou not heare me ſweare I would not do it?
Qu. I, but thou vſeſt to forſweare thy ſelfe.
'Twas Sin before, but now 'tis Charity.
What wilt ÿ not? Where is that diuels butcher *Richard*?
Hard fauor'd *Richard*? *Richard*, where art thou?
Thou art not heere; Murther is thy Almeſ-deed:
Petitioners for Blood, thou ne're put'ſt backe.
Ed. Away I ſay, I charge ye beare her hence.
Qu. So come to you, and yours, as to this Prince.
Exit Queene
Ed. Where's *Richard* gone.
Cla. To London all in poſt, and as I gueſſe,
To make a bloody Supper in the Tower.
Ed. He's ſodaine if a thing comes in his head.
Now march we hence, diſcharge the common ſort
With Pay and Thankes, and let's away to London,
And ſee our gentle Queene how well ſhe fares,
By this (I hope) ſhe hath a Sonne for me. *Exit.*

Enter Henry the ſixt, and Richard, with the Lieutenant on the Walles.

Rich. Good day, my Lord, what at your Booke ſo hard?
Hen. I my good Lord: my Lord I ſhould ſay rather,
Tis ſinne to flatter, Good was little better:
'Good Gloſter, and good Deuill, were alike,
And both prepoſterous: therefore, not Good Lord.
Rich. Sirra, leaue vs to our ſelues, we muſt conferre.
Hen. So flies the wreakleſſe ſhepherd from ÿ Wolfe:
So firſt the harmleſſe Sheepe doth yeeld his Fleece,
And next his Throate, vnto the Butchers Knife.
What Scene of death hath *Roſcius* now to Acte?
Rich. Suſpition alwayes haunts the guilty minde,
The Theefe doth feare each buſh an Officer,
Hen. The Bird that hath bin limed in a buſh,
With trembling wings miſdoubteth euery buſh;
And I the hapleſſe Male to one ſweet Bird,
Haue now the fatall Obiect in my eye,
Where my poore yong was lim'd, was caught, and kill'd.
Rich. Why what a peeuiſh Foole was that of Creet,
That taught his Sonne the office of a Fowle,
And yet for all his wings, the Foole was drown'd.
Hen. I *Dedalus*, my poore Boy *Icarus*,
Thy Father *Minos*, that deni'de our courſe,
The Sunne that ſear'd the wings of my ſweet Boy.
Thy Brother *Edward*, and thy Selfe, the Sea
Whoſe enuious Gulfe did ſwallow vp his life:
Ah, kill me with thy Weapon, not with words,
My breſt can better brooke thy Daggers point,
Then can my eares that Tragicke Hiſtory.
But wherefore doſt thou come? Is't for my Life?
Rich. Think'ſt thou I am an Executioner?
Hen. A Perſecutor I am ſure thou art,
If murthering Innocents be Executing,
Why then thou art an Executioner.
Rich Thy Son I kill'd for his preſumption.
Hen. Hadſt thou bin kill'd, when firſt ÿ didſt preſume,
Thou had'ſt not liu'd to kill a Sonne of mine:
And thus I propheſie, that many a thouſand,
Which now miſtruſt no parcell of my feare,
And many an old mans ſighe, and many a Widdowes,
And many an Orphans water-ſtanding-eye,
Men for their Sonnes, Wiues for their Husbands,
Orphans, for their Parents timeles death,
Shall rue the houre that euer thou was't borne.
The Owle ſhriek'd at thy birth, an euill ſigne,
The Night-Crow cry'de, aboding luckleſſe time,
Dogs howl'd, and hiddeous Tempeſt ſhook down Trees:
The Rauen rook'd her on the Chimnies top,
And chatt'ring Pies in diſmall Diſcords ſung:
Thy Mother felt more then a Mothers paine,
And yet brought forth leſſe then a Mothers hope,
To wit, an indigeſted and deformed lumpe,
Not like the fruit of ſuch a goodly Tree.
Teeth had'ſt thou in thy head, when thou was't borne,
To ſignifie, thou cam'ſt to bite the world:
And if the reſt be true, which I haue heard,
Thou cam'ſt——
Rich. Ile heare no more:
Dye Prophet in thy ſpeech, *Stabbes him.*
For this (among'ſt the reſt) was I ordain'd.
Hen. I, and for much more ſlaughter after this.
O God forgiue my ſinnes, and pardon thee. *Dyes.*
Rich. What? will the aſpiring blood of Lancaſter
Sinke in the ground? I thought it would haue mounted.
See how my ſword weepes for the poore Kings death.
O may ſuch purple teares be alway ſhed
From thoſe that wiſh the downfall of our houſe.
If any ſparke of Life be yet remaining,
Downe, downe to hell, and ſay I ſent thee thither.
Stabs him againe.
I that haue neyther pitty, loue, nor feare,
Indeed 'tis true that *Henrie* told me of:
For I haue often heard my Mother ſay,
I came into the world with my Legges forward.
Had I not reaſon (thinke ye) to make haſt,
And ſeeke their Ruine, that vſurp'd our Right?
The Midwife wonder'd, and the Women cri'de
O Ieſus bleſſe vs, he is borne with teeth,
And

And so I was, which plainly signified,
That I should snarle, and bite, and play the dogge:
Then since the Heauens haue shap'd my Body so,
Let Hell make crook'd my Minde to answer it.
I haue no Brother, I am like no Brother:
And this word [Loue] which Gray-beards call Diuine,
Be resident in men like one another,
And not in me: I am my selfe alone.
Clarence beware, thou keept'st me from the Light,
But I will sort a pitchy day for thee:
For I will buzze abroad such Prophesies,
That *Edward* shall be fearefull of his life,
And then to purge his feare, Ile be thy death.
King *Henry*, and the Prince his Son are gone,
Clarence thy turne is next, and then the rest,
Counting my selfe but bad, till I be best.
Ile throw thy body in another roome,
And Triumph *Henry*, in thy day of Doome. *Exit*

Flourish. Enter King, Queene, Clarence, Richard, Hastings, Nurse, and Attendants.

King. Once more we sit in Englands Royall Throne,
Re-purchac'd with the Blood of Enemies:
What valiant Foe-men, like to Autumnes Corne,
Haue we mow'd downe in tops of all their pride?
Three Dukes of Somerset, threefold Renowne,
For hardy and vndoubted Champions:
Two *Cliffords*, as the Father and the Sonne,
And two Northumberlands: two brauer men,
Ne're spurr'd their Coursers at the Trumpets sound.
With them, the two braue Beares, *Warwick* & *Montague*,
That in their Chaines fetter'd the Kingly Lyon,
And made the Forrest tremble when they roar'd.
Thus haue we swept Suspicion from our Seate,
And made our Footstoole of Security.
Come hither *Besse*, and let me kisse my Boy:
Kong *Ned*, for thee, thine Vnckles, and my selfe,
Haue in our Armors watcht the Winters night,
Went all afoote in Summers scalding heate,
That thou might'st repossesse the Crowne in peace,
And of our Labours thou shalt reape the gaine.
Rich. Ile blast his Haruest, if your head were laid,
For yet I am not look'd on in the world.
This shoulder was ordain'd so thicke, to heaue,
And heaue it shall some waight, or breake my backe,
Worke thou the way, add that shalt execute.
King. *Clarence* and *Gloster*, loue my louely Queene,
And 'tis your Princely Nephew Brothers both.
Cla. The duty that I owe vnto your Maiesty,
I Seale vpon the lips of this sweet Babe.
Cla. Thanke Noble *Clarence*, worthy brother thanks.
Rich. And that I loue the tree frō whence ẏ sprang'st:
Witnesse the louing kisse I giue the Fruite,
To say the truth, so *Iudas* kist his master,
And cried all haile, when as he meant all harme.
King. Now am I seated as my soule delights,
Hauing my Countries peace, and Brothers loues.
Cla. What will your Grace haue done with *Margaret*,
Reynard her Father, to the King of France
Hath pawn'd the Sicils and Ierusalem,
And hither haue they sent it for her ransome.
King. Away with her, and waft her hence to France:
And now what rests, but that we spend the time
With stately Triumphes, mirthfull Comicke shewes,
Such as befits the pleasure of the Court.
Sound Drums and Trumpets, farwell sowre annoy,
For heere I hope begins our lasting ioy. *Exeunt omnes*

FINIS.

The Tragedy of Richard the Third: with the Landing of Earle Richmond, and the Battell at Bosworth Field.

Actus Primus. Scœna Prima.

Enter Richard Duke of Gloster, solus.

NOw is the Winter of our Discontent,
Made glorious Summer by this Son of Yorke:
And all the clouds that lowr'd vpon our house
In the deepe bosome of the Ocean buried.
Now are our browes bound with Victorious Wreathes,
Our bruised armes hung vp for Monuments;
Our sterne Alarums chang'd to merry Meetings;
Our dreadfull Marches, to delightfull Measures.
Grim-visag'd Warre, hath smooth'd his wrinkled Front:
And now, in stead of mounting Barbed Steeds,
To fright the Soules of fearfull Aduersaries,
He capers nimbly in a Ladies Chamber,
To the lasciuious pleasing of a Lute.
But I, that am not shap'd for sportiue trickes,
Nor made to court an amorous Looking-glasse:
I, that am Rudely stampt, and want loues Maiesty,
To strut before a wonton ambling Nymph:
I, that am curtail'd of this faire Proportion,
Cheated of Feature by dissembling Nature,
Deform'd, vn-finish'd, sent before my time
Into this breathing World, scarse halfe made vp,
And that so lamely and vnfashionable,
That dogges barke at me, as I halt by them.
Why I (in this weake piping time of Peace)
Haue no delight to passe away the time,
Vnlesse to see my Shadow in the Sunne,
And descant on mine owne Deformity.
And therefore, since I cannot proue a Louer,
To entertaine these faire well spoken dayes,
I am determined to proue a Villaine,
And hate the idle pleasures of these dayes.
Plots haue I laide, Inductions dangerous,
By drunken Prophesies, Libels, and Dreames,
To set my Brother *Clarence* and the King
In deadly hate, the one against the other:
And if King *Edward* be as true and iust,
As I am Subtle, False, and Treacherous,
This day should *Clarence* closely be mew'd vp:
About a Prophesie, which sayes that G,
Of *Edwards* heyres the murtherer shall be.
Diue thoughts downe to my soule, here *Clarence* comes.

Enter Clarence and Brakenbury, guarded.

Brother, good day: What meanes this armed guard
That waites vpon your Grace?
Cla. His Maiesty tendring my persons safety,
Hath appointed this Conduct, to conuey me to th'Tower
Rich. Vpon what cause?
Cla. Because my name is *George*.
Rich. Alacke my Lord, that fault is none of yours:
He should for that commit your Godfathers.
O belike, his Maiesty hath some intent,
That you should be new Christned in the Tower.
But what's the matter *Clarence*, may I know?
Cla. Yea *Richard*, when I know: but I protest
As yet I do not: But as I can learne,
He hearkens after Prophesies and Dreames,
And from the Crosse-row pluckes the letter G:
And sayes, a Wizard told him, that by G,
His issue disinherited should be.
And for my name of *George* begins with G,
It followes in his thought, that I am he.
These (as I learne) and such like toyes as these,
Hath moou'd his Highnesse to commit me now.
Rich. Why this it is, when men are rul'd by Women
'Tis not the King that sends you to the Tower,
My Lady *Grey* his Wife, *Clarence* 'tis shee,
That tempts him to this harsh Extremity.
Was it not shee, and that good man of Worship,
Anthony Woodeuille her Brother there,
That made him send Lord *Hastings* to the Tower?
From whence this present day he is deliuered?
We are not safe *Clarence*, we are not safe.
Cla. By heauen, I thinke there is no man secure
But the Queenes Kindred, and night-walking Heralds,
That trudge betwixt the King, and Mistris *Shore*.
Heard you not what an humble Suppliant
Lord *Hastings* was, for her deliuery?
Rich. Humbly complaining to her Deitie,
Got my Lord Chamberlaine his libertie
Ile tell you what, I thinke it is our way,
If we will keepe in fauour with the King,
To be her men, and weare her Liuery.
The iealous ore-worne Widdow, and her selfe,
Since that our Brother dub'd them Gentlewomen,
Are mighty Gossips in our Monarchy.
Bra I beseech your Graces both to pardon me,
His Maiesty hath straightly giuen in charge,
That no man shall haue priuate Conference
(Of what degree soeuer) with your Brother.

Rich

Rich. Euen so, and please your Worship *Brakenbury*,
You may partake of any thing we say:
We speake no Treason man; We say the King
Is wise and vertuous, and his Noble Queene
Well strooke in yeares, faire, and not iealious.
We say, that *Shores* Wife hath a pretty Foot,
A cherry Lip, a bonny Eye, a passing pleasing tongue:
And that the Queenes Kindred are made gentle Folkes.
How say you sir? can you deny all this?

Bra. With this (my Lord) my selfe haue nought to doo.

Rich. Naught to do with Mistris *Shore*?
I tell thee Fellow, he that doth naught with her
(Excepting one) were best to do it secretly alone.

Bra. What one, my Lord?

Rich. Her Husband Knaue, would'st thou betray me?

Bra. I do beseech your Grace
To pardon me, and withall forbeare
Your Conferenee with the Noble Duke.

Cla. We know thy charge *Brakenbury*, and wil obey.

Rich. We are the Queenes abiects, and must obey.
Brother farewell, I will vnto the King,
And whatsoe're you will imploy me in,
Were it to call King *Edwards* Widdow, Sister,
I will performe it to infranchise you.
Meane time, this deepe disgrace in Brotherhood,
Touches me deeper then you can imagine.

Cla. I know it pleaseth neither of vs well.

Rich. Well, your imprisonment shall not be long,
I will deliuer you, or else lye for you:
Meane time, haue patience.

Cla. I must perforce: Farewell. *Exit Clar.*

Rich Go treade the path that thou shalt ne're return:
Simple plaine *Clarence*, I do loue thee so,
That I will shortly send thy Soule to Heauen,
If Heauen will take the present at our hands.
But who comes heere? the new deliuered *Hastings*?

Enter Lord Hastings.

Hast. Good time of day vnto my gracious Lord.

Rich. As much vnto my good Lord Chamberlaine:
Well are you welcome to this open Ayre,
How hath your Lordship brook'd imprisonment?

Hast. With patience (Noble Lord) as prisoners must:
But I shall liue (my Lord) to giue them thankes
That were the cause of my imprisonment.

Rich. No doubt, no doubt, and so shall *Clarence* too,
For they that were your Enemies, are his,
And haue preuail'd as much on him, as you,

Hast. More pitty, that the Eagles should be mew'd,
Whiles Kites and Buzards play at liberty.

Rich. What newes abroad?

Hast. No newes so bad abroad, as this at home:
The King is sickly, weake, and melancholly,
And his Physitians feare him mightily.

Rich. Now by S. Iohn, that Newes is bad indeed
O he hath kept an euill Diet long,
And ouer-much consum'd his Royall Person:
'Tis very greeuous to be thought vpon.
Where is he, in his bed?

Hast. He is.

Rich. Go you before, and I will follow you.
Exit Hastings.
He cannot liue I hope, and must not dye,
Till *George* be pack'd with post-horse vp to Heauen.
Ile in to vrge his hatred more to *Clarence*,
With Lyes well steel'd with weighty Arguments,
And if I faile not in my deepe intent,
Clarence hath not another day to liue:
Which done, God take King *Edward* to his mercy,
And leaue the world for me to bussle in.
For then, Ile marry Warwickes yongest daughter.
What though I kill'd her Husband, and her Father,
The readiest way to make the Wench amends,
Is to become her Husband, and her Father:
The which will I, not all so much for loue,
As for another secret close intent,
By marrying her, which I must reach vnto.
But yet I run before my horse to Market:
Clarence still breathes, *Edward* still liues and raignes,
When they are gone, then must I count my gaines. *Exit*

Scena Secunda.

Enter the Coarse of Henrie the sixt with Halberds to guard it, Lady Anne being the Mourner.

Anne. Set downe, set downe your honourable load,
If Honor may be shrowded in a Herse;
Whil'st I a-while obsequiously lament
Th'vntimely fall of Vertuous Lancaster.
Poore key-cold Figure of a holy King,
Pale Ashes of the House of Lancaster;
Thou bloodlesse Remnant of that Royall Blood,
Be it lawfull that I inuocate thy Ghost,
To heare the Lamentations of poore *Anne*,
Wife to thy *Edward*, to thy slaughtred Sonne,
Stab'd by the selfesame hand that made these wounds.
Loe, in these windowes that let forth thy life,
I powre the helplesse Balme of my poore eyes.
O cursed be the hand that made these holes:
Cursed the Heart, that had the heart to do it:
Cursed the Blood, that let this blood from hence:
More direfull hap betide that hated Wretch
That makes vs wretched by the death of thee,
Then I can wish to Wolues, to Spiders, Toades,
Or any creeping venom'd thing that liues.
If euer he haue Childe, Abortiue be it,
Prodigeous, and vntimely brought to light,
Whose vgly and vnnaturall Aspect
May fright the hopefull Mother at the view,
And that be Heyre to his vnhappinesse.
If euer he haue Wife, let her be made
More miserable by the death of him,
Then I am made by my young Lord, and thee.
Come now towards Chertsey with your holy Lode,
Taken from Paules, to be interred there.
And still as you are weary of this waight,
Rest you, whiles I lament King *Henries* Coarse.

Enter Richard Duke of Glouster

Rich. Stay you that beare the Coarse, & set it down.

An. What blacke Magitian coniures vp this Fiend,
To stop deuoted charitable deeds?

Rich. Villaines set downe the Coarse, or by S. Paul,
Ile make a Coarse of him that disobeyes.

Gen

Gen. My Lord ſtand backe, and let the Coffin paſſe.
Rich. Vnmanner'd Dogge,
Stand'ſt thou when I commaund:
Aduance thy Halbert higher then my breſt,
Or by S. Paul Ile ſtrike thee to my Foote,
And ſpurne vpon thee Begger for thy boldneſſe.
Anne. What do you tremble? are you all affraid?
Alas, I blame you not, for you are Mortall,
And Mortall eyes cannot endure the Diuell.
Auant thou dreadfull miniſter of Hell;
Thou had'ſt but power ouer his Mortall body,
His Soule thou canſt not haue: Therefore be gone.
Rich. Sweet Saint, for Charity, be not ſo curſt.
An. Foule Diuell,
For Gods ſake hence, and trouble vs not,
For thou haſt made the happy earth thy Hell:
Fill'd it with curſing cries, and deepe exclaimes:
If thou delight to view thy heynous deeds,
Behold this patterne of thy Butcheries.
Oh Gentlemen, ſee, ſee dead *Henries* wounds,
Open their congeal'd mouthes, and bleed afreſh.
Bluſh, bluſh, thou lumpe of fowle Deformitie:
For 'tis thy preſence that exhales this blood
From cold and empty Veines where no blood dwels.
Thy Deeds inhumane and vnnaturall,
Prouokes this Deluge moſt vnnaturall.
O God! which this Blood mad'ſt, reuenge his death:
O Earth! which this Blood drink'ſt, reuenge his death.
Either Heau'n with Lightning ſtrike the murth'rer dead:
Or Earth gape open wide, and eate him quicke,
As thou doſt ſwallow vp this good Kings blood,
Which his Hell-gouern'd arme hath butchered.
Rich. Lady, you know no Rules of Charity,
Which renders good for bad, Bleſſings for Curſes.
An. Villaine, thou know'ſt nor law of God nor Man,
No Beaſt ſo fierce, but knowes ſome touch of pitty.
Rich. But I know none, and therefore am no Beaſt.
An. O wonderfull, when diuels tell the truth!
Rich. More wonderfull, when Angels are ſo angry:
Vouchſafe (diuine perfection of a Woman)
Of theſe ſuppoſed Crimes, to giue me leaue
By circumſtance, but to acquit my ſelfe.
An. Vouchſafe (defus'd infection of man)
Of theſe knowne euils, but to giue me leaue
By circumſtance, to curſe thy curſed Selfe.
Rich. Fairer then tongue can name thee, let me haue
Some patient leyſure to excuſe my ſelfe.
An. Fouler then heart can thinke thee,
Thou can'ſt make no excuſe currant,
But to hang thy ſelfe.
Rich. By ſuch diſpaire, I ſhould accuſe my ſelfe.
An. And by diſpairing ſhalt thou ſtand excuſed,
For doing worthy Vengeance on thy ſelfe,
That did'ſt vnworthy ſlaughter vpon others.
Rich. Say that I ſlew them not.
An. Then ſay they were not ſlaine:
But dead they are, and diuelliſh ſlaue by thee.
Rich. I did not kill your Husband.
An. Why then he is aliue.
Rich. Nay, he is dead, and ſlaine by *Edwards* hands.
An. In thy foule throat thou Ly'ſt,
Queene *Margaret* ſaw
Thy murd'rous Faulchion ſmoaking in his blood:
The which, thou once didd'ſt bend againſt her breſt,
But that thy Brothers beate aſide the point.
Rich. I was prouoked by her ſland'rous tongue,
That laid their guilt, vpon my guiltleſſe Shoulders.
An. Thou was't prouoked by thy bloody minde,
That neuer dream'ſt on ought but Butcheries:
Did'ſt thou not kill this King?
Rich. I graunt ye.
An. Do'ſt grant me Hedge-hogge,
Then God graunt me too
Thou may'ſt be damned for that wicked deede,
O he was gentle, milde, and vertuous.
Rich. The better for the King of heauen that hath him.
An. He is in heauen, where thou ſhalt neuer come.
Rich. Let him thanke me, that holpe to ſend him thither:
For he was fitter for that place then earth.
An. And thou vnfit for any place, but hell.
Rich. Yes one place elſe, if you will heare me name it.
An. Some dungeon.
Rich. Your Bed-chamber.
An. Ill reſt betide the chamber where thou lyeſt.
Rich. So will it Madam, till I lye with you.
An. I hope ſo.
Rich. I know ſo. But gentle Lady *Anne*,
To leaue this keene encounter of our wittes,
And fall ſomething into a ſlower method.
Is not the cauſer of the timeleſſe deaths
Of theſe *Plantagenets*, *Henrie* and *Edward*,
As blamefull as the Executioner.
An. Thou was't the cauſe, and moſt accurſt effect.
Rich. Your beauty was the cauſe of that effect:
Your beauty, that did haunt me in my ſleepe,
To vndertake the death of all the world,
So I might liue one houre in your ſweet boſome.
An. If I thought that, I tell thee Homicide,
Theſe Nailes ſhould rent that beauty from my Cheekes.
Rich. Theſe eyes could not endure ẏ beauties wrack,
You ſhould not blemiſh it, if I ſtood by;
As all the world is cheared by the Sunne,
So I by that: It is my day, my life.
An. Blacke night ore-ſhade thy day, & death thy life.
Rich. Curſe not thy ſelfe faire Creature,
Thou art both.
An. I would I were, to be reueng'd on thee.
Rich. It is a quarrell moſt vnnaturall,
To be reueng'd on him that loueth thee.
An. It is a quarrell iuſt and reaſonable,
To be reueng'd on him that kill'd my Husband.
Rich. He that bereft the Lady of thy Husband,
Did it to helpe thee to a better Husband.
An. His better doth not breath vpon the earth.
Rich. He liues, that loues thee better then he could.
An. Name him.
Rich. *Plantagenet.*
An. Why that was he.
Rich. The ſelfeſame name, but one of better Nature.
An. Where is he?
Rich. Heere: *Spits at him.*
Why doſt thou ſpit at me.
An. Would it were mortall poyſon, for thy ſake.
Rich. Neuer came poyſon from ſo ſweet a place.
An. Neuer hung poyſon on a fowler Toade.
Out of my ſight, thou doſt infect mine eyes.
Rich. Thine eyes (ſweet Lady) haue infected mine.
An. Would they were Baſiliskes, to ſtrike thee dead.
Rich. I would they were, that I might dye at once:
For now they kill me with a liuing death.
Thoſe eyes of thine, from mine haue drawne ſalt Teares;
For

Sham'd their Aſpects with ſtore of childiſh drops:
Theſe eyes, which neuer ſhed remorſefull teare,
No, when my Father Yorke, and *Edward* wept,
To heare the pittious moane that Rutland made
When black-fac'd *Clifford* ſhooke his ſword at him.
Nor when thy warlike Father like a Childe,
Told the ſad ſtorie of my Fathers death,
And twenty times, made pauſe to ſob and weepe:
That all the ſtanders by had wet their cheekes
Like Trees bedaſh'd with raine. In that ſad time,
My manly eyes did ſcorne an humble teare:
And what theſe ſorrowes could not thence exhale,
Thy Beauty hath, and made them blinde with weeping.
I neuer ſued to Friend, nor Enemy:
My Tongue could neuer learne ſweet ſmoothing word.
But now thy Beauty is propos'd my Fee,
My proud heart ſues, and prompts my tongue to ſpeake.
She lookes ſcornfully at him.
Teach not thy lip ſuch Scorne; for it was made
For kiſſing Lady, not for ſuch contempt.
If thy reuengefull heart cannot forgiue,
Loe heere I lend thee this ſharpe-pointed Sword,
Which if thou pleaſe to hide in this true breſt,
And let the Soule forth that adoreth thee,
I lay it naked to the deadly ſtroke,
And humbly begge the death vpon my knee,
He layes his breſt open, ſhe offers at with his ſword.
Nay do not pauſe: For I did kill King *Henrie*,
But 'twas thy Beauty that prouoked me.
Nay now diſpatch: 'Twas I that ſtabb'd yong *Edward*,
But 'twas thy Heauenly face that ſet me on.
She fals the Sword.
Take vp the Sword againe, or take vp me.
An. Ariſe Diſſembler, though I wiſh thy death,
I will not be thy Executioner.
Rich. Then bid me kill my ſelfe, and I will do it.
An. I haue already.
Rich. That was in thy rage:
Speake it againe, and euen with the word,
This hand, which for thy loue, did kill thy Loue,
Shall for thy loue, kill a farre truer Loue,
To both their deaths ſhalt thou be acceſſary.
An. I would I knew thy heart.
Rich. 'Tis figur'd in my tongue.
An. I feare me, both are falſe.
Rich. Then neuer Man was true.
An. Well, well, put vp your Sword.
Rich. Say then my Peace is made.
An. That ſhalt thou know heereafter.
Rich. But ſhall I liue in hope.
An. All men I hope liue ſo.
Vouchſafe to weare this Ring.
Rich. Looke how my Ring incompaſſeth thy Finger,
Euen ſo thy Breſt incloſeth my poore heart:
Weare both of them, for both of them are thine.
And if thy poore deuoted Seruant may
But beg one fauour at thy gracious hand,
Thou doſt confirme his happineſſe for euer.
An. What is it?
Rich. That it may pleaſe you leaue theſe ſad deſignes,
To him that hath moſt cauſe to be a Mourner,
And preſently repayre to Crosbie Houſe:
Where (after I haue ſolemnly interr'd
At Chertſey Monaſt'ry this Noble King,
And wet his Graue with my Repentant Teares)
I will with all expedient duty ſee you,
For diuers vnknowne Reaſons, I beſeech you,
Grant me this Boon.
An. With all my heart, and much it ioyes me too,
To ſee you are become ſo penitent.
Treſſel and *Barkley*, go along with me.
Rich. Bid me farwell.
An. 'Tis more then you deſerue:
But ſince you teach me how to flatter you,
Imagine I haue ſaide farewell already.
Exit two with Anne.
Gent. Towards Chertſey, Noble Lord?
Rich. No: to White Friars, there attend my comming
Exit Coarſe
Was euer woman in this humour woo'd?
Was euer woman in this humour wonne?
Ile haue her, but I will not keepe her long.
What? I that kill'd her Husband, and his Father,
To take her in her hearts extreameſt hate,
With curſes in her mouth, Teares in her eyes,
The bleeding witneſſe of my hatred by,
Hauing God, her Conſcience, and theſe bars againſt me,
And I, no Friends to backe my ſuite withall,
But the plaine Diuell, and diſſembling lookes?
And yet to winne her? All the world to nothing.
Hah!
Hath ſhe forgot alreadie that braue Prince,
Edward, her Lord, whom I (ſome three monthes ſince)
Stab'd in my angry mood, at Tewkesbury?
A ſweeter, and a louelier Gentleman,
Fram'd in the prodigallity of Nature:
Yong, Valiant, Wiſe, and (no doubt) right Royal,
The ſpacious World cannot againe affoord:
And will ſhe yet abaſe her eyes on me,
That cropt the Golden prime of this ſweet Prince,
And made her Widdow to a wofull Bed?
On me, whoſe All not equals *Edwards* Moytie?
On me, that halts, and am miſhapen thus?
My Dukedome, to a Beggerly denier!
I do miſtake my perſon all this while:
Vpon my life ſhe findes (although I cannot)
My ſelfe to be a maru'llous proper man.
Ile be at Charges for a Looking-glaſſe,
And entertaine a ſcore or two of Taylors,
To ſtudy faſhions to adorne my body:
Since I am crept in fauour with my ſelfe,
I will maintaine it with ſome little coſt.
But firſt Ile turne yon Fellow in his Graue,
And then returne lamenting to my Loue.
Shine out faire Sunne, till I haue bought a glaſſe,
That I may ſee my Shadow as I paſſe. *exit.*

Scena Tertia.

Enter the Queene Mother, Lord Riuers, and Lord Gray.

Riu. Haue patience Madam, ther's no doubt his Maieſty
Will ſoone recouer his accuſtom'd health.
Gray. In that you brooke it ill, it makes him worſe,
Therefore for Gods ſake entertaine good comfort,
And cheere his Grace with quicke and merry eyes
Qu. If he were dead, what would betide on me?
Gray.

If he were dead, what would betide on me?
Gray. No other harme, but losse of such a Lord.
Qu. The losse of such a Lord, includes all harmes.
Gray. The Heauens haue blest you with a goodly Son,
To be your Comforter, when he is gone.
Qu. Ah! he is yong; and his minority
Is put vnto the trust of *Richard Glouster*,
A man that loues not me, nor none of you.
Riu. Is it concluded he shall be Protector?
Qu. It is determin'd, not concluded yet:
But so it must be, if the King miscarry.

Enter Buckingham and Derby.

Gray. Here comes the Lord of Buckingham & Derby.
Buc. Good time of day vnto your Royall Grace.
Der. God make your Maiesty ioyful, as you haue bin
Qu. The Countesse *Richmond*, good my L. of *Derby*.
To your good prayer, will scarsely say, Amen.
Yet *Derby*, notwithstanding shee's your wife,
And loues not me, be you good Lord assur'd,
I hate not you for her proud arrogance.
Der. I do beseech you, either not beleeue
The enuious slanders of her false Accusers:
Or if she be accus'd on true report,
Beare with her weaknesse, which I thinke proceeds
From wayward sicknesse, and no grounded malice.
Qu. Saw you the King to day my Lord of *Derby*.
Der. But now the Duke of Buckingham and I,
Are come from visiting his Maiesty.
Que. What likelyhood of his amendment Lords.
Buc. Madam good hope, his Grace speaks chearfully.
Qu. God grant him health, did you confer with him?
Buc. I Madam, he desires to make attonement
Betweene the Duke of Glouster, and your Brothers,
And betweene them, and my Lord Chamberlaine,
And sent to warne them to his Royall presence.
Qu. Would all were well, but that will neuer be,
I feare our happinesse is at the height.

Enter Richard.

Rich. They do me wrong and I will not indure it,
Who is it that complaines vnto the King,
That I (forsooth) am sterne, and loue them not?
By holy *Paul*, they loue his Grace but lightly,
That fill his eares with such dissentious Rumors.
Because I cannot flatter, and looke faire,
Smile in mens faces, smooth, deceiue, and cogge,
Ducke with French nods, and Apish curtesie,
I must be held a rancorous Enemy.
Cannot a plaine man liue, and thinke no harme,
But thus his simple truth must be abus'd,
With silken, slye, insinuating Iackes?
Grey. To who in all this presence speaks your Grace?
Rich. To thee, that hast not Honesty, nor Grace:
When haue I iniur'd thee? When done thee wrong?
Or thee? or thee? or any of your Faction?
A plague vpon you all. His Royall Grace
(Whom God preserue better then you would wish)
Cannot be quiet scarse a breathing while,
But you must trouble him with lewd complaints.
Qu. Brother of Glouster, you mistake the matter:
The King on his owne Royall disposition,
(And not prouok'd by any Sutor else)
Ayming (belike) at your interiour hatred,
That in your outward action shewes it selfe
Against my Children, Brothers, and my Selfe,
Makes him to send, that he may learne the ground.
Rich. I cannot tell, the world is growne so bad,
That Wrens make prey, where Eagles dare not pearch.
Since euerie Iacke became a Gentleman,
There's many a gentle person made a Iacke.
Qu. Come, come, we know your meaning Brother
You enuy my aduancement, and my friends: (Gloster
God grant we neuer may haue neede of you.
Rich. Meane time, God grants that I haue need of you.
Our Brother is imprison'd by your meanes,
My selfe disgrac'd, and the Nobilitie
Held in contempt, while great Promotions
Are daily giuen to ennoble those
That scarse some two dayes since were worth a Noble.
Qu. By him that rais'd me to this carefull height,
From that contented hap which I inioy'd,
I neuer did incense his Maiestie
Against the Duke of *Clarence*, but haue bin
An earnest aduocate to plead for him.
My Lord you do me shamefull iniurie,
Falsely to draw me in these vile suspects.
Rich. You may deny that you were not the meane
Of my Lord *Hastings* late imprisonment.
Riu. She may my Lord, for——
Rich. She may Lord *Riuers*, why who knowes not so?
She may do more sir then denying that:
She may helpe you to many faire preferments,
And then deny her ayding hand therein,
And lay those Honors on your high desert.
What may she not, she may, I marry may she.
Riu. What marry may she?
Ric. What marrie may she? Marrie with a King,
A Batcheller, and a handsome stripling too,
I wis your Grandam had a worser match.
Qu. My Lord of Glouster, I haue too long borne
Your blunt vpbraidings, and your bitter scoffes:
By heauen, I will acquaint his Maiestie
Of those grosse taunts that oft I haue endur'd.
I had rather be a Countrie seruant maide
Then a great Queene, with this condition,
To be so baited, scorn'd, and stormed at,
Small ioy haue I in being Englands Queene.

Enter old Queene Margaret.

Mar. And lesned be that small, God I beseech him,
Thy honor, state, and seate, is due to me.
Rich. What? threat you me with telling of the King?
I will auouch't in presence of the King:
I dare aduenture to be sent to th' Towre.
'Tis time to speake,
My paines are quite forgot.
Margaret. Out Diuell,
I do remember them too well:
Thou killd'st my Husband *Henrie* in the Tower,
And *Edward* my poore Son, at Tewkesburie.
Rich. Ere you were Queene,
I, or your Husband King:
I was a packe-horse in his great affaires:
A weeder out of his proud Aduersaries,
A liberall rewarder of his Friends,
To royalize his blood, I spent mine owne.
Margaret. I and much better blood
Then his, or thine.

Rich.

Rich. In all which time, you and your Husband *Grey*
Were factious, for the House of *Lancaster*;
And *Riuers*, so were you: Was not your Husband,
In *Margarets* Battaile, at Saint *Albons*, slaine?
Let me put in your mindes, if you forget
What you haue beene ere this, and what you are:
Withall, what I haue beene, and what I am.
Q.M. A murth'rous Villaine, and so still thou art.
Rich. Poore *Clarence* did forsake his Father *Warwicke*,
I, and forswore himselfe (which Iesu pardon.)
Q.M. Which God reuenge.
Rich. To fight on *Edwards* partie, for the Crowne,
And for his meede, poore Lord, he is mewed vp:
I would to God my heart were Flint, like *Edwards*,
Or *Edwards* soft and pittifull, like mine;
I am too childish foolish for this World.
Q.M. High thee to Hell for shame, & leaue this World
Thou Cacodemon, there thy Kingdome is.
Riu. My Lord of Gloster: in those busie dayes,
Which here you vrge, to proue vs Enemies,
We follow'd then our Lord, our Soueraigne King,
So should we you, if you should be our King.
Rich. If I should be? I had rather be a Pedler.
Farre be it from my heart, the thought thereof.
Qu. As little ioy (my Lord) as you suppose
You should enioy, were you this Countries King,
As little ioy you may suppose in me,
That I enioy, being the Queene thereof.
Q.M. A little ioy enioyes the Queene thereof,
For I am shee, and altogether ioylesse:
I can no longer hold me patient.
Heare me, you wrangling Pyrates, that fall out,
In sharing that which you haue pill'd from me:
Which off you trembles not, that lookes on me?
If not, that I am Queene, you bow like Subiects;
Yet that by you depos'd, you quake like Rebells.
Ah gentle Villaine, doe not turne away. (sight?
Rich. Foule wrinckled Witch, what mak'st thou in my
Q.M. But repetition of what thou hast marr'd,
That will I make, before I let thee goe.
Rich. Wert thou not banished, on paine of death?
Q.M. I was: but I doe find more paine in banishment,
Then death can yeeld me here, by my abode.
A Husband and a Sonne thou ow'st to me,
And thou a Kingdome; all of you, allegeance:
This Sorrow that I haue, by right is yours,
And all the Pleasures you vsurpe, are mine.
Rich. The Curse my Noble Father layd on thee,
When thou didst Crown his Warlike Brows with Paper
And with thy scornes drew'st Riuers from his eyes,
And then to dry them, gau'st the Duke a Clowt,
Steep'd in the faultlesse blood of prettie *Rutland*:
His Curses then, from bitternesse of Soule,
Denounc'd against thee, are all falne vpon thee:
And God, not we, hath plagu'd thy bloody deed.
Qu. So iust is God, to right the innocent.
Hast. O, 'twas the foulest deed to slay that Babe,
And the most mercilesse, that ere was heard of.
Riu. Tyrants themselues wept when it was reported.
Dors. No man but prophecied reuenge for it.
Buck. *Northumberland*, then present, wept to see it.
Q.M. What? were you snarling all before I came,
Ready to catch each other by the throat,
And turne you all your hatred now on me?
Did *Yorkes* dread Curse preuaile so much with Heauen,
That *Henries* death, my louely *Edwards* death,
Their Kingdomes losse, my wofull Banishment,
Should all but answer for that peeuish Brat?
Can Curses pierce the Clouds, and enter Heauen?
Why then giue way dull Clouds to my quick Curses.
Though not by Warre, by Surfet dye your King,
As ours by Murther, to make him a King.
Edward thy Sonne, that now is Prince of Wales,
For *Edward* our Sonne, that was Prince of Wales,
Dye in his youth, by like vntimely violence.
Thy selfe a Queene, for me that was a Queene,
Out-liue thy glory, like my wretched selfe:
Long may'st thou liue, to wayle thy Childrens death,
And see another, as I see thee now,
Deck'd in thy Rights, as thou art stall'd in mine.
Long dye thy happie dayes, before thy death,
And after many length'ned howres of griefe,
Dye neyther Mother, Wife, nor Englands Queene.
Riuers and *Dorset*, you were standers by,
And so wast thou, Lord *Hastings*, when my Sonne
Was stab'd with bloody Daggers: God, I pray him,
That none of you may liue his naturall age,
But by some vnlook'd accident cut off.
Rich. Haue done thy Charme, ŷ hateful wither'd Hagge.
Q.M. And leaue out thee? stay Dog, for ŷ shalt heare me.
If Heauen haue any grieuous plague in store,
Exceeding those that I can wish vpon thee,
O let them keepe it, till thy sinnes be ripe,
And then hurle downe their indignation
On thee, the troubler of the poore Worlds peace.
The Worme of Conscience still begnaw thy Soule,
Thy Friends suspect for Traytors while thou liu'st,
And take deepe Traytors for thy dearest Friends.
No sleepe close vp that deadly Eye of thine,
Vnlesse it be while some tormenting Dreame
Affrights thee with a Hell of ougly Deuills.
Thou eluish mark'd, abortiue rooting Hogge,
Thou that wast seal'd in thy Natiuitie
The slaue of Nature, and the Sonne of Hell:
Thou slander of thy heauie Mothers Wombe,
Thou loathed Issue of thy Fathers Loynes,
Thou Ragge of Honor, thou detested--
Rich. *Margaret.*
Q.M *Richard.* *Rich* Ha.
Q.M. I call thee not.
Rich. I cry thee mercie then: for I did thinke,
That thou hadst call'd me all these bitter names.
Q.M. Why so I did, but look'd for no reply.
Oh let me make the Period to my Curse.
Rich. 'Tis done by me, and ends in *Margaret*.
Qu. Thus haue you breath'd your Curse against your self.
Q.M. Poore painted Queen, vain flourish of my fortune,
Why strew'st thou Sugar on that Bottel'd Spider,
Whose deadly Web ensnareth thee about?
Foole, foole, thou whet'st a Knife to kill thy selfe:
The day will come, that thou shalt wish for me,
To helpe thee curse this poysonous Bunch-backt Toade.
Hast. False boding Woman, end thy frantick Curse,
Least to thy harme, thou moue our patience.
Q.M. Foule shame vpon you, you haue all mou'd mine.
Ri. Were you wel seru'd, you would be taught your duty.
Q.M To serue me well, you all should do me duty,
Teach me to be your Queene, and you my Subiects:
O serue me well, and teach your selues that duty.
Dors. Dispute not with her, shee is lunaticke.
Q.M. Peace Master Marquesse, you are malapert,
Your fire-new stampe of Honor is scarce currant.
Q

O that your yong Nobility could iudge
What 'twere to lose it, and be miserable.
They that stand high, haue many blasts to shake them,
And if they fall, they dash themselues to peeces.
Rich. Good counsaile marry, learne it, learne it Marquesse.
Dor. It touches you my Lord, as much as me.
Rich. I, and much more: but I was borne so high:
Our ayerie buildeth in the Cedars top,
And dallies with the winde, and scornes the Sunne.
Mar. And turnes the Sun to shade: alas, alas,
Witnesse my Sonne, now in the shade of death,
Whose bright out-shining beames, thy cloudy wrath
Hath in eternall darknesse folded vp.
Your ayery buildeth in our ayeries Nest:
O God that seest it, do not suffer it,
As it is wonne with blood, lost be it so.
Buc. Peace, peace for shame: If not, for Charity.
Mar. Vrge neither charity, nor shame to me:
Vncharitably with me haue you dealt,
And shamefully my hopes (by you) are butcher'd.
My Charity is outrage, Life my shame,
And in that shame, still liue my sorrowes rage.
Buc. Haue done, haue done.
Mar. O Princely Buckingham, Ile kisse thy hand,
In signe of League and amity with thee:
Now faire befall thee, and thy Noble house:
Thy Garments are not spotted with our blood:
Nor thou within the compasse of my curse.
Buc. Nor no one heere: for Curses neuer passe
The lips of those that breath them in the ayre.
Mar. I will not thinke but they ascend the sky,
And there awake Gods gentle sleeping peace.
O Buckingham, take heede of yonder dogge:
Looke when he fawnes, he bites; and when he bites,
His venom tooth will rankle to the death.
Haue not to do with him, beware of him,
Sinne, death, and hell haue set their markes on him,
And all their Ministers attend on him.
Rich. What doth she say, my Lord of Buckingham.
Buc. Nothing that I respect my gracious Lord.
Mar. What dost thou scorne me
For my gentle counsell?
And sooth the diuell that I warne thee from.
O but remember this another day:
When he shall split thy very heart with sorrow:
And say (poore *Margaret*) was a Prophetesse:
Liue each of you the subiects to his hate,
And he to yours, and all of you to Gods. *Exit.*
Buc. My haire doth stand an end to heare her curses.
Riu. And so doth mine, I muse why she's at libertie.
Rich. I cannot blame her, by Gods holy mother,
She hath had too much wrong, and I repent
My part thereof, that I haue done to her.
Mar I neuer did her any to my knowledge.
Rich. Yet you haue all the vantage of her wrong:
I was too hot, to do somebody good,
That is too cold in thinking of it now:
Marry as for *Clarence*, he is well repayed:
He is frank'd vp to fatting for his paines,
God pardon them, that are the cause thereof.
Riu A vertuous, and a Christian-like conclusion
To pray for them that haue done scath to vs.
Rich. So do I euer, being well aduis'd.
Speakes to himselfe.
For had I curst now, I had curst my selfe

Enter Catesby.

Cates. Madam, his Maiesty doth call for you,
And for your Grace, and yours my gracious Lord.
Qu. Catesby I come, Lords will you go with mee.
Riu. We wait vpon your Grace.
Exeunt all but Gloster.
Rich. I do the wrong, and first begin to brawle.
The secret Mischeefes that I set abroach,
I lay vnto the greeuous charge of others.
Clarence, who I indeede haue cast in darknesse,
I do beweepe to many simple Gulles,
Namely to *Derby*, *Hastings*, *Buckingham*,
And tell them 'tis the Queene, and her Allies,
That stirre the King against the Duke my Brother.
Now they beleeue it, and withall whet me
To be reueng'd on *Riuers*, *Dorset*, *Grey*.
But then I sigh, and with a peece of Scripture,
Tell them that God bids vs do good for euill:
And thus I cloath my naked Villanie
With odde old ends, stolne forth of holy Writ,
And seeme a Saint, when most I play the deuill.

Enter two murtherers.

But soft, heere come my Executioners,
How now my hardy stout resolued Mates,
Are you now going to dispatch this thing?
Vil. We are my Lord, and come to haue the Warrant,
That we may be admitted where he is.
Ric. Well thought vpon, I haue it heare about me:
When you haue done, repayre to *Crosby* place;
But sirs be sodaine in the execution,
Withall obdurate, do not heare him pleade;
For *Clarence* is well spoken, and perhappes
May moue your hearts to pitty, if you marke him.
Vil. Tut, tut, my Lord, we will not stand to prate,
Talkers are no good dooers, be assur'd:
We go to vse our hands, and not our tongues.
Rich. Your eyes drop Mill-stones, when Fooles eyes fall Teares:
I like you Lads, about your businesse straight.
Go, go, dispatch.
Vil. We will my Noble Lord.

Scena Quarta.

Enter Clarence and Keeper.

Keep. Why lookes your Grace so heauily to day.
Cla. O, I haue past a miserable night,
So full of fearefull Dreames, of vgly sights,
That as I am a Christian faithfull man,
I would not spend another such a night
Though 'twere to buy a world of happy daies:
So full of dismall terror was the time.
Keep. What was your dream my Lord, I pray you tel me
Cla. Me thoughts that I had broken from the Tower,
And was embark'd to crosse to Burgundy,
And in my company my Brother Glouster,
Who from my Cabin tempted me to walke,
Vpon the Hatches: There we look'd toward England,
And cited vp a thousand heauy times,

t 2 During

During the warres of Yorke and Lancaster
That had befalne vs. As we pac'd along
Vpon the giddy footing of the Hatches,
Me thought that Glouster stumbled, and in falling
Strooke me (that thought to stay him) ouer-boord,
Into the tumbling billowes of the maine.
O Lord, me thought what paine it was to drowne,
What dreadfull noise of water in mine eares,
What sights of vgly death within mine eyes.
Me thoughts, I saw a thousand fearfull wrackes:
A thousand men that Fishes gnaw'd vpon:
Wedges of Gold, great Anchors, heapes of Pearle,
Inestimable Stones, vnvalewed Iewels,
All scattred in the bottome of the Sea,
Some lay in dead-mens Sculles, and in the holes
Where eyes did once inhabit, there were crept
(As 'twere in scorne of eyes) reflecting Gemmes,
That woo'd the slimy bottome of the deepe,
And mock'd the dead bones that lay scattred by.
Keep. Had you such leysure in the time of death
To gaze vpon these secrets of the deepe?
Cla. Me thought I had, and often did I striue
To yeeld the Ghost: but still the enuious Flood
Stop'd in my soule, and would not let it forth
To find the empty, vast, and wand'ring ayre:
But smother'd it within my panting bulke,
Who almost burst, to belch it in the Sea.
Keep. Awak'd you not in this sore Agony?
Clar. No, no, my Dreame was lengthen'd after life.
O then, began the Tempest to my Soule.
I past (me thought) the Melancholly Flood,
With that sowre Ferry-man which Poets write of,
Vnto the Kingdome of perpetuall Night.
The first that there did greet my Stranger-soule,
Was my great Father-in-Law, renowned Warwicke,
Who spake alowd: What scourge for Periurie,
Can this darke Monarchy affoord false *Clarence*?
And so he vanish'd. Then came wand'ring by,
A Shadow like an Angell, with bright hayre
Dabbel'd in blood, and he shriek'd out alowd
Clarence is come, false, fleeting, periur'd *Clarence*,
That stabb'd me in the field by Tewkesbury:
Seize on him Furies, take him vnto Torment.
With that (me thought) a Legion of foule Fiends
Inuiron'd me, and howled in mine eares
Such hiddeous cries, that with the very Noise,
I (trembling) wak'd, and for a season after,
Could not beleeue, but that I was in Hell,
Such terrible Impression made my Dreame.
Keep No maruell Lord, though it affrighted you,
I am affraid (me thinkes) to heare you tell it.
Cla. Ah Keeper, Keeper, I haue done these things
(That now giue euidence against my Soule)
For *Edwards* sake, and see how he requits mee.
O God! if my deepe prayres cannot appease thee,
But thou wilt be aueng'd on my misdeeds,
Yet execute thy wrath in me alone:
O spare my guiltlesse Wife, and my poore children.
Keeper, I prythee sit by me a-while,
My Soule is heauy, and I faine would sleepe.
Keep. I will my Lord, God giue your Grace good rest.

Enter Brakenbury the Lieutenant.

Bra. Sorrow breakes Seasons, and reposing houres,
Makes the Night Morning, and the Noon-tide night:
Princes haue but their Titles for their Glories,
An outward Honor, for an inward Toyle,
And for vnfelt Imaginations
They often feele a world of restlesse Cares:
So that betweene their Titles, and low Name,
There's nothing differs, but the outward fame.

Enter two Murtherers.

1. *Mur.* Ho, who's heere?
Bra. What would'st thou Fellow? And how camm'st thou hither.
2. *Mur.* I would speak with *Clarence*, and I came hither on my Legges.
Bra. What so breefe?
1. 'Tis better (Sir) then to be tedious:
Let him see our Commission, and talke no more. *Reads*
Bra. I am in this, commanded to deliuer
The Noble Duke of *Clarence* to your hands.
I will not reason what is meant heereby,
Because I will be guiltlesse from the meaning.
There lies the Duke asleepe, and there the Keyes.
Ile to the King, and signifie to him,
That thus I haue resign'd to you my charge. *Exit.*
1 You may sir, 'tis a point of wisedome:
Far you well.
2 What, shall we stab him as he sleepes.
1 No: hee'l say 'twas done cowardly, when he wakes
2 Why he shall neuer wake, vntill the great Iudgement day.
1 Why then hee'l say, we stab'd him sleeping.
2 The vrging of that word Iudgement, hath bred a kinde of remorse in me.
1 What? art thou affraid?
2 Not to kill him, hauing a Warrant,
But to be damn'd for killing him, from the which
No Warrant can defend me.
1 I thought thou had'st bin resolute.
2 So I am, to let him liue.
1 Ile backe to the Duke of Glouster, and tell him so.
2 Nay, I prythee stay a little:
I hope this passionate humor of mine, will change,
It was wont to hold me but while one tels twenty.
1 How do'st thou feele thy selfe now?
2 Some certaine dregges of conscience are yet within mee.
1 Remember our Reward, when the deed's done.
2 Come, he dies: I had forgot the Reward.
1 Where's thy conscience now.
2 O, in the Duke of Glousters purse.
1 When hee opens his purse to giue vs our Reward, thy Conscience flyes out.
2 'Tis no matter, let it goe: There's few or none will entertaine it.
1 What if it come to thee againe?
2 Ile not meddle with it, it makes a man a Coward: A man cannot steale, but it accuseth him: A man cannot Sweare, but it Checkes him: A man cannot lye with his Neighbours Wife, but it detects him. 'Tis a blushing shamefac'd spirit, that mutinies in a mans bosome: It filles a man full of Obstacles. It made me once restore a Pursse of Gold that (by chance) I found. It beggars any man that keepes it: It is turn'd out of Townes and Cities for a dangerous thing, and euery man that means to liue well, endeuours to trust to himselfe, and liue without it.

1 'Tis

1 'Tis euen now at my elbow, perſwading me not to
kill the Dkue.
2 Take the diuell in thy minde, and beleeue him not:
He would inſinuate with thee but to make thee ſigh.
1 I am ſtrong fram'd, he cannot preuaile with me.
2 Spoke like a tall man, that reſpects thy reputation.
Come, ſhall we fall to worke?
1 Take him on the Coſtard, with the hiltes of thy
Sword, and then throw him into the Malmeſey-Butte in
the next roome.
2 O excellent deuice; and make a ſop of him.
1 Soft, he wakes.
2 Strike.
1 No, wee'l reaſon with him.
Cla. Where art thou Keeper? Giue me a cup of wine.
2 You ſhall haue Wine enough my Lord anon.
Cla. In Gods name, what art thou?
1 A man, as you are.
Cla. But not as I am Royall.
1 Nor you as we are, Loyall.
Cla. Thy voice is Thunder, but thy looks are humble.
1 My voice is now the Kings, my lookes mine owne.
Cla. How darkly, and how deadly doſt thou ſpeake?
Your eyes do menace me: why looke you pale?
Who ſent you hither? Wherefore do you come?
2 To, to, to——
Cla. To murther me?
Both. I, I.
Cla. You ſcarſely haue the hearts to tell me ſo,
And therefore cannot haue the hearts to do it.
Wherein my Friends haue I offended you?
1 Offended vs you haue not, but the King.
Cla. I ſhall be reconcil'd to him againe.
2 Neuer my Lord, therefore prepare to dye.
Cla. Are you drawne forth among a world of men
To ſlay the innocent? What is my offence?
Where is the Euidence that doth accuſe me?
What lawfull Queſt haue giuen their Verdict vp
Vnto the frowning Iudge? Or who pronounc'd
The bitter ſentence of poore *Clarence* death,
Before I be conuict by courſe of Law?
To threaten me with death, is moſt vnlawfull.
I charge you, as you hope for any goodneſſe,
That you depart, and lay no hands on me:
The deed you vndertake is damnable.
1 What we will do, we do vpon command.
2 And he that hath commanded, is our King.
Cla. Erroneous Vaſſals, the great King of Kings
Hath in the Table of his Law commanded
That thou ſhalt do no murther. Will you then
Spurne at his Edict, and fulfill a Mans?
Take heed: for he holds Vengeance in his hand,
To hurle vpon their heads that breake his Law.
2 And that ſame Vengeance doth he hurle on thee,
For falſe Forſwearing, and for murther too:
Thou did'ſt receiue the Sacrament, to fight
In quarrell of the Houſe of Lancaſter.
1 And like a Traitor to the name of God,
Did'ſt breake that Vow, and with thy treacherous blade,
Vnrip'ſt the Bowels of thy Sou'raignes Sonne.
2 Whom thou was't ſworne to cheriſh and defend.
1 How canſt thou vrge Gods dreadfull Law to vs,
When thou haſt broke it in ſuch deere degree?
Cla. Alas! for whoſe ſake did I that ill deede?
For *Edward*, for my Brother, for his ſake.
He ſends you not to murther me for this:
For in that ſinne, he is as deepe as I.
If God will be auenged for the deed,
O know you yet, he doth it publiquely,
Take not the quarrell from his powrefull arme:
He needs no indirect, or lawleſſe courſe,
To cut off thoſe that haue offended him.
1 Who made thee then a bloudy miniſter,
When gallant ſpringing braue *Plantagenet*,
That Princely Nouice was ſtrucke dead by thee?
Cla. My Brothers loue, the Diuell, and my Rage.
1 Thy Brothers Loue, our Duty, and thy Faults,
Prouoke vs hither now, to ſlaughter thee.
Cla. If you do loue my Brother, hate not me:
I am his Brother, and I loue him well.
If you are hyr'd for meed, go backe againe,
And I will ſend you to my Brother Glouſter:
Who ſhall reward you better for my life,
Then *Edward* will for tydings of my death.
2 You are deceiu'd,
Your Brother Glouſter hates you.
Cla. Oh no, he loues me, and he holds me deere:
Go you to him from me.
1 I ſo we will.
Cla. Tell him, when that our Princely Father Yorke,
Bleſt his three Sonnes with his victorious Arme,
He little thought of this diuided Friendſhip:
Bid Glouſter thinke on this, and he will weepe.
1 I Milſtones, as he leſſoned vs to weepe.
Cla. O do not ſlander him, for he is kinde.
1 Right, as Snow in Harueſt:
Come, you deceiue your ſelfe,
'Tis he that ſends vs to deſtroy you heere.
Cla. It cannot be, for he bewept my Fortune,
And hugg'd me in his armes, and ſwore with ſobs,
That he would labour my deliuery.
1 Why ſo he doth, when he deliuers you
From this earths thraldome, to the ioyes of heauen.
2 Make peace with God, for you muſt die my Lord.
Cla. Haue you that holy feeling in your ſoules,
To counſaile me to make my peace with God,
And are you yet to your owne ſoules ſo blinde,
That you will warre with God, by murd'ring me.
O ſirs conſider, they that ſet you on
To do this deede, will hate you for the deede.
2 What ſhall we do?
Clar. Relent, and ſaue your ſoules:
Which of you, if you were a Princes Sonne,
Being pent from Liberty, as I am now,
If two ſuch murtherers as your ſelues came to you,
Would not intreat for life, as you would begge
Were you in my diſtreſſe.
1 Relent? no: 'Tis cowardly and womaniſh.
Cla. Not to relent, is beaſtly, ſauage, diueliſh:
My Friend, I ſpy ſome pitty in thy lookes:
O, if thine eye be not a Flatterer,
Come thou on my ſide, and intreate for mee,
A begging Prince, what begger pitties not.
2 Looke behinde you, my Lord.
1 Take that, and that, if all this will not do, *Stabs him.*
Ile drowne you in the Malmeſey-But within. *Exit.*
2 A bloody deed, and deſperately diſpatcht:
How faine (like *Pilate*) would I waſh my hands
Of this moſt greeuous murther. *Enter 1. Murtherer*
1 How now? what mean'ſt thou that thou help'ſt me
not? By Heauen the Duke ſhall know how ſlacke you
haue beene.

r 3 2 I

2.*Mur* I would he knew that I had sau'd his brother,
Take thou the Fee, and tell him what I say,
For I repent me that the Duke is slaine. *Exit.*

1.*Mur.* So do not I: go Coward as thou art.
Well, Ile go hide the body in some hole,
Till that the Duke giue order for his buriall:
And when I haue my meede, I will away,
For this will out, and then I must not stay. *Exit*

Actus Secundus. Scœna Prima.

Flourish.
Enter the King sicke, the Queene, Lord Marquesse Dorset, Riuers, Hastings, Catesby, Buckingham, Wooduill.

King. Why so: now haue I done a good daies work.
You Peeres, continue this vnited League:
I, euery day expect an Embassage
From my Redeemer, to redeeme me hence.
And more to peace my soule shall part to heauen,
Since I haue made my Friends at peace on earth.
Dorset and *Riuers*, take each others hand,
Dissemble not your hatred, Sweare your loue.

Riu. By heauen, my soule is purg'd from grudging hate
And with my hand I seale my true hearts Loue.

Hast. So thriue I, as I truly sweare the like.

King. Take heed you dally not before your King,
Lest he that is the supreme King of Kings
Confound your hidden falshood, and award
Either of you to be the others end.

Hast. So prosper I, as I sweare perfect loue.

Ri. And I, as I loue *Hastings* with my heart,

King. Madam, your selfe is not exempt from this:
Nor you Sonne *Dorset*, *Buckingham* nor you;
You haue bene factious one against the other.
Wife, loue Lord *Hastings*, let him kisse your hand,
And what you do, do it vnfeignedly.

Qu. There *Hastings*, I will neuer more remember
Our former hatred, so thriue I, and mine.

King. Dorset, imbrace him:
Hastings, loue Lord Marquesse.

Dor. This interchange of loue, I heere protest
Vpon my part, shall be inuiolable.

Hast. And so sweare I.

King. Now Princely *Buckingham*, seale ÿ this league
With thy embracements to my wiues Allies,
And make me happy in your vnity.

Buc. When euer *Buckingham* doth turne his hate
Vpon your Grace, but with all dutious loue,
Doth cherish you, and yours, God punish me
With hate in those where I expect most loue,
When I haue most need to imploy a Friend,
And most assured that he is a Friend,
Deepe, hollow, treacherous, and full of guile,
Be he vnto me: This do I begge of heauen,
When I am cold in loue, to you, or yours. *Embrace*

King. A pleasing Cordiall, Princely *Buckingham*,
Is this thy Vow, vnto my sickely heart:
There wanteth now our Brother Gloster heere,
To make the blessed period of this peace.

Buc. And in good time,
Heere comes Sir *Richard Ratcliffe*, and the Duke.

Enter Ratcliffe, and Gloster.

Rich. Good morrow to my Soueraigne King & Queen
And Princely Peeres, a happy time of day.

King, Happy indeed, as we haue spent the day:
Gloster, we haue done deeds of Charity,
Made peace of enmity, faire loue of hate,
Betweene these swelling wrong incensed Peeres.

Rich. A blessed labour my most Soueraigne Lord:
Among this Princely heape, if any heere
By false intelligence, or wrong surmize
Hold me a Foe. If I vnwillingly, or in my rage,
Haue ought committed that is hardly borne,
To any in this presence, I desire
To reconcile me to his Friendly peace:
'Tis death to me to be at enmitie:
I hate it, and desire all good mens loue,
First Madam, I intreate true peace of you,
Which I will purchase with my dutious seruice.
Of you my Noble Cosin Buckingham,
If euer any grudge were lodg'd betweene vs.
Of you and you, Lord *Riuers* and of *Dorset*,
That all without desert haue frown'd on me:
Of you Lord *Wooduill*, and Lord *Scales* of you,
Dukes, Earles, Lords, Gentlemen, indeed of all.
I do not know that Englishman aliue,
With whom my soule is any iot at oddes,
More then the Infant that is borne to night:
I thanke my God for my Humility.

Qu. A holy day shall this be kept heereafter:
I would to God all strifes were well compounded.
My Soueraigne Lord, I do beseech your Highnesse
To take our Brother *Clarence* to your Grace.

Rich. Why Madam, haue I offred loue for this,
To be so flowted in this Royall presence?
Who knowes not that the gentle Duke is dead? *They*
You do him iniurie to scorne his Coarse. *all start.*

King. Who knowes not he is dead? Who knowes he is?

Qu. All-seeing heauen, what a world is this?

Buc. Looke I so pale Lord *Dorset*, as the rest?

Dor. I my good Lord, and no man in the presence,
But his red colour hath forsooke his cheekes.

King. Is *Clarence* dead? The Order was reuerst.

Rich. But he (poore man) by your first order dyed,
And that a winged Mercurie did beare:
Some tardie Cripple bare the Countermand,
That came too lagge to see him buried.
God grant, that some lesse Noble, and lesse Loyall,
Neerer in bloody thoughts, and not in blood,
Deserue not worse then wretched *Clarence* did,
And yet go currant from Suspition.

Enter Earle of Derby.

Der. A boone my Soueraigne for my seruice done.

King. I prethee peace, my soule is full of sorrow.

Der. I will not rise, vnlesse your Highnes heare me.

King Then say at once, what is it thou requests.

Der. The forfeit (Soueraigne) of my seruants life.
Who slew to day a Riotous Gentleman,
Lately attendant on the Duke of Norfolke.

King. Haue I a tongue to doome my Brothers death?
And shall that tongue giue pardon to a slaue?
My Brother kill'd no man, his fault was Thought,
And yet his punishment was bitter death.

Who

Who sued to me for him? Who (in my wrath)
Kneel'd and my feet, and bid me be aduis'd?
Who spoke of Brother-hood? who spoke of loue?
Who told me how the poore soule did forsake
The mighty Warwicke, and did fight for me?
Who told me in the field at Tewkesbury,
When Oxford had me downe, he rescued me:
And said deare Brother liue, and be a King?
Who told me, when we both lay in the Field,
Frozen (almost) to death, how he did lap me
Euen in his Garments, and did giue himselfe
(All thin and naked) to the numbe cold night?
All this from my Remembrance, brutish wrath
Sinfully pluckt, and not a man of you
Had so much grace to put it in my minde.
But when your Carters, or your wayting Vassalls
Haue done a drunken Slaughter, and defac'd
The precious Image of our deere Redeemer,
You straight are on your knees for Pardon, pardon,
And I (vniustly too) must grant it you.
But for my Brother, not a man would speake,
Nor I (vngracious) speake vnto my selfe
For him poore Soule. The proudest of you all,
Haue bin beholding to him in his life:
Yet none of you, would once begge for his life.
O God! I feare thy iustice will take hold
On me, and you; and mine, and yours for this.
Come *Hastings* helpe me to my Closset.
Ah poore *Clarence*. *Exeunt some with K. & Queen.*

Rich. This is the fruits of rashnes: Markt you not,
How that the guilty Kindred of the Queene
Look'd pale, when they did heare of *Clarence* death.
O! they did vrge it still vnto the King,
God will reuenge it. Come Lords will you go,
To comfort *Edward* with our company.

Buc. We wait vpon your Grace. *exeunt.*

Scena Secunda.

Enter the old Dutchesse of Yorke, with the two children of Clarence.

Edw. Good Grandam tell vs, is our Father dead?

Dutch. No Boy.

Daugh. Why do weepe so oft? And beate your Brest?
And cry, O *Clarence*, my vnhappy Sonne.

Boy. Why do you looke on vs, and shake your head,
And call vs Orphans, Wretches, Castawayes,
If that our Noble Father were aliue?

Dut. My pretty Cosins, you mistake me both,
I do lament the sicknesse of the King,
As loath to lose him, not your Fathers death:
It were lost sorrow to waile one that's lost.

Boy. Then you conclude, (my Grandam) he is dead:
The King mine Vnckle is too blame for it.
God will reuenge it, whom I will importune
With earnest prayers, all to that effect.

Daugh. And so will I.

Dut. Peace children peace, the King doth loue you wel.
Incapeable, and shallow Innocents,
You cannot guesse who caus'd your Fathers death.

Boy. Grandam we can: for my good Vnkle Gloster
Told me, the King prouok'd to it by the Queene,
Deuis'd impeachments to imprison him;
And when my Vnckle told me so, he wept,
And pittied me, and kindly kist my cheeke:
Bad me rely on him, as on my Father,
And he would loue me deerely as a childe.

Dut. Ah! that Deceit should steale such gentle shape,
And with a vertuous Vizor hide deepe vice.
He is my sonne, I, and therein my shame,
Yet from my dugges, he drew not this deceit.

Boy. Thinke you my Vnkle did dissemble Grandam?

Dut. I Boy.

Boy. I cannot thinke it. Hearke, what noise is this?

Enter the Queene with her haire about her ears, Riuers & Dorset after her.

Qu. Ah! who shall hinder me to waile and weepe?
To chide my Fortune, and torment my Selfe.
Ile ioyne with blacke dispaire against my Soule,
And to my selfe, become an enemie.

Dut. What meanes this Scene of rude impatience?

Qu. To make an act of Tragicke violence.
Edward my Lord, thy Sonne, our King is dead.
Why grow the Branches, when the Roote is gone?
Why wither not the leaues that want their sap?
If you will liue, Lament: if dye, be breefe,
That our swift-winged Soules may catch the Kings,
Or like obedient Subiects follow him,
To his new Kingdome of nere-changing night.

Dut. Ah so much interest haue in thy sorrow,
As I had Title in thy Noble Husband:
I haue bewept a worthy Husbands death,
And liu'd with looking on his Images:
But now two Mirrors of his Princely semblance,
Are crack'd in peeces, by malignant death,
And I for comfort, haue but one false Glasse,
That greeues me, when I see my shame in him.
Thou art a Widdow: yet thou art a Mother,
And hast the comfort of thy Children left,
But death hath snatch'd my Husband from mine Armes,
And pluckt two Crutches from my feeble hands,
Clarence, and *Edward*. O, what cause haue I,
(Thine being but a moity of my moane)
To ouer-go thy woes, and drowne thy cries.

Boy. Ah Aunt! you wept not for our Fathers death:
How can we ayde you with our Kindred teares?

Daugh. Our fatherlesse distresse was left vnmoan'd,
Your widdow-dolour, likewise be vnwept.

Qu. Giue me no helpe in Lamentation,
I am not barren to bring forth complaints:
All Springs reduce their currents to mine eyes,
That I being gouern'd by the waterie Moone,
May send forth plenteous teares to drowne the World.
Ah, for my Husband, for my deere Lord *Edward*.

Chil. Ah for our Father, for our deere Lord *Clarence*.

Dut. Alas for both, both mine *Edward* and *Clarence*.

Qu. What stay had I but *Edward*, and hee's gone?

Chil. What stay had we but *Clarence*? and he's gone.

Dut. What stayes had I, but they? and they are gone.

Qu. Was neuer widdow had so deere a losse.

Chil. Were neuer Orphans had so deere a losse.

Dut. Was neuer Mother had so deere a losse.
Alas! I am the Mother of these Greefes,
Their woes are parcell'd, mine is generall.
She for an *Edward* weepes, and so do I:

I

I for a *Clarence* weepes, so doth not shee:
These Babes for *Clarence* weepe, so do not they.
Alas! you three, on me threefold distrest:
Power all your teares, I am your sorrowes Nurse,
And I will pamper it with Lamentation.
Dor. Comfort deere Mother, God is much displeas'd,
That you take with vnthankfulnesse his doing.
In common worldly things, 'tis call'd vngratefull,
With dull vnwillingnesse to repay a debt,
Which with a bounteous hand was kindly lent:
Much more to be thus opposite with heauen,
For it requires the Royall debt it lent you.
Riuers. Madam, bethinke you like a carefull Mother
Of the young Prince your sonne: send straight for him,
Let him be Crown'd, in him your comfort liues.
Drowne desperate sorrow in dead *Edwards* graue,
And plant your ioyes in liuing *Edwards* Throne.

Enter Richard, Buckingham, Derbie, Hastings, and Ratcliffe.

Rich. Sister haue comfort, all of vs haue cause
To waile the dimming of our shining Starre:
But none can helpe our harmes by wayling them.
Madam, my Mother, I do cry you mercie,
I did not see your Grace. Humbly on my knee,
I craue your Blessing.
Dut. God blesse thee, and put meeknes in thy breast,
Loue Charity, Obedience, and true Dutie.
Rich. Amen, and make me die a good old man,
That is the butt-end of a Mothers blessing;
I maruell that her Grace did leaue it out.
Buc. You clowdy-Princes, & hart-sorowing-Peeres,
That beare this heauie mutuall loade of Moane,
Now cheere each other, in each others Loue:
Though we haue spent our Haruest of this King,
We are to reape the Haruest of his Sonne.
The broken rancour of your high-swolne hates,
But lately splinter'd, knit, and ioyn'd together,
Must gently be preseru'd, cherisht, and kept:
Me seemeth good, that with some little Traine,
Forthwith from Ludlow, the young Prince be fet
Hither to London, to be crown'd our King.
Riuers. Why with some little Traine,
My Lord of Buckingham?
Buc. Marrie my Lord, least by a multitude,
The new-heal'd wound of Malice should breake out,
Which would be so much the more dangerous,
By how much the estate is greene, and yet vngouern'd.
Where euery Horse beares his commanding Reine,
And may direct his course as please himselfe,
As well the feare of harme, as harme apparant,
In my opinion, ought to be preuented.
Rich. I hope the King made peace with all of vs,
And the compact is firme, and true in me.
Riu. And so in me, and so (I thinke) in all.
Yet since it is but greene, it should be put
To no apparant likely-hood of breach,
Which haply by much company might be vrg'd:
Therefore I say with Noble Buckingham,
That it is meete so few should fetch the Prince.
Hast. And so say I.
Rich. Then be it so, and go we to determine
Who they shall be that strait shall poste to London.
Madam, and you my Sister, will you go
To giue your censures in this businesse. *Exeunt*

Manet Buckingham, and Richard.

Buc. My Lord, who euer iournies to the Prince,
For God sake let not vs two stay at home:
For by the way, Ile sort occasion,
As Index to the story we late talk'd of,
To part the Queenes proud Kindred from the Prince.
Rich. My other selfe, my Counsailes Consistory,
My Oracle, My Prophet, my deere Cosin,
I, as a childe, will go by thy direction,
Toward London then, for wee'l not stay behinde. *Exeunt*

Scena Tertia.

Enter one Citizen at one doore, and another at the other.

1 Cit. Good morrow Neighbour, whether away so fast?
2 Cit. I promise you, I scarsely know my selfe:
Heare you the newes abroad?
1. Yes, that the King is dead.
2. Ill newes byrlady, seldome comes the better:
I feare, I feare, 'twill proue a giddy world.

Enter another Citizen.

3. Neighbours, God speed.
1. Giue you good morrow sir.
3. Doth the newes hold of good king *Edwards* death
2. I sir, it is too true, God helpe the while.
3. Then Masters looke to see a troublous world.
1. No, no, by Gods good grace, his Son shall reigne.
3. Woe to that Land that's gouern'd by a Childe.
2. In him there is a hope of Gouernment,
Which in his nonage, counsell vnder him,
And in his full and ripened yeares, himselfe
No doubt shall then, and till then gouerne well.
1. So stood the State, when *Henry* the sixt
Was crown'd in Paris, but at nine months old.
3. Stood the State so? No, no, good friends, God wot
For then this Land was famously enrich'd
With politike graue Counsell; then the King
Had vertuous Vnkles to protect his Grace.
1. Why so hath this, both by his Father and Mother
3. Better it were they all came by his Father:
Or by his Father there were none at all:
For emulation, who shall now be neerest,
Will touch vs all too neere, if God preuent not.
O full of danger is the Duke of Glouster,
And the Queenes Sons, and Brothers, haught and proud
And were they to be rul'd, and not to rule,
This sickly Land, might solace as before.
1. Come, come, we feare the worst: all will be well.
3. When Clouds are seen, wisemen put on their clokes;
When great leaues fall, then Winter is at hand;
When the Sun sets, who doth not looke for night?
Vntimely stormes, makes men expect a Dearth:
All may be well; but if God sort it so,
'Tis more then we deserue, or I expect.
2. Truly, the hearts of men are full of feare:
You cannot reason (almost) with a man,
That lookes not heauily, and full of dread
3. Before the dayes of Change, still is it so,
By a diuine instinct, mens mindes mistrust

Ensuing

Purſuing danger: as by proofe we ſee
The Water ſwell before a boyſt'rous ſtorme:
But leaue it all to God. Whither away?
2 Marry we were ſent for to the Iuſtices.
3 And ſo was I: Ile beare you company. *Exeunt*

Scena Quarta.

Enter Arch-biſhop, yong Yorke, the Queene, and the Dutcheſſe

Arch. Laſt night I heard they lay at Stony Stratford,
And at Northampton they do reſt to night:
To morrow, or next day, they will be heere.
Dut. I long with all my heart to ſee the Prince:
I hope he is much growne ſince laſt I ſaw him.
Qu. But I heare no, they ſay my ſonne of Yorke
Ha's almoſt ouertane him in his growth.
Yorke. I Mother, but I would not haue it ſo.
Dut. Why my good Coſin, it is good to grow.
Yor. Grandam, one night as we did ſit at Supper,
My Vnkle *Riuers* talk'd how I did grow
More then my Brother. I, quoth my Vnkle Glouſter,
Small Herbes haue grace, great Weeds do grow apace.
And ſince, me thinkes I would not grow ſo faſt,
Becauſe ſweet Flowres are ſlow, and Weeds make haſt.
Dut. Good faith, good faith, the ſaying did not hold
In him that did obiect the ſame to thee.
He was the wretched'ſt thing when he was yong,
So long a growing, and ſo leyſurely,
That if his rule were true, he ſhould be gracious.
Yor. And ſo no doubt he is, my gracious Madam.
Dut. I hope he is, but yet let Mothers doubt.
Yor. Now by my troth, if I had beene remembred,
I could haue giuen my Vnkles Grace, a flout,
To touch his growth, neerer then he toucht mine.
Dut. How my yong Yorke,
I prythee let me heare it.
Yor. Marry (they ſay) my Vnkle grew ſo faſt,
That he could gnaw a cruſt at two houres old,
'Twas full two yeares ere I could get a tooth.
Grandam, this would haue beene a byting Ieſt.
Dut. I prythee pretty Yorke, who told thee this?
Yor. Grandam, his Nurſſe.
Dut. His Nurſe? why ſhe was dead, ere y wast borne.
Yor. If 'twere not ſhe, I cannot tell who told me.
Qu. A parlous Boy: go too, you are too ſhrew'd.
Dut. Good Madam, be not angry with the Childe.
Qu. Pitchers haue eares.

Enter a Meſſenger.

Arch. Heere comes a Meſſenger: What Newes?
Meſ. Such newes my Lord, as greeues me to report.
Qu. How doth the Prince?
Meſ. Well Madam, and in health.
Dut. What is thy Newes?
Meſſ. Lord *Riuers*, and Lord *Grey*,
Are ſent to Pomfret, and with them,
Sir *Thomas Vaughan*, Priſoners.
Dut. Who hath committed them?
Meſ. The mighty Dukes, *Glouſter* and *Buckingham.*
Arch. For what offence?
Meſ. The ſumme of all I can, I haue diſclos'd:
Why, or for what, the Nobles were committed,
Is all vnknowne to me, my gracious Lord.
Qu. Aye me! I ſee the ruine of my Houſe:
The Tyger now hath ſeiz'd the gentle Hinde,
Inſulting Tiranny beginnes to Iutt
Vpon the innocent and aweleſſe Throne:
Welcome Deſtruction, Blood, and Maſſacre,
I ſee (as in a Map) the end of all.
Dut. Accurſed, and vnquiet wrangling dayes,
How many of you haue mine eyes beheld?
My Husband loſt his life, to get the Crowne,
And often vp and downe my ſonnes were toſt
For me to ioy, and weepe, their gaine and loſſe.
And being ſeated, and Domeſticke broyles
Cleane ouer-blowne, themſelues the Conquerors,
Make warre vpon themſelues, Brother to Brother;
Blood to blood, ſelfe againſt ſelfe: O prepoſterous
And franticke outrage, end thy damned ſpleene,
Or let me dye, to looke on earth no more.
Qu. Come, come my Boy, we will to Sanctuary.
Madam, farwell.
Dut. Stay, I will go with you.
Qu. You haue no cauſe.
Arch. My gracious Lady go,
And thether beare your Treaſure and your Goodes,
For my part, Ile reſigne vnto your Grace
The Seale I keepe, and ſo betide to me,
As well I tender you, and all of yours.
Go, Ile conduct you to the Sanctuary. *Exeunt*

Actus Tertius. Scœna Prima.

The Trumpets ſound.
Enter yong Prince, the Dukes of Glouceſter, and Buckingham, Lord Cardinall, with others.

Buc. Welcome ſweete Prince to London,
To your Chamber.
Rich. Welcome deere Coſin, my thoughts Soueraign
The wearie way hath made you Melancholly.
Prin. No Vnkle, but our croſſes on the way,
Haue made it tedious, weariſome, and heauie.
I want more Vnkles heere to welcome me.
Rich. Sweet Prince, the vntainted vertue of your yeers
Hath not yet diu'd into the Worlds deceit:
No more can you diſtinguiſh of a man,
Then of his outward ſhew, which God he knowes,
Seldome or neuer iumpeth with the heart.
Thoſe Vnkles which you want, were dangerous:
Your Grace attended to their Sugred words,
But look'd not on the poyſon of their hearts:
God keepe you from them, and from ſuch falſe Friends.
Prin. God keepe me from falſe Friends,
But they were none.
Rich. My Lord, the Maior of London comes to greet you.

Enter Lord Maior.

Lo. Maior. God bleſſe your Grace, with health and happie dayes.
Prin. I thanke you, good my Lord, and thank you all:

I thought my Mother, and my Brother *Yorke*,
Would long, ere this, haue met vs on the way.
Fie, what a Slug is *Haſtings*, that he comes not
To tell vs, whether they will come, or no.

Enter Lord Haſtings.

Buck. And in good time, heere comes the ſweating Lord.
Prince. Welcome, my Lord: what, will our Mother come?
Haſt. On what occaſion God he knowes, not I;
The Queene your Mother, and your Brother *Yorke*,
Haue taken Sanctuarie: The tender Prince
Would faine haue come with me, to meet your Grace,
But by his Mother was perforce with-held.
Buck. Fie, what an indirect and peeuiſh courſe
Is this of hers? Lord Cardinall, will your Grace
Perſwade the Queene, to ſend the Duke of Yorke
Vnto his Princely Brother preſently?
If ſhe denie, Lord *Haſtings* goe with him,
And from her iealous Armes pluck him perforce.
Card. My Lord of Buckingham, if my weake Oratorie
Can from his Mother winne the Duke of Yorke,
Anon expect him here: but if ſhe be obdurate
To milde entreaties, God forbid
We ſhould infringe the holy Priuiledge
Of bleſſed Sanctuarie: not for all this Land,
Would I be guiltie of ſo great a ſinne.
Buck. You are too ſenceleſſe obſtinate, my Lord,
Too ceremonious, and traditionall.
Weigh it but with the groſſeneſſe of this Age,
You breake not Sanctuarie, in ſeizing him:
The benefit thereof is alwayes granted
To thoſe, whoſe dealings haue deſeru'd the place,
And thoſe who haue the wit to clayme the place:
This Prince hath neyther claym'd it, nor deſeru'd it,
And therefore, in mine opinion, cannot haue it.
Then taking him from thence, that is not there,
You breake no Priuiledge, nor Charter there:
Oft haue I heard of Sanctuarie men,
But Sanctuarie children, ne're till now.
Card. My Lord, you ſhall o're-rule my mind for once.
Come on, Lord *Haſtings*, will you goe with me?
Haſt. I goe, my Lord. *Exit Cardinall and Haſtings.*
Prince. Good Lords, make all the ſpeedie haſt you may.
Say, Vnckle *Glocester*, if our Brother come,
Where ſhall we ſoiourne, till our Coronation?
Glo. Where it think'ſt beſt vnto your Royall ſelfe.
If I may counſaile you, ſome day or two
Your Highneſſe ſhall repoſe you at the Tower:
Then where you pleaſe, and ſhall be thought moſt fit
For your beſt health, and recreation.
Prince. I doe not like the Tower, of any place:
Did *Iulius Cæſar* build that place, my Lord?
Buck. He did, my gracious Lord, begin that place,
Which ſince, ſucceeding Ages haue re-edify'd.
Prince. Is it vpon record? or elſe reported
Succeſſiuely from age to age, he built it?
Buck. Vpon record, my gracious Lord.
Prince. But ſay, my Lord, it were not regiſtred,
Me thinkes the truth ſhould liue from age to age,
As 'twere retayl'd to all poſteritie,
Euen to the generall ending day.
Glo. So wiſe, ſo young, they ſay doe neuer liue long.
Prince. What ſay you, Vnckle?
Glo. I ſay, without Characters, Fame liues long.
Thus, like the formall Vice, Iniquitie,
I moralize two meanings in one word.
Prince. That *Iulius Cæſar* was a famous man,
With what his Valour did enrich his Wit,
His Wit ſet downe, to make his Valour liue:
Death makes no Conqueſt of his Conqueror,
For now he liues in Fame, though not in Life.
Ile'tell you what, my Couſin *Buckingham*.
Buck. What, my gracious Lord?
Prince. And if I liue vntill I be a man,
Ile win our ancient Right in France againe,
Or dye a Souldier, as I liu'd a King.
Glo. Short Summers lightly haue a forward Spring.

Enter young Yorke, Haſtings, and Cardinall.

Buck. Now in good time, heere comes the Duke of Yorke.
Prince. *Richard* of Yorke, how fares our Noble Brother?
Yorke. Well, my deare Lord, ſo muſt I call you now.
Prince. I, Brother, to our griefe, as it is yours:
Too late he dy'd, that might haue kept that Title,
Which by his death hath loſt much Maieſtie.
Glo. How fares our Couſin, Noble Lord of Yorke?
Yorke. I thanke you, gentle Vnckle. O my Lord,
You ſaid, that idle Weeds are faſt in growth:
The Prince, my Brother, hath out-growne me farre.
Glo. He hath, my Lord.
Yorke. And therefore is he idle?
Glo. Oh my faire Couſin, I muſt not ſay ſo.
Yorke. Then he is more beholding to you, then I.
Glo. He may command me as my Soueraigne,
But you haue power in me, as in a Kinſman.
Yorke. I pray you, Vnckle, giue me this Dagger.
Glo. My Dagger, little Couſin? with all my heart.
Prince. A Begger, Brother?
Yorke. Of my kind Vnckle, that I know will giue,
And being but a Toy, which is no griefe to giue.
Glo. A greater gift then that, Ile giue my Couſin.
Yorke. A greater gift? O, that's the Sword to it.
Glo. I, gentle Couſin, were it light enough.
Yorke. O then I ſee, you will part but with light gifts,
In weightier things you'le ſay a Begger nay.
Glo. It is too weightie for your Grace to weare.
Yorke. I weigh it lightly, were it heauier.
Glo. What, would you haue my Weapon, little Lord?
Yorke. I would that I might thanke you, as, as, you call me.
Glo. How?
Yorke. Little.
Prince. My Lord of Yorke will ſtill be croſſe in talke:
Vnckle, your Grace knowes how to beare with him.
Yorke. You meane to beare me, not to beare with me:
Vnckle, my Brother mockes both you and me,
Becauſe that I am little, like an Ape,
He thinkes that you ſhould beare me on your ſhoulders.
Buck. With what a ſharpe prouided wit he reaſons:
To mittigate the ſcorne he giues his Vnckle,
He prettily and aptly taunts himſelfe:
So cunning, and ſo young, is wonderfull.
Glo. My Lord, wilt pleaſe you paſſe along?
My ſelfe, and my good Couſin *Buckingham*,
Will to your Mother, to entreat of her
To meet you at the Tower, and welcome you.
Yorke. What,

Yorke. What, will you goe vnto the Tower, my Lord?
Prince. My Lord Protector will haue it ſo.
Yorke. I ſhall not ſleepe in quiet at the Tower.
Glo. Why, what ſhould you feare?
Yorke. Marry, my Vnckle *Clarence* angry Ghoſt:
My Grandam told me he was murther'd there.
Prince. I feare no Vnckles dead.
Glo. Nor none that liue, I hope.
Prince. And if they liue, I hope I need not feare.
But come my Lord: and with a heauie heart,
Thinking on them, goe I vnto the Tower.
A Senet. Exeunt Prince, Yorke, Haſtings, and Dorſet.

Manet Richard, Buckingham, and Catesby.

Buck. Thinke you, my Lord, this little prating *Yorke*
Was not incenſed by his ſubtile Mother,
To taunt and ſcorne you thus opprobriouſly?
Glo. No doubt, no doubt: Oh 'tis a perillous Boy,
Bold, quicke, ingenious, forward, capable:
Hee is all the Mothers, from the top to toe.
Buck. Well, let them reſt: Come hither *Catesby*,
Thou art ſworne as deepely to effect what we intend,
As cloſely to conceale what we impart:
Thou know'ſt our reaſons vrg'd vpon the way.
What think'ſt thou? is it not an eaſie matter,
To make *William* Lord *Haſtings* of our minde,
For the inſtallment of this Noble Duke
In the Seat Royall of this famous Ile?
Cates. He for his fathers ſake ſo loues the Prince,
That he will not be wonne to ought againſt him.
Buck. What think'ſt thou then of *Stanley*? Will not hee?
Cates. Hee will doe all in all as *Haſtings* doth.
Buck. Well then, no more but this:
Goe gentle *Catesby*, and as it were farre off,
Sound thou Lord *Haſtings*,
How he doth ſtand affected to our purpoſe,
And ſummon him to morrow to the Tower,
To ſit about the Coronation.
If thou do'ſt finde him tractable to vs,
Encourage him, and tell him all our reaſons:
If he be leaden, ycie, cold, vnwilling,
Be thou ſo too, and ſo breake off the talke,
And giue vs notice of his inclination:
For we to morrow hold diuided Councels,
Wherein thy ſelfe ſhalt highly be employ'd.
Rich. Commend me to Lord *William*: tell him *Catesby*,
His ancient Knot of dangerous Aduerſaries
To morrow are let blood at Pomfret Caſtle,
And bid my Lord, for ioy of this good newes,
Giue Miſtreſſe *Shore* one gentle Kiſſe the more.
Buck. Good *Catesby*, goe effect this buſineſſe ſoundly.
Cates. My good Lords both, with all the heed I can.
Rich. Shall we heare from you, *Catesby*, ere we ſleepe?
Cates. You ſhall, my Lord.
Rich. At *Crosby* Houſe, there ſhall you find vs both.
Exit Catesby.
Buck. Now, my Lord,
What ſhall wee doe, if wee perceiue
Lord *Haſtings* will not yeeld to our Complots?
Rich. Chop off his Head:
Something wee will determine:
And looke when I am King, clayme thou of me
The Earledome of Hereford, and all the moueables
Whereof the King, my Brother, was poſſeſt.
Buck. Ile clayme that promiſe at your Graces hand.
Rich. And looke to haue it yeelded with all kindneſſe.
Come, let vs ſuppe betimes, that afterwards
Wee may digeſt our complots in ſome forme.
Exeunt.

Scena Secunda.

Enter a Meſſenger to the Doore of Haſtings.

Meſſ. My Lord, my Lord.
Haſt. Who knockes?
Meſſ. One from the Lord *Stanley*.
Haſt. What is't a Clocke?
Meſſ. Vpon the ſtroke of foure.

Enter Lord Haſtings.

Haſt. Cannot my Lord *Stanley* ſleepe theſe tedious Nights?
Meſſ. So it appeares, by that I haue to ſay:
Firſt, he commends him to your Noble ſelfe.
Haſt. What then?
Meſſ. Then certifies your Lordſhip, that this Night
He dreamt, the Bore had raſed off his Helme:
Beſides, he ſayes there are two Councels kept;
And that may be determin'd at the one,
Which may make you and him to rue at th'other.
Therefore he ſends to know your Lordſhips pleaſure,
If you will preſently take Horſe with him,
And with all ſpeed poſt with him toward the North,
To ſhun the danger that his Soule diuines.
Haſt. Goe fellow, goe, returne vnto thy Lord,
Bid him not feare the ſeperated Councell:
His Honor and my ſelfe are at the one,
And at the other, is my good friend *Catesby*;
Where nothing can proceede, that toucheth vs,
Whereof I ſhall not haue intelligence:
Tell him his Feares are ſhallow, without inſtance.
And for his Dreames, I wonder hee's ſo ſimple,
To truſt the mock'ry of vnquiet ſlumbers.
To flye the Bore, before the Bore purſues,
Were to incenſe the Bore to follow vs,
And make purſuit, where he did meane no chaſe.
Goe, bid thy Maſter riſe, and come to me,
And we will both together to the Tower,
Where he ſhall ſee the Bore will vſe vs kindly
Meſſ. Ile goe, my Lord, and tell him what you ſay.
Exit.

Enter Catesby.

Cates. Many good morrowes to my Noble Lord.
Haſt. Good morrow *Catesby*, you are early ſtirring:
What newes, what newes, in this our tott'ring State?
Cates. It is a reeling World indeed, my Lord:
And I beleeue will neuer ſtand vpright,
Till *Richard* weare the Garland of the Realme.
Haſt. How weare the Garland?
Doeſt thou meane the Crowne?
Cates. I, my good Lord.
Haſt. Ile haue this Crown of mine cut frō my ſhoulders,
Before Ile ſee the Crowne ſo foule miſ-plac'd:
But canſt thou gueſſe, that he doth ayme at it?
Cates. I,

Cates. I,on my life, and hopes to find you forward,
Vpon his partie,for the gaine thereof:
And thereupon he ſends you this good newes,
That this ſame very day your enemies,
The Kindred of the Queene,muſt dye at Pomfret.
Haſt. Indeed I am no mourner for that newes,
Becauſe they haue beene ſtill my aduerſaries:
But,that Ile giue my voice on *Richards* ſide,
To barre my Maſters Heires in true Deſcent,
God knowes I will not doe it,to the death.
Cates. God keepe your Lordſhip in that gracious minde.
Haſt. But I ſhall laugh at this a twelue-month hence,
That they which brought me in my Maſters hate,
I liue to looke vpon their Tragedie.
Well *Catesby*,ere a fort-night make me older,
Ile ſend ſome packing,that yet thinke not on't.
Cates. 'Tis a vile thing to dye,my gracious Lord,
When men are vnprepar'd,and looke not for it.
Haſt. O monſtrous,monſtrous! and ſo falls it out
With *Riuers,Vaughan,Grey*: and ſo 'twill doe
With ſome men elſe,that thinke themſelues as ſafe
As thou and I,who(as thou know'ſt) are deare
To Princely *Richard*, and to *Buckingham*.
Cates. The Princes both make high account of you,
For they account his Head vpon the Bridge.
Haſt. I know they doe,and I haue well deſeru'd it.

Enter Lord Stanley.

Come on,come on,where is your Bore-ſpeare man?
Feare you the Bore,and goe ſo vnprouided?
Stan. My Lord good morrow,good morrow *Catesby*:
You may ieaſt on, but by the holy Rood,
I doe not like theſe ſeuerall Councels,I.
Haſt. My Lord,I hold my Life as deare as yours,
And neuer in my dayes,I doe proteſt,
Was it ſo precious to me,as 'tis now.
Thinke you,but that I know our ſtate ſecure,
I would be ſo triumphant as I am?
*Sta.*The Lords at Pomfret,whē they rode from London,
Were iocund,and ſuppos'd their ſtates were ſure,
And they indeed had no cauſe to miſtruſt:
But yet you ſee,how ſoone the Day o're-caſt.
This ſudden ſtab of Rancour I miſdoubt:
Pray God (I ſay) I proue a needleſſe Coward.
What,ſhall we toward the Tower? the day is ſpent.
Haſt. Come,come,haue with you:
Wot you what,my Lord,
To day the Lords you talke of,are beheaded.
*Sta.*They,for their truth,might better wear their Heads,
Then ſome that haue accus'd them,weare their Hats.
But come,my Lord,let's away.

Enter a Purſuivant.

Haſt. Goe on before,Ile talke with this good fellow.
Exit Lord Stanley,and Catesby.
How now,Sirrha? how goes the World with thee?
*Purſ.*The better,that your Lordſhip pleaſe to aske.
Haſt. I tell thee man,'tis better with me now,
Then when thou met'ſt me laſt,where now we meet:
Then was I going Priſoner to the Tower,
By the ſuggeſtion of the Queenes Allyes.
But now I tell thee (keepe it to thy ſelfe)
This day thoſe Enemies are put to death,
And I in better ſtate then ere I was.
Purſ. God hold it, to your Honors good content.
Haſt. Gramercie fellow: there,drinke that for me.
Throwes him his Purſe.
Purſ. I thanke your Honor. *Exit Purſuivant.*

Enter a Prieſt.

Prieſt. Well met,my Lord,I am glad to ſee your Honor.
Haſt. I thanke thee,good Sir *Iohn*,with all my heart.
I am in your debt,for your laſt Exerciſe:
Come the next Sabboth,and I will content you.
Prieſt. Ile wait vpon your Lordſhip.

Enter Buckingham.

Buc. What,talking with a Prieſt,Lord Chamberlaine?
Your friends at Pomfret,they doe need the Prieſt,
Your Honor hath no ſhriuing worke in hand.
Haſt. Good faith,and when I met this holy man,
The men you talke of,came into my minde.
What,goe you toward the Tower?
Buc. I doe,my Lord,but long I cannot ſtay there:
I ſhall returne before your Lordſhip,thence.
Haſt Nay like enough,for I ſtay Dinner there.
Buc. And Supper too,although thou know'ſt it not.
Come,will you goe?
Haſt. Ile wait vpon your Lordſhip. *Exeunt.*

Scena Tertia.

Enter Sir Richard Ratcliffe,with Halberds,carrying the Nobles to death at Pomfret.

Riuers. Sir *Richard Ratcliffe*,let me tell thee this,
To day ſhalt thou behold a Subiect die,
For Truth,for Dutie,and for Loyaltie.
Grey. God bleſſe the Prince from all the Pack of you,
A Knot you are,of damned Blood-ſuckers.
Vaugh. You liue, that ſhall cry woe for this heereafter.
Rat. Diſpatch,the limit of your Liues is out.
Riuers. O Pomfret,Pomfret! O thou bloody Priſon!
Fatall and ominous to Noble Peeres:
Within the guiltie Cloſure of thy Walls,
Richard the Second here was hackt to death:
And for more ſlander to thy diſmall Seat,
Wee giue to thee our guiltleſſe blood to drinke.
Grey. Now *Margarets* Curſe is falne vpon our Heads,
When ſhee exclaim'd on *Haſtings*,you,and I,
For ſtanding by,when *Richard* ſtab'd her Sonne.
Riuers. Then curs'd ſhee *Richard*,
Then curs'd ſhee *Buckingham*,
Then curs'd ſhee *Haſtings*. Oh remember God,
To heare her prayer for them,as now for vs:
And for my Siſter,and her Princely Sonnes,
Be ſatisfy'd,deare God,with our true blood,
Which,as thou know'ſt,vniuſtly muſt be ſpilt.
Rat. Make haſte,the houre of death is expiate.
Riuers. Come *Grey*,come *Vaughan*,let vs here embrace.
Farewell,vntill we meet againe in Heauen.
Exeunt.

Scena

Scæna Quarta.

Enter Buckingham Darby, Haſtings, Biſhop of Ely, Norfolke, Ratcliffe, Louell, with others, at a Table.

Haſt. Now Noble Peeres, the cauſe why we are met,
Is to determine of the Coronation:
In Gods Name ſpeake, when is the Royall day?
Buck. Is all things ready for the Royall time?
Darb. It is, and wants but nomination.
Ely. To morrow then I iudge a happie day.
Buck. Who knowes the Lord Protectors mind herein?
Who is moſt inward with the Noble Duke?
Ely. Your Grace, we thinke, ſhould ſooneſt know his minde.
Buck. We know each others Faces: for our Hearts,
He knowes no more of mine, then I of yours,
Or I of his, my Lord, then you of mine:
Lord *Haſtings*, you and he are neere in loue.
Haſt. I thanke his Grace, I know he loues me well:
But for his purpoſe in the Coronation,
I haue not ſounded him, nor he deliuer'd
His gracious pleaſure any way therein:
But you, my Honorable Lords, may name the time,
And in the Dukes behalfe Ile giue my Voice,
Which I preſume hee'le take in gentle part.

Enter Glouceſter.

Ely. In happie time, here comes the Duke himſelfe.
Rich. My Noble Lords, and Couſins all, good morrow:
I haue beene long a ſleeper: but I truſt,
My abſence doth neglect no great deſigne,
Which by my preſence might haue beene concluded.
Buck. Had you not come vpon your Q my Lord,
William, Lord *Haſtings*, had pronounc'd your part;
I meane your Voice, for Crowning of the King.
Rich. Then my Lord *Haſtings*, no man might be bolder,
His Lordſhip knowes me well, and loues me well.
My Lord of Ely, when I was laſt in Holborne,
I ſaw good Strawberries in your Garden there,
I doe beſeech you, ſend for ſome of them.
Ely. Mary and will, my Lord, with all my heart.
Exit Biſhop.
Rich. Couſin of Buckingham, a word with you.
Catesby hath ſounded *Haſtings* in our buſineſſe,
And findes the teſtie Gentleman ſo hot,
That he will loſe his Head, ere giue conſent
His Maſters Child, as worſhipfully he tearmes it,
Shall loſe the Royaltie of Englands Throne.
Buck. Withdraw your ſelfe a while, Ile goe with you.
Exeunt.
Darb. We haue not yet ſet downe this day of Triumph:
To morrow, in my iudgement, is too ſudden,
For I my ſelfe am not ſo well prouided,
As elſe I would be, were the day prolong'd.

Enter the Biſhop of Ely.

Ely. Where is my Lord, the Duke of Gloſter?
I haue ſent for theſe Strawberries.
Ha. His Grace looks chearfully & ſmooth this morning,
There's ſome conceit or other likes him well,
When that he bids good morrow with ſuch ſpirit.
I thinke there's neuer a man in Chriſtendome
Can leſſer hide his loue, or hate, then hee,
For by his Face ſtraight ſhall you know his Heart.
Derb. What of his Heart perceiue you in his Face,
By any liuelyhood he ſhew'd to day?
Haſt. Mary, that with no man here he is offended:
For were he, he had ſhewne it in his Lookes.

Enter Richard, and Buckingham.

Rich. I pray you all, tell me what they deſerue,
That doe conſpire my death with diuelliſh Plots
Of damned Witchcraft, and that haue preuail'd
Vpon my Body with their Helliſh Charmes.
Haſt. The tender loue I beare your Grace, my Lord,
Makes me moſt forward, in this Princely preſence,
To doome th'Offendors, whoſoe're they be:
I ſay, my Lord, they haue deſerued death.
Rich. Then be your eyes the witneſſe of their euill.
Looke how I am bewitch'd: behold, mine Arme
Is like a blaſted Sapling, wither'd vp:
And this is *Edwards* Wife, that monſtrous Witch,
Conſorted with that Harlot, Strumpet *Shore*,
That by their Witchcraft thus haue marked me.
Haſt. If they haue done this deed, my Noble Lord.
Rich. If? thou Protector of this damned Strumpet,
Talk'ſt thou to me of Ifs: thou art a Traytor,
Off with his Head; now by Saint *Paul* I ſweare,
I will not dine, vntill I ſee the ſame.
Louell and *Ratcliffe*, looke that it be done: *Exeunt.*
The reſt that loue me, riſe, and follow me.

Manet Louell and Ratcliffe, with the Lord Haſtings.

Haſt. Woe, woe for England, not a whit for me,
For I, too fond, might haue preuented this:
Stanley did dreame, the Bore did rowſe our Helmes,
And I did ſcorne it, and diſdaine to flye:
Three times to day my Foot-Cloth-Horſe did ſtumble,
And ſtarted, when he look'd vpon the Tower,
As loth to beare me to the ſlaughter-houſe.
O now I need the Prieſt, that ſpake to me:
I now repent I told the Purſuiuant,
As too triumphing, how mine Enemies
To day at Pomfret bloodily were butcher'd,
And I my ſelfe ſecure, in grace and fauour.
Oh *Margaret*, *Margaret*, now thy heauie Curſe
Is lighted on poore *Haſtings* wretched Head.
Ra. Come, come, diſpatch, the Duke would be at dinner:
Make a ſhort Shrift, he longs to ſee your Head.
Haſt. O momentarie grace of mortall men,
Which we more hunt for, then the grace of God!
Who builds his hope in ayre of your good Lookes,
Liues like a drunken Sayler on a Maſt,
Readie with euery Nod to tumble downe,
Into the fatall Bowels of the Deepe.
Lou. Come, come, diſpatch, 'tis bootleſſe to exclaime.
Haſt. O bloody *Richard*: miſerable England,
I prophecie the fearefull'ſt time to thee,
That euer wretched Age hath look'd vpon.
Come, lead me to the Block, beare him my Head,
They ſmile at me, who ſhortly ſhall be dead.
Exeunt.

ſ *Enter*

Enter Richard, and Buckingham, in rotten Armour, maruellous ill-fauoured.

Richard. Come Couſin,
Canſt thou quake, and change thy colour,
Murther thy breath in middle of a word,
And then againe begin, and ſtop againe,
As if thou were diſtraught, and mad with terror?
Buck. Tut, I can counterfeit the deepe Tragedian,
Speake, and looke backe, and prie on euery ſide,
Tremble and ſtart at wagging of a Straw:
Intending deepe ſuſpition, gaſtly Lookes
Are at my ſeruice, like enforced Smiles;
And both are readie in their Offices,
At any time to grace my Stratagemes.
But what, is *Catesby* gone?
Rich. He is, and ſee he brings the Maior along.

Enter the Maior, and Catesby.

Buck. Lord Maior.
Rich. Looke to the Draw-Bridge there.
Buck. Hearke, a Drumme.
Rich. *Catesby*, o're-looke the Walls.
Buck. Lord Maior, the reaſon we haue ſent.
Rich. Looke back, defend thee, here are Enemies.
Buck. God and our Innocencie defend, and guard vs.

Enter Louell and Ratcliffe, with Haſtings Head.

Rich. Be patient, they are friends: *Ratcliffe*, and *Louell.*
Louell. Here is the Head of that ignoble Traytor,
The dangerous and vnſuſpected *Haſtings.*
Rich. So deare I lou'd the man, that I muſt weepe:
I tooke him for the plaineſt harmeleſſe Creature,
That breath'd vpon the Earth, a Chriſtian.
Made him my Booke, wherein my Soule recorded
The Hiſtorie of all her ſecret thoughts.
So ſmooth he dawb'd his Vice with ſhew of Vertue,
That his apparant open Guilt omitted,
I meane, his Conuerſation with *Shores* Wife,
He liu'd from all attainder of ſuſpects.
Buck. Well, well, he was the couertſt ſheltred Traytor
That euer liu'd.
Would you imagine, or almoſt beleeue,
Wert not, that by great preſeruation
We liue to tell it, that the ſubtill Traytor
This day had plotted, in the Councell-Houſe,
To murther me, and my good Lord of Gloſter.
Maior. Had he done ſo?
Rich. What? thinke you we are Turkes, or Infidels?
Or that we would, againſt the forme of Law,
Proceed thus raſhly in the Villaines death,
But that the extreme perill of the caſe,
The Peace of England, and our Perſons ſafetie,
Enforc'd vs to this Execution.
Maior. Now faire befall you, he deſeru'd his death,
And your good Graces both haue well proceeded,
To warne falſe Traytors from the like Attempts.
Buck. I neuer look'd for better at his hands,
After he once fell in with Miſtreſſe *Shore:*
Yet had we not determin'd he ſhould dye,
Vntill your Lordſhip came to ſee his end,
Which now the louing haſte of theſe our friends,
Something againſt our meanings, haue preuented;
Becauſe, my Lord, I would haue had you heard
The Traytor ſpeake, and timorouſly confeſſe
The manner and the purpoſe of his Treaſons:
That you might well haue ſignify'd the ſame
Vnto the Citizens, who haply may
Miſconſter vs in him, and wayle his death.
Ma. But, my good Lord, your Graces words ſhal ſerue,
As well as I had ſeene, and heard him ſpeake:
And doe not doubt, right Noble Princes both,
But Ile acquaint our dutious Citizens
With all your iuſt proceedings in this caſe.
Rich. And to that end we wiſh'd your Lordſhip here,
T'auoid the Cenſures of the carping World.
Buck. Which ſince you come too late of our intent,
Yet witneſſe what you heare we did intend:
And ſo, my good Lord Maior, we bid farwell.

Exit Maior.

Rich. Goe after, after, Couſin *Buckingham.*
The Maior towards Guild-Hall hyes him in all poſte:
There, at your meeteſt vantage of the time,
Inferre the Baſtardie of *Edwards* Children:
Tell them, how *Edward* put to death a Citizen,
Onely for ſaying, he would make his Sonne
Heire to the Crowne, meaning indeed his Houſe,
Which, by the Signe thereof, was tearmed ſo.
Moreouer, vrge his hatefull Luxurie,
And beaſtiall appetite in change of Luſt,
Which ſtretcht vnto their Seruants, Daughters, Wiues,
Euen where his raging eye, or ſauage heart,
Without controll, luſted to make a prey.
Nay, for a need, thus farre come neere my Perſon:
Tell them, when that my Mother went with Child
Of that inſatiate *Edward*; Noble *Yorke*,
My Princely Father, then had Warres in France,
And by true computation of the time,
Found, that the Iſſue was not his begot:
Which well appeared in his Lineaments,
Being nothing like the Noble Duke, my Father:
Yet touch this ſparingly, as 'twere farre off,
Becauſe, my Lord, you know my Mother liues.
Buck. Doubt not, my Lord, Ile play the Orator,
As if the Golden Fee, for which I plead,
Were for my ſelfe: and ſo, my Lord, adue.
Rich. If you thriue wel, bring them to Baynards Caſtle,
Where you ſhall finde me well accompanied
With reuerend Fathers, and well-learned Biſhops.
Buck. I goe, and towards three or foure a Clocke
Looke for the Newes that the Guild-Hall affoords.

Exit Buckingham.

Rich. Goe *Louell* with all ſpeed to Doctor *Shaw*,
Goe thou to Fryer *Peuker*, bid them both
Meet me within this houre at Baynards Caſtle. *Exit.*
Now will I goe to take ſome priuie order,
To draw the Brats of *Clarence* out of ſight,
And to giue order, that no manner perſon
Haue any time recourſe vnto the Princes. *Exeunt.*

Enter a Scriuener.

Scr. Here is the Indictment of the good Lord *Haſtings*,
Which in a ſet Hand fairely is engroſs'd,
That it may be to day read o're in *Paules.*
And marke how well the ſequell hangs together:
Eleuen houres I haue ſpent to write it ouer,
For yeſter-night by *Catesby* was it ſent me,
The Precedent was full as long a doing,
And yet within theſe fiue houres *Haſtings* liu'd,
Vntainted, vnexamin'd, free, at libertie.
Here's a good World the while.
Who is ſo groſſe, that cannot ſee this palpable deuice?
Yet

Yet who ſo bold, but ſayes he ſees it not?
Bad is the World, and all will come to nought,
When ſuch ill dealing muſt be ſeene in thought. *Exit.*

Enter Richard and Buckingham at ſeuerall Doores.

Rich. How now, how now, what ſay the Citizens?
Buck. Now by the holy Mother of our Lord,
The Citizens are mum, ſay not a word.
Rich. Toucht you the Baſtardie of *Edwards* Children?
Buck. I did, with his Contract with Lady *Lucy*,
And his Contract by Deputie in France,
Th'vnſatiate greedineſſe of his deſire,
And his enforcement of the Citie Wiues,
His Tyrannie for Trifles, his owne Baſtardie,
As being got, your Father then in France,
And his reſemblance, being not like the Duke.
Withall, I did inferre your Lineaments,
Being the right *Idea* of your Father,
Both in your forme, and Nobleneſſe of Minde:
Layd open all your Victories in Scotland,
Your Diſcipline in Warre, Wiſdome in Peace,
Your Bountie, Vertue, faire Humilitie:
Indeed, left nothing fitting for your purpoſe,
Vntoucht, or ſleightly handled in diſcourſe.
And when my Oratorie drew toward end,
I bid them that did loue their Countries good,
Cry, God ſaue *Richard*, Englands Royall King.
Rich. And did they ſo?
Buck. No, ſo God helpe me, they ſpake not a word,
But like dumbe Statues, or breathing Stones,
Star'd each on other, and look'd deadly pale:
Which when I ſaw, I reprehended them,
And ask'd the Maior, what meant this wilfull ſilence?
His anſwer was, the people were not vſed
To be ſpoke to, but by the Recorder.
Then he was vrg'd to tell my Tale againe:
Thus ſayth the Duke, thus hath the Duke inferr'd,
But nothing ſpoke, in warrant from himſelfe.
When he had done, ſome followers of mine owne,
At lower end of the Hall, hurld vp their Caps,
And ſome tenne voyces cry'd, God ſaue King *Richard*:
And thus I tooke the vantage of thoſe few,
Thankes gentle Citizens, and friends, quoth I,
This generall applauſe, and chearefull ſhowt,
Argues your wiſdome, and your loue to *Richard*:
And euen here brake off, and came away.
Rich. What tongue-leſſe Blockes were they,
Would they not ſpeake?
Will not the Maior then, and his Brethren, come?
Buck. The Maior is here at hand: intend ſome feare,
Be not you ſpoke with, but by mightie ſuit:
And looke you get a Prayer-Booke in your hand,
And ſtand betweene two Church-men, good my Lord,
For on that ground Ile make a holy Deſcant:
And be not eaſily wonne to our requeſts,
Play the Maids part, ſtill anſwer nay, and take it.
Rich. I goe: and if you plead as well for them,
As I can ſay nay to thee for my ſelfe,
No doubt we bring it to a happie iſſue.
Buck. Go, go vp to the Leads, the Lord Maior knocks.

Enter the Maior, and Citizens.

Welcome, my Lord, I dance attendance here,
I thinke the Duke will not be ſpoke withall.

Enter Catesby.

Buck. Now *Catesby*, what ſayes your Lord to my requeſt?
Catesby. He doth entreat your Grace, my Noble Lord,
To viſit him to morrow, or next day:
He is within, with two right reuerend Fathers,
Diuinely bent to Meditation,
And in no Worldly ſuites would he be mou'd,
To draw him from his holy Exerciſe.
Buck. Returne, good *Catesby*, to the gracious Duke,
Tell him, my ſelfe, the Maior and Aldermen,
In deepe deſignes, in matter of great moment,
No leſſe importing then our generall good,
Are come to haue ſome conference with his Grace.
Catesby. Ile ſignifie ſo much vnto him ſtraight. *Exit.*
Buck. Ah ha, my Lord, this Prince is not an *Edward*,
He is not lulling on a lewd Loue-Bed,
But on his Knees, at Meditation:
Not dallying with a Brace of Curtizans,
But meditating with two deepe Diuines:
Not ſleeping, to engroſſe his idle Body,
But praying, to enrich his watchfull Soule.
Happie were England, would this vertuous Prince
Take on his Grace the Soueraigntie thereof.
But ſure I feare we ſhall not winne him to it.
Maior. Marry God defend his Grace ſhould ſay vs nay.
Buck. I feare he will: here *Catesby* comes againe.

Enter Catesby.

Now *Catesby*, what ſayes his Grace?
Catesby. He wonders to what end you haue aſſembled
Such troopes of Citizens, to come to him,
His Grace not being warn'd thereof before:
He feares, my Lord, you meane no good to him.
Buck. Sorry I am, my Noble Couſin ſhould
Suſpect me, that I meane no good to him:
By Heauen, we come to him in perfit loue,
And ſo once more returne, and tell his Grace. *Exit.*
When holy and deuout Religious men
Are at their Beades, 'tis much to draw them thence,
So ſweet is zealous Contemplation.

Enter Richard aloft, betweene two Biſhops.

Maior. See where his Grace ſtands, tweene two Clergie men.
Buck. Two Props of Vertue, for a Chriſtian Prince,
To ſtay him from the fall of Vanitie:
And ſee a Booke of Prayer in his hand,
True Ornaments to know a holy man.
Famous *Plantagenet*, moſt gracious Prince,
Lend fauourable eare to our requeſts,
And pardon vs the interruption
Of thy Deuotion, and right Chriſtian Zeale.
Rich. My Lord, there needes no ſuch Apologie:
I doe beſeech your Grace to pardon me,
Who earneſt in the ſeruice of my God,
Deferr'd the viſitation of my friends.
But leauing this, what is your Graces pleaſure?
Buck. Euen that (I hope) which pleaſeth God aboue,
And all good men, of this vngouern'd Ile.
Rich. I doe ſuſpect I haue done ſome offence,
That ſeemes diſgracious in the Cities eye,
And that you come to reprehend my ignorance.

Buck. You haue, my Lord:
Would it might please your Grace,
On our entreaties, to amend your fault.
Rich. Else wherefore breathe I in a Christian Land.
Buck. Know then, it is your fault, that you resigne
The Supreme Seat, the Throne Maiesticall,
The Sceptred Office of your Ancestors,
Your State of Fortune, and your Deaw of Birth,
The Lineall Glory of your Royall House,
To the corruption of a blemisht Stock;
Whiles in the mildnesse of your sleepie thoughts,
Which here we waken to our Countries good,
The Noble Ile doth want his proper Limmes:
His Face defac'd with skarres of Infamie,
His Royall Stock graft with ignoble Plants,
And almost shouldred in the swallowing Gulfe
Of darke Forgetfulnesse, and deepe Obliuion.
Which to recure, we heartily solicite
Your gracious selfe to take on you the charge
And Kingly Gouernment of this your Land:
Not as Protector, Steward, Substitute,
Or lowly Factor, for anothers gaine;
But as successiuely, from Blood to Blood,
Your Right of Birth, your Empyrie, your owne.
For this, consorted with the Citizens,
Your very Worshipfull and louing friends,
And by their vehement instigation,
In this iust Cause come I to moue your Grace.
Rich. I cannot tell, if to depart in silence,
Or bitterly to speake in your reproofe,
Best fitteth my Degree, or your Condition.
If not to answer, you might haply thinke,
Tongue-ty'd Ambition, not replying, yeelded
To beare the Golden Yoake of Soueraigntie,
Which fondly you would here impose on me.
If to reproue you for this suit of yours,
So season'd with your faithfull loue to me,
Then on the other side I check'd my friends.
Therefore to speake, and to auoid the first,
And then in speaking, not to incurre the last,
Definitiuely thus I answer you.
Your loue deserues my thankes, but my desert
Vnmeritable, shunnes your high request.
First, if all Obstacles were cut away,
And that my Path were euen to the Crowne,
As the ripe Reuenue, and due of Birth:
Yet so much is my pouertie of spirit,
So mightie, and so manie my defects,
That I would rather hide me from my Greatnesse,
Being a Barke to brooke no mightie Sea;
Then in my Greatnesse couet to be hid,
And in the vapour of my Glory smother'd.
But God be thank'd, there is no need of me,
And much I need to helpe you, were there need:
The Royall Tree hath left vs Royall Fruit,
Which mellow'd by the stealing howres of time,
Will well become the Seat of Maiestie,
And make (no doubt) vs happy by his Reigne.
On him I lay that, you would lay on me,
The Right and Fortune of his happie Starres,
Which God defend that I should wring from him.
Buck. My Lord, this argues Conscience in your Grace,
But the respects thereof are nice, and triuiall,
All circumstances well considered.
You say, that *Edward* is your Brothers Sonne,
So say we too, but not by *Edwards* Wife:
For first was he contract to Lady *Lucie*,
Your Mother liues a Witnesse to his Vow;
And afterward by substitute betroth'd
To *Bona*, Sister to the King of France.
These both put off, a poore Petitioner,
A Care-cras'd Mother to a many Sonnes,
A Beautie-waining, and distressed Widow,
Euen in the after-noone of her best dayes,
Made prize and purchase of his wanton Eye,
Seduc'd the pitch, and height of his degree,
To base declension, and loath'd Bigamie.
By her, in his vnlawfull Bed, he got
This *Edward*, whom our Manners call the Prince.
More bitterly could I expostulate,
Saue that for reuerence to some aliue,
I giue a sparing limit to my Tongue.
Then good, my Lord, take to your Royall selfe
This proffer'd benefit of Dignitie;
If not to blesse vs and the Land withall,
Yet to draw forth your Noble Ancestrie
From the corruption of abusing times,
Vnto a Lineall true deriued course.
Maior. Do good my Lord, your Citizens entreat you.
Buck. Refuse not, mightie Lord, this proffer'd loue.
Catesb. O make them ioyfull, grant their lawfull suit.
Rich. Alas, why would you heape this Care on me?
I am vnfit for State, and Maiestie:
I doe beseech you take it not amisse,
I cannot, nor I will not yeeld to you.
Buck. If you refuse it, as in loue and zeale,
Loth to depose the Child, your Brothers Sonne,
As well we know your tendernesse of heart,
And gentle, kinde, effeminate remorse,
Which we haue noted in you to your Kindred,
And egally indeede to all Estates:
Yet know, where you accept our suit, or no,
Your Brothers Sonne shall neuer reigne our King,
But we will plant some other in the Throne,
To the disgrace and downe-fall of your House:
And in this resolution here we leaue you.
Come Citizens, we will entreat no more. *Exeunt.*
Catesb. Call him againe, sweet Prince, accept their suit:
If you denie them, all the Land will rue it.
Rich. Will you enforce me to a world of Cares.
Call them againe, I am not made of Stones,
But penetrable to your kinde entreaties,
Albeit against my Conscience and my Soule.
Enter Buckingham, and the rest.
Cousin of Buckingham, and sage graue men,
Since you will buckle fortune on my back,
To beare her burthen, where I will or no.
I must haue patience to endure the Load:
But if black Scandall, or foule-fac'd Reproach,
Attend the sequell of your Imposition,
Your meere enforcement shall acquittance me
From all the impure blots and staynes thereof;
For God doth know, and you may partly see,
How farre I am from the desire of this.
Maior. God blesse your Grace, wee see it, and will say it.
Rich. In saying so, you shall but say the truth.
Buck. Then I salute you with this Royall Title,
Long liue King *Richard*, Englands worthie King.
All. Amen.
Buck. To morrow may it please you to be Crown'd.
Rich. Euen when you please, for you will haue it so.
Buck, To

Buck. To morrow then we will attend your Grace.
And so most ioyfully we take our leaue.
Rich. Come, let vs to our holy Worke againe.
Farewell my Cousins, farewell gentle friends. *Exeunt.*

Actus Quartus. Scena Prima.

Enter the Queene, Anne Duchesse of Gloucester, the Duchesse of Yorke, and Marquesse Dorset.

Duch.Yorke. Who meetes vs heere?
My Neece *Plantagenet,*
Led in the hand of her kind Aunt of Gloster?
Now, for my Life, shee's wandring to the Tower,
On pure hearts loue, to greet the tender Prince.
Daughter, well met.
Anne. God giue your Graces both, a happie
And a ioyfull time of day.
Qu. As much to you, good Sister: whither away?
Anne. No farther then the Tower, and as I guesse,
Vpon the like deuotion as your selues,
To gratulate the gentle Princes there.
Qu. Kind Sister thankes, wee'le enter all together:

Enter the Lieutenant.

And in good time, here the Lieutenant comes.
Master Lieutenant, pray you, by your leaue,
How doth the Prince, and my young Sonne of *Yorke*?
Lieu. Right well, deare Madame: by your patience,
I may not suffer you to visit them,
The King hath strictly charg'd the contrary.
Qu. The King? who's that?
Lieu. I meane, the Lord Protector.
Qu. The Lord protect him from that Kingly Title.
Hath he set bounds betweene their loue, and me?
I am their Mother, who shall barre me from them?
Duch.Yorke. I am their Fathers Mother, I will see them.
Anne. Their Aunt I am in law, in loue their Mother:
Then bring me to their sights, Ile beare thy blame,
And take thy Office from thee, on my perill.
Lieu. No, Madame, no; I may not leaue it so:
I am bound by Oath, and therefore pardon me.
Exit Lieutenant.

Enter Stanley.

Stanley. Let me but meet you Ladies one howre hence,
And Ile salute your Grace of Yorke as Mother,
And reuerend looker on of two faire Queenes.
Come Madame, you must straight to Westminster,
There to be crowned *Richards* Royall Queene.
Qu. Ah, cut my Lace asunder,
That my pent heart may haue some scope to beat,
Or else I swoone with this dead-killing newes.
Anne. Despightfull tidings, O vnpleasing newes.
Dors. Be of good cheare: Mother, how fares your Grace?
Qu. O *Dorset*, speake not to me, get thee gone,
Death and Destruction dogges thee at thy heeles,
Thy Mothers Name is ominous to Children.
If thou wilt out-strip Death, goe crosse the Seas,
And liue with *Richmond*, from the reach of Hell.
Goe hye thee, hye thee from this slaughter-house,
Lest thou encrease the number of the dead,
And make me dye the thrall of *Margarets* Curse,
Nor Mother, Wife, nor Englands counted Queene.
Stanley. Full of wise care, is this your counsaile, Madame:
Take all the swift aduantage of the howres:
You shall haue Letters from me to my Sonne,
In your behalfe, to meet you on the way:
Be not ta'ne tardie by vnwise delay.
Duch. Yorke. O ill dispersing Winde of Miserie,
O my accursed Wombe, the Bed of Death:
A Cockatrice hast thou hatcht to the World,
Whose vnauoided Eye is murtherous.
Stanley. Come, Madame, come, I in all haste was sent.
Anne. And I with all vnwillingnesse will goe.
O would to God, that the inclusiue Verge
Of Golden Mettall, that must round my Brow,
Were red hot Steele, to seare me to the Braines,
Anoynted let me be with deadly Venome,
And dye ere men can say, God saue the Queene.
Qu. Goe, goe, poore soule, I enuie not thy glory,
To feed my humor, wish thy selfe no harme.
Anne. No: why? When he that is my Husband now,
Came to me, as I follow'd *Henries* Corse,
When scarce the blood was well washt from his hands,
Which issued from my other Angell Husband,
And that deare Saint, which then I weeping follow'd:
O, when I say I look'd on *Richards* Face,
This was my Wish: Be thou (quoth I) accurst,
For making me, so young, so old a Widow:
And when thou wed'st, let sorrow haunt thy Bed;
And be thy Wife, if any be so mad,
More miserable, by the Life of thee,
Then thou hast made me, by my deare Lords death.
Loe, ere I can repeat this Curse againe,
Within so small a time, my Womans heart
Grossely grew captiue to his honey words,
And prou'd the subiect of mine owne Soules Curse,
Which hitherto hath held mine eyes from rest:
For neuer yet one howre in his Bed
Did I enioy the golden deaw of sleepe,
But with his timorous Dreames was still awak'd.
Besides, he hates me for my Father *Warwicke*,
And will (no doubt) shortly be rid of me.
Qu. Poore heart adieu, I pittie thy complaining.
Anne. No more, then with my soule I mourne for yours.
Dors. Farewell, thou wofull welcommer of glory.
Anne. Adieu, poore soule, that tak'st thy leaue of it.
Du.Y. Go thou to *Richmond*, & good fortune guide thee,
Go thou to *Richard*, and good Angels tend thee,
Go thou to Sanctuarie, and good thoughts possesse thee,
I to my Graue, where peace and rest lye with mee.
Eightie odde yeeres of sorrow haue I seene,
And each howres ioy wrackt with a weeke of teene.
Qu. Stay, yet looke backe with me vnto the Tower.
Pitty, you ancient Stones, those tender Babes,
Whom Enuie hath immur'd within your Walls,
Rough Cradle for such little prettie ones,
Rude ragged Nurse, old sullen Play-fellow,
For tender Princes: vse my Babies well;
So foolish Sorrowes bids your Stones farewell.
Exeunt.

t 3 *Sound*

Scena Secunda.

Sound a Sennet. Enter Richard in pompe, Buckingham, Catesby, Ratcliffe, Louel.

Rich. Stand all apart. Cousin of Buckingham.
Buck. My gracious Soueraigne.
Rich. Giue me thy hand. *Sound.*
Thus high, by thy aduice, and thy assistance,
Is King *Richard* seated:
But shall we weare these Glories for a day?
Or shall they last, and we reioyce in them?
Buck. Still liue they, and for euer let them last.
Rich. Ah *Buckingham*, now doe I play the Touch,
To trie if thou be currant Gold indeed:
Young *Edward* liues, thinke now what I would speake.
Buck. Say on my louing Lord.
Rich. Why *Buckingham*, I say I would be King.
Buck. Why so you are, my thrice-renowned Lord.
Rich. Ha? am I King? 'tis so: but *Edward* liues.
Buck. True, Noble Prince.
Rich. O bitter consequence!
That *Edward* still should liue true Noble Prince.
Cousin, thou wast not wont to be so dull.
Shall I be plaine? I wish the Bastards dead,
And I would haue it suddenly perform'd.
What say'st thou now? speake suddenly, be briefe.
Buck. Your Grace may doe your pleasure.
Rich. Tut, tut, thou art all Ice, thy kindnesse freezes:
Say, haue I thy consent, that they shall dye?
Buc. Giue me some litle breath, some pawse, deare Lord,
Before I positiuely speake in this:
I will resolue you herein presently. *Exit Buck.*
Catesby. The King is angry, see he gnawes his Lippe.
Rich. I will conuerse with Iron-witted Fooles,
And vnrespectiue Boyes: none are for me,
That looke into me with considerate eyes,
High-reaching *Buckingham* growes circumspect.
Boy.
Page. My Lord.
Rich. Know'st thou not any, whom corrupting Gold
Will tempt vnto a close exploit of Death?
Page. I know a discontented Gentleman,
Whose humble meanes match not his haughtie spirit:
Gold were as good as twentie Orators,
And will (no doubt) tempt him to any thing.
Rich. What is his Name?
Page. His Name, my Lord, is *Tirrell.*
Rich. I partly know the man: goe call him hither,
Boy. *Exit.*
The deepe reuoluing wittie *Buckingham*,
No more shall be the neighbor to my counsailes.
Hath he so long held out with me, vntyr'd,
And stops he now for breath? Well, be it so.

Enter Stanley.

How now, Lord *Stanley*, what's the newes?
Stanley. Know my louing Lord, the Marquesse *Dorset*
As I heare, is fled to *Richmond*,
In the parts where he abides.
Rich. Come hither *Catesby*, rumor it abroad,
That *Anne* my Wife is very grieuous sicke,
I will take order for her keeping close.
Inquire me out some meane poore Gentleman,
Whom I will marry straight to *Clarence* Daughter:
The Boy is foolish, and I feare not him.
Looke how thou dream'st: I say againe, giue out,
That *Anne*, my Queene, is sicke, and like to dye.
About it, for it stands me much vpon
To stop all hopes, whose growth may dammage me.
I must be marryed to my Brothers Daughter,
Or else my Kingdome stands on brittle Glasse:
Murther her Brothers, and then marry her,
Vncertaine way of gaine. But I am in
So farre in blood, that sinne will pluck on sinne,
Teare-falling Pittie dwells not in this Eye.

Enter Tyrrel.

Is thy Name *Tyrrel*?
Tyr. *Iames Tyrrel*, and your most obedient subiect.
Rich. Art thou indeed?
Tyr. Proue me, my gracious Lord.
Rich. Dar'st thou resolue to kill a friend of mine?
Tyr. Please you:
But I had rather kill two enemies.
Rich. Why then thou hast it: two deepe enemies,
Foes to my Rest, and my sweet sleepes disturbers,
Are they that I would haue thee deale vpon:
Tyrrel, I meane those Bastards in the Tower.
Tyr. Let me haue open meanes to come to them,
And soone Ile rid you from the feare of them.
Rich. Thou sing'st sweet Musique:
Hearke, come hither *Tyrrel*,
Goe by this token: rise, and lend thine Eare, *Whispers.*
There is no more but so: say it is done,
And I will loue thee, and preferre thee for it.
Tyr. I will dispatch it straight. *Exit.*

Enter Buckingham.

Buck. My Lord, I haue consider'd in my minde,
The late request that you did sound me in.
Rich. Well, let that rest: *Dorset* is fled to *Richmond.*
Buck. I heare the newes, my Lord.
Rich. *Stanley*, hee is your Wiues Sonne: well, looke vnto it.
Buck. My Lord, I clayme the gift, my due by promise,
For which your Honor and your Faith is pawn'd,
Th'Earledome of Hertford, and the moueables,
Which you haue promised I shall possesse.
Rich. *Stanley* looke to your Wife: if she conuey
Letters to *Richmond*, you shall answer it.
Buck. What sayes your Highnesse to my iust request?
Rich. I doe remember me, *Henry* the Sixt
Did prophecie, that *Richmond* should be King,
When *Richmond* was a little peeuish Boy.
A King perhaps.
Buck. May it please you to resolue me in my suit.
Rich. Thou troublest me, I am not in the vaine. *Exit.*
Buck. And is it thus? repayes he my deepe seruice
With such contempt? made I him King for this?
O let me thinke on *Hastings*, and be gone
To Brecnock, while my fearefull Head is on. *Exit.*

Enter Tyrrel.

Tyr. The tyrannous and bloodie Act is done,
The most arch deed of pittious massacre

That

That euer yet this Land was guilty of:
Dighton and *Forreſt*, who I did ſuborne
To do this peece of ruthfull Butchery,
Albeit they were fleſht Villaines, bloody Dogges,
Melted with tenderneſſe, and milde compaſſion,
Wept like to Children, in their deaths ſad Story.
O thus (quoth *Dighton*) lay the gentle Babes:
Thus, thus (quoth *Forreſt*) girdling one another
Within their Alablaſter innocent Armes:
Their lips were foure red Roſes on a ſtalke,
And in their Summer Beauty kiſt each other.
A Booke of Prayers on their pillow lay,
Which one (quoth *Forreſt*) almoſt chang'd my minde:
But oh the Diuell, there the Villaine ſtopt:
When *Dighton* thus told on, we ſmothered
The moſt repleniſhed ſweet worke of Nature,
That from the prime Creation ere ſhe framed.
Hence both are gone with Conſcience and Remorſe,
They could not ſpeake, and ſo I left them both,
To beare this tydings to the bloody King.

Enter Richard.

And heere he comes. All health my Soueraigne Lord.
Ric. Kinde *Tirrell*, am I happy in thy Newes.
Tir. If to haue done the thing you gaue in charge,
Beget your happineſſe, be happy then,
For it is done.
Rich. But did'ſt thou ſee them dead.
Tir. I did my Lord.
Rich. And buried gentle *Tirrell*.
Tir. The Chaplaine of the Tower hath buried them,
But where (to ſay the truth) I do not know.
Rich. Come to me *Tirrel* ſoone, and after Supper,
When thou ſhalt tell the proceſſe of their death.
Meane time, but thinke how I may do the good,
And be inheritor of thy deſire.
Farewell till then.
Tir. I humbly take my leaue.
Rich. The Sonne of *Clarence* haue I pent vp cloſe,
His daughter meanly haue I matcht in marriage,
The Sonnes of *Edward* ſleepe in *Abrahams* boſome,
And *Anne* my wife hath bid this world good night.
Now for I know the Britaine *Richmond* aymes
At yong *Elizabeth* my brothers daughter,
And by that knot lookes proudly on the Crowne,
To her go I, a iolly thriuing wooer.

Enter Ratcliffe.

Rat. My Lord.
Rich. Good or bad newes, that thou com'ſt in ſo bluntly?
Rat. Bad news my Lord, *Mourton* is fled to Richmond,
And Buckingham backt with the hardy Welſhmen
Is in the field, and ſtill his power encreaſeth.
Rich. Ely with Richmond troubles me more neere,
Then Buckingham and his raſh leuied Strength.
Come, I haue learn'd, that fearfull commenting
Is leaden ſeruitor to dull delay.
Delay leds impotent and Snaile-pac'd Beggery:
Then fierie expedition be my wing,
Ioues Mercury, and Herald for a King:
Go muſter men: My counſaile is my Sheeld,
We muſt be breefe, when Traitors braue the Field.
Exeunt.

Scena Tertia.

Enter old Queene Margaret.

Mar. So now proſperity begins to mellow,
And drop into the rotten mouth of death:
Heere in theſe Confines ſlily haue I lurkt,
To watch the waining of mine enemies.
A dire induction, am I witneſſe to,
And will to France, hoping the conſequence
Will proue as bitter, blacke, and Tragicall.
Withdraw thee wretched *Margaret*, who comes heere?

Enter Dutcheſſe and Queene.

Qu. Ah my poore Princes! ah my tender Babes:
My vnblowed Flowres, new appearing ſweets:
If yet your gentle ſoules flye in the Ayre,
And be not fixt in doome perpetuall,
Houer about me with your ayery wings,
And heare your mothers Lamentation.
Mar. Houer about her, ſay that right for right
Hath dim'd your Infant morne, to Aged night
Dut. So many miſeries haue craz'd my voyce,
That my woe-wearied tongue is ſtill and mute.
Edward Plantagenet, why art thou dead?
Mar. Plantagenet doth quit *Plantagenet*,
Edward for *Edward*, payes a dying debt.
Qu. Wilt thou, O God, flye from ſuch gentle Lambs,
And throw them in the intrailes of the Wolfe?
When didſt thou ſleepe, when ſuch a deed was done?
Mar. When holy *Harry* dyed, and my ſweet Sonne.
Dut Dead life, blind ſight, poore mortall liuing ghoſt,
Woes Scene, Worlds ſhame, Graues due, by life vſurpt,
Breefe abſtract and record of tedious dayes,
Reſt thy vnreſt on Englands lawfull earth,
Vnlawfully made drunke with innocent blood.
Qu. Ah that thou would'ſt aſſoone affoord a Graue,
As thou canſt yeeld a melancholly ſeate:
Then would I hide my bones, not reſt them heere,
Ah who hath any cauſe to mourne but wee?
Mar. If ancient ſorrow be moſt reuerent,
Giue mine the benefit of ſigneurie,
And let my greefes frowne on the vpper hand
If ſorrow can admit Society.
I had an *Edward*, till a *Richard* kill'd him:
I had a Husband, till a *Richard* kill'd him:
Thou had'ſt an *Edward*, till a *Richard* kill'd him:
Thou had'ſt a *Richard*, till a *Richard* kill'd him.
Dut. I had a *Richard* too, and thou did'ſt kill him;
I had a *Rutland* too, thou hop'ſt to kill him.
Mar. Thou had'ſt a *Clarence* too,
And *Richard* kill'd him.
From forth the kennell of thy wombe hath crept
A Hell-hound that doth hunt vs all to death:
That Dogge, that had his teeth before his eyes,
To worry Lambes, and lap their gentle blood:
That foule defacer of Gods handy worke:
That reignes in gauled eyes of weeping ſoules:
That excellent grand Tyrant of the earth,
Thy wombe let looſe to chaſe vs to our graues.
O vpright, iuſt, and true-diſpoſing God,
How do I thanke thee, that this carnall Curre

Prayes

Prayes on the issue of his Mothers body,
And makes her Pue-fellow with others mone.
Dut. Oh *Harries* wife, triumph not in my woes:
God witnesse with me, I haue wept for thine.
Mar. Beare with me: I am hungry for reuenge,
And now I cloy me with beholding it.
Thy *Edward* he is dead, that kill'd my *Edward*,
The other *Edward* dead, to quit my *Edward*:
Yong Yorke, he is but boote, because both they
Matcht not the high perfection of my losse.
Thy *Clarence* he is dead, that stab'd my *Edward*,
And the beholders of this franticke play,
Th'adulterate *Hastings*, *Riuers*, *Vaughan*, *Gray*,
Vntimely smother'd in their dusky Graues.
Richard yet liues, Hels blacke Intelligencer,
Onely reseru'd their Factor, to buy soules,
And send them thither: But at hand, at hand
Insues his pittious and vnpittied end.
Earth gapes, Hell burnes, Fiends roare, Saints pray,
To haue him sodainly conuey'd from hence:
Cancell his bond of life, deere God I pray,
That I may liue and say, The Dogge is dead.
Qu. O thou did'st prophesie, the time would come,
That I should wish for thee to helpe me curse
That bottel'd Spider, that foule bunch-back'd Toad.
Mar. I call'd thee then, vaine flourish of my fortune:
I call'd thee then, poore Shadow, painted Queen,
The presentation of but what I was;
The flattering Index of a direfull Pageant;
One heau'd a high, to be hurl'd downe below:
A Mother onely mockt with two faire Babes;
A dreame of what thou wast, a garish Flagge
To be the ayme of euery dangerous Shot,
A signe of Dignity, a Breath, a Bubble;
A Queene in ieast, onely to fill the Scene.
Where is thy Husband now? Where be thy Brothers?
Where be thy two Sonnes? Wherein dost thou Ioy?
Who sues, and kneeles, and sayes, God saue the Queene?
Where be the bending Peeres that flattered thee?
Where be the thronging Troopes that followed thee?
Decline all this, and see what now thou art.
For happy Wife, a most distressed Widdow:
For ioyfull Mother, one that wailes the name:
For one being sued too, one that humbly sues:
For Queene, a very Caytiffe, crown'd with care:
For she that scorn'd at me, now scorn'd of me;
For she being feared of all, now fearing one:
For she commanding all, obey'd of none.
Thus hath the course of Iustice whirl'd about,
And left thee but a very prey to time,
Hauing no more but Thought of what thou wast.
To torture thee the more, being what thou art,
Thou didst vsurpe my place, and dost thou not
Vsurpe the iust proportion of my Sorrow?
Now thy proud Necke, beares halfe my burthen'd yoke,
From which, euen heere I slip my wearied head,
And leaue the burthen of it all, on thee.
Farwell Yorkes wife, and Queene of sad mischance,
These English woes, shall make me smile in France.
Qu. O thou well skill'd in Curses, stay a-while,
And teach me how to curse mine enemies.
Mar. Forbeare to sleepe the night, and fast the day:
Compare dead happinesse, with liuing woe:
Thinke that thy Babes were sweeter then they were,
And he that slew them fowler then he is:
Bett'ring thy losse, makes the bad causer worse,
Reuoluing this, will teach thee how to Curse.
Qu. My words are dull, O quicken them with thine.
Mar. Thy woes will make them sharpe,
And pierce like mine. *Exit Margaret.*
Dut. Why should calamity be full of words?
Qu. Windy Atturnies to their Clients Woes,
Ayery succeeders of intestine ioyes,
Poore breathing Orators of miseries,
Let them haue scope, though what they will impart,
Helpe nothing els, yet do they ease the hart.
Dut. If so then, be not Tongue-ty'd: go with me,
And in the breath of bitter words, let's smother
My damned Son, that thy two sweet Sonnes smother'd.
The Trumpet sounds, be copious in exclaimes.

Enter King Richard, and his Traine.

Rich. Who intercepts me in my Expedition?
Dut. O she, that might haue intercepted thee
By strangling thee in her accursed wombe,
From all the slaughters (Wretch) that thou hast done.
Qu. Hid'st thou that Forhead with a Golden Crowne
Where't should be branded, if that right were right?
The slaughter of the Prince that ow'd that Crowne,
And the dyre death of my poore Sonnes, and Brothers.
Tell me thou Villaine-slaue, where are my Children?
Dut. Thou Toad, thou Toade,
Where is thy Brother *Clarence*?
And little *Ned Plantagenet* his Sonne?
Qu. Where is the gentle *Riuers*, *Vaughan*, *Gray*?
Dut. Where is kinde *Hastings*?
Rich. A flourish Trumpets, strike Alarum Drummes:
Let not the Heauens heare these Tell-tale women
Raile on the Lords Annointed. Strike I say.
Flourish. Alarums.
Either be patient, and intreat me fayre,
Or with the clamorous report of Warre,
Thus will I drowne your exclamations.
Dut. Art thou my Sonne?
Rich. I, I thanke God, my Father, and your selfe.
Dut. Then patiently heare my impatience.
Rich. Madam, I haue a touch of your condition,
That cannot brooke the accent of reproofe.
Dut. O let me speake.
Rich. Do then, but Ile not heare.
Dut. I will be milde, and gentle in my words.
Rich. And breefe (good Mother) for I am in hast.
Dut. Art thou so hasty? I haue staid for thee
(God knowes) in torment and in agony.
Rich. And came I not at last to comfort you?
Dut. No by the holy Rood, thou know'st it well,
Thou cam'st on earth, to make the earth my Hell.
A greeuous burthen was thy Birth to me,
Tetchy and wayward was thy Infancie.
Thy School-daies frightfull, desp'rate, wilde, and furious,
Thy prime of Manhood, daring, bold, and venturous:
Thy Age confirm'd, proud, subtle, slye, and bloody,
More milde, but yet more harmfull; Kinde in hatred:
What comfortable houre canst thou name,
That euer grac'd me with thy company?
Rich. Faith none, but *Humfrey Hower*,
That call'd your Grace
To Breakefast once, forth of my company.
If I be so disgracious in your eye,
Let me march on, and not offend you Madam.
Strike vp the Drumme.
Dut. I prythee heare me speake.
Rich.

Rich. You speake too bitterly.
Dut. Heare me a word:
For I shall neuer speake to thee againe.
Rich. So.
Dut. Either thou wilt dye, by Gods iust ordinance
Ere from this warre thou turne a Conqueror:
Or I with greefe and extreame Age shall perish,
And neuer more behold thy face againe.
Therefore take with thee my most greeuous Curse,
Which in the day of Battell tyre thee more
Then all the compleat Armour that thou wear'st.
My Prayers on the aduerse party fight,
And there the little soules of *Edwards* Children,
Whisper the Spirits of thine Enemies,
And promise them Successe and Victory:
Bloody thou art, bloody will be thy end:
Shame serues thy life, and doth thy death attend. *Exit.*
Qu. Though far more cause, yet much lesse spirit to curse
Abides in me, I say Amen to her.
Rich. Stay Madam, I must talke a word with you.
Qu. I haue no more sonnes of the Royall Blood
For thee to slaughter. For my Daughters (*Richard*)
They shall be praying Nunnes, not weeping Queenes:
And therefore leuell not to hit their liues.
Rich. You haue a daughter call'd *Elizabeth*,
Vertuous and Faire, Royall and Gracious?
Qu. And must she dye for this? O let her liue,
And Ile corrupt her Manners, staine her Beauty,
Slauder my Selfe, as false to *Edwards* bed:
Throw ouer her the vaile of Infamy,
So she may liue vnscarr'd of bleeding slaughter,
I will confesse she was not *Edwards* daughter.
Rich. Wrong not her Byrth, she is a Royall Princesse.
Qu. To saue her life, Ile say she is not so.
Rich. Her life is safest onely in her byrth.
Qu. And onely in that safety, dyed her Brothers.
Rich. Loe at their Birth, good starres were opposite.
Qu. No, to their liues, ill friends were contrary.
Rich. All vnauoyded is the doome of Destiny.
Qu. True: when auoyded grace makes Destiny.
My Babes were destin'd to a fairer death,
If grace had blest thee with a fairer life.
Rich. You speake as if that I had slaine my Cosins?
Qu. Cosins indeed, and by their Vnckle couzend,
Of Comfort, Kingdome, Kindred, Freedome, Life,
Whose hand soeuer lanch'd their tender hearts,
Thy head (all indirectly) gaue direction.
No doubt the murd'rous Knife was dull and blunt,
Till it was whetted on thy stone-hard heart,
To reuell in the Intrailes of my Lambes.
But that still vse of greefe, makes wilde greefe tame,
My tongue should to thy eares not name my Boyes,
Till that my Nayles were anchor'd in thine eyes:
And I in such a desp'rate Bay of death,
Like a poore Barke, of sailes and tackling reft,
Rush all to peeces on thy Rocky bosome.
Rich. Madam, so thriue I in my enterprize
And dangerous successe of bloody warres,
As I intend more good to you and yours,
Then euer you and yours by me were harm'd.
Qu. What good is couer'd with the face of heauen,
To be discouered, that can do me good.
Rich. Th'aduancement of your children, gentle Lady
Qu. Vp to some Scaffold, there to lose their heads.
Rich. Vnto the dignity and height of Fortune,
The high Imperiall Type of this earths glory.

Qu. Flatter my sorrow with report of it:
Tell m , what State, what Dignity, what Honor,
Canst thou demise to any childe of mine.
Rich. Euen all I haue; I, and my selfe and all,
Will I withall indow a childe of thine:
So in the Lethe of thy angry soule,
Thou drowne the sad remembrance of those wrongs,
Which thou supposest I haue done to thee.
Qu. Be breefe, least that the processe of thy kindnesse
Last longer telling then thy kindnesse date.
Rich. Then know,
That from my Soule, I loue thy Daughter.
Qu. My daughters Mother thinkes it with her soule.
Rich. What do you thinke?
Qu. That thou dost loue my daughter from thy soule
So from thy Soules loue didst thou loue her Brothers,
And from my hearts loue, I do thanke thee for it.
Rich. Be not so hasty to confound my meaning:
I meane that with my Soule I loue thy daughter,
And do intend to make her Queene of England.
Qu. Well then, who dost ÿ meane shallbe her King.
Rich. Euen he that makes her Queene:
Who else should bee?
Qu. What, thou?
Rich. Euen so: How thinke you of it?
Qu. How canst thou woo her?
Rich. That I would learne of you,
As one being best acquainted with her humour.
Qu. And wilt thou learne of me?
Rich. Madam, with all my heart.
Qu. Send to her by the man that slew her Brothers,
A paire of bleeding hearts: thereon ingraue
Edward and *Yorke*, then haply will she weepe:
Therefore present to her, as sometime *Margaret*
Did to thy Father, steept in Rutlands blood,
A hand-kercheefe, which say to her did dreyne
The purple sappe from her sweet Brothers body,
And bid her wipe her weeping eyes withall.
If this inducement moue her not to loue,
Send her a Letter of thy Noble deeds:
Tell her, thou mad'st away her Vnckle *Clarence*,
Her Vnckle *Riuers*, I (and for her sake)
Mad'st quicke conueyance with her good Aunt *Anne*.
Rich. You mocke me Madam, this not the way
To win your daughter.
Qu. There is no other way,
Vnlesse thou could'st put on some other shape,
And not be *Richard*, that hath done all this.
Ric. Say that I did all this for loue of her.
Qu. Nay then indeed she cannot choose but hate thee
Hauing bought loue, with such a bloody spoyle.
Rich. Looke what is done, cannot be now amended:
Men shall deale vnaduisedly sometimes,
Which after-houres giues leysure to repent.
If I did take the Kingdome from your Sonnes,
To make amends, Ile giue it to your daughter:
If I haue kill'd the issue of your wombe,
To quicken your encrease, I will beget
Mine yssue of your blood, vpon your Daughter:
A Grandams name is little lesse in loue,
Then is the doting Title of a Mother;
They are as Children but one steppe below,
Euen of your mettall, of your very blood:
Of all one paine, saue for a night of groanes
Endur'd of her, for whom you bid like sorrow.
Your Children were vexation to your youth,
But

But mine ſhall be a comfort to your Age,
The loſſe you haue, is but a Sonne being King,
And by that loſſe, your Daughter is made Queene.
I cannot make you what amends I would,
Therefore accept ſuch kindneſſe as I can.
Dorſet your Sonne, that with a fearfull ſoule
Leads diſcontented ſteppes in Forraine ſoyle,
This faire Alliance, quickly ſhall call home
To high Promotions, and great Dignity.
The King that calles your beauteous Daughter Wife,
Familiarly ſhall call thy *Dorſet*, Brother:
Againe ſhall you be Mother to a King:
And all the Ruines of diſtreſſefull Times,
Repayr'd with double Riches of Content.
What? we haue many goodly dayes to ſee:
The liquid drops of Teares that you haue ſhed,
Shall come againe, transform'd to Orient Pearle,
Aduantaging their Loue, with intereſt
Often-times double gaine of happineſſe.
Go then (my Mother) to thy Daughter go,
Make bold her baſhfull yeares, with your experience,
Prepare her eares to heare a Woers Tale.
Put in her tender heart, th'aſpiring Flame
Of Golden Soueraignty: Acquaint the Princeſſe
With the ſweet ſilent houres of Marriage ioyes:
And when this Arme of mine hath chaſtiſed
The petty Rebell, dull-brain'd *Buckingham*,
Bound with Triumphant Garlands will I come,
And leade thy daughter to a Conquerors bed:
To whom I will retaile my Conqueſt wonne,
And ſhe ſhalbe ſole Victoreſſe, *Cæſars Cæſar*.
Qu. What were I beſt to ſay, her Fathers Brother
Would be her Lord? Or ſhall I ſay her Vnkle?
Or he that ſlew her Brothers, and her Vnkles?
Vnder what Title ſhall I woo for thee,
That God, the Law, my Honor, and her Loue,
Can make ſeeme pleaſing to her tender yeares?
Rich. Inferre faire Englands peace by this Alliance.
Qu. Which ſhe ſhall purchaſe with ſtil laſting warre.
Rich. Tell her, the King that may command, intreats.
Qu. That at her hands, which the kings King forbids.
Rich. Say ſhe ſhall be a High and Mighty Queene.
Qu. To vaile the Title, as her Mother doth.
Rich. Say I will loue her euerlaſtingly.
Qu. But how long ſhall that title euer laſt?
Rich. Sweetly in force, vnto her faire liues end.
Qu. But how long fairely ſhall her ſweet life laſt?
Rich. As long as Heauen and Nature lengthens it.
Qu. As long as Hell and *Richard* likes of it.
Rich. Say, I her Soueraigne, am her Subiect low.
Qu. But ſhe your Subiect, lothes ſuch Soueraignty.
Rich. Be eloquent in my behalfe to her.
Qu. An honeſt tale ſpeeds beſt, being plainly told.
Rich. Then plainly to her, tell my louing tale.
Qu. Plaine and not honeſt, is too harſh a ſtyle.
Rich. Your Reaſons are too ſhallow, and to quicke.
Qu. O no, my Reaſons are too deepe and dead,
Too deepe and dead (poore Infants) in their graues,
Harpe on it ſtill ſhall I, till heart-ſtrings breake.
Rich. Harpe not on that ſtring Madam, that is paſt.
Now by my George, my Garter, and my Crowne.
Qu. Prophan'd, diſhonor'd, and the third vſurpt.
Rich. I ſweare.
Qu. By nothing, for this is no Oath:
Thy George prophan'd, hath loſt his Lordly Honor;
Thy Garter blemiſh'd, pawn'd his Knightly Vertue;
Thy Crowne vſurp'd, diſgrac'd his Kingly Glory:
If ſomething thou would'ſt ſweare to be beleeu'd,
Sweare then by ſomething, that thou haſt not wrong'd.
Rich. Then by my Selfe.
Qu. Thy Selfe, is ſelfe-miſvs'd.
Rich. Now by the World.
Qu. 'Tis full of thy foule wrongs.
Rich. My Fathers death.
Qu. Thy life hath it diſhonor'd.
Rich. Why then, by Heauen.
Qu. Heauens wrong is moſt of all:
If thou didd'ſt feare to breake an Oath with him,
The vnity the King my husband made,
Thou had'ſt not broken, nor my Brothers died.
If thou had'ſt fear'd to breake an oath by him,
Th'Imperiall mettall, circling now thy head,
Had grac'd the tender temples of my Child,
And both the Princes had bene breathing heere,
Which now two tender Bed-fellowes for duſt,
Thy broken Faith hath made the prey for Wormes.
What can'ſt thou ſweare by now.
Rich. The time to come.
Qu. That thou haſt wronged in the time ore-paſt:
For I my ſelfe haue many teares to waſh
Heereafter time, for time paſt, wrong'd by thee.
The Children liue, whoſe Fathers thou haſt ſlaughter'd,
Vngouern'd youth, to waile it with their age:
The Parents liue, whoſe Children thou haſt butcher'd,
Old barren Plants, to waile it with their Age.
Sweare not by time to come, for that thou haſt
Miſvs'd ere vs'd, by times ill-vs'd repaſt.
Rich. As I entend to proſper, and repent:
So thriue I in my dangerous Affayres
Of hoſtile Armes: My ſelfe, my ſelfe confound:
Heauen, and Fortune barre me happy houres:
Day, yeeld me not thy light; nor Night, thy reſt.
Be oppoſite all Planets of good lucke
To my proceeding, if with deere hearts loue,
Immaculate deuotion, holy thoughts,
I tender not thy beautious Princely daughter.
In her, conſiſts my Happineſſe, and thine:
Without her, followes to my ſelfe, and thee;
Her ſelfe, the Land, and many a Chriſtian ſoule,
Death, Deſolation, Ruine, and Decay;
It cannot be auoyded, but by this:
It will not be auoyded, but by this.
Therefore deare Mother (I muſt call you ſo)
Be the Atturney of my loue to her:
Pleade what I will be, not what I haue beene;
Not my deſerts, but what I will deſerue:
Vrge the Neceſſity and ſtate of times,
And be not peeuiſh found, in great Deſignes.
Qu. Shall I be tempted of the Diuel thus?
Rich. I, if the Diuell tempt you to do good.
Qu. Shall I forget my ſelfe, to be my ſelfe.
Rich. I, if your ſelfes remembrance wrong your ſelfe.
Qu. Yet thou didſt kil my Children.
Rich. But in your daughters wombe I bury them.
Where in that Neſt of Spicery they will breed
Selues of themſelues, to your recomforture.
Qu. Shall I go win my daughter to thy will?
Rich. And be a happy Mother by the deed.
Qu. I go, write to me very ſhortly,
And you ſhal vnderſtand from me her mind. *Exit Q.*
Rich. Beare her my true loues kiſſe, and ſo farewell.
Relenting Foole, and ſhallow-changing Woman.

How

How now, what newes?

Enter Ratcliffe.

Rat. Moſt mightie Soueraigne, on the Weſterne Coaſt
Rideth a puiſſant Nauie: to our Shores
Throng many doubtfull hollow-hearted friends,
Vnarm'd, and vnreſolu'd to beat them backe.
'Tis thought, that *Richmond* is their Admirall:
And there they hull, expecting but the aide
Of *Buckingham*, to welcome them aſhore.
Rich. Some light-foot friend poſt to ÿ Duke of Norfolk:
Ratcliffe thy ſelfe, or *Catesby*, where is hee?
Cat. Here, my good Lord.
Rich. *Catesby*, flye to the Duke.
Cat. I will, my Lord, with all conuenient haſte.
Rich. *Catesby* come hither, poſte to Salisbury:
When thou com'ſt thither: Dull vnmindfull Villaine,
Why ſtay'ſt thou here, and go'ſt not to the Duke?
Cat. Firſt, mighty Liege, tell me your Highneſſe pleaſure,
What from your Grace I ſhall deliuer to him.
Rich. O true, good *Catesby*, bid him leuie ſtraight
The greateſt ſtrength and power that he can make,
And meet me ſuddenly at Salisbury.
Cat. I goe. *Exit.*
Rat. What, may it pleaſe you, ſhall I doe at Salisbury?
Rich. Why, what would'ſt thou doe there, before I goe?
Rat. Your Highneſſe told me I ſhould poſte before.
Rich. My minde is chang'd:

Enter Lord Stanley.

Stanley, what newes with you?
Sta. None, good my Liege, to pleaſe you with ÿ hearing,
Nor none ſo bad, but well may be reported.
Rich. Hoyday, a Riddle, neither good nor bad:
What need'ſt thou runne ſo many miles about,
When thou mayeſt tell thy Tale the neereſt way?
Once more, what newes?
Stan. *Richmond* is on the Seas.
Rich. There let him ſinke, and be the Seas on him,
White-liuer'd Runnagate, what doth he there?
Stan. I know not, mightie Soueraigne, but by gueſſe.
Rich. Well, as you gueſſe.
Stan. Stirr'd vp by *Dorſet*, *Buckingham*, and *Morton*,
He makes for England, here to clayme the Crowne.
Rich. Is the Chayre emptie? is the Sword vnſway'd?
Is the King dead? the Empire vnpoſſeſt?
What Heire of *Torke* is there aliue, but wee?
And who is Englands King, but great *Torkes* Heire?
Then tell me, what makes he vpon the Seas?
Stan. Vnleſſe for that, my Liege, I cannot gueſſe.
Rich. Vnleſſe for that he comes to be your Liege,
You cannot gueſſe wherefore the Welchman comes.
Thou wilt reuolt, and flye to him, I feare.
Stan. No, my good Lord, therefore miſtruſt me not.
Rich. Where is thy Power then, to beat him back?
Where be thy Tenants, and thy followers?
Are they not now vpon the Weſterne Shore,
Safe-conducting the Rebels from their Shippes?
Stan. No, my good Lord, my friends are in the North.
Rich. Cold friends to me: what do they in the North,
When they ſhould ſerue their Soueraigne in the Weſt?
Stan. They haue not been commanded, mighty King:
Pleaſeth your Maieſtie to giue me leaue,
Ile muſter vp my friends, and meet your Grace,
Where, and what time your Maieſtie ſhall pleaſe.
Rich. I, thou would'ſt be gone, to ioyne with *Richmond*:
But Ile not truſt thee.
Stan. Moſt mightie Soueraigne,
You haue no cauſe to hold my friendſhip doubtfull,
I neuer was, nor neuer will be falſe.
Rich. Goe then, and muſter men: but leaue behind
Your Sonne *George Stanley*: looke your heart be firme,
Or elſe his Heads aſſurance is but fraile.
Stan. So deale with him, as I proue true to you.
Exit Stanley.

Enter a Meſſenger.

Meſſ. My gracious Soueraigne, now in Deuonſhire,
As I by friends am well aduertiſed,
Sir *Edward Courtney*, and the haughtie Prelate,
Biſhop of Exeter, his elder Brother,
With many moe Confederates, are in Armes.

Enter another Meſſenger.

Meſſ. In Kent, my Liege, the *Guilfords* are in Armes,
And euery houre more Competitors
Flocke to the Rebels, and their power growes ſtrong.

Enter another Meſſenger.

Meſſ. My Lord, the Armie of great *Buckingham*.
Rich. Out on ye, Owles, nothing but Songs of Death,
He ſtriketh him.
There, take thou that, till thou bring better newes.
Meſſ. The newes I haue to tell your Maieſtie,
Is, that by ſudden Floods, and fall of Waters,
Buckinghams Armie is diſpers'd and ſcatter'd,
And he himſelfe wandred away alone,
No man knowes whither.
Rich. I cry thee mercie:
There is my Purſe, to cure that Blow of thine.
Hath any well-aduiſed friend proclaym'd
Reward to him that brings the Traytor in?
Meſſ. Such Proclamation hath been made, my Lord.

Enter another Meſſenger.

Meſſ. Sir *Thomas Louell*, and Lord Marqueſſe *Dorſet*,
'Tis ſaid, my Liege, in Yorkeſhire are in Armes:
But this good comfort bring I to your Highneſſe,
The Brittaine Nauie is diſpers'd by Tempeſt.
Richmond in Dorſetſhire ſent out a Boat
Vnto the ſhore, to aske thoſe on the Banks,
If they were his Aſſiſtants, yea, or no?
Who anſwer'd him, they came from *Buckingham*,
Vpon his partie: he miſtruſting them,
Hoys'd ſayle, and made his courſe againe for Brittaine.
Rich. March on, march on, ſince we are vp in Armes,
If not to fight with forraine Enemies,
Yet to beat downe theſe Rebels here at home.

Enter Catesby.

Cat. My Liege, the Duke of Buckingham is taken,
That is the beſt newes: that the Earle of Richmond
Is

Is with a mighty power Landed at Milford,
Is colder Newes, but yet they must be told.
Rich. Away towards Salsbury, while we reason here,
A Royall batteil might be wonne and lost:
Some one take order Buckingham be brought
To Salsbury, the rest march on with me. *Florish. Exeunt*

Scena Quarta.

Enter Derby, and Sir Christopher.

Der. Sir *Christopher*, tell *Richmond* this from me,
That in the stye of the most deadly Bore,
My Sonne *George Stanley* is frankt vp in hold:
If I reuolt, off goes yong *Georges* head,
The feare of that, holds off my present ayde.
So get thee gone: commend me to thy Lord.
Withall say, that the Queene hath heartily consented
He should espouse *Elizabeth* hir daughter.
But tell me, where is Princely Richmond now?
Chri. At Penbroke, or at Hertford West in Wales.
Der. What men of Name resort to him.
Chri, Sir *Walter Herbert*, a renowned Souldier,
Sir *Gilbert Talbot*, Sir *William Stanley*,
Oxford, redoubted *Pembroke*, Sir *Iames Blunt*,
And *Rice ap Thomas*, with a valiant Crew,
And many other of great name and worth:
And towards London do they bend their power,
If by the way they be not fought withall.
Der. Well hye thee to thy Lord: I kisse his hand,
My Letter will resolue him of my minde.
Farewell. *Exeunt*

Actus Quintus. Scena Prima.

Enter Buckingham with Halberds, led to Execution

Buc. Will not King *Richard* let me speake with him?
Sher. No my good Lord, therefore be patient
Buc. *Hastings*, and *Edwards* children, *Gray* & *Riuers*,
Holy King *Henry*, and thy faire Sonne *Edward*,
Vaughan, and all that haue miscarried
By vnder-hand corrupted foule iniustice,
If that your moody discontented soules,
Do through the clowds behold this present houre,
Euen for reuenge mocke my destruction.
This is All-soules day (Fellow) is it not?
Sher. It is.
Buc. Why then Al-soules day, is my bodies doomsday
This is the day, which in King *Edwards* time
I wish'd might fall on me, when I was found
False to his Children, and his Wiues Allies.
This is the day, wherein I wisht to fall
By the false Faith of him whom most I trusted.
This, this All-soules day to my fearfull Soule,
Is the determin'd respit of my wrongs.
That high All-seer, which I dallied with,
Hath turn'd my fained Prayer on my head,
And giuen in earnest, what I begg'd in iest.
Thus doth he force the swords of wicked men
To turne their owne points in their Masters bosomes.
Thus *Margarets* curse falles heauy on my necke:
When he (quoth she) shall split thy heart with sorrow,
Remember *Margaret* was a Prophetesse:
Come leade me Officers to the blocke of shame,
Wrong hath but wrong, and blame the due of blame.
Exeunt Buckingham with Officers.

Scena Secunda.

Enter Richmond, Oxford, Blunt, Herbert, and others, with drum and colours.

Richm Fellowes in Armes, and my most louing Frends
Bruis'd vnderneath the yoake of Tyranny,
Thus farre into the bowels of the Land,
Haue we marcht on without impediment;
And heere receiue we from our Father *Stanley*
Lines of faire comfort and encouragement:
The wretched, bloody, and vsurping Boare,
(That spoyl'd your Summer Fields, and fruitfull Vines)
Swilles your warm blood like wash, & makes his trough
In your embowel'd bosomes: This foule Swine
Is now euen in the Centry of this Isle,
Ne're to the Towne of Leicester, as we learne:
From Tamworth thither, is but one dayes march.
In Gods name cheerely on, couragious Friends,
To reape the Haruest of perpetuall peace,
By this one bloody tryall of sharpe Warre.
Oxf. Euery mans Conscience is a thousand men,
To fight against this guilty Homicide.
Her. I doubt not but his Friends will turne to vs.
Blunt. He hath no friends, but what are friends for fear
Which in his deerest neede will flye from him.
Richm. All for our vantage, then in Gods name march,
True Hope is swift, and flyes with Swallowes wings,
Kings it makes Gods, and meaner creatures Kings.
Exeunt Omnes.

Enter King Richard in Armes with Norfolke, Ratcliffe, and the Earle of Surrey.

Rich. Here pitch our Tent, euen here in Bosworth field,
My Lord of Surrey, why looke you so sad?
Sur. My heart is ten times lighter then my lookes.
Rich. My Lord of Norfolke.
Nor. Heere most gracious Liege.
Rich. Norfolke, we must haue knockes:
Ha, must we not?
Nor. We must both giue and take my louing Lord.
Rich. Vp with my Tent, heere wil I lye to night,
But where to morrow? Well, all's one for that.
Who hath descried the number of the Traitors?
Nor Six or seuen thousand is their vtmost power.
Rich. Why our Battalia trebbles that account:
Besides, the Kings name is a Tower of strength,
Which they vpon the aduerse Faction want.
Vp with the Tent: Come Noble Gentlemen,
Let vs suruey the vantage of the ground.
Call for some men of sound direction:
Let's

Let's lacke no Discipline, make no delay,
For Lords, to morrow is a busie day. *Exeunt*

Enter Richmond, Sir William Branden, Oxford, and Dorset.

Richm. The weary Sunne, hath made a Golden set,
And by the bright Tract of his fiery Carre,
Giues token of a goodly day to morrow.
Sir *William Brandon*, you shall beare my Standard:
Giue me some Inke and Paper in my Tent:
Ile draw the Forme and Modell of our Battaile,
Limit each Leader to his seuerall Charge,
And part in iust proportion our small Power.
My Lord of Oxford, you Sir *William Brandon*,
And your Sir *Walter Herbert* stay with me;
The Earle of Pembroke keepes his Regiment;
Good Captaine *Blunt*, beare my goodnight to him,
And by the second houre in the Morning,
Desire the Earle to see me in my Tent:
Yet one thing more (good Captaine) do for me:
Where is Lord *Stanley* quarter'd, do you know?
Blunt. Vnlesse I haue mistane his Colours much,
(Which well I am assur'd I haue not done)
His Regiment lies halfe a Mile at least
South, from the mighty Power of the King.
Richm. If without perill it be possible,
Sweet *Blunt*, make some good meanes to speak with him
And giue him from me, this most needfull Note.
Blunt. Vpon my life, my Lord, Ile vndertake it,
And so God giue you quiet rest to night.
Richm. Good night good Captaine *Blunt*:
Come Gentlemen,
Let vs consult vpon to morrowes Businesse;
Into my Tent, the Dew is rawe and cold.
They withdraw into the Tent.

Enter Richard, Ratcliffe, Norfolke, & Catesby.

Rich. What is't a Clocke?
Cat. It's Supper time my Lord, it's nine a clocke.
King. I will not sup to night,
Giue me some Inke and Paper:
What, is my Beauer easier then it was?
And all my Armour laid into my Tent?
Cat. It is my Liege: and all things are in readinesse.
Rich. Good Norfolke, hye thee to thy charge,
Vse carefull Watch, choose trusty Centinels,
Nor. I go my Lord.
Rich. Stir with the Larke to morrow, gentle Norfolk.
Nor. I warrant you my Lord. *Exit*
Rich. *Ratcliffe.*
Rat. My Lord.
Rich. Send out a Pursuiuant at Armes
To *Stanleys* Regiment: bid him bring his power
Before Sun-rising, least his Sonne *George* fall
Into the blinde Caue of eternall night.
Fill me a Bowle of Wine: Giue me a Watch,
Saddle white Surrey for the Field to morrow:
Look that my Staues be sound, & not too heauy. *Ratcliff.*
Rat. My Lord.
Rich Saw'st the melancholly Lord Northumberland?
Rat. *Thomas* the Earle of Surrey, and himselfe,
Much about Cockshut time, from Troope to Troope
Went through the Army, chearing vp the Souldiers.
King. So, I am satisfied: Giue me a Bowle of Wine,
I haue not that Alacrity of Spirit,
Nor cheere of Minde that I was wont to haue.
Set it downe. Is Inke and Paper ready?
Rat. It is my Lord.
Rich. Bid my Guard watch. Leaue me.
Ratcliffe, about the mid of night come to my Tent
And helpe to arme me. Leaue me I say. *Exit Ratclif.*

Enter Derby to Richmond in his Tent.

Der. Fortune, and Victory sit on thy Helme.
Rich. All comfort that the darke night can affoord,
Be to thy Person, Noble Father in Law.
Tell me, how fares our Noble Mother?
Der. I by Attourney, blesse thee from thy Mother,
Who prayes continually for Richmonds good:
So much for that. The silent houres steale on,
And flakie darkenesse breakes within the East.
In breefe, for so the season bids vs be,
Prepare thy Battell early in the Morning,
And put thy Fortune to th'Arbitrement
Of bloody stroakes, and mortall staring Warre:
I, as I may, that which I would, I cannot,
With best aduantage will deceiue the time,
And ayde thee in this doubtfull shocke of Armes.
But on thy side I may not be too forward,
Least being seene, thy Brother, tender *George*
Be executed in his Fathers sight.
Farewell: the leysure, and the fearfull time
Cuts off the ceremonious Vowes of Loue,
And ample enterchange of sweet Discourse,
Which so long sundred Friends should dwell vpon:
God giue vs leysure for these rites of Loue.
Once more Adieu, be valiant, and speed well.
Richm. Good Lords conduct him to his Regiment:
Ile striue with troubled noise, to take a Nap,
Lest leaden slumber peize me downe to morrow,
When I should mount with wings of Victory:
Once more, good night kinde Lords and Gentlemen.
Exeunt. Manet Richmond.
O thou, whose Captaine I account my selfe,
Looke on my Forces with a gracious eye:
Put in their hands thy bruising Irons of wrath,
That they may crush downe with a heauy fall,
Th'vsurping Helmets of our Aduersaries:
Make vs thy ministers of Chasticement,
That we may praise thee in thy victory:
To thee I do commend my watchfull soule,
Ere I let fall the windowes of mine eyes:
Sleeping, and waking, oh defend me still. *Sleeps.*
Enter the Ghost of Prince Edward, Sonne to Henry the sixt.
Gh. to Ri. Let me sit heauy on thy soule to morrow:
Thinke how thou stab'st me in my prime of youth
At Teukesbury: Dispaire therefore, and dye.
Ghost to Richm. Be chearefull Richmond,
For the wronged Soules
Of butcher'd Princes, fight in thy behalfe:
King *Henries* issue Richmond comforts thee.
Enter the Ghost of Henry the sixt.
Ghost. When I was mortall, my Annointed body
By thee was punched full of holes;
Thinke on the Tower, and me: Dispaire, and dye,
Harry the sixt, bids thee dispaire, and dye.
To Richm. Vertuous and holy be thou Conqueror:
Harry that prophesied thou should'st be King,
Doth comfort thee in sleepe: Liue, and flourish.

t *Enter*

Enter the Ghost of Clarence.
Ghost. Let me sit heauy in thy soule to morrow.
I that was wash'd to death with Fulsome Wine:
Poore *Clarence* by thy guile betray'd to death:
To morrow in the battell thinke on me,
And fall thy edgelesse Sword, dispaire and dye.
To Richm. Thou off-spring of the house of Lancaster
The wronged heyres of Yorke do pray for thee,
Good Angels guard thy battell, Liue and Flourish.
Enter the Ghosts of Riuers, Gray, and Vaughan.
Riu Let me sit heauy in thy soule to morrow,
Riuers, that dy'de at Pomfret: dispaire, and dye.
Grey. Thinke vpon *Grey*, and let thy soule dispaire.
Vaugh. Thinke vpon *Vaughan*, and with guilty feare
Let fall thy Lance, dispaire and dye.
All to Richm. Awake,
And thinke our wrongs in *Richards* Bosome,
Will conquer him. Awake, and win the day.
Enter the Ghost of Lord Hastings.
Gho. Bloody and guilty: guiltily awake,
And in a bloody Battell end thy dayes.
Thinke on Lord Hastings: dispaire, and dye.
Hast. to Rich. Quiet vntroubled soule,
Awake, awake:
Arme, fight, and conquer, for faire Englands sake.
Enter the Ghosts of the two yong Princes.
Ghosts. Dreame on thy Cousins
Smothered in the Tower:
Let vs be laid within thy bosome *Richard*,
And weigh thee downe to ruine, shame, and death,
Thy Nephewes soule bids thee dispaire and dye.
Ghosts to Richm. Sleepe Richmond,
Sleepe in Peace, and wake in Ioy,
Good Angels guard thee from the Boares annoy,
Liue, and beget a happy race of Kings,
Edwards vnhappy Sonnes, do bid thee flourish.
Enter the Ghost of Anne, his Wife.
Ghost to Rich. Richard, thy Wife,
That wretched *Anne* thy Wife,
That neuer slept a quiet houre with thee,
Now filles thy sleepe with perturbations,
To morrow in the Battaile, thinke on me,
And fall thy edgelesse Sword, dispaire and dye:
Ghost to Richm. Thou quiet soule,
Sleepe thou a quiet sleepe:
Dreame of Successe, and Happy Victory,
Thy Aduersaries Wife doth pray for thee.
Enter the Ghost of Buckingham.
Ghost to Rich. The first was I
That help'd thee to the Crowne:
The last was I that felt thy Tyranny.
O, in the Battaile think on Buckingham,
And dye in terror of thy guiltinesse.
Dreame on, dreame on, of bloody deeds and death,
Fainting dispaire; dispairing yeeld thy breath.
Ghost to Richm. I dyed for hope
Ere I could lend thee Ayde;
But cheere thy heart, and be thou not dismayde:
God, and good Angels fight on Richmonds side,
And *Richard* fall in height of all his pride.
Richard starts out of his dreame.
Rich. Giue me another Horse, bind vp my Wounds:
Haue mercy Iesu. Soft, I did but dreame.
O coward Conscience! how dost thou afflict me?
The Lights burne blew. It is not dead midnight.
Cold fearefull drops stand on my trembling flesh.
What? do I feare my Selfe? There's none else by,
Richard loues *Richard*, that is, I am I.
Is there a Murtherer heere? No; Yes, I am:
Then flye; What from my Selfe? Great reason: why?
Lest I Reuenge. What? my Selfe vpon my Selfe?
Alacke, I loue my Selfe. Wherefore? For any good
That I my Selfe, haue done vnto my Selfe?
O no. Alas, I rather hate my Selfe,
For hatefull Deeds committed by my Selfe.
I am a Villaine: yet I Lye, I am not.
Foole, of thy Selfe speake well: Foole, do not flatter.
My Conscience hath a thousand seuerall Tongues,
And euery Tongue brings in a seuerall Tale,
And euerie Tale condemnes me for a Villaine;
Periurie, in the high'st Degree,
Murther, sterne murther, in the dyr'st degree,
All seuerall sinnes, all vs'd in each degree,
Throng all to'th'Barre, crying all, Guilty, Guilty.
I shall dispaire, there is no Creature loues me;
And if I die, no soule shall pittie me.
Nay, wherefore should they? Since that I my Selfe,
Finde in my Selfe, no pittie to my Selfe.
Me thought, the Soules of all that I had murther'd
Came to my Tent, and euery one did threat
To morrowes vengeance on the head of *Richard.*

Enter Ratcliffe.

Rat. My Lord.
King Who's there?
Rat. Ratcliffe my Lord, 'tis I: the early Village Cock
Hath twice done salutation to the Morne,
Your Friends are vp, and buckle on their Armour.
King. O *Ratcliffe*, I feare, I feare.
Rat. Nay good my Lord, be not affraid of Shadows.
King. By the Apostle *Paul*, shadowes to night
Haue stroke more terror to the soule of *Richard*,
Then can the substance of ten thousand Souldiers
Armed in proofe, and led by shallow *Richmond*.
'Tis not yet neere day. Come go with me,
Vnder our Tents Ile play the Ease-dropper,
To heare if any meane to shrinke from me.
Exeunt Richard & Ratliffe.

Enter the Lords to Richmond sitting in his Tent.

Richm. Good morrow Richmond.
Rich. Cry mercy Lords, and watchfull Gentlemen,
That you haue tane a tardie sluggard heere?
Lords. How haue you slept my Lord?
Rich. The sweetest sleepe,
And fairest boading Dreames,
That euer entred in a drowsie head,
Haue I since your departure had my Lords.
Me thought their Soules, whose bodies *Rich.* murther'd,
Came to my Tent, and cried on Victory:
I promise you my Heart is very iocond,
In the remembrance of so faire a dreame,
How farre into the Morning is it Lords?
Lor. Vpon the stroke of foure.
Rich. Why then 'tis time to Arme, and giue direction.
His Oration to his Souldiers.
More then I haue said, louing Countrymen,
The leysure and inforcement of the time
Forbids to dwell vpon: yet remember this,
God

God, and our good cause, fight vpon our side,
The Prayers of holy Saints and wronged soules,
Like high rear'd Bulwarkes, stand before our Faces,
(*Richard* except) those whom we fight against,
Had rather haue vs win, then him they follow.
For, what is he they follow? Truly Gentlemen,
A bloudy Tyrant, and a Homicide:
One rais'd in blood, and one in blood establish'd;
One that made meanes to come by what he hath,
And slaughter'd those that were the meanes to help him:
A base foule Stone, made precious by the foyle
Of Englands Chaire, where he is falsely set:
One that hath euer beene Gods Enemy.
Then if you fight against Gods Enemy,
God will in iustice ward you as his Soldiers.
If you do sweare to put a Tyrant downe,
You sleepe in peace, the Tyrant being slaine:
If you do fight against your Countries Foes,
Your Countries Fat shall pay your paines the hyre.
If you do fight in safegard of your wiues,
Your wiues shall welcome home the Conquerors.
If you do free your Children from the Sword,
Your Childrens Children quits it in your Age.
Then in the name of God and all these rights,
Aduance your Standards, draw your willing Swords.
For me, the ransome of my bold attempt,
Shall be this cold Corpes on the earth's cold face.
But if I thriue, the gaine of my attempt,
The least of you shall share his part thereof.
Sound Drummes and Trumpets boldly, and cheerefully,
God, and Saint *George*, *Richmond*, and Victory.

Enter King Richard, Ratcliffe, and Catesby.

K. What said Northumberland as touching Richmond?
Rat. That he was neuer trained vp in Armes.
King. He said the truth: and what said Surrey then?
Rat. He smil'd and said, the better for our purpose.
King. He was in the right, and so indeed it is.
Tell the clocke there. *Clocke strikes.*
Giue me a Kalender: Who saw the Sunne to day?
Rat. Not I my Lord.
King. Then he disdaines to shine: for by the Booke
He should haue bran'd the East an houre ago,
A blacke day will it be to somebody. *Ratcliffe.*
Rat. My Lord.
King. The Sun will not be seene to day,
The sky doth frowne, and lowre vpon our Army.
I would these dewy teares were from the ground.
Not shine to day? Why, what is that to me
More then to Richmond? For the selfe-same Heauen
That frownes on me, lookes sadly vpon him.

Enter Norfolke.

Nor. Arme, arme, my Lord: the foe vaunts in the field.
King. Come, bustle, bustle. Caparison my horse.
Call vp Lord *Stanley*, bid him bring his power,
I will leade forth my Soldiers to the plaine,
And thus my Battell shal be ordred.
My Foreward shall be drawne in length,
Consisting equally of Horse and Foot:
Our Archers shall be placed in the mid'st;
Iohn Duke of Norfolke, *Thomas* Earle of Surrey,
Shall haue the leading of the Foot and Horse.
They thus directed, we will follow
In the maine Battell, whose puissance on either side
Shall be well-winged with our cheefest Horse:
This, and Saint George to boote.
What think'st thou Norfolke.
Nor. A good direction warlike Soueraigne,
This found I on my Tent this Morning.
Iockey of Norfolke, be not so bold,
For Dickon thy maister is bought and sold.
King. A thing deuised by the Enemy.
Go Gentlemen, euery man to his Charge,
Let not our babling Dreames affright our soules:
For Conscience is a word that Cowards vse,
Deuis'd at first to keepe the strong in awe,
Our strong armes be our Conscience, Swords our Law.
March on, ioyne brauely, let vs too't pell mell,
If not to heauen, then hand in hand to Hell.
What shall I say more then I haue inferr'd?
Remember whom you are to cope withall,
A sort of Vagabonds, Rascals, and Run-awayes,
A scum of Brittaines, and base Lackey Pezants,
Whom their o're-cloyed Country vomits forth
To desperate Aduentures, and assur'd Destruction.
You sleeping safe, they bring you to vnrest:
You hauing Lands, and blest with beauteous wiues,
They would restraine the one, distaine the other,
And who doth leade them, but a paltry Fellow?
Long kept in Britaine at our Mothers cost,
A Milke-sop, one that neuer in his life
Felt so much cold, as ouer shooes in Snow:
Let's whip these straglers o're the Seas againe,
Lash hence these ouer-weening Ragges of France,
These famish'd Beggers, weary of their liues,
Who (but for dreaming on this fond exploit)
For want of meanes (poore Rats) had hang'd themselues.
If we be conquered, let men conquer vs,
And not these bastard Britaines, whom our Fathers
Haue in their owne Land beaten, bobb'd, and thump'd,
And on Record, left them the heires of shame.
Shall these enioy our Lands? lye with our Wiues?
Rauish our daughters? *Drum afarre off*
Hearke, I heare their Drumme,
Right Gentlemen of England, fight boldly yeomen,
Draw Archers draw your Arrowes to the head,
Spurre your proud Horses hard, and ride in blood,
Amaze the welkin with your broken staues.

Enter a Messenger.

What sayes Lord *Stanley*, will he bring his power?
Mes. My Lord, he doth deny to come.
King. Off with his sonne *Georges* head.
Nor. My Lord, the Enemy is past the Marsh:
After the battaile, let *George Stanley* dye.
King. A thousand hearts are great within my bosom.
Aduance our Standards, set vpon our Foes,
Our Ancient word of Courage, faire S. *George*
Inspire vs with the spleene of fiery Dragons:
Vpon them, Victorie sits on our helpes.

Alarum, excursions. Enter Catesby.

Cat. Rescue my Lord of Norfolke,
Rescue, Rescue:
The King enacts more wonders then a man,
Daring an opposite to euery danger:
His horse is slaine, and all on foot he fights,
Seeking for Richmond in the throat of death:
Rescue faire Lord, or else the day is lost.
Alarums.

c 2 Enter

Enter Richard.

Rich. A Horſe, a Horſe, my Kingdome for a Horſe.
Cates. Withdraw my Lord, Ile helpe you to a Horſe
Rich. Slaue, I haue ſet my life vpon a caſt,
And I will ſtand the hazard of the Dye:
I thinke there be ſixe Richmonds in the field,
Fiue haue I ſlaine to day, in ſtead of him.
A Horſe, a Horſe, my Kingdome for a Horſe.

Alarum, Enter Richard and Richmond, they fight, Richard is ſlaine.

Retreat, and Flouriſh. Enter Richmond, Derby bearing the Crowne, with diuers other Lords.

Richm. God, and your Armes
Be prais'd Victorious Friends;
The day is ours, the bloudy Dogge is dead.
Der. Couragious Richmond,
Well haſt thou acquit thee: Loe,
Heere theſe long vſurped Royalties,
From the dead Temples of this bloudy Wretch,
Haue I pluck'd off, to grace thy Browes withall.
Weare it, and make much of it.
Richm. Great God of Heauen, ſay Amen to all.
But tell me, is yong *George Stanley* liuing?
Der. He is my Lord, and ſafe in Leiceſter Towne,
Whither (if you pleaſe) we may withdraw vs.
Richm. What men of name are ſlaine on either ſide?
Der. *Iohn* Duke of Norfolke, *Walter* Lord Ferris,
Sir *Robert Brokenbury*, and Sir *William Brandon.*
Richm. Interre their Bodies, as become their Births,
Proclaime a pardon to the Soldiers fled,
That in ſubmiſſion will returne to vs,
And then as we haue tane the Sacrament,
We will vnite the White Roſe, and the Red.
Smile Heauen vpon this faire Coniunction,
That long haue frown'd vpon their Enmity:
What Traitor heares me, and ſayes not Amen?
England hath long beene mad, and ſcarr'd her ſelfe;
The Brother blindely ſhed the Brothers blood;
The Father, raſhly ſlaughtered his owne Sonne;
The Sonne compell'd, beene Butcher to the Sire;
All this diuided Yorke and Lancaſter,
Diuided, in their dire Diuiſion.
O now, let *Richmond* and *Elizabeth*,
The true Succeeders of each Royall Houſe,
By Gods faire ordinance, conioyne together:
And let thy Heires (God if thy will be ſo)
Enrich the time to come, with Smooth-fac'd Peace,
With ſmiling Plenty, and faire Proſperous dayes.
Abate the edge of Traitors, Gracious Lord,
That would reduce theſe bloudy dayes againe,
And make poore England weepe in Streames of Blood;
Let them not liue to taſte this Lands increaſe,
That would with Treaſon, wound this faire Lands peace.
Now Ciuill wounds are ſtopp'd, Peace liues agen;
That ſhe may long liue heere, God ſay, Amen. *Exeu*

FINIS.

The Famous History of the Life of King HENRY the Eight.

THE PROLOGUE.

I Come no more to make you laugh, Things now,
That beare a Weighty, and a Serious Brow,
Sad, high, and working, full of State and Woe:
Such Noble Scœnes, as draw the Eye to flow
We now present. Those that can Pitty, heere
May (if they thinke it well) let fall a Teare,
The Subiect will deserue it. Such as giue
Their Money out of hope they may beleeue,
May heere finde Truth too. Those that come to see
Onely a show or two, and so agree,
The Play may passe: If they be still, and willing,
Ile vndertake may see away their shilling
Richly in two short houres. Onely they
That come to heare a Merry, Bawdy Play,
A noyse of Targets: Or to see a Fellow
In a long Motley Coate, garded with Yellow,
Will be deceyu'd. For gentle Hearers, know
To ranke our chosen Truth with such a show
As Foole, and Fight is, beside forfeyting
Our owne Braines, and the Opinion that we bring
To make that onely true, we now intend,
Will leaue vs neuer an vnderstanding Friend.
Therefore, for Goodnesse sake, and as you are knowne
The First and Happiest Hearers of the Towne,
Be sad, as we would make ye. Thinke ye see
The very Persons of our Noble Story,
As they were Liuing: Thinke you see them Great,
And follow'd with the generall throng, and sweat
Of thousand Friends: Then, in a moment, see
How soone this Mightinesse, meets Misery:
And if you can be merry then, Ile say,
A Man may weepe vpon his Wedding day.

Actus Primus. Scœna Prima.

Enter the Duke of Norfolke at one doore. At the other, the Duke of Buckingham, and the Lord Aburgauenny.

Buckingham.

GOod morrow, and well met. How haue ye done
Since last we saw in France?
Norf. I thanke your Grace:
Healthfull, and euer since a fresh Admirer
Of what I saw there.
Buck. An vntimely Ague
Staid me a Prisoner in my Chamber, when
Those Sunnes of Glory, those two Lights of Men
Met in the vale of Andren.
Nor. 'Twixt Guynes and Arde,
I was then present, saw them salute on Horsebacke,
Beheld them when they lighted, how they clung
In their Embracement, as they grew together,
Which had they,
What foure Thron'd ones could haue weigh'd
Such a compounded one?
Buck. All the whole time
I was my Chambers Prisoner.
Nor. Then you lost
The view of earthly glory: Men might say
Till this time Pompe was single, but now married
To one aboue it selfe. Each following day
Became the next dayes master, till the last
Made former Wonders, it's. To day the French,
All Clinquant all in Gold, like Heathen Gods
Shone downe the English; and to morrow, they
Made Britaine, India: Euery man that stood,
Shew'd like a Mine. Their Dwarfish Pages were
As Cherubins, all gilt: the Madams too,
Not vs'd to toyle, did almost sweat to beare
The Pride vpon them, that their very labour
Was to them, as a Painting. Now this Maske
Was cry'de incompareable; and th'ensuing night
Made it a Foole, and Begger. The two Kings
Equall in lustre, were now best, now worst
As presence did present them Him in eye,
Still him in praise, and being present both,
'Twas said they saw but one, and no Discerner
Durst wagge his Tongue in censure, when these Sunnes
(For so they phrase 'em) by their Heralds challeng'd
The Noble Spirits to Armes, they did performe

t 3 Beyond

Beyond thoughts Compasse, that former fabulous Storie
Being now seene, possible enough, got credit
That *Beuis* was beleeu'd.
Buc. Oh you go farre.
Nor. As I belong to worship, and affect
In Honor, Honesty, the tract of eu'ry thing,
Would by a good Discourser loose some life,
Which Actions selfe, was tongue too.
Buc. All was Royall,
To the disposing of it nought rebell'd,
Order gaue each thing view. The Office did
Distinctly his full Function: who did guide,
I meane who set the Body, and the Limbes
Of this great Sport together?
Nor. As you guesse:
One certes, that promises no Element
In such a businesse.
Buc. I pray you who, my Lord?
Nor. All this was ordred by the good Discretion
Of the right Reuerend Cardinall of Yorke.
Buc. The diuell speed him: No mans Pye is freed
From his Ambitious finger. What had he
To do in these fierce Vanities? I wonder,
That such a Keech can with his very bulke
Take vp the Rayes o'th'beneficiall Sun,
And keepe it from the Earth.
Nor. Surely Sir,
There's in him stuffe, that put's him to these ends:
For being not propt by Auncestry, whose grace
Chalkes Successors their way; nor call'd vpon
For high feats done to'th'Crowne; neither Allied
To eminent Assistants; but Spider-like
Out of his Selfe-drawing Web. O giues vs note,
The force of his owne merit makes his way
A guift that heauen giues for him, which buyes
A place next to the King.
Abur. I cannot tell
What Heauen hath giuen him: let some Grauer eye
Pierce into that, but I can see his Pride
Peepe through each part of him: whence ha's he that,
If not from Hell? The Diuell is a Niggard,
Or ha's giuen all before, and he begins
A new Hell in himselfe.
Buc. Why the Diuell,
Vpon this French going out, tooke he vpon him
(Without the priuity o'th'King) t'appoint
Who should attend on him? He makes vp the File
Of all the Gentry; for the most part such
To whom as great a Charge, as little Honor
He meant to lay vpon: and his owne Letter
The Honourable Boord of Councell, out
Must fetch him in, he Papers.
Abur. I do know
Kinsmen of mine, three at the least, that haue
By this, so sicken'd their Estates, that neuer
They shall abound as formerly.
Buc. O many
Haue broke their backes with laying Mannors on 'em
For this great Iourney. What did this vanity
But minister communication of
A most poore issue.
Nor. Greeuingly I thinke,
The Peace betweene the French and vs, not valewes
The Cost that did conclude it.
Buc. Euery man,
After the hideous storme that follow'd, was
A thing Inspir'd, and not consulting, broke
Into a generall Prophesie; That this Tempest
Dashing the Garment of this Peace, aboaded
The sodaine breach on't.
Nor. Which is budded out,
For France hath flaw'd the League, and hath attach'd
Our Merchants goods at Burdeux.
Abur. Is it therefore
Th'Ambassador is silenc'd?
Nor. Marry is't.
Abur. A proper Title of a Peace, and purchas'd
At a superfluous rate.
Buc. Why all this Businesse
Our Reuerend Cardinall carried.
Nor. Like it your Grace,
The State takes notice of the priuate difference
Betwixt you, and the Cardinall. I aduise you
(And take it from a heart, that wishes towards you
Honor, and plenteous safety) that you reade
The Cardinals Malice, and his Potency
Together; To consider further, that
What his high Hatred would effect, wants not
A Minister in his Power. You know his Nature,
That he's Reuengefull; and I know, his Sword
Hath a sharpe edge: It's long, and't may be saide
It reaches farre, and where 'twill not extend,
Thither he darts it. Bosome vp my counsell,
You'l finde it wholesome. Loe, where comes that Rock
That I aduice your shunning.

Enter Cardinall Wolsey, the Purse borne before him, certaine of the Guard, and two Secretaries with Papers: The Cardinall in his passage, fixeth his eye on Buckham, and Buckingham on him, both full of disdaine.

Car. The Duke of *Buckinghams* Surueyor? Ha?
Where's his Examination?
Secr. Heere so please you.
Car. Is he in person, ready?
Secr. I, please your Grace.
Car. Well, we shall then know more, & *Buckingham*
Shall lessen this bigge looke.
Exeunt Cardinall, and his Traine.
Buc. This Butchers Curre is venom'd-mouth'd, and I
Haue not the power to muzzle him, therefore best
Not wake him in his slumber. A Beggers booke,
Out-worths a Nobles blood.
Nor. What are you chaff'd?
Aske God for Temp'rance, that's th'appliance onely
Which your disease requires.
Buc. I read in's looks
Matter against me, and his eye reuil'd
Me as his abiect obiect, at this instant
He bores me with some tricke; He's gone to'th King:
Ile follow, and out-stare him.
Nor. Stay my Lord,
And let your Reason with your Choller question
What 'tis you go about: to climbe steepe hilles
Requires slow pace at first. Anger is like
A full hot Horse, who being allow'd his way
Selfe-mettle tyres him: Not a man in England
Can aduise me like you: Be to your selfe,
As you would to your Friend.
Buc. Ile to the King,
And from a mouth of Honor, quite cry downe
This

This *Ipſwich* fellowes inſolence; or proclaime,
There's difference in no perſons.
Norf. Be aduiſ'd;
Heat not a Furnace for your foe ſo hot
That it do ſindge your ſelfe. We may out-runne
By violent ſwiftneſſe that which we run at;
And loſe by ouer-running: know you not,
The fire that mounts the liquor til't run ore,
In ſeeming to augment it, waſts it: be aduiſ'd;
I ſay againe there is no Engliſh Soule
More ſtronger to direct you then your ſelfe;
If with the ſap of reaſon you would quench,
Or but allay the fire of paſſion.
Buck. Sir,
I am thankfull to you, and Ile goe along
By your preſcription: but this top-proud fellow,
Whom from the flow of gall I name not, but
From ſincere motions, by Intelligence,
And prooſes as cleere as Founts in *Iuly*, when
Wee ſee each graine of grauell; I doe know
To be corrupt and treaſonous.
Norf. Say not treaſonous.
Buck. To th'King Ile ſay't, & make my vouch as ſtrong
As ſhore of Rocke: attend. This holy Foxe,
Or Wolfe, or both (for he is equall rau'nous
As he is ſubtile, and as prone to miſchiefe,
As able to perform't) his minde, and place
Infecting one another, yea reciprocally,
Only to ſhew his pompe, as well in France,
As here at home, ſuggeſts the King our Maſter
To this laſt coſtly Treaty: Th'enterview,
That ſwallowed ſo much treaſure, and like a glaſſe
Did breake ith'wrenching.
Norf. Faith, and ſo it did.
Buck. Pray giue me fauour Sir: This cunning Cardinall
The Articles o'th' Combination drew
As himſelfe pleas'd; and they were ratified
As he cride thus let be, to as much end,
As giue a Crutch to th'dead. But our Count-Cardinall
Has done this, and tis well: for worthy *Wolſey*
(Who cannot erre) he did it. Now this followes,
(Which as I take it, is a kinde of Puppie
To th'old dam Treaſon) *Charles* the Emperour,
Vnder pretence to ſee the Queene his Aunt,
(For twas indeed his colour, but he came
To whiſper *Wolſey*) here makes viſitation,
His feares were that the Interview betwixt
England and France, might through their amity
Breed him ſome preiudice; for from this League,
Peep'd harmes that menac'd him. Priuily
Deales with our Cardinal, and as I troa
Which I doe well; for I am ſure the Emperour
Paid ere he promis'd, whereby his Suit was granted
Ere it was ask'd. But when the way was made
And pau'd with gold: the Emperor thus deſir'd,
That he would pleaſe to alter the Kings courſe,
And breake the foreſaid peace. Let the King know
(As ſoone he ſhall by me) that thus the Cardinall
Does buy and ſell his Honour as he pleaſes,
And for his owne aduantage.
Norf. I am ſorry
To heare this of him; and could wiſh he were
Something miſtaken in't.
Buck. No, not a ſillable:
I doe pronounce him in that very ſhape
He ſhall appeare in proofe.

Enter Brandon, a Sergeant at Armes before him, and two or three of the Guard.

Brandon. Your Office Sergeant: execute it.
Sergeant. Sir,
My Lord the Duke of *Buckingham* and Earle
Of *Hertford Stafford* and *Northampton*, I
Arreſt thee of High Treaſon, in the name
Of our moſt Soueraigne King.
Buck. Lo you my Lord,
The net has falne vpon me, I ſhall periſh
Vnder deuice, and practiſe.
Bran. I am ſorry,
To ſee you tane from liberty, to looke on
The buſines preſent. Tis his Highnes pleaſure
You ſhall to th'Tower.
Buck. It will helpe me nothing
To plead mine Innocence; for that dye is on me
Which makes my whit'ſt part, black. The will of Heau'n
Be done in this and all things: I obey.
O my Lord *Aburgany*: Fare you well.
Bran. Nay, he muſt beare you company. The King
Is pleas'd you ſhall to th'Tower, till you know
How he determines further.
Abur. As the Duke ſaid,
The will of Heauen be done, and the Kings pleaſure
By me obey'd.
Bran. Here is a warrant from
The King, t'attach Lord *Mountacute*, and the Bodies
Of the Dukes Confeſſor, *Iohn de la Car*,
One *Gilbert Pecke*, his Councellour.
Buck. So, ſo;
Theſe are the limbs o'th' Plot: no more I hope.
Bra. A Monke o'th' *Chartreux*.
Buck. O *Michaell Hopkins*?
Bra. He.
Buck. My Surueyor is falce. The ore-great *Cardinall*
Hath ſhew'd him gold; my life is ſpand already:
I am the ſhadow of poore *Buckingham*,
Whoſe Figure euen this inſtant Clowd puts on,
By Darkning my cleere Sunne. My Lords farewell. *Exe.*

Scena Secunda.

Cornets. Enter King Henry, leaning on the Cardinals ſhoulder, the Nobles, and Sir Thomas Louell: the Cardinall places himſelfe vnder the Kings feete on his right ſide.

King. My life it ſelfe, and the beſt heart of it,
Thankes you for this great care: I ſtood i'th' leuell
Of a full-charg'd confederacie, and giue thankes
To you that choak'd it. Let be cald before vs
That Gentleman of *Buckinghams*, in perſon,
Ile heare him his confeſſions iuſtifie,
And point by point the Treaſons of his Maſter,
He ſhall againe relate.

A noyſe within crying roome for the Queene, vſher'd by the Duke of Norfolke. Enter the Queene, Norfolke and Suffolke: ſhe kneels. King riſeth from his State, takes her vp, kiſſes and placeth her by him.

Queen. Nay, we muſt longer kneele; I am a Suitor.
King. Ariſe, and take place by vs; halfe your Suit
Neuer name to vs; you haue halfe our power:

The

The other moity ere you aske is giuen,
Repeat your will,and take it.
Queen. Thanke your Maieſty
That you would loue your ſelfe,and in that loue
Not vnconſidered leaue your Honour,nor
The dignity of your Office; is the poynt
Of my Petition.
Kin. Lady mine proceed.
Queen. I am ſolicited not by a few,
And thoſe of true condition; That your Subiects
Are in great grieuance: There haue beene Commiſſions
Sent downe among 'em, which hath flaw'd the heart
Of all their Loyalties; wherein, although
My good Lord Cardinall, they vent reproches
Moſt bitterly on you,as putter on
Of theſe exactions: yet the King,our Maiſter (not
Whoſe Honor Heauen ſhield from ſoile;euen he eſcapes
Language vnmannerly;yea,ſuch which breakes
The ſides of loyalty,and almoſt appeares
In lowd Rebellion.
Norf. Not almoſt appeares,
It doth appeare; for, vpon theſe Taxations,
The Clothiers all not able to maintaine
The many to them longing, haue put off
The Spinſters, Carders, Fullers, Weauers, who
Vnfit for other life,compeld by hunger
And lack of other meanes, in deſperate manner
Daring th'euent too th'teeth,are all in vprore,
And danger ſerues among them.
Kin. Taxation?
Wherein?and what Taxation? My Lord Cardinall,
You that are blam'd for it alike with vs,
Know you of this Taxation?
Card. Pleaſe you Sir,
I know but of a ſingle part in ought
Pertaines to th'State; and front but in that File
Where others tell ſteps with me.
Queen. No,my Lord?
You know no more then others? But you frame
Things that are knowne alike, which are not wholſome
To thoſe which would not know them, and yet muſt
Perforce be their acquaintance. Theſe exactions
(Whereof my Soueraigne would haue note) they are
Moſt peſtilent to th'hearing,and to beare 'em,
The Backe is Sacrifice to th'load; They ſay
They are deuis'd by you, or elſe you ſuffer
Too hard an exclamation.
Kin. Still Exaction:
The nature of it, in what kinde let's know,
Is this Exaction?
Queen. I am much too venturous
In tempting of your patience; but am boldned
Vnder your promis'd pardon. The Subiects griefe
Comes through Commiſſions,which compels from each
The ſixt part of his Subſtance,to be leuied
Without delay; and the pretence for this
Is nam'd,your warres in France:this makes bold mouths,
Tongues ſpit their duties out, and cold hearts freeze
Allegeance in them; their curſes now
Liue where their prayers did: and it's come to paſſe,
This tractable obedience is a Slaue
To each incenſed Will: I would your Highneſſe
Would giue it quicke conſideration; for
There is no primer baſeneſſe.
Kin. By my life,
This is againſt our pleaſure.
Card. And for me,
I haue no further gone in this, then by
A ſingle voice,and that not paſt me,but
By learned approbation of the Iudges: If I am
Traduc'd by ignorant Tongues,which neither know
My faculties nor perſon,yet will be
The Chronicles of my doing: Let me ſay,
'Tis but the fate of Place,and the rough Brake
That Vertue muſt goe through: we muſt not ſtint
Our neceſſary actions, in the feare
To cope malicious Cenſurers, which euer,
As rau'nous Fiſhes doe a Veſſell follow
That is new trim'd; but benefit no further
Then vainly longing. What we oft doe beſt,
By ſicke Interpreters (once weake ones) is
Not ours,or not allow'd; what worſt,as oft
Hitting a groſſer quality, is cride vp
For our beſt Act: if we ſhall ſtand ſtill,
In feare our motion will be mock'd,or carp'd at,
We ſhould take roote here, where we ſit;
Or ſit State-Statues onely.
Kin. Things done well,
And with a care, exempt themſelues from feare:
Things done without example,in their iſſue
Are to be fear'd. Haue you a Preſident
Of this Commiſſion? I beleeue,not any.
We muſt not rend our Subiects from our Lawes,
And ſticke them in our Will. Sixt part of each?
A trembling Contribution; why we take
From euery Tree, lop, barke,and part o'th' Timber:
And though we leaue it with a roote thus hackt,
The Ayre will drinke the Sap. To euery County
Where this is queſtion'd,ſend our Letters, with
Free pardon to each man that has deny'de
The force of this Commiſſion: pray looke too't;
I put it to your care.
Card. A word with you.
Let there be Letters writ to euery Shire,
Of the Kings grace and pardon: the greeued Commons
Hardly conceiue of me. Let it be nois'd,
That through our Interceſſion, this Reuokement
And pardon comes: I ſhall anon aduiſe you
Further in the proceeding. *Exit Secret.*

Enter Surueyor.

Queen. I am ſorry, that the Duke of *Buckingham*
Is run in your diſpleaſure.
Kin. It grieues many:
The Gentleman is Learn'd,and a moſt rare Speaker,
To Nature none more bound; his trayning ſuch,
That he may furniſh and inſtruct great Teachers,
And neuer ſeeke for ayd out of himſelfe: yet ſee,
When theſe ſo Noble benefits ſhall proue
Not well diſpos'd, the minde growing once corrupt,
They turne to vicious formes, ten times more vgly
Then euer they were faire. This man ſo compleat,
Who was enrold 'mongſt wonders; and when we
Almoſt with rauiſh'd liſtning,could not finde
His houre of ſpeech,a minute: He, (my Lady)
Hath into monſtrous habits put the Graces
That once were his,and is become as blacke,
As if beſmear'd in hell. Sit by Vs,you ſhall heare
(This was his Gentleman in truſt) of him
Things to ſtrike Honour ſad. Bid him recount
The fore-recited practiſes, whereof
We cannot feele too little, heare too much.

Card.

Card. Stand forth, & with bold ſpirit relate what you
Moſt like a carefull Subiect haue collected
Out of the Duke of *Buckingham.*
Kin. Speake freely.
Sur. Firſt, it was vſuall with him; euery day
It would infect his Speech: That if the King
Should without iſſue dye; hee'l carry it ſo
To make the Scepter his. Theſe very words
I'ue heard him vtter to his Sonne in Law,
Lord *Aburgany*, to whom by oth he menac'd
Reuenge vpon the *Cardinall.*
Card. Pleaſe your Highneſſe note
This dangerous conception in this point,
Not frended by his wiſh to your High perſon;
His will is moſt malignant, and it ſtretches
Beyond you to your friends.
Queen. My learn'd Lord *Cardinall*,
Deliuer all with Charity.
Kin. Speake on;
How grounded hee his Title to the Crowne
Vpon our faile; to this poynt haſt thou heard him,
At any time ſpeake ought?
Sur. He was brought to this,
By a vaine Propheſie of *Nicholas Henton.*
Kin. What was that *Henton*?
Sur. Sir, a *Chartreux* Fryer,
His Confeſſor, who fed him euery minute
With words of Soueraignty.
Kin. How know'ſt thou this?
Sur. Not long before your Higneſſe ſped to France,
The Duke being at the Roſe, within the Pariſh
Saint *Laurence Poultney*, did of me demand
What was the ſpeech among the Londoners,
Concerning the French Iourney. I replide,
Men feare the French would proue perfidious
To the Kings danger: preſently, the Duke
Said, 'twas the feare indeed, and that he doubted
'Twould proue the verity of certaine words
Spoke by a holy Monke, that oft, ſayes he,
Hath ſent to me, wiſhing me to permit
Iohn de la Car, my Chaplaine, a choyce howre
To heare from him a matter of ſome moment:
Whom after vnder the Commiſſions Seale,
He ſollemnly had ſworne, that what he ſpoke
My Chaplaine to no Creature liuing, but
To me, ſhould vtter, with demure Confidence,
This pauſingly enſu'de; neither the King, nor's Heyres
(Tell you the Duke) ſhall proſper, bid him ſtriue
To the loue o'th' Commonalty, the Duke
Shall gouerne England.
Queen. If I know you well,
You were the Dukes Surueyor, and loſt your Office
On the complaint o'th' Tenants; take good heed
You charge not in your ſpleene a Noble perſon,
And ſpoyle your nobler Soule; I ſay, take heed;
Yes, heartily beſeech you.
Kin. Let him on: Goe forward.
Sur. On my Soule, Ile ſpeake but truth.
I told my Lord the Duke, by th'Diuels illuſions
The Monke might be deceiu'd, and that 'twas dangerous
For this to ruminate on this ſo farre, vntill
It forg'd him ſome deſigne, which being beleeu'd
It was much like to doe: He anſwer'd, Tuſh,
It can doe me no damage; adding further,
That had the King in his laſt Sickneſſe faild,
The Cardinals and Sir *Thomas Louels* heads
Should haue gone off.
Kin. Ha? What, ſo rancke? Ah, ha,
There's miſchiefe in this man; canſt thou ſay further?
Sur. I can my Liedge.
Kin. Proceed.
Sur. Being at *Greenwich*,
After your Highneſſe had reprou'd the Duke
About Sir *William Blumer*
Kin. I remember of ſuch a time, being my ſworn ſer- (uant,
The Duke retein'd him his. But on: what hence?
Sur. If (quoth he) I for this had beene committed,
As to the Tower, I thought; I would haue plaid
The Part my Father meant to act vpon
Th'Vſurper *Richard*, who being at *Salsbury*,
Made ſuit to come in's preſence; which if granted,
(As he made ſemblance of his duty) would
Haue put his knife into him.
Kin. A Gyant Traytor.
Card. Now Madam, may his Highnes liue in freedome,
And this man out of Priſon.
Queen. God mend all.
Kin. Ther's ſomething more would out of thee; what (ſay'ſt?
Sur. After the Duke his Father, with the knife
He ſtretch'd him, and with one hand on his dagger,
Another ſpread on's breaſt, mounting his eyes,
He did diſcharge a horrible Oath, whoſe tenor
Was, were he euill vs'd, he would outgoe
His Father, by as much as a performance
Do's an irreſolute purpoſe.
Kin. There's his period,
To ſheath his knife in vs: he is attach'd,
Call him to preſent tryall: if he may
Finde mercy in the Law, 'tis his; if none,
Let him not ſeek't of vs: By day and night
Hee's Traytor to th' height. *Exeunt.*

Scæna Tertia.

Enter L. Chamberlaine, and L. Sandys.

L. Ch. Is't poſſible the ſpels of France ſhould iuggle
Men into ſuch ſtrange myſteries?
L. San. New cuſtomes,
Though they be neuer ſo ridiculous,
(Nay let 'em be vnmanly) yet are follow'd.
L. Ch. As farre as I ſee, all the good our Engliſh
Haue got by the late Voyage, is but meerely
A fit or two o'th' face, (but they are ſhrewd ones)
For when they hold 'em, you would ſweare directly
Their very noſes had been Councellours
To *Pepin* or *Clotharius*, they keepe State ſo.
L. San. They haue all new legs,
And lame ones; one would take it,
That neuer ſee 'em pace before, the Spauen
A Spring-halt rain'd among 'em.
L. Ch. Death my Lord,
Their cloathes are after ſuch a Pagan cut too't,
That ſure th'haue worne out Chriſtendome: how now?
What newes, Sir *Thomas Louell*?

Enter Sir Thomas Louell.

Louell. Faith my Lord,
I heare of none but the new Proclamation,
That's clapt vpon the Court Gate.
L. Cham.

L. Cham. What is't for?
Lou The reformation of our trauel'd Gallants,
That fill the Court with quarrels, talke, and Taylors.
L. Cham. I'm glad 'tis there;
Now I would pray our Monſieurs
To thinke an Engliſh Courtier may be wiſe,
And neuer ſee the *Louure.*
Lou: They muſt either
(For ſo run the Conditions) leaue thoſe remnants
Of Foole and Feather, that they got in France,
With all their honourable points of ignorance
Pertaining thereunto; as Fights and Fire-workes,
Abuſing better men then they can be
Out of a forreigne wiſedome, renouncing cleane
The faith they haue in Tennis and tall Stockings,
Short bliſtred Breeches, and thoſe types of Trauell;
And vnderſtand againe like honeſt men,
Or pack to their old Playfellowes; there, I take it,
They may *Cum Priuilegio,* wee away
The lag end of their lewdneſſe, and be laugh'd at.
L. San. Tis time to giue 'em Phyſicke, their diſeaſes
Are growne ſo catching.
L. Cham What a loſſe our Ladies
Will haue of theſe trim vanities?
Louell. I marry,
There will be woe indeed Lords, the ſlye whorſons
Haue got a ſpeeding tricke to lay downe Ladies.
A French Song, and a Fiddle, has no Fellow.
L. San. The Diuell fiddle 'em,
I am glad they are going,
For ſure there's no conuerting of 'em: now
An honeſt Country Lord as I am, beaten
A long time out of play, may bring his plaine ſong,
And haue an houre of hearing, and by'r Lady
Held currant Muſicke too.
L. Cham. Well ſaid Lord *Sands,*
Your Colts tooth is not caſt yet?
L San. No my Lord,
Nor ſhall not while I haue a ſtumpe.
L. Cham. Sir *Thomas,*
Whither were you a going?
Lou To the Cardinals;
Your Lordſhip is a gueſt too.
L Cham O, 'tis true;
This night he makes a Supper, and a great one,
To many Lords and Ladies; there will be
The Beauty of this Kingdome Ile aſſure you.
Lou. That Churchman
Beares a bounteous minde indeed,
A hand as fruitfull as the Land that feeds vs,
His dewes fall euery where.
L. Cham. No doubt hee's Noble;
He had a blacke mouth that ſaid other of him.
L. San. He may my Lord,
Ha's wherewithall in him;
Sparing would ſhew a worſe ſinne, then ill Doctrine,
Men of his way, ſhould be moſt liberall,
They are ſet heere for examples.
L. Cham. True, they are ſo;
But few now giue ſo great ones:
My Barge ſtayes;
Your Lordſhip ſhall along: Come, good Sir *Thomas,*
We ſhall be late elſe, which I would not be,
For I was ſpoke to, with Sir *Henry Guilford*
This night to be Comptrollers.
L. San. I am your Lordſhips. *Exeunt.*

Scena Quarta.

Hoboies. A ſmall Table vnder a State for the Cardinall, a longer Table for the Gueſts. Then Enter Anne Bullen, and diuers other Ladies, & Gentlemen, as Gueſts at one Doore; at an other Doore enter Sir Henry Guilford.

S. Hen. Guilf. Ladyes,
A generall welcome from his Grace
Salutes ye all; This Night he dedicates
To faire content, and you: None heere he hopes
In all this Noble Beuy, has brought with her
One care abroad: hee would haue all as merry:
As first, good Company, good wine, good welcome,
Can make good people.

Enter L. Chamberlaine L. Sands and Louell.

O my Lord, y'are tardy;
The very thought of this faire Company,
Clapt wings to me.
Cham. You are young Sir *Harry Guilford.*
San. Sir *Thomas Louell,* had the Cardinall
But halfe my Lay-thoughts in him, ſome of theſe
Should finde a running Banket, ere they reſted,
I thinke would better pleaſe 'em: by my life,
They are a ſweet ſociety of faire ones.
Lou O that your Lordſhip were but now Confeſſor,
To one or two of theſe.
San. I would I were,
They ſhould finde eaſie pennance.
Lou. Faith how eaſie?
San. As eaſie as a downe bed would affoord it.
Cham. Sweet Ladies will it pleaſe you ſit; Sir *Harry*
Place you that ſide, Ile take the charge of this:
His Grace is entring. Nay, you muſt not freeze,
Two women plac'd together, makes cold weather:
My Lord *Sands,* you are one will keepe 'em waking:
Pray ſit betweene theſe Ladies.
San By my faith,
And thanke your Lordſhip: by your leaue ſweet Ladies,
If I chance to talke a little wilde, forgiue me:
I had it from my Father.
An. Bul. Was he mad Sir?
San. O, very mad, exceeding mad, in loue too;
But he would bite none, iuſt as I doe now,
He would Kiſſe you Twenty with a breath.
Cham. Well ſaid my Lord:
So now y'are fairely ſeated: Gntlemen,
The pennance lyes on you; if theſe faire Ladies
Paſſe away frowning.
San. For my little Cure,
Let me alone.

Hoboyes. Enter Cardinall Wolſey, and takes his State.

Card Y'are welcome my faire Gueſts; that noble Lady
Or Gentleman that is not freely merry
Is not my Friend. This to confirme my welcome,
And to you all good health.
San. Your Grace is Noble,
Let me haue ſuch a Bowle may hold my thankes,
And ſaue me ſo much talking.
Card. My Lord *Sands,*
I

I am beholding to you : cheere your neighbours.
Ladies you are not merry ; Gentlemen.
Whose fault is this?
San. The red wine first must rise
In their faire cheekes my Lord, then wee shall haue 'em,
Talke vs to silence.
An.B. You are a merry Gamster
My Lord *Sands.*
San. Yes, if I make my play:
Heer's to your Ladiship, and pledge it Madam:
For tis to such a thing.
An.B. You cannot shew me.
Drum and Trumpet, Chambers dischargd.
San. I told your Grace, they would talke anon.
Card. What's that?
Cham. Looke out there, some of ye.
Card. What warlike voyce,
And to what end is this? Nay, Ladies, feare not;
By all the lawes of Warre y'are priuiledg'd.
Enter a Seruant.
Cham. How now, what is't?
Seru. A noble troupe of Strangers,
For so they seeme; th'haue left their Barge and landed,
And hither make, as great Embassadors
From forraigne Princes.
Card. Good Lord Chamberlaine,
Go, giue 'em welcome; you can speake the French tongue
And pray receiue 'em Nobly, and conduct 'em
Into our presence, where this heauen of beauty
Shall shine at full vpon them. Some attend him.
All rise, and Tables remou'd.
You haue now a broken Banket, but wee'l mend it.
A good digestion to you all; and once more
I showre a welcome on yee : welcome all.

Hoboyes. Enter King and others as Maskers, habited like Shepheards, vsher'd by the Lord Chamberlaine. They passe directly before the Cardinall, and gracefully salute him.

A noble Company : what are their pleasures?
Cham. Because they speak no English, thus they praid
To tell your Grace: That hauing heard by fame
Of this so Noble and so faire assembly,
This night to meet heere they could doe no lesse,
(Out of the great respect they beare to beauty)
But leaue their Flockes, and vnder your faire Conduct
Craue leaue to view these Ladies, and entreat
An houre of Reuels with 'em.
Card. Say, Lord *Chamberlaine,*
They haue done my poore house grace:
For which I pay 'em a thousand thankes,
And pray 'em take their pleasures.
Choose Ladies, King and An Bullen.
King The fairest hand I euer touch'd: O Beauty,
Till now I neuer knew thee.
Musicke, Dance.
Card. My Lord.
Cham. Your Grace.
Card. Pray tell 'em thus much from me:
There should be one amongst 'em by his person
More worthy this place then my selfe, to whom
(If I but knew him) with my loue aud duty
I would surrender it. *Whisper.*
Cham. I will my Lord.
Card. What say they?
Cham. Such a one, they all confesse
There is indeed, which they would haue your Grace
Find out, and he will take it.
Card. Let me see then,
By all your good leaues Gentlemen; heere Ile make
My royall choyce.
Kin. Ye haue found him Cardinall,
You hold a faire Assembly; you doe well Lord:
You are a Churchman, or Ile tell you Cardinall,
I should iudge now vnhappily.
Card. I am glad
Your Grace is growne so pleasant.
Kin. My Lord Chamberlaine,
Prethee come hither, what faire Ladie's that?
Cham. An't please your Grace,
Sir *Thomas Bullens* Daughter, the Viscount *Rochford,*
One of her Highnesse women.
Kin. By Heauen she is a dainty one. Sweet heart,
I were vnmannerly to take you out,
And not to kisse you. A health Gentlemen,
Let it goe round.
Card. Sir *Thomas Louell,* is the Banket ready
I'th' Priuy Chamber?
Lou. Yes, my Lord.
Card. Your Grace
I feare, with dancing is a little heated.
Kin. I feare too much.
Card. There's fresher ayre my Lord,
In the next Chamber.
Kin. Lead in your Ladies eu'ry one: Sweet Partner,
I must not yet forsake you: Let's be merry,
Good my Lord Cardinall: I haue halfe a dozen healths,
To drinke to these faire Ladies, and a measure
To lead 'em once againe, and then let's dreame
Who's best in fauour. Let the Musicke knock it.
Exeunt with Trumpets.

Actus Secundus. Scena Prima.

Enter two Gentlemen at seuerall Doores.
1. Whether away so fast?
2. O, God saue ye:
Eu'n to the Hall, to heare what shall become
Of the great Duke of Buckingham.
1. Ile saue you
That labour Sir. All's now done but the Ceremony
Of bringing backe the Prisoner.
2. Were you there?
1. Yes indeed was I.
2. Pray speake what ha's happen'd.
1. You may guesse quickly what.
2. Is he found guilty?
1. Yes truely is he,
And condemn'd vpon't.
2. I am sorry fort.
1. So are a number more.
2. But pray how past it?
1. Ile tell you in a little. The great Duke
Came to the Bar; where, to his accusations
He pleaded still not guilty, and alleadged
Many sharpe reasons to defeat the Law.
The Kings Atturney on the contrary,
Vrg'd on the Examinations, proofes, confessions
Of

Of diuers witnesses, which the Duke desir'd
To him brought *viua voce* to his face;
At which appear'd against him, his Surueyor
Sir *Gilbert Pecke* his Chancellour, and *Iohn Car*,
Confessor to him, with that Diuell Monke,
Hopkins, that made this mischiefe.
   2 That was hee
That fed him with his Prophecies.
   1. The same,
All these accus'd him strongly, which he faine
Would haue flung from him; but indeed he couldnot;
And so his Peeres vpon this euidence,
Haue found him guilty of high Treason. Much
He spoke, and learnedly for life: But all
Was either pittied in him, or forgotten.
   2. After all this, how did he beare himselfe?
   1. When he was brought agen to th' Bar, to heare
His Knell rung out, his Iudgement, he was stir'd
With such an Agony, he sweat extreamly,
And somthing spoke in choller, ill, and hasty:
But he fell to himselfe againe, and sweetly,
In all the rest shew'd a most Noble patience.
   2. I doe not thinke he feares death.
   1. Sure he does not,
He neuer was so womanish, the cause
He may a little grieue at.
   2. Certainly,
The Cardinall is the end of this.
   1. Tis likely,
By all coniectures: First *Kildares* Attendure;
Then Deputy of Ireland, who remou'd
Earle *Surrey*, was sent thither, and in hast too,
Least he should helpe his Father.
   2. That tricke of State
Was a deepe enuious one,
   1. At his returne,
No doubt he will requite it; this is noted
(And generally) who euer the King fauours,
The Cardnall instantly will finde imployment,
And farre enough from Court too.
   2. All the Commons
Hate him perniciously, and o' my Conscience
Wish him ten faddom deepe: This Duke as much
They loue and doate on: call him bounteous *Buckingham*,
The Mirror of all courtesie.

Enter Buckingham from his Arraignment, Tipstaues before him, the Axe with the edge towards him, Halberds on each side, accompanied with Sir Thomas Louell, Sir Nicholas Vaux, Sir Walter Sands, and common people, &c.

   1. Stay there Sir,
And see the noble ruin'd man you speake of.
   2 Let's stand close and behold him.
Buck. All good people,
You that thus farre haue come to pitty me;
Heare what I say, and then goe home and lose me.
I haue this day receiu'd a Traitors iudgement,
And by that name must dye; yet Heauen beare witnes,
And if I haue a Conscience, let it sincke me,
Euen as the Axe falls, if I be not faithfull.
The Law I beare no mallice for my death,
T'has done vpon the premises, but Iustice:
But those that sought it, I could wish more Christians:
(Be what they will) I heartily forgiue 'em;
Yet let 'em looke they glory not in mischiefe;
Nor build their euils on the graues of great men;
For then, my guiltlesse blood must cry against 'em.
For further life in this world I ne're hope,
Nor will I sue, although the King haue mercies
More then I dare make faults.
You few that lou'd me,
And dare be bold to weepe for *Buckingham*,
His Noble Friends and Fellowes; whom to leaue
Is only bitter to him, only dying:
Goe with me like good Angels to my end,
And as the long diuorce of Steele fals on me,
Make of your Prayers one sweet Sacrifice,
And lift my Soule to Heauen.
Lead on a Gods name.
   Louell. I doe beseech your Grace, for charity
If euer any malice in your heart
Were hid against me, now to forgiue me frankly.
   Buck. Sir *Thomas Louell*, I as free forgiue you
As I would be forgiuen: I forgiue all.
There cannot be those numberlesse offences
Gainst me, that I cannot take peace with:
No blacke Enuy shall make my Graue,
Commend mee to his Grace.
And if he speake of *Buckingham*; pray tell him,
You met him halfe in Heauen: my vowes and prayers
Yet are the Kings; and till my Soule forsake,
Shall cry for blessings on him. May he liue
Longer then I haue time to tell his yeares;
Euer belou'd and louing, may his Rule be;
And when old Time shall lead him to his end,
Goodnesse and he, fill vp one Monument.
   Lou To th' water side I must conduct your Grace:
Then giue my Charge vp to Sir *Nicholas Vaux*,
Who vndertakes you to your end.
   Vaux. Prepare there,
The Duke is comming. See the Barge be ready;
And fit it with such furniture as suites
The Greatnesse of his Person.
   Buck. Nay, Sir *Nicholas*,
Let it alone; my State now will but mocke me.
When I came hither, I was Lord High Constable,
And Duke of *Buckingham*: now poore *Edward Bohun*;
Yet I am richer then my base Accusers,
That neuer knew what Truth meant: I now seale it;
And with that bloud will make 'em one day groane for't
My noble Father *Henry of Buckingham*,
Who first rais'd head against Vsurping *Richard*,
Flying for succour to his Seruant *Banister*,
Being distrest; was by that wretch betraid,
And without Tryall, fell; Gods peace be with him.
Henry the Seauenth succeeding, truly pittying
My Fathers losse; like a most Royall Prince
Restor'd me to my Honours: and out of ruines
Made my Name once more Noble. Now his Sonne,
Henry the Eight, Life, Honour, Name and all
That made me happy; at one stroake ha's taken
For euer from the World. I had my Tryall,
And must needs say a Noble one; which makes me
A little happier then my wretched Father:
Yet thus farre we are one in Fortunes; both
Fell by our Seruants, by those Men we lou'd most:
A most vnnaturall and faithlesse Seruice.
Heauen ha's an end in all: yet, you that heare me,
This from a dying man receiue as certaine:
Where you are liberall of your loues and Councels,
Be sure you be not loose; for those you make friends,
And

And giue your hearts to; when they once perceiue
The least rub in your fortunes, fall away
Like water from ye, neuer found againe
But where they meane to sinke ye: all good people
Pray for me, I must now forsake ye; the last houre
Of my long weary life is come vpon me:
Farewell; and when you would say somthing that is sad,
Speake how I fell.
I haue done; and God forgiue me.

Exeunt Duke and Traine.

1. O, this is full of pitty; Sir, it cals
I feare, too many curses on their heads
That were the Authors.
2. If the Duke be guiltlesse,
'Tis full of woe: yet I can giue you inckling
Of an ensuing euill, if it fall,
Greater then this
1. Good Angels keepe it from vs:
What may it be? you doe not doubt my faith Sir?
2. This Secret is so weighty, 'twill require
A strong faith to conceale it.
1. Let me haue it:
I doe not talke much.
2. I am confident;
You shall Sir: Did you not of late dayes heare
A buzzing of a Separation
Betweene the King and *Katherine*?
1. Yes, but it held not;
For when the King once heard it, out of anger
He sent command to the Lord Mayor straight
To stop the rumor; and allay those tongues
That durst disperse it.
2. But that slander Sir,
Is found a truth now: for it growes agen
Fresher then e're it was; and held for certaine
The King will venture at it. Either the Cardinall,
Or some about him neere, haue out of malice
To the good Queene, possest him with a scruple
That will vndoe her. To confirme this too,
Cardinall *Campeius* is arriu'd, and lately,
As all thinke for this busines.
1. Tis the Cardinall;
And meerely to reuenge him on the Emperour,
For not bestowing on him at his asking,
The Archbishopricke of *Toledo*, this is purpos'd.
2. I thinke
You haue hit the marke; but is't not cruell,
That she should feele the smart of this: the Cardinall
Will haue his will, and she must fall.
1. 'Tis wofull.
Wee are too open heere to argue this:
Let's thinke in priuate more. *Exeunt.*

Scena Secunda.

Enter Lord Chamberlaine, reading this Letter.

MY Lord, the Horses your Lordship sent for, with all the care I had, I saw well chosen, ridden, and furnish'd. They were young and handsome, and of the best breed in the North. When they were ready to set out for London, a man of my Lord Cardinalls, by Commission, and maine power tooke 'em from me, with this reason: his maister would bee seru'd before a Subiect, if not before the King, which stop'd our mouthes Sir.

I feare he will indeede; well, let him haue them; hee will haue all I thinke

Enter to the Lord Chamberlaine, the Dukes of Norfolke and Suffolke.

Norf. Well met my Lord Chamberlaine.
Cham. Good day to both your Graces.
Suff. How is the King imployd?
Cham. I left him priuate,
Full of sad thoughts and troubles.
Norf. What's the cause?
Cham. It seemes the Marriage with his Brothers Wife
Ha's crept too neere his Conscience.
Suff. No, his Conscience
Ha's crept too neere another Ladie.
Norf. Tis so;
This is the Cardinals doing: The King-Cardinall,
That blinde Priest, like the eldest Sonne of Fortune,
Turnes what he list. The King will know him one day.
Suff. Pray God he doe,
Hee'l neuer know himselfe else.
Norf. How holily he workes in all his businesse,
And with what zeale? For now he has crackt the League
Betweeen vs & the Emperor (the Queens great Nephew)
He diues into the Kings Soule, and there scatters
Dangers, doubts, wringing of the Conscience,
Feares, and despaires, and all these for his Marriage.
And out of all these, to restore the King,
He counsels a Diuorce, a losse of her
That like a Iewell, ha's hung twenty yeares
About his necke, yet neuer lost her lustre;
Of her that loues him with that excellence,
That Angels loue good men with: Euen of her,
That when the greatest stroake of Fortune falls
Will blesse the King: and is not this course pious?
Cham. Heauen keep me from such councel: tis most true
These newes are euery where, euery tongue speaks 'em,
And euery true heart weepes for't. All that dare
Looke into these affaires, see this main end,
The French Kings Sister. Heauen will one day open
The Kings eyes, that so long haue slept vpon
This bold bad man.
Suff. And free vs from his slauery.
Norf. We had need pray,
And heartily, for our deliuerance;
Or this imperious man will worke vs all
From Princes into Pages: all mens honours
Lie like one lumpe before him, to be fashion'd
Into what pitch he please.
Suff. For me, my Lords,
I loue him not, nor feare him, there's my Creede:
As I am made without him, so Ile stand,
If the King please: his Curses and his blessings
Touch me alike: th'are breath I not beleeue in.
I knew him, and I know him: so I leaue him
To him that made him proud; the Pope.
Norf. Let's in;
And with some other busines, put the King
From these sad thoughts, that work too much vpon him:
My Lord, youle beare vs company?
Cham. Excuse me,
The King ha's sent me otherwhere: Besides
You'l finde a most vnfit time to disturbe him:
Health to your Lordships.

v *Nor.*

Norfolke. Thankes my good Lord Chamberlaine.

Exit Lord Chamberlaine, and the King drawes the Curtaine and ſits reading penſiuely.

Suff. How ſad he lookes; ſure he is much afflicted.
Kin. Who's there? Ha?
Norff. Pray God he be not angry.
Kin. Who's there I ſay? How dare you thruſt your ſelues
Into my priuate Meditations?
Who am I? Ha?
Norff. A gracious King, that pardons all offences
Malice ne're meant: Our breach of Duty this way.
Is buſineſſe of Eſtate; in which, we come
To know your Royall pleaſure.
Kin. Ye are too bold:
Go too; Ile make ye know your times of buſineſſe:
Is this an howre for temporall affaires? Ha?

Enter Wolſey and Campeius with a Commiſſion.

Who's there? my good Lord Cardinall? O my Wolſey,
The quiet of my wounded Conſcience;
Thou art a cure fit for a King; you'r welcome
Moſt learned Reuerend Sir, into our Kingdome,
Vſe vs, and it: My good Lord, haue great care,
I be not found a Talker.
Wol. Sir, you cannot;
I would your Grace would giue vs but an houre
Of priuate conference.
Kin. We are buſie; goe.
Norff. This Prieſt ha's no pride in him?
Suff. Not to ſpeake of:
I would not be ſo ſicke though for his place:
But this cannot continue.
Norff. If it doe, Ile venture one; haue at him.
Suff. I another.

Exeunt Norfolke and Suffolke.

Wol. Your Grace ha's giuen a Preſident of wiſedome
Aboue all Princes, in committing freely
Your ſcruple to the voyce of Chriſtendome:
Who can be angry now? What Enuy reach you?
The Spaniard tide by blood and fauour to her,
Muſt now confeſſe, if they haue any goodneſſe,
The Tryall, iuſt and Noble. All the Clerkes,
(I meane the learned ones in Chriſtian Kingdomes)
Haue their free voyces. Rome (the Nurſe of Iudgement)
Inuited by your Noble ſelfe, hath ſent
One generall Tongue vnto vs. This good man,
This iuſt and learned Prieſt, Cardnall Campeius,
Whom once more, I preſent vnto your Highneſſe.
Kin. And once more in mine armes I bid him welcome,
And thanke the holy Conclaue for their loues,
They haue ſent me ſuch a Man, I would haue wiſh'd for.
Cam. Your Grace muſt needs deſerue all ſtrangers loues,
You are ſo Noble: To your Highneſſe hand
I tender my Commiſſion; by whoſe vertue,
The Court of Rome commanding. You my Lord
Cardinall of Yorke, are ioyn'd with me their Seruant,
In the vnpartiall iudging of this Buſineſſe.
Kin. Two equall men: The Queene ſhall be acquainted
Forthwith for what you come. Where's Gardiner?
Wol. I know your Maieſty, ha's alwayes lou'd her
So deare in heart, not to deny her that
A Woman of leſſe Place might aske by Law;
Schollers allow'd freely to argue for her.
Kin. I, and the beſt ſhe ſhall haue; and my fauour
To him that does beſt, God forbid els: Cardinall,
Prethee call Gardiner to me, my new Secretary.
I find him a fit fellow.

Enter Gardiner.

Wol. Giue me your hand: much ioy & fauour to you;
You are the Kings now.
Gard. But to be commanded
or euer by your Grace, whoſe hand ha's rais'd me.
Kin. Come hither Gardiner.

Walkes and whiſpers.

Camp. My Lord of Yorke, was not one Doctor Pace
In this mans place before him?
Wol. Yes, he was.
Camp. Was he not held a learned man?
Wol. Yes ſurely.
Camp. Beleeue me, there's an ill opinion ſpread then,
Euen of your ſelfe Lord Cardinall.
Wol. How? of me?
Camp. They will not ſticke to ſay, you enuide him;
And fearing he would riſe (he was ſo vertuous)
Kept him a forraigne man ſtill, which ſo greeu'd him,
That he ran mad, and dide.
Wol. Heau'ns peace be with him:
That's Chriſtian care enough: for liuing Murmurers,
There's places of rebuke. He was a Foole;
For he would needs be vertuous. That good Fellow,
If I command him followes my appointment,
I will haue none ſo neere els. Learne this Brother,
We liue not to be grip'd by meaner perſons.
Kin. Deliuer this with modeſty to th' Queene.

Exit Gardiner.

The moſt conuenient place, that I can thinke of
For ſuch receipt of Learning, is Black-Fryers:
There ye ſhall meete about this waighty buſines.
My Wolſey, ſee it furniſh'd, O my Lord,
Would it not grieue an able man to leaue
So ſweet a Bedfellow? But Conſcience, Conſcience;
O 'tis a tender place, and I muſt leaue her. *Exeunt.*

Scena Tertia.

Enter Anne Bullen, and an old Lady.

An. Not for that neither; here's the pang that pinches.
His Highneſſe, hauing liu'd ſo long with her, and ſhe
So good a Lady, that no Tongue could euer
Pronounce diſhonour of her; by my life,
She neuer knew harme-doing: Oh, now after
So many courſes of the Sun enthroaned,
Still growing in a Maieſty and pompe, the which
To leaue, a thouſand fold more bitter, then
'Tis ſweet at firſt t'acquire. After this Proceſſe.
To giue her the auaunt, it is a pitty
Would moue a Monſter.
Old La. Hearts of moſt hard temper
Melt and lament for her.
An. Oh Gods will, much better
She ne're had knowne pompe; though't be temporall,
Yet if that quarrell. Fortune, do diuorce
It from the bearer, 'tis a ſufferance, panging
As ſoule and bodies ſeuering.
Old L. Alas poore Lady,
Shee's a ſtranger now againe.
An. So much the more
Muſt pitty drop vpon her; verily
I ſweare, tis better to be lowly borne,
And

And range with humble liuers in Content,
Then to be perk'd vp in a glistring griefe,
And weare a golden sorrow.
Old L. Our content
Is our best hauing.
Anne: By my troth, and Maidenhead,
I would not be a Queene.
Old.L. Beshrew me, I would,
And venture Maidenhead for't,and so would you
For all this spice of your Hipocrisie:
You that haue so faire parts of Woman on you,
Haue (too) a Womans heart, which euer yet
Affected Eminence, Wealth, Soueraignty;
Which, to say sooth, are Blessings; and which guifts
(Sauing your mincing) the capacity
Of your soft Chiuerell Conscience, would receiue,
If you might please to stretch it
Anne. Nay, good troth.
Old L. Yes troth, & troth; you would not be a Queen?
Anne. No, not for all the riches vnder Heauen.
Old.L. Tis strange; a threepence bow'd would hire me
Old as I am, to Queene it: but I pray you,
What thinke you of a Dutchesse? Haue you limbs
To beare that load of Title?
An. No in truth.
Old. L Then you are weakly made; plucke off a little,
I would not be a young Count in your way,
For more then blushing comes to: If your backe
Cannot vouchsafe this burthen, tis too weake
Euer to get a Boy.
An. How you doe talke;
I sweare againe, I would not be a Queene,
For all the world:
Old. L. In faith, for little England
You'ld venture an emballing: I my selfe
Would for *Carnaruanshire*, although there long'd
No more to th' Crowne but that: Lo, who comes here?

Enter Lord Chamberlaine. (know

L.Cham. Good morrow Ladies; what wer't worth to
The secret of your conference?
An. My good Lord,
Not your demand; it values not your asking:
Our Mistris Sorrowes we were pittying.
Cham. It was a gentle businesse, and becomming
The action of good women, there is hope
All will be well.
An. Now I pray God, *Amen.*
Cham. You beare a gentle minde, & heau'nly blessings
Follow such Creatures. That you may, faire Lady
Perceiue I speake sincerely, and high notes
Tane of your many vertues; the Kings Maiesty
Commends his good opinion of you, to you; and
Doe's purpose honour to you no lesse flowing,
Then Marchionesse of *Pembrooke*; to which Title,
A Thousand pound a yeare, Annuall support,
Out of his Grace, he addes.
An I doe not know
What kinde of my obedience, I should tender;
More then my All, is Nothing: Nor my Prayers
Are not words duely hallowed; nor my Wishes
More worth, then empty vanities: yet Prayers & Wishes
Are all I can returne. Beseech your Lordship,
Vouchsafe to speake my thankes, and my obedience,
As from a blushing Handmaid, to his Highnesse;
Whose health and Royalty I pray for.
Cham. Lady;
I shall not faile t'approue the faire conceit
The King hath of you. I haue perus'd her well,
Beauty and Honour in her are so mingled,
That they haue caught the King: and who knowes yet
But from this Lady, may proceed a Iemme,
To lighten all this Ile. I'le to the King,
And say I spoke with you.

Exit Lord Chamberlaine

An. My honour'd Lord.
Old L. Why this it is: See, see,
I haue beene begging sixteene yeares in Court
(Am yet a Courtier beggerly) nor could
Come pat betwixt too early, and too late
For any suit of pounds: and you, (oh fate)
A very fresh Fish heere; fye, fye, fye vpon
This compel'd fortune: haue your mouth fild vp,
Before you open it.
An. This is strange to me.
Old L. How tasts it? Is it bitter? Forty pence, no:
There was a Lady once (tis an old Story)
That would not be a Queene, that would she not
For all the mud in Egypt; haue you heard it?
An. Come you are pleasant.
Old. L. With your Theame, I could
O're-mount the Larke: The Marchionesse of *Pembrooke*?
A thousand pounds a yeare, for pure respect?
No other obligation? by my Life,
That promises mo thousands: Honours traine
Is longer then his fore-skirt; by this time
I know your backe will beare a Dutchesse. Say,
Are you not stronger then you were?
An. Good Lady,
Make your selfe mirth with your particular fancy,
And leaue me out on't. Would I had no being
If this salute my blood a iot; it faints me
To thinke what followes.
The Queene is comfortlesse, and wee forgetfull
In our long absence: pray doe not deliuer,
What heere y'haue heard to her.
Old L. What doe you thinke me —— *Exeunt*

Scena Quarta.

Trumpets, Sennet, and Cornets.

Enter two Vergers, with short siluer wands; next them two Scribes in the habite of Doctors; after them, the Bishop of Canterbury alone; after him, the Bishops of Lincolne, Ely, Rochester, and S. Asaph: Next them, with some small distance, followes a Gentleman bearing the Purse, with the great Seale, and a Cardinals Hat: Then two Priests bearing each a Siluer Crosse: Then a Gentleman Vsher bareheaded, accompanyed with a Sergeant at Armes, bearing a Siluer Mace: Then two Gentlemen bearing two great Siluer Pillers: After them, side by side, the two Cardinals, two Noblemen, with the Sword and Mace. The King takes place vnder the Cloth of State. The two Cardinalls sit vnder him as Iudges. The Queene takes place some distance from the King. The Bishops place themselues on each side the Court in manner of a Consistory: Below them the Scribes. The Lords sit next the Bishops. The rest of the Attendants stand in conuenient order about the Stage.

Car. Whil'ſt our Commiſſion from Rome is read,
Let ſilence be commanded.
King. What's the need?
It hath already publiquely bene read,
And on all ſides th'Authority allow'd,
You may then ſpare that time.
Car. Bee't ſo, proceed.
Scri. Say, *Henry* K. of England, come into the Court.
Crier. *Henry* King of England, &c.
King. Heere.
Scribe. Say, *Katherine* Queene of England,
Come into the Court.
Crier. *Katherine* Queene of England, &c.
The Queene makes no anſwer, riſes out of her Chaire, goes about the Court, comes to the King, and kneeles at his Feete. Then ſpeakes.
Sir, I deſire you do me Right and Iuſtice,
And to beſtow your pitty on me; for
I am a moſt poore Woman, and a Stranger,
Borne out of your Dominions: hauing heere
No Iudge indifferent, nor no more aſſurance
Of equall Friendſhip and Proceeding. Alas Sir
In what haue I offended you? What cauſe
Hath my behauiour giuen to your diſpleaſure,
That thus you ſhould proceede to put me off.
And take your good Grace from me? Heauen witneſſe,
I haue bene to you, a true and humble Wife,
At all times to your will conformable:
Euer in feare to kindle your Diſlike,
Yea, ſubiect to your Countenance: Glad, or ſorry,
As I ſaw it inclin'd? When was the houre
I euer contradicted your Deſire?
Or made it not mine too? Or which of your Friends
Haue I not ſtroue to loue, although I knew
He were mine Enemy? What Friend of mine,
That had to him deriu'd your Anger, did I
Continue in my Liking? Nay, gaue notice
He was from hence diſcharg'd? Sir, call to minde,
That I haue beene your Wife, in this Obedience,
Vpward of twenty yeares, and haue bene bleſt
With many Children by you. If in the courſe
And proceſſe of this time, you can report,
And proue it too, againſt mine Honor, aught;
My bond to Wedlocke, or my Loue and Dutie
Againſt your Sacred Perſon; in Gods name
Turne me away: and let the fowl'ſt Contempt
Shut doore vpon me, and ſo giue me vp
To the ſharp'ſt kinde of Iuſtice. Pleaſe you, Sir,
The King your Father, was reputed for
A Prince moſt Prudent; of an excellent
And vnmatch'd Wit, and Iudgement. *Ferdinand*
My Father, King of Spaine, was reckon'd one
The wiſeſt Prince, that there had reign'd, by many
A yeare before. It is not to be queſtion'd,
That they had gather'd a wiſe Councell to them
Of euery Realme, that did debate this Buſineſſe,
Who deem'd our Marriage lawful. Wherefore I humbly
Beſeech you Sir, to ſpare me, till I may
Be by my Friends in Spaine, aduis'd; whoſe Counſaile
I will implore. If not, i'th'name of God
Your pleaſure be fulfill'd.
Wol. You haue heere Lady,
(And of your choice) theſe Reuerend Fathers, men
Of ſingular Integrity, and Learning;
Yea, the elect o'th'Land, who are aſſembled
To pleade your Cauſe. It ſhall be therefore bootleſſe,
That longer you deſire the Court, as well
For your owne quiet, as to rectifie
What is vnſetled in the King.
Camp. His Grace
Hath ſpoken well, and iuſtly: Therefore Madam,
It's fit this Royall Seſſion do proceed,
And that (without delay) their Arguments
Be now produc'd, and heard.
Qu. Lord Cardinall, to you I ſpeake.
Wol. Your pleaſure, Madam.
Qu. Sir, I am about to weepe; but thinking that
We are a Queene (or long haue dream'd ſo) certaine
The daughter of a King, my drops of teares,
Ile turne to ſparkes of fire.
Wol. Be patient yet.
Qu. I will, when you are humble; Nay before,
Or God will puniſh me. I do beleeue
(Induc'd by potent Circumſtances) that
You are mine Enemy, and make my Challenge,
You ſhall not be my Iudge. For it is you
Haue blowne this Coale, betwixt my Lord, and me;
(Which Gods dew quench) therefore, I ſay againe,
I vtterly abhorre; yea, from my Soule
Refuſe you for my Iudge, whom yet once more
I hold my moſt malicious Foe, and thinke not
At all a Friend to truth.
Wol. I do profeſſe
You ſpeake not like your ſelfe: who euer yet
Haue ſtood to Charity, and diſplayd th'effects
Of diſpoſition gentle, and of wiſedome,
Ore-topping womans powre. Madam, you do me wrong
I haue no Spleene againſt you, nor iniuſtice
For you, or any: how farre I haue proceeded,
Or how farre further (Shall) is warranted
By a Commiſſion from the Conſiſtorie,
Yea, the whole Conſiſtorie of Rome. You charge me,
That I haue blowne this Coale: I do deny it,
The King is preſent: If it be knowne to him,
That I gainſay my Deed, how may he wound,
And worthily my Falſehood, yea, as much
As you haue done my Truth. If he know
That I am free of your Report, he knowes
I am not of your wrong. Therefore in him
It lies to cure me, and the Cure is to
Remoue theſe Thoughts from you. The which before
His Highneſſe ſhall ſpeake in, I do beſeech
You (gracious Madam) to vnthinke your ſpeaking,
And to ſay ſo no more.
Queen. My Lord, my Lord,
I am a ſimple woman, much too weake
T'oppoſe your cunning. Y'are meek, & humble-mouth'd
You ſigne your Place, and Calling, in full ſeeming,
With Meekeneſſe and Humilitie: but your Heart
Is cramm'd with Arrogancie, Spleene, and Pride.
You haue by Fortune, and his Highneſſe fauors,
Gone ſlightly o're lowe ſteppes, and now are mounted
Where Powres are your Retainers, and your words
(Domeſtickes to you) ſerue your will, as't pleaſe
Your ſelfe pronounce their Office. I muſt tell you,
You tender more your perſons Honor, then
Your high profeſſion Spirituall. That agen
I do refuſe you for my Iudge, and heere
Before you all, Appeale vnto the Pope,
To bring my whole Cauſe 'fore his Holineſſe,
And to be iudg'd by him.
She Curtſies to the King, and offers to depart.

Camp.

Camp. The Queene is obstinate,
Stubborne to Iustice, apt to accuse it,and
Disdainfull to be tride by't; tis not well.
Shee's going away.
Kin. Call her againe.
Crier. Katherine. Q of England,come into the Court.
Gent.Vsh. Madam ,you are cald backe.
Que. What need you note it?pray you keep your way,
When you are cald returne. Now the Lord helpe,
They vexe me past my patience,pray you passe on;
I will not tarry:no, nor euer more
Vpon this businesse my appearance make,
In any of their Courts.
Exit Queene, and her Attendants.
Kin. Goe thy wayes *Kate*,
That man i'th' world,who shall report he ha's
A better Wife,let him in naught be trusted,
For speaking false in that ; thou art alone
(If thy rare qualities, sweet gentlenesse,
Thy meeknesse Saint-like, Wife-like Gouernment,
Obeying in commanding,and thy parts
Soueraigne and Pious els,could speake thee out)
The Queene of earthly Queenes : Shee's Noble borne;
And like her true Nobility,she ha's
Carried her selfe towards me.
Wol. Most gracious Sir,
In humblest manner I require your Highnes,
That it shall please you to declare in hearing
Of all these eares(for where I am rob'd and bound,
There must I be vnloos'd, although not there
At once,and fully satisfide) whether euer I
Did broach this busines to your Highnes,or
Laid any scruple in your way, which might
Induce you to the question on't:or euer
Haue to you, but with thankes to God for such
A Royall Lady, spake one, the least word that might
Be to the preiudice of her present State,
Or touch of her good Person ?
Kin. My Lord Cardinall,
I doe excuse you ; yea, vpon mine Honour,
I free you from't : You are not to be taught
That you haue many enemies,that know not
Why they are so; but like to Village Curres,
Barke when their fellowes doe By some of these
The Queene is put in anger; y'are excus'd:
But will you be more iustifi'de? You euer
Haue wish'd the sleeping of this busines,neuer desir'd
It to be stir'd; but oft haue hindred,oft
The pass ges made toward it; on my Honour,
I speake my good Lord Cardnall, to this point;
And thus farre cleare him.
Now, what mou'd me too't,
I will be bold with time and your attention : (too't:
Then marke th'inducement Thus it came; giue heede
My Conscience first receiu'd a tendernes,
Scruple,and pricke,on certaine Speeches vtter'd
By th'Bishop of *Bayon*,then French Embassador,
Who had beene hither sent on the debating
And Marriage 'twixt the Duke of *Orleance*,and
Our Daughter *Mary* : I'th' Progresse of this busines,
Ere a determinate resolution, hee
(I meane the Bishop) did require a respite,
Wherein he might the King his Lord aduertise,
Whether our Daughter were legitimate,
Respecting this our Marriage with the Dowager,
Sometimes our Brothers Wife. This respite shooke
The bosome of my Conscience, enter'd me;
Yea, with a spitting power and made to tremble
The region of my Breast, which forc'd such way,
That many maz'd considerings, did throng
And prest in with this Caution. First,me thought
I stood not in the smile of Heauen, who had
Commanded Nature, that my Ladies wombe
If it conceiu'd a male-child by me, should
Doe no more Offices of life too't; then
The Graue does to th' dead: For her Male Issue,
Or di'de where they were made, or shortly after
This world had ayr'd them. Hence I tooke a thought,
This was a Iudgement on me,that my Kingdome
(Well worthy the best Heyre o'th' World) should not
Be gladded in't by me. Then followes,that
I weigh'd the danger which my Realmes stood in
By this my Issues faile,and that gaue to me
Many a groaning throw : thus hulling in
The wild Sea of my Conscience,I did steere
Toward this remedy, whereupon we are
Now present heere together:that's to say,
I meant to rectifie my Conscience, which
I then did feele full sicke,and yet not well,
By all the Reuerend Fathers of the Land,
And Doctors learn'd. First I began in priuate,
With you my Lord of *Lincolne*; you remember
How vnder my oppression I did reeke
When I first mou'd you.
B. Lin. Very well my Liedge.
Kin I haue spoke long, be pleas'd your selfe to say
How farre you satisfide me.
Lin. So please your Highnes,
The question did at first so stagger me,
Bearing a State of mighty moment in't,
And consequence of dread, that I committed
The daringst Counsaile which I had to doubt,
And did entreate your Highnes to this course,
Which you are running heere.
Kin. I then mou'd you,
My Lord of *Canterbury*,and got your leaue
To make this present Summons vnsolicited.
I left no Reuerend Person in this Court;
But by particular consent proceeded
Vnder your hands and Seales; therefore goe on,
For no dislike i'th' world against the person
Of the good Queene; but the sharpe thorny points
Of my alleadged reasons, driues this forward :
Proue but our Marriage lawfull, by my Life
And Kingly Dignity, we are contented
To weare our mortall State to come, with her,
(*Katherine* our Queene) before the primest Creature
That's Parragon'd o'th' World
Camp. So please your Highnes,
The Queene being absent, 'tis a needfull fitnesse,
That we adiourne this Court till further day;
Meane while, must be an earnest motion
Made to the Queene to call backe her Appeale
She intends vnto his Holinesse.
Kin. I may perceiue
These Cardinals trifle with me : I abhorre
This dilatory sloth, and trickes of Rome.
My learn'd and welbeloued Seruant *Cranmer*,
Prethee returne,with thy approch: I know,
My comfort comes along : breake vp the Court ;
I say, set on.
Exeunt, in manner as they enter'd.

v 3

Actus Tertius. Scena Prima.

Enter Queene and her Women as at worke.

Queen. Take thy Lute wench,
My Soule growes sad with troubles,
Sing, and disperse 'em if thou canst: leaue working:

SONG.

Orpheus with his Lute made Trees,
And the Mountaine tops that freeze,
Bow themselues when he did sing.
To his Musicke, Plants and Flowers
Euer sprung; as Sunne and Showers,
There had made a lasting Spring.
Euery thing that heard him play,
Euen the Billowes of the Sea,
Hung their heads, & then lay by.
In sweet Musicke is such Art,
Killing care, & griefe of heart,
Fall asleepe, or hearing dye.

Enter a Gentleman.

Queen. How now?
Gent. And't please your Grace, the two great Cardinals
Wait in the presence.
Queen. Would they speake with me?
Gent. They wil'd me say so Madam.
Queen. Pray their Graces
To come neere: what can be their busines
With me, a poore weake woman, falne from fauour?
I doe not like their comming; now I thinke on't,
They should bee good men, their affaires as righteous:
But all Hoods, make not Monkes.

Enter the two Cardinalls, Wolsey & Campian.

Wolf. Peace to your Highnesse.
Queen. Your Graces find me heere part of a Houswife,
(I would be all) against the worst may happen:
What are your pleasures with me, reuerent Lords?
Wol. May it please you Noble Madam, to withdraw
Into your priuate Chamber; we shall giue you
The full cause of our comming.
Queen. Speake it heere.
There's nothing I haue done yet o' my Conscience
Deserues a Corner: would all other Women
Could speake this with as free a Soule as I doe.
My Lords, I care not (so much I am happy
Aboue a number) if my actions
Were tri'de by eu'ry tongue, eu'ry eye saw 'em,
Enuy and base opinion set against 'em,
I know my life so euen. If your busines
Seeke me out, and that way I am Wife in;
Out with it boldly: Truth loues open dealing.
Card. Tanta est erga te mentis integritas Regina serenissima.
Queen. O good my Lord, no Latin;
I am not such a Truant since my comming,
As not to know the Language I haue liu'd in: (ous:
A strange Tongue makes my cause more strange, suspiti-
Pray speake in English; heere are some will thanke you,
If you speake truth, for their poore Mistris sake;
Beleeue me she ha's had much wrong. Lord Cardinall,
The willing'st sinne I euer yet committed,
May be absolu'd in English.
Card. Noble Lady,
I am sorry my integrity should breed,
(And seruice to his Maiesty and you)
So deepe suspition, where all faith was meant;
We come not by the way of Accusation,
To taint that honour euery good Tongue blesses;
Nor to betray you any way to sorrow;
You haue too much good Lady: But to know
How you stand minded in the waighty difference
Betweene the King and you, and to deliuer
(Like free and honest men) our iust opinions,
And comforts to our cause.
Camp. Most honour'd Madam,
My Lord of Yorke, out of his Noble nature,
Zeale and obedience he still bore your Grace,
Forgetting (like a good man) your late Censure
Both of his truth and him (which was too farre)
Offers, as I doe, in a signe of peace,
His Seruice, and his Counsell.
Queen. To betray me.
My Lords, I thanke you both for your good wills,
Ye speake like honest men, (pray God ye proue so)
But how to make ye sodainly an Answere
In such a poynt of weight, so neere mine Honour,
(More neere my Life I feare) with my weake wit;
And to such men of grauity and learning;
In truth I know not. I was set at worke,
Among my Maids, full little (God knowes) looking
Either for such men, or such businesse;
For her sake that I haue beene, for I feele
The last fit of my Greatnesse; good your Graces
Let me haue time and Councell for my Cause:
Alas, I am a Woman frendlesse, hopelesse.
Wol. Madam,
You wrong the Kings loue with these feares,
Your hopes and friends are infinite.
Queen. In England,
But little for my profit can you thinke Lords,
That any English man dare giue me Councell?
Or be a knowne friend 'gainst his Highnes pleasure,
(Though he be growne so desperate to be honest)
And liue a Subiect? Nay forsooth, my Friends,
They that must weigh out my afflictions,
They that my trust must grow to, liue not heere,
They are (as all my other comforts) far hence
In mine owne Countrey Lords.
Camp. I would your Grace
Would leaue your greefes, and take my Counsell.
Queen. How Sir?
Camp. Put your maine cause into the Kings protection,
Hee's louing and most gracious. 'Twill be much,
Both for your Honour better, and your Cause:
For if the tryall of the Law o'retake ye,
You'l part away disgrac'd.
Wol. He tels you rightly.
Queen. Ye tell me what ye wish for both, my ruine:
Is this your Christian Councell? Out vpon ye.
Heauen is aboue all yet; there sits a Iudge,
That no King can corrupt.
Camp. Your rage mistakes vs.
Queen. The more shame for ye; holy men I thought ye,
Vpon my Soule two reuerend Cardinall Vertues:
But Cardinall Sins, and hollow hearts I feare ye:
Mend 'em for shame my Lords: Is this your comfort?
The Cordiall that ye bring a wretched Lady?
A woman lost among ye, laugh't at, scornd?
I will not wish ye halfe my miseries,

I haue more Charity. But ſay I warn'd ye;
Take heed, for heauens ſake take heed, leaſt at once
The burthen of my ſorrowes, fall vpon ye.
Car. Madam, this is a meere diſtraction,
You turne the good we offer, into enuy.
Quee. Ye turne me into nothing. Woe vpon ye,
And all ſuch falſe Profeſſors. Would you haue me
(If you haue any Iuſtice, any Pitty,
If ye be any thing but Churchmens habits)
Put my ſicke cauſe into his hands, that hates me?
Alas, ha's baniſh'd me his Bed already,
His Loue, too long ago. I am old my Lords,
And all the Fellowſhip I hold now with him
Is onely my Obedience. What can happen
To me, aboue this wretchedneſſe? All your Studies
Make me a Curſe, like this.
Camp. Your feares are worſe.
Qu. Haue I liu'd thus long (let me ſpeake my ſelfe,
Since Vertue findes no friends) a Wife, a true one?
A Woman (I dare ſay without Vainglory)
Neuer yet branded with Suſpition?
Haue I, with all my full Affections
Still met the King? Lou'd him next Heau'n? Obey'd him?
Bin (out of fondneſſe) ſuperſtitious to him?
Almoſt forgot my Prayres to content him?
And am I thus rewarded? 'Tis not well Lords.
Bring me a conſtant woman to her Husband,
One that ne're dream'd a Ioy, beyond his pleaſure;
And to that Woman (when ſhe has done moſt)
Yet will I adde an Honor; a great Patience.
Car. Madam, you wander from the good
We ayme at.
Qu. My Lord,
I dare not make my ſelfe ſo guiltie,
To giue vp willingly that Noble Title
Your Maſter wed me to: nothing but death
Shall e're diuorce my Dignities.
Car. Pray heare me.
Qu. Would I had neuer trod this Engliſh Earth,
Or felt the Flatteries that grow vpon it:
Ye haue Angels Faces; but Heauen knowes your hearts.
What will become of me now, wretched Lady?
I am the moſt vnhappy Woman liuing.
Alas (poore Wenches) where are now your Fortunes?
Shipwrack'd vpon a Kingdome, where no Pitty,
No Friends, no Hope, no Kindred weepe for me?
Almoſt no Graue allow'd me? Like the Lilly
That once was Miſtris of the Field, and flouriſh'd,
Ile hang my head, and periſh.
Car. If your Grace
Could but be brought to know, our Ends are honeſt,
Youl'd feele more comfort. Why ſhold we (good Lady)
Vpon what cauſe wrong you? Alas, our Places,
The way of our Profeſſion is againſt it;
We are to Cure ſuch ſorrowes, not to ſowe 'em.
For Goodneſſe ſake, conſider what you do,
How you may hurt your ſelfe: I, vtterly
Grow from the Kings Acquaintance, by this Carriage.
The hearts of Princes kiſſe Obedience,
So much they loue it. But to ſtubborne Spirits,
They ſwell and grow, as terrible as ſtormes.
I know you haue a Gentle, Noble temper,
A Soule as euen as a Calme; Pray thinke vs,
Thoſe we profeſſe, Peace-makers, Friends, and Seruants.
Camp. Madam, you'l finde it ſo:
You wrong your Vertues
With theſe weake Womens feares. A Noble Spirit
As yours was, put into you, euer caſts
Such doubts as falſe Coine from it. The King loues you,
Beware you looſe it not: For vs (if you pleaſe
To truſt vs in your buſineſſe) we are ready
To vſe our vtmoſt Studies, in your ſeruice.
Qu. Do what ye will, my Lords:
And pray forgiue me;
If I haue vs'd my ſelfe vnmannerly,
You know I am a Woman, lacking wit
To make a ſeemely anſwer to ſuch perſons.
Pray do my ſeruice to his Maieſtie,
He ha's my heart yet, and ſhall haue my Prayers
While I ſhall haue my life. Come reuerend Fathers,
Beſtow your Councels on me. She now begges
That little thought when ſhe ſet footing heere,
She ſhould haue bought her Dignities ſo deere. *Exeunt*

Scena Secunda.

Enter the Duke of Norfolke, Duke of Suffolke, Lord Surrey, and Lord Chamberlaine.

Norf. If you will now vnite in your Complaints,
And force them with a Conſtancy, the Cardinall
Cannot ſtand vnder them. If you omit
The offer of this time, I cannot promiſe,
But that you ſhall ſuſtaine moe new diſgraces,
With theſe you beare alreadie.
Sur. I am ioyfull
To meete the leaſt occaſion, that may giue me
Remembrance of my Father-in-Law, the Duke,
To be reueng'd on him.
Suf. Which of the Peeres
Haue vncontemn'd gone by him, or at leaſt
Strangely neglected? When did he regard
The ſtampe of Nobleneſſe in any perſon
Out of himſelfe?
Cham. My Lords, you ſpeake your pleaſures:
What he deſerues of you and me, I know:
What we can do to him (though now the time
Giues way to vs) I much feare. If you cannot
Barre his acceſſe to'th'King, neuer attempt
Any thing on him: for he hath a Witchcraft
Ouer the King in's Tongue.
Nor. O feare him not,
His ſpell in that is out: the King hath found
Matter againſt him, that for euer marres
The Hony of his Language. No, he's ſetled
(Not to come off) in his diſpleaſure.
Sur. Sir,
I ſhould be glad to heare ſuch Newes as this
Once euery houre.
Nor. Beleeue it, this is true.
In the Diuorce, his contrarie proceedings
Are all vnfolded: wherein he appeares,
As I would wiſh mine Enemy.
Sur. How came
His practiſes to light?
Suf. Moſt ſtrangely.
Sur. O how? how?
Suf. The Cardinals Letters to the Pope miſcarried,
And

And came to th'eye o'th'King, wherein was read
How that the Cardinall did intreat his Holinesse
To stay the Iudgement o'th'Diuorce; for if
It did take place, I do (quoth he) perceiue
My King is tangled in affection, to
A Creature of the Queenes, Lady *Anne Bullen*,

Sur. Ha's the King this?

Suf. Beleeue it.

Sur. Will this worke?

Cham. The King in this perceiues him, how he coasts
And hedges his owne way. But in this point,
All his trickes founder, and he brings his Physicke
After his Patients death; the King already
Hath married the faire Lady.

Sur. Would he had.

Suf. May you be happy in your wish my Lord,
For I professe you haue it.

Sur. Now all my ioy
Trace the Coniunction.

Suf. My Amen too't.

Nor. All mens.

Suf. There's order giuen for her Coronation:
Marry this is yet but yong, and may be left
To some eares vnrecounted. But my Lords
She is a gallant Creature, and compleate
In minde and feature. I perswade me, from her
Will fall some blessing to this Land, which shall
In it be memoriz'd.

Sur. But will the King
Digest this Letter of the Cardinals?
The Lord forbid.

Nor. Marry Amen.

Suf. No, no:
There be moe Waspes that buz about his Nose,
Will make this sting the sooner. Cardinall *Campeius*,
Is stolne away to Rome, hath 'tane no leaue,
Ha's left the cause o'th'King vnhandled, and
Is posted as the Agent of our Cardinall,
To second all his plot. I do assure you,
The King cry'de Ha, at this.

Cham. Now God incense him,
And let him cry Ha, lowder.

Norf. But my Lord
When returnes *Cranmer*?

Suf. He is return'd in his Opinions, which
Haue satisfied the King for his Diuorce,
Together with all famous Colledges
Almost in Christendome: shortly (I beleeue)
His second Marriage shall be publishd, and
Her Coronation. *Katherine* no more
Shall be call'd Queene, but Princesse Dowager,
And Widdow to Prince *Arthur*.

Nor. This same *Cranmer's*
A worthy Fellow, and hath tane much paine
In the Kings businesse.

Suf. He ha's, and we shall see him
For it, an Arch-byshop.

Nor. So I heare.

Suf. Tis so

Enter Wolsey and Cromwell.

The Cardinall.

Nor. Obserue, obserue, hee's moody.

Car. The Packet Cromwell,
Gau't you the King?

Crom. To his owne hand, in's Bed-chamber.

Card. Look'd he o'th'inside of the Paper?

Crom. Presently
He did vnseale them, and the first he view'd,
He did it with a Serious minde: a heede
Was in his countenance. You he bad
Attend him heere this Morning.

Card. Is he ready to come abroad?

Crom. I thinke by this he is.

Card. Leaue me a while. *Exit Cromwell.*
It shall be to the Dutches of Alanson,
The French Kings Sister; He shall marry her.
Anne Bullen? No: Ile no *Anne Bullens* for him,
There's more in't then faire Visage. *Bullen*?
No, wee'l no *Bullens*: Speedily I wish
To heare from Rome. The Marchionesse of Penbroke?

Nor. He's discontented.

Suf. May be he heares the King
Does whet his Anger to him.

Sur. Sharpe enough,
Lord for thy Iustice.

Car. The late Queenes Gentlewoman?
A Knights Daughter
To be her Mistris Mistris? The Queenes, Queene?
This Candle burnes not cleere, 'tis I must snuffe it,
Then out it goes. What though I know her vertuous
And well deseruing? yet I know her for
A spleeny Lutheran, and not wholsome to
Our cause, that she should lye i'th'bosome of
Our hard rul'd King. Againe, there is sprung vp
An Heretique, an Arch-one; *Cranmer*, one
Hath crawl'd into the fauour of the King,
And is his Oracle.

Nor. He is vex'd at something

Enter King, reading of a Scedule.

Sur. I would 'twer somthing ỳ would fret the string,
The Master-cord on's heart.

Suf. The King, the King.

King. What piles of wealth hath he accumulated
To his owne portion? And what expence by'th'houre
Seemes to flow from him? How, i'th'name of Thrift
Does he rake this together? Now my Lords,
Saw you the Cardinall?

Nor. My Lord, we haue
Stood heere obseruing him. Some strange Commotion
Is in his braine: He bites his lip, and starts,
Stops on a sodaine, lookes vpon the ground,
Then layes his finger on his Temple: straight
Springs out into fast gate, then stops againe,
Strikes his brest hard, and anon, he casts
His eye against the Moone: in most strange Postures
We haue seene him set himselfe.

King. It may well be,
There is a mutiny in's minde. This morning,
Papers of State he sent me, to peruse
As I requir'd: and wot you what I found
There (on my Conscience put vnwittingly)
Forsooth an Inuentory, thus importing
The seuerall parcels of his Plate, his Treasure,
Rich Stuffes and Ornaments of Houshold, which
I finde at such proud Rate, that it out-speakes
Possession of a Subiect.

Nor. It's Heauens will,
Some Spirit put this paper in the Packet,
To blesse your eye withall.

King. If we did thinke

His

His Contemplation were aboue the earth,
And fixt on Spirituall obiect, he ſhould ſtill
Dwell in his Muſings, but I am affraid
His Thinkings are below the Moone, not worth
His ſerious conſidering.
King takes his Seat, whiſpers Louell, who goes to the Cardinall.
Car. Heauen forgiue me,
Euer God bleſſe your Highneſſe.
King. Good my Lord,
You are full of Heauenly ſtuffe, and beare the Inuentory
Of your beſt Graces, in your minde; the which
You were now running o're: you haue ſcarſe time
To ſteale from Spirituall leyſure, a briefe ſpan
To keepe your earthly Audit, ſure in that
I deeme you an ill Husband, and am gald
To haue you therein my Companion.
Car. Sir,
For Holy Offices I haue a time; a time
To thinke vpon the part of buſineſſe, which
I beare i'th'State: and Nature does require
Her times of preſeruation, which perforce
I her fraile ſonne, among'ſt my Brethren mortall,
Muſt giue my tendance to
King. You haue ſaid well.
Car. And euer may your Highneſſe yoake together,
(As I will lend you cauſe) my doing well,
With my well ſaying.
King. 'Tis well ſaid agen,
And 'tis a kinde of good deede to ſay well,
And yet words are no deeds. My Father lou'd you,
He ſaid he did, and with his deed did Crowne
His word vpon you. Since I had my Office,
I haue kept you next my Heart, haue not alone
Imploy'd you where high Profits might come home,
But par'd my preſent Hauings, to beſtow
My Bounties vpon you.
Car. What ſhould this meane?
Sur. The Lord increaſe this buſineſſe.
King. Haue I not made you
The prime man of the State? I pray you tell me,
If what I now pronounce, you haue found true:
And if you may confeſſe it, ſay withall
If you are bound to vs, or no. What ſay you?
Car. My Soueraigne, I confeſſe your Royall graces
Showr'd on me daily, haue bene more then could
My ſtudied purpoſes requite, which went
Beyond all mans endeauors. My endeauors,
Haue euer come too ſhort of my Deſires,
Yet fill'd with my Abilities: Mine owne ends
Haue beene mine ſo, that euermore they pointed
To'th'good of your moſt Sacred Perſon, and
The profit of the State. For your great Graces
Heap'd vpon me (poore Vndeſeruer) I
Can nothing render but Allegiant thankes,
My Prayres to heauen for you; my Loyaltie
Which euer ha's, and euer ſhall be growing,
Till death (that Winter) kill it.
King. Fairely anſwer'd:
A Loyall, and obedient Subiect is
Therein illuſtrated, the Honor of it
Does pay the Act of it, as i'th'contrary
The fowleneſſe is the puniſhment. I preſume,
That as my hand ha's open'd Bounty to you,
My heart drop'd Loue, my powre rain'd Honor, more
On you, then any: So your Hand, and Heart,
Your Braine, and euery Function of your power,
Should, notwithſtanding that your bond of duty,
As 'twer in Loues particular, be more
To me your Friend, then any.
Car. I do profeſſe,
That for your Highneſſe good, I euer labour'd
More then mine owne: that am, haue, and will be
(Though all the world ſhould cracke their duty to you,
And throw it from their Soule, though perils did
Abound, as thicke as thought could make 'em, and
Appeare in formes more horrid) yet my Duty,
As doth a Rocke againſt the chiding Flood,
Should the approach of this wilde Riuer breake,
And ſtand vnſhaken yours.
King. 'Tis Nobly ſpoken:
Take notice Lords, he ha's a Loyall breſt,
For you haue ſeene him open't. Read o're this,
And after this, and then to Breakfaſt with
What appetite you haue.
Exit King, frowning vpon the Cardinall, the Nobles throng after him ſmiling, and whiſpering.
Car. What ſhould this meane?
What ſodaine Anger's this? How haue I reap'd it?
He parted Frowning from me, as if Ruine
Leap'd from his Eyes. So lookes the chafed Lyon
Vpon the daring Huntſman that has gall'd him:
Then makes him nothing. I muſt reade this paper:
I feare the Story of his Anger. 'Tis ſo:
This paper ha's vndone me: 'Tis th'Accompt
Of all that world of Wealth I haue drawne together
For mine owne ends, (Indeed to gaine the Popedome,
And fee my Friends in Rome.) O Negligence!
Fit for a Foole to fall by: What croſſe Diuell
Made me put this maine Secret in the Packet
I ſent the King? Is there no way to cure this?
No new deuice to beate this from his Braines?
I know 'twill ſtirre him ſtrongly; yet I know
A way, if it take right, in ſpight of Fortune
Will bring me off againe. What's this? *To th'Pope?*
The Letter (as I liue) with all the Buſineſſe
I writ too's Holineſſe. Nay then, farewell:
I haue touch'd the higheſt point of all my Greatneſſe,
And from that full Meridian of my Glory,
I haſte now to my Setting. I ſhall fall
Like a bright exhalation in the Euening,
And no man ſee me more.

Enter to Woolſey, the Dukes of Norfolke and Suffolke, the Earle of Surrey, and the Lord Chamberlaine.

Nor. Heare the Kings pleaſure Cardinall,
Who commands you
To render vp the Great Seale preſently
Into our hands, and to Confine your ſelfe
To Aſher-houſe, my Lord of Wincheſters,
Till you heare further from his Highneſſe.
Car. Stay:
Where's your Commiſſion? Lords, words cannot carrie
Authority ſo weighty.
Suf. Who dare croſſe 'em,
Bearing the Kings will from his mouth expreſſely?
Car. Till I finde more then will, or words to do it,
(I meane your malice) know, Officious Lords,
I dare, and muſt deny it. Now I feele
Of what courſe Mettle ye are molded, Enuy,
How eagerly ye follow my Diſgraces
As

As if it fed ye, and how sleeke and wanton
Ye appeare in euery thing may bring my ruine?
Follow your enuious courses, men of Malice;
You haue Christian warrant for 'em, and no doubt
In time will finde their fit Rewards. That Seale
You aske with such a Violence, the King
(Mine, and your Master) with his owne hand, gaue me:
Bad me enioy it, with the Place, and Honors
During my life; and to confirme his Goodnesse,
Ti'de it by Letters Patents. Now, who'll take it?
Sur. The King that gaue it.
Car. It must be himselfe then.
Sur. Thou art a proud Traitor, Priest.
Car. Proud Lord, thou lyest:
Within these fortie houres, Surrey durst better
Haue burnt that Tongue, then saide so.
Sur. Thy Ambition
(Thou Scarlet sinne) robb'd this bewailing Land
Of Noble Buckingham, my Father-in-Law,
The heads of all thy Brother-Cardinals,
(With thee, and all thy best parts bound together)
Weigh'd not a haire of his. Plague of your policie,
You sent me Deputie for Ireland,
Farre from his succour; from the King, from all
That might haue mercie on the fault, thou gau'st him:
Whil'st your great Goodnesse, out of holy pitty,
Absolu'd him with an Axe.
Wol. This, and all else
This talking Lord can lay vpon my credit,
I answer, is most false. The Duke by Law
Found his deserts. How innocent I was
From any priuate malice in his end,
His Noble Iurie, and foule Cause can witnesse.
If I lou'd many words, Lord, I should tell you,
You haue as little Honestie, as Honor,
That in the way of Loyaltie, and Truth,
Toward the King, my euer Roiall Master,
Dare mate a sounder man then Surrie can be,
And all that loue his follies.
Sur. By my Soule,
Your long Coat (Priest) protects you,
Thou should'st feele
My Sword i'th'life blood of thee else. My Lords,
Can ye endure to heare this Arrogance?
And from this Fellow? If we liue thus tamely,
To be thus Iaded by a peece of Scarlet,
Farewell Nobilitie: let his Grace go forward,
And dare vs with his Cap, like Larkes.
Card. All Goodnesse
Is poyson to thy Stomacke.
Sur. Yes, that goodnesse
Of gleaning all the Lands wealth into one,
Into your owne hands (Card'nall) by Extortion:
The goodnesse of your intercepted Packets
You writ to'th Pope, against the King: your goodnesse
Since you prouoke me, shall be most notorious.
My Lord of Norfolke, as you are truly Noble,
As you respect the common good, the State
Of our despis'd Nobilitie, our Issues,
(Whom if he liue, will scarse be Gentlemen)
Produce the grand summe of his sinnes, the Articles
Collected from his life. Ile startle you
Worse then the Sacring Bell, when the browne Wench
Lay kissing in your Armes, Lord Cardinall.
Car. How much me thinkes, I could despise this man,
But that I am bound in Charitie against it.
Nor. Those Articles, my Lord, are in the Kings hand:
But thus much, they are foule ones.
Wol. So much fairer
And spotlesse, shall mine Innocence arise,
When the King knowes my Truth.
Sur. This cannot saue you:
I thanke my Memorie, I yet remember
Some of these Articles, and out they shall.
Now, if you can blush, and crie guiltie Cardinall,
You'l shew a little Honestie.
Wol. Speake on Sir,
I dare your worst Obiections: If I blush,
It is to see a Nobleman want manners.
Sur. I had rather want those, then my head;
Haue at you.
First, that without the Kings assent or knowledge,
You wrought to be a Legate, by which power
You maim'd the Iurisdiction of all Bishops.
Nor. Then, That in all you writ to Rome, or else
To Forraigne Princes, *Ego & Rex meus*
Was still inscrib'd: in which you brought the King
To be your Seruant.
Suf. Then, that without the knowledge
Either of King or Councell, when you went
Ambassador to the Emperor, you made bold
To carry into Flanders, the Great Seale.
Sur. Item, You sent a large Commission
To *Gregory de Cassado*, to conclude
Without the Kings will, or the States allowance,
A League betweene his Highnesse, and *Ferrara*.
Suf. That out of meere Ambition, you haue caus'd
Your holy-Hat to be stampt on the Kings Coine.
Sur Then, That you haue sent inumerable substance,
(By what meanes got, I leaue to your owne conscience)
To furnish Rome, and to prepare the wayes
You haue for Dignities, to the meere vndooing
Of all the Kingdome. Many more there are,
Which since they are of you, and odious,
I will not taint my mouth with.
Cham. O my Lord,
Presse not a falling man too farre: 'tis Vertue:
His faults lye open to the Lawes, let them
(Not you) correct him. My heart weepes to see him
So little, of his great Selfe.
Sur. I forgiue him.
Suf. Lord Cardinall, the Kings further pleasure is,
Because all those things you haue done of late
By your power Legatiue within this Kingdome,
Fall into'th'compasse of a Premunire;
That therefore such a Writ be sued against you,
To forfeit all your Goods, Lands, Tenements,
Castles, and whatsoeuer, and to be
Out of the Kings protection. This is my Charge.
Nor. And so wee'l leaue you to your Meditations
How to liue better. For your stubborne answer
About the giuing backe the Great Seale to vs,
The King shall know it, and (no doubt) shal thanke you.
So fare you well, my little good Lord Cardinall.
Exeunt all but Wolsey.
Wol. So farewell, to the little good you beare me.
Farewell? A long farewell to all my Greatnesse.
This is the state of Man; to day he puts forth
The tender Leaues of hopes, to morrow Blossomes,
And beares his blushing Honors thicke vpon him:
The third day, comes a Frost; a killing Frost,
And when he thinkes, good easie man, full surely
His

His Greatnesse is a ripening, nippes his roote,
And then he fals as I do. I haue ventur'd
Like little wanton Boyes that swim on bladders:
This many Summers in a Sea of Glory,
But farre beyond my depth: my high-blowne Pride
At length broke vnder me, and now ha's left me
Weary, and old with Seruice, to the mercy
Of a rude streame, that must for euer hide me.
Vaine pompe, and glory of this World, I hate ye,
I feele my heart new open'd. Oh how wretched
Is that poore man, that hangs on Princes fauours?
There is betwixt that smile we would aspire too,
That sweet Aspect of Princes, and their ruine,
More pangs, and feares then warres, or women haue;
And when he falles, he falles like Lucifer,
Neuer to hope againe.

Enter Cromwell, standing amazed.

Why how now *Cromwell*?
Crom. I haue no power to speake Sir.
Car. What, amaz'd
At my misfortunes? Can thy Spirit wonder
A great man should decline. Nay, and you weep
I am falne indeed.
Crom. How does your Grace.
Card. Why well:
Neuer so truly happy, my good *Cromwell*,
I know my selfe now, and I feele within me,
A peace aboue all earthly Dignities,
A still, and quiet Conscience. The King ha's cur'd me,
I humbly thanke his Grace: and from these shoulders
These ruin'd Pillers, out of pitty, taken
A loade, would sinke a Nauy, (too much Honor.)
O 'tis a burden *Cromwel*, 'tis a burden
Too heauy for a man, that hopes for Heauen.
Crom. I am glad your Grace,
Ha's made that right vse of it.
Card. I hope I haue:
I am able now (me thinkes)
(Out of a Fortitude of Soule, I feele)
To endure more Miseries, and greater farre
Then my Weake-hearted Enemies, dare offer.
What Newes abroad?
Crom. The heauiest, and the worst,
Is your displeasure with the King.
Card. God blesse him.
Crom. The next is, that Sir *Thomas Moore* is chosen
Lord Chancellor, in your place.
Card. That's somewhat sodain.
But he's a Learned man. May he continue
Long in his Highnesse fauour, and do Iustice
For Truths-sake, and his Conscience; that his bones,
When he ha's run his course, and sleepes in Blessings,
May haue a Tombe of Orphants teares wept on him.
What more?
Crom. That *Cranmer* is return'd with welcome;
Install'd Lord Arch-byshop of Canterbury.
Card. That's Newes indeed.
Crom. Last, that the Lady *Anne*,
Whom the King hath in secrecie long married,
This day was view'd in open, as his Queene,
Going to Chappell: and the voyce is now
Onely about her Corronation.
Card There was the waight that pull'd me downe.
O *Cromwell*,
The King ha's gone beyond me: All my Glories
In that one woman, I haue lost for euer.
No Sun, shall euer vsher forth mine Honors,
Or gilde againe the Noble Troopes that waighted
Vpon my smiles. Go get thee from me *Cromwel*,
I am a poore falne man, vnworthy now
To be thy Lord, and Master. Seeke the King
(That Sun, I pray may neuer set) I haue told him,
What, and how true thou art; he will aduance thee.
Some little memory of me, will stirre him
(I know his Noble Nature) not to let
Thy hopefull seruice perish too. Good *Cromwell*
Neglect him not; make vse now, and prouide
For thine owne future safety.
Crom. O my Lord,
Must I then leaue you? Must I needes forgo
So good, so Noble, and so true a Master?
Beare witnesse, all that haue not hearts of Iron,
With what a sorrow *Cromwel* leaues his Lord.
The King shall haue my seruice; but my prayres
For euer, and for euer shall be yours.
Card. *Cromwel*, I did not thinke to shed a teare
In all my Miseries: But thou hast forc'd me
(Out of thy honest truth) to play the Woman.
Let's dry our eyes: And thus farre heare me *Cromwel*,
And when I am forgotten, as I shall be,
And sleepe in dull cold Marble, where no mention
Of me, more must be heard of: Say I taught thee;
Say *Wolsey*, that once trod the wayes of Glory,
And sounded all the Depths, and Shoales of Honor,
Found thee a way (out of his wracke) to rise in:
A sure, and safe one, though thy Master mist it.
Marke but my Fall, and that that Ruin'd me:
Cromwel, I charge thee, fling away Ambition,
By that sinne fell the Angels: how can man then
(The Image of his Maker) hope to win by it?
Loue thy selfe last, cherish those hearts that hate thee;
Corruption wins not more then Honesty.
Still in thy right hand, carry gentle Peace
To silence enuious Tongues. Be iust, and feare not;
Let all the ends thou aym'st at, be thy Countries,
Thy Gods, and Truths. Then if thou fall'st (O *Cromwell*)
Thou fall'st a blessed Martyr.
Serue the King: And prythee leade me in:
There take an Inuentory of all I haue,
To the last peny, 'tis the Kings. My Robe,
And my Integrity to Heauen, is all,
I dare now call mine owne. O *Cromwel*, *Cromwel*,
Had I but seru'd my God, with halfe the Zeale
I seru'd my King: he would not in mine Age
Haue left me naked to mine Enemies.
Crom. Good Sir, haue patience.
Card. So I haue. Farewell
The Hopes of Court, my Hopes in Heauen do dwell.

Exeunt.

Actus Quartus. Scena Prima.

Enter two Gentlemen, meeting one another.

1 Y'are well met once againe.
2 So are you.
1 You come to take your stand heere, and behold
The Lady *Anne*, passe from her Corronation.

2 'Tis

2 'Tis all my businesse. At our last encounter,
The Duke of Buckingham came from his Triall.
1 'Tis very true. But that time offer'd sorrow,
This generall ioy.
2 Tis well: The Citizens
I am sure haue shewne at full their Royall minds,
As let 'em haue their rights, they are euer forward
In Celebration of this day with Shewes,
Pageants, and Sights of Honor.
1 Neuer greater,
Nor Ile assure you better taken Sir.
2 May I be bold to aske what that containes,
That Paper in your hand.
1 Yes, 'tis the List
Of those that claime their Offices this day,
By custome of the Coronation.
The Duke of Suffolke is the first, and claimes
To be high Steward; Next the Duke of Norfolke,
He to be Earle Marshall: you may reade the rest.
1 I thanke you Sir: Had I not known those customs,
I should haue beene beholding to your Paper:
But I beseech you, what's become of *Katherine*
The Princesse Dowager? How goes her businesse?
1 That I can tell you too. The Archbishop
Of Canterbury, accompanied with other
Learned, and Reuerend Fathers of his Order,
Held a late Court at Dunstable; sixe miles off
From Ampthill, where the Princesse lay, to which
She was often cyted by them, but appear'd not:
And to be short, for not Appearance, and
The Kings late Scruple, by the maine assent
Of all these Learned men, she was diuorc'd,
And the late Marriage made of none effect:
Since which, she was remou'd to Kymmalton,
Where she remaines now sicke.
2 Alas good Lady.
The Trumpets sound: Stand close,
The Queene is comming. *Ho-boyes.*

The Order of the Coronation.

1 *A liuely Flourish of Trumpets.*
2 *Then, two Iudges*
3 *Lord* Chancellor, *with Purse and Mace before him.*
4 Quirristers *singing.* Musicke
5 Maior of London, *bearing the Mace. Then* Garter, *in his Coate of Armes, and on his head he wore a Gilt Copper Crowne.*
6 Marquesse Dorset, *bearing a Scepter of Gold, on his head, a Demy Coronall of Gold. With him, the Earle of* Surrey, *bearing the Rod of Siluer with the Doue, Crowned with an Earles Coronet. Collars of Esses.*
7 Duke of Suffolke, *in his Robe of Estate, his Coronet on his head, bearing a long white Wand, as High Steward. With him, the Duke of* Norfolke, *with the Rod of Marshalship, a Coronet on his head. Collars of Esses.*
8 *A Canopy, borne by foure of the* Cinque-Ports, *vnder it the Queene in her Robe, in her haire, richly adorned with Pearle, Crowned. On each side her, the Bishops of* London, *and* Winchester.
9 *The* Olde Dutchesse of Norfolke, *in a Coronall of Gold, wrought with Flowers, bearing the Queenes Traine.*
10 *Certaine* Ladies *or* Countesses, *with plaine Circlets of Gold, without Flowers.*

Exeunt, *first passing ouer the Stage in Order and State, and then, A great Flourish of Trumpets.*

2 A Royall Traine beleeue me: These I know:
Who's that that beares the Scepter?
1 Marquesse Dorset,
And that the Earle of Surrey, with the Rod.
2 A bold braue Gentleman. That should bee
The Duke of Suffolke.
1 'Tis the same: high Steward.
2 And that my Lord of Norfolke?
1 Yes.
2 Heauen blesse thee,
Thou hast the sweetest face I euer look'd on.
Sir, as I haue a Soule, she is an Angell;
Our King has all the Indies in his Armes,
And more, and richer, when he straines that Lady,
I cannot blame his Conscience.
1 They that beare
The Cloath of Honour ouer her, are foure Barons
Of the Cinque Ports.
2 Those men are happy,
And so are all, are neere her.
I take it, she that carries vp the Traine,
Is that old Noble Lady, Dutchesse of Norfolke.
1 It is, and all the rest are Countesses.
2 Their Coronets say so. These are Starres indeed,
And sometimes falling ones.
2 No more of that.
Enter a third Gentleman.
1 God saue you Sir. Where haue you bin broiling?
3 Among the crow'd i'th'Abbey, where a finger
Could not be wedg'd in more: I am stifled
With the meere ranknesse of their ioy.
2 You saw the Ceremony?
3 That I did.
1 How was it?
3 Well worth the seeing.
2 Good Sir, speake it to vs?
3 As well as I am able. The rich streame
Of Lords, and Ladies, hauing brought the Queene
To a prepar'd place in the Quire, fell off
A distance from her; while her Grace sate downe
To rest a while, some halfe an houre, or so,
In a rich Chaire of State, opposing freely
The Beauty of her Person to the People.
Beleeue me Sir, she is the goodliest Woman
That euer lay by man: which when the people
Had the full view of, such a noyse arose,
As the shrowdes make at Sea, in a stiffe Tempest,
As lowd, and to as many Tunes. Hats, Cloakes,
(Doublets, I thinke) flew vp, and had their Faces
Bin loose, this day they had beene lost. Such ioy
I neuer saw before. Great belly'd women,
That had not halfe a weeke to go, like Rammes
In the old time of Warre, would shake the prease
And make 'em reele before 'em. No man liuing
Could say this is my wife there, all were wouen
So strangely in one peece.
2 But what follow'd?
3 At length, her Grace rose, and with modest paces
Came to the Altar, where she kneel'd, and Saint-like
Cast her faire eyes to Heauen and pray'd deuoutly.
Then rose againe, and bow'd her to the people:
When by the Arch-byshop of Canterbury,
She had all the Royall makings of a Queene;
As holy Oyle, *Edward* Confessors Crowne,
The Rod, and Bird of Peace, and all such Emblemes
Laid Nobly on her: which perform'd, the Quire

With

With all the choyſeſt Muſicke of the Kingdome,
Together ſung *To Deum*. So ſhe parted,
And with the ſame full State pac'd backe againe
To Yorke-Place, where the Feaſt is held.
1 Sir,
You muſt no more call it Yorke-place, that's paſt:
For ſince the Cardinall fell, that Titles loſt,
'Tis now the Kings, and call'd White-Hall.
3 I know it:
But 'tis ſo lately alter'd, that the old name
Is freſh about me.
2 What two Reuerend Byſhops
Were thoſe that went on each ſide of the Queene?
3 *Stokeley* and *Gardiner*, the one of Wincheſter,
Newly preferr'd from the Kings Secretary:
The other London.
2 He of Wincheſter
Is held no great good louer of the Archbiſhops,
The vertuous *Cranmer*.
3 All the Land knowes that:
How euer, yet there is no great breach, when it comes
Cranmer will finde a Friend will not ſhrinke from him.
2 Who may that be, I pray you.
3 *Thomas Cromwell*,
A man in much eſteeme with th'King, and truly
A worthy Friend. The King ha's made him
Maſter o'th'Iewell Houſe,
And one already of the Priuy Councell.
2 He will deſerue more.
3 Yes without all doubt.
Come Gentlemen, ye ſhall go my way,
Which is to'th Court, and there ye ſhall be my Gueſts:
Something I can command. As I walke thither,
Ile tell ye more.
Both. You may command vs Sir. *Exeunt.*

Scena Secunda.

Enter Katherine Dowager, ſicke, lead betweene Griffith, her Gentleman Vſher, and Patience her Woman.

Grif. How do's your Grace?
Kath. O *Griffith*, ſicke to death:
My Legges like loaden Branches bow to'th'Earth,
Willing to leaue their burthen: Reach a Chaire,
So now (me thinkes) I feele a little eaſe.
Did'ſt thou not tell me *Griffith*, as thou lead'ſt mee,
That the great Childe of Honor, Cardinall *Wolſey*
Was dead?
Grif. Yes Madam: but I thanke your Grace
Out of the paine you ſuffer'd, gaue no eare too't.
Kath. Pre'thee good *Griffith*, tell me how he dy'de.
If well, he ſtept before me happily
For my example.
Grif. Well, the voyce goes Madam,
For after the ſtout Earle Northumberland
Arreſted him at Yorke, and brought him forward
As a man ſorely tainted, to his Anſwer,
He fell ſicke ſodainly, and grew ſo ill
He could not ſit his Mule.
Kath. Alas poore man.
Grif. At laſt, with eaſie Rodes, he came to Leiceſter,
Lodg'd in the Abbey; where the reuerend Abbot
With all his Couent, honourably receiu'd him;
To whom he gaue theſe words. O Father Abbot,
An old man, broken with the ſtormes of State,
Is come to lay his weary bones among ye;
Giue him a little earth for Charity.
So went to bed; where eagerly his ſickneſſe
Purſu'd him ſtill, and three nights after this,
About the houre of eight, which he himſelſe
Foretold ſhould be his laſt, full of Repentance,
Continuall Meditations, Teares, and Sorrowes,
He gaue his Honors to the world agen,
His bleſſed part to Heauen, and ſlept in peace.
Kath. So may he reſt,
His Faults lye gently on him:
Yet thus farre *Griffith*, giue me leaue to ſpeake him,
And yet with Charity. He was a man
Of an vnbounded ſtomacke, euer ranking
Himſelfe with Princes. One that by ſuggeſtion
Ty'de all the Kingdome. Symonie, was faire play,
His owne Opinion was his Law. I'th'preſence
He would ſay vntruths, and be euer double
Both in his words, and meaning. He was neuer
(But where he meant to Ruine) pittifull.
His Promiſes, were as he then was, Mighty:
But his performance, as he is now, Nothing:
Of his owne body he was ill, and gaue
The Clergy ill example.
Grif. Noble Madam:
Mens euill manners, liue in Braſſe, their Vertues
We write in Water. May it pleaſe your Highneſſe
To heare me ſpeake his good now?
Kath. Yes good *Griffith*,
I were malicious elſe.
Grif. This Cardinall,
Though from an humble Stocke, vndoubtedly
Was faſhion'd to much Honor. From his Cradle
He was a Scholler, and a ripe, and good one:
Exceeding wiſe, faire ſpoken, and perſwading:
Lofty, and ſowre to them that lou'd him not:
But, to thoſe men that ſought him, ſweet as Summer.
And though he were vnſatiſfied in getting,
(Which was a ſinne) yet in beſtowing, Madam,
He was moſt Princely: Euer witneſſe for him
Thoſe twinnes of Learning, that he rais'd in you,
Ipſwich and Oxford: one of which, fell with him,
Vnwilling to out-liue the good that did it.
The other (though vnfiniſh'd) yet ſo Famous,
So excellent in Art, and ſtill ſo riſing,
That Chriſtendome ſhall euer ſpeake his Vertue.
His Ouerthrow, heap'd Happineſſe vpon him:
For then, and not till then, he felt himſelfe,
And found the Bleſſedneſſe of being little.
And to adde greater Honors to his Age
Then man could giue him; he dy'de, fearing God.
Kath. After my death, I wiſh no other Herald,
No other ſpeaker of my liuing Actions,
To keepe mine Honor, from Corruption,
But ſuch an honeſt Chronicler as *Griffith*.
Whom I moſt hated Liuing, thou haſt made mee
With thy Religious Truth, and Modeſtie,
(Now in his Aſhes) Honor: Peace be with him.
Patience, be neere me ſtill, and ſet me lower,
I haue not long to trouble thee. Good *Griffith*,
Cauſe the Muſitians play me that ſad note
I nam'd my Knell; whil'ſt I ſit meditating

x On

On that Cœlestiall Harmony I go too.

Sad and solemne Musicke.

Grif. She is asleep: Good wench, let's sit down quiet,
For feare we wake her. Softly, gentle *Patience.*

The Vision.

Enter solemnely tripping one after another, sixe Personages, clad in white Robes, wearing on their heades Garlands of Bayes, and golden Vizards on their faces, Branches of Bayes or Palme in their hands. They first Conge vnto her, then Dance: and at certaine Changes, the first two hold a spare Garland ouer her Head, at which the other foure make reuerend Curtsies. Then the two that held the Garland, deliuer the same to the other next two, who obserue the same order in their Changes, and holding the Garland ouer her head. Which done, they deliuer the same Garland to the last two: who likewise obserue the same Order. At which (as it were by inspiration) she makes (in her sleepe) signes of reioycing, and holdeth vp her hands to heauen. And so, in their Dancing vanish, carrying the Garland with them. The Musicke continues.

Kath. Spirits of peace, where are ye? Are ye all gone
And leaue me heere in wretchednesse, behinde ye?
Grif. Madam, we are heere.
Kath. It is not you I call for,
Saw ye none enter since I slept?
Grif. None Madam.
Kath. No? Saw you not euen now a blessed Troope
Inuite me to a Banquet, whose bright faces
Cast thousand beames vpon me, like the Sun?
They promis'd me eternall Happinesse,
And brought me Garlands (*Griffith*) which I feele
I am not worthy yet to weare: I shall assuredly.
Grif. I am most ioyfull Madam, such good dreames
Possesse your Fancy.
Kath. Bid the Musicke leaue,
They are harsh and heauy to me. *Musicke ceases.*
Pati. Do you note
How much her Grace is alter'd on the sodaine?
How long her face is drawne? How pale she lookes,
And of an earthy cold? Marke her eyes?
Grif. She is going Wench. Pray, pray.
Pati. Heauen comfort her.

Enter a Messenger.

Mes. And't like your Grace——
Kath. You are a sawcy Fellow,
Deserue we no more Reuerence?
Grif. You are too blame,
Knowing she will not loose her wonted Greatnesse
To vse so rude behauiour. Go too, kneele.
Mes. I humbly do entreat your Highnesse pardon,
My hast made me vnmannerly. There is staying
A Gentleman sent from the King, to see you.
Kath. Admit him entrance *Griffith.* But this Fellow
Let me ne're see againe. *Exit Messeng.*

Enter Lord Capuchius.

If my sight faile not,
You should be Lord Ambassador from the Emperor,
My Royall Nephew, and your name *Capuchius.*
Cap. Madam the same. Your Seruant.
Kath. O my Lord,
The Times and Titles now are alter'd strangely
With me, since first you knew me.
But I pray you,
What is your pleasure with me?
Cap. Noble Lady,
First mine owne seruice to your Grace, the next
The Kings request, that I would visit you,
Who greeues much for your weaknesse, and by me
Sends you his Princely Commendations,
And heartily entreats you take good comfort.
Kath. O my good Lord, that comfort comes too late,
'Tis like a Pardon after Execution;
That gentle Physicke giuen in time, had cur'd me:
But now I am past all Comforts heere, but Prayers.
How does his Highnesse?
Cap. Madam, in good health.
Kath. So may he euer do, and euer flourish,
When I shall dwell with Wormes, and my poore name
Banish'd the Kingdome. *Patience*, is that Letter
I caus'd you write, yet sent away?
Pat. No Madam.
Kath. Sir, I most humbly pray you to deliuer
This to my Lord the King.
Cap. Most willing Madam.
Kath. In which I haue commended to his goodnesse
The Modell of our chaste loues: his yong daughter,
The dewes of Heauen fall thicke in Blessings on her,
Beseeching him to giue her vertuous breeding.
She is yong, and of a Noble modest Nature,
I hope she will deserue well; and a little
To loue her for her Mothers sake, that lou'd him,
Heauen knowes how deerely.
My next poore Petition,
Is, that his Noble Grace would haue some pittie
Vpon my wretched women, that so long
Haue follow'd both my Fortunes, faithfully,
Of which there is not one, I dare auow
(And now I should not lye) but will deserue
For Vertue, and true Beautie of the Soule,
For honestie, and decent Carriage
A right good Husband (let him be a Noble)
And sure those men are happy that shall haue 'em.
The last is for my men, they are the poorest,
(But pouerty could neuer draw 'em from me)
That they may haue their wages, duly paid 'em,
And something ouer to remember me by.
If Heauen had pleas'd to haue giuen me longer life
And able meanes, we had not parted thus.
These are the whole Contents, and good my Lord,
By that you loue the deerest in this world,
As you wish Christian peace to soules departed,
Stand these poore peoples Friend, and vrge the King
To do me this last right.
Cap. By Heauen I will,
Or let me loose the fashion of a man.
Kath. I thanke you honest Lord. Remember me
In all humilitie vnto his Highnesse:
Say his long trouble now is passing
Out of this world. Tell him in death I blest him
(For so I will) mine eyes grow dimme. Farewell
My Lord. *Griffith* farewell. Nay *Patience*,
You must not leaue me yet. I must to bed,
Call in more women. When I am dead, good Wench,
Let me be vs'd with Honor; strew me ouer
With Maiden Flowers, that all the world may know
I was a chaste Wife, to my Graue: Embalme me,
Then lay me forth (although vnqueen'd) yet like
A Queene, and Daughter to a King enterre me.
I can no more.

Exeunt leading Katherine.

Scena

Actus Quintus. Scena Prima.

Enter Gardiner Bishop of Winchester, a Page with a Torch before him, met by Sir Thomas Louell.

Gard. It's one a clocke Boy, is't not.
Boy. It hath strooke.
Gard. These should be houres for necessities,
Not for delights: Times to repayre our Nature
With comforting repose, and not for vs
To waste these times. Good houre of night Sir *Thomas*:
Whether so late?
Lou. Came you from the King, my Lord?
Gar. I did Sir *Thomas* and left him at Primero
With the Duke of Suffolke.
Lou. I must to him too
Before he go to bed. Ile take my leaue.
Gard. Not yet Sir *Thomas Louell*: what's the matter?
It seemes you are in hast: and if there be
No great offence belongs too't, giue your Friend
Some touch of your late businesse: Affaires that walke
(As they say Spirits do) at midnight, haue
In them a wilder Nature, then the businesse
That seekes dispatch by day.
Lou. My Lord, I loue you;
And durst commend a secret to your eare
Much waightier then this worke. The Queens in Labor
They say in great Extremity, and fear'd
Shee'l with the Labour, end.
Gard. The fruite she goes with
I pray for heartily, that it may finde
Good time, and liue: but for the Stocke Sir *Thomas*,
I wish it grubb'd vp now.
Lou. Me thinkes I could
Cry the Amen, and yet my Conscience sayes
Shee's a good Creature, and sweet-Ladie do's
Deserue our better wishes.
Gard. But Sir, Sir,
Heare me Sir *Thomas*, y'are a Gentleman
Of mine owne way. I know you Wise, Religious,
And let me tell you, it will ne're be well,
'Twill not Sir *Thomas Louell*, tak't of me,
Till *Cranmer*, *Cromwel*, her two hands, and shee
Sleepe in their Graues.
Louell. Now Sir, you speake of two
The most remark'd i'th'Kingdome: as for *Cromwell*,
Beside that of the Iewell-House, is made Master
O'th'Rolles, and the Kings Secretary. Further Sir,
Stands in the gap and Trade of moe Preferments,
With which the Lime will loade him. Th'Archbyshop
Is the Kings hand, and tongue, and who dare speak
One syllable against him?
Gard. Yes, yes, Sir *Thomas*,
There are that Dare, and I my selfe haue ventur'd
To speake my minde of him: and indeed this day,
Sir (I may tell it you) I thinke I haue
Incenst the Lords o'th'Councell, that he is
(For so I know he is, they know he is)
A most Arch-Heretique, a Pestilence
That does infect the Land: with which, they moued
Haue broken with the King, who hath so farre
Giuen eare to our Complaint, of his great Grace,
And Princely Care, fore-seeing those fell Mischiefes,
Our Reasons layd before him, hath commanded
To morrow Morning to the Councell Boord
He be conuented. He's a ranke weed Sir *Thomas*,
And we must root him out. From your Affaires
I hinder you too long: Good night, Sir *Thomas*.
Exit Gardiner and Page.
Lou. Many good nights, my Lord, I rest your seruant.
Enter King and Suffolke.
King. *Charles*, I will play no more to night,
My mindes not on't, you are too hard for me.
Suff. Sir, I did neuer win of you before.
King. But little *Charles*,
Nor shall not when my Fancies on my play.
Now *Louel*, from the Queene what is the Newes.
Lou. I could not personally deliuer to her
What you commanded me, but by her woman,
I sent your Message, who return'd her thankes
In the great'st humblenesse, and desir'd your Highnesse
Most heartily to pray for her.
King. What say'st thou? Ha?
To pray for her? What, is she crying out?
Lou. So said her woman, and that her suffrance made
Almost each pang, a death.
King. Alas good Lady.
Suf. God safely quit her of her Burthen, and
With gentle Trauaile, to the gladding of
Your Highnesse with an Heire.
King. 'Tis midnight *Charles*,
Prythee to bed, and in thy Prayres remember
Th'estate of my poore Queene. Leaue me alone,
For I must thinke of that, which company
Would not be friendly too.
Suf. I wish your Highnesse
A quiet night, and my good Mistris will
Remember in my Prayers.
King. *Charles* good night. *Exit Suffolke.*
Well Sir, what followes?
Enter Sir Anthony Denny.
Den. Sir, I haue brought my Lord the Arch-byshop,
As you commanded me.
King. Ha? Canterbury?
Den. I my good Lord.
King. 'Tis true: where is he *Denny*?
Den. He attends your Highnesse pleasure.
King. Bring him to Vs.
Lou. This is about that, which the Byshop spake,
I am happily come hither.
Enter Cranmer and Denny.
King. Auoyd the Gallery. *Louel seemes to stay.*
Ha? I haue said. Be gone.
What? *Exeunt Louell and Denny.*
Cran. I am fearefull: Wherefore frownes he thus?
'Tis his Aspect of Terror. All's not well.
King. How now my Lord?
You do desire to know wherefore
I sent for you.
Cran. It is my dutie
T'attend your Highnesse pleasure.
King. Pray you arise
My good and gracious Lord of Canterburie:
Come, you and I must walke a turne together:
I haue Newes to tell you.
Come, come, giue me your hand.
Ah my good Lord, I greeue at what I speake,
And am right sorrie to repeat what followes.
I haue, and most vnwillingly of late

Heard many greeuous. I do ſay my Lord
Greeuous complaints of you; which being conſider'd,
Haue mou'd Vs, and our Councell, that you ſhall
This Morning come before vs, where I know
You cannot with ſuch freedome purge your ſelfe,
But that till further Triall, in thoſe Charges
Which will require your Anſwer, you muſt take
Your patience to you, and be well contented
To make your houſe our Towre: you, a Brother of vs
It fits we thus proceed, or elſe no witneſſe
Would come againſt you.
Cran. I humbly thanke your Highneſſe,
And am right glad to catch this good occaſion
Moſt throughly to be winnowed, where my Chaffe
And Corne ſhall flye aſunder. For I know
There's none ſtands vnder more calumnious tongues,
Then I my ſelfe, poore man.
King. Stand vp, good Canterbury,
Thy Truth, and thy Integrity is rooted
In vs thy Friend. Giue me thy hand, ſtand vp,
Prythee let's walke. Now by my Holydame,
What manner of man are you? My Lord, I look'd
You would haue giuen me your Petition, that
I ſhould haue tane ſome paines, to bring together
Your ſelfe, and your Accuſers, and to haue heard you
Without indurance further.
Cran. Moſt dread Liege,
The good I ſtand on, is my Truth and Honeſtie:
If they ſhall faile, I with mine Enemies
Will triumph o're my perſon, which I waigh not,
Being of thoſe Vertues vacant. I feare nothing
What can be ſaid againſt me.
King. Know you not
How your ſtate ſtands i'th'world, with the whole world?
Your Enemies are many, and not ſmall; their practiſes
Muſt beare the ſame proportion, and not euer
The Iuſtice and the Truth o'th'queſtion carries
The dew o'th'Verdict with it; at what eaſe
Might corrupt mindes procure, Knaues as corrupt
To ſweare againſt you: Such things haue bene done.
You are Potently oppos'd, and with a Malice
Of as great Size. Weene you of better lucke,
I meane in periur'd Witneſſe, then your Maſter,
Whoſe Miniſter you are, whiles heere he liu'd
Vpon this naughty Earth? Go too, go too,
You take a Precepit for no leape of danger,
And woe your owne deſtruction.
Cran. God, and your Maieſty
Protect mine innocence, or I fall into
The trap is laid for me.
King. Be of good cheere,
They ſhall no more preuaile, then we giue way too:
Keepe comfort to you, and this Morning ſee
You do appeare before them. If they ſhall chance
In charging you with matters, to commit you:
The beſt perſwaſions to the contrary
Faile not to vſe, and with what vehemencie
Th'occaſion ſhall inſtruct you. If intreaties
Will render you no remedy, this Ring
Deliuer them, and your Appeale to vs
There make before them. Looke, the goodman weeps:
He's honeſt on mine Honor. Gods bleſt Mother,
I ſweare he is true-hearted, and a ſoule
None better in my Kingdome. Get you gone,
And do as I haue bid you. *Exit Cranmer.*
He ha's ſtrangled his Language in his teares.

Enter Olde Lady.

Gent. within. Come backe: what meane you?
Lady. Ile not come backe, the tydings that I bring
Will make my boldneſſe, manners. Now good Angels
Fly o're thy Royall head, and ſhade thy perſon
Vnder their bleſſed wings.
King. Now by thy lookes
I geſſe thy Meſſage. Is the Queene deliuer'd?
Say I, and of a boy.
Lady. I, I my Liege,
And of a louely Boy: the God of heauen
Both now, and euer bleſſe her: 'Tis a Gyrle
Promiſes Boyes heereafter. Sir, your Queen
Deſires your Viſitation, and to be
Acquainted with this ſtranger; 'tis as like you,
As Cherry, is to Cherry.
King. Louell.
Lou. Sir.
King. Giue her an hundred Markes.
Ile to the Queene. *Exit King.*
Lady. An hundred Markes? By this light, Ile ha more.
An ordinary Groome is for ſuch payment.
I will haue more, or ſcold it out of him.
Said I for this, the Gyrle was like to him? Ile
Haue more, or elſe vnſay't: and now, while 'tis hot,
Ile put it to the iſſue. *Exit Ladie.*

Scena Secunda.

Enter Cranmer, Archbyſhop of Canterbury.

Cran. I hope I am not too late, and yet the Gentleman
That was ſent to me from the Councell, pray'd me
To make great haſt. All faſt? What meanes this? Hoa?
Who waites there? Sure you know me?
Enter Keeper.
Keep. Yes, my Lord:
But yet I cannot helpe you.
Cran. Why?
Keep. Your Grace muſt waight till you be call'd for.
Enter Doctor Buts.
Cran. So.
Buts. This is a Peere of Malice: I am glad
I came this way ſo happily. The King
Shall vnderſtand it preſently. *Exit Buts*
Cran. 'Tis *Buts.*
The Kings Phyſitian, as he paſt along
How earneſtly he caſt his eyes vpon me:
Pray heauen he ſound not my diſgrace: for certaine
This is of purpoſe laid by ſome that hate me,
(God turne their hearts, I neuer ſought their malice)
To quench mine Honor; they would ſhame to make me
Wait elſe at doore: a fellow Councellor
'Mong Boyes, Groomes, and Lackeyes.
But their pleaſures
Muſt be fulfill'd, and I attend with patience.

Enter the King, and Buts, at a Windowe aboue.

Buts. Ile ſhew your Grace the ſtrangeſt ſight.
King. What's that *Buts?*

Buts

Butts. I thinke your Highnesse saw this many a day.
Kin. Body a me: where is it?
Butts. There my Lord:
The high promotion of his Grace of *Canterbury,*
Who holds his State at dore 'mongst Purseuants,
Pages, and Foot-boyes.
Kin. Ha! 'Tis he indeed.
Is this the Honour they doe one another?
'Tis well there's one aboue 'em yet; I had thought
They had parted so much honesty among 'em,
At least good manners; as not thus to suffer
A man of his Place, and so neere our fauour
To dance attendance on their Lordships pleasures,
And at the dore too, like a Post with Packets:
By holy *Mary* (*Butts*) there's knauery;
Let 'em alone, and draw the Curtaine close:
We shall heare more anon.

A Councell Table brought in with Chayres and Stooles, and placed vnder the State. Enter Lord Chancellour, places himselfe at the vpper end of the Table, on the left hand: A Seate being left void aboue him, as for Canterburies Seate. Duke of Suffolke, Duke of Norfolke, Surrey, Lord Chamberlaine, Gardiner, seat themselues in Order on each side. Cromwell at lower end, as Secretary.

Chan. Speake to the businesse, M. Secretary;
Why are we met in Councell?
Crom. Please your Honours,
The chiefe cause concernes his Grace of *Canterbury.*
Gard. Ha's he had knowledge of it?
Crom. Yes.
Norf. Who waits there?
Keep. Without my Noble Lords?
Gard. Yes.
Keep. My Lord Archbishop:
And ha's done halfe an houre to know your pleasures.
Chan. Let him come in.
Keep. Your Grace may enter now.
Cranmer approches the Councell Table.
Chan. My good Lord Archbishop, I'm very sorry
To sit heere at this present, and behold
That Chayre stand empty: But we all are men
In our owne natures fraile, and capable
Of our flesh, few are Angels; out of which frailty
And want of wisedome, you that best should teach vs,
Haue misdemean'd your selfe, and not a little:
Toward the King first, then his Lawes, in filling
The whole Realme, by your teaching & your Chaplaines
(For so we are inform'd) with new opinions,
Diuers and dangerous; which are Heresies;
And not reform'd, may proue pernicious.
Gard. Which Reformation must be sodaine too
My Noble Lords; for those that tame wild Horses,
Pace 'em not in their hands to make 'em gentle;
But stop their mouthes with stubborn Bits & spurre 'em,
Till they obey the mannage. If we suffer
Out of our easinesse and childish pitty
To one mans Honour, this contagious sicknesse;
Farewell all Physicke: and what followes then?
Commotions, vprores, with a generall Taint
Of the whole State; as of late dayes our neighbours,
The vpper *Germany* can deerely witnesse:
Yet freshly pittied in our memories.
Cran. My good Lords; Hitherto, in all the Progresse
Both of my Life and Office, I haue labour'd,
And with no little study, that my teaching
And the strong course of my Authority,
Might goe one way, and safely; and the end
Was euer to doe well: nor is there liuing,
(I speake it with a single heart, my Lords)
A man that more detests, more stirres against,
Both in his priuate Conscience, and his place,
Defacers of a publique peace then I doe:
Pray Heauen the King may neuer find a heart
With lesse Allegeance in it. Men that make
Enuy, and crooked malice, nourishment;
Dare bite the best. I doe beseech your Lordships,
That in this case of Iustice, my Accusers,
Be what they will, may stand forth face to face,
And freely vrge against me.
Suff. Nay, my Lord,
That cannot be; you are a Counsellor,
And by that vertue no man dare accuse you.
Gard. My Lord, because we haue busines of more moment,
We will be short with you. 'Tis his Highnesse pleasure
And our consent, for better tryall of you,
From hence you be committed to the Tower,
Where being but a priuate man againe,
You shall know many dare accuse you boldly,
More then (I feare) you are prouided for.
Cran. Ah my good Lord of *Winchester*: I thanke you,
You are alwayes my good Friend, if your will passe,
I shall both finde your Lordship, Iudge and Iuror,
You are so mercifull. I see your end,
'Tis my vndoing. Loue and meekenesse, Lord
Become a Churchman, better then Ambition:
Win straying Soules with modesty againe,
Cast none away: That I shall cleere my selfe,
Lay all the weight ye can vpon my patience,
I make as little doubt as you doe conscience,
In doing dayly wrongs. I could say more,
But reuerence to your calling, makes me modest.
Gard. My Lord, my Lord, you are a Sectary,
That's the plaine truth; your painted glosse discouers
To men that vnderstand you, words and weaknesse.
Crom. My Lord of *Winchester*, y'are a little,
By your good fauour, too sharpe; Men so Noble,
How euer faulty, yet should finde respect
For what they haue beene: 'tis a cruelty,
To load a falling man.
Gard. Good M. Secretary,
I cry your Honour mercie; you may worst
Of all this Table say so.
Crom. Why my Lord?
Gard. Doe not I know you for a Fauourer
Of this new Sect? ye are not sound.
Crom. Not sound?
Gard. Not sound I say.
Crom. Would you were halfe so honest:
Mens prayers then would seeke you, not their feares.
Gard. I shall remember this bold Language.
Crom. Doe.
Remember your bold life too.
Cham. This is too much;
Forbeare for shame my Lords.
Gard. I haue done.
Crom. And I.
Cham. Then thus for you my Lord, it stands agreed
I take it, by all voyces: That forthwith,
You be conuaid to th' Tower a Prisoner;
There to remaine till the Kings further pleasure
Be knowne vnto vs: are you all agreed Lords.
All

All. We are.
Cran. Is there no other way of mercy,
But I must needs to th' Tower my Lords?
Gard. What other,
Would you expect? You are strangely troublesome:
Let some o'th' Guard be ready there.

Enter the Guard.

Cran. For me?
Must I goe like a Traytor thither?
Gard. Receiue him,
And see him safe i'th' Tower.
Cran. Stay good my Lords,
I haue a little yet to say. Looke there my Lords,
By vertue of that Ring, I take my cause
Out of the gripes of cruell men, and giue it
To a most Noble Iudge, the King my Maister.
Cham. This is the Kings Ring.
Sur. 'Tis no counterfeit.
Suff. 'Ts the right Ring, by Heau'n: I told ye all,
When we first put this dangerous stone a rowling,
'Twold fall vpon our selues.
Norf. Doe you thinke my Lords
The King will suffer but the little finger
Of this man to be vex'd?
Cham. 'Tis now too certaine;
How much more is his Life in value with him?
Would I were fairely out on't.
Crom. My mind gaue me,
In seeking tales and Informations
Against this man, whose honesty the Diuell
And his Disciples onely enuy at,
Ye blew the fire that burnes ye: now haue at ye.

Enter King frowning on them, takes his Seate.

Gard Dread Soueraigne,
How much are we bound to Heauen,
In dayly thankes; that gaue vs such a Prince;
Not onely good and wise, but most religious:
One that in all obedience, makes the Church
The cheefe ayme of his Honour, and to strengthen
That holy duty out of deare respect,
His Royall selfe in Iudgement comes to heare
The cause betwixt her, and this great offender.
Kin. You were euer good at sodaine Commendations,
Bishop of *Winchester*. But know I come not
To heare such flattery now, and in my presence
They are too thin, and base to hide offences,
To me you cannot reach. You play the Spaniell,
And thinke with wagging of your tongue to win me:
But whatsoere thou tak'st me for; I'm sure
Thou hast a cruell Nature and a bloody.
Good man sit downe: Now let me see the proudest
Hee, that dares most, but wag his finger at thee.
By all that's holy, he had better starue,
Then but once thinke his place becomes thee not.
Sur. May it please your Grace; ———
Kin. No Sir, it doe's not please me,
I had thought, I had had men of some vnderstanding,
And wisedome of my Councell; but I finde none:
Was it discretion Lords, to let this man,
This good man (few of you deserue that Title)
This honest man, wait like a lowsie Foot-boy
At Chamber dore? and one, as great as you are?
Why, what a shame was this? Did my Commission
Bid ye so farre forget your selues? I gaue ye
Power, as he was a Counsellour to try him,
Not as a Groome: There's some of ye, I see,
More out of Malice then Integrity,
Would trye him to the vtmost, had ye meane,
Which ye shall neuer haue while I liue.
Chan. Thus farre
My most dread Soueraigne, may it like your Grace,
To let my tongue excuse all. What was purpos'd
Concerning his Imprisonment, was rather
(If there be faith in men) meant for his Tryall,
And faire purgation to the world then malice,
I'm sure in me.
Kin. Well, well my Lords respect him,
Take him, and vse him well; hee's worthy of it,
I will say thus much for him, if a Prince
May be beholding to a Subiect; I
Am for his loue and seruice, so to him.
Make me no more adoe, but all embrace him;
Be friends for shame my Lords: My Lord of *Canterbury*
I haue a Suite which you must not deny mee.
That is, a faire young Maid that yet wants Baptisme,
You must be Godfather, and answere for her.
Cran. The greatest Monarch now aliue may glory
In such an honour: how may I deserue it,
That am a poore and humble Subiect to you?
Kin. Come, come my Lord, you'd spare your spoones;
You shall haue two noble Partners with you: the old
Duchesse of *Norfolke*, and Lady Marquesse *Dorset*? will
these please you?
Once more my Lord of *Winchester*, I charge you
Embrace, and loue this man.
Gard. With a true heart,
And Brother; loue I doe it.
Cran. And let Heauen
Witnesse how deare, I hold this Confirmation. (hearts,
Kin. Good Man, those ioyfull teares shew thy true
The common voyce I see is verified
Of thee, which sayes thus: Doe my Lord of *Canterbury*
A shrewd turne, and hee's your friend for euer:
Come Lords, we trifle time away: I long
To haue this young one made a Christian.
As I haue made ye one Lords, one remaine:
So I grow stronger, you more Honour gaine. *Exeunt.*

Scena Tertia.

Noyse and Tumult within: Enter Porter and his man.

Port. You'l leaue your noyse anon ye Rascals: doe you take the Court for Parish Garden: ye rude Slaues, leaue your gaping.
Within. Good M. Porter I belong to th' Larder.
Port Belong to th' Gallowes, and be hang'd ye Rogue: Is this a place to roare in? Fetch me a dozen Crab-tree staues, and strong ones; these are but switches to 'em: Ile scratch your heads; you must be seeing Christenings? Do you looke for Ale, and Cakes heere, you rude Raskalls?
Man. Pray Sir be patient; 'tis as much impossible,
Vnlesse wee sweepe 'em from the dore with Cannons,
To scatter 'em, as 'tis to make 'em sleepe
On May-day Morning, which will neuer be:
We may as well push against Powles as stirre 'em.
Por. How got they in, and be hang'd?

Man.

Man. Alas I know not, how gets the Tide in?
As much as one sound Cudgell of foure foote,
(You see the poore remainder) could distribute,
I made no spare Sir.

Port. You did nothing Sir.

Man. I am not *Sampson*, nor Sir *Guy*, nor *Colebrand*,
To mow 'em downe before me: but if I spar'd any
That had a head to hit, either young or old,
He or shee, Cuckold or Cuckold-maker:
Let me ne're hope to see a Chine againe,
And that I would not for a Cow, God saue her.

Within. Do you heare M. Porter?

Port. I shall be with you presently, good M. *Puppy*, Keepe the dore close Sirha.

Man. What would you haue me doe?

Por. What should you doe,
But knock 'em downe by th' dozens? Is this More fields to muster in? Or haue wee some strange Indian with the great *Toole*, come to Court, the women so besiege vs? Blesse me, what a fry of Fornication is at dore? On my Christian Conscience this one Christening will beget a thousand, here will bee Father, God-father, and all together.

Man. The Spoones will be the bigger Sir: There is a fellow somewhat neere the doore, he should be a Brasier by his face, for o' my conscience twenty of the Dog-dayes now reigne in's Nose; all that stand about him are vnder the Line, they need no other pennance: that Fire-Drake did I hit three times on the head, and three times was his Nose discharged against mee; hee stands there like a Morter-piece to blow vs. There was a Habberdashers Wife of small wit, neere him, that rail'd vpon me, till her pinck'd porrenger fell off her head, for kindling such a combustion in the State. I mist the Meteor once, and hit that Woman, who cryed out Clubbes, when I might see from farre, some forty Truncheoners draw to her succour, which were the hope o'th' Strond where she was quartered; they fell on, I made good my place; at length they came to th' broome staffe to me, I defide 'em stil, when sodainly a File of Boyes behind 'em, loose shot, deliuer'd such a showre of Pibbles, that I was faine to draw mine Honour in, and let 'em win the Worke, the Diuell was amongst 'em I thinke surely.

Por. These are the youths that thunder at a Playhouse, and fight for bitten Apples, that no Audience but the tribulation of Tower Hill, or the Limbes of Limehouse, their deare Brothers are able to endure. I haue some of 'em in *Limbo Patrum*, and there they are like to dance these three dayes; besides the running Banquet of two Beadles, that is to come.

Enter Lord Chamberlaine.

Cham. Mercy o' me: what a Multitude are heere?
They grow still too; from all Parts they are comming,
As if we kept a Faire heere? Where are these Porters?
These lazy knaues? Y'haue made a fine hand fellowes?
Theres a trim rabble let in: are all these
Your faithfull friends o'th' Suburbs? We shall haue
Great store of roome no doubt, left for the Ladies,
When they passe backe from the Christening?

Por. And't please your Honour,
We are but men; and what so many may doe,
Not being torne a pieces, we haue done:
An Army cannot rule 'em.

Cham. As I liue,
If the King blame me for't; Ile lay ye all
By th' heeles, and sodainly: and on your heads
Clap round Fines for neglect: y'are lazy knaues,
And heere ye lye baiting of Bombards, when
Ye should doe Seruice. Harke the Trumpets sound,
Th'are come already from the Christening,
Go breake among the preasse, and finde away out
To let the Troope passe fairely; or Ile finde
A Marshallsey, shall hold ye play these two Monthes.

Por Make way there, for the Princesse.

Man. You great fellow,
Stand close vp, or Ile make your head ake.

Por. You i'th' Chamblet, get vp o'th' raile,
Ile pecke you o're the pales else. *Exeunt*.

Scena Quarta.

Enter Trumpets sounding: Then two Aldermen, L. Maior, Garter, Cranmer, Duke of Norfolke with his Marshals Staffe, Duke of Suffolke, two Noblemen, bearing great standing Bowles for the Christening Guifts: Then foure Noblemen bearing a Canopy, vnder which the Dutchesse of Norfolke, Godmother, bearing the Childe richly habited in a Mantle, &c. Traine borne by a Lady: Then followes the Marchionesse Dorset, the other Godmother, and Ladies. The Troope passe once about the Stage, and Garter speakes.

Gart. Heauen
From thy endlesse goodnesse, send prosperous life,
Long, and euer happie, to the high and Mighty
Princesse of England *Elizabeth*.

Flourish. Enter King and Guard.

Cran. And to your Royall Grace, & the good Queen,
My Noble Partners, and my selfe thus pray
All comfort, ioy in this most gracious Lady,
Heauen euer laid vp to make Parents happy,
May hourely fall vpon ye.

Kin. Thanke you good Lord Archbishop:
What is her Name?

Cran *Elizabeth*.

Kin. Stand vp Lord,
With this Kisse, take my Blessing: God protect thee,
Into whose hand, I giue thy Life.

Cran. *Amen*.

Kin. My Noble Gossips, y'haue beene too Prodigall;
I thanke ye heartily: So shall this Lady,
When she ha's so much English.

Cran. Let me speake Sir,
For Heauen now bids me; and the words I vtter,
Let none thinke Flattery; for they'l finde 'em Truth.
This Royall Infant, Heauen still moue about her;
Though in her Cradle; yet now promises
Vpon this Land a thousand thousand Blessings,
Which Time shall bring to ripenesse: She shall be,
(But few now liuing can behold that goodnesse)
A Patterne to all Princes liuing with her,
And all that shall succeed: *Saba* was neuer
More couetous of Wisedome, and faire Vertue
Then this pure Soule shall be. All Princely Graces
That mould vp such a mighty Piece as this is,
With all the Vertues that attend the good,
Shall still be doubled on her. Truth shall Nurse her,
Holy

Holy and Heauenly thoughts still Counsell her.
She shall be lou'd and fear'd. Her owne shall blesse her;
Her Foes shake like a Field of beaten Corne,
And hang their heads with sorrow.
Good growes with her
In her dayes, Euery Man shall eate in safety,
Vnder his owne Vine what he plants; and sing
The merry Songs of Peace to all his Neighbours.
God shall be truely knowne, and those about her,
From her shall read the perfect way of Honour,
And by those claime their greatnesse; not by Blood.
Nor shall this peace sleepe with her: But as when
The Bird of Wonder dyes, the Mayden Phoenix,
Her Ashes new create another Heyre,
As great in admiration as her selfe.
So shall she leaue her Blessednesse to One,
(When Heauen shal call her from this clowd of darknes)
Who, from the sacred Ashes of her Honour
Shall Star-like rise, as great in fame as she was,
And so stand fix'd. Peace, Plenty, Loue, Truth, Terror,
That were the Seruants to this chosen Infant,
Shall then be his, and like a Vine grow to him;
Where euer the bright Sunne of Heauen shall shine,
His Honour, and the greatnesse of his Name,
Shall be, and make new Nations. He shall flourish,
And like a Mountaine Cedar, reach his branches,
To all the Plaines about him: Our Childrens Children
Shall see this, and blesse Heauen.

Kin. Thou speakest wonders.

Cran. She shall be to the happinesse of England,
An aged Princesse; many dayes shall see her,
And yet no day without a deed to Crowne it.
Would I had knowne no more: But she must dye,
She must, the Saints must haue her; yet a Virgin,
A most vnspotted Lilly shall she passe
To th' ground, and all the World shall mourne her.

Kin. O Lord Archbishop
Thou hast made me now a man, neuer before
This happy Child, did I get any thing.
This Oracle of comfort, ha's so pleas'd me,
That when I am in Heauen, I shall desire
To see what this Child does, and praise my Maker.
I thanke ye all. To you my good Lord Maior,
And you good Brethren, I am much beholding:
I haue receiu'd much Honour by your presence,
And ye shall find me thankfull. Lead the way Lords,
Ye must all see the Queene, and she must thanke ye,
She will be sicke els. This day, no man thinke
'Has businesse at his house; for all shall stay:
This Little-One shall make it Holy-day. *Exeunt.*

THE EPILOGVE.

TIs ten to one, this Play can neuer please
All that are heere. Some come to take their ease,
And sleepe an Act or two; but those we feare
W'haue frighted with our Tumpets: so 'tis cleare,
They'l say tis naught. Others to heare the City
Abus'd extreamly, and to cry that's witty.
Which wee haue not done neither; that I feare
All the expected good w'are like to heare.
For this Play at this time, is onely in
The mercifull construction of good women,
For such a one we shew'd 'em. If they smile,
And say twill doe; I know within a while,
All the best men are ours; for 'tis ill hap,
If they hold, when their Ladies bid 'em clap.

FINIS.

The Prologue.

IN Troy there lyes the Scene: From Iles of Greece
The Princes Orgillous, their high blood chaf'd
Haue to the Port of Athens sent their shippes
Fraught with the ministers and instruments
Of cruell Warre: Sixty and nine that wore
Their Crownets Regall, from th' Athenian bay
Put forth toward Phrygia, and their vow is made
To ransacke Troy, within whose strong emures
The rauish'd Helen, Menelaus Queene,
With wanton Paris sleepes, and that's the Quarrell.
To Tenedos they come,
And the deepe-drawing Barke do there disgorge
Their warlike frautage: now on Dardan Plaines
The fresh and yet vnbruised Greekes do pitch
Their braue Pauillions. Priams six-gated City,
Dardan and Timbria, Helias, Chetas, Troien.
And Antenonidus with massie Staples
And corresponsiue and fulfilling Bolts
Stirre vp the Sonnes of Troy.
Now Expectation tickling skittish spirits,
On one and other side, Troian and Greeke,
Sets all on hazard And hither am J come,
A Prologue arm'd, but not in confidence
Of Authors pen, or Actors voyce; but suited
Jn like conditions, as our Argument,
To tell you (faire Beholders) that our Play
Leapes ore the vaunte and firstlings of those broyles,
Beginning in the middle. starting thence away,
To what may be digested in a Play:
Like, or finde fault, do as your pleasures are,
Now good, or bad, 'tis but the chance of Warre.

THE TRAGEDIE OF
Troylus and Creſsida.

Actus Primus. Scœna Prima.

Enter Pandarus and Troylus.

Troylus.

CAll here my Varlet, Ile vnarme againe.
Why ſhould I warre without the wals of Troy
That finde ſuch cruell battell here within?
Each Troian that is maſter of his heart,
Let him to field, *Troylus* alas hath none.

Pan. Will this geere nere be mended?

Troy. The Greeks are ſtrong, & skilful to their ſtrength,
Fierce to their skill, and to their fierceneſſe Valiant:
But I am weaker then a womans teare;
Tamer then ſleepe, fonder then ignorance;
Leſſe valiant then the Virgin in the night,
And skilleſſe as vnpractis'd Infancie.

Pan. Well, I haue told you enough of this: For my part, Ile not meddle nor make no farther. Hee that will haue a Cake out of the Wheate, muſt needes tarry the grinding.

Troy. Haue I not tarried?

Pan. I the grinding, but you muſt tarry the bolting.

Troy. Haue I not tarried?

Pan. I the boulting; but you muſt tarry the leau'ing.

Troy Still haue I tarried.

Pan. I, to the leauening: but heeres yet in the word hereafter, the Kneading, the making of the Cake, the heating of the Ouen, and the Baking; nay, you muſt ſtay the cooling too, or you may chance to burne your lips.

Troy. Patience her ſelfe, what Goddeſſe ere ſhe be,
Doth leſſer blench at ſufferance, then I doe:
At *Priams* Royall Table doe I ſit;
And when faire *Creſſid* comes into my thoughts,
So (Traitor) then ſhe comes, when ſhe is thence.

Pan. Well:
She look'd yeſternight fairer, then euer I ſaw her looke,
Or any woman elſe.

Troy. I was about to tell thee, when my heart,
As wedged with a ſigh, would riue in twaine,
Leaſt *Hector*, or my Father ſhould perceiue me:
I haue (as when the Sunne doth light a-ſcorne)
Buried this ſigh, in wrinkle of a ſmile:
But ſorrow, that is couch'd in ſeeming gladneſſe,
Is like that mirth, Fate turnes to ſudden ſadneſſe.

Pan. And her haire were not ſomewhat darker then *Helens*, well go too, there were no more compariſon betweene the Women. But for my part ſhe is my Kinſwoman, I would not (as they tearme it) praiſe it, but I wold ſome-body had heard her talke yeſterday as I did: I will not diſpraiſe your ſiſter *Caſſandra's* wit, but——

Troy. Oh *Pandarus*! I tell thee *Pandarus*;
When I doe tell thee, there my hopes lye drown'd:
Reply not in how many Fadomes deepe
They lye indrench'd. I tell thee, I am mad
In *Creſſids* loue. Thou anſwer'ſt ſhe is Faire,
Powr'ſt in the open Vlcer of my heart,
Her Eyes, her Haire, her Cheeke, her Gate, her Voice,
Handleſt in thy diſcourſe. O that her Hand
(In whoſe compariſon, all whites are Inke)
Writing their owne reproach; to whoſe ſoft ſeizure,
The Cignets Downe is harſh, and ſpirit of Senſe
Hard as the palme of Plough-man. This thou tel'ſt me;
As true thou tel'ſt me, when I ſay I loue her:
But ſaying thus, inſtead of Oyle and Balme,
Thou lai'ſt in euery gaſh that loue hath giuen me,
The Knife that made it.

Pan. I ſpeake no more then truth.

Troy Thou do'ſt not ſpeake ſo much.

Pan Faith, Ile not meddle in't: Let her be as ſhee is, if ſhe be faire, 'tis the better for her, and ſhe be not, ſhe ha's the mends in her owne hands.

Troy. Good *Pandarus*: How now *Pandarus*?

Pan. I haue had my Labour for my trauell, ill thought on of her, and ill thought on of you; Gone betweene and betweene, but ſmall thankes for my labour.

Troy. What art thou angry *Pandarus*? what with me?

Pan. Becauſe ſhe's Kinne to me, therefore ſhee's not ſo faire as *Helen*, and ſhe were not kin to me, ſhe would be as faire on Friday, as *Helen* is on Sunday. But what care I? I care not and ſhe were a Black-a Moore, 'tis all one to me.

Troy. Say I ſhe is not faire?

Troy. I doe not care whether you doe or no. Shee's a Foole to ſtay behinde her Father: Let her to the Greeks, and ſo Ile tell her the next time I ſee her: for my part, Ile meddle nor make no more i'th' matter

Troy. *Pandarus*? *Pan.* Not I.

Troy. Sweete *Pandarus*.

Pan. Pray you ſpeake no more to me, I will leaue all as I found it, and there an end. *Exit Pand.*

Sound Alarum.

Tro. Peace you vngracious Clamors, peace rude ſounds,
Fooles on both ſides, *Helen* muſt needs be faire,
When with your bloud you daily paint her thus.
I cannot fight vpon this Argument:

It

It is too staru'd a subiect for my Sword,
But *Pandarus*. O Gods! How do you plague me?
I cannot come to *Cressid* but by *Pandar*,
And he's as teachy to be woo'd to woe,
As she is stubborne, chast, against all suite.
Tell me *Apollo* for thy *Daphnes* Loue
What *Cressid* is, what *Pandar*, and what we:
Her bed is *India*, there she lies, a Pearle,
Between our Ilium, and where shee recides
Let it be cald the wild and wandring flood,
Our selfe the Merchant, and this sayling *Pandar*,
Our doubtfull hope, our conuoy and our Barke.

Alarum. Enter Æneas.

Æne. How now Prince *Troylus*?
Wherefore not a field?

Troy. Because not there; this womans answer sorts.
For womanish it is to be from thence:
What newes *Æneas* from the field to day?

Æne. That *Paris* is returned home, and hurt.

Troy. By whom *Æneas*?

Æne. *Troylus* by *Menelaus*.

Troy. Let *Paris* bleed, 'tis but a scar to scorne,
Paris is gor'd with *Menelaus* horne. *Alarum.*

Æne. Harke what good sport is out of Towne to day.

Troy. Better at home, if would I might were may:
But to the sport abroad, are you bound thither?

Æne. In all swift hast.

Troy. Come goe wee then togither. *Exeunt.*

Enter Cressid and her man.

Cre. Who were those went by?

Man. Queene *Hecuba*, and *Hellen*.

Cre. And whether go they?

Man. Vp to the Easterne Tower,
Whose height commands as subiect all the vaile,
To see the battell: *Hector* whose pacience,
Is as a Vertue fixt, to day was mou'd.
He chides *Andromache* and strooke his Armorer,
And like as there were husbandry in Warre
Before the Sunne rose, hee was harnest lyte,
And to the field goe's he; where euery flower
Did as a Prophet weepe what it forsaw,
In *Hectors* wrath.

Cre. What was his cause of anger?

Man. The noise goe's this;
There is among the Greekes,
A Lord of Troian blood, Nephew to *Hector*,
They call him *Aiax*.

Cre. Good; and what of him?

Man. They say he is a very man *per se* and stands alone.

Cre. So do all men, vnlesse they are drunke, sicke, or haue no legges.

Man. This man Lady, hath rob'd many beasts of their particular additions, he is as valiant as the Lyon, churlish as the Beare, slow as the Elephant: a man into whom nature hath so crowded humors, that his valour is crusht into folly, his folly sauced with discretion: there is no man hath a vertue, that he hath not a glimpse of, nor any man an attaint, but he carries some staine of it. He is melancholy without cause, and merry against the haire, hee hath the ioynts of euery thing, but euery thing so out of ioynt, that hee is a gowtie *Briareus*, many hands and no vse; or purblinded *Argus*, all eyes and no sight.

Cre. But how should this man that makes me smile, make *Hector* angry?

Man. They say he yesterday cop'd *Hector* in the battell and stroke him downe, the' disdaind & shame whereof, hath euer since kept *Hector* fasting and waking.

Enter Pandarus.

Cre. Who comes here?

Man. Madam your Vncle *Pandarus*.

Cre. *Hectors* a gallant man.

Man. As may be in the world Lady.

Pan. What's that? what's that?

Cre. Good morrow Vncle *Pandarus*.

Pan. Good morrow Cozen *Cressid*: what do you talke of? good morrow *Alexander*. how do you Cozen? when were you at Ilium?

Cre. This morning Vncle.

Pan. What were you talking of when I came? Was *Hector* arm'd and gon ere yea came to Ilium? *Hellen* was not vp? was she?

Cre. *Hector* was gone but *Hellen* was not vp?

Pan. E'ene so; *Hector* was stirring early.

Cre. That were we talking of, and of his anger.

Pan. Was he angry?

Cre. So he saies here.

Pan True he was so; I know the cause too, heele lay about him to day I can tell them that, and there's *Troylus* will not come farre behind him, let them take heede of *Troylus*; I can tell them that too.

Cre. What is he angry too?

Pan. Who *Troylus*?
Troylus is the better man of the two.

Cre. Oh *Iupiter*; there's no comparison.

Pan. What not betweene *Troylus* and *Hector*? do you know a man if you see him?

Cre. I, if I euer saw him before and knew him.

Pan. Well I say *Troylus* is *Troylus*.

Cre. Then you say as I say,
For I am sure he is not *Hector*.

Pan. No not *Hector* is not *Troylus* in some degrees.

Cre. Tis iust, to each of them he is himselfe.

Pan. Himselfe? alas poore *Troylus* I would he were.

Cre. So he is.

Pan. Condition I had gone bare-foote to India.

Cre. He is not *Hector*.

Pan. Himselfe? no? hee's not himselfe, would a were himselfe: well, the Gods are aboue, time must friend or end: well *Troylus* well, I would my heart were in her body; no, *Hector* is not a better man then *Troylus*.

Cre. Excuse me.

Pan. He is elder.

Cre. Pardon me, pardon me.

Pan. Th'others not come too't, you shall tell me another tale when th'others come too't: *Hector* shall not haue his will this yeare.

Cre. He shall not neede it if he haue his owne.

Pan. Nor his qualities.

Cre. No matter.

Pan. Not his beautie.

Cre. 'Twould not become him, his own's better.

Pan. You haue no iudgement Neece; *Hellen* her selfe swore th'other day that *Troylus* for a browne fauour (for so 'tis I must confesse) not browne neither.

Cre. No, but browne.

Pan. Faith to say truth, browne and not browne

Cre. To say the truth, true and not true

Pan. She prais'd his complexion aboue *Paris*.

Cre. Why *Paris* hath colour inough.

Pan So he has.

Cre. Then *Troylus* should haue too much, if she prasi'd him aboue, his complexion is higher then his, he hauing colour

colour enough, and the other higher, is too flaming a praiſe for a good complexion, I had as lieue *Hellens* golden tongue had commended *Troylus* for a copper noſe.

Pan. I ſweare to you,
I thinke *Hellen* loues him better then *Paris*.

Cre. Then ſhee's a merry Greeke indeed.

Pan. Nay I am ſure ſhe does, ſhe came to him th'other day into the compaſt window, and you know he has not paſt three or foure haires on his chinne.

Creſ. Indeed a Tapſters Arithmetique may ſoone bring his particulars therein, to a totall.

Pand. Why he is very yong, and yet will he within three pound liſt as much as his brother *Hector*.

Creſ. Is he is ſo young a man, and ſo old a lifter?

Pan. But to prooue to you that *Hellen* loues him, ſhe came and puts me her white hand to his clouen chin.

Creſ. *Iuno* haue mercy, how came it clouen?

Pan. Why, you know 'tis dimpled,
I thinke his ſmyling becomes him better then any man in all Phrigia.

Cre. Oh he ſmiles valiantly.

Pan. Dooes hee not?

Cre. Oh yes, and 'twere a clow'd in *Autumne*.

Pan. Why go to then, but to proue to you that *Hellen* loues *Troylus*.

Cre. *Troylus* wil ſtand to thee
Proofe, if youle prooue it ſo.

Pan. *Troylus*? why he eſteemes her no more then I eſteeme an addle egge.

Cre. If you loue an addle egge as well as you loue an idle head, you would eate chickens i'th'ſhell.

Pan. I cannot chuſe but laugh to thinke how ſhe tickled his chin, indeed ſhee has a maruel's white hand I muſt needs confeſſe.

Cre. Without the racke.

Pan. And ſhee takes vpon her to ſpie a white haire on his chinne.

Cre. Alas poore chin? many a wart is richer.

Pand. But there was ſuch laughing, Queene *Hecuba* laught that her eyes ran ore.

Cre. With Milſtones.

Pan. And *Caſſandra* laught.

Cre. But there was more temperate fire vnder the pot of her eyes: did her eyes run ore too?

Pan. And *Hector* laught.

Cre. At what was all this laughing?

Pand. Marry at the white haire that *Hellen* ſpied on *Troylus* chin.

Creſ. And t'had beene a greene haire, I ſhould haue laught too.

Pand. They laught not ſo much at the haire, as at his pretty anſwere.

Cre. What was his anſwere?

Pan. Quoth ſhee, heere's but two and fifty haires on your chinne; and one of them is white.

Cre. This is her queſtion.

Pand. That's true, make no queſtion of that, two and fiftie haires quoth hee, and one white, that white haire is my Father, and all the reſt are his Sonnes. *Iupiter* quoth ſhe, which of theſe haires is *Paris* my husband? The forked one quoth he, pluckt out and giue it him: but there was ſuch laughing, and *Hellen* ſo bluſht, and *Paris* ſo chaft, and all the reſt ſo laught, that it paſt.

Cre. So let it now,
For is has beene a great while going by.

Pan. Well Cozen,
I told you a thing yeſterday, think on't.

Cre. So I does.

Pand. Ile be ſworne 'tis true, he will weepe you an'twere a man borne in Aprill. *Sound a retreate.*

Creſ. And Ile ſpring vp in his teares, an'twere a nettle againſt May.

Pan. Harke they are comming from the field, ſhal we ſtand vp here and ſee them, as they paſſe toward Illium, good Neece do, ſweet Neece *Creſſida*.

Cre. At your pleaſure.

Pan. Heere, heere, here's an excellent place, heere we may ſee moſt brauely, Ile tel you them all by their names, as they paſſe by, but marke *Troylus* aboue the reſt.

Enter Æneas.

Cre. Speake not ſo low'd.

Pan. That's *Æneas*, is not that a braue man, hee's one of the flowers of Troy I can you, but merke *Troylus* you ſhal ſee anon.

Cre. Who's that?

Enter Antenor.

Pan. That's *Antenor*, he has a ſhrow'd wit I can tell you, and hee's a man good inough, hee's one o'th ſoundeſt iudgement in Troy whoſoeuer, and a proper man of perſon: when comes *Troylus*? Ile ſhew you *Troylus* anon, if hee ſee me, you ſhall ſee him him nod at me.

Cre. Will he giue you the nod?

Pan. You ſhall ſee.

Cre. If he do, the rich ſhall haue, more.

Enter Hector.

Pan. That's *Hector*, that, that, looke you, that there's a fellow. Goe thy way *Hector*, there's a braue man Neece, O braue *Hector*! Looke how hee lookes? there's a countenance; iſt not a braue man?

Cre. O braue man!

Pan. Is a not? It dooes a mans heart good, looke yon what hacks are on his Helmet, looke you yonder, do you ſee? Looke you there? There's no ieſting, laying on, tak't off, who ill as they ſay, there be hacks.

Cre. Be thoſe with Swords?

Enter Paris.

Pan. Swords, any thing he cares not, and the diuell come to him, it's all one, by Gods lid it dooes ones heart good. Yonder comes *Paris*, yonder comes *Paris*: looke yee yonder Neece, iſt not a gallant man to, iſt not? Why this is braue now: who ſaid he came hurt home to day? Hee's not hurt, why this will do *Hellens* heart good now, ha? Would I could ſee *Troylus* now, you ſhall *Troylus* anon.

Cre. Whoſe that?

Enter Hellenus.

Pan. That's *Hellenus*, I maruell where *Troylus* is, that's *Helenus*, I thinke he went not forth to day: that's *Hellenus*.

Cre. Can *Hellenus* fight Vncle?

Pan. *Hellenus* no: yes heele fight indifferent, well, I maruell where *Troylus* is; harke, do you not haere the people crie *Troylus*? *Hellenus* is a Prieſt.

Cre. What ſneaking fellow comes yonder?

Enter Trylus

Pan. Where? Yonder? That's *Daphobus*. 'Tis *Troylus*! Ther's a man Neece, hem? Braue *Troylus*, the Prince of Chiualrie.

Cre. Peace, for ſhame peace.

Pand. Marke him, not him: O braue *Troylus*: looke well vpon him Neece, looke you how his Sword is bloudied, and his Helme more hackt then *Hectors*, and how he lookes,

lookes, and how he goes. O admirable youth! he ne're saw three and twenty. Go thy way *Troylus*, go thy way, had I a sister were a *Grace*, or a daughter a Goddesse, hee should take his choice. O admirable man! *Paris*? *Paris* is durt to him, and I warrant, *Helen* to change, would giue money to boot.

Enter common Souldiers.

Cres. Heere come more.

Pan. Asses, fooles, dolts, chaffe and bran, chaffe and bran; porredge after meat. I could liue and dye i'th'eyes of *Troylus*. Ne're looke, ne're looke; the Eagles are gon, Crowes and Dawes, Crowes and Dawes: I had rather be such a man as *Troylus*, then *Agamemnon* and all Greece.

Cres There is among the Greekes *Achilles*, a better man then *Troylus*.

Pan. Achilles? a Dray-man, a Porter, a very Camell.

Cres. Well well.

Pan. Well, well? Why haue you any discretion? haue you any eyes? Do you know what a man is? Is not birth, b auty, good shape, discourse, manhood, learning, gentlenesse, vertue, youth, liberality, and so forth: the Spice, and salt that seasons a man?

Cres. I, a minc'd man and then to be bak'd with no Date in the pye, for then the mans dates out.

Pan. You are such another woman, one knowes not at what ward you lye.

Cres. Vpon my backe, to defend my belly; vpon my wit, to defend my wiles; vppon my secrecy, to defend mine honesty; my Maske, to defend my beauty, and you to defend all these: and at all these wardes I lye at, at a thousand watches.

Pan. Say one of your watches.

Cres. Nay Ile watch you for that, and that's one of the cheefest of them too: If I cannot ward what I would not haue hit, I can watch you for telling how I took the blow, vnlesse it swell past hiding, and then it's past watching

Enter Boy.

Pan You are such another.

Boy Sir, my Lord would instantly speake with you.

Pan. Where?

Boy. At your owne house

Pan. Good Boy tell him I come, I doubt he bee hurt Fare ye well good Neece.

Cres. Adieu Vnkle

Pan. Ile be with you Neece by and by

Cres. To bring Vnkle.

Pan. I, a token from *Troylus*.

Cres. By the same token, you are a Bawd. *Exit Pand*

Words, vowes, gifts, teares, & loues full sacrifice,
He offers in anothers enterprise:
But more in *Troylus* thousand fold I see,
Then in the glasse of *Pandar's* praise may be;
Yet hold I off. Women are Angels wooing,
Things won are done, ioyes soule lyes in the dooing:
That she belou'd, knowes nought, that knowes not this;
Men prize the thing vngain'd, more then it is.
That she was neuer yet, that euer knew
Loue got so sweet, as when desire did sue:
Therefore this maxime out of loue I teach;
" *Atchieuement, is command; vngain'd, beseech.*
That though my hearts Contents firme loue doth beare,
Nothing of that shall from mine eyes appeare. *Exit.*

Senet. Enter Agamemnon, Nestor, Vlysses, Diomedes, Menelaus, with others.

Agam. Princes:
What greefe hath set the Iaundies on your cheekes?
The ample proposition that hope makes
In all designes, begun on earth below
Fayles in the promist largenesse: checkes and disasters
Grow in the veines of actions highest rear'd.
As knots by the conflux of meeting sap,
Infect the sound Pine, and diuerts his Graine
Tortiue and erant from his course of growth.
Nor Princes, is it matter new to vs,
That we come short of our suppose so farre,
That after seuen yeares siege, yet Troy walles stand,
Sith euery action that hath gone before,
Whereof we haue Record, Triall did draw
Bias and thwart, not answering the ayme:
And that vnbodied figure of the thought
That gaue't surmised shape. Why then (you Princes)
Do you with cheekes abash'd, behold our workes,
And thinke them shame, which are (indeed) nought else
But the protractiue trials of great Ioue,
To finde persistiue constancie in men?
The finenesse of which Mettall is not found
In Fortunes loue: for then, the Bold and Coward,
The Wise and Foole, the Artist and vn-read,
The hard and soft, seeme all affin'd, and kin.
But in the Winde and Tempest of her frowne,
Distinction with a lowd and powrefull fan,
Puffing at all, winnowes the light away;
And what hath masse, or matter by it selfe,
Lies rich in Vertue, and vnmingled.

Nestor With due Obseruance of thy godly seat,
Great *Agamemnon*, *Nestor* shall apply
Thy latest words.
In the reproofe of Chance,
Lies the true proofe of men: The Sea being smooth,
How many shallow bauble Boates dare saile
Vpon her patient brest, making their way
With those of Nobler bulke?
But let the Ruffian *Boreas* once enrage
The gentle *Thetis*, and anon behold
The strong ribb'd Barke through liquid Mountaines cut,
Bounding betweene the two moyst Elements
Like *Perseus* Horse. Where's then the sawcy Boate,
Whose weake vntimber'd sides but euen now
Co-riual'd Greatnesse? Either to harbour fled,
Or made a Toste for Neptune. Euen so,
Doth valours shew, and valours worth diuide
In stormes of Fortune.
For, in her ray and brightnesse,
The Heard hath more annoyance by the Brieze
Then by the Tyger: But, when the splitting winde
Makes flexible the knees of knotted Oakes,
And Flies fled vnder shade, why then
The thing of Courage,
As rowz'd with rage, with rage doth sympathize,
And with an accent tun'd in selfe-same key,
Retyres to chiding Fortune.

Vlys. Agamemnon.
Thou great Commander, Nerue, and Bone of Greece,
Heart of our Numbers, soule, and onely spirit,
In whom the tempers, and the mindes of all
Should be shut vp: Heare what *Vlysses* speakes,
Besides the applause and approbation
The which most mighty for thy place and sway,

G And

And thou moſt reuerend for thy ſtretcht-out life,
I giue to both your ſpeeches : which were ſuch,
As *Agamemnon* and the hand of Greece
Should hold vp high in Braſſe : and ſuch againe
As venerable *Neſtor* (hatch'd in Siluer)
Should with a bond of ayre, ſtrong as the Axletree
In which the Heauens ride, knit all Greekes eares
To his experienc'd tongue : yet let it pleaſe both
(Thou Great, and Wiſe) to heare *Vlyſſes* ſpeake.
Aga. Speak Prince of *Ithaca*, and be't of leſſe expect :
That matter needleſſe of importleſſe burthen
Diuide thy lips ; then we are confident
When ranke *Therſites* opes his Maſticke iawes,
We ſhall heare Muſicke, Wit, and Oracle.
Vlyſ. Troy yet vpon his baſis had bene downe,
And the great *Hectors* ſword had lack'd a Maſter
But for theſe inſtances.
The ſpecialty of Rule hath beene neglected ;
And looke how many Grecian Tents do ſtand
Hollow vpon this Plaine, ſo many hollow Factions.
When that the Generall is not like the Hiue,
To whom the Forragers ſhall all repaire,
What Hony is expected? Degree being vizarded,
Th'vnworthieſt ſhewes as fairely in the Maske.
The Heauens themſelues, the Planets, and this Center,
Obſerue degree, priority, and place,
Inſiſture, courſe, proportion, ſeaſon, forme,
Office, and cuſtome, in all line of Order :
And therefore is the glorious Planet Sol
In noble eminence, enthron'd and ſphear'd
Amid'ſt the other, whoſe med'cinable eye
Corrects the ill Aſpects of Planets euill,
And poſtes like the Command'ment of a King,
Sans checke, to good and bad. But when the Planets
In euill mixture to diſorder wander,
What Plagues, and what portents, what mutiny?
What raging of the Sea? ſhaking of Earth?
Commotion in the Windes? Frights, changes, horrors,
Diuert, and cracke, rend and deracinate
The vnity, and married calme of States
Quite from their fixure? O, when Degree is ſhak'd,
(Which is the Ladder to all high deſignes)
The enterprize is ſicke. How could Communities,
Degrees in Schooles, and Brother-hoods in Cities,
Peacefull Commerce from diuidable ſhores,
The primogenitiue, and due of Byrth,
Prerogatiue of Age, Crownes, Scepters, Lawrels,
(But by Degree) ſtand in Authentique place?
Take but Degree away, vn-tune that ſtring,
And hearke what Diſcord followes : each thing meetes
In meere oppugnancie. The bounded Waters,
Should lift their boſomes higher then the Shores,
And make a ſoppe of all this ſolid Globe :
Strength ſhould be Lord of imbecility,
And the rude Sonne ſhould ſtrike his Father dead :
Force ſhould be right, or rather, right and wrong,
(Betweene whoſe endleſſe iarre, Iuſtice recides)
Should looſe her names, and ſo ſhould Iuſtice too.
Then euery thing includes it ſelfe in Power.
Power into Will, Will into Appetite,
And Appetite (an vniuerſall Wolfe,
So doubly ſeconded with Will, and Power)
Muſt make perforce an vniuerſall prey,
And laſt, eate vp himſelfe.
Great *Agamemnon* :
This Chaos, when Degree is ſuffocate,
Followes the choaking :
And this neglection of Degree, is it
That by a pace goes backward in a purpoſe
It hath to climbe. The Generall's diſdain'd
By him one ſtep below ; he, by the next,
That next, by him beneath : ſo euery ſtep
Exampled by the firſt pace that is ſicke
Of his Superiour, growes to an enuious Feauer
Of pale, and bloodleſſe Emulation.
And 'tis this Feauer that keepes Troy on foote,
Not her owne ſinewes. To end a tale of length,
Troy in our weakneſſe liues, not in her ſtrength.
Neſt. Moſt wiſely hath *Vlyſſes* heere diſcouer'd
The Feauer, whereof all our power is ſicke.
Aga. The Nature of the ſickneſſe found (*Vlyſſes*)
What is the remedie?
Vlyſ. The great *Achilles*, whom Opinion crownes,
The ſinew, and the fore-hand of our Hoſte,
Hauing his eare full of his ayery Fame,
Growes dainty of his worth, and in his Tent
Lyes mocking our deſignes. With him, *Patroclus*,
Vpon a lazie Bed, the liue-long day
Breakes ſcurrill Ieſts,
And with ridiculous and aukward action,
(Which Slanderer, he imitation call's)
He Pageants vs. Sometime great *Agamemnon*,
Thy topleſſe deputation he puts on ;
And like a ſtrutting Player, whoſe conceit
Lies in his Ham-ſtring, and doth thinke it rich
To heare the woodden Dialogue and ſound
'Twixt his ſtretcht footing, and the Scaffolage,
Such to be pittied, and ore-reſted ſeeming
He acts thy Greatneſſe in : and when he ſpeakes,
'Tis like a Chime a mending. With tearmes vnſquar'd,
Which from the tongue of roaring *Typhon* dropt,
Would ſeemes Hyperboles. At this fuſty ſtuffe,
The large *Achilles* (on his preſt-bed lolling)
From his deepe Cheſt, laughes out a lowd applauſe,
Cries excellent, 'tis *Agamemnon* iuſt.
Now play me *Neſtor* ; hum, and ſtroke thy Beard
As he, being dreſt to ſome Oration :
That's done, as neere as the extreameſt ends
Of paralels ; as like, as *Vulcan* and his wife,
Yet god *Achilles* ſtill cries excellent,
'Tis *Neſtor* right. Now play him (me) *Patroclus*,
Arming to anſwer in a night-Alarme,
And then (forſooth) the faint defects of Age
Muſt be the Scene of myrth, to cough, and ſpit,
And with a palſie fumbling on his Gorget,
Shake in and out the Riuet : and at this ſport
Sir Valour dies ; cries, O enough *Patroclus*,
Or, giue me ribs of Steele, I ſhall ſplit all
In pleaſure of my Spleene. And in this faſhion,
All our abilities, gifts, natures, ſhapes,
Seuerals and generals of grace exact,
Atchieuments, plots, orders, preuentions,
Excitements to the field, or ſpeech for truce,
Succeſſe or loſſe, what is, or is not, ſerues
As ſtuffe for theſe two, to make paradoxes.
Neſt. And in the imitation of theſe twaine,
Who (as *Vlyſſes* ſayes) Opinion crownes
With an Imperiall voyce, many are infect :
Aiax is growne ſelfe-will'd, and beares his head
In ſuch a reyne in full as proud a place
As broad *Achilles*, and keepes his Tent like him ;
Makes factious Feaſts, railes on our ſtate of Warre

Bold

Bold as an Oracle, and sets *Thersites*
A slaue, whose Gall coines slanders like a Mint,
To match vs in comparisons with durt,
To weaken and discredit our exposure,
How ranke soeuer rounded in with danger.
Vlys. They taxe our policy, and call it Cowardice,
Count Wisedome as no member of the Warre,
Fore-stall prescience, and esteeme no acte
But that of hand: The still and mentall parts,
That do contriue how many hands shall strike
When fitnesse call them on, and know by measure
Of their obseruant toyle, the Enemies waight,
Why this hath not a fingers dignity:
They call this Bed-worke, Mapp'ry, Closset-Warre:
So that the Ramme that batters downe the wall,
For the great swing and rudenesse of his poize,
They place before his hand that made the Engine,
Or those that with the finenesse of their soules,
By Reason guide his execution.
Nest. Let this be granted, and *Achilles* horse
Makes many *Thetis* sonnes. *Tucket*
Aga. What Trumpet? Looke *Menelaus.*
Men. From Troy. *Enter Æneas.*
Aga. What would you 'fore our Tent?
Æne. Is this great *Agamemnons* Tent, I pray you?
Aga. Euen this.
Æne. May one that is a Herald, and a Prince,
Do a faire message to his Kingly eares?
Aga. With surety stronger then *Achilles* arme,
'Fore all the Greekish heads, which with one voyce
Call *Agamemnon* Head and Generall.
Æne. Faire leaue, and large security. How may
A stranger to those most Imperial lookes,
Know them from eyes of other Mortals?
Aga. How?
Æne. I: I aske, that I might waken reuerence,
And on the cheeke be ready with a blush
Modest as morning, when she coldly eyes
The youthfull Phœbus:
Which is that God in office guiding men?
Which is the high and mighty *Agamemnon?*
Aga. This Troyan scornes vs, or the men of Troy
Are ceremonious Courtiers.
Æne. Courtiers as free, as debonnaire; vnarm'd,
As bending Angels: that's their Fame, in peace:
But when they would seeme Souldiers, they haue galles,
Good armes, strong ioynts, true swords, & *Ioues* accord,
Nothing so full of heart. But peace *Æneas*,
Peace Troyan, lay thy finger on thy lips,
The worthinesse of praise distaines his worth:
If that he prais'd himselfe, bring the praise forth.
But what the repining enemy commends,
That breath Fame blowes, that praise sole pure transce͂ds.
Aga. Sir, you of Troy, call you your selfe *Æneas?*
Æne. I Greeke, that is my name.
Aga. What's your affayre I pray you?
Æne. Sir pardon, 'tis for *Agamemnons* eares.
Aga. He heares nought priuatly
That comes from Troy.
Æne. Nor I from Troy come not to whisper him,
I bring a Trumpet to awake his eare,
To set his sence on the attentiue bent,
And then to speake.
Aga. Speake frankely as the winde,
It is not *Agamemnons* sleeping houre;
That thou shalt know Troyan he is awake,
He tels thee so himselfe.
Æne. Trumpet blow loud,
Send thy Brasse voyce through all these lazie Tents,
And euery Greeke of mettle, let him know,
What Troy meanes fairely, shall be spoke alowd.
The Trumpets sound.
We haue great *Agamemnon* heere in Troy,
A Prince calld *Hector, Priam* is his Father:
Who in this dull and long-continew'd Truce
Is rusty growne. He bad me take a Trumpet,
And to this purpose speake: Kings, Princes, Lords,
If there be one among'st the fayr'st of Greece,
That holds his Honor higher then his ease,
That seekes his praise, more then he feares his perill,
That knowes his Valour, and knowes not his feare,
That loues his Mistris more then in confession,
(With truant vowes to her owne lips he loues)
And dare avow her Beauty, and her Worth,
In other armes then hers: to him this Challenge.
Hector, in view of Troyans, and of Greekes,
Shall make it good, or do his best to do it.
He hath a Lady, wiser, fairer, truer,
Then euer Greeke did compasse in his armes,
And will to morrow with his Trumpet call,
Midway betweene your Tents, and walles of Troy,
To rowze a Grecian that is true in loue.
If any come, *Hector* shal honour him:
If none, hee'l say in Troy when he retyres,
The Grecian Dames are sun-burnt, and not worth
The splinter of a Lance: Euen so much.
Aga. This shall be told our Louers Lord *Æneas*,
If none of them haue soule in such a kinde,
We left them all at home: But we are Souldiers,
And may that Souldier a meere recreant proue,
That meanes not, hath not, or is not in loue:
If then one is, or hath, or meanes to be,
That one meets *Hector*; if none else, Ile be he.
Nest. Tell him of *Nestor*, one that was a man
When *Hectors* Grandsire suckt: he is old now,
But if there be not in our Grecian mould,
One Noble man, that hath one sparke of fire
To answer for his Loue; tell him from me,
Ile hide my Siluer beard in a Gold Beauer,
And in my Vantbrace put this wither'd brawne,
And meeting him, wil tell him, that my Lady
Was fayrer then his Grandame, and as chaste
As may be in the world: his youth in flood,
Ile pawne this truth with my three drops of blood.
Æne. Now heauens forbid such scarsitie of youth.
Vlys. Amen.
Aga. Faire Lord *Æneas*,
Let me touch your hand:
To our Pauillion shal I leade you first:
Achilles shall haue word of this intent,
So shall each Lord of Greece from Tent to Tent:
Your selfe shall Feast with vs before you goe,
And finde the welcome of a Noble Foe. *Exeunt.*
Manet Vlysses, and Nestor.
Vlys. *Nestor.*
Nest. What sayes *Vlysses?*
Vlys. I haue a young conception in my braine,
Be you my time to bring it to some shape.
Nest. What is't?
Vlysses. This 'tis:
Blunt wedges riue hard knots: the seeded Pride
That hath to this maturity blowne vp

¶ 2 In

In ranke *Achilles*, muſt or now be cropt,
Or ſhedding breed a Nurſery of like euil
To ouer-bulke vs all.
Neſt. Wel, and how?
Vlyſ. This challenge that the gallant *Hector* ſends,
How euer it is ſpred in general name,
Relates in purpoſe onely to *Achilles*.
Neſt. The purpoſe is perſpicuous euen as ſubſtance,
Whoſe groſſeneſſe little charracters ſumme vp,
And in the publication make no ſtraine,
But that *Achilles*, were his braine as barren
As bankes of Lybia, though (*Apollo* knowes)
'Tis dry enough, wil with great ſpeede of iudgement,
I, with celerity, finde *Hectors* purpoſe
Pointing on him.
Vlyſ. And wake him to the anſwer, thinke you?
Neſt. Yes, 'tis moſt meet; who may you elſe oppoſe
That can from *Hector* bring his Honor off,
If not *Achilles*; though't be a ſportfull Combate,
Yet in this triall, much opinion dwels.
For heere the Troyans taſte our deer'ſt repute
With their fin'ſt Pallate: and truſt to me *Vlyſſes*,
Our imputation ſhall be oddely poiz'd
In this wilde action. For the ſucceſſe
(Although particular) ſhall giue a ſcantling
Of good or bad, vnto the Generall:
And in ſuch Indexes, although ſmall prickes
To their ſubſequent Volumes, there is ſeene
The baby figure of the Gyant-maſſe
Of things to come at large. It is ſuppos'd,
He that meets *Hector*, iſſues from our choyſe;
And choiſe being mutuall acte of all our ſoules,
Makes Merit her election, and doth boyle
As 'twere, from forth vs all: a man diſtill'd
Out of our Vertues; who miſcarrying,
What heart from hence receyues the conqu'ring part,
To ſteele a ſtrong opinion to themſelues,
Which entertain'd, Limbes are in his inſtruments,
In no leſſe working, then are Swords and Bowes
Directiue by the Limbes.
Vlyſ. Giue pardon to my ſpeech.
Therefore 'tis meet, *Achilles* meet not *Hector*:
Let vs (like Merchants) ſhew our fowleſt Wares,
And thinke perchance they'l ſell: If not,
The luſter of the better yet to ſhew,
Shall ſhew the better. Do not conſent,
That euer *Hector* and *Achilles* meete:
For both our Honour, and our Shame in this,
Are dogg'd with two ſtrange Followers.
Neſt. I ſee them not with my old eies: what are they?
Vlyſ. What glory our *Achilles* ſhares from *Hector*,
(Were he not proud) we all ſhould weare with him:
But he already is too inſolent,
And we were better parch in Affricke Sunne,
Then in the pride and ſalt ſcorne of his eyes
Should he ſcape *Hector* faire. If he were foyld,
Why then we did our maine opinion cruſh
In taint of our beſt man. No, make a Lott'ry,
And by deuice let blockiſh *Aiax* draw
The ſort to fight with *Hector*: Among our ſelues,
Giue him allowance as the worthier man,
For that will phyſicke the great Myrmidon
Who broyles in lowd applauſe, and make him fall
His Creſt, that prouder then blew Iris bends.
If the dull brainleſſe *Aiax* come ſafe off,
Wee'l dreſſe him vp in voyces: if he faile,
Yet go we vnder our opinion ſtill,
That we haue better men. But hit or miſſe,
Our proiects life this ſhape of ſence aſſumes,
Aiax imploy'd, pluckes downe *Achilles* Plumes.
Neſt. Now *Vlyſſes*, I begin to relliſh thy aduice,
And I wil giue a taſte of it forthwith
To *Agamemnon*, go we to him ſtraight:
Two Curres ſhal tame each other, Pride alone
Muſt tarre the Maſtiffes on, as 'twere their bone. *Exeunt*

Enter Aiax, and Therſites.

Aia. Therſites?
Ther. Agamemnon, how if he had Biles (ful) all ouer generally.
Aia. Therſites?
Ther. And thoſe Byles did runne, ſay ſo; did not the General run, were not that a botchy core?
Aia. Dogge.
Ther. Then there would come ſome matter from him: I ſee none now.
Aia. Thou Bitch-Wolfes-Sonne, canſt y not heare? Feele then. *Strikes him.*
Ther. The plague of Greece vpon thee thou Mungrel beefe-witted Lord.
Aia. Speake then you whinid'ſt leauen ſpeake, I will beate thee into handſomneſſe.
Ther. I ſhal ſooner rayle thee into wit and holineſſe: but I thinke thy Horſe wil ſooner con an Oration, then ỷ learn a prayer without booke: Thou canſt ſtrike, canſt thou? A red Murren o'th thy Iades trickes.
Aia. Toads ſtoole, learne me the Proclamation.
Ther. Doeſt thou thinke I haue no ſence thou ſtrik'ſt (me thus?
Aia. The Proclamation.
Ther. Thou art proclaim'd a foole, I thinke.
Aia. Do not Porpentine, do not; my fingers itch.
Ther. I would thou didſt itch from head to foot, and I had the ſcratching of thee, I would make thee the lothſom'ſt ſcab in Greece.
Aia. I ſay the Proclamation.
Ther. Thou grumbleſt & raileſt euery houre on *Achilles*, and thou art as ful of enuy at his greatnes, as *Cerberus* is at *Proſerpina's* beauty. I, that thou barkſt at him.
Aia. Miſtreſſe *Therſites*.
Ther. Thou ſhould'ſt ſtrike him.
Aia. Cobloſe.
Ther. He would pun thee into ſhiuers with his fiſt, as a Sailor breakes a bisket.
Aia. You horſon Curre. *Ther.* Do, do.
Aia. Thou ſtoole for a Witch.
Ther. I, do, do, thou ſodden-witted Lord: thou haſt no more braine then I haue in mine elbows: An Aſinico may tutor thee. Thou ſcuruy valiant Aſſe, thou art heere but to threſh Troyans, and thou art bought and ſolde among thoſe of any wit, like a Barbarian ſlaue. If thou vſe to beat me, I wil begin at thy heele and tel what thou art by inches, thou thing of no bowels thou.
Aia. You dogge.
Ther. You ſcuruy Lord.
Aia. You Curre.
Ther. *Mars* his Ideot: do rudenes, do Camell, do, do.

Enter Achilles, and Patroclus.

Achil. Why how now *Aiax*? wherefore do you this? How now *Therſites*? what's the matter man?
Ther. You ſee him there, do you?
Achil. I, what's the matter.
Ther. Nay looke vpon him.
Achil. So I do: what's the matter?

Ther.

Ther. Nay but regard him well.

Achil. Well, why I do ſo.

Ther. But yet you looke not well vpon him: for who ſome euer you take him to be, he is *Aiax*.

Achil. I know that foole.

Ther. I, but that foole knowes not himſelfe.

Aiax. Therefore I beate thee.

Ther. Lo, lo, lo, lo, what *modicums* of wit he vtters: his euaſions haue eares thus long. I haue bobb'd his Braine more then he has beate my bones: I will buy nine Sparrowes for a peny, and his *Piamater* is not worth the ninth part of a Sparrow. This Lord (*Achilles*) *Aiax* who wears his wit in his belly, and his guttes in his head, Ile tell you what I ſay of him.

Achil. What?

Ther. I ſay this *Aiax* ——

Achil. Nay good *Aiax*.

Ther. Has not ſo much wit.

Achil. Nay, I muſt hold you.

Ther. As will ſtop the eye of *Helens* Needle, for whom he comes to fight.

Achil. Peace foole.

Ther. I would haue peace and quietnes, but the foole will not: he there, that he, looke you there.

Aiax. O thou damn'd Curre, I ſhall——

Achil. Will you ſet your wit to a Fooles.

Ther. No I warrant you, for a fooles will ſhame it.

Pat. Good words *Therſites*.

Achil. What's the quarrell?

Aiax. I bad thee vile Owle, goe learne me the tenure of the Proclamation, and he rayles vpon me.

Ther. I ſerue thee not.

Aiax. Well, go too, go too.

Ther. I ſerue heere voluntary.

Achil. Your laſt ſeruice was ſufferance, 'twas not voluntary, no man is beaten voluntary: *Aiax* was heere the voluntary, and you as vnder an Impreſſe.

Ther. E'ne ſo, a great deale of your wit too lies in your ſinnewes, or elſe there be Liars. *Hector* ſhall haue a great catch, if he knocke out either of your braines, he were as good cracke a fuſtie nut with no kernell.

Achil. What with me to *Therſites*?

Ther. There's *Vlyſſes*, and old *Neſtor*, whoſe Wit was mouldy ere their Grandſires had nails on their toes, yoke you like draft-Oxen, and make you plough vp the warre.

Achil. What? what?

Ther. Yes good ſooth, to *Achilles*, to *Aiax*, to——

Aiax. I ſhall cut out your tongue.

Ther. 'Tis no matter, I ſhall ſpeake as much as thou afterwards.

Pat. No more words *Therſites*.

Ther. I will hold my peace when *Achilles* Brooch bids me, ſhall I?

Achil. There's for you *Patroclus*.

Ther. I will ſee you hang'd like Clotpoles ere I come any more to your Tents; I will keepe where there is wit ſtirring, and leaue the faction of fooles. *Exit.*

Pat. A good riddance.

Achil. Marry this Sir is proclaim'd through al our hoſt,
That *Hector* by the fift houre of the Sunne,
Will with a Trumpet, 'twixt our Tents and Troy
To morrow morning call ſome Knight to Armes,
That hath a ſtomacke, and ſuch a one that dare
Maintaine I know not what: 'tis traſh. Farewell.

Aiax. Farewell: who ſhall anſwer him?

Achil. I know not, 'tis put to Lottry: otherwiſe
He knew his man.

Aiax. O meaning you, I wil go learne more of it. *Exit.*

Enter Priam, Hector, Troylus, Paris and Helenus.

Pri. After ſo many houres, liues, ſpeeches ſpent,
Thus once againe ſayes *Neſtor* from the Greekes,
Deliuer *Helen*, and all damage elſe
(As honour, loſſe of time, trauaile, expence,
Wounds, friends, and what els deere that is conſum'd
In hot digeſtion of this comorant Warre)
Shall be ſtroke off. *Hector*, what ſay you too't.

Hect. Though no man leſſer feares the Greeks then I,
As farre as touches my particular: yet dread *Priam*,
There is no Lady of more ſofter bowels,
More ſpungie, to ſucke in the ſenſe of Feare,
More ready to cry out, who knowes what followes
Then *Hector* is: the wound of peace is ſurety,
Surety ſecure: but modeſt Doubt is cal'd
The Beacon of the wiſe: the tent that ſearches
To'th'bottome of the worſt. Let *Helen* go,
Since the firſt ſword was drawne about this queſtion,
Euery tythe ſoule 'mongſt many thouſand diſmes,
Hath bin as deere as *Helen*: I meane of ours:
If we haue loſt ſo many tenths of ours
To guard a thing not ours, nor worth to vs
(Had it our name) the valew of one ten;
What merit's in that reaſon which denies
The yeelding of her vp.

Troy. Fie, fie, my Brother;
Weigh you the worth and honour of a King
(So great as our dread Father) in a Scale
Of common Ounces? Wil you with Counters ſumme
The paſt propor tion of his infinite,
And buckle in a waſte moſt fathomleſſe,
With ſpannes and inches ſo diminutiue,
As feares and reaſons? Fie for godly ſhame?

Hel. No maruel though you bite ſo ſharp at reaſons,
You are ſo empty of them, ſhould not our Father
Beare the great ſway of his affayres with reaſons,
Becauſe your ſpeech hath none that tels him ſo.

Troy. You are for dreames & ſlumbers brother Prieſt
You furre your gloues with reaſon: here are your reaſons
You know an enemy intends you harme,
You know, a ſword imploy'd is perillous,
And reaſon flyes the obiect of all harme.
Who maruels then when *Helenus* beholds
A Grecian and his ſword, if he do ſet
The very wings of reaſon to his heeles:
Or like a Starre diſorb'd. Nay, if we talke of Reaſon,
And flye like chidden Mercurie from Ioue,
Let's ſhut our gates and ſleepe: Manhood and Honor
Should haue hard hearts, wold they but fat their thoghts
With this cramm'd reaſon: reaſon and reſpect,
Makes Liuers pale, and luſtyhood deiect.

Hect. Brother, ſhe is not worth
What ſhe doth coſt the holding.

Troy. What's aught, but as 'tis valew'd?

Hect. But value dwels not in particular will,
It holds his eſtimate and dignitie
As well, wherein 'tis precious of it ſelfe,
As in the prizer: 'Tis made Idolatrie,
To make the ſeruice greater then the God,
And the will dotes that is inclineable
To what infectiouſly it ſelfe affects,
Without ſome image of th'affected merit.

Troy. I take to day a Wife, and my election
Is led on in the conduct of my Will;

My

My Will enkindled by mine eyes and eares,
Two traded Pylots 'twixt the dangerous ſhores
Of Will, and Iudgement. How may I auoyde
(Although my will diſtaſte what it elected)
The Wife I choſe, there can be no euaſion
To blench from this, and to ſtand firme by honour.
We turne not backe the Silkes vpon the Merchant
When we haue ſpoyl'd them; nor the remainder Viands
We do not throw in vnreſpectiue ſame,
Becauſe we now are full. It was thought meete
Paris ſhould do ſome vengeance on the Greekes;
Your breath of full conſent bellied his Sailes,
The Seas and Windes (old Wranglers) tooke a Truce,
And did him ſeruice; he touch'd the Ports deſir'd,
And for an old Aunt whom the Greekes held Captiue,
He brought a Grecian Queen, whoſe youth & freſhneſſe
Wrinkles *Apolloes*, and makes ſtale the morning.
Why keepe we her? the Grecians keepe our Aunt:
Is ſhe worth keeping? Why ſhe is a Pearle,
Whoſe price hath launch'd aboue a thouſand Ships,
And turn'd Crown'd Kings to Merchants.
If you'l auouch, 'twas wiſedome *Paris* went,
(As you muſt needs, for you all cride, Go, go:)
If you'l confeſſe, he brought home Noble prize,
(As you muſt needs) for you all clapt your hands,
And cride ineſtimable; why do you now
The iſſue of your proper Wiſedomes rate,
And do a deed that Fortune neuer did?
Begger the eſtimation which you priz'd,
Richer then Sea and Land? O Theft moſt baſe!
That we haue ſtolne what we do feare to keepe
But Theeues vnworthy of a thing ſo ſtolne,
That in their Country did them that diſgrace,
We feare to warrant in our Natiue place.

Enter Caſſandra with her haire about her eares

Caſ. Cry *Troyans*, cry.
Priam. What noyſe? what ſhreeke is this?
Troy. 'Tis our mad ſiſter, I do know her voyce.
Caſ. Cry Troyans.
Hect. It is *Caſſandra.*
Caſ. Cry Troyans cry; lend me ten thouſand eyes,
And I will fill them with Propheticke teares.
Hect. Peace ſiſter, peace.
Caſ. Virgins, and Boyes; mid-age & wrinkled old,
Soft infancie, that nothing can but cry,
Adde to my clamour: let vs pay betimes
A moity of that maſſe of moane to come.
Cry Troyans cry, practiſe your eyes with teares,
Troy muſt not be, nor goodly Illion ſtand,
Our fire-brand Brother *Paris* burnes vs all.
Cry Troyans cry, a *Helen* and a woe;
Cry, cry, Troy burnes, or elſe let *Helen* goe. *Exit.*
Hect. Now youthfull *Troylus*, do not theſe hie ſtrains
Of diuination in our Siſter, worke
Some touches of remorſe? Or is your bloud
So madly hot, that no diſcourſe of reaſon,
Nor feare of bad ſucceſſe in a bad cauſe,
Can qualifie the ſame?
Troy Why Brother *Hector*,
We may not thinke the iuſtneſſe of each acte
Such, and no other then euent doth forme it,
Nor once deiect the courage of our mindes;
Becauſe *Caſſandra's* mad, her brainſicke raptures
Cannot diſtaſte the goodneſſe of a quarrell,
Which hath our ſeuerall Honours all engag'd
To make it gracious. For my priuate part,
I am no more touch'd, then all *Priams* ſonnes,
And Ioue forbid there ſhould be done among'ſt vs
Such things as might offend the weakeſt ſpleene,
To fight for, and maintaine.
Par. Elſe might the world conuince of leuitie,
As well my vnder-takings as your counſels:
But I atteſt the gods, your full conſent
Gaue wings to my propenſion, and cut off
All feares attending on ſo dire a proiect.
For what (alas) can theſe my ſingle armes?
What propugnation is in one mans valour
To ſtand the puſh and enmity of thoſe
This quarrell would excite? Yet I proteſt,
Were I alone to paſſe the difficulties,
And had as ample power, as I haue will,
Paris ſhould ne're retract what he hath done,
Nor faint in the purſuite.
Pri. *Paris*, you ſpeake
Like one be-ſotted on your ſweet delights;
You haue the Hony ſtill but theſe the Gall,
So to be valiant, is no praiſe at all.
Par. Sir, I propoſe not meerely to my ſelfe,
The pleaſures ſuch a beauty brings with it:
But I would haue the ſoyle of her faire Rape
Wip'd off in honourable keeping her.
What Treaſon were it to the ranſack'd Queene,
Diſgrace to your great worths, and ſhame to me,
Now to deliuer her poſſeſsion vp
On termes of baſe compulſion? Can it be,
That ſo degenerate a ſtraine as this,
Should once ſet footing in your generous boſomes?
There's not the meaneſt ſpirit on our partie,
Without a heart to dare, or ſword to draw,
When *Helen* is defended: nor none ſo Noble,
Whoſe life were ill beſtow'd, or death vnfam'd,
Where *Helen* is the ſubiect. Then (I ſay)
Well may we fight for her, whom we know well,
The worlds large ſpaces cannot paralell.
Hect. *Paris* and *Troylus*, you haue both ſaid well:
And on the cauſe and queſtion now in hand,
Haue gloz'd, but ſuperficially; not much
Vnlike young men, whom *Ariſtotle* thought
Vnfit to heare Morall Philoſophie.
The Reaſons you alledge, do more conduce
To the hot paſſion of diſtemp'red blood,
Then to make vp a free determination
'Twixt right and wrong: For pleaſure, and reuenge,
Haue eares more deafe then Adders, to the voyce
Of any true deciſion. Nature craues
All dues be rendred to their Owners: now
What neerer debt in all humanity,
Then Wife is to the Husband? If this law
Of Nature be corrupted through affection,
And that great mindes of partiall indulgence,
To their benummed wills reſiſt the ſame,
There is a Law in each well-ordred Nation,
To curbe thoſe raging appetites that are
Moſt diſobedient and refracturie.
If *Helen* then be wife to Sparta's King
(As it is knowne ſhe is) theſe Morall Lawes
Of Nature, and of Nation, ſpeake alowd
To haue her backe return'd. Thus to perſiſt
In doing wrong, extenuates not wrong,
But makes it much more heauie. *Hectors* opinion

Is

Is this in way of truth : yet nere the lesse,
My spritely brethren, I propend to you
In resolution to keepe *Helen* still ;
For 'tis a cause that hath no meane dependance,
Vpon our ioynt and seuerall dignities.

Tro. Why? there you toucht the life of our designe:
Were it not glory that we more affected,
Then the performance of our heauing spleenes,
I would not wish a drop of *Troian* blood,
Spent more in her defence. But worthy *Hector*,
She is a theame of honour and renowne,
A spurre to valiant and magnanimous deeds,
Whose present courage may beate downe our foes,
And fame in time to come canonize vs.
For I presume braue *Hector* would not loose
So rich aduantage of a promis'd glory,
As smiles vpon the fore-head of this action,
For the wide worlds reuenew.

Hect. I am yours,
You valiant off-spring of great *Priamus*,
I haue a roisting challenge sent among'st
The dull and factious nobles of the Greekes,
Will strike amazement to their drowsie spirits,
I was aduertiz'd, their Great generall slept,
Whil'st emulation in the armie crept:
This I presume will wake him. *Exeunt.*

Enter Thersites *solus.*

How now *Thersites*? what lost in the Labyrinth of thy furie? shall the Elephant *Aiax* carry it thus? he beates me, and I raile at him: O worthy satisfaction, would it were otherwise: that I could beate him, whil'st he rail'd at me: Sfoote, Ile learne to coniure and raise Diuels, but Ile see some issue of my spitefull execrations. Then ther's *Achilles*, a rare Enginer. If *Troy* be not taken till these two vndermine it, the wals will stand till they fall of themselues. O thou great thunder-darter of Olympus, forget that thou art *Ioue* the King of gods: and *Mercury*, loose all the Serpentine craft of thy Caduceus, if thou take not that little little lesse then little wit from them that they haue, which short-arm'd ignorance it selfe knowes, is so abundant scarse, it will not in circumuention deliuer a Flye from a Spider, without drawing the massie Irons and cutting the web: after this, the vengeance on the whole Camp, or rather the bone-ach, for that me thinkes is the curse dependant on those that warre for a placket. I haue said my prayers and diuell, enuie, say Amen: What ho? my Lord *Achilles*?

Enter Patroclus.

Patr. Who's there? *Thersites.* Good *Thersites* come in and raile.

Ther. If I could haue remembred a guilt counterfeit, thou would'st not haue slipt out of my contemplation; but it is no matter, thy selfe vpon thy selfe. The common curse of mankinde, follie and ignorance be thine in great reuenew; heauen blesse thee from a Tutor, and Discipline come not neere thee. Let thy bloud be thy direction till thy death, then if she that laies thee out sayes thou art a faire coarse, Ile be sworne and sworne vpon't she neuer shrowded any but Lazars, Amen. Wher's *Archilles*?

Patr. What art thou deuout? wast thou in a prayer?

Ther. I, the heauens heare me.

Enter Achilles.

Achil. Who's there?

Patr. *Thersites*, my Lord.

Achil. Where, where, art thou come? why my cheese, my digestion, why hast thou not seru'd thy selfe into my Table, so many meales? Come, what's *Agamemnon*?

Ther. Thy Commander *Achilles*, then tell me *Patroclus*, what's *Achilles*?

Patr. Thy Lord *Thersites*: then tell me I pray thee, what's thy selfe?

Ther. Thy knower *Patroclus*: then tell me *Patroclus*, what art thou?

Patr. Thou maist tell that know'st.

Achil. O tell, tell.

Ther. Ile declin the whole question: *Agamemnon* commands *Archilles, Achilles* is my Lord, I am *Patroclus* knower, and *Patroclus* is a foole.

Patro. You rascall.

Ter. Peace foole, I haue not done.

Achil. He is a priuiledg'd man, proceede *Thersites*.

Ther. *Agamemnon* is a foole, *Achilles* is a foole, *Thersites* is a foole, and as aforesaid, *Patroclus* is a foole.

Achil. Deriue this? come?

Ther. *Agamemnon* is a foole to offer to command *Achilles*, *Achilles* is a foole to be commanded of *Agamemnon*, *Thersites* is a foole to serue such a foole: and *Patroclus* is a foole positiue.

Patr. Why am I a foole?

Enter Agamemnon, Vlisses, Nestor, Diomedes, Aiax, and Chalcas.

Ther. Make that demand to the Creator, it suffises me thou art. Looke you, who comes here?

Achil. *Patroclus*, Ile speake with no body: come in with me *Thersites*. *Exit.*

Ther. Here is such patcherie, such iugling, and such knauerie: all the argument is a Cuckold and a Whore, a good quarrel to draw emulations, factions, and bleede to death vpon: Now the dry Suppeago on the Subiect, and Warre and Lecherie confound all.

Agam. Where is *Achilles*?

Patr. Within his Tent, but ill dispos'd my Lord.

Agam. Let it be knowne to him that we are here:
He sent our Messengers, and we lay by
Our appertainments, visiting of him:
Let him be told of, so perchance he thinke
We dare not moue the question of our place,
Or know not what we are.

Pat. I shall so say to him.

Vlis. We saw him at the opening of his Tent,
He is not sicke.

Aia. Yes, Lyon sicke, sicke of proud heart; you may call it Melancholly if will fauour the man, but by my head, it is pride; but why, why, let him show vs the cause? A word my Lord.

Nes. What moues *Aiax* thus to bay at him?

Vlis. *Achillis* hath inueigled his Foole from him.

Nes. Who, *Thersites*?

Vlis. He.

Nes. Then will *Aiax* lacke matter, if he haue lost his A gument.

Vlis. No, you see he is his argument that has his argument *Achilles*.

Nes. All the better, their fraction is more our wish then their faction; but it was a strong counsell that a Foole could disunite.

Vlis. The amitie that wisedome knits, not folly may easily vntie. *Enter Patroclus.*

Here

Here comes *Patroclus*.
Nes. No *Achilles* with him?
Vlis. The Elephant hath ioynts, but none for curtesie:
His legge are legs for necessitie, not for flight.
Patro. *Achilles* bids me say he is much sorry:
If any thing more then your sport and pleasure,
Did moue your greatnesse, and this noble State,
To call vpon him; he hopes it is no other,
But for your health, and your digestion sake;
An after Dinners breath.
Aga. Heare you *Patroclus*:
We are too well acquainted with these answers:
But his euasion winged thus swift with scorne,
Cannot outflye our apprehensions.
Much attribute he hath, and much the reason,
Why we ascribe it to him, yet all his vertues,
Not vertuously of his owne part beheld,
Doe in our eyes, begin to loose their glosse;
Yea, and like faire Fruit in an vnholdsome dish,
Are like to rot vntasted: goe and tell him,
We came to speake with him; and you shall not sinne,
If you doe say, we thinke him ouer proud,
And vnder honest; in selfe-assumption greater
Then in the note of iudgement: & worthier then himselfe
Here tends the sauage strangenesse he puts on,
Disguise the holy strength of their command:
And vnder write in an obseruing kinde
His humorous predominance, yea watch
His pettish lines, his ebs, his flowes, as if
The passage and whole carriage of this action
Rode on his tyde. Goe tell him this, and adde,
That if he ouerhold his price so much,
Weele none of him; but let him, like an Engin
Not portable, lye vnder this report.
Bring action hither, this cannot goe to warre:
A stirring Dwarfe, we doe allowance giue,
Before a sleeping Gyant: tell him so.
Pat. I shall, and bring his answere presently.
Aga. In second voyce weele not be satisfied,
We come to speake with him, *Vlisses* enter you.
Exit Vlisses.
Aiax. What is he more then another?
Aga. No more then what he thinkes he is.
Aia. Is he so much, doe you not thinke, he thinkes himselfe a better man then I am?
Ag. No question.
Aiax. Will you subscribe his thought, and say he is?
Ag. No, Noble *Aiax*, you are as strong, as valiant, as wise, no lesse noble, much more gentle, and altogether more tractable.
Aiax. Why should a man be proud? How doth pride grow? I know not what it is.
Aga. Your minde is the cleerer *Aiax*, and your vertues the fairer; he that is proud, eates vp himselfe; Pride is his owne Glasse, his owne trumpet, his owne Chronicle, and what euer praises it selfe but in the deede, deuoures the deede in the praise.
Enter Vlysses.
Aiax, I do hate a proud man, as I hate the ingendring of Toades.
Nest. Yet he loues himselfe: is't not strange?
Vlis. *Achilles* will not to the field to morrow.
Ag. What's his excuse?
Vlis. He doth relye on none,
But carries on the streame of his dispose,
Without obseruance or respect of any,
In will peculiar, and in selfe admission.
Aga. Why, will he not vpon our faire request,
Vntent his person, and share the ayre with vs?
Vlis. Things small as nothing, for requests sake onely
He makes important; possest he is with greatnesse,
And speakes not to himselfe, but with a pride
That quarrels at selfe-breath. Imagin'd wroth
Holds in his bloud such swolne and hot discourse,
That twixt his mentall and his actiue parts,
Kingdom'd *Achilles* in commotion rages,
And batters gainst it selfe; what should I say?
He is so plaguy proud, that the death tokens of it,
Cry no recouery.
Ag. Let *Aiax* goe to him.
Deare Lord, goe you and greete him in his Tent;
'Tis said he holds you well, and will be led
At your request a little from himselfe.
Vlis. O *Agamemnon*, let it not be so.
Weele consecrate the steps that *Aiax* makes,
When they goe from *Achilles*; shall the proud Lord,
That bastes his arrogance with his owne seame,
And neuer suffers matter of the world,
Enter his thoughts: saue such as doe reuolue
Aud ruminate himselfe. Shall he be worshipt,
Of that we hold an Idoll, more then hee?
No, this thrice worthy and right valiant Lord,
Must not so staule his Palme, nobly acquir'd,
Nor by my will assubiugate his merit,
As amply titled as *Achilles* is: by going to *Achilles*,
That were to enlard his fat already, pride,
And adde more Coles to Cancer, when he burnes
With entertaining great *Hiperion*.
This L. goe to him? *Iupiter* forbid,
And say in thunder, *Achilles* goe to him.
Nest O this is well, he rubs the veine of him.
Dio. And how his silence drinkes vp this applause.
Aia. If I goe to him, with my armed fist, Ile pash him ore the face.
Ag. O no, you shall not goe.
Aia. And a be proud with me, ile phese his pride: let me goe to him.
Vlis. Not for the worth that hangs vpon our quarrel.
Aia. A paultry insolent fellow.
Nest. How he describes himselfe.
Aia. Can he not be sociable?
Vlis. The Rauen chides blacknesse.
Aia. Ile let his humours bloud.
Ag. He will be the Physitian that should be the patient.
Aia. And all men were a my minde.
Vlis. Wit would be out of fashion.
Aia. A should not beare it so, a should eate Swords first: shall pride carry it?
Nest. And 'twould, you'ld carry halfe.
Vlis. A would haue ten shares.
Aia. I will knede him, Ile make him supple, hee's not yet through warme.
Nest. Force him with praises, poure in, poure in: his ambition is dry.
Vlis. My L. you feede too much on this dislike.
Nest. Our noble Generall, doe not doe so.
Diom. You must prepare to fight without *Achilles*.
Vlis. Why, 'tis this naming of him doth him harme.
Here is a man, but 'tis before his face,
I will be silent.
Nest. Wherefore should you so?

He

He is not emulous, as *Achilles* is.
Vlis. Know the whole world, he is as valiant.
Aia. A horson dog, that shal palter thus with vs, would he were a *Troian*.
Nest. What a vice were it in *Aiax* now———
Vlis. If he were proud.
Dio. Or couetous of praise
Vlis. I, or surley borne
Dio. Or strange, or selfe affected.
Vl. Thank the heauens L. thou art of sweet composure;
Praise him that got thee, she that gaue thee sucke:
Fame be thy Tutor, and thy parts of nature
Thrice fam'd beyond, beyond all erudition;
But he that disciplin'd thy armes to fight,
Let *Mars* deuide Eternity in twaine,
And giue him halfe, and for thy vigour,
Bull-bearing *Milo*: his addition yeelde
To sinnowie *Aiax*: I will not praise thy wisdome,
Which like a bourne, a pale, a shore confines
Thy spacious and dilated parts; here's *Nestor*
Instructed by the Antiquary times:
He must, he is, he cannot but be wise
But pardon Father *Nestor*, were your dayes
As greene as *Aiax* and your braine so temper'd,
You should not haue the eminence of him,
But be as *Aiax*.
Aia. Shall I call you Father?
Ulis. I my good Sonne.
Dio. Be rul'd by him Lord *Aiax*.
Vlis. There is no tarrying here, the Hart *Achilles*
Keepes thicket: please it our Generall,
To call together all his state of warre,
Fresh Kings are come to *Troy*; to morrow
We must with all our maine of power stand fast.
And here's a Lord, come Knights from East to West,
And cull their flowre, *Aiax* shall cope the best.
Ag. Goe we to Counsaile, let *Achilles* sleepe;
Light Botes may saile swift, though greater bulkes draw deepe. *Exeunt.*

Musicke sounds within.

Enter Pandarus and a Seruant.

Pan. Friend, you, pray you a word: Doe not you follow the yong Lord *Paris*?
Ser. I sir, when he goes before me.
Pan. You depend vpon him I meane?
Ser. Sir, I doe depend vpon the Lord.
Pan. You depend vpon a noble Gentleman: I must needes praise him.
Ser. The Lord be praised.
Pa. You know me, doe you not?
Ser. Faith sir, superficially.
Pa. Friend know me better, I am the Lord *Pandarus*.
Ser. I hope I shall know your honour better.
Pa. I doe desire it.
Ser. You are in the state of Grace?
Pa. Grace, not so friend, honor and Lordship are my title: What Musique is this?
Ser. I doe but partly know sir: it is Musicke in parts.
Pa. Know you the Musitians.
Ser. Wholly sir
Pa. Who play they to?
Ser. To the hearers sir.
Pa. At whose pleasure friend?
Ser. At mine sir, and theirs that loue Musicke.
Pa. Command, I meane friend.
Ser. Who shall I command sir?
Pa. Friend, we vnderstand not one another: I am too courtly, and thou art too cunning. At whose request doe these men play?
Ser. That's too't indeede sir: marry sir, at the request of *Paris* my L. who's there inperson: with him the mortall *Venus*, the heart bloud of beauty, loues inuisible soule.
Pa. Who? my Cosin *Cressida*.
Ser. No sir, *Helen*, could you not finde out that by her attributes?
Pa. It should seeme fellow, that thou hast not seen the Lady *Cressida*. I come to speake with *Paris* from the Prince *Troylus*: I will make a complementall assault vpon him, for my businesse seethes.
Ser. Sodden businesse, there's a stewed phrase indeede.

Enter Paris and Helena.

Pan. Faire be to you my Lord, and to all this faire company: faire desires in all faire measure fairely guide them, especially to you faire Queene, faire thoughts be your faire pillow.
Hel. Deere L. you are full of faire words.
Pan You speake your faire pleasure sweete Queene: faire Prince, here is good broken Musicke.
Par. You haue broke it cozen: and by my life you shall make it whole againe, you shall peece it out with a peece of your performance. *Nel*, he is full of harmony.
Pan. Truely Lady no.
Hel. O sir
Pan. Rude in sooth, in good sooth very rude.
Paris. Well said my Lord: well, you say so in fits.
Pan. I haue businesse to my Lord, deere Queene: my Lord will you vouchsafe me a word.
Hel. Nay, this shall not hedge vs out, weele heare you sing certainely.
Pan. Well sweete Queene you are pleasant with me, but, marry thus my Lord, my deere Lord, and most esteemed friend your brother *Troylus*
Hel. My Lord *Pandarus*, hony sweete Lord.
Pan. Go too sweete Queene, goe to.
Commends himselfe most affectionately to you.
Hel You shall not bob vs out of our melody:
If you doe, our melancholly vpon your head.
Pan Sweete Queene, sweete Queene, that's a sweete Queene Ifaith———
Hel. And to make a sweet Lady sad, is a sower offence.
Pan. Nay, that shall not serue your turne, that shall it not in truth la. Nay, I care not for such words, no, no. And my Lord he desires you, that if the King call for him at Supper, you will make his excuse.
Hel. My Lord *Pandarus*?
Pan. What saies my sweete Queene, my very, very sweete Queene?
Par. What exploit's in hand, where sups he to night?
Hel. Nay but my Lord?
Pan. What saies my sweete Queene? my cozen will fall out with you.
Hel. You must not know where he sups.
Par. With my disposer *Cressida*.
Pan. No, no; no such matter, you are wide, come your disposer is sicke.
Par. Well, Ile make excuse.
Pan. I good my Lord: why should you say *Cressida*? no, your poore disposer's sicke.
Par. I spie.

Pan. You

Pan. You ſpie, what doe you ſpie : come, giue me an Inſtrument now ſweete Queene.

Hel. Why this is kindely done?

Pan. My Neece is horrible in loue with a thing you haue ſweete Queene.

Hel. She ſhall haue it my Lord, if it be not my Lord *Paris.*

Pand. Hee? no, ſheele none of him, they two are twaine.

Hel. Falling in after falling out, may make them three.

Pan. Come, come, Ile heare no more of this, Ile ſing you a ſong now.

Hel. I, I, prethee now: by my troth ſweet Lord thou haſt a fine fore-head.

Pan. I you may, you may.

Hel. Let thy ſong be loue: this loue will vndoe vs all Oh *Cupid, Cupid, Cupid.*

Pan. Loue? I that it ſhall yfaith.

Par. I, good now loue, leue, no thing but loue.

Pan. In good troth it begins ſo.

Loue, loue, nothing but loue, ſtill more:
For O loues Bow,
Shootes Bucke and Doe:
The Shaft confounds not that it wounds,
But tickles ſtill the ſore:
Theſe Louers cry, oh ho they dye;
Yet that which ſeemes the wound to kill,
Doth turne oh ho, to ha ha he:
So dying loue liues ſtill,
O ho a while, but ha ha ha,
O ho grones out for ha ha ha——hey ho.

Hel. In loue yfaith to the very tip of the noſe.

Par. He eates nothing but doues loue, and that breeds hot bloud, and hot bloud begets hot thoughts, and hot thoughts beget hot deedes, and hot deedes is loue.

Pan. Is this the generation of loue? Hot bloud, hot thoughts, and hot deedes, why they are Vipers, is Loue a generation of Vipers?
Sweete Lord whoſe a field to day?

Par. *Hector, Deiphœbus, Helenus, Anthenor,* and all the gallantry of *Troy.* I would faine haue arm'd to day, but my *Nell* would not haue it ſo.
How chance my brother *Troylus* went not?

Hel. He hangs the lippe at ſomething; you know all Lord *Pandarus?*

Pan. Not I hony ſweete Queene: I long to heare how they ſped to day:
Youle remember your brothers excuſe?

Par. To a hayre.

Pan. Farewell ſweete Queene.

Hel. Commend me to your Neece.

Pan. I will ſweete Queene. *Sound a retreat.*

Par. They're come from fielde: let vs to *Priams* Hall
To greete the Warriers. Sweet *Hellen,* I muſt woe you,
To helpe vnarme our *Hector*: his ſtubborne Buckles,
With theſe your white enchanting fingers toucht,
Shall more obey then to the edge of Steele,
Or force of Greekiſh ſinewes: you ſhall doe more
Then all the Iland Kings, diſarme great *Hector.*

Hel. 'Twill make vs proud to be his ſeruant *Paris*:
Yea what he ſhall receiue of vs in duetie,
Giues vs more palme in beautie then we haue:
Yea ouerſhines our ſelfe.
Sweete aboue thought I loue thee. *Exeunt.*

Enter Pandarus and Troylus Man.

Pan. How now, where's thy Maiſter, at my Couzen *Creſsidas?*

Man. No ſir, he ſtayes for you to conduct him thither.

Enter Troylus.

Pan. O here he comes: How now, how now?

Troy. Sirra walke off.

Pan. Haue you ſeene my Couſin?

Troy. No *Pandarus*: I ſtalke about her doore
Like a ſtrange ſoule vpon the Stigian bankes
Staying for waftage. O be thou my *Charon,*
And giue me ſwift tranſportance to thoſe fields,
Where I may wallow in the Lilly beds
Propos'd for the deſeruer. O gentle *Pandarus,*
From *Cupids* ſhoulder plucke his painted wings,
And flye with me to *Creſsid.*

Pan. Walke here ith' Orchard, Ile bring her ſtraight. *Exit Pandarus.*

Troy. I am giddy; expectation whirles me round,
Th'imaginary reliſh is ſo ſweete,
That it inchants my ſence: what will it be
When that the watry pallats taſte indeede
Loues thrice reputed Nectar? Death I feare me
Sounding diſtruction, or ſome ioy too fine,
Too ſubtile, potent, and too ſharpe in ſweetneſſe,
For the capacitie of my ruder powers;
I feare it much, and I doe feare beſides,
That I ſhall looſe diſtinction in my ioyes,
As doth a battaile, when they charge on heapes
The enemy flying. *Enter Pandarus.*

Pan. Shee's making her ready, ſheele come ſtraight; you muſt be witty now, ſhe does ſo bluſh, & fetches her winde ſo ſhort, as if ſhe were fraid with a ſprite: Ile fetch her; it is the prettieſt villaine, ſhe fetches her breath ſo ſhort as a new tane Sparrow. *Exit Pand.*

Troy. Euen ſuch a paſſion doth imbrace my boſome:
My heart beates thicker then a feauorous pulſe,
And all my powers doe their beſtowing looſe,
Like vaſſalage at vnawares encountring
The eye of Maieſtie.

Enter Pandarus and Creſsida.

Pan. Come, come, what neede you bluſh? Shames a babie; here ſhe is now, ſweare the oathes now to her, that you haue ſworne to me. What are you gone againe, you muſt be watcht ere you be made tame, muſt you? come your wayes, come your wayes, and you draw backward weele put you i'th fils: why doe you not ſpeak to her? Come draw this curtaine, & let's ſee your picture. Alaſſe the day, how loath you are to offend day light? and 'twere darke you'ld cloſe ſooner: So, ſo, rub on, and kiſſe the miſtreſſe; how now, a kiſſe in fee-farme? build there Carpenter, the ayre is ſweete. Nay, you ſhall fight your hearts out ere I part you. The Faulcon, as the Tercell, for all the Ducks ith Riuer: go too, go too.

Troy. You haue bereft me of all words Lady.

Pan. Words pay no debts; giue her deedes: but ſheele bereaue you 'oth' deeds too, if ſhee call your actiuity in queſtion: what billing againe? here's in witneſſe whereof the Parties interchangeably. Come in, come in, Ile go get a fire?

Cres. Will you walke in my Lord?

Troy. O *Creſsida,* how often haue I wiſht me thus?

Cres. Wiſht my Lord? the gods grant? O my Lord.

Troy. What ſhould they grant? what makes this pretty abruption: what too curious dreg eſpies my ſweete Lady in the fountaine of our loue?

Cres. More

Creſ. More dregs then water, if my teares haue eyes.

Troy. Feares make diuels of Cherubins, they neuer ſee truely.

Creſ. Blinde feare, that ſeeing reaſon leads, findes ſafe footing, then blinde reaſon, ſtumbling without feare: to feare the worſt, oft cures the worſe.

Troy. Oh let my Lady apprehend no feare,
In all *Cupids* Pageant there is preſented no monſter

Creſ. Not nothing monſtrous neither?

Troy. Nothing but our vndertakings, when we vowe to weepe ſeas, liue in fire, eate rockes, tame Tygers; thinking it harder for our Miſtreſſe to deuiſe impoſition inough, then for vs to vndergoe any difficultie impoſed. This is the monſtruoſitie in loue Lady, that the will is infinite, and the execution confin'd; that the deſire is boundleſſe, and the act a ſlaue to limit.

Creſ. They ſay all Louers ſweare more performance then they are able, and yet reſerue an ability that they neuer performe: vowing more then the perfection of ten; and diſcharging leſſe then the tenth part of one. They that haue the voyce of Lyons, and the act of Hares: are they not Monſters?

Troy. Are there ſuch? ſuch are not we: Praiſe vs as we are taſted, allow vs as we proue: our head ſhall goe bare till merit crowne it: no perfection in reuerſion ſhall haue a praiſe in preſent: wee will not name deſert before his birth, and being borne his addition ſhall be humble: few words to faire faith. *Troylus* ſhall be ſuch to *Creſſid*, as what enuie can ſay worſt, ſhall be a mocke for his truth; and what truth can ſpeake trueſt, not truer then *Troylus*.

Creſ. Will you walke in my Lord?

Enter Pandarus.

Pan. What bluſhing ſtill? haue you not done talking yet?

Creſ. Well Vnckle, what folly I commit, I dedicate to you.

Pan. I thanke you for that: if my Lord get a Boy of you, youle giue him me: be true to my Lord, if he flinch, chide me for it.

Tro. You know now your hoſtages: your Vnckles word and my firme faith.

Pan. Nay, Ile giue my word for her too: our kindred though they be long ere they are wooed, they are conſtant being wonne: they are Burres I can tell you, they'le ſticke where they are throwne.

Creſ. Boldneſſe comes to mee now, and brings mee heart: Prince *Troylus*, I haue lou'd you night and day, for many weary moneths.

Troy. Why was my *Creſſid* then ſo hard to win?

Creſ Hard to ſeeme won: but I was won my Lord
With the firſt glance; that euer pardon me,
If I confeſſe much you will play the tyrant:
I loue you now, but not till now ſo much
But I might maiſter it; infaith I lye:
My thoughts were like vnbrideled children grow
Too head-ſtrong for their mother: ſee we fooles,
Why haue I blab'd: who ſhall be true to vs
When we are ſo vnſecret to our ſelues?
But though I lou'd you well, I woed you not,
And yet good faith I-wiſht my ſelfe a man;
Or that we women had mens priuiledge
Of ſpeaking firſt. Sweet, bid me hold my tongue,
For in this rapture I ſhall ſurely ſpeake
The thing I ſhall repent: ſee, ſee, your ſilence
Comming in dumbneſſe, from my weakeneſſe drawes
My ſoule of counſell from me. Stop my mouth.

Troy. And ſhall, albeit ſweete Muſicke iſſues thence.

Pan. Pretty yfaith.

Creſ. My Lord, I doe beſeech you pardon me,
'Twas not my purpoſe thus to beg a kiſſe:
I am aſham'd; O Heauens, what haue I done!
For this time will I take my leaue my Lord.

Troy. Your leaue ſweete *Creſſid*?

Pan. Leaue: and you take leaue till to morrow morning.

Creſ. Pray you content you.

Troy. What offends yo Lady?

Creſ. Sir, mine owne company.

Troy. You cannot ſhun your ſelfe.

Creſ. Let me goe and try.
I haue a kinde of ſelfe recides with you:
But an vnkinde ſelfe, that it ſelfe will leaue,
To be anothers foole. Where is my wit?
I would be gone: I ſpeake I know not what.

Troy. Well know they what they ſpeake, that ſpeakes ſo wiſely.

Cre. Perchance my Lord, I ſhew more craft then loue,
And fell ſo roundly to a large confeſſion,
To Angle for your thoughts: but you are wiſe,
Or elſe you loue not: for to be wiſe and loue,
Exceedes mans might, that dwels with gods aboue.

Troy. O that I thought it could be in a woman:
As if it can, I will preſume in you,
To feede for aye her lampe and flames of loue.
To keepe her conſtancie in plight and youth,
Out-liuing beauties outward, with a minde
That doth renew ſwifter then blood decaies:
Or that perſwaſion could but thus conuince me,
That my integritie and truth to you,
Might be affronted with the match and waight
Of ſuch a winnowed puriritie in loue:
How were I then vp-lifted! but alas,
I am as true, as truths ſimplicitie,
And ſimpler then the infancie of truth.

Creſ. In that Ile warre with you.

Troy. O vertuous fight,
When right with right wars who ſhall be moſt right:
True ſwaines in loue, ſhall in the world to come
Approue their truths by *Troylus*, when their rimes,
Full of proteſt, of oath and big compare;
Wants ſimiles, truth tir'd with iteration,
As true as ſteele, as plantage to the Moone:
As Sunne to day: as Turtle to her mate:
As Iron to Adamant: as Earth to th'Center:
Yet after all compariſons of truth,
(As truths authenticke author to be cited)
As true as *Troylus*, ſhall crowne vp the Verſe,
And ſanctifie the numbers.

Creſ Prophet may you be:
If I be falſe, or ſwerue a haire from truth,
When time is old and hath forgot it ſelfe:
When water drops haue worne the Stones of *Troy*;
And blinde obliuion ſwallow'd Cities vp;
And mightie States characterleſſe are grated
To duſtie nothing; yet let memory,
From falſe to falſe, among falſe Maids in loue,
Vpbraid my falſehood, when they'aue ſaid as falſe,
As Aire, as Water, as Winde, as ſandie earth;
As Foxe to Lambe; as Wolfe to Heifers Calfe;
Pard to the Hinde, or Stepdame to her Sonne;
Yea, let them ſay, to ſticke the heart of falſehood,

As

As false as *Cressid.*

Pand. Go too, a bargaine made: seale it, seale it, Ile be the witnesse here I hold your hand: here my Cousins, if euer you proue false one to another, since I haue taken such paines to bring you together, let all pittifull goers betweene be cal'd to the worlds end after my name: call them all Panders; let all constant men be *Troylusses*, all false women *Cressids*, and all brokers betweene, Panders: say, Amen.

Troy. Amen.

Cres. Amen.

Pan. Amen.

Whereupon I will shew you a Chamber, which bed, because it shall not speake of your prettie encounters, presse it to death: away.

And *Cupid* grant all tong-tide Maidens heere,
Bed, Chamber, and Pander, to prouide this geere. *Exeunt.*

Enter Vlysses, Diomedes, Nestor, Agamemnon, Menelaus and Chalcas. Florish.

Cal. Now Princes for the seruice I haue done you,
Th'aduantage of the time promps me aloud,
To call for recompence: appeare it to your minde,
That through the sight I beare in things to loue,
I haue abandon'd Troy, left my possession,
Incur'd a Traitors name, expos'd my selfe,
From certaine and possest conueniences,
To doubtfull fortunes, sequestring from me all
That time, acquaintance, custome and condition,
Made tame, and most familiar to my nature:
And here to doe you seruice am become,
As new into the world, strange, vnacquainted.
I doe beseech you, as in way of taste,
To giue me now a little benefit:
Out of those many registred in promise,
Which you say, liue to come in my behalfe.

Agam. What would'st thou of vs Troian? make demand?

Cal. You haue a Troian prisoner, cal'd *Anthenor*,
Yesterday tooke: Troy holds him very deere.
Oft haue you (often haue you, thankes therefore)
Desir'd my *Cressia* in right great exchange.
Whom Troy hath still deni'd: but this *Anthenor*,
I know is such a wrest in their affaires;
That their negotiations all must slacke,
Wanting his mannage: and they will almost,
Giue vs a Prince of blood, a Sonne of *Priam*,
In change of him. Let him be sent great Princes,
And he shall buy my Daughter: and her presence,
Shall quite strike off all seruice I haue done,
In most accepted paine.

Aga. Let *Diomedes* beare him,
And bring vs *Cressid* hither: *Calcas* shall haue
What he requests of vs: good *Diomed*
Furnish you fairely for this enterchange;
Withall bring word, if *Hector* will to morrow
Be answer'd in his challenge. *Aiax* is ready.

Dio. This shall I vndertake, and 'tis a burthen
Which I am proud to beare. *Exit.*

Enter Achilles *and* Patroclus *in their Tent.*

Vlis. *Achilles* stands i'th entrance of his Tent;
Please it our Generall to passe strangely by him,
As if he were forgot: and Princes all,
Lay negligent and loose regard vpon him;
I will come last, 'tis like heele question me,
Why such vnplausiue eyes are bent? why turn'd on him?
If so, I haue derision medicinable,
To vse betweene your strangenesse and his pride,
Which his owne will shall haue desire to drinke;
It may doe good, pride hath no other glasse
To show it selfe, but pride: for supple knees,
Feede arrogance, and are the proud mans fees.

Agam. Weele execute your purpose, and put on
A forme of strangenesse as we passe along,
So doe each Lord, and either greete him not,
Or else disdainfully, which shall shake him more,
Then if not lookt on. I will lead the way.

Achil. What comes the Generall to speake with me?
You know my minde, Ile fight no more 'gainst Troy.

Aga. What saies *Achilles*, would he ought with vs?

Nes. Would you my Lord ought with the Generall?

Achil. No.

Nes. Nothing my Lord.

Aga. The better.

Achil. Good day, good day.

Men. How doe you? how doe you?

Achi. What, do's the Cuckold scorne me?

Aiax. How now *Patroclus*?

Achil. Good morrow *Aiax*?

Aiax. Ha.

Achil. Good morrow.

Aiax. I, and good next day too. *Exeunt.*

Achil. What meane these fellowes? know they not *Achilles*?

Patr. They passe by strangely: they were vs'd to bend
To send their smiles before them to *Achilles*:
To come as humbly as they vs'd to creepe to holy Altars.

Achil. What am I poore of late?
Tis certaine, greatnesse once falne out with fortune,
Must fall out with men too: what the declin'd is,
He shall as soone reade in the eyes of others,
As feele in his owne fall: for men like butter-flies,
Shew not their mealie wings, but to the Summer:
And not a man for being simply man,
Hath any honour; but honour'd for those honours
That are without him; as place, riches, and fauour,
Prizes of accident, as oft as merit:
Which when they fall, as being slippery standers;
The loue that leand on them as slippery too,
Doth one plucke downe another, and together
Dye in the fall. But 'tis not so with me;
Fortune and I are friends, I doe enioy
At ample point, all that I did possesse,
Saue these mens lookes: who do me thinkes finde out
Something not worth in me such rich beholding,
As they haue often giuen. Here is *Vlisses*,
Ile interrupt his reading: how now *Vlisses*?

Vlis. Now great *Thetis* Sonne.

Achil. What are you reading?

Vlis. A strange fellow here
Writes me, that man, how dearely euer parted,
How much in hauing, or without, or in,
Cannot make boast to haue that which he hath;
Nor feeles not what he owes, but by reflection:
As when his vertues shining vpon others,
Heate them, and they retort that heate againe
To the first giuer.

Achil. This is not strange *Vlisses*:
The beautie that is borne here in the face,
The bearer knowes not, but commends it selfe,
Not going from it selfe: but eye to eye oppos'd,

Salutes

Salutes each other with each others forme
For speculation turnes not to it selfe,
Till it hath trauail'd, and is married there
Where it may see it selfe : this is not strange at all.
Vlis. I doe not straine it at the position,
It is familiar ; but at the Authors drift,
Who in his circumstance, expresly proues
That no may is the Lord of any thing,
(Though in and of him there is much consisting,)
Till he communicate his parts to others :
Nor doth he of himselfe know them for ought,
Till he behold them formed in th'applause,
Where they are extended : who like an arch reuerb'rate
The voyce againe ; or like a gate of steele,
Fronting the Sunne, receiues and renders backe
His figure, and his heate. I was much rapt in this,
And apprehended here immediately :
The vnknowne *Aiax* ;
Heauens what a man is there? a very Horse, (are
That has he knowes not what. Nature, what things there
Most abiect in regard, and deare in vse.
What things againe most deere in the esteeme,
And poore in worth : now shall we see to morrow,
An act that very chance doth throw vpon him?
Aiax renown'd ? O heauens, what some men doe,
While some men leaue to doe !
How some men creepe in skittish fortunes hall,
Whiles others play the Ideots in her eyes :
How one man eates into anothers pride,
While pride is feasting in his wantonnesse
To see these Grecian Lords ; why, euen already,
They clap the lubber *Aiax* on the shoulder,
As if his foote were on braue *Hectors* brest,
And great *Troy* shrinking.
Achil. I doe beleeue it :
For they past by me, as mysers doe by beggars,
Neither gaue to me good word, nor looke:
What are my deedes forgot?
Vlis. Time hath (my Lord) a wallet at his backe,
Wherein he puts almes for obliuion :
A great siz'd monster of ingratitudes :
Those scraps are good deedes past,
Which are deuour'd as fast as they are made,
Forgot as soone as done : perseuerance, deere my Lord,
Keepes honor bright, to haue done, is to hang
Quite out of fashion, like a rustie male,
In monumentall mockrie : take the instant way,
For honour trauels in a straight so narrow,
Where one but goes a breast, keepe then the path:
For emulation hath a thousand Sonnes,
That one by one pursue ; if you giue way,
Or hedge aside from the direct forth right ;
Like to an entred Tyde, they all rush by,
And leaue you hindmost :
Or like a gallant Horse falne in first ranke,
Lye there for pauement to the abiect, neere
Ore-run and trampled on : then what they doe in present,
Though lesse then yours in past, must ore-top yours :
For time is like a fashionable Hoste,
That slightly shakes his parting Guest by th'hand;
And with his armes out-stretcht, as he would flye,
Graspes in the commer : the welcome euer smiles,
And farewels goes out sighing : O let not vertue seeke
Remuneration for the thing it was : for beautie, wit,
High birth, vigor of bone, desert in seruice,
Loue, friendship, charity, are subiects all
To enuious and calumniating time:
One touch of nature makes the whole world kin :
That all with one consent praise new borne gaudes,
Though they are made and moulded of things past,
And goe to dust, that is a little guilt,
More laud then guilt oredusted.
The present eye praises the present obiect :
Then maruell not thou great and compleat man,
That all the Greekes begin to worship *Aiax* ;
Since things in motion begin to catch the eye,
Then what not stirs : the cry went out on thee,
And still it might, and yet it may againe,
If thou would'st not entombe thy selfe aliue,
And case thy reputation in thy Tent ;
Whose glorious deedes, but in these fields of late,
Made emulous missions 'mongst the gods themselues,
And draue great *Mars* to faction.
Achil. Of this my priuacie,
I haue strong reasons.
Vlis. But 'gainst your priuacie
The reasons are more potent and heroycall :
'Tis knowne *Achilles*, that you are in loue
With one of *Priams* daughters.
Achil. Ha ? knowne ?
Vlis. Is that a wonder ?
The prouidence that's in a watchfull State,
Knowes almost euery graine of Plutoes gold ;
Findes bottome in th'vncomprehensiue deepes ;
Keepes place with thought ; and almost like the gods,
Doe thoughts vnuaile in their dumbe cradles :
There is a mysterie (with whom relation
Durst neuer meddle) in the soule of State ;
Which hath an operation more diuine,
Then breath or pen can giue expressure to :
All the commerse that you haue had with Troy,
As perfectly is ours, as yours, my Lord.
And better would it fit *Achilles* much,
To throw downe *Hector* then *Polixena*.
But it must grieue yong *Pirhus* now at home,
When fame shall in her Hand sound her trumpe ;
And all the Greekish Girles shall tripping sing,
Great *Hectors* sister did *Achilles* winne ;
But our great *Aiax* brauely beate downe him.
Farewell my Lord : I as your louer speake ;
The foole slides ore the Ice that you should breake.
Patr. To this effect *Achilles* haue I mou'd you ;
A woman impudent and mannish growne,
Is not more loth'd, then an effeminate man,
In time of action : I stand condemn'd for this ;
They thinke my little stomacke to the warre,
And your great loue to me, restraines you thus :
Sweete, rouse your selfe; and the weake wanton *Cupid*
Shall from your necke vnloose his amorous fould,
And like a dew drop from the Lyons mane,
Be shooke to ayrie ayre.
Achil. Shall *Aiax* fight with *Hector* ?
Patr. I, and perhaps receiue much honor by him.
Achil. I see my reputation is at stake,
My fame is shrowdly gored.
Patr. O then beware :
Those wounds heale ill, that men doe giue themselues
Omission to doe what is necessary,
Seales a commission to a blanke of danger,
And danger like an ague subtly taints
Euen then when we sit idely in the sunne.
Achil. Goe call *Thersites* hither sweet *Patroclus*,

¶ ¶ Ile

Ile send the foole to *Aiax*, and desire him
T'inuite the Troian Lords after the Combat
To see vs here vnarm'd: I haue a womans longing,
An appetite that I am sicke withall,
To see great *Hector* in his weedes of peace; *Enter Thersi.*
To talke with him, and to behold his visage,
Euen to my full of view. A labour sau'd.

Ther. A wonder.

Achil. What?

Ther. *Aiax* goes vp and downe the field, asking for himselfe.

Achil. How so?

Ther. Hee must fight singly to morrow with *Hector*, and is so prophetically proud of an heroicall cudgelling, that he raues in saying nothing.

Achil. How can that be?

Ther. Why he stalkes vp and downe like a Peacock, a stride and a stand: ruminates like an hostesse, that hath no Arithmatique but her braine to set downe her reckoning: bites his lip with a politique regard, as who should say, there were wit in his head and twoo'd out; and so there is: but it lyes as coldly in him, as fire in a flint, which will not shew without knocking. The mans vndone for euer; for if *Hector* breake not his necke i'th'combat, heele break't himselfe in vaine-glory. He knowes not mee: I said, good morrow *Aiax*; And he replyes, thankes *Agamemnon*. What thinke you of this man, that takes me for the Generall? Hee's growne a very land-fish, languagelesse, a monster: a plague of opinion, a man may weare it on both sides like a leather Ierkin.

Achil. Thou must be my Ambassador to him *Thersites*.

Ther. Who, I: why, heele answer no body: he professes notanswering; speaking is for beggers: he weares his tongue in's armes: I will put on his presence; let *Patroclus* make his demands to me, you shall see the Pageant of *Aiax*.

Achil. To him *Patroclus*; tell him, I humbly desire the valiant *Aiax*, to inuite the most valorous *Hector*, to come vnarm'd to my Tent, and to procure safe conduct for his person, of the magnanimious and most illustrious, sixe or seauen times honour'd Captaine, Generall of the Grecian Armie *Agamemnon*, &c. doe this.

Patro. *Ioue* blesse great *Aiax*.

Ther. Hum.

Patr. I come from the worthy *Achilles*.

Ther. Ha?

Patr. Who most humbly desires you to inuite *Hector* to his Tent.

Ther. Hum.

Patr. And to procure safe conduct from *Agamemnon*.

Ther. *Agamemnon*?

Patr. I my Lord.

Ther. Ha?

Patr. What say you too't.

Ther. God buy you with all my heart

Patr. Your answer sir.

Ther. If to morrow be a faire day, by eleuen a clocke it will goe one way or other; howsoeuer, he shall pay for me ere he has me.

Patr Your answer sir.

Ther Fare you well withall my heart.

Achil. Why, but he is not in this tune, is he?

Ther. No, but he's out a tune thus: what musicke will be in him when *Hector* has knockt out his braines, I know not: but I am sure none, vnlesse the Fidler *Apollo* get his sinewes to make catlings on.

Achil. Come, thou shalt beare a Letter to him straight.

Ther Let me carry another to his Horse; for that's the more capable creature.

Achil. My minde is troubled like a Fountaine stir'd,
And I my selfe see not the bottome of it.

Ther. Would the Fountaine of your minde were cleere againe, that I might water an Asse at it: I had rather be a Ticke in a Sheepe, then such a valiant ignorance.

Enter at one doore Æneas with a Torch, at another Paris, Diephœbus, Anthenor, Diomed the Grecian, with Torches.

Par. See hoa, who is that there?

Dieph. It is the Lord *Æneas*.

Æne. Is the Prince there in person?
Had I so good occasion to lye long
As you Prince *Paris*, nothing but heauenly businesse,
Should rob my bed-mate of my company.

Diom. That's my minde too: good morrow Lord *Æneas*.

Par. A valiant Greeke *Æneas*, take his hand,
Witnesse the processe of your speech within;
You told how *Diomed* in a whole weeke by dayes
Did haunt you in the Field.

Æne. Health to you valiant sir,
During all question of the gentle truce:
But when I meete you arm'd, as blacke defiance,
As heart can thinke, or courage execute.

Diom. The one and other *Diomed* embraces,
Our bloods are now in calme; and so long health.
But when contention, and occasion meetes,
By *Ioue*, Ile play the hunter for thy life,
With all my force, pursuite and pollicy.

Æne. And thou shalt hunt a Lyon that will flye
With his face backward, in humaine gentlenesse:
Welcome to Troy; now by *Anchises* life,
Welcome indeede: by *Venus* hand I sweare,
No man aliue can loue in such a sort,
The thing he meanes to kill, more excellently.

Diom. We simpathize. *Ioue* let *Æneas* liue
(If to my sword his fate be not the glory)
A thousand compleate courses of the Sunne,
But in mine emulous honor let him dy
With euery ioynt a wound, and that to morrow.

Æne. We know each other well.

Dio. We doe, and long to know each other worse.

Par. This is the most, despightful'st gentle greeting;
The noblest hatefull loue, that ere I heard of.
What businesse Lord so early?

Æne. I was sent for to the King; but why, I know not.

Par. His purpose meets you; it was to bring this Greek
To *Calcha's* house; and there to render him,
For the enfreed *Anthenor*, the faire *Cressid*:
Lets haue your company; or if you please,
Haste there before vs. I constantly doe thinke
(Or rather call my thought a certaine knowledge)
My brother *Troylus* lodges there to night.
Rouse him, and giue him note of our approach,
With the whole quality whereof, I feare
We shall be much vnwelcome.

Æne. That I assure you:
Troylus had rather Troy were borne to Greece,
Then *Cressid* borne from Troy.

Par. There

Par. There is no helpe:
The bitter disposition of the time will haue it so.
On Lord, weele follow you.
Æne. Good morrow all. *Exit Æneas*
Par. And tell me noble *Diomed*; faith tell me true,
Euen in the soule of sound good fellow ship,
Who in your thoughts merits faire *Helen* most?
My selfe, or *Menelaus*?
Diom. Both alike.
He merits well to haue her, that doth seeke her,
Not making any scruple of her soylure,
With such a hell of paine, and world of charge.
And you as well to keepe her, that defend her,
Not pallating the taste of her dishonour,
With such a costly losse of wealth and friends:
He like a puling Cuckold, would drinke vp
The lees and dregs of a flat tamed peece:
You like a letcher, out of whorish loynes,
Are pleas'd to breede out your inheritors:
Both merits poyz'd, each weighs no lesse nor more,
But he as he, which heauier for a whore.
Par. You are too bitter to your country-woman.
Dio. Shee's bitter to her countrey: heare me *Paris*,
For euery false drop in her baudy veines,
A Grecians life hath sunke: for euery scruple
Of her contaminated carrion weight,
A Troian hath beene slaine. Since she could speake,
She hath not giuen so many good words breath,
As for her, Greekes and Troians suffred death.
Par. Faire *Diomed*, you doe as chapmen doe,
Dispraise the thing that you desire to buy:
But we in silence hold this vertue well;
Weele not commend, what we intend to sell.
Here lyes our way. *Exeunt.*

Enter Troylus and Cressida.

Troy. Deere trouble not your selfe: the morne is cold.
Cres. Then sweet my Lord, Ile call mine Vnckle down;
He shall vnbolt the Gates.
Troy. Trouble him not:
To bed, to bed: sleepe kill those pritty eyes,
And giue as soft attachment to thy sences,
As Infants empty of all thought.
Cres. Good morrow then.
Troy. I prithee now to bed.
Cres. Are you a weary of me?
Troy. O *Cressida*! but that the busie day
Wak't by the Larke, hath rouz'd the ribauld Crowes,
And dreaming night will hide our eyes no longer:
I would not from thee.
Cres. Night hath beene too briefe.
Troy. Beshrew the witch! with venemous wights she (stayes,
As hidiously as hell; but flies the graspes of loue,
With wings more momentary, swift then thought:
You will catch cold, and curse me.
Cres. Prithee tarry you men will neuer tarry;
O foolish *Cressid*, I might haue still held off,
And then you would haue tarried. Harke, ther's one vp?
Pand. within. What's all the doores open here?
Troy. It is your Vnckle. *Enter Pandarus.*
Cres. A pestilence on him: now will he be mocking:
I shall haue such a life.
Pan. How now, how now? how goe maiden-heads?
Heare you Maide: wher's my cozin *Cressid*?
Cres. Go hang your self, you naughty mocking Vnckle:
You bring me to doo----and then you floute me too.
Pan. To do what? to do what? let her say what:
What haue I brought you to doe?
Cres. Come, come, beshrew your heart: youle nere be good, nor suffer others.
Pan. Ha, ha: alas poore wretch: a poore *Chipochia*, hast not slept to night? would he not (a naughty man) let it sleepe: a bug-beare take him. *One knocks.*
Cres. Did not I tell you? would he were knockt ith' head. Who's that at doore? good Vnckle goe and see.
My Lord, come you againe into my Chamber:
You smile and mocke me, as if I meant naughtily.
Troy. Ha, ha.
Cre. Come you are deceiu'd, I thinke of no such thing.
How earnestly they knocke: pray you come in. *Knocke.*
I would not for halfe *Troy* haue you seene here. *Exeunt.*
Pan. Who's there? what's the matter? will you beate downe the doore? How now, what's the matter?
Æne. Good morrow Lord, good morrow
Pan. Who's there my Lord *Æneas*? by my troth I knew you not: what newes with you so early?
Æne Is not Prince *Troylus* here?
Pan. Here? what should he doe here?
Æne. Come he is here, my Lord, doe not deny him:
It doth import him much to speake with me.
Pan. Is he here say you? 'tis more then I know, Ile be sworne: For my owne part I came in late: what should he doe here?
Æne. Who, nay then: Come, come, youle doe him wrong, ere y'are ware: youle be so true to him, to be false to him: Doe not you know of him, but yet goe fetch him hither, goe.

Enter Troylus.

Troy. How now, what's the matter?
Æne. My Lord, I scarce haue leisure to salute you,
My matter is so rash: there is at hand,
Paris your brother, and *Deiphœbus*,
The Grecian *Diomed*, and our *Anthenor*
Deliuer'd to vs, and for him forth-with,
Ere the first sacrifice, within this houre,
We must giue vp to *Diomeds* hand
The Lady *Cressida*.
Troy. Is it concluded so?
Æne. By *Priam*, and the generall state of *Troy*,
They are at hand, and ready to effect it.
Troy. How my atchieuements mocke me;
I will goe meete them: and my Lord *Æneas*,
We met by chance; you did not finde me here.
Æn. Good, good, my Lord, the secrets of nature
Haue not more gift in taciturnitie. *Exeunt.*

Enter Pandarus and Cressid.

Pan. Is't possible? no sooner got but lost: the diuell take *Anthenor*; the yong Prince will goe mad: a plague vpon *Anthenor*: I would they had brok's necke.
Cres. How now? what's the matter? who was here?
Pan. Ah, ha!
Cres. Why sigh you so profoundly? wher's my Lord? gone? tell me sweet Vnckle, what's the matter?
Pan. Would I were as deepe vnder the earth as I am aboue.
Cres. O the gods! what's the matter?
Pan. Prythee get thee in: would thou had'st nere been borne; I knew thou would'st be his death. O poore Gentleman: a plague vpon *Anthenor*.

¶ ¶ 2 *Cres.* Good

Cres. Good Vnckle I beſeech you, on my knees, I beſeech you what's the matter?

Pan. Thou muſt be gone wench, thou muſt be gone; thou art chang'd for *Anthenor*: thou muſt to thy Father, and be gone from *Troylus*: 'twill be his death: 'twill be his baine, he cannot beare it..

Cres. O you immortall gods! I will not goe.

Pan. Thou muſt.

Cres. I will not Vnckle: I haue forgot my Father:
I know no touch of conſanguinitie:
No kin, no loue, no bloud, no ſoule, ſo neere me,
As the ſweet *Troylus*: O you gods diuine!
Make *Creſsids* name the very crowne of falſhood!
If euer ſhe leaue *Troylus*: time, orce and death,
Do to this body what extremitie you can;
But the ſtrong baſe and building of my loue,
Is as the very Center of the earth,
Drawing all things to it. I will goe in and weepe.

Pan. Doe, doe.

Cres. Teare my bright heire, and ſcratch my praiſed cheekes,
Cracke my cleere voyce with ſobs, and breake my heart
With ſounding *Troylus*. I will not goe from *Troy*. *Exeunt.*

Enter Paris, Troylus, Æneas, Deiphebus, Anthenor and Diomedes.

Par. It is great morning, and the houre prefixe
Of her deliuerie to this valiant Greeke
Comes faſt vpon: good my brother *Troylus*,
Tell you the Lady what ſhe is to doe,
And haſt her to the purpoſe.

Troy. Walke into her houſe:
Ile bring her to the Grecian preſently;
And to his hand, when I deliuer her,
Thinke it an Altar, and thy brother *Troylus*
A Prieſt, there offring to it his heart.

Par. I know what 'tis to loue,
And would, as I ſhall pittie, I could helpe.
Pleaſe you walke in, my Lords. *Exeunt.*

Enter Pandarus and Creſsid.

Pan. Be moderate, be moderate.

Cres. Why tell you me of moderation?
The griefe is fine, full perfect that I taſte,
And no leſſe in a ſenſe as ſtrong
As that which cauſeth it. How can I moderate it?
If I could temporiſe with my affection,
Or brew it to a weake and colder pallat,
The like alaiment could I giue my griefe:
My loue admits no qualifying croſſe; *Enter Troylus.*
No more my griefe, in ſuch a precious loſſe.

Pan. Here, here, here, he comes, a ſweet ducke.

Cres. O *Troylus*, *Troylus*!

Pan. What a paire of ſpectacles is here? let me embrace too: oh hart, as the goodly ſaying is; O heart, heauie heart, why ſigheſt thou without breaking? where he anſwers againe; becauſe thou canſt not eaſe thy ſmart by friendſhip, nor by ſpeaking: there was neuer a truer rime; let vs caſt away nothing, for we may liue to haue neede of ſuch a Verſe: we ſee it, we ſee it: how now Lambs?

Troy. *Creſsid*: I loue thee in ſo ſtrange a puritie;
That the bleſt gods, as angry with my fancie,
More bright in zeale, then the deuotion which
Cold lips blow to their Deities: take thee from me.

Cres. Haue the gods enuie?

Pan. I, I, I, I, 'tis too plaine a caſe.

Cres. And is it true, that I muſt goe from Troy?

Troy. A hatefull truth.

Cres. What, and from *Troylus* too?

Troy. From Troy, and *Troylus*.

Cres. Iſt poſsible?

Troy. And ſodainely, where iniurie of chance
Puts backe leaue-taking, iuſtles roughly by
All time of pauſe; rudely beguiles our lips
Of all reioyndure: forcibly preuents
Our lockt embraſures; ſtrangles our deare vowes,
Euen in the birth of our owne laboring breath.
We two, that with ſo many thouſand ſighes
Did buy each other, muſt poorely ſell our ſelues,
With the rude breuitie and diſcharge of our
Iniurious time; now with a robbers haſte
Crams his rich theeuerie vp, he knowes not how.
As many farwels as be ſtars in heauen,
With diſtinct breath, and conſign'd kiſſes to them,
He fumbles vp into a looſe adiew;
And ſcants vs with a ſingle famiſht kiſſe,
Diſtaſting with the ſalt of broken teares. *Enter Æneus.*

Æneas within. My Lord, is the Lady ready?

Troy. Harke, you are call'd: ſome ſay the genius ſo
Cries, come to him that inſtantly muſt dye.
Bid them haue patience: ſhe ſhall come anon.

Pan. Where are my teares? raine, to lay this winde, or my heart will be blowne vp by the root.

Cres. I muſt then to the Grecians?

Troy. No remedy.

Cres. A wofull *Creſsid* 'mong'ſt the merry Greekes.

Troy. When ſhall we ſee againe?

Troy. Here me my loue: be thou but true of heart.

Cres. I true? how now? what wicked deeme is this?

Troy. Nay, we muſt vſe expoſtulation kindely,
For it is parting from vs:
I ſpeake not, be thou true, as fearing thee:
For I will throw my Gloue to death himſelfe,
That there's no maculation in thy heart:
But be thou true, ſay I, to faſhion in
My ſequent proteſtation: be thou true,
And I will ſee thee.

Cres. O you ſhall be expos'd, my Lord to dangers
As infinite, as imminent: but Ile be true.

Troy. And Ile grow friend with danger;
Weare this Sleeue.

Cres. And you this Gloue.
When ſhall I ſee you?

Troy. I will corrupt the Grecian Centinels,
To giue thee nightly viſitation.
But yet be true.

Cres. O heauens: be true againe?

Troy. Heare why I ſpeake it; Loue:
The Grecian youths are full of qualitie,
Their louing well compos'd, with guiſt of nature,
Flawing and ſwelling ore with Arts and exerciſe:
How nouelties may moue, and parts with perſon.
Alas, a kinde of godly iealouſie;
Which I beſeech you call a vertuous ſinne:
Makes me affraid.

Cres. O heauens, you loue me not!

Troy. Dye I a villaine then:
In this I doe not call your faith in queſtion
So mainely as my merit: I cannot ſing,
Nor heele the high Lauolt; nor ſweeten talke;
Nor play at ſubtill games; faire vertues all;

To

To which the Grecians are moſt prompt and pregnant:
But I can tell that in each grace of theſe,
There lurkes a ſtill and dumb-diſcourſiue diuell,
That tempts moſt cunningly: but be not tempted.
Creſ. Doe you thinke I will:
Troy. No, but ſomething may be done that we wil not:
And ſometimes we are diuels to our ſelues,
When we will tempt the frailtie of our powers,
Preſuming on their changefull potencie.
Æneas within. Nay, good my Lord?
Troy. Come kiſſe, and let vs part.
Paris within. Brother *Troylus*?
Troy. Good brother come you hither,
And bring *Æneas* and the Grecian with you,
Creſ. My Lord, will you be true? *Exit*
Troy. Who I? alas it is my vice, my fault:
Whiles others fiſh with craft for great opinion,
I, with great truth, catch meere ſimplicitie;
Whil'ſt ſome with cunning guild their copper crownes,
With truth and plaineſſe I doe weare mine bare:
Enter the Greekes.
Feare not my truth; the morrall of my wit
Is plaine and true, ther's all the reach of it.
Welcome ſir *Diomed*, here is the Lady
Which for *Antenor*, we deliuer you.
At the port (Lord) Ile giue her to thy hand,
And by the way poſſeſſe thee what ſhe is
Entreate her faire; and by my ſoule, faire Greeke,
If ere thou ſtand at mercy of my Sword,
Name *Creſſid*, and thy life ſhall be as ſafe
As *Priam* is in Illion?
Diom. Faire Lady *Creſſid*,
So pleaſe you ſaue the thankes this Prince expects:
The luſtre in your eye, heauen in your cheeke,
Pleades your faire viſage, and to *Diomed*
You ſhall be miſtreſſe, and command him wholly.
Troy. Grecian, thou do'ſt not vſe me curteouſly,
To ſhame the ſeale of my petition towards,
I praiſing her. I tell thee Lord of Greece:
Shee is as farre high ſoaring o're thy praiſes,
As thou vnworthy to be cal'd her ſeruant:
I charge thee vſe her well, euen for my charge:
For by the dreadfull *Pluto*, if thou do'ſt not,
(Though the great bulke *Achilles* be thy guard)
Ile cut thy throate.
Diom. Oh be not mou'd Prince *Troylus*;
Let me be priuiledg'd by my place and meſſage,
To be a ſpeaker free? when I am hence,
Ile anſwer to my luſt: and know my Lord;
Ile nothing doe on charge: to her owne worth
She ſhall be priz'd: but that you ſay, be't ſo;
Ile ſpeake it in my ſpirit and honor, no.
Troy. Come to the Port. Ile tell thee *Diomed*,
This braue, ſhall oft make thee to hide thy head:
Lady giue me your hand, and as we walke,
To our owne ſelues bend we our needefull talke.
Sound Trumpet.
Par. Harke, *Hectors* Trumpet.
Æne. How haue we ſpent this morning
The Prince muſt thinke me tardy and remiſſe,
That ſwore to ride before him in the field.
Par. 'Tis *Troylus* fault: come, come, to field with him.
Exeunt.
Dio. Let vs make ready ſtraight.
Æne. Yea, with a Bridegroomes freſh alacritie
Let vs addreſſe to tend on *Hectors* heeles:
The glory of our *Troy* doth this day lye
On his faire worth, and ſingle Chiualrie.

Enter Aiax armed, Achilles, Patroclus, Agamemnon, Menelaus, Vliſſes, Neſter, Calcas, &c.

Aga. Here art thou in appointment freſh and faire,
Anticipating time. With ſtarting courage,
Giue with thy Trumpet a loud note to Troy
Thou dreadfull *Aiax*, that the appauled aire
May pierce the head of the great Combatant,
And hale him hither.
Aia. Thou, Trumpet, ther's my purſe;
Now cracke thy lungs, and ſplit thy braſen pipe:
Blow villaine, till thy ſphered Bias cheeke
Out-ſwell the collicke of puft *Aquilon*:
Come, ſtretch thy cheſt, and let thy eyes ſpout bloud:
Thou bloweſt for *Hector*.
Vliſ. No Trumpet anſwers.
Achil. 'Tis but early dayes.
Aga. Is not yong *Diomed* with *Calcas* daughter?
Vliſ. 'Tis he, I ken the manner of his gate,
He riſes on the toe: that ſpirit of his
In aſpiration lifts him from the earth.
Aga. Is this the Lady *Creſſid*?
Dio. Euen ſhe.
Aga. Moſt deerely welcome to the Greekes, ſweete Lady.
Neſt. Our Generall doth ſalute you with a kiſſe.
Vliſ. Yet is the kindeneſſe but particular; 'twere better ſhe were kiſt in generall.
Neſt. And very courtly counſell: Ile begin. So much for *Neſtor*.
Achil. Ile take that winter from your lips faire Lady *Achilles* bids you welcome.
Mene. I had good argument for kiſſing once.
Patro. But that's no argument for kiſſing now;
For thus pop't *Paris* in his hardiment.
Vliſ. Oh deadly gall, and theame of all our ſcornes,
For which we looſe our heads, to gild his hornes.
Patro. The firſt was *Menelaus* kiſſe, this mine:
Patroclus kiſſes you.
Mene. Oh this is trim.
Patr. *Paris* and I kiſſe euermore for him.
Mene. Ile haue my kiſſe ſir: Lady by your leaue.
Creſ. In kiſſing doe you render, or receiue.
Patr. Both take and giue.
Creſ. Ile make my match to liue,
The kiſſe you take is better then you giue: therefore no kiſſe.
Mene. Ile giue you boote, Ile giue you three for one.
Creſ. You are an odde man, giue euen, or giue none.
Mene. An odde man Lady, euery man is odde.
Creſ. No, *Paris* is not; for you know 'tis true,
That you are odde, and he is euen with you.
Mene. You fillip me a'th' head.
Creſ. No, Ile be ſworne.
Vliſ. It were no match, your naile againſt his horne:
May I ſweete Lady beg a kiſſe of you?
Creſ. You may.
Vliſ. I doe deſire it.
Creſ. Why begge then?
Vliſ. Why then for *Venus* ſake, giue me a kiſſe:
When *Hellen* is a maide againe, and his——
Creſ. I am your debtor, claime it when 'tis due.

¶ g 3 *Vliſ.* Neuer's

Vliſ. Neuer's my day, and men a kiſſe of you.
Diom. Lady a word, Ile bring you to your Father
Neſt. A woman of quicke ſence.
Vliſ. Fie, fie, vpon her:
Ther's a language in her eye, her cheeke, her lip;
Nay, her foote ſpeakes, her wanton ſpirites looke out
At euery ioynt, and motiue of her body:
Oh theſe encounterers ſo glib of tongue,
That giue a coaſting welcome ete it comes;
And wide vnclaſpe the tables of their thoughts,
To euery tickling reader: ſet them downe,
For ſluttiſh ſpoyles of opportunitie;
And daughters of the game. *Exennt.*

Enter all of Troy, Hector, Paris, Æneas, Helenus and Attendants. Floriſh.

All. The Troians Trumpet.
Aga. Yonder comes the troope.
Æne. Haile all you ſtate of Greece: what ſhalbe done
To him that victory commands? or doe you purpoſe,
A victor ſhall be knowne: will you the Knights
Shall to the edge of all extremitie
Purſue each other, or ſhall be diuided
By any voyce, or order of the field: *Hector* bad aske?
Aga. Which way would *Hector* haue it?
Æne. He cares not, heele obey conditions.
Aga. 'Tis done like *Hector*, but ſecurely done,
A little proudly, and great deale diſpriſing
The Knight oppos'd.
Æne. If not *Achilles* ſir, what is your name?
Achil. If not *Achilles*, nothing.
Æne. Therefore *Achilles*: but what ere, know this,
In the extremity of great and little:
Valour and pride excell themſelues in *Hector*;
The one almoſt as infinite as all;
The other blanke as nothing: weigh him well:
And that which lookes like pride, is curteſie:
This *Aiax* is halfe made of *Hectors* bloud;
In loue whereof, halfe *Hector* ſtaies at home:
Halfe heart, halfe hand, halfe *Hector*, comes to ſeeke
This blended Knight, halfe Troian, and halfe Greeke.
Achil. A maiden battaile then? O I perceiue you.
Aga. Here is ſir, *Diomed*: goe gentle Knight,
Stand by our *Aiax*: as you and Lord *Æneas*
Conſent vpon the order of their fight,
So be it: either to the vttermoſt,
Or elſe a breach: the Combatants being kin,
Halfe ſtints their ſtrife, before their ſtrokes begin.
Vliſ. They are oppos'd already.
Aga. What Troian is that ſame that lookes ſo heauy?
Vliſ. The yongeſt Sonne of *Priam*;
A true Knight; they call him *Troylus*;
Not yet mature, yet matchleſſe, firme of word,
Speaking in deedes, and deedeleſſe in his tongue;
Not ſoone prouok't, nor being prouok't, ſoone calm'd;
His heart and hand both open, and both free:
For what he has, he giues; what thinkes, he ſhewes;
Yet giues he not till iudgement guide his bounty,
Nor dignifies an impaire thought with breath:
Manly as *Hector*, but more dangerous;
For *Hector* in his blaze of wrath ſubſcribes
To tender obiects; but he, in heate of action,
Is more vindecatiue then iealous loue.
They call him *Troylus*; and on him erect,
A ſecond hope, as fairely built as *Hector*.
Thus ſaies *Æneas*, one that knowes the youth,
Euen to his inches: and with priuate ſoule,
Did in great Illion thus tranſlate him to me. *Alarum.*
Aga. They are in action.
Neſt. Now *Aiax* hold thine owne.
Troy. *Hector*, thou ſleep'ſt, awake thee.
Aga. His blowes are wel diſpos'd there *Aiax*. *trũpets ceaſe.*
Diom. You muſt no more.
Æne. Princes enough, ſo pleaſe you.
Aia. I am not warme yet, let vs fight againe.
Diom. As *Hector* pleaſes.
Hect. Why then will I no more:
Thou art great Lord, my Fathers ſiſters Sonne;
A couſen german to great *Priams* ſeede:
The obligation of our bloud forbids
A gorie emulation 'twixt vs twaine:
Were thy commixion, Greeke and Troian ſo,
That thou could'ſt ſay, this hand is Grecian all,
And this is Troian: the ſinewes of this Legge,
All Greeke, and this all Troy: my Mothers bloud
Runs on the dexter cheeke, and this ſiniſter
Bounds in my fathers: by *Ioue* multipotent,
Thou ſhould'ſt not beare from me a Greekiſh member
Wherein my ſword had not impreſſure made
Of our ranke feud: but the iuſt gods gainſay,
That any drop thou borrwd'ſt from thy mother,
My ſacred Aunt, ſhould by my mortall Sword
Be drained. Let me embrace thee *Aiax*:
By him that thunders, thou haſt luſtie Armes;
Hector would haue them fall vpon him thus.
Cozen, all honor to thee.
Aia. I thanke thee *Hector*:
Thou art too gentle, and too free a man:
I came to kill thee Cozen, and beare hence
A great addition, earned in thy death.
Hect. Not *Neoptolymus* ſo mirable,
On whoſe bright creſt, fame with her lowd'ſt (O yes)
Cries, This is he; could'ſt promiſe to himſelfe,
A thought of added honor, torne from *Hector*.
Æne. There is expectance here from both the ſides,
What further you will doe?
Hect. Weele anſwere it:
The iſſue is embracement: *Aiax*, farewell.
Aia. If I might in entreaties finde ſucceſſe,
As ſeld I haue the chance; I would deſire
My famous Couſin to our Grecian Tents.
Diom. 'Tis *Agamemnons* wiſh, and great *Achilles*
Doth long to ſee vnarm'd the valiant *Hector*.
Hect. *Æneas*, call my brother *Troylus* to me:
And ſignifie this louing enterview
To the expecters of our Troian part:
Deſire them home. Giue me thy hand, my Couſin:
I will goe eate with thee, and ſee your Knights.

Enter Agamemnon and the reſt.

Aia. Great *Agamemnon* comes to meete vs here.
Hect. The worthieſt of them, tell me name by name:
But for *Achilles*, mine owne ſerching eyes
Shall finde him by his large and portly ſize.
Aga. Worthy of Armes: as welcome as to one
That would be rid of ſuch an enemie.
But that's no welcome: vnderſtand more cleere
What's paſt, and what's to come, is ſtrew'd with huskes,
And formeleſſe ruine of obliuion:
But in this extant moment, faith and troth,
Strain'd purely from all hollow bias drawing:
Bids thee with moſt diuine integritie,
From heart of very heart, great *Hector* welcome.
Hect. I thanke thee moſt imperious *Agamemnon*.

Aga. My

Aga. My well-fam'd Lord of Troy, no lesse to you.
Men. Let me confirme my Princely brothers greeting,
You brace of warlike Brothers, welcome hither.
Hect. Who must we answer?
Æne. The Noble *Menelaus.*
Hect. O, you my Lord, by *Mars* his gauntlet thanks,
Mocke not, that I affect th'vntraded Oath,
Your *quondam* wife sweares still by *Venus* Gloue
Shee's well, but bad me not commend her to you.
Men. Name her not now sir, she's a deadly Theame.
Hect. O pardon, I offend.
Nest. I haue (thou gallant Troyan) seene thee oft
Labouring for destiny, make cruell way
Through rankes of Greekish youth: and I haue seen thee
As hot as *Perseus*, spurre thy Phrygian Steed,
And seene thee scorning forfeits and subduments,
When thou hast hung thy aduanced sword i'th'ayre,
Not letting it decline, on the declined:
That I haue said vnto my standers by,
Loe Iupiter is yonder, dealing life.
And I haue seene thee pause, and take thy breath,
When that a ring of Greekes haue hem'd thee in,
Like an Olympian wrestling. This haue I seene,
But this thy countenance (still lockt in steele)
I neuer saw till now. I knew thy Grandsire,
And once fought with him; he was a Souldier good,
But by great Mars, the Captaine of vs all,
Neuer like thee. Let an oldman embrace thee,
And (worthy Warriour) welcome to our Tents.
Æne. 'Tis the old *Nestor*.
Hect. Let me embrace thee good old Chronicle,
That hast so long walk'd hand in hand with time:
Most reuerend *Nestor*, I am glad to claspe thee
Ne. I would my armes could match thee in contention
As they contend with thee in courtesie.
Hect. I would they could.
Nest. Ha? by this white beard I'ld fight with thee to morrow. Well, welcom, welcome: I haue seen the time.
Vlys. I wonder now, how yonder City stands,
When we haue heere her Base and pillar by vs.
Hect. I know your fauour Lord *Vlysses* well.
Ah sir, there's many a Greeke and Troyan dead,
Since first I saw your selfe, and *Diomed*
In Illion, on your Greekish Embassie.
Vlys. Sir, I foretold you then what would ensue,
My prophesie is but halfe his iourney yet;
For yonder wals that pertly front your Towne,
Yond Towers, whose wanton tops do busse the clouds,
Must kisse their owne feet.
Hect. I must not beleeue you:
There they stand yet: and modestly I thinke,
The fall of euery Phrygian stone will cost
A drop of Grecian blood: the end crownes all,
And that old common Arbitrator, Time,
Will one day end it.
Vlys. So to him we leaue it.
Most gentle, and most valiant *Hector*, welcome;
After the Generall, I beseech you next
To Feast with me, and see me at my Tent.
Achil. I shall forestall thee Lord *Vlysses*, thou:
Now *Hector* I haue fed mine eyes on thee,
I haue with exact view perus'd thee *Hector*,
And quoted ioynt by ioynt.
Hect. Is this *Achilles*?
Achil. I am *Achilles*.
Hect. Stand faire I prythee, let me looke on thee.
Achil. Behold thy fill.
Hect. Nay, I haue done already.
Achil. Thou art to breefe, I will the second time,
As I would buy thee, view thee, limbe by limbe.
Hect. O like a Booke of sport thou'lt reade me ore:
But there's more in me then thou vnderstand'st.
Why doest thou so oppresse me with thine eye?
Achil. Tell me you Heauens, in which part of his body
Shall I destroy him? Whether there, or there, or there,
That I may giue the locall wound a name,
And make distinct the very breach, where-out
Hectors great spirit flew. Answer me heauens.
Hect. It would discredit the blest Gods, proud man,
To answer such a question: Stand againe;
Think'st thou to catch my life so pleasantly,
As to prenominate in nice coniecture
Where thou wilt hit me dead?
Achil. I tell thee yea.
Hect. Wert thou the Oracle to tell me so,
I'ld not beleeue thee: henceforth guard thee well,
For Ile not kill thee there, nor there, nor there,
But by the forge that stythied Mars his helme,
Ile kill thee euery where, yea, ore and ore.
You wisest Grecians, pardon me this bragge,
His insolence drawes folly from my lips,
But Ile endeuour deeds to match these words,
Or may I neuer——
Aiax. Do not chafe thee Cosin:
And you *Achilles*, let these threats alone
Till accident, or purpose bring you too't.
You may euery day enough of *Hector*
If you haue stomacke. The generall state I feare,
Can scarse intreat you to be odde with him.
Hect. I pray you let vs see you in the field,
We haue had pelting Warres since you refus'd
The Grecians cause.
Achil. Dost thou intreat me *Hector*?
To morrow do I meete thee fell as death,
To night, all Friends.
Hect. Thy hand vpon that match.
Aga. First, all you Peeres of Greece go to my Tent,
There in the full conuiue you: Afterwards,
As *Hectors* leysure, and your bounties shall
Concurre together, seuerally intreat him.
Beate lowd the Taborins, let the Trumpets blow,
That this great Souldier may his welcome know. *Exeunt*
Troy. My Lord *Vlysses*, tell me I beseech you,
In what place of the Field doth *Calchas* keepe?
Vlys. At *Menelaus* Tent, most Princely *Troylus*,
There *Diomed* doth feast with him to night,
Who neither lookes on heauen, nor on earth,
But giues all gaze and bent of amorous view
On the faire *Cressid*.
Troy. Shall I (sweet Lord) be bound to thee so much,
After we part from *Agamemnons* Tent,
To bring me thither?
Vlys. You shall command me sir:
As gentle tell me, of what Honour was
This *Cressida* in Troy, had she no Louer there
That wailes her absence?
Troy. O sir, to such as boasting shew their scarres,
A mocke is due: will you walke on my Lord?
She was belou'd, she lou'd; she is, and dooth;
But still sweet Loue is food for Fortunes tooth. *Exeunt.*

Enter Achilles, and Patroclus.

Achil. Ile heat his blood with Greekish wine to night
Which

Which with my Cemitar Ile coole to morrow:
Patroclus, let vs Feaſt him to the hight.

Pat. Heere comes *Therſites*. *Enter Therſites.*

Achil. How now, thou core of Enuy?
Thou cruſty batch of Nature, what's the newes?

Ther. Why thou picture of what thou ſeem'ſt, & Idoll of Ideot-worſhippers, here's a Letter for thee.

Achil. From whence, Fragment?

Ther. Why thou full diſh of Foole, from Troy.

Pat. Who keepes the Tent now?

Ther. The Surgeons box, or the Patients wound.

Patr. Well ſaid aduerſity, and what need theſe tricks?

Ther. Prythee be ſilent boy, I profit not by thy talke, thou art thought to be *Achilles* male Varlot.

Patro. Male Varlot you Rogue: What's that?

Ther. Why his maſculine Whore. Now the rotten diſeaſes of the South, guts-griping Ruptures, Catarres, Loades a grauell i'th'backe, Lethargies, cold Palſies, and the like, take and take againe, ſuch prepoſtrous diſcoueries.

Pat. Why thou damnable box of enuy thou, what mean'ſt thou to curſe thus?

Ther. Do I curſe thee?

Patr. Why no, you ruinous But, you whorſon indiſtinguiſhable Curre.

Ther. No? why art thou then exaſperate, thou idle, immateriall skiene of Sleyd ſilke; thou greene Sarcenet flap for a ſore eye, thou taſſell of a Prodigals purſe thou: Ah how the poore world is peſtred with ſuch water-flies, diminutiues of Nature.

Pat. Out gall.

Ther. Finch Egge.

Ach. My ſweet *Patroclus*, I am thwarted quite
From my great purpoſe in to morrowes battell:
Heere is a Letter from Queene *Hecuba*,
A token from her daughter, my faire Loue,
Both taxing me, and gaging me to keepe
An Oath that I haue ſworne. I will not breake it,
Fall Greekes, faile Fame, Honor or go, or ſtay,
My maior vow lyes heere; this Ile obay:
Come, come *Therſites*, helpe to trim my Tent,
This night in banquetting muſt all be ſpent.
Away *Patroclus*. *Exit.*

Ther. With too much bloud, and too little Brain, theſe two may run mad: but if with too much braine, and too little blood, they do, Ile be a curer of madmen. Heere's *Agamemnon*, an honeſt fellow enough, and one that loues Quailes, but he has not ſo much Braine as eare-wax; and the goodly transformation of Iupiter there his Brother, the Bull, the primatiue Statue, and oblique memoriall of Cuckolds, a thrifty ſhooing-horne in a chaine, hanging at his Brothers legge, to what forme but that he is, ſhold wit larded with malice, and malice forced with wit, turne him too: to an Aſſe were nothing; hee is both Aſſe and Oxe; to an Oxe were nothing, hee is both Oxe and Aſſe: to be a Dogge, a Mule, a Cat, a Fitchew, a Toade, a Lizard, an Owle, a Puttocke, or a Herring without a Roe, I would not care: but to be *Menelaus*, I would conſpire againſt Deſtiny. Aske me not what I would be, if I were not *Therſites*: for I care not to bee the lowſe of a Lazar, ſo I were not *Menelaus*. Hoy-day, ſpirits and fires.

Enter Hector, Aiax, Agamemnon, Vlyſſes, Neſtor, Diomed, with Lights.

Aga. We go wrong, we go wrong.

Aiax. No yonder 'tis, there where we ſee the light.

Hect. I trouble you.

Aiax. No, not a whit.

Enter Achilles.

Vlyſ. Heere comes himſelfe to guide you?

Achil. Welcome braue *Hector*, welcome Princes all.

Agam. So now faire Prince of Troy, I bid goodnight,
Aiax commands the guard to tend on you.

Hect. Thanks, and goodnight to the Greeks general.

Men. Goodnight my Lord.

Hect. Goodnight ſweet Lord *Menelaus*.

Ther. Sweet draught: ſweet quoth-a? ſweet ſinke, ſweet ſure.

Achil. Goodnight and welcom, both at once, to thoſe that go, or tarry.

Aga. Goodnight.

Achil. Old *Neſtor* tarries, and you too *Diomed*,
Keepe *Hector* company an houre, or two.

Dio. I cannot Lord, I haue important buſineſſe,
The tide whereof is now, goodnight great *Hector*.

Hect. Giue me your hand.

Vlyſ. Follow his Torch, he goes to *Chalcas* Tent,
Ile keepe you company

Troy. Sweet ſir, you honour me.

Hect. And ſo good night.

Achil. Come, come, enter my Tent. *Exeunt.*

Ther. That ſame *Diomed's* a falſe-hearted Rogue, a moſt vniuſt Knaue; I will no more truſt him when hee leeres, then I will a Serpent when he hiſſes: he will ſpend his mouth & promiſe, like Brabler the Hound; but when he performes, Aſtronomers foretell it, that it is prodigious, there will come ſome change: the Sunne borrowes of the Moone when *Diomed* keepes his word. I will rather leaue to ſee *Hector*, then not to dogge him: they ſay, he keepes a Troyan Drab, and vſes the Traitour *Chalcas* his Tent. Ile after—— Nothing but Letcherie? All incontinent Varlets. *Exeunt*

Enter Diomed.

Dio. What are you vp here ho? ſpeake?

Chal. Who cals?

Dio. *Diomed*, *Chalcas* (I thinke) wher's you Daughter?

Chal. She comes to you.

Enter Troylus and Vliſſes.

Vliſ. Stand where the Torch may not diſcouer vs.

Enter Creſsid.

Troy. *Creſsid* comes forth to him.

Dio. How now my charge?

Creſ. Now my ſweet gardian: harke a word with you.

Troy. Yea, ſo familiar?

Vliſ. She will ſing any man at firſt ſight.

Ther. And any man may finde her, if he can take her life: ſhe's noted.

Dio. Will you remember?

Cal. Remember? yes.

Dio. Nay, but doe then; and let your minde be coupled with your words.

Troy. What ſhould ſhe remember?

Vliſ. Liſt?

Creſ. Sweete hony Greek, tempt me no more to folly.

Ther. Roguery.

Dio. Nay then.

Creſ. Ile tell you what.

Dio. Fo, fo, come tell a pin, you are a forſworne.——

Creſ. In faith I cannot: what would you haue me do?

Ther. A iugling tricke, to be ſecretly open.

Dio. What did you ſweare you would beſtow on me?

Creſ. I prethee do not hold me to mine oath,
Bid me doe not any thing but that ſweete Greeke.

Dio. Good

Dio. Good night.
Troy. Hold, patience.
Vliſ. How now Troian ?
Creſ. *Diomed.*
Dio. No, no, good night : Ile be your foole no more.
Troy. Thy better muſt.
Creſ. Harke one word in your eare.
Troy. O plague and madneſſe :
Vliſ. You are moued Prince, let vs depart I pray yóu,
Leſt your diſpleaſure ſhould enlarge it ſelfe
To wrathfull tearmes : this place is dangerous ;
The time right deadly : I beſeech you goe.
Troy. Behold, I pray you.
Vliſ. Nay, good my Lord goe off :
You flow to great diſtraction : come my Lord ?
Troy. I pray thee ſtay ?
Vliſ. You haue not patience, come.
Troy. I pray you ſtay ? by hell and hell torments,
I will not ſpeake a word.
Dio. And ſo good night.
Creſ. Nay, but you part in anger.
Troy. Doth that grieue thee ? O withered truth !
Vliſ. Why, how now Lord ?
Troy. By *Ioue* I will be patient.
Creſ. Gardian ? why Greeke ?
Dio. Fo, fo, adew, you palter.
Creſ. In faith I doe not : come hither once againe.
Vliſ. You ſhake my Lord at ſomething, will you goe
you will breake out.
Troy. She ſtroakes his cheeke.
Vliſ. Come, come.
Troy. Nay ſtay, by *Ioue* I will not ſpeake a word.
There is betweene my will, and all offences,
A guard of patience ; ſtay a little while.
Ther. How the diuell Luxury with his fat rumpe and
potato finger, tickles theſe together : frye lechery, frye.
Dio. But will you then ?
Creſ. In faith I will lo ; neuer truſt me elſe.
Dio. Giue me ſome token for the ſurety of it.
Creſ. Ile fetch you one. *Exit.*
Vliſ. You haue ſworne patience.
Troy. Feare me not ſweete Lord.
I will not be my ſelfe, nor haue cognition
Of what I feele : I am all patience. *Enter Creſſid.*
Ther. Now the pledge, now, now, now.
Creſ. Here *Diomed*, keepe this Sleeue.
Troy. O beautie ! where is thy Faith ?
Vliſ. My Lord.
Troy. I will be patient, outwardly I will.
Creſ. You looke vpon that Sleeue ? behold it well :
He lou'd me : O falſe wench : giue't me againe.
Dio. Whoſe was't ?
Creſ. It is no matter now I haue't againe.
I will not meete with you to morrow night :
I prythee *Diomed* viſite me no more.
Ther. Now ſhe ſharpens : well ſaid Whetſtone.
Dio. I ſhall haue it.
Creſ. What, this ?
Dio. I that.
Creſ. O all you gods ! O prettie, prettie pledge ;
Thy Maiſter now lies thinking in his bed
Of thee and me, and ſighes, and takes my Gloue,
And giues memoriall daintie kiſſes to it ;
As I kiſſe thee.
Dio. Nay, doe not ſnatch it from me.
Creſ. He that takes that, rakes my heart withall.
Dio. I had your heart before, this followes it.
Troy. I did ſweare patience.
Creſ. You ſhall not haue it *Diomed* ; faith you ſhall not ;
Ile giue you ſomething elſe.
Dio. I will haue this : whoſe was it ?
Creſ. It is no matter.
Dio. Come tell me whoſe it was ?
Creſ. 'Twas one that lou'd me better then you will.
But now you haue it, take it.
Dio. Whoſe was it ?
Creſ. By all *Dianas* waiting women yond :
And by her ſelfe, I will not tell you whoſe.
Dio. To morrow will I weare it on my Helme,
And grieue his ſpirit that dares not challenge it.
Troy. Wert thou the diuell, and wor'ſt it on thy horne,
It ſhould be challeng'd.
Creſ. Well, well, 'tis done, 'tis paſt ; and yet it is not :
I will not keepe my word.
Dio. Why then farewell,
Thou neuer ſhalt mocke *Diomed* againe.
Creſ. You ſhall not goe : one cannot ſpeake a word,
But it ſtrait ſtarts you.
Dio. I doe not like this fooling.
Ther. Nor I by *Pluto* : but that that likes not me, plea-
ſes me beſt.
Dio. What ſhall I come ? the houre.
Creſ. I ; come : O *Ioue* ! doe, come : I ſhall be plagu'd.
Dio. Farewell till then. *Exit.*
Creſ. Good night : I prythee come :
Troylus farewell ; one eye yet lookes on thee ;
But with my heart, the other eye, doth ſee.
Ah poore our ſexe ; this fault in vs I finde :
The errour of our eye, directs our minde.
What errour leads, muſt erre : O then conclude,
Mindes ſwai'd by eyes, are full of turpitude. *Exit.*
Ther. A proofe of ſtrength ſhe could not publiſh more ;
Vnleſſe ſhe ſay, my minde is now turn'd whore.
Vliſ. Al's done my Lord.
Troy. It is.
Vliſ. Why ſtay we then ?
Troy. To make a recordation to my ſoule
Of euery ſyllable that here was ſpoke :
But if I tell how theſe two did coact ;
Shall I not lye, in publiſhing a truth ?
Sith yet there is a credence in my heart :
An eſperance ſo obſtinately ſtrong,
That doth inuert that teſt of eyes and eares ;
As if thoſe organs had deceptio us functions,
Created onely to calumniate.
Was *Creſſed* here ?
Vliſ. I cannot coniure Troian.
Troy. She was not ſure.
Vliſ. Moſt ſure ſhe was.
Troy. Why my negation hath no taſte of madneſſe ?
Vliſ. Nor mine my Lord : *Creſſid* was here but now.
Troy. Let it not be beleeu'd for womanhood :
Thinke we had mothers ; doe not giue aduantage
To ſtubborne Criticks, apt without a theame
For deprauation, to ſquare the generall ſex
By *Creſſids* rule. Rather thinke this not *Creſſid.*
Vliſ. What hath ſhe done Prince, that can ſoyle our
mothers ?
Troy. Nothing at all, vnleſſe that this were ſhe.
Ther. Will he ſwagger himſelfe out on's owne eyes ?
Troy. This ſhe ? no, this is *Diomids Creſſida* :
If beautie haue a ſoule, this is not ſhe :

H

If ſoules guide vowes; if vowes are ſanctimonie;
If ſanctimonie be the gods delight;
If there be rule in vnitie it ſelfe,
This is not ſhe: O madneſſe of diſcourſe!
That cauſe ſets vp, with, and againſt thy ſelfe
By foule authoritie: where reaſon can reuolt
Without perdition, and loſſe aſſume all reaſon,
Without reuolt. This is, and is not *Creſſid*:
Within my ſoule, there doth conduce a fight
Of this ſtrange nature, that a thing inſeperate,
Diuides more wider then the skie and earth:
And yet the ſpacious bredth of this diuiſion,
Admits no Orifex for a point as ſubtle,
As *Ariachnes* broken woofe to enter:
Inſtance, O inſtance! ſtrong as *Plutoes* gates:
Creſſid is mine, tied with the bonds of heauen;
Inſtance, O inſtance, ſtrong as heauen it ſelfe:
The bonds of heauen are ſlipt, diſſolu'd, and looſ'd,
And with another knot fiue finger tied,
The fractions of her faith, orts of her loue:
The fragments, ſcraps, the bits, and greazie reliques,
Of her ore-eaten faith, are bound to *Diomed*.
Vliſ. May worthy *Troylus* be halfe attached
With that which here his paſſion doth expreſſe?
Troy. I Greeke: and that ſhall be divulged well
In Characters, as red as *Mars* his heart
Inflam'd with *Venus*: neuer did yong man fancy
With ſo eternall, and ſo fixt a ſoule.
Harke Greek: as much I doe *Creſſida* loue;
So much by weight, hate I her *Diomed*,
That Sleeue is mine, that heele beare in his Helme:
Were it a Caske compos'd by *Vulcans* skill,
My Sword ſhould bite it: Not the dreadfull ſpout,
Which Shipmen doe the Hurricano call,
Conſtring'd in maſſe by the almighty Fenne,
Shall dizzie with more clamour Neptunes eare
In his diſcent; then ſhall my prompted ſword,
Falling on *Diomed*.
Ther. Heele tickle it for his concupie.
Troy. O *Creſſid*! O falſe *Creſſid*! falſe, falſe, falſe:
Let all vntruths ſtand by thy ſtained name,
And theyle ſeeme glorious.
Vliſ. O containe your ſelfe:
Your paſſion drawes eares hither.

Enter Æneas.

Æne. I haue beene ſeeking you this houre my Lord:
Hector by this is arming him in Troy.
Aiax your Guard, ſtaies to conduct you home.
Troy. Haue with you Prince: my curteous Lord adew:
Farewell reuolted faire: and *Diomed*,
Stand faſt and weare a Caſtle on thy head.
Vli. Ile bring you to the Gates.
Troy. Accept diſtracted thankes.

Exeunt Troylus, Æneas, and Vliſſes.

Ther. Would I could meete that roague *Diomed*, I would croke like a Rauen: I would bode, I would bode: *Patroclus* will giue me any thing for the intelligence of this whore: the Parrot will not doe more for an Almond, then he for a commodious drab: Lechery, lechery, ſtill warres and lechery, nothing elſe holds faſhion. A burning diuell take them.

Enter Hector and Andromache.

And. When was my Lord ſo much vngently temper'd,
To ſtop his eares againſt admoniſhment?
Vnarme, vnarme, and doe not fight to day.
Hect. You traine me to offend you: get you gone.
By the euerlaſting gods, Ile goe.
And. My dreames will ſure proue ominous to the day.
Hect. No more I ſay. *Enter Caſſandra.*
Caſſa. Where is my brother *Hector*?
And. Here ſiſter, arm'd, and bloudy in intent:
Conſort with me in loud and deere petition:
Purſue we him on knees: for I haue dreampt
Of bloudy turbulence; and this whole night
Hath nothing beene but ſhapes, and formes of ſlaughter.
Caſſ. O, 'tis true.
Hect. Ho? bid my Trumpet ſound
Caſſ. No notes of ſallie, for the heauens, ſweet brother.
Hect. Begon I ſay: the gods haue heard me ſweare.
Caſſ. The gods are deafe to hot and peeuiſh vowes;
They are polluted offrings, more abhord
Then ſpotted Liuers in the ſacrifice.
And. O be perſwaded, doe not count it holy,
To hurt by being iuſt; it is as lawfull:
For we would count giue much to as violent thefts,
And rob in the behalfe of charitie.
Caſſ. It is the purpoſe that makes ſtrong the vowe;
But vowes to euery purpoſe muſt not hold:
Vnarme ſweete *Hector*.
Hect. Hold you ſtill I ſay;
Mine honour keepes the weather of my fate:
Life euery man holds deere, but the deere man
Holds honor farre more precious, deere, then life.

Enter Troylus.

How now yong man? mean'ſt thou to fight to day?
And. *Caſſandra*, call my father to perſwade.

Exit Caſſandra.

Hect. No faith yong *Troylus*; doffe thy harneſſe youth:
I am to day ith'vaine of Chiualrie:
Let grow thy Sinews till their knots be ſtrong;
And tempt not yet the bruſhes of the warre.
Vnarme thee, goe; and doubt thou not braue boy,
Ile ſtand to day, for thee, and me, and Troy.
Troy. Brother, you haue a vice of mercy in you;
Which better fits a Lyon, then a man.
Hect. What vice is that? good *Troylus* chide me for it.
Troy. When many times the captiue Grecian fals,
Euen in the fanne and winde of your faire Sword:
You bid them riſe, and liue.
Hect. O 'tis faire play.
Troy. Fooles play, by heauen *Hector*.
Hect. How now? how now?
Troy. For th'loue of all the gods
Let's leaue the Hermit Pitty with our Mothers;
And when we haue our Armors buckled on,
The venom'd vengeance ride vpon our ſwords,
Spur them to ruthfull worke, reine them from ruth.
Hect. Fie ſauage, fie.
Troy. *Hector*, then 'tis warres.
Hect. *Troylus*, I would not haue you fight to day.
Troy. Who ſhould with-hold me?
Not fate, obedience, nor the hand of *Mars*,
Beckning with fierie trunchion my retire;
Not *Priamus*, and *Hecuba* on knees;
Their eyes ore-galled with recourſe of teares;
Nor you my brother, with your true ſword drawne
Oppoſ'd to hinder me, ſhould ſtop my way:
But by my ruine.

Enter Priam and Caſſandra.

Caſſ. Lay hold vpon him *Priam*, hold him faſt:
He is thy crutch; now if thou looſe thy ſtay,
Thou on him leaning, and all Troy on thee,

Fall

Fall all together.
Priam. Come *Hector*, come, goe backe:
Thy wife hath dreampt: thy mother hath had visions;
Cassandra doth foresee; and I my selfe,
Am like a Prophet suddenly enrapt,
to tell thee that this day is ominous:
Therefore come backe.
Hect. *Æneas* is a field,
And I do stand engag'd to many Greekes,
Euen in the faith of valour, to appeare
This morning to them.
Priam. I, but thou shalt not goe.
Hect. I must not breake my faith:
You know me dutifull, therefore deare sir,
Let me not shame respect; but giue me leaue
To take that course by your consent and voice,
Which you doe here forbid me, Royall *Priam.*
Cass. O *Priam*, yeelde not to him.
And. Doe not deere father.
Hect. *Andromache* I am offended with you:
Vpon the loue you beare me, get you in.
Exit Andromache.
Troy. This foolish, dreaming, superstitious girle,
Makes all these bodements.
Cass. O farewell, deere *Hector*:
Looke how thou diest; looke how thy eye turnes pale:
Looke how thy wounds doth bleede at many vents:
Harke how Troy roares; how *Hecuba* cries out;
How poore *Andromache* shrils her dolour forth;
Behold distraction, frenzie, and amazement,
Like witlesse Antickes one another meete,
And all cry *Hector*, *Hectors* dead: O *Hector*!
Troy. Away, away.
Cas. Farewell: yes, soft: *Hector* I take my leaue;
Thou do'st thy selfe, and all our Troy deceiue. *Exit.*
Hect. You are amaz'd, my Liege, at her exclaime:
Goe in and cheere the Towne, weele forth and fight:
Doe deedes of praise, and tell you them at night.
Priam. Farewell: the gods with safetie stand about
thee. *Alarum.*
Troy. They are at it, harke: proud *Diomed*, beleeue
I come to loose my arme, or winne my sleeue.

Enter Pandar.

Pand. Doe you heare my Lord? do you heare?
Troy. What now?
Pand. Here's a Letter come from yond poore girle.
Troy. Let me reade.
Pand. A whorson tisicke, a whorson rascally tisicke, so troubles me; and the foolish fortune of this girle, and what one thing, what another, that I shall leaue you one o'th's dayes: and I haue a rheume in mine eyes too; and such an ache in my bones; that vnlesse a man were curst, I cannot tell what to thinke on't. What sayes shee there?
Troy. Words, words, meere words, no matter from the heart;
Th'effect doth operate another way.
Goe winde to winde, there turne and change together:
My loue with words and errors still she feedes;
But edifies another with her deedes.
Pand. Why, but heare you?
Troy. Hence brother lackie; ignomie and shame
Pursue thy life, and liue aye with thy name.
A Larum. *Exeunt.*

Enter Thersites in excursion.

Ther. Now they are clapper-clawing one another, Ile goe looke on: that dissembling abhominable varlet *Diomede*, has got that same scuruie, doting, foolish yong knaues Sleeue of Troy, there in his Helme. I would faine see them meet; that, that same yong Troian asse, that loues the whore there, might send that Greekish whore-maisterly villaine, with the Sleeue, backe to the dissembling luxurious drabbe, of a sleeuelesse errant. O'th' tother side, the pollicie of those craftie swearing rascals; that stole old Mouse-eaten dry cheese, *Nestor*: and that same dog-foxe *Vlisses'* is not prou'd worth a Black-berry. They set me vp in pollicy, that mungrill curre *Aiax*, against that dogge of as bad a kinde, *Achilles* And now is the curre *Aiax* prouder then the curre *Achilles*, and will not arme to day. Whereupon, the Grecians began to proclaime barbarisme; and pollicie growes into an ill opinion.
Enter Diomed and Troylus.
Soft, here comes Sleeue, and th'other.
Troy. Flye not: for should'st thou take the Riuer Stix,
I would swim after.
Diom. Thou do'st miscall retire:
I doe not flye; but aduantagious care
Withdrew me from the oddes of multitude:
Haue at thee?
Ther. Hold thy whore Grecian: now for thy whore
Troian: Now the Sleeue, now the Sleeue.
Enter Hector.
Hect. What art thou Greek? art thou for *Hectors* match?
Art thou of bloud, and honour?
Ther. No, no: I am a rascall: a scuruie railing knaue:
a very filthy roague.
Hect. I doe beleeue thee, liue.
Ther God a mercy, that thou wilt beleeue me; but a plague breake thy necke---for frighting me: what's become of the wenching rogues? I thinke they haue swallowed one another. I would laugh at that miracle----yet in a sort, lecherie eates it selfe: Ile seeke them.
Exit

Enter Diomed and Seruants.
Dio. Goe, goe, my seruant, take thou *Troylus* Horse;
Present the faire Steede to my Lady *Cressid*:
Fellow, commend my seruice to her beauty;
Tell her, I haue chastis'd the amorous Troyan.
And am her Knight by proofe.
Ser. I goe my Lord. *Enter Agamemnon.*
Aga. Renew, renew, the fierce *Polidamus*
Hath beate downe *Menon* bastard *Margarelon*
Hath *Doreus* prisoner.
And stands Calossus-wise wauing his beame,
Vpon the pashed courses of the Kings:
Epistropus and *Cedus*, *Polixines* is slaine;
Amphimacus, and *Thous* deadly hurt;
Patroclus tane or slaine, and *Palamedes*
Sore hurt and bruised; the dreadfull Sagittary
Appauls our numbers, haste we *Diomed*
To re-enforcement, or we perish all.
Enter Nestor.
Nest. Goe beare *Patroclus* body to *Achilles*,
And bid the snaile-pac'd *Aiax* arme for shame;
There is a thousand *Hectors* in the field:
Now here he fights on *Galathe* his Horse,
And there lacks worke: anon he's there a foote,
And there they flye or dye, like scaled sculs,
Before

Before the belching Whale; then is he yonder,
And there the strawing Greekes, ripe for his edge,
Fall downe before him, like the mowers swath;
Here, there, and euery where, he leaues and takes;
Dexteritie so obaying appetite,
That what he will, he does, and does so much,
That proofe is call'd impossibility.

Enter Vlisses.

Vlis. Oh, courage, courage Princes: great *Achilles*
Is arming, weeping, cursing, vowing vengeance;
Patroclus wounds haue rouz'd his drowzie bloud,
Together with his mangled *Myrmidons*,
That noselesse, handlesse, hackt and chipt, come to him;
Crying on *Hector*. *Aiax* hath lost a friend,
And foames at mouth, and he is arm'd, and at it:
Roaring for *Troylus*; who hath done to day.
Mad and fantasticke execution;
Engaging and redeeming of himselfe,
With such a carelesse force, and forcelesse care,
As if that luck in very spight of cunning, bad him win all.

Enter Aiax.

Aia. *Troylus*, thou coward *Troylus* *Exit.*

Dio. I, there, there.

Nest. So, so, we draw together. *Exit.*

Enter Achilles

Achil. Where is this *Hector*?
Come, come, thou boy-queller, shew thy face:
Know what it is to meete *Achilles* angry.
Hector, wher's *Hector*? I will none but *Hector* *Exit.*

Enter Aiax.

Aia. *Troylus*, thou coward *Troylus*, shew thy head.

Enter Diomed.

Diom. *Troylus*, I say, wher's *Troylus*?

Aia. What would'st thou?

Diom. I would correct him.

Aia. Were I the Generall,
Thou should'st haue my office,
Ere that correction: *Troylus* I say, what *Troylus*?

Enter Troylus.

Troy. Oh traitour *Diomed*!
Turne thy false face thou traytor,
And pay thy life thou owest me for my horse.

Dio. Ha, art thou there?

Aia. Ile fight with him alone, stand *Diomed*.

Dio. He is my prize, I will not looke vpon.

Troy. Come both you coging Greekes, haue at you both. *Exit Troylus.*

Enter Hector.

Hect. Yea *Troylus*? O well fought my yongest Brother.

Enter Achilles.

Achil. Now doe I see thee; haue at thee *Hector*.

Hect. Pause if thou wilt.

Achil. I doe disdaine thy curtesie, proud Troian;
Be happy that my armes are out of vse:
My rest and negligence befriends thee now,
But thou anon shalt heare of me againe:
Till when, goe seeke thy fortune. *Exit.*

Hect. Fare thee well:
I would haue beene much more a fresher man,
Had I expected thee: how now my Brother?

Enter Troylus.

Troy. *Aiax* hath tane *Æneas*; shall it be?
No, by the flame of yonder glorious heauen,
He shall not carry him: Ile be tane too,
Or bring him off: Fate heare me what I say;
I wreake not, though thou end my life to day. *Exit*

Enter one in Armour.

Hect. Stand, stand, thou Greeke,
Thou art a goodly marke:
No? wilt thou not? I like thy armour well,
Ile frush it, and vnlocke the riuets all,
But Ile be maister of it: wilt thou not beast abide?
Why then flye on, Ile hunt thee for thy hide. *Exit.*

Enter Achilles with Myrmidons.

Achil. Come here about me you my *Myrmidons*
Marke what I say; attend me where I wheele:
Strike not a stroake, but keepe your selues in breath,
And when I haue the bloudy *Hector* found,
Empale him with your weapons round about:
In fellest manner execute your arme.
Follow me sirs, and my proceedings eye;
It is decreed, *Hector* the great must dye. *Exit.*

Enter Thersites, Menelaus, and Paris.

Ther The Cuckold and the Cuckold maker are at it: now bull, now dogge, lowe; *Paris* lowe; now my double hen'd sparrow; lowe *Paris*, lowe; the bull has the game: ware hornes ho?

Exit Paris and Menelaus.

Enter Bastard.

Bast. Turne slaue and fight.

Ther. What art thou?

Bast. A Bastard Sonne of *Priams*

Ther. I am a Bastard too, I loue Bastards, I am a Bastard begot, Bastard instructed, Bastard in minde, Bastard in valour, in euery thing illegitimate: one Beare will not bite another, and wherefore should one Bastard? take heede, the quarrel's most ominous to vs: if the Sonne of a whore fight for a whore, he tempts iudgement: farewell Bastard.

Bast. The diuell take thee coward. *Exeunt.*

Enter Hector.

Hect. Most putrified core so faire without:
Thy goodly armour thus hath cost thy life.
Now is my daies worke done; Ile take good breath:
Rest Sword, thou hast thy fill of bloud and death.

Enter Achilles and his Myrmidons.

Achil. Looke *Hector* how the Sunne begins to set;
How vgly night comes breathing at his heeles,
Euen with the vaile and darking of the Sunne.
To close the day vp, *Hectors* life is done.

Hect. I am vnarm'd, forgoe this vantage Greeke.

Achil Strike fellowes, strike, this is the man I seeke.
So Illion fall thou: now Troy sinke downe;
Here lyes thy heart, thy sinewes, and thy bone.
On *Myrmidons*, cry you all a maine,
Achilles hath the mighty *Hector* slaine. *Retreat.*
Harke, a retreat vpon our Grecian part.

Gree. The Troian Trumpets sounds the like my Lord.

Achi. The dragon wing of night ore-spreds the earth
And stickler-like the Armies seperates
My halfe supt Sword, that frankly would haue fed,
Pleas'd with this dainty bed; thus goes to bed.
Come, tye his body to my horses tayle;
Along the field, I will the Troian traile. *Exeunt.*

Sound Retreat. Shout.

Enter Agamemnon, Aiax, Menelaus, Nestor Diomed, and the rest marching.

Aga. Harke, harke, what shout is that?

Nest. Peace Drums.

Sol. Achilles

Sold. *Achilles, Achilles, Hector's* slaine. *Achilles.*
Dio. The bruite is, *Hector's* slaine, and by *Achilles.*
Aia. If it be so yet braglesse let it be:
Great *Hector* was a man as good as he.
Agam. March patiently along; let one be sent
To pray *Achilles* see vs at our Tent.
If in his death the gods haue vs befrended,
Great Troy is ours, and our sharpe wars are ended.
Exeunt

Enter Æneas, Paris, Anthenor and Deipoebus.

Æne. Stand hoe, yet are we maisters of the field,
Neuer goe home; here starue we out the night.

Enter Troylus.

Troy. *Hector* is slaine.
All. *Hector*? the gods forbid
Troy. Hee's dead: and at the murtherers Horses taile,
In beastly sort, drag'd through the shamefull Field.
Frowne on you heauens, effect your rage with speede:
Sit gods vpon your throanes, and smile at Troy.
I say at once, let your briefe plagues be mercy,
And linger not our sure destructions on.
Æne. My Lord, you doe discomfort all the Hoste.
Troy. You vnderstand me not, that tell me so:
I doe not speake of flight, of feare, of death,
But dare all imminence that gods and men,
Addresse their dangers in. *Hector* is gone:
Who shall tell *Priam* so? or *Hecuba*?
Let him that will a screechoule aye be call'd,
Goe in to Troy, and say there, *Hector's* dead:
There is a word will *Priam* turne to stone;
Make wels, and *Niobes* of the maides and wiues;
Coole statues of the youth: and in a word,
Scarre Troy out of it selfe. But march away,
Hector is dead: there is no more to say.
Stay yet: you vile abhominable Tents,
Thus proudly pight vpon our Phrygian plaines:
Let Titan rise as early as he dare,
Ile through, and through you; & thou great siz'd coward:
No space of Earth shall sunder our two hates,
Ile haunt thee, like a wicked conscience still,
That mouldeth goblins swift as frensies thoughts.
Strike a free march to Troy, with comfort goe:
Hope of reuenge, shall hide our inward woe.

Enter Pandarus.

Pand. But heare you? heare you?
Troy. Hence broker, lackie, ignomy, and shame
Pursue thy life and liue aye with thy name. *Exeunt.*

Pan. A goodly medcine for mine akingbones: oh world, world, world! thus is the poore agent dispisde: Oh traitours and bawdes; how earnestly are you set aworke, and how ill requited? why should our indeuour be so desir'd, and the performance so loath'd? What Verse for it? what instance for it? let me see.

Full merrily the humble Bee doth sing,
Till he hath lost his hony, and his sting.
And being once subdu'd in armed taile,
Sweete hony, and sweete notes together faile.
Good traders in the flesh, set this in your painted cloathes;
As many as be here of Panders hall,
Your eyes halfe out, weepe out at *Pandar's* fall:
Or if you cannot weepe, yet giue some grones;
Though not for me, yet for your akingbones:
Brethren and sisters of the hold-dore trade,
Some two months hence, my will shall here be made:
It should be now, but that my feare is this:
Some galled Goose of Winchester would hisse:
Till then, Ile sweate, and seeke about for eases;
And at that time bequeath you my diseases. *Exeunt.*

¶ ¶ ¶

FINIS.

The Tragedy of Coriolanus.

Actus Primus. Scœna Prima.

Enter a Company of Mutinous Citizens, with Staues, Clubs, and other weapons.

1. *Citizen.*

BEfore we proceed any further, heare me speake.

All. Speake, speake.

1.*Cit.* You are all resolu'd rather to dy then to famish?

All. Resolu'd, resolu'd.

1.*Cit.* First you know, *Caius Martius* is chiefe enemy to the people.

All. We know't, we know't.

1.*Cit.* Let vs kill him, and wee'l haue Corne at our own price. Is't a Verdict?

All. No more talking on't; Let it be done, away, away

2.*Cit.* One word, good Citizens.

1.*Cit.* We are accounted poore Citizens, the Patricians good: what Authority surfets one, would releeue vs. If they would yeelde vs but the superfluitie while it were wholsome, wee might guesse they releeued vs humanely: But they thinke we are too deere, the leannesse that afflicts vs, the obiect of our misery, is as an inuentory to particularize their abundance, our sufferance is a gaine to them. Let vs reuenge this with our Pikes, ere we become Rakes. For the Gods know, I speake this in hunger for Bread, not in thirst for Reuenge.

2.*Cit.* Would you proceede especially against *Caius Martius.*

All. Against him first: He's a very dog to the Commonalty.

2.*Cit.* Consider you what Seruices he ha's done for his Country?

1.*Cit.* Very well, and could bee content to giue him good report for't, but that hee payes himselfe with beeing proud.

All. Nay, but speak not maliciously.

1.*Cit.* I say vnto you, what he hath done Famouslie, he did it to that end: though soft conscienc'd men can be content to say it was for his Countrey, he did it to please his Mother, and to be partly proud, which he is, euen to the altitude of his vertue.

2.*Cit.* What he cannot helpe in his Nature, you account a Vice in him: You must in no way say he is couetous.

1.*Cit.* If I must not, I neede not be barren of Accusations he hath faults (with surplus) to tyre in repetition.

Showts within.

What showts are these? The other side a'th City is risen: why stay we prating heere? To th Capitoll.

All. Come, come.

1 *Cit.* Soft, who comes heere?

Enter Menenius Agrippa.

2 *Cit.* Worthy *Menenius Agrippa,* one that hath alwayes lou'd the people.

1 *Cit.* He's one honest enough, wold al the rest wer so.

Men. What work's my Countrimen in hand?
Where go you with Bats and Clubs? The matter
Speake I pray you.

2 *Cit.* Our busines is not vnknowne to th Senat, they haue had inkling this fortnight what we intend to do, & now wee'l shew em in deeds: they say poore Suters haue strong breaths, they shal know we haue strong arms too.

Menen. Why Masters, my good Friends, mine honest Neighbours, will you vndo your selues?

2 *Cit.* We cannot Sir, we are vndone already.

Men. I tell you Friends, most charitable care
Haue the Patricians of you for your wants.
Your suffering in this dearth, you may as well
Strike at the Heauen with your staues, as lift them
Against the Roman State, whose course will on
The way it takes: cracking ten thousand Curbes
Of more strong linke assunder, then can euer
Appeare in your impediment. For the Dearth,
The Gods, not the Patricians make it, and
Your knees to them (not armes) must helpe. Alacke,
You are transported by Calamity
Thether, where more attends you, and you slander
The Helmes o'th State; who care for you like Fathers,
When you curse them, as Enemies.

2 *Cit.* Care for vs? True indeed, they nere car'd for vs yet. Suffer vs to famish, and their Store-houses cramm'd with Graine: Make Edicts for Vsurie, to support Vsurers; repeale daily any wholsome Act established against the rich, and prouide more piercing Statutes daily, to chaine vp and restraine the poore. If the Warres eate vs not vppe, they will; and there's all the loue they beare vs.

Menen. Either you must
Confesse your selues wondrous Malicious,
Or be accus'd of Folly. I shall tell you
A pretty Tale, it may be you haue heard it,
But since it serues my purpose, I will venture
To scale't a little more.

2 *Citizen.* Well,
Ile heare it Sir: yet you must not thinke
To fobbe off our disgrace with a tale:
But and't please you deliuer.

Men. There was a time, when all the bodies members
Rebell'd against the Belly; thus accus'd it:
That onely like a Gulfe it did remaine

a a I'th

I'th midd'ſt a th'body, idle and vnactiue,
Still cubbording the Viand, neuer bearing
Like labour with the reſt, where th'other Inſtruments
Did ſee, and heare, deuiſe, inſtruct, walke, feele,
And mutually participate, did miniſter
Vnto the appetite; and affection common
Of the whole body, the Belly anſwer'd.
2. Cit. Well ſir, what anſwer made the Belly.
Men. Sir, I ſhall tell you with a kinde of Smile,
Which ne're came from the Lungs, but euen thus:
For looke you I may make the belly Smile,
As well as ſpeake, it taintingly replyed
To'th'diſcontented Members, the mutinous parts
That enuied his receite: euen ſo moſt fitly,
As you maligne our Senators, for that
They are not ſuch as you.
2. Cit. Your Bellies anſwer: What
The Kingly crown'd head, the vigilant eye,
The Counſailor Heart, the Arme our Souldier,
Our Steed the Legge, the Tongue our Trumpeter,
With other Muniments and petty helpes
In this our Fabricke, if that they
Men. What then? Foreme, this Fellow ſpeakes.
What then? What then?
2 Cit. Should by the Cormorant belly be reſtrain'd,
Who is the ſinke a th'body.
Men. Well, what then?
2. Cit. The former Agents, if they did complaine,
What could the Belly anſwer?
Men. I will tell you,
If you'l beſtow a ſmall (of what you haue little)
Patience awhile; you'ſt heare the Bellies anſwer
2. Cit. Y'are long about it.
Men. Note me this good Friend;
Your moſt graue Belly was deliberate,
Not raſh like his Accuſers, and thus anſwered.
True is it my Incorporate Friends (quoth he)
That I receiue the generall Food at firſt
Which you do liue vpon: and fit it is,
Becauſe I am the Store-houſe, and the Shop
Of the whole Body. But, if you do remember,
I ſend it through the Riuers of your blood
Euen to the Court, the Heart, to th'ſeate o th'Braine,
And through the Crankes and Offices of man,
The ſtrongeſt Nerues, and ſmall inferiour Veines
From me receiue that naturall competencie
Whereby they liue. And though that all at once
(You my good Friends, this ſayes the Belly) marke me.
2. Cit. I ſir, well, well.
Men. Though all at once, cannot
See what I do deliuer out to each,
Yet I can make my Awdit vp, that all
From me do backe receiue the Flowre of all,
And leaue me but the Bran. What ſay you too't?
2 Cit. It was an anſwer, how apply you this?
Men. The Senators of Rome, are this good Belly,
And you the mutinous Members: For examine
Their Counſailes, and their Cares; diſgeſt things rightly,
Touching the Weale a'th Common, you ſhall finde
No publique benefit which you receiue
But it proceeds, or comes from them to you,
And no way from your ſelues. What do you thinke?
You, the great Toe of this Aſſembly?
2. Cit. I the great Toe? Why the great Toe?
Men. For that being one o'th loweſt, baſeſt, pooreſt
Of this moſt wiſe Rebellion, thou goeſt formoſt:
Thou Raſcall, that art worſt in blood to run,
Lead'ſt firſt to win ſome vantage.
But make you ready your ſtiffe bats and clubs,
Rome, and her Rats, are at the point of battell,
The one ſide muſt haue baile.

Enter Caius Martius.

Hayle, Noble *Martius.*
Mar. Thanks. What's the matter you diſſentious rogues
That rubbing the poore Itch of your Opinion,
Make your ſelues Scabs.
2. Cit. We haue euer your good word.
Mar. He that will giue good words to thee, wil flatter
Beneath abhorring. What would you haue, you Curres,
That like not Peace, nor Warre? The one affrights you,
The other makes you proud. He that truſts to you,
Where he ſhould finde you Lyons, findes you Hares:
Where Foxes, Geeſe you are: No ſurer, no,
Then is the coale of fire vpon the Ice,
Or Hailſtone in the Sun. Your Vertue is,
To make him worthy, whoſe offence ſubdues him,
And curſe that Iuſtice did it. Who deſerues Greatnes,
Deſerues your Hate: and your Affections are
A ſickmans Appetite; who deſires moſt that
Which would encreaſe his euill. He that depends
Vpon your fauours, ſwimmes with finnes of Leade,
And hewes downe Oakes, with ruſhes. Hang ye: truſt ye?
With euery Minute you do change a Minde,
And call him Noble, that was now your Hate:
Him vilde, that was your Garland. What's the matter,
That in theſe ſeuerall places of the Citie,
You cry againſt the Noble Senate, who
(Vnder the Gods) keepe you in awe, which elſe
Would feede on one another? What's their ſeeking?
Men. For Corne at their owne rates, wherof they ſay
The Citie is well ſtor'd.
Mar. Hang 'em: They ſay?
They'l ſit by th'fire, and preſume to know
What's done i'th Capitoll: Who's like to riſe,
Who thriues, & who declines: Side factions, & giue out
Coniecturall Marriages, making parties ſtrong,
And feebling ſuch as ſtand not in their liking,
Below their cobled Shooes. They ſay ther's grain enough?
Would the Nobility lay aſide their ruth,
And let me vſe my Sword, I'de make a Quarrie
With thouſands of theſe quarter'd ſlaues, as high
As I could picke my Lance.
Menen. Nay theſe are almoſt thoroughly perſwaded:
For though abundantly they lacke diſcretion
Yet are they paſſing Cowardly. But I beſeech you,
What ſayes the other Troope?
Mar. They are diſſolu'd: Hang em;
They ſaid they were an hungry, ſigh'd forth Prouerbes
That Hunger-broke ſtone wals: that dogges muſt eate
That meate was made for mouths. That the gods ſent not
Corne for the Richmen onely: With theſe ſhreds
They vented their Complainings, which being anſwer'd
And a petition granted them, a ſtrange one,
To breake the heart of generoſity,
And make bold power looke pale, they threw their caps
As they would hang them on the hornes a'th Moone,
Shooting their Emulation.
Menen. What is graunted them?
Mar. Fiue Tribunes to defend their vulgar wiſdoms
Of their owne choice. One's *Iunius Brutus,*
Sicinius Velutus, and I know not. Sdeath,

The

The rabble should haue first vnroo'st the City
Ere so preuayl'd with me; it will in time
Win vpon power, and throw forth greater Theames
For Insurrections arguing.
Menen. This is strange.
Mar. Go get you home you Fragments.
Enter a Messenger hastily.
Mess. Where's *Caius Martius*?
Mar. Heere: what's the matter?
Mes. The newes is sir, the Volcies are in Armes.
Mar. I am glad on't, then we shall ha meanes to vent
Our mustie superfluity. See our best Elders.

Enter Sicinius Velutus, Annius Brutus Cominius, Titus Lartius, with other Senatours.

1. Sen. *Martius* 'tis true, that you haue lately told vs,
The Volces are in Armes.
Mar. They haue a Leader,
Tullus Auffidius that will put you too't:
I sinne in enuying his Nobility:
And were I any thing but what I am,
I would wish me onely he.
Com. You haue fought together?
Mar. Were halfe to halfe the world by th'eares, & he
vpon my partie, I'de reuolt to make
Onely my warres with him. He is a Lion
That I am proud to hunt.
1. Sen. Then worthy *Martius*,
Attend vpon *Cominius* to these Warres.
Com. It is your former promise.
Mar. Sir it is,
And I am constant: *Titus Lucius*, thou
Shalt see me once more strike at *Tullus* face.
What art thou stiffe? Stand'st out?
Tit. No *Caius Martius*,
Ile leane vpon one Crutch, and fight with tother,
Ere stay behinde this Businesse.
Men. Oh true-bred.
Sen. Your Company to'th Capitoll, where I know
Our greatest Friends attend vs.
Tit. Lead you on: Follow *Cominius*, we must followe
you, right worthy you Priority.
Com. Noble *Martius*.
Sen. Hence to your homes, be gone.
Mar. Nay let them follow,
The Volces haue much Corne: take these Rats thither,
To gnaw their Garners. Worshipfull Mutiners,
Your valour puts well forth: Pray follow. *Exeunt.*
Citizens steale away. Manet Sicin. & Brutus.
Sicin. Was euer man so proud as is this *Martius*?
Bru. He has no equall.
Sicin. When we were chosen Tribunes for the people.
Bru. Mark'd you his lip and eyes.
Sicin. Nay, but his taunts.
Bru. Being mou'd, he will not spare to gird the Gods.
Sicin. Bemocke the modest Moone.
Bru. The present Warres deuoure him, he is growne
Too proud to be so valiant.
Sicin. Such a Nature, tickled with good successe, disdaines the shadow which he treads on at noone, but I do wonder, his insolence can brooke to be commanded vnder *Cominius*?
Bru Fame, at the which he aymes,
In whom already he's well grac'd, cannot
Better be held, nor more attain'd then by
A place below the first: for what miscarries
Shall be the Generals fault, though he performe
To th'vtmost of a man, and giddy censure
Will then cry out of *Martius*: Oh, if he
Had borne the businesse.
Sicin. Besides, if things go well,
Opinion that so stickes on *Martius*, shall
Of his demerits rob *Cominius*.
Bru. Come: halfe all *Cominius* Honors are to *Martius*
Though *Martius* earn'd them not: and all his faults
To *Martius* shall be Honors, though indeed
In ought he merit not.
Sicin. Let's hence, and heare
How the dispatch is made, and in what fashion
More then his singularity, he goes
Vpon this present Action.
Bru. Let's along. *Exeunt*

Enter Tullus Auffidius with Senators of Coriolus.

1. Sen. So, your opinion is *Auffidius*,
That they of Rome are entred in our Counsailes,
And know how we proceede.
Auf. Is it not yours?
What euer haue bin thought one in this State
That could be brought to bodily act, ere Rome
Had circumuention: 'tis not foure dayes gone
Since I heard thence, these are the words, I thinke
I haue the Letter heere: yes, heere it is;
They haue prest a Power, but it is not knowne
Whether for East or West: the Dearth is great,
The people Mutinous: And it is rumour'd,
Cominius, *Martius* your old Enemy
(Who is of Rome worse hated then of you)
And *Titus Lartius*, a most valiant Roman,
These three leade on this Preparation
Whether 'tis bent: most likely, 'tis for you:
Consider of it.
1. Sen. Our Armie's in the Field:
We neuer yet made doubt but Rome was ready
To answer vs.
Auf Nor did you thinke it folly,
To keepe your great pretences vayl'd, till when
They needs must shew themselues, which in the hatching
It seem'd appear'd to Rome. By the discouery,
We shalbe shortned in our ayme, which was
To take in many Townes, ere (almost) Rome
Should know we were a-foot.
2. Sen. Noble *Auffidius*,
Take your Commission, hye you to your Bands,
Let vs alone to guard *Corioles*
If they set downe before's: for the remoue
Bring vp your Army: but (I thinke) you'l finde
Th'haue not prepar'd for vs.
Auf. O doubt not that,
I speake from Certainties. Nay more,
Some parcels of their Power are forth already,
And onely hitherward. I leaue your Honors.
If we, and *Caius Martius* chance to meete,
'Tis sworne betweene vs, we shall euer strike
Till one can do no more.
All. The Gods assist you.
Auf. And keepe your Honors safe.
1. Sen. Farewell.
2. Sen. Farewell.
All. Farewell. *Exeunt omnes.*

aa2 *Enter*

Enter Volumnia and Virgilia, mother and wife to Martius: They set them downe on two lowe stooles and sowe.

Volum. I pray you daughter sing, or expresse your selfe in a more comfortable sort: If my Sonne were my Husband, I should freelier reioyce in that absence wherein he wonne Honor, then in the embracements of his Bed, where he would shew most loue. When yet hee was but tender-bodied, and the onely Sonne of my womb; when youth with comelinesse pluck'd all gaze his way; when for a day of Kings entreaties, a Mother should not sel him an houre from her beholding; I considering how Honour would become such a person, that it was no better then Picture-like to hang by th'wall, if renowne made it not stirre, was pleas'd to let him seeke danger, where he was like to finde fame: To a cruell Warre I sent him, from whence he return'd, his browes bound with Oake. I tell thee Daughter, I sprang not more in ioy at first hearing he was a Man-child, then now in first seeing he had proued himselfe a man.

Virg. But had he died in the Businesse Madame, how then?

Volum. Then his good report should haue beene my Sonne, I therein would haue found issue. Heare me professe sincerely, had I a dozen sons each in my loue alike, and none lesse deere then thine, and my good *Martius*, I had rather had eleuen dye Nobly for their Countrey, then one voluptuously surfet out of Action.

Enter a Gentlewoman.

Gent. Madam, the Lady *Valeria* is come to visit you.
Virg. Beseech you giue me leaue to retire my selfe.
Volum. Indeed you shall not:
Me thinkes, I heare hither your Husbands Drumme:
See him plucke *Auffidius* downe by th'haire:
(As children from a Beare) the *Volces* shunning him:
Me thinkes I see him stampe thus, and call thus,
Come on you Cowards, you were got in feare
Though you were borne in Rome; his bloody brow
With his mail'd hand, then wiping, forth he goes
Like to a Haruest man, that task'd to mowe
Or all, or loose his hyre.
Virg. His bloody Brow? Oh Iupiter, no blood.
Volum. Away you Foole; it more becomes a man
Then gilt his Trophe. The brests of *Hecuba*
When she did suckle *Hector*, look'd not louelier
Then *Hectors* forhead, when it spit forth blood
At Grecian sword. *Contenning*, tell *Valeria*
We are fit to bid her welcome. *Exit Gent.*
Vir. Heauens blesse my Lord from fell *Auffidius*.
Vol. Hee'l beat *Auffidius* head below his knee,
And treade vpon his necke.

Enter Valeria with an Vsher, and a Gentlewoman.

Val. My Ladies both good day to you.
Vol. Sweet Madam.
Vir. I am glad to see your Ladyship.
Val. How do you both? You are manifest house-keepers. What are you sowing heere? A fine spotte in good faith. How does your little Sonne?
Vir. I thanke your Lady-ship: Well good Madam.
Vol. He had rather see the swords, and heare a Drum, then looke vpon his Schoolmaster.
Val. A my word the Fathers Sonne: Ile sweare 'tis a very pretty boy. A my troth, I look'd vpon him a Wensday halfe an houre together: ha's such a confirm'd countenance. I saw him run after a gilded Butterfly, & when he caught it, he let it go againe, and after it againe, and ouer and ouer he comes, and vp againe: catcht it again: or whether his fall enrag'd him, or how 'twas, hee did so set his teeth, and teare it. Oh, I warrant how he mammockt it.
Vol. One on's Fathers moods.
Val. Indeed la, tis a Noble childe.
Virg. A Cracke Madam.
Val. Come, lay aside your stitchery, I must haue you play the idle Huswife with me this afternoone.
Virg. No (good Madam)
I will not out of doores.
Val. Not out of doores?
Volum. She shall, she shall.
Virg. Indeed no, by your patience; Ile not ouer the threshold, till my Lord returne from the Warres.
Val. Fye, you confine your selfe most vnreasonably: Come, you must go visit the good Lady that lies in.
Virg. I will wish her speedy strength, and visite her with my prayers: but I cannot go thither.
Volum. Why I pray you.
Vlug. Tis not to saue labour, nor that I want loue.
Val. You would be another *Penelope*: yet they say, all the yearne she spun in *Vlisses* absence, did but fill *Athica* full of Mothes. Come, I would your Cambrick were sensible as your finger, that you might leaue pricking it for pitie. Come you shall go with vs.
Vir. No good Madam, pardon me, indeed I will not foorth.
Val. In truth la go with me, and Ile tell you excellent newes of your Husband.
Virg. Oh good Madam, there can be none yet.
Val. Verily I do not iest with you: there came newes from him last night.
Vir. Indeed Madam.
Val. In earnest it's true; I heard a Senatour speake it. Thus it is: the Volcies haue an Army forth, against whõ *Cominius* the Generall is gone, with one part of our Romane power. Your Lord, and *Titus Lartius*, are set down before their Citie *Carioles*, they nothing doubt preuailing, and to make it breefe Warres. This is true on mine Honor, and so I pray go with vs.
Virg. Giue me excuse good Madame, I will obey you in euery thing heereafter.
Vol. Let her alone Ladie, as she is now:
She will but disease our better mirth.
Valeria. In troth I thinke she would:
Fare you well then. Come good sweet Ladie.
Prythee *Virgilia* turne thy solemnesse out a doore,
And go along with vs.
Virgil. No
At a word Madam; Indeed I must not,
I wish you much mirth.
Val. Well, then farewell. *Exeunt Ladies*

Enter Martius, Titus Lartius, with Drumme and Colours, with Captaines and Souldiers, as before the City Corialus: to them a Messenger.

Martius. Yonder comes Newes:
A Wager they haue met.
Lar. My horse to yours, no.
Mar. Tis done.
Lart. Agreed.

Mar.

Mar. Say, ha's our Generall met the Enemy?
Meſſ. They lye in view, but haue not ſpoke as yet.
Lart. So, the good Horſe is mine.
Mart. Ile buy him of you.
Lart. No, Ile not ſel, nor giue him: Lend you him I will
For halfe a hundred yeares: Summon the Towne.
Mar. How farre off lie theſe Armies?
Meſſ. Within this mile and halfe.
Mar. Then ſhall we heare their Larum, & they Ours.
Now Mars, I prythee make vs quicke in worke,
That we with ſmoaking ſwords may march from hence
To helpe our fielded Friends. Come, blow thy blaſt.

They Sound a Parley: Enter two Senators with others on the Walles of Corialus.

Tullus Auffidious, is he within your Walles?
1 Senat. No, nor a man that feares you leſſe then he,
That's leſſer then a little: *Drum a farre off.*
Hearke, our Drummes
Are bringing forth our youth: Wee'l breake our Walles
Rather then they ſhall pound vs vp our Gates,
Which yet ſeeme ſhut, we haue but pin'd with Ruſhes,
They'le open of themſelues. Harke you, farre off
Alarum farre off.
There is *Auffidious.* Liſt what worke he makes
Among'ſt your clouen Army.
Mart. Oh they are at it.
Lart. Their noiſe be our inſtruction. Ladders hoa.

Enter the Army of the Volces.

Mar. They feare vs not, but iſſue forth their Citie.
Now put your Shields before your hearts, and fight
With hearts more proofe then Shields.
Aduance braue *Titus,*
They do diſdaine vs much beyond our Thoughts,
which makes me ſweat with wrath. Come on my fellows
He that retires, Ile take him for a *Volce,*
And he ſhall feele mine edge.
Alarum, the Romans are beat back to their Trenches
Enter Martius Curſing.
Mar. All the contagion of the South, light on you,
You Shames of Rome: you Heard of Byles and Plagues
Plaiſter you o're, that you may be abhorr'd
Farther then ſeene, and one infect another
Againſt the Winde a mile: you ſoules of Geeſe,
That beare the ſhapes of men, how haue you run
From Slaues, that Apes would beate; *Pluto* and Hell,
All hurt behinde, backes red, and faces pale
With flight and agued feare, mend and charge home,
Or by the fires of heauen, Ile leaue the Foe,
And make my Warres on you: Looke too't: Come on,
If you'l ſtand faſt, wee'l beate them to their Wiues,
As they vs to our Trenches followes.
Another Alarum, and Martius followes them to gates, and is ſhut in.
So, now the gates are ope: now proue good Seconds,
'Tis for the followers Fortune, widens them,
Not for the flyers: Marke me, and do the like.
Enter the Gati.
1.Sol. Foole-hardineſſe, not I.
2.Sol. Nor I.
1.Sol. See they haue ſhut him in. *Alarum continues*
All. To th'pot I warrant him. *Enter Titus Lartius*
Tit. What is become of *Martius*?
All. Slaine (Sir) doubtleſſe.
1.Sol. Following the Flyers at the very heeles,
With them he enters: who vpon the ſodaine
Clapt to their Gates, he is himſelfe alone,
To anſwer all the City.
Lar. Oh Noble Fellow!
Who ſenſibly out-dares his ſenceleſſe Sword,
And when it bowes, ſtand'ſt vp: Thou art left *Martius,*
A Carbuncle intire: as big as thou art
Weare not ſo rich a Iewell. Thou was't a Souldier
Euen to *Calues* wiſh, not fierce and terrible
Onely in ſtrokes, but with thy grim lookes, and
The Thunder-like percuſſion of thy ſounds
Thou mad'ſt thine enemies ſhake, as if the World
Were Feauorous, and did tremble.

Enter Martius bleeding, aſſaulted by the Enemy.

1 Sol. Looke Sir.
Lar. O 'tis *Martius.*
Let's fetch him off, or make remaine alike.
They fight, and all enter the City.
Enter certaine Romanes with ſpoiles.
1.Rom. This will I carry to *Rome.*
2.Rom. And I this.
3 Rom. A Murrain on't, I tooke this for Siluer. *exeunt.*
Alarum continues ſtill a-farre off.
Enter Martius, and Titus with a Trumpet.
Mar. See heere theſe mouers, that do prize their hours
At a crack'd Drachme: Cuſhions, Leaden Spoones,
Irons of a Doit, Dublets that Hangmen would
Bury with thoſe that wore them. Theſe baſe ſlaues,
Ere yet the fight be done, packe vp, downe with them.
And harke, what noyſe the Generall makes: To him
There is the man of my ſoules hate, *Auffidious,*
Piercing our Romanes: Then Valiant *Titus* take
Conuenient Numbers to make good the City,
Whil'ſt I with thoſe that haue the ſpirit, wil haſte
To helpe *Cominius.*
Lar. Worthy Sir, thou bleed'ſt,
Thy exerciſe hath bin too violent,
For a ſecond courſe of Fight.
Mar. Sir, praiſe me not:
My worke hath yet not warm'd me. Fare you well:
The blood I drop, is rather Phyſicall
Then dangerous to me: To *Auffidious* thus, I will appear (and fight.
Lar. Now the faire Goddeſſe Fortune,
Fall deepe in loue with thee, and her great charmes
Miſguide thy Oppoſers ſwords, Bold Gentleman:
Proſperity be thy Page.
Mar. Thy Friend no leſſe,
Then thoſe ſhe placeth higheſt: So farewell.
Lar. Thou worthieſt *Martius,*
Go ſound thy Trumpet in the Market place,
Call thither all the Officers a'th'Towne,
Where they ſhall know our minde. Away. *Exeunt*
Enter Cominius as it were in retire, with ſoldiers.
Com. Breath you my friends, wel fought, we are come (off,
Like Romans, neither fooliſh in our ſtands,
Nor Cowardly in retyre: Beleeue me Sirs,
We ſhall be charg'd againe. Whiles we haue ſtrooke
By Interims and conueying guſts, we haue heard
The Charges of our Friends. The Roman Gods,
Leade their ſucceſſes, as we wiſh our owne,
That both our powers, with ſmiling Fronts encountring,
May giue you thankfull Sacrifice. Thy Newes?
Enter a Meſſenger.
Meſſ. The Cittizens of *Corioles* haue yſſued,
And giuen to *Lartius* and to *Martius* Battaile:

I ſaw our party to their Trenches driuen,
And then I came away.
Com. Though thou ſpeakeſt truth,
Me thinkes thou ſpeak'ſt not well. How long is't ſince?
Meſ. Aboue an houre, my Lord.
Com. 'Tis not a mile: briefely we heard their drummes.
How could'ſt thou in a mile confound an houre,
And bring thy Newes ſo late?
Meſ. Spies of the *Volces*
Held me in chace, that I was forc'd to wheele
Three or foure miles about, elſe had I ſir
Halfe an houre ſince brought my report.

Enter Martius.

Com. Whoſe yonder,
That doe's appeare as he were Flead? O Gods,
He has the ſtampe of *Martius*, and I haue
Before time ſeene him thus.
Mar. Come I too late?
Com. The Shepherd knowes not Thunder frõ a Taber,
More then I know the ſound of *Martius* Tongue
From euery meaner man.
Martius. Come I too late?
Com. I, if you come not in the blood of others,
But mantled in your owne.
Mart. Oh! let me clip ye
In Armes as ſound, as when I woo'd in heart;
As merry, as when our Nuptiall day was done,
And Tapers burnt to Bedward.
Com. Flower of Warriors, how is't with *Titus Lartius*?
Mar. As with a man buſied about Decrees:
Condemning ſome to death, and ſome to exile,
Ranſoming him, or pittying, threatning th'other;
Holding *Corioles* in the name of Rome,
Euen like a fawning Grey-hound in the Leaſh,
To let him ſlip at will.
Com. Where is that Slaue
Which told me they had beate you to your Trenches?
Where is he? Call him hither.
Mar. Let him alone,
He did informe the truth: but for our Gentlemen,
The common file, (a plague Tribunes for them)
The Mouſe ne're ſhunn'd the Cat, as they did budge
From Raſcals worſe then they.
Com. But how preuail'd you?
Mar. Will the time ſerue to tell, I do not thinke:
Where is the enemy? Are you Lords a'th Field?
If not, why ceaſe you till you are ſo?
Com. *Martius*, we haue at diſaduantage fought,
And did retyre to win our purpoſe.
Mar. How lies their Battell? Know you on ẇ ſide
They haue plac'd their men of truſt?
Com. As I gueſſe *Martius*,
Their Bands i'th Vaward are the Antients
Of their beſt truſt: O're them *Auffidious*,
Their very heart of Hope.
Mar. I do beſeech you,
By all the Battailes wherein we haue fought,
By th'Blood we haue ſhed together,
By th'Vowes we haue made
To endure Friends, that you directly ſet me
Againſt *Affidious*, and his *Antiats*,
And that you not delay the preſent (but
Filling the aire with Swords aduanc'd) and Darts,
We proue this very houre.
Com. Though I could wiſh,
You were conducted to a gentle Bath,
And Balmes applyed to you, yet dare I neuer
Deny your asking, take your choice of thoſe
That beſt can ayde your action.
Mar. Thoſe are they
That moſt are willing; if any ſuch be heere,
(As it were ſinne to doubt) that loue this painting
Wherein you ſee me ſmear'd, if any feare
Leſſen his perſon, then an ill report.
If any thinke, braue death out-weighes bad life,
And that his Countries deerer then himſelfe,
Let him alone: Or ſo many ſo minded,
Waue thus to expreſſe his diſpoſition,
And follow *Martius*.

They all ſhout and waue their ſwords, take him vp in their Armes, and caſt vp their Caps.

Oh me alone, make you a ſword of me:
If theſe ſhewes be not outward, which of you
But is foure *Volces*? None of you, but is
Able to beare againſt the great *Auffidious*
A Shield, as hard as his. A certaine number
(Though thankes to all) muſt I ſelect from all:
The reſt ſhall beare the buſineſſe in ſome other fight
(As cauſe will be obey'd:) pleaſe you to March,
And foure ſhall quickly draw out my Command,
Which men are beſt inclin'd.
Com. March on my Fellowes:
Make good this oſtentation, and you ſhall
Diuide in all, with vs. *Exeunt*

Titus Lartius, hauing ſet a guard vpon Carioles, going with Drum and Trumpet toward Cominius, and Caius Martius, Enters with a Lieutenant, other Souldiours, and a Scout.

Lar. So, let the Ports be guarded; keepe your Duties
As I haue ſet them downe. If I do ſend, diſpatch
Thoſe Centuries to our ayd, the reſt will ſerue
For a ſhort holding, if we looſe the Field,
We cannot keepe the Towne.
Lieu. Feare not our care Sir.
Lart Hence; and ſhut your gates vpon's:
Our Guider come, to th'Roman Campe conduct vs. *Exit*

Alarum, as in Battaile.

Enter Martius and Auffidius at ſeueral doores.

Mar. Ile fight with none but thee, for I do hate thee
Worſe then a Promiſe-breaker.
Auffid. We hate alike:
Not Affricke ownes a Serpent I abhorre
More then thy Fame and Enuy: Fix thy foot.
Mar. Let the firſt Budger dye the others Slaue,
And the Gods doome him after.
Auf. If I flye *Martius*, hollow me like a Hare.
Mar. Within theſe three houres *Tullus*
Alone I fought in your *Corioles* walles,
And made what worke I pleas'd: 'Tis not my blood,
Wherein thou ſeeſt me maskt, for thy Reuenge
Wrench vp thy power to th'higheſt.
Auf. Wer't thou the *Hector*,
That was the whip of your bragg'd Progeny,
Thou ſhould'ſt not ſcape me heere.

Heere they fight, and certaine Volces come in the ayde of Auffi. Martius fights til they be driuen in breathles.

Officious and not valiant, you haue ſham'd me
In your condemned Seconds.

Flouriſh.

Flourish. Alarum. A Retreat is sounded. Enter at one Doore Cominius, with the Romanes: At another Doore Martius, with his Arme in a Scarfe.

Com. If I should tell thee o're this thy dayes Worke,
Thou't not beleeue thy deeds: but Ile report it,
Where Senators shall mingle teares with smiles,
Where great Patricians shall attend, and shrug,
I'th'end admire: where Ladies shall be frighted,
And gladly quak'd, heare more: where the dull Tribunes,
That with the fustie Plebeans, hate thine Honors,
Shall say against their hearts, We thanke the Gods
Our Rome hath such a Souldier.
Yet cam'st thou to a Morsell of this Feast,
Hauing fully din'd before.

Enter Titus with his Power, from the Pursuit.

Titus Lartius. Oh Generall:
Here is the Steed, wee the Caparison:
Hadst thou beheld——

Martius. Pray now, no more:
My Mother, who ha's a Charter to extoll her Bloud,
When she do's prayse me, grieues me:
I haue done as you haue done, that's what I can,
Induc'd as you haue beene, that's for my Countrey:
He that ha's but effected his good will,
Hath ouerta'ne mine Act.

Com. You shall not be the Graue of your deseruing,
Rome must know the value of her owne:
'Twere a Concealement worse then a Theft,
No lesse then a Traducement,
To hide your doings, and to silence that,
Which to the spire, and top of prayses vouch'd,
Would seeme but modest: therefore I beseech you,
In signe of what you are, not to reward
What you haue done, before our Armie heare me.

Martius. I haue some Wounds vpon me, and they smart
To heare themselues remembred.

Com. Should they not:
Well might they fester 'gainst Ingratitude,
And tent themselues with death: of all the Horses,
Whereof we haue ta'ne good, and good store of all,
The Treasure in this field atchieued, and Citie,
We render you the Tenth, to be ta'ne forth,
Before the common distribution,
At your onely choyse.

Martius. I thanke you Generall:
But cannot make my heart consent to take
A Bribe, to pay my Sword: I doe refuse it,
And stand vpon my common part with those,
That haue beheld the doing.

A long flourish. They all cry, Martius, Martius, cast vp their Caps and Launces: Cominius and Lartius stand bare.

Mar. May these same Instruments, which you prophane,
Neuer sound more: when Drums and Trumpets shall
I'th'field proue flatterers, let Courts and Cities be
Made all of false-fac'd soothing:
When Steele growes soft, as the Parasites Silke,
Let him be made an Ouerture for th' Warres:
No more I say, for that I haue not wash'd
My Nose that bled, or foyl'd some debile Wretch,
Which without note, here's many else haue done,
You shoot me forth in acclamations hyperbolicall,
As if I lou'd my little should be dieted
In prayses, sawc'st with Lyes.

Com. Too modest are you:
More cruell to your good report, then gratefull
To vs, that giue you truly: by your patience,
If 'gainst your selfe you be incens'd, wee'le put you
(Like one that meanes his proper harme) in Manacles,
Then reason safely with you: Therefore be it knowne,
As to vs, to all the World, That *Caius Martius*
Weares this Warres Garland: in token of the which,
My Noble Steed, knowne to the Campe, I giue him,
With all his trim belonging; and from this time,
For what he did before *Corioles*, call him,
With all th'applause and Clamor of the Hoast,
Marcus Caius Coriolanus. Beare th'addition Nobly euer?

Flourish. Trumpets sound, and Drums.

Omnes. Marcus Caius Coriolanus.

Martius. I will goe wash:
And when my Face is faire, you shall perceiue
Whether I blush, or no: howbeit, I thanke you,
I meane to stride your Steed, and at all times
To vnder-crest your good Addition,
To th'fairenesse of my power.

Com. So, to our Tent:
Where ere we doe repose vs, we will write
To Rome of our successe: you *Titus Lartius*
Must to *Corioles* backe, send vs to Rome
The best, with whom we may articulate,
For their owne good, and ours.

Lartius. I shall, my Lord.

Martius. The Gods begin to mocke me:
I that now refus'd most Princely gifts,
Am bound to begge of my Lord Generall.

Com. Tak't, 'tis yours: what is't?

Martius. I sometime lay here in *Corioles*,
At a poore mans house: he vs'd me kindly,
He cry'd to me: I saw him Prisoner:
But then *Auffidius* was within my view,
And Wrath o're-whelm'd my pittie: I request you
To giue my poore Host freedome.

Com. Oh well begg'd:
Were he the Butcher of my Sonne, he should
Be free, as is the Winde: deliuer him, *Titus*.

Lartius. Martius, his Name.

Martius. By *Iupiter* forgot:
I am wearie, yea, my memorie is tyr'd:
Haue we no Wine here?

Com. Goe we to our Tent:
The bloud vpon your Visage dryes, 'tis time
It should be lookt too: come. *Exeunt.*

A flourish. Cornets. Enter Tullus Auffidius bloudie, with two or three Souldiors.

Auff. The Towne is ta'ne.

Sould. 'Twill be deliuer'd backe on good Condition.

Auffid. Condition?
I would I were a Roman, for I cannot,
Being a *Volce*, be that I am. Condition?
What good Condition can a Treatie finde
I'th'part that is at mercy? fiue times, *Martius*,
I haue fought with thee; so often hast thou beat me:
And would'st doe so, I thinke, should we encounter

his

As often as we eate. By th'Elements.
If ere againe I meet him beard to beard,
He's mine, or I am his: Mine Emulation
Hath not that Honor in't it had: For where
I thought to crush him in an equall Force,
True Sword to Sword: Ile potche at him some way,
Or Wrath, or Craft may get him.

Sol. He's the diuell.

Auf. Bolder, though not so subtle: my valors poison'd,
With onely suff'ring staine by him: for him
Shall flye out of it selfe, nor sleepe, nor sanctuary,
Being naked, sicke; nor Phane, nor Capitoll,
The Prayers of Priests, nor times of Sacrifice:
Embarquements all of Fury, shall lift vp
Their rotten Priuiledge, and Custome 'gainst
My hate to *Martius*. Where I finde him, were it
At home, vpon my Brothers Guard, euen there
Against the hospitable Canon, would I
Wash my fierce hand in's heart. Go you to th'Citie,
Learne how 'tis held, and what they are that must
Be Hostages for Rome.

Soul. Will not you go?

Auf. I am attended at the Cyprus groue. I pray you
('Tis South the City Mils) bring me word thither
How the world goes: that to the pace of it
I may spurre on my iourney.

Soul. I shall sir.

Actus Secundus.

Enter Menenius with the two Tribunes of the people, Sicinius & Brutus.

Men. The Agurer tels me, wee shall haue Newes to night.

Bru. Good or bad?

Men. Not according to the prayer of the people, for they loue not *Martius*.

Sicin. Nature teaches Beasts to know their Friends.

Men. Pray you, who does the Wolfe loue?

Sicin. The Lambe.

Men. I, to deuour him, as the hungry Plebeians would the Noble *Martius*.

Bru. He's a Lambe indeed, that baes like a Beare.

Men. Hee's a Beare indeede, that liues like a Lambe. You two are old men, tell me one thing that I shall aske you.

Both. Well sir.

Men. In what enormity is *Martius* poore in, that you two haue not in abundance?

Bru. He's poore in no one fault, but stor'd withall.

Sicin. Especially in Pride.

Bru. And topping all others in boasting.

Men. This is strange now: Do you two know, how you are censured heere in the City, I mean of vs a'th'right hand File, do you?

Both. Why? ho ware we censur'd?

Men. Because you talke of Pride now, will you not be angry.

Both. Well, well sir, well.

Men. Why 'tis no great matter: for a very little theefe of Occasion, will rob you of a great deale of Patience: Giue your dispositions the reines, and bee angry at your pleasures (at the least) if you take it as a pleasure to you, in being so: you blame *Martius* for being proud.

Brut. We do it not alone, sir.

Men. I know you can doe very little alone, for your helpes are many, or else your actions would growe wondrous single: your abilities are to Infant-like, for dooing much alone. You talke of Pride: Oh, that you could turn your eyes toward the Napes of your neckes, and make but an Interiour suruey of your good selues. Oh that you could.

Both. What then sir?

Men. Why then you should discouer a brace of vnmeriting, proud, violent, testie Magistrates (alias Fooles) as any in Rome.

Sicin. *Menenius*, you are knowne well enough too.

Men. I am knowne to be a humorous *Patritian*, and one that loues a cup of hot Wine, with not a drop of alaying Tiber in't: Said, to be something imperfect in fauouring the first complaint, hasty and Tinder-like vppon, to triuiall motion: One, that conuerses more with the Buttocke of the night, then with the forhead of the morning. What I think, I vtter, and spend my malice in my breath. Meeting two such Weales men as you are (I cannot call you *Licurgusses*,) if the drinke you giue me, touch my Palat aduersly, I make a crooked face at it, I can say, your Worshippes haue deliuer'd the matter well, when I finde the Asse in compound, with the Maior part of your syllables. And though I must be content to beare with those, that say you are reuerend graue men, yet they lye deadly, that tell you haue good faces, if you see this in the Map of my Microcosme, followes it that I am knowne well enough too? What harme can your beesome Conspectuities gleane out of this Charracter, if I be knowne well enough too.

Bru. Come sir come, we know you well enough.

Menen. You know neither mee, your selues, nor any thing: you are ambitious, for poore knaues cappes and legges: you weare out a good wholesome Forenoone, in hearing a cause betweene an Orendge wife, and a Forsetseller, and then reiourne the Controuersie of three-pence to a second day of Audience. When you are hearing a matter betweene party and party, if you chaunce to bee pinch'd with the Collicke, you make faces like Mummers, set vp the bloodie Flagge against all Patience, and in roaring for a Chamber-pot, dismisse the Controuersie bleeding, the more intangled by your hearing: All the peace you make in their Cause, is calling both the parties Knaues. You are a payre of strange ones.

Bru. Come, come, you are well vnderstood to bee a perfecter gyber for the Table, then a necessary Bencher in the Capitoll.

Men. Our very Priests must become Mockers, if they shall encounter such ridiculous Subiects as you are, when you speake best vnto the purpose. It is not woorth the wagging of your Beards, and your Beards deserue not so honourable a graue, as to stuffe a Botchers Cushion, or to be intomb'd in an Asses Packe-saddle; yet you must bee saying, *Martius* is proud: who in a cheape estimation, is worth all your predecessors, since *Deucalion*, though peraduenture some of the best of 'em were hereditarie hangmen. Godden to your Worships, more of your conuersation would infect my Braine, being the Heardsmen of the Beastly Plebeans. I will be bold to take my leaue of you.

Bru. and Scic. *Aside.*

Enter

Enter Volumnia, Virgilia, and Valeria.

How now (my as faire as Noble) Ladyes, and the Moone were shee Earthly, no Nobler; whither doe you follow your Eyes so fast?

Volum. Honorable *Menenius*, my Boy *Martius* approches: for the loue of *Iuno* let's goe.

Menen. Ha? *Martius* comming home?

Volum. I, worthy *Menenius*, and with most prosperous approbation.

Menen. Take my Cappe *Iupiter*, and I thanke thee: hoo, *Martius* comming home?

2. *Ladies.* Nay, 'tis true.

Volum. Looke, here's a Letter from him, the State hath another, his Wife another, and (I thinke) there's one at home for you.

Men. I will make my very house reele to night: A Letter for me?

Virgil. Yes certaine, there's a Letter for you, I saw't.

Menen. A Letter for me? it giues me an Estate of seuen yeeres health; in which time, I will make a Lippe at the Physician: The most soueraigne Prescription in *Galen*, is but Emperickqutique; and to this Preseruatiue, of no better report then a Horse-drench. Is he not wounded? he was wont to come home wounded?

Virgil. Oh no, no, no.

Volum. Oh, he is wounded, I thanke the Gods for't.

Menen. So doe I too, if it be not too much: brings a Victorie in his Pocket? the wounds become him.

Volum. On's Browes: *Menenius*, hee comes the third time home with the Oaken Garland.

Menen. Ha's he disciplin'd *Auffidius* soundly?

Volum. *Titus Lartius* writes, they fought together, but *Auffidius* got off.

Menen. And 'twas time for him too, Ile warrant him that: and he had stay'd by him, I would not haue been so fiddious'd, for all the Chests in Carioles, and the Gold that's in them. Is the Senate possest of this?

Volum. Good Ladies let's goe. Yes yes, yes: The Senate ha's Letters from the Generall, wherein hee giues my Sonne the whole Name of the Warre: he hath in this action out-done his former deeds doubly.

Valer. In troth, there's wondrous things spoke of him.

Menen. Wondrous: I, I warrant you, and not without his true purchasing.

Virgil. The Gods graunt them true.

Volum. True? pow waw.

Mene. True? Ile be sworne they are true: where is hee wounded, God saue your good Worships? *Martius* is comming home: hee ha's more cause to be prowd: where is he wounded?

Volum. Ith' Shoulder, and ith' left Arme: there will be large Cicatrices to shew the People, when hee shall stand for his place: he receiued in the repulse of *Tarquin* seuen hurts ith' Body.

Mene. One ith' Neck, and two ith' Thigh, there's nine that I know.

Volum. Hee had, before this last Expedition, twentie fiue Wounds vpon him.

Mene. Now it's twentie seuen; euery gash was an Enemies Graue. Hearke, the Trumpets.

A Showt, and flourish.

Volum. These are the Vshers of *Martius*:
Before him, hee carryes Noyse;
And behinde him, hee leaues Teares:
Death, that darke Spirit, in's neruie Arme doth lye,
Which being aduanc'd, declines, and then men dye.

A Sennet. Trumpets sound.
Enter Cominius the Generall, and Titus Latius: betweene them Coriolanus, crown'd with an Oaken Garland, with Captaines and Souldiers, and a Herauld.

Herauld. Know Rome, that all alone *Martius* did fight
Within Corioles Gates: where he hath wonne,
With Fame, a Name to *Martius Caius*:
These in honor followes *Martius Caius Coriolanus.*
Welcome to Rome, renowned *Coriolanus.*

Sound. Flourish.

All. Welcome to Rome, renowned *Coriolanus.*

Coriol. No more of this, it does offend my heart: pray now no more.

Com. Looke, Sir, your Mother.

Coriol. Oh! you haue, I know, petition'd all the Gods for my prosperitie. *Kneeles.*

Volum. Nay, my good Souldier, vp:
My gentle *Martius*, worthy *Caius*,
And by deed-atchieuing Honor newly nam'd,
What is it (*Coriolanus*) must I call thee?
But oh, thy Wife.

Corio. My gracious silence, hayle:
Would'st thou haue laugh'd, had I come Coffin'd home,
That weep'st to see me triumph? Ah my deare,
Such eyes the Widowes in Carioles were,
And Mothers that lacke Sonnes.

Mene. Now the Gods Crowne thee.

Com. And liue you yet? Oh my sweet Lady, pardon.

Volum. I know not where to turne.
Oh welcome home: and welcome Generall,
And y'are welcome all.

Mene. A hundred thousand Welcomes:
I could weepe, and I could laugh,
I am light, and heauie; welcome:
A Curse begin at very root on's heart,
That is not glad to see thee.
You are three, that Rome should dote on:
Yet by the faith of men, we haue
Some old Crab-trees here at home,
That will not be grafted to your Rallish.
Yet welcome Warriors:
Wee call a Nettle, but a Nettle;
And the faults of fooles, but folly.

Com. Euer right.

Cor. *Menenius*, euer, euer.

Herauld. Giue way there, and goe on.

Cor. Your Hand, and yours?
Ere in our owne house I doe shade my Head,
The good Patricians must be visited,
From whom I haue receiu'd not onely greetings,
But with them, change of Honors.

Volum. I haue liued,
To see inherited my very Wishes,
And the Buildings of my Fancie:
Onely there's one thing wanting,
Which (I doubt not) but our Rome
Will cast vpon thee.

Cor. Know, good Mother,
I had rather be their seruant in my way,
Then sway with them in theirs.

Com. On, to the Capitall. *Flourish. Cornets.*
Exeunt in State, as before.

Enter

Enter Brutus and Scicinius.

Bru. All tongues ſpeake of him,and the bleared ſights
Are ſpectacled to ſee him. Your pratling Nurſe
Into a rapture lets her Baby crie,
While ſhe chats him: the Kitchin *Malkin* pinnes
Her richeſt Lockram 'bout her reechie necke,
Clambring the Walls to eye him:
Stalls,Bulkes,Windowes,are ſmother'd vp,
Leades fill'd, and Ridges hors'd
With variable Complexions; all agreeing
In earneſtneſſe to ſee him: ſeld-ſhowne Flamins
Doe preſſe among the popular Throngs,and puffe
To winne a vulgar ſtation: our veyl'd Dames
Commit the Warre of White and Damaske
In their nicely gawded Cheekes,toth' wanton ſpoyle
Of *Phœbus* burning Kiſſes: ſuch a poother,
As if that whatſoeuer God, who leades him,
Were ſlyly crept into his humane powers,
And gaue him gracefull poſture.

Scicin. On the ſuddaine,I warrant him Conſull.

Brutus. Then our Office may, during his power, goe ſleepe.

Scicin. He cannot temp'rately tranſport his Honors,
From where he ſhould begin,and end,but will
Loſe thoſe he hath wonne.

Brutus In that there's comfort.

Scici. Doubt not,
The Commoners,for whom we ſtand, but they
Vpon their ancient mallice,will forget
With the leaſt cauſe,theſe his new Honors,
Which that he will giue them,make I as little queſtion,
As he is prowd to doo't.

Brutus. I heard him ſweare,
Were he to ſtand for Conſull,neuer would he
Appeare i'th' Market place,nor on him put
The Naples Veſture of Humilitie,
Nor ſhewing(as the manner is)his Wounds
Toth' People,begge their ſtinking Breaths.

Scicin. 'Tis right.

Brutus. It was his word:
Oh he would miſſe it, rather then carry it,
But by the ſuite of the Gentry to him,
And the deſire of the Nobles.

Scicin. I wiſh no better,then haue him hold that purpoſe,and to put it in execution.

Brutus. 'Tis moſt like he will.

Scicin. It ſhall be to him then, as our good wills; a ſure deſtruction.

Brutus. So it muſt fall out
To him,or our Authorities,for an end.
We muſt ſuggeſt the People,in what hatred
He ſtill hath held them: that to's power he would
Haue made them Mules,ſilenc'd their Pleaders,
And diſpropertied their Freedomes; holding them,
In humane Action,and Capacitie,
Of no more Soule,nor fitneſſe for the World,
Then Cammels in their Warre, who haue their Prouand
Onely for bearing Burthens,and ſore blowes
For ſinking vnder them

Scicin. This(as you ſay)ſuggeſted,
At ſome time,when his ſoaring Inſolence
Shall reach the People,which time ſhall not want,
If he be put vpon't,and that's as eaſie,
As to ſet Dogges on Sheepe,will be his fire
To kindle their dry Stubble: and their Blaze
Shall darken him for euer.

Enter a Meſſenger.

Brutus: What's the matter?

Meſſ. You are ſept for to the Capitoll:
'Tis thought,that *Martius* ſhall be Conſull:
I haue ſeene the dumbe men throng to ſee him,
And the blind to heare him ſpeak: Matrons flong Gloues,
Ladies and Maids their Scarffes,and Handkerchers,
Vpon him as he paſ'd: the Nobles bended
As to *Ioues* Statue,and the Commons made
A Shower,and Thunder,with their Caps,and Showts:
I neuer ſaw the like.

Brutus. Let's to the Capitoll,
And carry with vs Eares and Eyes for th' time,
But Hearts for the euent.

Scicin Haue with you. *Exeunt*

Enter two Officers, to lay Cuſhions, as it were, in the Capitoll.

1. *Off* Come,come,they are almoſt here: how many ſtand for Conſulſhips?

2. *Off.* Three,they ſay: but 'tis thought of euery one, *Coriolanus* will carry it.

1. *Off.* That's a braue fellow: but hee's vengeance prowd,and loues not the common people

2. *Off.* 'Faith,there hath beene many great men that haue flatter'd the people,who ne're loued them;and there be many that they haue loued,they know not wherefore: ſo that if they loue they know not why, they hate vpon no better a ground. Therefore, for *Coriolanus* neyther to care whether they loue, or hate him, manifeſts the true knowledge he ha's in their diſpoſition,and out of his Noble careleſneſſe lets them plainely ſee't.

1. *Off.* If he did not care whether he had their loue,or no, hee waued indifferently,'twixt doing them neyther good,nor harme: but hee ſeekes their hate with greater deuotion,then they can render it him; and leaues nothing vndone,that may fully diſcouer him their oppoſite. Now to ſeeme to affect the mallice and diſpleaſure of the People,is as bad,as that which he diſlikes, to flatter them for their loue.

2. *Off.* Hee hath deſerued worthily of his Countrey, and his aſſent is not by ſuch eaſie degrees as thoſe, who hauing beene ſupple and courteous to the People, Bonnetted,without any further deed,to haue them at all into their eſtimation,and report: but hee hath ſo planted his Honors in their Eyes,and his actions in their Hearts, that for their Tongues to be ſilent,and not confeſſe ſo much, were a kinde of ingratefull Iniurie: to report otherwiſe, were a Mallice, that giuing it ſelfe the Lye,would plucke reproofe and rebuke from euery Eare that heard it.

1. *Off* No more of him, hee's a worthy man: make way,they are comming.

A Sennet. Enter the Patricians, and the Tribunes of the People, Lictors before them: Coriolanus, Menenius, Cominius the Conſul: Scicinius and Brutus take their places by themſelues: Coriolanus ſtands.

Menen. Hauing determin'd of the Voices,
And to ſend for *Titus Lartius* it remaines,
As the maine Point of this our after-meeting,

To

To gratifie his Noble ſeruice, that hath
Thus ſtood for his Countrey. Therefore pleaſe you,
Moſt reuerend and graue Elders, to deſire
The preſent Conſull, and laſt Generall,
In our well-found Succeſſes, to rep ort
A little of that worthy Worke, perform'd
By *Martius Caius Coriolanus*: whom
We met here, both to thanke, and to remember,
With Honors like himſelfe.
1.Sen. Speake, good *Cominius*:
Leaue nothing out for length, and make vs thinke
Rather our ſtates defectiue for requitall,
Then we to ſtretch it out. Maſters a'th' People,
We doe requeſt your kindeſt eares: and after
Your louing motion toward the common Body,
To yeeld what paſſes here.
Scicin. We are conuented vpon a pleaſing Treatie, and haue hearts inclinable to honor and aduance the Theame of our Aſſembly.
Brutus. Which the rather wee ſhall be bleſt to doe, if he remember a kinder value of the People, then he hath hereto priz'd them at.
Menen. That's off, that's off: I would you rather had been ſilent: Pleaſe you to heare *Cominius* ſpeake?
Brutus Moſt willingly: but yet my Caution was more pertinent then the rebuke you giue it.
Menen. He loues your People, but tye him not to be their Bed-fellow: Worthie *Cominius* ſpeake.
Coriolanus riſes, and offers to goe away.
Nay, keepe your place.
Senat. Sit *Coriolanus*: neuer ſhame to heare
What you haue Nobly done.
Coriol. Your Honors pardon:
I had rather haue my Wounds to heale againe,
Then heare ſay how I got them.
Brutus. Sir, I hope my words dis-bench'd you not?
Coriol. No Sir: yet oft,
When blowes haue made me ſtay, I fled from words.
You ſooth'd not, therefore hurt not: but your People,
I loue them as they weigh--
Menen. Pray now ſit downe.
Corio. I had rather haue one ſcratch my Head i'th' Sun,
When the Alarum were ſtrucke, then idly ſit
To heare my Nothings monſter'd. *Exit Coriolanus*
Menen. Maſters of the People,
Your multiplying Spawne, how can he flatter?
That's thouſand to one good one, when you now ſee
He had rather venture all his Limbes for Honor,
Then on ones Eares to heare it. Proceed *Cominius*.
Com. I ſhall lacke voyce: the deeds of *Coriolanus*
Should not be vtter'd feebly: it is held,
That Valour is the chiefeſt Vertue,
And moſt dignifies the hauer: if it be,
The man I ſpeake of, cannot in the World
Be ſingly counter-poys'd. At ſixteene yeeres,
When *Tarquin* made a Head for Rome, he fought
Beyond the marke of others: our then Dictator,
Whom with all prayſe I point at, ſaw him fight,
When with his Amazonian Shinne he droue
The brizled Lippes before him: he beſtrid
An o're-preſt Roman, and i'th' Conſuls view
Slew three Oppoſers: *Tarquins* ſelfe he met,
And ſtrucke him on his Knee: in that dayes feates,
When he might act the Woman in the Scene,
He prou'd beſt man i'th' field, and for his meed
Was Brow-bound with the Oake. His Pupill age
Man-entred thus, he waxed like a Sea,
And in the brunt of ſeuenteene Battailes ſince,
He lurcht all Swords of the Garland: for this laſt,
Before, and in Corioles, let me ſay
I cannot ſpeake him home: he ſtopt the flyers,
And by his rare example made the Coward
Turne terror into ſport: as Weeds before
A Veſſell vnder ſayle, ſo men obey'd,
And fell below his Stem: his Sword, Deaths ſtampe,
Where it did marke, it tooke from face to foot:
He was a thing of Blood, whoſe euery motion
Was tim'd with dying Cryes: alone he entred
The mortall Gate of th' Citie, which he painted
With ſhunleſſe deſtinie: aydeleſſe came off,
And with a ſudden re-inforcement ſtrucke
Catioles like a Planet: now all's his,
When by and by the dinne of Warre gan pierce
His readie ſence: then ſtraight his doubled ſpirit
Requickned what in fleſh was fatigate,
And to the Battaile came he, where he did
Runne reeking o're the liues of men, as if 'twere
A perpetuall ſpoyle: and till we call'd
Both Field and Citie ours, he neuer ſtood
To eaſe his Breſt with panting.
Menen Worthy man.
Senat He cannot but with meaſure fit the Honors which we deuiſe him.
Com. Our ſpoyles he kickt at,
And look'd vpon things precious, as they were
The common Muck of the World: he couets leſſe
Then Miſerie it ſelfe would giue, rewards his deeds
With doing them, and is content
To ſpend the time, to end it.
Menen. Hee's right Noble, let him be call'd for.
Senat. Call *Coriolanus*.
Off He doth appeare.
Enter Coriolanus.
Menen. The Senate, *Coriolanus*, are well pleas'd to make thee Conſull.
Corio. I doe owe them ſtill my Life, and Seruices.
Menen. It then remaines, that you doe ſpeake to the People.
Corio. I doe beſeech you,
Let me o're-leape that cuſtome: for I cannot
Put on the Gowne, ſtand naked, and entreat them
For my Wounds ſake, to giue their ſufferage:
Pleaſe you that I may paſſe this doing.
Scicin. Sir, the People muſt haue their Voyces,
Neyther will they bate one iot of Ceremonie.
Menen. Put them not too't:
Pray you goe fit you to the Cuſtome,
And take to you, as your Predeceſſors haue,
Your Honor with your forme.
Corio. It is a part that I ſhall bluſh in acting,
And might well be taken from the People.
Brutus. Marke you that.
Corio. To brag vnto them, thus I did, and thus
Shew them th'vnaking Skarres, which I ſhould hide,
As if I had receiu'd them for the hyre
Of their breath onely.
Menen. Doe not ſtand vpon't:
We recommend to you Tribunes of the People
Our purpoſe to them, and to our Noble Conſull
Wiſh we all Ioy, and Honor.
Senat. To

Senat. To *Coriolanus* come all ioy and Honor.

Flourish Cornets.

Then Exeunt. Manet Sicinius and Brutus.

Bru. You see how he intends to vse the people.

Scicin. May they perceiue's intent: he wil require them
As if he did contemne what he requested,
Should be in them to giue.

Bru. Come, wee'l informe them
Of our proceedings heere on th'Market place,
I know they do attend vs.

Enter seuen or eight Citizens.

1.Cit. Once if he do require our voyces, wee ou ght not to deny him.

2.Cit. We may Sir if we will.

3.Cit. We haue power in our selues to do it, but it is a power that we haue no power to do: For, if hee shew vs his wounds, and tell vs his deeds; we are to put our tongues into those wounds, and speake for them: So if he tel vs his Noble deeds, we must also tell him our Noble acceptance of them. Ingratitude is monstrous, and for the multitude to be ingratefull, were to make a Monster of the multitude; of the which, we being members, should bring our selues to be monstrous members.

1.Cit. And to make vs no better thought of a little helpe will serue: for once we stood vp about the Corne, he himselfe stucke not to call vs the many-headed Multitude.

3.Cit. We haue beene call'd so of many, not that our heads are some browne, some blacke, some Abram, some bald; but that our wits are so diuersly Coulord; and truely I thinke, if all our wittes were to issue out of one Scull, they would flye East, West, North, South, and their consent of one direct way, should be at once to all the points a'th Compasse.

2.Cit. Thinke you so? Which way do you iudge my wit would flye.

3.Cit. Nay your wit will not so soone out as another mans will, 'tis strongly wadg'd vp in a blocke head: but if it were at liberty, 'twould sure Southward.

2 Cit. Why that way?

3 Cit. To loose it selfe in a Fogge, where being three parts melted away with rotten Dewes, the fourth would returne for Conscience sake, to helpe to get thee a Wife.

2 Cit. You are neuer without your trickes, you may, you may.

3 Cit. Are you all resolu'd to giue your voyces? But that's no matter, the greater part carries it, I say. If hee would incline to the people, there was neuer a worthier man.

Enter Coriolanus in a gowne of Humility, with Menenius.

Heere he comes, and in the Gowne of humility, marke his behauiour: we are not to stay altogether, but to come by him where he stands, by ones, by twoes, & by threes. He's to make his requests by particulars, wherein euerie one of vs ha's a single Honor, in giuing him our own voices with our owne tongues, therefore follow me, and Ile direct you how you shall go by him.

All. Content, content.

Men. Oh Sir, you are not right: haue you not knowne
The worthiest men haue done't?

Corio. What must I say, I pray Sir?
Plague vpon't, I cannot bring
My tougne to such a pace. Looke Sir, my wounds,
I got them in my Countries Seruice, when
Some certaine of your Brethren roar'd, and ranne
From th'noise of our owne Drummes.

Menen. Oh me the Gods, you must not speak of that,
You must desire them to thinke vpon you.

Coriol. Thinke vpon me? Hang 'em,
I would they would forget me, like the Vertues
Which our Diuines lose by em.

Men. You'l marre all,
Ile leaue you: Pray you speake to em, I pray you
In wholsome manner. *Exit*

Enter three of the Citizens.

Corio. Bid them wash their Faces,
And keepe their teeth cleane: So, heere comes a brace,
You know the cause (Sir) of my standing heere.

3 Cit. We do Sir, tell vs what hath brought you too't.

Corio. Mine owne desert.

2 Cit. Your owne desert.

Corio. I, but mine owne desire.

3 Cit. How not your owne desire?

Corio. No Sir, 'twas neuer my desire yet to trouble the poore with begging.

3 Cit. You must thinke if we giue you any thing, we hope to gaine by you.

Corio. Well then I pray, your price a'th'Consulship.

1 Cit. The price is, to aske it kindly.

Corio. Kindly sir, I pray let me ha't: I haue wounds to shew you, which shall bee yours in priuate: your good voice Sir, what say you?

2 Cit. You shall ha't worthy Sir.

Corio. A match Sir, there's in all two worthie voyces begg'd: I haue your Almes, Adieu.

3 Cit. But this is something odde.

2 Cit. And 'twere to giue againe: but 'tis no matter.

Exeunt. Enter two other Citizens.

Coriol. Pray you now, if it may stand with the tune of your voices, that I may bee Consull, I haue heere the Customarie Gowne.

1. You haue deserued Nobly of your Countrey, and you haue not deserued Nobly.

Coriol. Your Ænigma.

1 You haue bin a scourge to her enemies, you haue bin a Rod to her Friends, you haue not indeede loued the Common people.

Coriol You should account mee the more Vertuous, that I haue not bin common in my Loue, I will sir flatter my sworne Brother the people to earne a deerer estimation of them, 'tis a condition they account gentle: & since the wisedome of their choice, is rather to haue my Hat, then my Heart, I will practice the insinuating nod, and be off to them most counterfetly, that is sir, I will counterfet the bewitchment of some popular man, and giue it bountifull to the desirers: Therefore beseech you, I may be Consull.

2. Wee hope to finde you our friend: and therefore giue you our voices heartily.

1. You haue receyued many wounds for your Countrey.

Coriol. I wil not Seale your knowledge with shewing them. I will make much of your voyces, and so trouble you no farther.

Both. The Gods giue you ioy Sir heartily.

Coriol. Most sweet Voyces:
Better it is to dye, better to sterue,
Then craue the higher, which first we do deserue.
Why in this Wooluish tongue should I stand heere,
To begge of Hob and Dicke, that does appeere

Their

Their needlesse Vouches: Custome calls me too't.
What Custome wills in all things, should we doo't?
The Dust on antique Time would lye vnswept,
And mountainous Error be too highly heapt,
For Truth to o're-peere. Rather then foole it so,
Let the high Office and the Honor go
To one that would doe thus. I am halfe through,
The one part suffered, the other will I doe.

Enter three Citizens more.

Here come moe Voyces.
Your Voyces? for your Voyces I haue fought,
Watcht for your Voyces: for your Voyces, beare
Of Wounds, two dozen odde: Battailes thrice six
I haue seene, and heard of: for your Voyces,
Haue done many things, some lesse, some more:
Your Voyces? Indeed I would be Consull.

1.Cit. Hee ha's done Nobly, and cannot goe without any honest mans Voyce.

2.Cit. Therefore let him be Consull: the Gods giue him ioy, and make him good friend to the People.

All. Amen, Amen. God saue thee, Noble Consull.

Corio. Worthy Voyces.

Enter Menenius, with Brutus and Scicinius.

Mene. You haue stood your Limitation:
And the Tribunes endue you with the Peoples Voyce,
Remaines, that in th'Officiall Markes inuested,
You anon doe meet the Senate.

Corio. Is this done?

Scicin. The Custome of Request you haue discharg'd:
The People doe admit you, and are summon'd
To meet anon, vpon your approbation.

Corio. Where? at the Senate-house?

Scicin. There, *Coriolanus.*

Corio. May I change these Garments?

Scicin. You may, Sir.

Cori. That Ile straight do: and knowing my selfe again,
Repayre toth' Senate-house.

Mene. Ile keepe you company. Will you along?

Brut. We stay here for the People.

Scicin. Fare you well. *Exeunt Coriol. and Mene.*
He ha's it now: and by his Lookes, me thinkes,
'Tis warme at's heart.

Brut. With a prowd heart he wore his humble Weeds:
Will you dismisse the People?

Enter the Plebeians.

Scici. How now, my Masters, haue you chose this man?

1.Cit. He ha's our Voyces, Sir.

Brut. We pray the Gods, he may deserue your loues.

2.Cit. Amen, Sir: to my poore vnworthy notice,
He mock'd vs, when he begg'd our Voyces.

3.Cit. Certainely, he flowted vs downe-right.

1.Cit. No, 'tis his kind of speech, he did not mock vs.

2.Cit. Not one amongst vs, saue your selfe, but sayes
He vs'd vs scornefully: he should haue shew'd vs
His Marks of Merit, Wounds receiu'd for's Countrey.

Scicin. Why so he did I am sure.

All. No, no: no man saw 'em.

3.Cit. Hee said hee had Wounds,
Which he could shew in priuate:
And with his Hat, thus wauing it in scorne,
I would be Consull, sayes he: aged Custome,
But by your Voyces, will not so permit me.
Your Voyces therefore: when we graunted that,
Here was, I thanke you for your Voyces, thanke you
Your most sweet Voyces: now you haue left your Voyces,
I haue no further with you. Was not this mockerie?

Scicin. Why eyther were you ignorant to see't?
Or seeing it, of such Childish friendlinesse,
To yeeld your Voyces?

Brut. Could you not haue told him,
As you were lesson'd: When he had no Power,
But was a pettie seruant to the State,
He was your Enemie, euer spake against
Your Liberties, and the Charters that you beare
I'th' Body of the Weale: and now arriuing
A place of Potencie, and sway o'th' State,
If he should still malignantly remaine
Fast Foe toth' *Plebeij*, your Voyces might
Be Curses to your selues. You should haue said,
That as his worthy deeds did clayme no lesse
Then what he stood for: so his gracious nature
Would thinke vpon you, for your Voyces,
And translate his Mallice towards you, into Loue,
Standing your friendly Lord.

Scicin. Thus to haue said,
As you were fore-aduis'd, had toucht his Spirit,
And try'd his Inclination: from him pluckt
Eyther his gracious Promise, which you might
As cause had call'd you vp, haue held him to;
Or else it would haue gall'd his surly nature,
Which easily endures not Article,
Tying him to ought, so putting him to Rage,
You should haue ta'ne th'aduantage of his Choller,
And pass'd him vnelected.

Brut. Did you perceiue,
He did sollicite you in free Contempt,
When he did need your Loues: and doe you thinke,
That his Contempt shall not be brusing to you,
When he hath power to crush? Why, had your Bodyes
No Heart among you? Or had you Tongues, to cry
Against the Rectorship of Iudgement?

Scicin. Haue you, ere now, deny'd the asker:
And now againe, of him that did not aske, but mock,
Bestow your su'd-for Tongues?

3.Cit. Hee's not confirm'd, we may deny him yet.

2.Cit. And will deny him:
Ile haue fiue hundred Voyces of that sound.

1.Cit. I twice fiue hundred, & their friends, to piece 'em.

Brut. Get you hence instantly, and tell those friends,
They haue chose a Consull, that will from them take
Their Liberties, make them of no more Voyce
Then Dogges, that are as often beat for barking,
As therefore kept to doe so.

Scici. Let them assemble: and on a safer Iudgement,
All reuoke your ignorant election: Enforce his Pride,
And his old Hate vnto you: besides, forget not
With what Contempt he wore the humble Weed,
How in his Suit he scorn'd you: but your Loues,
Thinking vpon his Seruices, tooke from you
Th'apprehension of his present portance,
Which most gibingly, vngrauely, he did fashion
After the inueterate Hate he beares you.

Brut. Lay a fault on vs, your Tribunes,
That we labour'd (no impediment betweene)
But that you must cast your Election on him.

Scici. Say you chose him, more after our commandment,
Then as guided by your owne true affections, and that
Your Minds pre-occupy'd with what you rather must do,
Then what you should, made you against the graine
To Voyce him Consull. Lay the fault on vs.

b b *Brut.* I,

Brut. I, ſpare vs not: Say, we read Lectures to you,
How youngly he began to ſerue his Countrey,
How long continued, and what ſtock he ſprings of,
The Noble Houſe o'th' *Martians*: from whence came
That *Ancus Martius*, *Numaes* Daughters Sonne.
Who after great *Hoſtilius* here was King,
Of the ſame Houſe *Publius* and *Quintus* were,
That our beſt Water, brought by Conduits hither,
And Nobly nam'd, ſo twice being Cenſor,
Was his great Anceſtor.
Scicin. One thus deſcended,
That hath beſide well in his perſon wrought,
To be ſet high in place, we did commend
To your remembrances: but you haue found,
Skaling his preſent bearing with his paſt,
That hee's your fixed enemie; and reuoke
Your ſuddaine approbation.
Brut. Say you ne're had don't,
(Harpe on that ſtill) but by our putting on:
And preſently, when you haue drawne your number,
Repaire toth' Capitoll.
All. We will ſo: almoſt all repent in their election.
Exeunt Plebeians.
Brut. Let them goe on:
This Mutinie were better put in hazard,
Then ſtay paſt doubt, for greater:
If, as his nature is, he fall in rage
With their refuſall, both obſerue and anſwer
The vantage of his anger.
Scicin. Toth' Capitoll, come:
We will be there before the ſtreame o'th' People:
And this ſhall ſeeme, as partly 'tis, their owne,
Which we haue goaded on-ward. *Exeunt.*

Actus Tertius.

Cornets. Enter Coriolanus, Menenius, all the Gentry, Cominius, Titus Latius, and other Senators.

Corio. *Tullus Auffidius* then had made new head.
Latius. He had, my Lord, and that it was which caus'd
Our ſwifter Compoſition.
Corio. So then the Volces ſtand but as at firſt,
Readie when time ſhall prompt them, to make roade
Vpon's againe.
Com. They are worne (Lord Conſull) ſo,
That we ſhall hardly in our ages ſee
Their Banners waue againe.
Corio. Saw you *Auffidius*?
Latius. On ſafegard he came to me, and did curſe
Againſt the Volces, for they had ſo vildly
Yeelded the Towne: he is retyred to Antium.
Corio. Spoke he of me?
Latius. He did, my Lord.
Corio. How? what?
Latius. How often he had met you Sword to Sword:
That of all things vpon the Earth, he hated
Your perſon moſt: That he would pawne his fortunes
To hopeleſſe reſtitution, ſo he might
Be call'd your Vanquiſher.
Corio. At Antium liues he?
Latius. At Antium.
Corio. I wiſh I had a cauſe to ſeeke him there,
To oppoſe his hatred fully. Welcome home.
Enter Scicinius and Brutus.
Behold, theſe are the Tribunes of the People,
The Tongues o'th' Common Mouth. I do deſpiſe them:
For they doe pranke them in Authoritie,
Againſt all Noble ſufferance.
Scicin. Paſſe no further.
Cor. Hah? what is that?
Brut. It will be dangerous to goe on-- No further.
Corio. What makes this change?
Mene. The matter?
Com. Hath he not paſs'd the Noble, and the Common?
Brut. *Cominius*, no.
Corio. Haue I had Childrens Voyces?
Senat. Tribunes giue way, he ſhall toth' Market place.
Brut. The People are incens'd againſt him.
Scicin. Stop, or all will fall in broyle.
Corio. Are theſe your Heard?
Muſt theſe haue Voyces, that can yeeld them now,
And ſtraight diſclaim their toungs? what are your Offices?
You being their Mouthes, why rule you not their Teeth?
Haue you not ſet them on?
Mene. Be calme, be calme.
Corio. It is a purpos'd thing, and growes by Plot,
To curbe the will of the Nobilitie:
Suffer't, and liue with ſuch as cannot rule,
Nor euer will be ruled.
Brut. Call't not a Plot:
The People cry you mockt them: and of late,
When Corne was giuen them *gratis*, you repin'd,
Scandal'd the Suppliants: for the People, call'd them
Time-pleaſers, flatterers, foes to Nobleneſſe.
Corio. Why this was knowne before.
Brut. Not to them all.
Corio. Haue you inform'd them ſithence?
Brut. How? I informe them?
Com. You are like to doe ſuch buſineſſe.
Brut. Not vnlike each way to better yours.
Corio. Why then ſhould I be Conſull? by yond Clouds
Let me deſerue ſo ill as you, and make me
Your fellow Tribune.
Scicin. You ſhew too much of that,
For which the People ſtirre: if you will paſſe
To where you are bound, you muſt enquire your way,
Which you are out of, with a gentler ſpirit,
Or neuer be ſo Noble as a Conſull,
Nor yoake with him for Tribune.
Mene. Let's be calme.
Com. The People are abus'd: ſet on, this paltring
Becomes not Rome: nor ha's *Coriolanus*
Deſeru'd this ſo diſhonor'd Rub, layd falſely
I'th' plaine Way of his Merit.
Corio. Tell me of Corne: this was my ſpeech,
And I will ſpeak't againe.
Mene. Not now, not now.
Senat. Not in this heat, Sir, now.
Corio. Now as I liue, I will.
My Nobler friends, I craue their pardons:
For the mutable ranke-ſented Meynie,
Let them regard me, as I doe not flatter,
And therein behold themſelues: I ſay againe,
In ſoothing them, we nouriſh 'gainſt our Senate
The Cockle of Rebellion, Inſolence, Sedition,
Which we our ſelues haue plowed for, ſow'd, & ſcatter'd,
By mingling them with vs, the honor'd Number,
Who lack not Vertue, no, nor Power, but that
Which they haue giuen to Beggers.
Mene. Well, no more.
Senat. No more words, we beſeech you.
Corio. How? no more?

As

As for my Country, I haue shed my blood,
Not fearing outward force: So shall my Lungs
Coine words till their decay, against those Meazels
Which we disdaine should Tetter vs, yet sought
The very way to catch them.
Bru. You speake a'th people, as if you were a God,
To punish; Not a man, of their Infirmity.
Sicin. 'Twere well we let the people know't.
Mene. What, what? His Choller?
Cor. Choller? Were I as patient as the midnight sleep,
By Ioue, 'twould be my minde.
Sicin. It is a minde that shall remain a poison
Where it is: not poyson any further.
Corio. Shall remaine?
Heare you this Triton of the *Minnowes*? Marke you
His absolute Shall?
Com. 'Twas from the Cannon.
Cor. Shall? O God! but most vnwise Patricians: why
You graue, but wreaklesse Senators, haue you thus
Giuen Hidra heere to choose an Officer,
That with his peremptory Shall, being but
The horne, and noise o'th' Monsters, wants not spirit
To say, hee'l turne your Current in a ditch,
And make your Channell his? If he haue power,
Then vale your Ignorance: If none, awake
Your dangerous Lenity: If you are Learn'd,
Be not as common Fooles; if you are not,
Let them haue Cushions by you. You are Plebeians,
If they be Senators: and they are no lesse,
When both your voices blended, the great'st taste
Most pallates theirs. They choose their Magistrate,
And such a one as he, who puts his Shall,
His popular Shall, against a grauer Bench
Then euer frown'd in Greece. By Ioue himselfe,
It makes the Consuls base; and my Soule akes
To know, when two Authorities are vp,
Neither Supreame: How soone Confusion
May enter 'twixt the gap of Both, and take
The one by th'other.
Com. Well, on to'th' Market place.
Corio. Who euer gaue that Counsell, to giue forth
The Corne a'th' Store-house gratis, as 'twas vs'd
Sometime in Greece.
Mene. Well, well, no more of that.
Cor. Thogh there the people had more absolute powre
I say they norisht disobedience: fed, the ruin of the State.
Bru. Why shall the people giue
One that speakes thus, their voyce?
Corio. Ile giue my Reasons,
More worthier then their Voyces. They know the Corne
Was not our recompence, resting well assur'd
They ne're did seruice for't; being prest to'th' Warre,
Euen when the Nauell of the State was touch'd,
They would not thred the Gates: This kinde of Seruice
Did not deserue Corne gratis. Being i'th' Warre,
There Mutinies and Reuolts, wherein they shew'd
Most Valour, spoke not for them. Th'Accusation
Which they haue often made against the Senate,
All cause vnborne, could neuer be the Natiue
Of our so franke Donation. Well, what then?
How shall this Bosome-multiplied, digest
The Senates Courtesie? Let deeds expresse
What's like to be their words, We did request it,
We are the greater pole, and in true feare
They gaue vs our demands. Thus we debase
The Nature of our Seats, and make the Rabble
Call our Cares, Feares; which will in time
Breake ope the Lockes a'th' Senate, and bring in
The Crowes to pecke the Eagles.
Mene. Come enough.
Bru. Enough, with ouer measure.
Corio. No, take more.
What may be sworne by, both Diuine and Humane,
Seale what I end withall. This double worship,
Whereon part do's disdaine with cause, the other
Insult without all reason: where Gentry, Title, wisedom
Cannot conclude, but by the yea and no
Of generall Ignorance, it must omit
Reall Necessities, and giue way the while
To vnstable Slightnesse. Purpose so barr'd, it followes,
Nothing is done to purpose. Therefore beseech you,
You that will be lesse fearefull, then discreet,
That loue the Fundamentall part of State
More then you doubt the change on't: That preferre
A Noble life, before a Long, and Wish,
To iumpe a Body with a dangerous Physicke,
That's sure of death without it: at once plucke out
The Multitudinous Tongue, let them not licke
The sweet which is their poyson. Your dishonor
Mangles true iudgement, and bereaues the State
Of that Integrity which should becom't:
Not hauing the power to do the good it would
For th'ill which doth controul't.
Bru. Has said enough.
Sicin. Ha's spoken like a Traitor, and shall answer
As Traitors do.
Corio. Thou wretch, despight ore-whelme thee:
What should the people do with these bald Tribunes?
On whom depending, their obedience failes
To'th' greater Bench, in a Rebellion:
When what's not meet, but what must be, was Law,
Then were they chosen: in a better houre,
Let what is meet, be saide it must be meet,
And throw their power i'th' dust.
Bru. Manifest Treason.
Sicin. This a Consull? No.
Enter an Ædile.
Bru. The Ediles hoe: Let him be apprehended:
Sicin. Go call the people, in whose name my Selfe
Attach thee as a Traitorous Innouator:
A Foe to'th' publike Weale. Obey I charge thee,
And follow to thine answer.
Corio. Hence old Goat.
All. Wee'l Surety him.
Com. Ag'd sir, hands off.
Corio. Hence rotten thing, or I shall shake thy bones
Out of thy Garments.
Sicin. Helpe ye Citizens.
Enter a rabble of Plebeians with the Ædiles.
Mene. On both sides more respect.
Sicin. Heere's hee, that would take from you all your power.
Bru. Seize him *Ædiles.*
All. Downe with him, downe with him.
2 Sen. Weapons, weapons, weapons:
They all bustle about Coriolanus.
Tribunes, Patricians, Citizens: what ho:
Sicinius, Brutus, Coriolanus, Citizens.
All. Peace, peace, peace, stay, hold, peace.
Mene. What is about to be? I am out of Breath,
Confusions neere, I cannot speake. You, Tribunes
To'th' people: *Coriolanus,* patience: Speak good *Sicinius.*

Scici. Heare me, People peace.
All. Let's here our Tribune: peace, ſpeake, ſpeake, ſpeake.
Scici. You are at point to loſe your Liberties:
Martius would haue all from you; *Martius*,
Whom late you haue nam'd for Conſull.
Mene. Fie, fie, fie, this is the way to kindle, not to quench.
Sena. To vnbuild the Citie, and to lay all flat.
Scici. What is the Citie, but the People?
All. True, the People are the Citie.
Brut. By the conſent of all, we were eſtabliſh'd the Peoples Magiſtrates.
All. You ſo remaine.
Mene. And ſo are like to doe.
Com. That is the way to lay the Citie flat,
To bring the Roofe to the Foundation,
And burie all, which yet diſtinctly raunges
In heapes, and piles of Ruine.
Scic. This deſerues Death.
Brut. Or let vs ſtand to our Authoritie,
Or let vs loſe it: we doe here pronounce,
Vpon the part o'th' People, in whoſe power
We were elected theirs, *Martius* is worthy
Of preſent Death.
Scici. Therefore lay hold of him:
Beare him toth' Rock Tarpeian, and from thence
Into deſtruction caſt him.
Brut. Ædiles ſeize him.
All Ple. Yeeld *Martius*, yeeld.
Mene. Heare me one word, 'beſeech you Tribunes, heare me but a word.
Ædiles. Peace, peace.
Mene. Be that you ſeeme, truly your Countries friend,
And temp'rately proceed to what you would
Thus violently redreſſe.
Brut. Sir, thoſe cold wayes,
That ſeeme like prudent helpes, are very poyſonous,
Where the Diſeaſe is violent. Lay hands vpon him,
And beare him to the Rock. *Corio. drawes his Sword.*
Corio. No, Ile die here:
There's ſome among you haue beheld me fighting,
Come trie vpon your ſelues, what you haue ſeene me.
Mene. Downe with that Sword, Tribunes withdraw a while.
Brut. Lay hands vpon him.
Mene. Helpe *Martius*, helpe: you that be noble, helpe him young and old.
All. Downe with him, downe with him. *Exeunt.*
In this Mutinie, the Tribunes, the Ædiles, and the People are beat in.
Mene. Goe, get you to our Houſe: be gone, away,
All will be naught elſe.
2. Sena. Get you gone.
Com. Stand faſt, we haue as many friends as enemies.
Mene. Shall it be put to that?
Sena. The Gods forbid:
I prythee noble friend, home to thy Houſe,
Leaue vs to cure this Cauſe.
Mene. For 'tis a Sore vpon vs,
You cannot Tent your ſelfe: be gone, 'beſeech you.
Corio. Come Sir, along with vs.
Mene. I would they were Barbarians, as they are,
Though in Rome litter'd: not Romans, as they are not,
Though calued i'th' Porch o'th' Capitoll:
Be gone, put not your worthy Rage into your Tongue,
One time will owe another.
Corio. On faire ground, I could beat fortie of them.
Mene. I could my ſelfe take vp a Brace o'th' beſt of them, yea, the two Tribunes.
Com. But now 'tis oddes beyond Arithmetick,
And Manhood is call'd Foolerie, when it ſtands
Againſt a falling Fabrick. Will you hence,
Before the Tagge returne? whoſe Rage doth rend
Like interrupted Waters, and o're-beare
What they are vs'd to beare.
Mene. Pray you be gone:
Ile trie whether my old Wit be in requeſt
With thoſe that haue but little: this muſt be patcht
With Cloth of any Colour.
Com. Nay, come away. *Exeunt Coriolanus and Cominius.*
Patri. This man ha's marr'd his fortune.
Mene. His nature is too noble for the World:
He would not flatter *Neptune* for his Trident,
Or *Ioue*, for's power to Thunder: his Heart's his Mouth:
What his Breſt forges, that his Tongue muſt vent,
And being angry, does forget that euer
He heard the Name of Death. *A Noiſe within.*
Here's goodly worke.
Patri. I would they were a bed.
Mene. I would they were in Tyber.
What the vengeance, could he not ſpeake 'em faire?
Enter Brutus and Sicinius with the rabble againe.
Sicin. Where is this Viper,
That would depopulate the city, & be euery man himſelf
Mene. You worthy Tribunes.
Sicin. He ſhall be throwne downe the Tarpeian rock
With rigorous hands: he hath reſiſted Law,
And therefore Law ſhall ſcorne him further Triall
Then the ſeuerity of the publike Power,
Which he ſo ſets at naught.
1 Cit. He ſhall well know the Noble Tribunes are
The peoples mouths, and we their hands.
All. He ſhall ſure ont.
Mene. Sir, ſir. *Sicin.* Peace.
Me. Do not cry hauocke, where you ſhold but hunt
With modeſt warrant.
Sicin. Sir, how com'ſt that you haue holpe
To make this reſcue?
Mene. Heere me ſpeake? As I do know
The Conſuls worthineſſe, ſo can I name his Faults.
Sicin. Conſull? what Conſull?
Mene. The Conſull *Coriolanus.*
Bru. He Conſull.
All. No, no, no, no, no.
Mene. If by the Tribunes leaue,
And yours good people,
I may be heard, I would craue a word or two,
The which ſhall turne you to no further harme,
Then ſo much loſſe of time.
Sic. Speake breefely then,
For we are peremptory to diſpatch
This Viporous Traitor: to eiect him hence
Were but one danger, and to keepe him heere
Our certaine death: therefore it is decreed,
He dyes to night.
Menen. Now the good Gods forbid,
That our renowned Rome, whoſe gratitude
Towards her deſerued Children, is enroll'd
In Ioues owne Booke, like an vnnaturall Dam
Should now eate vp her owne.
Sicin.

Sicin. He's a Diſeaſe that muſt be cut away.
Mene. Oh he's a Limbe, that ha's but a Diſeaſe
Mortall, to cut it off: to cure it, eaſie.
What ha's he done to Rome, that's worthy death?
Killing our Enemies, the blood he hath loſt
(Which I dare vouch, is more then that he hath
By many an Ounce) he dropp'd it for his Country:
And what is left, to looſe it by his Countrey,
Were to vs all that doo't, and ſuffer it
A brand to th'end a'th World.
Sicin. This is cleane kamme.
Brut. Meerely awry:
When he did loue his Country, it honour'd him.
Menen. The ſeruice of the foote
Being once gangren'd, is not then reſpected
For what before it was.
Bru. Wee'l heare no more:
Purſue him to his houſe, and plucke him thence,
Leaſt his infection being of catching nature,
Spred further.
Menen. One word more, one word:
This Tiger-footed-rage, when it ſhall find
The harme of vnskan'd ſwiftneſſe, will (too late)
Tye Leaden pounds too's heeles. Proceed by Proceſſe,
Leaſt parties (as he is belou'd) breake out,
And ſacke great Rome with Romanes.
Brut. If it were ſo?
Sicin. What do ye talke?
Haue we not had a taſte of his Obedience?
Our Ediles ſmot: our ſelues reſiſted: come.
Mene. Conſider this: He ha's bin bred i'th'Warres
Since a could draw a Sword, and is ill-ſchool'd
In boulted Language: Meale and Bran together
He throwes without diſtinction. Giue me leaue,
Ile go to him, and vndertake to bring him in peace,
Where he ſhall anſwer by a lawfull Forme
(In peace) to his vtmoſt perill.
1.Sen. Noble Tribunes,
It is the humane way: the other courſe
Will proue to bloody: and the end of it,
Vnknowne to the Beginning.
Sic. Noble *Menenius*, be you then as the peoples officer:
Maſters, lay downe your Weapons.
Bru. Go not home.
Sic. Meet on the Market place: wee'l attend you there:
Where if you bring not *Martius*, wee'l proceede
In our firſt way.
Menen. Ile bring him to you.
Let me deſire your company: he muſt come,
Or what is worſt will follow.
Sena. Pray you let's to him. *Exeunt Omnes.*

Enter Coriolanus with Nobles.

Corio. Let them pull all about mine eares, preſent me
Death on the Wheele, or at wilde Horſes heeles,
Or pile ten hilles on the Tarpeian Rocke,
That the precipitation might downe ſtretch
Below the beame of ſight; yet will I ſtill
Be thus to them.

Enter Volumnia.

Noble. You do the Nobler.
Corio. I muſe my Mother
Do's not approue me further, who was wont
To call them Wollen Vaſſailes, things created
To buy and ſell with Groats, to ſhew bare heads
In Congregations, to yawne, be ſtill, and wonder,
When one but of my ordinance ſtood vp
To ſpeake of Peace, or Warre. I talke of you,
Why did you wiſh me milder? Would you haue me
Falſe to my Nature? Rather ſay, I play
The man I am.
Volum. Oh ſir, ſir, ſir,
I would haue had you put your power well on
Before you had worne it out.
Corio. Let go.
Vol. You might haue beene enough the man you are,
With ſtriuing leſſe to be ſo: Leſſer had bin
The things of your diſpoſitions, if
You had not ſhew'd them how ye were diſpos'd
Ere they lack'd power to croſſe you.
Corio. Let them hang.
Volum. I, and burne too.

Enter Menenius with the Senators.

Men. Come, come, you haue bin too rough, ſomthing too rough: you muſt returne, and mend it.
Sen. There's no remedy,
Vnleſſe by not ſo doing, our good Citie
Cleaue in the midd'ſt, and periſh.
Volum. Pray be counſail'd;
I haue a heart as little apt as yours,
But yet a braine, that leades my vſe of Anger
To better vantage.
Mene. Well ſaid, Noble woman:
Before he ſhould thus ſtoope to'th'heart, but that
The violent fit a'th'time craues it as Phyſicke
For the whole State; I would put mine Armour on,
Which I can ſcarſely beare.
Corio. What muſt I do?
Mene. Returne to th'Tribunes.
Corio. Well, what then? what then?
Mene. Repent, what you haue ſpoke.
Corio. For them, I cannot do it to the Gods,
Muſt I then doo't to them?
Volum. You are too abſolute,
Though therein you can neuer be too Noble,
But when extremities ſpeake. I haue heard you ſay,
Honor and Policy, like vnſeuer'd Friends,
I'th'Warre do grow together: Grant that, and tell me
In Peace, what each of them by th'other looſe,
That they combine not there?
Corio. Tuſh, tuſh.
Mene. A good demand.
Volum. If it be Honor in your Warres, to ſeeme
The ſame you are not, which for your beſt ends
You adopt your policy: How is it leſſe or worſe
That it ſhall hold Companionſhip in Peace
With Honour, as in Warre; ſince that to both
It ſtands in like requeſt.
Corio. Why force you this?
Volum. Becauſe, that
Now it lyes you on to ſpeake to th'people:
Not by your owne inſtruction, nor by'th'matter
Which your heart prompts you, but with ſuch words
That are but roated in your Tongue;
Though but Baſtards, and Syllables
Of no allowance, to your boſomes truth.
Now, this no more diſhonors you at all,
Then to take in a Towne with gentle words,
Which elſe would put you to your fortune, and
The hazard of much blood.
I would diſſemble with my Nature, where
My Fortunes and my Friends at ſtake, requir'd
I ſhould do ſo in Honor. I am in this

Your Wife,your Sonne:These Senators,the Nobles,
And you,will rather shew our generall Lowts,
How you can frowne,then spend,a fawne vpon'em,
For the inheritance of their loues, and safegard
Of what that want might ruine.
Menen. Noble Lady.
Come goe with vs,speake faire: you may salue so,
Not what is dangerous present,but the losse
Of what is past.
Volum. I pry thee now,my Sonne,
Goe to them,with this Bonnet in thy hand,
And thus farre hauing stretcht it(here be with them)
Thy Knee bussing the stones: for in such businesse
Action is eloquence,and the eyes of th'ignorant
More learned then the eares,wauing thy head,
Which often thus correcting thy stout heart,
Now humble as the ripest Mulberry,
That will not hold the handling : or say to them,
Thou art their Souldier,and being bred in broyles,
Hast not the soft way,which thou do'st confesse
Were fit for thee to vse,as they to clayme,
In asking their good loues, but thou wilt frame
Thy selfe (forsooth) hereafter theirs so farre,
As thou hast power and person.
Menen This but done,
Euen as she speakes,why their hearts were yours:
For they haue Pardons,being ask'd,as free,
As words to little purpose.
Volum. Prythee now,
Goe,and be rul'd : although I know thou hadst rather
Follow thine Enemie in a fierie Gulfe,
Then flatter him in a Bower. *Enter Cominius.*
Here is *Cominius.*
Com I haue beene i'th' Market place: and Sir 'tis fit
You make strong partie,or defend your selfe
By calmenesse,or by absence: all's in anger.
Menen. Onely faire speech.
Com. I thinke 'twill serue,if he can thereto frame his spirit.
Volum. He must,and will:
Prythee now say you will,and goe about it.
Corio. Must I goe shew them my vnbarb'd Sconce?
Must I with my base Tongue giue to my Noble Heart
A Lye, that it must beare well? I will doo't:
Yet were there but this single Plot,to loose
This Mould of *Martius*,they to dust should grinde it,
And throw't against the Winde. Toth' Market place:
You haue put me now to such a part,which neuer
I shall discharge toth' Life.
Com Come,come,wee'le prompt you.
Volum. I prythee now sweet Son,as thou hast said
My praises made thee first a Souldier; so
To haue my praise for this, performe a part
Thou hast not done before
Corio. Well,I must doo't:
Away my disposition, and possesse me
Some Harlots spirit: My throat of Warre be turn'd,
Which quier'd with my Drumme into a Pipe,
Small as an Eunuch, or the Virgin voyce
That Babies lull a-sleepe: The smiles of Knaues
Tent in my cheekes, and Schoole-boyes Teares take vp
The Glasses of my sight: A Beggars Tongue
Make motion through my Lips,and my Arm'd knees
Who bow'd but in my Stirrop, bend like his
That hath receiu'd an Almes. I will not doo't,
Least I surcease to honor mine owne truth,
And by my Bodies action, teach my Minde
A most inherent Basenesse.
Volum. At thy choice then:
To begge of thee, it is my more dis-honor,
Then thou of them. Come all to ruine, let
Thy Mother rather feele thy Pride, then feare
Thy dangerous Stoutnesse: for I mocke at death
With as bigge heart as thou. Do as thou list,
Thy Valiantnesse was mine, thou suck'st it from me:
But owe thy Pride thy selfe.
Corio. Pray be content:
Mother, I am going to the Market place
Chide me no more. Ile Mountebanke their Loues,
Cogge their Hearts from them,and come home belou'd
Of all the Trades in Rome. Looke,I am going:
Commend me to my Wife, Ile returne Consull,
Or neuer trust to what my Tongue can do
I'th way of Flattery further.
Volum. Do your will. *Exit Volumnia*
Com. Away,the Tribunes do attend you:arm your self
To answer mildely: for they are prepar'd
With Accusations, as I heare more strong
Then are vpon you yet.
Corio. The word is, Mildely. Pray you let vs go,
Let them accuse me by inuention: I
Will answer in mine Honor.
Menen. I, but mildely.
Corio. Well mildely be it then, Mildely. *Exeunt*

Enter Sicinius and Brutus.

Bru. In this point charge him home,that he affects
Tyrannicall power: If he euade vs there,
Inforce him with his enuy to the people,
And that the Spoile got on the *Antiats*
Was ne're distributed. What,will he come?

Enter an Edile.

Edile. Hee's comming.
Bru. How accompanied?
Edile. With old *Menenius*,and those Senators
That alwayes fauour'd him.
Sicin. Haue you a Catalogue
Of all the Voices that we haue procur'd,set downe by'th (Pole?
Edile. I haue: 'tis ready.
Sicin. Haue you collected them by Tribes?
Edile. I haue.
Sicin. Assemble presently the people hither:
And when they heare me say, it shall be so,
I'th'right and strength a'th'Commons: be it either
For death, for fine,or Banishment, then let them
If I say Fine,cry Fine; if Death, cry Death,
Insisting on the olde prerogatiue
And power i'th Truth a'th Cause.
Edile. I shall informe them.
Bru. And when such time they haue begun to cry,
Let them not cease. but with a dinne confus'd
Inforce the present Execution
Of what we chance to Sentence
Edi. Very well.
Sicin. Make them be strong,and ready for this hint
When we shall hap to giu't them.
Bru. Go about it.
Put him to Choller straite, he hath bene vs'd
Euer to conquer, and to haue his worth
Of contradiction. Being once chaft, he cannot
Be rein'd againe to Temperance, then he speakes
What's

What's in his heart, and that is there which lookes
With vs to breake his necke.

Enter Coriolanus, Menenius, and Cominius, with others.

Sicin. Well, heere he comes.
Mene. Calmely, I do beſeech you.
Corio. I, as an Hoſtler, that fourth pooreſt peece
Will beare the Knaue by'th Volume:
Th'honor'd Goddes
Keepe Rome in ſafety, and the Chaires of Iuſtice
Supplied with worthy men, plant loue amongs
Through our large Temples with ẏ ſhewes of peace
And not our ſtreets with Warre.
1 Sen. Amen, Amen.
Mene. A Noble wiſh.

Enter the Edile with the Plebeians.

Sicin. Draw neere ye people.
Edile. Liſt to your Tribunes. Audience:
Peace I ſay.
Corio. Firſt heare me ſpeake.
Both Tri. Well, ſay: Peace hoe.
Corio. Shall I be charg'd no further then this preſent?
Muſt all determine heere?
Sicin. I do demand,
If you ſubmit you to the peoples voices,
Allow their Officers, and are content
To ſuffer lawfull Cenſure for ſuch faults
As ſhall be prou'd vpon you.
Corio. I am Content.
Mene. Lo Citizens, he ſayes he is Content.
The warlike Seruice he ha's done, conſider: Thinke
Vpon the wounds his body beares, which ſhew
Like Graues i'th holy Church-yard.
Corio. Scratches with Briars, ſcarres to moue
Laughter onely.
Mene. Conſider further:
That when he ſpeakes not like a Citizen,
You finde him like a Soldier: do not take
His rougher Actions for malicious ſounds:
But as I ſay, ſuch as become a Soldier,
Rather then enuy you.
Com. Well, well, no more.
Corio. What is the matter,
That being paſt for Conſull with full voyce:
I am ſo diſhonour'd, that the very houre
You take it off againe.
Sicin. Anſwer to vs.
Corio. Say then: 'tis true, I ought ſo.
Sicin. We charge you, that you haue contriu'd to take
From Rome all ſeaſon'd Office, and to winde
Your ſelfe into a power tyrannicall,
For which you are a Traitor to the people.
Corio. How? Traytor?
Mene. Nay temperately: your promiſe.
Corio. The fires i'th'loweſt hell. Fould in the people:
Call me their Traitor, thou iniurious Tribune.
Within thine eyes ſate twenty thouſand deaths
In thy hands clutcht: as many Millions in
Thy lying tongue, both numbers. I would ſay
Thou lyeſt vnto thee, with a voice as free,
As I do pray the Gods.
Sicin. Marke you this people?
All. To'th'Rocke, to'th'Rocke with him.
Sicin. Peace:
We neede not put new matter to his charge:
What you haue ſeene him do, and heard him ſpeake:
Beating your Officers, curſing your ſelues,
Oppoſing Lawes with ſtroakes, and heere defying
Thoſe whoſe great power muſt try him.
Euen this ſo criminall, and in ſuch capitall kinde
Deſerues th'extreameſt death.
Bru. But ſince he hath ſeru'd well for Rome.
Corio. What do you prate of Seruice.
Brut. I talke of that, that know it.
Corio. You?
Mene. Is this the promiſe that you made your mother.
Com. Know, I pray you.
Corio. Ile know no further:
Let them pronounce the ſteepe Tarpeian death,
Vagabond exile, Fleaing, pent to linger
But with a graine a day, I would not buy
Their mercie, at the price of one faire word,
Nor checke my Courage for what they can giue,
To haue't with ſaying, Good morrow.
Sicin. For that he ha's
(As much as in him lies) from time to time
Enui'd againſt the people; ſeeking meanes
To plucke away their power: as now at laſt,
Giuen Hoſtile ſtrokes, and that not in the preſence
Of dreaded Iuſtice, but on the Miniſters
That doth diſtribute it. In the name a'th'people,
And in the power of vs the Tribunes, wee
(Eu'n from this inſtant) baniſh him our Citie
In perill of precipitation
From off the Rocke Tarpeian, neuer more
To enter our Rome gates. I'th'Peoples name,
I ſay it ſhall bee ſo.
All. It ſhall be ſo, it ſhall be ſo: let him away:
Hee's baniſh'd, and it ſhall be ſo.
Com. Heare me my Maſters, and my common friends.
Sicin. He's ſentenc'd: No more hearing.
Com. Let me ſpeake:
I haue bene Conſull, and can ſhew from Rome
Her Enemies markes vpon me. I do loue
My Countries good, with a reſpect more tender,
More holy, and profound, then mine owne life,
My deere Wiues eſtimate, her wombes encreaſe,
And treaſure of my Loynes: then if I would
Speake that.
Sicin. We know your drift. Speake what?
Bru. There's no more to be ſaid, but he is baniſh'd
As Enemy to the people, and his Countrey.
It ſhall bee ſo.
All. It ſhall be ſo, it ſhall be ſo.
Corio. You common cry of Curs, whoſe breath I hate,
As reeke a'th rotten Fennes: whoſe Loues I prize,
As the dead Carkaſſes of vnburied men,
That do corrupt my Ayre: I baniſh you,
And heere remaine with your vncertaintie.
Let euery feeble Rumor ſhake your hearts:
Your Enemies, with nodding of their Plumes
Fan you into diſpaire: Haue the power ſtill
To baniſh your Defenders, till at length
Your ignorance (which findes not till it feeles,
Making but reſeruation of your ſelues,
Still your owne Foes) deliuer you
As moſt abated Captiues, to ſome Nation
That wonne you without blowes, deſpiſing
For you the City. Thus I turne my backe;
There is a world elſewhere.

Exeunt Coriolanus, Cominius, with Cumalijs.
They all ſhout, and throw vp their Caps.

Edile

Edile. The peoples Enemy is gone, is gone.
All. Our enemy is banish'd, he is gone: Hoo, oo.
Sicin. Go see him out at Gates, and follow him
As he hath follow'd you, with all despight
Giue him deseru'd vexation. Let a guard
Attend vs through the City.
All. Come, come, lets see him out at gates, come:
The Gods preserue our Noble Tribunes, come. *Exeunt.*

Actus Quartus.

Enter Coriolanus Volumnia, Virgilia, Menenius, Cominius, with the yong Nobility of Rome.

Corio. Come leaue your teares: a brief farwel: the beast
With many heads butts me away. Nay Mother,
Where is your ancient Courage? You were vs'd
To say, Extreamities was the trier of spirits,
That common chances. Common men could beare,
That when the Sea was calme, all Boats alike
Shew'd Mastership in floating. Fortunes blowes,
When most strooke home, being gentle wounded, craues
A Noble cunning. You were vs'd to load me
With Precepts that would make inuincible
The heart that conn'd them.
Virg. Oh heauens! O heauens!
Corio. Nay, I prythee woman.
Vol. Now the Red Pestilence strike al Trades in Rome,
And Occupations perish.
Corio. What, what, what:
I shall be lou'd when I am lack'd. Nay Mother,
Resume that Spirit, when you were wont to say,
If you had beene the Wife of *Hercules*,
Six of his Labours youl'd haue done, and sau'd
Your Husband so much swet. *Cominius*,
Droope not, Adieu: Farewell my Wife, my Mother,
Ile do well yet. Thou old and true *Menenius*,
Thy teares are salter then a yonger mans,
And venomous to thine eyes. My (sometime) Generall,
I haue seene the Sterne, and thou hast oft beheld
Heart-hardning spectacles. Tell these sad women,
Tis fond to waile ineuitable strokes,
As 'tis to laugh at 'em. My Mother, you wot well
My hazards still haue beene your solace, and
Beleeu't not lightly, though I go alone
Like to a lonely Dragon, that his Fenne
Makes fear'd, and talk'd of more then seene: your Sonne
Will or exceed the Common, or be caught
With cautelous baits and practice.
Volum. My first sonne,
Whether will thou go? Take good *Cominius*
With thee awhile: Determine on some course
More then a wilde exposture, to each chance
That start's i'th' way before thee.
Corio. O the Gods!
Com. Ile follow thee a Moneth, deuise with thee
Where thou shalt rest, that thou may'st heare of vs,
And we of thee. So if the time thrust forth
A cause for thy Repeale, we shall not send
O're the vast world, to seeke a single man,
And loose aduantage, which doth euer coole
Ith'absence of the needer.
Corio. Fare ye well:
Thou hast yeares vpon thee, and thou art too full
Of the warres surfets, to go roue with one
That's yet vnbruis'd: bring me but out at gate.
Come my sweet wife, my deerest Mother, and
My Friends of Noble touch: when I am forth,
Bid me farewell, and smile. I pray you come:
While I remaine aboue the ground, you shall
Heare from me still, and neuer of me ought
But what is like me formerly.
Menen. That's worthily
As any eare can heare. Come, let's not weepe,
If I could shake off but one seuen yeeres
From these old armes and legges, by the good Gods
I'ld with thee, euery foot.
Corio. Giue me thy hand, come. *Exeunt*

Enter the two Tribunes, Sicinius, and Brutus, with the Edile.

Sicin. Bid them all home, he's gone: & wee'l no further
The Nobility are vexed, whom we see haue sided
In his behalfe.
Brut. Now we haue shewne our power,
Let vs seeme humbler after it is done,
Then when it was a dooing.
Sicin Bid them home: say their great enemy is gone
And they, stand in their ancient strength.
Brut. Dismisse them home. Here comes his Mother

Enter Volumnia, Virgilia, and Menenius.

Sicin. Let's not meet her.
Brut Why?
Sicin. They say she's mad.
Brut. They haue tane note of vs: keepe on your way
Volum. Oh y'are well met:
Th'hoorded plague a'th'Gods requit your loue.
Menen. Peace, peace, be not so loud.
Volum. If that I could for weeping, you should heare
Nay, and you shall heare some. Will you be gone?
Virg. You shall stay too. I would I had the power
To say so to my Husband.
Sicin. Are you mankinde?
Volum. I foole, is that a shame. Note but this Foole,
Was not a man my Father? Had'st thou Foxship
To banish him that strooke more blowes for Rome
Then thou hast spoken words.
Sicin. Oh blessed Heauens!
Volum. Moe Noble blowes, then euer ÿ wise words.
And for Romes good, Ile tell thee what: yet goe:
Nay but thou shalt stay too: I would my Sonne
Were in Arabia, and thy Tribe before him,
His good Sword in his hand.
Sicin. What then?
Virg. What then? Hee'ld make an end of thy posterity
Volum. Bastards, and all.
Good man, the Wounds that he does beare for Rome!
Menen. Come, come, peace.
Sicin. I would he had continued to his Country
As he began, and not vnknit himselfe
The Noble knot he made.
Bru. I would he had.
Volum. I would he had? Twas you incenst the rable.
Cats, that can iudge as fitly of his worth,
As I can of those Mysteries which heauen
Will not haue earth to know.
Brut. Pray let's go.
Volum. Now pray sir get you gone.
You haue done a braue deede: Ere you go, heare this:
As farre as doth the Capitoll exceede
[illegible] house in Rome; so farre my Sonne

This

This Ladies Husband heere; this (do you see)
Whom you haue banish'd, does exceed you all.

Bru. Well, well, wee'l leaue you.

Sicin. Why stay we to be baited
With one that wants her Wits. *Exit Tribunes.*

Volum. Take my Prayers with you.
I would the Gods had nothing else to do,
But to confirme my Cursses. Could I meete 'em
But once a day, it would vnclogge my heart
Of what lyes heauy too't.

Mene. You haue told them home,
And by my troth you haue cause: you'l Sup with me.

Volum. Angers my Meate: I suppe vpon my selfe,
And so shall sterue with Feeding: Come, let's go,
Leaue this faint-puling, and lament as I do,
In Anger, *Iuno*-like: Come, come, come. *Exeunt*

Mene. Fie, fie, fie. *Exit.*

Enter a Roman, and a Volce.

Rom. I know you well sir, and you know mee: your name I thinke is *Adrian*.

Volce. It is so sir, truly I haue forgot you.

Rom. I am a Roman, and my Seruices are as you are, against 'em. Know you me yet.

Volce. Nicanor: no.

Rom. The same sir.

Volce. You had more Beard when I last saw you, but your Fauour is well appear'd by your Tongue. What's the Newes in Rome: I haue a Note from the Volcean state to finde you out there. You haue well saued mee a dayes iourney.

Rom. There hath beene in Rome straunge Insurrections: The people, against the Senatours, Patricians, and Nobles.

Vol. Hath bin; is it ended then? Our State thinks not so, they are in a most warlike preparation, & hope to com vpon them, in the heate of their diuision

Rom. The maine blaze of it is past, but a small thing would make it flame againe. For the Nobles receyue so to heart, the Banishment of that worthy *Coriolanus*, that they are in a ripe aptnesse, to take al power from the people, and to plucke from them their Tribunes for euer. This lyes glowing I can tell you, and is almost mature for the violent breaking out.

Vol. Coriolanus Banisht?

Rom. Banish'd sir.

Vol. You will be welcome with this intelligence *Nicanor*.

Rom. The day serues well for them now. I haue heard it saide, the fittest time to corrupt a mans Wife, is when shee's falne out with her Husband. Your Noble *Tullus Auffidius* well appeare well in these Warres, his great Opposer *Coriolanus* being now in no request of his countrey.

Volce. He cannot choose: I am most fortunate, thus accidentally to encounter you. You haue ended my Businesse, and I will merrily accompany you home.

Rom. I shall betweene this and Supper, tell you most strange things from Rome: all tending to the good of their Aduersaries. Haue you an Army ready say you?

Vol. A most Royall one: The Centurions, and their charges distinctly billetted already in th'entertainment, and to be on foot at an houres warning.

Rom. I am ioyfull to heare of their readinesse, and am the man I thinke, that shall set them in present Action. So sir, heartily well met, and most glad of your Company.

Volce. You take my part from me sir, I haue the most cause to be glad of yours.

Rom. Well, let vs go together. *Exe*

Enter Coriolanus in meane Apparrell, Disguisd, and muffled.

Corio. A goodly City is this *Antium*. Citty,
'Tis I that made thy Widdowes: Many an heyre
Of these faire Edifices fore my Warres
Haue I heard groane, and drop: Then know me not,
Least that thy Wiues with Spits, and Boyes with stones
In puny Battell slay me. Saue you sir.

Enter a Citizen.

Cit. And you.

Corio. Direct me, if it be your will, where great *Aufidius* lies: Is he in *Antium*?

Cit. He is, and Feasts the Nobles of the State, at his house this night.

Corio. Which is his house, beseech you?

Cit. This heere before you.

Corio. Thanke you sir, farewell. *Exit Citizen*
Oh World, thy slippery turnes! Friends now fast sworn,
Whose double bosomes seemes to weare one heart,
Whose Houres, whose Bed, whose Meale and Exercise
Are still together: who Twin (as 'twere) in Loue,
Vnseparable, shall within this houre,
On a dissention of a Doit, breake out
To bitterest Enmity: So fellest Foes,
Whose Passions, and whose Plots haue broke their sleep
To take the one the other, by some chance,
Some tricke not worth an Egge, shall grow deere friends
And inter-ioyne their yssues. So with me,
My Birth-place haue I, and my loues vpon
This Enemie Towne: Ile enter, if he slay me
He does faire Iustice: if he giue me way,
Ile do his Country Seruice. *Exit.*

Musicke playes. Enter a Seruingman.

1 *Ser.* Wine, Wine, Wine: What seruice is heere? I thinke our Fellowes are asleepe.

Enter another Seruingman.

2 *Ser.* Where's *Cotus*: my M. cals for him: *Cotus*. *Exit*

Enter Coriolanus.

Corio. A goodly House:
The Feast smels well: but I appeare not like a Guest.

Enter the first Seruingman.

1 *Ser.* What would you haue Friend? whence are you? Here's no place for you: Pray go to the doore? *Exit*

Corio. I haue deseru'd no better entertainment, in being *Coriolanus*. *Enter second Seruant.*

2 *Ser.* Whence are you sir? Ha's the Porter his eyes in his head, that he giues entrance to such Companions? Pray get you out.

Corio. Away.

2 *Ser.* Away? Get you away.

Corio. Now th'art troublesome.

2 *Ser.* Are you so braue: Ile haue you talkt with anon

Enter 3 Seruingman, the 1 meets him.

3 What Fellowes this?

1 A strange one as euer I look'd on: I cannot get him out o'th'house: Prythee call my Master to him.

3 What haue you to do here fellow? Pray you auoid the house.

Corio. Let me but stand, I will not hurt your Harth.

3 What are you?

Corio. A Gentleman.

3 A maru'llous poore one.

Corio. True, so I am.

3 Pray you poore Gentleman, take vp some other station

tion : Heere's no place for you, pray you auoid: Come.

Corio. Follow your Function, go, and batten on colde bits. *Pushes him away from him.*

3 What you will not? Prythee tell my Maister what a strange Guest he ha's heere.

2 And I shall. *Exit second Seruingman.*

3 Where dwel'st thou?

Corio. Vnder the Canopy.

3 Vnder the Canopy?

Corio. I.

3 Where's that?

Corio. I'th City of Kites and Crowes.

3 I'th City of Kites and Crowes? What an Asse it is, then thou dwel'st with Dawes too?

Corio. No, I serue not thy Master.

3 How sir? Do you meddle with my Master?

Corio. I, tis an honester seruice, then to meddle with thy Mistris : Thou prat'st, and prat'st, serue with thy trencher : Hence. *Beats him away*

Enter Auffidius with the Seruingman.

Auf. Where is this Fellow?

2 Here sir, I'de haue beaten him like a dogge, but for disturbing the Lords within.

Auf. Whence com'st thou? What woldst ÿ? Thy name? Why speak'st not? Speake man : What's thy name?

Corio. If *Tullus* not yet thou know'st me, and seeing me, dost not thinke me for the man I am, necessitie commands me name my selfe.

Auf. What is thy name?

Corio. A name vnmusicall to the Volcians eares,
And harsh in sound to thine.

Auf. Say, what's thy name?
Thou hast a Grim apparance, and thy Face
Beares a Command in't : Though thy Tackles torne,
Thou shew'st a Noble Vessell : What's thy name?

Corio. Prepare thy brow to frowne: knowst ÿ me yet?

Auf. I know thee not? Thy Name?

Corio My name is *Caius Martius*, who hath done
To thee particularly, and to all the Volces
Great hurt and Mischiefe : thereto witnesse may
My Surname *Coriolanus*. The painfull Seruice,
The extreme Dangers, and the droppes of Blood
Shed for my thanklesse Country, are requitted :
But with that Surname, a good memorie
And witnesse of the Malice and Displeasure
Which thou should'st beare me, only that name remains.
The Cruelty and Enuy of the people,
Permitted by our dastard Nobles, who
Haue all forsooke me, hath deuour'd the rest :
And suffer'd me by th'voyce of Slaues to be
Hoop'd out of Rome. Now this extremity,
Hath brought me to thy Harth, not out of Hope
(Mistake me not) to saue my life : for if
I had fear'd death, of all the Men i'th' World
I would haue voided thee. But in meere spight
To be full quit of those my Banishers,
Stand I before thee heere : Then if thou hast
A heart of wreake in thee, that wilt reuenge
Thine owne particular wrongs, and stop those maimes
Of shame seene through thy Country, speed thee straight
And make my misery serue thy turne : So vse it,
That my reuengefull Seruices may proue
As Benefits to thee. For I will fight
Against my Cankred Countrey, with the Spleene
Of all the vnder Fiends. But if so be,
Thou dar'st not this, and that to proue more Fortunes
Th'art tyr'd, then in a word, I also am
Longer to liue most wearie : and present
My throat to thee, and to thy Ancient Malice :
Which not to cut, would shew thee but a Foole,
Since I haue euer followed thee with hate,
Drawne Tunnes of Blood out of thy Countries brest,
And cannot liue but to thy shame, vnlesse
It be to do thee seruice.

Auf. Oh *Martius*, *Martius*;
Each word thou hast spoke, hath weeded from my heart
A roote of Ancient Enuy. If Iupiter
Should from yond clowd speake diuine things,
And say 'tis true; I'de not beleeue them more
Then thee all-Noble *Martius*. Let me twine
Mine armes about that body, where against
My grained Ash an hundred times hath broke,
And scarr'd the Moone with splinters : heere I cleep
The Anuile of my Sword, and do contest
As hotly, and as Nobly with thy Loue,
As euer in Ambitious strength, I did
Contend against thy Valour. Know thou first,
I lou'd the Maid I married : neuer man
Sigh'd truer breath. But that I see thee heere
Thou Noble thing, more dances my rapt heart,
Then when I first my wedded Mistris saw
Bestride my Threshold. Why, thou Mars I tell thee,
We haue a Power on foote : and I had purpose
Once more to hew thy Target from thy Brawne,
Or loose mine Arme for't : Thou hast beate mee out
Twelue seuerall times, and I haue nightly since
Dreamt of encounters 'twixt thy selfe and me :
We haue beene downe together in my sleepe,
Vnbuckling Helmes, fisting each others Throat,
And wak'd halfe dead with nothing. Worthy *Martius*,
Had we no other quarrell else to Rome, but that
Thou art thence Banish'd, we would muster all
From twelue, to seuentie : and powring Warre
Into the bowels of vngratefull Rome,
Like a bold Flood o're-beate. Oh come, go in,
And take our Friendly Senators by'th'hands
Who now are heere, taking their leaues of mee,
Who am prepar'd against your Territories,
Though not for Rome it selfe.

Corio. You blesse me Gods.

Auf. Therefore most absolute Sir, if thou wilt haue
The leading of thine owne Reuenges, take
Th'one halfe of my Commission, and set downe
As best thou art experienc'd, since thou know'st
Thy Countries strength and weaknesse, thine own waies
Whether to knocke against the Gates of Rome,
Or rudely visit them in parts remote,
To fright them, ere destroy. But come in,
Let me commend thee first, to those that shall
Say yea to thy desires. A thousand welcomes,
And more a Friend, then ere an Enemie,
Yet *Martius* that was much. Your hand: most welcome.
Exeunt

Enter two of the Seruingmen.

1 Heere's a strange alteration?

2 By my hand, I had thoght to haue stroken him with a Cudgell, and yet my minde gaue me, his cloathes made a false report of him.

1 What an Arme he has, he turn'd me about with his finger and his thumbe, as one would set vp a Top.

2 Nay, I knew by his face that there was some-thing in him. He had sir, a kinde of face me thought, I cannot tell

ceu now to tearme it.

1 He had so, looking as it were, would I were hang'd but I thought there was more in him, then I could think.

2 So did I, Ile be sworne: He is simply the rarest man i'th'world.

1 I thinke he is: but a greater soldier then he, You wot one.

2 Who my Master?

1 Nay, it's no matter for that.

2 Worth six on him.

1 Nay not so neither: but I take him to be the greater Souldiour.

2 Faith looke you, one cannot tell how to say that: for the Defence of a Towne, our Generall is excellent.

1 I, and for an assault too.

Enter the third Seruingman.

3 Oh Slaues, I can tell you Newes, News you Rascals

Both. What, what, what? Let's partake.

3 I would not be a Roman of all Nations; I had as liue be a condemn'd man.

Both. Wherefore? Wherefore?

3 Why here's he that was wont to thwacke our Generall, *Caius Martius.*

1 Why do you say, thwacke our Generall?

3 I do not say thwacke our Generall, but he was alwayes good enough for him

2 Come we are fellowes and friends: he was euer too hard for him, I haue heard him say so himselfe.

1 He was too hard for him directly, to say the Troth on't before *Corioles*, he scotcht him, and notcht him like a Carbinado.

2 And hee had bin Cannibally giuen, hee might haue boyld and eaten him too.

1 But more of thy Newes.

3 Why he is so made on heere within, as if hee were Son and Heire to Mars, set at vpper end o'th'Table: No question askt him by any of the Senators, but they stand bald before him. Our Generall himselfe makes a Mistris of him, Sanctifies himselfe with's hand, and turnes vp the white o'th'eye to his Discourse. But the bottome of the Newes is, our Generall is cut i'th'middle, & but one halfe of what he was yesterday. For the other ha's halfe, by the intreaty and graunt of the whole Table. Hee'l go he sayes, and sole the Porter of Rome Gates by th'eares. He will mowe all downe before him, and leaue his passage poul'd.

2 And he's as like to do't, as any man I can imagine.

3 Doo't? he will doo't: for look you sir, he has as many Friends as Enemies: which Friends sir as it were, durst not (looke you sir) shew themselues (as we terme it) his Friends, whilest he's in Directitude.

1 Directitude? What's that?

3 But when they shall see sir, his Crest vp againe, and the man in blood, they will out of their Burroughes (like Conies after Raine) and reuell all with him.

1 But when goes this forward:

3 To morrow, to day, presently, you shall haue the Drum strooke vp this afternoone: 'Tis as it were a parcel of their Feast, and to be executed ere they wipe their lips.

2 Why then wee shall haue a stirring World againe: This peace is nothing, but to rust Iron, encrease Taylors, and breed Ballad-makers.

1 Let me haue Warre say I, it exceeds peace as farre as day do's night: It's sprightly walking, audible, and full of Vent. Peace, is a very Apoplexy, Lethargie, mull'd, deafe, sleepe, insensible, a getter of more bastard Children, then warres a destroyer of men.

2 'Tis so, and as warres in some sort may be saide to be a Rauisher, so it cannot be denied, but peace is a great maker of Cuckolds.

1 I, and it makes men hate one another.

3 Reason, because they then lesse neede one another: The Warres for my money. I hope to see Romanes as cheape as Volcians. They are rising, they are rising.

Both. In, in, in, in. *Exeunt*

Enter the two Tribunes, Sicinius, and Brutus.

Sicin. We heare not of him, neither need we fear him,
His remedies are tame, the present peace,
And quietnesse of the people, which before
Were in wilde hurry. Heere do we make his Friends
Blush, that the world goes well: who rather had,
Though they themselues did suffer by't, behold
Dissentious numbers pestring streets, then see
Our Tradesmen singing in their shops, and going
About their Functions friendly.

Enter Menenius.

Bru. We stood too't in good time. Is this *Menenius*?

Sicin. 'Tis he, 'tis he: O he is grown most kind of late:
Haile Sir. *Mene.* Haile to you both.

Sicin. Your *Coriolanus* is not much mist, but with his Friends: the Commonwealth doth stand, and so would do, were he more angry at it.

Mene. All's well, and might haue bene much better, if he could haue temporiz'd.

Sicin. Where is he, heare you?

Mene. Nay I heare nothing:
His Mother and his wife, heare nothing from him.

Enter three or foure Citizens.

All. The Gods preserue you both.

Sicin. Gooden our Neighbours.

Bru. Gooden to you all, gooden to you all.

1 Our selues, our wiues, and children, on our knees,
Are bound to pray for you both.

Sicin. Liue, and thriue.

Bru. Farewell kinde Neighbours:
We wisht *Coriolanus* had lou'd you as we did.

All. Now the Gods keepe you.

Both Tri. Farewell, farewell. *Exeunt Citizens*

Sicin. This is a happier and more comely time,
Then when these Fellowes ran about the streets,
Crying Confusion.

Bru. *Caius Martius* was
A worthy Officer i'th'Warre, but Insolent,
O'recome with Pride, Ambitious, past all thinking
Selfe-louing.

Sicin. And affecting one sole Throne, without assista͂ce

Mene. I thinke not so.

Sicin. We should by this, to all our Lamention,
If he had gone forth Consull, found it so.

Bru. The Gods haue well preuented it, and Rome
Sits safe and still, without him.

Enter an Ædile.

Ædile. Worthy Tribunes,
There is a Slaue whom we haue put in prison,
Reports the Volces with two seuerall Powers
Are entred in the Roman Territories,
And with the deepest malice of the Warre,
Destroy, what lies before 'em.

Mene. 'Tis *Auffidius*,
Who hearing of our *Martius* Banishment,
Thrusts forth his hornes againe into the world
Which were In-shell'd, when *Martius* stood for Rome,

And

And durst not once peepe out.
Sicin. Come, what talke you of *Martius*.
Bru. Go see this Rumorer whipt, it cannot be,
The Volces dare breake with vs.
Mene. Cannot be?
We haue Record, that very well it can,
And three examples of the like, hath beene
Within my Age. But reason with the fellow
Before you punish him, where he heard this,
Least you shall chance to whip your Information,
And beate the Messenger, who bids beware
Of what is to be dreaded.
Sicin. Tell not me: I know this cannot be.
Bru. Not possible.
Enter a Messenger.
Mes. The Nobles in great earnestnesse are going
All to the Senate-house: some newes is comming
That turnes their Countenances.
Sicin. 'Tis this Slaue:
Go whip him fore the peoples eyes: His raising,
Nothing but his report.
Mes. Yes worthy Sir,
The Slaues report is seconded, and more
More fearfull is deliuer'd.
Sicin. What more fearefull?
Mes. It is spoke freely out of many mouths,
How probable I do not know, that *Martius*
Ioyn'd with *Auffidius*, leads a power 'gainst Rome,
And vowes Reuenge as spacious, as betweene
The yong'st and oldest thing.
Sicin. This is most likely.
Bru. Rais'd onely, that the weaker sort may wish
Good *Martius* home againe.
Sicin. The very tricke on't.
Mene. This is vnlikely,
He, and *Auffidius* can no more attone
Then violent'st Contrariety.
Enter Messenger.
Mes. You are sent for to the Senate:
A fearefull Army, led by *Caius Martius*,
Associated with *Auffidius*, Rages
Vpon our Territories, and haue already
O're-borne their way, consum'd with fire, and tooke
What lay before them.
Enter Cominius.
Com. Oh you haue made good worke.
Mene. What newes? What newes?
Com. You haue holp to rauish your owne daughters, &
To melt the Citty Leades vpon your pates,
To see your Wiues dishonour'd to your Noses.
Mene. What's the newes? What's the newes?
Com. Your Temples burned in their Ciment, and
Your Franchises, whereon you stood, confin'd
Into an Augors boare.
Mene. Pray now, your Newes:
You haue made faire worke I feare me: pray your newes,
If *Martius* should be ioyn'd with Volceans.
Com. If? He is their God, he leads them like a thing
Made by some other Deity then Nature,
That shapes man Better: and they follow him
Against vs Brats, with no lesse Confidence,
Then Boyes pursuing Summer Butter-flies,
Or Butchers killing Flyes.
Mene. You haue made good worke,
You and your Apron men: you, that stood so much
Vpon the voyce of occupation, and
The breath of Garlicke-eaters.
Com. Hee'l shake your Rome about your eares.
Mene. As *Hercules* did shake downe Mellow Fruite:
You haue made faire worke.
Brut. But is this true sir?
Com. I, and you'l looke pale
Before you finde it other. All the Regions
Do smilingly Reuolt, and who resists
Are mock'd for valiant Ignorance,
And perish constant Fooles: who is't can blame him?
Your Enemies and his, finde something in him.
Mene. We are all vndone, vnlesse
The Noble man haue mercy.
Com. Who shall aske it?
The Tribunes cannot doo't for shame; the people
Deserue such pitty of him, as the Wolfe
Doe's of the Shepheards: For his best Friends, if they
Should say be good to Rome, they charg'd him, euen
As those should do that had deseru'd his hate,
And therein shew'd like Enemies.
Me. 'Tis true, if he were putting to my house, the brand
That should consume it, I haue not the face
To say, beseech you cease. You haue made faire hands,
You and your Crafts, you haue crafted faire.
Com. You haue brought
A Trembling vpon Rome, such as was neuer
S'incapeable of helpe.
Tri. Say not, we brought it.
Mene. How? Was't we? We lou'd him,
But like Beasts, and Cowardly Nobles,
Gaue way vnto your Clusters, who did hoote
Him out o'th'Citty.
Com. But I feare
They'l roare him in againe. *Tullus Auffidius*,
The second name of men, obeyes his points
As if he were his Officer: Desperation,
Is all the Policy, Strength, and Defence
That Rome can make against them.
Enter a Troope of Citizens.
Mene Heere come the Clusters.
And is *Auffidius* with him? You are they
That made the Ayre vnwholsome, when you cast
Your stinking, greasie Caps, in hooting
At *Coriolanus* Exile. Now he's comming,
And not a haire vpon a Souldiers head
Which will not proue a whip: As many Coxcombes
As you threw Caps vp, will he tumble downe,
And pay you for your voyces. 'Tis no matter,
If he could burne vs all into one coale,
We haue deseru'd it.
Omnes. Faith, we heare fearfull Newes.
1 Cit. For mine owne part,
When I said banish him, I said 'twas pitty.
2 And so did I.
3 And so did I: and to say the truth, so did very many of vs, that we did we did for the best, and though wee willingly consented to his Banishment, yet it was against our will.
Com. Y'are goodly things, you Voyces.
Mene. You haue made good worke
You and your cry. Shal's to the Capitoll?
Com. Oh I, what else? *Exeunt both.*
Sicin. Go Masters get you home, be not dismaid,
These are a Side, that would be glad to haue
This true, which they so seeme to feare. Go home,
And shew no signe of Feare.
1. *Cit.*

1 Cit. The Gods bee good to vs: Come Masters let's home, I euer said we were i'th wrong, when we banish'd him.

2 Cit. So did we all. But come, let's home. *Exit Cit.*

Bru. I do not like this Newes.

Sicin. Nor I.

Bru. Let's to the Capitoll: would halfe my wealth
Would buy this for a lye.

Sicin. Pray let's go. *Exeunt Tribunes.*

Enter Auffidius with his Lieutenant.

Auf. Do they still flye to'th'Roman?

Lieu. I do not know what Witchcraft's in him: but
Your Soldiers vse him as the Grace 'fore meate,
Their talke at Table, and their Thankes at end,
And you are darkned in this action Sir,
Euen by your owne.

Auf. I cannot helpe it now,
Vnlesse by vsing meanes I lame the foote
Of our designe. He beares himselfe more proudlier,
Euen to my person, then I thought he would
When first I did embrace him. Yet his Nature
In that's no Changeling, and I must excuse
What cannot be amended.

Lieu. Yet I wish Sir,
(I meane for your particular) you had not
Ioyn'd in Commission with him: but either haue borne
The action of your selfe, or else to him, had left it soly.

Auf. I vnderstand thee well, and be thou sure
When he shall come to his account, he knowes not
What I can vrge against him, although it seemes
And so he thinkes, and is no lesse apparant
To th'vulgar eye, that he beares all things fairely:
And shewes good Husbandry for the Volcian State,
Fights Dragon-like, and does atcheeue as soone
As draw his Sword: yet he hath left vndone
That which shall breake his necke, or hazard mine,
When ere we come to our account.

Lieu. Sir, I beseech you, think you he'l carry Rome?

Auf. All places yeelds to him ere he sits downe,
And the Nobility of Rome are his:
The Senators and Patricians loue him too:
The Tribunes are no Soldiers: and their people
Will be as rash in the repeale, as hasty
To expell him thence. I thinke hee'l be to Rome
As is the Aspray to the Fish, who takes it
By Soueraignty of Nature. First, he was
A Noble seruant to them, but he could not
Carry his Honors eeuen: whether 'was Pride
Which out of dayly Fortune euer taints
The happy man; whether detect of iudgement,
To faile in the disposing of those chances
Which he was Lord of: or whether Nature,
Not to be other then one thing, not moouing
From th'Caske to th'Cushion: but commanding peace
Euen with the same austerity and garbe,
As he controll'd the warre. But one of these
(As he hath spices of them all) not all,
For I dare so farre free him, made him fear'd,
So hated, and so banish'd: but he ha's a Merit
To choake it in the vtt'rance: So our Vertue,
Lie in th'interpretation of the time,
And power vnto it selfe most commendable,
Hath not a Tombe so euident as a Chaire
T'extoll what it hath done.
One fire driues out one fire; one Naile, one Naile;
Rights by rights fouler, strengths by strengths do faile.
Come let's away: when Caius Rome is thine,
Thou art poor'st of all; then shortly art thou mine. *exeunt*

Actus Quintus.

Enter Menenius, Cominius, Sicinius, Brutus, the two Tribunes, with others.

Menen. No, Ile not go: you heare what he hath said
Which was sometime his Generall: who loued him
In a most deere particular. He call'd me Father:
But what o'that? Go you that banish'd him
A Mile before his Tent, fall downe, and knee
The way into his mercy: Nay, if he coy'd
To heare Cominius speake, Ile keepe at home.

Com. He would not seeme to know me.

Menen. Do you heare?

Com. Yet one time he did call me by my name:
I vrg'd our old acquaintance, and the drops
That we haue bled together. *Coriolanus*
He would not answer too: Forbad all Names,
He was a kinde of Nothing, Titlelesse,
Till he had forg'd himselfe a name a'th'fire
Of burning Rome.

Menen. Why so: you haue made good worke:
A paire of Tribunes, that haue wrack'd for Rome,
To make Coales cheape: A Noble memory.

Com. I minded him, how Royall 'twas to pardon
When it was lesse expected. He replyed
It was a bare petition of a State
To one whom they had punish'd.

Menen. Very well, could he say lesse.

Com. I offered to awaken his regard
For's priuate Friends. His answer to me was
He could not stay to picke them, in a pile
Of noysome musty Chaffe. He said, 'twas folly
For one poore graine or two, to leaue vnburnt
And still to nose th'offence.

Menen. For one poore graine or two?
I am one of those: his Mother, Wife, his Childe,
And this braue Fellow too: we are the Graines,
You are the musty Chaffe, and you are smelt
Aboue the Moone. We must be burnt for you.

Sicin. Nay, pray be patient: If you refuse your ayde
In this so neuer-needed helpe, yet do not
Vpbraid's with our distresse. But sure if you
Would be your Countries Pleader, your good tongue
More then the instant Armie we can make
Might stop our Countryman.

Mene. No: Ile not meddle.

Sicin. Pray you go to him.

Mene. What should I do?

Bru. Onely make triall what your Loue can do,
For Rome, towards *Martius*.

Mene. Well, and say that *Martius* returne mee,
As *Cominius* is return'd, vnheard: what then?
But as a discontented Friend, greefe-shot
With his vnkindnesse. Say't be so?

Sicin. Yet your good will
Must haue that thankes from Rome, after the measure
As you intended well.

Mene. Ile vndertak't:
I thinke hee'l heare me. Yet to bite his lip,
And humme at good *Cominius*, much vnhearts mee.

He was not taken well, he had not din'd,
The Veines vnfill'd, our blood is cold, and then
We powt vpon the Morning, are vnapt
To giue or to forgiue; but when we haue stufft
These Pipes, and these Conueyances of our blood
With Wine and Feeding, we haue suppler Soules
Then in our Priest-like Fasts: therefore Ile watch him
Till he be dieted to my request,
And then Ile set vpon him.

Bru. You know the very rode into his kindnesse,
And cannot lose your way.

Mene. Good faith Ile proue him,
Speed how it will. I shall ere long, haue knowledge
Of my successe. *Exit.*

Com. Hee'l neuer heare him.

Sicin. Not.

Com. I tell you, he doe's sit in Gold, his eye
Red as 'twould burne Rome: and his Iniury
The Gaoler to his pitty. I kneel'd before him,
'Twas very faintly he said Rise: dismist me
Thus with his speechlesse hand. What he would do
He sent in writing after me: what he would not,
Bound with an Oath to yeeld to his conditions:
So that all hope is vaine, vnlesse his Noble Mother,
And his Wife, who (as I heare) meane to solicite him
For mercy to his Countrey: therefore let's hence,
And with our faire intreaties hast them on. *Exeunt*

Enter Menenius to the Watch or Guard.

1.*Wat.* Stay: whence are you.

2.*Wat.* Stand, and go backe.

Me. You guard like men, 'tis well. But by your leaue,
I am an Officer of State, & come to speak with *Coriolanus*

1 From whence? *Mene.* From Rome.

1 You may not passe, you must returne: our Generall will no more heare from thence.

2 You'l see your Rome embrac'd with fire, before
You'l speake with *Coriolanus.*

Mene. Good my Friends,
If you haue heard your Generall talke of Rome,
And of his Friends there, it is Lots to Blankes,
My name hath touch't your eares: it is *Menenius.*

1 Be it so, go back: the vertue of your name,
Is not heere passable.

Mene. I tell thee Fellow,
Thy Generall is my Louer: I haue beene
The booke of his good Acts, whence men haue read
His Fame vnparalell'd, happely amplified:
For I haue euer verified my Friends,
(Of whom hee's cheefe) with all the size that verity
Would without lapsing suffer: Nay, sometimes,
Like to a Bowle vpon a subtle ground
I haue tumbled past the throw: and in his praise
Haue (almost) stampt the Leasing. Therefore Fellow,
I must haue leaue to passe.

1 Faith Sir, if you had told as many lies in his behalfe, as you haue vttered words in your owne, you should not passe heere: no, though it were as vertuous to lye, as to liue chastly. Therefore go backe.

Men. Prythee fellow, remember my name is *Menenius*, alwayes factionary on the party of your Generall.

2 Howsoeuer you haue bin his Lier, as you say you haue, I am one that telling true vnder him, must say you cannot passe. Therefore go backe.

Mene. Ha's he din'd can'st thou tell? For I would not speake with him, till after dinner.

1 You are a Roman, are you?

Mene. I am as thy Generall is.

1 Then you should hate Rome, as he do's. Can you, when you haue pusht out your gates, the very Defender of them, and in a violent popular ignorance, giuen your enemy your shield, thinke to front his reuenges with the easie groanes of old women, the Virginall Palms of your daughters, or with the palsied intercession of such a decay'd Dotant as you seeme to be? Can you think to blow out the intended fire, your City is ready to flame in, with such weake breath as this? No, you are deceiu'd, therfore backe to Rome, and prepare for your execution: you are condemn'd, our Generall has sworne you out of repreeue and pardon.

2. *me.* Sirra, if thy Captaine knew I were heere,
He would vse me with estimation.

1 Come, my Captaine knowes you not.

Mene. I meane thy Generall.

1 My Generall cares not for you. Back I say, go: least I let forth your halfe pinte of blood. Backe, that's the vtmost of your hauing, backe.

Mene. Nay but Fellow, Fellow.

Enter Coriolanus with Auffidius.

Corio. What's the matter?

Mene. Now you Companion: Ile say an arrant for you: you shall know now that I am in estimation: you shall perceiue, that a Iacke gardant cannot office me from my Son *Coriolanus*, guesse but my entertainment with him: if thou stand'st not i'th state of hanging, or of some death more long in Spectatorship, and crueller in suffering, behold now presently, and swoond for what's to come vpon thee. The glorious Gods sit in hourely Synod about thy particular prosperity, and loue thee no worse then thy old Father *Menenius* do's. O my Son, my Son! thou art preparing fire for vs: looke thee, heere's water to quench it. I was hardly moued to come to thee: but beeing assured none but my selfe could moue thee, I haue bene blowne out of your Gates with sighes: and coniure thee to pardon Rome, and thy petitionary Countrimen. The good Gods asswage thy wrath, and turne the dregs of it, vpon this Varlet heere: This, who like a blocke hath denyed my accesse to thee.

Corio. Away.

Mene. How? Away?

Corio. Wife, Mother, Child I know not. My affaires
Are Seruanted to others: Though I owe
My Reuenge properly, my remission lies
In Volcean brests. That we haue beene familiar,
Ingrate forgetfulnesse shall poison rather
Then pitty: Note how much, therefore be gone.
Mine eares against your suites, are stronger then
Your gates against my force. Yet for I loued thee,
Take this along, I writ it for thy sake,
And would haue sent it. Another word *Menenius*,
I will not heare thee speake. This man *Auffidius*
Was my belou'd in Rome: yet thou behold'st.

Auffid. You keepe a constant temper. *Exeunt*

Manet the Guard and Menenius.

1 Now sir, is your name *Menenius*?

2 'Tis a spell you see of much power:
You know the way home againe.

1 Do you heare how wee are shent for keeping your greatnesse backe?

2 What cause do you thinke I haue to swoond?

Menen. I neither care for th' world, nor your General: for such things as you, I can scarse thinke ther's any, y'are so slight. He that hath a will to die by himselfe, feares it not

not from another: Let your Generall do his worst. For you, bee that you are, long; and your misery encreafe with your age. I fay to you, as I was faid to, Away. *Exit*

1 A Noble Fellow I warrant him.

2 The worthy Fellow is our General. He's the Rock,
The Oake not to be winde-shaken. *Exit Watch.*

Enter Coriolanus and Auffidius.

Corio. We will before the walls of Rome to morrow
Set downe our Hoaft. My partner in this Action,
You muft report to th'Volcian Lords, how plainly
I haue borne this Bufineffe.

Auf. Onely their ends you haue refpected,
Stopt your eares against the generall fuite of Rome:
Neuer admitted a priuat whifper, no not with fuch frends
That thought them fure of you.

Corio. This laft old man,
Whom with a crack'd heart I haue fent to Rome,
Lou'd me, aboue the meafure of a Father,
Nay godded me indeed. Their lateft refuge
Was to fend him: for whofe old Loue I haue
(Though I fhew'd fowrely to him) once more offer'd
The firft Conditions which they did refufe,
And cannot now accept, to grace him onely,
That thought he could do more: A very little
I haue yeelded too. Frefh Embaffes, and Suites,
Nor from the State, nor priuate friends heereafter
Will I lend eare to. Ha? what fhout is this? *Shout within*
Shall I be tempted to infringe my vow
In the fame time 'tis made? I will not.

Enter Virgilia, Volumnia, Valeria, yong Martius with Attendants.

My wife comes formoft, then the honour'd mould
Wherein this Trunke was fram'd, and in her hand
The Grandchilde to her blood. But out affection,
All bond and priuiledge of Nature breake;
Let it be Vertuous to be Obftinate.
What is that Curt'fie worth? Or thofe Doues eyes,
Which can make Gods forfworne? I melt, and am not
Of ftronger earth then others: my Mother bowes,
As if Olympus to a Mole-hill fhould
In fupplication Nod: and my yong Boy
Hath an Afpect of intercefsion, which
Great Nature cries, Deny not. Let the Volces
Plough Rome, and harrow Italy, Ile neuer
Be fuch a Gofling to obey inftinct; but ftand
As if a man were Author of himfelf, & knew no other kin

Virgil. My Lord and Husband.

Corio. Thefe eyes are not the fame I wore in Rome.

Virg. The forrow that deliuers vs thus chang'd,
Makes you thinke fo.

Corio Like a dull Actor now, I haue forgot my part,
And I am out, euen to a full Difgrace. Beft of my Flefh,
Forgiue my Tyranny: but do not fay,
For that forgiue our Romanes. O a kiffe
Long as my Exile, fweet as my Reuenge!
Now by the iealous Queene of Heauen, that kiffe
I carried from thee deare; and my true Lippe
Hath Virgin'd it ere fince. You Gods, I pray,
And the moft noble Mother of the world
Leaue vnfaluted: Sinke my knee i'th'earth, *Kneeles*
Of thy deepe duty, more impresfion fhew
Then that of common Sonnes.

Volum. Oh ftand vp bleft!
Whil'ft with no fofter Cufhion then the Flint
I kneele before thee, and vnproperly
Shew duty as miftaken, all this while,
Betweene the Childe, and Parent.

Corio. What's this? your knees to me?
To your Corrected Sonne?
Then let the Pibbles on the hungry beach
Fillop the Starres: Then, let the mutinous windes
Strike the proud Cedars 'gainft the fiery Sun:
Murd'ring Impoffibility, to make
What cannot be, flight worke.

Volum. Thou art my Warriour, I hope to frame thee
Do you know this Lady?

Corio. The Noble Sifter of *Publicola*;
The Moone of Rome: Chafte as the Ificle
That's curdied by the Froft, from pureft Snow,
And hangs on *Dians* Temple: Deere *Valeria*.

Volum. This is a poore Epitome of yours,
Which by th'interpretation of full time,
May fhew like all your felfe.

Corio. The God of Souldiers:
With the confent of fupreame Ioue, informe
Thy thoughts with Nobleneffe, that thou mayft proue
To fhame vnvulnerable, and fticke i'th Warres
Like a great Sea-marke ftanding euery flaw,
And fauing thofe that eye thee.

Volum. Your knee, Sirrah.

Corio. That's my braue Boy.

Volum. Euen he, your wife, this Ladie, and my felfe,
Are Sutors to you.

Corio. I befeech you peace:
Or if you'ld aske, remember this before;
The thing I haue forfworne to graunt, may neuer
Be held by you denials. Do not bid me
Difmiffe my Soldiers, or capitulate
Againe, with Romes Mechanickes. Tell me not
Wherein I feeme vnnaturall: Defire not t'allay
My Rages and Reuenges, with your colder reafons.

Volum. Oh no more, no more:
You haue faid you will not grant vs any thing:
For we haue nothing elfe to aske, but that
Which you deny already: yet we will aske,
That if you faile in our requeft, the blame
May hang vpon your hardneffe, therefore heare vs.

Corio. *Auffidius*, and you Volces marke, for wee'l
Heare nought from Rome in priuate. Your requeft?

Volum. Should we be filent & not fpeak, our Raiment
And ftate of Bodies would bewray what life
We haue led fince thy Exile. Thinke with thy felfe,
How more vnfortunate then all liuing women
Are we come hither; fince that thy fight, which fhould
Make our eies flow with ioy, harts dance with comforts,
Conftraines them weepe, and fhake with feare & forow,
Making the Mother, wife, and Childe to fee,
The Sonne, the Husband, and the Father tearing
His Countries Bowels out; and to poore we
Thine enmities moft capitall: Thou barr'ft vs
Our prayers to the Gods, which is a comfort
That all but we enioy. For how can we?
Alas! how can we, for our Country pray?
Whereto we are bound, together with thy victory:
Whereto we are bound: Alacke, or we muft loofe
The Countrie our deere Nurfe, or elfe thy perfon
Our comfort in the Country. We muft finde
An euident Calamity, though we had
Our wifh, which fide fhould win. For either thou
Muft as a Forraine Recreant be led
With Manacles through our ftreets, or elfe
Triumphantly treade on thy Countries ruine,

cc 2 And

And beare the Palme, for hauing brauely shed
Thy Wife and Childrens blood: For my selfe, Sonne,
I purpose not to waite on Fortune, till
These warres determine: If I cannot perswade thee,
Rather to shew a Noble grace to both parts,
Then seeke the end of one; thou shalt no sooner
March to assault thy Country, then to treade
(Trust too't, thou shalt not) on thy Mothers wombe
That brought thee to this world.

Virg. I, and mine, that brought you forth this boy,
To keepe your name liuing to time.

Boy. A shall not tread on me: Ile run away
Till I am bigger, but then Ile fight.

Corio. Not of a womans tendernesse to be,
Requires nor Childe, nor womans face to see:
I haue sate too long.

Volum. Nay, go not from vs thus:
If it were so, that our request did tend
To saue the Romanes, thereby to destroy
The Volces whom you serue, you might condemne vs
As poysonous of your Honour. No, our suite
Is that you reconcile them: While the Volces
May say, this mercy we haue shew'd: the Romanes,
This we receiu'd, and each in either side
Giue the All-haile to thee, and cry be Blest
For making vp this peace. Thou know'st (great Sonne)
The end of Warres vncertaine: but this certaine,
That if thou conquer Rome, the benefit
Which thou shalt thereby reape, is such a name
Whose repetition will be dogg'd with Curses:
Whose Chronicle thus writ, The man was Noble,
But with his last Attempt, he wip'd it out:
Destroy'd his Country, and his name remaines
To th'insuing Age, abhorr'd. Speake to me Son:
Thou hast affected the fiue straines of Honor,
To imitate the graces of the Gods.
To teare with Thunder the wide Cheekes a'th'Ayre,
And yet to change thy Sulphure with a Boult
That should but riue an Oake. Why do'st not speake?
Think'st thou it Honourable for a Nobleman
Still to remember wrongs? Daughter, speake you:
He cares not for your weeping. Speake thou Boy,
Perhaps thy childishnesse will moue him more
Then can our Reasons. There's no man in the world
More bound to's Mother, yet heere he let's me prate
Like one i'th'Stockes. Thou hast neuer in thy life,
Shew'd thy deere Mother any curtesie,
When she (poore Hen) fond of no second brood,
Ha's clock'd thee to the Warres: and safelie home
Loden with Honor. Say my Request's vniust,
And spurne me backe: But, if it be not so
Thou art not honest, and the Gods will plague thee
That thou restrain'st from me the Duty, which
To a Mothers part belongs. He turnes away:
Down Ladies: let vs shame him with him with our knees
To his sur-name *Coriolanus* longs more pride
Then pitty to our Prayers. Downe: an end,
This is the last. So, we will home to Rome,
And dye among our Neighbours: Nay, behold's,
This Boy that cannot tell what he would haue,
But kneeles, and holds vp hands for fellowship,
Doe's reason our Petition with more strength
Then thou hast to deny't. Come, let vs go:
This Fellow had a Volcean to his Mother:
His Wife is in *Corioles*, and his Childe
Like him by chance: yet giue vs our dispatch:
I am husht vntill our City be afire, & then Ile speak a litle

Holds her by the hand silent.

Corio. O Mother, Mother!
What haue you done? Behold, the Heauens do ope,
The Gods looke downe, and this vnnaturall Scene
They laugh at. Oh my Mother, Mother: Oh!
You haue wonne a happy Victory to Rome.
But for your Sonne, beleeue it: Oh beleeue it,
Most dangerously you haue with him preuail'd,
If not most mortall to him. But let it come:
Auffidius, though I cannot make true Warres,
Ile frame conuenient peace. Now good *Auffidius*,
Were you in my steed, would you haue heard
A Mother lesse? or granted lesse *Auffidius*?

Auf. I was mou'd withall.

Corio. I dare be sworne you were:
And sir, it is no little thing to make
Mine eyes to sweat compassion. But (good sir)
What peace you'l make, aduise me: For my part,
Ile not to Rome, Ile backe with you, and pray you
Stand to me in this cause. Oh Mother! Wife!

Auf. I am glad thou hast set thy mercy, & thy Honor
At difference in thee: Out of that Ile worke
My selfe a former Fortune.

Corio. I by and by; But we will drinke together:
And you shall beare
A better witnesse backe then words, which we
On like conditions, will haue Counter-seal'd.
Come enter with vs: Ladies you deserue
To haue a Temple built you: All the Swords
In Italy, and her Confederate Armes
Could not haue made this peace. *Exeunt.*

Enter Menenius and Sicinius.

Mene. See you yon'd Coin a'th Capitol, yon'd corner stone?

Sicin. Why what of that?

Mene. If it be possible for you to displace it with your little finger, there is some hope the Ladies of Rome, especially his Mother, may preuaile with him. But I say, there is no hope in't, our throats are sentenc'd, and stay vppon execution.

Sicin. Is't possible, that so short a time can alter the condition of a man.

Mene. There is differency between a Grub & a Butterfly, yet your Butterfly was a Grub: this *Martius*, is growne from Man to Dragon: He has wings, hee's more then a creeping thing.

Sicin. He lou'd his Mother deerely.

Mene So did he mee: and he no more remembers his Mother now, then an eight yeare old horse. The tartnesse of his face, sowres ripe Grapes. When he walks, he moues like an Engine, and the ground shrinkes before his Treading. He is able to pierce a Corslet with his eye: Talkes like a knell, and his hum is a Battery. He sits in his State, as a thing made for *Alexander*. What he bids bee done, is finisht with his bidding. He wants nothing of a God but Eternity, and a Heauen to Throne in.

Sicin. Yes, mercy, if you report him truly.

Mene. I paint him in the Character. Mark what mercy his Mother shall bring from him: There is no more mercy in him, then there is milke in a male-Tyger, that shall our poore City finde: and all this is long of you.

Sicin. The Gods be good vnto vs.

Mene. No, in such a case the Gods will not bee good vnto vs. When we banish'd him, we respected not them: and he returning to breake our necks, they respect not vs.

Enter a Messenger.

Mess.

Mes. Sir, if you'ld saue your life, flye to your House,
The Plebeians haue got your Fellow Tribune,
And hale him vp and downe; all swearing, if
The Romane Ladies bring not comfort home,
They'l giue him death by Inches.

Enter another Messenger.

Sicin. What's the Newes?

Mess. Good Newes, good newes, the Ladies haue (preuayl'd,
The Volcians are dislodg'd, and *Martius* gone:
A merrier day did neuer yet greet Rome,
No, not th'expulsion of the *Tarquins*

Sicin. Friend, art thou certaine this is true?
Is't most certaine.

Mes. As certaine as I know the Sun is fire:
Where haue you lurk'd that you make doubt of it:
Ne're through an Arch so hurried the blowne Tide,
As the recomforted through th'gates. Why harke you:

Trumpets, Hoboyes, Drums beate, altogether.

The Trumpets, Sack-buts, Psalteries, and Fifes,
Tabors, and Symboles, and the showting Romans
Make the Sunne dance. Hearke you. *A shout within*

Mene. This is good Newes:
I will go meete the Ladies. This *Volumnia*,
Is worth of Consuls, Senators, Patricians,
A City full: Of Tribunes such as you,
A Sea and Land full: you haue pray'd well to day:
This Morning, for ten thousand of your throates,
I'de not haue giuen a doit. Harke, how they ioy.

Sound still with the Shouts.

Sicin. First, the Gods blesse you for your tydings:
Next, accept my thankefulnesse.

Mess. Sir, we haue all great cause to giue great thanks.

Sicin. They are neere the City.

Mes. Almost at point to enter.

Sicin. Wee'l meet them, and helpe the ioy. *Exeunt.*

Enter two Senators, with Ladies, passing ouer the Stage, with other Lords.

Sena. Behold our Patronnesse, the life of Rome:
Call all your Tribes together, praise the Gods,
And make triumphant fires, strew Flowers before them:
Vnshoot the noise that Banish'd *Martius*;
Repeale him, with the welcome of his Mother:
Cry welcome Ladies, welcome.

All. Welcome Ladies, welcome.

A Flourish with Drummes & Trumpets.

Enter Tullus Auffidius, with Attendants.

Auf. Go tell the Lords a'th'City, I am heere:
Deliuer them this Paper: hauing read it,
Bid them repayre to th'Market place, where I
Euen in theirs, and in the Commons eares
Will vouch the truth of it. Him I accuse:
The City Ports by this hath enter'd, and
Intends t'appeare before the People, hoping
To purge himselfe with words. Dispatch.

Enter 3 or 4 Conspiratorr of Auffidius Faction.

Most Welcome.

1. Con. How is it with our Generall?

Auf. Euen so, as with a man by his owne Almes impoyson'd, and with his Charity slaine.

2. Con. Most Noble Sir, If you do hold the same intent
Wherein you wisht vs parties: Wee'l deliuer you
Of your great danger.

Auf Sir, I cannot tell,
We must proceed as we do finde the People.

3. Con. The People will remaine vncertaine, whil'st
'Twixt you there's difference: but the fall of either
Makes the Suruiuor heyre of all.

Auf. I know it:
And my pretext to strike at him, admits
A good construction. I rais'd him, and I pawn'd
Mine Honor for his truth: who being so heighten'd,
He watered his new Plants with dewes of Flattery,
Seducing so my Friends: and to this end,
He bow'd his Nature, neuer knowne before,
But to be rough, vnswayable, and free.

3. Consp. Sir, his stoutnesse
When he did stand for Consull, which he lost
By lacke of stooping.

Auf. That I would haue spoke of:
Being banish'd for't, he came vnto my Harth,
Presented to my knife his Throat: I tooke him,
Made him ioynt-seruant with me: Gaue him way
In all his owne desires: Nay, let him choose
Out of my Files, his proiects, to accomplish
My best and freshest men, seru'd his designements
In mine owne person: holpe to reape the Fame
Which he did end all his; and tooke some pride
To do my selfe this wrong: Till at the last
I seem'd his Follower, not Partner; and
He wadg'd me with his Countenance, as if
I had bin Mercenary.

.Con. So he did my Lord:
The Army marueyl'd at it, and in the last,
When he had carried Rome, and that we look'd
For no lesse Spoile, then Glory.

Auf. There was it:
For which my sinewes shall be stretcht vpon him,
At a few drops of Womens rhewme, which are
As cheape as Lies; he sold the Blood and Labour
Of our great Action; therefore shall he dye,
And Ile renew me in his fall. But hearke

Drummes and Trumpets sounds, with great showts of the people.

1. Con. Your Natiue Towne you enter'd like a Poste,
And had no welcomes home, but he returnes
Splitting the Ayre with noyse.

2. Con. And patient Fooles,
Whose children he hath slaine, their base throats teare
With giuing him glory.

3. Con. Therefore at your vantage,
Ere he expresse himselfe, or moue the people
With what he would say, let him feele your Sword:
Which we will second, when he lies along
After your way. His Tale pronounc'd, shall bury
His Reasons, with his Body.

Auf. Say no more. Heere come the Lords,

Enter the Lords of the City.

All Lords. You are most welcome home.

Auff. I haue not deseru'd it.
But worthy Lords, haue you with heede perused
What I haue written to you?

All. We haue.

1. Lord. And greeue to heare't:
What faults he made before the last, I thinke
Might haue found easie Fines: But there to end
Where he was to begin, and giue away
The benefit of our Leuies, answering vs
With our owne charge: making a Treatie, where
There was a yeelding; this admits no excuse.

cc3 *Auf.*

Auf. He approaches, you shall heare him.

Enter Coriolanus marching with Drumme, and Colours. The Commoners being with him.

Corio. Haile Lords, I am return'd your Souldier:
No more infected with my Countries loue
Then when I parted hence: but still subsisting
Vnder your great Cōmmand. You are to know,
That prosperously I haue attempted, and
With bloody passage led your Warres, euen to
The gates of Rome: Our spoiles we haue brought home
Doth more then counterpoize a full third part
The charges of the Action. We haue made peace
With no lesse Honor to the *Antiates*
Then shame to th'Romaines. And we heere deliuer
Subscrib'd by'th'Consuls, and Patricians,
Together with the Seale a'th Senat, what
We haue compounded on.

Auf. Read it not Noble Lords,
But tell the Traitor in the highest degree
He hath abus'd your Powers.

Corio. Traitor? How now?

Auf. I Traitor, *Martius.*

Corio. *Martius?*

Auf. I *Martius, Caius Martius*: Do'st thou thinke
Ile grace thee with that Robbery, thy stolne name
Coriolanus in *Corioles*?
You Lords and Heads a'th'State, perfidiously
He ha's betray'd your businesse, and giuen vp
For certaine drops of Salt, your City Rome:
I say your City to his Wife and Mother,
Breaking his Oath and Resolution, like
A twist of rotten Silke, neuer admitting
Counsaile a'th'warre: But at his Nurses teares
He whin'd and roar'd away your Victory,
That Pages blush'd at him, and men of heart
Look'd wond'ring each at others.

Corio. Hear'st thou Mars?

Auf. Name not the God, thou boy of Teares.

Corio. Ha?

Aufid. No more.

Corio. Measurelesse Lyar, thou hast made my heart
Too great for what containes it. Boy? Oh Slaue,
Pardon me Lords, 'tis the first time that euer
I was forc'd to scoul'd. Your iudgments my graue Lords
Must giue this Curre the Lye: and his owne Notion,
Who weares my stripes imprest vpon him, that
Must beare my beating to his Graue, shall ioyne
To thrust the Lye vnto him.

1 Lord. Peace both, and heare me speake.

Corio. Cut me to peeces Volces men and Lads,
Staine all your edges on me. Boy, false Hound:
If you haue writ your Annales true, 'tis there,
That like an Eagle in a Doue-coat, I
Flatter'd your Volcians in *Corioles.*
Alone I did it, Boy.

Auf. Why Noble Lords,
Will you be put in minde of his blinde Fortune,
Which was your shame, by this vnholy Braggart?
'Fore your owne eyes, and eares?

All Consp. Let him dye for't.

All People. Teare him to peeces, do it presently:
He kill'd my Sonne, my daughter, he kill'd my Cosine
Marcus, he kill'd my Father.

2 Lord. Peace hoe: no outrage, peace:
The man is Noble, and his Fame folds in
This Orbe o'th'earth: His last offences to vs
Shall haue Iudicious hearing. Stand *Auffidius*,
And trouble not the peace.

Corio. O that I had him, with six *Auffidiusses*, or more:
His Tribe, to vse my lawfull Sword.

Auf. Insolent Villaine.

All Consp. Kill, kill, kill, kill, kill him.

Draw both the Conspirators, and kils Martius, who falles, Auffidius stands on him.

Lords. Hold, hold, hold, hold.

Auf. My Noble Masters, heare me speake.

1. Lord. O *Tullus.*

2. Lord. Thou hast done a deed, whereat
Valour will weepe.

3. Lord. Tread not vpon him Masters, all be quiet,
Put vp your Swords.

Auf. My Lords,
When you shall know (as in this Rage
Prouok'd by him, you cannot) the great danger
Which this mans life did owe you, you'l reioyce
That he is thus cut off. Please it your Honours
To call me to your Senate, Ile deliuer
My selfe your loyall Seruant, or endure
Your heauiest Censure.

1. Lord. Beare from hence his body,
And mourne you for him. Let him be regarded
As the most Noble Coarse, that euer Herald
Did follow to his Vrne.

2. Lord. His owne impatience,
Takes from *Auffidius* a great part of blame:
Let's make the Best of it.

Auf. My Rage is gone,
And I am strucke with sorrow. Take him vp:
Helpe three a'th'cheefest Souldiers, Ile be one.
Beate thou the Drumme that it speake mournfully:
Traile your steele Pikes. Though in this City hee
Hath widdowed and vnchilded many a one,
Which to this houre bewaile the Iniury,
Yet he shall haue a Noble Memory. Assist.

Exeunt bearing the Body of Martius. A dead March Sounded.

FINIS.

The Lamentable Tragedy of
Titus Andronicus.

Actus Primus. Scœna Prima.

Flourish. Enter the Tribunes and Senators aloft And then enter Saturninus and his Followers at one doore, and Bassianus and his Followers at the other, with Drum & Colours.

Saturninus.

NOble Patricians, Patrons of my right,
Defend the iustice of my Cause with Armes.
And Countrey-men, my louing Followers,
Pleade my Successiue Title with your Swords.
I was the first borne Sonne, that was the last
That wore the Imperiall Diadem of Rome:
Then let my Fathers Honours liue in me,
Nor wrong mine Age with this indignitie.
Bassianus. Romaines, Friends, Followers,
Fauourers of my Right:
If euer *Bassianus, Cæsars* Sonne,
Were gracious in the eyes of Royall Rome,
Keepe then this passage to the Capitoll:
And suffer not Dishonour to approach
Th'Imperiall Seate to Vertue: consecrate
To Iustice, Continence, and Nobility:
But let Desert in pure Election shine;
And Romanes, fight for Freedome in your Choice.

Enter Marcus Andronicus aloft with the Crowne.

Princes, that striue by Factions, and by Friends,
Ambitiously for Rule and Empery:
Know, that the people of Rome for whom we stand
A speciall Party, haue by Common voyce
In Election for the Romane Emperie,
Chosen *Andronicus*, Sur-named *Pious*,
For many good and great deserts to Rome.
A Nobler man, a brauer Warriour,
Liues not this day within the City Walles.
He by the Senate is accited home
From weary Warres against the barbarous Gothes,
That with his Sonnes (a terror to our Foes)
Hath yoak'd a Nation strong, train'd vp in Armes.
Ten yeares are spent, since first he vndertooke
This Cause of Rome, and chasticed with Armes
Our Enemies pride. Fiue times he hath return'd
Bleeding to Rome, bearing his Valiant Sonnes
In Coffins from the Field.
And now at last, laden with Honours Spoyles,
Returnes the good *Andronicus* to Rome,
Renowned *Titus*, flourishing in Armes.
Let vs intreat, by Honour of his Name,
Whom (worthily) you would haue now succeede,
And in the Capitoll and Senates right,
Whom you pretend to Honour and Adore,
That you withdraw you, and abate your Strength,
Dismisse your Followers, and as Suters should,
Pleade your Deserts in Peace and Humblenesse.
Saturnine. How fayre the Tribune speakes,
To calme my thoughts.
Bassia. *Marcus Andronicus*, so I do affie
In thy vprightnesse and Integrity:
And so I Loue and Honor thee, and thine,
Thy Noble Brother *Titus*, and his Sonnes,
And Her (to whom my thoughts are humbled all)
Gracious *Lauinia*, Romes rich Ornament,
That I will heere dismisse my louing Friends:
And to my Fortunes, and the Peoples Fauour,
Commit my Cause in ballance to be weigh'd.
Exit Souldiours.
Saturnine. Friends, that haue beene
Thus forward in my Right,
I thanke you all, and heere Dismisse you all,
And to the Loue and Fauour of my Countrey,
Commit my Selfe, my Person, and the Cause.
Rome, be as iust and gracious vnto me,
As I am confident and kinde to thee.
Open the Gates, and let me in.
Bassia. Tribunes, and me, a poore Competitor.
Flourish. They go vp into the Senat house.

Enter a Captaine.

Cap. Romanes make way: the good *Andronicus*,
Patron of Vertue, Romes best Champion,
Successefull in the Battailes that he fights,
With Honour and with Fortune is return'd,
From whence he circumscribed with his Sword,
And brought to yoke the Enemies of Rome.

Sound Drummes and Trumpets. And then enter two of Titus Sonnes; After them, two men bearing a Coffin couered with blacke, then two other Sonnes. After them, Titus Andronicus, and then Tamora the Queene of Gothes, & her two Sonnes Chiron and Demetrius, with Aaron the Moore, and others, as many as can bee: They set downe the Coffin, and Titus speakes.

Andronicus. Haile Rome:
Victorious in thy Mourning Weedes:
Loe,

Loe as the Barke that hath discharg'd his fraught,
Returnes with precious lading to the Bay,
From whence at first she wegih'd her Anchorage:
Commeth *Andronicus* bound with Lawrell bowes,
To resalute his Country with his teares,
Teares of true ioy for his returne to Rome,
Thou great defender of this Capitoll,
Stand gracious to the Rites that we intend.
Romaines, of fiue and twenty Valiant Sonnes,
Halfe of the number that King *Priam* had,
Behold the poore remaines aliue and dead!
These that Suruiue, let Rome reward with Loue:
These that I bring vnto their latest home,
With buriall amongst their Auncestors.
Heere Gothes haue giuen me leaue to sheath my Sword:
Titus vnkinde, and carelesse of thine owne,
Why suffer'st thou thy Sonnes vnburied yet,
To houer on the dreadfull shore of Stix?
Make way to lay them by their Bretheren.

They open the Tombe.

There greete in silence as the dead are wont,
And sleepe in peace, slaine in your Countries warres:
O sacred receptacle of my ioyes,
Sweet Cell of vertue and Noblitie,
How many Sonnes of mine hast thou in store,
That thou wilt neuer render to me more?
Luc. Giue vs the proudest prisoner of the Gothes,
That we may hew his limbes, and on a pile
Ad manus fratrum, sacrifice his flesh:
Before this earthly prison of their bones,
That so the shadowes be not vnappeas'd.
Nor we disturb'd with prodigies on earth.
Tit. I giue him you, the Noblest that Suruiues,
The eldest Son of this distressed Queene.
Tam. Stay Romaine Bretheren, gracious Conqueror,
Victorious *Titus*, rue the teares I shed,
A Mothers teares in passion for her sonne:
And if thy Sonnes were euer deere to thee,
Oh thinke my sonnes to be as deere to mee.
Sufficeth not, that we are brought to Rome
To beautifie thy Triumphs, and returne
Captiue to thee, and to thy Romaine yoake,
But must my Sonnes be slaughtred in the streetes,
For Valiant doings in their Countries cause?
O! If to fight for King and Common-weale,
Were piety in thine, it is in these:
Andronicus, staine not thy Tombe with blood.
Wilt thou draw neere the nature of the Gods?
Draw neere them then in being mercifull.
Sweet mercy is Nobilities true badge,
Thrice Noble *Titus*, spare my first borne sonne.
Tit. Patient your selfe Madam, and pardon me.
These are the Brethren, whom you Gothes beheld
Aliue and dead, and for their Bretheren slaine,
Religiously they aske a sacrifice:
To this your sonne is markt, and die he must,
T'appease their groaning shadowes that are gone.
Luc. Away with him, and make a fire straight,
And with our Swords vpon a pile of wood,
Let's hew his limbes till they be cleane consum'd.

Exit Sonnes with Alarbus.

Tamo. O cruell irreligious piety.
Chi. Was euer Scythia halfe so barbarous?
Dem. Oppose me Scythia to ambitious Rome,
Alarbus goes to rest, and we suruiue,
To tremble vnder *Titus* threatning lookes,
Then Madam stand resolu'd, but hope withall,
The selfe same Gods that arm'd the Queene of Troy
With opportunitie of sharpe reuenge
Vpon the Thracian Tyrant in his Tent,
May fauour *Tamora* the Queene of Gothes,
(When Gothes were Gothes, and *Tamora* was Queene)
To quit the bloody wrongs vpon her foes.

Enter the Sonnes of Andronicus againe.

Luci. See Lord and Father, how we haue perform'd
Our Romaine rightes, *Alarbus* limbs are lopt,
And intrals feede the sacrifising fire,
Whose smoke like incense doth perfume the skie.
Remaineth nought but to interre our Brethren,
And with low'd Larums welcome them to Rome.
Tit. Let it be so, and let *Andronicus*
Make this his latest farewell to their soules.

Flourish.

Then Sound Trumpets, and lay the Coffins in the Tombe.

In peace and Honour rest you heere my Sonnes,
Romes readiest Champions, repose you heere in rest,
Secure from worldly chaunces and mishaps:
Heere lurks no Treason, heere no enuie swels,
Heere grow no damned grudges, heere are no stormes,
No noyse, but silence and Eternall sleepe,
In peace and Honour rest you heere my Sonnes.

Enter Lauinia.

Laui. In peace and Honour, liue Lord *Titus* long,
My Noble Lord and Father, liue in Fame:
Loe at this Tombe my tributarie teares,
I render for my Bretherens Obsequies:
And at thy feete I kneele, with teares of ioy
Shed on the earth for thy returne to Rome.
O blesse me heere with thy victorious hand,
Whose Fortune Romes best Citizens applau'd.
Ti. Kind Rome,
That hast thus louingly reseru'd
The Cordiall of mine age to glad my hart,
Lauinia liue, out-liue thy Fathers dayes:
And Fames eternall date for vertues praise.
Marc. Long liue Lord *Titus*, my beloued brother,
Gracious Triumpher in the eyes of Rome.
Tit. Thankes Gentle Tribune,
Noble brother *Marcus*.
Mar. And welcome Nephews from succesfull wars,
You that suruiue and you that sleepe in Fame:
Faire Lords your Fortunes are all alike in all,
That in your Countries seruice drew your Swords.
But safer Triumph is this Funerall Pompe,
That hath aspir'd to *Solons* Happines,
And Triumphs ouer chaunce in honours bed.
Titus Andronicus, the people of Rome,
Whose friend in iustice thou hast euer bene,
Send thee by me their Tribune and their trust,
This Palliament of white and spotlesse Hue,
And name thee in Election for the Empire,
With these our late deceased Emperours Sonnes:
Be *Candidatus* then and put it on,
And helpe to set a head on headlesse Rome.
Tit. A better head her Glorious body fits,
Then his that shakes for age and feeblenesse.

What

What ſhould I d'on this Robe and trouble you,
Be choſen with proclamations to day,
To morrow yeeld vp rule, reſigne my life,
And ſet abroad new buſineſſe for you all.
Rome I haue bene thy Souldier forty yeares,
And led my Countries ſtrength ſucceſſefully,
And buried one and twenty Valiant Sonnes,
Knighted in Field, ſlaine manfully in Armes,
In right and Seruice of their Noble Countrie:
Giue me a ſtaffe of Honour for mine age,
But not a Scepter to controule the world,
Vpright he held it Lords, that held it laſt.
Mar. *Titus*, thou ſhalt obtaine and aske the Emperie
Sat. Proud and ambitious Tribune can'ſt thou tell?
Titus. Patience Prince *Saturninus*.
Sat. Romaines do me right.
Patricians draw your Swords, and ſheath them not
Till *Saturninus* be Romes Emperour:
Andronicus would thou wert ſhipt to hell,
Rather then rob me of the peoples harts.
Luc. Proud *Saturnine*, interrupter of the good
That Noble minded *Titus* meanes to thee.
Tit. Content thee Prince, I will reſtore to thee
The peoples harts, and weane them from themſelues.
Baſs. *Andronicus*, I do not flatter thee
But Honour thee, and will doe till I die:
My Faction if thou ſtrengthen with thy Friend?
I will moſt thankefull be, and thankes to men
Of Noble mindes, is Honourable Meede.
Tit. People of Rome, and Noble Tribunes heere,
I aske your voyces and your Suffrages,
Will you beſtow them friendly on *Andronicus*?
Tribunes. To gratifie the good *Andronicus*,
And Gratulate his ſafe returne to Rome,
The people will accept whom he admits.
Tit. Tribunes I thanke you, and this ſure I make,
That you Create your Emperours eldeſt ſonne,
Lord *Saturnine*, whoſe Vertues will I hope,
Reflect on Rome as Tytans Rayes on earth
And ripen Iuſtice in this Common-weale:
Then if you will elect by my aduiſe,
Crowne him, and ſay: Long liue our Emperour.
Mar. An. With Voyces and applauſe of euery ſort,
Patricians and Plebeans we Create
Lord *Saturninus* Romes Great Emperour.
And ſay, *Long liue our Emperour Saturnine.*
A long Flouriſh till they come downe.
Satu. *Titus Andronicus*, for thy Fauours done,
To vs in our Election this day,
I giue thee thankes in part of thy Deſerts,
And will with Deeds requite thy gentleneſſe:
And for an Onſet *Titus* to aduance
Thy Name, and Honorable Familie,
Lauinia will I make my Empreſſe,
Romes Royall Miſtris, Miſtris of my hart
And in the Sacred *Pathan* her eſpouſe:
Tell me *Andronicus* doth this motion pleaſe thee?
Tit. It doth my worthy Lord, and in this match,
I hold me Highly Honoured of your Grace,
And heere in ſight of Rome, to *Saturnine*,
King and Commander of our Common-weale,
The Wide-worlds Emperour, do I Conſecrate,
My Sword, my Chariot, and my Priſonerss,
Preſents well Worthy Romes Imperiall Lord:
Receiue them then, the Tribute that I owe,
Mine Honours Enſignes humbled at my feete.
Satu. Thankes Noble *Titus*, Father of my life,
How proud I am of thee, and of thy gifts
Rome ſhall record, and when I do forget
The leaſt of theſe vnſpeakable Deſerts,
Romans forget your Fealtie to me.
Tit. Now Madam are your priſoner to an Emperour,
To him that for you Honour and your State,
Will vſe you Nobly and your followers.
Satu. A goodly Lady, truſt me of the Hue
That I would chooſe, were I to thooſe a new:
Cleere vp Faire Queene that cloudy countenance,
Though chance of warre
Hath wrought this change of cheere,
Thou com'ſt not to be made a ſcorne in Rome:
Princely ſhall be thy vſage euery way.
Reſt on my word, and let not diſcontent
Daunt all your hopes: Madam he comforts you,
Can make your Greater then the Queene of Gothes?
Lauinia you are not diſpleas'd with this?
Lau. Not I my Lord, ſith true Nobilitie,
Warrants theſe words in Princely curteſie.
Sat. Thankes ſweete *Lauinia* Romans let vs goe:
Ranſomleſſe heere we ſet our Priſoners free,
Proclaime our Honors Lords with Trumpe and Drum.
Baſs. Lord *Titus* by your leaue, this Maid is mine.
Tit. How ſir? Are you in earneſt then my Lord?
Baſs. I Noble *Titus*, and reſolu'd withall,
To doe my ſelfe this reaſon, and this right.
Marc. *Suum cuiquam*, is our Romane Iuſtice,
This Prince in Iuſtice ceazeth but his owne.
Luc. And that he will and ſhall, if *Lucius* liue.
Tit. Traytors auant, where is the Emperours Guarde?
Treaſon my Lord, *Lauinia* is ſurpris'd.
Sat. Surpris'd, by whom?
Baſs. By him that iuſtly may
Beare his Betroth'd, from all the world away.
Muti. Brothers helpe to conuey her hence away,
And with my Sword Ile keepe this doore ſafe.
Tit. Follow my Lord, and Ile ſoone bring her backe.
Mut. My Lord you paſſe not heere.
Tit. What villaine Boy, bar'ſt me my way in Rome?
Mut. Helpe *Lucius* helpe. *He kils him.*
Luc. My Lord you are vniuſt, and more then ſo,
In wrongfull quarrell, you haue ſlaine your ſon.
Tit. Nor thou, nor he are any ſonnes of mine,
My ſonnes would neuer ſo diſhonour me.
Traytor reſtore *Lauinia* to the Emperour.
Luc. Dead if you will, but not to be his wife,
That is anothers lawfull promiſt Loue.

Enter aloft the Emperour with Tamora and her two ſonnes, and Aaron the Moore.

Empe. No *Titus*, no, the Emperour needs her not,
Nor her, nor thee, nor any of thy ſtocke:
Ile truſt by Leiſure him that mocks me once.
Thee neuer: nor thy Trayterous haughty ſonnes,
Confederates all, thus to diſhonour me.
Was none in Rome to make a ſtale
But *Saturnine*? Full well *Andronicus*
Agree theſe Deeds, with that proud bragge of thine,
That ſaid'ſt, I beg'd the Empire at thy hands.
Tit. O monſtrous, what reproachfull words are theſe?
Sat. But goe thy wayes, goe giue that changing peece,
To him that flouriſht for her with his Sword:
A Valliant ſonne in-law thou ſhalt enioy:
One, fit to bandy with thy lawleſſe Sonnes,
To

To ruffle in the Common-wealth of Rome.
Tit. These words are Razors to my wounded hart.
Sat. And therefore louely *Tamora* Queene of Gothes,
That like the stately *Thebe* mong'st her Nimphs
Dost ouer-shine the Gallant'st Dames of Rome,
If thou be pleas'd with this my sodaine choyse,
Behold I choose thee *Tamora* for my Bride,
And will Create thee Empresse of Rome.
Speake Queene of Goths dost thou applau'd my choyse?
And heere I sweare by all the Romaine Gods,
Sith Priest and Holy-water are so neere,
And Tapers burne so bright, and euery thing
In readines for *Hymeneus* stand,
I will not resalute the streets of Rome,
Or clime my Pallace, till from forth this place,
I leade espous'd my Bride along with me.
Tamo. And heere in sight of heauen to Rome I sweare,
If *Saturnine* aduance the Queen of Gothes,
Shee will a Hand-maid be to his desires,
A louing Nurse, a Mother to his youth.
Satur. Ascend Faire Qeene,
Panthean Lords, accompany
Your Noble Emperour and his louely Brid,e
Sent by the heauens for Prince *Saturnine*,
Whose wisedome hath her Fortune Conquered,
There shall we Consummate our Spousall rites.
Exeunt omnes.
Tit. I am not bid to waite vpon this Bride:
Titus when wer't thou wont to walke alone,
Dishonoured thus and Challenged of wrongs?

Enter Marcus and Titus Sonnes.

Mar O *Titus* see! O see what thou hast done'
In a bad quarrell, slaine a Vertuous sonne.
Tit. No foolish Tribune, no: No sonne of mine,
Nor thou, nor these Confedrates in the deed,
That hath dishonoured all our Family,
Vnworthy brother, and vnworthy Sonnes.
Luci. But let vs giue him buriall as becomes:
Giue *Mutius* buriall with our Bretheren.
Tit. Traytors away, he rest's not in this Tombe:
This Monument fiue hundreth yeares hath stood,
Which I haue Sumptuously re-edified:
Heere none but Souldiers, and Romes Seruitors,
Repose in Fame: None basely slaine in braules,
Bury him where you can, he comes not heere.
Mar. My Lord this is impiety in you,
My Nephew *Mutius* deeds do plead for him,
He must be buried with his bretheren.
Titus two Sonnes speakes.
And shall, or him we will accompany.
Ti. And shall! What villaine was it spake that word?
Titus sonne speakes.
He that would vouch'd it in any place but heere.
Tit. What would you bury him in my despight?
Mar. No Noble *Titus*, but intreat of thee,
To pardon *Mutius*, and to bury him.
Tit. *Marcus*, Euen thou hast stroke vpon my Crest,
And with these Boyes mine Honour thou hast wounded,
My foes I doe repute you euery one.
So trouble me no more, but get you gone.
1.Sonne. He is not himselfe, let vs withdraw.
2.Sonne. Not I tell *Mutius* bones be buried.
The Brother and the sonnes kneele.
Mar. Brother, for in that name doth nature plea'd.
2.Sonne. Father, and in that name doth nature speake.
Tit. Speake thou no more if all the rest will speede.
Mar. Renowned *Titus* more then halfe my soules.
Luc. Deare Father, soule and substance of vs all.
Mar. Suffer thy brother *Marcus* to interre
His Noble Nephew heere in vertues nest,
That died in Honour and *Lauinia's* cause.
Thou art a Romaine, be not barbarous:
The Greekes vpon aduise did bury *Aiax*
That slew himselfe: And *Laertes* sonne,
Did graciously plead for his Funerals:
Let not young *Mutius* then that was thy ioy,
Be bar'd his entrance heere.
Tit. Rise *Marcus*, rise,
The dismall'st day is this that ere I saw,
To be dishonored by my Sonnes in Rome:
Well, bury him, and bury me the next.
They put him in the Tombe.
Luc. There lie thy bones sweet *Mutius* with thy
Till we with Trophees do adorne thy Tombe. (friends
They all kneele and say.
No man shed teares for Noble *Mutius*,
He liues in Fame, that di'd in vertues cause. *Exit.*
Mar. My Lord to step out of these sudden dumps,
How comes it that the subtile Queene of Gothes,
Is of a sodaine thus aduanc'd in Rome?
Ti. I know not *Marcus*: but I know it is,
(Whether by deuise or no) the heauens can tell,
Is she not then beholding to the man,
That brought her for this high good turne so farre?
Yes, and will Nobly him remunerate.

Flourish.
Enter the Emperor, Tamora, and her two sons, with the Moore at one doore. Enter at the other doore Bassianus and Lauinia with others.

Sat. So *Bassianus*, you haue plaid your prize,
God giue you ioy sir of your Gallant Bride.
Bass. And you of yours my Lord: I say no more,
Nor wish no lesse, and so I take my leaue.
Sat. Traytor, if Rome haue law, or we haue power,
Thou and thy Faction shall repent this Rape.
Bass. Rape call you it my Lord, to cease my owne,
My true betrothed Loue, and now my wife?
But let the lawes of Rome determine all,
Meane while I am possest of that is mine.
Sat. 'Tis good sir: you are very short with vs,
But if we liue, weele be as sharpe with you.
Bass. My Lord, what I haue done as best I may,
Answere I must, and shall do with my life,
Onely thus much I giue your Grace to know,
By all the duties that I owe to Rome,
This Noble Gentleman Lord *Titus* heere,
Is in opinion and in honour wrong'd,
That in the rescue of *Lauinia*,
With his owne hand did slay his youngest Son,
In zeale to you, and highly mou'd to wrath.
To be controul'd in that he frankly gaue:
Recieue him then to fauour *Saturnine*,
That hath expre'st himselfe in all his deeds,
A Father and a friend to thee, and Rome.
Tit. Prince *Bassianus* leaue to plead my Deeds,
'Tis thou, and those, that haue dishonoured me.
Rome and the righteous heauens be my iudge,
How I haue lou'd and Honour'd *Saturnine*.
Tam. My worthy Lord if euer *Tamora*,
Were

Were gracious in those Princely eyes of thine,
Then heare me speake indifferently for all:
And at my sute (sweet) pardon what is past.
Satu. What Madam, be dishonoured openly,
And basely put it vp without reuenge?
Tam. Not so my Lord,
The Gods of Rome for-fend,
I should be Authour to dishonour you.
But on mine honour dare, I vndertake
For good Lord *Titus* innocence in all:
Whose fury not dissembled speakes his griefes:
Then at my sute looke graciously on him,
Loose not so noble a friend on vaine suppose,
Nor with sowre lookes afflict his gentle heart.
My Lord, be rul'd by me, be wonne at last,
Dissemble all your griefes and discontents,
You are but newly planted in your Throne,
Least then the people, and Patricians too,
Vpon a iust suruey take *Titus* part,
And so supplant vs for ingratitude,
Which Rome reputes to be a hainous sinne.
Yeeld at intreats, and then let me alone:
Ile finde a day to massacre them all,
And race their faction, and their familie,
The cruell Father, and his trayt'rous sonnes,
To whom I sued for my deare sonnes life.
And make them know what 'tis to let a Queene.
Kneele in the streetes, and beg for grace in vaine.
Come, come, sweet Emperour, (come *Andronicus*)
Take vp this good old man, and cheere the heart,
That dies in tempest of thy angry frowne.
King. Rise *Titus*, rise,
My Empresse hath preuail'd.
Titus. I thanke your Maiestie,
And her my Lord.
These words, these lookes,
Infuse new life in me.
Tamo. *Titus*, I am incorparate in Rome,
A Roman now adopted happily.
And must aduise the Emperour for his good,
This day all quarrels die *Andronicus*.
And let it be mine honour good my Lord,
That I haue reconcil'd your friends and you.
For you Prince *Bassianus*, I haue past
My word and promise to the Emperour,
That you will be more milde and tractable.
And feare not Lords:
And you *Lauinia*,
By my aduise all humbled on your knees,
You shall aske pardon of his Maiestie.
Son. We doe,
And vow to heauen, and to his Highnes,
That what we did, was mildly, as we might,
Tendring our sisters honour and our owne.
Mar. That on mine honour heere I do protest.
King. Away and talke not, trouble vs no more.
Tamora. Nay, nay,
Sweet Emperour, we must all be friends,
The Tribune and his Nephews kneele for grace,
I will not be denied, sweet hart looke back.
King. *Marcus*,
For thy sake and thy brothers heere,
And at my louely *Tamora's* intreats,
I doe remit these young mens haynous faults.
Stand vp: *Lauinia*, though you left me like a churle,
I found a friend, and sure as death I sware,
I would not part a Batchellour from the Priest.
Come, if the Emperours Court can feast two Brides,
You are my guest *Lauinia*, and your friends:
This day shall be a Loue-day *Tamora*.
Tit. To morrow and it please your Maiestie,
To hunt the Panther and the Hart with me,
With horne and Hound,
Weele giue your Grace *Bon iour*.
Satur. Be it so *Titus*, and Gramercy to. *Exeunt.*

Actus Secunda.

Flourish. *Enter Aaron alone.*

Aron. Now climbeth *Tamora* Olympus toppe,
Safe out of Fortunes shot, and sits aloft,
Secure of Thunders cracke or lightning flash,
Aduanc'd about pale enuies threatning reach:
As when the golden Sunne salutes the morne,
And hauing gilt the Ocean with his beames,
Gallops the Zodiacke in his glistering Coach,
And ouer-lookes the highest piering hills:
So *Tamora*:
Vpon her wit doth earthly honour waite,
And vertue stoopes and trembles at her frowne.
Then *Aaron* arme thy hart, and fit thy thoughts,
To mount aloft with thy Emperiall Mistris,
And mount her pitch, whom thou in triumph long
Hast prisoner held, fettred in amorous chaines,
And faster bound to *Aarons* charming eyes,
Then is *Prometheus* ti'de to *Caucasus*.
Away with slauish weedes, and idle thoughts,
I will be bright and shine in Pearle and Gold,
To waite vpon this new made Empresse.
To waite said I? To wanton with this Queene,
This Goddesse, this *Semerimis*, this Queene,
This Syren, that will charme Romes *Saturnine*,
And see his shipwracke, and his Common weales.
Hollo, what storme is this?

Enter Chiron and Demetrius brauing.

Dem. *Chiron* thy yeres wants wit, thy wit wants edge
And manners to intru'd where I am grac'd,
And may for ought thou know'st affected be.
Chi. *Demetrius*, thou doo'st ouer-weene in all,
And so in this, to beare me downe with braues,
'Tis not the difference of a yeere or two
Makes me lesse gracious, or thee more fortunate:
I am as able, and as fit, as thou,
To serue, and to deserue my Mistris grace,
And that my sword vpon thee shall approue,
And plead my passions for *Lauinia's* loue.
Aron. Clubs, clubs, these louers will not keep the peace.
Dem. Why Boy, although our mother (vnaduised)
Gaue you a daunsing Rapier by your side,
Are you so desperate growne to threat your friends?
Goe too: haue your Lath glued within your sheath,
Till you know better how to handle it.
Chi. Meane while sir, with the little skill I haue,
Full well shalt thou perceiue how much I dare.
Deme. I Boy, grow ye so braue? *They drawe.*
Aron. Why how now Lords?
So nere the Emperours Pallace dare you draw,

And

And maintaine such a quarrell openly?
Full well I wote, the ground of all this grudge.
I would not for a million of Gold,
The cause were knowne to them it most concernes.
Nor would your noble mother for much more
Be so dishonored in the Court of Rome:
For shame put vp.
Deme. Not I, till I haue sheath'd
My rapier in his bosome, and withall
Thrust these reprochfull speeches downe his throat,
That he hath breath'd in my dishonour heere.
Chi. For that I am prepar'd, and full resolu'd,
Foule spoken Coward,
That thundrest with thy tongue,
And with thy weapon nothing dar'st performe.
Aron. A way I say.
Now by the Gods that warlike Gothes adore,
This pretty brabble will vndoo vs all:
Why Lords, and thinke you not how dangerous
It is to set vpon a Princes right?
What is *Lauinia* then become so loose,
Or *Bassianus* so degenerate,
That for her loue such quarrels may be broacht,
Without controulement, Iustice, or reuenge?
Young Lords beware, and should the Empresse know,
This discord ground, the musicke would not please.
Chi. I care not I, knew she and all the world,
I loue *Lauinia* more then all the world.
Demet. Youngling,
Learne thou to make some meaner choise,
Lauinia is thine elder brothers hope.
Aron. Why are ye mad? Or know ye not in Rome,
How furious and impatient they be,
And cannot brooke Competitors in loue?
I tell you Lords, you doe but plot your deaths,
By this deuise.
Chi. *Aaron*, a thousand deaths would I propose,
To atchieue her whom I do loue.
Aron. To atcheiue her, how?
Deme. Why, mak'st thou it so strange?
Shee is a woman, therefore may be woo'd,
Shee is a woman, therfore may be wonne,
Shee is *Lauinia* therefore must be lou'd.
What man, more water glideth by the Mill
Then wots the Miller of, and easie it is
Of a cut loafe to steale a shiue we know:
Though *Bassianus* be the Emperours brother,
Better then he haue worne *Vulcans* badge.
Aron. I, and as good as *Saturnius* may.
Deme. Then why should he dispaire that knowes to
With words, faire lookes, and liberality: (court it
What hast not thou full often strucke a Doe,
And borne her cleanly by the Keepers nose?
Aron. Why then it seemes some certaine snatch or so
Would serue your turnes.
Chi. I so the turne were serued.
Deme. *Aaron* thou hast hit it.
Aron. Would you had hit it too,
Then should not we be tir'd with this adoo:
Why harke yee, harke yee, aud are you such fooles,
To square for this? Would it offend you then?
Chi. Faith not me.
Deme. Nor me, so I were one.
Aron. For shame be friends, & ioyne for that you iar:
'Tis pollicie, and stratageme must doe
That you affect, and so must you resolue,
That what you cannot as you would atcheiue,
You must perforce accomplish as you may:
Take this of me, *Lucrece* was not more chast
Then this *Lauinia*, *Bassianus* loue,
A speedier course this lingring languishment
Must we pursue, and I haue found the path:
My Lords, a solemne hunting is in hand.
There will the louely Roman Ladies troope:
The Forrest walkes are wide and spacious,
And many vnfrequented plots there are,
Fitted by kinde for rape and villanie:
Single you thither then this dainty Doe,
And strike her home by force, if not by words:
This way or not at all, stand you in hope.
Come, come, our Empresse with her sacred wit
To villainie and vengance consecrate,
Will we acquaint with all that we intend,
And she shall file our engines with aduise,
That will not suffer you to square your selues,
But to your wishes height aduance you both.
The Emperours Court is like the house of Fame,
The pallace full of tongues, of eyes, of eares:
The Woods are ruthlesse, dreadfull, deafe, and dull:
There speake, and strike braue Boyes, & take your turnes.
There serue your lusts, shadow'd from heauens eye,
And reuell in *Lauinia's* Treasurie.
Chi. Thy counsell Lad smells of no cowardise.
Deme. *Sy fas aut nefas*, till I finde the streames,
To coole this heat, a Charme to calme their fits,
Per Stigia per manes Vehor. *Exeunt.*

Enter Titus Andronicus and his three sonnes, making a noyse with hounds and hornes, and Marcus.

Tit. The hunt is vp, the morne is bright and gray,
The fields are fragrant, and the Woods are greene,
Vncouple heere, and let vs make a bay,
And wake the Emperour, and his louely Bride,
And rouze the Prince, and ring a hunters peale,
That all the Court may eccho with the noyse.
Sonnes let it be your charge, as it is ours,
To attend the Emperours person carefully:
I haue bene troubled in my sleepe this night,
But dawning day new comfort hath inspir'd.

Winde Hornes.

Heere a cry of houndes, and winde hornes in a peale, then Enter Saturninus, Tamora, Bassianus, Lauinia, Chiron, Demetrius, and their Attendants.

Ti. Many good morrowes to your Maiestie,
Madam to you as many and as good.
I promised your Grace, a Hunters peale.
Satur. And you haue rung it lustily my Lords,
Somewhat to earely for new married Ladies.
Bass. *Lauinia*, how say you?
Laui. I say no:
I haue bene awake two houres and more.
Satur. Come on then, horse and Chariots let vs haue,
And to our sport: Madam, now shall ye see,
Our Romaine hunting.
Mar. I haue dogges my Lord,
Will rouze the proudest Panther in the Chase,
And clime the highest Pomontary top.
Tit. And I haue horse will follow where the game
Makes way, and runnes likes Swallowes ore the plaine
Deme. Chiron

Deme. Chiron we hunt not we, with Horse nor Hound
But hope to plucke a dainty Doe to ground. *Exeunt*

Enter Aaron alone.

Aron. He that had wit, would thinke that I had none,
To bury so much Gold vnder a Tree,
And neuer after to inherit it.
Let him that thinks of me so abiectly,
Know that this Gold must coine a stratageme,
Which cunningly effected, will beget
A very excellent peece of villany:
And so repose sweet Gold for their vnrest,
That haue their Almes out of the Empresse Chest.

Enter Tamora to the Moore.

Tamo. My louely *Aaron*,
Wherefore look'st thou sad,
When euery thing doth make a Gleefull boast?
The Birds chaunt melody on euery bush,
The Snake lies rolled in the chearefull Sunne,
The greene leaues quiuer, with the cooling winde,
And make a chequer'd shadow on the ground:
Vnder their sweete shade, *Aaron* let vs sit,
And whil'st the babling Eccho mock's the Hounds,
Replying shrilly to the well tun'd-Hornes,
As if a double hunt were heard at once,
Let vs sit downe, and marke their yelping noyse:
And after conflict, such as was suppos'd.
The wandring Prince and *Dido* once enioy'd,
When with a happy storme they were surpris'd,
And Curtain'd with a Counsaile-keeping Caue,
We may each wreathed in the others armes,
(Our pastimes done) possesse a Golden slumber,
Whiles Hounds and Hornes, and sweet Melodious Birds
Be vnto vs, as is a Nurses Song
Of Lullabie, to bring her Babe asleepe.

Aron. Madame,
Though *Venus* gouerne your desires,
Saturne is Dominator ouer mine:
What signifies my deadly standing eye,
My silence, and my Cloudy Melancholie,
My fleece of Woolly haire, that now vncurles,
Euen as an Adder when she doth vnrowle
To do some fatall execution?
No Madam, these are no Veneriall signes,
Vengeance is in my heart, death in my hand,
Blood, and reuenge, are Hammering in my head.
Harke *Tamora*, the Empresse of my Soule,
Which neuer hopes more heauen, then rests in thee,
This is the day of Doome for *Bassianus*;
His *Philomel* must loose her tongue to day,
Thy Sonnes make Pillage of her Chastity,
And wash their hands in *Bassian* blood.
Seest thou this Letter, take it vp I pray thee,
And giue the King this fatall plotted Scrowle,
Now question me no more, we are espied,
Heere comes a parcell of our hopefull Booty,
Which dreads not yet their liues destruction.

Enter Bassianus and Lauinia.

Tamo. Ah my sweet *Moore*:
Sweeter to me then life.

Aron. No more great Empresse, *Bassianus* comes,
Be crosse with him, and Ile goe fetch thy Sonnes
To backe thy quarrell what so ere they be.

Bassi. Whom haue we heere?
Romes Royall Empresse,
Vnfurnisht of our well beseeming troope?
Or is it *Dian* habited like her,
Who hath abandoned her holy Groues,
To see the generall Hunting in this Forrest?

Tamo. Sawcie controuler of our priuate steps:
Had I the power, that some say *Dian* had,
Thy Temples should be planted presently.
With Hornes, as was *Acteons*, and the Hounds
Should driue vpon his new transformed limbes,
Vnmannerly Intruder as thou art.

Laui. Vnder your patience gentle Empresse,
'Tis thought you haue a goodly gift in Horning,
And to be doubted, that your *Moore* and you
Are singled forth to try experiments:
Ioue sheild your husband from his Hounds to day,
'Tis pitty they should take him for a Stag.

Bassi. Beleeue me Queene, your swarth Cymerion,
Doth make your Honour of his bodies Hue,
Spotted, detested, and abhominable.
Why are you sequestred from all your traine?
Dismounted from your Snow-white goodly Steed,
And wandred hither to an obscure plot,
Accompanied with a barbarous *Moore*,
If foule desire had not conducted you?

Laui. And being intercepted in your sport,
Great reason that my Noble Lord, be rated
For Saucinesse, I pray you let vs hence,
And let her ioy her Rauen coloured loue,
This valley fits the purpose passing well.

Bassi. The King my Brother shall haue notice of this.

Laui. I, for these slips haue made him noted long,
Good King, to be so mightily abused.

Tamora. Why I haue patience to endure all this?

Enter Chiron and Demetrius.

Dem. How now deere Soueraigne
And our gracious Mother,
Why doth your Highnes looke so pale and wan?

Tamo. Haue I not reason thinke you to looke pale.
These two haue tic'd me hither to this place,
A barren, detested vale you see it is.
The Trees though Sommer, yet forlorne and leane,
Ore-come with Mosse, and balefull Misselto.
Heere neuer shines the Sunne, heere nothing breeds,
Vnlesse the nightly Owle, or fatall Rauen:
And when they shew'd me this abhorred pit,
They told me heere at dead time of the night,
A thousand Fiends, a thousand hissing Snakes,
Ten thousand swelling Toades, as many Vrchins,
Would make such fearefull and confused cries,
As any mortall body hearing it,
Should straite fall mad, or else die suddenly.
No sooner had they told this hellish tale,
But strait they told me they would binde me heere,
Vnto the body of a dismall yew,
And leaue me to this miserable death.
And then they call'd me foule Adulteresse,
Lasciuious Goth, and all the bitterest tearmes
That euer eare did heare to such effect.
And had you not by wondrous fortune come,
This vengeance on me had they executed:
Reuenge it, as you loue your Mothers life,
Or be ye not henceforth cal'd my Children.

Dem. This is a witnesse that I am thy Sonne. *stab him.*

Chi. And this for me,
Strook home to shew my strength.

Laui. I come *Semeramis*, nay Barbarous *Tamora*.

d d For

For no name fits thy nature but thy owne.
Tam. Giue me thy poyniard, you shal know my boyes
Your Mothers hand shall right your Mothers wrong.
Deme. Stay Madam heere is more belongs to her,
First thrash the Corne, then after burne the straw:
This Minion stood vpon her chastity,
Vpon her Nuptiall vow, her loyaltie.
And with that painted hope, braues your Mightinesse,
And shall she carry this vnto her graue?
Chi. And if she doe,
I would I were an Eunuch,
Drag hence her husband to some secret hole,
And make his dead Trunke-Pillow to our lust.
Tamo. But when ye haue the hony we desire,
Let not this Waspe out-liue vs both to sting.
Chir. I warrant you Madam we will make that sure:
Come Mistris, now perforce we will enioy,
That nice-preserued honesty of yours.
Laui. Oh *Tamora*, thou bear'st a woman face.
Tamo. I will not heare her speake, away with her.
Lasi. Sweet Lords intreat her heare me but a word
Demet. Listen faire Madam, let it be your glory
To see her teares, but be your hart to them,
As vnrelenting flint to drops of raine.
Laui. When did the Tigers young-ones teach the dam?
O doe not learne her wrath, she taught it thee,
The milke thou suck'st from her did turne to Marble,
Euen at thy Teat thou had'st thy Tyranny,
Yet euery Mother breeds not Sonnes alike,
Do thou intreat her shew a woman pitty.
Chiro. What,
Would'st thou haue me proue my selfe a bastard?
Lau. 'Tis true,
The Rauen doth not hatch a Larke,
Yet haue I heard, Oh could I finde it now,
The Lion mou'd with pitty, did indure
To haue his Princely pawes par'd all away.
Some say, that Rauens foster forlorne children,
The whil'st their owne birds famish in their nests:
Oh be to me though thy hard hart say no,
Nothing so kind but something pittifull.
Tamo. I know not what it meanes, away with her.
Lauia. Oh let me teach thee for my Fathers sake,
That gaue thee life when well he might haue slaine thee:
Be not obdurate, open thy deafe eares.
Tame. Had'st thou in person nere offended me.
Euen for his sake am I pittilesse:
Remember Boyes I powr'd forth teares in vaine,
To saue your brother from the sacrifice,
But fierce *Andronicus* would not relent,
Therefore away with her, and vse her as you will,
The worse to her, the better lou'd of me.
Laui. Oh *Tamora*,
Be call'd a gentle Queene,
And with thine owne hands kill me in this place,
For 'tis not life that I haue beg'd so long,
Poore I was slaine, when *Bassianus* dy'd.
Tam. What beg'st thou then? fond woman let me go?
Laui. 'Tis present death I beg, and one thing more,
That womanhood denies my tongue to tell:
Oh keepe me from their worse then killing lust,
And tumble me into some loathsome pit,
Where neuer mans eye may behold my body,
Doe this, and be a charitable murderer.
Tam. So should I rob my sweet Sonnes of their fee,
No let them satisfie their lust on thee.
Deme. Away,
For thou hast staid vs heere too long.
Lauinia. No Garace,
No womanhood? Ah beastly creature,
The blot and enemy to our generall name,
Confusion fall——
Chi. Nay then Ile stop your mouth
Bring thou her husband,
This is the Hole where *Aaron* bid vs hide him.
Tam. Farewell my Sonnes, see that you make her sure,
Nere let my heart know merry cheere indeed,
Till all the *Andronici* be made away:
Now will I hence to seeke my louely *Moore*,
And let my spleenefull Sonnes this Trull defloure. *Exit.*

Enter Aaron with two of Titus Sonnes.

Aron. Come on my Lords, the better foote before,
Straight will I bring you to the lothsome pit,
Where I espied the Panther fast asleepe.
Quin. My sight is very dull what ere it bodes.
Marti. And mine I promise you, were it not for shame,
Well could I leaue our sport to sleepe a while.
Quin. What art thou fallen?
What subtile Hole is this,
Whose mouth is couered with Rude growing Briers,
Vpon whose leaues are drops of new-shed-blood,
As fresh as mornings dew distil'd on flowers,
A very fatall place it seemes to me
Speake Brother hast thou hurt thee with the fall?
Martius. Oh Brother,
With the dismal'st obiect
That euer eye with sight made heart lament.
Arone. Now will I fetch the King to finde them heere,
That he thereby may haue a likely gesse,
How these were they that made away his Brother.
Exit Aaron.
Marti. Why dost not comfort me and helpe me out,
From this vnhallow'd and blood-stained Hole?
Quintus. I am surprised with an vncouth feare,
A chilling sweat ore-runs my trembling ioynts,
My heart suspects more then mine eie can see.
Marti. To proue thou hast a true diuining heart,
Aaron and thou looke downe into this den,
And see a fearefull sight of blood and death.
Quintus. *Aaron* is gone,
And my compassionate heart
Will not permit mine eyes once to behold
The thing whereat it trembles by surmise:
Oh tell me how it is, for nere till now
Was I a child, to feare I know not what.
Marti. Lord *Bassianus* lies embrewed heere,
All on a heape like to the slaughtred Lambe,
In this detested, darke, blood-drinking pit.
Quin. If it be darke, how doost thou know 'tis he?
Mart. Vpon his bloody finger he doth weare
A precious Ring, that lightens all the Hole:
Which like a Taper in some Monument,
Doth shine vpon the dead mans earthly cheekes,
And shewes the ragged intrailes of the pit:
So pale did shine the Moone on *Piramus*,
When he by night lay bath'd in Maiden blood:
O Brother helpe me with thy fainting hand.
If feare hath made thee faint, as mee it hath,
Out of this fell deuouring receptacle,
As hatefull as *Ocitus* mistie mouth
Quint. Reach me thy hand, that I may helpe thee out,
Or

Or wanting ſtrength to doe thee ſo much good,
I may be pluckt into the ſwallowing wombe,
Of this deepe pit, poore *Baſsianus* graue:
I haue no ſtrength to plucke thee to the brinke.
Martius. Nor I no ſtrength to clime without thy help.
Quin. Thy hand once more, I will not looſe againe,
Till thou art heere aloft, or I below,
Thou can'ſt not come to me, I come to thee. *Boths fall in.*

Enter the Emperour, Aaron the Moore.

Satur. Along with me, Ile ſee what hole is here,
And what he is that now is leapt into it.
Say, who art thou that lately did'ſt deſcend,
Into this gaping hollow of the earth?
Marti. The vnhappie ſonne of old *Andronicus*,
Brought hither in a moſt vnluckie houre,
To finde thy brother *Baſsianus* dead.
Satur. My brother dead? I know thou doſt but ieſt,
He and his Lady both are at the Lodge,
Vpon the North-ſide of this pleaſant Chaſe,
'Tis not an houre ſince I left him there.
Marti. We know not where you left him all aliue,
But out alas, heere haue we found him dead.

Enter Tamora, Andronicus, and Lucius.

Tamo. Where is my Lord the King?
King. Heere *Tamora*, though grieu'd with killing griefe.
Tam. Where is thy brother *Baſsianus*?
King. Now to the bottome doſt thou ſearch my wound,
Poore *Baſsianus* heere lies murthered.
Tam. Then all too late I bring this fatall writ,
The complot of this timeleſſe Tragedie,
And wonder greatly that mans face can fold,
In pleaſing ſmiles ſuch murderous Tyrannie.
She giueth Saturnine a Letter.

Saturninus reads the Letter.

And if we miſſe to meete him handſomely,
Sweet huntſman, Baſsianus 'tis we meane,
Doe thou ſo much as dig the graue for him,
Thou know'ſt our meaning, looke for thy reward
Among the Nettles at the Elder tree:
Which ouer-ſhades the mouth of that ſame pit:
Where we decreed to bury Baſsianus
Doe this and purchaſe vs thy laſting friends.

King. Oh *Tamora*, was euer heard the like?
This is the pit, and this the Elder tree,
Looke ſirs, if you can finde the huntſman out,
That ſhould haue murthered *Baſsianus* heere.
Aron. My gracious Lord heere is the bag of Gold.
King. Two of thy whelpes, fell Curs of bloody kind
Haue heere bereft my brother of his life:
Sirs drag them from the pit vnto the priſon,
There let them bide vntill we haue deuis'd
Some neuer heard-of torturing paine for them.
Tamo. What are they in this pit,
Oh wondrous thing!
How eaſily murder is diſcouered?
Tit. High Emperour, vpon my feeble knee,
I beg this boone, with teares, not lightly ſhed,
That this fell fault of my accurſed Sonnes,
Accurſed, if the faults be prou'd in them.
King. If it be prou'd? you ſee it is apparant,
Who found this Letter, *Tamora* was it you?
Tamora. *Andronicus* himſelfe did take it vp.
Tit. I did my Lord,
Yet let me be their baile,
For by my Fathers reuerent Tombe I vow
They ſhall be ready at your Highnes will,
To anſwere their ſuſpition with their liues.
King. Thou ſhalt not baile them, ſee thou follow me.
Some bring the murthered body, ſome the murtherers,
Let them not ſpeake a word, the guilt is plaine,
For by my ſoule, were there worſe end then death,
That end vpon them ſhould be executed.
Tamo. *Andronicus* I will entreat the King,
Feare not thy Sonnes, they ſhall do well enough.
Tit. Come *Lucius* come,
Stay not to talke with them. *Exeunt.*

Enter the Empreſſe Sonnes, with Lauinia, her hands cut off and her tongue cut out, and rauiſht.

Deme. So now goe tell and if thy tongue can ſpeake,
Who t'was that cut thy tongue and rauiſht thee.
Chi. Write downe thy mind, bewray thy meaning ſo,
And if thy ſtumpes will let thee play the Scribe.
Dem. See how with ſignes and tokens ſhe can ſcowle.
Chi. Goe home,
Call for ſweet water, waſh thy hands.
Dem. She hath no tongue to call, nor hands to waſh.
And ſo let's leaue her to her ſilent walkes.
Chi. And t'were my cauſe, I ſhould goe hang my ſelfe.
Dem. If thou had'ſt hands to helpe thee knit the cord.
Exeunt.

Winde Hornes.

Enter Marcus from hunting to Lauinia.

Who is this, my Neece that flies away ſo faſt?
Coſen a word, where is your husband?
If I do dreame, would all my wealth would wake me;
If I doe wake, ſome Planet ſtrike me downe,
That I may ſlumber in eternall ſleepe.
Speake gentle Neece, what ſterne vngentle hands
Hath lopt, and hew'd, and made thy body bare
Of her two branches, thoſe ſweet Ornaments.
Whoſe circkling ſhadowes, Kings haue ſought to ſleep in
And might not gaine ſo great a happines
As halfe thy Loue: Why dooſt not ſpeake to me?
Alas, a Crimſon riuer of warme blood,
Like to a bubling fountaine ſtir'd with winde,
Doth riſe and fall betweene thy Roſed lips,
Comming and going with thy hony breath.
But ſure ſome *Tereus* hath defloured thee,
And leaſt thou ſhould'ſt detect them, cut thy tongue.
Ah, now thou turn'ſt away thy face for ſhame:
And notwithſtanding all this loſſe of blood,
As from a Conduit with their iſſuing Spouts,
Yet doe thy cheekes looke red as *Titans* face,
Bluſhing to be encountred with a Cloud,
Shall I ſpeake for thee? ſhall I ſay 'tis ſo?
Oh that I knew thy hart, and knew the beaſt
That I might raile at him to eaſe my mind.
Sorrow concealed, like an Ouen ſtopt,
Doth burne the hart to Cinders where it is.
Faire *Philomela* ſhe but loſt her tongue,
And in a tedious Sampler ſowed her minde.
But louely Neece, that meane is cut from thee,
A craftier *Tereus* haſt thou met withall,
And he hath cut thoſe pretty fingers off,

dd 2 That

That could haue better sowed then *Philomel.*
Oh had the monster seene those Lilly hands,
Tremble like Aspen leaues vpon a Lute,
And make the silken strings delight to kisse them,
He would not then haue toucht them for his life.
Or had he heard the heauenly Harmony,
Whic h that sweet tongue hath made:
He would haue dropt his knife and fell asleepe,
As *Cerberus* at the Thracian Poets feete.
Come, let vs goe, and make thy father blinde,
For such a sight will blinde a fathers eye.
One houres storme will drowne the fragrant meades,
What, will whole months of teares thy Fathers eyes?
Doe not draw backe, for we will mourne with thee:
Oh could our mourning ease thy misery. *Exeunt*

Actus Tertius.

Enter the Iudges and Senatours with Titus two sonnes bound, passing on the Stage to the place of executon, and Titus going before pleading.

Ti. Heare me graue fathers, noble Tribunes stay,
For pitty of mine age, whose youth was spent
In dangerous warres, whilst you securely slept:
For all my blood in Romes great quarrell shed,
For all the frosty nights that I haue watcht,
And for these bitter teares, which now you see,
Filling the aged wrinkles in my cheekes,
Be pittifull to my condemned Sonnes,
Whose soules is not corrupted as 'tis thought:
For two and twenty sonnes I neuer wept,
Because they died in honours lofty bed.
Andronicus lyeth downe, and the Iudges passe by him.
For these, Tribunes, in the dust I write
My harts deepe languor, and my soules sad teares:
Let my teares stanch the earths drie appetite.
My sonnes sweet blood, will make it shame and blush:
O earth! I will be friend thee more with raine *Exeunt*
That shall distill from these two ancient ruines,
Then youthfull Aprill shall with all his showres
In summers drought: Ile drop vpon thee still,
In Winter with warme teares Ile melt the snow,
And keepe eternall spring time on thy face,
So thou refuse to drinke my deare sonnes blood.

Enter Lucius, with his weapon drawne.

Oh reuerent Tribunes, oh gentle aged men,
nbinde my sonnes, reuerse the doome of death,
And let me say (that neuer wept before)
My teares are now preualing Oratours.
L. Oh noble father, you lament in vaine,
The Tribunes heare not, no man is by,
And you recount your sorrowes to a stone.
Ti. Ah *Lucius* for thy brothers let me plead,
Graue Tribunes, once more I intreat of you.
Lu. My gracious Lord, no Tribune heares you speake.
Ti. Why 'tis no matter man, if they did heare
They would not marke me: oh if they did heare
They would not pitty me.
Therefore I tell my sorrowes bootles to the stones.
Who though they cannot answere my distresse,
Yet in some sort they are better then the Tribunes,
For that they will not intercept my tale;
When I doe weepe, they humbly at my feete
Receiue my teares, and seeme to weepe with me,
And were they but attired in graue weedes,
Rome could afford no Tribune like to these,
A stone is as soft waxe,
Tribunes more hard then stones:
A stone is silent, and offendeth not,
And Tribunes with their tongues doome men to death.
But wherefore stand'st thou with thy weapon drawne?
Lu. To rescue my two brothers from their death,
For which attempt the Iudges haue pronounc'st
My euerlasting doome of banishment.
Ti. O happy man, they haue befriended thee:
Why foolish *Lucius*, dost thou not perceiue
That Rome is but a wildernes of Tigers?
Tigers must pray, and Rome affords no prey
But me and and mine: how happy art thou then,
From these deuourers to be banished?
But who comes with our brother *Marcus* heere?

Enter Marcus and Lauinia.

Mar. *Titus*, prepare thy noble eyes to weepe,
Or if not so, thy noble heart to breake:
I bring consuming sorrow to thine age.
Ti. Will it consume me? Let me see it then.
Mar. This was thy daughter.
Ti. Why *Marcus* so she is.
Luc. Aye me this obiect kils me.
Ti. Faint-harted boy, arise and looke vpon her,
Speake *Lauinia*, what accursed hand
Hath made thee handlesse in thy Fathers sight?
What foole hath added water to the Sea?
Or brought a faggot to bright burning Troy?
My griefe was at the height before thou cam'st,
And now like *Nylus* it disdaineth bounds:
Giue me a sword, Ile chop off my hands too,
For they haue fought for Rome, and all in vaine:
And they haue nur'st this woe,
In feeding life:
In bootelesse prayer haue they bene held vp,
And they haue seru'd me to effectlesse vse.
Now all the seruice I require of them,
Is that the one will helpe to cut the other:
'Tis well *Lauinia*, that thou hast no hands,
For hands to do Rome seruice, is but vaine.
Luci. Speake gentle sister, who hath martyr'd thee?
Mar. O that delightfull engine of her thoughts,
That blab'd them with such pleasing eloquence,
Is torne from forth that pretty hollow cage,
Where like a sweet mellodius bird it sung,
Sweet varied notes inchanting euery eare.
Luci. Oh say thou for her,
Who hath done this deed?
Marc. Oh thus I found her straying in the Parke,
Seeking to hide herselfe as doth the Deare
That hath receiude some vnrecuring wound.
Tit. It was my Deare,
And he that wounded her,
Hath hurt me more, then had he kild me dead:
For now I stand as one vpon a Rocke,
Inuiron'd with a wildernesse of Sea.
Who markes the waxing tide,
Grow waue by waue,

Expecting

Expecting euer when ſome enuious ſurge,
Will in his briniſh bowels ſwallow him.
This way to death my wretched ſonnes are gone:
Heere ſtands my other ſonne, a baniſht man,
And heere my brother weeping at my woes.
But that which giues my ſoule the greateſt ſpurne,
Is deere *Lauinia*, deerer then my ſoule.
Had I but ſeene thy picture in this plight,
It would haue madded me. What ſhall I doe?
Now I behold thy liuely body ſo?
Thou haſt no hands to wipe away thy teares,
Nor tongue to tell me who hath martyr'd thee:
Thy husband he is dead, and for his death
Thy brothers are condemn'd, and dead by this.
Looke *Marcus*, ah ſonne *Lucius* looke on her:
When I did name her brothers, then freſh teares
Stood on her cheekes, as doth the hony dew,
Vpon a gathred Lillie almoſt withered.

Mar. Perchance ſhe weepes becauſe they kil'd her husband,
Perchance becauſe ſhe knowes him innocent.

Ti. If they did kill thy husband then be ioyfull
Becauſe the law hath tane reuenge on them.
No, no, they would not doe ſo foule a deede,
Witnes the ſorrow that their ſiſter makes.
Gentle *Lauinia* let me kiſſe thy lips,
Or make ſome ſignes how I may do thee eaſe:
Shall thy good Vncle, and thy brother *Lucius*,
And thou and I ſit round about ſome Fountaine,
Looking all downewards to behold our cheekes
How they are ſtain'd in meadowes, yet not dry
With miery ſlime left on them by a flood:
And in the Fountaine ſhall we gaze ſo long,
Till the freſh taſte be taken from that cleerenes,
And made a brine pit with our bitter teares?
Or ſhall we cut away our hands like thine?
Or ſhall we bite our tongues, and in dumbe ſhewes
Paſſe the remainder of our hatefull dayes?
What ſhall we doe? Let vs that haue our tongues
Plot ſome deuiſe of further miſeries
To make vs wondred at in time to come.

Lu. Sweet Father ceaſe your teares, for at your griefe
See how my wretched ſiſter ſobs and weeps.

Mar. Patience deere Neece, good *Titus* drie thine eyes.

Ti. Ah *Marcus, Marcus*, Brother well I wot,
Thy napkin cannot drinke a teare of mine,
For thou poore man haſt drown'd it with thine owne.

Lu. Ah my *Lauinia* I will wipe thy cheekes.

Ti Marke *Marcus* marke, I vnderſtand her ſignes,
Had ſhe a tongue to ſpeake, now would ſhe ſay
That to her brother which I ſaid to thee.
His Napkin with hertrue teares all bewet,
Can do no ſeruice on her ſorrowfull cheekes.
Oh what a ſimpathy of woe is this!
As farre from helpe as Limbo is from bliſſe,

Enter Aron the Moore alone.

Moore. *Titus Andronicus*, my Lord the Emperour,
Sends thee this word, that if thou loue thy ſonnes,
Let *Marcus*, *Lucius*, or thy ſelfe old *Titus*,
Or any one of you, chop off your hand,
And ſend it to the King: he for the ſame,
Will ſend thee hither both thy ſonnes aliue,
And that ſhall be the ranſome for their fault.

Ti. Oh gracious Emperour, oh gentle *Aaron*.
Did euer Rauen ſing ſo like a Larke,
That giues ſweet tydings of the Sunnes vpriſe?
With all my heart, Ile ſend the Emperour my hand,
Good *Aron* wilt thou help to chop it off?

Lu. Stay Father, for that noble hand of thine,
That hath throwne downe ſo many enemies,
Shall not be ſent: my hand will ſerue the turne,
My youth can better ſpare my blood then you,
And therfore mine ſhall ſaue my brothers liues.

Mar. Which of your hands hath not defended Rome
And rear'd aloft the bloody Battleaxe,
Writing deſtruction on the enemies Caſtle?
Oh none of both but are of high deſert:
My hand hath bin but idle, let it ſerue
To ranſome my two nephewes from their death,
Then haue I kept it to a worthy end.

Moore. Nay come agree, whoſe hand ſhall goe along
For feare they die before their pardon come.

Mar. My hand ſhall goe.

Lu. By heauen it ſhall not goe.

Ti. Sirs ſtriue no more, ſuch withered hearbs as theſe
Are meete for plucking vp, and therefore mine.

Lu. Sweet Father, if I ſhall be thought thy ſonne,
Let me redeeme my brothers both from death.

Mar. And for our fathers ſake, and mothers care,
Now let me ſhew a brothers loue to thee.

Ti. Agree betweene you, I will ſpare my hand.

Lu. Then Ile goe fetch an Axe.

Mar. But I will vſe the Axe. *Exeunt*

Ti. Come hither *Aaron*, Ile deceiue them both,
Lend me thy hand, and I will giue thee mine,

Moore. If that be cal'd deceit, I will be honeſt,
And neuer whil'ſt I liue deceiue men ſo:
But Ile deceiue you in another ſort,
And that you'l ſay ere halfe an houre paſſe.

He cuts off Titus hand.

Enter Lucius and Marcus againe.

Ti. Now ſtay you ſtrife, what ſhall be, is diſpatcht:
Good *Aron* giue his Maieſtie me hand,
Tell him, it was a hand that warded him
From thouſand dangers: bid him bury it:
More hath it merited: That let it haue.
As for for my ſonnes, ſay I account of them,
As iewels purchaſt at an eaſie price,
And yet deere too, becauſe I bought mine owne.

Aron. I goe *Andronicus*, and for thy hand,
Looke by and by to haue thy ſonnes with thee:
Their heads I meane: Oh how this villany
Doth fat me with the very thoughts of it.
Let fooles doe good, and faire men call for grace,
Aron will haue his ſoule blacke like his face. *Exit.*

Ti. O heere I lift this one hand vp to heauen,
And bow this feeble ruine to the earth,
If any power pitties wretched teares,
To that I call: what wilt thou kneele with me?
Doe then deare heart, for heauen ſhall heare our prayers,
Or with our ſighs weele breath the welkin dimme,
And ſtaine the Sun with fogge as ſomtime cloudes,
When they do hug him in their melting boſomes.

Mar. Oh brother ſpeake with poſſibilities,
And do not breake into theſe deepe extreames.

Ti. Is not my ſorrow deepe, hauing no bottome?

dd 2 Then

Then be my paſſions bottomleſſe with them.
Mar. But yet let reaſon gouerne thy lament.
Titus. If there were reaſon for theſe miſeries,
Then into limits could I binde my woes:
When heauen doth weepe, doth not the earth oreflow?
If the windes rage, doth not the Sea wax mad,
Threatning the welkin with his big-ſwolne face?
And wilt thou haue a reaſon for this coile?
I am the Sea. Harke how her ſighes doe flow:
Shee is the weeping welkin, I the earth:
Then muſt my Sea be moued with her ſighes,
Then muſt my earth with her continuall teares,
Become a deluge: ouerflow'd and drown'd:
For why, my bowels cannot hide her woes,
But like a drunkard muſt I vomit them:
Then giue me leaue, for looſers will haue leaue,
To eaſe their ſtomackes with their bitter tongues,

Enter a meſſenger with two heads and a hand.

Meſſ. Worthy *Andronicus*, ill art thou repaid,
For that good hand thou ſentſt the Emperour:
Heere are the heads of thy two noble ſonnes.
And heeres thy hand in ſcorne to thee ſent backe:
Thy griefes, their ſports: Thy reſolution mockt,
That woe is me to thinke vpon thy woes,
More then remembrance of my fathers death. *Exit.*
Marc. Now let hot Ætna coole in Cicilie,
And be my heart an euer-burning hell:
Theſe miſeries are more then may be borne
To weepe with them that weepe, doth eaſe ſome deale,
But ſorrow flouted at, is double death.
Luci. Ah that this ſight ſhould make ſo deep a wound,
And yet deteſted life not ſhrinke thereat:
That euer death ſhould let life beare his name,
Where life hath no more intereſt but to breath.
Mar. Alas poore hart that kiſſe is comfortleſſe,
As frozen water to a ſtarued ſnake.
Titus. When will this fearefull ſlumber haue an end?
Mar. Now farwell flatterie, die *Andronicus*,
Thou doſt not ſlumber, ſee thy two ſons heads,
Thy warlike hands, thy mangled daughter here:
Thy other baniſht ſonnes with this deere ſight
Strucke pale and bloodleſſe, and thy brother I,
Euen like a ſtony Image, cold and numme.
Ah now no more will I controule my griefes,
Rent off thy ſiluer haire, thy other hand
Gnawing with thy teeth, and be this diſmall ſight
The cloſing vp of our moſt wretched eyes:
Now is a time to ſtorme, why art thou ſtill?
Titus. Ha, ha, ha,
Mar. Why doſt thou laugh? it fits not with this houre.
Ti. Why I haue not another teare to ſhed:
Beſides, this ſorrow is an enemy,
And would vſurpe vpon my watry eyes,
And make them blinde with tributarie teares.
Then which way ſhall I finde Reuenges Caue?
For theſe two heads doe ſeeme to ſpeake to me,
And threat me, I ſhall neuer come to bliſſe,
Till all theſe miſchiefes be returned againe,
Euen in their throats that haue committed them.
Come let me ſee what taske I haue to doe,
You heauie people, circle me about,
That I may turne me to each one of you,
And ſweare vnto my ſoule to right your wrongs.
The vow is made, come Brother take a head,
And in this hand the other will I beare.
And *Lauinia* thou ſhalt be employd in theſe things:
Beare thou my hand ſweet wench betweene thy teeth:
As for thee boy, goe get thee from my ſight,
Thou art an Exile, and thou muſt not ſtay,
Hie to the *Gothes*, and raiſe an army there,
And if you loue me, as I thinke you doe,
Let's kiſſe and part, for we haue much to doe. *Exeunt*

Manet Lucius.

Luci. Farewell *Andronicus* my noble Father:
The woful'ſt man that euer liu'd in Rome:
Farewell proud Rome, til *Lucius* come againe,
He loues his pledges dearer then his life:
Farewell *Lauinia* my noble ſiſter,
O would thou wert as thou to fore haſt beene,
But now, nor *Lucius* nor *Lauinia* liues
But in obliuion and hateful griefes:
If *Lucius* liue, he will requit your wrongs,
And make proud *Saturnine* and his Empreſſe
Beg at the gates likes *Tarquin* and his Queene.
Now will I to the Gothes and raiſe a power,
To be reueng'd on Rome and *Saturnine*. *Exit Lucius*

A Banket.
Enter Andronicus, Marcus, Lauinia, and the Boy.

An. So, ſo, now ſit, and looke you eate no more
Then will preſerue iuſt ſo much ſtrength in vs
As will reuenge theſe bitter woes of ours.
Marcus vnknit that ſorrow-wreathen knot:
Thy Neece and I (poore Creatures) want our hands
And cannot paſſionate our tenfold griefe,
With foulded Armes. This poore right hand of mine,
Is left to tirranize vppon my breaſt.
Who when my hart all mad with miſery,
Beats in this hollow priſon of my fleſh,
Then thus I thumpe it downe.
Thou Map of woe, that thus doſt talk in ſignes,
When thy poore hart beates without ragious beating,
Thou canſt not ſtrike it thus to make it ſtill?
Wound it with ſighing girle, kil it with grones:
Or get ſome little knife betweene thy teeth,
And iuſt againſt thy hart make thou a hole,
That all the teares that thy poore eyes let fall
May run into that ſinke, and ſoaking in,
Drowne the lamenting foole, in Sea ſalt teares.
Mar. Fy brother fy, teach her not thus to lay
Such violent hands vppon her tender life.
An. How now! Has ſorrow made thee doate already?
Why *Marcus*, no man ſhould be mad but I:
What violent hands can ſhe lay on her life:
Ah wherefore doſt thou vrge the name of hands,
To bid *Æneas* tell the tale twice ore
How Troy was burnt, and he made miſerable?
O handle not the theame, to talke of hands,
Leaſt we remember ſtill that we haue none.
Fie, fie, how Frantiquely I ſquare my talke
As if we ſhould forget we had no hands:
If *Marcus* did not name the word of hands.
Come, lets fall too, and gentle girle eate this,
Heere is no drinke? Harke *Marcus* what ſhe ſaies,
I can interpret all her martir'd ſignes,
She ſaies, ſhe drinkes no other drinke but teares
Breu'd with her ſorrow: meſh'd vppon her cheekes,
Speech.

Speechleſſe complayne, I will learne thy thought:
In thy dumb action, will I be as perfect
As begging Hermits in their holy prayers.
Thou ſhalt not ſighe nor hold thy ſtumps to heauen,
Nor winke, nor nod, nor kneele, nor make a ſigne,
But I (of theſe) will wreſt an Alphabet,
And by ſtill practice, learne to know thy meaning.
Boy. Good grandſire leaue theſe bitter deepe laments,
Make my Aunt merry, with ſome pleaſing tale.
Mar. Alas, the tender boy in paſſion mou'd,
Doth weepe to ſee his grandſires heauineſſe.
An. Peace tender Sapling, thou art made of teares,
And teares will quickly melt thy life away.
Marcus ſtrikes the diſh with a knife.
What doeſt thou ſtrike at *Marcus* with knife.
Mar. At that that I haue kil'd my Lord, a Flys
An. Out on the murderour: thou kil'ſt my hart,
Mine eyes cloi'd with view of Tirranie:
A deed of death done on the Innocent
Becoms not *Titus* broher: get thee gone,
I ſee thou art not for my company:
Mar. Alas (my Lord) I haue but kild a flie.
An. But? How: if that Flie had a father and mother?
How would he hang his ſlender gilded wings
And buz lamenting doings in the ayer,
Poore harmeleſſe Fly,
That with his pretty buzing melody,
Came heere to make vs merry,
And thou haſt kil'd him.
Mar. Pardon me ſir,
It was a blacke illfauour'd Fly,
Like to the Empreſſe Moore, therefore I kild him.
An. O, o, o,
Then pardon me for reprehending thee,
For thou haſt done a Charitable deed:
Giue me thy knife, I will inſult on him,
Flattering my ſelfes, as if it were the Moore,
Come hither purpoſely to poyſon me.
There's for thy ſelfe, and thats for *Tamira*: Ah ſirra,
Yet I thinke we are not brought ſo low,
But that betweene vs, we can kill a Fly,
That comes in likeneſſe of a Cole-blacke Moore.
Mar. Alas poore man, griefe ha's ſo wrought on him,
He takes falſe ſhadowes, for true ſubſtances.
And. Come, take away: *Lauinia*, goe with me,
Ile to thy cloſſet, and goe read with thee
Sad ſtories, chanced in the times of old.
Come boy, and goe with me, thy ſight is young,
And thou ſhalt read, when mine begin to dazell. *Exeunt*

Actus Quartus.

Enter young Lucius and Lauinia running after him, and the Boy flies from her with his bookes vnder his arme.
Enter Titus and Marcus.

Boy. Helpe Grandſier helpe, my Aunt *Lauinia*,
Followes me euery where I know not why.
Good Vncle *Marcus* ſee how ſwift ſhe comes,
Alas ſweet Aunt, I know not what you meane.
Mar. Stand by me *Lucius*, doe not feare thy Aunt.
Titus. She loues thee boy too well to doe thee harme
Boy I when my father was in Rome ſhe did.
Mar. What meanes my Neece *Lauinia* by theſe ſignes?
Ti. Feare not *Lucius*, ſome what doth ſhe meane:
See *Lucius* ſee, how much ſhe makes of thee:
Some whether would ſhe haue thee goe with her.
Ah boy, *Cornelia* neuer with more care
Read to her ſonnes, then ſhe hath read to thee,
Sweet Poetry, and Tullies Oratour:
Canſt thou not geſſe wherefore ſhe plies thee thus?
Boy. My Lord I know not I, nor can I geſſe,
Vnleſſe ſome fit or frenzie do poſſeſſe her:
For I haue heard my Grandſier ſay full oft,
Extremitie of griefes would make men mad.
And I haue read that *Hecuba* of Troy,
Ran mad through ſorrow, that made me to feare,
Although my Lord, I know my noble Aunt,
Loues me as deare as ere my mother did,
And would not but in fury fright my youth,
Which made me downe to throw my bookes, and flie
Cauſles perhaps, but pardon me ſweet Aunt,
And Madam, if my Vncle *Marcus* goe,
I will moſt willingly attend your Ladyſhip.
Mar. *Lucius* I will.
Ti. How now *Lauinia*, *Marcus* what meanes this?
Some booke there is that ſhe deſires to ſee,
Which is it girle of theſe? Open them boy,
But thou art deeper read and better ſkild,
Come and take choyſe of all my Library,
And ſo beguile thy ſorrow, till the heauens
Reueale the damn'd contriuer of this deed.
What booke?
Why lifts ſhe vp her armes in ſequence thus?
Mar. I thinke ſhe meanes that ther was more then one
Confederate in the fact, I more there was:
Or elſe to heauen ſhe heaues them to reuenge.
Ti. *Lucius* what booke is that ſhe toſſeth ſo?
Boy. Grandſier 'tis Ouids Metamorphoſis,
My mother gaue it me.
Mar. For loue of her that's gone,
Perhahs ſhe culd it from among the reſt.
Ti. Soft, ſo buſily ſhe turnes the leaues,
Helpe her, what would ſhe finde? *Lauinia* ſhall I read?
This is the tragicke tale of *Philomel*?
And treates of *Tereus* treaſon and his rape,
And rape I feare was roote of thine annoy.
Mar. See brother ſee, note how ſhe quotes the leaues
Ti. *Lauinia*, wert thou thus ſurpriz'd ſweet girle,
Rauiſht and wrong'd as *Philomela* was?
Forc'd in the ruthleſſe, vaſt, and gloomy woods?
See, ſee, I ſuch a place there is where we did hunt,
(O had we neuer, neuer hunted there)
Patern'd by that the Poet heere deſcribes,
By nature made for murthers and for rapes.
Mar. O why ſhould nature build ſo foule a den,
Vnleſſe the Gods delight in tragedies?
Ti. Giue ſignes ſweet girle, for heere are none but friend.
What Romaine Lord it was durſt do the deed?
Or ſlunke not *Saturnine*, as *Tarquin* erſts,
That left the Campe to ſinne in *Lucrece* bed.
Mar. Sit downe ſweet Neece, brother ſit downe by me,
Appollo, Pallas, Ioue, or *Mercury*,
Inſpire me that I may this treaſon finde.
My Lord looke heere, looke heere *Lauinia*.

He writes his Name with his ſtaffe, and guides it with feete and mouth.

This ſandie plot is plaine, guide if thou canſt
This

This after me, I haue writ my name,
Without the helpe of any hand at all.
Curst be that hart that forc'st vs to that shift:
Write thou good Neece, and heere display at last,
What God will haue discouered for reuenge,
Heauen guide thy pen to print thy sorrowes plaine,
That we may know the Traytors and the truth.

She takes the staffe in her mouth, and guides it with her stumps and writes.

Ti. Oh doe ye read my Lord what she hath writs?
Stuprum, Chiron, Demetrius

Mar. What, what, the lustfull sonnes of *Tamora*,
Performers of this hainous bloody deed?

Ti. *Magni Dominator poli,*
Tam lentus audis scelera, tam lentus vides?

Mar. Oh calme thee gentle Lord: Although I know
There is enough written vpon this earth,
To stirre a mutinie in the mildest thoughts,
And arme the mindes of infants to exclaimes.
My Lord kneele downe with me: *Lauinia* kneele,
And kneele sweet boy, the Romaine *Hectors* hope,
And sweare with me, as with the wofull Feere
And father of that chast dishonoured Dame,
Lord *Iunius Brutus* sweare for *Lucrece* rape,
That we will prosecute (by good aduise)
Mortall reuenge vpon these traytorous Gothes,
And see their blood, or die with this reproach

Ti. Tis sure enough, and you knew how.
But if you hunt these Beare-whelpes, then beware
The Dam will wake, and if she winde you once,
Shee's with the Lyon deepely still in league.
And lulls him whilst she palyeth on her backe,
And when he sleepes will she do what she list.
You are a young huntsman *Marcus*, let it alone:
And come, I will goe get a leafe of brasse,
And with a Gad of steele will write these words,
And lay it by: the angry Northerne winde
Will blow these sands like *Sibels* leaues abroad,
And wheres your lesson then. Boy what say you?

Boy. I say my Lord, that if I were a man,
Their mothers bed-chamber should not be safe,
For these bad bond-men to the yoake of Rome.

Mar. I that's my boy, thy father hath full oft,
For his vngratefull country done the like

Boy. And Vncle so will I, and if I liue.

Ti. Come goe with me into mine Armorie,
Lucius Ile fit thee, and withall, my boy
Shall carry from me to the Empresse sonnes,
Presents that I intend to send them both,
Come, come, thou'lt do thy message, wilt thou not?

Boy. I with my dagger in their bosomes Grandsire:

Ti. No boy not so, Ile teach thee another course,
Lauinia come, *Marcus* looke to my house,
Lucius and Ile goe braue it at the Court,
I marry will we sir, and weele be waited on. *Exeunt.*

Mar. O heauens! Can you heare a good man grone
And not relent, or not compassion him?
Marcus attend him in his extasie,
That hath more scars of sorrow in his heart,
Then foe-mens markes vpon his batter'd shield,
But yet so iust, that he will not reuenge,
Reuenge the heauens for old *Andronicus*. *Exit*

Enter Aron, Chiron and Demetrius at one dore: and at another dore young Lucius and another, with a bundle of weapons, and verses writ vpon them.

Chi. *Demetrius* heeres the sonne of *Lucius*,
He hath some message to deliuer vs.

Aron. I some mad message from his mad Grandfather.

Boy. My Lords, with all the humblenesse I may,
I greete your honours from *Andronicus*,
And pray the Romane Gods confound you both.

Deme. Gramercie louely *Lucius*, what's the newes?
For villanie's markt with rape. May it please you,
My Grandsire well aduis'd hath sent by me,
The goodliest weapons of his Armorie,
To gratifie your honourable youth,
The hope of Rome, for so he bad me say:
And so I do and with his gifts present
Your Lordships, when euer you haue need,
You may be armed and appointed well,
And so I leaue you both: like bloody villaines. *Exit*

Deme. What's heere? a scrole, & written round about?
Let's see.
Integer vitæ scelerisque purus, non egit maury iaculis nec arcus.

Chi. O 'tis a verse in *Horace*, I know it well.
I read it in the Grammer long agoe.

Moore. I iust, a verse in *Horace*: right, you haue it,
Now what a thing it is to be an Asse?
Heer's no sound iest, the old man hath found their guilt,
And sends the weapons wrapt about with lines,
That wound (beyond their feeling) to the quick:
But were our witty Empresse well a foot,
She would applaud *Andronicus* conceit:
But let her rest, in her vnrest a while.
And now young Lords, wa'st not a happy starre
Led vs to Rome strangers, and more then so;
Captiues, to be aduanced to this height?
It did me good before the Pallace gate,
To braue the Tribune in his brothers hearing.

Deme. But me more good, to see so great a Lord
Basely insinuate, and send vs gifts.

Moore. Had he not reason Lord *Demetrius*?
Did you not vse his daughter very friendly?

Deme. I would we had a thousand Romane Dames
At such a bay, by turne to serue our lust.

Chi. A charitable wish, and full of loue.

Moore. Heere lack's but you mother for to say, Amen.

Chi. And that would she for twenty thousand more.

Deme. Come, let vs go, and pray to all the Gods
For our beloued mother in her paines.

Moore. Pray to the deuils, the gods haue giuen vs ouer.
Flourish.

Dem. Why do the Emperors trumpets flourish thus?

Chi. Belike for ioy the Emperour hath a sonne.

Deme. Soft, who comes heere?

Enter Nurse with a blacke a Moore childe.

Nur. Good morrow Lords:
O tell me, did you see *Aaron* the Moore?

Aron. Well, more or lesse, or nere a whit at all,
Heere *Aaron* is, and what with *Aaron* now?

Nurse. Oh gentle *Aaron*, we are all vndone,
Now helpe, or woe betide thee euermore.

Aron. Why, what a catterwalling dost thou keepe?
What dost thou wrap and fumble in thine armes?

Nurse. O that which I would hide from heauens eye,
Our Empresse shame, and stately Romes disgrace,
She is deliuered Lords, she is deliuered.

Aron To whom?

Nurse. I meane she is brought a bed?

Aron. Wel God giue her good rest,

What

What hath he ſent her?
Nurſe. A deuill.
Aron. Why then ſhe is the Deuils Dam: a ioyfull iſſue.
Nurſe. A ioyleſſe, diſmall, blacke & ſorrowfull iſſue,
Heere is the babe as loathſome as a toad,
Among'ſt the faireſt breeders of our clime,
The Empreſſe ſends it thee, thy ſtampe, thy ſeale,
And bids thee chriſten it with thy daggers point.
Aron. Out you whore, is black ſo baſe a hue?
Sweet blowſe, you are a beautious bloſſome ſure.
Deme. Villaine what haſt thou done?
Aron. That which thou canſt not vndoe.
Chi. Thou haſt vndone our mother.
Deme. And therein helliſh dog, thou haſt vndone,
Woe to her chance, and damn'd her loathed choyce,
Accur'ſt the off-ſpring of ſo foule a fiend.
Chi. It ſhall not liue.
Aron. It ſhall not die.
Nurſe. *Aaron* it muſt, the mother wils it ſo.
Aron. What, muſt it *Nurſe*? Then let no man but I
Doe execution on my fleſh and blood.
Deme. Ile broach the Tadpole on my Rapiers point:
Nurſe giue it me, my ſword ſhall ſoone diſpatch it
Aron. Sooner this ſword ſhall plough thy bowels vp.
Stay murtherous villaines, will you kill your brother?
Now by the burning Tapers of the skie,
That ſh'one ſo brightly when this Boy was got,
He dies vpon my Semitars ſharpe point,
That touches this my firſt borne ſonne and heire.
I tell you young-lings, not *Enceladus*
With all his threatning band of *Typhons* broode,
Nor great *Alcides*, nor the God of warre,
Shall ceaze this prey out of his fathers hands:
What, what, ye ſanguine ſhallow harted Boyes,
Ye white-limb'd walls, ye Ale-houſe painted ſignes,
Cole-blacke is better then another hue,
In that it ſcornes to beare another hue:
For all the water in the Ocean,
Can neuer turne the Swans blacke legs to white,
Although ſhe laue them hourely in the flood:
Tell the Empreſſe from me, I am of age
To keepe mine owne, excuſe it how ſhe can.
Deme. Wilt thou betray thy noble miſtris thus?
Aron. My miſtris is my miſtris: this my ſelfe,
The vigour, and the picture of my youth:
This, before all the world do I preferre,
This mauger all the world will I keepe ſafe,
Or ſome of you ſhall ſmoake for it in Rome.
Deme By this our mother is for euer ſham'd.
Chi. Rome will deſpiſe her for this foule eſcape.
Nur. The Emperour in his rage will doome her death.
Chi. I bluſh to thinke vpon this ignominie.
Aron. Why ther's the priuiledge your beauty beares:
Fie trecherous hue, that will betray with bluſhing
The cloſe enacts and counſels of the hart:
Heer's a young Lad fram'd of another leere,
Looke how the blacke ſlaue ſmiles vpon the father,
As who ſhould ſay, old Lad I am thine owne.
He is your brother Lords, ſenſibly fed
Of that ſelfe blood that firſt gaue life to you,
And from that wombe where you impriſoned were
He is infranchiſed and come to light:
Nay he is your brother by the ſurer ſide,
Although my ſeale be ſtamped in his face.
Nurſe. *Aaron* what ſhall I ſay vnto the Empreſſe?
Dem. Aduiſe thee *Aaron*, what is to be done,
And we will all ſubſcribe to thy aduiſe:
Saue thou the child, ſo we may all be ſafe.
Aron. Then ſit we downe and let vs all conſult.
My ſonne and I will haue the winde of you:
Keepe there, now talke at pleaſure of your ſafety.
Deme. How many women ſaw this childe of his?
Aron. Why ſo braue Lords, when we ioyne in league
I am a Lambe: but if you braue the *Moore*,
The chafed Bore, the mountaine Lyoneſſe,
The Ocean ſwells not ſo as *Aaron* ſtormes:
But ſay againe, how many ſaw the childe?
Nurſe. *Cornelia*, the midwife, and my ſelfe,
And none elſe but the deliuered Empreſſe.
Aron. The Empreſſe, the Midwife, and your ſelfe,
Two may keepe counſell, when the the third's away:
Goe to the Empreſſe, tell her this I ſaid, *He kils her*
Weeke, weeke, ſo cries a Pigge prepared to th'ſpit
Deme. What mean'ſt thou *Aaron*?
Wherefore did'ſt thou this?
Aron. O Lord ſir, 'tis a deed of pollicie?
Shall ſhe liue to betray this guilt of our's:
A long tongu'd babling Goſſip? No Lords no:
And now be it knowne to you my full intent.
Not farre, one *Muliteus* my Country-man
His wife but yeſternight was brought to bed,
His childe is like to her, faire as you are:
Goe packe with him, and giue the mother gold,
And tell them both the circumſtance of all,
And how by this their Childe ſhall be aduaunc'd,
And be receiued for the Emperours heyre,
And ſubſtituted in the place of mine,
To calme this tempeſt whirling in the Court,
And let the Emperour dandle him for his owne.
Harke ye Lords, ye ſee I haue giuen her phyſicke,
And you muſt needs beſtow her funerall,
The fields are neere, and you are gallant Groomes:
This done, ſee that you take no longer daies
But ſend the Midwife preſently to me.
The Midwife and the Nurſe well made away,
Then let the Ladies tattle what they pleaſe.
Chi. *Aaron* I ſee thou wilt not truſt the ayre with ſe-
Deme. For this care of *Tamora*, (crets.
Her ſelfe, and hers are highly bound to thee. *Exeunt.*
Aron. Now to the Gothes, as ſwift as Swallow flies,
There to diſpoſe this treaſure in mine armes,
And ſecretly to greete the Empreſſe friends:
Come on you thick-lipt-ſlaue, Ile beare you hence,
For it is you that puts vs to our ſhifts:
Ile make you feed on berries, and on rootes,
And feed on curds and whay, and ſucke the Goate,
And cabbin in a Caue, and bring you vp
To be a warriour, and command a Campe. *Exit*

Enter Titus, old Marcus, young Lucius and other gentlemen with bowes, and Titus beares the arrowes with Letters on the end of them.

Tit. Come *Marcus* come, kinſmen this is the way.
Sir Boy let me ſee your Archerie,
Looke yee draw home enough, and 'tis there ſtraight:
Terras Aſtrea reliquit, be you remembred *Marcus*.
She's gone, ſhe's fled, ſirs take you to your tooles,
You Coſens ſhall goe ſound the Ocean:
And caſt your nets, haply you may find her in the Sea,
Yet ther's as little iuſtice as at Land.
No *Publius* and *Sempronius*, you muſt doe it,
Tis

'Tis you must dig with Mattocke, and with Spade,
And pierce the inmost Center of the earth:
Then when you come to *Plutoes* Region,
I pray you deliuer him this petition,
Tell him it is for iustice, and for aide,
And that it comes from old *Andronicus*,
Shaken with sorrowes in vngratefull Rome.
Ah Rome! Well, well, I made thee miserable,
What time I threw the peoples suffrages
On him that thus doth tyrannize ore me.
Goe get you gone, and pray be carefull all,
And leaue you not a man of warre vnsearcht,
This wicked Emperour may haue shipt her hence,
And kinsmen then we may goe pipe for iustice.

Marc. O *Publius* is not this a heauie case
To see thy Noble Vnckle thus distract?

Publ. Therefore my Lords it highly vs concernes,
By day and night t'attend him carefully:
And feede his humour kindely as we may,
Till time beget some carefull remedie.

Marc. Kinsmen, his sorrowes are past remedie.
Ioyne with the Gothes, and with reuengefull warre,
Take wreake on Rome for this ingratitude,
And vengeance on the Traytor *Saturnine*.

Tit. *Publius* how now? how now my Maisters?
What haue you met with her?

Publ. No my good Lord, but *Pluto* sends you word,
If you will haue reuenge from hell you shall,
Marrie for iustice she is so imploy'd,
He thinkes with *Ioue* in heauen, or some where else:
So that perforce you must needs stay a time.

Tit. He doth me wrong to feed me with delayes,
Ile diue into the burning Lake below,
And pull her out of *Acaron* by the heeles.
Marcus we are but shrubs, no Cedars we,
No big-bon'd-men, fram'd of the Cyclops size,
But mettall *Marcus* steele to the very backe,
Yet wrung with wrongs more then our backe can beare:
And sith there's no iustice in earth nor hell,
We will sollicite heauen, and moue the Gods
To send downe Iustice for to wreake our wongs:
Come to this geare, you are a good Archer *Marcus*.

He giues them the Arrowes.

Ad Iouem, that's for you: here *ad Appollonem*,
Ad Martem, that's for my selfe,
Heere Boy to *Pallas*, heere to *Mercury*,
To *Saturnine*, to *Caius*, not to *Saturnine*,
You were as good to shoote against the winde.
Too it Boy, *Marcus* loose when I bid:
Of my word, I haue written to effect,
Ther's not a God left vnsollicited.

Marc. Kinsmen, shoot all your shafts into the Court,
We will afflict the Emperour in his pride.

Tit. Now Maisters draw, Oh well said *Lucius*:
Good Boy in *Virgoes* lap, giue it *Pallas*.

Marc. My Lord, I aime a Mile beyond the Moone,
Your letter is with *Iupiter* by this.

Tit. Ha, ha, *Publius*, *Publius*, what hast thou done?
See, see, thou hast shot off one of *Taurus* hornes.

Mar. This was the sport my Lord, when *Publius* shot,
The Bull being gal'd, gaue *Aries* such a knocke,
That downe fell both the Rams hornes in the Court,
And who should finde them but the Empresse villaine:
She laught, and told the Moore he should not choose
But giue them to his Maister for a present.

Tit. Why there it goes, God giue your Lordship ioy.

Enter the Clowne with a basket and two Pigeons in it.

Titus. Newes, newes, from heauen,
Marcus the poast is come.
Sirrah, what tydings? haue you any letters?
Shall I haue Iustice, what sayes *Iupiter*?

Clowne. Ho the Iibbetmaker, he sayes that he hath taken them downe againe, for the man must not be hang'd till the next weeke.

Tit. But what sayes *Iupiter* I aske thee?

Clowne. Alas sir I know not *Iupiter*:
I neuer dranke with him in all my life.

Tit. Why villaine art not thou the Carrier?

Clowne. I of my Pigious sir, nothing else.

Tit. Why, did'st thou not come from heauen?

Clowne. From heauen? Alas sir, I neuer came there, God forbid I should be so bold, to presse to heauen in my young dayes. Why I am going with my pigeons to the Tribunall Plebs, to take vp a matter of brawle, betwixt my Vncle, and one of the Emperialls men.

Mar. Why sir, that is as fit as can be to serue for your Oration, and let him deliuer the Pigions to the Emperour from you.

Tit. Tell mee, can you deliuer an Oration to the Emperour with a Grace?

Clowne. Nay truely sir, I could neuer say grace in all my life.

Tit. Sirrah come hither, make no more adoe,
But giue your Pigeons to the Emperour,
By me thou shalt haue Iustice at his hands.
Hold, hold, meane while her's money for thy charges.
Giue me pen and inke.
Sirrah, can you with a Grace deliuer a Supplication?

Clowne. I sir.

Titus. Then here is a Supplication for you, and when you come to him, at the first approach you must kneele, then kisse his foote, then deliuer vp your Pigeons, and then looke for your reward. Ile be at hand sir, see you do it brauely.

Clowne. I warrant you sir, let me alone.

Tit. Sirrha hast thou a knife? Come let me see it.
Heere *Marcus*, fold it in the Oration,
For thou hast made it like an humble Suppliant:
And when thou hast giuen it the Emperour,
Knocke at my dore, and tell me what he sayes.

Clowne. God be with you sir, I will. *Exit.*

Tit. Come *Marcus* let vs goe, *Publius* follow me.

Exeunt.

Enter Emperour and Empresse, and her two sonnes, the Emperour brings the Arrowes in his hand that Titus shot at him.

Satur. Why Lords,
What wrongs are these? was euer seene
An Emperour in Rome thus ouerborne,
Troubled, Confronted thus, and for the extent
Of egall iustice, vs'd in such contempt?
My Lords, you know the mightfull Gods,
(How euer these disturbers of our peace
Buz in the peoples eares) there nought hath past,
But euen with law against the willfull Sonnes
Of old *Andronicus*. And what and if
His sorrowes haue so ouerwhelm'd his wits,
Shall we be thus afflicted in his wreakes,
His fits, his frenzie, and his bitternesse?
And now he writes to heauen for his redresse.
See, heeres to *Ioue*, and this to *Mercury*,

Thi

This to *Apollo*, this to the God of warre:
Sweet ſcrowles to flie about the ſtreets of Rome:
What's this but Libelling againſt the Senate,
And blazoning our Iniuſtice euery where?
A goodly humour, is it not my Lords?
As who would ſay, in Rome no Iuſtice were.
But if I liue, his fained extaſies
Shall be no ſhelter to theſe outrages:
But he and his ſhall know, that Iuſtice liues
In *Saturninus* health; whom if he ſleepe,
Hee'l ſo awake, as he in fury ſhall
Cut off the proud'ſt Conſpirator that liues.

Tamo. My gracious Lord, my louely *Saturnine*,
Lord of my life, Commander of my thoughts,
Calme thee, and beare the faults of *Titus* age,
Th'effects of ſorrow for his valiant Sonnes,
Whoſe loſſe hath pier'ſt him deepe, and ſcar'd his heart;
And rather comfort his diſtreſſed plight,
Then proſecute the meaneſt or the beſt
For theſe contempts. Why thus it ſhall become
High witted *Tamora* to gloſe with all: *Aſide.*
But *Titus*, I haue touch'd thee to the quicke,
Thy life blood out: If *Aaron* now be wiſe,
Then is all ſafe, the Anchor's in the Port.

Enter Clowne.

How now good fellow, would'ſt thou ſpeake with vs?

Clow. Yea forſooth, and your Miſterſhip be Emperiall.

Tam. Empreſſe I am, but yonder ſits the Emperour.

Clo. 'Tis he; God & Saint Stephen giue you good den;
I haue brought you a Letter, & a couple of Pigions heere.

He reads the Letter.

Satu. Goe take him away, and hang him preſently.

Clowne. How much money muſt I haue?

Tam. Come ſirrah you muſt be hang'd.

Clow. Hang'd? ber Lady, then I haue brought vp a neck
to a faire end. *Exit.*

Satu. Deſpightfull and intollerable wrongs,
Shall I endure this monſtrous villany?
I know from whence this ſame deuiſe proceedes:
May this be borne? As if his traytrous Sonnes,
That dy'd by law for murther of our Brother,
Haue by my meanes beene butcher'd wrongfully?
Goe dragge the villaine hither by the haire,
Nor Age, nor Honour, ſhall ſhape priuiledge:
For this proud mocke, Ile be thy ſlaughter man:
Sly franticke wretch, that holp'ſt to make me great,
In hope thy ſelfe ſhould gouerne Rome and me.

Enter Nuntius Emillius.

Satur. What newes with thee *Emillius*?

Emil. Arme my Lords, Rome neuer had more cauſe,
The Gothes haue gather'd head, and with a power
Of high reſolued men, bent to the ſpoyle
They hither march amaine, vnder conduct
Of *Lucius*, Sonne to old *Andronicus*:
Who threats in courſe of this reuenge to do
As much as euer *Coriolanus* did.

King. Is warlike *Lucius* Generall of the Gothes?
Theſe tydings nip me, and I hang the head
As flowers with froſt, or graſſe beat downe with ſtormes:
I, now begins our ſorrowes to approach,
'Tis he the common people loue ſo much,
My ſelfe hath often heard them ſay,
(When I haue walked like a priuate man)
That *Lucius* baniſhment was wrongfully,
And they haue wiſht that *Lucius* were their Emperour.

Tam. Why ſhould you feare? Is not our City ſtrong?

King. I, but the Cittizens fauour *Lucius*,
And will reuolt from me, to ſuccour him.

Tam. *King*, be thy thoughts Imperious like thy name.
Is the Sunne dim'd, that Gnats do flie in it?
The Eagle ſuffers little Birds to ſing,
And is not carefull what they meane thereby,
Knowing that with the ſhadow of his wings,
He can at pleaſure ſtint their melodie.
Euen ſo mayeſt thou, the giddy men of Rome,
Then cheare thy ſpirit, for know thou Emperour,
I will enchaunt the old *Andronicus*,
With words more ſweet, and yet more dangerous
Then baites to fiſh, or hony ſtalkes to ſheepe,
When as the one is wounded with the baite,
The other rotted with delicious foode.

King. But he will not entreat his Sonne for vs.

Tam. If *Tamora* entreat him, then he will,
For I can ſmooth and fill his aged eare,
With golden promiſes, that were his heart
Almoſt Impregnable, his old eares deafe,
Yet ſhould both eare and heart obey my tongue.
Goe thou before to our Embaſſadour,
Say, that the Emperour requeſts a parly
Of warlike *Lucius*, and appoint the meeting.

King. *Emillius* do this meſſage Honourably,
And if he ſtand in Hoſtage for his ſafety,
Bid him demaund what pledge will pleaſe him beſt.

Emill. Your bidding ſhall I do effectually. *Exit.*

Tam. Now will I to that old *Andronicus*,
And temper him with all the Art I haue,
To plucke proud *Lucius* from the warlike Gothes.
And now ſweet Emperour be blithe againe,
And bury all thy feare in my deuiſes.

Satu. Then goe ſucceſſantly and plead for him. *Exit.*

Actus Quintus.

Flouriſh. Enter Lucius with an Army of Gothes, with Drum and Souldiers.

Luci. Approued warriours, and my faithfull Friends,
I haue receiued Letters from great Rome,
Which ſignifies what hate they beare their Emperour,
And how deſirous of our ſight they are.
Therefore great Lords, be as your Titles witneſſe,
Imperious and impatient of your wrongs,
And wherein Rome hath done you any ſcathe,
Let him make treble ſatiſfaction.

Goth. Braue ſlip, ſprung from the Great *Andronicus*,
Whoſe name was once our terrour, now our comfort,
Whoſe high exploits, and honourable Deeds,
Ingratefull Rome requites with foule contempt:
Behold in vs, weele follow where thou lead'ſt,
Like ſtinging Bees in hotteſt Sommers day,
Led by their Maiſter to the flowred fields,
And be aueng'd on curſed *Tamora*:
And as he ſaith, ſo ſay we all with him.

Luci. I humbly thanke him, and I thanke you all.
But who comes heere, led by a luſty *Goth*?

Enter a Goth leading of Aaron with his child in his armes.

Goth. Renowned *Lucius*, from our troups I ſtraid,
To gaze vpon a ruinous Monaſterie,

And

And as I earneſtly did fixe mine eye
Vpon the waſted building, ſuddainely
I heard a childe cry vnderneath a wall:
I made vnto the noyſe, when ſoone I heard,
The crying babe control'd with this diſcourſe:
Peace Tawny ſlaue, halfe me, and halfe thy Dam,
Did not thy Hue bewray whoſe brat thou art?
Had nature lent thee, but thy Mothers looke,
Villaine thou might'ſt haue bene an Emperour.
But where the Bull and Cow are both milk-white,
They neuer do beget a cole-blacke-Calfe:
Peace, villaine peace, euen thus he rates the babe,
For I muſt beare thee to a truſty Goth,
Who when he knowes thou art the Empreſſe babe,
Will hold thee dearely for thy Mothers ſake.
With this, my weapon drawne I ruſht vpon him,
Surpriz'd him ſuddainely, and brought him hither
To vſe, as you thinke neeedefull of the man.
Luci. Oh worthy Goth, this is the incarnate deuill,
That rob'd *Andronicus* of his good hand:
This is the Pearle that pleas'd your Empreſſe eye,
And heere's the Baſe Fruit of his burning luſt.
Say wall-ey'd ſlaue, whether would'ſt thou conuay
This growing Image of thy fiend-like face?
Why doſt not ſpeake? what deafe? Not a word?
A halter Souldiers, hang him on this Tree,
And by his ſide his Fruite of Baſtardie.
Aron. Touch not the Boy, he is of Royall blood.
Luci. Too like the Syre for euer being good.
Firſt hang the Child that he may ſee it ſprall,
A ſight to vexe the Fathers ſoule withall.
Aron. Get me a Ladder *Lucius*, ſaue the Childe,
And beare it from me to the Empreſſe:
If thou do this, Ile ſhew thee wondrous things,
That highly may aduantage thee to heare;
If thou wilt not, befall what may befall,
Ile ſpeake no more: but vengeance rot you all.
Luci. Say on, and if it pleaſe me which thou ſpeak'ſt,
Thy child ſhall liue, and I will ſee it Nouriſht.
Aron. And if it pleaſe thee? why aſſure thee *Lucius*,
'Twill vexe thy ſoule to heare what I ſhall ſpeake:
For I muſt talke of Murthers, Rapes, and Maſſacres,
Acts of Blacke-night, abhominable Deeds,
Complots of Miſchiefe, Treaſon, Villanies
Ruthfull to heare, yet pittiouſly preform'd,
And this ſhall all be buried by my death,
Vnleſſe thou ſweare to me my Childe ſhall liue.
Luci. Tell on thy minde,
I ſay thy Childe ſhall liue.
Aron. Sweare that he ſhall, and then I will begin.
Luci. Who ſhould I ſweare by,
Thou beleeueſt no God,
That graunted, how can'ſt thou beleeue an oath?
Aron. What if I do not, as indeed I do not,
Yet for I know thou art Religious,
And haſt a thing within thee, called Conſcience,
With twenty Popiſh trickes and Ceremonies,
Which I haue ſeene thee carefull to obſerue:
Therefore I vrge thy oath, for that I know
An Ideot holds his Bauble for a God,
And keepes the oath which by that God he ſweares,
To that Ile vrge him: therefore thou ſhalt vow
By that ſame God, what God ſo ere it be
That thou adoreſt, and haſt in reuerence,
To ſaue my Boy, to nouriſh and bring him vp,
Ore elſe I will diſcouer nought to thee.
Luci. Euen by my God I ſweare to to thee I will.
Aron. Firſt know thou,
I be got him on the Empreſſe.
Luci. Oh moſt Inſatiate luxurious woman!
Aron. Tut *Lucius*, this was but a deed of Charitie,
To that which thou ſhalt heare of me anon,
'Twas her two Sonnes that murdered *Baſſianus*,
They cut thy Siſters tongue, and rauiſht her,
And cut her hands off, and trim'd her as thou ſaw'ſt.
Lucius. Oh deteſtable villaine!
Call'ſt thou that Trimming?
Aron. Why ſhe was waſht, and cut, and trim'd,
And 'twas trim ſport for them that had the doing of it.
Luci. Oh barbarous beaſtly villaines like thy ſelfe!
Aron. Indeede, I was their Tutor to inſtruct them,
That Codding ſpirit had they from their Mother,
As ſure a Card as euer wonne the Set:
That bloody minde I thinke they learn'd of me,
As true a Dog as euer fought at head.
Well, let my Deeds be witneſſe of my worth:
I trayn'd thy Bretheren to that guilefull Hole,
Where the dead Corps of *Baſſianus* lay:
I wrote the Letter, that thy Father found,
And hid the Gold within the Letter mention'd.
Confederate with the Queene, and her two Sonnes,
And what not done, that thou haſt cauſe to rue,
Wherein I had no ſtroke of Miſcheife in it.
I play'd the Cheater for thy Fathers hand,
And when I had it, drew my ſelfe apart,
And almoſt broke my heart with extreame laughter.
I pried me through the Creuice of a Wall,
When for his hand, he had his two Sonnes heads,
Beheld his teares, and laught ſo hartily,
That both mine eyes were rainie like to his:
And when I told the Empreſſe of this ſport,
She ſounded almoſt at my pleaſing tale,
And for my tydings, gaue me twenty kiſſes.
Goth. What canſt thou ſay all this, and neuer bluſh?
Aron. I, like a blacke Dogge, as the ſaying is.
Luci. Art thou not ſorry for theſe hainous deedes?
Aron. I, that I had not done a thouſand more:
Euen now I curſe the day, and yet I thinke
Few come within few compaſſe of my curſe,
Wherein I did not ſome Notorious ill,
As kill a man, or elſe deuiſe his death,
Rauiſh a Maid, or plot the way to do it,
Accuſe ſome Innocent, and forſweare my ſelfe,
Set deadly Enmity betweene two Friends,
Make poore mens Cattell breake their neckes,
Set fire on Barnes and Hayſtackes in the night,
And bid the Owners quench them with the teares:
Oft haue I dig'd vp dead men from their graues,
And ſet them vpright at their deere Friends doore,
Euen when their ſorrowes almoſt was forgot,
And on their ſkinnes, as on the Barke of Trees,
Haue with my knife carued in Romaine Letters,
Let not your ſorrow die, though I am dead.
Tut, I haue done a thouſand dreadfull things
As willingly, as one would kill a Fly,
And nothing greeues me hartily indeede,
But that I cannot doe ten thouſand more.
Luci. Bring downe the diuell, for he muſt not die
So ſweet a death as hanging preſently.
Aron. If there be diuels, would I were a deuill,
To liue and burne in euerlaſting fire,
So I might haue your company in hell,
But

But to torment you with my bitter tongue.
Luci. Sirs ſtop his mouth,& let him ſpeake no more.
Enter Emillius.
Goth. My Lord,there is a Meſſenger from Rome
Deſires to be admitted to your preſence.
Luc. Let him come neere.
Welcome *Emillius*, what the newes from Rome?
Emi. Lord *Lucius*,and you Princes of the Gothes,
The Romaine Emperour greetes you all by me,
And for he vnderſtands you are in Armes,
He craues a parly at your Fathers houſe
Willing you to demand your Hoſtages,
And they ſhall be immediately deliuered.
Goth. What ſaies our Generall?
Luc. *Emillius*,let the Emperour giue his pledges
Vnto my Father,and my Vncle *Marcus*, *Flouriſh.*
And we will come: march away. *Exeunt.*

Enter Tamora,and her two Sonnes diſguiſed.

Tam. Thus in this ſtrange and ſad Habilliament,
I will encounter with *Andronicus*,
And ſay,I am Reuenge ſent from below,
To ioyne with him and right his hainous wrongs:
Knocke at his ſtudy where they ſay he keepes,
To ruminate ſtrange plots of dire Reuenge,
Tell him Reuenge is come to ioyne with him,
And worke confuſion on his Enemies.
They knocke and Titus opens his ſtudy dore.
Tit. Who doth moleſt my Contemplation?
Is it your tricke to make me ope the dore,
That ſo my ſad decrees may flie away,
And all my ſtudie be to no effect?
You are deceiu'd,for what I meane to do,
See heere in bloody lines I haue ſet downe:
And what is written ſhall be executed.
Tam. *Titus*,I am come to talke with thee,
Tit. No not a word: how can I grace my talke,
Wanting a hand to giue it action,
Thou haſt the ods of me,therefore no more.
Tam. If thou did'ſt know me,
Thou would'ſt talke with me.
Tit. I am not mad,I know thee well enough,
Witneſſe this wretched ſtump,
Witneſſe theſe crimſon lines,
Witneſſe theſe Trenches made by griefe and care,
Witneſſe the tyring day, andheauie night,
Witneſſe all ſorrow,that I know thee well
For our proud Empreſſe,Mighty *Tamora*:
Is not thy comming for my other hand?
Tamo. Know thou ſad man,I am not *Tamora*,
She is thy Enemie,and I thy Friend,
I am Reuenge ſent from th'infernall Kingdome,
To eaſe the gnawing Vulture of the mind,
By working wreakefull vengeance on my Foes:
Come downe and welcome me to this worlds light,
Conferre with me of Murder and of Death,
Ther's not a hollow Caue or lurking place,
No Vaſt obſcurity,or Miſty vale,
Where bloody Murther or deteſted Rape,
Can couch for feare,but I will finde them out,
And in their eares tell them my dreadfull name,
Reuenge,which makes the foule offenders quake
Tit. Art thou Reuenge?and art thou ſent to me,
To be a torment to mine Enemies?
Tam. I am,therefore come downe and welcome me.
Tit. Doe me ſome ſeruice ere I come to thee:
Loe by thy ſide where Rape and Murder ſtands,
Now giue ſome ſurance that thou art Reuenge,
Stab them,or teare them on thy Chariot wheeles,
And then Ile come and be thy Waggoner,
And whirle along with thee about the Globes.
Prouide thee two proper Palfries,as blacke as Iet.
To hale thy vengefull Waggon ſwift away,
And finde out Murder in their guilty cares.
And when thy Car is loaden with their heads,
I will diſmount,and by the Waggon wheele,
Trot like a Seruile footeman all day long,
Euen from *Eptons* riſing in the Eaſt,
Vntill his very downefall in the Sea.
And day by day Ile do this heauy taske,
So thou deſtroy Rapine and Murder there.
Tam. Theſe are my Miniſters,and come with me.
Tit. Are them thy Miniſters, what are they call'd?
Tam. Rape and Murder,therefore called ſo,
Cauſe they take vengeance of ſuch kind of men.
Tit. Good Lord how like the Empreſſe Sons they are.
And you the Empreſſe: But we worldly men,
Haue miſerable mad miſtaking eyes:
Oh ſweet Reuenge,now do I come to thee,
And if one armes imbracement will content thee,
I will imbrace thee in it by and by.
Tam. This cloſing with him,fits his Lunacie,
What ere I forge to feede his braine-ſicke fits,
Do you vphold,and maintaine in your ſpeeches,
For now he firmely takes me for Reuenge,
And being Credulous in this mad thought,
Ile make him ſend for *Lucius* his Sonne,
And whil'ſt I at a Banquet hold him ſure,
Ile find ſome cunning practiſe out of hand
To ſcatter and diſperſe the giddie Gothes,
Or at the leaſt make them his Enemies:
See heere he comes,and I muſt play my theame.
Tit. Long haue I bene forlorne,and all for thee,
Welcome dread Fury to my woefull houſe,
Rapine and Murther,you are welcome too,
How like the Empreſſe and her Sonnes you are.
Well are you fitted,had you but a Moore,
Could not all hell afford you ſuch a deuill?
For well I wote the Empreſſe neuer wags;
But in her company there is a Moore,
And would you repreſent our Queene aright
It were conuenient you had ſuch a deuill:
But welcome as you are,what ſhall we doe?
Tam. What would'ſt thou haue vs doe *Andronicus*?
Dem. Shew me a Murtherer,Ile deale with him.
Chi. Shew me a Villaine that hath done a Rape,
And I am ſent to be reueng'd on him.
Tam. Shew me a thouſand that haue done thee wrong,
And Ile be reuenged on them all.
Tit. Looke round about the wicked ſtreets of Rome,
And when thou find'ſt a man that's like thy ſelfe,
Good Murder ſtab him,hee's a Murtherer.
Goe thou with him,and when it is thy hap
To finde another that is like to thee,
Good Rapine ſtab him,he is a Rauiſher.
Go thou with them,and in the Emperours Court,
There is a Queene attended by a Moore,
Well maiſt thou know her by thy owne proportion,
For vp and downe ſhe doth reſemble thee.
I pray thee doe on them ſome violent death,
They haue bene violent to me and mine.

ee *Tamora.*

Tam. Well haſt thou leſſon'd vs,this ſhall we do.
But would it pleaſe thee good *Andronicus*,
To ſend for *Lucius* thy thrice Valiant Sonne,
Who leades towards Rome a Band of Warlike Gothes,
And bid him come and Banquet at thy houſe.
When he is heere,euen at thy Solemne Feaſt,
I will bring in the Empreſſe and her Sonnes,
The Emperour himſelfe,and all thy Foes,
And at thy mercy ſhall they ſtoop,and kneele,
And on them ſhalt thou eaſe,thy angry heart :
What ſaies *Andronicus* to this deuiſe?

Enter Marcus.

Tit. Marcus my Brother, 'tis ſad *Titus* calls,
Go gentle *Marcus* to thy Nephew *Lucius*,
Thou ſhalt enquire him out among the Gothes,
Bid him repaire to me,and bring with him
Some of the chiefeſt Princes of the Gothes,
Bid him encampe his Souldiers where they are,
Tell him the Emperour,and the Empreſſe too,
Feaſts at my houſe,and he ſhall Feaſt with them,
This do thou for my loue,and ſo let him,
As he regards his aged Fathers life.
Mar. This will I do,and ſoone returne againe.
Tam. Now will I hence about thy buſineſſe,
And take my Miniſters along with me.
Tit. Nay,nay,let Rape and Murder ſtay with me,
Or els Ile call my Brother backe againe,
And cleaue to no reuenge but *Lucius*.
Tam. What ſay you Boyes,will you bide with him,
Whiles I goe tell my Lord the Emperour,
How I haue gouern'd our determined ieſt?
Yeeld to his Humour,ſmooth and ſpeake him faire,
And tarry with him till I turne againe.
Tit. I know them all,though they ſuppoſe me mad,
And will ore-reach them in their owne deuiſes,
A payre of curſed hell-hounds and their Dam.
Dem. Madam depart at pleaſure,leaue vs heere.
Tam. Farewell *Andronicus*,reuenge now goes
To lay a complot to betray thy Foes.
Tit. I know thou doo'ſt,and ſweet reuenge farewell.
Chi. Tell vs old man,how ſhall we be imploy'd?
Tit. Tut,I haue worke enough for you to doe,
Publius come hither,*Caius*,and *Valentine*.
Pub. What is your will?
Tit. Know you theſe two?
Pub. The Empreſſe Sonnes
I take them,*Chiron*,*Demetrius*.
Titus. Fie *Publius*,fie,thou art too much deceau'd,
The one is Murder,Rape is the others name,
And therefore bind them gentle *Publius*,
Caius,and *Valentine*,lay hands on them,
Oft haue you heard me wiſh for ſuch an houre,
And now I find it,therefore binde them ſure,
Chi. Villaines forbeare,we are the Empreſſe Sonnes.
Pub. And therefore do we,what we are commanded.
Stop cloſe their mouthes,let them not ſpeake a word,
Is he ſure bound,looke that you binde them faſt. *Exeunt.*

Enter Titus Andronicus with a knife,and Lauinia with a Baſon.

Tit. Come,come *Lauinia*,looke,thy Foes are bound,
Sirs ſtop their mouthes,let them not ſpeake to me,
But let them heare what fearefull words I vtter.
Oh Villaines,*Chiron*,and *Demetrius*,
Here ſtands the ſpring whom you haue ſtain'd with mud,
This goodly Sommer with your Winter mixt,
You kil'd her husband,and for that vil'd fault,
Two of her Brothers were condemn'd to death,
My hand cut off,and made a merry ieſt,
Both her ſweet Hands,her Tongue,and that more deere
Then Hands or tongue,her ſpotleſſe Chaſtity,
Inhumaine Traytors,you conſtrain'd and forc't.
What would you ſay,if I ſhould let you ſpeake?
Villaines for ſhame you could not beg for grace.
Harke Wretches,how I meane to martyr you,
This one Hand yet is left,to cut your throats,
Whil'ſt that *Lauinia* tweene her ſtumps doth hold:
The Baſon that receiues your guilty blood.
You know your Mother meanes to feaſt with me,
And calls herſelfe Reuenge,and thinkes me mad.
Harke Villaines,I will grin'd your bones to duſt,
And with your blood and it,Ile make a Paſte,
And of the Paſte a Coffen I will reare,
And make two Paſties of your ſhamefull Heads,
And bid that ſtrumpet your vnhallowed Dam,
Like to the earth ſwallow her increaſe.
This is the Feaſt,that I haue bid her to,
And this the Banquet ſhe ſhall ſurfet on,
For worſe then *Philomel* you vs'd my Daughter,
And worſe then *Progne*,I will be reueng'd,
And now prepare your throats: *Lauinia* come.
Receiue the blood,and when that they are dead,
Let me goe grin'd their Bones to powder ſmall,
And with this hatefull Liquor temper it,
And in that Paſte let their vil'd Heads be bakte,
Come,come,be euery one officious,
To make this Banket,which I wiſh might proue,
More ſterne and bloody then the Centaures Feaſt.
He cuts their throats.
So now bring them in,for Ile play the Cooke,
And ſee them ready,gainſt their Mother comes. *Exeunt.*

Enter Lucius,Marcus,and the Gothes.

Luc. Vnckle *Marcus*,ſince 'tis my Fathers minde
That I repair to Rome,I am content.
Goth. And ours with thine befall,what Fortune will.
Luc. Good Vnckle take you in this barbarous *Moore*,
This Rauenous Tiger,this accurſed deuill,
Let him receiue no ſuſtenance,fetter him,
Till he be brought vnto the Emperous face,
For teſtimony of her foule proceedings.
And ſee the Ambuſh of our Friends be ſtrong,
If ere the Emperour meanes no good to vs.
Aron. Some deuill whiſper curſes in my eare,
And prompt me that my tongue may vtter forth,
The Venemous Mallice of my ſwelling heart.
Luc. Away Inhumaine Dogge,Vnhallowed Slaue,
Sirs,helpe our Vnckle,to conuey him in, *Flouriſh.*
The Trumpets ſhew the Emperour is at hand.

Sound Trumpets. Enter Emperour and Empreſſe,with Tribunes and others.

Sat. What,hath the Firemament more Suns then one?
Luc. What bootes it thee to call thy ſelfe a Sunne?
Mar. Romes Emperour & Nephewe breake the parle
Theſe quarrels muſt be quietly debated,
The Feaſt is ready which the carefull *Titus*,

Hath

Hath ordained to an Honourable end,
For Peace, for Loue, for League, and good to Rome :
Please you therfore draw nie and take your places.
Satur. *Marcus* we will. *Hoboyes.*

A Table brought in.
Enter Titus like a Cooke, placing the meat on the Table, and Lauinia with a vale ouer her face.

Titus. Welcome my gracious Lord,
Welcome Dread Queene,
Welcome ye Warlike Gothes, welcome *Lucius*,
And welcome all: although the cheere be poore,
'Twill fill your stomacks, please you eat of it.
Sat. Why art thou thus attir'd *Andronicus*?
Tit. Because I would be sure to haue all well,
To entertaine your Highnesse, and your Empresse.
Tam. We are beholding to you good *Andronicus*?
Tit. And if your Highnesse knew my heart, you were:
My Lord the Emperour resolue me this,
Was it well done of rash *Virginius*,
To slay his daughter with his owne right hand,
Because she was enfor'st, stain'd, and deflowr'd?
Satur. It was *Andronicus*.
Tit. Your reason, Mighty Lord?
Sat. Because the Girle, should not suruiue her shame,
And by her presence still renew his sorrowes.
Tit. A reason mighty, strong, and effectuall,
A patterne, president, and liuely warrant,
For me (most wretched) to performe the like:
Die, die, *Lauinia*, and thy shame with thee,
And with thy shame, thy Fathers sorrow die.
He kils her.
Sat. What hast done, vnnaturall and vnkinde?
Tit. Kil'd her for whom my teares haue made me blind.
I am as wofull as *Virginius* was,
And haue a thousand times more cause then he.
Sat. What was she rauisht? tell who did the deed,
Tit. Wilt please you eat,
Wilt please your Highnesse feed?
Tam. Why hast thou slaine thine onely Daughter?
Titus. Not I, 'twas *Chiron* and *Demetrius*,
They rauisht her, and cut away her tongue,
And they, 'twas they, that did her all this wrong.
Satu. Go fetch them hither to vs presently.
Tit. Why there they are both, baked in that Pie,
Whereof their Mother dantily hath fed,
Eating the flesh that she herselfe hath bred.
'Tis true, 'tis true, witnesse my kniues sharpe point.
He stabs the Empresse.
Satu. Die franticke wretch, for this accursed deed.
Luc. Can the Sonnes eye, behold his Father bleed?
There's meede for meede, death for a deadly deed.
Mar. You sad fac'd men, people and Sonnes of Rome,
By vprores seuer'd like a flight of Fowle,
Scattred by windes and high tempestuous gusts:
Oh let me teach you how, to knit againe
This scattred Corne, into one mutuall sheafe,
These broken limbs againe into one body.
Goth. Let Rome herselfe be bane vnto herselfe,
And shee whom mightie kingdomes curtsie too,
Like a forlorne and desperate castaway,
Doe shamefull execution on her selfe.
But if my frostie signes and chaps of age,
Graue witnesses of true experience,
Cannot induce you to attend my words,
Speake Romes deere friend, as 'erst our Auncestor,
When with his solemne tongue he did discourse
To loue-sicke *Didoes* sad attending eare,
The story of that balefull burning night,
When subtil Greekes surpriz'd King *Priams* Troy:
Tell vs what *Sinon* hath bewicht our eares,
Or who hath brought the fatall engine in,
That giues our Troy, our Rome the ciuill wound.
My heart is not compact of flint nor steele,
Nor can I vtter all our bitter griefe,
But floods of teares will drowne my Oratorie,
And breake my very vtterance, euen in the time
When it should moue you to attend me most,
Lending your kind hand Commiseration.
Heere is a Captaine, let him tell the tale,
Your hearts will throb and weepe to heare him speake.
Luc. This Noble Auditory, be it knowne to you,
That cursed *Chiron* and *Demetrius*
Were they that murdred our Emperours Brother,
And they it were that rauished our Sister,
For their fell faults our Brothers were beheaded,
Our Fathers teares despis'd, and basely cousen'd,
Of that true hand that fought Romes quarrell out,
And sent her enemies vnto the graue.
Lastly, my selfe vnkindly banished,
The gates shut on me, and turn'd weeping out,
To beg reliefe among Romes Enemies,
Who drown'd their enmity in my true teares,
And op'd their armes to imbrace me as a Friend:
And I am turned forth, be it knowne to you,
That haue preseru'd her welfare in my blood,
And from her bosome tooke the Enemies point,
Sheathing the steele in my aduentrous body.
Alas you know, I am no Vaunter I,
My scars can witnesse, dumbe although they are,
That my report is iust and full of truth:
But soft, me thinkes I do digresse too much,
Cyting my worthlesse praise: Oh pardon me,
For when no Friends are by, men praise themselues,
Marc. Now is my turne to speake: Behold this Child,
Of this was *Tamora* deliuered,
The issue of an Irreligious *Moore*,
Chiefe Architect and plotter of these woes,
The Villaine is aliue in *Titus* house,
And as he is, to witnesse this is true.
Now iudge what course had *Titus* to reuenge
These wrongs, vnspeakeable past patience,
Or more then any liuing man could beare.
Now you haue heard the truth, what say you Romaines?
Haue we done ought amisse? shew vs wherein,
And from the place where you behold vs now,
The poore remainder of *Andronici*,
Will hand in hand all headlong cast vs downe,
And on the ragged stones beat forth our braines,
And make a mutuall closure of our house:
Speake Romaines speake, and if you say we shall,
Loe hand in hand, *Lucius* and I will fall.
Emilli. Come come, thou reuerent man of Rome,
And bring our Emperour gently in thy hand,
Lucius our Emperour: for well I know,
The common voyce do cry it shall be so.
Mar. *Lucius*, all haile Romes Royall Emperour,
Goe, goe into old *Titus* sorrowfull house,
And hither hale that misbelieuing *Moore*,
To be adiudg'd some direfull slaughtering death,
As punishment for his most wicked life.
Lucius all haile to Romes gracious Gouernour.

ee 2 *Lucius*

Luc. Thankes gentle Romanes, may I gouerne so,
To heale Romes harmes, and wipe away her woe.
But gentle people, giue me ayme a-while,
For Nature puts me to a heauy taske:
Stand all aloofe, but Vnokle draw you neere,
To shed obsequious teares vpon this Trunke:
Oh take this warme kisse on thy pale cold lips,
These sorrowfull drops vpon thy bloud-slaine face,
The last true Duties of thy Noble Sonne.
Mar. Teare for teare, and louing kisse for kisse,
Thy Brother *Marcus* tenders on thy Lips:
O were the summe of these that I should pay
Countlesse, and infinit, yet would I pay them.
Luc. Come hither Boy, come, come, and learne of vs
To melt in showres: thy Grandsire lou'd thee well:
Many a time he danc'd thee on his knee:
Sung thee asleepe, his Louing Brest, thy Pillow
Many a matter hath he told to thee,
IMeete, and agreeing with thine Infancie.
n that respect then, like a louing Childe,
Shed yet some small drops from thy tender Spring,
Because kinde Nature doth require it so:
Friends, should associate Friends, in Greefe and Wo.
Bid him farwell, commit him to the Graue,
Do him that kindnesse, and take leaue of him.
Boy. O Grandsire, Grandsire: euen with all my heart
Would I were Dead, so you did Liue againe.
O Lord, I cannot speake to him for weeping,
My teares will choake me, if I ope my mouth.
Romans. You sad *Andronici*, haue done with woes,
Giue sentence on this exectable Wretch,
That hath beene breeder of these dire euents.
Luc. Set him brest deepe in earth, and famish him:
There let him stand, and raue, and cry for foode:
If any one releeues, or pitties him,
For the offence, he dyes. This is our doome:
Some stay, to see him fast'ned in the earth.
Aron. O why should wrath be mute, & Fury dumbe?
I am no Baby I, that with base Prayers
I should repent the Euils I haue done.
Ten thousand worse, then euer yet I did,
Would I performe if I might haue my will:
If one good Deed in all my life I did,
I do repent it from my very Soule.
Lucius. Some louing Friends conuey the Emp. hence,
And giue him buriall in his Fathers graue.
My Father, and *Lauinia*, shall forthwith
Be closed in our Housholds Monument:
As for that heynous Tyger *Tamora*,
No Funerall Rite, nor man in mournfull Weeds:)
No mournfull Bell shall ring her Buriall:
But throw her foorth to Beasts and Birds of prey:
Her life was Beast-like, and deuoid of pitty,
And being so, shall haue like want of pitty.
See Iustice done on *Aaron* that damn'd Moore,
From whom, our heauy happes had their beginning:
Then afterwards, to Order well the State,
That like Euents, may ne're it Ruinate. *Exeunt omnes.*

FINIS.

THE TRAGEDIE OF ROMEO and IVLIET.

Actus Primus. Scœna Prima.

Enter Sampson and Gregory, with Swords and Bucklers, of the House of Capulet.

Sampson.

Gregory: A my word wee'l not carry coales.
Greg. No, for then we should be Colliars.
Samp. I mean, if we be in choller, wee'l draw.
Greg. I, While you liue, draw your necke out o'th Collar.
Samp. I strike quickly, being mou'd.
Greg. But thou art not quickly mou'd to strike.
Samp. A dog of the house of *Mountague*, moues me.
Greg. To moue, is to stir: and to be valiant, is to stand: Therefore, if thou art mou'd, thou runst away.
Samp. A dogge of that house shall moue me to stand. I will take the wall of any Man or Maid of *Mountagues*.
Greg. That shewes thee a weake slaue, for the weakest goes to the wall.
Samp. True, and therefore women being the weaker Vessels, are euer thrust to the wall: therefore I will push *Mountagues* men from the wall, and thrust his Maides to the wall. (their men.
Greg. The Quarrell is betweene our Masters, and vs
Samp. 'Tis all one, I will shew my selfe a tyrant: when I haue fought with the men, I will bee ciuill with the Maids, and cut off their heads.
Greg. The heads of the Maids?
Sam. I, the heads of the Maids, or their Maiden-heads, Take it in what sence thou wilt.
Greg. They must take it sence, that feele it.
Samp. Me they shall feele while I am able to stand: And 'tis knowne I am a pretty peece of flesh.
Greg. 'Tis well thou art not Fish: If thou had'st, thou had'st beene poore Iohn. Draw thy Toole, here comes of the House of the *Mountagues*.

Enter two other Seruingmen.

Sam. My naked weapon is out: quarrel, I wil back thee
Gre. How? Turne thy backe, and run.
Sam. Feare me not.
Gre. No marry: I feare thee.
Sam. Let vs take the Law of our sides: let them begin.
Gr. I wil frown as I passe by, & let thē take it as they list
Sam. Nay, as they dare. I wil bite my Thumb at them, which is a disgrace to them, if they beare it.
Abra. Do you bite your Thumbe at vs sir?
Samp. I do bite my Thumbe, sir.
Abra. Do you bite your Thumb at vs, sir?
Sam. Is the Law of our side, if I say I? *Gre.* No.
Sam. No sir, I do not bite my Thumbe at you sir: but I bite my Thumbe sir.
Greg. Do you quarrell sir?
Abra. Quarrell sir? no sir. (as you
Sam. If you do sir, I am for you, I serue as good a man
Abra. No better? *Samp.* Well sir.

Enter Benuolio.

Gr. Say better: here comes one of my masters kinsmen.
Samp. Yes, better.
Abra. You Lye.
Samp. Draw if you be men. *Gregory*, remember thy washing blow. *They Fight.*
Ben. Part Fooles, put vp your Swords, you know not what you do.

Enter Tibalt.

Tyb. What art thou drawne, among these heartlesse Hindes? Turne thee *Benuolio*, looke vpon thy death.
Ben. I do but keepe the peace, put vp thy Sword,
Or manage it to part these men with me.
Tyb. What draw, and talke of peace? I hate the word
As I hate hell, all *Mountagues*, and thee:
Haue at thee Coward. *Fight.*

Enter three or foure Citizens with Clubs.

Offi. Clubs, Bils, and Partisons, strike, beat them down
Downe with the *Capulets*, downe with the *Mountagues*.

Enter old Capulet in his Gowne, and his wife.

Cap. What noise is this? Giue me my long Sword ho.
Wife. A crutch, a crutch: why call you for a Sword?
Cap. My Sword I say: Old *Mountague* is come,
And flourishes his Blade in spight of me.

Enter old Mountague, & his wife.

Moun. Thou villaine *Capulet*. Hold me not, let me go
2. Wife. Thou shalt not stir a foote to seeke a Foe.

Enter Prince Eskales, with his Traine.

Prince. Rebellious Subiects, Enemies to peace,
Prophaners of this Neighbor-stained Steele,
Will they not heare? What hoe, you Men, you Beasts,
That quench the fire of your pernitious Rage,
With purple Fountaines issuing from your Veines:
On paine of Torture, from those bloody hands
Throw your mistemper'd Weapons to the ground,
And heare the Sentence of your mooued Prince.
Three ciuill Broyles, bred of an Ayery word,
By thee old *Capulet* and *Mountague*,
Haue thrice disturb'd the quiet of our streets,
And made *Verona's* ancient Citizens
Cast by their Graue beseeming Ornaments,
To wield old Partizans, in hands as old,

ee 3 Cankred

Cankred with peace, to part your Cankred hate,
If euer you diſturbe our ſtreets againe,
Your liues ſhall pay the forfeit of the peace.
For this time all the reſt depart away.
You *Capulet* ſhall goe along with me,
And *Mountague* come you this afternoone,
To know our Fathers pleaſure in this caſe:
To old Free-towne, our common iudgement place:
Once more on paine of death, all men depart. *Exeunt.*
Moun. Who ſet this auncient quarrell new abroach?
Speake Nephew, were you by, when it began:
Ben. Heere were the ſeruants of your aduerſarie,
And yours cloſe fighting ere I did approach,
I drew to part them, in the inſtant came
The fiery *Tibalt*, with his ſword prepar'd,
Which as he breath'd defiance to my eares,
He ſwong about his head, and cut the windes,
Who nothing hurt withall, hiſt him in ſcorne.
While we were enterchanging thruſts and blowes,
Came more and more, and fought on part and part,
Till the Prince came, who parted either part.
Wife. O where is *Romeo*, ſaw you him to day?
Right glad am I, he was not at this fray.
Ben Madam, an houre before the worſhipt Sun
Peer'd forth the golden window of the Eaſt,
A troubled mind draue me to walke abroad,
Where vnderneath the groue of Sycamour,
That Weſt-ward rooteth from this City ſide:
So earely walking did I ſee your Sonne:
Towards him I made, but he was ware of me,
And ſtole into the couert of the wood,
I meaſuring his affections by my owne,
Which then moſt ſought, wher moſt might not be found:
Being one too many by my weary ſelfe,
Purſued my Honour, not purſuing his
And gladly ſhunn'd, who gladly fled from me.
Mount. Many a morning hath he there beene ſeene,
With teares augmenting the freſh mornings deaw,
Adding to cloudes, more cloudes with his deepe ſighes,
But all ſo ſoone as the all-cheering Sunne,
Should in the fartheſt Eaſt begin to draw
The ſhadie Curtaines from *Auroras* bed,
Away from light ſteales home my heauy Sonne,
And priuate in his Chamber pennes himſelfe,
Shuts vp his windowes, lockes faire day-light out,
And makes himſelfe an artificiall night:
Blacke and portendous muſt this humour proue,
Vnleſſe good counſell may the cauſe remoue.
Ben. My Noble Vncle doe you know the cauſe?
Moun. I neither know it, nor can learne of him.
Ben. Haue you importun'd him by any meanes?
Moun. Both by my ſelfe and many others Friends,
But he his owne affections counſeller,
Is to himſelfe (I will not ſay how true)
But to himſelfe ſo ſecret and ſo cloſe,
So farre from ſounding and diſcouery,
As is the bud bit with an enuious worme,
Ere he can ſpread his ſweete leaues to the ayre,
Or dedicate his beauty to the ſame.
Could we but learne from whence his ſorrowes grow,
We would as willingly giue cure, as know.
Enter Romeo.
Ben. See where he comes, ſo pleaſe you ſtep aſide,
Ile know his greeuance, or be much denide.
Moun. I would thou wert ſo happy by thy ſtay,
To heare true ſhrift. Come Madam let's away. *Exeunt.*

Ben. Good morrow Couſin.
Rom. Is the day ſo young?
Ben. But new ſtrooke nine.
Rom. Aye me, ſad houres ſeeme long.
Was that my Father that went henec ſo faſt?
Ben. It was: what ſadnes lengthens *Romeo*'s houres?
Ro. Not hauing that, which hauing, makes them ſhort
Ben. In loue.
Romeo. Out.
Ben. Of loue.
Rom. Out of her fauour where I am in loue.
Ben. Alas that loue ſo gentle in his view,
Should be ſo tyrannous and rough in proofe.
Rom. Alas that loue, whoſe view is muffled ſtill,
Should without eyes, ſee path-wayes to his will
Where ſhall we dine? O me: what fray was heere?
Yet tell me not, for I haue heard it all:
Heere's much to do with hate, but more with loue:
Why then, O brawling loue, O louing hate,
O any thing, of nothing firſt created:
O heauie lightneſſe, ſerious vanity,
Miſhapen Chaos of welſeeing formes,
Feather of lead, bright ſmoake, cold fire, ſicke health,
Still waking ſleepe, that is not what it is.
This loue feele I, that feele no loue in this.
Doeſt thou not laugh?
Ben. No Coze, I rather weepe.
Rom. Good heart, at what?
Ben. At thy good hearts oppreſsion.
Rom. Why ſuch is loues tranſg reſsion.
Griefes of mine owne lie heauie in my breaſt,
Which thou wilt propagate to haue it preaſt
With more of thine, this loue that thou haſt ſhowne,
Doth adde more griefe, to too much of mine owne.
Loue, is a ſmoake made with the fume of ſighes,
Being purg'd, a fire ſparkling in Louers eyes,
Being vext, a Sea nouriſht with louing teares,
What is it elſe? a madneſſe, moſt diſcreet,
A choking gall, and a preſeruing ſweet:
Farewell my Coze.
Ben. Soft I will goe along.
And if you leaue me ſo, you do me wrong.
Rom. Tut I haue loſt my ſelfe, I am not here,
This is not *Romeo*, hee's ſome other where.
Ben. Tell me in ſadneſſe, who is that you loue?
Rom. What ſhall I grone and tell thee?
Ben. Grone, why no: but ſadly tell me who.
Rom. A ſicke man in ſadneſſe makes his will:
A word ill vrg'd to one that is ſo ill:
In ſadneſſe Cozin, I do loue a woman.
Ben. I aym'd ſo neare, when I ſuppoſ'd you lou'd.
Rom. A right good marke man, and ſhee's faire I loue
Ben. A right faire marke, faire Coze, is ſooneſt hit.
Rom. Well in that hit you miſſe, ſheel not be hit
With Cupids arrow, ſhe hath *Dians* wit:
And in ſtrong proofe of chaſtity well arm'd:
From loues weake childiſh Bow, ſhe liues vncharm'd.
Shee will not ſtay the ſiege of louing tearmes,
Nor bid th'incounter of aſſailing eyes.
Nor open her lap to Sainct-ſeducing Gold:
O ſhe is rich in beautie, onely poore,
That when ſhe dies, with beautie dies her ſtore.
Ben. Then ſhe hath ſworne, that ſhe will ſtill liue chaſt?
Rom. She hath, and in that ſparing make huge waſt?
For beauty ſteru'd with her ſeuerity,
Cuts beauty off from all poſteritie.
She

She is too faire, too wisewi: sely too faire,
To merie blisse by making me dispaire:
She hath forsworne to loue, and in that vow
Do I liue dead, that liue to tell it now.
Ben. Be rul'd by me, forget to thinke of her.
Rom. O teach me how I should forget to thinke.
Ben. By giuing liberty vnto thine eyes,
Examine other beauties,
Ro. Tis the way to cal hers (exquisit) in question more,
These happy maskes that kisse faire Ladies browes,
Being blacke, puts vs in mind they hide the faire:
He that is strooken blind, cannot forget
The precious treasure of his eye-sight lost:
Shew me a Mistresse that is passing faire,
What doth her beauty serue but as a note,
Where I may read who past that passing faire.
Farewell thou can'st not teach me to forget,
Ben. Ile pay that doctrine, or else die in debt. *Exeunt*

Enter Capulet, Countie Paris, and the Clowne.

Capu. *Mountague* is bound as well as I,
In penalty alike, and tis not hard I thinke,
For men so old as wee, to keepe the peace.
Par. Of Honourable reckoning are you both,
And pittie tis you liu'd at ods so long:
But now my Lord, what say you to my sute?
Capu. But saying ore what I haue said before,
My Child is yet a stranger in the world,
Shee hath not seene the change of fourteene yeares,
Let two more Summers wither in their pride
Ere we may thinke her ripe to be a Bride.
Pari. Younger then she, are happy mothers made.
Capu And too soone mar'd are those so early made:
Earth hath swallowed all my hopes but she,
Shee's the hopefull Lady of my earth:
But wooe her gentle *Paris*, get her heart,
My will to her consent, is but a part,
And shee agree, within her scope of choise,
Lyes my consent, and faire according voice:
This night I hold an old accustom'd Feast,
Whereto I haue inuited many a Guest,
Such as I loue, and you among the store,
One more, most welcome makes my number more.
At my poore house, looke to behold this night,
Earth treading starres, that make darke heauen light,
Such comfort as do lusty young men feele,
When well apparrel'd Aprill on the heele
Of limping Winter treads, euen such delight
Among fresh Fennell buds shall you this night
Inherit at my house: heare all all see:
And like her most, whose merit most shall be:
Which one more veiw, of many, mine being one,
May stand in number, though in reckning none.
Come, goe with me: goe sirrah trudge about,
Through faire *Verona*, find those persons out,
Whose names are written there, and to them say,
My house and welcome, on their pleasure stay. *Exit.*

Ser. Find them out whose names are written. Heere it is written, that the Shoo-maker should meddle with his Yard, and the Tayler with his Last, the Fisher with his Pensill, and the Painter with his Nets. But I am sent to find those persons whose names are writ, & can neuer find what names the writing person hath here writ (I must to the learned) in good time.

Enter Benuolio, and Romeo.

Ben. Tut man, one fire burnes out anothers burning,
One paine is lesned by anothers anguish:
Turne giddie, and be holpe by backward turning:
One desparate greefe, cures with anothers languish:
Take thou some new infection to the eye,
And the rank poyson of the old wil die.
Rom. Your Plantan leafe is excellent for that
Ben. For what I pray thee?
Rom. For your broken shin.
Ben. Why *Romeo* art thou mad?
Rom. Not mad, but bound more then a mad man is:
Shut vp in prison, kept without my foode,
Whipt and tormented: and Godden good fellow,
Ser. Godgigoden, I pray sir can you read?
Rom. I mine owne fortune in my miserie.
Ser. Perhaps you haue learn'd it without booke:
But I pray can you read any thing you see
Rom. I, if I know the Letters and the Language.
Ser. Ye say honestly, rest you merry.
Rom. Stay fellow, I can read.

He reades the Letter.

Seigneur Martino, and his wife and daughter: County Anselme and his beautious sisters: the Lady widdow of Utruuio, Seigneur Placentio, and his louely Neeces: Mercutio and his brother Valentine: mine vncle Capulet his wife and daughters: my faire Neece Rosaline, Liuia, Seigneur Valentio, & his Cosen Tybalt: Lucio and the liuely Helena.

A faire assembly, whither should they come?
Ser. Vp.
Rom. Whither? to supper?
Ser. To our house.
Rom. Whose house?
Ser. My Maisters.
Rom. Indeed I should haue askt you that before.

Ser Now Ile tell you without asking. My maister is the great rich *Capulet*, and if you be not of the house of *Mountagues* I pray come and crush a cup of wine. Rest you merry. *Exit.*

Ben. At this same auncient Feast of *Capulets*
Sups the faire *Rosaline*, whom thou so loues:
With all the admired Beauties of *Verona*,
Go thither and with vnattainted eye,
Compare her face with some that I shall show,
And I will make thee thinke thy Swan a Crow.
Rom. When the deuout religion of mine eye
Maintaines such falshood, then turne teares to fire:
And these who often drown'd could neuer die,
Transparent Heretiques be burnt for liers.
One fairer then my loue the all-seeing Sun
Nere saw her match, since first the world begun.
Ben. Tut, you saw her faire, none else being by,
Herselfe poys'd with herselfe in either eye:
But in that Christall scales, let there be waid,
Your Ladies loue against some other Maid
That I will show you, shining at this Feast,
And she shew scant shell, well, that now shewes best.
Rom. Ile goe along, no such sight to be showne,
But to reioyce in splendor of mine owne.

Enter Capulets Wife and Nurse.

Wife Nurse wher's my daughter? call her forth to me.
Nurse. Now by my Maidenhead, at twelue yeare old
I bad her come, what Lamb: what Ladi-bird, God forbid,
Where's this Girle? what *Iuliet*?

Enter Iuliet.

Iuliet. How now, who calls?
Nur. Your Mother.
Iuliet. Madam I am heere, what is your will?
Wife. This is the matter: Nurse giue leaue awhile, we
must

muſt talke in ſecret. Nurſe come backe againe, I haue remembred me, thou'ſe heare our counſell. Thou knoweſt my daughter's of a pretty age.

Nurſe. Faith I can tell her age vnto an houre.

Wife. Shee's not fourteene.

Nurſe. Ile lay fourteene of my teeth,
And yet to my teene be it ſpoken,
I haue but foure, ſhee's not fourteene.
How long is it now to *Lammas* tide?

Wife. A fortnight and odde dayes.

Nurſe. Euen or odde, of all daies in the yeare come *Lammas* Eue at night ſhall ſhe be fourteene. *Suſan* & ſhe, God reſt all Chriſtian ſoules, were of an age. Well *Suſan* is with God, ſhe was too good for me. But as I ſaid, on *Lamas* Eue at night ſhall ſhe be fourteene, that ſhall ſhe marie, I remember it well. 'Tis ſince the Earth-quake now eleuen yeares, and ſhe was wean'd I neuer ſhall forget it, of all the daies of the yeare, vpon that day: for I had then laid Worme-wood to my Dug ſitting in the Sunne vnder the Douehouſe wall, my Lord and you were then at *Mantua*, nay I doe beare a braine. But as I ſaid, when it did taſt the Worme-wood on the nipple of my Dugge, and felt it bitter, pretty foole, to ſee it teachie, and fall out with the Dugge, Shake quoth the Doue-houſe, 'twas no neede I trow to bid mee trudge: and ſince that time it is a eleuen yeares, for then ſhe could ſtand alone, nay bi'th' roode ſhe could haue runne & wadled all about: for euen the day before ſhe broke her brow, & then my Husband God be with his ſoule, a was a merrie man, tooke vp the Child, yea quoth hee, doeſt thou fall vpon thy face? thou wilt fall backeward when thou haſt more wit, wilt thou not *Iule*? And by my holy-dam, the pretty wretch leſte crying, & ſaid I: to ſee now how a Ieſt ſhall come about. I warrant, & I ſhall liue a thouſand yeares, I neuer ſhould forget it: wilt thou not *Iulet* quoth he? and pretty foole it ſtinted, and ſaid I.

Old La. Inough of this, I pray thee hold thy peace.

Nurſe. Yes Madam, yet I cannot chuſe but laugh, to thinke it ſhould leaue crying, & ſay I: and yet I warrant it had vpon it brow, a bumpe as big as a young Cockrels ſtone? A perilous knock, and it cryed bitterly. Yea quoth my husband, fall'ſt vpon thy face, thou wilt fall backward when thou commeſt to age: wilt thou not *Iule*? It ſtinted: and ſaid I.

Iule. And ſtint thou too, I pray thee *Nurſe*, ſay I.

Nur. Peace I haue done: God marke thee too his grace thou waſt the pretties Babe that ere I nurſt, and I might liue to ſee thee married once, I haue my wiſh.

Old La. Marry that marry is the very theame
I came to talke of, tell me daughter *Iuliet*,
How ſtands your diſpoſition to be Married?

Iuli. It is an houre that I dreame not of.

Nur. An houre, were not I thine onely Nurſe, I would ſay thou had'ſt ſuckt wiſedome from thy teat.

Old La. Well thinke of marriage now, yonger then you
Heere in *Verona*, Ladies of eſteeme,
Are made already Mothers. By my count
I was your Mother, much vpon theſe yeares
That you are now a Maide, thus then in briefe:
The valiant *Paris* ſeekes you for his loue.

Nurſe. A man young Lady, Lady, ſuch a man as all the world. Why hee's a man of waxe.

Old La. *Veronas* Summer hath not ſuch a flower.

Nurſe. Nay hee's a flower, infaith a very flower.

Old La. What ſay you, can you loue the Gentleman?
This night you ſhall behold him at our Feaſt,
Read ore the volume of young *Paris* face,
And find delight, writ there with Beauties pen:
Examine euery ſeuerall liniament,
And ſee how one another lends content:
And what obſcur'd in this faire volume lies,
Find written in the Margent of his eyes.
This precious Booke of Loue, this vnbound Louer,
To Beautifie him, onely lacks a Couer.
The fiſh liues in the Sea, and 'tis much pride
For faire without, the faire within to hide:
That Booke in manies eyes doth ſhare the glorie,
That in Gold claſpes, Lockes in the Golden ſtorie:
So ſhall you ſhare all that he doth poſſeſſe,
By hauing him, making your ſelfe no leſſe.

Nurſe. No leſſe, nay bigger: women grow by men.

Old La. Speake briefly, can you like of *Paris* loue?

Iuli. Ile looke to like, if looking liking moue.
But no more deepe will I endart mine eye,
Then your conſent giues ſtrength to make flye.

Enter a Seruing man.

Ser. Madam, the gueſts are come, ſupper ſeru'd vp, you cal'd, my young Lady askt for, the Nurſe cur'ſt in the Pantery, and euery thing in extremitie: I muſt hence to wait, I beſeech you follow ſtraight. *Exit.*

Mo. We follow thee, *Iuliet*, the Countie ſtaies.

Nurſe. Goe Gyrle, ſeeke happie nights to happy daies. *Exeunt.*

Enter Romeo, Mercutio, Benuolio, with fiue or ſixe other Maskers, Torch-bearers.

Rom. What ſhall this ſpeeh be ſpoke for our excuſe
Or ſhall we on without Apologie?

Ben. The date is out of ſuch prolixitie,
Weele haue no *Cupid*, hood winkt with a ſkarfe,
Bearing a Tartars painted Bow of lath,
Skaring the Ladies like a Crow-keeper.
But let them meaſure vs by what they will,
Weele meaſure them a Meaſure, and be gone.

Rom. Giue me a Torch, I am not for this ambling.
Being but heauy I will beare the light.

Mer. Nay gentle *Romeo*, we muſt haue you dance.

Rom. Not I beleeue me, you haue dancing ſhooes
With nimble ſoles, I haue a ſoale of Lead
So ſtakes me to the ground, I cannot moue.

Mer. You are a Louer, borrow *Cupids* wings,
And ſoare with them aboue a common bound.

Rom. I am too ſore enpearced with his ſhaft,
To ſoare with his light feathers, and to bound:
I cannot bound a pitch aboue dull woe,
Vnder loues heauy burthen doe I ſinke.

Hora. And to ſinke in it ſhould you burthen loue,
Too great oppreſſion for a tender thing.

Rom. Is loue a tender thing? it is too rough,
Too rude, too boyſterous, and it pricks like thorne.

Mer. If loue be rough with you, be rough with loue,
Pricke loue for pricking, and you beat loue downe,
Giue me a Caſe to put my viſage in,
A Viſor for a Viſor, what care I
What curious eye doth quote deformities:
Here are the Beetle-browes ſhall bluſh for me.

Ben. Come knocke and enter, and no ſooner in,
But euery man betake him to his legs.

Rom. A Torch for me, let wantons light of heart
Tickle the ſenceleſſe ruſhes with their heeles:
For I am prouerb'd with a Grandſier Phraſe,
Ile be a Candle-holder and looke on,
The game was nere ſo faire, and I am done.

Mer. Tut,

Mer. Tut, duns the Mouſe, the Conſtables owne word,
If thou art dun, weele draw thee from the mire.
Or ſaue your reuerence loue, wherein thou ſtickeſt
Vp to the eares, come we burne day-light ho.

Rom. Nay that's not ſo.

Mer. I meane ſir I delay,
We waſt our lights in vaine, lights, lights, by day;
Take our good meaning, for our Iudgement ſits
Fiue times in that, ere once in our fine wits.

Rom. And we meane well in going to this Maske,
But 'tis no wit to go.

Mer. Why may one aske?

Rom. I dreampt a dreame to night.

Mer. And ſo did I.

Rom. Well what was yours?

Mer. That dreamers often lye.

Ro. In bed a ſleepe while they do dreame things true.

Mer. O then I ſee Queene Mab hath beene with you: She is the Fairies Midwife, & ſhe comes in ſhape no bigger then Agat-ſtone, on the fore-finger of an Alderman, drawne with a teeme of little Atomies, ouer mens noſes as they lie aſleepe: her Waggon Spokes made of long Spinners legs: the Couer of the wings of Graſhoppers, her Traces of the ſmalleſt Spiders web, her coullers of the Moonſhines watry Beames, her Whip of Crickets bone, the Laſh of Philome, her Waggoner, a ſmall gray-coated Gnat, not halfe ſo bigge as a round little Worme, prickt from the Lazie-finger of a man. Her Chariot is an emptie Haſelnut, made by the Ioyner Squirrel or old Grub, time out a mind, the Faries Coach-makers: & in this ſtate ſhe gallops night by night, through Louers braines: and then they dreame of Loue. On Courtiers knees, that dreame on Curſies ſtrait: ore Lawyers fingers, who ſtrait dreamt on Fees, ore Ladies lips, who ſtrait on kiſſes dreame, which oft the angry Mab with bliſters plagues, becauſe their breath with Sweet meats tainted are. Sometime ſhe gallops ore a Courtiers noſe, & then dreames he of ſmelling out a ſute: & ſomtime comes ſhe with Tith pigs tale, tickling a Parſons noſe as a lies aſleepe, then he dreames of another Benefice. Sometime ſhe driueth ore a Souldiers necke, & then dreames he of cutting Forraine throats, of Breaches, Ambuſcados, Spaniſh Blades: Of Healths fiue Fadome deepe, and then anon drums in his eares, at which he ſtartes and wakes; and being thus frighted, ſweares a prayer or two & ſleepes againe: this is that very Mab that plats the manes of Horſes in the night: & bakes the Elklocks in foule ſluttiſh haires, which once vntangled, much misfortune bodes,
This is the hag, when Maides lie on their backs,
That preſſes them, and learnes them firſt to beare,
Making them women of good carriage:
This is ſhe.

Rom. Peace, peace, *Mercutio* peace,
Thou talk'ſt of nothing.

Mer. True, I talke of dreames:
Which are the children of an idle braine,
Begot of nothing, but vaine phantaſie,
Which is as thin of ſubſtance as the ayre,
And more inconſtant then the wind, who wooes
Euen now the frozen boſome of the North:
And being anger'd, puffes away from thence,
Turning his ſide to the dew dropping South.

Ben. This wind you talke of blowes vs from our ſelues,
Supper is done, and we ſhall come too late.

Rom. I feare too early, for my mind misgiues,
Some conſequence yet hanging in the ſtarres,
Shall bitterly begin his fearefull date
With this nights reuels, and expire the tearme
Of a deſpiſed life cloſ'd in my breſt:
By ſome vile forfeit of vntimely death.
But he that hath the ſtirrage of my courſe,
Direct my ſute: on luſtie Gentlemen.

Ben. Strike Drum.

They march about the Stage, and Seruingmen come forth with their napkins.

Enter Seruant.

Ser. Where's *Potpan*, that he helpes not to take away? He ſhift a Trencher? he ſcrape a Trencher?

1. When good manners, ſhall lie in one or two mens hands, and they vnwaſht too, 'tis a foule thing.

Ser. Away with the Ioynſtooles, remoue the Courtcubbord, looke to the Plate: good thou, ſaue mee a piece of Marchpane, and as thou loueſt me, let the Porter let in *Suſan Grindſtone* and *Nell*, *Anthonie* and *Potpan*.

2. I Boy readie.

Ser. You are lookt for, and cal'd for, askt for, & ſought for, in the great Chamber.

1 We cannot be here and there too, chearly Boyes, Be brisk a while, and the longer liuer take all.

Exeunt.

Enter all the Gueſts and Gentlewomen to the Maskers.

1. *Capu.* Welcome Gentlemen,
Ladies that haue their toes
Vnplagu'd with Cornes, will walke about with you:
Ah my Miſtreſſes, which of you all
Will now deny to dance? She that makes dainty,
She Ile ſweare hath Cornes: am I come neare ye now?
Welcome Gentlemen, I haue ſeene the day
That I haue worne a Viſor, and could tell
A whiſpering tale in a faire Ladies eare:
Such as would pleaſe: 'tis gone, 'tis gone, 'tis gone,
You are welcome Gentlemen, come Muſitians play:

Muſicke plaies: and the dance.

A Hall, Hall, giue roome, and foote it Girles,
More light you knaues, and turne the Tables vp:
And quench the fire, the Roome is growne too hot.
Ah ſirrah, this vnlookt for ſport comes well:
Nay ſit, nay ſit, good Cozin *Capulet*,
For you and I are paſt our dauncing daies:
How long 'iſt now ſince laſt your ſelfe and I
Were in a Maske?

2. *Capu.* Berlady thirty yeares.

1. *Capu.* What man: 'tis not ſo much, 'tis not ſo much,
'Tis ſince the Nuptiall of *Lucentio*,
Come Pentycoſt as quickely as it will,
Some fiue and twenty yeares, and then we Maskt.

2. *Cap.* 'Tis more, 'tis more, his Sonne is elder ſir:
His Sonne is thirty.

3. *Cap.* Will you tell me that?
His Sonne was but a Ward two yeares agoe.

Rom. What Ladie is that which doth inrich the hand
Of yonder Knight?

Ser. I know not ſir.

Rom. O ſhe doth teach the Torches to burne bright:
It ſeemes ſhe hangs vpon the cheeke of night,
As a rich Iewel in an Æthiops eare:
Beauty too rich for vſe, for earth too deare:
So ſhewes a Snowy Doue trooping with Crowes,
As yonder Lady ore her fellowes ſhowes;
The meaſure done, Ile watch her place of ſtand,
And touching hers, make bleſſed my rude hand.

Did

Did my heart loue till now, forſweare it ſight,
For I neuer ſaw true Beauty till this night.
Tib. This by his voice, ſhould be a *Mountague.*
Fetch me my Rapier Boy, what dares the ſlaue
Come hither couer'd with an antique face,
To fleere and ſcorne at our Solemnitie?
Now by the ſtocke and Honour of my kin,
To ſtrike him dead I hold it not a ſin.
Cap. Why how now kinſman,
Wherefore ſtorme you ſo?
Tib. Vncle this is a *Mountague*, our foe:
A Villaine that is hither come in ſpight,
To ſcorne at our Solemnitie this night.
Cap. Young *Romeo* is it?
Tib. 'Tis he, that Villaine *Romeo.*
Cap. Content thee gentle Coz, let him alone,
A beares him like a portly Gentleman:
And to ſay truth, *Verona* brags of him,
To be a vertuous and well gouern'd youth:
I would not for the wealth of all the towne,
Here in my houſe do him diſparagement:
Therfore be patient, take no note of him,
It is my will, the which if thou reſpect,
Shew a faire preſence, and put off theſe frownes,
An ill beſeeming ſemblance for a Feaſt.
Tib. It fits when ſuch a Villaine is a gueſt,
Ile not endure him.
Cap. He ſhall be endu'rd.
What goodman boy, I ſay he ſhall, go too,
Am I the Maiſter here or you? go too,
Youle not endure him, God ſhall mend my ſoule,
Youle make a Mutinie among the Gueſts:
You will ſet cocke a hoope, youle be the man.
Tib. Why Vncle, 'tis a ſhame.
Cap. Go too, go too,
You are a ſawcy Boy, 'iſt ſo indeed?
This tricke may chance to ſcath you, I know what,
You muſt contrary me, marry 'tis time.
Well ſaid my hearts, you are a Princox, goe,
Be quiet, or more light, more light for ſhame,
Ile make you quiet. What, chearely my hearts.
Tib. Patience perforce, with wilfull choler meeting,
Makes my fleſh tremble in their different greeting:
I will withdraw, but this intruſion ſhall
Now ſeeming ſweet, conuert to bitter gall. *Exit.*
Rom. If I prophane with my vnworthieſt hand,
This holy ſhrine, the gentle ſin is this,
My lips to bluſhing Pilgrims did ready ſtand,
To ſmooth that rough touch, with a tender kiſſe.
Iul. Good Pilgrime,
You do wrong your hand too much.
Which mannerly deuotion ſhewes in this,
For Saints haue hands, that Pilgrims hands do tuch,
And palme to palme, is holy Palmers kiſſe.
Rom. Haue not Saints lips, and holy Palmers too?
Iul. I Pilgrim, lips that they muſt vſe in prayer.
Rom. O then deare Saint, let lips do what hands do,
They pray (grant thou) leaſt faith turne to diſpaire.
Iul. Saints do not moue,
Though grant for prayers ſake.
Rom. Then moue not while my prayers effect I take:
Thus from my lips, by thine my ſin is purg'd.
Iul. Then haue my lips the ſin that they haue tooke.
Rom. Sin from my lips? O treſpaſſe ſweetly vrg'd:
Giue me my ſin againe.
Iul. You kiſſe by'th'booke.
Nur. Madam your Mother craues a word with you.
Rom. What is her Mother?
Nurſ. Marrie Batcheler,
Her Mother is the Lady of the houſe,
And a good Lady, and a wiſe, and Vertuous,
I Nur'ſt her Daughter that you talkt withall:
I tell you, he that can lay hold of her,
Shall haue the chincks.
Rom. Is ſhe a *Capulet*?
O deare account! My life is my foes debt.
Ben. Away, be gone, the ſport is at the beſt.
Rom. I ſo I feare, the more is my vnreſt.
Cap. Nay Gentlemen prepare not to be gone,
We haue a trifling fooliſh Banquet towards:
Is it e'ne ſo? why then I thanke you all.
I thanke you honeſt Gentlemen, good night:
More Torches here: come on, then let's to bed.
Ah ſirrah, by my faie it waxes late,
Ile to my reſt.
Iuli. Come hither Nurſe,
What is yond Gentleman:
Nur. The Sonne and Heire of old *Tyberio.*
Iuli. What's he that now is going out of doore?
Nur. Marrie that I thinke be young *Petruchio.*
Iul. What's he that follows here that would not dance?
Nur. I know not.
Iul. Go aske his name: if he be married,
My graue is like to be my wedded bed.
Nur. His name is *Romeo*, and a *Mountague*,
The onely Sonne of your great Enemie.
Iul. My onely Loue ſprung from my onely hate,
Too early ſeene, vnknowne, and knowne too late,
Prodigious birth of Loue it is to me,
That I muſt loue a loathed Enemie.
Nur. What's this? whats this?
Iul. A rime, I learne euen now
Of one I dan'ſt withall.
One cals within, Iuliet.
Nur. Anon, anon:
Come let's away, the ſtrangers all are gone.
Exeunt.

Chorus.

Now old deſire doth in his death bed lie,
And yong affection gapes to be his Heire,
That faire, for which Loue gron'd for and would die,
With tender *Iuliet* matcht, is now not faire.
Now *Romeo* is beloued, and Loues againe,
A like bewitched by the charme of lookes:
But to his foe ſuppos'd he muſt complaine,
And ſhe ſteale Loues ſweet bait from fearefull hookes:
Being held a foe, he may not haue acceſſe
To breath ſuch vowes as Louers vſe to ſweare,
And ſhe as much in Loue, her meanes much leſſe,
To meete her new Beloued any where:
But paſſion lends them Power, time, meanes to meete,
Temp'ring extremities with extreame ſweete.

Enter Romeo alone.

Rom. Can I goe forward when my heart is here?
Turne backe dull earth, and find thy Center out.

Enter Benuolio, with Mercutio.

Ben. *Romeo*, my Cozen *Romeo*, *Romeo*.
Merc. He is wiſe,
And on my life hath ſtolne him home to bed.
Ben. He ran this way and leapt this Orchard wall.
Call good *Mercutio*:
Nay, Ile coniure too.

Mer. Romeo, Humours, Madman, Paſſion, Louer,
Appeare thou in the likeneſſe of a ſigh,
Speake but one rime, and I am ſatisfied:
Cry me but ay me, Prouant, but Loue and day,
Speake to my goſhip *Venus* one faire word,
One Nickname for her purblind Sonne and her,
Young *Abraham* *Cupid* he that ſhot ſo true,
When King *Cophetua* lou'd the begger Maid,
He heareth not, he ſtirreth not, he mouethn ot,
The Ape is dead, I muſt coniure him,
I coniure thee by *Roſalines* bright eyes,
By her High forehead, and her Scarlet lip,
By her Fine foote, Straight leg, and Quiuering thigh,
And the Demeanes, that there Adiacent lie,
That in thy likeneſſe thou appeare to vs.
Ben. And if he heare thee thou wilt anger him.
Mer. This cannot anger him, t'would anger him
To raiſe a ſpirit in his Miſtreſſe circle,
Of ſome ſtrange nature, letting it ſtand
Till ſhe had laid it, and coniured it downe,
That were ſome ſpight.
My inuocation is faire and honeſt, & in his Miſtris name,
I coniure onely but to raiſe vp him.
Ben. Come, he hath hid himſelfe among theſe Trees
To be conſorted with the Humerous night:
Blind is his Loue, and beſt befits the darke.
Mer. If Loue be blind, Loue cannot hit the marke,
Now will he ſit vnder a Medler tree,
And wiſh his Miſtreſſe were that kind of Fruite,
As Maides call Medlers when they laugh alone,
O *Romeo* that ſhe were, O that ſhe were
An open, or thou a Poprin Peare,
Romeo goodnight, Ile to my Truckle bed,
This Field-bed is to cold for me to ſleepe,
Come ſhall we go?
Ben. Go then, for 'tis in vaine to ſeeke him here
That meanes not to be found. *Exeunt.*
Rom. He ieaſts at Scarres that neuer felt a wound,
But ſoft, what light through yonder window breaks?
It is the Eaſt, and *Iuliet* is the Sunne,
Ariſe faire Sun and kill the enuious Moone,
Who is already ſicke and pale with griefe,
That thou her Maid art far more faire then ſhe:
Be not her Maid ſince ſhe is enuious,
Her Veſtal liuery is but ſicke and greene,
And none but fooles do weare it, caſt it off:
It is my Lady, O it is my Loue, O that ſhe knew ſhe were,
She ſpeakes, yet ſhe ſayes nothing, what of that?
Her eye diſcourſes, I will anſwere it:
I am too bold 'tis not to me ſhe ſpeakes:
Two of the faireſt ſtarres in all the Heauen,
Hauing ſome buſineſſe do entreat her eyes,
To twinckle in their Spheres till they returne.
What if her eyes were there, they in her head,
The brightneſſe of her cheeke would ſhame thoſe ſtarres,
As day-light doth a Lampe, her eye in heauen,
Would through the ayrie Region ſtreame ſo bright,
That Birds would ſing, and thinke it were not night:
See how ſhe leanes her cheeke vpon her hand.
O that I were a Gloue vpon that hand,
That I might touch that cheeke.
Iul. Ay me.
Rom. She ſpeakes.
Oh ſpeake againe bright Angell, for thou art
As glorious to this night being ore my head,
As is a winged meſſenger of heauen
Vnto the white vpturned wondring eyes
Of mortalls that fall backe to gaze on him,
When he beſtrides the lazie puffing Cloudes,
And ſailes vpon the boſome of the ayre.
Iul. O *Romeo, Romeo,* wherefore art thou *Romeo*?
Denie thy Father and refuſe thy name:
Or if thou wilt not, be but ſworne my Loue,
And Ile no longer be a *Capulet*.
Rom. Shall I heare more, or ſhall I ſpeake at this?
Iu. 'Tis but thy name that is my Enemy:
Thou art thy ſelfe, though not a *Mountague*,
What's *Mountague*? it is nor hand nor foote,
Nor arme, nor face, O be ſome other name
Belonging to a man.
What? in a names that which we call a Roſe,
By any other word would ſmell as ſweete,
So *Romeo* would, were he not *Romeo* cal'd,
Retaine that deare perfection which he owes,
Without that title *Romeo*, doffe thy name,
And for thy name which is no part of thee,
Take all my ſelfe.
Rom. I take thee at thy word:
Call me but Loue, and Ile be new baptiz'd,
Hence foorth I neuer will be *Romeo*.
Iuli. What man art thou, that thus beſcreen'd in night
So ſtumbleſt on my counſell?
Rom. By a name,
I know not how to tell thee who I am:
My name deare Saint, is hatefull to my ſelfe,
Becauſe it is an Enemy to thee,
Had I it written, I would teare the word.
Iuli. My eares haue yet not drunke a hundred words
Of thy tongues vttering, yet I know the ſound.
Art thou not *Romeo*, and a *Montague*?
Rom. Neither faire Maid, if either thee diſlike.
Iul. How cam'ſt thou hither,
Tell me, and wherefore?
The Orchard walls are high, and hard to climbe,
And the place death, conſidering who thou art,
If any of my kinſmen find thee here,
Rom. With Loues light wings
Did I ore-perch theſe Walls,
For ſtony limits cannot hold Loue out,
And what Loue can do, that dares Loue attempt:
Therefore thy kinſmen are no ſtop to me.
Iul. If they do ſee thee, they will murther thee.
Rom. Alacke there lies more perill in thine eye,
Then twenty of their Swords, looke thou but ſweete,
And I am proofe againſt their enmity.
Iul. I would not for the world they ſaw thee here.
Rom. I haue nights cloake to hide me from their eyes
And but thou loue me, let them finde me here,
My life were better ended by their hate,
Then death proroged wanting of thy Loue.
Iul. By whoſe direction found'ſt thou out this place?
Rom. By Loue that firſt did promp me to enquire,
He lent me counſell, and I lent him eyes,
I am no Pylot, yet wert thou as far
As that vaſt-ſhore-waſhet with the fartheſt Sea,
I ſhould aduenture for ſuch Marchandiſe.
Iul. Thou knoweſt the maske of night is on my face,
Elſe would a Maiden bluſh bepaint my cheeke,
For that which thou haſt heard me ſpeake to night,
Faine would I dwell on forme, faine, faine, denie
What I haue ſpoke, but farewell Complement,
Doeſt thou Loue? I know thou wilt ſay I,
And

And I will take thy word, yet it thou swear'st,
Thou maiest proue false: at Louers periuries
They say *Ioue* laught, oh gentle *Romeo*,
If thou dost Loue, pronounce it faithfully :
Or if thou thinkest I am too quickly woone,
Ile frowne and be peruerse, and say thee nay,
So thou wilt wooe : But else not for the world.
In truth faire *Mountague* I am too fond :
And therefore thou maiest thinke my behauiour light,
But trust me Gentleman, Ile proue more true,
Then those that haue coying to be strange,
I should haue beene more strange, I must confesse,
But that thou ouer heard'st ere I was ware
My true Loues passion, therefore pardon me,
And not impute this yeelding to light Loue,
Which the darke night hath so discouered.
Rom. Lady, by yonder Moone I vow,
That tips with siluer all these Fruite tree tops.
Iul. O sweare not by the Moone, th'inconstant Moone,
That monethly changes in her circled Orbe,
Least that thy Loue proue likewise variable.
Rom. What shall I sweare by ?
Iul. Do not sweare at all :
Or if thou wilt sweare by thy gratious selfe,
Which is the God of my Idolatry,
And Ile beleeue thee.
Rom. If my hearts deare loue.
Iuli. Well do not sweare, although I ioy in thee:
I haue no ioy of this contract to night,
It is too rash, too vnaduis'd, too sudden,
Too like the lightning which doth cease to be
Ere, one can say, it lightens, Sweete good night:
This bud of Loue by Summers ripening breath,
May proue a beautious Flower when next we meete:
Goodnight, goodnight, as sweete repose and rest,
Come to thy heart, as that within my brest.
Rom. O wilt thou leaue me so vnsatisfied ?
Iuli. What satisfaction can'st thou haue to night ?
Ro. Th'exchange of thy Loues faithfull vow for mine.
Iul. I gaue thee mine before thou did'st request it :
And yet I would it were to giue againe.
Rom. Would'st thou withdraw it,
For what purpose Loue ?
Iul. But to be franke and giue it thee againe,
And yet I wish but for the thing I haue,
My bounty is as boundlesse as the Sea,
My Loue as deepe, the more I giue to thee
The more I haue, for both are Infinite :
I heare some noyse within deare Loue adue :
Cals within.
Anon good Nurse, sweet *Mountague* be true :
Stay but alittle, I will come againe.
Rom. O blessed blessed night, I am afear'd
Being in night, all this is but a dreame,
Too flattering sweet to be substantiall.
Iul. Three words deare *Romeo*,
And goodnight indeed,
If that thy bent of Loue be Honourable,
Thy purpose marriage, send me word to morrow,
By one that Ile procure to come to thee,
Where and what time thou wilt performe the right,
And all my Fortunes at thy foote Ile lay,
And follow thee my Lord throughout the world.
Within : Madam.
I come, anon : but if thou meanest not well,
I do beseech theee *Within*: Madam.
(By and by I come)
To cease thy strife, and leaue me to my griefe,
To morrow will I send.
Rom. So thriue my soule.
Iu. A thousand times goodnight. *Exit.*
Rome. A thousand times the worse to want thy light,
Loue goes toward Loue as school-boyes frō thier books
But Loue frō Loue, towards schoole with heauie lookes.

Enter Iuliet againe.

Iul. Hist *Romeo* hist: O for a Falkners voice,
To lure this Tassell gentle backe againe,
Bondage is hoarse, and may not speake aloud,
Else would I teare the Caue where Eccho lies,
And make her ayrie tongue more hoarse, then
With repetition of my *Romeo*.
Rom. It is my soule that calls vpon my name.
How siluer sweet, sound Louers tongues by night,
Like softest Musicke to attending eares.
Iul. *Romeo.*
Rom. My Neece.
Iul. What a clock to morrow
Shall I send to thee?
Rom. By the houre of nine.
Iul. I will not faile, 'tis twenty yeares till then,
I haue forgot why I did call thee backe.
Rom. Let me stand here till thou remember it.
Iul. I shall forget, to haue thee still stand there,
Remembring how I Loue thy company.
Rom. And Ile still stay, to haue thee still forget,
Forgetting any other home but this.
Iul. 'Tis almost morning, I would haue thee gone,
And yet no further then a wantons Bird,
That let's it hop a little from his hand,
Like a poore prisoner in his twisted Gyues,
And with a silken thred plucks it backe againe,
So louing Iealous of his liberty.
Rom. I would I were thy Bird.
Iul. Sweet so would I,
Yet I should kill thee with much cherishing:
Good night, good night.
Rom. Parting is such sweete sorrow,
That I shall say goodnight, till it be morrow.
Iul. Sleepe dwell vpon thine eyes, peace in thy brest.
Rom. Would I were sleepe and peace so sweet to rest,
The gray ey'd morne smiles on the frowning night,
Checkring the Easterne Clouds with streakes of light,
And darknesse fleckel'd like a drunkard reeles,
From forth dayes pathway, made by *Titans* wheeles.
Hence will I to my ghostly Fries close Cell,
His helpe to craue, and my deare hap to tell. *Exit.*

Enter Frier alone with a basket.

Fri. The gray ey'd morne smiles on the frowning night,
Checkring the Easterne Cloudes with streaks of light :
And fleckled darknesse like a drunkard reeles,
From forth daies path, and *Titans* burning wheeles :
Now ere the Sun aduance his burning eye,
The day to cheere, and nights danke dew to dry,
I must vpfill this Osier Cage of ours,
With balefull weedes, and precious Iuiced flowers,
The earth that's Natures mother, is her Tombe,
What is her burying graue that is her wombe :
And from her wombe children of diuers kind
We

We ſucking on her naturall boſome find:
Many for many vertues excellent:
None but for ſome, and yet all different.
Omickle is the powerfull grace that lies
In Plants, Hearbs, ſtones, and their true qualities:
For nought ſo vile, that on the earth doth liue,
But to the earth ſome ſpeciall good doth giue.
Nor ought ſo good, but ſtrain'd from that faire vſe,
Reuolts from true birth, ſtumbling on abuſe.
Vertue it ſelfe turnes vice being miſapplied,
And vice ſometime by action dignified.

Enter Romeo.

Within the infant rin'd of this weake flower,
Poyſon hath reſidence, and medicine power:
For this being ſmelt, with that part cheares each part,
Being taſted ſlayes all ſences with the heart.
Two ſuch oppoſed Kings encampe them ſtill,
In man as well as Hearbes grace and rude will:
And where the worſer is predominant,
Full ſoone the Canker death eates vp that Plant.

Rom. Good morrow Father.

Fri. Benedecite.
What early tongue ſo ſweet ſaluteth me?
Young Sonne, it argues a diſtempered head,
So ſoone to bid goodmorrow to thy bed;
Care keepes his watch in euery old mans eye,
And where Care lodges, ſleepe will neuer lye:
But where vnbruſed youth with vnſtuft braine
Doth couch his lims, there, golden ſleepe doth raigne;
Therefore thy earlineſſe doth me aſſure,
Thou art vprous'd with ſome diſtemprature;
Or if not ſo, then here I hit it right.
Our *Romeo* hath not beene in bed to night.

Rom That laſt is true, the ſweeter reſt was mine.

Fri. God pardon ſin: waſt thou with *Roſaline*?

Rom. With *Roſaline*, my ghoſtly Father? No,
I haue forgot that name, and that names woe.

Fri. That's my good Son, but wher haſt thou bin then?

Rom Ile tell thee ere thou aske it me agen.
I haue beene feaſting with mine enemie,
Where on a ſudden one hath wounded me,
That's by me wounded: both our remedies
Within thy helpe and holy phiſicke lies:
I beare no hatred, bleſſed man: for loe
My interceſſion likewiſe ſteads my foe.

Fri. Be plaine good Son, reſt homely in thy drift,
Ridling confeſſion, findes but ridling ſhrift.

Rom. Then plainly know my hearts deare Loue is ſet,
On the faire daughter of rich *Capulet*;
As mine on hers, ſo hers is ſet on mine;
And all combin'd, ſaue what thou muſt combine
By holy marriage: when and where, and how,
We met, we wooed, and made exchange of vow:
Ile tell thee as we paſſe, but this I pray,
That thou conſent to marrie vs to day.

Fri. Holy S. *Francis*, what a change is heere?
Is *Roſaline* that thou didſt Loue ſo deare
So ſoone forſaken? young mens Loue then lies
Not truely in their hearts, but in their eyes.
Ieſu *Maria*, what a deale of brine
Hath waſht thy ſallow cheekes for *Roſaline*?
How much ſalt water throwne away in waſt,
To ſeaſon Loue that of it doth not taſt.
The Sun not yet thy ſighes, from heauen cleares,
Thy old grones yet ringing in my auncient eares:
Lo here vpon thy cheeke the ſtaine doth ſit,
Of an old teare that is not waſht off yet.
If ere thou waſt thy ſelfe, and theſe woes thine,
Thou and theſe woes, were all for *Roſaline*.
And art thou chang'd? pronounce this ſentence then,
Women may fall, when there's no ſtrength in men.

Rom. Thou chid'ſt me oft for louing *Roſaline*.

Fri. For doting, not for louing pupill mine.

Rom. And bad'ſt me bury Loue.

Fri. Not in a graue,
To lay one in, another out to haue.

Rom. I pray thee chide me not, her I Loue now
Doth grace for grace, and Loue for Loue allow:
The other did not ſo.

Fri. O ſhe knew well,
Thy Loue did read by rote, that could not ſpell:
But come young wauerer, come goe with me,
In one reſpect, Ile thy aſſiſtant be:
For this alliance may ſo happy proue,
To turne your houſhould rancor to pure Loue.

Rom. O let vs hence, I ſtand on ſudden haſt.

Fri. Wiſely and ſlow, they ſtumble that run faſt.

Exeunt

Enter Benuolio and Mercutio.

Mer. Where the deule ſhould this *Romeo* be? came he not home to night?

Ben. Not to his Fathers, I ſpoke with his man.

Mer. Why that ſame pale hard-harted wench, that *Roſaline* torments him ſo, that he will ſure run mad.

Ben. *Tibalt*, the kinſman to old *Capulet*, hath ſent a Letter to his Fathers houſe.

Mer. A challenge on my life.

Ben. *Romeo* will anſwere it.

Mer. Any man that can write, may anſwere a Letter.

Ben. Nay, he will anſwere the Letters Maiſter how he dares, being dared.

Mer Alas poore *Romeo*, he is already dead ſtab'd with a white wenches blacke eye, runne through the eare with a Loue ſong, the very pinne of his heart, cleft with the blind Bowe-boyes but-ſhaft, and is he a man to encounter *Tybalt*?

Ben. Why what is *Tibalt*?

Mer. More then Prince of Cats. Oh hee's the Couragious Captaine of Complements: he fights as you ſing prickſong, keeps time, diſtance, and proportion, he reſts his minum, one, two, and the third in your boſom: the very butcher of a ſilk button a Dualiſt, a Dualiſt: a Gentleman of the very firſt houſe of the firſt and ſecond cauſe: ah the immortall Paſſado the Punto reuerſo, the Hay.

Ben. The what?

Mer. The Pox of ſuch antique liſping affecting phantacies, theſe new tuners of accent: Ieſu a very good blade, a very tall man, a very good whore. Why is not this a lamentable thing Grandſire, that we ſhould be thus afflicted with theſe ſtrange flies: theſe faſhion Mongers, theſe pardon-mee's, who ſtand ſo much on the new form, that they cannot ſit at eaſe on the old bench. O their bones, their bones.

Enter Romeo.

Ben. Here comes *Romeo*, here comes *Romeo*.

Mer. Without his Roe, like a dryed Hering. O fleſh, fleſh, how art thou fiſhified? Now is he for the numbers that *Petrarch* flowed in: *Laura* to his Lady, was a kitchen wench, marrie ſhe had a better Loue to berime her: *Dido* a dowdie, *Cleopatra* a Gipſie, *Hellen* and *Hero*, hildings and Harlots: *Thisbie* a gray eie or ſo, but not to the purpoſe. Signior *Romeo*, *Bon iour*, there's a French ſalutation to your

ff French

French ſlop: you gaue vs the the counterfait fairely laſt night.

Romeo. Good morrow to you both, what counterfeit did I giue you?

Mer. The ſlip ſir, the ſlip, can you not conceiue?

Rom. Pardon *Mercutio*, my buſineſſe was great, and in ſuch a caſe as mine, a man may ſtraine curteſie.

Mer. That's as much as to ſay, ſuch a caſe as yours conſtrains a man to bow in the hams.

Rom. Meaning to curſie.

Mer. Thou haſt moſt kindly hit it.

Rom. A moſt curteous expoſition.

Mer. Nay, I am the very pinck of curteſie.

Rom. Pinke for flower.

Mer. Right.

Rom. Why then is my Pump well flowr'd.

Mer. Sure wit, follow me this ieaſt, now till thou haſt worne out thy Pump, that when the ſingle ſole of it is worne, the ieaſt may remaine after the wearing, ſole-ſingular.

Rom. O ſingle ſol'd ieaſt,
Soly ſingular for the ſingleneſſe.

Mer. Come betweene vs good *Benuolio*, my wits faints.

Rom Swits and ſpurs,
Swits and ſpurs, or Ile crie a match.

Mer. Nay, if our wits run the Wild-Gooſe chaſe, I am done: For thou haſt more of the Wild-Gooſe in one of thy wits, then I am ſure I haue in my whole fiue. Was I with you there for the Gooſe?

Rom. Thou waſt neuer with mee for any thing, when thou waſt not there for the Gooſe.

Mer. I will bite thee by the eare for that ieſt.

Rom. Nay, good Gooſe bite not.

Mer. Thy wit is a very Bitter-ſweeting,
It is a moſt ſharpe ſawce.

Rom. And is it not well ſeru'd into a Sweet-Gooſe?

Mer. Oh here's a wit of Cheuerell, that ſtretches from vnch narrow, to an ell broad.

Rom. I ſtretch it out for that word, broad, which added to the Gooſe, proues thee farre and wide, abroad Gooſe.

Mer. Why is not this better now, then groning for Loue, now art thou ſociable, now art thou *Romeo*: now art thou what thou art by Art as well as by Nature, for this driueling Loue is like a great Naturall, that runs lolling vp and downe to hid his bable in a hole.

Ben. Stop there, ſtop there.

Mer. Thou deſir'ſt me to ſtop in my tale againſt the haire.

Ben. Thou would'ſt elſe haue made thy tale large.

Mer. O thou art deceiu'd, I would haue made it ſhort, or I was come to the whole depth of my tale, and meant indeed to occupie the argument no longer.

Enter Nurſe and her man.

Rom. Here's goodly geare.
A ſayle, a ſayle.

Mer. Two, two: a Shirt and a Smocke.

Nur. *Peter?*

Peter. Anon.

Nur. My Fan *Peter?*

Mer. Good *Peter* to hide her face?
For her Fans the fairer face?

Nur. God ye good morrow Gentlemen.

Mer God ye gooden faire Gentlewoman.

Nur. Is it gooden?

Mer. Tis no leſſe I tell you: for the bawdy hand of the Dyall is now vpon the pricke of Noone.

Nur. Out vpon you: what a man are you?

Rom. One Gentlewoman,
That God hath made, himſelfe to mar.

Nur. By my troth it is ſaid, for himſelfe to, mar quatha Gentleman: can any of you tel me where I may find the young *Romeo?*

Romeo. I can tell you: but young *Romeo* will be older when you haue found him, then he was when you ſought him: I am the youngeſt of that name, for fault of a worſe.

Nur. You ſay well.

Mer. Yea is the worſt well,
Very well tooke: Iſaith, wiſely, wiſely.

Nur. If you be he ſir,
I deſire ſome confidence with you?

Ben. She will endite him to ſome Supper.

Mer. A baud, a baud, a baud. So ho.

Rom. What haſt thou found?

Mer. No Hare ſir, vnleſſe a Hare ſir in a Lenten pie, that is ſomething ſtale and hoare ere it be ſpent.
An old Hare hoare, and an old Hare hoare is very good meat in Lent.
But a Hare that is hoare is too much for a ſcore, when it hoares ere it be ſpent,
Romeo will you come to your Fathers? Weele to dinner thither.

Rom. I will follow you.

Mer. Farewell auncient Lady:
Farewell Lady, Lady, Lady.

Exit. Mercutio, Benuolio.

Nur. I pray you ſir, what ſawcie Merchant was this that was ſo full of his roperie?

Rom. A Gentleman Nurſe, that loues to heare himſelfe talke, and will ſpeake more in a minute, then he will ſtand to in a Moneth.

Nur. And a ſpeake any thing againſt me, Ile take him downe, & a were luſtier then he is, and twentie ſuch Iacks: and if I cannot, Ile finde thoſe that ſhall: ſcuruie knaue, I am none of his flurt-gils, I am none of his skaines mates, and thou muſt ſtand by too and ſuffer euery knaue to vſe me at his pleaſure.

Pet. I ſaw no man vſe you at his pleaſure: if I had, my weapon ſhould quickly haue beene out, I warrant you, I dare draw aſſoone as another man, if I ſee occaſion in a good quarrell, and the law on my ſide.

Nur. Now afore God, I am ſo vext, that euery part about me quiuers, skuruy knaue: pray you ſir a word: and as I told you, my young Lady bid me enquire you out, what ſhe bid me ſay, I will keepe to my ſelfe: but firſt let me tell ye, if ye ſhould leade her in a fooles paradiſe, as they ſay, it were a very groſſe kind of behauiour, as they ſay: for the Gentlewoman is yong: & therefore, if you ſhould deale double with her, truely it were an ill thing to be offered to any Gentlewoman, and very weake deſling.

Nur. Nurſe commend me to thy Lady and Miſtreſſe, I proteſt vnto thee.

Nur. Good heart, and yfaith I will tell her as much: Lord, Lord ſhe will be a ioyfull woman.

Rom. What wilt thou tell her Nurſe? thou doeſt not marke me?

Nur. I will tell her ſir, that you do proteſt, which as I take it, is a Gentleman-like offer.

Rom. Bid her deuiſe ſome meanes to come to ſhrift this afternoone,
And there ſhe ſhall at Frier *Lawrence* Cell
Beſhriu'd and married: here is for thy paines.

Nur. No truly ſir not a penny.

Rom. Go too, I ſay you ſhall.

Nurſe

Nur. This afternoone ſir? well ſhe ſhall be there.
Ro. And ſtay thou good Nurſe behind the Abbey wall,
Within this houre my man ſhall be with thee,
And bring thee Cords made like a tackled ſtaire,
Which to the high top gallant of my ioy,
Muſt be my conuoy in the ſecret night.
Farewell, be truſtie and Ile quite thy paines:
Farewell, commend me to thy Miſtreſſe.
Nur. Now God in heauen bleſſe thee: harke you ſir,
Rom. What ſaiſt thou my deare Nurſe?
Nurſe. Is your man ſecret, did you nere heare ſay two may keepe counſell putting one away.
Ro. Warrant thee my man as true as ſteele.
Nur. Well ſir, my Miſtreſſe is the ſweeteſt Lady, Lord, Lord, when 'twas a little prating thing. O there is a Noble man in Towne one *Paris*, that would faine lay knife aboard: but ſhe good ſoule had as leeue a ſee Toade, a very Toade as ſee him: I anger her ſometimes, and tell her that *Paris* is the properer man, but Ile warrant you, when I ſay ſo, ſhee lookes as pale as any clout in the verſall world. Doth not Roſemarie and *Romeo* begin both with a letter?
Rom. I Nurſe, what of that? Both with an *R*
Nur. A mocker that's the dogsname. *R.* is for the no, I know it begins with ſome other letter, and ſhe hath the pretties ſententious of it, of you and Roſemary, that it would do you good to heare it.
Rom. Commend me to thy Lady.
Nur. I a thouſand times. *Peter?*
Pet. Anon.
Nur. Before and apace. *Exit Nurſe and Peter.*

Enter Iuliet.

Iul. The clocke ſtrook nine, when I did ſend the Nurſe,
In halfe an houre ſhe promiſed to returne,
Perchance ſhe cannot meete him: that's not ſo:
Oh ſhe is lame, Loues Herauld ſhould be thoughts,
Which ten times faſter glides then the Sunnes beames,
Driuing backe ſhadowes ouer lowring hils.
Therefore do nimble Pinion'd Doues draw Loue,
And therefore hath the wind-ſwift *Cupid* wings:
Now is the Sun vpon the highmoſt hill
Of this daies iourney, and from nine till twelue,
I three long houres, yet ſhe is not come.
Had ſhe affections and warme youthfull blood,
She would be as ſwift in motion as a ball,
My words would bandy her to my ſweete Loue,
And his to me, but old folkes,
Many faine as they were dead,
Vnwieldie, ſlow, heauy, and pale as lead.

Enter Nurſe.

O God ſhe comes, O hony Nurſe what newes?
Haſt thou met with him? ſend thy man away.
Nur. *Peter* ſtay at the gate.
Iul. Now good ſweet Nurſe:
O Lord, why lookeſt thou ſad?
Though newes, be ſad, yet tell them merrily.
If good thou ſham'ſt the muſicke of ſweet newes,
By playing it to me, with ſo ſower a face.
Nur. I am a weary, giue me leaue awhile,
Fie how my bones ake, what a iaunt haue I had?
Iul. I would thou had'ſt my bones, and I thy newes:
Nay come I pray thee ſpeake, good good Nurſe ſpeake.
Nur. Ieſu what haſt? can you not ſtay a while?
Do you not ſee that I am out of breath?
Iul How art thou out of breath, when thou haſt breth
To ſay to me, that thou art out of breath?
The excuſe that thou doſt make in this delay,
Is longer then the tale thou doſt excuſe.
Is thy newes good or bad? anſwere to that,
Say either, and Ile ſtay the circuſtance:
Let me be ſatisfied, iſt good or bad?
Nur. Well, you haue made a ſimple choice, you know not how to chuſe a man: *Romeo*, no not he though his face be better then any mans, yet his legs excels all mens, and for a hand, and a foote, and a body, though they be not to be talkt on, yet they are paſt compare: he is not the flower of curteſie, but Ile warrant him as gentle a Lambe. go thy waies wench, ſerue God. What haue you din'd at home?
Iul. No no: but all this this did I know before
What ſaies he of our marriage? what of that?
Nur. Lord how my head akes, what a head haue I?
It beates as it would fall in twenty peeces.
My backe a tother ſide: o my backe, my backe:
Beſhrew your heart for ſending me about
To catch my death with iaunting vp and downe.
Iul. Ifaith: I am ſorrie that that thou art ſo well.
Sweet ſweet, ſweet Nurſe, tell me what ſaies my Loue?
Nur. Your Loue ſaies like an honeſt Gentleman,
And a courteous, and a kind, and a handſome,
And I warrant a vertuous: where is your Mother?
Iul. Where is my Mother?
Why ſhe is within, where ſhould ſhe be?
How odly thou repli'ſt:
Your Loue ſaies like an honeſt Gentleman:
Where is your Mother?
Nur. O Gods Lady deare,
Are you ſo hot? marrie come vp I trow,
Is this the Poultis for my aking bones?
Henceforward do your meſſages your ſelfe.
Iul. Heere's ſuch a coile, come what ſaies *Romeo?*
Nur. Haue you got leaue to go to ſhrift to day?
Iul. I haue.
Nur. Then high you hence to Frier *Lawrence* Cell,
There ſtaies a Husband to make you a wife:
Now comes the wanton bloud vp in your cheekes,
Thei'le be in Scarlet ſtraight at any newes:
Hie you to Church, I muſt an other way,
To fetch a Ladder by the which your Loue
Muſt climde a birds neſt Soone when it is darke:
I am the drudge, and toile in your delight:
But you ſhall beare the burthen ſoone at night.
Go Ile to dinner hie you to the Cell.
Iul. Hie to high Fortune, honeſt Nurſe, farewell. *Exeunt.*

Enter Frier and Romeo.

Fri. So ſmile the heauens vpon this holy act,
That after houres, with ſorrow chide vs not.
Rom. Amen, amen, but come what ſorrow can,
It cannot counteruaile the exchange of ioy
That one ſhort minute giues me in her ſight:
Do thou but cloſe our hands with holy words,
Then Loue-deuouring death do what he dare,
It is inough. I may but call her mine.
Fri. Theſe violent delights haue violent endes,
And in their triumph: die like fire and powder;
Which as they kiſſe conſume. The ſweeteſt honey
Is loathſome in his owne deliciouſneſſe,
And in the taſte confoundes the appetite.
Therefore Loue moderately, long Loue doth ſo,
Too ſwift arriues as tardie as too ſlow.

Enter Iuliet.

Here comes the Lady. Oh ſo light a foot
Will nere weare out the euerlaſting flint,

A Louer may beſtride the Goſſamours,
That ydles in the wanton Summer ayre,
And yet not fall,ſo light is vanitie.
Iul. Good euen to my ghoſtly Confeſſor.
Fri. Romeo ſhall thanke thee Daughter for vs both.
Iul. As much to him,elſe in his thanks too much.
Fri. Ah Iuliet,if the meaſure of thy ioy
Be heapt like mine,and that thy ſkill be more
To blaſon it,then ſweeten with thy breath
This neighbour ayre,and let rich muſickes tongue,
Vnfold the imagin'd happineſſe that both
Receiue in either,by this deere encounter.
Iul. Conceit more rich in matter then in words,
Brags of his ſubſtance,not of Ornament:
They are but beggers that can count their worth,
But my true Loue is growne to ſuch ſuch exceſſe,
I cannot ſum vp ſome of halfe my wealth.
Fri. Come,come with me,& we will make ſhort worke,
For by your leaues,you ſhall not ſtay alone,
Till holy Church incorporate two in one.
Enter Mercutio,Benuolio,and men.
Ben. I pray thee good Mercutio lets retire,
The day is hot,the Capulets abroad:
And if we meet, we ſhal not ſcape a brawle,for now theſe
hot dayes,is the mad blood ſtirring.
Mer. Thou art like one of theſe fellowes,that when he
enters the confines of a Tauerne,claps me his Sword vpon
the Table,and ſayes,God ſend me no need of thee: and by
the operation of the ſecond cup,drawes him on the Drawer,when indeed there is no need.
Ben. Am I like ſuch a Fellow?
Mer. Come,come,thou art as hot a Iacke in thy mood,
as any in Italie: and aſſoone moued to be moodie, and aſſoone moodie to be mou'd.
Ben. And what too?
Mer. Nay, and there were two ſuch, we ſhould haue
none ſhortly,for one would kill the other:thou, why thou
wilt quarrell with a man that hath a haire more, or a haire
leſſe in his beard,then thou haſt:thou wilt quarrell with a
man for cracking Nuts, hauing no other reaſon, but becauſe thou haſt haſell eyes: what eye, but ſuch an eye,
would ſpie out ſuch a quarrell? thy head is as full of quarrels,as an egge is full of meat, and yet thy head hath bin
beaten as addle as an egge for quarreling: thou haſt quarrel'd with a man for coffing in the ſtreet, becauſe he hath
wakened thy Dog that hath laine aſleepe in the Sun. Did'ſt
thou not fall out with a Tailor for wearing his new Doublet before Eaſter? with another,for tying his new ſhooes
with old Riband,and yet thou wilt Tutor me from quarrelling?
Ben. And I were ſo apt to quarell as thou art,any man
ſhould buy the Fee-ſimple of my life, for an houre and a
quarter.
Mer. The Fee-ſimple? O ſimple.
Enter Tybalt,Petruchio,and others.
Ben. By my head here comes the Capulets.
Mer. By my heele I care not.
Tyb. Follow me cloſe,for I will ſpeake to them.
Gentlemen,Good den,a word with one of you.
Mer. And but one word with one of vs? couple it with
ſomething,make it a word and a blow.
Tib. You ſhall find me apt inough to that ſir, and you
will giue me occaſion.
Mercu. Could you not take ſome occaſion without
giuing?
Tib. Mercutio thou conſort'ſt with Romeo.
Mer. Conſort? what doſt thou make vs Minſtrels? &
thou make Minſtrels of vs,looke to heare nothing but diſ-
cords: heere's my fiddleſticke,heere's that ſhall make you
daunce. Come conſort.
Ben. We talke here in the publike haunt of men
Either withdraw vnto ſome priuate place,
Or reaſon coldly of your greeuances:
Or elſe depart,here all eies gaze on vs.
Mer. Mens eyes were made to looke,and let them gaze.
I will not budge for no mans pleaſure I.
Enter Romeo.
Tib. Well peace be with you ſir,here comes my man
Mer. But Ile be hang'd ſir if he weare your Liuery.
Marry go before to field,heele be your follower,
Your worſhip in that ſenſe,may call him man.
Tib. Romeo,the loue I beare thee,can affoord
No better terme then this: Thou art a Villaine.
Rom. Tibalt,the reaſon that I haue to loue thee,
Doth much excuſe the appertaining rage
To ſuch a greeting: Villaine am I none;
Therefore farewell,I ſee thou know'ſt me not.
Tib. Boy,this ſhall not excuſe the iniuries
That thou haſt done me,therefore turne and draw.
Rom. I do proteſt I neuer iniur'd thee,
But lou'd thee better then thou can'ſt deuiſe:
Till thou ſhalt know the reaſon of my loue,
And ſo good Capulet,which name I tender
As dearely as my owne,be ſatisfied.
Mer. O calme,diſhonourable,vile ſubmiſſion:
Alla ſtucatho carries it away.
Tybalt,you Rat-catcher,will you walke?
Tib. What wouldſt thou haue with me?
Mer. Good King of Cats,nothing but one of your nine
liues,that I meane to make bold withall,and as you ſhall
vſe me hereafter dry beate the reſt of the eight. Will you
pluck your Sword out of his Pilcher by the eares? Make
haſt,leaſt mine be about your eares ere it be out.
Tib. I am for you.
Rom. Gentle Mercutio,put thy Rapier vp.
Mer. Come ſir,your Paſſado.
Rom. Draw Benuolio,beat downe their weapons:
Gentlemen,for ſhame forbeare this outrage,
Tibalt,Mercutio,the Prince expreſly hath
Forbidden bandying in Verona ſtreetes.
Hold Tybalt,good Mercutio.
Exit Tybalt.
Mer. I am hurt.
A plague a both the Houſes,I am ſped:
Is he gone and hath nothing?
Ben. What art thou hurt?
Mer. I,I,a ſcratch,a ſcratch,marry 'tis inough,
Where is my Page? go Villaine fetch a Surgeon.
Rom. Courage man,the hurt cannot be much.
Mer. No: 'tis not ſo deepe as a well, nor ſo wide as a
Church doore,but 'tis inough, 'twill ſerue: aske for me to
morrow,and you ſhall find me a graue man. I am pepper'd
I warrant,for this world: a plague a both your houſes.
What, a Dog, a Rat, a Mouſe,a Cat to ſcratch a man to
death: a Braggart,a Rogue,a Villaine, that fights by the
booke of Arithmeticke, why the deu'le came you be-
tweene vs? I was hurt vnder your arme.
Rom. I thought all for the beſt.
Mer. Helpe me into ſome houſe Benuolio,
Or I ſhall faint: a plague a both your houſes.
They haue made wormes meat of me,
I

I haue it, and ſoundly to your Houſes. *Exit.*

Rom. This Gentleman the Princes neere Alie,
My very Friend hath got his mortall hurt
In my behalfe, my reputation ſtain'd
With *Tybalts* ſlaunder, *Tybalt* that an houre
Hath beene my Cozin: O Sweet *Iuliet*,
Thy Beauty hath made me Effeminate,
And in my temper ſoftned Valours ſteele.

Enter Bennolio.

Ben. O Romeo, Romeo, braue *Mercutio's* is dead,
That Gallant ſpirit hath aſpir'd the Cloudes,
Which too vntimely here did ſcorne the earth.

Rom. This daies blacke Fate, on mo daies doth depend,
This but begins, the wo others muſt end.

Enter Tybalt.

Ben. Here comes the Furious *Tybalt* backe againe.

Rom. He gon in triumph, and *Mercutio* ſlaine?
Away to heauen reſpectiue Lenitie,
And fire and Fury, be my conduct now.
Now *Tybalt* take the Villaine backe againe
That late thou gau'ſt me, for *Mercutios* ſoule
Is but a little way aboue our heads,
Staying for thine to keepe him companie:
Either thou or I, or both, muſt goe with him.

Tib. Thou wretched Boy that didſt conſort him here,
Shalt with him hence.

Rom. This ſhall determine that.

They fight. Tybalt falles.

Ben. Romeo, away be gone:
The Citizens are vp, and *Tybalt* ſlaine,
Stand not amaz'd, the Prince will Doome thee death
If thou art taken: hence, be gone, away.

Rom. O! I am Fortunes foole.

Ben. Why doſt thou ſtay?

Exit Romeo.

Enter Citizens.

Citi. Which way ran he that kild *Mercutio*?
Tibalt that Murtherer, which way ran he?

Ben. There lies that *Tybalt*.

Citi. Vp ſir go with me:
I charge thee in the Princes names obey.

Enter Prince, old Montague, Capulet, their Wiues and all.

Prin. Where are the vile beginners of this Fray?

Ben. O Noble Prince, I can diſcouer all
The vnluckie Mannage of this fatall brall:
There lies the man ſlaine by young *Romeo*,
That ſlew thy kinſman braue *Mercutio*.

Cap. Wi. *Tybalt*, my Cozin? O my Brothers Child,
O Prince, O Cozin, Husband, O the blood is ſpild
Of my deare kinſman. Prince as thou art true,
For bloud of ours, ſhed bloud of *Mountague*.
O Cozin, Cozin.

Prin. Benuolio, who began this Fray?

Ben. *Tybalt* here ſlaine, whom *Romeo's* hand did ſlay,
Romeo that ſpoke him faire, bid him bethinke
How nice the Quarrell was, and vrg'd withall
Your high diſpleaſure: all this vttered,
With gentle breath, calme looke, knees humbly bow'd
Could not take truce with the vnruly ſpleene
Of *Tybalts* deafe to peace, but that he Tilts
With Peireing ſteele at bold *Mercutio's* breaſt,
Who all as hot, turnes deadly point to point,
And with a Martiall ſcorne, with one hand beates
Cold death aſide, and with the other ſends
It back to *Tybalt*, whoſe dexterity
Retorts it: *Romeo* he cries aloud,
Hold Friends, Friends part, and ſwifter then his tongue,
His aged arme, beats downe their fatall points,
And twixt them ruſhes, vnderneath whoſe arme,
An enuious thruſt from *Tybalt*, hit the life
Of ſtout *Mercutio*, and then *Tybalt* fled.
But by and by comes backe to *Romeo*,
Who had but newly entertained Reuenge,
And too't they goe like lightning, for ere I
Could draw to part them, was ſtout *Tybalt* ſlaine:
And as he fell, did *Romeo* turne and flie:
This is the truth, or let *Benuolio* die.

Cap. Wi. He is a kinſman to the *Mountague*,
Affection makes him falſe, he ſpeakes not true:
Some twenty of them fought in this blacke ſtrife,
And all thoſe twenty could but kill one life.
I beg for Iuſtice, which thou Prince muſt giue:
Romeo ſlew *Tybalt*, *Romeo* muſt not liue.

Prin. Romeo ſlew him, he ſlew *Mercutio*,
Who now the price of his deare blood doth owe.

Cap. Not *Romeo* Prince, he was *Mercutios* Friend,
His fault concludes, but what the law ſhould end,
The life of *Tybalt*.

Prin. And for that offence,
Immediately we doe exile him hence:
I haue an intereſt in your hearts proceeding:
My bloud for your rude brawles doth lie a bleeding.
But Ile Amerce you with ſo ſtrong a fine,
That you ſhall all repent the loſſe of mine.
It will be deafe to pleading and excuſes,
Nor teares, nor prayers ſhall purchaſe our abuſes.
Therefore vſe none, let *Romeo* hence in haſt,
Elſe when he is found, that houre is his laſt.
Beare hence this body, and attend our will:
Mercy not Murders, pardoning thoſe that kill.

Exeunt.

Enter Iuliet alone.

Iul. Gallop apace, you fiery footed ſteedes,
Towards *Phœbus* lodging, ſuch a Wagoner
As *Phaeton* would whip you to the weſt,
And bring in Cloudie night immediately.
Spred thy cloſe Curtaine Loue-performing night,
That run-awayes eyes may wincke, and *Romeo*
Leape to theſe armes, vntalkt of and vnſeene,
Louers can ſee to doe their Amorous rights,
And by their owne Beauties: or if Loue be blind,
It beſt agrees with night: come ciuill night,
Thou ſober ſuted Matron all in blacke,
And learne me how to looſe a winning match,
Plaid for a paire of ſtainleſſe Maidenhoods,
Hood my vnman'd blood bayting in my Cheekes,
With thy Blacke mantle, till ſtrange Loue grow bold,
Thinke true Loue acted ſimple modeſtie:
Come night, come *Romeo*, come thou day in night,
For thou wilt lie vpon the wings of night
Whiter then new Snow vpon a Rauens backe:
Come gentle night, come louing blackebrow'd night.
Giue me my *Romeo*, and when I ſhall die,
Take him and cut him out in little ſtarres,
And he will make the Face of heauen ſo fine,
That all the world will be in Loue with night,
And pay no worſhip to the Gariſh Sun.
O I haue bought the Manſion of a Loue,
But not poſſeſt it, and though I am ſold,
Not yet enioy'd, ſo tedious is this day,
As is the night before ſome Feſtiuall,

ff 3 To

To an impatient child that hath new robes
And may not weare them, O here comes my Nurſe.
Enter Nurſe with cords.
And ſhe brings newes and euery tongue that ſpeaks
But *Romeos*, name, ſpeakes heauenly eloquence:
Now Nurſe, what newes? what haſt thou there?
The Cords that *Romeo* bid thee fetch?
Nur. I, I, the Cords.
Iuli. Ay me, what newes?
Why doſt thou wring thy hands.
Nur. A weladay, hee's dead, hee's dead,
We are vndone Lady, we are vndone.
Alacke the day, hee's gone, hee's kil'd, he's dead.
Iul. Can heauen be ſo enuious?
Nur. *Romeo* can,
Though heauen cannot. O *Romeo, Romeo*.
Who euer would haue thought it *Romeo*.
Iuli. What diuell art thou,
That doſt torment me thus?
This torture ſhould be roar'd in diſmall hell,
Hath *Romeo* ſlaine himſelfe? ſay thou but I,
And that bare vowell I ſhall poyſon more
Then the death-darting eye of Cockatrice,
I am not I, if there be ſuch an I.
Or thoſe eyes ſhot, that makes thee anſwere I:
If he be ſlaine ſay I, or if not, no.
Briefe, ſounds, determine of my weale or wo.
Nur. I ſaw the wound, I ſaw it with mine eyes,
God ſaue the marke, here on his manly breſt,
A pitteous Coarſe, a bloody piteous Coarſe:
Pale, pale as aſhes, all bedawb'd in blood,
All in gore blood, I ſounded at the ſight.
Iul O breake my heart,
Poore Banckrout breake at once,
To priſon eyes, nere looke on libertie.
Vile earth to earth reſigne, end motion here,
And thou and *Romeo* preſſe on heauie beere.
Nur. O *Tybalt, Tybalt*, the beſt Friend I had:
O curteous *Tybalt* honeſt Gentleman,
That euer I ſhould liue to ſee thee dead.
Iul What ſtorme is this that blowes ſo contrarie?
Is *Romeo* ſlaughtred? and is *Tybalt* dead?
My deareſt Cozen, and my dearer Lord:
Then dreadfull Trumpet ſound the generall doome,
For who is liuing, if thoſe two are gone?
Nur. *Tybalt* is gone, and *Romeo* baniſhed,
Romeo that kil'd him, he is baniſhed.
Iul. O God!
Did *Rom'os* hand ſhed *Tybalts* blood
It did, it did, alas the day, it did.
Nur. O Serpent heart, hid with a flowring face.
Iul. Did euer Dragon keepe ſo faire a Caue?
Beautifull Tyrant, fiend Angelicall:
Rauenous Doue-feather'd Rauen,
Woluiſh-rauening Lambe,
Diſpiſed ſubſtance of Diuineſt ſhow:
Iuſt oppoſite to what thou iuſtly ſeem'ſt,
A dimne Saint, an Honourable Villaine:
O Nature! what had'ſt thou to doe in hell,
When thou did'ſt bower the ſpirit of a fiend
In mortall paradiſe of ſuch ſweet fleſh?
Was euer booke containing ſuch vile matter
So fairely bound? O that deceit ſhould dwell
In ſuch a gorgeous Pallace.
Nur. There's no truſt, no faith, no honeſtie in men,
All periur'd, all forſworne, all naught, all diſſemblers,
Ah where's my man? giue me ſome Aqua-vitæ?
Theſe griefes, theſe woes, theſe ſorrowes make me old:
Shame come to *Romeo*.
Iul. Bliſter'd be thy tongue
For ſuch a wiſh, he was not borne to ſhame:
Vpon his brow ſhame is aſham'd to ſit;
For 'tis a throane where Honour may be Crown'd
Sole Monarch of the vniuerſall earth:
O what a beaſt was I to chide him?
Nur. Will you ſpeake well of him,
That kil'd your Cozen?
Iul. Shall I ſpeake ill of him that is my husband?
Ah poore my Lord, what tongue ſhall ſmooth thy name,
When I thy three houres wife haue mangled it.
But wherefore Villaine did'ſt thou kill my Cozin?
That Villaine Cozin would haue kil'd my husband:
Backe fooliſh teares, backe to your natiue ſpring,
Your tributarie drops belong to woe,
Which you miſtaking offer vp to ioy:
My husband liues that *Tibalt* would haue ſlaine,
And *Tibalt* dead that would haue ſlaine my husband:
All this is comfort, wherefore weepe I then?
Some words there was worſer then *Tybalts* death
That murdered me, I would forget it feine,
But oh, it preſſes to my memory,
Like damned guilty deedes to ſinners minds,
Tybalt is dead and *Romeo* baniſhed:
That baniſhed, that one word baniſhed,
Hath ſlaine ten thouſand *Tibalts*: *Tibalts* death
Was woe inough if it had ended there:
Or if ſower woe delights in fellowſhip,
And needly will be rankt with other griefes,
Why followed not when ſhe ſaid *Tibalts* dead,
Thy Father or thy Mother, nay or both,
Which moderne lamentation might haue mou'd.
But which a rere-ward following *Tybalts* death
Romeo is baniſhed to ſpeake that word,
Is Father, Mother, *Tybalt, Romeo, Iuliet*,
All ſlaine, all dead. *Romeo* is baniſhed,
There is no end, no limit, meaſure, bound,
In that words death, no words can that woe ſound.
Where is my Father and my Mother Nurſe?
Nur. Weeping and wailing ouer *Tybalts* Coarſe,
Will you go to them? I will bring you thither.
Iu. Waſh they his wounds with tears: mine ſhal be ſpent
When theirs are drie for *Romeo's* baniſhment.
Take vp thoſe Cordes, poore ropes you are beguil'd,
Both you and I for *Romeo* is exild:
He made you for a high-way to my bed,
But I a Maid, die Maiden widowed.
Come Cord, come Nurſe, Ile to my wedding bed,
And death not *Romeo*, take my Maiden head.
Nur. Hie to your Chamber, Ile find *Romeo*
To comfort you, I wot well where he is:
Harke ye your *Romeo* will be heere at night,
Ile to him, he is hid at *Lawrence* Cell.
Iul. O find him, giue this Ring to my true Knight,
And bid him come, to take his laſt farewell.
Exit.

Enter Frier and Romeo.

Fri. *Romeo* come forth,
Come forth thou fearfull man,
Affliction is enamor'd of thy parts:
And thou art wedded to calamitie.
Rom. Father what newes?
What

What is the Princes Doome?
What ſorrow craues acquaintance at my hand,
That I yet know not?
Fri. Too familiar
Is my deare Sonne with ſuch ſowre Company:
I bring thee tydings of the Princes Doome.
Rom. What leſſe then Doomeſday,
Is the Princes Doome?
Fri. A gentler iudgement vaniſht from his lips,
Not bodies death, but bodies baniſhment.
Rom. Ha, baniſhment? be mercifull, ſay death:
For exile hath more terror in his looke,
Much more then death: do not ſay baniſhment.
Fri. Here from *Verona* art thou baniſhed:
Be patient, for the world is broad and wide.
Rom. There is no world without *Verona* walles,
But Purgatorie, Torture, hell it ſelfe:
Hence baniſhed, is baniſht from the world,
And worlds exile is death. Then baniſhed,
Is death, miſtearm'd, calling death baniſhed,
Thou cut'ſt my head off with a golden Axe,
And ſmileſt vpon the ſtroke that murders me.
Fri. O deadly ſin, O rude vnthankefulneſſe!
Thy falt our Law calles death, but the kind Prince
Taking thy part, hath ruſht aſide the Law,
And turn'd that blacke word death, to baniſhment.
This is deare mercy, and thou ſeeſt it not.
Rom. 'Tis Torture and not mercy, heauen is here
Where *Iuliet* liues, and euery Cat and Dog,
And little Mouſe, euery vnworthy thing
Liue here in Heauen and may looke on her,
But *Romeo* may not. More Validitie,
More Honourable ſtate, more Courtſhip liues
In carrion Flies, then *Romeo*: they may ſeaze
On the white wonder of deare *Iuliets* hand,
And ſteale immortall bleſſing from her lips,
Who euen in pure and veſtall modeſtie
Still bluſh, as thinking their owne kiſſes ſin.
This may Flies doe, when I from this muſt flie,
And ſaiſt thou yet, that exile is not death?
But *Romeo* may not, hee is baniſhed.
Had'ſt thou no poyſon mixt, no ſharpe ground knife,
No ſudden meane of death, though nere ſo meane,
But baniſhed to kill me? Baniſhed?
O Frier, the damned vſe that word in hell:
Howlings attends it, how haſt thou the hart
Being a Diuine, a Ghoſtly Confeſſor,
A Sin-Abſoluer, and my Friend profeſt:
To mangle me with that word, baniſhed?
Fri. Then fond Mad man, heare me ſpeake.
Rom. O thou wilt ſpeake againe of baniſhment.
Fri. Ile giue thee Armour to keepe off that word,
Aduerſities ſweete milke, Philoſophie,
To comfort thee, though thou art baniſhed.
Rom. Yet baniſhed? hang vp Philoſophie:
Vnleſſe Philoſohpie can make a *Iuliet*,
Diſplant a Towne, reuerſe a Princes Doome,
It helpes not, it preuailes not, talke no more.
Fri. O then I ſee, that Mad men haue no eares.
Rom. How ſhould they,
When wiſemen haue no eyes?
Fri. Let me diſpaire with thee of thy eſtate,
Rom. Thou can'ſt not ſpeake of that yͭ doſt not feele,
Wert thou as young as *Iuliet* my Loue:
An houre but married, *Tybalt* murdered,
Doting like me, and like me baniſhed,
Then mighteſt thou ſpeake,
Then mighteſt thou teare thy hayre,
And fall vpon the ground as I doe now,
Taking the meaſure of an vnmade graue.
Enter Nurſe, and knockes.
Frier. Ariſe one knockes,
Good *Romeo* hide thy ſelfe.
Rom. Not I,
Vnleſſe the breath of Hartſicke groanes
Miſt-like infold me from the ſearch of eyes.
Knocke
Fri. Harke how they knocke:
(Who's there) *Romeo* ariſe,
Thou wilt be taken, ſtay a while, ſtand vp:
Knocke.
Run to my ſtudy: by and by, Gods will
What ſimpleneſſe is this. I come, I come.
Knocke
Who knocks ſo hard?
Whence come you? what's your will?
Enter Nurſe.
Nur. Let me come in,
And you ſhall know my errand:
I come from Lady *Iuliet*.
Fri. Welcome then.
Nur. O holy Frier, O tell me holy Frier,
Where's my Ladies Lord? where's *Romeo*?
Fri. There on the ground,
With his owne teares made drunke.
Nur. O he is euen in my Miſtreſſe caſe,
Iuſt in her caſe. O wofull ſimpathy:
Pittious predicament, euen ſo lies ſhe,
Blubbring and weeping, weeping and blubbring,
Stand vp, ſtand vp, ſtand and you be a man,
For *Iuliets* ſake, for her ſake riſe and ſtand:
Why ſhould you fall into ſo deepe an O.
Rom. Nurſe.
Nur. Ah ſir, ah ſir, deaths the end of all.
Rom. Speak'ſt thou of *Iuliet*? how is it with her?
Doth not ſhe thinke me an old Murtherer,
Now I haue ſtain'd the Childhood of our ioy,
With blood remoued, but little from her owne?
Where is ſhe? and how doth ſhe? and what ſayes
My conceal'd Lady to our conceal'd Loue?
Nur. Oh ſhe ſayes nothing ſir, but weeps and weeps,
And now fals on her bed, and then ſtarts vp,
And *Tybalt* calls, and then on *Romeo* cries,
And then downe falls againe.
Ro. As if that name ſhot from the dead leuell of a Gun,
Did murder her, as that names curſed hand
Murdred her kinſman. Oh tell me Frier, tell me,
In what vile part of this Anatomie
Doth my name lodge? Tell me, that I may ſacke
The hatefull Manſion.
Fri. Hold thy deſperate hand:
Art thou a man? thy forme cries out thou art:
Thy teares are womaniſh, thy wild acts denote
The vnreaſonable Furie of a beaſt.
Vnſeemely woman, in a ſeeming man,
And ill beſeeming beaſt in ſeeming both,
Thou haſt amaz'd me. By my holy order,
I thought thy diſpoſition better temper'd.
Haſt thou ſlaine *Tybalt*? wilt thou ſlay thy ſelfe?
And ſlay thy Lady, that in thy life lies,
By doing damned hate vpon thy ſelfe?
Why rayl'ſt thou on thy birth? the heauen and earth?
Since

Since birth, and heauen and earth, all three do meete
In thee at once, which thou at once would'st loose.
Fie, fie, thou sham'st thy shape, thy loue, thy wit,
Which like a Vsurer abound'st in all:
And vsest none in that true vse indeed,
Which should bedecke thy shape, thy loue, thy wit:
Thy Noble shape, is but a forme of waxe,
Digressing from the Valour of a man,
Thy deare Loue sworne but hollow periurie,
Killing that Loue which thou hast vow'd to cherish.
Thy wit, that Ornament, to shape and Loue,
Mishapen in the conduct of them both
Like powder in a skillesse Souldiers flaske,
Is set a fire by thine owne ignorance,
And thou dismembred with thine owne defence.
What, rowse thee man, thy *Iuliet* is aliue,
For whose deare sake thou wast but lately dead.
There art thou happy. *Tybalt* would kill thee,
But thou slew'st *Tybalt*, there art thou happie.
The law that threatned death became thy Friend,
And turn'd it to exile, there art thou happy.
A packe or blessing light vpon thy backe,
Happinesse Courts thee in her best array,
But like a mishaped and sullen wench,
Thou puttest vp thy Fortune and thy Loue:
Take heed, take heed, for such die miserable.
Goe get thee to thy Loue as was decreed,
Ascend her Chamber, hence and comfort her:
But looke thou stay not till the watch be set,
For then thou canst not passe to *Mantua*,
Where thou shalt liue till we can finde a time
To blaze your marriage, reconcile your Friends,
Beg pardon of thy Prince, and call thee backe,
With twenty hundred thousand times more ioy
Then thou went'st forth in lamentation.
Goe before Nurse, commend me to thy Lady,
And bid her hasten all the house to bed,
Which heauy sorrow makes them apt vnto.
Romeo is comming.

Nur. O Lord, I could haue staid here all night,
To heare good counsell: oh what learning is;
My Lord Ile tell my Lady you will come.

Rom. Do so, and bid my Sweete prepare to chide.

Nur. Heere sir, a Ring she bid me giue you sir:
Hie you, make hast, for it growes very late.

Rom. How well my comfort is reuiu'd by this.

Fri. Go hence,
Goodnight, and here stands all your state:
Either be gone before the watch be set,
Or by the breake of day disguis'd from hence,
Soiourne in *Mantua*, Ile find out your man,
And he shall signifie from time to time,
Euery good hap to you, that chaunces heere:
Giue me thy hand, 'tis late, farewell, goodnight.

Rom. But that a ioy past ioy, calls out on me,
It were a griefe, so briefe to part with thee:
Farewell. *Exeunt.*

Enter old Capulet, his Wife and Paris.

Cap. Things haue falne out sir so vnluckily,
That we haue had no time to moue our Daughter:
Looke you, she Lou'd her kinsman *Tybalt* dearely,
And so did I. Well, we were borne to die.
'Tis very late, she'l not come downe to night:
I promise you, but for your company,
I would haue bin a bed an houre ago.

Par. These times of wo, affoord no times to wooe:
Madam goodnight, commend me to your Daughter.

Lady. I will, and know her mind early to morrow,
To night, she is mewed vp to her heauinesse.

Cap. Sir *Paris*, I will make a desperate tender
Of my Childes loue: I thinke she will be rul'd
In all respects by me: nay more, I doubt it not.
Wife, go you to her ere you go to bed,
Acquaint her here, of my Sonne *Paris* Loue,
And bid her, marke you me, on Wendsday next,
But soft, what day is this?

Par. Monday my Lord.

Cap. Monday, ha ha: well Wendsday is too soone,
A Thursday let it be: a Thursday tell her,
She shall be married to this Noble Earle:
Will you be ready? do you like this hast?
Weele keepe no great adoe, a Friend or two,
For harke you, *Tybalt* being slaine so late,
It may be thought we held him carelesly,
Being our kinsman, if we reuell much:
Therefore weele haue some halfe a dozen Friends,
And there an end. But what say you to Thursday?

Paris. My Lord,
I would that Thursday were to morrow.

Cap. Well, get you gone, a Thursday, be it then:
Go you to *Iuliet* ere you go to bed,
Prepare her wife, against this wedding day.
Farewell my Lord, light to my Chamber hoa,
Afore me, it is so late, that we may call it early by and by,
Goodnight. *Exeunt*

Enter Romeo and Iuliet aloft.

Iul. Wilt thou be gone? It is not yet neere day:
It was the Nightingale, and not the Larke,
That pier'st the fearefull hollow of thine eare,
Nightly she sings on yond Pomgranet tree,
Beleeue me Loue, it was the Nightingale.

Rom. It was the Larke the Herauld of the Morne:
No Nightingale: looke Loue what enuious streakes
Do lace the seuering Cloudes in yonder East:
Nights Candles are burnt out, and Iocond day
Stands tipto on the mistie Mountaines tops,
I must be gone and liue, or stay and die.

Iul. Yond light is not daylight, I know it I:
It is some Meteor that the Sun exhales,
To be to thee this night a Torch-bearer,
And light thee on thy way to *Mantua*.
Therefore stay yet, thou need'st not to be gone.

Rom. Let me be tane, let me be put to death,
I am content, so thou wilt haue it so.
Ile say yon gray is not the mornings eye,
'Tis but the pale reflexe of *Cinthias* brow.
Nor that is not Larke whose noates do beate
The vaulty heauen so high aboue our heads,
I haue more care to stay, then will to go:
Come death and welcome, *Iuliet* wills it so.
How ist my soule, lets talke, it is not day.

Iuli. It is, it is, hie hence be gone away:
It is the Larke that sings so out of tune,
Straining harsh Discords, and vnpleasing Sharpes.
Some say the Larke makes sweete Diuision;
This doth not so: for she diuideth vs.
Some say, the Larke and loathed Toad change eyes,
O now I would they had chang'd voyces too:

s

Since arme from arme that voyce doth vs affray,
Hunting thee hence, with Hunt ſ-vp to the day,
O now be gone, more light and itlı ght growes.

Rom. More light & light, more darke & darke our woes.

Enter Madam and Nurſe.

Nur. Madam.

Iul. Nurſe.

Nur. Your Lady Mother is comming to your chamber,
The day is broke, be wary, looke about.

Iul. Then window let day in, and let life out.

Rom. Farewell, farewell, one kiſſe and Ile deſcend.

Iul. Art thou gone ſo? Loue, Lord, ay Husband, Friend,
I muſt heare from thee euery day in the houre,
For in a minute there are many dayes,
O by this count I ſhall be much in yeares,
Ere I againe behold my *Romeo*.

Rom. Farewell:
I will omit no oportunitie,
That may conuey my greetings Loue, to thee.

Iul. O thinkeſt thou we ſhall euer meet againe?

Rom. I doubt it not, and all theſe woes ſhall ſerue
For ſweet diſcourſes in our time to come.

Iuilet. O God! I haue an ill Diuining ſoule,
Me thinkes I ſee thee now, thou art ſo lowe,
As one dead in the bottome of a Tombe,
Either my eye-ſight failes, or thou look'ſt pale.

Rom. And truſt me Loue, in my eye ſo do you:
Drie ſorrow drinkes our blood. Adue, adue. *Exit.*

Iul. O Fortune, Fortune, all men call thee fickle,
If thou art fickle, what doſt thou with him
That is renown'd for faith? be fickle Fortune:
For then I hope thou wilt not keepe him long,
But ſend him backe.

Enter Mother.

Lad. Ho Daughter, are you vp?

Iul: Who iſt that calls? Is it my Lady Mother.
Is ſhe not downe ſo late, or vp ſo early?
What vnaccuſtom'd cauſe procures her hither?

Lad. Why how now *Iuliet*?

Iul. Madam I am not well.

Lad. Euermore weeping for your Cozins death?
What wilt thou waſh him from his graue with teares?
And if thou could'ſt, thou could'ſt not make him liue:
Therefore haue done, ſome griefe ſhewes much of Loue,
But much of griefe, ſhewes ſtill ſome want of wit.

Iul. Yet let me weepe, for ſuch a feeling loſſe.

Lad. So ſhall you feele the loſſe, but not the Friend
Which you weepe for.

Iul. Feeling ſo the loſſe,
I cannot chuſe but euer weepe the Friend.

La. Well Girle, thou weep'ſt not ſo much for his death,
As that the Villaine liues which ſlaughter'd him.

Iul. What Villaine, Madam?

Lad. That ſame Villaine *Romeo*.

Iul. Villaine and he, be many Miles aſſunder:
God pardon, I doe with all my heart:
And yet no man like he, doth grieue my heart.

Lad. That is becauſe the Traitor liues.

Iul. I Madam from the reach of theſe my hands:
Would none but I might venge my Cozins death.

Lad. We will haue vengeance for it, feare thou not.
Then weepe no more, Ile ſend to one in *Mantua*,
Where that ſame baniſht Run-agate doth liue,
Shall giue him ſuch an vnaccuſtom'd dram,
That he ſhall ſoone keepe *Tybalt* company:
And then I hope thou wilt be ſatisfied.

Iul. Indeed I neuer ſhall be ſatisfied
With *Romeo*, till I behold him. Dead
Is my poore heart ſo for a kinſman vext:
Madam if you could find out but a man
To beare a poyſon, I would temper it;
That *Romeo* ſhould vpon receit thereof,
Soone ſleepe in quiet. O how my heart abhors
To heare him nam'd, and cannot come to him,
To wreake the Loue I bore my Cozin,
Vpon his body that hath ſlaughter'd him.

Mo. Find thou the meanes, and Ile find ſuch a man.
But now Ile tell thee ioyfull tidings Gyrle.

Iul. And ioy comes well, in ſuch a needy time,
What are they, beſeech your Ladyſhip?

Mo. Well, well, thou haſt a carefull Father Child?
One who to put thee from thy heauineſſe,
Hath ſorted out a ſudden day of ioy,
That thou expects not, nor I lookt not for.

Iul. Madam in happy time, what day is this?

Mo. Marry my Child, early next Thurſday morne,
The gallant, young, and Noble Gentleman,
The Countie *Paris* at Saint *Peters* Church,
Shall happily make thee a ioyfull Bride.

Iul. Now by Saint *Peters* Church, and *Peter* too,
He ſhall not make me there a ioyfull Bride.
I wonder at this haſt, that I muſt wed
Ere he that ſhould be Husband comes to woe:
I pray you tell my Lord and Father Madam,
I will not marrie yet, and when I doe, I ſweare
It ſhallbe *Romeo*, whom you know I hate
Rather then *Paris*. Theſe are newes indeed.

Mo. Here comes your Father, tell him ſo your ſelfe,
And ſee how he will take it at your hands.

Enter Capulet and Nurſe.

Cap. When the Sun ſets, the earth doth drizzle daew
But for the Sunſet of my Brothers Sonne.
It raines downright.
How now? A Conduit Gyrle, what ſtill in teares?
Euermore ſhowring in one little body?
Thou counterfaits a Barke, a Sea, a Wind:
For ſtill thy eyes, which I may call the Sea,
Do ebbe and flow with teares, the Barke thy body is
Sayling in this ſalt floud, the windes thy ſighes,
Who raging with the teares and they with them,
Without a ſudden calme will ouer ſet
Thy tempeſt toſſed body. How now wife?
Haue you deliuered to her our decree?

Lady. I ſir;
But ſhe will none, ſhe giues you thankes,
I would the foole were married to her graue.

Cap. Soft, take me with you, take me with you wife,
How, will ſhe none? doth ſhe not giue vs thanks?
Is ſhe not proud? doth ſhe not count her bleſt,
Vnworthy as ſhe is, that we haue wrought
So worthy a Gentleman, to be her Bridegroome

Iul. Not proud you haue,
But thankfull that you haue:
Proud can I neuer be of what I haue,
But thankfull euen for hate, that is meant Loue.

Cap. How now?
How now? Chopt Logicke? what is this?
Proud, and I thanke you: and I thanke you not.
Thanke me no thankings, nor proud me no prouds,
But fettle your fine ioints 'gainſt Thurſday next,

To

To go with *Paris* to Saint *Peters* Church:
Or I will drag thee, on a Hurdle thither.
Out you greene ſickneſſe carrion, out you baggage,
You tallow face.
Lady. Fie, fie, what are you mad?
Iul. Good Father, I beſeech you on my knees
Heare me with patience, but to ſpeake a word.
Fa. Hang thee young baggage, diſobedient wretch,
I tell thee what, get thee to Church a Thurſday,
Or neuer after looke me in the face.
Speake not, reply not, do not anſwere me.
My fingers itch, wife: we ſcarce thought vs bleſt,
That God had lent vs but this onely Child,
But now I ſee this one is one too much,
And that we haue a curſe in hauing her:
Out on her Hilding.
Nur. God in heauen bleſſe her,
You are too blame my Lord to rate her ſo.
Fa. And why my Lady wiſedome? hold your tongue,
Good Prudence, ſmatter with your goſſip, go.
Nur. I ſpeake no treaſon,
Father, O Godigoden,
May not one ſpeake?
Fa. Peace you mumbling foole,
Vtter your grauitie ore a Goſſips bowles
For here we need it not.
La. You are too hot.
Fa. Gods bread, it makes me mad:
Day, night, houre, ride, time, worke, play,
Alone in companie, ſtill my care hath bin
To haue her matcht, and hauing now prouided
A Gentleman of Noble Parentage,
Of faire Demeanes, Youthfull, and Nobly Allied,
Stuft as they ſay with Honourable parts,
Proportion'd as ones thought would wiſh a man,
And then to haue a wretched puling foole,
A whining mammet, in her Fortunes tender,
To anſwer, Ile not wed, I cannot Loue:
I am too young, I pray you pardon me.
But, and you will not wed, Ile pardon you.
Graze where you will, you ſhall not houſe with me:
Looke too't, thinke on't, I do not vſe to ieſt.
Thurſday is neere, lay hand on heart, aduiſe,
And you be mine, Ile giue you to my Friend:
And you be not, hang, beg, ſtraue, die in the ſtreets,
For by my ſoule, Ile nere acknowledge thee,
Nor what is mine ſhall neuer do thee good:
Truſt too't, bethinke you, Ile not be forſworne. *Exit*.
Iuli. Is there no pittie ſitting in the Cloudes,
That ſees into the bottome of my griefe?
O ſweet my Mother caſt me not away,
Delay this marriage, for a month, a weeke,
Or if you do not, make the Bridall bed
In that dim Monument where *Tybalt* lies.
Mo. Talke not to me, for Ile not ſpeake a word,
Do as thou wilt, for I haue done with thee. *Exit*.
Iul. O God!
O Nurſe, how ſhall this be preuented?
My Husband is on earth, my faith in heauen,
How ſhall that faith returne againe to earth,
Vnleſſe that Husband ſend it me from heauen,
By leauing earth? Comfort me, counſaile me:
Hlacke, alacke, that heauen ſhould practiſe ſtratagems
Vpon ſo ſoft a ſubiect as my ſelfe.
What ſaiſt thou? haſt thou not a word of ioy?
Some comfort Nurſe.
Nur. Faith here it is,
Romeo is baniſhed, and all the world to nothing,
That he dares nere come backe to challenge you:
Or if he do, it needs muſt be by ſtealth.
Then ſince the caſe ſo ſtands as now it doth,
I thinke it beſt you married with the Countie,
O hee's a Louely Gentleman:
Romeos a diſh-clout to him: an Eagle Madam
Hath not ſo greene, ſo quicke, ſo faire an eye
As *Paris* hath, beſhrow my very heart,
I thinke you are happy in this ſecond match,
For it excels your firſt: or if it did not,
Your firſt is dead, or 'twere as good he were,
As liuing here and you no vſe of him.
Iul. Speakeſt thou from thy heart?
Nur. And from my ſoule too,
Or elſe beſhrew them both.
Iul. Amen.
Nur. What?
Iul. Well, thou haſt comforted me maruellous much,
Go in, and tell my Lady I am gone,
Hauing diſpleas'd my Father, to *Lawrence* Cell,
To make confeſſion, and to be abſolu'd.
Nur. Marrie I will, and this is wiſely done.
Iul. Auncient damnation, O moſt wicked fiend!
It is more ſin to wiſh me thus forſworne,
Or to diſpraiſe my Lord with that ſame tongue
Which ſhe hath prais'd him with aboue compare,
So many thouſand times? Go Counſellor,
Thou and my boſome henceforth ſhall be twaine:
Ile to the Frier to know his remedie,
If all elſe faile, my ſelfe haue power to die. *Exeunt*.

Enter Frier and Countie Paris.

Fri. On Thurſday ſir? the time is very ſhort.
Par. My Father *Capulet* will haue it ſo,
And I am nothing ſlow to ſlack his haſt.
Fri. You ſay you do not know the Ladies mind?
Vneuen is the courſe, I like it not.
Pa. Immoderately ſhe weepes for *Tybalts* death,
And therfore haue I little talke of Loue,
For *Venus* ſmiles not in a houſe of teares.
Now ſir, her Father counts it dangerous
That ſhe doth giue her ſorrow ſo much ſway:
And in his wiſedome, haſts our marriage,
To ſtop the inundation of her teares,
Which too much minded by her ſelfe alone,
May be put from her by ſocietie.
Now doe you know the reaſon of this haſt?
Fri. I would I knew not why it ſhould be ſlow'd.
Looke ſir, here comes the Lady towards my Cell.
Enter Iuliet.
Par. Happily met, my Lady and my wife.
Iul. That may be ſir, when I may be a wife.
Par. That may be, muſt be Loue, on Thurſday next.
Iul. What muſt be ſhall be.
Fri. That's a certaine text.
Par. Come you to make confeſſion to this Father?
Iul. To anſwere that, I ſhould confeſſe to you.
Par. Do not denie to him, that you Loue me.
Iul. I will confeſſe to you that I Loue him.
Par. So will ye, I am ſure that you Loue me.
Iul. If I do ſo, it will be of more price,
Benig ſpoke behind your backe, then to your face.
Par. Poore ſoule, thy face is much abuſ'd with teares.
Iuli. The

Iul. The teares haue got ſmall victorie by that:
For it was bad inough before their ſpight.
Pa. Thou wrong'ſt it more then teares with that report.
Iul. That is no ſlaunder ſir, which is a truth,
And what I ſpake, I ſpake it to thy face.
Par. Thy face is mine, and thou haſt ſlaundred it.
Iul. It may be ſo, for it is not mine owne.
Are you at leiſure, Holy Father now,
Or ſhall I come to you at euening Maſſe?
Fri. My leiſure ſerues me penſiue daughter now.
My Lord you muſt intreat the time alone.
Par. Godſheild: I ſhould diſturbe Deuotion,
Iuliet, on Thurſday early will I rowſe yee,
Till then adue, and keepe this holy kiſſe. *Exit Paris.*
Iul. O ſhut the doore, and when thou haſt done ſo,
Come weepe with me, paſt hope, paſt care, paſt helpe.
Fri. O *Iuliet*, I alreadie know thy griefe,
It ſtreames me paſt the compaſſe of my wits:
I heare thou muſt and nothing may prorogue it,
On Thurſday next be married to this Countie.
Iul. Tell me not Frier that thou heareſt of this,
Vnleſſe thou tell me how I may preuent it:
If in thy wiſedome, thou canſt giue no helpe,
Do thou but call my reſolution wiſe,
And with' his knife, Ile helpe it preſently.
God ioyn'd my heart, and *Romeos*, thou our hands,
And ere this hand by thee to *Romeo* ſeal'd:
Shall be the Labell to another Deede,
Or my true heart with trecherous reuolt,
Turne to another; this ſhall ſlay them both:
Therefore out of thy long experien'ſt time,
Giue me ſome preſent counſeil, or behold
Twixt my extreames and me, this bloody knife
Shall play the vmpeere, arbitrating that,
Which the commiſſion of thy yeares and art,
Could to no iſſue of true honour bring:
Be not ſo long to ſpeak, I long to die,
If what thou ſpeak'ſt, ſpeake not of remedy.
Fri. Hold Daughter, I doe ſpie a kind of hope,
Which craues as deſperate an execution,
As that is deſperate which we would preuent.
If rather then to marrie Countie *Paris*
Thou haſt the ſtrength of will to ſtay thy ſelfe,
Then is it likely thou wilt vndertake
A thing like death to chide away this ſhame,
That coap'ſt with death himſelfe, to ſcape fro it:
And if thou dar'ſt, Ile giue thee remedie.
Iul. Oh bid me leape, rather then marrie *Paris*,
From of the Battlements of any Tower,
Or walke in theeuiſh waies, or bid me lurke
Where Serpents are: chaine me with roaring Beares
Or hide me nightly in a Charnell houſe,
Orecouered quite with dead mens ratling bones,
With reckie ſhankes and yellow chappels ſculls:
Or bid me go into a new made graue,
And hide me with a dead man in his graue,
Things that to heare them told, haue made me tremble,
And I will doe it without feare or doubt,
To liue an vnſtained wife to my ſweet Loue.
Fri. Hold then: goe home be merrie, giue conſent,
To marrie *Paris*: wenſday is to morrow,
To morrow night looke that thou lie alone,
Let not thy Nurſe lie with thee in thy Chamber:
Take thou this Violl being then in bed,
And this diſtilling liquor drinke thou off,
When preſently through all thy veines ſhall run,
A cold and drowſie humour: for no pulſe
Shall keepe his natiue progreſſe, but ſurceaſe:
No warmth, no breath ſhall teſtifie thou liueſt,
The Roſes in thy lips and cheekes ſhall fade
To many aſhes, the eyes windowes fall
Like death when he ſhut vp the day of life:
Each part depriu'd of ſupple gouernment,
Shall ſtiffe and ſtarke, and cold appeare like death,
And in this borrowed likeneſſe of ſhrunke death
Thou ſhalt continue two and forty houres,
And then awake, as from a pleaſant ſleepe.
Now when the Bridegroome in the morning comes,
To rowſe thee from thy bed, there art thou dead:
Then as the manner of our country is,
In thy beſt Robes vncouer'd on the Beere,
Be borne to buriall in thy kindreds graue:
Thou ſhalt be borne to that ſame ancient vault,
Where all the kindred of the *Capulets* lie,
In the meane time againſt thou ſhalt awake,
Shall *Romeo* by my Letters know our drift,
And hither ſhall he come, and that very night
Shall *Romeo* beare thee hence to *Mantua*.
And this ſhall free thee from this preſent ſhame,
If no inconſtant toy nor womaniſh feare,
Abate thy valour in the acting it.
Iul. Giue me, giue me, O tell not me of care.
Fri. Hold get you gone, be ſtrong and proſperous:
In this reſolue, Ile ſend a Frier with ſpeed
To *Mantua* with my Letters to thy Lord.
Iu. Loue giue me ſtrength,
And ſtrength ſhall helpe afford:
Farewell deare father. *Exit*

Enter Father Capulet, Mother, Nurſe, and Seruing men, two or three.

Cap So many gueſts inuite as here are writ,
Sirrah, go hire me twenty cunning Cookes.
Ser. You ſhall haue none ill ſir, for Ile trie if they can licke their fingers
Cap. How canſt thou trie them ſo?
Ser. Marrie ſir, 'tis an ill Cooke that cannot licke his owne fingers therefore he that cannot licke his fingers goes not with me
Cap. Go be gone, we ſhall be much vnfurniſht for this time what is my Daughter gone to Frier *Laurence*?
Nur I forſooth
Cap. Well he may chance to do ſome good on her,
A peeuiſh ſelfe-wild harlotry it is.
Enter Iuliet.
Nur See where ſhe comes from ſhrift
With merrie looke.
Cap. How now my headſtrong,
Where haue you bin gadding?
Iul. Where I haue learnt me to repent the ſin
Of diſobedient oppoſition:
To you and your beheſts, and am enioyn'd
By holy *Lawrence*, to fall proſtrate here,
To beg your pardon: pardon I beſeech you.
Henceforward I am euer rul'd by you.
Cap. Send for the Countie, goe tell him of this,
Ile haue this knot knit vp to morrow morning.
Iul. I met the youthfull Lord at *Lawrence* Cell,
And gaue him what becomed Loue I might.
Not ſtepping ore the bounds of modeſtie.
Cap. Why I am glad on't, this is well, ſtand vp,
Thit

This is as't should be,let me see the County:
I marrie go I say,and fetch him hither.
Now afore God,this reuerend holy Frier,
All our whole Cittie is much bound to him.
Iul. Nurse will you goe with me into my Closet,
To helpe me sort such needfull ornaments,
As you thinke fit to furnish me to morrow?
Mo. No not till Thursday,there's time inough.
Fa. Go Nurse,go with her,
Weele to Church to morrow.

Exeunt Iuliet and Nurse.

Mo. We shall be short in our prouision,
Tis now neere night.
Fa Tush,I will stirre about,
And all things shall be well,I warrant thee wife:
Go thou to *Iuliet*,helpe to deckevp her,
Ile not to bed to night,let me alone:
Ile play the huswife for this once. What ho?
They are all forth,well I will walke my selfe
To Countie *Paris*,to prepare him vp
Against to morrow,my heart is wondrous light,
Since this same way-ward Gyrle is so reclaim'd.

Exeunt Father and Mother

Enter Iuliet and Nurse.

Iul. I those attires are best,but gentle Nurse
I pray thee leaue me to my selfe to night:
For I haue need of many Orysons,
To moue the heauens to smile vpon my state,
Which well thou know'st,is crosse and full of sin.

Enter Mother.

Mo. What are you busie ho?need you my help?
Iul. No Madam,we haue cul'd such necessaries
As are behoouefull for our state to morrow:
So please you,let me now be left alone;
And let the Nurse this night sit vp with you,
For I am sure,you haue your hands full all,
In this so sudden businesse.
Mo. Goodnight.
Get thee to bed and rest,for thou hast need. *Exeunt.*
Iul Farewell:
God knowes when we shall meete againe.
I haue a faint cold feare thrills through my veines,
That almost freezes vp the heate of fire:
Ile call them backe againe to comfort me.
Nurse,what should she do here?
My dismall Sceane,I needs must act alone:
Come Viall what if this mixture do not worke at all?
Shall I be married then to morrow morning?
No,no,this shall forbid it. Lie thou there,
What if it be a poyson which the Frier
Subtilly hath ministred to haue me dead,
Least in this marriage he should be dishonour'd,
Because he married me before to *Romeo*?
I feare it is,and yet me thinkes it should not,
For he hath still beene tried a holy man.
How,if when I am laid into the Tombe,
I wake before the time that *Romeo*
Come to redeeme me? There's a fearefull point:
Shall I not then be stifled in the Vault?
To whose foule mouth no healthsome ayre breaths in,
And there die strangled ere my *Romeo* comes.
Or if I liue,is it not very like,
The horrible conceit of death and night,
Together with the terror of the place,
As in a Vaulte,an ancient receptacle,
Where for these many hundred yeeres the bones
Of all my buried Auncestors are packt,
Where bloody *Tybalt*,yet but greene in earth,
Lies festring in his shrow'd,where as they say,
At some houres in the night,Spirits resort:
Alacke,alacke,is it not like that I
So early waking,what with loathsome smels,
And shrikes like Mandrakes torne out of the earth,
That liuing mortalls hearing them,run mad.
O if I walke,shall I not be distraught,
Inuironed with all these hidious feares,
And madly play with my forefathers ioynts?
And plucke the mangled *Tybalt* from his shrow'd?
And in this rage,with some great kinsmans bone,
As (with a club) dash out my desperate braines.
O looke,me thinks I see my Cozins Ghost,
Seeking out *Romeo* that did spit his body
Vpon my Rapiers point: stay *Tybalt*,stay;
Romeo,*Romeo*,*Romeo*,here's drinke: I drinke to thee.

Enter Lady of the house,and Nurse.

Lady. Hold,
Take these keies,and fetch more spices Nurse.
Nur. They call for Dates and Quinces in the Pastrie.

Enter old Capulet.

Cap. Come,stir,stir,stir,
The second Cocke hath Crow'd,
The Curphew Bell hath rung,'tis three a clocke:
Looke to the bakte meates,good *Angelica*,
Spare not for cost.
Nur. Go you Cot-queane,go,
Get you to bed,faith youle be sicke to morrow
For this nights watching.
Cap. No not a whit:what? I haue watcht ere now
All night for lesse cause,and nere beene sicke.
La. I you haue bin a Mouse-hunt in your time,
But I will watch you from such watching now.

Exit Lady and Nurse.

Cap. A iealous hood,a iealous hood,
Now fellow,what there?

Enter three or foure with spits,and logs,and baskets.

Fel. Things for the Cooke sir,but I know not what.
Cap. Make hast,make hast,sirrah,fetch drier Logs.
Call *Peter*,he will shew thee where they are.
Fel. I haue a head sir,that will find out logs,
And neuer trouble *Peter* for the matter.
Cap. Masse and well said,a merrie horson,ha,
Thou shalt be loggerhead; good Father,'tis day.

Play Musicke

The Countie will be here with Musicke straight,
For so he said he would,I heare him neere,
Nurse,wife,what ho? what Nurse I say?

Enter Nurse.

Go waken *Iuliet*,go and trim her vp,
Ile go and chat with *Paris*:hie,make hast,
Make hast,the Bridegroome,he is come already:
Make hast I say.
Nur. Mistris,what Mistris? *Iuliet*? Fast I warrant her she.
Why Lambe,why Lady,fie you sluggabed,
Why Loue I say? Madam,sweet heart: why Bride?
What not a word? You take your peniworths now.
Sleepe for a weeke,for the next night I warrant
The Countie *Paris* hath set vp his rest,
That you shall rest but little,God forgiue me:
Marrie and Amen: how sound is she a sleepe?

I must needs wake her : Madam, Madam, Madam,
I, let the Countie take you in your bed,
Heele fright you vp yfaith. Will it not be ?
What drest, and in your clothes, and downe againe ?
I must needs wake you : Lady, Lady, Lady ?
Alas, alas, helpe, helpe, my Ladyes dead,
Oh weladay, that euer I was borne,
Some Aqua-vitæ ho, my Lord, my Lady ?
Mo. What noise is heere ? *Enter Mother.*
Nur. O lamentable day.
Mo. What is the matter ?
Nur. Looke, looke, oh heauie day.
Mo. O me, O me, my Child, my onely life :
Reuiue, looke vp, or I will die with thee :
Helpe, helpe, call helpe.

Enter Father.

Fa. For shame bring *Iuliet* forth, her Lord is come.
Nur. Shee's dead: deceast, shee's dead: alacke the day.
M. Alacke the day, shee's dead, shee's dead, shee's dead.
Fa. Ha ? Let me see her: out alas shee's cold,
Her blood is setled and her ioynts are stiffe :
Life and these lips haue long bene sep erated:
Death lies on her like an vntimely frost
Vpon the sweetest flower of all the field.
Nur. O Lamentable day !
Mo. O wofull time.
Fa. Death that hath tane her hence to make me waile,
Ties vp my tongue, and will not let me speake.

Enter Frier and the Countie.

Fri. Come, is the Bride ready to go to Church ?
Fa. Ready to go, but neuer to returne.
O Sonne, the night before thy wedding day,
Hath death laine with thy wife : there she lies,
Flower as she was, deflowred by him.
Death is my Sonne in law, death is my Heire,
My Daughter he hath wedded. I will die,
And leaue him all life liuing, all is deaths.
Pa. Haue I thought long to see this mornings face,
And doth it giue me such a sight as this ?
Mo. Accur'st, vnhappie, wretched hatefull day,
Most miserable houre, that ere time saw
In lasting labour of his Pilgrimage.
But one, poore one, one poore and louing Child,
But one thing to reioyce and solace in,
And cruell death hath catcht it from my sight.
Nur. O wo, O wofull, wofull, wofull day,
Most lamentable day, most wofull day,
That euer, euer, I did yet behold.
O day, O day, O day, O hatefull day,
Neuer was seene so blacke a day as this :
O wofull day, O wofull day.
Pa. Beguild, diuorced, wronged, spighted, slaine,
Most detestable death, by thee beguil'd,
By cruell, cruell thee quite ouerthrowne :
O loue, O life; not life, but loue in death.
Fat. Despis'd, distressed, hated, martir'd, kil'd,
Vncomfortable time, why cam'st thou now
To murther, murther our solemnitie ?
O Child, O Child; my soule, and not my Child,
Dead art thou, alacke my Child is dead,
And with my Child, my ioyes are buried.
Fri. Peace ho for shame, confusions : Care liues not
In these confusions, heauen and your selfe
Had part in this faire Maid, now heauen hath all,
And all the better is it for the Maid :
Your part in her, you could not keepe from death,
But heauen keepes his part in eternall life :
The most you sought was her promotion,
For 'twas your heauen, she shouldst be aduan'st,
And weepe ye now, seeing she is aduan'st
Aboue the Cloudes, as high as Heauen it selfe ?
O in this loue, you loue your Child so ill,
That you run mad, seeing that she is well :
Shee's not well married, that liues married long,
But shee's best married, that dies married yong.
Drie vp your teares, and sticke your Rosemarie
On this faire Coarse, and as the custome is,
And in her best array beare her to Church :
For though some Nature bids all vs lament,
Yet Natures teares are Reasons merriment.
Fa. All things that we ordained Festiuall,
Turne from their office to blacke Funerall :
Our instruments to melancholy Bells,
Our wedding cheare, to a sad buriall Feast :
Our solemne Hymnes, to sullen Dyrges change :
Our Bridall flowers serue for a buried Coarse :
And all things change them to the contrarie.
Fri. Sir go you in ; and Madam, go with him,
And go sir *Paris*, euery one prepare
To follow this faire Coarse vnto her graue :
The heauens do lowre vpon you, for some ill :
Moue them no more, by crossing their high will. *Exeunt*
Mu. Faith we may put vp our Pipes and be gone.
Nur. Honest goodfellowes : Ah put vp, put vp,
For well you know, this is a pitifull case.
Mu. I by my troth, the case may be amended.

Enter Peter.

Pet. Musitions, oh Musitions,
Hearts ease, hearts ease,
O, and you will haue me liue, play hearts ease.
Mu. Why hearts ease ;
Pet O Musitions,
Because my heart it selfe plaies, my heart is full.
Mu. Not a dump we, 'tis no time to play now.
Pet. You will not then ?
Mu. No.
Pet. I will then giue it you soundly.
Mu What will you giue vs ?
Pet. No money on my faith, but the gleeke.
I will giue you the Minstrell.
Mu. Then will I giue you the Seruing creature.
Peter. Then will I lay the seruing Creatures Dagger on your pate. I will carie no Crochets, Ile Re you, Ile Fa you, do you note me ?
Mu. And you Re vs, and Fa vs, you Note vs.
2 *M.* Pray you put vp your Dagger,
And put out your wit.
Then haue at you with my wit.
Peter. I will drie-beate you with an yron wit,
And put vp my yron Dagger.
Answere me like men :
When griping griefes the heart doth wound, then Musicke with her siluer sound.
Why siluer sound ? why Musicke with her siluer sound :
what say you *Simon Catling* ?
Mu. Mary sir, because siluer hath a sweet sound.
Pet. Pratest, what say you *Hugh Rebicke* ?
2. *M.* I say siluer sound, because Musitions sound for siluer.
Pet. Pratest to, what say you *Iames Sound-Post* ?
3. *Mu.* Faith I know not what to say.
Pet. O I cry you mercy, you are the Singer.
I will say for you ; it is Musicke with her siluer sound,

g g Be

Becauſe Muſitions haue no gold for ſounding:
Then Muſicke with her ſiluer ſound with ſpeedy helpe
doth lend redreſſe. *Exit.*
Mu. What a peſtilent knaue is this ſame?
M. 2. Hang him Iacke, come weele in here, tarrie for
the Mourners, and ſtay dinner. *Exit.*

Enter Romeo.

Rom. If I may truſt the flattering truth of ſleepe,
My dreames preſage ſome ioyfull newes at hand:
My boſomes L. ſits lightly in his throne:
And all thiſan day an vccuſtom'd ſpirit,
Lifts me aboue the ground with cheerefull thoughts.
I dreamt my Lady came and found me dead,
(Strange dreame that giues a dead man leaue to thinke,)
And breath'd ſuch life with kiſſes in my lips,
That I reuiu'd and was an Emperour.
Ah me, how ſweet is loue it ſelfe poſſeſt,
When but loues ſhadowes are ſo rich in ioy.

Enter Romeo's man.

Newes from *Verona*, how now *Balthazer*?
Doſt thou not bring me Letters from the Frier?
How doth my Lady? Is my Father well?
How doth my Lady *Iuliet*? that I aske againe,
For nothing can be ill, if ſhe be well.
Man. Then ſhe is well, and nothing can be ill.
Her body ſleepes in *Capels* Monument,
And her immortall part with Angels liue,
I ſaw her laid low in her kindreds Vault,
And preſently tooke Poſte to tell it you:
O pardon me for bringing theſe ill newes,
Since you did leaue it for my office Sir.
Rom. Is it euen ſo?
Then I denie you Starres.
Thou knoweſt my lodging, get me inke and paper,
And hire Poſt-Horſes, I will hence to night.
Man. I do beſeech you ſir, haue patience:
Your lookes are pale and wild, and do import
Some miſaduenture.
Rom. Tuſh, thou art deceiu'd,
Leaue me, and do the thing I bid thee do.
Haſt thou no Letters to me from the Frier?
Man. No my good Lord.
Exit Man.
Rom. Mo matter: Get thee gone,
And hyre thoſe Horſes, Ile be with thee ſtraight.
Well *Iuliet*, I will lie with thee to night:
Lets ſee for meanes: O miſchiefe thou art ſwift,
To enter in the thoughts of deſperate men:
I do remember an Appothecarie,
And here abouts dwells, which late I noted
In tattred weeds, with ouerwhelming browes,
Culling of Simples, meager were his lookes,
Sharpe miſerie had worne him to the bones:
And in his needie ſhop a Tortoyrs hung,
An Allegater ſtuft, and other skins
Of ill ſhap'd fiſhes, and about his ſhelues,
A beggerly account of emptie boxes,
Greene earthen pots, Bladders, and muſtie ſeedes,
Remnants of packthred, and old cakes of Roſes
Were thinly ſcattered, to make vp a ſhew.
Noting this penury, to my ſelfe I ſaid,
An if a man did need a poyſon now,
Whoſe ſale is perſent death in *Mantua*,
Here liues a Caitiffe wretch would ſell it him.
O this ſame thought did but fore-run my need,
And this ſame needie man muſt ſell it me.
As I remember, this ſhould be the houſe,
Being holy day, the beggers ſhop is ſhut.
What ho? Appothecarie?

Enter Appothecarie.

App. Who call's ſo low'd?
Rom. Come hither man, I ſee that thou art poore,
Hold, there is fortie Duckets, let me haue
A dram of poyſon, ſuch ſoone ſpeeding geare,
As will diſperſe it ſelfe through all the veines,
That the life-wearie-taker may fall dead,
And that the Trunke may be diſcharg'd of breath,
As violently, as haſtie powder fier'd
Doth hurry from the fatall Canons wombe.
App. Such mortall drugs I haue, but *Mantuas* law
Is death to any he, that vtters them.
Rom. Art thou ſo bare and full of wretchedneſſe,
And fear'ſt to die? Famine is in thy cheekes,
Need and opreſſion ſtarueth in thy eyes,
Contempt and beggery hangs vpon thy backe:
The world is not thy friend, nor the worlds law:
The world affords no law to make thee rich.
Then be not poore, but breake it, and take this.
App. My pouerty, but not my will conſents.
Rom. I pray thy pouerty, and not thy will.
App. Put this in any liquid thing you will
And drinke it off, and if you had the ſtrength
Of twenty men, it would diſpatch you ſtraight.
Rom. There's thy Gold,
Worſe poyſon to mens ſoules,
Doing more murther in this loathſome world,
Then theſe poore compounds that thou maieſt not ſell.
I ſell thee poyſon, thou haſt ſold me none,
Farewell, buy food, and get thy ſelfe in fleſh.
Come Cordiall, and not poyſon, go with me
To *Iuliets* graue, for there muſt I vſe thee.
Exeunt

Enter Frier Iohn to Frier Lawrence.

Iohn. Holy *Franciſcan* Frier, Brother, ho?

Enter Frier Lawrence.

Law. This ſame ſhould be the voice of Frier *Iohn.*
Welcome from *Mantua*, what ſayes *Romeo*?
Or if his mind be writ, giue me his Letter.
Iohn. Going to find a bare-foote Brother out,
One of our order to aſſociate me,
Here in this Citie viſiting the ſick,
And finding him, the Searchers of the Towne
Suſpecting that we both were in a houſe
Where the infectious peſtilence did raigne,
Seal'd vp the doores, and would not let vs forth,
So that my ſpeed to *Mantua* there was ſtaid.
Law. Who bare my Letter then to *Romeo*?
Iohn. I could not ſend it, here it is againe,
Nor get a meſſenger to bring it thee,
So fearefull were they of infection.
Law. Vnhappie Fortune: by my Brotherhood
The Letter was not nice, but full of charge,
Of deare import, and the neglecting it
May do much danger: Frier *Iohn* go hence,
Get me an Iron Crow, and bring it ſtraight
Vnto my Cell.
Iohn. Brother Ile go and bring it thee. *Exit.*
Law. Now muſt I to the Monument alone,
Within this three houres will faire *Iuliet* wake,
Shee will beſhrew me much that *Romeo*
Hath had no notice of theſe accidents:
But I will write againe to *Mantua*,

And

And keepe her at my Cell till *Romeo* come,
Poore liuing Coarse, clos'd in a dead mans Tombe,
Exit.

Enter Paris and his Page.

Par. Giue me thy Torch Boy, hence and stand aloft,
Yet put it out, for I would not be seene:
Vnder yond young Trees lay thee all along,
Holding thy eare close to the hollow ground,
So shall no foot vpon the Churchyard tread,
Being loose, vnfirme with digging vp of Graues,
But thou shalt heare it: whistle then to me,
As signall that thou hearest some thing approach,
Giue me those flowers. Do as I bid thee, go.
Page. I am almost afraid to stand alone
Here in the Churchyard, yet I will aduenture.
Pa. Sweet Flower with flowers thy Bridall bed I strew:
O woe, thy Canopie is dust and stones,
Which with sweet water nightly I will dewe,
Or wanting that, with teares destil'd by mones;
The obsequies that I for thee will keepe,
Nightly shall be, to strew thy graue, and weepe.
Whistle Boy.
The Boy giues warning, something doth approach,
What cursed foot wanders this wayes to night,
To crosse my obsequies, and true loues right?
What with a Torch? Muffle me night a while.

Enter Romeo, and Peter.

Rom. Giue me that Mattocke, & the wrenching Iron,
Hold take this Letter, early in the morning
See thou deliuer it to my Lord and Father,
Giue me the light; vpon thy life I charge thee,
What ere thou hear'st or seest, stand all aloofe,
And do not interrupt me in my course.
Why I descend into this bed of death,
Is partly to behold my Ladies face:
But chiefly to take thence from her dead finger,
A precious Ring: a Ring that I must vse,
In deare employment, therefore hence be gone:
But if thou iealous dost returne to prie
In what I further shall intend to do,
By heauen I will teare thee ioynt by ioynt,
And strew this hungry Churchyard with thy limbs:
The time, and my intents are sauage wilde:
More fierce and more inexorable farre,
Then emptie Tygers, or the roaring Sea.
Pet. I will be gone sir, and not trouble you
Ro. So shalt thou shew me friendship: take thou that,
Liue and be prosperous, and farewell good fellow.
Pet. For all this same, Ile hide me here about,
His lookes I feare, and his intents I doubt.
Rom. Thou detestable mawe, thou wombe of death,
Gorg'd with the dearest morsell of the earth:
Thus I enforce thy rotten Iawes to open,
And in despight, Ile cram thee with more food.
Par. This is that banisht haughtie *Mountague*,
That murdred my Loues Cozin; with which griefe,
It is supposed the faire Creature died,
And here is come to do some villanous shame
To the dead bodies: I will apprehend him.
Stop thy vnhallowed toyle, vile *Mountague*:
Can vengeance be pursued further then death?
Condemned villaine, I do apprehend thee.
Obey and go with me, for thou must die,
Rom. I must indeed, and therfore came I hither:
Good gentle youth, tempt not a desperate man,
Flie hence and leaue me, thinke vpon those gone,
Let them affright thee. I beseech thee Youth,
Put not an other sin vpon my head,
By vrging me to furie. O be gone,
By heauen I loue thee better then my selfe,
For I come hither arm'd against my selfe:
Stay not, be gone, liue, and hereafter say,
A mad mans mercy bid thee run away.
Par. I do defie thy commisseration,
And apprehend thee for a Fellon here.
Ro. Wilt thou prouoke me? Then haue at thee Boy.
Pet. O Lord they fight, I will go call the Watch.
Pa. O I am slaine, if thou be mercifull,
Open the Tombe, lay me with *Iuliet*.
Rom. In faith I will, let me peruse this face:
Mercutius kinsman, Noble Countie *Paris*,
What said my man, when my betossed soule
Did not attend him as we rode? I thinke
He told me *Paris* should haue married *Iuliet*.
Said he not so? Or did I dreame it so?
Or am I mad, hearing him talke of *Iuliet*,
To thinke it was so? O giue me thy hand,
One, writ with me in sowre misfortunes booke.
Ile burie thee in a triumphant graue.
A Graue; O no, a Lanthorne; slaughtred Youth:
For here lies *Iuliet*, and her beautie makes
This Vault a feasting presence full of light.
Death lie thou there, by a dead man inter'd.
How oft when men are at the point of death,
Haue they beene merrie? Which their Keepers call
A lightning before death? Oh how may I
Call this a lightning? O my Loue, my Wife,
Death that hath suckt the honey of thy breath,
Hath had no power yet vpon thy Beautie:
Thou are not conquer'd: Beauties ensigne yet
Is Crymson in thy lips, and in thy cheekes,
And Deaths pale flag is not aduanced there.
Tybalt, ly'st thou there in thy bloudy sheet?
O what more fauour can I do to thee,
Then with that hand that cut thy youth in twaine,
To sunder his that was thy enemie?
Forgiue me Cozen. Ah deare *Iuliet*:
Why art thou yet so faire? I will beleeue,
Shall I beleeue, that vnsubstantiall death is amorous?
And that the leane abhorred Monster keepes
Thee here in darke to be his Paramour?
For feare of that, I still will stay with thee,
And neuer from this Pallace of dym night
Depart againe: come lie thou in my armes,
Heere's to thy health, where ere thou tumblest in.
O true Appothecarie!
Thy drugs are quicke. Thus with a kisse I die.
Depart againe; here, here will I remaine,
With Wormes that are thy Chambermaides: O here
Will I set vp my euerlasting rest:
And shake the yoke of inauspicious starres
From this world-wearied flesh: Eyes looke your last:
Armes take your last embrace: And lips, O you
The doores of breath, seale with a righteous kisse
A datelesse bargaine to ingrossing death:
Come bitter conduct, come vnsauoury guide,
Thou desperate Pilot, now at once run on
The dashing Rocks, thy Sea-sicke wearie Barke:
Heere's to my Loue. O true Appothecary:

Thy drugs are quicke. Thus with a kisse I die.
Enter Frier with Lanthorne, Crow, and Spade.
Fri. St. Francis be my speed, how oft to night
Haue my old feet stumbled at graues? Who's there?
Man. Here's one, a Friend, & one that knowes you well.
Fri. Blisse be vpon you. Tell me good my Friend
What Torch is yond that vainely lends his light
To grubs, and eyelesse Sculles? As I discerne,
It burneth in the *Capels* Monument.
Man. It doth so holy sir,
And there's my Master, one that you loue.
Fri. Who is it?
Man. *Romeo.*
Fri. How long hath he bin there?
Man. Full halfe an houre.
Fri. Go with me to the Vault.
Man. I dare not Sir:
My Master knowes not but I am gone hence,
And fearefully did menace me with death,
If I did stay to looke on his entents.
Fri. Stay, then Ile go alone, feares comes vpon me.
O much I feare some ill vnluckie thing.
Man. As I did sleepe vnder this young tree here,
I dreamt my maister and another fought,
And that my Maister slew him.
Fri. *Romeo.*
Alacke, alacke, what blood is this which staines
The stony entrance of this Sepulcher?
What meane these Masterlesse, and goarie Swords
To lie discolour'd by this place of peace?
Romeo, oh pale: who else? what *Paris* too?
And steept in blood? Ah what an vnknd houre
Is guiltie of this lamentable chance?
The Lady stirs.
Iul. O comfortable Frier, where's my Lord?
I do remember well where I should be:
And there I am, where is my *Romeo*?
Fri. I heare some noyse Lady, come from that nest
Of death, contagion, and vnnaturall sleepe,
A greater power then we can contradict
Hath thwarted our entents, come, come away,
Thy husband in thy bosome there lies dead:
And *Paris* too: come Ile dispose of thee,
Among a Sisterhood of holy Nunnes:
Stay not to question, for the watch is comming.
Come, go good *Iuliet*, I dare no longer stay. *Exit.*
Iul. Go get thee hence, for I will notuaway,
What's here? A cup clos'd in my true lo:es hand?
Poyson I see hath bin his timelesse end
O churle, drinke all? and left no friendly drop,
To helpe me after, I will kisse thy lips,
Happlie some poyson yet doth hang on them,
To make me die wth a restoratiue.
Thy lips are warme.
Enter Boy and Watch.
Watch. Lead Boy, which way?
Iul. Yea noise?
Then ile be briefe. O happy Dagger.
'Tis in thy sheath, there rust and let me die *Kils herselfe.*
Boy. This is the place,
There where the Torch doth burne
Watch. The ground is bloody,
Search about the Churchyard.
Go some of you, who ere you find attach.
Pittifull sight, here lies the Countie slaine,
And *Iuliet* bleeding, warme and newly dead
Who here hath laine these two dayes buried.
Go tell the Prince, runne to the *Capulets*,
Raise vp the *Mountagues*, some others search,
We see the ground whereon these woes do lye,
But the true ground of all these piteous woes,
We cannot without circumstance descry.
Enter Romeo's man.
Watch. Here's *Romeo's* man,
We found him in the Churchyard.
Con. Hold him in safety, till the Prince come hither.
Enter Frier, and another Watchman.
3. *Wat.* Here is a Frier that trembles, sighes, and weepes
We tooke this Mattocke and this Spade from him,
As he was comming from this Church-yard side.
Con. A great suspition, stay the Frier too.
Enter the Prince.
Prin. What misaduenture is so earely vp,
That calls our person from our mornings rest?
Enter Capulet and his Wife.
Cap. What should it be that they so shrike abroad?
Wife. O the people in the streete crie *Romeo.*
Some *Iuliet*, and some *Paris*, and all runne
With open outcry toward out Monument.
Pri. What feare is this which starties in your eares?
Wat. Soueraigne, here lies the Countie *Paris* slaine,
And *Romeo* dead, and *Iuliet* dead before,
Warme and new kil'd.
Prin. Search,
Seeke, and know how, this foule murder comes.
Wat. Here is a Frier, and Slaughter'd *Romeos* man,
With Instruments vpon them fit to open
These dead mens Tombes.
Cap. O heauen!
O wife looke how our Daughter bleedes!
This Dagger hath mistaine, for loe his house
Is empty on the backe of *Mountague*,
And is misheathed in my Daughters bosome.
Wife. O me, this sight of death, is as a Bell
That warnes my old age to a Sepulcher.
Enter Mountague.
Pri. Come *Mountague*, for thou art early vp
To see thy Sonne and Heire, now early downe.
Moun. Alas my liege, my wife is dead to night,
Griefe of my Sonnes exile hath stopt her breath:
What further woe conspires against my age?
Prin. Looke: and thou shalt see.
Moun. O thou vntaught, what manners in is this,
To presse before thy Father to a graue?
Prin. Seale vp the mouth of outrage for a while,
Till we can cleare these ambiguities,
And know their spring, their head, their true descent,
And then will I be generall of your woes,
And lead you euen to death? meane time forbeare,
And let mischance be slaue to patience,
Bring forth the parties of suspition.
Fri. I am the greatest, able to doe least,
Yet most suspected as the time and place
Doth make against me of this direfull murther:
And heere I stand both to impeach and purge
My selfe condemned, and my selfe excus'd.
Prin. Then say at once, what thou dost know in this?
Fri. I will be briefe, for my short date of breath
Is not so long as is a tedious tale.
Romeo there dead, was husband to that *Iuliet*,
And she there dead, that's *Romeo's* faithfull wife:

I

I married them; and their ſtolne marriage day
Was *Tybalts* Doomeſday: whoſe vntimely death
Baniſh'd the new-made Bridegroome from this Citie:
For whom (and not for *Tybalt*) *Iuliet* pinde.
You, to remoue that ſiege of Greefe from her,
Betroth'd, and would haue married her perforce
To Countie *Paris* Then comes ſhe to me,
And (with wilde lookes) bid me deuiſe ſome meanes
To rid her from this ſecond Marriage,
Or in my Cell there would ſhe kill her ſelfe
Then gaue I her (ſo Tutor'd by my Art)
A ſleeping Potion, which ſo tooke effect
As I intended, for it wrought on her
The forme of death. Meane time, I writ to *Romeo*,
That he ſhould hither come, as this dyre night,
To helpe to take her from her borrowed graue,
Being the time the Potions force ſhould ceaſe.
But he which bore my Letter, Frier *Iohn*,
Was ſtay'd by accident; and yeſternight
Return'd my Letter backe. Then all alone,
At the prefixed houre of her waking,
Came I to take her from her Kindreds vault,
Meaning to keepe her cloſely at my Cell,
Till I conueniently could ſend to *Romeo*.
But when I came (ſome Minute ere the time
Of her awaking) heere vntimely lay
The Noble *Paris*, and true *Romeo* dead.
Shee wakes, and I intreated her come foorth,
And beare this worke of Heauen, with patience:
But then, a noyſe did ſcarre me from the Tombe,
And ſhe (too deſperate) would not go with me,
But (as it ſeemes) did violence on her ſelfe.
All this I know, and to the Marriage her Nurſe is priuy:
And if ought in this miſcarried by my fault,
Let my old life be ſacrific'd, ſome houre before the time,
Vnto the rigour of ſeuereſt Law.
Prin. We ſtill haue knowne thee for a Holy man.
Where's *Romeo's* man? What can he ſay to this?
Boy. I brought my Maſter newes of *Iuliets* death,
And then in poſte he came from *Mantua*
To this ſame place, to this ſame Monument.
This Letter he early bid me giue his Father,
And threatned me with death, going in the Vault,
If I departed not, and left him there
Prin. Giue me the Letter, I will look on it
Where is the Counties Page that rais'd the Watch?
Sirra, what made your Maſter in this place?
Page. He came with flowres to ſtrew his Ladies graue,
And bid me ſtand aloofe, and ſo I did:
Anon comes one with light to ope the Tombe,
And by and by my Maiſter drew on him,
And then I ran away to call the Watch.
Prin. This Letter doth make good the Friers words,
ir courſe of Loue, the tydings of her death·
And heere he writes, that he did buy a poyſon
Of a poore Pothecarie, and therewithall
Came to this Vault to dye, and lye with *Iuliet*.
Where be theſe Enemies? *Capulet*, *Mountague*,
See what a ſcourge is laide vpon your hate,
That Heauen finds meanes to kill your ioyes with Loue;
And I, for winking at your diſcords too,
Haue loſt a brace of Kinſmen: All are puniſh'd.
Cap. O Brother *Mountague*, giue me thy hand,
This is my Daughters ioynture, for no more
Can I demand.
Moun But I can giue thee more·
For I will raiſe her Statue in pure Gold,
That whiles *Verona* by that name is knowne,
There ſhall no figure at that Rate be ſet,
As that of True and Faithfull *Iuliet*.
Cap As rich ſhall *Romeo* by his Lady ly,
Poore ſacrifices of our enmity.
Prin. A glooming peace this morning with it brings,
The Sunne for ſorrow will not ſhew his head;
Go hence, to haue more talke of theſe ſad things,
Some ſhall be pardon'd, and ſome puniſhed·
For neuer was a Storie of more Wo,
Then this of *Iuliet*, and her *Romeo*.
Exeunt omnes

Gg

FINIS.

THE LIFE OF TYMON OF ATHENS.

Actus Primus. Scœna Prima.

Enter Poet, Painter, Ieweller, Merchant, and Mercer, at seuerall doores.

Poet.

Ood day Sir.
Pain. I am glad y'are well.
Poet. I haue not seene you long, how goes the World?
Pain. It weares sir, as it growes.
Poet. I that's well knowne:
But what particular Rarity? What strange,
Which manifold record not matches: see
Magicke of Bounty, all these spirits thy power
Hath coniur'd to attend.
I know the Merchant.
Pain. I know them both: th'others a Ieweller.
Mer. O 'tis a worthy Lord.
Iew. Nay that's most fixt.
Mer. A most incomparable man, breath'd as it were,
To an vntyreable and continuate goodnesse:
He passes.
Iew. I haue a Iewell heere.
Mer. O pray let's see't. For the Lord *Timon*, sir?
Iewel. If he will touch the estimate. But for that——
Poet. When we for recompence haue prais'd the vild,
It staines the glory in that happy Verse,
Which aptly sings the good.
Mer. 'Tis a good forme.
Iewel. And rich: heere is a Water looke ye.
Pain. You are rapt sir, in some worke, some Dedication to the great Lord.
Poet. A thing slipt idlely from me.
Our Poesie is as a Gowne, which vses
From whence 'tis nourisht: the fire i'th Flint
Shewes not, till it be strooke: our gentle flame
Prouokes it selfe, and like the currant flyes
Each bound it chases. What haue you there?
Pain. A Picture sir: when comes your Booke forth?
Poet. Vpon the heeles of my presentment sir.
Let's see your peece.
Pain. 'Tis a good Peece.
Poet. So 'tis, this comes off well, and excellent.
Pain. Indifferent.
Poet. Admirable: How this grace
Speakes his owne standing: what a mentall power
This eye shootes forth? How bigge imagination
Moues in this Lip, to th'dumbnesse of the gesture,
One might interpret.
Pain. It is a pretty mocking of the life:
Heere is a touch: Is't good?
Poet. I will say of it,
It Tutors Nature, Artificiall strife
Liues in these toutches, liuelier then life.

Enter certaine Senators.

Pain. How this Lord is followed.
Poet. The Senators of Athens, happy men.
Pain. Looke moe.
Po. You see this confluence, this great flood of visitors,
I haue in this rough worke, shap'd out a man
Whom this beneath world doth embrace and hugge
With amplest entertainment: My free drift
Halts not particularly, but moues it selfe
In a wide Sea of wax, no leuell'd malice
Infects one comma in the course I hold,
But flies an Eagle flight, bold, and forth on,
Leauing no Tract behinde.
Pain. How shall I vnderstand you?
Poet. I will vnboult to you.
You see how all Conditions, how all Mindes,
As well of glib and slipp'ry Creatures, as
Of Graue and austere qualitie, tender downe
Their seruices to Lord *Timon*: his large Fortune,
Vpon his good and gracious Nature hanging,
Subdues and properties to his loue and tendance
All sorts of hearts; yea, from the glasse-fac'd Flatterer
To *Apemantus*, that few things loues better
Then to abhorre himselfe; euen hee drops downe
The knee before him, and returnes in peace
Most rich in *Timons* nod.
Pain. I saw them speake together.
Poet. Sir, I haue vpon a high and pleasant hill
Feign'd Fortune to be thron'd.
The Base o'th' Mount
Is rank'd with all deserts, all kinde of Natures
That labour on the bosome of this Sphere,
To propagate their states; among'st them all,
Whose eyes are on this Soueraigne Lady fixt,
One do I personate of Lord *Timons* frame,
Whom Fortune with her Iuory hand wafts to her,
Whose present grace, to present slaues and seruants
Translates his Riuals.
Pain. 'Tis conceyu'd, to scope
This Throne, this Fortune, and this Hill me thinkes
With

With one man becken'd from the reſt below,
Bowing his head againſt the ſteepy Mount
To climbe his happineſſe, would be well expreſt
In our Condition.
Poet. Nay Sir, but heare me on:
All thoſe which were his Fellowes but of late,
Some better then his valew; on the moment
Follow his ſtrides, his Lobbies fill with tendance,
Raine Sacrificiall whiſperings in his eare,
Make Sacred euen his ſtyrrop, and through him
Drinke the free Ayre.
Pain. I marry, what of theſe?
Poet. When Fortune in her ſhift and change of mood
Spurnes downe her late beloued; all his Dependants
Which labour'd after him to the Mountaines top,
Euen on their knees and hand, let him ſit downe,
Not one accompanying his declining foot.
Pain. Tis common:
A thouſand morall Paintings I can ſhew,
That ſhall demonſtrate theſe quicke blowes of Fortunes,
More pregnantly then words. Yet you do well,
To ſhew Lord *Timon*, that meane eyes haue ſeene
The foot aboue the head.

Trumpets ſound.
Enter Lord Timon, addreſſing himſelfe curteouſly to euery Sutor.

Tim. Impriſon'd is he, ſay you?
Meſ. I my good Lord, fiue Talents is his debt,
His meanes moſt ſhort, his Creditors moſt ſtraite:
Your Honourable Letter he deſires
To thoſe haue ſhut him vp, which failing,
Periods his comfort.
Tim. Noble *Ventidius* well:
I am not of that Feather, to ſhake off
My Friend when he muſt neede me. I do know him
A Gentleman, that well deſerues a helpe,
Which he ſhall haue. Ile pay the debt, and free him.
Meſ. Your Lordſhip euer bindes him.
Tim. Commend me to him, I will ſend his ranſome,
And being enfranchized bid him come to me;
'Tis not enough to helpe the Feeble vp,
But to ſupport him after. Fare you well.
Meſ. All happineſſe to your Honor. *Exit.*

Enter an old Athenian.

Oldm. Lord *Timon*, heare me ſpeake.
Tim. Freely good Father.
Oldm. Thou haſt a Seruant nam'd *Lucilius.*
Tim. I haue ſo: What of him?
Oldm. Moſt Noble *Timon*, call the man before thee.
Tim. Attends he heere, or no? *Lucillius.*
Luc Heere at your Lordſhips ſeruice.
Oldm. This Fellow heere, L. *Timon*, this thy Creature,
By night frequents my houſe. I am a man
That from my firſt haue beene inclin'd to thrift,
And my eſtate deſerues an Heyre more rais'd,
Then one which holds a Trencher.
Tim. Well: what further?
Old. One onely Daughter haue I, no Kin elſe,
On whom I may conferre what I haue got:
The Maid is faire, a'th'youngeſt for a Bride,
And I haue bred her at my deereſt coſt
In Qualities of the beſt. This man of thine
Attempts her loue: I prythee (Noble Lord)
Ioyne with me to forbid him her reſort,
My ſelfe haue ſpoke in vaine.
Tim. The man is honeſt.
Oldm. Therefore he will be *Timon*,
His honeſty rewards him in it ſelfe,
It muſt not beare my Daughter.
Tim. Does ſhe loue him?
Oldm. She is yong and apt:
Our owne precedent paſſions do inſtruct vs
What leuities in youth.
Tim. Loue you the Maid?
Luc. I my good Lord, and ſhe accepts of it.
Oldm. If in her Marriage my conſent be miſſing,
I call the Gods to witneſſe, I will chooſe
Mine heyre from forth the Beggers of the world,
And diſpoſſeſſe her all.
Tim. How ſhall ſhe be endowed,
If ſhe be mated with an equall Husband?
Oldm. Three Talents on the preſent; in future, all.
Tim. This Gentleman of mine
Hath ſeru'd me long:
To build his Fortune, I will ſtraine a little,
For 'tis a Bond in men. Giue him thy Daughter,
What you beſtow, in him Ile counterpoize,
And make him weigh with her.
Oldm. Moſt Noble Lord,
Pawne me to this your Honour, ſhe is his.
Tim My hand to thee,
Mine Honour on my promiſe.
Luc. Humbly I thanke your Lordſhip, neuer may
That ſtate or Fortune fall into my keeping,
Which is not owed to you. *Exit*
Poet. Vouchſafe my Labour,
And long liue your Lordſhip.
Tim. I thanke you, you ſhall heare from me anon:
Go not away. What haue you there, my Friend?
Pain. A peece of Painting, which I do beſeech
Your Lordſhip to accept.
Tim. Painting is welcome.
The Painting is almoſt the Naturall man:
For ſince Diſhonor Trafickes with mans Nature,
He is but out-ſide: Theſe Penſil'd Figures are
Euen ſuch as they giue out. I like your worke,
And you ſhall finde I like it; Waite attendance
Till you heare further from me.
Pain. The Gods preſerue ye.
Tim. Well fare you Gentleman: giue me your hand,
We muſt needs dine together: ſir your Iewell
Hath ſuffered vnder praiſe.
Iewel. What my Lord, diſpraiſe?
Tim. A meere ſaciety of Commendations,
If I ſhould pay you for't as 'tis extold,
It would vnclew me quite.
Iewel. My Lord, 'tis rated
As thoſe which ſell would giue: but you well know,
Things of like valew differing in the Owners,
Are prized by their Maſters. Beleeu't deere Lord,
You mend the Iewell by the wearing it.
Tim. Well mock'd. *Enter Apermantus.*
Mer. No my good Lord, he ſpeakes ỳ common toong
Which all men ſpeake with him.
Tim. Looke who comes heere, will you be chid?
Iewel. Wee'l beare with your Lordſhip.
Mer. Hee'l ſpare none.
Tim. Good morrow to thee,
Gentle *Apermantus.*

Ape. Till I be gentle, stay thou for thy good morrow.
When thou art *Timons* dogge, and these Knaues honest.
Tim. Why dost thou call them Knaues, thou know'st them not.
Ape. Are they not Athenians?
Tim. Yes.
Ape. Then I repent not.
Iew. You know me, *Apemantus*?
Ape. Thou know'st I do, I call'd thee by thy name.
Tim. Thou art proud *Apemantus*?
Ape. Of nothing so much, as that I am not like *Timon*
Tim. Whether art going?
Ape. To knocke out an honest Athenians braines.
Tim. That's a deed thou't dye for.
Ape. Right, if doing nothing be death by th'Law.
Tim. How lik'st thou this picture *Apemantus*?
Ape. The best, for the innocence.
Tim. Wrought he not well that painted it.
Ape. He wrought better that made the Painter, and yet he's but a filthy peece of worke.
Pain. Y'are a Dogge.
Ape. Thy Mothers of my generation: what's she, if I be a Dogge?
Tim. Wilt dine with me *Apemantus*?
Ape. No: I eate not Lords.
Tim. And thou should'st, thoud'st anger Ladies.
Ape. O they eate Lords;
So they come by great bellies.
Tim. That's a lasciuious apprehension.
Ape. So, thou apprehend'st it,
Take it for thy labour.
Tim. How dost thou like this Iewell, *Apemantus*?
Ape. Not so well as plain-dealing, which wil not cast a man a Doit.
Tim. What dost thou thinke 'tis worth?
Ape. Not worth my thinking.
How now Poet?
Poet. How now Philosopher?
Ape. Thou lyest.
Poet. Art not one?
Ape. Yes.
Poet. Then I lye not.
Ape. Art not a Poet?
Poet. Yes.
Ape. Then thou lyest:
Looke in thy last worke, where thou hast fegin'd him a worthy Fellow.
Poet. That's not feign'd, he is so.
Ape. Yes he is worthy of thee, and to pay thee for thy labour. He that loues to be flattered, is worthy o'th flatterer. Heauens, that I were a Lord.
Tim. What wouldst do then *Apemantus*?
Ape. E'ne as *Apemantus* does now, hate a Lord with my heart.
Tim. What thy selfe?
Ape. I.
Tim. Wherefore?
Ape. That I had no angry wit to be a Lord.
Art not thou a Merchant?
Mer. I *Apemantus*.
Ape. Traffick confound thee, if the Gods will not.
Mer. If Trafficke do it, the Gods do it.
Ape. Traffickes thy God, & thy God confound thee.

Trumpet sounds. Enter a Messenger.

Tim. What Trumpets that?
Mes. 'Tis *Alcibiades*, and some twenty Horse
All of Companionship.
Tim. Pray entertaine them, giue them guide to vs.
You must needs dine with me: go not you hence
Till I haue thankt you: when dinners done
Shew me this peece, I am ioyfull of your sights.

Enter Alcibiades with the rest.

Most welcome Sir.
Ape. So, so; their Aches contract, and sterue your supple ioynts: that there should bee small loue amongest these sweet Knaues, and all this Curtesie. The straine of mans bred out into Baboon and Monkey.
Alc. Sir, you haue sau'd my longing, and I feed
Most hungerly on your sight.
Tim. Right welcome Sir:
Ere we depatt, wee'l share a bounteous time
In different pleasures.
Pray you let vs in. *Exeunt.*

Enter two Lords.

1. Lord What time a day is't *Apemantus*?
Ape. Time to be honest.
1 That time serues still.
Ape. The most accursed thou that still omitst it.
2 Thou art going to Lord *Timons* Feast.
Ape. I, to see meate fill Knaues, and Wine heat fooles.
2 Farthee well, farthee well.
Ape. Thou art a Foole to bid me farewell twice.
2 Why *Apemantus*?
Ape. Should'st haue kept one to thy selfe, for I meane to giue thee none.
1 Hang thy selfe.
Ape. No I will do nothing at thy bidding:
Make thy requests to thy Friend.
2 Away vnpeaceable Dogge,
Or Ile spurne thee hence.
Ape. I will flye like a dogge, the heeles a'th'Asse.
1 Hee's opposite to humanity.
Comes shall we in,
And taste Lord *Timons* bountie: he out-goes
The verie heart of kindnesse.
2 He powres it out: *Plutus* the God of Gold
Is but his Steward: no meede but he repayes
Seuen-fold aboue it selfe: No guift to him,
But breeds the giuer a returne: exceeding
All vse of quittance.
1 The Noblest minde he carries,
That euer gouern'd man.
2 Long may he liue in Fortunes. Shall we in?
Ile keepe you Company. *Exeunt.*

Hoboyes Playing lowd Musicke.

A great Banquet seru'd in: and then, Enter Lord Timon, the States, the Athenian Lords, Ventigius which Timon redeem'd from prison. Then comes dropping after all Apemantus discontentedly like himselfe.

Ventig. Most honoured *Timon*,
It hath pleas'd the Gods to remember my Fathers age,
And call him to long peace:
He is gone happy, and has left me rich:
Then, as in gratefull Vertue I am bound
To your free heart, I do returne those Talents
Doubled with thankes and seruice, from whose helpe
I deriu'd libertie.
Tim. O by no meanes,
Honest *Ventigius*: You mistake my loue,
I gaue

I gaue it freely euer, and ther's none
Can truely say he giues, if he receiues:
If our betters play at that game, we must not dare
To imitate them: faults that are rich are faire.

Vint. A Noble spirit.

Tim. Nay my Lords, Ceremony was but deuis'd at first
To set a glosse on faint deeds, hollow welcomes,
Recanting goodnesse, sorry ere 'tis showne:
But where there is true friendship, there needs none.
Pray sit, more welcome are ye to my Fortunes,
Then my Fortunes to me.

1. Lord. My Lord, we alwaies haue confest it.

Aper. Ho ho, confest it? Handg'd it? Haue you not?

Timo. O *Apermantus*, you are welcome.

Aper. No: You shall not make me welcome:
I come to haue thee thrust me out of doores.

Tim. Fie, th'art a churle, ye haue got a humour there
Does not become a man, 'tis much too blame:
They say my Lords, *Ira furor breuis est*,
But yond man is verie angrie.
Go, let him haue a Table by himselfe:
For he does neither affect companie,
Nor is he fit for't indeed.

Aper. Let me stay at thine apperill *Timon*,
I come to obserue, I giue thee warning on't.

Tim. I take no heede of thee: Th'art an *Athenian*, therefore welcome: I my selfe would haue no power, prythee let my meate make thee silent.

Aper. I scorne thy meate, 'twould choake me: for I should nere flatter thee. Oh you Gods! What a number of men eats *Timon*, and he sees 'em not? It greeues me to see so many dip there meate in one mans blood, and all the madnesse is, he cheeres them vp too.
I wonder men dare trust themselues with men.
Me thinks they should enuite them without kniues,
Good for there meate, and safer for their liues.
There's much example for't, the fellow that sits next him, now parts bread with him, pledges the breath of him in a diuided draught: is the readiest man to kill him. 'Tas beene proued, if I were a huge man I should feare to drinke at meales, least they should spie my wind-pipes dangerous noates, great men should drinke with harnesse on their throates.

Tim. My Lord in heart: and let the health go round.

2. Lord. Let it flow this way my good Lord.

Aper. Flow this way? A braue fellow. He keepes his tides well, those healths will make thee and thy state looke ill, *Timon*.
Heere's that which is too weake to be a sinner,
Honest water, which nere left man i'th'mire:
This and my food are equals, there's no ods,
Feasts are to proud to giue thanks to the Gods.

Apermantus Grace.

Immortall Gods, I craue no pelfe,
I pray for no man but my selfe,
Graunt I may neuer proue so fond,
To trust man on his Oath or Bond.
Or a Harlot for her weeping,
Or a Dogge that seemes asleeping,
Or a keeper with my freedome,
Or my friends if I should need 'em.
Amen. So fall too't:
Richmen sin, and I eat root.

Much good dich thy good heart, *Apermantus*

Tim. Captaine,
Alcibiades, your hearts in the field now.

Alci. My heart is euer at your seruice, my Lord.

Tim. You had rather be at a breakefast of Enemies, then a dinner of Friends.

Alc. So they were bleeding new my Lord there's no meat like 'em, I could wish my best friend at such a Feast.

Aper. Would all those Flatterers were thine Enemies then, that then thou might'st kill 'em: & bid me to 'em.

1. Lord. Might we but haue that happinesse my Lord, that you would once vse our hearts, whereby we might expresse some part of our zeales, we should thinke our selues for euer perfect.

Timon. Oh no doubt my good Friends, but the Gods themselues haue prouided that I shall haue much helpe from you: how had you beene my Friends else. Why haue you that charitable title from thousands? Did not you chiefely belong to my heart? I haue told more of you to my selfe, then you can with modestie speake in your owne behalfe. And thus farre I confirme you. Oh you Gods (thinke I,) what need we haue any Friends; if we should nere haue need of 'em? They were the most needlesse Creatures liuing; should we nere haue vse for 'em? And would most resemble sweete Instruments hung vp in Cases, that keepes there sounds to themselues. Why I haue often wisht my selfe poorer, that I might come neerer to you: we are borne to do benefits. And what better or properer can we call our owne, then the riches of our Friends? Oh what a pretious comfort 'tis, to haue so many like Brothers commanding one anothers Fortunes. Oh ioyes, e'ne made away er't can be borne: mine eies cannot hold out water me thinks. to forget their Faults. I drinke to you.

Aper. Thou weep'st to make them drinke, *Timon*.

2. Lord. Ioy had the like conception in our eies,
And at that instant, like a babe sprung vp.

Aper. Ho, ho: I laugh to thinke that babe a bastard

3. Lord. I promise you my Lord you mou'd me much.

Aper. Much.

Sound Tucket. Enter the Maskers of Amazons, with Lutes in their hands, dauncing and playing.

Tim. What meanes that Trumpe? How now?

Enter Seruant.

Ser. Please you my Lord, there are certaine Ladies
Most desirous of admittance.

Tim. Ladies? what are their wils?

Ser. There comes with them a fore-runner my Lord, which beares that office, to signifie their pleasures.

Tim. I pray let them be admitted.

Enter Cupid with the Maske of Ladies.

Cup. Haile to thee worthy *Timon* and to all that of his Bounties taste: the fiue best Sences acknowledge thee their Patron, and come freely to gratulate thy plentious bosome.
There tast, touch all pleas'd from thy Table rise:
They onely now come but to Feast thine eies.

Timo. They'r wecome all, let 'em haue kind admittance. Musicke make their welcome.

Luc. You see my Lord, how ample y'are belou'd.

Aper. Hoyday,
What a sweepe of vanitie comes this way.
They daunce? They are madwomen,

gg3 Like

Like Madnesse is the glory of this life,
As this pompe shewes to a little oyle and roote.
We make our selues Fooles, to disport our selues,
And spend our Flatteries, to drinke those men,
Vpon whose Age we voyde it vp agen
With poysonous Spight and Enuy.
Who liues, that's not depraued, or depraues;
Who dyes, that beares not one spurne to their graues
Of their Friends guift:
I should feare, those that dance before me now,
Would one day stampe vpon me: 'Tas bene done,
Men shut their doores against a setting Sunne.

The Lords rise from Table, with much adoring of Timon, and to shew their loues, each single out an Amazon, and all Dance, men with women, a loftie straine or two to the Hoboyes, and cease.

Tim. You haue done our pleasures
Much grace (faire Ladies)
Set a faire fashion on our entertainment,
Which was not halfe so beautifull, and kinde:
You haue added worth vntoo't, and luster,
And entertain'd me with mine owne deuice.
I am to thanke you for't.

1 Lord. My Lord you take vs euen at the best.

Aper. Faith for the worst is filthy, and would not hold taking, I doubt me.

Tim. Ladies, there is an idle banquet attends you,
Please you to dispose your selues.

All La. Most thankfully, my Lord. *Exeunt.*

Tim. *Flauius.*

Fla. My Lord.

Tim. The little Casket bring me hither.

Fla. Yes, my Lord. More Iewels yet?
There is no crossing him in's humor,
Else I should tell him well, yfaith I should;
When all's spent, hee'ld be crost then, and he could.
'Tis pitty Bounty had not eyes behinde,
That man might ne're be wretched for his minde. *Exit.*

1 Lord. Where be our men?

Ser. Heere my Lord, in readinesse.

2 Lord. Our Horses.

Tim. O my Friends:
I haue one word to say to you: Looke you, my good L.
I must intreat you honour me so much,
As to aduance this Iewell, accept it, and weare it,
Kinde my Lord.

1 Lord. I am so farre already in your guifts.

All. So are we all.

Enter a Seruant.

Ser. My Lord, there are certaine Nobles of the Senate newly alighted, and come to visit you.

Tim. They are fairely welcome.

Enter Flauius.

Fla. I beseech your Honor, vouchsafe me a word, it does concerne you neere.

Tim. Neere? why then another time Ile heare thee.
I prythee let's be prouided to shew them entertainment.

Fla. I scarse know how.

Enter another Seruant.

Ser. May it please your Honor, Lord *Lucius*
(Out of his free loue) hath presented to you
Foure Milke-white Horses, trapt in Siluer.

Tim. I shall accept them fairely: let the Presents
Be worthily entertain'd.

Enter a third Seruant.

How now? What newes?

3. Ser. Please you my Lord, that honourable Gentleman Lord *Lucullus*, entreats your companie to morrow, to hunt with him, and ha's sent your Honour two brace of Grey-hounds.

Tim. Ile hunt with him,
And let them be receiu'd, not without faire Reward.

Fla. What will this come to?
He commands vs to prouide, and giue great guifts, and all out of an empty Coffer:
Nor will he know his Purse, or yeeld me this,
To shew him what a Begger his heart is,
Being of no power to make his wishes good.
His promises flye so beyond his state,
That what he speaks is all in debt, he ows for eu'ry word:
He is so kinde, that he now payes interest for't;
His Land's put to their Bookes. Well, would I were
Gently put out of Office, before I were forc'd out:
Happier is he that has no friend to feede,
Then such that do e'ne Enemies exceede.
I bleed inwardly for my Lord. *Exit*

Tim. You do your selues much wrong,
You bate too much of your owne merits.
Heere my Lord, a trifle of our Loue.

2 Lord. With more then common thankes
I will receyue it.

3. Lord. O he's the very soule of Bounty

Tim. And now I remember my Lord, you gaue good words the other day of a Bay Courser I rod on. Tis yours because you lik'd it.

1. L. Oh, I beseech you pardon mee, my Lord, in that.

Tim. You may take my word my Lord: I know no man can iustly praise, but what he does affect. I weighe my Friends affection with mine owne: Ile tell you true, Ile call to you.

All Lor. O none so welcome.

Tim I take all, and your seuerall visitations
So kinde to heart, 'tis not enough to giue.
Me thinkes, I could deale Kingdomes to my Friends,
And nere be wearie. *Alcibiades*,
Thou art a Soldiour, therefore sildome rich,
It comes in Charitie to thee: for all thy liuing
Is mong'st the dead: and all the Lands thou hast
Lye in a pitcht field.

Alc. I, defil'd Land, my Lord.

1. Lord. We are so vertuously bound.

Tim. And so am I to you.

2. Lord. So infinitely endeer'd.

Tim. All to you. Lights, more Lights.

1 Lord. The best of Happines, Honor, and Fortunes
Keepe with you Lord *Timon*.

Tim. Ready for his Friends. *Exeunt Lords*

Aper. What a coiles heere, seruing of beckes, and iutting out of bummes. I doubt whether their Legges be worth the summes that are giuen for 'em.
Friendships full of dregges,
Me thinkes false hearts, should neuer haue sound legges.
Thus honest Fooles lay out their wealth on Curtsies.

Tim. Now *Apermantus* (if thou wert not sullen)
I would be good to thee.

Aper. No, Ile nothing; for if I should be brib'd too, there would be none left to raile vpon thee, and then thou wouldst sinne the faster. Thou giu'st so long *Timon* (I feare me) thou wilt giue away thy selfe in paper shortly. What needs these Feasts, pompes, and Vaine-glories?

Tim.

Tim. Nay, and you begin to raile on Societie once, I am sworne not to giue regard to you. Farewell, & come with better Musicke. *Exit*

Aper. So: Thou wilt not heare mee now, thou shalt not then. Ile locke thy heauen from thee:
Oh that mens eares should be
To Counsell deafe, but not to Flatterie. *Exit*

Enter a Senator.

Sen. And late fiue thousand: to *Varro* and to *Isidore*
He owes nine thousand, besides my former summe,
Which makes it fiue and twenty. Still in motion
Of raging waste? It cannot hold, it will not.
If I want Gold, steale but a beggers Dogge,
And giue it *Timon*, why the Dogge coines Gold.
If I would sell my Horse, and buy twenty moe
Better then he; why giue my Horse to *Timon*.
Aske nothing, giue it him, it Foles me straight
And able Horses: No Porter at his gate,
But rather one that smiles, and still inuites
All that passe by. It cannot hold, no reason
Can sound his state in safety. *Caphis* hoa,
Caphis I say.

Enter Caphis.

Ca. Heere sir, what is your pleasure.

Sen. Get on your cloake, & hast you to Lord *Timon*,
Importune him for my Moneyes, be not ceast
With slight deniall; nor then silenc'd, when
Commend me to your Master, and the Cap
Playes in the right hand, thus: but tell him,
My Vses cry to me; I must serue my turne
Out of mine owne, his dayes and times are past,
And my reliances on his fracted dates
Haue smit my credit. I loue, and honour him,
But must not breake my backe, to heale his finger.
Immediate are my needs, and my releefe
Must not be tost and turn'd to me in words,
But finde supply immediate. Get you gone,
Put on a most importunate aspect,
A visage of demand: for I do feare
When euery Feather stickes in his owne wing,
Lord *Timon* will be left a naked gull,
Which flashes now a Phœnix, get you gone.

Ca. I go sir.

Sen. I go sir?
Take the Bonds along with you,
And haue the dates in. Come.

Ca. I will Sir.

Sen. Go. *Exeunt*

Enter Steward, with many billes in his hand.

Stew. No care, no stop, so senselesse of expence,
That he will neither know how to maintaine it,
Nor cease his flow of Riot. Takes no accompt
How things go from him, nor resume no care
Of what is to continue: neuer minde,
Was to be so vnwise, to be so kinde.
What shall be done, he will not heare, till feele:
I must be round with him, now he comes from hunting.
Fye, fie, fie, fie.

Enter Caphis, Isidore, and Varro.

Cap. Good euen *Varro*: what, you come for money?

Var. Is't not your businesse too?

Cap. It is, and yours too, *Isidore*?

Isid. It is so.

Cap. Would we were all discharg'd.

Var. I feare it,

Cap. Heere comes the Lord.

Enter Timon, and his Traine.

Tim. So soone as dinners done, wee'l forth againe
My *Alcibiades*. With me, what is your will?

Cap. My Lord, heere is a note of certaine dues.

Tim. Dues? whence are you?

Cap. Of Athens heere, my Lord.

Tim. Go to my Steward.

Cap. Please it your Lordship, he hath put me off
To the succession of new dayes this moneth:
My Master is awak'd by great Occasion,
To call vpon his owne, and humbly prayes you,
That with your other Noble parts, you'l suite,
In giuing him his right.

Tim. Mine honest Friend,
I prythee but repaire to me next morning.

Cap. Nay, good my Lord.

Tim. Containe thy selfe, good Friend.

Var. One *Varroes* seruant, my good Lord.

Isid From *Isidore*, he humbly prayes your speedy payment.

Cap. If you did know my Lord, my Masters wants.

Var. 'Twas due on forfeyture my Lord, sixe weekes, and past.

Isi. Your Steward puts me off my Lord, and I
Am sent expressely to your Lordship.

Tim. Giue me breath:
I do beseech you good my Lords keepe on,
Ile waite vpon you instantly. Come hither. pray you
How goes the world, that I am thus encountred
With clamorous demands of debt, broken Bonds,
And the detention of long since due debts
Against my Honor?

Stew. Please you Gentlemen,
The time is vnagreeable to this businesse:
Your importunacie cease, till after dinner,
That I may make his Lordship vnderstand:
Wherefore you are not paid.

Tim. Do so my Friends, see them well entertain'd.

Stew. Pray draw neere. *Exit.*

Enter Apemantus and Foole.

Caph. Stay, stay, here comes the Foole with *Apemantus*, let's ha some sport with 'em.

Var. Hang him, hee'l abuse vs.

Isid. A plague vpon him dogge.

Var. How dost Foole?

Ape. Dost Dialogue with thy shadow?

Var. I speake not to thee.

Ape. No 'tis to thy selfe. Come away.

Isi. There's the Foole hangs on your backe already.

Ape. No thou stand'st single, th'art not on him yet.

Cap. Where's the Foole now?

Ape. He last ask'd the question. Poore Rogues, and Vsurers men, Bauds betweene Gold and want.

Al. What are we *Apemantus*?

Ape. Asses.

All. Why?

Ape. That you ask me what you are, & do not know your selues. Speake to 'em Foole.

Foole. How do you Gentlemen?

All. Gramercies good Foole:
How does your Mistris?

Foole.

Foole. She's e'ne setting on water to scal'd such Chickens as you are. Would we could see you at Corinth.
Ape. Good, Gramercy.

Enter Page.

Foole. Looke you, heere comes my Masters Page.
Page. Why how now Captaine? what do you in this
wise Company.
How dost thou *Apermantus*?
Ape. Would I had a Rod in my mouth, that I might
answer thee profitably
Boy. Prythee *Apemantus* reade me the superscripti-
on of these Letters, I know not which is which.
Ape. Canst not read?
Page No.
Ape There will litle Learning dye then that day thou
art hang'd. This is to Lord *Timon*, this to *Alcibiades*. Go
thou was't borne a Bastard, and thou't dye a Bawd.
Page. Thou was't whelpt a Dogge, and thou shalt
famish a Dogges death.
Answer not, I am gone. *Exit*
Ape. E'ne so thou out-runst Grace,
Foole I will go with you to Lord *Timons.*
Foole. Will you leaue me there?
Ape. If *Timon* stay at home.
You three serue three Vsurers?
All. I would they seru'd vs.
Ape. So would I:
As good a tricke as euer Hangman seru'd Theefe.
Foole. Are you three Vsurers men?
All. I Foole.
Foole. I thinke no Vsurer, but ha's a Foole to his Ser-
uant. My Mistris is one, and I am her Foole: when men
come to borrow of your Masters, they approach sadly,
and go away merry: but they enter my Masters house
merrily, and go away sadly. The reason of this?
Var. I could render one.
Ap. Do it then, that we may account thee a Whore-
master, and a Knaue, which notwithstanding thou shalt
be no lesse esteemed.
Varro. What is a Whoremaster Foole?
Foole. A Foole in good cloathes, and something like
thee. 'Tis a spirit, sometime t'appeares like a Lord, somtime like a Lawyer, sometime like a Philosopher, with
two stones moe then's artificiall one. Hee is verie often
like a Knight; and generally, in all shapes that man goes
vp and downe in, from fourescore to thirteen, this spirit
walkes in.
Var. Thou art not altogether a Foole.
Foole. Nor thou altogether a Wise man,
As much foolerie as I haue, so much wit thou lack'st.
Ape. That answer might haue become *Apemantus.*
All. Aside, aside, heere comes Lord *Timon.*

Enter Timon and Steward.

Ape. Come with me (Foole) come.
Foole. I do not alwayes follow Louer, elder Brother,
and Woman, sometime the Philosopher.
Stew. Pray you walke neere,
Ile speake with you anon. *Exeunt.*
Tim. You make me meruell wherefore ere this time
Had you not fully laide my state before me,
That I might so haue rated my expence
As I had leaue of meanes.
Stew. You would not heare me:
At many leysures I propose.
Tim. Go too:
Perchance some single vantages you tooke,
When my indisposition put you backe,
And that vnaptnesse made your minister
Thus to excuse your selfe.
Stew. O my good Lord,
At many times I brought in my accompts,
Laid them before you, you would throw them off,
And say you found them in mine honestie,
When for some trifling present you haue bid me
Returne so much, I haue shooke my head, and wept:
Yea 'gainst th' Authoritie of manners, pray'd you
To hold your hand more close: I did indure
Not sildome, nor no slight checkes, when I haue
Prompted you in the ebbe of your estate,
And your great flow of debts; my lou'd Lord,
Though you heare now (too late) yet nowes a time,
The greatest of your hauing, lackes a halfe,
To pay your present debts.
Tim. Let all my Land be sold.
Stew. Tis all engag'd, some forfeyted and gone,
And what remaines will hardly stop the mouth
Of present dues; the future comes apace:
What shall defend the interim, and at length
How goes our reck'ning?
Tim. To Lacedemon did my Land extend.
Stew. O my good Lord, the world is but a word,
Were it all yours, to giue it in a breath,
How quickely were it gone.
Tim. You tell me true.
Stew. If you suspect my Husbandry or Falshood,
Call me before th'exactest Auditors,
And set me on the proofe. So the Gods blesse me,
When all our Offices haue beene opprest
With riotous Feeders, when our Vaults haue wept
With drunken spilth of Wine; when euery roome
Hath blaz'd with Lights, and braid with Minstrelsie,
I haue retyr'd me to a wastefull cocke,
And set mine eyes at flow.
Tim. Prythee no more.
Stew. Heauens, haue I said, the bounty of this Lord:
How many prodigall bits haue Slaues and Pezants
This night englutted: who is not *Timons*,
What heart, head, sword, force, meanes, but is L. *Timons*:
Great *Timon*, Noble, Worthy, Royall *Timon*:
Ah, when the meanes are gone, that buy this praise,
The breath is gone, whereof this praise is made:
Feast won, fast lost; one cloud of Winter showres,
These flyes are coucht.
Tim. Come sermon me no further.
No villanous bounty yet hath past my heart;
Vnwisely, not ignobly haue I giuen.
Why dost thou weepe, canst thou the conscience lacke,
To thinke I shall lacke friends: secure thy heart,
If I would broach the vessels of my loue,
And try the argument of hearts, by borrowing,
Men, and mens fortunes could I frankely vse
As I can bid thee speake.
Ste. Assurance blesse your thoughts.
Tim. And in some sort these wants of mine are crown'd,
That I account them blessings. For by these
Shall I trie Friends. You shall perceiue
How you mistake my Fortunes:
I am wealthie in my Friends.
Within there, *Flauius, Seruilius*?

Enter

Enter three Seruants.

Ser. My Lord, my Lord.

Tim. I will dispatch you seuerally.
You to Lord *Lucius*, to Lord *Lucullus* you, I hunted with his Honor to day; you to *Sempronius*; commend me to their loues ; and I am proud say, that my occasions haue found time to vse 'em toward a supply of mony : let the request be fifty Talents.

Flam. As you haue said, my Lord.

Stew. Lord *Lucius* and *Lucullus*? Humh.

Tim. Go you sir to the Senators;
Of whom, euen to the States best health ; I haue
Deseru'd this Hearing : bid 'em send o'th'instant
A thousand Talents to me.

Ste. I haue beene bold
(For that I knew it the most generall way)
To them, to vse your Signet, and your Name,
But they do shake their heads, and I am heere
No richer in returne.

Tim. Is't true? Can't be?

Stew. They answer in a ioynt and corporate voice,
That now they are at fall, want Treature cannot
Do what they would, are sorrie : you are Honourable,
But yet they could haue wisht, they know not,
Something hath beene amisse ; a Noble Nature
May catch a wrench ; would all were well ; tis pitty,
And so intending other serious matters,
After distastefull lookes ; and these hard Fractions
With certaine halfe-caps, and cold mouing nods,
They froze me into Silence.

Tim. You Gods reward them :
Prythee man looke cheerely. These old Fellowes
Haue their ingratitude in them Hereditary :
Their blood is cak'd, 'tis cold, it sildome flowes,
'Tis lacke of kindely warmth, they are not kinde ;
And Nature, as it growes againe toward earth,
Is fashion'd for the iourney, dull and heauy.
Go to *Ventiddius* (prythee be not sad,
Thou art true, and honest ; Ingeniously I speake,
No blame belongs to thee :) *Ventiddius* lately
Buried his Father, by whose death hee's stepp'd
Into a great estate : When he was poore,
Imprison'd, and in scarsitie of Friends,
I cleer'd him with fiue Talents : Greet him from me,
Bid him suppose, some good necessity
Touches his Friend, which craues to be remembred
With those fiue Talents ; that had, giue't these Fellowes
To whom 'tis instant due. Neu'r speake, or thinke,
That *Timons* fortunes 'mong his Friends can sinke.

Stew. I would I could not thinke it :
That thought is Bounties Foe ;
Being free it selfe, it thinkes all others so. *Exeunt*

Flaminius waiting to speake with a Lord from his Master, enters a seruant to him.

Ser. I haue told my Lord of you, he is comming down to you.

Flam. I thanke you Sir.

Enter Lucullus.

Ser. Heere's my Lord.

Luc. One of Lord *Timons* men? A Guift I warrant. Why this hits right : I dreampt of a Siluer Bason & Ewre to night. *Flaminius*, honest *Flaminius*, you are verie respectiuely welcome sir. Fill me some Wine. And how does that Honourable, Compleate, Free-hearted Gentleman of Athens, thy very bountifull good Lord and Mayster?

Flam. His health is well sir.

Luc. I am right glad that his health is well sir : and what hast thou there vnder thy Cloake, pretty *Flaminius*?

Flam. Faith, nothing but an empty box Sir, which in my Lords behalfe, I come to intreat your Honor to supply : who hauing great and instant occasion to vse fiftie Talents, hath sent to your Lordship to furnish him : nothing doubting your present assistance therein.

Luc. La, la, la, la : Nothing doubting sayes hee? Alas good Lord, a Noble Gentleman 'tis, if he would not keep so good a house. Many a time and often I ha din'd with him, and told him on't, and come againe to supper to him of purpose, to haue him spend lesse, and yet he wold embrace no counsell, take no warning by my comming, euery man has his fault, and honesty is his. I ha told him on't, but I could nere get him from't.

Enter Seruant with Wine.

Ser. Please your Lordship, heere is the Wine.

Luc. *Flaminius*, I haue noted thee alwayes wise. Heere's to thee.

Flam. Your Lordship speakes your pleasure.

Luc. I haue obserued thee alwayes for a towardlie prompt spirit, giue thee thy due, and one that knowes what belongs to reason; and canst vse the time wel, if the time vse thee well. Good parts in thee ; get you gone sirrah. Draw neerer honest *Flaminius*. Thy Lords a bountifull Gentleman, but thou art wise, and thou know'st well enough (although thou com'st to me) that this is no time to lend money, especially vpon bare friendshippe without securitie. Here's three *Solidares* for thee, good Boy winke at me, and say thou saw'st mee not. Fare thee well.

Flam. Is't possible the world should so much differ,
And we aliue that liued? Fly damned basenesse
To him that worships thee.

Luc. Ha? Now I see thou art a Foole, and fit for thy Master. *Exit L.*

Flam May these adde to the number ỳ may scald thee:
Let moulten Coine be thy damnation,
Thou disease of a friend, and not himselfe :
Has friendship such a faint and milkie heart,
It turnes in lesse then two nights? O you Gods!
I feele my Masters passion. This Slaue vnto his Honor,
Has my Lords meate in him :
Why should it thriue, and turne to Nutriment,
When he is turn'd to poyson?
O may Diseases onely worke vpon't :
And when he's sicke to death, let not that part of Nature
Which my Lord payd for, be of any power
To expell sicknesse, but prolong his hower. *Exit.*

Enter Lucius, with three strangers.

Luc. Who the Lord *Timon*? He is my very good friend and an Honourable Gentleman.

1 We know him for no lesse, thogh we are but strangers to him. But I can tell you one thing my Lord, and which I heare from common rumours, now Lord *Timons* happie howres are done and past, and his estate shrinkes from him.

Lucius. Fye no, doe not beleeue it : hee cannot want for money.

2 But beleeue you this my Lord, that not long agoe, one of his men was with the Lord *Lucullus*, to borrow so many Talents, nay vrg'd extreamly for't, and shewed what

what neceſſity belong'd too't, and yet was deny'de.

Luci. How?

2 I tell you, deny'de my Lord.

Luci. What a ſtrange caſe was that? Now before the Gods I am aſham'd on't. Denied that honourable man? There was verie little Honour ſhew'd in't. For my owne part, I muſt needes confeſſe, I haue receyued ſome ſmall kindneſſes from him, as Money, Plate, Iewels, and ſuch like Trifles; nothing comparing to his: yet had hee miſtooke him, and ſent to me, I ſhould ne're haue denied his Occaſion ſo many Talents.

Enter Seruilius.

Seruil. See, by good hap yonders my Lord, I haue ſwet to ſee his Honor. My Honor'd Lord.

Lucil. *Seruilius*? You are kindely met ſir. Farthewell, commend me to thy Honourable vertuous Lord, my very exquiſite Friend.

Seruil. May it pleaſe your Honour, my Lord hath ſent ——

Luci. Ha? what ha's he ſent? I am ſo much endeered to that Lord; hee's euer ſending: how ſhall I thank him think'ſt thou? And what has he ſent now?

Seruil. Has onely ſent his preſent Occaſion now my Lord: requeſting your Lordſhip to ſupply his inſtant vſe with ſo many Talents.

Lucil. I know his Lordſhip is but merry with me,
He cannot want fifty fiue hundred Talents.

Seruil. But in the mean time he wants leſſe my Lord.
If his occaſion were not vertuous,
I ſhould not vrge it halfe ſo faithfully.

Luc. Doſt thou ſpeake ſeriouſly *Seruilius*?

Seruil. Vpon my ſoule 'tis true Sir.

Luci. What a wicked Beaſt was I to disfurniſh my ſelf againſt ſuch a good time, when I might ha ſhewn my ſelfe Honourable? How vnluckily it hapned, that I ſhold Purchaſe the day before for a little part, and vndo a great deale of Honour? *Seruilius*, now before the Gods I am not able to do (the more beaſt I ſay) I was ſending to vſe Lord *Timon* my ſelfe, theſe Gentlemen can witneſſe; but I would not for the wealth of Athens I had done't now. Commend me bountifully to his good Lordſhip, and I hope his Honor will conceiue the faireſt of mee, becauſe I haue no power to be kinde. And tell him this from me, I count it one of my greateſt afflictions ſay, that I cannot pleaſure ſuch an Honourable Gentleman. Good *Seruilius*, will you befriend mee ſo farre, as to vſe mine owne words to him?

Ser. Yes ſir, I ſhall. *Exit Seruil.*

Lucil. Ile looke you out a good turne *Seruilius*.
True as you ſaid, *Timon* is ſhrunke indeede,
And he that's once deny'de, will hardly ſpeede. *Exit.*

1 Do you obſerue this *Hoſtilius*?

2 I, to well.

1 Why this is the worlds ſoule,
And iuſt of the ſame peece
Is euery Flatterers ſport: who can call him his Friend
That dips in the ſame diſh? For in my knowing
Timon has bin this Lords Father,
And kept his credit with his purſe:
Supported his eſtate, nay *Timons* money
Has paid his men their wages. He ne're drinkes,
But *Timons* Siluer treads vpon his Lip,
And yet, oh ſee the monſtrouſneſſe of man,
When he lookes out in an vngratefull ſhape;
He does deny him (in reſpect of his)
What charitable men affoord to Beggers.

3 Religion grones at it.

1 For mine owne part, I neuer taſted *Timon* in my life
Nor came any of his bounties ouer me,
To marke me for his Friend. Yet I proteſt,
For his right Noble minde, illuſtrious Vertue,
And Honourable Carriage,
Had his neceſſity made vſe of me,
I would haue put my wealth into Donation,
And the beſt halfe ſhould haue return'd to him,
So much I loue his heart: But I perceiue,
Men muſt learne now with pitty to diſpence,
For Policy ſits aboue Conſcience. *Exeunt.*

Enter a third ſeruant with Sempronius, another of Timons Friends.

Semp. Muſt he needs trouble me in't? Hum.
'Boue all others?
He might haue tried Lord *Lucius*, or *Lucullus*,
And now *Ventidgius* is wealthy too,
Whom he redeem'd from priſon. All theſe
Owes their eſtates vnto him.

Ser. My Lord,
They haue all bin touch'd, and found Baſe-Mettle,
For they haue all denied him.

Semp. How? Haue they deny'de him?
Has *Ventidgius* and *Lucullus* deny'de him,
And does he ſend to me? Three? Humh?
It ſhewes but little loue, or iudgement in him.
Muſt I be his laſt Refuge? His Friends (like Phyſitians)
Thriue, giue him ouer: Muſt I take th'Cure vpon me?
Has much diſgrac'd me in't, I'me angry at him,
That might haue knowne my place. I ſee no ſenſe for't,
But his Occaſions might haue wooed me firſt:
For in my conſcience, I was the firſt man
That ere receiued guift from him.
And does he thinke ſo backwardly of me now,
That Ile requite it laſt? No:
So it may proue an Argument of Laughter
To th'reſt, and 'mong'ſt Lords be thought a Foole:
I'de rather then the worth of thrice the ſumme,
Had ſent to me firſt, but for my mindes ſake:
I'de ſuch a courage to do him good. But now returne,
And with their faint reply, this anſwer ioyne;
Who bates mine Honor, ſhall not know my Coyne. *Exit*

Ser. Excellent: Your Lordſhips a goodly Villain: the diuell knew not what he did, when hee made man Politicke; he croſſed himſelfe by't: and I cannot thinke, but in the end, the Villanies of man will ſet him cleere. How fairely this Lord ſtriues to appeare foule? Takes Vertuous Copies to be wicked: like thoſe, that vnder hotte ardent zeale, would ſet whole Realmes on fire, of ſuch a nature is his politike loue.
This was my Lords beſt hope, now all are fled
Saue onely the Gods. Now his Friends are dead,
Doores that were ne're acquainted with their Wards
Many a bounteous yeere, muſt be imploy'd
Now to guard ſure their Maſter:
And this is all a liberall courſe allowes,
Who cannot keepe his wealth, muſt keep his houſe. *Exit.*

Enter Varro's man, meeting others. All Timons Creditors to wait for his comming out. Then enter Lucius and Hortenſius.

Var.man. Well met, goodmorrow *Titus* & *Hortenſius*

Titus

Tit. The like to you kinde Varro.
Hort. Lucius, what do we meet together?
Luci. I, and I think one businesse do's command vs all.
For mine is money.
Tit. So is theirs, and ours.

Enter Philotus.

Luci. And sir Philotus too.
Phil. Good day at once.
Luci. Welcome good Brother.
What do you thinke the houre?
Phil. Labouring for Nine.
Luci. So much?
Phil. Is not my Lord seene yet?
Luci. Not yet.
Phil. I wonder on't, he was wont to shine at seauen.
Luci. I, but the dayes are waxt shorter with him:
You must consider, that a Prodigall course
Is like the Sunnes, but not like his recouerable, I feare:
'Tis deepest Winter in Lord Timons purse, that is: One may reach deepe enough, and yet finde little.
Phil. I am of your feare, for that.
Tit. Ile shew you how t'obserue a strange euent:
Your Lord sends now for Money?
Hort. Most true, he doe's.
Tit. And he weares Iewels now of Timons guift,
For which I waite for money.
Hort. It is against my heart.
Luci. Marke how strange it showes,
Timon in this, should pay more then he owes:
And e'ne as if your Lord should weare rich Iewels,
And send for money for 'em.
Hort. I'me weary of this Charge,
The Gods can witnesse:
I know my Lord hath spent of Timons wealth,
And now Ingratitude, makes it worse then stealth.
Varro. Yes, mine's three thousand Crownes:
What's yours?
Luci. Fiue thousand mine.
Varro. 'Tis much deepe, and it should seem by th'sum
Your Masters confidence was aboue mine,
Else surely his had equall'd.

Enter Flaminius.

Tit. One of Lord Timons men.
Luc. Flaminius? Sir, a word: Pray is my Lord readie to come forth?
Flam. No, indeed he is not.
Tit. We attend his Lordship: pray signifie so much.
Flam. I need not tell him that, he knowes you are too (diligent.

Enter Steward in a Cloake, muffled

Luci. Ha: is not that his Steward muffled so?
He goes away in a Clowd: Call him, call him.
Tit. Do you heare, sir?
2.Varro. By your leaue, sir.
Stew. What do ye aske of me, my Friend.
Tit. We waite for certaine Money heere, sir.
Stew. I, if Money were as certaine as your waiting,
T'were sure enough.
Why then preferr'd you not your summes and Billes
When your false Masters eate of my Lords meat?
Then they could smile, and fawne vpon his debts,
And take downe th'Intrest into their glutt'nous Mawes.
You do your selues but wrong, to stirre me vp,
Let me passe quietly:
Beleeue't, my Lord and I haue made an end,
I haue no more to reckon, he to spend.
Luci. I, but this answer will not serue.
Stew. If't 'twill not serue, 'tis not so base as you,
For you serue Knaues.
1.Varro. How? What does his casheer'd Worship mutter?
2.Varro. No matter what, hee's poore, and that's reuenge enough. Who can speake broader, then hee that has no house to put his head in? Such may rayle against great buildings.

Enter Seruilius.

Tit. Oh heere's Seruilius: now wee shall know some answere.
Seru. If I might beseech you Gentlemen, to repayre some other houre, I should deriue much from't. For tak't of my soule, my Lord leanes wondrously to discontent: His comfortable temper has forsooke him, he's much out of health, and keepes his Chamber.
Luci. Many do keepe their Chambers, are not sick:
And if it be so farre beyond his health,
Me thinkes he should the sooner pay his debts,
And make a cleere way to the Gods.
Seruil. Good Gods.
Titus We cannot take this for answer, sir.
Flaminius within. Seruilius helpe, my Lord, my Lord.

Enter Timon in a rage.

Tim What, are my dores oppos'd against my passage?
Haue I bin euer free, and must my house
Be my retentiue Enemy? My Gaole?
The place which I haue Feasted, does it now
(Like all Mankinde) shew me an Iron heart?
Luci. Put in now Titus.
Tit. My Lord, heere is my Bill.
Luci. Here's mine.
1 Var. And mine, my Lord.
2.Var. And ours, my Lord.
Philo. All our Billes.
Tim. Knocke me downe with 'em, cleaue mee to the Girdle.
Luc. Alas, my Lord.
Tim. Cut my heart in summes.
Tit. Mine, fifty Talents.
Tim. Tell out my blood.
Luc. Fiue thousand Crownes, my Lord.
Tim. Fiue thousand drops payes that.
What yours? and yours?
1.Var. My Lord.
2.Var. My Lord.
Tim. Teare me, take me, and the Gods fall vpon you.

Exit Timon.

Hort. Faith I perceiue our Masters may throwe their caps at their money, these debts may well be call'd desperate ones, for a madman owes 'em. Exeunt.

Enter Timon.

Timon. They haue e'ne put my breath from mee the slaues. Creditors? Diuels.
Stew. My deere Lord.
Tim. What if it should be so?
Stew. My Lord.
Tim. Ile haue it so. My Steward?
Stew. Heere my Lord.
Tim. So fitly? Go, bid all my Friends againe
Lucius, Lucullus, and Sempronius Vllorxa: All,
Ile once more feast the Rascals.
Stew. O my Lord, you onely speake from your distracted soule; there's not so much left to, furnish out a moderate Table.

Timon

Tim. Be it not in thy care:
Go I charge thee, inuite them all, let in the tide
Of Knaues once more: my Cooke and Ile prouide. *Exeunt*

Enter three Senators at one doore, Alcibiades meeting them, with Attendants.

1.Sen. My Lord, you haue my voyce, too't,
The faults Bloody:
'Tis necessary he should dye:
Nothing imboldens sinne so much, as Mercy.
2 Most true; the Law shall bruise 'em.
Alc Honor, health, and compassion to the Senate.
1 Now Captaine.
Alc, I am an humble Sutor to your Vertues;
For pitty is the vertue of the Law,
And none but Tyrants vse it cruelly.
It pleases time and Fortune to lye heauie
Vpon a Friend of mine, who in hot blood
Hath stept into the Law: which is past depth
To those that (without heede) do plundge intoo't.
He is a Man (setting his Fate aside) of comely Vertues,
Nor did he soyle the fact with Cowardice,
(And Honour in him, which buyes out his fault)
But with a Noble Fury, and faire spirit,
Seeing his Reputation touch'd to death,
He did oppose his Foe:
And with such sober and vnnoted passion
He did behooue his anger ere 'twas spent,
As if he had but prou'd an Argument
1 Sen. You vndergo too strict a Paradox,
Striuing to make an vgly deed looke faire:
Your words haue tooke such paines, as if they labour'd
To bring Man-slaughter into forme, and set Quarrelling
Vpon the head of Valour; which indeede
Is Valour mis-begot, and came into the world,
When Sects, and Factions were newly borne.
Hee's truly Valiant, that can wisely suffer
The worst that man can breath,
And make his Wrongs, his Out-sides,
To weare them like his Rayment, carelessely,
And ne're preferre his iniuries to his heart,
To bring it into danger.
If Wrongs be euilles, and inforce vs kill,
What Folly 'tis, to hazard life for Ill.
Alci. My Lord.
1.Sen. You cannot make grosse finnes looke cleare,
To reuenge is no Valour, but to beare.
Alci. My Lords, then vnder fauour, pardon me,
If I speake like a Captaine.
Why do fond men expose themselues to Battell,
And not endure all threats? Sleepe vpon't,
And let the Foes quietly cut their Throats
Without repugnancy? If there be
Such Valour in the bearing, what make wee
Abroad? Why then, Women are more valiant
That stay at home, if Bearing carry it:
And the Asse, more Captaine then the Lyon?
The fellow loaden with Irons, wiser then the Iudge?
If Wisedome be in suffering, Oh my Lords,
As you are great, be pittifully Good,
Who cannot condemne rashnesse in cold blood?
To kill, I grant, is sinnes extreamest Gust,
But in defence, by Mercy, 'tis most iust.
To be in Anger, is impietie:
But who is Man, that is not Angrie.
Weigh but the Crime with this.

2.Sen. You breath in vaine.
Alci. In vaine?
His seruice done at Lacedemon, and Bizantium,
Were a sufficient briber for his life.
1 What's that?
Alc. Why say my Lords ha's done faire seruice,
And slaine in fight many of your enemies:
How full of valour did he beare himselfe
In the last Conflict, and made plenteous wounds?
2 He has made too much plenty with him:
He's a sworne Riotor, he has a sinne
That often drownes him, and takes his valour prisoner.
If there were no Foes, that were enough
To ouercome him. In that Beastly furie,
He has bin knowne to commit outrages,
And cherrish Factions. 'Tis inferr'd to vs,
His dayes are foule, and his drinke dangerous.
1 He dyes.
Alci. Hard fate: he might haue dyed in warre.
My Lords, if not for any parts in him,
Though his right arme might purchase his owne time,
And be in debt to none: yet more to moue you,
Take my deserts to his, and ioyne 'em both.
And for I know, your reuerend Ages loue Security,
Ile pawne my Victories, all my Honour to you
Vpon his good returnes.
If by this Crime, he owes the Law his life,
Why let the Warre receiue't in valiant gore,
For Law is strict, and Warre is nothing more.
1 We are for Law, he dyes, vrge it no more
On height of our displeasure: Friend, or Brother,
He forfeits his owne blood, that spilles another.
Alc. Must it be so? It must not bee:
My Lords, I do beseech you know mee.
2 How?
Alc. Call me to your remembrances.
3 What.
Alc I cannot thinke but your Age has forgot me,
It could not else be, I should proue so bace,
To sue and be deny'de such common Grace.
My wounds ake at you.
1 Do you dare our anger?
'Tis in few words, but spacious in effect:
We banish thee for euer.
Alc. Banish me?
Banish your dotage, banish vsurie,
That makes the Senate vgly.
1 If after two dayes shine, Athens containe thee,
Attend our waightier Iudgement.
And not to swell our Spirit,
He shall be executed presently. *Exeunt.*
Alc. Now the Gods keepe you old enough,
That you may liue
Onely in bone, that none may looke on you.
I'm worse then mad: I haue kept backe their Foes
While they haue told their Money, and let out
Their Coine vpon large interest. I my selfe,
Rich onely in large hurts. All those, for this?
Is this the Balsome, that the vsuring Senat
Powres into Captaines wounds? Banishment.
It comes not ill: I hate not to be banisht,
It is a cause worthy my Spleene and Furie,
That I may strike at Athens. Ile cheere vp
My discontented Troopes, and lay for hearts;
'Tis Honour with most Lands to be at ods,
Souldiers should brooke as little wrongs as Gods. *Exit.*

Enter

Enter diuers Friends at seuerall doores.

1 The good time of day to you, sir.

2 I also wish it to you: I thinke this Honorable Lord did but try vs this other day.

1 Vpon that were my thoughts tyring when wee encountred. I hope it is not so low with him as he made it seeme in the triall of his seuerall Friends.

2 It should not be, by the perswasion of his new Feasting.

1 I should thinke so. He hath sent mee an earnest inuiting, which many my neere occasions did vrge mee to putoff: but he hath coniur'd mee beyond them, and I must needs appeare.

2 In like manner was I in debt to my importunat businesse, but he would not heare my excuse. I am sorrie, when he sent to borrow of mee, that my Prouision was out.

1 I am sicke of that greefe too, as I vnderstand how all things go.

2 Euery man heares so: what would hee haue borrowed of you?

1 A thousand Peeces.

2 A thousand Peeces?

1 What of you?

2 He sent to me sir —— Heere he comes.

Enter Timon and Attendants.

Tim. With all my heart Gentlemen both; and how fare you?

1 Euer at the best, hearing well of your Lordship.

2 The Swallow followes not Summer more willing, then we your Lordship.

Tim. Nor more willingly leaues Winter, such Summer Birds are men. Gentlemen, our dinner will not recompence this long stay: Feast your eares with the Musicke awhile: If they will fare so harshly o'th' Trumpets sound: we shall too't presently.

1 I hope it remaines not vnkindely with your Lordship, that I return'd you an empty Messenger.

Tim. O sir, let it not trouble you.

2 My Noble Lord.

Tim. Ah my good Friend, what cheere?

The Banket brought in.

2 My most Honorable Lord, I am e'ne sick of shame, that when your Lordship this other day sent to me, I was so vnfortunate a Beggar.

Tim. Thinke not on't, sir.

2 If you had sent but two houres before.

Tim. Let it not cumber your better remembrance.
Come bring in all together.

2 All couer'd Dishes.

1 Royall Cheare, I warrant you.

3 Doubt not that, if money and the season can yeild it

1 How do you? What's the newes?

3 *Alcibiades* is banish'd: heare you of it?

Both. *Alcibiades* banish'd?

3 'Tis so, be sure of it.

1 How? How?

2 I pray you vpon what?

Tim. My worthy Friends, will you draw neere?

3 Ile tell you more anon. Here's a Noble feast toward

2 This is the old man still.

3 Wilt hold? Wilt hold?

2 It do's: but time will, and so.

3 I do conceyue.

Tim. Each man to his stoole, with that spurre as hee would to the lip of his Mistris: your dyet shall bee in all places alike. Make not a Citie Feast of it, to let the meat coole, ere we can agree vpon the first place. Sit, sit.
The Gods require our Thankes.

You great Benefactors, sprinkle our Society with Thankefulnesse. For your owne guifts, make your selues prais'd: But reserue still to giue, least your Deities be despised. Lend to each man enough, that one neede not lend to another. For were your Godheads to borrow of men, men would forsake the Gods. Make the Meate be beloued, more then the Man that giues it. Let no Assembly of Twenty, be without a score of Villaines. If there sit twelue Women at the Table, let a dozen of them bee as they are. The rest of your Fees, O Gods, the Senators of Athens, together with the common legge of People, what is amisse in them, you Gods, make suteable for destruction. For these my present Friends, as they are to mee nothing, so in nothing blesse them, and to nothing are they welcome.

Vncouer Dogges, and lap.

Some speake. What do's his Lordship meane?

Some other. I know not.

Timon. May you a better Feast neuer behold
You knot of Mouth-Friends: Smoke, & lukewarm water
Is your perfection. This is *Timons* last,
Who stucke and spangled you with Flatteries,
Washes it off and sprinkles in your faces
Your reeking villany. Liue loath'd, and long
Most smiling, smooth, detested Parasites,
Curteous Destroyers, affable Wolues, meeke Beares:
You Fooles of Fortune, Trencher-friends, Times Flyes,
Cap and knee-Slaues, vapours, and Minute Iackes.
Of Man and Beast, the infinite Maladie
Crust you quite o're. What do'st thou go?
Soft, take thy Physicke first; thou too, and thou:
Stay I will lend thee money, borrow none.
What? All in Motion? Henceforth be no Feast,
Whereat a Villaine's not a welcome Guest.
Burne house, sinke Athens, henceforth hated be
Of *Timon* Man, and all Humanity. *Exit*

Enter the Senators, with other Lords.

1 How now, my Lords?

2 Know you the quality of Lord *Timons* fury?

3 Push, did you see my Cap?

4 I haue lost my Gowne.

1 He's but a mad Lord, & nought but humors swaies him. He gaue me a Iewell th'other day, and now hee has beate it out of my hat.
Did you see my Iewell?

2 Did you see my Cap.

3 Heere 'tis.

4 Heere lyes my Gowne.

1 Let's make no stay.

2 Lord *Timons* mad.

3 I feel't vpon my bones.

4 One day he giues vs Diamonds, next day stones.

Exeunt the Senators.

Enter Timon.

Tim. Let me looke backe vpon thee. O thou Wall
That girdles in those Wolues, diue in the earth,
And fence not Athens. Matrons, turne incontinent,
Obedience fayle in Children: Slaues and Fooles

h h Plucke

Plucke the graue wrinkled Senate from the Bench,
And minister in their steeds, to generall Filthes.
Conuert o'th'Instant greene Virginity,
Doo't in your Parents eyes. Bankrupts, hold fast
Rather then render backe; out with your Kniues,
And cut your Trusters throates. Bound Seruants, steale,
Large-handed Robbers your graue Masters are,
And pill by Law. Maide, to thy Masters bed,
Thy Mistris is o'th'Brothell. Some of sixteen,
Plucke the lyn'd Crutch from thy old limping Sire,
With it, beate out his Braines. Piety, and Feare,
Religion to the Gods, Peace, Iustice, Truth,
Domesticke awe, Night-rest, and Neighbour-hood,
Instruction, Manners, Mysteries, and Trades,
Degrees, Obseruances, Customes, and Lawes,
Decline to your confounding contraries.
And yet Confusion liue: Plagues incident to men,
Your potent and infectious Feauors, heape
On Athens ripe for stroke. Thou cold Sciatica,
Cripple our Senators, that their limbes may halt
As lamely as their Manners. Lust, and Libertie
Creepe in the Mindes and Marrowes of our youth,
That 'gainst the streame of Vertue they may striue,
And drowne themselues in Riot. Itches, Blaines,
Sowe all th'Athenian bosomes, and their crop
Be generall Leprosie: Breath, infect breath,
That their Society (as their Friendship) may
Be meerely poyson. Nothing Ile beare from thee
But nakednesse, thou detestable Towne,
Take thou that too, with multiplying Bannes:
Timon will to the Woods, where he shall finde
Th'vnkindest Beast, more kinder then Mankinde.
The Gods confound (heare me you good Gods all)
Th'Athenians both within and out that Wall:
And graunt as *Timon* growes, his hate may grow
To the whole race of Mankinde, high and low.
Amen. *Exit.*

Enter Steward with two or three Seruants.

1 Heare you M. Steward, where's our Master?
Are we vndone, cast off, nothing remaining?
Stew. Alack my Fellowes, what should I say to you?
Let me be recorded by the righteous Gods,
I am as poore as you.
1 Such a House broke?
So Noble a Master falne, all gone, and not
One Friend to take his Fortune by the arme,
And go along with him.
2 As we do turne our backes
From our Companion, throwne into his graue,
So his Familiars to his buried Fortunes
Slinke all away, leaue their false vowes with him
Like empty purses pickt; and his poore selfe
A dedicated Beggar to the Ayre,
With his disease, of all shunn'd pouerty,
Walkes like contempt alone. More of our Fellowes.
Enter other Seruants.
Stew. All broken Implements of a ruin'd house.
3 Yet do our hearts weare *Timons* Liuery,
That see I by our Faces: we are Fellowes still,
Seruing alike in sorrow: Leak'd is our Barke,
And we poore Mates, stand on the dying Decke,
Hearing the Surges threat: we must all part
Into this Sea of Ayre.
Stew. Good Fellowes all,
The latest of my wealth Ile share among'st you
Where euer we shall meete, for *Timons* sake,
Let's yet be Fellowes. Let's shake our heads, and say
As 'twere a Knell vnto our Masters Fortunes,
We haue seene better dayes. Let each take some:
Nay put out all your hands: Not one word more,
Thus part we rich in sorrow, parting poore.
Embrace and part seuerall wayes.
Oh the fierce wretchednesse that Glory brings vs!
Who would not wish to be from wealth exempt,
Since Riches point to Misery and Contempt?
Who would be so mock'd with Glory, or to liue
But in a Dreame of Friendship,
To haue his pompe, and all what state compounds,
But onely painted like his varnisht Friends:
Poore honest Lord, brought lowe by his owne heart,
Vndone by Goodnesse: Strange vnvsuall blood,
When mans worst sinne is, He do's too much Good.
Who then dares to be halfe so kinde agen?
For Bounty that makes Gods, do still marre Men.
My deerest Lord, blest to be most accurst,
Rich onely to be wretched; thy great Fortunes
Are made thy cheefe Afflictions. Alas (kinde Lord)
Hee's flung in Rage from this ingratefull Seate
Of monstrous Friends:
Nor ha's he with him to supply his life,
Or that which can command it:
Ile follow and enquire him out.
Ile euer serue his minde, with my best will,
Whilst I haue Gold, Ile be his Steward still. *Exit.*

Enter Timon in the woods.

Tim. O blessed breeding Sun, draw from the earth
Rotten humidity: below thy Sisters Orbe
Infect the ayre. Twin'd Brothers of one wombe,
Whose procreation, residence, and birth,
Scarse is diuidant: touch them with seuerall fortunes,
The greater scornes the lesser. Not Nature
(To whom all sores lay siege) can beare great Fortune
But by contempt of Nature.
Raise me this Begger, and deny't that Lord,
The Senators shall beare contempt Hereditary,
The Begger Natiue Honor.
It is the Pastour Lards, the Brothers sides,
The want that makes him leaue: who dares? who dares
In puritie of Manhood stand vpright
And say, this mans a Flatterer. If one be,
So are they all: for euerie grize of Fortune
Is smooth'd by that below. The Learned pate
Duckes to the Golden Foole. All's obliquie;
There's nothing leuell in our cursed Natures
But direct villanie. Therefore be abhorr'd,
All Feasts, Societies, and Throngs of men.
His semblable, yea himselfe *Timon* disdaines,
Destruction phang mankinde; Earth yeeld me Rootes,
Who seekes for better of thee, sawce his pallate
With thy most operant Poyson. What is heere?
Gold? Yellow, glittering, precious Gold?
No Gods, I am no idle Votarist,
Roots you cleere Heauens. Thus much of this will make
Blacke, white; fowle, faire; wrong, right;
Base, Noble; Old, young; Coward, valiant.
Ha you Gods! why this? what this, you Gods? why this
Will lugge your Priests and Seruants from your sides:
Plucke stout mens pillowes from below their heads.
This

This yellow Slaue,
Will knit and breake Religions, blesse th'accurst,
Make the hoare Leprosie ador'd, place Theeues,
And giue them Title, knee, and approbation
With Senators on the Bench: This is it
That makes the wappen'd Widdow wed againe;
Shee, whom the Spittle-house, and vlcerous sores,
Would cast the gorge at. This Embalmes and Spices
To'th'Aprill day againe. Come damn'd Earth,
Thou common whore of Mankinde, that puttes oddes
Among the rout of Nations, I will make thee
Do thy right Nature. *March afarre off.*
Ha? A Drumme? Th'art quicke,
But yet Ile bury thee: Thou't go (strong Theefe)
When Gowty keepers of thee cannot stand:
Nay stay thou out for earnest.

Enter Alcibiades with Drumme and Fife in warlike manner, and Phryn a and Timandra.

Alc. What art thou there? speake.
Tim. A Beast as thou art. The Canker gnaw thy hart
For shewing me againe the eyes of Man.
Alc. What is thy name? Is man so hatefull to thee,
That art thy selfe a Man?
Tim. I am *Misantropos*, and hate Mankinde.
For thy part, I do wish thou wert a dogge,
That I might loue thee something.
Alc. I know thee well:
But in thy Fortunes am vnlearn'd, and strange.
Tim. I know thee too, and more then that I know thee
I not desire to know. Follow thy Drumme,
With mans blood paint the ground Gules, Gules:
Religious Cannons, ciuill Lawes are cruell,
Then what should warre be? This fell whore of thine,
Hath in her more destruction then thy Sword,
For all her Cherubin looke.
Phrin. Thy lips rot off.
Tim. I will not kisse thee, then the rot returnes
To thine owne lippes againe.
Alc. How came the Noble *Timon* to this change?
Tim. As the Moone do's, by wanting light to giue:
But then renew I could not like the Moone,
There were no Sunnes to borrow of.
Alc. Noble *Timon*, what friendship may I do thee?
Tim. None, but to maintaine my opinion.
Alc. What is it *Timon*?
Tim. Promise me Friendship, but performe none. If thou wilt not promise, the Gods plague thee, for thou art a man: if thou do'st performe, confound thee, for thou art a man.
Alc. I haue heard in some sort of thy Miseries.
Tim. Thou saw'st them when I had prosperitie.
Alc. I see them now, then was a blessed time.
Tim. As thine is now, held with a brace of Harlots.
Timan. Is this th'Athenian Minion, whom the world
Voic'd so regardfully?
Tim. Art thou *Timandra*? *Timan.* Yes.
Tim. Be a whore still, they loue thee not that vse thee, giue them diseases, leauing with thee their Lust. Make vse of thy salt houres, season the slaues for Tubbes and Bathes, bring downe Rose-cheekt youth to the Fubfast, and the Diet.
Timan Hang thee Monster.
Alc. Pardon him sweet *Timandra*, for his wits
Are drown'd and lost in his Calamities.
I haue but little Gold of late, braue *Timon*,
The want whereof, doth dayly make reuolt
In my penurious Band. I haue heard and greeu'd
How cursed Athens, mindelesse of thy worth,
Forgetting thy great deeds, when Neighbour states
But for thy Sword and Fortune trod vpon them.
Tim. I prythee beate thy Drum, and get thee gone.
Alc. I am thy Friend, and pitty thee deere *Timon*.
Tim. How doest thou pitty him whom ỳ dost troble,
I had rather be alone.
Alc. Why fare thee well:
Heere is some Gold for thee.
Tim. Keepe it, I cannot eate it.
Alc. When I haue laid proud Athens on a heape.
Tim. Warr'st thou 'gainst Athens.
Alc. I *Timon*, and haue cause.
Tim. The Gods confound them all in thy Conquest,
And thee after, when thou hast Conquer'd.
Alc. Why me, *Timon*?
Tim. That by killing of Villaines
Thou was't borne to conquer my Country.
Put vp thy Gold. Go on, heeres Gold, go on;
Be as a Plannetary plague, when Ioue
Will o're some high-Vic'd City, hang his poyson
In the sicke ayre: let not thy sword skip one:
Pitty not honour'd Age for his white Beard,
He is an Vsurer. Strike me the counterfet Matron,
It is her habite onely, that is honest,
Her selfe's a Bawd. Let not the Virgins cheeke
Make soft thy trenchant Sword: for those Milke pappes
That through the window Barne bore at mens eyes,
Are not within the Leafe of pitty writ,
But set them down horrible Traitors. Spare not the Babe
Whose dimpled smiles from Fooles exhaust their mercy;
Thinke it a Bastard, whom the Oracle
Hath doubtfully pronounced, the throat shall cut,
And mince it sans remorse. Sweare against Obiects,
Put Armour on thine eares, and on thine eyes,
Whose proofe, nor yels of Mothers, Maides, nor Babes,
Nor sight of Priests in holy Vestments bleeding,
Shall pierce a iot. There's Gold to pay thy Souldiers,
Make large confusion: and thy fury spent,
Confounded be thy selfe. Speake not, be gone.
Alc. Hast thou Gold yet, Ile take the Gold thou giuest me, not all thy Counsell.
Tim. Dost thou or dost thou not, Heauens curse vpon thee.
Both. Giue vs some Gold good *Timon*, hast ỳ more?
Tim. Enough to make a Whore forsweare her Trade,
And to make Whores, a Bawd. Hold vp you Sluts
Your Aprons mountant; you are not Othable,
Although I know you'l sweare, terribly sweare
Into strong shudders, and to heauenly Agues
Th'immortall Gods that heare you. Spare your Oathes:
Ile trust to your Conditions, be whores still.
And he whose pious breath seekes to conuert you,
Be strong in Whore, allure him, burne him vp,
Let your close fire predominate his smoke,
And be no turne-coats: yet may your paines six months
Be quite contrary, And Thatch
Your poore thin Roofes with burthens of the dead,
(Some that were hang'd) no matter:
Weare them, betray with them; Whore still,
Paint till a horse may myre vpon your face:
A pox of wrinkles.
Both. Well, more Gold, what then?

hh 2 Beleeue't

Beleeue't that wee'l do any thing for Gold.
Tim. Conſumptions ſowe
In hollow bones of man, ſtrike their ſharpe ſhinnes,
And marre mens ſpurring. Cracke the Lawyers voyce,
That he may neuer more falſe Title pleade,
Nor ſound his Quillets ſhrilly: Hoare the Flamen,
That ſcold'ſt againſt the quality of fleſh,
And not beleeues himſelfe. Downe with the Noſe,
Downe with it flat, take the Bridge quite away
Of him, that his particular to foreſee (bald
Smels from the generall weale. Make curld'pate Ruffians
And let the vnſcarr'd Braggerts of the Warre
Deriue ſome paine from you. Plague all,
That your Actiuity may defeate and quell
The ſourſe of all Erection. There's more Gold.
Do you damne others, and let this damne you,
And ditches graue you all.
Both. More counſell with more Money, bounteous
Timon.
Tim. More whore, more Miſcheefe firſt, I haue gi-
uen you earneſt.
Alc. Strike vp the Drum towardes Athens, farewell
Timon: if I thriue well, Ile viſit thee againe.
Tim. If I hope well, Ile neuer ſee thee more.
Alc. I neuer did thee harme.
Tim. Yes, thou ſpok'ſt well of me.
Alc. Call'ſt thou that harme?
Tim. Men dayly finde it. Get thee away,
And take thy Beagles with thee.
Alc. We but offend him, ſtrike. *Exeunt.*
Tim. That Nature being ſicke of mans vnkindneſſe
Should yet be hungry: Common Mother, thou
Whoſe wombe vnmeaſureable, and infinite breſt
Teemes and feeds all. whoſe ſelfeſame Mettle
Whereof thy proud Childe (arrogant man) is puft,
Engenders the blacke Toad, and Adder blew,
The gilded Newt, and eyeleſſe venom'd Worme,
With all th'abhorred Births below Criſpe Heauen,
Whereon *Hyperions* quickning fire doth ſhine:
Yeeld him, who all the humane Sonnes do hate,
From foorth thy plenteous boſome, one poore roote:
Enſeare thy Fertile and Conceptious wombe,
Let it no more bring out ingratefull man.
Goe great with Tygers, Dragons, Wolues, and Beares,
Teeme with new Monſters, whom thy vpward face
Hath to the Marbled Manſion all aboue
Neuer preſented. O, a Root, deare thankes:
Dry vp thy Marrowes, Vines, and Plough-torne Leas,
Whereof ingratefull man with Licouriſh draughts
And Morſels Vnctious, greaſes his pure minde,
That from it all Conſideration ſlippes ——
Enter Apemantus.
More man? Plague, plague.
Ape. I was directed hither. Men report,
Thou doſt affect my Manners, and doſt vſe them.
Tim. 'Tis then, becauſe thou doſt not keepe a dogge
Whom I would imitate. Conſumption catch thee.
Ape. This is in thee a Nature but infected,
A poore vnmanly Melancholly ſprung
From change of future. Why this Spade? this place?
This Slaue-like Habit, and theſe lookes of Care?
Thy Flatterers yet weare Silke, drinke Wine, lye ſoft,
Hugge their diſeas'd Perfumes, and haue forgot
That euer *Timon* was. Shame not theſe Woods,
By putting on the cunning of a Carper.
Be thou a Flatterer now, and ſeeke to thriue
By that which ha's vndone thee; hindge thy knee,
And let his very breath whom thou'lt obſerue
Blow off thy Cap: praiſe his moſt vicious ſtraine,
And call it excellent: thou waſt told thus:
Thou gau'ſt thine eares (like Tapſters, that bad welcom)
To Knaues, and all approachers: 'Tis moſt iuſt
That thou turne Raſcall, had'ſt thou wealth againe,
Raſcals ſhould haue't. Do not aſſume my likeneſſe.
Tim. Were I like thee, I'de throw away my ſelfe.
Ape. Thou haſt caſt away thy ſelfe, being like thy ſelf
A Madman ſo long, now a Foole: what think'ſt
That the bleake ayre, thy boyſterous Chamberlaine
Will put thy ſhirt on warme? Will theſe moyſt Trees,
That haue out-liu'd the Eagle, page thy heeles
And skip when thou point'ſt out? Will the cold brooke
Candied with Ice, Cawdle thy Morning taſte
To cure thy o're-nights ſurfet? Call the Creatures,
Whoſe naked Natures liue in all the ſpight
Of wrekefull Heauen, whoſe bare vnhouſed Trunkes,
To the conflicting Elements expos'd
Anſwer meere Nature: bid them flatter thee.
O thou ſhalt finde.
Tim. A Foole of thee: depart.
Ape. I loue thee better now, then ere I did.
Tim. I hate thee worſe.
Ape. Why?
Tim. Thou flatter'ſt miſery.
Ape. I flatter not, but ſay thou art a Caytiffe.
Tim. Why do'ſt thou ſeeke me out?
Ape. To vex thee.
Tim. Alwayes a Villaines Office, or a Fooles.
Doſt pleaſe thy ſelfe in't?
Ape. I.
Tim. What, a Knaue too?
Ape. If thou did'ſt put this ſowre cold habit on
To caſtigate thy pride, 'twere well: but thou
Doſt it enforcedly: Thou'dſt Courtier be againe
Wert thou not Beggar: willing miſery
Out-liues: incertaine pompe, is crown'd before:
The one is filling ſtill, neuer compleat:
The other, at high wiſh: beſt ſtate Contentleſſe,
Hath a diſtracted and moſt wretched being,
Worſe then the worſt, Content.
Thou ſhould'ſt deſire to dye, being miſerable.
Tim. Not by his breath, that is more miſerable.
Thou art a Slaue, whom Fortunes tender arme
With fauour neuer claſpt: but bred a Dogge.
Had'ſt thou like vs from our firſt ſwath proceeded,
The ſweet degrees that this breefe world affords,
To ſuch as may the paſſiue drugges of it
Freely command'ſt: thou would'ſt haue plung'd thy ſelf
In generall Riot, melted downe thy youth
In different beds of Luſt, and neuer learn'd
The Icie precepts of reſpect, but followed
The Sugred game before thee. But my ſelfe,
Who had the world as my Confectionarie,
The mouthes, the tongues, the eyes, and hearts of men,
At duty more then I could frame employment;
That numberleſſe vpon me ſtucke, as leaues
Do on the Oake, haue with one Winters bruſh
Fell from their boughes, and left me open, bare,
For euery ſtorme that blowes. I to beare this,
That neuer knew but better, is ſome burthen:
Thy Nature, did commence in ſufferance, Time
Hath made thee hard in't. Why ſhould'ſt yͤ hate Men?
They neuer flatter'd thee. What haſt thou giuen?
If

If thou wilt curse; thy Father (that poore ragge)
Must be thy subiect; who in spight put stuffe
To some shee-Begger, and compounded thee
Poore Rogue, hereditary. Hence, be gone,
If thou hadst not bene borne the worst of men,
Thou hadst bene a Knaue and Flatterer.

Ape. Art thou proud yet?

Tim. I, that I am not thee.

Ape. I, that I was no Prodigall.

Tim. I, that I am one now.
Were all the wealth I haue shut vp in thee,
I'ld giue thee leaue to hang it. Get thee gone:
That the whole life of Athens were in this,
Thus would I eate it.

Ape. Heere, I will mend thy Feast.

Tim. First mend thy company, take away thy selfe.

Ape. So I shall mend mine owne, by'th'lacke of thine

Tim. 'Tis not well mended so, it is but botcht;
If not, I would it were.

Ape. What would'st thou haue to Athens?

Tim. Thee thither in a whirlewind: if thou wilt,
Tell them there I haue Gold, looke, so I haue.

Ape. Heere is no vse for Gold.

Tim. The best, and truest:
For heere it sleepes, and do's no hyred harme.

Ape. Where lyest a nights *Timon*?

Tim. Vnder that's aboue me.
Where feed'st thou a-dayes *Apemantus*?

Ape. Where my stomacke findes meate, or rather where I eate it.

Tim. Would poyson were obedient, & knew my mind

Ape. Where would'st thou send it?

Tim. To sawce thy dishes.

Ape. The middle of Humanity thou neuer knewest, but the extremitie of both ends. When thou wast in thy Gilt, and thy Perfume, they mockt thee for too much Curiositie: in thy Ragges thou know'st none, but art despis'd for the contrary. There's a medler for thee, eate it.

Tim. On what I hate, I feed not.

Ape. Do'st hate a Medler?

Tim. I, though it looke like thee.

Ape. And th'hadst hated Medlers sooner, ÿ should'st haue loued thy selfe better now. What man didd'st thou euer know vnthrift, that was beloued after his meanes?

Tim. Who without those meanes thou talk'st of, didst thou euer know belou'd?

Ape. My selfe.

Tim. I vnderstand thee: thou had'st some meanes to keepe a Dogge.

Apem. What things in the world canst thou neerest compare to thy Flatterers?

Tim. Women neerest, but men: men are the things themselues. What would'st thou do with the world *Apemantus*, if it lay in thy power?

Ape. Giue it the Beasts, to be rid of the men.

Tim Would'st thou haue thy selfe fall in the confusion of men, and remaine a Beast with the Beasts.

Ape. I *Timon.*

Tim. A beastly Ambition, which the Goddes graunt thee t'attaine to. If thou wert the Lyon, the Fox would beguile thee: if thou wert the Lambe, the Foxe would eate thee: if thou wert the Fox, the Lion would suspect thee, when peraduenture thou wert accus'd by the Asse: If thou wert the Asse, thy dulnesse would torment thee; and still thou liu'dst but as a Breakefast to the Wolfe. If thou wert the Wolfe, thy greedinesse would afflict thee, & oft thou should'st hazard thy life for thy dinner. Wert thou the Vnicorne, pride and wrath would confound thee, and make thine owne selfe the conquest of thy fury. Wert thou a Beare, thou would'st be kill'd by the Horse: wert thou a Horse, thou would'st be seaz'd by the Leopard: wert thou a Leopard, thou wert Germane to the Lion, and the spottes of thy Kindred, were Iurors on thy life. All thy safety were remotion, and thy defence absence. What Beast could'st thou bee, that were not subiect to a Beast: and what a Beast art thou already, that seest not thy losse in transformation.

Ape. If thou could'st please me
With speaking to me, thou might'st
Haue hit vpon it heere.
The Commonwealth of Athens, is become
A Forrest of Beasts.

Tim. How ha's the Asse broke the wall, that thou art out of the Citie.

Ape. Yonder comes a Poet and a Painter:
The plague of Company light vpon thee:
I will feare to catch it, and giue way.
When I know not what else to do,
Ile see thee againe.

Tim. When there is nothing liuing but thee,
Thou shalt be welcome.
I had rather be a Beggers Dogge,
Then *Apemantus*.

Ape. Thou art the Cap
Of all the Fooles aliue.

Tim. Would thou wert cleane enough
To spit vpon.

Ape. A plague on thee,
Thou art too bad to curse.

Tim. All Villaines
That do stand by thee, are pure.

Ape. There is no Leprosie,
But what thou speak'st.

Tim. If I name thee, Ile beate thee;
But I should infect my hands.

Ape. I would my tongue
Could rot them off.

Tim. Away thou issue of a mangie dogge,
Choller does kill me,
That thou art aliue, I swoond to see thee.

Ape. Would thou would'st burst.

Tim. Away thou tedious Rogue, I am sorry I shall lose a stone by thee.

Ape. Beast.

Tim. Slaue.

Ape. Toad.

Tim. Rogue, Rogue, Rogue.
I am sicke of this false world, and will loue nought
But euen the meere necessities vpon't:
Then *Timon* presently prepare thy graue:
Lye where the light Fome of the Sea may beate
Thy graue stone dayly, make thine Epitaph,
That death in me, at others liues may laugh.
O thou sweete King-killer, and deare diuorce
Twixt naturall Sunne and fire: thou bright defiler
of *Himens* purest bed, thou valiant Mars,
Thou euer, yong, fresh, loued, and delicate wooer,
Whose blush doth thawe the consecrated Snow
That lyes on Dians lap.
Thou visible God,
That souldrest close Impossibilities,
And mak'st them kisse; that speak'st with euerie Tongue

To euerie purpose: O thou touch of hearts,
Thinke thy slaue-man rebels, and by thy vertue
Set them into confounding oddes, that Beasts
May haue the world in Empire.

Ape. Would'twere so,
But not till I am dead. Ile say th'hast Gold:
Thou wilt be throng'd too shortly.

Tim. Throng'd too?

Ape. I.

Tim. Thy backe I prythee.

Ape. Liue, and loue thy misery.

Tim. Long liue so, and so dye. I am quit.

Ape. Mo things like men,
Eate *Timon*, and abhorre then. *Exit Apeman.*

Enter the Bandetti.

1 Where should he haue this Gold? It is some poore Fragment, some slender Ort of his remainder: the meere want of Gold, and the falling from of his Friendes, droue him into this Melancholly.

2 It is nois'd
He hath a masse of Treasure.

3 Let vs make the assay vpon him, if he care not for't, he will supply vs easily: if he couetously reserue it, how shall's get it?

2 True: for he beares it not about him:
'Tis hid.

1 Is not this hee?

All. Where?

2 'Tis his description.

3 He? I know him.

All. Saue thee *Timon.*

Tim. Now Theeues.

All. Soldiers, not Theeues.

Tim. Both too, and womens Sonnes.

All. We are not Theeues, but men
That much do want.

Tim. Your greatest want is, you want much of meat:
Why should you want? Behold, the Earth hath Rootes:
Within this Mile breake forth a hundred Springs:
The Oakes beare Mast, the Briars Scarlet Heps,
The bounteous Huswife Nature, on each bush,
Layes her full Messe before you. Want? why Want?

1 We cannot liue on Grasse, on Berries, Water,
As Beasts, and Birds, and Fishes.

Ti. Nor on the Beasts themselues, the Birds & Fishes,
You must eate men. Yet thankes I must you con,
That you are Theeues profest: that you worke not
In holier shapes: For there is boundlesse Theft
In limited Professions. Rascall Theeues
Heere's Gold. Go, sucke the subtle blood o'th' Grape,
Till the high Feauor seeth your blood to froth,
And so scape hanging. Trust not the Physitian,
His Antidotes are poyson, and he slayes
[illegible]e then you Rob: Take wealth, and liues together,
Do Villaine do, since you protest to doo't.
Like Workemen, Ile example you with Theeuery:
The Sunnes a Theefe, and with his great attraction
Robbes the vaste Sea. The Moones an arrant Theefe,
And her pale fire, she snatches from the Sunne.
The Seas a Theefe, whose liquid Surge, resolues
The Moone into Salt teares. The Earth's a Theefe,
That feeds and breeds by a composture stolne
From gen'rall excrement: each thing's a Theefe.
The Lawes, your curbe and whip, in their rough power
Ha's vncheck'd Theft. Loue not your selues, away,
Rob one another, there's more Gold, cut throates,
All that you meete are Theeues: to Athens go,
Breake open shoppes, nothing can you steale
But Theeues do loose it: steale lesse, for this I giue you,
And Gold confound you howsoere: Amen.

3 Has almost charm'd me from my Profession, by perswading me to it.

1 'Tis in the malice of mankinde, that he thus aduises vs not to haue vs thriue in our mystery.

2 Ile beleeue him as an Enemy,
And giue ouer my Trade.

1 Let vs first see peace in Athens, there is no time so miserable, but a man may be true. *Exit Theeues.*

Enter the Steward to Timon.

Stew. Oh you Gods!
Is yon'd despis'd and ruinous man my Lord?
Full of decay and fayling? Oh Monument
And wonder of good deeds, euilly bestow'd!
What an alteration of Honor has desp'rate want made?
What vilder thing vpon the earth, then Friends,
Who can bring Noblest mindes, to basest ends.
How rarely does it meete with this times guise,
When man was wisht to loue his Enemies:
Grant I may euer loue, and rather woo
Those that would mischeefe me, then those that doo.
Has caught me in his eye, I will present my honest griefe
vnto him; and as my Lord, still serue him with my life.
My deerest Master.

Tim. Away: what art thou?

Stew. Haue you forgot me, Sir?

Tim. Why dost aske that? I haue forgot all men.
Then, if thou grunt'st, th'art a man.
I haue forgot thee.

Stew. An honest poore seruant of yours.

Tim. Then I know thee not:
I neuer had honest man about me, I all
I kept were Knaues, to serue in meate to Villaines.

Stew. The Gods are witnesse,
Neu'r did poore Steward weare a truer greefe
For his vndone Lord, then mine eyes for you.

Tim. What, dost thou weepe?
Come neerer, then I loue thee
Because thou art a woman, and disclaim'st
Flinty mankinde: whose eyes do neuer giue,
But thorow Lust and Laughter: pittie's sleeping:
Strange times ẏ weepe with laughing, not with weeping.

Stew. I begge of you to know me, good my Lord,
T'accept my greefe, and whil'st this poore wealth lasts,
To entertaine me as your Steward still.

Tim. Had I a Steward
So true, so iust, and now so comfortable?
It almost turnes my dangerous Nature wilde.
Let me behold thy face: Surely, this man
Was borne of woman.
Forgiue my generall, and exceptlesse rashnesse
You perpetuall sober Gods. I do proclaime
One honest man: Mistake me not, but one:
No more I pray, and hee's a Steward.
How faine would I haue hated all mankinde,
And thou redeem'st thy selfe. But all saue thee,
I fell with Curses.
Me thinkes thou art more honest now, then wise:
For, by oppressing and betraying mee,

Thou

Thou might'ſt haue ſooner got another Seruice:
For many ſo arriue at ſecond Maſters,
Vpon their firſt Lords necke. But tell me true,
(For I muſt euer doubt, though ne're ſo ſure)
Is not thy kindneſſe ſubtle, couetous,
If not a Vſuring kindneſſe, and as rich men deale Guifts,
Expecting in returne twenty for one?
Stew. No my moſt worthy Maſter, in whoſe breſt
Doubt, and ſuſpect (alas) are plac'd too late:
You ſhould haue fear'd falſe times, when you did Feaſt.
Suſpect ſtill comes, where an eſtate is leaſt.
That which I ſhew, Heauen knowes, is meerely Loue,
Dutie, and Zeale, to your vnmatched minde;
Care of your Food and Liuing, and beleeue it,
My moſt Honour'd Lord,
For any benefit that points to mee,
Either in hope, or preſent, I'de exchange
For this one wiſh, that you had power and wealth
To requite me, by making rich your ſelfe.
Tim. Looke thee, 'tis ſo: thou ſingly honeſt man,
Heere take: the Gods out of my miſerie
Ha's ſent thee Treaſure. Go, liue rich and happy.
But thus condition'd: Thou ſhalt build from men:
Hate all, curſe all, ſhew Charity to none,
But let the famiſht fleſh ſlide from the Bone,
Ere thou releeue the Begger. Giue to dogges
What thou denyeſt to men. Let Priſons ſwallow 'em,
Debts wither 'em to nothing, be men like blaſted woods
And may Diſeaſes licke vp their falſe bloods,
And ſo farewell, and thriue.
Stew. O let me ſtay, and comfort you, my Maſter.
Tim. If thou hat'ſt Curſes
Stay not: flye, whil'ſt thou art bleſt and free:
Ne're ſee thou man, and let me ne're ſee thee. *Exit*

Enter Poet, and Painter.

Pain. As I tooke note of the place, it cannot be farre where he abides.
Poet. What's to be thought of him?
Does the Rumor hold for true,
That hee's ſo full of Gold?
Painter. Certaine.
Alcibiades reports it: *Phrinica* and *Timandylo*
Had Gold of him. He likewiſe enrich'd
Poore ſtragling Souldiers, with great quantity
'Tis ſaide, he gaue vnto his Steward
A mighty ſumme.
Poet. Then this breaking of his,
Ha's beene but a Try for his Friends?
Painter Nothing elſe:
You ſhall ſee him a Palme in Athens againe,
And flouriſh with the higheſt:
Therefore, 'tis not amiſſe, we tender our loues
To him, in this ſuppos'd diſtreſſe of his:
It will ſhew honeſtly in vs,
And is very likely, to loade our purpoſes
With what they trauaile for,
If it be a iuſt and true report, that goes
Of his hauing.
Poet. What haue you now
To preſent vnto him?
Painter. Nothing at this time
But my Viſitation: onely I will promiſe him
An excellent Peece.
Poet. I muſt ſerue him ſo too;
Tell him of an intent that's comming toward him.
Painter. Good as the beſt.
Promiſing, is the verie Ayre o'th'Time;
It opens the eyes of Expectation.
Performance, is euer the duller for his acte,
And but in the plainer and ſimpler kinde of people,
The deede of Saying is quite out of vſe.
To Promiſe, is moſt Courtly and faſhionable;
Performance, is a kinde of Will or Teſtament
Which argues a great ſickneſſe in his iudgement
That makes it.

Enter Timon from his Caue.

Timon. Excellent Workeman,
Thou canſt not paint a man ſo badde
As is thy ſelfe.
Poet. I am thinking
What I ſhall ſay I haue prouided for him:
It muſt be a perſonating of himſelfe:
A Satyre againſt the ſoftneſſe of Proſperity,
With a Diſcouerie of the infinite Flatteries
That follow youth and opulencie.
Timon. Muſt thou needes
Stand for a Villaine in thine owne Worke?
Wilt thou whip thine owne faults in other men?
Do ſo, I haue Gold for thee.
Poet. Nay let's ſeeke him.
Then do we ſinne againſt our owne eſtate,
When we may profit meete, and come too late.
Painter. True:
When the day ſerues before blacke-corner'd night;
Finde what thou want'ſt, by free and offer'd light.
Come.
Tim. Ile meete you at the turne:
What a Gods Gold, that he is worſhipt
In a baſer Temple, then where Swine feede?
'Tis thou that rigg'ſt the Barke, and plow'ſt the Fome,
Setleſt admired reuerence in a Slaue,
To thee be worſhipt, and thy Saints for aye:
Be crown'd with Plagues, that thee alone obay.
Fit I meet them.
Poet. Haile worthy *Timon.*
Pain. Our late Noble Maſter.
Timon. Haue I once liu'd
To ſee two honeſt men?
Poet. Sir:
Hauing often of your open Bounty taſted,
Hearing you were retyr'd, your Friends falne off,
Whoſe thankeleſſe Natures (O abhorred Spirits)
Not all the Whippes of Heauen, are large enough.
What, to you,
Whoſe Starre-like Nobleneſſe gaue life and influence
To their whole being? I am rapt, and cannot couer
The monſtrous bulke of this Ingratitude
With any ſize of words.
Timon. Let it go,
Naked men may ſee't the better:
You that are honeſt, by being what you are,
Make them beſt ſeene, and knowne.
Pain. He, and my ſelfe
Haue trauail'd in the great ſhowre of your guifts,
And ſweetly felt it.
Timon. I, you are honeſt man.
Painter. We are hither come
To offer you our ſeruice
Timon. Moſt honeſt men:

Why

Why how ſhall I requite you?
Can you eate Roots, and drinke cold water, no?
Both. What we can do,
Wee'l do to do you ſeruice.
Tim. Y'are honeſt men,
Y'haue heard that I haue Gold,
I am ſure you haue, ſpeake truth, y'are honeſt men.
Pain. So it is ſaid my Noble Lord, but therefore
Came not my Friend, nor I.
Timon. Good honeſt men: Thou draw'ſt a counterfet
Beſt in all Athens, th'art indeed the beſt,
Thou counterfet'ſt moſt liuely.
Pain. So, ſo, my Lord.
Tim. E'ne ſo ſir as I ſay. And for thy fiction,
Why thy Verſe ſwels with ſtuffe ſo fine and ſmooth,
That thou art euen Naturall in thine Art.
But for all this (my honeſt Natur'd friends)
I muſt needs ſay you haue a little fault,
Marry 'tis not monſtrous in you, neither wiſh I
You take much paines to mend.
Both. Beſeech your Honour
To make it knowne to vs.
Tim. You'l take it ill.
Both. Moſt thankefully, my Lord.
Timon. Will you indeed?
Both. Doubt it not worthy Lord.
Tim. There's neuer a one of you but truſts a Knaue,
That mightily deceiues you.
Both. Do we, my Lord?
Tim. I, and you heare him cogge,
See him diſſemble,
Know his groſſe patchery, loue him, feede him,
Keepe in your boſome, yet remaine aſſur'd
That he's a made-vp-Villaine
Pain. I know none ſuch, my Lord.
Poet. Nor I.
Timon. Looke you,
I loue you well, Ile giue you Gold
Rid me theſe Villaines from your companies;
Hang them, or ſtab them, drowne them in a draught
Confound them by ſome courſe, and come to me,
Ile giue you Gold enough.
Both. Name them my Lord, let's know them.
Tim. You that way, and you this:
But two in Company:
Each man a part, all ſingle, and alone,
Yet an arch Villaine keepes him company:
If where thou art, two Villaines ſhall not be,
Come not neere him. If thou would'ſt not recide
But where one Villaine is, then him abandon.
Hence, packe, there's Gold, you came for Gold ye ſlaues.
You haue worke for me; there's payment, hence,
You are an Alcumiſt, make Gold of that:
Out Raſcall dogges. *Exeunt*

Enter Steward, and two Senators

Stew. It is vaine that you would ſpeake with *Timon*:
For he is ſet ſo onely to himſelfe,
That nothing but himſelfe, which lookes like man,
Is friendly with him.
1.Sen. Bring vs to his Caue.
It is our part and promiſe to th'Athenians
To ſpeake with *Timon.*
2.Sen. At all times alike
Men are not ſtill the ſame: 'twas Time and Greefes
That fram'd him thus. Time with his fairer hand,
Offering the Fortunes of his former dayes,
The former man may make him: bring vs to him
And chanc'd it as it may.
Stew. Heere is his Caue:
Peace and content be heere. Lord *Timon, Timon,*
Looke out, and ſpeake to Friends: Th'Athenians
By two of their moſt reuerend Senate greet thee:
Speake to them Noble *Timon.*

Enter Timon out of his Caue.

Tim. Thou Sunne that comforts burne,
Speake and be hang'd:
For each true word, a bliſter, and each falſe
Be as a Cantherizing to the root o'th'Tongue,
Conſuming it with ſpeaking.
1 Worthy *Timon.*
Tim. Of none but ſuch as you,
And you of *Timon.*
1 The Senators of Athens, greet thee *Timon.*
Tim. I thanke them,
And would ſend them backe the plague,
Could I but catch it for them.
1 O forget
What we are ſorry for our ſelues in thee:
The Senators, with one conſent of loue,
Intreate thee backe to Athens, who haue thought
On ſpeciall Dignities, which vacant lye
For thy beſt vſe and wearing.
2 They confeſſe
Toward thee, forgetfulneſſe too generall groſſe;
Which now the publike Body, which doth ſildome
Play the re-canter, feeling in it ſelfe
A lacke of *Timons* ayde, hath ſince withall
Of it owne fall, reſtraining ayde to *Timon*,
And ſend forth vs, to make their ſorrowed render,
Together, with a recompence more fruitfull
Then their offence can weigh downe by the Dramme,
I euen ſuch heapes and ſummes of Loue and Wealth,
As ſhall to thee blot out, what wrongs were theirs,
And write in thee the figures of their loue,
Euer to read them thine.
Tim. You witch me in it;
Surprize me to the very brinke of teares;
Lend me a Fooles heart, and a womans eyes,
And Ile beweepe theſe comforts, worthy Senators.
1 Therefore ſo pleaſe thee to returne with vs,
And of our Athens, thine and ours to take
The Captainſhip, thou ſhalt be met with thankes,
Allowed with abſolute power, and thy good name
Liue with Authoritie: ſo ſoone we ſhall driue backe
Of *Alcibiades* th'approaches wild,
Who like a Bore too ſauage, doth root vp
His Countries peace.
2 And ſhakes his threatning Sword
Againſt the walles of *Athens.*
1 Therefore *Timon*
Tim. Well ſir, I will: therefore I will ſir thus
If *Alcibiades* kill my Countrymen,
Let *Alcibiades* know this of *Timon*,
That *Timon* cares not. But if he ſacke faire Athens,
And take our goodly aged men by th'Beards,
Giuing our holy Virgins to the ſtaine
Of contumelious, beaſtly, mad-brain'd warre:
Then let him know, and tell him *Timon* ſpeakes it,
In

In pitty of our aged, and our youth,
I cannot choose but tell him that I care not,
And let him tak't at worst: For their Kniues care not.
While you haue throats to answer. For my selfe,
There's not a whittle, in th'vnruly Campe,
But I do prize it at my loue, before
The reuerends Throat in Athens. So I leaue you
To the protection of the prosperous Gods,
As Theeues to Keepers.
Stew. Stay not, all's in vaine.
Tim. Why I was writing of my Epitaph,
It will be seene to morrow. My long sicknesse
Of Health, and Liuing, now begins to mend,
And nothing brings me all things. Go, liue still,
Be *Alcibiades* your plague; you his,
And last so long enough.
1 We speake in vaine.
Tim. But yet I loue my Country, and am not
One that reioyces in the common wracke,
As common bruite doth put it.
1 That's well spoke.
Tim. Commend me to my louing Countreymen.
1 These words become your lippes as they passe thorow them.
2 And enter in our eares, like great Triumphers
In their applauding gates.
Tim. Commend me to them,
And tell them, that to ease them of their greefes,
Their feares of Hostile strokes, their Aches losses,
Their pangs of Loue, with other incident throwes
That Natures fragile Vessell doth sustaine
In lifes vncertaine voyage, I will some kindnes do them,
Ile teach them to preuent wilde *Alcibiades* wrath.
1 I like this well, he will returne againe.
Tim. I haue a Tree which growes heere in my Close,
That mine owne vse inuites me to cut downe,
And shortly must I fell it. Tell my Friends,
Tell Athens, in the sequence of degree,
From high to low throughout, that who so please
To stop Affliction, let him take his haste;
Come hither ere my Tree hath felt the Axe,
And hang himselfe. I pray you do my greeting.
Stew. Trouble him no further, thus you still shall
Finde him.
Tim. Come not to me againe, but say to Athens,
Timon hath made his euerlasting Mansion
Vpon the Beached Verge of the salt Flood,
Who once a day with his embossed Froth
The turbulent Surge shall couer; thither come,
And let my graue-stone be your Oracle:
Lippes, let foure words go by, and Language end:
What is amisse, Plague and Infection mend.
Graues onely be mens workes, and Death their gaine;
Sunne, hide thy Beames, *Timon* hath done his Raigne.
Exit Timon.
1 His discontents are vnremoueably coupled to Nature.
2 Our hope in him is dead: let vs returne,
And straine what other meanes is left vnto vs
In our deere perill.
1 It requires swift foot. *Exeunt.*

Enter two other Senators, with a Messenger.

1 Thou hast painfully discouer'd: are his Files
As full as thy report?
Mes. I haue spoke the least.
Besides his expedition promises present approach.
2 We stand much hazard, if they bring not *Timon*.
Mes. I met a Currier, one mine ancient Friend,
Whom though in generall part we were oppos'd,
Yet our old loue made a particular force,
And made vs speake like Friends. This man was riding
From *Alcibiades* to *Timons* Caue,
With Letters of intreaty, which imported
His Fellowship i'th'cause against your City,
In part for his sake mou'd.

Enter the other Senators.

1 Heere come our Brothers.
3 No talke of *Timon*, nothing of him expect,
The Enemies Drumme is heard, and fearefull scouring
Doth choake the ayre with dust: In, and prepare,
Ours is the fall I feare, our Foes the Snare. *Exeunt*

Enter a Souldier in the Woods, seeking Timon.

Sol. By all description this should be the place.
Whose heere? Speake hoa. No answer? What is this?
Tymon is dead, who hath out-stretcht his span,
Some Beast reade this; There do's not liue a Man.
Dead sure, and this his Graue, what's on this Tomb,
I cannot read: the Charracter Ile take with wax,
Our Captaine hath in euery Figure skill;
An ag'd Interpreter, though yong in dayes:
Before proud Athens hee's set downe by this,
Whose fall the marke of his Ambition is. *Exit.*

Trumpets sound. Enter Alcibiades with his Powers before Athens.

Alc. Sound to this Coward, and lasciuious Towne,
Our terrible approach.
Sounds a Parly.
The Senators appeare vpon the wals.
Till now you haue gone on, and fill'd the time
With all Licentious measure, making your willes
The scope of Iustice. Till now, my selfe and such
As slept within the shadow of your power
Haue wander'd with our trauerst Armes, and breath'd
Our sufferance vainly: Now the time is flush,
When crouching Marrow in the bearer strong
Cries (of it selfe) no more: Now breathlesse wrong,
Shall sit and pant in your great Chaires of ease,
And pursie Insolence shall breake his winde
With feare and horrid flight.
1. Sen. Noble, and young;
When thy first greefes were but a meere conceit,
Ere thou had'st power, or we had cause of feare,
We sent to thee, to giue thy rages Balme,
To wipe out our Ingratitude, with Loues
Aboue their quantitie.
2 So did we wooe
Transformed *Timon*, to our Citties loue
By humble Message, and by promist meanes:
We were not all vnkinde, nor all deserue
The common stroke of warre.
1 These walles of ours,
Were not erected by their hands, from whom
You haue receyu'd your greefe: Nor are they such,
That these great Towres, Trophees, & Schools shold fall
For priuate faults in them.
2 Nor are they liuing
Who

Who were the motiues that you first went out,
(Shame that they wanted, cunning in excesse)
Hath broke their hearts. March, Noble Lord,
Into our City with thy Banners spred,
By decimation and a tythed death;
If thy Reuenges hunger for that Food
Which Nature loathes, take thou the destin'd tenth,
And by the hazard of the spotted dye,
Let dye the spotted.
1 All haue not offended:
For those that were, it is not square to take
On those that are, Reuenge: Crimes, like Lands
Are not inherited, then deere Countryman,
Bring in thy rankes, but leaue without thy rage,
Spare thy Athenian Cradle, and those Kin
Which in the bluster of thy wrath must fall
With those that haue offended; like a Shepheard,
Approach the Fold, and cull th'infected forth,
But kill not altogether.
2 What thou wilt,
Thou rather shalt inforce it with thy smile,
Then hew too't, with thy Sword.
1 Set but thy foot
Against our rampyr'd gates, and they shall ope:
So thou wilt send thy gentle heart before,
To say thou't enter Friendly.
2 Throw thy Gloue,
Or any Token of thine Honour else,
That thou wilt vse the warres as thy redresse,
And not as our Confusion: All thy Powers
Shall make their harbour in our Towne, till wee
Haue seal'd thy full desire.
Alc. Then there's my Gloue,
Descend and open your vncharged Ports,
Those Enemies of *Timons*, and mine owne
Whom you your selues shall set out for reproofe,
Fall and no more; and to attone your feares
With my more Noble meaning, not a man
Shall passe his quarter, or offend the streame
Of Regular Iustice in your Citties bounds,
But shall be remedied to your publique Lawes
At heauiest answer.
Both. 'Tis most Nobly spoken.
Alc. Descend, and keepe your words.
Enter a Messenger.
Mes. My Noble Generall, *Timon* is dead,
Entomb'd vpon the very hemme o'th'Sea,
And on his Grauestone, this Insculpture which
With wax I brought away: whose soft Impression
Interprets for my poore ignorance.

Alcibiades reades the Epitaph.

Heere lies a wretched Coarse, of wretched Soule bereft,
Seek not my name: A Plague consume you, wicked Caitifs left:
Heere lye I Timon, who aliue, all liuing men did hate,
Passe by, and curse thy fill, but passe and stay not here thy gate.
These well expresse in thee thy latter spirits:
Though thou abhorr'dst in vs our humane griefes,
Scornd'st our Braines flow, and those our droplets, which
From niggard Nature fall; yet Rich Conceit
Taught thee to make vast Neptune weepe for aye
On thy low Graue, on faults forgiuen. Dead
Is Noble *Timon*, of whose Memorie
Heereafter more. Bring me into your Citie,
And I will vse the Oliue, with my Sword:
Make war breed peace; make peace stint war, make each
Prescribe to other, as each others Leach.
Let our Drummes strike. *Exeunt.*

FINIS.

THE ACTORS NAMES.

YMON of *Athens*.
Lucius, *And*
Lucullus, *two Flattering Lords*.
Appemantus, a Churlish Philosopher.
Sempronius another flattering Lord.
Alcibiades, an Athenian Captaine.
Poet.
Painter.
Jeweller.
Merchant.
Certaine Senatours.
Certaine Maskers.
Certaine Theeues.

Flaminius, one of Tymons Seruants.
Seruilius, another.
Caphis.
Varro.
Philo.
Titus.
Lucius.
Hortensis } *Seuerall Seruants to Vsurers*.
Ventigius. one of Tymons false Friends.
Cupid.
Sempronius.
With diuers other Seruants,
And Attendants.

THE TRAGEDIE OF IVLIVS CÆSAR.

Actus Primus. Scœna Prima.

Enter Flauius, Murellus, and certaine Commoners ouer the Stage.

Flauius.

HEnce: home you idle Creatures, get you home:
Is this a Holiday? What, know you not
(Being Mechanicall) you ought not walke
Vpon a labouring day, without the signe
Of your Profession? Speake, what Trade art thou?

Car. Why Sir, a Carpenter.

Mur. Where is thy Leather Apron, and thy Rule?
What dost thou with thy best Apparrell on?
You sir, what Trade are you?

Cobl. Truely Sir, in respect of a fine Workman, I am but as you would say, a Cobler.

Mur. But what Trade art thou? Answer me directly.

Cob. A Trade Sir, that I hope I may vse, with a safe Conscience, which is indeed Sir, a Mender of bad soules

Fla. What Trade thou knaue? Thou naughty knaue, what Trade?

Cobl. Nay I beseech you Sir, be not out with me: yet if you be out Sir, I can mend you.

Mur. What mean'st thou by that? Mend mee, thou sawcy Fellow?

Cob. Why sir, Cobble you.

Fla. Thou art a Cobler, art thou?

Cob. Truly sir, all that I liue by, is with the Aule: I meddle with no Tradesmans matters, nor womens matters; but withal I am indeed Sir, a Surgeon to old shooes: when they are in great danger, I recouer them. As proper men as euer trod vpon Neats Leather, haue gone vpon my handy-worke.

Fla. But wherefore art not in thy Shop to day?
Why do'st thou leade these men about the streets?

Cob. Truly sir, to weare out their shooes, to get my selfe into more worke. But indeede sir, we make Holyday to see *Cæsar*, and to reioyce in his Triumph.

Mur. Wherefore reioyce?
What Conquest brings he home?
What Tributaries follow him to Rome,
To grace in Captiue bonds his Chariot Wheeles?
You Blockes, you stones, you worse then senslesse things:
O you hard hearts, you cruell men of Rome,
Knew you not *Pompey* many a time and oft?
Haue you climb'd vp to Walles and Battlements,
To Towres and Windowes? Yea, to Chimney tops,
Your Infants in your Armes, and there haue sate
The liue-long day, with patient expectation,
To see great *Pompey* passe the streets of Rome:
And when you saw his Chariot but appeare,
Haue you not made an Vniuersall shout,
That Tyber trembled vnderneath her bankes
To heare the replication of your sounds,
Made in her Concaue Shores?
And do you now put on your best attyre?
And do you now cull out a Holyday?
And do you now strew Flowers in his way,
That comes in Triumph ouer *Pompeyes* blood?
Be gone,
Runne to your houses, fall vpon your knees,
Pray to the Gods to intermit the plague
That needs must light on this Ingratitude.

Fla. Go, go, good Countrymen, and for this fault
Assemble all the poore men of your sort;
Draw them to Tyber bankes, and weepe your teares
Into the Channell, till the lowest streame
Do kisse the most exalted Shores of all.

Exeunt all the Commoners.

See where their basest mettle be not mou'd,
They vanish tongue-tyed in their guiltinesse:
Go you downe that way towards the Capitoll,
This way will I: Disrobe the Images,
If you do finde them deckt with Ceremonies.

Mur. May we do so?
You know it is the Feast of Lupercall.

Fla. It is no matter, let no Images
Be hung with *Cæsars* Trophees: Ile about,
And driue away the Vulgar from the streets;
So do you too, where you perceiue them thicke.
These growing Feathers, pluckt from *Cæsars* wing,
Will make him flye an ordinary pitch,
Who else would soare aboue the view of men,
And keepe vs all in seruile fearefulnesse.

Exeunt

Enter Cæsar, Antony for the Course, Calphurnia, Portia, Decius, Cicero, Brutus, Cassius, Caska, a Soothsayer: after them Murellus and Flauius.

Cæs. Calphurnia.

Cask. Peace ho, *Cæsar* speakes.

Cæs. Calphurnia.

Calp. Heere my Lord.

Cæs. Stand you directly in *Antonio's* way,
When he doth run his course. *Antonio.*

Ant. *Cæsar*, my Lord.

Cæs. Forget not in your speed *Antonio*,
To touch *Calphurnia*: for our Elders say,

k k The-

The Barren touched in this holy chace,
Shake off their sterrile curse.
Ant. I shall remember,
When *Cæsar* sayes, Do this; it is perform'd.
Cæs. Set on, and leaue no Ceremony out.
Sooth. *Cæsar.*
Cæs. Ha? Who calles?
Cask. Bid euery noyse be still: peace yet againe.
Cæs. Who is it in the presse, that calles on me?
I heare a Tongue shriller then all the Musicke
Cry, *Cæsar*: Speake. *Cæsar* is turn'd to heare.
Sooth. Beware the Ides of March.
Cæs. What man is that?
Br. A Sooth-sayer bids you beware the Ides of March
Cæs. Set him before me, let me see his face.
Cassi. Fellow, come from the throng, look vpon *Cæsar.*
Cæs. What sayst thou to me now? Speak once againe.
Sooth. Beware the Ides of March.
Cæs. He is a Dreamer, let vs leaue him: Passe.
Sennet. Exeunt. Manet Brut. & Cass.
Cassi. Will you go see the order of the course?
Brut. Not I.
Cassi. I pray you do.
Brut. I am not Gamesom: I do lacke some part
Of that quicke Spirit that is in *Antony*:
Let me not hinder *Cassius* your desires;
Ile leaue you.
Cassi. *Brutus*, I do obserue you now of late:
I haue not from your eyes, that gentlenesse
And shew of Loue, as I was wont to haue:
You beare too stubborne, and too strange a hand
Ouer your Friend, that loues you.
Bru. *Cassius,*
Be not deceiu'd: If I haue veyl'd my looke,
I turne the trouble of my Countenance
Meerely vpon my selfe. Vexed I am
Of late, with passions of some difference,
Conceptions onely proper to my selfe,
Which giue some soyle (perhaps) to my Behauiours:
But let not therefore my good Friends be greeu'd
(Among which number *Cassius* be you one)
Nor construe any further my neglect,
Then that poore *Brutus* with himselfe at warre,
Forgets the shewes of Loue to other men
Cassi. Then *Brutus*, I haue much mistook your passion,
By meanes whereof, this Brest of mine hath buried
Thoughts of great value, worthy Cogitations.
Tell me good *Brutus*, Can you see your face?
Brutus. No *Cassius*:
For the eye sees not it selfe but by reflection,
By some other things.
Cassius. 'Tis iust,
And it is very much lamented *Brutus*,
That you haue no such Mirrors, as will turne
Your hidden worthinesse into your eye,
That you might see your shadow:
I haue heard,
Where many of the best respect in Rome,
(Except immortall *Cæsar*) speaking of *Brutus*,
And groaning vnderneath this Ages yoake,
Haue wish'd, that Noble *Brutus* had his eyes.
Bru. Into what dangers, would you
Leade me *Cassius*?
That you would haue me seeke into my selfe,
For that which is not in me?
Cas. Therefore good *Brutus*, be prepar'd to heare
And since you know, you cannot see your selfe
So well as by Reflection; I your Glasse,
Will modestly discouer to your selfe.
That of your selfe, which you yet know not of.
And be not iealous on me, gentle *Brutus*:
Were I a common Laughter, or did vse
To stale with ordinary Oathes my loue
To euery new Protester: if you know,
That I do fawne on men, and hugge them hard,
And after scandall them: Or if you know,
That I professe my selfe in Banquetting
To all the Rout, then hold me dangerous.

Flourish, and Shout.

Bru. What meanes this Showting?
I do feare, the People choose *Cæsar*
For their King.
Cassi. I, do you feare it?
Then must I thinke you would not haue it so.
Bru. I would not *Cassius*, yet I loue him well:
But wherefore do you hold me heere so long?
What is it, that you would impart to me?
If it be ought toward the generall good,
Set Honor in one eye, and Death i'th other,
And I will looke on both indifferently:
For let the Gods so speed mee, as I loue
The name of Honor, more then I feare death.
Cassi. I know that vertue to be in you *Brutus*,
As well as I do know your outward fauour.
Well, Honor is the subiect of my Story:
I cannot tell, what you and other men
Thinke of this life: But for my single selfe,
I had as liefe not be, as liue to be
In awe of such a Thing, as I my selfe.
I was borne free as *Cæsar*, so were you,
We both haue fed as well, and we can both
Endure the Winters cold, as well as hee.
For once, vpon a Rawe and Gustie day,
The troubled Tyber, chafing with her Shores,
Cæsar saide to me, Dar'st thou *Cassius* now
Leape in with me into this angry Flood,
And swim to yonder Point? Vpon the word,
Accoutred as I was, I plunged in,
And bad him follow: so indeed he did.
The Torrent roar'd, and we did buffet it
With lusty Sinewes, throwing it aside,
And stemming it with hearts of Controuersie.
But ere we could arriue the Point propos'd,
Cæsar cride, Helpe me *Cassius*, or I sinke.
I (as *Æneas*, our great Ancestor,
Did from the Flames of Troy, vpon his shoulder
The old *Anchyses* beare) so, from the waues of Tyber
Did I the tyred *Cæsar*: And this Man,
Is now become a God, and *Cassius* is
A wretched Creature, and must bend his body,
If *Cæsar* carelesly but nod on him.
He had a Feauer when he was in Spaine,
And when the Fit was on him, I did marke
How he did shake: Tis true, this God did shake,
His Coward lippes did from their colour flye,
And that same Eye, whose bend doth awe the World,
Did loose his Lustre: I did heare him grone:
I, and that Tongue of his, that bad the Romans
Marke him, and write his Speeches in their Bookes,
Alas, it cried, Giue me some drinke *Titinius*,
Ar

As a ſicke Girle: Ye Gods, it doth amaze me,
A man of ſuch a feeble temper ſhould
So get the ſtart of the Maieſticke world,
And beare the Palme alone.

Shout. Flouriſh.

Bru. Another generall ſhout?
I do beleeue, that theſe applauſes are
For ſome new Honors, that are heap'd on *Cæſar*.

Caſſi. Why man, he doth beſtride the narrow world
Like a Coloſſus, and we petty men
Walke vnder his huge legges, and peepe about
To finde our ſelues diſhonourable Graues.
Men at ſometime, are Maſters of their Fates.
The fault (deere *Brutus*) is not in our Starres,
But in our Selues, that we are vnderlings.
Brutus and *Cæſar*: What ſhould be in that *Cæſar*?
Why ſhould that name be ſounded more then yours
Write them together: Yours, is as faire a Name:
Sound them, it doth become the mouth aſwell:
Weigh them, it is as heauy: Coniure with 'em,
Brutus will ſtart a Spirit as ſoone as *Cæſar*.
Now in the names of all the Gods at once,
Vpon what meate doth this our *Cæſar* feede,
That he is growne ſo great? Age, thou art ſham'd.
Rome, thou haſt loſt the breed of Noble Bloods.
When went there by an Age, ſince the great Flood,
But it was fam'd with more then with one man?
When could they ſay (till now) that talk'd of Rome,
That her wide Walkes incompaſt but one man?
Now is it Rome indeed, and Roome enough
When there is in it but one onely man.
O! you and I, haue heard our Fathers ſay,
There was a *Brutus* once, that would haue brook'd
Th'eternall Diuell to keepe his State in Rome,
As eaſily as a King.

Bru. That you do loue me, I am nothing iealous:
What you would worke me too, I haue ſome ayme:
How I haue thought of this, and of theſe times
I ſhall recount heereafter. For this preſent,
I would not ſo (with loue I might intreat you)
Be any further moou'd: What you haue ſaid,
I will conſider: what you haue to ſay
I will with patience heare, and finde a time
Both meete to heare, and anſwer ſuch high things.
Till then, my Noble Friend, chew vpon this:
Brutus had rather be a Villager,
Then to repute himſelfe a Sonne of Rome
Vnder theſe hard Conditions, as this time
Is like to lay vpon vs.

Caſſi. I am glad that my weake words
Haue ſtrucke but thus much ſhew of fire fro[illegible] *tus*,

Enter Cæſar and his Traine.

Bru. The Games are done,
And *Cæſar* is returning.

Caſſi As they paſſe by,
Plucke *Caska* by the Sleeue,
And he will (after his ſowre faſhion) tell you
What hath proceeded worthy note to day.

Bru. I will do ſo: but looke you *Caſſius*,
The angry ſpot doth glow on *Cæſars* brow,
And all the reſt, looke like a chidden Traine;
Calphurnia's Cheeke is pale, and *Cicero*
Lookes with ſuch Ferret, and ſuch fiery eyes
As we haue ſeene him in the Capitoll
Being croſt in Conference, by ſome Senators.

Caſſi. *Caska* will tell vs what the matter is.

Cæſ. *Antonio.*

Ant. *Cæſar.*

Cæſ. Let me haue men about me, that are fat,
Sleeke-headed men, and ſuch as ſleepe a-nights:
Yond *Caſſius* has a leane and hungry looke,
He thinkes too much: ſuch men are dangerous.

Ant. Feare him not *Cæſar*, he's not dangerous,
He is a Noble Roman, and well giuen.

Cæſ. Would he were fatter; But I feare him not:
Yet if my name were lyable to feare,
I do not know the man I ſhould auoyd
So ſoone as that ſpare *Caſſius*. He reades much,
He is a great Obſeruer, and he lookes
Quite through the Deeds of men. He loues no Playes,
As thou doſt *Antony*: he heares no Muſicke;
Seldome he ſmiles, and ſmiles in ſuch a ſort
As if he mock'd himſelfe, and ſcorn'd his ſpirit
That could be mou'd to ſmile at any thing.
Such men as he, be neuer at hearts eaſe,
Whiles they behold a greater then themſelues,
And therefore are they very dangerous.
I rather tell thee what is to be fear'd,
Then what I feare: for alwayes I am *Cæſar*.
Come on my right hand, for this eare is deafe,
And tell me truely, what thou think'ſt of him, *Sennit.*

Exeunt Cæſar and his Traine.

Cask. You pul'd me by the cloake, would you ſpeake with me?

Bru. I *Caska*, tell vs what hath chanc'd to day
That *Cæſar* lookes ſo ſad.

Cask. Why you were with him, were you not?

Bru. I ſhould not then aske *Caska* what had chanc'd

Cask. Why there was a Crowne offer'd him; & being offer'd him, he put it by with the backe of his hand thus, and then the people fell a ſhouting.

Bru What was the ſecond noyſe for?

Cask. Why for that too.

Caſſi. They ſhouted thrice: what was the laſt cry for?

Cask. Why for that too.

Bru Was the Crowne offer'd him thrice?

Cask. I marry was't, and hee put it by thrice, euerie time gentler then other; and at euery putting by, mine honeſt Neighbors ſhowted.

Caſſi. Who offer'd him the Crowne?

Cask. Why *Antony*.

Bru Tell vs the manner of it, gentle *Caska*.

Caska. I can as well bee hang'd as tell the manner of it: It was meere Foolerie, I did not marke it. I ſawe *Marke Antony* offer him a Crowne, yet 'twas not a Crowne neyther, 'twas one of theſe Coronets: and as I told you, hee put it by once: but for all that, to my thinking, he would faine haue had it. Then hee offered it to him againe: then hee put it by againe: but to my thinking, he was very loath to lay his fingers off it. And then he offered it the third time; hee put it the third time by, and ſtill as hee refus'd it, the rabblement howted, and clapp'd their chopt hands, and threw vppe their ſweatie Night-cappes, and vttered ſuch a deale of ſtinking breath, becauſe *Cæſar* refus'd the Crowne, that it had (almoſt) choaked *Cæſar*: for hee ſwoonded, and fell downe at it: And for mine owne part, I durſt not laugh, for feare of opening my Lippes, and receyuing the bad Ayre.

kk 2 *Caſſi.*

Cassi. But soft I pray you: what, did *Cæsar* swound?

Cask. He fell downe in the Market-place, and foam'd at mouth, and was speechlesse.

Brut. 'Tis very like he hath the Falling sicknesse.

Cassi. No, *Cæsar* hath it not: but you, and I,
And honest *Caska*, we haue the Falling sicknesse.

Cask. I know not what you meane by that, but I am sure *Cæsar* fell downe. If the tag-ragge people did not clap him, and hisse him, according as he pleas'd, and displeas'd them, as they vse to doe the Players in the Theatre, I am no true man.

Brut. What said he, when he came vnto himselfe?

Cask. Marry, before he fell downe, when he perceiu'd the common Heard was glad he refus'd the Crowne, he pluckt me ope his Doublet, and offer'd them his Throat to cut: and I had beene a man of any Occupation, if I would not haue taken him at a word, I would I might goe to Hell among the Rogues, and so hee fell. When he came to himselfe againe, hee said, If hee had done, or said any thing amisse, he desir'd their Worships to thinke it was his infirmitie. Three or foure Wenches where I stood, cryed, Alasse good Soule, and forgaue him with all their hearts: But there's no heed to be taken of them; if *Cæsar* had stab'd their Mothers, they would haue done no lesse.

Brut. And after that, he came thus sad away.

Cask. I.

Cassi. Did *Cicero* say any thing?

Cask. I, he spoke Greeke.

Cassi. To what effect?

Cask. Nay, and I tell you that, Ile ne're looke you i'th' face againe. But those that vnderstood him, smil'd at one another, and shooke their heads: but for mine owne part, it was Greeke to me. I could tell you more newes too: *Murrellus* and *Flauius*, for pulling Scarffes off *Cæsars* Images, are put to silence. Fare you well. There was more Foolerie yet, if I could remember it.

Cassi. Will you suppe with me to Night, *Caska*?

Cask. No, I am promis'd forth.

Cassi. Will you Dine with me to morrow?

Cask. I, if I be aliue, and your minde hold, and your Dinner worth the eating.

Cassi. Good, I will expect you.

Cask. Doe so: farewell both. *Exit.*

Brut. What a blunt fellow is this growne to be?
He was quick Mettle, when he went to Schoole.

Cassi. So is he now, in execution
Of any bold, or Noble Enterprize,
How-euer he puts on this tardie forme:
This Rudenesse is a Sawce to his good Wit,
Which giues men stomacke to disgest his words
With better Appetite.

Brut. And so it is:
For this time I will leaue you:
To morrow, if you please to speake with me,
I will come home to you: or if you will,
Come home to me, and I will wait for you.

Cassi. I will doe so: till then, thinke of the World.

Exit Brutus.

Well *Brutus*, thou art Noble: yet I see,
Thy Honorable Mettle may be wrought
From that it is dispos'd: therefore it is meet,
That Noble mindes keepe euer with their likes:
For who so firme, that cannot be seduc'd?
Cæsar doth beare me hard, but he loues *Brutus*.
If I were *Brutus* now, and he were *Cassius*,
He should not humor me. I will this Night,
In seuerall Hands, in at his Windowes throw,
As if they came from seuerall Citizens,
Writings, all tending to the great opinion
That Rome holds of his Name: wherein obscurely
Cæsars Ambition shall be glanced at.
And after this, let *Cæsar* seat him sure,
For wee will shake him, or worse dayes endure.

Exit.

Thunder, and Lightning. Enter Caska, and Cicero.

Cic. Good euen, *Caska*: brought you *Cæsar* home?
Why are you breathlesse, and why stare you so?

Cask. Are not you mou'd, when all the sway of Earth
Shakes, like a thing vnfirme? O *Cicero*,
I haue seene Tempests, when the scolding Winds
Haue riu'd the knottie Oakes, and I haue seene
Th'ambitious Ocean swell, and rage, and foame,
To be exalted with the threatning Clouds:
But neuer till to Night, neuer till now,
Did I goe through a Tempest-dropping-fire.
Eyther there is a Ciuill strife in Heauen,
Or else the World, too sawcie with the Gods,
Incenses them to send destruction.

Cic. Why, saw you any thing more wonderfull?

Cask. A common slaue, you know him well by sight,
Held vp his left Hand, which did flame and burne
Like twentie Torches ioyn'd; and yet his Hand,
Not sensible of fire, remain'd vnscorch'd.
Besides, I ha'not since put vp my Sword,
Against the Capitoll I met a Lyon,
Who glaz'd vpon me, and went surly by,
Without annoying me. And there were drawne
Vpon a heape, a hundred gastly Women,
Transformed with their feare, who swore, they saw
Men, all in fire, walke vp and downe the streetes.
And yesterday, the Bird of Night did sit,
Euen at Noone-day, vpon the Market place,
Howting, and shreeking. When these Prodigies
Doe so conioyntly meet, let not men say,
These are their Reasons, they are Naturall:
For I beleeue, they are portentous things
Vnto the Clymate, that they point vpon.

Cic. Indeed, it is a strange disposed time:
But men may construe things after their fashion,
Cleane from the purpose of the things themselues.
Comes *Cæsar* to the Capitoll to morrow?

Cask. He doth: for he did bid *Antonio*
Send word to you, he would be there to morrow.

Cic. Good-night then, *Caska*:
This disturbed Skie is not to walke in.

Cask. Farewell *Cicero*. *Exit Cicero.*

Enter Cassius.

Cassi. Who's there?

Cask. A Romane.

Cassi. *Caska*, by your Voyce.

Cask. Your Eare is good.
Cassius, what Night is this?

Cassi. A very pleasing Night to honest men.

Cask. Who euer knew the Heauens menace so?

Cassi. Those that haue knowne the Earth so full of faults.

For

For my part, I haue walk'd about the ſtreets,
Submitting me vnto the perillous Night;
And thus vnbraced, *Caska*, as you ſee,
Haue bar'd my Boſome to the Thunder-ſtone:
And when the croſſe blew Lightning ſeem'd to open
The Breſt of Heauen, I did preſent my ſelfe
Euen in the ayme, and very flaſh of it. (uens

Cask. But wherefore did you ſo much tempt the Hea
It is the part of men, to feare and tremble,
When the moſt mightie Gods, by tokens ſend
Such dreadfull Herauld ſ, to aſtoniſh vs.

Caſſi. You are dull, *Caska*.
And thoſe ſparkes of Life, that ſhould be in a Roman,
You doe want, or elſe you vſe not.
You looke pale, and gaze, and put on feare,
And caſt your ſelfe in wonder,
To ſee the ſtrange impatience of the Heauens:
But if you would conſider the true cauſe,
Why all theſe Fires, why all theſe gliding Ghoſts,
Why Birds and Beaſts, from qualitie and kinde,
Why Old men, Fooles, and Children calculate,
Why all theſe things change from their Ordinance,
Their Natures, and pre-formed Faculties,
To monſtrous qualitie; why you ſhall finde,
That Heauen hath infus'd them with theſe Spirits,
To make them Inſtruments of feare, and warning,
Vnto ſome monſtrous State.
Now could I (*Caska*) name to thee a man,
Moſt like this dreadfull Night,
That Thunders, Lightens, opens Graues, and roares,
As doth the Lyon in the Capitoll:
A man no mightier then thy ſelfe, or me,
In perſonall action; yet prodigious growne,
And fearefull, as theſe ſtrange eruptions are.

Cask. 'Tis *Cæſar* that you meane:
Is it not, *Caſſius*?

Caſſi. Let it be who it is: for Romans now
Haue Thewes, and Limbes, like to their Anceſtors;
But woe the while, our Fathers mindes are dead,
And we are gouern'd with our Mothers ſpirits,
Our yoake, and ſufferance, ſhew vs Womaniſh.

Cask. Indeed, they ſay, the Senators to morrow
Meane to eſtabliſh *Cæſar* as a King:
And he ſhall weare his Crowne by Sea, and Land,
In euery place, ſaue here in Italy.

Caſſi. I know where I will weare this Dagger then;
Caſſius from Bondage will deliuer *Caſſius*:
Therein, yee Gods, you make the weake moſt ſtrong;
Therein, yee Gods, you Tyrants doe defeat.
Nor Stonie Tower, nor Walls of beaten Braſſe,
Nor ayre-leſſe Dungeon, nor ſtrong Linkes of Iron,
Can be retentiue to the ſtrength of ſpirit:
But Life being wearie of theſe worldly Barres,
Neuer lacks power to diſmiſſe it ſelfe.
If I know this, know all the World beſides,
That part of Tyrannie that I doe beare,
I can ſhake off at pleaſure. *Thunder ſtill.*

Cask. So can I:
So euery Bond-man in his owne hand beares
The power to cancell his Captiuitie.

Caſſi. And why ſhould *Cæſar* be a Tyrant then?
Poore man, I know he would not be a Wolfe,
But that he ſees the Romans are but Sheepe:
He were no Lyon, were not Romans Hindes.
Thoſe that with haſte will make a mightie fire,
Begin it with weake Strawes. What traſh is Rome?
What Rubbiſh, and what Offall? when it ſerues
For the baſe matter, to illuminate
So vile a thing as *Cæſar*. But oh Griefe,
Where haſt thou led me? I (perhaps) ſpeake this
Before a willing Bond-man: then I know
My anſwere muſt be made. But I am arm'd,
And dangers are to me indifferent.

Cask. You ſpeake to *Caska*, and to ſuch a man,
That is no flearing Tell-tale. Hold, my Hand:
Be factious for redreſſe of all theſe Griefes,
And I will ſet this foot of mine as farre,
As who goes fartheſt.

Caſſi. There's a Bargaine made.
Now know you, *Caska*, I haue mou'd already
Some certaine of the Nobleſt minded Romans
To vnder-goe, with me, an Enterprize,
Of Honorable dangerous conſequence;
And I doe know by this, they ſtay for me
In *Pompeyes* Porch: for now this fearefull Night,
There is no ſtirre, or walking in the ſtreetes;
And the Complexion of the Element
Is Fauors, like the Worke we haue in hand,
Moſt bloodie, fierie, and moſt terrible.

Enter Cinna.

Caska. Stand cloſe a while, for heere comes one in haſte.

Caſſi. 'Tis *Cinna*, I doe know him by his Gate,
He is a friend. *Cinna*, where haſte you ſo?

Cinna. To finde out you: Who's that, *Metellus Cymber*?

Caſſi. No, it is *Caska*, one incorporate
To our Attempts. Am I not ſtay'd for, *Cinna*?

Cinna. I am glad on't.
What a fearefull Night is this?
There's two or three of vs haue ſeene ſtrange ſights.

Caſſi. Am I not ſtay'd for? tell me.

Cinna. Yes, you are. O *Caſſius*,
If you could but winne the Noble *Brutus*
To our party——

Caſſi. Be you content. Good *Cinna*, take this Paper,
And looke you lay it in the Pretors Chayre,
Where *Brutus* may but finde it: and throw this
In at his Window; ſet this vp with Waxe
Vpon old *Brutus* Statue: all this done,
Repaire to *Pompeyes* Porch, where you ſhall finde vs.
Is *Decius Brutus* and *Trebonius* there?

Cinna. All, but *Metellus Cymber*, and hee's gone
To ſeeke you at your houſe. Well, I will hie,
And ſo beſtow theſe Papers as you bad me.

Caſſi. That done, repayre to *Pompeyes* Theater.

Exit Cinna.

Come *Caska*, you and I will yet, ere day,
See *Brutus* at his houſe: three parts of him
Is ours alreadie, and the man entire
Vpon the next encounter, yeelds him ours.

Cask. O, he ſits high in all the Peoples hearts:
And that which would appeare Offence in vs,
His Countenance, like richeſt Alchymie,
Will change to Vertue, and to Worthineſſe.

Caſſi. Him, and his worth, and our great need of him,
You haue right well conceited: let vs goe,
For it is after Mid-night, and ere day,
We will awake him, and be ſure of him.

Exeunt.

Actus Secundus.

Enter Brutus in his Orchard.

Brut. What *Lucius*, hoe?
I cannot, by the progresse of the Starres,
Giue guesse how neere to day.-- *Lucius*, I say?
I would it were my fault to sleepe so soundly.
When *Lucius*, when? awake, I say: what *Lucius*?

Enter Lucius.

Luc. Call'd you my Lord?
Brut. Get me a Tapor in my Study, *Lucius*:
When it is lighted, come and call me here.
Luc. I will, my Lord. *Exit*
Brut. It must be by his death: and for my part,
I know no personall cause, to spurne at him,
But for the generall. He would be crown'd:
How that might change his nature, there's the question?
It is the bright day, that brings forth the Adder,
And that craues warie walking: Crowne him that,
And then I graunt we put a Sting in him,
That at his will he may doe danger with.
Th'abuse of Greatnesse, is, when it dis-ioynes
Remorse from Power: And to speake truth of *Cæsar*,
I haue not knowne, when his Affections sway'd
More then his Reason. But 'tis a common proofe,
That Lowlynesse is young Ambitions Ladder,
Whereto the Climber vpward turnes his Face:
But when he once attaines the vpmost Round,
He then vnto the Ladder turnes his Backe,
Lookes in the Clouds, scorning the base degrees
By which he did ascend: so *Cæsar* may;
Then least he may, preuent. And since the Quarrell
Will beare no colour, for the thing he is,
Fashion it thus; that what he is, augmented,
Would runne to these, and these extremities:
And therefore thinke him as a Serpents egge,
Which hatch'd, would as his kinde grow mischieuous;
And kill him in the shell.

Enter Lucius.

Luc. The Taper burneth in your Closet, Sir:
Searching the Window for a Flint, I found
This Paper, thus seal'd vp, and I am sure
It did not lye there when I went to Bed.

Giues him the Letter.

Brut. Get you to Bed againe, it is not day:
Is not to morrow (Boy) the first of March?
Luc. I know not, Sir.
Brut. Looke in the Calender, and bring me word.
Luc. I will, Sir. *Exit.*
Brut. The exhalations, whizzing in the ayre,
Giue so much light, that I may reade by them.

Opens the Letter, and reades.

Brutus thou sleep'st; awake, and see thy selfe:
Shall Rome, &c. speake, strike, redresse.
Brutus, thou sleep'st: awake.
Such instigations haue beene often dropt,
Where I haue tooke them vp:
Shall Rome, &c. Thus must I piece it out:
Shall Rome stand vnder one mans awe? What Rome?
My Ancestors did from the streetes of Rome
The *Tarquin* driue, when he was call'd a King.
Speake, strike, redresse. Am I entreated
To speake, and strike? O Rome, I make thee promise,
If the redresse will follow, thou receiuest
Thy full Petition at the hand of *Brutus*.

Enter Lucius.

Luc. Sir, March is wasted fifteene dayes.

Knocke within.

Brut. 'Tis good. Go to the Gate, some body knocks:
Since *Cassius* first did whet me against *Cæsar*,
I haue not slept.
Betweene the acting of a dreadfull thing,
And the first motion, all the *Interim* is
Like a *Phantasma*, or a hideous Dreame:
The *Genius*, and the mortall Instruments
Are then in councell; and the state of a man,
Like to a little Kingdome, suffers then
The nature of an Insurrection.

Enter Lucius.

Luc. Sir, 'tis your Brother *Cassius* at the Doore,
Who doth desire to see you.
Brut. Is he alone?
Luc. No, Sir, there are moe with him.
Brut. Doe you know them?
Luc. No, Sir, their Hats are pluckt about their Eares,
And halfe their Faces buried in their Cloakes,
That by no meanes I may discouer them,
By any marke of fauour.
Brut. Let'em enter:
They are the Faction. O Conspiracie,
Sham'st thou to shew thy dang'rous Brow by Night,
When euills are most free? O then, by day
Where wilt thou finde a Cauerne darke enough,
To maske thy monstrous Visage? Seek none Conspiracie,
Hide it in Smiles, and Affabilitie:
For if thou path thy natiue semblance on,
Not *Erebus* it selfe were dimme enough,
To hide thee from preuention.

Enter the Conspirators, Cassius, Caska, Decius, Cinna, Metellus, and Trebonius.

Cass. I thinke we are too bold vpon your Rest:
Good morrow *Brutus*, doe we trouble you?
Brut. I haue beene vp this howre, awake all Night:
Know I these men, that come along with you?
Cass. Yes, euery man of them; and no man here
But honors you: and euery one doth wish,
You had but that opinion of your selfe,
Which euery Noble Roman beares of you.
This is *Trebonius*.
Brut. He is welcome hither.
Cass. This, *Decius Brutus*.
Brut. He is welcome too.
Cass. This, *Caska*; this, *Cinna*; and this, *Metellus Cymber*.
Brut. They are all welcome.
What watchfull Cares doe interpose themselues
Betwixt your Eyes, and Night?
Cass. Shall I entreat a word? *They whisper.*
Decius. Here lyes the East: doth not the Day breake heere?
Cask. No.
Cin. O pardon, Sir, it doth; and yon grey Lines,
That fret the Clouds, are Messengers of Day.
Cask. You shall confesse, that you are both deceiu'd:
Heere, as I point my Sword, the Sunne arises,
Which is a great way growing on the South,
Weigh-

Weighing the youthfull Season of the yeare.
Some two moneths hence, vp higher toward the North
He first presents his fire, and the high East
Stands as the Capitoll, directly heere.
Bru. Giue me your hands all ouer, one by one.
Cas. And let vs sweare our Resolution.
Brut. No, not an Oath: if not the Face of men,
The sufferance of our Soules, the times Abuse;
If these be Motiues weake, breake off betimes,
And euery man hence, to his idle bed:
So let high-sighted-Tyranny range on,
Till each man drop by Lottery. But if these
(As I am sure they do) beare fire enough
To kindle Cowards, and to steele with valour
The melting Spirits of women. Then Countrymen,
What neede we any spurre, but our owne cause
To pricke vs to redresse? What other Bond,
Then secret Romans, that haue spoke the word,
And will not palter? And what other Oath,
Then Honesty to Honesty ingag'd,
That this shall be, or we will fall for it.
Sweare Priests and Cowards, and men Cautelous
Old feeble Carrions, and such suffering Soules
That welcome wrongs: Vnto bad causes, sweare
Such Creatures as men doubt; but do not staine
The euen vertue of our Enterprize,
Nor th'insuppressiue Mettle of our Spirits,
To thinke, that or our Cause, or our Performance
Did neede an Oath. When euery drop of blood
That euery Roman beares, and Nobly beares
Is guilty of a seuerall Bastardie,
If he do breake the smallest Particle
Of any promise that hath past from him.
Cas. But what of *Cicero*? Shall we sound him?
I thinke he will stand very strong with vs.
Cask. Let vs not leaue him out.
Cyn. No, by no meanes.
Metel. O let vs haue him, for his Siluer haires
Will purchase vs a good opinion:
And buy mens voyces, to commend our deeds:
It shall be sayd, his iudgement rul'd our hands,
Our youths, and wildenesse, shall no whit appeare,
But all be buried in his Grauity.
Bru. O name him not; let vs not breake with him,
For he will neuer follow any thing
That other men begin.
Cas. Then leaue him out.
Cask. Indeed, he is not fit.
Decius. Shall no man else be toucht, but onely *Cæsar*?
Cas. *Decius* well vrg'd: I thinke it is not meet,
Marke Antony, so well belou'd of *Cæsar*,
Should out-liue *Cæsar*, we shall finde of him
A shrew'd Contriuer. And you know, his meanes
If he improue them, may well stretch so farre
As to annoy vs all: which to preuent,
Let *Antony* and *Cæsar* fall together.
Bru. Our course will seeme too bloody, *Caius Cassius*,
To cut the Head off, and then hacke the Limbes:
Like Wrath in death, and Enuy afterwards:
For *Antony*, is but a Limbe of *Cæsar*.
Let's be Sacrificers, but not Butchers *Caius*:
We all stand vp against the spirit of *Cæsar*,
And in the Spirit of men, there is no blood:
O that we then could come by *Cæsars* Spirit,
And not dismember *Cæsar*! But (alas)
Cæsar must bleed for it. And gentle Friends,
Let's kill him Boldly, but not Wrathfully:
Let's carue him, as a Dish fit for the Gods,
Not hew him as a Carkasse fit for Hounds:
And let our Hearts, as subtle Masters do,
Stirre vp their Seruants to an acte of Rage,
And after seeme to chide 'em. This shall make
Our purpose Necessary, and not Enuious.
Which so appearing to the common eyes,
We shall be call'd Purgers, not Murderers.
And for *Marke Antony*, thinke not of him:
For he can do no more then *Cæsars* Arme,
When *Cæsars* head is off.
Cas. Yet I feare him,
For in the ingrafted loue he beares to *Cæsar*.
Bru. Alas, good *Cassius*, do not thinke of him:
If he loue *Cæsar*, all that he can do
Is to himselfe; take thought, and dye for *Cæsar*,
And that were much he should: for he is giuen
To sports, to wildenesse, and much company.
Treb. There is no feare in him; let him not dye,
For he will liue, and laugh at this heereafter.

Clocke strikes.

Bru. Peace, count the Clocke.
Cas. The Clocke hath stricken three.
Treb. 'Tis time to part.
Cass. But it is doubtfull yet,
Whether *Cæsar* will come forth to day, or no:
For he is Superstitious growne of late,
Quite from the maine Opinion he held once,
Of Fantasie, of Dreames, and Ceremonies:
It may be, these apparant Prodigies,
The vnaccustom'd Terror of this night,
And the perswasion of his Augurers,
May hold him from the Capitoll to day.
Decius. Neuer feare that: If he be so resolu'd,
I can ore-sway him: For he loues to heare,
That Vnicornes may be betray'd with Trees,
And Beares with Glasses, Elephants with Holes,
Lyons with Toyles, and men with Flatterers.
But, when I tell him, he hates Flatterers,
He sayes, he does; being then most flattered.
Let me worke:
For I can giue his humour the true bent;
And I will bring him to the Capitoll.
Cas. Nay, we will all of vs, be there to fetch him.
Bru. By the eight houre, is that the vttermost?
Cin. Be that the vttermost, and faile not then.
Met. *Caius Ligarius* doth beare *Cæsar* hard,
Who rated him for speaking well of *Pompey*;
I wonder none of you haue thought of him.
Bru. Now good *Metellus* go along by him:
He loues me well, and I haue giuen him Reasons,
Send him but hither, and Ile fashion him.
Cas. The morning comes vpon's:
Wee'l leaue you *Brutus*,
And Friends disperse your selues; but all remember
What you haue said, and shew your selues true Romans.
Bru. Good Gentlemen, looke fresh and merrily,
Let not our lookes put on our purposes,
But beare it as our Roman Actors do,
With vntyr'd Spirits, and formall Constancie,
And so good morrow to you euery one. *Exeunt.*

Manet Brutus.

Boy: *Lucius*: Fast asleepe? It is no matter,
Enioy the hony-heauy-Dew of Slumber:
Thou hast no Figures, nor no Fantasies,

Which

Which busie care drawes, in the braines of men;
Therefore thou sleep'st so sound.

Enter Portia.

Por. *Brutus*, my Lord.
Bru. *Portia:* What meane you? wherfore rise you now?
It is not for your health, thus to commit
Your weake condition, to the raw cold morning.
Por. Nor for yours neither. Y'haue vngently *Brutus*
Stole from my bed: and yesternight at Supper
You sodainly arose, and walk'd about,
Musing, and sighing, with your armes a-crosse:
And when I ask'd you what the matter was,
You star'd vpon me, with vngentle lookes.
I vrg'd you further, then you scratch'd your head,
And too impatiently stampt with your foote:
Yet I insisted, yet you answer'd not,
But with an angry wafter of your hand
Gaue signe for me to leaue you: So I did,
Fearing to strengthen that impatience
Which seem'd too much inkindled; and withall,
Hoping it was but an effect of Humor,
Which sometime hath his houre with euery man.
It will not let you eate, nor talke, nor sleepe;
And could it worke so much vpon your shape,
As it hath much preuayl'd on your Condition,
I should not know you *Brutus*. Deare my Lord,
Make me acquainted with your cause of greefe.
Bru. I am not well in health, and that is all.
Por. *Brutus* is wise, and were he not in health,
He would embrace the meanes to come by it.
Bru. Why so I do: good *Portia* go to bed.
Por. Is *Brutus* sicke? And is it Physicall
To walke vnbraced, and sucke vp the humours
Of the danke Morning? What, is *Brutus* sicke?
And will he steale out of his wholsome bed
To dare the vile contagion of the Night?
And tempt the Rhewmy, and vnpurged Ayre,
To adde vnto his sicknesse? No my *Brutus*,
You haue some sicke Offence within your minde,
Which by the Right and Vertue of my place
I ought to know of: And vpon my knees,
I charme you, by my once commended Beauty,
By all your vowes of Loue, and that great Vow
Which did incorporate and make vs one,
That you vnfold to me, your selfe; your halfe
Why you are heauy: and what men to night
Haue had resort to you: for heere haue beene
Some sixe or seuen, who did hide their faces
Euen from darknesse.
Bru. Kneele not gentle *Portia*.
Por. I should not neede, if you were gentle *Brutus*.
Within tho Bond of Marriage, tell me *Brutus*,
Is it excepted, I should know no Secrets
That appertaine to you? Am I your Selfe,
But as it were in sort, or limitation?
To keepe with you at Meales, comfort your Bed,
And talke to you sometimes? Dwell I but in the Suburbs
Of your good pleasure? If it be no more,
Portia is *Brutus* Harlot, not his Wife.
Bru. You are my true and honourable Wife,
As deere to me, as are the ruddy droppes
That visit my sad heart.
Por. If this were true, then should I know this secret.
I graunt I am a Woman; but withall,
A Woman that Lord *Brutus* tooke to Wife:
I graunt I am a Woman; but withall,
A Woman well reputed: *Cato's* Daughter.
Thinke you, I am no stronger then my Sex
Being so Father'd, and so Husbanded?
Tell me your Counsels, I will not disclose 'em:
I haue made strong proofe of my Constancie,
Giuing my selfe a voluntary wound
Heere, in the Thigh: Can I beare that with patience,
And not my Husbands Secrets?
Bru. O ye Gods!
Render me worthy of this Noble Wife. *Knocke.*
Harke, harke, one knockes: *Portia* go in a while,
And by and by thy bosome shall partake
The secrets of my Heart.
All my engagements, I will construe to thee,
All the Charractery of my sad browes:
Leaue me with hast. *Exit Portia.*

Enter Lucius and Ligarius.

Lucius, who's that knockes.
Luc. Heere is a sicke man that would speak with you.
Bru. *Caius Ligarius*, that *Metellus* spake of.
Boy, stand aside. *Caius Ligarius*, how?
Cai. Vouchsafe good morrow from a feeble tongue.
Bru. O what a time haue you chose out braue *Caius*
To weare a Kerchiefe? Would you were not sicke.
Cai. I am not sicke, if *Brutus* haue in hand
Any exploit worthy the name of Honor.
Bru. Such an exploit haue I in hand *Ligarius*,
Had you a healthfull eare to heare of it.
Cai. By all the Gods that Romans bow before,
I heere discard my sicknesse. Soule of Rome,
Braue Sonne, deriu'd from Honourable Loines,
Thou like an Exorcist, hast coniur'd vp
My mortified Spirit. Now bid me runne,
And I will striue with things impossible,
Yea get the better of them. What's to do?
Bru. A peece of worke,
That will make sicke men whole.
Cai. But are not some whole, that we must make sicke?
Bru. That must we also. What it is my *Caius*,
I shall vnfold to thee, as we are going,
To whom it must be done.
Cai. Set on your foote,
And with a heart new-fir'd, I follow you,
To do I know not what: but it sufficeth
That *Brutus* leads me on. *Thunder.*
Bru. Follow me then. *Exeunt*

Thunder & Lightning.
Enter Iulius Cæsar in his Night-gowne.

Cæsar. Nor Heauen, nor Earth,
Haue beene at peace to night:
Thrice hath *Calphurnia*, in her sleepe cryed out,
Helpe, ho: They murther *Cæsar*. Who's within?

Enter a Seruant.

Ser. My Lord.
Cæs. Go bid the Priests do present Sacrifice,
And bring me their opinions of Successe.
Ser. I will my Lord. *Exit*

Enter Calphurnia.

Cal. What mean you *Cæsar*? Think you to walk forth?
You shall not stirre out of your house to day.
Cæs. *Cæsar* shall forth; the things that threaten'd me,
Ne're look'd but on my backe: When they shall see
The face of *Cæsar*, they are vanished.

Calp.

Calp. *Cæſar*, I neuer ſtood on Ceremonies,
Yet now they fright me: There is one within,
Beſides the things that we haue heard and ſeene,
Recounts moſt horrid ſights ſeene by the Watch.
A Lionneſſe hath whelped in the ſtreets,
And Graues haue yawn'd, and yeelded vp their dead;
Fierce fiery Warriours fight vpon the Clouds
In Rankes and Squadrons, and right forme of Warre
Which drizel'd blood vpon the Capitoll:
The noiſe of Battell hurtled in the Ayre:
Horſſes do neigh, and dying men did grone,
And Ghoſts did ſhrieke and ſqueale about the ſtreets.
O *Cæſar*, theſe things are beyond all vſe,
And I do feare them.

Cæſ. What can be auoyded
Whoſe end is purpos'd by the mighty Gods?
Yet *Cæſar* ſhall go forth: for theſe Predictions
Are to the world in generall, as to *Cæſar*.

Calp. When Beggers dye, there are no Comets ſeen,
The heauens themſelues blaze forth the death of Princes

Cæſ. Cowards dye many times before their deaths,
The valiant neuer taſte of death but once:
Of all the Wonders that I yet haue heard,
It ſeemes to me moſt ſtrange that men ſhould feare,
Seeing that death, a neceſſary end
Will come, when it will come.

Enter a Seruant.

What ſay the Augurers?

Ser. They would not haue you to ſtirre forth to day.
Plucking the intrailes of an Offering forth,
They could not finde a heart within the beaſt.

Cæſ. The Gods do this in ſhame of Cowardice:
Cæſar ſhould be a Beaſt without a heart
If he ſhould ſtay at home to day for feare:
No *Cæſar* ſhall not; Danger knowes full well
That *Cæſar* is more dangerous then he.
We heare two Lyons litter'd in one day,
And I the elder and more terrible,
And *Cæſar* ſhall go foorth.

Calp. Alas my Lord,
Your wiſedome is conſum'd in confidence:
Do not go forth to day: Call it my feare,
That keepes you in the houſe, and not your owne.
Wee'l ſend *Mark Antony* to the Senate houſe,
And he ſhall ſay, you are not well to day:
Let me vpon my knee, preuaile in this.

Cæſ. *Mark Antony* ſhall ſay I am not well,
And for thy humor, I will ſtay at home.

Enter Decius.

Heere's *Decius Brutus*, he ſhall tell them ſo.

Deci. *Cæſar*, all haile: Good morrow worthy *Cæſar*,
I come to fetch you to the Senate houſe.

Cæſ. And you are come in very happy time,
To beare my greeting to the Senators,
And tell them that I will not come to day:
Cannot, is falſe: and that I dare not, falſer:
I will not come to day, tell them ſo *Decius*.

Calp. Say he is ſicke.

Cæſ. Shall *Cæſar* ſend a Lye?
Haue I in Conqueſt ſtretcht mine Arme ſo farre,
To be afear'd to tell Gray-beards the truth:
Decius, go tell them, *Cæſar* will not come.

Deci. Moſt mighty *Cæſar* let me know ſome cauſe,
Leſt I be laught at when I tell them ſo.

Cæſ. The cauſe is in my Will, I will not come,
That is enough to ſatisfie the Senate.
But for your priuate ſatisfaction,
Becauſe I loue you, I will let you know.
Calphurnia heere my wife, ſtayes me at home:
She dreampt to night, ſhe ſaw my Statue,
Which like a Fountaine, with an hundred ſpouts
Did run pure blood: and many luſty Romans
Came ſmiling, & did bathe their hands in it:
And theſe does ſhe apply, for warnings and portents,
And euils imminent; and on her knee
Hath begg'd, that I will ſtay at home to day.

Deci. This Dreame is all amiſſe interpreted,
It was a viſion, faire and fortunate:
Your Statue ſpouting blood in many pipes,
In which ſo many ſmiling Romans bath'd,
Signifies, that from you great Rome ſhall ſucke
Reuiuing blood, and that great men ſhall preſſe
For Tinctures, Staines, Reliques, and Cogniſance.
This by *Calphurnia's* Dreame is ſignified.

Cæſ. And this way haue you well expounded it.

Deci. I haue, when you haue heard what I can ſay:
And know it now, the Senate haue concluded
To giue this day, a Crowne to mighty *Cæſar*.
If you ſhall ſend them word you will not come,
Their mindes may change. Beſides, it were a mocke
Apt to be render'd, for ſome one to ſay,
Breake vp the Senate, till another time:
When *Cæſars* wife ſhall meete with better Dreames.
If *Cæſar* hide himſelfe, ſhall they not whiſper
Loe *Cæſar* is affraid?
Pardon me *Cæſar*, for my deere deere loue
To your proceeding, bids me tell you this:
And reaſon to my loue is liable.

Cæſ. How fooliſh do your fears ſeeme now *Calphurnia*?
I am aſhamed I did yeeld to them.
Giue me my Robe, for I will go.

Enter Brutus, Ligarius, Metellus, Caska, Trebonius, Cynna, and Publius.

And looke where *Publius* is come to fetch me.

Pub. Good morrow *Cæſar*.

Cæſ. Welcome *Publius*.
What *Brutus*, are you ſtirr'd ſo earely too?
Good morrow *Caska*: *Caius Ligarius*,
Cæſar was ne're ſo much your enemy,
As that ſame Ague which hath made you leane.
What is't a Clocke?

Bru. *Cæſar*, 'tis ſtrucken eight.

Cæſ. I thanke you for your paines and curteſie.

Enter Antony.

See, *Antony* that Reuels long a-nights
Is notwithſtanding vp. Good morrow *Antony*.

Ant. So to moſt Noble *Cæſar*.

Cæſ. Bid them prepare within:
I am too blame to be thus waited for.
Now *Cynna*, now *Metellus*: what *Trebonius*,
I haue an houres talke in ſtore for you:
Remember that you call on me to day:
Be neere me, that I may remember you.

Treb. *Cæſar* I will: and ſo neere will I be,
That your beſt Friends ſhall wiſh I had beene further.

Cæſ. Good Friends go in, and taſte ſome wine with me
And we (like Friends) will ſtreight way go together.

Bru. That euery like is not the ſame, O *Cæſar*,
The heart of *Brutus* earnes to thinke vpon. *Exeunt*

Enter Artemidorus.

Cæſar, beware of Brutus, take heede of Caſsius; come not neere

neere Caska, haue an eye to Cynna, truſt not Trebonius, marke well Metellus Cymber, Decius Brutus loues thee not: Thou haſt wrong'd Caius Ligarius. There is but one minde in all theſe men, and it is bent againſt Cæſar: If thou beeſt not Immortall, looke about you: Security giues way to Conſpiracie. The mighty Gods defend thee.

Thy Louer, *Artemidorus.*

Heere will I ſtand, till *Cæſar* paſſe along,
And as a Sutor will I giue him this:
My heart laments, that Vertue cannot liue
Out of the teeth of Emulation.
If thou reade this, O *Cæſar*, thou mayeſt liue;
If not, the Fates with Traitors do contriue. *Exit.*

Enter Portia and Lucius.

Por. I prythee Boy, run to the Senate-houſe,
Stay not to anſwer me, but get thee gone.
Why doeſt thou ſtay?
Luc. To know my errand Madam.
Por. I would haue had thee there and heere agen
Ere I can tell thee what thou ſhould'ſt do there:
O Conſtancie, be ſtrong vpon my ſide,
Set a huge Mountaine 'tweene my Heart and Tongue:
I haue a mans minde, but a womans might:
How hard it is for women to keepe counſell.
Art thou heere yet?
Luc. Madam, what ſhould I do?
Run to the Capitoll, and nothing elſe?
And ſo returne to you, and nothing elſe?
Por. Yes, bring me word Boy, if thy Lord look well,
For he went ſickly forth: and take good note
What *Cæſar* doth, what Sutors preſſe to him.
Hearke Boy, what noyſe is that?
Luc. I heare none Madam.
Por. Prythee liſten well:
I heard a buſling Rumor like a Fray,
And the winde brings it from the Capitoll.
Luc. Sooth Madam, I heare nothing.

Enter the Soothſayer.

Por. Come hither Fellow, which way haſt thou bin?
Sooth. At mine owne houſe, good Lady.
Por. What is't a clocke?
Sooth. About the ninth houre Lady.
Por. Is *Cæſar* yet gone to the Capitoll?
Sooth. Madam not yet, I go to take my ſtand,
To ſee him paſſe on to the Capitoll.
Por. Thou haſt ſome ſuite to *Cæſar*, haſt thou not?
Sooth. That I haue Lady, if it will pleaſe *Cæſar*
To be ſo good to *Cæſar*, as to heare me:
I ſhall beſeech him to befriend himſelfe.
Por. Why know'ſt thou any harme's intended towards him?
Sooth. None that I know will be,
Much that I feare may chance:
Good morrow to you: heere the ſtreet is narrow:
The throng that followes *Cæſar* at the heeles,
Of Senators, of Prætors, common Sutors,
Will crowd a feeble man (almoſt) to death:
Ile get me to a place more voyd, and there
Speake to great *Cæſar* as he comes along. *Exit*
Por. I muſt go in:
Aye me: How weake a thing
The heart of woman is? O *Brutus*,
The Heauens ſpeede thee in thine enterprize.
Sure the Boy heard me: *Brutus* hath a ſuite
That *Cæſar* will not grant. O, I grow faint:
Run *Lucius*, and commend me to my Lord,
Say I am merry; Come to me againe
And bring me word what he doth ſay to thee. *Exeunt*

Actus Tertius.

Flouriſh.

Enter Cæſar, Brutus, Caſſius, Caska, Decius, Metellus, Trebonius, Cynna, Antony, Lepidus, Artimedorus, Publius, and the Soothſayer.

Cæſ. The Ides of March are come.
Sooth. I *Cæſar*, but not gone.
Art. Haile *Cæſar*: Read this Scedule.
Deci. *Trebonius* doth deſire you to ore-read
(At your beſt leyſure) this his humble ſuite.
Art. O *Cæſar*, reade mine firſt: for mine's a ſuite
That touches *Cæſar* neerer. Read it great *Cæſar*.
Cæſ. What touches vs our ſelfe, ſhall be laſt ſeru'd.
Art. Delay not *Cæſar*, read it inſtantly.
Cæſ. What, is the fellow mad?
Pub Sirra, giue place.
Caſſi. What, vrge you your Petitions in the ſtreet?
Come to the Capitoll.
Popil. I wiſh your enterprize to day may thriue.
Caſſi. What enterprize *Popillius*?
Popil. Fare you well.
Bru. What ſaid *Popillius Lena*?
Caſſi. He wiſht to day our enterprize might thriue:
I feare our purpoſe is diſcouered.
Bru. Looke how he makes to *Cæſar*: marke him.
Caſſi. *Caska* be ſodaine, for we feare preuention.
Brutus what ſhall be done? If this be knowne,
Caſſius or *Cæſar* neuer ſhall turne backe,
For I will ſlay my ſelfe.
Bru. *Caſſius* be conſtant:
Popillius Lena ſpeakes not of our purpoſes,
For looke he ſmiles, and *Cæſar* doth not change.
Caſſi. *Trebonius* knowes his time: for look you *Brutus*.
He drawes *Mark Antony* out of the way.
Deci. Where is *Metellus Cimber*, let him go,
And preſently preferre his ſuite to *Cæſar*.
Bru. He is addreſt: preſſe neere, and ſecond him.
Cin. *Caska*, you are the firſt that reares your hand.
Cæſ. Are we all ready? What is now amiſſe,
That *Cæſar* and his Senate muſt redreſſe?
Metel. Moſt high, moſt mighty, and moſt puiſant *Cæſar*
Metellus Cymber throwes before thy Seate
An humble heart.
Cæſ. I muſt preuent thee *Cymber*:
Theſe couchings, and theſe lowly courteſies
Might fire the blood of ordinary men,
And turne pre-Ordinance, and firſt Decree
Into the lane of Children. Be not fond,
To thinke that *Cæſar* beares ſuch Rebell blood
That will be thaw'd from the true quality
With that which melteth Fooles, I meane ſweet words,
Low-crooked-curtſies, and baſe Spaniell fawning:
Thy Brother by decree is baniſhed:
If thou doeſt bend, and pray, and fawne for him,
I ſpurne thee like a Curre out of my way:
Know, *Cæſar* doth not wrong, nor without cauſe
Will he be ſatisfied.
Metel. Is there no voyce more worthy then my owne,

To ſound more ſweetly in great *Cæſars* eare,
For the repealing of my baniſh'd Brother?
Bru. I kiſſe thy hand, but not in flattery *Cæſar*:
Deſiring thee, that *Publius Cymber* may
Haue an immediate freedome of repeale.
Cæſ. What *Brutus*?
Caſſi. Pardon *Cæſar*: *Cæſar* pardon:
As lowe as to thy foote doth *Caſſius* fall,
To begge infranchiſement for *Publius Cymber*.
Cæſ. I could be well mou'd, if I were as you,
If I could pray to moooue, Prayers would mooue me:
But I am conſtant as the Northerne Starre,
Of whoſe true fixt, and reſting quality,
There is no fellow in the Firmament.
The Skies are painted with vnnumbred ſparkes,
They are all Fire, and euery one doth ſhine:
But, there's but one in all doth hold his place.
So, in the World; 'Tis furniſh'd well with Men,
And Men are Fleſh and Blood, and apprehenſiue;
Yet in the number, I do know but One
That vnaſſayleable holds on his Ranke,
Vnſhak'd of Motion: and that I am he,
Let me a little ſhew it, euen in this:
That I was conſtant *Cymber* ſhould be baniſh'd,
And conſtant do remaine to keepe him ſo.
Cinna. O *Cæſar*.
Cæſ. Hence: Wilt thou lift vp Olympus?
Decius. Great *Cæſar*.
Cæſ. Doth not *Brutus* bootleſſe kneele?
Cask. Speake hands for me.

They ſtab Cæſar.

Cæſ. Et Tu Brutè?——Then fall *Cæſar*. *Dyes*
Cin. Liberty, Freedome; Tyranny is dead,
Run hence, proclaime, cry it about the Streets.
Caſſi. Some to the common Pulpits, and cry out
Liberty, Freedome, and Enfranchiſement.
Bru. People and Senators, be not affrighted:
Fly not, ſtand ſtill: Ambitions debt is paid.
Cask. Go to the Pulpit *Brutus*.
Dec. And *Caſſius* too.
Bru. Where's *Publius*?
Cin. Heere, quite confounded with this mutiny.
Met. Stand faſt together, leaſt ſome Friend of *Cæſars*
Should chance——
Bru. Talke not of ſtanding. *Publius* good cheere,
There is no harme intended to your perſon,
Nor to no Roman elſe: ſo tell them *Publius*.
Caſſi. And leaue vs *Publius*, leaſt that the people
Ruſhing on vs, ſhould do your Age ſome miſchiefe.
Bru. Do ſo, and let no man abide this deede,
But we the Doers.

Enter Trebonius.

Caſſi. Where is *Antony*?
Treb. Fled to his Houſe amaz'd:
Men, Wiues, and Children, ſtare, cry out, and run,
As it were Doomeſday.
Bru. Fates, we will know your pleaſures:
That we ſhall dye we know, 'tis but the time
And drawing dayes out, that men ſtand vpon.
Cask. Why he that cuts off twenty yeares of life,
Cuts off ſo many yeares of fearing death.
Bru. Grant that, and then is Death a Benefit:
So are we *Cæſars* Friends, that haue abridg'd
His time of fearing death. Stoope Romans, ſtoope,
And let vs bathe our hands in *Cæſars* blood
Vp to the Elbowes, and beſmeare our Swords:
Then walke we forth, euen to the Market place,
And wauing our red Weapons o're our heads,
Let's all cry Peace, Freedome, and Liberty.
Caſſi. Stoop then, and waſh. How many Ages hence
Shall this our lofty Scene be acted ouer,
In State vnborne, and Accents yet vnknowne?
Bru. How many times ſhall *Cæſar* bleed in ſport,
That now on *Pompeyes* Baſis lye along,
No worthier then the duſt?
Caſſi. So oft as that ſhall be,
So often ſhall the knot of vs be call'd,
The Men that gaue their Country liberty.
Dec. What, ſhall we forth?
Caſſi. I, euery man away.
Brutus ſhall leade, and we will grace his heeles
With the moſt boldeſt, and beſt hearts of Rome.

Enter a Seruant.

Bru. Soft, who comes heere? A friend of *Antonies*.
Ser. Thus *Brutus* did my Maſter bid me kneele;
Thus did *Mark Antony* bid me fall downe,
And being proſtrate, thus he bad me ſay:
Brutus is Noble, Wiſe, Valiant, and Honeſt;
Cæſar was Mighty, Bold, Royall, and Louing:
Say, I loue *Brutus*, and I honour him;
Say, I fear'd *Cæſar*, honour'd him, and lou'd him.
If *Brutus* will vouchſafe, that *Antony*
May ſafely come to him, and be reſolu'd
How *Cæſar* hath deſeru'd to lye in death,
Mark Antony, ſhall not loue *Cæſar* dead
So well as *Brutus* liuing; but will follow
The Fortunes and Affayres of Noble *Brutus*,
Thorough the hazards of this vntrod State,
With all true Faith. So ſayes my Maſter *Antony*.
Bru. Thy Maſter is a Wiſe and Valiant Romane,
I neuer thought him worſe:
Tell him, ſo pleaſe him come vnto this place
He ſhall be ſatisfied: and by my Honor
Depart vntouch'd.
Ser. Ile fetch him preſently. *Exit Seruant.*
Bru. I know that we ſhall haue him well to Friend.
Caſſi. I wiſh we may: But yet haue I a minde
That feares him much: and my miſgiuing ſtill
Falles ſhrewdly to the purpoſe.

Enter Antony.

Bru. But heere comes *Antony*:
Welcome *Mark Antony*.
Ant. O mighty *Cæſar*! Doſt thou lye ſo lowe?
Are all thy Conqueſts, Glories, Triumphes, Spoiles,
Shrunke to this little Meaſure? Fare thee well.
I know not Gentlemen what you intend,
Who elſe muſt be let blood, who elſe is ranke:
If I my ſelfe, there is no houre ſo fit
As *Cæſars* deaths houre; nor no Inſtrument
Of halfe that worth, as thoſe your Swords; made rich
With the moſt Noble blood of all this World.
I do beſeech yee, if you beare me hard,
Now, whil'ſt your purpled hands do reeke and ſmoake,
Fulfill your pleaſure. Liue a thouſand yeeres,
I ſhall not finde my ſelfe ſo apt to dye.
No place will pleaſe me ſo, no meane of death,
As heere by *Cæſar*, and by you cut off,
The Choice and Maſter Spirits of this Age.
Bru. O *Antony*! Begge not your death of vs:
Though now we muſt appeare bloody and cruell,
As by our hands, and this our preſent Acte
You ſee we do: Yet ſee you but our hands,

And

And this, the bleeding buſineſſe they haue done:
Our hearts you ſee not, they are pittifull:
And pitty to the generall wrong of Rome,
As fire driues out fire, ſo pitty, pitty
Hath done this deed on *Cæſar*. For your part,
To you, our Swords haue leaden points *Marke Antony*:
Our Armes in ſtrength of malice, and our Hearts
Of Brothers temper, do receiue you in,
With all kinde loue, good thoughts, and reuerence.
Caſſi. Your voyce ſhall be as ſtrong as any mans,
In the diſpoſing of new Dignities.
Bru. Onely be patient, till we haue appeas'd
The Multitude, beſide themſelues with feare,
And then, we will deliuer you the cauſe,
Why I, that did loue *Cæſar* when I ſtrooke him,
Haue thus proceeded.
Ant. I doubt not of your Wiſedome.
Let each man render me his bloody hand.
Firſt *Marcus Brutus* will I ſhake with you;
Next *Caius Caſſius* do I take your hand;
Now *Decius Brutus* yours; now yours *Metellus*,
Yours *Cinna*; and my valiant *Caska* yours;
Though laſt, not leaſt in loue, yours good *Trebonius*.
Gentlemen all: Alas, what ſhall I ſay,
My credit now ſtands on ſuch ſlippery ground,
That one of two bad wayes you muſt conceit me,
Either a Coward, or a Flatterer.
That I did loue thee *Cæſar* O 'tis true:
If then thy Spirit looke vpon vs now,
Shall it not greeue thee deerer then thy death,
To ſee thy *Antony* making his peace,
Shaking the bloody fingers of thy Foes?
Moſt Noble, in the preſence of thy Coarſe,
Had I as many eyes, as thou haſt wounds,
Weeping as faſt as they ſtreame forth thy blood,
It would become me better, then to cloſe
In tearmes of Friendſhip with thine enemies.
Pardon me *Iulius*, heere was't thou bay'd braue Hart,
Heere did'ſt thou fall, and heere thy Hunters ſtand
Sign'd in thy Spoyle, and Crimſon'd in thy Lethee.
O World! thou waſt the Forreſt to this Hart,
And this indeed, O World, the Hart of thee.
How like a Deere, ſtroken by many Princes,
Doſt thou heere lye?
Caſſi. Mark Antony.
Ant. Pardon me *Caius Caſſius*:
The Enemies of *Cæſar*, ſhall ſay this:
Then, in a Friend, it is cold Modeſtie.
Caſſi. I blame you not for praiſing *Cæſar* ſo,
But what compact meane you to haue with vs?
Will you be prick'd in number of our Friends,
Or ſhall we on, and not depend on you?
Ant. Therefore I tooke your hands, but was indeed
Sway'd from the point, by looking downe on *Cæſar*.
Friends am I with you all, and loue you all,
Vpon this hope, that you ſhall giue me Reaſons,
Why, and wherein, *Cæſar* was dangerous.
Bru Or elſe were this a ſauage Spectacle:
Our Reaſons are ſo full of good regard,
That were you *Antony*, the Sonne of *Cæſar*,
You ſhould be ſatisfied.
Ant. That's all I ſeeke,
And am moreouer ſutor, that I may
Produce his body to the Market-place,
And in the Pulpit as becomes a Friend,
Speake in the Order of his Funerall.
Bru. You ſhall *Marke Antony*.
Caſſi. Brutus, a word with you:
You know not what you do; Do not conſent
That *Antony* ſpeake in his Funerall:
Know you how much the people may be mou'd
By that which he will vtter.
Bru. By your pardon:
I will my ſelfe into the Pulpit firſt,
And ſhew the reaſon of our *Cæſars* death.
What *Antony* ſhall ſpeake, I will proteſt
He ſpeakes by leaue, and by permiſſion:
And that we are contented *Cæſar* ſhall
Haue all true Rites, and lawfull Ceremonies,
It ſhall aduantage more, then do vs wrong.
Caſſi. I know not what may fall, I like it not.
Bru. Mark Antony, heere take you *Cæſars* body:
You ſhall not in your Funerall ſpeech blame vs,
But ſpeake all good you can deuiſe of *Cæſar*,
And ſay you doo't by our permiſſion:
Elſe ſhall you not haue any hand at all
About his Funerall. And you ſhall ſpeake
In the ſame Pulpit whereto I am going,
After my ſpeech is ended.
Ant. Be it ſo:
I do deſire no more.
Bru. Prepare the body then, and follow vs. *Exeunt.*
Manet Antony.
O pardon me, thou bleeding peece of Earth:
That I am meeke and gentle with theſe Butchers.
Thou art the Ruines of the Nobleſt man
That euer liued in the Tide of Times.
Woe to the hand that ſhed this coſtly Blood.
Ouer thy wounds, now do I Propheſie,
(Which like dumbe mouthes do ope their Ruby lips,
To begge the voyce and vtterance of my Tongue)
A Curſe ſhall light vpon the limbes of men;
Domeſticke Fury, and fierce Ciuill ſtrife,
Shall cumber all the parts of Italy:
Blood and deſtruction ſhall be ſo in vſe,
And dreadfull Obiects ſo familiar,
That Mothers ſhall but ſmile, when they behold
Their Infants quartered with the hands of Warre:
All pitty choak'd with cuſtome of fell deeds,
And *Cæſars* Spirit ranging for Reuenge,
With *Ate* by his ſide, come hot from Hell,
Shall in theſe Confines, with a Monarkes voyce,
Cry hauocke, and let ſlip the Dogges of Warre,
That this foule deede, ſhall ſmell aboue the earth
With Carrion men, groaning for Buriall.
Enter Octauio's Seruant.
You ſerue *Octauius Cæſar*, do you not?
Ser. I do *Marke Antony*.
Ant. Cæſar did write for him to come to Rome.
Ser. He did receiue his Letters, and is comming,
And bid me ſay to you by word of mouth———
O *Cæſar*!
Ant. Thy heart is bigge: get thee a-part and weepe:
Paſſion I ſee is catching from mine eyes,
Seeing thoſe Beads of ſorrow ſtand in thine,
Began to water. Is thy Maſter comming?
Ser. He lies to night within ſeuen Leagues of Rome.
Ant. Poſt backe with ſpeede,
And tell him what hath chanc'd:
Heere is a mourning Rome, a dangerous Rome,
No Rome of ſafety for *Octauius* yet,
Hie hence, and tell him ſo. Yet ſtay a-while,
The

Thou shalt not backe, till I haue borne this course
Into the Market place: There shall I try
In my Oration, how the People take
The cruell issue of these bloody men,
According to the which, thou shalt discourse
To yong *Octauius*, of the state of things.
Lend me your hand. *Exeunt*

Enter Brutus and goes into the Pulpit, and Cassius, with the Plebeians.

Ple. We will be satisfied: let vs be satisfied.
Bru. Then follow me, and giue me Audience friends.
Cassius go you into the other streete,
And part the Numbers.
Those that will heare me speake, let'em stay heere;
Those that will follow *Cassius*, go with him,
And publike Reasons shall be rendred
Of *Cæsars* death.
1.*Ple.* I will heare *Brutus* speake.
2. I will heare *Cassius*, and compare their Reasons,
When seuerally we heare them rendred.
3. The Noble *Brutus* is ascended: Silence.
Bru. Be patient till the last.

Romans, Countrey-men, and Louers, heare mee for my cause, and be silent, that you may heare. Beleeue me for mine Honor, and haue respect to mine Honor, that you may beleeue. Censure me in your Wisedom, and awake your Senses, that you may the better Iudge. If there bee any in this Assembly, any deere Friend of *Cæsars*, to him I say, that *Brutus* loue to *Cæsar*, was no lesse then his. If then, that Friend demand, why *Brutus* rose against *Cæsar*, this is my answer: Not that I lou'd *Cæsar* lesse, but that I lou'd Rome more. Had you rather *Cæsar* were liuing, and dye all Slaues; then that *Cæsar* were dead, to liue all Free-men? As *Cæsar* lou'd mee, I weepe for him; as he was Fortunate, I reioyce at it; as he was Valiant, I honour him: But, as he was Ambitious, I slew him. There is Teares, for his Loue: Ioy, for his Fortune: Honor, for his Valour: and Death, for his Ambition. Who is heere so base, that would be a Bondman? If any, speak, for him haue I offended. Who is heere so rude, that would not be a Roman? If any, speak, for him haue I offended. Who is heere so vile, that will not loue his Countrey? If any, speake, for him haue I offended. I pause for a Reply.

All. None *Brutus*, none.

Brutus. Then none haue I offended. I haue done no more to *Cæsar*, then you shall do to *Brutus*. The Question of his death, is inroll'd in the Capitoll: his Glory not extenuated, wherein he was worthy; nor his offences enforc'd, for which he suffered death.

Enter Mark Antony, with Cæsars body.

Heere comes his Body, mourn'd by *Marke Antony*, who though he had no hand in his death, shall receiue the benefit of his dying, a place in the Comonwealth, as which of you shall not. With this I depart, that as I slewe my best Louer for the good of Rome, I haue the same Dagger for my selfe, when it shall please my Country to need my death.

All. Liue *Brutus*, liue, liue.
1. Bring him with Triumph home vnto his house.
2. Giue him a Statue with his Ancestors.
3. Let him be *Cæsar*.
4 *Cæsars* better parts,
Shall be Crown'd in *Brutus*.
Wee'l bring him to his House
With Showts and Clamors.
Bru. My Country-men.
2. Peace, silence, *Brutus* speakes.
1. Peace ho.
Bru. Good Countrymen, let me depart alone,
And (for my sake) stay heere with *Antony*:
Do grace to *Cæsars* Corpes, and grace his Speech
Tending to *Cæsars* Glories, which *Marke Antony*
(By our permission) is allow'd to make.
I do intreat you, not a man depart,
Saue I alone, till *Antony* haue spoke. *Exit*
1 Stay ho, and let vs heare *Mark Antony*.
3 Let him go vp into the publike Chaire,
Wee'l heare him: Noble *Antony* go vp.
Ant. For *Brutus* sake, I am beholding to you.
4 What does he say of *Brutus*?
3 He sayes, for *Brutus* sake
He findes himselfe beholding to vs all.
4 'Twere best he speake no harme of *Brutus* heere?
1 This *Cæsar* was a Tyrant.
3 Nay that's certaine:
We are blest that Rome is rid of him.
2 Peace, let vs heare what *Antony* can say.
Ant. You gentle Romans.
All. Peace hoe, let vs heare him.
An. Friends, Romans, Countrymen, lend me your ears
I come to bury *Cæsar*, not to praise him:
The euill that men do, liues after them,
The good is oft enterred with their bones,
So let it be with *Cæsar*. The Noble *Brutus*,
Hath told you *Cæsar* was Ambitious
If it were so, it was a greeuous Fault,
And greeuously hath *Cæsar* answer'd it.
Heere, vnder leaue of *Brutus*, and the rest
(For *Brutus* is an Honourable man,
So are they all; all Honourable men)
Come I to speake in *Cæsars* Funerall.
He was my Friend, faithfull, and iust to me;
But *Brutus* sayes, he was Ambitious,
And *Brutus* is an Honourable man.
He hath brought many Captiues home to Rome,
Whose Ransomes, did the generall Coffers fill:
Did this in *Cæsar* seeme Ambitious?
When that the poore haue cry'de, *Cæsar* hath wept:
Ambition should be made of sterner stuffe,
Yet *Brutus* sayes, he was Ambitious:
And *Brutus* is an Honourable man.
You all did see, that on the *Lupercall*,
I thrice presented him a Kingly Crowne,
Which he did thrice refuse. Was this Ambition?
Yet *Brutus* sayes, he was Ambitious:
And sure he is an Honourable man.
I speake not to disprooue what *Brutus* spoke,
But heere I am, to speake what I do know;
You all did loue him once, not without cause,
What cause with-holds you then, to mourne for him?
O Iudgement! thou are fled to brutish Beasts,
And Men haue lost their Reason. Beare with me,
My heart is in the Coffin there with *Cæsar*,
And I must pawse, till it come backe to me.
1 Me thinkes there is much reason in his sayings.
2 If thou consider rightly of the matter,
Cæsar ha's had great wrong.
Ha's hee Masters? I feare there will a worse come in his place.

4. Mark'd ye his words? he would not take ỹ Crown,
Therefore 'tis certaine, he was not Ambitious.
1. If it be found ſo, ſome will deere abide it.
2. Poore ſoule, his eyes are red as fire with weeping.
3. There's not a Nobler man in Rome then *Antony*.
4. Now marke him, he begins againe to ſpeake.
Ant. But yeſterday, the word of *Cæſar* migh
Haue ſtood againſt the World: Now lies he there,
And none ſo poore to do him reuerence.
O Maiſters! If I were diſpos'd to ſtirre
Your hearts and mindes to Mutiny and Rage,
I ſhould do *Brutus* wrong, and *Caſſius* wrong:
Who (you all know) are Honourable men.
I will not do them wrong: I rather chooſe
To wrong the dead, to wrong my ſelfe and you,
Then I will wrong ſuch Honourable men.
But heere's a Parchment, with the Seale of *Cæſar*,
I found it in his Cloſſet, 'tis his Will:
Let but the Commons heare this Teſtament:
(Which pardon me) I do not meane to reade,
And they would go and kiſſe dead *Cæſars* wounds,
And dip their Napkins in his Sacred Blood;
Yea, begge a haire of him for Memory,
And dying, mention it within their Willes,
Bequeathing it as a rich Legacie
Vnto their iſſue.
4 Wee'l heare the Will, reade it *Marke Antony*.
All. The Will, the Will; we will heare *Cæſars* Will
Ant. Haue patience gentle Friends, I muſt not read it,
It is not meete you know how *Cæſar* lou'd you:
You are not Wood, you are not Stones, but men:
And being men, hearing the Will of *Cæſar*,
It will inflame you, it will make you mad:
'Tis good you know not that you are his Heires,
For if you ſhould, O what would come of it?
4 Read the Will, wee'l heare it *Antony*:
You ſhall reade vs the Will, *Cæſars* Will.
Ant. Will you be Patient? Will you ſtay a-while?
I haue o're-ſhot my ſelfe to tell you of it,
I feare I wrong the Honourable men,
Whoſe Daggers haue ſtabb'd *Cæſar*: I do feare it.
4 They were Traitors: Honourable men?
All. The Will, the Teſtament.
2 They were Villaines, Murderers: the Will, read the Will.
Ant. You will compell me then to read the Will:
Then make a Ring about the Corpes of *Cæſar*,
And let me ſhew you him that made the Will:
Shall I deſcend? And will you giue me leaue?
All. Come downe.
2 Deſcend.
3 You ſhall haue leaue.
4 A Ring, ſtand round.
1 Stand from the Hearſe, ſtand from the Body.
2 Roome for *Antony*, moſt Noble *Antony*.
Ant. Nay preſſe not ſo vpon me, ſtand farre off.
All. Stand backe: roome, beare backe.
Ant. If you haue teares, prepare to ſhed them now.
You all do know this Mantle, I remember
The firſt time euer *Cæſar* put it on,
'Twas on a Summers Euening in his Tent,
That day he ouercame the *Neruij*.
Looke, in this place ran *Caſſius* Dagger through:
See what a rent the enuious *Caska* made:
Through this, the wel-beloued *Brutus* ſtabb'd,
And as he pluck'd his curſed Steele away:
Marke how the blood of *Cæſar* followed it,
As ruſhing out of doores, to be reſolu'd
If *Brutus* ſo vnkindely knock'd, or no:
For *Brutus*, as you know, was *Cæſars* Angel.
Iudge, O you Gods, how deerely *Cæſar* lou'd him:
This was the moſt vnkindeſt cut of all.
For when the Noble *Cæſar* ſaw him ſtab,
Ingratitude, more ſtrong then Traitors armes,
Quite vanquiſh'd him: then burſt his Mighty heart,
And in his Mantle, muffling vp his face,
Euen at the Baſe of *Pompeyes* Statue
(Which all the while ran blood) great *Cæſar* fell.
O what a fall was there, my Countrymen?
Then I, and you, and all of vs fell downe,
Whil'ſt bloody Treaſon flouriſh'd ouer vs.
O now you weepe, and I perceiue you feele
The dint of pitty: Theſe are gracious droppes.
Kinde Soules, what weepe you, when you but behold
Our *Cæſars* Veſture wounded? Looke you heere,
Heere is Himſelfe, marr'd as you ſee with Traitors.
1. O pitteous ſpectacle!
2. O Noble *Cæſar*!
3. O wofull day!
4. O Traitors, Villaines!
1. O moſt bloody ſight!
2. We will be reueng'd: Reuenge
About, ſeeke, burne, fire, kill, ſlay,
Let not a Traitor liue.
Ant. Stay Country-men.
1. Peace there, heare the Noble *Antony*.
2. Wee'l heare him, wee'l follow him, wee'l dy with him.
Ant. Good Friends, ſweet Friends, let me not ſtirre you vp
To ſuch a ſodaine Flood of Mutiny:
They that haue done this Deede, are honourable.
What priuate greefes they haue, alas I know not,
That made them do it: They are Wiſe, and Honourable,
And will no doubt with Reaſons anſwer you.
I come not (Friends) to ſteale away your hearts,
I am no Orator, as *Brutus* is;
But (as you know me all) a plaine blunt man
That loue my Friend, and that they know full well,
That gaue me publike leaue to ſpeake of him:
For I haue neyther writ nor words, nor worth,
Action, nor Vtterance, nor the power of Speech,
To ſtirre mens Blood. I onely ſpeake right on:
I tell you that, which you your ſelues do know,
Shew you ſweet *Cæſars* wounds, poor poor dum mouths
And bid them ſpeake for me: But were I *Brutus*,
And *Brutus Antony*, there were an *Antony*
Would ruffle vp your Spirits, and put a Tongue
In euery Wound of *Cæſar*, that ſhould moue
The ſtones of Rome, to riſe and Mutiny.
All. Wee'l Mutiny.
1 Wee'l burne the houſe of *Brutus*.
3 Away then, come, ſeeke the Conſpirators.
Ant. Yet heare me Countrymen, yet heare me ſpeake
All. Peace hoe, heare *Antony*, moſt Noble *Antony*.
Ant. Why Friends, you go to do you know not what:
Wherein hath *Cæſar* thus deſeru'd your loues?
Alas you know not, I muſt tell you then:
You haue forgot the Will I told you of.
All. Moſt true, the Will, let's ſtay and heare the Wil.
Ant. Heere is the Will, and vnder *Cæſars* Seale:
To euery Roman Citizen he giues,
To euery ſeuerall man, ſeuenty fiue Drachmaes.
2. *Ple.*

2 Ple. Moſt Noble *Cæſar*, wee'l reuenge his death.
3 Ple. O Royall *Cæſar*.
Ant. Heare me with patience.
All. Peace hoe
Ant. Moreouer, he hath left you all his Walkes,
His priuate Arbors, and new-planted Orchards,
On this ſide Tyber, he hath left them you,
And to your heyres for euer: common pleaſures
To walke abroad, and recreate your ſelues.
Heere was a *Cæſar*: when comes ſuch another?
1.Ple. Neuer, neuer: come, away, away:
Wee'l burne his body in the holy place,
And with the Brands fire the Traitors houſes.
Take vp the body.
2.Ple. Go fetch fire.
3.Ple. Plucke downe Benches.
4.Ple. Plucke downe Formes, Windowes, any thing.
Exit Plebeians.
Ant. Now let it worke: Miſcheefe thou art a-foot,
Take thou what courſe thou wilt.
How now Fellow?
Enter Seruant.
Ser. Sir, *Octauius* is already come to Rome.
Ant. Where is hee?
Ser. He and *Lepidus* are at *Cæſars* houſe.
Ant. And thither will I ſtraight, to viſit him:
He comes vpon a wiſh. Fortune is merry,
And in this mood will giue vs any thing.
Ser. I heard him ſay, *Brutus* and *Caſſius*
Are rid like Madmen through the Gates of Rome.
Ant. Belike they had ſome notice of the people
How I had moued them. Bring me to *Octauius*. *Exeunt*

Enter Cinna the Poet, and after him the Plebeians.

Cinna. I dreamt to night, that I did feaſt with *Cæſar*,
And things vnluckily charge my Fantaſie:
I haue no will to wander foorth of doores,
Yet ſomething leads me foorth.
1. What is your name?
2. Whether are you going?
3. Where do you dwell?
4. Are you a married man, or a Batchellor?
2. Anſwer euery man directly.
1. I, and breefely.
4. I, and wiſely.
3. I, and truly, you were beſt.
Cin. What is my name? Whether am I going? Where do I dwell? Am I a married man, or a Batchellour? Then to anſwer euery man, directly and breefely, wiſely and truly: wiſely I ſay, I am a Batchellor.
2 That's as much as to ſay, they are fooles that marrie: you'l beare me a bang for that I feare: proceede directly.
Cinna. Directly I am going to *Cæſars* Funerall.
1. As a Friend, or an Enemy?
Cinna. As a friend.
2. That matter is anſwered directly.
4. For your dwelling: breefely.
Cinna. Breefely, I dwell by the Capitoll.
3. Your name ſir, truly.
Cinna. Truly, my name is *Cinna*.
1. Teare him to peeces, hee's a Conſpirator.
Cinna. I am *Cinna* the Poet, I am *Cinna* the Poet.
4. Teare him for his bad verſes, teare him for his bad Verſes.
Cin. I am not *Cinna* the Conſpirator.
4. It is no matter, his name's *Cinna*, plucke but his name out of his heart, and turne him going.
3. Teare him, tear him; Come Brands hoe, Firebrands: to *Brutus*, to *Caſſius*, burne all. Some to *Decius* Houſe, and ſome to *Caska's*; ſome to *Ligarius*: Away, go.
Exeunt all the Plebeians.

Actus Quartus.

Enter Antony, Octauius, and Lepidus.
Ant. Theſe many then ſhall die, their names are prickt
Octa. Your Brother too muſt dye: conſent you *Lepidus*?
Lep. I do conſent.
Octa. Pricke him downe *Antony*.
Lep Vpon condition *Publius* ſhall not liue,
Who is your Siſters ſonne, *Marke Antony*.
Ant. He ſhall not liue; looke, with a ſpot I dam him.
But *Lepidus*, go you to *Cæſars* houſe:
Fetch the Will hither, and we ſhall determine
How to cut off ſome charge in Legacies.
Lep. What? ſhall I finde you heere?
Octa. Or heere, or at the Capitoll. *Exit Lepidus*
Ant. This is a ſlight vnmeritable man,
Meet to be ſent on Errands: is it fit
The three-fold World diuided, he ſhould ſtand
One of the three to ſhare it?
Octa. So you thought him,
And tooke his voyce who ſhould be prickt to dye
In our blacke Sentence and Proſcription.
Ant. *Octauius*, I haue ſeene more dayes then you,
And though we lay theſe Honours on this man,
To eaſe our ſelues of diuers ſland'rous loads,
He ſhall but beare them, as the Aſſe beares Gold,
To groane and ſwet vnder the Buſineſſe,
Either led or driuen, as we point the way:
And hauing brought our Treaſure, where we will,
Then take we downe his Load, and turne him off
(Like to the empty Aſſe) to ſhake his eares,
And graze in Commons.
Octa. You may do your will:
But hee's a tried, and valiant Souldier.
Ant. So is my Horſe *Octauius*, and for that
I do appoint him ſtore of Prouender.
It is a Creature that I teach to fight,
To winde, to ſtop, to run directly on:
His corporall Motion, gouern'd by my Spirit,
And in ſome taſte, is *Lepidus* but ſo:
He muſt be taught, and train'd, and bid go forth:
A barren ſpirited Fellow; one that feeds
On Obiects, Arts, and Imitations.
Which out of vſe, and ſtal'de by other men
Begin his faſhion. Do not talke of him,
But as a property: and now *Octauius*,
Liſten great things. *Brutus* and *Caſſius*
Are leuying Powers; We muſt ſtraight make head:
Therefore let our Alliance be combin'd,
Our beſt Friends made, our meanes ſtretcht,
And let vs preſently go ſit in Councell,
How couert matters may be beſt diſclos'd,
And open Perils ſureſt anſwered.
Octa. Let vs do ſo: for we are at the ſtake,

ll 2 And

And bayed about with many Enemies,
And ſome that ſmile haue in their hearts I feare
Millions of Miſcheefes. *Exeunt*

Drum. Enter Brutus, Lucillius, and the Army. Titinius and Pindarus meete them.

Bru. Stand ho.
Lucil. Giue the word ho, and Stand.
Bru. What now *Lucillius*, is *Caſſius* neere?
Lucil. He is at hand, and *Pindarus* is come
To do you ſalutation from his Maſter.
Bru. He greets me well. Your Maſter *Pindarus*
In his owne change, or by ill Officers,
Hath giuen me ſome worthy cauſe to wiſh
Things done, vndone: But if he be at hand
I ſhall be ſatisfied.
Pin. I do not doubt
But that my Noble Maſter will appeare
Such as he is, full of regard, and Honour.
Bru. He is not doubted. A word *Lucillius*
How he receiu'd you: let me be reſolu'd.
Lucil. With courteſie, and with reſpect enough,
But not with ſuch familiar inſtances,
Nor with ſuch free and friendly Conference
As he hath vs'd of old.
Bru. Thou haſt deſcrib'd
A hot Friend, cooling: Euer note *Lucillius*,
When Loue begins to ſicken and decay
It vſeth an enforced Ceremony.
There are no trickes, in plaine and ſimple Faith:
But hollow men, like Horſes hot at hand,
Make gallant ſhew, and promiſe of their Mettle:
Low March within.
But when they ſhould endure the bloody Spurre,
They fall their Creſts, and like deceitfull Iades
Sinke in the Triall. Comes his Army on?
Lucil. They meane this night in Sardis to be quarter'd:
The greater part, the Horſe in generall
Are come with *Caſſius*.

Enter Caſſius and his Powers.

Bru. Hearke, he is arriu'd:
March gently on to meete him.
Caſſi. Stand ho.
Bru. Stand ho, ſpeake the word along.
Stand.
Stand.
Stand.
Caſſi. Moſt Noble Brother, you haue done me wrong.
Bru. Iudge me you Gods; wrong I mine Enemies?
And if not ſo, how ſhould I wrong a Brother.
Caſſi. *Brutus*, this ſober forme of yours, hides wrongs,
And when you do them———
Brut. *Caſſius*, be content,
Speake your greefes ſoftly, I do know you well.
Before the eyes of both our Armies heere
(Which ſhould perceiue nothing but Loue from vs)
Let vs not wrangle. Bid them moue away:
Then in my Tent *Caſſius* enlarge your Greefes,
And I will giue you Audience.
Caſſi. *Pindarus*,
Bid our Commanders leade their Charges off
A little from this ground.
Bru. *Lucillius*, do you the like, and let no man
Come to our Tent, till we haue done our Conference.
Let *Lucius* and *Titinius* guard our doore. *Exeunt*

Manet Brutus and Caſſius.

Caſſi. That you haue wrong'd me, doth appear in this:
You haue condemn'd, and noted *Lucius Pella*
For taking Bribes heere of the Sardians;
Wherein my Letters, praying on his ſide,
Becauſe I knew the man was ſlighted off.
Bru. You wrong'd your ſelfe to write in ſuch a caſe.
Caſſi. In ſuch a time as this, it is not meet
That euery nice offence ſhould beare his Comment.
Bru. Let me tell you *Caſſius*, you your ſelfe
Are much condemn'd to haue an itching Palme,
To ſell, and Mart your Offices for Gold
To Vndeſeruers.
Caſſi. I, an itching Palme?
You know that you are *Brutus* that ſpeakes this,
Or by the Gods, this ſpeech were elſe your laſt.
Bru. The name of *Caſſius* Honors this corruption,
And Chaſticement doth therefore hide his head.
Caſſi. Chaſticement?
Bru. Remember March, the Ides of March reme̅ber:
Did not great *Iulius* bleede for Iuſtice ſake?
What Villaine touch'd his body, that did ſtab,
And not for Iuſtice? What? Shall one of Vs,
That ſtrucke the Formoſt man of all this World,
But for ſupporting Robbers: ſhall we now,
Contaminate our fingers, with baſe Bribes?
And ſell the mighty ſpace of our large Honors
For ſo much traſh, as may be graſped thus?
I had rather be a Dogge, and bay the Moone,
Then ſuch a Roman.
Caſſi. *Brutus*, baite not me,
Ile not indure it: you forget your ſelfe
To hedge me in. I am a Souldier, I,
Older in practice, Abler then your ſelfe
To make Conditions.
Bru. Go too: you are not *Caſſius*.
Caſſi. I am.
Bru. I ſay, you are not.
Caſſi. Vrge me no more, I ſhall forget my ſelfe:
Haue minde vpon your health: Tempt me no farther.
Bru. Away ſlight man.
Caſſi. Is't poſſible?
Bru. Heare me, for I will ſpeake.
Muſt I giue way, and roome to your raſh Choller?
Shall I be frighted, when a Madman ſtares?
Caſſi. O ye Gods, ye Gods, Muſt I endure all this?
Bru. All this? I more: Fret till your proud hart break.
Go ſhew your Slaues how Chollericke you are,
And make your Bondmen tremble. Muſt I bouge?
Muſt I obſerue you? Muſt I ſtand and crouch
Vnder your Teſtie Humour? By the Gods,
You ſhall digeſt the Venom of your Spleene
Though it do Split you. For, from this day forth,
Ile vſe you for my Mirth, yea for my Laughter
When you are Waſpiſh.
Caſſi. Is it come to this?
Bru. You ſay, you are a better Souldier:
Let it appeare ſo; make your vaunting true,
And it ſhall pleaſe me well. For mine owne part,
I ſhall be glad to learne of Noble men.
Caſſ. You wrong me euery way:
You wrong me *Brutus*:
I ſaide, an Elder Souldier, not a Better.
Did I ſay Better?
Bru. If you did, I care not.
Caſſ. When *Cæſar* liu'd, he durſt not thus haue mou'd (me.
Brut. Peace, peace, you durſt not ſo haue tempted him.
Caſſ.

Caſſi. I durſt not.
Bru. No.
Caſſi. What? durſt not tempt him?
Bru. For your life you durſt not.
Caſſi. Do not preſume too much vpon my Loue,
I may do that I ſhall be ſorry for.
Bru. You haue done that you ſhould be ſorry for.
There is no terror *Caſſius* in your threats:
For I am Arm'd ſo ſtrong in Honeſty,
That they paſſe by me, as the idle winde,
Which I reſpect not. I did ſend to you
For certaine ſummes of Gold, which you deny'd me,
For I can raiſe no money by vile meanes:
By Heauen, I had rather Coine my Heart,
And drop my blood for Drachmaes, then to wring
From the hard hands of Peazants, their vile traſh
By any indirection. I did ſend
To you for Gold to pay my Legions,
Which you deny'd me: was that done like *Caſſius*?
Should I haue anſwer'd *Caius Caſſius* ſo?
When *Marcus Brutus* growes ſo Couetous,
To locke ſuch Raſcall Counters from his Friends,
Be ready Gods with all your Thunder-bolts,
Daſh him to peeces.
Caſſi. I deny'd you not.
Bru. You did.
Caſſi. I did not. He was but a Foole
That brought my anſwer back. *Brutus* hath riu'd my hart:
A Friend ſhould beare his Friends infirmities;
But *Brutus* makes mine greater then they are.
Bru. I do not, till you practice them on me.
Caſſi. You loue me not.
Bru. I do not like your faults.
Caſſi. A friendly eye could neuer ſee ſuch faults.
Bru. A Flatterers would not, though they do appeare
As huge as high Olympus.
Caſſi. Come *Antony*, and yong *Octauius* come,
Reuenge your ſelues alone on *Caſſius*,
For *Caſſius* is a-weary of the World:
Hated by one he loues, brau'd by his Brother,
Check'd like a bondman, all his faults obſeru'd,
Set in a Note-booke, learn'd, and con'd by roate
To caſt into my Teeth. O I could weepe
My Spirit from mine eyes. There is my Dagger,
And heere my naked Breaſt: Within, a Heart
Deerer then *Pluto's* Mine, Richer then Gold:
If that thou bee'ſt a Roman, take it foorth.
I that deny'd thee Gold, will giue my Heart:
Strike as thou did'ſt at *Cæſar*: For I know,
When thou did'ſt hate him worſt, ỳ loued'ſt him better
Then euer thou loued'ſt *Caſſius*.
Bru. Sheath your Dagger:
Be angry when you will, it ſhall haue ſcope:
Do what you will, Diſhonor, ſhall be Humour.
O *Caſſius*, you are yoaked with a Lambe
That carries Anger, as the Flint beares fire,
Who much inforced, ſhewes a haſtie Sparke,
And ſtraite is cold agen.
Caſſi. Hath *Caſſius* liu'd
To be but Mirth and Laughter to his *Brutus*,
When greefe and blood ill temper'd, vexeth him?
Bru. When I ſpoke that, I was ill temper'd too.
Caſſi. Do you confeſſe ſo much? Giue me your hand.
Bru. And my heart too.
Caſſi. O *Brutus*!
Bru. What's the matter?
Caſſi. Haue not you loue enough to beare with me,
When that raſh humour which my Mother gaue me
Makes me forgetfull.
Bru. Yes *Caſſius*, and from henceforth
When you are ouer-earneſt with your *Brutus*,
Hee'l thinke your Mother chides, and leaue you ſo.

Enter a Poet.

Poet. Let me go in to ſee the Generals,
There is ſome grudge betweene 'em, 'tis not meete
They be alone.
Lucil. You ſhall not come to them.
Poet. Nothing but death ſhall ſtay me.
Caſ. How now? What's the matter?
Poet. For ſhame you Generals; what do you meane?
Loue, and be Friends, as two ſuch men ſhould bee,
For I haue ſeene more yeeres I'me ſure then yee.
Caſ. Ha, ha, how vildely doth this Cynicke rime?
Bru. Get you hence ſirra: Sawcy Fellow, hence.
Caſ. Beare with him *Brutus*, 'tis his faſhion.
Brut. Ile know his humor, when he knowes his time:
What ſhould the Warres do with theſe Iigging Fooles?
Companion, hence.
Caſ. Away, away be gone. *Exit Poet*
Bru. *Lucillius* and *Titinius* bid the Commanders
Prepare to lodge their Companies to night.
Caſ. And come your ſelues, & bring *Meſſala* with you
Immediately to vs.
Bru. *Lucius*, a bowle of Wine.
Caſ. I did not thinke you could haue bin ſo angry.
Bru. O *Caſſius*, I am ſicke of many greefes.
Caſ. Of your Philoſophy you make no vſe,
If you giue place to accidentall euils.
Bru. No man beares ſorrow better. *Portia* is dead.
Caſ. Ha? *Portia*?
Bru. She is dead.
Caſ. How ſcap'd I killing, when I croſt you ſo?
O inſupportable, and touching loſſe!
Vpon what ſickneſſe?
Bru. Impatient of my abſence,
And greefe, that yong *Octauius* with *Mark Antony*
Haue made themſelues ſo ſtrong: For with her death
That tydings came. With this ſhe fell diſtract,
And (her Attendants abſent) ſwallow'd fire.
Caſ. And dy'd ſo?
Bru. Euen ſo.
Caſ. O ye immortall Gods!

Enter Boy with Wine, and Tapers.

Bru. Speak no more of her: Giue me a bowl of wine,
In this I bury all vnkindneſſe *Caſſius*. *Drinkes*
Caſ. My heart is thirſty for that Noble pledge.
Fill *Lucius*, till the Wine ore-ſwell the Cup:
I cannot drinke too much of *Brutus* loue.

Enter Titinius and Meſſala.

Brutus. Come in *Titinius*:
Welcome good *Meſſala*:
Now ſit we cloſe about this Taper heere,
And call in queſtion our neceſſities.
Caſſ. *Portia*, art thou gone?
Bru. No more I pray you.
Meſſala, I haue heere receiued Letters,
That yong *Octauius*, and *Marke Antony*
Come downe vpon vs with a mighty power,
Bending their Expedition toward *Philippi*.

ll 3 *Meſſ.*

Meſſ. My ſelfe haue Letters of the ſelfe-ſame Tenure.
Bru With what Addition.
Meſſ. That by proſcription, and billes of Outlarie,
Octauius, Antony, and *Lepidus,*
Haue put to death, an hundred Senators.
Bru. Therein our Letters do not well agree:
Mine ſpeake of ſeuenty Senators, that dy'de
By their proſcriptions, *Cicero* being one.
Caſſi. *Cicero* one?
Meſſa. *Cicero* is dead, and by that order of proſcription;
Had you your Letters from your wife, my Lord?
Bru. No *Meſſala.*
Meſſa. Nor nothing in your Letters writ of her?
Bru. Nothing *Meſſala.*
Meſſa. That me thinkes is ſtrange.
Bru. Why aske you?
Heare you ought of her, in yours?
Meſſa. No my Lord
Bru. Now as you are a Roman tell me true.
Meſſa. Then like a Roman, beare the truth I tell,
For certaine ſhe is dead, and by ſtrange manner.
Bru. Why farewell *Portia:* We muſt die *Meſſala:*
With meditating that ſhe muſt dye once,
I haue the patience to endure it now
Meſſa Euen ſo great men, great loſſes ſhold indure.
Caſſi. I haue as much of this in Art as you
But yet my Nature could not beare it ſo.
Bru. Well, to our worke aliue What do you thinke
Of marching to *Philippi* preſently.
Caſſi I do not thinke it good.
Bru. Your reaſon?
Caſſi. This it is:
'Tis better that the Enemie ſeeke vs,
So ſhall he waſte his meanes, weary his Souldiers,
Doing himſelfe offence, whil'ſt we lying ſtill,
Are full of reſt, defence, and nimbleneſſe
Bru. Good reaſons muſt of force giue place to better
The people 'twixt *Philippi*, and this ground
Do ſtand but in a forc'd affection:
For they haue grug'd vs Contribution.
The Enemy, marching along by them,
By them ſhall make a fuller number vp,
Come on refreſht, new added, and encourag'd
From which aduantage ſhall we cut him off.
If at *Philippi* we do face him there,
Theſe people at our backe
Caſſi. Heare me good Brother
Bru. Vnder your pardon. You muſt note beſide,
That we haue tride the vtmoſt of our Friends:
Our Legions are brim full, our cauſe is ripe,
The Enemy encreaſeth euery day,
We at the height, are readie to decline
There is a Tide in the affayres of men,
Which taken at the Flood, leades on to Fortune:
Omitted, all the voyage of their life,
Is bound in Shallowes, and in Miſeries
On ſuch a full Sea are we now a-float,
And we muſt take the current when it ſerues,
Or looſe our Ventures
Caſſi: Then with your will go on: wee'l along
Our ſelues, and meet them at *Philippi*
Bru. The deepe of night is crept vpon our talke,
And Nature muſt obey Neceſſitie,
Which we will niggard with a little reſt:
There is no more to ſay
Caſſi. No more, good night,
Early to morrow will we riſe, and hence.
Enter Lucius.
Bru. *Lucius* my Gowne: farewell good *Meſſala,*
Good night *Titinius*: Noble, Noble *Caſſius,*
Good night, and good repoſe.
Caſſi. O my deere Brother:
This was an ill beginning of the night:
Neuer come ſuch diuiſion 'tweene our ſoules:
Let it not *Brutus.*
Enter Lucius with the Gowne
Bru. Euery thing is well.
Caſſi. Good night my Lord.
Bru. Good night good Brother.
Tit. Meſſa. Good night Lord *Brutus.*
Bru. Farwell euery one. *Exeunt*
Giue me the Gowne. Where is thy Inſtrument?
Luc. Heere in the Tent.
Bru. What, thou ſpeak'ſt drowſily?
Poore knaue I blame thee not, thou art ore-watch'd.
Call *Claudio,* and ſome other of my men,
Ile haue them ſleepe on Cuſhions in my Tent.
Luc. *Varrus,* and *Claudio.*
Enter Varrus and Claudio.
Var. Cals my Lord?
Bru. I pray you ſirs, lye in my Tent and ſleepe,
It may be I ſhall raiſe you by and by
On buſineſſe to my Brother *Caſſius.*
Var. So pleaſe you, we will ſtand,
And watch your pleaſure.
Bru. I will it not haue it ſo: Lye downe good ſirs,
It may be I ſhall otherwiſe bethinke me.
Looke *Lucius,* heere's the booke I ſought for ſo
I put it in the pocket of my Gowne.
Luc. I was ſure your Lordſhip did not giue it me.
Bru. Beare with me good Boy, I am much forgetfull.
Canſt thou hold vp thy heauie eyes a-while,
And touch thy Inſtrument a ſtraine or two
Luc. I my Lord, an't pleaſe you.
Bru. It does my Boy:
I trouble thee too much, but thou art willing.
Luc. It is my duty Sir
Brut. I ſhould not vrge thy duty paſt thy might,
I know yong bloods looke for a time of reſt
Luc. I haue ſlept my Lord already.
Bru. It was well done, and thou ſhalt ſleepe againe:
I will not hold thee long. If I do liue,
I will be good to thee.
Muſicke, and a Song.
This is a ſleepy Tune: O Murd'rous ſlumbler!
Layeſt thou thy Leaden Mace vpon my Boy,
That playes thee Muſicke? Gentle knaue good night:
I will not do thee ſo much wrong to wake thee:
If thou do'ſt nod, thou break'ſt thy Inſtrument,
Ile take it from thee, and (good Boy) good night
Let me ſee, let me ſee; is not the Leafe turn'd downe
Where I left reading? Heere it is I thinke.
Enter the Ghoſt of Cæſar.
How ill this Taper burnes. Ha! Who comes heere?
I thinke it is the weakeneſſe of mine eyes
That ſhapes this monſtrous Apparition.
It comes vpon me: Art thou any thing?
Art thou ſome God, ſome Angell, or ſome Diuell,
That mak'ſt my blood cold, and my haire to ſtare?
Speake to me, what thou art.
Ghoſt Thy euill Spirit *Brutus*?
Bru. Why com'ſt thou?
Ghoſt.

Ghost. To tell thee thou shalt see me at *Philippi.*
Brut. Well: then I shall see thee againe?
Ghost. I, at *Philippi.*
Brut. Why I will see thee at *Philippi* then:
Now I haue taken heart, thou vanishest.
Ill Spirit, I would hold more talke with thee.
Boy, *Lucius, Varrus, Claudio,* Sirs: Awake:
Claudio.
Luc. The strings my Lord, are false.
Bru. He thinkes he still is at his Instrument.
Lucius, awake.
Luc. My Lord.
Bru. Did'st thou dreame *Lucius,* that thou so cryedst out?
Luc. My Lord, I do not know that I did cry.
Bru. Yes that thou did'st: Did'st thou see any thing?
Luc. Nothing my Lord.
Bru. Sleepe againe *Lucius*: Sirra *Claudio,* Fellow,
Thou: Awake.
Var. My Lord.
Clau. My Lord.
Bru. Why did you so cry out sirs, in your sleepe?
Both. Did we my Lord?
Bru. I: saw you any thing?
Var. No my Lord, I saw nothing.
Clau. Nor I my Lord.
Bru. Go, and commend me to my Brother *Cassius*:
Bid him set on his Powres betimes before,
And we will follow.
Both. It shall be done my Lord. *Exeunt*

Actus Quintus.

Enter Octauius, Antony, and their Army.

Octa. Now *Antony,* our hopes are answered,
You said the Enemy would not come downe,
But keepe the Hilles and vpper Regions:
It proues not so: their battailes are at hand,
They meane to warne vs at *Philippi* heere:
Answering before we do demand of them.
Ant. Tut I am in their bosomes, and I know
Wherefore they do it: They could be content
To visit other places, and come downe
With fearefull brauery: thinking by this face
To fasten in our thoughts that they haue Courage;
But 'tis not so.

Enter a Messenger.

Mes. Prepare you Generals,
The Enemy comes on in gallant shew:
Their bloody signe of Battell is hung out,
And something to be done immediately.
Ant. *Octauius,* leade your Battaile softly on
Vpon the left hand of the euen Field.
Octa. Vpon the right hand I. keepe thou the left.
Ant. Why do you crosse me in this exigent.
Octa. I do not crosse you: but I will do so. *March.*

Drum. Enter Brutus, Cassius, & their Army.

Bru. They stand, and would haue parley.
Cassi. Stand fast *Titinius,* we must out and talke.
Octa. *Mark Antony,* shall we giue signe of Battaile?
Ant. No *Cæsar,* we will answer on their Charge.
Make forth, the Generals would haue some words.
Oct. Stirre not vntill the Signall.
Bru. Words before blowes: is it so Countrymen?
Octa. Not that we loue words better, as you do.
Bru. Good words are better then bad strokes *Octauius.*
An. In your bad strokes *Brutus,* you giue good words
Witnesse the hole you made in *Cæsars* heart,
Crying long liue, Haile *Cæsar.*
Cassi. *Antony,*
The posture of your blowes are yet vnknowne;
But for your words, they rob the *Hibla* Bees,
And leaue them Hony-lesse.
Ant. Not stinglesse too.
Bru. O yes, and soundlesse too:
For you haue stolne their buzzing *Antony,*
And very wisely threat before you sting.
Ant. Villains: you did not so, when your vile daggers
Hackt one another in the sides of *Cæsar*:
You shew'd your teethes like Apes,
And fawn'd like Hounds,
And bow'd like Bondmen, kissing *Cæsars* feete;
Whil'st damned *Caska,* like a Curre, behinde
Strooke *Cæsar* on the necke. O you Flatterers.
Cassi Flatterers? Now *Brutus* thanke your selfe,
This tongue had not offended so to day,
If *Cassius* might haue rul'd.
Octa. Come, come, the cause. If arguing make vs swet,
The proofe of it will turne to redder drops:
Looke, I draw a Sword against Conspirators,
When thinke you that the Sword goes vp againe?
Neuer till *Cæsars* three and thirtie wounds
Be well aueng'd; or till another *Cæsar*
Haue added slaughter to the Sword of Traitors.
Brut. *Cæsar,* thou canst not dye by Traitors hands,
Vnlesse thou bring'st them with thee.
Octa. So I hope:
I was not borne to dye on *Brutus* Sword.
Bru. O if thou wer't the Noblest of thy Straine,
Yong-man, thou could'st not dye more honourable.
Cassi. A peeuish School-boy, worthles of such Honor
Ioyn'd with a Masker, and a Reueller.
Ant. Old *Cassius* still.
Octa. Come *Antony*: away:
Defiance Traitors, hurle we in your teeth.
If you dare fight to day, come to the Field;
If not, when you haue stomackes.
Exit Octauius, Antony, and Army
Cassi Why now blow winde, swell Billow,
And swimme Barke:
The Storme is vp, and all is on the hazard.
Bru. Ho *Lucillius,* hearke, a word with you.
Lucillius and Messala stand forth.
Luc My Lord.
Cassi *Messala.*
Messa. What sayes my Generall?
Cassi. *Messala,* this is my Birth-day: as this very day
Was *Cassius* borne. Giue me thy hand *Messala*:
Be thou my witnesse, that against my will
(As *Pompey* was) am I compell'd to set
Vpon one Battell all our Liberties.
You know, that I held *Epicurus* strong,
And his Opinion: Now I change my minde,
And partly credit things that do presage.
Comming from *Sardis,* on our former Ensigne
Two mighty Eagles fell, and there they pearch'd,
Gorging and feeding from our Soldiers hands,
Who

Who to *Philippi* heere consorted vs:
This Morning are they fled away, and gone,
And in their steeds, do Rauens, Crowes, and Kites
Fly ore our heads, and downward looke on vs
As we were sickely prey; their shadowes seeme
A Canopy most fatall, vnder which
Our Army lies, ready to giue vp the Ghost.
Messa. Beleeue not so.
Cassi. I but beleeue it partly,
For I am fresh of spirit, and resolu'd
To meete all perils, very constantly.
Bru. Euen so *Lucillius.*
Cassi. Now most Noble *Brutus,*
The Gods to day stand friendly, that we may
Louers in peace, leade on our dayes to age.
But since the affayres of men rests still incertaine,
Let's reason with the worst that may befall.
If we do lose this Battaile, then is this
The very last time we shall speake together:
What are you then determined to do?
Bru. Euen by the rule of that Philosophy,
By which I did blame *Cato,* for the death
Which he did giue himselfe, I know not how:
But I do finde it Cowardly, and vile,
For feare of what might fall, so to preuent
The time of life, arming my selfe with patience,
To stay the prouidence of some high Powers,
That gouerne vs below.
Cassi. Then, if we loose this Battaile,
You are contented to be led in Triumph
Thorow the streets of Rome.
Bru. No *Cassius,* no:
Thinke not thou Noble Romane,
That euer *Brutus* will go bound to Rome,
He beares too great a minde. But this same day
Must end that worke, the Ides of March begun.
And whether we shall meete againe, I know not:
Therefore our euerlasting farewell take:
For euer, and for euer, farewell *Cassius,*
If we do meete againe, why we shall smile;
If not, why then this parting was well made.
Cassi. For euer, and for euer, farewell *Brutus:*
If we do meete againe, wee'l smile indeede;
If not, 'tis true, this parting was well made.
Bru. Why then leade on. O that a man might know
The end of this dayes businesse, ere it come:
But it sufficeth, that the day will end,
And then the end is knowne. Come ho, away. *Exeunt.*

Alarum. Enter Brutus and Messala.

Bru. Ride, ride *Messala,* ride and giue these Billes
Vnto the Legions, on the other side.
Lowd Alarum.
Let them set on at once: for I perceiue
But cold demeanor in *Octauio's* wing:
And sodaine push giues them the ouerthrow:
Ride, ride *Messala,* let them all come downe. *Exeunt*

Alarums. Enter Cassius and Titinius.

Cassi. O looke *Titinius,* looke, the Villaines flye:
My selfe haue to mine owne turn'd Enemy:
This Ensigne heere of mine was turning backe,
I slew the Coward, and did take it from him.
Titin. O *Cassius, Brutus* gaue the word too early,
Who hauing some aduantage on *Octauius,*
Tooke it too eagerly: his Soldiers fell to spoyle,
Whil'st we by *Antony* are all inclos'd.

Enter Pindarus.

Pind. Fly further off my Lord: flye further off,
Mark Antony is in your Tents my Lord:
Flye therefore Noble *Cassius,* flye farre off.
Cassi. This Hill is farre enough. Looke, look *Titinius*
Are those my Tents where I perceiue the fire?
Tit. They are, my Lord.
Cassi. Titinius, if thou louest me,
Mount thou my horse, and hide thy spurres in him,
Till he haue brought thee vp to yonder Troopes
And heere againe, that I may rest assur'd
Whether yond Troopes, are Friend or Enemy.
Tit. I will be heere againe, euen with a thought. *Exit.*
Cassi. Go *Pindarus,* get higher on that hill,
My sight was euer thicke: regard *Titinius,*
And tell me what thou not'st about the Field.
This day I breathed first, Time is come round,
And where I did begin, there shall I end,
My life is run his compasse. Sirra, what newes?
Pind. Aboue. O my Lord.
Cassi. What newes?
Pind. Titinius is enclosed round about
With Horsemen, that make to him on the Spurre,
Yet he spurres on. Now they are almost on him:
Now *Titinius.* Now some light: O he lights too.
Hee's tane. *Showt.*
And hearke, they shout for ioy.
Cassi. Come downe, behold no more:
O Coward that I am, to liue so long,
To see my best Friend tane before my face.
Enter Pindarus.
Come hither sirrah: In Parthia did I take thee Prisoner,
And then I swore thee, sauing of thy life,
That whatsoeuer I did bid thee do,
Thou should'st attempt it. Come now, keepe thine oath,
Now be a Free-man, and with this good Sword
That ran through *Cæsars* bowels, search this bosome.
Stand not to answer: Heere, take thou the Hilts,
And when my face is couer'd, as 'tis now,
Guide thou the Sword —— *Cæsar,* thou art reueng'd,
Euen with the Sword that kill'd thee.
Pin. So, I am free,
Yet would not so haue beene
Durst I haue done my will. O *Cassius,*
Farre from this Country *Pindarus* shall run,
Where neuer Roman shall take note of him.

Enter Titinius and Messala.

Messa. It is but change, *Titinius:* for *Octauius*
Is ouerthrowne by Noble *Brutus* power,
As *Cassius* Legions are by *Antony.*
Titin. These tydings will well comfort *Cassius.*
Messa. Where did you leaue him.
Titin. All disconsolate,
With *Pindarus* his Bondman, on this Hill.
Messa. Is not that he that lyes vpon the ground?
Titin. He lies not like the Liuing. O my heart!
Messa. Is not that hee?
Titin. No, this was he *Messala,*
But *Cassius* is no more. O setting Sunne:
As in thy red Rayes thou doest sinke to night;
So

So in his red blood *Caſſius* day is ſet.
The Sunne of Rome is ſet. Our day is gone,
Clowds, Dewes, and Dangers come; our deeds are done:
Miſtruſt of my ſucceſſe hath done this deed.
Meſſa. Miſtruſt of good ſucceſſe hath done this deed.
O hatefull Error, Melancholies Childe:
Why do'ſt thou ſhew to the apt thoughts of men
The things that are not? O Error ſoone conceyu'd,
Thou neuer com'ſt vnto a happy byrth,
But kil'ſt the Mother that engendred thee.
Tit. What *Pindarus*? Where art thou *Pindarus*?
Meſſa. Seeke him *Titinius*, whilſt I go to meet
The Noble *Brutus*, thruſting this report
Into his eares; I may ſay thruſting it:
For piercing Steele, and Darts inuenomed,
Shall be as welcome to the eares of *Brutus*,
As tydings of this ſight.
Tit. Hye you *Meſſala*,
And I will ſeeke for *Pindarus* the while:
Why did'ſt thou ſend me forth braue *Caſſius*?
Did I not meet thy Friends, and did not they
Put on my Browes this wreath of Victorie,
And bid me giue it thee? Did'ſt thou not heare their
Alas, thou haſt miſconſtrued euery thing. (ſhowts
But hold thee, take this Garland on thy Brow,
Thy *Brutus* bid me giue it thee, and I
Will do his bidding. *Brutus*, come apace,
And ſee how I regarded *Caius Caſſius*:
By your leaue Gods: This is a Romans part,
Come *Caſſius* Sword, and finde *Titinius* hart. *Dies*

Alarum. Enter Brutus, Meſſala, yong Cato, Strato, Volumnius, and Lucillius.

Bru. Where, where *Meſſala*, doth his body lye?
Meſſa. Loe yonder, and *Titinius* mourning it.
Bru. *Titinius* face is vpward.
Cato He is ſlaine.
Bru. O *Iulius Cæſar*, thou art mighty yet,
Thy Spirit walkes abroad, and turnes our Swords
In our owne proper Entrailes. *Low Alarums.*
Cato. Braue *Titinius*,
Looke where he haue not crown'd dead *Caſſius*.
Bru. Are yet two Romans liuing ſuch as theſe?
The laſt of all the Romans, far thee well:
It is impoſſible, that euer Rome
Should breed thy fellow. Friends I owe mo teares
To this dead man, then you ſhall ſee me pay.
I ſhall finde time, *Caſſius*: I ſhall finde time.
Come therefore, and to *Tharſus* ſend his body,
His Funerals ſhall not be in our Campe,
Leaſt it diſcomfort vs. *Lucillius* come,
And come yong *Cato*, let vs to the Field,
Labio and *Flauio* ſet our Battailes on:
'Tis three a clocke, and Romans yet ere night,
We ſhall try Fortune in a ſecond fight. *Exeunt.*

Alarum. Enter Brutus, Meſſala, Cato, Lucillius, and Flauius.

Bru. Yet Country-men: O yet, hold vp your heads.
Cato What Baſtard doth not? Who will go with me?
I will proclaime my name about the Field.
I am the Sonne of *Marcus Cato*, hoe.
A Foe to Tyrants, and my Countries Friend.
I am the Sonne of *Marcus Cato*, hoe.
Enter Souldiers, and fight.
And I am *Brutus*, *Marcus Brutus*, I,
Brutus my Countries Friend: Know me for *Brutus*.
Luc. O yong and Noble *Cato*, art thou downe?
Why now thou dyeſt, as brauely as *Titinius*,
And may'ſt be honour'd, being *Cato's* Sonne.
Sold. Yeeld, or thou dyeſt.
Luc. Onely I yeeld to dye:
There is ſo much, that thou wilt kill me ſtraight:
Kill *Brutus*, and be honour'd in his death.
Sold. We muſt not: a Noble Priſoner.

Enter Antony.

2.Sold. Roome hoe: tell *Antony*, *Brutus* is tane.
1.Sold. Ile tell thee newes. Heere comes the Generall,
Brutus is tane, *Brutus* is tane my Lord.
Ant. Where is hee?
Luc. Safe *Antony*, *Brutus* is ſafe enough:
I dare aſſure thee, that no Enemy
Shall euer take aliue the Noble *Brutus*:
The Gods defend him from ſo great a ſhame,
When you do finde him, or aliue, or dead,
He will be found like *Brutus*, like himſelfe.
Ant. This is not *Brutus* friend, but I aſſure you,
A prize no leſſe in worth; keepe this man ſafe,
Giue him all kindneſſe. I had rather haue
Such men my Friends, then Enemies. Go on,
And ſee where *Brutus* be aliue or dead,
And bring vs word, vnto *Octauius* Tent:
How euery thing is chanc'd. *Exeunt.*

Enter Brutus, Dardanius, Clitus, Strato, and Volumnius.

Brut. Come poore remaines of friends, reſt on this Rocke.
Clit. *Statillius* ſhew'd the Torch-light, but my Lord
He came not backe: he is or tane, or ſlaine.
Brut. Sit thee downe, *Clitus*: ſlaying is the word,
It is a deed in faſhion. Hearke thee, *Clitus*.
Clit What I, my Lord? No, not for all the World.
Brut. Peace then, no words.
Clit. Ile rather kill my ſelfe.
Brut Hearke thee, *Dardanius*.
Dard. Shall I doe ſuch a deed?
Clit. O *Dardanius*.
Dard. O *Clitus*.
Clit. What ill requeſt did *Brutus* make to thee?
Dard. To kill him, *Clitus*: looke he meditates.
Clit. Now is that Noble Veſſell full of griefe,
That it runnes ouer euen at his eyes.
Brut. Come hither, good *Volumnius*, liſt a word.
Volum. What ſayes my Lord?
Brut. Why this, *Volumnius*:
The Ghoſt of *Cæſar* hath appear'd to me
Two ſeuerall times by Night: at Sardis, once;
And this laſt Night, here in Philippi fields:
I know my houre is come.
Volum. Not ſo, my Lord.
Brut Nay, I am ſure it is, *Volumnius*.
Thou ſeeſt the World, *Volumnius*, how it goes,
Our Enemies haue beat vs to the Pit: *Low Alarums.*
It is more worthy, to leape in our ſelues,
Then tarry till they puſh vs. Good *Volumnius*,
Thou know'ſt, that we two went to Schoole together:
Euen for that our loue of old, I prethee
Hold thou my Sword Hilts, whileſt I runne on it.
Vol. That's not an Office for a friend, my Lord.
Alarum ſtill.
Clit. Fly,

Cly. Fly, flye my Lord, there is no tarrying heere.
Bru. Farewell to you, and you, and you *Volumnius.*
Strato, thou haſt bin all this while aſleepe:
Farewell to thee, to *Strato*, Countrymen:
My heart doth ioy, that yet in all my life,
I found no man, but he was true to me.
I ſhall haue glory by this looſing day
More then *Octauius*, and *Marke Antony*,
By this vile Conqueſt ſhall attaine vnto
So fare you well at once, for *Brutus* tongue
Hath almoſt ended his liues Hiſtory.
Night hangs vpon mine eyes, my Bones would reſt,
That haue but labour'd, to attaine this houre.

Alarum. Cry within, Flye, flye, flye.

Cly. Fly my Lord, flye.
Bru. Hence: I will follow.
I prythee *Strato*, ſtay thou by thy Lord,
Thou art a Fellow of a good reſpect:
Thy life hath had ſome ſmatch of Honor in it,
Hold then my Sword, and turne away thy face,
While I do run vpon it. Wilt thou *Strato*?
Stra. Giue me your hand firſt. Fare you wel my Lord.
Bru. Farewell good *Strato*. —— *Cæſar*, now be ſtill,
I kill'd not thee with halfe ſo good a will. *Dyes.*

Alarum. Retreat. Enter Antony, Octauius, Meſſala, Lucillius, and the Army.

Octa. What man is that?
Meſſa. My Maſters man. *Strato*, where is thy Maſter?
Stra. Free from the Bondage you are in *Meſſala*,
The Conquerors can but make a fire of him:
For *Brutus* onely ouercame himſelfe,
And no man elſe hath Honor by his death.
Lucil. So *Brutus* ſhould be found. I thank thee *Brutus*
That thou haſt prou'd *Lucillius* ſaying true,
Octa. All that ſeru'd *Brutus*, I will entertaine them.
Fellow, wilt thou beſtow thy time with me?
Stra. I, if *Meſſala* will preferre me to you.
Octa. Do ſo, good *Meſſala*.
Meſſa. How dyed my Maſter *Strato*?
Stra. I held the Sword, and he did run on it.
Meſſa. *Octauius*, then take him to follow thee,
That did the lateſt ſeruice to my Maſter.
Ant. This was the Nobleſt Roman of them all:
All the Conſpirators ſaue onely hee,
Did that they did, in enuy of great *Cæſar*:
He, onely in a generall honeſt thought,
And common good to all, made one of them.
His life was gentle, and the Elements
So mixt in him, that Nature might ſtand vp,
And ſay to all the world; This was a man.
Octa. According to his Vertue, let vs vſe him
Withall Reſpect, and Rites of Buriall.
Within my Tent his bones to night ſhall ly,
Moſt like a Souldier ordered Honourably:
So call the Field to reſt, and let's away,
To part the glories of this happy day. *Exeunt omnes.*

FINIS.

THE TRAGEDIE OF MACBETH.

Actus Primus. Scœna Prima

Thunder and Lightning. Enter three Witches.

1. Hen shall we three meet againe?
In Thunder, Lightning, or in Raine?
2. When the Hurley-burley's done,
When the Battaile's lost, and wonne.
3. That will be ere the set of Sunne.
1 Where the place?
2. Vpon the Heath.
3. There to meet with *Macbeth*
1 I come, *Gray-Malkin.*
All. *Padock* calls anon: faire is foule, and foule is faire,
Houer through the fogge and filthie ayre. *Exeunt.*

Scena Secunda.

Alarum within. Enter King Malcome, Donalbaine, Lenox, with attendants, meeting a bleeding Captaine.

King. What bloody man is that? he can report,
As seemeth by his plight, of the Reuolt
The newest state.
Mal. This is the Serieant,
Who like a good and hardie Souldier fought
'Gainst my Captiuitie: Haile braue friend;
Say to the King, the knowledge of the Broyle,
As thou didst leaue it.
Cap. Doubtfull it stood,
As two spent Swimmers, that doe cling together,
And choake their Art. The mercilesse *Macdonwald*
(Worthie to be a Rebell, for to that
The multiplying Villanies of Nature
Doe swarme vpon him) from the Westerne Isles
Of Kernes and Gallowgrosses is supply'd,
And Fortune on his damned Quarry smiling,
Shew'd like a Rebells Whore: but all's too weake:
For braue *Macbeth* (well hee deserues that Name)
Disdayning Fortune, with his brandisht Steele,
Which smoak'd with bloody execution
(Like Valours Minion) caru'd out his passage,
Till hee fac'd the Slaue:
Which neu'r shooke hands, nor bad farwell to him,
Till he vnseam'd him from the Naue toth' Chops,
And fix'd his Head vpon our Battlements.
King O valiant Cousin, worthy Gentleman.
Cap. As whence the Sunne gins his reflection,
Shipwracking Stormes, and direfull Thunders
So from that Spring, whence comfort seem'd to come,
Discomfort swells: Marke King of Scotland, marke,
No sooner Iustice had, with Valour arm'd,
Compell'd these skipping Kernes to trust their heeles
But the Norweyan Lord, surueying vantage,
With furbusht Armes, and new supplyes of men,
Began a fresh assault.
King. Dismay'd not this our Captaines, *Macbeth* and *Banquoh*?
Cap. Yes, as Sparrowes, Eagles;
Or the Hare, the Lyon:
If I say sooth, I must report they were
As Cannons ouer-charg'd with double Cracks,
So they doubly redoubled stroakes vpon the Foe:
Except they meant to bathe in recking Wounds,
Or memorize another *Golgotha*,
I cannot tell: but I am faint,
My Gashes cry for helpe.
King. So well thy words become thee, as thy wounds,
They smack of Honor both: Goe get him Surgeons.

Enter Rosse and Angus.

Who comes here?
Mal. The worthy *Thane* of Rosse.
Lenox. What a haste lookes through his eyes?
So should he looke, that seemes to speake things strange.
Rosse God saue the King.
King. Whence cam'st thou, worthy *Thane*?
Rosse. From Fiffe, great King,
Where the Norweyan Banners flowt the Skie,
And fanne our people cold.
Norway himselfe, with terrible numbers,
Assisted by that most disloyall Traytor,
The *Thane* of Cawdor, began a dismall Conflict,
Till that *Bellona's* Bridegroome, lapt in proofe,
Confronted him with selfe-comparisons,
Point against Point, rebellious Arme 'gainst Arme,
Curbing his lauish spirit: and to conclude,
The Victorie fell on vs.
King Great happinesse.
Rosse. That now *Sweno*, the Norwayes King,
Craues composition:
Nor would we deigne him buriall of his men,
Till he disbursed, at Saint *Colmes* ynch,
Ten thousand Dollars, to our generall vse.

King No

King. No more that *Thane* of Cawdor shall deceiue
Our Bosome interest: Goe pronounce his present death,
And with his former Title greet *Macbeth.*
Rosse. Ile see it done.
King. What he hath lost, Noble *Macbeth* hath wonne.
Exeunt.

Scena Tertia.

Thunder. Enter the three Witches.

1. Where hast thou beene, Sister?
2. Killing Swine.
3. Sister, where thou?
1. A Saylors Wife had Chestnuts in her Lappe,
And mouncht, & mouncht, and mouncht:
Giue me, quoth I.
Aroynt thee, Witch, the rumpe-fed Ronyon cryes.
Her Husband's to Aleppo gone, Master o'th' *Tiger:*
But in a Syue Ile thither sayle,
And like a Rat without a tayle,
Ile doe, Ile doe, and Ile doe.
2. Ile giue thee a Winde.
1. Th'art kinde.
3. And I another.
1. I my selfe haue all the other,
And the very Ports they blow,
All the Quarters that they know,
I'th' Ship-mans Card.
Ile dreyne him drie as Hay:
Sleepe shall neyther Night nor Day
Hang vpon his Pent-house Lid:
He shall liue a man forbid:
Wearie Seu'nights, nine times nine,
Shall he dwindle, peake, and pine:
Though his Barke cannot be lost,
Yet it shall be Tempest-tost.
Looke what I haue.
2. Shew me, shew me.
1. Here I haue a Pilots Thumbe,
Wrackt, as homeward he did come. *Drum within.*
3. A Drumme, a Drumme:
Macbeth doth come.
All. The weyward Sisters, hand in hand,
Posters of the Sea and Land,
Thus doe goe, about, about,
Thrice to thine, and thrice to mine,
And thrice againe, to make vp nine.
Peace, the Charme's wound vp.

Enter Macbeth and Banquo.

Macb. So foule and faire a day I haue not seene.
Banquo. How farre is't call'd to Soris? What are these,
So wither'd, and so wilde in their attyre,
That looke not like th'Inhabitants o'th'Earth,
And yet are on't? Liue you, or are you aught
That man may question? you seeme to vnderstand me,
By each at once her choppie finger laying
Vpon her skinnie Lips: you should be Women,
And yet your Beards forbid me to interprete
That you are so.
Mac. Speake if you can: what are you?
1. All haile *Macbeth*, haile to thee *Thane* of Glamis.
2. All haile *Macbeth*, haile to thee *Thane* of Cawdor.
3. All haile *Macbeth*, that shalt be King hereafter.
Banq. Good Sir, why doe you start, and seeme to feare
Things that doe sound so faire? i'th' name of truth
Are ye fantasticall, or that indeed
Which outwardly ye shew? My Noble Partner
You greet with present Grace, and great prediction
Of Noble hauing, and of Royall hope,
That he seemes wrapt withall: to me you speake not.
If you can looke into the Seedes of Time,
And say, which Graine will grow, and which will not,
Speake then to me, who neyther begge, nor feare
Your fauors, nor your hate.
1. Hayle.
2. Hayle.
3. Hayle.
1 Lesser then *Macbeth*, and greater.
2 Not so happy, yet much happyer.
3. Thou shalt get Kings, though thou be none:
So all haile *Macbeth*, and *Banquo*
1. *Banquo*, and *Macbeth*, all haile.
Macb. Stay you imperfect Speakers, tell me more
By *Sinells* death, I know I am *Thane* of Glamis,
But how, of Cawdor? the *Thane* of Cawdor liues
A prosperous Gentleman: And to be King,
Stands not within the prospect of beleefe,
No more then to be Cawdor. Say from whence
You owe this strange Intelligence, or why
Vpon this blasted Heath you stop our way
With such Prophetique greeting?
Speake, I charge you *Witches vanish.*
Banq. The Earth hath bubbles, as the Water ha's,
And these are of them: whither are they vanish'd?
Macb. Into the Ayre: and what seem'd corporall,
Melted, as breath into the Winde.
Would they had stay'd
Banq Were such things here, as we doe speake about?
Or haue we eaten on the insane Root,
That takes the Reason Prisoner?
Macb. Your Children shall be Kings.
Banq. You shall be King.
Macb And *Thane* of Cawdor too: went it not so?
Banq. Toth' selfe-same tune and words: who's here?

Enter Rosse and Angus.

Rosse. The King hath happily receiu'd, *Macbeth*,
The newes of thy successe: and when he reades
Thy personall Venture in the Rebels fight,
His Wonders and his Prayses doe contend,
Which should be thine, or his: silenc'd with that,
In viewing o're the rest o'th' selfe-same day,
He findes thee in the stout Norweyan Rankes,
Nothing afeard of what thy selfe didst make
Strange Images of death, as thick as Tale
Can post with post, and euery one did beare
Thy prayses in his Kingdomes great defence,
And powr'd them downe before him.
Ang. Wee are sent,
To giue thee from our Royall Master thanks,
Onely to harrold thee into his sight,
Not pay thee.
Rosse. And for an earnest of a greater Honor,
He bad me, from him, call thee *Thane* of Cawdor:
In

In which addition, haile most worthy *Thane*,
For it is thine.
Banq. What, can the Deuill speake true?
Macb. The *Thane* of Cawdor liues:
Why doe you dresse me in borrowed Robes?
Ang. Who was the *Thane*, liues yet,
But vnder heauie Iudgement beares that Life,
Which he deserues to loose
Whether he was combin'd with those of Norway,
Or did lyne the Rebell with hidden helpe,
And vantage; or that with both he labour'd
In his Countreyes wracke, I know not
But Treasons Capitall, confess'd, and prou'd,
Haue ouerthrowne him.
Macb. Glamys, and *Thane* of Cawdor:
The greatest is behinde. Thankes for your paines.
Doe you not hope your Children shall be Kings,
When those that gaue the *Thane* of Cawdor to me,
Promis'd no lesse to them.
Banq. That trusted home,
Might yet enkindle you vnto the Crowne,
Besides the *Thane* of Cawdor. But 'tis strange:
And oftentimes, to winne vs to our harme,
The Instruments of Darknesse tell vs Truths,
Winne vs with honest Trifles, to betray's
In deepest consequence.
Cousins, a word, I pray you.
Macb. Two Truths are told,
As happy Prologues to the swelling Act
Of the Imperiall Theame. I thanke you Gentlemen.
This supernaturall solliciting
Cannot be ill; cannot be good
If ill? why hath it giuen me earnest of successe,
Commencing in a Truth? I am *Thane* of Cawdor.
If good? why doe I yeeld to that suggestion,
Whose horrid Image doth vnfixe my Heire,
And make my seated Heart knock at my Ribbes,
Against the vse of Nature? Present Feares
Are lesse then horrible Imaginings
My Thought, whose Murther yet is but fantasticall,
Shakes so my single state of Man,
That Function is smother'd in surmise,
And nothing is, but what is not
Banq Looke how our Partner's rapt
Macb. If Chance will haue me King,
Why Chance may Crowne me,
Without my stirre
Banq New Honors come vpon him
Like our strange Garments, cleaue not to their mould,
But with the aid of vse
Macb Come what come may,
Time, and the Houre, runs through the roughest Day.
Banq Worthy *Macbeth*, wee stay vpon your ley sure
Macb Giue me your fauour.
My dull Braine was wrought with things forgotten
Kinde Gentlemen, your paines are registred,
Where euery day I turne the Leafe,
To reade them.
Let vs toward the King: thinke vpon
What hath chanc'd: and at more time,
The *Interim* hauing weigh'd it, let vs speake
Our free Hearts each to other
Banq. Very gladly.
Macb Till then enough:
Come friends *Exeunt.*

Scena Quarta.

Flourish. Enter King, Lenox, Malcolme, Donalbaine, and Attendants.

King. Is execution done on *Cawdor*?
Or not those in Commission yet return'd?
Mal. My Liege, they are not yet come back.
But I haue spoke with one that saw him die:
Who did report, that very frankly hee
Confess'd his Treasons, implor'd your Highnesse Pardon,
And set forth a deepe Repentance:
Nothing in his Life became him,
Like the leauing it. Hee dy'de,
As one that had beene studied in his death,
To throw away the dearest thing he ow'd,
As 'twere a carelesse Trifle.
King. There's no Art,
To finde the Mindes construction in the Face:
He was a Gentleman, on whom I built
An absolute Trust
Enter Macbeth, Banquo, Rosse, and Angus.
O worthyest Cousin,
The sinne of my Ingratitude euen now
Was heauie on me. Thou art so farre before,
That swiftest Wing of Recompence is slow,
To ouertake thee. Would thou hadst lesse deseru'd,
That the proportion both of thanks, and payment,
Might haue beene mine: onely I haue left to say,
More is thy due, then more then all can pay.
Macb The seruice, and the loyaltie I owe,
In doing it, payes it selfe.
Your Highnesse part, is to receiue our Duties:
And our Duties are to your Throne, and State,
Children, and Seruants; which doe but what they should,
By doing euery thing safe toward your Loue
And Honor
King. Welcome hither:
I haue begun to plant thee, and will labour
To make thee full of growing. Noble *Banquo*,
That hast no lesse deseru'd, nor must be knowne
No lesse to haue done so: Let me enfold thee,
And hold thee to my Heart.
Banq There if I grow,
The Haruest is your owne
King My plenteous Ioyes,
Wanton in fulnesse, seeke to hide themselues
In drops of sorrow Sonnes, Kinsmen, *Thanes*,
And you whose places are the nearest, know,
We will establish our Estate vpon
Our eldest, *Malcolme*, whom we name hereafter,
The Prince of Cumberland: which Honor must
Not vnaccompanied, inuest him onely,
But signes of Noblenesse, like Starres, shall shine
On all deseruers. From hence to Envernes,
And binde vs further to you.
Macb. The Rest is Labor, which is not vs'd for you:
Ile be my selfe the Herbenger, and make ioyfull
The hearing of my Wife, with your approach:
So humbly take my leaue.
King. My worthy *Cawdor*.
Macb. The Prince of Cumberland: that is a step,
On which I must fall downe, or else o're-leape,

mm For

For in my way it lyes. Starres hide your fires,
Let not Light see my black and deepe desires:
The Eye winke at the Hand; yet let that bee,
Which the Eye feares, when it is done to see. *Exit.*

King. True, worthy *Banquo*: he is full so valiant,
And in his commendations, I am fed:
It is a Banquet to me. Let's after him,
Whose care is gone before, to bid vs welcome:
It is a peerelesse Kinsman. *Flourish. Exeunt.*

Scena Quinta.

Enter Macbeths Wife alone with a Letter.

Lady. They met me in the day of successe: and I haue learn'd by the perfect'st report, they haue more in them, then mortall knowledge. When I burnt in desire to question them further, they made themselues Ayre, into which they vanish'd. Whiles I stood rapt in the wonder of it, came Missiues from the King, who all-hail'd me Thane of *Cawdor, by which Title before, these weyward Sisters saluted me, and referr'd me to the comming on of time, with haile King that shalt be. This haue I thought good to deliuer thee (my dearest Partner of Greatnesse) that thou might'st not loose the dues of reioycing by being ignorant of what Greatnesse is promis'd thee. Lay it to thy heart, and farewell.*

Glamys thou art, and Cawdor, and shalt be
What thou art promis'd: yet doe I feare thy Nature,
It is too full o'th' Milke of humane kindnesse,
To catch the neerest way. Thou would'st be great,
Art not without Ambition, but without
The illnesse should attend it. What thou would'st highly,
That would'st thou holily: would'st not play false,
And yet would'st wrongly winne.
Thould'st haue, great Glamys, that which cryes,
Thus thou must doe, if thou haue it;
And that which rather thou do'st feare to doe,
Then wishest should be vndone. High thee hither,
That I may powre my Spirits in thine Eare,
And chastise with the valour of my Tongue
All that impeides thee from the Golden Round,
Which Fate and Metaphysicall ayde doth seeme
To haue thee crown'd withall. *Enter Messenger.*
What is your tidings?

Mess. The King comes here to Night.

Lady. Thou'rt mad to say it.
Is not thy Master with him? who, wer't so,
Would haue inform'd for preparation.

Mess. So please you, it is true: our *Thane* is comming:
One of my fellowes had the speed of him;
Who almost dead for breath, had scarcely more
Then would make vp his Message.

Lady. Giue him tending,
He brings great newes. *Exit Messenger.*
The Rauen himselfe is hoarse,
That croakes the fatall entrance of *Duncan*
Vnder my Battlements. Come you Spirits,
That tend on mortall thoughts, vnsex me here,
And fill me from the Crowne to the Toe, top-full
Of direst Crueltie: make thick my blood,
Stop vp th'accesse, and passage to Remorse,
That no compunctious visitings of Nature
Shake my fell purpose, nor keepe peace betweene
Th'effect, and hit. Come to my Womans Brests,
And take my Milke for Gall, you murth'ring Ministers,
Where-euer, in your sightlesse substances,
You wait on Natures Mischiefe. Come thick Night,
And pall thee in the dunnest smoake of Hell,
That my keene Knife see not the Wound it makes,
Nor Heauen peepe through the Blanket of the darke,
To cry, hold, hold. *Enter Macbeth.*
Great Glamys, worthy Cawdor,
Greater then both, by the all-haile hereafter,
Thy Letters haue transported me beyond
This ignorant present, and I feele now
The future in the instant.

Macb. My dearest Loue,
Duncan comes here to Night.

Lady. And when goes hence?

Macb. To morrow, as he purposes.

Lady. O neuer,
Shall Sunne that Morrow see.
Your Face, my *Thane*, is as a Booke, where men
May reade strange matters, to beguile the time.
Looke like the time, beare welcome in your Eye,
Your Hand, your Tongue: looke like th'innocent flower,
But be the Serpent vnder't. He that's comming,
Must be prouided for: and you shall put
This Nights great Businesse into my dispatch,
Which shall to all our Nights, and Dayes to come,
Giue solely soueraigne sway, and Masterdome.

Macb. We will speake further.

Lady. Onely looke vp cleare:
To alter fauor, euer is to feare:
Leaue all the rest to me. *Exeunt.*

Scena Sexta.

Hoboyes, and Torches. Enter King, Malcolme, Donalbaine, Banquo, Lenox, Macduff, Rosse, Angus, and Attendants.

King. This Castle hath a pleasant seat,
The ayre nimbly and sweetly recommends it selfe
Vnto our gentle sences.

Banq. This Guest of Summer,
The Temple-haunting Barlet does approue,
By his loued Mansonry, that the Heauens breath
Smells wooingly here: no Iutty frieze,
Buttrice, nor Coigne of Vantage, but this Bird
Hath made his pendant Bed, and procreant Cradle,
Where they must breed, and haunt: I haue obseru'd
The ayre is delicate. *Enter Lady.*

King. See, see, our honor'd Hostesse:
The Loue that followes vs, sometime is our trouble,
Which still we thanke as Loue. Herein I teach you,
How you shall bid God-eyld vs for your paines,
And thanke vs for your trouble.

Lady. All our seruice,
In euery point twice done, and then done double,
Were poore, and single Businesse, to contend
Against those Honors deepe, and broad,
Wherewith your Maiestie loades our House:
For those of old, and the late Dignities,
Heap'd vp to them, we rest your Ermites.

King. Where's

King. Where's the Thane of Cawdor?
We courst him at the heeles, and had a purpose
To be his Purueyor: But he rides well,
And his great Loue (sharpe as his Spurre) hath holp him
To his home before vs: Faire and Noble Hostesse
We are your guest to night.
La. Your Seruants euer,
Haue theirs, themselues, and what is theirs in compt,
To make their Audit at your Highnesse pleasure,
Still to returne your owne.
King. Giue me your hand:
Conduct me to mine Host we loue him highly,
And shall continue, our Graces towards him.
By your leaue Hostesse. *Exeunt*

Scena Septima.

Ho-boyes. Torches.
Enter a Sewer, and diuers Seruants with Dishes and Seruice ouer the Stage. Then enter Macbeth.

Macb. If it were done, when 'tis done, then 'twer well,
It were done quickly: If th' Assassination
Could trammell vp the Consequence, and catch
With his surcease, Successe: that but this blow
Might be the be all, and the end all. Heere,
But heere, vpon this Banke and Schoole of time,
Wee'ld iumpe the life to come. But in these Cases,
We still haue iudgement heere, that we but teach
Bloody Instructions, which being taught, returne
To plague th' Inuenter. This euen-handed Iustice
Commends th' Ingredience of our poyson'd Challice
To our owne lips. Hee's heere in double trust;
First, as I am his Kinsman, and his Subiect,
Strong both against the Deed: Then, as his Host,
Who should against his Murtherer shut the doore,
Not beare the knife my selfe. Besides, this *Duncane*
Hath borne his Faculties so meeke; hath bin
So cleere in his great Office, that his Vertues
Will pleade like Angels, Trumpet-tongu'd against
The deepe damnation of his taking off:
And Pitty, like a naked New-borne-Babe,
Striding the blast, or Heauens Cherubin, hors'd
Vpon the sightlesse Curriors of the Ayre,
Shall blow the horrid deed in euery eye,
That teares shall drowne the winde. I haue no Spurre
To pricke the sides of my intent, but onely
Vaulting Ambition, which ore-leapes it selfe,
And falles on th'other. *Enter Lady.*
How now? What Newes?
La. He has almost supt: why haue you left the chamber?
Mac. Hath he ask'd for me?
La. Know you not, he ha's?
Mac. We will proceed no further in this Businesse:
He hath Honour'd me of late, and I haue bought
Golden Opinions from all sorts of people,
Which would be worne now in their newest glosse,
Not cast aside so soone.
La. Was the hope drunke,
Wherein you drest your selfe? Hath it slept since?
And wakes it now to looke so greene, and pale,
At what it did so freely? From this time,
Such I account thy loue. Art thou affear'd
To be the same in thine owne Act, and Valour,
As thou art in desire? Would'st thou haue that
Which thou esteem'st the Ornament of Life,
And liue a Coward in thine owne Esteeme?
Letting I dare not, wait vpon I would,
Like the poore Cat i'th' Addage.
Macb. Prythee peace:
I dare do all that may become a man,
Who dares no more, is none.
La. What Beast was't then
That made you breake this enterprize to me?
When you durst do it, then you were a man:
And to be more then what you were, you would
Be so much more the man. Nor time, nor place
Did then adhere, and yet you would make both:
They haue made themselues, and that their fitnesse now
Do's vnmake you. I haue giuen Sucke, and know
How tender 'tis to loue the Babe that milkes me,
I would, while it was smyling in my Face,
Haue pluckt my Nipple from his Bonelesse Gummes,
And dasht the Braines out, had I so sworne
As you haue done to this.
Macb. If we should faile?
Lady. We faile?
But screw your courage to the sticking place,
And wee'le not fayle: when *Duncan* is asleepe,
(Whereto the rather shall his dayes hard Iourney
Soundly inuite him) his two Chamberlaines
Will I with Wine, and Wassell, so conuince,
That Memorie, the Warder of the Braine,
Shall be a Fume, and the Receit of Reason
A Lymbeck onely: when in Swinish sleepe,
Their drenched Natures lyes as in a Death,
What cannot you and I performe vpon
Th' vnguarded *Duncan*? What not put vpon
His spungie Officers? who shall beare the guilt
Of our great quell.
Macb. Bring forth Men-Children onely:
For thy vndaunted Mettle should compose
Nothing but Males. Will it not be receiu'd,
When we haue mark'd with blood those sleepie two
Of his owne Chamber, and vs'd their very Daggers,
That they haue don't?
Lady. Who dares receiue it other,
As we shall make our Griefes and Clamor rore,
Vpon his Death?
Macb. I am settled, and bend vp
Each corporall Agent to this terrible Feat.
Away, and mock the time with fairest show,
False Face must hide what the false Heart doth know.
Exeunt.

Actus Secundus. Scena Prima.

Enter Banquo, and Fleance, with a Torch before him.

Banq. How goes the Night, Boy?
Fleance. The Moone is downe: I haue not heard the Clock.
Banq. And she goes downe at Twelue.
Fleance. I take't, 'tis later, Sir.
Banq. Hold, take my Sword:
There's Husbandry in Heauen,
Their Candles are all out: take thee that too.

mm 2

A heauie Summons lyes like Lead vpon me,
And yet I would not ſleepe:
Mercifull Powers, reſtraine in me the curſed thoughts
That Nature giues way to in repoſe.

Enter Macbeth, and a Seruant with a Torch.

Giue me my Sword: who's there?
Macb. A Friend.
Banq. What Sir, not yet at reſt? the King's a bed.
He hath beene in vnuſuall Pleaſure,
And ſent forth great Largeſſe to your Offices.
This Diamond he greetes your Wife withall,
By the name of moſt kind Hoſteſſe.
And ſhut vp in meaſureleſſe content.
Mac. Being vnprepar'd,
Our will became the ſeruant to defect,
Which elſe ſhould free haue wrought.
Banq. All's well.
I dreamt laſt Night of the three weyward Siſters
To you they haue ſhew'd ſome truth.
Macb. I thinke not of them
Yet when we can entreat an houre to ſerue,
We would ſpend it in ſome words vpon that Buſineſſe
If you would graunt the time.
Banq. At your kind'ſt leyſure.
Macb. If you ſhall cleaue to my conſent,
When 'tis, it ſhall make Honor for you.
Banq. So I loſe none,
In ſeeking to augment it, but ſtill keepe
My Boſome franchis'd, and Allegeance cleare,
I ſhall be counſail'd.
Macb Good repoſe the while.
Banq. Thankes Sir: the like to you. *Exit Banquo.*
Macb Goe bid thy Miſtreſſe, when my drinke is ready
She ſtrike vpon the Bell. Get thee to bed. *Exit.*
Is this a Dagger, which I ſee before me,
The Handle toward my Hand? Come, let me clutch thee
I haue thee not, and yet I ſee thee ſtill.
Art thou not fatall Viſion, ſenſible
To feeling, as to ſight? or art thou but
A Dagger of the Minde, a falſe Creation,
Proceeding from the heat-oppreſſed Braine?
I ſee thee yet, in forme as palpable,
As this which now I draw.
Thou marſhall'ſt me the way that I was going,
And ſuch an Inſtrument I was to vſe.
Mine Eyes are made the fooles o'th'other Sences,
Or elſe worth all the reſt: I ſee thee ſtill;
And on thy Blade, and Dudgeon, Gouts of Blood,
Which was not ſo before. There's no ſuch thing:
It is the bloody Buſineſſe, which informes
Thus to mine Eyes. Now o're the one halfe World
Nature ſeemes dead, and wicked Dreames abuſe
The Curtain'd ſleepe: Witchcraft celebrates
Pale *Heccats* Offrings: and wither'd Murther,
Alarum'd by his Centinell, the Wolfe,
Whoſe howle's his Watch, thus with his ſtealthy pace,
With *Tarquins* rauiſhing ſides, towards his deſigne
Moues like a Ghoſt. Thou ſowre and firme-ſet Earth
Heare not my ſteps, which they may walke, for feare
Thy very ſtones prate of my where-about,
And take the preſent horror from the time,
Which now ſutes with it. Whiles I threat, he liues:
Words to the heat of deedes too cold breath giues.
A Bell rings.
I goe, and it is done: the Bell inuites me.
Heare it not, *Duncan*, for it is a Knell,
That ſummons thee to Heauen, or to Hell. *Exit.*

Scena Secunda.

Enter Lady.

La. That which hath made thē drunk, hath made me bold:
What hath quench'd them, hath giuen me fire.
Hearke, peace: it was the Owle that ſhriek'd,
The fatall Bell-man, which giues the ſtern'ſt good-night.
He is about it, the Doores are open:
And the ſurfeted Groomes doe mock their charge
With Snores. I haue drugg'd their Poſſets,
That Death and Nature doe contend about them,
Whether they liue, or dye.
Enter Macbeth
Macb Who's there? what hoa?
Lady. Alack, I am afraid they haue awak'd,
And 'tis not done: th'attempt, and not the deed,
Confounds vs: hearke: I lay'd their Daggers ready,
He could not miſſe 'em. Had he not reſembled
My Father as he ſlept, I had don't.
My Husband?
Macb. I haue done the deed:
Didſt thou not heare a noyſe?
Lady. I heard the Owle ſchreame, and the Crickets cry.
Did not you ſpeake?
Macb. When?
Lady Now.
Macb. As I deſcended?
Lady. I.
Macb. Hearke, who lyes i'th' ſecond Chamber?
Lady. *Donalbaine.*
Mac. This is a ſorry ſight.
Lady. A fooliſh thought, to ſay a ſorry ſight.
Macb. There's one did laugh in's ſleepe,
And one cry'd Murther, that they did wake each other:
I ſtood, and heard them: But they did ſay their Prayers,
And addreſt them againe to ſleepe.
Lady. There are two lodg'd together.
Macb. One cry'd God bleſſe vs, and Amen the other,
As they had ſeene me with theſe Hangmans hands:
Liſtning their feare, I could not ſay Amen,
When they did ſay God bleſſe vs
Lady. Conſider it not ſo deepely
Mac. But wherefore could not I pronounce Amen?
I had moſt need of Bleſſing, and Amen ſtuck in my throat.
Lady. Theſe deeds muſt not be thought
After theſe wayes: ſo, it will make vs mad.
Macb Me thought I heard a voyce cry, Sleep no more:
Macbeth does murther Sleepe, the innocent Sleepe,
Sleepe that knits vp the rauel'd Sleeue of Care,
The death of each dayes Life, ſore Labors Bath,
Balme of hurt Mindes, great Natures ſecond Courſe,
Chiefe nouriſher in Life's Feaſt
Lady What doe you meane?
Macb Still it cry'd, Sleepe no more to all the Houſe:
Glamis hath murther'd Sleepe, and therefore *Cawdor*
Shall ſleepe no more: *Macbeth* ſhall ſleepe no more.
Lady. Who was it, that thus cry'd? why worthy *Thane*,
You doe vnbend your Noble ſtrength, to thinke
So braine-ſickly of things: Goe get ſome Water,
And

And wash this filthie Witnesse from your Hand.
Why did you bring these Daggers from the place?
They must lye there: goe carry them, and smeare
The sleepie Groomes with blood.
Macb. Ile goe no more:
I am afraid, to thinke what I haue done:
Looke on't againe, I dare not.
Lady. Infirme of purpose:
Giue me the Daggers: the sleeping, and the dead,
Are but as Pictures: 'tis the Eye of Child-hood,
That feares a painted Deuill. If he doe bleed,
Ile guild the Faces of the Groomes withall,
For it must seeme their Guilt. *Exit.*
Knocke within.
Macb. Whence is that knocking?
How is't with me, when euery noyse appalls me?
What Hands are here? hah: they pluck out mine Eyes.
Will all great *Neptunes* Ocean wash this blood
Cleane from my Hand? no: this my Hand will rather
The multitudinous Seas incarnardine,
Making the Greene one, Red.

Enter Lady.

Lady. My Hands are of your colour: but I shame
To weare a Heart so white. *Knocke.*
I heare a knocking at the South entry:
Retyre we to our Chamber:
A little Water cleares vs of this deed.
How easie is it then? your Constancie
Hath left you vnattended. *Knocke.*
Hearke, more knocking.
Get on your Night-Gowne, least occasion call vs,
And shew vs to be Watchers: be not lost
So poorely in your thoughts.
Macb. To know my deed, *Knocke.*
'Twere best not know my selfe.
Wake *Duncan* with thy knocking:
I would thou could'st. *Exeunt.*

Scena Tertia.

Enter a Porter.

Knocking within.

Porter. Here's a knocking indeede: if a man were Porter of Hell Gate, hee should haue old turning the Key. *Knock.* Knock, Knock, Knock. Who's there i'th' name of *Belzebub*? Here's a Farmer, that hang'd himselfe on th'expectation of Plentie: Come in time, haue Napkins enow about you, here you'le sweat for't. *Knock.* Knock, knock. Who's there in th'other Deuils Name? Faith here's an Equiuocator, that could sweare in both the Scales against eyther Scale, who committed Treason enough for Gods sake, yet could not equiuocate to Heauen: oh come in, Equiuocator. *Knock.* Knock, Knock, Knock. Who's there? Faith here's an English Taylor come hither, for stealing out of a French Hose: Come in Taylor, here you may rost your Goose. *Knock.* Knock, Knock. Neuer at quiet: What are you? but this place is too cold for Hell. Ile Deuill-Porter it no further: I had thought to haue let in some of all Professions, that goe the Primrose way to th'euerlasting Bonfire. *Knock.* Anon, anon, I pray you remember the Porter.

Enter Macduff, and Lenox.

Macd. Was it so late, friend, ere you went to Bed,
That you doe lye so late?
Port. Faith Sir, we were carowsing till the second Cock:
And Drinke, Sir, is a great prouoker of three things.
Macd. What three things does Drinke especially prouoke?
Port. Marry, Sir, Nose-painting, Sleepe, and Vrine. Lecherie, Sir, it prouokes, and vnprouokes: it prouokes the desire, but it takes away the performance. Therefore much Drinke may be said to be an Equiuocator with Lecherie: it makes him, and it marres him; it sets him on, and it takes him off; it perswades him, and dis-heartens him; makes him stand too, and not stand too: in conclusion, equiuocates him in a sleepe, and giuing him the Lye, leaues him.
Macd. I beleeue, Drinke gaue thee the Lye last Night.
Port. That it did, Sir, i'the very Throat on me: but I requited him for his Lye, and (I thinke) being too strong for him, though he tooke vp my Legges sometime, yet I made a Shift to cast him.

Enter Macbeth.

Macd. Is thy Master stirring?
Our knocking ha's awak'd him: here he comes.
Lenox. Good morrow, Noble Sir.
Macb. Good morrow both.
Macd. Is the King stirring, worthy *Thane*?
Macb. Not yet.
Macd. He did command me to call timely on him,
I haue almost slipt the houre.
Ma b. Ile bring you to him.
Macd. I know this is a ioyfull trouble to you:
But yet 'tis one.
Macb. The labour we delight in, Physicks paine:
This is the Doore.
Macd. Ile make so bold to call, for 'tis my limitted seruice. *Exit Macduffe.*
Lenox. Goes the King hence to day?
Macb. He does: he did appoint so.
Lenox. The Night ha's been vnruly:
Where we lay, our Chimneys were blowne downe,
And (as they say) lamentings heard i'th' Ayre;
Strange Schreemes of Death,
And Prophecying, with Accents terrible,
Of dyre Combustion, and confus'd Euents,
New hatch'd toth' wofull time.
The obscure Bird clamor'd the liue-long Night.
Some say, the Earth was feuorous,
And did shake.
Macb. 'Twas a rough Night.
Lenox. My young remembrance cannot paralell
A fellow to it.

Enter Macduff.

Macd. O horror, horror, horror,
Tongue nor Heart cannot conceiue, nor name thee.
Macb. and Lenox. What's the matter?
Macd. Confusion now hath made his Master-peece:
Most sacrilegious Murther hath broke ope
The Lords anoynted Temple, and stole thence
The Life o'th' Building.
Macb. What is't you say, the Life?
Lenox. Meane you his Maiestie?
Macd. Approch the Chamber, and destroy your sight
With a new *Gorgon*. Doe not bid me speake:
See,

See,and then speake your selues: awake,awake,
Exeunt Macbeth and Lenox.
Ring the Alarum Bell: Murther,and Treason,
Banquo,and *Donalbaine*: *Malcolme* awake,
Shake off this Downey sleepe,Deaths counterfeit,
And looke on Death it selfe: vp,vp,and see
The great Doomes Image: *Malcolme,Banquo*,
As from your Graues rise vp,and walke like Sprights,
To countenance this horror. Ring the Bell.
Bell rings. Enter Lady.
Lady. What's the Businesse?
That such a hideous Trumpet calls to parley
The sleepers of the House? speake,speake.
Macd. O gentle Lady,
'Tis not for you to heare what I can speake:
The repetition in a Womans eare,
Would murther as it fell.
Enter Banquo.
O *Banquo,Banquo*, Our Royall Master's murther'd.
Lady. Woe,alas:
What,in our House?
Ban. Too cruell,any where.
Deare *Duff*, I prythee contradict thy selfe,
And say,it is not so.

Enter Macbeth,Lenox,and Rosse.

Macb. Had I but dy'd an houre before this chance,
I had liu'd a blessed time: for from this instant,
There's nothing serious in Mortalitie:
All is but Toyes: Renowne and Grace is dead,
The Wine of Life is drawne,and the meere Lees
Is left this Vault,to brag of.

Enter Malcolme and Donalbaine.

Donal. What is amisse?
Macb. You are,and doe not know't:
The Spring,the Head,the Fountaine of your Blood
Is stopt,the very Source of it is stopt.
Macd. Your Royall Father's murther'd.
Mal. Oh,by whom?
Lenox. Those of his Chamber,as it seem'd,had don't:
Their Hands and Faces were all badg'd with blood,
So were their Daggers,which vnwip'd,we found
Vpon their Pillowes: they star'd,and were distracted,
No mans Life was to be trusted with them.
Macb. O,yet I doe repent me of my furie,
That I did kill them.
Macd. Wherefore did you so?
Macb. Who can be wise,amaz'd,temp'rate,& furious,
Loyall,and Neutrall,in a moment? No man:
Th'expedition of my violent Loue
Out-run the pawser,Reason. Here lay *Duncan*,
His Siluer skinne,lac'd with his Golden Blood,
And his gash'd Stabs,look'd like a Breach in Nature,
For Ruines wastfull entrance: there the Murtherers,
Steep'd in the Colours of their Trade; their Daggers
Vnmannerly breech'd with gore: who could refraine,
That had a heart to loue; and in that heart,
Courage,to make's loue knowne?
Lady. Helpe me hence,hoa.
Macd. Looke to the Lady.
Mal. Why doe we hold our tongues,
That most may clayme this argument for ours?
Donal. What should be spoken here,
Where our Fate hid in an augure hole,
May rush,and seize vs? Let's away,
Our Teares are not yet brew'd.
Mal. Nor our strong Sorrow
Vpon the foot of Motion.
Banq. Looke to the Lady:
And when we haue our naked Frailties hid,
That suffer in exposure; let vs meet,
And question this most bloody piece of worke,
To know it further. Feares and scruples shake vs:
In the great Hand of God I stand,and thence,
Against the vndivulg'd pretence,I fight
Of Treasonous Mallice.
Macd. And so doe I.
All. So all.
Macb. Let's briefely put on manly readinesse,
And meet i'th' Hall together.
All. Well contented. *Exeunt.*
Malc. What will you doe?
Let's not consort with them:
To shew an vnfelt Sorrow,is an Office
Which the false man do's easie.
Ile to England.
Don. To Ireland, I:
Our seperated fortune shall keepe vs both the safer:
Where we are,there's Daggers in mens Smiles;
The neere in blood,the neerer bloody.
Malc. This murtherous Shaft that's shot,
Hath not yet lighted:and our safest way,
Is to auoid the ayme. Therefore to Horse,
And let vs not be daintie of leaue-taking,
But shift away: there's warrant in that Theft,
Which steales it selfe,when there's no mercie left.
Exeunt.

Scena Quarta.

Enter Rosse,with an Old man.

Old man. Threescore and ten I can remember well,
Within the Volume of which Time,I haue seene
Houres dreadfull,and things strange: but this sore Night
Hath trifled former knowings.
Rosse. Ha,good Father,
Thou seest the Heauens,as troubled with mans Act,
Threatens his bloody Stage: byth' Clock 'tis Day,
And yet darke Night strangles the trauailing Lampe:
Is't Nights predominance,or the Dayes shame,
That Darknesse does the face of Earth intombe,
When liuing Light should kisse it?
Old man. 'Tis vnnaturall,
Euen like the deed that's done: On Tuesday last,
A Faulcon towring in her pride of place,
Was by a Mowsing Owle hawkt at,and kill'd.
Rosse. And *Duncans* Horses,
(A thing most strange,and certaine)
Beauteous,and swift,the Minions of their Race,
Turn'd wilde in nature,broke their stalls,flong out,
Contending 'gainst Obedience,as they would
Make Warre with Mankinde.
Old man. 'Tis said,they eate each other.
Rosse. They did so:

To th'amazement of mine eyes that look'd vpon't.
Enter Macduffe.
Heere comes the good *Macduffe*.
How goes the world Sir, now?
Macd. Why ſee you not?
Roſſ. Is't known who did this more then bloody deed?
Macd. Thoſe that *Macbeth* hath ſlaine.
Roſſ. Alas the day,
What good could they pretend?
Macd. They were ſubborned,
Malcolme, and *Donalbaine* the Kings two Sonnes
Are ſtolne away and fled, which puts vpon them
Suſpition of the deed.
Roſſe. 'Gainſt Nature ſtill,
Thriftleſſe Ambition, that will rauen vp
Thine owne liues meanes: Then 'tis moſt like,
The Soueraignty will fall vpon *Macbeth*.
Macd. He is already nam'd, and gone to Scone
To be inueſted.
Roſſe. Where is *Duncans* body?
Macd. Carried to Colmekill,
The Sacred Store-houſe of his Predeceſſors,
And Guardian of their Bones.
Roſſe. Will you to Scone?
Macd. No Coſin, Ile to Fife.
Roſſe Well, I will thither.
Macd. Well may you ſee things wel done there: Adieu
Leaſt our old Robes ſit eaſier then our new.
Roſſe. Farewell, Father.
Old M. Gods benyſon go with you, and with thoſe
That would make good of bad, and Friends of Foes.
Exeunt omnes

Actus Tertius. Scena Prima.

Enter Banquo.
Banq. Thou haſt it now, King, Cawdor, Glamis, all,
As the weyard Women promis'd, and I feare
Thou play'dſt moſt fowly for't: yet it was ſaide
It ſhould not ſtand in thy Poſterity,
But that my ſelfe ſhould be the Roote, and Father
Of many Kings. If there come truth from them,
As vpon thee *Macbeth*, their Speeches ſhine,
Why by the verities on thee made good,
May they not be my Oracles as well,
And ſet me vp in hope. But huſh, no more.

Senit ſounded. Enter Macbeth as King, Lady Lenox, Roſſe, Lords, and Attendants.

Macb. Heere's our chiefe Gueſt.
La. If he had beene forgotten,
It had bene as a gap in our great Feaſt,
And all-thing vnbecomming.
Macb. To night we hold a ſolemne Supper ſir,
And Ile requeſt your preſence.
Banq. Let your Highneſſe
Command vpon me, to the which my duties
Are with a moſt indiſſoluble tye
For euer knit.
Macb Ride you this afternoone?
Ban. I, my good Lord.
Macb We ſhould haue elſe deſir'd your good aduice
(Which ſtill hath been both graue, and proſperous)
In this dayes Councell: but wee'le take to morrow.
Is't farre you ride?
Ban. As farre, my Lord, as will fill vp the time
'Twixt this, and Supper. Goe not my Horſe the better,
I muſt become a borrower of the Night,
For a darke houre, or twaine.
Macb. Faile not our Feaſt.
Ban. My Lord, I will not.
Macb. We heare our bloody Cozens are beſtow'd
In England, and in Ireland, not confeſsing
Their cruell Parricide, filling their hearers
With ſtrange inuention. But of that to morrow,
When therewithall, we ſhall haue cauſe of State,
Crauing vs ioyntly. Hye you to Horſe:
Adieu, till you returne at Night.
Goes *Fleance* with you?
Ban. I, my good Lord: our time does call vpon's.
Macb I wiſh your Horſes ſwift, and ſure of foot:
And ſo I doe commend you to their backs.
Farwell. *Exit Banquo.*
Let euery man be maſter of his time,
Till ſeuen at Night, to make ſocietie
The ſweeter welcome:
We will keepe our ſelfe till Supper time alone:
While then, God be with you. *Exeunt Lords.*
Sirrha, a word with you: Attend thoſe men
Our pleaſure?
Seruant. They are, my Lord, without the Pallace Gate.
Macb Bring them before vs. *Exit Seruant.*
To be thus, is nothing, but to be ſafely thus:
Our feares in *Banquo* ſticke deepe,
And in his Royaltie of Nature reignes that
Which would be fear'd. 'Tis much he dares,
And to that dauntleſſe temper of his Minde,
He hath a Wiſdome, that doth guide his Valour,
To act in ſafetie. There is none but he,
Whoſe being I doe feare: and vnder him,
My *Genius* is rebuk'd, as it is ſaid
Mark Anthonies was by *Cæſar*. He chid the Siſters,
When firſt they put the Name of King vpon me,
And bad them ſpeake to him. Then Prophet-like,
They hayl'd him Father to a Line of Kings.
Vpon my Head they plac'd a fruitleſſe Crowne,
And put a barren Scepter in my Gripe,
Thence to be wrencht with an vnlineall Hand,
No Sonne of mine ſucceeding: if't be ſo,
For *Banquo's* Iſſue haue I fil'd my Minde,
For them, the gracious *Duncan* haue I murther'd,
Put Rancours in the Veſſell of my Peace
Onely for them, and mine eternall Iewell
Giuen to the common Enemie of Man,
To make them Kings, the Seedes of *Banquo* Kings.
Rather then ſo, come Fate into the Lyſt,
And champion me to th'vtterance.
Who's there?

Enter Seruant, and two Murtherers.

Now goe to the Doore, and ſtay there till we call.
Exit Seruant.
Was it not yeſterday we ſpoke together?
Murth. It was, ſo pleaſe your Highneſſe.
Macb. Well then,
Now haue you conſider'd of my ſpeeches:
Know,

Know, that it was he, in the times past,
Which held you so vnder fortune,
Which you thought had been our innocent selfe.
This I made good to you, in our last conference,
Past in probation with you:
How you were borne in hand, how crost:
The Instruments: who wrought with them:
And all things else, that might
To halfe a Soule, and to a Notion craz'd,
Say, Thus did *Banquo*.

1. Murth. You made it knowne to vs.

Macb. I did so:
And went further, which is now
Our point of second meeting.
Doe you finde your patience so predominant,
In your nature, that you can let this goe?
Are you so Gospell'd, to pray for this good man,
And for his Issue, whose heauie hand
Hath bow'd you to the Graue, and begger'd
Yours for euer?

1. Murth. We are men, my Liege.

Macb. I, in the Catalogue ye goe for men,
As Hounds, and Greyhounds, Mungrels, Spaniels, Curres,
Showghes, Water-Rugs, and Demy-Wolues are clipt
All by the Name of Dogges: the valued file
Distinguishes the swift, the slow, the subtle,
The House-keeper, the Hunter, euery one
According to the gift, which bounteous Nature
Hath in him clos'd: whereby he does receiue
Particular addition, from the Bill,
That writes them all alike: and so of men.
Now, if you haue a station in the file,
Not i'th' worst ranke of Manhood, say't,
And I will put that Businesse in your Bosomes,
Whose execution takes your Enemie off,
Grapples you to the heart; and loue of vs,
Who weare our Health but sickly in his Life,
Which in his Death were perfect.

2. Murth. I am one, my Liege,
Whom the vile Blowes and Buffets of the World
Hath so incens'd, that I am recklesse what I doe,
To spight the World.

1. Murth. And I another,
So wearie with Disasters, tugg'd with Fortune,
That I would set my Life on any Chance,
To mend it, or be rid on't.

Macb. Both of you know *Banquo* was your Enemie.

Murth. True, my Lord.

Macb. So is he mine: and in such bloody distance,
That euery minute of his being, thrusts
Against my neer'st of Life: and though I could
With bare-fac'd power sweepe him from my sight,
And bid my will auouch it; yet I must not,
For certaine friends that are both his, and mine,
Whose loues I may not drop, but wayle his fall,
Who I my selfe struck downe: and thence it is,
That I to your assistance doe make loue,
Masking the Businesse from the common Eye,
For sundry weightie Reasons.

2. Murth. We shall, my Lord,
Performe what you command vs.

1. Murth. Though our Liues--

Macb. Your Spirits shine through you.
Within this houre, at most,
I will aduise you where to plant your selues,
Acquaint you with the perfect Spy o'th' time,
The moment on't, for't must be done to Night,
And something from the Pallace: alwayes thought,
That I require a clearenesse; and with him,
To leaue no Rubs nor Botches in the Worke:
Fleans, his Sonne, that keepes him companie,
Whose absence is no lesse materiall to me,
Then is his Fathers, must embrace the fate
Of that darke houre: resolue your selues apart,
Ile come to you anon.

Murth. We are resolu'd, my Lord.

Macb. Ile call vpon you straight: abide within,
It is concluded: *Banquo*, thy Soules flight,
If it finde Heauen, must finde it out to Night. *Exeunt.*

Scena Secunda.

Enter Macbeths Lady, and a Seruant.

Lady. Is *Banquo* gone from Court?

Seruant. I, Madame, but returnes againe to Night.

Lady. Say to the King, I would attend his leysure,
For a few words.

Seruant. Madame, I will. *Exit.*

Lady. Nought's had, all's spent,
Where our desire is got without content:
'Tis safer, to be that which we destroy,
Then by destruction dwell in doubtfull ioy.

Enter Macbeth.

How now, my Lord, why doe you keepe alone?
Of sorryest Fancies your Companions making,
Vsing those Thoughts, which should indeed haue dy'd
With them they thinke on: things without all remedie
Should be without regard: what's done, is done.

Macb. We haue scorch'd the Snake, not kill'd it:
Shee'le close, and be her selfe, whilest our poore Mallice
Remaines in danger of her former Tooth.
But let the frame of things dis-ioynt,
Both the Worlds suffer,
Ere we will eate our Meale in feare, and sleepe
In the affliction of these terrible Dreames,
That shake vs Nightly: Better be with the dead,
Whom we, to gayne our peace, haue sent to peace,
Then on the torture of the Minde to lye
In restlesse extasie.
Duncane is in his Graue:
After Lifes fitfull Feuer, he sleepes well,
Treason ha's done his worst: nor Steele, nor Poyson,
Mallice domestique, forraine Leuie, nothing,
Can touch him further.

Lady. Come on:
Gentle my Lord, sleeke o're your rugged Lookes,
Be bright and Iouiall among your Guests to Night.

Macb. So shall I Loue, and so I pray be you:
Let your remembrance apply to *Banquo*,
Present him Eminence, both with Eye and Tongue:
Vnsafe the while, that wee must laue
Our Honors in these flattering streames,
And make our Faces Vizards to our Hearts,
Disguising what they are.

Lady. You must leaue this.

Macb. O, full of Scorpions is my Minde, deare Wife:
Thou know'st, that *Banquo* and his *Fleans* liues.

Lady. But

Lady. But in them, Natures Coppie's not eterne.
Macb. There's comfort yet, they are assaileable,
Then be thou iocund: ere the Bat hath flowne
His Cloyster'd flight, ere to black *Heccats* summons
The shard-borne Beetle, with his drowsie hums,
Hath rung Nights yawning Peale,
There shall be done a deed of dreadfull note.
Lady. What's to be done?
Macb Be innocent of the knowledge, dearest Chuck,
Till thou applaud the deed: Come, seeling Night,
Skarfe vp the tender Eye of pittifull Day,
And with thy bloodie and inuisible Hand
Cancell and teare to pieces that great Bond,
Which keepes me pale. Light thickens,
And the Crow makes Wing toth' Rookie Wood:
Good things of Day begin to droope, and drowse,
Whiles Nights black Agents to their Prey's doe rowse.
Thou maruell'st at my words: but hold thee still,
Things bad begun, make strong themselues by ill:
So prythee goe with me. *Exeunt.*

Scena Tertia.

Enter three Murtherers.

1. But who did bid thee ioyne with vs?
3. *Macbeth.*
2. He needes not our mistrust, since he deliuers
Our Offices, and what we haue to doe,
To the direction iust.
1. Then stand with vs:
The West yet glimmers with some streakes of Day.
Now spurres the lated Traueller apace,
To gayne the timely Inne, end neere approches
The subiect of our Watch.
3. Hearke, I heare Horses.
Banquo within. Giue vs a Light there, hoa.
2. Then 'tis hee:
The rest, that are within the note of expectation,
Alreadie are i'th'Court.
1. His Horses goe about.
3. Almost a mile: but he does vsually,
So all men doe, from hence toth' Pallace Gate
Make it their Walke.

Enter Banquo and Fleans, with a Torch.

2. A Light, a Light.
3. 'Tis hee.
1. Stand too't.
Ban. It will be Rayne to Night.
1. Let it come downe.
Ban. O, Trecherie!
Flye good *Fleans*, flye, flye, flye,
Thou may'st reuenge. O Slaue!
3. Who did strike out the Light?
1. Was't not the way?
3. There's but one downe: the Sonne is fled.
2. We haue lost
Best halfe of our Affaire.
1. Well, let's away, and say how much is done.
Exeunt.

Scæna Quarta.

Banquet prepar'd. Enter Macbeth, Lady, Rosse, Lenox, Lords, and Attendants.

Macb. You know your owne degrees, sit downe:
At first and last, the hearty welcome.
Lords. Thankes to your Maiesty.
Macb. Our selfe will mingle with Society,
And play the humble Host:
Our Hostesse keepes her State, but in best time
We will require her welcome.
La. Pronounce it for me Sir, to all our Friends,
For my heart speakes, they are welcome.
Enter first Murtherer.
Macb. See they encounter thee with their harts thanks
Both sides are euen: heere Ile sit i'th'mid'st,
Be large in mirth, anon wee'l drinke a Measure
The Table round. There's blood vpon thy face.
Mur. 'Tis *Banquo's* then.
Macb. 'Tis better thee without, then he within.
Is he dispatch'd?
Mur. My Lord his throat is cut, that I did for him.
Mac. Thou art the best o'th'Cut-throats,
Yet hee's good that did the like for *Fleans*:
If thou did'st it, thou art the Non-pareill.
Mur. Most Royall Sir
Fleans is scap'd.
Macb. Then comes my Fit againe:
I had else beene perfect;
Whole as the Marble, founded as the Rocke,
As broad, and generall, as the casing Ayre:
But now I am cabin'd, crib'd, confin'd, bound in
To sawcy doubts, and feares. But *Banquo's* safe?
Mur. I, my good Lord: safe in a ditch he bides,
With twenty trenched gashes on his head;
The least a Death to Nature.
Macb. Thankes for that:
There the growne Serpent lyes, the worme that's fled
Hath Nature that in time will Venom breed,
No teeth for th'present. Get thee gone, to morrow
Wee'l heare our selues againe. *Exit Murderer.*
Lady. My Royall Lord,
You do not giue the Cheere, the Feast is sold
That is not often vouch'd, while 'tis a making:
'Tis giuen, with welcome: to feede were best at home:
From thence, the sawce to meate is Ceremony,
Meeting were bare without it.

Enter the Ghost of Banquo, and sits in Macbeths place.

Macb. Sweet Remembrancer:
Now good digestion waite on Appetite,
And health on both.
Lenox. May't please your Highnesse sit.
Macb. Here had we now our Countries Honor, roof'd,
Were the grac'd person of our *Banquo* present:
Who, may I rather challenge for vnkindnesse,
Then pitty for Mischance.
Rosse. His absence (Sir)
Layes blame vpon his promise. Pleas't your Highnesse
To grace vs with your Royall Company?
Mcab.

Macb. The Table's full.
Lenox. Heere is a place reseru'd Sir,
Macb. Where?
Lenox. Heere my good Lord.
What is't that moues your Highnesse?
Macb. Which of you haue done this?
Lords. What, my good Lord?
Macb. Thou canst not say I did it: neuer shake
Thy goary lockes at me.
Rosse. Gentlemen rise, his Highnesse is not well.
Lady. Sit worthy Friends: my Lord is often thus,
And hath beene from his youth. Pray you keepe Seat,
The fit is momentary, vpon a thought
He will againe be well. If much you note him
You shall offend him, and extend his Passion,
Feed, and regard him not. Are you a man?
Macb. I, and a bold one, that dare looke on that
Which might appall the Diuell.
La. O proper stuffe:
This is the very painting of your feare:
This is the Ayre-drawne-Dagger which you said
Led you to *Duncan.* O, these flawes and starts
(Impostors to true feare) would well become
A womans story, at a Winters fire
Authoriz'd by her Grandam: shame it selfe,
Why do you make such faces? When all's done
You looke but on a stoole.
Macb. Prythee see there:
Behold, looke, loe, how say you:
Why what care I, if thou canst nod, speake too.
If Charnell houses, and our Graues must send
Those that we bury, backe; our Monuments
Shall be the Mawes of Kytes.
La. What? quite vnmann'd in folly.
Macb. If I stand heere, I saw him.
La. Fie for shame.
Macb. Blood hath bene shed ere now, i'th'olden time
Ere humane Statute purg'd the gentle Weale:
I, and since too, Murthers haue bene perform'd
Too terrible for the eare. The times has bene,
That when the Braines were out, the man would dye,
And there an end: But now they rise againe
With twenty mortall murthers on their crownes,
And push vs from our stooles. This is more strange
Then such a murther is.
La. My worthy Lord
Your Noble Friends do lacke you.
Macb. I do forget:
Do not muse at me my most worthy Friends,
I haue a strange infirmity, which is nothing
To those that know me. Come, loue and health to all,
Then Ile sit downe: Giue me some Wine, fill full:
Enter Ghost.
I drinke to th'generall ioy o'th'whole Table,
And to our deere Friend *Banquo*, whom we misse:
Would he were heere: to all, and him we thirst,
And all to all.
Lords. Our duties, and the pledge.
Mac. Auant, & quit my sight, let the earth hide thee:
Thy bones are marrowlesse, thy blood is cold:
Thou hast no speculation in those eyes
Which thou dost glare with.
La. Thinke of this good Peeres
But as a thing of Custome: 'Tis no other,
Onely it spoyles the pleasure of the time.
Macb. What man dare, I dare:
Approach thou like the rugged Russian Beare,
The arm'd Rhinoceros, or th'Hircan Tiger,
Take any shape but that, and my firme Nerues
Shall neuer tremble. Or be aliue againe,
And dare me to the Desart with thy Sword:
If trembling I inhabit then, protest mee
The Baby of a Girle. Hence horrible shadow,
Vnreall mock'ry hence. Why so, being gone
I am a man againe: pray you sit still.
La. You haue displac'd the mirth,
Broke the good meeting, with most admir'd disorder.
Macb. Can such things be,
And ouercome vs like a Summers Clowd,
Without our speciall wonder? You make me strange
Euen to the disposition that I owe,
When now I thinke you can behold such sights,
And keepe the naturall Rubie of your Cheekes,
When mine is blanch'd with feare.
Rosse. What sights, my Lord?
La. I pray you speake not: he growes worse & worse
Question enrages him: at once, goodnight.
Stand not vpon the order of your going,
But go at once.
Len. Good night, and better health
Attend his Maiesty.
La. A kinde goodnight to all. *Exit Lords.*
Macb. It will haue blood they say:
Blood will haue Blood:
Stones haue beene knowne to moue, & Trees to speake:
Augures, and vnderstood Relations, haue
By Maggot Pyes, & Choughes, & Rookes brought forth
The secret'st man of Blood. What is the night?
La. Almost at oddes with morning, which is which.
Macb. How say'st thou that *Macduff* denies his person
At our great bidding.
La: Did you send to him Sir?
Macb. I heare it by the way: But I will send:
There's not a one of them but in his house
I keepe a Seruant Feed. I will to morrow
(And betimes I will) to the weyard Sisters.
More shall they speake: for now I am bent to know
By the worst meanes, the worst, for mine owne good,
All causes shall giue way. I am in blood
Stept in so farre, that should I wade no more,
Returning were as tedious as go ore:
Strange things I haue in head, that will to hand,
Which must be acted, ere they may be scand.
La. You lacke the season of all Natures, sleepe.
Macb. Come, wee'l to sleepe: My strange & self-abuse
Is the initiate feare, that wants hard vse:
We are yet but yong indeed. *Exeunt.*

Scena Quinta.

Thunder. Enter the three Witches, meeting Hecat.

1. Why how now *Hecat*, you looke angerly?
Hec. Haue I not reason (Beldams) as you are?
Sawcy, and ouer-bold, how did you dare
To Trade, and Trafficke with *Macbeth*,
In Riddles, and Affaires of death;
And

And I the Mistris of your Charmes,
The close contriuer of all harmes,
Was neuer call'd to beare my part,
Or shew the glory of our Art?
And which is worse, all you haue done
Hath bene but for a wayward Sonne,
Spightfull, and wrathfull, who (as others do)
Loues for his owne ends, not for you.
But make amends now: Get you gon,
And at the pit of Acheron
Meete me i'th'Morning: thither he
Will come, to know his Destinie.
Your Vessels, and your Spels prouide,
Your Charmes, and euery thing beside;
I am for th'Ayre: This night Ile spend
Vnto a dismall, and a Fatall end.
Great businesse must be wrought ere Noone.
Vpon the Corner of the Moone
There hangs a vap'rous drop, profound,
Ile catch it ere it come to ground;
And that distill'd by Magicke slights,
Shall raise such Artificiall Sprights,
As by the strength of their illusion,
Shall draw him on to his Confusion.
He shall spurne Fate, scorne Death, and beare
His hopes 'boue Wisedome, Grace, and Feare:
And you all know, Security
Is Mortals cheefest Enemie.
Musicke, and a Song.
Hearke, I am call'd: my little Spirit see
Sits in a Foggy cloud, and stayes for me.
Sing within. Come away, come away, &c.
1 Come, let's make hast, shee'l soone be
Backe againe. *Exeunt.*

Scæna Sexta.

Enter Lenox, and another Lord.

Lenox. My former Speeches,
Haue but hit your Thoughts
Which can interpret farther: Onely I say
Things haue bin strangely borne. The gracious *Duncan*
Was pittied of *Macbeth*: marry he was dead:
And the right valiant *Banquo* walk'd too late,
Whom you may say (if't please you) *Fleans* kill'd,
For *Fleans* fled: Men must not walke too late.
Who cannot want the thought, how monstrous
It was for *Malcolme*, and for *Donalbane*
To kill their gracious Father? Damned Fact,
How it did greeue *Macbeth*? Did he not straight
In pious rage, the two delinquents teare,
That were the Slaues of drinke, and thralles of sleepe?
Was not that Nobly done? I, and wisely too:
For 'twould haue anger'd any heart aliue
To heare the men deny't. So that I say,
He ha's borne all things well, and I do thinke,
That had he *Duncans* Sonnes vnder his Key,
(As, and't please Heauen he shall not) they should finde
What 'twere to kill a Father: So should *Fleans*.
But peace; for from broad words, and cause he fayl'd
His presence at the Tyrants Feast, I heare
Macduffe liues in disgrace. Sir, can you tell
Where he bestowes himselfe?
Lord. The Sonnes of *Duncane*
(From whom this Tyrant holds the due of Birth)
Liues in the English Court, and is receyu'd
Of the most Pious *Edward*, with such grace,
That the maleuolence of Fortune, nothing
Takes from his high respect. Thither *Macduffe*
Is gone, to pray the Holy King, vpon his ayd
To wake Northumberland, and warlike *Seyward*,
That by the helpe of these (with him aboue)
To ratifie the Worke) we may againe
Giue to our Tables meate, sleepe to our Nights:
Free from our Feasts, and Banquets bloody kniues;
Do faithfull Homage, and receiue free Honors,
All which we pine for now. And this report
Hath so exasperate their King, that hee
Prepares for some attempt of Warre.
Len. Sent he to *Macduffe*?
Lord. He did: and with an absolute Sir, not I
The clowdy Messenger turnes me his backe,
And hums; as who should say, you'l rue the time
That clogges me with this Answer.
Lenox. And that well might
Aduise him to a Caution, t' hold what distance
His wisedome can prouide. Some holy Angell
Flye to the Court of England, and vnfold
His Message ere he come, that a swift blessing
May soone returne to this our suffering Country,
Vnder a hand accurs'd.
Lord. Ile send my Prayers with him. *Exeunt*

Actus Quartus. Scena Prima.

Thunder. Enter the three Witches.

1 Thrice the brinded Cat hath mew'd.
2 Thrice, and once the Hedge-Pigge whin'd.
3 Harpier cries, 'tis time, 'tis time.
1 Round about the Caldron go:
In the poysond Entrailes throw
Toad, that vnder cold stone,
Dayes and Nights, ha's thirty one:
Sweltred Venom sleeping got,
Boyle thou first i'th'charmed pot.
All. Double, double, toile and trouble;
Fire burne, and Cauldron bubble.
2 Fillet of a Fenny Snake,
In the Cauldron boyle and bake:
Eye of Newt, and Toe of Frogge,
Wooll of Bat, and Tongue of Dogge:
Adders Forke, and Blinde-wormes Sting,
Lizards legge, and Howlets wing:
For a Charme of powrefull trouble,
Like a Hell-broth, boyle and bubble.
All. Double, double, toyle and trouble,
Fire burne, and Cauldron bubble.
3 Scale of Dragon, Tooth of Wolfe,
Witches Mummey, Maw, and Gulfe
Of the rauin'd salt Sea sharke:
Roote of Hemlocke, digg'd i'th'darke:
Liuer of Blaspheming Iew,
Gall of Goate, and Slippes of Yew,
Sliuer'd in the Moones Ecclipse:
Nose

Noſe of Turke,and Tartars lips:
Finger of Birth-ſtrangled Babe,
Ditch-deliuer'd by a Drab,
Make the Grewell thicke, and ſlab.
Adde thereto a Tigers Chawdron,
For th'Ingredience of our Cawdron.
All. Double, double, toyle and trouble,
Fire burne,and Cauldron bubble.
2 Coole it with a Baboones blood,
Then the Charme is firme and good.

Enter Hecat, and the other three Witches.

Hec. O well done: I commend your paines,
And euery one ſhall ſhare i'th'gaines:
And now about the Cauldron ſing
Like Elues and Fairies in a Ring,
Inchanting all that you put in.
Muſicke and a Song. Blacke Spirits, &c.
2 By the pricking of my Thumbes,
Something wicked this way comes:
Open Lockes, who euer knockes.
Enter Macbeth.
Macb. How now you ſecret, black, & midnight Hags?
What is't you do?
All. A deed without a name.
Macb. I coniure you, by that which you Profeſſe,
(How ere you come to know it) anſwer me:
Though you vntye the Windes, and let them fight
Againſt the Churches: Though the yeſty Waues
Confound and ſwallow Nauigation vp:
Though bladed Corne be lodg'd, & Trees blown downe,
Though Caſtles topple on their Warders heads:
Though Pallaces, and Pyramids do ſlope
Their heads to their Foundations: Though the treaſure
Of Natures Germaine, tumble altogether,
Euen till deſtruction ſicken: Anſwer me
To what I aske you.
1 Speake.
2 Demand.
3 Wee'l anſwer.
1 Say, if th'hadſt rather heare it from our mouthes,
Or from our Maſters.
Macb. Call 'em: let me ſee 'em.
1 Powre in Sowes blood, that hath eaten
Her nine Farrow: Greaze that's ſweaten
From the Murderers Gibbet, throw
Into the Flame.
All. Come high or low:
Thy Selfe and Office deaftly ſhow. *Thunder.*
1. Apparation, an Armed Head.
Macb. Tell me, thou vnknowne power.
1 He knowes thy thought:
Heare his ſpeech, but ſay thou nought.
1 Appar. Macbeth, Macbeth, Macbeth:
Beware *Macduffe,*
Beware the Thane of Fife: diſmiſſe me. Enough.
He Deſcends.
Macb. What ere thou art, for thy good caution, thanks
Thou haſt harp'd my feare aright. But one word more.
1 He will not be commanded: heere's another
More potent then the firſt. *Thunder.*
2 Apparition, a Bloody Childe.
2 Appar. Macbeth, Macbeth, Macbeth.
Macb. Had I three eares, Il'd heare thee.
2 Appar. Be bloody, bold, & reſolute:
Laugh to ſcorne
The powre of man: For none of woman borne
Shall harme *Macbeth.* *Deſcends.*
Mac. Then liue *Macduffe*: what need I feare of thee?
But yet Ile make aſſurance: double ſure,
And take a Bond of Fate: thou ſhalt not liue,
That I may tell pale-hearted Feare, it lies;
And ſleepe in ſpight of Thunder. *Thunder*
3 Apparation, a Childe Crowned, with a Tree in his hand.
What is this, that riſes like the iſſue of a King,
And weares vpon his Baby-brow, the round
And top of Soueraignty?
All. Liſten, but ſpeake not too't.
3 Appar. Be Lyon metled, proud, and take no care:
Who chafes, who frets, or where Conſpirers are:
Macbeth ſhall neuer vanquiſh'd be, vntill
Great Byrnam Wood, to high Dunſmane Hill
Shall come againſt him. *Deſcend.*
Macb. That will neuer bee:
Who can impreſſe the Forreſt, bid the Tree
Vnfixe his earth-bound Root? Sweet boadments, good:
Rebellious dead, riſe neuer till the Wood
Of Byrnan riſe, and our high plac'd *Macbeth*
Shall liue the Leaſe of Nature, pay his breath
To time, and mortall Cuſtome. Yet my Hart
Throbs to know one thing: Tell me, if your Art
Can tell ſo much: Shall *Banquo's* iſſue euer
Reigne in this Kingdome?
All. Seeke to know no more.
Macb. I will be ſatisfied. Deny me this,
And an eternall Curſe fall on you: Let me know.
Why ſinkes that Caldron? & what noiſe is this? *Hoboyes*
1 Shew.
2 Shew.
3 Shew.
All. Shew his Eyes, and greeue his Hart,
Come like ſhadowes, ſo depart.
A ſhew of eight Kings, and Banquo laſt, with a glaſſe in his hand.
Macb. Thou art too like the Spirit of *Banquo*: Down:
Thy Crowne do's ſeare mine Eye-bals. And thy haire
Thou other Gold-bound-brow, is like the firſt:
A third, is like the former. Filthy Hagges,
Why do you ſhew me this? —— A fourth? Start eyes!
What will the Line ſtretch out to'th'cracke of Doome?
Another yet? A ſeauenth? Ile ſee no more:
And yet the eight appeares, who beares a glaſſe,
Which ſhewes me many more: and ſome I ſee,
That two-fold Balles, and trebble Scepters carry.
Horrible ſight: Now I ſee 'tis true,
For the Blood-bolter'd *Banquo* ſmiles vpon me,
And points at them for his. What? is this ſo?
1 I Sir, all this is ſo. But why
Stands *Macbeth* thus amazedly?
Come Siſters, cheere we vp his ſprights,
And ſhew the beſt of our delights.
Ile Charme the Ayre to giue a ſound,
While you performe your Antique round:
That this great King may kindly ſay,
Our duties, did his welcome pay. *Muſicke.*
The Witches Dance, and vaniſh.
Macb. Where are they? Gone?
Let this pernitious houre,
Stand aye accurſed in the Kalender.
Come in, without there. *Enter Lenox.*
Lenox. What's your Graces will.
Macb.

Macb. Saw you the Weyard Sisters?
Lenox. No my Lord.
Macb. Came they not by you?
Lenox. No indeed my Lord.
Macb. Infected be the Ayre whereon they ride,
And damn'd all those that trust them. I did heare
The gallopping of Horse. Who was't came by?
Len. 'Tis two or three my Lord, that bring you word:
Macduff is fled to England.
Macb. Fled to England?
Len. I, my good Lord.
Macb. Time, thou anticipat'st my dread exploits:
The flighty purpose neuer is o're-tooke
Vnlesse the deed go with it. From this moment,
The very firstlings of my heart shall be
The firstlings of my hand. And euen now
To Crown my thoughts with Acts: be it thoght & done:
The Castle of *Macduff*, I will surprize,
Seize vpon Fife; giue to th'edge o'th'Sword
His Wife, his Babes, and all vnfortunate Soules
That trace him in his Line. No boasting like a Foole,
This deed Ile do, before this purpose coole,
But no more sights. Where are these Gentlemen?
Come bring me where they are. *Exeunt*

Scena Secunda.

Enter Macduffes Wife, her Son, and Rosse.

Wife. What had he done, to make him fly the Land?
Rosse. You must haue patience Madam.
Wife. He had none:
His flight was madnesse: when our Actions do not,
Our feares do make vs Traitors.
Rosse. You know not
Whether it was his wisedome, or his feare.
Wife. Wisedom? to leaue his wife, to leaue his Babes,
His Mansion, and his Titles, in a place
From whence himselfe do's flye? He loues vs not,
He wants the naturall touch. For the poore Wren
(The most diminitiue of Birds) will fight,
Her yong ones in her Nest, against the Owle:
All is the Feare, and nothing is the Loue;
As little is the Wisedome, where the flight
So runnes against all reason.
Rosse. My deerest Cooz,
I pray you schoole your selfe. But for your Husband,
He is Noble, Wise, Iudicious, and best knowes
The fits o'th'Season. I dare not speake much further,
But cruell are the times, when we are Traitors
And do not know our selues: when we hold Rumor
From what we feare, yet know not what we feare,
But floate vpon a wilde and violent Sea
Each way, and moue. I take my leaue of you:
Shall not be long but Ile be heere againe:
Things at the worst will cease, or else climbe vpward,
To what they were before. My pretty Cosine,
Blessing vpon you.
Wife. Father'd he is,
And yet hee's Father-lesse.
Rosse. I am so much a Foole, should I stay longer
It would be my disgrace, and your discomfort.
I take my leaue at once. *Exit Rosse.*
Wife. Sirra, your Fathers dead,
And what will you do now? How will you liue?
Son. As Birds do Mother.
Wife. What with Wormes, and Flyes?
Son. With what I get I meane, and so do they.
Wife. Poore Bird,
Thou'dst neuer Feare the Net, nor Lime,
The Pitfall, nor the Gin.
Son. Why should I Mother?
Poore Birds they are not set for:
My Father is not dead for all your saying.
Wife. Yes, he is dead:
How wilt thou do for a Father?
Son. Nay how will you do for a Husband?
Wife. Why I can buy me twenty at any Market.
Son. Then you'l by 'em to sell againe.
Wife. Thou speak'st withall thy wit,
And yet I'faith with wit enough for thee.
Son. Was my Father a Traitor, Mother?
Wife. I, that he was.
Son. What is a Traitor?
Wife. Why one that sweares, and lyes.
Son. And be all Traitors, that do so.
Wife. Euery one that do's so, is a Traitor,
And must be hang'd.
Son. And must they all be hang'd, that swear and lye?
Wife. Euery one.
Son. Who must hang them?
Wife. Why, the honest men.
Son. Then the Liars and Swearers are Fools: for there are Lyars and Swearers enow, to beate the honest men, and hang vp them.
Wife. Now God helpe thee, poore Monkie:
But how wilt thou do for a Father?
Son. If he were dead, youl'd weepe for him: if you would not, it were a good signe, that I should quickely haue a new Father.
Wife. Poore pratler, how thou talk'st?

Enter a Messenger.

Mes. Blesse you faire Dame: I am not to you known,
Though in your state of Honor I am perfect;
I doubt some danger do's approach you neerely.
If you will take a homely mans aduice,
Be not found heere: Hence with your little ones
To fright you thus. Me thinkes I am too sauage:
To do worse to you were fell Cruelty,
Which is too nie your person. Heauen preserue you,
I dare abide no longer. *Exit Messenger*
Wife. Whether should I flye?
I haue done no harme. But I remember now
I am in this earthly world: where to do harme
Is often laudable, to do good sometime
Accounted dangerous folly. Why then (alas)
Do I put vp that womanly defence,
To say I haue done no harme?
What are these faces?

Enter Murtherers.

Mur. Where is your Husband?
Wife. I hope in no place so vnsanctified,
Where such as thou may'st finde him.
Mur. He's a Traitor.
Son. Thou ly'st thou shagge-ear'd Villaine.
Mur. What you Egge?
Yong fry of Treachery?
Son. He ha's kill'd me Mother,
Run away I pray you. *Exit crying Murther.*

N n Scena

Scæna Tertia.

Enter Malcolme and Macduffe.

Mal. Let vs ſeeke out ſome deſolate ſhade, & there
Weepe our ſad boſomes empty.
Macd. Let vs rather
Hold faſt the mortall Sword: and like good men,
Beſtride our downfall Birthdome: each new Morne,
New Widdowes howle, new Orphans cry, new ſorowes
Strike heauen on the face, that it reſounds
As if it felt with Scotland, and yell'd out
Like Syllable of Dolour.
Mal. What I beleeue, Ile waile;
What know, beleeue; and what I can redreſſe,
As I ſhall finde the time to friend: I wil.
What you haue ſpoke, it may be ſo perchance.
This Tyrant, whoſe ſole name bliſters our tongues,
Was once thought honeſt: you haue lou'd him well,
He hath not touch'd you yet. I am yong, but ſomething
You may diſcerne of him through me, and wiſedome
To offer vp a weake, poore innocent Lambe
T'appeaſe an angry God.
Macd. I am not treacherous.
Malc. But *Macbeth* is.
A good and vertuous Nature may recoyle
In an Imperiall charge. But I ſhall craue your pardon:
That which you are, my thoughts cannot tranſpoſe;
Angels are bright ſtill, though the brighteſt fell.
Though all things foule, would wear the brows of grace
Yet Grace muſt ſtill looke ſo.
Macd. I haue loſt my Hopes.
Malc. Perchance euen there
Where I did finde my doubts.
Why in that rawneſſe left you Wife, and Childe?
Thoſe precious Motiues, thoſe ſtrong knots of Loue,
Without leaue-taking. I pray you,
Let not my Iealouſies, be your Diſhonors,
But mine owne Safeties: you may be rightly iuſt,
What euer I ſhall thinke.
Macd. Bleed, bleed poore Country,
Great Tyrrany, lay thou thy baſis ſure,
For goodneſſe dare not check thee: wear ỹ thy wrongs,
The Title, is affear'd. Far thee well Lord,
I would not be the Villaine that thou think'ſt,
For the whole Space that's in the Tyrants Graſpe,
And the rich Eaſt to boot.
Mal. Be not offended:
I ſpeake not as in abſolute feare of you:
I thinke our Country ſinkes beneath the yoake,
It weepes, it bleeds, and each new day a gaſh
Is added to her wounds. I thinke withall,
There would be hands vplifted in my right:
And heere from gracious England haue I offer
Of goodly thouſands. But for all this,
When I ſhall treade vpon the Tyrants head,
Or weare it on my Sword; yet my poore Country
Shall haue more vices then it had before,
More ſuffer, and more ſundry wayes then euer,
By him that ſhall ſucceede.
Macd. What ſhould he be?
Mal. It is my ſelfe I meane: in whom I know
All the particulars of Vice ſo grafted,
That when they ſhall be open'd, blacke *Macbeth*
Will ſeeme as pure as Snow, and the poore State
Eſteeme him as a Lambe, being compar'd
With my confineleſſe harmes.
Macd. Not in the Legions
Of horrid Hell, can come a Diuell more damn'd
In euils, to top *Macbeth*.
Mal. I grant him Bloody,
Luxurious, Auaricious, Falſe, Deceitfull,
Sodaine, Malicious, ſmacking of euery ſinne
That ha's a name. But there's no bottome, none
In my Voluptuouſneſſe: Your Wiues, your Daughters,
Your Matrons, and your Maides, could not fill vp
The Ceſterne of my Luſt, and my Deſire
All continent Impediments would ore-beare
That did oppoſe my will. Better *Macbeth*,
Then ſuch an one to reigne.
Macd. Boundleſſe intemperance
In Nature is a Tyranny: It hath beene
Th'vntimely emptying of the happy Throne,
And fall of many Kings. But feare not yet
To take vpon you what is yours: you may
Conuey your pleaſures in a ſpacious plenty,
And yet ſeeme cold. The time you may ſo hoodwinke:
We haue willing Dames enough: there cannot be
That Vulture in you, to deuoure ſo many
As will to Greatneſſe dedicate themſelues,
Finding it ſo inclinde.
Mal. With this, there growes
In my moſt ill-compos'd Affection, ſuch
A ſtancheleſſe Auarice, that were I King,
I ſhould cut off the Nobles for their Lands,
Deſire his Iewels, and this others Houſe,
And my more-hauing, would be as a Sawce
To make me hunger more, that I ſhould forge
Quarrels vniuſt againſt the Good and Loyall,
Deſtroying them for wealth.
Macd. This Auarice
ſtickes deeper: growes with more pernicious roote
Then Summer-ſeeming Luſt: and it hath bin
The Sword of our ſlaine Kings: yet do not feare,
Scotland hath Foyſons, to fill vp your will
Of your meere Owne. All theſe are portable,
With other Graces weigh'd.
Mal. But I haue none. The King-becoming Graces,
As Iuſtice, Verity, Temp'rance, Stableneſſe,
Bounty, Perſeuerance, Mercy, Lowlineſſe,
Deuotion, Patience, Courage, Fortitude,
I haue no relliſh of them, but abound
In the diuiſion of each ſeuerall Crime,
Acting it many wayes. Nay, had I powre, I ſhould
Poure the ſweet Milke of Concord, into Hell,
Vprore the vniuerſall peace, confound
All vnity on earth.
Macd. O Scotland, Scotland.
Mal. If ſuch a one be fit to gouerne, ſpeake:
I am as I haue ſpoken.
Mac. Fit to gouern? No not to liue. O Natiō miſerable!
With an vntitled Tyrant, bloody Sceptred,
When ſhalt thou ſee thy wholſome dayes againe?
Since that the trueſt Iſſue of thy Throne
By his owne Interdiction ſtands accuſt,
And do's blaſpheme his breed? Thy Royall Father
Was a moſt Sainted-King: the Queene that bore thee,
Oftner vpon her knees, then on her feet,
Dy'de euery day ſhe liu'd. Fare thee well,

These

These Euils thou repeat'st vpon thy selfe,
Hath banish'd me from Scotland. O my Brest,
Thy hope ends heere.
Mal. *Macduff*, this Noble passion
Childe of integrity, hath from my soule
Wip'd the blacke Scruples, reconcil'd my thoughts
To thy good Truth, and Honor. Diuellish *Macbeth*,
By many of these traines, hath sought to win me
Into his power : and modest Wisedome pluckes me
From ouer-credulous hast : but God aboue
Deale betweene thee and me; For euen now
I put my selfe to thy Direction, and
Vnspeake mine owne detraction. Heere abiure
The taints, and blames I laide vpon my selfe,
For strangers to my Nature. I am yet
Vnknowne to Woman, neuer was forsworne,
Scarsely haue coueted what was mine owne.
At no time broke my Faith, would not betray
The Deuill to his Fellow, and delight
No lesse in truth then life. My first false speaking
Was this vpon my selfe. What I am truly
Is thine, and my poore Countries to command :
Whither indeed, before they heere approach
Old *Seyward* with ten thousand warlike men
Already at a point, was setting foorth :
Now wee'l together, and the chance of goodnesse
Be like our warranted Quarrell. Why are you silent ?
Macd Such welcome, and vnwelcom things at once
'Tis hard to reconcile.

Enter a Doctor

Mal. Well, more anon. Comes the King forth
I pray you ?
Doct. I Sir : there are a crew of wretched Soules
That stay his Cure : their malady conuinces
The great assay of Art. But at his touch,
Such sanctity hath Heauen giuen his hand,
They presently amend. *Exit.*
Mal. I thanke you Doctor.
Macd. What's the Disease he meanes ?
Mal. 'Tis call'd the Euill.
A most myraculous worke in this good King,
Which often since my heere remaine in England,
I haue seene him do : How he solicites heauen
Himselfe best knowes: but strangely visited people
All swolne and Vlcerous, pittifull to the eye,
The meere dispaire of Surgery, he cures,
Hanging a golden stampe about their neckes,
Put on with holy Prayers, and 'tis spoken
To the succeeding Royalty he leaues
The healing Benediction. With this strange vertue,
He hath a heauenly guift of Prophesie,
And sundry Blessings hang about his Throne,
That speake him full of Grace.

Enter Rosse.

Macd. See who comes heere.
Malc. My Countryman : but yet I know him not
Macd. My euer gentle Cozen, welcome hither.
Malc. I know him now. Good God betimes remoue
The meanes that makes vs Strangers.
Rosse. Sir, Amen.
Macd. Stands Scotland where it did ?
Rosse. Alas poore Countrey,
Almost affraid to know it selfe. It cannot
Be call'd our Mother, but our Graue ; where nothing
But who knowes nothing, is once seene to smile:
Where sighes, and groanes, and shrieks that rent the ayre
Are made, not mark'd : Where violent sorrow seemes
A Moderne extasie : The Deadmans knell,
Is there scarse ask'd for who, and good mens liues
Expire before the Flowers in their Caps,
Dying, or ere they sicken.
Macd. Oh Relation; too nice, and yet too true.
Malc. What's the newest griefe ?
Rosse. That of an houres age, doth hisse the speaker,
Each minute teemes a new one.
Macd. How do's my Wife ?
Rosse. Why well.
Macd. And all my Children ?
Rosse. Well too.
Macd. The Tyrant ha's not batter'd at their peace ?
Rosse. No, they were wel at peace, when I did leaue 'em
Macd. Be not a niggard of your speech : How gos't ?
Rosse. When I came hither to transport the Tydings
Which I haue heauily borne, there ran a Rumour
Of many worthy Fellowes, that were out,
Which was to my beleefe witnest the rather,
For that I saw the Tyrants Power a-foot.
Now is the time of helpe : your eye in Scotland
Would create Soldiours, make our women fight,
To doffe their dire distresses.
Malc. Bee't their comfort
We are comming thither : Gracious England hath
Lent vs good *Seyward*, and ten thousand men,
An older, and a better Souldier, none
That Christendome giues out.
Rosse. Would I could answer
This comfort with the like. But I haue words
That would be howl'd out in the desert ayre,
Where hearing should not latch them.
Macd. What concerne they,
The generall cause, or is it a Fee-griefe
Due to some single brest ?
Rosse. No minde that's honest
But in it shares some woe, though the maine part
Pertaines to you alone.
Macd. If it be mine
Keepe it not from me, quickly let me haue it.
Rosse. Let not your eares dispise my tongue for euer,
Which shall possesse them with the heauiest sound
That euer yet they heard.
Macd. Humh : I guesse at it.
Rosse. Your Castle is surpriz'd : your Wife, and Babes
Sauagely slaughter'd : To relate the manner
Were on the Quarry of these murther'd Deere
To adde the death of you.
Malc. Mercifull Heauen :
What man, ne're pull your hat vpon your browes :
Giue sorrow words ; the griefe that do's not speake,
Whispers the o're-fraught heart, and bids it breake.
Macd. My Children too ?
Ro. Wife, Children, Seruants, all that could be found.
Macd. And I must be from thence? My wife kil'd too?
Rosse. I haue said.
Malc. Be comforted.
Let's make vs Med'cines of our great Reuenge,
To cure this deadly greefe.
Macd. He ha's no Children. All my pretty ones ?
Did you say All ? Oh Hell-Kite ! All ?
What, All my pretty Chickens, and their Damme
At one fell swoope ?
Malc. Dispute it like a man.
Macd. I shall do so :

Nn 2 But

But I muſt alſo feele it as a man;
I cannot but remember ſuch things were
That were moſt precious to me: Did heauen looke on,
And would not take their part? Sinfull *Macduff*,
They were all ſtrooke for thee: Naught that I am,
Not for their owne demerits, but for mine
Fell ſlaughter on their ſoules: Heauen reſt them now.

Mal. Be this the Whetſtone of your ſword, let griefe
Conuert to anger: blunt not the heart, enrage it.

Macd. O I could play the woman with mine eyes,
And Braggart with my tongue. But gentle Heauens,
Cut ſhort all intermiſſion: Front to Front,
Bring thou this Fiend of Scotland, and my ſelfe
Within my Swords length ſet him, if he ſcape
Heauen forgiue him too.

Mal. This time goes manly:
Come go we to the King, our Power is ready,
Our lacke is nothing but our leaue. *Macbeth*
Is ripe for ſhaking, and the Powres aboue
Put on their inſtruments: Receiue what cheere you may,
The Night is long, that neuer findes the Day. *Exeunt*

Actus Quintus. Scena Prima.

Enter a Doctor of Phyſicke, and a Wayting Gentlewoman.

Doct. I haue too Nights watch'd with you, but can perceiue no truth in your report. When was it ſhee laſt walk'd?

Gent. Since his Maieſty went into the Field, I haue ſeene her riſe from her bed, throw her Night-Gown vppon her, vnlocke her Cloſſet, take foorth paper, folde it, write vpon't, read it, afterwards Seale it, and againe returne to bed; yet all this while in a moſt faſt ſleepe.

Doct. A great perturbation in Nature, to receyue at once the benefit of ſleep, and do the effects of watching. In this ſlumbry agitation, beſides her walking, and other actuall performances, what (at any time) haue you heard her ſay?

Gent. That Sir, which I will not report after her.

Doct. You may to me, and 'tis moſt meet you ſhould.

Gent. Neither to you, nor any one, hauing no witneſſe to confirme my ſpeech. *Enter Lady, with a Taper.*
Lo you, heere ſhe comes: This is her very guiſe, and vpon my life faſt aſleepe: obſerue her, ſtand cloſe.

Doct. How came ſhe by that light?

Gent. Why it ſtood by her: ſhe ha's light by her continually, 'tis her command.

Doct. You ſee her eyes are open.

Gent. I but their ſenſe are ſhut.

Doct. What is it ſhe do's now?
Looke how ſhe rubbes her hands.

Gent. It is an accuſtom'd action with her, to ſeeme thus waſhing her hands: I haue knowne her continue in this a quarter of an houre.

Lad. Yet heere's a ſpot.

Doct. Heark, ſhe ſpeaks, I will ſet downe what comes from her, to ſatisfie my remembrance the more ſtrongly.

La. Out damned ſpot: out I ſay. One: Two: Why then 'tis time to doo't: Hell is murky. Fye, my Lord, fie, a Souldier, and affear'd? what need we feare? who knowes it, when none can call our powre to accompt: yet who would haue thought the olde man to haue had ſo much blood in him.

Doct. Do you marke that?

Lad. The Thane of Fife, had a wife: where is ſhe now? What will theſe hands ne're be cleane? No more o'that my Lord, no more o'that: you marre all with this ſtarting.

Doct. Go too, go too:
You haue knowne what you ſhould not.

Gent. She ha's ſpoke what ſhee ſhould not, I am ſure of that: Heauen knowes what ſhe ha's knowne.

La. Heere's the ſmell of the blood ſtill: all the perfumes of Arabia will not ſweeten this little hand. Oh, oh, oh.

Doct. What a ſigh is there? The hart is ſorely charg'd.

Gent. I would not haue ſuch a heart in my boſome, for the dignity of the whole body.

Doct. Well, well, well.

Gent. Pray God it be ſir.

Doct. This diſeaſe is beyond my practiſe: yet I haue knowne thoſe which haue walkt in their ſleep, who haue dyed holily in their beds.

Lad. Waſh your hands, put on your Night-Gowne, looke not ſo pale: I tell you yet againe *Banquo's* buried; he cannot come out on's graue.

Doct. Euen ſo?

Lady. To bed, to bed: there's knocking at the gate: Come, come, come, come, giue me your hand: What's done, cannot be vndone. To bed, to bed, to bed. *Exit Lady.*

Doct. Will ſhe go now to bed?

Gent. Directly.

Doct. Foule whiſp'rings are abroad: vnnaturall deeds
Do breed vnnaturall troubles: infected mindes
To their deafe pillowes will diſcharge their Secrets:
More needs ſhe the Diuine, then the Phyſitian:
God, God forgiue vs all. Looke after her,
Remoue from her the meanes of all annoyance,
And ſtill keepe eyes vpon her: So goodnight,
My minde ſhe ha's mated, and amaz'd my ſight.
I thinke, but dare not ſpeake.

Gent. Good night good Doctor. *Exeunt.*

Scena Secunda.

Drum and Colours. Enter Menteth, Cathnes, Angus, Lenox, Soldiers.

Ment. The Engliſh powre is neere, led on by *Malcolm*,
His Vnkle *Seyward*, and the good *Macduff*.
Reuenges burne in them: for their deere cauſes
Would to the bleeding, and the grim Alarme
Excite the mortified man.

Ang. Neere Byrnan wood
Shall we well meet them, that way are they comming.

Cath. Who knowes if *Donalbane* be with his brother?

Len. For certaine Sir, he is not: I haue a File
Of all the Gentry; there is *Seywards* Sonne,
And many vnruffe youths, that euen now
Proteſt their firſt of Manhood.

Ment. What do's the Tyrant.

Cath. Great Dunſinane he ſtrongly Fortifies:
Some ſay hee's mad: Others, that leſſer hate him,
Do call it valiant Fury, but for certaine

He

He cannot buckle his distemper'd cause
Within the belt of Rule.
Ang. Now do's he feele
His secret Murthers sticking on his hands,
Now minutely Reuolts vpbraid his Faith-breach:
Those he commands, moue onely in command,
Nothing in loue: Now do's he feele his Title
Hang loose about him, like a Giants Robe
Vpon a dwarfish Theefe.
Ment. Who then shall blame
His pester'd Senses to recoyle, and start,
When all that is within him, do's condemne
It selfe, for being there.
Cath. Well, march we on,
To giue Obedience, where 'tis truly ow'd:
Meet we the Med'cine of the sickly Weale,
And with him poure we in our Countries purge,
Each drop of vs.
Lenox. Or so much as it needes,
To dew the Soueraigne Flower, and drowne the Weeds:
Make we our March towards Birnan. *Exeunt marching.*

Scæna Tertia.

Enter Macbeth, Doctor, and Attendants.

Macb. Bring me no more Reports, let them flye all:
Till Byrnane wood remoue to Dunsinane,
I cannot taint with Feare. What's the Boy *Malcolme*?
Was he not borne of woman? The Spirits that know
All mortall Consequences, haue pronounc'd me thus:
Feare not *Macbeth*, no man that's borne of woman
Shall ere haue power vpon thee. Then fly false Thanes,
And mingle with the English Epicures,
The minde I sway by, and the heart I beare,
Shall neuer sagge with doubt, nor shake with feare.
Enter Seruant.
The diuell damne thee blacke, thou cream-fac'd Loone:
Where got'st thou that Goose-looke.
Ser. There is ten thousand.
Macb. Geese Villaine?
Ser. Souldiers Sir.
Macb. Go pricke thy face, and ouer-red thy feare
Thou Lilly-liuer'd Boy. What Soldiers, Patch?
Death of thy Soule, those Linnen cheekes of thine
Are Counsailers to feare. What Soldiers Whay-face?
Ser. The English Force, so please you.
Macb. Take thy face hence. *Seyton*, I am sick at hart,
When I behold: *Seyton*, I say, this push
Will cheere me euer, or dis-eate me now.
I haue liu'd long enough: my way of life
Is falne into the Seare, the yellow Leafe,
And that which should accompany Old-Age,
As Honor, Loue, Obedience, Troopes of Friends,
I must not looke to haue: but in their steed,
Curses, not lowd but deepe, Mouth-honor, breath
Which the poore heart would faine deny, and dare not.
Seyton?
Enter Seyton.
Ser. What's your gracious pleasure?
Macb. What Newes more?
Sey. All is confirm'd my Lord, which was reported.
Macb. Ile fight, till from my bones, my flesh be hackt.
Giue me my Armor.
Seyt. 'Tis not needed yet.
Macb. Ile put it on:
Send out moe Horses, skirre the Country round,
Hang those that talke of Feare. Giue me mine Armor:
How do's your Patient, Doctor?
Doct. Not so sicke my Lord,
As she is troubled with thicke-comming Fancies
That keepe her from her rest.
Macb. Cure of that:
Can'st thou not Minister to a minde diseas'd,
Plucke from the Memory a rooted Sorrow,
Raze out the written troubles of the Braine,
And with some sweet Obliuious Antidote
Cleanse the stufft bosome, of that perillous stuffe
Which weighes vpon the heart?
Doct. Therein the Patient
Must minister to himselfe.
Macb. Throw Physicke to the Dogs, Ile none of it.
Come, put mine Armour on: giue me my Staffe:
Seyton, send out: Doctor, the Thanes flye from me:
Come sir, dispatch. If thou could'st Doctor, cast
The Water of my Land, finde her Disease,
And purge it to a sound and pristiue Health,
I would applaud thee to the very Eccho,
That should applaud againe. Pull't off I say,
What Rubarb, Cyme, or what Purgatiue drugge
Would scowre these English hence: hear'st ỹ of them?
Doct. I my good Lord: your Royall Preparation
Makes vs heare something.
Macb. Bring it after me:
I will not be affraid of Death and Bane,
Till Birnane Forrest come to Dunsinane.
Doct. Were I from Dunsinane away, and cleere,
Profit againe should hardly draw me heere. *Exeunt*

Scena Quarta.

Drum and Colours. Enter Malcolme, Seyward, Macduffe, Seywards Sonne, Menteth, Cathnes, Angus, and Soldiers Marching.

Malc. Cosins, I hope the dayes are neere at hand
That Chambers will be safe.
Ment. We doubt it nothing.
Syew. What wood is this before vs?
Ment. The wood of Birnane.
Malc. Let euery Souldier hew him downe a Bough,
And bear't before him, thereby shall we shadow
The numbers of our Hoast, and make discouery
Erre in report of vs.
Sold. It shall be done.
Syw. We learne no other, but the confident Tyrant
Keepes still in Dunsinane, and will indure
Our setting downe befor't.
Malc. 'Tis his maine hope:
For where there is aduantage to be giuen,
Both more and lesse haue giuen him the Reuolt,
And none serue with him, but constrained things,
Whose hearts are absent too.
Macd. Let our iust Censures
Attend the true euent, and put we on

nn 2 Industrious

Industrious Souldiership.
Sey. The time approaches,
That will with due decision make vs know
What we shall say we haue, and what we owe:
Thoughts speculatiue, their vnsure hopes relate,
But certaine issue, stroakes must arbitrate,
Towards which, aduance the warre. *Exeunt marching*

Scena Quinta.

Enter Macbeth, Seyton, & Souldiers, with Drum and Colours.

Macb. Hang out our Banners on the outward walls,
The Cry is still, they come: our Castles strength
Will laugh a Siedge to scorne: Heere let them lye,
Till Famine and the Ague eate them vp:
Were they not forc'd with those that should be ours,
We might haue met them dareful, beard to beard,
And beate them backward home. What is that noyse?
A Cry within of Women.
Sey. It is the cry of women, my good Lord.
Macb. I haue almost forgot the taste of Feares:
The time ha's beene, my sences would haue cool'd
To heare a Night-shrieke, and my Fell of haire
Would at a dismall Treatise rowze, and stirre
As life were in't. I haue supt full with horrors,
Direnesse familiar to my slaughterous thoughts
Cannot once start me. Wherefore was that cry?
Sey. The Queene (my Lord) is dead.
Macb. She should haue dy'de heereafter;
There would haue beene a time for such a word:
To morrow, and to morrow, and to morrow,
Creepes in this petty pace from day to day,
To the last Syllable of Recorded time:
And all our yesterdayes, haue lighted Fooles
The way to dusty death. Out, out, breefe Candle,
Life's but a walking Shadow, a poore Player,
That struts and frets his houre vpon the Stage,
And then is heard no more. It is a Tale
Told by an Ideot, full of sound and fury
Signifying nothing. *Enter a Messenger.*
Thou com'st to vse thy Tongue: thy Story quickly.
Mes. Gracious my Lord,
I should report that which I say I saw,
But know not how to doo't.
Macb. Well, say sir.
Mes. As I did stand my watch vpon the Hill
I look'd toward Byrnane, and anon me thought
The Wood began to moue.
Macb. Lyar, and Slaue.
Mes. Let me endure your wrath, if't be not so:
Within this three Mile may you see it comming.
I say, a mouing Groue.
Macb. If thou speak'st false,
Vpon the next Tree shall thou hang aliue
Till Famine cling thee: If thy speech be sooth,
I care not if thou dost for me as much.
I pull in Resolution, and begin
To doubt th'Equiuocation of the Fiend,
That lies like truth. Feare not, till Byrnane Wood
Do come to Dunsinane, and now a Wood
Comes toward Dunsinane. Arme, Arme, and out,
If this which he auouches, do's appeare,
There is nor flying hence, nor tarrying here.
I'ginne to be a-weary of the Sun,
And wish th'estate o'th' world were now vndon.
Ring the Alarum Bell, blow Winde, come wracke,
At least wee'l dye with Harnesse on our backe. *Exeunt*

Scena Sexta.

Drumme and Colours.
Enter Malcolme, Seyward, Macduffe, and their Army, with Boughes.

Mal. Now neere enough:
Your leauy Skreenes throw downe,
And shew like those you are: You (worthy Vnkle)
Shall with my Cosin your right Noble Sonne
Leade our first Battell. Worthy *Macduffe*, and wee
Shall take vpon's what else remaines to do,
According to our order.
Sey. Fare you well:
Do we but finde the Tyrants power to night,
Let vs be beaten, if we cannot fight.
Macd. Make all our Trumpets speak, giue the all breath
Those clamorous Harbingers of Blood, & Death. *Exeunt*
Alarums continued.

Scena Septima.

Enter Macbeth.

Macb. They haue tied me to a stake, I cannot flye,
But Beare-like I must fight the course. What's he
That was not borne of Woman? Such a one
Am I to feare, or none.
Enter young Seyward.
Y. Sey. What is thy name?
Macb. Thou'lt be affraid to heare it.
Y. Sey. No: though thou call'st thy selfe a hoter name
Then any is in hell.
Macb. My name's *Macbeth.*
Y. Sey. The diuell himselfe could not pronounce a Title
More hatefull to mine eare.
Macb. No: nor more fearefull.
Y. Sey. Thou lyest abhorred Tyrant, with my Sword
Ile proue the lye thou speak'st.
Fight, and young Seyward slaine.
Macb. Thou was't borne of woman;
But Swords I smile at, Weapons laugh to scorne,
Brandish'd by man that's of a Woman borne. *Exit.*
Alarums. Enter Macduffe.
Macd. That way the noise is: Tyrant shew thy face,
If thou beest slaine, and with no stroake of mine,
My Wife and Childrens Ghosts will haunt me still:
I cannot strike at wretched Kernes, whose armes
Are hyr'd to beare their Staues; either thou *Macbeth*,
Or else my Sword with an vnbattered edge
I sheath againe vndeeded. There thou should'st be,
By this great clatter, one of greatest note
Seemes

Seemes bruited. Let me finde him Fortune,
And more I begge not. *Exit.* *Alarums.*

Enter Malcolme and Seyward.

Sey. This way my Lord, the Caſtles gently rendred:
The Tyrants people, on both ſides do fight,
The Noble Thanes do brauely in the Warre,
The day almoſt it ſelfe profeſſes yours,
And little is to do.
Malc. We haue met with Foes
That ſtrike beſide vs.
Sey. Enter Sir, the Caſtle. *Exeunt.* *Alarum*

Enter Macbeth.

Macb. Why ſhould I play the Roman Foole, and dye
On mine owne ſword? whiles I ſee liues, the gaſhes
Do better vpon them.

Enter Macduffe.

Macd. Turne Hell-hound, turne.
Macb. Of all men elſe I haue auoyded thee:
But get thee backe, my ſoule is too much charg'd
With blood of thine already.
Macd. I haue no words,
My voice is in my Sword, thou bloodier Villaine
Then tearmes can giue thee out. *Fight: Alarum*
Macb. Thou looſeſt labour,
As eaſie may'ſt thou the intrenchant Ayre
With thy keene Sword impreſſe, as make me bleed:
Let fall thy blade on vulnerable Creſts,
I beare a charmed Life, which muſt not yeeld
To one of woman borne.
Macd. Diſpaire thy Charme,
And let the Angell whom thou ſtill haſt ſeru'd
Tell thee, *Macduffe* was from his Mothers womb
Vntimely ript.
Macb. Accurſed be that tongue that tels mee ſo;
For it hath Cow'd my better part of man:
And be theſe Iugling Fiends no more beleeu'd,
That palter with vs in a double ſence,
That keepe the word of promiſe to our eare,
And breake it to our hope. Ile not fight with thee.
Macd. Then yeeld thee Coward,
And liue to be the ſhew, and gaze o'th' time.
Wee'l haue thee, as our rarer Monſters are
Painted vpon a pole, and vnder-writ,
Heere may you ſee the Tyrant.
Macb. I will not yeeld
To kiſſe the ground before young *Malcolmes* feet,
And to be baited with the Rabbles curſe.
Though Byrnane wood be come to Dunſinane,
And thou oppos'd, being of no woman borne,
Yet I will try the laſt. Before my body,
I throw my warlike Shield: Lay on *Macduffe*,
And damn'd be him, that firſt cries hold, enough.
Exeunt fighting. *Alarums.*

Enter Fighting, and Macbeth ſlaine.

Retreat, and Flouriſh. Enter with Drumme and Colours, Malcolm, Seyward, Roſſe, Thanes, & Soldiers.

Mal. I would the Friends we miſſe, were ſafe arriu'd.
Sey. Some muſt go off: and yet by theſe I ſee,
So great a day as this is cheapely bought.
Mal. *Macduffe* is miſſing, and your Noble Sonne.
Roſſe Your ſon my Lord, ha's paid a ſouldiers debt,
He onely liu'd but till he was a man,
The which no ſooner had his Proweſſe confirm'd
In the vnſhrinking ſtation where he fought,
But like a man he dy'de.
Sey. Then he is dead?
Roſſe. I, and brought off the field: your cauſe of ſorrow
Muſt not be meaſur'd by his worth, for then
It hath no end.
Sey. Had he his hurts before?
Roſſe. I, on the Front.
Sey. Why then, Gods Soldier be he:
Had I as many Sonnes, as I haue haires,
I would not wiſh them to a fairer death:
And ſo his Knell is knoll'd.
Mal. Hee's worth more ſorrow,
And that Ile ſpend for him.
Sey. He's worth no more,
They ſay he parted well, and paid his ſcore,
And ſo God be with him. Here comes newer comfort.

Enter Macduffe, with Macbeths head.

Macd. Haile King, for ſo thou art.
Behold where ſtands
Th' Vſurpers curſed head: the time is free:
I ſee thee compaſt with thy Kingdomes Pearle,
That ſpeake my ſalutation in their minds:
Whoſe voyces I deſire alowd with mine.
Haile King of Scotland.
All. Haile King of Scotland. *Flouriſh.*
Mal. We ſhall not ſpend a large expence of time,
Before we reckon with your ſeuerall loues,
And make vs euen with you. My Thanes and Kinſmen
Henceforth be Earles, the firſt that euer Scotland
In ſuch an Honor nam'd: What's more to do,
Which would be planted newly with the time,
As calling home our exil'd Friends abroad,
That fled the Snares of watchfull Tyranny,
Producing forth the cruell Miniſters
Of this dead Butcher, and his Fiend-like Queene;
Who (as 'tis thought) by ſelfe and violent hands,
Tooke off her life. This, and what needfull elſe
That call's vpon vs, by the Grace of Grace,
We will performe in meaſure, time, and place:
So thankes to all at once, and to each one,
Whom we inuite, to ſee vs Crown'd at Scone.
Flouriſh. *Exeunt Omnes.*

FINIS.

THE TRAGEDIE OF HAMLET, Prince of Denmarke.

Actus Primus. Scœna Prima.

Enter Barnardo and Franciſco two Centinels.

Barnardo.

WHo's there?
Fran. Nay anſwer me: Stand & vnfold your ſelfe.
Bar. Long liue the King.
Fran. *Barnardo?*
Bar. He.
Fran. You come moſt carefully vpon your houre.
Bar. 'Tis now ſtrook twelue, get thee to bed *Franciſco.*
Fran. For this releefe much thankes: 'Tis bitter cold,
And I am ſicke at heart.
Barn. Haue you had quiet Guard?
Fran. Not a Mouſe ſtirring.
Barn. Well, goodnight. If you do meet *Horatio* and
Marcellus, the Riuals of my Watch, bid them make haſt.

Enter Horatio and Marcellus.

Fran. I thinke I heare them. Stand: who's there?
Hor. Friends to this ground.
Mar. And Leige-men to the Dane.
Fran. Giue you good night.
Mar. O farwel honeſt Soldier, who hath relieu'd you?
Fra. *Barnardo* ha's my place: giue you goodnight.

Exit Fran.

Mar. Holla *Barnardo.*
Bar. Say, what is *Horatio* there?
Hor. A peece of him.
Bar. Welcome *Horatio*, welcome good *Marcellus.*
Mar. What, ha's this thing appear'd againe to night.
Bar. I haue ſeene nothing.
Mar. *Horatio* ſaies, 'tis but our Fantaſie,
And will not let beleefe take hold of him
Touching this dreaded ſight, twice ſeene of vs,
Therefore I haue intreated him along
With vs, to watch the minutes of this Night,
That if againe this Apparition come,
He may approue our eyes, and ſpeake to it.
Hor. Tuſh, tuſh, 'twill not appeare.
Bar. Sit downe a-while,
And let vs once againe aſſaile your eares,
That are ſo fortified againſt our Story,
What we two Nights haue ſeene.
Hor. Well, ſit we downe,
And let vs heare *Barnardo* ſpeake of this.
Barn. Laſt night of all,
When yond ſame Starre that's Weſtward from the Pole
Had made his courſe t'illume that part of Heauen
Where now it burnes, *Marcellus* and my ſelfe,
The Bell then beating one.
Mar. Peace, breake thee of: *Enter the Ghoſt.*
Looke where it comes againe.
Barn. In the ſame figure, like the King that's dead.
Mar. Thou art a Scholler; ſpeake to it *Horatio.*
Barn. Lookes it not like the King? Marke it *Horatio.*
Hora. Moſt like: It harrowes me with fear & wonde
Barn. It would be ſpoke too.
Mar. Queſtion it *Horatio.*
Hor. What art thou that vſurp'ſt this time of night,
Together with that Faire and Warlike forme
In which the Maieſty of buried Denmarke
Did ſometimes march: By Heauen I charge thee ſpeake.
Mar. It is offended.
Barn. See, it ſtalkes away.
Hor. Stay: ſpeake; ſpeake: I Charge thee, ſpeake.

Exit the Ghoſt.

Mar. 'Tis gone, and will not anſwer.
Barn. How now *Horatio*? You tremble & look pale:
Is not this ſomething more then Fantaſie?
What thinke you on't?
Hor. Before my God, I might not this beleeue
Without the ſenſible and true auouch
Of mine owne eyes.
Mar. Is it not like the King?
Hor. As thou art to thy ſelfe,
Such was the very Armour he had on,
When th'Ambitious Norwey combatted:
So frown'd he once, when in an angry parle
He ſmot the ſledded Pollax on the Ice.
'Tis ſtrange.
Mar. Thus twice before, and iuſt at this dead houre,
With Martiall ſtalke, hath he gone by our Watch.
Hor. In what particular thought to work, I know not:
But in the groſſe and ſcope of my Opinion,
This boades ſome ſtrange erruption to our State.
Mar. Good now ſit downe, & tell me he that knowes
Why this ſame ſtrict and moſt obſeruant Watch,
So nightly toyles the ſubiect of the Land,
And why ſuch dayly Caſt of Brazon Cannon
And Forraigne Mart for Implements of warre:
Why ſuch impreſſe of Ship-wrights, whoſe ſore Taſke
Do's not diuide the Sunday from the weeke,
What might be toward, that this ſweaty haſt
Doth make the Night ioynt-Labourer with the day:
Who is't that can informe m
Hor. That can I,

At

At leaſt the whiſper goes ſo: Our laſt King,
Whoſe Image euen but now appear'd to vs,
Was (as you know) by *Fortinbras* of Norway,
(Thereto prick'd on by a moſt emulate Pride)
Dar'd to the Combate. In which, our Valiant *Hamlet*,
(For ſo this ſide of our knowne world eſteem'd him)
Did ſlay this *Fortinbras*: who by a Seal'd Compact,
Well ratified by Law, and Heraldrie,
Did forfeite (with his life) all thoſe his Lands
Which he ſtood ſeiz'd on, to the Conqueror:
Againſt the which, a Moity competent
Was gaged by our King: which had return'd
To the Inheritance of *Fortinbras*,
Had he bin Vanquiſher, as by the ſame Cou'nant
And carriage of the Article deſigne,
His fell to *Hamlet*. Now ſir, young *Fortinbras*,
Of vnimproued Mettle, hot and full,
Hath in the skirts of Norway, heere and there,
Shark'd vp a Liſt of Landleſſe Reſolutes,
For Foode and Diet, to ſome Enterprize
That hath a ſtomacke in't: which is no other
(And it doth well appeare vnto our State)
But to recouer of vs by ſtrong hand
And termes Compulſatiue, thoſe foreſaid Lands
So by his Father loſt: and this (I take it)
Is the maine Motiue of our Preparations,
The Sourſe of this our Watch, and the cheefe head
Of this poſt-haſt, and Romage in the Land.
Enter Ghoſt againe.
But ſoft, behold: Loe, where it comes againe:
Ile croſſe it, though it blaſt me. Stay Illuſion:
If thou haſt any ſound, or vſe of Voyce,
Speake to me. If there be any good thing to be done,
That may to thee do eaſe, and grace to me; ſpeak to me.
If thou art priuy to thy Countries Fate
(Which happily foreknowing may auoyd) Oh ſpeake.
Or, if thou haſt vp-hoorded in thy life
Extorted Treaſure in the wombe of Earth,
(For which, they ſay, you Spirits oft walke in death)
Speake of it. Stay, and ſpeake. Stop it *Marcellus*.
Mar. Shall I ſtrike at it with my Partizan?
Hor. Do, if it will not ſtand.
Barn. 'Tis heere.
Hor. 'Tis heere.
Mar. 'Tis gone. *Exit Ghoſt.*
We do it wrong, being ſo Maieſticall
To offer it the ſhew of Violence,
For it is as the Ayre, invulnerable,
And our vaine blowes, malicious Mockery.
Barn. It was about to ſpeake, when the Cocke crew.
Hor. And then it ſtarted, like a guilty thing
Vpon a fearfull Summons. I haue heard,
The Cocke that is the Trumpet to the day,
Doth with his lofty and ſhrill-ſounding Throate
Awake the God of Day: and at his warning,
Whether in Sea, or Fire, in Earth, or Ayre,
Th'extrauagant, and erring Spirit, hyes
To his Confine. And of the truth heerein,
This preſent Obiect made probation.
Mar. It faded on the crowing of the Cocke.
Some ſayes, that euer 'gainſt that Seaſon comes
Wherein our Sauiours Birth is celebrated,
The Bird of Dawning ſingeth all night long:
And then (they ſay) no Spirit can walke abroad,
The nights are wholſome, then no Planets ſtrike,
No Faiery talkes, nor Witch hath power to Charme:
So hallow'd, and ſo gracious is the time.
Hor. So haue I heard, and do in part beleeue it.
But looke, the Morne in Ruſſet mantle clad,
Walkes o're the dew of yon high Eaſterne Hill,
Breake we our Watch vp, and by my aduice
Let vs impart what we haue ſeene to night
Vnto yong *Hamlet*. For vpon my life,
This Spirit dumbe to vs, will ſpeake to him:
Do you conſent we ſhall acquaint him with it,
As needfull in our Loues, fitting our Duty?
Mar. Let do't I pray, and I this morning know
Where we ſhall finde him moſt conueniently. *Exeunt*

Scena Secunda.

Enter Claudius King of Denmarke, Gertrude the Queene, Hamlet, Polonius, Laertes, and his Siſter Ophelia, Lords Attendant.

King. Though yet of *Hamlet* our deere Brothers death
The memory be greene: and that it vs befitted
To beare our hearts in greefe, and our whole Kingdome
To be contracted in one brow of woe:
Yet ſo farre hath Diſcretion fought with Nature,
That we with wiſeſt ſorrow thinke on him,
Together with remembrance of our ſelues.
Therefore our ſometimes Siſter, now our Queen,
Th'Imperiall Ioyntreſſe of this warlike State,
Haue we, as 'twere, with a defeated ioy,
With one Auſpicious, and one Dropping eye,
With mirth in Funerall, and with Dirge in Marriage,
In equall Scale weighing Delight and Dole
Taken to Wife; nor haue we heerein barr'd
Your better Wiſedomes, which haue freely gone
With this affaire along, for all our Thankes.
Now followes, that you know young *Fortinbras*,
Holding a weake ſuppoſall of our worth;
Or thinking by our late deere Brothers death,
Our State to be diſioynt, and out of Frame,
Colleagued with the dreame of his Aduantage;
He hath not fayl'd to peſter vs with Meſſage,
Importing the ſurrender of thoſe Lands
Loſt by his Father: with all Bonds of Law
To our moſt valiant Brother. So much for him.
Enter Voltemand and Cornelius.
Now for our ſelfe, and for this time of meeting
Thus much the buſineſſe is. We haue heere writ
To Norway, Vncle of young *Fortinbras*,
Who Impotent and Bedrid, ſcarſely heares
Of this his Nephewes purpoſe, to ſuppreſſe
His further gate heerein. In that the Leuies,
The Liſts, and full proportions are all made
Out of his ſubiect: and we heere diſpatch
You good *Cornelius*, and you *Voltemand*,
For bearing of this greeting to old Norway,
Giuing to you no further perſonall power
To buſineſſe with the King, more then the ſcope
Of theſe dilated Articles allow:
Farewell and let your haſt commend your duty.
Volt. In that, and all things, will we ſhew our duty.
King. We doubt it nothing, heartily farewell.
Exit Voltemand and Cornelius
And now *Laertes*, what's the newes with you?

You

You told vs of ſome ſuite. What is't *Laertes*?
You cannot ſpeake of Reaſon to the Dane,
And looſe your voyce. What would'ſt thou beg *Laertes*,
That ſhall not be my Offer, not thy Asking?
The Head is not more Natiue to the Heart,
The Hand more Inſtrumentall to the Mouth,
Then is the Throne of Denmarke to thy Father.
What would'ſt thou haue *Laertes*?
Laer. Dread my Lord,
Your leaue and fauour to returne to France,
From whence, though willingly I came to Denmarke
To ſhew my duty in your Coronation,
Yet now I muſt confeſſe, that duty done,
My thoughts and wiſhes bend againe towards France,
And bow them to your gracious leaue and pardon.
King. Haue you your Fathers leaue?
What ſayes *Pollonius*?
Pol. He hath my Lord:
I do beſeech you giue him leaue to go.
King. Take thy faire houre *Laertes*, time be thine,
And thy beſt graces ſpend it at thy will:
But now my Coſin *Hamlet*, and my Sonne?
Ham. A little more then kin, and leſſe then kinde.
King. How is it that the Clouds ſtill hang on you?
Ham. Not ſo my Lord, I am too much i'th'Sun.
Queen. Good *Hamlet* caſt thy nightly colour off,
And let thine eye looke like a Friend on Denmarke.
Do not for euer with thy veyled lids
Seeke for thy Noble Father in the duſt;
Thou know'ſt 'tis common, all that liues muſt dye,
Paſſing through Nature, to Eternity.
Ham. I Madam, it is common.
Queen. If it be;
Why ſeemes it ſo particular with thee.
Ham. Seemes Madam? Nay, it is: I know not Seemes:
'Tis not alone my Inky Cloake (good Mother)
Nor Customary ſuites of ſolemne Blacke,
Nor windy ſuſpiration of forc'd breath,
No, nor the fruitfull Riuer in the Eye,
Nor the deiected hauiour of the Viſage,
Together with all Formes, Moods, ſhewes of Griefe,
That can denote me truly. Theſe indeed Seeme,
For they are actions that a man might play:
But I haue that Within, which paſſeth ſhow;
Theſe, but the Trappings, and the Suites of woe.
King. 'Tis ſweet and commendable
In your Nature *Hamlet*,
To giue theſe mourning duties to your Father:
But you muſt know, your Father loſt a Father,
That Father loſt, loſt his, and the Suruiuer bound
In filiall Obligation, for ſome terme
To do obſequious Sorrow. But to perſeuer
In obſtinate Condolement, is a courſe
Of impious ſtubbornneſſe. 'Tis vnmanly greefe,
It ſhewes a will moſt incorrect to Heauen,
A Heart vnfortified, a Minde impatient,
An Vnderſtanding ſimple, and vnſchool'd:
For, what we know muſt be, and is as common
As any the moſt vulgar thing to ſence,
Why ſhould we in our peeuiſh Oppoſition
Take it to heart? Fye, 'tis a fault to Heauen,
A fault againſt the Dead, a fault to Nature,
To Reaſon moſt abſurd, whoſe common Theame
Is death of Fathers, and who ſtill hath cried,
From the firſt Coarſe, till he that dyed to day,
This muſt be ſo. We pray you throw to earth
This vnpreuayling woe, and thinke of vs
As of a Father; For let the world take note,
You are the moſt immediate to our Throne,
And with no leſſe Nobility of Loue,
Then that which deereſt Father beares his Sonne,
Do I impart towards you. For your intent
In going backe to Schoole in Wittenberg,
It is moſt retrograde to our deſire:
And we beſeech you, bend you to remaine
Heere in the cheere and comfort of our eye,
Our cheefeſt Courtier Coſin, and our Sonne.
Qu. Let not thy Mother loſe her Prayers *Hamlet*:
I prythee ſtay with vs, go not to Wittenberg.
Ham. I ſhall in all my beſt
Obey you Madam.
King. Why 'tis a louing, and a faire Reply,
Be as our ſelfe in Denmarke. Madam come,
This gentle and vnforc'd accord of *Hamlet*
Sits ſmiling to my heart; in grace whereof,
No iocond health that Denmarke drinkes to day,
But the great Cannon to the Clowds ſhall tell,
And the Kings Rouce, the Heauens ſhall bruite againe,
Reſpeaking earthly Thunder. Come away. *Exeunt*

Manet Hamlet.

Ham. Oh that this too too ſolid Fleſh, would melt,
Thaw, and reſolue it ſelfe into a Dew:
Or that the Euerlaſting had not fixt
His Cannon 'gainſt Selfe-ſlaughter. O God, O God!
How weary, ſtale, flat, and vnprofitable
Seemes to me all the vſes of this world?
Fie on't? Oh fie, fie, 'tis an vnweeded Garden
That growes to Seed: Things rank, and groſſe in Nature
Poſſeſſe it meerely. That it ſhould come to this:
But two months dead: Nay, not ſo much; not two,
So excellent a King, that was to this
Hiperion to a Satyre: ſo louing to my Mother,
That he might not beteene the windes of heauen
Viſit her face too roughly. Heauen and Earth
Muſt I remember: why ſhe would hang on him,
As if encreaſe of Appetite had growne
By what it fed on; and yet within a month?
Let me not thinke on't: Frailty, thy name is woman.
A little Month, or ere thoſe ſhooes were old,
With which ſhe followed my poore Fathers body
Like *Niobe*, all teares. Why ſhe, euen ſhe.
(O Heauen! A beaſt that wants diſcourſe of Reaſon
Would haue mourn'd longer) married with mine Vnkle,
My Fathers Brother: but no more like my Father,
Then I to *Hercules*. Within a Moneth?
Ere yet the ſalt of moſt vnrighteous Teares
Had left the fluſhing of her gauled eyes,
She married. O moſt wicked ſpeed, to poſt
With ſuch dexterity to Inceſtuous ſheets:
It is not, nor it cannot come to good.
But breake my heart, for I muſt hold my tongue.

Enter Horatio, Barnard, and Marcellus.

Hor. Haile to your Lordſhip.
Ham. I am glad to ſee you well:
Horatio, or I do forget my ſelfe.
Hor. The ſame my Lord,
And your poore Seruant euer.
Ham. Sir my good friend,
Ile change that name with you:
And what make you from Wittenberg *Horatio*?

Mar.

Marcellus.
Mar. My good Lord.
Ham. I am very glad to see you: good euen Sir.
But what in faith make you from *Wittemberge*?
Hor. A truant disposition, good my Lord.
Ham. I would not haue your Enemy say so;
Nor shall you doe mine eare that violence,
To make it truster of your owne report
Against your selfe. I know you are no Truant:
But what is your affaire in *Elsenour*?
Wee'l teach you to drinke deepe, ere you depart.
Hor. My Lord, I came to see your Fathers Funerall.
Ham. I pray thee doe not mock me (fellow Student
I thinke it was to see my Mothers Wedding.
Hor. Indeed my Lord, it followed hard vpon.
Ham. Thrift, thrift *Horatio*: the Funerall Bake-meats
Did coldly furnish forth the Marriage Tables;
Would I had met my dearest foe in heauen,
Ere I had euer seene that day *Horatio*.
My father, me thinkes I see my father.
Hor. Oh where my Lord?
Ham. In my minds eye (*Horatio*)
Hor. I saw him once; he was a goodly King.
Ham. He was a man, take him for all in all:
I shall not look vpon his like againe.
Hor. My Lord, I thinke I saw him yesternight.
Ham. Saw? Who?
Hor. My Lord, the King your Father.
Ham. The King my Father?
Hor. Season your admiration for a while
With an attent eare; till I may deliuer
Vpon the witnesse of these Gentlemen,
This maruell to you.
Ham. For Heauens loue let me heare.
Hor. Two nights together, had these Gentlemen
(*Marcellus* and *Barnardo*) on their Watch
In the dead wast and middle of the night
Beene thus encountred. A figure like your Father,
Arm'd at all points exactly, *Cap a Pe*,
Appeares before them, and with sollemne march
Goes slow and stately: By them thrice he walkt,
By their opprest and feare-surprized eyes,
Within his Truncheons length; whilst they bestil'd
Almost to Ielly with the Act of feare,
Stand dumbe and speake not to him. This to me
In dreadfull secrecie impart they did,
And I with them the third Night kept the Watch,
Whereas they had deliuer'd both in time,
Forme of the thing; each word made true and good,
The Apparition comes. I knew your Father:
These hands are not more like.
Ham. But where was this?
Mar. My Lord, vpon the platforme where we watcht
Ham. Did you not speake to it?
Hor. My Lord, I did;
But answere made it none: yet once me thought
It lifted vp it head, and did addresse
It selfe to motion, like as it would speake:
But euen then, the Morning Cocke crew lowd;
And at the sound it shrunke in hast away,
And vanisht from our sight.
Ham. Tis very strange.
Hor. As I doe liue my honourd Lord 'tis true;
And we did thinke it writ downe in our duty
To let you know of it.
Ham. Indeed, indeed Sirs; but this troubles me.
Hold you the watch to Night?
Both. We doe my Lord.
Ham. Arm'd, say you?
Both. Arm'd, my Lord.
Ham. From top to toe?
Both. My Lord, from head to foote.
Ham. Then saw you not his face?
Hor. O yes, my Lord, he wore his Beauer vp.
Ham. What, lookt he frowningly?
Hor. A countenance more in sorrow then in anger.
Ham. Pale, or red?
Hor. Nay very pale.
Ham. And fixt his eyes vpon you?
Hor. Most constantly.
Ham. I would I had beene there.
Hor. It would haue much amaz'd you.
Ham. Very like, very like: staid it long? (dred.
Hor. While one with moderate hast might tell a hun-
All. Longer, longer.
Hor. Not when I saw't.
Ham. His Beard was grisly? no.
Hor. It was, as I haue seene it in his life,
A Sable Siluer'd. (gaine.
Ham. Ile watch to Night; perchance 'twill wake a-
Hor. I warrant you it will.
Ham. If it assume my noble Fathers person,
Ile speake to it, though Hell it selfe should gape
And bid me hold my peace. I pray you all,
If you haue hitherto conceald this sight;
Let it bee treble in your silence still:
And whatsoeuer els shall hap to night,
Giue it an vnderstanding but no tongue;
I will requite your loues; so, fare ye well:
Vpon the Platforme twixt eleuen and twelue,
Ile visit you.
All. Our duty to your Honour. *Exeunt.*
Ham. Your loue, as mine to you: farewell.
My Fathers Spirit in Armes? All is not well:
I doubt some foule play: would the Night were come;
Till then sit still my soule; foule deeds will rise,
Though all the earth orewhelm them to mens eies. *Exit.*

Scena Tertia.

Enter Laertes and Ophelia.
Laer. My necessaries are imbark't; Farewell:
And Sister, as the Winds giue Benefit,
And Conuoy is assistant; doe not sleepe,
But let me heare from you.
Ophel. Doe you doubt that?
Laer. For *Hamlet*, and the trifling of his fauours,
Hold it a fashion and a toy in Bloud;
A Violet in the youth of Primy Nature;
Froward, not permanent; sweet not lasting
The suppliance of a minute? No more.
Ophel. No more but so.
Laer. Thinke it no more.
For nature cressant does not grow alone,
In thewes and Bulke: but as his Temple waxes,
The inward seruice of the Minde and Soule
Growes wide withall. Perhaps he loues you now,
And now no soyle nor cautell doth besmerch
The vertue of his feare: but you must feare
His

His greatneſſe weigh'd, his will is not his owne;
For hee himſelfe is ſubiect to his Birth:
Hee may not, as vnuallued perſons doe,
Carue for himſelfe; for, on his choyce depends
The ſanctity and health of the weole State.
And therefore muſt his choyce be circumſcrib'd
Vnto the voyce and yeelding of that Body,
Whereof he is the Head. Then if he ſayes he loues you,
It fits your wiſedome ſo farre to beleeue it;
As he in his peculiar Sect and force
May giue his ſaying deed: which is no further,
Then the maine voyce of *Denmarke* goes withall.
Then weigh what loſſe your Honour may ſuſtaine,
If with too credent eare you liſt his Songs;
Or loſe your Heart; or your chaſt Treaſure open
To his vnmaſtred importunity.
Feare it *Ophelia*, feare it my deare Siſter,
And keepe within the reare of your Affection;
Out of the ſhot and danger of Deſire.
The chariest Maid is Prodigall enough,
If ſhe vnmaske her beauty to the Moone:
Vertue it ſelfe ſcapes not calumnious ſtroakes,
The Canker Galls, the Infants of the Spring
Too oft before the buttons be diſclos'd,
And in the Morne and liquid dew of Youth,
Contagious blaſtments are moſt imminent.
Be wary then, beſt ſafety lies in feare;
Youth to it ſelfe rebels, though none elſe neere.
Ophe. I ſhall th'effect of this good Leſſon keepe,
As watchmen to my heart: but good my Brother
Doe not as ſome vngracious Paſtors doe,
Shew me the ſteepe and thorny way to Heauen;
Whilſt like a puſt and reckleſſe Libertine
Himſelfe, the Primroſe path of dalliance treads,
And reaks not his owne reade.
Laer. Oh, feare me not.
Enter Polonius.
I ſtay too long; but here my Father comes:
A double bleſſing is a double grace;
Occaſion ſmiles vpon a ſecond leaue.
Polon. Yet heere *Laertes*? Aboord, aboord for ſhame,
The winde ſits in the ſhoulder of your ſaile,
And you are ſtaid for there: my bleſſing with you;
And theſe few Precepts in thy memory.
See thou Character. Giue thy thoughts no tongue,
Nor any vnproportion'd thought his Act:
Be thou familiar; but by no meanes vulgar:
The friends thou haſt, and their adoption tride,
Grapple them to thy Soule, with hoopes of Steele:
But doe not dull thy palme, with entertainment
Of each vnhatch't, vnfledg'd Comrade. Beware
Of entrance to a quarrell: but being in
Bear't that th'oppoſed may beware of thee.
Giue euery man thine eare; but few thy voyce:
Take each mans cenſure; but reſerue thy iudgement:
Coſtly thy habit as thy purſe can buy;
But not expreſt in fancie; rich, not gawdie:
For the Apparell oft proclaimes the man.
And they in France of the beſt ranck and ſtation,
Are of a moſt ſelect and generous cheff in that.
Neither a borrower, nor a lender be;
For lone oft loſes both it ſelfe and friend:
And borrowing duls the edge of Husbandry.
This aboue all; to thine owne ſelfe be true:
And it muſt follow, as the Night the Day,
Thou canſt not then be falſe to any man.
Farewell: my Bleſſing ſeaſon this in thee.
Laer. Moſt humbly doe I take my leaue, my Lord.
Polon. The time inuites you, goe, your ſeruants tend
Laer. Farewell *Ophelia*, and remember well
What I haue ſaid to you.
Ophe. Tis in my memory lockt,
And you your ſelfe ſhall keepe the key of it.
Laer. Farewell. *Exit Laer.*
Polon. What iſt *Ophelia* he hath ſaid to you?
Ophe. So pleaſe you, ſomthing touching the L *Hamlet*.
Polon. Marry, well bethought:
Tis told me he hath very oft of late
Giuen priuate time to you; and you your ſelfe
Haue of your audience beene moſt free and bounteous.
If it be ſo, as ſo tis put on me;
And that in way of caution: I muſt tell you,
You doe not vnderſtand your ſelfe ſo cleerely,
As it behoues my Daughter, and your Honour.
What is betweene you, giue me vp the truth?
Ophe He hath my Lord of late, made many tenders
Of his affection to me.
Polon. Affection, puh. You ſpeake like a greene Girle,
Vnſifted in ſuch perillous Circumſtance.
Doe you beleeue his tenders, as you call them?
Ophe. I do not know, my Lord, what I ſhould thinke.
Polon. Marry Ile teach you; thinke your ſelfe a Baby,
That you haue tane his tenders for true pay,
Which are not ſterling. Tender your ſelfe more dearly;
Or not to crack the winde of the poore Phraſe,
Roaming it thus, you'l tender me a foole.
Ophe. My Lord, he hath importun'd me with loue,
In honourable faſhion.
Polon. I, faſhion you may call it, go too, go too.
Ophe. And hath giuen countenance to his ſpeech,
My Lord, with all the vowes of Heauen.
Polon. I, Springes to catch Woodcocks. I doe know
When the Bloud burnes, how Prodigall the Soule
Giues the tongue vowes: theſe blazes, Daughter,
Giuing more light then heate; extinct in both,
Euen in their promiſe, as it is a making;
You muſt not take for fire. For this time Daughter,
Be ſomewhat ſcanter of your Maiden preſence;
Set your entreatments at a higher rate,
Then a command to parley. For Lord *Hamlet*,
Beleeue ſo much in him, that he is young,
And with a larger tether may he walke,
Then may be giuen you. In few, *Ophelia*,
Doe not beleeue his vowes; for they are Broakers,
Not of the eye, which their Inueſtments ſhow:
But meere implorators of vnholy Sutes,
Breathing like ſanctified and pious bonds,
The better to beguile. This is for all.
I would not, in plaine tearmes, from this time forth,
Haue you ſo ſlander any moment leiſure,
As to giue words or talke with the Lord *Hamlet*:
Looke too't, I charge you; come your wayes.
Ophe. I ſhall obey my Lord. *Exeunt.*

Enter Hamlet, Horatio, Marcellus.
Ham. The Ayre bites ſhrewdly: is it very cold?
Hor. It is a nipping and an eager ayre.
Ham. What hower now?
Hor. I thinke it lacks of twelue.
Mar. No, it is ſtrooke. (ſeaſon,
Hor. Indeed I heard it not: then it drawes neere the
Wherein the Spirit held his wont to walke.
What

What does this meane my Lord? (rouſe,
Ham. The King doth wake to night, and takes his
Keepes waſſels and the ſwaggering vpſpring reeles,
And as he dreines his draughts of Reniſh downe,
The kettle Drum and Trumpet thus bray out
The triumph of his Pledge.
Horat. Is it a cuſtome?
Ham. I marry iſt;
And to my mind, though I am natiue heere,
And to the manner borne: It is a Cuſtome
More honour'd in the breach, then the obſeruance.
Enter Ghoſt.
Hor. Looke my Lord, it comes.
Ham. Angels and Miniſters of Grace defend vs:
Be thou a Spirit of health, or Goblin damn'd,
Bring with thee ayres from Heauen, or blaſts from Hell
Be thy euents wicked or charitable,
Thou com'ſt in ſuch a queſtionable ſhape
That I will ſpeake to thee. Ile call thee *Hamlet*,
King, Father, Royall Dane: Oh, oh, anſwer me,
Let me not burſt in Ignorance; but tell
Why thy Canoniz'd bones Hearſed in death,
Haue burſt their cerments, why the Sepulcher
Wherein we ſaw thee quietly enurn'd,
Hath op'd his ponderous and Marble iawes,
To caſt thee vp againe? What may this meane?
That thou dead Coarſe againe in compleat ſteele,
Reuiſits thus the glimpſes of the Moone,
Making Night hidious? And we fooles of Nature,
So horridly to ſhake our diſpoſition,
With thoughts beyond thee; reaches of our Soules,
Say, why is this? wherefore? what ſhould we doe?
Ghoſt beckens Hamlet.
Hor It beckons you to goe away with it,
As if it ſome impartment did deſire
To you alone.
Mar. Looke with what courteous action
It wafts you to a more remoued ground:
But doe not goe with it.
Hor. No, by no meanes.
Ham. It will not ſpeake: then will I follow it.
Hor. Doe not my Lord.
Ham. Why, what ſhould be the feare?
I doe not ſet my life at a pins fee;
And for my Soule, what can it doe to that?
Being a thing immortall as it ſelfe.
It waues me forth againe; Ile follow it.
Hor. What if it tempt you toward the Floud my Lord?
Or to the dreadfull Sonnet of the Cliffe,
That beetles o're his baſe into the Sea,
And there aſſumes ſome other horrible forme,
Which might depriue your Soueraignty of Reaſon,
And draw you into madneſſe thinke of it?
Ham. It wafts me ſtill: goe on, Ile follow thee.
Mar. You ſhall not goe my Lord.
Ham. Hold off your hand.
Hor. Be rul'd, you ſhall not goe.
Ham. My fate cries out,
And makes each petty Artire in this body,
As hardy as the Nemian Lions nerue:
Still am I cal'd? Vnhand me Gentlemen:
By Heau'n, Ile make a Ghoſt of him that lets me:
I ſay away, goe on, Ile follow thee.
Exeunt Ghoſt & Hamlet.
Hor He waxes deſperate with imagination.
Mar. Let's follow; 'tis not fit thus to obey him.
Hor. Haue after, to what iſſue will this come?
Mar. Something is rotten in the State of Denmarke.
Hor. Heauen will direct it.
Mar. Ney, let's follow him. *Exeunt.*
Enter Ghoſt and Hamlet.
Ham Where wilt thou lead me? ſpeak; Ile go no fur- (ther.
Gho. Marke me
Ham. I will.
Gho. My hower is almoſt come,
When I to ſulphurous and tormenting Flames
Muſt render vp my ſelfe.
Ham. Alas poore Ghoſt.
Gho. Pitty me not, but lend thy ſerious hearing
To what I ſhall vnfold.
Ham. Speake, I am bound to heare.
Gho. So art thou to reuenge, when thou ſhalt heare.
Ham. What?
Gho. I am thy Fathers Spirit,
Doom'd for a certaine terme to walke the night;
And for the day confin'd to faſt in Fiers,
Till the foule crimes done in my dayes of Nature
Are burnt and purg'd away? But that I am forbid
To tell the ſecrets of my Priſon-Houſe;
I could a Tale vnfold, whoſe lighteſt word
Would harrow vp thy ſoule, freeze thy young blood,
Make thy two eyes like Starres, ſtart from their Spheres,
Thy knotty and combined locks to part,
And each particular haire to ſtand an end,
Like Quilles vpon the fretfull Porpentine:
But this eternall blaſon muſt not be
To eares of fleſh and bloud; liſt *Hamlet*, oh liſt,
If thou didſt euer thy deare Father loue.
Ham. Oh Heauen!
Gho. Reuenge his foule and moſt vnnaturall Murther.
Ham. Murther?
Ghoſt. Murther moſt foule, as in the beſt it is;
But this moſt foule, ſtrange, and vnnaturall.
Ham. Haſt, haſt me to know it,
That with wings as ſwift
As meditation, or the thoughts of Loue,
May ſweepe to my Reuenge.
Ghoſt. I finde thee apt,
And duller ſhould'ſt thou be then the fat weede
That rots it ſelfe in eaſe, on Lethe Wharfe,
Would'ſt thou not ſtirre in this. Now *Hamlet* heare:
It's giuen out, that ſleeping in mine Orchard,
A Serpent ſtung me: ſo the whole eare of Denmarke,
Is by a forged proceſſe of my death
Rankly abus'd: But know thou Noble youth,
The Serpent that did ſting thy Fathers life,
Now weares his Crowne.
Ham O my Propheticke ſoule: mine Vncle?
Ghoſt. I that inceſtuous, that adulterate Beaſt
With witchcraft of his wits, hath Traitorous guifts.
Oh wicked Wit, and Gifts, that haue the power
So to ſeduce? Won to to this ſhamefull Luſt
The will of my moſt ſeeming vertuous Queene:
Oh *Hamlet*, what a falling off was there,
From me, whoſe loue was of that dignity,
That it went hand in hand, euen with the Vow
I made to her in Marriage; and to decline
Vpon a wretch, whoſe Naturall gifts were poore
To thoſe of mine. But Vertue, as it neuer wil be moued,
Though Lewdneſſe court it in a ſhape of Heauen:
So Luſt, though to a radiant Angell link'd,
Will ſate it ſelfe in a Celeſtiall bed, & prey on Garbage.
O o
But

But ſoft, me thinkes I ſent the Mornings Ayre;
Briefe let me be: Sleeping within mine Orchard,
My cuſtome alwayes in the afternoone;
Vpon my ſecure hower thy Vncle ſtole
With iuyce of curſed Hebenon in a Violl,
And in the Porches of mine eares did poure
The leaperous Diſtilment; whoſe effect
Holds ſuch an enmity with bloud of Man,
That ſwift as Quick-ſiluer, it courſes through
The naturall Gates and Allies of the Body;
And with a ſodaine vigour it doth poſſet
And curd, like Aygre droppings into Milke,
The thin and wholſome blood: ſo did it mine;
And a moſt inſtant Tetter bak'd about,
Moſt Lazar-like, with vile and loathſome cruſt,
All my ſmooth Body.
Thus was I, ſleeping, by a Brothers hand,
Of Life, of Crowne, and Queene at once diſpatcht;
Cut off euen in the Bloſſomes of my Sinne,
Vnhouzzled, diſappointed, vnnaneld,
No reckoning made, but ſent to my account
With all my imperfections on my head;
Oh horrible, Oh horrible, moſt horrible:
If thou haſt nature in thee beare it not;
Let not the Royall Bed of Denmarke be
A Couch for Luxury and damned Inceſt.
But howſoeuer thou purſueſt this Act,
Taint not thy mind; nor let thy Soule contriue
Againſt thy Mother ought; leaue her to heauen,
And to thoſe Thornes that in her boſome lodge,
To pricke and ſting her. Fare thee well at once;
The Glow-worme ſhowes the Matine to be neere,
And gins to pale his vneffectuall Fire:
Adue, adue, *Hamlet*: remember me. *Exit.*

Ham Oh all you hoſt of Heauen! Oh Earth: what els?
And ſhall I couple Hell? Oh fie: hold my heart;
And you my ſinnewes, grow not inſtant Old;
But beare me ſtiffely vp: Remember thee?
I, thou poore Ghoſt, while memory holds a ſeate
In this diſtracted Globe: Remember thee?
Yea, from the Table of my Memory,
Ile wipe away all triuiall fond Records,
All ſawes of Bookes, all formes, all preſures paſt,
That youth and obſeruation coppied there;
And thy Commandment all alone ſhall liue
Within the Booke and Volume of my Braine,
Vnmixt with baſer matter; yes, yes, by Heauen:
Oh moſt pernicious woman!
Oh Villaine, Villaine, ſmiling damned Villaine!
My Tables, my Tables; meet it is I ſet it downe,
That one may ſmile, and ſmile and be a Villaine;
At leaſt I'm ſure it may be ſo in Denmarke;
So Vnckle there you are: now to my word;
It is; Adue, Adue, Remember me: I haue ſworn't.

Hor & Mar. within. My Lord, my Lord.

Enter Horatio and Marcellus.

Mar. Lord *Hamlet.*

Hor. Heauen ſecure him.

Mar. So be it.

Hor. Illo, ho, ho, my Lord.

Ham. Hillo, ho, ho, boy; come bird, come.

Mar. How iſt't my Noble Lord?

Hor. What newes, my Lord?

Ham. Oh wonderfull!

Hor. Good my Lord tell it.

Ham. No you'l reueale it.

Hor. Not I, my Lord, by Heauen.

Mar. Nor I, my Lord.

Ham. How ſay you then, would heart of man once (think it?
But you'l be ſecret?

Both. I, by Heau'n, my Lord.

Ham. There's nere a villaine dwelling in all Denmarke
But hee's an arrant knaue.

Hor. There needs no Ghoſt my Lord, come from the
Graue, to tell vs this.

Ham. Why right, you are i'th' right;
And ſo, without more circumſtance at all,
I hold it fit that we ſhake hands, and part:
You, as your buſines and deſires ſhall point you:
For euery man ha's buſineſſe and deſire,
Such as it is: and for mine owne poore part,
Looke you, Ile goe pray.

Hor. Theſe are but wild and hurling words, my Lord.

Ham. I'm ſorry they offend you heartily:
Yes faith, heartily.

Hor. There's no offence my Lord.

Ham. Yes, by Saint *Patricke*, but there is my Lord,
And much offence too, touching this Viſion heere:
It is an honeſt Ghoſt, that let me tell you:
For your deſire to know what is betweene vs,
O'remaſter't as you may. And now good friends,
As you are Friends, Schollers and Soldiers,
Giue me one poore requeſt.

Hor. What is't my Lord? we will.

Ham Neuer make known what you haue ſeen to night.

Both. My Lord, we will not.

Ham Nay, but ſwear't.

Hor. Infaith my Lord, not I.

Mar. Nor I my Lord: in faith.

Ham. Vpon my ſword.

Marcell. We haue ſworne my Lord already.

Ham Indeed, vpon my ſword, Indeed.

Gho. Sweare. *Ghoſt cries vnder the Stage.*

Ham. Ah ha boy, ſayeſt thou ſo. Art thou there true-
penny? Come one you here this fellow in the ſellerage
Conſent to ſweare.

Hor. Propoſe the Oath my Lord.

Ham. Neuer to ſpeake of this that you haue ſeene.
Sweare by my ſword.

Gho. Sweare.

Ham. *Hic & vbique?* Then wee'l ſhift for grownd,
Come hither Gentlemen,
And lay your hands againe vpon my ſword,
Neuer to ſpeake of this that you haue heard:
Sweare by my Sword.

Gho. Sweare.

Ham. Well ſaid old Mole, can'ſt worke i'th' ground ſo (faſt?
A worthy Pioner, once more remoue good friends.

Hor. Oh day and night: but this is wondrous ſtrange.

Ham. And therefore as a ſtranger giue it welcome.
There are more things in Heauen and Earth, *Horatio*,
Then are dream't of in our Philoſophy. But come,
Here as before, neuer ſo helpe you mercy,
How ſtrange or odde ſo ere I beare my ſelfe;
(As I perchance heereafter ſhall thinke meet
To put an Anticke diſpoſition on:)
That you at ſuch time ſeeing me, neuer ſhall
With Armes encombred thus, or thus, head ſhake;
Or by pronouncing of ſome doubtfull Phraſe;
As well, we know, or we could and if we would,
Or if we liſt to ſpeake; or there be and if there might,
Or ſuch ambiguous giuing out to note,
That

That you know ought of me; this not to doe.
So grace and mercy at your most neede helpe you:
Sweare.
Ghost. Sweare.
Ham. Rest, rest perturbed Spirit: so Gentlemen,
With all my loue I doe commend me to you;
And what so poore a man as *Hamlet* is,
May doe t'expresse his loue and friending to you,
God willing shall not lacke: let vs goe in together,
And still your fingers on your lippes I pray,
The time is out of ioynt: Oh cursed spight,
That euer I was borne to set it right.
Nay, come let's goe together. *Exeunt*

Actus Secundus.

Enter Polonius, and Reynoldo.

Polon. Giue him his money, and these notes *Reynoldo*
Reynol I will my Lord.
Polon. You shall doe maruels wisely: good *Reynoldo,*
Before you visite him you make inquiry
Of his behauiour.
Reynol. My Lord, I did intend it.
Polon. Marry, well said;
Very well said. Looke you Sir,
Enquire me first what Danskers are in Paris;
And how, and who; what meanes; and where they keepe:
What company, at what expence: and finding
By this encompassement and drift of question,
That they doe know my sonne. Come you more neerer
Then your particular demands will touch it,
Take you as 'twere some distant knowledge of him,
And thus I know his father and his friends,
And in part him. Doe you marke this *Reynoldo?*
Reynol. I, very well my Lord
Polon. And in part him, but you may say not well;
But if't be hee I meane, hees very wilde;
Addicted so and so; and there put on him
What forgeries you please: marry, none so ranke,
As may dishonour him; take heed of that:
But Sir, such wanton, wild, and vsuall slips,
As are Companions noted and most knowne
To youth and liberty
Reynol. As gaming my Lord.
Polon. I, or drinking, fencing, swearing,
Quarelling, drabbing. You may goe so farre.
Reynol. My Lord that would dishonour him.
Polon. Faith no, as you may season it in the charge;
You must not put another scandall on him,
That hee is open to Incontinencie;
That's not my meaning: but breath his faults so quaintly,
That they may seeme the taints of liberty;
The flash and out-breake of a fiery minde,
A sauagenes in vnreclaim'd bloud of generall assault.
Reynol. But my good Lord.
Polon. Wherefore should you doe this?
Reynol. I my Lord, I would know that.
Polon. Marry Sir, heere's my drift,
And I belieue it is a fetch of warrant:
You laying these slight sulleyes on my Sonne,
As 'twere a thing a little soil'd i'th' working: (sound,
Marke you your party in conuerse; him you would
Hauing euer seene. In the prenominate crimes,
The youth you breath of guilty, be assur'd
He closes with you in this consequence:
Good sir, or so, or friend, or Gentleman.
According to the Phrase and the Addition,
Of man and Country.
Reynol. Very good my Lord.
Polon. And then Sir does he this?
He does: what was I about to say?
I was about to say somthing: where did I leaue?
Reynol. At closes in the consequence:
At friend, or so, and Gentleman.
Polon. At closes in the consequence, I marry,
He closes with you thus. I know the Gentleman,
I saw him yesterday, or tother day;
Or then or then, with such and such; and as you say,
There was he gaming, there o'retooke in's Rouse,
There falling out at Tennis; or perchance,
I saw him enter such a house of saile;
Videlicet, a Brothell, or so forth. See you now;
Your bait of falshood, takes this Cape of truth;
And thus doe we of wisedome and of reach
With windlesses, and with assaies of Bias,
By indirections finde directions out:
So by my former Lecture and aduice
Shall you my Sonne; you haue me, haue you not?
Reynol. My Lord I haue.
Polon. God buy you; fare you well.
Reynol. Good my Lord.
Polon Obserue his inclination in your selfe
Reynol. I shall my Lord.
Polon. And let him plye his Musicke
Reynol Well, my Lord *Exit.*

Enter Ophelia.

Polon Farewell:
How now *Ophelia,* what's the matter?
Ophe. Alas my Lord, I haue beene so affrighted.
Polon. With what, in the name of Heauen?
Ophe. My Lord, as I was sowing in my Chamber,
Lord *Hamlet* with his doublet all vnbrac'd,
No hat vpon his head, his stockings foul'd,
Vngartred, and downe giued to his Anckle,
Pale as his shirt, his knees knocking each other,
And with a looke so pitious in purport,
As if he had been loosed out of hell,
To speake of horrors: he comes before me.
Polon. Mad for thy Loue?
Ophe. My Lord, I doe not know: but truly I do feare it.
Polon. What said he?
Ophe. He tooke me by the wrist, and held me hard;
Then goes he to the length of all his arme;
And with his other hand thus o're his brow,
He fals to such perusall of my face,
As he would draw it. Long staid he so,
At last, a little shaking of mine Arme:
And thrice his head thus wauing vp and downe;
He rais'd a sigh, so pittious and profound,
That it did seeme to shatter all his bulke,
And end his being. That done, he lets me goe,
And with his head ouer his shoulders turn'd,
He seem'd to finde his way without his eyes,
For out adores he went without their helpe;
And to the last, bended their light on me.
Polon. Goe with me, I will goe seeke the King,
This is the very extasie of Loue,
Whose violent property foredoes it selfe,
And

And leads the will to desperate Vndertakings,
As oft as any passion vnder Heauen,
That does afflict our Natures. I am sorrie.
What haue you giuen him any hard words of late?

Opha. No my good Lord: but as you did command,
I did repell his Letters, and deny'de
His accesse to me.

Pol. That hath made him mad.
I am sorrie that with better speed and iudgement
I had not quoted him. I feare he did but trifle,
And meant to wracke thee: but beshrew my iealousie:
It seemes it is as proper to our Age,
To cast beyond our selues in our Opinions,
As it is common for the yonger sort
To lacke discretion. Come, go we to the King,
This must be knowne, w being kept close might moue
More greefe to hide, then hate to vtter loue. *Exeunt*

Scena Secunda.

Enter King, Queene, Rosincrane, and Guildensterne Cumalijs.

King. Welcome deere *Rosincrance* and *Guildensterne.*
Moreouer, that we much did long to see you,
The neede we haue to vse you, did prouoke
Our hastie sending. Something haue you heard
Of *Hamlets* transformation: so I call it,
Since not th'exterior, nor the inward man
Resembles that it was. What it should bee
More then his Fathers death, that thus hath put him
So much from th'vnderstanding of himselfe,
I cannot deeme of. I intreat you both,
That being of so young dayes brought vp with him
And since so Neighbour'd to his youth, and humour,
That you vouchsafe your rest heere in our Court
Some little time: so by your Companies
To draw him on to pleasures, and to gather
So much as from Occasions you may gleane,
That open'd lies within our remedie.

Qu. Good Gentlemen, he hath much talk'd of you,
And sure I am, two men there are not liuing,
To whom he more adheres. If it will please you
To shew vs so much Gentrie, and good will,
As to expend your time with vs a-while,
For the supply and profit of our Hope,
Your Visitation shall receiue such thankes
As fits a Kings remembrance.

Rosin. Both your Maiesties
Might by the Soueraigne power you haue of vs,
Put your dread pleasures, more into Command
Then to Entreatie.

Guil. We both obey,
And here giue vp our selues, in the full bent,
To lay our Seruices freely at your feete,
To be commanded.

King. Thankes *Rosincrance*, and gentle *Guildensterne.*

Qu. Thankes *Guildensterne* and gentle *Rosincrance.*
And I beseech you instantly to visit
My too much changed Sonne.
Go some of ye,
And bring the Gentlemen where *Hamlet* is.

Guil. Heauens make our presence and our practises
Pleasant and helpfull to him. *Exit.*

Queene. Amen.

Enter Polonius.

Pol. Th'Ambassadors from Norwey, my good Lord,
Are ioyfully return'd.

King. Thou still hast bin the Father of good Newes

Pol. Haue I, my Lord? Assure you, my good Liege,
I hold my dutie, as I hold my Soule,
Both to my God, one to my gracious King:
And I do thinke, or else this braine of mine
Hunts not the traile of Policie, so sure
As I haue vs'd to do: that I haue found
The very cause of *Hamlets* Lunacie.

King Oh speake of that, that I do long to heare.

Pol Giue first admittance to th'Ambassadors,
My Newes shall be the Newes to that great Feast.

King. Thy selfe do grace to them, and bring them in.
He tels me my sweet Queene, that he hath found
The head and sourse of all your Sonnes distemper.

Qu. I doubt it is no other, but the maine,
His Fathers death, and our o're-hasty Marriage.

Enter Polonius, Voltumand, and Cornelius.

King. Well, we shall sift him. Welcome good Frends:
Say *Voltumand*, what from our Brother Norwey?

Volt. Most faire returne of Greetings, and Desires.
Vpon our first, he sent out to suppresse
His Nephewes Leuies, which to him appear'd
To be a preparation 'gainst the Poleak:
But better look'd into, he truly found
It was against your Highnesse, whereat greeued,]
That so his Sicknesse, Age, and Impotence
Was falsely borne in hand, sends out Arrests
On *Fortinbras*, which he (in breefe) obeyes,
Receiues rebuke from Norwey: and in fine,
Makes Vow before his Vnkle, neuer more
To giue th'assay of Armes against your Maiestie.
Whereon old Norwey, ouercome with ioy,
Giues him three thousand Crownes in Annuall Fee,
And his Commission to imploy those Soldiers
So leuied as before, against the Poleak:
With an intreaty heerein further shewne,
That it might please you to giue quiet passe
Through your Dominions, for his Enterprize,
On such regards of safety and allowance,
As therein are set downe.

King. It likes vs well:
And at our more consider'd time wee'l read,
Answer, and thinke vpon this Businesse.
Meane time we thanke you, for your well-tooke Labour.
Go to your rest, at night wee'l Feast together.
Most welcome home. *Exit Ambass*

Pol. This businesse is very well ended
My Liege, and Madam, to expostulate
What Maiestie should be, what Dutie is,
Why day is day; night, night; and time is time.
Were nothing but to waste Night, Day and Time.
Therefore, since Breuitie is the Soule of Wit,
And tediousnesse, the limbes and outward flourishes,
I will be breefe. Your Noble Sonne is mad.
Mad call I it; for to define true Madnesse,
What is't, but to be nothing else but mad.
But let that go.

Qu. More matter, with lesse Art.

Pol. Madam, I sweare I vse no Art at all:
That he is mad, 'tis true: 'Tis true 'tis pittie,
And pittie it is true: A foolish figure,
But farewell it: for I will vse no Art.

Mad

Mad let vs grant him then: and now remaines
That we finde out the cauſe of this effect,
Or rather ſay, the cauſe of this defect;
For this effect defectiue, comes by cauſe,
Thus it remaines, and the remainder thus. Perpend,
I haue a daughter: haue, whil'ſt ſhe is mine,
Who in her Dutie and Obedience, marke,
Hath giuen me this: now gather, and ſurmiſe.

The Letter.

To the Celeſtiall, and my Soules Idoll, the moſt beautified Ophelia

That's an ill Phraſe, a vilde Phraſe, beautified is a vilde Phraſe: but you ſhall heare theſe in her excellent white boſome, theſe.

Qu. Came this from *Hamlet* to her.

Pol. Good Madam ſtay awhile, I will be faithfull.

Doubt thou, the Starres are fire,
Doubt, that the Sunne doth moue:
Doubt Truth to be a Lier,
But neuer Doubt, I loue.

O deere Ophelia, I am ill at theſe Numbers: I haue not Art to reckon my grones; but that I loue thee beſt, oh moſt Beſt beleeue it. Adieu.

Thine euermore moſt deere Lady, whilſt this Machine is to him, Hamlet.

This in Obedience hath my daughter ſhew'd me:
And more aboue hath his ſoliciting,
As they fell out by Time, by Meanes, and Place,
All giuen to mine eare.

King. But how hath ſhe receiu'd his Loue?

Pol. What do you thinke of me?

King. As of a man, faithfull and Honourable.

Pol. I wold faine proue ſo. But what might you think?
When I had ſeene this hot loue on the wing,
As I perceiued it, I muſt tell you that
Before my Daughter told me, what might you
Or my deere Maieſtie your Queene heere, think,
If I had playd the Deske or Table-booke,
Or giuen my heart a winking, mute and dumbe,
Or look'd vpon this Loue, with idle ſight,
What might you thinke? No, I went round to worke,
And (my yong Miſtris) thus I did beſpeake
Lord *Hamlet* is a Prince out of thy Starre,
This muſt not be: and then, I Precepts gaue her,
That ſhe ſhould locke her ſelfe from his Reſort,
Admit no Meſſengers, receiue no Tokens:
Which done, ſhe tooke the Fruites of my Aduice,
And he repulſed. A ſhort Tale to make,
Fell into a Sadneſſe, then into a Faſt,
Thence to a Watch, thence into a Weakneſſe,
Thence to a Lightneſſe, and by this declenſion
Into the Madneſſe whereon now he raues,
And all we waile for.

King. Do you thinke 'tis this?

Qu. It may be very likely.

Pol. Hath there bene ſuch a time, I'de fain know that,
That I haue poſitiuely ſaid, 'tis ſo,
When it prou'd otherwiſe?

King. Not that I know.

Pol. Take this from this; if this be otherwiſe,
If Circumſtances leade me, I will finde
Where truth is hid, though it were hid indeede
Within the Center.

King. How may we try it further?

Pol. You know ſometimes
He walkes foure houres together, heere
In the Lobby.

Qu. So he ha's indeed.

Pol. At ſuch a time Ile looſe my Daughter to him,
Be you and I behinde an Arras then,
Marke the encounter: If he loue her not,
And be not from his reaſon falne thereon;
Let me be no Aſſiſtant for a State,
And keepe a Farme and Carters.

King. We will try it.

Enter Hamlet reading on a Booke.

Qu. But looke where ſadly the poore wretch
Comes reading.

Pol. Away I do beſeech you, both away,
Ile boord him preſently. *Exit King & Queen.*
Oh giue me leaue. How does my good Lord *Hamlet*?

Ham. Well, God-a-mercy.

Pol. Do you know me, my Lord?

Ham. Excellent, excellent well: y'are a Fiſhmonger.

Pol. Not I my Lord.

Ham. Then I would you were ſo honeſt a man.

Pol. Honeſt, my Lord?

Ham. I ſir, to be honeſt as this world goes, is to bee one man pick'd out of two thouſand.

Pol. That's very true, my Lord.

Ham. For if the Sun breed Magots in a dead dogge, being a good kiſsing Carrion——
Haue you a daughter?

Pol. I haue my Lord.

Ham. Let her not walke i'th'Sunne: Conception is a bleſsing, but not as your daughter may conceiue. Friend looke too't.

Pol. How ſay you by that? Still harping on my daughter: yet he knew me not at firſt; he ſaid I was a Fiſhmonger: he is farre gone, farre gone: and truly in my youth, I ſuffred much extreamity for loue: very neere this. Ile ſpeake to him againe. What do you read my Lord?

Ham. Words, words, words.

Pol. What is the matter, my Lord?

Ham. Betweene who?

Pol. I meane the matter you meane, my Lord.

Ham. Slanders Sir: for the Satyricall ſlaue ſaies here, that old men haue gray Beards; that their faces are wrinkled; their eyes purging thicke Amber, or Plum-Tree Gumme: and that they haue a plentifull locke of Wit, together with weake Hammes. All which Sir, though I moſt powerfully, and potently beleeue; yet I holde it not Honeſtie to haue it thus ſet downe: For you your ſelfe Sir, ſhould be old as I am, if like a Crab you could go backward.

Pol. Though this be madneſſe,
Yet there is Method in't: will you walke
Out of the ayre my Lord?

Ham. Into my Graue?

Pol. Indeed that is out o'th'Ayre:
How pregnant (ſometimes) his Replies are?
A happineſſe,
That often Madneſſe hits on,
Which Reaſon and Sanitie could not
So proſperouſly be deliuer'd of.
I will leaue him,
And ſodainely contriue the meanes of meeting
Betweene him, and my daughter.
My Honourable Lord, I will moſt humbly
Take my leaue of you.

oo 3 *Ham.*

Ham. You cannot Sir take from me any thing, that I will more willingly part withall, except my life, my life.

Polon. Fare you well my Lord.

Ham. These tedious old fooles.

Polon. You goe to seeke my Lord *Hamlet*; there hee is.

Enter Rosincran and Guildensterne.

Rosin. God saue you Sir.

Guild. Mine honour'd Lord?

Rosin. My most deare Lord?

Ham. My excellent good friends? How do'st thou *Guildensterne*? Oh, *Rosincrane*; good Lads: How doe ye both?

Rosin. As the indifferent Children of the earth.

Guild. Happy, in that we are not ouer-happy: on Fortunes Cap, we are not the very Button.

Ham. Nor the Soales of her Shoo?

Rosin. Neither my Lord.

Ham. Then you liue about her waste, or in the middle of her fauour?

Guil. Faith, her priuates, we.

Ham. In the secret parts of Fortune? Oh, most true: she is a Strumpet. What's the newes?

Rosin. None my Lord; but that the World's growne honest.

Ham. Then is Doomesday neere: But your newes is not true. Let me question more in particular: what haue you my good friends, deserued at the hands of Fortune, that she sends you to Prison hither?

Guil. Prison, my Lord?

Ham. Denmark's a Prison.

Rosin. Then is the World one.

Ham. A goodly one, in which there are many Confines, Wards, and Dungeons; *Denmarke* being one o'th' worst.

Rosin. We thinke not so my Lord.

Ham. Why then 'tis none to you; for there is nothing either good or bad, but thinking makes it so: to me it is a prison.

Rosin. Why then your Ambition makes it one: 'tis too narrow for your minde.

Ham. O God, I could be bounded in a nutshell, and count my selfe a King of infinite space; were it not that I haue bad dreames.

Guil. Which dreames indeed are Ambition: for the very substance of the Ambitious, is meerely the shadow of a Dreame.

Ham. A dreame it selfe is but a shadow.

Rosin. Truely, and I hold Ambition of so ayry and light a quality, that it is but a shadowes shadow.

Ham. Then are our Beggers bodies; and our Monarchs and out-stretcht Heroes the Beggers Shadowes: shall wee to th' Court: for, by my fey I cannot reason?

Both. Wee'l wait vpon you.

Ham. No such matter. I will not sort you with the rest of my seruants: for to speake to you like an honest man: I am most dreadfully attended; but in the beaten way of friendship, What make you at *Elsonower*?

Rosin. To visit you my Lord, no other occasion.

Ham. Begger that I am, I am euen poore in thankes; but I thanke you: and sure deare friends my thanks are too deare a halfepeny; were you not sent for? Is it your owne inclining? Is it a free visitation? Come, deale iustly with me: come, come; nay speake.

Guil. What should we say my Lord?

Ham. Why any thing. But to the purpose; you were sent for; and there is a kinde confession in your lookes; which your modesties haue not craft enough to color, I know the good King & Queene haue sent for you.

Rosin. To what end my Lord?

Ham. That you must teach me: but let mee coniure you by the rights of our fellowship, by the consonancy of our youth, by the Obligation of our euer-preserued loue, and by what more deare, a better proposer could charge you withall; be euen and direct with me, whether you were sent for or no.

Rosin. What say you?

Ham. Nay then I haue an eye of you: if you loue me hold not off.

Guil. My Lord, we were sent for.

Ham. I will tell you why; so shall my anticipation preuent your discouery of your secricie to the King and Queene: moult no feather, I haue of late, but wherefore I know not, lost all my mirth, forgone all custome of exercise; and indeed, it goes so heauenly with my disposition; that this goodly frame the Earth, seemes to me a sterrill Promontory; this most excellent Canopy the Ayre, look you, this braue ore-hanging, this Maiesticall Roofe, fretted with golden fire: why, it appeares no other thing to mee, then a foule and pestilent congregation of vapours. What a piece of worke is a man! how Noble in Reason? how infinite in faculty? in forme and mouing how expresse and admirable? in Action, how like an Angel? in apprehension, how like a God? the beauty of the world, the Parragon of Animals; and yet to me, what is this Quintessence of Dust? Man delights not me; no, nor Woman neither; though by your smiling you seeme to say so.

Rosin. My Lord, there was no such stuffe in my thoughts.

Ham. Why did you laugh, when I said, Man delights not me?

Rosin. To thinke, my Lord, if you delight not in Man, what Lenton entertainment the Players shall receiue from you: wee coated them on the way, and hither are they comming to offer you Seruice.

Ham. He that playes the King shall be welcome; his Maiesty shall haue Tribute of mee: the aduenturous Knight shal vse his Foyle and Target: the Louer shall not sigh *gratis*, the humorous man shall end his part in peace: the Clowne shall make those laugh whose lungs are tickled a'th' sere: and the Lady shall say her minde freely; or the blanke Verse shall halt for't: what Players are they?

Rosin. Euen those you were wont to take delight in the Tragedians of the City.

Ham. How chances it they trauaile? their residence both in reputation and profit was better both wayes.

Rosin. I thinke their Inhibition comes by the meanes of the late Innouation?

Ham. Doe they hold the same estimation they did when I was in the City? Are they so follow'd?

Rosin. No indeed, they are not.

Ham How comes it? doe they grow rusty?

Rosin. Nay, their indeauour keepes in the wonted pace; But there is Sir an ayrie of Children, little Yases, that crye out on the top of question; and are most tyrannically clap't for't: these are now the fashi-

fashiou, and so be-ratled the common Stages (so they call them) that many wearing Rapiers, are affraide of Goose-quils, and dare scarse come thither.

Ham. What are they Children? Who maintains 'em? How are they escoted? Will they pursue the Quality no longer then they can sing? Will they not say afterwards if they should grow themselues to common Players (as it is like most if their meanes are no better) their Writers do them wrong, to make them exclaim against their owne Succession.

Rosin. Faith there ha's bene much to do on both sides: and the Nation holds it no sinne, to tarre them to Controuersie. There was for a while, no mony bid for argument, vnlesse the Poet and the Player went to Cuffes in the Question.

Ham. Is't possible?

Guild. Oh there ha's beene much throwing about of Braines.

Ham. Do the Boyes carry it away?

Rosin. I that they do my Lord, *Hercules* & his load too.

Ham. It is not strange: for mine Vnckle is King of Denmarke, and those that would make mowes at him while my Father liued; giue twenty, forty, an hundred Ducates a peece, for his picture in Little. There is something in this more then Naturall, if Philosophie could finde it out.

Flourish for the Players.

Guil. There are the Players.

Ham. Gentlemen, you are welcom to *Elsonower*: your hands, come: The appurtenance of Welcome, is Fashion and Ceremony. Let me comply with you in the Garbe, lest my extent to the Players (which I tell you must shew fairely outward) should more appeare like entertainment then yours. You are welcome: but my Vnckle Father, and Aunt Mother are deceiu'd.

Guil. In what my deere Lord?

Ham. I am but mad North, North-West: when the Winde is Southerly, I know a Hawke from a Handsaw.

Enter Polonius.

Pol. Well be with you Gentlemen.

Ham. Hearke you *Guildensterne*, and you too: at each eare a hearer: that great Baby you see there, is not yet out of his swathing clouts.

Rosin. Happily he's the second time come to them: for they say, an old man is twice a childe.

Ham. I will Prophesie. Hee comes to tell me of the Players. Mark it, you say right Sir: for a Monday morning 'twas so indeed.

Pol. My Lord, I haue Newes to tell you.

Ham. My Lord, I haue Newes to tell you.
When *Rossius* an Actor in Rome——

Pol. The Actors are come hither my Lord.

Ham. Buzze, buzze.

Pol. Vpon mine Honor.

Ham. Then can each Actor on his Asse——

Polon. The best Actors in the world, either for Tragedie, Comedie, Historie, Pastorall: Pastoricall-Comicall-Historicall-Pastorall: Tragicall-Historicall: Tragicall-Comicall-Historicall-Pastorall: Scene indiuible, or Poem vnlimited. *Seneca* cannot be too heauy, nor *Plautus* too light, for the law of Writ, and the Liberty. These are the onely men.

Ham. O *Iephta* Iudge of Israel, what a Treasure had'st thou?

Pol. What a Treasure had he, my Lord?

Ham. Why one faire Daughter, and no more,
The which he loued passing well.

Pol. Still on my Daughter.

Ham. Am I not i'th'right old *Iephta*?

Polon. If you call me *Iephta* my Lord, I haue a daughter that I loue passing well.

Ham. Nay that followes not.

Polon What followes then, my Lord?

Ha. Why, As by lot, God wot: and then you know, It came to passe, as most like it was: The first rowe of the *Pons Chanson* will shew you more. For looke where my Abridgements come.

Enter foure or fiue Players.

Y'are welcome Masters, welcome all. I am glad to see thee well: Welcome good Friends. O my olde Friend? Thy face is valiant since I saw thee last: Com'st thou to beard me in Denmarke? What, my yong Lady and Mistris? Byrlady your Ladiship is neerer Heauen then when I saw you last, by the altitude of a Choppine. Pray God your voice like a peece of vncurrant Gold be not crack'd within the ring. Masters, you are all welcome: wee'l e'ne to't like French Faulconers, flie at any thing we see: wee'l haue a Speech straight. Come giue vs a tast of your quality: come, a passionate speech.

1. Play. What speech, my Lord?

Ham. I heard thee speak me a speech once, but it was neuer Acted. or if it was, not aboue once, for the Play I remember pleas'd not the Million, 'twas *Cauiarie* to the Generall: but it was (as I receiu'd it, and others, whose iudgement in such matters, cried in the top of mine) an excellent Play; well digested in the Scoenes, set downe with as much modestie, as cunning. I remember one said there was no Sallets in the lines, to make the matter sauoury; nor no matter in the phrase, that might indite the Author of affectation, but cal'd it an honest method. One cheefe Speech in it, I cheefely lou'd, 'twas *Æneas* Tale to *Dido*, and thereabout of it especially, where he speaks of *Priams* slaughter. If it liue in your memory, begin at this Line, let me see, let me see: The rugged *Pyrrhus* like th'*Hyrcanian* Beast. It is not so: it begins with *Pyrrhus*
The rugged *Pyrrhus*, he whose Sable Armes
Blacke as his purpose, did the night resemble
When he lay couched in the Ominous Horse,
Hath now this dread and blacke Complexion smear'd
With Heraldry more dismall: Head to foote
Now is he to take Geulles, horridly Trick'd
With blood of Fathers, Mothers, Daughters, Sonnes,
Bak'd and impasted with the parching streets,
That lend a tyrannous, and damned light
To their vilde Murthers, roasted in wrath and fire,
And thus o're-sized with coagulate gore,
VVith eyes like Carbuncles, the hellish *Pyrrhus*
Old Grandsire *Priam* seekes.

Pol. Fore God, my Lord, well spoken, with good accent, and good discretion.

1. Player. Anon he findes him,
Striking too short at Greekes. His anticke Sword,
Rebellious to his Arme, lyes where it falles
Repugnant to command: vnequall match,
Pyrrhus at *Priam* driues, in Rage strikes wide:
But with the whiffe and winde of his fell Sword,
Th'vnnerued Father fals. Then senselesse *Illium*,
Seeming to feele his blow, with flaming top
Stoopes to his Bace, and with a hideous crash
Takes Prisoner *Pyrrhus* eare. For loe, his Sword
Which was declining on the Milkie head
Of Reuerend *Priam*, seem'd i'th'Ayre to sticke:

So

So as a painted Tyrant *Pyrrhus* stood,
And like a Newtrall to his will and matter, did nothing.
But as we often see against some storme,
A silence in the Heauens, the Racke stand still,
The bold windes speechlesse, and the Orbe below
As hush as death : Anon the dreadfull Thunder
Doth rend the Region. So after *Pyrrhus* pause,
A ro wsed Vengeance sets him new a-worke,
And neuer did the Cyclops hammers fall
On Mars his Armours, forg'd for proofe Eterne,
With lesse remorse then *Pyrrhus* bleeding sword
Now falles on *Priam*.
Out, out, thou Strumpet-Fortune, all you Gods,
In generall Synod take away her power :
Breake all the Spokes and Fallies from her wheele,
And boule the round Naue downe the hill of Heauen,
As low as to the Fiends.

Pol. This is too long.

Ham. It shall to'th Barbars, with your beard. Prythee say on : He's for a Iigge, or a tale of Baudry, or hee sleepes. Say on ; come to *Hecuba*.

1. Play. But who, O who, had seen the inobled Queen.

Ham. The inobled Queene?

Pol. That's good : Inobled Queene is good.

1. Play. Run bare-foot vp and downe,
Threatning the flame
With Bisson Rheume : A clout about that head,
Where late the Diadem stood, and for a Robe
About her lanke and all ore-teamed Loines,
A blanket in th'Alarum of feare caught vp.
Who this had seene, with tongue in Venome steep'd,
'Gainst Fortunes State, would Treason haue pronounc'd?
But if the Gods themselues did see her then,
When she saw *Pyrrhus* make malicious sport
In mincing with his Sword her Husbands limbes,
The instant Burst of Clamour that she made
(Vnlesse things mortall moue them not at all)
Would haue made milche the Burning eyes of Heauen,
And passion in the Gods.

Pol. Looke where he ha's not turn'd his colour, and ha's teares in's eyes. Pray you no more.

Ham. 'Tis well, Ile haue thee speake out the rest, soone. Good my Lord, will you see the Players wel bestow'd. Do ye heare, let them be well vs'd : for they are the Abstracts and breefe Chronicles of the time. After your death, you were better haue a bad Epitaph, then their ill report while you liued.

Pol. My Lord, I will vse them according to their desart.

Ham. Gods bodykins man, better. Vse euerie man after his desart, and who should scape whipping : vse them after your own Honor and Dignity. The lesse they deserue, the more merit is in your bountie. Take them in.

Pol. Come sirs. *Exit Polon.*

Ham. Follow him Friends: wee'l heare a play to morrow. Dost thou heare me old Friend, can you play the murther of *Gonzago*?

Play. I my Lord.

Ham. Wee'l ha't to morrow night. You could for a need study a speech of some dosen or sixteene lines, which I would set downe, and insert in't? Could ye not?

Play. I my Lord.

Ham. Very well. Follow that Lord, and looke you mock him not. My good Friends, Ile leaue you til night you are welcome to *Elsonower*?

Rosin. Good my Lord. *Exeunt.*

Manet Hamlet.

Ham. I so, God buy'ye : Now I am alone.
Oh what a Rogue and Pesant slaue am I?
Is it not monstrous that this Player heere,
But in a Fixion, in a dreame of Passion,
Could force his soule so to his whole conceit,
That from her working, all his visage warm'd;
Teares in his eyes, distraction in's Aspect,
A broken voyce, and his whole Function suiting
With Formes, to his Conceit? And all for nothing?
For *Hecuba*?
What's *Hecuba* to him, or he to *Hecuba*,
That he should weepe for her? What would he doe,
Had he the Motiue and the Cue for passion
That I haue? He would drowne the Stage with teares,
And cleaue the generall eare with horrid speech :
Make mad the guilty, and apale the free,
Confound the ignorant, and amaze indeed,
The very faculty of Eyes and Eares. Yet I,
A dull and muddy-metled Rascall, peake
Like Iohn a-dreames, vnpregnant of my cause,
And can say nothing : No, not for a King,
Vpon whose property, and most deere life,
A damn'd defeate was made. Am I a Coward?
Who calles me Villaine? breakes my pate a-crosse?
Pluckes off my Beard, and blowes it in my face?
Tweakes me by'th'Nose? giues me the Lye i'th'Throate,
As deepe as to the Lungs? Who does me this?
Ha? Why I should take it : for it cannot be,
But I am Pigeon-Liuer'd, and lacke Gall
To make Oppression bitter, or ere this,
I should haue fatted all the Region Kites
With this Slaues Offall, bloudy : a Bawdy villaine,
Remorselesse, Treacherous, Letcherous, kindles villaine!
Oh Vengeance!
Who? What an Asse am I? I sure, this is most braue,
That I, the Sonne of the Deere murthered,
Prompted to my Reuenge by Heauen, and Hell,
Must (like a Whore) vnpacke my heart with words,
And fall a Cursing like a very Drab,
A Scullion? Fye vpon't : Foh. About my Braine.
I haue heard, that guilty Creatures sitting at a Play,
Haue by the very cunning of the Scœne,
Bene strooke so to the soule, that presently
They haue proclaim'd their Malefactions.
For Murther, though it haue no tongue, will speake
With most myraculous Organ. Ile haue these Players,
Play something like the murder of my Father,
Before mine Vnkle. Ile obserue his lookes,
Ile tent him to the quicke : If he but blench
I know my course. The Spirit that I haue seene
May be the Diuell, and the Diuel hath power
T'assume a pleasing shape, yea and perhaps
Out of my Weaknesse, and my Melancholly,
As he is very potent with such Spirits,
Abuses me to damne me. Ile haue grounds
More Relatiue then this : The Play's the thing,
Wherein Ile catch the Conscience of the King. *Exit*

Enter King, Queene, Polonius, Ophelia, Rosincrance, Guildenstern, and Lords.

King. And can you by no drift of circumstance
Get from him why he puts on this Confusion :
Grating so harshly all his dayes of quiet

With

With turbulent and dangerous Lunacy.
Roſin. He does confeſſe he feeles himſelfe diſtracted,
But from what cauſe he will by no meanes ſpeake.
Guil. Nor do we finde him forward to be ſounded,
But with a crafty Madneſſe keepes aloofe:
When we would bring him on to ſome Confeſſion
Of his true ſtate.
Qu. Did he receiue you well?
Roſin. Moſt like a Gentleman.
Guild. But with much forcing of his diſpoſition.
Roſin. Niggard of queſtion, but of our demands
Moſt free in his reply.
Qu. Did you aſſay him to any paſtime?
Roſin. Madam, it ſo fell out, that certaine Players
We ore-wrought on the way: of theſe we told him,
And there did ſeeme in him a kinde of ioy
To heare of it. They are about the Court,
And (as I thinke) they haue already order
This night to play before him.
Pol. 'Tis moſt true:
And he beſeech'd me to intreate your Maieſties
To heare, and ſee the matter.
King. With all my heart, and it doth much content me
To heare him ſo inclin'd. Good Gentlemen,
Giue him a further edge, and driue his purpoſe on
To theſe delights.
Roſin. We ſhall my Lord. *Exeunt.*
King. Sweet *Gertrude* leaue vs too,
For we haue cloſely ſent for *Hamlet* hither,
That he, as 'twere by accident, may there
Affront *Ophelia*. Her Father, and my ſelfe (lawful eſpials)
Will ſo beſtow our ſelues, that ſeeing vnſeene
We may of their encounter frankely iudge,
And gather by him, as he is behaued,
If't be th'affliction of his loue, or no.
That thus he ſuffers for.
Qu. I ſhall obey you,
And for your part *Ophelia*, I do wiſh
That your good Beauties be the happy cauſe
Of *Hamlets* wildeneſſe: ſo ſhall I hope your Vertues
Will bring him to his wonted way againe,
To both your Honors.
Ophe. Madam, I wiſh it may.
Pol. *Ophelia*, walke you heere. Gracious ſo pleaſe ye
We will beſtow our ſelues: Reade on this booke,
That ſhew of ſuch an exerciſe may colour
Your lonelineſſe. We are oft too blame in this,
'Tis too much prou'd, that with Deuotions viſage,
And pious Action, we do ſurge o're
The diuell himſelfe.
King. Oh 'tis true:
How ſmart a laſh that ſpeech doth giue my Conſcience?
The Harlots Cheeke beautied with plaiſt'ring Art
Is not more vgly to the thing that helpes it,
Then is my deede, to my moſt painted word.
Oh heauie burthen!
Pol. I heare him comming, let's withdraw my Lord.
Exeunt.

Enter Hamlet.

Ham. To be, or not to be, that is the Queſtion:
Whether 'tis Nobler in the minde to ſuffer
The Slings and Arrowes of outragious Fortune,
Or to take Armes againſt a Sea of troubles,
And by oppoſing end them: to dye, to ſleepe
No more; and by a ſleepe, to ſay we end
The Heart-ake, and the thouſand Naturall ſhockes
That Fleſh is heyre too? 'Tis a conſummation
Deuoutly to be wiſh'd. To dye to ſleepe,
To ſleepe, perchance to Dreame; I, there's the rub,
For in that ſleepe of death, what dreames may come,
When we haue ſhuffel'd off this mortall coile,
Muſt giue vs pawſe. There's the reſpect
That makes Calamity of ſo long life:
For who would beare the Whips and Scornes of time,
The Oppreſſors wrong, the poore mans Contumely,
The pangs of diſpriz'd Loue, the Lawes delay,
The inſolence of Office, and the Spurnes
That patient merit of the vnworthy takes,
When he himſelfe might his *Quietus* make
With a bare Bodkin? Who would theſe Fardles beare
To grunt and ſweat vnder a weary life,
But that the dread of ſomething after death,
The vndiſcouered Countrey, from whoſe Borne
No Traueller returnes, Puzels the will,
And makes vs rather beare thoſe illes we haue,
Then flye to others that we know not of.
Thus Conſcience does make Cowards of vs all,
And thus the Natiue hew of Reſolution
Is ſicklied o're, with the pale caſt of Thought,
And enterprizes of great pith and moment,
With this regard their Currants turne away,
And looſe the name of Action. Soft you now,
The faire *Ophelia*? Nimph, in thy Orizons
Be all my ſinnes remembred.
Ophe. Good my Lord,
How does your Honor for this many a day?
Ham. I humbly thanke you: well, well, well.
Ophe. My Lord, I haue Remembrances of yours,
That I haue longed long to re-deliuer.
I pray you now, receiue them.
Ham. No, no, I neuer gaue you ought.
Ophe. My honor'd Lord, I know right well you did,
And with them words of ſo ſweet breath compos'd,
As made the things more rich, then perfume left:
Take theſe againe, for to the Noble minde
Rich gifts wax poore, when giuers proue vnkinde.
There my Lord.
Ham. Ha, ha: Are you honeſt?
Ophe. My Lord.
Ham. Are you faire?
Ophe. What meanes your Lordſhip?
Ham. That if you be honeſt and faire, your Honeſty ſhould admit no diſcourſe to your Beautie.
Ophe. Could Beautie my Lord, haue better Comerce then your Honeſtie?
Ham. I trulie: for the power of Beautie, will ſooner transforme Honeſtie from what it is, to a Bawd, then the force of Honeſtie can tranſlate Beautie into his likeneſſe. This was ſometime a Paradox, but now the time giues it proofe. I did loue you once.
Ophe. Indeed my Lord, you made me beleeue ſo.
Ham. You ſhould not haue beleeued me. For vertue cannot ſo innocculate our old ſtocke, but we ſhall relliſh of it. I loued you not.
Ophe. I was the more deceiued.
Ham. Get thee to a Nunnerie. Why would'ſt thou be a breeder of Sinners? I am my ſelfe indifferent honeſt, but yet I could accuſe me of ſuch things, that it were better my Mother had not borne me. I am very prowd, reuengefull, Ambitious, with more offences at my becke, then I haue thoughts to put them in imagination, to giue them ſhape, or time to acte them in. What ſhould ſuch
Fel-

Fellowes as I do, crawling betweene Heauen and Earth. We are arrant Knaues all, beleeue none of vs. Goe thy wayes to a Nunnery. Where's your Father?

Ophe. At home, my Lord.

Ham. Let the doores be ſhut vpon him, that he may play the Foole no way, but in's owne houſe. Farewell.

Ophe. O helpe him, you ſweet Heauens.

Ham. If thou doeſt Marry, Ile giue thee this Plague for thy Dowrie. Be thou as chaſt as Ice, as pure as Snow, thou ſhalt not eſcape Calumny. Get thee to a Nunnery. Go, Farewell. Or if thou wilt needs Marry, marry a fool: for Wiſe men know well enough, what monſters you make of them. To a Nunnery go, and quickly too. Farwell.

Ophe. O heauenly Powers, reſtore him.

Ham. I haue heard of your pratlings too wel enough. God has giuen you one pace, and you make your ſelfe another: you gidge, you amble, and you liſpe, and nickname Gods creatures, and make your Wantonneſſe, your Ignorance. Go too, Ile no more on't, it hath made me mad. I ſay, we will haue no more Marriages. Thoſe that are married already, all but one ſhall liue, the reſt ſhall keep as they are. To a Nunnery, go. *Exit Hamlet*

Ophe. O what a Noble minde is heere o're-throwne?
The Courtiers, Soldiers, Schollers: Eye, tongue, ſword,
Th'expectanſie and Roſe of the faire State,
The glaſſe of Faſhion, and the mould of Forme,
Th'obſeru'd of all Obſeruers, quite, quite downe.
Haue I of Ladies moſt deiect and wretched,
That ſuck'd the Honie of his Muſicke Vowes:
Now ſee that Noble, and moſt Soueraigne Reaſon,
Like ſweet Bels iangled out of tune, and harſh,
That vnmatch'd Forme and Feature of blowne youth,
Blaſted with extaſie. Oh woe is me,
T'haue ſeene what I haue ſeene: ſee what I ſee.

Enter King, and Polonius.

King. Loue? His affections do not that way tend,
Nor what he ſpake, though it lack'd Forme a little,
Was not like Madneſſe. There's ſomething in his ſoule?
O're which his Melancholly ſits on brood,
And I do doubt the hatch, and the diſcloſe
Will be ſome danger, which to preuent
I haue in quicke determination
Thus ſet it downe. He ſhall with ſpeed to England
For the demand of our neglected Tribute:
Haply the Seas and Countries different
With variable Obiects, ſhall expell
This ſomething ſetled matter in his heart:
Whereon his Braines ſtill beating, puts him thus
From faſhion of himſelfe. What thinke you on't?

Pol. It ſhall do well. But yet do I beleeue
The Origin and Commencement of this greefe
Sprung from neglected loue. How now *Ophelia*?
You neede not tell vs, what Lord *Hamlet* ſaide,
We heard it all. My Lord, do as you pleaſe,
But if you hold it fit after the Play,
Let his Queene Mother all alone intreat him
To ſhew his Greefes: let her be round with him,
And Ile be plac'd ſo, pleaſe you in the eare
Of all their Conference. If ſhe finde him not,
To England ſend him: Or confine him where
Your wiſedome beſt ſhall thinke.

King. It ſhall be ſo:
Madneſſe in great Ones, muſt not vnwatch'd go.

Exeunt.

Enter Hamlet, and two or three of the Players.

Ham. Speake the Speech I pray you, as I pronounc'd it to you trippingly on the Tongue: But if you mouth it, as many of your Players do, I had as liue the Town-Cryer had ſpoke my Lines: Nor do not ſaw the Ayre too much your hand thus, but vſe all gently; for in the verie Torrent, Tempeſt, and (as I may ſay) the Whirle-winde of Paſſion, you muſt acquire and beget a Temperance that may giue it Smoothneſſe. O it offends mee to the Soule, to ſee a robuſtious Pery-wig-pated Fellow, teare a Paſſion to tatters, to verie ragges, to ſplit the eares of the Groundlings: who (for the moſt part) are capeable of nothing, but inexplicable dumbe ſhewes, & noiſe: I could haue ſuch a Fellow whipt for o're-doing Termagant: it out-*Herod's Herod*. Pray you auoid it.

Player. I warrant your Honor.

Ham. Be not too tame neyther: but let your owne Diſcretion be your Tutor. Sute the Action to the Word, the Word to the Action, with this ſpeciall obſeruance: That you ore-ſtop not the modeſtie of Nature; for any thing ſo ouer-done, is frō the purpoſe of Playing, whoſe end both at the firſt and now, was and is, to hold as 'twer the Mirrour vp to Nature; to ſhew Vertue her owne Feature, Scorne her owne Image, and the verie Age and Bodie of the Time, his forme and preſſure. Now, this ouer-done, or come tardie off, though it make the vnskilfull laugh, cannot but make the Iudicious greeue; The cenſure of the which One, muſt in your allowance o're-way a whole Theater of Others. Oh, there bee Players that I haue ſeene Play, and heard others praiſe, and that highly (not to ſpeake it prophanely) that neyther hauing the accent of Chriſtians, nor the gate of Chriſtian, Pagan, or Norman, haue ſo ſtrutted and bellowed, that I haue thought ſome of Natures Iourney-men had made men, and not made them well, they imitated Humanity ſo abhominably.

Play. I hope we haue reform'd that indifferently with vs, Sir.

Ham. O reforme it altogether. And let thoſe that play your Clownes, ſpeake no more then is ſet downe for them. For there be of them, that will themſelues laugh, to ſet on ſome quantitie of barren Spectators to laugh too, though in the meane time, ſome neceſſary Queſtion of the Play be then to be conſidered: that's Villanous, & ſhewes a moſt pittifull Ambition in the Foole that vſes it. Go make you readie. *Exit Players.*

Enter Polonius, Roſincrance, and Guildensterne.

How now my Lord,
Will the King heare this peece of Worke?

Pol. And the Queene too, and that preſently.

Ham. Bid the Players make haſt. *Exit Polonius.*
Will you two helpe to haſten them?

Both. We will my Lord. *Exeunt.*

Enter Horatio.

Ham. What hoa, *Horatio*?

Hora. Heere ſweet Lord, at your Seruice.

Ham. *Horatio*, thou art eene as iuſt a man
As ere my Conuerſation coap'd withall.

Hora. O my deere Lord.

Ham. Nay do not thinke I flatter:
For what aduancement may I hope from thee,
That no Reuennew haſt, but thy good ſpirits

To

To feed & cloath thee. Why ſhold the poor be flatter'd?
No, let the Candied tongue, like abſurd pompe,
And crooke the pregnant Hindges of the knee,
Where thrift may follow faining? Doſt thou heare,
Since my deere Soule was Miſtris of my choyſe,
And could of men diſtinguiſh, her election
Hath ſeal'd thee for her ſelfe. For thou haſt bene
As one in ſuffering all, that ſuffers nothing.
A man that Fortunes buffets, and Rewards
Hath 'tane with equall Thankes. And bleſt are thoſe,
Whoſe Blood and Iudgement are ſo well co-mingled,
That they are not a Pipe for Fortunes finger,
To ſound what ſtop ſhe pleaſe. Giue me that man,
That is not Paſſions Slaue, and I will weare him
In my hearts Core: I, in my Heart of heart,
As I do thee. Something too much of this.
There is a Play to night before the King,
One Scoene of it comes neere the Circumſtance
Which I haue told thee, of my Fathers death.
I prythee, when thou ſee'ſt that Acte a-foot,
Euen with the verie Comment of my Soule
Obſerue mine Vnkle: If his occulted guilt,
Do not it ſelfe vnkennell in one ſpeech,
It is a damned Ghoſt that we haue ſeene:
And my Imaginations are as foule
As Vulcans Stythe. Giue him needfull note,
For I mine eyes will riuet to his Face:
And after we will both our iudgements ioyne,
To cenſure of his ſeeming.

Hora. Well my Lord.
If he ſteale ought the whil'ſt this Play is Playing,
And ſcape detecting, I will pay the Theft.

Enter King, Queene, Polonius, Ophelia, Roſincrance, Guildenſterne, and other Lords attendant, with his Guard carrying Torches. Daniſh March. Sound a Flouriſh.

Ham. They are comming to the Play: I muſt be idle
Get you a place.

King. How fares our Coſin *Hamlet*?

Ham. Excellent Ifaith, of the Camelions diſh: I eate the Ayre promiſe-cramm'd, you cannot feed Capons ſo.

King. I haue nothing with this anſwer *Hamlet*, theſe words are not mine.

Ham. No, nor mine. Now my Lord, you plaid once i'th'Vniuerſity, you ſay?

Polon. That I did my Lord, and was accounted a good Actor.

Ham. And what did you enact?

Pol. I did enact *Iulius Cæſar*, I was kill'd i'th'Capitol: *Brutus* kill'd me.

Ham. It was a bruite part of him, to kill ſo Capitall a Calfe there. Be the Players ready?

Roſin. I my Lord, they ſtay vpon your patience.

Qu. Come hither my good *Hamlet*, ſit by me.

Ha. No good Mother, here's Mettle more attractiue.

Pol. Oh ho, do you marke that?

Ham. Ladie, ſhall I lye in your Lap?

Ophe. No my Lord.

Ham. I meane, my Head vpon your Lap?

Ophe. I my Lord.

Ham. Do you thinke I meant Country matters?

Ophe. I thinke nothing, my Lord.

Ham. That's a faire thought to ly between Maids legs

Ophe. What is my Lord?

Ham. Nothing.

Ophe. You are merrie, my Lord?

Ham. Who I?

Ophe. I my Lord.

Ham. Oh God, your onely Iigge-maker: what ſhould a man do, but be merrie. For looke you how cheerefully my Mother lookes, and my Father dyed within's two Houres.

Ophe. Nay, 'tis twice two moneths, my Lord.

Ham. So long? Nay then let the Diuel weare blacke, for Ile haue a ſuite of Sables. Oh Heauens! dye two moneths ago, and not forgotten yet? Then there's hope, a great mans Memorie, may out-liue his life halfe a yeare: But byrlady he muſt builde Churches then: or elſe ſhall he ſuffer not thinking on, with the Hoby-horſſe, whoſe Epitaph is, For o, For o, the Hoby-horſe is forgot.

Hoboyes play. The dumbe ſhew enters.

Enter a King and Queene, very louingly; the Queene embracing him. She kneeles, and makes ſhew of Proteſtation vnto him. He takes her vp, and declines his head vpon her neck. Layes him downe vpon a Banke of Flowers. She ſeeing him a-ſleepe, leaues him. Anon comes in a Fellow, takes off his Crowne, kiſſes it, and powres poyſon in the Kings eares, and Exits. The Queene returnes, findes the King dead, and makes paſſionate Action. The Poyſoner, with ſome two or three Mutes comes in againe, ſeeming to lament with her. The dead body is carried away: The Poyſoner Wooes the Queene with Gifts, ſhe ſeemes loath and vnwilling awhile, but in the end, accepts his loue. Exeunt

Ophe. What meanes this, my Lord?

Ham. Marry this is Miching *Malicho*, that meanes Miſcheefe.

Ophe. Belike this ſhew imports the Argument of the Play?

Ham. We ſhall know by theſe Fellowes: the Players cannot keepe counſell, they'l tell all.

Ophe. Will they tell vs what this ſhew meant?

Ham. I, or any ſhew that you'l ſhew him. Bee not you aſham'd to ſhew, hee'l not ſhame to tell you what it meanes.

Ophe. You are naught, you are naught, Ile marke the Play

Enter Prologue.

For vs, and for our Tragedie,
Heere ſtooping to your Clemencie:
We begge your hearing Patientlie.

Ham. Is this a Prologue, or the Poeſie of a Ring?

Ophe. 'Tis briefe my Lord.

Ham. As Womans loue.

Enter King and his Queene.

King. Full thirtie times hath Phœbus Cart gon round,
Neptunes ſalt Waſh, and *Tellus* Orbed ground:
And thirtie dozen Moones with borrowed ſheene,
About the World haue times twelue thirties beene,
Since loue our hearts, and *Hymen* did our hands
Vnite comutuall, in moſt ſacred Bands.

Bap. So many iournies may the Sunne and Moone
Make vs againe count o're, ere loue be done.
But woe is me, you are ſo ſicke of late,
So farre from cheere, and from your forme ſtate,
That I diſtruſt you: yet though I diſtruſt,
Diſcomfort you (my Lord) it nothing muſt:
For womens Feare and Loue, holds quantitie,

In

In neither ought, or in extremity:
Now what my loue is, proofe hath made you know,
And as my Loue is ſiz'd, my Feare is ſo.

King. Faith I muſt leaue thee Loue, and ſhortly too:
My operant Powers my Functions leaue to do:
And thou ſhalt liue in this faire world behinde,
Honour'd, belou'd, and haply, one as kinde.
For Husband ſhalt thou———

Bap. Oh confound the reſt:
Such Loue, muſt needs be Treaſon in my breſt:
In ſecond Husband, let me be accurſt,
None wed the ſecond, but who kill'd the firſt.

Ham. Wormwood, Wormwood.

Bapt. The inſtances that ſecond Marriage moue,
Are baſe reſpects of Thrift, but none of Loue.
A ſecond time, I kill my Husband dead,
When ſecond Husband kiſſes me in Bed.

King. I do beleeue you. Think what now you ſpeak:
But what we do determine, oft we breake:
Purpoſe is but the ſlaue to Memorie,
Of violent Birth, but poore validitie:
Which now like Fruite vnripe ſtickes on the Tree,
But fall vnſhaken, when they mellow bee.
Moſt neceſſary 'tis, that we forget
To pay our ſelues, what to our ſelues is debt:
What to our ſelues in paſſion we propoſe,
The paſſion ending, doth the purpoſe loſe.
The violence of other Greefe or Ioy,
Their owne ennactors with themſelues deſtroy:
Where Ioy moſt Reuels, Greefe doth moſt lament;
Greefe ioyes, Ioy greeues on ſlender accident.
This world is not for aye, nor 'tis not ſtrange
That euen our Loues ſhould with our Fortunes change.
For 'tis a queſtion left vs yet to proue,
Whether Loue lead Fortune, or elſe Fortune Loue.
The great man downe, you marke his fauourites flies,
The poore aduanc'd, makes Friends of Enemies:
And hitherto doth Loue on Fortune tend.
For who not needs, ſhall neuer lacke a Frend:
And who in want a hollow Friend doth try,
Directly ſeaſons him his Enemie.
But orderly to end, where I begun,
Our Willes and Fates do ſo contrary run,
That our Deuices ſtill are ouerthrowne,
Our thoughts are ours, their ends none of our owne.
So thinke thou wilt no ſecond Husband wed.
But die thy thoughts, when thy firſt Lord is dead.

Bap. Nor Earth to giue me food, nor Heauen light,
Sport and repoſe locke from me day and night:
Each oppoſite that blankes the face of ioy,
Meet what I would haue well, and it deſtroy:
Both heere, and hence, purſue me laſting ſtrife,
If once a Widdow, euer I be Wife.

Ham. If ſhe ſhould breake it now.

King. 'Tis deepely ſworne:
Sweet, leaue me heere a while,
My ſpirits grow dull, and faine I would beguile
The tedious day with ſleepe.

Qu. Sleepe rocke thy Braine, *Sleepes*
And neuer come miſchance betweene vs twaine. *Exit*

Ham. Madam, how like you this Play?

Qu. The Lady proteſts to much me thinkes.

Ham. Oh but ſhee'l keepe her word.

King. Haue you heard the Argument, is there no Offence in't?

Ham. No, no, they do but ieſt, poyſon in ieſt, no Offence i'th' world.

King. What do you call the Play?

Ham. The Mouſe-trap: Marry how? Tropically: This Play is the Image of a murder done in *Vienna*: *Gonzago* is the Dukes name, his wife *Baptiſta*: you ſhall ſee anon: 'tis a knauiſh peece of worke: But what o'that? Your Maieſtie, and wee that haue free ſoules, it touches vs not: let the gall'd iade winch: our withers are vnrung.

Enter Lucianus.

This is one *Lucianus* nephew to the King.

Ophe. You are a good Chorus, my Lord.

Ham. I could interpret betweene you and your loue: if I could ſee the Puppets dallying.

Ophe. You are keene my Lord, you are keene.

Ham. It would coſt you a groaning, to take off my edge.

Ophe. Still better and worſe.

Ham. So you miſtake Husbands. Begin Murderer. Pox, leaue thy damnable Faces, and begin. Come, the croaking Rauen doth bellow for Reuenge.

Lucian. Thoughts blacke, hands apt,
Drugges fit, and Time agreeing:
Confederate ſeaſon, elſe, no Creature ſeeing:
Thou mixture ranke, of Midnight Weeds collected,
With Hecats Ban, thrice blaſted, thrice infected,
Thy naturall Magicke, and dire propertie,
On wholſome life, vſurpe immediately.

Powres the poyſon in his eares.

Ham. He poyſons him i'th Garden for's eſtate: His name's *Gonzago*: the Story is extant and writ in choyce Italian. You ſhall ſee anon how the Murtherer gets the loue of *Gonzago's* wiſe.

Ophe. The King riſes.

Ham. What, frighted with falſe fire.

Qu. How fares my Lord?

Pol. Giue o're the Play.

King. Giue me ſome Light. Away.

All. Lights, Lights, Lights. *Exeunt*

Manet Hamlet & Horatio.

Ham. Why let the ſtrucken Deere go weepe,
The Hart vngalled play:
For ſome muſt watch, while ſome muſt ſleepe;
So runnes the world away.
Would not this Sir, and a Forreſt of Feathers, if the reſt of my Fortunes turne Turke with me; with two Prouinciall Roſes on my rac'd Shooes, get me a Fellowſhip in a crie of Players ſir.

Hor. Halfe a ſhare.

Ham. A whole one I,
For thou doſt know: Oh *Damon* deere,
This Realme diſmantled was of Ioue himſelfe,
And now reignes heere.
A verie verie Paiocke.

Hora. You might haue Rim'd.

Ham. Oh good *Horatio*, Ile take the Ghoſts word for a thouſand pound. Did'ſt perceiue?

Hora. Verie well my Lord.

Ham. Vpon the talke of the poyſoning?

Hora. I did verie well note him.

Enter Roſincrance and Guildenſterne.

Ham. Oh, ha? Come ſome Muſick. Come ÿ Recorders:
For if the King like not the Comedie,
Why then belike he likes it not perdie.
Come ſome Muſicke.

Guild. Good my Lord, vouchſafe me a word with you.

Ham.

Ham. Sir,a whole History.

Guild. The King, sir.

Ham. I sir,what of him ?

Guild. Is in his retyrement, maruellous distemper'd.

Ham. With drinke Sir ?

Guild. No my Lord,rather with choller.

Ham. Your wisedome should shew it selfe more richer, to signifie this to his Doctor. for for me to put him to his Purgation, would perhaps plundge him into farre more Choller.

Guild. Good my Lord put your discourse into some frame,and start not so wildely from my affayre.

Ham. I am tame Sir,pronounce.

Guild. The Queene your Mother, in most great affliction of spirit, hath sent me to you.

Ham. You are welcome.

Guild. Nay, good my Lord, this courtesie is not of the right breed. If it shall please you to make me a wholsome answer, I will doe your Mothers command'ment : if not, your pardon, and my returne shall bee the end of my Businesse.

Ham. Sir, I cannot.

Guild What,my Lord?

Ham. Make you a wholsome answere : my wits diseas'd. But sir, such answers as I can make,you shal command : or rather you say, my Mother : therfore no more but to the matter. My Mother you say.

Rosin. Then thus she sayes : your behauior hath stroke her into amazement,and admiration.

Ham. Oh wonderfull Sonne, that can so astonish a Mother. But is there no sequell at the heeles of this Mothers admiration ?

Rosin. She desires to speake with you in her Closset, ere you go to bed.

Ham. We shall obey, were she ten times our Mother. Haue you any further Trade with vs ?

Rosin. My Lord,you once did loue me.

Ham. So I do still, by these pickers and stealers.

Rosin. Good my Lord, what is your cause of distemper ? You do freely barre the doore of your owne Libertie, if you deny your greefes to your Friend.

Ham. Sir I lacke Aduancement.

Rosin. How can that be, when you haue the voyce of the King himselfe, for your Succession in Denmarke ?

Ham. I,but while the grasse growes, the Prouerbe is something musty.

Enter one with a Recorder.

O the Recorder. Let me see,to withdraw with you,why do you go about to recouer the winde of mee, as if you would driue me into a toyle ?

Guild. O my Lord, if my Dutie be too bold,my loue is too vnmannerly.

Ham. I do not well vnderstand that. Will you play vpon this Pipe?

Guild. My Lord, I cannot.

Ham. I pray you.

Guild. Beleeue me,I cannot.

Ham. I do beseech you.

Guild. I know no touch of it,my Lord.

Ham. 'Tis as easie as lying : gouerne these Ventiges with your finger and thumbe, giue it breath with your mouth, and it will discourse most excellent Musicke. Looke you, these are the stoppes.

Guild. But these cannot I command to any vtterance of hermony. I haue not the skill.

Ham. Why looke you now, how vnworthy a thing you make of me : you would play vpon mee; you would seeme to know my stops : you would pluck out the heart of my Mysterie ; you would sound mee from my lowest Note,to the top of my Compasse: and there is much Musicke, excellent Voice, in this little Organe, yet cannot you make it. Why do you thinke, that I am easier to bee plaid on, then a Pipe? Call me what Instrument you will, though you can fret me, you cannot play vpon me. God blesse you Sir.

Enter Polonius.

Polon. My Lord;the Queene would speak with you, and presently.

Ham. Do you see that Clowd? that's almost in shape like a Camell.

Polon. By'th'Misse, and it's like a Camell indeed.

Ham. Me thinkes it is like a Weazell.

Polon. It is back'd like a Weazell.

Ham. Or like a Whale ?

Polon. Verie like a Whale.

Ham. Then will I come to my Mother, by and by :
They foole me to the top of my bent.
I will come by and by.

Polon. I will say so. *Exit.*

Ham. By and by, is easily said. Leaue me Friends :
'Tis now the verie witching time of night,
When Churchyards yawne,and Hell it selfe breaths out
Contagion to this world. Now could I drink hot blood,
And do such bitter businesse as the day
Would quake to looke on. Soft now,to my Mother :
Oh Heart, loose not thy Nature ; let not euer
The Soule of *Nero*, enter this firme bosome :
Let me be cruell, not vnnaturall,
I will speake Daggers to her, but vse none :
My Tongue and Soule in this be Hypocrites.
How in my words someuer she be shent,
To giue them Seales, neuer my Soule consent.

Enter King, Rosincrance, and Guildensterne.

King. I like him not, nor stands it safe with vs,
To let his madnesse range. Therefore prepare you,
I your Commission will forthwith dispatch,
And he to England shall along with you :
The termes of our estate, may not endure
Hazard so dangerous as doth hourely grow
Out of his Lunacies.

Guild. We will our selues prouide :
Most holie and Religious feare it is
To keepe those many many bodies safe
That liue and feede vpon your Maiestie.

Rosin. The single
And peculiar life is bound
With all the strength and Armour of the minde,
To keepe it selfe from noyance : but much more,
That Spirit, vpon whose spirit depends and rests
The liues of many, the cease of Maiestie
Dies not alone; but like a Gulfe doth draw
What's neere it, with it. It is a massie wheele
Fixt on the Somnet of the highest Mount,
To whose huge Spoakes, ten thousand lesser things
Are mortiz'd and adioyn'd : which when it falles,
Each small annexment, pettie consequence
Attends the boystrous Ruine. Neuer alone
Did the King sighe, but with a generall grone.

King. Arme you, I pray you to this speedie Voyage;
For we will Fetters put vpon this feare,

PP Which

Which now goes too free-footed.
Both. We will haste vs. *Exeunt Gent.*
Enter Polonius.
Pol. My Lord, he's going to his Mothers Closset:
Behinde the Arras Ile conuey my ſelfe
To heare the Proceſſe. Ile warrant ſhee'l tax him home,
And as you ſaid, and wiſely was it ſaid,
'Tis meete that ſome more audience then a Mother,
Since Nature makes them partiall, ſhould o're-heare
The ſpeech of vantage. Fare you well my Liege,
Ile call vpon you ere you go to bed,
And tell you what I know.
King. Thankes deere my Lord.
Oh my offence is ranke, it ſmels to heauen,
It hath the primall eldeſt curſe vpon't,
A Brothers murther. Pray can I not,
Though inclination be as ſharpe as will:
My ſtronger guilt, defeats my ſtrong intent,
And like a man to double buſineſſe bound,
I ſtand in pauſe where I ſhall firſt begin,
And both neglect; what if this curſed hand
Were thicker then it ſelfe with Brothers blood,
Is there not Raine enough in the ſweet Heauens
To waſh it white as Snow? Whereto ſerues mercy,
But to confront the viſage of Offence?
And what's in Prayer, but this two-fold force,
To be fore-ſtalled ere we come to fall,
Or pardon'd being downe? Then Ile looke vp,
My fault is paſt. But oh, what forme of Prayer
Can ſerue my turne? Forgiue me my foule Murther:
That cannot be, ſince I am ſtill poſſeſt
Of thoſe effects for which I did the Murther.
My Crowne, mine owne Ambition, and my Queene:
May one be pardon'd, and retaine th'offence?
In the corrupted currants of this world,
Offences gilded hand may ſhoue by Iuſtice,
And oft 'tis ſeene, the wicked prize it ſelfe
Buyes out the Law; but 'tis not ſo aboue,
There is no ſhuffling, there the Action lyes
In his true Nature, and we our ſelues compell'd
Euen to the teeth and forehead of our faults,
To giue in euidence. What then? What reſts?
Try what Repentance can. What can it not?
Yet what can it, when one cannot repent?
Oh wretched ſtate! Oh boſome, blacke as death!
Oh limed ſoule, that ſtrugling to be free,
Art more ingag'd: Helpe Angels, make aſſay:
Bow ſtubborne knees, and heart with ſtrings of Steele,
Be ſoft as ſinewes of the new-borne Babe,
All may be well.
Enter Hamlet.

Ham. Now might I do it pat, now he is praying,
And now Ile doo't, and ſo he goes to Heauen,
And ſo am I reueng'd: that would be ſcann'd,
A Villaine killes my Father, and for that
I his foule Sonne, do this ſame Villaine ſend
To heauen. Oh this is hyre and Sallery, not Reuenge.
He tooke my Father groſſely, full of bread,
With all his Crimes broad blowne, as freſh as May,
And how his Audit ſtands, who knowes, ſaue Heauen:
But in our circumſtance and courſe of thought
'Tis heauie with him: and am I then reueng'd,
To take him in the purging of his Soule,
When he is fit and ſeaſon'd for his paſſage? No.
Vp Sword, and know thou a more horrid hent
When he is drunke aſleepe: or in his Rage,
Or in th'inceſtuous pleaſure of his bed,
At gaming, ſwearing, or about ſome acte
That ha's no reliſh of Saluation in't,
Then trip him, that his heeles may kicke at Heauen,
And that his Soule may be as damn'd and blacke
As Hell, whereto it goes. My Mother ſtayes,
This Phyſicke but prolongs thy ſickly dayes. *Exit.*
King. My words flye vp, my thoughts remain below,
Words without thoughts, neuer to Heauen go. *Exit.*

Enter Queene and Polonius.
Pol. He will come ſtraight:
Looke you lay home to him,
Tell him his prankes haue been too broad to beare with,
And that your Grace hath ſcree'nd, and ſtoode betweene
Much heate, and him. Ile ſilence me e'ene heere:
Pray you be round with him.
Ham. within. Mother, mother, mother.
Qu. Ile warrant you, feare me not.
Withdraw, I heare him comming.
Enter Hamlet.
Ham. Now Mother, what's the matter?
Qu. Hamlet, thou haſt thy Father much offended.
Ham. Mother, you haue my Father much offended.
Qu. Come, come, you anſwer with an idle tongue.
Ham. Go, go, you queſtion with an idle tongue.
Qu. Why how now *Hamlet*?
Ham. Whats the matter now?
Qu. Haue you forgot me?
Ham. No by the Rood, not ſo:
You are the Queene, your Husbands Brothers wife,
But would you were not ſo. You are my Mother.
Qu. Nay, then Ile ſet thoſe to you that can ſpeake.
Ham. Come, come, and ſit you downe, you ſhall not boudge:
You go not till I ſet you vp a glaſſe,
Where you may ſee the inmoſt part of you?
Qu. What wilt thou do? thou wilt not murther me?
Helpe, helpe, hoa.
Pol. What hoa, helpe, helpe, helpe.
Ham. How now, a Rat? dead for a Ducate, dead.
Pol. Oh I am ſlaine. *Killes Polonius.*
Qu. Oh me, what haſt thou done?
Ham. Nay I know not, is it the King?
Qu. Oh what a raſh, and bloody deed is this?
Ham. A bloody deed, almoſt as bad good Mother,
As kill a King, and marrie with his Brother.
Qu. As kill a King?
Ham. I Lady, 'twas my word.
Thou wretched, raſh, intruding foole farewell,
I tooke thee for thy Betters, take thy Fortune,
Thou find'ſt to be too buſie, is ſome danger.
Leaue wringing of your hands, peace, ſit you downe,
And let me wring your heart, for ſo I ſhall
If it be made of penetrable ſtuffe;
If damned Cuſtome haue not braz'd it ſo,
That it is proofe and bulwarke againſt Senſe.
Qu. What haue I done, that thou dar'ſt wag thy tong,
In noiſe ſo rude againſt me?
Ham. Such an Act
That blurres the grace and bluſh of Modeſtie,
Cals Vertue Hypocrite, takes off the Roſe
From the faire forehead of an innocent loue,
And makes a bliſter there. Makes marriage vowes
As falſe as Dicers Oathes. Oh ſuch a deed,
As

As from the body of Contraction pluckes
The very soule, and sweete Religion makes
A rapsidie of words. Heauens face doth glow,
Yea this solidity and compound masse,
With tristfull visage as against the doome,
Is thought-sicke at the act.

Qu. Aye me; what act, that roares so lowd, & thunders in the Index.

Ham. Looke heere vpon this Picture, and on this,
The counterfet presentment of two Brothers:
See what a grace was seated on his Brow.
Hyperions curles, the front of Ioue himselfe,
An eye like Mars, to threaten or command
A Station, like the Herald Mercurie
New lighted on a heauen kissing hill:
A Combination, and a forme indeed,
Where euery God did seeme to set his Seale,
To giue the world assurance of a man.
This was your Husband. Looke you now what followes.
Heere is your Husband, like a Mildew'd eare
Blasting his wholsom breath. Haue you eyes?
Could you on this faire Mountaine leaue to feed,
And batten on this Moore? Ha? Haue you eyes?
You cannot call it Loue: For at your age,
The hey-day in the blood is tame, it's humble,
And waites vpon the Iudgement: and what Iudgement
Would step from this, to this? What diuell was't,
That thus hath cousend you at hoodman-blinde?
O Shame! where is thy Blush? Rebellious Hell,
If thou canst mutine in a Matrons bones,
To flaming youth, let Vertue be as waxe.
And melt in her owne fire. Proclaime no shame,
When the compulsiue Ardure giues the charge,
Since Frost it selfe, as actiuely doth burne,
As Reason panders Will.

Qu. O *Hamlet*, speake no more.
Thou turn'st mine eyes into my very soule,
And there I see such blacke and grained spots,
As will not leaue their Tinct.

Ham. Nay, but to liue
In the ranke sweat of an enseamed bed,
Stew'd in Corruption; honying and making loue
Ouer the nasty Stye.

Qu. Oh speake to me, no more,
These words like Daggers enter in mine eares.
No more sweet *Hamlet*

Ham. A Murderer, and a Villaine:
A Slaue, that is not twentieth part the tythe
Of your precedent Lord. A vice of Kings,
A Cutpurse of the Empire and the Rule.
That from a shelfe, the precious Diadem stole,
And put it in his Pocket.

Qu. No more.

Enter Ghost.

Ham. A King of shreds and patches.
Saue me; and houer o're me with your wings
You heauenly Guards. What would you gracious figure?

Qu. Alas he's mad

Ham. Do you not come your tardy Sonne to chide,
That laps't in Time and Passion, lets go by
Th'important acting of your dread command? Oh say.

Ghost. Do not forget: this Visitation
Is but to whet thy almost blunted purpose.
But looke, Amazement on thy Mother sits;
O step betweene her, and her fighting Soule,
Conceit in weakest bodies, strongest workes.
Speake to her *Hamlet*.

Ham. How is it with you Lady?

Qu. Alas, how is't with you?
That you bend your eye on vacancie,
And with their corporall ayre do hold discourse.
Forth at your eyes, your spirits wildely peepe,
And as the sleeping Soldiours in th'Alarme,
Your bedded haire, like life in excrements,
Start vp, and stand an end. Oh gentle Sonne,
Vpon the heate and flame of thy distemper
Sprinkle coole patience. Whereon do you looke?

Ham. On him, on him: look you how pale he glares,
His forme and cause conioyn'd, preaching to stones,
Would make them capeable. Do not looke vpon me,
Least with this pitteous action you conuert
My sterne effects: then what I haue to do,
Will want true colour; teares perchance for blood.

Qu. To who do you speake this?

Ham. Do you see nothing there?

Qu. Nothing at all, yet all that is I see

Ham. Nor did you nothing heare?

Qu. No, nothing but our selues.

Ham. Why look you there: looke how it steals away:
My Father in his habite, as he liued,
Looke where he goes euen now out at the Portall. *Exit.*

Qu. This is the very coynage of your Braine,
This bodilesse Creation extasie is very cunning in.

Ham. Extasie?
My Pulse as yours doth temperately keepe time,
And makes as healthfull Musicke. It is not madnesse
That I haue vttered; bring me to the Test
And I the matter will re-word which madnesse
Would gamboll from. Mother, for loue of Grace,
Lay not a flattering Vnction to your soule,
That not your trespasse, but my madnesse speakes:
It will but skin and filme the Vlcerous place,
Whil'st ranke Corruption mining all within,
Infects vnseene. Confesse your selfe to Heauen,
Repent what's past, auoyd what is to come,
And do not spred the Compost or the Weedes,
To make them ranke. Forgiue me this my Vertue,
For in the fatnesse of this pursie times,
Vertue it selfe, of Vice must pardon begge,
Yea courb, and woe, for leaue to do him good.

Qu. Oh *Hamlet*,
Thou hast cleft my heart in twaine.

Ham. O throw away the worser part of it,
And liue the purer with the other halfe.
Good night, but go not to mine Vnkles bed,
Assume a Vertue, if you haue it not, refraine to night,
And that shall lend a kinde of easinesse
To the next abstinence. Once more goodnight,
And when you are desirous to be blest,
Ile blessing begge of you. For this same Lord,
I do repent: but heauen hath pleas'd it so,
To punish me with this, and this with me,
That I must be their Scourge and Minister.
I will bestow him, and will answer well
The death I gaue him: so againe, good night.
I must be cruell, onely to be kinde;
Thus bad begins, and worse remaines behinde.

Qu. What shall I do?

Ham. Not this by no meanes that I bid you do:
Let the blunt King tempt you againe to bed,
Pinch Wanton on your cheeke, call you his Mouse,
And let him for a paire of reechie kisses,

Or padling in your necke with his damn'd Fingers,
Make you to rauell all this matter out,
That I essentially am not in madnesse.
But made in craft. 'Twere good you let him know,
For who that's but a Queene, faire, sober, wise,
Would from a Paddocke, from a Bat, a Gibbe,
Such deere concernings hide. Who would do so,
No in despight of Sense and Secrecie,
Vnpegge the Basket on the houses top:
Let the Birds flye, and like the famous Ape
To try Conclusions in the Basket, creepe
And breake your owne necke downe.

Qu. Be thou assur'd, if words be made of breath,
And breath of life: I haue no life to breath
What thou hast saide to me.

Ham. I must to England, you know that?

Qu. Alacke I had forgot: 'Tis so concluded on.

Ham. This man shall set me packing:
Ile lugge the Guts into the Neighbor roome,
Mother goodnight. Indeede this Counsellor
Is now most still, most secret, and most graue,
Who was in life, a foolish prating Knaue.
Come sir, to draw toward an end with you.
Good night Mother.

Exit Hamlet tugging in Polonius.

Enter King.

King. There's matters in these sighes.
These profound heaues
You must translate; Tis fit we vnderstand them.
Where is your Sonne?

Qu. Ah my good Lord, what haue I seene to night?

King. What *Gertrude*? How do's *Hamlet*?

Qu. Mad as the Seas, and winde, when both contend
Which is the Mightier, in his lawlesse fit
Behinde the Arras, hearing something stirre,
He whips his Rapier out, and cries a Rat, a Rat,
And in his brainish apprehension killes
The vnseene good old man.

King. Oh heauy deed:
It had bin so with vs had we beene there:
His Liberty is full of threats to all,
To you your selfe, to vs, to euery one.
Alas, how shall this bloody deede be answered?
It will be laide to vs, whose prouidence
Should haue kept short, restrain'd, and out of haunt,
This mad yong man. But so much was our loue,
We would not vnderstand what was most fit,
But like the Owner of a foule disease,
To keepe it from divulging, let's it feede
Euen on the pith of life. Where is he gone?

Qu. To draw apart the body he hath kild,
O're whom his very madnesse like some Oare
Among a Minerall of Mettels base
Shewes it selfe pure. He weepes for what is done.

King. Oh *Gertrude*, come away:
The Sun no sooner shall the Mountaines touch,
But we will ship him hence, and this vilde deed,
We must with all our Maiesty and Skill
Both countenance, and excuse. *Enter Ros. & Guild.*
Ho *Guildenstern*:
Friends both go ioyne you with some further ayde:
Hamlet in madnesse hath *Polonius* slaine,
And from his Mother Clossets hath he drag'd him.
Go seeke him out, speake faire, and bring the body
Into the Chappell. I pray you hast in this. *Exit Gent.*
Come *Gertrude*, wee'l call vp our wisest friends,
To let them know both what we meane to do,
And what's vntimely done. Oh come away,
My soule is full of discord and dismay. *Exeunt*

Enter Hamlet.

Ham. Safely stowed.

Gentlemen within. Hamlet, Lord Hamlet.

Ham. What noise? Who cals on *Hamlet*?
Oh heere they come. *Enter Ros. and Guildensterne.*

Ro. What haue you done my Lord with the dead body?

Ham. Compounded it with dust, whereto 'tis Kinne.

Rosin. Tell vs where 'tis, that we may take it thence,
And beare it to the Chappell.

Ham. Do not beleeue it.

Rosin. Beleeue what?

Ham. That I can keepe your counsell, and not mine owne. Besides, to be demanded of a Spundge, what replication should be made by the Sonne of a King.

Rosin. Take you me for a Spundge, my Lord?

Ham. I sir, that sokes vp the Kings Countenance, his Rewards, his Authorities (but such Officers do the King best seruice in the end. He keepes them like an Ape in the corner of his iaw, first mouth'd to be last swallowed, when he needes what you haue glean'd, it is but squeezing you, and Spundge you shall be dry againe.

Rosin. I vnderstand you not my Lord.

Ham. I am glad of it: a knauish speech sleepes in a foolish eare.

Rosin. My Lord, you must tell vs where the body is, and go with vs to the King.

Ham. The body is with the King, but the King is not with the body. The King, is a thing ——

Guild. A thing my Lord?

Ham. Of nothing: bring me to him, hide Fox, and all after. *Exeunt*

Enter King.

King. I haue sent to seeke him, and to find the bodie:
How dangerous is it that this man goes loose:
Yet must not we put the strong Law on him:
Hee's loued of the distracted multitude,
Who like not in their iudgement, but their eyes:
And where 'tis so, th'Offenders scourge is weigh'd
But neerer the offence: to beare all smooth, and euen,
This sodaine sending him away, must seeme
Deliberate pause, diseases desperate growne,
By desperate appliance are releeued,
Or not at all. *Enter Rosincrane.*
How now? What hath befalne?

Rosin. Where the dead body is bestow'd my Lord,
We cannot get from him.

King. But where is he?

Rosin. Without my Lord, guarded to know your pleasure.

King. Bring him before vs.

Rosin. Hoa, *Guildensterne*? Bring in my Lord.

Enter Hamlet and Guildensterne.

King. Now *Hamlet*, where's *Polonius*?

Ham. At Supper.

King. At Supper? Where?

Ham. Not where he eats, but where he is eaten, a certaine conuocation of wormes are e'ne at him. Your worm is your onely Emperor for diet. We fat all creatures else to fat vs, and we fat our selfe for Magots. Your fat King, and your leane Begger is but variable seruice to dishes, but to one Table that's the end.

King. What dost thou meane by this?

Ham.

Ham. Nothing but to ſhew you how a King may go
a Progreſſe through the guts of a Begger.
King. Where is *Polonius*.
Ham. In heauen, ſend thither to ſee. If your Meſſen-
ger finde him not there, ſeeke him i'th other place your
ſelfe : but indeed, if you finde him not this moneth, you
ſhall noſe him as you go vp the ſtaires into the Lobby.
King. Go ſeeke him there.
Ham. He will ſtay till ye come.
K. Hamlet, this deed of thine, for thine eſpecial ſafety
Which we do tender, as we deerely greeue
For that which thou haſt done, muſt ſend thee hence
With fierie Quickneſſe. Therefore prepare thy ſelfe,
The Barke is readie, and the winde at helpe,
Th'Aſſociates tend, and euery thing at bent
For England.
Ham. For England?
King. I *Hamlet*.
Ham. Good.
King. So is it, if thou knew'ſt our purpoſes.
Ham. I ſee a Cherube that ſee's him: but come, for
England. Farewell deere Mother.
King. Thy louing Father *Hamlet*.
Hamlet. My Mother : Father and Mother is man and
wife : man & wife is one fleſh, and ſo my mother. Come,
for England. *Exit*
King. Follow him at foote,
Tempt him with ſpeed aboord :
Delay it not, Ile haue him hence to night.
Away, for euery thing is Seal'd and done
That elſe leanes on th'Affaire pray you make haſt
And England, if my loue thou holdſt at ought,
As my great power thereof may giue thee ſenſe,
Since yet thy Cicatrice lookes raw and red
After the Daniſh Sword, and thy free awe
Payes homage to vs; thou maiſt not coldly ſet
Our Soueraigne Proceſſe, which imports at full
By Letters coniuring to that effect
The preſent death of *Hamlet*. Do it England,
For like the Hecticke in my blood he rages,
And thou muſt cure me: Till I know 'tis done,
How ere my happes, my ioyes were ne're begun. *Exit*

Enter Fortinbras with an Armie.

For. Go Captaine, from me greet the Daniſh King,
Tell him that by his licenſe, *Fortinbras*
Claimes the conueyance of a promis'd March
Ouer his Kingdome. You know the Rendeuous :
If that his Maieſty would ought with vs,
We ſhall expreſſe our dutie in his eye,
And let him know ſo.
Cap. I will doo't, my Lord.
For. Go ſafely on. *Exit.*

Enter Queene and Horatio.

Qu. I will not ſpeake with her.
Hor. She is importunate, indeed diſtract, her moode
will needs be pittied.
Qu. What would ſhe haue?
Hor. She ſpeakes much of her Father; ſaies ſhe heares
There's trickes i'th'world, and hems, and beats her heart,
Spurnes enuiouſly at Strawes, ſpeakes things in doubt,
That carry but halfe ſenſe : Her ſpeech is nothing,
Yet the vnſhaped vſe of it doth moue
The hearers to Collection; they ayme at it,
And botch the words vp fit to their owne thoughts,
Which as her winkes, and nods, and geſtures yeeld them,
Indeed would make one thinke there would be thought,
Though nothing ſure, yet much vnhappily.
Qu. 'Twere good ſhe were ſpoken with,
For ſhe may ſtrew dangerous coniectures
In ill breeding minds. Let her come in.
To my ſicke ſoule (as ſinnes true Nature is)
Each toy ſeemes Prologue, to ſome great amiſſe,
So full of Artleſſe iealouſie is guilt,
It ſpill's it ſelfe, in fearing to be ſpilt.

Enter Ophelia diſtracted.

Ophe. Where is the beauteous Maieſty of Denmark.
Qu. How now *Ophelia*?
Ophe. *How ſhould I your true loue know from another one?*
By his Cockle hat and ſtaffe, and his Sandal ſhoone.
Qu. Alas ſweet Lady: what imports this Song?
Ophe. Say you? Nay pray you marke.
He is dead and gone Lady, he is dead and gone,
At his head a graſſe-greene Turfe, at his heeles a ſtone.

Enter King.

Qu Nay but *Ophelia*.
Ophe Pray you marke.
White his Shrow'd as the Mountaine Snow.
Qu Alas looke heere my Lord.
Ophe. *Larded with ſweet flowers :*
Which bewept to the graue did not go,
With true-loue ſhowres.
King. How do ye, pretty Lady?
Ophe. Well, God dil'd you. They ſay the Owle was
a Bakers daughter. Lord, wee know what we are, but
know not what we may be. God be at your Table.
King. Conceit vpon her Father
Ophe Pray you let's haue no words of this: but when
they aske you what it meanes, ſay you this :
To morrow is S. Valentines day, all in the morning betime,
And I a Maid at your Window to be your Valentine
Then vp he roſe, & don'd his clothes, & dupt the chamber dore,
Let in the Maid, that out a Maid, neuer departed more.
King. Pretty *Ophelia*.
Ophe. Indeed la? without an oath Ile make an end ont.
By gis, and by S. Charity,
Alacke, and fie for ſhame :
Yong men wil doo't, if they come too't,
By Cocke they are too blame
Quoth ſhe before you tumbled me,
You promis'd me to Wed.
So would I ha done by yonder Sunne,
And thou hadſt not come to my bed.
King. How long hath ſhe bin this?
Ophe. I hope all will be well. We muſt bee patient,
but I cannot chooſe but weepe, to thinke they ſhould
lay him i'th'cold ground : My brother ſhall knowe of it,
and ſo I thanke you for your good counſell. Come, my
Coach : Goodnight Ladies : Goodnight ſweet Ladies :
Goodnight, goodnight. *Exit.*
King. Follow her cloſe,
Giue her good watch I pray you :
Oh this is the poyſon of deepe greefe, it ſprings
All from her Fathers death. Oh *Gertrude*, *Gertrude*,
When ſorrowes comes, they come not ſingle ſpies,
But in Battaliaes. Firſt, her Father ſlaine,
Next your Sonne gone, and he moſt violent Author
Of his owne iuſt remoue : the people muddied,
Thicke and vnwholſome in their thoughts, and whiſpers
For good *Polonius* death; and we haue done but greenly
In hugger mugger to interre him. Poore *Ophelia*
Diuided from her ſelfe, and her faire iudgement

pp 3 Without

Without the which we are Pictures, or meere Beasts.
Last, and as much containing as all these,
Her Brother is in secret come from France,
Keepes on his wonder, keepes himselfe in clouds,
And wants not Buzzers to infect his eare
With pestilent Speeches of his Fathers death,
Where in necessitie of matter Beggard,
Will nothing sticke our persons to Arraigne
In eare and eare. O my deere *Gertrude*, this,
Like to a murdering Peece in many places,
Giues me superfluous death. *A Noise within.*

Enter a Messenger.

Qu. Alacke, what noyse is this?
King. Where are my *Switzers*?
Let them guard the doore. What is the matter?
Mes. Saue your selfe, my Lord.
The Ocean (ouer-peering of his List)
Eates not the Flats with more impittious haste
Then young *Laertes*, in a Riotous head,
Ore-beares your Officers, the rabble call him Lord,
And as the world were now but to begin,
Antiquity forgot, Custome not knowne,
The Ratifiers and props of euery word,
They cry choose we? *Laertes* shall be King,
Caps, hands, and tongues, applaud it to the clouds,
Laertes shall be King, *Laertes* King.
Qu. How cheerefully on the false Traile they cry,
Oh this is Counter you false Danish Dogges.

Noise within. Enter Laertes.

King. The doores are broke.
Laer. Where is the King, sirs? Stand you all without.
All. No, let's come in.
Laer. I pray you giue me leaue.
Al. We will, we will.
Laer. I thanke you: Keepe the doore.
Oh thou vilde King, giue me my Father.
Qu. Calmely good *Laertes*.
Laer. That drop of blood, that calmes
Proclaimes me Bastard:
Cries Cuckold to my Father, brands the Harlot
Euen heere betweene the chaste vnsmirched brow
Of my true Mother.
King. What is the cause *Laertes*,
That thy Rebellion lookes so Gyant-like?
Let him go *Gertrude*: Do not feare our person:
There's such Diuinity doth hedge a King,
That Treason can but peepe to what it would,
Acts little of his will. Tell me *Laertes*,
Why thou art thus Incenst? Let him go *Gertrude*.
Speake man.
Laer. Where's my Father?
King. Dead.
Qu. But not by him.
King. Let him demand his fill.
Laer. How came he dead? Ile not be Iuggel'd with.
To hell Allegeance: Vowes, to the blackest diuell.
Conscience and Grace, to the profoundest Pit.
I dare Damnation: to this point I stand,
That both the worlds I giue to negligence,
Let come what comes: onely Ile be reueng'd
Most throughly for my Father.
King. Who shall stay you?
Laer. My Will, not all the world,
And for my meanes, Ile husband them so well,
They shall go farre with little.
King. Good *Laertes*:
If you desire to know the certaintie
Of your deere Fathers death, if writ in your reuenge,
That Soop-stake you will draw both Friend and Foe,
Winner and Looser.
Laer. None but his Enemies.
King. Will you know them then.
La. To his good Friends, thus wide Ile ope my Armes:
And like the kinde Life-rend'ring Politician,
Repast them with my blood.
King. Why now you speake
Like a good Childe, and a true Gentleman.
That I am guiltlesse of your Fathers death,
And am most sensible in greefe for it,
It shall as leuell to your Iudgement pierce
As day do's to your eye.

A noise within. Let her come in.
Enter Ophelia.

Laer. How now? what noise is that?
Oh heate drie vp my Braines, teares seuen times salt,
Burne out the Sence and Vertue of mine eye.
By Heauen, thy madnesse shall be payed by waight,
Till our Scale turnes the beame. Oh Rose of May,
Deere Maid, kinde Sister, sweet *Ophelia*:
Oh Heauens, is't possible, a yong Maids wits,
Should be as mortall as an old mans life?
Nature is fine in Loue, and where 'tis fine,
It sends some precious instance of it selfe
After the thing it loues.
Ophe. They bore him bare fac'd on the Beer,
Hey non nony, nony, hey nony:
And on his graue raines many a teare,
Fare you well my Doue.
Laer. Had'st thou thy wits, and did'st perswade Reuenge, it could not moue thus.
Ophe. You must sing downe a-downe, and you call him a-downe-a. Oh, how the wheele becomes it? It is the false Steward that stole his masters daughter.
Laer. This nothings more then matter.
Ophe. There's Rosemary, that's for Remembraunce. Pray loue remember: and there is Paconcies, that's for Thoughts.
Laer. A document in madnesse, thoughts & remembrance fitted.
Ophe. There's Fennell for you, and Columbines: ther's Rew for you, and heere's some for me. Wee may call it Herbe-Grace a Sundaies: Oh you must weare your Rew with a difference. There's a Daysie, I would giue you some Violets, but they wither'd all when my Father dyed: They say, he made a good end;
For bonny sweet Robin is all my ioy.
Laer. Thought, and Affliction, Passion, Hell it selfe:
She turnes to Fauour, and to prettinesse.
Ophe. And will he not come againe,
And will he not come againe:
No, no, he is dead, go to thy Death-bed,
He neuer wil come againe.
His Beard as white as Snow,
All Flaxen was his Pole.
He is gone, he is gone, and we cast away mone,
Gramercy on his Soule.
And of all Christian Soules, I pray God.
God buy ye. *Exeunt Ophelia*
Laer. Do you see this, you Gods?
King. *Laertes*, I must common with your greefe,
Or you deny me right: go but apart,

Make

Make choice of whom your wisest Friends you will,
And they shall heare and iudge 'twixt you and me;
If by direct or by Colaterall hand
They finde vs touch'd, we will our Kingdome giue,
Our Crowne, our Life, and all that we call Ours
To you in satisfaction. But if not,
Be you content to lend your patience to vs,
And we shall ioyntly labour with your soule
To giue it due content.

Laer. Let this be so:
His meanes of death, his obscure buriall;
No Trophee, Sword, nor Hatchment o're his bones,
No Noble rite, nor formall ostentation,
Cry to be heard, as 'twere from Heauen to Earth,
That I must call in question.

King. So you shall:
And where th'offence is, let the great Axe fall.
I pray you go with me. *Exeunt*

Enter Horatio, with an Attendant.

Hora. What are they that would speake with me?

Ser. Saylors sir, they say they haue Letters for you.

Hor. Let them come in,
I do not know from what part of the world
I should be greeted, if not from Lord *Hamlet*.

Enter Saylor.

Say. God blesse you Sir.

Hor. Let him blesse thee too.

Say. Hee shall Sir, and't please him. There's a Letter for you Sir: It comes from th'Ambassadours that was bound for England, if your name be *Horatio*, as I am let to know it is.

Reads the Letter.

HOratio, *When thou shalt haue ouerlook'd this, giue these Fellowes some meanes to the King: They haue Letters for him. Ere we were two dayes old at Sea, a Pyrate of very Warlicke appointment gaue vs Chace. Finding our selues too slow of Saile, we put on a compelled Valour. In the Grapple, I boorded them. On the instant they got cleare of our Shippe, so I alone became their Prisoner. They haue dealt with mee, like Theeues of Mercy, but they knew what they did. I am to doe a good turne for them. Let the King haue the Letters I haue sent, and repaire thou to me with as much hast as thou wouldest flye death. I haue words to speake in your eare, will make thee dumbe, yet are they much too light for the bore of the Matter. These good Fellowes will bring thee where I am.* Rosincrance and Guildensterne, *hold their course for England. Of them I haue much to tell thee, Farewell.*

He that thou knowest thine,
Hamlet.

Come, I will giue you way for these your Letters,
And do't the speedier, that you may direct me
To him from whom you brought them. *Exit.*

Enter King and Laertes.

King. Now must your conscience my acquittance seal,
And you must put me in your heart for Friend,
Sith you haue heard, and with a knowing eare,
That he which hath your Noble Father slaine,
Pursued my life.

Laer. It well appeares. But tell me,
Why you proceeded not against these feates,
So crimefull, and so Capitall in Nature,
As by your Safety, Wisedome, all things else,
You mainly were stirr'd vp?

King. O for two speciall Reasons,
Which may to you (perhaps) seeme much vnsinnowed,
And yet to me they are strong. The Queen his Mother,
Liues almost by his lookes: and for my selfe,
My Vertue or my Plague, be it either which,
She's so coniunctiue to my life and soule;
That as the Starre moues not but in his Sphere,
I could not but by her. The other Motiue,
Why to a publike count I might not go,
Is the great loue the generall gender beare him,
Who dipping all his Faults in their affection,
Would like the Spring that turneth Wood to Stone,
Conuert his Gyues to Graces. So that my Arrowes
Too slightly timbred for so loud a Winde,
Would haue reuerted to my Bow againe,
And not where I had arm'd them.

Laer. And so haue I a Noble Father lost,
A Sister driuen into desperate tearmes,
Who was (if praises may go backe againe)
Stood Challenger on mount of all the Age
For her perfections. But my reuenge will come.

King. Breake not your sleepes for that,
You must not thinke
That we are made of stuffe, so flat, and dull,
That we can let our Beard be shooke with danger,
And thinke it pastime. You shortly shall heare more,
I lou'd your Father, and we loue our Selfe,
And that I hope will teach you to imagine.——

Enter a Messenger.

How now? What Newes?

Mes. Letters my Lord from *Hamlet*. This to your Maiesty: this to the Queene.

King. From *Hamlet*? Who brought them?

Mes. Saylors my Lord they say, I saw them not:
They were giuen me by *Claudio*, he receiu'd them.

King. *Laertes* you shall heare them:
Leaue vs. *Exit Messenger*

High and Mighty, you shall know I am set naked on your Kingdome. To morrow shall I begge leaue to see your Kingly Eyes. When I shall (first asking your Pardon thereunto) recount th'Occasions of my sodaine and more strange returne.
Hamlet.

What should this meane? Are all the rest come backe?
Or is it some abuse? Or no such thing?

Laer. Know you the hand?

Kin. 'Tis *Hamlets* Character, naked and in a Postscript here he sayes alone: Can you aduise me?

Laer. I'm lost in it my Lord; but let him come,
It warmes the very sicknesse in my heart,
That I shall liue and tell him to his teeth;
Thus diddest thou.

Kin. If it be so *Laertes*, as how should it be so:
How otherwise will you be rul'd by me?

Laer. If so you'l not o'rerule me to a peace.

Kin. To thine owne peace: if he be now return'd,
As checking at his Voyage, and that he meanes
No more to vndertake it; I will worke him
To an exployt now ripe in my Deuice,
Vnder the which he shall not choose but fall;
And for his death no winde of blame shall breath,
But euen his Mother shall vncharge the practice,
And call it accident: Some two Monthes hence
Here was a Gentleman of *Normandy*,
I'ue seene my selfe, and seru'd against the French,
And they ran well on Horsebacke; but this Gallant
Had

Had witchcraft in't; he grew into his Seat,
And to such wondrous doing brought his Horse,
As had he beene encorps't and demy-Natur'd
With the braue Beast, so farre he past my thought,
That I in forgery of shapes and trickes,
Come short of what he did.

Laer. A Norman was't?

Kin. A Norman.

Laer. Vpon my life *Lamound.*

Kin. The very same.

Laer. I know him well, he is the Brooch indeed,
And Iemme of all our Nation.

Kin. Hee mad confession of you,
And gaue you such a Masterly report,
For Art and exercise in your defence;
And for your Rapier most especially,
That he cryed out, t'would be a sight indeed,
If one could match you Sir. This report of his
Did *Hamlet* so envenom with his Enuy,
That he could nothing doe but wish and begge,
Your sodaine comming ore to play with him;
Now out of this.

Laer. Why out of this, my Lord?

Kin *Laertes* was your Father deare to you?
Or are you like the painting of a sorrow,
A face without a heart?

Laer. Why aske you this?

Kin. Not that I thinke you did not loue your Father,
But that I know Loue is begun by Time:
And that I see in passages of proofe,
Time qualifies the sparke and fire of it:
Hamlet comes backe: what would you vndertake,
To show your selfe your Fathers sonne indeed,
More then in words?

Laer. To cut his throat i'th' Church.

Kin. No place indeed should murder Sancturize;
Reuenge should haue no bounds: but good *Laertes*
Will you doe this, keepe close within your Chamber,
Hamlet return'd, shall know you are come home:
Wee'l put on those shall praise your excellence,
And set a double varnish on the fame
The Frenchman gaue you, bring you in fine together,
And wager on your heads, he being remisse,
Most generous, and free from all contriuing,
Will not peruse the Foiles? So that with ease,
Or with a little shuffling, you may choose
A Sword vnbaited, and in a passe of practice,
Requit him for your Father.

Laer. I will doo't,
And for that purpose Ile annoint my Sword:
I bought an Vnction of a Mountebanke
So mortall, I but dipt a knife in it,
Where it drawes blood, no Cataplasme so rare,
Collected from all Simples that haue Vertue
Vnder the Moone, can saue the thing from death,
That is but scratcht withall: Ile touch my point,
With this contagion, that if I gall him slightly,
It may be death.

Kin Let's further thinke of this,
Weigh what conuenience both of time and meanes
May fit vs to our shape, if this should faile;
And that our drift looke through our bad performance,
'Twere better not assaid; therefore this Proiect
Should haue a backe or second, that might hold,
If this should blast in proofe: Soft, let me see
Wee'l make a solemne wager on your commings,
I ha't: when in your motion you are hot and dry,
As make your bowts more violent to the end,
And that he cals for drinke; Ile haue prepar'd him
A Challice for the nonce; whereon but sipping,
If he by chance escape your venom'd stuck,
Our purpose may hold there; how sweet Queene.

Enter Queene.

Queen. One woe doth tread vpon anothers heele,
So fast they'l follow: your Sister's drown'd *Laertes.*

Laer. Drown'd! O where?

Queen. There is a Willow growes aslant a Brooke,
That shewes his hore leaues in the glassie streame:
There with fantasticke Garlands did she come,
Of Crow-flowers, Nettles, Daysies, and long Purples,
That liberall Shepheards giue a grosser name;
But our cold Maids doe Dead Mens Fingers call them:
There on the pendant boughes, her Coronet weeds
Clambring to hang; an enuious sliuer broke,
When downe the weedy Trophies, and her selfe,
Fell in the weeping Brooke, her cloathes spred wide,
And Mermaid-like, a while they bore her vp,
Which time she chaunted snatches of old tunes,
As one incapable of her owne distresse,
Or like a creature Natiue, and indued
Vnto that Element: but long it could not be,
Till that her garments, heauy with her drinke,
Pul'd the poore wretch from her melodious buy,
To muddy death.

Laer. Alas then, is she drown'd?

Queen. Drown'd, drown'd.

Laer. Too much of water hast thou poore *Ophelia*,
And therefore I forbid my teares: but yet
It is our tricke, Nature her custome holds,
Let shame say what it will; when these are gone
The woman will be out: Adue my Lord,
I haue a speech of fire, that faine would blaze,
But that this folly doubts it. *Exit.*

Kin. Let's follow, *Gertrude:*
How much I had to doe to calme his rage?
Now feare I this will giue it start againe;
Therefore let's follow. *Exeunt.*

Enter two Clownes.

Clown. Is she to bee buried in Christian buriall, that wilfully seekes her owne saluation?

Other. I tell thee she is, and therefore make her Graue straight, the Crowner hath sate on her, and finds it Christian buriall.

Clo. How can that be, vnlesse she drowned her selfe in her owne defence?

Other. Why 'tis found so.

Clo. It must be *Se offendendo*, it cannot bee else: for heere lies the point; If I drowne my selfe wittingly, it argues an Act: and an Act hath three branches. It is an Act to doe and to performe; argall she drown'd her selfe wittingly.

Other. Nay but heare you Goodman Deluer.

Clown. Giue me leaue; heere lies the water; good: heere stands the man; good: If the man goe to this water and drowne himsele; it is will he nill he, he goes; marke you that? But if the water come to him & drowne him; hee drownes not himselfe. Argall, hee that is not guilty of his owne death, shortens not his owne life.

Other. But is this law?

Clo. I marry is't, Crowners Quest Law.

Other

Other. Will you ha the truth on't: if this had not beene a Gentlewoman, ſhee ſhould haue beene buried out of Chriſtian Buriall.

Clo. Why there thou ſay'ſt. And the more pitty that great folke ſhould haue countenance in this world to drowne or hang themſelues, more then their euen Chriſtian. Come, my Spade; there is no ancient Gentlemen, but Gardiners, Ditchers and Graue-makers; they hold vp *Adams* Profeſſion.

Other. Was he a Gentleman?

Clo. He was the firſt that euer bore Armes.

Other. Why he had none.

Clo. What, ar't a Heathen? how doſt thou vnderſtand the Scripture? the Scripture ſayes *Adam* dig'd; could hee digge without Armes? Ile put another queſtion to thee; if thou anſwereſt me not to the purpoſe, confeſſe thy ſelfe——

Other. Go too.

Clo. What is he that builds ſtronger then either the Maſon, the Shipwright, or the Carpenter?

Other. The Gallowes maker; for that Frame outliues a thouſand Tenants.

Clo. I like thy wit well in good faith, the Gallowes does well; but how does it well? it does well to thoſe that doe ill: now, thou doſt ill to ſay the Gallowes is built ſtronger then the Church: Argall, the Gallowes may doe well to thee. Too't againe, Come.

Other. Who builds ſtronger then a Maſon, a Shipwright, or a Carpenter?

Clo. I, tell me that, and vnyoake.

Other. Marry, now I can tell.

Clo. Too't.

Other. Maſſe, I cannot tell.

Enter Hamlet and Horatio a farre off.

Clo. Cudgell thy braines no more about it; for your dull Aſſe will not mend his pace with beating, and when you are ask't this queſtion next, ſay a Graue-maker: the Houſes that he makes, laſts till Doomeſday: go, get thee to *Yaughan*, fetch me a ſtoupe of Liquor.

Sings.

In youth when I did loue, did loue,
me thought it was very ſweete:
To contract O the time for a my behoue,
O me thought there was nothing meete.

Ham. Ha's this fellow no feeling of his buſineſſe, that he ſings at Graue-making?

Hor. Cuſtome hath made it in him a property of eaſineſſe.

Ham. Tis ee'n ſo; the hand of little Imployment hath the daintier ſenſe.

Clowne ſings.

But Age with his ſtealing ſteps
hath caught me in his clutch:
And hath ſhipped me intill the Land,
as if I had neuer beene ſuch.

Ham. That Scull had a tongue in it, and could ſing once: how the knaue iowles it to th' grownd, as if it were *Caines* Iaw-bone, that did the firſt murther: It might be the Pate of a Politician which this Aſſe o're Offices: one that could circumuent God, might it not?

Hor. It might, my Lord.

Ham. Or of a Courtier, which could ſay, Good Morrow ſweet Lord: how doſt thou, good Lord? this might be my Lord ſuch a one, that prais'd my Lord ſuch a ones Horſe, when he meant to begge it; might it not?

Hor. I, my Lord.

Ham. Why ee'n ſo: and now my Lady Wormes, Chapleſſe, and knockt about the Mazard with a Sextons Spade; heere's fine Reuolution, if wee had the tricke to ſee't. Did theſe bones coſt no more the breeding, but to play at Loggets with 'em? mine ake to thinke on't.

Clowne ſings.

A Pickhaxe and a Spade, a Spade
for and a ſhrowding-Sheete:
O a Pit of Clay for to be made,
for ſuch a Gueſt is meete.

Ham. There's another: why might not that bee the Scull of of a Lawyer? where be his Quiddits now? his Quillets? his Caſes? his Tenures, and his Tricks? why doe's he ſuffer this rude knaue now to knocke him about the Sconce with a dirty Shouell, and will not tell him of his Action of Battery? hum. This fellow might be in's time a great buyer of Land, with his Statutes, his Recognizances, his Fines, his double Vouchers, his Recoueries: Is this the fine of his Fines, and the recouery of his Recoueries, to haue his fine Pate full of fine Dirt? will his Vouchers vouch him no more of his Purchaſes, and double ones too, then the length and breadth of a paire of Indentures? the very Conueyances of his Lands will hardly lye in this Boxe; and muſt the Inheritor himſelfe haue no more? ha?

Hor. Not a iot more, my Lord.

Ham. Is not Parchment made of Sheep-skinnes?

Hor. I my Lord, and of Calue-skinnes too.

Ham. They are Sheepe and Calues that ſeek out aſſurance in that. I will ſpeake to this fellow: whoſe Graue's this Sir?

Clo. Mine Sir:

O a Pit of Clay for to be made,
for ſuch a Gueſt is meete.

Ham. I thinke it be thine indeed: for thou lieſt in't.

Clo. You lye out on't Sir, and therefore it is not yours: for my part, I doe not lye in't; and yet it is mine.

Ham. Thou doſt lye in't, to be in't and ſay 'tis thine: 'tis for the dead, not for the quicke, therefore thou lyeſt.

Clo. 'Tis a quicke lye Sir, 'twill away againe from me to you.

Ham. What man doſt thou digge it for?

Clo. For no man Sir.

Ham. What woman then?

Clo For none neither.

Ham. Who is to be buried in't?

Clo. One that was a woman Sir; but reſt her Soule, ſhee's dead.

Ham. How abſolute the knaue is? wee muſt ſpeake by the Carde, or equiuocation will vndoe vs: by the Lord *Horatio*, theſe three yeares I haue taken note of it, the Age is growne ſo picked, that the toe of the Peſant comes ſo neere the heeles of our Courtier, hee galls his Kibe. How long haſt thou been a Graue-maker?

Clo. Of all the dayes i'th' yeare, I came too't that day that our laſt King *Hamlet* o'recame *Fortinbras*.

Ham. How long is that ſince?

Clo. Cannot you tell that? euery foole can tell that: It was the very day, that young *Hamlet* was borne, hee that was mad, and ſent into England.

Ham. I marry, why was he ſent into England?

Clo. Why, becauſe he was mad; hee ſhall recouer his wits there; or if he do not, it's no great matter there.

Ham.

Ham. Why?

Clo. 'Twill not be seene in him, there the men are as mad as he.

Ham. How came he mad?

Clo. Very strangely they say

Ham. How strangely?

Clo. Faith e'ene with loosing his wits.

Ham. Vpon what ground?

Clo. Why heere in Denmarke: I haue bin sixeteene heere, man and Boy thirty yeares.

Ham. How long will a man lie 'ith' earth ere he rot?

Clo. Ifaith, if he be not rotten before he die (as we haue many pocky Coarses now adaies, that will scarce hold the laying in) he will last you some eight yeare, or nine yeare. A Tanner will last you nine yeare.

Ham. Why he, more then another?

Clo. Why sir, his hide is so tan'd with his Trade, that he will keepe out water a great while. And your water, is a sore Decayer of your horson dead body. Heres a Scull now: this Scul, has laine in the earth three & twenty years.

Ham. Whose was it?

Clo. A whoreson mad Fellowes it was; Whose doe you thinke it was?

Ham. Nay, I know not.

Clo. A pestlence on him for a mad Rogue, a pou'rd a Flaggon of Renish on my head once. This same Scull Sir, this same Scull sir, was *Yoricks* Scull, the Kings Iester.

Ham. This?

Clo. E'ene that.

Ham. Let me see. Alas poore *Yorick*, I knew him *Horatio*, a fellow of infinite Iest; of most excellent fancy, he hath borne me on his backe a thousand times: And how abhorred my Imagination is, my gorge rises at it. Heere hung those lipps, that I haue kist I know not how oft. VVhere be your Iibes now? Your Gambals? Your Songs? Your flashes of Merriment that were wont to set the Table on a Rore) No one now to mock your own Ieering? Quite chopfalne? Now get you to my Ladies Chamber, and tell her, let her paint an inch thicke, to this fauour she must come. Make her laugh at that: prythee *Horatio* tell me one thing.

Hor. What's that my Lord?

Ham. Dost thou thinke *Alexander* lookt o'this fashion i'th' earth?

Hor. E'ene so.

Ham. And smelt so? Puh.

Hor. E'ene so, my Lord.

Ham. To what base vses we may returne *Horatio*. Why may not Imagination trace the Noble dust of *Alexander*, till he find it stopping a bunghole.

Hor. 'Twere to consider: to curiously to consider so.

Ham. No faith, not a iot. But to follow him thether with modestie enough, & likeliehood to lead it; as thus. *Alexander* died: *Alexander* was buried: *Alexander* returneth into dust; the dust is earth; of earth we make Lome, and why of that Lome (whereto he was conuerted) might they not stopp a Beere-barrell?
Imperiall *Cæsar*, dead and turn'd to clay,
Might stop a hole to keepe the winde away.
Oh, that that earth, which kept the world in awe,
Should patch a Wall, t'expell the winters flaw.
But soft, but soft, aside; heere comes the King.

Enter King, Queene, Laertes, and a Coffin, with Lords attendant.

The Queene, the Courtiers. Who is that they follow,
And with such maimed rites? This doth betoken,
The Coarse they follow, did with disperate hand,
Fore do it owne life; 'twas some Estate.
Couch we a while, and mark.

Laer. What Cerimony else?

Ham. That is *Laertes*, a very Noble youth: Marke.

Laer. What Cerimony else?

Priest. Her Obsequies haue bin as farre inlarg'd,
As we haue warrantis, her death was doubtfull,
And but that great Command, o're-swaies the order,
She should in ground vnsanctified haue lodg'd,
Till the last Trumpet. For charitable praier,
Shardes, Flints, and Peebles, should be throwne on her:
Yet heere she is allowed her Virgin Rites,
Her Maiden strewments, and the bringing home
Of Bell and Buriall,

Laer. Must there no more be done?

Priest. No more be done:
We should prophane the seruice of the dead,
To sing sage *Requiem*, and such rest to her
As to peace-parted Soules.

Laer. Lay her i'th' earth,
And from her faire and vnpolluted flesh,
May Violets spring. I tell thee (churlish Priest)
A Ministring Angell shall my Sister be,
When thou liest howling?

Ham. What, the faire *Ophelia*?

Queene. Sweets, to the sweet farewell.
I hop'd thou should'st haue bin my *Hamlets* wife:
I thought thy Bride-bed to haue deckt (sweet Maid)
And not t'haue strew'd thy Graue.

Laer. Oh terrible woer,
Fall ten times trebble, on that cursed head
Whose wicked deed, thy most Ingenious sence
Depriu'd thee of. Hold off the earth a while,
Till I haue caught her once more in mine armes:

Leaps in the graue.

Now pile your dust, vpon the quicke, and dead,
Till of this flat a Mountaine you haue made,
To o're top old *Pelion*, or the skyish head
Of blew *Olympus*.

Ham. What is he, whose griefes
Beares such an Emphasis? whose phrase of Sorrow
Coniure the wandring Starres, and makes them stand
Like wonder-wounded hearers? This is I,
Hamlet the Dane.

Laer. The deuill take thy soule.

Ham. Thou prai'st not well,
I prythee take thy fingers from my throat;
Sir though I am not Spleenatiue, and rash,
Yet haue I something in me dangerous,
Which let thy wisenesse feare. Away thy hand.

King. Pluck them asunder.

Qu. *Hamlet, Hamlet*

Gen. Good my Lord be quiet.

Ham. Why I will fight with him vppon this Theme,
Vntill my eielids will no longer wag.

Qu. Oh my Sonne, what Theame?

Ham. I lou'd *Ophelia*; fortie thousand Brothers
Could not (with all there quantitie of Loue)
Make vp my summe. What wilt thou do for her?

King. Oh he is mad *Laertes*,

Qu. For loue of God forbeare him.

Ham. Come show me what thou'lt doe.
Woo't weepe? Woo't fight? Woo't teare thy selfe?
Woo't drinke vp *Esile*, eate a Crocodile?

Ile

Ile doo't. Doſt thou come heere to whine;
To outface me with leaping in her Graue?
Be buried quicke with her, and ſo will I.
And if thou prate of Mountaines; let them throw
Millions of Akers on vs; till our ground
Sindging his pate againſt the burning Zone,
Make *Oſſa* like a wart. Nay, and thoul't mouth,
Ile rant as well as thou.
Kin. This is meere Madneſſe:
And thus awhile the fit will worke on him:
Anon as patient as the female Doue,
When that her golden Cuplet are diſclos'd;
His ſilence will ſit drooping.
Ham. Heare you Sir:
What is the reaſon that you vſe me thus?
I lou'd' you euer; but it is no matter:
Let *Hercules* himſelfe doe what he may,
The Cat will Mew, and Dogge will haue his day *Exit.*
Kin. I pray you good *Horatio* wait vpon him,
Strengthen you patience in our laſt nights ſpeech,
Wee'l put the matter to the preſent puſh:
Good *Gertrude* ſet ſome watch ouer your Sonne,
This Graue ſhall haue a liuing Monument:
An houre of quiet ſhortly ſhall we ſee;
Till then, in patience our proceeding be. *Exeunt.*

Enter Hamlet and Horatio.

Ham. So much for this Sir; now let me ſee the other,
You doe remember all the Circumſtance.
Hor. Remember it my Lord?
Ham. Sir, in my heart there was a kinde of fighting,
That would not let me ſleepe; me thought I lay
Worſe then the mutines in the Bilboes, raſhly,
(And praiſe be raſhneſſe for it) let vs know,
Our indiſcretion ſometimes ſerues vs well,
When our deare plots do paule, and that ſhould teach vs,
There's a Diuinity that ſhapes our ends,
Rough-hew them how we will.
Hor. That is moſt certaine.
Ham. Vp from my Cabin
My ſea-gowne ſcarft about me in the darke,
Grop'd I to finde out them; had my deſire,
Finger'd their Packet, and in fine, withdrew
To mine owne roome againe, making ſo bold,
(My feares forgetting manners) to vnſeale
Their grand Commiſſion, where I found *Horatio*,
Oh royall knauery: An exact command,
Larded with many ſeuerall ſorts of reaſon;
Importing Denmarks health, and Englands too,
With hoo, ſuch Bugges and Goblins in my life,
That on the ſuperuize no leaſure bated,
No not to ſtay the grinding of the Axe,
My head ſhoud be ſtruck off.
Hor. Iſt poſſible?
Ham. Here's the Commiſſion, read it at more leyſure:
But wilt thou heare me how I did proceed?
Hor. I beſeech you.
Ham. Being thus benetted round with Villaines,
Ere I could make a Prologue to my braines,
They had begun the Play. I ſate me downe,
Deuis'd a new Commiſſion, wrote it faire,
I once did hold it as our Statiſts doe,
A baſeneſſe to write faire; and laboured much
How to forget that learning: but Sir now,
It did me Yeomans ſeruice: wilt thou know
The effects of what I wrote?
Hor. I, good my Lord.
Ham. An earneſt Coniuration from the King,
As England was his faithfull Tributary,
As loue betweene them, as the Palme ſhould flouriſh,
As Peace ſhould ſtill her wheaten Garland weare,
And ſtand a Comma 'tweene their amities,
And many ſuch like Aſſis of great charge,
That on the view and know of theſe Contents,
Without debatement further, more or leſſe,
He ſhould the bearers put to ſodaine death,
Not ſhriuing time allowed.
Hor. How was this ſeal'd?
Ham. Why, euen in that was Heauen ordinate;
I had my fathers Signet in my Purſe,
Which was the Modell of that Daniſh Seale:
Folded the Writ vp in forme of the other,
Subſcrib'd it, gau't th' impreſſion, plac't it ſafely,
The changeling neuer knowne: Now, the next day
Was our Sea Fight, and what to this was ſement,
Thou know'ſt already.
Hor. So *Guildenſterne* and *Roſincrance*, go too't.
Ham. Why man, they did make loue to this imployment
They are not neere my Conſcience; their debate
Doth by their owne inſinuation grow:
'Tis dangerous, when the baſer nature comes
Betweene the paſſe, and fell incenſed points
Of mighty oppoſites.
Hor. Why, what a King is this?
Ham. Does it not, thinkſt thee, ſtand me now vpon
He that hath kil'd my King, and whor'd my Mother,
Popt in betweene th'election and my hopes,
Throwne out his Angle for my proper life,
And with ſuch coozenage; is't not perfect conſcience,
To quit him with this arme? And is't not to be damn'd
To let this Canker of our nature come
In further euill.
Hor. It muſt be ſhortly knowne to him from England
What is the iſſue of the buſineſſe there.
Ham. It will be ſhort,
The *interim's* mine, and a mans life's no more
Then to ſay one: but I am very ſorry good *Horatio*,
That to *Laertes* I forgot my ſelfe;
For by the image of my Cauſe, I ſee
The Portraiture of his; Ile count his fauours:
But ſure the brauery of his griefe did put me
Into a Towring paſſion.
Hor. Peace, who comes heere?

Enter young Oſricke.

Oſr. Your Lordſhip is right welcome back to Den-(marke.
Ham. I humbly thank you Sir, doſt know this waterflie?
Hor. No my good Lord.
Ham. Thy ſtate is the more gracious; for 'tis a vice to know him: he hath much Land, and fertile; let a Beaſt be Lord of Beaſts, and his Crib ſhall ſtand at the Kings Meſſe; 'tis a Chowgh; but as I ſaw ſpacious in the poſſeſſion of dirt.
Oſr. Sweet Lord, if your friendſhip were at leyſure, I ſhould impart a thing to you from his Maieſty.
Ham. I will receiue it with all diligence of ſpirit; pu your Bonet to his right vſe, 'tis for the head.
Oſr. I thanke your Lordſhip, 'tis very hot.
Ham. No, beleeue mee 'tis very cold, the winde is Northerly.
Oſr. It is indifferent cold my Lord indeed.
Ham. Mee thinkes it is very ſoultry, and hot for my Complexion.

Oſricke.

Osr. Exceedingly, my Lord, it is very soultry, as 'twere I cannot tell how: but my Lord, his Maiesty bad me signifie to you, that he ha's laid a great wager on your head: Sir, this is the matter.

Ham. I beseech you remember.

Osr. Nay, in good faith, for mine ease in good faith: Sir, you are not ignorant of what excellence *Laertes* is at his weapon.

Ham. What's his weapon?

Osr. Rapier and dagger.

Ham. That's two of his weapons; but well.

Osr. The sir King ha's wag'd with him six Barbary Horses, against the which he impon'd as I take it, sixe French Rapiers and Poniards, with their assignes, as Girdle, Hangers or so: three of the Carriages infaith are very deare to fancy, very responsiue to the hilts, most delicate carriages, and of very liberall conceit.

Ham. What call you the Carriages?

Osr. The Carriages Sir, are the hangers.

Ham. The phrase would bee more Germaine to the matter: If we could carry Cannon by our sides; I would it might be Hangers till then; but on sixe Barbary Horses against sixe French Swords: their Assignes, and three liberall conceited Carriages, that's the French but against the Danish; why is this impon'd as you call it?

Osr. The King Sir, hath laid that in a dozen passes betweene you and him, hee shall not exceed you three hits; He hath one twelue for mine, and that would come to imediate tryall, if your Lordship would vouchsafe the Answere.

Ham. How if I answere no?

Osr. I meane my Lord, the opposition of your person in tryall.

Ham. Sir, I will walke heere in the Hall; if it please his Maiestie, 'tis the beathing time of day with me; let the Foyles bee brought, the Gentleman willing, and the King hold his purpose; I will win for him if I can: if not, Ile gaine nothing but my shame, and the odde hits.

Osr. Shall I redeliuer you ee'n so?

Ham. To this effect Sir, after what flourish your nature will.

Osr. I commend my duty to your Lordship.

Ham. Yours, yours; hee does well to commend it himselfe, there are no tongues else for's tongue.

Hor. This Lapwing runs away with the shell on his head.

Ham. He did Complie with his Dugge before hee suck't it: thus had he and mine more of the same Beauy that I know the drossie age dotes on; only got the tune of the time, and outward habite of encounter, a kinde of yesty collection, which carries them through & through the most fond and winnowed opinions; and doe but blow them to their tryalls: the Bubbles are out.

Hor. You will lose this wager, my Lord.

Ham. I doe not thinke so, since he went into France, I haue beene in continuall practice; I shall winne at the oddes: but thou wouldest not thinke how all heere about my heart: but it is no matter.

Hor. Nay, good my Lord.

Ham. It is but foolery; but it is such a kinde of gain-giuing as would perhaps trouble a woman.

Hor. If your minde dislike any thing, obey. I will forestall their repaire hither, and say you are not fit.

Ham. Not a whit, we defie Augury; there's a speciall Prouidence in the fall of a sparrow. If it be now, 'tis not to come: if it bee not to come, it will bee now. : if it be not now; yet it will come; the readinesse is all, since no man ha's ought of what he leaues. What is't to leaue betimes?

Enter King, Queene, Laertes and Lords, with other Attendants with Foyles, and Gauntlets, a Table and Flagons of Wine on it.

Kin. Come Hamlet, come, and take this hand from me.

Ham. Giue me your pardon Sir, I'ue done you wrong,
But pardon't as you are a Gentleman.
This presence knowes,
And you must needs haue heard how I am punisht
With sore distraction? What I haue done
That might your nature honour, and exception
Roughly awake, I heere proclaime was madnesse:
Was't *Hamlet* wrong'd *Laertes*? Neuer *Hamlet*.
If *Hamlet* from himselfe be tane away:
And when he's not himselfe, do's wrong *Laertes*,
Then *Hamlet* does it not, *Hamlet* denies it:
Who does it then? His Madnesse? If't be so,
Hamlet is of the Faction that is wrong'd,
His madnesse is poore *Hamlets* Enemy.
Sir, in this Audience,
Let my disclaiming from a purpos'd euill,
Free me so farre in your most generous thoughts,
That I haue shot mine Arrow o're the house,
And hurt my Mother.

Laer. I am satisfied in Nature,
Whose motiue in this case should stirre me most
To my Reuenge. But in my termes of Honor
I stand aloofe, and will no reconcilement,
Till by some elder Masters of knowne Honor,
I haue a voyce, and president of peace
To keepe my name vngorg'd. But till that time,
I do receiue your offer'd loue like loue,
And wil not wrong it.

Ham. I do embrace it freely,
And will this Brothers wager frankely play.
Giue vs the Foyles: Come on.

Laer. Come one for me.

Ham. Ile be your foile *Laertes*, in mine ignorance,
Your Skill shall like a Starre i'th' darkest night,
Sticke fiery off indeede.

Laer. You mocke me Sir.

Ham. No by this hand.

King. Giue them the Foyles yong *Osricke*,
Cousen *Hamlet*, you know the wager.

Ham. Verie well my Lord,
Your Grace hath laide the oddes a'th' weaker side.

King. I do not feare it,
I haue seene you both:
But since he is better'd, we haue therefore oddes.

Laer. This is too heauy,
Let me see another.

Ham. This likes me well,
These Foyles haue all a length. *Prepare to play.*

Osricke. I my good Lord.

King. Set me the Stopes of wine vpon that Table:
If *Hamlet* giue the first, or second hit,
Or quit in answer of the third exchange,
Let all the Battlements their Ordinance fire,
The King shal drinke to *Hamlets* better breath,
And in the Cup an vnion shal he throw
Richer then that, which foure successiue Kings
In Denmarkes Crowne haue worne.

Giue

Giue me the Cups,
And let the Kettle to the Trumpets ſpeake,
The Trumpet to the Cannoneer without,
The Cannons to the Heauens, the Heauen to Earth,
Now the King drinkes to *Hamlet*. Come, begin,
And you the Iudges beare a wary eye.
Ham. Come on ſir.
Laer. Come on ſir. *They play.*
Ham. One.
Laer. No.
Ham. Iudgement.
Oſr. A hit, a very palpable hit.
Laer. Well: againe.
King. Stay, giue me drinke.
Hamlet, this Pearle is thine,
Here's to thy health. Giue him the cup,
Trumpets ſound, and ſhot goes off.
Ham. Ile play this bout firſt, ſet by a-while.
Come: Another hit; what ſay you?
Laer. A touch, a touch, I do confeſſe.
King. Our Sonne ſhall win.
Qu. He's fat, and ſcant of breath.
Heere's a Napkin, rub thy browes,
The Queene Carowſes to thy fortune, *Hamlet*.
Ham. Good Madam.
King. *Gertrude*, do not drinke.
Qu. I will my Lord;
I pray you pardon me.
King. It is the poyſon'd Cup, it is too late.
Ham. I dare not drinke yet Madam,
By and by.
Qu. Come, let me wipe thy face.
Laer. My Lord, Ile hit him now.
King. I do not thinke't.
Laer. And yet 'tis almoſt 'gainſt my conſcience.
Ham. Come for the third.
Laertes, you but dally,
I pray you paſſe with your beſt violence,
I am affear'd you make a wanton of me.
Laer. Say you ſo? Cōme on. *Play.*
Oſr. Nothing neither way.
Laer. Haue at you now.
In ſcuffling they change Rapiers.
King. Part them, they are incens'd.
Ham. Nay come, againe.
Oſr. Looke to the Queene there hoa.
Hor. They bleed on both ſides. How is't my Lord?
Oſr. How is't *Laertes*?
Laer. Why as a Woodcocke
To mine Sprindge, *Oſricke*,
I am iuſtly kill'd with mine owne Treacherie.
Ham. How does the Queene?
King. She ſounds to ſee them bleede.
Qu. No, no, the drinke, the drinke.
Oh my deere *Hamlet*, the drinke, the drinke,
I am poyſon'd.
Ham. Oh Villany! How? Let the doore be lock'd.
Treacherie, ſeeke it out.
Laer. It is heere *Hamlet*.
Hamlet, thou art ſlaine,
No Medicine in the world can do thee good.
In thee, there is not halfe an houre of life;
The Treacherous Inſtrument is in thy hand,
Vnbated and envenom'd: the foule practiſe
Hath turn'd it ſelfe on me. Loe, heere I lye,
Neuer to riſe againe: Thy Mothers poyſon'd:
I can no more, the King, the King's too blame.
Ham. The point envenom'd too,
Then venome to thy worke.
Hurts the King.
All. Treaſon, Treaſon.
King. O yet defend me Friends, I am but hurt.
Ham. Heere thou inceſtuous, murdrous,
Damned Dane,
Drinke off this Potion: Is thy Vnion heere?
Follow my Mother. *King Dyes.*
Laer. He is iuſtly ſeru'd.
It is a poyſon temp'red by himſelfe:
Exchange forgiueneſſe with me, Noble *Hamlet*;
Mine and my Fathers death come not vpon thee,
Nor thine on me. *Dyes.*
Ham. Heauen make thee free of it, I follow thee.
I am dead *Horatio*, wretched Queene adiew,
You that looke pale, and tremble at this chance,
That are but Mutes or audience to this acte:
Had I but time (as this fell Sergeant death
Is ſtrick'd in his Arreſt) oh I could tell you.
But let it be: *Horatio*, I am dead,
Thou liu'ſt, report me and my cauſes right
To the vnſatisfied.
Hor. Neuer beleeue it.
I am more an Antike Roman then a Dane:
Heere's yet ſome Liquor left.
Ham. As th'art a man, giue me the Cup.
Let go, by Heauen Ile haue't.
Oh good *Horatio*, what a wounded name,
(Things ſtanding thus vnknowne) ſhall liue behind me.
If thou did'ſt euer hold me in thy heart,
Abſent thee from felicitie awhile,
And in this harſh world draw thy breath in paine,
To tell my Storie.
March afarre off, and ſhout within.
What warlike noyſe is this?

Enter Oſricke.

Oſr. Yong *Fortinbras*, with conqueſt come fro Poland
To th'Ambaſſadors of England giues this warlike volly.
Ham. O I dye *Horatio*:
The potent poyſon quite ore-crowes my ſpirit,
I cannot liue to heare the Newes from England,
But I do propheſie th'election lights
On *Fortinbras*, he ha's my dying voyce,
So tell him with the occurrents more and leſſe,
Which haue ſolicited. The reſt is ſilence. O,o,o,o. *Dyes*
Hora. Now cracke a Noble heart:
Goodnight ſweet Prince,
And flights of Angels ſing thee to thy reſt,
Why do's the Drumme come hither?

Enter Fortinbras and Engliſh Ambaſſador, with Drumme, Colours, and Attendants.

Fortin. Where is this ſight?
Hor. What is it ye would ſee;
If ought of woe, or wonder, ceaſe your ſearch.
For. His quarry cries on hauocke. Oh proud death,
What feaſt is toward in thine eternall Cell,
That thou ſo many Princes, at a ſhoote,
So bloodily haſt ſtrooke.
Amb. The ſight is diſmall,
And our affaires from England come too late,
The eares are ſenſeleſſe that ſhould giue vs hearing,
To tell him his command'ment is fulfill'd,

qq That

That *Roſincrance* and *Guildenſterne* are dead :
Where ſhould we haue our thankes ?
Hor. Not from his mouth,
Had it th'abilitie of life to thanke you :
He neuer gaue command'ment for their death.
But ſince ſo iumpe vpon this bloodie queſtion,
You from the Polake warres, and you from England
Are heere arriued. Giue order that theſe bodies
High on a ſtage be placed to the view,
And let me ſpeake to th'yet vnknowing world,
How theſe things came about. So ſhall you heare
Of carnall, bloudie, and vnnaturall acts,
Of accidentall iudgements, caſuall ſlaughters
Of death's put on by cunning, and forc'd cauſe,
And in this vpſhot, purpoſes miſtooke,
Falne on the Inuentors heads. All this can I
Truly deliuer.
For. Let vs haſt to heare it,
And call the Nobleſt to the Audience.
For me, with ſorrow, I embrace my Fortune,
I haue ſome Rites of memory in this Kingdome,
Which are to claime, my vantage doth
Inuite me,
Hor. Of that I ſhall haue alwayes cauſe to ſpeake,
And from his mouth
Whoſe voyce will draw on more :
But let this ſame be preſently perform'd,
Euen whiles mens mindes are wilde,
Leſt more miſchance
On plots, and errors happen.
For. Let foure Captaines
Beare *Hamlet* like a Soldier to the Stage,
For he was likely, had he beene put on
To haue prou'd moſt royally :
And for his paſſage,
The Souldiours Muſicke, and the rites of Warre
Speake lowdly for him.
Take vp the body ; Such a ſight as this
Becomes the Field, but heere ſhewes much amis.
Go, bid the Souldiers ſhoote.
Exeunt Marching: after the which, a Peale of Ordenance are ſhot off.

FINIS.

THE TRAGEDIE OF KING LEAR.

Actus Primus. Scœna Prima.

Enter Kent, Glouceſter, and Edmond.

Kent.

I Thought the King had more affected the Duke of *Albany*, then *Cornwall*.

Glou. It did alwayes ſeeme ſo to vs: But now in the diuiſion of the Kingdome, it appeares not which of the Dukes hee valewes moſt, for qualities are ſo weigh'd, that curioſity in neither, can make choiſe of eithers moity.

Kent. Is not this your Son, my Lord?

Glou. His breeding Sir, hath bin at my charge. I haue ſo often bluſh'd to acknowledge him, that now I am braz'd too't.

Kent. I cannot conceiue you.

Glou. Sir, this yong Fellowes mother could; whereupon ſhe grew round womb'd, and had indeede (Sir) a Sonne for her Cradle, ere ſhe had a husband for her bed. Do you ſmell a fault?

Kent. I cannot wiſh the fault vndone, the iſſue of it, being ſo proper.

Glou. But I haue a Sonne, Sir, by order of Law, ſome yeere elder then this; who, yet is no deerer in my account, though this Knaue came ſomthing ſawcily to the world before he was ſent for: yet was his Mother fayre, there was good ſport at his making, and the horſon muſt be acknowledged. Doe you know this Noble Gentleman, *Edmond*?

Edm. No, my Lord.

Glou. My Lord of Kent:
Remember him heereafter, as my Honourable Friend.

Edm. My ſeruices to your Lordſhip.

Kent. I muſt loue you, and ſue to know you better.

Edm. Sir, I ſhall ſtudy deſeruing.

Glou. He hath bin out nine yeares, and away he ſhall againe. The King is comming.

Sennet. Enter King Lear, Cornwall, Albany, Gonerill, Regan, Cordelia, and attendants.

Lear. Attend the Lords of France & Burgundy, Gloſter.

Glou. I ſhall, my Lord. *Exit.*

Lear. Meane time we ſhal expreſſe our darker purpoſe.
Giue me the Map there. Know, that we haue diuided
In three our Kingdome: and 'tis our faſt intent,
To ſhake all Cares and Buſineſſe from our Age,
Conferring them on yenger ſtrengths, while we
Vnburthen'd crawle toward death. Our ſon of *Cornwal*,
And you our no leſſe louing Sonne of *Albany*,
We haue this houre a conſtant will to publiſh
Our daughters ſeuerall Dowers, that future ſtrife
May be preuented now. The Princes, *France & Burgundy*,
Great Riuals in our yongeſt daughters loue,
Long in our Court, haue made their amorous ſoiourne,
And heere are to be anſwer'd. Tell me my daughters
(Since now we will diueſt vs both of Rule,
Intereſt of Territory, Cares of State)
Which of you ſhall we ſay doth loue vs moſt,
That we, our largeſt bountie may extend
Where Nature doth with merit challenge. *Gonerill*,
Our eldeſt borne, ſpeake firſt.

Gon. Sir, I loue you more then word can weild yͤ matter,
Deerer then eye-ſight, ſpace, and libertie,
Beyond what can be valewed, rich or rare,
No leſſe then life, with grace, health, beauty, honor:
As much as Childe ere lou'd, or Father found.
A loue that makes breath poore, and ſpeech vnable,
Beyond all manner of ſo much I loue you.

Cor. What ſhall *Cordelia* ſpeake? Loue, and be ſilent.

Lear. Of all theſe bounds euen from this Line, to this,
With ſhadowie Forreſts, and with Champains rich'd
With plenteous Riuers, and wide-skirted Meades
We make thee Lady. To thine and *Albanies* iſſues
Be this perpetuall. What ſayes our ſecond Daughter?
Our deereſt *Regan*, wife of *Cornwall*?

Reg. I am made of that ſelfe-mettle as my Siſter,
And prize me at her worth. In my true heart,
I finde ſhe names my very deede of loue:
Onely ſhe comes too ſhort, that I profeſſe
My ſelfe an enemy to all other ioyes,
Which the moſt precious ſquare of ſenſe profeſſes,
And finde I am alone felicitate
In your deere Highneſſe loue.

Cor. Then poore *Cordelia*,
And yet not ſo, ſince I am ſure my loue's
More ponderous then my tongue.

Lear. To thee, and thine hereditarie euer,
Remaine this ample third of our faire Kingdome,
No leſſe in ſpace, validitie, and pleaſure
Then that conferr'd on *Gonerill*. Now our Ioy,
Although our laſt and leaſt; to whoſe yong loue,
The Vines of France, and Milke of Burgundie,
Striue to be intereſt. What can you ſay, to draw
A third, more opilent then your Siſters? ſpeake.

Cor. Nothing my Lord.

Lear. Nothing?

Cor. Nothing.
Lear. Nothing will come of nothing, speake againe
Cor. Vnhappie that I am, I cannot heaue
My heart into my mouth: I loue your Maiesty
According to my bond, no more nor lesse.
Lear. How, how *Cordelia*? Mend your speech a little,
Least you may marre your Fortunes.
Cor. Good my Lord,
You haue begot me, bred me, lou'd me.
I returne those duties backe as are right fit,
Obey you, Loue you, and most Honour you.
Why haue my Sisters Husbands, if they say
They loue you all? Happily when I shall wed,
That Lord, whose hand must take my plight, shall carry
Halfe my loue with him, halfe my Care, and Dutie,
Sure I shall neuer marry like my Sisters.
Lear But goes thy heart with this?
Cor. I my good Lord.
Lear. So young, and so vntender?
Cor. So young my Lord, and true.
Lear. Let it be so, thy truth then be thy dowre:
For by the sacred radience of the Sunne,
The miseries of *Heccat* and the night:
By all the operation of the Orbes,
From whom we do exist, and cease to be,
Heere I disclaime all my Paternall care,
Propinquity and property of blood,
And as a stranger to my heart and me,
Hold thee from this for euer. The barbarous *Scythian*,
Or he that makes his generation messes
To gorge his appetite, shall to my bosome
Be as well neighbour'd, pittied, and releeu'd,
As thou my sometime Daughter.
Kent Good my Liege.
Lear. Peace *Kent*,
Come not betweene the Dragon and his wrath,
I lou'd her most, and thought to set my rest
On her kind nursery. Hence and avoid my sight:
So be my graue my peace, as here I giue
Her Fathers heart from her; call *France*, who stirres?
Call *Burgundy*, *Cornwall*, and *Albanie*,
With my two Daughters Dowres, digest the third,
Let pride which she cals plainnesse, marry her:
I doe inuest you ioyntly with my power,
Preheminence, and all the large effects
That troope with Maiesty Our selfe by Monthly course,
With reseruation of an hundred Knights,
By you to be sustain'd, shall our abode
Make with you by due turne, onely we shall retaine
The name, and all th'addition to a King: the Sway,
Reuennew, Execution of the rest,
Beloued Sonnes be yours, which to confirme,
This Coronet part betweene you.
Kent. Royall *Lear*,
Whom I haue euer honor'd as my King,
Lou'd as my Father, as my Master follow'd,
As my great Patron thought on in my praiers.
Le. The bow is bent & drawne, make from the shaft.
Kent. Let it fall rather, though the forke inuade
The region of my heart, be *Kent* vnmannerly,
When *Lear* is mad, what wouldest thou do old man?
Think'st thou that dutie shall haue dread to speake,
When power to flattery bowes?
To plainnesse honour's bound,
When Maiesty falls to folly, reserue thy state,
And in thy best consideration checke
This hideous rashnesse, answere my life, my iudgement:
Thy yongest Daughter do's not loue thee least,
Nor are those empty hearted, whose low sounds
Reuerbe no hollownesse.
Lear. *Kent*, on thy life no more.
Kent. My life I neuer held but as pawne
To wage against thine enemies, nere feare to loose it,
Thy safety being motiue.
Lear. Out of my sight.
Kent. See better *Lear*, and let me still remaine
The true blanke of thine eie.
Kear. Now by *Apollo*,
Lent. Now by *Apollo*, King
Thou swear'st thy Gods in vaine.
Lear. O Vassall! Miscreant.
Alb. Cor. Deare Sir forbeare.
Kent. Kill thy Physition, and thy fee bestow
Vpon the foule disease, reuoke thy guift,
Or whil'st I can vent clamour from my throate,
Ile tell thee thou dost euill.
Lea. Heare me recreant, on thine allegeance heare me;
That thou hast sought to make vs breake our vowes,
Which we durst neuer yet; and with strain'd pride,
To come betwixt our sentences, and our power,
Which, nor our nature, nor our place can beare;
Our potencie made good, take thy reward.
Fiue dayes we do allot thee for prouision,
To shield thee from disasters of the world,
And on the sixt to turne thy hated backe
Vpon our kingdome; if on the tenth day following,
Thy banisht trunke be found in our Dominions,
The moment is thy death, away. By *Iupiter*,
This shall not be reuok'd,
Kent Fare thee well King, sith thus thou wilt appeare,
Freedome liues hence, and banishment is here;
The Gods to their deere shelter take thee Maid,
That iustly think'st, and hast most rightly said:
And your large speeches, may your deeds approue,
That good effects may spring from words of loue:
Thus *Kent*, O Princes, bids you all adew,
Hee'l shape his old course, in a Country new. *Exit.*

Flourish. Enter Gloster with France, and Burgundy, Attendants.

Cor Heere's *France* and *Burgundy*, my Noble Lord
Lear. My Lord of *Bugundie*,
We first addresse toward you, who with this King
Hath riuald for our Daughter; what in the least
Will you require in present Dower with her,
Or cease your quest of Loue?
Bur. Most Royall Maiesty,
I craue no more then hath your Highnesse offer'd,
Nor will you tender lesse?
Lear. Right Noble *Burgundy*,
When she was deare to vs, we did hold her so,
But now her price is fallen: Sir, there she stands,
If ought within that little seeming substance,
Or all of it with our displeasure piec'd,
And nothing more may fitly like your Grace,
Shee's there, and she is yours.
Bur. I know no answer.
Lear. Will you with those infirmities she owes,
Vnfriended, new adopted to our hate,
Dow'rd with our curse, and stranger'd with our oath,
Take her or, leaue her.
Bur. Par-

Bur. Pardon me Royall Sir,
Election makes not vp in ſuch conditions.
Le. Then leaue her ſir, for by the powre that made me,
I tell you all her wealth. For you great King,
I would not from your loue make ſuch a ſtray,
To match you where I hate, therefore beſeech you
T'auert your liking a more worthier way,
Then on a wretch whom Nature is aſham'd
Almoſt t'acknowledge hers.
Fra. This is moſt ſtrange,
That ſhe whom euen but now, was your obiect,
The argument of your praiſe, balme of your age,
The beſt, the deereſt, ſhould in this trice of time
Commit a thing ſo monſtrous, to diſmantle
So many folds of fauour: ſure her offence
Muſt be of ſuch vnnaturall degree,
That monſters it: Or your fore-voucht affection
Fall into taint, which to beleeue of her
Muſt be a faith that reaſon without miracle
Should neuer plant in me.
Cor. I yet beſeech your Maieſty.
If for I want that glib and oylie Art,
To ſpeake and purpoſe not, ſince what I will intend,
Ile do't before I ſpeake, that you make knowne
It is no vicious blot, murther, or fouleneſſe,
No vnchaſte action or diſhonoured ſtep
That hath depriu'd me of your Grace and fauour,
But euen for want of that, for which I am richer,
A ſtill ſoliciting eye, and ſuch a tongue,
That I am glad I haue not, though not to haue it,
Hath loſt me in your liking.
Lear. Better thou had'ſt
Not beene borne, then not t haue pleas'd me better.
Fra. Is it but this? A tardineſſe in nature,
Which often leaues the hiſtory vnſpoke
That it intends to do: my Lord of *Burgundy*,
What ſay you to the Lady? Loue's not loue
When it is mingled with regards, that ſtands
Alooſe from th'intire point, will you haue her?
She is herſelfe a Dowrie.
Bur. Royall King,
Giue but that portion which your ſelfe propos'd,
And here I take *Cordelia* by the hand,
Dutcheſſe of *Burgundie*.
Lear. Nothing, I haue ſworne, I am firme.
Bur. I am ſorry then you haue ſo loſt a Father,
That you muſt looſe a husband.
Cor. Peace be with *Burgundie*,
Since that reſpect and Fortunes are his loue,
I ſhall not be his wife.
Fra. Faireſt *Cordelia*, that art moſt rich being poore,
Moſt choiſe forſaken, and moſt lou'd deſpis'd,
Thee and thy vertues here I ſeize vpon,
Be it lawfull I take vp what's caſt away.
Gods, Gods! 'Tis ſtrange, that from their cold'ſt neglect
My Loue ſhould kindle to enflam'd reſpect.
Thy dowreleſſe Daughter King, throwne to my chance,
Is Queene of vs, of ours, and our faire *France*:
Not all the Dukes of watriſh *Burgundy*,
Can buy this vnpriz'd precious Maid of me.
Bid them farewell *Cordelia*, though vnkinde,
Thou looſeſt here a better where to finde.
Lear. Thou haſt her *France*, let her be thine, for we
Haue no ſuch Daughter, nor ſhall euer ſee
That face of hers againe, therfore be gone,
Without our Grace, our Loue, our Benizon:
Come Noble *Burgundie*. *Flouriſh. Exeunt.*
Fra. Bid farwell to your Siſters.
Cor. The Iewels of our Father, with waſh'd eies
Cordelia leaues you, I know you what you are,
And like a Siſter am moſt loth to call
Your faults as they are named. Loue well our Father:
To your profeſſed boſomes I commit him,
But yet alas, ſtood I within his Grace,
I would prefer him to a better place,
So farewell to you both.
Regn. Preſcribe not vs our dutie.
Gon. Let your ſtudy
Be to content your Lord, who hath receiu'd you
At Fortunes almes, you haue obedience ſcanted,
And well are worth the want that you haue wanted.
Cor. Time ſhall vnfold what plighted cunning hides,
Who couers faults, at laſt with ſhame derides:
Well may you proſper.
Fra. Come my faire *Cordelia*. *Exit France and Cor.*
Gon. Siſter, it is not little I haue to ſay,
Of what moſt neerely appertaines to vs both,
I thinke our Father will hence to night.
Reg. That's moſt certaine, and with you: next moneth with vs.

Gon. You ſee how full of changes his age is, the obſeruation we haue made of it hath beene little; he alwaies lou'd our Siſter moſt, and with what poore iudgement he hath now caſt her off, appeares too groſſely.

Reg. 'Tis the infirmity of his age, yet he hath euer but ſlenderly knowne himſelfe.

Gon. The beſt and ſoundeſt of his time hath bin but raſh, then muſt we looke from his age, to receiue not alone the imperfections of long ingraffed condition, but therewithall the vnruly way-wardneſſe, that infirme and cholericke yeares bring with them.

Reg. Such vnconſtant ſtarts are we like to haue from him, as this of *Kents* baniſhment.

Gon. There is further complement of leaue-taking betweene *France* and him, pray you let vs ſit together, if our Father carry authority with ſuch diſpoſition as he beares, this laſt ſurrender of his will but offend vs.

Reg. We ſhall further thinke of it.

Gon. We muſt do ſomething, and i'th' heate. *Exeunt.*

Scena Secunda.

Enter Baſtard.

Baſt. Thou Nature art my Goddeſſe, to thy Law
My ſeruices are bound, wherefore ſhould I
Stand in the plague of cuſtome, and permit
The curioſity of Nations, to depriue me?
For that I am ſome twelue, or fourteene Moonſhines
Lag of a Brother? Why Baſtard? Wherefore baſe?
When my Dimenſions are as well compact,
My minde as generous, and my ſhape as true
As honeſt Madams iſſue? Why brand they vs
With Baſe? With baſenes Barſtadie? Baſe, Baſe?
Who in the luſtie ſtealth of Nature, take
More compoſition, and fierce qualitie,
Then doth within a dull ſtale tyred bed
Goe to th'creating a whole tribe of Fops
Got'tweene a ſleepe, and wake? Well then,
Legitimate *Edgar*, I muſt haue your land,
Our Fathers loue, is to the Baſtard *Edmond*,
As to th'legitimate: fine word: Legitimate.

qq3 Well

Well, my Legittimate, if this Letter ſpeed,
And my inuention thriue, *Edmond* the baſe
Shall to'th'Legitimate: I grow, I proſper:
Now Gods, ſtand vp for Baſtards.

Enter Glouceſter

Glo Kent baniſh'd thus? and France in choller parted?
And the King gone to night? Preſcrib'd his powre,
Confin'd to exhibition? All this done
Vpon the gad? *Edmond*, how now? What newes?

Baſt. So pleaſe your Lordſhip, none.

Glou. Why ſo earneſtly ſeeke you to put vp ẏ Letter?

Baſt. I know no newes, my Lord.

Glou. What Paper were you reading?

Baſt. Nothing my Lord.

Glou. No? what needed then that terrible diſpatch of it into your Pocket? The quality of nothing, hath not ſuch neede to hide it ſelfe. Let's ſee: come, if it bee nothing, I ſhall not neede Spectacles.

Baſt. I beſeech you Sir, pardon mee; it is a Letter from my Brother, that I haue not all ore-read; and for ſo much as I haue perus'd, I finde it not fit for your ore-looking.

Glou. Giue me the Letter, Sir.

Baſt. I ſhall offend, either to detaine, or giue it:
The Contents, as in part I vnderſtand them,
Are too blame.

Glou. Let's ſee, let's ſee.

Baſt. I hope for my Brothers iuſtification, hee wrote this but as an eſſay, or taſte of my Vertue.

Glou. reads. *This policie, and reuerence of Age, makes the world bitter to the beſt of our times: keepes our Fortunes from vs, till our oldneſſe cannot relliſh them. I begin to finde an idle and fond bondage, in the oppreſſion of aged tyranny, who ſwayes not as it hath power, but as it is ſuffer'd. Come to me, that of this I may ſpeake more. If our Father would ſleepe till I wak'd him, you ſhould enioy halfe his Reuennew for euer, and liue the beloued of your Brother.* Edgar.

Hum? Conſpiracy? Sleepe till I wake him, you ſhould enioy halfe his Reuennew: my Sonne *Edgar*, had hee a hand to write this? A heart and braine to breede it in? When came you to this? Who brought it?

Baſt. It was not brought mee, my Lord; there's the cunning of it. I found it throwne in at the Caſement of my Cloſſet.

Glou. You know the character to be your Brothers?

Baſt. If the matter were good my Lord, I durſt ſwear it were his: but in reſpect of that, I would faine thinke it were not.

Glou. It is his.

Baſt. It is his hand, my Lord: but I hope his heart is not in the Contents.

Glo. Has he neuer before ſounded you in this buſines?

Baſt. Neuer my Lord. But I haue heard him oft maintaine it to be fit, that Sonnes at perfect age, and Fathers declin'd, the Father ſhould bee as Ward to the Son, and the Sonne manage his Reuennew.

Glou. O Villain, villain: his very opinion in the Letter. Abhorred Villaine, vnnaturall, deteſted, brutiſh Villaine; worſe then brutiſh: Go ſirrah, ſeeke him: Ile apprehend him. Abhominable Villaine, where is he?

Baſt. I do not well know my L. If it ſhall pleaſe you to ſuſpend your indignation againſt my Brother, til you can deriue from him better teſtimony of his intent, you ſhold run a certaine courſe: where, if you violently proceed againſt him, miſtaking his purpoſe, it would make a great gap in your owne Honor, and ſhake in peeces, the heart of his obedience. I dare pawne downe my life for him, that he hath writ this to feele my affection to your Honor, & to no other pretence of danger.

Glou. Thinke you ſo?

Baſt. If your Honor iudge it meete, I will place you where you ſhall heare vs conferre of this, and by an Auricular aſſurance haue your ſatisfaction, and that without any further delay, then this very Euening.

Glou. He cannot bee ſuch a Monſter. *Edmond* ſeeke him out: winde me into him, I pray you: frame the Buſineſſe after your owne wiſedome. I would vnſtate my ſelfe, to be in a due reſolution.

Baſt. I will ſeeke him Sir, preſently: conuey the buſineſſe as I ſhall find meanes, and acquaint you withall.

Glou. Theſe late Eclipſes in the Sun and Moone portend no good to vs: though the wiſedome of Nature can reaſon it thus, and thus, yet Nature finds it ſelfe ſcourg'd by the ſequent effects. Loue cooles, friendſhip falls off, Brothers diuide. In Cities, mutinies; in Countries, diſcord; in Pallaces, Treaſon; and the Bond crack'd, 'twixt Sonne and Father. This villaine of mine comes vnder the prediction; there's Son againſt Father, the King fals from byas of Nature, there's Father againſt Childe. We haue ſeene the beſt of our time. Machinations, hollowneſſe, treacherie, and all ruinous diſorders follow vs diſquietly to our Graues. Find out this Villain, *Edmond*, it ſhall loſe thee nothing, do it carefully: and the Noble & true-harted Kent baniſh'd; his offence, honeſty. 'Tis ſtrange. *Exit*

Baſt. This is the excellent foppery of the world, that when we are ſicke in fortune, often the ſurfets of our own behauiour, we make guilty of our diſaſters, the Sun, the Moone, and Starres, as if we were villaines on neceſſitie, Fooles by heauenly compulſion, Knaues, Theeues, and Treachers by Sphericall predominance. Drunkards, Lyars, and Adulterers by an inforc'd obedience of Planatary influence; and all that we are euill in, by a diuine thruſting on. An admirable euaſion of Whore-maſter-man, to lay his Goatiſh diſpoſition on the charge of a Starre, My father compounded with my mother vnder the Dragons taile, and my Natiuity was vnder *Vrſa Maior*, ſo that it followes, I am rough and Leacherous. I ſhould haue bin that I am, had the maidenleſt Starre in the Firmament twinkled on my baſtardizing.

Enter Edgar.

Pat: he comes like the Cataſtrophe of the old Comedie: my Cue is villanous Melancholly, with a ſighe like *Tom* o'Bedlam. —— O theſe Eclipſes do portend theſe diuiſions. Fa, Sol, La, Me.

Edg. How now Brother *Edmond*, what ſerious contemplation are you in?

Baſt. I am thinking Brother of a prediction I read this other day, what ſhould follow theſe Eclipſes.

Edg. Do you buſie your ſelfe with that?

Baſt. I promiſe you, the effects he writes of, ſucceede vnhappily.
When ſaw you my Father laſt?

Edg. The night gone by.

Baſt. Spake you with him?

Edg. I, two houres together.

Baſt. Parted you in good termes? Found you no diſpleaſure in him, by word, nor countenance?

Edg. None at all,

Baſt. Bethink your ſelfe wherein you may haue offended him: and at my entreaty forbeare his preſence, vntill ſome little time hath qualified the heat of his diſpleaſure, which at this inſtant ſo rageth in him, that with the miſchiefe

chiefe of your person, it would scarsely alay.

Edg. Some Villaine hath done me wrong.

Edm. That's my feare, I pray you haue a continent forbearance till the speed of his rage goes slower: and as I say, retire with me to my lodging, from whence I will fitly bring you to heare my Lord speake: pray ye goe, there's my key: if you do stirre abroad, goe arm'd.

Edg. Arm'd, Brother?

Edm. Brother, I aduise you to the best, I am no honest man, if ther be any good meaning toward you: I haue told you what I haue seene, and heard: But faintly. Nothing like the image, and horror of it, pray you away.

Edg. Shall I heare from you anon? *Exit.*

Edm. I do serue you in this businesse:
A Credulous Father, and a Brother Noble,
Whose nature is so farre from doing harmes,
That he suspects none: on whose foolish honestie
My practises ride easie: I see the businesse.
Let me, if not by birth, haue lands by wit,
All with me's meete, that I can fashion fit. *Exit.*

Scena Tertia.

Enter Gonerill, and Steward.

Gon. Did my Father strike my Gentleman for chiding of his Foole?

Ste. I Madam.

Gon. By day and night, he wrongs me, euery howre
He flashes into one grosse crime, or other,
That sets vs all at ods: Ile not endure it;
His Knights grow riotous, and himselfe vpbraides vs
On euery trifle. When he returnes from hunting,
I will not speake with him, say I am sicke,
If you come slacke of former seruices,
You shall do well, the fault of it Ile answer.

Ste. He's comming Madam, I heare him.

Gon. Put on what weary negligence you please,
You and your Fellowes: I'de haue it come to question;
If he distaste it, let him to my Sister,
Whose mind and mine I know in that are one,
Remember what I haue said.

Ste. Well Madam.

Gon. And let his Knights haue colder lookes among you: what growes of it no matter, aduise your fellowes so, Ile write straight to my Sister to hold my course; prepare for dinner. *Exeunt*

Scena Quarta.

Enter Kent.

Kent. If but as will I other accents borrow,
That can my speech defuse, my good intent
May carry through it selfe to that full issue
For which I raiz'd my likenesse. Now banisht *Kent*,
If thou canst serue where thou dost stand condemn'd,
So may it come, thy Master whom thou lou'st,
Shall find thee full of labours.

Hornes within. Enter Lear and Attendants.

Lear. Let me not stay a iot for dinner, go get it ready: how now, what art thou?

Kent. A man Sir.

Lear. What dost thou professe? What would'st thou with vs?

Kent. I do professe to be no lesse then I seeme; to serue him truely that will put me in trust, to loue him that is honest, to conuerse with him that is wise and saies little, to feare iudgement, to fight when I cannot choose, and to eate no fish.

Lear. What art thou?

Kent. A very honest hearted Fellow, and as poore as the King.

Lear. If thou be'st as poore for a subiect, as hee's for a King, thou art poore enough. What wouldst thou?

Kent. Seruice.

Lear. Who wouldst thou serue?

Kent. You.

Lear. Do'st thou know me fellow?

Kent. No Sir, but you haue that in your countenance, which I would faine call Master.

Lear. What's that?

Kent. Authority.

Lear. What seruices canst thou do?

Kent. I can keepe honest counsaile, ride, run, marre a curious tale in telling it, and deliuer a plaine message bluntly: that which ordinary men are fit for, I am qualified in, and the best of me, is Dilligence.

Lear. How old art thou?

Kent. Not so young Sir to loue a woman for singing, nor so old to dote on her for any thing. I haue yeares on my backe forty eight.

Lear. Follow me, thou shalt serue me, if I like thee no worse after dinner, I will not part from thee yet. Dinner ho, dinner, where's my knaue? my Foole? Go you and call my Foole hither. You you Sirrah, where's my Daughter?

Enter Steward.

Ste. So please you —— *Exit.*

Lear. What saies the Fellow there? Call the Clotpole backe: wher's my Foole? Ho, I thinke the world's asleepe, how now? Where's that Mungrell?

Knigh. He saies my Lord, your Daughters is not well.

Lear. Why came not the slaue backe to me when I call'd him?

Knigh. Sir, he answered me in the roundest manner, he would not.

Lear. He would not?

Knight. My Lord, I know not what the matter is, but to my iudgement your Highnesse is not entertain'd with that Ceremonious affection as you were wont, theres a great abatement of kindnesse appeares as well in the generall dependants, as in the Duke himselfe also, and your Daughter.

Lear. Ha? Saist thou so?

Knigh. I beseech you pardon me my Lord, if I bee mistaken, for my duty cannot be silent, when I thinke your Highnesse wrong'd.

Lear. Thou but remembrest me of mine owne Conception, I haue perceiued a most faint neglect of late, which I haue rather blamed as mine owne iealous curiositie, then as a very pretence and purpose of vnkindnesse; I will looke further intoo't: but where's my Foole? I haue not seene him this two daies.

Knight. Since my young Ladies going into *France* Sir,

Sir,the Foole hath much pined away.

Lear. No more of that, I haue noted it well, goe you and tell my Daughter,I would speake with her. Goe you call hither my Foole; Oh you Sir,you, come you hither Sir,who am I Sir?

Enter Steward.

Ste. My Ladies Father.

Lear. My Ladies Father? my Lords knaue,you whorson dog,you slaue,you curre.

Ste. I am none of these my Lord,
I beseech your pardon.

Lear. Do you bandy lookes with me,you Rascall?

Ste. Ile not be strucken my Lord.

Kent. Nor tript neither,you base Foot-ball plaier.

Lear. I thanke thee fellow.
Thou seru'st me,and Ile loue thee.

Kent. Come sir,arise,away,Ile teach you differences: away, away, if you will measure your lubbers length againe,tarry,but away,goe too,haue you wisedome,so.

Lear. Now my friendly knaue I thanke thee, there's earnest of thy seruice.

Enter Foole.

Foole. Let me hire him too,here's my Coxcombe.

Lear. How now my pretty knaue,how dost thou?

Foole. Sirrah,you were best take my Coxcombe.

Lear. Why my Boy?

Foole. Why? for taking ones part that's out of fauour, nay, & thou canst not smile as the wind sits,thou'lt catch colde shortly,there take my Coxcombe; why this fellow ha's banish'd two on's Daughters, and did the third a blessing against his will,if thou follow him, thou must needs weare my Coxcombe. How now Nunckle? would I had two Coxcombes and two Daughters.

Lear. Why my Boy?

Fool. If I gaue them all my liuing,I'ld keepe my Coxcombes my selfe, there's mine, beg another of thy Daughters.

Lear. Take heed Sirrah,the whip.

Foole. Truth's a dog must to kennell, hee must bee whipt out,. when the Lady Brach may stand by'th'fire and stinke.

Lear. A pestilent gall to me.

Foole. Sirha,Ile teach thee a speech.

Lear. Do.

Foole. Marke it Nuncle;
Haue more then thou showest,
Speake lesse then thou knowest,
Lend lesse then thou owest,
Ride more then thou goest,
Learne more then thou trowest,
Set lesse then thou throwest;
Leaue thy drinke and thy whore,
And keepe in a dore,
And thou shalt haue more,
Then two tens to a score.

Kent. This is nothing Foole.

Foole. Then 'tis like the breath of an vnfeed Lawyer, you gaue me nothing for't,can you make no vse of nothing Nuncle?

Lear. Why no Boy,
Nothing can be made out of nothing.

Foole. Prythee tell him, so much the rent of his land comes to,he will not beleeue a Foole.

Lear. A bitter Foole.

Foole. Do'st thou know the difference my Boy, betweene a bitter Foole,and a sweet one.

Lear. No Lad,teach me.

Foole. Nunckle, giue me an egge, and Ile giue thee two Crownes.

Lear. What two Crownes shall they be?

Foole. Why after I haue cut the egge i'th'middle and eate vp the meate,the two Crownes of the egge: when thou clouest thy Crownes i'th'middle, and gau'st away both parts, thou boar'st thine Asse on thy backe o're the durt,thou had'st little wit in thy bald crowne, when thou gau'st thy golden one away; if I speake like my selfe in this, let him be whipt that first findes it so.
Fooles had nere lesse grace in a yeere,
For wisemen are growne foppish,
And know not how their wits to weare,
Their manners are so apish.

Le. When were you wont to be so full of Songs sirrah?

Foole. I haue vsed it Nunckle, ere since thou mad'st thy Daughters thy Mothers, for when thou gau'st them the rod,and put'st downe thine owne breeches,then they
For sodaine ioy did weepe,
And I for sorrow sung,
That such a King should play bo-peepe,
And goe the Foole among.
Pry'thy Nunckle keepe a Schoolemaster that can teach thy Foole to lie,I would faine learne to lie.

Lear. And you lie sirrah,wee'l haue you whipt.

Foole. I maruell what kin thou and thy daughters are, they'l haue me whipt for speaking true: thou'lt haue me whipt for lying, and sometimes I am whipt for holding my peace. I had rather be any kind o'thing then a foole, and yet I would not be thee Nunckle,thou hast pared thy wit o'both sides, and left nothing i'th'middle; heere comes one o'the parings.

Enter Gonerill.

Lear. How now Daughter? what makes that Frontlet on? You are too much of late i'th'frowne.

Foole. Thou wast a pretty fellow when thou hadst no need to care for her frowning, now thou art an O without a figure,I am better then thou art now,I am a Foole, thou art nothing. Yes forsooth I will hold my tongue,so your face bids me,though you say nothing.
Mum,mum,he that keepes nor crust,not crum,
Weary of all,shall want some. That's a sheal'd Pescod.

Gon. Not only Sir this,your all-lycenc'd Foole,
But other of your insolent retinue
Do hourely Carpe and Quarrell,breaking forth
In ranke,and(not to be endur'd) riots Sir.
I had thought by making this well knowne vnto you,
To haue found a safe redresse,but now grow fearefull
By what your selfe too late haue spoke and done,
That you protect this course,and put it on
By your allowance,which if you should,the fault
Would not scape censure,nor the redresses sleepe,
Which in the tender of a wholesome weale,
Might in their working do you that offence,
Which else were shame,that then necessitie
Will call discreet proceeding.

Foole. For you know Nunckle, the Hedge-Sparrow fed the Cuckoo so long, that it's had it head bit off by it young,so out went the Candle,and we were left darkling.

Lear Are you our Daughter?

Gon. I would you would make vse of your good wisedome
(Whereof I know you are fraught),and put away
These dispositions,which of late transport you
From what you rightly are.

Foole. May

Poole. May not an Aſſe know, when the Cart drawes
the Horſe?
Whoop Iugge I loue thee.
Lear. Do's any heere know me?
This is not *Lear*:
Do's *Lear* walke thus? Speake thus? Where are his eies?
Either his Notion weakens, his Diſcernings
Are Lethargied. Ha! Waking? 'Tis not ſo?
Who is it that can tell me who I am?
Foole. *Lears* ſhadow.
Lear. Your name, faire Gentlewoman?
Gon. This admiration Sir, is much o'th'ſauour
Of other your new prankes. I do beſeech you
To vnderſtand my purpoſes aright:
As you are Old, and Reuerend, ſhould be Wiſe.
Heere do you keepe a hundred Knights and Squires,
Men ſo diſorder'd, ſo deboſh'd, and bold,
That this our Court infected with their manners,
Shewes like a riotous Inne; Epicuriſme and Luſt
Makes it more like a Tauerne, or a Brothell,
Then a grac'd Pallace. The ſhame it ſelfe doth ſpeake
For inſtant remedy. Be then deſir'd
By her, that elſe will take the thing ſhe begges,
A little to diſquantity your Traine,
And the remainders that ſhall ſtill depend,
To be ſuch men as may beſort your Age,
Which know themſelues, and you.
Lear. Darkneſſe, and Diuels.
Saddle my horſes: call my Traine together.
Degenerate Baſtard, Ile not trouble thee;
Yet haue I left a daughter.
Gon. You ſtrike my people, and your diſorder'd rable,
make Seruants of their Betters.

Enter Albany.

Lear. Woe, that too late repents:
Is it your will, ſpeake Sir? Prepare my Horſes.
Ingratitude! thou Marble-hearted Fiend,
More hideous when thou ſhew'ſt thee in a Child,
Then the Sea-monſter.
Alb. Pray Sir be patient.
Lear. Deteſted Kite, thou lyeſt.
My Traine are men of choice, and rareſt parts,
That all particulars of dutie know,
And in the moſt exact regard, ſupport
The worſhips of their name. O moſt ſmall fault,
How vgly did'ſt thou in *Cordelia* ſhew?
Which like an Engine, wrencht my frame of Nature
From the fixt place: drew from my heart all loue,
And added to the gall. O *Lear, Lear, Lear*!
Beate at this gate that let thy Folly in,
And thy deere Iudgement out. Go, go, my people.
Alb My Lord, I am guiltleſſe, as I am ignorant
Of what hath moued you.
Lear. It may be ſo, my Lord.
Heare Nature, heare deere Goddeſſe, heare:
Suſpend thy purpoſe, if thou did'ſt intend
To make this Creature fruitfull:
Into her Wombe conuey ſtirrility,
Drie vp in her the Organs of increaſe,
And from her derogate body, neuer ſpring
A Babe to honor her. If ſhe muſt teeme,
Create her childe of Spleene, that it may liue
And be a thwart diſnatur'd torment to her.
Let it ſtampe wrinkles in her brow of youth,
With cadent Teares fret Channels in her cheekes,
Turne all her Mothers paines, and benefits
To laughter, and contempt: That ſhe may feele,
How ſharper then a Serpents tooth it is,
To haue a thankleſſe Childe. Away, away. *Exit.*
Alb. Now Gods that we adore,
Whereof comes this?
Gon. Neuer afflict your ſelfe to know more of it:
But let his diſpoſition haue that ſcope
As dotage giues it.

Enter Lear.

Lear. What fiftie of my Followers at a clap?
Within a fortnight?
Alb. What's the matter, Sir?
Lear. Ile tell thee:
Life and death, I am aſham'd
That thou haſt power to ſhake my manhood thus,
That theſe hot teares, which breake from me perforce
Should make thee worth them.
Blaſtes and Fogges vpon thee:
Th'vntented woundings of a Fathers curſe
Pierce euerie ſenſe about thee. Old fond eyes,
Beweepe this cauſe againe, Ile plucke ye out,
And caſt you with the waters that you looſe
To temper Clay. Ha? Let it be ſo.
I haue another daughter,
Who I am ſure is kinde and comfortable:
When ſhe ſhall heare this of thee, with her nailes
Shee'l flea thy Woluiſh viſage. Thou ſhalt finde,
That Ile reſume the ſhape which thou doſt thinke
I haue caſt off for euer. *Exit*
Gon. Do you marke that?
Alb. I cannot be ſo partiall *Gonerill*,
To the great loue I beare you.
Gon. Pray you content. What *Oſwald*, hoa?
You Sir, more Knaue then Foole, after your Maſter.
Foole. Nunkle *Lear*, Nunkle *Lear*,
Tarry, take the Foole with thee:
A Fox, when one has caught her,
And ſuch a Daughter,
Should ſure to the Slaughter,
If my Cap would buy a Halter,
So the Foole followes after. *Exit*
Gon. This man hath had good Counſell,
A hundred Knights?
'Tis politike, and ſafe to let him keepe
At point a hundred Knights: yes, that on euerie dreame,
Each buz, each fancie, each complaint, diſlike,
He may enguard his dotage with their powres,
And hold our liues in mercy. *Oſwald*, I ſay.
Alb. Well, you may feare too farre.
Gon. Safer then truſt too farre;
Let me ſtill take away the harmes I feare,
Not feare ſtill to be taken. I know his heart,
What he hath vtter'd I haue writ my Siſter:
If ſhe ſuſtaine him, and his hundred Knights
When I haue ſhew'd th'vnfitneſſe.

Enter Steward.

How now *Oſwald*?
What haue you writ that Letter to my Siſter?
Stew. I Madam.
Gon. Take you ſome company, and away to horſe,
Informe her full of my particular feare,
And thereto adde ſuch reaſons of your owne,
As may compact it more. Get you gone,
And

And hasten your returne; no,no,my Lord,
This milky gentlenesse,and course of yours
Though I condemne not,yet vnder pardon
Your are much more at task for want of wisedome,
Then prai'sd for harmefull mildnesse.
Alb. How farre your eies may pierce I cannot tell;
Striuing to better, oft we marre what's well.
Gon. Nay then ——
Alb. Well,well,the'uent. *Exeunt*

Scena Quinta.

Enter Lear, Kent, Gentleman, and Foole.

Lear. Go you before to *Gloster* with these Letters; acquaint my Daughter no further with any thing you know, then comes from her demand out of the Letter, if your Dilligence be not speedy, I shall be there afore you.
Kent. I will not sleepe my Lord, till I haue deliuered your Letter. *Exit.*
Foole. If a mans braines were in's heeles, wert not in danger of kybes?
Lear. I Boy.
Foole. Then I prythee be merry, thy wit shall not go slip-shod.
Lear. Ha,ha,ha.
Fool. Shalt see thy other Daughter will vse thee kindly, for though she's as like this, as a Crabbe's like an Apple,yet I can tell what I can tell.
Lear. What can'st tell Boy?
Foole. She will taste as like this as, a Crabbe do's to a Crab: thou canst tell why ones nose stands i'th'middle on's face?
Lear. No.
Foole. Why to keepe ones eyes of either side's nose, that what a man cannot smell out,he may spy into.
Lear. I did her wrong.
Foole. Can'st tell how an Oyster makes his shell?
Lear. No.
Foole. Nor I neither; but I can tell why a Snaile ha's a house.
Lear. Why?
Foole. Why to put's head in,not to giue it away to his daughters,and leaue his hornes without a case.
Lear. I will forget my Nature, so kind a Father? Be my Horsses ready?
Foole. Thy Asses are gone about 'em; the reason why the seuen Starres are no mo then seuen, is a pretty reason.
Lear. Because they are not eight.
Foole. Yes indeed,thou would'st make a good Foole.
Lear. To tak't againe perforce; Monster Ingratitude!
Foole. If thou wert my Foole Nunckle, Il'd haue thee beaten for being old before thy time.
Lear. How's that?
Foole. Thou shouldst not haue bin old, till thou hadst bin wise.
Lear. O let me not be mad, not mad sweet Heauen: keepe me in temper,I would not be mad. How now are the Horses ready?
Gent. Ready my Lord.
Lear. Come Boy.
Fool. She that's a Maid now,& laughs at my departure
Shall not be a Maid long, vnlesse things be cut shorter.
Exeunt.

Actus Secundus. Scena Prima.

Enter Bastard, and Curan seuerally.

Bast. Saue thee *Curan.*
Cur. And your Sir,I haue bin
With your Father,and giuen him notice
That the Duke of *Cornwall*,and *Regan* his Duchesse
Will be here with him this night.
Bast. How comes that?
Cur. Nay I know not, you haue heard of the newes abroad,I meane the whisper'd ones, for they are yet but ear-kissing arguments.
Bast. Not I: pray you what are they?
Cur. Haue you heard of no likely Warres toward,
Twixt the Dukes of *Cornwall*,and *Albany*?
Bast. Not a word.
Cur. You may do then in time.
Fare you well Sir. *Exit.*
Bast. The Duke be here to night? The better best,
This weaues it selfe perforce into my businesse,
My Father hath set guard to take my Brother,
And I haue one thing of a queazie question
Which I must act, Briefenesse,and Fortune worke.
Enter Edgar.
Brother, a word, discend; Brother I say,
My Father watches: O Sir, fly this place,
Intelligence is giuen where you are hid;
You haue now the good aduantage of the night,
Haue you not spoken 'gainst the Duke of *Cornewall*?
Hee's comming hither,now i'th' night,i'th' haste,
And *Regan* with him,haue you nothing said
Vpon his partie 'gainst the Duke of *Albany*?
Aduise your selfe.
Edg. I am sure on't,not a word.
Bast. I heare my Father comming,pardon me:
In cunning,I must draw my Sword vpon you:
Draw,seeme to defend your selfe,
Now quit you well.
Yeeld,come before my Father,light hoa,here,
Fly Brother,Torches,Torches,so farewell.
Exit Edgar.
Some blood drawne on me,would beget opinion
Of my more fierce endeauour. I haue seene drunkards
Do more then this in sport; Father,Father,
Stop,stop,no helpe?

Enter Gloster, and Seruants with Torches.

Glo. Now *Edmund*,where's the villaine?
Bast. Here stood he in the dark,his sharpe Sword out,
Mumbling of wicked charmes,coniuring the Moone
To stand auspicious Mistris.
Glo. But where is he?
Bast. Looke Sir,I bleed.
Glo. Where is the villaine,*Edmund*?
Bast. Fled this way Sir,when by no meanes he could.
Glo. Pursue him,ho: go after. By no meanes,what?
Bast. Perswade me to the murther of your Lordship,
But

But that I told him the reuenging Gods,
'Gainst Paricides did all the thunder bend,
Spoke with how manifold,and strong aBond
The Child was bound to'th' Father; Sir in fine,
Seeing how lothly opposite I stood
To his vnnaturall purpose,in fell motion
With his prepared Sword,he charges home
My vnprouided body,latch'd mine arme;
And when he saw my best alarum'd spirits
Bold in the quarrels right,rouz'd to th'encounter,
Or whether gasted by the noyse I made,
Full sodainely he fled.

Glost. Let him fly farre:
Not in this Land shall he remaine vncaught
And found; dispatch,the Noble Duke my Master,
My worthy Arch and Patron comes to night,
By his authoritie I will proclaime it,
That he which finds him shall deserue our thankes,
Bringing the murderous Coward to the stake:
He that conceales him death.

Bast. When I disswaded him from his intent,
And found him pight to doe it,with curst speech
I threaten'd to discouer him; he replied,
Thou vnpossessing Bastard,dost thou thinke,
If I would stand against thee,would the reposall
Of any trust,vertue,or worth in thee
Make thy words faith'd? No,what should I denie,
(As this I would, though thou didst produce
My very Character) I'ld turne it all
To thy suggestion,plot,and damned practise:
And thou must make a dullard of the world,
If they not thought the profits of my death
Were very pregnant and potentiall spirits
To make thee seeke it. *Tucket within.*

Glo. O strange and fastned Villaine,
Would he deny his Letter,said he?
Harke,the Dukes Trumpets,I know not wher he comes;
All Ports Ile barre,the villaine shall not scape,
The Duke must grant me that; besides,his picture
I will send farre and neere,that all the kingdome
May haue due note of him,and of my land,
(Loyall and naturall Boy) Ile worke the meanes
To make thee capable.

Enter Cornewall,Regan,and Attendants.

Corn. How now my Noble friend,since I came hither
(Which I can call but now,)I haue heard strangenesse.

Reg. If it be true,all vengeance comes too short
Which can pursue th'offender; how dost my Lord?

Glo. O Madam,my old heart is crack'd,it's crack'd.

Reg. What,did my Fathers Godsonne seeke your life?
He whom my Father nam'd,your *Edgar*?

Glo. O Lady,Lady,shame would haue it hid.

Reg. Was he not companion with the riotous Knights
That tended vpon my Father?

Glo I know not Madam,'tis too bad,too bad.

Bast. Yes Madam,he was of that consort.

Reg. No maruaile then,though he were ill affected,
'Tis they haue put him on the old mans death,
To haue th'expence and wast of his Reuenues:
I haue this present euening from my Sister
Beene well inform'd of them,and with such cautions,
That if they come to soiourne at my house,
Ile not be there.

Cor. Nor I,assure thee *Regan*;
Edmund,I heare that you haue shewne your Father
A Child-like Office.

Bast. It was my duty Sir.

Glo. He did bewray his practise,and receiu'd
This hurt you see,striuing to apprehend him.

Cor. Is he pursued?

Glo. I my good Lord.

Cor. If he be taken,he shall neuer more
Be fear'd of doing harme,make your owne purpose,
How in my strength you please: for you *Edmund*,
Whose vertue and obedience doth this instant
So much commend it selfe,you shall be ours,
Nature's of such deepe trust,we shall much need:
You we first seize on.

Bast. I shall serue you Sir truely,how euer else.

Glo. For him I thanke your Grace.

Cor. You know not why we came to visit you?

Reg. Thus out of season,thredding darke ey'd night,
Occasions Noble *Gloster* of some prize,
Wherein we must haue vse of your aduise.
Our Father he hath writ,so hath our Sister,
Of differences,which I best though it fit
To answere from our home: the seuerall Messengers
From hence attend dispatch,our good old Friend,
Lay comforts to your bosome,and bestow
Your needfull counsaile to our businesses,
Which craues the instant vse.

Glo. I serue you Madam,
Your Graces are right welcome. *Exeunt. Flourish.*

Scena Secunda.

Enter Kent,and Steward seuerally.

Stew. Good dawning to thee Friend,art of this house?

Kent. I.

Stew. Where may we set our horses?

Kent. I'th'myre.

Stew. Prythee,if thou lou'st me,tell me.

Kent. I loue thee not.

Ste. Why then I care not for thee.

Kent. If I had thee in *Lipsbury* Pinfold,I would make thee care for me.

Ste. Why do'st thou vse me thus? I know thee not.

Kent. Fellow I know thee.

Ste. What do'st thou know me for?

Kent. A Knaue,a Rascall, an eater of broken meates,a base, proud, shallow, beggerly, three-suited-hundred pound, filthy woosted-stocking knaue,a Lilly-liuered, action-taking,whoreson glasse-gazing super-seruiceable finicall Rogue, one Trunke-inheriting slaue, one that would'st be a Baud in way of good seruice, and art nothing but the composition of a Knaue, Begger, Coward, Pandar, and the Sonne and Heire of a Mungrill Bitch, one whom I will beate into clamours whining, if thou deny'st the least sillable of thy addition.

Stew. Why,what a monstrous Fellow art thou, thus to raile on one, that is neither knowne of thee, nor knowes thee?

Kent. What a brazen-fac'd Varlet art thou, to deny thou knowest me? Is it two dayes since I tript vp thy heeles,and beate thee before the King? Draw you rogue, for

for though it be night, yet the Moone shines, Ile make a sop oth' Moonshine of you, you whoreson Cullyenly Barber-monger, draw.

Stew. Away, I haue nothing to do with thee.

Kent. Draw you Rascall, you come with Letters against the King, and take Vanitie the puppets part, against the Royaltie of her Father: draw you Rogue, or Ile so carbonado your shanks, draw you Rascall, come your waies.

Ste. Helpe, ho, murther, helpe.

Kent. Strike you slaue: stand rogue, stand you neat slaue, strike.

Stew. Helpe hoa, murther, murther.

Enter Bastard, Cornewall, Regan, Gloster, Seruants.

Bast. How now, what's the matter? Part.

Kent. With you goodman Boy, if you please, come, Ile flesh ye, come on yong Master.

Glo. Weapons? Armes? what's the matter here?

Cor. Keepe peace vpon your liues, he dies that strikes againe, what is the matter?

Reg. The Messengers from our Sister, and the King

Cor. What is your difference, speake?

Stew. I am scarce in breath my Lord.

Kent. No Maruell, you haue so bestir'd your valour, you cowardly Rascall, nature disclaimes in thee: a Taylor made thee.

Cor. Thou art a strange fellow, a Taylor make a man?

Kent. A Taylor Sir, a Stone-cutter, or a Painter, could not haue made him so ill, though they had bin but two yeares oth'trade.

Cor. Speake yet, how grew your quarrell?

Ste. This ancient Ruffian Sir, whose life I haue spar'd at sute of his gray-beard.

Kent. Thou whoreson Zed, thou vnnecessary letter: my Lord, if you will giue me leaue, I will tread this vnboulted villaine into morter, and daube the wall of a Iakes with him. Spare my gray-beard, you wagtaile?

Cor. Peace sirrah,
You beastly knaue, know you no reuerence?

Kent. Yes Sir, but anger hath a priuiledge.

Cor. Why art thou angrie?

Kent. That such a slaue as this should weare a Sword,
Who weares no honesty: such smiling rogues as these,
Like Rats oft bite the holy cords a twaine,
Which are t'intrince, t'vnloose: smooth euery passion
That in the natures of their Lords rebell,
Being oile to fire, snow to the colder moodes,
Reuenge, affirme, and turne their Halcion beakes
With euery gall, and varry of their Masters,
Knowing naught (like dogges) but following:
A plague vpon your Epilepticke visage,
Smoile you my speeches, as I were a Foole?
Goose, if I had you vpon *Sarum* Plaine,
I'ld driue ye cackling home to *Camelot*.

Corn. What art thou mad old Fellow?

Glost. How fell you out, say that?

Kent. No contraries hold more antipathy,
Then I, and such a knaue.

Corn. Why do'st thou call him Knaue?
What is his fault?

Kent. His countenance likes me not.

Cor. No more perchance do's mine, nor his, nor hers.

Kent. Sir, 'tis my occupation to be plaine,
I haue seene better faces in my time,
Then stands on any shoulder that I see
Before me, at this instant.

Corn. This is some Fellow,
Who hauing beene prais'd for bluntnesse, doth affect
A saucy roughnes, and constraines the garb
Quite from his Nature. He cannot flatter he,
An honest mind and plaine, he must speake truth,
And they will take it so, if not, hee's plaine.
These kind of Knaues I know, which in this plainnesse
Harbour more craft, and more corrupter ends,
Then twenty silly ducking obseruants,
That stretch their duties nicely.

Kent. Sir, in good faith, in sincere verity,
Vnder th'allowance of your great aspect,
Whose influence like the wreath of radient fire
On flicking *Phœbus* front.

Corn. What mean'st by this?

Kent. To go out of my dialect, which you discommend so much; I know Sir, I am no flatterer, he that beguild you in a plaine accent, was a plaine Knaue, which for my part I will not be, though I should win your displeasure to entreat me too't.

Corn. What was th'offence you gaue him?

Ste. I neuer gaue him any:
It pleas'd the King his Master very late
To strike at me vpon his misconstruction,
When he compact, and flattering his displeasure
Tript me behind: being downe, insulted, rail'd,
And put vpon him such a deale of Man,
That worthied him, got praises of the King,
For him attempting, who was selfe-subdued,
And in the fleshment of this dead exploit,
Drew on me here againe.

Kent. None of these Rogues, and Cowards
But *Aiax* is there Foole.

Corn. Fetch forth the Stocks?
You stubborne ancient Knaue, you reuerent Bragart,
Wee'l teach you.

Kent. Sir, I am too old to learne:
Call not your Stocks for me, I serue the King.
On whose imployment I was sent to you,
You shall doe small respects, show too bold malice
Against the Grace, and Person of my Master,
Stocking his Messenger.

Corn. Fetch forth the Stocks;
As I haue life and Honour, there shall he sit till Noone.

Reg. Till noone? till night my Lord, and all night too.

Kent. Why Madam, if I were your Fathers dog,
You should not vse me so.

Reg. Sir, being his Knaue, I will. *Stocks brought out.*

Cor. This is a Fellow of the selfe same colour,
Our Sister speakes of. Come, bring away the Stocks.

Glo. Let me beseech your Grace, not to do so,
The King his Master, needs must take it ill
That he so slightly valued in his Messenger,
Should haue him thus restrained.

Cor. Ile answere that.

Reg. My Sister may recieue it much more worsse,
To haue her Gentleman abus'd, assaulted.

Corn. Come my Lord, away. *Exit.*

Glo. I am sorry for thee friend, 'tis the Duke pleasure,
Whose disposition all the world well knowes
Will not be rub'd nor stopt, Ile entreat for thee.

Kent. Pray do not Sir, I haue watch'd and trauail'd hard,
Some time I shall sleepe out, the rest Ile whistle.
A good mans fortune may grow out at heeles:

Giue

Giue you good morrow.

Glo. The Duke's too blame in this,
'Twill be ill taken. *Exit.*

Kent. Good King, that must approue the common saw,
Thou out of Heauens benediction com'st
To the warme Sun.
Approach thou Beacon to this vnder Globe,
That by thy comfortable Beames I may
Peruse this Letter. Nothing almost sees miracles
But miserie. I know 'tis from *Cordelia*,
Who hath most fortunately beene inform'd
Of my obscured course. And shall finde time
From this enormous State, seeking to giue
Losses their remedies. All weary and o're-watch'd,
Take vantage heauie eyes, not to behold
This shamefull lodging. Fortune goodnight,
Smile once more, turne thy wheele.

Enter Edgar.

Edg. I heard my selfe proclaim'd,
And by the happy hollow of a Tree,
Escap'd the hunt. No Port is free, no place
That guard, and most vnusall vigilance
Do's not attend my taking. Whiles I may scape
I will preserue myselfe: and am bethought
To take the basest, and most poorest shape
That euer penury in contempt of man,
Brought neere to beast; my face Ile grime with filth,
Blanket my loines, else all my haires in knots,
And with presented nakednesse out-face
The Windes, and persecutions of the skie;
The Country giues me proofe, and president
Of Bedlam beggers, who with roaring voices,
Strike in their num'd and mortified Armes.
Pins, Wodden-prickes, Nayles, Sprigs of Rosemarie:
And with this horrible obiect, from low Farmes,
Poore pelting Villages, Sheeps-Coates, and Milles,
Sometimes with Lunaticke bans, sometime with Praiers
Inforce their charitie: poore *Turlygod*, poore *Tom*,
That's something yet: *Edgar* I nothing am. *Exit.*

Enter Lear, Foole, and Gentleman.

Lea. 'Tis strange that they should so depart from home,
And not send backe my Messengers.

Gent. As I learn'd,
The night before, there was no purpose in them
Of this remoue.

Kent. Haile to thee Noble Master.

Lear. Ha? Mak'st thou this shame thy pastime?

Kent. No my Lord.

Foole. Hah, ha, he weares Cruell Garters Horses are tide by the heads, Dogges and Beares, by'th'necke, Monkies by'th'loynes, and Men by'th' legs: when a man ouerlustie at legs, then he weares wodden nether-stocks.

Lear. What's he,
That hath so much thy place mistooke
To set thee heere?

Kent. It is both he and she,
Your Son, and Daughter.

Lear. No.

Kent. Yes.

Lear. No I say.

Kent. I say yea.

Lear. By *Iupiter* I sweare no.

Kent. By *Iuno*, I sweare I.

Lear. They durst not do't:
They could not, would not do't: 'tis worse then murther,
To do vpon respect such violent outrage:
Resolue me with all modest haste, which way
Thou might'st deserue, or they impose this vsage,
Comming from vs.

Kent. My Lord, when at their home
I did commend your Highnesse Letters to them,
Ere I was risen from the place, that shewed
My dutie kneeling, came there a reeking Poste,
Stew'd in his haste, halfe breathlesse, painting forth
From *Gonerill* his Mistris, salutations;
Deliuer'd Letters spight of intermission,
Which presently they read; on those contents
They summon'd vp their meiney, straight tooke Horse,
Commanded me to follow, and attend
The leisure of their answer, gaue me cold lookes,
And meeting heere the other Messenger,
Whose welcome I perceiu'd had poison'd mine,
Being the very fellow which of late
Displaid so sawcily against your Highnesse,
Hauing more man then wit about me, drew;
He rais'd the house, with loud and coward cries,
Your Sonne and Daughter found this trespasse worth
The shame which heere it suffers.

Foole. Winters not gon yet, if the wil'd Geese fly that way,
Fathers that weare rags, do make their Children blind,
But Fathers that beare bags, shall see their children kind.
Fortune that arrant whore, nere turns the key toth' poore.
But for all this thou shalt haue as many Dolors for thy Daughters, as thou canst tell in a yeare.

Lear. Oh how this Mother swels vp toward my heart!
Historica passio, downe thou climing sorrow,
Thy Elements below where is this Daughter?

Kent. With the Earle Sir, here within.

Lear. Follow me not, stay here. *Exit.*

Gen. Made you no more offence,
But what you speake of?

Kent. None:
How chance the the King comes with so small a number?

Foole. And thou hadst beene set i'th' Stockes for that question, thoud'st well deseru'd it.

Kent. Why Foole?

Foole. Wee'l set thee to schoole to an Ant, to teach thee ther's no labouring i'th' winter. All that follow their noses, are led by their eyes, but blinde men, and there's not a nose among twenty, but can smell him that's stinking; let go thy hold, when a great wheele runs downe a hill, least it breake thy necke with following. But the great one that goes vpward, let him draw thee after: when a wiseman giues thee better counsell giue me mine againe, I would haue none but knaues follow it, since a Foole giues it.
That Sir, which serues and seekes for gaine,
And follo wes but for forme;
Will packe, when it begins to raine,
And leaue thee in the storme.
But I will tarry, the Foole will stay,
And let the wiseman flie:
The knaue turnes Foole that runnes away,
The Foole no knaue perdie.

Enter Lear, and Gloster:

Kent. Where learn'd you this Foole?

Foole. Not i'th' Stocks Foole.

Lear.

Lear. Deny to ſpeake with me?
They are ſicke, they are weary,
They haue trauail'd all the night? meere fetches,
The images of reuolt and flying off.
Fetch me a better anſwer.
Glo. My deere Lord,
You know the fiery quality of the Duke,
How vnremoueable and fixt he is
In his owne courſe.
Lear. Vengeance, Plague, Death, Confuſion:
Fiery? What quality? Why *Gloſter*, *Gloſter*,
I'ld ſpeake with the Duke of *Cornewall*, and his wife.
Glo. Well my good Lord, I haue inform'd them ſo.
Lear. Inform'd them? Do'ſt thou vnderſtand me man.
Glo. I my good Lord.
Lear. The King would ſpeake with *Cornwall*,
The deere Father
Would with his Daughter ſpeake, commands, tends, ſer-
Are they inform'd of this? My breath and blood: (uice,
Fiery? The fiery Duke, tell the hot Duke that ——
No, but not yet, may be he is not well,
Infirmity doth ſtill neglect all office,
Whereto our health is bound, we are not our ſelues,
When Nature being oppreſt, commands the mind
To ſuffer with the body; Ile forbeare,
And am fallen out with my more headier will,
To take the indiſpos'd and ſickly fit,
For the ſound man. Death on my ſtate: wherefore
Should he ſit heere? This act perſwades me,
That this remotion of the Duke and her
Is practiſe only. Giue me my Seruant forth;
Goe tell the Duke, and's wife, Il'd ſpeake with them:
Now, preſently: bid them come forth and heare me,
Or at their Chamber doore Ile beate the Drum,
Till it crie ſleepe to death.
Glo. I would haue all well betwixt you. *Exit.*
Lear Oh me my heart! My riſing heart! But downe.
Foole. Cry to it Nunckle, as the Cockney did to the Eeles, when ſhe put 'em i'th' Paſte aliue, ſhe knapt 'em o'th' coxcombs with a ſticke, and cryed downe wantons, downe; 'twas her Brother, that in pure kindneſſe to his Horſe buttered his Hay.

Enter Cornewall, Regan, Gloſter, Seruants.

Lear. Good morrow to you both.
Corn. Haile to your Grace. *Kent here ſet at liberty.*
Reg. I am glad to ſee your Highneſſe.
Lear *Regan*, I thinke your are. I know what reaſon
I haue to thinke ſo, if thou ſhould'ſt not be glad,
I would diuorce me from thy Mother Tombe,
Sepulchring an Adultreſſe. O are you free?
Some other time for that. Beloued *Regan*,
Thy Siſters naught: oh *Regan*, ſhe hath tied
Sharpe-tooth'd vnkindneſſe, like a vulture heere,
I can ſcarce ſpeake to thee, thou'lt not beleeue
With how deprau'd a quality. Oh *Regan*.
Reg I pray you Sir, take patience, I haue hope
You leſſe know how to value her deſert,
Then ſhe to ſcant her dutie.
Lear. Say? How is that?
Reg. I cannot thinke my Siſter in the leaſt
Would faile her Obligation. If Sir perchance
She haue reſtrained the Riots of your Followres,
'Tis on ſuch ground, and to ſuch wholeſome end,
As cleeres her from all blame.
Lear. My curſes on her.
Reg. O Sir, you are old,
Nature in you ſtands on the very Verge
Of his confine: you ſhould be rul'd, and led
By ſome diſcretion, that diſcernes your ſtate
Better then you your ſelfe: therefore I pray you,
That to our Siſter, you do make returne,
Say you haue wrong'd her.
Lear. Aske her forgiueneſſe?
Do you but marke how this becomes the houſe?
Deere daughter, I confeſſe that I am old;
Age is vnneceſſary: on my knees I begge,
That you'l vouchſafe me Rayment, Bed, and Food.
Reg. Good Sir, no more: theſe are vnſightly trickes:
Returne you to my Siſter.
Lear. Neuer *Regan*:
She hath abated me of halfe my Traine;
Look'd blacke vpon me, ſtrooke me with her Tongue
Moſt Serpent-like, vpon the very Heart.
All the ſtor'd Vengeances of Heauen, fall
On her ingratefull top: ſtrike her yong bones
You taking Ayres, with Lameneſſe.
Corn. Fye ſir, fie.
Le. You nimble Lightnings, dart your blinding flames
Into her ſcornfull eyes: Infect her Beauty,
You Fen-ſuck'd Fogges, drawne by the powrfull Sunne,
To fall, and bliſter.
Reg. O the bleſt Gods!
So will you wiſh on me, when the raſh moode is on.
Lear. No *Regan*, thou ſhalt neuer haue my curſe:
Thy tender-hefted Nature ſhall not giue
Thee o're to harſhneſſe: Her eyes are fierce, but thine
Do comfort, and not burne. 'Tis not in thee
To grudge my pleaſures, to cut off my Traine,
To bandy haſty words, to ſcant my ſizes,
And in concluſion, to oppoſe the bolt
Againſt my comming in. Thou better know'ſt
The Offices of Nature, bond of Childhood,
Effects of Curteſie, dues of Gratitude:
Thy halfe o'th' Kingdome haſt thou not forgot,
Wherein I thee endow'd.
Reg. Good Sir, to'th' purpoſe. *Tucket within.*
Lear. Who put my man i'th' Stockes?

Enter Steward.

Corn. What Trumpet's that?
Reg. I know't, my Siſters: this approues her Letter,
That ſhe would ſoone be heere. Is your Lady come?
Lear. This is a Slaue, whoſe eaſie borrowed pride
Dwels in the fickly grace of her he followes.
Out Varlet, from my ſight.
Corn. What meanes your Grace?

Enter Gonerill.

Lear. Who ſtockt my Seruant? *Regan*, I haue good hope
Thou did'ſt not know on't.
Who comes here? O Heauens!
If you do loue old men; if your ſweet ſway
Allow Obedience; if you your ſelues are old,
Make it your cauſe: Send downe, and take my part.
Art not aſham'd to looke vpon this Beard?
O *Regan*, will you take her by the hand?
Gon. Why not by'th' hand Sir? How haue I offended?
All's not offence that indiſcretion findes,
And dotage termes ſo.
Lear. O ſides, you are too tough!
Will you yet hold?
How came my man i'th' Stockes?
Corn. I ſet him there, Sir: but his owne Diſorders
Deſeru'd

Deseru'd much lesse aduancement.
Lear. You? Did you?
Reg. I pray you Father being weake, seeme so.
If till the expiration of your Moneth
You will returne and soiourne with my Sister,
Dismissing halfe your traine, come then to me,
I am now from home, and out of that prouision
Which shall be needfull for your entertainement.
Lear. Returne to her? and fifty men dismiss'd?
No, rather I abiure all roofes, and chuse
To wage against the enmity oth'ayre,
To be a Comrade with the Wolfe, and Owle,
Necessities sharpe pinch. Returne with her?
Why the hot-bloodied *France*, that dowerlesse tooke
Our yongest borne, I could as well be brought
To knee his Throne, and Squire-like pension beg,
To keepe base life a foote; returne with her?
Perswade me rather to be slaue and sumpter
To this detested groome.
Gon. At your choice Sir.
Lear. I prythee Daughter do not make me mad,
I will not trouble thee my Child; farewell:
Wee'l no more meete, no more see one another.
But yet thou art my flesh, my blood, my Daughter,
Or rather a disease that's in my flesh,
Which I must needs call mine. Thou art a Byle,
A plague sore, or imbossed Carbuncle
In my corrupted blood. But Ile not chide thee,
Let shame come when it will, I do not call it,
I do not bid the Thunder-bearer shoote,
Nor tell tales of thee to high-iudging *Ioue*.
Mend when thou can'st, be better at thy leisure,
I can be patient, I can stay with *Regan*,
I and my hundred Knights.
Reg. Not altogether so,
I look'd not for you yet, nor am prouided
For your fit welcome, giue eare Sir to my Sister,
For those that mingle reason with your passion,
Must be content to thinke you old, and so,
But she knowes what she doe's.
Lear. Is this well spoken?
Reg. I dare auouch it Sir, what fifty Followers?
Is it not well? What should you need of more?
Yea, or so many? Sith that both charge and danger,
Speake 'gainst so great a number? How in one house
Should many people, vnder two commands
Hold amity? 'Tis hard, almost impossible.
Gon. Why might not you my Lord, receiue attendance
From those that she cals Seruants, or from mine?
Reg. Why not my Lord?
If then they chanc'd to slacke ye,
We could comptroll them; if you will come to me,
(For now I spie a danger) I entreate you
To bring but fiue and twentie, to no more
Will I giue place or notice.
Lear. I gaue you all.
Reg. And in good time you gaue it.
Lear. Made you my Guardians, my Depositaries,
But kept a reseruation to be followed
With such a number? What, must I come to you
With fiue and twenty? *Regan*, said you so?
Reg. And speak't againe my Lord, no more with me.
Lea. Those wicked Creatures yet do look wel fauor'd
When others are more wicked, not being the worst
Stands in some ranke of praise, Ile go with thee,
Thy fifty yet doth double fiue and twenty,
And thou art twice her Loue.
Gon. Heare me my Lord;
What need you fiue and twenty? Ten? Or fiue?
To follow in a house, where twice so many
Haue a command to tend you?
Reg. What need one?
Lear. O reason not the need: our basest Beggers
Are in the poorest thing superfluous,
Allow not Nature, more then Nature needs:
Mans life is cheape as Beastes. Thou art a Lady;
If onely to go warme were gorgeous,
Why Nature needs not what thou gorgeous wear'st,
Which scarcely keepes thee warme, but for true need:
You Heauens, giue me that patience, patience I need,
You see me heere (you Gods) a poore old man,
As full of griefe as age, wretched in both,
If it be you that stirres these Daughters hearts
Against their Father, foole me not so much,
To beare it tamely: touch me with Noble anger,
And let not womens weapons, water drops,
Staine my mans cheekes. No you vnnaturall Hags,
I will haue such reuenges on you both,
That all the world shall——I will do such things,
What they are yet, I know not, but they shalbe
The terrors of the earth? you thinke Ile weepe,
No, Ile not weepe, I haue full cause of weeping.

Storme and Tempest.

But this heart shal break into a hundred thousand flawes
Or ere Ile weepe; O Foole, I shall go mad. *Exeunt.*
Corn. Let vs withdraw, 'twill be a Storme.
Reg. This house is little, the old man an'ds people,
Cannot be well bestow'd.
Gon. Tis his owne blame hath put himselfe from rest,
And must needs taste his folly.
Reg. For his particular, Ile receiue him gladly,
But not one follower.
Gon. So am I purpos'd.
Where is my Lord of *Gloster*?

Enter Gloster.

Corn. Followed the old man forth, he is return'd.
Glo. The King is in high rage.
Corn. Whether is he going?
Glo. He cals to Horse, but will I know not whether.
Corn. 'Tis best to giue him way, he leads himselfe.
Gon. My Lord, entreate him by no meanes to stay.
Glo. Alacke the night comes on, and the high windes
Do sorely ruffle, for many Miles about
There's scarce a Bush.
Reg. O Sir, to wilfull men,
The iniuries that they themselues procure,
Must be their Schoole-Masters: shut vp your doores,
He is attended with a desperate traine,
And what they may incense him too, being apt,
To haue his eare abus'd, wisedome bids feare.
Cor. Shut vp your doores my Lord, 'tis a wil'd night,
My *Regan* counsels well: come out oth'storme. *Exeunt.*

Actus Tertius. Scena Prima.

Storme still. Enter Kent, and a Gentleman, seuerally.

Kent. Who's there besides foule weather?
Gen. One minded like the weather, most vnquietly

rr 2 *Kent.*

Kent. I know you: Where's the King?
Gent. Contending with the fretfull Elements;
Bids the winde blow the Earth into the Sea,
Or swell the curled Waters 'boue the Maine,
That things might change, or cease.
Kent. But who is with him?
Gent. None but the Foole, who labours to out-iest
His heart-strooke iniuries.
Kent. Sir, I do know you,
And dare vpon the warrant of my note
Commend a deere thing to you. There is diuision
(Although as yet the face of it is couer'd
With mutuall cunning) 'twixt Albany, and Cornwall:
Who haue, as who haue not, that their great Starres
Thron'd and set high; Seruants, who seeme no lesse,
Which are to France the Spies and Speculations
Intelligent of our State. What hath bin seene,
Either in snuffes, and packings of the Dukes,
Or the hard Reine which both of them hath borne
Against the old kinde King; or something deeper,
Whereof (perchance) these are but furnishings.
Gent. I will talke further with you.
Kent. No, do not:
For confirmation that I am much more
Then my out-wall; open this Purse, and take
What it containes. If you shall see *Cordelia*,
(As feare not but you shall) shew her this Ring,
And she will tell you who that Fellow is
That yet you do not know. Fye on this Storme,
I will go seeke the King.
Gent. Giue me your hand,
Haue you no more to say?
Kent. Few words, but to effect more then all yet;
That when we haue found the King, in which your pain
That way, Ile this: He that first lights on him,
Holla the other. *Exeunt.*

Scena Secunda.

Storme still. Enter Lear, and Foole.

Lear. Blow windes, & crack your cheeks; Rage, blow
You Cataracts, and Hyrricano's spout,
Till you haue drench'd our Steeples, drown the Cockes.
You Sulph'rous and Thought-executing Fires,
Vaunt-curriors of Oake-cleauing Thunder-bolts,
Sindge my white head. And thou all-shaking Thunder,
Strike flat the thicke Rotundity o'th'world,
Cracke Natures moulds, all germaines spill at once
That makes ingratefull Man.
Foole. O Nunkle, Court holy-water in a dry house, is better then this Rain-water out o'doore. Good Nunkle, in, aske thy Daughters blessing, heere's a night pitties neither Wisemen, nor Fooles.
Lear. Rumble thy belly full: spit Fire, spowt Raine:
Nor Raine, Winde, Thunder, Fire are my Daughters;
I taxe not you, you Elements with vnkindnesse.
I neuer gaue you Kingdome, call'd you Children;
You owe me no subscription. Then let fall
Your horrible pleasure. Heere I stand your Slaue,
A poore, infirme, weake, and dispis'd old man:
But yet I call you Seruile Ministers,
That will with two pernicious Daughters ioyne
Your high-engender'd Battailes, 'gainst a head
So old, and white as this. O, ho! 'tis foule.
Foole. He that has a house to put's head in, has a good Head-peece:
The Codpiece that will house, before the head has any;
The Head, and he shall Lowse: so Beggers marry many.
The man ẏ makes his Toe, what he his Hart shold make,
Shall of a Corne cry woe, and turne his sleepe to wake.
For there was neuer yet faire woman, but shee made mouthes in a glasse.

Enter Kent.

Lear. No, I will be the patterne of all patience,
I will say nothing.
Kent. Who's there?
Foole. Marry here's Grace, and a Codpiece, that's a Wiseman, and a Foole.
Kent. Alas Sir are you here? Things that loue night,
Loue not such nights as these: The wrathfull Skies
Gallow the very wanderers of the darke
And make them keepe their Caues: Since I was man,
Such sheets of Fire, such bursts of horrid Thunder,
Such groanes of roaring Winde, and Raine, I neuer
Remember to haue heard. Mans Nature cannot carry
Th'affliction, nor the feare.
Lear. Let the great Goddes
That keepe this dreadfull pudder o're our heads,
Finde out their enemies now. Tremble thou Wretch,
That hast within thee vndivulged Crimes
Vnwhipt of Iustice. Hide thee, thou Bloudy hand;
Thou Periur'd, and thou Simular of Vertue
That art Incestuous. Caytiffe, to peeces shake
That vnder couert, and conuenient seeming
Ha's practis'd on mans life. Close pent-vp guilts,
Riue your concealing Continents, and cry
These dreadfull Summoners grace. I am a man,
More sinn'd against, then sinning.
Kent. Alacke, bare-headed?
Gracious my Lord, hard by heere is a Houell,
Some friendship will it lend you 'gainst the Tempest:
Repose you there, while I to this hard house,
(More harder then the stones whereof 'tis rais'd,
Which euen but now, demanding after you,
Deny'd me to come in) returne, and force
Their scanted curtesie.
Lear. My wits begin to turne.
Come on my boy. How dost my boy? Art cold?
I am cold my selfe. Where is this straw, my Fellow?
The Art of our Necessities is strange,
And can make vilde things precious. Come, your Houel;
Poore Foole, and Knaue, I haue one part in my heart
That's sorry yet for thee.
Foole. He that has and a little-tyne wit,
With heigh-ho, the Winde and the Raine,
Must make content with his Fortunes fit,
Though the Raine it raineth euery day.
Le. True Boy: Come bring vs to this Houell. *Exit.*
Foole. This is a braue night to coole a Curtizan:
Ile speake a Prophesie ere I go:
When Priests are more in word, then matter;
When Brewers marre their Malt with water;
When Nobles are their Taylors Tutors,
No Heretiques burn'd, but wenches Sutors;
When euery Case in Law, is right;
No Squire in debt, nor no poore Knight;
When Slanders do not liue in Tongues;
Nor Cut-purses come not to throngs;
When Vsurers tell their Gold i'th'Field,
And

And Baudes, and whores, do Churches build,
Then shal the Realme of *Albion*, come to great confusion:
Then comes the time, who liues to see't,
That going shalbe vs'd with feet.
This prophecie *Merlin* shall make, for I liue before his (time.
Exit.

Scæna Tertia.

Enter Gloster, and Edmund.

Glo. Alacke, alacke *Edmund*, I like not this vnnaturall dealing; when I desired their leaue that I might pity him, they tooke from me the vse of mine owne house, charg'd me on paine of perpetuall displeasure, neither to speake of him, entreat for him, or any way sustaine him.

Bast. Most sauage and vnnaturall.

Glo. Go too; say you nothing. There is diuision betweene the Dukes, and a worsse matter then that: I haue receiued a Letter this night, 'tis dangerous to be spoken, I haue lock'd the Letter in my Closset, these iniuries the King now beares, will be reuenged home; ther is part of a Power already footed, we must incline to the King, I will looke him, and priuily relieue him; goe you and maintaine talke with the Duke, that my charity be not of him perceiued; If he aske for me, I am ill, and gone to bed, if I die for it, (as no lesse is threatned me) the King my old Master must be relieued. There is strange things toward *Edmund*, pray you be carefull. *Exit.*

Bast. This Curtesie forbid thee, shall the Duke
Instantly know, and of that Letter too;
This seemes a faire deseruing, and must draw me
That which my Father looses: no lesse then all,
The yonger rises, when the old doth fall. *Exit.*

Scena Quarta.

Enter Lear, Kent, and Foole.

Kent Here is the place my Lord, good my Lord enter,
The tirrany of the open night's too rough
For Nature to endure. *Storme still*

Lear. Let me alone.

Kent. Good my Lord enter heere.

Lear. Wilt breake my heart?

Kent. I had rather breake mine owne,
Good my Lord enter.

Lear. Thou think'st 'tis much that this contentious (storme
Inuades vs to the skin so: 'tis to thee,
But where the greater malady is fixt,
The lesser is scarce felt. Thou'dst shun a Beare,
But if they flight lay toward the roaring Sea,
Thou'dst meete the Beare i'th' mouth, when the mind's (free,
The bodies delicate: the tempest in my mind,
Doth from my sences take all feeling else,
Saue what beates there, Filliall ingratitude,
Is it not as this mouth should teare this hand
For lifting food too't? But I will punish home;
No, I will weepe no more; in such a night,
To shut me out? Poure on, I will endure:
In such a night as this? O *Regan, Gonerill*,
Your old kind Father, whose franke heart gaue all,
O that way madnesse lies, let me shun that;
No more of that.

Kent. Good my Lord enter here.

Lear. Prythee go in thy selfe, seeke thine owne ease,
This tempest will not giue me leaue to ponder
On things would hurt me more, but Ile goe in,
In Boy, go first. You houselesse pouertie, *Exit.*
Nay get thee in; Ile pray, and then Ile sleepe.
Poore naked wretches, where so ere you are
That bide the pelting of this pittilesse storme,
How shall your House-lesse heads, and vnfed sides,
Your lop'd, and window'd raggednesse defend you
From seasons such as these? O I haue tane
Too little care of this: Take Physicke, Pompe,
Expose thy selfe to feele what wretches feele,
That thou maist shake the superflux to them,
And shew the Heauens more iust.

Enter Edgar, and Foole.

Edg. Fathom, and halfe, Fathom and halfe; poore *Tom.*

Foole. Come not in heere Nuncle, here's a spirit, helpe me, helpe me.

Kent. Giue me thy hand, who's there?

Foole. A spirite, a spirite, he sayes his name's poore *Tom.*

Kent. What art thou that dost grumble there i'th' straw? Come forth.

Edg Away, the foule Fiend followes me, through the sharpe Hauthorne blow the windes. Humh, goe to thy bed and warme thee.

Lear. Did'st thou giue all to thy Daughters? And art thou come to this?

Edgar. Who giues any thing to poore *Tom*? Whom the foule fiend hath led though Fire, and through Flame, through Sword, and Whirle-Poole, o're Bog, and Quagmire, that hath laid Kniues vnder his Pillow, and Halters in his Pue, set Rats-bane by his Porredge, made him Proud of heart, to ride on a Bay trotting Horse, ouer foure inch'd Bridges, to course his owne shadow for a Traitor. Blisse thy fiue Wits, *Toms* a cold. O do, de, do, de, do de, blisse thee from Whirle-Windes, Starre-blasting, and taking, do poore *Tom* some charitie, whom the foule Fiend vexes. There could I haue him now, and there, and there againe, and there. *Storme still.*

Lear. Ha's his Daughters brought him to this passe?
Could'st thou saue nothing? Would'st thou giue 'em all?

Foole. Nay, he reseru'd a Blanket, else we had bin all sham'd.

Lea. Now all the plagues that in the pendulous ayre
Hang fated o're mens faults, light on thy Daughters.

Kent. He hath no Daughters Sir.

Lear. Death Traitor, nothing could haue subdu'd (Nature
To such a lownesse, but his vnkind Daughters.
Is it the fashion, that discarded Fathers,
Should haue thus little mercy on their flesh:
Iudicious punishment, 'twas this flesh begot
Those Pelicane Daughters.

Edg. Pillicock sat on Pillicock hill, alow: alow, loo, loo.

Foole. This cold night will turne vs all to Fooles, and Madmen.

Edgar. Take heed o'th' foole Fiend, obey thy Parents, keepe thy words Iustice, sweare not, commit not, with

with mans sworne Spouse; set not thy Sweet-heart on proud array. *Tom's* a cold.

Lear. What hast thou bin?

Edg. A Seruingman? Proud in heart, and minde; that curl'd my haire, wore Gloues in my cap; seru'd the Lust of my Mistris heart, and did the acte of darkenesse with her. Swore as many Oathes, as I spake words, & broke them in the sweet face of Heauen. One, that slept in the contriuing of Lust, and wak'd to doe it. Wine lou'd I deerely, Dice deerely; and in Woman, out-Paramour'd the Turke. False of heart, light of eare, bloody of hand Hog in sloth, Foxe in stealth, Wolfe in greedinesse, Dog in madnes, Lyon in prey. Let not the creaking of shooes, Nor the rustling of Silkes, betray thy poore heart to woman. Keepe thy foote out of Brothels, thy hand out of Plackets, thy pen from Lenders Bookes, and defye the foule Fiend. Still through the Hauthorne blowes the cold winde: Sayes suum, mun, nonny, Dolphin my Boy, Boy *Sesey*: let him trot by. *Storme still.*

Lear. Thou wert better in a Graue, then to answere with thy vncouer'd body, this extremitie of the Skies. Is man no more then this? Consider him well. Thou ow'st the Worme no Silke; the Beast, no Hide; the Sheepe, no Wooll, the Cat, no perfume. Ha? Here's three on's are sophisticated. Thou art the thing it selfe; vnaccommodated man, is no more but such a poore, bare, forked Animall as thou art. Off, off you Lendings: Come, vnbutton heere.

Enter Gloucester, with a Torch.

Foole. Prythee Nunckle be contented, 'tis a naughtie night to swimme in. Now a little fire in a wilde Field, were like an old Letchers heart, a small spark, all the rest on's body, cold: Looke, heere comes a walking fire.

Edg. This is the foule Flibbertigibbet; hee begins at Curfew, and walkes at first Cocke: Hee giues the Web and the Pin, squints the eye, and makes the Hare-lippe; Mildewes the white Wheate, and hurts the poore Creature of earth.

Swithold footed thrice the old,
He met the Night-Mare, and her nine-fold;
Bid her a-light, and her troth-plight,
And aroynt thee Witch, aroynt thee.

Kent. How fares your Grace?

Lear. What's he?

Kent. Who's there? What is't you seeke?

Glou. What are you there? Your Names?

Edg. Poore Tom, that eates the swimming Frog, the Toad, the Tod-pole, the wall-Neut, and the water: that in the furie of his heart, when the foule Fiend rages, eats Cow-dung for Sallets; swallowes the old Rat, and the ditch-Dogge; drinkes the green Mantle of the standing Poole: who is whipt from Tything to Tything, and stockt, punish'd, and imprison'd: who hath three Suites to his backe, sixe shirts to his body:

Horse to ride, and weapon to weare:
But Mice, and Rats, and such small Deare,
Haue bin Toms food, for seuen long yeare:

Beware my Follower. Peace Smulkin, peace thou Fiend.

Glou What, hath your Grace no better company?

Edg. The Prince of Darkenesse is a Gentleman. *Modo* he's call'd, and *Mahu.*

Glou. Our flesh and blood, my Lord, is growne so vilde, that it doth hate what gets it.

Edg. Poore Tom's a cold.

Glou. Go in with me; my duty cannot suffer
T'obey in all your daughters hard commands:
Though their Iniunction be to barre my doores,
And let this Tyrannous night take hold vpon you,
Yet haue I ventured to come seeke you out,
And bring you where both fire, and food is ready.

Lear. First let me talke with this Philosopher,
What is the cause of Thunder?

Kent. Good my Lord take his offer,
Go into th'house.

Lear. Ile talke a word with this same lerned Theban:
What is your study?

Edg. How to preuent the Fiend, and to kill Vermine.

Lear. Let me aske you one word in priuate.

Kent. Importune him once more to go my Lord,
His wits begin t'vnsettle.

Glou. Canst thou blame him? *Storm still*
His Daughters seeke his death: Ah, that good Kent,
He said it would be thus: poore banish'd man:
Thou sayest the King growes mad, Ile tell thee Friend
I am almost mad my selfe. I had a Sonne,
Now out-law'd from my blood: he sought my life
But lately: very late: I lou'd him (Friend)
No Father his Sonne deerer: true to tell thee,
The greefe hath craz'd my wits. What a night's this?
I do beseech your grace.

Lear. O cry you mercy, Sir:
Noble Philosopher, your company.

Edg. Tom's a cold.

Glou. In fellow there, into th'Houel; keep thee warm.

Lear. Come, let's in all.

Kent. This way, my Lord.

Lear. With him;
I will keepe still with my Philosopher.

Kent. Good my Lord, sooth him:
Let him take the Fellow.

Glou. Take him you on.

Kent. Sirra, come on: go along with vs.

Lear. Come, good Athenian.

Glou. No words, no words, hush.

Edg. Childe *Rowland* to the darke Tower came,
His word was still, fie, foh, and fumme,
I smell the blood of a Brittish man. *Exeunt*

Scena Quinta.

Enter Cornwall, and Edmund.

Corn. I will haue my reuenge, ere I depart his house.

Bast. How my Lord, I may be censured, that Nature thus giues way to Loyaltie, something feares mee to thinke of.

Cornw. I now perceiue, it was not altogether your Brothers euill disposition made him seeke his death: but a prouoking merit set a-worke by a reprouable badnesse in himselfe.

Bast. How malicious is my fortune, that I must repent to be iust? This is the Letter which hee spoake of; which approues him an intelligent partie to the aduantages of France O Heauens! that this Treason were not; or not I the detector.

Corn. Go with me to the Dutchesse.

Bast. If the matter of this Paper be certain, you haue mighty businesse in hand.

Corn.

Corn. True or false, it hath made thee Earle of Glou-cester: seeke out where thy Father is, that hee may bee ready for our apprehension.

Bast. If I finde him comforting the King, it will stuffe his suspition more fully. I will perseuer in my course of Loyalty, though the conflict be sore betweene that, and my blood.

Corn. I will lay trust vpon thee: and thou shalt finde a deere Father in my loue. *Exeunt.*

Scena Sexta.

Enter Kent, and Gloucester.

Glou. Heere is better then the open ayre, take it thank-fully: I will peece out the comfort with what addition I can: I will not be long from you. *Exit*

Kent. All the powre of his wits, haue giuen way to his impatience: the Gods reward your kindnesse.

Enter Lear, Edgar, and Foole.

Edg. Fraterretto cals me, and tells me *Nero* is an Angler in the Lake of Darknesse: pray Innocent, and beware the foule Fiend.

Foole. Prythee Nunkle tell me, whether a madman be a Gentleman, or a Yeoman.

Lear. A King, a King.

Foole. No, he's a Yeoman, that ha's a Gentleman to his Sonne: for hee's a mad Yeoman that sees his Sonne a Gentleman before him.

Lear. To haue a thousand with red burning spits
Come hizzing in vpon 'em.

Edg. Blesse thy fiue wits.

Kent. O pitty: Sir, where is the patience now
That you so oft haue boasted to retaine?

Edg. My teares begin to take his part so much,
They marre my counterfetting.

Lear. The little dogges, and all;
Trey, Blanch, and Sweet-heart: see, they barke at me.

Edg. Tom, will throw his head at them: Auaunt you
Curres, be thy mouth or blacke or white:
Tooth that poysons if it bite:
Mastiffe, Grey-hound, Mongrill, Grim,
Hound or Spaniell, Brache, or Hym:
Or Bobtaile tight, or Troudle taile,
Tom will make him weepe and waile,
For with throwing thus my head;
Dogs leapt the hatch, and all are fled.
Do, de, de, de: sese: Come, march to Wakes and Fayres,
And Market Townes: poore Tom thy horne is dry.

Lear Then let them Anatomize *Regan*: See what breeds about her heart. Is there any cause in Nature that make these hard-hearts. You sir, I entertaine for one of my hundred; only, I do not like the fashion of your gar-ments. You will say they are Persian; but let them bee chang'd.

Enter Gloster.

Kent. Now good my Lord, lye heere, and rest awhile.

Lear. Make no noise, make no noise, draw the Cur-taines: so, so, wee'l go to Supper i'th'morning.

Foole. And Ile go to bed at noone.

Glou. Come hither Friend:
Where is the King my Master?

Kent. Here Sir, but trouble him not, his wits are gon.

Glou. Good friend, I prythee take him in thy armes;
I haue ore-heard a plot of death vpon him:
There is a Litter ready, lay him in't,
And driue toward Douer friend, where thou shalt meete
Both welcome, and protection. Take vp thy Master,
If thou should'st dally halfe an houre, his life
With thine, and all that offer to defend him,
Stand in assured losse. Take vp, take vp,
And follow me, that will to some prouision
Giue thee quicke conduct. Come, come, away. *Exeunt*

Scena Septima.

Enter Cornwall, Regan, Gonerill, Bastard, and Seruants.

Corn. Poste speedily to my Lord your husband, shew him this Letter, the Army of France is landed: seeke out the Traitor Glouster.

Reg. Hang him instantly.

Gon. Plucke out his eyes.

Corn. Leaue him to my displeasure. *Edmond*, keepe you our Sister company: the reuenges wee are bound to take vppon your Traitorous Father, are not fit for your beholding. Aduice the Duke where you are going, to a most festiuate preparation: we are bound to the like. Our Postes shall be swift, and intelligent betwixt vs. Fare-well deere Sister, farewell my Lord of Glouster.

Enter Steward.

How now? Where's the King?

Stew. My Lord of Glouster hath conuey'd him hence
Some fiue or six and thirty of his Knights
Hot Questrists after him, met him at gate,
Who, with some other of the Lords, dependants,
Are gone with him toward Douer; where they boast
To haue well armed Friends.

Corn. Get horses for your Mistris.

Gon. Farewell sweet Lord, and Sister. *Exit*

Corn. Edmund farewell: go seek the Traitor Gloster,
Pinnion him like a Theefe, bring him before vs:
Though well we may not passe vpon his life
Without the forme of Iustice: yet our power
Shall do a curt'sie to our wrath, which men
May blame, but not comptroll.

Enter Gloucester, and Seruants.

Who's there? the Traitor?

Reg. Ingratefull Fox, 'tis he.

Corn. Binde fast his corky armes.

Glou. What meanes your Graces?
Good my Friends consider you are my Ghests:
Do me no foule play, Friends.

Corn. Binde him I say.

Reg. Hard, hard: O filthy Traitor.

Glou. Vnmercifull Lady, as you are, I'me none.

Corn. To this Chaire binde him,
Villaine, thou shalt finde.

Glou. By the kinde Gods, 'tis most ignobly done
To plucke me by the Beard.

Reg. So white, and such a Traitor?

Glou. Naughty Ladie,
These haires which thou dost rauish from my chin
Will quicken and accuse thee. I am your Host,
With Robbers hands, my hospitable fauours

You

You should not ruffle thus. What will you do?
Corn. Come Sir.
What Letters had you late from France?
Reg. Be simple answer'd, for we know the truth.
Corn. And what confederacie haue you with the Traitors, late footed in the Kingdome?
Reg. To whose hands
You haue sent the Lunaticke King: Speake.
Glou. I haue a Letter guessingly set downe
Which came from one that's of a newtrall heart,
And not from one oppos'd.
Corn. Cunning.
Reg. And false.
Corn. Where hast thou sent the King?
Glou. To Douer.
Reg. Wherefore to Douer?
Was't thou not charg'd at perill.
Corn. Wherefore to Douer? Let him answer that.
Glou. I am tyed to'th'Stake,
And I must stand the Course.
Reg Wherefore to Douer?
Glou Because I would not see thy cruell Nailes
Plucke out his poore old eyes: nor thy fierce Sister,
In his Annointed flesh, sticke boarish phangs.
The Sea, with such a storme as his bare head,
In Hell-blacke-night indur'd, would haue buoy'd vp
And quench'd the Stelled fires:
Yet poore old heart, he holpe the Heauens to raine.
If Wolues had at thy Gate howl'd that sterne time,
Thou should'st haue said, good Porter turne the Key.
All Cruels else subscribe: but I shall see
The winged Vengeance ouertake such Children.
Corn. See't shalt thou neuer. Fellowes hold ẏ Chaire,
Vpon these eyes of thine, Ile set my foote.
Glou. He that will thinke to liue, till he be old,
Giue me some helpe. ——O cruell! O you Gods.
Reg One side will mocke another: Th'other too.
Corn If you see vengeance
Seru Hold your hand, my Lord:
I haue seru'd you euer since I was a Childe
But better seruice haue I neuer done you,
Then now to bid you hold.
Reg. How now, you dogge?
Ser If you did weare a beard vpon your chin,
I'ld shake it on this quarrell. What do you meane?
Corn. My Villaine?
Seru. Nay then come on, and take the chance of anger.
Reg. Giue me thy Sword. A pezant stand vp thus?
Killes him
Ser Oh I am slaine: my Lord, you haue one eye left
To see some mischefe on him. Oh.
Corn. Lest it see more, preuent it; Out vilde gelly:
Where is thy luster now?
Glou. All darke and comfortlesse?
Where's my Sonne *Edmund*?
Edmund, enkindle all the sparkes of Nature
To quit this horrid acte.
Reg. Out treacherous Villaine,
Thou call'st on him, that hates thee. It was he
That made the ouerture of thy Treasons to vs:
Who is too good to pitty thee.
Glou. O my Follies! then *Edgar* was abus'd,
Kinde Gods, forgiue me that, and prosper him
Reg. Go thrust him out at gates, and let him smell
His way to Douer. *Exit with Glouster.*
How is't my Lord? How looke you?
Corn. I haue receiu'd a hurt: Follow me Lady;
Turne out that eyelesse Villaine: throw this Slaue
Vpon the Dunghill: *Regan*, I bleed apace,
Vntimely comes this hurt. Giue me your arr . *Exeunt.*

Actus Quartus. Scena Prima.

Enter Edgar.

Edg. Yet better thus, and knowne to be contemn'd,
Then still contemn'd and flatter'd, to be worst
The lowest, and most dejected thing of Fortune,
Stands still in esperance, liues not in feare:
The lamentable change is from the best,
The worst returnes to laughter. Welcome then,
Thou vnsubstantiall ayre that I embrace:
The Wretch that thou hast blowne vnto the worst,
Owes nothing to thy blasts.
Enter Glouster, and an Oldman.
But who comes heere? My Father poorely led?
World, World, O world!
But that thy strange mutations make vs hate thee,
Life would not yeelde to age.
Oldm. O my good Lord, I haue bene your Tenant,
And your Fathers Tenant, these fourescore yeares.
Glou. Away, get thee away: good Friend be gone,
Thy comforts can do me no good at all,
Thee, they may hurt.
Oldm. You cannot see your way.
Glou. I haue no way, and therefore want no eyes:
I stumbled when I saw. Full oft 'tis seene,
Our meanes secure vs, and our meere defects
Proue our Commodities. Oh deere Sonne *Edgar*,
The food of thy abused Fathers wrath:
Might I but liue to see thee in my touch,
I'ld say I had eyes againe.
Oldm. How now? who's there?
Edg. O Gods! Who is't can say I am at the worst?
I am worse then ere I was.
Old. 'Tis poore mad Tom.
Edg And worse I may be yet: the worst is not,
So long as we can say this is the worst
Oldm. Fellow, where goest?
Glou. Is it a Beggar-man?
Oldm. Madman, and beggar too.
Glou. He has some reason, else he could not beg.
I'th'last nights storme, I such a fellow saw;
Which made me thinke a Man, a Worme. My Sonne
Came then into my minde, and yet my minde
Was then scarse Friends with him.
I haue heard more since:
As Flies to wanton Boyes, are we to th'Gods,
They kill vs for their sport.
Edg. How should this be?
Bad is the Trade that must play Foole to sorrow,
Ang'ring it selfe, and others. Blesse thee Master.
Glou. Is that the naked Fellow?
Oldm. I, my Lord.
Glou. Get thee away: If for my sake
Thou wilt ore-take vs hence a mile or twaine
I'th'way toward Douer, do it for ancient loue,
And bring some couering for this naked Soule,
Which Ile intreate to leade me.
Old. Alacke sir, he is mad

Glou.

Glou. 'Tis the times plague,
When Madmen leade the blinde:
Do as I bid thee, or rather do thy pleaſure:
Aboue the reſt, be gone.
Oldm. Ile bring him the beſt Parrell that I haue
Come on't, what will. *Exit*
Glou. Sirrah, naked fellow.
Edg. Poore Tom's a cold. I cannot daub it further.
Glou. Come hither fellow.
Edg. And yet I muſt:
Bleſſe thy ſweete eyes, they bleede.
Glou. Know'ſt thou the way to Douer?
Edg. Both ſtyle, and gate; Horſeway, and foot-path: poore Tom hath bin ſcarr'd out of his good wits. Bleſſe thee good mans ſonne, from the foule Fiend.
Glou. Here take this purſe, ŷ whom the heau'ns plagues
Haue humbled to all ſtrokes: that I am wretched
Makes thee the happier: Heauens deale ſo ſtill:
Let the ſuperfluous, and Luſt-dieted man,
That ſlaues your ordinance, that will not ſee
Becauſe he do's not feele, feele your powre quickly:
So diſtribution ſhould vndoo exceſſe,
And each man haue enough. Doſt thou know Douer?
Edg. I Maſter.
Glou. There is a Cliffe, whoſe high and bending head
Lookes fearfully in the confined Deepe:
Bring me but to the very brimme of it,
And Ile repayre the miſery thou do'ſt beare
With ſomething rich about me: from that place,
I ſhall no leading neede.
Edg. Giue me thy arme;
Poore Tom ſhall leade thee. *Exeunt.*

Scena Secunda.

Enter Gonerill, Baſtard, and Steward.

Gon. Welcome my Lord. I meruell our mild husband
Not met vs on the way. Now, where's your Maſter?
Stew. Madam within, but neuer man ſo chang'd:
I told him of the Army that was Landed:
He ſmil'd at it. I told him you were comming,
His anſwer was, the worſe. Of Gloſters Treachery,
And of the loyall Seruice of his Sonne
When I inform'd him, then he call'd me Sot,
And told me I had turn'd the wrong ſide out:
What moſt he ſhould diſlike, ſeemes pleaſant to him;
What like, offenſiue.
Gon. Then ſhall you go no further.
It is the Cowiſh terror of his ſpirit
That dares not vndertake: Hee'l not feele wrongs
Which tye him to an anſwer: our wiſhes on the way
May proue effects. Backe *Edmond* to my Brother,
Haſten his Muſters, and conduct his powres.
I muſt change names at home, and giue the Diſtaffe
Into my Husbands hands. This truſtie Seruant
Shall paſſe betweene vs: ere long you are like to heare
(If you dare venture in your owne behalfe)
A Miſtreſſes command. Weare this; ſpare ſpeech,
Decline your head. This kiſſe, if it durſt ſpeake
Would ſtretch thy Spirits vp into the ayre:
Conceiue, and fare thee well.
Baſt. Yours in the rankes of death. *Exit.*
Gon. My moſt deere Gloſter.
Oh, the difference of man, and man,
To thee a Womans ſeruices are due,
My Foole vſurpes my body.
Stew. Madam, here come's my Lord.

Enter Albany.

Gon. I haue beene worth the whiſtle.
Alb. Oh *Gonerill*,
You are not worth the duſt which the rude winde
Blowes in your face.
Gon. Milke-Liuer'd man,
That bear'ſt a cheeke for blowes, a head for wrongs,
Who haſt not in thy browes an eye-diſcerning
Thine Honor, from thy ſuffering.
Alb. See thy ſelfe diuell:
Proper deformitie ſeemes not in the Fiend
So horrid as in woman.
Gon. Oh vaine Foole.

Enter a Meſſenger.

Meſ. Oh my good Lord, the Duke of *Cornwals* dead,
Slaine by his Seruant, going to put out
The other eye of Glouſter.
Alb. Glouſters eyes.
Meſ. A Seruant that he bred, thrill'd with remorſe,
Oppos'd againſt the act: bending his Sword
To his great Maſter, who, threat-enrag'd
Flew on him, and among'ſt them fell'd him dead,
But not without that harmefull ſtroke, which ſince
Hath pluckt him after.
Alb. This ſhewes you are aboue
You Iuſtices, that theſe our neather crimes
So ſpeedily can venge. But (O poore Glouſter)
Loſt he his other eye?
Meſ. Both, both, my Lord.
This Leter Madam, craues a ſpeedy anſwer:
'Tis from your Siſter.
Gon. One way I like this well,
But being widdow, and my Glouſter with her,
May all the building in my fancie plucke
Vpon my hatefull life. Another way
The Newes is not ſo tart. Ile read, and anſwer.
Alb. Where was his Sonne,
When they did take his eyes?
Meſ. Come with my Lady hither.
Alb. He is not heere.
Meſ. No my good Lord, I met him backe againe.
Alb. Knowes he the wickedneſſe?
Meſ. I my good Lord: 'twas he inform'd againſt him
And quit the houſe on purpoſe, that their puniſhment
Might haue the freer courſe.
Alb. Glouſter, I liue
To thanke thee for the loue thou ſhew'dſt the King,
And to reuenge thine eyes. Come hither Friend,
Tell me what more thou know'ſt. *Exeunt.*

Scena Tertia.

Enter with Drum and Colours, Cordelia, Gentlemen, and Souldiours.

Cor. Alacke, 'tis he: why he was met euen now
As mad as the vext Sea, ſinging alowd.
Crown'd with ranke Fenitar, and furrow weeds,
With Hardokes, Hemlocke, Nettles, Cuckoo flowres,
Darnell

Darnell, and all the idle weedes that grow
In our ſuſtaining Corne. A Centery ſend forth;
Search euery Acre in the high-growne field,
And bring him to our eye. What can mans wiſedome
In the reſtoring his bereaued Senſe; he that helpes him,
Take all my outward worth.
Gent. There is meanes Madam:
Our foſter Nurſe of Nature, is repoſe,
The which he lackes: that to prouoke in him
Are many Simples operatiue, whoſe power
Will cloſe the eye of Anguiſh.
Cord. All bleſt Secrets,
All you vnpubliſh'd Vertues of the earth
Spring with my teares; be aydant, and remediate
In the Goodmans deſires: ſeeke, ſeeke for him,
Leaſt his vngouern'd rage, diſſolue the life
That wants the meanes to leade it.
Enter Meſſenger.
Meſ. Newes Madam,
The Brittiſh Powres are marching hitherward.
Cor. 'Tis knowne before. Our preparation ſtands
In expectation of them. O deere Father,
It is thy buſineſſe that I go about: Therfore great France
My mourning, and importun'd teares hath pittied:
No blowne Ambition doth our Armes incite,
But loue, deere loue, and our ag'd Fathers Rite:
Soone may I heare, and ſee him *Exeunt.*

Scena Quarta.

Enter Regan, and Steward.
Reg. But are my Brothers Powres ſet forth?
Stew. I Madam.
Reg. Himſelfe in perſon there?
Stew. Madam with much ado:
Your Siſter is the better Souldier.
Reg. Lord *Edmund* ſpake not with your Lord at home?
Stew. No Madam.
Reg. What might import my Siſters Letter to him?
Stew I know not, Lady.
Reg. Faith he is poaſted hence on ſerious matter:
It was great ignorance, Glouſters eyes being out
To let him liue. Where he arriues, he moues
All hearts againſt vs: *Edmund*, I thinke is gone
In pitty of his miſery, to diſpatch
His nighted life: Moreouer to deſcry
The ſtrength o'th'Enemy.
Stew. I muſt needs after him, Madam, with my Letter.
Reg. Our troopes ſet forth to morrow, ſtay with vs:
The wayes are dangerous.
Stew. I may not Madam:
My Lady charg'd my dutie in this buſines.
Reg. Why ſhould ſhe write to *Edmund*?
Might not you tranſport her purpoſes by word? Belike,
Some things, I know not what. Ile loue thee much
Let me vnſeale the Letter.
Stew. Madam, I had rather———
Reg. I know your Lady do's not loue her Husband,
I am ſure of that: and at her late being heere,
She gaue ſtrange Eliads, and moſt ſpeaking lookes
To Noble *Edmund*. I know you are of her boſome.
Stew. I, Madam?
Reg. I ſpeake in vnderſtanding: Y'are: I know't,
Therefore I do aduiſe you take this note:
My Lord is dead: *Edmond*, and I haue talk'd,
And more conuenient is he for my hand
Then for your Ladies: You may gather more:
If you do finde him, pray you giue him this;
And when your Miſtris heares thus much from you,
I pray deſire her call her wiſedome to her.
So fare you well:
If you do chance to heare of that blinde Traitor,
Preferment fals on him, that cuts him off.
Stew. Would I could meet Madam, I ſhould ſhew
What party I do follow.
Reg. Fare thee well *Exeunt*

Scena Quinta.

Enter Glouceſter, and Edgar.
Glou. When ſhall I come to th'top of that ſame hill?
Edg. You do climbe vp it now. Look how we labor.
Glou. Me thinkes the ground is euen.
Edg. Horrible ſteepe.
Hearke, do you heare the Sea?
Glou. No truly.
Edg. Why then your other Senſes grow imperfect
By your eyes anguiſh.
Glou. So may it be indeed.
Me thinkes thy voyce is alter'd, and thou ſpeak'ſt
In better phraſe, and matter then thou did'ſt.
Edg. Y'are much deceiu'd: In nothing am I chang'd
But in my Garments.
Glou. Me thinkes y'are better ſpoken.
Edg. Come on Sir,
Heere's the place: ſtand ſtill: how fearefull
And dizie 'tis, to caſt ones eyes ſo low,
The Crowes and Choughes, that wing the midway ayre
Shew ſcarſe ſo groſſe as Beetles. Halfe way downe
Hangs one that gathers Sampire: dreadfull Trade:
Me thinkes he ſeemes no bigger then his head.
The Fiſhermen, that walk'd vpon the beach
Appeare like Mice: and yond tall Anchoring Barke,
Diminiſh'd to her Cocke: her Cocke, a Buoy
Almoſt too ſmall for ſight. The murmuring Surge,
That on th'vnnumbred idle Pebble chaſes
Cannot be heard ſo high. Ile looke no more,
Leaſt my braine turne, and the deficient ſight
Topple downe headlong.
Glou Set me where you ſtand.
Edg. Giue me your hand:
You are now within a foote of th'extreme Verge:
For all beneath the Moone would I not leape vpright.
Glou. Let go my hand.
Heere Friend's another purſe: in it, a Iewell
Well worth a poore mans taking. Fayries, and Gods
Proſper it with thee. Go thou further off,
Bid me farewell, and let me heare thee going.
Edg. Now fare ye well, good Sir.
Glou. With all my heart.
Edg. Why I do trifle thus with his diſpaire,
Is done to cure it.
Glou. O you mighty Gods!
This world I do renounce, and in your ſights
Shake

Shake patiently my great affliction off:
If I could beare it longer, and not fall
To quarrell with your great opposelesse willes,
My snuffe, and loathed part of Nature should
Burne it selfe out. If *Edgar* liue, O blesse him:
Now Fellow, fare thee well.

Edg. Gone Sir, farewell:
And yet I know not how conceit may rob
The Treasury of life, when life it selfe
Yeelds to the Theft. Had he bin where he thought,
By this had thought bin past. Aliue, or dead?
Hoa, you Sir: Friend, heare you Sir, speake:
Thus might he passe indeed: yet he reuiues.
What are you Sir?

Glou. Away, and let me dye.

Edg. Had'st thou beene ought
But Gozemore, Feathers, Ayre,
(So many fathome downe precipitating)
Thou'dst shiuer'd like an Egge: but thou do'st breath:
Hast heauy substance, bleed'st not, speak'st, art sound,
Ten Masts at each, make not the altitude
Which thou hast perpendicularly fell,
Thy life's a Myracle. Speake yet againe.

Glou. But haue I falne, or no?

Edg. From the dread Somnet of this Chalkie Bourne
Looke vp a height, the shrill-gorg'd Larke so farre
Cannot be seene, or heard: Do but looke vp.

Glou. Alacke, I haue no eyes:
Is wretchednesse depriu'd that benefit
To end it selfe by death? 'Twas yet some comfor
When misery could beguile the Tyrants rage,
And frustrate his proud will.

Edg. Giue me your arme.
Vp, so: How is't? Feele you your Legges? You stand.

Glou. Too well, too well.

Edg. This is aboue all strangenesse,
Vpon the crowne o'th'Cliffe. What thing was that
Which parted from you?

Glou. A poore vnfortunate Beggar.

Edg. As I stood heere below, me thought his eyes
Were two full Moones: he had a thousand Noses,
Hornes wealk'd, and waued like the enraged Sea:
It was some Fiend: Therefore thou happy Father,
Thinke that the cleerest Gods, who make them Honors
Of mens Impossibilities, haue preserued thee.

Glou. I do remember now: henceforth Ile beare
Affliction, till it do cry out it selfe
Enough, enough, and dye. That thing you speake of,
I tooke it for a man: often 'twould say
The Fiend, the Fiend, he led me to that place.

Edgar. Beare free and patient thoughts.

Enter Lear.

But who comes heere?
The safer sense will ne're accommodate
His Master thus.

Lear. No, they cannot touch me for crying. I am the King himselfe.

Edg. O thou side-piercing sight!

Lear. Nature's aboue Art, in that respect. Ther's your Presse-money. That fellow handles his bow, like a Crow-keeper: draw mee a Cloathiers yard. Looke, looke, a Mouse: peace, peace, this peece of toasted Cheese will doo't. There's my Gauntlet, Ile proue it on a Gyant. Bring vp the browne Billes. O well flowne Bird: i'th' clout, i'th' clout: Hewgh. Giue the word.

Edg. Sweet Marjorum.

Lear. Passe.

Glou. I know that voice.

Lear. Ha! *Gonerill* with a white beard? They flatter'd me like a Dogge, and told mee I had the white hayres in my Beard, ere the blacke ones were there. To say I, and no, to euery thing that I said: I, and no too, was no good Diuinity. When the raine came to wet me once, and the winde to make me chatter: when the Thunder would not peace at my bidding, there I found 'em, there I smelt 'em out. Go too, they are not men o'their words; they told me, I was euery thing: 'Tis a Lye, I am not Agu-proofe.

Glou. The tricke of that voyce, I do well remember:
Is't not the King?

Lear. I, euery inch a King.
When I do stare, see how the Subiect quakes.
I pardon that mans life. What was thy cause?
Adultery? thou shalt not dye: dye for Adultery?
No, the Wren goes too't, and the small gilded Fly
Do's letcher in my sight. Let Copulation thriue:
For Glousters bastard Son was kinder to his Father,
Then my Daughters got 'tweene the lawfull sheets.
Too't Luxury pell-mell, for I lacke Souldiers.
Behold yond simpring Dame, whose face betweene her Forkes presages Snow; that minces Vertue, & do's shake the head to heare of pleasures name. The Fitchew, nor the soyled Horse goes too't with a more riotous appetite: Downe from the waste they are Centaures, though Women all aboue: but to the Girdle do the Gods inherit, beneath is all the Fiends. There's hell, there's darkenes, there is the sulphurous pit; burning, scalding stench, consumption: Fye, fie, fie; pah, pah: Giue me an Ounce of Ciuet; good Apothecary sweeten my immagination: There's money for thee.

Glou. O let me kisse that hand.

Lear. Let me wipe it first,
It smelles of Mortality.

Glou. O ruin'd peece of Nature, this great world
Shall so weare out to naught.
Do'st thou know me?

Lear. I remember thine eyes well enough: dost thou squiny at me? No, doe thy worst blinde Cupid, Ile not loue. Reade thou this challenge, marke but the penning of it.

Glou. Were all thy Letters Sunnes, I could not see.

Edg. I would not take this from report,
It is, and my heart breakes at it.

Lear. Read.

Glou. What with the Case of eyes?

Lear. Oh ho, are you there with me? No eies in your head, nor no mony in your purse? Your eyes are in a heauy case, your purse in a light, yet you see how this world goes.

Glou. I see it feelingly.

Lear. What, art mad? A man may see how this world goes, with no eyes. Looke with thine eares: See how yond Iustice railes vpon yond simple theefe. Hearke in thine eare: Change places, and handy-dandy, which is the Iustice, which is the theefe: Thou hast seene a Farmers dogge barke at a Beggar?

Glou. I Sir.

Lear. And the Creature run from the Cur: there thou might'st behold the great image of Authoritie, a Dogg's obey'd in Office. Thou, Rascall Beadle, hold thy bloody hand: why dost thou lash that Whore? Strip thy owne backe, thou hotly lusts to vse her in that kind, for which thou whip'st her. The Vsurer hangs the Cozener. Thro-

rough

rough tatter'd cloathes great Vices do appeare: Robes, and Furr'd gownes hide all. Place sinnes with Gold, and the strong Lance of Iustice, hurtlesse breakes: Arme it in ragges, a Pigmies straw do's pierce it. None do's offend, none, I say none, Ile able 'em; take that of me my Friend, who haue the power to seale th'accusers lips. Get thee glasse-eyes, and like a scuruy Politician, seeme to see the things thou dost not. Now, now, now, now. Pull off my Bootes: harder, harder, so.

Edg. O matter, and impertinency mixt,
Reason in Madnesse.

Lear. If thou wilt weepe my Fortunes, take my eyes.
I know thee well enough, thy name is Glouster:
Thou must be patient; we came crying hither:
Thou know'st, the first time that we smell the Ayre
We wawle, and cry. I will preach to thee: Marke.

Glou. Alacke, alacke the day.

Lear. When we are borne, we cry that we are come
To this great stage of Fooles. This a good blocke:
It were a delicate stratagem to shoo
A Troope of Horse with Felt: Ile put't in proofe,
And when I haue stolne vpon these Son in Lawes,
Then kill, kill, kill, kill, kill, kill.

Enter a Gentleman.

Gent. Oh heere he is: lay hand vpon him, Sir.
Your most deere Daughter ——

Lear. No rescue? What, a Prisoner? I am euen
The Naturall Foole of Fortune. Vse me well,
You shall haue ransome. Let me haue Surgeons,
I am cut to'th'Braines.

Gent. You shall haue any thing.

Lear. No Seconds? All my selfe?
Why, this would make a man, a man of Salt
To vse his eyes for Garden water-pots. I wil die brauely,
Like a smugge Bridegroome. What? I will be Iouiall:
Come, come, I am a King, Masters, know you that?

Gent. You are a Royall one and we obey you.

Lear. Then there's life in't. Come, and you get it,
You shall get it by running: Sa, sa, sa, sa. *Exit.*

Gent. A sight most pittifull in the meanest wretch,
Past speaking of in a King. Thou hast a Daughter
Who redeemes Nature from the generall curse
Which twaine haue brought her to.

Edg. Haile gentle Sir.

Gent. Sir, speed you: what's your will?

Edg. Do you heare ought (Sir) of a Battell toward.

Gent. Most sure, and vulgar:
Euery one heares that, which can distinguish sound.

Edg. But by your fauour:
How neere's the other Army?

Gent. Neere, and on speedy foot: the maine descry
Stands on the hourely thought.

Edg. I thanke you Sir, that's all.

Gent. Though that the Queen on special cause is here
Her Army is mou'd on. *Exit.*

Edg. I thanke you Sir

Glou. You euer gentle Gods, take my breath from me,
Let not my worser Spirit tempt me againe
To dye before you please.

Edg. Well pray you Father.

Glou. Now good sir, what are you?

Edg. A most poore man, made tame to Fortunes blows
Who, by the Art of knowne, and feeling sorrowes,
Am pregnant to good pitty. Giue me your hand,
Ile leade you to some biding.

Glou. Heartie thankes:
The bountie, and the benizon of Heauen
To boot, and boot.

Enter Steward.

Stew. A proclaim'd prize: most happie
That eyelesse head of thine, was first fram'd flesh
To raise my fortunes. Thou old, vnhappy Traitor,
Breefely thy selfe remember: the Sword is out
That must destroy thee.

Glou. Now let thy friendly hand
Put strength enough too't.

Stew. Wherefore, bold Pezant,
Dar'st thou support a publish'd Traitor? Hence,
Least that th'infection of his fortune take
Like hold on thee. Let go his arme.

Edg. Chill not let go Zir,
Without vurther 'casion.

Stew. Let go Slaue, or thou dy'st.

Edg. Good Gentleman goe your gate, and let poore volke passe: and 'chud ha' bin zwaggerd out of my life, 'twould not ha'bin zo long as 'tis, by a vortnight. Nay, come not neere th'old man: keepe out che vor'ye, or ice try whither your Costard, or my Ballow be the harder; chill be plaine with you.

Stew. Out Dunghill.

Edg. Chill picke your teeth Zir: come, no matter vor your foynes.

Stew. Slaue thou hast slaine me: Villain, take my purse;
If euer thou wilt thriue, bury my bodie,
And giue the Letters which thou find'st about me,
To *Edmund* Earle of Glouster: seeke him out
Vpon the English party. Oh vntimely death, death.

Edg. I know thee well. A seruiceable Villaine,
As duteous to the vices of thy Mistris,
As badnesse would desire.

Glou. What, is he dead?

Edg. Sit you downe Father: rest you.
Let's see these Pockets; the Letters that he speakes of
May be my Friends: hee's dead; I am onely sorry
He had no other Deathsman. Let vs see:
Leaue gentle waxe, and manners: blame vs not
To know our enemies mindes, we rip their hearts,
Their Papers is more lawfull.

Reads the Letter.

Let our reciprocall vowes be remembred. You haue manie opportunities to cut him off: if your will want not, time and place will be fruitfully offer'd. There is nothing done. If hee returne the Conqueror, then am I the Prisoner, and his bed, my Gaole, from the loathed warmth whereof, deliuer me, and supply the place for your Labour.

Your (Wife, so I would say) affectionate Seruant. Gonerill.

Oh indinguish'd space of Womans will,
A plot vpon her vertuous Husbands life,
And the exchange my Brother: heere in the sands
Thee Ile rake vp, the poste vnsanctified
Of murtherous Letchers: and in the mature time,
With this vngracious paper strike the sight
Of the death-practis'd Duke: for him 'tis well,
That of thy death, and businesse, I can tell.

Glou. The King is mad:
How stiffe is my vilde sense
That I stand vp, and haue ingenious feeling
Of my huge Sorrowes? Better I were distract,
So should my thoughts be seuer'd from my greefes,
Drum afarre off.
And woes, by wrong imaginations loose

The

The knowledge of themselues.
Edg. Giue me your hand :
Farre off methinkes I heare the beaten Drumme.
Come Father, Ile bestow you with a Friend. *Exeunt.*

Scæna Septima.

Enter Cordelia, Kent, and Gentleman.

Cor. O thou good *Kent*,
How shall I liue and worke
To match thy goodnesse?
My life will be too short,
And euery measure faile me.
Kent. To be acknowledg'd Madam is ore-pai'd,
All my reports go with the modest truth,
Nor more, nor clipt, but so.
Cor. Be better suited,
These weedes are memories of those worser houres :
I prythee put them off.
Kent. Pardon deere Madam,
Yet to be knowne shortens my made intent,
My boone I make it, that you know me not,
Till time, and I, thinke meet.
Cor. Then be't so my good Lord :
How do's the King?
Gent. Madam sleepes still.
Cor. O you kind Gods!
Cure this great breach in his abused Nature,
Th'vntun'd and iarring senses, O winde vp,
Of this childe-changed Father.
Gent. So please your Maiesty,
That we may wake the King, he hath slept long?
Cor. Be gouern'd by your knowledge, and proceede
I'th'sway of your owne will : is he array'd?

Enter Lear in a chaire carried by Seruants

Gent. I Madam: in the heauinesse of sleepe,
We put fresh garments on him.
Be by good Madam when we do awake him,
I doubt of his Temperance.
Cor. O my deere Father, restauratian hang
Thy medicine on my lippes, and let this kisse
Repaire those violent harmes, that my two Sisters
Haue in thy Reuerence made.
Kent. Kind and deere Princesse.
Cor. Had you not bin their Father, these white flakes
Did challenge pitty of them. Was this a face
To be oppos'd against the iarring windes?
Mine Enemies dogge, though he had bit me,
Should haue stood that night against my fire,
And was't thou faine (poore Father)
To houell thee with Swine and Rogues forlorne,
In short, and musty straw? Alacke, alacke,
'Tis wonder that thy life and wits, at once
Had not concluded all. He wakes, speake to him.
Gen. Madam do you, 'tis fittest.
Cor. How does my Royall Lord?
How fares your Maiesty?
Lear. You do me wrong to take me out o'th'graue,
Thou art a Soule in blisse, but I am bound
Vpon a wheele of fire, that mine owne teares
Do scal'd, like molten Lead.
Cor. Sir, do you know me?
Lear. You are a spirit I know, where did you dye?
Cor. Still, still, farre wide.
Gen. He's scarse awake,
Let him alone a while.
Lear. Where haue I bin?
Where am I? Faire day light?
I am mightily abus'd; I should eu'n dye with pitty
To see another thus. I know not what to say :
I will not sweare these are my hands: let's see,
I feele this pin pricke, would I were assur'd
Of my condition.
Cor. O looke vpon me Sir,
And hold your hand in benediction o're me,
You must not kneele.
Lear. Pray do not mocke me:
I am a very foolish fond old man,
Fourescore and vpward,
Not an houre more, nor lesse:
And to deale plainely,
I feare I am not in my perfect mind.
Me thinkes I should know you, and know this man,
Yet I am doubtfull : For I am mainely ignorant
What place this is: and all the skill I haue
Remembers not these garments : nor I know not
Where I did lodge last night. Do not laugh at me,
For (as I am a man) I thinke this Lady
To be my childe *Cordelia.*
Cor. And so I am : I am.
Lear. Be your teares wet?
Yes faith : I pray weepe not,
If you haue poyson for me, I will drinke it :
I know you do not loue me, for your Sisters
Haue (as I do remember) done me wrong.
You haue some cause, they haue not.
Cor. No cause, no cause.
Lear. Am I in France?
Kent. In your owne kingdome Sir.
Lear. Do not abuse me.
Gent. Be comforted good Madam, the great rage
You see is kill'd in him: desire him to go in,
Trouble him no more till further setling.
Cor. Wilt please your Highnesse walke?
Lear. You must beare with me :
Pray you now forget, and forgiue,
I am old and foolish. *Exeunt*

Actus Quintus. Scena Prima.

Enter with Drumme and Colours, Edmund, Regan, Gentlemen, and Souldiers.

Bast. Know of the Duke if his last purpose hold,
Or whether since he is aduis'd by ought
To change the course, he's full of alteration,
And selfereprouing, bring his constant pleasure.
Reg. Our Sisters man is certainely miscarried.
Bast. 'Tis to be doubted Madam.
Reg. Now sweet Lord,

ff You

You know the goodnesse I intend vpon you:
Tell me but truly, but then speake the truth,
Do you not loue my Sister?

Bast. In honour'd Loue.

Reg. But haue you neuer found my Brothers way,
To the fore-fended place?

Bast. No by mine honour, Madam.

Reg. I neuer shall endure her, deere my Lord
Be not familiar with her.

Bast. Feare not, she and the Duke her husband.

Enter with Drum and Colours, Albany, Gonerill, Soldiers.

Alb. Our very louing Sister, well be-met:
Sir, this I heard, the King is come to his Daughter
With others, whom the rigour of our State
Forc'd to cry out.

Regan. Why is this reasond?

Gone. Combine together 'gainst the Enemie:
For these domesticke and particurlar broiles,
Are not the question heere.

Alb. Let's then determine with th'ancient of warre
On our proceeding.

Reg. Sister you'le go with vs?

Gon. No.

Reg. 'Tis most conuenient, pray go with vs.

Gon. Oh ho, I know the Riddle, I will goe.

Exeunt both the Armies.

Enter Edgar.

Edg. If ere your Grace had speech with man so poore,
Heare me one word.

Alb. Ile ouertake you, speake.

Edg. Before you fight the Battaile, ope this Letter:
If you haue victory, let the Trumpet sound
For him that brought it: wretched though I seeme,
I can produce a Champion, that will proue
What is auouched there. If you miscarry,
Your businesse of the world hath so an end,
And machination ceases. Fortune loues you.

Alb. Stay till I haue read the Letter.

Edg. I was forbid it:
When time shall serue, let but the Herald cry,
And Ile appeare againe. *Exit.*

Alb. Why farethee well, I will o're-looke thy paper

Enter Edmund.

Bast. The Enemy's in view, draw vp your powers,
Heere is the guesse of their true strength and Forces,
By dilligent discouerie, but your hast
Is now vrg'd on you.

Alb. We will greet the time *Exit.*

Bast. To both these Sisters haue I sworne my loue:
Each iealous of the other, as the stung
Are of the Adder. Which of them shall I take?
Both? One? Or neither? Neither can be enioy'd
If both remaine aliue: To take the Widdow,
Exasperates, makes mad her Sister *Gonerill*,
And hardly shall I carry out my side,
Her husband being aliue. Now then, wee'l vse
His countenance for the Battaile, which being done,
Let her who would be rid of him, deuise
His speedy taking off. As for the mercie
Which he intends to *Lear* and to *Cordelia*,
The Battaile done, and they within our power,
Shall neuer see his pardon: for my state,
Stands on me to defend, not to debate. *Exit.*

Scena Secunda.

Alarum within. Enter with Drumme and Colours, Lear, Cordelia, and Souldiers, ouer the Stage, and Exeunt.

Enter Edgar, and Gloster.

Edg. Heere Father, take the shadow of this Tree
For your good hoast: pray that the right may thriue:
If euer I returne to you againe,
Ile bring you comfort.

Glo. Grace go with you Sir. *Exit.*

Alarum and Retreat within.

Enter Edgar.

Egdar. Away old man, giue me thy hand, away:
King *Lear* hath lost, he and his Daughter tane,
Giue me thy hand: Come on.

Glo. No further Sir, a man may rot euen heere.

Edg. What in ill thoughts againe?
Men must endure
Their going hence, euen as their comming hither,
Ripenesse is all come on.

Glo. And that's true too. *Exeunt.*

Scena Tertia.

Enter in conquest with Drum and Colours, Edmund, Lear, and Cordelia, as prisoners, Souldiers, Captaine.

Bast. Some Officers take them away: good guard,
Vntill their greater pleasures first be knowne
That are to censure them.

Cor. We are not the first,
Who with best meaning haue incurr'd the worst:
For thee oppressed King I am cast downe,
My selfe could else out-frowne false Fortunes frowne.
Shall we not see these Daughters, and these Sisters?

Lear. No, no, no, no: come let's away to prison,
We two alone will sing like Birds i'th'Cage:
When thou dost aske me blessing, Ile kneele downe
And aske of thee forgiuenesse: So wee'l liue,
And pray, and sing, and tell old tales, and laugh
At gilded Butterflies: and heere (poore Rogues)
Talke of Court newes, and wee'l talke with them too,
Who looses, and who wins; who's in, who's out;
And take vpon's the mystery of things,
As if we were Gods spies: And wee'l weare out
In a wall'd prison, packs and sects of great ones,
That ebbe and flow by th'Moone.

Bast. Take them away.

Lear. Vpon such sacrifices my *Cordelia*,
The Gods themselues throw Incense.
Haue I caught thee?
He that parts vs, shall bring a Brand from Heauen,
And fire vs hence, like Foxes: wipe thine eyes,
The good yeares shall deuoure them, flesh and fell,

Ere

Ere they ſhall make vs weepe?
Weele ſee e'm ſtaru'd firſt: come. *Exit.*
Baſt. Come hither Captaine, hearke.
Take thou this note, go follow them to priſon,
One ſtep I haue aduanc'd thee, if thou do'ſt
As this inſtructs thee, thou doſt make thy way
To Noble Fortunes: know thou this, that men
Are as the time is; to be tender minded
Do's not become a Sword, thy great imployment
Will not beare queſtion: either ſay thou'lt do't,
Or thriue by other meanes.
Capt. Ile do't my Lord.
Baſt. About it, and write happy, when th'haſt done,
Marke I ſay inſtantly, and carry it ſo
As I haue ſet it downe. *Exit Captaine.*

Flouriſh. Enter Albany, Generill, Regan, Soldiers.

Alb. Sir, you haue ſhew'd to day your valiant ſtraine
And Fortune led you well: you haue the Captiues
Who were the oppoſites of this dayes ſtrife:
I do require them of you ſo to vſe them,
As we ſhall find their merites, and our ſafety
May equally determine.
Baſt. Sir, I thought it fit,
To ſend the old and miſerable King to ſome retention,
Whoſe age had Charmes in it, whoſe Title more,
To plucke the common boſome on his ſide,
And turne our impreſt Launces in our eies
Which do command them. With him I ſent the Queen:
My reaſon all the ſame, and they are ready
To morrow, or at further ſpace, t'appeare
Where you ſhall hold your Seſſion.
Alb. Sir, by your patience,
I hold you but a ſubiect of this Warre,
Not as a Brother.
Reg. That's as we liſt to grace him.
Methinkes our pleaſure might haue bin demanded
Ere you had ſpoke ſo farre. He led our Powers,
Bore the Commiſſion of my place and perſon,
The which immediacie may well ſtand vp,
And call it ſelfe your Brother.
Gon. Not ſo hot:
In his owne grace he doth exalt himſelfe,
More then in your addition.
Reg. In my rights,
By me inueſted, he compeeres the beſt.
Alb. That were the moſt, if he ſhould husband you.
Reg. Ieſters do oft proue Prophets.
Gon. Hola, hola,
That eye that told you ſo, look'd but a ſquint.
Rega. Lady I am not well, elſe I ſhould anſwere
From a full flowing ſtomack. Generall,
Take thou my Souldiers, priſoners, patrimony,
Diſpoſe of them, of me, the walls is thine:
Witneſſe the world, that I create thee heere
My Lord, and Maſter.
Gon. Meane you to enioy him?
Alb. The let alone lies not in your good will.
Baſt. Nor in thine Lord.
Alb. Halfe-blooded fellow, yes.
Reg. Let the Drum ſtrike, and proue my title thine.
Alb. Stay yet, heare reaſon: *Edmund*, I arreſt thee
On capitall Treaſon; and in thy arreſt,
This guilded Serpent: for your claime faire Siſters,
I bare it in the intereſt of my wife,
'Tis ſhe is ſub-contracted to this Lord,
And I her husband contradict your Banes.
If you will marry, make your loues to me,
My Lady is beſpoke.
Gon. An enterlude.
Alb. Thou art armed *Gloſter*,
Let the Trmpet ſound:
If none appeare to proue vpon thy perſon,
Thy heynous, manifeſt, and many Treaſons,
There is my pledge: Ile make it on thy heart
Ere I taſte bread, thou art in nothing leſſe
Then I haue heere proclaim'd thee.
Reg. Sicke, O ſicke.
Gon. If not, Ile nere truſt medicine.
Baſt. There's my exchange, what in the world hes
That names me Traitor, villain-like he lies,
Call by the Trumpet: he that dares approach;
On him, on you, who not, I will maintaine
My truth and honor firmely.

Enter a Herald.

Alb. A Herald, ho.
Truſt to thy ſingle vertue, for thy Souldiers
All leuied in my name, haue in my name
Tooke their diſcharge.
Regan. My ſickneſſe growes vpon me.
Alb. She is not well, conuey her to my Tent.
Come hither Herald, let the Trumper ſound,
And read out this. *A Tumpet ſounds.*

Herald reads.

IF any man of qualitie or degree, within the liſts of the Army, will maintaine vpon Edmund, ſuppoſed Earle of Gloſter, that he is a manifold Traitor, let him appeare by the third ſound of the Trumpet: he is bold in his defence. 1 *Trumpet.*
Her. Againe. 2 *Trumpet.*
Her. Againe. 3 *Trumpet.*
Trumpet anſwers within.

Enter Edgar armed.

Alb. Aske him his purpoſes, why he appeares
Vpon this Call o'th'Trumpet.
Her. What are you?
Your name, your quality, and why you anſwer
This preſent Summons?
Edg. Know my name is loſt
By Treaſons tooth: bare-gnawne, and Canker-bit,
Yet am I Noble as the Aduerſary
I come to cope.
Alb. Which is that Aduerſary?
Edg. What's he that ſpeakes for *Edmund* Earle of Glo-(ſter?
Baſt. Himſelfe, what ſaiſt thou to him?
Edg. Draw thy Sword,
That if my ſpeech offend a Noble heart,
Thy arme may do thee Iuſtice, heere is mine:
Behold it is my priuiledge,
The priuiledge of mine Honours,
My oath, and my profeſſion. I proteſt,
Maugre thy ſtrength, place, youth, and eminence,
Deſpiſe thy victor-Sword, and fire new Fortune,
Thy valor, and thy heart, thou art a Traitor:
Falſe to thy Gods, thy Brother, and thy Father,
Conſpirant 'gainſt this high illuſtrious Prince,
And from th'extremeſt vpward of thy head,
To the diſcent and duſt below thy foote,

ſſ2

A moſt Toad-ſpotted Traitor. Say thou no,
This Sword, this arme, and my beſt ſpirits are bent
To proue vpon thy heart, whereto I ſpeake,
Thou lyeſt.
Baſt. In wiſedome I ſhould aske thy name,
But ſince thy out-ſide lookes ſo faire and Warlike,
And that thy tongue (ſome ſay) of breeding breathes,
What ſafe, and nicely I might well delay,
By rule of Knight-hood, I diſdaine and ſpurne:
Backe do I toſſe theſe Treaſons to thy head,
With the hell-hated Lye, ore-whelme thy heart,
Which for they yet glance by, and ſcarely bruiſe,
This Sword of mine ſhall giue them inſtant way,
Where they ſhall reſt for euer. Trumpets ſpeake.
Alb. Saue him, ſaue him. *Alarums. Fights.*
Gon. This is practiſe *Gloſter*,
By th'law of Warre, thou waſt not bound to anſwer
An vnknowne oppoſite: thou art not vanquiſh'd,
But cozend, and beguild.
Alb. Shut your mouth Dame,
Or with this paper ſhall I ſtop it: hold Sir,
Thou worſe then any name, reade thine owne euill:
No tearing Lady, I perceiue you know it.
Gon. Say if I do, the Lawes are mine not thine,
Who can araigne me for't? *Exit.*
Alb. Moſt monſtrous! O, know'ſt thou this paper?
Baſt. Aske me not what I know.
Alb. Go after her, ſhe's deſperate, gouerne her.
Baſt. What you haue charg'd me with,
That haue I done,
And more, much more, the time will bring it out.
'Tis paſt, and ſo am I: But what art thou
That haſt this Fortune on me? If thou'rt Noble,
I do forgiue thee.
Edg. Let's exchange charity:
I am no leſſe in blood then thou art *Edmond*,
If more, the more th'haſt wrong'd me.
My name is *Edgar* and thy Fathers Sonne,
The Gods are iuſt, and of our pleaſant vices
Make inſtruments to plague vs:
The darke and vitious place where thee he got
Coſt him his eyes.
Baſt. Th'haſt ſpoken right, 'tis true,
The Wheele is come full circle, I am heere.
Alb. Me thought thy very gate did propheſie
A Royall Nobleneſſe: I muſt embrace thee,
Let ſorrow ſplit my heart, if euer I
Did hate thee, or thy Father.
Edg. Worthy Prince I know't.
Alb. Where haue you hid your ſelfe?
How haue you knowne the miſeries of your Father?
Edg. By nurſing them my Lord. Liſt a breefe tale,
And when 'tis told, O that my heart would burſt.
The bloody proclamation to eſcape
That follow'd me ſo neere, (O our liues ſweetneſſe,
That we the paine of death would hourely dye,
Rather then die at once) taught me to ſhift
Into a mad-mans rags, t'aſſume a ſemblance
That very Dogges diſdain'd: and in this habit
Met I my Father with his bleeding Rings,
Their precious Stones new loſt: became his guide,
Led him, begg'd for him, ſau'd him from diſpaire.
Neuer (O fault) reueal'd my ſelfe vnto him,
Vntill ſome halfe houre paſt when I was arm'd,
Not ſure, though hoping of this good ſucceſſe,
I ask'd his bleſſing, and from firſt to laſt
Told him our pilgrimage. But his flaw'd heart
(Alacke too weake the conflict to ſupport)
Twixt two extremes of paſſion, ioy and greefe,
Burſt ſmilingly.
Baſt. This ſpeech of yours hath mou'd me,
And ſhall perchance do good, but ſpeake you on,
You looke as you had ſomething more to ſay.
Alb. If there be more, more woſull, hold it in,
For I am almoſt ready to diſſolue,
Hearing of this.

Enter a Gentleman.

Gen. Helpe, helpe: O helpe.
Edg. What kinde of helpe?
Alb. Speake man.
Edg. What meanes this bloody Knife?
Gen. 'Tis hot, it ſmoakes, it came euen from the heart
of—— O ſhe's dead.
Alb. Who dead? Speake man.
Gen. Your Lady Sir, your Lady; and her Siſter
By her is poyſon'd: ſhe confeſſes it.
Baſt. I was contracted to them both, all three
Now marry in an inſtant.
Edg. Here comes *Kent*.

Enter Kent.

Alb. Produce the bodies, be they aliue or dead;
Gonerill and Regans bodies brought out.
This iudgement of the Heauens that makes vs tremble.
Touches vs not with pitty: O, is this he?
The time will not allow the complement
Which very manners vrges.
Kent. I am come
To bid my King and Maſter aye good night.
Is he not here?
Alb. Great thing of vs forgot,
Speake *Edmund*, where's the King? and where's *Cordelia*?
Seeſt thou this obiect *Kent*?
Kent. Alacke, why thus?
Baſt Yet *Edmund* was belou'd:
The one the other poiſon'd for my ſake,
And after ſlew herſelfe.
Alb. Euen ſo: couer their faces.
Baſt. I pant for life: ſome good I meane to do
Deſpight of mine owne Nature. Quickly ſend,
(Be briefe in it) to'th Caſtle, for my Writ
Is on the life of *Lear*, and on *Cordelia*:
Nay, ſend in time.
Alb. Run, run, O run.
Edg. To who my Lord? Who ha's the Office?
Send thy token of repreeue.
Baſt. Well thought on, take my Sword,
Giue it the Captaine.
Edg. Haſt thee for thy life.
Baſt. He hath Commiſſion from thy Wife and me,
To hang *Cordelia* in the priſon, and
To lay the blame vpon her owne diſpaire,
That ſhe for-did her ſelfe.
Alb. The Gods defend her, beare him hence awhile.

Enter Lear with Cordelia in his armes.

Lear. Howle, howle, howle: O your are men of ſtones,
Had I your tongues and eyes, Il'd vſe them ſo,
That Heauens vault ſhould crack: ſhe's gone for euer.
I know when one is dead, and when one liues,
She's dead as earth: Lend me a Looking-glaſſe,
If

If that her breath will mist or staine the stone,
Why then she liues.
Kent. Is this the promis'd end?
Edg. Or image of that horror.
Alb. Fall and cease.
Lear. This feather stirs, she liues: if it be so,
It is a chance which do's redeeme all sorrowes
That euer I haue felt.
Kent. O my good Master.
Lear. Prythee away.
Edg. 'Tis Noble *Kent* your Friend.
Lear. A plague vpon you Murderors, Traitors all,
I might haue sau'd her, now she's gone for euer:
Cordelia, Cordelia, stay a little. Ha:
What is't thou saist? Her voice was euer soft,
Gentle, and low, an excellent thing in woman.
I kill'd the Slaue that was a hanging thee.
Gent. 'Tis true (my Lords) he did.
Lear. Did I not fellow?
I haue seene the day, with my good biting Faulchion
I would haue made him skip: I am old now,
And these same crosses spoile me. Who are you?
Mine eyes are not o'th'best, Ile tell you straight.
Kent. If Fortune brag of two, she lou'd and hated,
One of them we behold.
Lear. This is a dull sight, are you not *Kent*?
Kent. The same: your Seruant *Kent*,
Where is your Seruant *Caius*?
Lear. He's a good fellow, I can tell you that,
He'le strike and quickly too, he's dead and rotten.
Kent. No my good Lord, I am the very man.
Lear. Ile see that straight.
Kent. That from your first of difference and decay,
Haue follow'd your sad steps.
Lear. Your are welcome hither.
Kent. Nor no man else.
All's cheerlesse, darke, and deadly,
Your eldest Daughters haue fore-done themselues,
And desperately are dead
Lear. I so I thinke.
Alb. He knowes not what he saies, and vaine is it
That we present vs to him.

Enter a Messenger.

Edg. Very bootlesse.
Mess. *Edmund* is dead my Lord.
Alb. That's but a trifle heere:
You Lords and Noble Friends, know our intent,
What comfort to this great decay may come,
Shall be appli'd. For vs we will resigne,
During the life of this old Maiesty
To him our absolute power, you to your rights,
With boote, and such addition as your Honours
Haue more then merited. All Friends shall
Taste the wages of their vertue, and all Foes
The cup of their deseruings: O see, see.
Lear. And my poore Foole is hang'd: no, no, no life?
Why should a Dog, a Horse, a Rat haue life,
And thou no breath at all? Thou'lt come no more,
Neuer, neuer, neuer, neuer, neuer.
Pray you vndo this Button. Thanke you Sir,
Do you see this? Looke on her? Looke her lips,
Looke there, looke there. *He dis.*
Edg. He faints, my Lord, my Lord.
Kent. Breake heart, I prythee breake.
Edg. Looke vp my Lord.
Kent. Vex not his ghost, O let him passe, he hates him,
That would vpon the wracke of this tough world
Stretch him out longer.
Edg. He is gon indeed.
Kent. The wonder is, he hath endur'd so long,
He but vsurpt his life.
Alb. Beare them from hence, our present businesse
Is generall woe: Friends of my soule, you twaine,
Rule in this Realme, and the gor'd state sustaine.
Kent. I haue a iourney Sir, shortly to go,
My Master calls me, I must not say no.
Edg. The waight of this sad time we must obey,
Speake what we feele, not what we ought to say:
The oldest hath borne most, we that are yong,
Shall neuer see so much, nor liue so long.

Exeunt with a dead March.

ss3

FINIS.

THE TRAGEDIE OF
Othello, the Moore of Venice.

Actus Primus. Scœna Prima.

Enter Rodorigo, and Iago.

Rodorigo.

NEuer tell me, I take it much vnkindly
That thou (*Iago*) who hast had my purse,
As if ŷ strings were thine, should'st know of this.
Ia. But you'l not heare me. If euer I did dream
Of such a matter, abhorre me.
Rodo. Thou told'st me,
Thou did'st hold him in thy hate.
Iago. Despise me
If I do not. Three Great-ones of the Cittie,
(In personall suite to make me his Lieutenant)
Off-capt to him: and by the faith of man
I know my price, I am worth no worsse a place.
But he (as louing his owne pride, and purposes)
Euades them, with a bumbast Circumstance,
Horribly stufft with Epithites of warre,
Non-suites my Mediators. For certes, saies he,
I haue already chose my Officer. And what was he?
For-sooth, a great Arithmatician,
One *Michaell Cassio*, a *Florentine*,
(A Fellow almost damn'd in a faire Wife)
That neuer set a Squadron in the Field,
Nor the deuision of a Battaile knowes
More then a Spinster. Vnlesse the Bookish Theoricke:
Wherein the Tongued Consuls can propose
As Masterly as he. Meere pratle (without practise)
Is all his Souldiership. But he (Sir) had th'election;
And I (of whom his eies had seene the proofe
At Rhodes, at Ciprus, and on others grounds
Christen'd, and Heathen) must be be-leed, and calm'd
By Debitor, and Creditor. This Counter-caster,
He (in good time) must his Lieutenant be,
And I (blesse the marke) his Mooreships Auntient.
Rod. By heauen, I rather would haue bin his hangman.
Iago. Why, there's no remedie.
'Tis the cursse of Seruice;
Preferment goes by Letter, and affection,
And not by old gradation, where each second
Stood Heire to'th'first. Now Sir, be iudge your selfe,
Whether I in any iust terme am Affin'd
To loue the *Moore*?
Rod. I would not follow him then.
Iago. O Sir content you.
I follow him to serue my turne vpon him.
We cannot all be Masters, nor all Masters
Cannot be truely follow'd. You shall marke
Many a dutious and knee-crooking knaue;
That (doting on his owne obsequious bondage)
Weares out his time, much like his Masters Asse,
For naught but Prouender, & when he's old Casheer'd.
Whip me such honest knaues. Others there are
Who trym'd in Formes, and visages of Dutie,
Keepe yet their hearts attending on themselues,
And throwing but showes of Seruice on their Lords
Doe well thriue by them.
And when they haue lin'd their Coates
Doe themselues Homage.
These Fellowes haue some soule,
And such a one do I professe my selfe. For (Sir)
It is as sure as you are *Rodorigo*,
Were I the Moore, I would not be *Iago*:
In following him, I follow but my selfe.
Heauen is my Iudge, not I for loue and dutie,
But seeming so, for my peculiar end:
For when my outward Action doth demonstrate
The natiue act, and figure of my heart
In Complement externe, 'tis not long after
But I will weare my heart vpon my sleeue
For Dawes to pecke at; I am not what I am.
Rod. What a fall Fortune do's the Thicks-lips owe
If he can carry't thus?
Iago. Call vp her Father:
Rowse him, make after him, poyson his delight,
Proclaime him in the Streets. Incense her kinsmen,
And though he in a fertile Clymate dwell,
Plague him with Flies: though that his Ioy be Ioy,
Yet throw such chances of vexation on't,
As it may loose some colour.
Rodo. Heere is her Fathers house, Ile call aloud.
Iago. Doe, with like timerous accent, and dire yell,
As when (by Night and Negligence) the Fire
Is spied in populus Citties.
Rodo. What hoa: *Brabantio*, Siginor *Brabantio*, hoa.
Iago. Awake: what hoa, *Brabantio*: Theeues, Theeues.
Looke to your house, your daughter, and your Bags,
Theeues, Theeues.
Bra. Aboue. What is the reason of this terrible
Summons? What is the matter there?
Rodo. Signior is all your Familie within?
Iago. Are your Doores lock'd?
Bra. Why? Wherefore ask you this?
Iago. Sir, y'are rob'd, for shame put on your Gowne,
Your

Your heart is burst, you haue lost halfe your soule
Euen now, now, very now, an old blacke Ram
Is tupping your white Ewe. Arise, arise,
Awake the snorting Cit.izens with the Bell,
Or else the deuill will make a Grand-sire of you.
Arise I say.

Bra. What, haue you lost your wits?

Rod. Most reuerend Signior, do you know my voice?

Bra. Not I: what are you?

Rod. My name is *Rodorigo.*

Bra. The worsser welcome:
I haue charg'd thee not to haunt about my doores:
In honest plainenesse thou hast heard me say,
My Daughter is not for thee. And now in madnesse
(Being full of Supper, and distempring draughtes)
Vpon malitious knauerie, dost thou come
To start my quiet.

Rod. Sir, Sir, Sir.

Bra. But thou must needs be sure,
My spirits and my place haue in their power
To make this bitter to thee.

Rodo. Patience good Sir.

Bra. What tell'st thou me of Robbing?
This is Venice: my house is not a Grange.

Rodo. Most graue *Brabantio,*
In simple and pure soule, I come to you

Ia. Sir: you are one of those that will not serue God, if the deuill bid you. Because we come to do you seruice, and you thinke we are Ruffians, you'le haue your Daughter couer'd with a Barbary horse, you'le haue your Nephewes neigh to you, you'le haue Coursers for Cozens: and Genners for Germaines.

Bra. What prophane wretch art thou?

Ia. I am one Sir, that comes to tell you, your Daughter and the Moore, are making the Beast with two backs.

Bra. Thou art a Villaine.

Iago. You are a Senator.

Bra. This thou shalt answere. I know thee *Rodorigo.*

Rod. Sir, I will answere any thing. But I beseech you
If't be your pleasure, and most wise consent,
(As partly I find it is) that your faire Daughter,
At this odde Euen and dull watch o'th'night
Transported with no worse nor better guard,
But with a knaue of common hire, a Gundelier,
To the grosse claspes of a Lasciuious Moore:
If this be knowne to you, and your Allowance,
We then haue done you bold, and saucie wrongs.
But if you know not this, my Manners tell me,
We haue your wrong rebuke. Do not beleeue
That from the sence of all Ciuilitie,
I thus would play and trifle with your Reuerence.
Your Daughter (if you haue not giuen her leaue)
I say againe, hath made a grosse reuolt,
Tying her Dutie, Beautie, Wit, and Fortunes
In an extrauagant, and wheeling Stranger,
Of here, and euery where: straight satisfie your selfe.
If she be in her Chamber, or your house,
Let loose on me the Iustice of the State
For thus deluding you.

Bra. Strike on the Tinder, hoa:
Giue me a Taper: call vp all my people,
This Accident is not vnlike my dreame,
Beleefe of it oppresses me alreadie.
Light, I say, light. *Exit.*

Iag. Farewell: for I must leaue you.
It seemes not meete, nor wholesome to my place
To be producted, (as if I stay, I shall,)
Against the Moore. For I do know the State,
(How euer this may gall him with some checke)
Cannot with safetie cast-him. For he's embark'd
With such loud reason to the Cyprus Warres,
(Which euen now stands in Act) that for their soules
Another of his Fadome, they haue none,
To lead their Businesse. In which regard,
Though I do hate him as I do hell apines,
Yet, for necessitie of present life,
I must show out a Flag, and signe of Loue,
(Which is indeed but signe) that you shal surely find him
Lead to the Sagitary the raised Search:
And there will I be with him. So farewell. *Exit.*

Enter Brabantio, with Seruants and Torches.

Bra. It is too true an euill. Gone she is,
And what's to come of my despised time,
Is naught but bitternesse. Now *Rodorigo,*
Where didst thou see her? (Oh vnhappie Girle)
With the Moore saist thou? (Who would be a Father?)
How didst thou know 'twas she? (Oh she deceaues me
Past thought:) what said she to you? Get moe Tapers:
Raise all my Kindred. Are they married thinke you?

Rodo. Truely I thinke they are.

Bra. Oh Heauen: how got she out?
Oh treason of the blood.
Fathers, from hence trust not your Daughters minds
By what you see them act. Is there not Charmes,
By which the propertie of Youth, and Maidhood
May be abus'd? Haue you not read *Rodorigo,*
Of some such thing?

Rod. Yes Sir: I haue indeed.

Bra. Call vp my Brother: oh would you had had her.
Some one way, some another. Doe you know
Where we may apprehend her, and the Moore?

Rod. I thinke I can discouer him, if you please
To get good Guard, and go along with me.

Bra. Pray you lead on. At euery house Ile call,
(I may command at most) get Weapons (hoa)
And raise some speciall Officers of might:
On good *Rodorigo,* I will deserue your paines. *Exeunt.*

Scena Secunda.

Enter Othello, Iago, Attendants, with Torches.

Ia. Though in the trade of Warre I haue slaine men,
Yet do I hold it very stuffe o'th'conscience
To do no contriu'd Murder: I lacke Iniquitie
Sometime to do me seruice. Nine, or ten times
I had thought t'haue yerk'd him here vnder the Ribbes.

Othello. 'Tis better as it is.

Iago. Nay but he prated,
And spoke such scuruy, and prouoking termes
Against your Honor, that with the little godlinesse I haue
I did full hard forbeare him. But I pray you Sir,
Are you fast married? Be assur'd of this,
That the Magnifico is much belou'd,
And hath in his effect a voice potentiall
As double as the Dukes: He will diuorce you.
Or put vpon you, what restraint or greeuance,

The

The Law (with all his might, to enforce it on)
Will giue him Cable.
Othel. Let him do his ſpight;
My Seruices, which I haue done the Signorie
Shall out-tongue his Complaints. 'Tis yet to know,
Which when I know, that boaſting is an Honour,
I ſhall promulgate. I fetch my life and being,
From Men of Royall Seige. And my demerites
May ſpeake (vnbonnetted) to as proud a Fortune
As this that I haue reach'd. For know *Iago*,
But that I loue the gentle *Deſdemona*,
I would not my vnhouſed free condition
Put into Circumſcription, and Confine,
For the Seas worth. But looke, what Lights come yond?

Enter Caſſio, with Torches.

Iago. Thoſe are the raiſed Father, and his Friends:
You were beſt go in.
Othel. Not I: I muſt be found.
My Parts, my Title, and my perfect Soule
Shall manifeſt me rightly. Is it they?
Iago. By *Ianus*, I thinke no.
Othel. The Seruants of the Dukes?
And my Lieutenant?
The goodneſſe of the Night vpon you (Friends)
What is the Newes?
Caſſio. The Duke do's greet you (Generall)
And he requires your haſte, Poſt-haſte appearance,
Enen on the inſtant.
Othello. What is the matter, thinke you?
Caſſio. Something from Cyprus, as I may diuine:
It is a buſineſſe of ſome heate. The Gallies
Haue ſent a dozen ſequent Meſſengers
This very night, at one anothers heeles:
And many of the Conſuls, rais'd and met,
Are at the Dukes already. You haue bin hotly call'd for,
When being not at your Lodging to be found,
The Senate hath ſent about three ſeuerall Queſts,
To ſearch you out.
Othel. 'Tis well I am found by you:
I will but ſpend a word here in the houſe,
And goe with you.
Caſſio. Aunciant, what makes he heere?
Iago. Faith, he to night hath boarded a Land Carract,
If it proue lawfull prize, he's made for euer.
Caſſio. I do not vnderſtand.
Iago. He's married.
Caſſio. To who?
Iago. Marry to —— Come Captaine, will you go?
Othel. Haue with you.
Caſſio. Here comes another Troope to ſeeke for you.

Enter Brabantio, Rodorigo, with Officers, and Torches.

Iago. It is *Brabantio*: Generall be aduis'd,
He comes to bad intent.
Othello. Holla, ſtand there.
Rodo. Signior, it is the Moore.
Bra. Downe with him, Theefe.
Iago. You, *Rodorigoe*? Cme Sir, I am for you.
Othe. Keepe vp your bright Swords, for the dew will ruſt them. Good Signior, you ſhall more command with yeares, then with your Weapons.
Bra. Oh thou foule Theefe,
Where haſt thou ſtow'd my Daughter?
Damn'd as thou art, thou haſt enchaunted her
For Ile referre me to all things of ſenſe,
(If ſhe in Chaines of Magick we're not bound)
Whether a Maid, ſo tender, Faire, and Happie,
So oppoſite to Marriage, that ſhe ſhun'd
The wealthy curled Deareling of our Nation,
Would euer haue (t'encurre a generall mocke)
Run from her Guardage to the ſootie boſome,
Of ſuch a thing as thou: to feare, not to delight
Iudge me the world, if 'tis not groſſe in ſenſe,
That thou haſt practis'd on her with foule Charmes,
Abus'd her delicate Youth, with Drugs or Minerals,
That weakens Motion. Ile haue't diſputed on,
'Tis probable, and palpable to thinking;
I therefore apprehend and do attach thee,
For an abuſer of the World, a practiſer
Of Arts inhibited, and out of warrant;
Lay hold vpon him, if he do reſiſt
Subdue him, at his perill.
Othe. Hold your hands
Both you of my inclining, and the reſt.
Were it my Cue to fight, I ſhould haue knowne it
Without a Prompter. Whether will you that I goe
To anſwere this your charge?
Bra. To Priſon, till fit time
Of Law, and courſe of direct Seſſion
Call thee to anſwer.
Othe. What if do obey?
How may the Duke be therewith ſatisf'd,
Whoſe Meſſengers are heere about my ſide,
Vpon ſome preſent buſineſſe of the State,
To bring me to him.
Officer. 'Tis true moſt worthy Signior,
The Dukes in Counſell, and your Noble ſelfe,
I am ſure is ſent for.
Bra. How? The Duke in Counſell?
In this time of the night? Bring him away;
Mine's not an idle Cauſe. The Duke himſelfe,
Or any of my Brothers of the State,
Cannot but feele this wrong, as 'twere their owne:
For if ſuch Actions may haue paſſage free,
Bond-ſlaues, and Pagans ſhall our Stateſmen be. *Exeunt*

Scæna Tertia.

Enter Duke, Senators, and Officers.

Duke. There's no compoſition in this Newes,
That giues them Credite.
1. Sen. Indeed, they are diſproportioned;
My Letters ſay, a Hundred and ſeuen Gallies.
Duke. And mine a Hundred fortie.
2. Sena. And mine two Hundred:
But though they iumpe not on a iuſt accompt,
(As in theſe Caſes where the ayme reports,
'Tis oft with difference) yet do they all confirme
A Turkiſh Fleete, and bearing vp to Cyprus.
Duke. Nay, it is poſſible enough to iudgement:
I do not ſo ſecure me in the Error,
But the maine Article I do approue
In fearefull ſenſe.
Saylor within. What hoa, what hoa, what hoa
Enter Saylor.

Officer A

Officer. A Meſſenger from the Gallies.
Duke. Now? What's the buſineſſe?
Sailor. The Turkiſh Preparation makes for Rhodes,
So was I bid report here to the State,
By Signior *Angelo.*
Duke. How ſay you by this change?
1. Sen. This cannot be
By no aſſay of reaſon. 'Tis a Pageant
To keepe vs in falſe gaze,when we conſider
Th'importancie of Cyprus to the Turke;
And let our ſelues againe but vnderſtand,
That as it more concernes the Turke then Rhodes,
So may he with more facile queſtion beare it,
For that it ſtands not in ſuch Warrelike brace,
But altogether lackes th'abilities
That Rhodes is dreſs'd in. If we make thought of this,
We muſt not thinke the Turke is ſo vnskillfull,
To leaue that lateſt,which concernes him firſt,
Neglecting an attempt of eaſe,and gaine
To wake,and wage a danger profitleſſe.
Duke. Nay,in all confidence he's not for Rhodes.
Officer. Here is more Newes.

Enter a Meſſenger.

Meſſen. The *Ottamites*,Reueren'd.and Gracious,
Steering with due courſe toward the Ile of Rhodes,
Haue there inioynted them with an after Fleete.
1. Sen. I,ſo I thought: how many,as you gueſſe?
Meſſ. Of thirtie Saile: and now they do re-ſtem
Their backward courſe,bearing with frank appearance
Their purpoſes toward Cyprus. Signior *Montano,*
Your truſtie and moſt Valiant Seruitour,
With his free dutie,recommends you thus,
And prayes you to beleeue him.
Duke. 'Tis certaine then for Cyprus:
Marcus Luccicos is not he in Towne?
1. Sen. He's now in Florence.
Duke. Write from vs,
To him,Poſt,Poſt-haſte,diſpatch.
1. Sen. Here comes *Brabantio*,and the Valiant Moore.

Enter Brabantio, Othello, Caſſio, Iago, Rodorego, and Officers.

Duke. Valiant *Othello*,we muſt ſtraight employ you,
Againſt the generall Enemy *Ottoman.*
I did not ſee you: welcome gentle Signior,
We lack't your Counſaile,and your helpe to night.
Bra. So did I yours: Good your Grace pardon me.
Neither my place,nor ought I heard of buſineſſe
Hath rais'd me from my bed; nor doth the generall care
Take hold on me. For my perticular griefe
Is of ſo flood-gate,and ore-bearing Nature,
That it engluts,snd ſwallowes other ſorrowes,
And it is ſtill it ſelfe.
Duke. Why? What's the matter?
Bra. My Daughter: oh my Daughter!
Sen. Dead?
Bra. I,to me.
She is abus'd,ſtolne from me,and corrupted
By Spels,and Medicines,bought of Mountebanks;
For Nature,ſo prepoſterouſly to erre,
(Being not deficient,blind,or lame of ſenſe,)
Sans witch-craft could not.
Duke. Who ere he be,that in this foule proceeding
Hath thus beguil'd your Daughter of her ſelfe,
And you of her; the bloodie Booke of Law,
You ſhall your ſelfe read,in the bitter letter,
After your owne ſenſe: yea,though our proper Son
Stood in your Action.
Bra. Humbly I thanke your Grace,
Here is the man; this Moore,whom now it ſeemes
Your ſpeciall Mandate,for the State affaires
Hath hither brought.
All. We are verie ſorry for't.
Duke. What in yonr owne part,cau you ſay to this?
Bra. Nothing,but this is ſo.
Othe. Moſt Potent,Graue,and Reueren'd Signiors,
My very Noble,and approu'd good Maſters;
That I haue tane away this old mans Daughter,
It is moſt true: true I haue married her;
The verie head,and front of my offending,
Hath this extent; no more. Rude am I,in my ſpeech,
And little bleſs'd with the ſoft phraſe of Peace;
For ſince theſe Armes of mine,had ſeuen yeares pith,
Till now,ſome nine Moones waſted,they haue vs'd
Their deereſt action,in the Tented Field:
And little of this great world can I ſpeake,
More then pertaines to Feats of Broiles,and Battaile,
And therefore little ſhall I grace my cauſe,
In ſpeaking for my ſelfe. Yet,(by your gratious patience)
I will a round vn-varniſh'd u Tale deliuer,
Of my whole courſe of Loue
What Drugges,what Charmes,
What Coniuration,and what mighty Magicke,
(For ſuch proceeding I am charg'd withall)
I won his Daughter.
Bra. A Maiden,neuer bold:
Of Spirit ſo ſtill,and quiet,that her Motion
Bluſh'd at her ſelfe,and ſhe,in ſpight of Nature,
Of Yeares,of Country,Credite,euery thing
To fall in Loue,with what ſhe fear'd to looke on;
It is a iudgement main'd,and moſt imperfect.
That will confeſſe Perfection ſo could erre
Againſt all rules of Nature,and muſt be driuen
To find out practiſes of cunning hell
Why this ſhould be. I therefore vouch againe,
That with ſome Mixtures,powrefull o're the blood,
Or with ſome Dram,(coniur'd to this effect)
He wrought vp on her.
To vouch this,is no proofe,
Without more wider,and more ouer Teſt
Then theſe thin habits and poore likely-hoods
Of moderne ſeeming,do prefer againſt him.
Sen. But *Othello*,ſpeake,
Did you,by indirect,and forced courſes
Subdue,and poyſon this yong Maides affections?
Or came it by requeſt,and ſuch faire queſtion
As ſoule,to ſoule affordeth?
Othel. I do beſeech you,
Send for the Lady to the Sagitary.
And let her ſpeake of me before her Father;
If you do finde me foule,in her report,
The Truſt,the Office,I do hold of you,
Not onely take away,but let your Sentence
Euen fall vpon my life.
Duke. Fetch *Deſdemona* hither.
Othe. Auncient,conduct them:
You beſt know the place.
And tell ſhe come,as truely as to heauen,
I do confeſſe the vices of my blood,
So iuſtly to your Graue eares,Ile preſent
How

How I did thriue in this faire Ladies loue,
And ſhe in mine.
Duke. Say it *Othello*.
Othe. Her Father lou'd me, oft inuited me:
Still queſtion'd me the Storie of my life,
From yeare to yeare: the Battaile, Sieges, Fortune,
That I haue paſt.
I ran it through, euen from my boyiſh daies,
Toth' very moment that he bad me tell it.
Wherein I ſpoke of moſt diſaſtrous chances:
Of mouing Accidents by Flood and Field,
Of haire-breadth ſcapes i'th'imminent deadly breach;
Of being taken by the Inſolent Foe,
And ſold to ſlauery. Of my redemption thence,
And portance in my Trauellours hiſtorie.
Wherein of Antars vaſt, and Deſarts idle,
Rough Quarries, Rocks, Hills, whoſe head touch heauen,
It was my hint to ſpeake. Such was my Proceſſe,
And of the Canibals that each others eate,
The *Antropophague*, and men whoſe heads
Grew beneath their ſhoulders. Theſe things to heare,
Would *Deſdemona* ſeriouſly incline
But ſtill the houſe Affaires would draw her hence:
Which euer as ſhe could with haſte diſpatch,
She'l'd come againe, and with a greedie eare
Deuoure vp my diſcourſe. Which I obſeruing,
Tooke once a pliant houre, and found good meanes
To draw from her a prayer of earneſt heart,
That I would all my Pilgrimage dilate,
Whereof by parcels ſhe had ſomething heard,
But not inſtinctiuely: I did conſent,
And often did beguile her of her teares,
When I did ſpeake of ſome diſtreſſefull ſtroke
That my youth ſuffer'd: My Storie being done,
She gaue me for my paines a world of kiſſes:
She ſwore in faith 'twas ſtrange: 'twas paſſing ſtrange,
'Twas pittifull: 'twas wondrous pittifull.
She wiſh'd ſhe had not heard it, yet ſhe wiſh'd
That Heauen had made her ſuch a man. She thank'd me,
And bad me, if I had a Friend that lou'd her,
I ſhould but teach him how to tell my Story,
And that would wooe her. Vpon this hint I ſpake,
She lou'd me for the dangers I had paſt,
And I lou'd her, that ſhe did pitty them.
This onely is the witch-craft I haue vs'd.
Here comes the Ladie: Let her witneſſe it.

Enter Deſdemona, Iago, Attendants.

Duke. I thinke this tale would win my Daughter too,
Good *Braba tio*, take vp this mangled matter at the beſt:
Men do their broken Weapons rather vſe,
Then their bare hands.
Bra. I pray you heare her ſpeake?
If ſhe confeſſe that ſhe was halfe the wooer,
Deſtruction on my head, if my bad blame
Light on the man. Come hither gentle Miſtris,
Do you perceiue in all this Noble Companie,
Where moſt you owe obedience?
Deſ. My Noble Father,
I do perceiue heere a diuided dutie.
To you I am bound for life, and education:
My life and education both do learne me,
How to reſpect you. You are the Lord of duty,
I am hitherto your Daughter. But heere's my Husband;
And ſo much dutie, as my Mother ſhew'd
To you, preferring you before her Father:
So much I challenge, that I may profeſſe
Due to the Moore my Lord.
Bra. God be with you: I haue done.
Pleaſe it your Grace, on to the State Affaires;
I had rather to adopt a Child, then get it.
Come hither Moore;
I here do giue thee that with all my heart,
Which but thou haſt already, with all my heart
I would keepe from thee. For your ſake (Iewell)
I am glad at ſoule, I haue no other Child,
For thy eſcape would teach me Tirranie
To hang clogges on them. I haue done my Lord.
Duke. Let me ſpeake like your ſelfe:
And lay a Sentence,
Which as a griſe, or ſtep may helpe theſe Louers.
When remedies are paſt, the griefes are ended
By ſeeing the worſt, which late on hopes depended.
To mourne a Miſcheefe that is paſt and gon,
Is the next way to draw new miſchiefe on.
What cannot be preſern'd, when Fortune takes:
Patience, her Iniury a mock'ry makes.
The rob'd that ſmiles, ſteales ſomething from the Thiefe,
He robs himſelfe, that ſpends a bootleſſe griefe.
Bra. So let the Turke of Cyprus vs beguile,
We looſe it not ſo long as we can ſmile:
He beares the Sentence well, that nothing beares,
But the free comfort which from thence he heares.
But he beares both the Sentence, and the ſorrow,
That to pay griefe, muſt of poore Patience borrow.
Theſe Sentences, to Sugar, or to Gall,
Being ſtrong on both ſides, are Equiuocall.
But words are words, I neuer yet did heare:
That the bruized heart was pierc'd through the eares.
I humbly beſeech you proceed to th'Affaires of State.

Duke. The Turke with a moſt mighty Preparation makes for Cyprus: *Othello*, the Fortitude of the place is beſt knowne to you. And though we haue there a Subſtitute of moſt allowed ſufficiencie; yet opinion, a more ſoueraigne Miſtris of Effects, throwes a more ſafer voice on you: you muſt therefore be content to ſlubber the gloſſe of your new Fortunes, with this more ſtubborne, and boyſtrous expedition.

Othe. The Tirant Cuſtome, moſt Graue Senators,
Hath made the flinty and Steele Coach of Warre
My thrice-driuen bed of Downe. I do agnize
A Naturall and prompt Alacartie,
I finde in hardneſſe: and do vndertake
This preſent Warres againſt the *Ottamites*.
Moſt humbly therefore bending to your State,
I craue fit diſpoſition for my Wife,
Due reference of Place, and Exhibition,
With ſuch Accomodation and beſort
As leuels with her breeding.
Duke. Why at her Fathers?
Bra. I will not haue it ſo.
Othe. Nor I.
Deſ. Nor would I there recide,
To put my Father in impatient thoughts
By being in his eye. Moſt Greaious Duke,
To my vnfolding, lend your proſperous eare,
And let me finde a Charter in your voice
T'aſſiſt my ſimpleneſſe.
Duke. What would you *Deſdemona*?
Deſ. That I loue the Moore, to liue with him,
My downe-right violence, and ſtorme of Fortunes,
May

May trumpet to the world. My heart's ſubdu'd
Euen to the very quality of my Lord;
I ſaw *Othello's* viſage in his mind,
And to his Honours and his valiant parts,
Did I my ſoule and Fortunes conſecrate.
So that (deere Lords) if I be left behind
A Moth of Peace, and he go to the Warre,
The Rites for why I loue him, are bereft me:
And I a heauie interim ſhall ſupport
By his deere abſence. Let me go with him.

Othe. Let her haue your voice.
Vouch with me Heauen, I therefore beg it not
To pleaſe the pallate of my Appetite:
Nor to comply with heat the yong affects
In my defunct, and proper ſatisfaction.
But to be free, and bounteous to her minde:
And Heauen defend your good ſoules, that you thinke
I will your ſerious and great buſineſſe ſcant
When ſhe is with me. No, when light wing'd Toyes
Of feather'd *Cupid*, ſeele with wanton dulneſſe
My ſpeculatiue, and offic'd Inſtrument:
That my Diſports corrupt, and taint my buſineſſe:
Let Houſe-wiues make a Skillet of my Helme,
And all indigne, and baſe aduerſities,
Make head againſt my Eſtimation.

Duke. Be it as you ſhall priuately determine,
Either for her ſtay, or going: th'Affaire cries haſt:
And ſpeed muſt anſwer it.

Sen. You muſt away to night.

Othe. With all my heart.

Duke. At nine i'th'morning, here wee'l meete againe.
Othello, leaue ſome Officer behind
And he ſhall our Commiſſion bring to you:
And ſuch things elſe of qualitie and reſpect
As doth import you.

Othe. So pleaſe your Grace, my Ancient,
A man he is of honeſty and truſt:
To his conueyance I aſſigne my wife,
With what elſe needfull, your good Grace ſhall think
To be ſent after me.

Duke. Let it be ſo:
Good night to euery one. And Noble Signior,
If Vertue no delighted Beautie lacke,
Your Son-in-law is farre more Faire then Blacke.

Sen. Adieu braue Moore, vſe *Deſdemona* well.

Bra. Looke to her (Moore) if thou haſt eies to ſee:
She ha's deceiu'd her Father, and may thee. *Exit.*

Othe. My life vpon her faith. Honeſt *Iago*,
My *Deſdemona* muſt I leaue to thee:
I prythee let thy wife attend on her,
And bring them after in the beſt aduantage.
Come *Deſdemona*, I haue but an houre
Of Loue, of wordly matter, and direction
To ſpend with thee. We muſt obey the the time. *Exit.*

Rod. Iago.

Iago. What ſaiſt thou Noble heart?

Rod. What will I do, think'ſt thou?

Iago. Why go to bed and ſleepe.

Rod. I will incontinently drowne my ſelfe.

Iago. If thou do'ſt, I ſhall neuer loue thee after. Why thou ſilly Gentleman?

Rod. It is ſillyneſſe to liue, when to liue is torment: and then haue we a preſcription to dye, when death is our Phyſition.

Iago. Oh villanous: I haue look'd vpon the world for foure times ſeuen yeares, and ſince I could diſtinguiſh betwixt a Benefit, and an Iniurie: I neuer found man that knew how to loue himſelfe. Ere I would ſay, I would drowne my ſelfe for the loue of a Gynney Hen, I would change my Humanity with a Baboone.

Rod. What ſhould I do? I confeſſe it is my ſhame to be ſo fond, but it is not in my vertue to amend it.

Iago. Vertue? A figge, 'tis in our ſelues that we are thus, or thus. Our Bodies are our Gardens, to the which, our Wills are Gardiners. So that if we will plant Nettels, or ſowe Lettice: Set Hiſope, and weede vp Time: Supplie it with one gender of Hearbes, or diſtract it with many: either to haue it ſterrill with idleneſſe, or manured with Induſtry, why the power, and Corrigeable authoritie of this lies in our Wills. If the braine of our liues had not one Scale of Reaſon, to poize another of Senſualitie, the blood, and baſeneſſe of our Natures would conduct vs to moſt prepoſtrous Concluſions. But we haue Reaſon to coole our raging Motions, our carnall Stings, or vnbitted Luſts: whereof I take this, that you call Loue, to be a Sect, or Seyen.

Rod. It cannot be.

Iago. It is meerly a Luſt of the blood, and a permiſſion of the will. Come, be a man: drowne thy ſelfe? Drown Cats, and blind Puppies. I haue profeſt me thy Friend, and I confeſſe me knit to thy deſeruing, with Cables of perdurable toughneſſe. I could neuer better ſteed thee then now. Put Money in thy purſe: follow thou the Warres, defeate thy fauour, with an vſurp'd Beard. I ſay put Money in thy purſe. It cannot be long that *Deſdemona* ſhould continue her loue to the Moore. Put Money in thy purſe: nor he his to her. It was a violent Commencement in her, and thou ſhalt ſee an anſwerable Sequeſtration, put but Money in thy purſe. Theſe Moores are changeable in their wils: fill thy purſe with Money. The Food that to him now is as luſhious as Locuſts, ſhalbe to him ſhortly, as bitter as Coloquintida. She muſt change for youth: when ſhe is ſated with his body ſhe will find the errors of her choice. Therefore, put Money in thy purſe. If thou wilt needs damne thy ſelfe, do it a more delicate way then drowning. Make all the Money thou canſt: If Sanctimonie, and a fraile vow, betwixt an erring Barbarian, and ſuper-ſubtle Venetian be not too hard for my wits, and all the Tribe of hell, thou ſhalt enioy her: therefore make Money: a pox of drowning thy ſelfe, it is cleane out of the way. Seeke thou rather to be hang'd in Compaſſing thy ioy, then to be drown'd, and go without her.

Rodo. Wilt thou be faſt to my hopes, if I depend on the iſſue?

Iago. Thou art ſure of me: Go make Money: I haue told thee often, and I re-tell thee againe, and againe, I hate the Moore. My cauſe is hearted; thine hath no leſſe reaſon. Let vs be coniunctiue in our reuenge, againſt him. If thou canſt Cuckold him, thou doſt thy ſelfe a pleaſure, me a ſport. There are many Euents in the Wombe of Time, which wilbe deliuered. Trauerſe, go, prouide thy Money. We will haue more of this to morrow. Adieu.

Rod. Where ſhall we meete i'th'morning?

Iago. At my Lodging.

Rod. Ile be with thee betimes.

Iago. Go too, farewell. Do you heare *Rodorigo*?

Rod. Ile ſell all my Land. *Exit.*

Iago. Thus do I euer make my Foole, my purſe:
For I mine owne gain'd knowledge ſhould prophane
If I would time expend with ſuch Snpe,

But

But for my Sport, and Profit: I hate the Moore,
And it is thought abroad, that 'twixt my ſheets
She ha's done my Office. I know not if't be true,
But I, for meere ſuſpition in that kinde,
Will do, as if for Surety. He holds me well,
The better ſhall my purpoſe worke on him:
Caſſio's a proper man: Let me ſee now,
To get his Place, and to plume vp my will
In double Knauery. How? How? Let's ſee.
After ſome time, to abuſe *Othello's* eares,
That he is too familiar with his wife:
He hath a perſon, and a ſmooth diſpoſe
To be ſuſpected: fram'd to make women falſe.
The Moore is of a free, and open Nature,
That thinkes men honeſt, that but ſeeme to be ſo,
And will as tenderly be lead by'th'Noſe
As Aſſes are:
I haue't: it is engendred: Hell, and Night,
Muſt bring this monſtrous Birth, to the worlds light.

Actus Secundus. Scena Prima.

Enter Montano, and two Gentlemen.

Mon. What from the Cape, can you diſcerne at Sea?
1 *Gent.* Nothing at all, it is a high wrought Flood:
I cannot 'twixt the Heauen, and the Maine,
Deſcry a Saile.
Mon. Me thinks, the wind hath ſpoke aloud at Land,
A fuller blaſt ne're ſhooke our Battlements:
If it hath ruffiand ſo vpon the Sea,
What ribbes of Oake, when Mountaines melt on them,
Can hold the Mortiſe. What ſhall we heare of this?
2 A Segregation of the Turkiſh Fleet:
For do but ſtand vpon the Foaming Shore,
The chidden Billow ſeemes to pelt the Clowds,
The winde-ſhak'd-Surge, with high & monſtrous Maine
Seemes to caſt water on the burning Beare,
And quench the Guards of th'euer-fixed Pole:
I neuer did like moleſtation view
On the enchafed Flood.
Mon. If that the Turkiſh Fleete
Be not enſhelter'd, and embay'd, they are drown'd,
It is impoſſible to beare it out.

Enter a Gentleman.

3 Newes Laddes: our warres are done:
The deſperate Tempeſt hath ſo bang'd the Turkes,
That their deſignement halts. A Noble ſhip of Venice,
Hath ſeene a greeuous wracke and ſufferance
On moſt part of their Fleet.
Mon. How? Is this true?
3 The Ship is heere put in: A *Verameſſa, Michael Caſſio*
Lieutenant to the warlike Moore, *Othello*,
Is come on Shore: the Moore himſelfe at Sea,
And is in full Commiſſion heere for Cyprus.
Mon. I am glad on't:
'Tis a worthy Gouernour.
3 But this ſame *Caſſio*, though he ſpeake of comfort,
Touching the Turkiſh loſſe, yet he lookes ſadly,
And praye the Moore be ſafe; for they were parted
With fowle and violent Tempeſt.
Mon. Pray Heauens he be:
For I haue ſeru'd him, and the man commands
Like a full Soldier. Let's to the Sea-ſide (hoa)
As well to ſee the Veſſell that's come in,
As to throw-out our eyes for braue *Othello*,
Euen till we make the Maine, and th'Eriall blew,
An indiſtinct regard.
Gent. Come, let's do ſo;
For euery Minute is expectancie
Of more Arriuancie.

Enter Caſſio.

Caſſi. Thankes you, the valiant of the warlike Iſle,
That ſo approoue the Moore: Oh let the Heauens
Giue him defence againſt the Elements,
For I haue loſt him on a dangerous Sea.
Mon. Is he well ſhip'd?
Caſſio. His Barke is ſtoutly Timber'd, and his Pylot
Of verie expert, and approu'd Allowance;
Therefore my hope's (not ſurfetted to death)
Stand in bold Cure.
Within. A Saile, a Saile, a Saile.
Caſſio. What noiſe?
Gent. The Towne is empty; on the brow o'th'Sea
Stand rankes of People, and they cry, a Saile.
Caſſio. My hopes do ſhape him for the Gouernor.
Gent. They do diſcharge their Shot of Courteſie,
Our Friends, at leaſt.
Caſſio. I pray you Sir, go forth,
And giue vs truth who 'tis that is arriu'd.
Gent. I ſhall. *Exit.*
Mon. But good Lieutenant, is your Generall wiu'd?
Caſſio. Moſt fortunately: he hath atchieu'd a Maid
That paragons deſcription, and wilde Fame:
One that excels the quirkes of Blazoning pens,
And in th'eſſentiall Veſture of Creation,
Do's tyre the Ingeniuer.
Enter Gentleman.
How now? Who ha's put in?
Gent. 'Tis one *Iago*, Auncient to the Generall.
Caſſio. Ha's had moſt fauourable, and happie ſpeed:
Tempeſts themſelues, high Seas, and howling windes,
The gutter'd-Rockes, and Congregated Sands,
Traitors enſteep'd, to enclogge the guiltleſſe Keele,
As hauing ſence of Beautie, do omit
Their mortall Natures, letting go ſafely by
The Diuine *Deſdemona*.
Mon. What is ſhe?
Caſſio. She that I ſpake of:
Our great Captains Captaine,
Left in the conduct of the bold *Iago*,
Whoſe footing heere anticipates our thoughts,
A Senights ſpeed. Great Ioue, *Othello* guard,
And ſwell his Saile with thine owne powrefull breath,
That he may bleſſe this Bay with his tall Ship,
Make loues quicke pants in *Deſdemonaes* Armes,
Giue renew'd fire to our extincted Spirits.

Enter Deſdemona, Iago, Rodorigo, and Æmilia.

Oh behold,
The Riches of the Ship is come on ſhore:
You men of Cyprus, let her haue your knees.
Haile to thee Ladie: and the grace of Heauen,
Before, behinde thee, and on euery hand
Enwheele thee round.
Def. I thanke you, Valiant *Caſſio*,
What tydings can you tell of my Lord?
Caſſio.

Caſ. He is not yet arriu'd, nor know I ought
But that he's well, and will be ſhortly heere.
Deſ. Oh, but I feare:
How loſt you company?
Caſſio. The great Contention of Sea, and Skies
Parted our fellowſhip. But hearke, a Saile.
Within. A Saile, a Saile.
Gent. They giue this greeting to the Cittadell:
This likewiſe is a Friend.
Caſſio. See for the Newes:
Good Ancient, you are welcome. Welcome Miſtris:
Let it not gaule your patience (good *Iago*)
That I extend my Manners. 'Tis my breeding,
That giues me this bold ſhew of Curteſie.
Iago. Sir, would ſhe giue you ſomuch of her lippes,
As of her tongue ſhe oft beſtowes on me,
You would haue enough.
Deſ. Alas: ſhe ha's no ſpeech.
Iago. Infaith too much:
I finde it ſtill, when I haue leaue to ſleepe.
Marry before your Ladyſhip, I grant,
She puts het tongue a little in her heart,
And chides with thinking.
Æmil. You haue little cauſe to ſay ſo.
Iago. Come on, come on: you are Pictures out of doore: Bells in your Parlours: Wilde-Cats in your Kitchens: Saints in your Iniuries: Diuels being offended: Players in your Huſwiferie, and Huſwiues in your Beds.
Deſ. Oh, fie vpon thee, Slanderer.
Iago. Nay, it is true: or elſe I am a Turke,
You riſe to play, and go to bed to worke.
Æmil. You ſhall not write my praiſe.
Iago. No, let me not.
Deſde. What would'ſt write of me, if thou ſhould'ſt praiſe me?
Iago. Oh, gentle Lady, do not put me too't,
For I am nothing, if not Criticall.
Deſ. Come on, aſſay.
There's one gone to the Harbour?
Iago. I Madam.
Deſ. I am not merry: but I do beguile
The thing I am, by ſeeming otherwiſe.
Come, how would'ſt thou praiſe me?
Iago. I am about it, but indeed my inuention comes from my pate, as Birdlyme do's from Freeze, it pluckes out Braines and all. But my Muſe labours, and thus ſhe is deliuer'd.
If ſhe be faire, and wiſe: faireneſſe and wit,
The ones for vſe, the other vſeth it.
Deſ. Well prais'd:
How if ſhe be Blacke and Witty?
Iago. *If ſhe be blacke, and thereto haue a wit,*
She'le find a white, that ſhall her blackneſſe fit.
Deſ. Worſe, and worſe.
Æmil. How if Faire, and Fooliſh?
Iago. *She neuer yet was fooliſh that was faire,*
For euen her folly helpt her to an heire.
Deſde. Theſe are old fond Paradoxes, to make Fooles laugh i'th'Alehouſe. What miſerable praiſe haſt thou for her that's Foule, and Fooliſh.
Iago. *There's none ſo foule and fooliſh thereunto,*
But do's foule prankes, which faire, and wiſe-ones do.
Deſde. Oh heauy ignorance: thou praiſeſt the worſt beſt. But what praiſe could'ſt thou beſtow on a deſeruing woman indeed? One, that in the authorithy of her merit, did iuſtly put on the vouch of very malice it ſelfe.

Iago. *She that was euer faire, and neuer proud,*
Had Tongue at will, and yet was neuer loud:
Neuer lackt Gold, and yet went neuer gay,
Fled from her wiſh, and yet ſaid now I may.
She that being angred, her reuenge being nie,
Bad her wrong ſtay, and her diſpleaſure flie:
She that in wiſedome neuer was ſo fraile,
To change the Cods-head for the Salmons taile:
She that could thinke, and neu'r diſcloſe her mind,
See Suiters following, and not looke behind:
She was a wight, (if euer ſuch wightes were)
Deſ. To do what?
Iago. *To ſuckle Fooles, and chronicle ſmall Beere.*

Deſde. Oh moſt lame and impotent concluſion. Do not learne of him *Æmillia*, though he be thy husband. How ſay you (*Caſſio*) is he not a moſt prophane, and liberall Counſailor?
Caſſio. He ſpeakes home (Madam) you may rellish him more in the Souldier, then in the Scholler.
Iago. He takes her by the palme: I, well ſaid, whiſper. With as little a web as this, will I enſnare as great a Fly as *Caſſio*. I ſmile vpon her, do: I will giue thee in thine owne Courtſhip. You ſay true, 'tis ſo indeed. If ſuch tricks as theſe ſtrip you out of your Lieutenantrie, it had beene better you had not kiſs'd your three fingers ſo oft, which now againe you are moſt apt to play the Sir, in. Very good: well kiſs'd, and excellent Curtſie: tis ſo indeed. Yet againe, your fingers to your lippes? Would they were Cluſter-pipes for your ſake.
The Moore I know his Trumpet.
Caſſio 'Tis truely ſo.
Deſ. Let's meete him, and recieue him.
Caſſio. Loe, where he comes.

Enter Othello, and Attendants.

Oth O, my faire Warriour.
Deſ. My deere *Othello.*
Othe. It giues me wonder great, as my content
To ſee you heere before me.
Oh my Soules Ioy:
If after euery Tempeſt, come ſuch Calmes,
May the windes blow, till they haue waken'd death:
And let the labouring Barke climbe hills of Seas
Olympus high: and duck againe as low,
As hell's from Heauen. If it were now to dye,
'Twere now to be moſt happy. For I feare,
My Soule hath her content ſo abſolute,
That not another comfort like to this,
Succeedes in vnknowne Fate.
Deſ. The Heauens forbid
But that our Loues
And Comforts ſhould encreaſe
Euen as our dayes do grow.
Othe. Amen to that (ſweet Powers)
I cannot ſpeake enough of this content,
It ſtoppes me heere: it is too much of ioy.
And this and this the greateſt diſcords be
That ere our hearts ſhall make.
Iago. Oh you are well tun'd now: But Ile ſet downe the peggs that make this Muſicke, as honeſt as I am.

t t *Othe.*

Othe. Come: let vs to the Castle.
Newes (Friends) our Warres are done:
The Turkes are drown'd.
How do's my old Acquaintance of this Isle?
(Hony) you shall be well desir'd in Cyprus,
I haue found great loue among'st them. Oh my Sweet,
I prattle out of fashion, and I doate
In mine owne comforts. I prythee, good *Iago*,
Go to the Bay, and disimbarke my Coffers:
Bring thou the Master to the Cittadell,
He is a good one, and his worthynesse
Do's challenge much respect. Come *Desdemona*,
Once more well met at Cyprus.

Exit Othello and Desdemona.

Iago. Do thou meet me presently at the Harbour. Come thither, if thou be'st Valiant, (as they say base men being in Loue, haue then a Nobilitie in their Natures, more then is natiue to them) list-me; the Lieutenant to night watches on the Court of Guard. First, I must tell thee this: *Desdemona*, is directly in loue with him.

Rod. With him? Why, 'tis not possible.

Iago. Lay thy finger thus: and let thy soule be instructed. Marke me with what violence she first lou'd the Moore, but for bragging, and telling her fantasticall lies. To loue him still for prating, let not thy discreet heart thinke it. Her eye must be fed. And what delight shall she haue to looke on the diuell? When the Blood is made dull with the Act of Sport, there should be a game to enflame it, and to giue Satiety a fresh appetite. Louelinesse in fauour, simpathy in yeares, Manners, and Beauties: all which the Moore is defectiue in. Now for want of these requir'd Conueniences, her delicate tendernesse wil finde it selfe abus'd, begin to heaue the, gorge, disrellish and abhorre the Moore, very Nature wil instruct her in it, and compell her to some second choice. Now Sir, this granted (as it is a most pregnant and vnforc'd position) who stands so eminent in the degree of this Forune, as *Cassio* do's: a knaue very voluble: no further conscionable, then in putting on the meere forme of Ciuill, and Humaine seeming, for the better compasse of his salt, and most hidden loose Affection? Why none, why none: A slipper, and subtle knaue, a finder of occasion: that he's an eye can stampe, and counterfeit Aduantages, though true Aduantage neuer present it selfe. A diuelish knaue: besides, the knaue is handsome, young: and hath all those requisites in him, that folly and greene mindes looke after. A pestilent compleat knaue, and the woman hath found him already.

Rodo. I cannot beleeue that in her, she's full of most bless'd condition.

Iago. Bless'd figges-end. The Wine she drinkes is made of grapes. If shee had beene bless'd, shee would neuer haue lou'd the Moore: Bless'd pudding. Didst thou not see her paddle with the palme of his hand? Didst not marke that?

Rod. Yes, that I did: but that was but curtesie.

Iago. Leacherie by this hand: an Index, and obscure prologue to the History of Lust and foule Thoughts. They met so neere with their lippes, that their breathes embrac'd together. Villanous thoughts *Rodorigo*, when these mutabilities so marshall the way, hard at hand comes the Master, and maine exercise, th'incorporate conclusion: Pish. But Sir, be you rul'd by me. I haue brought you from Venice. Watch you to night: for the Command, Ile lay't vpon you. *Cassio* knowes you not: Ile not be farre from you. Do you finde some occasion to anger *Cassio*, either by speaking too loud, or tainting his discipline, or from what other course you please, which the time shall more fauorably minister.

Rod. Well.

Iago. Sir, he's rash, and very sodaine in Choller: and happely may strike at you, prouoke him that he may: for euen out of that will I cause these of Cyprus to Mutiny. Whose qualification shall come into no true taste againe, but by the displanting of *Cassio*. So shall you haue a shorter iourney to your desires, by the meanes I shall then haue to preferre them. And the impediment most profitably remoued, without the which there were no expectation of our prosperitie.

Rodo. I will do this, if you can bring it to any opportunity.

Iago. I warrant thee. Meete me by and by at the Cittadell. I must fetch his Necessaries a Shore. Farewell.

Rodo. Adieu. *Exit.*

Iago. That *Cassio* loues her, I do well beleeu't:
That she loues him, 'tis apt, and of great Credite.
The Moore (how beit that I endure him not)
Is of a constant, louing Noble Nature,
And I dare thinke, he'le proue to *Desdemona*
A most deere husband. Now I do loue her too,
Not out of absolute Lust, (though peraduenture
I stand accomptant for as great a sin)
But partely led to dyet my Reuenge,
For that I do suspect the lustie Moore
Hath leap'd into my Seate. The thought whereof,
Doth (like a poysonous Minerall) gnaw my Inwardes:
And nothing can, or shall content my Soule
Till I am euen'd with him, wife, for wift.
Or fayling so, yet that I put the Moore,
At least into a Ielouzie so strong
That iudgement cannot cure. Which thing to do,
If this poore Trash of Venice, whom I trace
For his quicke hunting, stand the putting on,
Ile haue our *Michael Cassio* on the hip,
Abuse him to the Moore, in the right garbe
(For I feare *Cassio* with my Night-Cape too)
Make the Moore thanke me, loue me, and reward me,
For making him egregiously an Asse,
And practising vpon his peace, and quiet,
Euen to madnesse. 'Tis heere: but yet confus'd,
Knaueries plaine face, is neuer seene, till vs'd. *Exit.*

Scena Secunda.

Enter Othello's, Herald with a Proclamation.

Herald. It is *Othello's* pleasure, our Noble and Valiant Generall. That vpon certaine tydings now arriu'd, importing the meere perdition of the Turkish Fleete: euery man put himselfe into Triumph. Some to daunce, some to make Bonfires, each man, to what Sport and Reuels his addition leads him. For besides these beneficiall Newes, it is the Celebration of his Nuptiall. So much was his pleasure should be proclaimed All offices are open, & there is full libertie of Feasting from this pre-

present houre of fiue, till the Bell haue told eleuen. Blesse the Isle of Cyprus, and our Noble Generall *Othello*. *Exit.*

Enter Othello, Desdemona, Cassio, and Attendants.

Othe. Good *Michael*, looke you to the guard to night.
Let's teach our selues that Honourable stop,
Not to out-sport discretion.

Cas. *Iago*, hath direction what to do.
But notwithstanding with my personall eye
Will I looke to't.

Othe. *Iago*, is most honest:
Michael, goodnight. To morrow with your earliest,
Let me haue speech with you. Come my deere Loue,
The purchase made, the fruites are to ensue,
That profit's yet to come 'tweene me, and you.
Goodnight.

Enter Iago.

Cas. Welcome *Iago*: we must to the Watch.

Iago. Not this houre Lieutenant: 'tis not yet ten o'th'clocke. Our Generall cast vs thus earely for the loue of his *Desdemona*: Who, let vs not therefore blame; he hath not yet made wanton the night with her: and she is sport for *Ioue*.

Cas. She's a most exquisite Lady.

Iago. And Ile warrant her, full of Game.

Cas. Indeed shes a most fresh and delicate creature.

Iago. What an eye she ha's?
Methinkes it sounds a parley to prouocation.

Cas. An inuiting eye:
And yet me thinkes right modest.

Iago. And when she speakes,
Is it not an Alarum to Loue?

Cas. She is indeed perfection.

Iago. Well: happinesse to their Sheetes. Come Lieutenant, I haue a stope of Wine, and neere without are a brace of Cyprus Gallants, that would faine haue a measure to the health of blacke *Othello*.

Cas. Not to night, good *Iago*, I haue very poore, and vnhappie Braines for drinking. I could well wish Curtesie would inuent some other Custome of entertainment.

Iago. Oh, they are our Friends: but one Cup, Ile drinke for you.

Cassio. I haue drunke but one Cup to night, and that was craftily qualified too: and behold what inouation it makes heere. I am infortunate in the infirmity, and dare not taske my weakenesse with any more.

Iago. What man? 'Tis a night of Reuels, the Gallants desire it.

Cas. Where are they?

Iago. Heere, at the doore: I pray you call them in.

Cas. Ile do't, but it dislikes me. *Exit.*

Iago. If I can fasten but one Cup vpon him
With that which he hath drunke to night alreadie,
He'l be as full of Quarrell, and offence
As my yong Mistris dogge.
Now my sicke Foole *Rodorigo*,
Whom Loue hath turn'd almost the wrong side out,
To *Desdemona* hath to night Carrows'd.
Potations, pottle-deepe; and he's to watch.
Three else of Cyprus, Noble swelling Spirites,
(That hold their Honours in a wary distance,
The very Elements of this Warrelike Isle)
Haue I to night fluster'd with flowing Cups,
And they Watch too.
Now 'mongst this Flocke of drunkards
Am I put to our *Cassio* in some Action
That may offend the Isle. But here they come.

Enter Cassio, Montano, and Gentlemen.

If Consequence do but approue my dreame,
My Boate sailes freely, both with winde and Streame.

Cas. 'Fore heauen, they haue giuen me a rowse already.

Mon. Good-faith a litle one: not past a pint, as I am a Souldier.

Iago. Some Wine hoa.
And let me the Cannakin clinke, clinke:
And let me the Cannakin clinke.
A Souldiers a man: Oh, mans life's but a span,
Why then let a Souldier drinke.
Some Wine Boyes.

Cas. 'Fore Heauen: an excellent Song.

Iago. I learn'd it in England: where indeed they are most potent in Potting. Your Dane, your Germaine, and your swag-belly'd Hollander, (drinke hoa) are nothing to your English.

Cassio. Is your Englishmen so exquisite in his drinking?

Iago. Why, he drinkes you with facillitie, your Dane dead drunke. He sweates not to ouerthrow your Almaine. He giues your Hollander a vomit, ere the next Pottle can be fill'd.

Cas. To the health of our Generall.

Mon. I am for it Lieutenant: and Ile do you Iustice.

Iago Oh sweet England.
King Stephen was and-a worthy Peere,
His Breeches cost him but a Crowne,
He held them Six pence all to deere,
With that he cal'd the Tailor Lowne:
He was a wight of high Renowne,
And thou art but of low degree:
'Tis Pride that pulls the Country downe,
And take thy awl'd Cloake about thee.
Some Wine hoa.

Cassio. Why this is a more exquisite Song then the other.

Iago. Will you heare't againe?

Cas. No: for I hold him to be vnworthy of his Place, that do's those things. Well: heau'ns aboue all: and there be soules must be saued, and there be soules must not be saued.

Iago. It's true, good Lieutenant.

Cas. For mine owne part, no offence to the Generall, nor any man of qualitie: I hope to be saued.

Iago. And so do I too Lieutenant.

Cassio. I: (but by your leaue) not before me. The Lieutenant is to be saued before the Ancient. Let's haue no more of this: let's to our Affaires. Forgiue vs our sinnes: Gentlemen let's looke to our businesse. Do not thinke Gentlemen, I am drunke: this is my Ancient, this is my right hand, and this is my left. I am not drunke now: I can stand well enough, and I speake well enough.

Gent. Excellent well.

Cas. Why very well then: you must not thinke then, that I am drunke. *Exit.*

Monta. To th'Platforme (Masters) come, let's set the Watch.

Iago. You see this Fellow, that is gone before,
He's a Souldier, fit to stand by *Cæsar*,
And giue direction. And do but see his vice,
'Tis to his vertue, a iust Equinox,

t t 3 The

The one as long as th'other. 'Tis pittie of him:
I feare the trust *Othello* puts him in,
On some odde time of his infirmitie
Will shake this Island.
Mont. But is he often thus?
Iago. 'Tis euermore his prologue to his sleepe,
He'le watch the Horologe a double Set,
If Drinke rocke not his Cradle.
Mont. It were well
The Generall were put in mind of it:
Perhaps he sees it not, or his good nature
Prizes the vertue that appeares in *Cassio*,
And lookes not on his euills: is not this true?
Enter Rodorigo.
Iago. How now *Rodorigo*?
I pray you after the Lieutenant, go.
Mon. And 'tis great pitty, that the Noble Moore
Should hazard such a Place, as his owne Second
With one of an ingraft Infirmitie,
It were an honest Action, to say so
To the Moore.
Iago. Not I, for this faire Island,
I do loue *Cassio* well: and would do much
To cure him of this euill. But hearke, what noise?
Enter Cassio pursuing Rodorigo.
Cas. You Rogue: you Rascall.
Mon. What's the matter Lieutenant?
Cas. A Knaue teach me my dutie? Ile beate the
Knaue into a Twiggen-Bottle.
Rod. Beate me?
Cas. Dost thou prate, Rogue?
Mon. Nay, good Lieutenant:
I pray you Sir, hold your hand.
Cassio Let me go (Sir)
Or Ile knocke you o're the Mazard.
Mon. Come, come: you're drunke.
Cassio. Drunke?
Iago. Away I say: go out and cry a Mutinie.
Nay good Lieutenant. Alas Gentlemen:
Helpe hoa. Lieutenant. Sir *Montano*:
Helpe Masters. Heere's a goodly Watch indeed.
Who's that which rings the Bell: Diablo, hoa:
The Towne will rise. Fie, fie Lieutenant,
You'le be asham'd for euer.

Enter Othello, and Attendants.
Othe. What is the matter heere?
Mon. I bleed still, I am hurt to th'death. He dies.
Othe. Hold for your liues.
Iag. Hold hoa: Lieutenant, Sir *Montano*, Gentlemen:
Haue you forgot all place of sense and dutie?
Hold. The Generall speaks to you: hold for shame.
Oth. Why how now hoa? From whence ariseth this?
Are we turn'd Turkes? and to our selues do that
Which Heauen hath forbid the *Ottamittes*.
For Christian shame, put by this barbarous Brawle:
He that stirs next, to carue for his owne rage,
Holds his soule light: He dies vpon his Motion.
Silence that dreadfull Bell, it frights the Isle,
From her propriety. What is the matter, Masters?
Honest *Iago*, that lookes dead with greeuing,
Speake: who began this? On thy loue I charge thee?
Iago. I do not know: Friends all, but now, euen now.
In Quarter, and in termes like Bride, and Groome
Deuesting them for Bed: and then, but now:
(As if some Planet had vnwitted men)
Swords out, and tilting one at others breastes,
In opposition bloody. I cannot speake
Any begining to this peeuish oddes.
And would, in Action glorious, I had lost
Those legges, that brought me to a part of it.
Othe. How comes it (*Michaell*) you are thus forgot?
Cas. I pray you pardon me, I cannot speake.
Othe. Worthy *Montano*, you were wont to be ciuill:
The grauitie, and stillnesse of your youth
The world hath noted. And your name is great
In mouthes of wisest Censure. What's the matter
That you vnlace your reputation thus,
And spend your rich opinion, for the name
Of a night-brawler? Giue me answer to it.
Mon. Worthy *Othello*, I am hurt to danger,
Your Officer *Iago*, can informe you.
While I spare speech which something now offends me.
Of all that I do know, nor know I ought
By me, that's said, or done amisse this night,
Vnlesse selfe-charitie be sometimes a vice,
And to defend our selues, it be a sinne
When violence assailes vs.
Othe. Now by Heauen,
My blood begins my safer Guides to rule,
And passion (hauing my best iudgement collied)
Assaies to leade the way. If I once stir,
Or do but lift this Arme, the best of you
Shall sinke in my rebuke. Giue me to know
How this foule Rout began: Who set it on,
And he that is approu'd in this offence,
Though he had twinn'd with me, both at a birth,
Shall loose me. What in a Towne of warre,
Yet wilde, the peoples hearts brim-full of feare,
To Manage priuate, and domesticke Quarrell?
In night, and on the Court and Guard of safetie?
'Tis monstrous: *Iago*, who began't?
Mon. If partially Affin'd, or league in office,
Thou dost deliuer more, or lesse then Truth,
Thou art no Souldier.
Iago. Touch me not so neere,
I had rather haue this tongue cut from my mouth,
Then it should do offence to *Michaell Cassio*.
Yet I perswade my selfe, to speake the truth
Shall nothing wrong him. This it is Generall:
Montano and my selfe being in speech,
There comes a Fellow, crying out for helpe,
And *Cassio* following him with determin'd Sword
To execute vpon him. Sir, this Gentleman,
Steppes in to *Cassio*, and entreats his pause:
My selfe, the crying Fellow did pursue,
Least by his clamour (as it so fell out)
The Towne might fall in fright. He, (swift of foote)
Out-ran my purpose: and I return'd then rather
For that I heard the clinke, and fall of Swords,
And *Cassio* high in oath: Which till to night
I nere might say before. When I came backe
(For this was briefe) I found them close together
At blow, and thrust, euen as againe they were
When you your selfe did part them.
More of this matter cannot I report.
But Men are Men: The best sometimes forget,
Though *Cassio* did some little wrong to him,
As men in rage strike those that wish them best,
Yet surely *Cassio* I beleeue receiu'd
From him that fled, some strange Indignitie,
Which patience could not passe.

Othe. I know *Iago*
Thy honestie, and loue doth mince this matter,
Making it light to *Cassio*: *Cassio*, I loue thee,
But neuer more be Officer of mine.

Enter Desdemona attended.

Looke if my gentle Loue be not rais'd vp:
Ile make thee an example.
Des. What is the matter (Deere?)
Othe. All's well, Sweeting:
Come away to bed. Sir for your hurts,
My selfe will be your Surgeon. Lead him off:
Iago, looke with care about the Towne,
And silence those whom this vil'd brawle distracted.
Come *Desdemona*, 'tis the Soldiers life,
To haue their Balmy slumbers wak'd with strife. *Exit.*

Iago. What are you hurt Lieutenant?

Cas. I, past all Surgery.

Iago. Marry Heauen forbid.

Cas. Reputation, Reputation, Reputation: Oh I haue lost my Reputation. I haue lost the immortall part of myselfe, and what remaines is bestiall. My Reputation, *Iago*, my Reputation.

Iago. As I am an honest man I had thought you had receiued some bodily wound; there is more sence in that then in Reputation. Reputation is an idle, and most false imposition; oft got without merit, aud lost without deseruing. You haue lost no Reputation at all, vnlesse you repute your selfe such a looser. What man, there are more wayes to recouer the Generall againe. You are but now cast in his moode, (a punishment more in policie, then in malice) euen so as one would beate his offencelesse dogge, to affright an Imperious Lyon. Sue to him againe, and he's yours.

Cas. I will rather sue to be despis'd, then to deceiue so good a Commander, with so slight, so drunken, and so indiscreet an Officer. Drunke? And speake Parrat? And squabble? Swagger? Sweare? And discourse Fustian with ones owne shadow? Oh thou inuisible spirit of Wine, if thou hast no name to be knowne by, let vs call thee Diuell.

Iago. What was he that you follow'd with your Sword? What had he done to you?

Cas. I know not.

Iago. Is't possible?

Cas. I remember a masse of things, but nothing distinctly: a Quarrell, but nothing wherefore. Oh, that men should put an Enemie in their mouthes, to steale away their Braines? that we should with ioy, pleasance, reuell and applause, transforme our selues into Beasts.

Iago. Why? But you are now well enough: how came you thus recouered?

Cas. It hath pleas'd the diuell drunkennesse, to giue place to the diuell wrath, one vnperfectnesse, shewes me another to make me frankly despise my selfe.

Iago. Come, you are too seuere a Moraller. As the Time, the Place, & the Condition of this Country stands I could hartily wish this had not befalne: but since it is, as it is, mend it for your owne good.

Cas. I will aske him for my Place againe, he shall tell me, I am a drunkard: had I as many mouthes as *Hydra*, such an answer would stop them all. To be now a sensible man, by and by a Foole, and presently a Beast. Oh strange! Euery inordinate cup is vnbless'd, and the Ingredient is a diuell.

Iago. Come, come: good wine, is a good famillar Creature, if it be well vs'd: exclaime no more against it. And good Lieutenant, I thinke, you thinke I loue you.

Cassio. I haue well approued it, Sir. I drunke?

Iago. You, or any man liuing, may be drunke at a time man. I tell you what you shall do: Our General's Wife, is now the Generall. I may say so, in this respect, for that he hath deuoted, and giuen vp himselfe to the Contemplation, marke: and deuotement of her parts and Graces. Confesse your selfe freely to her: Importune her helpe to put you in your place againe. She is of so free, so kinde, so apt, so blessed a disposition, she holds it a vice in her goodnesse, not to do more then she is requested. This broken ioynt betweene you, and her husband, entreat her to splinter. And my Fortunes against any lay worth naming, this cracke of your Loue, shall grow stonger, then it was before.

Cassio. You aduise me well.

Iago. I protest in the sinceritie of Loue, and honest kindnesse.

Cassio. I thinke it freely: and betimes in the morning, I will beseech the vertuous *Desdemona* to vndertake for me: I am desperate of my Fortunes if they check me.

Iago. You are in the right: good night Lieutenant, I must to the Watch.

Cassio. Good night, honest *Iago.*

Exit Cassio.

Iago. And what's he then,
That saies I play the Villaine?
When this aduise is free I giue, and honest,
Proball to thinking, and indeed the course
To win the Moore againe.
For 'tis most easie
Th'inclyning *Desdemona* to subdue
In any honest Suite. She's fram'd as fruitefull
As the free Elements. And then for her
To win the Moore, were to renownce his Baptisme,
All Seales, and Simbols of redeemed sin:
His Soule is so enfetter'd to her Loue,
That she may make, vnmake, do what she list,
Euen as her Appetite shall play the God,
With his weake Function. How am I then a Villaine,
To Counsell *Cassio* to this paralell course,
Directly to his good? Diuinitie of hell,
When diuels will the blackest sinnes put on,
They do suggest at first with heauenly shewes,
As I do now. For whiles this honest Foole
Plies *Desdemona*, to repaire his Fortune,
And she for him, pleades strongly to the Moore,
Ile powre this pestilence into his eare:
That she repeales him, for her bodies Lust'
And by how much she striues to do him good,
She shall vndo her Credite with the Moore.
So will I turne her vertue into pitch,
And out of her owne goodnesse make the Net,
That shall en-mash them all.
How now *Rodorigo*?

Enter Rodorigo.

Rodorigo. I do follow heere in the Chace, not like a Hound that hunts, but one that filles vp the Crie. My Money is almost spent; I haue bin to night exceedingly well Cudgell'd: And I thinke the issue

t t 3 will

will bee, I ſhall haue ſo much experience for my paines; And ſo, with no money at all, and a little more Wit, returne againe to Venice.

Iago. How poore are they that haue not Patience?
What wound did euer heale but by degrees?
Thou know'ſt we worke by Wit, and not by Witchcraft
And Wit depends on dilatory time:
Do'ſt not go well? *Caſſio* hath beaten thee,
And thou by that ſmall hurt hath caſheer'd *Caſſio:*
Though other things grow faire againſt the Sun,
Yet Fruites that bloſſome firſt, will firſt be ripe:
Content thy ſelfe, a-while. Introth 'tis Morning;
Pleaſure, and Action, make the houres ſeeme ſhort.
Retire thee, go where thou art Billited:
Away, I ſay, thou ſhalt know more heereafter:
Nay get thee gone. *Exit Rodorigo.*
Two things are to be done:
My Wife muſt moue for *Caſſio* to her Miſtris:
Ile ſet her on my ſelfe, a while, to draw the Moor apart,
And bring him iumpe, when he may *Caſſio* finde
Soliciting his wife: I, that's the way:
Dull not Deuice, by coldneſſe, and delay. *Exit.*

Actus Tertius. Scena Prima.

Enter Caſſio, Muſitians, and Clowne.

Caſſio. Maſters, play heere, I wil content your paines, Something that's brieſe: and bid, goodmorrow General.

Clo. Why Maſters, haue your Inſtruments bin in Naples, that they ſpeake i'th' Noſe thus?

Muſ. How Sir? how?

Clo. Are theſe I pray you, winde Inſtruments?

Muſ. I marry are they ſir.

Clo. Oh, thereby hangs a tale.

Muſ. Whereby hangs a tale, ſir?

Clow. Marry ſir, by many a winde Inſtrument that I know. But Maſters, heere's money for you: and the Generall ſo likes your Muſick, that he deſires you for loues ſake to make no more noiſe with it.

Muſ. Well Sir, we will not.

Clo. If you haue any Muſicke that may not be heard, too't againe. But (as they ſay) to heare Muſicke, the Generall do's not greatly care.

Muſ. We haue none ſuch, ſir.

Clow. Then put vp your Pipes in your bagge, for Ile away. Go, vaniſh into ayre, away. *Exit Mu.*

Caſſio Doſt thou heare me, mine honeſt Friend?

Clo. No, I heare not your honeſt Friend: I heare you.

Caſſio. Prythee keepe vp thy Quillets, ther's a poore peece of Gold for thee: if the Gentlewoman that attends the Generall be ſtirring, tell her, there's one *Caſſio* entreats her a little fauour of Speech. Wilt thou do this?

Clo. She is ſtirring ſir: if ſhe will ſtirre hither, I ſhall ſeeme to notifie vnto her. *Exit Clo.*

Enter Iago.

In happy time, *Iago.*

Iago You haue not bin a-bed then?

Caſſio. Why no: the day had broke before we parted.
I haue made bold (*Iago*) to ſend in to your wife:
My ſuite to her is, that ſhe will to vertuous *Deſdemona*
Procure me ſome acceſſe.

Iago. Ile ſend her to you preſently:
And Ile deuiſe a meane to draw the Moore
Out of the way, that your conuerſe and buſineſſe
May be more free. *Exit.*

Caſſio. I humbly thanke you for't. I neuer knew
A Florentine more kinde, and honeſt.

Enter Æmilia.

Æmil. Goodmorrow (good Lieutenant) I am ſorrie
For your diſpleaſure: but all will ſure be well.
The Generall and his wife are talking of it,
And ſhe ſpeakes for you ſtoutly. The Moore replies,
That he you hurt is of great Fame in Cyprus,
And great Affinitie: and that in wholſome Wiſedome
He might not but refuſe you. But he proteſts he loues you
And needs no other Suitor, but his likings
To bring you in againe.

Caſſio. Yet I beſeech you,
If you thinke fit, or that it may be done,
Giue me aduantage of ſome breefe Diſcourſe
With *Deſdemon* alone.

Æmil. Pray you come in:
I will beſtow you where you ſhall haue time
To ſpeake your boſome freely.

Caſſio. I am much bound to you.

Scœna Secunda.

Enter Othello, Iago, and Gentlemen.

Othe. Theſe Letters giue (*Iago*) to the Pylot,
And by him do my duties to the Senate:
That done, I will be walking on the Workes,
Repaire there to mee.

Iago. Well, my good Lord, Ile doo't.

Oth. This Fortification (Gentlemen) ſhall we ſee't?

Gent. Well waite vpon your Lordſhip. *Exeunt*

Scœna Tertia.

Enter Deſdemona, Caſſio, and Æmilia.

Deſ. Be thou aſſur'd (good *Caſſio*) I will do
All my abilities in thy behalfe.

Æmil. Good Madam do:
I warrant it greeues my Husband,
As if the cauſe were his.

Deſ. Oh that's an honeſt Fellow, Do not doubt *Caſſio*
But I will haue my Lord, and you againe
As friendly as you were.

Caſſio. Bounteous Madam,
What euer ſhall become of *Michael Caſſio*,
He's neuer any thing but your true Seruant.

Deſ. I know't: I thanke you: you do loue my Lord:
You haue knowne him long, and be you well aſſur'd
He ſhall in ſtrangeneſſe ſtand no farther off,
Then in a politique diſtance.

Caſſio. I, but Lady,
That policie may either laſt ſo long,
Or feede vpon ſuch nice and wateriſh diet,
Or breede it ſelfe ſo out of Circumſtances,
That I being abſent, and my place ſupply'd,
My Generall will forget my Loue, and Seruice.

Deſ. Do not doubt that: before *Æmilia* here,

t

I giue thee warrant of thy place. Assure thee,
If I do vow a friendship, Ile performe it
To the last Article. My Lord shall neuer rest,
Ile watch him tame, and talke him out of patience;
His Bed shall seeme a Schoole, his Boord a Shrift,
Ile intermingle euery thing he do's
With *Cassio's* suite: Therefore be merry *Cassio*,
For thy Solicitor shall rather dye,
Then giue thy cause away.

Enter Othello, and Iago.

Æmil. Madam, heere comes my Lord.
Cassio. Madam, Ile take my leaue.
Des. Why stay, and heare me speake.
Cassio. Madam, not now: I am very ill at ease,
Vnfit for mine owne purposes.
Des. Well, do your discretion. *Exit Cassio.*
Iago. Hah? I like not that.
Othel. What dost thou say?
Iago. Nothing my Lord; or if——I know not what.
Othel. Was not that *Cassio* parted from my wife?
Iago. *Cassio* my Lord? No sure, I cannot thinke it
That he would steale away so guilty-like,
Seeing your comming.
Oth. I do beleeue 'twas he.
Des. How now my Lord?
I haue bin talking with a Suitor heere,
A man that languishes in your displeasure.
Oth. Who is't you meane?
Des. Why your Lieutenant *Cassio*: Good my Lord,
If I haue any grace, or power to moue you,
His present reconciliation take.
For if he be not one, that truly loues you,
That erres in Ignorance, and not in Cunning,
I haue no iudgement in an honest face.
I prythee call him backe.
Oth. Went he hence now?
Des. I sooth; so humbled,
That he hath left part of his greefe with mee
To suffer with him. Good Loue, call him backe.
Othel. Not now (sweet *Desdemon*) some other time.
Des. But shall't be shortly?
Oth. The sooner (Sweet) for you.
Des. Shall't be to night, at Supper?
Oth. No, not to night.
Des. To morrow Dinner then?
Oth. I shall not dine at home:
I meete the Captaines at the Cittadell.
Des. Why then to morrow night, on Tuesday morne,
On Tuesday noone, or night; on Wensday Morne.
I prythee name the time, but let it not
Exceed three dayes. Infaith hee's penitent:
And yet his Trespasse, in our common reason
(Saue that they say the warres must make example)
Out of her best, is not almost a fault
T'encurre a priuate checke. When shall he come?
Tell me *Othello*. I wonder in my Soule
What you would aske me, that I should deny,
Or stand so mam'ring on? What? *Michael Cassio*,
That came a woing with you? and so many a time
(When I haue spoke of you dispraisingly)
Hath tane your part, to haue so much to do
To bring him in? Trust me, I could do much.
Oth. Prythee no more: Let him come when he will:
I will deny thee nothing.
Des. Why, this is not a Boone:
'Tis as I should entreate you weare your Gloues,
Or feede on nourishing dishes, or keepe you warme,
Or sue to you, to do a peculiar profit
To your owne person. Nay, when I haue a suite
Wherein I meane to touch your Loue indeed,
It shall be full of poize, and difficult waight,
And fearefull to be granted.
Oth. I will deny thee nothing.
Whereon, I do beseech thee, grant me this,
To leaue me but a little to my selfe.
Des. Shall I deny you? No: farewell my Lord.
Oth. Farewell my *Desdemona*, Ile come to thee strait.
Des. *Æmilia* come; be as your Fancies teach you:
What ere you be, I am obedient. *Exit.*
Oth. Excellent wretch: Perdition catch my Soule
But I do loue thee: and when I loue thee not,
Chaos is come againe.
Iago. My Noble Lord.
Oth. What dost thou say, *Iago*?
Iago. Did *Michael Cassio*
When he woo'd my Lady, know of your loue?
Oth. He did, from first to last:
Why dost thou aske?
Iago. But for a satisfaction of my Thought,
No further harme.
Oth Why of thy thought, *Iago*?
Iago. I did not thinke he had bin acquainted with hir.
Oth. O yes, and went betweene vs very oft.
Iago. Indeed?
Oth. Indeed? I indeed. Discern'st thou ought in that?
Is he not honest?
Iago. Honest, my Lord?
Oth. Honest? I, Honest.
Iago. My Lord, for ought I know.
Oth. What do'st thou thinke?
Iago. Thinke, my Lord?
Oth. Thinke, my Lord? Alas, thou ecchos't me;
As if there were some Monster in thy thought
Too hideous to be shewne. Thou dost mean somthing:
I heard thee say euen now, thou lik'st not that,
When *Cassio* left my wife. What didd'st not like?
And when I told thee, he was of my Counsaile,
Of my whole course of wooing; thou cried'st, Indeede?
And didd'st contract, and purse thy brow together,
As if thou then hadd'st shut vp in thy Braine
Some horrible Conceite. If thou do'st loue me,
Shew me thy thought.
Iago. My Lord, you know I loue you.
Oth. I thinke thou do'st:
And for I know thou'rt full of Loue, and Honestie,
And weigh'st thy words before thou giu'st them breath,
Therefore these stops of thine, fright me the more:
For such things in a false disloyall Knaue
Are tricks of Custome: but in a man that's iust,
They're close dilations, working from the heart,
That Passion cannot rule.
Iago. For *Michael Cassio*,
I dare be sworne, I thinke that he is honest.
Oth. I thinke so too.
Iago. Men should be what they seeme,
Or those that be not, would they might seeme none.
Oth. Certaine, men should be what they seeme.
Iago. Why then I thinke *Cassio's* an honest man.
Oth. Nay, yet there's more in this?
I prythee speake to me, as to thy thinkings,
As thou dost ruminate, and giue thy worst of thoughts
The

The worſt of words.
Iago Good my Lord pardon me,
Though I am bound to euery Acte of dutie,
I am not bound to that: All Slaues are free:
Vtter my Thoughts? Why ſay, they are vild, and falce?
As where's that Palace, whereinto foule things
Sometimes intrude not? Who ha's that breaſt ſo pure,
Wherein vncleanly Apprehenſions
Keepe Leetes, and Law-dayes, and in Seſſions ſit
With meditations lawfull?
Oth. Thou do'ſt conſpire againſt thy Friend (*Iago*)
If thou but think'ſt him wrong'd, and mak'ſt his eare
A ſtranger to thy Thoughts.
Iago. I do beſeech you,
Though I perchance am vicious in my gueſſe
(As I confeſſe it is my Natures plague
To ſpy into Abuſes, and of my iealouſie
Shapes faults that are not) that your wiſedome
From one, that ſo imperfectly conceits,
Would take no notice, nor build your ſelfe a trouble
Out of his ſcattering, and vnſure obſeruance:
It were not for your quiet, nor your good,
Nor for my Manhood, Honeſty, and Wiſedome,
To let you know my thoughts.
Oth. What doſt thou meane?
Iago. Good name in Man, & woman (deere my Lord)
Is the immediate Iewell of their Soules;
Who ſteales my purſe, ſteales traſh:
'Tis ſomething, nothing;
'Twas mine, 'tis his, and has bin ſlaue to thouſands:
But he that filches from me my good Name,
Robs me of that, which not enriches him,
And makes me poore indeed.
Oth. Ile know thy Thoughts.
Iago. You cannot, if my heart were in your hand,
Nor ſhall not, whil'ſt 'tis in my cuſtodie.
Oth. Ha?
Iago. Oh, beware my Lord, of iealouſie,
It is the greene-ey'd Monſter, which doth mocke
The meate it feeds on. That Cuckold liues in bliſſe,
Who certaine of his Fate, loues not his wronger:
But oh, what damned minutes tels he ore,
Who dotes, yet doubts: Suſpects, yet ſoundly loues?
Oth. O miſerie.
Iago Poore, and Content, is rich, and rich enough,
But Riches fineleſſe, is as poore as Winter,
To him that euer feares he ſhall be poore:
Good Heauen, the Soules of all my Tribe defend
From Iealouſie.
Oth. Why? why is this?
Think'ſt thou, I'ld make a Life of Iealouſie;
To follow ſtill the changes of the Moone
With freſh ſuſpitions? No: to be once in doubt,
Is to be reſolu'd: Exchange me for a Goat,
When I ſhall turne the buſineſſe of my Soule
To ſuch exufflicate, and blow'd Surmiſes,
Matching thy inference. 'Tis not to make me Iealious,
To ſay my wife is faire, feeds well, loues company,
Is free of Speech, Sings, Playes, and Dances:
Where Vertue is, theſe are more vertuous.
Nor from mine owne weake merites, will I draw
The ſmalleſt feare, or doubt of her reuolt,
For ſhe had eyes, and choſe me. No *Iago*,
Ile ſee before I doubt; when I doubt, proue;
And on the proofe, there is no more but this,
Away at once with Loue, or Iealouſie.
Ia. I am glad of this: For now I ſhall haue reaſon
To ſhew the Loue and Duty that I beare you
With franker ſpirit. Therefore (as I am bound)
Receiue it from me. I ſpeake not yet of proofe:
Looke to your wife, obſerue her well with *Caſſio*,
Weare your eyes, thus: not Iealious, nor Secure:
I would not haue your free, and Noble Nature,
Out of ſelfe-Bounty, be abus'd: Looke too't:
I know our Country diſpoſition well:
In Venice, they do let Heauen ſee the prankes
They dare not ſhew their Husbands.
Their beſt Conſcience,
Is not to leaue't vndone, but kept vnknowne.
Oth. Doſt thou ſay ſo?
Iago. She did deceiue her Father, marrying you,
And when ſhe ſeem'd to ſhake, and feare your lookes,
She lou'd them moſt.
Oth. And ſo ſhe did.
Iago. Why go too then:
Shee that ſo young could giue out ſuch a Seeming
To ſeele her Fathers eyes vp, cloſe as Oake,
He thought 'twas Witchcraft.
But I am much too blame:
I humbly do beſeech you of your pardon
For too much louing you.
Oth. I am bound to thee for euer.
Iago. I ſee this hath a little daſh'd your Spirits:
Oth. Not a iot, not a iot.
Iago. Truſt me, I feare it has:
I hope you will conſider what is ſpoke
Comes from your Loue.
But I do ſee, y'are mou'd:
I am to pray you, not to ſtraine my ſpeech
To groſſer iſſues, nor to larger reach,
Then to Suſpition.
Oth. I will not.
Iago. Should you do ſo (my Lord)
My ſpeech ſhould fall into ſuch vilde ſucceſſe,
Which my Thoughts aym'd not.
Caſſio's my worthy Friend:
My Lord, I ſee y'are mou'd.
Oth. No, not much mou'd:
I do not thinke but *Deſdemona's* honeſt.
Iago. Long liue ſhe ſo;
And long liue you to thinke ſo.
Oth. And yet how Nature erring from it ſelfe.
Iago. I, there's the point:
As (to be bold with you)
Not to affect many propoſed Matches
Of her owne Clime, Complexion, and Degree,
Whereto we ſee in all things, Nature tends:
Foh, one may ſmel in ſuch, a will moſt ranke,
Foule diſproportions, Thoughts vnnaturall.
But (pardon me) I do not in poſition
Diſtinctly ſpeake of her, though I may feare
Her will, recoyling to her better iudgement,
May fal to match you with her Country formes,
And happily repent.
Oth. Farewell, farewell:
If more thou doſt perceiue, let me know more:
Set on thy wife to obſerue.
Leaue me *Iago*.
Iago. My Lord, I take my leaue.
Othel. Why did I marry?
This honeſt Creature (doubtleſſe)
Sees, and knowes more, much more then he vnfolds.
Iago

Iago. My Lord, I would I might intreat your Honor
To ſcan this thing no farther: Leaue it to time,
Although 'tis fit that *Caſſio* haue his Place;
For ſure he filles it vp with great Ability;
Yet if you pleaſe, to him off a-while:
You ſhall by that perceiue him, and his meanes:
Note if your Lady ſtraine his Entertainment
With any ſtrong, or vehement importunitie,
Much will be ſeene in that: In the meane time,
Let me be thought too buſie in my feares,
(As worthy cauſe I haue to feare I am)
And hold her free, I do beſeech your Honor.
Oth. Feare not my gouernment.
Iago. I once more take my leaue. *Exit.*
Oth. This Fellow's of exceeding honeſty,
And knowes all Quantities with a learn'd Spirit
Of humane dealings. If I do proue her Haggard,
Though that her ieſſes were my deere heart-ſtrings,
I'ld whiſtle her off, and let her downe the winde
To prey at Fortune. Haply, for I am blacke,
And haue not thoſe ſoft parts of Conuerſation
That Chamberers haue: Or for I am declin'd
Into the vale of yeares (yet that's not much)
Shee's gone. I am abus'd, and my releefe
Muſt be to loath her. Oh Curſe of Marriage!
That we can call theſe delicate Creatures ours,
And not their Appetites? I had rather be a Toad,
And liue vpon the vapour of a Dungeon,
Then keepe a corner in the thing I loue
For others vſes. Yet 'tis the plague to Great-ones,
Prerogatiu'd are they leſſe then the Baſe,
'Tis deſtiny vnſhunnable, like death:
Euen then, this forked plague is Fated to vs,
When we do quicken. Looke where ſhe comes:

Enter Deſdemona and Æmilia.

If ſhe be falſe, Heauen mock'd it ſelfe:
Ile not beleeue't.
Deſ. How now, my deere *Othello*?
Your dinner, and the generous Iſlanders
By you inuited, do attend your preſence.
Oth. I am too blame.
Deſ. Why do you ſpeake ſo faintly?
Are you not well?
Oth. I haue a paine vpon my Forehead, heere.
Deſ. Why that's with watching, 'twill away againe.
Let me but binde it hard, within this houre
It will be well.
Oth. Your Napkin is too little:
Let it alone: Come, Ile go in with you. *Exit.*
Deſ. I am very ſorry that you are not well.
Æmil. I am glad I haue found this Napkin:
This was her firſt remembrance from the Moore,
My wayward Husband hath a hundred times
Woo'd me to ſteale it. But ſhe ſo loues the Token,
(For he coniur'd her, ſhe ſhould euer keepe it)
That ſhe reſerues it euermore about her,
To kiſſe, and talke too. Ile haue the worke tane out,
And giu't *Iago*: what he will do with it
Heauen knowes, not I:
I nothing, but to pleaſe his Fantaſie.

Enter Iago.

Iago. How now? What do you heere alone?
Æmil. Do not you chide: I haue a thing for you.
Iago. You haue a thing for me?
It is a common thing ——
Æmil. Hah?
Iago. To haue a fooliſh wife.
Æmil. Oh, is that all? What will you giue me now
For that ſame Handkerchiefe.
Iago. What Handkerchiefe?
Æmil. What Handkerchiefe?
Why that the Moore firſt gaue to *Deſdemona*,
That which ſo often you did bid me ſteale.
Iago. Haſt ſtolne it from her?
Æmil. No: but ſhe let it drop by negligence,
And to th'aduantage, I being heere, took't vp:
Looke, heere 'tis.
Iago. A good wench, giue it me.
Æmil. What will you do with't, that you haue bene
ſo earneſt to haue me filch it?
Iago. Why, what is that to you?
Æmil. If it be not for ſome purpoſe of import,
Giu't me againe. Poore Lady, ſhee'l run mad
When ſhe ſhall lacke it.
Iago. Be not acknowne on't:
I haue vſe for it. Go, leaue me. *Exit Æmil.*
I will in *Caſſio's* Lodging looſe this Napkin,
And let him finde it. Trifles light as ayre,
Are to the iealious, confirmations ſtrong,
As proofes of holy Writ. This may do ſomething.
The Moore already changes with my poyſon:
Dangerous conceites, are in their Natures poyſons,
Which at the firſt are ſcarſe found to diſtaſte:
But with a little acte vpon the blood,
Burne like the Mines of Sulphure. I did ſay ſo.

Enter Othello.

Looke where he comes: Not Poppy, nor Mandragora,
Nor all the drowſie Syrrups of the world
Shall euer medicine thee to that ſweete ſleepe
Which thou owd'ſt yeſterday.
Oth. Ha, ha, falſe to mee?
Iago. Why how now Generall? No more of that.
Oth. Auant, be gone: Thou haſt ſet me on the Racke:
I ſweare 'tis better to be much abus'd,
Then but to know't a little.
Iago. How now, my Lord?
Oth. What ſenſe had I, in her ſtolne houres of Luſt?
I ſaw't not, thought it not: it harm'd not me:
I ſlept the next night well, fed well, was free, and merrie.
I found not *Caſſio's* kiſſes on her Lippes:
He that is robb'd, not wanting what is ſtolne,
Let him not know't, and he's not robb'd at all.
Iago. I am ſorry to heare this?
Oth. I had beene happy, if the generall Campe,
Pyoners and all, had taſted her ſweet Body,
So I had nothing knowne. Oh now, for euer
Farewell the Tranquill minde; farewell Content;
Farewell the plumed Troopes, and the bigge Warres,
That makes Ambition, Vertue! Oh farewell,
Farewell the neighing Steed, and the ſhrill Trumpe,
The Spirit-ſtirring Drum, th'Eare-piercing Fife,
The Royall Banner, and all Qualitie,
Pride, Pompe, and Circumſtance of glorious Warre:
And O you mortall Engines, whoſe rude throates
Th'immortall Ioues dread Clamours, counterfet,
Farewell: *Othello's* Occupation's gone.
Iago. Is't poſſible my Lord?
Oth. Villaine, be ſure thou proue my Loue a Whore;
Be ſure of it: Giue me the Occular proofe,

Or

Or by the worth of mine eternall Soule,
Thou had'ſt bin better haue bin borne a Dog
Then anſwer my wak'd wrath.
Iago. Is't come to this?
Oth. Make me to ſee't: or (at the leaſt) ſo proue it,
That the probation beare no Hindge, nor Loope,
To hang a doubt on: Or woe vpon thy life.
Iago. My Noble Lord.
Oth. If thou doſt ſlander her, and torture me,
Neuer pray more: Abandon all remorſe
On Horrors head, Horrors accumulate:
Do deeds to make Heauen weepe, all Earth amaz'd;
For nothing canſt thou to damnation adde,
Greater then that.
Iago. O Grace! O Heauen forgiue me!
Are you a Man? Haue you a Soule? or Senſe?
God buy you: take mine Office. Oh wretched Foole,
That lou'ſt to make thine Honeſty, a Vice!
Oh monſtrous world! Take note, take note (O World)
To be direct and honeſt, is not ſafe.
I thanke you for this profit, and from hence
Ile loue no Friend, ſith Loue breeds ſuch offence.
Oth. Nay ſtay: thou ſhould'ſt be honeſt.
Iago. I ſhould be wiſe; for Honeſtie's a Foole,
And looſes that it workes for.
Oth. By the World,
I thinke my Wife be honeſt, and thinke ſhe is not:
I thinke that thou art iuſt, and thinke thou art not:
Ile haue ſome proofe. My name that was as freſh
As *Dians* Viſage, is now begrim'd and blacke
As mine owne face. If there be Cords, or Kniues,
Poyſon, or Fire, or ſuffocating ſtreames,
Ile not indure it. Would I were ſatis fied.
Iago. I ſee you are eaten vp with Paſſion:
I do repent me, that I put it to you.
You would be ſatisfied?
Oth. Would? Nay, and I will.
Iago. And may: but how? How ſatisfied, my Lord
Would you the ſuper-viſion groſſely gape on?
Behold her top'd?
Oth. Death, and damnation. Oh!
Iago. It were a tedious difficulty, I thinke,
To bring them to that Proſpect: Damne them then,
If euer mortall eyes do ſee them boulſter
More then their owne. What then? How then?
What ſhall I ſay? Where's Satisfaction?
It is impoſſible you ſhould ſee this,
Were they as prime as Goates, as hot as Monkeyes,
As ſalt as Wolues in pride, and Fooles as groſſe
As Ignorance, made drunke. But yet, I ſay,
If imputation, and ſtrong circumſtances,
Which leade directly to the doore of Truth,
Will giue you ſatisfaction, you might haue't.
Oth. Giue me a liuing reaſon ſhe's diſloyall.
Iago. I do not like the Office.
But ſith I am entred in this cauſe ſo farre
(Prick'd too't by fooliſh Honeſty, and Loue)
I will go on. I lay with *Caſſio* lately,
And being troubled with a raging tooth,
I could not ſleepe. There are a kinde of men,
So looſe of Soule, that in their ſleepes will mutter
Their Affayres: one of this kinde is *Caſſio*:
In ſleepe I heard him ſay, ſweet *Deſdemona*,
Let vs be wary, let vs hide our Loues,
And then (Sir) would he gripe, and wring my hand:
Cry, oh ſweet Creature: then kiſſe me hard,
As if he pluckt vp kiſſes by the rootes,
That grew vpon my lippes, laid his Leg ore my Thigh,
And ſigh, and kiſſe, and then cry curſed Fate,
That gaue thee to the Moore.
Oth. O monſtrous! monſtrous!
Iago. Nay, this was but his Dreame.
Oth. But this denoted a fore-gone concluſion,
'Tis a ſhrew'd doubt, though it be but a Dreame.
Iago. And this may helpe to thicken other proofes,
That do demonſtrate thinly.
Oth. Ile teare her all to peeces.
Iago. Nay yet be wiſe; yet we ſee nothing done,
She may be honeſt yet: Tell me but this,
Haue you not ſometimes ſeene a Handkerchiefe
Spotted with Strawberries, in your wiues hand?
Oth. I gaue her ſuch a one: 'twas my firſt gift.
Iago. I know not that: but ſuch a Handkerchiefe
(I am ſure it was your wiues) did I to day
See *Caſſio* wipe his Beard with.
Oth. If it be that.
Iago. If it be that, or any, it was hers.
It ſpeakes againſt her with the other proofes.
Othel. O that the Slaue had forty thouſand liues:
One is too poore, too weake for my reuenge.
Now do I ſee 'tis true. Looke heere *Iago*,
All my fond loue thus do I blow to Heauen. 'Tis gone.
Ariſe blacke vengeance, from the hollow hell,
Yeeld vp (O Loue) thy Crowne, and hearted Throne
To tyrannous Hate. Swell boſome with thy fraught,
For 'tis of Aſpickes tongues.
Iago. Yet be content.
Oth. Oh blood, blood, blood.
Iago. Patience I ſay: your minde may change.
Oth. Neuer *Iago*. Like to the Ponticke Sea,
Whoſe Icie Current, and compulſiue courſe,
Neu'r keepes retyring ebbe, but keepes due on
To the Proponticke, and the Helleſpont:
Euen ſo my bloody thoughts, with violent pace
Shall neu'r looke backe, neu'r ebbe to humble Loue,
Till that a capeable, and wide Reuenge
Swallow them vp. Now by yond Marble Heauen,
In the due reuerence of a Sacred vow,
I heere engage my words.
Iago. Do not riſe yet:
Witneſſe you euer-burning Lights aboue,
You Elements, that clip vs round about,
Witneſſe that heere *Iago* doth giue vp
The execution of his wit, hands, heart,
To wrong'd *Othello's* Seruice. Let him command,
And to obey ſhall be in me remorſe,
What bloody buſineſſe euer.
Oth. I greet thy loue,
Not with vaine thanks, but with acceptance bounteous,
And will vpon the inſtant put thee too't.
Within theſe three dayes let me heare thee ſay,
That *Caſſio's* not aliue.
Iago. My Friend is dead:
'Tis done at your Requeſt.
But let her liue.
Oth. Damne her lewde Minx:
O damne her, damne her.
Come go with me a-part, I will withdraw
To furniſh me with ſome ſwift meanes of death
For the faire Diuell.
Now art thou my Lieutenant.
Iago. I am your owne for euer. *Exeunt.*

Scena

Scæna Quarta.

Enter Desdemona, Æmilia and Clown.

Des. Do you know Sirrah, where Lieutenant *Cassio* lyes?

Clow. I dare not say he lies any where.

Des. Why man?

Clo. He's a Soldier, and for me to say a Souldier lyes, 'tis stabbing.

Des. Go too: where lodges he?

Clo. To tell you where he lodges, is to tel you where I lye.

Des. Can any thing be made of this?

Clo. I know not where he lodges, and for mee to deuise a lodging, and say he lies heere, or he lies there, were to lye in mine owne throat.

Des. Can you enquire him out? and be edified by report?

Clo. I will Catechize the world for him, that is, make Questions, and by them answer.

Des. Seeke him, bidde him come hither: tell him, I haue mou'd my Lord on his behalfe, and hope all will be well.

Clo. To do this, is within the compasse of mans Wit, and therefore I will attempt the doing it. *Exit Clo.*

Des. Where should I loose the Handkerchiefe, *Æmilia?*

Æmil. I know not Madam.

Des. Beleeue me, I had rather haue lost my purse
Full of Cruzadoes. And but my Noble Moore
Is true of minde, and made of no such basenesse,
As iealious Creatures are, it were enough
To put him to ill thinking.

Æmil. Is he not iealious?

Des. Who, he? I thinke the Sun where he was borne,
Drew all such humors from him.

Æmil. Looke where he comes.

Enter Othello.

Des. I will not leaue him now, till *Cassio* be
Call'd to him. How is't with you, my Lord?

Oth. Well my good Lady. Oh hardnes to dissemble!
How do you, *Desdemona?*

Des. Well, my good Lord.

Oth. Giue me your hand.
This hand is moist, my Lady.

Des. It hath felt no age, nor knowne no sorrow.

Oth. This argues fruitfulnesse, and liberall heart:
Hot, hot, and moyst. This hand of yours requires
A sequester from Liberty: Fasting, and Prayer,
Much Castigation, Exercise deuout,
For heere's a yong, and sweating Diuell heere
That commonly rebels: 'Tis a good hand,
A franke one.

Des. You may (indeed) say so:
For 'twas that hand that gaue away my heart.

Oth. A liberall hand. The hearts of old, gaue hands:
But our new Heraldry is hands, not hearts.

Des. I cannot speake of this:
Come, now your promise.

Oth. What promise, Chucke?

Des. I haue sent to bid *Cassio* come speake with you.

Oth. I haue a salt and sorry Rhewme offends me:
Lend me thy Handkerchiefe.

Des. Heere my Lord.

Oth. That which I gaue you.

Des. I haue it not about me.

Oth. Not?

Des. No indeed, my Lord.

Oth. That's a fault: That Handkerchiefe
Did an Ægyptian to my Mother giue:
She was a Charmer, and could almost read
The thoughts of people. She told her, while she kept it,
'T would make her Amiable, and subdue my Father
Intirely to her loue: But if she lost it,
Or made a Guift of it, my Fathers eye
Should hold her loathed, and his Spirits should hunt
After new Fancies. She dying, gaue it me,
And bid me (when my Fate would haue me Wiu'd)
To giue it her. I did so; and take heede on't,
Make it a Darling, like your precious eye
To loose't, or giue't away, were such perdition,
As nothing else could match.

Des. Is't possible?

Oth. 'Tis true: There's Magicke in the web of it:
A *Sybill* that had numbred in the world
The Sun to course, two hundred compasses,
In her Prophetticke furie sow'd the Worke:
The Wormes were hallowed, that did breede the Silke,
And it was dyde in Mummey, which the Skilfull
Conseru'd of Maidens hearts.

Des. Indeed? Is't true?

Oth. Most veritable, therefore looke too't well.

Des. Then would to Heauen, that I had neuer seene't?

Oth. Ha? wherefore?

Des. Why do you speake so startingly, and rash?

Oth. Is't lost? Is't gon? Speak, is't out o'th'way?

Des. Blesse vs.

Oth. Say you?

Des. It is not lost: but what and if it were?

Oth. How?

Des. I say it is not lost.

Oth. Fetcht, let me see't.

Des. Why so I can: but I will not now:
This is a tricke to put me from my suite,
Pray you let *Cassio* be receiu'd againe.

Oth. Fetch me the Handkerchiefe.
My minde mis-giues.

Des. Come, come: you'l neuer meete a more sufficient man.

Oth. The Handkerchiefe.

Des. A man that all his time
Hath founded his good Fortunes on your loue;
Shar'd dangers with you.

Oth. The Handkerchiefe.

Des. Insooth, you are too blame.

Oth. Away. *Exit Othello.*

Æmil. Is not this man iealious?

Des. I neu'r saw this before.
Sure, there's some wonder in this Handkerchiefe,
I am most vnhappy in the losse of it.

Æmil. 'Tis not a yeare or two shewes vs a man:
They are all but Stomackes, and we all but Food,
They eate vs hungerly, and when they are full
They belch vs.

Enter Iago, and Cassio.

Looke you, *Cassio* and my Husband.

Iago. There is no other way: 'tis she must doo't:
And loe the happinesse: go, and importune her.

Des.

Des. How now (good *Cassio*) what's the newes with
you?

Cassio. Madam, my former suite. I do beseech you,
That by your vertuous meanes, I may againe
Exist, and be a member of his loue,
Whom I, with all the Office of my heart
Intirely honour, I would not be delayd.
If my offence, be of such mortall kinde,
That nor my Seruice past, nor present Sorrowes,
Nor purpos'd merit in futurity,
Can ransome me into his loue againe,
But to know so, must be my benefit:
So shall I cloath me in a forc'd content,
And shut my selfe vp in some other course
To Fortunes Almes.

Des. Alas (thrice-gentle *Cassio*)
My Aduocation is not now in Tune;
My Lord, is not my Lord; nor should I know him,
Were he in Fauour, as in Humour alter'd.
So helpe me euery spirit sanctified,
As I haue spoken for you all my best,
And stood within the blanke of his displeasure
For my free speech. You must awhile be patient:
What I can do, I will: and more I will
Then for my selfe, I dare. Let that suffice you.

Iago. Is my Lord angry?

Æmil. He went hence but now:
And certainly in strange vnquietnesse.

Iago. Can he be angry? I haue seene the Cannon
When it hath blowne his Ranks into the Ayre,
And like the Diuell from his very Arme
Puff't his owne Brother: And is he angry?
Something of moment then: I will go meet him,
There's matter in't indeed, if he be angry. *Exit*

Des. I prythee do so. Something sure of State,
Either from Venice, or some vnhatch'd practise
Made demonstrable heere in Cyprus, to him,
Hath pudled his cleare Spirit: and in such cases,
Mens Natures wrangle with inferiour things,
Though great ones are their obiect. 'Tis euen so.
For let our finger ake, and it endues
Our other healthfull members, euen to a sense
Of paine. Nay, we must thinke men are not Gods,
Nor of them looke for such obseruancie
As fits the Bridall. Beshrew me much, *Æmilia*,
I was (vnhandsome Warrior, as I am)
Arraigning his vnkindnesse with my soule:
But now I finde, I had suborn'd the Witnesse,
And he's Indited falsely.

Æmil. Pray heauen it bee
State matters, as you thinke, and no Conception,
Nor no Iealious Toy, concerning you.

Des Alas the day, I neuer gaue him cause.

Æmil. But Iealious soules will not be answer'd so;
They are not euer iealious for the cause,
But iealious, for they're iealious. It is a Monster
Begot vpon it selfe, borne on it selfe.

Des. Heauen keepe the Monster from *Othello's* mind.

Æmil. Lady, Amen.

Des I will go seeke him. *Cassio*, walke heere about:
If I doe finde him fit, Ile moue your suite,
And seeke to effect it to my vttermost. *Exit*

Cas. I humbly thanke your Ladyship.

Enter Bianca.

Bian. Saue you (Friend *Cassio.*)

Cassio. What make you from home?
How is't with you, my most faire *Bianca*?
Indeed (sweet Loue) I was comming to your house.

Bian. And I was going to your Lodging, *Cassio.*
What? keepe a weeke away? Seuen dayes, and Nights?
Eight score eight houres? And Louers absent howres
More tedious then the Diall, eight score times?
Oh weary reck'ning.

Cassio. Pardon me, *Bianca*:
I haue this while with leaden thoughts beene prest,
But I shall in a more continuate time
Strike off this score of absence. Sweet *Bianca*
Take me this worke out.

Bianca. Oh *Cassio*, whence came this?
This is some Token from a newer Friend,
To the felt-Absence: now I feele a Cause:
Is't come to this? Well, well.

Cassio. Go too, woman:
Throw your vilde gesses in the Diuels teeth,
From whence you haue them. You are iealious now,
That this is from some Mistris, some remembrance;
No, in good troth *Bianca*.

Bian. Why, who's is it?

Cassio. I know not neither:
I found it in my Chamber,
I like the worke well; Ere it be demanded
(As like enough it will) I would haue it coppied:
Take it, and doo't, and leaue me for this time.

Bian. Leaue you? Wherefore?

Cassio. I do attend heere on the Generall,
And thinke it no addition nor my wish
To haue him see me woman'd.

Bian. Why, I pray you?

Cassio. Not that I loue you not.

Bian. But that you do not loue me.
I pray you bring me on the way a little,
And say, if I shall see you soone at night?

Cassio. 'Tis but a little way that I can bring you,
For I attend heere: But Ile see you soone.

Bian. 'Tis very good: I must be circumstanc'd.

Exeunt omnes.

Actus Quartus. Scena Prima.

Enter Othello, and Iago.

Iago. Will you thinke so?

Oth. Thinke so, *Iago*?

Iago. What, to kisse in priuate?

Oth. An vnauthoriz'd kisse?

Iago. Or to be naked with her Friend in bed,
An houre, or more, not meaning any harme?

Oth. Naked in bed (*Iago*) and not meane harme?
It is hypocrisie against the Diuell:
They that meane vertuously, and yet do so,
The Diuell their vertue tempts, and they tempt Heauen.

Iago. If they do nothing, 'tis a Veniall slip:
But if I giue my wife a Handkerchiefe.

Oth. What then?

Iago. Why then 'tis hers (my Lord) and being hers,
She may (I thinke) bestow't on any man.

Oth. She is Protectresse of her honor too:
May she giue that?

Iago.

Iago. Her honor is an Essence that's not seene,
They haue it very oft, that haue it not.
But for the Handkerchiefe.

Othe. By heauen, I would most gladly haue forgot it:
Thou saidst (oh, it comes ore my memorie,
As doth the Rauen o're the infectious house:
Boading to all) he had my Handkerchiefe.

Iago. I: what of that?

Othe. That's not so good now.

Iag. What if I had said, I had seene him do you wrong?
Or heard him say (as Knaues be such abroad,
Who hauing by their owne importunate suit,
Or voluntary dotage of some Mistris,
Conuinced or supply'd them, cannot chuse
But they must blab.)

Oth. Hath he said any thing?

Iago. He hath (my Lord) but be you well assur'd,
No more then he'le vn-sweare.

Oth. What hath he said?

Iago. Why, that he did: I know not what he did.

Othe. What? What?

Iago. Lye.

Oth. With her?

Iago. With her? On her: what you will.

Othe. Lye with her? lye on her? We say lye on her, when they be-lye-her. Lye with her: that's fullsome: Handkerchiefe: Confessions: Handkerchiefe. To confesse, and be hang'd for his labour. First, to be hang'd, and then to confesse: I tremble at it. Nature would not inuest her selfe in such shadowing passion, without some Instruction. It is not words that shakes me thus, (pish) Noses, Eares, and Lippes: is't possible. Confesse? Handkerchiefe? O diuell. *Falls in a Traunce.*

Iago. Worke on,
My Medicine workes. Thus credulous Fooles are caught,
And many worthy, and chast Dames euen thus,
(All guiltlesse) meete reproach: what hoa? My Lord?
My Lord, I say: *Othello.*

Enter Cassio.

How now *Cassio?*

Cas. What's the matter?

Iago. My Lord is falne into an Epilepsie,
This is his second Fit: he had one yesterday

Cas. Rub him about the Temples.

Iago. The Lethargie must haue his quyet course:
If not, he foames at mouth: and by and by
Breakes out to sauage madnesse. Looke, he stirres:
Do you withdraw your selfe a little while,
He will recouer straight: when he is gone,
I would on great occasion, speake with you.
How is it Generall? Haue you not hurt your head?

Othe. Dost thou mocke me?

Iago. I mocke you not, by Heauen:
Would you would beare your Fortune like a Man.

Othe. A Horned man's a Monster, and a Beast.

Iago. Ther's many a Beast then in a populous Citty,
And many a ciuill Monster.

Othe. Did he confesse it?

Iago. Good Sir, be a man:
Thinke euery bearded fellow that's but yoak'd
May draw with you. There's Millions now aliue,
That nightly lye in those vnproper beds,
Which they dare sweare peculiar. Your case is better.
Oh, 'tis the spight of hell, the Fiends Arch-mock,
To lip a wanton in a secure Cowch;
And to suppose her chast. No, let me know,
And knowing what I am, I know what she shallbe.

Oth. Oh, thou art wise: 'tis certaine.

Iago. Stand you a while apart,
Confine your selfe but in a patient List,
Whil'st you were heere, o're-whelmed with your griefe
(A passion most resulting such a man)
Cassio came hither. I shifted him away,
And layd good scuses vpon your Extasie,
Bad him anon returne: and heere speake with me,
The which he promis'd. Do but encaue your selfe,
And marke the Fleeres, the Gybes, and notable Scornes
That dwell in euery Region of his face
For I will make him tell the Tale anew;
Where, how, how oft, how long ago, and when
He hath, and is againe to cope your wife.
I say, but marke his gesture: marry Patience,
Or I shall say y'are all in all in Spleene,
And nothing of a man.

Othe. Do'st thou heare, *Iago,*
I will be found most cunning in my Patience:
But (do'st thou heare) most bloody.

Iago. That's not amisse,
But yet keepe time in all: will you withdraw?
Now will I question *Cassio* of *Bianca,*
A Huswife, that by selling her desires
Buyes her selfe Bread, and Cloath. It is a Creature
That dotes on *Cassio,* (as 'tis the Strumpets plague
To be-guile many, and be be-guil'd by one)
He, when he heares of her, cannot restraine
From the excesse of Laughter. Heere he comes.

Enter Cassio.

As he shall smile, *Othello* shall go mad:
And his vnbookish Ielousie must conserue
Poore *Cassio's* smiles, gestures, and light behauiours
Quite in the wrong. How do you Lieutenant?

Cas. The worser, that you giue me the addition,
Whose want euen killes me.

Iago. Ply *Desdemona* well, and you are sure on't:
Now, if this Suit lay in *Bianca's* dowre,
How quickely should you speed?

Cas. Alas poore Caitiffe.

Oth. Looke how he laughes already.

Iago. I neuer knew woman loue man so.

Cas. Alas poore Rogue, I thinke indeed she loues me

Oth. Now he denies it faintly: and laughes it out.

Iago. Do you heare *Cassio?*

Oth. Now he importunes him
To tell it o're: go too, well said, well said.

Iago. She giues it out, that you shall marry her.
Do you intend it?

Cas. Ha, ha, ha.

Oth. Do ye triumph, Romaine? do you triumph?

Cas. I marry. What? A customer; prythee beare
Some Charitie to my wit, do not thinke it
So vnwholesome. Ha, ha, ha.

Oth. So, so, so, so: they laugh, that winnes.

Iago. Why the cry goes, that you marry her.

Cas. Prythee say true.

Iago. I am a very Villaine else.

Oth. Haue you scoar'd me? Well.

Cas. This is the Monkeys owne giuing out:
She is perswaded I will marry her
Out of her owne loue & flattery, not out of my promise.

Oth. *Iago* becomes me: now he begins the story.

Cassio. She was heere euen now: she haunts me in euery place. I was the other day talking on the Sea-banke with certaine Venetians, and thither comes the Bauble, and falls me thus about my neck.

Oth. Crying oh deere *Cassio*, as it were: his iesture imports it.

Cassio. So hangs, and lolls, and weepes vpon me.
So shakes, and pulls me. Ha, ha, ha.

Oth. Now he tells how she pluckt him to my Chamber: oh, I see that nose of yours, but not that dogge, I shall throw it to.

Cassio. Well, I must leaue her companie.

Iago. Before me: looke where she comes.

Enter Bianca.

Cas. 'Tis such another Fitchew: marry a perfum'd one?
What do you meane by this haunting of me?

Bian. Let the diuell, and his dam haunt you: what did you meane by that same Handkerchiefe, you gaue me euen now? I was a fine Foole to take it: I must take out the worke? A likely piece of worke, that you should finde it in your Chamber, and know not who left it there. This is some Minxes token, & I must take out the worke? There, giue it your Hobbey-horse, wheresoeuer you had it, Ile take out no worke on't.

Cassio. How now, my sweete *Bianca*?
How now? How now?

Othe. By Heauen, that should be my Handkerchiefe.

Bian. If you'le come to supper to night you may, if you will not, come when you are next prepar'd for. *Exit*

Iago. After her: after her.

Cas. I must, shee'l rayle in the streets else.

Iago. Will you sup there?

Cassio. Yes, I intend so.

Iago. Well, I may chance to see you: for I would very faine speake with you.

Cas. Prythee come: will you?

Iago. Go too: say no more.

Oth. How shall I murther him, *Iago*.

Iago. Did you perceiue how he laugh'd at his vice?

Oth. Oh, *Iago*

Iago. And did you see the Handkerchiefe?

Oth. Was that mine?

Iago. Yours by this hand: and to see how he prizes the foolish woman your wife: she gaue it him, and he hath giu'n it his whore.

Oth. I would haue him nine yeeres a killing:
A fine woman, a faire woman, a sweete woman?

Iago. Nay, you must forget that.

Othello. I, let her rot and perish, and be damn'd to night, for she shall not liue. No, my heart is turn'd to stone: I strike it, and it hurts my hand. Oh, the world hath not a sweeter Creature: she might lye by an Emperours side, and command him Taskes.

Iago. Nay, that's not your way.

Othe. Hang her, I do but say what she is: so delicate with her Needle: an admirable Musitian. Oh she will sing the Sauagenesse out of a Beare: of so high and plenteous wit, and inuention?

Iago. She's the worse for all this.

Othe. Oh, a thousand, a thousand times:
And then of so gentle a condition?

Iago. I too gentle.

Othe. Nay that's certaine:
But yet the pitty of it, *Iago*: oh *Iago*, the pitty of it *Iago*.

Iago. If you are so fond ouer her iniquitie: giue her pattent to offend, for if it touch not you, it comes neere no body.

Oth. I will chop her into Messes: Cuckold me?

Iago. Oh, 'tis foule in her.

Oth. With mine Officer?

Iago. That's fouler.

Othe. Get me some poyson, *Iago*, this night. Ile not expostulate with her: least her body and beautie vnprouide my mind againe: this night *Iago*.

Iago. Do it not with poyson, strangle her in her bed,
Euen the bed she hath contaminated.

Oth. Good, good:
The Iustice of it pleases: very good.

Iago. And for *Cassio*, let me be his vndertaker:
You shall heare more by midnight.

Enter Lodouico, Desdemona, and Attendants.

Othe. Excellent good: What Trumpet is that same?

Iago. I warrant something from Venice,
'Tis *Lodouico* this, comes from the Duke.
See, your wife's with him.

Lodo. Saue you worthy Generall.

Othe. With all my heart Sir.

Lod. The Duke, and the Senators of Venice greet you.

Othe. I kisse the Instrument of their pleasures.

Des. And what's the newes, good cozen *Lodouico*?

Iago. I am very glad to see you Signior:
Welcome to Cyprus.

Lod. I thanke you: how do's Lieutenant *Cassio*?

Iago. Liues Sir,

Des. Cozen, there's falne betweene him, & my Lord,
An vnkind breach: but you shall make all well.

Othe. Are you sure of that?

Des. My Lord?

Othe. This faile you not to do, as you will ——

Lod. He did not call: he's busie in the paper,
Is there deuision 'twixt my Lord, and *Cassio*?

Des. A most vnhappy one: I would do much
T'attone them for the loue I beare to *Cassio*.

Oth. Fire, and brimestone.

Des. My Lord.

Oth. Are you wise?

Des. What is he angrie?

Lod. May be th Letter mou'd him.
For as I thinke, they do command him home,
Deputing *Cassio* in his Gouernment.

Des. Trust me, I am glad on't.

Othe. Indeed?

Des. My Lord?

Othe. I am glad to see you mad.

Des. Why, sweete *Othello*?

Othe. Diuell.

Des. I haue not deseru'd this.

Lod. My Lord, this would not be beleeu'd in Venice,
Though I should sweare I saw't. 'Tis very much,
Make her amends: she weepes.

Othe. Oh diuell, diuell:
If that the Earth could teeme with womans teares,
Each drop she falls, would proue a Crocodile:
Out of my sight.

Des. I will not stay to offend you.

Lod. Truely obedient Lady:
I do beseech your Lordship call her backe.

Oth

Othe. Miſtris.
Deſ. My Lord.
Othe. What would you with her, Sir?
Lod. Who I, my Lord?
Othe. I, you did wiſh, that I would make her turne:
Sir, ſhe can turne, and turne: and yet go on
And turne againe. And ſhe can weepe, Sir, weepe.
And ſhe's obedient: as you ſay obedient.
Very obedient: proceed you in your teares.
Concerning this Sir, (oh well-painted paſſion)
I am commanded home: get you away:
Ile ſend for you anon. Sir I obey the Mandate,
And will returne to Venice. Hence, auaunt:
Caſſio ſhall haue my Place. And Sir, to night
I do entreat, that we may ſup together.
You are welcome Sir to Cyprus.
Goates, and Monkeys. *Exit.*
Lod. Is this the Noble Moore, whom our full Senate
Call all in all ſufficient? Is this the Nature
Whom Paſſion could not ſhake? Whoſe ſolid vertue
The ſhot of Accident, nor dart of Chance
Could neither graze, nor pierce?
Iago. He is much chang'd.
Lod. Are his wits ſafe? Is he not light of Braine?
Iago. He's that he is: I may not breath my cenſure.
What he might be: if what he might, he is not,
I would to heauen he were.
Lod. What? Strike his wife?
Iago. 'Faith that was not ſo well: yet would I knew
That ſtroke would proue the worſt.
Lod. Is it his vſe?
Or did the Letters, worke vpon his blood,
And new create his fault?
Iago. Alas, alas:
It is not honeſtie in me to ſpeake
What I haue ſeene, and knowne. You ſhall obſerue him,
And his owne courſes will deonte him ſo,
That I may ſaue my ſpeech: do but go after
And marke how he continues.
Lod. I am ſorry that I am deceiu'd in him. *Exeunt.*

Scena Secunda.

Enter Othello and Æmilia.

Othe. You haue ſeene nothing then?
Æmil. Nor euer heard: nor euer did ſuſpect.
Othe. Yes, you haue ſeene *Caſſio*, and ſhe together.
Æmi. But then I ſaw no harme: and then I heard,
Each ſyllable that breath made vp betweene them.
Othe. What? Did they neuer whiſper?
Æmil. Neuer my Lord.
Othe. Nor ſend you out o'th' way?
Æmil. Neuer.
Othe. To fetch her Fan, her Gloues, her Mask, nor no- (thing?
Æmil. Neuer my Lord.
Othe. That's ſtrange.
Æmil. I durſt (my Lord) to wager, ſhe is honeſt:
Lay downe my Soule at ſtake: If you thinke other,
Remoue your thought. It doth abuſe your boſome:
If any wretch haue put this in your head,
Let Heauen requit it with the Serpents curſe,
For if ſhe be not honeſt, chaſte, and true,
There's no man happy. The pureſt of their Wiues
Is foule as Slander.
Othe. Bid her come hither: go. *Exit Æmilia.*
She ſaies enough: yet ſhe's a ſimple Baud
That cannot ſay as much. This is a ſubtile Whore:
A Cloſſet Locke and Key of Villanous Secrets,
And yet ſhe'le kneele, and pray: I haue ſeene her do't.

Enter Deſdemona and Æmilia.

Deſ. My Lord, what is your will?
Othe. Pray you Chucke come hither.
Deſ. What is your pleaſure?
Oth. Let me ſee your eyes: looke in my face.
Deſ. What horrible Fancie's this?
Othe. Some of your Function Miſtris:
Leaue Procreants alone, and ſhut the doore:
Cough, or cry hem; if any body come:
Your Myſtery, your Myſtery: May diſpatch. *Exit Æmi.*
Deſ. Vpon my knee, what doth your ſpeech import?
I vnderſtand a Fury in your words.
Othe. Why? What art thou?
Deſ. Your wife my Lord: your true and loyall wife.
Othello. Come ſweare it: damne thy ſelfe, leaſt
being like one of Heauen, the diuells themſelues ſhould
feare to ceaze thee. Therefore be double damn'd: ſweare
thou art honeſt.
Deſ. Heauen doth truely know it.
Othe. Heauen truely knowes, that thou art falſe as hell.
Deſ. To whom my Lord?
With whom? How am I falſe?
Othe. Ah *Deſdemon*, away, away, away.
Deſ. Alas the heauy day: why do you weepe?
Am I the motiue of theſe teares my Lord?
If happely you my Father do ſuſpect,
An Inſtrument of this your calling backe,
Lay not your blame on me: if you haue loſt him,
I haue loſt him too.
Othe. Had it pleas'd Heauen,
To try me with Affliction, had they rain'd
All kind of Sores, and Shames on my bare-head:
Steep'd me in pouertie to the very lippes.
Giuen to Captiuitie, me, and my vtmoſt hopes,
I ſhould haue found in ſome place of my Soule
A drop of patience. But alas, to make me
The fixed Figure for the time of Scorne,
To point his ſlow, and mouing finger at.
Yet could I beare that too, well, very well:
But there where I haue garnerd vp my heart,
Where either I muſt liue, or beare no life,
The Fountaine from the which my currant runnes,
Or elſe dries vp: to be diſcarded thence,
Or keepe it as a Ceſterne, for foule Toades
To knot and gender in. Turne thy complexion there:
Patience, thou young and Roſe-lip'd Cherubin,
I heere looke grim as hell.
Deſ. I hope my Noble Lord eſteemes me honeſt.
Othe. Oh I, as Sommer Flyes are in the Shambles,
That quicken euen with blowing. Oh thou weed:
Who art ſo louely faire, and ſmell'ſt ſo ſweete,
That the Senſe akes at thee,
Would thou had'ſt neuer bin borne.
Deſ. Alas, what ignorant ſin haue I committed?
Othe. Was this faire Paper? This moſt goodly Booke
Made to write Whore vpon? What commited,
Com-

Committed? Oh, thou publicke Commoner,
I should make very Forges of my cheekes,
That would to Cynders burne vp Modestie,
Did I but speake thy deedes. What commited?
Heauen stoppes the Nose at it, and the Moone winks:
The baudy winde that kisses all it meetes,
Is hush'd within the hollow Myne of Earth
And will not hear't. What commited?

Des. By Heauen you do me wrong.

Othe. Are not you a Strumpet?

Des. No, as I am a Christian.
If to preserue this vessell for my Lord,
From any other foule vnlawfull touch
Be not to be a Strumpet, I am none.

Othe. What, not a Whore?

Des. No, as I shall be sau'd.

Othe. Is't possible?

Des. Oh Heauen forgiue vs.

Othe. I cry you mercy then.
I tooke you for that cunning Whore of Venice,
That married with *Othello*. You Mistris,

Enter Æmilia.

That haue the office opposite to Saint *Peter*,
And keepes the gate of hell. You, you: I you.
We haue done our course: there's money for your paines:
I pray you turne the key, and keepe our counsaile. *Exit.*

Æmil. Alas, what do's this Gentleman conceiue?
How do you Madam? how do you my good Lady?

Des. Faith, halfe a sleepe.

Æmi. Good Madam,
What's the matter with my Lord?

Des. With who?

Æmil. Why, with my Lord, Madam?

Des. Who is thy Lord?

Æmil. He that is yours, sweet Lady

Des. I haue none: do not talke to me, *Æmilia*,
I cannot weepe: nor answeres haue I none,
But what should go by water. Prythee to night,
Lay on my bed my wedding sheetes, remember,
And call thy husband hither.

Æmil. Heere's a change indeed. *Exit.*

Des. 'Tis meete I should be vs'd so: very meete.
How haue I bin behau'd, that he might sticke
The small'st opinion on my least misvse?

Enter Iago, and Æmilia.

Iago. What is your pleasure Madam?
How is't with you?

Des. I cannot tell: those that do teach yong Babes
Do it with gentle meanes, and easie taskes
He might haue chid me so: for in good faith
I am a Child to chiding.

Iago. What is the matter Lady?

Æmil. Alas (*Iago*) my Lord hath so bewhor'd her,
Throwne such dispight, and heauy termes vpon her
That true hearts cannot beare it.

Des. Am I that name, *Iago*?

Iago. What name, (faire Lady?)

Des. Such as she said my Lord did say I was.

Æmil. He call'd her whore: a Begger in his drinke:
Could not haue laid such termes vpon his Callet.

Iago. Why did he so?

Des. I do not know: I am sure I am none such

Iago Do not weepe, do not weepe: alas the day.

Æmil. Hath she forsooke so many Noble Matches?
Her Father? And her Country? And her Friends?
To be call'd Whore? Would it not make one weepe?

Des. It is my wretched Fortune.

Iago. Beshrew him for't:
How comes this Tricke vpon him?

Des. Nay, Heauen doth know.

Æmi. I will be hang'd, if some eternall Villaine,
Some busie and insinuating Rogue,
Some cogging, cozening Slaue, to get some Office,
Haue not deuis'd this Slander: I will be hang'd else.

Iago. Fie, there is no such man: it is impossible.

Des. If any such there be, Heauen pardon him.

Æmil. A halter pardon him:
A nd hell gnaw his bones.
Why should he call her Whore?
Who keepes her companie?
What Place? What Time?
What Forme? What liklyhood?
The Moore's abus'd by some most villanous Knaue,
Some base notorious Knaue, some scuruy Fellow
Oh Heauens, that such companions thou'd'st vnfold,
And put in euery honest hand a whip
To lash the Rascalls naked through the world,
Euen from the East to th'West.

Iago. Speake within doore.

Æmil. Oh fie vpon them: some such Squire he was
That turn'd your wit, the seamy-side without,
And made you to suspect me with the Moore.

Iago. You are a Foole: go too.

Des. Alas *Iago*,
What shall I do to win my Lord againe?
Good Friend, go to him: for by this light of Heauen,
I know not how I lost him. Heere I kneele:
If ere my will did trespasse 'gainst his Loue,
Either in discourse of thought, or actuall deed,
Or that mine Eyes, mine Eares, or any Sence
Delighted them: or any other Forme.
Or that I do not yet, and euer did,
And euer will, (though he do shake me off
To beggerly diuorcement) Loue him deerely,
Comfort forsweare me. Vnkindnesse may do much,
And his vnkindnesse may defeat my life,
But neuer taynt my Loue. I cannot say Whore,
It do's abhorre me now I speake the word,
To do the Act, that might the addition earne,
Not the worlds Masse of vanitie could make me.

Iago. I pray you be content: 'tis but his humour:
The businesse of the State do's him offence.

Des. If 'twere no other.

Iago. It is but so, I warrant,
Hearke how these Instruments summon to supper:
The Messengers of Venice staies the meate,
Go in, and weepe not: all things shall be well.

Exeunt Desdemona and Æmilia.

Enter Rodorigo.

How now *Rodorigo*?

Rod. I do not finde
That thou deal'st iustly with me.

Iago. What in the contrarie?

Rodori. Euery day thou dafts me with some deuise *Iago*, and rather, as it seemes to me now, keep'st from me all conueniencie, then suppliest me with the least aduantage of hope: I will indeed no longer endure it. Nor am I yet perswaded to put vp in peace, what already I haue foolishly suffred.

Iago. Will you heare me *Rodorigo*?

Rodori.

Rodori. I haue heard too much: and your words and Performanc es are no kin together.

Iago. You charge me most vniustly.

Rodo. With naught but truth: I haue wasted my selfe out of my meanes. The Iewels you haue had from me to deliuer *Desdemona,* would halfe haue corrupted a Votarist. You haue told me she hath receiu'd them, and return'd me expectations and comforts of sodaine respect, and acquaintance, but I finde none.

Iago. Well, go too: very well.

Rod. Very well, go too: I cannot go too, (man) nor tis not very well. Nay I think it is scuruy: and begin to finde my selfe fopt in it.

Iago. Very well.

Rodor. I tell you, 'tis not very well: I will make my selfe knowne to *Desdemona.* If she will returne me my Iewels, I will giue ouer my Suit, and repent my vnlawfull solicitation. If not, assure your selfe, I will seeke satisfaction of you.

Iago. You haue said now.

Rodo. I: and said nothing but what I protest intendment of doing.

Iago. Why, now I see there's mettle in thee: and euen from this instant do build on thee a better opinion then euer before: giue me thy hand *Rodorigo.* Thou hast taken against me a most iust exception: but yet I protest I haue dealt most directly in thy Affaire.

Rod. It hath not appeer'd.

Iago. I grant indeed it hath not appeer'd: and your suspition is not without wit and iudgement. But *Rodorigo,* if thou hast that in thee indeed, which I haue greater reason to beleeue now then euer (I meane purpose, Courage, and Valour) this night shew it. If thou the next night following enioy not *Desdemona,* take me from this world with Treacherie, and deuise Engines for my life.

Rod. Well: what is it? Is it within, reason and compasse?

Iago. Sir, there is especiall Commission come from Venice to depute *Cassio* in *Othello's* place.

Rod. Is that true? Why then *Othello* and *Desdemona* returne againe to Venice.

Iago. Oh no: he goes into Mauritania and taketh away with him the faire *Desdemona,* vnlesse his abode be lingred heere by some accident. Wherein none can be so determinate, as the remouing of *Cassio.*

Rod. How do you meane remouing him?

Iago. Why, by making him vncapable of *Othello's* place: knocking out his braines.

Rod. And that you would haue me to do.

Iago. I: if you dare do your selfe a profit, and a right. He sups to night with a Harlotry: and thither will I go to him. He knowes not yet of his Honourable Fortune, if you will watch his going thence (which I will fashion to fall out betweene twelue and one) you may take him at your pleasure. I will be neere to second your Attempt, and he shall fall betweene vs. Come, stand not amaz'd at it, but go along with me: I will shew you such a necessitie in his death, that you shall thinke your selfe bound to put it on him. It is now high supper time: and the night growes to wast. About it.

Rod. I will heare further reason for this.

Iago. And you shalbe satisfi'd. *Exeunt.*

Scena Tertia.

Enter Othello, Lodouico, Desdemona Æmilia, and Atendants.

Lod. I do beseech you Sir, trouble your selfe no further.

Oth. Oh pardon me: 'twill do me good to walke.

Lodoui. Madam, good night: I humbly thanke your Ladyship.

Des. Your Honour is most welcome.

Oth. Will you walke Sir? Oh *Desdemona.*

Des. My Lord.

Othello. Get you to bed on th'instant, I will be return'd forthwith: dismisse your Attendant there: look't be done. *Exit.*

Des. I will my Lord.

Æm. How goes it now? He lookes gentler then he did.

Des. He saies he will returne incontinent,
And hath commanded me to go to bed,
And bid me to dismisse you.

Æmi. Dismisse me?

Des. It was his bidding: therefore good *Æmilia,*
Giue me my nightly wearing, and adieu.
We must not now displease him.

Æmil. I, would you had neuer seene him.

Des. So would not I: my loue doth so approue
That euen his stubbornesse, his checks, his frownes,
(Prythee vn-pin me) haue grace and fauour.

Æmi. I haue laid those Sheetes you bad me on the be

Des. All's one: good Father, how foolish are our minds:
If I do die before, prythee shrow'd me
In one of these same Sheetes.

Æmil. Come, come: you talke.

Des. My Mother had a Maid call'd *Barbarie,*
She was in loue: and he she lou'd prou'd mad,
And did forsake her. She had a Song of Willough,
An old thing 'twas: but it express'd her Fortune,
And she dy'd singing it. That Song to night,
Will not go from my mind: I haue much to do,
But to go hang my head all at one side
And sing it like poore *Brabarie:* prythee dispatch.

Æmi. Shall I go fetch your Night-gowne?

Des. No, vn-pin me here,
This *Lodouico* is a proper man.

Æmil. A very handsome m ...

Des. He speakes well.

Æmil. I know a Lady in Venice would haue walk'd barefoot to Palestine for a touch of his nether lip.

Des. The poore Soule sat singing, by a Sicamour tree.
Sing all a greene Willough:
Her hand on her bosome her head on her knee,
Sing Willough, Willough, Willough.
The fresh Streames ran by her, and murmur'd her meanes
Sing Willough, &c.
Her salt teares fell from her, and softned the stones,
Sing Willough, &c. (Lay by these)
Willough, Willough. (Prythee high thee: he'le come anon)
Sing all a greene Willough must be my Garland.
Let no body blame him, his scorne I approue.
(Nay that's not next. Harke, who is't that knocks?

Æmil. It's the wind.

Des. I call'd my Loue false Loue: but what said he then?
Sing Willough, &c.
If I court mo women, you'le couch with mo men.

v v 3 So

So get thee gone, good night: mine eyes do itch:
Doth that boade weeping?

Æmil, 'Tis neyther heere, nor there

Def. I haue heard it said so. O these Men, these men!
Do'st thou in conscience thinke (tell me *Æmilia*)
That there be women do abuse their husbands
In such grosse kinde?

Æmil. There be some such, no question.

Def. Would'st thou do such a deed for all the world?

Æmil. Why, would not you?

Def. No, by this Heauenly light.

Æmil. Nor I neither, by this Heauenly light:
I might doo't as well i'th'darke.

Def. Would'st thou do such a deed for al the world?

Æmil. The world's a huge thing:
It is a great price, for a small vice.

Def. Introth, I thinke thou would'st not.

Æmil. Introth I thinke I should, and vndoo't when I had done. Marry, I would not doe such a thing for a ioynt Ring, nor for measures of Lawne, nor for Gownes, Petticoats, nor Caps, nor any petty exhibition. But for all the whole world: why, who would not make her husband a Cuckold, to make him a Monarch? I should venture Purgatory for't.

Def. Beshrew me, if I would do such a wrong
For the whole world.

Æmil. Why, the wrong is but a wrong i'th'world; and hauing the world for your labour, 'tis a wrong in your owne world, and you might quickly make it right.

Def. I do not thinke there is any such woman.

Æmil. Yes, a dozen: and as many to'th'vantage, as would store the world they plaid for.
But I do thinke it is their Husbands faults
If Wiues do fall: (Say, that they slacke their duties,
And powre our Treasures into forraigne laps;
Or else breake out in peeuish Iealousies,
Throwing restraint vpon vs: Or say they strike vs,
Or scant our former hauing in despight)
Why we haue galles: and though we haue some Grace,
Yet haue we some Reuenge. Let Husbands know,
Their wiues haue sense like them: They see, and smell,
And haue their Palats both for sweet, and sowre,
As Husbands haue. What is it that they do,
When they change vs for others? Is it Sport?
I thinke it is: and doth Affection breed it?
I thinke it doth. Is't Frailty that thus erres?
It is so too. And haue not we Affections?
Desires for Sport? and Frailty, as men haue?
Then let them vse vs well: else let them know,
The illes we do, their illes instruct vs so.

Def. Good night, good night:
Heauen me such vses send,
Not to picke bad, from bad; but by bad, mend. *Exeunt*

Actus Quintus. Scena Prima.

Enter Iago, and Rodorigo,

Iago. Heere, stand behinde this Barke,
Straight will he come:
Weare thy good Rapier bare, and put it home:
Quicke, quicke, feare nothing; Ile be at thy Elbow,
It makes vs, or it marres vs, thinke on that,
And fixe most firme thy Resolution.

Rod. Be neere at hand, I may miscarry in't.

Iago. Heere, at thy hand: Be bold, & take thy stand.

Rod. I haue no great deuotion to the deed,
And yet he hath giuen me satisfying Reasons:
'Tis but a man gone. Forth my Sword: he dies.

Iago. I haue rub'd this yong Quat almost to the sense,
And he growes angry. Now, whether he kill *Cassio*,
Or *Cassio* him, or each do kill the other,
Euery way makes my gaine. Liue *Rodorigo*,
He calles me to a restitution large
Of Gold, and Iewels, that I bob'd from him,
As Guifts to *Desdemona*.
It must not be: If *Cassio* do remaine,
He hath a dayly beauty in his life,
That makes me vgly: and besides, the Moore
May vnfold me to him: there stand I in much perill:
No, he must dye. But so, I heard him comming.

Enter Cassio.

Rod. I know his gate, 'tis he: Villaine thou dyest.

Cas. That thrust had beene mine enemy indeed,
But that my Coate is better then thou know'st:
I will make proofe of thine.

Rod. Oh, I am slaine.

Cassio. I am maym'd for euer:
Helpe hoa: Murther, murther.

Enter Othello.

Oth. The voyce of *Cassio*, *Iago* keepes his word.

Rod. O Villaine that I am.

Oth. It is euen so.

Cas. Oh helpe hoa: Light, a Surgeon.

Oth. 'Tis he: O braue *Iago*, honest, and iust,
That hast such Noble sense of thy Friends wrong,
Thou teachest me. Minion, your deere lyes dead,
And your vnblest Fate highes: Strumpet I come:
For of my heart, those Charmes thine Eyes, are blotted.
Thy Bed lust-stain'd, shall with Lusts blood bee spotted.

Exit Othello.

Enter Lodouico and Gratiano.

Cas. What hoa? no Watch? No passage?
Murther, Murther.

Gra. 'Tis some mischance, the voyce is very direfull.

Cas Oh helpe.

Lodo. Hearke.

Rod. Oh wretched Villaine.

Lod. Two or three groane. 'Tis heauy night;
These may be counterfeits: Let's think't vnsafe
To come into the cry, without more helpe.

Rod. Nobody come: then shall I bleed to death.

Enter Iago.

Lod. Hearke.

Gra Here's one comes in his shirt, with Light, and Weapons.

Iago. Who's there?
Who's noyse is this that cries on murther?

Lodo. We do not know.

Iago. Do not you heare a cry?

Cas. Heere, heere: for heauen sake helpe me.

Iago. What's the matter?

Gra. This is *Othello*'s Ancient, as I take it.

Lodo. The same indeede, a very valiant Fellow.

Iago. What are you heere, that cry so greeuously?

Cas. *Iago*? Oh I am spoyl'd, vndone by Villaines:
Giue me some helpe.

Iago. O mee, Lieutenant!
What Villaines haue done this?

Cas. I thinke that one of them is heereabout,

And

And cannot make away.
Iago. Oh treacherous Villaines:
What are you there? Come in, and giue some helpe.
Rod. O helpe me there.
Cassio. That's one of them.
Iago. Oh murd'rous Slaue! O Villaine!
Rod. O damn'd *Iago*! O inhumaine Dogge!
Iago. Kill men i'th'darke?
Where be these bloody Theeues?
How silent is this Towne? Hoa, murther, murther.
What may you be? Are you of good, or euill?
Lod. As you shall proue vs, praise vs.
Iago. Signior *Lodouico*?
Lod. He Sir.
Iago. I cry you mercy: here's *Cassio* hurt by Villaines.
Gra. *Cassio*?
Iago. How is't Brother?
Cas. My Legge is cut in two.
Iago. Marry heauen forbid:
Light Gentlemen, Ile binde it with my shirt.
Enter Bianca.
Bian. What is the matter hoa? Who is't that cry'd
Iago. Who is't that cry'd?
Bian. Oh my deere *Cassio*,
My sweet *Cassio*: Oh *Cassio*, *Cassio*, *Cassio*.
Iago. O notable Strumpet. *Cassio*, may you suspect
Who they should be, that haue thus mangled you?
Cas. No.
Gra. I am sorry to finde you thus;
I haue beene to seeke you.
Iago. Lend me a Garter. So:——Oh for a Chaire
To beare him easily hence.
Bian. Alas he faints. Oh *Cassio*, *Cassio*, *Cassio*.
Iago. Gentlemen all, I do suspect this Trash
To be a party in this Iniurie.
Patience awhile, good *Cassio*. Come, come;
Lend me a Light: know we this face, or no?
Alas my Friend, and my deere Countryman
Rodorigo? No: Yes sure: Yes, 'tis *Roderigo*.
Gra. What, of Venice?
Iago. Euen he Sir: Did you know him?
Gra. Know him? I.
Iago. Signior *Gratiano*? I cry your gentle pardon:
These bloody accidents must excuse my Manners,
That so neglected you.
Gra. I am glad to see you.
Iago. How do you *Cassio*? Oh, a Chaire, a Chaire.
Gra. *Rodorigo*?
Iago. He, he, 'tis he:
Oh that's well said, the Chaire.
Some good man beare him carefully from hence,
Ile fetch the Generall's Surgeon. For you Mistris,
Saue you your labour. He that lies slaine heere (*Cassio*)
Was my deere friend. What malice was between you?
Cas. None in the world: nor do I know the man?
Iago. What? looke you pale? Oh beare him o'th'Ayre.
Stay you good Gentlemen. Looke you pale, Mistris?
Do you perceiue the gastnesse of her eye?
Nay, if you stare, we shall heare more anon.
Behold her well: I pray you looke vpon her:
Do you see Gentlemen? Nay, guiltinesse will speake
Though tongues were out of vse.
Æmil. Alas, what is the matter?
What is the matter, Husband?
Iago. *Cassio* hath heere bin set on in the darke
By *Rodorigo*, and Fellowes that are scap'd:
He's almost slaine, and *Rodorigo* quite dead.
Æmil. Alas good Gentleman: alas good *Cassio*.
Iago. This is the fruits of whoring. Prythe *Æmilia*,
Go know of *Cassio* where he supt to night.
What, do you shake at that?
Bian. He supt at my house, but I therefore shake not.
Iago. O did he so? I charge you go with me.
Æmil. Oh fie vpon thee Strumpet.
Bian. I am no Strumpet, but of life as honest,
As you that thus abuse me.
Æmil. As I? Fie vpon thee.
Iago. Kinde Gentlemen:
Let's go see poore *Cassio* drest.
Come Mistris, you must tel's another Tale.
Æmilia, run you to the Cittadell,
And tell my Lord and Lady, what hath happ'd:
Will you go on afore? This is the night
That either makes me, or foredoes me quight. *Exeunt*

Scœna Secunda.

Enter Othello, and Desdemona in her bed.

Oth. It is the Cause, it is the Cause (my Soule)
Let me not name it to you, you chaste Starres,
It is the Cause. Yet Ile not shed her blood,
Nor scarre that whiter skin of hers, then Snow,
And smooth as Monumentall Alablaster:
Yet she must dye, else shee'l betray more men:
Put out the Light, and then put out the Light:
If I quench thee, thou flaming Minister,
I can againe thy former light restore,
Should I repent me. But once put out thy Light,
Thou cunning'st Patterne of excelling Nature,
I know not where is that *Promethaan* heate
That can thy Light re-Lume.
When I haue pluck'd thy Rose,
I cannot giue it vitall growth againe,
It needs must wither. Ile smell thee on the Tree.
Oh Balmy breath, that dost almost perswade
Iustice to breake her Sword. One more, one more:
Be thus when thou art dead, and I will kill thee,
And loue thee after. One more, and that's the last.
So sweet, was ne're so fatall. I must weepe,
But they are cruell Teares: This sorrow's heauenly,
It strikes, where it doth loue. She wakes.
Des. Who's there? *Othello*?
Othel. I *Desdemona*.
Des. Will you come to bed, my Lord?
Oth. Haue you pray'd to night, *Desdemon*?
Des. I my Lord.
Oth. If you bethinke your selfe of any Crime
Vnreconcil'd as yet to Heauen, and Grace,
Solicite for it straight.
Des. Alacke, my Lord,
What may you meane by that?
Oth. Well, do it, and be breefe, I will walke by:
I would not kill thy vnprepared Spirit,
No, Heauens fore-fend) I would not kill thy Soule.
Des. Talke you of killing?
Oth. I, I do.
Des. Then Heauen haue mercy on mee.

Oth.

Oth. Amen, with all my heart.
Def. If you say, I hope you will not kill me.
Oth. Humh.
Def. And yet I feare you: for you're fatall then
When your eyes rowle so.
Why I should feare, I know not,
Since guiltinesse I know not: But yet I feele I feare.
Oth. Thinke on thy sinnes.
Def They are Loues I beare to you.
Oth. I and for that thou dy'st.
Def. That death's vnnaturall, that kils for louing.
Alas, why gnaw you so your nether-lip?
Some bloody passion shakes your very Frame:
These are portents: but yet I hope, I hope,
They do not point on me.
Oth. Peace, and be still.
Def. I will so: What's the matter?
Oth. That Handkerchiefe
Which I so lou'd, and gaue thee, thou gau'st to *Cassio.*
Def. No by my Life, and Soule: send for the man,
And aske him.
Oth. Sweet Soule, take heed, take heed of Periury,
Thou art on thy death-bed.
Def. I, but not yet to dye.
Oth. Presently.
Therefore confesse thee freely of thy sinne:
For to deny each Article with Oath,
Cannot remoue, nor choake the strong Conception
That I do grone withall. Thou art to dye.
Def. O Heauen haue mercy on me.
Oth. I say, Amen.
Def. And haue you mercy too. I neuer did
Offend you in my life: neuer lou'd *Cassio,*
But with such generall warrantie of Heauen,
As I might loue. I neuer gaue him Token.
Oth. By Heauen I saw my Handkerchiefe in's hand.
O periur'd woman, thou do'st stone my heart,
And makes me call, what I intend to do,
A Murther, which I thought a Sacrifice.
I saw the Handkerchiefe.
Def. He found it then:
I neuer gaue it him: Send, for him hither:
Let him confesse a truth.
Oth. He hath confest.
Def. What, my Lord?
Oth. That he hath vs'd thee.
Def. How? vnlawfully?
Oth. I.
Def. He will not say so.
Oth. No: his mouth is stopp'd:
Honest *Iago* hath 'tane order for't.
Def. Oh, my feare interprets. What is he dead?
Oth. Had all his haires bin liues, my great Reuenge
Had stomacke for them all.
Def. Alas, he is betray'd, and I vndone.
Oth. Out Strumpet: weep'st thou for him to my face?
Def. O banish me, my Lord, but kill me not.
Oth. Downe Strumpet.
Def. Kill me to morrow, let me liue to night.
Oth. Nay, if you striue.
Def. But halfe an houre.
Oth. Being done, there is no pawse.
Def. But while I say one prayer.
Oth. It is too late. *Smothers her.*
Æmilia at the doore.
Æmil. My Lord, my Lord? What hoa?
My Lord, my Lord.
Oth. What noise is this? Not dead? not yet quite dead?
I that am cruell, am yet mercifull,
I would not haue thee linger in thy paine?
So, so.
Æmil. within. What hoa? my Lord, my Lord?
Oth. Who's there?
Æmil. Oh good my Lord, I would speake a word
with you.
Oth. Yes: 'Tis *Æmilia*: by and by. Shee's dead.
'Tis like she comes to speake of *Cassio's* death:
The noise was high. Hah, no more moouing?
Still as the Graue. Shall she come in? Wer't good?
I thinke she stirres againe. No, what's best to do?
If she come in, shee'l sure speake to my wife:
My wife, my wife: what wife? I haue no wife.
Oh insupportable! Oh heauy houre!
Me thinkes, it should be now a huge Eclipse
Of Sunne, and Moone; and that th'affrighted Globe
Did yawne at Alteration.
Æmil. I do beseech you
That I may speake with you. Oh good my Lord.
Oth. I had forgot thee: oh come in *Æmilia.*
Soft, by and by, let me the Curtaines draw.
Where art thou? What's the matter with thee now?
Enter Æmilia.
Æmil. Oh my good Lord, yonders foule Murthers
done.
Oth. What? now?
Æmil. But now, my Lord.
Oth. It is the very error of the Moone,
She comes more neerer Earth then she was wont,
And makes men mad.
Æmil. *Cassio,* my Lord, hath kill'd
A young Venetian, call'd *Rodorigo.*
Oth *Rodorigo* kill'd? and *Cassio* kill'd?
Æmil No. *Cassio* is not kill'd.
Oth. Not *Cassio* kill'd? Then Murther's out of tune,
And sweet Reuenge growes harsh.
Def. O falsely, falsely murder'd.
Æmil. Alas! what cry is that?
Oth. That? What?
Æmil. Out, and alas, that was my Ladies voice.
Helpe, helpe hoa, helpe. Oh Ladie speake againe,
Sweet *Desdemona,* oh sweet Mistris, speake.
Def. A guiltlesse death, I dye.
Æmil. Oh who hath done this deed?
Def No body: I my selfe, farewell:
Commend me to my kinde Lord: oh farewell.
Oth. Why, how should she be murdred?
Æmil. Alas: who knowes?
Oth You heare her say her selfe, it was not I.
Æmil. She said so: I must needs report the truth.
Oth. She's like a Liar gone to burning hell,
'Twas I that kill'd her.
Æmil. Oh the more Angell she, and you the blacker
Diuell.
Oth. She turn'd to folly: and she was a whore.
Æmil. Thou do'st bely her, and thou art a diuell.
Oth. She was false as water.
Æmil. Thou art rash as fire, to say
That she was false. Oh she was heauenly true.
Oth. *Cassio* did top her: Ask thy husband else.
O, I were damn'd beneath all depth in hell:
But that I did proceed vpon iust grounds
To this extremity. Thy Husband knew it all.

Æmil.

Æmil. My Husband?
Oth. Thy Husband.
Æmil. That she was false to Wedlocke?
Oth. I, with *Cassio*: had she bin true,
If Heauen would make me such another world,
Of one entyre and perfect Chrysolite,
I'ld not haue sold her for it
Æmil. My Husband?
Oth. I, 'twas he that told me on her first,
An honest man he is, and hates the slime
That stickes on filthy deeds.
Æmil. My Husband?
Oth. What needs this itterance, Woman?
I say, thy Husband.
Æmil. Oh Mistris,
Villany hath made mockes with loue:
My Husband say she was false?
Oth. He, Woman;
I say thy Husband: Do'st vnderstand the word?
My Friend, thy Husband; honest, honest *Iago*.
Æmil. If he say so, may his pernicious Soule
Rot halfe a graine a day: he lyes to'th'heart,
She was too fond of her most filthy Bargaine.
Oth. Hah?
Æmil. Do thy worst:
This deede of thine is no more worthy Heauen,
Then thou was't worthy her.
Oth. Peace, you were best.
Æmil. Thou hast not halfe that powre to do me harm,
As I haue to be hurt. Oh Gull, oh dolt,
As ignorant as durt: thou hast done a deed
(I care not for thy Sword) Ile make thee known,
Though I lost twenty liues. Helpe, helpe, hoa, helpe:
The Moore hath kill'd my Mistris. Murther, murther.

Enter Montano, Gratiano, and Iago.

Mon. What is the matter? How now Generall?
Æmil. Oh, are you come, *Iago*: you haue done well,
That men must lay their Murthers on your necke.
Gra. What is the matter?
Æmil. Disproue this Villaine, if thou bee'st a man:
He sayes, thou told'st him that his wife was false:
I know thou did'st not: thou't not such a Villain.
Speake, for my heart is full.
Iago. I told him what I thought,
And told no more
Then what he found himselfe was apt, and true.
Æmil. But did you euer tell him,
She was false?
Iago. I did.
Æmil. You told a Lye an odious damned Lye:
Vpon my Soule, a Lye; a wicked Lye.
Shee false with *Cassio*?
Did you say with *Cassio*?
Iago. With *Cassio*, Mistris?
Go too, charme your tongue.
Emil. I will not charme my Tongue;
I am bound to speake,
My Mistris heere lyes murthered in her bed.
All. Oh Heauens, forefend.
Emil. And your reports haue set the Murder on.
Othello. Nay stare not Masters,
It is true indeede.
Gra. 'Tis a strange Truth.
Mont. O monstrous Acte.
Emil. Villany, villany, villany:
I thinke vpon't, I thinke: I smel't: O Villany:
I thought so then: Ile kill my selfe for greefe.
O villany! villany!
Iago. What, are you mad?
I charge you get you home.
Emil. Good Gentlemen, let me haue leaue to speake:
'Tis proper I obey him; but not now:
Perchance *Iago*, I will ne're go home.
Oth Oh, oh, oh.
Emil. Nay, lay thee downe, and roare:
For thou hast kill'd the sweetest innocent,
That ere did lift vp eye.
Oth. Oh she was fowle!
I scarse did know you Vnkle, there lies your Neece,
Whose breath (indeed) these hands haue newly stopp'd:
I know this acte shewes horrible and grim.
Gra. Poore *Desdemon*:
I am glad thy Father's dead,
Thy Match was mortall to him: and pure greefe
Shore his old thred in twaine. Did he liue now,
This sight would make him do a desperate turne:
Yea, curse his better Angell from his side,
And fall to Reprobance.
Oth. 'Tis pittifull: but yet *Iago* knowes
That she with *Cassio*, hath the Act of shame,
A thousand times committed. *Cassio* confest it,
And she did gratifie his amorous workes
With that Recognizance and pledge of Loue
Which I first gaue her: I saw it in his hand:
It was a Handkerchiefe, an Antique Token
My Father gaue my Mother.
Emil. Oh Heauen! oh heauenly Powres
Iago. Come, hold your peace.
Emil. 'Twill out, 'twill out. I peace?
No, I will speake as liberall as the North;
Let Heauen, and Men, and Diuels, let them all,
All, all, crie shame against me, yet Ile speake.
Iago. Be wise, and get you home.
Emil. I will not.
Gra. Fye, your Sword vpon a Woman.
Emil. Oh thou dull Moore,
That Handkerchiefe thou speak'st of
I found by Fortune, and did giue my Husband:
For often, with a solemne earnestnesse,
(More then indeed belong'd to such a Trifle)
He begg'd of me, to steale't.
Iago. Villanous Whore.
Emil. She giue it *Cassio*? No, alas I found it,
And I did giu't my Husband.
Iago. Filth, thou lyest.
Emil. By Heauen I do not, I do not Gentlemen:
Oh murd'rous Coxcombe, what should such a Foole
Do with so good a wife?
Oth. Are there no stones in Heauen,
But what serues for the Thunder?
Precious Villaine.
Gra. The woman falles:
Sure he hath kill'd his Wife.
Emil. I, I: oh lay me by my Mistris side.
Gra. Hee's gone, but his wife's kill'd.
Mon. 'Tis a notorious Villain: take you this weapon
Which I haue recouer'd from the Moore:
Come guard the doore without, let him not passe,
But kill him rather. Ile after that same villaine,
For 'tis a damned Slaue. *Exit.*

Oth.

Oth. I am not valiant neither:
But euery Punie whipſter gets my Sword.
But why ſhould Honor out-liue Honeſty?
Let it go all.
Æmil. What did thy Song boad Lady?
Hearke, canſt thou heare me? I will play the Swan,
And dye in Muſicke: *Willough, Willough, Willough.*
Moore, ſhe was chaſte: She lou'd thee, cruell Moore,
So come my Soule to bliſſe, as I ſpeake true:
So ſpeaking as I thinke, alas, I dye.
Oth. I haue another weapon in this Chamber,
It was a Sword of Spaine, the Ice brookes temper:
Oh heere it is: Vnkle I muſt come forth.
Gra. If thou attempt it, it will coſt thee deere;
Thou haſt no weapon, and perforce muſt ſuffer.
Oth. Looke in vpon me then, and ſpeake with me,
Or naked as I am I will aſſault thee.
Gra. What is the matter?
Othel. Behold, I haue a weapon:
A better neuer did it ſelfe ſuſtaine
Vpon a Soldiers Thigh. I haue ſeene the day,
That with this little Arme, and this good Sword,
I haue made my way through more impediments
Then twenty times your ſtop. But (oh vaine boaſt)
Who can controll his Fate? 'Tis not ſo now.
Be not affraid, though you do ſee me weapon'd:
Heere is my iournies end, heere is my butt
And verie Sea-marke of my vtmoſt Saile.
Do you go backe diſmaid? 'Tis a loſt feare:
Man but a Ruſh againſt *Othello's* breſt,
And he retires. Where ſhould *Othello* go?
Now: how doſt thou looke now? Oh ill-Starr'd wench,
Pale as thy Smocke: when we ſhall meete at compt,
This looke of thine will hurle my Soule from Heauen,
And Fiends will ſnatch at it. Cold, cold, my Girle?
Euen like thy Chaſtity. O curſed, curſed Slaue!
Whip me ye Diuels,
From the poſſeſſion of this Heauenly ſight:
Blow me about in windes, roaſt me in Sulphure,
Waſh me in ſteepe-downe gulfes of Liquid fire.
Oh *Deſdemon*! dead *Deſdemon*: dead. Oh, oh!

Enter Lodouico, Caſſio, Montano, and Iago, with Officers.

Lod. Where is this raſh, and moſt vnfortunate man?
Oth. That's he that was *Othello*: heere I am.
Lod. Where is that Viper?
Bring the Villaine forth.
Oth. I look down towards his feet; but that's a Fable,
If that thou bee'ſt a Diuell, I cannot kill thee.
Lod. Wrench his Sword from him.
Iago. I bleed Sir, but not kill'd.
Othel. I am not ſorry neither, Il'd haue thee liue:
For in my ſenſe, 'tis happineſſe to die.
Lod. Oh thou *Othello*, that was once ſo good,
Falne in the practiſe of a curſed Slaue,
What ſhall be ſaide to thee.
Oth. Why any thing:
An honourable Murderer, if you will:
For nought I did in hate, but all in Honour.
Lod. This wretch hath part confeſt his Villany:
Did you and he conſent in *Caſſio's* death.
Oth. I.
Caſ. Deere Generall, I neuer gaue you cauſe.
Oth. I do beleeue it, and I aske your pardon:
Will you, I pray, demand that demy-Diuell,
Why he hath thus enſnar'd my Soule and Body.
Iag. Demand me nothing: what you know, you know:
From this time forth, I neuer will ſpeake word.
Lod. What? not to pray?
Gra. Torments will ope your lips.
Oth. Well, thou doſt beſt.
Lod. Sir,
You ſhall vnderſtand what hath befalne,
(Which, as I thinke, you know not) heere is a Letter
Found in the pocket of the ſlaine *Rodorigo*,
And heere another, the one of them imports
The death of *Caſſio*, to be vndertooke
By *Rodorigo*.
Oth. O Villaine!
Caſſio. Moſt Heatheniſh, and moſt groſſe.
Lod. Now, heere's another diſcontented paper
Found in his pocket too: and this it ſeemes
Rodorigo meant t'haue ſent this damned villaine:
But that (belike) *Iago* in the interim
Came in, and ſatiſfi'd him.
Oth. Oh thou pernitious Caitiffe;
How came you (*Caſſio*) by that Handkerchiefe
That was my wiues?
Caſſio. I found it in my Chamber:
And he himſelfe confeſt it but euen now,
That there he dropt it for a ſpeciall purpoſe,
Which wrought to his deſire.
Othel. O Foole, foole, foole!
Caſſio. There is beſides, in *Rodorigo's* Letter,
How he vpbraides *Iago*, that he made him
Braue me vpon the Watch: whereon it came
That I was caſt: and euen but now he ſpake
(After long ſeeming dead) *Iago* hurt him,
Iago ſet him on.
Lod. You muſt forſake this roome, and go with vs:
Your Power, and your Command is taken off,
And *Caſſio* rules in Cyprus. For this Slaue,
If there be any cunning Crueltie,
That can torment him much, and hold him long,
It ſhall be his. You ſhall cloſe Priſoner reſt,
Till that the Nature of your fault be knowne
To the Venetian State. Come, bring away.
Oth. Soft you; a word or two before you goe:
I haue done the State ſome ſeruice, and they know't:
No more of that. I pray you in your Letters,
When you ſhall theſe vnluckie deeds relate,
Speake of me, as I am. Nothing extenuate,
Nor ſet downe ought in malice.
Then muſt you ſpeake,
Of one that lou'd not wiſely, but too well:
Of one, not eaſily Iealious, but being wrought,
Perplexed in the extreame: Of one, whoſe hand
(Like the baſe Iudean) threw a Pearle away
Richer then all his Tribe: Of one, whoſe ſubdu'd Eyes,
Albeit vn-vſed to the melting moode,
Drops teares as faſt as the Arabian Trees
Their Medicinable gumme. Set you downe this:
And ſay beſides, that in *Aleppo* once,
Where a malignant, and a Turbond-Turke
Beate a Venetian, and traduc'd the State,
I tooke by th'throat the circumciſed Dogge,
And ſmoate him, thus.
Lod. Oh bloody period.
Gra. All that is ſpoke, is marr'd.
Oth. I kiſt thee, ere I kill'd thee: No way but this,
Killing my ſelfe, to dye vpon a kiſſe. *Dyes*

Caſſio.

Cas. This did I feare, but thought he had no weapon:
For he was great of heart.
Lod. Oh Sparton Dogge:
More fell then Anguish, Hunger, or the Sea:
Looke on the Tragicke Loading of this bed:
This is thy worke:
The Obiect poysons Sight,
Let it be hid. *Gratiano*, keepe the house,
And seize vpon the Fortunes of the Moore,
For they succeede on you. To you, Lord Gouernor,
Remaines th eCensure of this hellish villaine:
The Time, the Place, the Torture, oh inforce it:
My selfe will straight aboord, and to the State,
This heauie Act, with heauie heart relate. *Exeunt.*

FINIS.

The Names of the Actors.

(:*.*:)

Othello, *the Moore.*
Brabantio, *Father to Desdemona.*
Cassio, *an Honourable Lieutenant.*
Iago, *a Villaine.*
Rodorigo, *a gull'd Gentleman.*
Duke of Venice.
Senators.
Montano, *Gouernour of Cyprus.*
Gentlemen of Cyprus.
Lodouico *and* Gratiano, *two Noble Venetians.*
Saylors.
Clowne.

Desdemona, *wife to Othello.*
Æmilia, *wife to Iago.*
Bianca, *a Curtezan.*

THE TRAGEDIE OF Anthonie, and Cleopatra.

Actus Primus. Scœna Prima.

Enter Demetrius and Philo.

Philo.
NAy, but this dotage of our Generals
Ore-flowes the measure: those his goodly eyes
That o're the Files and Musters of the Warre,
Haue glow'd like plated Mars:
Now bend, now turne
The Office and Deuotion of their view
Vpon a Tawny Front. His Captaines heart,
Which in the scuffles of great Fights hath burst
The Buckles on his brest, reneages all temper,
And is become the Bellowes and the Fan
To coole a Gypsies Lust.

Flourish. Enter Anthony, Cleopatra, her Ladies, the Traine, with Eunuchs fanning her

Looke where they come:
Take but good note, and you shall see in him
(The triple Pillar of the world) transform'd
Into a Strumpets Foole. Behold and see.
Cleo. If it be Loue indeed, tell me how much.
Ant. There's beggery in the loue that can be reckon'd
Cleo. Ile set a bourne how farre to be belou'd.
Ant. Then must thou needes finde out new Heauen, new Earth.

Enter a Messenger.

Mes. Newes (my good Lord) from Rome.
Ant. Grates me, the summe.
Cleo. Nay heare them *Anthony*.
Fuluia perchance is angry: Or who knowes,
If the scarse-bearded *Cæsar* haue not sent
His powrefull Mandate to you, Do this, or this;
Take in that Kingdome, and Infranchise that:
Perform't, or else we damne thee.
Ant. How, my Loue?
Cleo. Perchance? Nay, and most like:
You must not stay heere longer, your dismission
Is come from *Cæsar*, therefore heare it *Anthony*.
Where's *Fuluias* Processe? (*Cæsars* I would say) both?
Call in the Messengers: As I am Egypts Queene,
Thou blushest *Anthony*, and that blood of thine
Is *Cæsars* homager: else so thy cheeke payes shame,
When shrill-tongu'd *Fuluia* scolds. The Messengers.
Ant. Let Rome in Tyber melt, and the wide Arch
Of the raing'd Empire fall: Heere is my space,
Kingdomes are clay: Our dungie earth alike
Feeds Beast as Man; the Noblenesse of life
Is to do thus: when such a mutuall paire,
And such a twaine can doo't, in which I binde
One paine of punishment, the world to weete
We stand vp Peerelesse.
Cleo. Excellent falshood:
Why did he marry *Fuluia*, and not loue her?
Ile seeme the Foole I am not. *Anthony* will be himselfe.
Ant. But stirr'd by *Cleopatra*.
Now for the loue of Loue, and her soft houres,
Let's not confound the time with Conference harsh;
There's not a minute of our liues should stretch
Without some pleasure now. What sport to night?
Cleo. Heare the Ambassadors.
Ant. Fye wrangling Queene:
Whom euery thing becomes, to chide, to laugh,
To weepe: who euery passion fully striues
To make it selfe (in Thee) faire, and admir'd.
No Messenger but thine, and all alone, to night
Wee'l wander through the streets, and note
The qualities of people. Come my Queene,
Last night you did desire it. Speake not to vs.

Exeunt with the Traine.

Dem. Is *Cæsar* with *Anthonius* priz'd so slight?
Philo. Sir sometimes when he is not *Anthony*,
He comes too short of that great Property
Which still should go with *Anthony*.
Dem. I am full sorry, that hee approues the common Lyar, who thus speakes of him at Rome; but I will hope of better deeds to morrow. Rest you happy. *Exeunt*

Enter Enobarbus, Lamprius, a Southsayer, Rannius, Lucillius, Charmian, Iras, Mardian the Eunuch, and Alexas.

Char. L. *Alexas*, sweet *Alexas*, most any thing *Alexas*, almost most absolute *Alexas*, where's the Soothsayer that you prais'd so to th' Queene? Oh that I knewe this Husband, which you say, must change his Hornes with Garlands.
Alex. Soothsayer.
Sooth. Your will?
Char. Is this the Man? Is't you sir that know things?
Sooth. In Natures infinite booke of Secrecie, a little I can read.
Alex. Shew him your hand.
Enob. Bring in the Banket quickly: Wine enough, Cleopa

Cleopatra's health to drinke.

Char. Good ſir, giue me good Fortune.

Sooth. I make not, but foreſee.

Char. Pray then, foreſee me one.

Sooth. You ſhall be yet farre fairer then you are.

Char. He meanes in fleſh.

Iras. No, you ſhall paint when you are old.

Char. Wrinkles forbid.

Alex. Vex not his preſcience, be attentiue.

Char. Huſh.

Sooth. You ſhall be more belouing, then beloued.

Char. I had rather heate my Liuer with drinking.

Alex. Nay, heare him.

Char. Good now ſome excellent Fortune: Let mee be married to three Kings in a forenoone, and Widdow them all: Let me haue a Childe at fifty, to whom *Herode* of Iewry may do Homage. Finde me to marrie me with *Octauius Cæſar*, and companion me with my Miſtris.

Sooth. You ſhall out-liue the Lady whom you ſerue.

Char. Oh excellent, I loue long life better then Figs.

Sooth. You haue ſeene and proued a fairer former fortune, then that which is to approach.

Char. Then belike my Children ſhall haue no names: Prythee how many Boyes and Wenches muſt I haue.

Sooth. If euery of your wiſhes had a wombe, & foretell euery wiſh, a Million.

Char. Out Foole, I forgiue thee for a Witch.

Alex. You thinke none but your ſheets are priuie to your wiſhes.

Char. Nay come, tell *Iras* hers.

Alex. Wee'l know all our Fortunes.

Enob. Mine, and moſt of our Fortunes to night, ſhall be drunke to bed.

Iras. There's a Palme preſages Chaſtity, if nothing els.

Char. E'ne as the o're-flowing Nylus preſageth Famine.

Iras. Go you wilde Bedfellow, you cannot Soothſay.

Char. Nay, if an oyly Palme bee not a fruitfull Prognoſtication, I cannot ſcratch mine eare. Prythee tel her but a worky day Fortune.

Sooth. Your Fortunes are alike.

Iras But how, but how, giue me particulars.

Sooth. I haue ſaid.

Iras. Am I not an inch of Fortune better then ſhe?

Char. Well, if you were but an inch of fortune better then I: where would you chooſe it.

Iras. Not in my Husbands noſe.

Char. Our worſer thoughts Heauens mend.

Alexas Come, his Fortune, his Fortune. Oh let him mary a woman that cannot go, ſweet *Iſis*, I beſeech thee, and let her dye too, and giue him a worſe, and let worſe follow worſe, till the worſt of all follow him laughing to his graue, fifty-fold a Cuckold. Good *Iſis* heare me this Prayer, though thou denie me a matter of more waight: good *Iſis* I beſeech thee.

Iras. Amen, deere Goddeſſe, heare that prayer of the people. For, as it is a heart-breaking to ſee a handſome man looſe-Wiu'd, ſo it is a deadly ſorrow, to beholde a foule Knaue vncuckolded: Therefore deere *Iſis* keep decorum, and Fortune him accordingly.

Char. Amen.

Alex Lo now, if it lay in their hands to make mee a Cuckold, they would make themſelues Whores, but they'ld doo't.

Enter Cleopatra.

Enob. Huſh, heere comes *Anthony*.

Char. Not he, the Queene.

Cleo. Saue you, my Lord.

Enob. No Lady.

Cleo. Was he not heere?

Char. No Madam.

Cleo. He was diſpos'd to mirth, but on the ſodaine
A Romane thought hath ſtrooke him.
Enobarbus?

Enob. Madam.

Cleo. Seeke him, and bring him hither: wher's *Alexias*?

Alex. Heere at your ſeruice.
My Lord approaches.

Enter Anthony, with a Meſſenger.

Cleo. We will not looke vpon him:
Go with vs. *Exeunt.*

Meſſen. *Fuluia* thy Wife,
Firſt came into the Field.

Ant. Againſt my Brother *Lucius*?

Meſſen. I: but ſoone that Warre had end,
And the times ſtate
Made friends of them, ioynting their force 'gainſt *Cæſar*,
Whoſe better iſſue in the warre from Italy,
Vpon the firſt encounter draue them.

Ant. Well, what worſt.

Meſſ. The Nature of bad newes infects the Teller.

Ant. When it concernes the Foole or Coward: On.
Things that are paſt, are done, with me. 'Tis thus,
Who tels me true, though in his Tale lye death,
I heare him as he flatter'd.

Meſ. *Labienus* (this is ſtiffe-newes)
Hath with his Parthian Force
Extended Aſia: from Euphrates his conquering
Banner ſhooke, from Syria to Lydia,
And to Ionia, whil'ſt——

Ant. *Anthony* thou would'ſt ſay.

Meſ. Oh my Lord.

Ant. Speake to me home,
Mince not the generall tongue, name
Cleopatra as ſhe is call'd in Rome:
Raile thou in *Fuluia's* phraſe, and taunt my faults
With ſuch full Licenſe, as both Truth and Malice
Haue power to vtter. Oh then we bring forth weeds,
When our quicke windes lye ſtill, and our illes told vs
Is as our earing: fare thee well awhile.

Meſ. At your Noble pleaſure. *Exit Meſſenger.*

Enter another Meſſenger.

Ant. From *Scicion* how the newes? Speake there.

1.*Meſ.* The man from *Scicion*,
Is there ſuch an one?

2.*Meſ.* He ſtayes vpon your will.

Ant. Let him appeare:
Theſe ſtrong Egyptian Fetters I muſt breake,
Or looſe my ſelfe in dotage.

Enter another Meſſenger with a Letter.

What are you?

3.*Meſ.* *Fuluia* thy wife is dead.

Ant. Where dyed ſhe.

Meſ In *Scicion*, her length of ſickneſſe,
With what elſe more ſerious,
Importeth thee to know, this beares.

Antho. Forbeare me
There's a great Spirit gone, thus did I deſire it:
What our contempts doth often hurle from vs,

x We

We with it ours againe. The present pleasure,
By reuolution lowring, does become
The opposite of it selfe: she's good being gon,
The hand could plucke her backe, that shou'd her on.
I must from this enchanting Queene breake off,
Ten thousand harmes, more then the illes I know
My idlenesse doth hatch.

Enter Enobarbus.

How now *Enobarbus.*

Eno. What's your pleasure, Sir?

Anth. I must with haste from hence.

Eno. Why then we kill all our Women. We see how mortall an vnkindnesse is to them, if they suffer our departure death's the word.

Ant. I must be gone.

Eno. Vnder a compelling an occasion, let women die. It were pitty to cast them away for nothing, though betweene them and a great cause, they should be esteemed nothing. *Cleopatra* catching but the least noyse of this, dies instantly: I haue seene her dye twenty times vppon farre poorer moment: I do think there is mettle in death, which commits some louing acte vpon her, she hath such a celerity in dying.

Ant. She is cunning past mans thought.

Eno. Alacke Sir no, her passions are made of nothing but the finest part of pure Loue. We cannot cal her winds and waters, sighes and teares: They are greater stormes and Tempests then Almanackes can report. This cannot be cunning in her; if it be, she makes a showre of Raine as well as Ioue.

Ant. Would I had neuer seene her.

Eno. Oh sir, you had then left vnseene a wonderfull peece of worke, which not to haue beene blest withall, would haue discredited your Trauaile.

Ant. *Fuluia* is dead.

Eno. Sir.

Ant. *Fuluia* is dead.

Eno. *Fuluia?*

Ant. Dead.

Eno. Why sir, giue the Gods a thankefull Sacrifice: when it pleaseth their Deities to take the wife of a man from him, it shewes to man the Tailors of the earth: comforting therein, that when olde Robes are worne out, there are members to make new. If there were no more Women but *Fuluia*, then had you indeede a cut, and the case to be lamented: This greefe is crown'd with Consolation, your old Smocke brings foorth a new Petticoate, and indeed the teares liue in an Onion, that should water this sorrow.

Ant. The businesse she hath broached in the State,
Cannot endure my absence.

Eno. And the businesse you haue broach'd heere cannot be without you, especially that of *Cleopatra's*, which wholly depends on your abode.

Ant. No more light Answeres.
Let our Officers
Haue notice what we purpose. I shall breake
The cause of our Expedience to the Queene,
And get her loue to part. For not alone
The death of *Fuluia*, with more vrgent touches
Do strongly speake to vs: but the Letters too
Of many our contriuing Friends in Rome,
Petition vs at home. *Sextus Pompeius*
Haue giuen the dare to *Cæsar*, and commands
The Empire of the Sea. Our slippery people,
Whose Loue is neuer link'd to the deseruer,
Till his deserts are past, begin to throw
Pompey the great, and all his Dignities
Vpon his Sonne, who high in Name and Power,
Higher then both in Blood and Life, stands vp
For the maine Souldier. Whose quality going on,
The sides o'th'world may danger. Much is breeding,
Which like the Coursers heire, hath yet but life,
And not a Serpents poyson. Say our pleasure,
To such whose places vnder vs, require
Our quicke remoue from hence.

Enob. I shall doo't.

Enter Cleopatra, Charmian, Alexas, and Iras.

Cleo. Where is he?

Char. I did not see him since.

Cleo. See where he is,
Whose with him, what he does:
I did not send you. If you finde him sad,
Say I am dauncing: if in Myrth, report
That I am sodaine sicke. Quicke, and returne.

Char. Madam, me thinkes if you did loue him deerly,
You do not hold the method, to enforce
The like from him.

Cleo. What should I do, I do not?

Ch. In each thing giue him way, crosse him in nothing.

Cleo. Thou teachest like a foole: the way to lose him.

Char. Tempt him not so too farre. I wish forbeare,
In time we hate that which we often feare.

Enter Anthony.

But heere comes *Anthony.*

Cleo. I am sicke, and sullen.

An. I am sorry to giue breathing to my purpose.

Cleo. Helpe me away deere *Charmian*, I shall fall,
It cannot be thus long, the sides of Nature
Will not sustaine it.

Ant. Now my deerest Queene.

Cleo. Pray you stand farther from mee.

Ant. What's the matter?

Cleo. I know by that same eye ther's some good news.
What sayes the married woman you may goe?
Would she had neuer giuen you leaue to come.
Let her not say 'tis I that keepe you heere,
I haue no power vpon you: Hers you are.

Ant. The Gods best know.

Cleo. Oh neuer was there Queene
So mightily betrayed: yet at the first
I saw the Treasons planted.

Ant. *Cleopatra.*

Cleo. Why should I thinke you can be mine, & true,
(Though you in swearing shake the Throaned Gods)
Who haue beene false to *Fuluia?*
Riotous madnesse,
To be entangled with those mouth-made vowes,
Which breake themselues in swearing.

Ant. Most sweet Queene.

Cleo. Nay pray you seeke no colour for your going.
But bid farewell, and goe:
When you sued staying,
Then was the time for words: No going then,
Eternity was in our Lippes, and Eyes,
Blisse in our browes bent: none our parts so poore,
But was a race of Heauen. They are so still,
Or thou the greatest Souldier of the world,
Art turn'd the greatest Lyar.

Ant. How now Lady?

Cleo

Cleo. I would I had thy inches, thou should'st know
There were a heart in Egypt.
Ant. Heare me Queene:
The strong necessity of Time, commands
Our Seruicles a-while: but my full heart
Remaines in vse with you. Our Italy,
Shines o're with ciuill Swords; *Sextus Pompeius*
Makes his approaches to the Port of Rome,
Equality of two Domesticke powers,
Breed scrupulous faction: The hated growne to strength
Are newly growne to Loue: The condemn'd *Pompey*,
Rich in his Fathers Honor, creepes apace
Into the hearts of such, as haue not thriued
Vpon the present state, whose Numbers threaten,
And quietnesse growne sicke of rest, would purge
By any desperate change: My more particular,
And that which most with you should safe my going,
Is *Fuluias* death.
Cleo. Though age from folly could not giue me freedom
It does from childishnesse. Can *Fuluia* dye?
Ant. She's dead my Queene.
Looke heere, and at thy Soueraigne leysure read
The Garboyles she awak'd: at the last, best,
See when, and where shee died.
Cleo. O most false Loue!
Where be the Sacred Violles thou should'st fill
With sorrowfull water? Now I see, I see,
In *Fuluias* death, how mine receiu'd shall be.
Ant. Quarrell no more, but bee prepar'd to know
The purposes I beare; which are, or cease,
As you shall giue th'aduice. By the fire
That quickens Nylus slime, I go from hence
Thy Souldier, Seruant, making Peace or Warre,
As thou affects.
Cleo. Cut my Lace, *Charmian* come,
But let it be, I am quickly ill, and well,
So *Anthony* loues.
Ant. My precious Queene forbeare,
And giue true euidence to his Loue, which stands
An honourable Triall.
Cleo. So *Fuluia* told me.
I prythee turne aside, and weepe for her,
Then bid adiew to me, and say the teares
Belong to Egypt. Good now, play one Scene
Of excellent dissembling, and let it looke
Like perfect Honor.
Ant. You'l heat my blood no more?
Cleo. You can do better yet: but this is meetly.
Ant. Now by Sword.
Cleo. And Target. Still he mends.
But this is not the best. Looke prythee *Charmian*,
How this Herculean Roman do's become
The carriage of his chafe.
Ant. Ile leaue you Lady.
Cleo. Courteous Lord, one word:
Sir, you and I must part, but that's not it:
Sir, you and I haue lou'd, but there's not it:
That you know well, something it is I would:
Oh, my Obliuion is a very *Anthony*,
And I am all forgotten.
Ant. But that your Royalty
Holds Idlenesse your subiect, I should take you
For Idlenesse it selfe.
Cleo 'Tis sweating Labour,
To beare such Idlenesse so neere the heart
As *Cleopatra* this. But Sir, forgiue me,
Since my becommings kill me, when they do not
Eye well to you. Your Honor calles you hence,
Therefore be deafe to my vnpittied Folly,
And all the Gods go with you. Vpon your Sword
Sit Lawrell victory, and smooth successe
Be strew'd before your feete.
Ant. Let vs go.
Come: Our separation so abides and flies,
That thou reciding heere, goes yet with mee;
And I hence fleeting, heere remaine with thee.
Away. *Exeunt.*

Enter Octauius reading a Letter, Lepidus, and their Traine.

Cæs. You may see *Lepidus*, and henceforth know,
It is not *Cæsars* Naturall vice, to hate
One great Competitor. From Alexandria
This is the newes: He fishes, drinkes, and wastes
The Lampes of night in reuell: Is not more manlike
Then *Cleopatra*: nor the Queene of *Ptolomy*
More Womanly then he. Hardly gaue audience
Or vouchsafe to thinke he had Partners. You
Shall finde there a man, who is th'abstracts of all faults,
That all men follow.
Lep. I must not thinke
There are, euils enow to darken all his goodnesse:
His faults in him, seeme as the Spots of Heauen,
More fierie by nights Blacknesse; Hereditarie,
Rather then purchaste: what he cannot change,
Then what he chooses.
Cæs. You are too indulgent. Let's graunt it is not
Amisse to tumble on the bed of *Ptolomy*,
To giue a Kingdome for a Mirth, to sit
And keepe the turne of Tipling with a Slaue,
To reele the streets at noone, and stand the Buffet
With knaues that smels of sweate: Say this becoms him
(As his composure must be rare indeed,
Whom these things cannot blemish) yet must *Anthony*
No way excuse his foyles, when we do beare
So great waight in his lightnesse. If he fill'd
His vacancie with his Voluptuousnesse,
Full surfets, and the drinesse of his bones,
Call on him for't. But to confound such time,
That drummes him from his sport, and speakes as lowd
As his owne State, and ours, 'tis to be chid:
As we rate Boyes, who being mature in knowledge,
Pawne their experience to their present pleasure,
And so rebell to iudgement.
Enter a Messenger.
Lep. Heere's more newes.
Mes. Thy biddings haue beene done, & euerie houre
Most Noble *Cæsar*, shalt thou haue report
How 'tis abroad. *Pompey* is strong at Sea,
And it appeares, he is belou'd of those
That only haue feard *Cæsar*: to the Ports
The discontents repaire, and mens reports
Giue him much wrong'd.
Cæs. I should haue knowne no lesse,
It hath bin taught vs from the primall state
That he which is was wisht, vntill he were:
And the ebb'd man,
Ne're lou'd, till ne're worth loue,
Comes fear'd, by being lack'd. This common bodie,
Like to a Vagabond Flagge vpon the Streame,
Goes too, and backe, lacking the varrying tyde

To rot it selfe with motion.
Mes. *Cæsar* I bring thee word,
Menacrates and *Menas* famous Pyrates
Makes the Sea serue them, which they eare and wound
With keeles of euery kinde. Many hot inrodes
They make in Italy, the Borders Maritime
Lacke blood to thinke on't, and flush youth reuolt,
No Vessell can peepe forth : but 'tis as soone
Taken as seene : for *Pompeyes* name strikes more
Then could his Warre resisted.
Cæsar. *Anthony*,
Leaue thy lasciuious Vassailes. When thou once
Was beaten from *Medena*, where thou slew'st
Hirsius, and *Pausa* Consuls, at thy heele
Did Famine follow, whom thou fought'st against,
(Though daintily brought vp) with patience more
Then Sauages could suffer. Thou did'st drinke
The stale of Horses, and the gilded Puddle
Which Beasts would cough at. Thy pallat the did daine
The roughest Berry, on the rudest Hedge.
Yea, like the Stagge, when Snow the Pasture sheets,
The barkes of Trees thou brows'd. On the Alpes,
It is reported thou did'st eate strange flesh,
Which some did dye to looke on : And all this
(It wounds thine Honor that I speake it now)
Was borne so like a Soldiour, that thy cheeke
So much as lank'd not.
Lep. Tis pitty of him.
Cæs. Let his shames quickely
Driue him to Rome, 'tis time we twaine
Did shew our selues i'th'Field, and to that end
Assemble me immediate counsell, *Pompey*
Thriues in our Idlenesse.
Lep. To morrow *Cæsar*,
I shall be furnisht to informe you rightly
Both what by Sea and Land I can be able
To front this present time.
Cæs. Til which encounter, it is my busines too. Farwell.
Lep. Farwell my Lord, what you shal know mean time
Of stirres abroad, I shall beseech you Sir
To let me be partaker.
Cæsar. Doubt not sir, I knew it for my Bond. *Exeunt*
Enter Cleopatra, Charmian, Iras, & Mardian.
Cleo. Charmian.
Char. Madam.
Cleo. Ha, ha, giue me to drinke *Mandragoru*.
Char. Why Madam ?
Cleo. That I might sleepe out this great gap of time :
My *Anthony* is away.
Char. You thinke of him too much.
Cleo. O'tis Treason.
Char. Madam, I trust not so.
Cleo. Thou, Eunuch *Mardian*?
Mar. What's your Highnesse pleasure?
Cleo. Not now to heare thee sing. I take no pleasure
In ought an Eunuch ha's : Tis well for thee,
That being vnseminar'd, thy freer thoughts
May not flye forth of Egypt. Hast thou Affections ?
Mar. Yes gracious Madam.
Cleo. Indeed?
Mar. Not in deed Madam, for I can do nothing
But what in deede is honest to be done :
Yet haue I fierce Affections, and thinke
What Venus did with Mars.
Cleo. Oh Charmion :
Where think'st thou he is now? Stands he, or sits he?
Or does he walke? Or is he on his Horse?
Oh happy horse to beare the weight of *Anthony* !
Do brauely Horse, for wot'st thou whom thou moou'st,
The demy *Atlas* of this Earth, the Arme
And Burganet of men. Hee's speaking now,
Or murmuring, where's my Serpent of old Nyle,
(For so he cals me :) Now I feede my selfe
With most delicious poyson. Thinke on me
That am with Phœbus amorous pinches blacke,
And wrinkled deepe in time. Broad-fronted *Cæsar*,
When thou was't heere aboue the ground, I was
A morsell for a Monarke : and great *Pompey*
Would stand and make his eyes grow in my brow,
There would he anchor his Aspect, and dye
With looking on his life.
Enter Alexas from Cæsar.
Alex. Soueraigne of Egypt, haile.
Cleo. How much vnlike art thou *Marke Anthony*?
Yet comming from him, that great Med'cine hath
With his Tinct gilded thee.
How goes it with my braue *Marke Anthonie*?
Alex. Last thing he did (deere Qu enc)
He kist the last of many doubled kisses
This Orient Pearle. His speech stickes in my heart
Cleo. Mine eare must plucke it thence.
Alex Good Friend, quoth he :
Say the firme Roman to great Egypt sends
This treasure of an Oyster : at whose foote
To mend the petty present, I will peece
Her opulent Throne, with Kingdomes. All the East,
(Say thou) shall call her Mistris. So he nodded,
And soberly did mount an Arme-gaunt Steede,
Who neigh'd so hye, that what I would haue spoke,
Was beastly dumbe by him.
Cleo. What was he sad, or merry ?
Alex. Like to the time o'th'yeare, between ÿ extremes
Of hot and cold, he was nor sad nor merrie.
Cleo. Oh well diuided disposition: Note him,
Note him good *Charmian*, 'tis the man ; but note him.
He was not sad, for he would shine on those
That make their lookes by his. He was not merrie,
Which seem'd to tell them, his remembrance lay
In Egypt with his ioy, but betweene both.
Oh heauenly mingle ! Bee'st thou sad, or merrie,
The violence of either thee becomes,
So do's it no mans else. Met'st thou my Posts ?
Alex. I Madam, twenty seuerall Messengers.
Why do you send so thicke?
Cleo. Who's borne that day, when I forget to send
to *Anthonie*, shall dye a Begger. Inke and paper *Charmian*. Welcome my good *Alexas*. Did I *Charmian*, euer loue *Cæsar* so?
Char. Oh that braue *Cæsar* !
Cleo. Be choak'd with such another Emphasis,
Say the braue *Anthony*.
Char. The valiant *Cæsar*.
Cleo. By *Isis*, I will giue thee bloody teeth,
If thou with *Cæsar* Parago nagaine :
My man of men.
Char. By your most gracious pardon,
I sing but after you.
Cleo. My Sallad dayes,
When I was greene in iudgement, cold in blood,
To say, as I saide then. But come, away,
Get me Inke and Paper,
Hee

he shall haue euery day a seuerall greeting, or Ile vnpeople Egypt. *Exeunt*

Enter Pompey, Menecrates, and Menas, in warlike manner.

Pom. If the great Gods be iust,they shall assist
The deeds of iustest men.
Mene. Know worthy Pompey, that what they do de-
lay,they not deny.
Pom. Whiles we are sutors to their Throne, decayes
the thing we sue for.
Mene. We ignorant of our selues,
Begge often our owne harmes,which the wise Powres
Deny vs for our good : so finde we profit
By loosing of our Prayers.
Pom. I shall do well :
The people loue me, and the Sea is mine;
My powers are Cressent, and my Auguring hope
Sayes it will come to'th'full. Marke Anthony
In Egypt sits at dinner, and will make
No warres without doores. Cæsar gets money where
He looses hearts : Lepidus flatters both,
Of both is flatter'd : but he neither loues,
Nor either cares for him.
Mene. Cæsar and Lepidus are in the field,
A mighty strength they carry
Pom. Where haue you this? 'Tis false
Mene. From Siluius, Sir
Pom. He dreames : I know they are in Rome together
Looking for Anthony : but all the charmes of Loue,
Salt Cleopatra soften thy wand lip,
Let Witchcraft ioyne with Beauty, Lust with both,
Tye vp the Libertine in a field of Feasts,
Keepe his Braine fuming. Epicurean Cookes,
Sharpen with cloylesse sawce his Appetite,
That sleepe and feeding may prorogue his Honour,
Euen till a Lethied dulnesse——

Enter Varrius.

How now Varrius?
Var. This is most certaine, that I shall deliuer:
Marke Anthony is euery houre in Rome
Expected. Since he went from Egypt, 'tis
A space for farther Trauaile.
Pom. I could haue giuen lesse matter
A better eare. Menas, I did not thinke
This amorous Surfetter would haue donn'd his Helme
For such a petty Warre : His Souldiership
Is twice the other twaine : But let vs reare
The higher our Opinion, that our stirring
Can from the lap of Egypts Widdow, plucke
The neere Lust-wearied Anthony.
Mene. I cannot hope,
Cæsar and Anthony shall well greet together;
His Wife that's dead, did trespasses to Cæsar,
His Brother wan'd vpon him,although I thinke
Not mou'd by Anthony
Pom. I know not Menas,
How lesser Enmities may giue way to greater,
Were't not that we stand vp against them all:
'Twer pregnant they should square between themselues,
For they haue entertained cause enough
To draw their swords : but how the feare of vs
May Ciment their diuisions, and binde vp
The petty difference, we yet not know:
Bee't as our Gods will haue't; it onely stands
Our liues vpon,to vse our strongest hands
Come Menas. *Exeunt.*

Enter Enobarbus and Lepidus

Lep. Good Enobarbus, 'tis a worthy deed,
And shall become you well,to intreat your Captaine
To soft and gentle speech.
Enob. I shall intreat him
To answer like himselfe : if Cæsar moue him,
Let Anthony looke ouer Cæsars head,
And speake as lowd as Mars. By Iupiter,
Were I the wearer of Anthonio's Beard,
I would not shaue't to day.
Lep. Tis not a time for priuate stomacking.
Eno. Euery time serues for the matter that is then
borne in't.
Lep. But small to greater matters must giue way.
Eno. Not if the small come first.
Lep. Your speech is passion : but pray you stirre
No Embers vp. Heere comes the Noble Anthony.

Enter Anthony and Ventidius.

Eno. And yonder Cæsar

Enter Cæsar, Mecenas, and Agrippa.

Ant. If we compose well heere, to Parthia:
Hearke Ventidius
Cæsar. I do not know Mecenas, aske Agrippa.
Lep Noble Friends:
That which combin'd vs was most great,and let not
A leaner action rend vs. What's amisse,
May it be gently heard. When we debate
Our triuiall difference loud, we do commit
Murther in healing wounds. Then Noble Partners,
The rather for I earnestly beseech,
Touch you the sowrest points with sweetest tearmes,
Nor curstnesse grow to'th'matter.
Ant. 'Tis spoken well:
Were we before our Armies,and to fight,
I should do thus. *Flourish.*
Cæs. Welcome to Rome.
Ant. Thanke you.
Cæs. Sit.
Ant, Sit sir.
Cæs. Nay then.
Ant. I learne, you take things ill, which are not so:
Or being,concerne you not.
Cæs. I must be laught at,if or for nothing,or a little, I
Should say my selfe offended, and with you
Chiefely i'th'world. More laught at,that I should
Once name you derogately : when to sound your name
It not concern'd me.
Ant. My being in Egypt Cæsar, what was't to you?
Cæs. No more then my reciding heere at Rome
Might be to you in Egypt : yet if you there
Did practise on my State,your being in Egypt
Might be my question.
Ant. How intend you, practis'd?
Cæs. You may be pleas'd to catch at mine intent,
By what did heere befall me. Your Wife and Brother
Made warres vpon me, and their contestation
Was Theame for you, you were the word of warre.
Ant. You do mistake your busines, my Brother neuer
Did vrge me in his Act : I did inquire it,
And haue my Learning from some true reports
That drew their swords with you, did he not rather
Discredit my authority with yours,
And make the warres alike against my stomacke,
Hauing alike your cause. Of this, my Letters
Before did satisfie you. If you'l patch a quarrell,
As matter whole you haue to make it with,

x 3 It

It muſt not be with this.
Caſ. You praiſe your ſelfe, by laying defects of iudge-
ment to me: but you patcht vp your excuſes.
Anth. Not ſo, not ſo:
I know you could not lacke, I am certaine on't,
Very neceſſity of this thought, that I
Your Partner in the cauſe 'gainſt which he fought,
Could not with gracefull eyes attend thoſe Warres
Which fronted mine owne peace. As for my wife,
I would you had her ſpirit, in ſuch another,
The third oth'world is yours, which with a Snaffle,
You may pace eaſie, but not ſuch a wife.
Enobar. Would we had all ſuch wiues, that the men
might go to Warres with the women.
Anth. So much vncurbable, her Garboiles (*Cæſar*)
Made out of her impatience: which not wanted
Shrodeneſſe of policie to: I greeuing grant,
Did you too much diſquiet, for that you muſt,
But ſay I could not helpe it?
Cæſar. I wrote to you, when rioting in Alexandria you
Did pocket vp my Letters: and with taunts
Did gibe my Miſsiue out of audience.
Ant. Sir, he fell vpon me, ere admitted, then:
Three Kings I had newly feaſted, and did want
Of what I was i'th'morning: but next day
I told him of my ſelfe, which was as much
As to haue askt him pardon. Let this Fellow
Be nothing of our ſtrife: if we contend
Out of our queſtion wipe him.
Cæſar. You haue broken the Article of your oath,
which you ſhall neuer haue tongue to charge me with.
Lep. Soft *Cæſar.*
Ant. No *Lepidus*, let him ſpeake,
The Honour is Sacred which he talks on now,
Suppoſing that I lackt it: but on *Cæſar*,
The Article of my oath.
Cæſar. To lend me Armes, and aide when I requir'd
them, the which you both denied.
Anth. Neglected rather:
And then when poyſoned houres had bound me vp
From mine owne knowledge, as neerely as I may,
Ile play the penitent to you. But mine honeſty,
Shall not make poore my greatneſſe, nor my power
Worke without it. Truth is, that *Fuluia*,
To haue me out of Egypt, made Warres heere,
For which my ſelfe, the ignorant motiue, do
farre aske pardon, as beſits mine Honour
To ſtoope in ſuch a caſe.
Lep. 'Tis Noble ſpoken.
Mece. If it might pleaſe you, to enforce no furthe
The griefes betweene ye: to forget them quite,
Were to remember: that the preſent neede,
Speakes to attone you.
Lep. Worthily ſpoken *Mecenas*.
Enobar. Or if you borrow one anothers Loue for the
inſtant, you may when you heare no more words of
Pompey returne it againe: you ſhall haue time to wrangle
in, when you haue nothing elſe to do.
Anth. Thou art a Souldier, onely, ſpeake no more.
Enob. That trueth ſhould be ſilent, I had almoſt for-
got.
Anth. You wrong this preſence, therefore ſpeake no
more.
Enob. Go too then: your Conſiderate ſtone.
Cæſar. I do not much diſlike the matter, but
The manner of his ſpeech: for't cannot be,
We ſhall remaine in friendſhip, our conditions
So diffring in their acts. Yet if I knew,
What Hoope ſhould hold vs ſtaunch from edge to edge
Ath'world: I would perſue it.
Agri. Giue me leaue *Cæſar.*
Cæſar. Speake *Agrippa.*
Agri. Thou haſt a Siſter by the Mothers ſide, admir'd
Octauia: Great *Mark Anthony* is now a widdower.
Cæſar. Say not, ſay *Agrippa*; if *Cleopater* heard you, your
proofe were well deſerued of raſhneſſe.
Anth. I am not marryed *Cæſar*: let me heere *Agrippa*
further ſpeake.
Agri. To hold you in perpetuall amitie,
To make you Brothers, and to knit your hearts
With an vn-ſlipping knot, take *Anthony*,
Octauia to his wife: whoſe beauty claimes
No worſe a husband then the beſt of men: whoſe
Vertue, and whoſe generall graces, ſpeake
That which none elſe can vtter. By this marriage,
All little Ielouſies which now ſeeme great,
And all great feares, which now import their dangers,
Would then be nothing. Truth's would be tales,
Where now halfe tales be truth's: her loue to both,
Would each to other, and all loues to both
Draw after her. Pardon what I haue ſpoke,
For 'tis a ſtudied not a preſent thought,
By duty ruminated.
Anth. Will *Cæſar* ſpeake?
Cæſar. Not till he heares how *Anthony* is toucht,
With what is ſpoke already.
Anth. What power is in *Agrippa*,
If I would ſay *Agrippe*, be it ſo,
To make this good?
Cæſar. The power of *Cæſar*,
And his power, vnto *Octauia*.
Anth. May I neuer
(To this good purpoſe, that ſo fairely ſhewes)
Dreame of impediment: let me haue thy hand
Further this act of Grace: and from this houre,
The heart of Brothers gouerne in our Loues,
And ſway our great Deſignes.
Cæſar. There's my hand:
A Siſter I bequeath you, whom no Brother
Did euer loue ſo deerely. Let her liue
To ioyne our kingdomes, and our hearts, and neuer
Flie off our Loues againe.
Lepi. Happily, Amen.
Ant. I did not think to draw my Sword 'gainſt *Pompey*,
For he hath laid ſtrange courteſies, and great
Of late vpon me. I muſt thanke him onely,
Leaſt my remembrance, ſuffer ill report:
At heele of that, defie him.
Lepi. Time cals vpon's,
Of vs muſt *Pompey* preſently be ſought,
Or elſe he ſeekes out vs
Anth. Where lies he?
Cæſar. About the Mount-Meſena.
Anth. What is his ſtrength by land?
Cæſar. Great, and encreaſing:
But by Sea he is an abſolute Maſter.
Anth. So is the Fame,
Would we had ſpoke together. Haſt we for it,
Yet ere we put our ſelues in Armes, diſpatch we
The buſineſſe we haue talke of.
Cæſar. With moſt gladneſſe,
And do inuite you to my Siſters view,
Whe

Whether ſtraight Ile lead you.

Anth. Let vs *Lepidus* not lacke your companie.

Lep. Noble *Anthony*, not ſickeneſſe ſhould detaine me.

Flouriſh. Exit omnes.

Manet Enobarbus, Agrippa, Mecenas.

Mec. Welcome from Ægypt Sir.

Eno. Halfe the heart of *Cæſar*, worthy *Mecenas*. My honourable Friend *Agrippa*.

Agri. Good *Enobarbus*.

Mece. We haue cauſe to be glad, that matters are ſo well diſgeſted: you ſtaid well by't in Egypt.

Enob. I Sir, we did ſleepe day out of countenaunce: and made the night light with drinking.

Mece. Eight Wilde-Boares roſted whole at a breakfaſt: and but twelue perſons there. Is this true?

Eno. This was but as a Flye by an Eagle: we had much more monſtrous matter of Feaſt, which worthily deſerued noting.

Mecenas. She's a moſt triumphant Lady, if report be ſquare to her.

Enob. When ſhe firſt met *Marke Anthony*, ſhe purſt vp his heart vpon the Riuer of Sidnis.

Agri. There ſhe appear'd indeed: or my reporter deuis'd well for her.

Eno. I will tell you,
The Barge ſhe ſat in, like a burniſht Throne
Burnt on the water: the Poope was beaten Gold,
Purple the Sailes: and ſo perfumed that
The Windes were Loue-ſicke.
With them the Owers were Siluer,
Which to the tune of Flutes kept ſtroke, and made
The water which they beate, to follow faſter;
As amorous of their ſtrokes. For her owne perſon,
It beggerd all diſcription, ſhe did lye
In her Pauillion, cloth of Gold, of Tiſſue,
O're-picturing that Venns, where we ſee
The fancie out-worke Nature. On each ſide her,
Stood pretty Dimpled Boyes, like ſmiling Cupids,
With diuers coulour'd Fannes whoſe winde did ſeeme,
To gloue the delicate cheekes which they did coole,
And what they vndid did.

Agrip. Oh rare for *Anthony*.

Eno. Her Gentlewoman, like the Nereides,
So many Mer-maides tended her i'th'eyes,
And made their bends adornings. At the Helme.
A ſeeming Mer-maide ſteeres: The Silken Tackle,
Swell with the touches of thoſe Flower-ſoft hands,
That yarely frame the office. From the Barge
A ſtrange inuiſible perfume hits the ſenſe
Of the adiacent Wharfes. The Citty caſt
Her people out vpon her: and *Anthony*
Enthron'd i'th'Market-place, did ſit alone,
Whiſling to'th'ayre: which but for vacancie,
Had gone to gaze on *Cleopater* too,
And made a gap in Nature.

Agri. Rare Egiptian.

Eno. Vpon her landing, *Anthony* ſent to her,
Inuited her to Supper: ſhe replyed,
It ſhould be better, he became her gueſt:
Which ſhe entreated, our Courteous *Anthony*,
Whom nere the word of no woman hard ſpeake,
Being barber'd ten times o're, goes to the Feaſt;
And for his ordinary, paies his heart,
For what his eyes eate onely.

Agri. Royall Wench:
She made great *Cæſar* lay his Sword to bed,
He ploughed her, and ſhe cropt.

Eno. I ſaw her once
Hop forty Paces through the publicke ſtreete,
And hauing loſt her breath, ſhe ſpoke, and panted,
That ſhe did make defect, perfection,
And breathleſſe powre breath forth.

Mece. Now *Anthony*, muſt leaue her vtterly.

Eno. Neuer he will not:
Age cannot wither her, nor cuſtome ſtale
Her infinite variety: other women cloy
The appetites they feede, but ſhe makes hungry,
Where moſt ſhe ſatisfies. For vildeſt things
Become themſelues in her, that the holy Prieſts
Bleſſe her, when ſhe is Riggiſh.

Mece If Beauty, Wiſedome, Modeſty, can ſettle
The heart of *Anthony*: *Octauia* is
A bleſſed Lottery to him.

Agrip. Let vs go. Good *Enobarbus*, make your ſelfe my gueſt, whilſt you abide heere.

Eno. Humbly Sir I thanke you. *Exeunt*

Enter Anthony, Cæſar, Octauia betweene them.

Anth. The world, and my great office, will
Sometimes deuide me from your boſome.

Octa. All which time, before the Gods my knee ſhall bowe my prayers to them for you.

Anth. Goodnight Sir. My *Octauia*
Read not my blemiſhes in the worlds report:
I haue not kept my ſquare, but that to come
Shall all be done byth'Rule: good night deere Lady:
Good night Sir.

Cæſar. Goodnight. *Exit.*

Enter Soothſaier.

Anth. Now ſirrah: you do wiſh your ſelfe in Egypt?

Sooth. Would I had neuer come from thence, nor you thither.

Ant. If you can, your reaſon?

Sooth. I ſee it in my motion: haue it not in my tongue,
But yet hie you to Egypt againe.

Antho. Say to me, whoſe Fortunes ſhall riſe higher
Cæſars or mine?

Soot. *Cæſars.* Therefore (oh *Anthony*) ſtay not by his ſide
Thy Dæmon that thy ſpirit which keepes thee, is
Noble, Couragious, high vnmatchable,
Where *Cæſars* is not. But neere him, thy Angell
Becomes a feare: as being o're-powr'd, therefore
Make ſpace enough betweene you.

Anth. Speake this no more.

Sooth. To none but thee no more but: when to thee,
If thou doſt play with him at any game,
Thou art ſure to looſe: And of that Naturall lucke,
He beats thee 'gainſt the oddes. Thy Luſter thickens,
When he ſhines by: I ſay againe, thy ſpirit
Is all affraid to gouerne thee neere him:
But he alway 'tis Noble.

Anth. Get thee gone:
Say to *Ventigius* I would ſpeake with him. *Exit.*
He ſhall to Parthia, be it Art or hap,
He hath ſpoken true. The very Dice obey him,
And in our ſports my better cunning faints,
Vnder his chance, if we draw lots he ſpeeds,
His Cocks do winne the Battaile, ſtill of mine,
When it is all to naught: and his Quailes euer
Beate mine (in hoopt) at odd's. I will to Egypte:

And

And though I make this marriage for my peace,
I'th'East my pleasure lies. Oh come *Ventigius*.

Enter Ventigius.

You must to Parthia, your Commissions ready:
Follow me, and reciue't. *Exeunt*

Enter Lepidus, Mecenas and Agrippa.

Lepidus. Trouble your selues no further: pray you
hasten your Generals after.
Agr. Sir, *Marke Anthony*, will e'ne but kisse *Octauia*,
and weele follow.
Lepi. Till I shall see you in your Souldiers dresse,
Which will become you both: Farewell.
Mece. We shall: as I conceiue the iourney, be at
Mount before you *Lepidus*.
Lepi. Your way is shorter, my purposes do draw me
much about, you'le win two dayes vpon me.
Both. Sir good successe.
Lepi. Farewell. *Exeunt*.

Enter Cleopater, Charmian, Iras, and Alexas.

Cleo. Giue me some Musicke: Musicke, moody foode
of vs that trade in Loue.
Omnes. The Musicke, hoa.

Enter Mardian the Eunuch.

Cleo. Let it alone, let's to Billards: come *Charmian*.
Char. My arme is sore, best play with *Mardian*.
Cleopa. As well a woman with an Eunuch plaide, as
with a woman. Come you'le play with me Sir?
Mardi. As well as I can Madam.
Cleo. And when good will is shewed,
Though't come to short
The Actor may pleade pardon. Ile none now,
Giue me mine Angle, weele to'th'Riuer there
My Musicke playing farre off. I will betray
Tawny fine fishes, my bended hooke shall pierce
Their slimy iawes. and as I draw them vp,
Ile thinke them euery one an *Anthony*,
And say, ah hay'are caught.
Char. 'Twas merry when you wager'd on your Ang-
ling, when your diuer did hang a salt fish on his hooke
which he with feruencie drew vp.
Cleo. That time? Oh times:
I laught him out of patience: and that night
I laught him into patience, and next morne,
Ere the ninth houre, I drunke him to his bed:
Then put my Tires and Mantles on him, whilst
I wore his Sword Phillippan. Oh from Italie,

Enter a Messenger.

Ramme thou thy fruitefull tidings in mine eares,
That long time haue bin barren.
Mes. Madam, Madam.
Cleo. *Anthonyo's* dead.
If thou say so Villaine, thou kil'st thy Mistris:
But well and free, if thou so yeild him.
There is Gold, and heere
My blewest vaines to kisse: a hand that Kings
Haue lipt, and trembled kissing.
Mes. First Madam, he is well.
Cleo Why there's more Gold.
But sirrah marke, we vse
To say, the dead are well: bring it to that,
The Gold I giue thee, will I melt and powr
Downe thy ill vttering throate.
Mes. Good Madam heare me.
Cleo. Well, go too I will:
But there's no goodnesse in thy face if *Anthony*
Be free and healthfull; so tart a fauour
To trumpet such good tidings. If not well,
Thou shouldst come like a Furie crown'd with Snakes,
Not like a formall man.
Mes. Wilt please you heare me?
Cleo. I haue a mind to strike thee ere thou speak'st:
Yet if thou say *Anthony* liues, 'tis well,
Or friends with *Cæsar*, or not Captiue to him,
Ile set thee in a shower of Gold, and haile
Rich Pearles vpon thee.
Mes. Madam, he's well.
Cleo. Well said.
Mes. And Friends with *Cæsar*.
Cleo. Th'art an honest man.
Mes. *Cæsar*, and he, are greater Friends then euer.
Cleo. Make thee a Fortune from me.
Mes. But yet Madam.
Cleo. I do not like but yet, it does alay
The good precedence, fie vpon but yet,
But yet is as a Iaylor to bring foorth
Some monstrous Malefactor. Prythee Friend,
Powre out the packe of matter to mine eare,
The good and bad together: he's friends with *Cæsar*,
In state of health thou saist, and thou saist, free.
Mes. Free Madam, no: I made no such report,
He's bound vnto *Octauia*.
Cleo. For what good turne?
Mes. For the best turne i'th'bed.
Cleo. I am pale *Charmian*.
Mes. Madam, he's married to *Octauia*.
Cleo. The most infectious Pestilence vpon thee.
Strikes him downe.
Mes. Good Madam patience.
Cleo. What say you? *Strikes him.*
Hence horrible Villaine, or Ile spurne thine eyes
Like balls before me: Ile vnhaire thy head,
She hales him vp and downe.
Thou shalt be whipt with Wyer, and stew'd in brine,
Smarting in lingring pickle.
Mes. Gratious Madam,
I that do bring the newes, made not the match.
Cleo. Say 'tis not so, a Prouince I will giue thee,
And make thy Fortunes proud: the blow thou had'st
Shall make thy peace, for mouing me to rage,
And I will boot thee with what guift beside
Thy modestie can begge.
Mes. He's married Madam.
Cleo. Rogue, thou hast liu'd too long. *Draw a knife.*
Mes. Nay then Ile runne:
What meane you Madam, I haue made no fault. *Exit.*
Char. Good Madam keepe your selfe within your selfe,
The man is innocent.
Cleo. Some Innocents scape not the thunderbolt:
Melt Egypt into Nyle: and kindly creatures
Turne all to Serpents. Call the slaue againe,
Though I am mad, I will not byte him: Call?
Char. He is afeard to come.
Cleo. I will not hurt him,
These hands do lacke Nobility, that they strike
A meaner then my selfe: since I my selfe
Haue giuen my selfe the cause. Come hither Sir.

Enter the Messenger againe.

Though it be honest, it is neuer good
To bring bad newes: giue to a gratious Message
An

An host of tongues, but let ill tydings tell
Themselues, when they be felt.
Mes. I haue done my duty.
Cleo. Is he married?
I cannot hate thee worser then I do,
If thou againe say yes.
Mes. He's married Madam.
Cleo. The Gods confound thee,
Dost thou hold there still?
Mes. Should I lye Madame?
Cleo. Oh, I would thou didst:
So halfe my Egypt were submerg'd and made
A Cesterne for scal'd Snakes. Go get thee hence,
Had'st thou *Narcissus* in thy face to me,
Thou would'st appeere most vgly: He is married?
Mes. I craue your Highnesse pardon.
Cleo. He is married?
Mes. Take no offence, that I would not offend you,
To punnish me for what you make me do
Seemes much vnequall, he's married to *Octauia*.
Cleo. Oh that his fault should make a knaue of thee,
That art not what th'art sure of. Get thee hence,
The Marchandize which thou hast brought from Rome
Are all too deere for me:
Lye they vpon thy hand, and be vndone by em.
Char. Good your Highnesse patience.
Cleo. In praysing *Anthony*, I haue disprais'd *Cæsar*.
Char. Many times Madam
Cleo. I am paid for't now: lead me from hence,
I faint, oh *Iras*, *Charmian*: 'tis no matter.
Go to the Fellow, good *Alexas* bid him
Report the feature of *Octauia*: her yeares,
Her inclination, let him not leaue out
The colour of her haire. Bring me word quickly,
Let him for euer go, let him not *Charmian*,
Though he be painted one way like a Gorgon,
The other wayes a Mars. Bid you *Alexas*
Bring me word, how tall she is: pitty me *Charmian*,
But do not speake to me. Lead me to my Chamber
Exeunt.

Flourish. Enter Pompey, at one doore with Drum and Trumpet: at another Cæsar, Lepidus, Anthony, Enobarbus, Mecenas, Agrippa, Menas with Souldiers Marching

Pom. Your Hostages I haue, so haue you mine:
And we shall talke before we fight.
Cæsar. Most meete that first we come to words,
And therefore haue we
Our written purposes before vs sent,
Which if thou hast considered, let vs know,
If't will tye vp thy discontented Sword,
And carry backe to Cicelie much tall youth,
That else must perish heere.
Pom. To you all three,
The Senators alone of this great world,
Chiefe Factors for the Gods. I do not know,
Wherefore my Father should reuengers want,
Hauing a Sonne and Friends, since *Julius Cæsar*,
Who at Phillippi the good *Brutus* ghosted,
There saw you labouring for him. What was't
That mou'd pale *Cassius* to conspire? And what
Made all-honor'd, honest, Romaine *Brutus*,
With the arm'd rest, Courtiers of beautious freedome,
To drench the Capitoll, but that they would
Haue one man but a man, and that his it
Hath made me rigge my Nauie. At whose burthen,
The anger'd Ocean fomes, with which I meant
To scourge th'ingratitude, that despightfull Rome
Cast on my Noble Father.
Cæsar. Take your time.
Ant. Thou can'st not feare vs *Pompey* with thy sailes.
Weele speake with thee at Sea. At land thou know'st
How much we do o're-count thee.
Pom. At Land indeed
Thou dost orecount me of my Fatherrs house:
But since the Cuckoo buildes not for himselfe,
Remaine in't as thou maist.
Lepi. Be pleas'd to tell vs,
(For this is from the present how you take)
The offers we haue sent you.
Cæsar. There's the point.
Ant. Which do not be entreated too,
But waigh what it is worth imbrac'd
Cæsar. And what may follow to try a larger Fortune.
Pom. You haue made me offer
Of Cicelie, Sardinia: and I must
Rid all the Sea of Pirats. Then, to send
Measures of Wheate to Rome: this greed vpon,
To part with vnhackt edges, and beare backe
Our Targes vndinted.
Omnes. That's our offer.
Pom. Know then I came before you heere,
A man prepar'd
To take this offer. But *Marke Anthony*,
Put me to some impatience: though I loose
The praise of it by telling. You must know
When *Cæsar* and your Brother were at blowes,
Your Mother came to Cicelie, and did finde
Her welcome Friendly.
Ant. I haue heard it *Pompey*,
And am well studied for a liberall thanks,
Which I do owe you.
Pom. Let me haue your hand:
I did not thinke Sir, to haue met you heere,
Ant. The beds i'th'East are soft, and thanks to you,
That cal'd me timelier then my purpose hither:
For I haue gained by't.
Cæsar. Since I saw you last, ther's a change vpon you.
Pom. Well, I know not,
What counts harsh Fotune cast's vpon my face,
But in my bosome shall she neuer come,
To make my heart her vassaile.
Lep. Well met heere.
Pom. I hope so *Lepidus*, thus we are agreed:
I craue our composion may be written
And seal'd betweene vs,
Cæsar. That's the next to do.
Pom. Weele feast each other, ere we part, and lett's
Draw lots who shall begin.
Ant. That will I *Pompey*.
Pompey. No *Anthony* take the lot: but first or last, your fine Egyptian cookerie shall haue the fame, I haue heard that *Julius Cæsar*, grew fat with feasting there.
Anth. You haue heard much.
Pom. I haue faire meaning Sir.
Ant. And faire words to them.
Pom. Then so much haue I heard,
And I haue heard *Appolodorus* carried——
Eno. No more that: he did so.
Pom. What I pray you?
Eno. A certaine Queene to *Cæsar* in a Matris.
Pom. I know thee now, how far'st thou Souldier?
Eno. Well, and well am like to do, for I perceiue
Four

Foure Feasts are toward.

Pom Let me shake thy hand,
I neuer hated thee: I haue seene thee fight,
When I haue enuied thy behauiour.

Enob. Sir, I neuer lou'd you much, but I ha' prais'd ye,
When you haue well deseru'd ten times as much,
As I haue said you did.

Pom. Inioy thy plainnesse,
It nothing ill becomes thee:
Aboord my Gally, I inuite you all.
Will you leade Lords?

All. Shew's the way, sir.

Pom. Come. *Exeunt. Manet Enob. & Menas*

Men. Thy Father *Pompey* would ne're haue made this Treaty. You, and I haue knowne sir.

Enob. At Sea, I thinke.

Men. We haue Sir.

Enob. You haue done well by water.

Men. And you by Land.

Enob. I will praise any man that will praise me, thogh it cannot be denied what I haue done by Land.

Men. Nor what I haue done by water.

Enob. Yes some-thing you can deny for your owne safety: you haue bin a great Theefe by Sea.

Men. And you by Land.

Enob. There I deny my Land seruice: but giue mee your hand *Menas*, if our eyes had authority, heere they might take two Theeues kissing.

Men. All mens faces are true, whatsomere their hands are.

Enob. But there is neuer a fayre Woman, ha's a true Face.

Men. No slander, they steale hearts.

Enob. We came hither to fight with you.

Men. For my part, I am sorry it is turn'd to a Drinking. *Pompey* doth this day laugh away his Fortune.

Enob. If he do, sure he cannot weep't backe againe.

Men. Y'haue said Sir, we look'd not for *Marke Anthony* heere, pray you, is he married to *Cleopatra*?

Enob. *Cæsars* Sister is call'd *Octauia*.

Men. True Sir, she was the wife of *Caius Marcellus*.

Enob. But she is now the wife of *Marcus Anthonius*.

Men. Pray'ye sir.

Enob. 'Tis true.

Men. Then is *Cæsar* and he, for euer knit together.

Enob. If I were bound to Diuine of this vnity, I wold not Prophesie so.

Men. I thinke the policy of that purpose, made more in the Marriage, then the loue of the parties.

Enob. I thinke so too. But you shall finde the band that seemes to tye their friendship together, will bee the very strangler of their Amity: *Octauia* is of a holy, cold, and still conuersation.

Men. Who would not haue his wife so?

Eno. Not he that himselfe is not so: which is *Marke Anthony*: he will to his Egyptian dish againe: then shall the sighes of *Octauia* blow the fire vp in *Cæsar*, and (as I said before) that which is the strength of their Amity, shall proue the immediate Author of their variance. *Anthony* will vse his affection where it is. Hee married but his occasion heere.

Men. And thus it may be. Come Sir, will you aboord? I haue a health for you.

Enob. I shall take it sir: we haue vs'd our Throats in Egypt.

Men. Come, let's away. *Exeunt.*

Musicke playes.
Enter two or three Seruants with a Banket.

1 Heere they'l be man: some o'th'their Plants are rooted already, the least winde i'th'world wil blow them downe.

2 *Lepidus* is high Conlord.

1 They haue made him drinke Almes drinke.

2 As they pinch one another by the disposition, hee cries out, no more; reconciles them to his entreatie, and himselfe to'th'drinke.

1 But it raises the greater warre betweene him & his discretion.

2 Why this it is to haue a name in great mens Fellowship: I had as liue haue a Reede that will doe me no seruice, as a Partizan I could not heaue.

1 To be call'd into a huge Sphere, and not to be seene to moue in't, are the holes where eyes should bee, which pittifully disaster the cheekes.

A Sennet sounded.
Enter Cæsar, Anthony, Pompey, Lepidus, Agrippa, Mecenas, Enobarbus, Menes, with other Captaines.

Ant. Thus do they Sir: they take the flow o'th'Nyle
By certaine scales i'th'Pyramid: they know
By'th'height, the lownesse, or the meane: If dearth
Or Foizon follow. The higher Nilus swels,
The more it promises: as it ebbes, the Seedsman
Vpon the slime and Ooze scatters his graine,
And shortly comes to Haruest.

Lep. Y'haue strange Serpents there?

Anth. I *Lepidus*.

Lep. Your Serpent of Egypt, is bred now of your mud by the operation of your Sun: so is your Crocodile.

Ant. They are so.

Pom. Sit, and some Wine: A health to *Lepidus*.

Lep. I am not so well as I should be:
But Ile ne're out.

Enob. Not till you haue slept: I feare me you'l bee in till then.

Lep. Nay certainly, I haue heard the *Ptolomies* Pyramisis are very goodly things: without contradiction I haue heard that.

Menas. *Pompey*, a word.

Pomp. Say in mine eare, what is't.

Men. Forsake thy seate I do beseech thee Captaine,
And heare me speake a word.

Pom. Forbeare me till anon. *Whispers in's Eare.*
This Wine for *Lepidus*.

Lep. What manner o'thing is your Crocodile?

Ant. It is shap'd sir like it selfe, and it is as broad as it hath bredth; It is iust so high as it is, and mooues with it owne organs. It liues by that which nourisheth it, and the Elements once out of it, it Transmigrates.

Lep. What colour is it of?

Ant. Of it owne colour too.

Lep. 'Tis a strange Serpent.

Ant. 'Tis so, and the teares of it are wet.

Cæs. Will this description satisfie him?

Ant. With the Health that *Pompey* giues him, else he is a very Epicure.

Pomp. Go hang sir, hang: tell me of that? Away:
Do as I bid you. Where's this Cup I call'd for?

Men. If for the sake of Merit thou wilt heare mee,

Rise

Rise from thy stoole.
Pom. I thinke th'art mad: the matter?
Men. I haue euer held my cap off to thy Fortunes.
Pom. Thou hast seru'd me with much faith: what's
else to say? Be iolly Lords.
Anth. These Quicke-sands *Lepidus*,
Keepe off, them for you sinke.
Men. Wilt thou be Lord of all the world?
Pom. What saist thou?
Men. Wilt thou be Lord of the whole world?
That's twice.
Pom. How should that be?
Men. But entertaine it, and though thou thinke me
poore, I am the man will giue thee all the world.
Pom. Hast thou drunke well.
Men. No *Pompey*, I haue kept me from the cup,
Thou art if thou dar'st be, the earthly Ioue:
What ere the Ocean pales, or skie inclippes,
Is thine, if thou wilt ha't.
Pom. Shew me which way?
Men. These three World-sharers, these Competitors
Are in thy vessell. Let me cut the Cable,
And when we are put off, fall to their throates:
All there is thine.
Pom. Ah, this thou shouldst haue done,
And not haue spoke on't. In me 'tis villanie,
In thee, 't had bin good seruice: thou must know,
'Tis not my profit that does lead mine Honour:
Mine Honour it, Repent that ere thy tongue,
Hath so betraide thine acte. Being done vnknowne,
I should haue found it afterwards well done,
But must condemne it now: desist, and drinke.
Men. For this, Ile neuer follow
Thy paul'd Fortunes more,
Who seekes and will not take, when once 'tis offer'd,
Shall neuer finde it more.
Pom. This health to *Lepidus*
Ant. Beare him ashore,
Ile pledge it for him *Pompey*.
Eno Heere's to thee *Menas*
Men. *Enobarbus*, welcome.
Pom. Fill till the cup be hid.
Eno. There's a strong Fellow *Menas*.
Men. Why?
Eno. A beares the third part of the world man: seest
not?
Men. The third part, then he is drunk: would it were
all, that it might go on wheeles.
Eno. Drinke thou: encrease the Reeles.
Men Come.
Pom. This is not yet an Alexandrian Feast.
Ant. It ripen's towards it: strike the Vesselles hoa.
Heere's to *Cæsar*
Cæsar. I could well forbear't, it's monstrous labour
when I wash my braine, and it grow fouler.
Ant. Be a Child o'th'time.
Cæsar. Possesse it, Ile make answer: but I had rather
fast from all, foure dayes, then drinke so much in one.
Enob. Ha my braue Emperour, shall we daunce now
the Egyptian Backenals, and celebrate our drinke?
Pom. Let's ha't good Souldier.
Ant. Come, let's all take hands,
Till that the conquering Wine hath steep't our sense,
In soft and delicate Lethe.
Eno. All take hands:
Make battery to our eares with the loud Musicke,
The while, Ile place you, then the Boy shall sing.
The holding euery man shall beate as loud,
As his strong sides can volly

Musicke Playes. Enobarbus places them hand in hand.

The Song.

Come thou Monarch of the Vine,
Plumpie Bacchus, with pinke eyne:
In thy Fattes our Cares be drown'd,
With thy Grapes our haires be Crown'd.
Cup vs till the world go round,
Cup vs till the world go round.

Cæsar. What would you more?
Pompey goodnight. Good Brother
Let me request you of our grauer businesse
Frownes at this leuitie. Gentle Lords let's part,
You see we haue burnt our cheekes. Strong *Enobarbe*
Is weaker then the Wine, and mine owne tongue
Spleet's what it speakes: the wilde disguise hath almost
Antickt vs all. What needs more words? goodnight.
Good *Anthony* your hand.
Pom. Ile try you on the shore.
Anth. And shall Sir, giues your hand.
Pom Oh *Anthony*, you haue my Father house.
But what, we are Friends?
Come downe into the Boate.
Eno Take heed you fall not *Menas*: Ile not on shore,
No to my Cabin: these Drummes,
These Trumpets, Flutes: what
Let Neptune heare, we bid aloud farewell
To these great Fellowes. Sound and be hang'd, sound out.
Sound a Flourish with Drummes.
Enor. Hoo saies a there's my Cap.
Men. Hoa, Noble Captaine, come. *Exeunt.*

Enter Ventidius as it were in triumph, the dead body of Pacorus borne before him.

Ven. Now darting Parthya art thou stroke, and now
Pleas'd Fortune does of *Marcus Crassus* death
Make me reuenger. Beare the Kings Sonnes body,
Before our Army thy *Pacorus Orades*,
Paies this for *Marcus Crassus*
Romaine. Noble *Ventidius*,
Whil'st yet with Parthian blood thy Sword is warme,
The Fugitiue Parthians follow. Spurre through Media,
Mesapotamia, and the shelters, whether
The routed flie. So thy grand Captaine *Anthony*
Shall set thee on triumphant Chariots, and
Put Garlands on thy head.
Ven. Oh *Sillius*, *Sillius*,
I haue done enough. A lower place note well
May make too great an act. For learne this *Sillius*,
Better to leaue vndone, then by our deed
Acquire too high a Fame, when him we serues away.
Cæsar and *Anthony*, haue euer wonne
More in their officer, then person. *Sossius*
One of my place in Syria, his Lieutenant,
For quicke accumulation of renowne,
Which he atchiu'd by'th'minute, lost his fauour.
Who does i'th'Warres more then his Captaine can,
Becomes his Captaines Captaine: and Ambition
(The Souldiers vertue) rather makes choise of losse
Then gaine, which darkens him.
I could do more to do *Anthonius* good,
But 'twould offend him. And in his offence,
Should

Should my performance perish.
Rom. Thou hast *Ventidius* that, without the which a
Souldier and his Sword graunts scarce distinction : thou
wilt write to *Anthony*.
Ven. Ile humbly signifie what in his name,
That magicall word of Warre we haue effected,
How with his Banners, and his well paid ranks,
The nere-yet beaten Horse of Parthia,
We haue iaded out o'th Field.
Rom Where is he now?
Ven. He purposeth to Athens, whither with what hast
The waight we must conuay with's, will permit :
We shall appeare before him. On there, passe along.
Exeunt.

Enter Agrippa at one doore, Enobarbus at another.

Agri. What are the Brothers parted?
Eno. They haue dispatcht with *Pompey*, he is gone,
The other three are Sealing. *Octauia* weepes
To part from Rome: *Cæsar* is sad, and *Lepidus*
Since *Pompey's* feast, as *Menas* saies, is troubled
With the Greene-Sicknesse.
Agri. 'Tis a Noble *Lepidus*.
Eno. A very fine one : oh, how he loues *Cæsar*.
Agri. Nay but how deerely he adores *Mark Anthony*.
Eno. *Cæsar*? why he's the Iupiter of men.
Ant. What's *Anthony*, the God of Iupiter?
Eno. Spake you of *Cæsar*? How, the non-pareill?
Agri. Oh *Anthony*, oh thou Arabian Bird!
Eno Would you praise *Cæsar*, say *Cæsar* go no further.
Agr Indeed he plied them both with excellent praises.
Eno. But he loues *Cæsar* best, yet he loues *Anthony* :
Hoo Hearts, Tongues, Figure,
Scribes, Bards, Poets, cannot
Thinke speake, cast, write, sing, number: hoo,
His loue to *Anthony*. But as for *Cæsar*,
Kneele downe, kneele downe, and wonder.
Agri. Both he loues.
Eno. They are his Shards, and he their Beetle, so:
This is to horse : Adieu, Noble *Agrippa*.
Agri. Good Fortune worthy Souldier, and farewell.

Enter Cæsar, Anthony, Lepidus, and Octauia.

Antho. No further Sir.
Cæsar. You take from me a great part of my selfe:
Vse me well in't. Sister, proue such a wife
As my thoughts make thee, and as my farthest Band
Shall passe on thy approofe : most Noble *Anthony*,
Let not the peece of Vertue which is set
Betwixt vs, as the Cyment of our loue
To keepe it builded, be the Ramme to batter
The Fortresse of it: for better might we
Haue lou'd without this meane, if on both parts
This be not cherisht.
Ant. Make me not offended, in your distrust.
Cæsar, I haue said.
Ant. You shall not finde,
Though you be therein curious, the lest cause
For what you seeme to feare, so the Gods keepe you,
And make the hearts of Romaines serue your ends :
We will heere part.
Cæsar. Farewell my deerest Sister, fare thee well,
The Elements be kind to thee, and make
Thy spirits all of comfort : fare thee well.
Octa. My Noble Brother.
Anth. The Aprill's in her eyes, it is Loues spring,
And these the showers to bring it on : be cheerfull.
Octa. Sir, looke well to my Husbands house : and —
Cæsar. What *Octauia*?
Octa. Ile tell you in your eare.
Ant. Her tongue will not obey her heart, nor can
Her heart informe her tougue,
The Swannes downe feather
That stands vpon the Swell at the of full Tide :
And neither way inclines.
Eno. Will *Cæsar* weepe?
Agr. He ha's a cloud in's face.
Eno. He were the worse for that, were he a Horse so is
he being a man
Agri. Why *Enobarbus* :
When *Anthony* found *Iulius Cæsar* dead,
He cried almost to roaring : And he wept,
When at Phillippi he found *Brutus* slaine.
Eno. That yeare indeed, he was troubled with a rume,
What willingly he did confound, he wail'd,
Beleeu't till I weepe too.
Cæsar. No sweet *Octauia*,
You shall heare from me still : the time shall not
Out-go my thinking on you.
Ant. Come Sir, come,
Ile wrastle with you in my strength of loue,
Looke heere I haue you, thus I let you go,
And giue you to the Gods.
Cæsar. Adieu be happy.
Lep. Let all the number of the Starres giue light
To thy faire way.
Cæsar. Farewell, farewell. *Kisses Octauia.*
Ant. Farewell. *Trumpets sound. Exeunt.*

Enter Cleopatra, Charmian, Iras, and Alexas.

Cleo. Where is the Fellow?
Alex. Halfe afeard to come.
Cleo. Go too, go too : Come hither Sir.
Enter the Messenger as before.
Alex. Good Maiestie: *Herod* of Iury dare not looke
vpon you, but when you are well pleas'd.
Cleo. That *Herods* head, Ile haue : but how? When
Anthony is gone, through whom I might commaund it:
Come thou neere.
Mes. Most gratious Maiestie.
Cleo. Did'st thou behold *Octauia*?
Mes I dread Queene.
Cleo. Where?
Mes. Madam in Rome, I lookt her in the face : and
saw her led betweene her Brother, and *Marke Anthony*.
Cleo. Is she as tall as me?
Mes. She is not Madam.
Cleo. Didst heare her speake?
Is she shrill tongu'd or low?
Mes. Madam, I heard her speake she is low voic'c.
Cleo. That's not so good : he cannot like her long.
Char. Like her? Oh *Isis* : 'tis impossible.
Cleo. I thinke so *Charmian*: dull of tongue, & dwarfish
What Maiestie is in her gate, remember
If ere thou look'st on Maiestie.
Mes. She creepes: her motion, & her station are as one.
She shewes a body, rather then a life,
A Statue, then a Breather.
Cleo. Is this certaine?
Mes. Or I haue no obseruance.
Cha. Three in Egypt cannot make better note.
Cleo. He's very knowing, I do perceiu't,
There's nothing in her yet.
The

The Fellow ha's good iudgement.
Char. Excellent.
Cleo. Guesse at her yeares, I prythee.
Messe. Madam, she was a widdow.
Cleo. Widdow? *Charmian*, hearke.
Mes. And I do thinke she's thirtie.
Cle. Bear'st thou her face in mind? is't long or round?
Mess. Round, euen to faultinesse.
Cleo. For the most part too, they are foolish that are so. Her haire what colour?
Mess. Browne Madam: and her forehead
As low as she would wish it.
Cleo. There's Gold for thee,
Thou must not take my former sharpenesse ill,
I will employ thee backe againe: I finde thee
Most fit for businesse. Go, make thee ready,
Our Letters are prepar'd.
Char. A proper man.
Cleo. Indeed he is so: I repent me much
That so I harried him. Why me think's by him,
This Creature's no such thing.
Char. Nothing Madam.
Cleo. The man hath seene some Maiesty, and should know.
Char. Hath he seene Maiestie? *Isis* else defend: and seruing you so long.
Cleopa. I haue one thing more to aske him yet good *Charmian*: but 'tis no matter, thou shalt bring him to me where I will write; all may be well enough.
Char. I warrant you Madam. *Exeunt.*

Enter Anthony and Octauia.

Ant. Nay, nay *Octauia*, not onely that,
That were excusable, that and thousands more
Of semblable import, but he hath wag'd
New Warres 'gainst *Pompey*. Made his will, and read it,
To publicke eare, spoke scantly of me,
When perforce he could not
But pay me tearmes of Honour: cold and sickly
He vented then most narrow measure: lent me,
When the best hint was giuen him: he not look't,
Or did it from his teeth.
Octaui. Oh my good Lord,
Beleeue not all, or if you must beleeue,
Stomacke not all. A more vnhappie Lady,
If this deuision chance, ne're stood betweene
Praying for both parts:
The good Gods wil mocke me presently,
When I shall pray: Oh blesse my Lord, and Husband,
Vndo that prayer, by crying out as loud,
Oh blesse my Brother. Husband winne, winne Brother,
Prayes, and distroyes the prayer, no midway
'Twixt these extreames at all.
Ant. Gentle *Octauia*,
Let your best loue draw to that point which seeks
Best to preserue it: if I loose mine Honour,
I loose my selfe: better I were not yours
Then your so branchlesse. But as you requested,
Your selfe shall go between's, the meane time Lady,
Ile raise the preparation of a Warre
Shall staine your Brother, make your soonest hast,
So your desires are yours.
Oct. Thanks to my Lord,
The Ioue of power make me most weake, most weake,
You reconciler: Warres 'twixt you twaine would be,
As if the world should cleaue, and that slaine men
Should soader vp the Rift.
Anth. When it appeeres to you where this begins,
Turne your displeasure that way, for our faults
Can neuer be so equall, that your loue
Can equally moue with them. Prouide your going,
Choose your owne company, and command what cost
Your heart he's mind too. *Exeunt.*

Enter Enobarbus, and Eros.

Eno. How now Friend *Eros*?
Eros. Ther's strange Newes come Sir.
Eno. What man?
Ero. *Cæsar* & *Lepidus* haue made warres vpon *Pompey*.
Eno. This is old, what is the successe?
Eros. *Cæsar* hauing made vse of him in the warres gainst *Pompey*: presently denied him riuality, would not let him partake in the glory of the action, and not resting here, accuses him of Letters he had formerly wrote to *Pompey*. Vpon his owne appeale seizes him, so the poore third is vp, till death enlarge his Confine.
Eno. Then would thou hadst a paire of chaps no more, and throw betweene them all the food thou hast, they'le grinde the other. Where's *Anthony*?
Eros. He's walking in the garden thus, and spurnes
The rush that lies before him. Cries Foole *Lepidus*,
And threats the throate of that his Officer,
That murdred *Pompey*.
Eno. Our great Nauies rig'd.
Eros. For Italy and *Cæsar*, more *Domitius*,
My Lord desires you presently: my Newes
I might haue told heareafter.
Eno. 'Twillbe naught, but let it be: bring me to *Anthony*.
Eros. Come Sir, *Exeunt.*

Enter Agrippa, Mecenas, and Cæsar.

Cæs. Contemning Rome he ha's done all this, & more
In Alexandria: heere's the manner of't:
I'th' Market-place on a Tribunall siluer'd,
Cleopatra and himselfe in Chaires of Gold
Were publikely enthron'd: at the feet, sat
Cæsarion whom they call my Fathers Sonne,
And all the vnlawfull issue, that their Lust
Since then hath made betweene them. Vnto her,
He gaue the stablishment of Egypt, made her
Of lower Syria, Cyprus, Lydia, absolute Queene.
Mece. This in the publike eye?
Cæsar. I'th' common shew place, where they exercise,
His Sonnes hither proclaimed the King of Kings,
Great Media, Parthia, and Armenia
He gaue to *Alexander*. To *Ptolomy* he assign'd,
Syria, Silicia, and Phœnetia: she
In th'abiliments of the Goddesse *Isis*
That day appeer'd, and oft before gaue audience,
As 'tis reported so.
Mece. Let Rome be thus inform'd.
Agri. Who queazie with his insolence already,
Will their good thoughts call from him.
Cæsar. The people knowes it,
And haue now receiu'd his accusations.
Agri. Who does he accuse?
Cæsar. *Cæsar*, and that hauing in Cicilie
Sextus Pompeius spoil'd, we had not rated him
His part o'th' Isle. Then does he say, he lent me
Some shipping vnrestor'd. Lastly, he frets
That *Lepidus* of the Triumpherate, should be depos'd,
And being that, we detaine all his Reuenue.
Agri. Sir, this should be answer'd.
Cæsar. 'Tis done already, and the Messenger gone:
I haue told him *Lepidus* was growne too cruell,

That he his high Authority abus'd,
And did deserue his change: for what I haue conquer'd,
I grant him part: but then in his Armenia,
And other of his conquer'd Kingdoms, I demand the like
Mec. Hee'l neuer yeeld to that.
Cæs. Nor must not then be yeelded to in this.
Enter Octauia with her Traine.
Octa. Haile *Cæsar*, and my L. haile most deere *Cæsar*.
Cæsar. That euer I should call thee Cast-away.
Octa. You haue not call'd me so, nor haue you cause.
Cæs. Why haue you stoln vpon vs thus? you come not
Like *Cæsars* Sister, The wife of *Anthony*
Should haue an Army for an Vsher, and
The neighes of Horse to tell of her approach,
Long ere she did appeare. The trees by th'way
Should haue borne men, and expectation fainted,
Longing for what it had not. Nay, the dust
Should haue ascended to the Roofe of Heauen,
Rais'd by your populous Troopes: But you are come
A Market-maid to Rome, and haue preuented
The ostentation of our loue; which left vnshewne,
Is often left vnlou'd: we should haue met you
By Sea, and Land, supplying euery Stage
With an augmented greeting.
Octa. Good my Lord,
To come thus was I not constrain'd, but did it
On my free-will. My Lord *Marke Anthony*,
Hearing that you prepar'd for Warre, acquainted
My greeued eare withall: whereon I begg'd
His pardon for returne.
Cæs. Which soone he granted,
Being an abstract 'tweene his Lust, and him.
Octa. Do not say so, my Lord.
Cæs. I haue eyes vpon him,
And his affaires come to me on the wind: wher is he now?
Octa. My Lord, in Athens.
Cæsar. No my most wronged Sister, *Cleopatra*
Hath nodded him to her. He hath giuen his Empire
Vp to a Whore, who now are leuying
The Kings o'th'earth for Warre. He hath assembled,
Bochus the King of Lybia, *Archilaus*
Of Cappadocia, *Philadelphos* King
Of Paphlagonia: the Thracian King *Adullas*,
King *Manchus* of Arabia, King of Pont,
Herod of Iewry, *Mithridates* King
Of Comageat, *Polemen* and *Amintas*,
The Kings of Mede, and Licoania,
With a more larger List of Scepters.
Octa. Aye me most wretched,
That haue my heart parted betwixt two Friends,
That does afflict each other. (breaking forth
Cæs. Welcom hither: your Letters did with-holde our
Till we perceiu'd both how you were wrong led,
And we in negligent danger: cheere your heart,
Be you not troubled with the time, which driues
O're your content, these strong necessities,
But let determin'd things to destinie
Hold vnbewayl'd their way. Welcome to Rome,
Nothing more deere to me. You are abus'd
Beyond the marke of thought: and the high Gods
To do you Iustice, makes his Ministers
Of vs, and those that loue you. Best of comfort,
And euer welcom to vs. *Agrip.* Welcome Lady.
Mec. Welcome deere Madam,
Each heart in Rome does loue and pitty you,
Onely th'adulterous *Anthony*, most large
In his abhominations, turnes you off,
And giues his potent Regiment to a Trull
That noyses it against vs.
Octa. Is it so sir?
Cæs. Most certaine: Sister welcome: pray you
Be euer knowne to patience. My deer'st Sister. *Exeunt*
Enter Cleopatra, and Enobarbus.
Cleo. I will be euen with thee, doubt it not.
Eno. But why, why, why?
Cleo. Thou hast forespoke my being in these warres,
And say'st it it not fit.
Eno. Well: is it, is it.
Cleo. If not, denounc'd against vs, why should not
we be there in person.
Enob. Well, I could reply: if wee should serue with
Horse and Mares together, the Horse were meerly lost:
the Mares would beare a Soldiour and his Horse.
Cleo. What is't you say?
Enob. Your presence needs must puzle *Anthony*,
Take from his heart, take from his Braine, from's time,
What should not then be spar'd. He is already
Traduc'd for Leuity, and 'tis said in Rome,
That *Photinus* an Eunuch, and your Maides
Mannage this warre.
Cleo. Sinke Rome, and their tongues rot
That speake against vs. A Charge we beare i'th'Warre,
And as the president of my Kingdome will
Appeare there for a man. Speake not against it,
I will not stay behinde.
Enter Anthony and Camidias.
Eno. Nay I haue done, here comes the Emperor.
Ant. Is it not strange *Camidius*,
That from Tarrentum, and Brandusium,
He could so quickly cut the Ionian Sea,
And take in Troine. You haue heard on't (Sweet?)
Cleo. Celerity is neuer more admir'd,
Then by the negligent.
Ant. A good rebuke,
Which might haue well becom'd the best of men
To taunt at slacknesse. *Camidius*, wee
Will fight with him by Sea.
Cleo. By Sea, what else?
Cam. Why will my Lord, do so?
Ant. For that he dares vs too't.
Enob. So hath my Lord, dar'd him to single fight.
Cam. I, and to wage this Battell at Pharsalia,
Where *Cæsar* fought with *Pompey*. But these offers
Which serue not for his vantage, he shakes off,
And so should you.
Enob. Your Shippes are not well mann'd,
Your Marriners are Militers, Reapers, people
Ingrost by swift Impresse. In *Cæsars* Fleete,
Are those, that often haue 'gainst *Pompey* fought,
Their shippes are yare, yours heauy no disgrace
Shall fall you for refusing him at Sea,
Being prepar'd for Land.
Ant. By Sea, by Sea.
Eno. Most worthy Sir, you therein throw away
The absolute Soldiership you haue by Land,
Distract your Armie, which doth most consist
Of Warre-markt-footmen, leaue vnexecuted
Your owne renowned knowledge, quite forgoe
The way which promises assurance, and
Giue vp your selfe meerly to chance and hazard,
From firme Securitie.
Ant. Ile fight at Sea.

Cleo

Cleo. I haue ſixty Sailes, *Cæſar* none better.
Ant. Our ouer-plus of ſhipping will we burne,
And with the reſt full mann'd, from th'head of Action
Beate th'approaching *Cæſar*. But if we faile,
We then can doo't at Land. *Enter a Meſſenger.*
Thy Buſineſſe?
Meſ. The Newes is true, my Lord, he is deſcried,
Cæſar ha's taken Toryne.
Ant. Can he be there in perſon? 'Tis impoſſible
Strange, that his power ſhould be. *Camidius,*
Our nineteene Legions thou ſhalt hold by Land,
And our twelue thouſand Horſe. Wee'l to our Ship,
Away my *Thetis.*
Enter a Soldiour.
How now worthy Souldier?
Soul. Oh Noble Emperor, do not fight by Sea,
Truſt not to rotten plankes: Do you miſdoubt
This Sword, and theſe my Wounds; let th'Egyptians
And the Phœnicians go a ducking: wee
Haue vs'd to conquer ſtanding on the earth,
And fighting foot to foot.
Ant. Well, well, away. *exit Ant. Cleo. & Enob.*
Soul. By *Hercules* I thinke I am i'th'right.
Cam. Souldier thou art: but his whole action growes
Not in the power on't: ſo our Leaders leade,
And we are Womens men.
Soul. You keepe by Land the Legions and the Horſe
whole, do you not?
Ven. Marcus Octauius, Marcus Iuſteus,
Publicola, and *Celius*, are for Sea:
But we keepe whole by Land. This ſpeede of *Cæſars*
Carries beyond beleefe.
Soul. While he was yet in Rome
His power went out in ſuch diſtractions,
As beguilde all Spies.
Cam. Who's his Lieutenant, heare you?
Soul. They ſay, one *Towrus.*
Cam. Well, I know the man.
Enter a Meſſenger.
Meſ. The Emperor cals *Camidius.*
Cam. With Newes the times with Labour,
And throwes forth each minute, ſome. *exeunt*

Enter Cæſar with his Army, marching.

Cæſ. Towrus?
Tow. My Lord.
Cæſ. Strike not by Land,
Keepe whole, prouoke not Battaile
Till we haue done at Sea. Do not exceede
The Preſcript of this Scroule: Our fortune lyes
Vpon this iumpe. *exit.*
Enter Anthony, and Enobarbus.
Ant Set we our Squadrons on yond ſide o'th'Hill,
In eye of *Cæſars* battaile, from which place
We may the number of the Ships behold,
And ſo proceed accordingly. *exit.*

Camidius Marcheth with his Land Army one way ouer the ſtage, and Towrus the Lieutenant of Cæſar the other way: After their going in, is heard the noiſe of a Sea fight.
Alarum. Enter Enobarbus and Scarus.

Eno. Naught, naught, al naught, I can behold no longer:
Thantoniad, the Egyptian Admirall,
With all their ſixty flye, and turne the Rudder:
To ſee't, mine eyes are blaſted.
Enter Scarrus.
Scar. Gods, & Goddeſſes, all the whol ſynod of them!
Eno. What's thy paſſion.
Scar. The greater Cantle of the world, is loſt
With very ignorance, we haue kiſt away
Kingdomes, and Prouinces.
Eno. How appeares the Fight?
Scar. On our ſide, like the Token'd Peſtilence,
Where death is ſure. Yon ribaudred Nagge of Egypt,
(Whom Leproſie o're-take) i'th'midſt o'th'fight,
When vantage like a payre of Twinnes appear'd
Both as the ſame, or rather ours the elder;
(The Breeze vpon her) like a Cow in Iune,
Hoiſts Sailes, and flyes.
Eno. That I beheld:
Mine eyes did ſicken at the ſight, and could not
Indure a further view.
Scar. She once being looft,
The Noble ruine of her Magicke, *Anthony*,
Claps on his Sea-wing, and (like a doting Mallard)
Leauing the Fight in heighth, flyes after her:
I neuer ſaw an Action of ſuch ſhame;
Experience, Man-hood, Honor, ne're before,
Did violate ſo it ſelfe.
Enob. Alacke, alacke.
Enter Camidius.
Cam. Our Fortune on the Sea is out of breath,
And ſinkes moſt lamentably. Had our Generall
Bin what he knew himſelfe, it had gone well:
Oh his ha's giuen example for our flight,
Moſt groſſely by his owne.
Enob. I, are you thereabouts? Why then goodnight
indeede.
Cam. Toward Peloponneſus are they fled.
Scar. 'Tis eaſie toot,
And there I will attend what further comes.
Camid. To *Cæſar* will I render
My Legions and my Horſe, ſixe Kings alreadie
Shew me the way of yeelding.
Eno. Ile yet follow
The wounded chance of *Anthony*, though my reaſon
Sits in the winde againſt me.
Enter Anthony with Attendants.
Ant. Hearke, the Land bids me tread no more vpon't,
It is aſham'd to beare me. Friends, come hither,
I am ſo lated in the world, that I
Haue loſt my way for euer. I haue a ſhippe,
Laden with Gold, take that, diuide it: flye,
And make your peace with *Cæſar*.
Omnes. Fly? Not wee.
Ant. I haue fled my ſelfe, and haue inſtructed cowards
To runne, and ſhew their ſhoulders. Friends be gone,
I haue my ſelfe reſolu'd vpon a courſe,
Which has no neede of you. Be gone,
My Treaſure's in the Harbour. Take it: Oh,
I follow'd that I bluſh to looke vpon,
My very haires do mutiny: for the white
Reproue the browne for raſhneſſe, and they them
For feare, and doting. Friends be gone, you ſhall
Haue Letters from me to ſome Friends, that will
Sweepe your way for you. Pray you looke not ſad,
Nor make replyes of loathneſſe, take the hint
Which my diſpaire proclaimes. Let them be left
Which leaues it ſelfe, to the Sea-ſide ſtraight way;
I will poſſeſſe you of that ſhip and Treaſure.

Leaue me, I pray a little: pray you now,
Nay do ſo: for indeede I haue loſt command,
Therefore I pray you, Ile ſee you by and by. *Sits downe*

Enter Cleopatra led by Charmian and Eros.

Eros. Nay gentle Madam, to him, comfort him.
Iras. Do moſt deere Queene.
Char. Do, why, what elſe?
Cleo. Let me ſit downe: Oh *Iuno.*
Ant. No,no,no,no,no.
Eros. See you heere, Sir?
Ant. Oh fie,fie,fie.
Char. Madam.
Iras. Madam, oh good Empreſſe.
Eros. Sir,ſir.
Ant. Yes my Lord, yes; he at Philippi kept
His ſword e'ne like a dancer, while I ſtrooke
The leane and wrinkled *Caſſius*, and 'twas I
That the mad *Brutus* ended: he alone
Dealt on Lieutenantry, and no practiſe had
In the braue ſquares of Warre: yet now: no matter.
Cleo. Ah ſtand by.
Eros. The Queene my Lord, the Queene.
Iras. Go to him, Madam, ſpeake to him,
Hee's vnqualited with very ſhame.
Cleo. Well then, ſuſtaine me: Oh.
Eros. Moſt Noble Sir ariſe, the Queene approaches,
Her head's declin'd, and death will ceaſe her, but
Your comfort makes the reſcue.
Ant. I haue offended Reputation,
A moſt vnnoble ſweruing.
Eros. Sir, the Queene.
Ant. Oh whether haſt thou lead me Egypt, ſee
How I conuey my ſhame, out of thine eyes,
By looking backe what I haue left behinde
Stroy'd in diſhonor.
Cleo. Oh my Lord, my Lord,
Forgiue my fearfull ſayles, I little thought
You would haue followed.
Ant. Egypt, thou knew'ſt too well,
My heart was to thy Rudder tyed by'th'ſtrings,
And thou ſhould'ſt ſtowe me after. O're my ſpirit
The full ſupremacie thou knew'ſt, and that
Thy becke, might from the bidding of the Gods
Command mee.
Cleo. Oh my pardon.
Ant. Now I muſt
To the young man ſend humble Treaties, dodge
And palter in the ſhifts of lownes, who
With halfe the bulke o'th'world plaid as I pleas'd,
Making, and marring Fortunes. You did know
How much you were my Conqueror, and that
My Sword, made weake by my affection, would
Obey it on all cauſe.
Cleo. Pardon, pardon.
Ant Fall not a teare I ſay, one of them rates
All that is wonne and loſt: Giue me a kiſſe,
Euen this repayes me.
We ſent our Schoolemaſter, is a come backe?
Loue I am full of Lead: ſome Wine
Within there, and our Viands: Fortune knowes,
We ſcorne her moſt, when moſt ſhe offers blowes. *Exeunt*

Enter Cæſar, Agrippa, and Dollabello, with others.

Cæſ. Let him appeare that's come from *Anthony.*
Know you him.
Dolla *Cæſar*, 'tis his Schoolemaſter,
An argument that he is pluckt, when hither
He ſends ſo poore a Pinnion of his Wing,
Which had ſuperfluous Kings for Meſſengers,
Not many Moones gone by.

Enter Ambaſſador from Anthony.

Cæſar. Approach, and ſpeake.
Amb. Such as I am, I come from *Anthony*:
I was of late as petty to his ends,
As is the Morne-dew on the Mertle leafe
To his grand Sea.
Cæſ. Bee't ſo, declare thine office.
Amb. Lord of his Fortunes he ſalutes thee, and
Requires to liue in Egypt, which not granted
He Leſſons his Requeſts, and to thee ſues
To let him breath betweene the Heauens and Earth
A priuate man in Athens: this for him.
Next, *Cleopatra* does confeſſe thy Greatneſſe,
Submits her to thy might, and of thee craues
The Circle of the *Ptolemies* for her heyres,
Now hazarded to thy Grace.
Cæſ. For *Anthony*,
I haue no eares to his requeſt. The Queene,
Of Audience, nor Deſire ſhall faile, ſo ſhee
From Egypt driue her all-diſgraced Friend,
Or take his life there. This if ſhee performe,
She ſhall not ſue vnheard. So to them both.
Amb. Fortune purſue thee.
Cæſ. Bring him through the Bands:
To try thy Eloquence, now 'tis time, diſpatch,
From *Anthony* winne *Cleopatra*, promiſe
And in our Name, what ſhe requires, adde more
From thine inuention, offers. Women are not
In their beſt Fortunes ſtrong; but want will periure
The ne're touch'd Veſtall. Try thy cunning *Thidias*,
Make thine owne Edict for thy paines, which we
Will anſwer as a Law.
Thid. *Cæſar*, I go.
Cæſar. Obſerue how *Anthony* becomes his flaw,
And what thou think'ſt his very action ſpeakes
In euery power that mooues.
Thid. *Cæſar*, I ſhall. *exeunt.*

Enter Cleopatra, Enobarbus, Charmian, & Iras.

Cleo. What ſhall we do, *Enobarbus*?
Eno. Thinke, and dye.
Cleo. Is *Anthony*, or we in fault for this?
Eno. *Anthony* onely, that would make his will
Lord of his Reaſon. What though you fled,
From that great face of Warre, whoſe ſeuerall ranges
Frighted each other? Why ſhould he follow?
The itch of his Affection ſhould not then
Haue nickt his Captain-ſhip, at ſuch a point,
When halfe to halfe the world oppos'd, he being
The meered queſtion? 'Twas a ſhame no leſſe
Then was his loſſe, to courſe your flying Flagges,
And leaue his Nauy gazing.
Cleo. Prythee peace.

Enter the Ambaſſador, with Anthony.

Ant. Is that his anſwer? *Amb.* I my Lord.
Ant. The Queene ſhall then haue courteſie,
So ſhe will yeeld vs vp.
Am. He ſayes ſo.
Antho. Let her know't. To the Boy *Cæſar* ſend this
grizled head, and he will fill thy wiſhes to the brimme,
With Principalities.
Cleo. That head my Lord?

Ant.

Ant. To him againe, tell him he weares the Roſe
Of youth vpon him: from which, the world ſhould note
Something particular: His Coine, Ships, Legions,
May be a Cowards, whoſe Miniſters would preuaile
Vnder the ſeruice of a Childe, as ſoone
As i'th'Command of *Cæſar.* I dare him therefore
To lay his gay Compariſons a-part,
And anſwer me declin'd, Sword againſt Sword,
Our ſelues alone: Ile write it: Follow me.
Eno. Yes like enough: hye battel'd *Cæſar* will
Vnſtate his happineſſe, and be Stag'd to th'ſhew
Againſt a Sworder. I ſee mens Iudgements are
A parcell of their Fortunes, and things outward
Do draw the inward quality after them
To ſuffer all alike, that he ſhould dreame,
Knowing all meaſures, the full *Cæſar* will
Anſwer his emptineſſe; *Cæſar* thou haſt ſubdu'de
His iudgement too.

Enter a Seruant.

Ser. A Meſſenger from *Cæſar.*
Cleo. What no more Ceremony? See my Women,
Againſt the blowne Roſe may they ſtop their noſe,
That kneel'd vnto the Buds. Admit him ſir.
Eno. Mine honeſty, and I, beginne to ſquare,
The Loyalty well held to Fooles, does make
Our Faith meere folly: yet he that can endure
To follow with Allegeance a falne Lord,
Does conquer him that did his Maſter conquer,
And earnes a place i'th'Story.

Enter Thidias.

Cleo. *Cæſars* will.
Thid. Heare it apart.
Cleo. None but Friends: ſay boldly.
Thid. So haply are they Friends to *Anthony.*
Enob. He needs as many (Sir) as *Cæſar* ha's,
Or needs not vs. If *Cæſar* pleaſe, our Maſter
Will leape to be his Friend: For vs you know,
Whoſe he is, we are, and that is *Cæſars.*
Thid. So. Thus then thou moſt renown'd, *Cæſar* intreats,
Not to conſider in what caſe thou ſtand'ſt
Further then he is *Cæſars.*
Cleo. Go on, right Royall.
Thid. He knowes that you embrace not *Anthony*
As you did loue, but as you feared him.
Cleo. Oh.
Thid. The ſcarre's vpon your Honor, therefore he
Does pitty, as conſtrained blemiſhes,
Not as deſerued.
Cleo. He is a God,
And knowes what is moſt right. Mine Honour
Was not yeelded, but conquer'd meerely.
Eno. To be ſure of that, I will aske *Anthony.*
Sir, ſir, thou art ſo leakie
That we muſt leaue thee to thy ſinking, for
Thy deereſt quit thee. *Exit Enob.*
Thid Shall I ſay to *Cæſar,*
What you require of him: for he partly begges
To be deſir'd to giue. It much would pleaſe him,
That of his Fortunes you ſhould make a ſtaffe
To leane vpon. But it would warme his ſpirits
To heare from me you had left *Anthony,*
And put your ſelfe vnder his ſhrowd, the vniuerſal Land- (lord.
Cleo. What's your name?
Thid. My name is *Thidias.*
Cleo. Moſt kinde Meſſenger,
Say to great *Cæſar* this in diſputation,
I kiſſe his conqu'ring hand: Tell him, I am prompt
To lay my Crowne at's feete, and there to kneele.
Tell him, from his all-obeying breath, I heare
The doome of Egypt.
Thid. Tis your Nobleſt courſe:
Wiſedome and Fortune combatting together,
If that the former dare but what it can,
No chance may ſhake it. Giue me grace to lay
My dutie on your hand.
Cleo. Your *Cæſars* Father oft,
(When he hath mus'd of taking kingdomes in)
Beſtow'd his lips on that vnworthy place,
As it rain'd kiſſes.

Enter Anthony and Enobarbus.

Ant. Fauours? By Ioue that thunders. What art thou (Fellow?
Thid. One that but performes
The bidding of the fulleſt man, and worthieſt
To haue command obey'd.
Eno You will be whipt.
Ant. Approch there: ah you Kite. Now Gods & diuels
Authority melts from me of late. When I cried hoa,
Like Boyes vnto a muſſe, Kings would ſtart forth,
And cry, your will. Haue you no eares?
I am *Anthony* yet. Take hence this Iack, and whip him.

Enter a Seruant.

Eno. Tis better playing with a Lions whelpe,
Then with an old one dying.
Ant. Moone and Starres,
Whip him: wer't twenty of the greateſt Tributaries
That do acknowledge *Cæſar,* ſhould I finde them
So ſawcy with the hand of ſhe heere, what's her name
Since ſhe was *Cleopatra?* Whip him Fellowes,
Till like a Boy you ſee him crindge his face,
And whine aloud for mercy. Take him hence.
Thid. Marke Anthony.
Ant. Tugge him away: being whipt
Bring him againe, the Iacke of *Cæſars* ſhall
Beare vs an arrant to him. *Exeunt with Thidius.*
You were halfe blaſted ere I knew you: Ha?
Haue I my pillow left vnpreſt in Rome,
Forborne the getting of a lawfull Race,
And by a Iem of women, to be abus'd
By one that lookes on Feeders?
Cleo. Good my Lord.
Ant. You haue beene a boggeler euer,
But when we in our viciouſneſſe grow hard
(Oh miſery on't) the wiſe Gods ſeele our eyes
In our owne filth, drop our cleare iudgements, make vs
Adore our errors, laugh at's while we ſtrut
To our confuſion.
Cleo. Oh, is't come to this?
Ant. I found you as a Morſell, cold vpon
Dead *Cæſars* Trencher: Nay, you were a Fragment
Of *Gneius Pompeyes,* beſides what hotter houres
Vnregiſtred in vulgar Fame, you haue
Luxuriouſly pickt out. For I am ſure,
Though you can gueſſe what Temperance ſhould be,
You know not what it is.
Cleo. Wherefore is this?
Ant. To let a Fellow that will take rewards,
And ſay, God quit you, be familiar with
My play-fellow, your hand; this Kingly Seale,
And plighter of high hearts. O that I were
Vpon the hill of *Baſan,* to out-roare
The horned Heard, for I haue ſauage cauſe,
And to proclaime it ciuilly, were like

A halter'd necke, which do's the Hangman thanke,
For being yare about him. Is he whipt?

Enter a Seruant with Thidias.

Ser. Soundly, my Lord.
Ant. Cried he? and begg'd a Pardon?
Ser. He did aske fauour.
Ant. If that thy Father liue, let him repent
Thou was't not made his daughter, and be thou sorrie
To follow *Cæsar* in his Triumph, since
Thou hast bin whipt. For following him, henceforth
The white hand of a Lady Feauer thee,
Shake thou to looke on't. Get thee backe to *Cæsar*,
Tell him thy entertainment: looke thou say
He makes me angry with him. For he seemes
Proud and disdainfull, harping on what I am,
Not what he knew I was. He makes me angry,
And at this time most easie 'tis to doo't:
When my good Starres, that were my former guides
Haue empty left their Orbes, and shot their Fires
Into th'Abisme of hell. If he mislike,
My speech, and what is done, tell him he has
Hiparchus, my enfranched Bondman, whom
He may at pleasure whip, or hang, or torture,
As he shall like to quit me. Vrge it thou:
Hence with thy stripes, be gone. *Exit Thid.*
Cleo. Haue you done yet?
Ant. Alacke our Terrene Moone is now Eclipst,
And it portends alone the fall of *Anthony*.
Cleo. I must stay his time?
Ant. To flatter *Cæsar*, would you mingle eyes
With one that tyes his points.
Cleo. Not know me yet?
Ant. Cold-hearted toward me?
Cleo. Ah (Deere) if I be so,
From my cold heart let Heauen ingender haile,
And poyson it in the sourse, and the first stone
Drop in my necke: as it determines so
Dissolue my life, the next Cæsarian smile,
Till by degrees the memory of my wombe,
Together with my braue Egyptians all,
By the discandering of this pelleted storme,
Lye graueless, till the Flies and Gnats of Nyle
Haue buried them for prey.
Ant. I am satisfied:
Cæsar sets downe in Alexandria, where
I will oppose his Fate. Our force by Land,
Hath Nobly held, our seuer'd Nauie too
Haue knit againe, and Fleete, threatning most Sea-like.
Where hast thou bin my heart? Dost thou heare Lady?
If from the Field I shall returne once more
To kisse these Lips, I will appeare in Blood,
I, and my Sword, will earne our Chronicle,
There's hope in't yet.
Cleo. That's my braue Lord.
Ant. I will be trebble-sinewed, hearted, breath'd,
And fight maliciously: for when mine houres
Were nice and lucky, men did ransome liues
Of me for iests: But now, Ile set my teeth,
And send to darkenesse all that stop me. Come,
Let's haue one other gawdy night: Call to me
All my sad Captaines, fill our Bowles once more:
Let's mocke the midnight Bell.
Cleo. It is my Birth-day,
I had thought t'haue held it poore. But since my Lord
Is *Anthony* againe, I will be *Cleopatra*.
Ant. We will yet do well.
Cleo. Call all his Noble Captaines to my Lord.
Ant. Do so, wee'l speake to them,
And to night Ile force
The Wine peepe through their scarres.
Come on (my Queene)
There's sap in't yet. The next time I do fight
Ile make death loue me: for I will contend
Euen with his pestilent Sythe. *Exeunt.*
Eno. Now hee'l out-stare the Lightning, to be furious
Is to be frighted out of feare, and in that moode
The Doue will pecke the Estridge; and I see still
A diminution in our Captaines braine,
Restores his heart; when valour prayes in reason,
It eates the Sword it fights with: I will seeke
Some way to leaue him. *Exeunt.*

Enter Cæsar, Agrippa, & Mecenas with his Army, Cæsar reading a Letter.

Cæs. He calles me Boy, and chides as he had power
To beate me out of Egypt. My Messenger
He hath whipt with Rods, dares me to personal Combat.
Cæsar to *Anthony*: let the old Ruffian know,
I haue many other wayes to dye: meane time
Laugh at his Challenge.
Mece. *Cæsar* must thinke,
When one so great begins to rage, hee's hunted
Euen to falling. Giue him no breath, but now
Make boote of his distraction: Neuer anger
Made good guard for it selfe.
Cæs. Let our best heads know,
That to morrow, the last of many Battailes
We meane to fight. Within our Files there are,
Of those that seru'd *Marke Anthony* but late,
Enough to fetch him in. See it done,
And Feast the Army, we haue store to doo't,
And they haue earn'd the waste. Poore *Anthony*. *Exeunt*

Enter Anthony, Cleopatra, Enobarbus, Charmian, Iras, Alexas, with others.

Ant. He will not fight with me, *Domitian*?
Eno. No?
Ant. Why should he not?
Eno. He thinks, being twenty times of better fortune,
He is twenty men to one.
Ant. To morrow Soldier,
By Sea and Land Ile fight: or I will liue,
Or bathe my dying Honor in the blood
Shall make it liue againe. Woo't thou fight well.
Eno. Ile strike, and cry, Take all.
Ant. Well said, come on:
Call forth my Houshold Seruants, lets to night

Enter 3 or 4 Seruitors.

Be bounteous at our Meale. Giue me thy hand,
Thou hast bin rightly honest, so hast thou,
Thou, and thou, and thou: you haue seru'd me well,
And Kings haue beene your fellowes.
Cleo. What meanes this?
Eno. 'Tis one of those odde tricks which sorow shoots
Out of the minde.
Ant. And thou art honest too:
I wish I could be made so many men,
And all of you clapt vp together, in
An *Anthony*: that I might do you seruice,
So good as you haue done.
Omnes.

Omnes. The Gods forbid.
Ant. Well, my good Fellowes, wait on me to night:
Scant not my Cups, and make as much of me
As when mine Empire was your Fellow too,
And suffer'd my command.
Cleo. What does he meane?
Eno. To make his Followers weepe.
Ant. Tend me to night;
May be, it is the period of your duty,
Haply you shall not see me more, or if,
A mangled shadow. Perchance to morrow,
You'l serue another Master. I looke on you,
As one that takes his leaue. Mine honest Friends,
I turne you not away, but like a Master
Married to your good seruice, stay till death:
Tend me to night two houres, I aske no more,
And the Gods yeeld you for't.
Eno. What meane you (Sir)
To giue them this discomfort? Looke they weepe,
And I an Asse, am Onyon-ey'd; for shame,
Transforme vs not to women.
Ant. Ho, ho, ho:
Now the Witch take me, if I meant it thus.
Grace grow where those drops fall (my hearty Friends)
You take me in too dolorous a sense,
For I spake to you for your comfort, did desire you
To burne this night with Torches: Know (my hearts)
I hope well of to morrow, and will leade you,
Where rather Ile expect victorious life,
Then death, and Honor. Let's to Supper, come,
And drowne consideration. *Exeunt.*

Enter a Company of Soldiours.

1.Sol. Brother, goodnight: to morrow is the day.
2.Sol. It will determine one way: Fare you well.
Heard you of nothing strange about the streets.
1 Nothing: what newes?
2 Belike 'tis but a Rumour, good night to you.
1 Well sir, good night.
They meete other Soldiers.
2 Souldiers, haue carefull Watch.
1 And you: Goodnight, goodnight.
They place themselues in euery corner of the Stage.
2 Heere we: and if to morrow
Our Nauie thriue, I haue an absolute hope
Our Landmen will stand vp.
1 'Tis a braue Army, and full of purpose.
Musicke of the Hoboyes is vnder the Stage.
2 Peace, what noise?
1 List list.
2 Hearke.
1 Musicke i'th'Ayre.
3 Vnder the earth.
4 It signes well, do's it not?
3 No.
1 Peace I say: What should this meane?
2 'Tis the God *Hercules*, whom *Anthony* loued,
Now leaues him.
1 Walke, let's see if other Watchmen
Do heare what we do?
2 How now Maisters? *Speak together.*
Omnes. How now? how now? do you heare this?
1 I, is't not strange?
3 Do you heare Masters? Do you heare?
1 Follow the noyse so farre as we haue quarter.
Let's see how it will giue off.
Omnes. Content: 'Tis strange. *Exeunt.*

Enter Anthony and Cleopatra, with others.

Ant. *Eros*, mine Armour *Eros.*
Cleo. Sleepe a little.
Ant. No my Chucke. *Eros*, come mine Armor *Eros.*
Enter Eros.
Come good Fellow, put thine Iron on,
If Fortune be not ours to day, it is
Because we braue her. Come.
Cleo. Nay, Ile helpe too, *Anthony.*
What's this for? Ah let be, let be, thou art
The Armourer of my heart: False, false: This, this,
Sooth-law Ile helpe: Thus it must bee.
Ant. Well, well, we shall thriue now.
Seest thou my good Fellow. Go, put on thy defences.
Eros. Briefely Sir.
Cleo. Is not this buckled well?
Ant. Rarely, rarely:
He that vnbuckles this, till we do please
To daft for our Repose, shall heare a storme.
Thou fumblest *Eros*, and my Queenes a Squire
More tight at this, then thou: Dispatch. O Loue,
That thou couldst see my Warres to day, and knew'st
The Royall Occupation, thou should'st see
A Workeman in't.
Enter an Armed Soldier.
Good morrow to thee, welcome,
Thou look'st like him that knowes a warlike Charge:
To businesse that we loue, we rise betime,
And go too't with delight.
Soul. A thousand Sir, early though't be, haue on their
Riueted trim, and at the Port expect you. *Showt.*
Trumpets Flourish.
Enter Captaines, and Souldiers.
Alex. The Morne is faire: Good morrow Generall.
All. Good morrow Generall.
Ant. 'Tis well blowne Lads.
This Morning, like the spirit of a youth
That meanes to be of note, begins betimes.
So, so: Come giue me that, this way, well-sed.
Fare thee well Dame, what ere becomes of me,
This is a Soldiers kisse: rebukeable,
And worthy shamefull checke it were, to stand
On more Mechanicke Complement, Ile leaue thee.
Now like a man of Steele, you that will fight,
Follow me close, Ile bring you too't: Adieu. *Exeunt.*
Char. Please you retyre to your Chamber?
Cleo. Lead me:
He goes forth gallantly: That he and *Cæsar* might
Determine this great Warre in single fight;
Then *Anthony*; but now. Well on. *Exeunt*

Trumpets sound. Enter Anthony, and Eros.

Eros. The Gods make this a happy day to *Anthony.*
Ant. Would thou, & those thy scars had once preuaild
To make me fight at Land.
Eros. Had'st thou done so,
The Kings that haue reuolted, and the Soldier
That has this morning left thee, would haue still
Followed thy heeles.
Ant. Whose gone this morning?
Eros. Who? one euer neere thee, call for *Enobarbus*,
Hee

He ſhall not heare thee, or from *Cæſars* Campe,
Say I am none of thine.
Ant. What ſayeſt thou?
Sold. Sir he is with *Cæſar.*
Eros. Sir, his Cheſts and Treaſure he has not with him.
Ant. Is he gone?
Sol. Moſt certaine.
Ant. Go *Eros,* ſend his Treaſure after, do it,
Detaine no iot I charge thee: write to him,
(I will ſubſcribe) gentle adieu's, and greetings;
Say, that I wiſh he neuer finde more cauſe
To change a Maſter. Oh my Fortunes haue
Corrupted honeſt men. Diſpatch *Enobarbus.* *Exit*

Flouriſh. Enter Agrippa, Cæſar, with Enobarbus, and Dollabella.

Cæſ. Go forth *Agrippa,* and begin the fight:
Our will is *Anthony* be tooke aliue:
Make it ſo knowne.
Agrip. *Cæſar,* I ſhall.
Cæſar. The time of vniuerſall peace is neere:
Proue this a proſp'rous day, the three nook'd world
Shall beare the Oliue freely.
Enter a Meſſenger.
Meſ. *Anthony* is come into the Field.
Cæſ. Go charge *Agrippa,*
Plant thoſe that haue reuolted in the Vant,
That *Anthony* may ſeeme to ſpend his Fury
Vpon himſelfe. *Exeunt.*
Enob. *Alexas* did reuolt, and went to *Iewry* on
Affaires of *Anthony,* there did diſſwade
Great *Herod* to incline himſelfe to *Cæſar,*
And leaue his Maſter *Anthony.* For this paines,
Cæſar hath hang'd him: *Camindius* and the reſt
That fell away, haue entertainment, but
No honourable truſt: I haue done ill,
Of which I do accuſe my ſelfe ſo ſorely,
That I will ioy no more.
Enter a Soldier of Cæſars.
Sol. *Enobarbus, Anthony*
Hath after thee ſent all thy Treaſure, with
His Bounty ouer-plus. The Meſſenger
Came on my guard, and at thy Tent is now
Vnloading of his Mules.
Eno. I giue it you.
Sol. Mocke not *Enobarbus,*
I tell you true: Beſt you ſaf't the bringer
Out of the hoaſt, I muſt attend mine Office,
Or would haue done't my ſelfe. Your Emperor
Continues ſtill a Ioue. *Exit*
Enob. I am alone the Villaine of the earth,
And feele I am ſo moſt. Oh *Anthony,*
Thou Mine of Bounty, how would'ſt thou haue payed
My better ſeruice, when my turpitude
Thou doſt ſo Crowne with Gold. This blowes my hart,
If ſwift thought breake it not: a ſwifter meane
Shall out-ſtrike thought, but thought will doo't. I feele
I fight againſt thee: No I will go ſeeke
Some Ditch, wherein to dye: the foul'ſt beſt fits
My latter part of life. *Exit.*
Alarum, Drummes and Trumpets.
Enter Agrippa.
Agrip. Retire, we haue engag'd our ſelues too farre:
Cæſar himſelfe ha's worke, and our oppreſſion
Exceeds what we expected. *Exit.*

Alarums.
Enter Anthony, and Scarrus wounded.

Scar. O my braue Emperor, this is fought indeed,
Had we done ſo at firſt, we had drouen them home
With clowts about their heads. *Far off.*
Ant. Thou bleed'ſt apace.
Scar. I had a wound heere that was like a T,
But now 'tis made an H.
Ant. They do retyre.
Scar. Wee'l beat 'em into Bench-holes, I haue yet
Roome for ſix ſcotches more.
Enter Eros.
Eros. They are beaten Sir, and our aduantage ſerues
For a faire victory.
Scar. Let vs ſcore their backes,
And ſnatch 'em vp, as we take Hares behinde,
'Tis ſport to maul a Runner.
Ant. I will reward thee
Once for thy ſprightly comfort, and ten-fold
For thy good valour. Come thee on.
Scar. Ile halt after. *Exeunt*

Alarum. Enter Anthony againe in a March. Scarrus, with others.

Ant. We haue beate him to his Campe: Runne one
Before, & let the Queen know of our gueſts: to morrow
Before the Sun ſhall ſee's, wee'l ſpill the blood
That ha's to day eſcap'd. I thanke you all,
For doughty handed are you, and haue fought
Not as you ſeru'd the Cauſe, but as't had beene
Each mans like mine: you haue ſhewne all *Hectors.*
Enter the Citty, clip your Wiues, your Friends,
Tell them your feats, whil'ſt they with ioyfull teares
Waſh the congealement from your wounds, and kiſſe
The Honour'd-gaſhes whole.
Enter Cleopatra.
Giue me thy hand,
To this great Faiery, Ile commend thy acts,
Make her thankes bleſſe thee. Oh thou day o'th'world,
Chaine mine arm'd necke, leape thou, Attyre and all
Through proofe of Harneſſe to my heart, and there
Ride on the pants triumphing.
Cleo. Lord of Lords.
Oh infinite Vertue, comm'ſt thou ſmiling from
The worlds great ſnare vncaught.
Ant. Mine Nightingale,
We haue beate them to their Beds.
What Gyrle, though gray
Do ſomthing mingle with our yonger brown, yet ha we
A Braine that nouriſhes our Nerues, and can
Get gole for gole of youth. Behold this man,
Commend vnto his Lippes thy fauouring hand,
Kiſſe it my Warriour: He hath fought to day,
As if a God in hate of Mankinde, had
Deſtroyed in ſuch a ſhape.
Cleo. Ile giue thee Friend
An Armour all of Gold: it was a Kings.
Ant. He has deſeru'd it, were it Carbunkled
Like holy Phœbus Carre. Giue me thy hand,
Through Alexandria make a iolly March,
Beare our hackt Targets, like the men that owe them.
Had our great Pallace the capacity
To Campe this hoaſt, we all would ſup together,
And drinke Carowſes to the next dayes Fate
Which

Which promises Royall perill, Trumpetters
With brazen dinne blast you the Citties eare,
Make mingle with our ratling Tabourines,
That heauen and earth may strike their sounds together,
Applauding our approach. *Exeunt.*

Enter a Centerie, and his Company, Enobarbus followes.

Cent. If we be not releeu'd within this houre,
We must returne to th'Court of Guard: the night
Is shiny, and they say, we shall embattaile
By th'second houre i'th'Morne.
1.Watch. This last day was a shrew'd one too's.
Enob. Oh beare me witnesse night.
2 What man is this?
1 Stand close, and list him.
Enob. Be witnesse to me (O thou blessed Moone)
When men reuolted shall vpon Record
Beare hatefull memory: poore *Enobarbus* did
Before thy face repent.
Cent. *Enobarbus*?
2 Peace: Hearke further.
Enob. Oh Soueraigne Mistris of true Melancholly,
The poysonous dampe of night dispunge vpon me,
That Life, a very Rebell to my will,
May hang no longer on me. Throw my heart
Against the flint and hardnesse of my fault,
Which being dried with greefe, will breake to powder,
And finish all foule thoughts. Oh *Anthony*,
Nobler then my reuolt is Infamous,
Forgiue me in thine owne particular,
But let the world ranke me in Register
A Master leauer, and a fugitiue:
Oh *Anthony*! Oh *Anthony*!
1 Let's speake to him.
Cent. Let's heare him, for the things he speakes
May concerne *Cæsar*.
2 Let's do so, but he sleepes.
Cent. Swoonds rather, for so bad a Prayer as his
Was neuer yet for sleepe.
1 Go we to him.
2 Awake sir, awake, speake to vs.
1 Heare you sir?
Cent. The hand of death hath raught him.
Drummes afarre off.
Hearke the Drummes demurely wake the sleepers:
Let vs beare him to'th'Court of Guard: he is of note:
Our houre is fully out.
2 Come on then, he may recouer yet. *exeunt*

Enter Anthony and Scarrus, with their Army.

Ant. Their preparation is to day by Sea,
We please them not by Land.
Scar. For both, my Lord.
Ant. I would they'ld fight i'th'Fire, or i'th'Ayre,
Wee'ld fight there too. But this it is, our Foote
Vpon the hilles adioyning to the Citty
Shall stay with vs. Order for Sea is giuen,
They haue put forth the Hauen:
Where their appointment we may best discouer,
And looke on their endeuour. *exeunt*

Enter Cæsar, and his Army.

Cæs. But being charg'd, we will be still by Land,
Which as I tak't we shall, for his best force
Is forth to Man his Gallies. To the Vales,
And hold our best aduantage. *exeunt.*

Alarum afarre off, as at a Sea-fight.
Enter Anthony, and Scarrus.

Ant. Yet they are not ioyn'd:
Where yon'd Pine does stand, I shall discouer all.
Ile bring thee word straight, how 'tis like to go. *exit*
Scar. Swallowes haue built
In *Cleopatra's* Sailes their nests. The Auguries
Say, they know not, they cannot tell, looke grimly,
And dare not speake their knowledge. *Anthony*,
Is valiant, and deiected, and by starts
His fretted Fortunes giue him hope and feare
Of what he has, and has not.
Enter Anthony.
Ant. All is lost:
This fowle Egyptian hath betrayed me:
My Fleete hath yeelded to the Foe, and yonder
They cast their Caps vp, and Carowse together
Like Friends long lost. Triple-turn'd Whore, 'tis thou
Hast sold me to this Nouice, and my heart
Makes onely Warres on thee. Bid them all flye:
For when I am reueng'd vpon my Charme,
I haue done all. Bid them all flye, be gone.
Oh Sunne, thy vprise shall I see no more,
Fortune, and *Anthony* part heere, euen heere
Do we shake hands? All come to this? The hearts
That pannelled me at heeles, to whom I gaue
Their wishes, do dis-Candie, melt their sweets
On blossoming *Cæsar*: And this Pine is barkt,
That ouer-top'd them all. Betray'd I am.
Oh this false Soule of Egypt! this graue Charme,
Whose eye beck'd forth my Wars, & cal'd them home:
Whose Bosome was my Crownet, my chiefe end,
Like a right Gypsie, hath at fast and loose
Beguil'd me, to the very heart of losse.
What *Eros, Eros*?
Enter Cleopatra.
Ah, thou Spell! Auaunt.
Cleo. Why is my Lord enrag'd against his Loue?
Ant. Vanish, or I shall giue thee thy deseruing,
And blemish *Cæsars* Triumph. Let him take thee,
And hoist thee vp to the shouting Plebeians,
Follow his Chariot, like the greatest spot
Of all thy Sex. Most Monster-like be shewne
For poor'st Diminitiues, for Dolts, and let
Patient *Octauia*, plough thy visage vp
With her prepared nailes. *exit Cleopatra.*
'Tis well th'art gone,
If it be well to liue. But better 'twere
Thou fell'st into my furie, for one death
Might haue preuented many. *Eros*, hoa?
The shirt of *Nessus* is vpon me, teach me
Alcides, thou mine Ancestor, thy rage.
Let me lodge *Licas* on the hornes o'th'Moone,
And with those hands that grasp't the heauiest Club,
Subdue my worthiest selfe: The Witch shall die,
To the young Roman Boy she hath sold me, and I fall
Vnder this plot: She dyes for't. *Eros* hoa? *exit*

Enter Cleopatra, Charmian, Iras, Mardian.

Cleo. Helpe me my women: Oh hee's more mad
Then *Telamon* for his Shield, the Boare of Thessaly
Was neuer so imbost.
Char. To'th'Monument there locke your selfe,
And send him word you are dead:

The

The Soule and Body riue not more in parting,
Then greatnesse going off.
Cleo. To'th'Monument:
Mardian, go tell him I haue slaine my selfe.
Say, that the last I spoke was *Anthony*,
And word it(prythee)pitteously. Hence *Mardian*,
And bring me how he takes my death to'th'Monument.
Exeunt.

Enter Anthony, and Eros.

Ant. *Eros*, thou yet behold'st me?
Eros. I Noble Lord.
Ant. Sometime we see a clowd that's Dragonish,
A vapour sometime, like a Beare, or Lyon,
A toward Cittadell, a pendant Rocke,
A forked Mountaine, or blew Promontorie
With Trees vpon't, that nodde vnto the world,
And mocke our eyes with Ayre.
Thou hast seene these Signes,
They are blacke Vespers Pageants.
Eros. I my Lord.
Ant. That which is now a Horse, euen with a thoght
the Racke dislimes, and makes it indistinct
As water is in water.
Eros It does my Lord.
Ant My good Knaue *Eros*, now thy Captaine is
Euen such a body: Heere I am *Anthony*,
Yet cannot hold this visible shape (my Knaue)
I made these warres for Egypt, and the Queene,
Whose heart I thought I had, for she had mine:
Which whil'st it was mine, had annext vntoo't
A Million moe, (now lost:) shee *Eros* has
Packt Cards with *Cæsars*, and false plaid my Glory
Vnto an Enemies triumph.
Nay, weepe not gentle *Eros*, there is left vs
Our selues to end our selues.

Enter Mardian.

Oh thy vilde Lady, she has rob'd me of my Sword.
Mar. No *Anthony*,
My Mistris lou'd thee, and her Fortunes mingled
With thine intirely.
Ant. Hence sawcy Eunuch peace, she hath betraid me,
And shall dye the death.
Mar. Death of one person, can be paide but once,
And that she ha's discharg'd. What thou would'st do
Is done vnto thy hand: the last she spake
Was *Anthony*, most Noble *Anthony*.
Then in the midd'st a tearing grone did breake
The name of *Anthony*: it was diuided
Betweene her heart, and lips: she rendred life
Thy name so buried in her.
Ant. Dead then?
Mar. Dead.
Ant Vnarme *Eros*, the long dayes taske is done,
And we must sleepe: That thou depart'st hence safe
Does pay thy labour richly: Go. *exit Mardian.*
Off, plucke off,
The seuen-fold shield of *Aiax* cannot keepe
The battery from my heart. Oh cleaue my sides.
Heart, once be stronger then thy Continent,
Cracke thy fraile Case. Apace *Eros*, apace;
No more a Soldier: bruised peeces go,
You haue bin Nobly borne. From me awhile. *exit Eros*
I will o're-take thee *Cleopatra*, and
Weepe for my pardon. So it must be, for now
All length is Torture: since the Torch is out,
Lye downe and stray no farther. Now all labour
Marres what it does: yea, very force entangles
It selfe with strength: Seale then, and all is done.
Eros? I come my Queene. *Eros*? Stay for me,
Where Soules do couch on Flowers, wee'l hand in hand,
And with our sprightly Port make the Ghostes gaze:
Dido, and her *Æneas* shall want Troopes,
And all the haunt be ours. Come *Eros*, *Eros*.

Enter Eros.

Eros. What would my Lord?
Ant. Since *Cleopatra* dyed,
I haue liu'd in such dishonour, that the Gods
Detest my basenesse. I, that with my Sword,
Quarter'd the World, and o're greene Neptunes backe
With Ships, made Cities; condemne my selfe, to lacke
The Courage of a Woman, lesse Noble minde
Then she which by her death, our *Cæsar* telles
I am Conqueror of my selfe. Thou art sworne *Eros*,
That when the exigent should come, which now
Is come indeed: When I should see behinde me
Th'ineuitable prosecution of disgrace and horror,
That on my command, thou then would'st kill me.
Doo't, the time is come: Thou strik'st not me,
'Tis *Cæsar* thou defeat'st. Put colour in thy Cheeke.
Eros. The Gods with-hold me,
Shall I do that which all the Parthian Darts,
(Though Enemy) lost ayme, and could not.
Ant. *Eros*,
Would'st thou be window'd in great Rome, and see
Thy Master thus with pleacht Armes, bending downe
His corrigible necke, his face subdu'de
To penetratiue shame; whil'st the wheel'd seate
Of Fortunate *Cæsar* drawne before him, branded
His Basenesse that ensued.
Eros. I would not see't.
Ant. Come then: for with a wound I must be cur'd.
Draw that thy honest Sword, which thou hast worne
Most vsefull for thy Country.
Eros. Oh sir, pardon me.
Ant. When I did make thee free, swor'st ŷ not then
To do this when I bad thee? Do it at once,
Or thy precedent Seruices are all
But accidents vnpurpos'd. Draw, and come.
Eros. Turne from me then that Noble countenance,
Wherein the worship of the whole world lyes.
Ant. Loe thee.
Eros. My sword is drawne.
Ant. Then let it do at once
The thing why thou hast drawne it.
Eros. My deere Master,
My Captaine, and my Emperor. Let me say
Before I strike this bloody stroke, Farwell.
Ant. 'Tis said man, and farewell.
Eros. Farewell great Chiefe. Shall I strike now?
Ant. Now *Eros*. *Killes himselfe.*
Eros. Why there then:
Thus I do escape the sorrow of *Anthonies* death.
Ant. Thrice-Nobler then my selfe,
Thou teachest me: Oh valiant *Eros*, what
I should, and thou could'st not, my Queene and *Eros*
Haue by their braue instruction got vpon me
A Noblenesse in Record. But I will bee
A Bride-groome in my death, and run intoo't
As to a Louers bed. Come then, and *Eros*,
Thy Master dies thy Scholler; to do thus
I learnt of thee. How, not dead? Not dead?
The Guard, how? Oh dispatch me.

Enter

Enter a Guard.
1.*Guard.* What's the noiſe?
Ant. I haue done my worke ill Friends:
Oh make an end of what I haue begun.
2 The Starre is falne.
1 And time is at his Period.
All. Alas, and woe.
Ant. Let him that loues me, ſtrike me dead.
1 Not I.
2 Nor I.
3 Nor any one. *exeunt*
Dercetus. Thy death and fortunes bid thy folowers fly
This ſword but ſhewne to *Cæſar* with this tydings,
Shall enter me with him.
Enter Diomedes.
Dio. Where's *Anthony*?
Decre. There *Diomed* there.
Diom. Liues he: wilt thou not anſwer man?
Ant. Art thou there *Diomed*?
Draw thy ſword, and giue mee,
Suffiſing ſtrokes for death.
Diom. Moſt abſolute Lord:
My Miſtris *Cleopatra* ſent me to thee.
Ant. When did ſhee ſend thee?
Diom. Now my Lord.
Anth. Where is ſhe?
Diom. Lockt in her Monument: ſhe had a Propheſying (feare
Of what hath come to paſſe: for when ſhe ſaw
(Which neuer ſhall be found) you did ſuſpect
She had diſpos'd with *Cæſar*, and that your rage
Would not be purg'd, ſhe ſent you word ſhe was dead:
But fearing ſince how it might worke, hath ſent
Me to proclaime the truth, and I am come
I dread, too late.
Ant. Too late good *Diomed*: call my Guard I prythee.
Dio. What hoa: the Emperors Guard,
The Guard, what hoa? Come, your Lord calles.
Enter 4. or 5. of the Guard of Anthony.
Ant. Beare me good Friends where *Cleopatra* bides,
'Tis the laſt ſeruice that I ſhall command you.
1 Woe, woe are we ſir, you may not liue to weare
All your true Followers out.
All. Moſt heauy day.
Ant Nay good my Fellowes, do not pleaſe ſharp fate
To grace it with your ſorrowes. Bid that welcome
Which comes to puniſh vs, and we puniſh it
Seeming to beare it lightly. Take me vp,
I haue led you oft, carry me now good Friends,
And haue my thankes for all. *Exit bearing Anthony*

Enter Cleopatra, and her Maides aloft, with Charmian & Iras.

Cleo. Oh *Charmian*, I will neuer go from hence.
Char. Be comforted deere Madam.
Cleo. No, I will not:
All ſtrange and terrible euents are welcome,
But comforts we diſpiſe; our ſize of ſorrow
Proportion'd to our cauſe, muſt be as great
As that which makes it.
Enter Diomed.
How now? is he dead?
Diom His death's vpon him, but not dead.
Looke out o'th other ſide your Monument,
His Guard haue brought him thither.
Enter Anthony, and the Guard.

Cleo. Oh Sunne,
Burne the great Sphere thou mou'ſt in, darkling ſtand
The varrying ſhore o'th'world. O *Antony*, *Antony*, *Antony*
Helpe *Charmian*, helpe *Iras* helpe: helpe Friends
Below, let's draw him hither.
Ant. Peace,
Not *Cæſars* Valour hath o'rethrowne *Anthony*,
But *Anthonie's* hath Triumpht on it ſelfe.
Cleo. So it ſhould be,
That none but *Anthony* ſhould conquer *Anthony*,
But woe 'tis ſo.
Ant. I am dying Egypt, dying; onely
I heere importune death a-while, vntill
Of many thouſand kiſſes, the poore laſt
I lay vpon thy lippes.
Cleo. I dare not Deere,
Deere my Lord pardon: I dare not,
Leaſt I be taken: not th'Imperious ſhew
Of the full-Fortun'd *Cæſar*, euer ſhall
Be brooch'd with me, if Knife, Drugges, Serpents haue
Edge, ſting, or operation. I am ſafe:
Your Wife *Octauia*, with her modeſt eyes,
And ſtill Concluſion, ſhall acquire no Honour
Demuring vpon me: but come, come *Anthony*,
Helpe me my women, we muſt draw thee vp:
Aſſiſt good Friends.
Ant. Oh quicke, or I am gone.
Cleo. Heere's ſport indeede:
How heauy weighes my Lord?
Our ſtrength is all gone into heauineſſe,
That makes the waight. Had I great *Iuno's* power,
The ſtrong wing'd Mercury ſhould fetch thee vp,
And ſet thee by Ioues ſide. Yet come a little,
Wiſhers were euer Fooles. Oh come, come, come,
They heaue Anthony aloft to Cleopatra.
And welcome, welcome. Dye when thou haſt liu'd,
Quicken with kiſſing: had my lippes that power,
Thus would I weare them out.
All. A heauy ſight.
Ant. I am dying Egypt, dying.
Giue me ſome Wine, and let me ſpeake a little.
Cleo. No, let me ſpeake, and let me rayle ſo hye,
That the falſe Huſwife Fortune, breake her Wheele,
Prouok'd by my offence.
Ant. One word (ſweet Queene)
Of *Cæſar* ſeeke your Honour, with your ſafety. Oh.
Cleo. They do not go together.
Ant. Gentle heare me,
None about *Cæſar* truſt, but *Proculeius*.
Cleo. My Reſolution, and my hands, Ile truſt,
None about *Cæſar*.
Ant. The miſerable change now at my end,
Lament nor ſorrow at: but pleaſe your thoughts
In feeding them with thoſe my former Fortunes
Wherein I liued. The greateſt Prince o'th'world,
The Nobleſt: and do now not baſely dye,
Not Cowardly put off my Helmet to
My Countreyman. A Roman, by a Roman
Valiantly vanquiſh'd. Now my Spirit is going,
I can no more.
Cleo. Nobleſt of men, woo't dye?
Haſt thou no care of me, ſhall I abide
In this dull world, which in thy abſence is
No better then a Stye? Oh ſee my women:
The Crowne o'th'earth doth melt. My Lord?
Oh wither'd is the Garland of the Warre,
The

The Souldiers pole is falne : young Boyes and Gyrles
Are leuell now with men : The oddes is gone,
And there is nothing left remarkeable
Beneath the visiting Moone.

Char. Oh quietnesse, Lady.
Iras. She's dead too, our Soueraigne.
Char. Lady.
Iras. Madam.
Char. Oh Madam, Madam, Madam.
Iras. Royall Egypt : Empresse.
Char. Peace, peace, *Iras.*
Cleo. No more but in a Woman, and commanded
By such poore passion, as the Maid that Milkes,
And doe's the meanest chares. It were for me,
To throw my Scepter at the iniurious Gods,
To tell them that this World did equall theyrs,
Till they had stolne our Iewell. All's but naught :
Patience is sottish, and impatience does
Become a Dogge that's mad : Then is it sinne,
To rush into the secret house of death,
Ere death dare come to vs. How do you Women?
What, what good cheere? Why how now *Charmian?*
My Noble Gyrles? Ah Women, women! Looke
Our Lampe is spent, it's out. Good sirs, take heart,
Wee'l bury him : And then, what's braue, what's Noble,
Let's doo't after the high Roman fashion,
And make death proud to take vs. Come, away,
This case of that huge Spirit now is cold.
Ah Women, Women! Come, we haue no Friend
But Resolution, and the breefest end.

Exeunt, bearing of Anthonies body.

Enter Cæsar, Agrippa, Dollabella, Menas, with his Counsell of Warre.

Cæsar. Go to him *Dollabella*, bid him yeeld,
Being so frustrate, tell him,
He mockes the pawses that he makes.
Dol. Cæsar, I shall

Enter Decretas with the sword of Anthony.

Cæs. Wherefore is that? And what art thou that dar'st
Appeare thus to vs?
Dec. I am call'd *Decretas*,
Marke Anthony I seru'd, who best was worthie
Best to be seru'd : whil'st he stood vp, and spoke
He was my Master, and I wore my life
To spend vpon his haters. If thou please
To take me to thee, as I was to him,
Ile be to *Cæsar* : if ỹ pleasest not, I yeild thee vp my life.
Cæsar. What is't thou say'st?
Dec. I say (Oh *Cæsar*) *Anthony* is dead.
Cæsar. The breaking of so great a thing, should make
A greater cracke. The round World
Should haue shooke Lyons into ciuill streets,
And Cittizens to their dennes. The death of *Anthony*
Is not a single doome, in the name lay
A moity of the world
Dec. He is dead *Cæsar*,
Not by a publike minister of Iustice,
Nor by a hyred Knife, but that selfe-hand
Which writ his Honor in the Acts it did,
Hath with the Courage which the heart did lend it,
Splitted the heart. This is his Sword,
I robb'd his wound of it : behold it stain'd
With his most Noble blood.
Cæs. Looke you sad Friends,
The Gods rebuke me, but it is Tydings
To wash the eyes of Kings.
Dol. And strange it is,
That Nature must compell vs to lament
Our most persisted deeds.
Mec. His taints and Honours, wag'd equal with him.
Dola. A Rarer spirit neuer
Did steere humanity : but you Gods will giue vs
Some faults to make vs men. *Cæsar* is touch'd.
Mec. When such a spacious Mirror's set before him,
He needes must see himselfe.
Cæsar. Oh *Anthony*,
I haue followed thee to this, but we do launch
Diseases in our Bodies. I must perforce
Haue shewne to thee such a declining day,
Or looke on thine : we could not stall together,
In the whole world. But yet let me lament
With teares as Soueraigne as the blood of hearts,
That thou my Brother, my Competitor,
In top of all designe ; my Mate in Empire,
Friend and Companion in the front of Warre,
The Arme of mine owne Body, and the Heart
Where mine his thoughts did kindle ; that our Starres
Vnreconciliable, should diuide our equalnesse to this.
Heare me good Friends,
But I will tell you at some meeter Season,
The businesse of this man lookes out of him,
Wee'l heare him what he sayes.

Enter an Ægyptian.

Whence are you?
Ægyp. A poore Egyptian yet, the Queen my mistris
Confin'd in all, she has her Monument
Of thy intents, desires, instruction,
That she preparedly may frame her selfe
To'th'way shee's forc'd too.
Cæsar. Bid her haue good heart,
She soone shall know of vs, by some of ours,
How honourable, and how kindely Wee
Determine for her. For *Cæsar* cannot leaue to be vngentle
Ægypt. So the Gods preserue thee. *Exit.*
Cæs. Come hither *Proculeius*. Go and say
We purpose her no shame : giue her what comforts
The quality of her passion shall require ;
Least in her greatnesse, by some mortall stroke
She do defeate vs. For her life in Rome,
Would be eternall in our Triumph : Go,
And with your speediest bring vs what she sayes,
And how you finde of her.
Pro. Cæsar I shall. *Exit Proculeius.*
Cæs. Gallus, go you along : where's *Dolabella*, to second *Proculeius*?
All. Dolabella.
Cæs. Let him alone : for I remember now
How hee's imployd : he shall in time be ready.
Go with me to my Tent, where you shall see
How hardly I was drawne into this Warre,
How calme and gentle I proceeded still
In all my Writings. Go with me, and see
What I can shew in this. *Exeunt.*

Enter Cleopatra, Charmian, Iras, and Mardian.

Cleo. My desolation does begin to make
A better life : Tis paltry to be *Cæsar* :
Not being Fortune, hee's but Fortunes knaue,
A minister of her will : and it is great

To

To do that thing that ends all other deeds,
Which ſhackles accedents, and bolts vp change;
Which ſleepes, and neuer pallates more the dung,
The beggers Nurſe, and *Cæſars*

Enter Proculeius

Pro. *Cæſar* ſends greeting to the Queene of Egypt,
And bids thee ſtudy on what faire demands
Thou mean'ſt to haue him grant thee.
Cleo. What's thy name?
Pro. My name is *Proculeius.*
Cleo. *Anthony*
Did tell me of you, bad me truſt you, but
I do not greatly care to be deceiu'd
That haue no vſe for truſting. If your Maſter
Would haue a Queece his begger, you muſt tell him,
That Maieſty to keepe *decorum*, muſt
No leſſe begge then a Kingdome: If he pleaſe
To giue me conquer'd Egypt for my Sonne,
He giues me ſo much of mine owne, as I
Will kneele to him with thankes.
Pro. Be of good cheere:
Y'are falne into a Princely hand, feare nothing,
Make your full reference freely to my Lord,
Who is ſo full of Grace, that it flowes ouer
On all that neede. Let me report to him
Your ſweet dependacie, and you ſhall finde
A Conqueror that will pray in ayde for kindneſſe,
Where he for grace is kneel'd too.
Cleo. Pray you tell him,
I am his Fortunes Vaſſall, and I ſend him
The Greatneſſe he has got. I hourely learne
A Doctrine of Obedience, and would gladly
Looke him i'th'Face.
Pro. This Ile report (deere Lady)
Haue comfort, for I know your plight is pittied
Of him that caus'd it.
Pro. You ſee how eaſily ſhe may be ſurpriz'd:
Guard her till *Cæſar* come.
Iras. Royall Queene.
Char. Oh *Cleopatra*, thou art taken Queene.
Cleo. Quicke, quicke, good hands.
Pro. Hold worthy Lady, hold:
Doe not your ſelfe ſuch wrong, who are in this
Releeu'd, but not betraid.
Cleo. What of death too that rids our dogs of languiſh
Pro. *Cleopatra*, do not abuſe my Maſters bounty, by
Th'vndoing of your ſelfe: Let the World ſee
His Nobleneſſe well acted, which your death
Will neuer let come forth.
Cleo. Where art thou Death?
Come hither come; Come, come, and take a Queene
Worth many Babes and Beggers.
Pro. Oh temperance Lady.
Cleo. Sir, I will eate no meate, Ile not drinke ſir,
If idle talke will once be neceſſary
Ile not ſleepe neither. This mortall houſe Ile ruine,
Do *Cæſar* what he can. Know ſir, that I
Will not waite pinnion'd at your Maſters Court,
Nor once be chaſtic'd with the ſober eye
Of dull *Octauia*. Shall they hoyſt me vp,
And ſhew me to the ſhowting Varlotarie
Of cenſuring Rome? Rather a ditch in Egypt.
Be gentle graue vnto me, rather on Nylus mudde
Lay me ſtarke-nak'd, and let the water-Flies
Blow me into abhorring; rather make
My Countries high pyramides my Gibbet,
And hang me vp in Chaines.
Pro. You do extend
These thoughts of horror further then you ſhall
Finde cauſe in *Cæſar*.

Enter Dolabella.

Dol. *Proculeius*,
What thou haſt done, thy Maſter *Cæſar* knowes,
And he hath ſent for thee: for the Queene,
Ile take her to my Guard.
Pro. So *Dolabella*,
It ſhall content me beſt: Be gentle to her,
To *Cæſar* I will ſpeake, what you ſhall pleaſe,
If you'l imploy me to him. *Exit Proculeius*
Cleo. Say, I would dye.
Dol. Moſt Noble Empreſſe, you haue heard of me.
Cleo. I cannot tell.
Dol. Aſſuredly you know me.
Cleo. No matter ſir, what I haue heard or knowne:
You laugh when Boyes or Women tell their Dreames,
Is't not your tricke?
Dol. I vnderſtand not, Madam.
Cleo I dreampt there was an Emperor *Anthony*.
Oh ſuch another ſleepe, that I might ſee
But ſuch another man.
Dol. If it might pleaſe ye.
Cleo. His face was as the Heau'ns, and therein ſtucke
A Sunne and Moone, which kept their courſe, & lighted
The little o'th'earth.
Dol. Moſt Soueraigne Creature.
Cleo. His legges beſtrid the Ocean, his rear'd arme
Creſted the world: His voyce was propertied
As all the tuned Spheres, and that to Friends:
But when he meant to quaile, and ſhake the Orbe,
He was as ratling Thunder. For his Bounty,
There was no winter in't. An *Anthony* it was,
That grew the more by reaping: His delights
Were Dolphin-like, they ſhew'd his backe aboue
The Element they liu'd in: In his Liuery
Walk'd Crownes and Crownets: Realms & Iſlands were
As plates dropt from his pocket.
Dol. *Cleopatra.*
Cleo. Thinke you there was, or might be ſuch a man
As this I dreampt of?
Dol. Gentle Madam, no.
Cleo. You Lye vp to the hearing of the Gods:
But if there be, nor euer were one ſuch
It's paſt the ſize of dreaming: Nature wants ſtuffe
To vie ſtrange formes with fancie, yet t'imagine
An *Anthony* were Natures peece, 'gainſt Fancie,
Condemning ſhadowes quite.
Dol. Heare me, good Madam:
Your loſſe is as your ſelfe, great; and you beare it
As anſwering to the waight, would I might neuer
Ore-take purſu'de ſucceſſe: But I do feele
By the rebound of yours, a greefe that ſuites
My very heart at roote.
Cleo. I thanke you ſir:
Know you what *Cæſar* meanes to do with me?
Dol. I am loath to tell you what, I would you knew.
Cleo. Nay pray you ſir.
Dol. Though he be Honourable.
Cleo. Hee'l leade me then in Triumph.
Dol. Madam he will, I know't. *Flouriſh.*

Enter Proculeius, Cæſar, Gallus, Mecenas, and others of his Traine.

All. Make way there *Cæſar*.

Caſ. Which is the Queene of Egypt.
Dol. It is the Emperor Madam. *Cleo. kneels.*
Cæſar. Ariſe, you ſhall not kneele:
I pray you riſe, riſe Egypt.
Cleo. Sir, the Gods will haue it thus,
My Maſter and my Lord I muſt obey,
Cæſar. Take to you no hard thoughts,
The Record of what iniuries you did vs,
Though written in our fleſh, we ſhall remember
As things but done by chance.
Cleo. Sole Sir o'th' World,
I cannot proiect mine owne cauſe ſo well
To make it cleare, but do confeſſe I haue
Bene laden with like frailties, which before
Haue often ſham'd our Sex.
Cæſar. *Cleopatra* know,
We will extenuate rather then inforce:
If you apply your ſelfe to our intents,
Which towards you are moſt gentle, you ſhall finde
A benefit in this change: but if you ſeeke
To lay on me a Cruelty, by taking
Anthonies courſe, you ſhall bereaue your ſelfe
Of my good purpoſes, and put your children
To that deſtruction which Ile guard them from.
If thereon you relye. Ile take my leaue.
Cleo. And may through all the world: tis yours, & we
your Scutcheons, and your ſignes of Conqueſt ſhall
Hang in what place you pleaſe. Here my good Lord.
Cæſar. You ſhall aduiſe me in all for *Cleopatra*.
Cleo. This is the breefe: of Money, Plate, & Iewels
I am poſſeſt of, 'tis exactly valewed,
Not petty things admitted. Where's *Seleucus*?
Seleu. Heere Madam.
Cleo. This is my Treaſurer, let him ſpeake (my Lord)
Vpon his perill, that I haue reſeru'd
To my ſelfe nothing. Speake the truth *Seleucus*.
Seleu. Madam, I had rather ſeele my lippes,
Then to my perill ſpeake that which is not.
Cleo. What haue I kept backe.
Sel. Enough to purchaſe what you haue made known
Cæſar. Nay bluſh not *Cleopatra*, I approue
Your Wiſedome in the deede.
Cleo. See *Cæſar*: Oh behold,
How pompe is followed: Mine will now be yours,
And ſhould we ſhift eſtates, yours would be mine
The ingratitude of this *Seleucus*, does
Euen make me wilde. Oh Slaue, of no more truſt
Then loue that's hyr'd? What goeſt thou backe, ŷ ſhalt
Go backe I warrant thee: but Ile catch thine eyes
Though they had wings. Slaue, Soule-leſſe, Villain, Dog.
O rarely baſe!
Cæſar. Good Queene, let vs intreat you.
Cleo. O *Cæſar*, what a wounding ſhame is this,
That thou vouchſafing heere to viſit me,
Doing the Honour of thy Lordlineſſe
To one ſo meeke, that mine owne Seruant ſhould
Parcell the ſumme of my diſgraces, by
Addition of his Enuy. Say (good *Cæſar*)
That I ſome Lady trifles haue reſeru'd,
Immoment toyes, things of ſuch Dignitie
As we greet moderne Friends withall, and ſay
Some Nobler token I haue kept apart
For *Liuia* and *Octauia*, to induce
Their mediation, muſt I be vnfolded
With one that I haue bred: The Gods! it ſmites me
Beneath the fall I haue. Prythee go hence,
Or I ſhall ſhew the Cynders of my ſpirits
Through th'Aſhes of my chance: Wer't thou a man,
Thou would'ſt haue mercy on me.
Cæſar. Forbeare *Seleucus*.
Cleo. Be it known, that we the greateſt are miſ-thoght
For things that others do: and when we fall,
We anſwer others merits, in our name
Are therefore to be pittied.
Cæſar. *Cleopatra*,
Not what you haue reſeru'd, nor what acknowledg'd
Put we i'th'Roll of Conqueſt: ſtill bee't yours,
Beſtow it at your pleaſure, and beleeue
Cæſars no Merchant, to make prize with you
Of things that Merchants ſold. Therefore be cheer'd,
Make not your thoughts your priſons: No deere Queen,
For we intend ſo to diſpoſe you, as
Your ſelfe ſhall giue vs counſell: Feede, and ſleepe
Our care and pitty is ſo much vpon you,
That we remaine your Friend, and ſo adieu.
Cleo. My Maſter, and my Lord.
Cæſar. Not ſo: Adieu. *Flouriſh.*
Exeunt Cæſar, and his Traine.
Cleo. He words me Gyrles, he words me,
That I ſhould not be Noble to my ſelfe.
But hearke thee *Charmian*.
Iras. Finiſh good Lady, the bright day is done,
And we are for the darke.
Cleo. Hye thee againe,
I haue ſpoke already, and it is prouided,
Go put it to the haſte.
Char. Madam, I will.
Enter Dolabella.
Dol. Where's the Queene?
Char. Behold ſir.
Cleo. *Dolabella*.
Dol. Madam, as thereto ſworne, by your command
(Which my loue makes Religion to obey)
I tell you this: *Cæſar* through Syria
Intends his iourney, and within three dayes,
You with your Children will he ſend before,
Make your beſt vſe of this. I haue perform'd
Your pleaſure, and my promiſe.
Cleo. *Dolabella*, I ſhall remaine your debter.
Dol. I your Seruant:
Adieu good Queene, I muſt attend on *Cæſar*. *Exit*
Cleo. Farewell, and thankes.
Now *Iras*, what think'ſt thou?
Thou, an Egyptian Puppet ſhall be ſhewne
In Rome aſwell as I: Mechanicke Slaues
With greazie Aprons, Rules, and Hammers ſhall
Vplift vs to the view. In their thicke breathes,
Ranke of groſſe dyet, ſhall we be enclowded.
And forc'd to drinke their vapour.
Iras. The Gods forbid.
Cleo. Nay, 'tis moſt certaine *Iras*: ſawcie Lictors
Will catch at vs like Strumpets, and ſcald Rimers
Ballads vs out a Tune. The quicke Comedians
Extemporally will ſtage vs, and preſent
Our Alexandrian Reuels: *Anthony*
Shall be brought drunken forth, and I ſhall ſee
Some ſqueaking *Cleopatra* Boy my greatneſſe
I'th'poſture of a Whore.
Iras. O the good Gods!
Cleo. Nay that's certaine.
Iras. Ile neuer ſee't? for I am ſure mine Nailes
Are ſtronger then mine eyes.
Cleo

Cleo. Why that's the way to foole their preparation,
And to conquer their moſt abſurd intents.
Enter Charmian.
Now *Charmian*.
Shew me my Women like a Queene: Go fetch
My beſt Attyres. I am againe for *Cidrus*,
To meete *Marke Anthony*. Sirra *Iras*, go
(Now Noble *Charmian*, wee'l diſpatch indeede,)
And when thou haſt done this chare, Ile giue thee leaue
To play till Doomeſday: bring our Crowne, and all.
A noiſe within.
Whereſore's this noiſe?
Enter a Guardſman.
Gardſ. Heere is a rurall Fellow,
That will not be deny'de your Highneſſe preſence,
He brings you Figges.
Cleo. Let him come in. *Exit Guardſman.*
What poore an Inſtrument
May do a Noble deede: he brings me liberty:
My Reſolution's plac'd, and I haue nothing
Of woman in me: Now from head to foote
I am Marble conſtant: now the fleeting Moone
No Planet is of mine.
Enter Guardſman, and Clowne.
Guardſ. This is the man.
Cleo. Auoid, and leaue him. *Exit Guardſman.*
Haſt thou the pretty worme of Nylus there,
That killes and paines not?
Clow. Truly I haue him: but I would not be the partie that ſhould deſire you to touch him, for his byting is immortall: thoſe that doe dye of it, doe ſeldome or neuer recouer.
Cleo. Remember'ſt thou any that haue dyed on't?
Clow. Very many, men and women too. I heard of one of them no longer then yeſterday, a very honeſt woman, but ſomething giuen to lye, as a woman ſhould not do, but in the way of honeſty, how ſhe dyed of the byting of it, what paine ſhe felt: Truely, ſhe makes a verie good report o'th'worme: but he that wil beleeue all that they ſay, ſhall neuer be ſaued by halfe that they do: but this is moſt falliable, the Worme's an odde Worme.
Cleo. Get thee hence, farewell.
Clow. I wiſh you all ioy of the Worme.
Cleo. Farewell.
Clow You muſt thinke this (looke you,) that the Worme will do his kinde.
Cleo. I, I, farewell.
Clow. Looke you, the Worme is not to bee truſted, but in the keeping of wiſe people: for indeede, there is no goodneſſe in the Worme.
Cleo. Take thou no care, it ſhall be heeded.
Clow. Very good: giue it nothing I pray you, for it is not worth the feeding.
Cleo. Will it eate me?
Clow. You muſt not think I am ſo ſimple, but I know the diuell himſelfe will not eate a woman: I know, that a woman is a diſh for the Gods, if the diuell dreſſe her not. But truly, theſe ſame whorſon diuels doe the Gods great harme in their women: for in euery tenne that they make, the diuels marre fiue.
Cleo. Well, get thee gone, farewell.
Clow. Yes forſooth: I wiſh you ioy o'th'worm. *Exit*
Cleo Giue me my Robe, put on my Crowne, I haue
Immortall longings in me. Now no more
The iuyce of Egypts Grape ſhall moyſt this lip.
Yare, yare, good *Iras*; quicke: Me thinkes I heare
Anthony call: I ſee him rowſe himſelfe
To praiſe my Noble Act. I heare him mock
The lucke of *Cæſar*, which the Gods giue men
To excuſe their after wrath. Husband, I come:
Now to that name, my Courage proue my Title.
I am Fire, and Ayre; my other Elements
I giue to baſer life. So, haue you done?
Come then, and take the laſt warmth of my Lippes.
Farewell kinde *Charmian*, *Iras*, long farewell.
Haue I the Aſpicke in my lippes? Doſt fall?
If thou, and Nature can ſo gently part,
The ſtroke of death is as a Louers pinch,
Which hurts, and is deſir'd. Doſt thou lye ſtill?
If thus thou vaniſheſt, thou tell'ſt the world,
It is not worth leaue-taking.
Char. Diſſolue thicke clowd, & Raine, that I may ſay
The Gods themſelues do weepe.
Cleo. This proues me baſe:
If ſhe firſt meete the Curled *Anthony*,
Hee'l make demand of her, and ſpend that kiſſe
Which is my heauen to haue. Come thou mortal wretch,
With thy ſharpe teeth this knot intrinſicate,
Of life at once vntye: Poore venomous Foole,
Be angry, and diſpatch. Oh could'ſt thou ſpeake,
That I might heare thee call great *Cæſar* Aſſe, vnpolicied.
Char. Oh Eaſterne Starre.
Cleo: Peace, peace:
Doſt thou not ſee my Baby at my breaſt,
That ſuckes the Nurſe aſleepe.
Char. O breake! O breake!
Cleo. As ſweet as Balme, as ſoft as Ayre, as gentle.
O *Anthony*! Nay I will take thee too.
What ſhould I ſtay——— *Dyes.*
Char. In this wilde World? So fare thee well:
Now boaſt thee Death, in thy poſſeſſion lyes
A Laſſe vnparalell'd. Downie Windowes cloze,
And golden Phœbus neuer be beheld
Of eyes againe ſo Royall: your Crownes away,
Ile mend it, and then play———
Enter the Guard ruſtling in, and Dolabella.
1 Guard. Where's the Queene?
Char. Speake ſoftly, wake her not.
1 Cæſar hath ſent
Char. Too ſlow a Meſſenger.
Oh come apace, diſpatch, I partly feele thee.
1 Approach hoa,
All's not well: *Cæſar's* beguild.
2 There's *Dolabella* ſent from *Cæſar*: call him.
1 What worke is heere *Charmian*?
Is this well done?
Char. It is well done, and fitting for a Princeſſe
Deſcended of ſo many Royall Kings.
Ah Souldier. *Charmian dyes*

Enter Dolabella.

Dol. How goes it heere?
2. Guard. All dead.
Dol. *Cæſar*, thy thoughts
Touch their effects in this: Thy ſelfe art comming
To ſee perform'd the dreaded Act which thou
So ſought'ſt to hinder.

Enter Cæſar and all his Traine, marching.

All. A way there, a way for *Cæſar*.

z z 2 *Dol*

Dol. Oh ſir, you are too ſure an Augurer:
That you did feare, is done.
Cæſar. Braueſt at the laſt,
She leuell'd at our purpoſes, and being Royall
Tooke her owne way: the manner of their deaths,
I do not ſee them bleede.
Dol. Who was laſt with them?
1 *Guard.* A ſimple Countryman, that broght hir Figs:
This was his Basket.
Cæſar. Poyſon'd then.
1 *.Guard.* Oh *Cæſar*:
This *Charmian* liu'd but now, ſhe ſtood and ſpake:
I found her trimming vp the Diadem;
On her dead Miſtris tremblingly ſhe ſtood,
And on the ſodaine dropt.
Cæſar. Oh Noble weakeneſſe:
If they had ſwallow'd poyſon, 'twould appeare
By externall ſwelling: but ſhe lookes like ſleepe,
As ſhe would catch another *Anthony*
In her ſtrong toyle of Grace.
Dol. Heere on her breſt,
There is a vent of Bloud, and ſomething blowne,
The like is on her Arme.
1 *.Guard.* This is an Aſpickes traile,
And theſe Figge-leaues haue ſlime vpon them, ſuch
As th'Aſpicke leaues vpon the Caues of Nyle.
Cæſar. Moſt probable
That ſo ſhe dyed: for her Phyſitian tels mee
She hath purſu'de Concluſions infinite
Of eaſie wayes to dye. Take vp her bed,
And beare her Women from the Monument,
She ſhall be buried by her *Anthony*.
No Graue vpon the earth ſhall clip in it
A payre ſo famous: high euents as theſe
Strike thoſe that make them: and their Story is
No leſſe in pitty, then his Glory which
Brought them to be lamented. Our Army ſhall
In ſolemne ſhew, attend this Funerall,
And then to Rome. Come *Dolabella*, ſee
High Order, in this great Solmemnity. *Exeunt omnes*

FINIS.

THE TRAGEDIE OF CYMBELINE.

Actus Primus. Scœna Prima.

Enter two Gentlemen.

1. Gent.
YOu do not meet a man but Frownes.
Our bloods no more obey the Heauens
Then our Courtiers:
Still seeme, as do's the Kings.
2 Gent. But what's the matter?
1. His daughter, and the heire of's kingdome (whom
He purpos'd to his wiues sole Sonne, a Widdow
That late he married) hath referr'd her selfe
Vnto a poore, but worthy Gentleman. She's wedded,
Her Husband banish'd; she imprison'd, all
Is outward sorrow, though I thinke the King
Be touch'd at very heart.
2 None but the King?
1 He that hath lost her too: so is the Queene,
That most desir'd the Match. But not a Courtier,
Although they weare their faces to the bent
Of the Kings lookes, hath a heart that is not
Glad at the thing they scowle at.
2 And why so?
1 He that hath miss'd the Princesse, is a thing
Too bad, for bad report: and he that hath her,
(I meane, that married her, alacke good man,
And therefore banish'd) is a Creature, such,
As to seeke through the Regions of the Earth
For one, his like; there would be something failing
In him, that should compare. I do not thinke,
So faire an Outward, and such stuffe Within
Endowes a man, but hee.
2 You speake him farre.
1 I do extend him (Sir) within himselfe,
Crush him together, rather then vnfold
His measure duly.
2 What's his name, and Birth?
1 I cannot delue him to the roote: His Father
Was call'd *Sicillius*, who did ioyne his Honor
Against the Romanes, with *Cassibulan*,
But had his Titles by *Tenantius*, whom
He seru'd with Glory, and admir'd Successe:
So gain'd the Sur-addition, *Leonatus*.
And had (besides this Gentleman in question)
Two other Sonnes, who in the Warres o'th'time
Dy'de with their Swords in hand. For which, their Father
Then old, and fond of yssue, tooke such sorrow
That he quit Being; and his gentle Lady
Bigge of this Gentleman (our Theame) deceast
As he was borne. The King he takes the Babe
To his protection, cals him *Posthumus Leonatus*,
Breedes him, and makes him of his Bed-chamber,
Puts to him all the Learnings that his time
Could make him the receiuer of, which he tooke
As we do ayre, fast as 'twas ministred,
And in's Spring, became a Haruest: Liu'd in Court
(Which rare it is to do) most prais'd, most lou'd,
A sample to the yongest: to th'more Mature,
A glasse that feated them: and to the grauer,
A Childe that guided Dotards. To his Mistris,
(For whom he now is banish'd) her owne price
Proclaimes how she esteem'd him; and his Vertue
By her electiō may be truly read, what kind of man he is.
2 I honor him, euen out of your report.
But pray you tell me, is she sole childe to'th'King?
1 His onely childe:
He had two Sonnes (if this be worth your hearing,
Marke it) the eldest of them, at three yeares old
I'th'swathing cloathes, the other from their Nursery
Were stolne, and to this houre, no ghesse in knowledge
Which way they went.
2 How long is this ago?
1 Some twenty yeares.
2 That a Kings Children should be so conuey'd,
So slackely guarded, and the search so slow
That could not trace them.
1 Howsoere, 'tis strange,
Or that the negligence may well be laugh'd at:
Yet is it true Sir.
2 I do well beleeue you.
1 We must forbeare. Heere comes the Gentleman,
The Queene, and Princesse. *Exeunt*

Scena Secunda.

Enter the Queene, Posthumus, and Imogen.

Qu. No, be assur'd you shall not finde me (Daughter)
After the slander of most Step-Mothers,
Euill-ey'd vnto you. You're my Prisoner, but
Your Gaoler shall deliuer you the keyes

That locke vp your restraint. For you *Posthumus*,
So soone as I can win th'offended King,
I will be knowne your Aduocate: marry yet
The fire of Rage is in him, and 'twere good
You lean'd vnto his Sentence, with what patience
Your wisedome may informe you.
Post. 'Please your Highnesse,
I will from hence to day.
Qu. You know the perill:
Ile fetch a turne about the Garden, pittying
The pangs of barr'd Affections, though the King
Hath charg'd you should not speake together. *Exit*
Imo. O dissembling Curtesie! How fine this Tyrant
Can tickle where she wounds? My deerest Husband,
I something feare my Fathers wrath, but nothing
(Alwayes reseru'd my holy duty) what
His rage can do on me. You must be gone,
And I shall heere abide the hourely shot
Of angry eyes: not comforted to liue,
But that there is this Iewell in the world,
That I may see againe.
Post. My Queene, my Mistris:
O Lady, weepe no more, least I giue cause
To be suspected of more tendernesse
Then doth become a man. I will remaine
The loyall'st husband, that did ere plight troth.
My residence in Rome, at one *Filorio's*,
Who, to my Father was a Friend, to me
Knowne but by Letter; thither write (my Queene)
And with mine eyes, Ile drinke the words you send,
Though Inke be made of Gall.
Enter Queene.
Qu. Be briefe, I pray you:
If the King come, I shall incurre, I know not
How much of his displeasure: yet Ile moue him
To walke this way: I neuer do him wrong,
But he do's buy my Iniuries, to be Friends:
Payes deere for my offences.
Post. Should we be taking leaue
As long a terme as yet we haue to liue,
The loathnesse to depart, would grow: Adieu.
Imo. Nay, stay a little:
Were you but riding forth to ayre your selfe,
Such parting were too petty. Looke heere (Loue)
This Diamond was my Mothers; take it (Heart)
But keepe it till you woo another Wife,
When *Imogen* is dead.
Post. How, how? Another?
You gentle Gods, giue me but this I haue,
And seare vp my embracements from a next,
With bonds of death. Remaine, remaine thou heere,
While sense can keepe it on: And sweetest, fairest,
As I (my poore selfe) did exchange for you
To your so infinite losse; so in our trifles
I still winne of you. For my sake weare this,
It is a Manacle of Loue, Ile place it
Vpon this fayrest Prisoner.
Imo. O the Gods!
When shall we see againe?
Enter Cymbeline, and Lords.
Post. Alacke, the King.
Cym. Thou basest thing, auoyd hence, from my sight:
If after this command thou fraught the Court
With thy vnworthinesse, thou dyest. Away,
Thou'rt poyson to my blood.
Post. The Gods protect you,
And blesse the good Remainders of the Court:
I am gone. *Exit.*
Imo. There cannot be a pinch in death
More sharpe then this is.
Cym. O disloyall thing,
That should'st repayre my youth, thou heap'st
A yeares age on mee.
Imo. I beseech you Sir,
Harme not your selfe with your vexation,
I am senselesse of your Wrath; a Touch more rare
Subdues all pangs, all feares.
Cym. Past Grace? Obedience?
Imo. Past hope, and in dispaire, that way past Grace.
Cym. That might'st haue had
The sole Sonne of my Queene.
Imo. O blessed, that I might not: I chose an Eagle,
And did auoyd a Puttocke.
Cym. Thou took'st a Begger, would'st haue made my
Throne, a Seate for basenesse.
Imo. No, I rather added a lustre to it.
Cym. O thou vilde one!
Imo. Sir,
It is your fault that I haue lou'd *Posthumus*:
You bred him as my Play-fellow, and he is
A man, worth any woman: Ouer-buyes mee
Almost the summe he payes.
Cym. What? art thou mad?
Imo. Almost Sir: Heauen restore me: would I were
A Neat-heards Daughter, and my *Leonatus*
Our Neighbour-Shepheards Sonne.
Enter Queene.
Cym. Thou foolish thing;
They were againe together: you haue done
Not after our command. Away with her,
And pen her vp.
Qu. Beseech your patience: Peace
Deere Lady daughter, peace. Sweet Soueraigne,
Leaue vs to our selues, and make your self some comfort
Out of your best aduice.
Cym. Nay let her languish
A drop of blood a day, and being aged
Dye of this Folly. *Exit.*
Enter Pisanio.
Qu. Fye, you must giue way:
Heere is your Seruant. How now Sir? What newes?
Pisa. My Lord your Sonne, drew on my Master.
Qu. Hah?
No harme I trust is done?
Pisa. There might haue beene,
But that my Master rather plaid, then fought,
And had no helpe of Anger: they were parted
By Gentlemen, at hand.
Qu. I am very glad on't.
Imo. Your Son's my Fathers friend, he takes his part
To draw vpon an Exile. O braue Sir,
I would they were in Affricke both together,
My selfe by with a Needle, that I might pricke
The goer backe. Why came you from your Master?
Pisa. On his command: he would not suffer mee
To bring him to the Hauen: left these Notes
Of what commands I should be subiect too,
When't pleas'd you to employ me.
Qu. This hath beene
Your faithfull Seruant: I dare lay mine Honour
He will remaine so
Pisa. I humbly thanke your Highnesse.
Qu.

Qu. Pray walke a-while.
Imo. About ſome halfe houre hence,
Pray you ſpeake with me;
You ſhall (at leaſt) go ſee my Lord aboord.
For this time leaue me. *Exeunt.*

Scena Tertia.

Enter Cloten, and two Lords.

1. Sir, I would aduiſe you to ſhift a Shirt; the Violence of Action hath made you reek as a Sacrifice: where ayre comes out, ayre comes in: There's none abroad ſo wholeſome as that you vent.

Clot. If my Shirt were bloody, then to ſhift it.
Haue I hurt him?

2 No faith: not ſo much as his patience.

1 Hurt him? His bodie's a paſſable Carkaſſe if he bee not hurt. It is a through-fare for Steele if it be not hurt.

2 His Steele was in debt, it went o'th'Backe-ſide the Towne.

Clot. The Villaine would not ſtand me.

2 No, but he fled forward ſtill, toward your face.

1 Stand you? you haue Land enough of your owne: But he added to your hauing, gaue you ſome ground.

2 As many Inches, as you haue Oceans (Puppies.)

Clot. I would they had not come betweene vs.

2 So would I, till you had meaſur'd how long a Foole you were vpon the ground.

Clot. And that ſhee ſhould loue this Fellow, and refuſe mee.

2 If it be a ſin to make a true election, ſhe is damn'd.

1 Sir, as I told you alwayes: her Beauty & her Braine go not together. Shee's a good ſigne, but I haue ſeene ſmall reflection of her wit.

2 She ſhines not vpon Fooles, leaſt the reflection Should hurt her.

Clot. Come, Ile to my Chamber: would there had beene ſome hurt done.

2 I wiſh not ſo, vnleſſe it had bin the fall of an Aſſe, which is no great hurt.

Clot. You'l go with vs?

1 Ile attend your Lordſhip.

Clot. Nay come, let's go together.

2 Well my Lord. *Exeunt.*

Scena Quarta.

Enter Imogen, and Piſanio.

Imo. I would thou grew'ſt vnto the ſhores o'th'Hauen,
And queſtioned'ſt euery Saile: if he ſhould write,
And I not haue it, 'twere a Paper loſt
As offer'd mercy is: What was the laſt
That he ſpake to thee?
Piſa. It was his Queene, his Queene.
Imo. Then wau'd his Handkerchiefe?
Piſa. And kiſt it, Madam.
Imo. Senſeleſſe Linnen, happier therein then I:
And that was all?
Piſa. No Madam: for ſo long
As he could make me with his eye, or eare,
Diſtinguiſh him from others, he did keepe
The Decke, with Gloue, or Hat, or Handkerchife,
Still wauing, as the fits and ſtirres of's mind
Could beſt expreſſe how ſlow his Soule ſayl'd on,
How ſwift his Ship.
Imo. Thou ſhould'ſt haue made him
As little as a Crow, or leſſe, ere left
To after-eye him.
Piſa. Madam, ſo I did.
Imo. I would haue broke mine eye-ſtrings;
Crack'd them, but to looke vpon him, till the diminution
Of ſpace, had pointed him ſharpe as my Needle:
Nay, followed him, till he had melted from
The ſmalneſſe of a Gnat, to ayre: and then
Haue turn'd mine eye, and wept. But good *Piſanio*,
When ſhall we heare from him.
Piſa. Be aſſur'd Madam,
With his next vantage.
Imo. I did not take my leaue of him, but had
Moſt pretty things to ſay: Ere I could tell him
How I would thinke on him at certaine houres,
Such thoughts, and ſuch: Or I could make him ſweare,
The Shees of Italy ſhould not betray
Mine Intereſt, and his Honour: or haue charg'd him
At the ſixt houre of Morne, at Noone, at Midnight,
T'encounter me with Oriſons, for then
I am in Heauen for him: Or ere I could,
Giue him that parting kiſſe, which I had ſet
Betwixt two charming words, comes in my Father,
And like the Tyrannous breathing of the North,
Shakes all our buddes from growing.

Enter a Lady.

La. The Queene (Madam)
Deſires your Highneſſe Company.
Imo. Thoſe things I bid you do, get them diſpatch'd,
I will attend the Queene.
Piſa. Madam, I ſhall. *Exeunt.*

Scena Quinta.

Enter Philario, Iachimo: a Frenchman, a Dutchman, and a Spaniard.

Iach. Beleeue it Sir, I haue ſeene him in Britaine; hee was then of a Creſſent note, expected to proue ſo woorthy, as ſince he hath beene allowed the name of. But I could then haue look'd on him, without the help of Admiration, though the Catalogue of his endowments had bin tabled by his ſide, and I to peruſe him by Items.

Phil. You ſpeake of him when he was leſſe furniſh'd, then now hee is, with that which makes him both without, and within.

French. I haue ſeene him in France: wee had very many there, could behold the Sunne, with as firme eyes as hee.

Iach. This matter of marrying his Kings Daughter, wherein he muſt be weighed rather by her valew, then his owne, words him (I doubt not) a great deale from the matter.

French. And then his baniſhment.

Iach. I, and the approbation of thoſe that weepe this lamentable diuorce vnder her colours, are wonderfully to to extend him,be it but to fortifie her iudgement, which elſe an eaſie battery might lay flat,for taking a Begger without leſſe quality. But how comes it,he is to ſoiourne with you? How creepes acquaintance ?

Phil. His Father and I were Souldiers together, to whom I haue bin often bound for no leſſe then my life.

Enter Poſthumus.

Heere comes the Britaine. Let him be ſo entertained among'ſt you,as ſuites with Gentlemen of your knowing, to a Stranger of his quality. I beſeech you all be better knowne to this Gentleman, whom I commend to you, as a Noble Friend of mine. How Worthy he is, I will leaue to appeare hereafter, rather then ſtory him in his owne hearing.

French. Sir we haue knowne togither in Orleance.

Poſt. Since when,I haue bin debtor to you for courteſies, which I will be euer to pay,and yet pay ſtill.

French. Sir,you o're-rate my poore kindneſſe,I was glad I did attone my Countryman and you:it had beene pitty you ſhould haue beene put together,with ſo mortall a purpoſe,as then each bore, vpon importance of ſo ſlight and triuiall a nature.

Poſt. By your pardon Sir, I was then a young Traueller, rather ſhun'd to go euen with what I heard, then in my euery action to be guided by others experiences: but vpon my mended iudgement (if I offend to ſay it is mended) my Quarrell was not altogether ſlight.

French. Faith yes, to be put to the arbiterment of Swords, and by ſuch two,that would by all likelyhood haue confounded one the other,or haue falne both.

Iach. Can we with manners, aske what was the difference?

French. Safely, I thinke, 'twas a contention in publicke, which may (without contradiction) ſuffer the report. It was much like an argument that fell out laſt night, where each of vs fell in praiſe of our Country-Miſtreſſes. This Gentleman,at that time vouching (and vpon warrant of bloody affirmation) his to be more Faire, Vertuous, Wiſe, Chaſte, Conſtant, Qualified,and leſſe attemptible then any, the rareſt of our Ladies in Fraunce.

Iach. That Lady is not now liuing; or this Gentlemans opinion by this,worne out.

Poſt. She holds her Vertue ſtill,and I my mind.

Iach. You muſt not ſo farre preferre her, 'fore ours of Italy.

Poſth. Being ſo farre prouok'd as I was in France: I would abate her nothing,though I profeſſe my ſelfe her Adorer,not her Friend.

Iach. As faire, and as good: a kind of hand in hand compariſon, had beene ſomething too faire, and too good for any Lady in Britanie; if ſhe went before others. I haue ſeene as that Diamond of yours out-luſters many I haue beheld, I could not beleeue ſhe excelled many: but I haue not ſeene the moſt pretious Diamond that is, nor you the Lady.

Poſt. I prais'd her,as I rated her: ſo do I my Stone.

Iach. What do you eſteeme it at?

Poſt. More then the world enioyes.

Iach. Either your vnparagon'd Miſtirs is dead, or ſhe's out-priz'd by a trifle.

Poſt. You are miſtaken: the one may be ſolde or giuen,or if there were wealth enough for the purchaſes,or merite for the guift. The other is not a thing for ſale, and onely the guift of the Gods.

Iach. Which the Gods haue giuen you?

Poſt. Which by their Graces I will keepe.

Iach. You may weare her in title yours: but you know ſtrange Fowle light vpon neighbouring Ponds. Your Ring may be ſtolne too,ſo your brace of vnprizeable Eſtimations,the one is but fraile, and the other Caſuall;. A cunning Thiefe, or a (that way) accompliſh'd Courtier, would hazzard the winning both of firſt and laſt.

Poſt. Your Italy, containes none ſo accompliſh'd a Courtier to conuince the Honour of my Miſtris: if in the holding or loſſe of that, you terme her fraile, I do nothing doubt you haue ſtore of Theeues,notwithſtanding I feare not my Ring.

Phil. Let vs leaue heere,Gentlemen?

Poſt. Sir, with all my heart. This worthy Signior I thanke him, makes no ſtranger of me, we are familiar at firſt.

Iach. With fiue times ſo much conuerſation,I ſhould get ground of your faire Miſtris; make her go backe, euen to the yeilding, had I admittance, and opportunitie to friend.

Poſt. No,no.

Iach. I dare thereupon pawne the moytie of my Eſtate, to your Ring, which in my opinion o're-values it ſomething: but I make my wager rather againſt your Confidence,then her Reputation. And to barre your offence heerein to, I durſt attempt it againſt any Lady in the world.

Poſt. You are a great deale abus'd in too bold a perſwaſion,and I doubt not you ſuſtaine what y'are worthy of,by your Attempt.

Iach. What's that?

Poſth. A Repulſe though your Attempt (as you call it) deſerue more; a puniſhment too.

Phi. Gentlemen enough of this, it came in too ſodainely,let it dye as it was borne,and I pray you be better acquainted.

Iach. Would I had put my Eſtate,and my Neighbors on th'approbation of what I haue ſpoke.

Poſt. What Lady would you chuſe to aſſaile?

Iach. Yours,whom in conſtancie you thinke ſtands ſo ſafe. I will lay you ten thouſands Duckets to your Ring, that commend me to the Court where your Lady is, with no more aduantage then the opportunitie of a ſecond conference, and I will bring from thence, that Honor of hers,which you imagine ſo reſeru'd.

Posthmus. I will wage againſt your Gold, Gold to it: My Ring I holde deere as my finger, 'tis part of it.

Iach. You are a Friend, and there in the wiſer: if you buy Ladies fleſh at a Million a Dram, you cannot preſeure it from tainting; but I ſee you haue ſome Religion in you,that you feare.

Poſthu. This is but a cuſtome in your tongue: you beare a grauer purpoſe I hope.

Iach. I am the Maſter of my ſpeeches,and would vnder-go what's ſpoken,I ſweare.

Poſthu. Will you? I ſhall but lend my Diamond till your returne: let there be Couenants drawne between's. My Miſtris exceedes in goodneſſe,the hugeneſſe of your vnworthy thinking. I dare you to this match: heere's my Ring.

Phil. I will haue it no lay.

Iach. By the Gods it is one: if I bring you no ſufficient teſtimony that I haue enioy'd the deereſt bodily part of your Miſtris: my ten thouſand Duckets are yours, ſo ſo is your Diamond too: if I come off, and leaue her in ſuch honour as you haue truſt in; Shee your Iewell, this your Iewell, and my Gold are yours: prouided, I haue your commendation, for my more free entertainment.

Poſt. I embrace theſe Conditions, let vs haue Articles betwixt vs: onely thus farre you ſhall anſwere, if you make your voyage vpon her, and giue me directly to vnderſtand, you haue preuayl'd, I am no further your Enemy, ſhee is not worth our debate. If ſhee remaine vnſeduc'd, you not making it appeare otherwiſe: for your ill opinion, and th'aſſault you haue made to her chaſtity, you ſhall anſwer me with your Sword.

Iach. Your hand, a Couenant: wee will haue theſe things ſet downe by lawfull Counſell, and ſtraight away for Britaine, leaſt the Bargaine ſhould catch colde, and ſterue: I will fetch my Gold, and haue our two Wagers recorded.

Poſt. Agreed.
French. Will this hold, thinke you.
Phil. Signior *Iachimo* will not from it.
Pray let vs follow 'em. *Exeunt*

Scena Sexta.

Enter Queene, Ladies, and Cornelius.

Qu. Whiles yet the dewe's on ground,
Gather thoſe Flowers,
Make haſte. Who ha's the note of them?
Lady. I Madam.
Queen. Diſpatch. *Exit Ladies.*
Now Maſter Doctor, haue you brought thoſe drugges?
Cor. Pleaſeth your Highnes, I: here they are, Madam:
But I beſeech your Grace, without offence
(My Conſcience bids me aske) wherefore you haue
Commanded of me theſe moſt poyſonous Compounds,
Which are the moouers of a languiſhing death:
But though ſlow, deadly.
Qu. I wonder, Doctor,
Thou ask'ſt me ſuch a Queſtion: Haue I not bene
Thy Pupill long? Haſt thou not learn'd me how
To make Perfumes? Diſtill? Preſerue? Yea ſo,
That our great King himſelfe doth woo me oft
For my Confections? Hauing thus farre proceeded,
(Vnleſſe thou think'ſt me diuelliſh) is't not meete
That I did amplifie my iudgement in
Other Concluſions? I will try the forces
Of theſe thy Compounds, on ſuch Creatures as
We count not worth the hanging (but none humane)
To try the vigour of them, and apply
Allayments to their Act, and by them gather
Their ſeuerall vertues, and effects.
Cor. Your Highneſſe
Shall from this practiſe, but make hard your heart:
Beſides, the ſeeing theſe effects will be
Both noyſome, and infectious.
Qu. O content thee.

Enter Piſanio.

Heere comes a flattering Raſcall, vpon him
Will I firſt worke: Hee's for his Maſter,
And enemy to my Sonne. How now *Piſanio*?
Doctor, your ſeruice for this time is ended,
Take your owne way.
Cor. I do ſuſpect you, Madam,
But you ſhall do no harme.
Qu. Hearke thee, a word.
Cor. I do not like her. She doth thinke ſhe ha's
Strange ling'ring poyſons: I do know her ſpirit,
And will not truſt one of her malice, with
A drugge of ſuch damn'd Nature. Thoſe ſhe ha's,
Will ſtupifie and dull the Senſe a-while,
Which firſt (perchance) ſhee'l proue on Cats and Dogs,
Then afterward vp higher: but there is
No danger in what ſhew of death it makes,
More then the locking vp the Spirits a time,
To be more freſh, reuiuing. She is fool'd
With a moſt falſe effect: and I, the truer,
So to be falſe with her.
Qu. No further ſeruice, Doctor,
Vntill I ſend for thee.
Cor. I humbly take my leaue. *Exit.*
Qu. Weepes ſhe ſtill (ſaiſt thou?)
Doſt thou thinke in time
She will not quench, and let inſtructions enter
Where Folly now poſſeſſes? Do thou worke:
When thou ſhalt bring me word ſhe loues my Sonne,
Ile tell thee on the inſtant, thou art then
As great as is thy Maſter: Greater, for
His Fortunes all lye ſpeechleſſe, and his name
Is at laſt gaſpe. Returne he cannot, nor
Continue where he is: To ſhift his being,
Is to exchange one miſery with another,
And euery day that comes, comes to decay
A dayes worke in him. What ſhalt thou expect
To be depender on a thing that leanes?
Who cannot be new built, nor ha's no Friends
So much, as but to prop him? Thou tak'ſt vp
Thou know'ſt not what: But take it for thy labour,
It is a thing I made, which hath the King
Fiue times redeem'd from death. I do not know
What is more Cordiall. Nay, I prythee take it,
It is an earneſt of a farther good
That I meane to thee. Tell thy Miſtris how
The caſe ſtands with her: doo't, as from thy ſelfe;
Thinke what a chance thou changeſt on, but thinke
Thou haſt thy Miſtris ſtill, to boote, my Sonne,
Who ſhall take notice of thee. Ile moue the King
To any ſhape of thy Preferment, ſuch
As thou'lt deſire: and then my ſelfe, I cheefely,
That ſet thee on to this deſert, am bound
To loade thy merit richly. Call my women. *Exit Piſa.*
Thinke on my words. A ſlye, and conſtant knaue,
Not to be ſhak'd: the Agent for his Maſter,
And the Remembrancer of her, to hold
The hand-faſt to her Lord. I haue giuen him that,
Which if he take, ſhall quite vnpeople her
Of Leidgers for her Sweete: and which, ſhe after
Except ſhe bend her humor, ſhall be aſſur'd
To taſte of too.

Enter Piſanio, and Ladies.

So, ſo: Well done, well done:
The Violets, Cowſlippes, and the Prime-Roſes
Beare to my Cloſſet: Fare thee well, *Piſanio.*
Thinke on my words. *Exit Qu. and Ladies*
Piſa. And ſhall do:
But when to my good Lord, I proue vntrue,
Ile choake my ſelfe: there's all Ile do for you. *Exit.*
Scena

Scena Septima.

Enter Imogen alone.

Imo. A Father cruell, and a Stepdame false,
A Foolish Suitor to a Wedded-Lady,
That hath her Husband banish'd: O, that Husband,
My supreame Crowne of griefe, and those repeated
Vexations of it. Had I bin Theefe-stolne,
As my two Brothers, happy: but most miserable
Is the desires that's glorious. Blessed be those
How meane so ere, that haue their honest wills,
Which seasons comfort. Who may this be? Fye.

Enter Pisanio, and Iachimo.

Pisa. Madam, a Noble Gentleman of Rome,
Comes from my Lord with Letters.
Iach. Change you, Madam:
The Worthy *Leonatus* is in safety,
And greetes your Highnesse deerely.
Imo. Thanks good Sir,
You're kindly welcome.
Iach. All of her, that is out of doore, most rich:
If she be furnish'd with a mind so rare
She is alone th'Arabian-Bird; and I
Haue lost the wager. Boldnesse be my Friend:
Arme me Audacitie from head to foote,
Orlike the Parthian I shall flying fight,
Rather directly fly.

Imogen reads.

He is one of the Noblest note, to whose kindnesses I am most infinitely tied. Reflect vpon him accordingly, as you value your trust. Leonatus.

So farre I reade aloud.
But euen the very middle of my heart
Is warm'd by'th'rest, and take it thankefully.
You are as welcome (worthy Sir) as I
Haue words to bid you, and shall finde it so
In all that I can do.
Iach. Thankes fairest Lady:
What are men mad? Hath Nature giuen them eyes
To see this vaulted Arch, and the rich Crop
Of Sea and Land, which can distinguish 'twixt
The firie Orbes aboue, and the twinn'd Stones
Vpon the number'd Beach, and can we not
Partition make with Spectales so pretious
Twixt faire, and foule?
Imo. What makes your admiration?
Iach. It cannot be i'th'eye: for Apes, and Monkeys
'Twixt two such She's, would chatter this way, and
Contemne with mowes the other. Nor i'th'iudgment
For Idiots in this case of fauour, would
Be wisely definit: Nor i'th'Appetite.
Sluttery to such neate Excellence, oppos'd
Should make desire vomit emptinesse,
Not so allur'd to feed.
Imo. What is the matter trow?
Iach. The Cloyed will:
That satiate yet vnsatisfi'd desire, that Tub
Both fill'd and running: Rauening first the Lambe,
Longs after for the Garbage.
Imo. What, deere Sir,
Thus rap's you? Are you well?
Iach. Thanks Madam well: Beseech you Sir,
Desire my Man's abode, where I did leaue him:
He's strange and peeuish.
Pisa. I was going Sir,
To giue him welcome. *Exit.*
Imo. Continues well my Lord?
His health beseech you?
Iach. Well, Madam.
Imo. Is he dispos'd to mirth? I hope he is.
Iach. Exceeding pleasant: none a stranger there,
So merry, and so gamesome: he is call'd
The Britaine Reueller.
Imo. When he was heere
He did incline to sadnesse, and oft times
Not knowing why.
Iach. I neuer saw him sad.
There is a Frenchman his Companion, one
An eminent Monsieur, that it seemes much loues
A Gallian-Girle at home. He furnaces
The thicke sighes from him; whiles the iolly Britaine,
(Your Lord I meane) laughes from's free lungs: cries oh,
Can my sides hold, to think that man who knowes
By History, Report, or his owne proofe
What woman is, yea what she cannot choose
But must be: will's free houres languish:
For assured bondage?
Imo. Will my Lord say so?
Iach. I Madam, with his eyes in flood with laughter,
It is a Recreation to be by
And heare him mocke the Frenchman:
But Heauen's know some men are much too blame.
Imo. Not he I hope.
Iach. Not he:
But yet Heauen's bounty towards him, might
Be vs'd more thankfully. In himselfe 'tis much;
In you, which I account his beyond all Talents.
Whil'st I am bound to wonder, I am bound
To pitty too.
Imo. What do you pitty Sir?
Iach. Two Creatures heartyly.
Imo. Am I one Sir?
You looke on me: what wrack discerne you in me
Deserues your pitty?
Iach. Lamentable: what
To hide me from the radiant Sun, and solace
I'th'Dungeon by a Snuffe.
Imo. I pray you Sir,
Deliuer with more opennesse your answeres
To my demands. Why do you pitty me?
Iach. That others do,
(I was about to say) enioy your —— but
It is an office of the Gods to venge it,
Not mine to speake on't.
Imo You do seeme to know
Something of me, or what concernes me; pray you
Since doubting things go ill, often hurts more
Then to be sure they do. For Certainties
Either are past remedies; or timely knowing,
The remedy then borne. Discouer to me
What both you spur and stop.
Iach' Had I this cheeke
To bathe my lips vpon: this hand, whose touch,
(Whose euery touch) would force the Feelers soule
To'th'oath of loyalty. This obiect, which
Takes prisoner the wild motion of mine eye,
Fixing it onely heere, should I (damn'd then)

Slauer

Slauuer with lippes as common as the ſtayres
That mount the Capitoll: Ioyne gripes, with hands
Made hard with hourely falſhood (falſhood as
With labour:) then by peeping in an eye
Baſe and illuſtrious as the ſmoakie light
That's fed with ſtinking Tallow: it were fit
That all the plagues of Hell ſhould at one time
Encounter ſuch reuolt.
Imo. My Lord, I feare
Has forgot Brittaine.
Iach. And himſelfe, not I
Inclin'd to this intelligence, pronounce
The Beggery of his change: but 'tis your Graces
That from my muteſt Conſcience, to my tongue,
Charmes this report out.
Imo. Let me heare no more.
Iach. O deereſt Soule: your Cauſe doth ſtrike my hart
With pitty, that doth make me ſicke. A Lady
So faire, and faſten'd to an Emperie
Would make the great'ſt King double, to be partner'd
With Tomboyes hyr'd, with that ſelfe exhibition
Which your owne Coffers yeeld: with diſeas'd ventures
That play with all Infirmities for Gold,
Which rottenneſſe can lend Nature. Such boyl'd ſtuffe
As well might poyſon Poyſon. Be reueng'd,
Or ſhe that bore you, was no Queene, and you
Recoyle from your great Stocke.
Imo. Reueng'd:
How ſhould I be reueng'd? If this be true,
(As I haue ſuch a Heart, that both mine eares
Muſt not in haſte abuſe) if it be true,
How ſhould I be reueng'd?
Iach. Should he make me
Liue like *Diana*'s Prieſt, betwixt cold ſheets,
Whiles he is vaulting variable Rampes
In your deſpight, vpon your purſe: reuenge it.
I dedicate my ſelfe to your ſweet pleaſure,
More Noble then that runnagate to your bed,
And will continue faſt to your Affection,
Still cloſe, as ſure.
Imo. What hoa, *Piſanio*?
Iach. Let me my ſeruice tender on your lippes.
Imo. Away, I do condemne mine eares, that haue
So long attended thee. If thou wert Honourable
Thou would'ſt haue told this tale for Vertue, not
For ſuch an end thou ſeek'ſt, as baſe, as ſtrange:
Thou wrong'ſt a Gentleman, who is as farre
From thy report, as thou from Honor: and
Solicites heere a Lady, that diſdaines
Thee, and the Diuell alike. What hoa, *Piſanio*?
The King my Father ſhall be made acquainted
Of thy Aſſault: if he ſhall thinke it fit,
A ſawcy Stranger in his Court, to Mart
As in a Romiſh Stew, and to expound
His beaſtly minde to vs; he hath a Court
He little cares for, and a Daughter, who
He not reſpects at all. What hoa, *Piſanio*?
Iach. O happy *Leonatus* I may ſay,
The credit that thy Lady hath of thee
Deſerues thy truſt, and thy moſt perfect goodneſſe
Her aſſur'd credit. Bleſſed liue you long,
A Lady to the worthieſt Sir, that euer
Country call'd his; and you his Miſtris, onely
For the moſt worthieſt fit. Giue me your pardon,
I haue ſpoke this to know if your Affiance
Were deeply rooted, and ſhall make your Lord,
That which he is, new o're: And he is one
The trueſt manner'd: ſuch a holy Witch,
That he enchants Societies into him:
Halfe all men hearts are his.
Imo. You make amends.
Iach. He ſits 'mongſt men, like a defended God;
He hath a kinde of Honor ſets him off,
More then a mortall ſeeming. Be not angrie
(Moſt mighty Princeſſe) that I haue aduentur'd
To try your taking of a falſe report, which hath
Honour'd with confirmation your great Iudgement,
In the election of a Sir, ſo rare,
Which you know, cannot erre. The loue I beare him,
Made me to fan you thus, but the Gods made you
(Vnlike all others) chaffeleſſe. Pray your pardon.
Imo. All's well Sir:
Take my powre i'th'Court for yours.
Iach. My humble thankes: I had almoſt forgot
T'intreat your Grace, but in a ſmall requeſt,
And yet of moment too, for it concernes:
Your Lord, my ſelfe, and other Noble Friends
Are partners in the buſineſſe.
Imo. Pray what is't?
Iach. Some dozen Romanes of vs, and your Lord
(The beſt Feather of our wing) haue mingled ſummes
To buy a Preſent for the Emperor.
Which I (the Factor for the reſt) haue done
In France: 'tis Plate of rare deuice, and Iewels
Of rich, and exquiſite forme, their valewes great,
And I am ſomething curious, being ſtrange
To haue them in ſafe ſtowage: May it pleaſe you
To take them in protection.
Imo. Willingly:
And pawne mine Honor for their ſafety, ſince
My Lord hath intereſt in them, I will keepe them
In my Bed-chamber.
Iach. They are in a Trunke
Attended by my men: I will make bold
To ſend them to you, onely for this night.
I muſt aboord to morrow.
Imo. O no, no.
Iach. Yes I beſeech: or I ſhall ſhort my word
By length'ning my returne. From Gallia,
I croſt the Seas on purpoſe, and on promiſe
To ſee your Grace.
Imo. I thanke you for your paines:
But not away to morrow.
Iach. O I muſt Madam.
Therefore I ſhall beſeech you, if you pleaſe
To greet your Lord with writing, doo't to night,
I haue out-ſtood my time, which is materiall
To'th'tender of our Preſent.
Imo. I will write:
Send your Trunke to me, it ſhall ſafe be kept,
And truely yeelded you: you're very welcome. *Exeunt.*

Actus Secundus. Scena Prima.

Enter Clotten, and the two Lords.

Clot. Was there euer man had ſuch lucke? when I kiſt the Iacke vpon an vp-caſt, to be hit away? I had a hundred pound on't: and then a whorſon Iacke-an-Apes, muſt

must take me vp for swearing, as if I borrowed mine oathes of him, and might not spend them at my pleasure.

1. What got he by that? you haue broke his pate with your Bowle.

2. If his wit had bin like him that broke it: it would haue run all out.

Clot. When a Gentleman is dispos'd to sweare: it is not for any standers by to curtall his oathes. Ha?

2. No my Lord; nor crop the eares of them.

Clot. Whorson dog: I gaue him satisfaction? would he had bin one of my Ranke.

2. To haue smell'd like a Foole.

Clot. I am not vext more at any thing in th'earth: a pox on't. I had rather not be so Noble as I am: they dare not fight with me, because of the Queene my Mother: euery Iacke-Slaue hath his belly full of Fighting, and I must go vp and downe like a Cock, that no body can match.

2. You are Cocke and Capon too, and you crow Cock, with your combe on.

Clot. Sayest thou?

2. It is not fit you Lordship should vndertake euery Companion, that you giue offence too.

Clot. No, I know that: but it is fit I should commit offence to my inferiors.

2. I, it is fit for your Lordship onely.

Clot. Why so I say.

1. Did you heere of a Stranger that's come to Court night?

Clot. A Stranger, and I not know on't?

2. He's a strange Fellow himselfe, and knowes it not.

1. There's an Italian come, and 'tis thought one of *Leonatus* Friends.

Clot. *Leonatus*? A banisht Rascall; and he's another, whatsoeuer he be. Who told you of this Stranger?

1. One of your Lordships Pages.

Clot. Is it fit I went to looke vpon him? Is there no derogation in't?

2. You cannot derogate my Lord.

Clot. Not easily I thinke.

2. You are a Foole graunted, therefore your Issues being foolish do not derogate.

Clot. Come, Ile go see this Italian: what I haue lost to day at Bowles, Ile winne to night of him. Come: go.

2. Ile attend your Lordship. *Exit.*

That such a craftie Diuell as is his Mother
Should yeild the world this Asse: A woman, that
Beares all downe with her Braine, and this her Sonne,
Cannot take two from twenty for his heart,
And leaue eighteene. Alas poore Princesse,
Thou diuine *Imogen*, what thou endur'st,
Betwixt a Father by thy Step-dame gouern'd,
A Mother hourely coyning plots: A Wooer,
More hatefull then the foule expulsion is
Of thy deere Husband. Then that horrid Act
Of the diuorce, heel'd make the Heauens hold firme
The walls of thy deere Honour. Keepe vnshak'd
That Temple thy faire mind, that thou maist stand
T'enioy thy banish'd Lord: and this great Land. *Exeunt.*

Scena Secunda.

Enter Imogen, in her Bed, and a Lady.

Imo. Who's there? My woman: *Helene*?
La. Please you Madam.
Imo. What houre is it?
Lady. Almost midnight, Madam.
Imo. I haue read three houres then:
Mine eyes are weake,
Fold downe the leafe where I haue left: to bed
Take not away the Taper, leaue it burning:
And if thou canst awake by foure o'th'clock,
I prythee call me: Sleepe hath ceiz'd me wholly.
To your protection I commend me, Gods,
From Fayries, and the Tempters of the night,
Guard me beseech yee. *Sleepes.*

Iachimo from the Trunke.

Iach. The Crickets sing, and mans ore-labor'd sense
Repaires it selfe by rest: Our *Tarquine* thus
Did softly presse the Rushes, ere he waken'd
The Chastitie he wounded. *Cytherea*,
How brauely thou becom'st thy Bed; fresh Lilly,
And whiter then the Sheetes: that I might touch,
But kisse, one kisse. Rubies vnparagon'd,
How deerely they doo't: 'Tis her breathing that
Perfumes the Chamber thus: the Flame o'th'Taper
Bowes toward her, and would vnder-peepe her lids,
To see th'inclosed Lights, now Canopied
Vnder these windowes, White and Azure lac'd
With Blew of Heauens owne tinct. But my designe.
To note the Chamber, I will write all downe,
Such, and such pictures: There the window, such
Th'adornement of her Bed; the Arras, Figures,
Why such, and such: and the Contents o'th'Story.
Ah, but some naturall notes about her Body,
Aboue ten thousand meaner Moueables
Would testifie, t'enrich mine Inuentorie.
O sleepe, thou Ape of death, lye dull vpon her,
And be her Sense but as a Monument,
Thus in a Chappell lying. Come off, come off;
As slippery as the Gordian-knot was hard.
'Tis mine, and this will witnesse outwardly,
As strongly as the Conscience do's within:
To th'madding of her Lord. On her left brest
A mole Cinque-spotted: Like the Crimson drops
I'th'bottome of a Cowslippe. Heere's a Voucher,
Stronger then euer Law could make; this Secret
Will force him thinke I haue pick'd the lock, and t'ane
The treasure of her Honour. No more: to what end?
Why should I write this downe, that's riueted,
Screw'd to my memorie. She hath bin reading late,
The Tale of *Tereus*, heere the leaffe's turn'd downe
Where *Philomele* gaue vp. I haue enough,
To th'Truncke againe, and shut the spring of it.
Swift, swift, you Dragons of the night, that dawning
May beare the Rauens eye: I lodge in feare,
Though this a heauenly Angell: hell is heere.
Clocke strikes
One, two, three: time, time. *Exit.*

Scena Tertia.

Enter Clotten, and Lords.

1. Your Lordship is the most patient man in losse, the most coldest that euer turn'd vp Ace.

Clot. It would make any man cold to loose.

1. But not euery man patient after the noble temper of your Lordship; You are most hot, and furious when you winne.

Clot

Winning will put any man into courage: if I could get this foolish *Imogen*, I should haue Gold enough: it's almost morning, is't not?

1 Day, my Lord.

Clot. I would this Musicke would come: I am aduised to giue her Musicke a mornings, they say it will penetrate. *Enter Musitians.*

Come on, tune: If you can penetrate her with your fingering, so: wee'l try with tongue too: if none will do, let her remaine: but Ile neuer giue o're. First, a very excellent good conceyted thing; after a wonderful sweet aire, with admirable rich words to it, and then let her consider.

SONG.

Hearke, hearke, the Larke at Heauens gate sings,
and Phœbus gins arise,
His Steeds to water at those Springs
on chalic'd Flowres that lyes:
And winking Mary-buds begin to ope their Golden eyes
With euery thing that pretty is, my Lady sweet arise:
Arise, arise.

So, get you gone: if this pen trate, I will consider your Musicke the better: if it do not, it is a voyce in her eares which Horse-haires, and Calues-guts, nor the voyce of vnpaued Eunuch to boot, can neuer amed.

Enter Cymbaline, and Queene.

2 Heere comes the King.

Clot. I am glad I was vp so late, for that's the reason I was vp so earely: he cannot choose but take this Seruice I haue done, fatherly. Good morrow to your Maiesty, and to my gracious Mother.

Cym. Attend you here the doore of our stern daughter
Will she not forth?

Clot. I haue assayl'd her with Musickes, but she vouchsafes no notice.

Cym. The Exile of her Minion is too new,
She hath not yet forgot him, some more time
Must weare the print of his remembrance on't,
And then she's yours.

Qu. You are most bound to'th'King,
Who let's go by no vantages, that may
Preferre you to his daughter: Frame your selfe
To orderly solicity, and be friended
With aptnesse of the season: make denials
Encrease your Seruices: so seeme, as if
You were inspir'd to do those duties which
You tender to her: that you in all obey her,
Saue when command to your dismission tends,
And therein you are senselesse.

Clot. Senselesse? Not so.

Mes. So like you (Sir) Ambassadors from Rome;
The one is *Caius Lucius*.

Cym. A worthy Fellow,
Albeit he comes on angry purpose now;
But that's no fault of his: we must receyue him
According to the Honor of his Sender,
And towards himselfe, his goodnesse fore-spent on vs
We must extend our notice: Our deere Sonne,
When you haue giuen good morning to your Mistris,
Attend the Queene, and vs, we shall haue neede
T'employ you towards this Romane.
Come our Queene. *Exeunt.*

Clot. If she be vp, Ile speake with her: if not
Let her lye still, and dreame: by your leaue hoa,
I know her women are about her: what
If I do line one of their hands, 'tis Gold
Which buyes admittance (oft it doth) yea, and makes
Diana's Rangers false themselues, yeeld vp
Their Deere to'th'stand o'th'Stealer: and 'tis Gold
Which makes the True-man kill'd, and saues the Theefe:
Nay, sometime hangs both Theefe, and True-man: what
Can it not do, and vndoo? I will make
One of her women Lawyer to me, for
I yet not vnderstand the case my selfe.
By your leaue. *Knockes.*

Enter a Lady.

La. Who's there that knockes?

Clot. A Gentleman.

La. No more.

Clot. Yes, and a Gentlewomans Sonne.

La That's more
Then some whose Taylors are as deere as yours,
Can iustly boast of: what's your Lordships pleasure?

Clot. Your Ladies person, is she ready?

La. I, to keepe her Chamber.

Clot. There is Gold for you,
Sell me your good report.

La. How, my good name? or to report of you
What I shall thinke is good, The Princesse.

Enter Imogen.

Clot. Good morrow fairest, Sister your sweet hand.

Imo. Good morrow Sir, you lay out too much paines
For purchasing but trouble: the thankes I giue,
Is telling you that I am poore of thankes,
And scarse can spare them.

Clot. Still I sweare I loue you.

Imo. If you but said so, 'twere as deepe with me:
If you sweare still, your recompence is still
That I regard it not.

Clot. This is no answer.

Imo. But that you shall not say, I yeeld being silent,
I would not speake. I pray you spare me, 'faith
I shall vnfold equall discourtesie
To your best kindnesse: one of your great knowing
Should learne (being taught) forbearance.

Clot. To leaue you in your madnesse, 'twere my sin,
I will not.

Imo. Fooles are not mad Folkes.

Clot. Do you call me Foole?

Imo. As I am mad I do:
If you'l be patient, Ile no more be mad,
That cures vs both. I am much sorry (Sir)
You put me to forget a Ladies manners
By being so verball: and learne now, for all,
That I which know my heart, do heere pronounce
By th'very truth of it, I care not for you,
And am so neere the lacke of Charitie
To accuse my selfe, I hate you: which I had rather
You felt, then make't my boast.

Clot. You sinne against
Obedience, which you owe your Father, for
The Contract you pretend with that base Wretch,
One, bred of Almes, and foster'd with cold dishes,
With scraps o'th'Court: It is no Contract, none;
And though it be allowed in meaner parties
(Yet who then he more meane) to knit their soules
(On whom there is no more dependancie
But Brats and Beggery) in selfe-figur'd knot,
Yet you are curb'd from that enlargement, by

The

The conſequence o th'Crowne,and muſt not foyle
The precious note of it; with a baſe Slaue,
A Hilding for a Liuorie,a Squires Cloth,
A Pantler; not ſo eminent.
Imo Prophane Fellow:
Wert thou the Sonne of *Iupiter*,and no more,
But what thou art beſides : thou wer't too baſe,
To be his Groome : thou wer't dignified enough
Euen to the point of Enuie. If 'twere made
Comparatiue for your Vertues,to be ſtil'd
The vnder Hangman of his Kingdome; and hated
For being prefer'd ſo well.
Clot. The South-Fog rot him.
Imo. He neuer can meete more miſchance,then come
To be but nam'd of thee. His mean'ſt Garment
That euer hath but clipt his body; is dearer
In my reſpect,then all the Heires aboue thee,
Were they all made ſuch men : How now *Piſanio*?
Enter Piſanio,
Clot. His Garments? Now the diuell.
Imo. To *Dorothy* my woman hie thee preſently.
Clot. His Garment?
Imo. I am ſprighted with a Foole,
Frighted,and angred worſe : Go bid my woman
Search for a Iewell, that too caſually
Hath left mine Arme : it was thy Maſters. Shrew me
If I would looſe it for a Reuenew,
Of any Kings in Europe. I do think,
I ſaw't this morning : Confident I am.
Laſt night 'twas on mine Arme; I kiſs'd it,
I hope it be not gone,to tell my Lord
That I kiſſe aught but he.
Piſ. 'Twill not be loſt.
Imo. I hope ſo : go and ſearch.
Clot. You haue abus'd me :
His meaneſt Garment?
Imo. I,I ſaid ſo Sir,
If you will make't an Action,call witneſſe to't.
Clot. I will enforme your Father.
Imo. Your Mother too :
She's my good Lady; and will concieue,I hope
But the worſt of me. So I leaue your Sir,
To th'worſt of diſcontent. *Exit.*
Clot. Ile be reueng'd:
His mean'ſt Garment? Well. *Exit.*

Scena Quarta.

Enter Poſthumus,and Philario.
Poſt. Feare it not Sir : I would I were ſo ſure
To winne the King, as I am bold, her Honour
Will remaine her's.
Phil. What meanes do you make to him?
Poſt. Not any : but abide the change of Time,
Quake in the preſent winters ſtate,and wiſh
That warmer dayes would come : In theſe fear'd hope
I barely gratifie your loue; they fayling
I muſt die much your debtor.
Phil. Your very goodneſſe,and your company,
Ore-payes all I can do. By this your King,
Hath heard of Great *Auguſtus* : *Caius Lucius*,
Will do's Commiſſion throughly. And I think
Hee'le grant the Tribute : ſend th'Arrerages,
Or looke vpon our Romaines,whoſe remembrance
Is yet freſh in their griefe.
Poſt. I do beleeue
(Statiſt though I am none,nor like to be)
That this will proue a Warre; and you ſhall heare
The Legion now in Gallia,ſooner landed
In our not-fearing-Britaine,then haue tydings
Of any penny Tribute paid. Our Countrymen
Are men more order'd,then when *Iulius Cæſar*
Smil'd at their lacke of skill,but found their courage
Worthy his frowning at. Their diſcipline,
(Now wing-led with their courages) will make knowne
To their Approuers, they are People,ſuch
That mend vpon the world. *Enter Iachimo.*
Phi. See *Iachimo*.
Poſt. The ſwifteſt Harts,haue poſted you by land;
And Windes of all the Corners kiſs'd your Sailes,
To make your veſſell nimble.
Phil. Welcome Sir.
Poſt. I hope the brieſeneſſe of your anſwere,made
The ſpeedineſſe of your returne.
Iachi. Your Lady,
Is one of the fayreſt that I haue look'd vpon
Poſt. And therewithall the beſt,or let her beauty
Looke thorough a Caſement to allure falſe hearts,
And be falſe with them.
Iachi. Heere are Letters for you.
Poſt. Their tenure good I truſt.
Iach. 'Tis very like.
Poſt. Was *Caius Lucius* in the Britaine Court,
When you were there?
Iach. He was expected then,
But not approach'd.
Poſt. All is well yet,
Sparkles this Stone as it was wont,or is't not
Too dull for your good wearing?
Iach. If I haue loſt it,
I ſhould haue loſt the worth of it in Gold,
Ile make a iourney twice as farre,t'enioy
A ſecond night of ſuch ſweet ſhortneſſe, which
Was mine in Britaine, for the Ring is wonne.
Poſt. The Stones too hard to come by.
Iach. Not a whit,
Your Lady being ſo eaſy.
Poſt. Make note Sir
Your loſſe,your Sport : I hope you know that we
Muſt not continue Friends.
Iach. Good Sir,we muſt
If you keepe Couenant : had I not brought
The knowledge of your Miſtris home,I grant
We were to queſtion farther; but I now
Profeſſe my ſelfe the winner of her Honor,
Together with your Ring; and not the wronger
Of her,or you hauing proceeded but
By both your willes.
Poſt. If you can mak't apparant
That you haue taſted her in Bed; my hand,
And Ring is yours. If not,the foule opinion
You had of her pure Honour; gaines,or looſes,
Your Sword,or mine,or Maſterleſſe leaue both
To who ſhall finde them.
Iach. Sir,my Circumſtances
Being ſo nere the Truth,as I will make them,
Muſt firſt induce you to beleeue; whoſe ſtrength
I will confirme with oath,which I doubt not
You'l

You'l giue me leaue to spare, when you shall finde
You neede it not.
Post. Proceed.
Iach. First, her Bed-chamber
(Where I confesse I slept not, but professe
Had that was well worth watching) it was hang'd
With Tapistry of Silke, and Siluer, the Story
Proud *Cleopatra*, when she met her Roman,
And *Sidnus* swell'd aboue the Bankes, or for
The presse of Boates, or Pride. A peece of Worke
So brauely done, so rich, that it did striue
In Workemanship, and Value, which I wonder'd
Could be so rarely, and exactly wrought
Since the true life on't was———
Post. This is true:
And this you might haue heard of heere, by me,
Or by some other.
Iach. More particulars
Must iustifie my knowledge.
Post. So they must,
Or doe your Honour iniury.
Iach. The Chimney
Is South the Chamber, and the Chimney-peece
Chaste *Dian*, bathing: neuer saw I figures
So likely to report themselues; the Cutter
Was as another Nature dumbe, out-went her,
Motion, and Breath left out.
Post. This is a thing
Which you might from Relation likewise reape,
Being, as it is, much spoke of.
Iach. The Roofe o'th Chamber,
With golden Cherubins is fretted. Her Andirons
(I had forgot them) were two winking Cupids
Of Siluer, each on one foote standing, nicely
Depending on their Brands.
Post. This is her Honor:
Let it be granted you haue seene all this (and praise
Be giuen to your remembrance) the description
Of what is in her Chamber, nothing saues
The wager you haue laid.
Iach. Then if you can
Be pale, I begge but leaue to ayre this Iewell: See,
And now 'tis vp againe: it must be married
To that your Diamond, Ile keepe them.
Post. Ioue———
Once more let me behold it: Is it that
Which I left with her?
Iach. Sir (I thanke her) that
She stript it from her Arme: I see her yet:
Her pretty Action, did out-sell her guift,
And yet enrich'd it too: she gaue it me,
And said, she priz'd it once.
Post. May be, she pluck'd it off
To send it me.
Iach. She writes so to you? doth shee?
Post. O no, no, no, 'tis true. Heere, take this too,
It is a Basiliske vnto mine eye,
Killes me to looke on't: Let there be no Honor,
Where there is Beauty: Truth, where semblance: Loue,
Where there's another man. The Vowes of Women,
Of no more bondage be, to where they are made,
Then they are to their Vertues, which is nothing:
O, aboue measure false.
Phil. Haue patience Sir,
And take your Ring againe, 'tis not yet wonne:
It may be probable she lost it: or
Who knowes if one her women, being corrupted
Hath stolne it from her.
Post. Very true,
And so I hope he came by't: backe my Ring,
Render to me some corporall signe about her
More euident then this: for this was stolne.
Iach. By Iupiter, I had it from her Arme.
Post. Hearke you, he sweares: by Iupiter he sweares.
'Tis true, nay keepe the Ring; 'tis true. I am sure
She would not loose it: her Attendants are
All sworne, and honourable: they induc'd to steale it?
And by a Stranger? No, he hath enioy'd her,
The Cognisance of her incontinencie
Is this: she hath bought the name of Whore, thus deerly
There, take thy hyre, and all the Fiends of Hell
Diuide themselues betweene you.
Phil. Sir, be patient:
This is not strong enough to be beleeu'd
Of one perswaded well of.
Post. Neuer talke on't:
She hath bin colted by him.
Iach. If you seeke
For further satisfying, vnder her Breast
(Worthy her pressing) lyes a Mole, right proud
Of that most delicate Lodging. By my life
I kist it, and it gaue me present hunger
To feede againe, though full. You do remember
This staine vpon her?
Post. I, and it doth confirme
Another staine, as bigge as Hell can hold,
Were there no more but it.
Iach. Will you heare more?
Post. Spare your Arethmaticke,
Neuer count the Turnes: Once, and a Million.
Iach. Ile be sworne.
Post. No swearing:
If you will sweare you haue not done't, you lye,
And I will kill thee, if thou do'st deny
Thou'st made me Cuckold.
Iach. Ile deny nothing.
Post. O that I had her heere, to teare her Limb-meale:
I will go there and doo't, i'th'Court, before
Her Father. Ile do something. *Exit.*
Phil. Quite besides
The gouernment of Patience. You haue wonne:
Let's follow him, and peruert the present wrath
He hath against himselfe.
Iach. With all my heart. *Exeunt.*

Enter Posthumus.

Post. Is there no way for Men to be, but Women
Must be halfe-workers? We are all Bastards,
And that most venerable man, which I
Did call my Father, was, I know not where
When I was stampt. Some Coyner with his Tooles
Made me a counterfeit: yet my Mother seem'd
The *Dian* of that time: so doth my Wife
The Non-pareill of this. Oh Vengeance, Vengeance!
Me of my lawfull pleasure she restrain'd,
And pray'd me oft forbearance: did it with
A pudencie so Rosie, the sweet view on't
Might well haue warm'd olde Saturne;
That I thought her
As Chaste, as vn-Sunn'd Snow. Oh, all the Diuels!
This yellow *Iachimo* in an houre, was't not?

aaa2 Or

Or lesse; at first? Perchance he spoke not, but
Like a full Acorn'd Boare, a Iarmen on,
Cry'de oh, and mounted; found no opposition
But what he look'd for, should oppose, and she
Should from encounter guard. Could I finde out
The Womans part in me, for there's no motion
That tends to vice in man, but I affirme
It is the Womans part: be it Lying, note it,
The womans: Flattering, hers; Deceiuing, hers:
Lust, and ranke thoughts, hers, hers: Reuenges hers:
Ambitions, Couetings, change of Prides, Disdaine,
Nice-longing, Slanders, Mutability;
All Faults that name, nay, that Hell knowes,
Why hers, in part, or all: but rather all For euen to Vice
They are not constant, but are changing still;
One Vice, but of a minute old, for one
Not halfe so old as that. Ile write against them,
Detest them, curse them: yet 'tis greater Skill
In a true Hate, to pray they haue their will:
The very Diuels cannot plague them better. *Exit.*

Actus Tertius. Scena Prima.

Enter in State, Cymbeline, Queene, Clotten, and Lords at one doore, and at another, Caius, Lucius, and Attendants.

Cym. Now say, what would *Augustus Cæsar* with vs?
Luc. When *Iulius Cæsar* (whose remembrance yet
Liues in mens eyes, and will to Eares and Tongues
Be Theame, and hearing euer) was in this Britain,
And Conquer'd it, *Cassibulan* thine Vnkle
(Famous in *Cæsars* prayses, no whit lesse
Then in his Feats deseruing it) for him,
And his Succession, granted Rome a Tribute,
Yeerely three thousand pounds; which (by thee) lately
Is left vntender'd.
Qu. And to kill the meruaile,
Shall be so euer.
Clot. There be many *Cæsars*,
Ere such another *Iulius*: Britaine's a world
By it selfe, and we will nothing pay
For wearing our owne Noses.
Qu. That opportunity
Which then they had to take from's, to resume
We haue againe. Remember Sir, my Liege,
The Kings your Ancestors, together with
The naturall brauery of your Isle, which stands
As Neptunes Parke, ribb'd, and pal'd in
With Oakes vnskaleable, and roaring Waters,
With Sands that will not beare your Enemies Boates,
But sucke them vp to'th' Top-mast. A kinde of Conquest
Cæsar made heere, but made not heere his bragge
Of Came, and Saw, and Ouer-came: with shame
(The first that euer touch'd him) he was carried
From off our Coast, twice beaten: and his Shipping
(Poore ignorant Baubles) on our terrible Seas
Like Egge-shels mou'd vpon their Surges, crack'd
As easily gainst our Rockes. For ioy whereof,
The fam'd *Cassibulan*, who was once at point
(Oh giglet Fortune) to master *Cæsars* Sword,
Made *Luds-Towne* with reioycing-Fires bright,
And Britaines strut with Courage.

Clot. Come, there's no more Tribute to be paid: our Kingdome is stronger then it was at that time: and (as I said) there is no mo such *Cæsars*, other of them may haue crook'd Noses, but to owe such straite Armes, none.

Cym. Son, let your Mother end.

Clot. We haue yet many among vs, can gripe as hard as *Cassibulan*, I doe not say I am one: but I haue a hand. Why Tribute? Why should we pay Tribute? If *Cæsar* can hide the Sun from vs with a Blanket, or put the Moon in his pocket, we will pay him Tribute for light: else Sir, no more Tribute, pray you now.

Cym. You must know,
Till the iniurious Romans, did extort
This Tribute from vs, we were free. *Cæsars* Ambition,
Which swell'd so much, that it did almost stretch
The sides o'th'World, against all colour heere,
Did put the yoake vpon's; which to shake off
Becomes a warlike people, whom we reckon
Our selues to be, we do. Say then to *Cæsar*,
Our Ancestor was that *Mulmutius*, which
Ordain'd our Lawes, whose vse the Sword of *Cæsar*
Hath too much mangled; whose repayre, and franchise,
Shall (by the power we hold) be our good deed,
Tho Rome be therfore angry. *Mulmutius* made our lawes
Who was the first of Britaine, which did put
His browes within a golden Crowne, and call'd
Himselfe a King.
Luc. I am sorry *Cymbeline*,
That I am to pronounce *Augustus Cæsar*
(*Cæsar*, that hath moe Kings his Seruants, then
Thy selfe Domesticke Officers) thine Enemy:
Receyue it from me then. Warre, and Confusion
In *Cæsars* name pronounce I 'gainst thee: Looke
For fury, not to be resisted. Thus defide,
I thanke thee for my selfe.
Cym. Thou art welcome *Caius*.
Thy *Cæsar* Knighted me; my youth I spent
Much vnder him; of him, I gather'd Honour,
Which he, to seeke of me againe, perforce,
Behooues me keepe at vtterance. I am perfect,
That the Pannonians and Dalmatians, for
Their Liberties are now in Armes: a President
Which not to reade, would shew the Britaines cold:
So *Cæsar* shall not finde them.
Luc. Let proofe speake.

Clot. His Maiesty biddes you welcome. Make pastime with vs, a day, or two, or longer: if you seek vs afterwards in other tearmes, you shall finde vs in our Salt-water-Girdle: if you beate vs out of it, it is yours: if you fall in the aduenture, our Crowes shall fare the better for you: and there's an end.

Luc. So sir.
Cym. I know your Masters pleasure, and he mine:
All the Remaine, is welcome. *Exeunt.*

Scena Secunda.

Enter Pisanio reading of a Letter.

Pis. How? of Adultery? Wherefore write you not
What Monsters her accuse? *Leonatus*:
Oh Master, what a strange infection

Is

Is falne into thy eare? What false Italian,
(As poysonous tongu'd,as handed)hath preuail'd
On thy too ready hearing? Disloyall? No.
She's punish'd for her Truth; and vndergoes
More Goddesse-like,then Wife-like; such Assaults
As would take in some Vertue. Oh my Master,
Thy mind to her,is now as lowe,as were
Thy Fortunes. How? That I should murther her,
Vpon the Loue,and Truth,and Vowes;which I
Haue made to thy command? I her? Her blood?
If it be so,to do good seruice,neuer
Let me be counted seruiceable. How looke I,
That I should seeme to lacke humanity,
So much as this Fact comes to? Doo't: The Letter.
That I haue sent her,by her owne command,
Shall giue thee opportunitie. Oh damn'd paper,
Blacke as the Inke that's on thee: senselesse bauble,
Art thou a Fœdarie for this Act; and look'st
So Virgin-like without? Loe here she comes.

Enter Imogen.

I am ignorant in what I am commanded.
Imo. How now *Pisanio*?
Pis. Madam,heere is a Letter from my Lord.
Imo. Who,thy Lord? That is my Lord *Leonatus*?
Oh,learn'd indeed were that Astronomer
That knew the Starres,as I his Characters,
Heel'd lay the Future open. You good Gods,
Let what is heere contain'd,rellish of Loue,
Of my Lords health,of his content: yet not
That we two are asunder, let that grieue him;
Some griefes are medcinable,that is one of them,
For it doth physicke Loue,of his content,
All but in that. Good Wax,thy leaue: blest be
You Bees that make these Lockes of counsaile. Louers,
And men in dangerous Bondes pray not alike,
Though Forfeytours you cast in prison,yet
You claspe young *Cupids* Tables: good Newes Gods.

IVstice and your Fathers wrath (should he take me in his Dominion) could not be so cruell to me,as you: (oh the deerest of Creatures) would euen renew me with your eyes. Take notice that I am in Cambria *at* Milford-Hauen: *what your owne Loue,will out of this aduise you, follow. So he wishes you all happinesse,that remaines loyall to his Vow,and your encreasing in Loue.* Leonatus Posthumus.

Oh for a Horse with wings: Hear'st thou *Pisanio*?
He is at Milford-Hauen: Read,and tell me
How farre 'tis thither. If one of meane affaires
May plod it in a weeke,why may not I
Glide thither in a day? Then true *Pisanio*,
Who long'st like me,to see thy Lord; who long'st
(Oh let me bate) but not like me: yet long'st
But in a fainter kinde. Oh not like me:
For mine's beyond,beyond: say,and speake thicke
(Loues Counsailor should fill the bores of hearing,
To th'smothering of the Sense) how farre it is
To this same blessed Milford. And by'th'way
Tell me how Wales was made so happy,as
T'inherite such a Hauen. But first of all,
How we may steale from hence: and for the gap
That we shall make in Time, from our hence-going,
And our returne, to excuse: but first,how get hence.
Why should excuse be borne or ere begot?
Weele talke of that heereafter. Prythee speake,
How many store of Miles may we well rid
Twixt houre,and houre?
Pis. One score 'twixt Sun,and Sun,
Madam's enough for you: and too much too.
Imo. Why,one that rode to's Excution Man,
Could neuer go so slow: I haue heard of Riding wagers,
Where Horses haue bin nimbler then the Sands
That run i'th'Clocks behalfe. But this is Foolrie,
Go,bid my Woman faigne a Sicknesse,say
She'le home to her Father; and prouide me presently
A Riding Suit: No costlier then would fit
A Franklins Huswife.
Pisa. Madam,you're best consider.
Imo. I see before me (Man) nor heere,not heere;
Nor what ensues but haue a Fog in them
That I cannot looke through. Away, I prythee,
Do as I bid thee: There's no more to say:
Accessible is none but Milford way. *Exeunt.*

Scena Tertia.

Enter Belarius, Guiderius, and Aruiragus.

Bel. A goodly day,not to keepe house with such,
Whose Roofe's as lowe as ours: Sleepe Boyes,this gate
Instructs you how t'adore the Heauens; and bowes you
To a mornings holy office. The Gates of Monarches
Are Arch'd so high,that Giants may iet through
And keepe their impious Turbonds on,without
Good morrow to the Sun. Haile thou faire Heauen,
We house i'th'Rocke,yet vse thee not so hardly
As prouder liuers do.
Guid. Haile Heauen.
Aruir. Haile Heauen.
Bela. Now for our Mountaine sport, vp to yond hill
Your legges are yong: Ile tread these Flats. Consider,
When you aboue perceiue me like a Crow,
That it is Place, which lessen's,and sets off,
And you may then reuolue what Tales,I haue told you,
Of Courts,of Princes; of the Tricks in Warre.
This Seruice,is not Seruice; so being done,
But being so allowed. To apprehend thus,
Drawes vs a profit from all things we see:
And often to our comfort, shall we finde
The sharded-Beetle,in a safer hold
Then is the full-wing'd Eagle. Oh this life,
Is Nobler,then attending for a checke:
Richer,then doing nothing for a Babe:
Prouder, then rustling in vnpayd-for Silke:
Such gaine the Cap of him,that makes him fine,
Yet keepes his Booke vncros'd: no life to ours.
Gui. Out of your proofe you speak: we poore vnfledg'd
Haue neuer wing'd from view o'th'nest; nor knowes not
What Ayre's from home. Hap'ly this life is best,
(If quiet life be best) sweeter to you
That haue a sharper knowne. Well corresponding
With your stiffe Age; but vnto vs,it is
A Cell of Ignorance: trauailing a bed,
A Prison,or a Debtor,that not dares
To stride a limit.
Arui. What should we speake of
When we are old as you? When we shall heare
The Raine and winde beate darke December? How
In this our pinching Caue,shall we discourse

The freezing houres away? We haue seene nothing:
We are beastly; subtle as the Fox for prey,
Like warlike as the Wolfe, for what we eate:
Our Valour is to chace what flyes: Our Cage
We make a Quire, as doth the prison'd Bird,
And sing our Bondage freely.

Bel. How you speake.
Did you but know the Citties Vsuries,
And felt them knowingly: the Art o'th Court,
As hard to leaue, as keepe: whose top to climbe
Is certaine falling: or so slipp'ry, that
The feare's as bad as falling. The toyle o'th'Warre,
A paine that onely seemes to seeke out danger
I'th'name of Fame, and Honor, which dyes i'th'search,
And hath as oft a sland'rous Epitaph,
As Record of faire Act. Nay, many times
Doth ill deserue, by doing well: what's worse
Must curt'sie at the Censure. Oh Boyes, this Storie
The World may reade in me: My bodie's mark'd
With Roman Swords; and my report, was once
First, with the best of Note. *Cymbeline* lou'd me,
And when a Souldier was the Theame, my name
Was not farre off: then was I as a Tree
Whose boughes did bend with fruit. But in one night,
A Storme, or Robbery (call it what you will)
Shooke downe my mellow hangings: nay my Leaues,
And left me bare to weather.

Gui. Vncertaine fauour.

Bel. My fault being nothing (as I haue told you oft)
But that two Villaines, whose false Oathes preuayl'd
Before my perfect Honor, swore to *Cymbeline*,
I was Confederate with the Romanes: so
Followed my Banishment, and this twenty yeeres,
This Rocke, and these Demesnes, haue bene my World,
Where I haue liu'd at honest freedome, payed
More pious debts to Heauen, then in all
The fore-end of my time. But, vp to'th'Mountaines,
This is not Hunters Language; he that strikes
The Venison first, shall be the Lord o'th'Feast,
To him the other two shall minister,
And we will feare no poyson, which attends
In place of greater State:
Ile meete you in the Valleyes. *Exeunt.*
How hard it is to hide the sparkes of Nature?
These Boyes know little they are Sonnes to'th'King,
Nor *Cymbeline* dreames that they are aliue.
They thinke they are mine,
And though train'd vp thus meanely
I'th'Caue, whereon the Bowe their thoughts do hit,
The Roofes of Palaces, and Nature prompts them
In simple and lowe things, to Prince it, much
Beyond the tricke of others. This *Paladour*,
The heyre of *Cymbeline* and Britaine, who
The King his Father call'd *Guiderius*. Ioue,
When on my three-foot stoole I sit, and tell
The warlike feats I haue done, his spirits flye out
Into my Story: say thus mine Enemy fell,
And thus I set my foote on's necke, euen then
The Princely blood flowes in his Cheeke, he sweats,
Straines his yong Nerues, and puts himselfe in posture
That acts my words. The yonger Brother *Cadwall*,
Once *Aruiragus*, in as like a figure
Strikes life into my speech, and shewes much more
His owne conceyuing. Hearke, the Game is rows'd,
Oh *Cymbeline*, Heauen and my Conscience knowes
Thou didd'st vniustly banish me: whereon
At three, and two yeeres old, I stole these Babes,
Thinking to barre thee of Succession, as
Thou refts me of my Lands. *Euriphile*,
Thou was't their Nurse, they took thee for their mother,
And euery day do honor to her graue:
My selfe *Belarius*, that am *Morgan* call'd
They take for Naturall Father. The Game is vp. *Exit.*

Scena Quarta.

Enter Pisanio and Imogen.

Imo. Thou told'st me when we came frō horse, ŷ place
Was neere at hand: Ne're long'd my Mother so
To see me first, as I haue now. *Pisanio*, Man:
Where is *Posthumus*? What is in thy mind
That makes thee stare thus? Wherefore breaks that sigh
From th'inward of thee? One, but painted thus
Would be interpreted a thing perplex'd
Beyond selfe-explication. Put thy selfe
Into a hauiour of lesse feare, ere wildnesse
Vanquish my stayder Senses. What's the matter?
Why tender'st thou that Paper to me, with
A looke vntender? If't be Summer Newes
Smile too't before: if Winterly, thou need'st
But keepe that count'nance stil. My Husbands hand?
That Drug-damn'd Italy, hath out-craftied him,
And hee's at some hard point. Speake man, thy Tongue
May take off some extreamitie, which to reade
Would be euen mortall to me.

Pis. Please you reade,
And you shall finde me (wretched man) a thing
The most disdain'd of Fortune

Imogen reades

Thy Mistris (Pisanio) hath plaide the Strumpet in my Bed: the Testimonies whereof, lyes bleeding in me. I speak not out of weake Surmises, but from proofe as strong as my greefe, and as certaine as I expect my Reuenge. That part, thou (Pisanio) must acte for me, if thy Faith be not tainted with the breach of hers; let thine owne hands take away her life: I shall giue thee opportunity at Milford Hauen. She hath my Letter for the purpose; where, if thou feare to strike, and to make mee certaine it is done, thou art the Pander to her dishonour, and equally to me disloyall.

Pis. What shall I need to draw my Sword, the Paper
Hath cut her throat alreadie? No, 'tis Slander,
Whose edge is sharper then the Sword, whose tongue
Out-venomes all the Wormes of Nyle, whose breath
Rides on the posting windes, and doth belye
All corners of the World. Kings, Queenes, and States,
Maides, Matrons, nay the Secrets of the Graue
This viperous slander enters. What cheere, Madam?

Imo. False to his Bed? What is it to be false?
To lye in watch there, and to thinke on him?
To weepe 'twixt clock and clock? If sleep charge Nature,
To breake it with a fearfull dreame of him,
And cry my selfe awake? That's false to's bed? Is it?

Pisa. Alas good Lady.

Imo. I false? Thy Conscience witnesse: *Iachimo*,
Thou didd'st accuse him of Incontinencie,
Thou then look'dst like a Villaine: now, me thinkes
Thy

Thy fauours good enough. Some Iay of Italy
(Whoſe mother was her painting) hath betraid him:
Poore I am ſtale, a Garment out of faſhion,
And for I am richer then to hang by th'walles,
I muſt be ript: To peeces with me: Oh!
Mens Vowes are womens Traitors. All good ſeeming
By thy reuolt (oh Husband) ſhall be thought
Put on for Villainy; not borne where't growes,
But worne a Baite for Ladies.
Piſa. Good Madam, heare me.
Imo. True honeſt men being heard, like falſe *Æneas*,
Were in his time thought falſe: and *Synons* weeping
Did ſcandall many a holy teare: tooke pitty
From moſt true wretchedneſſe. So thou, *Poſthumus*
Wilt lay the Leauen on all proper men;
Goodly, and gallant, ſhall be falſe and periur'd
From thy great faile: Come Fellow, be thou honeſt,
Do thou thy Maſters bidding. When thou ſeeſt him,
A little witneſſe my obedience. Looke
I draw the Sword my ſelfe, take it, and hit
The innocent Manſion of my Loue (my Heart:)
Feare not, 'tis empty of all things, but Greefe:
Thy Maſter is not there, who was indeede
The riches of it. Do his bidding, ſtrike,
Thou mayſt be valiant in a better cauſe;
But now thou ſeem'ſt a Coward.
Piſ. Hence vile Inſtrument,
Thou ſhalt not damne my hand.
Imo. Why, I muſt dye:
And if I do not by thy hand, thou art
No Seruant of thy Maſters. Againſt Selfe-ſlaughter,
There is a prohibition ſo Diuine,
That crauens my weake hand: Come, heere's my heart:
Something's a-foot: Soft, ſoft, wee'l no defence,
Obedient as the Scabbard. What is heere,
The Scriptures of the Loyall *Leonatus*,
All turn'd to Hereſie? Away, away.
Corrupters of my Faith, you ſhall no more
Be Stomachers to my heart: thus may poore Fooles
Beleeue falſe Teachers: Though thoſe that are betraid
Do feele the Treaſon ſharpely, yet the Traitor
Stands in worſe caſe of woe. And thou *Poſthumus*,
That didd'ſt ſet vp my diſobedience 'gainſt the King
My Father, and makes me put into contempt the ſuites
Of Princely Fellowes, ſhalt heereafter finde
It is no acte of common paſſage, but
A ſtraine of Rareneſſe: and I greeue my ſelfe,
To thinke, when thou ſhalt be diſedg'd by her,
That now thou tyreſt on, how thy memory
Will then be pang'd by me. Prythee diſpatch,
The Lambe entreats the Butcher. Wher's thy knife?
Thou art too ſlow to do thy Maſters bidding
When I deſire it too.
Piſ. Oh gracious Lady:
Since I receiu'd command to do this buſineſſe,
I haue not ſlept one winke.
Imo. Doo't, and to bed then.
Piſ. Ile wake mine eye-balles firſt.
Imo. Wherefore then
Didd'ſt vndertake it? Why haſt thou abus'd
So many Miles, with a pretence? This place?
Mine Action? and thine owne? Our Horſes labour?
The Time inuiting thee? The perturb'd Court
For my being abſent? whereunto I neuer
Purpoſe returne. Why haſt thou gone ſo farre
To be vn-bent? when thou haſt tane thy ſtand,
Th'elected Deere before thee?
Piſ. But to win time
To looſe ſo bad employment, in the which
I haue conſider'd of a courſe: good Ladie
Heare me with patience.
Imo. Talke thy tongue weary, ſpeake:
I haue heard I am a Strumpet, and mine eare
Therein falſe ſtrooke, can take no greater wound,
Nor tent, to bottome that. But ſpeake.
Piſ. Then Madam,
I thought you would not backe againe.
Imo. Moſt like,
Bringing me heere to kill me.
Piſ. Not ſo neither:
But if I were as wiſe, as honeſt, then
My purpoſe would proue well: it cannot be,
But that my Maſter is abus'd. Some Villaine,
I, and ſingular in his Art, hath done you both
This curſed iniurie.
Imo. Some Roman Curtezan?
Piſa. No, on my life:
Ile giue but notice you are dead, and ſend him
Some bloody ſigne of it. For 'tis commanded
I ſhould do ſo: you ſhall be miſt at Court,
And that will well confirme it.
Imo. Why good Fellow,
What ſhall I do the while? Where bide? How liue?
Or in my life, what comfort, when I am
Dead to my Husband?
Piſ. If you'l backe to'th'Court.
Imo. No Court, no Father, nor no more adoe
With that harſh, noble, ſimple nothing:
That *Ciotten*, whoſe Loue-ſuite hath bene to me
As fearefull as a Siege.
Piſ. If not at Court,
Then not in Britaine muſt you bide.
Imo. Where then?
Hath Britaine all the Sunne that ſhines? Day? Night?
Are they not but in Britaine? I'th'worlds Volume
Our Britaine ſeemes as of it, but not in't:
In a great Poole, a Swannes-neſt, prythee thinke
There's liuers out of Britaine.
Piſ. I am moſt glad
You thinke of other place: Th'Ambaſſador,
Lucius the Romane comes to Milford-Hauen
To morrow. Now, if you could weare a minde
Darke, as your Fortune is, and but diſguiſe
That which t'appeare it ſelfe, muſt not yet be,
But by ſelfe-danger, you ſhould tread a courſe
Pretty, and full of view: yea, happily, neere
The reſidence of *Poſthumus*; ſo nie (at leaſt)
That though his Actions were not viſible, yet
Report ſhould render him hourely to your eare,
As truely as he mooues.
Imo. Oh for ſuch meanes,
Though perill to my modeſtie, not death on't
I would aduenture.
Piſ. Well then, heere's the point:
You muſt forget to be a Woman: change
Command, into obedience. Feare, and Niceneſſe
(The Handmaides of all Women, or more truely
Woman it pretty ſelfe) into a waggiſh courage,
Ready in gybes, quicke-anſwer'd, ſawcie, and
As quarrellous as the Weazell: Nay, you muſt
Forget that rareſt Treaſure of your Cheeke,
Expoſing it (but oh the harder heart,

Alacke

Alacke no remedy) to the greedy touch
Of common-kissing *Titan*: and forget
Your laboursome and dainty Trimmes, wherein
You made great *Iuno* angry.
Imo. Nay be breefe?
I see into thy end, and am almost
A man already.
Pis. First, make your selfe but like one,
Fore-thinking this. I haue already fit
('Tis in my Cloake-bagge) Doublet, Hat, Hose, all
That answer to them: Would you in their seruing,
(And with what imitation you can borrow
From youth of such a season) 'fore Noble *Lucius*
Present your selfe, desire his seruice: tell him
Wherein you're happy; which will make him know,
If that his head haue eare in Musicke, doubtlesse
With ioy he will imbrace you: for hee's Honourable,
And doubling that, most holy. Your meanes abroad:
You haue me rich, and I will neuer faile
Beginning, nor supplyment.
Imo. Thou art all the comfort
The Gods will diet me with. Prythee away,
There's more to be consider'd: but wee'l euen
All thet good time will giue vs. This attempt,
I am Souldier too, and will abide it with
A Princes Courage. Away, I prythee.
Pis. Well Madam, we must take a short farewell,
Least being mist, I be suspected of
Your carriage from the Court. My Noble Mistris,
Heere is a boxe, I had it from the Queene,
What's in't is precious: if you are sicke at Sea,
Or Stomacke-qualm'd at Land, a Dramme of this
Will driue away distemper. To some shade,
And fit you to your Manhood: may the Gods
Direct you to the best.
Imo. Amen: I thanke thee. *Exeunt.*

Scena Quinta.

Enter Cymbeline, Queene, Cloten, Lucius, and Lords.

Cym. Thus farre and so farewell.
Luc. Thankes, Royall Sir
My Emperor hath wrote, I must from hence,
And am right sorry, that I must report ye
My Masters Enemy.
Cym. Our Subiects (Sir)
Will not endure his yoake; and for our selfe
To shew lesse Soueraignty then they, must needs
Appeare vn-Kinglike.
Luc. So Sir: I desire of you
A Conduct ouer Land, to Milford-Hauen.
Madam, all ioy befall your Grace, and you.
Cym. My Lords, you are appointed for that Office:
The due of Honor, in no point omit:
So farewell Noble *Lucius*.
Luc. Your hand, my Lord.
Clot. Receiue it friendly: but from this time forth
I weare it as your Enemy.
Luc. Sir, the Euent
Is yet to name the winner. Fare you well.
Cym. Leaue not the worthy *Lucius*, good my Lords
Till he haue crost the Seuern. Happines. *Exit Lucius, &c*
Qu. He goes hence frowning: but it honours vs
That we haue giuen him cause.
Clot. 'Tis all the better,
Your valiant Britaines haue their wishes in it.
Cym. *Lucius* hath wrote already to the Emperor
How it goes heere. It fits vs therefore ripely
Our Chariots, and our Horsemen be in readinesse:
The Powre that he already hath in Gallia
Will soone be drawne to head, from whence he moues
His warre for Britaine.
Qu. 'Tis not sleepy businesse,
But must be look'd too speedily, and strongly.
Cym. Our expectation that it would be thus
Hath made vs forward. But my gentle Queene,
Where is our Daughter? She hath not appear'd
Before the Roman, nor to vs hath tender'd
The duty of the day. She looke vs like
A thing more made of malice, then of duty,
We haue noted it. Call her before vs, for
We haue beene too slight in sufferance.
Qu. Royall Sir,
Since the exile of *Posthumus*, most retyr'd
Hath her life bin: the Cure whereof, my Lord,
'Tis time must do. Beseech your Maiesty,
Forbeare sharpe speeches to her. Shee's a Lady
So tender of rebukes, that words are stroke;
And strokes death to her.
Enter a Messenger.
Cym. Where is she Sir? How
Can her contempt be answer'd?
Mes. Please you Sir,
Her Chambers are all lock'd, and there's no answer
That will be giuen to'th'lowd of noise, we make.
Qu. My Lord, when last I went to visit her,
She pray'd me to excuse her keeping close,
Whereto constrain'd by her infirmitie,
She should that dutie leaue vnpaide to you
Which dayly she was bound to proffer: this
She wish'd me to make knowne: but our great Court
Made me too blame in memory.
Cym Her doores lock'd?
Not seene of late? Grant Heauens, that which I
Feare, proue false. *Exit.*
Qu. Sonne, I say, follow the King.
Clot That man of hers, *Pisanio*, her old Seruant
I haue not seene these two dayes. *Exit.*
Qu Go, looke after:
Pisanio, thou that stand'st so for *Posthumus*,
He hath a Drugge of mine: I pray, his absence
Proceed by swallowing that. For he beleeues
It is a thing most precious. But for her,
Where is she gone? Haply dispaire hath seiz'd her:
Or wing'd with feruour of her loue, she's flowne
To her desir'd *Posthumus*: gone she is,
To death, or to dishonor, and my end
Can make good vse of either. Shee being downe,
I haue the placing of the Brittish Crowne.
Enter Cloten.
How now, my Sonne?
Clot. 'Tis certaine she is fled:
Go in and cheere the King, he rages, none
Dare come about him.
Qu. All the better: may
This night fore-stall him of the comming day. *Exit Qu.*
Clo. I loue, and hate her: for she's Faire and Royall,
And that she hath all courtly parts more exquisite
Then

Then Lady, Ladies, Woman, from euery one
The beſt ſhe hath, and ſhe of all compounded
Out-ſelles them all. I loue her therefore, but
Diſdaining me, and throwing Fauours on
The low *Poſthumus*, ſlanders ſo her iudgement,
That what's elſe rare, is choak'd: and in that point
I will conclude to hate her, nay indeede,
To be reueng'd vpon her. For, when Fooles ſhall—

Enter Piſanio.

Who is heere? What, are you packing ſirrah?
Come hither: Ah you precious Pandar, Villaine,
Where is thy Lady? In a word, or elſe
Thou art ſtraightway with the Fiends.

Piſ. Oh, good my Lord.

Clo. Where is thy Lady? Or, by Iupiter,
I will not aske againe. Cloſe Villaine,
Ile haue this Secret from thy heart, or rip
Thy heart to finde it. Is ſhe with *Poſthumus*?
From whoſe ſo many waights of baſeneſſe, cannot
A dram of worth be drawne.

Piſ. Alas, my Lord,
How can ſhe be with him? When was ſhe miſs'd?
He is in Rome.

Clot. Where is ſhe Sir? Come neerer:
No farther halting: ſatisfie me home,
What is become of her?

Piſ. Oh, my all-worthy Lord.

Clo. All-worthy Villaine,
Diſcouer where thy Miſtris is, at once,
At the next word: no more of worthy Lord:
Speake, or thy ſilence on the inſtant, is
Thy condemnation, and thy death.

Piſ. Then Sir:
This Paper is the hiſtorie of my knowledge
Touching her flight.

Clo. Let's ſee't: I will purſue her
Euen to *Auguſtus* Throne.

Piſ. Or this, or periſh.
She's farre enough, and what he learnes by this,
May proue his trauell, not her danger.

Clo. Humh.

Piſ. Ile write to my Lord ſhe's dead: Oh *Imogen*,
Safe mayſt thou wander, ſafe returne agen.

Clot. Sirra, is this Letter true?

Piſ. Sir, as I thinke.

Clot. It is *Poſthumus* hand, I know't. Sirrah, if thou would'ſt not be a Villain, but do me true ſeruice: vndergo thoſe Imployments wherin I ſhould haue cauſe to vſe thee with a ſerious induſtry, that is, what villainy ſoere I bid thee do to performe it, directly and truely, I would thinke thee an honeſt man: thou ſhould'ſt neither want my meanes for thy releefe, nor my voyce for thy preferment.

Piſ. Well, my good Lord.

Clot. Wilt thou ſerue mee? For ſince patiently and conſtantly thou haſt ſtucke to the bare Fortune of that Begger *Poſthumus*, thou canſt not in the courſe of gratitude, but be a diligent follower of mine. Wilt thou ſerue mee?

Piſ. Sir, I will.

Clo. Giue mee thy hand, heere's my purſe. Haſt any of thy late Maſters Garments in thy poſſeſſion?

Piſan. I haue (my Lord) at my Lodging, the ſame Suite he wore, when he tooke leaue of my Ladie & Miſtreſſe.

Clo. The firſt ſeruice thou doſt mee, fetch that Suite hither, let it be thy firſt ſeruice, go.

Piſ. I ſhall my Lord. *Exit.*

Clo. Meet thee at Milford-Hauen: (I forgot to aske him one thing, Ile remember't anon:) euen there, thou villaine *Poſthumus* will I kill thee. I would theſe Garments were come. She ſaide vpon a time (the bitterneſſe of it, I now belch from my heart) that ſhee held the very Garment of *Poſthumus*, in more reſpect, then my Noble and naturall perſon; together with the adornement of my Qualities. With that Suite vpon my backe wil I rauiſh her: firſt kill him, and in her eyes; there ſhall ſhe ſee my valour, which wil then be a torment to hir contempt. He on the ground, my ſpeech of inſulment ended on his dead bodie, and when my Luſt hath dined (which, as I ſay, to vex her, I will execute in the Cloathes that ſhe ſo prais'd:) to the Court Ile knock her backe, foot her home againe. She hath deſpis'd mee reioycingly, and Ile bee merry in my Reuenge.

Enter Piſanio.

Be thoſe the Garments?

Piſ. I, my Noble Lord.

Clo. How long is't ſince ſhe went to Milford-Hauen?

Piſ. She can ſcarſe be there yet.

Clo. Bring this Apparrell to my Chamber, that is the ſecond thing that I haue commanded thee. The third is, that thou wilt be a voluntarie Mute to my deſigne. Be but dutious, and true preferment ſhall tender it ſelfe to thee. My Reuenge is now at Milford, would I had wings to follow it. Come, and be true. *Exit*

Piſ. Thou bid'ſt me to my loſſe: for true to thee,
Were to proue falſe, which I will neuer bee
To him that is moſt true. To Milford go,
And finde not her, whom thou purſueſt. Flow, flow
You Heauenly bleſſings on her: This Fooles ſpeede
Be croſt with ſlowneſſe; Labour be his meede. *Exit*

Scena Sexta.

Enter Imogen alone.

Imo. I ſee a mans life is a tedious one,
I haue tyr'd my ſelfe: and for two nights together
Haue made the ground my bed. I ſhould be ſicke,
But that my reſolution helpes me: Milford,
When from the Mountaine top, *Piſanio* ſhew'd thee,
Thou was't within a kenne. Oh Ioue, I thinke
Foundations flye the wretched: ſuch I meane,
Where they ſhould be releeu'd. Two Beggers told me,
I could not miſſe my way. Will poore Folkes lye
That haue Afflictions on them, knowing 'tis
A puniſhment, or Triall? Yes; no wonder,
When Rich-ones ſcarſe tell true. To lapſe in Fulneſſe
Is ſorer, then to lye for Neede: and Falſhood
Is worſe in Kings, then Beggers. My deere Lord,
Thou art one o'th'falſe Ones: Now I thinke on thee,
My hunger's gone; but euen before, I was
At point to ſinke, for Food. But what is this?
Heere is a path too't: 'tis ſome ſauage hold:
I were beſt not call; I dare not call: yet Famine
Ere cleane it o're-throw Nature, makes it valiant.
Plentie, and Peace breeds Cowards: Hardneſſe euer
Of Hardineſſe is Mother. Hoa? who's heere?
If any thing that's ciuill, ſpeake: if ſauage,

Take,

Take, or lend. Hoa? No answer? Then Ile enter.
Best draw my Sword; and if mine Enemy
But feare the Sword like me, hee'l scarsely looke on't.
Such a Foe, good Heauens. *Exit.*

Scena Septima.

Enter Belarius, Guiderius, and Aruiragus.

Bel. You *Polidore* haue prou'd best Woodman, and
Are Master of the Feast: *Cadwall*, and I
Will play the Cooke, and Seruant, 'tis our match:
The sweat of industry would dry, and dye
But for the end it workes too. Come, our stomackes
Will make what's homely, sauoury: Wearinesse
Can snore vpon the Flint, when restie Sloth
Findes the Downe-pillow hard. Now peace be heere,
Poore house, that keep'st thy selfe.
Gui. I am throughly weary.
Arui. I am weake with toyle, yet strong in appetite.
Gui. There is cold meat i'th'Caue, we'l brouz on that
Whil'st what we haue kill'd, be Cook'd.
Bel. Stay, come not in:
But that it eates our victualles, I should thinke
Heere were a Faiery.
Gui. What's the matter, Sir?
Bel. By Iupiter an Angell: or if not
An earthly Paragon. Behold Diuinenesse
No elder then a Boy.

Enter Imogen.

Imo. Good masters harme me not:
Before I enter'd heere, I call'd, and thought
To haue begg'd, or bought, what I haue took: good troth
I haue stolne nought, nor would not, though I had found
Gold strew'd i'th'Floore. Heere's money for my Meate,
I would haue left it on the Boord, so soone
As I had made my Meale; and parted
With Pray'rs for the Prouider.
Gui. Money? Youth.
Aru. All Gold and Siluer rather turne to durt,
As 'tis no better reckon'd, but of those
Who worship durty Gods.
Imo. I see you're angry:
Know, if you kill me for my fault, I should
Haue dyed, had I not made it.
Bel. Whether bound?
Imo. To Milford-Hauen.
Bel. What's your name?
Imo. *Fidele* Sir: I haue a Kinsman, who
Is bound for Italy; he embark'd at Milford,
To whom being going, almost spent with hunger,
I am falne in this offence.
Bel. Prythee (faire youth)
Thinke vs no Churles: nor measure our good mindes
By this rude place we liue in. Well encounter'd,
'Tis almost night, you shall haue better cheere
Ere you depart; and thankes to stay, and eate it:
Boyes, bid him welcome.
Gui. Were you a woman, youth,
I should woo hard, but be your Groome in honesty:
I bid for you, as I do buy.
Arui. Ile make't my Comfort
He is a man, Ile loue him as my Brother:
And such a welcome as I'ld giue to him
(After long absence) such is yours. Most welcome:
Be sprightly, for you fall 'mongst Friends.
Imo. 'Mongst Friends?
If Brothers: would it had bin so, that they
Had bin my Fathers Sonnes, then had my prize
Bin lesse, and so more equall ballasting
To thee *Posthumus*.
Bel. He wrings at some distresse.
Gui. Would I could free't.
Arui. Or I, what ere it be,
What paine it cost, what danger: Gods!
Bel. Hearke Boyes.
Imo. Great men
That had a Court no bigger then this Caue,
That did attend themselues, and had the vertue
Which their owne Conscience seal'd them: laying by
That nothing-guift of differing Multitudes
Could not out-peere these twaine. Pardon me Gods,
I'ld change my sexe to be Companion with them,
Since *Leonatus* false.
Bel. It shall be so:
Boyes wee'l go dresse our Hunt. Faire youth come in;
Discourse is heauy, fasting: when we haue supp'd
Wee'l mannerly demand thee of thy Story,
So farre as thou wilt speake it.
Gui. Pray draw neere.
Arui. The Night to'th'Owle,
And Morne to th'Larke lesse welcome.
Imo. Thankes Sir
Arui. I pray draw neere. *Exeunt.*

Scena Octaua.

Enter two Roman Senators, and Tribunes.

1.Sen. This is the tenor of the Emperors Writ;
That since the common men are now in Action
'Gainst the Pannonians, and Dalmatians,
And that the Legions now in Gallia, are
Full weake to vndertake our Warres against
The falne-off Britaines, that we do incite
The Gentry to this businesse. He creates
Lucius Pro-Consull: and to you the Tribunes
For this immediate Leuy, he commands
His absolute Commission. Long liue *Cæsar*.
Tri. Is *Lucius* Generall of the Forces?
2.Sen I.
Tri. Remaining now in Gallia?
1.Sen. With those Legions
Which I haue spoke of, whereunto your leuie
Must be suppliant: the words of your Commission
Will tye you to the numbers, and the time
Of their dispatch.
Tri. We will discharge our duty. *Exeunt.*

Actus Quartus. Scena Prima.

Enter Clotten alone.

Clot. I am neere to'th'place where they should meet,
if *Pisanio* haue mapp'd it truely. How fit his Garments
serue me? Why should his Mistris who was made by him
that

that made the Taylor, not be fit too? The rather (sauing reuerence of the Word) for 'tis saide a Womans fitnesse comes by fits: therein I must play the Workman, I dare speake it to my selfe, for it is not Vainglorie for a man, and his Glasse, to confer in his owne Chamber; I meane, the Lines of my body are as well drawne as his; no lesse young, more strong, not beneath him in Fortunes, beyond him in the aduantage of the time, aboue him in Birth, alike conuersant in generall seruices, and more remarkeable in single oppositions; yet this imperseuerant Thing loues him in my despight. What Mortalitie is? *Posthumus*, thy head (which now is growing vppon thy shoulders) shall within this houre be off, thy Mistris inforced, thy Garments cut to peeces before thy face: and all this done, spurne her home to her Father, who may (happily) be a little angry for my so rough vsage: but my Mother hauing power of his testinesse, shall turne all into my commendations. My Horse is tyed vp safe, out Sword, and to a sore purpose: Fortune put them into my hand: This is the very description of their meeting place and the Fellow dares not deceiue me. *Exit.*

Scena Secunda.

Enter Belerius, Guiderius, Arusragus, and Imogen from the Caue.

Bel. You are not well: Remaine heere in the Caue,
Wee'l come to you after Hunting.
Arui. Brother, stay heere:
Are we not Brothers?
Imo. So man and man should be,
But Clay and Clay, differs in dignitie,
Whose dust is both alike. I am very sicke,
Gui. Go you to Hunting, Ile abide with him.
Imo. So sicke I am not, yet I am not well:
But not so Citizen a wanton, as
To seeme to dye, ere sicke: So please you, leaue me,
Sticke to your Iournall course: the breach of Custome,
Is breach of all. I am ill, but your being by me
Cannot amend me. Society, is no comfort
To one not sociable: I am not very sicke,
Since I can reason of it: pray you trust me heere,
Ile rob none but my selfe, and let me dye
Stealing so poorely.
Gui. I loue thee: I haue spoke it,
How much the quantity, the waight as much,
As I do loue my Father.
Bel. What? How? how?
Arui. If it be sinne to say so (Sir) I yoake mee
In my good Brothers fault: I know not why
I loue this youth, and I haue heard you say,
Loue's reason's, without reason. The Beere at doore,
And a demand who is't shall dye, I'ld say
My Father, not this youth.
Bel. Oh noble straine!
O worthinesse of Nature, breed of Greatnesse!
"Cowards father Cowards, & Base things Syre Bace;
"Nature hath Meale, and Bran; Contempt, and Grace.
I'me not their Father, yet who this should bee,
Doth myracle it selfe, lou'd before mee.
'Tis the ninth houre o'th' Morne.
Arui. Brother, farewell.
Imo. I wish ye sport.
Arui. You health. —— So please you Sir.
Imo. These are kinde Creatures.
Gods, what lyes I haue heard:
Our Courtiers say, all's sauage, but at Court;
Experience, oh thou disproou'st Report.
Th'emperious Seas breeds Monsters; for the Dish,
Poore Tributary Riuers, as sweet Fish:
I am sicke still, heart-sicke; *Pisanio*,
Ile now taste of thy Drugge.
Gui. I could not stirre him:
He said he was gentle, but vnfortunate;
Dishonestly afflicted, but yet honest.
Arui. Thus did he answer me: yet said heereafter,
I might know more.
Bel. To'th'Field, to'th'Field:
Wee'l leaue you for this time, go in, and rest.
Arui. Wee'l not be long away.
Bel. Pray be not sicke,
For you must be our Huswife.
Imo. Well, or ill,
I am bound to you. *Exit.*
Bel. And shal't be euer.
This youth, how ere distrest, appeares he hath had
Good Ancestors.
Arui. How Angell-like he sings?
Gui. But his neate Cookerie?
Arui. He cut our Rootes in Charracters,
And sawc'st our Brothes, as *Iuno* had bin sicke,
And he her Dieter.
Arui. Nobly he yoakes
A smiling, with a sigh; as if the sighe
Was that it was, for not being such a Smile:
The Smile, mocking the Sigh, that it would flye
From so diuine a Temple, to commix
With windes, that Saylors raile at.
Gui. I do note,
That greefe and patience rooted in them both,
Mingle their spurres together.
Arui. Grow patient,
And let the stinking-Elder (Greefe) vntwine
His perishing roote, with the encreasing Vine.
Bel. It is great morning. Come away: Who's there?
Enter Cloten.
Clo. I cannot finde those Runnagates, that Villaine
Hath mock'd me. I am faint.
Bel. Those Runnagates?
Meanes he not vs? I partly know him, 'tis
Cloten, the Sonne o'th' Queene. I feare some Ambush:
I saw him not these many yeares, and yet
I know 'tis he: We are held as Out-Lawes: Hence.
Gui. He is but one: you, and my Brother search
What Companies are neere: pray you away,
Let me alone with him.
Clot. Soft, what are you
That flye me thus? Some villaine-Mountainers?
I haue heard of such. What Slaue art thou?
Gui. A thing
More slauish did I ne're, then answering
A Slaue without a knocke.
Clot. Thou art a Robber,
A Law-breaker, a Villaine: yeeld thee Theefe.
Gui. To who? to thee? What art thou? Haue not I
An arme as bigge as thine? A heart, as bigge:
Thy words I grant are bigger: for I weare not
My Dagger in my mouth. Say what thou art:
Why

Why I should yeeld to thee?
Clot. Thou Villaine base,
Know'st me not by my Cloathes?
Gui. No, nor thy Taylor, Rascall:
Who is thy Grandfather? He made those cloathes,
Which (as it seemes) make thee.
Clo. Thou precious Varlet,
My Taylor made them not.
Gui. Hence then, and thanke
The man that gaue them thee. Thou art some Foole,
I am loath to beate thee.
Clot. Thou iniurious Theefe,
Heare but my name, and tremble.
Gui. What's thy name?
Clo. Cloten, thou Villaine.
Gui. Cloten, thou double Villaine be thy name,
I cannot tremble at it, were it Toad, or Adder, Spider,
'Twould moue me sooner.
Clot. To thy further feare,
Nay, to thy meere Confusion, thou shalt know
I am Sonne to'th'Queene.
Gui. I am sorry for't: not seeming
So worthy as thy Birth.
Clot. Art not afeard?
Gui. Those that I reuerence, those I feare: the Wise:
At Fooles I laugh: not feare them.
Clot. Dye the death:
When I haue slaine thee with my proper hand,
Ile follow those that euen now fled hence:
And on the Gates of *Luds-Towne* set your heads:
Yeeld Rusticke Mountaineer. *Fight and Exeunt.*

Enter Belarius and Aruiragus.

Bel. No Companie's abroad?
Arui. None in the world: you did mistake him sure.
Bel. I cannot tell: Long is it since I saw him,
But Time hath nothing blurr'd those lines of Fauour
Which then he wore: the snatches in his voice,
And burst of speaking were as his: I am absolute
'Twas very *Cloten*.
Arui. In this place we left them;
I wish my Brother make good time with him,
You say he is so fell.
Bel. Being scarse made vp,
I meane to man; he had not apprehension
Of roaring terrors: For defect of iudgement
Is oft the cause of Feare.

Enter Guiderius.

But see thy Brother.
Gui. This *Cloten* was a Foole, an empty purse,
There was no money in't: Not *Hercules*
Could haue knock'd out his Braines, for he had none:
Yet I not doing this, the Foole had borne
My head, as I do his.
Bel. What hast thou done?
Gui. I am perfect what: cut off one *Clotens* head,
Sonne to the Queene (after his owne report)
Who call'd me Traitor, Mountaineer, and swore
With his owne single hand heel'd take vs in,
Displace our heads, where (thanks the Gods) they grow
And set them on *Luds-Towne*.
Bel. We are all vndone.
Gui. Why, worthy Father, what haue we to loose,
But that he swore to take, our Liues? the Law
Protects not vs, then why should we be tender,
To let an arrogant peece of flesh threat vs?
Play Iudge, and Executioner, all himselfe?
For we do feare the Law. What company
Discouer you abroad?
Bel. No single soule
Can we set eye on: but in all safe reason
He must haue some Attendants. Though his Honor
Was nothing but mutation, I, and that
From one bad thing to worse: Not Frenzie,
Not absolute madnesse could so farre haue rau'd
To bring him heere alone: although perhaps
It may be heard at Court, that such as wee
Caue heere, hunt heere, are Out-lawes, and in time
May make some stronger head, the which he hearing,
(As it is like him) might breake out, and sweare
Heel'd fetch vs in, yet is't not probable
To come alone, either he so vndertaking,
Or they so suffering: then on good ground we feare,
If we do feare this Body hath a taile
More perillous then the head.
Arui. Let Ord'nance
Come as the Gods fore-say it: howsoere,
My Brother hath done well.
Bel. I had no minde
To hunt this day: The Boy *Fideles* sickenesse
Did make my way long forth.
Gui. With his owne Sword,
Which he did waue against my throat, I haue tane
His head from him: Ile throw't into the Creeke
Behinde our Rocke, and let it to the Sea,
And tell the Fishes, hee's the Queenes Sonne, *Cloten*,
That's all I reake. *Exit.*
Bel. I feare 'twill be reueng'd:
Would (*Polidore*) thou had'st not done't: though valour
Becomes thee well enough.
Arui. Would I had done't:
So the Reuenge alone pursu'de me: *Polidore*
I loue thee brotherly, but enuy much
Thou hast robb'd me of this deed: I would Reuenges
That possible strength might meet, wold seek vs through
And put vs to our answer.
Bel. Well, 'tis done:
Wee'l hunt no more to day, nor seeke for danger,
Where there's no profit. I prythee to our Rocke,
You and *Fidele* play the Cookes: Ile stay
Till hasty *Polidore* returne, and bring him
To dinner presently.
Arui. Poore sicke *Fidele.*
Ile willingly to him, to gaine his colour,
Il'd let a parish of such *Clotens* blood,
And praise my selfe for charity. *Exit.*
Bel. Oh thou Goddesse,
Thou diuine Nature; thou thy selfe thou blazon'st
In these two Princely Boyes: they are as gentle
As Zephires blowing below the Violet,
Not wagging his sweet head; and yet, as rough
(Their Royall blood enchaf'd) as the rud'st winde,
That by the top doth take the Mountaine Pine,
And make him stoope to th'Vale. 'Tis wonder
That an inuisible instinct should frame them
To Royalty vnlearn'd, Honor vntaught,
Ciuility not seene from other: valour
That wildely growes in them, but yeelds a crop
As if it had beene sow'd: yet still it's strange
What *Clotens* being heere to vs portends,
Or what his death will bring vs.

Enter Guidereus.

Gui. Where's my Brother?

I

I haue sent *Clotens* Clot-pole downe the streame,
In Embassie to his Mother; his Bodie's hostage
For his returne. *Solemn Musick.*

Bel. My ingenuous Instrument,
(Hearke *Polidore*) it sounds: but what occasion
Hath *Cadwal* now to giue it motion? Hearke.

Gui. Is he at home?

Bel. He went hence euen now.

Gui. What does he meane?
Since death of my deer'st Mother
It did not speake before. All solemne things
Should answer solemne Accidents. The matter?
Triumphes for nothing, and lamenting Toyes,
Is iollity for Apes, and greefe for Boyes.
Is *Cadwall* mad?

Enter Aruiragus, with Imogen dead, bearing her in his Armes.

Bel. Looke, heere he comes,
And brings the dire occasion in his Armes,
Of what we blame him for.

Arui. The Bird is dead
That we haue made so much on. I had rather
Haue skipt from sixteene yeares of Age, to sixty:
To haue turn'd my leaping time into a Crutch,
Then haue seene this.

Gui. Oh sweetest, fayrest Lilly:
My Brother weares thee not the one halfe so well,
As when thou grew'st thy selfe.

Bel. Oh Melancholly,
Who euer yet could sound thy bottome? Finde
The Ooze, to shew what Coast thy sluggish care
Might'st easileST harbour in. Thou blessed thing,
Ioue knowes what man thou might'st haue made: but I,
Thou dyed'st a most rare Boy, of Melancholly
How found you him?

Arui. Starke, as you see:
Thus smiling, as some Fly had tickled slumber,
Not as deaths dart, being laugh'd at: his right Cheeke
Reposing on a Cushion.

Gui. Where?

Arui. O'th'floore:
His armes thus leagu'd, I thought he slept, and put
My clowted Brogues from off my feete, whose rudenesse
Answer'd my steps too lowd.

Gui. Why, he but sleepes:
If he be gone, hee'l make his Graue, a Bed:
With female Fayries will his Tombe be haunted,
And Wormes will not come to thee.

Arui. With fayrest Flowers
Whil'st Sommer lasts, and I liue heere, *Fidele*,
Ile sweeten thy sad graue: thou shalt not lacke
The Flower that's like thy face. Pale-Primrose, nor
The azur'd Hare-bell, like thy Veines: no, nor
The leafe of Eglantine, whom not to slander,
Out-sweetned not thy breath: the Raddocke would
With Charitable bill (Oh bill sore shaming
Those rich-left-heyres, that let their Fathers lye
Without a Monument) bring thee all this,
Yea, and furr'd Mosse besides. When Flowres are none
To winter-ground thy Coarse———

Gui. Prythee haue done,
And do not play in Wench-like words with that
Which is so serious. Let vs bury him,
And not protract with admiration, what
Is now due debt. To'th'graue.

Arui. Say, where shall's lay him?

Gui. By good *Euriphile*, our Mother.

Arui. Bee't so:
And let vs (*Polidore*) though now our voyces
Haue got the mannish cracke, sing him to'th'ground
As once to our Mother: vse like note, and words,
Saue that *Euriphile*, must be *Fidele*.

Gui. *Cadwall*,
I cannot sing: Ile weepe, and word it with thee;
For Notes of sorrow, out of tune, are worse
Then Priests, and Phanes that lye.

Arui. Wee'l speake it then.

Bel. Great greefes I see med'cine the lesse: For *Cloten*
Is quite forgot. He was a Queenes Sonne, Boyes,
And though he came our Enemy, remember
He was paid for that: though meane, and mighty rotting
Together haue one dust, yet Reuerence
(That Angell of the world) doth make distinction
Of place 'tweene high, and low. Our Foe was Princely,
And though you tooke his life, as being our Foe,
Yet bury him, as a Prince.

Gui. Pray you fetch him hither,
Thersites body is as good as *Aiax*,
When neyther are aliue.

Arui. If you'l go fetch him,
Wee'l say our Song the whil'st: Brother begin.

Gui. Nay *Cadwall*, we must lay his head to th'East,
My Father hath a reason for't.

Arui. 'Tis true.

Gui. Come on then, and remoue him.

Arui. So, begin.

SONG.

Guid. *Feare no more the heate o'th'Sun,*
Nor the furious Winters rages,
Thou thy worldly task hast don,
Home art gon, and tane thy wages.
Golden Lads, and Girles all must,
As Chimney-Sweepers come to dust.

Arui. *Feare no more the frowne o'th'Great,*
Thou art past the Tirants stroake,
Care no more to cloath and eate,
To thee the Reede is as the Oake:
The Scepter, Learning, Physicke must,
All follow this and come to dust.

Guid. *Feare no more the Lightning flash.*
Arui. *Nor th'all-dreaded Thunderstone*
Gui. *Feare not Slander, Censure rash.*
Arui. *Thou hast finish'd Ioy and mone.*
Both. *All Louers young, all Louers must,*
Consigne to thee and come to dust.

Guid. *No Exorcisor harme thee,*
Arui. *Nor no witch-craft charme thee.*
Guid. *Ghost vnlaid forbeare thee.*
Arui. *Nothing ill come neere thee.*
Both. *Quiet consumation haue,*
And renowned be thy graue.

Enter Belarius with the body of Cloten.

Gui. We haue done our obsequies:
Come lay him downe.

Bel. Heere's a few Flowres, but 'bout midnight more:
The hearbes that haue on them cold dew o'th'night
Are strewings fit'st for Graues: vpon their Faces.
You were as Flowres, now wither'd: euen so
These Herbelets shall, which we vpon you strew.
Come on, away, apart vpon our knees:
The ground that gaue them first, ha's them againe:
Their pleasures here are past, so are their paine. *Exeunt.*

bbb *Imogen*

Imogen awakes.

Yes Sir, to Milford-Hauen, which is the way?
I thanke you: by yond bush? pray how farre thether?
'Ods pittikins: can it be sixe mile yet?
I haue gone all night: 'Faith, Ile lye downe, and sleepe.
But soft; no Bedfellow? Oh Gods, and Goddesses!
These Flowres are like the pleasures of the World;
This bloody man the care on't. I hope I dreame:
For so I thought I was a Caue-keeper,
And Cooke to honest Creatures. But 'tis not so:
'Twas but a bolt of nothing, shot at nothing,
Which the Braine makes of Fumes. Our very eyes,
Are sometimes like our Iudgements, blinde. Good faith
I tremble still with feare: but if there be
Yet left in Heauen, as small a drop of pittie
As a Wrens eye; fear'd Gods, a part of it.
The Dreame's heere still: euen when I wake it is
Without me, as within me: not imagin'd, felt.
A headlesse man? The Garments of *Posthumus*?
I know the shape of's Legge: this is his Hand:
His Foote Mercuriall: his martiall Thigh
The brawnes of *Hercules*: but his Iouiall face——
Murther in heauen? How? 'tis gone. *Pisanio*,
All Curses madded *Hecuba* gaue the Greekes,
And mine to boot, be darted on thee: thou
Conspir'd with that Irregulous diuell *Cloten*,
Hath heere cut off my Lord. To write, and read,
Be henceforth treacherous. Damn'd *Pisanio*,
Hath with his forged Letters (damn'd *Pisanio*)
From this most brauest vessell of the world
Strooke the maine top! Oh *Posthumus*, alas,
Where is thy head? where's that? Aye me! where's that?
Pisanio might haue kill'd thee at the heart,
And left this head on. How should this be, *Pisanio*?
'Tis he, and *Cloten*: Malice, and Lucre in them
Haue laid this Woe heere. Oh 'tis pregnant, pregnant!
The Drugge he gaue me, which hee said was precious
And Cordiall to me, haue I not found it
Murd'rous to th'Senses? That confirmes it home:
This is *Pisanio's* deede, and *Cloten*: Oh!
Giue colour to my pale cheeke with thy blood,
That we the horrider may seeme to those
Which chance to finde vs. Oh, my Lord! my Lord!

Enter Lucius, Captaines, and a Soothsayer.

Cap. To them, the Legions garrison'd in Gallia
After your will, haue crost the Sea, attending
You heere at Milford-Hauen, with your Shippes:
They are heere in readinesse.

Luc. But what from Rome?

Cap. The Senate hath stirr'd vp the Confiners,
And Gentlemen of Italy, most willing Spirits,
That promise Noble Seruice: and they come
Vnder the Conduct of bold *Iachimo*,
Syenna's Brother.

Luc. When expect you them?

Cap With the next benefit o'th'winde.

Luc. This forwardnesse
Makes our hopes faire. Command our present numbers
Be muster'd: bid the Captaines looke too't. Now Sir,
What haue you dream'd of late of this warres purpose.

Sooth. Last night the very Gods shew'd me a vision
(I fast, and pray'd for their Intelligence) thus:
I saw Ioues Bird, the Roman Eagle wing'd
From the spungy South, to this part of the West,
There vanish'd in the Sun-beames, which portends
(Vnlesse my sinnes abuse my Diuination)
Successe to th'Roman hoast.

Luc. Dreame often so,
And neuer false. Soft hoa, what truncke is heere?
Without his top? The ruine speakes, that sometime
It was a worthy building. How? a Page?
Or dead, or sleeping on him? But dead rather:
For Nature doth abhorre to make his bed
With the defunct, or sleepe vpon the dead.
Let's see the Boyes face.

Cap. Hee's aliue my Lord.

Luc. Hee'l then instruct vs of this body: Young one,
Informe vs of thy Fortunes, for it seemes
They craue to be demanded: who is this
Thou mak'st thy bloody Pillow? Or who was he
That (otherwise then noble Nature did)
Hath alter'd that good Picture? What's thy interest
In this sad wracke? How came't? Who is't?
What art thou?

Imo. I am nothing; or if not,
Nothing to be were better: This was my Master,
A very valiant Britaine, and a good,
That heere by Mountaineers lyes slaine: Alas,
There is no more such Masters: I may wander
From East to Occident, cry out for Seruice,
Try many, all good: serue truly: neuer
Finde such another Master.

Luc. 'Lacke, good youth:
Thou mou'st no lesse with thy complaining, then
Thy Maister in bleeding: say his name, good Friend.

Imo. Richard du Champ: If I do lye, and do
No harme by it, though the Gods heare, I hope
They'l pardon it. Say you Sir?

Luc. Thy name?

Imo. *Fidele* Sir.

Luc. Thou doo'st approue thy selfe the very same:
Thy Name well fits thy Faith; thy Faith, thy Name:
Wilt take thy chance with me? I will not say
Thou shalt be so well master'd, but be sure
No lesse belou'd. The Romane Emperors Letters
Sent by a Consull to me, should not sooner
Then thine owne worth preferre thee: Go with me.

Imo. Ile follow Sir. But first, and't please the Gods,
Ile hide my Master from the Flies, as deepe
As these poore Pickaxes can digge: and when
With wild wood-leaues & weeds, I ha' strew'd his graue
And on it said a Century of prayers
(Such as I can) twice o're, Ile weepe, and sighe,
And leauing so his seruice, follow you,
So please you entertaine mee.

Luc. I good youth,
And rather Father thee, then Master thee: My Friends,
The Boy hath taught vs manly duties: Let vs
Finde out the prettiest Dazied-Plot we can,
And make him with our Pikes and Partizans
A Graue: Come, Arme him: Boy hee's preferr'd
By thee, to vs, and he shall be interr'd
As Souldiers can. Be cheerefull; wipe thine eyes,
Some Falles are meanes the happier to arise. *Exeunt*

Scena Tertia.

Enter Cymbeline, Lords, and Pisanio.

Cym. Againe: and bring me word how 'tis with her,
A Feauour with the absence of her Sonne;

A

A madnesse, of which her life's in danger : Heauens,
How deeply you at once do touch me. *Imogen,*
The great part of my comfort, gone : My Queene
Vpon a desperate bed, and in a time
When fearefull Warres point at me : Her Sonne gone,
So needfull for this present ? It strikes me, past
The hope of comfort. But for thee, Fellow,
Who needs must know of her departure, and
Dost seeme so ignorant, wee'l enforce it from thee
By a sharpe Torture.
Pis. Sir, my life is yours,
I humbly set it at your will : But for my Mistris,
I nothing know where she remaines : why gone,
Nor when she purposes returne. Beseech your Highnes,
Hold me your loyall Seruant.
Lord. Good my Liege,
The day that she was missing, he was heere;
I dare be bound hee's true, and shall performe
All parts of his subiection loyally. For *Cloten,*
There wants no diligence in seeking him,
And will no doubt be found.
Cym. The time is troublesome :
Wee'l slip you for a season, but our iealousie
Do's yet depend.
Lord. So please your Maiesty,
The Romaine Legions, all from Gallia drawne,
Are landed on your Coast, with a supply
Of Romaine Gentlemen, by the Senate sent.
Cym. Now for the Counsaile of my Son and Queen,
I am amaz'd with matter.
Lord. Good my Liege,
Your preparation can affront no lesse (ready :
Then what you heare of. Come more, for more you're
The want is, but to put those Powres in motion,
That long to moue.
Cym. I thanke you : let's withdraw
And meete the Time, as it seekes vs. We feare not
What can from Italy annoy vs, but
We greeue at chances heere. Away. *Exeunt*
Pisa. I heard no Letter from my Master, since
I wrote him *Imogen* was slaine. Tis strange :
Nor heare I from my Mistris, who did promise
To yeeld me often tydings. Neither know I
What is betide to *Cloten*, but remaine
Perplext in all. The Heauens still must worke
Wherein I am false, I am honest : not true, to be true.
These present warres shall finde I loue my Country,
Euen to the note o'th'King, or Ile fall in them :
All other doubts, by time let them be cleer'd,
Fortune brings in some Boats, that are not steer'd. *Exit.*

Scena Quarta.

Enter Belarius, Guiderius, & Aruiragus.

Gui. The noyse is round about vs.
Bel. Let vs from it.
Arui. What pleasure Sir, we finde in life, to locke it
From Action, and Aduenture.
Gui. Nay, what hope
Haue we in hiding vs? This way the Romaines
Must, or for Britaines slay vs or receiue vs
For barbarous and vnnaturall Reuolts
During their vse, and slay vs after.
Bel. Sonnes,
Wee'l higher to the Mountaines, there secure vs.
To the Kings party there's no going : newnesse
Of *Clotens* death (we being not knowne, not muster'd
Among the Bands) may driue vs to a render
Where we haue liu'd; and so extort from's that
Which we haue done, whose answer would be death
Drawne on with Torture.
Gui. This is (Sir) a doubt
In such a time, nothing becomming you,
Nor satisfying vs.
Arui. It is not likely,
That when they heare their Roman horses neigh,
Behold their quarter'd Fires; haue both their eyes
And eares so cloyd importantly as now,
That they will waste their time vpon our note,
To know from whence we are.
Bel. Oh, I am knowne
Of many in the Army : Many yeeres
(Though *Cloten* then but young) you see, not wore him
From my remembrance. And besides, the King
Hath not deseru'd my Seruice, nor your Loues,
Who finde in my Exile, the want of Breeding;
The certainty of this heard life, aye hopelesse
To haue the courtesie your Cradle promis'd,
But to be still hot Summers Tanlings, and
The shrinking Slaues of Winter.
Gui. Then be so,
Better to cease to be. Pray Sir, to'th'Army :
I, and my Brother are not knowne; your selfe
So out of thought, and thereto so ore-growne,
Cannot be question'd.
Arui. By this Sunne that shines
Ile thither : What thing is't, that I neuer
Did see man dye, scarse euer look'd on blood,
But that of Coward Hares, hot Goats, and Venison?
Neuer bestrid a Horse saue one, that had
A Rider like my selfe, who ne're wore Rowell,
Nor Iron on his heele? I am asham'd
To looke vpon the holy Sunne, to haue
The benefit of his blest Beames, remaining
So long a poore vnknowne.
Gui. By heauens Ile go,
If you will blesse me Sir, and giue me leaue,
Ile take the better care : but if you will not,
The hazard therefore due fall on me, by
The hands of Romaines.
Arui. So say I, Amen.
Bel. No reason I (since of your liues you set
So slight a valewation) should reserue
My crack'd one to more care. Haue with you Boyes :
If in your Country warres you chance to dye,
That is my Bed too (Lads) and there Ile lye.
Lead, lead; the time seems long, their blood thinks scorn
Till it flye out, and shew them Princes borne. *Exeunt.*

Actus Quintus. Scena Prima.

Enter Posthumus alone.

Post. Yea bloody cloth, Ile keep thee : for I am wisht
Thou should'st be colour'd thus. You married ones,
If each of you should take this course, how many
Must murther Wiues much better then themselues
bbb 2 For

For wrying but a little? Oh *Pisanio*,
Euery good Seruant do's not all Commands:
No Bond, but to do iust ones. Gods, if you
Should haue 'tane vengeance on my faults, I neuer
Had liu'd to put on this: so had you saued
The noble *Imogen*, to repent, and strooke
Me (wretch) more worth your Vengeance. But alacke,
You snatch some hence for little faults; that's loue
To haue them fall no more: you some permit
To second illes with illes, each elder worse,
And make them dread it, to the dooers thrift.
But *Imogen* is your owne, do your best willes,
And make me blest to obey. I am brought hither
Among th'Italian Gentry, and to fight
Against my Ladies Kingdome: 'Tis enough
That (Britaine) I haue kill'd thy Mistris: Peace,
Ile giue no wound to thee: therefore good Heauens,
Heare patiently my purpose. Ile disrobe me
Of these Italian weedes, and suite my selfe
As do's a *Britaine* Pezant: so Ile fight
Against the part I come with: so Ile dye
For thee (O *Imogen*) euen for whom my life
Is euery breath, a death: and thus, vnknowne,
Pittied, nor hated, to the face of perill
My selfe Ile dedicate. Let me make men know
More valour in me, then my habits show.
Gods, put the strength o'th' *Leonati* in me:
To shame the guize o'th'world, I will begin,
The fashion lesse without, and more within. *Exit.*

Scena Secunda.

Enter Lucius, Iachimo, and the Romane Army at one doore: and the Britaine Army at another: Leonatus Posthumus following like a poore Souldier. They march ouer, and goe out. Then enter againe in Skirmish Iachimo and Posthumus: he vanquisheth and disarmeth Iachimo, and then leaues him.

Iac. The heauinesse and guilt within my bosome,
Takes off my manhood: I haue belyed a Lady,
The Princesse of this Country; and the ayre on't
Reuengingly enfeebles me, or could this Carle,
A very drudge of Natures, haue subdu'de me
In my profession? Knighthoods, and Honors borne
As I weare mine) are titles but of scorne.
If that thy Gentry (Britaine) go before
This Lowt, as he exceeds our Lords, the oddes
Is, that we scarse are men, and you are Goddes. *Exit.*

The Battaile continues, the Britaines fly, Cymbeline is taken: Then enter to his rescue, Bellarius, Guiderius, and Aruiragus.

Bel. Stand, stand, we haue th'aduantage of the ground,
The Lane is guarded: Nothing rowts vs, but
The villany of our feares.

Gui. Arui. Stand, stand, and fight.

Enter Posthumus, and seconds the Britaines. They Rescue Cymbeline, and Exeunt.

Then enter Lucius, Iachimo, and Imogen.

Luc. Away boy from the Troopes, and saue thy selfe:
For friends kil friends, and the disorder's such
As warre were hood-wink'd.

Iac. 'Tis their fresh supplies.

Luc. It is a day turn'd strangely: or betimes
Let's re-inforce, or fly. *Exeunt*

Scena Tertia.

Enter Posthumus, and a Britaine Lord.

Lor. Cam'st thou from where they made the stand?

Post. I did.
Though you it seemes come from the Fliers?

Lo. I did.

Post. No blame be to you Sir, for all was lost,
But that the Heauens fought: the King himselfe
Of his wings destitute, the Army broken,
And but the backes of Britaines seene; all flying
Through a strait Lane, the Enemy full-hearted,
Lolling the Tongue with slaught'ring: hauing worke
More plentifull, then Tooles to doo't: strooke downe
Some mortally, some slightly touch'd, some falling
Meerely through feare, that the strait passe was damm'd
With deadmen, hurt behinde, and Cowards liuing
To dye with length'ned shame.

Lo. Where was this Lane?

Post. Close by the battell, ditch'd, & wall'd with turph,
Which gaue aduantage to an ancient Soldiour
(An honest one I warrant) who deseru'd
So long a breeding, as his white beard came to,
In doing this for's Country. Athwart the Lane,
He, with two striplings (Lads more like to run
The Country base, then to commit such slaughter,
With faces fit for Maskes, or rather fayrer
Then those for preseruation cas'd, or shame)
Made good the passage, cryed to those that fled.
Our *Britaines* hearts dye flying, not our men,
To darknesse fleete soules that flye backwards; stand,
Or we are Romanes, and will giue you that
Like beasts, which you shun beastly, and may saue
But to looke backe in frowne: Stand, stand. These three,
Three thousand confident, in acte as many:
For three performers are the File, when all
The rest do nothing. With this word stand, stand,
Accomodated by the Place; more Charming
With their owne Noblenesse, which could haue turn'd
A Distaffe, to a Lance, guilded pale lookes;
Part shame, part spirit renew'd, that some turn'd coward
But by example (Oh a sinne in Warre,
Damn'd in the first beginners) gan to looke
The way that they did, and to grin like Lyons
Vpon the Pikes o'th'Hunters. Then beganne
A stop i'th'Chaser; a Retyre: Anon
A Rowt, confusion thicke: forthwith they flye
Chickens, the way which they stopt Eagles: Slaues
The strides the Victors made: and now our Cowards
Like Fragments in hard Voyages became
The life o'th'need: hauing found the backe doore open
Of the vnguarded hearts: heauens, how they wound,
Some slaine before some dying; some their Friends
Ore-borne i'th'former waue, ten chac'd by one,
Are now each one the slaughter-man of twenty:
Those that would dye, or ere resist, are growne
The mortall bugs o'th'Field.

Lor

Lord. This was strange chance:
A narrow Lane, an old man, and two Boyes.
Post. Nay, do not wonder at it: you are made
Rather to wonder at the things you heare,
Then to worke any. Will you Rime vpon't,
And vent it for a Mock'rie? Heere is one:
"*Two Boyes, an Oldman (twice a Boy) a Lane,*
"*Preseru'd the Britaines, was the Romanes bane.*
Lord. Nay, be not angry Sir.
Post. Lacke, to what end?
Who dares not stand his Foe, Ile be his Friend:
For if hee'l do, as he is made to doo,
I know hee'l quickly flye my friendship too.
You haue put me into Rime.
Lord. Farewell, you're angry. *Exit.*
Post. Still going? This is a Lord: Oh Noble misery
To be i'th'Field, and aske what newes of me:
To day, how many would haue giuen their Honours
To haue sau'd their Carkasses? Tooke heele to doo't,
And yet dyed too. I, in mine owne woe charm'd
Could not finde death, where I did heare him groane,
Nor feele him where he strooke. Being an vgly Monster,
'Tis strange he hides him in fresh Cups, soft Beds,
Sweet words; or hath moe ministers then we
That draw his kniues i'th'War. Well I will finde him:
For being now a Fauourer to the Britaine,
No more a Britaine, I haue resum'd againe
The part I came in. Fight I will no more,
But yeeld me to the veriest Hinde, that shall
Once touch my shoulder. Great the slaughter is
Heere made by'th'Romane; great the Answer be
Britaines must take. For me, my Ransome's death,
On eyther side I come to spend my breath;
Which neyther heere Ile keepe, nor beare agen,
But end it by some meanes for *Imogen.*

Enter two Captaines, and Soldiers.

1 Great Iupiter be prais'd, *Lucius* is taken,
'Tis thought the old man, and his sonnes, were Angels.
2 There was a fourth man, in a silly habit,
That gaue th'Affront with them.
1 So 'tis reported:
But none of 'em can be found. Stand, who's there?
Post. A Roman,
Who had not now beene drooping heere, if Seconds
Had answer'd him.
2 Lay hands on him: a Dogge,
A legge of Rome shall not returne to tell
What Crows haue peckt them here: he brags his seruice
As if he were of note: bring him to'th'King.

Enter Cymbeline, Belarius, Guiderius, Aruiragus, Pisanio, and Romane Captiues. The Captaines present Posthumus to Cymbeline, who deliuers him ouer to a Gaoler.

Scena Quarta.

Enter Posthumus, and Gaoler.

Gao. You shall not now be stolne,
You haue lockes vpon you:
So graze, as you finde Pasture.
2. *Gao.* I, or a stomacke.
Post. Most welcome bondage; for thou art a way
(I thinke) to liberty: yet am I better
Then one that's sicke o'th'Gowt, since he had rather
Groane so in perpetuity, then be cur'd
By'th'sure Physitian, Death; who is the key
T'vnbarre these Lockes. My Conscience, thou art fetter'd
More then my shanks, & wrists: you good Gods giue me
The penitent Instrument to picke that Bolt,
Then free for euer. Is't enough I am sorry?
So Children temporall Fathers do appease;
Gods are more full of mercy. Must I repent,
I cannot do it better then in Gyues,
Desir'd, more then constrain'd, to satisfie
If of my Freedome 'tis the maine part, take
No stricter render of me, then my All.
I know you are more clement then vilde men,
Who of their broken Debtors take a third,
A sixt, a tenth, letting them thriue againe
On their abatement; that's not my desire.
For *Imogens* deere life, take mine, and though
'Tis not so deere, yet 'tis a life; you coyn'd it,
'Tweene man, and man, they waigh not euery stampe:
Though light, take Peeces for the figures sake.
(You rather) mine being yours: and so great Powres,
If you will take this Audit, take this life,
And cancell these cold Bonds. Oh *Imogen,*
Ile speake to thee in silence.

Solemne Musicke. Enter (as in an Apparation) Sicillius Leonatus, Father to Posthumus, an old man, attyred like a warriour, leading in his hand an ancient Matron (his wife, & Mother to Posthumus) with Musicke before them. Then, after other Musicke, followes the two young Leonati (Brothers to Posthumus) with wounds as they died in the warrs. They circle Posthumus round as he lies sleeping.

Sicil. No more thou Thunder-Master
shew thy spight, on Mortall Flies:
With Mars fall out with *Iuno* chide, that thy Adulteries
Rates, and Reuenges.
Hath my poore Boy done ought but well,
whose face I neuer saw:
I dy'de whil'st in the Wombe he staide,
attending Natures Law.
Whose Father then (as men report,
thou Orphanes Father art)
Thou should'st haue bin, and sheelded him,
from this earth-vexing smart.
Moth. Lucina lent not me her ayde,
but tooke me in my Throwes,
That from me was *Posthumus* ript,
came crying 'mong'st his Foes.
A thing of pitty.
Sicil. Great Nature like his Ancestrie,
moulded the stuffe so faire:
That he d seru'd the praise o'th'World,
as great *Sicilius* heyre.
1. *Bro.* When once he was mature for man,
in Britaine where was hee
That could stand vp his paralell?
Or fruitfull obiect bee?
In eye of *Imogen*, that best could deeme
his dignitie.
Mo. With Marriage wherefore was he mockt
to be exil'd, and throwne
From *Leonati* Seate, and cast from her,
his deerest one:
Sweete *Imogen*?
Sic. Why did you suffer *Iachimo*, slight thing of Italy,

To taint his Nobler hart & braine, with needlesse ielousy,
And to become the geeke and scorne o'th'others vilany?

2 Bro. For this, from stiller Seats we came,
our Parents, and vs twaine,
That striking in our Countries cause,
fell brauely, and were slaine,
Our Fealty, & *Tenantius* right, with Honor to maintaine.

1 Bro. Like hardiment *Posthumus* hath
to *Cymbeline* perform'd:
Then Iupiter, yͧ King of Gods, why hast yͧ thus adiourn'd
The Graces for his Merits due, being all to dolors turn'd?

Sicil. Thy Christall window ope; looke,
looke out, no longer exercise
Vpon a valiant Race, thy harsh, and potent iniuries:

Moth. Since (Iupiter) our Son is good,
take off his miseries.

Sicil. Peepe through thy Marble Mansion, helpe,
or we poore Ghosts will cry
To'th'shining Synod of the rest, against thy Deity.

Brothers. Helpe (Iupiter) or we appeale,
and from thy iustice flye.

Iupiter descends in Thunder and Lightning, sitting vppon an Eagle: hee throwes a Thunder-bolt. The Ghostes fall on their knees.

Iupiter. No more you petty Spirits of Region low
Offend our hearing: hush. How dare you Ghostes
Accuse the Thunderer, whose Bolt (you know)
Sky-planted, batters all rebelling Coasts.
Poore shadowes of Elizium, hence, and rest
Vpon your neuer-withering bankes of Flowres.
Be not with mortall accidents opprest,
No care of yours it is, you know 'tis ours.
Whom best I loue, I crosse; to make my guift
The more delay'd, delighted. Be content,
Your low-laide Sonne, our Godhead will vplift:
His Comforts thriue, his Trials well are spent:
Our Iouiall Starre reign'd at his Birth, and in
Our Temple was he married: Rise, and fade,
He shall be Lord of Lady *Imogen*,
And happier much by his Affliction made.
This Tablet lay vpon his Brest, wherein
Our pleasure, his full Fortune, doth confine,
And so away: no farther with your dinne
Expresse Impatience, least you stirre vp mine:
Mount Eagle, to my Palace Christalline. *Ascends*

Sicil. He came in Thunder, his Celestiall breath
Was sulphurous to smell: the holy Eagle
Stoop'd, as to foote vs: his Ascension is
More sweet then our blest Fields: his Royall Bird
Prunes the immortall wing, and cloyes his Beake,
As when his God is pleas'd.

All. Thankes Iupiter.

Sic. The Marble Pauement clozes, he is enter'd
His radiant Roofe: Away, and to be blest
Let vs with care performe his great behest. *Vanish*

Post. Sleepe, thou hast bin a Grandsire, and begot
A Father to me: and thou hast created
A Mother, and two Brothers. But (oh scorne)
Gone, they went hence so soone as they were borne:
And so I am awake. Poore Wretches, that depend
On Greatnesse, Fauour; Dreame as I haue done,
Wake, and finde nothing. But (alas) I swerue:
Many Dreame not to finde, neither deserue,
And yet are steep'd in Fauours; so am I
That haue this Golden chance, and know not why:
What Fayeries haunt this ground? A Book? Oh rare one,
Be not, as is our fangled world, a Garment
Nobler then that it couers. Let thy effects
So follow, to be most vnlike our Courtiers,
As good, as promise.

Reades.

When as a Lyons whelpe, shall to himselfe vnknown, without seeking finde, and bee embrac'd by a peece of tender Ayre: And when from a stately Cedar shall be lopt branches, which being dead many yeares, shall after reuiue, bee ioynted to the old Stocke, and freshly grow, then shall Posthumus end his miseries, Britaine be fortunate, and flourish in Peace and Plentie.

'Tis still a Dreame: or else such stuffe as Madmen
Tongue, and braine not: either both, or nothing,
Or senselesse speaking, or a speaking such
As sense cannot vntye. Be what it is,
The Action of my life is like it, which Ile keepe
If but for simpathy.

Enter Gaoler.

Gao. Come Sir, are you ready for death?

Post. Ouer-roasted rather: ready long ago.

Gao. Hanging is the word, Sir, if you bee readie for that, you are well Cook'd.

Post. So if I proue a good repast to the Spectators, the dish payes the shot.

Gao. A heauy reckoning for you Sir: But the comfort is you shall be called to no more payments, fear no more Tauerne Bils, which are often the sadnesse of parting, as the procuring of mirth: you come in faint for want of meate, depart reeling with too much drinke: sorrie that you haue payed too much, and sorry that you are payed too much: Purse and Braine, both empty: the Brain the heauier, for being too light; the Purse too light, being drawne of heauinesse. Oh, of this contradiction you shall now be quit: Oh the charity of a penny Cord, it summes vp thousands in a trice: you haue no true Debitor, and Creditor but it: of what's past, is, and to come, the discharge: your necke (Sir) is Pen, Booke, and Counters; so the Acquittance followes.

Post. I am merrier to dye, then thou art to liue.

Gao. Indeed Sir, he that sleepes, feeles not the Tooth-Ache: but a man that were to sleepe your sleepe, and a Hangman to helpe him to bed, I think he would change places with his Officer: for, look you Sir, you know not which way you shall go.

Post. Yes indeed do I, fellow.

Gao. Your death has eyes in's head then: I haue not seene him so pictur'd: you must either bee directed by some that take vpon them to know, or to take vpon your selfe that which I am sure you do not know. or iump the after-enquiry on your owne perill: and how you shall speed in your iournies end, I thinke you'l neuer returne to tell one.

Post. I tell thee, Fellow, there are none want eyes, to direct them the way I am going, but such as winke, and will not vse them.

Gao. What an infinite mocke is this, that a man shold haue the best vse of eyes, to see the way of blindnesse: I am sure hanging's the way of winking.

Enter a Messenger.

Mes. Knocke off his Manacles, bring your Prisoner to the King.

Post. Thou bring'st good newes, I am call'd to bee made free.

Gao. Ile be hang'd then.

Post. Thou shalt be then freer then a Gaoler; no bolts for

for the dead.

Gao. Vnlesse a man would marry a Gallowes, & beget yong Gibbets, I neuer saw one so prone: yet on my Conscience, there are verier Knaues desire to liue, for all he be a Roman; and there be some of them too that dye against their willes; so should I, if I were one. I would we were all of one minde, and one minde good: O there were desolation of Gaolers and Galowses: I speake against my present profit, but my wish hath a preferment in't. *Exeunt.*

Scena Quinta.

Enter Cymbeline, Bellarius, Guiderius, Aruiragus, Pisanio, and Lords.

Cym. Stand by my side you, whom the Gods haue made
Preseruers of my Throne: woe is my heart,
That the poore Souldier that so richly fought,
Whose ragges, sham'd gilded Armes, whose naked brest
Stept before Targes of proofe, cannot be found:
He shall be happy that can finde him, if
Our Grace can make him so.

Bel. I neuer saw
Such Noble fury in so poore a Thing;
Such precious deeds, in one that promist nought
But beggery, and poore lookes.

Cym. No tydings of him?

Pisa. He hath bin search'd among the dead, & liuing;
But no trace of him.

Cym. To my greefe, I am
The heyre of his Reward, which I will adde
To you (the Liuer, Heart, and Braine of Britaine)
By whom (I grant) she liues. 'Tis now the time
To aske of whence you are. Report it.

Bel. Sir,
In Cambria are we borne, and Gentlemen:
Further to boast, were neyther true, nor modest,
Vnlesse I adde, we are honest.

Cym. Bow your knees:
Arise my Knights o'th'Battell, I create you
Companions to our person, and will fit you
With Dignities becomming your estates.

Enter Cornelius and Ladies.

There's businesse in these faces: why so sadly
Greet you our Victory? you looke like Romaines,
And not o'th'Court of Britaine.

Corn. Hayle great King,
To sowre your happinesse, I must report
The Queene is dead.

Cym. Who worse then a Physitian
Would this report become? But I consider,
By Med'cine life may be prolong'd, yet death
Will seize the Doctor too. How ended she?

Cor. With horror, madly dying, like her life,
Which (being cruell to the world) concluded
Most cruell to her selfe. What she confest,
I will report, so please you. These her Women
Can trip me, if I erre, who with wet cheekes
Were present when she finish'd.

Cym. Prythee say.

Cor. First, she confest she neuer lou'd you: onely
Affected Greatnesse got by you: not you:
Married your Royalty, was wife to your place:
Abhorr'd your person.

Cym. She alone knew this:
And but she spoke it dying, I would not
Beleeue her lips in opening it. Proceed.

Corn. Your daughter, whom she bore in hand to loue
With such integrity, she did confesse
Was as a Scorpion to her sight, whose life
(But that her flight preuented it) she had
Tane off by poyson.

Cym. O most delicate Fiend!
Who is't can reade a Woman? Is there more?

Corn. More Sir, and worse. She did confesse she had
For you a mortall Minerall, which being tooke,
Should by the minute feede on life, and ling'ring,
By inches waste you. In which time, she purpos'd
By watching, weeping, tendance, kissing, to
Orecome you with her shew; and in time
(When she had fitted you with her craft, to worke
Her Sonne into th'adoption of the Crowne:
But fayling of her end by his strange absence,
Grew shamelesse desperate, open'd (in despight
Of Heauen, and Men) her purposes: repented
The euils she hatch'd, were not effected: so
Dispayring, dyed.

Cym. Heard you all this, her Women?

La. We did, so please your Highnesse

Cym. Mine eyes
Were not in fault, for she was beautifull:
Mine eares that heare her flattery, nor my heart,
That thought her like her seeming. It had beene vicious
To haue mistrusted her: yet (Oh my Daughter)
That it was folly in me, thou mayst say,
And proue it in thy feeling. Heauen mend all.

Enter Lucius, Iachimo, and other Roman prisoners, Leonatus behind, and Imogen.

Thou comm'st not *Caius* now for Tribute, that
The Britaines haue rac'd out, though with the losse
Of many a bold one: whose Kinsmen haue made suite
That their good soules may be appeas'd, with slaughter
Of you their Captiues, which our selfe haue granted,
So thinke of your estate.

Luc. Consider Sir, the chance of Warre, the day
Was yours by accident: had it gone with vs,
We should not when the blood was cool, haue threatend
Our Prisoners with the Sword. But since the Gods
Will haue it thus, that nothing but our liues
May be call'd ransome, let it come: Sufficeth,
A Roman, with a Romans heart can suffer:
Augustus liues to thinke on't: and so much
For my peculiar care. This one thing onely
I will entreate, my Boy (a Britaine borne)
Let him be ransom'd: Neuer Master had
A Page so kinde, so duteous, diligent,
So tender ouer his occasions, true,
So feate, so Nurse-like: let his vertue ioyne
With my request, which Ile make bold your Highnesse
Cannot deny: he hath done no Britaine harme,
Though he haue seru'd a Roman. Saue him (Sir)
And spare no blood beside.

Cym. I haue surely seene him:
His fauour is familiar to me: Boy,
Thou hast look'd thy selfe into my grace,
And art mine owne. I know not why, wherefore,
To say, liue boy: ne're thanke thy Master, liue;
And aske of *Cymbeline* what Boone thou wilt,
Fitting my bounty, and thy state, Ile giue it:

Yea

Yes, though thou do demand a Prisoner
The Noblest tane.
Imo. I humbly thanke your Highnesse.
Luc. I do not bid thee begge my life, good Lad,
And yet I know thou wilt.
Imo. No,no,alacke,
There's other worke in hand: I see a thing
Bitter to me, as death: your life,good Master,
Must shuffle for it selfe.
Luc. The Boy disdaines me,
He leaues me,scornes me: briefely dye their ioyes,
That place them on the truth of Gyrles,and Boyes.
Why stands he so perplexe?
Cym. What would'st thou Boy?
I loue thee more,and more: thinke more and more
What's best to aske. Know'st him thou look'st on?speak
Wilt haue him liue? Is he thy Kin? thy Friend?
Imo. He is a Romane, no more kin to me,
Then I to your Highnesse, who being born your vassaile
Am something neerer.
Cym. Wherefore ey'st him so?
Imo. Ile tell you (Sir) in priuate, if you please
To giue me hearing.
Cym. I,with all my heart,
And lend my best attention. What's thy name?
Imo. *Fidele* Sir.
Cym. Thou'rt my good youth: my Page
Ile be thy Master: walke with me: speake freely.
Bel. Is not this Boy reuiu'd from death?
Arui. One Sand another
Not more resembles that sweet Rosie Lad:
Who dyed, and was *Fidele*: what thinke you?
Gui. The same dead thing aliue.
Bel. Peace,peace, see further: he eyes vs not, forbeare
Creatures may be alike: were't he, I am sure
He would haue spoke to vs.
Gui. But we see him dead.
Bel. Be silent: let's see further.
Pisa. It is my Mistris:
Since she is liuing, let the time run on,
To good,or bad.
Cym. Come, stand thou by our side,
Make thy demand alowd. Sir, step you forth,
Giue answer to this Boy, and do it freely,
Or by our Greatnesse, and the grace of it
(Which is our Honor) bitter torture shall
Winnow the truth from falshood. One speake to him.
Imo. My boone is that this Gentleman may render
Of whom he had this Ring.
Post. What's that to him?
Cym. That Diamond vpon your Finger, say
How came it yours?
Iach. Thou'lt torture me to leaue vnspoken, that
Which to be spoke, wou'd torture thee.
Cym. How? me?
Iach. I am glad to be constrain'd to vtter that
Which torments me to conceale. By Villany
I got this Ring: 'twas *Leonatus* Iewell,
Whom thou did'st banish: and which more may greeue (thee,
As it doth me: a Nobler Sir, ne're liu'd
'Twixt sky and ground. Wilt thou heare more my Lord?
Cym. All that belongs to this.
Iach. That Paragon, thy daughter,
For whom my heart drops blood, and my false spirits
Quaile to remember. Giue me leaue, I faint.
Cym. My Daughter? what of hir? Renew thy strength
I had rather thou should'st liue, while Nature will,
Then dye ere I heare more: striue man, and speake.
Iach. Vpon a time, vnhappy was the clocke
That strooke the houre: it was in Rome, accurst
The Mansion where: 'twas at a Feast, oh would
Our Viands had bin poyson'd (or at least
Those which I heau'd to head:) the good *Posthumus*,
(What should I say? he was too good to be
Where ill men were, and was the best of all
Among'st the rar'st of good ones) sitting sadly,
Hearing vs praise our Loues of Italy
For Beauty, that made barren the swell'd boast
Of him that best could speake: for Feature, laming
The Shrine of *Venus*, or straight-pight *Minerua*,
Postures, beyond breefe Nature. For Condition,
A shop of all the qualities, that man
Loues woman for, besides that hooke of Wiuing,
Fairenesse, which strikes the eye.
Cym. I stand on fire. Come to the matter.
Iach. All too soone I shall,
Vnlesse thou would'st greeue quickly. This *Posthumus*,
Most like a Noble Lord, in loue, and one
That had a Royall Louer, tooke his hint,
And (not dispraising whom we prais'd, therein
He was as calme as vertue) he began
His Mistris picture, which, by his tongue, being made,
And then a minde put in't, either our bragges
Were crak'd of Kitchin-Trulles, or his description
Prou'd vs vnspeaking sottes.
Cym. Nay, nay, to'th'purpose.
Iach. Your daughters Chastity, (there it beginnes)
He spake of her, as *Dian* had hot dreames,
And she alone, were cold: Whereat, I wretch
Made scruple of his praise, and wager'd with him
Peeces of Gold, 'gainst this, which then he wore
Vpon his honour'd finger) to attaine
In suite the place of's bed, and winne this Ring
By hers, and mine Adultery: he (true Knight)
No lesser of her Honour confident
Then I did truly finde her, stakes this Ring,
And would so, had it beene a Carbuncle
Of Phoebus Wheele; and might so safely, had it
Bin all the worth of's Carre. Away to Britaine
Poste I in this designe: Well may you (Sir)
Remember me at Court, where I was taught
Of your chaste Daughter, the wide difference
'Twixt Amorous, and Villanous. Being thus quench'd
Of hope, not longing; mine Italian braine,
Gan in your duller Britaine operare
Most vildely: for my vantage excellent.
And to be breefe, my practise so preuayl'd
That I return'd with simular proofe enough,
To make the Noble *Leonatus* mad,
By wounding his beleefe in her Renowne,
With Tokens thus, and thus: auerring notes
Of Chamber-hanging, Pictures, this her Bracelet
(Oh cunning how I got) nay some markes
Of secret on her person, that he could not
But thinke her bond of Chastity quite crack'd,
I hauing 'tane the forfeyt. Whereupon,
Me thinkes I see him now.
Post. I so thou do'st,
Italian Fiend. Aye me, most credulous Foole,
Egregious murtherer, Theefe, any thing
That's due to all the Villaines past, in being
To come. Oh giue me Cord, or knife, or poyson,
Some

Some vpright Iusticer. Thou King, send out
For Torturors ingenious: it is I
That all th'abhorred things o'th'earth amend
By being worse then they. I am *Posthumus*,
That kill'd thy Daughter: Villain-like, I lye,
That caus'd a lesser villaine then my selfe,
A sacrilegious Theefe to doo't. The Temple
Of Vertue was she; yea, and she her selfe.
Spit, and throw stones, cast myre vpon me, set
The dogges o'th'street to bay me: euery villaine
Be call'd *Posthumus Leonatus*, and
Be villany lesse then 'twas. Oh *Imogen*!
My Queene, my life, my wife: oh *Imogen*,
Imogen, *Imogen*.
Imo. Peace my Lord, heare, heare.
Post. Shall's haue a play of this?
Thou scornfull Page, there lye thy part.
Pis. Oh Gentlemen, helpe,
Mine and your Mistris: Oh my Lord *Posthumus*,
You ne're kill'd *Imogen* till now: helpe, helpe,
Mine honour'd Lady.
Cym. Does the world go round?
Posth. How comes these staggers on mee?
Pisa. Wake my Mistris.
Cym. If this be so, the Gods do meane to strike me
To death, with mortall ioy.
Pisa. How fares my Mistris?
Imo. Oh get thee from my sight,
Thou gau'st me poyson: dangerous Fellow hence,
Breath not where Princes are.
Cym. The tune of *Imogen*.
Pisa. Lady, the Gods throw stones of sulpher on me, if
That box I gaue you, was not thought by mee
A precious thing, I had it from the Queene.
Cym. New matter still.
Imo. It poyson'd me.
Corn. Oh Gods!
I left out one thing which the Queene confest,
Which must approue thee honest. If *Pasanio*
Haue (said she) giuen his Mistris that Confection
Which I gaue him for Cordiall, she is seru'd,
As I would serue a Rat.
Cym. What's this, *Cornelius*?
Corn. The Queene (Sir) very oft importun'd me
To temper poysons for her, still pretending
The satisfaction of her knowledge, onely
In killing Creatures vilde, as Cats and Dogges
Of no esteeme. I dreading, that her purpose
Was of more danger, did compound for her
A certaine stuffe, which being tane, would cease
The present powre of life, but in short time,
All Offices of Nature, should againe
Do their due Functions. Haue you tane of it?
Imo. Most like I did, for I was dead.
Bel. My Boyes, there was our error.
Gui. This is sure *Fidele*.
Imo. Why did you throw your wedded Lady fro you?
Thinke that you are vpon a Rocke, and now
Throw me againe.
Post. Hang there like fruite, my soule,
Till the Tree dye.
Cym. How now, my Flesh? my Childe?
What, mak'st thou me a dullard in this Act?
Wilt thou not speake to me?
Imo. Your blessing, Sir.
Bel. Though you did loue this youth, I blame ye not,
You had a motiue for't.
Cym. My teares that fall
Proue holy-water on thee; *Imogen*,
Thy Mothers dead.
Imo. I am sorry for't, my Lord.
Cym. Oh, she was naught; and long of her it was
That we meet heere so strangely: but her Sonne
Is gone, we know not how, nor where.
Pisa. My Lord,
Now feare is from me, Ile speake troth. Lord *Cloten*
Vpon my Ladies missing, came to me
With his Sword drawne, foam'd at the mouth, and swore
If I discouer'd not which way she was gone,
It was my instant death. By accident,
I had a feigned Letter of my Masters
Then in my pocket, which directed him
To seeke her on the Mountaines neere to Milford,
Where in a frenzie, in my Masters Garments
(Which he inforc'd from me) away he postes
With vnchaste purpose, and with oath to violate
My Ladies honor, what became of him,
I further know not.
Gui. Let me end the Story: I slew him there.
Cym. Marry, the Gods forefend.
I would not thy good deeds, should from my lips
Plucke a hard sentence: Prythee valiant youth
Deny't againe.
Gui. I haue spoke it, and I did it.
Cym. He was a Prince.
Gui. A most inciuill one. The wrongs he did mee
Were nothing Prince-like; for he did prouoke me
With Language that would make me spurne the Sea,
If it could so roare to me. I cut off's head,
And am right glad he is not standing heere
To tell this tale of mine.
Cym. I am sorrow for thee:
By thine owne tongue thou art condemn'd, and must
Endure our Law: Thou'rt dead.
Imo. That headlesse man I thought had bin my Lord
Cym. Binde the Offender,
And take him from our presence.
Bel. Stay, Sir King.
This man is better then the man he slew,
As well descended as thy selfe, and hath
More of thee merited, then a Band of *Clotens*
Had euer scarre for. Let his Armes alone,
They were not borne for bondage.
Cym. Why old Soldier:
Wilt thou vndoo the worth thou art vnpayd for
By tasting of our wrath? How of descent
As good as we?
Arui. In that he spake too farre.
Cym. And thou shalt dye for't.
Bel. We will dye all three,
But I will proue that two one's are as good
As I haue giuen out him. My Sonnes, I must
For mine owne part, vnfold a dangerous speech,
Though haply well for you.
Arui. Your danger's ours.
Guid. And our good his.
Bel. Haue at it then, by leaue
Thou hadd'st (great King) a Subiect, who
Was call'd *Belarius*.
Cym. What of him? He is a banish'd Traitor.
Bel. He it is, that hath
Assum'd this age: indeed a banish'd man,

I

I know not how, a Traitor.
Cym. Take him hence,
The whole world shall not saue him.
Bel. Not too hot;
First pay me for the Nursing of thy Sonnes,
And let it be confiscate all, so soone
As I haue receyu'd it.
Cym. Nursing of my Sonnes?
Bel. I am too blunt, and sawcy: heere's my knee:
Ere I arise, I will preferre my Sonnes,
Then spare not the old Father. Mighty Sir,
These two young Gentlemen that call me Father,
And thinke they are my Sonnes, are none of mine,
They are the yssue of your Loynes, my Liege,
And blood of your begetting.
Cym. How? my Issue.
Bel. So sure as you, your Fathers: I (old *Morgan*)
Am that *Belarius*, whom you sometime banish'd:
Your pleasure was my neere offence, my punishment
It selfe, and all my Treason that I suffer'd,
Was all the harme I did. These gentle Princes
(For such, and so they are) these twenty yeares
Haue I train'd vp; those Arts they haue, as I
Could put into them. My breeding was (Sir)
As your Highnesse knowes: Their Nurse *Euriphile*
(Whom for the Theft I wedded) stole these Children
Vpon my Banishment: I moou'd her too't,
Hauing receyu'd the punishment before
For that which I did then. Beaten for Loyaltie,
Excited me to Treason. Their deere losse,
The more of you 'twas felt, the more it shap'd
Vnto my end of stealing them. But gracious Sir,
Heere are your Sonnes againe, and I must loose
Two of the sweet'st Companions in the World.
The benediction of these couering Heauens
Fall on their heads like dew, for they are worthie
To in-lay Heauen with Starres.
Cym. Thou weep'st, and speak'st:
The Seruice that you three haue done, is more
Vnlike, then this thou tell'st. I lost my Children,
If these be they, I know not how to wish
A payre of worthier Sonnes.
Bel. Be pleas'd awhile;
This Gentleman, whom I call *Polidore*,
Most worthy Prince, as yours, is true *Guiderius*:
This Gentleman, my *Cadwall*, *Aruiragus*.
Your yonger Princely Son, he Sir, was lapt
In a most curious Mantle, wrought by th'hand
Of his Queene Mother, which for more probation
I can with ease produce.
Cym. *Guiderius* had
Vpon his necke a Mole, a sanguine Starre,
It was a marke of wonder.
Bel. This is he,
Who hath vpon him still that naturall stampe:
It was wise Natures end, in the donation
To be his euidence now.
Cym. Oh, what am I
A Mother to the byrth of three? Nere Mother
Reioyc'd deliuerance more: Blest, pray you be,
That after this strange starting from your Orbes,
You may reigne in them now: Oh *Imogen*,
Thou hast lost by this a Kingdome.
Imo. No, my Lord:
I haue got two Worlds by't. Oh my gentle Brothers,
Haue we thus met? Oh neuer say heereafter
But I am truest speaker. You call'd me Brother
When I was but your Sister: I you Brothers,
When we were so indeed.
Cym. Did you ere meete?
Arui. I my good Lord.
Gui. And at first meeting lou'd,
Continew'd so, vntill we thought he dyed.
Corn. By the Queenes Dramme she swallow'd.
Cym. O rare instinct!
When shall I heare all through? This fierce abridgment,
Hath to it Circumstantiall branches, which
Distinction should be rich in. Where? how liu'd you?
And when came you to serue our Romane Captiue?
How parted with your Brother? How first met them?
Why fled you from the Court? And whether these?
And your three motiues to the Battaile? with
I know not how much more should be demanded,
And all the other by-dependances
From chance to chance? But nor the Time, nor Place
Will serue our long Interrogatories. See,
Posthumus Anchors vpon *Imogen*;
And she (like harmlesse Lightning) throwes her eye
On him: her Brothers, Me: her Master hitting
Each obiect with a Ioy: the Counter-change
Is seuerally in all. Let's quit this ground,
And smoake the Temple with our Sacrifices.
Thou art my Brother, so wee'l hold thee euer.
Imo. You are my Father too, and did releeue me:
To see this gracious season.
Cym. All ore-ioy'd
Saue these in bonds, let them be ioyfull too,
For they shall taste our Comfort.
Imo. My good Master, I will yet do you seruice.
Luc. Happy be you.
Cym. The forlorne Souldier, that no Nobly fought
He would haue well becom'd this place, and grac'd
The thankings of a King.
Post. I am Sir
The Souldier that did company these three
In poore beseeming: 'twas a fitment for
The purpose I then follow'd. That I was he,
Speake *Iachimo*, I had you downe, and might
Haue made you finish.
Iach. I am downe againe:
But now my heauie Conscience sinkes my knee,
As then your force did. Take that life, beseech you
Which I so often owe: but your Ring first,
And heere the Bracelet of the truest Princesse
That euer swore her Faith.
Post. Kneele not to me:
The powre that I haue on you, is to spare you:
The malice towards you, to forgiue you. Liue
And deale with others better.
Cym. Nobly doom'd:
Wee'l learne our Freenesse of a Sonne-in-Law:
Pardon's the word to all.
Arui. You holpe vs Sir,
As you did meane indeed to be our Brother,
Ioy'd are we, that you are.
Post. Your Seruant Princes. Good my Lord of Rome
Call forth your Sooth-sayer: As I slept, me thought
Great Iupiter vpon his Eagle back'd
Appear'd to me, with other sprightly shewes
Of mine owne Kindred. When I wak'd, I found
This Labell on my bosome; whose containing
Is so from sense in hardnesse, that I can

Make

Make no Collection of it. Let him ſhew
His skill in the conſtruction.

Luc. *Philarmonus.*

Sooth. Heere,my good Lord.

Luc Read,and declare the meaning.

Reades.

WHen as a Lyons whelpe, ſhall to himſelfe vnknown, without ſeeking finde, and bee embrac'd by a peece of tender Ayre: And when from a ſtately Cedar ſhall be lopt branches, which being dead many yeares, ſhall after reuiue, bee ioynted to the old Stocke, and freſhly grow, then ſhall Poſthumus end his miſeries, Britaine be fortunate, and flouriſh in Peace and Plentie.

Thou *Leonatus* art the Lyons Whelpe,
The fit and apt Conſtruction of thy name
Being *Leonatus*, doth import ſo much:
The peece of tender Ayre, thy vertuous Daughter,
Which we call *Mollis Aer*, and *Mollis Aer*
We terme it *Mulier*; which *Mulier* I diuine
Is this moſt conſtant Wife, who euen now
Anſwering the Letter of the Oracle,
Vnknowne to you vnſought, were clipt about
With this moſt tender Aire.

Cym. This hath ſome ſeeming.

Sooth. The lofty Cedar, Royall *Cymbeline*
Perſonates thee: And thy lopt Branches, point
Thy two Sonnes forth: who by *Belarius* ſtolne
For many yeares thought dead, are now reuiu'd
To the Maieſticke Cedar ioyn'd; whoſe Iſſue
Promiſes Britaine, Peace and Plenty.

Cym. Well,
My Peace we will begin: And *Caius Lucius*,
Although the Victor, we ſubmit to *Cæſar*,
And to the Romane Empire; promiſing
To pay our wonted Tribute, from the which
We were diſſwaded by our wicked Queene,
Whom heauens in Iuſtice both on her, and hers,
Haue laid moſt heauy hand.

Sooth. The fingers of the Powres aboue, do tune
The harmony of this Peace: the Viſion
Which I made knowne to *Lucius* ere the ſtroke
Of yet this ſcarſe-cold-Battaile, at this inſtant
Is full accompliſh'd. For the Romaine Eagle
From South to Weſt, on wing ſoaring aloft
Leſſen'd her ſelfe, and in the Beames o'th Sun
So vaniſh'd; which fore-ſhew'd our Princely Eagle
Th'Imperiall *Cæſar*, ſhould againe vnite
His Fauour, with the Radiant *Cymbeline*,
Which ſhines heere in the Weſt.

Cym. Laud we the Gods,
And let our crooked Smoakes climbe to their Noſtrils
From our bleſt Altars. Publiſh we this Peace
To all our Subiects. Set we forward: Let
A Roman, and a Brittiſh Enſigne waue
Friendly together: ſo through *Luds-Towne* march,
And in the Temple of great Iupiter
Our Peace wee'l ratifie: Seale it with Feaſts.
Set on there: Neuer was a Warre did ceaſe
(Ere bloodie hands were waſh'd) with ſuch a Peace.

Exeunt.

FINIS.